INDEX TO
CD AND RECORD REVIEWS
1987-1997

Based on material originally published in
*Notes: Quarterly Journal of
the Music Library Association*
between 1987 and 1997

Compiled by
MARK PALKOVIC and PAUL CAUTHEN
Incorporating material
supplied by
RICHARD LESUEUR

Compilation of this cumulation was funded in part by a grant
from the National Academy of Recording Arts and Sciences, Inc.

G.K. Hall & Co.
An Imprint of Simon & Schuster Macmillan
New York

Prentice Hall International
London • Mexico City • New Delhi • Singapore • Sydney • Toronto

G.K. Hall & Co.

1633 Broadway 7th Floor
New York, NY 10019

Manufactured in the United States of America.

The paper used in this publication meets the minimum requirements of American
National Standards for Information Sciences–Permanence of Paper for Printed
Library Materials, ANSI Z39.48-1984∞™

ISBN   0-7838-8191-6   (set)
ISBN   0-7838-0369-9   (vol. 1)
ISBN   0-7838-0370-2   (vol. 2)
ISBN   0-7838-8487-7   (vol. 3)

CONTENTS

IBS

18540. 1007: Music of Turrin, Jeanjean, Bitsch, Rizetto, and others. *Few, trumpet; Loewen, McDonald, piano.*
+ ARG 1-2/95: 231

IMAGES

18541. 001: Music of Zelesny, Prokofiev, Zuckert, Messiaen, and Fisher. *Fisher, clarinet; Stephens, piano; Franciscan Quartet; Penderecki Quartet.*
+ ARG 11-12/95: 248

IMAGINARY ROAD

18542. 314 528 869-2: The chant of Christmas midnight. *Schola Cantorum of St. Peter's in the Loop (Chicago); Thompson, cond.*
+ Fa 11-12/96: 443

IMC

18543. 205002 (2 discs): BELLINI—Il pirata. *Caballé, Labò, Cappuccilli; Florence Opera; Ghiglia, cond.* Recorded live 1967.
+ ARG 11-12/95: 86

IMG

18544. IMGCD 1601: *Tchaikovsky gala.* TCHAIKOVSKY—Capriccio italien; Romeo and Juliet overture; Francesca da Rimini; 1812 overture. *Royal Phil. Orch.; Serebrier, cond.*
- Fa 11-12/93: 423

18545. IMGCD 1602: VIVALDI—Four seasons. MOZART—Eine kleine Nachtmusik. *Guttman, violin; Scottish National Orch.; Serebrier, cond.*
• Fa 3-4/94: 360

18546. IMGCD 1603: PROKOFIEV—Love for three oranges: Suite; Symphony no. 1; Lt. Kijé: Suite. *London Phil. Orch.; Bátiz, cond.*
- Fa 3-4/94: 276

18547. IMGCD 1605: RACHMANINOFF—Piano concerto no. 3; Vocalise; Prince Rostislav. *Prats, piano; Phil. Orch. of Mexico City; Bátiz, cond.*
• Fa 9-10/94: 302
• Gr 2/94: 52

18548. IMGCD 1606: BERLIOZ—Symphonie fantastique; Roman carnival overture; Le corsaire overture. *Royal Phil. Orch.; Bátiz, cond.*
• Fa 9-10/94: 144
- Gr 7/94: 41

18549. IMGCD 1607: ALBÉNIZ—Iberia suite; Navarra; Piano concerto no. 1; Catalonia folk suite. *Ciccolini, piano; London Symphony Orch.; Royal Phil. Orch.; Phil. Orch. of Mexico City; Bátiz, cond.* Reissue.

+ ARG 11-12/94: 60
• Fa 9-10/94: 110

18550. IMGCD 1608: TURINA—Danzas fantásticas; Rapsodia sinfónica; Sinfonia Sevillana; La procesión del rocio; La oración del torero. *Wibaut, piano; London Phil. Orch.; Phil. Orch. of Mexico City; Bátiz, cond.*
+ ARG 11-12/94: 204
+ Fa 9-10/94: 358

18551. IMGCD 1609: SHOSTAKOVICH—Symphony no. 5; Overture, op. 115; Novorossiisk chimes; October. *Royal Phil. Orch.; Bátiz, cond.*
• Gr 2/95: 56

18552. IMGCD 1613: GROFÉ—Grand Canyon suite; Mississippi suite. COPLAND—Red pony: Suite. *Royal Phil. Orch.; Mexico City Phil. Orch.; Bátiz, cond.*
+ ARG 7-8/95: 116

18553. IMGCD 1801: BERNSTEIN—West side story. *Bonney, Ball, Williams, Howard; Royal Phil. Orch.; Wordsworth, cond.*
• Fa 3-4/94: 134
• Gr 10/93: 111

18554. 30368 00025 (5 discs): BEETHOVEN—Symphonies. *Sinfonia Varsovia; Menuhin, cond.*
+ Fi 11/96: 120
• Gr 4/96: 41

IMP

18555. MCD 16: DEBUSSY—Préludes, books I and II. *Tirimo, piano.*
+ Fa 1-2/92: 200

18556. MCD 19, 20, 29, 33, 35-36 (6 separate discs): SCHUBERT—Complete piano sonatas. *Kuerti, piano.*
+ ARG 7-8/92: 217 (v. 2-5)
+ ARG 1-2/93: 146 (v. 6)
• Fa 1-2/93: 231 (v. 1, 6)
• Gr 2/92: 64 (v. 1-4)
• Gr 4/92: 116 (v. 5)
• Gr 4/93: 95 (v. 6)

18557. MCD 21: SHERIFF—Revival of the dead. *Dutch Men's Choir; Ankor Children's Choir; Israel Phil. Orch.; Porcelijn, cond.*
+ ARG 11-12/91: 147

18558. MCD 22: SCHUMANN—Liederkreis, op. 39; Frauenliebe und Leben; Lieder: Aus den östlichen Rosen; Die Soldatenbraut; Der Nussbaum; Widmung; Mignon; Meine Rose; Requiem. *Lott, soprano; Johnson, piano.*
+ ARG 5-6/92: 130
+ Fa 1-2/92: 325
+ Gr 10/91: 174

18559. MCD 23: DEBUSSY—Chamber works. *Various performers.*
+ Gr 8/91: 59

18560. MCD 24: DEBUSSY—Piano works, vol. 3. *Tirimo, piano.*
+ ARG 11-12/91: 57
+ Gr 7/91: 87

18561. MCD 25: STRAVINSKY—Le sacre du printemps (orchestral version and piano version arr. by the composer). *Boston Phil. Orch.; Zander, cond.; Lawson, player piano.*
• ARG 5-6/92: 143
+ Fa 1-2/92: 343
+ St 4/93: 289

18562. MCD 26: *20th century flute classics.* Sonatas by Prokofieff and Martinù; Bartok's Suite paysanne hongroise (arr.). *Hall, flute; Jacobson, piano.*
- ARG 1-2/92: 153
+ Gr 11/91: 111

18563. MCD 27: JOACHIM—Violin concerto no. 2 "In the Hungarian manner"; Overture to Hamlet; Overture to Henry IV. *Oliveira, violin; London Phil. Orch.; Botstein, cond.*
• ARG 11-12/91: 86
+ Fa 1-2/92: 243
+ Gr 8/91: 55

18564. MCD 28: BACH—*Flute works and arrangements.* Harpsichord concertos BWV 1052, 1056; Italian concerto; Orchestra suite no 2. *Dower, flute; London Bach Orch.; Layfield, cond.*
+ Gr 4/92: 43

18565. MCD 30: BRAHMS—Piano quintet; Quartet no. 3. *Han, piano; New World Quartet.*
+ ARG 7-8/92: 106
• Gr 3/92: 64

18566. MCD 31: *Horn music.* HANDEL—Concerto in F. BARSANTI—Concerto grosso in D. HAENSEL—Concerto in F. FRANZ—Concert piece. HUBLER—Concerto in F. SCHUMANN—Konzertstück. *Members of Israel Phil. Orch.; Rimon, horns.*
+ ARG 5-6/92: 166
+ Gr 2/92: 43

18567. MCD 32: DEBUSSY—Piano music, vol. 4. *Tirimo, piano.*
+ Gr 10/92: 139

18568. MCD 37: FAURÉ—Violin sonata no. 1. DEBUSSY—Violin sonata. FRANCK—Violin sonata. *Hasson, violin; Ivaldi, piano.*
+ Fa 9-10/92: 233
+ Gr 6/92: 56

18569. MCD 38: Music of Ibert, Poulenc, Milhaud, Tomasi and Villa-Lobos. *London Wind Trio.*
+ Gr 9/92: 120

18570. MCD 39: LISZT—Piano music. *Llewelyn-Jones, piano.*
• Gr 10/92: 140

18571. MCD 40: BEETHOVEN—Symphony no. 9. *Labelle, soprano; Fortunato, mezzo-soprano; Cresswell, tenor; Arnold, baritone; Boston Phil. Orch. and Chorus Pro Musica; Zander, cond.*
  + ARG 11-12/92: 84
  + Fa 9-10/92: 185
  • Gr 9/92: 41

18572. MCD 41: DEBUSSY—Piano trio. FAURÉ—Piano trio. RAVEL—Piano trio. *Solomon Trio.*
  + Gr 7/92: 69

18573. MCD 44: BEETHOVEN—Piano trios op. 70. *Solomon Trio.*
  + Gr 11/92: 118

18574. MCD 45: Gala de Reyes. *Vocal soloists; Madrid Symphony Orch.; García Asensio, cond.*
  • Gr 11/92: 196

18575. MCD 46: MENDELSSOHN—Trios for violin, cello and piano no. 1-2. *Solomon Trio.*
  • Fa 3-4/93: 221
  + Gr 12/92: 97

18576. MCD 49: KABALEVSKY—Cello sonata, op. 71. SHOSTAKOVICH—Cello sonata, op. 40. SCHNITTKE—Cello sonata. *Hugh, cello; Sturrock, piano.*
  + ARG 5-6/93: 161
  + Fa 5-6/93: 237

18577. MCD 50: BRAHMS—Viola sonatas; Cello sonata no. 1. *Vardi,viola; Sturrock, piano.*
  • ARG 7-8/93: 71

18578. MCD 52: ARENSKY—Piano trio no. 1. TCHAIKOVSKY—Piano trio. *Solomon Trio.*
  + Gr 5/93: 60

18579. MCD 53: BRAHMS—String quartets no. 1-2. *New World String Quartet.*
  + Fa 3-4/93: 127
  • Gr 4/93: 77

18580. MCD 55: *Romeo and Juliet.* Music of Bellini, Tchaikovsky, Svendsen, and Kabalevsky. *Philharmonia Orch.; Atlas, cond.*
  + Fa 11-12/93: 519
  • Gr 6/93: 57

18581. MCD 56 : SMETANA—Má vlast. *Philharmonia Orch.; D'Avalos, cond.*
  • Fa 9-10/93: 293

18582. MCD 57: BRITTEN—Folk songs; Six Chinese songs; Canticle no. 2. *Esswood, alto; Griffett, tenor; Ridgway, piano; Walker, guitar.*
  + Gr 1/94: 81

18583. MCD 58: SHOSTAKOVICH—Violin sonata, op. 134. PROKOFIEV—Violin sonata no. 2. *Sushanskaya, violin; Vignoles, piano.*

  - ARG 11-12/93: 171
  - Fa 11-12/93: 394

18584. MCD 59: STRAUSS—Oboe concerto. VAUGHAN WILLIAMS—Oboe concerto; Studies in English folk song (arr.). *Canter, oboe; London Symphony Orch.; Judd, cond.*
  + Gr 10/93: 56

18585. MCD 60: *English string music.* Music of Berkeley, Holst, Tippett, and Britten. *English Sinfonia; Farrer, cond.*
  • Fa 9-10/95: 421

18586. MCD 61: ROSSINI—Petite messe solennelle. *Schmitt, Gregoire, Garin, Golven; Chorus of l' Opéra-Comique; Hatton, harmonium; Maciocchi, piano; Brain, cond.*
  + Fa 1-2/94: 292
  • Gr 10/93: 100

18587. MCD 62: *Classical flute à la jazz.* Music of Bolling, Gershwin, Debussy, Correa, Milhaud, Martinů, Lloyd, Heath, Joplin, Jacobson, Previn, and Piazzolla. *Hall, flute; other instrumentalists.*
  + Fa 11-12/93: 483

18588. MCD 63: *Huapango: music of Mexican composers.* Music of Chávez, Galindo, R. Halffter, Moncayo, and Revueltas. *Xalapa Symphony Orch.; Mineria Symphony Orch.; Herrera de la Fuente, cond.*
  + ARG 11-12/93: 227
  + Fa 11-12/93: 522
  + Gr 12/93: 68

18589. MCD 64: TCHAIKOVSKY—Soprano arias. *Farley, soprano; Melbourne Symphony Orch.; Orch. Sinfonica Siciliana; Serebrier, cond.*
  + Fa 11-12/93: 415

18590. MCD 66: FAURÉ—Piano quartets. *Los Angeles Piano Quartet.*
  + ARG 1-2/94: 99
  + Gr 10/93: 70

18591. MCD 67: SCRIABIN—Piano sonatas no. 1, 5. PROKOFIEV—Piano sonatas no. 1-3. *Shin'ar, piano.*
  + Fa 11-12/93: 393

18592. MCD 68: MENDELSSOHN—Symphony no. 5; Die erste Walpurgisnacht. *Rigby, Tear, Michaels-Moore, Allan; Philharmonia Chorus & Orch.; D'Avalos, cond.*
  • ARG 5-6/94: 113
  + Fa 11-12/93: 322
  + Fa 5-6/94: 191 (Burke)
  • Fa 5-6/94: 193 (Hurwitt)
  + Gr 3/94: 56

18593. MCD 69: BEETHOVEN—Piano trio op. 97; Variations on Ich bin der Schneider Kakadu; Trio movement in E♭. *Solomon Trio.*
  • Fa 9-10/94: 141
  + Gr 3/94: 69

18594. MCD 70: IBARRA—Cello concerto. ZYMAN—Cello concerto. PIAZZOLLA—Grand tango. *Prieto, cello; Philharmonia International of Mexico; Medina, cond.; National Symphony Orch. of Mexico; Diemecke, cond.*
  + ARG 3-4/94: 200
  + Fa 3-4/94: 220

18595. MCD 71: INDY—Symphony on a French mountain air. FAURÉ—Ballade. SAINT-SAËNS—Piano concerto no. 2. *Traficante, piano; Royal Phil. Orch.; Serebrier, cond.*
  • Fa 3-4/94: 175
  - Gr 6/94: 50

18596. MCD 72: GRIEG—Cello sonata. RACHMANINOFF—Cello sonata; 2 transcriptions. *Hugh, cello; Solomon, piano.*
  + ARG 3-4/94: 104
  • Gr 2/94: 61

18597. MCD 74: MOZART—Piano concertos no. 21, 27. *Fou, piano & cond.; Sinfonia Varsovia.*
  - Fa 3-4/94: 253
  • Gr 3/94: 58

18598. MCD 75: COPLAND—Rodeo: four dance episodes; Billy the Kid: suite. GERSHWIN (arr. BENNETT)—Porgy and Bess: symphonic picture. *Bournemouth Symphony Orch.; Farrer, cond.*
  + ARG 9-10/95: 127
  • Fa 9-10/94: 173
  • Gr 8/94: 46

18599. MCD 76: *Nettle and Markham in America.* Music of Bernstein, Bennett, and Gershwin. *Nettle, Markham, pianos.*
  + Fa 11-12/94: 490

18600. TCD 77 (3 discs): MOZART—Wind concertos. *Peck, clarinet; Kamins, bassoon; Dorough, flute; Atherholt, oboe; Ver Meulen, horn; Houston Symphony Orch.; Eschenbach, cond.*
  • ARG 9-10/95: 180
  + Fa 5-6/94: 199
  • Gr 4/94: 52

18601. MCD 78: MENDELSSOHN—Midsummer night's dream; Fair Melusine. *Howarth, soprano; Rigby, mezzo- soprano; Bach Choir; Philharmonia Orch.; D'Avalos, cond.*
  • ARG 11-12/94: 154
  + Gr 7/94: 51

18602. MCD 79: MOZART—Piano concertos no. 22, 24. *Fou, piano & cond.; Sinfonia Varsovia.*
  • Gr 6/94: 56

18603. MCD 80: BEETHOVEN—Cello sonatas, no. 1-3. *Hugh, cello; Y. Solomon, piano.*
  + Fa 9-10/94: 139
  + Gr 9/94: 71

18604. MCD 81: MENDELSSOHN—
Symphony no. 1; Overtures: Die
Hochzeit des Camacho; The Hebrides;
Calm sea and prosperous voyage;
Athalie; Overture in C major "Trumpet".
Philharmonia Orch.; D'Avalos, cond.
  - ARG 7-8/95: 156
  + Fa 3-4/95: 229

18605. MCD 82: *Russian masterpieces.*
Music of Mussorgsky, Rimsky-Korsakov,
Balakirev, and Rachmaninoff.
Philharmonia Orch.; Yu, cond.
  • Fa 11-12/94: 503
  + Gr 1/95: 64

18606. MCD 83: MENDELSSOHN—
Symphony no. 2; St. Paul overture.
*Wiens, Howarth, sopranos; Tear, tenor;
Bach Choir; Philharmonia Orch.;
D'Avalos, cond.*
  + ARG 3-4/95: 141
  + Fa 9-10/94: 255

18607. MCD 84: MOZART—Piano
concertos no. 9, 12. *Fou, piano & cond.;
Polish Chamber Orch.* Recorded 1986.
  • Fa 1-2/95: 208
  • Gr 9/94: 58

18608. MCD 87: BEETHOVEN—Piano
concerto no. 4. HAYDN—Piano concerto in
D. *T'song, piano; Sinfonia Varsovia;
Swoboda, cond.; Polish Chamber Orch.*
  • Gr 11/94: 63

18609. MCD 88: MENDELSSOHN—
Symphonies no. 3-4; Son and stranger
overture; Ruy Blas overture.
Philharmonia Orch.; D'Avalos, cond.
  + Fa 11-12/94: 302

18610. MCD 89: TCHAIKOVSKY—Serenade
for strings; Souvenir de Florence (arr.
Yu). *Philharmonia Orch.; Yu, cond.*
  - Gr 11/94: 88

18611. MCD 93 (2 discs): MAHLER—
Symphony no. 6. *Boston Phil. Orch.;
Zander, cond.*
  + ARG 11-12/95: 149
  + Fa 1-2/97: 200
  - Gr 2/96: 50

18612. MCD 122: PROKOFIEV—Zdravitsa.
TCHAIKOVSKY—Ode to joy. *Geoffrey
Mitchell Choir; London Phil. Orch.;
Gleeson, cond.*
  + ARG 7-8/96: 172

18613. PCD 821: *Trumpet concertos.*
Works by J. & M. Haydn, Torelli,
Telemann, Neruda and Humphries.
*Steele- Perkins, trumpet; English
Chamber Orch.; Halstead, cond.*
  + ARG 9-10/91: 267

18614. PCD 822: *Italian madrigals.*
Works by Arcadelt, Caimo, A. Gabrieli,
Gastoldi, Gesualdo, Lasso, Mainerio,
Marenzio, Monte, Monteverdi, Negri,
Vecchi and Wert. *Amaryllis Consort.*
  + ARG 11-12/91: 198

18615. PCD 825: *A Florentine carnival.*
Festival music for Lorenzo da Medici.
London Pro Musica; Thomas, cond.
  + ARG 9-10/91: 170

18616. PCD 832: MOZART—Piano
concertos no. 21, 24. *Shelley, piano &
cond.; City of London Sinfonia.*
  • ARG 1-2/92: 82

18617. PCD 834: CHOPIN—Piano music.
Ogdon, piano.
  - ARG 1-2/92: 43

18618. PCD 857: BRAHMS—Symphony
no. 2 in D; Tragic overture. *Hallé Orch.;
Skrowaczewski, cond.*
  + ARG 11-12/91: 47

18619. PCD 858: *Great piano
transcriptions.* Works by Gounod-Liszt,
Strauss-Grainger, Strauss-Gieseking,
Wagner-Moszkowski, Ravel, Offenbach-
Moszkowski, Tchaikovsky-Grainger,
Gershwin-Grainger. *Saba, piano.*
  • ARG 11-12/91: 191

18620. PCD 860: WAGNER—Overtures:
Rienzi; Lohengrin; Meistersinger; Flying
Dutchman; Tannhäuser; Ride of the
Valkyries. *London Symphony Orch.;
Tuckwell, cond.*
  + ARG 11-12/91: 168

18621. PCD 862: CHOPIN—Twenty-four
preludes; Piano sonata no. 2. *Shelley,
piano.*
  + ARG 1-2/92: 43

18622. PCD 863: PALESTRINA—Missa
Papae Marcelli; Stabat Mater. *Pro
Cantione Antiqua; Brown, cond.*
  + ARG 11-12/91: 130

18623. PCD 867: TCHAIKOVSKY—
Symphony no. 4; Marche slave. *London
Symphony Orch.; Rozhdestvensky, cond.*
Reissue.
  • ARG 1-2/92: 128

18624. PCD 873: *English madrigals.*
Morley, Ramsay, East, Gibbons, Bennet,
Weelkes, Ford, Ward, Farmer, Tomkins,
Byrd, Greaves and Wilbye. *Amaryllis
Consort.*
  + ARG 11-12/91: 199

18625. PCD 875: TCHAIKOVSKY—
Symphony no. 5; Capriccio italien.
*London Symphony Orch.;
Rozhdestvensky, cond.*
  • ARG 1-2/92: 128

18626. PCD 878: TCHAIKOVSKY—
Symphony no. 6; The storm. *London
Symphony Orch.; Rozhdestvensky, cond.*
  • ARG 1-2/92: 128

18627. PCD 881: MONTEVERDI—
Madrigals; Motets. *Kirkby, Tubb,
sopranos; Consort of Musicke; Rooley,
cond.*
  + ARG 3-4/92: 104

18628. PCD 904: RACHMANINOFF—
Symphony no. 2. *London Symphony
Orch.; Rozhdestvensky, cond.*
  - ARG 1-2/95: 158

18629. PCD 914: MOZART—Symphonies
no. 35, 41. *Orch. of St. John's Smith
Square; Gilmour, cond.*
  - ARG 1-2/92: 85

18630. PCD 915: DEBUSSY—La mer;
Nocturnes; Prelude to the afternoon of a
faun. *London Symphony Orch.; Burgos,
cond.*
  + ARG 3-4/95: 92

18631. PCD 919: *Great occasions at
Westminster Abbey.* Works by Bliss,
Parry, Walton, Wesley, Stanford,
Vaughan Williams, Hilton, Adcock and
Widor. *Choir of Westminster Abbey;
London Brass; Neary, cond.*
  + ARG 11-12/91: 199

18632. PCD 927: SIBELIUS—Symphony
no. 2; Swan of Tuonela. *London
Symphony Orch.; Mackerras, cond.*
  + ARG 11-12/94: 191

18633. PCD 928: DVOŘÁK—Serenade for
strings; Romance. WAGNER—Siegfried
Idyll. *Scottish Chamber Orch.; Laredo,
cond.*
  + ARG 1-2/92: 51

18634. PCD 932: SAINT-SAËNS—Carnival
of the animals. BIZET—Jeux d'enfants.
RAVEL—Ma mère l'oye. *Jacobson,
Hutchinson, pianos; London Symphony
Orch.; Wordsworth, cond.*
  + ARG 3-4/92: 129

18635. PCD 936: SCHUBERT—
Symphonies no. 4, 6. *Orch. of St. John's,
Smith Square; Gilmour, cond.*
  + ARG 5-6/92: 126

18636. PCD 940: SHOSTAKOVICH—
Symphony no. 5. *Hallé Orch.;
Skrowaczewski, cond.*
  + ARG 9-10/91: 128
  + Fa 1-2/92: 330
  + Gr 8/91: 58

18637. PCD 941: MAHLER—Symphony
no. 1. *London Symphony Orch.; Butt,
cond.*
  - ARG 9-10/91: 89
  - Gr 12/91: 72

18638. PCD 942: SCHUMANN—
Symphonies no. 2, 4. *English Sinfonia;
Gilmour, cond.*
  + ARG 9-10/91: 124
  • Gr 2/91: 1517

18639. PCD 943: SCHUBERT—Symphony
no. 9. *English Sinfonia; Groves, cond.*
  + ARG 5-6/92: 127

18640. PCD 944: SCHUBERT—
Symphonies no. 1, 5; Overture in D in the
Italian style; Des Teufels Lustschloss.

English Sinfonia; Groves, cond.
+ ARG 5-6/92: 126
+ Gr 11/91: 101

18641. PCD 946: Mozart—Violin concertos no. 1, 3, K. 271a. *Kovacic, violin & cond.; Scottish Chamber Orch.*
● Fa 1-2/92: 275
● Gr 6/91: 46

18642. PCD 948: Mozart—Violin concertos no. 2, 5; Adagio. *Kovacic, violin; Scottish Chamber Orch.*
● ARG 9-10/92: 135

18643. PCD 949: *Piano recital.* Works by Brahms, Mendelssohn and Schumann. *Servadei, piano.*
● Gr 7/91: 91

18644. PCD 950: Schubert—Piano sonatas D. 625, D. 959; Impromptus, D. 899, no. 2-3. *Saba, piano.*
+ Gr 9/91: 105

18645. PCD 951: Schubert—Symphony no. 8; Rosamunde: Excerpts. *English Sinfonia; Groves, cond.*
+ Gr 9/91: 70

18646. PCD 952: Palestrina—Missa l'Homme armé; Missa Assumpta est Maria. *Pro Cantione Antiqua; Brown, cond.*
● EM 8/92: 499

18647. PCD 953: Mendelssohn—Piano concertos, no. 1-2; Capriccio brilliant. *Kuerti, piano; London Phil. Orch.; Freeman, cond.*
+ Gr 12/91: 75

18648. PCD 954: Strauss—Don Juan; Till Eulenspiegel; Death and transfiguration. *London Symphony Orch.; Butt, cond.*
+ ARG 11-12/91: 150
● Gr 9/91: 73

18649. PCD 955: Shostakovich—Symphony no. 10. *Hallé Orch.; Skrowaczewski, cond.*
● ARG 5-6/92: 134
+ Gr 10/91: 110

18650. PCD 956: Elgar—Symphony no. 1. *Hallé Orch.; Judd, cond.*
+ ARG 5-6/92: 57
+ Gr 1/92: 52

18651. PCD 957: Schubert—Octet in F major, D. 803. *Musicfest Octet.*
+ Gr 10/91: 133

18652. PCD 959: Beethoven—Clarinet trio, op. 11. Brahms—Clarinet trio. *Musicfest Trio.*
+ Gr 11/91: 112

18653. PCD 961: Vivaldi—Flute concertos op. 10. *Hall, flute; Divertimenti of London; Barritt, cond.*
+ Gr 12/91: 83

18654. PCD 963: Liszt—Piano sonata; Scherzo and march; Après une lecture de Dante. *Cohen, piano.*
+ Fa 3-4/96: 204
+ Gr 6/92: 68

18655. PCD 964: Bach—Harpsichord concerto, BWV 1052. Haydn—Keyboard concerto, H. XVIII, 2. Mozart—Piano concerto, K. 246. *Maione, Atri, Bruni, pianos; European Community Chamber Orch.; Aadland, cond.*
+ Gr 3/92: 38

18656. PCD 966: *Works for violin and orchestra.* Music of Glazunov, Tchaikovsky, Chausson, Sarasate, and Saint-Saëns. *Udagawa, violin; London Phil. Orch.; Klein, cond.*
- Fa 5-6/93: 391
+ Gr 3/92: 58

18657. PCD 967: Schubert—Symphonies no. 3-4; Overtures: Der häusliche Krieg; Der Teufel als Hydraulicus; In C in the Italian style. *English Sinfonia; Groves, cond.*
+ ARG 9-10/92: 157
● Gr 5/92: 48

18658. PCD 968: Schubert—Symphonies no. 2, 6; Die Zwillingsbrüder: overture. *English Sinfonia; Groves, cond.*
- Fa 3-4/93: 277
- Gr 3/93: 52

18659. PCD 970: Victoria—Surge propera Mass, Alma redemptoris mater. Gutierrez de Padilla—Ego flos campi Mass, Stabat mater. *Mixolydian; Schmidt, cond.*
+ ARG 5-6/92: 173
● EM 8/92: 499
+ Gr 5/92: 99

18660. PCD 972: Mahler—Symphony no. 4. *Hargan, soprano; Hallé Orch.; Skrowaczewski, cond.*
+ ARG 9-10/92: 126
- Gr 9/92: 75

18661. PCD 976: Tchaikovsky—The seasons; Romance; Valse-scherzo. *Lisney, piano.*
+ Gr 6/92: 70

18662. PCD 977: Beethoven—Violin concerto; Romances no. 1-2. *J. Laredo, violin & cond.; Scottish Chamber Orch.*
+ Gr 4/92: 44

18663. PCD 978: Haydn—Symphonies no. 28, 34, 43. *European Community Chamber Orch.; Aadland, cond.*
+ ARG 11-12/92: 132
+ Gr 9/92: 68

18664. PCD 979: Vivaldi—Concertos, RV 428 "Il gardellino;" RV 93; RV 413; RV 444; RV 498; RV 535. *Various performers.*
● Gr 3/92: 71

18665. PCD 988: Khachaturian—Spartacus excerpts. *Bolshoi Theater Orch.; Žiuraitis, cond.*
+ ARG 3-4/94: 112

18666. PCD 991: Music of Gaubert, Caplet, Fauré, Poulenc, Roussel and others. *Lloyd, flute; Holt, piano.*
+ Gr 9/92: 122

18667. PCD 992 (2 discs): Khachaturian—Spartacus. *Bolshoi Theater Orch.; Žiuraitis, cond.*
+ ARG 1-2/93: 109

18668. PCD 996: Tchaikovsky—Souvenir de Florence. Borodin—Quartet no. 2. *I Solisti di Zagreb; Ninic, cond.*
● ARG 11-12/92: 219

18669. PCD 999: Barrios—Guitar music. Ponce—Guitar music. *Kayath, guitar.*
- ARG 1-2/93: 73

18670. PCD 0001: Saint-Saëns—Symphony no. 3; Carnival of the animals; Cyprès et lauriers. *Y. Kim, J. Kim, pianos; Kynaston, organ; Philharmonia Orch; Yu, cond.*
+ Gr 3/96: 50

18671. PCD 0010: Arias by Rossini and Donizetti. *Lavender, tenor; Bournemouth Symphony Orch.; Williams, cond.*
+ Gr 3/96: 99

18672. PCD 1000: Bartók—Romanian folk dances. Shostakovich—Scherzo from op. 11; Chamber symphony op. 110a. *I Solisti di Zagreb; Ninic, cond.*
+ Gr 11/92: 55

18673. PCD 1001: Music for string orchestra by Hindemith, Britten, Warlock, Puccini, and Bartók. *European Community Chamber Orch.; Aadland, cond.*
+ ARG 3-4/93: 157

18674. PCD 1003: Sibelius—Karelia overture; Karelia suite; En saga; King Christian II: suite; The swan of Tuonela. *New Finnish Symphony Orch.; Engstrom, cond.*
+ ARG 3-4/93: 139
+ Fa 5-6/93: 323

18675. PCD 1004: Music of Martinů, Janáček, Roussel, and Grieg. *Zagreb Soloists.*
● ARG 5-6/93: 157
+ Fa 5-6/93: 405
- Gr 3/93: 58

18676. PCD 1006: Schubert—Trio no. 1 for piano, violin, and cello, D. 898. Dvořák—Trio no. 4 for violin, cello, and piano "Dumky". *London Mozart Trio.*
- Fa 3-4/93: 277
+ Gr 11/92: 137

18677. PCD 1007 (2 discs): Adam—Giselle. *Bolshoi Theater Orch.; Zhuraitis,*

cond.
+ Fa 3-4/93: 99

18678. PCD 1009: BEETHOVEN—Piano sonatas no. 30-32. *Papadopoulos, piano.*
• Gr 11/92: 150

18679. PCD 1011: *The Dolmetsch years: program 5.* Music of Bach and Walther. *C., M., & J. Dolmetsch, recorders; assisting instrumentalists.*
• Fa 3-4/93: 399

18680. PCD 1012: SVENDSEN—Romance for violin and piano, op. 26. SAINT-SAËNS—Havanaise; Introduction and rondo capriccioso. DVOŘÁK—Romance for violin and orchestra, op. 11. BEETHOVEN—Romances for violin and orchestra no. 1-2. BLOCH—Baal shem. *Sushanskaya, violin; English String Orch.; Boughton, cond.*
- Fa 5-6/93: 391

18681. PCD 1013: BARTÓK—Concerto for orchestra; The miraculous mandarin: suite; Kossuth. *Hungarian State Orch.; Ferenc, cond.*
+ Fa 3-4/93: 115
• Gr 7/93: 34

18682. PCD 1015 (2 discs): Karaoke opera. *Prague Radio Symphony Orch.; Prague Phil. Choir; Bigg, cond.*
+ ARG 5-6/93: 178
• ON 2/13/93: 33

18683. PCD 1016: TCHAIKOVSKY—Suite no. 3: Theme and variations. KODÁLY—Háry János: suite. JANÁČEK—Sinfonietta. *Hungarian State Orch.; Ferenc, cond.*
+ Fa 5-6/93: 340
• Gr 6/93: 48

18684. PCD 1018: *The Arnold Dolmetsch years: programme 6.* Music of Picchi, Cabanilles, Vitali, C.P.E. Bach, Howells, and Bach. *C., J., & M. Dolmetsch, recorders; assisting instrumentalists.* Recorded live.
+ Fa 5-6/93: 396

18685. DPCD 1019 (2 discs): MAHLER—Symphony no. 8 "Symphony of a thousand". *Vocalists; Symphonica of London; Morris, cond.*
+ Fa 5-6/93: 259

18686. PCD 1020: PROKOFIEV—Peter and the wolf. BRITTEN—The young person's guide to the orchestra. *McShane, narrator; Royal Phil. Orch.; Bátiz, cond.*
+ Fa 5-6/93: 282

18687. PCD 1021: BARTÓK—Dance suite; Two pictures; Four pieces. *Hungarian State Orch.; Ferenc, cond.*
+ ARG 5-6/93: 66
• Gr 5/93: 38

18688. PCD 1022: MOZART—Requiem (Süssmayr ed.). *Mirgová, KoŽená, Griffett, Klecker; Prague Concertino*

Notturno; Brno Academic Choir; Kröper, cond.
• Fa 5-6/93: 274

18689. PCD 1023: *Favorite overtures.* Music of Berlioz, Borodin, Mendelssohn, Wagner, Brahms, and Von Suppé. *BBC Phil. Orch.; Downes, cond.*
+ Fa 5-6/93: 405

18690. PCD 1024: BRAHMS—Serenades no. 1-2. *Westdeutsche Sinfonia; Joeres, cond.*
+ Fa 5-6/93: 175
+ Gr 5/93: 40

18691. PCD 1026: Carol concert. *Royal Choral Society; Royal Marines Fanfare Trumpeters; Birch, organ; Heltay, cond.*
- Fa 5-6/93: 373

18692. PCD 1027: *Violin favorites.* Music of Wieniawski, Prokofiev, Debussy, Bartók, Poulenc, Elgar, Massenet, Dvořák, Paganini, Saint-Saëns, Hemsi, and Bazzini. *Hasson, violin; Brown, piano.*
+ Fa 5-6/93: 391

18693. PCD 1028: BARTÓK—Suites no. 1-2 for orchestra. *Hungarian State Orch.; Ferenc, cond.*
+ Fa 5-6/93: 148

18694. PCD 1029: *My heart is like a singing bird.* Music of Parry, Stanford, Quilter, Warlock, and Gurney. *Leonard, soprano; Martineau, piano.*
+ Fa 5-6/93: 360

18695. PCD 1035: MAHLER—Lieder aus Des Knaben Wunderhorn; Lieder eines fahrenden Gesellen. *Baker, Evans, Hermann; London Phil. Orch; Symphonica of London; Morris, cond.* Reissues.
+ Gr 5/93: 87

18696. PCD 1036: *Guitar favorites.* Music of Barrios, Ponce, Villa-Lobos, Brouwer, Nobre, and others. *Kayath, guitar.*
• ARG 9-10/93: 234

18697. PCD 1039 (2 discs): ELGAR—Works for violin and piano. *Bouton, violin; Hall, piano.*
- Gr 10/93: 70

18698. PCD 1041: *Brahms and his friends.* Music of Brahms, Schumann, Dietrich, Grimm, and Kirchner. *Joeres, piano.*
• Fa 11-12/93: 493

18699. PCD 1042: WAGNER—Liebesmahl der Apostel. BRUCKNER—Helgoland. *Ambrosian Male Chorus; Symphonica of London; Morris, cond.*
+ ARG 11-12/93: 217
+ Fa 1-2/94: 346

18700. PCD 1043: *Opera favourites.* Music of Bizet, Saint-Saëns, Offenbach, Puccini, Rossini, Verdi, Mozart, and Leoncavallo. *McCulloch, soprano; Owens, mezzo-soprano; Oakman, tenor; Page, baritone; Prague Phil. Choir; Czech Symphony Orch.; Judd, cond.*
- Fa 11-12/93: 470

18701. PCD 1045: STRAVINSKY—Symphony in E♭; Firebird suite. *Royal Phil. Orch.; Atlas, cond.* Reissue.
+ ARG 9-10/93: 201
+ Fa 11-12/93: 411
+ Gr 6/94: 64

18702. PCD 1047: Hear my prayer: choirboy and choirgirl of the year. *Moralee, treble; Wight, soprano; Rosebery Chamber Orch.; Rosebery Chorus; Choristers of St. Barnabas, Dulwich; McVicker, cond.*
+ Fa 11-12/93: 475

18703. DPCD 1048 (2 discs): SCHUMANN—Symphonies (complete). *Philharmonia Orch.; Woods, cond.*
- Gr 12/93: 78

18704. PCD 1050: BRAHMS—Violin sonatas no. 1-3. *Wakbayashi, violin; Sturrock, piano.*
+ Gr 10/93: 62

18705. PCD 1051: RACHMANINOFF—Transcriptions. *Weber, piano; Michel, trumpet.*
• Fa 11-12/93: 354
• Gr 12/93: 89

18706. PCD 1052: VORISEK—Symphony, op. 24. SCHUBERT—Symphony no. 2. *Westdeutsche Sinfonia; Joeres, cond.*
+ Fa 9-10/94: 373
+ Gr 8/94: 56

18707. PCD 1054: MOZART—Bassoon concerto; Oboe concerto, K. 314; Clarinet concerto. *Azzolini, bassoon; Baccini, oboe; Carulli, clarinet; European Community Chamber Orch.; Aadland, cond.*
• Fa 1-2/94: 242
+ Gr 12/93: 72

18708. PCD 1057: GERSHWIN—Crazy for Gershwin. *Soloists; Orquestra Sinfonica de Mineria; Herrera de la Fuente, cond.; Xalapa Symphony Orch.; Brooks, Levine, conds.*
- Fa 11-12/93: 241

18709. PCD 1058: GERSHWIN—Piano music. *Bennett, piano.*
• Gr 5/94: 80

18710. PCD 1059: BRUCKNER Symphony no. 4. *Hallé Orch.; Skrowaczewski, cond.*
+ ARG 5-6/94: 81
• Fa 3-4/94: 153
+ Gr 3/94: 44

18711. PCD 1060: Music of Canteloube, Albinoni, Rodrigo, Vivaldi, Puccini, Prokofiev, Satie, Mozart, Haydn, and others. *Loew, cello; National Arts Centre Orch.; Casey, cond.*
- ARG 3-4/94: 202

18712. PCD 1062: BRAHMS—Violin concerto. SCHUMANN—Violin concerto. *Wanami, violin; London Phil. Orch.; Leaper, cond.*
- Fa 3-4/94: 144
+ Gr 4/94: 40

18713. PCD 1063: GRIEG—Piano concerto. DOHNÁNYI—Variations on a nursery song. LITOLFF—Concerto symphonique no. 4: scherzo. *Prats, piano; Royal Phil. Orch.; Bátiz, cond.*
• Fa 9-10/94: 302

18714. PCD 1064: The best of British song. *Ritchie, soprano; Purvis, piano.*
+ Fa 3-4/94: 277
• Gr 7/94: 102

18715. PCD 1065: Songs by Vaughan Williams, Butterworth, Ireland, Gurney, and Warlock. *Rolfe Johnson, tenor; Willison, piano.* Reissue.
+ ARG 5-6/94: 198
+ Fa 3-4/94: 376
+ Gr 4/94: 94

18716. DPCD 1068 (2 discs): HANDEL—Messiah. *Holton, Williamson, Griffett, Albert; Gioia della Musica Prague; Brown, cond.*
- Gr 5/94: 95

18717. PCD 1071: LISZT—A Faust symphony. *Necolescu, tenor; Hungarian State Orch.; D'Avalos, cond.*
+ Fa 3-4/94: 232
• Fa 5-6/94: 180
• Gr 5/94: 56

18718. PCD 1074: FALLA—Nights in the gardens of Spain. RACHMANINOFF—Rhapsody on a theme of Paganini. TCHAIKOVSKY—Piano concerto no. 1. *Osorio, piano; Orquesta Sinfonica de Xalapa; Orquestra Sinfonica de Mineria; Herrera de la Fuente, cond.* Reissue.
+ Fa 9-10/94: 188

18719. PCD 1075: *Opera intermezzi.* Music of Bizet, Ponchielli, Mascagni, Puccini, Offenbach, Leoncavallo, Massenet, and Verdi. *Philharmonia Orch.; Westrip, cond.*
+ Fa 9-10/94: 434

18720. PCD 1076: PALESTRINA—Missa brevis; Missa Lauda Sion; Motets. *Pro Cantione Antiqua; Brown, cond.*
- ARG 11-12/94: 167
• Gr 10/94: 183

18721. PCD 1077: *Twentieth-century English choral classics.* Music of Vaughan Williams, Elgar, Stanford, Britten, Rutter, Holst, James, Tippett, and

Warlock. *National Youth Chamber Choir; Brewer, cond.*
+ ARG 11-12/94: 249
+ Fa 9-10/94: 399

18722. PCD 1080: ELGAR—Enigma variations. STRAUSS—Sinfonia domestica. *National Youth Orch. of Great Britain; Seaman, cond.*
+ Gr 8/94: 46

18723. PCD 1081: RACHMANINOFF—Preludes. *Katin, piano.*
+ ARG 3-4/95: 161
- Fa 9-10/94: 304
+ Gr 1/95: 79

18724. PCD 1083: TCHAIKOVSKY—Serenade for strings. ARENSKY—Variations on a theme of Tchaikovsky. SUK—Serenade for strings. *Camerata Atlas; Atlas, cond.*
- ARG 1-2/95: 65
+ Fa 11-12/94: 400

18725. PCD 1084: SHOSTAKOVICH—Cello concerto no. 1; Cello sonata, op. 40. SAINT-SAËNS—Cello concerto no. 1. *Prieto, cello; Stevenson, piano; Orquestra Sinfonica de Xalapa; Orquestra Sinfonica de Mineria; Herrera de la Fuente, cond.*
• Fa 11-12/94: 379

18726. PCD 1095: BEETHOVEN—Piano sonatas no. 14, 21, 23, 26. *Osorio, piano.*
• ARG 5-6/95: 84

18727. PCD 1105: WEBER—Overtures. *Hallé Orch.; Skrowaczewski, cond.*
+ ARG 7-8/95: 224

18728. PCD 1106 (2 discs): HANDEL—Messiah. *Kenny, Rigby, Randle, White; Royal Choral Society; Royal Phil. Orch.; Hughes, cond.*
• ARG 3-4/95: 110

18729. PCD 1108: Music of Sibelius, Tchaikovsky, Dvořák, Elgar, and Grieg. *Serenata of London; Wilde, cond.*
+ Gr 2/95: 60

18730. PCD 1150: BEETHOVEN—Symphony no. 9 "Choral"; Fidelio overture. *Sutherland, Procter, Dermota, Mill; Chorale Du Brassus; Suisse romande Orch.; Ansermet, cond.*
+ ARG 1-2/92: 29

18731. PCD 1153: BEETHOVEN—Piano concertos no. 3-4. *Katchen, piano; London Symphony Orch.; Gamba, cond.* Reissue.
+ ARG 3-4/92: 26

18732. PCD 1154: MENDELSSOHN-BARTHOLDY—Piano concerto no. 1. LISZT—Piano concerto no. 2. *Katin, Katchen, piano; London Symphony Orch.; Collins, Argenta, conds.*
+ ARG 1-2/92: 76

18733. PCD 2028: FALLA—El amor brujo; La vida breve: interlude and dance; Three-cornered hat. *Herrera, mezzo-soprano; Sallinas, soprano; Mexico Symphony Orch.; Bátiz, cond.*
+ ARG 3-4/96: 112

18734. PCD 2032: BEETHOVEN—Piano sonatas no. 8, 14, 23. *Ogdon, piano.* Recorded 1986.
• ARG 5-6/96: 81

18735. IMPX 9028: MOZART—Divertimento, K. 136; Eine kleine Nachtmusik; A musical joke. *Stuttgart Chamber Orch.; Münchinger, cond.*
+ ARG 11-12/91: 108

18736. IMPX 9031: MENDELSSOHN—Violin concerto. BRUCH—Scottish fantasy. *Campoli, violin; London Phil. Orch.; Boult, cond.*
+ ARG 5-6/92: 84

18737. IMPX 9035: DVOŘÁK—Cello concerto. TCHAIKOVSKY—Rococo variations. *Walevska, cello; London Phil. Orch.; Gibson, cond.* Reissue.
+ ARG 3-4/92: 51

18738. IMPX 9039—9040 (2 separate discs): BRAHMS—Piano concertos no. 1-2; Rhapsodies op. 79. *Kovacevich, piano; London Symphony Orch.; C. Davis, cond.* Reissues.
• Gr 10/92: 56

18739. 30366 0003-2: LISZT—Organ music. *Kynaston, organ.*
+ Gr 7/96: 75

18740. 30366 0004-2: BARTÓK—Forty-four duos. *Mordkovitch, violin (both parts).*
• Gr 5/96: 72

18741. 30366 0006/7-2 (2 discs): GLAZUNOV—Raymonda; Concert waltz no. 1. *Kirov Orch.; Fedotov, cond.*
• ARG 1-2/97: 112
+ Gr 8/96: 46

18742. 30366 0072-2: *Russian opera dance spectacular.* Music of Glinka, Rimsky-Korsakov, Rubinstein, and others. *Kirov Orch.; Fedotov, cond.*
+ ARG 1-2/97: 112

INA-GRM

18743. C 1001: BAYLE—Motion-emotion; Couleurs de la nuit. *Electronic composition.*
+ Fa 1-2/87: 63

18744. C 1002: PARMEGIANI—La création du monde; Lumière noire; Métamorphose du vide; Signe de vie. *Parmegiani, electronics.*
• Fa 3-4/91: 319

18745. C 1004: SCHWARZ—Quatre saisons. *Schwarz, electronics & electro*

acoustics; Chaminé, baritone.
+ Fa 3-4/91: 380

18746. C 1005: REDOLFI—Too much sky; Desert tracks; Pacific tubular waves. *Redolfi, electronics & electro- acoustics.*
□ Fa 3-4/91: 337

INA MEMOIRE VIVE

18747. 252020: Music of Machaut, Isaac, Sermisy, Dowland, and others. *Cuénod, tenor; Cohen, lute; Dobos, piano.* Recorded 1960, 1976, 1980.
+ ARG 1-2/97: 226

18748. 262002: Music of Bizet, Gounod, Berlioz, Chausson, and others. *Danco, soprano; Boutry, Agosti, piano.* Recorded 1955.
+ ARG 11-12/94: 261

18749. 262003: FRANCK—Piano quintet, op. 14. FAURÉ—Piano quintet no. 2. *Perlemuter, piano; Quatuor Parrenin.* Reissue.
+ Fa 3-4/95: 170

18750. 262005: HAYDN—Piano sonatas no. 4, 47, 54, 60. *Planès, piano.*
+ ARG 1-2/95: 113
• Fa 3-4/93: 184
+ Fa 3-4/95: 186

18751. 262006: TOURNEMIRE—Poème mystique; La sagesse; Sonate-poème; Musique orante. *Puig-Roget, piano; Plantey, tenor; Erlih, violin; Quatuor de l' O.R.T.F.*
+ Fa 11-12/94: 404

18752. 262007: BRAHMS—Violin concerto (2 performances). *Oistrakh, Ferras, violin; ORTF Phil. Orch.; Bruck, cond.* Recorded 1967, 1966.
• Fa 3-4/95: 140
+ Gr 9/93: 43

18753. 262008: *Teresa Stich-Randall: recital au Festival d' Aix-en-Provence 1956.* Music of Mozart, Brahms, R. Strauss, Debussy, and Schumann. *Stich-Randall, soprano; Rosbaud, piano.* Recorded live 1956.
+ Fa 3-4/95: 347

18754. 262010: DEBUSSY—Songs. *Kruysen, baritone; Poulenc, Richard, piano.* Recorded 1962-1965.
• ARG 11-12/95: 111
• Fa 9-10/95: 186

18755. 262012: PROKOFIEV—Cello sonata, op. 119. CASSADÓ—Cello suite. BEETHOVEN—Cello sonata no. 3. HINDEMITH—Cello sonata, op. 25, no. 3. *Starker, cello; Planès, piano.* Recorded 1978-1983.
+ ARG 3-4/95: 234
+ Fa 3-4/95: 369

18756. 262014: Music of Debussy, Ravel, Fauré, and Honegger. *Kolassi,*

mezzo-soprano; Collard, Bienvenu, Gallay, piano; instrumental ensemble; Chabrun, cond. Recorded 1957-62.
+ Fa 9-10/95: 373

18757. 262015 (2 discs): MOZART—Così fan tutte. *Stich-Randall, Berganza, Adani, Alva, Panerai, Cortis; Aix-en- Provence Festival Chorus; Paris Conservatoire Orch.; Rosbaud, cond.* Recorded live 1957.
+ Fa 3-4/95: 237

18758. 262016 (2 discs): BEETHOVEN—Six bagatelles, op. 126. LISZT—Piano sonata. BACH—The art of the fugue. SCRIABIN—Piano sonata no. 9 "Black mass"; Desire; Poem, op. 59, no. 1. *Vieru, piano.* Recorded live.
+ Fa 3-4/95: 385

18759. 262017: *Xavier Darasse.* Music of Lebègue, Nivers, M. Lanes, Raison, and Bach. *Darasse, organ.*
+ Fa 5-6/95: 409

18760. 262018: *Paul Derenne.* Music of Gounod, Satie, Rosenthal, Milhaud, Sauguet, Debussy, Ravel, Roussel, and Poulenc. *Derenne, tenor; Sauguet, piano.* Recorded live 1957-1959.
+ Fa 3-4/95: 352

18761. 262019: POULENC—La voix humaine. *Rhodes, soprano; Orch. National de France; Marty, cond.* Broadcast recording 1976.
+ ARG 7-8/95: 169
• Fa 5-6/95: 292

18762. 262021: Music of Forqueray, Duphly, and Bach. *Ross, harpsichord.*
+ ARG 9-10/96: 244

INAK

18763. 849: SCHUMANN—Symphonic etudes, op. 13; Arabeske, op. 18; Toccata, op. 7. *Ohmen, piano.*
+ Fa 7-8/88: 251

18764. 862: HANDEL—Suite no. 7; Xerxes: Ombra mai fù. LAWALL—Guitar music. *Lawall, guitar.*
- Fa 7-8/88: 173

18765. 8617: PERGOLESI—Stabat Mater. *Cohen, Rolef; Ankor Conservatory Children's Choir; Roloff, organ; Israel Sinfonietta Beer Sheva; Rodan, cond.*
• Fa 7-8/88: 217

18766. 8619: BACH—Toccatas and fugues; Prelude and fugue in E major, BWV 566. *Kaunzinger, organ.*
• ARG 11-12/88: 11
• Fa 7-8/88: 109

18767. 8703: PAGANINI—Guitar music. *Legnani, guitar.*
+ Fa 7-8/88: 215

18768. 8704: Music of Bach, Meranger, Bohm, Zehm, and Vivaldi. *Heidelberger Kammerduo.*
• Fa 1-2/89: 107

18769. 8707: SCRIABIN—Piano music. *Margulis, piano.*
+ Fa 1-2/89: 264

18770. 8811: SOR—Preludes, op. 29, no. 5, 12; Grand sonata, op. 25. LAWALL—Three Asiatic pictures, op. 27; Big bang, from op. 29. *Lawall, guitar.*
+ Fa 9-10/89: 421

INDEPENDENT ARTIST GUILD

18771. VT 22560: *Rosamund.* Music of anon., Dowland, De Countie, Rosseter, Ferrabosco, Daniel, Byrd, Phillips, Marchant, Bacheler, and Gilbert. *Gilbert, lute.*
- Fa 7-8/93: 296

INDIANA UNIVERSITY SCHOOL OF MUSIC

18772. IUSM 01: WEIGL—String quartet no. 1. TURINA—Oracion del torero. MALIPIERO—Rispetti e strambotti. *Christopher Quartet.*
• Fa 9-10/89: 377

18773. IUSM 02: ORREGO-SALAS— Tangos; Glosas; Serenata; Mobili; Violin concerto. *Indiana University New Music Ensemble; Sollberger, cond.; Indiana University Symphony; Baldner, cond.*
+ ARG 7-8/94: 147

INNOVA

18774. 002 (LP): *The Minnesota Composers Forum presents the Minneapolis Artists Ensemble.* Music of Proto, Larsen, Tartaglia, and Ives. *Minneapolis Artists Ensemble.*
+ Fa 7-8/88: 325
+ Opus 4/88: 41

18775. 106: *Free fall.* TIBBETTS—Four letters. OLSON—Three days in the Arrowhead. GWIAZDA—Sinfony. DEVINE—Stop thinking or get out of the way. MORIARTY—Out of touch-Albert. *Minnesota Composers Forum.*
+ DA 3/89: 59
+ Fa 7-8/88: 203

18776. 107: *Building higher nests.* Music of Kinney, Price, Wegren, Phillips, and Kosch. *Kinney, Cora, cellos; Mensah, Anderson, percussion; Price, violin, violectra, mandolin & synthesizers; Wegren, Johnson, piano; Lark Quartet.*
+ ARG 7-8/90: 128

18777. 110: Music of Childs, Paulus, S. Barnett, C. Barnett, Franklin, Hodkinson, and Larsen. *Dale Warland Singers; Rubino, piano.*
+ ARG 7-8/92: 279

INNOVA

18778. 111: *Sur pointe*. Music of Greenberg, Dzubay, Hess, and Peterson. *Alexander Quartet.*
+ ARG 7-8/95: 268

18779. 401 (4 discs): PARTCH— Compositions. *Various performers.* Reissues.
+ ARG 9-10/96: 176

18780. 500: *Heartbeats: new songs from Minnesota for the AIDS quilt songbook.* Music of Harbison, Houtz, Vandervelde, Larsen, Barnett, Bolcom, Olsen, Carnahan, Jennings, Wilson, Kallman, Kernis, Musto, Franklin, and DeBlasio. *Various performers.*
+ Fa 9-10/95: 430

18781. 502: *Music of the next moment.* Music of Mason, Burrier, Marth, Nielson, Hultgren, Ross, and Paredes. *Hultgren, cello; Geary, percussion; Collins, guitar; Lecuona, piano.*
+ ARG 1-2/97: 245

18782. 503: MACY—Reflections; Solstice and equinox; Maria music; Ostinato studies. *Jensen, Dahl, piano; Bogorad, Kuenzel, flute.*
+ ARG 11-12/96: 307

INTAGLIO

18783. INCD 7011: ELGAR—Sea pictures; Symphony no. 1. *K. Meyer, mezzo-soprano; Hallé Orch., Barbirolli, cond.* Recorded live 1970.
+ ARG 5-6/92: 54
+ St 5/92: 203

18784. INCD 7021 (2 discs): DELIUS—A mass of life; Requiem. *Te Kanawa, Bowden, Dowd, Shirley-Quirk, vocalists; BBC Symphony Orch. & Chorus; Del Mar, cond.; Harper, Hemley, vocalists; Liverpool Phil. Orch. & Choir; Groves, cond.* Reissue.
+ ARG 5-6/92: 46

18785. INCD 7031: L. BOULANGER— Psalm 24; Pie Jesu; Du fond de l'abime. FAURÉ—Requiem. *BBC Symphony Orch.; BBC Chorus; N. Boulanger, cond.* Recorded live 1968.
+ ARG 7-8/92: 103

18786. INCD 7041: BANTOCK—Hebridean symphony; Pagan symphony. *BBC Scottish Symphony Orch.; Boult, cond.; BBC Northern Symphony Orch.; Hanford, cond.* Reissue.
- ARG 5-6/92: 29
+ Fa 5-6/92: 118

18787. INCD 7061: BRAHMS—Violin concerto. BERG—Violin concerto. *Francescatti, violin; Vienna Phil. Orch.; Szigeti, violin; NBC Symphony Orch.; Mitropoulos, cond.* Recorded live.
• Fa 5-6/92: 127

18788. INCD 7071: MOZART—Piano concerto no. 17. LISZT—Piano concerto no. 2. CHOPIN—Andante spianato and grand polonaise. *Richter, piano; Philadelphia Orch.; Ormandy, cond.; Hungarian State Orch.; Ferencsik, cond.; London Symphony Orch.; Kondrashin, cond.* Recorded live 1970, 1961.
+ ARG 5-6/92: 95

18789. INCD 7081: HINDEMITH—Cello concerto. LALO—Cello concerto. TCHAIKOVSKY—Variations on a rococo theme. *Rostropovich, cello; London Symphony Orch.; Rozhdestvensky, cond.* Recorded live 1967.
+ Fa 9-10/92: 260

18790. INCD 7091: BRUCKNER— Symphony no. 9. *BBC Symphony Orch.; Horenstein, cond.* Recorded live.
+ ARG 9-10/92: 92

18791. INCD 7111: BEETHOVEN—Piano sonatas no. 17, 18, 31. *Richter, piano.* Recorded live 1965.
+ Fa 9-10/92: 176

18792. INCD 7131: BRAHMS—Violin concerto; Double concerto. *Perlman, violin; Rostropovich, cello; St. Louis Symphony Orch.; Carvalho, cond; London Symphony Orch.; Rozhdestvensky, cond.* Recorded live 1968, 1967.
+ Fa 11-12/92: 206

18793. INCD 7151: BLISS—Cello concerto. BRITTEN—Cello symphony. *Rostropovich, cello; English Chamber Orch.; Britten, cond.; London Symphony Orch.; Rozhdestvensky, cond.* Recorded live 1970, 1967.
+ ARG 11-12/92: 90

18794. INCD 7161: BEETHOVEN—Piano sonatas no. 27-28; Variations in F; Variations in D; Eroica variations. *Richter, piano.* Recorded live 1965, 1970.
+ ARG 11-12/92: 82
+ Fa 1-2/93: 107

18795. INCD 7171: SCHOENBERG—Pelleas und Melisande. SIBELIUS—Symphony no. 7. *Hallé Orch.; Helsinki Symphony Orch.; Barbirolli, cond.* Recorded live 1968.
- ARG 11-12/92: 206
+ Fa 11-12/92: 356

18796. INCD 7201: BACH—Concerto for two violins. MOZART—Violin concerto no. 3. SIBELIUS—Violin concerto. *Szeryng, violin & cond.; García, violin; English Chamber Orch.; Helsinki Chamber Orch.; Barbirolli, cond.* Recorded live.
• Fa 11-12/92: 186

18797. INCD 7231: WALTON—Symphony no. 1. WAGNER—A Faust overture. *Royal Phil. Orch.; BBC Northern Symphony Orch.; Horenstein, cond.* Recorded 1971.

+ ARG 1-2/93: 166
• Fa 1-2/93: 271

18798. INCD 7241: SHOSTAKOVICH— Violin concertos no. 1-2. *D. Oistrakh, violin; Philharmonia Orch.; M. Shostakovich, cond.; USSR State Symphony Orch.; Svetlanov, cond.*
+ ARG 3-4/93: 137

18799. INCD 7251: SHOSTAKOVICH—Cello concertos no. 1-2. *Rostropovich, cello; Czech Phil. Orch.;Kondrashin, cond.; London Symphony Orch.; Rozhdestvensky, cond.* Recorded live 1960, 1967.
+ Fa 1-2/93: 237

18800. INCD 7272 (2 discs): BRUCKNER—Symphony no. 8. SIMPSON— Symphony no. 3 (rehearsal). *London Symphony Orch.; Royal Phil. Orch.; Horenstein, cond.* Recorded live 1970, 1966.
+ ARG 1-2/93: 84
+ Fa 1-2/93: 120

18801. INCD 7291: MAHLER—Symphony no. 4. *Harper, soprano; BBC Symphony Orch.; Barbirolli, cond.* Recordee live 1967.
- ARG 3-4/93: 106
+ Fa 1-2/93: 183

18802. INCD 7301: ELGAR—Cello concerto. PROKOFIEV—Cello concertino. TCHAIKOVSKY—Pezzo capriccioso. *Rostropovich, cello; London Symphony Orch.; Rozhdestvensky, cond.* Recorded live 1967.
• ARG 3-4/93: 76

18803. INCD 7311: RUBBRA— Symphonies, no. 6, 8. *Royal Phil. Orch.; Boult, cond.; Royal Liverpool Phil. Orch.; Groves, cond.* Recorded 1971.
+ ARG 5-6/93: 127
+ Fa 1-2/93: 224

18804. INCD 7331: SCHOENBERG— Chamber symphony no. 1, op. 9b. SIBELIUS—Symphony no. 5. *BBC Northern Symphony Orch.; Horenstein, cond.*
- ARG 5-6/93: 137
- Fa 5-6/93: 312

18805. INCD 7342 (2 discs): CHERUBINI—Les deux journées (The water carrier). *Vocalists; Royal Phil. Orch.; Beecham, cond.* Recorded live, 1947.
+ ARG 5-6/93: 181
+ Fa 5-6/93: 184
+ ON 3/5/94: 36
+ Op 8/93: 1002

18806. INCD 7351: ELGAR—Cello concerto; The music makers. *Du Pré, cello; Thomas, contralto; BBC Symphony Orch.; London Symphony Orch.; Sargent, cond.*
+ ARG 5-6/93: 83

18807. INCD 7361: BEETHOVEN—Cantata on the death of Emperor Joseph II, WoO 87; Grosse Fuge, op. 133. *Te Kanawa; Newman; Barrett; Langdon; BBC Chorus & Choral Society; BBC Symphony Orch.; Colin Davis, cond.* Recorded live 1968-70.
• ARG 9-10/93: 92
+ Fa 5-6/93: 149

18808. INCD 7381: NIELSEN—Symphonies no. 3, 6. *BBC Northern Symphony Orch.; Hallé Orch.; Horenstein, cond.*
• ARG 9-10/93: 165

18809. INCD 7401: HOLST—Choral symphony; Choral fantasia. *Harper, soprano; BBC Symphony Orch. & Chorus; Sargent, cond.; Coster, mezzo-soprano; London Phil. Orch.; John Alldis Choir; Boult, cond.* Recorded live 1964 and 1967.
+ Fa 7-8/93: 155

18810. INCD 7491: MAHLER—Symphony no. 2. *Woodland, soprano; Baker, alto; choruses; London Symphony Orch.; Stokowski, cond.* Recorded live 1963.
+ ARG 1-2/94: 119
+ Fa 11-12/93: 304

18811. INCD 7511: DVOŘÁK—Piano concerto. GRIEG—Piano concerto. *Richter, piano; London Symphony Orch.; Kondrashin, cond.; Bergen Phil. Orch.; Oistrakh, cond.* Recorded 1961, 1968.
+ ARG 5-6/94: 89

18812. INCD 7521: NABOKOV—Tchaikovsky variations. LEVITIN—Suite. B. TCHAIKOVSKY—Partita. *Rostropovich, cello; Philadelphia Orch.; Ormandy, cond.; London Symphony Orch.; Rozhdestvensky, cond.*
+ ARG 11-12/93: 232
+ Fa 1-2/94: 328

18813. INCD 7541: BRUCKNER—Symphony no. 5. *BBC Symphony Orch.; Horenstein, cond.*
• ARG 1-2/94: 89

18814. INCD 7552: BLISS—The olympians. *Minty, Dickerson, Robinson; other vocalists; Ambrosian Singers; Polyphonia Orch.; Fairfax, cond.*
+ ARG 1-2/94: 82
+ Fa 11-12/93: 190

18815. INCD 7561: SHOSTAKOVICH—Piano quintet; String quartet no. 12. *Richter, piano; Borodin Quartet.*
+ ARG 1-2/94: 154
+ Fa 1-2/94: 311

18816. INCD 7571: VAUGHAN WILLIAMS—Tudor portraits; Thanksgiving for victory. *Sudaby, Harrison, Walker; BBC Northern Singers; BBC Symphony; Boult, cond.*
+ ARG 1-2/94: 168

INTAVOLATURA

18817. GLP CD-4003: PETTERSEN—Sogno de Orfeo; A Niente; Canon liber. BRINDLE—Polifemo de oro. *Pettersen, guitar, lute, & percussion.*
- ARG 7-8/90: 84
• Fa 9-10/90: 332

INTEGRA

18818. IMCD 951: *Sing me to heaven.* GAWTHROP—Choral music. *Utah State University Chamber Singers; Kesling, cond.*
+ Fa 3-4/96: 168

18819. IMCD 953: *Hornpipes.* Music of Handel, Mouret, Bach, Gounod, Mozart, Pettit, Mathias, Purcell, Clarke, Ravel, Pezel, and Debussy. *Siebert, trumpet; Pettit, organ.*
+ Fa 3-4/96: 365

INTERCORD SAPHIR

18820. 160.857 (LP): *Welte-Philharmonie-Orgel.* Music of Reger, Dupré, Bonnet, and Gigout. *Reger, Bonnet, Dupré, Gigout, organ.*
+ Fa 3-4/87: 264

18821. 160.858 (LP): *Welte-Philharmonie-Orgel.* BACH—Organ music. *Straube, Dupré, Fischer, Hindermann, organ.*
+ Fa 11-12/87: 89

18822. 180.824 (2 LPs): BACH—Kunst der Fuge. *Bell' Arte Ensemble.*
- Fa 9-10/86: 84

18823. 180.834 (2 LPs): BRAHMS—String sextets (complete). *Stuttgarter Solisten.*
• Fa 9-10/86: 117

18824. 180.844 (2 LPs): BACH—French suites, BWV 812-817; Duets, BWV 802-05. *Jaccottet, harpsichord.*
• Fa 9-10/86: 88

18825. 180.846 (2 LPs): BACH—Italian concerto; Chromatic fantasy and fugue; Partita in B minor; Goldberg variations. *Jaccottet, harpsichord.*
• Fa 9-10/86: 88

18826. 180.858 (2 LPs): BACH—Anna Magdalena notebook. *Scheurich, harpsichord; Schädle, soprano; Brachmann, cello; Die Stuttgart Hymnus Chorknaben.*
+ Fa 9-10/86: 84

18827. 185.703 (3 LPs): *Die Flötensonaten.* HANDEL—Flute and recorder sonatas. *Linde, recorder; Möhring, flute; Scheidegger, harpsichord; Koch, viola da gamba; Michel, cello.*
+ Fa 9-10/86: 157

18828. 185.704 (3 LPs): CORELLI—Concerti grossi, op. 6. *Egger, Schmidt, violin; Muckel, cello; Southwest German Chamber Orch.; Wich, cond.*
+ Fa 9-10/86: 130

18829. 185.709 (3 LPs): BACH—Harpsichord music. *Jaccottet, harpsichord.*
• Fa 9-10/86: 88

18830. 185.756 (4 LPs): SCHUBERT—Schöne Müllerin; Winterreise; Schwanengesang. *Jelden, baritone; Wagner, Čech, piano.*
- Fa 9-10/86: 221

18831. 820.510: BACH—Masses, BWV 233-234. *Speiser, Russ, Kesteren, Stämpfli; Gächinger Kantorei; Bach Collegium Stuttgart; Rilling, cond.*
• ARG 5-6/95: 74

18832. 820.546—820.548 (3 separate discs): MOZART—Piano concertos no. 9, 16, 18, 20, 24, 26. *Firkušný, piano; Southwest German Radio Symphony Orch.; Bour, cond.*
+ ARG 3-4/95: 148 (820.546)
+ Fa 3-4/95: 237 (820.546)
+ Gr 8/94: 50

18833. 820.574: BEETHOVEN—Symphony no. 6. *Radio-Sinfonieorchester Stuttgart; Münchinger, cond.*
• Fa 9-10/95: 142

18834. 820.725: BACH—Masses: in F major, BWV 233; in A major, BWV 234. *Speiser, Russ, Van Kesteren, Faulstich, Stämpfli; Gächinger Kantorei; Bach-Collegium Stuttgart; Rilling, cond.*
+ Fa 9-10/88: 89

18835. 820.726: HANDEL—Concerti grossi, op. 3. *Sous, Schnell, oboes; Lautenbacher, Lutz, violins; Galling, harpsichord; Süddeutsche Kammerphilharmonie Stuttgart; Wich, cond.*
+ Fa 9-10/88: 162

18836. 820.728: MOZART—Symphonies no. 28-29, 33. *Stuttgart Chamber Orch.; Münchinger, cond.*
• Fa 9-10/88: 218

18837. 820.730: MOZART—String quartets no. 21-23. *Melos Quartet Stuttgart.*
- Fa 9-10/88: 216

18838. 820.731: SCHUBERT—Piano quintet, D. 667; Piano trio no. 1. *Stuttgart Piano Trio; Kussmaul, viola; Hörtnagel, double bass.*
• Fa 9-10/88: 252 (Quintet)
+ Fa 9-10/88: 252 (Trio)

18839. 820.732: BRAHMS—String sextets no. 1-2. *Stuttgarter Solisten.*
+ Fa 9-10/88: 119

INTERCORD SAPHIR

18840. 820.733: BRAHMS—Liebeslieder Waltzes; Neue Liebeslieder Waltzes. *Gächinger Kantorei; Uhde, Werner, pianos; Rilling, cond.*
- Fa 9-10/88: 119

18841. 820.735—820.736 (2 discs): VIVALDI—L'estro armonico, op. 3. *Terebesi, Muroya, Fülöp, Egger, violins; Muckel, cello; Southwest German Chamber Orch. Pforzheim.*
• Fa 3-4/89: 332

18842. 820.737—820.738 (2 separate discs): BACH—Harpsichord concertos. *Kipnis, Schell-Pluth, Schrader, Hertzberg, harpsichord; Stuttgart Chamber Orch.; Münchinger, cond.*
+ ARG 9-10/89: 19
+ Fa 3-4/89: 74

18843. 820.739: BACH—Kunst der Fuge. *Bell' Arte Ensemble.*
• Fa 3-4/89: 72

18844. 820.740: TELEMANN—Twelve fantasies for solo violin. *Kalafusz, violin.*
+ ARG 9-10/89: 110
+ Fa 3-4/89: 314

18845. 820.741: MOZART—Serenade for winds no. 10, K. 361. *Mozart-Ensemble Stuttgart; Wich, cond.*
- Fa 3-4/89: 226

18846. 820.742: ROSSINI—Flute quartets no. 1-4. *Nicolet, Aurèle; German String Trio.*
• Fa 3-4/89: 253

18847. 820.743: SMETANA—String quartet no. 1. JANÁČEK—String quartet no. 2. WOLF—Italian serenade. *Melos Quartet Stuttgart.*
- Fa 3-4/89: 283

18848. 820.744: BRUCKNER—String quintet in F major. HAYDN—String quartet, op. 20, no. 4. *Melos Quartet Stuttgart; Santiago, 2nd viola.*
+ ARG 7-8/89: 31
- Fa 3-4/89: 126

18849. 820.749: Guitar music of Tárrega, Carulli, Sanz, Albéniz, Sor, Bach, Newsidler, Handel, and Anon. *Lawall, guitar.*
• Fa 3-4/89: 284

18850. 820.759—820.762 (4 separate discs): BACH—Well-tempered clavier. *Jaccottet, harpsichord.*
+ ARG 1-2/90: 18
• Fa 1-2/90: 105

18851. 820.763: BACH—Goldberg variations; Italian concerto; Chromatic fantasy and fugue. *Jaccottet, harpsichord.*
+ ARG 1-2/90: 18
+ Fa 1-2/90: 105

18852. 820.764—820.765 (2 separate discs): BACH—French suites; Clavier-Übung, pt. 3: 4 duets, BWV 802-806; Clavierübung, pt. 2: Partita in B minor. *Jaccottet, harpsichord.*
+ ARG 1-2/90: 18
+ Fa 1-2/90: 105

18853. 820.767: BACH—Harpsichord concertos no. 3, 6-7; Concerto for 2 harpsichords. *Kipnis, Schell-Pluth; Stuttgart Chamber Orch.; Münchinger, cond.*
+ ARG 1-2/90: 16
- Fa 3-4/90: 110

18854. 820.768: HANDEL—Water music: Suite. HAYDN—Symphony no. 88. MOZART—Symphony no. 25. *Stuttgart Chamber Orch.; Münchinger, cond.*
• Fa 3-4/90: 187

18855. 820.769: HANDEL—Sonatas for flute and recorder. *Möhring, flute; Linde, recorder; Scheidegger, harpsichord; Koch, viola da gamba; Michel, cello.*
+ ARG 3-4/90: 57
+ Fa 3-4/90: 187

18856. 820.770—820.771 (2 discs): CORELLI—Concerti grossi, op. 6. *Egger, Schmidt, Muckel, Lehrndorfer; South German Chamber Orch.; Wich, cond.*
+ ARG 1-2/90: 41
• Fa 3-4/90: 168

18857. 820.772—820.773 (2 separate discs): HAYDN—Paris symphonies. *South German Chamber Orch.; Wich, cond.*
• Fa 3-4/90: 194

18858. 820.774: SCHUBERT—Winterreise. *Jelden, tenor; Wagner, piano.*
• Fa 3-4/90: 287

18859. 820.775: ORFF—Carmina Burana. *Hartmann, Brünner, Knoll; Salzburg Mozarteum Chorus & Orch.; Prestel, cond.*
- Fa 3-4/90: 252

18860. 820.778: MOZART—Piano concertos no. 18, 25. *Firkušný, piano; Southwest German Radio Orch.; Bour, cond.*
• ARG 1-2/92: 82

18861. 830.616: Music of Smetana, Dvořák, and Tchaikovsky. *London Festival Orch.; Warren, cond.*
- Fa 11-12/86: 222

18862. 830.802: MOZART—Serenade no. 13, K. 525. SCHUBERT—Symphony no. 8. *Stuttgart Chamber Orch.; Münchinger, cond.*
• ARG 7-8/86: 78
+ Fa 5-6/86: 198

18863. 830.809: BRAHMS—Quartets for 4 voices and piano: op. 31, no. 1-3; op. 64, no. 1-3; op. 92, no. 1-4; op. 112, no. 1-2. *Stuttgart Chamber Choir; Bernius,*
Rothkopf, piano.
+ ARG 1-2/87: 19
+ Fa 5-6/86: 122

18864. 830.810: BACH—Inventions and sinfonias BWV 772-801; Toccatas BWV 914-916. *Jaccottet, harpsichord.*
• Fa 9-10/86: 90

18865. 830.811: BACH—Preludes BWV 924-928, 930-931, 933-943, 999; Toccatas BWV 910-913. *Jaccottet, harpsichord.*
• Fa 9-10/86: 91

18866. 830.832: SCHUBERT—Mirjams Siegesgesang; Gott im Ungewitter; Der 23 Psalm; An die Sonne; Coronach; Hymne an den Unendlichen; Gott der Weltschöpfer. *Laki, soprano; Rothkopf, piano; Stuttgart Chamber Choir; Bernius, cond.*
• ARG 1-2/90: 84
+ Fa 11-12/89: 345

18867. 830.833: TCHAIKOVSKY—Symphony no. 5. *Bamberg Symphony Orch.; Bertini, cond.*
+ ARG 1-2/90: 97
- Fa 11-12/89: 381

18868. 830.834: DVOŘÁK—Piano quartets (complete). *Odeon Trio; Moog, viola.*
+ ARG 3-4/90: 45
• Fa 11-12/89: 195

18869. 830.835: BRAHMS—Liebeslieder. *Prey, baritone; Deutsch, piano.* Recorded 1982.
+ ARG 1-2/95: 88
+ Fa 5-6/88: 92

18870. 830.836: LOEWE—Ballads. *Prey, baritone; Deutsch, piano.*
+ ARG 9-10/91: 88

18871. 830.837: SCHUBERT—Lieder. *Prey, baritone; Deutsch, cond.* Recorded live 1982.
+ ARG 3-4/92: 134

18872. 830.846: BARRIOS—La catedral; Julia Florida; Confesion; Choro da Saudade; Un sueno en la Floresta; Preludio in G minor; Mazurka apasionada; Vals de la primavera; Vals no. 3-4. *Lieske, guitar.*
+ Fa 5-6/88: 75

18873. 830.847: *Italienische Barockmusik.* Music of Corelli, Boni, Vivaldi, Pasquini, and Mancini. *Hannover Baroque Ensemble.*
+ Fa 5-6/88: 267

18874. 830.848: BACH—Fantasy and fugue in G minor; Toccata and fugue in F; Passacaglia and fugue in C minor; Trio in D minor, S. 583; Canzona in D minor; Fugues in B minor and C minor, S. 579 and 574. *Bossert, organ.*
+ ARG 5-6/92: 23
+ Fa 5-6/88: 72

18875. 830.849: DVOŘÁK—Piano trios no. 3-4. *Odeon Trio.*
+ ARG 3-4/89: 33
+ Fa 11-12/88: 179

18876. 830.850: BACH—Harpsichord music. *Jaccottet, theorbo-harpsichord.*
+ Fa 11-12/88: 119

18877. 830.851: BEETHOVEN—Songs. *Schreier, tenor; Shetler, piano.*
+ Fa 11-12/88: 134

18878. 830.852: BACH—Ich habe genug, BWV 82; Ich will den Kreuzstab gerne tragen, BWV 56. *Prey, baritone; Kammerchor der Frankfurter Singakademie; Deutsche Bachsolisten; Winschermann, cond.*
+ Fa 11-12/88: 117

18879. 830.853: MOZART—Serenade no. 7; March, K. 249. *Kalafusz, violin; Stuttgart Chamber Orch.; Münchinger, cond.*
+ Fa 11-12/88: 235

18880. 830.860: MENDELSSOHN—Six preludes and fugues op. 35 (arr. Bossert). *Bossert, organ.*
• Fa 11-12/89: 278

18881. 830.861—830.862 (2 separate discs): BACH—English suites. *Jaccottet, harpsichord.*
+ ARG 11-12/89: 30
• Fa 11-12/89: 117-118

18882. 830.863: DVOŘÁK—Piano quintet no. 2; Piano trio no. 2. *Leonhard, piano; Panocha String Quartet; Odeon Trio.*
• ARG 3-4/90: 45
+ Fa 11-12/89: 196

18883. 830.864: BRUCKNER—Symphony no. 7 (Haas ed.). *Southwest German Radio Symphony Orch.; Gielen, cond.*
• ARG 11-12/89: 50
+ Fa 11-12/89: 162

18884. 830.867: BRAHMS—Concerto for violin and cello; Symphony no. 4. *Kaplan, violin; Geringas, cello; Southwest German Radio Symphony Orch.; Gielen, cond.*
+ ARG 5-6/90: 32
• Fa 5-6/90: 131

18885. 830.868: MOZART—Clarinet concerto; Piano concerto K. 503 . *Pencz, clarinet; Bishop-Kovacevich, piano; Southwest German Radio Symphony Orch.; Gielen, cond.*
- ARG 5-6/90: 80
• Fa 5-6/90: 224

18886. 830.869: STRAVINSKY—Oedipus Rex. *Schreckenbach, Hollweg, Baldin, Hermann, Bracht, Bartels; RIAS Chamber Choir; Southwest German Radio Symphony Orch., Baden-Baden; Leitner, cond.*

• ARG 7-8/90: 114
• Fa 7-8/90: 285

18887. 830.870: MOZART—Symphonies no. 36, 40. *Southwest German Radio Symphony Orch.; Gielen, cond.*
- ARG 3-4/90: 84
- Fa 5-6/90: 236

18888. 830.872: BRUCKNER—Symphony no. 5. *Southwest German Radio Symphony Orch.; Gielen, cond.*
• ARG 11-12/90: 42

18889. 830.874: BACH—Sonatas for viola da gamba and harpsichord. *Pank, viola da gamba; Bernstein, harpsichord.*
+ ARG 3-4/92: 23

18890. 830.899: *Virtuoso orchestral music.* Opera overtures of Mozart, Rossini, Weber, Glinka, and Smetana. *Polish Chamber Orch.; Rajski, cond.*
+ Fa 5-6/95: 433

18891. 845,198: *Adios Nonino: Tango nuevo: in memoriam Astor Piazzolla.* Music of Piazzolla and Rivero. *Lieske, guitar; Rivero, bandonéon; Kurec, violin; Modern Strings; Sodemann, cond.*
+ Fa 3-4/95: 253

18892. 860.815: *My favorite Spanish encores.* Music of Narvaez, Valderrábano, Pisador, Mudarra, Sor, Llobet, Tarrega, Moreno Torroba, and Albéniz. *Segovia, guitar.*
• Fa 1-2/88: 81

18893. 860.850: LOEWE—Songs. *Prey, baritone; Deutsch, piano.*
+ ARG 7-8/86: 69
+ Fa 1-2/86: 166

18894. 860.851: SCHUMANN—Piano trio, op. 63; Fantasy pieces, op. 88. *Abegg Trio.*
+ ARG 11-12/88: 83

18895. 860.860—860.861 (2 seprate discs): BEETHOVEN—Piano trios no. 1-4. *Abegg Trio.*
+ ARG 11-12/88: 16
+ Fa 7-8/88: 123

18896. 860.862—860.863 (2 separate discs): BEETHOVEN—Piano trio no. 5-6; Variations; Trio movements. *Abegg Trio.*
+ ARG 11-12/89: 39
+ Fa 9-10/89: 144

18897. 860.864: *Welte-Mignon digital: Vladimir Horowitz 1926.* Music of Bach, Liszt, Schubert, Chopin, Rachmaninoff, and Horowitz. *Horowitz, Welte-Mignon piano rolls.*
+ Fa 1-2/89: 325
□ MA 5/89: 85

18898. 860.865: SCHUMANN—Piano trios no. 2-3. *Abegg Trio.*
+ Fa 7-8/90: 263
+ NYT 5/13/90: H32

18899. 860.866: RAVEL—Piano trio in A minor. DEBUSSY—Piano trio in G major. *Abegg Trio.*
+ Fa 7-8/90: 235

18900. 860.867: GOETZ—Piano trio in G minor. KIEL—Piano trio no. 5. *Abegg Trio.*
+ ARG 11-12/90: 61
+ Fa 11-12/90: 237

18901. 860.900: MAHLER—Symphony no. 4. *Whittlesey, voice; Southwest German Radio Orch.; Gielen, cond.*
+ ARG 11-12/92: 152

18902. 860.901: BRUCKNER—Symphony no. 7. *Southwest German Radio Symphony Orch.; Gielen, cond. Recorded 1986.*
• Gr 5/94: 48

18903. 860.902: JANÁČEK—Slavonic mass; Taras Bulba. *E. Shade, Szirmay, Moser, Reich; Southwest German Radio Orch.; Gielen, cond.*
• ARG 1-2/95: 122

18904. 860.908: MAHLER—Symphony no. 10: Adagio. WAGNER—Tristan und Isolde: Prelude and Liebestod. *Southwest German Radio Symphony Orch.; Gielen, cond.*
+ ARG 1-2/93: 115

18905. 860.912: BEETHOVEN—Violin concerto; Fidelio overture; Consecration of the house overture. *Tetzlaff, violin; Southwest German Radio Orch.; Gielen, cond.*
+ ARG 11-12/92: 80

18906. 860.913: MAHLER—Symphony no. 9. *Southwest German Radio Orch.; Gielen, cond.*
+ ARG 9-10/92: 126
+ Fa 3-4/95: 218
• Gr 2/94: 46

18907. 860.914 (2 discs): BRUCKNER—Symphony no. 8. *Southwest German Radio Orch.; Gielen, cond.*
+ ARG 11-12/92: 99

18908. 860.915: SCHOENBERG—Erwartung. GIELEN—Die Glocken sind auf Falscher Spur. *Bryn-Julson, soprano; other soloists; Southwest German Radio Orch.; Gielen, cond.*
• ARG 11-12/92: 196

18909. 860.916: BEETHOVEN—Missa solemnis. *Bryn-Julson, Lipovsek, Protschka, Rydl; Phil. Choir Prague; SWF- Sinfonieorchester Baden-Baden; Gielen, cond. Recorded 1987.*
• ARG 11-12/92: 81
• Fa 11-12/95: 203

18910. 860.924: MAHLER—Symphony no. 7. *Southwest German Radio Orch.; Gielen, cond.*
+ ARG 3-4/95: 133

INTERCORD SAPHIR

+ Fa 3-4/95: 217
+ Gr 6/94: 52

18911. 870.766: BACH—Masses, BWV 235, BWV 236. *Speiser, Russ, Rütgers, Equiluz, Kesteren, Wenk, Stämpfli; Gächinger Kantorei; Figuralchor der Gedächtniskirche Stuttgart; Bach-Collegium Stuttgart; Rilling, cond.*
• Fa 3-4/90: 116

18912. 885.750—885.752 (3 3-disc sets): BEETHOVEN—String quartets. *Melos String Quartet.*
• Fa 1-2/88: 86

18913. 885.855 (2 discs): BACH—Mass in B minor. *Sonntag, Lipovsek, Crook, Schmidt; Gächinger Kantorei; Stuttgart Chamber Orch.; Rilling, cond.*
• ARG 7-8/89: 15
+ SR 5/90: 88

18914. 885.929: *Famous overtures and intermezzi.* Music of Mozart, Rossini, Nicolai, Glinka, Wagner, J. Strauss, Jr., Beethoven, Smetana, Weber, Verdi, and Wagner. *Various orchs. & conds.* Reissues.
• Fa 11-12/95: 497

INTERNATIONAL PIANO ARCHIVES

18915. IPAM 1037 (2 discs): Music of Chopin, Godowsky, and Albeniz. *Saperton, piano.* Recorded 1952, 1957.
+ ARG 5-6/94: 213

18916. IPAM 1066 (2 discs): LISZT—Hungarian rhapsodies. *19 pianists.*
+ ARG 9-10/94: 269

18917. IPAM 1102/3 (2 LPs): *Master pianist: The artistry of Carl Friedberg.* Music of Schumann, Beethoven, Brahms, Chopin, Mendelssohn, Kramer, Pauer, Paradies, and Friedberg. *Friedberg, Carl; Perole Quartet.*
+ Opus 12/86: 34

18918. IPAM 1202: *Gina Bachauer plays French music.* Music of Saint-Saëns, Couperin, Debussy, and Ravel. *Bachauer, piano.*
- Fa 9-10/92: 427

18919. IPAM 1203: *Hungerford plays Schubert. Hungerford, piano.*
+ ARG 9-10/92: 156
+ Fa 9-10/92: 427

18920. IPAM 1204 (2 discs): *Ovation to Sidney Foster.* Music of Mendelssohn, Beethoven, Chopin, Liszt, Palmgren, Delibes, Prokofiev, Godowsky, Bach, Schumann, Bartók, Albeniz, Scriabin, and Weber. *Foster, piano.*
+ ARG 3-4/94: 210

INTERNATIONAL RECORD COLLECTOR'S CLUB

18921. CD 810: American singers. *White, Homer, Althouse, Whitehill, Marsh, vocalists.* Historical reissues.
+ ARG 11-12/94: 262
• Fa 11-12/94: 451
+ ARG 3-4/96: 266

18922. CD 811: *American singers, vol. 2.* Music of Gounod, Arditi, Thomas, Bizet, Bayly, Tosti, Puccini, Verdi, Flotow, Rossini, Massenet, Brogi, Meyerbeer, Donizetti, and Saint-Saëns. *Mario, Chamlee, Bonelli, Lazzari, vocalists.* Recorded 1920-1926.
+ ARG 3-4/95: 279
+ Fa 3-4/95: 358

18923. CD 812: *Souvenirs from verismo operas, vol. 1.* Music of Franchetti, Pacchierotti, Mascagni, and D'Erlanger. *Various singers and accs.*
+ ARG 11-12/95: 297
+ Fa 7-8/95: 388

18924. CD 813: *Souvenirs from verismo operas, vol. 2.* Music of Wolf-Ferrari, Virgilio, and Mascagni . *Various singers and acc.*
+ Fa 11-12/95: 445

18925. CD 814: *Souvenirs of opera and song, vol. 2.* Music of Donizetti, Ricci, Cadman, Proch, Meyerbeer, Gounod, Robert, Tosti, Thomas, Verdi, Wagner, Rubinstein, Rossini, Ponchielli, and Wilson . *Various vocalists.*
+ ARG 3-4/96: 266
+ Fa 1-2/96: 367

18926. CD 815: Souvenirs from Verismo operas, vol. 3. *Various performers.*
+ ARG 7-8/96: 296
+ Fa 5-6/96: 333

INTERSOUND

18927. 3449: RACHMANINOFF—Symphony no. 2. *Symphony Orch. of Russia; Freeman, cond.*
• ARG 3-4/94: 140

18928. 3450: RACHMANINOFF—Isle of the dead; Vocalise; Caprice bohémien; 5 études tableaux. *San Diego Symphony Orch.; Talmi, cond.*
• ARG 3-4/94: 139

18929. 3534: WILLIAMS—Symphony for the sons of Nam. HAILSTORK—An American port of call; Epitaph. CORDERO—Eight miniatures. *Chicago Sinfonietta; Freeman, cond.*
+ ARG 3-4/96: 218

18930. 3535: GLAZUNOV—Violin concerto, op. 82. TCHAIKOVSKY—Violin concerto, op. 35. *Kim, violin; Moscow Phil. Orch.; Symphony Orch. of Russia; Freeman, cond.*

• ARG 3-4/96: 192
• Fa 1-2/96: 207

18931. 3537: MOZART—*The complete piano concertos, vol. 6.* Concertos no. 8, 16, 19. *Han, piano; Philharmonia Orch.; Freeman, cond.*
- ARG 5-6/96: 152
- Fa 5-6/96: 215

18932. 3539: GRIEG—Piano concerto. LISZT—Sonata. *Graf, piano; Moscow Phil. Orch.; Won, cond.*
- ARG 7-8/96: 121

18933. 3836 (3 discs): BEETHOVEN—The 5 piano concertos; Fifteen variations with fugue, op. 35. *Han, piano; Berlin Symphony Orch.; Freeman, cond.*
- Fa 5-6/96: 94

INTIM

18934. IMCD 008: BACH—Flute sonatas, BWV 1030-32; Partita for flute solo. *G. Schaub, flute; Svahn-Schaub, harpsichord.*
• Fa 3-4/94: 111

18935. IMCD 009: Music of Roussel, Fauré, Sancan, Dutilleux, Gaubert, and Poulenc. *Haraldsdottir, flute; Derwinger, piano.*
+ Fa 3-4/94: 397

18936. IMCD 015: *Swedish bassoon concertos.* Music of Berwald, Brendler, Fernström, and Crusell. *Engström, bassoon; Gothenburg Symphony Orch.; Svedlund, cond.*
+ Fa 3-4/94: 392

18937. IMCD 016: MOZART—Clarinet quintet; Quintet for piano and winds. *Nyberg, piano; Members of the Gothenburg Symphony Orch.*
• Fa 3-4/94: 254

18938. IMCD 018 : Music of Alfvén, Peterson-Berger, Atterberg, Nystroem, and De Frumerie. *Marcusson, flute; Gothenburg Symphony Orch.; Svedlund, cond.*
+ Fa 3-4/94: 394

18939. IMCD 019: NORGÅRD—For a change. MÁSSON—Marimba concerto . SALLINEN—Symphony no. 2. *Carlsson, percussion; Gothenburg Symphony Orch.; Willén, Hirokami, conds.*
+ ARG 3-4/95: 175
+ Fa 3-4/94: 259

18940. IMCD 020: Music of Schubert, Reinecke, Saint-Saëns, and Gounod. *Haraldsdottir, flute; Derwinger, piano.*
+ Fa 3-4/94: 395

18941. IMCD 021: *Music around the Baltic Sea.* Music of Eller, Nielsen, Sibelius, and Rangström. *Camerata Roman.*
+ Fa 3-4/94: 419

18942. IMCD 023: Music of Grieg, Roman, Lindberg, Simai, and Larsson. *Marcusson, flute; Camerata Roman.*
+ Fa 3-4/94: 396

18943. IMCD 030: LARSSON— Concertinos no. 1-7. *Camerata Roman.*
+ ARG 3-4/96: 141

INTRADA

18944. 7055: RÓZSA (RECONSTRUCTED ROBBINS)—Ivanhoe. *Sinfonia of London; Broughton, cond.*
+ ARG 9-10/95: 205
+ Gr 5/95: 58

18945. 7056: RÓZSA—Julius Caesar. *Emmanuel, soprano; Sinfonia of London; Broughton, cond.*
+ Gr 12/95: 90

IRCC

18946. IRCC-CD 800: MEYERBEER— Arias, duets and scenes. *Various vocalists.* Historical reissue.
+ ARG 5-6/92: 86
+ Gr 9/92: 174
+ Op 9/92: 1131

18947. IRCC-CD 802: *Souvenirs of rare French opera.* Music of Donizetti, Reyer, Leroux, Duvernoy, Massenet, Gounod, and others. *Various performers.* Historical reissues.
□ ARG 9-10/92: 224
+ ARG 1-2/95: 268
+ Fa 9-10/92: 406

18948. IRCC-CD 804: *Souvenirs from Rossini operas.* Historical vocal recordings from Le barbier de Seville; Cenerentola; Comte Ory, Semiramide, Mosé and Guillaume e Tell. *Various performers.*
+ Fa 11-12/92: 423

18949. IRCC-CD 805: *Geraldine Farrar: 60th anniversary issue.* Music of Schumann, Massenet, Humperdinck, Gounod, Boito, Mozart, Verdi, Horn, Bemberg, R. Strauss, Gluck, Heuberger, Lehár, Wolf-Ferrari, Leoncavallo, Mattei, Wagner, and Farrar. *Farrar, soprano; orch. acc.*
+ ARG 5-6/93: 182
+ Fa 3-4/93: 334

18950. IRCC-CD 806—807 (2 separate discs): A 1940's radio hour, vol. 1-2. *Various artists.* Opera excerpts.
+ ARG 7-8/93: 217
+ Fa 1-2/94: 381

18951. IRCC-CD 808: *Souvenirs of nineteenth century Italian opera.* Music of Apolloni, Petrella, Ruggi, Faccio, Usiglio, Marchetti, Campana, Gomes, Ponchielli, Bottesini. *Various performers.*
• Fa 1-2/94: 380
+ Fa 5-6/94: 303
+ Op 10/94: 1241

18952. IRCC-CD 809: A 1940s radio hour, vol. 3. *Various performers.*
+ Fa 3-4/94: 386

IRIDISC

18953. 53713: BEATTY—Symphony no. 6 "Oceanic". *Computer generated sounds.*
□ ARG 1-2/97: 245

IRON NEEDLE

18954. IN 1301: *The golden years, vol. 1.* Music of Borodin, Rimsky-Korsakov, Verdi, Puccini, Meyerbeer, Ponchielli, Massenet, Rossini, Gounod, Flotow, Leoncavallo, and Donizetti. *Björling, tenor; orch.; Grevillius, cond.*
+ Fa 11-12/95: 440

18955. IN 1306: MOZART—Clarinet quintet. GERSHWIN—Rhapsody in blue; An American in Paris. *Goodman, clarinet; Wild, piano; Budapest String Quartet; NBC Symphony Orch.; Toscanini, cond.* Recorded 1942.
+ ARG 1-2/96: 245

18956. IN 1313: Rubinstein's early recordings, 1928-37. *Rubinstein, piano.*
• ARG 3-4/96: 262

18957. IN 1325: BEETHOVEN—Symphony no. 3. WAGNER—Tannhäuser overture. *New York Phil.; Concertgebouw Orch.; Mengelberg, cond.*
+ ARG 9-10/96: 270

18958. IN 1326: Music of Beethoven, Weber, Wagner, Brahms, and Liszt. *Concertgebouw Orch.; Mengelberg, cond.*
□ ARG 9-10/96: 270

18959. IN 1327: SCHUMANN—Symphony no. 2. CHOPIN—Chopiniana. *Minneapolis Symphony Orch.; Mitropoulos, cond.*
+ ARG 9-10/96: 270

18960. IN 1328: BEETHOVEN—Violin concerto. MENDELSSOHN—Violin concerto. *Kreisler, violin; London Phil. Orch.; Barbirolli, cond.; Berlin State Opera Orch.; Blech, cond.* Recorded 1936 and 1926.
□ Fa 7-8/96: 100

ISBA

18961. 2070: Music of Gounod, Saint-Saëns, Verdi, Gershwin, and others. *Choquette, soprano; Orch. de La Scala de Montreal; Lagacé, cond.*
• ARG 1-2/97: 225

ISIS

18962. ISISCD 001: HANDEL—Suites, no. 5, 7. SCARLATTI—Sonatas. *Souter, harpsichord.*
+ Gr 3/93: 72

18963. ISISCD 002: BACH—Organ music. *Souter, organ.*
+ Fa 3-4/94: 108
+ Gr 10/94: 154

18964. ISISCD 003: HANDEL—Harpsichord suites. *Souter, harpsichord.*
+ Fa 3-4/94: 207
+ Gr 7/93: 66

18965. ISISCD 004: PURCELL—Suites for harpsichord no. 1-8. *Souter, harpsichord.*
• Fa 3-4/94: 283

18966. ISISCD 007/8 (2 discs): BACH—Organ music. *Souter, organ.*
+ Gr 5/95: 78

18967. ISISCD 010: *The royal harpsichord of George III.* Music of Handel, Arne, J.C. Bach, Chilcot, and Mozart. *Souter, harpsichord.*
• Gr 12/95: 122

ITALIA

18968. CDC 10: SALIERI—Piano concertos in B♭ and in C. *Ciccolini, piano; I Solisti Veneti; Scimone, cond.*
+ Fa 11-12/93: 371

18969. CDC 11: VIVALDI—Mass in C, RV 586; Credo RV 591; Concerto for 2 flutes, 2 oboes, 2 bassoons and violin, RV 577; Concerto for oboe, English horn, violin, 2 violas and cello, RV 579. *Bima, soprano; Rizzi, alto; Sai, tenor; Turicchi, bass; Coro da Camera della Radiotelevisione Italiana; I Solisti Veneti; Scimone, cond.; Cappella Coloniensis; Ferro, cond.*
+ Fa 11-12/93: 439

18970. CDC 13: PAGANINI—Serenade in C for viola, cello, and guitar; Quartets for violin, viola, cello, and guitar no. 14-15. *Bonell, guitar; Accardo, Gazeau, violins; Ghedin, viola; Filippini, cello.*
+ Fa 11-12/93: 339

18971. CDC 17: MERCADANTE—Flute concerto, op. 57; Clarinet concerto, op. 101; Horn concerto. *Larrieu, flute; Leister, clarinet; Baumann, horn; Masterplayers; Schumacher, cond.*
+ Fa 11-12/93: 323

18972. CDC 22: PAGANINI—String quartets no. 1-3. *Accardo, Gazeau, violins; Ghedin, viola; Filippini, cello.*
+ ARG 11-12/93: 163
+ Fa 11-12/93: 339

18973. CDC 40: ALBINONI—Pimpinone. MARCELLO—Flute sonatas, op. 2: no. 7, 10, 12. *Zilio, mezzo-soprano; Trimarchi, bass; I Solisti Veneti; Scimone, cond.; Persichilli, flute; De Robertis, harpsichord; Bevers, cello.* Reissue.
• Fa 1-2/94: 108

18974. CDC 44 (3 discs): ROSSINI—La gazza ladra. *Pizzo, Müller-Molinari,*

ITALIA

Condo, Bottazzo, Romero, Ambrosian Opera Chorus; Royal Phil. Orch.; Zedda, cond. Reissue.
   • ARG 1-2/94: 142
   + Fa 1-2/94: 289

18975. CDC 64 (2 discs): ROSSINI—Adelaide di Borgogna. *Devia, Dupuy, Caforio, Bertolo; Festival di Martina Franca; Zedda, cond.* Recorded 1984.
   • ARG 1-2/94: 140
   + Fa 1-2/94: 282

18976. CDC 75 (2 discs): AUBER—Fra diavolo (sung in Italian). *Raffanti, Serra, Dupily, Portella; Festival di Martina Franca; Zedda, cond.* Recorded 1981.
   • ARG 7-8/94: 61

18977. CDC 77 (2 discs): PUCCINI—La rondine. *Gasdia, Scarabelli, Cupido, Cosotti; RAI Milan; Gelmetti, cond.*
   • ARG 9-10/94: 176
   • Fa 9-10/94: 293
   + ON 1/7/95: 36

18978. CDC 82 (2 discs): MERCADANTE—Il giuramento. *Gonzales, Omilian, Visconti; Valle d'Istria Festival; Campanella, cond.* Recorded 1984.
   • ARG 3-4/95: 143

18979. CDC 92: PAISIELLO—Missa defunctorum. *Dessì, Gonzales, Barbacini, Tadeo; Cambridge University Chamber Choir; Orch. of the Martina Franca Festival; Zedda, cond.*
   + ARG 7-8/95: 166
   + Fa 7-8/95: 267

ITALIAN OPERA RARITIES

18980. L07716/18 (3 discs): DONIZETTI—Les martyrs (sung in Italian). *Gencer, Garaventa, Furlanetto, Bruson; Teatro La Fenice Venice; Gelmetti, cond.* Recorded 1978.
   - Gr 10/94: 188

ITM

18981. 6-04: LEIFS—Geysir; Landsyn; Three images; Hekla. *Iceland Symphony Orch.; Zukofsky, cond.; Reykjavik Male Choir.*
   - ARG 3-4/92: 84
   + Fa 11-12/91: 367

18982. 7-05: THORÁRINSSON—String quartet; Styr; Io; Mót; För. *Miami String Quartet; Sigurdsson, piano; Iceland Symphony Orch.; Leifsson, Sakari, conds.*
   + ARG 3-4/93: 149

18983. 7-07: TÓMASSON—Spiral; Echo of the past; Octet; String quartet no. 2; Offspring; Strati. *Caput Ensemble; Haraldsdottir, flute; Magnusdottir, harpsichord; Danish Radio Symphony Orch.; Segerstam, cond.; Iceland Symphony Orch.; Pálsson, cond.*
   + ARG 9-10/95: 231

18984. 8-07: PÁL PÁLLSON—Gudis-Mana-Hasi; Crystals; Tomorrow; August sonnet; September sonnet; Lantao; Six thoughtful songs. *Saemundsdóttir, soprano; Bragadóttir, mezzo-soprano; Reykjavik Chamber Orch.; Pálsson, cond.*
   + ARG 11-12/95: 170
   + Fa 9-10/95: 272

18985. 8-08: *Icelandic chamber works.* Music of Leifs, Másson, Grímsson, Birgisson, Tómasson, Ingólfsson, and Ragnarsson. *Caput Animato.*
   • Fa 3-4/96: 376

18986. 804: *Icelandic cello.* Music of Masson, Tomasson, Sveinsson, Hauksson, H. I. Sigurbjornsson, and Nordal. *Gylfadóttir, cello; Birgisson, piano; Halldorsdottir, soprano.*
   + ARG 3-4/94: 201

18987. 1424: SATIE—Quatre preludes; Petite ouverture à danser; Danses gothiques. *Gumpert, piano.*
   • Fa 7-8/92: 268

18988. 1451: SATIE—Trois gymnopédies; Pages mystiques; Sonneries de la rose et crois; Ogives; Pièces froides. *Gumpert, piano.*
   • Fa 7-8/92: 268

18989. 950005: SCHUBERT—String quintet (arr.). *Atlas Camerata; Atlas, cond.*
   + ARG 5-6/93: 129

J. MARTIN STAFFORD

18990. JMSCD 1: *English organ music.* Music of Byrd, Bull, Gibbons, Tomkins, Blow, Locke, Purcell, Greene, Handel, Nares, Boyce, and Stanley. *Dart, organ.*
   + Gr 5/95: 87

18991. JMSCD 2: MOERAN—Piano works. *Parkin, piano.*
   + Gr 5/96: 89

JADE

18992. JACD 004: Music of Dumont, Lully, Charpentier, Lalande, and Boëly. *Les Petits Chanteurs de Saint- François de Versailles.*
   + ARG 11-12/92: 254
   + Fa 9-10/92: 413

18993. JACD 005: The proper of masses of the Christmas cycle. *Choir of Monks of the Montserrat Abbey; Estrada, cond.* Reissue.
   + Fa 1-2/93: 290

18994. JACD 006: BRITTEN—A ceremony of carols. MENDELSSOHN—Three motets, op. 39. *Escolanía Montserrat; Segarra, cond.*
   + ARG 11-12/92: 265
   + Fa 9-10/92: 203

18995. JACD 008: Music of Allegri, Josquin des Prez, Palestrina, and Victoria. *Les Petits Chanteurs de Saint- François de Versailles.*
   - Fa 9-10/92: 413

18996. JACD 009: *Music and chants at the Abbey of Einsiedeln and the Cathedral of St. Gall.* Music of Victoria, Clérambault, Aichinger, Sicher, Speth, Barbarini, Stehle, Scheel, Hildenbrand, Huber, and Gregorian chant. *Choral groups; Bannwart, Meier, Scherer, Fuchs, conds.* Reissue.
   + Fa 9-10/92: 412

18997. JACD 020: Music of Dumont, Moulinié, and Charpentier. *Les Petits Chanteurs de Saint-François de Versailles.*
   + Fa 9-10/92: 413

18998. JACD 022: GARCIA—Matins for Christmas day. OLIVEIRA—Magnificat. *Valadao, Passos, Tutman, Costa; Camerata de Rio de Janeiro; Morelenbaum, cond.*
   • ARG 11-12/92: 123

18999. JACD 026: Nuit de Noel. *Les Petits Chanteurs of St. François, Versailles.*
   □ ARG 11-12/92: 264

19000. JACD 030: *Nuit de Noel à Bethleem.* Midnight Mass at St. Catherine's, Bethlehem, 1967. *Unidentified performers.*
   • ARG 11-12/92: 264

19001. JACD 031: GARCIA—Missa de Nossa Senhora do Carmo. *Vocal soloists; Associação de Canto Coral; Camerata Rio de Janeiro; Morelenbaum, cond.*
   • ARG 9-10/92: 107

19002. JACD 033: DURUFLÉ—Requiem; Four motets on Gregorian chants. *Apanaviciute, soprano; Azuoliukas Boys Choir of Vilnius; Lithuanian State Phil. Symphony Orch.; Miskinis, cond.*
   • Fa 1-2/94: 171

19003. JACD 041: STRAVINSKY—Mass. CAPLET—Messe à trois voix. *Vocal soloists; Belgrade Radio Chamber Orch. & Choir; Simić, cond.; Collegium Musicum Chamber Choir; Matic-Marovic, cond.*
   • ARG 11-12/92: 214

19004. JACD 056: EKMALIAN—Armenian liturgical chants. *Armenian Choir of Sofia; Papazian, cond.*
   + ARG 9-10/93: 116

19005. JACD 062: GRECHANINOFF—Liturgia domestica. *Christoff, bass; Svetoslav Obretenov Choir; Bulgarian Radio Chamber Orch.; Robev, cond.* Recorded 1979.
   + ARG 11-12/94: 121

19006. JACD 063 (2 discs): RACHMANINOFF—Liturgy of St. John Chrysostom. *Mixed Choir of Bulgarian Radio; Mikov, cond.* Reissue.
+ Fa 7-8/93: 208

19007. JACD 099: MESSIAEN—Eclairs sur l'au-délà. *Polish National Radio Orch. of Katowice; Wit, cond.*
+ Fa 9-10/94: 256
+ Gr 6/94: 54

19008. JACD 102: LASSO—Lamentations. *Jean-Paul Gipon Ensemble.*
• ARG 9-10/94: 151
- Gr 10/94: 174

19009. JACD 111: Toussaint: All Saint's Day: Requiem. *Choeur Grégorien de Paris; Chancerelle, cond.; Schola Gregoriana Pragensis; D. Eben, cond.*
- EM 2/95: 161

19010. JACD 122: Chant mozarabe. *Schola Antiqua de España; Saenz de Buruaga, cond.*
+ Fa 11-12/95: 452

19011. JACD 131: *Plainchant.* Masses: Lux et origo; Fons bonitatis; De angelis; Cum jubilo; Orbis factor. *Santo Domingo de Silos Monastery Choir; Angulo, cond.* Recorded 1956-62.
• Gr 9/95: 98

19012. JACD 1222.14: HAYDN—The seven last words from the cross. *M.K. Ciurlionis Quartet.*
+ Fa 9-10/93: 178

19013. 74321-29490-2: Les mystères du rosaire. *Benedictine Nuns of the Abbey of Notre Dame d'Argentan; Gajard, cond.*
+ Gr 2/96: 97

19014. 74321-29491-2 (7 discs): MESSIAEN—Complete organ music. *Bate, Gillock, Hakim, Thiry, Schlee, Ericsson, organs.*
+ ARG 7-8/96: 153 (as 491)
+ Gr 7/96: 76

JAPIS MILLENIUM

19015. P. 006: *Implosions.* Music of Hallgrímsson, Hauksson, Sollberger, Huber, Ferneyhough, and Lavista. *Bjarnason, flutes.*
+ Fa 3-4/96: 357

JAZZMANIA

19016. 6003: *Ragtime classics.* Music of Arndt, Gottschalk, Krell, Lamb, Joplin, Debussy, Marshall, Aufderheide, Pratt, Gershwin, Nazareth, and Jenks. *Ikemiya, piano.*
- ARG 3-4/94: 211

JECKLIN

19017. JD 236 (LP): BEETHOVEN—Piano sonatas no. 8, 20, 26; Albumblatt für

Elise, WoO 59. *Kukorelly, piano.*
• Fa 9-10/86: 103

19018. JD 239 (LP): BRITTEN—Six metamorphoses after Ovid. POULENC—Oboe sonata. SAINT-SAËNS—Oboe sonata, op. 166. SCHUMANN—Three pieces for oboe and piano, op. 94. *Paradise, oboe; Rütti, piano.*
• Fa 9-10/86: 300

19019. JS 240-2: BACH—Cello suite no. 3 (arr. Duarte). GIULIANI—Rossiniana, no. 1, op. 119; Grande ouverture, op. 61. *Mariotti, guitar.* Issued also as LP: 240.
• ARG 1-2/90: 18
• Fa 11-12/86: 98
+ Fa 3-4/90: 115

19020. JD 248 (LP): HAYDN—Horn concertos no. 1-2. MOZART—Horn concerto no. 1. *Hefti, horn; Glarner Musikkollegium; Aschmann, cond.*
• Fa 9-10/86: 160

19021. JD 250 (LP): SCHOECK—Frühe Lieder. *Steiner, tenor; Fueter, piano.*
+ Fa 9-10/88: 247

19022. JS 263-2: Guitar music of Mangoré, Molleda, and Rodrigo. *Mariotti, guitar.*
+ ARG 7-8/89: 116
+ Fa 3-4/89: 375
• Fa 5-6/89: 397

19023. JS 268-2: SCHUBERT—Winterreise. *Loosli, bass-baritone; Grenacher, piano.*
- ARG 11-12/89: 112
- Fa 11-12/89: 349

19024. JS 269-2: MOZART—Divertimento for string trio, K. 563. ROLLA—Trio concertante no. 2. *Novák Trio.*
+ Fa 9-10/90: 305

19025. JD 272-2: *Le spleen de Paris.* Music of Debussy, Honegger, Poulenc, Milhaud, Benjamin, Auric, Durey, Tailleferre. *Blattmann, clarinet; Schwaar, piano.*
+ Fa 9-10/90: 485

19026. JS 275-2: PORTENIER—Klavierstücke, 1982-1988. *Eberhard, Portenier, pianos.*
□ Fa 3-4/91: 323

19027. JS 276-2: WEHRLI—Weltliches Requiem. *Vocal soloists; Aargau Pro Musica Chamber Orch.; Girod, cond.*
• ARG 9-10/93: 220

19028. JD 279-2: GROSSMANN—Il President da Valdel. *Dudas, Verhouning, Danuser, Muoth; Kammerorchester "Opera mobile Basel"; Stern, cond.*
- Fa 11-12/91: 330

19029. JD 289-2: *Tétraclavier.* Music of Glaus, Stockhausen, Pepi, Zimmerlin, and Dünki. *Reymond, piano & cembalo; Dünki, piano & clavichord; Sublet,*

celesta; *Clemann, piano.*
+ Fa 11-12/93: 511

19030. JD 293-2: MERTZ—Guitar music. REGONDI—Guitar music. *Mariotti, guitar.*
+ ARG 1-2/95: 140

19031. JD 296-2: *New music from Switzerland.* Music of Huber, Pagliarani, Lehmann, Robert-George, Danuser, and others. *Ensemble Mobile.*
+ ARG 1-2/95: 210

19032. JD 297-2: *Aargau composers.* MIEG—double concerto. WEHRLI—Sinfonietta. BLUM—Symphony no. 8. *Kolly, piano; Riniker, cello; Rumpel, flute; Andres, piano; South Bohemian Chamber Orch.; Schmid, cond.*
+ ARG 7-8/94: 199

19033. JD 301-2: WEHRLI—String quartet no. 2-3; Trio; Cello sonata. *Euler Quartet; Larsens, violin; Hefti, horn; Dadelsen, piano; Pawlica, cello.*
+ ARG 3-4/95: 223

19034. JD 303-2: HUMMEL—Flute trio. RIES—Flute trio. DUSSEK—Flute sonata, op. 65. KUHLAU—Capriccios. *Kronjäger, flute; Degen, cello; Desponds, piano.*
+ ARG 5-6/96: 231

19035. JD 306-2: VOGEL—Horformen; Varietude; Intervalle. SCHOECK—Consolation; Toccata. MAREK—Toccata; Rural scenes. *Fischer, soprano; Bärtschi, Tschupp, piano; Camerata Zürich.*
+ ARG 3-4/96: 221

19036. JD 504-2: SCHOECK—Selections. *Haefliger, tenor; Grenacher, piano; Seminarchor Wettingen; Wettinger Kammerchor; Winds of the Tonhalle Orch., Zürich; Wettinger Kammerorchester.*
+ ARG 9-10/89: 99
+ Fa 7-8/89: 235

19037. JD 510-2: SCHOECK—Elegie. *Loosli, bass-baritone; Berner Kammerensemble; Hug, cond.*
+ ARG 9-10/89: 99
+ Fa 7-8/89: 235

19038. JD 529-2: MARTIN—Harpsichord concerto; Ballade for trombone and orchestra; Ballade for piano and orchestra . *Jaccottet, harpsichord; Rosin, trombone; Benda, piano; Lausanne Chamber Orch.; Martin, cond.*
+ ARG 1-2/90: 61
+ Fa 11-12/89: 268
+ Gr 9/89: 456

19039. JD 530 (LP): PFISTER—Agäisches Tagebuch; Ottobeuren-Quintett. *Fuchs, oboe; Dyk, percussion; Camerata Zürich; Tschupp, cond.; Stadler Wind Quintet.*
+ Fa 5-6/86: 204

19040. JD 535-2: SCHOECK—Nachhall, op. 70; Hesse Lieder. *A. Loosli, bass-*

baritone; Kammerensemble von Radio Bern; T. Loosli, cond.; Grenacher, piano.
  + ARG 9-10/89: 99
  + Fa 7-8/89: 235

19041. JD 541-2: Bach—Piano concerto no. 1, BWV 1052 (arr. Busoni). Chopin—Piano concerto no. 1; Piano music. *Lipatti, piano; Concertgebouw Orch.; Beinum, cond.; Tonhalle Orch.; Ackermann, cond.*
  + Fa 3-4/90: 111

19042. JD 543-2: Reger—String sextet, op. 118. *Die Kammermusiker Zürich.*
  + ARG 11-12/89: 104
  - Fa 11-12/89: 332

19043. JD 549-2: Mozart—Music for clarinet and basset horn. *Leister, Geisler, clarinet; Stalder, Hofer, Kubli, Leuthold, Schmid, basset horns; Meyer, bassoon; Speiser, Gohl, Widmer, vocalists.*
  + Fa 5-6/88: 172

19044. JD 560-2: *Musik aus der Blutezeit des Bassetthorns.* Music of Danzi, Backofen, Beerhalter, and Mendelssohn. *Stalder, basset horn & clarinet; Leuthold, basset horn; Sirokay, Vintschger, piano; Holliger, harp; Schmid, cello.*
  + ARG 11-12/89: 156
  + Fa 5-6/89: 403

19045. JD 561-2: Songs of Berg, Schoenberg, and Schreker. *Speiser, soprano, Gage, piano.*
  + ARG 7-8/89: 26
  • Fa 7-8/89: 97
  • Gr 1/89: 1202

19046. JD 563-2: Martin—Selections. *Rehfuss, baritone; Ameling, soprano; Willoughby, flute; H. Honegger, cello; Martin, piano.*
  + ARG 1-2/90: 61
  + Fa 11-12/89: 269
  + Gr 3/90: 1669

19047. JD 570-2: Liszt—Lenore; Der blinde Sänger; Der traurige Mönch; Des toten Dichters Liebe. Strauss—Das Schloss am Meere. Nietzsche—Das zerbrochene Ringlein. *Westphal, speaker; Studer, piano.*
  + Fa 9-10/90: 466

19048. JD 577-2: Flute music of Kuhlau, Ries, Czerny, and Molique. *Graf, flute; Sirokay, piano.*
  + Fa 5-6/88: 261

19049. JD 578-2: *Virtuose Klarinettenmusik der Romantik, II.* Music of Boieldieu, Crusell, Cavallini, Berr, Fessy, Ponchielli, and Rossini. *Stalder, Hofer, clarinets; Sirokay, Vintschger, piano.*
  + Fa 5-6/88: 262

19050. JD 579-2: Busoni—Improvisation über das Bachsche Choralied Wie wohl ist mir; Fantasia contrappuntistica.

Mozart—Fantasia in F minor for mechanical organ, K. 608 (arr. Busoni); Duettino concertante (arr. Busoni). *I. & J. Vintschger, pianos.*
  + ARG 7-8/89: 116
  + Fa 3-4/89: 127

19051. JD 581/82-2 (2 discs): Martin—Le vin herbé. *Vocal soloists; instrumental chamber ensemble; Desarzens, cond.*
  • ARG 3-4/90: 70
  + Fa 5-6/90: 211
  + Gr 12/89: 1185

19052. JD 588-2: Gutzwiller—Der wahre Geist der Leere. *Gutzwiller, shakuhachi.*
  + Fa 5-6/88: 136

19053. JD 590 (LP): *Klaviermusik aus Böhmen, Mähren und der Slowakei.* Music of Dvořák, Smetana, Novák, Suchon, Martinů, Janáček, and Hilmar. *Schmid-Wyss, piano.*
  + Fa 3-4/86: 284
  + NR 6/87: 18

19054. JD 592-2: Strauss—Enoch Arden. *Westphal, speaker; Buttrick, piano.*
  + Fa 3-4/91: 398

19055. JD 594-2: Zemlinsky—Songs. *Widmer, baritone; Dünki, piano.*
  • Fa 3-4/89: 344

19056. JD 601-2: Reger—Six intermezzos, op. 45; Träume am Kamin. *Buttrick, piano.*
  + Fa 3-4/91: 338

19057. JD 608-2: Czerny—Grand variations on Haydn's Gott erhalte Franz den Kaiser, op. 73. Hänsel—String quintet in G major. *Jones, piano; Die Kammermusiker Zürich.*
  • Fa 5-6/88: 111
  + Gr 8/87: 316

19058. JD 609-2: Reger—Piano music. *I. & J. Vitschger, pianos.*
  + ARG 7-8/89: 33
  + Fa 7-8/89: 221

19059. JD 615-2: Halfhide—Movements of mind; Five overtone movements. *Halfhide, voice, tambura & harmonium.*
  + Fa 5-6/88: 137

19060. JD 616-2: *Musiques utiles aux mélancholiques.* Corrette—Selections. *Ensemble Festes Galantes.*
  + Fa 9-10/87: 185

19061. JD 618-2: T. Kirchner—Preludes, op. 9; Lieder ohne Worte, op. 13. *Ungerer, piano.*
  - Fa 9-10/88: 177
  • Fa 3-4/89: 195

19062. JD 620-2: Shostakovich—String quartets no. 3, 7. *Amati Quartet.*
  + Fa 11-12/88: 279

19063. JD 621-2: Haydn—The wanderer; She never told her love; Spirit's song; O tuneful voice; Arianna a Naxos; Piano sonata, H. XVI:50; Andante con variazioni in F minor. *Speiser, soprano; Buttrick, piano.*
  + Fa 1-2/89: 175
  + Fa 3-4/89: 179

19064. JD 622-2: *Melpo.* Music of Lorenzo da Firenze, Gherardello da Firenza, Machaut, Caccini, Eyck, Irman, Steinmann, Moser, and Anon. *Steinmann, recorders.*
  + Fa 7-8/89: 313

19065. JD 623-2: Busoni—Piano music. *Buttrick, piano.*
  + Fa 3-4/89: 127

19066. JD 624-2: Giuliani—Ariette, Lieder, musiche da camera. *Meister Consort.*
  • ARG 1-2/90: 51
  - Fa 3-4/90: 184

19067. JD 627-2: *Romantische Chormusik.* Fröhlich—Choral music. *Speiser, soprano; Steiner, tenor; Krattiger, bass; Spring, piano; Vokalensemble Pro Musica Winterthur; Sarbach, cond.*
  + ARG 9-10/89: 55
  + Fa 5-6/89: 198

19068. JD 629-2: Music of Bach, Beethoven, Chopin, Bärtschi, Janáček, and Franck. *Bärtschi, piano.* Recorded live.
  + Fa 9-10/89: 415

19069. JD 630-2: Schubert—Songs. *Speiser, soprano; Buttrick, piano.*
  + Fa 7-8/90: 249

19070. JD 631-2: Martin—Requiem. *Speiser, Bollen, Tappy, Lagger; Union Chorale; Lausanne Women's Choir; Vocal Group Ars Laeta; Luy, organ; Orch. de la Suisse romande; Martin, cond.*
  + ARG 3-4/90: 70
  + Fa 5-6/90: 211
  + Gr 1/90: 1362

19071. JD 632-2: Martin—Violin concerto; Piano concerto no. 2. *Schneiderhan, violin; Badura-Skoda, piano; Radio Luxembourg Symphony Orch.; Martin, cond.*
  + ARG 3-4/90: 70
  + Fa 5-6/90: 211
  • Gr 1/90: 1334

19072. JD 633-2: Ries—Quintet in B minor for flute and strings. A.J. Romberg—Quintets for flute and strings, op. 21: Nos. 4-5. *Bennett, flute; Novšak Trio; Kosi, 2nd viola.*
  + Fa 1-2/92: 307

19073. JD 637-2: VETTER—Flowers. *Vetter, piano & voice.*
+ Fa 9-10/90: 425

19074. JD 640-2: VETTER—Light. *Vetter, instruments & voice.*
+ Fa 9-10/90: 425

19075. JD 643-2: BERG—Early piano music. *Dünki, piano.*
+ Fa 5-6/91: 133

19076. JD 644-2: HINDEMITH—Piano music. *Billeter, piano.*
+ Fa 3-4/91: 240

19077. JD 645-2: MARTIN—Petite symphonie concertante; Maria-triptychon; Passacaglia. *Instrumental soloists; Suisse romande Orch.; Berlin Phil. Orch.; Martin, cond.* Reissue.
+ Fa 3-4/91: 267
+ Gr 10/91: 90

19078. JD 646-2: MARTIN—Pavane couleur du temps; Piano quintet; String trio; Trio sur des mélodies populaires irlandaises. *Zürich Chamber Ensemble; Schmid-Wyss, piano.*
+ Fa 3-4/91: 267
+ Gr 10/91: 129

19079. JD 647-2: BURKHARD—Viola concerto; Chamber music. *Schiller, viola; Schneeberger, violin; Gärtner, flute; Meienberg, clarinet; Stavicek, bassoon; Gugel, horn; Paccagnella, harp; Wyganth, double bass; Swiss Italian Radio-Television Orch.; Venzago, Kelterborn, cond.*
+ ARG 11-12/91: 48
+ Fa 7-8/91: 131

19080. JD 648-2: BARTÓK—Rhapsody for piano and orchestra; Piano concerto no. 2. *Foldes, piano; Lamoureux Orch.; Bigot, cond.*
+ Fa 7-8/91: 108

19081. JD 649-2: REGER—Violin sonatas no. 6-7. *Schneeberger, violin; Dünki, piano.*
+ Fa 5-6/92: 230
+ Gr 5/93: 67

19082. JD 661-2: MENDELSSOHN—Piano sonatas no. 1, 3; Character pieces op. 7. *Meyer, piano.*
+ Fa 9-10/93: 215
• Fa 11-12/92: 302

19083. JD 663-2: MÜLLER-ZÜRICH—Sinfonietta 1-2; Consenso. *Zürich Symphony Orch.; Schweizer, cond.*
• ARG 11-12/92: 173
+ Fa 11-12/92: 317

19084. JD 667-2: SCHROEDER—Lasciando. *Schroeder, piano.*
+ Fa 5-6/93: 313

19085. JD 668-2: FRITZ—Flute sonatas op. 2. *Graf, flute; Baltenspeger,*

harpsichord.
+ ARG 9-10/93: 122

19086. JD 671-2: SCHOECK—Songs, vol. 1. *Schäfer, soprano; Rieger, piano.*
+ ARG 11-12/96: 199

19087. JD 672-2: SCHOECK—Songs, vol. 2. *Berg, bass; Drake, piano; Birchmeier, organ.*
+ ARG 11-12/96: 199

19088. JD 673, 677-2 (2 separate discs): SCHOECK—Complete songs, vol. 3, 7. *Töller, baritone; Keller, piano; Banse, soprano; Henschel, tenor; Rieger, piano.*
+ Fa 9-10/93: 264
+ Gr 3/94: 95

19089. JD 674-2: SCHOECK—Songs, vol. 4. *Kallisch, mezzo-soprano; Körber, piano.*
• ARG 5-6/96: 184

19090. JD 675-2: SCHOECK—Songs, vol. 5. *Banse, soprano; Henschel, baritone; Rieger, piano.*
• ARG 5-6/96: 184

19091. JD 680-2: SCHOECK—Songs, vol. 10. *Fassbender, mezzo-soprano; Kortel, piano.*
• ARG 5-6/96: 184

19092. JD 682-2: SCHOECK—Das Schloss Dürande: Excerpts. *Anders, Cebotari, Domgraf-Fassbaender; Berlin State Opera; Heger, cond.* Recorded 1943.
+ ARG 5-6/96: 268

19093. JD 684-2: BERIO—Folk songs; Chamber music. DENISOV—La vie enrouge. *H. Fassbender, mezzo-soprano; Zürich Ensemble for New Music.*
□ ARG 7-8/94: 73

19094. JD 686-2: KARG-ELERT—Suite pointillistique; Symphonic canzone; Cello sonata; Little violin sonata. *Bosshart, flute; Schneeberger, violin; Grimmer, cello; Fahmi, piano.*
+ ARG 3-4/95: 120

19095. JD 687-2: BURKHARD—Mass, op. 85. *Beiler, Brodard; Gabrieli Choir; Bern Symphony Orch.; Gafner, cond.*
+ ARG 11-12/94: 86

19096. JD 690-2: SUTER—Nocturnes; String quartet no. 2; Ballade des Cortez Leuten. *Fukai, viola; Basel Symphony Orch.; Meier, cond.; Amati Quartet; Frankfurt Radio Symphony Orch.; Tschupp, cond.*
• ARG 11-12/94: 197

19097. JD 691-2: HINDEMITH—Piano music. *Bärtschi, piano.*
+ ARG 3-4/95: 114

19098. JD 693-2 (2 discs): MENDELSSOHN—Songs without words.

Meyer, piano.
• ARG 5-6/96: 149

19099. JD 700-2: BERTONI—Orfeo ed Euridice. *Juon, Fischer, Davislim, New Canton School Choir; Aargau Symphony Orch.; Tschupp, cond.*
• ARG 5-6/96: 84

19100. JD 702-2: SCHOENBERG—Verklärte Nacht. SCHULHOFF—Sextet. *Kammermusik Zürich.*
+ ARG 5-6/96: 185

19101. JS 266/67-2 (2 discs): BACH—Sonatas and partitas for solo violin. *Schneeberger, violin.*
+ Fa 5-6/89: 76

19102. JS 270/71-2 (2 discs): *Zürcher Liederbuch 1986.* Music of Schoeck, Boesch, Wettstein, Jordi, Haselbach, Derungs, and Irman. *Various performers.*
+ Fa 11-12/89: 343

19103. D 1006/07 (2 LPs): BACH—The flute sonatas. *Graf, flute; Barbé, harpsichord; Koch, viola da gamba.*
+ Fa 5-6/86: 92

19104. J 4400/01-2 (2 discs): BACH—Flute music. *Graf, flute; Barbé, harpsichord; Koch, viola da gamba.*
+ Fa 11-12/89: 114

19105. J 4402-2: Music of Bach, Dowland, Eyck, Telemann, Handel, and Anon. *Linde, recorder; Ragossnig, lute.*
+ ARG 1-2/90: 126
+ DA 12/89: 88
+ Fa 11-12/89: 118

19106. J 4403-2: TELEMANN—Six partitas for recorder and continuo; Sonatas for recorder and continuo: in C major; in F minor. *Zürcher, recorder; Barbé, harpsichord.*
+ ARG 3-4/90: 117
+ Fa 11-12/89: 383

19107. J 4404-2: MOZART—Cassations, K. 63, K. 99. *Collegium Musicum Zürich; Sacher, cond.*
+ ARG 3-4/90: 76
+ Fa 11-12/89: 285

19108. J 4405-2: MOZART—Sonatas for piano 4 hands, K. 358, K. 381, K. 497, K. 521; Andante with variations, K. 501. *I. & J. Vintschger, piano.*
+ ARG 11-12/89: 87

19109. J 4406-2: HOLZBAUER—Notturni no. 1-3; Quintet for flute, violin, viola, bassoon and harpsichord in G major. *Winterthur Baroque Quintet; Weber, viola; Frei, double bass.*
□ ARG 11-12/89: 68
- Fa 11-12/89: 285

19110. J 4407-2: HAYDN—Feldparthien, H.II:41-46. *Winds of the Zürich Tonhalle Orch.*

JECKLIN

+ ARG 11-12/89: 66
+ Fa 11-12/89: 232

19111. J 4408-2: VANHAL—Symphony in G minor. KROMMER—Concertino for flute and oboe in C major. J.C. BACH—Symphony op. 6, no. 6. *Rumpel, flute; Raoult, oboe; Camerata Zürich; Tschupp, cond.*
 • Fa 11-12/89: 255

19112. J 4409-2: *Virtuose Flötenquartette.* Flute quartets of Fürstenau, Haydn, and Hoffmeister. *Rumpel, flute; Kurtz, violin; Onozaki, viola; Hopkins, cello.*
 + Fa 11-12/89: 476

19113. J 4411-2: Flute music of Rossini, Czerny, Donizetti, and Kreutzer. *Rumpel, flute; Andres, piano.*
 + Fa 11-12/89: 114

19114. J 4420/21-2 (2 discs): SCHUBERT—Piano sonatas, D. 784, D. 845, D. 894, D. 959. *Leonhardt, fortepiano.*
 - Fa 3-4/90: 285
 + Gr 11/91: 131

19115. J 4422/23-2 (2 discs): SCHUBERT—Piano sonatas, D. 958, D. 960, D. 664, D. 850. *Leonhardt, fortepiano.*
 - Fa 3-4/90: 373

19116. J 4424/25-2 (2 discs): SCHUBERT—Piano sonatas, D. 557, D. 568, D. 537, D. 575, D. 566, D. 459. *Leonhardt, fortepiano.*
 - Fa 3-4/91: 365

19117. JD 5001-2: MARCELLO—Harpsichord sonatas. BACH—Harpsichord concerto after Marcello, BWV 981. *Hirsch, harpsichord.*
 + Fa 5-6/89: 229

19118. JD 5004-2: CARISSIMI—Lamento della Maria Stuarda; In un mar di pensieri; Amor mio; Deh, memoria; Suonerà l'ultima tromba. *Speiser, soprano; Hirsch, harpsichord & organ.*
 + ARG 9-10/89: 40
 + Fa 5-6/89: 155
 + Gr 3/89: 1470

JERUSALEM

19119. SCD 8005: VAÏNBERG—Symphony no. 6. SHOSTAKOVICH—From Jewish folk poetry. *Tuneh, Zakai, Jenkins; Neve-Shir Children's Choir; Jerusalem Symphony Orch.; Ahronovitch, cond.*
 + Fa 9-10/89: 378

19120. ATD 8507/08 (2 LPs): DEBUSSY—Preludes for piano, bk. 1-2. *Haimovsky, piano.*
 + Fa 1-2/87: 88

19121. CATD 8701: VÁRKONYI—Piano trio, op. 17; Leda, op. 42a. *Seraphim Trio; Shumsky, viola; Reisman, piano.*
 + Fa 9-10/87: 331

+ Gr 9/87: 436
+ Opus 12/87: 47

19122. CATD 8702: *Italian love songs from the 15th to 18th centuries.* Music of Bassini, Bononcini, Caccini, Caldara, Carissimi, Cesti, Del Leuto, Durante, Giordani, Lotti, Paisiello, Pergolesi, Rontani, and A. Scarlatti. *Kohn, baritone; English Chamber Orch.; Halstead, cond.*
 - ARG 7-8/88: 85
 - Fa 3-4/88: 243

JOHN MARKS RECORDS

19123. JMR 2: BRAHMS—Violin sonata no. 1. BEACH—Violin sonata. *Delmoni, violin; Funahashi, piano.*
 • ARG 1-2/97: 82
 + Fi 4/97: 103

19124. JMR 3: TCHAIKOVSKY—Variations on a rococo theme; Pezzo capriccioso; Nocturne, op. 19, no. 4. SHOSTAKOVICH—Cello concerto no. 1. *Rosen, cello; Sofia Phil. Orch.; Tabakov, cond.*
 - ARG 9-10/94: 211
 + Fa 7-8/94: 261

19125. JMR 4: *Transylvanian softwear.* Music of Klucevsek, Zorn, Duckworth, and Frith. *Klucevsek, free bass accordion.*
 + Fa 11-12/94: 472

19126. JMR 5: BRAHMS—Cello sonatas no. 1-2. SCHUMANN—Fantasy pieces, op. 73. MENDELSSOHN—Song without words, op. 109. *Rosen, cello; Stevenson, piano.*
 + ARG 1-2/95: 89
 + Fa 11-12/94: 186
 + Gr 3/95: 61

19127. JMR 6/7 (2 discs): BACH—Cello suites, BWV 1007-1012. *Rosen, cello.*
 + ARG 3-4/95: 69
 + Fa 1-2/95: 102
 • Gr 4/95: 89

LE JOUEUR

20397. LJD 001: *Duo Lengyel.* Music of Hubay, Farkas, Veress, and Kovach. *A. Lengyel, piano; G. Lengyel, violin.*
 + Fa 1-2/97: 330

JSL

19128. 143 (3 discs): VILLA-LOBOS—Bachianas brasileiras (complete). *Brazil Symphony Orch.; Karabtchevsky, cond.* Reissue.
 + ARG 1-2/96: 192

JUPITER

19129. 3107: HENSELT—Préambules. Music of Beethoven, Chopin, Rubinstein, and others. *Moyer, piano.*
 + ARG 9-10/96: 136

JUSTICE

19130. JR 1802-2: *Papal concert to commemorate the Holocaust.* Music of Bruch, Beethoven, Schubert, and Bernstein. *Royal Phil. Orch.; Coro "Cappella Giulia" della Basilica di San Pietro; Coro Dell' Accademia Filarmonica Romana; Harrell, cello; Dreyfuss, narrator; Nevison, cantor; Rodriguez, boy soprano; G. Levine, cond.*
 • ARG 1-2/95: 206
 + Fa 1-2/95: 375

JVC/MELODYIA

19131. VDC-540: SHOSTAKOVICH—Symphony no. 11. *USSR Ministry of Culture Symphony Orch.; Rozhdestvensky, cond.*
 - DA 10/86: 48

K RECORDS

19132. KOCO-2: BROCK—Berlin symphony; Largo from Three cinematographic scenes from The last laugh. *Beck, cello; Olympia Chamber Orch.; Brock, cond.*
 □ ARG 1-2/96: 249

K617

19133. K617004: BACH—Orgelbüchlein. *Petry, organ.*
 • Fa 11-12/92: 442

19134. K617007 (2 discs): *Orgues de Moselle.* Music of Bull, Frescobaldi, Valente, Roberday, Guilain and others. *Various performers.*
 + Fa 11-12/92: 442

19135. K617011: MOZART—Church sonatas. *Ferran, organ; Ensemble Stradivaria.*
 • Fa 11-12/92: 312

19136. K617012 (2 discs): *L'Orgue historique de Fénétrange.* Music of Purcell, De Grigny, Böhm, Bach, Mozart, Liszt and Brahms. *Petry, organ.*
 + Fa 11-12/92: 442

19137. K617014: *Glosses and variations for organ around 1620.* Music of Sweelinck, Frescobaldi, Schildt, Scheidemann, De Arauxo and Scheidt. *Petry, organ.*
 + Fa 11-12/92: 442

19138. K617015: Music of Frescobaldi, Monteverdi, Lotti, Allegri, Scheidemann, Gasparini and Charpentier. *Maîtrise de garçons de Colmar; Steyer, cond.*
 + Fa 11-12/92: 434

19139. K617016: *Festival de Musique Ancienne de Saintes.* Music of Cavalli, Rossi, Lassus, Schütz, Haydn, Mendelssohn and Bach. *Various performers.*

+ Fa 11-12/92: 431
□ Fa 11-12/92: 452

19140. K617017: CHARPENTIER—Leçons de ténèbres. TRAD.—Three ragas. *Zaepffel, countertenor; Dietschy, soprano; Ensemble Gradiva; Brahaspati, vocalist.*
• Fa 11-12/92: 216

19141. K617018: MENDELSSOHN—Oeuvre sacrée pour choeur et orgue. *Garreau De Labarre, organ; L'Ensemble vocal de Terville; Baltes, cond.*
- ARG 11-12/93: 148
- Fa 11-12/93: 321

19142. K617019: Music of Scriabin, Rachmaninoff, Balanchine, Nabokov, Lourié, Shostakovich, Prokofiev and Stravinsky. *Malraux, piano.*
• Fa 11-12/92: 446

19143. K617020: BENOÎT—Pâcques; Le chant intérieur. *Hommel, organ; Monks of Abbey of Clervaux.*
+ Fa 11-12/92: 199

19144. K617024: *Les chemins du baroque, vol. 3.* Music of Guerrero, Fernandez, Lienas, Aguilera de Heredia, Victoria, and Gregorian chant. *La Fenice ensemble; Cabré, cond.; Compañia Musical de las Americas.*
• ARG 5-6/93: 174
+ Fa 3-4/93: 359
+ Gr 9/93: 106

19145. K617025: *Les chemins du baroque, vol. 1.* Music of Juan de Araujo, Zipoli, Torrejon y Velasco, and Diego J. de Salazar. *Boys Choir of Cordoba (Argentina); Ensemble Elyma; Garrido, cond.*
+ Fa 3-4/93: 359
+ Gr 9/93: 106

19146. K617026: *Les chemins du baroque, vol. 2.* Music of M.A. Charpentier, Juan de Araujo, and Manuel de Sumaya. *Grande Ecurie et La Chambre du Roi; Malgoire, cond.; Compañia Musical de las Americas; Maîtrise nationale de Versailles.*
+ Fa 3-4/93: 359
+ Gr 9/93: 106

19147. K617027: ZIPOLI—Vespers of St. Ignatius. *Cordoba Boys Choir; Ensemble Elyma; Garrido, cond.*
+ ARG 9-10/93: 222
+ Fa 5-6/93: 358
+ Gr 9/93: 106

19148. K617028: MOZART—Vesperae solennes de Dominica/Litaniae Lauretanae B.M.V. *Choir of New College, Oxford; Hanover Band; Higginbottom, cond.*
- ARG 11-12/93: 155
+ Fa 11-12/93: 334

19149. K617030: MOZART—Clarinet concerto; Clarinet quintet. *Veilhan, basset-clarinet; Member of the Stadler Quintet; La Grande Ecurie et la chambre du roy; Malgoire, cond.*
• ARG 11-12/93: 155
+ Fa 11-12/93: 331

19150. K617031: DEBUSSY—Cello sonata. CHAUSSON—Piano trio. EMMANUEL—Cello sonata, op. 2. *Coppey, cello; Le Sage, piano; Wanderer Trio.*
+ ARG 11-12/93: 98
+ Fa 11-12/93: 215

19151. K617032: KUSSER—Six ouvertures de théâtre. *Musica Aeterna Bratislava; Les Menus Plaisirs; Zajíček, cond.*
+ Fa 11-12/93: 291

19152. K617033: Salga el torillo. *Ensemble Elyma; Garrido, cond.; various other groups.*
+ Fa 11-12/93: 477

19153. K617034: LEMÊTRE—Songes pour une nuit d'été. *Lemêtre, clarinet, percussion, voice; supporting instrumentalists.*
□ Fa 3-4/94: 231

19154. K617035: TORREJÓN Y VELASCO—Musique à la cité des rois. *Córdoba Boys Choir; Ensemble Elyma; Garrido, cond.*
+ ARG 3-4/94: 174
+ Fa 3-4/94: 348

19155. K617036: ZIPOLI—Sacred music. *Ensemble Elyma; Affetti Musicali; Cordoba Boys Choir; García Banegas, organ; Garrido, cond.*
+ ARG 5-6/94: 168
+ Fa 5-6/94: 288

19156. K617037: ZIPOLI—Cantatas; Organ music; Violin sonata. *Ensemble Elyma; Garrido, cond.; Ferran, organ.*
• ARG 9-10/94: 221

19157. K617038: ARAUJO—Villancicos; Lamentations; Magnificat. *Ensemble Elyma; Maîtrise Boréale; Garrido, cond.*
+ ARG 3-4/95: 65

19158. K617040 (2 discs): BACH—The art of fugue. *Grande Ecurie et la chambre du roy; Malgoire, cond.*
+ ARG 7-8/94: 63

19159. K617043: Missa Corsica. *A Cumpagnia; Casalonga, organ, harpsichord.*
□ ARG 11-12/94: 249
+ Fa 11-12/94: 461

19160. K617046: GOUVY—Requiem; Le printemps. *Greenawald, Maurus, Garino, Hemm; Chorus of the Schola de Vienne; Men's Chorus of Hombourg-Haut; Philarmonique de Lorraine Orch.; Houtmann, cond.*
+ ARG 3-4/95: 108
+ Fa 3-4/95: 177

19161. K617050 (2 discs): RUBINO—Vespers for the Stellario of Palermo. CAVALLI—Sonata a 12. DEL BUONO—Ave maris stella. *Ensemble Elyma; Nightingales of Poznan; Ensemble vocale dello Studio di Musica Antica Antonio Il Verso; Ensemble Eufonia; Ensemble Mille Regretz; Coro "Giovanni Pierluigi da Palestrina" di Messina; Garrido, cond.*
+ ARG 7-8/95: 183
+ Fa 5-6/95: 316
+ Fa 7-8/95: 296

19162. K617051: ESSYAD—Le collier des ruses. *Agoumi, Roukhe, Lorrain; other vocalists; instrumental ensemble; Nahon, cond.*
□ Fa 11-12/95: 250

19163. K617052: Le chant de la Jerusalem des terres froides. *Studio de Musique Ancienne de Montréal; Jackson, cond.*
+ Fa 1-2/96: 380

19164. K617053 (2 discs): DESMARETS—Marche Lorraine; Motets. *Fouchécourt, Procyshyn, Hoeven, Léonard, Richard, vocalists; Studio de Musique Ancienne de Montréal; Violons du Roy; Jackson, cond.*
+ ARG 7-8/96: 103
+ Fa 5-6/96: 136

19165. K617054: GOUVY—String quartet no. 5; Piano quintet; Songs. *Denis Clavier Quartet; Saroglou, piano; Gerstenhaber, soprano; Lucas, piano.*
+ ARG 5-6/96: 117
+ Fa 3-4/96: 170

19166. K617055 (2 discs): *L'orgue en Lorraine.* Music of Scheidt, Lebègue, Balbastre, Kerll, Buxtehude, Böhm, Back, Mendelssohn, Rheinberger, Ropartz, Liszt, Karg-Elert, and Camonin. *Various performers.*
+ Fa 7-8/96: 377

19167. K617056: *Chapel of the Dukes of Lorraine.* Music of Compère, Pierquin, Josquin, and others. *Ensemble Cantus Figuratus; La Traditora; Vellard, cond.*
+ ARG 9-10/96: 257
+ Fa 9-10/96: 364

19168. K617059: *Autour du livre d'orgue de Mexico.* Music of Torres, Olague, Carlston, Turk, and others. *Parra, Castellanos, organ.*
+ Fa 5-6/96: 350

19169. K617062: VIVALDI—Concertos with chalmeaux and clarinets. *Veilhan, clarinet, chalmeau; Accademia di Santa Cecilia; Couvert, cond.*
+ ARG 11-12/96: 229

19170. K617063 (2 discs): JOMMELLI—La passione di nostro signore Gesù Cristo. *Hermann, Beronesi, Francis, Picconi, vocal soloists; Ensemble Vocale*

Sigismondo D'India; Ensemble Vocale Eufonia; Berliner Barock Akademie; De Marchi, cond.
+ Fa 1-2/97: 182

19171. K617070: *Motets en espace.* Music of Lassus, Victoria, Caurroy, Guerrero, De Monte, Philips, Palestrina, Striggio and Tallis. *Matrise Nationale de Versailles; Choir of New College, Oxford; Gervais, Higginbottom, conds.*
+ Fa 11-12/92: 427

KAMELEON

19172. 9001: Music of Albeniz, Ibert, Marais, McGuire, and Piazzolla. *Kamrin, viola, viola; Goldberg, guitar.*
+ ARG 5-6/95: 208

KELLY HILL

19173. 430: Irish country airs. *Haggerty, soprano; Varley, piano; Ravnan, cello; Thompson, harp.*
+ ARG 11-12/95: 271

KEMDISC

19174. 1003: Music of Bizet, Massenet, Saint-Saëns, Offenbach, Gounod, and Delibes. *Adelaide Symphony Orch.; Serebrier, cond.*
+ Fa 5-6/87: 246

KEYBOARD RECORDS

19175. KGR 1027—1028 (2 separate discs): SCARLATTI—Keyboard sonatas, vol. 27-28. *Rowland, harpsichord.*
+ Gr 11/92: 161

19176. KGR 1043: FISCHER—Harpsichord suites. *Rowland, harpsichord.*
+ Gr 7/93: 65

KICCO CLASSIC

19177. 296 (2 discs): MASCAGNI—Amica. *Ricciarelli, Armiliato, Donati, Padovan; Hungarian Radio-TV Chorus & Orch.; Pace, cond.*
- ARG 11-12/96: 159
• Fa 11-12/96: 302
• Gr 2/97: 108
• ON 11/96: 45

19178. 396: DURANTE—Piano concerto. PRATI—Piano concerto. RAGAZZI—Concertos. *Solisti Partenopei; Caiazza, cond.; Cristiano, piano; Rogliano, violin.*
• ARG 1-2/97: 197

19179. 1195: *Desolation and despair.* Music of Ruta, Campana, Donizetti, Mercadante, and others. *Adkins-Chiti, mezzo-soprano; Sato, piano.*
+ ARG 1-2/97: 224

KING

19180. 39: Music of Cabezon, Praetorius, Hindemith, Bozza, and others. *Berlin Phil. Horn Quartet.*
+ ARG 11-12/96: 245

19181. 135: Music of Machaut, Dowland, Caccini, Guedron, Boesset, Bataille, Richard, Lefevre, Legrenzio Ciampi, Handel, Scarlatti, Schubert, Fererro, Poulenc, Offenbach, Satie, and Berio. *Visse, countertenor; Bellocq, lute; Fujii, piano.*
+ ARG 1-2/96: 238

19182. 137: SCHUBERT—Impromptus. *Schiff, piano.* Recorded 1978.
+ ARG 11-12/96: 200

KINGDOM

19183. KCLCD 2001: BALAKIREV—Piano sonata in B♭ minor. GLINKA—The lark (arr. Balakirev). SCRIABIN—Piano sonata no. 3; Vers la flamme, op. 72. *Fergus-Thompson, piano.*
+ ARG 11-12/89: 101
- Fa 11-12/89: 319

19184. KCLCD 2003: Piano music of Liszt, Debussy, Albéniz, Schumann, Bartók, Chopin, Schubert, Brahms, Rachmaninoff, and Beethoven. *Tirimo, piano.*
+ ARG 7-8/90: 122

19185. KCLCD 2004: SPOHR—Piano trios no. 1-2. *Beethoven Broadwood Trio.*
+ ARG 9-10/89: 108
• Fa 9-10/89: 333
+ Gr 3/89: 1448

19186. KCLCD 2005: *20th century harpsichord music.* Music of Persicetti, Adler, Albright, Martinů, Templeton, Sowash, and Thomson. *Harbach, harpsichord.*
+ Fa 11-12/90: 435

19187. KCLCD 2006: SCHUBERT—Violin sonatas no. 1-3. *Mason, violin; Freyhan, piano.*
+ Fa 7-8/89: 240

19188. KCLCD 2007: RACHMANINOFF—Piano sonatas no. 1-2. *Fergus-Thompson, piano.*
+ ARG 11-12/89: 101
- Fa 7-8/89: 178
+ Gr 6/89: 65

19189. KCLCD 2008: *Russian trinkets.* Music of Glinka, Dargomizhsky, Borodin, Tchaikovsky, Mussorgsky, Scriabin, Ilyinsky, Cui, and Balakirev. *Headington, piano.*
+ ARG 3-4/90: 137
- Fa 11-12/89: 451

19190. KCLCD 2010: *Harpsichord solos by 18th century women composers.* Music of Barthélemon, Martinez, Auenbrugg,

Gambarini, and Park. *Harbach, harpsichord.*
• Fa 11-12/89: 276
+ Gr 12/89: 1170

19191. KCLCD 2014/15 (2 discs): HAYDN—String quartets op. 33. *Bingham String Quartet.*
+ Gr 9/92: 110

19192. KCLCD 2027: *South American flute music.* Music of Ginastera, Villa-Lobos, and Piazzolla. *Various performers.*
+ Gr 12/92: 98

19193. KCLCD 2031: CHOPIN—Piano sonatas no. 2-3; Nocturne; Berceuse. *Lear, piano.*
• Gr 4/93: 87

19194. KLCD 5005, 5007 (2 2-disc sets): SCARLATTI—Keyboard sonatas. *Rowland, harpsichord.*
+ Gr 12/95: 117

KIWI-PACIFIC RECORDS

19195. CDSLD-90: LILBURN—Symphonies no. 1-3. *New Zealand Symphony Orch.; Hopkins, Heenan, conds.* Partly reissues.
+ Gr 3/94: 54

19196. CDSLD 100: LILBURN—Drysdale overture; A song of islands; Suite for orchestra; A birthday offering; Prodigal country. *Griffiths, baritone; Wellington Orpheus Choir; New Zealand Symphony Orch.; Hopkins, Groves, conds.*
+ Gr 5/96: 70

KLAVIER

19197. KCD-11007: Music of Massenet, Offenbach, and Berlioz. *Birmingham Symphony; Frémaux, cond.*
+ ARG 1-2/90: 62
+ Fa 5-6/91: 215
+ St 5/91: 175

19198. KCD-11012: BIZET—Symphony in C major; Roma suite. *Birmingham Symphony; Frémaux, cond.*
+ ARG 1-2/90: 32

19199. KCD-11016: *Enchanting Ravel.* RAVEL—Piano music. *Anderson, piano.*
• ARG 7-8/90: 90 m.f.

19200. KCD-11018: *Ignace Paderewski plays Beethoven, Liszt, Schubert, Debussy, vol. 1 (recital).* Music of Beethoven, Schubert, Liszt, Debussy, Mendelssohn, and Wagner. *Paderewski, piano.*
+ ARG 7-8/90: 145

19201. KCD-11019: PERSICHETTI—Serenade no. 10. BADINGS—Ballade; Cavatina. LAUBER—Four medieval dances. RENIE—Légende. *Di Tullio, flute;*

McDonald, harp.
+ Fa 5-6/91: 246

19202. KCD-11026: *Classical lute.* Music of Bach, Weiss, Visée, Gaultier, and Baron. *Satoh, lute.*
• ARG 11-12/92: 242

19203. KCD-11030: Piston—Turnbridge Fair. Dahl—Sinfonietta. Copland—Emblems. Maslanka—A child's garden of dreams. Bernstein—Slava. *Cincinnati College-Conservatory of Music Wind Symphony; Corporon, cond.*
+ ARG 7-8/92: 275
+ Fa 3-4/92: 418

19204. KCD-11032: Jongen—Two pieces, op. 33; Clair de lune; Soleil à midi; Sarabande triste, op. 58; Préludes, op. 69; Suite en forme de sonate, op. 60. *Stegall, piano.*
+ ARG 5-6/93: 99
+ Fa 1-2/93: 172

19205. KCD-11033: Sullivan—The tempest; Merchant of Venice; In memoriam. *City of Birmingham Symphony Orch.; Dunn, cond.* Reissue.
□ ARG 9-10/92: 170

19206. KCD-11034: Vaughan Williams—Toward the unknown region; Norfolk rhapsody no. 1; Fantasia on a theme of Tallis; Five variants of Dives and Lazarus. Mendelssohn—Hebrides overture. *City of Birmingham Symphony Orch.; Del Mar, cond.; Royal Liverpool Phil. Orch.; Tjeknavorian, cond.*
+ Fa 3-4/94: 350

19207. KCD-11036: *Pipe organ spectacular.* Music of Liszt, Reger, Reubke, and Franck. *Rawsthorne, organ.*
+ Fa 3-4/94:
+ Fa 3-4/94

19208. KCD-11037: *The romantic violin.* Music of Falla, Ravel, Dvořák, Brahms, Mussorgsky, Sarasate, and others. *Zsigmondy, violin; Nissen, piano; Vienna Kohonaden Orch.; Hagen, cond.*
+ Fa 3-4/94: 417

19209. KCD-11038: Stravinsky—The firebird. Prokofiev—Piano pieces. *Stravinsky, Prokofiev, piano.* Recorded using reproducing piano rolls.
+ Fa 7-8/94: 254

19210. KCD-11040: Offenbach—Overtures. Berlioz—Overtures. *City of Birmingham Symphony Orch.; Frémaux, cond.* Reissue.
+ ARG 3-4/93: 119

19211. KCD-11041: A.-L. Couperin—Pièces de clavecin. *Paul, harpsichord.*
• ARG 9-10/94: 120
+ EM 5/95: 335
+ Fa 3-4/94: 166
+ Gr 7/94: 79

19212. KCD-11042: Music of Reicha, McTee, Gillingham, Ives, and Gould. *CCM Wind Symphony; Corporon, cond.*
+ ARG 7-8/93: 197
+ Fa 3-4/94: 440

19213. KCD-11043: Cello encores. *Drinkall, cello; Baker, piano.*
+ ARG 11-12/93: 232
- Fa 3-4/94: 287

19214. KCD-11044: Music of Vierne, Elmore, Kabalevsky, Mendelssohn, and others. *Christiansen, organ.*
+ ARG 11-12/93: 238
+ Fa 3-4/94: 402

19215. KCD-11045: Music of Falla, Plaza, Troilo, Mores, Heinze, Guastavino, and others. *Santa Fe Guitar Quartet.*
• ARG 9-10/94: 237
+ Fa 3-4/94: 430

19216. KCD-11046: Mozart—Violins concertos no. 3, 5; Cassation, K. 99. *Maazel, violin & cond.; English Chamber Orch.; Dutch-English Mozart Ensemble.*
• Fa 11-12/94: 310

19217. KCD-11047: *Soundings.* Persichetti—Symphony no. 6. Gregson—Celebration. Maw—American games. Schoenberg—Theme and variations. Gershwin—Rhapsody in blue. *Black, piano; Cincinnati College-Conservatory Wind Symphony; Corporon, cond.*
+ ARG 7-8/94: 222
+ Fa 9-10/95: 273

19218. KCD-11048: *American dreams.* Music of Bernstein, Schuman, Copland, and Reed. *Cincinnati College-Conservatory of Music Wind Symphony; Corporon, cond.*
+ Fa 3-4/94: 439

19219. KCD-11049: *Opening night.* Music of Thomas, Massenet, Grétry, Hérold, Adam, and Offenbach. *American Promenade Orch.; Graham, cond.*
- ARG 9-10/94: 224
+ Fa 9-10/94: 433

19220. KCD-11050: Reinecke—Trio for oboe, horn, and piano, op. 188; Trio for clarinet, viola, and piano, op. 264; Trio for clarinet, horn, and piano, op. 274. *Dallas Chamber Players.*
+ ARG 11-12/94: 176
+ Fa 11-12/94: 355

19221. KCD-11051: Druckman—Paean; In memoriam Vincent Persichetti. Wilson—Piece of mind. Kurka—The good soldier Schweik suite. Diamond—Tantivy. *Cincinnati Wind Symphony; Corporon, cond.*
□ Fa 7-8/94: 331

19222. KCD-11052: *Shenandoah: American chorister 1890-1990.* Music of

MacDowell, Barber, Stevens, Mechem, Rutenberg, and Erb. *Los Angeles Chamber Singers; Rutenberg, cond.*
+ ARG 1-2/95: 238
• Fa 1-2/95: 339

19223. KCD-11054: *The Bach boys.* W.F. Bach—Sinfonia, F. 65. C.P.E. Bach—Sinfonias, H. 659; H. 663. J.C.F. Bach—Sinfonia in D minor. J.C. Bach—Sinfonias, op. 6 no. 3, 6. *Ensemble for Eighteenth Century Music; Hashimoto, cond.*
+ ARG 7-8/95: 72
+ Fa 7-8/95: 110

19224. KCD-11055: *Tryptych.* Harp trios by Mathias, Ravel, and Beethoven. *Dallas Tryptych Players.*
+ ARG 7-8/95: 241
+ Fa 7-8/95: 436

19225. KCD-11056: Bartók—Violin sonatas no. 1-2; Sonata for solo violin. *Zsigmondy, violin; Nissen, piano.*
+ Fa 3-4/96: 119

19226. KCD-11057: Music of Beethoven, Brahms, Debussy, and Farkas. *Kalamos Clarinet Quartet.*
+ ARG 1-2/97: 203
• Fa 9-10/96: 422

19227. KCD-11058: *Postcards.* Music of Adams, Nelson, Milhaud, Ticheli, and Margolis. *Cincinnati College-Conservatory of Music Wind Symphony; Corporon, cond.*
+ Fa 5-6/95: 444

19228. KCD-11059: *Paradigm.* Music of Stravinsky, Rands, Freund, Hindemith, Harbison, and Gregson. *CCM Wind Symphony; Corporon, cond.*
+ ARG 3-4/95: 245
+ Fa 5-6/95: 439

19229. KCD-11060: *American variations.* Music of Gould, Ticheli, Clarke, Ives, Picchi, Romberg, Bennett, Goldman, Bellstedt, Reeves, Rogers, and Simon. *Bowman, euphonium; Cincinnati College-Conservatory of Music Wind Symphony; Corporon, cond.*
+ ARG 11-12/95: 258
+ Fa 9-10/95: 425

19230. KCD-11062: Boccherini—Symphonies no. 6, 8, 26. *University of Cincinnati Ensemble for 18th Century Music; Hashimoto, cond.*
+ ARG 7-8/96: 85
+ Fa 7-8/96: 118

19231. KCD-11063: *Musical colors.* Music of Lauber, Donizetti, Paradis, Marais, Miyagi, Ibert, Krumpholtz, Bach, Rossini, Fauré, Chopin, and Anon. *Hedrick, flute; Bennett, harp.*
- ARG 1-2/97: 204
+ Fa 11-12/96: 453

KLAVIER

19232. KCD-11064: *Hearts music.* Music of Diamond, Hartley, Murray, Colgrass, and Nelson. *Cincinnati Wind Symphony; Corporon, cond.*
+ Fa 1-2/96: 413

19233. KCD-11065: RACHMANINOFF—Vespers. *Master Chorale of Orange County; Hall, cond.*
● ARG 3-4/96: 170
- Fa 3-4/96: 255

19234. KCD-11066: Music of Persichetti, Gillingham, Gilmore, Zappa, and Schmitt. *CCM Wind Symphony; Corporon, cond.*
+ Fa 5-6/96: 233

19235. KCD-11067: *In concert.* Music of Stamp, Tcherepnin, Tippett, Grainger, Weinstein, and Skalkottas. *Cincinnati Wind Symphony; Corporon, Milligan, conds.*
+ ARG 1-2/97: 216
+ Fa 11-12/96: 471

19236. KCD-11068: BEETHOVEN—Cello sonata no. 3. SAINT-SAËNS—Cello sonata no. 1; Suite for cello and piano, op. 16. *Drinkall-Baker Duo.*
- ARG 5-6/96: 181
- Fa 5-6/96: 104

19237. KCD-11069: *Romantic French fantasies.* Music of Vierne, Boëllmann, Alain, Franck, Dupré, and Widor. *Longhurst, organ.*
● ARG 1-2/96: 217
+ Fa 1-2/96: 390

19238. KCD-11070: *Tributes.* Music of Stamp, Tull, Grantham, Gould, Cichy, Holst, McTee, and Welcher. *North Texas Wind Symphony; Corporon, cond.*
+ ARG 3-4/96: 239
+ Fa 1-2/96: 413

19239. KCD-11071: *Bird songs: romantic chamber music of Arthur Bird.* BIRD—Serenade, op. 40; Suite in D major, op. 29; Marche miniature. TULL—Concertino for oboe and small orchestra. TICHELI—Pacific fanfare. *Veazey, oboe; North Texas Chamber Players; Corporon, cond.*
+ ARG 3-4/96: 239
+ Fa 1-2/96: 154

19240. KCD-11072: GLINKA—Trio pathétique. MOZART—Piano quintet, K. 452. BARTÓK—Contrasts. *Bilyeu, piano; West, clarinet; Hammel, bassoon; Teachey, oboe; Paterson, horn; Roelofs, violin.*
+ Fa 11-12/96: 256

19241. KCD-11073: *Piano and clarinet.* Music of Lutosławski, Faith, Genzmer, Delmas, Muczynski, and Alwyn. *West, clarinet; Grace, piano.*
+ ARG 11-12/96: 246
+ Fa 11-12/96: 452

19242. KCD-77006: Stairway to the stars: the San Sylmar Wurlitzer pipe organ. *Hazleton, organ.*
+ ARG 1-2/95: 225

19243. KCD-77007: An old-fashioned Christmas. *St. Amant Consort; Watts, cond.*
+ Fa 11-12/94: 508

19244. KCD-77008: *Whiplash.* Music of Bach, Tchaikovsky, Debussy, Bizet, Stamp, Green, Bolcom, Joel, and Levy. *O-Zone Percussion Group; Olmstead, cond.*
+ Fa 7-8/94: 326

19245. KCD-77009: *Please don't shoot the piano player, again!* Music for player piano.
□ Fa 1-2/95: 360

19246. KCD-77014: *The pipes of the mighty Wurlitzer.* Music of Berlin, Arlen, Kern, Rodgers, Torch, Ellington, Sullivan, Blane, Edwards and Rose. *Hazleton, organ.*
+ Fa 1-2/96: 387

KOCH INTERNATIONAL CLASSICS

19247. 3-7700/7704-2 (3 discs): *Albert Coates conducts, vol. 1-2.* Music of Glinka, Borodin, Liadov, Liszt, Weber, Wagner and others. *London Symphony Orch.; Coates, cond.* Recorded 1926-30.
+ Fa 1-2/93: 316
+ Gr 12/92: 148

19248. 3-7000-2: BERNSTEIN—Arias and barcarolles; Musical comedies: Songs and duets. *Kay, soprano; Sharp, baritone; Barrett, Blier, pianos.*
+ ARG 7-8/90: 28
+ DA 11/90: 69
+ Fa 7-8/90: 100
+ Gr 6/90: 93
+ MA 11/90: 70
+ NYT 6/3/90: H22
+ SR 7/90: 91

19249. 3-7001-2: Music of Bergsma, Tovey, Villa-Lobos, and Beach. *Dwyer, flute; Manhattan String Quartet.*
+ ARG 9-10/90: 140
+ Fa 7-8/90: 367
+ NYT 6/3/90: H22

19250. 3-7002-2: GOULD—Dance variations for 2 pianos and orchestra. PISTON—Concerto for 2 pianos and orchestra. COPLAND—Danzón cubano; Rodeo: Hoedown; Saturday night waltz; El salón México. *Pierce, Jonas, pianos; Royal Phil. Orch.; Amos, cond.*
- ARG 7-8/90: 147
+ DA 11/90: 70
+ Fa 7-8/90: 157
- Gr 10/90: 752
+ NYT 6/3/90: H22
+ SR 8/90: 89

19251. 3-7003-2: GRAINGER—Warriors; Beautiful fresh flower; Hill-song no. 12; Irish tune from County Derry; Hill-song no. 2; Colleen Dhas; Danish folk music suite. *Melbourne Symphony Orch.; Simon, cond.*
+ ARG 9-10/90: 68
□ Fa 11-12/90: 239
+ Gr 11/90: 976
+ St 1/91: 255

19252. 3-7004-2: MOZART—Sinfonia concertante, K. 364; Divertimento, K. 563. *J. Fuchs, violin; L. Fuchs, viola; Tortelier, cello; Prades Festival Orch.; Casals, cond.*
+ ARG 9-10/90: 95
- Fa 7-8/90: 212

19253. 3-7005-2: BARBER—Souvenirs. MENOTTI—Amahl and the night visitors: Introduction; March; Shepherd's dance; Sebastian suite. *New Zealand Symphony Orch.; Schenck, cond.*
+ ARG 7-8/90: 71
+ Fa 9-10/90: 162
+ Gr 9/90: 507
+ MA 5/91: 67

19254. 3-7007-2: DVOŘÁK—Symphonies no. 7-8. *Czech Phil. Orch.; Talich, cond.*
+ Fa 9-10/90: 235 m.f.

19255. 3-7008-2: *Romantic French & German organ music.* Music of Jongen, Karg-Elert, Dupré, Vierne, and Reger. *Long, organ.*
+ Fa 9-10/90: 480

19256. 3-7009-2: FRANCK—Violin sonata. FAURÉ—Berceuse. YSAŸE—Solo sonata no. 6. RAVEL—Violin sonata. SAINT-SAËNS—Caprice. *Kavakos, violin; Epperson, piano.*
- ARG 9-10/91: 167
+ Fa 11-12/90: 300

19257. 3-7010-2: BARBER—Medea: Suite; Essay no. 3; Fadograph of a yestern scene. *New Zealand Symphony Orch.; Schenck, cond.*
+ ARG 7-8/91: 24
+ Fa 3-4/91: 142
+ Gr 1/91: 1369
+ MA 5/91: 67
+ SR 1/91: 98

19258. 3-7011-2: HAYDN—Symphony no. 88. MOZART—Symphony no. 39. GLUCK—Alceste: Overture. BEETHOVEN—Leonore overture no. 3. *Vienna Phil. Orch.; Krauss, Walter, cond.; Berlin State Opera Orch.; Kleiber, cond.; Concertgebouw Orch.; Mengelberg, cond.*
+ ARG 11-12/184
+ Fa 11-12/90: 471
+ Gr 1/91: 1417

19259. 3-7012-2: *Twenty fanfares for the common man.* Music of Copland, Hanson, Harris, Cowell, Wagenaar, Gould, Taylor, Bernstein, Fuleihan,

Thomson, Piston, Creston, and Goossens. *London Phil. Orch.; Mester cond.*
+ ARG 1-2/91: 127
• Fa 11-12/90: 472
+ Gr 7/91: 74
+ SR 1/91: 104

19260. 3-7013-2: Music of Saint-Saëns, Rachmaninoff, Britten, Bax, Benjamin, Debussy, and Lutosławski. *Pierce, Jonas, pianos.*
- ARG 1-2/91: 140
• Fa 11-12/90: 433

19261. 3-7014-2: SCARLATTI— Harpsichord sonatas. *Thornburgh, harpsichord.*
+ ARG 11-12/91: 140
+ DA 2/91: 60
+ Fa 1-2/91: 299
+ Gr 10/91: 144

19262. 3-7015-2: GLINKA—Trio pathétique for piano, clarinet, and cello in D minor. BEETHOVEN—Trio for piano, clarinet, and cello in E♭ major. *Trio d'Amsterdam.*
+ ARG 3-4/91: 149
+ Fa 3-4/91: 219

19263. 3-7016-2: JONGEN—Concert à cinq. DEBUSSY—Sonata for flute, viola, and harp. JOLIVET—Chant de Linos. *Atlantic Sinfonietta.*
+ DA 4/91: 60
+ Fa 1-2/91: 393

19264. 3-7017-2: SHOSTAKOVICH— Execution of Stepan Razin. SVIRIDOV— Oratorio pathétique. *Vasilev, bass; Varna Phil. Chorus & Orch.; Andreev, cond.*
+ ARG 1-2/91: 97
- Fa 1-2/91: 316
- Gr 3/91: 1713
- MA 5/91: 84

19265. 3-7018-2: VAUGHAN WILLIAMS— Symphony no. 4. HOLST—Planets. *BBC Symphony Orch.; Vaughan Williams, cond.; London Symphony Orch.; Holst, cond.*
+ ARG 3-4/91: 182
+ Fa 5-6/81: 304
+ St 7/91: 187

19266. 3-7019-2: BARBER—Medea (original ballet). COPLAND—Appalachian spring. *Atlantic Sinfonietta.*
+ ARG 7-8/91: 24
+ Fa 3-4/91: 142
+ Gr 4/92: 43
+ MA 5/91: 67
+ SR 1/91: 98

19267. 3-7020-2: DELLO JOIO—Air power. GOULD—Holocaust suite. *Cracow Phil. Orch.; Amos, cond.*
• ARG 5-6/91: 50
+ Fa 3-4/91: 197

19268. 3-7021-2: Music of Ravel, Mahler, Berg, Webern, and Handel. *Zakai, alto; Zak, piano; Biron, flute;*

Haran, cello; Shalev, harpsichord.
- ARG 5-6/91: 167
• Fa 3-4/91: 450
• Gr 5/91: 2056

19269. 3-7022-2: BRUCKNER—Symphony no. 7. *Berlin Phil. Orch.; Horenstein, cond.*
+ Fa 5-6/91: 146

19270. 3-7023-2: BARBER—Canzonetta for oboe and string orchestra. R. STRAUSS—Oboe concerto. WOLF-FERRARI—Idillio-concertino. VAUGHAN WILLIAMS—Oboe concerto. *Lucarelli, oboe; Lehigh Valley Chamber Orch.; Spieth, cond.*
• Fa 11-12/91: 253

19271. 3-7024-2: DUBOIS—Saxophone quartet. SINGELÉE—Saxophone quartet no. 1. LEVY—Tenor indigo; Quartet; Lament. WOODS—Three improvisations for saxophone quartet. PECK—Drastic measures. *Prism Quartet.*
+ ARG 3-4/91: 160
+ Fa 3-4/91: 496

19272. 3-7025-2: IVES—Country band march; Four ragtime dances; Postlude in F; Calcium light night; Yale- Princeton football game; Set for theater orchestra; Largo cantabile; Three places in New England (version for small orchestra). *Orch. of New England; Sinclair, cond.*
+ ARG 1-2/91: 58
+ DA 5/91: 72
+ Fa 3-4/91: 245
+ Gr 2/91: 1506
+ MA 3/91: 77
+ SR 4/91: 97

19273. 3-7026-2: GOULD—Quotations; A capella; Of time and the river. *New York Choral Society and Orch.; Goodwin, cond.; Gregg Smith Singers; Smith, cond.*
- ARG 3-4/91: 71
+ Fa 3-4/91: 222
+ Gr 4/91: 1882

19274. 3-7027-2: HARBISON—Twilight music; Variations for clarinet, violin, and piano. ROCHBERG—Piano quartet. *American Chamber Players; Battersby, piano.*
+ Fa 3-4/91: 233
+ Gr 7/91: 77

19275. 3-7028-2: GERSHWIN—*He loves and she loves*. Songs and duets. *Kay, soprano; Sharp, baritone; Blier, piano.*
+ Gr 7/91: 96

19276. 3-7029-2: BRUCH—Eight pieces for clarinet, viola, and piano, op. 83. MOZART—Trio for clarinet, viola and piano, K. 498. *American Chamber Players.*
+ ARG 5-6/91: 38
+ Fa 5-6/91: 143
- MA 7/91: 69

19277. 3-7031-2: TELEMANN—Fourth book of quartets. *American Baroque.*
• ARG 9-10/91: 137
+ DA 10/91: 52
+ Fa 7-8/91: 310
+ Gr 12/91: 70

19278. 3-7032-2: SMETANA—Má vlast. *Czech Phil. Orch.; Talich, cond.*
+ ARG 5-6/91: 111
• Fa 5-6/91: 287

19279. 3-7033-2: STOYANOV—Liturgia solemnis. *Vasilev, bass; Slavonic Voices Male Chamber Choir; Varna Phil. Orch.; Matakiev, cond.*
+ ARG 5-6/91: 156
+ Fa 5-6/91: 289

19280. 3-7034-2: BRAHMS—Sonatas arr. for horn: op. 120, no. 2 (originally for clarinet), op. 38 (originally for cello). *Brubaker, horn; Levy, piano.*
+ ARG 1-2/92: 36
+ Fa 7-8/91: 127

19281. 3-7035-2: Music of Beethoven, Liszt, Metner, Prokofiev, and Godowsky. *Moiseiwitsch, piano; London Phil. Orch.; Szell, Lambert, cond.*
+ ARG 7-8/91: 172
+ Fa 7-8/91: 361

19282. 3-7036-2: CRESTON—Symphony no. 2; Walt Whitman; Corinthians XIII. *Cracow Phil. Orch.; Amos, cond.*
- ARG 7-8/91: 172
+ Fa 7-8/91: 235
+ Gr 4/92: 46

19283. 3-7037-2: *Suites for dancing*. BACH—Orchestral suites (complete). *Boston Early Music Soloists; Malloch, cond.*
+ Fa 5-6/91: 114
+ Gr 10/91: 74

19284. 3-7038-2: *Music from Washington*. Music by Vecchi, Monteverdi, Haydn, Mendelssohn, Vaughan Williams, Copland and Ives. *National Gallery Vocal Arts Ensemble.*
+ ARG 11-12/91: 199

19285. 3-7040-2: MOZART—Piano sonatas 4, 14; Fantasy, K. 475. *Tomšič, piano.*
• ARG 7-8/91: 120
+ ARG 11-12/91: 120
+ Fa 7-8/91: 235

19286. 3-7041-2: BLOCH—Quintets for piano and strings, no. 1-2. *American Chamber Players.*
• ARG 3-4/92: 34
+ Fa 11-12/91: 276

19287. 3-7042-2: KABALEVSKY—The Comedians. GLINKA—Kamarinskaya. PROKOFIEV—A Summer day. TCHAIKOVSKY—Orchestral suite no. 4. *San Diego Chamber Orch.; Barra, cond.*
+ ARG 9-10/91: 151

KOCH INTERNATIONAL CLASSICS

19288. 3-7043-2: *Twilight fancies.*
DELIUS—Songs. *Golden, soprano; Sulich, piano.*
+ ARG 7-8/91: 51
+ Fa 7-8/91: 148
• HPR v.8, no.3/91: 71

19289. 3-7044-2: HAYDN—Arianna a Naxos; Ten English canzonettas. *Nelson, soprano; Thornburgh, fortepiano.*
+ Fa 7-8/92: 176
+ Gr 11/91: 139

19290. 3-7045-2: GRIFFES—Three fantasy pieces; Piano sonata; Three tone pictures. MACDOWELL—Piano sonata no. 4. *Landes, piano.*
+ ARG 1-2/92: 60
+ Fa 7-8/91: 167
+ Gr 7/91: 87

19291. 3-7046-2: BACH—Toccatas, BWV 912, BWV 910; Sonata in D minor, BWV 964; Partita no. 4, BWV 828 . *Mattax, harpsichord.*
+ ARG 7-8/91: 18 m.f
+ Fa 7 8/91: 103

19292. 3-7047-2: BOLCOM—Casino Paradise. *Nolen; Metz; Korbich; American Music Theater Festival; Barrett, cond.*
+ Fa 1-2/92: 179

19293. 3-7048-2: WALLACE—Kabbalah. *Soloists; Instrumental ensemble; Barrett, cond.*
+ ARG 11-12/91: 168
+ Fa 1-2/92: 372

19294. 3-7050-2: BLITZSTEIN—Zipperfly and other songs. *Sharp, baritone; Holvick, soprano; Blier, piano.*
+ ARG 11-12/91: 36
+ Fa 7-8/91: 123

19295. 3-7051-2: *More music for Martha Graham.* MENOTTI—Errand into the maze. HINDEMITH—Hérodiade. SCHUMAN—Night journey. *Atlantic Sinfonietta; Schenck, cond.*
+ ARG 1-2/92: 144
+ Fa 9-10/91: 444
+ Gr 4/92: 43

19296. 3-7053-2: *The young Otto Klemperer.* WEILL—Kleine Dreigroschenmusik. R. STRAUSS—Till Eulenspiegels lustige Streiche, op. 26; Salome: Dance of the seven veils. BRAHMS—Symphony no. 1 in C minor, op. 68. *Berlin State Opera Orch.; Klemperer, cond.*
+ Fa 9-10/91: 442

19297. 3-7055-2: GENZMER—Trio. NIELSEN—3 Short pieces from The Mother. DEBUSSY—6 Epigraphes antiques. GUBAIDULINA—Garden of joys and sorrows. *Auréole.*
+ ARG 11-12/91: 179

19298. 3-7056-2: COLERIDGE-TAYLOR— Clarinet quintet; Petite suite de concert; Ballade in D minor; Spirituals for piano. *Wright, clarinet; Hawthorne Quartet; Eskin, piano; Ludwig, violin.*
+ ARG 7-8/92: 120
+ Fa 9-10/92: 218
+ Gr 10/92: 127

19299. 3-7057-2: BYRD—Keyboard music. *Thornburgh, keyboard.*
• ARG 11-12/91: 50
+ Gr 4/92: 110

19300. 3-7058-2: HOLST—Brook Green suite; Lyric movement for viola and orchestra; A fugal concerto; Morris dance tunes; St. Paul's suite. *New Zealand Chamber Orch.; Braithwaite, cond.; Yendoll, viola; Still, flute; Popperwell, oboe.*
+ ARG 11-12/91: 82
• Fa 1-2/92: 240
- Gr 4/92: 50

19301. 3-7059-2 (2 discs): *Wilhelm Furtwängler: the early recordings, vol. 1.* Works by J.S. Bach, Mozart, Schubert, Beethoven, Weber and Rossini. *Berlin Phil. Orch.; Furtwängler, cond.* Recorded 1926-37.
+ Fa 11-12/91: 472

19302. 3-7060-2: DVOŘÁK—Symphony no. 6. SUK—Serenade for strings. *Czech Phil. Orch.; Talich, cond.*
+ ARG 11-12/91: 62
□ Fa 1-2/92: 204

19303. 3-7061-2: SIBELIUS—Symphony no. 4; Orchestral works. *London Phil. Orch.; Beecham, cond.* Recorded 1938.
+ Fa 3-4/92: 326

19304. 3-7062-2: GRANADOS—Goyescas. NIN—Tonadas (Selections). *Battersby, piano.*
+ ARG 1-2/92: 59

19305. 3-7063-2: GRIFFES—Poem. HANSON—Serenade. HOVHANESS—Elibris. BLOCH—Suite modale. KENNAN—Night soliloquy. FOOTE—Night piece. ARNOLD—Concerto. *Still, flute; New Zealand Chamber Orch.; Braithwaite, cond.*
+ ARG 1-2/92: 152
+ Fa 1-2/92: 417

19306. 3-7065-2: HAYDN—Die Jahreszeiten. *Augér, Aler, Hagegård; Minnesota Chorale; St. Paul Chamber Orch.; Revzen, cond.*
+ ARG 3-4/92: 72
• Fa 11-12/91: 343
• Gr 1/92: 84

19307. 3-7066-2: BEETHOVEN—Piano sonatas no. 23, 26, 31. *Tomšič, piano.*
+ ARG 3-4/92: 31
+ Fa 1-2/92: 162

19308. 3-7067-2: GOUNOD—Petite symphonie for winds. DEBUSSY (ORCH. FALDNER)—Symphony in B minor. MILHAUD—Symphonies pour petit orchestre, no. 1-3, 5. *Sinfonia Orch. of Chicago; Faldner, cond.*
+ ARG 3-4/93: 157
• Fa 1-2/93: 156

19309. 3-7068-2: SCHUMANN—Songs and duets. *Hunt, mezzo-soprano; Ollmann, baritone; Barrett, piano.*
- ARG 5-6/92: 131
- Fa 5-6/92: 251

19310. 3-7069-2: PORTER—String quartet no. 3. BARBER—String quartet no. 1. PISTON—String quartet no. 1. *Chester Quartet.*
+ ARG 3-4/92: 177
+ Fa 5-6/92: 224
+ Gr 11/92: 118

19311. 3-7070-2: BARBER—Cello sonata. FOSS—Capriccio. ORNSTEIN—Cello sonata. *Hanani, cello; Levin, piano.*
• ARG 11-12/93: 231
+ Fa 9-10/93: 115
+ Gr 10/93: 61

19312. 3-7072-2: SCHUBERT—Symphony no. 9 "The great." BERLIOZ—Roman carnival overture. LISZT—Hungarian rhapsody no. 1. SMETANA—The Moldau. *London Symphony Orch.; Berlin Phil. Orch.; Berlin State Opera Orch.; Blech, cond.* Recorded 1927.
- Fa 1-2/92: 322

19313. 3-7073-2 (2 discs): *Wilhelm Furtwängler: the early recordings, vol. 2.* Works by Weber, Mendelssohn, Berlioz, Wagner, Brahms, J. Strauss, Jr., R. Strauss. *Berlin Phil. Orch.; Furtwängler, cond.* Recorded 1926-37.
+ Fa 11-12/91: 472

19314. 3-7074-2: THOMPSON— Symphonies no. 2-3. *New Zealand Symphony Orch.; Schenck, cond.*
+ ARG 11-12/91: 162
+ Fa 11-12/91: 511
+ Fa 3-4/93: 153
+ Gr 9/92: 94

19315. 3-7076-2: MOZART—Symphonies no. 39-41. *Staatskapelle Berlin; Strauss, cond.* Recorded 1928.
+ Fa 1-2/92: 168

19316. 3-7077-2: *The young John Barbirolli.* Music of Haydn, Mozart, Purcell, Tchaikovsky, and Grieg. *London Phil. Orch.; Barbirolli, cond.* Recorded 1928-33.
+ Fa 1-2/92: 436

19317. 3-7078-2: STRAVINSKY—L'Histoire du soldat: Suite; Duo concertante; Three pieces for clarinet; Elegy; Six pieces for violin & piano; Baiser de la fée: Ballad; Pastorale; Firebird: Excerpts. *American*

Chamber Players.
+ Fa 3-4/92: 338

19318. 3-7081-2: *The Sylvan winds.*
Music of Jongen, Bernard, Schmitt, and
d'Indy. *The Sylvan Winds.*
+ Fa 9-10/92: 437

19319. 3-7082-2: ARCHDUKE RUDOLPH OF
AUSTRIA—Variations on a theme by
Prince Louis Ferdinand of Prussia; Violin
sonata. *Suk, violin; Kagan, piano.*
+ ARG 1-2/93: 141
+ Gr 7/93: 61

19320. 3-7084-2: STILL—Bells; Seven
traceries; Lenox Avenue; Swanee River;
Five preludes; Three visions: Africa.
Oldham, piano.
+ ARG 7-8/92: 228
+ Fa 7-8/92: 287

19321. 3-7085-2: SCHÜTZ—Motets.
Chorus of Emmanuel Music; Smith, cond.
• ARG 5-6/92: 132
+ Fa 3-4/92: 320
• Gr 5/92: 96

19322. 3-7086-2: *Unquiet peace: the Lied
between the wars.* Music of Weill, Eisler,
R. Strauss, Pfitzner, Busoni, Zemlinsky,
Schoeck, and Bienert. *New York Festival
of Song.*
+ ARG 5-6/93: 180
+ Fa 3-4/93: 350
+ Gr 7/93: 84

19323. 3-7087-2: WEILL—Stranger here
myself: songs. *Réaux, soprano;
Schimmel, accordion; Ruyle, percussion;
Kapilow, piano.*
+ ARG 7-8/92: 244
- Fa 7-8/92: 324
+ Gr 6/92: 83

19324. 3-7091-2: KURKA—Good soldier
Schweik: Suite. MILHAUD—Création du
monde. WEILL—Kleine
Dreigroschenmusik. *Atlanta Sinfonietta;
Schenck, cond.*
+ ARG 5-6/92: 78
+ Fa 7-8/92: 196

19325. 3-7092-2: COPLAND—The tender
land: suite; Three Latin-American
sketches; The red pony: suite. *Phoenix
Symphony Orch.; Sedares, cond.*
+ ARG 3-4/92: 48
+ Fa 1-2/92: 199
+ Gr 4/92: 46
+ St 5/92: 195

19326. 3-7093-2: BAIRSTOW—Choral
music. *Choir of St. Thomas Church, New
York; Hancock, cond.*
+ ARG 5-6/92: 25
+ Fa 3-4/92: 139
+ St 3/93: 179

19327. 3-7094-2: IBERT—Divertissement;
Concertino da camera. POULENC—
Sinfonietta. *San Diego Chamber Orch.;
Barra, cond.*

+ ARG 3-4/92: 119
+ Fa 3-4/92: 216
- Gr 4/92: 52

19328. 3-7096-2: MONTÉCLAIR—Cantatas:
La bergère; La mort de Didon; Pan et
Sirinx. CLÉRAMBAULT—Médée. *Baird,
soprano; American Baroque; Schultz,
cond.*
+ ARG 3-4/92: 103
+ EM 2/93: 152
+ Fa 3-4/92: 246
+ Gr 9/92: 142

19329. 3-7098-2: RACHMANINOFF—
Preludes, op. 23, 32: selections; Études
tableaux, op. 39: selections. *Battersby,
piano.*
- ARG 9-10/93: 173
• Fa 7-8/93: 209
• Gr 10/93: 85

19330. 3-7100-2: DANIELPOUR—Urban
dances; Psalms; The enchanted garden;
Piano quintet. *Saturday Brass Quintet;
O'Riley, piano; Chamber Music Society
of Lincoln Center.*
□ ARG 11-12/92: 109
+ Fa 1-2/93: 136

19331. 3-7102-2: DEBUSSY—Sonata for
flute, viola, and harp. FAURÉ—Morceau
de concours for flute and harp. IBERT—
Deux interludes for flute, viola, and harp.
DEVIENNE—Duo for flute and viola. RAVEL
(ARR. SALZEDO)—Sonatine en trio for flute,
viola, and harp. *Auréole.*
+ ARG 7-8/93: 188
+ Fa 5-6/93: 402
+ Gr 7/93: 62

19332. 3-7103-2: *Romance of the rose.*
Feminine voices from medieval France.
HelioTrope; Todd, cond.
+ ARG 3-4/96: 240
+ Fa 1-2/96: 375

19333. 3-7104-2: CAGE—A room; Tossed
as it is untroubled; Root of an unfocus;
Primitive; Two pieces for piano (1935);
in a landscape; Ophelia; ASLSP; The
wonderful widow of eighteen springs;
Nowth upon Nacht. MONK—Travel song;
Paris; The tale; Gamemaster's song;
Memory song; Double fiesta. *De Mare,
piano and vocals.*
□ ARG 11-12/92: 101
+ Fa 9-10/92: 209

19334. 3-7105-2: PROKOFIEV—Flute
sonata; Five melodies; Visions fugitives.
Gilbert, flute; Tahmizian, piano.
+ ARG 1-2/94: 135
+ Fa 1-2/94: 263

19335. 3-7106-2: SESSIONS—Complete
works for solo piano. *Salwen, piano.*
+ ARG 9-10/92: 161
+ Fa 9-10/92: 352
+ Gr 12/92: 106

19336. 3-7109-2: ULLMANN—Piano
sonatas no. 5-7; String quartet no. 3.

*Kolben, Kraus, piano; Group for New
Music.*
• ARG 7-8/92: 240
+ Fa 7-8/92: 315
• Gr 10/92: 135

19337. 3-7110-2: WUORINEN—Five;
Archangel; Archaeopteryx; Hyperion.
*Instrumental soloists; Orch. of St. Luke's;
St. Luke's Chamber Ensemble; Wuorinen,
cond.*
+ Fa 5-6/93: 356
□ Gr 7/93: 62

19338. 3-7111-2: STRAUSS—Friedenstag.
*Marc, Roloff, Cassilly, Shirley; New York
City Gay Men's Chorus; Collegiate
Chorale & Orch.; Bass, cond.* Recorded
live.
• ARG 3-4/92: 145
• Fa 3-4/92: 331 (North)
+ Fa 3-4/92: 332 (Lucano)
+ Gr 1/92: 94
+ ON 3/28/92: 41
• OQ spring 93: 183
+ St 9/92: 195

19339. 3-7112-2: WOLPE—Quartet for
oboe, cello, piano, and percussion; Violin
sonata; Flute trio. *Group for
Contemporary Music.*
+ ARG 1-2/94: 171
+ Fa 1-2/94: 359
+ Gr 2/94: 66

19340. 3-7113-2: SESSIONS—String
quintet; Canons to the memory of I.
Stravinsky; Six pieces for cello; String
quartet no. 1. *Group for Contemporary
Music.*
+ ARG 3-4/94: 154
+ Fa 3-4/94: 317
+ Gr 2/95: 68

19341. 3-7115-2: BEETHOVEN—
Symphonies no. 5, 7. *Staatskapelle
Berlin; R. Strauss, cond.* Recorded 1928.
+ Fa 1-2/92: 168
+ Gr 10/92: 197

19342. 3-7116-2: BLOCH—Baal Shem;
Abodah. SHOSTAKOVICH—Violin sonata. *P.
Berman, violin; Epperson, piano.*
+ ARG 5-6/94: 71
• Fa 3-4/94: 138

19343. 3-7117-2: HUMMEL—Mass in B♭,
op. 77; Tantum ergo (after Gluck).
*Westminster Oratorio Choir; New
Brunswick Chamber Orch.; Floreen,
cond.*
+ ARG 5-6/92: 73
+ Fa 5-6/92: 176

19344. 3-7118-2: WARLOCK—My own
country: songs. *Golden, soprano,
Rothfuss, piano.*
- ARG 5-6/92: 156
+ Fa 5-6/92: 285
• Gr 10/92: 168

19345. 3-7119-2: *Richard Strauss
conducts.* Music of Cornelius, Gluck,

KOCH INTERNATIONAL CLASSICS

Mozart, Wagner and Weber. *Berlin Phil. Orch.; Berlin State Opera Orch.; Strauss, cond.* Recorded 1928.
+ Fa 3-4/92: 429

19346. 3-7120-2: BRAHMS—Symphonies no. 3-4. *Vienna Phil. Orch.; BBC Symphony Orch.; Walter, cond.* Recorded 1934-36.
● Fa 3-4/92: 164

19347. 3-7121-2: WUORINEN—String quartet no. 2. HARVEY—String quartet no. 1. PETERSON—String quartet no. 1. *The Group for Contemporary Music.*
+ ARG 3-4/94: 186
+ Fa 5-6/93: 357
□ Gr 7/93: 62

19348. 3-7123-2: WUORINEN—Horn trio; Horn trio continued; Trio for brass instruments; Trio for violin, cello, and piano; Double solo for horn trio; Trombone trio. *The Group for Contemporary Music.*
+ ARG 11-12/93: 223
+ Fa 9-10/93: 333

19349. 3-7124-2 (2 discs): THOMSON—Lord Byron. *Vocalists; Monadnock & Orch.; Bolle, cond.*
+ ARG 7-8/93: 170
+ Fa 7-8/93: 258
● Gr 5/93: 109
+ ON 5/93: 52
+ Op 7/93: 874

19350. 3-7125-2: BARBER—The lovers; Prayers of Kierkegaard. *Duesing, baritone; Reese, soprano; Chicago Symphony Orch.; Schenck, cond.*
+ ARG 7-8/92: 88
+ Fa 7-8/92: 110
+ Gr 3/92: 92
+ ON 1/30/93: 36
+ St 8/92: 181

19351. 3-7126-2: *Victor de Sabata conducts the Berlin Philharmonic Orchestra.* Music of Verdi, Wagner, Kodály and Respighi. *Berlin Phil. Orch.; De Sabata, cond.* Recorded 1939.
+ Fa 5-6/92: 346

19352. 3-7127-2: SIBELIUS—Symphony no. 1; Tapiola; Pohjola's daughter. *London Symphony Orch.; Kajanus, cond.* Reissues.
+ Fa 7-8/92: 286

19353. 3-7128-2: BEETHOVEN—Piano concerto no. 3. BRAHMS—Symphony no. 1. *Long, piano; Paris Conservatory Orch.; Royal Phil. Orch.; Weingartner, cond.* Recorded 1939, 1928.
+ ARG 5-6/92: 191
● Fa 5-6/92: 121

19354. 3-7129-2: BRAHMS—Symphony no. 3. R. STRAUSS—Le bourgeois gentilhomme: Suite; Salome: Dance of the seven veils. *Vienna Phil. Orch.;*

Krauss, cond. Recorded 1929-49.
● Fa 7-8/92: 127

19355. 3-7130-2: CAGE—Thirteen harmonies. ZAHAB—Verging lightfall. *Zahab, violin; Moe, piano.*
● ARG 9-10/95: 120
+ Fa 11-12/95: 231
+ Gr 11/95: 105

19356. 3-7131-2: SIBELIUS—Symphony no. 2; Belshazzar's feast: Suite; Karelia suite. *London Symphony Orch.; Kajanus, cond.* Reissues.
+ Fa 7-8/92: 286

19357. 3-7132-2: STRAUSS—Der Rosenkavalier: Suite; An Alpine symphony. *Tivoli Orch.; Bavarian State Orch.; R. Strauss, cond.* Recorded 1926-41.
+ ARG 5-6/92: 195
+ Fa 7-8/92: 296
+ Gr 1/93: 69

19358. 3-7133-2: SIBELIUS—Symphonies no. 3, 5; March of the Finnish Jaeger Battalion. *London Symphony Orch.; Kajanus, cond.*
+ ARG 9-10/92: 221
+ Fa 9-10/92: 356

19359. 3-7134-2: ARNOLD—Serenade for small orchestra; Sinfoniettas no. 1-2; Concerto for two violins and string orchestra. *I. & V. Gruppman, violins; San Diego Chamber Orch.; Barra, cond.*
+ ARG 9-10/92: 75
+ Fa 7-8/92: 99
+ Gr 6/92: 37

19360. 3-7135-2: HERRMANN—Symphony no. 1. SCHUMAN—New England triptych. *Phoenix Symphony Orch.; Sedares, cond.*
+ ARG 9-10/92: 159
+ Fa 9-10/92: 259
+ Gr 9/92: 71
+ St 4/93: 283

19361. 3-7137-2: *The art of Harold Samuel.* Music of J.S., C.P.E. and J.C. Bach, Clementi, Schubert, Gluck and Brahms. *Samuel, piano; with Stopak, Mendes, violin; Lora, flute.* Recorded 1923-35.
+ Fa 7-8/92: 348

19362. 3-7138-2: BACH—Solo cantatas: Widerstehe doch der Sünde; Ich habe genug; Ich, armer Mensch, Ich Sündenknecht. *Baird, Minter, Thomas, Sharp; American Bach Soloists.*
+ ARG 11-12/92: 73
+ Fa 7-8/92: 103
+ Gr 12/92: 113

19363. 3-7139-2: BRIDGE—Suite for strings; Roger de Coverly; Cherry ripe; There is a willow grows aslant a brook. DELIUS—Sonata for strings (arr. Fenby). *New Zealand Chamber Orch.; Braithwaite, cond.*
+ ARG 1-2/93: 83

+ Fa 1-2/93: 119
+ Gr 11/92: 57

19364. 3-7140-2: JACOB—Concerto for flute and orchestra. ARNOLD—Concerto no. 2 for flute and orchestra. MUSGRAVE—Orfeo II. *Still, flute; New Zealand Chamber Orch.; Braithwaite, cond.*
□ ARG 11-12/93: 160
+ Fa 7-8/93: 160

19365. 3-7141-2: WOLPE—Chamber music. *Members of Parnassus; Korf, cond.*
+ ARG 1-2/93: 169
+ Fa 11-12/92: 402
+ Gr 12/92: 98

19366. 3-7142-2: ZWILICH—Flute concerto. PISTON—Flute concerto. BERNSTEIN—Halil. *Dwyer, flute; London Symphony Orch.; Sedares, cond.*
+ ARG 1-2/93: 171
+ Fa 1-2/93: 274
+ Gr 3/93: 35

19367. 3-7143-2: GRIEG—Lyric pieces. *Margalit, piano.*
● ARG 5-6/93: 88
+ Fa 3-4/93: 174
+ Gr 3/93: 71

19368. 3-7144-2: Music of Bloch, Muczynski, Copland, E. Burton, Rochberg, Barber, and Q. Porter. *Still, flute; Smith, piano.*
+ ARG 11-12/93: 233
+ Fa 7-8/93: 293
+ Gr 4/94: 66

19369. 3-7145-2: SESSIONS—Solo violin sonata. HOFFMAN—Partenze. ADOLPHE—Soliloquy. *Macomber, violin.*
+ ARG 1-2/93: 188
+ Fa 1-2/93: 308

19370. 3-7146-2: RIMSKY-KORSAKOV—Scheherazade. LISZT—Les préludes. STRAVINSKY—The firebird: suite. *Berlin Phil. Orch.; Fried, cond.*
- ARG 9-10/92: 213
+ Fa 9-10/92: 331
● Gr 2/93: 79

19371. 3-7147-2: HOOVER—Quintet: Da pacem. STEVENS—Quintet. LOEFFLER—Music for 4 stringed instruments. *Montclaire String Quartet; Pettys, piano; Dobbs, flute.*
● ARG 3-4/95: 232
● Fa 3-4/95: 192

19372. 3-7148-2: *Hermit songs.* Music of Bernstein, Barber, Copland, Ives, and Gershwin. *Palmer, clarinet; Archer, piano.*
+ ARG 9-10/95: 256
+ Fa 7-8/95: 415

19373. 3-7149-2: GINASTERA—Glosses on themes of Pablo Casals, op. 46 & 48; Variaciones concertantes. *London*

Symphony Orch.; Israel Chamber Orch.; Ben-Dor, cond.
+ ARG 3-4/96: 115
+ Fa 1-2/96: 205
+ Fi 4/96: 125

19374. 3-7151-2: KRÁSA—Anna's song; Theme with variations; Three Rimbaud songs; Tanec; Passacaglia and fugue; Overture for small orchestra; Brundibár. *Various performers.*
+ ARG 1-2/97: 129
• Fa 1-2/97: 186

19375. 3-7152-2: HERRMANN—Sinfonietta for string orchestra. RÓSZA—Andante for string orchestra; Concerto for string orchestra. WAXMAN—Sinfonietta for strings and timpani. *Berlin Symphony Orch.; Jackson, cond.*
+ ARG 11-12/92: 234
- Fa 11-12/92: 255
+ Gr 7/93: 40

19376. 3-7153-2: SESSIONS—Duo; Cello pieces; Violin and piano duo; Violin sonata. *Macomber, violin; Krosnick, cello; Salwen, piano.*
• ARG 11-12/94: 190
+ Fa 11-12/94: 378

19377. 3-7154-2: STILL—La guiablesse; Quit dat fool'nish; Summerland; Danzas de Panama. *Berlin Symphony Orch.; Jackson, cond.; A. Still, flute; Smith, piano.*
+ ARG 9-10/93: 196
+ Fa 7-8/93: 248
+ Gr 11/93: 82

19378. 3-7156-2: MENOTTI—Apocalypse. LO PRESTI—The masks. DELLO JOIO—Mediations on Ecclesiastes. *Oregon Symphony Orch.; De Preist, cond.*
+ ARG 3-4/93: 111
• Fa 3-4/93: 222 (Snook)
+ Fa 3-4/93: 222 (Simmons)
+ Gr 1/93: 43

19379. 3-7159-2: SCHNITTKE—Piano concerto no. 2. SHOSTAKOVICH—Piano concerto no. 1; Piano music. *Margalit, piano; Moscow Phil. Symphony Orch.; Barra, cond.*
+ ARG 11-12/93: 184
+ Fa 9-10/93: 263
• Gr 9/93: 58

19380. 3-7160-2: TURINA—Rapsodia sinfónica; La oración del torero. RODRIGO—Cuatro madrigales amatorios; Tres viejas aires de danza; Zarabanda lejana y villancico. *Romero, piano; Golden, soprano; San Diego Chamber Orch.; Barra, cond.*
+ ARG 5-6/93: 125
• Fa 3-4/93: 315

19381. 3-7162-2: ARNOLD—Complete music for solo piano. *Frith, piano.*
+ ARG 3-4/95: 66
+ Fa 3-4/95: 105
+ Gr 2/95: 70

19382. 3-7163-2: BACH—Cantatas: Ich steh mit einem Fuss im Grabe, BWV 156; Lass, Fürstin, lass noch einem Strahl, BWV 198 "Trauerode"; Liebster Gott, wann werd ich sterben, BWV 8. *J. Nelson, Baird, J. Thomas, Rickards; American Bach Soloists; Thomas, cond.*
+ ARG 5-6/93: 60
+ Fa 3-4/93: 105
+ Gr 4/93: 102

19383. 3-7164-2: BACH—Cantatas: Gottes Zeit ist die allerbeste Zeit, BWV 106; Tritt auf die Glaubensbahn, BWV 152; Komm du süsse Todesstunde, BWV 161. *Brandes, Minter, Thomas, Sharp; American Bach Soloists; Thomas, cond.*
• Fa 3-4/94: 104
- Gr 4/94: 78

19384. 3-7165-2: KASEMETS—Requiem Renga; Palestrina on Devil's Staircase; The eight houses of I Ching. *Lyra Borealis Ensemble; P. Järvi, cond.*
+ ARG 3-4/95: 263
☐ Fa 3-4/95: 202
+ Gr 4/95: 56

19385. 3-7166-2: COPLAND—Dance panels. LIPKIS—Scaramouche. *Brey, cello; Lehigh Valley Chamber Orch.; Spieth, cond.*
• ARG 3-4/94: 87
+ Fa 5-6/94: 179
• Gr 7/94: 50

19386. 3-7167-2: DELLO JOIO—*Music for Martha Graham, vol. 3.* Diversion of angels; Seraphic dialogues; Exaltation of larks. *Atlantic Sinfonietta; Tchivzhel, cond.*
• ARG 11-12/94: 99
+ Fa 9-10/94: 178
+ Gr 1/95: 64

19387. 3-7168-2: VAUGHAN WILLIAMS—Songs. *R. Golden, soprano; Woodman, baritone; Bean, violin; Rothfuss, piano.*
• ARG 1-2/94: 167
+ Fa 1-2/94: 341
• Gr 5/94: 100

19388. 3-7169-2: HENSEL—Overture. C. SCHUMANN—Piano concerto. TAILLEFERRE—Concertino for harp. L. BOULANGER—D'un soir triste; D'un matin de printemps. *Cheng, piano; Benet, harp; Women's Phil.; Falletta, cond.*
+ ARG 3-4/93: 158
+ Fa 1-2/93: 314
+ Gr 2/93: 48

19389. 3-7170-2: DOWLAND—*Fortune my foe.* Vocal music. *Echos Muse.*
+ ARG 3-4/93: 74
+ Fa 1-2/93: 143
• Gr 7/93: 74

19390. 3-7172-2: *The Malinova sisters piano duo.* TCHAIKOVSKY—The nutcracker suite. PROKOFIEV—Romeo and Juliet. KHACHATURIAN—Spartacus. *M. & O.*

Malinova.
+ Fa 3-4/93: 371

19391. 3-7174-2: SCHÜTZ—Geistliche Chormusik: the 6-part motets. *Chorus of Emmanuel Music; Smith, cond.*
+ ARG 11-12/93: 194
+ Fa 11-12/93: 390
+ Gr 11/93: 133

19392. 3-7176-2: *O God, my heart is ready.* Music of Barnby, Barstow, Thalben-Ball, Hancock, Parry, Turle, Atkins, Wesley, Goss, Lloyd, Noble, and Talbot. *St. Thomas' Choir of Men and Boys; Hancock, cond.*
+ ARG 5-6/93: 176
+ Fa 3-4/93: 355

19393. 3-7177-2: HARRISON—Mass to St. Anthony. PÄRT—Berlin mass. *Oregon Repertory Singers; Seeley, cond.*
+ ARG 1-2/94: 107
• Fa 3-4/94: 269
+ Fa 5-6/94: 213
+ Gr 4/94: 80

19394. 3-7178-2: CARTER—Emblems; The harmony of morning; Heart not so heavy as mine; Musicians wrestle everywhere. SHENG—Two folk songs from Chinhai. AMLIN—Time's cavern. McKINLEY—Four text settings. *John Oliver Chorale.*
+ ARG 5-6/95: 232
+ Fa 5-6/95: 165
+ Gr 5/95: 91

19395. 3-7179-2: PINKHAM—Serenades for trumpet and wind ensemble; Symphonies no. 3-4; Sonata no. 3 for organ and strings. *Murphy, trumpet; Christie, organ; London Symphony Orch.; Sedares, cond.*
☐ ARG 9-10/95: 192
+ Fa 9-10/95: 276
+ Gr 8/95: 78

19396. 3-7180-2: PINKHAM—Christmas cantata; Introduction, nocturne, and rondo; Advent cantata; Wedding cantata; String quartet. *Boston Cecilia; Teeters, cond.; Lenox Brass; Christie, organ; Baum, harp; Ariel Wind Quintet; Buonocore, mandolin; Curtis, guitar; Boston Composers String Quartet.*
+ ARG 11-12/93: 167
+ Fa 11-12/93: 343
+ Gr 1/94: 88

19397. 3-7181-2: THOMPSON—Symphony no. 1. GOULD—Fall River legend: Suite. *New Zealand Symphony Orch.; Sedares, cond.*
+ ARG 9-10/93: 125
+ Fa 9-10/93: 312

19398. 3-7182-2: IVES—Remembrance: A Charles Ives collection. *Detroit Chamber Winds; Reynolds, cond.*
• Fa 3-4/94: 221

KOCH INTERNATIONAL CLASSICS

19399. 3-7185-2: Mompou—Cançiones y danzas no. 1-12; Impresiones intimas. *Romero, piano.*
+ ARG 3-4/97: 181
+ Fa 11-12/96: 309
+ Gr 4/97: 78

19400. 3-7186-2: Duvernoy—Clarinet concerto no. 3. Françaix—Theme with variations for clarinet and piano. Auric—Imaginées no. 3. Devienne—Clarinet sonata no. 1. *Samuels, clarinet; Renzi, piano; Collaborative Arts Chamber Orch.; Meena, cond.*
+ ARG 5-6/95: 206
+ Fa 3-4/95: 370
+ Gr 7/95: 48

19401. 3-7187-2: Music of Barlow, Wilder, Bloom, and Corigliano. *Lucarelli, oboe; Brooklyn Phil.; Barrett, cond.*
+ ARG 7-8/94: 213
+ Fa 7-8/94: 314
+ Gr 7/94: 69

19402. 3-7188-2: Moross—Symphony no. 1; The last judgement; Variations on a waltz. *London Symphony Orch.; Falletta, cond.*
+ ARG 11-12/93: 154
+ Fa 11-12/93: 329
+ Gr 10/93: 46

19403. 3-7191-2: Rózsa—Theme, variations and finale; Three Hungarian sketches; Overture to a symphony concert; Hungarian nocturne. *New Zealand Symphony Orch.; Sedares, cond.*
+ ARG 9-10/93: 181
+ Fa 9-10/93: 258
+ Gr 9/93: 58

19404. 3-7192-2: Still—Chamber music. *A. Still, flute; Smith, piano; New Zealand Quartet.*
+ ARG 9-10/94: 202
+ Gr 11/94: 103

19405. 3-7194-2 (2 discs): Bach—Mass in B minor, BWV 232. *Baird, J. Nelson, Rickards, Sharp; American Bach Soloists; Thomas, cond.*
• ARG 5-6/93: 60
+ Fa 3-4/93: 108
+ Gr 4/93: 102

19406. 3-7195-2: Hovhaness—Piano music. *Rosen, piano.*
• ARG 7-8/93: 102
• Fa 7-8/93: 158
• Gr 6/93: 76

19407. 3-7196-2: Bloch—Concerti grossi no. 1-2. Porter—Ukranian suite. *San Diego Chamber Orch.; Barra, cond.*
+ ARG 9-10/94: 105
+ Fa 11-12/94: 178
+ Gr 12/94: 76

19408. 3-7197-2: Mendelssohn—Piano concerto in E minor (reconstructed by R.L. Todd). Schumann—Konzertsatz for piano and orchestra. C. Schumann—Piano sonata in G minor. Hensel—The year: February; March; May; September; December. *Eley, piano; English Chamber Orch.; Stone, cond.*
+ ARG 9-10/96: 162
+ Fa 9-10/96: 447
+ Gr 10/96: 58

19409. 3-7201-2 (2 discs): *A royal gala concert.* Music of Parry, Tchaikovsky, Popper, Rimsky-Korsakov, Gershwin, R. Strauss, Saint-Saëns, Verdi, Collins, Puccini, Benet, Frost, Doyle, and Handel. *Soloists; English Chamber Orch.; Armstrong, cond.*
- Fa 3-4/93: 403

19410. 3-7202-2: *Essentially Christmas.* Music of Bliss, Walton, Rutter, Vaughan Williams, Grainger, Arnell, Edwards, Kelly, and Gregson. *Doyle, soprano; Liley, tenor; Ayres, organ; Lister, harp; Locke Brass Consort; East London Chorus; Kibblewhite, cond.*
+ Fa 3-4/93: 398

19411. 3-7203-2: *A Gilbert and Sullivan gallery.* Twenty-three selections from Gilbert and Sullivan operettas. *D'Oyly Carte Opera Company.*
- Fa 7-8/93: 252

19412. 3-7204-2: Berlioz—Messe solennelle. *Lamoreaux, Tucker, Cook; Washington Cathedral Choral Society; Lewis, cond.*
- ARG 1-2/95: 84
+ Fa 1-2/95: 121
• Gr 3/95: 81

19413. 3-7205-2: Cowell—Set of five; Trio in 9 short movements; Four combinations; Hymn and fuguing tune no. 9. *Trio Phoenix.*
+ ARG 9-10/95: 128
+ Fa 7-8/95: 159

19414. 3-7206-2: Barber—Horizon; Summer music; Knoxville, summer of 1915; Serenade; Capricorn concerto; Adagio. *Arioso Wind Quintet; Golden, soprano; San Diego Chamber Orch.; Barra, cond.*
• ARG 9-10/95: 101
+ Fa 11-12/95: 193

19415. 3-7207-2: Becker—Concerto arabesque; At Dieppe; Sound pieces no. 1, 5. *De Mare, piano; Narucki, soprano; Romanul, piano; Monadnock Music Festival Orch.; Bolle, cond.*
+ ARG 3-4/95: 72
+ Fa 3-4/95: 120

19416. 3-7208-2: Hovhaness—Symphonies no. 39, 46. *Long, guitar; Korean Broadcasting Symphony Orch.; Jordania, cond.*
+ ARG 11-12/93: 128
+ Fa 1-2/94: 206
+ Gr 7/94: 48

19417. 3-7211-2: Stravinsky—Symphonies of wind instruments; Septet; Octet for wind instruments; Tango for piano; Piano-rag-music; Concerto for piano and wind instruments. *Tocco, piano; Detroit Chamber Winds; Reynolds, cond.*
+ Fa 11-12/96: 388

19418. 3-7213-2: Persichetti—Piano concerto (four hands); Sonata for two pianos; Serenade no. 8. Barber—Souvenirs. *Malinova Sisters, piano duo.*
+ ARG 9-10/96: 179
• Fa 5-6/96: 233

19419. 3-7215-2: Respighi—Poema autunnale; Suite for string orchestra and organ; Il tramonto. Menotti—Cantilena e scherzo. *Gruppman, violin; Koman, organ; Trakas, baritone; Hays, harp; San Diego Chamber Orch.; Barra, cond.*
+ ARG 11-12/94: 176
+ Fa 5-6/94: 227
+ Gr 8/94: 56

19420. 3-7216-2: Griffes—The Kairn of Koridwen. *Ensemble M; DeCou, cond.*
+ ARG 1-2/95: 110
+ Fa 1-2/95: 166

19421. 3-7220-2: Cowell—American melting pot; Persian set; Old American country set; Hymn and fuguing tune no. 2; Air; Ensemble: Adagio. *Sutton, violin; Manhattan Chamber Orch.; Clark, cond.*
+ ARG 11-12/93: 97
+ Fa 11-12/93: 211

19422. 3-7221-2: Hovhaness—Symphony no. 6; Music for trumpet and orchestra. *Gekker, trumpet; Manhattan Chamber Orch.; Clark, cond.*
+ ARG 7-8/94: 115
+ Gr 7/94: 48

19423. 3-7223-2: Beach—Violin sonata, op. 34; Invocation; Romance. Corigliano—Violin sonata. *Macomber, violin; Walsh, piano.*
+ ARG 7-8/95: 103
+ Fa 7-8/95: 114
+ Gr 8/95: 91

19424. 3-7224-2: Herrmann—Film music. *New Zealand Symphony Orch.; Sedares, cond.*
• ARG 9-10/94: 144
+ Fa 9-10/94: 211
+ Gr 6/94: 50

19425. 3-7225-2: Waxman—Rhapsody for piano and orchestra (from The Paradine case); The charm bracelet. Herrmann—Concerto macabre (from Hangover Square); Prelude for piano. North—Concerto for piano and orchestra with trumpet obbligato. *Buechner, piano; New Zealand Symphony Orch.; Sedares, cond.*
+ ARG 3-4/96: 125
+ Fa 11-12/95: 425

19426. 3-7226-2; FRANCHOMME—Caprices, op. 7; Études, op. 35. *Ruede, cello.*
  + ARG 3-4/95: 101
  + Fa 1-2/95: 158

19427. 3-7228-2: *Most sacred banquet.* Music of Poulenc, Messiaen, Franck, Duruflé, and others. *St. Thomas' Choir; G. Hancock, cond.; J. Hancock, organ.*
  + ARG 7-8/96: 270
  + Fa 7-8/96: 352
  + Gr 9/96: 100

19428. 3-7230-2: KLEIN—Fantasie and fugue; Piano sonata; String trio; Two madrigals; Pvrni hrich; Seven folk songs. *Members of the Group for New Music; Sternfield, piano; Prague Phil. Choir; Kühn, cond.; Doležal, tenor.*
  + Fa 11-12/93: 285
  + Gr 8/94: 68

19429. 3-7231-2: VORISEK—Impromptus, op. 7: no. 1, 4. SUK—Life and dreams. JANÁČEK—In the mist. HAAS—Suite, op. 13. *Kraus, piano.*
  + ARG 1-2/94: 182
  + Fa 11-12/93: 285

19430. 3-7232-2: BLOCH—Three Jewish poems; Two last poems. *Still, flute; New Zealand Symphony Orch.; Sedares, cond.*
  + ARG 11-12/94: 79
  + Fa 9-10/94: 148
  + Gr 9/94: 48

19431. 3-7234-2: BACH—Cantatas, vol. 6. *Bott, Taylor, Thomas, Sharp; American Bach Soloists; Thomas, cond.*
  + Fa 11-12/96: 167
  + Fi 12/96: 131

19432. 3-7235-2: BACH—Cantatas: Himmelskönig, sei willkommen, BWV 182; Aus der Tiefen rufe ich, Herr, zu dir, BWV 131; Christ lag in Todesbanden, BWV 4. *American Bach Soloists; Thomas, cond.*
  • ARG 11-12/95: 69
  • Fa 11-12/95: 178
  • Gr 3/96: 78

19433. 3-7237-2: BACH—Concerto for 4 harpsichords, BWV 1065; Psalm 51: Tilge, Höchster, meine Sünden. *Valente, soprano; Malafronte, alto; American Bach Soloists; Thomas, J. cond.*
  + ARG 9-10/95: 97
  + Fa 9-10/95: 124
  - Fa 11-12/95: 415

19434. 3-7238-2 (3 discs): *A chance operation: a Cage tribute.* Music of Cage, Tardos, Mac Low, Wolff, Nordine, Anderson, and others. *Various performers.*
  + ARG 7-8/94: 202
  + Gr 8/94: 72

19435. 3-7239-2: L. COUPERIN—Pièces de clavecin. *Roberts, harpsichord.*
  + ARG 9-10/93: 111

  + EM 5/94: 350
  + Fa 9-10/93: 149

19436. 3-7240-2: *Women at an exposition: music composed by women and performed at the 1893 World's Fair in Chicago.* Music of Arne-Liza Lehmann, Beach, Chaminade, Lehmann, Rogers, C. Schumann, Vannah, White, and Wood. *Schmidt, piano; Langton, soprano; Mentzer, mezzo-soprano; Skorodin, violin.*
  + Fa 9-10/93: 373
  • Gr 12/93: 112

19437. 3-7242-2: WUORINEN—Fortune; Cello variations II; Album leaf; Violin variations; Tashi. *Group for Contemporary Music.*
  + ARG 9-10/94: 220
  + Fa 7-8/94: 288
  • Gr 9/94: 78

19438. 3-7243-2: DELLO JOIO—Triumph of St. Joan; Variations, chaconne and fugue. BARBER—Adagio. *New Zealand Symphony Orch.; Sedares, cond.*
  + Fa 3-4/94: 173
  + Gr 9/94: 52

19439. 3-7244-2: ROZSA—Symphony; Vintner's daughter. *New Zealand Symphony Orch.; Sedares, cond.*
  + ARG 5-6/94: 134
  + Fa 9-10/94: 315
  + Gr 6/94: 60

19440. 3-7245-2: MARTINO—Notturno; Quodlibets II; From the other side. *Group for Contemporary Music.*
  + ARG 7-8/94: 128
  + Fa 7-8/94: 171

19441. 3-7247-2: *Watch and pray: spirituals and art songs by African-American women composers.* Music of Bonds, King, Moore, Perry, and Price. *Dillard, mezzo-soprano; Hamilton, alto; Honeysucker, baritone; Taylor, piano.*
  + ARG 9-10/94: 258
  + Fa 7-8/94: 293

19442. 3-7248-2: *The art of Arleen Augér.* Music of Larsen, Purcell, Schumann, and Mozart. *Augér, soprano; Revzen, piano & cond.*
  + ARG 3-4/94: 224
  + Gr 4/94: 94

19443. 3-7250-2: CORIGLIANO—Piano concerto. TICHELI—Radiant voices; Postcard. *Lefevre, piano; Pacific Symphony Orch.; St. Clair, cond.*
  + ARG 1-2/95: 97
  + Fa 11-12/94: 205

19444. 3-7251-2: FELDMAN—String quartet. *The Group for Contemporary Music.*
  □ ARG 9-10/94: 130
  + Fa 7-8/94: 135
  + Gr 8/94: 67

19445. 3-7252-2: *Sweet torment: virtuoso duets of seventeenth-century Italy and Germany.* Music of Monteverdi, Luzzaschi, Pesenti, D'India, and Schutz. *Favella Lyrica.*
  + ARG 5-6/95: 220
  + Fa 3-4/95: 369

19446. 3-7254-2: BEACH—Piano music. *Eskin, Supové, pianos.*
  + ARG 5-6/96: 78
  + Fa 3-4/96: 121
  • Fa 5-6/96: 94

19447. 3-7256-2: RÓZSA—Variations on a Hungarian peasant song; North Hungarian peasant songs and dances; Duo for violin and piano; Sonata for solo violin. *Lippi, violin; Novacek, piano.*
  + ARG 11-12/95: 189
  + Fa 9-10/95: 300
  + Gr 11/95: 113

19448. 3-7258-2: GUBAIDULINA—In croce; Preludes. USTVOLSKAYA—Grand duet. *Beiser, cello; Papadakos, organ; Oldfather, piano.*
  + ARG 7-8/95: 117
  + Fa 9-10/95: 214
  + Gr 11/95: 106

19449. 3-7260-2: LILBURN—Diversions for string orchestra; Landfall in unknown seas; Allegro for strings. WATSON—Introduction and allegro for strings. PRUDEN—Soliloquy for strings. *Hillary, narrator; New Zealand Chamber Orch.; Armstrong, cond. Reissue.*
  + ARG 7-8/95: 141
  + Fa 7-8/95: 222
  + Gr 9/95: 58

19450. 3-7261-2: MATHIAS—Harp concerto. GINASTERA—Harp concerto. *Pilot, harp; English Chamber Orch.; Jackson, cond.*
  • ARG 1-2/95: 107
  + Fa 11-12/94: 295
  + Gr 12/94: 82

19451. 3-7262-2: HARBISON—Quintet for winds. ROCHBERG—To the dark wood; Trio for clarinet, horn, and piano. *Arioso Wind Quintet; Darby, piano.*
  + ARG 7-8/94: 160
  + Fa 5-6/94: 161

19452. 3-7263-2: SCHOENBERG—Pieces for orchestra, op. 16; A survivor from Warsaw; Accompaniment to a cinematographic scene; Herzgewächse; Serenade, op. 24. *Callow, speaker; Hulse, soprano; Varcoe, baritone; London Voices; London Symphony Orch.; Twentieth Century Classics Ensemble; Craft, cond.*
  • ARG 11-12/95: 191
  + Fa 5-6/95: 321
  + Gr 6/95: 98

19453. 3-7265-2: *The peaceful western wind.* Music of Dowland, Pilkington, Jones, Campion, Corkine, Ferrabosco,

KOCH INTERNATIONAL CLASSICS

Johnson, and Anon. *Thomas, tenor; Tayler, lute.*
+ ARG 5-6/94: 189
+ Fa 5-6/94: 298

19454. 3-7266-2: ARNOLD—Hobson's choice; Homage to the Queen; Five pieces; Cello fantasy; Trio. *St. Clair Trio.*
+ ARG 1-2/96: 71

19455. 3-7267-2: MESSIAEN—Petites esquisses d'oiseaux; Cantéyodjayâ; Quatre études de rythme; Pièce pour le tombeau de Paul Dukas. *Cheng, piano.*
• ARG 9-10/95: 176
+ Fa 5-6/95: 264
+ Gr 9/95: 84

19456. 3-7269-2: RAN—Fantasy movements; String quartet no. 3. BOULANGER—Cello pieces. *Flyer, cello; Lee, piano; Manhattan String Quartet; English Chamber Orch.; Falletta, cond.*
+ ARG 9-10/95: 199
+ Fa 11-12/95: 339

19457. 3-7270-2: BRITTEN—Lachrymae: reflections on a song of Dowland. HINDEMITH—Viola sonata, op. 11, no. 4. SHOSTAKOVICH—Viola sonata, op. 147. *Silverstone, viola; Constable, piano.*
+ ARG 5-6/95: 94
+ Fa 3-4/95: 144
• Fa 5-6/95: 342

19458. 3-7272-2: WUORINEN—A winter's tale; Album leaf; String sextet; New York notes. *Bryn-Julson, soprano; Winn, piano; Chamber Music Society of Lincoln Center; Wuorinen, cond.*
+ ARG 3-4/95: 224
+ Fa 1-2/95: 312
+ Gr 2/95: 60

19459. 3-7274-2: SHOSTAKOVICH—The gadfly (suite); King Lear (suite); Hamlet (excerpts). *KBS Symphony Orch.; Jordania, cond.*
+ ARG 1-2/95: 176
+ Fa 11-12/94: 379
+ Gr 12/94: 93

19460. 3-7277-2: KORNGOLD—Der Schneemann; Potpourri on the Ring of Polykrates. *Woolley, piano.*
+ ARG 3-4/95: 121
+ Fa 3-4/95: 202
- Gr 4/95: 89

19461. 3-7278-2: ZWILICH—Symphony no. 3; Oboe concerto; Concerto grosso. *Mack, oboe; Louisville Orch.; Sedares, cond.*
+ ARG 11-12/95: 298
+ Fa 9-10/95: 371
• Gr 12/95: 97

19462. 3-7279-2: LARSEN—Missa gaia. PAULUS—Echoes between the silent peaks. BARBER—To be sung on the water; 12th night. *Oregon Repertory Singers; Seeley, cond.*
+ ARG 9-10/95: 166

19463. 3-7280-2: INDY—Symphony no. 2; Souvenirs. *Monte Carlo Phil. Orch.; De Preist, cond.*
+ ARG 9-10/95: 159
+ Fa 11-12/95: 283
+ Gr 8/96: 50

19464. 3-7281-2: CLARKE—Cello sonata; Epilogue. BEACH—Cello sonata; Pieces, op. 40. *Frame, cello; Snyder, Weirich, piano.*
+ ARG 1-2/95: 231
• Fa 3-4/95: 154
+ Gr 3/95: 62

19465. 3-7282-2: COWELL—Concerto grosso; Hymn and fuguing tune no. 10; Air and scherzo; Fiddler's jig. PERSICHETTI—The hollow men. MACDOWELL—To a wild rose (arr. Luck). *Lucarelli, oboe; Louie, saxophone; Horne, violin; Gekker, trumpet; Manhattan Chamber Orch.; Clark, cond.*
+ ARG 3-4/95: 90
+ Fa 3-4/95: 156
+ Gr 7/95: 48

19466. 3-7283-2: THOMPSON—Frostiana; Testament of freedom. *New York Choral Society; Manhattan Chamber Orch.; Clark, cond.*
+ Fa 11-12/95: 400
• Fi 3/96: 126

19467. 3-7285-2: *Evensong. Music of Hancock, Hayes, Noble, Rorem, Monk, and Candlyn. St. Thomas' Choir of Men and Boys, New York; Hancock, cond.*
- Fa 1-2/96: 373

19468. 3-7287-2: *Celtic keyboards: Duets by 19th and 20th century Irish composers. Music of Osborne, Field, and Trimble. Posner, Garvelmann, pianos.*
+ Fa 1-2/95: 359

19469. 3-7288-2: HOVHANESS—Vision of a starry night. *Rosen, piano.*
• ARG 1-2/95: 118
+ Fa 11-12/94: 261

19470. 3-7289-2: HOVHANESS—Khrimian Hairig; The holy city; Psalm et fugue; Kohar; Symphony for metal orchestra. *Gecker, trumpet; Manhattan Chamber Orch.; Clark, cond.*
+ ARG 5-6/96: 128
+ Fa 1-2/96: 230

19471. 3-7291-2: RAID—Symphony no. 2 "Stockholm". TUBIN—Elegy (arr. for strings); Symphony no. 11: 1st movement (orchestration completed by Raid). *Estonian State Symphony Orch.; Volmer, cond.*
• ARG 1-2/95: 159
+ Fa 9-10/95: 286
+ Gr 1/96: 60

19472. 3-7293-2: FLAGELLO—Passion of Martin Luther King. SCHWANTNER—New morning for the world. *Bazemore, bass & narrator; Oregon Symphony Orch.;*

Portland Symphonic Choir; De Preist, cond.
+ Fa 5-6/95: 188

19473. 3-7294-2 (2 discs): BACH—Brandenburg concertos no. 1-6. *Bargemusic.*
• Fa 7-8/96: 84

19474. 3-7296-2: CHOPIN—Piano music. *Romero, piano.*
+ Fa 1-2/96: 179

19475. 3-7301-2: GÓRECKI—Piano sonata no. 1; Four preludes. PÄRT—Für Alina; Variationen zur Gesundung von Arinushka. USTVOLSKAYA—Twelve preludes; Piano sonata no. 6. *Arden, piano.*
+ ARG 11-12/95: 126
+ Fa 11-12/95: 263 (Carl)
+ Fa 11-12/95: 327 (Rapoport)

19476. 3-7303-2: *Castles in the sky. Celtic music for lute and percussion. Syncope.*
+ Fa 7-8/95: 421

19477. 3-7304-2: RÓZSA—Viola concerto; Sinfonia concertante. *Gruppman, violin; Silverthorne, viola; Boch, cello; New Zealand Symphony Orch.; Sedares, cond.*
+ ARG 7-8/96: 182
• Fa 7-8/96: 277
+ Fi 6/96: 125
+ Gr 10/96: 62

19478. 3-7307-2: SCHUBERT—Sonata for piano four hands "Grand Duo" (arr. Joachim); Fantasia for piano four hands, D. 940 (arr. Mottl); Six German dances, D. 820 (arr. Webern). *American Symphony Orch.; Botstein, cond.*
+ ARG 9-10/95: 209
- Fa 9-10/95: 312
• Gr 3/96: 52

19479. 3-7308-2: WUORINEN—Piano sonata no. 3; Bagatelle; Capriccio. FELDMAN—Palais de Mari. *Feinberg, piano.*
+ Fa 9-10/96: 359
+ Gr 9/96: 80

19480. 3-7311-2: HOVHANESS—Prayer of St. Gregory; Elibris; Mystic flute; Aria, hymn and fugue; Mountain idylls; Adagio; Sonata Fred the cat; Aria from Haroutiun. *Gecker, trumpet; Still, flute; Rosen, piano; Long, guitar; Manhattan Chamber Orch.; Clark, cond.; New Zealand Chamber Orch.; Braithwaite, cond.; KBS Symphony Orch.; Jordaria, cond.*
□ ARG 3-4/96: 129

19481. 3-7312-2: *Home sweet home: parlor music from the Civil War era. Music of Foster, Kummer, Winner, Nicholson, Maria J. Jones, Kothe, and Schreiner. Boland, flute; Dowdall, guitar.*
+ Fa 9-10/95: 391

19482. 3-7313-2: ASIA—Scherzo sonata; Piano quartet; Why (?) Jacob. *Shames, piano; Bridge Ensemble.*
+ ARG 7-8/95: 71
+ Fa 9-10/95: 118
+ Fa 11-12/95: 174

19483. 3-7315-2: WOLPE—The man from Midian; Second piece for violin alone; String quartet. SCHOENBERG (ARR. WEBERN)—Five pieces for orchestra. *Group for Contemporary Music.*
+ ARG 9-10/96: 227
+ Fa 9-10/96: 359

19484. 3-7316-2: SCHOENBERG—Pelleas und Melisande. WEBERN—Passacaglia. *Houston Symphony Orch.; Eschenbach, cond.*
- ARG 3-4/96: 177
- Gr 4/96: 50

19485. 3-7317-3 (3 discs): BEETHOVEN—Piano concertos (complete). *Romero, piano; English Chamber Orch.; Sedares, cond.*
• ARG 3-4/96: 86
• Fa 1-2/96: 136

19486. 3-7322-2: TURINA—Piano music. *Conti, piano.*
+ ARG 7-8/96: 216
+ Fa 5-6/96: 302
+ Gr 10/96: 87

19487. 3-7325-2: KREISLER—String quartet. KORNGOLD—String quartet no. 3. *Angeles String Quartet.*
+ ARG 5-6/96: 131
+ Fa 11-12/95: 287

19488. 3-7326-2: MATHIAS—Violin sonatas no. 1-2; Little suite for piano; Piano trio; Divertimento for violin and viola; Toccata alla danza. *Davis, violin; Adelson, viola; Conable, cello; Harper, piano.*
+ ARG 1-2/97: 137
+ Fa 1-2/97: 205

19489. 3-7331-2 (2 discs): ARMER—Uses of music in uttermost parts. *Women's Phil. Orch.; Falletta, cond.*
+ Fa 5-6/96: 64

19490. 3-7332-2: BACH—Cantatas no. 12, 18, 61. *Baird, Minter, Butterfield, Weaver; American Bach Soloists; Thomas, cond.*
+ ARG 3-4/96: 78

19491. 3-7335-2: BABBITT—Soli e duettini. *Group for Contemporary Music.*
+ ARG 3-4/97: 75
+ Fa 11-12/96: 162

19492. 3-7336-2: WUORINEN—Mass for the Restoration of St. Luke in the Fields; A solis ortu; Genesis. JOSQUIN—Ave Christe (arr. Wuorinen). *New York Virtuoso Singers; Wuorinen, cond. & piano; Minnesota Orch.; Waart, cond.*
+ ARG 7-8/96: 226

+ Fa 5-6/96: 321
+ Gr 7/96: 94

19493. 3-7337-2: SCHOENBERG—Wind quintet, op. 26. BERG—Piano sonata, op. 1. WEBERN—Concerto, op. 24; Three little pieces for cello and piano, op. 11; Four pieces for violin and piano, op. 7. *Eschenbach, piano; Houston Symphony Chamber Players.*
+ ARG 11-12/96: 234
+ Fa 9-10/96: 315
+ Gr 12/96: 95

19494. 3-7340-2: RÓZSA—El Cid. *New Zealand Symphony Orch.; Sedares, cond.*
+ ARG 7-8/96: 182
+ Fi 6/96: 125
+ Gr 6/96: 54

19495. 3-7343-2: BOWLES—Chamber music. *Herrmann, McGushin, pianos; Brandenburg, clarinet; Staufembiel, tenor; Waller, flute; Weismayer, organ.*
+ ARG 7-8/96: 87
• Fa 7-8/96: 118
+ Gr 10/96: 70

19496. 3-7344-2: *Stokowski transcriptions.* Music of Mussorgsky and Bach. *New Zealand Symphony Orch.; Sedares, cond.*
• ARG 3-4/96: 222
+ Fa 3-4/96: 389
• Fi 4/96: 113

19497. 3-7358-2: *Diamond settings: hommage à Satie.* Music of Satie, Diamond, Debussy, and Ravel. *Seattle Symphony Orch.; Schwarz, cond.*
□ ARG 9-10/96: 191
+ Fa 9-10/96: 443
+ Fi 10/96: 141

19498. 3-7361-2: BARBER—Capricorn concerto; Canzone; Fadograph; Cave of the heart; Adagio; Souvenirs; Hermit songs; To be sung on water; The lovers; Summer music. *Various performers.*
+ ARG 7-8/96: 72

19499. 3-7363-2: CAVALIERI—La rappresentazione di anima e di corpo. *Nelson, soprano; Hillier, baritone; Magnificat ensemble; The Whole Noyse ensemble.*
+ Fa 1-2/97: 134

19500. 3-7702-2: *Piero Coppola conducts.* Music of Ravel, Honegger, and Saint-Saëns. *Orch. de la Société des Concerts du Conservatoire, Paris; Orch. symphonique du Gramophone; Coppola, cond.* Recorded 1927-34.
+ ARG 9-10/93: 257
+ Fa 5-6/93: 413

19501. 3-7703-2 (2 discs): HANDEL—A collector's Messiah. *Various performers.* Recorded 1908-26.
+ ARG 11-12/93: 271
+ Fa 7-8/93: 146

19502. 3-7705-2 (2 discs): COUPERIN—Concert dans le gout theatral. BACH—Brandenburg concertos. BRAHMS—Double concerto. *Thibaud, violin; Casals, cello & cond.; Ecole Normale Orch.; Casals Orch. of Barcelona.*
+ ARG 9-10/93: 257
+ Fa 9-10/93: 385
+ Gr 11/93: 186

19503. 3-7708-2: HANDEL—Concertos, op. 6 (selections). *Decca String Orch.; Ansermet, cond.* Recorded 1929.
+ ARG 9-10/96: 270
+ Fa 7-8/96: 185

19504. 3-7721-2: HOVHANESS—Mountains and rivers without end; Prayer of St. Gregory; Haroutiun: Aria; Symphony no. 6; Return and rebuild the desolate places. *Gekker, trumpet; Manhattan Chamber Orch.; Clark, cond.*
+ Fa 5-6/94: 168 (Lange)
+ Fa 5-6/94: 168 (Simmons)

19505. 3-7909-2: SCOTT—Selections. *Beau Hunks Sextette.*
+ Fa 11-12/95: 371

19506. 3-7939-2: SCHUMANN—Symphonies no. 2, 4. *Berlin State Opera Orch.; New Symphonic Orch., Berlin; Pfitzner, cond.*
- Fa 7-8/91: 286

19507. 3-8708-2: ROGER—Orchestra music. *Metropole Orch.; Stulen, cond.*
+ Fa 3-4/96: 261

19508. 3-8900-2: KAPILOW—Green eggs and ham; You and Hugh. *Réaux, soprano; Kapilow, piano; Tabisel, Costanzo, boy sopranos; Sokol, baritone; New Jersey Chamber Music Society; Kapilow, cond.*
+ Fa 3-4/96: 189

KOCH SCHWANN

19509. 3-1006-2: VIEUXTEMPS—Violin and piano music. *Godhoff, violin; Kontarsky, piano.*
+ ARG 11-12/94: 208
+ Fa 11-12/94: 412

19510. 3-1008-2 (2 discs): HASSE—Piramo e Tisbe. *Schlick, Gari, Lecocq; Capella Clementina; Müller-Brühl, cond.*
+ Fa 5-6/94: 164

19511. 3-1010-2 (3 discs): MARTINŮ—Piano music. *Leichner, piano.*
+ ARG 1-2/93: 118

19512. 3-1020-2: DU MONT—Messe royale; Motets. *Les Demoiselles de Saint-Cyr; Mandrin, cond.*
+ ARG 5-6/94: 88
+ Fa 3-4/94: 177

19513. 3-1023-2: GOMEZANDA—Lagos; Mexican dances; Mexican fantasy; Xiuhzitzquilo. *Marks, piano; Boettcher,*

KOCH SCHWANN

cello; Berlin Symphony Orch.; Velazco, cond.
  + ARG 5-6/96: 116
  + Fa 7-8/96: 177

19514. 3-1026-2: *Clarinet concertos.* Music of Rivier, Mihalovici, Tomasi, and Françaix. *Brunner, clarinet; I Fiamminghi; Werthen, cond.*
  + Fa 11-12/96: 481

19515. 3-1027-2 : R. STRAUSS—Bourgeois gentilhomme: Suite. STRAVINSKY—Pulcinella: Suite. *Limburg Symphony Orch.; Conde, cond.*
  + Fa 7-8/92: 293
  + Gr 10/92: 122

19516. 3-1028-2: F.X. MOZART—Variations on a romance by Méhul; Six melancholy polonaises. HUMMEL—Bagatelles, no. 3, 6; Rondo, op. 11; Polonaise, op. 55. *Hellwig, piano.*
  + ARG 7-8/95: 157
  + Fa 7-8/95: 252

19517. 3-1029-2: *Kempff on the radio.* Music of Bach, Mozart, Liszt, Fauré, and Kempff. *Kempff, piano.* Recorded 1945-56.
  + ARG 7-8/95: 275

19518. 3-1030-2 (3 discs): FRANCHETTI—Cristoforo Colombo. *Vocal soloists; Hungarian Radio and Television Choir; Frankfurt Radio Symphony Orch.; Viotti, cond.*
  + ARG 9-10/92: 105
  + Fa 9-10/92: 235
  + Gr 7/92: 101
  + ON 10/92: 44
  + Op 7/92: 875
  • OQ spring 93: 175
  + St 1/93: 271

19519. 3-1031-2: DANIÉLIS—Motets. *Les Talens Lyriques.*
  + ARG 3-4/94: 88
  + Fa 3-4/94: 171

19520. 3-1032-2 (2 discs): MASSENET—Cléopatre. *Harries, Streff, Henry; Nouvel Orch. de Saint-Etienne; Fournillier, cond.* Recorded live 1990.
  + ARG 11-12/92: 158
  + Fa 11-12/92: 294
  + Gr 10/92: 175
  + ON 11/92: 46

19521. 3-1033-2: REGER—Piano music. *Urban, piano.*
  + ARG 5-6/95: 157

19522. 3-1034-2: MILHAUD—Carnaval d'Aix. SVENDSON—Norwegian artists' carnival. BRITTEN—Canadian carnival. *Hellwig, piano; Berlin Radio Symphony Orch.; Gülke, cond.*
  + ARG 1-2/93: 123
  + Fa 3-4/93: 225

19523. 3-1035-2: MILHAUD—Scaramouche; Clarinet concerto.

HINDEMITH—Clarinet concerto. COPLAND—Clarinet concerto. *Brunner, clarinet; Bavarian Radio Orch.; Schneider, cond.*
  • ARG 3-4/93: 112

19524. 3-1037-2: *E dame jolie.* Music of princes knights and thieves. *Capella Antiqua of Bamberg.*
  + ARG 1-2/93: 189

19525. 3-1039-2: PONCE—Concierto del Sur. VILLA-LOBOS—Guitar concerto. CASTELNUOVO-TEDESCO—Serenade, op. 118. *Wieggle, guitar; Virtuosi di Praga; Schmelzer, cond.*
  + ARG 1-2/96: 162

19526. 3-1040-2: *Guitar music from the age of Viennese classicism.* Music of Giuliani, Carulli, Coste, Mertz, and Rossini. *Duo Tedesco.*
  + Fa 3-4/93: 363

19527. 3-1041-2: GÓRECKI—Symphony no. 1; Chorus I, op. 20; Three pieces in the old style. *Cracow Phil. Orch.; Bader, cond.*
  + Fa 11-12/93: 245
  + Gr 11/93: 68

19528. 3-1044-2: FRANCK—Mass, op. 12. *Devos, tenor; Belgian Radio Choirs; Bartholomée, cond.* Reissue.
  • ARG 1-2/93: 97

19529. 3-1048-2 (2 discs): J.C.F. BACH—Symphonies no. 1-4, 6, 10, 20. *Cologne Chamber Orch.; Müller-Brühl, cond.* Reissue.
  + ARG 7-8/93: 58

19530. 3-1049-2: KROMMER—Three quintets for flute, violin, 2 violas, and cello, op. 55, 58, 109. *Meier, flute; Stamitz Quartet.*
  + ARG 3-4/93: 102
  + Fa 3-4/93: 201

19531. 3-1050-2: MACMILLAN—The confession of Isobel Gowdie; Tryst. *BBC Scottish Symphony Orch.; Maksymiuk, cond.*
  + ARG 7-8/93: 116
  + Fa 3-4/93: 211
  + Gr 10/92: 63

19532. 3-1053-2: FRANCK—String quartet. *Ensemble César Franck.*
  • ARG 7-8/94: 102

19533. 3-1054-2: *Concertos for two guitars and orchestra.* Music of Baumann, Domeniconi, and Petit. *Duo Tedesco; Cracow Phil. Orch.; Bader, cond.*
  + ARG 7-8/94: 211
  + Fa 1-2/94: 399

19534. 3-1055-2: FRANCK—Piano quintet; Viola sonata (arr.). *Ensemble César Franck.*
  • ARG 7-8/94: 102

19535. 3-1058-2: Music of Brahms, Britten, Egk, Mozart, Pfitzner and others. *Berger, soprano; Weissenborn, Raucheisen, piano.* Recorded live 1950-51.
  + ARG 3-4/93: 196
  + Gr 8/93: 92

19536. 3-1059-2: KOZELUH—Sonatas for fortepiano: op. 15, no. 1; op. 20, no. 3; op. 26, no. 3; op. 38, no. 3. *Faron, piano.*
  • EM 8/94: 531
  + Fa 11-12/93: 289

19537. 3-1060-2: GRANDI MOTETS; WITH SONATAS BY BUONAMENTE, CASTELLO, UCCELLINI, AND BERTALI. *COLOGNE VOCAL CONSORT; ROVATKAY, COND; MUSICA ANTIQUA KÖLN; GOEBEL, COND.*
  + ARG 3-4/93: 83

19538. 3-1063-2: GLOBOKAR—Accord; Voix instrumentalisés; Discours III, IV; Toucher. *Vilotijević, soprano; Holliger, oboe; Riessler, bass clarinet; Drouet, percussion; Domus Quartet.*
  + ARG 3-4/93: 82
  + Gr 7/93: 58

19539. 3-1065-2: FUMET—La nuit. HONEGGER—Le dit des jeux du monde. INDY—Concerto for piano, flute, cello, and strings. *Dechorgnat, piano; Ferrandis, flute; Noël, trumpet; Wiederker, cello; Jean-Jacques Wiederker Chamber Orch.; Bouaniche, cond.*
  + Gr 6/95: 44

19540. 3-1069-2: WEBERN—Im Sommerwind; Passacaglia; Pieces for orchestra, op. 6, op. 10; Variations; Ricercata from Bach's Musical Offering. *Netherlands Ballet Orch.; Driesten, cond.*
  + ARG 1-2/93: 167
  + Fa 11-12/92: 406

19541. 3-1072-2: BERGER—Variations and fugue on an original theme; Serenade, op. 102. *Bamberg Symphony Orch.; Michaels, cond.*
  • ARG 1-2/95: 83
  + Fa 11-12/94: 174

19542. 3-1074-2: DEVIENNE—Symphonies concertantes. *Consortium Classicum; NDR Symphony Orch.; Hauschild, cond.*
  + ARG 3-4/93: 73
  + Fa 3-4/93: 153

19543. 3-1075-2: HARTMANN—Concerto funèbre. ZIMMERMANN—Violin concerto. EGK—Violin music. *Maile, violin; Berlin Radio Symphony Orch.; Sander, cond.*
  + ARG 11-12/95: 131

19544. 3-1080-2: *Hubertus-Messe: hunting and forest songs for male chorus.* Music of Wolters, Anton, and Schumann. *Quartettverein "Die Räuber" (Camerata Vocale Gummersbach); Anton, cond.; Bleese, baritone; Althoff, piano; Gehring, organ; Waldhorngruppe "Freischütz".*

• ARG 11-12/96: 248
□ Fa 9-10/96: 388

19545. 3-1083-2: MARTIN—Concerto for seven wind instruments; Petite symphonie concertante; Ballade. *Brown, flute; Philharmonia Virtuosi; Kapp, cond.*
• Gr 3/94: 54

19546. 3-1084-2: SCHUBERT—Rosamunde; The magic harp. *Klöcker, clarinet & cond.; Consortium Classicum.*
+ Fa 3-4/96: 272

19547. 3-1086-2: CORNELIUS—Stabat Mater; Requiem. REGER—Motet: Mein odem ist schwach. *Soloists; Cologne Radio Chorus; Cologne Radio Symphony Orch.; RIAS Chamber Choir; Gronostay, cond.*
+ ARG 3-4/93: 70
+ Fa 1-2/93: 134

19548. 3-1088-2 (2 discs): HASSE—Piramo e Tisbe. *Schlick, Gari, Lecocq; Capella Clementina; Müller-Brühl, cond.*
+ Gr 4/94: 97

19549. 3-1089-2: SCHUMANN—Manfred. *Soloists; RIAS Chorus; RIAS Symphony Orch.; Albrecht, cond.*
+ ARG 5-6/94: 139

19550. 3-1090-2: GRÉTRY—Jugement de Midas (excerpts). *Devos, Degelin, Clini; Belgian Radio Orch.; Zollman, cond.* Recorded 1978.
• ARG 9-10/94: 135

19551. 3-1091-2: SCHOECK—Der Sänger. *Lang, tenor; Oester-Lang, piano.*
• ARG 5-6/94: 137
+ Fa 5-6/94: 237
+ Gr 10/94: 184

19552. 3-1092-2: E.T.A. HOFFMANN—Undine. *Laki, Mekler, Hermann, Ridderbusch; Berlin Radio Symphony Orch.; Bader, cond.*
• ARG 9-10/93: 137
• Fa 9-10/93: 185
+ Gr 10/93: 114
• ON 12/11/93: 46

19553. 3-1094-2: Music of Schoenberg, Weigl, Schreker, and Korngold. *Kimbrough, baritone; Baldwin, piano.*
• Gr 2/95: 91

19554. 3-1099-2: Music of Hasse, Fesch, and Vivaldi. *Rosin, trombone; Lehrndorfer, organ.*
+ ARG 11-12/92: 248

19555. 3-1123-2: MESSIAEN—Oiseaux exotiques; La ville en haut; Un sourire; Un vitrail et des oiseaux; Et expecto resurrectionem mortuorum. *Loriod, piano; Bavarian Radio Symphony Orch.; Berlin Radio Symphony Orch.; Rickenbacher, cond.* Recorded 1985.
• ARG 3-4/95: 144

+ Fa 3-4/95: 230
+ Gr 12/94: 90

19556. 3-1124-2: RESPIGHI—Concerto gregoriano; Concerto all'antica. *Cappelletti, violin; Philharmonia Orch.; Bamert, cond.*
+ Gr 8/94: 56

19557. 3-1125-2: DRUSCHETZKY—Sinfonia concertante for oboe, timpani, and orchestra. DROSTE-HÜLSHOFF—Sinfonia concertante for 3 flutes and orchestra. SCHINDELMEISSER—Sinfonia concertante for 4 clarinets and orchestra, op. 2. *Schmalfuss, oboe; Sadlo, timpani; Adorján, Henkel, Larieu, flutes; Klöcker, Wandel, Stier, Hubert, clarinets; Bamberger Symphoniker; Stadlmair, cond.*
+ ARG 7-8/95: 255
+ Fa 7-8/95: 173

19558. 3-1126-2: TARTINI—Eight piccole sonate for violin solo. *Cappelletti, violin.*
+ ARG 5-6/94: 152
+ Fa 3-4/94: 332

19559. 3-1127-2 : SUK—Piano quartet, op. 1. R. STRAUSS—Piano quartet, op. 13. *Berlin Phil. Piano Quartet.*
+ ARG 3-4/94: 162

19560. 3-1134-2: HINDEMITH—Mathis der Maler (symphony); String trio no. 2; String quartet no. 3. *Berlin Phil. Orch.; Hindemith, cond.; Hindemith Trio; Amar Quartet.* Recorded 1934+.
• ARG 5-6/94: 204
+ Gr 5/94: 129

19561. 3-1135-2: TANEEV—Suite de concert; Canzona. *Thomas-Mifune, cello; Bavarian Radio Orch.; Tang, cond.*
+ ARG 1-2/93: 155
• Fa 3-4/93: 309
+ Gr 4/93: 62

19562. 3-1136-2: BAIRD—Psychodrama; Canzona; Concerto lugubre; Oboe concerto; Scenes for cello, harp, and orchestra. *Leek, oboe; Rheinland-Pfalz Phil. Orch.; Gülke, cond.; Schmidt, viola; H. Storck, harp; K. Storck, cello; Lorraine Phil. Orch.; Houtmann, cond.*
+ ARG 3-4/94: 68

19563. 3-1138-2: MILHAUD—Saudades do Brazil; Le carnaval de Londres; Trois rag-caprices. *Capella Cracoviensis; Rickenbacher, cond.*
+ ARG 3-4/93: 112
+ Fa 3-4/93: 228
+ Gr 12/92: 85

19564. 3-1139-2: MILHAUD—Six little symphonies. *Capella Cracoviensis; Rickenbacher, cond.*
+ ARG 3-4/93: 112
+ Fa 3-4/93: 228
+ Gr 5/93: 48

19565. 3-1141-2: REGER—Mozart variations; Beethoven variations. *Bamberg Symphony Orch.; Stein, cond.*
+ ARG 1-2/93: 136

19566. 3-1143-2: BACEWICZ—Concerto for string orchestra; Symphony no. 3. *Cracow Phil. Orch.; Bader, cond.*
• Fa 7-8/94: 42
- Gr 2/95: 40

19567. 3-1145-2: PADEREWSKI—Piano concerto; Polish fantasy. *Radziwonowicz, Smendzianka, pianos; Cracow Phil. Orch.; Bader, cond.*
+ ARG 9-10/93: 166

19568. 3-1146-2: DVOŘÁK—Cello concertos no. 1-2. *Thomas-Mifune, cello; Bamberg Symphony Orch.; Krecmer, cond.*
+ Fa 5-6/94: 141

19569. 3-1147-2: VANHAL—Flute concertos no. 1-2. J. REICHA—Flute concerto. *Meier, flute; Prague Chamber Orch.*
+ ARG 5-6/94: 158

19570. 3-1150-2: REGER—Clarinet quintet. BRAHMS—Clarinet quintet. *Woudenberg, clarinet; Schoenberg Quartet.*
+ ARG 11-12/96: 187

19571. 3-1152-2: *Cellicatissimo: Light tunes for serious cellists.* Music of D'Hervelois, Saint-Saëns, Rimsky-Korsakov, Gretchaninov, Offenbach, Fauré, Françaix, Stravinsky, Hiller, Benjamin, Anderson, and Weiner. *Philharmonische Cellisten Köln.*
+ Fa 3-4/93: 361

19572. 3-1153-2: Music of Barber, Carter, Cage, and Schuller. *Aulos Wind Quintet.*
+ ARG 11-12/93: 245

19573. 3-1154-2: *Méditation hébraique.* Music of Bloch, Moscheles, Cervetto, and Bernstein. *Jaffe, cello; Fröhlich, piano.*
+ ARG 5-6/96: 233

19574. 3-1155-2: SZYMANOWSKI—Mythes; Notturno e tarantella; String quartets no. 1-2. *Gadzina, violin; M. Paderewski, piano; Wilanów Quartet.*
+ Fa 11-12/93: 411

19575. 3-1156-2: DIABELLI—Grandes sérénades, op. 66; op. 95; op. 105. *Neues KammerTrio.*
+ ARG 9-10/94: 122
+ Fa 5-6/94: 134

19576. 3-1161-2: SHOSTAKOVICH—Viola sonata. BARTÓK—Solo viola sonata. STRAVINSKY—Elegy. *Hillyer, viola; Leeuw, piano.*
• ARG 7-8/95: 196

+ Fa 5-6/95: 342
+ Gr 5/95: 66

19577. 3-1167-2: SCHULHOFF—Duo for violin and cello; Violin sonata no. 2; Cello sonata. *Wagner, violin; Gmelin, cello; Lamke, piano.*
+ Fa 5-6/96: 266
+ Gr 9/95: 77

19578. 3-1170-2: GUBAIDULINA—Flute quartet; Quasi hoquetus. FIRSOVA—Viola suite, op. 2; Meditation in a Japanese garden. USTVOLSKAYA—Composition no. 1. *Ritter, Osten, Heinzmann, Barner, flutes; Hilgers, tuba; Schoberansky, bassoon; Oepen, viola; Hagen, piano.*
+ Fa 7-8/95: 354

19579. 3-1171-2: HAYDN—Viennese harpsichord music. *Dengler, harpsichord.*
• EM 5/93: 323

19580. 3-1173-2: Music of Koetsier, Brown, and Schmidt. *Giles, harp; Budapest Brass Quintet.*
+ ARG 9-10/96: 238

19581. 3-1174-2 (2 discs): BROUWER—Guitar music. *Beer, Draper, Ljungstrom, Patterson, guitars.*
+ ARG 7-8/95: 95

19582. 3-1176-2: PADEREWSKI—Piano music. *Kupiec, piano.*
+ ARG 7-8/96: 167
• Fa 7-8/96: 262

19583. 3-1178-2: MOSCHELES—Septet; Introduction and rondo ecossais; Terpsichore; Etude; Flute sonata. *Heinzmann, flute; Weichert, piano; Shimizu, violin; Zeijl, viola; Groth, cello; Donandt, double bass; Hermann, clarinet; Monian, horn.*
+ ARG 5-6/96: 152

19584. 3-1182-2: Music of Villa-Lobos, Nazareth, Santoro, Guarnieri, and others. *Verzoni, piano.*
+ ARG 5-6/95: 214

19585. 3-1186-2: SCHULHOFF—Variations and fugate; Nine little dances; Piano sonata no. 3. *Urban, piano.*
+ ARG 3-4/96: 180
+ Fa 5-6/96: 266

19586. 3-1187-2: SCHUBERT—Arpeggione sonata. BRAHMS—Cello sonata no. 1. Music of Weber, Mendelssohn, and Schumann. *Bauer, cello; Kupiec, cello.*
+ Fa 7-8/93: 233

19587. 3-1188-2: MESSIAEN—Quartet for the end of time. DUNSER—Tage- und Nachtbücher. *Schelling, clarinet; Mumelter, violin; Nothas, cello; Kontarsky, piano.*
• ARG 11-12/96: 163

19588. 3-1197-2: HUMPERDINCK—Shakespeare suites no. 1-2; Die Heirat wider Willen: overture (2nd version); Humoreske in E major. *Bamberg Symphony; Rickenbacher, cond.*
+ ARG 3-4/95: 117
• Fa 3-4/95: 193
+ Gr 4/95: 54

19589. 3-1198-2: BAUR—Moments musicaux; Quintetto pittoresco; Abbreviaturen; Ostinato senza fine. *Ozim, violin; Ludwig, piano; Aulos Quintet; Amati Ensemble; Koelble, cond.; Cologne Radio Wind Sextet.*
+ Fa 11-12/93: 176

19590. 3-1202-2: HINDEMITH—Organ concerto; Kammermusik no. 7; Suite for mechanical organ "The triadic ballet". *Haselbock, organ; Vienna Symphony Orch.; Frühbeck de Burgos, cond.; Welte mechanical organ.*
• Fa 7-8/96: 197
+ Gr 1/96: 52

19591. 3-1207-2: WUORINEN—Piano concerto no. 3; Golden dance. *Ohlsson, piano; San Francisco Symphony Orch.; Blomstedt, cond.*
+ Gr 4/93: 73

19592. 3-1208-2: *Coronation music for Napoleon I.* Music of Paisiello, Le Sueur, and Roze. *Vocal soloists; St. Petersburg Capella Choir & Orch.; Guy Touvron Brass Ensemble; Tchernuchenko, cond.*
- ARG 11-12/96: 269
• Fa 11-12/96: 438

19593. 3-1209-2: REGER—Die Weihe der Nacht; Psalm 100; Weihegesang. *Braun, Kunz, contraltos; Bamberg Symphony; Stein, cond.*
+ ARG 3-4/96: 171
• Gr 3/96: 86

19594. 3-1210-2: Music of Scarlatti, Caccini, Giordani, Monteverdi, Gluck, Martini, and others. *Bruson, baritone; Juffinger, piano & organ.*
- ARG 7-8/94: 223

19595. 3-1213-2: Bohemian Baroque songs. *Music Bohemica Prague; Krček, cond.*
• ARG 3-4/95: 255

19596. 3-1217-2: Russian requiem. *Novospassky Monastery Choir; Mitrofan, cond.*
+ ARG 3-4/94: 223

19597. 3-1218-2 (2 discs): BARTÓK—Mikrokosmos. *Jandó, piano.*
+ ARG 7-8/94: 66
• Fa 7-8/94: 58

19598. 3-1219-2: DOHNÁNYI—Piano music. *Jandó, piano.*
• ARG 5-6/96: 105

19599. 3-1220-2: HONEGGER—Toccata and variations; Deux esquisses; La cahier romand; Prelude on BACH; Three pieces; Seven brief pieces; Roussel homage; Chopin souvenir; Sarabande. *Middelbeek, piano.*
• ARG 9-10/92: 119
+ Fa 1-2/93: 169

19600. 3-1221-2: MARTIN—Piano music. *Mathé, piano.*
+ ARG 3-4/94: 119
• Fa 1-2/94: 230
• Gr 8/94: 76

19601. 3-1223-2: SALZEDO—Harp music. *Giles, harp.*
+ ARG 9-10/94: 189
+ Fa 9-10/94: 322

19602. 3-1224-2: CASTELNUOVO-TEDESCO—Les guitares bien tempérées: 24 preludes for 2 guitars, op. 199. *Duo Tedesco.*
• Fa 9-10/96: 175

19603. 3-1231-2: DUTILLEUX—String quartet "Ainsi la nuit." DEBUSSY—Violin sonata. CHAUSSON—Concerto for piano, violin, and string quartet. *Schönberg Quartet; Kussmaul, violin; Meinders, piano.*
• Fa 5-6/94: 140

19604. 3-1232-2: SCHULHOFF—Concertino; Divertissement; Flute sonata; Jazz sonata. *NDR Players.*
+ ARG 11-12/95: 199
+ Fa 5-6/96: 266
+ Gr 9/95: 77

19605. 3-1233-2: SCHULHOFF—String sextet; Five pieces for string quartet; String quartets no. 1-2. *Schönberg Quartet; Regteren, 2nd viola; Kooistra, 2nd cello.*
+ ARG 1-2/95: 170
+ Fa 11-12/94: 372

19606. 3-1236-2: BENGUEREL—Tempo. MARCO—Concierto guadiana. CASTRO—Guitar concerto. *Weigel, guitar; European Masters Orch.; Schmelzer, cond.*
+ ARG 1-2/95: 82
+ Gr 5/95: 44

19607. 3-1237-2: Concertos by Forster, Telemann, Fick, Knechtel, and Quantz. *Komischke, corno da caccia; Philharmonic String Soloists; Schloter, cond.*
- ARG 5-6/95: 210

19608. 3-1239-2: MOSZKOWSKI—Spanish album; Polish folk dances; Dances from different countries; German round dances. *Cologne Piano Duo.*
- ARG 1-2/97: 142
- Fa 11-12/96: 313

19609. 3-1242-2: SCHROETER—Piano concertos no. 1, 3-4, 6. *Angerer, fortepiano; Concilium Musicum Wien.*
+ ARG 7-8/95: 187
+ Fa 9-10/95: 309

19610. 3-1246-2: VIOLA—Missa Alma redemptoris Mater; Beatus vir; Laetatus sum; Magnificat; Organ sonata; Partido for organ. *Choirboys and Monks of Montserrat; Segarra, cond.*
- ARG 3-4/93: 153
- Fa 11-12/92: 399

19611. 3-1251-2: BACH—Mass in B minor. *Venuti, Kallisch, Prégardien, Scharinger; Arnold Schönberg Chor Wien; Salzburger Barockensemble; Ortner, cond.*
- Fa 9-10/94: 126

19612. 3-1252-2: *Austrian church music.* Music of Hoffmann, Esterhazy, Fux, Caldara, Werner, M. and J. Haydn. *Khittl-Muhr, Solzbacher, Equiluz; Concilium Musicum of Vienna; Angerer, cond.*
+ ARG 3-4/95: 255

19613. 3-1257-2: *Live recordings.* Music of Verdi, Offenbach, Weber, Boito, Wallace, Meyerbeer, Adam, Donizetti, Schubert, Leoncavallo, J. Strauss, Jr., Lehár, Gounod, O. Straus, Wagner, and Puccini. *Schmidt, tenor; various acc.*
+ Fa 5-6/93: 369

19614. 3-1259-2: Music of Brahms, Dvořák, and Reger. *Banse, soprano; Fassbaender, mezzo-soprano; Garben, piano.*
+ ARG 1-2/96: 239
+ Gr 8/95: 109

19615. 3-1263-2: MAHLER—Lieder eines fahrenden Gesellen (arr. Schoenberg). BUSONI—Berceuse élégiaque; Kindertotenlieder (arr. de Leeuw). *Nes, alto; Bröcheler, baritone; Schoenberg Ensemble; Leeuw, cond.*
+ ARG 3-4/94: 117
+ Fa 3-4/94: 238
- Gr 5/94: 98

19616. 3-1265-2: SZYMANOWSKI—Symphony no. 3; Stabat Mater; Triptych. *Woytowicz, Szostek-Radkowa, Hiolski; Cracow Radio Orch.; Wisłocki, Strugala, conds.; Katowice Radio Orch.; Maksymiuk, cond.*
- ARG 9-10/94: 205
+ Gr 4/94: 92

19617. 3-1267-2: WOLF-FERRARI—La vita nuova. *Lindsley, soprano; Fortune, baritone; Boys Chorus of St. Hedwigs Cathedral; Chorus of St. Hedwigs Cathedral; Berlin Radio Symphony Orch.; Bader, cond.*
+ ARG 7-8/95: 231
+ Fa 7-8/95: 369

19618. 3-1269-2 (3 discs): MASSENET—Esclarmonde. *Gavazzeni-Mazzola, Sempere, Perraguin, Tréguier, Courtis, Gabelle; Choeurs du Festival Massenet; Maîtrise du Centre de Création Lyrique de Saint-Étienne; Franz Liszt Symphony Orch.; Fournillier, cond.*

- ARG 7-8/95: 153
+ Fa 7-8/95: 237
+ Fa 9-10/95: 257
- ON 8/95: 36

19619. 3-1270-2 (2 discs): MASSENET—Griséldis. *Command, Larcher, Desnoues; Franz Liszt Symphony Orch.; Foumillier, cond.* Recorded live 1992.
- ARG 1-2/95: 138
- Fa 3-4/95: 224
- Gr 12/94: 156
+ ON 4/1/95: 42

19620. 3-1278-2: CHAUMONT—Organ suites. *Schoonbroodt, organ.* Reissue.
+ ARG 1-2/93: 86

19621. 3-1286-2: HAYDN—Divertimenti. *Haydn Sinfonietta; Huss, cond.*
+ ARG 5-6/96: 122
+ Gr 1/96: 52

19622. 3-1291-2: LISZT—Saint Elisabeth. *Szechowska, Millmann, Lapins, Bercewy; Warsaw Radio Orch.; Heinrich, cond.*
- ARG 9-10/93: 148

19623. 3-1292-2: HONEGGER—Jeanne d'Arc au bûcher (sung in German). *Altschul, speaker; Claus, Remmert, Hees, Paul; Cracow Radio Symphony Orch.; Heinrich, cond.* Recorded 1991.
+ ARG 7-8/94: 115
- Gr 12/93: 100

19624. 3-1293-2: COUPERIN—Tenebrae lessons; Motets. *Ensemble Lyra Wien.*
- ARG 3-4/96: 104

19625. 3-1295-2: HARTMANN—Symphony no. 2; Gesangsszene to words from Giraudoux's Sodom and Gomorrah; Sinfonia tragica. *Nimsgern, baritone; Bamberg Symphony Orch.; Rickenbacher, cond.*
+ ARG 7-8/94: 110
+ Fa 5-6/94: 161
+ Gr 5/94: 52

19626. 3-1296-2: LICKL—Requiem in C minor; Missa solemnis in F major. *Zádori, Németh, Keönch, Bátor, vocalists; Pécs Chamber Chorus & Symphony Orch.; Williams, cond.*
+ ARG 11-12/96: 151
+ Fa 9-10/96: 238

19627. 3-1298-2: TAN—On Taoism; Orchestral theatre I; Death and fire: dialogue with Paul Klee. *BBC Scottish Symphony Orch.; Tan, cond.*
+ ARG 7-8/94: 96
+ Fa 5-6/94: 139
+ Gr 4/94: 56

19628. 3-1299-2: HINDEMITH—French dance suite; Nobilissima visione. *Bamberg Symphony Orch.; Rickenbacher, cond.*
- ARG 3-4/96: 127
+ Fi 5/96: 129

19629. 3-1310-2: MILHAUD—Le voyageur sans bagages; Suite for violin, clarinet, and piano; Le printemps; Sonata no. 2 for violin and piano; Petit concert; Sonatine for clarinet and piano; Caprice for clarinet and piano. *Trio Bellerive.*
+ ARG 3-4/93: 112
+ Fa 3-4/93: 228

19630. 3-1311-2: GOUNOD—Sapho. *Command, Coste, Papis, Faury, Sarrazin; Lyric Chorus of Saint-Étienne; New Orch. of Saint-Etienne; Fournillier, cond.* Recorded live 1992.
- ARG 7-8/94: 105
- Fa 5-6/94: 152
+ Gr 7/94: 109
- Op 10/94: 1235

19631. 3-1319-2: SOMMERLATTE—Old western suite; Dream ballet; The rose of Shiraz; Traumulus; Romanesca; Doina; Venetian suite; Metropolis; Nightexpress; Adieu, Mona Lisa. *Thüringen Philharmonie; Koch, cond.*
+ Fa 11-12/93: 399

19632. 3-1328-2: BRAHMS—Piano sonata no. 3; Intermezzo in A, op. 118, no. 2; Romanze in F, op. 118, no. 5. *Lahusen, piano.*
- ARG 3-4/93: 63
- Fa 3-4/93: 130
+ Gr 5/92: 76

19633. 3-1329-2: BRAHMS—Sonata for cello and piano, op. 38. R. STRAUSS—Sonata for cello and piano, op. 6. *Amann, cello; Merkle, piano.*
- ARG 5-6/93: 74
+ Fa 5-6/93: 175

19634. 3-1340-2: Music of Ponce, Weiner, Brouwer, Boccherini, and Baumann. *Bader, guitar.*
+ ARG 1-2/94: 179

19635. 3-1344-2: *Symphony for the spire.* Music of Parry, Popper, Tchaikovsky, Rimsky-Korsakov and others. *Soloists; English Chamber Orch.; Armstrong, cond.*
- Gr 9/92: 98

19636. 3-1345-2: ROSSINI—Petite messe solennelle. *Cruz, soprano; Gilles, alto; Saretzki, tenor; Grimm, bass; Städische Musikverein Paderborn; Chor der Nordwestdeutschen Philharmonie Herford; Nordwestdeutsche Philharmonie; Albert, cond.*
+ Fa 3-4/93: 263

19637. 3-1347-2: CASANOVES—Christmas responsories. *Chorus & Orch. D'Antics Escolans; Segarra, cond.*
+ Fa 3-4/93: 140

19638. 3-1348-2 (4 discs): WAGNER—Parsifal. *Schröter, Kollo, Adam, Cold; Leipzig Radio Symphony Orch. & Chorus; Kegel, cond.* Recorded 1975.
+ Gr 1/94: 98

KOCH SCHWANN

19639. 3-1350-2: Saygun—Piano concertos no. 1-2. *Onay, piano; NDR Rundfunkorchester Hannover; Aykal, cond.*
+ ARG 1-2/95: 166
+ Fa 11-12/94: 366

19640. 3-1354-2: Reger—Concerto in F "in olden style"; Sinfonietta, op. 90. *Bamberg Symphony Orch.; Stein, cond.*
+ ARG 9-10/94: 181
+ Fa 7-8/94: 211
+ Gr 8/94: 54

19641. 3-1357-2: Glière—Horn concerto, op. 91; Pieces for horn and piano, op. 35: no. 6-7, 10-11. Glazunov—Rêverie, op. 24; Serenade, op. 11, no. 2; Idyll. Shebalin—Horn concertino, op. 14, no. 2. *Neunecker, horn; Rivinius, piano; Bamberg Symphony Orch.; Albert, cond.*
+ ARG 7-8/95: 246
+ Fa 5-6/95: 198

19642. 3-1361—1362-2 (2 separate discs): Wagner—Complete piano music. *Möller, pinao.*
+ Gr 6/93: 78

19643. 3-1365-2: Brahms—String sextets arr. for piano trio. *Höxter, piano; Harding, violin; Feile, cello.*
+ ARG 1-2/96: 91

19644. 3-1371-2: *Music by Jewish composers (of Bohemia and Moravia).* Music of Haas, Karel, Klein, and Schulhoff. *Zoon, flute; Gutman, piano; Bavarian Chamber Phil.; Yinon, cond.*
□ ARG 3-4/95: 231
+ Fa 3-4/95: 292

19645. 3-1377-2: Franck—Music for two pianos. *Blumenthal, Bogaart, pianos.*
□ ARG 9-10/93: 121
● Fa 9-10/93: 163

19646. 3-1378-2: Pàque—String quartets no. 2, 5, 7. *Quatuor à cordes du Théâtre Royal de la Monnaie, Brussels.*
+ ARG 3-4/94: 130
● Fa 1-2/94: 255

19647. 3-1379-2: Haydn—Concertos for 2 lire organizzate, no. 1-5. *Peasgood, Czasch, flutes; Goodwin, oboe; Haydn Sinfonietta; Huss, cond.*
+ Fa 9-10/94: 205

19648. 3-1383-2: *New Russian organ music.* Gubaidulina—Light and dark. Schnittke—Zwei kleine Stücke. Suslin—Poco a poco no. 2; In my end is my beginning. *Herz, organ.*
+ Fa 1-2/94: 403

19649. 3-1389-2: *Zeitgenössische Orgelmusik.* Rihm—Bann, Nachtschwärmerei. Růžička—Z-Zeit. Feldman—Principal sound. Scelsi—In nomine Lucis. Hespos—SNS. *Herz, organ.*
+ Fa 1-2/94: 403

19650. 3-1391-2: Kagel—Exotica. *Ensemble Modern; Kagel, cond.*
+ Fa 11-12/93: 281

19651. 3-1392-2: Kagel—Rrrrrr: 8 pieces for organ; Der Tribun: 10 marches to miss the victory. *Zacher, organ; military band; Kagel, cond.*
+ Fa 11-12/93: 281

19652. 3-1393-2: Shostakovich—Symphony no. 13. *Shirley-Quirk, baritone; Düsseldorf Musikverein Symphony Orch.; Shallon, cond.* Recorded live 1991.
● Gr 8/95: 86

19653. 3-1397-2: Britten—Curlew River. *Jones, Milhofer, Evans, Hargreaves, Ticciati; Guildhall Chamber Ensemble; Angus, cond.*
+ ARG 11-12/96: 102
+ Fa 9-10/96: 163
● Gr 5/96: 115
● Op 4/96: 424

19654. 3-1409-2: Haydn—Applausus. *Erdl, Graf, Wildhaber, Tichy, Fussi; Concilium Musicum Wien; Angerer, cond.*
- ARG 11-12/96: 140
- Fa 11-12/96: 267

19655. 3-1413-2: Benguerel—Llibre vermell. *Rudnjewa, mezzo-soprano; Belarus Chorus; Minsk Phil. Orch.; Kramer, cond.*
+ ARG 7-8/96: 80
- Fa 9-10/96: 151

19656. 3-1417-2: Hölszky—Space; Miserere; Decorum; Nouns to nouns 1; Hinere Welten; Sonnet. *Hussong, accordion; Grossmann, harpsichord; Hölszky-Wiedemann, violin; German String Trio; Ascher, mezzo-soprano; Freiburg Guitar Duo; Saarbrücken Radio Orch.; Davies, cond.*
+ ARG 3-4/95: 115

19657. 3-1419-2: Rossini—Petite messe solennelle. *Potthoff, Most, Mavrak, Langshaw; Cologne Currende Chorus; Blankenburg, cond.*
● ARG 11-12/93: 181

19658. 3-1420-2: Fleischer—Choral music. *Israel Kibbutz Choir; Cameran Singers; Itai, cond.*
+ ARG 11-12/94: 111

19659. 3-1422-2: *Harpsichord concertos of the twentieth century.* Music of Françaix, Martinů, Farkas, and Jelinek. *Braito, harpsichord; Chamber Orch. of the Bratislava Opera; Artemis Ensemble of Vorarlberg; Kantschieder, cond.*
+ ARG 11-12/96: 248
● Fa 9-10/96: 431
- Gr 8/96: 60

19660. 3-1425-2: *Les trois Maries.* Liturgical play. *Madrigal de Paris;*

Académie internationale de Sées; Gagnepain, cond Baernard.
+ ARG 9-10/95: 275

19661. 3-1428-2: Mendelssohn—Athalia. *Borst, Desnoues, Watkinson, Avocat; Lorraine Phil. Orch.; Têtu, cond.* Live recording.
+ ARG 5-6/95: 137
+ Fa 5-6/95: 259

19662. 3-1432-2: *Cocaine Lil.* Music of Eisler, Rihm, Schwehr, and Van de Vate. *Bel Canto Ensemble; Spohr, cond.*
+ ARG 3-4/95: 233
+ Gr 3/95: 82

19663. 3-1435-2: Beethoven—Cantata on the death of Emperor Joseph II; Cantata on the elevation of Emperor Leopold II. *Arnesen, Schäfer, Titus; Berlin Radio Symphony Orch. & Chorus; Rickenbacher, cond.*
+ ARG 3-4/96: 85
● Fa 1-2/96: 135
● Gr 10/95: 104

19664. 3-1436-2: Shostakovich—Cello sonata. Prokofiev—Sonata. Stravinsky—Suite italienne. *Bauer, cello; Kupiec, piano.*
+ ARG 7-8/96: 197
● Fa 7-8/96: 304

19665. 3-1437-2: Schulhoff—Festive prelude; Symphony no. 1; Suite for chamber orchestra. *Brno Symphony Orch.; Yinon, cond.*
+ ARG 11-12/95: 199
● Fa 5-6/96: 266
+ Gr 8/95: 82

19666. 3-1438-2: Stravinsky—Concerto for two pianos; Rite of spring. *A. & J. Paratore, pianos.*
● ARG 5-6/96: 206

19667. 3-1439-2: Gershwin—Porgy and Bess fantasy; Concerto in F; Rhapsody in blue. *A. & J. Paratore, piano.*
● ARG 1-2/96: 111

19668. 3-1443-2: Haydn—Scherzandi, H. II, 33-38. *Haydn Sinfonietta of Vienna; Huss, cond.*
+ ARG 9-10/95: 153
+ Fa 7-8/95: 204
+ Gr 11/95: 86

19669. 3-1447-2: *My heritage.* American melodies and Negro spirituals. *Pickens, soprano; Sulzen, piano.*
+ ARG 9-10/94: 258

19670. 3-1448-2: Bruckner—Symphony no. 8 (first movement missing). *Preussische Staatskapelle; Karajan, cond.* Recorded 1944.
+ ARG 5-6/95: 239
● Fa 5-6/95: 157
+ Gr 12/94: 78

19671. 3-1450-2: *Edition Wiener Staatsoper: excerpts.* Music of Bizet, Wagner, R. Strauss, Verdi, Mozart, Borodin, Schmidt, and Mascagni. *Various singers & conds.; Vienna State Opera Chorus & Orch.* Recorded 1933-43.
+ ARG 11-12/94: 262
+ Fa 7-8/94: 298
+ Gr 6/94: 132

19672. 3-1451-2 (2 discs): *Vienna State Opera: live, 1933-36: vol. 1.* Music of R. Strauss, Tchaikovsky, Verdi, Rossini, Bellini, Wagner, Gounod, D'Albert, and Lehár. *Vienna State Opera.*
+ Fa 9-10/94: 397
+ Gr 7/94: 135

19673. 3-1452-2 (2 discs): *Vienna State Opera: historic recordings.* WAGNER—Parsifal: highlights; Die Meistersinger: highlights. *Grahl, Alsen, Konetzni, Wiedemann; Wiener Staatsoper; Knappertsbusch, cond.; Bockelmann, Maniwarda, Fuchs, Hann, Lemnitz; Wiener Staatsoper; Furtwängler, cond.* Recorded live 1939, 1938.
+ Fa 9-10/94: 379
+ Gr 8/94: 124

19674. 3-1453-2 (2 discs): *Vienna State Opera: historic recordings, vol. 3.* Excerpts from Salome, Siegfried, Idomeneo, Freischütz, Meistersinger, and Götterdämmerung. *Various performers.*
+ ARG 11-12/94: 262
• Fa 11-12/94: 445
+ ON 3/18/95: 34

19675. 3-1454-2 (2 discs): *Vienna State Opera: historic recordings, vol. 4.* Excerpts from Aida, Don Carlo, Pagliacci, Faust, Tannhäuser, Fliegende Holländer, Tosca, Turandot, and Samson et Dalila. *Various performers.*
+ ARG 11-12/94: 262
• Fa 11-12/94: 447
• Gr 12/94: 184
+ ON 3/18/95: 34

19676. 3-1455-2 (2 discs): *Vienna State Opera: historic recordings, vol. 5.* Excerpts from Ägyptische Helena, Frau ohne Schatten, and Daphne. *Various performers.*
+ ARG 11-12/94: 262
• Fa 11-12/94: 448
+ ON 3/18/95: 34

19677. 3-1456-2 (2 discs): *Vienna State Opera: historic recordings, vol. 6.* Excerpts from Tristan und Isolde, Parsifal, Götterdämmerung, Aida, Walküre, Siegfried, and Meistersinger. *Various performers.*
+ ARG 11-12/94: 262
• Fa 11-12/94: 449
+ Gr 1/95: 115
+ ON 3/18/95: 34

19678. 3-1457-2 (2 discs): *Vienna State Opera: historic recordings, vol. 7.* Music

of Bizet, Pfitzner, Schmidt, Verdi, and Smetana. *Vienna State Opera; Walter, Moralt, conds.*
+ Fa 1-2/95: 336
+ Gr 2/95: 115
+ ON 3/18/95: 34

19679. 3-1458-2 (2 discs): *Vienna State Opera: historic recordings, vol. 8.* VERDI—Music from Un ballo in maschera, Aida, and Falstaff. *Vienna State Opera; Böhm, Gui, Krauss, conds.*
+ Fa 1-2/95: 337
+ Gr 4/95: 143
+ ON 3/18/95: 34

19680. 3-1459-2 (2 discs): *Vienna State Opera: historic recordings, vol. 9.* WAGNER—Der Ring des Nibelungen (highlights). *Various artists of the Vienna State Opera, 1933-1937.*
+ Fa 1-2/95: 307
• ON 3/18/95: 34

19681. 3-1461-2 (2 discs): *Edition Wiener Staatsoper, vol. 11.* WAGNER—Tristan und Isolde (excerpts). *Lorenz, Konetzni, Alsen, Schöffler, Klose, Monthy, Ettl, Franter, Gallos; Vienna State Opera; Furtwängler, cond.* Recorded 1941, 1943.
• ARG 5-6/95: 252
- Fa 3-4/95: 335
+ Gr 5/95: 133
• ON 3/18/95: 34

19682. 3-1462-2 (2 discs): *Edition Wiener Staatsoper, vol. 12.* Music of R. Strauss, Wagner, Gounod, Giordano, Mascagni, and Leoncavallo. *Lehmann, Jeritza, sopranos; Rosvænge, tenor; other artists; Vienna State Opera.* Recorded live 1933-1936.
• ARG 5-6/95: 252
+ Fa 3-4/95: 355

19683. 3-1464-2 (2 discs): *Edition Wiener Staatsoper, vol. 14.* WAGNER—Selections from Das Rheingold, Die Walküre, Götterdämmerung, Parsifal, and Die Meistersinger von Nürnberg. *Various vocalists; Vienna State Opera; Krauss, cond.* Recorded 1933.
+ Fa 3-4/95: 336
+ Gr 8/95: 136
• ON 3/2/96: 40

19684. 3-1465-2: *The Vienna State Opera, live, vol. 15.* STRAUSS—Excerpts from Arabella, Friedenstag, and Ariadne auf Naxos. *Vienna State Opera; various soloists & conds.* Recorded 1933-1941.
+ ARG 7-8/95: 273
• Fa 5-6/95: 393
+ Gr 10/95: 164
+ ON 3/2/96: 40

19685. 3-1466-2 (2 discs): *The Vienna State Opera, live, vol. 16.* Music of Wagner, Leoncavallo, R. Strauss, and Verdi. *Ursuleac, soprano; Rünger, mezzo-soprano & soprano; Völker, tenor; Manowarda, bass; Vienna State Opera;*

various conds. Recorded live 1933-1938.
+ Fa 5-6/95: 394
+ Gr 9/95: 128
+ ON 3/2/96: 40

19686. 3-1467-2 (2 discs): *The Vienna State Opera live, vol. 17.* Music of Mozart, Weber, Wagner, R. Strauss, Wolf-Ferrari, and R. Strauss. *Various singers; Knappertsbusch, cond.*
+ Fa 7-8/95: 392
+ Gr 12/95: 178
+ ON 3/30/96: 37

19687. 3-1468-2 (2 discs): *The Vienna State Opera live, vol. 18.* WAGNER—Selections from Die Meistersinger von Nürnberg and Lohengrin. *Various singers; Böhm, Tietjen, conds.*
• Fa 7-8/95: 394
+ ON 3/30/96: 37

19688. 3-1469-2 (2 discs): *The Vienna State Opera live, vol. 19.* Music of Gluck, Wagner, Weber, and Smetana. *Various singers & conds.*
+ Fa 7-8/95: 394
+ ON 3/30/96: 37

19689. 3-1470-2 (2 discs): *The Vienna State Opera live, vol. 20.* WAGNER—Selections from operas. *Various singers; Furtwängler, cond.*
+ Fa 7-8/95: 396
- ON 3/30/96: 37

19690. 3-1471-2 (2 discs): *The Vienna State Opera live, vol. 21.* Music of R. Strauss, Pfitzner, Orff, Borodin, and Egk. *Various singers & conds.*
• Fa 7-8/95: 397

19691. 3-1472-2 (2 discs): *The Vienna State Opera live, vol. 22.* WAGNER—Selections from operas. *Various singers; Knappertsbusch, Krauss, conds.*
+ Fa 7-8/95: 397
+ ON 4/13/96: 53

19692. 3-1473-2 (2 discs): *Vienna State Opera live, vol. 23.* STRAUSS—Ariadne auf Naxos. WAGNER—Die Meistersinger von Nürnberg (excerpts). *Vocal soloists; Vienna State Opera Orch.; Böhm, cond.* Recorded live 1944 and 1943.
+ ARG 9-10/95: 301
+ Fa 1-2/96: 311
+ Gr 5/96: 132

19693. 3-1474-2 (2 discs): *Vienna State Opera live, vol. 24.* WAGNER—Der Ring des Nibelungen (selections). *Vocal soloists; Vienna State Opera; Knappertsbusch, cond.* Recorded 1937-43.
+ Fa 11-12/95: 418
+ Gr 5/96: 132

19694. 3-1475-2: GARNIER—Simphonies concertantes for 2 oboes and orchestra no. 1-2. GARNIER (ATTRIB.)—Oboe concerto. R. KREUTZER—Oboe concerto. *Villevielle, Kolář, oboes; Talich Chamber*

KOCH SCHWANN

Orch.
+ Fa 11-12/94: 231

19695. 3-1481-2: HAYDN—Divertimenti H. 2, 2, 17; Variations. *Haydn Sinfonietta Wien; Huss, cond.*
+ Gr 4/96: 46

19696. 3-1485-2: BEETHOVEN—Works for chorus and orchestra. *Arnesen, soprano; Lehner, speaker; Erxleben, harp; Restle, glass harmonica; Berlin Radio Chorus & Symphony Orch.; Rickenbacher, cond.*
+ ARG 9-10/96: 89
• Fa 9-10/96: 144
+ Gr 4/96: 85

19697. 3-1509-2: BEETHOVEN—Symphony no. 3. *Prussian State Orch.; Karajan, cond.* Recorded 1944.
+ Fa 7-8/95: 119

19698. 3-1510-2: SANTOS—Staccato brillante; Divertimento no. 2; Concerto in D major; Sinfonietta; Elegia a Vianna da Motta. *Orquesta Classica do Porto; Minsky, cond.*
+ ARG 9-10/96: 98
+ Fa 9-10/96: 308
+ Fa 11-12/96: 199

19699. 3-1511-2: Music of Carvalho, Portugal, Moreira, and Bomtempo. *Orquestra Clássica do Porto; Minsky, cond.*
+ ARG 1-2/97: 196
+ Fa 9-10/96: 443

19700. 3-1522-2 (2 discs): CORNELIUS—Der Cid. *Ottenthal, Johansen, Wottrich, Schopper; Rundfunk Chor Berlin; Rundfunk Sinfonie Orch. Berlin; Kuhn, cond.*
+ ARG 1-2/97: 91
• Fa 1-2/97: 144
□ Gr 12/96: 138
+ Op 5/97: 615

19701. 3-1523-2: SCHNITTKE—Viola concerto. LUTOSŁAWSKI—Chain II. *Keulen, violin, viola; Philharmonia Orch.; Schiff, cond.*
+ ARG 7-8/96: 185
+ Fa 7-8/96: 286
+ Gr 11/95: 88

19702. 3-1524-2: PETRASSI—Flute concerto; Souffle; Romanzetta; Ala; dialogo angelico. *Ancillotti, flute; Bartelloni, piano; Tristano, flute; Sicilian Symphony Orch.; Soudant, cond.*
+ ARG 11-12/96: 178

19703. 3-1526-2: CASTÉRÈDE—Quatre etudes; Diagrammes; Impromptu; Variations; Homage to Thelonius Monk; Sonata. *Mathé, piano.*
• ARG 1-2/96: 96

19704. 3-1527-2: DEBUSSY—Violin sonata. FAURÉ—Violin sonata no. 1. POULENC—Violin sonata. *Keulen, violin; Brautigam, piano.*
+ ARG 1-2/96: 221
+ Fi 4/96: 131
+ Gr 10/95: 81

19705. 3-1535-2: Music of Hindemith, Engel, Pirchner, Tcherepnin, Schwetsik, and Eder. *Mozarteum Horn Ensemble; Angerer, cond.*
+ ARG 5-6/95: 211

19706. 3-1539-2: LOEWE—Symphony in D minor; Piano concerto. *Kupiec, piano; Lorraine Concerto Orch.; Houtmann, cond.*
+ ARG 9-10/95: 169
+ Fa 7-8/95: 225

19707. 3-1543-2: SCHULHOFF—Concerto for string quartet and winds; Symphonies no. 2-3. *Kyncl Quartet; Brno Symphony Orch.; Yinon, cond.*
+ ARG 11-12/95: 199
• Fa 5-6/96: 266
+ Gr 2/96: 58

19708. 3-1544-2: Music of Pittoni, Ortiz, Dowland, Leroux, and others. *Robert, lute; Tramier, harpsichord.*
- ARG 7-8/95: 247

19709. 3-1545-2: GODARD—Trios. *Trio Ma Non Troppo.*
- ARG 5-6/95: 115

19710. 3-1556-2: Spiritual concert from Russia. *Moscow Men's Chorus; Popov, cond.*
+ ARG 1-2/97: 222

19711. 3-1558-2: GEHOT—String quartets, trios, and duo. *The Smithson String Quartet.*
+ Fa 9-10/94: 193

19712. 3-1565-2: *Viennese mélange.* Music of J. Strauss, Sr., J. Strauss, Jr., Drdla, Poliakin, Fibich, Jeral, Hellmesberger, Offenbach, Josef Strauss, Wiener, Weinlich-Amman, and Emilie, Countess Komarowsky. *Vienna Boheme Quartet.*
• Fa 5-6/96: 189

19713. 3-1566-2: REGER—Serenade, op. 95; Suite in the old style. *Bamberg Symphony Orch.; Stein, cond.*
+ ARG 5-6/96: 175
- Fa 7-8/96: 272

19714. 3-1572-2: HAYDN—Six lost piano sonatas. *Badura-Skoda, piano.*
- ARG 3-4/96: 123
+ Gr 10/95: 94

19715. 3-1574-2: BOWLES—Huapango no. 1-2; Songs; Six piano preludes; Concerto for two pianos, winds, and percussion. *Various performers.*
+ ARG 1-2/97: 78
+ Fa 9-10/96: 158
+ Gr 7/96: 84

19716. 3-1580-2: MENDELSSOHN—Allegro brilliant. MOSZKOWSKI—New Spanish dances; Waltzes, no. 8. MOSCHELES—Sonata. *Cologne Piano Duo.*
• ARG 7-8/95: 250

19717. 3-1587-2: STADLMAIR—Five novelettes for strings; Essay for clarinet and strings; Capriccio for flute and strings; Sinfonia for alphorn, tube bells and strings. *Brunner, clarinet; Grininelli, flute; Moltz, alphorn; Munich Chamber Orch.; Stadlmair, cond.*
□ ARG 1-2/96: 178

19718. 3-1592-2 (2 discs): PUCCINI—La bohème. *Ricciarelli, Broglia, Araiza, Antonucci, Noli, Burchuladze, Mariotti, Giombi; Verona Arena; Guadagno, cond.* Recorded live 1995.
- ARG 5-6/96: 166
- Fa 3-4/96: 251
- Gr 11/95: 155
- ON 3/2/96: 38

19719. 3-1594-2: WAGNER—Transcriptions for horns. *German Horn Ensemble.*
+ ARG 7-8/96: 221

19720. 3-1597-2: SCHULHOFF—Piano concerto no. 2; Symphony no. 5. *Rische, piano; Cologne Radio Symphony Orch.; Schuller, cond.*
+ ARG 5-6/96: 189
+ Fa 5-6/96: 266
- Gr 4/96: 50

19721. 3-1608-2: M. HAYDN—Requiem in C minor. ADLGASSER—Requiem in C minor. *Vocal soloists; Salzburg Radio Choir; Salzburg Mozarteum Orch.; Hinreiner, cond.* Reissue.
• Fa 11-12/92: 252

19722. 3-1610-2: Music of Holst, Bridge, Parry, Warlock and Britten. *RIAS Sinfonietta; Atherton, cond.* Reissue.
+ ARG 1-2/93: 174

19723. 3-1612-2: BOCCHERINI—Sinfonia concertante. GRAGNANI—Quartet for two guitars, clarinet and viola. TANSMAN—Musique de coeur. *Prunnbauer, Turngoel, guitars; Ganz, viola; Klöcker, clarinet; Consortium Classicum; RIAS Sinfonietta; Stárek, cond.* Reissue.
+ ARG 3-4/93: 163

19724. 3-1617-2: CORRETTE—Ballet des ages. VEJVANOVSKY—Balletti pro tabula. BEETHOVEN—Ritterballet. ANON.—Dances from the Löwen dancebook. *Cartigny, cond.*
+ ARG 11-12/92: 108

19725. 3-1618-2: MOZART—Masses, K. 66, K. 427; Aria Et incarnatus est. *Wise, Aoyama, Baillie, Müller, vocalists; Kuppelwieser, organ; Salzburg Radio Choir; Mozarteum Choir; Camerata Academica Salzburg; Hinreiner, cond.; Meinardus, soprano; Möhring, flute;*

Passin, oboe; Essmann, bassoon; Cologne Chamber Orch.; Müller-Brühl, cond.
• Fa 7-8/95: 254

19726. 3-1619-2: MARTIN—Maria Triptychon. FAURÉ—Messe de requiem. *Mathis, soprano; Widmer, baritone; Schneiderhan, violin; Kühner, organ; Lucerne Festival Choir; Swiss Festival Orch.; Fournet, cond.* Recorded live.
+ Fa 3-4/93: 214

19727. 3-1621-2: GAY-PEPUSCH— Beggar's opera. *Rogers, Jenkins, Minty, Fleet; Accademia Monteverdiana; Stevens, cond.* Reissue.
• ARG 5-6/93: 86
- ON 2/19/94: 33

19728. 3-1622-2: MENDELSSOHN— Concerto for violin, piano and string orchestra; Sonata for violin and piano. *Gulli, violin; Cavallo, piano; Orch. da camera del Angelicum Milano; Urbini, cond.*
• Fa 3-4/93: 218

19729. 3-1623-2: ONSLOW—Quartet, op. 8, no. 1; Quintet, op. 78, no. 1. *French String Trio.* Reissue.
• ARG 5-6/93: 117

19730. 3-1624-2: BRITTEN—Ceremony of carols. MENDELSSOHN—3 Latin motets. CEREROLS—Sacred romances. *Escalonía Montserrat.*
+ ARG 11-12/93: 251

19731. 3-1627-2: SCHUMANN—Etudes in the form of free variations on themes by Beethoven, WoO 31; Andante and variations in B♭; Quartet for piano and strings, WoO. *Badura-Skoda, piano; A. & J. Paratore, duo-piano; Levine, piano; Cologne Classic Ensemble.* Reissue.
+ Fa 3-4/93: 281

19732. 3-1631-2: CEREROLS—Vespers of the Blessed Virgin. *Montserrat Choirs; Ars Musicae; Segarra, cond.*
- ARG 3-4/94: 83

19733. 3-1635-2: DOHNÁNYI—String quartets no. 1-2. *Artis Quartet Vienna.* Reissue.
+ ARG 3-4/94: 90
+ Fa 3-4/94: 175

19734. 3-1713-2: Music of Gismonti, Dyens, Brouwer, and Pereira. *Abt, guitar.*
+ ARG 3-4/96: 230

19735. 3-1718 2: ROGISTER—Violin concerto, Fantasie concertante; Viola concerto. *Koch, violin; Gilissen, viola; Pecs Symphony Orch.; Trautmann, cond.*
• ARG 7-8/96: 180
+ Fa 7-8/96: 276

19736. 3-1719-2: PAQUE—Piano sonatas no. 1-5. *Anderson, piano.*
+ ARG 3-4/96: 164

19737. 3-1720-2: VIEUXTEMPS—String quartets no. 2-3. *Maurice Raskin Quartet.*
• ARG 3-4/96: 202

19738. 3-1721-2: YSAŸE—Poeme nocturne; Sonata for 2 violins; Cello sonata. *Jarry, Toyoda, violins; Lodéon, cello; Pludermacher, piano.*
• ARG 1-2/96: 201

19739. 3-1723-2: HAYDN—Complete overtures, vol. 1. *Haydn Sinfonietta Wien; Huss, cond.*
+ ARG 9-10/96: 133
+ Fa 9-10/96: 214
+ Gr 9/96: 54

19740. 3-1727-2: GLIÈRE—Eight duets, op. 39. KODÁLY—Duo for violin and cello, op. 7. RAVEL—Sonata for violin and cello. *Sebestyén, violin; Ostertag, cello.*
+ ARG 11-12/96: 245
+ Fa 11-12/96: 254

19741. 3-1730—1732-2 (3 separate discs): SOLER—Piano sonatas. *Barrio, piano.*
+ ARG 1-2/97: 173 (v.1-2)
- Gr 5/97: 93

19742. 3-1768-2: LISZT—Funeral odes; Tasso. *Berlin Radio Symphony & Chorus; Rickenbacher, cond.*
+ ARG 1-2/97: 131

19743. 3-1773-2: Geistliche Hymnen. *Zagorsk Monastery Choir.*
- ARG 9-10/96: 260

19744. 3-1774-2 (2 discs): SAINT-SAËNS—Samson et Dalila. *Cossutta, Lipovsek, Fondary, Bisson; Vienna Symphony Orch.; Cambreling, cond.* Recorded 1988.
+ Gr 4/96: 114

19745. 3-1786-2: SIBELIUS—String orchestra music. *Kauppinen, violin; Folkwang Kammerorchester Essen; Tumela, cond.*
• ARG 5-6/96: 199
+ Fa 5-6/96: 278

19746. 3-1787-2: MEDTNER—Sonata romantica; Forgotten melodies, book 3; Improvisation, op. 31, no. 1. *Balser, piano.*
+ Fa 11-12/96: 304

19747. 3-1788-2: MARTINEZ—In exitu Israel; Dixit Dominus. *Cologne Kurrende; Clara Schumann Orch.; Blankenburg, cond.*
• ARG 1-2/97: 136

19748. 3-1800-2 (2 discs): SCHULTZE— Das kalte Herz. *Kruse, Jüten, Steiner, Zywietz, Bendt, Blochwitz, Janssen, Wewel, Altmeyer, Fäth; Handel Collegium of Cologne; Cologne Radio Orch.; Schultze, cond.*
+ Fa 7-8/95: 307
+ ON 7/95: 46

19749. 3-1805-2: WÜSTHOFF—Light music, vol. 1. Die Schelde; Voyage to Greece; Old England suite; Street scenes. *Berlin Radio Orch.; Smola, cond.*
+ ARG 7-8/95: 232
+ Fa 5-6/95: 380

19750. 3-1806-2: WÜSTHOFF—Three Russian fantasies; Concertino; A little harp serenade; Transatlantic rhapsody. *Quelle, piano; Erxleben, harp; Berlin Radio Symphony Orch.; Falk, cond.*
+ Fa 9-10/96: 360

19751. 3-1807-2: WÜSTHOFF—All my animals; Spanish dance scene; The merry cyclist; The rain fairy: ballet music; Golf games; Slavonic rhapsody. *Berlin Radio Symphony Orch.; Falk, Smola, conds.*
+ Fa 9-10/96: 360

19752. 3-1809-2: MOZART—Clarinet quintet. REGER—Clarinet quintet. *Klein, clarinet; Amadeus String Quartet; Heutling Quartet.*
• ARG 7-8/96: 161

19753. 3-1811-2: DOHNÁNYI—Ruralia hungarica; Rhapsodies, op. 11. *Jandó, paino.*
+ ARG 7-8/94: 95

19754. 3-1823-2: BRAHMS—Cello sonatas. *Thomas-Mifune, cello; Piazzini, piano.*
+ ARG 7-8/96: 90
• Fa 7-8/96: 123

19755. 3-1832-2: WOLFRAM VON ESCHENBACH—Titurel. *Wiedenmann, baritone; Parisi, lute.*
+ ARG 3-4/96: 212

19756. SC 100 308 (2 discs): HANDEL (ARR. MOZART)—Messiah. *Altmann, Davidson, Price, Murphy, Elvin; Oratorio Society of New York; Sinfonia Rubinstein, Łód; Woodside, cond.*
- ARG 3-4/92: 66

19757. CD 310 000: BRAHMS—Serenade no. 2. WAGNER—Siegfried Idyll. *Linos Ensemble.*
- Fa 9-10/89: 157

19758. CD 310 001: Music of Weigl, Ries, Riotte, and Rossini. *Consortium Classicum.*
+ ARG 3-4/90: 135
+ Fa 11-12/89: 462

19759. CD 310 002: Music of M. Haydn, Mozart, Wölfl, Neukomm, Aamayer, and Anon. *Consortium Classicum.*
+ Fa 3-4/90: 387

19760. CD 310 003: STAMITZ—Quartets for clarinet, violin, viola, and cello, op. 19, no. 1-3. *Brunner, clarinet; Schneider, violin; Baader, viola; Veihelmann, cello.*
+ ARG 11-12/89: 122
+ Fa 3-4/89: 284

KOCH SCHWANN

19761. CD 310 005: BERG—String quartet, op. 3; Lyric suite. *Schoenberg Quartet.*
+ ARG 3-4/90: 28
+ Fa 1-2/90: 126
• Gr 12/89: 1151

19762. CD 310 006: HUMMEL—Grand serenades for guitar, piano, violin, clarinet, and bassoon: no. 1-2. GRAGNANI—Quartet for 2 guitars, clarinet, and viola, op. 8. *Consortium Classicum.*
+ ARG 9-10/89: 64
+ Fa 7-8/89: 164

19763. CD 310 007: HINDEMITH—Piano music. *Schenck, piano.*
+ ARG 7-8/89: 78
+ Fa 5-6/89: 217

19764. CD 310 008: REGER—Variations and fugue on a theme of Bach, op. 81; Variations and fugue on a theme of Telemann, op. 134. *Levine, piano.*
+ ARG 7-8/89: 49
+ Fa 5-6/89: 286

19765. CD 310 009: STOCKHAUSEN—Klavierstücke, v. 2: no. 9-11. *Wambach, piano.*
• Fa 11-12/90: 365

19766. CD 310 011: REICHA—Wind quintet, op. 100, no. 5. CAMBINI—Wind quintet no. 3. DANZI—Wind quintet, op. 67, no. 2. *Aulos Wind Quintet.*
+ Fa 11-12/89: 332
+ Gr 10/89: 684

19767. CD 310 015: STOCKHAUSEN—Klavierstücke XII, XIII, and XIV. *Wambach, piano.*
□ Fa 3-4/90: 304
+ Gr 5/90: 2023

19768. CD 310 016: STOCKHAUSEN—Klavierstücke, v. 1, no. 1-8. *Wambach, piano.*
• Fa 7-8/89: 255

19769. CD 310 019: *Brazilian piano music.* Music of Villa-Lobos, Guarnieri, and Nazareth. *Verzoni, piano.*
+ ARG 3-4/90: 136
+ Fa 3-4/90: 363
+ Gr 4/90: 1840

19770. CD 310 020: STOCKHAUSEN—Zyklus (2 versions); Refrain; Kontakte. *Ardeleanu, percussion; Wambach, piano; Rensch, celeste.*
+ ARG 1-2/90: 92
• Fa 11-12/89: 365

19771. CD 310 022: FRANÇAIS—Wind quintets no. 1-2; Divertissement for wind trio; Wind quartet. *Aulos Wind Quintet.*
+ ARG 11-12/89: 59
+ Fa 7-8/89: 148
+ Gr 10/89: 684

19772. CD 310 023: HENSELT—Piano music. *Steinfatt, piano.*
+ Fa 11-12/90: 248

19773. CD 310 026: WEBER—Violin sonatas, op. 10, no. 4-6. SCHUBERT—Violin sonatas: in D major; in G minor. *Danszczowska, violin; Malicki, piano.*
+ Fa 9-10/90: 373

19774. CD 310 028: DEVIENNE—Quartets for flute and strings, op. 66: vol. 1, no. 2; vol. 2, no. 1. MOZART—Quartet for flute and strings, K. 497. *Quatuor de Jean.*
• Fa 7-8/89: 128

19775. CD 310 030: HUYBRECHTS—String quartets no. 1-2; Concertino for cello and piano; Two poemes of Emil Verhaeren for mezzo-soprano and string quartet. *Lange, mezzo-soprano; Quartet of the Belgian National Opera; Zanlonghi, cello; Sakai, piano.*
+ ARG 9-10/89: 65
□ Fa 3-4/89: 191

19776. CD 310 031: WEINER—Chamber music. *Katharina Hempel, Klaus Hempel, guitar; Sauveur, flute; Weiner, violin & viola.*
□ ARG 7-8/90: 123
+ Fa 3-4/90: 339

19777. CD 310 033: SCHOENBERG—String quartet no. 1. *Schoenberg String Quartet.*
- ARG 7-8/89: 84
+ Fa 7-8/89: 236
- Gr 7/88: 200

19778. CD 310 034: GLINKA—Piano sextet in E♭ major. RIMSKY-KORSAKOV—String sextet in A major. *Ensemble Classique Köln.*
+ ARG 11-12/89: 107
+ Fa 3-4/89: 169

19779. CD 310 035: GOTTSCHALK—Piano music. *Kaufmann, Klaus.*
- ARG 7-8/90: 51
- Fa 7-8/90: 157
+ Gr 8/90: 390

19780. CD 310 038: JANÁČEK—On an overgrown path; In the mist. *Betz, piano.*
• Fa 11-12/90: 252

19781. CD 310 041: *Trio Basso, vol. 3.* Music of Kröll, Riehm, Goldmann, Brandmüller and Satie. *Trio Basso.*
+ Fa 3-4/92: 416

19782. CD 310 042: VIEUXTEMPS—Pieces for violin and piano, vol. 1. *Godhoff, violin; Ingwersen, piano.*
+ ARG 11-12/89: 132
- Fa 1-2/90: 334

19783. CD 310 043: RAMEAU—Harpsichord music (complete). *Chapelin-Dubar, harpsichord.*
+ ARG 5-6/92: 115
• EM 8/92: 515
+ Fa 3-4/92: 184

19784. CD 310 046: BEETHOVEN—Piano sonata no. 29. *Hendel, piano.*
• ARG 11-12/89: 36
• Fa 9-10/89: 136

19785. CD 310 047—310 048 (2 separate discs): KRENEK—Piano sonatas. *Madge, piano.*
+ ARG 3-4/92: 83
+ Fa 3-4/92: 221
+ Gr 6/92: 67

19786. CD 310 049: BEETHOVEN—Two preludes, op. 39; Piano sonata no. 4; Thirty-two variations in C minor, WoO 80. *Rische, piano.*
• ARG 11-12/89: 36
+ Fa 9-10/89: 133

19787. CD 310 051: FOERSTER—Wind quintet. HAAS—Quintet, op. 10. JANÁČEK—Mládi. *Aulos Wind Quintet.*
+ Fa 9-10/90: 496
+ Gr 6/93: 63

19788. CD 310 054: BARTÓK—Duos for 2 violins (complete). *Mumelter, Lefor, violins.*
• Fa 3-4/91: 144

19789. CD 310 055: Music of Glazunov, Moulaert, Bumcke, and Français. *Berlin Saxophone Quartet.*
+ ARG 7-8/90: 147
+ Fa 5-6/90: 382

19790. CD 310 056: BERWALD—Quartet for piano, clarinet, horn, and bassoon in E♭ major; Piano quintet in C minor; Septet in E♭ major. *Consortium Classicum.*
• ARG 3-4/90: 30
• Fa 11-12/89: 148

19791. CD 310 059: POULENC—Cello sonata. HONEGGER—Cello sonata; Cello sonatina. AURIC—Imaginées, for cello. MILHAUD—Elégie; Cello sonata. *Nyikos, cello; Smykal, piano.*
+ ARG 3-4/91: 148
+ Fa 7-8/91: 374

19792. CD 310 060: LEKEU—Piano trio in C minor. *Trio à Clavier de la Monnaie.*
• ARG 3-4/90: 65
- Fa 3-4/90: 209

19793. CD 310 061: ROSSINI—Barbiere di Siviglia. Excerpts (arr. Trautner). *Munich Rococo Soloists.*
+ Fa 9-10/90: 355
• Gr 9/90: 562

19794. CD 310 063: M. HAYDN—Notturno in F major. PLEYEL—Notturno in B♭ major. DITTERSDORF—Notturno in F major. FUSZ—Notturno in A♭ major. *Concilium Musicum, Vienna.*
+ Fa 11-12/90: 469

19795. CD 310 064: BEETHOVEN—Piano sonatas no. 10, 15, 17. *Faron, fortepiano.*
- Fa 7-8/91: 115

19796. CD 310 065: MOZART—Piano sonatas no. 4, 14-15; Fantasia in C minor. *Faron, fortepiano.*
- Fa 7-8/91: 235

19797. CD 310 066: SCHUBERT—Ländler and waltzes. *Betz, piano.*
+ ARG 11-12/91: 142

19798. CD 310 067: UHL—Divertimento. JELINEK—Divertimento, op. 15, no. 8. STARK—Serenade, op. 55. JETTEL—Quartet . *Württemberg Clarinet Quartet.*
+ ARG 7-8/90: 133
• Fa 7-8/90: 364

19799. CD 310 068: REGER—String quartets no. 5-6. *Joachim Quartet.*
+ Fa 9-10/92: 327

19800. CD 310 077: *Piano music of the Netherlands.* Works by Van Boom, Van Eijken, Lubeck, Schlegel, Buys and Schafer. *Bie, piano.*
□ ARG 11-12/91: 190

19801. CD 310 081: GOSSEC—Flute quartets, op. 14. *Bocquillon, flute; Millière String Trio.*
+ Fa 3-4/91: 221

19802. CD 310 082: PÂQUE—String quartets no. 3-4. *String Quartet of the Theatre Royale de la Monnaie, Brussels.*
+ Fa 3-4/91: 318

19803. CD 310 084: M. HAYDN—String quintets P. 109-110. *Concilium Musicum.*
- ARG 5-6/92: 72
• Fa 11-12/91: 349

19804. CD 310 087: BRICCIALDI—Wind quintet, op. 124. LEFÉBURE—Suite, op. 57. ROSSINI—Wind quartet no. 6. TAFFANEL—Wind quintet. *Aulos Quintet.*
+ Gr 10/91: 137

19805. CD 310 088: *Variations for four hands.* Music of Schumann, Mendelssohn, Beethoven, Saint-Saëns, and Lutosławski. *A. & J. Paratore, pianos.*
+ Fa 1-2/91: 381

19806. CD 310 090: KROL—Ballade Notre Pere des Chausseurs; Taugenichts suite. EDER—Three intermezzos. KOETSIER—Konzertante Musik. *Horns of the Mozarteum, Salzburg; H. Angerer, cond.*
+ ARG 1-2/92: 149

19807. CD 310 091: *In croce: Russian chamber music.* SCHNITTKE—Cello sonata. GUBAIDULINA In croce, for cello and organ. SUSLIN—Sonata for cello and percussion. PÄRT—Spiegel im Spiegel. *Geringas, cello; assisting artists.*
+ Fa 9-10/91: 432

19808. CD 310 094: HAYDN—Keyboard sonatas H. XVI, 2, 4-6, 14. *Faron, fortepiano.*

+ Fa 7-8/91: 174
+ Gr 9/92: 129

19809. CD 310 100: JOLIVET—Serenade. P. PIERNÉ—Suite pittoresque. NIELSEN—Wind quintet. HOLST—Quintet, op. 14. ZEMLINSKY—Humoresque. *Aulos Woodwind Quintet.*
+ Fa 1-2/91: 199

19810. CD 310 103: STRAUSS—Stimmungsbilder; Fünf Klavierstücke. *Salomé, piano.*
- Fa 5-6/91: 212

19811. CD 310 104: Music of Turina, Falla, Toldra, and Granados. *Larrea, violin; Protopopescu, piano.*
• Fa 3-4/91: 489

19812. CD 310 106: CLEMENTI—Piano sonatas. *Faron, piano.*
+ Fa 9-10/91: 190

19813. CD 310 107: MARTINŮ—Trio for flute, cello and piano; Cello sonata no. 1; Flute sonata. *Renggli, flute; Brady, cello; Hedinger, piano.*
+ Fa 5-6/91: 212

19814. CD 310 116: PETIT—Toccata; Tarantelle. SATIE—Gymnopédies. BENGUEREL—Stella splendens. BROUWER—Micro piezas. PIAZZOLLA—Tango suite. *Duo Tedesco, guitars.*
+ ARG 7-8/92: 261

19815. CD 310 117: SCHOENBERG—Pierrot lunaire; Suite, op. 29. *Sukowa, voice; Leeuw, cond.*
• ARG 11-12/92: 196

19816. CD 310 118: ZEMLINSKY—String quartets no. 2-3. *Schönberg Quartet.*
+ Gr 3/92: 72

19817. CD 310 120: *Almost Mozart.* Music of Schubert, Ries, Hummel, Kuhlau, Reinecke and Czerny. *Lambour, piano.*
+ ARG 3-4/92: 190
+ Fa 3-4/92: 402

19818. CD 310 121: SCHNYDER—Flute trio; Winds; Soprano saxophone sonata; Trio for Palladio. *Schnyder, saxophone; other performers.*
□ ARG 7-8/92: 215

19819. CD 310 122: WEISS—Suite in A; Sonata in A; Capriccio; Tombeau; Passacaglia; Fantasie. *Klee, guitar.*
+ Fa 1-2/92: 376

19820. CD 310 133: *Music for piano duet.* MOZART—Sonata, K. 381. BEETHOVEN—Variations on a theme by Count Waldstein. SCHUBERT—Fantasy in F minor. *McChesney, Rae-Gerrard, piano.*
• Fa 5-6/92: 321

19821. CD 310 150: *New Spanish guitar music.* Music of Cruz de Castro, Marco,

Chaviano, and Laborda. *Weigel, guitar.*
• ARG 11-12/92: 239
+ Fa 1-2/93: 295

19822. CD 310 153: WISSER—Alles Walzer. SCHWERTSIK—Blechpartie; Keulenwicht. BREIT—Als ich an einem Sonntagmorgen Frau Müller traf. BAKSA—Triptychon. *Vienna Brass.*
+ ARG 1-2/92: 149

19823. CD 310 165: SHOSTAKOVICH—String quartets no. 6-8. *Manhattan String Quartet.*
• Gr 6/93: 70

19824. CD 310 173: LISZT—Années de pèlerinage. Italie, no. 1, 5, 7; Bagatelle sans tonalité; Rhapsodie espagnole; Transcriptions of Schubert songs. *Glemser, piano.*
+ Fa 3-4/92: 226

19825. CD 310 185: LEKEU—Piano quartet (unfinished); Cello sonata. *Adamopoulos, violin; Desjardins, viola; Zanlonghi, cello; D. Blumenthal, piano.*
+ ARG 9-10/92: 124
• Fa 7-8/92: 198 (North)
+ Fa 7-8/92: 199 (Corleonis)

19826. CD 311 001: C. STAMITZ—Concerto for 2 clarinets in B♭ major. BACKOFEN—Concertante for 2 clarinets, op. 10. *F. Klein, E. Klein, clarinets; Cologne Radio Symphony Orch.; Schneider, cond.*
• Fa 1-2/90: 311

19827. CD 311 002: SAYGUN—Viola concerto. ELGAR—Overture In the south. *Günes, viola; London Phil. Orch.; Aykal, cond.*
+ ARG 1-2/90: 82
+ Fa 3-4/90: 280
- Gr 4/90: 1778 (Elgar)
+ Gr 4/90: 1778 (Saygun)

19828. CD 311 003: SIBELIUS—Serious melodies, op. 77; Serenades, op. 69; Humoresques, op. 87, op. 89. *Holmes, violin; Berlin Radio Symphony Orch.; Handley, cond.*
- ARG 5-6/89: 90
+ Fa 3-4/89: 279

19829. CD 311 004: REGER—Requiem; Latin requiem; Dies irae. *Kawahara, Höffgen, H. Bader, Hillebrand; North German Radio Chorus & Symphony Orch.; R. Bader, cond.*
+ Fa 5-6/89: 286

19830. CD 311 005: Trumpet concertos by Haydn, Reutter, L. Mozart, and Telemann. *Basch, trumpet; Bamberg Symphony Orch.; Andreae, cond.*
• Fa 11-12/88: 344

19831. CD 311 008: GRECHANINOV—Suite for cello and orchestra. KHATCHATURIAN—Cello concerto. *Thomas, cello; Bamberg Symphony Orch.; Symeonides, cond.*

KOCH SCHWANN

+ ARG 7-8/90: 51
- Fa 7-8/90: 158

19832. CD 311 009: SCHOENBERG—
Chamber symphony no. 1; Three pieces
for chamber orchestra; Gurrelieder: Song
of the wooddove; Five orchestral pieces,
op. 16 (arr. Greissle). *Nes, mezzo-
soprano; Schoenberg Ensemble; Leeuw,
cond.*
+ ARG 11-12/89: 110
+ Gr 8/89: 308

19833. CD 311 010: BURGMÜLLER—
Symphony no. 2. SCHUMANN—Symphony
no. 4. *Berlin Radio Symphony Orch.;
Schmöhe, cond.*
□ ARG 11-12/89: 116
□ Fa 3-4/89: 127
+ Gr 11/89: 893

19834. CD 311 011: REGER—Eine
Romantische Suite; Vier Tondichtung
nach Arnold Böcklin. *Berlin Radio
Symphony Orch.; Albrecht, cond.*
+ ARG 11-12/88: 73
+ Fa 3-4/89: 246
+ Gr 4/88: 1458
+ Gr 8/89: 308

19835. CD 311 012: SCHUBERT—
Symphony no. 7 (arr. Newbould). *Berlin
Radio Symphony Orch.; Chmura, cond.*
• Fa 3-4/89: 267

19836. CD 311 013: RAFF—Symphony
no. 5. *Berlin Radio Symphony Orch.;
Bamert, cond.*
• ARG 7-8/89: 76

19837. CD 311 021: SCHUMANN—
Konzertstück for 4 horns and orchestra.
GENZMER—Concerto for 4 horns.
COENEN—Variations for 4 horns. *Berlin
Phil. Horn Quartet; Bamberg Symphony
Orch.; Boder, cond.*
+ ARG 7-8/91: 160
+ Fa 5-6/91: 281

19838. CD 311 022: WEINER—Violin
concerto no. 4; Viola concerto. *Weiner,
violin & viola; NOS Chamber Orch. of
Hilversum; Stulen, cond.*
+ ARG 11-12/89: 137
• Fa 7-8/89: 283

19839. CD 311 025: *Virtuoso saxophone
concertos.* Music of Glazunov, Martin,
Rivier, and Villa-Lobos. *Bensmann,
saxophone; Send, trumpet; RIAS
Sinfonietta, Berlin; Shallon, cond.*
+ Fa 1-2/90: 406

19840. CD 311 027: NEUNER—Oboe
concerto in C major. WINTER—Oboe
concerto in F major. *Feit, oboe;
Württemberg Chamber Orch.; Faerber,
cond.*
+ ARG 3-4/90: 84
+ Fa 11-12/89: 304
• Gr 10/89: 671

19841. CD 311 029: RESPIGHI—
Rossiniana. TCHAIKOVSKY—Suite no. 4.
*Berlin Radio Symphony Orch.; Albrecht,
cond.*
+ ARG 7-8/89: 79
+ Fa 3-4/89: 248 (Respighi)
• Fa 3-4/89: 248 (Tchaikovsky)

19842. CD 311 030: SCHUMANN—
Carnaval (arr. for orch.); Carnaval: 3
excerpts (orch. Ravel). *Berlin Radio
Symphony Orch.; Gülke, cond.*
+ ARG 11-12/89: 114
• Fa 11-12/89: 351

19843. CD 311 031: S. WAGNER—
Symphony in C major. *Berlin Radio
Symphony Orch.; Hollreiser, cond.*
□ ARG 9-10/89: 116
+ Fa 7-8/89: 281

19844. CD 311 032: BACH—Kunst der
Fuge (arr. Stiedry). *Hellwig, Weber,
pianos; Berlin Radio Symphony Orch.;
Zender, cond.*
□ Fa 11-12/89: 104

19845. CD 311 033: SHOSTAKOVICH—
Symphony no. 14. *Hartwig, soprano;
Meven, bass; Saarbrücken Radio
Symphony Orch.; Chung, cond.*
+ ARG 7-8/89: 92
• Fa 5-6/89: 321

19846. CD 311 034: BRAHMS—Piano
quartet, op. 25 (orch. Schoenberg).
SCHOENBERG—Chamber symphony, op. 9
(arr. Berg). *A. & J. Paratore, pianos;
Cologne Radio Symphony Orch.; Gielen,
cond.*
+ ARG 11-12/90: 38
• Fa 9-10/90: 194
- Gr 9/90: 508

19847. CD 311 035: ARRIAGA—
Symphony in D major. SARRIER—
Symphony in D major. SOLER—Three
sonatas (orch. Halffter). *RIAS Sinfonietta,
Berlin; Velazco, cond.*
- Fa 1-2/90: 87
• Gr 12/89: 1148

19848. CD 311 039: POPPER—Cello
concerto in E minor. AUBER—Rondo for
cello and orchestra. MASSENET—Fantaisie
for cello and orchestra. *Ostertag, cello;
Berlin Radio Symphony Orch.;
Paternostro, cond.*
+ ARG 9-10/90: 138
+ Fa 9-10/90: 335

19849. CD 311 041: GÓRECKI—
Symphony no. 3; Three pieces in old
style. *Woytowicz, soprano; Berlin Radio
Symphony Orch.; Kamirski, cond.;
National Phil. Chamber Orch.; Teutsch,
cond. Reissues.*
+ Gr 4/93: 44

19850. CD 311 043: DOHNÁNYI—Violin
concerto no. 1; String quartet no. 1.
*Schneider, violin; Bamberg Symphony
Orch.; Levi, cond.; Artis String Quartet.*

+ ARG 7-8/89: 38
+ Fa 7-8/89: 130
• Gr 9/88: 283 (Concerto)

19851. CD 311 047: MENDELSSOHN—
Concerto for piano and violin in D minor.
VIOTTI—Concerto for piano and violin in
A major. *Entremont, piano; Rudner,
violin; Vienna Chamber Orch.*
+ ARG 7-8/90: 71
+ Fa 1-2/90: 227

19852. CD 311 050: BEETHOVEN—Septet
in E♭ major, op. 20. M. HAYDN—Violin
concerto in A major. *Wiener
Kammermusiker; Schubert, violin;
Wiener Concert-Verein.*
- ARG 3-4/90: 23
- Fa 11-12/89: 132

19853. CD 311 056: GENZMER—Concerto
for cello, double bass, and string
orchestra. Duos for cello and double bass
by Dall'Abacco, Boismortier, Kraft,
Offenbach, and Paganini. *Baumann,
cello; Stoll, double bass; Munich
Chamber Orch.; Stadlmair, cond.*
+ Fa 1-2/91: 199

19854. CD 311 058: REGER—Piano
concerto, op. 114. *Oppitz, piano;
Bamberg Symphony Orch.; Stein, cond.*
+ ARG 11-12/89: 104
+ Fa 11-12/89: 330

19855. CD 311 060: CHOPIN—Preludes
op. 28, no. 1-24 (arr. Françaix). *Berlin
Radio Symphony Orch.; Rickenbacher,
cond.*
+ ARG 9-10/89: 43
+ Fa 7-8/89: 148

19856. CD 311 064: SZYMANOWKSI—
Harnasie, op. 53; Mandragora, op. 43.
*Orch. & Chorus of the Polish National
Opera, Warsaw; Satanowski, cond.*
+ ARG 11-12/91: 157
+ Fa 9-10/91: 369
+ Gr 12/91: 118

19857. CD 311 065: BRUCH—Concerto
for clarinet and viola. LUTOSŁAWSKI—
Double concerto for clarinet and harp.
STRAUSS—Duet-concertino for clarinet
and bassoon. *Brunner, clarinet;
Zimmermann, viola; Turković, bassoon;
Graf, harp; Bamberg Symphony Orch.;
Zagrosek, cond.*
+ ARG 3-4/90: 36
+ Fa 3-4/90: 160
+ Gr 4/90: 1772

19858. CD 311 066: *A serenade for you
from France.* GODARD—Suite in B♭ for
flute and orchestra. OFFENBACH—Serenade
in C for string orchestra. GOUNOD—Petite
symphonie for winds. *Sebon, flute;
Passin, Hollerbühl, oboes; Fadle,
Hartmann, clarinets; Lemke, Schmidt,
bassoons; Bacon, Schmid, horns; RIAS
Sinfonietta; Stárek, cond.*
• ARG 9-10/89: 122
- Fa 5-6/89: 409

19859. CD 311 067: SCHUBERT—Overture in C minor, D. 8. VOLKMANN—Serenade no. 1, op. 62. WEBER—Sechs ecossaisen (arr. De Kresz). REGER—Lyrical andante. BRUCH—Serenade on Swedish melodies. *RIAS Sinfonietta; Stárek, cond.*
+ ARG 9-10/89: 122
+ Fa 7-8/89: 332

19860. CD 311 080: WEINER—Concierto de Sanlucar no. 1-2; Recuerdos de España; Music for Sanlucar. *Katharina Hempel, Klaus Hempel, guitar; Weiner, violin; Schneider, oboe; Sinfonietta Hamburg; Rodríguez Romero, cond.*
+ Fa 1-2/90: 351

19861. CD 311 081: W.F. BACH—Symphony in F major, F. 67. C.P.E. BACH—Sonata for 2 harpsichords and orchestra in B♭ major. J.C.F. BACH—Sinfonia no. 3. J.C. BACH—Flute concerto in D major. *Sebon, flute; Fetz, Scheidegger, harpsichord; Cologne Chamber Orch.; Müller-Brühl, cond.*
+ Fa 7-8/89: 79

19862. CD 311 082: RŮŽIČKA—Fünf Bruchstücke; Satyagraha; Annaherung und Stille, for piano and 42 strings; Six preludes for piano. *Levine, piano; Berlin Radio Symphony Orch.; Růžička, cond.*
+ Fa 3-4/91: 352

19863. CD 311 085: DEBUSSY—Piano music. *Rische, piano.*
+ Fa 11-12/89: 187

19864. CD 311 088: SPOHR—Concerto for string quartet, op. 131; Variations for violin and string trio no. 2-3. *Sebestyén, Granz, violins; Beyerle, Strehle, violas; Ostertag, cello; Berlin Radio Symphony Orch.; Albrecht, cond.*
+ ARG 5-6/90: 112
+ Fa 1-2/90: 309
☐ Gr 1/90: 1338

19865. CD 311 097: FÉTIS—Symphony no. 1; Symphonic fantasy for organ and orchestra. *Froidebise, organ; Orch. Symphonique de la RTBF; Priestman, cond.*
+ ARG 3-4/90: 51
+ Fa 1-2/90: 180

19866. CD 311 098: FRANCK—Symphony (arr. Valach); Prelude, chorale and fugue (orch. Pierné). *Valach, organ; Orch. Symphonique de la RTBF; Vandernoot, cond.*
- ARG 3-4/90: 52
- Fa 1-2/90: 181
- Gr 4/90· 1778

19867. CD 311 099: YSAŸE—Poème élégiaque; Scène au rouet; Andante; Exit; Chant d'hiver; Extase. *Rubenstein, violin; Belgian National Orch.; Rodan, cond.*
- Fa 1-2/90: 335

19868. CD 311 100: MAHAUT—Flute concertos: in E minor; in D minor;

Sinfonias. *Giaux, flute; Huybrechts, viola; Camerata Leodiensis; Schoonbroodt, cond.*
- Fa 3-4/90: 219

19869. CD 311 101: BOCCHERINI—Cello concerto no. 3. DANZI—Cello concerto in A major. *Boettcher, cello; RIAS Sinfonietta; Velazco, cond.*
● ARG 3-4/90: 41
- Fa 1-2/90: 113

19870. CD 311 103: RUBINSTEIN—Cello concertos no. 1-2. *Thomas, cello; Bamberg Symphony Orch.; Ahronovitch, cond.*
● ARG 9-10/90: 109
+ Fa 9-10/90: 359

19871. CD 311 104: MYSLIVEČEK—Flute concerto in D major. VANHAL—Flute concerto in E♭ major. WITT—Flute concerto, op. 8. *Meier, flute; Prague Chamber Orch.*
+ Fa 3-4/90: 375

19872. CD 311 106: GHEDINI—Concerto for two cellos. ROMBERG—Concertino for two cellos. *Menses, Thomas- Mifune, cellos; Bamberg Symphony Orch.; Schmöhe, cond.*
+ ARG 9-10/92: 108
+ Fa 7-8/92: 162

19873. CD 311 109: MOZART—Violin concertos, K. 185, 203, 204, 250. *Schneider, violin; Munich Chamber Orch.; Stadlmair, cond.*
+ Fa 5-6/91: 221

19874. CD 311 110: SKALKOTTAS—Symphony in one movement. KALOMIRIS—Symphony no. 1. *Danish Radio Symphony Orch.; Singverein der Gesellschaft der Musikfreude, Wien; ORF Symphony Orch.; Cardis, cond.*
+ ARG 7-8/90: 61
+ Fa 7-8/90: 275
+ Gr 10/90: 740 (Skalkottas)
- Gr 10/90: 740 (Kalomiris)

19875. CD 311 111: FRANCK—Piano concerto no. 2; Variations brilliantes sur la ronde favorite de Gustave III, op. 8. *Vanden Eynden, piano; Nouvel Orch. Symphonique de la RTBF; Doneux, cond.*
- ARG 3-4/90: 52
+ Fa 3-4/90: 180
● Gr 3/90: 1603

19876. CD 311 112: BOTTESINI—Concerto for double bass in B minor; Introduction and gavotte in A major; Melody in E minor; Gran duo concertante for violin, double bass, and strings. *Harrer, double bass; Altenburger, violin; New Vienna Soloists.*
- Fa 3-4/90: 152

19877. CD 311 113: WOLF-FERRARI—Idillio concertino, op. 15; Concertino, op. 34. *Zoboli, oboe, English horn; Folkwang Chamber Orch.; Maxym, cond.*

+ ARG 3-4/92: 167
+ Fa 9-10/91: 399

19878. CD 311 114: BRAHMS—Serenade no. 1 (nonet version). *Berlin Scharoun Ensemble.*
+ Gr 9/91: 83

19879. CD 311 121: LINDPAINTNER—Sinfonie concertanti, op. 36, 44. DONIZETTI—Concertinos: For flute; For oboe; For oboe d'amore; For clarinet. *Aulos Wind Quintet; Stuttgart Radio Symphony Orch.; Güller, cond.; Sebon, flute; Passin, oboe, oboe d'amore; Fadle, clarinet; RIAS Sinfonietta; Stárek, cond.*
+ ARG 9-10/90: 81
+ Fa 9-10/90: 273

19880. CD 311 122: ZEMLINSKY—Sinfonietta. STEPHAN—Music for 7 string instruments. REGER—Suite for violin and orchestra in A minor. *Maile, violin; Berlin Radio Symphony Orch.; Klee, Lajovic, cond.*
+ ARG 11-12/90: 137
+ Fa 9-10/90: 441

19881. CD 311 128: REZNICEK—Violin concerto in E minor; Serenade for string orchestra in G major. *Davis, violin; Philharmonia Hungarica; Wright, cond.; RIAS Sinfonietta; Stárek, cond.*
+ ARG 11-12/90: 105
- Fa 9-10/90: 353

19882. CD 311 136: MOZART—Piano concerto no. 17. DOHNÁNYI—Variations on a nursery tune; Ruralia hungarica. *Dohnányi, piano; Budapest Phil. Orch.; London Symphony Orch.; Collingwood, cond.*
+ Fa 9-10/91: 281

19883. CD 311 140: J. HAYDN—Violin concerto in A. M. HAYDN—Violin concerto in B♭. *Godhoff, violin; BBC Scottish Symphony Orch.; Trabichoff, cond.*
+ ARG 3-4/92: 70

19884. CD 311 146: HAMAL—Six ouvertures da camera a quattro, op. 1. *Camerata Leodiensis; Schoonbroodt, cond.*
+ Fa 11-12/91: 332

19885. CD 311 147: WEILL—Symphonies no. 1-2. *Cracow Phil. Orch.; Bader, cond.*
● ARG 7-8/92: 244
● Fa 11-12/91: 521
● Gr 10/91: 117

19886. CD 311 149: SHOSTAKOVICH—Chamber symphony, op. 118a. GLAZUNOV—Suite for strings, op. 35. *Camerata Assindia, Essen; Maxym, cond.*
● ARG 5-6/92: 133
● Fa 3-4/92: 235

19887. CD 311 150: REGER—Variations and fugue on a humorous theme by J.A.

KOCH SCHWANN

Hiller; Ballet suite. *Bamberg Symphony Orch.; Stein, cond.*
   + ARG 3-4/92: 125
   • Fa 3-4/92: 294
   • Gr 3/92: 52

19888. CD 311 157: MOZART—Piano concertos no. 12, 14. *Entremont, piano & cond.; Vienna Chamber Orch.*
   - Fa 7-8/92: 225

19889. CD 311 159: MENDELSSOHN— Symphony no. 3. BERLIOZ—Rob Roy overture. GADE—Echoes of Ossian. DEBUSSY—Marche écossaise sur un thème populaire. *BBC Scottish Symphony Orch.; Maksymiuk, cond.*
   • ARG 9-10/91: 152
   • Fa 7-8/91: 392

19890. CD 311 160: BUSONI—Piano concerto. *Lively, piano; Freiburg Vocal Ensemble; Baden-Baden Symphony Orch.; Gielen, cond.*
   + Gr 4/92: 46

19891. CD 311 164 (2 discs): MOZART— Violin concertos. *Cappelletti, violin; European Community Chamber Orch.; Aadland, cond.*
   + Gr 5/92: 43

19892. CD 311 166: THOMSON—The river; The plow that broke the plains. *Philharmonia Virtuosi; Kapp, cond.*
   + Gr 8/92: 42

19893. CD 311 167: BARTÓK—Orchestral suite no. 1. RINGGER—...vagheggi il mar e l'arenoso lido... *Slovenian Phil. Orch.; Jenny, cond.*
   + ARG 11-12/91: 28

19894. CD 311 170: Viennese Ladies' Opera Ball Orchestra plays music of Schrammel, J. Strauss Jr. Lanner, Drdla, Jos. Strauss, J. Strauss Sr., and Kreisler. *Viennese Ladies' Opera Ball Orch.*
   + ARG 1-2/92: 147
   - Fa 3-4/92: 330

19895. CD 311 175: LANDOWSKI—Piano concerto; Concertino for trombone and strings; Flute concerto; Concerto for ondes Martenot, percussion and orchestra. *Philharmonie de Lorraine; Houtmann, cond.*
   + ARG 7-8/92: 160
   + Fa 3-4/92: 224

19896. CD 311 177: STRAUSS—Till Eulenspiegel; Don Quixote; Don Juan. *Tsutsumi, cello; Tokyo Symphony Orch.; Paternostro, cond.*
   • ARG 3-4/92: 143
   • Fa 3-4/92: 336

19897. CD 311 186: REGER—Violin concerto. *Forchert, piano; Bamberg Symphony Orch.; Stein, cond.*
   • ARG 5-6/92: 116
   • Fa 3-4/92: 294

19898. CD 311 193: VIVALDI—Sonatas and concerto, RV 86, RV 58, RV 83, RV 42, RV 269. *Palladio Ensemble.*
   + Fa 3-4/92: 359

19899. CD 311 197: GRETRY—Suite rococo. YSAŸE—Les neiges d'Antan. VIEUXTEMPS AND SERVAIS—Duo on themes from Meyerbeer's Huguenots. GOSSEC— Gavotte. LEONARD AND SERVAIS— Variations on themes by Beethoven. LEKEU—Adagio. *Springuel, cello; Werthen, violin and conductor; Raudales, violin; I Flamminghi.*
   + ARG 1-2/92: 148

19900. CD 311 198: MARSICK—Stèle; La source; Scènes de montagne. *Orch. Phil. de Lorraine; Houtmann, cond.*
   □ ARG 1-2/92: 75
   + Fa 1-2/92: 255

19901. CD 311 202: SHOSTAKOVICH— Symphony no. 6. RIMSKY-KORSAKOV—The legend of the invisible city of Kitezh: suite. *Saar Radio Symphony Orch.; Chung, cond.*
   • ARG 1-2/92: 113
   • Fa 1-2/92: 330
   • Gr 2/92: 40

19902. CD 311 254: WEINER—Conciertos de Sanlucar no. 3-5. *Weiner, violin; Sauveur, flute; Maintz, cello; Seiger, piano; Berlin Symphony Orch.; Rodríguez Romero, cond.*
   □ Fa 3-4/91: 430

19903. CD 313 010: HOFFMANN— Miserere in B minor. REICHARDT—Funeral cantata on the death of Frederick the Great. *Laki, Killebrew, Baldin, Hillebrand; Cologne Radio Chorus & Symphony Orch.; Bader, cond.; Resick, Schreckenbach, Laubenthal, Stamm; RIAS Chamber Chorus; Berlin Radio Symphony Orch.; Albrecht, cond.*
   + ARG 11-12/89: 68
   + Fa 3-4/89: 185

19904. CD 313 013: WOLF—Christnacht. BRUCH—Gruss an die heilige Nacht; Die Flucht der heiligen Familie. *Inoue-Heller, Schreckenbach, Wilke, Thiem; Philharmonische Chor Berlin; Berlin Radio Symphony Orch.; Gronostay, cond.*
   • Fa 5-6/90: 349

19905. CD 313 014: GRUBER—Stille Nacht! Heilige Nacht (3 versions); Mass in D major (Hornmesse); Mass in D major (Hochzeitsmesse); Heiligste Nacht. *Damisch, Mayr, Roider, Habringer, Müller; Voggenberger, guitar; Mayr, Binniker, horns; Kuppelwieser, organ; Salzburg Radio Chorus; Mozarteum Chorus; Salzburg Mozart Players; Hinreiner, cond.*
   + Fa 5-6/91: 178

19906. CD 313 015: DIABELLI—Pastoral mass in F major. *Degler, Linden, Rauschkolb, Clayton, Müller; St.*

Michael's Church, Munich Choir & Orch.; Ehret, cond.
   + ARG 11-12/89: 54
   + Fa 7-8/89: 129

19907. CD 313 019: Russian Gregorian chants. *Monasteries of Zagorsk and Pjetschory.*
   + ARG 9-10/89: 135

19908. CD 313 028: L. MOZART—Missa solemnis in C major. *Augér, Schreckenbach, Laubenthal, McDaniel; St. Hedwigs Cathedral, Berlin Chorus; Domkapelle Berlin; Bader, cond.*
   + ARG 1-2/90: 67
   + Fa 1-2/90: 233

19909. CD 313 031: DONIZETTI—Messa di gloria e credo. *Mané, Vighi, Maus, Machi; St. Hedwigs Cathedral, Berlin Chorus; Berlin Radio Symphony Orch.; Bader, cond.*
   • ARG 5-6/90: 47
   + Fa 3-4/90: 171

19910. CD 313 032: KIEL—The star of Bethlehem; Six motets, op. 82. *Schiml, mezzo-soprano; Laubenthal, tenor; St Hedwigs Cathedral Choir; Berlin Radio Symphony Orch.; Bader, cond.*
   □ ARG 11-12/92: 141
   + Fa 5-6/92: 182

19911. CD 313 038 (2 discs): BLARR— Passion. *Vocal soloists; Choirs; Neander Sinfonietta; Blarr, cond.*
   □ ARG 3-4/92: 33

19912. CD 313 041 (2 discs): GOSSEC— Grande messe des morts; Symphony in 17 parts. *Chorus of the RTB; Liège Symphony Orch.; Houtmann, cond.*
   + ARG 9-10/91: 76
   • Fa 7-8/91: 163

19913. CD 313 043: ZELENKA—Te Deum in D; Magnificat in C; Haec dies. *Meyer, Hickman, Urrey, Riley; Westminster Oratorio Choir; Zelenka Chamber Orch.; Floreen, cond.*
   + ARG 11-12/91: 171

19914. CD 313 052: NICOLAI—Mass in D. RIGHINI—Te Deum. *Various performers. Reissues.*
   + ARG 5-6/92: 102
   + Fa 3-4/92: 277

19915. CD 313 055: SCHUBERT—Stabat Mater, D. 383. WEBER—Gloria et honore; In die solemnitatis. *RSO Berlin; RIAS Kammerchor; Bader, cond.; Taborsky, soprano; Chorus & Orch. of St. Michael, Munich; Ehret, cond. Reissue.*
   + ARG 3-4/92: 135
   • Fa 1-2/92: 322

19916. CD 313 062: CASALS—Sacred choral music. *Escolanía Montserrat; Segarra, cond.*
   + ARG 1-2/92: 42
   □ Gr 1/92: 84

19917. CD 313 075: TCHAIKOVSKY—
Liturgy of St. John Chrysostom, op. 41.
*A.A. Yurlov Chapel Choir; Verhoeff,
cond.*
+ Fa 11-12/91: 505

19918. CD 313 078: GOSSEC—Dernière
messe des vivants. *Parès-Reyna, Mayeur,
Laiter, Piquemal; Choeur Régional
Vittoria d'Ile de France; La Sinfonietta,
Orch. Régional de Picardie; Rouits,
cond.*
• ARG 9-10/91: 76
+ Fa 7-8/91: 163

19919. CD 313 081: GRAUN—Der Tod
Jesu. *Cuccaro, Markus, Shirley-Quirk;
RIAS Choir; RIAS Sinfonietta;
Gronostay, cond.* Recorded 1981.
+ ARG 3-4/92: 63

19920. CD 313 084 (2 discs):
MASSENET—La Vierge. *Command,
Olmeda, Keller, Salmon; Choeurs de
l'Orch. National de Lyon; Prague
Symphony Orch.; Fournillier, cond.*
+ ARG 3-4/92: 100
+ Fa 3-4/92: 240
+ Gr 5/92: 90

19921. CD 314 001: SZYMANOWSKI—
Songs. *Klosinska, Rorbach, Zagórzanka,
Szostek-Radkowa; Polish National
Opera; Satanowski, cond.*
• Fa 9-10/89: 338
+ Gr 12/89: 1186

19922. CD 314 002: *Early songs by
famous composers.* Music of Haydn,
Mozart, Beethoven, Weber, Schubert,
Mendelssohn, Schumann, Liszt, Brahms,
Wolf, Mahler, Strauss, Pfitzner,
Schoenberg, Webern, Marx, Hauer, Berg,
Krenek, Blacher, Einem, and Orff.
Klepper, soprano; Werba, piano.
+ ARG 9-10/89: 146
+ Fa 7-8/89: 285

19923. CD 314 004: WOLF-FERRARI—
From the Italienisches Liederbuch;
Edelwild. *Francesca-Cavazza, soprano;
Göbel, piano.*
+ ARG 3-4/90: 126
• Fa 1-2/90: 351
• Gr 4/90: 1858

19924. CD 314 005: WEBERN—Vocal
chamber music (complete). *Dorow,
soprano; Niederländischer
Kammerchoir; Schönberg Ensemble;
Leeuw, Reinbert de.*
+ Fa 3-4/90: 338
• Gr 5/90: 2037
+ MA 9/90: 91

19925. CD 314 006 (2 discs): HENZE—
The Bassarids. *Armstrong, Lindsley,
Wenkel, Riegel, Tear, Burt, Schmidt,
Murray; RIAS-Kammerchor;
Südfunkchor; Radio-Symphonie-Orch.
Berlin; Albrecht, cond.*
+ ARG 11-12/91: 81
+ Fa 11-12/91: 351

+ Gr 10/91: 187
+ ON 11/91: 41
+ Op 11/91: 1369

19926. CD 314 011: Music of Lassus,
Brandt, Senfl, Bruck, and Anon. *Musica
Canterey Bamberg; Dechant, cond.*
- Fa 7-8/90: 345

19927. CD 314 014 (2 discs):
SZYMANOWSKI—King Roger. *Zagórzanka,
Kowalski, Skulski; Chorus & Orch. of the
Teatr Wielki (Warsaw); Satanowski,
cond.*
• ARG 3-4/92: 150
- Fa 11-12/91: 499
+ ON 11/91: 41

19928. CD 314 020: KIENZL—Songs.
Kimbrough, baritone; Baldwin, piano.
• ARG 7-8/91: 73
• Fa 7-8/91: 185

19929. CD 314 021: ORFF—Catulli
carmina. STRAVINSKY—Les noces.
Soloists; ensembles; Schäfer, cond.
+ Fa 3-4/91: 314
• Gr 7/91: 100

19930. CD 314 022—314 023 (2 separate
discs): SCHUBERT—Part songs for men's
chorus, vol. 1-2. *Gus-Anton-
Konzertchor; Städtisches Orch.
Remscheid; Anton, cond.* Reissues.
+ Fa 5-6/92: 242

19931. CD 314 024: BRAHMS—Songs.
Blegen, soprano; Katz, piano.
+ Fa 3-4/91: 134

19932. CD 314 025 (2 discs): SCHOECK—
Massimilla Doni. *Mathis, Lindsley,
Protschka, Hermann; with assisting
soloists; Cologne Radio Chorus &
Symphony Orch.; Albrecht, cond.*
+ ARG 1-2/90: 83
+ Fa 11-12/89: 343
+ Gr 11/89: 971
+ ON 2/3/90: 30

19933. CD 314 027/28 (2 discs):
PFITZNER—Von deutscher Seele.
*Habereder, Most, Protschka, Halem;
Düsseldorf Municipal Music Society
Chorus; Düsseldorf Symphony Orch.;
Hollreiser, cond.*
• Fa 5-6/90: 246
+ Gr 10/89: 727

19934. CD 314 030 (2 discs): HENZE—El
cimarrón. *Yoder, baritone; Faust, flutes;
Evers, guitar; Ardeleanu, percussion.*
□ ARG 3-4/92: 75
+ Fa 1-2/92: 236
+ Gr 1/92: 86
+ Op 7/92: 876

19935. CD 314 033: *Songs of the Age of
Romanticism.* Music of Schumann,
Reger, Reinecke, Cornelius, Jensen, and
Mendelssohn. *Grossmeyer, soprano;
Silver, piano.*

+ ARG 3-4/91: 178
• Fa 1-2/91: 361

19936. CD 314 037: BEETHOVEN—Three
hymns, op. 86 (based on Mass in C).
*Vogel, Alder-Alford, Elsner, Köhler;
Cracow Phil. Chorus & Orch.; Bader,
cond.*
• ARG 11-12/90: 28
- Fa 9-10/90: 171

19937. CD 314 042 (2 discs):
MENDELSSOHN—Hochzeit des Camacho.
*Schudel, Swanson, Bieber, Mok, Horn,
Lukas, Becker, Murray, Molsberger;
RIAS Chamber Choir; Berlin Radio
Symphony Orch.; Klee, cond.*
• ARG 9-10/91: 97
+ Fa 7-8/91: 212

19938. CD 314 050: WEILL—Recordare;
Legende vom toten Soldaten; Zu Potsdam
unter den Eichen; Berliner Requiem; Four
Walt Whitman songs; Kiddush. *Wagner,
tenor; Holzmair, baritone; Robert
Schumann Chamber Orch.; Düsseldorf
Symphony Orch.; Schmidt,
Schlingensiepen, conds.*
+ ARG 3-4/92: 164
+ Gr 4/92: 140

19939. CD 314 056: PEPUSCH—Beggar's
opera. *Soloists; Hüsch, Hans Dieter;
Accademia Monteverdiana Chorus &
Orch.; Stevens, cond.*
+ Fa 3-4/91: 214

19940. CD 314 063: Songs by Giuliani,
Spohr, Beethoven, Schubert and Brahms.
Parcells, soprano; Justen, guitar.
+ ARG 3-4/92: 203
+ Gr 5/92: 99

19941. CD 314 069 (2 discs):
ZEMLINSKY—Kleider machen Leute.
*Winkler, Mathis, Slabbert; Zürich Opera;
Weikert, cond.* Recorded live.
+ ARG 3-4/92: 168
+ Gr 1/92: 96
+ ON 9/95: 58
+ Op 5/92: 616

19942. CD 314 074 (2 discs): VERDI—
Otello. *Guleghina, Murgu, Bruson; Tokyo
Phil. Orch.; Kuhn, cond.*
- ARG 7-8/92: 242
+ Fa 7-8/92: 317
+ Gr 6/92: 85
+ ON 1/30/93: 37
• Op 8/92: 998

19943. CD 314 081: STRAUSS—Vier letzte
Lieder; Orchestral songs. *Jones, soprano;
Tokyo Symphony Orch.; Paternostro,
cond.* Recorded live.
• ARG 3-4/92: 144
- Fa 3-4/92: 337
- Gr 6/92: 78

19944. CD 314 088 (3 discs): MOZART—
Don Giovanni. *Dohmen, Pedaci,
Galgani, Turco; Orch. Filarmonica
Marchigiana; Kuhn, cond.*

KOCH SCHWANN

• ARG 7-8/92: 185
- Fa 7-8/92: 229
• Gr 5/92: 109

19945. CD 315 003: *The Buxtehude organ in Torrlosa.* Organ music of Buxtehude, Bruhns, and Bach. *Tillmanns, organ.*
+ DA 12/89: 90
+ Fa 11-12/89: 167

19946. CD 315 006: *Organ, bagpipe, shawm, and flute.* Music of Purcell, Praetorius, Bach, Widor, Hasse, Rachmaninoff, Roewer, and Anon. *Ensemble Musica Variata.*
+ Fa 7-8/89: 318

19947. CD 315 009 (2 discs): VIERNE—Twenty-four pieces in free style, op. 31. *Kaunzinger, organ.*
+ ARG 1-2/90: 102
+ Fa 11-12/89: 397

19948. CD 315 011: BLARR—Organ sonata; Songs for soprano, harp, and organ. *Grossmeyer, soprano; Rohrmus, harp; Blarr, organ.*
+ ARG 7-8/90: 30
+ Fa 7-8/90: 102

19949. CD 315 012: JONGEN—Symphonie concertante for organ and orchestra, op. 81; Suite for viola and orchestra, op. 48; Allegro appassionato, op. 79. *Schoonbroodt, organ; Symphony Orch. of Liège; Defossez, cond.; Gilissen, viola; Symphony Orch. of the RTBF; Priestman, cond.* Reissues.
+ ARG 1-2/92: 67
+ Fa 3-4/92: 217
• Gr 8/92: 32

19950. CD 315 014: Organ book: Mass on the 8th mode; Suites: in A major, in C major, in F major, in D minor, in D major; Elévation; Plein jeu; Oh dites-nous Marie. *Schoonbroodt, organ.*
+ Fa 1-2/91: 130

19951. CD 315 017: Music of Bellini, Berlioz, Smetana, Weber, and others. *Haselböck, organ.*
• ARG 1-2/92: 159

19952. CD 315 019: *Transcriptions for organ four-hands and percussion.* Music of Handel, Corelli, Bach, Vivaldi, Langlais, Rachmaninoff, Stravinsky, and Satie. *Timporg Trio.*
□ Fa 1-2/92: 40

19953. CD 315 023: MESSIAEN—Les corps glorieux; Messe de la Pentacôte. *Rössler, organ.*
• Fa 3-4/91: 279

19954. CD 315 024: MESSIAEN—Livre d'orgue; L'Ascension; Verset pour la fête de la dédicace. *Rössler, organ.* Reissue.
• ARG 7-8/92: 178
+ Fa 1-2/92: 266

19955. CD 315 027: *Buxtehude und seine Schüler.* Music of Buxtehude, Lübeck, Bruhns, and Bach. *Tillmanns, organ.*
- Fa 3-4/91: 173

19956. CD 315 065: MOZART—Die Schuldigkeit des ersten Gebots. *Augér, Laki, Geszty, Hollweg, Ahnsjö, Berliner Domkapelle; Bader, cond.* Recorded 1980.
+ Fa 5-6/92: 209

19957. CD 316 001: HAYDN—Concerto for 2 horns in E♭ major; Symphony no. 72 in D; Cassation in D major. *Cologne Chamber Orch.; Müller-Brühl, cond.*
+ ARG 1-2/89: 55

19958. CD 316 003: DVOŘÁK—Piano concerto in G minor. *Frantz, piano; Northwest German Phil. Orch.; Müller-Brühl, cond.*
+ ARG 11-12/88: 32

19959. CD 316 006: C.P.E. BACH—Sonatinas, Wq. 108-110. *Trimborn, Fetz, Scheidegger, harpsichord; Cologne Chamber Orch.; Müller-Brühl, cond.*
+ ARG 11-12/88: 9

19960. CD 316 007: HOFFMEISTER—Flute concerto in D major. J.C. BACH—Flute concerto in D major. *Mohring, Sebon, flute; Cologne Chamber Orch.; Müller-Brühl, cond.*
• ARG 1-2/89: 57

19961. CD 316 008: STAMITZ—Clarinet concerto in E♭ major. MOLTER—Clarinet concerto in A major. ROLLA—Basset horn concerto in F major. *Stalder, clarinet & basset horn; Cologne Chamber Orch.; Müller-Brühl, cond.*
+ ARG 1-2/89: 90

19962. CD 316 011: MOZART—Harpsichord concertos after J.C. Bach, K. 107, no. 1-3. J.C. BACH—Harpsichord sonata, op. 5, no. 2. *Trimborn, harpsichord; Cologne Chamber Orch.; Müller-Brühl, cond.*
+ Fa 9-10/89: 257

19963. CD 316 012: W.F. BACH—Symphonies, F. 64-65, F. 67. *Cologne Chamber Orch.; Müller-Brühl, cond.*
+ Fa 3-4/89: 119
+ Fa 7-8/89: 80

19964. CD 316 013: HAYDN—Piano concertos, H. 14:12, H. 18:F2, H. 18:5, H. 18:7. *Frager, piano; RIAS Sinfonietta.*
- ARG 1-2/90: 53
+ Fa 3-4/89: 178

19965. CD 316 014: *Serenades for flute and guitar.* Music of Caruli, Böhm, Gänsbacher, and Call. *Pastor, guitar; Sebon, flute; Sebestyén, violin; Ganz, viola.*
• Fa 3-4/89: 375

19966. CD 316 015: AVISON—Concertos after Scarlatti, no. 1-6. *L'Ensemble Berlin.*
+ ARG 9-10/89: 16
• Fa 9-10/89: 115

19967. CD 316 015, 316 029 (2 separate discs): AVISON—Concertos in 7 parts from lessons by D. Scarlatti. *Berlin Ensemble.*
• Gr 3/92: 37

19968. CD 316 016: *Les vendredis.* Music of Glazunov, Artzibushev, Sokolov, Lyadov, Glazunov, Vītols, Osten-Sacken, Blumenfeld, Rimsky-Korsakov, Borodin, and Kopilov. *Haydn String Quartet.*
+ ARG 7-8/89: 125
□ Fa 5-6/89: 407

19969. CD 316 017: VANHAL—Organ concerto in F major. SALIERI—Organ concerto in C major. GRAUN—Organ concerto in F major. *Haselböck, organ; Capella Academica Wien; Hinreiner, cond.*
- Fa 5-6/89: 339

19970. CD 316 018: DEVIENNE—Bassoon concerto in B♭ major. DANZI—Bassoon concerto in F major. *Sax, bassoon; Cologne Chamber Orch.; Müller-Brühl, cond.*
- ARG 5-6/89: 40
+ Fa 5-6/89: 175

19971. CD 316 019: J.C. BACH—Flute concerto in D major; Bassoon concerto in E♭ major. *Sebon, flute; Thunemann, bassoon; Cologne Chamber Orch.; Müller-Brühl, cond.*
+ ARG 7-8/89: 12

19972. CD 316 022: HAYDN—Symphonies no. 6-8. *Capella Clementina; Müller-Brühl, cond.*
• Fa 3-4/89: 182

19973. CD 316 023: *Concerti d'amore.* TELEMANN—Concerto for flute, oboe d'amore, viola d'amore, strings, and continuo in E major. DONIZETTI—Concerto for oboe d'amore in G major. SCHUBERT—Sonata for arpeggione (arr.). *Labko, viola d'amore; Senn, flute; Zorn, Passin, oboe d'amore; RIAS Sinfonietta; Stárek, cond.*
+ Fa 1-2/90: 414

19974. CD 316 024: HAYDN—Cello concertos. C. STAMITZ—Cello concerto in A major. *Nyffenegger, Starck, cello; Cologne Chamber Orch.; Müller-Brühl, cond.*
+ Fa 5-6/89: 212

19975. CD 316 025: Trumpet sonatas and concertos of Torelli, Telemann, and Vejvanovsky. *Schneidewind, trumpet; Mayer-Schierning, violin; Musici Pragenses; Cologne Chamber Orch.; Müller-Brühl, cond.*

● ARG 11-12/89: 162
+ Fa 9-10/89: 432

19976. CD 316 026: HAYDN—Concerto for 2 horns in E♭ major; Cassation in D major, H.II:D22. REICHA—Four trios for 3 horns, op. 82. *Penzel, Lexutt, Grüger, Raspe, H. Alfing, K. Alfing, horns; Cologne Chamber Orch.; Müller-Brühl, cond.*
● ARG 5-6/90: 50
+ Fa 1-2/90: 198

19977. CD 316 027: HOFFMEISTER—Piano concerto, op. 24. HAYDN—Piano concerto in F major, H.18:3. *Neuhaus, Schröter, piano; Cologne Chamber Orch.; Müller-Brühl, cond.*
+ ARG 7-8/90: 58
● Fa 3-4/90: 199

19978. CD 316 028: HAYDN—Violin concerto no. 4. TOMASINI—Violin concerto in A major. *Melkus, violin; Capella Academica Wien; Müller-Brühl, cond.*
+ ARG 5-6/90: 58
● Fa 1-2/90: 199

19979. CD 316 035: *String quartets by famous opera composers.* String quartets by Humperdinck, Gounod, and Donizetti. E.T.A. HOFFMANN—Piano trio in E major. *Tonhalle Quartet, Zürich; Joste, piano; Jarry, violin; Tournus, cello.*
+ ARG 3-4/91: 146
● Fa 3-4/91: 498

19980. CD 316 038: PLEYEL—Sinfonia concertante no. 5 in F major; Symphonie périodique no. 6 in F major; Oboe quartet in D major . *Möhring, flute; Passin, oboe; Gode, bassoon; Lexutt, horn; Feit, oboe; Volmer, violin; Skabar, viola; Skerjanec, cello; Cologne Chamber Orch.; Müller-Brühl, cond.*
+ ARG 7-8/90: 84
- Fa 9-10/90: 334

19981. CD 316 039: *Serenades from Austria.* HEUBERGER—Nachtmusik: serenade for strings. FUCHS—Serenade in E minor, op. 21, no. 3. O. STRAUS—Serenade for strings in G minor. *RIAS Sinfonietta; Stárek, cond.*
□ ARG 9-10/90: 136
□ Fa 7-8/90: 172
+ Gr 9/90: 514

19982. CD 316 051: L. MOZART—Cassation in G major. HAYDN—Symphony no. 55. M. HAYDN—Dream: Excerpts. *Orch of the Hürth Youth Music School; Read, cond.; Cologne Chamber Orch.; Müller-Brühl, cond.; Camerata Academica Salzburg; Hinreiner, cond.*
● Fa 7-8/91: 395

19983. CD 316 070: BEETHOVEN—Creatures of Prometheus. *Basel Symphony Orch.; Müller-Brühl, cond.*
+ ARG 3-4/92: 27
+ Fa 3-4/92: 144

19984. CD 317 003: MOZART—Music for organ. *Haselböck, organ.*
- ARG 11-12/91: 114
+ Fa 1-2/91: 255
+ Gr 10/91: 140

19985. CD 317 006: *Sacred choral music.* Music of Schein, Verdi, Wolf, Distler, Schütz, Gasparini, Handl, Poulenc, and Brahms. *Concentus Vocalis Wien; Böck, cond.*
+ Fa 7-8/89: 297

19986. CD 317 007: *Chorwerke a capella.* Music of Kodály, David, Monteverdi, Bennet, Debussy, and Poulenc. *Concentus Vocalis Wien; Böck, cond.*
● Fa 9-10/89: 397

19987. CD 317 008: BRUCKNER—Motets. DISTLER—Totentanz. *Concentus Vocalis Wien; Böck, cond.*
+ ARG 11-12/89: 48
+ Da 10/89: 98
+ Fa 11-12/89: 161

19988. CD 321 451: *Wiener Strauss Capelle, vol. 1.* Music of J. Strauss, Jr., J. Strauss, Sr., E. Strauss, Josef Strauss, and Lanner. *Vienna Strauss Capelle; Karlinger, cond.*
● Fa 11-12/88: 289

19989. CD 321 758: *Laudate Dominum.* Music of Haydn, Schütz, Cimarosa, Handel, and Hammerschmidt. *Ensemble Pro Musica Divina; Amtmann, cond.*
● Fa 1-2/90: 413

19990. CD 321 760: HAYDN—Piano trios no. 12, 24; Variations of Gott Erhalte; Variations on Scottish folksongs for piano, violin, and flute; Trio for 2 flutes and cello. *Gamerith Consort.*
+ ARG 3-4/90: 61

19991. CD 321 761: *Una notte in Italia.* Music of Bellini, Boito, Cilea, Donizetti, Mascagni, Ponchielli, and Verdi. *Ciurca, Terranova, Hurny, Elenkov; Graz Opera Chorus; Graz Symphony Orch.; Quadri, cond.*
- Fa 3-4/88: 245

19992. CD 330 035 (2 discs): BACH—Organ music. *Tillmanns, organ.*
- Fa 1-2/90: 99

19993. CD 340 172: MOZART—Canons. MENDELSSOHN—Veni, domine; Laudate pueri; Surrexit pastor bonus. *Tölzer Knabenchor; Schmidt-Gaden, cond.*
+ ARG 7-8/94: 138

19994. CD 350 224 (4 discs): FRANCK—Harmonium music: complete edition. *Sacchetti, harmonium.*
+ Fa 1-2/92: 212

19995. CD 350 237: MONTEVERDI—Sacred and secular music. *Accademia Monteverdi; Hirsch, cond.*
- ARG 5-6/92: 87

KOKOPELLI

19996. 1310: STRAYHORN—Portrait of a silk thread. *Dutch Jazz Orch.; Rooijen, cond.*
+ Fa 11-12/96: 389

KONTRAPUNKT

19997. 32001: LA RUE—Requiem. WERT—Adesto dolori; Ascendente; Amen, amen, dico vobis; Egressus Jesus; Vox in Rama. *Ars Nova; Holton, cond.*
+ Fa 11-12/88: 212
+ Gr 11/87: 801

19998. 32002: *Summer music.* Music of Knussen, Fine, Barber, Cage, and Nielsen. *Winds of the Esbjerg Ensemble.*
+ Fa 11-12/88: 346

19999. 32003: TALLIS—Selections. *Mortensen, harpsichord; Ars Nova; Holton, cond.*
+ Fa 1-2/89: 275
+ Gr 12/88: 1049

20000. 32004: HAYDN—Piano sonatas no. 33, 39, 46-47, 50. *Mortensen, harpsichord.*
+ Fa 3-4/89: 182

20001. 32005: NORHOLM—Hearing Andersen; The shadow: Suite; Symphony no. 5. *Danish Radio Symphony Orch.; Schønwandt, Vetö, Latham-Koenig, conds.*
+ Fa 11-12/88: 243

20002. 32006: LECLAIR—Sonatas for transverse flute and continuo. *Flora Danica.*
● Fa 11-12/88: 213

20003. 32007: MENDELSSOHN—Variations concertantes; Cello sonatas no. 1-2; Song without words for cello and piano. *Brendstrup, cello; Edwards, piano.*
+ Fa 1-2/89: 327
+ Fa 3-4/91: 277

20004. 32008: LA RUE—Missa l'homme armé. GOMBERT—Musae Jovis; Lugebat David Absalon. *Ars Nova; Holton, cond.*
+ Fa 1-2/89: 188

20005. 32009/11 (3 discs): KUHLAU—Lulu. *Frellesvig, Kiberg, Saarman, Harbo, Cold; with assisting soloists; Danish Radio Choir & Symphony Orch.; Schønwandt, cond.*
● ARG 7-8/89: 51
+ Fa 3-4/89: 196
+ Gr 5/89: 1778
+ ON 5/89: 48

20006. 32012: BACH—Harpsichord music. *Mortensen, harpsichord.*
● Fa 1-2/89: 109

KONTRAPUNKT

20007. 32013: FRANCK—Cello sonata in A major. DVOŘÁK—Rondo for cello in G minor. GRIEG—Cello sonata in A minor. TCHAIKOVSKY—Pezzo capriccioso. *Fukačová, cello; Klánský, piano.*
+ Fa 1-2/89: 327

20008. 32014: TELEMANN—Recorder sonatas. *Boeckman, recorder; Hansen, viola da gamba; Mortensen, harpsichord.*
+ ARG 3-4/90: 117
+ Fa 9-10/89: 344
+ Gr 11/89: 922

20009. 32015: NORGÅRD—String quartets (complete). *Kontra Quartet.*
+ ARG 11-12/89: 92
+ Fa 9-10/89: 273

20010. 32016: SANDSTRÖM—A new heaven and a new earth. GUDMUNDSEN-HOLMGREEN—Statements. RUDERS—Preghiera semplice; Psalm 86. HOLTEN—Five Gruntvig motets. ABRAHAMSEN—Universe birds. NORGÅRD—Wie ein Kind. *Rilke Ensemble; Christensen, organ; Ars Nova; Holton, Hansen, conds.*
+ Fa 9-10/89: 400

20011. 32017: BENTZON—Sonatina for alto saxophone, op. 498; Sonata for soprano saxophone, op. 478; Emancipatio, op. 471; Sonata for alto saxophone, op. 320. *Egholm, saxophones; Bentzon, piano.*
+ ARG 1-2/90: 29
+ Fa 9-10/89: 149

20012. 32019: NORHOLM—Chamber music, vol. 1. *Christiansen, flute; Vitek, violin; Rorbech, violin; H. Olsen, viola; I. Olsen, guitar; Ullner, cello; Øland, piano.*
+ Fa 11-12/89: 307

20013. 32020/21 (2 discs): BEETHOVEN—Piano concerto no. 5. BRAHMS—Piano concerto no. 1. *Richter-Haaser, piano; Danish Radio Symphony Orch.; Sanderling, cond.* Recorded live 1980, 1979.
• ARG 11-12/89: 34
+ Fa 11-12/89: 127

20014. 32023: BACH—Goldberg variations. *Mortensen, harpsichord.*
• ARG 3-4/90: 18
+ ARG 5-6/91: 18
+ Gr 10/89: 696
+ St 3/90: 183

20015. 32026: CHOPIN—Cello sonata; Polonaise brillante. LISZT—Élegies, no 1-2; Romance oubliées; Lugubre gondola. *Brendstrup, cello; Edwards, piano.*
+ Fa 1-2/91: 179

20016. 32027: BRAHMS—Cello sonatas no. 1-2; Violin sonata no. 1 (arr. for cello). *Fukačová, cello; Klánský, piano.*
+ Fa 1-2/91: 163

20017. 32028/30 (3 discs): SCHOENBERG—Lieder (complete). *Lange, mezzo-soprano; Bertelsen, baritone; Lonskov, piano.*
• Fa 1-2/91: 303
• Gr 2/90: 1510

20018. 32031: MESSIAEN—Visions de l'Amen. *Lonskov, Llambias, pianos.*
+ Fa 1-2/91: 243

20019. 32032: *Wind chamber music, vol. 1.* Music of Debussy, Pierné, Bozza, Bentzon, Hoffding, Riisager, and Françaix. *Selandia Ensemble.*
+ Fa 1-2/91: 400
+ Gr 6/90: 76

20020. 32033/34 (2 discs): BRAHMS—String quartets no. 1-3. *Danish Quartet.*
+ ARG 5-6/91: 24
+ Fa 3-4/91: 135
• Gr 9/90: 555

20021. 32035: *Iberian organ music.* Organ music of Heredia, Concieçao, Cabézon, Carreira, Arauxo, Seixas, and Soler. *Christensen, organ.*
+ Fa 3-4/91: 482

20022. 32036 (2 discs): MUSSORGSKY—Boris Godunov. *Haugland, Moller, Zednik, Nyhus; Danish National Radio Chamber Choir & Orch.; Kitaenko, cond.* Recorded live 1986.
• ARG 5-6/92: 88

20023. 32036/37 (2 discs): MUSSORGSKY—Boris Godunov. *Haugland; with assisting soloists; Danish Radio Choir & Symphony Orch.; Kitaenko, cond.* Version based on original 1868/69 edition.
+ Fa 1-2/91: 265
• Gr 4/90: 1813

20024. 32047: NIELSON—Songs. *Westi, tenor; Metz, piano.*
• Gr 7/91: 103

20025. 32057: BUSONI—Piano concerto. *Thiollier, piano; Nice Phil. Orch.; Schønwandt, cond.*
+ ARG 11-12/91: 49

20026. 32060 (2 discs): MATTHESON—Der brauchbare Virtuoso. *T. Christiansen, flute; J. Christensen, harpsichord.*
+ ARG 9-10/91: 96

20027. 32066: *From the time of the Kronan.* Music from 17th-century Sweden. *Ensemble Mare Balticum.*
+ ARG 11-12/91: 197

20028. 32067: VIERNE—Organ symphony no. 1; Berceuse; Carillon. *Stewart, organ.*
• ARG 3-4/92: 158

20029. 32068: Danish choral music. *Canzone Choir; Rasmussen, cond.*
+ ARG 3-4/92: 201

20030. 32070: GADE—The Erl-King's daughter. *Balslev, Guillaume, Melbye; Canzone Choir; Collegium Musicum; Rasmussen, cond.*
+ ARG 3-4/92: 60

20031. 32072: GADE—Kalanus. *Rørholm, Gedda, Mroz; Canzone Choir; Collegium Musicum; Rasmussen, cond.* Reissue.
+ ARG 3-4/92: 60

20032. 32074: HAMERIK—Requiem; Concert-romance; Symphonie spirtuelle; Piano quintet. *Nyhus, mezzo-soprano; Danish Radio Orch. & Choir; Schmidt, cond.*
• ARG 5-6/92: 66

20033. 32076: SCHUBERT—Five songs, op. 55; Four songs, op. 59; Romances and ballads. *Hinz, Paaske, Binzer, Hansen, vocalists; Canzone Choir; Rasmussen, cond.*
+ ARG 5-6/92: 129

20034. 32077: GADE—Piano trios in F and B♭; Novelettes, op. 29. *Copenhagen Trio.*
+ ARG 3-4/92: 60

20035. 32088: SYBERG—Sinfonietta; Adagio for strings; Symphony. *Odense Symphony Orch.; Vetö, cond.*
+ ARG 7-8/92: 234
+ Fa 5-6/92: 263

20036. 32098: GADE—Violin sonatas no. 1-3. *Elbæk, violin; Westenholz, piano.*
+ Gr 3/93: 63

20037. 32099: NORHOLM—Violin concerto; Cello concerto. *Suzumi, violin; Bengtsson, cello; Aalborg Symphony Orch.; Vetö, cond.*
+ Gr 9/93: 57

20038. 32101/o2 (2 discs): BRITTEN—Complete works for cello. *Dinitzen, cello; Sulo, piano.*
• ARG 11-12/92: 97
+ Gr 2/93: 52

20039. 32106: Kronborg motets. *Capella Hafniensis; Kongsted, cond.*
+ ARG 1-2/93: 189

20040. 32110: JOSQUIN—Missa De Beata Virgine; Motets; Chansons. *Ars Nova; Holton, cond.*
+ ARG 3-4/93: 98

20041. 32111: BENTZON—Piano sonata no. 7; Woodcuts; Partita; Hoffmann-sonata. *Salo, piano.*
+ ARG 1-2/93: 77

20042. 32112: NORHOLM—Symphonies no. 7, 9. *Odense Symphony Orch.; Serov, cond.*
+ Fa 3-4/93: 244
+ Gr 9/93: 57

20043. 32113: BACH—Italian concerto; Overture in the French style. *Mortensen, harpsichord.*
+ Gr 12/92: 100

20044. 32118: BEETHOVEN—33 variations on a waltz by Diabelli; Six variations on an original theme. *Westenholz, piano.*
+ Fa 7-8/93: 109

20045. 32120: BRAHMS—Symphony no. 2; Academic festival overture. *Lonskov, Llambias, pianos.*
+ Gr 2/93: 52

20046. 32121: GADE—String quintet no. 1; String sextet. *Johannes Ensemble.*
• Gr 2/93: 53

20047. 32124: GADE—*Piano music, vol. 2.* 4 folk dances; Folk dance and romance; 4 idylls; From the sketchbook; 4 arabesques. *Westenholz, piano.*
+ ARG 7-8/93: 90
+ Gr 5/93: 71

20048. 32125: SEGERSTAM—Symphony no. 15; Waiting for ... *Tampere Phil. Orch.; Avanti Chamber Orch.; Segerstam, cond.*
+ ARG 7-8/93: 156

20049. 32132: NORHOLM—Symphonies no. 1, 3. *Odense Symphony Orch.; Serov, cond.*
+ Gr 9/93: 57

20050. 32135: SYBERG—Music for oboe and string orchestra; Quartet for oboe, violin, viola, and cello; Concertino for oboe and 5 strings; Quintet for winds. *Moller, oboe; Odense Symphony Orch.; Vetö, cond.*
+ Fa 7-8/93: 254

20051. 32146: SCHNITTKE—Cello sonata; Klingende Buchstaben. PROKOFIEV—Cello sonata. *Dinitzen, cello; Coker, cond.*
• ARG 3-4/94: 147

20052. 32147: NORGÅRD—Piano music. *Sale, piano.*
+ Gr 8/93: 59

20053. 32149: GADE—Zion; The holy night; Gefion. *Hoyer, baritone; Dolberg, alto; Canzone Choir; Aalborg Symphony Orch.; Rasmussen, cond.*
+ ARG 1-2/94: 100

20054. 32150/51 (2 discs): NIELSEN—String quartets. *Danish Quartet.*
+ Gr 10/93: 71

20055. 32153: KODÁLY—Hary Janos: Suite; Galanta dances; Marosszek dances; Peacock variations; Summer evening; Symphony. *Helsinki Phil. Orch.; Fürst, cond.*
+ ARG 7-8/95: 137

20056. 32156: STRAUSS—Four last songs. WAGNER—Wesendonck Lieder. *Meyer-*

Topsoe, soprano; Copenhagen Phil. Orch.; Bihlmaier, cond.
+ Gr 1/94: 88

20057. 32159: MOZART—Piano concertos no. 17-18. *Francesch, piano; Nice Phil. Orch.; Weise, ocnd.*
+ ARG 1-2/94: 126

20058. 32160: KUHLAU—Flute quintets, op. 51. BEETHOVEN—Quintet after op. 30, no. 3. *Christiansen, flute; Olsen, Dolgin, violin; Hansen, viola; Hermansen, cello.*
+ ARG 1-2/94: 116

20059. 32162: NORHOLM—Symphonies no. 6, 8. *Odense Symphony Orch.; Serov, cond.*
□ ARG 7-8/94: 146
+ Gr 2/94: 48

20060. 32165: SEGERSTAM—Impressions of nature no. 1-2; Nocturnal thoughts. *Tampere Phil. Orch.; Malmö Symphony Orch.; Segerstam, cond.*
+ ARG 7-8/94: 169

20061. 32170: HEISE—Songs. *Bjerno, soprano; Lonskov, piano.*
+ ARG 9-10/94: 143

20062. 32171: NIELSEN—Symphony no. 5; Bohemian-Danish folk tune; Symphonic rhapsody. *Odense Symphony Orch.; Serov, cond.*
+ ARG 1-2/96: 150
• Gr 9/95: 64

20063. 32176: GUBAIDULINA—Detto II; In croce; Ten preludes. *Cristensen, organ; Brendstrup, cello; Athelas Ensemble; Windekilde, cond.*
+ ARG 11-12/94: 122

20064. 32177: BRAHMS—Violin sonatas (complete); FAE sonata: Scherzo. *Elbæk, violin; Mogensen, piano.*
• ARG 11-12/94: 83

20065. 32178: NIELSEN—Symphony no. 2; Snefrid; Cupid and the poet. *Odense Symphony Orch.; Serov, cond.*
- ARG 11-12/94: 165
• Gr 11/94: 82

20066. 32180: GADE—Comala. *Dahl, Halling, Mannov; Sønderjylland Symphony; Rasmussen, cond.*
+ ARG 11-12/94: 113

20067. 32181: SCHUMANN—Manfred. *Berlin Radio Chorus; Berlin Radio Symphony Orch.; Schønwandt, cond.*
• ARG 1-2/96: 170
• Gr 4/95: 70

20068. 32182: NORHOLM—Symphony no. 2; Isola Bella. *Nyborg, narrator; Odense Symphony Orch.; Serov, cond.*
+ ARG 3-4/95: 151

20069. 32184: SEGERSTAM—Concertino-fantasia; Piano concerto no. 1; Orchestral

diary sheet 34. *H. Segerstam, violin; Kreuschnig, piano; Austrian Radio Orch.; Segerstam, cond.*
+ ARG 1-2/95: 175

20070. 32185: PROKOFIEV—Violin sonatas; Melodies. *Madojan, violin; Westenholz, piano.*
+ ARG 1-2/95: 155
• Gr 9/94: 74

20071. 32187: RACHMANINOFF—Trios élégiaques. *Copenhagen Trio.*
+ Gr 12/94: 122

20072. 32188: NIELSEN—Hagbarth and Signe; Ebbe Skammelsen; St. John's Eve play. *Vocal soloists; Odense Symphony Orch. & Choir; Vetö, cond.*
+ ARG 7-8/95: 162
+ Gr 3/95: 88

20073. 32189: MOZART—Piano concertos no. 21-22. *Francesch, piano; Nice Phil. Orch.; Weise, cond.* Recorded live 1991.
• Gr 2/95: 50

20074. 32190: REGER—Clarinet sonatas; Albumblatt; Tarantella. *Chen-Zion, clarinet; Ishay, piano.*
+ ARG 9-10/95: 200

20075. 32191: SYBERG—String quartets no. 1-2; Piano trio. *Carl Nielsen Quartet; Copenhagen Trio.*
- ARG 7-8/95: 208

20076. 32192: SCHUBERT—Lebensstürme; Marches, D. 819. *Lonskov, Llambias, piano.*
+ ARG 3-4/95: 179

20077. 32193: NIELSEN—Symphony no. 4; Pan and Syrinx; At the bier of a young artist; Saga-dream. *Odense Symphony Orch.; Serov, cond.*
• ARG 3-4/95: 150

20078. 32194: GADE—Ossian overture. HORNEMAN—Gurre suite. NORGÅRD—Twilight. ABRAHAMSEN—Symphony. *Aarhus Royal Academy of Music Orch.; Schmidt, Hansen, conds.*
+ ARG 7-8/95: 238
• Gr 7/95: 74

20079. 32195: GRIEG—Violin sonatas no. 1-3. *Madojan, violin; Westenholz, piano.*
• Gr 5/95: 68

20080. 32197: SYBERG—Allegro sonatissimo; Scherzando; String trio. *Christiansen, flute; Moller, oboe; Elbæk, violin; Zelazny, viola; Hermansen, cello; Mogensen, piano.*
• Gr 6/95: 72

20081. 32200: NIELSEN—Violin sonatas no. 1-2; Music for violin and piano. *Elbæk, violin; Morgensen, piano.*
• ARG 9-10/95: 183
• Gr 7/95: 80

KONTRAPUNKT

20082. 32202: IBERT—Chamber music with flute. *Christiansen, flute; Collegium Musicum Soloists.*
+ Gr 12/95: 106

20083. 32203: NIELSEN—Symphony no. 3; Andante tranquillo & scherzo; Maskarade suite. *Odense Symphony Orch.; Serov, cond.*
+ ARG 1-2/96: 150
- Gr 11/95: 89

20084. 32204: TCHAIKOVSKY—Symphony no. 6; Festival overture on the Danish national anthem. *Lonskov, Llambias, piano duet.*
+ Gr 10/95: 90

20085. 32205: MARTINŮ—Flute sonata; Sonata for flute and violin; Promenade; Madrigal sonata. *Arnheim, flute; Rub-Levi, piano; Saltzman, violin; Singer, harpsichord; Bergman, cello.*
+ ARG 1-2/96: 140

20086. 32208: LANGE-MÜLLER—Chamber music. *Copenhagen Trio; Carl Nielsen Quartet.*
• Gr 1/96: 72

20087. 32210: NIELSEN—Symphony no. 6; Fantasy-journey to the Faroe Islands; Interlude from Willemoes; Four pieces from The mother. *Odense Symphony Orch.; Serov, cond.*
• ARG 5-6/96: 159

20088. 32211: NØRGÅRD—Trio; Spell; Cao shu; Lin. *Lin Ensemble.*
+ ARG 9-10/96: 174
+ Gr 3/96: 64

20089. 32212: NORHOLM—Symphonies no. 4-5. *Pavslovski, Dahlberg, Hoyer, vocalists; Nørholm, narrator; Danish Radio Choir; Odense Symphony Orch.; Serov, cond.*
+ ARG 1-2/96: 150
+ Gr 10/95: 63

20090. 32215: GRIFFES—Tone pictures, op. 5; Fantasy pieces, op. 6; Roman sketches; Three preludes; Piano sonata in F# minor. *Rosenbaum, piano.*
• Gr 5/96: 81

20091. 32216: SHOSTAKOVICH—Cello sonata. PROKOFIEV—Cello sonata. STRAVINSKY—Suite italienne. *Fukačová, cello; Klánský, piano.*
• Gr 8/96: 67

20092. 32218/19 (2 discs): ROUSSEL—Complete chamber music with flute. *Various performers.*
+ Gr 3/96: 66

20093. 32220: FAURÉ—Music for cello and piano. *Dinitzen, cello; Westenholz, piano.*
• Gr 3/96: 64

20094. 32223: GÓRECKI—O Domina nostra; Cantata. GUBAIDULINA—Light and shadow; Detto I. *Bernstein, soprano; Christensen, organ; Danish Royal Academy Percussion.*
+ ARG 9-10/96: 127

KOSEI

20095. KOCD-3008: *La mer.* Music of Saint-Saëns, Glazunov, Rimsky-Korsakov, and Debussy. *Tokyo Kosei Wind Orch.; Fujita, cond.*
+ Fa 3-4/90: 388

20096. KOCD-3009: REED—Salutations, a northern legend; El camino real; Might and majesty; Praise Jerusalem. *Tokyo Kosei Wind Orch.; Reed, cond.*
+ Fa 3-4/90: 388

20097. KOCD-3010: REED—Celebration fanfare; Wapawekka; Symphony no. 3. SHOSTAKOVICH—Three symphonic preludes (arr. Reed). *Tokyo Kosei Wind Orch.; Reed, cond.*
+ Fa 3-4/90: 388

20098. KOCD-3011: BARNES—Fantasy variations on a theme by Paganini; Trailridge saga; Invocation and Toccata; Autumn soliloquy, Appalachian overture; Stone meadows; Breckenridge. *Tokyo Kosei Wind Orch.; Barnes, cond.*
+ Fa 7-8/90: 376

20099. KOCD-3014: BARNES—Centennial celebration overture; Poetic intermezzo; Pagan dances; Yorkshire ballad; Alvamar overture; Romanza; Chorale prelude on a German folk tune; March: We the people. *Tokyo Kosei Wind Orch.; Barnes, cond.*
+ Fa 11-12/91: 256

20100. KOCD-3015: C.T. SMITH—Overture on an early American folk hymn; Variations on a revolutionary hymn; Danse folâtre; Legacy for band; Symphony no. 1 for band; Variations on a hymn by Louis Bourgeois. *Tokyo Kosei Wind Orch.; Bankhead, cond.*
+ Fa 11-12/91: 256

20101. KOCD-3017: *Curtain up!* REED—Curtain up!; Rahoon; Golden jubilee; Ode for trumpet; Mr. Music!; First suite for band; Alleluia!; Laudamus te. WILLSON—Music man: Highlights. *Tokyo Kosei Wind Orch.; Reed, cond.*
+ Fa 7-8/92: 359

20102. KOCD-3101: Music of Persichetti, Milhaud, Khachaturian, and Rossini. *Tokyo Kosei Wind Orch.; Fennell, cond.*
+ Fa 5-6/91: 246

20103. KOCD-3313: Music of Debussy, Mozart, Graffeuil, Bassi, and Khachaturian. *Dangain, clarinet; Tokyo Kosei Wind Orch.; Fennell, cond.*
+ Fa 7-8/90: 372

20104. KOCD-3564: Music of Verdi, Andriessen, Lancen, Soderman, and Horovitz. *Tokyo Kosei Wind Orch.; Fennell, cond.*
+ Fa 3-4/90: 387

20105. KOCD-3565: STRAVINSKY—Firebird: Suite (arr. Earles and Fennell). MUSSORGSKY—Pictures at an exhibition (arr. Hindsley). *Tokyo Kosei Wind Orch.; Fennell, cond.*
+ Fa 9-10/90: 401

20106. KOCD-3566: *Peer Gynt.* KABALEVSKY (ARR. FUJITA)—The Comedians: Suite. CHANCE—Elegy. MENDELSSOHN (ARR. BOYD)—Overture for winds, op. 24. RACHMANINOFF—Italian polka ; Vocalise, op. 34, no. 14. GRIEG—Peer Gynt: Excerpts. GRAINGER—Molly on the shore; Irish tune from County Derry. *Tokyo Kosei Wind Orch.; Fennell, cond.*
+ Fa 11-12/91: 329

20107. KOCD-3567: MOZART—Wind serenades, K. 361, K. 388. *Tokyo Kosei Wind Orch.; Fennell, cond.*
• Fa 7-8/92: 234

20108. KOCD-3568: *Hungarian rhapsody!* Music of Liszt, Humperdinck, Gounod, J. Strauss, Jr., Tchaikovsky and Sibelius. *Tokyo Kosei Wind Orch.; Fennell, cond.*
+ Fa 7-8/92: 359

20109. KOCD-3901: *Spartacus.* Music of de Lijnschooten, Brossé, Halvorsen, Sparke, Cesarini and Ven der Roost. *Tokyo Kosei Wind Orch.; Haan, cond.*
+ Fa 7-8/92: 359

20110. KMYD-5101: YAMASH'TA—Solar dream, vol. 2. *Yamash'ta, percussion, electronics, voice.*
- Fa 7-8/92: 326

KOSS CLASSICS

20111. KC-1001: DVOŘÁK—Symphony no. 6; Husitska overture. *Milwaukee Symphony Orch.; Macal, cond.*
+ ARG 1-2/90: 46
+ Au 1/90: 144
+ DA 11/89: 68
+ Fa 11-12/89: 200
+ NYT 11/5/89: H29

20112. KC-1002: DVOŘÁK—Symphony no. 8; Czech suite. *Milwaukee Symphony Orch.; Macal, cond.*
+ ARG 11-12/89: 56
• DA 11/89: 68
+ Fa 11-12/89: 200
+ NYT 11/5/89: H29

20113. KC-1003: BEETHOVEN—Symphony no. 9. *Valente, Taylor, West, Plishka; Milwaukee Symphony Chorus & Orch.; Macal, cond.*
+ ARG 9-10/90: 49
+ DA 6/90: 60

+ Fa 3-4/90: 142
• NYT 11/5/89: H29

20114. KC-1004: Foss—Ode for orchestra; Song of songs; With music strong. *Page, soprano; Milwaukee Symphony Chorus & Orch.; Foss, cond.*
+ DA 12/90: 88
+ Fa 11-12/90: 226
- SR 1/91: 98

20115. KC-1005: Berlioz—Symphonie fantastique. *Milwaukee Symphony Orch.; Macal, cond.*
• Fa 9-10/91: 164

20116. KC-1006: Foss—Early song; Dedication; Composer's holiday; Thirteen ways of looking at a blackbird; Paradigm; Curriculum vitae with time bomb. *Milwaukee Symphony Orch.; Foss Festival Players; Foss, cond. & piano.*
□ ARG 7-8/91: 56
+ Fa 9-10/91: 218

20117. KC-1008: Kodály—Háry János: Suite; Dances of Galanta; Variations on a Hungarian folksong (The peacock). *Milwaukee Symphony Orch.; Macal, cond.*
- ARG 5-6/91: 71
+ Fa 7-8/91: 186
+ MA 7/91: 76

20118. KC-1009: Dvořák—Wood dove; Symphony no. 7. *Milwaukee Symphony Orch.; Macal, cond.*
+ Fa 9-10/91: 207

20119. KC-1010: Dvořák—The water goblin; Symphony no. 9. *Milwaukee Symphony Orch.; Macal, cond.*
• ARG 7-8/91: 54
- Fa 9-10/91: 207

20120. KC-1011: *A Chicago brass tradition.* Plog—Concerto for trumpet and brass ensemble. Wilbye—Three madrigals (arr. Baldwin). Franzetti—Overture for brass. Hornoff—Suite for 4 trombones. Rautavaara—Requiem in our time. Berners—What birds see. *Millar Brass Ensemble.*
+ Fa 5-6/91: 139
+ Fa 7-8/91: 381

20121. KC-1013: Organ music by Guilmant, Duruflé, Bossi, Vierne, Langlais, Widor, Bach, Parker, Yon, Dandrieu, Reger, Gigout, Jongen, Whitlock, and Lefébure-Wély. *Weir, organ.*
+ ARG 5-6/92: 168
+ Gr 12/92: 108

20122. KC-1014: Elgar—The wand of youth suites; Nursery suite; Starlight Express overture and finale. *Indianapolis Symphony Orch.; Leppard, cond.*
+ ARG 5-6/92: 58
+ Fa 11-12/93: 230
+ St 4/93: 281

20123. KC-1015: Dvořák—Symphony no. 4; The noon witch. *Milwaukee Symphony Orch.; Macal, cond.*
+ Fa 11-12/93: 225

20124. KC-1016: Prokofiev—Alexander Nevsky; Lieutenant Kije suite. *J. Taylor, mezzo-soprano; Milwaukee Symphony Orch.; Macal, cond.*
- ARG 11-12/93: 169
• Fa 11-12/93: 347

20125. KC-1017: Berlioz—Lélio. *Klemperer, narrator; Siebert, tenor; Diana, baritone; Milwaukee Symphony Orch.; Macal, cond.*
• ARG 11-12/94: 75

20126. KC-1018: Music of Villa-Lobos, Nazareth, Sauer, Scriabin, Ravel, and Lorenzo-Fernandez. *Feghali, piano.*
• ARG 7-8/94: 214
+ ARG 9-10/95: 267

20127. KC-1019: Dvořák—Symphony no. 3; A hero's song. *Milwaukee Symphony Orch.; Macal, cond.*
+ Fa 11-12/93: 225

20128. KC-1021: Sierra—Orchestra music. *Milwaukee Symphony Orch.; Macal, cond.*
+ ARG 11-12/94: 192

20129. KC-1023: Ott—The water garden; Concerto for 2 cellos and orchestra; Music of the canvas. *D. & W. Laufer, cellos; Milwaukee Symphony Orch.; Macal, cond.*
+ ARG 1-2/96: 153

20130. KC-2214: Vaughan Williams—Sinfonia Antarctica; Fantasia on a theme of Thomas Tallis. *Indianapolis Symphony Orch.; Leppard, cond.*
• Fa 9-10/93: 314
• Gr 10/93: 56

20131. KC-2215: Beethoven—Symphony no. 7; Coriolan; String quartet no. 11 (arr. Mahler). *Indianapolis Symphony Orch.; Leppard, cond.*
• ARG 5-6/95: 87

20132. KC-2216: Tchaikovsky—Manfred; Elegy; Cossack dance. *Indianapolis Symphony Orch.; Leppard, cond.*
• ARG 3-4/95: 203

20133. KC-2221: Schubert—Symphony no. 3; Grand duo, D. 812 (orch. Leppard); Overture in the Italian style, D. 597. *Indianapolis Symphony Orch.; Leppard, cond.*
+ ARG 11-12/91: 145
+ Fa 11-12/91: 476

20134. KC-3301: Ott—Symphonies no. 2-3. *Grand Rapids Symphony Orch.; Comet, cond.*
+ ARG 9-10/94: 170

+ Fa 9-10/93: 229 (Zagorski)
• Fa 9-10/93: 229 (North)

20135. KC-3302: Erb—Clarinet concerto; Violin concerto; Trombone concerto. *Stoltzman, clarinet; Fried, violin; Ordman, trombone; Grand Rapids Symphony Orch.; Comet, cond.*
+ ARG 3-4/96: 268

20136. KC-3303: *Encores.* Music of Järnefelt, Borodin, Harty, Bach, Haydn, and others. *Indianapolis Symphony Orch.; Leppard, cond.*
+ ARG 11-12/96: 239

LABEL BLEU

20137. LBLC 6506: Shostakovich—Cello concerto no. 1; Sinfonietta for strings in C minor. *Strauch, cello; Le Sinfonietta; Myrat, cond.*
• Fa 1-2/88: 209

LABOR

20138. LAB 6/10 (5 LPs): Kotík—Many, many women. *S.E.M. Ensemble.*
+ Fa 9-10/88: 178

20139. LAB 7001—7002-2 (2 2-disc sets): Bach—The well-tempered clavier. *Martins, piano.*
• ARG 5-6/95: 78
+ Fa 7-8/95: 110

20140. LAR 7006-2: Bach—Six partitas, BWV 825-830. *Martins, piano.*
+ ARG 5-6/95: 77
- Fa 5-6/95: 128

20141. LAB 7008-2: Bach—Goldberg variations. *Martins, piano.*
- ARG 5-6/95: 77
• Gr 9/95: 80

20142. LAB 7010-2: Bach—Two- and three-part inventions. *Martins, piano.*
+ ARG 5-6/95: 78
• Fa 7-8/95: 105

20143. LAB 7013-2: Bach—The notebook of Anna Magdalena Bach; Twelve little preludes, BWV 924-930, 937- 942, 999; Six little preludes, BWV 933-938; Italian concerto, BWV 971. *Martins, piano.*
• ARG 7-8/95: 73
• Fa 5-6/95: 125

20144. LAB 7014-2: Spasov—Canti dei morti. *Various performers.*
+ ARG 3-4/95: 263
+ Fa 5-6/95: 350

20145. LAB 7015-2: Bach—Piano concertos no. 1, 3, 5. *Martins, piano; Sofia Soloists; Djurov, cond.*
+ ARG 5-6/95: 71
+ Fa 5-6/95: 124

20146. LAB 7017-2: Bach—Preludes. Chopin—Preludes. *Martins, Moreira-*

LABOR

Lima, pianos. Recorded live.
- • ARG 5-6/96: 74
- + Fa 11-12/95: 187

20147. LAB 7018-2: VIVALDI—The four seasons (arr. Prado). *Martins, Corvisier, piano duet.*
- + ARG 1-2/96: 194
- - Fa 11-12/95: 416

20148. LAB 7022-2 (2 discs): BACH—French suites; French overture. *Martins, piano.* Reissue.
- + Fa 1-2/96: 120

LANDOR BARCELONA

20149. CTLCD 111: VOLANS—White man sleeps (2 versions); Mbira; She who sleeps with a small blanket. *Volans, James, Hill, harpsichords; Tindemans, viola da gamba; Schulkowsky, percussion; Smith Quartet.*
- + Gr 10/91: 137

LARGO

5002 see 5102.

5003 see 5103.

5004 see 5104.

20150. 5006 (LP): OCKENFELS—Trio for clarinet, cello and piano; Nine miniatures for wind quintet; Three small piano pieces; Three pieces for 3 clarinets. *Unnamed performers.*
- - Fa 11-12/86: 191

5007 see 5107.

20151. 5101: *Guitar duets.* Music of Scarlatti, Haydn, Mendelssohn, and Grieg. *Schöllmann-Abiton Duo.*
- + ARG 9-10/92: 193

20152. 5102: CADLER—Piano music. *Ockenfels, piano.* Issued also as LP: 5002.
- • Fa 11-12/86: 207
- - Fa 1-2/88: 205

20153. 5103: CLARKE—Piano trio. FANNY MENDELSSOHN—Piano trio, op. 11. *Clementi Trio.* Issued also as LP: 5003.
- + ARG 5-6/92: 84
- + Fa 3-4/87: 160
- + Fa 1-2/88: 108
- + Fa 3-4/92: 178
- + Gr 3/87: 1287

20154. 5104: SCHUBERT—Piano sonata, D. 960. *Joeres, piano.* Issued also as LP: 5004.
- - Fa 9-10/86: 224
- - Fa 11-12/86: 213

20155. 5105: Music of Fauré, Saint-Saëns, Paganini, Koussevitzky, Glière, Vivaldi, Bottesini, Gounod, and Mozart. *Kawahara, double bass; Hoffmann,*

piano.
- + Fa 9-10/92: 417

20156. 5107: SCHUBERT—Introduction and variations on Ihr Blümlein alle, D. 802. RIETZ—Flute sonata, op. 42. *Meier, flute; Brugger, piano.* Issued also as LP: 5007.
- + Fa 1-2/87: 175
- - Fa 3-4/88: 190

20157. 5108: McGUIRE—Forty-eight variations for two pianos. *Henck, Richards, pianos.*
- + Fa 7-8/92: 215

20158. 5109: PAGANINI—Sonata in A major. SCARLATTI—Sonatas. *Schollmann, guitar.*
- • Fa 1-2/89: 227

20159. 5110: BORODIN—Petite suite; Scherzo in A♭. RAVEL—Waltz in the style of Borodin; Paraphrase of Gounod in the style of Chabrier. CHABRIER—Suite pastorale. *Joeres, piano.*
- + ARG 9-10/92: 86
- + Fa 1-2/89: 133
- □ Fa 9-10/92: 425

20160. 5111: SCHOENBERG—Verklärte Nacht (arr. Steuermann). ZEMLINSKY—Piano trio, op. 3. *Clementi Trio.*
- • ARG 7-8/92: 245
- + Fa 1-2/89: 256

20161. 5112: TAILLEFERRE—Piano trio. MILHAUD—Piano trio. SHOSTAKOVICH—Piano trio no. 2. ROSLAVETS—Piano trio. *Clementi Trio.*
- + ARG 11-12/89: 49
- + Fa 11-12/90: 481

20162. 5114: WEILL—Berlin im Licht; Slow fox and algi-song; Klopslied; Ach, wär mein Lieb ein Brünnlein kalt; Frauentanz, op. 10; Bastille Musik; Öl-Musik; Suite panaméenne; Johnny Johnson: Cowboy-song; Captain Valentine's song; Die stille Stadt. *Hardy, soprano; Gruber, vocalist & cond.; Wiget, piano; Ensemble Modern.*
- + ARG 3-4/92: 164
- + Fa 1-2/92: 375

20163. 5115: GOLDSCHMIDT—Letzte Kapitel; Belsatzar; String quartets, no. 2-3. *Ars nova Ensemble Berlin; Mandelring Quartet.*
- □ ARG 304/92: 63
- + Fa 3-4/92: 197
- + Gr 11/91: 116

20164. 5116: Music of Wahren, Humel, Siebert and Rubbert. *Universal Ensemble Berlin; Wahren, Humel, conds.*
- + Fa 7-8/92: 353

20165. 5117: GOLDSCHMIDT—String quartet no. 1; Piano sonata, op. 10; Quintet for clarinet and strings. *Mandelring Quartet; Hausmann, clarinet; Lessing, piano.*

- + Fa 9-10/92: 248
- + Gr 11/92: 138

20166. 5118: LLOYD—Mass for six solo voices; Symphony no. 2. *London Sinfonietta Voices; Edwards, cond.; SWF-Sinfonienorchester Baden-Baden; Zagrosek, cond.*
- □ Fa 3-4/93: 210

20167. 5119: GERHARD—Alegrias; Soirées de Barcelone; Pandora; 2 sketches; 3 impromptus. *Ball, Jacobson, pianos; Benjafield, percussion.*
- + ARG 7-8/93: 92
- + Fa 9-10/93: 167

20168. 5120: WOLPE—Remembering the dancemaster: early piece; Passacaglia; Zemach suite; Studies, part I; Two studies for piano, part 2; Form for piano; Form IV. *K. Wolpe, piano.*
- + ARG 11-12/93: 223
- + Fa 9-10/93: 332

20169. 5121: WAHREN—Bye-bye Bayreuth; Toccata appassionata; Paradiesvogel; Tango-rag; Klassizistische Sonatine; Romantische Rapsodie. HARTMANN—Kleine Suite I; Sonatine. *Roggenkamp, piano.*
- + Fa 3-4/94: 362

20170. 5122: GINASTERA—Estancia; Ollantay; Panambi. *Poznan Phil. Orch.; Borejko, cond.*
- + ARG 3-4/94: 99
- + Fa 3-4/94: 191

20171. 5123: Music of Rachmaninoff, Glazunov, Bottesini, Schumann, Glière, and Vivaldi. *Kawahara, double bass; Hoffmann, piano.*
- + ARG 3-4/94: 202
- + Fa 3-4/94: 394

20172. 5124: GRUBER—The red carpet; Violin concerto no. 1; Six episodes; Bossa nova; Four pieces. *Kovacic, violin; Crossley, piano; London Sinfonietta; Gruber, cond.*
- □ ARG 11-12/94: 122
- • Fa 11-12/94: 243
- + Gr 9/94: 68

20173. 5125: SCHWERTSIK—Für Christa. *C. Schwertsik, voice; K. Schwertsik, piano; Van Kampen, cello; Meecham, piano.*
- + Fa 9-10/94: 335
- + Gr 9/94: 68

20174. 5126: CERHA—Eine art chansons. *Gruber, chansonnier; M. Jones, piano; McGee, double bass; Holland, percussion.*
- + Fa 9-10/94: 163
- + Gr 9/94: 68

20175. 5127: MARKEVITCH—Galop; Noces; Serenade; The flight of Icarus. *Lessing, Lyndon-Gee, pianos; Markevitch Ensemble; Fritz Lang Percussion*

Ensemble.
+ ARG 9-10/94: 158
+ Fa 9-10/94: 248
+ Gr 10/95: 60

20176. 5128: GOLDSCHMIDT—
Retrospectrum; Variations on a
Palestinian song; String quartet no. 4;
From the ballet; Encore; Piano music.
*Gaede Trio; Mandelring Quartet;
Lessing, piano; Schneeberger, violin.*
+ ARG 1-2/95: 109
+ Fa 3-4/95: 174
+ Gr 3/95: 64

20177. 5130 (2 discs): *Testimonies of war
1914-1945: Music of Boris Blacher and
his contemporaries.* Music of Blacher,
Shortall, Weill, Goldschmidt, Milhaud,
and Vaughan Williams. *Various
performers.*
• Fa 11-12/95: 213
+ Gr 7/95: 74

20178. 5131: BOWLES—Concerto for 2
pianos, winds, and percussion; Sonata for
flute and piano; Music for a farce; Sonata
for oboe and piano; Hippolytos and
Salome; Scenes d'Anabise; Night waltz.
*Kretzschmar, Balakleets, pianos; HCD
Ensemble of Frankfurt; Wiesner, flute;
Hausmann, clarinet; Nockles, trumpet;
Römer, Wiersma, percussion; Miliken,
oboe; Hill, tenor.*
+ ARG 3-4/96: 94
+ Fa 3-4/96: 135
• Gr 6/96: 65

20179. 5132: CAGE—Four walls.
McAlpine, piano; Griffith, voice.
• ARG 9-10/96: 106
+ Fa 7-8/96: 139

20180. 5133: M. AND S. STOCKHAUSEN—
Cologne music fantasy. *M. Stockhausen,
trumpets & flugelhorn; Stockhausen,
synthesizers, soprano saxophone;
Thönes, drums.*
• Fa 11-12/96: 385

20181. 5134: GERHARD—Libra; Concert
for 8; Gemini; Leo; Impromptus. *Nieuw
Ensemble; Spanjaard, cond.*
+ ARG 1-2/97: 108
+ Fa 3-4/97: 177
+ Gr 2/97: 50

LASERLIGHT

20182. 14 001: BRAHMS—Symphony no.
4; Tragic overture. *Netherlands Phil.
Orch.; Haenchen, cond.*
+ Fa 11-12/91: 285

20183. 14 002: BRUCKNER—Symphony
no. 3. *Netherlands Phil. Orch.;
Haenchen, cond.*
• Fa 11-12/91: 290

20184. 14 003: CHOPIN—Piano concertos,
no. 1-2. *Falvai, piano; Budapest Phil.
Orch.; Kórodi, cond.; Harasiewicz,
piano; Warsaw National Phil. Orch.;*

Kord, cond.
• Fa 11-12/91: 299

20185. 14 004: DEBUSSY—La mer;
Nocturnes; Prélude à l'après-midi d'un
faune. *Leipzig Radio Symphony Orch. &
Chorus; Pommer, cond.*
+ Fa 11-12/91: 309

20186. 14 005: DVOŘÁK—Symphony no.
5; Husitská overture. *Plovdiv Phil. Orch.;
Ghiaurov, cond.*
• Fa 11-12/91: 316

20187. 14 006: HANDEL—Concerti grossi,
op. 3. *New Bach Collegium Musicum
Leipzig; Pommer, cond.*
+ Fa 11-12/91: 336

20188. 14 007: HAYDN—Symphonies no.
82, 94. *Hungarian State Orch.;
Ferencsik, cond.*
+ Fa 11-12/91: 345

20189. 14 008: HAYDN—Symphonies no.
88, 100. *Hungarian State Orch.; Fischer,
cond.*
- Fa 11-12/91: 346

20190. 14 009: HAYDN—Cello concertos
no. 1-2. *Perényi, cello; Franz Liszt
Chamber Orch.; Rolla, cond.*
+ Fa 11-12/91: 342

20191. 14 010: HOLST—The planets, op.
32. PAGANINI—Introduction and variations
on a theme by Rossini. *Karr, double
bass; London Symphony Orch.; Simon,
cond.*
+ Fa 11-12/91: 354

20192. 14 011: LISZT—Fantasy on
Beethoven's Ruins of Athens;
Malédiction; Grande fantaisie
symphonique on Berlioz's Lélio. *Jandó,
piano; Budapest Symphony Orch.; Ligeti,
cond.*
+ Fa 11-12/91: 375

20193. 14 012: MUSSORGSKY—Pictures at
an exhibition (arr. Ravel); A night on the
Bare Mountain (arr. Rimsky-Korsakov);
Khovanshchina: intermezzo; dance of the
Persian slaves (arr. Rimsky-Korsakov).
Various performers.
- Fa 11-12/91: 423

20194. 14 013: RAVEL—Daphnis and
Chloé: Suite, no. 1; Ma mère l'oye: Suite;
Shéhérazade; La valse. *Various
performers.*
+ Fa 11-12/91: 453

20195. 14 020: ORFF—Carmina Burana.
*Prague Festival Orch. & Chorus;
Urbanek, cond.*
- Fa 11-12/92: 318

20196. 14 036: *Baroque dreams for flute.*
Music of Vivaldi, Telemann, Frederick
the Great and C.P.E. Bach. *Various
performers.*
+ Fa 11-12/92: 437

20197. 14 037: MOZART—Flute concertos
no. 1-2. MERCADANTE—Flute concerto in
E minor. *Tast, flute; C.P.E. Bach
Chamber Orch.; Haenchen, cond.*
• Fa 11-12/92: 308

20198. 14 038: *Flute daydreams.* Music
of Grieg, Gluck, Tchaikovsky, Bizet,
Mozart and others. *Various performers.*
+ Fa 1-2/93: 294

20199. 14 039: *Classical favorites for
strings.* Music of Sarasate, Chopin, De
Curtis, Mendelssohn, Baradazewska-
Baranowska, Wieniawski and Liszt.
*Budapest Strings; Bánfalvi, violin &
cond.*
+ Fa 11-12/92: 464

20200. 14 040: *Classical favorites for
strings: songs, romances and dances.*
Music of Schubert, Grieg, Brahms,
Rubinstein, Wieniawski, Sarasate,
Giordani, Tchaikovsky and Elgar.
*Budapest Strings; Bánfalvi, violin &
cond.*
+ Fa 11-12/92: 461

20201. 14 091: BRUCKNER—Symphony
no. 0; Motets. *Stuttgart Radio Symphony
Orch.; Marriner, cond.; Dresden
Kreuzchor; Flämig, cond.*
+ Fa 11-12/93: 200

20202. 14 092: DVOŘÁK—Cello concerto,
op. 104. HINDEMITH—Cello concerto.
*Perényi, cello; Budapest Festival Orch.;
Fischer, Lehel, conds.*
• Fa 11-12/93: 223

20203. 14 093: *Oboe concertos.* Music
of Haydn, Hummel, Bellini, and
Telemann. *Glaetzner, oboe; Leipzig
Radio Chamber Orch.; Hauschild, cond.*
+ Fa 11-12/93: 486

20204. 14 094: VIVALDI—Concertos for
flute, strings, and continuo, RV 433, 439,
428, 434; Concertos for flautino, strings,
and continuo, RV 443, 444. *Gyöngyössy,
flute & piccolo; Budapest Strings;
Botvay, cond.*
+ Fa 11-12/93: 437

20205. 14 095: BACH—St. Matthew
Passion (excerpts). *Kalmár, Hamari,
Vandersteene, Gulyás, Schramm;
Jeunesses Musicales Chorus; Franz Liszt
Chamber Orch.; Sándor, cond.*
- Fa 11-12/93: 172

20206. 14 096: BRUCKNER—Symphony
no. 7. *Netherlands Phil. Orch.;
Haenchen, cond.*
- Fa 11-12/93: 201

20207. 14 097: SCHUMANN—Piano
concerto; Introduction and allegro
appassionato; Introduction and allegro,
op. 134. *Holtmann, piano; Berlin Radio
Symphony Orch.; Soltesz, cond.*
• Fa 11-12/93: 385

20208. 14 098: MOZART—Mass in C, K. 317; Mass in C, K. 259; Exsultate, jubilate. *Vocal soloists; Slovak Phil. Chorus & Orch.; Ferencsik, cond.; Linz Sinfonietta; Salzburg Camerata; Hinreiner, cond.*
- Fa 11-12/93: 334

20209. 14 099: VIVALDI—Violin concertos RV 253, 180, 242, 362; Concerto for 2 violins, RV 522; Concerto for 2 violins and cello, RV 565. *Bánfalvi, violin; Budapest Strings; Botvay, cond.; Prague Festival Strings; Urbanek, cond.*
• Fa 11-12/93: 438

20210. 14 100: BACH—St. John Passion (excerpts). *Hamari, Réti, Abel; Franz Liszt Academy Budapest Chamber Chorus & Orch.; Lehel, cond.*
- Fa 11-12/93: 172

20211. 14 108: BIZET—Carmen excerpts. *Szostek-Radkowa, Molnár, Kincses, Ghiaurov; Budapest Phil. Orch.; Sándor, cond.*
• Fa 7-8/94: 75

20212. 14 109: VERDI—La traviata (excerpts). *Aliberti, Dvorský, Bruson; Fujiwara Opera Chorus; Tokyo Phil. Orch.; Paternostro, cond.*
- Fa 7-8/94: 271

20213. 14 110: VERDI—Macbeth (excerpts). *Sass, Cappuccilli, Kelen, Bándi, Kováts, Christoff; various orchs. and conds.*
- Fa 7-8/94: 269

20214. 14 112: PUCCINI—Madama Butterfly (excerpts). *Tomowa-Sintow, Aragall, Rinaldi, Mineva; Sofia National Opera Chorus & Orch.; Raĭchev, cond.*
• Fa 7-8/94: 202

20215. 14 113: GLUCK—Orfeo ed Euridice (excerpts). *Hamari, Kincses, Zempléni; Hungarian State Orch.; Lukacs, cond.*
• ARG 7-8/94: 104
• Fa 7-8/94: 140

20216. 14 116: MUSSORGSKY—Boris Godunov (excerpts, arr. Rimsky-Korsakov). *Kotcherga, Pustelak, Ostapiuk, Tarastchenko, Racewicz, Szmyt; Warsaw National Opera Orch. & Chorus; Satanowski, cond.*
• Fa 7-8/94: 194

20217. 14 117: MOZART—Die Entführung aus dem Serail (excerpts). *Greenberg, Thames, Schaaf, Gahmlich; Frankfurt Radio Symphony; Viotti, cond.*
+ ARG 7-8/94: 137
- Fa 7-8/94: 186

20218. 14 120 (2 discs): MAHLER—Symphony no. 6. *Netherlands Phil. Orch.; Haenchen, cond.*
• ARG 11-12/94: 151
+ Fa 11-12/94: 287

20219. 14 121: VERDI—Aida (excerpts). *Tomowa-Sintow, Simándi; Bulgarian National Chorus; Sofia National Opera Chorus; Sofia Phil. Orch.; Raĭchev, Robev, conds.*
- Fa 7-8/94: 267

20220. 14 122: VERDI—Nabucco (excerpts). *Tomowa-Sintow, Miller, Kováts, Schenk; various orchs. & conds.*
• ARG 7-8/94: 185
- Fa 7-8/94: 270

20221. 14 134: BACH—Concertos for violin and orchestra, BWV 1041-1042; Concerto for 2 violins and orchestra, BWV 1043; Concerto for flute, violin, harpsichord, and orchestra, BWV 1044. *Altenburger, Mayer-Schierning, Kussmaul, violins; Meisen, flute; Asperen, harpsichord; Deutsche Bachsolisten; Winschermann, cond.*
+ Fa 3-4/94: 106

20222. 14 135: BACH—Cantatas: Mein Herze schwimmt im Blut, BWV 199; Jauchzet Gott in allen Landen, BWV 51; Concerto for flute, oboe, violin, strings, and continuo, BWV 1064; Concerto for 2 recorders, harpsichord, strings, and continuo, BWV 1057. *Various soloists; Deutsche Bachsolisten; Winschermann, cond.*
• Fa 3-4/94: 104

20223. 14 136: BEETHOVEN—Missa solemnis. *Fiedler, Hölzl, Hollweg, Stämpfli; Knaben- und Männerchor "Sveshnikov"; Rundfunk-Kinderchor Moskau; Barshai, cond.* Recorded live 1993.
• Fa 11-12/94: 168

20224. 14 138: BRUCKNER—Symphony no. 9. *Netherlands Phil. Orch.; Haenchen, cond.*
• Fa 11-12/94: 192

20225. 14 139: MAHLER—Symphony no. 4; Blumine. *Coku, soprano; Netherlands Phil. Orch.; Haenchen, cond.*
+ Fa 11-12/94: 287

20226. 14 141 (2 discs): MAHLER—Symphony no. 7. *Netherlands Phil. Orch.; Haenchen, cond.*
+ Fa 11-12/94: 287

20227. 14 142: MENDELSSOHN—Violin concerto. TCHAIKOVSKY—Violin concerto. *Hagner, violin; Radio- Symphonie-Orchester Berlin; Schneidt, cond.*
+ Fa 11-12/94: 297

20228. 14 143: MOZART—Piano sonatas no. 10-12; Variations on Ah, vous dirai-je, Maman. *Babinsky, piano.*
• Fa 11-12/94: 317

20229. 14 144: *Virtuoso guitar: classical masterpieces for guitar.* Music of Dowland, Newsidler, Duarte, Tarrega, Ruiz-Pipo, Carcassi, Mozzani, Vinas,

Gomez, Albéniz, Mangoré, Villa-Lobos, Semenzato, and Anon. *Honti, guitar.*
+ Fa 11-12/94: 480

20230. 14 145 (2 discs): HAYDN—The creation. *Seidl, Elsner, Volle; Krakau National Phil. Orch. & Chorus; Bader, cond.*
• Fa 11-12/94: 250

20231. 14 146: MUSSORGSKY—Pictures at an exhibition. BRAHMS—Intermezzos, op. 117; Pieces, op. 118. *Várjon, piano.*
• Fa 11-12/94: 320

20232. 14 157—14 158 (2 separate discs): *Lost in meditation.* Gregorian chant. *Capella Gregoriana.*
+ Fa 1-2/95: 343

20233. 14 164: Gregorian chants. *Benedictine Monks of St. Michael's de Laudes; Monks of the Benedictine Abbey of St. Benoit; Ambrosian Singers; Stevins, cond.*
- Fa 1-2/95: 343

20234. 14 201—14 206 (6 separate discs): *Composers at the piano.* Music by Ravel, Gershwin, Prokofiev, Granados, and others. *Various performers.*
+ ARG 11-12/95: 289
- Fa 9-10/95: 289 (201, 203)

20235. 14 263: Arias by Verdi, Mozart, Wagner, Beethoven, and others. *Crespin, soprano.*
+ ARG 1-2/97: 225

20236. 14 265: Music of Donizetti, Bellini, Gounod, Verdi, Vivaldi, and others. *Robin, soprano.* Recorded live.
+ ARG 11-12/96: 274

20237. 14 131—14 133 (3 separate discs): BACH—Brandenburg concertos; Orchestral suites; Concerto for violin, oboe, strings, and continuo, BWV 1060; Concerto for 3 violins, strings, and continuo, BWV 1063. *Deutsche Bachsolisten; Winschermann, cond.*
+ Fa 5-6/94: 97

20238. 15 386: PROKOFIEV—Peter and the wolf. L. MOZART—Children's symphony. *Lemmon, narrator; Prague Festival Orch.; Urbanek, cond.*
• ARG 9-10/91: 107
+ Fa 9-10/91: 313

20239. 15 501: BRAHMS—Hungarian dances. *Hungarian Phil. Orch.; Sándor, cond.*
+ ARG 5-6/89: 26

20240. 15 506: ROSSINI—Overtures. *Plovdiv Phil. Orch.; Raĭchev, cond.*
- ARG 5-6/89: 80

20241. 15 508: BACH—Brandenburg concertos no. 1-3; Harpsichord concerto in D major. *Berlin Chamber Orch.;*

Wohlert, cond.
* ARG 5-6/89: 11

20242. 15 511: Mozart—Symphonies no. 40-41; Zauberflöte: Overture. *Hungarian Chamber Orch.; Tátrai, cond.; London Phil. Orch.; Sándor, cond.*
+ ARG 11-12/89: 91

20243. 15 602: Rodrigo—Concierto de Aranjuez. Music of Sor, Granados, Albéniz, and Falla. *Tokos, M. Rost, J. Rost, guitars; Budapest Strings; Bánfalvi, cond.*
+ Fa 3-4/90: 275

20244. 15 605: Dvořák—Slavonic dances, op. 72; Serenade for strings in E minor. *Berlin Chamber Orch.; Wohlert, cond.*
* Fa 5-6/90: 159

20245. 15 606: Gershwin—Rhapsody in blue; Porgy and Bess: Suite; American in Paris. *Jandó, piano; Budapest Phil. Orch.; Budapest Strings; Sándor, cond.*
* Fa 5-6/90: 169

20246. 15 607: Handel—Water music; Solomon: Act 3 sinfonia; Ode for St. Cecilia's day: Minuet. *Budapest Strings; Bánfalvi, cond.*
* Fa 5-6/90: 185

20247. 15 608: Rimsky-Korsakov— Scheherazade; Capriccio espagnol. *Hungarian State Orch.; Sándor, cond.*
* Fa 3-4/90: 320

20248. 15 609: Schubert—Four impromptus, D. 899; Impromptu no. 3, D. 935; Moments musicaux, D. 780. *Jandó, piano.*
- Fa 3-4/90: 283

20249. 15 611: Suppé—Overtures. *Hungarian State Opera Orch.; Sándor, cond.*
+ Fa 3-4/90: 315

20250. 15 614: Bizet—Carmen: Suites no. 1-2; L'Arlésienne: Suites no. 1-2. *Budapest Phil. Orch.; Sándor, cond.*
* Fa 5-6/90: 128

20251. 15 615: Mendelssohn—Violin concerto in E minor. Bruch—Violin concerto no. 1. *Verhey, violin; Szenthelyi, violin; Budapest Symphony Orch.; Joó, cond.; Sándor, cond.*
* Fa 3-4/90: 232

20252. 15 616: Delibes—Sylvia: Excerpts; Coppélia: Excerpts. Gounod— Faust: Ballet music. *Budapest Phil. Orch.; Sándor, cond.; Berlin Radio Symphony Orch.; Fricke, cond.*
* Fa 3-4/90: 170

20253. 15 617: Grieg—Peer Gynt: Suites no. 1-2; Piano concerto in A minor. *Jandó, piano; Budapest Phil. Orch.; Sándor, cond.; Vienna Symphony Orch.;*

Ahronovitch, cond.
* Fa 5-6/90: 169

20254. 15 618: Mozart—Piano concertos no. 17, 21. *Fischer, piano; Vienna Mozart Ensemble; Kraus, cond.*
* Fa 3-4/90: 232

20255. 15 620: Tchaikovsky—Symphony no. 5; Marche slave. *Prague Festival Orch.; Urbanek, cond.; Hungarian State Orch.; Fischer, cond.*
* Fa 3-4/90: 319

20256. 15 623: Mendelssohn— Midsummer night's dream: Excerpts; Song without words, op. 109; Spinning song; Spring song; Hebrides overture. *Kocsis, piano; Dubourg, piano; Perényi, cello; Budapest Strings; Budapest Phil. Orch.; Kovács, cond.; Hungarian State Orch.; Fischer, cond.*
* Fa 3-4/90: 232

20257. 15 624: Mozart—Flute concertos no. 1-2; Horn concertos no. 1, 3. *Berger, flute; Heiser, horn; Vienna Mozart Ensemble; Kraus, cond.*
* Fa 5-6/90: 225

20258. 15 810: Verdi—Overtures and preludes. *Sofia Phil. Orch.; Stefanov, cond.*
- Fa 1-2/89: 284

20259. 15 824: Dvořák—Symphony no. 9; Romance for violin and orchestra, op. 11; Carnival overture. *Prague Festival Orch.; Urbanek, cond.; Szenthelyi, violin; Hungarian State Orch.; Pal, cond.*
* Fa 1-2/89: 161

20260. 15 833 (10 discs): Masters of the opera. *Various artists.*
+ Fa 11-12/93: 471

20261. 15 900 (5 discs): Beethoven— Symphonies (complete). *Andor, Szirmay, Korondi, Sólyom-Nagy; Budapest Phil. Chorus; Hungarian State Orch.; Ferencsik, cond.*
* Fa 3-4/89: 98

20262. 15 902: Beethoven—Symphonies no. 3, 8. *Hungarian Phil. Orch.; Ferencsik, cond.*
* ARG 5-6/89: 21 m.f.

20263. 15 903: Beethoven—Symphonies no. 1, 7. *Hungarian Phil. Orch.; Ferencsik, cond.*
* ARG 5-6/89: 21 m.f.

20264. 15 947 (5 discs): Beethoven— Symphonies (complete). *Hargan, Walther, Büchner, Kováts, vocalists; Dresden Concerto Orch.; Berlin Radio Chorus; Leipzig Radio Chorus; Kegel, cond.* Reissues.
* Fa 9-10/95: 141

20265. 15 961 (5 discs): Great Chopin performers. *Various pianists, in part with*

orch. acc.
+ Fa 7-8/93: 125

LAUDIS

20266. LCD3 4001 (3 discs): Mozart— Don Giovanni. *Welitsch, Schwarzkopf, Seefried, Dermota, Gobbi; Vienna State Opera Chorus; Vienna Phil. Orch.; Furtwängler, Wilhelm.* Recorded live 1950.
* Fa 7-8/89: 196

20267. LCD3 4002—4005 (15 discs (4 sets)): Wagner—Ring des Nibelungen. *Varnay, Resnik, Windgassen, Vinay, Hotter, Greindl; with assisting soloists; Bayreuth Festival; Krauss, cond.* Recorded live 1953.
+ ARG 1-2/89: 103
+ Fa 7-8/88: 278
+ Gr 6/88: 78
+ ON 2/27/88: 42

20268. LCD4 4009 (4 discs): Wagner— Tristan und Isolde. *Braun, Klose, Treptow, Schoeffler, Frantz; Bavarian State Opera Chorus & Orch.; Knappertsbusch, cond.* Recorded live 1950.
* Fa 9-10/89: 368

20269. LCD3 4010 (3 discs): Wagner— Rheingold. *Milinkovic, Kuen, Suthaus, Hotter, Greindl; with assisting soloists; Bayreuth Festival Orch.; Knappertsbusch, cond.* Recorded live 1957.
□ Fa 9-10/89: 362

20270. LCD4 4011 (4 discs): Wagner— Walküre. *Varnay, Nilsson, Vinay, Hotter, Greindl; with assisting soloists; Bayreuth Festival Orch.; Knappertsbusch, cond.* Recorded live 1957.
□ Fa 9-10/89: 362

20271. LCD4 4012 (4 discs): Wagner— Siegfried. *Varnay, Aldenhoff, Hotter, Greindl; with assisting soloists; Bayreuth Festival Orch.; Knappertsbusch, cond.* Recorded live 1957.
□ Fa 9-10/89: 362

20272. LCD4 4013 (4 discs): Wagner— Götterdämmerung. *Varnay, Windgassen, Uhde, Greindl; with assisting soloists; Bayreuth Festival; Knappertsbusch, cond.* Recorded live 1957.
□ Fa 9-10/89: 362

20273. LCD2 4016 (2 discs): Wagner— Rienzi (abridged). *Christiansen, Ludwig, Svanholm, Schoeffler, Berry; with assisting soloists; Vienna Symphony Orch.; Krips, cond.* Recorded live.
* ARG 9-10/89: 115
* St 8/89: 185

LAUREL

20274. LR-135 (LP): Martin—Eight preludes. Busoni—Seven short pieces for

LAUREL

the cultivation of polyphonic playing;
Prelude and etude; Perpetuum mobile.
Jochum, piano.
- Fa 3-4/87: 157
- NR 2/87: 26

20275. LR-137 CD: CORIGLIANO—Violin
sonata. FLAGELLO—Declamation; Violin
sonata. *Fodor, violin; Portney, piano.*
Issued also as LP: LR 137.
+ ARG 7-8/89: 36
+ Fa 5-6/87: 120
- NR 4/87: 20

20276. LR-139 (LP): SCHRADER—Lost
Atlantis. *Electronic composition.*
+ Fa 1-2/87: 63

20277. LR-826 CD: BLOCH—String
quartet no. 2; Prelude; Night; Two pieces.
Pro Arte Quartet.
+ ARG 1-2/89: 35
+ Fa 9-10/88: 114
+ MA 1/89: 52

20278. LR-828 CD: BLOCH—Quintets for
piano and strings, no. 1-2; Suite no. 1 for
cello solo. *Pro Arte Quartet; H. Karp,
piano; P. Karp, cello.* Reissue.
+ ARG 3-4/92: 34
+ Fa 11-12/91: 276

20279. LR-838 CD: PERSICHETTI—Sonatas
for harpsichord no. 2-5. SCARLATTI—
Sonatas for harpsichord, L. 138, 157,
160, 178, 268, 457, 474. *Comparone,
harpsichord.*
+ ARG 1-2/93: 131
+ Fa 9-10/92: 311

20280. LR-840 CD: MORROW—Birth of
the war god; Cloud will break; Canticle
for Brother Sun. *Western Wind.*
+ ARG 1-2/89: 43
□ ARG 7-8/89: 63
- Fa 7-8/88: 203
+ Fa 9-10/88: 206

20281. LR-841 CD: BLOCH—String
quartets no 3-4; Paysages; In the
mountains. *Pro Arte Quartet*
+ ARG 1-2/89: 35
+ Fa 9-10/88: 114

20282. LR-842 CD: RÓZSA—String
quartets no. 1-2; Rhapsody for cello and
piano, op. 3. *Pro Arte Quartet; P. Karp,
cello; H. Karp, piano.*
+ Fa 3-4/89: 255 (2 reviews)
+ MA 9/89: 66

20283. LR-843 CD: LAZAROF—Music for
strings. *Members of the Chamber Music-
LA Festival; Kamei, cond.*
+ Fa 11-12/89: 260

20284. LR-844 CD: LAZAROF—
Sinfonietta; Volo; Intonazione e
variazioni; Chamber symphony. *Thomas,
viola; P. Schwarz, organ; Los Angeles
Chamber Orch.; G. Schwarz, cond.;
String ensemble; Lazarof, cond.*
+ Fa 11-12/89: 260

20285. LR-845 CD: LAZAROF—Momenti
for solo cello; Duo for cello and piano;
Piano trio; Wind trio. *Matsuo, violin;
Solow, cello; Lowenthal, piano; Stokes,
flute; Winter, oboe; Gray, clarinet.*
+ ARG 7-8/92: 162
+ Fa 9-10/92: 274
+ St 9/93: 183

20286. LR-846 CD: LOPATNIKOFF—Music
for piano and for violin and piano. *N.
Solomon, piano; Lefkowitz, violin.*
+ ARG 3-4/94: 116
+ Fa 11-12/93: 299

20287. LR-847 CD: BOLCOM—String
quartet no. 10. JOHNSTON—String quartet
no. 9. NEIKRUG—Stars the mirror.
Stanford String Quartet.
+ ARG 3-4/93: 159
+ Fa 9-10/92: 106
+ St 6/93: 257

20288. LR-849 CD: ROSNER—Concerto
grosso no. 1; Chronicle of nine: Prelude
to act 2; Five meditations; Gentle Musick;
Magnificat. *Cathedral Church of St.
Paul; Clarion Brass of San Diego;
Jerusalem Symphony Orch.; Amos, cond.*
+ ARG 7-8/90: 91
+ Fa 1-2/90: 279
+ MA 7/90: 84

20289. LR-850 CD: TOCH—String
quartets op. 26, op. 70; Divertimenti, op.
37; Dedication. *Mendelssohn String
Quartet.*
+ Fa 9-10/91: 377
+ ARG 11-12/91: 162

20290. LR-851 CD: BLOCH—Concerto
symphonique; Scherzo fantasque;
Concerto grosso no. 2. *Yui, piano;
London Symphony Orch.; Amos, cond.*
● ARG 11-12/91: 38
● Fa 9-10/91: 170

20291. LR-852 CD: BERGSMA—Tangents;
3 fantasies; Variations. *Timmons, piano.*
- ARG 1-2/94: 79
+ Fa 3-4/94: 131

20292. LR-855 CD: WEILL—Songs (arr.
Rosenblum). *P. Alexander, soprano;
Wolford, saxophone; Rosenblum,
keyboard.*
● Fa 1-2/97: 303

LAWRENCE UNIVERSITY

20293. 301690: Music of Maslanka,
Frank, Levitan, and Ginastera. *Lawrence
University Percussion Ensemble;
Richeson, cond.; Bedi, soprano.*
+ Fa 7-8/96: 392

LDR

20294. LDRC 1001: *British masters, vol.
1.* Music of Ireland, Jacob, Lloyd,
Cabezón, Bourgeois, and Holst . *Fry,
timpani; City of London Wind Ensemble;
Brand, cond.*

+ Fa 7-8/89: 315
+ Gr 7/89: 189

20295. LDRC 1002: Music of Arnold,
Danzi, Holst, Reicha, and Patterson. *Vega
Wind Quintet.*
+ Fa 7-8/89: 319

20296. LDRC 1006: *The well-tempered
trumpet.* Music of Handel, Puccini, Bach,
and Pearson. *Steele-Perkins, trumpets &
flugel horn; Pearson, organ.*
+ DA 8/90: 36
+ Fa 5-6/90: 382

20297. LDRCD 1008: BEETHOVEN—String
quartet no. 13; Grosse Fuge. SCHNITTKE—
String quartet no. 3. *Britten Quartet.*
● Fa 11-12/90: 339
+ Gr 4/90: 1813

20298. LDRCD 1009: DEBUSSY—The
complete music for 2 pianos. *Coombs,
Scott, pianos.*
● ARG 5-6/90: 44
● Fa 9-10/90: 222
+ Gr 1/90: 1344

20299. LDRCD 1010: HAYDN—Piano
sonatas no. 31, 33, 60; Andante con
variazione, H. XVII:6. *Mei, piano.*
- Fa 5-6/90: 187
● Gr 5/90: 2011

20300. LDRCD 1011: MOZART—Oboe
quartet, K. 370; Clarinet quintet, K. 581 .
*Caird, oboe; Malsbury, clarinet; Coull
Quartet.*
+ Fa 9-10/90: 310

20301. LDRCD 1012: *British masters,
vol. 2.* Music of Ireland, Bourgeois, Bach,
Holst, and Horovitz. *Lindberg, trombone;
City of London Wind Ensemble; City of
London Brass Quartet; Brand, cond.*
+ ARG 7-8/90: 130
+ Fa 7-8/90: 370

LEGATO

20302. 101: *Gala operatic concert.* Music
of Boito, Donizetti, Giordano, Massenet,
Meyerbeer, Puccini, Rossini, Tosti, and
Verdi. *Caballé, soprano; Corelli, tenor;
Giaiotti, bass; unidentified orchestra;
Antonioni, cond.* Recorded live 1968.
+ Fa 7-8/87: 212
+ Fa 9-10/88: 309

20303. 102 (2 discs): PUCCINI—Tosca.
*Milanov, Corelli, Guelfi; unidentified
chorus & orchestra; Gibson, cond.*
+ ARG 3/87: 50
+ Fa 7-8/87: 164

20304. 103: *Jussi Björling: live
recordings 1929-1960.* Music of Verdi,
Meyerbeer, Bizet, Massenet, Gounod,
Puccini, Speaks, Beach, Herbert, Handel,
Stradella, Mascagni, De Curtis, and
Lehár. *Björling, tenor; various
supporting artists, orchs. & conds.*
● Fa 9-10/88: 307

20305. 104: *Richard Tucker: live recordings 1950-1972.* Music of Verdi, Mascagni, Puccini, Giordano, Handel, Meyerbeer, Ponchielli, Hardelot, and Lehár. *Tucker, tenor; various supporting artists, orchs. & conds.*
• Fa 9-10/88: 307

20306. 105: VERDI—I lombardi (excerpts). *Millo, Bergonzi, Plishka; Orch.; Queler, cond.* Recorded live 1986.
+ ARG 1-2/94: 169
+ Fa 1-2/88: 224
• ON 1/8/94: 35

20307. 106: *Beniamino Gigli: live recordings 1935-1955.* Music of Verdi, Puccini, Massenet, Cilea, Millocker, Schubert, De Curtis, Bach, Mascagni, Pietri, Brahms, Wagner, Caccini, Di Capua, Bixio, Humperdinck, Melichar, and Anon. *Gigli, Beniamino; various supporting artists, orchs. & conds.*
• Fa 9-10/88: 307

20308. 108: DONIZETTI—Roberto Devereux: Abridged. *Caballé, Marsee, Carreras, Sardinero; with assisting soloists; unidentified chorus & orch.; Rudel, cond.* Recorded live 1977.
+ Fa 9-10/88: 141

20309. 109: *Anita Cerquetti: portrait of the artist.* Music of Spontini, Cherubini, Weber, Rossini, Verdi, Catalani, and Giordano. *Cerquetti, soprano; various assisting soloists, orchs. & conds.* All selections sung in Italian. Recorded live.
+ Fa 5-6/88: 238

20310. 111 (2 discs): CILEA—Adriana Lecouvreur. *Caballé, Cossotto, Carreras, D'Orazi; with assisting soloists; unidentified chorus & orch.; Masini, cond.*
+ Fa 9-10/88: 131
• ON 12/10/88: 65

20311. 112: ROSSINI—Semiramide: Highlights. *Caballé, Horne, Ramey; with assisting soloists; Scottish Chamber Orch.; López Cobos, cond.* Recorded live 1980.
+ Fa 7-8/88: 234
+ ON 5/88: 46

20312. 113 (2 discs): PUCCINI—Manon Lescaut. BOITO—Mefistofele: L'altra notte. VERDI—Il trovatore: Ah si ben mio; Di quella pira. *Olivero, Tucker, Sardinero; with assisting soloists; unidentified chorus & orchestra; Veltri, cond.* Recorded live 1972.
- Fa 7-8/88: 225

20313. 114 (3 discs): Operatic excerpts of Mozart, Puccini, Gluck, Rossini, Halévy, and Mussorgsky. *Rethberg, Helletsgruber, Bokor, Borgioli, Pinza, Lazzari, Ettl, Alsen; Vienna Phil. Orch.; Walter, cond.* Recorded at Salzburg, 1937.
+ Fa 9-10/88: 211

20314. 115: *Renata Tebaldi: a portrait of the artist, 1949-1958.* Music of Giordano, Boito, Cilea, Verdi, Puccini, Charpentier, Rossini, Turina, Catalani, and Mascagni. *Tebaldi, soprano; unidentified soloists, orchs. & conds.*
+ Fa 9-10/88: 320

20315. 116 (3 discs): MEYERBEER—L'Africaine. SAINT-SAËNS—Samson et Dalila: Excerpts. *Mandac, Verrett, Domingo, Mittelmann, Estes; with assisting soloists; San Francisco Opera; Perrison, cond.* Africaine recorded in 1972.
+ Fa 9-10/88: 204

20316. 118: VERDI—Forza del destino. *Milanov, Del Monaco, Warren; with assisting soloists; unidentified chorus & orch.; Herbert, cond.* Recorded live 1953.
+ Fa 11-12/88: 303

20317. 120 (2 discs): HALÉVY—Juive. *Hayashi, Tucker, Gwynne; with assisting soloists; unidentified chorus & orch.; Guadagno, cond.* Recorded live 1973.
+ Fa 11-12/88: 195 (Tucker)
• Fa 11-12/88: 195 (others)
+ ON 3/18/89: 43 (Tucker)
- ON 3/18/89: 43 (others)

20318. 121 (2 discs): DONIZETTI—Linda di Chamounix. *Rinaldi, Zilio, Kraus, Bruson, Dara, Cava; with assisting soloists; unidentified chorus & orch.; Gavazzeni, cond.* Recorded live 1975.
+ Fa 3-4/89: 150
• ON 11/88: 64

20319. 122 (2 discs): DONIZETTI—Maria Stuarda. VERDI—Traviata: excerpts. *Caballé, Vilma, Carreras, Mazzieri; with assisting soloists; unidentified chorus & orch.; Santi, cond.* Recorded live 1972, 1973.
• Fa 1-2/89: 157 (Donizetti)
+ Fa 1-2/89: 157 (Verdi)

20320. 123 (2 discs): VERDI—Trovatore; Ballo in maschera: Excerpts. *Caballé, Mattiucci, Tucker, Zanasi, Vinco; with assisting soloists; unidentified chorus & orch.; Schippers, cond.* Recorded live 1968, 1971.
+ Fa 1-2/89: 286

20321. 129 (2 discs): DONIZETTI—Poliuto. Operatic excerpts from Tosti, Puccini, Verdi, Giordano, and Mercadante. *Ricciarelli, Carreras, Pons; Vienna Symphony Orch.; Caetani, cond.* Poliuto recorded live in 1986.
• Fa 5-6/89: 177

20322. 130 (2 discs): BELLINI—Norma. *Callas, Stignani, Picchi, Vaghi; with assisting soloists; Royal Opera House Covent Garden; Gui, cond.* Recorded live 1952.
+ Fa 1-2/89: 126

20323. 133: WAGNER—Walküre: Act 2. *Flagstad, Lehmann, Melchior, Schorr; unnamed orch.; Reiner, cond.* Recorded live 1936.
+ Fa 5-6/89: 357
+ ON 4/1/89: 66

20324. 134 (2 discs): BELLINI—Straniera; Bianca e Fernando: La mia scelta a voi sia grata. STRAUSS—Vier letzte Lieder. *Caballé, Zambon, Sardinero; with assisting soloists; American Opera Society Chorus & Orch.; Guadagno, cond.* La straniera recorded live 1969.
+ Fa 5-6/89: 137

20325. 135 (2 discs): ROSSINI—Assedio di Corinto. *Sills, Horne, Bonisolli, Diaz; with assisting soloists; Teatro alla Scala;Schippers, cond.* Recorded live 1969. Issued also as Melodram MEL 27043.
+ ARG 9-10/89: 96
+ Fa 5-6/89: 292
+ ON 2/18/89: 42

20326. 136: BEETHOVEN—Symphony no. 9. VERDI—Luisa Miller: Overture; Forza del destino: Overture. *Novotná, Thorborg, Peerce, Moscona; Westminster Choir; NBC Symphony Orch.; Toscanini, cond.* Recorded live 1939, 1943, 1952.
□ Fa 7-8/89: 96

20327. 138 (3 discs): ROSSINI—Bianca e Falliero; Tancredi: Excerpts. *Ricciarelli, Horne, Merritt, Surian; with assisting soloists; Pesaro Festival Chorus & Orch.; Renzetti, cond. Aix-en-Provence Festival; Weikert, cond.* Recorded live 1986, 1981.
• ARG 9-10/89: 95
• Fa 7-8/89: 226

20328. 144: WAGNER—Parsifal: Act 2. *Flagstad, Lechleitner, Kraus; with assisting soloists; Royal Opera House Covent Garden; Rankl, cond.* Recorded live 1951.
+ ARG 1-2/90: 104 m.f.
+ Fa 11-12/89: 404

20329. 145: WAGNER—Tristan und Isolde: Act 2. *Flagstad, Meisle, Melchior, List; with assisting soloists; San Francisco Opera Orch.; Reiner, cond.* Recorded live 1937.
+ ARG 1-2/90: 104
- Fa 11-12/89: 405

20330. 148 (2 discs): VERDI—Lombardi alla prima crociata; Traviata: Excerpts. *Scotto, Pavarotti, Grilli, Umberto; Rome Opera Chorus & Orch., Gavazzeni, cond., Royal Opera House Covent Garden; Cillario, cond.* Recorded live 1969, 1965.
+ ARG 1-2/90: 100

20331. 149 (3 discs): DONIZETTI—Anna Bolena. *Souliotis, Horne, Baker, Domingo, Cava; with assisting soloists; unnamed chorus and orch.; Lewis, cond.*

LEGATO

Recorded live 1966.
- ARG 3-4/90: 41

20332. 150: VERDI—Traviata: Excerpts; I Lombardi: Giselda! O ciel traveggo. PUCCINI—Madama Butterfly: Excerpts. *Scotto; Carreras; with assisting soloists; unidentified orchs. & conds.* Recorded live 1973, 1974.
+ ARG 9-10/90: 151
+ Fa 11-12/90: 421

20333. 151: *Ettore Bastianini: opera arias, 1955-1962.* Music of Verdi, Giordano, Puccini, and Mascagni. *Bastianini, baritone; with assisting soloists; various accs.* Recorded live.
+ ARG 9-10/90: 162
+ Fa 11-12/90: 430

20334. 152 (2 discs): BELLINI—Beatrice di Tenda. *Freni, Gonzales, Desderi, Casellato; Bologna Opera; Arena, cond.* Recorded 1967.
+ ARG 9-10/92: 81
• ON 11/93: 42

20335. 153 (2 discs): PUCCINI—Turandot. Opera excerpts of Puccini, Verdi, and Cilea. *Nilsson, Price, Di Stefano; with assisting soloists; Vienna State Opera Chorus & Orch.; Molinari-Pradelli, cond.* Turandot recorded live 1961.
• Fa 1-2/91: 279

20336. 154: VERDI—Ballo in maschera: Abridged. *Morris, Larrimore, Björling, Rothmüller; with assisting soloists; New Orleans Opera Chorus & Orch.; Herbert, cond.* Recorded live 1950.
• ARG 9-10/90: 127 m.f.
- Fa 11-12/90: 381 m.f.

20337. 155: LEONCAVALLO—I Pagliacci. *Björling, Moberg, Sundquist; Stockholm Opera; Gardelli, cond.* Recorded 1954.
+ ARG 3-4/93: 192

20338. 156: *José Carreras in recital, 1989.* Music of A. Scarlatti, Bellini. Stradella, Fauré, Duparc, Massenet, Tosti, Turina, Falla, Ginastera, Guastavino, Nacho, Puccini, Cardillo, and Lara. *Carreras, tenor; Bavaj, piano.*
□ Fa 11-12/90: 416

20339. 157 (2 discs): PUCCINI—Tosca; Tosca: Act 2. *Tebaldi, Tagliavini, Gobbi, Di Stefano, Bastianini; with assisting soloists; Royal Opera House Covent Garden; Molinari-Pradelli, cond.; Théâtre de la Monnaie; unnamed conductor (probably Gianadrea Gavazzeni).* Recorded live 1955, 1958.
+ ARG 9-10/90: 99
+ Fa 11-12/90: 322

20340. 158 (2 discs): GIORDANO—Fedora. PUCCINI—Opera excerpts. *Tebaldi, Di Stefano, Sereni; Teatro San Carlo, Naples; Basile, cond.; various orchestras and conductors.* Recorded live 1961.

- Fa 11-12/90: 234 (Giordano)
+ Fa 11-12/90: 234 (Puccini)

20341. 159 (2 discs): ROSSINI—Ermione. *Caballé, Horne, Merritt, Blake, Morino, Surian; Teatro Rossini Pesaro; Kuhn, cond.* Recorded live 1987.
+ ARG 11-12/92: 191

20342. 160: VERDI—La traviata. *Scotto, Carreras, Bruscantini; Verchi, cond.* Recorded live 1973.
+ ARG 9-10/92: 177
+ ON 8/93: 37

20343. 162: Music of Puccini, Rossini, Bellini, Spontini, Verdi, Boito, Massenet, and Proch. *Callas; with acc.* Recorded live 1951-61.
+ ARG 11-12/92: 259

20344. 163 (2 discs): TCHAIKOVSKY—Eugene Onegin. *Vishnevskaya, Avedyeva, Lemeshev, Belov, Petrov; with assisting soloists; Bolshoi Theater; Khaikin, cond.*
+ ARG 9-10: 120
• Fa 1-2/91: 333
• Gr 10/90: 819
+ ON 6/91: 43
• Op 9/90: 1137 (Vishnevskaya)
• Op 9/90: 1137 (others)

20345. 167 (2 discs): GOUNOD—Faust. *Angeles, Tucker, Moscona; New Orleans Opera; Herbert, cond.* Recorded 1953.
+ ARG 9-10/93: 263
+ ON 1/8/94: 34

20346. 168 (2 discs): PUCCINI—Madama Butterfly. *Angeles, Nadell, Fredericks, Torigi; New Orleans Opera; Herbert, cond.* Recorded 1954.
+ ARG 9-10/93: 263
+ ON 1/8/94: 34

20347. 170 (2 discs): PONCHIELLI—La gioconda. *Caballé, Nave, Payne, Carreras; Orch.; López Cobos, cond.* Recorded 1979.
+ ARG 11-12/93: 168
• ON 2/4/95: 41

20348. 172: *Victoria de los Angeles.* Music of Bizet, Flotow, Gounod, Mozart, and others. *Angeles, soprano.* Recorded 1944-93.
+ ARG 9-10/94: 276

20349. 174: PUCCINI—Il tabarro. *Olivero, Bottion, Rafanelli; Florence Opera; Delogu, cond.* Recorded 1970.
+ ARG 5-6/94: 125
+ ON 3/19/94: 30

20350. 175 (2 discs): DONIZETTI—Anna Bolena. *Scotto, Ramey, Marsee, Kolk, Ciesinski; Philadelphia Opera; Rudel, cond.* Recorded 1975.
• ARG 5-6/94: 87

20351. 176 (2 discs): BELLINI—I Puritani. *Sills, Pavarotti, Quilico, Plishka; Philadelphia Opera; Guadagno, cond.*

Recorded 1972.
+ ARG 5-6/94: 68
+ ON 5/94: 50

20352. 179: *Rosa Ponselle.* Music of Porter, Rodgers, and others; and traditional songs. *Ponselle, soprano.*
+ ARG 9-10/94: 276

20353. 180 (2 discs): VERDI—Luisa Miller. *Ricciarelli, Carreras, Bruson, Rinaudo; Turin Opera; Previtali, cond.* Recorded 1976.
+ ARG 3-4/95: 212
• ON 2/18/95: 38

20354. 182 (2 discs): MASSENET—Hérodiade. *Vejzovic, Caballé, Carreras, Pons; Barcelona Opera; Delacôte, cond.* Recorded 1984.
+ ARG 3-4/95: 135
+ ON 2/18/95: 38

20355. 183: Arias from Trovatore, Forza del destino, Aida, Traviata, Otello, and others. *Tebaldi, soprano.* Recorded 1953-66.
+ ARG 5-6/95: 231

20356. 185: VERDI—Simon Boccanegra: Excerpts. *Warren, Garcia, Filippeschi, Silva; Mexico City Opera; Cellini, cond.* Recorded 1950.
• ARG 5-6/95: 241
+ ON 10/95: 46

20357. 186 (2 discs): ZANDONAI—Francesca da Rimini. *Olivero, Monaco, Malaspina, De Palma; Teatro La Scala; Gavazzeni, cond.* Recorded 1959.
+ ARG 7-8/95: 233
+ ON 3/2/96: 39

20358. 187 (2 discs): VERDI—Aida. *Callas, Simionato, Baum, Walter, Neri; Royal Opera Covent Garden; Barbirolli, cond.* Recorded 1953.
+ ARG 7-8/95: 215

20359. 188 (2 discs): PUCCINI—Turandot. *Caballé, Pavarotti, Mitchell, Tozzi; San Francisco Opera; Chailly, cond.* Recorded 1977.
+ ARG 7-8/95: 171

20360. 189 (2 discs): VERDI—Simon Boccanegra. *MacNeil, Tebaldi, Tucker, Flagello; Miami Opera; Levine, cond.*
• ARG 5-6/95: 190
• ON 10/95: 46

20361. 190 (2 discs): DONIZETTI—Dom Sébastien. *Leech, Takács, Miller, Koptchak; Opera Orch. of New York; Queler, cond.* Recorded live 1984.
• ARG 11-12/95: 112
• ON 2/3/96: 36

20362. 191 (2 discs): DELIBES—Lakmé. *Devia, Gedda, Plishka; Opera Orch. of New York; Queler, cond.* Recorded live 1981.

+ ARG 11-12/95: 111
• ON 1/6/96: 39

20363. 192: *Great tenor cabalettas.* Arias by Bellini, Verdi, Meyerbeer, and others. *Various performers.*
+ ARG 11-12/95: 275

20364. 193 (2 discs): VERDI—Giovanna d'Arco. *Tebaldi, Penno, Savarese; Naples Opera; Santini, cond.* Recorded live 1951.
• ARG 1-2/96: 244
+ ON 3/2/96: 39

20365. 194 (2 discs): BIZET—Carmen. *Resnik, Domingo, Vinay, Stokes; Santiago Teatro Municipal; Guadagno, cond.* Recorded live 1967.
• ARG 1-2/96: 88
+ ON 3/16/96: 40

20366. 195 (2 discs): BELLINI—I puritani. *Freni, Kraus, D'Orazi, Arié; Modena Opera; Verchi, cond.* Recorded live 1962.
+ ARG 1-2/96: 87

20367. 196: Music of Mozart, Handel, Rachmaninoff, Poulenc, and others. *E. Di Tullio, soprano; A. Di Tullio, piano.*
+ ARG 11-12/95: 267

20368. 197 (3 discs): STRAUSS—Der Rosenkavalier. HUMPERDINCK—Hänsel und Gretel (selections; sung in Italian). *Schwarzkopf, Jurinac, Della Casa, Edelmann, Kunz; Teatro alla Scala; Karajan, cond.* Recorded live 1952, 1954.
+ ARG 1-2/96: 243
• ON 3/30/96: 37

20369. 198 (2 discs): VERDI—Rigoletto. *MacNeil, Scotto, Tucker, Wildermann; Teatro Colon; Previtali, cond.* Recorded live 1967.
+ ARG 1-2/96: 191
• ON 3/2/96: 39

20370. 202 (2 discs): MASCAGNI—Cavalleria rusticana. *Rysanek, Domingo, Bella, Varnay; Munich Opera; Santi, cond.* Recorded 1978.
+ ARG 7-8/96: 150

20371. 203 (2 discs): BELLINI—Norma. *Scotto, Rinaldi, Mauro, Ferrin; Florence Opera; Muti, cond.* Recorded 1978.
• ARG 7-8/96: 79

20372. 708 (2 discs): *Jussi Björling.* Music of Althen, Beethoven, Bizet, Cilea, Donizetti, Geehl, Giordano, and others. *Björling, tenor; with assisting soloists; various orchs. & conds.* Recorded live.
+ ARG 9-10/90: 127
+ Fa 1-2/91: 368

20373. 709 (2 discs): *In memoriam (recital).* Music of Verdi, Mozart, Ponchielli, Puccini, Mascagni, Strauss, and Anon. *Milanov, soprano; with assisting soloists; various orchs. &*

conds. Recorded live 1938-1966.
• Fa 1-2/91: 357

20374. 713: Arias from Enfant prodigue, Reine de Saba, Ernani, Cavalleria rusticana, Andrea Chénier, Zaza, Walküre, Boris Godounov, Don Carlo, Le Cid, La favorite, Maid of Orleans, Le prophète, and Aïda. *Resnik, soprano.* Recorded 1944-61.
+ ARG 5-6/92: 189

20375. 714: Anna Moffo: the early years, 1956-60. *Moffo, soprano; with orch. acc.*
+ ARG 5-6/93: 183

20376. 826: VERDI—La forza del destino. *Farrell, Corelli, Colzani, Flagello; Guadagno, cond.* Recorded live 1963.
+ ARG 11-12/91: 40

20377. 836 (2 discs): DONIZETTI—Parisina d'Este. *Caballé, Pruett, Quilico, Morris; Opera Orch. of New York; Queler, cond.* Recorded live 1974.
+ ARG 7-8/92: 123
+ ON 1/16/93: 32

20378. 838 (2 discs): BELLINI—I Puritani. *Sutherland, Gedda, Blanc, Díaz; American Opera Society; Bonynge, cond.* Recorded 1963.
• ARG 1-2/93: 77

20379. 839: ALFANO—Resurrection. *Olivero, Gismondo, Boyer; RAI Turin; Boncompagni, cond.*
• ARG 3-4/93: 48

20380. 840 (2 discs): ZANDONAI—Francesca da Rimini. *Kabaivanska, Domingo, Manuguerra, Saetta; Opera Orch. of New York; Queler, cond.* Recorded 1973.
+ ARG 9-10/93: 221
• ON 9/94: 60

20381. 841 (2 discs): BELLINI—La sonnambula; I Puritani: Excerpts. *Sutherland, Cioni, Flagello, Tullio; orch.; Rescigno, cond.* Recorded 1961.
+ ARG 5-6/93: 69
+ ON 1/22/94: 40

20382. 842: VERDI—Requiem. *Price, Merriman, Tucker, Tozzi; Philadelphia Orch.; Ormandy, cond.* Recorded 1957.
+ ARG 5-6/93: 182

20383. 843 (2 discs): VERDI—Rigoletto. *Carreras, Wise, Quilico; New York City Opera; Rudel, cond.* Recorded 1973.
+ ARG 5-6/94: 164

20384. 844: Duets from Forza del destino, Simon Boccanegra, Andrea Chenier, and Manon Lescaut. *Tebaldi, soprano; Tucker, tenor; with orch. accomp.* Recorded 1956-63.
+ ARG 11-12/93: 254

20385. 845: Jussi Björling at the Hollywood Bowl. *Björling, tenor; with*

accomp. Recorded 1949.
+ ARG 5-6/94: 213

20386. 846: Arias and songs by Bononcini, A. Scarlatti, Bellini, Verdi, and others. *Pavarotti, tenor; with accomp.* Recorded 1974.
+ ARG 1-2/94: 193

20387. 847: Arias and songs by Rameau, Donizetti, Verdi, Puccini, Tosti, and others. *Domingo, tenor; with accomp.* Recorded 1960/69.
+ ARG 1-2/94: 193

20388. 850 (2 discs): VERDI—Don Carlo. *Jurinac, Cossotto, Domingo, Sereni; Vienna State Opera; Varviso, cond.* Recorded 1968.
+ ARG 5-6/94: 208

LEGENDARY RECORDINGS

20389. LRCD 1002-2: *Ettore Bastianini in recital.* Music of Durante, Gluck, Rossini, Verdi, Mozart, Giordano, Tosti, Denza, De Curtis, Cardillo, Di Capua, and Billi. *Bastianini, baritone; Miura, piano.* Recorded live 1965.
• Fa 9-10/88: 306

20390. LRCD 1003-2 (2 discs): VERDI—Macbeth. *Callas, Penno, Mascherini, Tajo; with assisting soloists; Teatro alla Scala; De Sabata, cond.* Recorded live 1952.
+ Fa 9-10/88: 286

20391. LRCD 1005-2 (2 discs): VERDI—Nabucco. *Callas, Sinimberghi, Bechi; with assisting soloists; Teatro di San Carlo; Gui, cond.* Recorded live 1949.
+ Fa 11-12/88: 304 m.f.

20392. LRCD 1006-2 (2 discs): VERDI—Rigoletto. *Callas, Di Stefano, Campolonghi; with assisting soloists; Mexico City National Opera; Mugnai, cond.* Recorded live 1952.
• Fa 3-4/89: 327

20393. LRCD 1007-2 (2 discs): VERDI—Il trovatore. *Callas, Stignani, Penno, Tagliabue, Modesti; with assisting soloists; Teatro alla Scala; Votto, cond.* Recorded live 1953.
+ Fa 1-2/89: 285 (Callas)
- Fa 1-2/89: 285 (others)

20394. LRCD 1008-2 (3 discs): VERDI—I vespri siciliani. *Callas, Kokolios, Mascherini, Christoff; with assisting soloists; Teatro Comunale (Firenze); Kleiber, cond.* Recorded live 1951.
• Fa 3-4/89: 327

20395. LRCD 1011-2: *The legendary Alma Gluck.* Music of Rimsky-Korsakov, Verdi, Charpentier, Leoncavallo, Rameau, Saint-Saëns, Bland, Monk-Lyte, Hahn, Cornelius, Sinding, Loewe, Tosti, Fuentes, and Anon. *Gluck, soprano;*

LEHMANN ARCHIVES

various accs.
+ Fa 5-6/89: 366

LEHMANN ARCHIVES

20396. LRT 1-3 (3 LPs): *Lotte Lehmann centennial album, 1888-1988.* Music of Beethoven, Mozart, Flies, Schubert, Schumann, Mendelssohn, Brahms, Strauss, Wagner, Wolf, Praetorius, Falk, Gruber, and Anon. *Lehmann, soprano; Ulanowsky, piano.*
+ Fa 5-6/89: 367

LEMAN CLASSICS

20398. LC 42501: CASTELNUOVO-TEDESCO—Guitar music. *Mebes, guitar.*
- Fa 11-12/90: 200

20399. LC 42601: PONCE—Variations and fugue on La folia. VILLA-LOBOS—5 preludes. GINASTERA—Guitar sonata. *Freire, guitar.*
+ Fa 7-8/91: 366

20400. LC 42602: GINASTERA—Sonata, op. 47. PONCE—Variations and fugue on La folia. VILLA-LOBOS—Five preludes. *Freire, guitar.*
+ Gr 7/92: 78

20401. LC 42701: PONCE—Guitar music. *Mebes, guitar.*
+ ARG 5 6/92: 106
+ Fa 11-12/93: 344

20402. LC 42801: *Oboe alone.* Music of Wagner, Telemann, Tomasi, Reade, Holliger, Berio, and M. Berkeley. *Daniel, oboe.*
+ Fa 11-12/93: 485

20403. LC 42901: YSAŸE—Six sonatas for solo violin, op. 27. *Popova, violin.*
+ Fa 3-4/92: 366

20404. LC 44100 (2 discs): NOBRE—Vocal and chamber music. *Various performers.*
+ ARG 9-10/94: 168
+ Fa 9-10/94: 278

20405. LC 44201: *Recital Catalan.* Music of Albéniz, Llobet, Asencio, and Mompou. *Mebes, guitar.*
+ ARG 5-6/93: 164
+ Fa 11-12/93: 344

20406. LC 44301: Music of Rossini, Woolrich, Destenay, Gardner, and Gilson. *Daniel Trio.*
+ Fa 9-10/94: 425

20407. LC 44401: *Fugas y fandangos: music for two guitars.* Music of Falla, Castelnuovo-Tedesco, and Granados. *Mebes, Freire, guitars.*
+ Fa 5-6/96: 348

20408. LC 44601: NOBRE—Reminiscencias, op. 83; Homenagem a Villa-Lobos, op. 46. VILLA-LOBOS—

Twelve etudes for guitar. *Freire, guitar.*
+ ARG 5-6/94: 176
+ Fa 5-6/94: 209

20409. LC 44801: FINZI—Interlude. PATTERSON—Duologue. HOWELLS—Oboe sonata. *Daniel, oboe; Drake, piano.*
+ Fa 11-12/93: 485
+ Gr 10/93: 70

LEONARDA

20410. LE-326: BRUCH—Pieces for viola, clarinet and piano, op. 83, no. 1-3, 5. BASSETT—Trio. HOAG—Inventions on the summer solstice. HOOVER—3 images. *Verdehr Trio.*
+ ARG 7-8/88: 78
● Fa 9-10/88: 338

20411. LE-327: *Journeys: Orchestral works by American women.* Music of Van de Vate, Gardner, Larsen, Richter, Hoover, Mamlok, and Brockman. *Bournemouth Sinfonietta; Arioso Chamber Orch.; Martin, cond.*
+ ARG 9-10/88: 108
+ Fa 9-10/88: 347

20412. LE-328: MUSGRAVE—Rorate coeli; 4 madrigals. ZAIMONT—Serenade; Parable. *Hilse, organ; Florilegium Chamber Choir; Rice, cond.*
+ ARG 11-12/89: 92
+ Fa 11-12/89: 302

20413. LE-329: ZAIMONT—From the great land. WEIGL—Songs of remembrance. HINDEMITH—Clarinet quartet. *Kingsbury, mezzo-soprano; Drucker, clarinet; Abram, piano; Baker, violin; Finckel, cello.*
+ ARG 7-8/90: 127
+ Fa 3-4/91: 240
+ Fa 1-2/92: 378

20414. LE-330: MARTINŮ—Trio. MARX—Divertimento à tre. LOEB—4 nocturnes. ROREM—Trio. *Huntington Trio.*
+ ARG 7-8/91: 150
□ Fa 7-8/91: 377

20415. LE-331: *The London Philharmonic celebrates American composers.* Music of Erb, Richter, Lundborg, and Bazelon. *Henegar, contrabassoon; London Phil. Orch.; Farberman, cond.*
+ ARG 7-8/91: 141
+ Fa 1-2/91: 403
+ HPR v. 8 n. 2/91: 64

20416. LE-332: KRAMER—Musica pro musica; Atlanta licks; Music for piano, no. 5; Renascence; Music for piano, no. 3. *Rehfeldt, clarinet; Weinstock, piano; Raley, piano; Atlanta Chamber Players; London Phil. Orch.; Farberman, cond.*
+ Fa 3-4/91: 252

20417. LE-333: *Let us break bread together.* Music of Ravel, Debussy, Saint-Saëns, Bach, Rogers, Colombier,

McNeill, Paget, Hanson, Massenet, Coleridge-Taylor, Mendelssohn, and Fauré. *Jones, flute; Valentine, piano.*
+ Fa 5-6/94: 315

20418. LE-334: Music of Bond, Léon, Brockman, Schonthal, Walker, and others. *N.K. Solomon, piano.*
+ ARG 1-2/95: 228
● Fa 3-4/95: 388

20419. LE-335: KARG-ELERT—Impressions exotiques; Flute sonata, op. 121; Jugend; Suite pointillistique. *Worthen, flute; Weber, piano; Shaughnessy, clarinet; Menual, horn.*
+ ARG 1-2/94: 114
+ Fa 11-12/93: 283

20420. LE-336: Music of Vellere, Aderholt, Schonthal, Beach, and Rainier. *Crescent Quartet; Alard Quartet.* Reissue.
+ ARG 1-2/95: 228
□ Fa 3-4/95: 388

20421. LE-337: RICHTER—Qhanri: Tibetan variations for cello and piano; Requiem for solo piano; Landscapes of the mind no. 2 for violin and piano. *Wells, cello; M. Richter, piano; Daniel Heifetz, violin; Skelly, piano.*
+ ARG 9-10/95: 201
+ Fa 3-4/95: 388

20422. LE 339: Music of Smith, Moore, Bonds, Eubanks, and others. *Walker, violin; Walker-Hill, piano.*
+ ARG 9-10/96: 253

20423. LE-341: *Ave Maria.* Music of Adam, Arcadelt, Cherubini, and others. *Chakoyan, soprano; Aivazian, organ.*
● ARG 7-8/96: 277

LEOPOLD STOKOWSKI SOCIETY OF AMERICA

20424. LSCD 03: BEETHOVEN—Symphony no. 9. Piano sonata no. 14 "Moonlight": Adagio sostenuto (arr. Stokowski). *A. Davis, Cahart, Betts, Loewenthal; Philadelphia Orch. Chorus; Philadelphia Orch.; Stokowski, cond.* Recorded 1934 & 1947.
● ARG 3-4/93: 190
+ Fa 3-4/93: 123
+ Fa 5-6/93: 162

20425. LSCD 04: BEETHOVEN—Symphony no. 5. BRAHMS—Symphony no. 1. *All-American Youth Symphony Orch.; Stokowski, cond.* Recorded 1940-41.
+ ARG 9-10/93: 257
+ Fa 11-12/93: 181

20426. LSCD 20: *Stokowski conducts Philadelphia rarities.* Music of Turina, Eicheim, Dubensky, McDonald, and Sousa. *Philadelphia Orch.; Stokowski, cond.; other performers.*

+ Fa 9-10/93: 384
+ Gr 10/93: 141

LIBRA

20427. LCD 1001/2 (2 separate discs): *Brynjar Off: oboe concertos, vol. 1-2.* Concertos by Marcello, D. Scarlatti, Albinoni, Corelli, Bach, Cimarosa, Handel, and Pergolesi. *Hoff, oboe; English Chamber Orch.; Watson, cond.*
+ Fa 5-6/95: 269

LIBRARY OF CONGRESS

20428. CLC-2: *Leopold Stokowski at the Library of Congress.* WAGNER—Siegfried-Idyll. VAUGHAN WILLIAMS—Fantasia on a theme by Thomas Tallis. SCHOENBERG—Verklärte Nacht. *Symphony of the Air; Stokowski, cond.*
- Fa 9-10/91: 445

20429. CLC-3: BRAHMS—Violin sonatas no. 1-3. *Francescatti, violin; R. Casadesus, piano.* Recorded live 1949, 1952.
+ Fa 5-6/92: 129

20430. LCM-2141: *Historic performances from the Library of Congress.* Music of Handel, Beethoven, Schumann, Brahms, Strauss, Schubert, Debussy, Bizet, G. Charpentier, Grovlez, Dett, Coleridge-Taylor, Cohen, and Anon. *Maynor, soprano; Sandor, piano.* Recorded live 1940.
+ ARG 9-10/91: 183
+ Fa 5-6/91: 330

LIGIA

20431. 0101005: C.P.E. BACH—Prussian sonatas. *Zylberajch, harpsichord.*
• ARG 1-2/95: 68
+ Fa 7-8/94: 42

20432. 0103006: DEBUSSY—Piano works, vol. 1. *Haguenauer, piano.*
• Fa 7-8/94: 120

20433. 0103009: MOMPOU—Piano music. *Martin, piano.*
• ARG 7-8/94: 134
+ Fa 7-8/94: 185

20434. 0103012: CHOPIN—Piano music. *Athanassova, piano.*
• Fa 9-10/94: 167

20435. 0103014: LISZT—Late piano works. *Martin, piano.*
• ARG 1-2/95: 133
• Fa 3-4/95: 210

20436. 0103018: SCHUMANN—Carnaval; Piano sonata no. 1. *Martin, piano.*
+ ARG 7-8/95: 191
+ Fa 7-8/95: 308

20437. 0103023/24 (2 discs): DEBUSSY—Piano preludes (complete). *Haguenauer,*

piano.
- Fa 9-10/95: 186

20438. 0103028: *The Five and their music.* Music of Mussorgsky, Borodin, Cui, Rimsky-Korsakov, and Balakirev. *Werchowska, piano.*
+ ARG 3-4/96: 234
• Fa 1-2/96: 395

20439. 0104001: BACH—Organ works. *Vernet, organ.*
+ ARG 11-12/94: 67
• Fa 9-10/94: 130

20440. 0104004: MENDELSSOHN—Organ sonatas, op. 65. *Vernet, organ.*
- Fa 7-8/94: 179

20441. 0104007: BUXTEHUDE—Organ works, vol. 1. *Vernet, organ.*
• Fa 7-8/94: 110
+ Fa 9-10/95: 158

20442. 0104013: BUXTEHUDE—Organ works, vol. 2. *Vernet, organ.*
• ARG 11-12/94: 87
• Fa 9-10/94: 130
+ Fa 9-10/95: 158

20443. 0104015: BUXTEHUDE—Organ works, vol. 3. *Vernet, organ.*
• Fa 11-12/94: 195
+ Fa 9-10/95: 158

20444. 0104019: BUXTEHUDE—Organ works, vol. 4. *Vernet, organ.*
+ Fa 7-8/95: 146
+ Fa 9-10/95: 158

20445. 0204022: BUXTEHUDE—Organ music, vol. 5. *Vernet, organ.*
+ Fa 9-10/95: 158

20446. 0104025 (5 discs): BUXTEHUDE—Organ music (complete). *Vernet, organ.*
+ ARG 11-12/95: 101

20447. 0104031: *Splendeurs de l'orgue français au XVIII siècle.* Music of Guilain, Piroye, Corrette, Calviere, Benaut, and Balbastre. *Vernet, organ.*
+ Fa 1-2/96: 391

20448. 0104041: COUPERIN—Messe pour les couvents. *Vernet, organ.*
+ ARG 1-2/97: 91
+ Fa 1-2/97: 147

20449. 0105002: *Dialogue.* Music of Bach, Handel, Loeillet, Corelli, and Zbinden. *Touvron, trumpet; Vernet, organ.*
+ Fa 7-8/94: 322

20450. 0105008: *Homage to Segovia.* Music of Ponce, Bach, Scarlatti, Torroba, Barrios, and others. *Regis, guitar.*
- ARG 7-8/94: 209
+ Fa 7-8/94: 313

20451. 0105030: *Rêverie.* Music of Vivaldi, Bach, Gounod, Fauré,

Schumann, Glinka, Rimsky-Korsakov, Massenet, Franck, Saint-Saëns, Schubert, Grieg, Tchaikovsky, Brahms, Tartini, and Telemann. *Touvron, trumpet; Vernet, organ.*
- Fa 1-2/96: 400

20452. 0105040: ARBAN—Verdi paraphrases. *Touvron, trumpet; Cottin, piano.*
+ ARG 1-2/97: 59

20453. 0106020: *The art of the viola bastarda: song and dance music for violin in Italy.* Music of Watillon, Ortiz, Sandrin, Ruffa, Rore, Dalla Casa, Bassani, Bonizzi, Selma y Salaverde, and Corelli. *Watillon, viola da gamba; Laethem, voice; Valetti, violin; Liegeois, Stryckers, violas da gamba; Leertouwer, cello; Devaere, harp; Noiri, lute; Stinders, harpsichord & organ.*
+ ARG 5-6/95: 215
+ Fa 3-4/95: 368

20454. 0201003: DUPARC—Songs. *Vernet, soprano; Séréo, piano.*
- ARG 9-10/94: 125
• Fa 9-10/94: 183

20455. 0201010: GOUNOD—Songs. *Vernet, soprano; Martin, piano.*
• ARG 7-8/94: 106
• Fa 7-8/94: 143

20456. 0201021: CHABRIER—Mélodies. *Freulon, baritone; Martin, piano.*
+ ARG 7-8/95: 99
- Fa 5-6/95: 171

20457. 0201033: Music of Strauss, Milhaud, Longas, Benedict, and others. *Hartglass, soprano; Leroy, piano.*
- ARG 9-10/96: 266

20458. 0202011: GOUNOD—Harmonies célestes: sacred music for voice, violin, piano, and organ. *Desnoues, mezzo-soprano; Massis, soprano; Gleusteen, violin; Martin, piano; Vernet, organ.*
• ARG 9-10/94: 134
+ Fa 7-8/94: 142

20459. 0202016: VIVALDI—La gloria e Imeneo; Two sinfonia concertos for strings and continuo in F major. *Estournet, violin & cond.; Nirouët, Expert, vocalists; Ensemble Jean-Marie Leclair.*
• ARG 11-12/95: 227
+ Fa 3-4/95: 330

20460. 0202026: *Petits motets de chapelle.* Music of Danelis, Charpentier, Bernier, Mouret, Boismortier, and Campra. *Ensemble Baroque de l'Ouest.*
+ ARG 3-4/96: 245
• Fa 11-12/95: 457

20461. 0301027: CORELLI—Recorder sonatas. *La Turbulente.*
+ ARG 11-12/95: 110
+ Fa 1-2/96: 181

20462. 0301036: ONSLOW—Symphonies no. 2, 4. *Hradec Králové Phil.; Leger, cond.*
- ARG 5-6/96: 160
- Fa 5-6/96: 229

LINDENBERG

20463. LBCD 11: Organ music of Bach, Vierne, Kee, Andriessen, and Van den Horst. *Jongepier, organ.*
+ Fa 7-8/90: 356

LINN RECORDS

20464. CKD 001: BACH—Violin concerto in A minor. BARTÓK—Divertimento. ELGAR—Introduction and Allegro. MOZART—Divertimento K. 138. VIVALDI—Concerto, op. 3, no. 10. *Polish Chamber Orch.; Stanienda, violin & cond.*
- Fa 9-10/92: 444
+ Gr 12/91: 86

20465. CKD 002: DEBUSSY—Cello sonata. MARTIN—Ballade (1949). POULENC—Cello sonata. *Conway, cello; Evans, piano.*
+ Fa 9-10/92: 192
+ Gr 11/91: 112

20466. CKD 003: MOZART—Symphony no. 40. SCHUBERT—Symphony no. 5. *English Classical Players; Brett, cond.*
+ Fa 9-10/92: 304
+ Gr 11/91: 92

20467. CKD 004: SHOSTAKOVICH—Symphony no. 5. *Leningrad Phil. Orch.; Dmitriev, cond.* Recorded live.
- Fa 9-10/92: 354

20468. CKD 005: *Udite amanti.* 17th-century italian love songs. *Feldman, soprano; North, theorbo, archlute.*
+ EM 8/92: 505

20469. CKD 006: Lute music of Weiss, Vivaldi, and Bach. *North, lute.*
+ EM 5/93: 312
+ Gr 12/92: 108

20470. CKD 007: Music from the time of Christopher Columbus. *Bott, soprano; New London Consort; Pickett, cond.*
- EM 11/92: 685
+ Gr 7/92: 95

20471. CKD 009: LUTOSŁAWSKI—Grave. RACHMANINOFF—Cello sonata. WEBERN—Little pieces, op. 11. *Conway, cello; Evans, piano.*
+ Gr 10/93: 71

20472. CKD 010: *An excess of pleasure.* Music of Uccellini, Matteis, Simpson, Marini, and others. *Palladian Ensemble.*
+ ARG 5-6/96: 250
+ Gr 7/93: 62

20473. CKD 011: *Elizabethan and Jacobean consort music.* Music of Byrd, Maynard, Brade, Jenkins, Lauder, Coleman, and others. *Bott, soprano; George, bass; New London Consort; Pickett, cond.*
+ Gr 4/94: 94

20474. CKD 013, 029 (2 separate discs): BACH—Sonatas and partitas. *North, lute.*
+ Gr 4/95: 89

20475. CKD 015: *The winged lion.* Music of Castello, Vitali, Uccello, Buonamente, Cavalli, and others. *Palladian Ensemble.*
+ EM 5/95: 331
+ Gr 1/95: 68

20476. CKD 035: PURCELL—The Indian queen. *Bonner, Bott, Covey-Crump, Harvey; Purcell Simfony Voices; Purcell Simfony; Mackintosh, cond.*
- ARG 5-6/96: 170
+ Gr 9/95: 105

20477. CKD 036: BACH—Trio sonatas (arr.); Duets, BWV 1087; Verschiedene Canones, BWV 1087. *Palladian Ensemble.*
+ Gr 8/95: 90

20478. HON 5041: *A choice collection.* Music of Locke, Matteis, Baltzar, Weldon, Blow, Butler, and J. Banister. *Palladian Ensemble.*
- ARG 11-2/96: 260
+ Gr 5/96: 78 (as CKD 041)

20479. HON 5047: BURNS—The complete songs, vol. 1. *Cuffe, Paterson, Ross, Kydd, Russell, Benzie, Reid; with various accs.*
- Gr 5/96: 93 (as CKD 047)

LIVE CLASSICS

20480. LCL 121: GUBAIDULINA—Rejoice! RAVEL—Violin and cello sonata. *Kagan, violin; Gutman, cello.* Recorded live 1988.
- ARG 1-2/96: 118

20481. LCL 122: MOZART—Violin sonatas, K. 304-306. *Kagan, violin; Richter, piano.*
+ ARG 3-4/96: 160

20482. LCL 145: BEETHOVEN—Violin sonatas no. 2, 4-5. *Kagan, violin; Richter, piano.*
+ ARG 3-4/96: 160

20483. LCL 161: HINDEMITH—Complete sonatas for violin and piano. *Kagan, violin; Richter, piano.* Recorded 1978.
□ ARG 1-2/97: 122

20484. LCL 352: SCHUMANN—Fantasy; Sonata no. 1; Widmung; Arabesque. *Wirssaladze, piano.*
+ ARG 1-2/97: 167

20485. LCL 431: Music of Haydn, Beethoven, Chopin, Scriabin, and Debussy. *Richter, piano.* Recorded live 1992.
+ ARG 1-2/96: 219

20486. LCL 441: Music of Chopin and Scriabin. *Richter, piano.* Recorded live 1992.
+ ARG 1-2/96: 219

20487. LCL 442: GRIEG—Lyric pieces. *Richter, piano.* Recorded 1993.
+ ARG 1-2/97: 116

20488. LCL 641: *Cello sonatas.* Music of Saint-Saëns, Britten, and Prokofiev. *Gutman, cello; Richter, piano.* Recorded live 1992.
- ARG 1-2/96: 208

LODIA

20489. 775: ROSSINI—*Overtures.* Semiramide; William Tell; L'Italiana in Algeri; La Cenerentola; Barber of Seville; La Gazza ladra. *Royal Phil. Orch.; Paita, cond.*
- ARG 9-10/91: 115

20490. 776: MAHLER—Symphony no. 1. *Royal Phil. Orch.; Païta, cond.*
- ARG 9-10/91: 89

20491. 789: DVOŘÁK—Symphonies no. 8-9. *Royal Phil. Orch.; Paita, cond.*
+ ARG 9-10/90: 62
+ DA 3/90: 66
- Gr 12/90: 1199

20492. 7702: DEBUSSY—String quartet. RAVEL—String quartet. *Fine Arts Quartet.*
- ARG 9-10/90: 60
- Fa 9-10/90: 224
- Gr 4/90: 1817

20493. 7703: MOZART—String quintets, K. 515, K. 516. *Fine Arts Quartet; Dupouy, viola.*
+ ARG 11-12/90: 89

LONDON

20494. 411 282-2: FRANCK—Symphony. SCHUMANN—Symphony no. 1. *Vienna Phil. Orch.; Furtwängler, cond.*
- Fa 1-2/87: 110 (Franck)
+ Fa 1-2/87: 110 (Schumann)
- Gr 10/86: 575 (Franck)
+ Gr 10/86: 575 (Schumann)

20495. 411 622-2 (2 discs): DONIZETTI—Lucia di Lammermoor. *Sutherland, Cioni, Merrill, Siepi; with assisting soloists; Accademia di Santa Cecilia; Pritchard, cond.*
- ARG 3-4/90: 155
+ Da 3/90: 66
- Gr 12/90: 1199

20496. 411 805-2 (3 discs): MOZART—Idomeneo. *Gruberová, Popp, Baltsa, Pavarotti; with assisting soloists; Vienna Phil. Orch.; Pritchard, cond.* Issued also as 3 LPs: 411 805-1.
- ARG 7-8/88: 45

+ DA 1/89: 37
• Fa 9-10/88: 212
- Gr 4/88: 1494
• ON 7/88: 42
+ Op 6/88: 752
+ SR 9/88: 110
• St 12/88: 189

20497. 411 862-2 (3 discs): MUSSORGSKY—Boris Godunov. *Vishnevskaya, Spiess, Ghiaurov, Diakov, Talvela; with assisting soloists; Vienna Choir Boys; Sofia Radio Chorus; Vienna State Opera Chorus; Vienna Phil. Orch.; Karajan, cond.*
• ARG 1-2/89: 73
- Fa 5-6/89: 256
• Gr 11/88: 861
☐ Op 1/89: 72

20498. 411 871-2 (2 discs): PUCCINI—Tosca. *Tebaldi, Del Monaco, London; Accademia di Santa Cecilia; Molinari-Pradelli, cond.* Reissue.
+ Gr 8/91: 78

20499. 411 940-2: SHOSTAKOVICH—Two pieces for string quartet; Romances on poems of Alexander Blok, op. 127; Piano quintet, op. 57. *Söderström, soprano; Ashkenazy, piano; Fitzwilliam String Quartet.*
• Fa 7-8/87: 183
+ Gr 2/87: 1150

20500. 414 073-1 (LP): HANDEL—Coronation anthems. *King's College Choir; English Chamber Orch.; Willcocks, cond.*
+ Fa 11-12/86: 147

20501. 414 087-2: VERDI—Aida. *Tebaldi, Simionato, Bergonzi, MacNeil, Van Mill; with assisting soloists; Gesellschaft der Musikfreunde Chorus; Vienna Phil. Orch.; Karajan, cond.*
+ Fa 7-8/89: 268
• Gr 1/89: 1210
+ Op 6/89: 754

20502. 414 095-1 (LP): CHAUSSON—Poème de l'amour et de la mer. BRAHMS—Vier ernste Gesänge (orch. Sargent; sung in English). BACH—Vergiss mein nicht; Ach, dass nicht die letzte Stunde. *Ferrier, alto; Hallé Orch.; Barbirolli, cond.; BBC Symphony Orch.; Sargent, cond.; Silver, harpsichord.*
+ ARG 3-4/86: 77
☐ Fa 3-4/87: 14
+ MA 3/87: 60
+ NYT 6/15/86: H29
+ Ov 2/86: 21

20503. 414 162-2: SHOSTAKOVICH—Cello concerto no. 1. BLOCH—Schelomo. *Harrell, cello; Concertgebouw Orch.; Haitink, cond.* Issued also as LP: 414 162-1.
• Fa 5-6/87: 194
+ Gr 2/87: 1121
+ NR 4/87: 11
+ SR 7/87: 101

20504. 414 204-2: CHOPIN—Songs, op. 74; Czary; Dumka. *Söderström, soprano; Ashkenazy, piano.* Issued also as LP: 414 204-1.
• Fa 1-2/87: 83
• Gr 7/86: 200

20505. 414 291-2: MOZART—Piano quintet, K. 452. BEETHOVEN—Piano quintet, op. 16. *Lupu, piano; Vries, oboe; Pieterson, clarinet; Zarzo, Vicente, horn; Pollard, bassoon.*
+ DA 4/87: 59
+ Fa 3-4/87: 172
+ Gr 9/86: 398
• Gr 12/86: 895
+ Ov 6/87: 38

20506. 414 335-2: MUSSORGSKY—Boris Godunov: Excerpts. VERDI—Opera excerpts. *Burchuladze, bass; London Opera Chorus; English Concert Orch.; Downes, cond.*
+ ARG 9-10/86: 28
- Fa 5-6/87: 222
+ NYT 8/2/87: H26

20507. 414 337-2: MOZART—Piano concertos no. 18, 20. *Ashkenazy, piano & cond.; Philharmonia Orch.* Issued also as LP: 414 337-1.
• Fa 3-4/87: 164
+ Gr 9/86: 381
• Gr 2/87: 1130
- Ov 7/87: 33

20508. 414 340-2: RACHMANINOFF—Cello sonata, op. 19; Cello and piano pieces. ALTSCHULER—Melodie on a theme by Rachmaninoff. *Harrell, cello; Ashkenazy, piano.* Issued also as LP: 414 340-1.
+ Fa 3-4/87: 188
+ Gr 8/86: 279
+ NR 287: 12

20509. 414 348-2: RACHMANINOFF—Piano concerto no. 2. ADDINSELL—Warsaw concerto. LITOLFF—Concerto symphonique no. 4: Scherzo. GOTTSCHALK—Grande fantaisie triomphale sur l'hymne national brésilien (arr. Hazell). *Ortiz, piano; Royal Phil. Orch.; Atzmon, cond.*
+ DA 12/86: 70
• Fa 11-12/86: 198
• Gr 5/86: 1424
+ Gr 9/86: 398
+ NYT 12/21/86: H24
+ SR 11/86: 161

20510. 414 353-2: SCRIABIN—Piano sonatas no. 1, 6, 8; Quatre morceaux, op. 51. *Ashkenazy, piano.*
+ Fa 5-6/92: 253

20511. 414 362-2 (3 discs): MOZART—The magic flute. *Gueden, Simoneau, Böhme, Berry, Loose, Lipp, Jaresch; Vienna Phil.; Böhm, cond.* Recorded 1955.
+ ARG 11-12/91: 106
• OQ autumn/91: 239

20512. 414 388-2: BACH—Well-tempered Clavier, bk. 1. *Schiff, piano.* Issued also as LP: 414 388-1.
+ Fa 11-12/86: 100
+ Gr 9/86: 415
• NR 9/86: 26
+ Ov 3/87: 32
+ SR 11/86: 102

20513. 414 391-2 (3 discs): BEETHOVEN—Piano concertos (complete); Fantasia in C minor, op. 80. *Larrocha, piano; RIAS Chamber Choir; Berlin Radio Symphony Orch.; Chailly, cond.* Issued also as LP: 414 391-1.
+ Fa 3-4/87: 71
• Gr 3/87: 1254
+ Gr 11/86: 705
+ NYT 10/19/86: H25
+ SR 11/86: 168

20514. 414 409-2: STRAVINSKY—Firebird; Scherzo fantastique; Feu d'artifice. *Montreal Symphony Orch.; Dutoit, cond.* Issued also as LP: 414 409-1.
+ Fa 3-4/87: 214
+ Gr 10/86: 585
+ Gr 12/86: 883
• Ov 5/87: 44
+ SR 3/87: 72

20515. 414 421-2: DVOŘÁK—Symphony no. 9. *Cleveland Orch.; Dohnanyi, cond.* Issued also as LP: 414 421-1.
+ Fa 3-4/87: 110
+ Gr 11/86: 711
+ Gr 12/86: 883
• Ov 10/87: 39

20516. 414 460-2: SAINT-SAËNS—Carnival of the animals; Phaéton; Le rouet d'Omphale; Danse macabre. *Rogé, Ortiz, pianos; London Sinfonietta; Philharmonia Orch.; Dutoit, cond.* Issued also as LP: 414 460-1.
• Fa 3-4/87: 196
- Gr 1/87: 1022

20517. 414 476-3 (3 discs): BELLINI—Norma. *Sutherland, Caballé, Pavarotti, Ramey; with assisting soloists; Welsh National Opera Orch.; Bonynge, cond.*
+ ARG 7-8/88: 14 (Caballé)
• ARG 7-8/88: 14 (others)
+ DA 11/88: 84: 84
- Fa 9-10/88: 110
• Gr 4/88: 1492
+ HPR 12/88: 74
• ON 4/9/88: 48
- Op 7/88: 839
+ OQ Winter/88: 141
• SR 8/88: 90

20518. 414 502-2 (2 discs): DELIBES—Coppélia. *National Phil. Orch.; Bonynge, cond.* Issued also as 2 LPs: 414 502-1.
• Fa 1-2/87: 89
- HF 4/87: 65
• NYT 12/28/86: H14

20519. 414 544-2 (LP): CHOPIN—Six waltzes (arr. Godowsky); GODOWSKY—Studies on the Chopin Etudes: no. 1, 5, 7,

LONDON

12-13, 15, 25, and 44. *Bolet, piano.*
+ Fa 9-10/86: 126

20520. 414 551-2 (2 discs): WAGNER—
Der fliegende Holländer. *Bailey, Talvela,
Martin, Kollo, Krenn, Jones; Chicago
Symphony Orch. & Chorus; Solti, cond.*
- Fa 9-10/94: 374

20521. 414 577-2 (3 discs): BRITTEN—
Peter Grimes. *Watson, Pears, Pease; with
assisting soloists; Royal Opera House
Covent Garden; Britten, cond.*
+ ARG 11-12/86: 57
+ Fa 9-10/86: 121
+ Gr 4/86: 1323
+ Ov 2/87: 45

20522. 414 581-2 (3 discs): WAGNER—
Tannhäuser. *Dernesch, Ludwig, Kollo,
Braun, Sotin; Vienna Choir Boys; Vienna
State Opera Chorus; Vienna Phil. Orch.;
Solti, cond.*
+ Fa 1-2/88: 235

20523. 414 585-2 (2 discs): MASSENET—
Manon (arr. Lucas). *Royal Opera House
Covent Garden; Bonynge, cond. Not
based on music from the opera of the
same name.*
+ Fa 7-8/88: 197
+ Gr 6/88: 30

20524. 414 597-2 (2 discs): PUCCINI—
Tosca. *Te Kanawa, Aragall, Nucci; with
assisting soloists; Welsh National Opera
Chorus; National Phil. Orch.; Solti, cond.
Issued also as 2 LPs: 414 597-1.*
● ARG 5-6/87: 48
- Fa 3-4/87: 184
● Gr 9/86: 439
● Gr 11/86: 748
+ NR 2/87: 20
+ ON 1/17/87: 44
● Op 2/87: 174
- OQ Spring/87: 151
- Ov 6/87: 42
● SR 3/87: 104

20525. 414 601-2: LISZT—Transcendental
études. *Bolet, piano. Issued also as LP:
414 601-2.*
+ Fa 3-4/87: 150
● Gr 9/86: 600
+ Ov 8/87: 20

20526. 414 604-2 (2 discs): HANDEL—
Organ concertos, op. 4 (complete); Organ
concertos no. 13-14; Sonata in D major.
*Hurford, organ; Concertgebouw
Chamber Orch.; Rifkin, cond.*
+ Fa 5-6/87: 126
+ Gr 11/86: 712
+ NR 4/87: 13

20527. 414 611-1 (LP): *The great voice
of Kathleen Ferrier. Music of Schubert,
Brahms, and Schumann. Ferrier,
contralto; Walter, piano.*
+ Fa 11-12/86: 256

20528. 414 612-1 (LP): *The great voice
of Teresa Berganza. Music of Haydn,*

Mozart, and Rossini. *Berganza, mezzo-
soprano; various orch. accs.*
+ Fa 9-10/86: 272

20529. 414 616-2: VILLA-LOBOS—Five
preludes for guitar; Twelve etudes for
guitar. GINASTERA—Guitar sonata, op. 47.
Fernandez, guitar.
+ Fa 7-8/87: 203
+ Gr 4/87: 1434

20530. 414 626-2: BEETHOVEN—
Symphony no. 3. *Vienna Phil. Orch.;
Kleiber, cond.*
+ Fa 9-10/86: 105
+ Gr 6/86: 48
+ NR 9/86: 2
● Ov 12/86: 44

20531. 414 667-2 (2 discs): HANDEL—
Rodelinda. *Sutherland, Nafé, Buchanan,
Tourangeau, Rayam, Ramey; Welsh
National Opera Orch.; Bonynge, cond.
Issued also as 2 LPs: 414 667-1.*
● ARG 3-4/88: 43
- Gr 4/87: 1457
- Op 7/87: 792
- Opus 12/87: 33
- OQ Winter 1987/88: 120

20532. 414 676-2: STRAUSS—
Alpensinfonie. *Bavarian Radio
Symphony Orch.; Solti, cond.*
+ ARG 1-2/87: 63

20533. 417 112-2: GRIEG—Piano concerto
in A minor. SCHUMANN—Piano concerto
in A minor. *Bolet, piano; Berlin Radio
Symphony Orch.; Chailly, cond. Issued
also as LP: 417 112-1.*
+ Fa 3-4/87: 123
+ Gr 12/86: 867
+ Ov 10/87: 41

20534. 417 143-2 (4 discs): WAGNER—
Parsifal. *Ludwig, Kollo, Fischer-Dieskau,
Hotter, Frick; with assisting soloists;
Vienna State Opera Chorus; Vienna Phil.
Orch.; Solti, cond.*
+ Fa 7-8/89: 278

20535. 417 164-2 (2 discs): ROSSINI—
Barbiere di Siviglia. *Ausensi, Berganza,
Benelli, Corena, Ghiaurov; Naples
Rossini Orch. & Chorus; Varviso, cond.
Reissue.*
● Gr 5/92: 114
+ OQ summer 93: 181

20536. 417 184-2: STRAUSS—Don
Quixote; Salome: Dance of the seven
veils. *Harrell, cello; Cleveland Orch.;
Ashkenazy, cond. Issued also as LP: 417
184-1.*
● Fa 3-4/87: 212
● Gr 12/86: 883
+ Opus 6/87: 50 (Quixote)
● Opus 6/87: 50 (Salome)
+ Ov 7/87: 35

20537. 417 190-2: MOZART—Piano
quartets no. 1-2. *Solti, piano; Members of
the Melos Quartet. Issued also as LP: 417*

190-1.
+ ARG 3-4/87: 36
- Fa 3-4/87: 170
● Gr 9/86: 593
● HF 6/87: 65
- NR 2/87: 14
● Ov 6/87: 38
● SR 4/87: 94

20538. 417 199-2: RODRIGO—Concierto
de Aranjuez; Fantasia para un
gentilhombre. CASTELNUOVO- TEDESCO—
Guitar concerto no. 1. *Fernandez, guitar;
English Chamber Orch.; Gómez
Martínez, cond. Issued also as LP: 417
199-1.*
● Fa 3-4/87: 193
+ Gr 12/86: 864
+ SR 4/87: 96

20539. 417 236-2 (2 discs): BACH—
Well-tempered clavier, book 2. *Schiff,
piano.*
● Fa 7-8/87: 54
+ Gr 3/87: 1295

20540. 417 239-2: RACHMANINOFF—Piano
concerto no. 3. *Ashkenazy, piano;
Concertgebouw Orch.; Haitink, cond.
Issued also as LP: 417 239-1.*
- Fa 3-4/87: 187
● Gr 11/86: 716
- MA 7/87: 61
- MA 11/87: 62
+ Ov 6/87: 43

20541. 417 261-2: SHOSTAKOVICH—
Symphony no. 13. *Rintzler, bass; Male
voices of the Choir of the Concertgebouw
Orch.; Concertgebouw Orch.; Haitink,
cond.*
+ Fa 11-12/86: 217
+ Gr 5/86: 1420
+ NR 9/86: 5

20542. 417 289-2: *Con amore.* Music of
Kreisler, Poldini, Wieniawski,
Chaminade, Elgar, Tchaikovsky,
Nováček, Debussy, Chopin, Gossec,
Saint-Saëns, and Brahms. *Chung, violin;
Moll, piano.*
+ ARG 1-2/88: 75
● DA 3/88: 56
+ Fa 1-2/88: 265
+ Gr 9/87: 438

20543. 417 294-2: TCHAIKOVSKY—Piano
concerto no. 1. DOHNÁNYI—Variations on
a nursery song, op. 25. *Schiff, piano;
Chicago Symphony Orch.; Solti, cond.*
+ DA 8/87: 56
● Fa 7-8/87: 193
+ Gr 10/86: 586
+ Gr 12/86: 884
● HF 5/87: 60
+ NR 4/87: 14
● Ov 2/87: 42
+ SR 3/87: 71

20544. 417 295-2: BRUCKNER—Symphony
no. 9. *Chicago Symphony Orch.; Solti,
cond. Issued also as LP: 417 295-1.*
+ Fa 3-4/87: 92

+ Gr 10/86: 564
+ Gr 11/86: 706
- NYT 3/15/87: H26
• Ov 6/87: 38

20545. 417 299-2: Mussorgsky—Pictures at an exhibition (arr. Ravel); Night on Bald Mountain; Khovanshchina: Prelude. Rimsky-Korsakov—Russian Easter overture. *Montreal Symphony Orch.; Dutoit, cond.*
+ Fa 9-10/88: 220
- Gr 5/88: 1602
• HPR 3/89: 83
- MA 1/89: 63
• SR 9/88: 110

20546. 417 300-2: Tchaikovsky—1812 overture; Capriccio italien; Nutcracker: Suite; Marche slave. *Montreal Symphony Orch.; Dutoit, cond.* Issued also as LP: 417 300-1.
- Fa 3-4/87: 221 (1812)
+ Fa 3-4/87: 221 (remainder)
+ Gr 10/86: 587
+ Gr 12/86: 884
+ NR 2/87: 1

20547. 417 301-2: Rimsky-Korsakov—Scheherazade; Tsar Saltan: Suite; Flight of the bumblebee. *Philharmonia Orch.; Ashkenazy, cond.*
• ARG 5-6/88: 57
+ DA 6/88: 60
+ Fa 3-4/88: 177
+ Gr 10/87: 584
+ HF 6/88: 60

20548. 417 302-2 (2 discs): Berlioz—Roméo et Juliette; Symphonie funèbre at triomphale. *Quivar, Cupido, Krause; Tudor Singers of Montreal; Montreal Symphony Choir & Orch.; Dutoit, cond.* Issued also as 2 LPs: 417 302-1.
+ Fa 3-4/87: 83
+ Gr 12/86: 915
+ NYT 11/16/86: H23
+ ON 1/3/87: 42
+ Ov 6/87: 40

20549. 417 314-2: Prokofiev—Symphony no. 5; Dreams, op. 6. *Concertgebouw Orch.; Ashkenazy, cond.*
- Fa 7-8/87: 162
+ Gr 3/87: 1269
- HF 7/87: 64

20550. 417 315-2 (3 discs): Mozart—Nozze di Figaro. *Della Casa, Güden, Danco, Pell, Siepi; with assisting soloists; Vienna Phil Orch.; Kleiber, cond.*
+ Fa 9-10/90: 308

20551. 417 319-2 (2 discs): Wagner—Der fliegende Holländer. *London, Tozzi, Rysanek, Liebl, Lewis, Elias; Royal Opera House, Covent Garden; Dorati, cond.*
- Fa 9-10/94: 373

20552. 417 325-2: Stravinsky—Rite of spring; Four Norwegian moods.

Cleveland Orch.; Chailly, cond. Issued also as LP: 417 325-1.
• DA 6/87: 84
+ Fa 7-8/87: 192
+ Gr 2/87: 1137
+ Gr 4/87: 1558
• HF 7/87: 65
+ SR 8/87: 91

20553. 417 326-2: Gershwin—Rhapsody in blue, for 2 pianos and orchestra; Lullaby, for string orchestra; An American in Paris; Cuban Overture. *K. & M. Labèque, pianos; Cleveland Orch.; Chailly, cond.*
+ Fa 7-8/87: 111
+ Gr 2/87: 1124

20554. 417 327-2: Schubert—Piano sonata, D. 960; Fantasia in C, D. 760. *Ashkenazy, piano.*
• Fa 11-12/87: 216
+ Gr 8/87: 327
+ SR 11/87: 192

20555. 417 329-2: *Grand march.* Marches. *Philip Jones Ensemble; Howarth, cond.*
• Fa 5-6/87: 239
+ Gr 4/87: 1466
+ NYT 8/16/87: H31

20556. 417 330-2: Haydn—Symphonies no. 95, 104. *London Phil. Orch.; Solti, cond.* Issued also as LP: 417 330-1.
- Fa 5-6/87: 136
+ Gr 1/87: 1014

20557. 417 354-2: Bernstein—West Side story: Suite. Weill—Little threepenny music: Suite. *Philip Jones Brass Ensemble.*
+ Fa 11-12/87: 108
+ Gr 7/87: 178

20558. 417 361-2: *Encores.* Music of Mendelssohn, Chopin, Debussy, Schubert, Albéniz, Strauss, Bizet, Godowsky, Moszkowsky, and Schlozer. *Bolet, piano.*
+ Fa 9-10/87: 291
+ Gr 7/87: 207

20559. 417 372-2: Handel—Suite no. 5. Mozart—Fantasy, K. 475; Piano sonata, K. 457. Bach—Violin partita no. 2: Chaconne (arr. Busoni). *Larrocha, piano.* Issued also as LP: 417 372-1.
• Fa 11-12/87: 279
+ Gr 9/87: 443

20560. 417 399-2: Liszt—Faust symphony. *Jerusalem; Chicago Symphony Chorus & Orch.; Solti, cond.* Issued also as LP: 417 399-1.
+ Fa 3-4/87: 146
+ Gr 9/86: 376
+ NR 2/87: 3
+ Ov 9/87: 40

20561. 417 400-2: Tchaikovsky—1812 overture; Romeo and Juliet; Nutcracker: Suite. *Chicago Symphony Orch.; Solti,*

cond. Issued also as LP: 417 400-1.
• Fa 9-10/87: 322
+ Gr 5/87: 1563
+ Ov 11/87: 43
+ SR 10/87: 144

20562. 417 401-2: Schumann—Carnaval, op. 9; Fantasie, op. 17 . *Bolet, piano.*
+ Fa 9-10/87: 291
+ Gr 4/87: 1434

20563. 417 402-2 (2 discs): Mozart—Entführung aus dem Serail. *Gruberová, Battle, Winbergh, Zednik, Talvela; Vienna State Opera Chorus; Vienna Phil. Orch.; Solti, cond.* Issued also as 2 LPs: 417 402-2.
• Fa 9-10/87: 244
• Gr 4/87: 1458
• NYT 8/2/87: H26
• ON 10/87: 64
+ Op 10/87: 1176
• Opus 12/87: 37
• Ov 4/88: 82

20564. 417 406-2: *Baroque horn concertos.* Music of Knechtl, Reinhardt, Quantz, Graun, and Rollig. *Tuckwell, horn; Academy of St. Martin-in-the-Fields; Brown, cond.* Issued also as LP: 417 406-1.
+ Fa 11-12/87: 288
+ Gr 7/87: 188
+ SR 3/88: 104

20565. 417 410-2 (2 discs): Gluck—Orfeo ed Euridice. *Horne, Lorengar, Donath; Royal Opera House Covent Garden; Solti, cond.*
+ Fa 1-2/90: 185
• Gr 8/89: 362

20566. 417 416-2 (3 discs): Verdi—Aida. *Price, Gorr, Vickers, Merrill, Tozzi; with assisting soloists; Rome Opera; Solti, cond.*
+ Fa 1-2/88: 225
• Gr 9/87: 482

20567. 417 420-2 (2 discs): Verdi—Luisa Miller. *Caballé, Reynolds, Pavarotti, Milnes, Giaiotti, Van Allan; with assisting soloists; London Opera Chorus; National Phil. Orch.; Maag, cond.*
+ ARG 1-2/89: 96
+ Gr 10/89: 676

20568. 417 428-2 (3 discs): Britten—Holy sonnets of John Donne; Songs and proverbs of William Blake; Billy Budd. *Pears, tenor; Fischer-Dieskau, baritone; with assisting soloists; Britten, piano; Ambrosian Opera Chorus; London Symphony Orch.; Britten, cond.*
+ DA 10/89: 90
+ Fa 11-12/89: 158
+ Gr 6/89: 81
+ MA 9/89: 75
+ St 2/90: 192

20569. 417 438-2: Poulenc—Piano music. *Rogé, piano.*
+ Fa 11-12/87: 197

LONDON

+ Gr 7/87: 204
+ HF 3/88: 64
+ SR 12/87: 141

20570. 417 439-2 (3 discs): VERDI—Aida. *Chiara, Dimitrova, Pavarotti, Nucci; with assisting soloists; Teatro alla Scala; Maazel, cond.*
- ARG 11-12/90: 131
• Fa 11-12/90: 380
• Gr 5/90: 2053
• ON 10/90: 42
- Op 7/90: 882
• SR 12/90: 136
- St 6/91: 255

20571. 417 450-2: ZEMLINSKY—Seejungfrau; Psalm XIII. *Kammerchor Ernst Senff; Berlin Radio Symphony Orch.; Chailly, cond.* Issued also as LP: 417 450-1.
+ Fa 11-12/87: 259
+ Gr 6/87: 56
□ NYT 1/10/88: H27
□ Opus 4/88: 22

20572. 417 452-2: DVOŘÁK—Serenades, op. 22, 44. *London Phil. Orch.; Hogwood, cond.*
+ Fa 9-10/88: 146
+ Gr 5/88: 1590
+ HF 11/88: 80

20573. 417 473-2: SCHUBERT—Winterreise. *Pears, tenor; Britten, piano.* Reissue.
+ Gr 10/91: 173

20574. 417 487-2: FRANCK—Symphony; Symphonic variations. *Bolet, piano; Concertgebouw Orch.; Chailly, cond.* Issued also as LP: 417 487-1.
• Fa 11-12/87: 138
• Gr 8/87: 292
• SR 12/87: 142

20575. 417 488-2: DEBUSSY—Prélude à l'après-midi d'un faune; Nocturnes for orchestra; La mer. *Cleveland Orch.; Ashkenazy, cond.*
+ DA 10/87: 88
+ Fa 7-8/87: 93
- Gr 2/87: 1122
- Gr 4/87: 1410
+ Opus 10/87: 512
- Ov 11/87: 39
+ SR 7/87: 97

20576. 417 497-2 (4 discs): WAGNER—Die Meistersinger. *Bode, Hamari, Kollo, Bailey, Weikl, Moll; with assisting soloists; Vienna State Opera Chorus; Vienna Phil. Orch.; Solti, cond.*
• Fa 7-8/89: 276

20577. 417 505-2 (2 discs): ADAM—Giselle. *Royal Opera House Covent Garden Orch.; Bonynge, cond.*
+ Fa 7-8/88: 92
+ Gr 6/88: 21

20578. 417 525-2 (2 discs): VERDI—Macbeth. *Verrett, Luchetti, Nucci,*

Ramey; with assisting soloists; Teatro comunale (Bologna); Chailly, cond.
• ARG 3-4/88: 94
• Fa 11-12/87: 245
• Gr 6/87: 103
- HPR 12/87: 102 (Verrett)
+ HPR 12/87: 102 (remainder)
• ON 1/16/88: 44
+ SR 11/87: 200

20579. 417 541-2: MENDELSSOHN—Midsummer night's dream: Excerpts; Hebrides overture; Fair Melusine overture; Ruy Blas overture. *Montreal Symphony Orch.; Dutoit, cond.* Issued also as LP: 417 541-1.
+ ARG 3-4/88: 54
- Fa 11-12/87: 175
+ Gr 7/87: 184
+ SR 11/87: 190

20580. 417 553-2: HOLST—Planets. *Montreal Symphony Orch.; Dutoit, cond.* Issued also as LP: 417 553-1.
+ Au 12/87: 146
+ Fa 11-12/87: 157
+ Gr 4/87: 142
+ HF 12/87: 77
+ NYT 9/2/87: H26

20581. 417 560-2 (2 discs): HANDEL—Organ concertos. *Hurford, organ; Concertgebouw Orch.; Rifkin, cond.*
+ Fa 3-4/88: 120
+ Gr 1/88: 1074

20582. 417 563-2: BEETHOVEN—Mass, op. 86; Calm sea and prosperous voyage. *Dunn, Zimmermann, Beccaria, Krause; Berlin Radio Chamber Choir; Ernst Senff Chamber Choir; Berlin Radio Symphony Orch.; Chailly, cond.*
- Fa 9-10/88: 99
+ Gr 11/87: 795
• Ov 1/89: 39

20583. 417 564-2: DVOŘÁK—Symphony no. 7. *Cleveland Orch.; Dohnányi, cond.*
+ DA 10/87: 78
+ Fa 7-8/87: 101
+ Gr 3/87: 1260
+ MA 11/87: 60
+ SR 8/87: 88

20584. 417 611-2: MUSSORGSKY—Pictures at an exhibition (arr. Ravel). DEBUSSY—Danse; Sarabande (arr. Ravel); RAVEL—Bolero. *Concertgebouw Orch.; Chailly, cond.* Issued also as LP: 417 611-1.
+ Fa 11-12/87: 188
• Gr 7/87: 178
- HF 12/87: 78

20585. 417 613-2: RACHMANINOFF—Piano concerto no. 1; Rhapsody on a theme of Paganini. *Ashkenazy, piano; Concertgebouw Orch.; Haitink, cond.*
+ Fa 9-10/88: 231
+ Gr 12/87: 955
+ SR 9/88: 114

20586. 417 617-2: *Guitar concertos.* Music of Giuliani and Vivaldi.

Fernandez, guitar; English Chamber Orch.; Malcolm, cond.
+ ARG 5-6/88: 30
+ Fa 3-4/88: 110
+ Gr 11/87: 734
+ SR 8/88: 91

20587. 417 618-2: Music of Albéniz, Llobet, Granados, Tarrega, Segovia, and Turina. *Fernandez, guitar.*
+ Fa 3-4/88: 259
+ Gr 2/88: 1216
+ Ov 6/88: 39

20588. 417 619-2: STRAVINSKY—Petrushka (1911); Chant du rossignol; 4 studies. *Montreal Symphony Orch.; Dutoit, cond.*
+ Fa 5-6/88: 222
• Gr 1/88: 1090 (Petrushka)
+ Gr 1/88: 1090 (Chant)

20589. 417 620-2: HAYDN—Symphonies no. 93, 99. *London Phil. Orch.; Solti, cond.*
- Fa 3-4/88: 126
+ Gr 11/87: 738
+ HF 11/88: 84

20590. 417 623-2 (3 discs): STRAUSS—Arabella. *Te Kanawa, Fontana, Seiffert, Grundheber, Gutstein; with assisting artists; Royal Opera House Covent Garden; Tate, cond.*
+ ARG 7-8/88: 58
+ Fa 7-8/88: 256
+ Gr 2/88: 1243
+ ON 3/12/88: 42
• Op 7/88: 839
+ OQ Win/88: 143
• SR 3/88: 102

20591. 417 627-2: MOZART—Piano concertos no. 11, 14. *Ashkenazy, piano & cond.; Philharmonia Orch.*
• Fa 5-6/89: 241
• Gr 12/88: 1007

20592. 417 628-2 (2 discs): BEETHOVEN—Cello sonatas (complete). *Harrell, cello; Ashkenazy, piano.*
- Fa 3-4/88: 70
+ Gr 11/87: 759

20593. 417 631-2: BRUCKNER—Symphony no. 7. *Chicago Symphony Orch.; Solti, cond.*
- ARG 11-12/88: 26
+ DA 1/89: 46
+ Fa 9-10/88: 124
• Gr 4/88: 1450
+ HPR 3/89: 73

20594. 417 637-2: BEETHOVEN—Symphonies no. 5-6. *Concertgebouw Orch.; Kleiber, cond.*
+ Fa 1-2/89: 124
+ Gr 9/87: 400

20595. 417 650-2: VILLA-LOBOS—Piano music. *Ortiz, piano.*
+ Fa 9-10/88: 290

+ Gr 12/87: 983
+ Ov 3/89: 53

20596. 417 671-2: Rachmaninoff—
Variations on a theme by Corelli;
Etudes-tableaux, op. 39. *Ashkenazy,
piano.*
   • Fa 11-12/88: 251
   + Gr 6/88: 52

20597. 417 672-2: Herbert—Cello
concertos no. 1-2; Five pieces for cello
and strings. *Harrell, cello; Academy of
St. Martin-in-the-Fields; Marriner, cond.*
   + ARG 5-6/89: 56
   + Fa 1-2/89: 182
   + Gr 10/88: 600
   + HF 1/89: 70
   + SR 6/89: 117

20598. 417 739-2: Brahms—Symphony
no. 1. *Vienna Phil. Orch.; Karajan, cond.*
   + ARG 1-2/90: 35

20599. 417 786-2: Albéniz—Suite
española (arr. Frühbeck de Burgos).
Granados—Goyescas: Intermezzo.
Falla—Amor brujo. *Mistral, mezzo-
soprano; New Philharmonia Orch.;
Frühbeck de Burgos, cond.*
   + Fa 11-12/89: 101

20600. 417 795-2: *Spanish fireworks.*
Music of Falla, M. Albéniz, I. Albéniz,
Mompou, Granados, and Turina.
Larrocha, piano.
   + Fa 7-8/89: 304

20601. 417 800-2: Beethoven—
Symphony no. 9. *Norman, Runkel,
Schunk, Sotin; Chicago Symphony
Chorus & Orch.; Solti, cond.*
   • Fa 3-4/88: 76
   • Gr 10/87: 574
   • Ov 5/88: 40
   + SR 4/88: 98

20602. 417 802-2: Dvořák—Piano
concerto, op. 33. Schumann—
Introduction and allegro appassionato for
piano and orchestra, op. 92. *Schiff,
piano; Vienna Phil. Orch.; Dohnányi,
cond.*
   + ARG 7-8/89: 40
   + Fa 5-6/89: 182
   + Gr 1/89: 1149
   + SR 5/89: 120

20603. 417 839-2: Bizet—L'arlésienne:
Suites 1-2; Carmen: Suites 1-2. *Montreal
Symphony Orch.; Dutoit, cond.*
   • ARG 11-12/88: 18
   + Fa 11-12/88: 146
   + Gr 6/88: 27
   - MA 1/89: 63

20604. 417 886-2: Mozart—Piano
concertos no. 12, 14. *Schiff, piano;
Camerata Academica of Salzburg; Végh,
Sándor.*
   + DA 9/90: 57
   + Fa 5-6/90: 225
   - Gr 12/89: 1141

20605. 417 887-2 (2 discs): Albéniz—
Iberia; Navarra; Suite espanola.
Larrocha, piano.
   + ARG 1-2/89: 13
   + Fa 11-12/88: 111
   + Gr 6/88: 47
   + MA 3/89: 50
   + SR 11/88: 133
   + St 2/89: 149

20606. 417 891-2: *Presenting Joshua
Bell.* Music of Wieniawski, Sibelius,
Brahms, Paganini, Bloch, Nováček,
Schumann, Falla, Grasse, and Sarasate.
Bell, violin; Sanders, piano.
   + ARG 9-10/88: 115
   + DA 9/88: 51
   + Fa 7-8/88: 140
   + Gr 5/88: 1618
   + Ov 6/88: 34

20607. 421 010-2: Schumann—Carnaval;
Humoreske; Novellettes. *Ashkenazy,
piano.*
   + Fa 11-12/88: 275
   - Gr 8/88: 320

20608. 421 053-2 (4 discs): Wagner—
Lohengrin. *Norman, Domingo, Nimsgern,
Sotin, Fischer-Dieskau; Vienna State
Opera Chorus; Vienna Phil. Orch.; Solti,
cond.*
   • ARG 9-10/88: 93
   + DA 6/88: 83
   • Fa 5-6/88: 235
   + Gr 10/87: 632
   • NYT 11/22/87: H27
   + ON 1/16/88: 44
   + Op 11/87: 1339
   • OQ Fall/88: 112 (reviewed by
Harris)
   • OQ Fall/88: 112 (reviewed by
Hamilton)
   + Ov 7/88: 40
   + SR 4/88: 84

20609. 421 061-2: Rachmaninoff—
Variations on a theme by Chopin;
Preludes: Selections; Melodie, op. 3, no.
3. Kreisler—Liebeslied; Liebesfreud.
Bolet, piano.
   • Fa 11-12/88: 251
   + Gr 8/88: 319
   + SR 12/88: 116

20610. 421 091-2: Bruckner—Symphony
no. 1 (Vienna version, 1890-91). *Berlin
Radio Symphony Orch.; Chailly, cond.*
   + Fa 11-12/88: 157
   + Gr 8/88: 319
   + SR 12/88: 116

20611. 421 096-2 (3 discs): Donizetti—
Anna Bolena. *Sutherland, Mentzer,
Hadley, Ramey; with assisting soloists;
Welsh National Opera Orch.; Bonynge,
cond.*
   + ARG 9-10/88: 37
   • Fa 1-2/89: 154 (Sutherland)
   + Fa 1-2/89: 154 (others)
   + Gr 7/89: 197
   + HPR 6/89: 75
   + ON 4/15/89: 42

   • Op 8/88: 968
   + Ov 2/89: 47
   • SR 12/88: 148

20612. 421 108-2: Ponce—Concierto del
sur. Villa-Lobos—Guitar concerto.
Lamarque-Pons—Concertino de invierno.
*Fernández, guitar; English Chamber
Orch.; García Asensio, cond.*
   + Fa 5-6/89: 269

20613. 421 114-2 (3 discs): Verdi—Don
Carlo. *Tebaldi, Bumbry, Bergonzi,
Fischer-Dieskau, Ghiaurov, Talvela; with
assisting soloists; Royal Opera House
Covent Garden; Solti, cond.*
   + ARG 1-12/89: 95
   + Gr 12/88: 1062

20614. 421 118-2: Dvořák—Piano trios
no. 1, 3. *Chung Trio.*
   + Fa 7-8/90: 136
   + Gr 2/90: 1479

20615. 421 119-2: Mendelssohn—Songs
without words: Selections. *Schiff, piano.*
   + Fa 9-10/88: 197
   • Gr 5/88: 1624
   - Ov 12/88: 50
   + SR 8/88: 72

20616. 421 120-2: Shostakovich—
Symphony no. 5; Five fragments, op. 42.
Royal Phil. Orch.; Ashkenazy, cond.
   + Fa 11-12/88: 278
   + Gr 6/88: 36
   • MA 3/89: 80

20617. 421 129-2: *Bel canto arias.* Music
of Bellini, Donizetti, Rossini, and Verdi.
*Nucci, baritone; English Chamber Orch.;
Masini, cond.*
   + ARG 1-2/90: 136
   + Fa 7-8/89: 295
   + Gr 12/88: 1065
   - NYT 2/30/89: H25
   • ON 9/89: 51

20618. 421 145-2: Bruch—Violin
concerto no. 1. Mendelssohn—Violin
concerto in E minor. *Bell, violin;
Academy of St. Martin-in-the-Fields;
Marriner, cond.*
   • ARG 11-12/88: 59
   • Fa 7-8/88: 140
   + Gr 5/88: 1589
   + Ov 6/88: 34

20619. 421 177-2 (3 discs): Bach—St.
Matthew passion. *Te Kanawa, Otter,
Rolfe Johnson, Krause, Blochwitz, Bär;
with assisting soloists; Chicago
Symphony Chorus & Orch.; Solti, cond.*
   - ARG 3-4/89: 17
   + DA 1/89: 49
   □ Fa 9-10/88: 93
   + Gr 4/88: 1483
   + St 12/88: 179

20620. 421 181-2: Rachmaninoff—Piano
concerto no. 2. Tchaikovsky—Piano
concerto, op. 23. *Bolet, piano; Montreal
Symphony Orch.; Dutoit, cond.*

LONDON

+ Fa 9-10/88: 231 (Rachmaninoff)
- Fa 9-10/88: 231 (Tchaikovsky)
- Gr 1/88: 1084
• HPR 12/88: 86
+ Ov 7/88: 37
+ SR 8/88: 74

20621. 421 182-2: MAHLER—Symphony no. 10 (ed. Cooke). SCHOENBERG—Verklärte Nacht. *Berlin Radio Symphony Orch.; Chailly, cond.*
• ARG 9-10/88: 59
+ DA 10/88: 62
+ Fa 11-12/88: 219

20622. 421 193-2: BERLIOZ—Harold en Italie; Rob Roy overture; Corsaire. *Zukerman, viola; Montreal Symphony Orch.; Dutoit, cond.*
• ARG 1-2/89: 32
- Fa 11-12/88: 145
• Gr 8/88: 280
+ HPR 4/89: 58
+ SR 11/88: 132

20623. 421 240-2 (3 discs): GOUNOD—Faust. *Sutherland, Corelli, Ghiaurov; Ambrosian Opera Chorus; London Symphony Orch.; Bonynge, cond. Reissue.*
+ Gr 12/91: 125

20624. 421 259-2: MOZART—Piano concertos no. 19, 27. *Schiff, piano; Camerata Academica Salzburg; Végh, cond.*
+ Fa 1-2/90: 237

20625. 421 290-2: SCHUMANN—Waldszenen; Kinderszenen; Piano sonata, op. 11. *Ashkenazy, piano.*
• Fa 11-12/89: 357

20626. 421 295-2: BRAHMS—Symphony no. 1; Academic festival overture. *Concertgebouw Orch.; Chailly, cond.*
• ARG 5-6/89: 30
+ DA 4/89: 64
• Fa 1-2/89: 138
+ Gr 9/88: 408
+ HPR 3/89: 73

20627. 421 360-2, 425 467-2 (2 separate discs): HAYDN—String quartets, op. 76. *Takacs Quartet.*
+ ARG 3-4/89: 44
+ DA 1/89: 40
- Fa 1-2/89: 132
- Gr 4/88: 439
+ MA 5/89: 60
• Fa 5-6/90: 186 (467)
+ Gr 1/90: 1344 (467)
+ MA 7/90: 75 (467)
+ St 10/90: 235 (467)

20628. 421 363-2: CHOPIN—Preludes, op. 28; Nocturnes. *Bolet, piano.*
+ Fa 3-4/89: 136
• Gr 11/88: 812

20629. 421 364-2: BEETHOVEN—String quartets no. 9-10. *Amadeus String Quartet.*

• Fa 7-8/89: 87
• Gr 3/89: 1444

20630. 421 369-2: MOZART—Piano music. *Schiff, piano.*
• Fa 1-2/89: 224
+ Gr 10/88: 642
+ SR 1/89: 127

20631. 421 384-2: ELGAR—Introduction and allegro; Serenade in E minor; Sospiri; Elegy; Spanish lady: Suite. WARLOCK—Serenade for Frederick Delius. *Academy of St. Martin-in-the-Fields; Marriner, cond.*
+ Fa 11-12/89: 202

20632. 421 385-2: ELGAR—Cello concerto. WALTON—Violin concerto. *Harrell, cello; Cleveland Orch.; Maazel, cond.; Chung, violin; London Symphony Orch.; Previn, cond.*
- Fa 11-12/89: 202 (Elgar)
+ Fa 11-12/89: 202 (Walton)

20633. 421 386-2: ELGAR—Symphony no. 2; Overture, In the south. *London Phil. Orch.; Solti, cond.*
+ Fa 11-12/89: 202

20634. 421 387-2: ELGAR—Symphony no. 1; Cockaigne overture. *London Phil. Orch,; Solti, cond.*
+ Fa 11-12/89: 202

20635. 421 388-2: ELGAR—Violin concerto in B minor; Salut d'amour; La capricieuse. *Chung, violin; Moll, piano; London Phil. Orch.; Solti, cond.*
+ Fa 11-12/89: 202

20636. 421 389-2: TIPPETT—Concerto for double string orchestra; Fantasia concertante on a theme of Corelli; Little music for string orchestra. *Academy of St. Martin-in-the-Fields; Marriner, cond.*
+ Fa 11-12/89: 384

20637. 421 390-2: DELIUS—Walk to paradise garden; Hassan; Intermezzo and serenade; Song before sunrise; Fennimore and Gerda; Intermezzo; On hearing the first cuckoo of spring; Summer night on the river; Air and dance; La calinda. *Academy of St. Martin-in-the-Fields; Marriner, cond.*
+ Fa 11-12/89: 188

20638. 421 391-2: BRITTEN—Variations on a theme of Frank Bridge. BUTTERWORTH—2 English idylls; Banks of green willow. WARLOCK—Capriol suite. *Academy of St. Martin-in-the-Fields; Marriner, cond.*
+ Fa 11-12/89: 160

20639. 421 417-2: *Russian songs.* Music of Dargomizhky, Tchaikovsky, Borodin, Rubinstein, Arensky, and Glinka. *Burchuladze, bass; Ivanova, piano; Smith, cello.*
• Fa 1-2/89: 312

• Gr 3/89: 1487
• NYT 3/5/89: H30

20640. 421 420-2: BEETHOVEN—Ah perfido. Opera arias of Wagner and Verdi. *Dunn, soprano; Teatro comunale (Bologna) Orch.; Chailly, cond.*
+ ARG 7-8/89: 128
+ Fa 11-12/89: 424
+ HPR v. 7, no. 1/90: 93
+ NYT 7/30/89: H25
+ ON 9/89: 51
+ Op 7/89: 888

20641. 421 422-2: SCARLATTI—Piano sonatas. *Schiff, piano.*
+ ARG 1-2/90: 82

20642. 421 423-2: DOHNÁNYI—Piano quintet no. 1; Sextet for piano, clarinet, horn and strings, op. 37. *Schiff, piano; Berkes, clarinet; Vlatković, horn; Takács Quartet.*
+ Fa 7-8/89: 130
• Gr 12/88: 1020
+ MA 5/89: 60

20643. 421 425-2: BRAHMS—Piano trio no. 1. MENDELSSOHN—Piano trio no. 1. *Chung Trio.*
+ Gr 4/95: 77

20644. 421 426-2 (2 discs): PUCCINI—Manon Lescaut. *Te Kanawa, Carreras, Coni; with assisting soloists; Teatro comunale (Bologna); Chailly, cond.*
- ARG 3-4/89: 72
+ Fa 1-2/89: 237
+ Gr 9/88: 477
+ HPR 3/89: 85
• ON 3/18/89: 42
+ Op 1/89: 69
- OQ Summer/89: 129 (Te Kanawa)
+ OQ Summer/89: 129 (others)
• SR 1/89: 129
+ St 2/89: 163

20645. 421 431-2 (2 discs): MINKUS AND DÉLIBES—La source. DRIGO—La flûte magique. *Royal Opera House Covent Garden Orch.; Bonynge, cond.*
+ Fa 7-8/91: 219
+ Gr 9/90: 510

20646. 421 434-2: BACH—Guitar music. *Fernandez, guitar.*
+ Fa 7-8/90: 75
+ Gr 1/90: 1349

20647. 421 439-2: SCHUMANN—Symphonies no. 1-2. *Cleveland Orch.; Dohnányi, cond.*
• DA 9/89: 76
• Fa 5-6/89: 317
• Gr 1/89: 1161
+ SR 4/89: 82

20648. 421 440-2: FAURÉ—Requiem; Pelléas et Mélisande: Suite; Pavane. *Te Kanawa, soprano; Milnes, baritone; Montreal Symphony Chorus & Orch.; Dutoit, cond.*
+ ARG 5-6/89: 49

+ Fa 3-4/89: 161
+ Gr 1/89: 1196
+ HF 5/89: 61
+ SR 6/89: 117

20649. 421 441-2: TCHAIKOVSKY—
Manfred symphony. *Concertgebouw
Orch.; Chailly, cond.*
  + ARG 3-4/89: 99
  • Fa 1-2/89: 277
  + Gr 9/88: 426
  • HF 2/89: 59
  + HPR 6/89: 88
  + Ov 4/89: 58
  + SR 3/89: 126

20650. 421 443-2: BARTÓK—Concerto for
orchestra; Music for strings, percussion
and celesta. *Montreal Symphony Orch.;
Dutoit, cond.*
  + ARG 5-6/89: 16
  + DA 4/89: 56
  + Fa 3-4/89: 86
  • Gr 12/88: 987
  + HF 3/89: 119

20651. 421 497-2 (2 discs): DONIZETTI—
Lucrezia Borgia. *Sutherland, Horne,
Aragall, Wixell; with assisting soloists;
London Opera Chorus; National Phil.
Orch. (London); Bonynge, cond.*
  + ARG 3-4/90: 156
  + DA 3/90: 66
  - Gr 3/90: 1678

20652. 421 523-2: HINDEMITH—Mathis
der Maler symphony; Trauermusik;
Symphonic metamorphoses on themes of
Weber . *San Francisco Symphony Orch.;
Blomstedt, cond.*
  + ARG 1-2/89: 56
  + Au 1/89: 166
  • Fa 11-12/88: 201
  + Gr 10/88: 600
  + HF 11/88: 81
  + HPR 3/89: 78
  + MA 11/88: 56
  + SR 12/88: 150
  + St 12/88: 187

20653. 421 524-2: NIELSEN—Symphonies
no. 4-5. *San Francisco Symphony Orch.;
Blomstedt, cond.*
  + ARG 3-4/89: 66
  + DA 10/88: 62
  + Fa 11-12/88: 241
  + Gr 10/88: 611
  + HF 12/88: 68
  + MA 11/88: 56
  + SR 11/88: 144

20654. 421 525-2: SCHUMANN—Carnaval;
Faschingsschwank aus Wien; Allegro in
B minor. *Larrocha, piano.*
  - Fa 11-12/89: 352
  • Gr 6/89: 65
  • SR 9/89: 154

20655. 421 527-2: Music of Chabrier,
Dukas, Satie, Saint-Saëns, Bizet,
Thomas, and Ibert. *Montreal Symphony
Orch.; Dutoit, cond.*
  + ARG 1-2/90: 109

+ DA 8/89: 62
+ Fa 9-10/89: 440
+ Gr 6/89: 48
+ SR 7/89: 96

20656. 421 580-2: BEETHOVEN—
Symphonies no. 4-5. *Chicago Symphony
Orch.; Solti, cond.*
  + ARG 1-2/89: 28
  + DA 3/89: 50
  + Fa 1-2/89: 124
  + Gr 11/88: 772
  + HPR 3/89: 70
  + MA 5/89: 54
  + HYT 1/8/89: H27
  + SR 1/89: 104
  + St 1/89: 207

20657. 421 581-2: POULENC—Sextet;
Clarinet sonata; Flute sonata; Oboe
sonata; Trio for oboe, bassoon, and piano.
*Rogé, piano; Gallois, flute; Bourgue,
oboe; Portal, clarinet; Wallez, bassoon;
Cazalet, horn.*
  - ARG 1-2/90: 74
  + DA 12/89: 76
  + Fa 1-2/90: 262
  + Gr 8/89: 330
  + SR 6/90: 114

20658. 421 593-2: BRUCKNER—Symphony
no. 0; Overture in G minor. *Berlin Radio
Symphony Orch; Chailly, cond.*
  • ARG 5-6/90: 37
  + Fa 5-6/90: 140
  + Gr 1/90: 1322

20659. 421 640-2: BACH—English suites,
BWV 806-811. *Schiff, piano.*
  + DA 8/89: 60
  + Fa 7-8/89: 78
  + Gr 12/88: 1031
  + Ov 6/89: 59
  + SR 8/89: 87
  + St 8/89: 171

20660. 421 643-2: SCHUMANN—
Symphonies no. 3-4. *Cleveland Orch.;
Dohnányi, cond.*
  • ARG 5-6/89: 87 (no. 3)
  + ARG 5-6/89: 87 (no. 4)
  + DA 9/89: 70
  + Fa 7-8/89: 246
  • Gr 2/89: 1298
  + SR 10/89: 146

20661. 421 644-2: ZEMLINSKY—
Symphony in B♭; Psalm 23. *Kammerchor
Ernst Senff; Berlin Radio Symphony
Orch.; Chailly, cond.*
  + ARG 1-2/90: 108
  • Fa 9-10/89: 383
  + Gr 3/89: 1443
  + SR 11/89: 163

20662. 421 713-2: SATIE—Piano music.
Rogé, piano.
  + Fa 11-12/89: 340
  + NYT 4/16/89: H30

20663. 421 714-2: FRANCK—Prelude,
chorale and fugue; Prelude, aria and
finale; Symphonic variations. *Bolet,*

piano; *Concertgebouw Orch.; Chailly,
cond.*
  + ARG 1-2/90: 50
  - Fa 11-12/89: 208
  + Gr 9/89: 450
  + NYT 8/20/89: H32
  + SR 11/89: 156

20664. 421 715-2: TCHAIKOVSKY—Romeo
and Juliet; Capriccio italien; Francesca da
Rimini. *Royal Phil. Orch.; Ashkenazy,
cond.*
  • Fa 11-12/90: 375

20665. 421 716-2: TCHAIKOVSKY—Violin
concerto, op. 35. WIENIAWSKI—Violin
concerto no. 2. *Bell, violin; Cleveland
Orch.; Ashkenazy, cond.*
  + DA 12/89: 95
  + Fa 5-6/89: 334 (2 reviews)
  + Gr 12/88: 1014
  • HF 6/89: 71

20666. 421 717-2: WALTON—Facade 1;
Facade 2. STRAVINSKY—Renard. *Ashcroft,
Irons, narrators; Langridge, Jenkins,
Hammond Stroud, Lloyd, vocalists;
London Sinfonietta; Chailly, cond.*
  + Fa 9-10/89: 373
  + Gr 7/89: 220
  + NYT 6/25/89: H28
  + SR 10/89: 150

20667. 421 718-2 (3 discs): BEETHOVEN—
Piano concertos (complete); Choral
fantasy. *Cleveland Chorus & Orch.;
Ashkenazy, piano & cond.*
  + Fa 6-7/89: 83
  + Gr 3/89: 1408

20668. 421 773-2: BEETHOVEN—
Symphony no. 6; Leonore overture no. 3.
Chicago Symphony Orch.; Solti, cond.
  • ARG 5-6/90: 27 (Symphony)
  + ARG 5-6/90: 27 (Overture)
  • Fa 3-4/90: 141

20669. 421 774-2: SHOSTAKOVICH—Cello
sonata; Moderato for cello and piano.
PROKOFIEV—Cello sonata in C major.
Harrell, cello; Ashkenazy, piano.
  • Fa 7-8/90: 270

20670. 421 814-2: TCHAIKOVSKY—
Symphony no. 4; Francesca da Rimini.
Montreal Symphony Orch.; Dutoit, cond.
  + ARG 9-10/90: 121
  • Fa 7-8/90: 291
  + Gr 2/90: 1471

20671. 421 815-2: STRAUSS—An Alpine
symphony; Don Juan. *San Francisco
Symphony; Blomstedt, cond.*
  + DA 12/90: 94
  + Fa 9-10/90: 395
  + Gr 6/90: 62
  + NYT 10/21/90: H36

20672. 421 816-2: PONCE—Variations and
fugue on La folia. BROUWER—Black
Decameron. TOSAR—Gandhara.
LAMARQUE-PONS—Sonatina. SAVIO—
Batucada. *Fernández, guitar.*

LONDON

+ Au 12/90: 140
+ Fa 7-8/90: 357
• Gr 12/89: 1170

20673. 421 817-2: FAURÉ—Violin sonata no. 1. DEBUSSY—Violin sonata. FRANCK—Violin sonata in A major. *Bell, violin; Thibaudet, piano.*
• ARG 1-2/90: 49
+ Fa 11-12/89: 206
+ Gr 11/89: 915
• SR 12/89: 150

20674. 421 818-2: *Ballet gala.* Music of Minkus, Drigo, Auber, Offenbach, Pugni, Scarlatti, and Thomas. *English Concert Orch.; Bonynge, cond.*
+ Fa 7-8/91: 393
+ Gr 11/90: 1056

20675. 421 831-2: PROKOFIEV—Symphonies no. 1, 5. *Montreal Symphony Orch.; Dutoit, cond.*
+ Fa 11-12/89: 321
+ Gr 7/89: 183
- MA 5/90: 79
+ SR 9/89: 150

20676. 421 849-2 (2 discs): BRITTEN—Albert Herring. *Pears, tenor; with assisting soloists; English Chamber Orch.; Britten, cond.*
+ DA 10/89: 90
+ Fa 11-12/89: 158
+ Gr 6/89: 81
+ MA 9/89: 75
+ St 2/90: 192

20677. 421 855-2 (2 discs): BRITTEN—Prince of the pagodas; Diversions for piano. *Royal Opera House Covent Garden; Katchen, piano; London Symphony Orch.; Britten, cond.*
+ DA 10/89: 90
+ Fa 11-12/89: 158
+ Gr 7/89: 171
+ MA 9/89: 75
+ St 2/90: 192

20678. 421 897-2: Regina Resnik, golden jubilee. *Resnik, mezzo-soprano; with orch. acc.* Recorded 1960-78.
+ Gr 3/93: 100

20679. 421 899-2: MOZART—Opera and concert arias. *Berganza, mezzo-soprano; with orch. acc.* Reissues.
+ Gr 4/93: 119

20680. 425 022-2: MUSSORGSKY (ARR. HOWARTH)—Pictures at an exhibition. SAINT-SAËNS (ARR. REEVE)—Carnival of the animals. *Philip Jones Brass Ensemble.* Reissue.
+ Gr 6/91: 49

20681. 425 030-2: BRAHMS—Rinaldo; Schicksalslied; Nänie. *King, tenor; Ambrosian Chorus; Philharmonia Orch.; Abbado, cond.; Lausanne Pro Arte Choir; Orch. de la Suisse romande; Ansermet, cond.* Reissues.
+ Gr 9/92: 141

20682. 425 033-2: BRUCKNER—Symphony no. 3. *Vienna Phil. Orch.; Böhm, cond.* Reissue.
+ Gr 3/93: 36

20683. 425 036-2: BRUCKNER—Symphony no. 4. *Vienna Phil. Orch.; Böhm, cond.* Reissue.
+ Gr 3/93: 36

20684. 425 037-2: Music of Buononcini, Handel, Scarlatti, Bellini, Tosti, Respighi, and Rossini. *Pavarotti, tenor; Teatro comunale (Bologna) Orch.; Bonynge, cond.* Reissue.
+ ARG 5-6/92: 189
+ Op 4/92: 491

20685. 425 048-2: *Home sweet home.* Music of Benedict, Arditi, Ricci, Tosti, Leoncavallo and others. *Sutherland, soprano; orchestras; Bonynge, cond.* Reissues.
+ ARG 3-4/93: 187

20686. 425 049-2: DEBUSSY—Jeux. RAVEL—Daphnis et Chloé. *Cleveland Orch.; Maazel, cond.* Reissues.
• Gr 9/93: 46

20687. 425 050-2: DEBUSSY—La mer; Nocturnes; Ibéria. *Cleveland Orch.; Maazel, cond.* Reissues.
• Gr 9/93: 46

20688. 425 053-2 (2 discs): BERLIOZ—Roméo et Juliette; Harold in Italy. *Ludwig, mezzo-soprano; Sénéchal, tenor; Ghiaurov, bass; Vernon, viola; Vienna Phil. Orch.; Cleveland Orch.; Maazel, cond.* Reissues.
• Gr 8/93: 66

20689. 425 056-2 (2 discs): BERLIOZ—Requiem; Choral songs. *Riegel, tenor; Cleveland Orch. & Chorus; Maazel, cond.; Schütz Choir of London; Norrington, cond.* Reissues.
• Gr 8/93: 66

20690. 425 063—425 074-2 (11 separate discs): SHOSTAKOVICH—Symphonies (complete). *London Phil. Orch.; Concertgebouw Orch.; Haitink, cond.* Reissues.
• Gr 11/93: 78

20691. 425 080-2: SIBELIUS—Violin concerto. TCHAIKOVSKY—Violin concerto. *Chung, violin; London Symphony Orch.; Previn, cond.* Reissue.
+ ARG 1-2/97: 181
+ Gr 5/95: 58

20692. 425 082-2: BRAHMS—Piano concerto no. 1. FRANCK—Symphonic variations. LITOLFF—Concerto symphonique no. 4: Scherzo. *Curzon, piano; London Symphony Orch.; Szell, cond.; London Phil. Orch.; Boult, cond.* Reissues.
+ Gr 4/95: 50

20693. 425 107-2: PREVIN—Piano concerto; Guitar concerto. *Ashkenazy, piano; Fernandez, guitar; Royal Phil. Orch.; Previn, cond.*
+ Fa 7-8/90: 227
+ Gr 4/90: 1786
+ NYT 6/10/90: H32
+ SR 7/90: 94

20694. 425 108-2: VERDI—Ballet music from the operas. *Teatro comunale orch. (Bologna); Chailly, cond.*
• Fa 3-4/90: 326
+ Gr 1/90: 1340

20695. 425 109-2: SCHUMANN—Phantasiestücke, op. 12; Blumenstück, op. 19; Davidsbündlertänze, op. 6. *Ashkenazy, piano.*
• Fa 11-12/90: 351
+ Gr 4/90: 1840

20696. 425 110-2: BRAHMS—Piano concerto no. 1; Variations on a theme of Schumann. *Schiff, piano; Vienna Phil. Orch.; Solti, piano & cond.*
• ARG 3-4/90: 32
+ Gr 10/89: 646
• HPR Winter/90-91: 63
• MA 5/90: 72 (Concerto)
+ MA 5/90: 72 (Variations)
• NYT 5/27/90: H19
+ SR 4/90: 95
+ St 10/90: 231

20697. 425 111-2: GERSHWIN—American in Paris; Rhapsody in blue; Porgy and Bess: Symphonic portrait; Cuban overture. *Lortie, piano; Montreal Symphony Orch.; Dutoit, cond.*
+ Fa 5-6/90: 169
+ Gr 3/90: 1603

20698. 425 112-2: STRAUSS—Alpine symphony; Till Eulenspiegels lustige Streiche. *Cleveland Orch.; Ashkenazy, cond.*
• Fa 3-4/90: 306
+ Gr 12/89: 1144

20699. 425 169-2 (3 discs): MOZART—Don Giovanni. *Weikl, Price, Burrows, Sass, Bacquier, Popp, Sramek, Moll; London Opera Chorus; London Phil. Orch.; Solti, cond.* Reissue.
+ ARG 11-12/91: 106
• Gr 3/91: 1727
- OQ autumn/91: 213

20700. 425 208-2: *Collected items from a silent dream.* SATIE—Piano music. *Marks, piano.*
- Fa 11-12/90: 339

20701. 425 211-2: WILBRANDT—Transforming V. *Royal Phil. Orch.; Wilbrandt, cond.*
- Fa 11-12/90: 405

20702. 425 221-2: SATIE—Vexations. *Marks, piano.*
+ Gr 7/91: 88

20703. 425 224-2: NYMAN—Prospero's books. *Vocal soloists; Michael Nyman Band; Nyman, cond.*
+ Gr 11/91: 166
+ St 7/92: 245

20704. 425 225-2: *Rags and tangos.* Music of Nazareth, Scott and Lamb. *Rifkin, piano.*
+ Gr 4/92: 120

20705. 425 227-2: NYMAN—Songs. *Lemper, vocalist; Michael Nyman Band.*
+ ARG 7-8/92: 196
+ St 6/93: 251

20706. 425 405-2: BRUCKNER—Symphony no. 9. *Cleveland Orch.; Dohnányi, cond.*
+ ARG 1-2/90: 38
+ Fa 1-2/90: 149
+ Gr 6/89: 26

20707. 425 410-2 (2 discs): DONIZETTI—Maria Stuarda. *Sutherland, Tourangeau, Pavarotti, Soyer, Morris; with assisting soloists; Bologna Teatro; Bonynge, cond.*
+ ARG 11-12/90: 48
- Gr 9/90: 605

20708. 425 417-2 (2 discs): CATALANI—La Wally. *Tebaldi, Marimpietri, Del Monaco, Cappuccilli, Díaz; with assisting soloists; Monte Carlo Opera; Cleva, cond.*
+ ARG 5-6/90: 40
+ Gr 2/90: 1519

20709. 425 430-2: ROSSINI—Arias. *Bartoli, mezzo-soprano; Arnold Schönberg-Chor; Vienna Volksopernorchester; Patanè, cond.*
● ARG 1-2/90: 79
+ Fa 5-6/90: 269
+ Gr 9/89: 538
● ON 1/6/90: 34
+ Op 1/90: 72

20710. 425 432-2: FRANCK—Symphony; Psyché: Excerpts; Djinns, for piano and orchestra. *Berlin Radio Symphony Orch.; Ashkenazy, piano & cond.*
● Fa 11-12/90: 228
+ MA 1/91: 74

20711. 425 448-2: GRIEG—Peer Gynt. *Hägander, soprano & speaker; Malmberg, baritone; San Francisco Symphony Chorus & Orch.; Blomstedt, cond.*
- ARG 5-6/90: 56
+ DA 6/90: 46
+ Fa 7-8/90: 160
+ Gr 3/90: 1658

20712. 425 466-2: MOZART—Piano concertos no. 9, 13. *Schiff, piano; Camerata Academica Salzburg; Végh, cond.*
+ ARG 11-12/90: 85
+ Fa 11-12/90: 287
+ Gr 7/90: 217

20713. 425 481-2 (2 discs): ROSSINI—Semiramide. *Sutherland, Horne, Serge, Rouleau; with assisting soloists; Ambrosian Chorus; London Symphony Orch.; Bonynge, cond.*
+ ARG 3-4/90: 156
+ DA 3/90: 66
+ Gr 2/90: 1526

20714. 425 485-2 (2 discs): DELIBES—Lakmé. *Sutherland, Berbié, Vanzo, Bacquier; with assisting soloists; Monte Carlo Opera; Bonynge, cond.*
● ARG 3-4/90: 155
+ DA 3/90: 66
+ Gr 12/89: 1196

20715. 425 488-2 (2 discs): BELLINI—Norma. *Sutherland, Horne, Alexander, Cross; with assisting soloists; London Symphony Chorus & Orch.; Bonynge, cond.*
● ARG 3-4/90: 156

20716. 425 501-2: LALO—Symphonie espagnole. SAINT-SAËNS—Violin concerto no. 3. *Bell, violin; Montreal Symphony Orch.; Dutoit, cond.*
+ ARG 3-4/90: 99
● Fa 5-6/90: 200
+ Gr 2/90: 1462 (Lalo)
+ Gr 2/90: 1462 (Saint-Saëns)
● MA 9/90: 82

20717. 425 502-2: DEBUSSY—Images for orchestra; Nocturnes. *Montreal Symphony Orch.; Dutoit, cond.*
● Fa 7-8/90: 128
+ Gr 6/90: 47

20718. 425 503-2: TCHAIKOVSKY—Symphony no. 5; Hamlet. *Montreal Symphony Orch.; Dutoit, cond.*
+ Fa 11-12/90: 379
+ Gr 7/90: 232

20719. 425 516-2: TCHAIKOVSKY—Symphony no. 5; Swan Lake: Suite. *Chicago Symphony Orch.; Solti, cond.*
● Fa 7-8/89: 265
+ Gr 5/89: 1738

20720. 425 518-2: DEBUSSY—Preludes for piano: bks. 1, 2 (selections). *Bolet, piano.*
- Fa 5-6/90: 154
- Gr 12/89: 1164

20721. 425 520-2 (3 discs): ROSSINI—Barbiere di Siviglia. *Bartoli, Matteuzzi, Nucci, Fissore, Burchuladze; with assisting soloists; Teatro comunale (Bologna); Patanè, cond.*
● Fa 5-6/90: 269
● Gr 9/89: 537
- NYT 2/25/90: H27
● ON 1/6/90: 34
+ Op 12/89: 1506
+ SR 4/90: 96
● St 11/90: 215

20722. 425 525-2: BEETHOVEN—Symphonies no. 7-8. *Chicago Symphony Orch.; Solti, cond.*

+ DA 8/90: 49
- Fa 9-10/90: 179
● Gr 3/90: 1596

20723. 425 526-2: BRAHMS—String quartets no. 1-2. *Takács Quartet.*
+ Fa 5-6/91: 135
+ Gr 9/90: 555

20724. 425 534-2 (2 discs): PUCCINI—La bohème. *Tebaldi, D'Angelo, Bergonzi, Bastianini, Siepi; with assisting soloists; Accademia di Santa Cecilia; Serafin, cond.*
+ ARG 5-6/90: 90

20725. 425 606-2: FAURÉ—Piano music. *Rogé, piano.*
+ Fa 11-12/93: 235

20726. 425 607-2: NIELSEN—Symphonies no. 1, 6. *San Francisco Symphony Orch.; Blomstedt, cond.*
+ ARG 7-8/90: 80 (no. 1)
● ARG 7-8/90: 80 (no. 6)
+ DA 12/90: 96
- Fa 9-10/90: 319
+ Gr 2/90: 1468
+ MA 7/90: 81
+ SR 6/90: 88

20727. 425 608-2: SCHUMANN—Symphonies no. 1, 4. *Concertgebouw Orch.; Chailly, cond.*
- Fa 3-4/91: 375
● MA 7/91: 88

20728. 425 609-2: SHOSTAKOVICH—Symphonies no. 1, 6. *Royal Phil. Orch.; Ashkenazy, cond.*
+ ARG 11-12/90: 116
+ DA 2/91: 52
● Fa 11-12/90: 355
+ Gr 6/90: 61

20729. 425 612-2: SCHUBERT—Schwanengesang; Herbst; Wanderer an den Mond; Am Fenster; Bei dir allein. *Schreier, tenor; Schiff, piano.*
● Fa 11-12/90: 343
+ Gr 6/90: 98
+ NYT 10/21/90: H33

20730. 425 613-2: BRUCKNER—Symphony no. 4 (Nowak edition). *Concertgebouw Orch.; Chailly, cond.*
+ Fa 7-8/90: 112
● Gr 3/90: 1598

20731. 425 614-2: STRAVINSKY—Pulcinella; Concerto in E♭. GALLO—Trio sonata excerpts. PERGOLESI—Sinfonia for cello and continuo. *Manca di Nissa, soprano; Gordon, tenor; Ostendorf, buss; St. Paul Chamber Orch.; Hogwood, cond.*
+ Fa 9-10/90: 402
+ Gr 6/90: 62

20732. 425 628-2: VERDI—Simon Boccanegra. *Te Kanawa, Aragall, Nucci, Coni, Burchuladze; with assisting soloists; Teatro alla Scala; Solti, cond.*

LONDON

- ARG 5-6/90: 126
- Gr 12/89: 1209
- ON 6/90: 53
+ Op 1/90: 69
- OQ Winter/90-91: 164
- St 2/91: 199

20733. 425 638-2: Schubert—Allegretto, D. 815; Drei Klavierstücke, D. 946; Ländler, D. 790; Impromptus, D. 935. *Schiff, piano.*
+ Au 6/91: 124
+ Fa 11-12/90: 342
- Gr 7/90: 252
+ MA 5/91: 83
+ SR 11/90: 170

20734. 425 651-2 (3 discs): Massenet—Esclarmonde. *Sutherland, Aragall, Quilico, Lloyd; John Alldis Choir; National Phil.; Bonynge, cond. Reissue.*
+ ARG 9-10/91: 96
+ OQ spring/91: 158

20735. 425 675-2: Shostakovich—Symphony no. 8. *Chicago Symphony Orch.; Solti, cond.*
+ ARG 3-4/90: 108
+ DA 4/90: 57
- Fa 3-4/90: 295
- Gr 9/98: 481
- St 4/90: 203

20736. 425 676-2: Bach—Concertos for keyboard and strings (complete). *Schiff, piano & cond.; Chamber Orch. of Europe.*
+ ARG 9-10/91: 37
+ Fa 7-8/91: 98
+ Gr 11/90: 973
+ SR 6/91: 89

20737. 425 693-2: Shostakovich—Symphony no. 4. *Royal Phil. Orch.; Ashkenazy, cond.*
- ARG 5-6/90: 107
+ DA 8/90: 38
+ Fa 7-8/90: 271
- Gr 12/89: 1143

20738. 425 694-2: Bartók—Concerto for orchestra. Lutosławski—Concerto for orchestra. *Cleveland Orch.; Dohnányi, cond.*
- ARG 11-12/90: 24 (Bartók)
+ ARG 11-12/90: 24 (Lutosławski)
- DA 9/90: 46
+ Fa 7-8/90: 81
+ Gr 3/90: 1596
+ MA 11/90: 69

20739. 425 718-2: Mahler—Symphony no. 1. *Cleveland Orch.; Dohnányi, cond.*
- ARG 1-2/91: 62
- Fa 11-12/90: 261
- Gr 7/90: 212

20740. 425 719-2: Mahler—Das klagende Lied. *Dunn, Fassbaender, Hollweg, Schmidt; Berlin Radio Symphony Orch.; Chailly, cond.*
- ARG 11-12/92: 151

+ Fa 7-8/92: 204
+ Gr 2/92: 68

20741. 425 790-2: Mahler—Kindertotenlieder; Lieder eines fahrenden Gesellen; Rückert-Lieder. *Fassbaender, mezzo-soprano; Deutsches Symphony Orch., Berlin; Chailly, cond.*
+ Gr 4/94: 83

20742. 425 791-2: Mozart—Piano concertos no. 24-25. *Schiff, piano; Camerata Academica Salzburg; Végh, cond.*
+ Gr 7/91: 51

20743. 425 792-2: Tchaikovsky—Symphony no. 4; 1812 overture. *Vienna Phil. Orch.; Dohnányi, cond.*
+ Fa 7-8/92: 309
- Gr 2/92: 40

20744. 425 816-2: Cilea—Adriana Lecouvreur. *Sutherland, Bergonzi, Nucci, Sénéchal; Welsh National Opera; Bonynge, cond.*
+ ARG 9-10/91: 61

20745. 425 821-2: Sor—Guitar music. *Fernández, guitar.*
+ Gr 11/91: 134

20746. 425 832-2: Berio—Formazioni; Folk songs; Sinfonia. *Nes, mezzo-soprano; Electric Phoenix; Royal Concertgebouw Orch.; Chailly, cond .*
- Fa 9-10/91: 160

20747. 425 833-2: Wagenaar—Overtures and other pieces. *Concertgebouw Orch.; Chailly, cond.*
+ ARG 9-10/91: 145
+ Fa 9-10/91: 386
+ Gr 6/91: 52

20748. 425 855-2: Mozart—Piano concertos no. 22-23. *Schiff, piano; Camerata Academica Salzburg; Végh, cond.*
+ Fa 11-12/91: 396

20749. 425 856-2: Mozart—Clarinet quintet. Weber—Clarinet quintet. *Members of the Vienna Octet.*
+ Gr 4/92: 100

20750. 425 857-2: Grieg—Peer Gynt: Suites, no. 1-2. Nielsen—Maskarade: Overture; Aladdin: Suite. *San Francisco Symphony Orch.; Blomstedt, cond.*
+ ARG 3-4/92: 64
+ Fa 3-4/92: 200
+ Gr 9/91: 62

20751. 425 858-2: Sibelius—Symphonies no. 4-5. *San Francisco Symphony Orch.; Blomstedt, cond.*
- ARG 1-2/92: 115
+ Fa 3-4/92: 327
+ Gr 7/91: 62

20752. 425 859-2: Chopin—Piano concertos no. 1-2. *Bolet, piano; Montreal*

Symphony Orch.; Dutoit, cond.
- Fa 5-6/91: 154
- Gr 12/90: 1202

20753. 425 860-2: Chausson—Concerto for violin, piano and string quartet. Ravel—Piano trio. *Bell, violin; Thibaudet, piano; Isserlis, cello; Takács Quartet.*
+ ARG 7-8/91: 45
+ Fa 7-8/91: 136
+ Gr 1/91: 1384
+ MA 7/91: 72
+ SR 6/91: 69

20754. 425 861-2: Music of Saint-Saëns, Indy, Roussel, Tansman, Françaix, Poulenc, and Milhaud. *Rogé, piano; Cantin, flute; Bourgue, oboe; Portal, clarinet; Cazalet, horn; Wallez, bassoon.*
+ Fa 7-8/91: 387

20755. 425 862-2: Poulenc—Piano music. *Rogé, piano.*
+ ARG 11-12/91: 135
+ DA 9/91: 60
+ Fa 7-8/91: 252

20756. 425 864-2 (2 discs): Verdi—Rigoletto. *Anderson, Verrett, Pavarotti, Nucci, Ghiaurov; with assisting soloists; Teatro comunale (Bologna); Chailly, cond.*
- ARG 5-6/90: 124
+ DA 4/90: 52
- Fa 5-6/90: 319
+ Gr 1/90: 1375 (Pavarotti)
- Gr 1/90: 1375 (others)
+ MA 7/90: 84
- NYT 2/25/90: H27
- ON 2/17/90: 38
+ Op 1/90: 68
- St 10/90: 249

20757. 425 940-2: Schumann—Kreisleriana; Sonata no. 2; Novelette no. 8. *Ashkenazy, piano.*
+ ARG 9-10/92: 160
+ Fa 11-12/92: 364
+ Gr 4/92: 119

20758. 425 941-2: Strauss—Don Juan; Aus Italien. *Cleveland Orch.; Ashkenazy, cond.*
+ ARG 1-2/92: 120
+ Fa 9-10/91: 365
+ Gr 6/91: 52

20759. 425 942-2: Strauss—Also sprach Zarathustra; Death and transfiguration. *Cleveland Orch.; Ashkenazy, cond.*
- Fa 3-4/91: 395
- Gr 11/90: 995

20760. 425 949-2: Schumann—*Lieder.* Dichterliebe, op. 48; Liederkreis, op. 24: Schöne Wiege meiner Leiden, Mit Myrten und Rosen; Lehn deine Wang an meine Wang, op. 142, no. 2; Mein Wangen rollet langsm, op. 142, no. 4. *Wächter, baritone; Brendel, piano. Reissue.*
+ Gr 6/91: 77

20761. 425 955-2: BEETHOVEN—
Symphony no. 9. *Güden, Wagner,
Dermota, Weber; Vienna Singverein;
Vienna Phil. Orch.; Kleiber, cond.*
+ ARG 11-12/90: 31
+ NYT 5/13/90: H29

20762. 425 956-2: RAVEL—Daphnis et
Chloé; Pavane; Rapsodie espagnole.
*Royal Opera House Covent Garden
Chorus; London Symphony Orch.;
Monteux, cond.*
+ ARG 11-12/90: 101
+ Gr 5/90: 1985
+ MA 11/90: 78
+ NYT 5/13/90: H29

20763. 425 957-2: SCHUBERT—Symphony
no. 9. SCHUMANN—Symphony no. 4.
London Symphony Orch.; Krips, cond.
• ARG 11-12/90: 111
+ Gr 10/90: 747
+ NYT 5/13/90: H29

20764. 425 959-2: STRAUSS—Vier letzte
Lieder; Arabella: Excerpts; Ariadne auf
Naxos: Es git ein Reich; Capriccio: Final
scene. *Della Casa, soprano; with
assisting soloists; Vienna Phil. Orch.;
Böhm, Moralt, Hollreiser, cond.*
+ ARG 11-12/90: 122
+ Gr 4/90: 1881 m.f.
+ NYT 5/13/90: H29

20765. 425 981-2 (3 discs): STRAUSS—Die
Frau ohne Schatten. *Hopf, Rysanek,
Höngen, Schoeffler, Goltz; Vienna State
Opera; Böhm, cond.* Reissue.
+ ARG 1-2/92: 122
+ Gr 10/91: 192

20766. 425 989-2: *Renata Tebaldi: the
early recordings.* Music of Gounod,
Puccini and Verdi. *Tebaldi, soprano;
Accademia di Santa Cecilia; Orch. de la
Suisse romande; Erede, cond.* Recorded
1950-52.
+ Gr 8/91: 78

20767. 425 990-2 (2 discs): J. STRAUSS,
JR.—Fledermaus; Waltzes and polkas.
*Patzak, Gueden, Wagner, Dermota;
Vienna State Opera; Krauss, cond.*
Recorded 1950.
+ ARG 11-12/92: 210
+ Fa 11-12/92: 379

20768. 425 995-2: MAHLER—
Kindertotenlieder. BRAHMS—Liebeslieder
waltzes, op. 52. *Ferrier, alto;
Concertgebouw Orch.; Klemperer, cond;
with Seefried, Patzak, and Günter,
vocalists; Curzon, Gál, pianos.* Recorded
live 1951-52.
+ Fa 11-12/92: 285

20769. 425 997-2: RAVEL—Rapsodie
espagnole; Alborada del gracioso; Pavane
pour une infante défunte; Valses nobles et
sentimentales; Ma mère l'oye: suite;
Daphnis et Chloé; Le tombeau de
Couperin. *L'Orch. de la Suisse romande;
Ansermet, cond.* Reissue.

+ ARG 9-10/92: 147
+ Fa 9-10/92: 325

20770. 427 596-2: DVOŘÁK—Symphony
no. 4; Golden spinning wheel. *London
Symphony Orch.; Kertész, cond.*
+ Fa 9-10/90: 235

20771. 427 597-2: DVOŘÁK—Symphony
no. 5; My home; Hustiská. *London
Symphony Orch.; Kertész, cond.*
+ Fa 9-10/90: 235

20772. 427 598-2: DVOŘÁK—Symphony
no. 6; Symphonic variations. *London
Symphony Orch.; Kertész, cond.*
+ Fa 9-10/90: 235

20773. 427 724-2: DVOŘÁK—Symphony
no. 9; Carnival; Scherzo capriccioso.
London Symphony Orch.; Kertész, cond.
+ Fa 9-10/90: 235

20774. 430 003-2: MARTIN—Concerto for
7 winds, timpani, percussion and string
orchestra; Etudes for string orchestra;
Petite symphonie concertante. *Orch. de la
Suisse romande; Ansermet, cond.*
+ Fa 5-6/91: 211

20775. 430 042-2 (3 discs): PONCHIELLI—
La Gioconda. *Tebaldi, Bergonzi, Merrill,
Horne, Ghiuselev, Domínguez; Santa
Cecila, Rome; Gardelli, cond.*
+ ARG 11-12/91: 135

20776. 430 046-2 (6 discs): DVOŘÁK—
Nine symphonies; My home; Scherzo
capriccioso; In nature's realm; Carnival
overture. *London Symphony Orch.;
Kertész, cond.* Reissues.
+ Fa 7-8/92: 147

20777. 430 075-2: WEILL—
Dreigroschenoper. *Lemper, Milva,
Dernesch, Kollo; with assisting soloists;
Berlin Radio Chamber Choir; Berlin
Radio Sinfonietta; Mauceri, cond.*
• Fa 7-8/90: 317
+ Gr 3/90: 1690
• SR 7/90: 94

20778. 430 077-2: DVOŘÁK—Five
bagatelles for harmonium and strings, op.
47; String quartets no. 12, 14. *Takács
String Quartet; Ormai, harmonium.*
+ Fa 3-4/92: 186

20779. 430 099-2: BRUCKNER—Symphony
no. 4 (ed. Haas). *Cleveland Orch.;
Dohnányi, cond.*
• Gr 10/91: 76

20780. 430 100-2 (32 discs): HAYDN—
Symphonies (Complete). *Philharmonia
Hungarica; Dorati, cond.* Reissue.
+ Gr 6/91: 40

20781. 430 101-2 (3 discs): MOZART—
Così fan tutte. *Lorengar, Berganza,
Davies, Krause, Bacquier, Berbié; Royal
Opera Chorus; London Phil. Orch.; Solti,
cond.* Reissue.

+ ARG 11-12/91: 106
• Gr 3/91: 1722
+ OQ autumn/91: 227

20782. 430 105-2 (2 discs): MOZART—La
clemenza di Tito. *Vienna State Opera;
Kertész, cond.*
+ ARG 11-12/91: 106
+ Fa 9-10/91: 278
+ Gr 5/91: 2061
+ OQ Autumn/91: 245

20783. 430 149-2: BRAHMS—Clarinet
sonatas. SCHUMANN—Fantasiestücke.
Cohen, clarinet; Ashkenazy, piano.
• ARG 5-6/94: 76
• Fa 3-4/94: 146
• Gr 10/93: 64

20784. 430 165-2 (2 discs): MAHLER—
Symphony no. 6. ZEMLINSKY—Six
Maeterlinck songs, op. 13. *Nes, mezzo-
soprano; Concertgebouw Orch.; Chailly,
cond.*
• ARG 3-4/91: 86 (Mahler)
+ ARG 3-4/91: 86 (Zemlinsky)
+ Fa 3-4/91: 263
+ MA 3/91: 78
• SR 5/91: 88
• St 6/91: 247 (Mahler)
+ St 6/91: 247 (Zemlinsky)

20785. 430 168-2: WEILL—The seven
deadly sins; Mahagonny Songspiel. *RIAS
Sinfonietta; Mauceri, cond.*
+ ARG 11-12/91: 170
+ Fa 9-10/91: 395

20786. 430 171-2: DVOŘÁK—Slavonic
dances, op. 46, 72. *Cleveland Orch.;
Dohnányi, cond.*
• ARG 5-6/91: 51
• Fa 5-6/91: 164
• Gr 12/90: 1203
+ MA 7/91: 73

20787. 430 196-2: HÉROLD—La fille mal
gardée: Excerpts (arr. Lanchberry). *Royal
Opera House Orch.; Lanchbery, cond.*
Reissue.
+ Gr 1/94: 48

20788. 430 198-2: MENDELSSOHN—Cello
sonatas no. 1-2; Variations concertantes;
Songs without words. *Harrell, cello;
Canino, piano.*
+ Gr 10/92: 128

20789. 430 199-2: HAYDN—String
quartets, op. 77, op. 103. *Takács String
Quartet.*
+ Fa 9-10/91: 231
+ Gr 5/91: 2033

20790. 430 201-2: BERLIOZ—Symphonie
fantastique; L'invitation á la valse.
Cleveland Orch.; Dohnányi, cond.
+ ARG 9-10/91: 48
• Fa 9-10/91:164
• Gr 5/91: 2005

20791. 430 204-2: DVOŘÁK—Symphony
no. 6. JANACEK—Taras Bulba. *Cleveland*

Orch.; Dohnányi, cond.
+ ARG 11-12/91: 62
+ Gr 7/91: 45

20792. 430 207-2: Mozart—Der Schauspieldirektor; Nozze di Figaro: Overture; Opera and concert arias. *Te Kanawa, Gruberova, Heilmann, Jungwirth; Vienna Phil.Orch.; Pritchard, cond.*
+ Fa 3-4/92: 265
+ Gr 8/91: 85
+ ON 2/1/92: 36

20793. 430 226-2: Verdi—Opera choruses. *Chicago Symphony Chorus & Orch.; Solti, cond.*
+ Fa 5-6/91: 307

20794. 430 227-2: Shostakovich—Symphonies no. 9, 15. *Royal Phil. Orch.; Ashkenazy, cond.*
+ Gr 10/92: 120

20795. 430 228-2: Bruckner—Symphony no. 8 (Nowak edition). *Chicago Symphony Orch.; Solti, cond.*
- ARG 3-4/93: 66
+ Fa 3-4/93: 136
+ Gr 10/92: 56

20796. 430 231-2: Gounod—Symphony no. 1; Petite symphonie. Bizet—L'Arlésienne: Excerpts. *St. Paul Chamber Orch.; Hogwood, cond.*
• ARG 11-12/91: 69
+ Fa 11-12/91: 328
+ Gr 7/91: 41

20797. 430 233-2: Arnold—Guitar concerto. Brouwer—Retrats catalans. Chappell—Caribbean concerto. *Fernandez; English Chamber Orch.; Wordsworth, cond.*
+ ARG 7-8/91: 16
+ Fa 9-10/91: 142
+ Gr 4/91: 1821

20798. 430 234-2 (4 discs): Wagner—Tristan und Isolde. *Nilsson, Uhl, Resnik, Krause; Vienna Phil. Orch.; Solti, cond.* Reissue.
+ ARG 11-12/92: 228
- Gr 6/92: 84

20799. 430 240-2: Debussy—La mer; Jeux; Martye de Saint Sébastien: Excerpts; Prélude à l'après-midi d'un faune. *Montreal Symphony Orch.; Dutoit, cond.*
+ Fa 5-6/91: 160
+ Gr 2/91: 1503
+ SR 4/91: 97

20800. 430 241-2: Elgar—Enigma variations; Falstaff. *Montreal Symphony Orch.; Dutoit, cond.*
• ARG 11-12/91: 64
+ Fa 9-10/91: 210
+ Gr 3/91: 1664

20801. 430 250-2 (2 discs): Verdi—La traviata. *Tebaldi, Poggi, Protti;*

Accademia di Santa Cecilia; Molinari-Pradelli, cond. Reissue.
- Gr 8/91: 78

20802. 430 253-2 (2 discs): Puccini—Manon Lescaut. *Tebaldi, Del Monaco, Boriello, Corena; Accademia di Santa Cecilia; Molinari-Pradelli, cond.* Reissue.
• Gr 8/91: 78

20803. 430 256-2 (2 discs): Cilea—Adriana Lecouvreur. *Tebaldi, Del Monaco, Simionato, Fioravanti; Accademia di Santa Cecilia; Capuana, cond.* Reissue.
+ Gr 8/91: 74

20804. 430 265-2: Telemann—Viola concerto; Don Quichotte; Hamburger Ebb und Flut; Suite in D. *Shingles, viola; Academy of St. Martin-in-the-Fields; Marriner, cond.* Reissue.
+ ARG 3-4/92: 153

20805. 430 278-2: Franck—Symphony in D minor. d'Indy—Symphonie sur un chant montagnard français. *Thibaudet, piano; Montreal Symphony Orch.; Dutoit, cond.*
+ Gr 1/92: 52

20806. 430 279-2: Prokofiev—Romeo and Juliet, op. 64: excerpts. *Montreal Symphony Orch.; Dutoit, cond.*
+ Fa 11-12/91: 443
+ Gr 9/91: 69

20807. 430 280-2: Nielsen—Symphonies no. 2-3. *Kromm, soprano; McMillan, baritone; San Francisco Symphony Orch.; Blomstedt, cond.*
+ ARG 3-4/91: 99
+ Au 7/91: 79
• Fa 5-6/91: 240
+ Gr 8/90: 376

20808. 430 281-2: Brahms—Schicksalslied; Alto rhapsody; Begräbnisgesang; Nänie; Gesang der Parzen. *Nes, mezzo-soprano; San Francisco Symphony Chorus & Orch.; Blomstedt, cond.*
+ ARG 3-4/91: 47
• Fa 3-4/91: 160 (Rhapsody)
+ Fa 3-4/91: 160 (others)
+ Gr 8/90: 399

20809. 430 285-2 (2 discs): Adam—Le corsaire. *English Chamber Orch.; Bonynge, cond.*
+ ARG 1-2/93: 64
□ Fa 3-4/93: 99
+ Gr 10/92: 53

20810. 430 295-2: Janáček—String quartets no. 1-2. Smetana—String quartet no. 1. *Gabrieli Quartet.*
+ Gr 8/92: 46

20811. 430 300-2 (5 discs): Mozart—Concert arias. *Various performers.* Reissues.

+ ARG 3-4/92: 104
+ Gr 10/91: 166

20812. 430 306-2 (4 discs): Mozart—Sonatas for violin and piano. *Goldberg, violin; Lupu, piano.* Reissues.
+ Gr 9/91: 91

20813. 430 320-2: Beethoven—Symphonies no. 1-2. *Chicago Symphony Orch.; Solti, cond.*
+ Fa 3-4/91: 154
• Gr 11/90: 974
+ St 6/91: 235

20814. 430 321-2 (2 discs): Schoenberg—Gurrelieder. *Chor der St. Hedwigs-Kathedrale Berlin; Städtischer Musikverein zu Düsseldorf; Radio-Symphonie-Orch. Berlin; Chailly, cond.*
+ ARG 1-2/92: 103
+ Fa 9-10/91: 341
+ Gr 3/91: 1710

20815. 430 333-2 (5 discs): Mozart—Piano sonatas (complete); Fantasy in C minor, K. 475. *Schiff, piano.* Reissues.
• Gr 2/92: 63

20816. 430 342-2: Brahms—Symphony no. 2. Webern—Im Sommerwind. *Concertgebouw Orch.; Chailly, cond.*
• ARG 5-6/91: 36
+ DA 5/91: 69
+ Fa 3-4/91: 166
+ Gr 12/90: 1198
+ SR 4/91: 84

20817. 430 343-2 (2 disc): Messiaen—Vingt regards sur l'Enfant-Jésus. *Ogdon, piano.* Reissue.
+ Gr 12/91: 100

20818. 430 346-2: Poulenc—Quatre motets pour un temps de pénitence. Stravinsky—Mass; Symphony of psalms; Canticum sacrum. *Vocal soloists; Christ Church Cathedral Choir, Oxford; London Sinfonietta; Philip Jones Ensemble; Preston, cond.* Reissues.
+ Gr 12/91: 117

20819. 430 347-2: Henze—Compases para preguntas ensimismadas; Violin concerto no. 2; Apollo et Hyazinthus. *Soloists; London Sinfonietta; Henze, cond.*
+ Fa 5-6/92: 173

20820. 430 348-2: Glazunov—The seasons; Concert waltzes no. 1-2; Stenka Razin. *Orch. de la Suisse romande; Ansermet, cond.* Reissues.
+ Gr 12/91: 66

20821. 430 350-2: Honegger—Symphonies no. 2, 4; Une cantate de Noël. *Mollet, baritone; Orch. de la Suisse romande; Ansermet, cond.* Reissues.
• Gr 12/91: 72

20822. 430 352-2: Bartók—Music for strings, percussion, and celesta;

Divertimento; The miraculous mandarin. *Chicago Symphony Orch.; Solti, cond.*
+ ARG 1-2/92: 26
+ Fa 9-10/91: 150
+ Gr 5/91: 2004

20823. 430 353-2 (2 discs): BACH—Mass in B minor. *Lott, Otter, Blochwitz, Shimell, Howell; Chicago Symphony Chorus; Chicago Symphony Orch.; Solti, cond.*
+ ARG 11-12/91: 22
- Fa 9-10/91: 145
• Gr 5/91: 2047e

20824. 430 370-2: STRAUSS—Horn concertos no. 1-2; Andante; Interlude from Capriccio; Alphorn; Introduction, theme and variations. *Tuckwell, cond; Royal Phil. Orch.; Ashkenazy, cond.*
+ Fa 11-12/91: 494
• Gr 9/92: 90

20825. 430 372-2 (2 discs): JANÁČEK—The Makropulos case; Lachian dances. *Söderström, Dvorský, Krejčík, Jedlička; Vienna Opera; Mackerras, cond.* Reissue.
+ ARG 3-4/93: 97
+ Gr 10/91: 188

20826. 430 375-2 (2 discs): JANÁČEK—From the house of the dead; Mladi; Nursery rhymes. *Vocal soloists; Vienna State Opera Chorus; Vienna Phil. Orch.; Mackerras, cond.; London Sinfonietta Chorus; London Sinfonietta; Atherton, cond.* Reissue.
+ Gr 10/91: 188

20827. 430 376-2 (2 discs): JANÁČEK—From the house of the dead; Mladi; Rikadla. *Vocal soloists; Vienna State Opera; Mackerras, cond.* Reissue.
+ ARG 5-6/93: 98

20828. 430 381-2 (2 discs): STRAUSS—Die aegyptische Helena. *Jones, Bryant, Kastu, White; Kenneth Jewell Chorale; Detroit Symphony Orch.; Dorati, cond.* Reissue.
• Gr 1/92: 92

20829. 430 384-2 (2 discs): STRAUSS—Ariadne auf Naxos. *L. Price, Kollo, Gruberova, Troyanos; London Phil. Orch.; Solti, cond.* Reissue.
• ARG 11-12/92: 211
• Gr 5/92: 116

20830. 430 387-2 (2 discs): STRAUSS—Arabella. *Della Casa, Gueden, London, Dermota; Vienna Phil. Orch.; Solti, cond.* Reissue.
+ ARG 9-10/92: 167
+ Gr 5/92: 115

20831. 430 391-2: WAGNER—Die Walküre. *Vickers, Brouwenstijn, Ward, London, Nilsson, Gorr; London Symphony Orch.; Leinsdorf, cond.*
• Fa 9-10/92: 389
• Gr 5/92: 117

20832. 430 411-2: STRAUSS—Four last songs; Thirteen songs. *Te Kanawa, soprano; Vienna Phil. Orch.; Solti, cond.*
+ ARG 3-4/92: 144
+ Gr 9/91: 114

20833. 430 413-2: RAVEL—La Valse; Ma mère l'oye; Rapsodie espagnole; Valses nobles et sentimentales. *Cleveland Orch.; Ashkenazy, cond.*
+ Gr 4/92: 72

20834. 430 414-2: SCHUBERT—Die schöne Müllerin. *Schreier, tenor; Schiff, piano.*
+ Fa 9-10/91: 346
+ Gr 5/91: 2055

20835. 430 434-2: DEBUSSY—String quartet. RAVEL—String quartet. *Ysaÿe Quartet.*
+ ARG 5-6/93: 81
+ Fa 3-4/92: 183
• Gr 10/91: 124

20836. 430 473-2 (2 discs): HAYDN—The creation. *Burrowes, Greenberg, Wohlers, Nimsgern, Morris; Chicago Symphony Orch. & Chorus; Solti, cond.* Reissue.
+ Gr 12/91: 112

20837. 430 481-2 (2 discs): *La Tebaldi: opera recital.* Music of Boito, Cilea, Giordano, Mascagni, Ponchielli, Puccini, Refice and Rossini. *Tebaldi, soprano; with various orchestras and conds.* Reissues.
+ Gr 8/91: 78

20838. 430 502-2 (2 discs): DEBUSSY—Pelléas et Mélisande. *Alliot-Lugaz, Henry, Cachemaille, Thau, Carlson, Golfier; Choeurs de l'OSM; Orch. symphonique de Montréal; Dutoit, cond.*
+ ARG 11-12/91: 56
+ Fa 9-10/91: 197
+ Gr 3/91: 1715
• ON 11-91: 40

20839. 430 505-2: SHOSTAKOVICH—Symphony no. 9. BEETHOVEN—Symphony no. 5. *Vienna Phil. Orch.; Solti, cond.* Live recording.
• Fa 11-12/91: 485
+ Gr 7/91: 40

20840. 430 506-2: PROKOFIEV—Alexander Nevsky; Lt. Kijé: Suite. *Nes, mezzo-soprano; Montreal Symphony Orch.; Dutoit, cond.*
• ARG 7-8/92: 199
• Fa 7-8/92: 248
• Gr 12/92: 123
• St 4/93: 287

20841. 430 507-2: TCHAIKOVSKY—Symphony no. 6; Romeo and Juliet. *Montreal Symphony Orch.; Dutoit, cond.*
• ARG 9-10/92: 174
• Fa 11-12/92: 387
• Gr 5/93: 52

20842. 430 509-2: ORFF—Carmina burana. *Dawson, Daniecki, McMillan;*

San Francisco Symphony Orch. & Chorus; Blomstedt, cond.
+ ARG 9-10/93: 166
+ Gr 12/91: 117

20843. 430 510-2: MOZART—Piano concertos no. 20-21. *Schiff, piano; Camerata Academica Salzburg; Végh, cond.*
+ Fa 3-4/92: 250
+ Gr 10/91: 93

20844. 430 512-2: LISZT—Songs. *Fassbaender, mezzo-soprano; Thibaudet, piano.*
+ ARG 1-2/93: 113
+ Gr 9/92: 147

20845. 430 513-2: MOZART—Arias. *Bartoli, soprano; Vienna Chamber Orch.; Fischer, cond.*
+ ARG 3-4/92: 104
+ Fa 7-8/92: 222
+ Gr 12/91: 133
• ON 12/5/92: 51
+ Op 3/92: 377

20846. 430 514-2: MOZART—Lieder. *Schreier, tenor; Schiff, piano.*
+ Gr 8/92: 62

20847. 430 515-2: BEETHOVEN—Symphonies no. 1, 3. *San Francisco Symphony Orch.; Blomstedt, cond.*
+ Fa 7-8/92: 116
+ Gr 12/91: 64

20848. 430 516-2: SCHUBERT—Octet; Minuet and finale. *Vienna Octet; Vienna Wind Soloists.*
+ Gr 2/93: 54

20849. 430 517-2: MOZART—Piano concertos no. 5-6; Rondo, K. 382. *Schiff, piano; Salzburg Mozarteum Camerata Academica; Végh, cond.*
+ ARG 3-4/93: 117
+ Fa 3-4/93: 236
+ Gr 8/92: 38

20850. 430 518-2: ROSSINI—Giovanna d'Arco; Songs. *Bartoli, mezzo-soprano; Spencer, piano.*
• Fa 9-10/91: 326
+ Gr 4/91: 1886
• ON 2/29/92: 35

20851. 430 529-2: BRAHMS—Piano quintet; Quartet no. 3. *Schiff, piano; Takács String Quartet.*
+ ARG 7-8/92: 106
+ Fa 1-2/93: 117
• Gr 11/91: 112

20852. 430 542-2: GERSHWIN—Piano concerto; Three preludes. COPLAND-BERNSTEIN EL SALÓN MÉXICO; PIANO BLUES NO. 3. BARBER—Ballade. *Jablonski, piano; Royal Phil. Orch.; Ashkenazy, cond.*
+ ARG 3-4/92: 61
• Fa 3-4/92: 192
• Gr 7/91:46

LONDON

20853. 430 549-2 (4 discs): MEYERBEER—Les Huguenots. *Sutherland, Arroyo, Tourangeau, Vrenios, Ghiuselev, Bacquier, Cossa; Ambrosian Opera Chorus; Philharmonia Orch.; Bonynge, cond.*
+ ARG 1-2/92: 78

20854. 430 555-2: BRAHMS—Violin sonatas no. 1-3; Scherzo in C minor. *Amoyal, violin; Rogé, piano.*
+ Gr 11/91: 112

20855. 430 628-2 (2 discs): VILLA-LOBOS—The five piano concertos. *Ortiz, piano; Royal Phil. Orch.; Gómez Martínez, cond.*
+ ARG 11-12/92: 226
+ Fa 11-12/92: 397
+ Gr 5/92: 57

20856. 430 636-2 (2 discs): MASSENET—Don Quichotte; Scènes alsaciennes. *Ghiaurov, Bacquier, Crespin; Orch. de la Suisse romande; Kord, cond.; National Phil. Orch.; Bonynge, cond. Reissues.*
+ ARG 3-4/92: 100
+ Gr 4/92: 156

20857. 430 694-2 (2 discs): VERDI—Il trovatore. *Pavarotti, Banaudi, Nucci, Verrett, Ellero d'Artegna, Frittoli, De Palma, Scaltriti, Facini; Maggio Musicale Fiorentino; Mehta, cond. Recorded 1990.*
● ARG 3-4/96: 201
- Fa 3-4/96: 311
- Fi 3/96: 119
● Gr 7/95: 118
● Op 7/95: 873

20858. 430 697-2: VIVALDI—Four seasons; Concertos. *Gulli, violin; Filarmonici del Teatro Comunale di Bologna; Chailly, cond.*
+ Gr 5/92: 58

20859. 430 698-2: SCHNITTKE—Concerti grossi, no. 3-4; Symphony no. 5. *Soloists; Concertgebouw Orch.; Chailly, cond.*
+ ARG 11-12/92: 195
+ Fa 11-12/92: 355
+ Gr 2/92: 38

20860. 430 723-2: RESPIGHI—La boutique fantasque. CHOPIN—Les sylphides. *National Phil. Orch.; Bonynge, cond. Reissue.*
+ ARG 9-10/92: 149

20861. 430 729-2: RESPIGHI—Roman trilogy. *Montreal Symphony Orch.; Dutoit, cond. Reissue.*
+ Gr 8/94: 54

20862. 430 738-2: PROKOFIEV—Alexander Nevsky. TCHAIKOVSKY—Francesca da Rimini. *Arkhipova, soprano; Cleveland Orch.; Chailly, cond. Reissue.*
● Gr 12/92: 123

20863. 430 742-2: *Great opera choruses.* Music of Boito, Verdi, Beethoven,

Bellini, and Wagner. *Various performers.*
+ ARG 9-10/92: 205

20864. 430 745-2: TCHAIKOVSKY—Symphony no. 4; Romeo and Juliet. *Chicago Symphony Orch.; Solti, cond.*
+ ARG 11-12/92: 220

20865. 430 771-2: BRAHMS—Piano sonata no. 3; Handel variations. *Ashkenazy, piano.*
- ARG 1-2/93: 81
● Fa 1-2/93: 116
● Gr 7/92: 77

20866. 430 772-2: MOZART—String quintets K. 515-516; Adagio and fugue, K. 546. *Takács String Quartet; Pauk, viola.*
● ARG 11-12/92: 171
+ Fa 11-12/92: 312
● Gr 5/92: 66

20867. 430 778-2 (3 discs): SIBELIUS—Symphonies. *Vienna Phil. Orch.; Maazel, cond. Reissues.*
+ Gr 2/92: 40

20868. 430 782-2 (4 discs): PROKOFIEV—Symphonies (complete); Russian overture; Scythian suite. *London Phil. Orch.; London Symphony Orch.; Weller, cond.*
+ ARG 7-8/92: 200

20869. 430 839-2. RACHMANINOFF—Prelude in G minor. FALLA—Dance from La vida breve. ALBENIZ—Granada. SARASATE—Zapateado. PAGANINI—Caprice. PARADIS—Sicilienne. BACH—Partita in D minor. *Hall, guitar.*
+ ARG 5-6/92: 162
● Gr 5/92: 79

20870. 430 841-2: BRUCKNER—Symphony no. 7. *Cleveland Orch.; Dohnanyi, cond.*
+ ARG 9-10/92: 91
+ Fa 11-12/92: 212
+ Gr 10/92: 56

20871. 430 843-2: SCRIABIN—Rêverie; Symphony no. 3 "Le divin poème"; Le poème de l'extase. *Berlin Radio Symphony Orch.; Ashkenazy, cond.*
+ Gr 11/91: 101

20872. 430 844-2: SHOSTAKOVICH—Symphony no. 10. LUTOSŁAWSKI—Musique funèbre. *Cleveland Orch.; Dohnányi, cond.*
- ARG 3-4/93: 138
● Fa 3-4/93: 292
+ Gr 9/92: 90

20873. 432 508-2: STRAUSS—Don Juan; Metamorphosen; Tod und Verklärung. *Vienna Philh. Orch.; Dohnányi, cond.*
+ ARG 11-12/92: 212
● Fa 11-12/92: 380
● Gr 6/92: 49

20874. 433 000-2 (2 discs): GLAZUNOV—Seasons. TCHAIKOVSKY—Nutcracker.

Royal Phil. Orch.; Ashkenazy, cond.
● ARG 3-4/93: 147
+ Fa 3-4/93: 311
+ Gr 4/92: 48
- St 8/93: 191

20875. 433 028-2: SHOSTAKOVICH—Symphony no. 10; Chamber symphony, op. 110. *Royal Phil. Orch.; Ashkenazy, cond.*
+ ARG 5-6/92: 134
● Gr 1/92: 60

20876. 433 030-2 (2 discs): ROSSINI—La Cenerentola. *Simionato, Benelli, Bruscantini, Montarsolo; Maggio Musicale, Florence; De Fabritiis, cond. Reissue.*
+ Gr 5/92: 113
● OQ summer 93: 204

20877. 433 033-2: GIORDANO—Fedora. ZANDONAI—Francesca da Rimini: excerpts. *Olivero, Del Monaco; Monte Carlo Opera; Gardelli, Rescigno, conds.*
+ ARG 5-6/92: 63
+ Gr 3/92: 110

20878. 433 036-2 (2 discs): DONIZETTI—Don Pasquale. CIMAROSA—Il maestro di capella. *Various performers. Reissues.*
● Gr 10/92: 175

20879. 433 039-2 (2 discs): VERDI—Macbeth. *Taddei, Nilsson, Foiani, Prevedi; Accademia di Santa Cecilia, Rome; Schippers, cond. Reissue.*
● Gr 5/92: 117

20880. 433 042-2: MOZART—Piano concertos no. 8, 11. *Schiff, piano; Camerata Academica Salzburg; Végh, cond.*
+ Fa 9-10/93: 219
+ Gr 5/93: 48

20881. 433 055-2: SHOSTAKOVICH—Twenty-four preludes, op. 34. ALKAN—Twenty-five preludes, op. 31. *Mustonen, piano.*
+ ARG 7-8/92: 82
+ Fa 3-4/92: 234
+ Gr 10/91: 144
+ St 7/92: 183

20882. 433 072-2: SCHUBERT—Symphonies no. 5, 8; Rosamunde overture. *San Francisco Symphony Orch.; Blomstedt, cond.*
● ARG 9-10/92: 157
+ Fa 11-12/92: 361
● Gr 5/92: 48

20883. 433 073-2: SHOSTAKOVICH—Symphony no. 10. *Chicago Symphony Orch.; Solti, cond.*
- ARG 11-12/92: 203
- Fa 11-12/92: 372
● Gr 6/92: 48
+ St 5/93: 183

20884. 433 074-2: ROSSINI—Overtures to Scala di seta; Semiramide; Gazza ladra;

William Tell; Barber of Seville; Italiana in Algeri; Signor Bruschino; Cenerentola. *Montreal Symphony Orch.; Dutoit, cond.*
- ARG 9-10/92: 151
+ Fa 11-12/92: 344
- Gr 10/92: 116

20885. 433 075-2: LISZT—Piano concertos no. 1-2. Hungarian fantasy; Totentanz. *Thibaudet, piano; Montreal Symphony Orch.; Dutoit, cond.*
- ARG 11-12/92: 147
+ Fa 7-8/92: 201
+ Gr 1/92: 55

20886. 433 076-2: Music of Berio, Britten, Brouwer, Takemitsu, Torres, and Yocoh. *Fernández, piano.*
+ Gr 7/93: 68

20887. 433 078-2 (6 discs): SHOSTAKOVICH—String quartets (Complete). *Fitzwilliam String Quartet.* Reissues.
+ Gr 6/92: 60

20888. 433 079-2: STRAVINSKY— Divertimento from Fairy's kiss; Suites, no. 1-2; Octet; Suite from L'histoire du soldat. *London Sinfonietta; Chailly, cond.* Reissues.
+ Gr 5/92: 57

20889. 433 081-2: HINDEMITH—Violin concerto; Symphonic metamorphoses on themes of Carl Maria von Weber; Mathis der Maler: symphony. *D. Oistrakh, violin; London Symphony Orch.; Hindemith, Abbado, conds.; Orch. de la Suisse romande; Kletzki, cond.* Reissues.
- Fa 11-12/92: 259
+ Gr 9/92: 72

20890. 433 082-2: BARTÓK—Duke Bluebeard's castle. *Sass, Kováts, Sztankay; London Phil. Orch.; Solti, cond.* Reissue.
+ Gr 5/92: 105

20891. 433 083-2: SCHOENBERG—Suite, op. 29; Wind quintet. *Members of the London Sinfonietta; Atherton, cond.* Reissues.
+ Gr 6/92: 60

20892. 433 086-2: MOZART—Piano concertos no. 23, 24. *Curzon, piano; London Symphony Orch.; Kertész, cond.* Reissue.
+ ARG 7-8/92: 181

20893. 433 087-2: ADAM—Giselle. SAINT-SAËNS—Danse macabre; Le rouet d'Omphale. BIZET—Jeux d'enfants. *Paris Conservatory Orch.; Martinon, cond.* Reissue.
+ ARG 9-10/92: 75

20894. 433 151-2: BRAHMS—Symphony no. 4. SCHOENBERG—Five pieces for orchestra, op. 16. *Concertgebouw Orch.; Chailly, cond.*
- ARG 11-12/92: 96

+ Fa 11-12/92: 210
- Gr 6/92: 38

20895. 433 181-2: RACHMANINOFF— Symphony no. 3; Symphonic dances. *Philadelphia Orch.; Dutoit, cond.*
+ ARG 7-8/92: 203
+ Fa 7-8/92: 253
- Gr 4/92: 72
- St 12/92: 245

20896. 433 182-2: BRAHMS—Lieder. *Holl, bass-baritone; Schiff, piano.*
+ Gr 6/93: 82

20897. 433 200-2 (2 discs): BRITTEN— Owen Wingrave; Hölderlin fragments; The poet's echo. *Vocal soloists; Wandsworth School Boys Choir; English Chamber Orch.; Britten, piano & cond.; Pears, tenor; Vishnevskaya, soprano; Rostropovich, piano.* Reissues.
+ Gr 11/93: 138
+ ON 2/19/94: 32

20898. 433 210-2 (2 discs): MOZART—Die Zauberflöte. *Ziesak, Jo, Heilmann, Kraus, Moll; Vienna Phil. Orch.; Solti, cond.*
- Fa 3-4/92: 272
+ Gr 10/91: 188
+ ON 6/92: 48
+ Op 10/91: 1239
+ St 8/92: 187

20899. 433 313-2 (2 discs): BACH— French suites. *Schiff, piano.*
- Gr 10/93: 76

20900. 433 316-2: Verismo arias. Music of Cilea, Giordano, Catalani, Alfano, Zandonai, Mascagni, and Puccini. *Freni, soprano; Teatro La Fenice, Venice; R. Abbado, cond.*
+ Gr 9/92: 164
+ ON 6/93: 44

20901. 433 318-2: BRUCKNER—Symphony no. 5. *Cleveland Orch.; Dohnányi, cond.*
+ ARG 1-2/94: 89
+ Fa 1-2/94: 149
+ Gr 8/93: 26

20902. 433 319-2: SHOSTAKOVICH—Suite on verses of Michelangelo; Four verses of Captain Lebyadkin. *Fischer-Dieskau, baritone; Berlin Radio Symphony Orch.; Ashkenazy, cond.*
+ ARG 9-10/93: 190
+ Fa 9-10/93: 287
+ Gr 7/93: 82

20903. 433 329-2: MAHLER—Symphony no. 5. *Chicago Symphony Orch.; Solti, cond.* Recorded live 1990.
- Gr 1/92: 55

20904. 433 371-2 (2 discs): WEILL— Street scene. *Barstow, Réaux, Hubbard, Ramey; Scottish Opera; Mauceri, cond.*
+ ARG 5-6/92: 157
+ Fa 5-6/92: 287
+ Op 11/91: 1370

20905. 433 374-2: MOZART—Concertos for piano and orchestra no. 15, 16. *Schiff, piano; Camerata Academica Salzburg; Végh, cond.*
- ARG 3-4/93: 117
+ Fa 3-4/93: 236
+ Gr 10/92: 113

20906. 433 396-2: HAYDN—Symphonies no. 97-98. *London Phil. Orch.; Solti, cond.*
+ ARG 5-6/93: 93
- Fa 3-4/93: 187
+ Gr 10/92: 62

20907. 433 403-2: BEETHOVEN— Symphony no. 7. DVOŘÁK—Symphony no. 7. *London Symphony Orch.; Monteux, cond.* Reissues.
+ Fa 9-10/93: 122
+ Gr 4/93: 41

20908. 433 486-2: SCHUMANN— Symphonies no. 2-3. *Concertgebouw Orch.; Chailly, cond.*
- Gr 9/93: 60

20909. 433 515-2 (2 discs): RAVEL— Complete works for solo piano. *Thibaudet, piano.*
+ ARG 5-6/93: 123
+ Fa 3-4/93: 256
+ Gr 11/92: 156

20910. 433 519-2: Music of Saint-Saëns, Massenet, Sarasate, Chausson and Ravel. *Bell, violin; Royal Phil. Orch.; Litton, cond.*
- ARG 9-10/92: 195
+ Fa 5-6/92: 329
+ Gr 1/92: 66

20911. 433 548-2: BRAHMS—Symphony no. 3; Variations on a theme of Haydn. DVOŘÁK—Carnival overture. *Cleveland Orch.; Ashkenazy, cond.*
+ Fa 11-12/94: 188
- Gr 6/94: 44

20912. 433 549-2: BRAHMS—Symphony no. 2. DVOŘÁK—Serenade for strings. *Cleveland Orch.; Ashkenazy, cond.*
- ARG 5-6/94: 78
- Gr 10/93: 44

20913. 433 625-2: Stokowski conducts. Music of Tchaikovsky, Mussorgsky, Borodin and Rimsky-Korsakov. *Various orchs.; Stokowski, cond.* Reissues.
+ Gr 4/92: 90

20914. 433 650—433 651-2 (2 separate discs): *Shura Cherkassky live, vol. 3-4.* Music of Chopin, Paderewski, Tchaikowsky, Shostakovich, and others. *Cherkassky, piano.*
+ ARG 5-6/95: 215 (v.4)
+ Fa 3-4/94: 408 (v.3)
+ Gr 6/93: 78

20915. 433 652-2: *Shura Cherkassky live, vol. 5.* SCHUMANN—Piano music.

LONDON

Cherkassky, piano. Recorded 1970-91.
+ Gr 1/95: 81

20916. 433 653-2: Music of Schubert, Scriabin, Rubinstein, Chopin, Albeniz, and Rachmaninoff. *Cherkassky, piano.* Recorded live.
+ ARG 7-8/92: 265
+ Gr 10/91: 146

20917. 433 654-2: *Shura Cherkassky: 80th birthday recital at Carnegie Hall.* Music of Bach, Schumann, Chopin, Ives, J. Hofmann, Tchaikovsky, and M. Gould. *Cherkassky, piano.* Recorded live 1991.
+ ARG 3-4/93: 169
+ Fa 3-4/93: 377
+ Gr 1/93: 50
+ St 8/93: 194

20918. 433 656-2: *Shura Cherkassky live, vol. 5.* Liszt—Piano music. *Cherkassky, piano.* Recorded 1970-91.
+ Gr 1/95: 81

20919. 433 657, 433 655-2 (2 separate discs): *Shura Cherkassky live, vol. 7-8.* Music of Scriabin, Stravinsky, Berg, and others. *Cherkassky, piano.* Recorded 1973-1989.
+ Gr 2/96: 80

20920. 433 660-2: Martinů—Sinfonietta "La jolla"; La revue de cuisine; Toccata e due canzoni; Merry Christmas 1941; Tre ricercari. *St. Paul Chamber Orch.; Hogwood, cond.*
+ ARG 7-8/93: 120
+ Fa 7-8/93: 176
+ Gr 3/93: 48

20921. 433 668-2: Tippett—Byzantium; Symphony no. 4. *Robinson, soprano; Chicago Symphony Orch.; Solti, cond.* Reissue.
+ ARG 7-8/93: 171
+ Fa 7-8/93: 260
+ Gr 4/93: 112

20922. 433 669-2 (2 discs): Verdi—Otello. *Pavarotti, Te Kanawa, Nucci; Chicago Symphony Orch.; Solti, cond.*
● ARG 3-4/92: 155
● Fa 5-6/92: 271
+ Gr 11/91: 161
● ON 2/1/92: 37
+ Op 12/91: 1494

20923. 433 680-2: Vivaldi—The four seasons; 2 other concertos. *Philharmonia Orch.; Stokowski, cond.*
+ ARG 9-10/92: 178

20924. 433 687-2: Tchaikovsky—Symphony no. 5; Romeo and Juliet. *Philharmonia Orch.; Orch. de la Suisse romande; Stokowski, cond.* Reissues.
+ ARG 1-2/93: 157

20925. 433 688-2: Mozart—Requiem. *Augér, Bartoli, Cole, Pape; Vienna Phil. Orch.; Solti, cond.* Recorded live 1991.
- ARG 9-10/92: 137

- Fa 7-8/92: 234
+ Gr 3/92: 104
- St 2/93: 197

20926. 433 694-2: Mozart—String quartets K. 458, 465, 590. *Musikverein Quartet.*
● Gr 10/92: 131

20927. 433 700-2: Messager—Les deux pigeons. *Welsh National Opera Orch.; Bonynge, cond.*
● ARG 1-2/94: 124
+ Fa 1-2/94: 237
+ Gr 10/93: 46

20928. 433 701-2, 436 832-2 (2 separate discs): Rossini—String sonatas. *Bologna Teatro Comunale Orch.; Chailly, cond.*
+ Gr 2/93: 47
● Gr 8/94: 56

20929. 433 702-2: Shostakovich—Suites for jazz no. 1-2; Concerto no. 1 for piano, trumpet, and strings; Tahiti trot. *Brautigam, piano; Masseurs, trumpet; Concertgebouw Orch.; Chailly, cond.*
+ ARG 7-8/93: 156
+ Fa 7-8/93: 243
● Gr 3/93: 52

20930. 433 703-2: Walton—Symphonies no. 1-2. *Royal Phil. Orch.; Ashkenazy, cond.*
● ARG 7-8/93: 178
+ Fa 9-10/93: 329
+ Gr 4/93: 64

20931. 433 706-2 (3 discs): Bellini—Excerpts from Beatrice di Tenda, Norma, I Puritani and La sonnambula. *Sutherland, soprano; with supporting soloists; London Symphony Orch.; Bonynge, cond.* Reissues.
+ ARG 3-4/93: 59
● Gr 2/93: 74

20932. 433 713-2: Berlioz—Symphonie fantastique; Corsaire; Roman carnival overture; Dance of the sylphs and March from The damnation of Faust. *Orch. de la Suisse romande; Ansermet, cond.*
● ARG 11-12/92: 88

20933. 433 716-2: Ravel—Bolero; Rapsodie espagnole; Pavane; Mother Goose; Valses nobles et sentimentales. *Orch. de la Suisse romande; Ansermet, cond.*
+ ARG 11-12/92: 183

20934. 433 717-2: Ravel—Daphnis and Chloe; La valse; Alborada del gracioso. *Orch. de la Suisse romande; Ansermet, cond.*
+ ARG 11-12/92: 183

20935. 433 719-2: Roussel—Symphonies, no. 3-4; The spider's feast. *Orch. de la Suisse romande; Ansermet, cond.* Reissue.
+ ARG 1-2/93: 140

20936. 433 727-2: Mozart—Clarinet concerto. Spohr—Clarinet concerto no. 1. Weber—Clarinet concerto no. 2. *De Peyer, clarinet; London Symphony Orch.; Maag, cond.* Reissues.
+ Gr 7/93: 45

20937. 433 728-2: Bach—Motets. *Louis Halsey Singers; Halsey, cond.; Lumsden, organ.* Reissue.
● Gr 6/93: 81

20938. 433 729-2: Mendelssohn—Concerto for two pianos in E major; Piano concerto in A minor; String symphony no. 12. *Ogdon, Lucas, pianos; Academy of St. Martin-in-the-Fields; Marriner, cond.* Reissues.
+ Gr 5/93: 48

20939. 433 731-2: The play of Daniel. *Pro Cantione Antiqua; Landini Consort; Brown, cond.* Reissue.
+ Gr 4/93: 102

20940. 433 733-2: Rameau—Temple de la gloire: Suites. Campra—Europe galante: Suites. *English Chamber Orch.; Leppard, cond.* Reissues.
● Gr 6/93: 52

20941. 433 734-2 (2 discs): Vivaldi—La cetra: concertos op. 9. *Academy of St. Martin-in-the-Fields; Brown, cond.* Reissue.
+ Gr 8/93: 42

20942. 433 737-2 (2 discs): Handel—L'Allegro, ed il penseroso; Cantatas. *Vocal soloists; St. Anthony Singers; Philomusica of London; Willcocks, cond.; English Chamber Orch.; Leppard, cond.* Reissues.
+ Gr 8/93: 70

20943. 433 749-2: Mozart—Mass in C minor, K. 427. *Norberg-Schulz, soprano; Otter, mezzo-soprano; Heilmann, tenor; Pape, bass; Vienna State Opera Concert Choir; Vienna Phil. Orch.; Solti, cond.*
● Gr 2/92: 68
- St 12/92: 241

20944. 433 762-2 (2 discs): Puccini—Turandot. *Borkh, Tebaldi, Corena, Del Monaco; Accademia di Santa Cecilia Chorus & Orch.; Erede, cond.* Reissue.
● Gr 8/93: 82

20945. 433 770-2 (2 discs): Ponchielli—La Gioconda. *Cerquetti, Simionato, Del Monaco, Siepi; Maggio Musicale Fiorentino; Gavazzeni, cond.* Reissue.
+ Gr 9/93: 110

20946. 433 802-2 (10 discs): Kathleen Ferrier edition. *Ferrier, contralto; with assisting artists.* Mono.
+ Gr 6/92: 78

20947. 433 809-2: Hindemith—Concert music for brass and strings, op. 50; Der Schwanendreher; Noblissima visione.

Walther, viola; San Francisco Symphony Orch.; Blomstedt, cond.
+ ARG 7-8/93: 101
+ Fa 7-8/93: 153
+ Gr 4/93: 48
+ St 10/93: 270

20948. 433 810-2: SIBELIUS—Symphony no. 2; Tapiola; Valse triste. *San Francisco Symphony Orch.; Blomstedt, cond.*
+ ARG 1-2/93: 151
+ Fa 1-2/93: 242
+ Gr 3/93: 54

20949. 433 811-2: MENDELSSOHN— Symphonies no. 3-4. *San Francisco Symphony Orch.; Blomstedt, cond.*
+ ARG 7-8/93: 125
+ Fa 7-8/93: 180
+ Gr 4/93: 55

20950. 433 812-2: BLITZSTEIN—Regina. *Ciesinski, Réaux, Kuebler, Maddalena, Ramey; Scottish Opera; Mauceri, cond.*
+ ARG 3-4/93: 60
• Fa 3-4/93: 125
+ Gr 3/93: 92
• ON 1/30/93: 36
+ Op 3/93: 374
+ St 5/93: 175

20951. 433 816-2: HINDEMITH— Kammermusiken. *Concertgebouw Orch.; Chailly, cond.; other instrumentalists.*
+ ARG 5-6/93: 94
+ Fa 5-6/93: 222
+ Gr 11/92: 62
+ St 10/93: 270

20952. 433 819-2: BRUCKNER—Symphony no. 5. *Concertgebouw Orch.; Chailly, cond.*
+ ARG 5-6/94: 82
+ Gr 11/93: 65

20953. 433 829-2: STRAVINSKY—Le sacre du printemps; Scherzo à la russe; Concerto for 2 pianos; Sonata for 2 pianos. *Ashkenazy, Gavrilov, pianos.*
+ Fa 7-8/93: 251
+ Gr 2/93: 54

20954. 433 849-2: BRAHMS—Handel variations; Rhapsodies, op. 79; Ballades, op. 10. *Rogé, piano.*
- ARG 9-10/93: 101
+ Fa 9-10/93: 137
+ Gr 4/93: 84

20955. 433 850-2: BRAHMS—Horn trio. SCHUMANN—Andante and variations; Andante and allegro. *Vlatković, horn; Maile, violin; G. & M. Doderer, cellos; Vl. & Vo. Ashkenazy, pianos.*
+ Gr 10/93: 64

20956. 433 851-2 (2 discs): MASSENET— Le roi de Lahore. *Sutherland, Lima, Milnes, Ghiaurov; National Phil. Orch.; Bonynge, cond.* Reissue.
+ Gr 2/93: 75

20957. 433 854-2 (2 discs): VERDI—I Masnadieri. *Sutherland, Bonisolli, Manuguerra, Ramey; Welsh National Opera; Bonynge, cond.* Reissue.
• Gr 7/93: 90

20958. 433 857-2 (3 discs): THOMAS— Hamlet. *Sutherland, Conrad, Milnes, Winbergh; Welsh National Opera; Bonynge, cond.* Reissue.
• Gr 5/93: 109

20959. 435 081-2: RAVEL—Piano music. DEBUSSY—Isle joyeuse. SCRIABIN—Piano music. *Ashkenazy, piano.* Reissue.
+ Gr 10/94: 160

20960. 436 075-2: ROSSINI—Heroines. Music from Zelmira, Maometto II, La donna del lago, Elisabetta, Regina d'Inghilterra, and Semiramide. *Bartoli, mezzo-soprano; Chorus & Orch. of the Teatro La Fenice, Venice; I. Marin, cond.*
+ Gr 2/92: 78
+ ON 12/5/92: 51
+ Op 4/92: 489

20961. 436 076-2: BEETHOVEN—Piano sonatas no. 30-32. *Ashkenazy, piano.*
+ ARG 5-6/93: 68
+ Fa 3-4/93: 120
• Gr 2/93: 60

20962. 436 077-2: RAMEAU—Pièces de clavecin. SCARLATTI—Sonatas. *Fernandez, guitar.*
• Gr 5/94: 87

20963. 436 115-2: SOLER—Concertos for two organs. *Hurford, Trotter, organs.*
+ Gr 6/93: 70

20964. 436 116-2: Liturgical music from Segovia. *Ensemble Alfonso el Sabio; Virumbrales, cond.*
• ARG 5-6/93: 172
• EM 8/93: 491

20965. 436 122-2: SCHUBERT— Winterreise. *Schreier, tenor; Schiff, piano.*
• ARG 9-10/94: 196
+ Fa 9-10/94: 330
+ Gr 5/94: 100

20966. 436 123-2: SCHUMANN— Liederkreis, op. 39; Songs. *Holl, bass; Schiff, piano.*
+ Gr 7/94: 100

20967. 436 129-2: BRUCKNER—Symphony no. 6 (Nowak edition). WAGNER— Siegfried Idyll. *San Francisco Symphony Orch.; Blomstedt, cond.*
• ARG 11-12/93: 88
- Fa 11-12/93: 201
• Gr 5/93: 40

20968. 436 153-2: BRUCKNER—Symphony no. 6. BACH-WEBERN—Ricercar a 6. *Cleveland Orch.; Dohnányi, cond.*
• ARG 9-10/94: 112

+ Fa 9-10/94: 159
+ Gr 10/94: 100

20969. 436 154-2: BRUCKNER—Symphony no. 2. *Concertgebouw Orch.; Chailly, cond.*
• ARG 7-8/94: 85
+ Fa 7-8/94: 104
• Gr 3/94: 44

20970. 436 201-2: SCHUBERT—Schöne Müllerin; Lieder. *Pears, tenor; Britten, piano.* Recorded 1960-61.
+ Gr 8/93: 72

20971. 436 202-2: Music of Scarlatti, Bellini, Cimara, Donizetti, Gluck, and Mascagni. *Tebaldi, soprano; Bonynge, piano.* Reissue.
• Gr 9/94: 100

20972. 436 203-2: SCHUBERT—Lieder. SCHUMANN—Lieder. *Prey, baritone; Engel, piano.* Reissues.
+ Gr 8/93: 73

20973. 436 204-2: TCHAIKOVSKY—Songs. *Söderström, soprano; Ashkenazy, piano.* Reissues.
+ Gr 5/94: 105

20974. 436 209-2: PERGOLESI—Stabat Mater; Salve Regina. SCARLATTI—Salve Regina. *Anderson, soprano; Bartoli, mezzo-soprano; Montreal Sinfonietta; Dutoit, cond.*
+ ARG 11-12/93: 165
+ ARG 3-4/94: 132
+ Fa 1-2/94: 258
• Gr 8/93: 72

20975. 436 210-2: BARTÓK—Miraculous mandarin; Two portraits; Divertimento for string orchestra. *Montreal Symphony Orch.; Dutoit, cond.*
+ ARG 3-4/94: 70
• Fa 3-4/94: 117
• Gr 3/94: 41

20976. 436 211-2: JANÁČEK—Slavonic mass; Sinfonietta. *Troitskaya, Randová, Kaludov, Leiferkus, vocalists; Trotter, organ; Orch. & Chorus symphonique de Montréal; Dutoit, cond.*
• Fa 9-10/94: 186
• Gr 4/94: 80

20977. 436 212-2 (2 discs): TCHAIKOVSKY—Swan lake. *Montreal Symphony Orch.; Dutoit, cond.*
- ARG 5-6/93: 145 (Vroon)
+ ARG 5-6/93: 146 (Haller)
+ Fa 5-6/93: 341
+ Gr 2/93: 48
+ St 8/93: 191

20978. 436 224-2: Concertos by Albinoni, Corelli, Gabrieli, Geminiani, Manfredini, Torelli, and Locatelli. *Academy of St. Martin-in-the-Fields; Marriner, cond.* Reissues.
+ Gr 9/93: 69

20979. 436 233-2: PROKOFIEV—Symphony-concerto; Cello concertino. *Harrell, cello; Royal Phil. Orch.; Ashkenazy, cond.*
+ Gr 5/94: 58

20980. 436 234-2 (3 discs): GLUCK—Alceste. HANDEL—Arias. *Flagstad, Jobin, Lowe; Geraint Jones Orch.; Jones, cond.; London Phil. Orch.; Boult, cond.* Recorded 1956.
+ Fa 3-4/94: 195
• Gr 11/93: 150

20981. 436 239-2: RACHMANINOFF—Rhapsody on a theme of Paganini. SHOSTAKOVICH—Concerto no. 1 for piano, trumpet and strings. LUTOSŁAWSKI—Paganini variations (version for piano and orchestra). *Jablonski, piano; Simmons, trumpet; Royal Phil. Orch.; Ashkenazy, cond.*
+ ARG 7-8/93: 139
• Fa 5-6/93: 285
+ Gr 12/92: 81

20982. 436 240-2 (2 discs): MAHLER—Symphony no. 6. SCHOENBERG—5 Orchesterstücke, op. 16. WEBERN—Im Sommerwind. *Cleveland Orch.; Dohnányi, cond.*
+ ARG 5-6/93: 105
• Fa 5-6/93: 257
• Gr 1/93: 43

20983. 436 243-2 (2 discs): STRAUSS—Die Frau ohne Schatten. *Varady, Behrens, Domingo, Van Dam; Vienna State Opera; Solti, cond.*
+ ARG 9-10/92: 167
+ Fa 7-8/92: 294
+ Gr 5/92: 114
• ON 7/92: 38
+ Op 7/92: 873

20984. 436 255-2: BALAKIREV—Islamey. TCHAIKOVSKY—Album for the young. MUSSORGSKY—Pictures at an exhibition. *Mustonen, piano.*
- Gr 2/93: 58

20985. 436 256—436 259-2 (4 separate discs): HANDEL—Anthems. BLOW—Anthems. *Vocal soloists; Academy of St. Martin-in-the-Fields; Marriner, cond.* Reissues.
+ Gr 8/93: 69

20986. 436 261-2 (3 discs): PUCCINI—Il trittico. *Freni, Giacomini, Pons, Nucci; Florence May Festival; Bartoletti, cond.*
+ ARG 11-12/94: 169
• Fa 11-12/94: 335
• Gr 8/94: 104
• ON 1/7/95: 36
• Op 8/94: 999

20987. 436 267-2: *If you love me.* Music of A. Scarlatti, Giordani, Lotti, Cesti, Paisiello and others. *Bartoli, soprano; Fischer, piano.*
+ ARG 3-4/93: 184
+ Fa 5-6/93: 364

+ Gr 12/92: 134
+ ON 12/25/93: 33

20988. 436 283-2: RACHMANINOFF—Symphony no. 1; Isle of the dead. *Philadelphia Orch.; Dutoit, cond.*
• Fa 7-8/94: 208
• Gr 2/94: 48

20989. 436 289-2: BRAHMS—Symphony no. 1. DVOŘÁK—Othello. *Cleveland Orch.; Ashkenazy, cond.*
• Fa 11-12/93: 195
• Gr 6/93: 38

20990. 436 290-2 (6 discs): HAYDN—London Symphonies. *London Phil. Orch.; Solti, cond.* Reissues.
+ Gr 3/93: 43

20991. 436 298-2: BRAHMS—Symphony no. 1. DVOŘÁK—Othello overture. *Cleveland Orch.; Ashkenazy, cond.*
- ARG 9-10/93: 105

20992. 436 320-2: Pavarotti in Hyde Park. *Pavarotti, tenor; Philharmonia Orch.; Magiera, cond.*
• ARG 11-12/92: 262

20993. 436 324-2: SCHUBERT—String quintet; Quartet movement D. 703. *Takács Quartet; Perényi, cello.*
+ Gr 6/93: 70

20994. 436 325-2: MENDELSSOHN—String quartets no. 1-2, 6. *Quatuor Ysaÿe.*
+ Fa 7-8/93: 181
• Gr 8/93: 49

20995. 436 359-2: LISZT—A Faust symphony. *Blochwitz, tenor; Groot Omroepkoor NOB; Royal Concertgebouw Orch.; Chailly, cond.*
• Gr 7/93: 45

20996. 436 376-2: MOZART—Concertos for violin and orchestra no. 3, 5; Adagio for violin and orchestra, K. 261; Rondo for violin and orchestra, K. 373. *Bell, violin; English Chamber Orch.; Maag, cond.*
+ Fa 5-6/93: 272
• Gr 3/93: 48

20997. 436 377-2: ROSSINI—Opera arias. *Anderson, soprano; Bologna Opera Orch.; Gatti, cond.*
• ARG 7-8/93: 144
+ Fa 9-10/93: 257
+ Gr 5/93: 106
+ ON 9/93: 53

20998. 436 393-2: BRITTEN—The little sweep; Gemini variations; Children's crusade. *Vocal soloists; English Opera Group Orch.; Britten, cond.; G. Jeney, flute, piano; Z. Jeney, violin, piano; Wandsworth School Boys Choir; Burgess, Britten, conds.* Reissues.
• Gr 11/93: 138

20999. 436 394-2: BRITTEN—Vocal music. *Harnett, treble; Simon, harp; Tunnard, piano; Choirs; Britten, cond.* Reissues.
+ Gr 9/93: 97

21000. 436 395-2: BRITTEN—Les illuminations; Serenade; Nocturne. *Pears, tenor; Tuckwell, horn; English Chamber Orch.; London Symphony Orch.; Britten, cond.* Reissues.
+ Gr 9/93: 97

21001. 436 396-2: BRITTEN—Spring symphony; Cantata academica; Hymn to St. Cecilia. *Vyvyan, Procter, Watts, Pears, Brannigan; Royal Opera House Covent Garden; Britten, cond.; London Symphony Orch.; Malcolm, cond.* Reissues.
+ Gr 9/93: 97

21002. 436 397-2: BRITTEN—Noye's fludde; The golden vanity. *Vocal soloists; English Opera Group Orch.; Del Mar, cond.; Wandsworth School Boys Choir; Burgess, cond.* Reissues.
+ Gr 11/93: 138

21003. 436 400-2: MESSIAEN—Organ music. *Trotter, organ.*
+ Gr 9/93: 90

21004. 436 415-2: STRAUSS—Violin concerto; Oboe concerto; Duett-concertino. *Belkin, violin; Hunt, oboe; D. Ashkenazy, clarinet; Walker, bassoon; Radio Symphonie Orch. Berlin; V. Ashkenazy, cond.*
• ARG 5-6/94: 146
+ Fa 3-4/94: 325
+ Gr 3/94: 62

21005. 436 416-2: STRAVINSKY—Symphony in C; Symphony in three movements; Symphonies of wind instruments. *Radio Symphonie Orch. Berlin; Ashkenazy, cond.*
• ARG 5-6/94: 147
• Fa 3-4/94: 326
+ Gr 9/93: 63

21006. 436 418-2 (2 discs): WAGNER—Flying Dutchman. *Behrens, Hale, Protschka, Rydl; Vienna Phil. Orch.; Dohnányi, cond.*
+ ARG 9-10/94: 219
• Fa 9-10/94: 373
+ Gr 4/94: 105
+ ON 9/94: 58

21007. 436 421-2 (3 discs): MOZART—Symphonies no. 35-41. WEBERN—Passcaglia; Variations, Symphony; Pieces, op. 6, 10. *Cleveland Orch.; Dohnányi, cond.* Reissues.
• ARG 11-12/93: 158
+ Fa 1-2/94: 248
+ Gr 10/93: 48

21008. 436 444-2: STRAUSS—Ein Heldenleben; Till Eulenspiegels lustige Streiche. *Cleveland Orch.; Dohnányi,*

cond.
+ ARG 3-4/94: 160
• Fa 1-2/94: 322
• Gr 10/93: 56

21009. 436 451-2 (2 discs): *Richter in Vienna.* Music of Prokofiev, Stravinsky, Shostakovich, Webern, Bartók, Szymanowski, and Hindemith. *Richter, piano.* Recorded live.
• ARG 11-12/93: 242
+ Fa 9-10/93: 362
- Gr 3/93: 76

21010. 436 454—436 455-2 (2 separate discs): HAYDN—Piano sonatas. *Richter, piano.* Recorded 1986-87.
• Gr 3/93: 76

21011. 436 456-2: SCHUMANN—Toccata; Blumenstück; Nachtstücke; Fugues, op. 72; March, op. 76, no. 2. *Richter, piano.* Reissue.
+ ARG 9-10/93: 188
+ Fa 9-10/93: 362
+ Gr 3/93: 76

21012. 436 457-2: BRAHMS—Piano sonatas no. 1-2. *Richter, piano.* Recorded live 1986.
+ ARG 9-10/93: 103
+ Fa 9-10/93: 362
+ Gr 3/93: 76

21013. 436 466-2: BRAHMS—Symphony no. 3. SCHOENBERG—Chamber symphony no. 1. *Concertgebouw Orch.; Chailly, cond.*
+ ARG 1-2/94: 84
• Fa 1-2/94: 142
+ Gr 9/93: 43

21014. 436 467-2: SCHOENBERG—Chamber symphony no. 1. WEBERN—Im Sommerwind; Passacaglia. *Concertgebouw Orch.; Chailly, cond.*
+ ARG 9-10/94: 192
+ Gr 4/94: 56

21015. 436 468-2: DEBUSSY—Nocturnes; Prelude to the afternoon of a faun; La mer. *Chicago Symphony Orch.; Solti, cond.*
- ARG 5-6/93: 80
+ Fa 5-6/93: 190
+ Gr 10/92: 58

21016. 436 469-2: SHOSTAKOVICH—Symphony no. 1. STRAVINSKY—Rite of spring. *Concertgebouw Orch.; Solti, cond.*
+ ARG 7-8/93: 157
- Fa 5-6/93: 323
• Gr 10/92: 119
• St 4/93: 289

21017. 436 470 2: HAYDN—Nelson mass. MOZART—Coronation mass. *Vocal soloists; London Symphony Chorus; City of London Sinfonia; Hickox, cond.; King's College Choir; English Chamber Orch.; Cleobury, cond.*

+ Gr 5/93: 84 (Haydn)
- Gr 5/93: 84 (Mozart)

21018. 436 474-2: STRAVINSKY—Symphony in C; Symphonies of wind instruments; Scherzo fantastique; Symphony in 3 movements. *Orch. de la Suisse romande; Montreal Symphony Orch.; Dutoit, cond.* Reissues.
+ Gr 5/94: 61

21019. 436 485-2: TCHAIKOVSKY—Piano concertos no. 2-3. *Postnikova, piano; Vienna Symphony Orch.; Rozhdestvensky, cond.* Reissues.
• Gr 6/94: 65

21020. 436 486-2 (2 discs): DURUFLÉ—Requiem; Motets; Prelude and fugue, op. 9. FAURÉ—Requiem. POULENC—Mass in G; Motets. *Luxon, Keyte; St. John's College Choir, Cambridge; Academy of St. Martin-in-the-Fields; Guest, cond.* Reissues.
+ ARG 3-4/96: 108
+ Gr 7/94: 94

21021. 436 546-2: POULENC—Piano concerto; Concerto for 2 pianos; Organ concerto. *Rogé, Deferne, pianos; Hurford, organ; Philharmonia Orch.; Dutoit, cond.*
+ ARG 9-10/94: 173
• Fa 9-10/94: 288
+ Gr 12/93: 74

21022. 436 547-2: MOZART—Violin sonatas K. 379, K. 304, K. 454; Variations, K. 360. *Shiokawa, violin; Schiff, fortepiano.*
+ ARG 5-6/93: 116
+ Gr 3/93: 63

21023. 436 566-2: SIBELIUS—Symphony no. 2; Romance; Valse triste; Finlandia. *Boston Symphony Orch.; Ashkenazy, cond.*
+ Fa 7-8/94: 245
+ Gr 10/93: 54

21024. 436 567-2: BERG—Seven early songs; Three pieces from the Lyric suite; Altenberg-Lieder; Pieces for orchestra, op. 6. *Balleys, soprano; Radio-Symphonie-Orch., Berlin; Ashkenazy, cond.*
+ ARG 5-6/94: 69
+ Gr 2/94: 78

21025. 436 596-2: STRAUSS—Ein Heldenleben; Metamorphosen. *San Francisco Symphony Orch.; Blomstedt, cond.*
+ ARG 9-10/94: 203
+ Fa 9-10/94: 346
• Gr 5/94: 61

21026. 436 597-2: BERWALD—Symphonies no. 1, 4. *San Francisco Symphony Orch; Blomstedt, cond.*
+ ARG 1-2/94: 80
+ Fa 3-4/94: 135
+ Gr 1/94: 41

21027. 436 598-2: SCHUBERT—Symphony no. 9; Overture in C, D. 991. *San Francisco Symphony Orch.; Blomstedt, cond.*
+ ARG 3-4/94: 150
+ Fa 1-2/94: 309
• Gr 10/93: 54

21028. 436 626-2: MESSIAEN—Turangalîla-symphonie. *Thibaudet, piano; Harada, ondes Martenot; Concertgebouw Orch.; Chailly, cond.*
+ Gr 11/93: 70
+ Fa 9-10/94: 257

21029. 436 627-2 (2 discs): BEETHOVEN—Fidelio. *Schnaut, Protschka, Welker, Rydl; Vienna State Opera; Dohnányi, cond.*
• ARG 1-2/94: 71
• Fa 1-2/94: 122
• Gr 7/93: 85
• ON 12/11/93: 45
• Op 10/93: 1254

21030. 436 631-2 (2 discs): KRENEK—Jonny spielt auf. *Kruse, Marc, St. Hill, Kraus; Gewandhaus Orch., Leipzig; Zagrosek, cond.*
+ ARG 9-10/93: 145
+ Gr 4/93: 116
+ ON 8/93: 36

21031. 436 636-2 (3 discs): KORNGOLD—Das Wunder der Heliane. *Tomowa-Sintow, Welker, Runkel, Gedda; Berlin Radio Symphony Orch.; Mauceri, cond.*
+ ARG 7-8/93: 110
+ Gr 4/93: 116
+ ON 8/93: 36
+ St 10/93: 273

21032. 436 640-2: MOSOLOV—Zavod: iron foundry. PROKOFIEV—Symphony no. 3. VARÈSE—Arcana. *Concertgebouw Orch.; Chailly, cond.*
• ARG 1-2/95: 143
+ Fa 11-12/94: 304
+ Gr 11/94: 82

21033. 436 648-2: FRANCK—Prélude, choral et fugue. LISZT—Réminiscences de Norma. MENDELSSOHN—Prelude and fugue, op. 35, no. 1. *Bolet, piano.* Recorded 1988.
+ Gr 4/94: 70

21034. 436 651-2: BORODIN—Symphonies no. 1-2; In the steppes of central Asia. *Royal Phil. Orch.; Ashkenazy, cond.*
• ARG 9-10/94: 106
+ Fa 11-12/94: 181
+ Gr 8/94: 42

21035. 436 654-2: BEETHOVEN—Octet, op. 103. MOZART—Serenades K. 375, K. 388. *Vienna Wind Soloists.*
+ Gr 3/95: 61

21036. 436 656-2: Music of Elgar, Gounod, Mendelssohn, Rossini, Suppé, Tchaikovsky, and Wagner. *Trotter,*

LONDON

organ.
+ Gr 4/94: 76

21037. 436 735-2: BEETHOVEN—Piano sonatas no. 28-29. *Ashkenazy, piano.*
• Fa 1-2/95: 114
+ Gr 4/94: 69

21038. 436 736-2: LISZT—Opera transcriptions. *Thibaudet, piano.*
+ Gr 2/94: 75

21039. 436 739-2 (2 discs): HAYDN— Paris symphonies. *Montreal Sinfonietta; Dutoit, cond.*
+ ARG 9-10/93: 134
+ Fa 9-10/93: 180
+ Gr 6/93: 44

21040. 436 760-2: SHOSTAKOVICH— Symphonies no. 3, 12. *Royal Phil. Orch.; Ashkenazy, cond.*
• Gr 11/94: 86

21041. 436 762-2: SHOSTAKOVICH— Symphony no. 2; Song of the forests; Festival overture. *Royal Phil. Orch.; Ashkenazy, cond.*
+ ARG 9-10/94: 198
+ Fa 9-10/94: 338
+ Gr 8/94: 60

21042. 436 763-2: SHOSTAKOVICH— Symphony no. 8; Funeral and triumphal prelude; Novorossii chimes. *Royal Phil. Orch.; Ashkenazy, cond.*
• ARG 9-10/94: 198
+ Fa 9-10/94: 338
• Gr 4/94: 56

21043. 436 798-2: LOUSSIER—Violin concerto; Trumpet concerto; Tableaux vénétiens. *Wallez, violin; Touvron, trumpet; Prague Chamber Orch.*
□ Gr 8/94: 48

21044. 436 821-2: CHOPIN—Piano sonata no. 3; Preludes, op. 28; Mazurka, op. 68, no. 4. *Ashkenazy, piano.*
• Fa 7-8/94: 113

21045. 436 834-2: BEETHOVEN—Piano variations. *Mustonen, piano.*
- ARG 7-8/94: 72
- Fa 7-8/94: 71
• Gr 10/93: 77

21046. 436 836-2: STRAUSS—Tanzsuite aus Klavierstücken von François Couperin; Le bourgeois gentilhomme. *Juillet, violin; Bertsch, piano; Montreal Symphony Orch.; Dutoit, cond.*
• Gr 10/95: 75

21047. 436 837-2: STRAVINSKY—Violin concerto. SZYMANOWSKI—Violin concertos no. 1-2. *Juillet, violin; Orch. Symphonique de Montréal; Dutoit, cond.*
• ARG 3-4/94: 163
- Fa 1-2/94: 324
+ Gr 10/93: 54

21048. 436 838-2: SHOSTAKOVICH— Symphonies no. 1, 10, 15. *Montreal Symphony Orch.; Dutoit, cond.*
• Gr 10/94: 122

21049. 436 839-2: BERLIOZ—Symphonie fantastique. LISZT—Les preludes. *Chicago Symphony Orch.; Solti, cond.*
- ARG 1-2/94: 79
+ Fa 3-4/94: 133
• Gr 11/93: 65

21050. 436 840-2 (2 discs): HAYDN—The seasons. *Ziesak, Heilmann, Pape; Chicago Symphony Orch. & Chorus; Solti, cond.* Recorded live 1992.
+ ARG 3-4/94: 108
+ Fa 3-4/94: 211
• Gr 2/94: 81

21051. 436 843-2: SCHUBERT—String quartets no. 13-14. *Takács String Quartet.*
+ Gr 12/93: 84

21052. 436 844-2: BRUCKNER—Symphony no. 2. *Chicago Symphony Orch.; Solti, cond.*
- ARG 1-2/94: 88
+ Fa 1-2/94: 148
+ Gr 8/93: 26

21053. 436 853-2: BRAHMS—Symphony no. 4; Variations and fugue on a theme by Handel (orch. Rubbra). *Cleveland Orch.; Ashkenazy, cond.*
+ ARG 7-8/95: 94
• Fa 7-8/95: 132
+ Gr 11/94: 68

21054. 436 866-2: FAURÉ—Violin sonatas; Morceau de concours; Andante; Romance; Berceuse. *Amoyal, violin; Rogé, piano.*
+ Gr 2/95: 64

21055. 436 902-2 (2 discs): ROSSINI—La Cenerentola. *Bartoli, Matteuzzi, Corbelli, Dara, Costa; Bologna Opera; Chailly, cond.*
+ ARG 1-2/94: 140
+ Fa 3-4/94: 292
+ Gr 11/93: 156
+ ON 12/25/93: 33
+ Op 11/93: 1366

21056. 436 917-2 (2 discs): MINKUS—La bayadère. *English Chamber Orch.; Bonynge, cond.*
+ Gr 7/94: 52

21057. 436 920-2 (3 discs): RACHMANINOFF—Songs. *Söderström, soprano; Ashkenazy, piano.* Reissues.
+ Gr 5/94: 100

21058. 436 991-2: POULENC—Songs. *Dubosc, soprano; Cachemaille, baritone; Rogé, piano.*
• Gr 11/94: 134

21059. 439 425-2: SCHUBERT—Piano music. *Schiff, piano.*

• ARG 5-6/93: 128
• Fa 7-8/93: 231
+ Gr 11/92: 161

21060. 440 038-2 (3 discs): HAYDN—Il ritorno di Tobia. *Hendricks, Zoghby, Jones, Langridge, Luxon; Brighton Festival Chorus; Royal Phil. Orch.; Dorati, cond.* Reissue.
+ Gr 10/94: 174

21061. 440 042-2 (2 discs): VERDI—Un ballo in maschera. *Tebaldi, Pavarotti, Milnes, Accademia di Santa Cecilia; Bartoletti, cond.* Recorded 1971.
• ARG 9-10/94: 215
• Gr 5/94: 115

21062. 440 045-2 (2 discs): VERDI— Otello. *Cossutta, M. Price, Bacquier, Dvorský; Vienna Phil. Orch.; Solti, cond.* Recorded 1978.
• Gr 5/94: 115

21063. 440 048-2 (2 discs): VERDI— Macbeth. *Suliotis, Fischer-Dieskau, Pavarotti, Ghiaurov; London Phil. Orch.; Gardelli, cond.* Recorded 1971.
• Gr 7/94: 120

21064. 440 051-2 (2 discs): PUCCINI— Tosca. *Nilsson, Corelli, Fischer-Dieskau; Academia di Santa Cecilia; Maazel, cond.* Reissue.
• ARG 9-10/94: 176
• Gr 4/94: 100

21065. 440 054-2 (2 discs): BOITO— Mefistofele. *Siepi, Del Monaco, Tebaldi, Cavalli; Orch. di Santa Cecilia; Serafin, cond.* Recorded 1958.
+ ARG 9-10/94: 105
+ Gr 4/94: 97

21066. 440 076-2: MOZART—String quartets no. 14-15. *Ysaÿe Quartet.*
• Gr 10/94: 142

21067. 440 077-2: MOZART—String quartets no. 16-17. *Ysaÿe Quartet.*
• Gr 4/95: 84

21068. 440 078-2: MOZART—String quartets no. 18-19. *Ysaÿe Quartet.*
• Gr 9/95: 76

21069. 440 200-2: PUCCINI—Manon Lescaut. *Freni, Pavarotti, Croft, Taddei, Vargas, Bartoli; Metropolitan Opera Orch. & Chorus; Levine, cond.*
+ ARG 3-4/94: 137
+ Fa 1-2/94: 265
+ Gr 11/93: 156
+ ON 1/8/94: 34
+ Op 1/94: 120

21070. 440 208-2: WOLF—Mörike Lieder. *Fassbaender, mezzo-soprano; Thibaudet, piano.*
+ ARG 5-6/94: 168
• Fa 3-4/94: 366
+ Gr 8/93: 77

21071. 440 229-2: STRAVINSKY—Concerto for piano and winds; Ebony concerto; Capriccio; Movements. *Mustonen, piano; D. Ashkenazy, clarinet; Deutsches Symphony Orch.; V. Ashkenazy, cond.*
- ARG 7-8/94: 177
+ Fa 9-10/94: 247
- Gr 1/94: 59

21072. 440 242-2 (2 discs): VERDI—Rigoletto. *Protti, Gueden, Del Monaco, Siepi; Academy of Santa Cecilia, Rome; Erede, cond.* Recorded 1955.
- Gr 7/94: 120

21073. 440 245-2 (2 discs): VERDI—Otello. *Del Monaco, Tebaldi, Protti, De Palma; Accademia di Santa Cecilia, Rome; Erede, cond.* Recorded 1954.
- Gr 5/94: 115

21074. 440 281-2: RACHMANINOFF—Piano sonata no. 2 (revised version). SCRIABIN—Piano sonatas no. 5, 9. PROKOFIEV—Piano sonata no. 7. *Jablonski, piano.*
- Fa 7-8/94: 207
- Gr 2/94: 76

21075. 440 283-2: LISZT—Organ music. *Trotter, organ.*
+ Gr 10/94: 159

21076. 440 293-2: PAGANINI—Violin concerto no. 2 (arr.). CASTELNUOVO-TEDESCO—Guitar concerto no. 1. SARASATE—Zigeunerweisen. *Hall, guitar; London Mozart Players; Litton, cond.*
+ ARG 7-8/94: 210
- Gr 3/94: 46

21077. 440 295-2: SCHUBERT—Piano sonatas D. 664, 960. *Lupu, piano.*
+ ARG 7-8/95: 188
+ Fa 1-2/96: 298
- Gr 11/94: 118

21078. 440 296-2: MENDELSSOHN—A midsummer night's dream; Octet. *Dawson, soprano; Schaechter, mezzo-soprano; Deutsches Symphony Orch.; Ashkenazy, cond.*
- Gr 8/94: 50

21079. 440 297-2: *The impatient lover.* Songs by Haydn, Mozart, Beethoven, and Schubert. *Bartoli, mezzo- soprano; Schiff, piano.*
+ ARG 3-4/94: 225
+ Fa 3-4/94: 373
+ Gr 11/93: 136

21080. 440 305—440 306-2 (2 separate discs): SCHUBERT—Piano sonatas, vol. 1-2. *Schiff, piano.*
+ ARG 3-4/94: 148
- Fa 3-4/94: 309
+ Gr 12/93: 91

21081. 440 307-2: SCHUBERT—Piano sonatas, vol. 3. *Schiff, piano.*
+ ARG 9-10/94: 194

- Fa 5-6/95: 327
+ Gr 6/94: 87

21082. 440 308-2: SCHUBERT—Piano sonatas D. 568, 958. *Schiff, piano.*
- ARG 1-2/95: 169
+ Fa 3-4/95: 291
+ Gr 10/94: 163

21083. 440 309-2: *Piano sonatas, vol. 5.* SCHUBERT—Sonatas D. 537, 959. *Schiff, piano.*
+ Fa 1-2/96: 298
- Gr 1/95: 79

21084. 440 310-2: SCHUBERT—Piano sonatas, D. 279, 625, 960. *Schiff, piano.*
+ ARG 1-2/96: 169
- Fa 11-12/95: 362
+ Gr 6/95: 83

21085. 440 311-2: SCHUBERT—Piano sonatas, D. 157, 459, 664. *Schiff, piano.*
- Fa 1-2/96: 297
+ Gr 11/95: 126

21086. 440 312—440 313-2 (2 separate discs): JANÁČEK—Chamber music. *Various performers.*
+ Fa 11-12/94: 264
+ Gr 1/94: 68

21087. 440 314-2: MAHLER—Das Lied von der Erde. *Lipovsek, soprano; Moser, tenor; Concertgebouw Orch.; Solti, cond.*
- ARG 9-10/94: 155
- Fa 9-10/94: 244
- Gr 5/94: 96

21088. 440 315-2: MAHLER—Symphony no. 4. *Upshaw, soprano; Cleveland Orch.; Dohnányi, cond.*
+ ARG 9-10/94: 157
+ Fa 9-10/94: 247
+ Gr 4/94: 50

21089. 440 316-2: BRUCKNER—Symphony no. 3 (1877 version, Nowak edition). *Chicago Symphony Orch.; Solti, cond.*
- ARG 9-10/94: 111
+ Fa 7-8/94: 105
- Gr 4/94: 42

21090. 440 327-2: STRAVINSKY—Apollo; Dumbarton Oaks; Danses concertantes; Concerto in D. *Sinfonietta de Montreal; Dutoit, cond.*
+ ARG 1-2/95: 185
+ Fa 1-2/95: 281
+ Gr 9/94: 64

21091. 440 331-2: PROKOFIEV—Violin concertos no. 1-2; The love for three oranges suite. *Bell, violin; Orch. Symphonique de Montréal; Dutoit, cond.*
- ARG 3-4/94: 135
+ Fa 1-2/94: 262
+ Gr 1/94: 48

21092. 440 332-2: IBERT—Escales; Flute concerto; Hommage à Mozart; Paris; Bacchanale Bostoniana; Louisville concerto. *Hutchins, flute; Montreal*

Symphony Orch.; Dutoit, cond.
+ ARG 11-12/94: 132
+ Fa 1-2/95: 180
+ Gr 6/94: 50

21093. 440 333-2: RAVEL—L'enfant et les sortilèges; Shéhérazade; Shéhérazade: fairy overture. *Alliot-Lugaz, Dubosc, Lefort, Beaupré, Carlson, Gautier, Henry, Sarrazin; Montreal Symphony Orch.; Dutoit, cond.*
+ Gr 10/95: 142

21094. 440 354-2: SCHUBERT—Die schöne Müllerin. *Heilmann, tenor; Levine, piano.*
- Gr 1/95: 90

21095. 440 355-2: RACHMANINOFF—The bells; Spring; Three Russian songs, op. 41. *Pendachanska, soprano; Kaludov, tenor; Leiferkus, baritone; Choral Arts Society of Philadelphia; Dutoit, cond.*
- Fa 11-12/94: 348
+ Gr 8/94: 92

21096. 440 369-2: MENDELSSOHN—String quartets no. 3-4. *Ysaÿe String Quartet.*
+ ARG 7-8/94: 132
+ Fa 7-8/94: 178
- Gr 5/94: 73

21097. 440 376-2: Music of Corelli, Bach, Tippett, and Holst. *St. Paul Chamber Orch.; Hogwood, cond.*
+ ARG 7-8/94: 199
+ Fa 7-8/94: 334
+ Gr 3/94: 41

21098. 440 410-2: Arias from Carmen, Lohengrin, Frau ohne Schatten, Tales of Hoffman, and Africaine. *Domingo, tenor.* Reissues.
+ ARG 5-6/95: 226

21099. 440 412-2: *Mirella Freni: 40th anniversary.* Arias from La Bohème, Butterfly, Tosca, Mefistofele, Pagliacci, Bianca e Fernando, Falstaff, and William Tell. *Freni, soprano.* Reissues.
+ ARG 3-4/95: 258

21100. 440 414-2: HAYDN—Cantatas. MOZART—Arias. *Augér, soprano; Handel and Haydn Society Orch.; Hogwood, cond.; Drottningholm Theater Orch.; Östman, cond.* Reissues.
+ ARG 5-6/95: 117

21101. 440 415-2: Arias by Handel, Gluck, Mozart, Rossini, Bizet, and Saint-Saëns. *Horne, mezzo-soprano.* Reissues.
+ ARG 5-6/95: 227

21102. 440 416-2: Arias from Iphigénie en Tauride, Damnation de Faust, Sapho, Carmen, and others. *Crespin, soprano.* Reissues.
+ ARG 5-6/95: 226

21103. 440 417-2: Arias from Aida, Luisa Miller, Forza del destino, Don Carlo, and others. *Bergonzi, tenor.*

LONDON

Reissues.
+ ARG 5-6/95: 225

21104. 440 474-2: Mozart—Four-hand piano music. *Schiff, Malcolm, fortepiano.*
+ ARG 7-8/94: 141
• Fa 7-8/94: 192
+ Gr 6/94: 73

21105. 440 476-2: Shostakovich—Symphony no. 5. Mendelssohn—Symphony no. 4. *Vienna Phil. Orch.; Solti, cond.* Recorded live.
+ Fa 5-6/95: 343
+ Gr 10/94: 110

21106. 440 477-2 (2 discs): Tchaikovsky—Nutcracker; Aurora's wedding. *Montreal Symphony Orch.; Dutoit, cond.*
• ARG 3-4/94: 166
+ Fa 3-4/94: 335
+ Gr 3/94: 64

21107. 440 490-2 (5 discs): Kirsten Flagstad edition. *Flagstad, soprano.* Reissues.
+ Gr 12/95: 139

21108. 440 496-2: Schumann—Humoreske; Kinderszenen; Kreisleriana. *Lupu, piano.*
+ ARG 7-8/96: 192
• Fa 5-6/96: 269
+ Fi 5/96: 130
+ Gr 4/95: 92

21109. 440 604-2: Rachmaninoff—Symphony no. 2; The rock. *Philadelphia Orch.; Dutoit, cond.*
- ARG 7-8/95: 177
• Fa 9-10/95: 285
• Gr 6/95: 54

21110. 440 605-2: Haydn—Oboe concerto. Mozart—Oboe concerto K. 314. Hummel—Introduction, theme and variations. *Rombout, oboe; Concertgebouw Chamber Orch.*
• Gr 12/94: 84

21111. 440 606-2 (2 discs): Wagner—Overtures. *Vienna Phil. Orch.; Solti, cond.*
- ARG 3-4/95: 220

21112. 440 612-2 (2 discs): Brahms—Piano concertos; Handel variations; Paganini variations. *Katchen, piano; London Symphony Orch.; Monteux, Ferencsik, conds.* Reissues.
+ ARG 3-4/95: 80
• Gr 10/95: 48

21113. 440 615-2 (2 discs): Mahler—Symphony no. 2. Schmidt—Symphony no. 4. *Vienna Phil. Orch.; Mehta, cond.* Reissues.
+ ARG 3-4/96: 147
□ ARG 5-6/96: 142

21114. 440 627-2 (2 discs): Beethoven—Symphonies no. 1, 3, 6, 8. *Vienna Phil.*

Orch.; Monteux, cond. Reissues.
+ ARG 5-6/95: 86
• Gr 12/94: 75

21115. 440 630-2 (2 discs): Tchaikovsky—Swan lake. Prokofiev—Romeo and Juliet: Suite. *Orch. de la Suisse Romande; Ansermet, cond.* Reissues.
+ ARG 9-10/96: 216

21116. 440 646-2 (2 discs): Auber—Le domino noir; Gustav III: ballet music. *Jo, Vemet, Ford, Power, Bastin; English Chamber Orch.; Bonynge, cond.*
+ ARG 3-4/96: 76
+ Gr 1/96: 102
+ ON 5/96: 60
+ Op 3/96: 344

21117. 440 650-2 (2 discs): Verdi—Falstaff. *Dam, Coni, Serra, Lipovsek; Berlin Phil. Orch.; Solti, cond.*
• ARG 5-6/94: 163
• Fa 3-4/94: 353
• Gr 12/93: 121
• ON 2/5/94: 39
- Op 1/94: 119

21118. 440 653-2: Rachmaninoff—Piano concerto no. 2; Paganini rhapsody. *Thibaudet, piano; Cleveland Orch.; Ashkenazy, cond.*
+ ARG 1-2/95: 157
• Gr 12/94: 90

21119. 440 679-2: *Carnaval!* Coloratura arias by Massenet, Offenbach, David, and others. *Jo, soprano; English Chamber Orch.; Bonynge, cond.*
+ ARG 1-2/95: 241
+ Gr 9/94: 119

21120. 440 680-2: *Great sacred arias.* Music of Handel, Bach, Mozart, Haydn, and Mendelssohn. *Heilmann, tenor; Leipzig Gewandhaus Orch.; Schreier, cond.*
+ Gr 3/95: 97

21121. 440 836-2 (2 discs): Ravel—Complete piano music. *P. & D.-F. Rogé, pianos.* Reissue.
+ ARG 3-4/95: 165
+ Gr 10/94: 160

21122. 440 839-2 (2 discs): Beethoven—Piano concertos no. 3-5; Choral fantasy. *Katchen, piano; London Symphony Orch.; Gamba, cond.* Recorded 1958-65.
+ ARG 7-8/96: 73

21123. 440 850-2 (2 discs): Goldschmidt—Der gewaltige Hahnrei; Mediterranean songs. *Alexander, Wörle, Petzold, Kraus, Otelli, Ainsley; Berlin Radio Chorus; Berlin Deutsches Symphony Orch.; Gewandhaus Orch.; Zagrosek, cond.*
+ ARG 9-10/94: 133
+ Fa 9-10/94: 196
+ Gr 3/94: 101

21124. 440 853-2: Haas—String quartets no. 2-3. Krása—String quartet. *Hawthorne String Quartet.*
+ ARG 9-10/94: 137
+ Fa 11-12/94: 372
+ Gr 3/94: 72

21125. 440 854-2: Ullmann—Der Kaiser von Atlantis; Hölderlin-Lieder. *Oelze, Vermillion, Lippert, Petzold, Kraus, Mazura, Berry; Leipzig Gewandhaus Orch.; Zagrosek, cond.; in Hölderlin-Lieder: Vermillion, mezzo-soprano; Alder, piano.*
+ ARG 5-6/95: 187
+ Fa 5-6/95: 365
+ Gr 12/94: 162
+ ON 3/4/95: 41
+ Op 3/95: 362

21126. 440 926-2: Prokofiev—Violin sonatas no. 1-2; Melodies. *Bell, violin; Mustonen, piano.*
- ARG 7-8/95: 170
• Gr 5/95: 73

21127. 440 935-2: Chopin—Allegro de concert; Sonata no. 3. Liszt—Dante sonata; Hungarian rhapsody no. 12. *Nebolsin, piano.*
- ARG 9-10/94: 117
+ Fa 9-10/94: 168
- Gr 7/94: 79

21128. 443 000-2 (2 discs): Verdi—La traviata. *Lorengar, Aragall, Fischer-Dieskau; Deutsche Oper Berlin; Maazel, cond.* Reissue.
+ ARG 3-4/95: 214

21129. 443 003-2 (2 discs): Tchaikovsky—Symphonic poems. *Detroit Symphony Orch.; National Symphony Orch.; Dorati, cond.* Reissues.
• ARG 3-4/95: 200

21130. 443 006-2 (2 discs): Kodály—Hary Janos: Suite; Galanta dances; Marosszek dances; Peacock variations; Summer evening; Symphony; Concerto for orchestra; Theatre overture. *Philharmonia Hungarica; Dorati, cond.* Reissues.
• ARG 7-8/95: 137

21131. 443 009-2 (2 discs): Mozart—Sacred music. *Soloists; Academy of St. Martin-in-the-Fields; Marriner, cond.* Reissues.
• ARG 9-10/95: 182

21132. 443 012-2: Beethoven—Piano sonatas no. 14-15, 17, 21-24, 32. *Gulda, piano.*
• ARG 9-10/95: 103

21133. 443 015-2 (2 discs): Smetana—Ma vlast; Bartered bride: Overture, polka, furiant; Haakon Jarl. Dvořák—Prague waltzes; Nocturne; Czech suite. *Israel Phil. Orch.; Weller, Kertész, conds.; Detroit Symphony Orch.; Dorati, cond.*

Reissues.
+ ARG 7-8/95: 199

21134. 443 018-2 (2 discs): *Pavarotti, Freni, Ricciarelli: Live!* Music of Verdi, Massenet, Ponchielli, Donizetti, Meyerbeer, and others. *Pavarotti, tenor; Freni, Ricciarelli, sopranos.* Recorded live.
+ ARG 3-4/95: 262

21135. 443 021-2 (2 discs): DEBUSSY— Piano music. *Rogé, piano.* Reissues.
+ ARG 3-4/95: 94

21136. 443 024-2 (2 discs): Music of Tchaikovsky, Borodin, Glinka, Rubinstein, and Dargomizhsky; Folk songs. *N. Ghiaurov, bass; Z. Ghiaurov, piano; Kaval Orch.; Margaritov, cond.* Recorded 1971, 1973.
+ ARG 7-8/95: 261

21137. 443 027-2 (2 discs): HAYDN— Creation; Salve Regina. *Soloists; Brighton Festival Chorus; Royal Phil. Orch.; Dorati, cond.; London Chamber Choir & Orch.; Heltay, cond.* Reissues.
• ARG 7-8/96: 126

21138. 443 030-2 (2 discs): MAHLER— Symphonies no. 1, 3. *Forrester, contralto; California Boys Choir; Los Angeles Master Chorale; Los Angeles Phil. Orch.; Israel Phil. Orch.; Mehta, cond.* Reissues.
+ ARG 9-10/95: 172

21139. 443 033-2 (2 discs): Music of Offenbach, Bizet, Chabrier, Dukas and Saint-Saëns. *Philharmonia Orch.; Munch, cond.; Paris Conservatory Orch.; Martinon, cond.; Orch. de la Suisse Romande; Ansermet, cond.; Israel Phil. Orch.; Solti, cond.* Reissues.
- ARG 7-8/96: 166

21140. 443 118-2: BEETHOVEN—Piano concerto no. 6. BACH—Piano concerto, BWV 1054. *Mustonen, piano; Deutsche Kammerphilharmonie; Saraste, cond.*
- ARG 5-6/95: 83
+ Fa 5-6/95: 134

21141. 443 171-2: DELIUS—Appalachia; Song of the high hills; Over the hills and far away. *Evans, soprano; Hoare, tenor; Washington, baritone; Welsh National Opera; Mackerras, cond.*
+ Gr 1/96: 88

21142. 443 172-2: IVES—Symphony no. 4; The unanswered question. VARÈSE— Amériques. *Cleveland Orch.; Dohnányi, cond.*
+ ARG 7-8/95: 131
+ Fa 5-6/95: 226
+ Gr 11/94: 78

21143. 443 173-2: BARTÓK—Music for strings, percussion, and celesta. MARTINŮ—Concerto for string quartet and orchestra. JANÁČEK—Capriccio for piano left-hand and chamber ensemble. *Majeske, Goldschmidt, violins; Vernon, viola; Geber, cello; Jones, piano; Cleveland Orch.; Dohnányi, cond.*
+ ARG 1-2/96: 79
• Fa 9-10/95: 135
• Gr 4/95: 47

21144. 443 174-2: GRIEG—Piano concerto. TCHAIKOVSKY—Piano concerto no. 1. *Jablonski, piano; Philharmonia Orch.; Maag, cond.*
- Gr 10/94: 106

21145. 443 175-2: MOZART—Eine kleine Nachtmusik; Concerto for flute and harp; Sinfonia concertante. *Majeske, violin; Vernon, viola; Smith, flute; Wellbaum, harp; Cleveland Orch.; Dohnányi, cond.*
+ ARG 7-8/95: 161
• Gr 2/95: 50

21146. 443 176-2: MOZART—Clarinet concerto; Oboe concerto; Bassoon concerto. *Mack, oboe; McGill, bassoon; Cohen, clarinet; Cleveland Orch.; Dohnanyi, cond.*
+ Gr 2/96: 52

21147. 443 322-2: SCHUMANN—Abegg variations; Fantasy, op. 17; Faschingsschwank aus Wien. *Ashkenazy, piano.*
+ Gr 2/95: 75

21148. 443 324-2: RESPIGHI—Concerto gregoriano; Poema autunnale. SAINT-SAËNS—Violin concerto no. 3. *Amoyal, violin; French National Orch.; Dutoit, cond.*
+ Gr 7/95: 64

21149. 443 325-2: PROKOFIEV— Symphonies no. 6-7. *Cleveland Orch.; Ashkenazy, cond.*
• Gr 4/95: 66

21150. 443 327-2: BRUCKNER—Symphony no. 4. *San Francisco Symphony Orch.; Blomstedt, cond.*
• Gr 7/95: 46

21151. 443 350-2 (2 discs): MAHLER— Symphony no. 2. *Ziesak, soprano; Hellekant, mezzo-soprano; San Francisco Symphony; San Francisco Chorus; Blomstedt, cond.*
+ ARG 3-4/95: 132
• Fa 3-4/95: 217
• Gr 12/94: 86

21152. 443 376-2: HARBISON—Oboe concerto; Symphony no. 2. SESSIONS— Symphony no. 2. *San Francisco Symphony Orch.; Blomstedt, cond.*
+ ARG 7-8/94: 110
+ Gr 7/94: 44

21153. 443 381-2: *Hallelujah!* Music of Handel, Beethoven, Mendelssohn, Franck, Mozart, Puccini, and others. *Mormon Tabernacle Choir; Ottley, cond.*
+ ARG 3-4/95: 257

21154. 443 444-2: *Mephisto magic.* Music of Bartók, Kodály, Liszt, and Weiner. *Chicago Symphony Orch.; Solti, cond.* Recorded live 1993.
+ ARG 3-4/95: 230
+ Gr 1/95: 64

21155. 443 445-2 (2 discs): HAYDN—The creation. *Ziesak, Lippert, Pape, Scharinger; Chicago Symphony Orch. & Chorus; Solti, cond.*
+ ARG 7-8/95: 121
• Fa 7-8/95: 201
+ Gr 5/95: 93
+ ON 11/95: 48

21156. 443 450-2: WALTON—Symphony no. 1; Cello concerto. *Cohen, cello; Bournemouth Symphony Orch.; Litton, cond.*
+ ARG 11-12/96: 233
• Fa 9-10/96: 354
+ Gr 10/95: 78

21157. 443 451-2: MOZART—Organ works. *Trotter, organ.*
+ Gr 10/95: 98

21158. 443 452-2: *Cecilia Bartoli: Mozart portraits.* Music from Così fan tutte, Le nozze di Figaro, Don Giovanni, Davidde penitente, and Exsultate, jubilate. *Bartoli, mezzo-soprano; Vienna Chamber Orch.; Fischer, cond.*
+ ARG 3-4/95: 147
• Fa 1-2/95: 322
+ Gr 11/94: 146
+ ON 1/21/95: 37
+ Op 2/95: 248

21159. 443 461-2 (2 discs): BERLIOZ— Enfance du Christ; Choral music; Mort de Cléopâtre. *Morison, Pashley, Pears, Fleet, Cameron; St. Anthony Singers; Goldsborough Orch.; English Chamber Orch.; C. Davis, cond.* Reissues.
+ Gr 12/94: 136

21160. 443 470-2 (2 discs): HANDEL— Israel in Egypt; Chandos anthem no. 10. *Gale, Watson, Bowman, Partridge, Watt; English Chamber Orch.; Preston, cond.; Academy of St. Martin-in-the-Fields; Willcocks, cond.* Reissues.
• ARG 7-8/96: 123

21161. 443 476-2 (2 discs): VIVALDI— Estro armonico; Wind concertos. *Academy of St. Martin-in-the-Fields; Marriner, cond.* Recorded 1973.
+ ARG 3-4/95: 216

21162. 443 482-2 (2 discs): MONTEVERDI—Vespers. BASSANO—Hodie Christus natus est. G. GABRIELI—Motets. *Gomez, Palmer, Bowman, Tear; Monteverdi Choir; Monteverdi Orch.; Gardiner, cond.* Reissue.
+ ARG 3-4/95: 146

21163. 443 488-2 (2 discs): KODÁLY— Háry János; Variations on a Hungarian folksong; The peacock; Psalmus

LONDON

Hungaricus. *Komlóssy, Palócz, Melis, Bende, Szőnyi, László, Ustinov, Kozma; Edinburgh Festival Chorus; Brighton Festival Chorus; Wandsworth School Boys' Choir; London Symphony Orch. & Chorus; Kertész, cond.* Reissue.
+ ARG 1-2/95: 126
+ Gr 10/95: 134

21164. 443 530-2 (2 discs): MOZART—Die Entführung aus dem Serail; Overtures. *Lipp, Loose, Ludwig, Klein, Koréh, Woester; Vienna State Opera Chorus; Vienna Phil. Orch.; London Symphony Orch.; Krips, cond.* Reissue; recorded 1951-52.
• Gr 7/95: 114

21165. 443 539-2 (2 discs): GOUNOD—Roméo et Juliette. *Jobin, Micheau, Rehfuss, Mollet, Collart, Cambon, Ricquier, Rialland, Roquetty, Philippe; Paris Opéra; Erede, cond.* Reissue; recorded 1954.
+ Gr 6/95: 109

21166. 443 542-2 (2 discs): DONIZETTI—L'elisir d'amore. *Güden, Di Stefano, Capecchi, Corena, Mandelli; Maggio Musicale Fiorentino; Molinari-Pradelli, cond.* Reissue.
+ Gr 7/95: 112

21167. 443 548-2 (2 discs): MOZART—Serenades. *Vienna Mozart Ensemble; Boskovsky, cond.* Reissues.
- ARG 7-8/96: 161

21168. 443 569-2: ZEMLINSKY—Lyrische Symphonie, op. 18; Symphonische Gesänge, op. 20. *Marc, soprano; Hagegård, baritone; White, bass-baritone; Royal Concertgebouw Orch.; Chailly, cond.*
+ ARG 1-2/96: 202
+ Fa 7-8/95: 375
+ Gr 12/94: 103

21169. 443 570-2: SCHUBERT—Piano sonata D. 850; Impromptus; Moments musicaux. *Curzon, piano.* Reissues.
+ Gr 4/95: 92

21170. 443 571-2: BARTÓK—Duke Bluebeard's castle. *Berry, Ludwig; London Symphony Orch.; Kertész, cond.* Reissue.
+ Gr 4/95: 119

21171. 443 575-2: BRIDGE—Cello sonata. SCHUBERT—Arpeggione sonata. *Rostropovich, cello; Britten, piano.* Recorded 1968.
+ ARG 1-2/97: 84
+ Gr 4/95: 77

21172. 443 577-2: STRAVINSKY—Pulcinella suite; Apollon musagète; Capriccio. *Ogdon, piano; Academy of St. Martin-in-the-Fields; Marriner, cond.* Reissues.
+ Gr 4/95: 72

21173. 443 578-2: MENDELSSOHN—Symphony no. 3; A midsummer night's dream: Excerpts; Hebrides. *London Symphony Orch.; Maag, cond.* Reissue.
+ ARG 1-2/97: 139
+ Gr 7/95: 60

21174. 443 579-2: SCHUBERT—Piano sonatas D. 664, 784; Ungarische Melodie; Waltzes, D. 145. *Ashkenazy, piano.* Reissue.
+ Gr 4/95: 92

21175. 443 581-2 (2 discs): WAGNER—Der Ring des Nibelungen: spoken introduction with 193 musical examples. *Cooke, narrator; various singers; Vienna Phil. Orch.; Solti, cond.* Reissue.
+ Gr 5/95: 117

21176. 443 672-2: WEBER—Der Freischütz. *Behrens, Kollo, Donath, Meven, Brendel, Moll, Grumbach, Boysen, Sapell; Bavarian Radio Chorus & Symphony Orch; Kubelik, cond.* Reissue.
+ Gr 8/95: 128

21177. 443 675-2: STRAUSS—Ariadne auf Naxos. *Rysanek, Jurinac, Peters, Berry; Vienna Phil. Orch.; Leinsdorf, cond.* Reissue.
+ Gr 12/95: 161

21178. 443 678-2 (3 discs): VERDI—La forza del destino. *Milanov, Di Stefano, Warren, Elias, Tozzi; Academia di Santa Cecilia; Previtali, cond.* Recorded 1958.
• ARG 11-12/96: 227

21179. 443 682-2 (4 discs): WAGNER—Tristan und Isolde. *Mitchinson, Gray, Wilkens, Howell, Joll, Folwell, Davies, Moses, Harris; Welsh National Opera; Goodall, cond.* Reissue.
+ Gr 5/95: 117

21180. 443 690-2 (2 discs): WAGNER—Rheingold. *Hale, Schwarz, Begley, Schreier, Kapellmann; Cleveland Orch.; Dohnányi, cond.*
+ ARG 7-8/96: 222
• Fa 5-6/96: 311
+ Fi 4/96: 126
• Gr 11/95: 161
• ON 4/13/96: 52
• Op 12/95: 1494

21181. 443 693-2 (4 discs): BERLIOZ—Les Troyens. *Voigt, Pollet, Lakes, Quilico; Choeur & Orch. Symphonique de Montreal; Dutoit, cond.*
+ ARG 3-4/95: 75
• Fa 3-4/95: 132
+ Gr 12/94: 150
+ ON 2/4/95: 40
- Op 4/95: 488

21182. 443 703-2: RIMSKY-KORSAKOV—Scheherazade. STRAVINSKY—Scherzo fantastique. *Concertgebouw Orch.; Chailly, cond.*
+ ARG 1-2/95: 162

• Fa 1-2/95: 244
+ Gr 10/94: 116

21183. 443 753-2 (2 discs): BRUCKNER—Symphonies no. 3, 8. *Cleveland Orch.; Dohnányi, cond.*
• Gr 5/96: 56

21184. 443 771-2: BRAHMS—German Requiem. *Norberg-Schulz, Holzmair; San Francisco Symphony Orch.; Blomstedt, cond.*
• ARG 11-12/95: 95
+ Gr 7/95: 93

21185. 443 772-2: STRAVINSKY—Agon; Orpheus; Jeu de cartes. *Deutsches Symphony Orch. Berlin; Ashkenazy, cond.*
• Gr 12/94: 94

21186. 443 773-2: BARTÓK—Concerto for orchestra; Kossuth. *San Francisco Symphony Orch.; Blomstedt, cond.*
+ ARG 1-2/96: 78
• Fa 1-2/96: 131
+ Gr 7/95: 43

21187. 443 774-2: STRAVINSKY—Petrushka (1947 version); Pulcinella. *Zoon, flute; Masseurs, trumpet; Brink, piano; Antonacci, soprano; Ballo, tenor; Shimell, bass; Royal Concertgebouw Orch.; Chailly, cond.*
+ ARG 9-10/95: 224
+ Fa 9-10/95: 331
+ Gr 6/95: 58

21188. 443 775-2: STRAVINSKY—Petrushka (1911); Jeu de cartes. *Chicago Symphony Orch.; Solti, cond.*
• ARG 9-10/96: 210
• Fa 9-10/96: 336
• Gr 1/96: 64

21189. 443 776-2: IVES—Orchestral sets no. 1-2. RUGGLES—Sun treader; Man and mountains. CRAWFORD—Andante. *Cleveland Orch.; Dohnanyi, cond.*
+ Gr 12/95: 82

21190. 443 785-2 (12 discs): HAYDN—Keyboard music. *McCabe, piano.* Reissues.
+ Gr 12/95: 114

21191. 443 838-2 (2 discs): ROSSINI—String sonatas. DONIZETTI—Quartet. CHERUBINI—Etude no. 2. BELLINI—Oboe concerto. *Tuckwell, horn; Lord, oboe; Academy of St. Martin-in-the-Fields; Marriner, cond.* Reissues.
+ ARG 11-12/95: 188

21192. 443 847-2 (2 discs): BACH—Brandenburg concertos; Concertos for violin and oboe, flute. *Caine, violin; Miller, oboe; Bennett, flute; English Chamber Orch.; Academy of St. Martin-in-the-Fields; Britten; Marriner, conds.* Reissues.
+ ARG 11-12/95: 69

21193. 443 850-2 (2 discs): Rossini—Overtures. *National Phil. Orch.; Chailly, cond.* Reissues.
+ ARG 9-10/95: 202

21194. 443 853-2 (2 discs): Verdi—Rigoletto. *MacNeil, Cioni, Sutherland, Siepi; Academy of Santa Cecilia; Sansogno, cond.* Recorded 1961.
• ARG 7-8/95: 216

21195. 443 856-2: Elgar—Symphonies no. 1-2; Cockaigne; In the South. *London Phil. Orch.; Solti, cond.* Reissue.
+ ARG 1-2/96: 106

21196. 443 859-2 (2 discs): Bach—St. John passion. *Pears, Howell, Shirley-Quirk, Harper, Hodgson, Tear; Wandsworth School Boys Choir; English Chamber Orch.; Britten, cond.* Sung in English; recorded 1971.
+ ARG 3-4/96: 83

21197. 443 862-2 (2 discs): Corelli—Concerti grossi op. 6. *Academy of St. Martin-in-the-Fields; Marriner, cond.* Recorded 1973.
• ARG 9-10/95: 128

21198. 443 871-2 (2 discs): Bizet—Carmen. *Resnik, Del Monaco, Sutherland, Krause; Orch. de la Suisse Romande; Schippers, cond.* Recorded 1963.
+ ARG 11-12/95: 91

21199. 443 877-2: Mozart—Piano concerto no. 26; Quintet for piano and winds. *Holliger, oboe; Schmid, clarinet; Thunemann, bassoon; Vlatković, horn; Schiff, piano; Salzburg Mozarteum Camerata Academica; Vegh, cond.*
+ Gr 4/95: 66

21200. 443 892-2: Beethoven—Quintet for piano and winds. Spohr—Septet. *Juillet, violin; Kampen, cello; Rogé, piano; London Winds.*
+ Gr 4/96: 61

21201. 443 893-2: Bartók—Violin sonata no. 2; Contrasts; Solo violin sonata. *Schmid, clarinet; Fenyves, Engegard, Heinz, violins; Schiff, piano.*
+ Gr 11/94: 97

21202. 443 894-2: Bartók—Violin sonata no. 1; Sonata for two pianos and percussion; Duos: Selections. *Fenyves, Heinz, violins; Schiff, Canino, pianos.*
+ Gr 11/94: 97

21203. 443 895-2: Herrmann—Hitchcock movie thrillers. Psucho; Marnie; North by Northwest; Vertigo; Portrait. *London Phil. Orch.; Herrmann, cond.* Reissues.
+ ARG 11-12/96: 144
+ Fi 9/96: 124

21204. 443 896-2: Music of Tchaikovsky, Mussorgsky, and Borodin. *Royal Phil. Orch.; London Symphony Orch.; Orch.*

de la Suisse Romande; Stokowski, cond. Reissues.
+ ARG 9-10/96: 230

21205. 443 897-2: Satie—Piano music. Milhaud—Saudades do Brasil. *London Festival Players; Hermann, cond.* Recorded 1972.
+ ARG 11-12/96: 194

21206. 443 899-2: Herrmann—Film music. Journey to the center of the Earth; Seventh voyage of Sinbad; The day the Earth stood still; Fahrenheit 451; Gulliver's travels. *Orch.; Herrmann, cond.* Reissues.
+ ARG 11-12/96: 144
+ Fi 9/96: 124

21207. 443 900-2: Gershwin—Girl crazy: Suite; Overtures; Preludes; Second rhapsody. *Votapek, piano; Boston Pops Orch.; Fiedler, cond.* Reissue.
+ ARG 1-2/97: 109

21208. 443 901-2: Wagner—Ring des Nibelungen: Orchestral excerpts. *London Symphony Orch.; Stokowski, cond.* Reissue.
+ ARG 9-10/96: 225

21209. 443 930-2: *Jussi Björling sings opera arias.* Music of Ponchielli, Puccini, Giordano, Cilea, Verdi, Mascagni, and Lehár. *Björling, tenor; Tebaldi, Corsi, sopranos; Dani, mezzo-soprano; Maggio Musicale Fiorentino; Erede, cond.; Vienna Phil. Orch.; Reiner, cond.* Reissue.
+ Gr 10/95: 146

21210. 443 933-2: Schumann—Dichterliebe. Schubert—Songs. *Pears, tenor; Britten, piano.* Reissue.
• Gr 10/95: 114

21211. 443 934-2: Debussy—Khamma. Ravel—Daphnis et Chloé. *Het Groot Omroepkoor; Royal Concertgebouw Orch.; Chailly, cond.*
+ ARG 9-10/96: 186
+ Fa 7-8/96: 271
+ Gr 10/95: 51

21212. 443 968-2: Poulenc—Capriccio; Sonata for 2 pianos; Élégie; Sonata for piano duet; L'embarquement pour Cythère; Sonata for violin and piano; Élégie. *Juillet, violin; Cazalet, horn; Rogé, Collard, piano.*
+ Gr 10/95: 86

21213. 444 105-2: Orff—Carmina Burana. *Soloists; Royal Phil. Orch.; Dorati, cond.* Reissue.
- ARG 9-10/96: 174

21214. 444 106-2: Respighi—Rines of Rome; Fountains of Rome; Rossiniana. *Philharmonia Orch.; Munch, cond.; Royal Phil. Orch.; Dorati, cond.* Reissues.
+ ARG 9-10/96: 188

21215. 444 107-2: *Spectacular dances.* Music of Strauss, Ponchielli, Tchaikovsky, Weber, and others. *Royal Phil. Orch.; London Symphony Orch.; Black, cond.* Reissues.
+ ARG 11-12/96: 240

21216. 444 114-2: Walton—Scapino; Violin concerto; Symphony no. 2. *Little, violin; Bournemouth Symphony Orch.; Litton, cond.*
+ ARG 11-12/96: 234
+ Fa 5-6/96: 315
+ Gr 10/95: 78

21217. 444 115-2: Mozart—Piano quartets. *Shiokawa, violin; Höbarth, viola; Perényi, cello; Schiff, piano.*
• Gr 4/95: 84

21218. 444 134-2: Rossini—Petite messe solennelle. *Dessì, Scalchi, Sabbatini, Pertusi; Teatro Comunale Bologna; Chailly, cond.*
+ Gr 2/95: 89

21219. 444 170-2: Korngold—Between two worlds: Judgement day; Symphonic serenade; Theme and variations. *Frey, piano; Deutsches Symphonie-Orchester Berlin; Mauceri, cond.*
+ ARG 1-2/96: 130
• Fa 1-2/96: 236

21220. 444 172-2: Franck—Violin sonata. Chausson—Concert for violin, piano, and string quartet. *Amoyal, violin; Rogé, piano; Ysaÿe Quartet.*
+ Gr 2/96: 65

21221. 444 174-2 (3 discs): Mozart—Così fan tutte. *Fleming, Otter, Bär, Lopardo, Scarabelli, Pertusi; Chamber Orch. of Europe; Solti, cond.*
+ ARG 9-10/96: 170
• Fa 9-10/96: 269
+ Gr 3/96: 97
+ Op 4/96: 423

21222. 444 178-2 (2 discs): Strauss—Salome. *Malfitano, Terfel, Riegel, Schwarz; Vienna Phil. Orch.; Dohnanyi, cond.*
+ ARG 11-12/95: 213
• Fa 11-12/95: 393
+ Gr 4/95: 126
• ON 11/95: 45
• Op 8/95: 1003

21223. 444 181-2: Britten—Solo cello suites. *Cohen, cello.*
+ Gr 6/96: 71

21224. 444 182-2: Schreker—Der Geburtstag der Infantin. Schulhoff—Die Mondsüchtige; Hindemith—Der Dämon. *Gewandhaus Orch.; Zagrosek, cond.*
+ ARG 11-12/95: 244
+ Fa 11-12/95: 367
+ Gr 5/95: 50

21225. 444 318-2: Ravel—Piano trio. Debussy—Violin sonata; Cello sonata.

LONDON

Perlman, violin; Harrell, cello;
Ashkenazy, piano.
- • ARG 5-6/96: 173
- + Fa 5-6/96: 245
- • Gr 12/95: 103

21226. 444 322-2: KODÁLY—Hary Janos
suite; Peacock variations; Galanta and
Marosszek dances. *Montreal Symphony*
Orch.; Dutoit, cond.
- - ARG 9-10/96: 145
- + Gr 4/96: 48

21227. 444 323-2 (2 discs): MOZART—
Symphonies no. 25, 29, 38, 40; Serenata
notturno. *English Chamber Orch.;*
Britten, cond. Reissue.
- + ARG 11-12/95: 168

21228. 444 335-2: LASSUS—Missa Vinum
bonum; Missa Triste depart; Missa
Quand'io pens'al martire; Vinum bonum
et suave. ARCADELT—Quand'io pens'al
martire. GOMBERT—Triste depart m'avoit.
King's College Choir, Cambridge;
Cleobury, cond.
- + Gr 7/96: 89

21229. 444 337-2: BEETHOVEN—Missa
solemnis. *Varady, Vermillion, Cole,*
Pape; Rundfunkchor Berlin; Berlin Phil.
Orch.; Solti, cond. Recorded live 1994.
- + ARG 1-2/96: 83
- • Fa 11-12/95: 203
- + Gr 6/95: 87

21230. 444 338-2: BRAHMS—Variations
on a theme of Paganini: books 1-2.
SCHUMANN—Arabeske, op. 18; Symphonic
etudes, op. 13 (with appendix).
Thibaudet, piano.
- • ARG 11-12/96: 101
- + Fa 9-10/96: 161
- + Gr 10/96: 93

21231. 444 386-2: DEBUSSY—Printemps
(arr. Busser); La boîte à joujoux (arr.
Caplet); Children's corner (arr. Caplet);
La plus que lente. *Orch. Symphonique de*
Montréal; Dutoit, cond.
- + ARG 9-10/95: 131
- + Fa 9-10/95: 186
- + Gr 8/95: 68

21232. 444 395-2: PUCCINI—Gianni
Schicchi. *Nucci, Freni, Alagna, Podles;*
Orch. del Maggio Musicale Fiorentino;
Bartoletti, cond. Reissue.
- + Gr 5/96: 120

21233. 444 398-2: DUTILLEUX—Violin
concerto; Cello concerto. *Amoyal, violin;*
Harrell, cello; French National Orch.;
Dutoit, cond.
- + Gr 3/95: 42

21234. 444 405-2: STRAUSS—Capriccio.
Te Kanawa, Hagegård, Heilmann, Bär;
Vienna Phil. Orch.; Schirmer, cond.
- + ARG 11-12/96: 215
- + Fa 9-10/96: 333
- • Gr 2/96: 105
- + ON 8/96: 42

21235. 444 408-2: PROKOFIEV—Piano
sonatas no. 6-8. *Ashkenazy, piano.*
- - Gr 6/95: 79

21236. 444 409-2: KREISLER—The
Kreisler album. *Bell, violin; Coker,*
piano.
- • ARG 9-10/96: 146
- + Fa 9-10/96: 231
- + Gr 4/96: 64

21237. 444 428-2: MENDELSSOHN—
Symphonies no. 1, 5. *Deutsches*
Symphony Orch., Berlin; Ashkenazy,
cond.
- + Gr 6/95: 52

21238. 444 442-2 (3 discs): SCHREKER—
Die Gezeichneten. *Connell, Kruse,*
Pederson, Muff; Rundfunkchor Berlin;
Deutsches Symphonie-Orchester Berlin;
Zagrosek, cond.
- • ARG 11-12/95: 194
- + Fa 11-12/95: 359
- + Gr 6/95: 112
- + Op 7/95: 874

21239. 444 446-2 (2 discs): MAHLER—
Symphony no. 7. DIEPENBROCK—Im
grossen Schweigen. *Hagegård, baritone;*
Concertgebouw Orch.; Chailly, cond.
- + ARG 11-12/95: 150
- - Fa 11-12/95: 295
- + Gr 5/95: 52

21240. 444 450-2: *Pavarotti in Central*
Park. Music of Verdi, Donizetti, Cilea,
Leoncavallo, and others. *Pavarotti, tenor;*
Harlem Boys' Choir; New York Phil.;
Magiera, cond. Recorded 1993.
- + Gr 2/95: 106

21241. 444 455-2: MARTIN—Ballades;
Concerto for 7 winds, timpani,
percussion, and strings . *Lindberg,*
trombone; Harle, saxophone; Brautigam,
piano; other soloists; Royal
Concertgebouw Orch., Amsterdam;
Chailly, cond.
- + Gr 10/95: 60

21242. 444 458-2: *Carnegie Hall project.*
Music of Wagner, Brahms, Shostakovich,
Strauss, and Smetana. *Solti Orchestral*
Project; Solti, cond. Recorded live 1994.
- + ARG 7-8/96: 232
- + Fa 1-2/96: 415
- + Gr 12/95: 98

21243. 444 494-2: *Gregorian chant.*
Liturgy of St. Antony. *Coro Gregoriano*
de Lisboa; Matos, cond.
- + Gr 7/95: 108

21244. 444 517-2: SCRIABIN—Symphony
no. 1; Prometheus. *Balleys, contralto;*
Larin, tenor; Jablonski, piano; Berlin
Radio Chorus; Deutsches Symphony
Orch. Berlin; Ashkenazy, cond.
- • Gr 1/96: 62

21245. 444 518-2: CHOPIN—Piano
concerto no. 1. GRIEG—Concerto.

Mustonen, piano; San Francisco
Symphony Orch.; Blomstedt, cond.
- - ARG 7-8/96: 100
- - Fa 7-8/96: 182
- + Gr 11/95: 80

21246. 444 526-2 (2 discs): RAMEAU—
Hippolyte et Aricie. *Tear, Hickey, Baker,*
Shirley-Quirk; St. Anthony Singers;
English Chamber Orch.; Lewis, cond.
Reissue.
- + Gr 5/96: 120

21247. 444 529-2 (2 discs): CAVALLI—
L'Ormindo. *Wakefield, Runge,*
Garcisanz, Bork, Van Allan; London
Phil. Orch.; Leppard, cond. Reissue;
recorded 1969.
- • Gr 9/95: 101

21248. 444 541-2: SIBELIUS—Symphonies
no. 1, 7. *San Francisco Symphony Orch.;*
Blomstedt, cond.
- + Gr 5/96: 66

21249. 444 594-2 (3 discs): MOZART—
Don Giovanni. *Siepi, Nilsson, L. Price,*
Corena; Vienna Phil. Orch.; Leinsdorf,
cond. Reissue.
- + ARG 9-10/96: 171

21250. 444 630-2 (2 discs): SCHULHOFF—
Flammen. *Eaglen, Vermillion, Westi,*
Wolf; Deutsches Sinfonie-Orch. Berlin;
Mauceri, cond.
- + ARG 7-8/96: 189
- + Fa 5-6/96: 265
- + Gr 1/96: 106
- + ON 4/13/96: 52
- + Op 2/96: 192

21251. 444 786-2: *In a monastery*
garden. Music of Ketèlbey, Hubay,
Godard, Massenet, and others. *London*
Festival Orch.; Royal Phil. Orch.;
Rogers, cond. Reissues.
- + ARG 9/96: 144
- + Gr 8/96: 60

21252. 444 791-2: SHOSTAKOVICH—
Symphony no. 13. *Hopkins, speaker;*
Aleksashkin, bass; Chicago Symphony
Chorus; Chicago Symphony Orch.; Solti,
cond.
- + ARG 1-2/96: 174
- + Fa 1-2/96: 306
- • Gr 8/95: 85

21253. 444 803-2: PROKOFIEV—Visions
fugitives. HINDEMITH—Ludus tonalis.
Mustonen, piano.
- + ARG 1-2/97: 121
- + Fa 1-2/97: 229
- + Gr 5/96: 81

21254. 444 811-2: BRAHMS—Violin
concerto. SCHUMANN—Violin concerto.
Bell, violin; Cleveland Orch.; Dohnányi,
cond.
- • ARG 1-2/97: 80
- + Fa 1-2/97: 118
- + Gr 5/96: 54

21255. 444 812-2 (2 discs): Berlioz—La damnation de Faust. *Pollet, Leech, Cachemaille, Philippe, vocalists; Choeur et Orch. symphonique de Montréal; Dutoit, cond.*
- ARG 3-4/97: 95
- Fa 1-2/97: 109
- Gr 10/96: 91

21256. 444 817-2: Beethoven—Lieder. *Schreier, tenor; Schiff, piano.*
+ Gr 8/96: 81

21257. 444 819-2: Schulhoff—Piano concerto no. 2. Concerto for flute and piano; Jazz-inspired compositions. *Wild, Madzer, Schulhoff, pianos; Hawthorne String Quartet; Deutsche Kammerphilharmonie; Delfs, cond.*
+ ARG 9-10/96: 196
+ Gr 12/95: 88

21258. 444 821-2 (2 discs): Vivaldi—Concertos, op. 4. *Academy of St. Martin-in-the-Fields; Marriner, cond.* Reissue.
+ ARG 5-6/96: 216

21259. 444 833-2 (2 discs): Verdi—Requiem; Four sacred pieces. *Price, Elias, Björling, Tozzi; Vienna Singverein; Vienna Phil. Orch.; Reiner, cond.; Minton, mezzo-soprano; Los Angeles Master Chorale; Los Angeles Phil. Orch.; Mehta, cond.* Reissue.
+ ARG 3-4/96: 200
- Gr 2/96: 95

21260. 444 839-2 (2 discs): Rachmaninoff—Piano concertos. *Ashkenazy, piano; London Symphony Orch.; Previn, cond.* Reissue.
+ ARG 7-8/96: 174
+ Gr 2/96: 56

21261. 444 845-2 (2 discs): Rachmaninoff—Suites no. 1-2; Symphonic dances; Russian rhapsody; Etudes tableaux, op. 33; Corelli variations. *Ashkenazy, Previn, pianos.* Reissues.
+ ARG 7-8/96: 175

21262. 444 851-2 (2 discs): Liszt—Piano music. *Bolet, piano.* Reissues.
+ ARG 5-6/96: 137

21263. 444 861-2: Haydn—Piano trios no. 12, 26, 28, 30. *Shiokawa, violin; Pergamenschikow, cello; Schiff, piano.*
+ Gr 6/96: 65

21264. 444 862-2: Haydn—Keyboard trios. *Shiokawa, violin; Pergamenschikow, cello; Schiff, piano.*
+ Gr 1/96: 70

21265. 444 867-2: Smetana—Orchestral excerpts. *Cleveland Orch.; Dohnanyi, cond.*
+ Gr 2/96: 60

21266. 444 958-2: Satie—Trois gymnopédies; Six gnossiennes; Cinq nocturnes; Avant-dernières pensées; Pièces froides. *Rogé, piano.* Reissue.
+ ARG 9/96: 191
+ Fa 11-12/96: 355

21267. 444 995-2 (2 discs): Canteloube—Songs of the Auvergne. Villa-Lobos—Bachianas brasileiras no. 5. *Te Kanawa, soprano; English Chamber Orch.; Tate, cond.* Reissue.
+ ARG 7-8/96: 94

21268. 448 000-2 (3 discs): Beethoven—Piano concertos. *Lupu, piano; Israel Phil Orch.; Mehta, cond.* Reissues.
+ Gr 3/96: 41

21269. 448 063-2: Rubinstein—Piano concerto no. 4; Encores. *Cherkassky, piano; Royal Phil. Orch.; Ashkenazy, cond.*
+ Gr 3/96: 50

21270. 448 064-2: Messiaen—Le banquet céleste; Les corps glorieux; Verset pour la fête. *Trotter, organ.*
• Gr 8/96: 74

21271. 448 086-2 (2 discs): Chopin—Nocturnes (complete). *Ashkenazy, piano.* Reissues.
• ARG 9-10/96: 108

21272. 448 098-2 (2 discs): Bruckner—Symphonies no. 3-4. *Vienna Phil. Orch.; Böhm, cond.* Reissues.
+ Gr 3/96: 42

21273. 448 104-2 (2 discs): Beethoven—Fidelio. *Nilsson, McCracken, Böhme, Krause; Vienna Phil. Orch.; Maazel, cond.* Recorded 1964.
+ ARG 7-8/96: 76
+ Gr 11/96: 161

21274. 448 116-2 (2 discs): Rachmaninoff—Symphonies no. 1-3. *Concertgebouw Orch.; Ashkenazy, cond.* Reissue.
+ Gr 7/96: 60

21275. 448 119-2 (2 discs): Verdi—La traviata. *Gheorghiu, Lopardo, Nucci; Royal Opera House, Covent Garden; Solti, cond.* Recorded live 1994.
• Fa 1-2/96: 336
+ Fi 5/96: 135
+ Gr 8/95: 128
○ ON 12/9/95: 46

21276. 448 122-2: Shostakovich—Symphonies no. 5, 9. *Montreal Symphony Orch.; Dutoit, cond.*
• Gr 11/95: 94

21277. 448 134-2: Walton—Belshazzar's feast; Henry V: Suite; Crown imperial. *Terfel, bass-baritone; Bournemouth Symphony Orch. & Chorus; Waynflete Singers; Inviti; Litton, cond.*
• ARG 3-4/96: 206
+ Fa 3-4/96: 319

+ Fi 5/96: 132
+ Gr 10/95: 78

21278. 448 138-2: Chopin—Piano concerto no. 1; Andante spianato and Grande polonaise; Variations on Là ci darem la mano. *Nebolsin, piano; Deutsches Symphony Orch., Berlin; Ashkenazy, cond.*
• Gr 7/96: 48

21279. 448 139-2: Poulenc—Gloria; Stabat Mater; Litanies à la vierge noire. *Pollet, soprano; French Radio Choir; French National Orch.; Dutoit, cond.*
+ Gr 4/96: 94

21280. 448 155-2: Wagner—Orchestral excerpts. *Concertgebouw Orch.; Chailly, cond.*
• ARG 7-8/96: 221
+ Fa 7-8/96: 335
• Gr 3/96: 56

21281. 448 177-2: Stravinsky—Ragtime; Octet; Pieces; Histoire du soldat; Pastorale; Concertino; Septet; Epitaphium. *European Soloists Ensemble; Ashkenazy, piano & cond.*
+ Gr 8/96: 58

21282. 448 179-2: Shostakovich—Symphony no. 11 "The year 1903". *St. Petersburg Phil. Orch.; Ashkenazy, cond.*
+ Gr 5/96: 64

21283. 448 180-2: Tchaikovsky—Piano concertos no. 2-3. *Jablonski, piano; Philharmonia Orch.; Dutoit, cond.*
• Gr 6/96: 60

21284. 448 191-2 (2 discs): Albéniz—Iberia; Navarra. Granados—Goyescas. *Larrocha, piano.* Reissues.
+ Gr 4/96: 72

21285. 448 194-2 (2 discs): Haydn—Symphonies no. 82-87. *Philharmonia Hungarica; Dorati, cond.* Reissue.
+ ARG 9-10/96: 135

21286. 448 197, 448 200-2 (2 2-disc sets): Brahms—Symphonies; Serenades; Haydn variations. *Vienna Phil. Orch.; Kertész, cond.* Reissues.
• ARG 9-10/96: 101
+ Fi 10/96: 140

21287. 448 218-2: Rossini—Overtures. *Orch. of La Scala, Milan; Chailly, cond.*
+ Gr 5/96: 64

21288. 448 219-2: Rachmaninoff—Piano concertos no. 1, 3. *Thibaudet, piano; Cleveland Orch.; Ashkenazy, cond.*
• ARG 7-8/96: 174
+ Fa 5-6/96: 244
+ Fa 7-8/96: 267
• Fi 6/96: 127
• Gr 10/95: 66

21289. 448 252-2 (2 discs): Khachaturian—Symphony no. 2 "The

bell"; Piano concerto; Violin concerto; Masquerade: Suite. *Ricci, violin; Larrocha, piano; Vienna Phil. Orch.; Khachaturian, cond.; London Phil. Orch.; Frühbeck de Burgos, Fistoulari, conds.; London Symphony Orch.; Black, cond.* Reissue.
+ Gr 6/96: 48

21290. 448 261-2 (2 discs): COPLAND—Orchestra music. *Various performers.* Reissues.
+ ARG 9-10/96: 111
+ Gr 8/96: 44

21291. 448 264-2 (2 discs): MARTIN—Concerto; Etudes; Petite symphonie concertante; Passacaglia; Violin concerto; In terra pax. *Various performers.* Reissues.
+ Gr 8/96: 50

21292. 448 270-2 (2 discs): POULENC—Piano concerto; Sextet for piano and winds; Sonata for 2 pianos; Concerto for 2 pianos and orchestra; Concerto for organ, strings, and percussion; Concert champêtre; Gloria. *Various performers.* Reissue.
• Gr 7/96: 60

21293. 448 279-2 (2 discs): SCHOENBERG—Verklärte Nacht; Chamber symphony no. 1; Variations for orchestra; Pieces, op.16; Lieder, op. 8; Erwartung. *Silja, soprano; Los Angeles Phil. Orch.; Mehta, cond.; Cleveland Orch.; Vienna Phil. Orch.; Dohnanyi, cond.* Reissues.
+ Gr 8/96: 56

21294. 448 282-2: *Opera lover's Broadway.* Music from My fair lady, Kiss me Kate, Show boat, Carousel, Too many girls, West Side story, One touch of Venus, and Fiddler on the roof. *Various performers.*
+ ARG 1-2/96: 239

21295. 448 293-2: MAHLER—Symphony no. 8. *Harper, Popp, Augér, Minton, Watts, Kollo, Shirley-Quirk, Talvela, vocalists; Vienna Boys' Choir; Vienna State Opera Chorus; Vienna Singverein; Chicago Symphony Orch.; Solti, cond.* Reissue.
+ Gr 5/96: 60

21296. 448 300-2: *Cecilia Bartoli: a portrait.* Music of Mozart, Parisotti, Giordani, Caccini, Schubert, and Rossini. *Bartoli, mezzo-soprano; various orch. accs.* Reissue.
+ ARG 1-2/96: 230
+ Fa 1-2/96: 357

21297. 448 389-2: EISLER—Deutsche Sinfonie. *Soloists; Leipzig Gewandhaus Orch.; Zagrosek, cond.*
+ ARG 7-8/96: 108
+ Fa 7-8/96: 163
+ Gr 12/95: 126

21298. 448 560-2: *Day's end: the soft sounds of the Spanish guitar.* Music of Tarrega, Albéniz, Anon., Segovia, Granados, Sainz, Torroba, and Llobet. *Fernandez, Hall, Gómez, Walker, Williams, guitars.*
+ ARG 1-2/97: 205
+ Fa 11-12/96: 454

21299. 448 570-2: MOZART—Symphony no. 36; Piano concerto no. 15. *Vienna Phil. Orch.; Bernstein, piano & cond.* Reissue.
+ ARG 11-12/96: 171

21300. 448 572-2 (2 discs): *New Year's day concert in Vienna, 1979.* Music of the Strausses, Ziehrer, and Suppé. *Vienna Phil. Orch.; Boskovsky, cond.* Reissues.
+ ARG 1-2/97: 193
+ Gr 4/96: 58

21301. 448 578-2: BRAHMS—Piano sonata no. 3; 2 intermezzi. SCHUBERT—Piano sonata D. 960. *Curzon, piano.* Recorded 1962, 1972.
+ ARG 1-2/97: 82
+ Gr 7/96: 74

21302. 448 581-2: BRUCKNER—Symphony no. 5 (Schalk ed.) WAGNER—Siegfried idyll. *Vienna Phil. Orch.; Knappertsbusch, cond.* Recorded 1956.
• ARG 1-2/97: 85
• Gr 2/96: 44

21303. 448 594-2 (2 discs): *The age of Bel canto.* Music of Handel, Bononcini, Arne, Shield, and others. *Sutherland, soprano; Horne, mezzo-soprano; New Symphony of London; London Symphony Orch.; Bonynge, cond.* Reissues.
+ ARG 11-12/96: 274
+ Gr 11/96: 178

21304. 448 616-2: LLOYD WEBBER—Requiem. *Domingo, Brightman, Miles-Kingston; Winchester Cathedral Choir; English Chamber Orch.; Maazel, cond.* Reissue.
+ Fa 3-4/96: 206

21305. 448 617-2: BEETHOVEN—Symphony no. 9. *Norman, Runkel, Schunk, Sotin; Chicago Symphony Orch. & Chorus; Solti, cond.* Recorded 1986.
- Fa 1-2/97: 150

21306. 448 618-2: RAVEL—Gaspard de la nuit; Miroirs; Pavane; Jeux d'eau; Haydn minuet; Prelude. *Thibaudet, piano.* Reissue.
• ARG 1-2/96: 159
- Fa 3-4/96: 258

21307. 448 629-2: MOZART—Piano sonatas, K. 311/284, 457, 570; Fantasia, K. 475; Adagio, K. 540. *Ashkenazy, piano.*
• Gr 7/96: 78

21308. 448 645-2: CHOPIN—Waltzes; Polonaise, op. 53. *Jablonski, piano.*
• Gr 8/96: 72

21309. 448 701-2: *Pavarotti plus.* Pavarotti 60th birthday album. *Pavarotti, tenor; Other vocal soloists; Philharmonia Orch.; Levine, cond.; Royal Phil. Orch.; Magiera, cond.*
• Gr 2/96: 107

21310. 448 897-2: MAHLER—Symphony no. 4. WAGNER—Siegfried's Rhine journey. *Hendricks, soprano; Israel Phil. Orch.; Mehta, cond.; English Chamber Orch.; Ashkenazy, cond.* Reissue.
• Gr 7/96: 56

21311. 448 898-2: BRUCKNER—Symphony no. 1. *Chicago Symphony Orch.; Solti, cond.*
+ Gr 4/96: 42

21312. 448 901-2: *United Nations 50th anniversary.* ROSSINI—William Tell overture. BARTÓK—Concerto for orchestra. BEETHOVEN—Fidelio: finale. *London Voices; World Orch. for Peace; Solti, cond.*
+ ARG 7-8/96: 233
• Fa 7-8/96: 403
+ Gr 3/96: 40

21313. 452 022-2 (2 discs): DEBUSSY—Complete piano works, vol. 1. *Thibaudet, piano.*
• ARG 1-2/97: 94
• Fa 1-2/97: 147
• Gr 8/96: 73

21314. 452 239-2: BORODIN—String quartet no. 2. SMETANA—String quartet no. 1. *Takács String Quartet.*
+ ARG 11-12/96: 96
- Fa 11-12/96: 383
+ Gr 7/96: 70

21315. 452 417-2: *Arias.* Music of Verdi, Massenet, Catalani, Bellini, Puccini, Boito, Gounod, Donizetti, and Grigoriu. *Gheorghiu, soprano; Orch. del Teatro Regio di Torino; Mauceri, cond.*
• ARG 9-10/96: 265
• Fa 9-10/96: 382 (Mandel)
+ Fa 9-10/96: 382 (Camner)
• Fi 10/96: 143
• Gr 6/96: 98
+ Op 6/96: 728

21316. 452 602-2: MOZART—Arias. *Fleming, soprano; Orch. of St. Luke's; Mackerras, cond.*
+ ARG 1-2/97: 144 (Arthur)
• ARG 1-2/97: 144 (Moses)
• Fa 1-2/97: 210
+ Gr 10/96: 106
+ ON 12/14/96: 52
• Op 10/96: 1246

21317. 452 667-2: *Chant d'amour.* Music of Bizet, Delibes, Viardot, Berlioz, and Ravel. *Bartoli, mezzo-soprano; Chung, piano.*

- ARG 1-2/97: 223
+ Fa 3-4/97: 352
+ Gr 12/96: 134
+ ON 12/14/96: 50

LORELT

21318. LNT 101: *British women composers, vol. 1.* Music of Wallen, Cooper, Maconchy and Lefanu. *Baines, Andoh, Minton, Manning, vocalists; Lontano; Martinez, cond.*
+ Fa 11-12/92: 415
+ Gr 9/92: 100

21319. LNT 104: BUTLER—Tin pan ballet; Bluegrass variations; Jazz machines; On the rocks; Going with the grain. *Lontano; Martinez, cond.*
+ ARG 7-8/94: 88
□ Gr 5/94: 48

21320. LNT 106: GINASTERA—Piano sonatas (complete); Piano music. *Petchersky, piano.*
+ ARG 7-8/95: 113

21321. LNT 108: BOULEZ—Le marteau sans maitre; Piano sonata no. 1. *Hirst, soprano; Ponthus, piano; Lontano; Martinez, cond.*
+ Gr 3/96: 79

LOTOS

21322. LT 0002, 0004, 0009, 0021 (4 separate discs): Romance; Lovely time; Lovely time 2; La follia. *Suk, violin.*
+ ARG 9-10/95: 273

21323. LT 0007 (2 discs): PERGOLESI—Six concertinos; Sinfonietta; Sonata in stile di concerto. *Suk, violin; Suk Chamber Orch.; Karr-Bertoli, cond.*
+ ARG 7-8/95: 166
- Fa 7-8/95: 268

21324. LT 0012: DVOŘÁK—Violin and piano music. SUK—Violin and piano music. O. DVOŘÁK (ARR. SUK)—Lullaby. *Suk, violin; Hála, piano.*
+ Fa 7-8/95: 178

21325. LT 0019: Music of Dvořák, Smetana, Janáček, and Suk. *Suk, violin; Hála, piano; Bárta, cello; Urbanová, soprano; Kriz, baritone; Czech, piano.*
● ARG 7-8/95: 254
● Fa 9-10/95: 408

LOUISIANA CONCERTS

21326. 1001: GADE—Novelettes for strings. *Louisiana Museum Art Ensemble.*
- ARG 9-10/96: 122

LOUISVILLE ORCHESTRA

21327. LCD 001: HODKINSON—Sinfonia concertante. JOSEPHS—Variations on a theme of Beethoven. KORTE—Symphony no. 3. *Louisville Orch.; Smith, Zimmermann, cond.*

● ARG 7-8/90: 125
+ DA 7/90: 52
+ Fa 7-8/90: 174

21328. LCD 002: HINDEMITH—Piano concerto. ZWILICH—Symphony no. 2. LAWHEAD—Aleost. *Luvisi, piano; Louisville Orch.; Smith, Zimmermann, cond.*
+ ARG 11-12/90: 143
+ Fa 7-8/90: 172

21329. LCD 003: HANLON—Cumulus nimbus. FENNELLY—Fantasy variations. SCHULLER—Farbenspiel-Concerto no. 3 for orchestra. *Louisville Orch.; Zimmermann, Smith, Schuller, cond.*
+ ARG 1-2/91: 128
+ Fa 1-2/91: 210

21330. LCD 005: CRESTON—Invocation and dance. HUSA—Apotheosis of this earth; Monodrama (Portrait of an artist). LUTOSŁAWSKI—Fanfare for Louisville. *Louisville Orch. University of Louisville Concert Choir; L.L. Smith, Husa, conds.*
□ ARG 11-12/91: 84
● Fa 9-10/92: 220

21331. LCD 006: TOWER—Island rhythms. GUBAIDULINA—Pro et contra. LUENING—Kentucky concerto. *Louisville Orch.; Smith, cond.*
□ ARG 3-4/92: 175

21332. LCD 007: BOLCOM—Symphonies, no. 1, 3; Seattle Slew: suite. *Louisville Orch.; L. L. Smith, cond.*
+ ARG 11-12/92: 92
+ Fa 11-12/92: 204

21333. LCD 008: CORIGLIANO—Piano concerto; Voyage; Summer fanfare; Promenade overture; Campane di Ravello. *Tocco, piano; Louisville Orch.; Smith, cond. Reissue.*
+ ARG 1-2/95: 97

21334. LCD 009: Music of Hailstork, Schuller, Zwilich, and Dzubay. *Laredo, violin; Robinson, cello; Louisville Orch.; Smith, Schuller, conds.*
+ ARG 7-8/96: 239
+ Fi 4/96: 114

21335. LCD 010: THOMAS—Triple concerto; Wind dance. LÉON—Carabali. *Debussy Trio; Louisville Orch.; Smith, Schuller, conds.*
□ ARG 7-8/96: 214
+ Fi 4/96: 115

21336. LS 785 (LP): RAMSIER—Divertimento concertante on a theme of Couperin, for double bass and orchestra; Road to Hamelin, for narrator, double bass and orchestra. *Karr, double bass and narrator; Louisville Orch.; Bernhardt, cond.*
- Fa 3-4/87: 189

21337. LS 786 (LP): HARRIS—Symphony 1933; Violin concerto. *Fulkerson, violin;*

Louisville Orch.; Mester, Smith, cond.
+ ARG 3-4/88: 45
+ Fa 11-12/87: 150

21338. LS 787 (LP): ROREM—Air music; Eagles. *Louisville Orch.; Leonard, Zimmermann, conds.*
+ ARG 3-4/88: 72
+ Fa 5-6/88: 193

21339. LS 788 (LP): GOULD—Viola concerto; Flourishes and Galop. CHIHARA—Forest music. *Glazer, viola; Louisville Orch.; Smith, Endo, cond.*
□ ARG 3-4/88: 38
+ Fa 5-6/88: 132

21340. LS 789 (LP): C. BAKER—Glass bead game. J. FOLEY—Movement for orchestra. PISTON—Ricercare. *Louisville Orch.; Bernhardt, Smith, cond.*
● ARG 7-8/88: 10
+ Fa 7-8/88: 110

21341. LS 790 (LP): SVOBODA—Symphony no. 4; Ex libris. GOOSSEN—Orpheus singing. *Louisville Orch.; Smith, Bernhardt, cond.*
+ Fa 11-12/88: 290

LOVELY MUSIC

21342. LCD 1001: ASHLEY—Private parts. *Ashley, voice; Tyranny, piano, polymoog, clavinet; Kris, tablas.*
+ Fa 3-4/91: 129

21343. LCD 1002: ASHLEY—Automatic writing; Purposeful lady slow afternoon; She was a visitor. *R. Ashley, Johnson, Liddell, M. Ashley, Lloyd, M. Lucier, vocalists; Brandeis University Chamber Chorus; A. Lucier, cond.*
+ ARG 3-4/97: 75
□ Fa 1-2/97: 78

21344. LCD 1003: ASHLEY—Yellow man with heart with wings. *Grenier, voice; Ashley, voice & instruments; Tyranny, clavinet.*
□ Fa 11-12/90: 140

21345. LCD 1004: ASHLEY—eL/ Aficionado. *R. Ashley, speaker; Buckner, baritone; Humbert, soprano; S. Ashley, tenor; R. Ashley, Hamilton, electronics.*
+ ARG 3-4/95: 66
+ Fa 3-4/95: 106

21346. LCD 1011: LUCIER—Music on a long thin wire. *Lucier, wire & oscillator.*
□ Fa 5-6/93: 250

21347. LCD 1013: LUCIER—I am sitting in a room, for voice on tape. *Lucier, voice & electronics.*
+ Fa 5-6/91: 207

21348. VR 1016 (LP): LUCIER—Still and moving lines of silence in families of hyperbolas, pt. 2. *Winant, vibraphone, xylophone, marimba & glockenspiel.*
+ Opus 12/86: 40

LOVELY MUSIC

21349. LCD 1019: Lucier—Clocker. *Lucier, electronics.*
+ ARG 7-8/95: 145
□ Fa 3-4/95: 213
• Fa 5-6/95: 246

21350. LCD 1042: Behrman—Leapday night; A traveller's dream journal; Interspecies smalltalk. *Neill, Chatham, trumpets; Mondshine, sound effects; Jakino, keyboards; Kosugi, violin.*
+ ARG 11-12/91: 30

21351. LCD 1051: Monk—Key: Porch; Understreet; What does it mean?; Visions; Fat stream; Do you be?; Change; Dungeon. *Monk, voice, electric organ; jews harp; with assisting instrumentalists.* Reissue.
+ ARG 7-8/96: 299
+ Fa 3-4/96: 226

21352. LCD 1064: Tyranny—Free delivery. *Tyranny, piano; Buckley, accordion.*
+ Fa 11-12/90: 380

21353. LCD 1065: Tyranny—Country boy country dog. *Tyranny, electronic keyboards; Buckley, accordion; Arch Ensemble for Experimental Music; Hughes, cond.*
□ Fa 9-10/94: 359

21354. LCD 1602 (2 discs): Tudor—Neural syntheses, no. 6-9. *Tudor, electronics.*
□ ARG 1-2/96: 249
+ Fa 11-12/95: 406

21355. LCD 1801: Reynolds—Voicespace (selections). *Larson, baritone.*
+ Fa 5-6/93: 293

21356. LCD 2011: Dresher—Liquid and stellar music; Destiny; Water dreams; This same temple. *Dresher, electronics & electric guitar; Rifkin, drums; Tilles, Neimann, pianos.*
□ ARG 1-2/97: 207
+ Fa 1-2/97: 155

21357. LCD 2022: Mitchell—Selections. Threadgill—He didn't give up/he was taken. *Mitchell, saxophones, winds, & percussion; Buckner, baritone; Kubera, piano; Manoogian, violin.*
+ ARG 1-2/96: 249
+ Fa 11-12/95: 310

21358. LCD 2031: *Buckner: Full spectrum voice.* Music of Ashley, Gibson, Vigeland, Gena, Lockwood, and Mitchell. *Buckner, baritone; with various accompaniments.*
+ Fa 3-4/92: 385

21359. LCD 2033: Duckworth—Southern harmony. *Gregg Smith Singers; Smith, cond.*
+ Fa 5-6/94: 138
+ Fa 11-12/94: 219

21360. LCD 2061: Payne—Crystal: Ahh-ahh (ver. 2.1); Subterranean network; Phase transitions; White night; Solar wind; Scirocco; Crystal. *Payne, computers & electronics.*
□ ARG 9-10/92: 142
+ Fa 3-4/92: 283

21361. LCD 2071: Kosugi—Violin improvisations. *Kosugi, violin.*
+ Fa 11-12/90: 256

21362. LCD 3001: La Barbara—Sound paintings. *La Barbara, voice & percussion.*
+ Fa 5-6/91: 202

21363. LCD 3002: La Barbara and Goldsmith—Seventy-three poems. *La Barbara, voice.*
□ ARG 11-12/94: 139
+ Fa 9-10/94: 229

21364. LCD 3011: De Marinis—Leçon par l'aiguille; Fonetica francese; Odd evening; An appeal; The sand clock; Cincinnati 1830-1850; The power of suggestion; Beneath the numbered sky. *De Marinis, concrete & electronic sounds.*
□ ARG 11-12/92: 111
□ Fa 3-4/92: 184

21365. LCD 3022: *Sign of the times.* Music of Gibson, Lockwood, Jenkins, Smith, and Ashley. *Buckner, vocalist.*
• ARG 11-12/94: 250
+ Fa 11-12/94: 441
+ Fa 11-12/94: 512

21366. LCD 3031: Music of Vigeland, Lucier, Tone and Held. *Held, flute; Kubera, piano.*
+ ARG 9-10/92: 191
+ Fa 7-8/92: 343

21367. LCD 3041: Tone—Musica iconologos. *Tone, electronics.*
+ Fa 3-4/94: 347

21368. LCD 3051: *Lois Svard: with and without memory.* Ashley—Van Cao's meditation. Duckworth—Imaginary dances. Tyranny—Nocturne with and without memory. *Svard, piano.*
+ ARG 1-2/95: 229
+ Fa 9-10/94: 115

21369. LCD 3071: Rosenboom and Braxton—Lineage; Enactment; Two lines; Transfiguration; Transference. *Rosenboom, electronics; Braxton, woodwinds.*
+ Fa 1-2/96: 287

21370. LCD 4917.3 (3 discs): Ashley—Perfect lives: an opera for television. *Ashley, voice; Tyranny, piano, electronic keyboards; Kroesen, Tieghem, voices.*
□ Fa 11-12/91: 238

LSSA

21371. 2: Brahms—Piano concerto no. 1 (with rehearsal excerpts). *Ogdon, piano; American Symphony Orch.; Stokowski, cond.* Recorded 1969.
+ ARG 7-8/92: 105

LYRA

21372. 52 (2 discs): Skalkottas—Thirty-six Greek dances for orchestra. *Urals State Orch.; Fidetzis, cond.*
+ ARG 9-10/92: 166

LYRA HOUSE

21373. LHL 1002: Rachmaninoff—Concerto no. 3 for piano and orchestra. Liszt—Rhapsodie espagnole; Two concert etudes. Mendelssohn—Variations sérieuses, op. 54. *Bolet, piano; Indiana University Phil. Orch.*
+ ARG 3-4/93: 169
+ Fa 3-4/93: 253

21374. LHL 1003: Mussorgsky—Pictures at an exhibition. Prokofiev—Piano sonata no. 6. *Atamian, piano.*
- Fa 5-6/93: 277

LYRICHORD

21375. LEMS 8001: *Troubadour and trouvère songs.* Music of Giraut de Bornelh, Guiraut Riquier, Arnaut Danile, Bernard de Ventadorn, Gautier d'Espinal, and Gace Brulé. *Oberlin, countertenor; Barab, viol.* Reissue.
+ ARG 1-2/95: 234
+ Fa 9-10/94: 407

21376. LEMS 8002: *Notre Dame organa.* Music of Leoninus and Perotinus. *Oberlin, countertenor; Bressler, Perry, tenors; Barab, viol.*
+ ARG 1-2/95: 234
+ Fa 9-10/94: 407

21377. LEMS 8003: Alfonso el Sabio—Las cantigas de Santa Maria (excerpts). *Oberlin, countertenor; Iadone, lute.*
+ ARG 1-2/95: 63
+ Fa 9-10/94: 407

21378. LEMS 8004: English polyphony (13th-14th centuries). *Oberlin, countertenor; Bressler, Perry, tenors; Barab, Blackman, viols.* Reissue.
+ Fa 11-12/94: 466

21379. LEMS 8005: English medieval songs (12th-13th centuries). *Oberlin, countertenor; Barab, viol.* Reissue.
+ Fa 11-12/94: 466

21380. LEMS 8006: English polyphony (14th-15th centuries). *Oberlin, countertenor; Bressler, tenor; Myers, baritone; Wolfe, organ.* Reissue.
+ Fa 11-12/94: 466

21381. LEMS 8007: The French Ars antiqua. *Oberlin, countertenor; Bressler, tenor; Myers, baritone; Wolfe, organ.* Reissue.
+ Fa 9-10/95: 384

21382. LEMS 8010: OCKEGHEM—Missa sine nomine à 3 (no. 2); Missa quinti toni à 3 (no. 1). *Schola Discantus; Moll, cond.*
+ ARG 1-2/95: 148
+ Fa 9-10/94: 280

21383. LEMS 8012: French sacred music of the fourteenth century. *Schola Discantus; Moll, cond.*
+ ARG 3-4/95: 248
+ Fa 3-4/95: 364

21384. LEMS 8013 (2 discs): DUFAY—Missa Se la face ay pale; Missa Sancti Jacobi; Vergine bella; Las que feray; Ma belle dame souveraine; Rite majorem; Ecclesiae militantis. *Capella Cordina; Planchart, cond.* Recoreded 1974.
● ARG 3-4/95: 95
● Fa 3-4/95: 164

21385. LEMS 8014: BYRD—Music for voice and viols. *Oberlin, countertenor; In Nomine Players; Stevens, cond.* Reissue.
- Fa 9-10/95: 159

21386. LEMS 8015: BYRD—Music of William Byrd. *Crout, soprano; Bagger, harpsichord; Lipnik, countertenor; Neely, viols; New York Consort of Viols.* Reissue.
● Fa 9-10/95: 159

21387. LEMS 8016: Istanpitta! vol. 1. *Velez, frame drums; New York's Ensemble for Early Music; Renz, cond.*
+ ARG 11-12/95: 259
+ Fa 11-12/95: 453

21388. LEMS 8017: BIBER—Mensa sonora. *La Follia Salzburg.*
+ ARG 11-12/95: 90
- Fa 11-12/95: 213

21389. LEMS 8018: Songs and dances of the Renaissance and Baroque. *Minstrelsy.*
+ ARG 5-6/96: 248
+ Fa 5-6/96: 336

21390. LEMS 8019: TELEMANN—Six sonatas for 2 flutes, TWV 40: 130-135. *Reighley, Moore, flutes.*
+ Fa 7-8/96: 324

21391. LEMS 8020: *The art of the lute.* Music of Milan, Capirola, Mudarra, Dalza, Narvaez, Milano, Lassus, Morely, Juan Ponce, Costeley, Di la Torre, Dufay, Craen, Isaac, Susato, Josquin, Brulé, and Anon. *Iadone, lute.*
+ Fa 3-4/96: 363

21392. LEMS 8021: LA RUE—Missa de Sancta Anna; Lamentationes Jeremiae. *Schola Discantus; Moll, cond.*

+ ARG 11-12/96: 114
+ Fa 11-12/96: 283

21393. LEMS 8022: Istanpitta II. *New York Ensemble for Early Music; Renz, cond.*
+ ARG 11-12/96: 262
+ Fa 11-12/96: 442

21394. LEMS 8023: *Vieni o cara.* Music of Castello, Monteverdi, Fontana, Steffani, Mancini, Weelkes, Purcell, Dowland, Bleier, and Arne. *Minstrelsy.*
+ ARG 1-2/97: 217
● Fa 11-12/96: 446

21395. LEMS 8024: PURCELL—Airs and duets. *Dooley, counter-tenor; Crook, tenor; Brewer, harpsichord; Shulman, Reed, violin; Carp, recorder; Springfels, viola da gamba; Godburn, recorder & bassoon.* Reissue.
● ARG 3-4/97: 199
+ Fa 1-2/97: 230

21396. LEMS 8025: LIEBERT—Missa de beata Virgine. *Schola Discantus; Moll, cond.*
+ Fa 1-2/97: 194

21397. LEMS 8026: *Love letters from Italy.* Music of Frescobaldi, d'India, Marco da Gagliano, Monteverdi, Sances, Mazzocchi, D. Gabrielli, and Cesti. *Minter, counter-tenor; Artek-458 Strings; Toth, cond.*
+ ARG 5-6/97: 281
+ Fa 1-2/97: 318

21398. LEMS 9002 (2 discs): MONTEVERDI—Orfeo. *Thomas, Hanchard, Brown, Shipper; ARTEK; Toth, cond.*
+ ARG 1-2/96: 144
● Fa 3-4/96: 227
● ON 2/17/96: 42

LYRINX

21399. LYRCD 005: DEBUSSY—Twelve études; Étude retrouvée; Masques; L'isle joyeuse. *Pludermacher, piano.*
● Fa 3-4/93: 150

21400. LYRCD 028: DVOŘÁK—Piano trio no. 4. SUK—Piano trio, op. 2. *Trio Gabriel Fauré.*
+ ARG 5-6/89: 44
- Fa 3-4/89: 152

21401. LYRCD 038: FRESCOBALDI—Arie musicali and Instrumental pieces. *Ensemble Hoc Opus; Ansermet, soprano; J. Rubin, lute; S. Rubin, viola da gamba; Volkonsky, harpsichord.*
+ ARG 3-4/89: 35
● ARG 1-2/92: 54
+ Fa 3-4/89: 165

21402. LYRCD 043: Music of India, Gesualdo, Macque, Kapsberger, and Anon. *Ensemble Hoc Opus.*
+ Fa 11-12/89: 248

21403. LYRCD 044: MOZART—Clarinet quintet, K. 581; Allegro for clarinet and strings, K. 516; Adagio for clarinet and strings, K. 580a; Trio for clarinet, viola and piano, K. 498. *Lethiec, clarinet; Mozarteum String Quartet; Engel, piano; Pasquier, viola.*
+ Fa 3-4/89: 224

21404. LYRCD 054: VIVALDI—Concertos, RV 429, 440, 441, 168, 581. *Marion, flute; Guglielmo, violin & cond.; Ensemble Strumentale di Venezia.*
□ Fa 3-4/89: 331

21405. LYRCD 055: DEBUSSY—12 études; Etude retrouvée; Masques; L'isle joyeuse. *Pludermacher, piano.*
+ Fa 3-4/89: 142

21406. LYRCD 056: BEETHOVEN—Piano sonata no. 32; Variations on a waltz by Diabelli. *Pludermacher, piano.*
● Fa 3-4/89: 92

21407. LYRCD 059: BEETHOVEN—Septet, op. 20; Clarinet trio, op. 11. *Pasquier, viola; Teulières, cello; Marder, double bass; Lethiec, clarinet; Del Vescovo, horn; Laroque, bassoon; Weber, piano.*
- Fa 5-6/89: 125
+ Fa 3-4/93: 118

21408. LYRCD 062: A. SCARLATTI—Vocal music. D. SCARLATTI—Vocal music. *Nascimento, male soprano; Foulon, baroque cello; Hasler, harpsichord.*
□ ARG 3-4/89: 76
● Fa 3-4/89: 259

21409. LYRCD 066: CHAMBONNIÈRES—Pavane; Drollerie; Printemps; Suites, C major and G major; Pavane; Gaillard. *Lengellé, harpsichord.*
+ ARG 3-4/93: 68
+ Fa 3-4/89: 131
● HF 5/89: 60

21410. LYRCD 069: CAMPRA—Fêtes vénitiennes: Suite. DESTOUCHES—Eléments: Suite; Carnaval et la folie: Suite. *Ensemble baroque de Limoges; Hasler, cond.*
+ ARG 5-6/89: 35
+ Fa 3-4/89: 129

21411. LYRCD 070: *Horszowski at Prades.* Music of Mozart, Beethoven, Chopin and Debussy. *Horszowski, piano.*
+ Fa 5-6/89: 252
+ Gr 4/92: 120

21412. LYRCD 071: *Prestige de la trompette* Music of Endler, Fasch, Telemann, Poglietti, Molter, Torelli, and Bononcini. *Ullrich, Petit, Porte, Messler, trumpets; La Follia Ensemble; Fuente, cond.*
+ Fa 3-4/89: 384

21413. LYRCD 073: *Leonard Rose: le dernier concert à Prades.* Music of Bach,

Beethoven, Barber, and Tchaikovsky. *Rose, cello; Wolf, piano.* Recorded live 1983.
+ Fa 1-2/94: 393

21414. LYRCD 074: SHOSTAKOVICH—Cello sonata, op. 40. RACHMANINOFF—Cello sonata, op. 19. *Sommer, cello; Adni, piano.*
• Fa 3-4/89: 276

21415. LYRCD 076: VIVALDI—Piccolo and oboe concertos. *Beaumadier, piccolo; Lencsés, oboe; Bianco, violin; La Follia Ensemble; Fuente, cond.*
+ Fa 7-8/89: 273

21416. LYRCD 077: GUÉRINEL—Contrechant; Soleil ployé; Ce chant de brume; Strophe 21 (Quartet no. 2). *Ensemble of bass instruments; Erlih, violin; Teulières, cello; Razoumovsky Quartet.*
+ Fa 5-6/89: 206

21417. LYRCD 079: MONTEVERDI—Combattimento de Tancredi e Clorinda; Lamento d'Arianna' Tempro la cetra. BIBER—Battaglia; Balletti. *Baroque Ensemble of Limoges; Hasler, cond.*
+ Fa 5-6/89: 238

21418. LYRCD 081: MOZART—Piano concertos no. 23-24. *Engel, piano; Gulbenkian Orch.; Fürst, cond.*
+ Fa 7-8/89: 191

21419. LYRCD 082: HAYDN—Piano sonatas no. 6, 13, 59, 62. *Collard, piano.*
+ Fa 11-12/89: 236

21420. LYRCD 082, 108, 126 (3 separate discs): HAYDN—Piano sonatas, vol. 1-3. *C. Collard, piano.*
+ Fa 1-2/94: 200

21421. LYRCD 083: SCHUMANN—Papillons; Arabeske; Kinderszenen; Piano sonata no. 1. *Collard, piano.*
+ Fa 11-12/89: 355

21422. LYRCD 091: CHAUSSON—Serres chaudes. FAURÉ—Melisande's song; Chanson d'Eve; Le jardin clos; Nocturne; Les présents; Arpège; Soir; Accompagnement; Le don silencieux. *Katz, mezzo-soprano; Talbot, piano.*
+ ARG 5-6/92: 44

21423. LYRCD 092: BRAHMS—Two rhapsodies, op. 79; Three intermezzi, op. 117; Six Klavierstücke, op. 118. *Collard, piano.*
• Fa 3-4/93: 128

21424. LYRCD 100: ELGAR—Cello concerto, op. 85. SCHUMANN—Cello concerto, op. 129. *Mørk, cello; Monte Carlo Phil. Orch.; Tabachnik, cond.*
+ Fa 1-2/94: 176

21425. LYRCD 102: *Prades Festival: the Casals years.* Music of Mozart. *Various performers; Casals, cond.* Recorded live

1950-62.
• Fa 1-2/94: 431

21426. LYRCD 104: FRANCK—Sonata in A for violin and piano; Quintet in F minor for piano and strings. *Pasquier, violin; Collard, piano; Quatuor Orlando.*
- Fa 3-4/93: 165

21427. LYRCD 107: MOZART—Piano concerto no. 27; Clarinet concerto. *Pennetier, piano; Lethiec, clarinet; Auvergne Chamber Orch.; Kantorow, cond.*
• Fa 3-4/93: 238

21428. LYRCD 110: LISZT—Piano music. *Rubackyté, piano.*
+ Fa 1-2/94: 227

21429. LYRCD 116: SAINT-SAËNS—Cello concerto no. 1. LALO—Cello concerto. FAURÉ—Élégie for cello and orchestra. *Mørk, cello; Monte Carlo Phil. Orch.; Tabachnik, cond.*
- Fa 1-2/94: 298

21430. LYRCD 117: SCHUBERT—Octet, D. 803. *Lethiec, clarinet; Vlatković, horn; Wallez, bassoon; Kantorow, Blakeslee, violins; Pasquier, viola; Noras, cello; Marder, double bass.*
+ Fa 3-4/93: 277

21431. LYRCD 122: BRAHMS—Gypsy songs; Six vocal quartets, op. 116; Five duets; Liebeslieder waltzes. *Soloists' Ensemble of the Chorus of the Lyon National Orch.; Têtu, cond.; Pludermacher, Barda, piano.*
- Fa 1-2/94: 137

21432. LYRCD 123: BRAHMS—Quintet for clarinet and strings, op. 115; Trio for clarinet, cello, and piano, op. 114. *Lethiec, clarinet; Lindsay String Quartet; Mørk, cello; Skanavi, piano.*
• Fa 1-2/94: 138

21433. LYRCD 124: RAVEL—Piano music. *Bianconi, piano.*
• ARG 1-2/94: 137
+ Fa 1-2/94: 274

21434. LYRCD 196/97 (2 discs): BEETHOVEN—Music for cello and piano. *Henkel, cello; Pludermacher, piano.*
+ Fa 3-4/93: 119

21435. LYRCD 199/20 (2 discs): *Horszowski à Prades.* Music of Bach, Mozart, Beethoven, and Brahms. *Horzowski, piano; London Collegium Musicum; Casals, cond.*
+ Fa 1-2/94: 413

LYRITA

21436. SRCD 200: ARNOLD—Symphony no. 4. *London Phil. Orch.; Arnold, cond.*
- Fa 5-6/91: 101
+ Gr 11/90: 973

21437. SRCD 202: RUBBRA—Symphonies no. 3-4; Tribute; Resurgam. *Philharmonia Orch.; Del Mar, cond.*
+ Fa 5-6/91: 270
+ Gr 11/90: 986

21438. SRCD 204: W. BENNETT—Piano concertos no. 1, 3; Caprice for piano and orchestra. *Binns, piano; London Phil. Orch.; Braithwaite, cond.*
+ ARG 3-4/91: 34
+ Fa 5-6/91: 130

21439. SRCD 205: W. BENNETT—Piano concertos no. 2, 5; Adagio for piano and orchestra in G minor. *Binns, piano; Philharmonia Orch.; Braithwaite, cond.*
+ ARG 3-4/91: 34
+ Fa 5-6/91: 130

21440. SRCD 207: WORDSWORTH—Symphonies no. 2-3. *London Phil Orch.; Braithwaite, cond.*
+ ARG 5-6/91: 128
+ Fa 5-6/91: 323
+ Gr 11/90: 995

21441. SRCD 208: HURLSTONE—Variations on an original theme; Magic mirror suite; Variations on a Hungarian air. *London Phil. Orch.; Braithwaite, cond.* Reissue.
+ Fa 9-10/93: 191
+ Gr 4/93: 48

21442. SRCD 209: HOLST—A winter idyll; The Cotswolds symphony: elegy; Indra; A song of the night; Sita: act 2 interlude; Invocation; The lure: ballet music; The morning of the year: dances. *McAslan, violin; Baillie, cello; London Phil. Orch.; London Symphony Orch.; Atherton, cond.*
+ Fa 11-12/93: 276
+ Gr 6/93: 48

21443. SRCD 211: VAUGHAN WILIAMS—Piano concerto. FOULDS—Dynamic dyptich. *Shelley, piano; Royal Phil. Orch.; Handley, cond.* Reissues.
+ ARG 7-8/93: 174
+ Gr 3/93: 39

21444. SRCD 212: FOULDS—Cabaret overture; April England; Pasquinade symphonique no. 2; Hellas; Three mantras. *London Phil. Orch.; Wordsworth, cond.*
+ Fa 9-10/93: 161
+ Gr 5/93: 43

21445. SRCD 219: STANFORD—Piano concerto no. 2; Irish rhapsody no. 4; Becket: Funeral march. *Binns, piano; London Phil. Orch.; Braithwaite, cond.; London Symphony Orch.; Boult, cond.* Reissue.
+ ARG 5-6/93: 140

21446. SRCD 220: PARRY—Overture to an unwritten tragedy; English suite; Lady Radnor's suite; Symphonic variations; Bridal March. *London Symphony Orch.;*

Boult, cond. Reissues.
+ ARG 7-8/93: 134

21447. SRCD 222: HOLST—Beni Mora; A fugal overture; Hammersmith; Japanese suite; Scherzo; A Somerset rhapsody. *London Phil. Orch.; London Symphony Orch.; Boult, cond.* Reissues.
+ Fa 1-2/93: 168
+ Gr 7/92: 57

21448. SRCD 223: HOLST—Orchestra music. *English Chamber Orch.; I. Holst, cond.* Reissues.
+ Gr 4/93: 51

21449. SRCD 224: WALTON—Capriccio burlesco; Music for children; Portsmouth Point; The quest: Suite; Scapino; Siesta; Sinfonia concertante. *Katin, piano; London Phil. Orch.; London Symphony Orch.; Walton, cond.* Reissues.
+ Fa 3-4/93: 329
+ Gr 7/92: 62

21450. SRCD 225: BLISS—Vocal and orchestral works. *Various performers.* Reissues.
+ ARG 7-8/93: 68
+ Gr 9/92: 140

21451. SRCD 226: BERKELEY—Serenade for strings; Divertimento; Partita for chamber orchestra; Canzonetta; Symphony no. 3. *London Phil. Orch.; Berkeley, cond.* Reissue.
+ ARG 7-8/93: 66
+ Gr 3/93: 35

21452. SRCD 227: ALWYN—Symphonies no. 1, 4. *London Phil. Orch.; Alwyn, cond.* Reissues.
+ Gr 7/92: 51

21453. SRCD 228: ALWYN—Symphonies, no. 2-3, 5. *London Phil. Orch.; Alwyn, cond.* Reissues.
+ Gr 10/92: 54

21454. SRCD 229: ALWYN—Overture Derby day; The magic island; Four Elizabethan dances; Sinfonietta for strings; Festival march. *London Phil. Orch.; Alwyn, cond.* Reissue.
+ ARG 5-6/93: 58
+ Gr 12/92: 71

21455. SRCD 230: ALWYN—Concerto grosso no. 2; Autumn legend; Lyra angelica. *London Phil. Orch.; Alwyn, cond.* Reissue.
+ Gr 12/92: 71

21456. SRCD 231: BAX—Tone poems. Northern ballad no. 1; Mediterranean; The garden of Fand; Tintagel; November woods. *London Phil. Orch.; Boult, cond.* Reissues.
+ Gr 9/92: 41

21457. SRCD 232: BAX—Symphonies, no. 1, 7. *London Phil. Orch.; Fredman, Leppard, conds.* Reissue.

+ ARG 5-6/93: 67
+ Gr 12/92: 72

21458. SRCD 234: RUBBRA—Symphonies no. 6, 8 "Hommage à Teilhard de Chardin"; Soliloquy for cello and orchestra. *Saram, cello; Philharmonia Orch.; Del Mar, cond.; London Symphony Orch.; Handley, cond.* Reissue.
+ Fa 3-4/93: 267
+ Gr 10/92: 116

21459. SRCD 235: RUBBRA— Symphonies, no. 2, 7; Festive overture. *Philharmonia Orch.; Handley,cond.; London Phil. Orch.; Boult, cond.* Reissues.
+ ARG 5-6/93: 126
+ Gr 12/92: 86

21460. SRCD 252: BUSH—Yorick overture; Music for orchestra; Symphonies no. 1-2. *Philharmonia Orch.; London Phil. Orch.; London Symphony Orch.; Royal Phil. Orch.; Handley, Braithwaite, Wordsworth, conds.* Reissues.
+ ARG 7-8/96: 94
+ Fi 5/96: 131
+ Gr 3/96: 42

21461. SRCD 291: RAWSTHORNE— Symphonies no. 1-3. *Chadwell, soprano; London Phil. Orch.; BBC Symphony Orch.; Pritchard, Braithwaite, Del Mar, cond.* Recorded 1967-1993.
+ ARG 7-8/96: 178
+ Fi /96: 131
+ Gr 2/96: 56

21462. SRCD 323: WILLIAMS—Fantasia on Welsh nursery tunes; Carillons; Penillion; Trumpet concerto; Sea sketches. *Camden, oboe; Snell, Allan, trumpets; London Symphony Orch.; Royal Phil. Orch.; Groves, cond.; English Chamber Orch.; Atherton, cond.* Reissue.
+ Gr 6/95: 64

21463. SRCD 324: MATHIAS—Ave Rex; Elegy for a prince; This worlde's joie. *Evans, J. Price, Bowen, Rippon; London Symphony Orch.; Philharmonia Orch.; Atherton, Willcocks, conds.* Reissues.
+ ARG 5-6/95: 137
+ Gr 2/95: 88

21464. SRCD 325: MATHIAS—Clarinet concerto; Harp concerto; Piano concerto no. 3. *Peyer, clarinet; Ellis, harp; Katin, piano; London Symphony Orch.; New Philharmonia Orch.; Atherton, cond.* Reissue.
+ Gr 7/95: 60

21465. SRCD 2217 (2 discs): TIPPETT— The midsummer marriage. *Remedios, Harwood, Burrows, Watts, Dean; Royal Opera House, Covent Garden; C. Davis, cond.* Reissue.

+ Fa 3-4/96: 304
+ Gr 1/96: 106

21466. SRCD 2218: ALWYN—Miss Julie. *Gomez, Jones, Mitchinson, Luxon; Philharmonia Orch.; Tausky, cond.* Reissue.
+ ARG 7-8/93: 56
+ Gr 3/93: 92
+ Op 6/93: 745

21467. SRCD 8020: Music of Milan, Capriola, Mudarra, Dalza, Narvaez, and others. *Iadone, lute.*
● ARG 5-6/96: 237

M RECORDS

21468. MCD 001: *European tour.* ELGAR—In Smyrna. RAVEL—Sonatine; La vallée des cloches. SCHUMANN—Piano sonata no. 2. SCRIABIN—Etudes. *Harel, piano.*
+ Fa 9-10/95: 323

21469. MCD 003: SHOSTAKOVICH— Preludes and fugues (selections). *Harel, piano.*
+ ARG 1-2/96: 171
+ Fa 9-10/95: 323

MAGNATONE

21470. 109: BEETHOVEN—Symphony no. 7. Music of Strauss, Dvořák, Schermerhorn, and Bernstein. *Nashville Symphony; Schermerhorn, cond.*
+ ARG 11-12/96: 93

MAGUELONE

21471. 519.202: MASSENET—Mélodies. *Duo de Paris.*
● ARG 7-8/96: 150
+ Fa 5-6/96: 205

21472. 519.232: LEGUERNEY—Songs. *Henry, baritone; Pondepeyre, piano.*
+ ARG 9-10/96: 151

MALARMÉ

21473. 002: BAX—Elegiac trio. CASTELNUOVO-TEDESCO—Sonata for cello and harp. LOCKLAIR—Dream steps. BACH—Eisteddfod. *Malarmé Chamber Players.*
+ ARG 5-6/95: 207

MANDALA

21474. MAN 4809: MOMPOU—Suburbis; Scènes d'enfants; Impressions intimes; Fêtes lointaines; Cants magics; Pessebres. *Colom, piano.*
+ ARG 7-8/95: 157
+ Fa 5-6/95: 264

21475. MAN 4810-4811 (2 separate discs): MOMPOU—Piano music. *Colom, piano.*

MANDALA

+ ARG 5-6/96: 150
+ Fa 3-4/96: 226

21476. MAN 4812: MOMPOU—Musica callada. *Colom, piano.* Reissue.
+ Fa 7-8/95: 249

21477. MAN 4816: FALLA—Music for piano. *Colom, piano.*
+ Fa 5-6/94: 144

21478. MAN 4882: SATIE—Complete works for piano duet. *Merlet, Armengaud, piano.*
• ARG 11-12/96: 194
• Fa 11-12/96: 356

MANU CLASSIC

21479. 1317: WAGNER—Opera excerpts. *Marc, Doig, McIntyre; New Zealand Symphony Orch.; Wallberg, cond.*
+ Gr 11/92: 192

21480. 1415: *New Zealand music.* Music of Carr, Rimmer, and Zagni. *Auckland Phil. Orch.; Hopkins, cond.*
• ARG 7-8/93: 187
+ Fa 5-6/93: 402

21481. 1478: *Music from New Zealand.* Music of Young, Hulford, Keay, De Castro, Holmes, and others. *Various performers.*
+ ARG 9-10/95: 247

MAP

21482. MAP CD 9024: BLOMDAHL—Preludio e allegro; Violin concerto; Concerto grosso; Concert overture; Symphony no. 2. *Rudner, violin; Helsingborg Symphony Orch.; Westerberg, cond.*
+ Fa 11-12/91: 278

21483. MAP CD 9026: *Scandinavian contemporary organ music.* Music of Moran, Hambraeus, Maros, Morthenson, Olson, Nilsson, and Sandstrom. *Welin, Lundkvist, organs.*
+ Fa 1-2/92: 40

21484. MAP CD 9130: SCHUMANN—Faschingsschwank aus Wien; Kinderszenen; Fantasy in C. *Negro, piano.*
- Fa 1-2/92: 324

21485. MAP CD 9131: HAMBRAEUS—Cadenza; Canvas with mirrors; Continuo. *Hellsten, Jacob, organ; Cherney, oboe; Sudwestfunk Symphony Orch.; Bour, cond.*
+ Fa 5-6/92: 165

21486. MAP CD 9132: SCHUMANN—Davidsbündlertänze. DEBUSSY—Estampes. SCRIABIN—Poèmes, op. 69; Piano sonata no. 5. *Backlund, piano.*
• Fa 5-6/92: 249

21487. MAP CD 9134: DVOŘÁK—Symphony no. 8. SALLINEN—Violin concerto. FRANKE-BLOM—Music for a mobile. *Norrköping Symphony Orch.; Kamu, violin; Welser-Möst, Andrén, Panula, conds.*
+ Fa 5-6/92: 343

21488. MAP CD 9235: *Flauto Dolce.* Music of Elgar, Haussmann, Coleman, Playford, Brade, Scheidt, Dowland, Ward, Holborne, Byrd, Bjerstedt, Karlsson, and Sjöberg. *Flauto Dolce.*
+ Fa 9-10/93: 381

MARCAL

21489. 951001: HOVHANESS—Lousadzak; Violin concerto no. 2; Violin pieces; Khirgiz suite. *Jodry, violin; Surmelian, piano; Leon Barzig Orch.; Werner, cond.*
+ ARG 1-2/97: 122

MARCATO

21490. MCD 068701: J. ZWART—Organ music. *D.J. Zwart, organ.*
+ ARG 11-12/90: 137
+ Fa 9-10/91: 402

21491. MCD 078801: Music of Gade, Hoepner, Mendelssohn, Merkel, and Liszt. *Zwart, organ.*
+ ARG 9-10/90: 144
+ Fa 3-4/91: 483

21492. MCD 088901: DURUFLÉ—Organ works. *Steen, organ.*
+ ARG 5-6/90: 48
• Fa 3-4/91: 203

21493. MCD 099001: *Ulrike Engelke, traverso.* Music of Telemann, Hotteterre, Handel, Boismortier, and Bach. *Engelke, flute; Oost, organ, harpsichord; Schwamberger, viola da gamba.*
+ Fa 1-2/92: 416

21494. MCD 109101: LISZT—Études d'exécution transcendante. *Oldenburg, piano.*
+ Fa 1-2/92: 250

MARCO POLO

21495. 8.220362: JANÁČEK—Danube; Schluck und Jau; Moravian dances; Suite, op. 3. *Slovak Phil. Orch.; Pešek, cond.* Reissue.
+ ARG 5-6/92: 75
+ Fa 7-8/92: 187

21496. 8.220392: SCHREKER—Orchestra music. *Slovak Phil. Orch.; Seipenbusch, cond.*
+ Fa 7-8/88: 244
+ Gr 8/88: 294

21497. 8.220417: GOLDMARK—Symphony no. 2; Penthesilea overture. *Rhenish State Phil. Orch.; Halász, cond.*
+ Fa 5-6/93: 212

21498. 8.220418: RESPIGHI—Sinfonia drammatica. *Slovak Phil. Orch.; Nazareth, cond.*
+ Fa 5-6/93: 293

21499. 8.220420: DVOŘÁK—The cunning peasant: overture; Rhapsody, op. 14; Dramatic overture, op. posth.; Vanda: overture. *Slovak Phil. Orch.; Gunzenhauser, Pešek, conds.*
+ ARG 7-8/93: 84
+ Fa 5-6/88: 119
+ Fa 5-6/93: 196

21500. 8.220438: RIMSKY-KORSAKOV—Night on Mount Triglav; Pan voyevoda. *Slovak Phil. Orch.; Režucha, cond.*
• Fa 3-4/92: 296

21501. 8.220469: SCHREKER—Prelude to Memnon; Romantic suite. *Tonkünstler Orch.; Mund, cond.*
+ ARG 5-6/89: 83
+ Fa 3-4/89: 262

21502. 8.220487: GLAZUNOV—Carnaval overture; Idylle; Reverie orientale; Serenades no. 1-2; Wedding March; Cortege solennel; Scene dansante. *Moldavian Phil. Orch.; Andreescu, cond.*
+ Fa 9-10/88: 158

21503. 8.223101: *Alphorn concertos.* Music of L. Mozart, Farkas, and Daetwyler. *Molnár, alphorn; Cappella Istropolitana; Slovak Phil. Orch.; Schneider, cond.*
□ Fa 9-10/88: 206

21504. 8.223102: BAX—Overture, elegy and rondo; Sinfonietta. *Slovak Phil. Orch.; Wordsworth, cond.*
+ ARG 7-8/88: 12
+ Fa 5-6/88: 77
• Gr 7/88: 152

21505. 8.223103: BLOCH—Symphony in C♯ minor. *Slovak Phil. Orch.; Gunzenhauser, cond.*
+ ARG 1-2/89: 36
+ Fa 5-6/89: 140
+ HF 1/89: 60
+ MA 1/89: 52

21506. 8.223104: BRUCH—Suite on Russian themes, op. 79b; Symphony no. 3. *Hungarian State Orch.; Honeck, cond.*
• ARG 11-12/88: 25
+ Fa 9-10/88: 123
• Fa 9-10/88: 123

21507. 8.223105: FURTWÄNGLER—Symphony no. 3. *RTBF Symphony Orch., Brussels; Walter, cond.*
• Fa 11-12/88: 186
+ Gr 2/89: 1282
• MA 1/89: 58
• St 10/88: 163

21508. 8.223106: GLIÈRE—Symphony no. 2; Zaporozhye cossacks, op. 64. *Czechoslovak Radio Orch.; Clark, cond.*
+ ARG 11-12/88: 37

+ Fa 11-12/88: 189
+ MA 1/89: 59

21509. 8.223107: HUMMEL—Piano concertos no. 6-7. *Chang, piano; Budapest Symphony Chamber Orch.; Pal, cond.*
    • ARG 5-6/88: 37
    • Fa 7-8/88: 179
    • Gr 7/88: 63
    + HF 10/88: 80

21510. 8.223113: MIASKOVSKY—Symphonies no. 7, 10. *Slovak Phil. Orch.; Halász, cond.*
    + ARG 7-8/88: 41
    + Fa 5-6/88: 166 (reviewed by R.S.B.)
    • Fa 5-6/88: 166 (reviewed by P.J.R.)

21511. 8.223115: PIERNÉ—Piano music. *Chang, piano.*
    + Fa 5-6/91: 247

21512. 8.223117: REINECKE—Symphony no. 1; King Manfred: Overture; Preludes to Acts 4 and 5; Ballet. *Rhenish State Phil. Orch.; Walter, cond.*
    • Fa 9-10/88: 237

21513. 8.223119: SCHMIDT—Symphony no. 1; Notre Dame: Introduction, Intermezzo, and Csardas. *Budapest Symphony Orch.; Halász, cond.*
    + ARG 5-6/88: 59
    - Fa 7-8/88: 242
    • Gr 11/88: 784
    □ HF 3/89: 59

21514. 8.223120: SMETANA—Festive symphony, op. 6. *Austrian Radio Orch.; Zagrosek, cond.*
    • ARG 7-8/88: 56
    • Fa 5-6/88: 216
    • HPR 7/88: 90

21515. 8.223122: SPOHR—Symphony no. 4; Faust: Overture; Jessonda: Overture. *Budapest Symphony Orch.; Walter, cond.*
    • ARG 5-6/90: 112
    • Fa 1-2/90: 310

21516. 8.223129: DVOŘÁK—Slavonic dances, op. 46; Slavonic rhapsodies, op. 45, no. 1, 3. *Slovak Phil. Orch.; Košler, cond.*
    + ARG 11-12/88: 32
    - Fa 5-6/88: 119
    - MA 5/88: 62

21517. 8.223131: DVOŘÁK—Slavonic dances, op. 72; Slavonic rhapsody no. 2; Scherzo capriccioso, op. 66. *Slovak Phil. Orch.; Košler, cond.*
    + ARG 7-8/89: 40
    - Fa 9 10/89: 195

21518. 8.223133: TANEEV—Symphony no. 2; Suite no. 2 in F major. *Philharmonia Hungarica; Albert, cond.*
    - Fa 1-2/90: 320

21519. 8.223135: KALINNIKOV—Tsar Boris; Bilina; Cedar and the palm; Nymphs . *Budapest Symphony Orch.; Jancsovics, cond.*
    • Fa 5-6/90: 197

21520. 8.223136: GLAZUNOV—Scènes de ballet; Seasons. *CSR Symphony Orch., Bratislava; Lenárd, cond.*
    • Fa 9-10/88: 159

21521. 8.223138: EINEM—Violin concerto, op. 33. MUSSORGSKY—Night on bare mountain (arr. Einem). SCHUBERT—Kuppelwieser-Walzer (arr. Einem). *Edinger, violin; North German Radio Symphony Orch.; Walter, cond.*
    + ARG 9-10/89: 114
    + Fa 7-8/89: 275

21522. 8.223139: MÉHUL—Symphonies no. 1-2. *Rhenish State Phil. Orch.; Rotter, cond.*
    + ARG 9-10/89: 78
    - Fa 9-10/89: 249
    + St 2/90: 197

21523. 8.223140: INDY—String quartets no. 1-2. *Kodály Quartet.*
    + ARG 1-2/91: 57
    + Fa 11-12/90: 251
    + Gr 10/91: 122

21524. 8.223141: ENESCO—Symphony no. 1; Sinfonia concertante for cello, op. 8. *Enesco State Phil. Orch., Brediceanu; Arcu, cello; Romanian Radio and Television Symphony Orch.; Conta, cond.*
    + ARG 5-6/89: 47
    + Fa 5-6/89: 192

21525. 8.223142: ENESCO—Symphony no. 2; Vox maris. *Enesco State Phil. Orch.; Andreescu, cond.; Muraru, soprano; Voineag, tenor; Moldava Phil. Chorus & Orch.; Baciu, cond.*
    + ARG 3-4/89: 47
    + Fa 3-4/89: 159

21526. 8.223143: ENESCO—Symphony no. 3; Chamber symphony for 12 solo instruments. *Cluj-Napoca Phil. Chorus & Orch.; Baciu, cond.*
    + ARG 3-4/89: 47
    • Fa 3-4/89: 159

21527. 8.223144: ENESCO—Orchestra suites no. 1-2; Concert overture, op. 32. *Romanian Radio and Television Symphony Orch.; Conta, Silvestri, cond.*
    + ARG 3-4/89: 47
    • Fa 5-6/89: 192

21528. 8.223145: ENESCO—Suite no. 3; Suite chatelaine; Voix de la nature. *Romanian Radio and Television Symphony Orch.; Conta, cond.; Timisoara Banatul Phil. Orch.; Georgescu, cond.*
    + ARG 5-6/89: 47
    • Fa 3-4/89: 159

21529. 8.223146: ENESCO—Romanian poem, op. 1; Romanian rhapsodies no. 1-2. *Romanian Radio and Television Symphony Chorus & Orch.; Conta, cond.*
    • ARG 3-4/89: 34
    + Fa 3-4/89: 158

21530. 8.223147: ENESCO—Octet for strings in C major; Dixtuor for winds in D major. *Voces String Quartet; Euterpe String Quartet; Winds of the Iasi Moldava Phil. Orch.; Baciu, cond.*
    • Fa 3-4/89: 159

21531. 8.223151, 8.223153 (2 separate discs): GLAZUNOV—Complete piano music (vol. 1, 3). *Franová, piano.*
    • ARG 9-10/93: 124
    + Fa 5-6/93: 210
    • Gr 7/93: 66

21532. 8.223152: GLAZUNOV—Piano music, vol. 2. *Franová, piano.*
    + ARG 1-2/94: 102
    • Fa 1-2/94: 187

21533. 8.223154: GLAZUNOV—Piano music, vol. 4. *Franová, Čápová, pianos.*
    + Fa 9-10/95: 207

21534. 8.223156: MIASKOVSKY—Piano sonatas no. 2-3, 5. *Hegedűs, piano.*
    + Fa 11-12/90: 282
    + Fa 11-12/93: 325
    • Gr 10/90: 789

21535. 8.223162: PFITZNER—Piano concerto, op. 31; Christelflein: Overture; Das Herz: Liebesmelodie. *Harden, piano; Bratislava Radio Symphony Orch.; Beissel, cond.*
    - ARG 3-4/90: 86
    - Fa 11-12/89: 315
    • Gr 7/89: 183

21536. 8.223163: GRECHANINOV—Symphonies no. 1-2. *Enesco State Phil. Orch.; Edlinger, cond.; Czechoslovak State Phil.; Wildner, cond.*
    + ARG 5-6/91: 61
    + Fa 5-6/91: 177

21537. 8.223165: RAFF—Symphony no. 1. *Rhenish State Phil. Orch.; Friedman, cond.*
    + ARG 9-10/89: 91
    + Fa 9-10/89: 293
    + Gr 11/89: 902

21538. 8.223166: ZEMLINSKY—Symphony no. 1; Das gläserne Herz: Suite. *Czecho-Slovak Radio Symphony Orch.; Rajter, cond.*
    + Gr 12/91: 84

21539. 8.223170: BERWALD—Piano trios no. 1-3. *Kiss, violin; Onczay, cello; Prunyi, piano.*
    + Fa 9-10/90: 186

21540. 8.223171: KIEL—Piano quintets no. 1-2. *New Budapest String Quartet;*

MARCO POLO

Prunyi, piano.
  + Fa 5-6/91: 196

21541. 8.223172: BORODIN—Cello sonata in B minor; String quintet in F minor; Piano quintet in C minor. *Kertész, cello; Prunyi, piano; New Budapest String Quartet.*
  + Fa 11-12/90: 179

21542. 8.223176: RUBINSTEIN—Album de Peterhof. *Banowetz, piano.*
  + ARG 9-10/90: 109
  + Fa 9-10/90: 359

21543. 8.223177: RUBINSTEIN—Soirées musicales. *Banowetz, piano.*
  + ARG 9-10/90: 109
  + Fa 9-10/90: 359
  • Gr 9/90: 578

21544. 8.223178: MIASKOVSKY—Piano sonatas no. 6-9. *Hegedűs, piano.*
  + Fa 11-12/90: 282
  + Fa 11-12/93: 325
  • Gr 10/90: 789

21545. 8.223181: HONEGGER—Misérables. *Bratislava Radio Symphony Orch.; Adriano, cond.*
  • Fa 7-8/91: 179

21546. 8.223182: VILLA-LOBOS—Piano trios no. 1, 3. *Spiller, violin; Duphil, piano; Humeston, cello.*
  + ARG 7-8/91: 133
  + Fa 5-6/91: 321

21547. 8.223189: PIERNÉ—Flute sonata; Piano trio. *Matuz, flute; Bánfalvi, violin; Vass, cello; Szelescényi, piano.*
  + ARG 11-12/90: 97
  + Fa 9-10/90: 333
  • Gr 10/90: 760

21548. 8.223190: RUBINSTEIN—Fantaisie, op. 84; Concertstück, op. 113. *Banowetz, piano; Czecho-Slovak Radio Symphony Orch.; O. Dohnányi, cond.*
  • ARG 1-2/92: 100
  + Fa 11-12/91: 463

21549. 8.223193: WIDOR—Piano trio, op. 19; Piano quintet, op. 7. *Prunyi, piano; Kiss, Balogh, violins; Botvay, Bároony, cellos.*
  + Fa 11-12/90: 405

21550. 8.223194: RAFF—Aus Thürigen: Suite; Italian suite. *Kosice State Phil. Orch.; Edlinger, cond.*
  + ARG 5-6/90: 93
  + Fa 1-2/90: 272

21551. 8.223195: LACHNER—Suites for orchestra no. 1, 7. *Polish State Phil. Orch., Katowice; Gunzenhauser, cond.*
  + ARG 1-2/91: 99
  + Fa 1-2/91: 225

21552. 8.223196: TANEYEV—Symphonies no. 2, 4. *Polish State Phil. Orch. (Katowice); Gunzenhauser, cond.*

  + ARG 5-6/91: 114
  • Fa 5-6/91: 295

21554. 8.223220—8.223221 (2 separate discs): J. STRAUSS, JR.—Complete orchestral music, vols. 20-21. *Czecho-Slovak State Phil. Orch., Kosice; Walter, Wildner, conds.*
  + ARG 1-2/92: 119
  + Fa 1-2/92: 337
  + Gr 5/91: 120

21555. 8.223222: J. STRAUSS, JR.—Complete orchestral music, vol. 22. *Czecho-Slovak State Phil. Orch.; Wildner, cond.*
  + Fa 5-6/92: 261
  • Gr 8/92: 72

21556. 8.223223—8.223227 (5 separate discs): J. STRAUSS, JR.—Complete orchestral music, vol. 23-27. *Czecho-Slovak State Phil. Orch., Kosice; Walter, Wildner; ORF Symphony Orch., Vienna; Guth, cond.*
  + ARG 11-12/93: 202 (v.25-27)
  + Fa 1-2/93: 246
  + Gr 10/92: 188

21557. 8.223228—8.223230 (3 separate discs): J. STRAUSS, JR.—Complete orchestral music, vol. 28-30. *Czechoslovak State Phil. Orch., Kosice; Wildner, A. Walter, conds.*
  + ARG 11-12/93: 202
  + Fa 11-12/93: 408
  + Gr 9/93: 63

21558. 8.223231—8.223233 (3 separate discs): J. STRAUSS, JR.—Complete orchestral music, vols. 31-33. *Slovak State Phil. Orch.,; Wildner, Walter, conds.*
  + ARG 5-6/94: 145
  + Fa 1-2/94: 320
  + Gr 6/94: 64

21559. 8.223234—8.223236 (3 separate discs): J. STRAUSS, JR.—Complete orchestral music vol. 34-36. *Slovak Radio Symphony Orch., Bratislava; Dittrich, cond.; Slovak State Phil. of Kosice; Wildner, Walter, conds.*
  + Fa 5-6/94: 256
  + Gr 7/94: 60

21560. 8.223237—8.223239 (3 separate discs): J. STRAUSS, JR.—The complete orchestra music, vol. 37-39. *Kosice State Phil. Orch.; Pollack, Walter, conds.*
  + ARG 9-10/95: 220
  + Fa 1-2/95: 276
  + Gr 9/95: 68

21561. 8.223240—8.223242 (3 separate discs): J. STRAUSS, JR.—Orchestra music vol. 40-42. *Kosice Phil. Orch.; Pollack, Walter, conds.; Slovak Radio Orch.; Bauer-Theussl, Dittrich, conds.*
  + ARG 9-10/95: 220
  + Fa 11-12/95: 390
  + Gr 12/95: 92

21562. 8.223243—8.223245 (3 separate discs): J. STRAUSS, JR.—The complete orchestra music, vol. 43-45. *Kosice State Phil. Orch.; Pollack, Walter, conds.*
  + ARG 9-10/96: 208
  + Fa 3-4/96: 293
  + Gr 3/96: 54

21563. 8.223246—8.223247 (2 separate discs): J. STRAUSS, JR.—Complete orchestra works, vol. 46-47. *Slovak Radio Symphony Orch. of Bratislava; Dittrich, Wildner, conds.; Slovak State Phil. Orch. of Kosice; Walter, cond.*
  + ARG 9-10/96: 208
  + Fa 9-10/96: 332

21564. 8.223248: SZYMANOWSKI—Symphonies no. 1-2. *Polish State Phil. Orch., Katowice; Stryja, cond.*
  □ ARG 1-2/91: 105
  • Fa 9-10/90: 404
  • Gr 7/90: 230

21565. 8.223249: J. STRAUSS, JR.—Complete orchestra works, vol. 49. Overtures, vol. 1. *Slovak State Phil. Orch. of Kosice; Walter, cond.*
  + ARG 9-10/96: 209

21566. 8.223250: J. STRAUSS, JR.—Works for male chorus. *Vienna Men's Chorus; Bratislava Radio Symphony Orch.; Wildner, Track, conds.*
  + ARG 1-2/93: 153
  + Fa 1-2/93: 247
  + Gr 10/92: 188

21567. 8.223251: SPOHR—String quartets no. 27-28. *New Budapest String Quartet.*
  • ARG 1-2/91: 99
  + Fa 1-2/91: 321

21568. 8.223252: SPOHR—String quartets no. 3, 29. *New Budapest String Quartet.*
  + Fa 5-6/91: 288

21569. 8.223253: SPOHR—Complete string quartets, vol. 3. *New Budapest String Quartet.*
  • Fa 11-12/91: 490
  + Gr 9/92: 120

21570. 8.223254: SPOHR—Complete string quartets, vol. 4. *New Budapest String Quartet.*
  + Fa 1-2/92: 334
  + Gr 9/92: 120

21571. 8.223255: SPOHR—Complete string quartets, vol. 5. *New Budapest String Quartet.*
  + Fa 1-2/92: 336
  + Gr 9/92: 120

21572. 8.223256: SPOHR—Complete string quartets, vol. 6. *New Budapest String Quartet.*
  + Fa 3-4/93: 301
  + Gr 1/93: 46

21573. 8.223257: SPOHR—Complete string quartets, vol. 7. *New Budapest*

String Quartet.
+ Fa 1-2/94: 315

21574. 8.223259: SPOHR—String quartets, vol. 9. *New Budapest String Quartet.*
+ Fa 3-4/96: 290

21575. 8.223268: MEDTNER—Piano sonata in F minor; Sonata-Triad. *Fellegi, piano.*
● Fa 1-2/91: 237

21576. 8.223270: SCHREKER—Der ferne Klang. *Grigorescu, Harper; with assisting soloists; Hagen Municipal Opera; Halász, cond.*
+ ARG 5-6/90: 100
+ Gr 8/90: 408
+ Op 11/90: 1376

21577. 8.223272: DVOŘÁK—Opera overtures and preludes. *Kosice State Phil. Orch.; Stankovsky, cond.*
+ Fa 9-10/90: 233

21578. 8.223273: COWEN—Symphony no. 3; Butterfly's all; Indian rhapsody. *Kosice State Phil. Orch.; Leaper, cond.*
+ ARG 1-2/91: 42
+ Fa 1-2/91: 183

21579. 8.223274: BANTOCK—Old English suite; Russian scenes; Hebridean orchestra. *Kosice State Phil. Orch.; Leaper, cond.*
+ Fa 9-10/90: 161
+ Gr 10/90: 732

21580. 8.223277: RUBINSTEIN—Symphony no. 1; Ivan the terrible. *Kosice State Phil. Orch.; Stankovsky, cond.*
● Fa 9-10/90: 359

21581. 8.223278: MOYZES—Dances from Gemer; Down the river Váh; Dances from Hron. *CSR Symphony Orch., Bratislava; Lenárd, cond.*
+ ARG 7-8/90: 73
● Fa 5-6/90: 222

21582. 8.223280/81 (2 discs): BRIAN—Symphony no. 1. *Bratislava Radio Symphony Orch.; Slovak Phil. Orch.; Lenárd, cond.*
+ Fa 11-12/90: 186
+ Gr 7/90: 208
+ MA 1/91: 73
+ NYT 10/3/90: H34
+ SR 1/91: 97

21583. 8.223282: LACHNER—Septet in E♭ (completed by Beyer). FUCHS—Quintet for clarinet and strings in E♭. *Villa Musica Ensemble.*
+ ARG 11-12/90: 72
+ Fa 11-12/90: 237

21584. 8.223283: SINDING—Piano trios no. 2-3. *Kiss, violin; Koó, cello; Prunyi, piano.*
+ Fa 9-10/90: 390

21585. 8.223284: ALKAN—Preludes, op. 31. *Martin, piano.*
● ARG 1-2/91: 20
● Fa 1-2/91: 128
+ Gr 4/91: 1862

21586. 8.223285: ALKAN—12 études in the minor keys, op. 39 (selections). *Ringeissen, piano.*
● ARG 1-2/91: 18
● Fa 3-4/91: 128
● Gr 4/91: 1862

21587. 8.223287: IBERT—Film music for Macbeth; Golgotha; Don Quichotte. *Kiichli, bass; Bratislava Radio Symphony Orch.; Adriano, cond.*
+ Fa 5-6/91: 189

21588. 8.223288: BLOCH—Poems of the sea; Five sketches in sepia; Nirvana; In the night; Enfantines; Four circus pieces. *Kassai, piano.*
+ Fa 9-10/90: 187
● Gr 6/90: 83

21589. 8.223289: BLOCH—Piano sonata; Visions and prophecies; Ex-voto; Danse sacrée. *Kassai, piano.*
+ Fa 9-10/90: 187
● Gr 6/90: 83

21590. 8.223290: SZYMANOWSKI—Symphonies no. 3-4; Concert overture. *Ochman, tenor; Polish State Phil. Chorus of Katowice; Zmudzinski, piano; Polish State Phil. Orch., Katowice; Stryja, cond.*
□ ARG 1-2/91: 105
- Fa 11-12/90: 370
● Gr 10/90: 748

21591. 8.223291: SZYMANOWSKI—Violin concertos no. 1-2; Notturno e tarantella for violin and orchestra. *Kulka, Lasocki, violins; Polish State Phil. Orch., Katowice; Stryja, cond.*
□ ARG 1-2/91: 105
● Fa 1-2/91: 330
+ Gr 4/91: 1845

21592. 8.223292: SZYMANOWSKI—Harnasie; Mandragora; Étude in B♭ minor. *Grychnik, Meus, tenor; Polish State Phil. Chorus & Orch., Katowice; Stryja, cond.*
□ ARG 1-2/91: 105
● Fa 1-2/91: 329

21593. 8.223293: SZYMANOWSKI—Stabat Mater; Veni Creator; Litany to the Virgin Mary; Demeter; Penthesilea. *Gadulanka, Owsinka, Zogórzanka, Szostek-Radkowa, Malewicz-Madey, Hoilski; Polish State Phil. Chorus & Orch.; Stryja, cond.*
□ ARG 1-2/91: 105
● Fa 1-2/91: 330

21594. 8.223294: SZYMANOWSKI—Love songs of Hafiz; Songs of the infatuated Muezzin; Songs of the fairytale princess; Three fragments after Jan Kasprowicz; King Roger: Roxana's song. *Gadulanka,*

Zogórzanka, Malewicz- Madey, Minkiewicz; Polish State Phil. Orch., Katowice; Stryja, cond.
+ ARG 1-2/91: 106
● Fa 1-2/91: 329
+ Gr 4/92: 134

21595. 8.223295: FURTWÄNGLER—Symphony no. 1. *Kosice State Phil. Orch.; Walter, cond.*
● ARG 7-8/91: 57
- Fa 7-8/91: 161
+ Gr 7/91: 45
● St 10/91: 215

21596. 8.223297: MIASKOVSKY—Symphony no. 8. *Czechoslovak Radio Symphony Orch., Bratislava; Stankovsky, cond.*
+ ARG 1-2/92: 79
- Fa 1-2/92: 268
● Gr 4/92: 66

21597. 8.223298: ENESCO—Cello sonata. VILLA-LOBOS—Divigaçao; O canto da Nossa terra; O canto do Capadocio; O canto do Cisne Negro; Sonhar; Berceuse, op. 50. *Rust, cello; Apter, piano.*
+ Fa 3-4/91: 210
+ Gr 10/90: 759

21598. 8.223301: MIASKOVSKY—Symphony no. 6. *Slovak Opera Choir; Bratislava Radio Symphony Orch.; Stankovsky, cond.*
● ARG 1-2/93: 122
- Fa 3-4/93: 224
- Gr 11/92: 90

21599. 8.223302: MIASKOVSKY—Symphony no. 12; Silence, op. 9. *Czecho-Slovak Radio Symphony Orch.; Stankovsky, cond.*
+ ARG 1-2/92: 79
+ Fa 9-10/91: 275
● Gr 10/91: 93

21600. 8.223304: BENNETT—Piano sextet; Sonata duo. *Kiss, Balogh, violins; Bársony, viola; Botvay, Kertész, cellos; Kubina, double bass; Prunyi, Dráfi, piano.*
+ Gr 11/94: 103

21601. 8.223306/07 (2 discs): MARSCHNER—Hans Heiling. *Seniglova, Markus, Mohr, Neshyba; Slovak Phil. Orch. & Chorus; Körner, cond.*
+ ARG 3-4/92: 96
+ Fa 11-12/91: 386
● Gr 11/91: 152

21602. 8.223312: GODOWSKI—Walzermasken. *Prunyi, piano.*
+ ARG 1-2/90: 52
+ Fa 11-12/90: 236
+ Fa 1-2/91: 203

21603. 8.223314: KHACHATURIAN—Battle of Stalingrad; Othello. *Bratislava Radio Orch.; Adriano, cond.*
+ ARG 1-2/94: 114
+ Fa 1-2/94: 215

MARCO POLO

21604. 8.223315: Bliss—Film music: Christopher Columbus; Seven waves away; Men of two worlds. *Bratislava Radio Symphony Orch.; Adriano, cond.*
  □ ARG 9-10/91: 49
  + Fa 7-8/91: 123

21605. 8.223316: Martinů—Epic of Gilgamesh. *Děpoltová, Margita, Kusnjer, Vele; Slovak Phil. Chorus & Orch.; Košler, cond.*
  + Fa 5-6/91: 214

21606. 8.223317: Erkel—Piano works and chamber music. *Kassai, piano; Szécsodi, violin; Lukács, viola.*
  + ARG 1-2/92: 53
  + Fa 1-2/92: 210

21607. 8.223318: Erkel—Opera transcriptions. *Kassai, piano.*
  + ARG 1-2/92: 53
  + Fa 1-2/92: 210

21608. 8.223319: Rubinstein—Symphony no. 4 "Dramatic". *Czechoslovak State Phil. Orch. (Kosice); Stankovsky, cond.*
  + ARG 5-6/92: 120
  - Fa 1-2/92: 311

21609. 8.223320: Rubinstein—Symphony no. 5; Dmitry Donskoy; Faust. *George Enescu State Phil.; Andreescu, cond.*
  + ARG 1-2/92: 100
  • Fa 9-10/91: 329

21610. 8.223321: Raff—Symphonies no. 3, 10. *Czecho-Slovak State Phil. Orch., Kosice; Schneider, cond.*
  + Fa 9-10/91: 319
  - ARG 9-10/91: 111

21611. 8.223323: Ciurlionis—Symphonic poems: The sea; In the forest. 5 Preludes for string orchestra. *Slovak Phil. Orch.; Domarkas, cond.*
  + Fa 3-4/91: 190
  + Gr 6/91: 38

21612. 8.223324: Schillings—Violin concerto; Harvest festival; Symphonic prologue to King Oedipus. *Rozsa, violin; Kosice State Phil. Orch.; Walter, cond.*
  + ARG 5-6/92: 122
  + Gr 4/92: 75

21613. 8.223325: Novák—Pan. *Slovak Phil. Orch.; Bílek, cond.*
  + Fa 9-10/91: 308
  + Gr 10/91: 96

21614. 8.223326: Smetana—Orchestral highlights from operas. *Czecho-Slovak State Phil. Orch., Kosice; Stankovsky, cond.*
  + ARG 11-12/91: 148
  + Fa 9-10/91: 360

21615. 8.223328/30 (3 discs): Schreker—Die Gezeichneten. *Schmiege, Cochran, Cowan, Oosterkamp, Tassel; Dutch Radio Phil. Chorus & Orch.; Waart, cond.*

  + Fa 9-10/91: 342
  + Gr 12/91: 134

21616. 8.223333: Furtwängler—Piano concerto. *Lively, piano; Czecho-Slovak State Phil. Orch. of Kosice; Walter, cond.*
  - ARG 3-4/92: 60
  • Fa 1-2/92: 214
  + Fa 9-10/92: 239
  - Gr 12/91: 66

21617. 8.223334: Schnittke—Cello concerto no. 1; Stille Musik; Cello sonata. *Kliegel, cello; Saarbrücken Radio Symphony Orch.; Markson, cond.; Havenith, piano.*
  + Fa 9-10/91: 338
  + Gr 1/92: 60

21618. 8.223335—8.223338 (4 separate discs): Hindemith—Piano works, vols. 1-4. *Petermandl, piano.*
  + Fa 9-10/91: 237

21619. 8.223339 (2 discs): Szymanowski—King Roger; Prince Potemkin: Act V. *Hiolski, Ochman, Grychnik; Katowice Phil. Orch.; Stryja, cond.; Katowice Radio Orch.; Wit, cond.*
  + ARG 1-2/95: 189
  • Fa 1-2/95: 284
  + Op 11/94: 1355

21620. 8.223342: Marschner—Overtures. *Kosice Phil. Orch.; Walter, cond.*
  • ARG 1-2/95: 136
  + Fa 3-4/95: 220
  + Gr 9/95: 60

21621. 8.223346: Respighi—Le astuzie di Colombina; Sèvres de la vieille France; La pentola magica. *Bratislava Radio Symphony Orch.; Adriano, cond.*
  + ARG 1-2/93: 136
  + Fa 3-4/93: 257
  • Gr 11/92: 98

21622. 8.223347: Respighi—Aretusa; La sensitiva; Il tramonto; Quattro liriche dal Poema paradisiaco di Gabriele d'Annunzio. *Subrata, mezzo-soprano; Czecho-Slovak Radio Symphony, Bratislava; Adriano, cond.*
  + ARG 5-6/92: 116
  + Fa 5-6/92: 231
  • Gr 9/92: 151

21623. 8.223348: Respighi—Variazioni sinfoniche; Preludio, corale, e fuga; Burlesca; Ouverture carnevalesca; Suite in E. *Czecho-Slovak Radio Symphony, Bratislava; Adriano, cond.*
  + ARG 5-6/92: 117
  + Fa 5-6/92: 232
  • Gr 5/92: 47

21624. 8.223350: Music of Ho Chan-hao, Jiao Jie, Sha Han Hun, Mao Yuen, and others. *Nishizaki, violin; Czecho-Slovak Radio Symphony Orch.; Jean, cond.*
  + Fa 9-10/91: 188

21625. 8.223351: Alkan—Etudes in all the major keys, op. 35; Scherzo diabolico, op. 39, no. 3; Le festin d'Ésope, op. 39, no. 12. *Ringeissen, piano.*
  + Fa 5-6/95: 116
  + Gr 11/93: 116

21626. 8.223352: Alkan—Esquisses, op. 63. *Martin, piano.*
  • ARG 11-12/92: 71
  + Fa 11-12/92: 175
  + Gr 4/95: 88

21627. 8.223354: Massenet—Esclarmonde: suite; Suite no. 1, op. 13; Cendrillon: suite. *Hong Kong Phil. Orch.; Jean, cond.*
  + ARG 11-12/91: 95
  + Fa 11-12/91: 388
  • Gr 1/92: 56

21628. 8.223355: Thalberg—Fantasias on operas by Bellini. *Nicolosi, piano.*
  • ARG 1-2/92: 131
  + Fa 1-2/92: 356

21629. 8.223356: Schubert—Octet, D. 72. Weber—Adagio and rondo for winds. Lachner—Octet in B♭. *German Wind Soloists.*
  + Fa 7-8/91: 387

21630. 8.223357: Villa-Lobos—Genesis; Erosao (Origem do rio Amazonas); Amazonas; Dawn in a tropical forest. *Czecho-Slovak Radio Symphony Orch., Bratislava; Duarte, cond.*
  + ARG 3-4/92: 158
  + Fa 1-2/92: 363
  + Gr 3/92: 56

21631. 8.223358: Glière—Symphony no. 3 "Ilya Murometz". *CSR Symphony Orch., Bratislava; Johanos.*
  • ARG 5-6/92: 63
  + Fa 3-4/92: 195
  • Gr 5/92: 33
  + St 6/92: 241

21632. 8.223362: Raff—Symphonies no. 8-9. *Kosice Phil. Orch.; Schneider, cond.*
  + ARG 1-2/93: 134
  + Fa 1-2/93: 215
  + Gr 11/92: 97

21633. 8.223363: Spohr—Symphonies no. 1, 5. *Kosice State Phil. Orch.; Walter, cond.*
  + Gr 12/92: 88

21634. 8.223365: Thalberg—Fantasies on themes from Donizetti operas. *Nicolosi, piano.*
  + ARG 11-12/93: 210
  • Fa 9-10/93: 311
  + Gr 7/94: 82

21635. 8.223366: Thalberg—Variations on operas by Rossini. *Nicolosi, piano.*
  + ARG 11-12/93: 210
  + Fa 11-12/93: 426

21636. 8.223367: Thalberg—Piano music, vol. 2. *Nicolosi, piano.*
    + ARG 5-6/95: 186
    + Fa 5-6/95: 361
    + Gr 1/96: 82

21637. 8.223369: Humperdinck—Moorish rhapsody; Sleeping Beauty: Tone pictures; Merchant of Venice: Love scene; Vivandière. Prelude. *Czecho-Slovak Radio Symphony Orch.; M. Fischer-Dieskau, cond.*
    - ARG 11-12/92: 137
    + Fa 11-12/92: 264

21638. 8.223370: German—Piano works. *Cuckston, piano.*
    + Fa 9-10/91: 222

21639. 8.223371: Medtner—Piano sonatas op. 22, op. 25. *Fellegi, piano.*
    • ARG 1-2/92: 75
    • Fa 11-12/91: 390
    - Gr 5/92: 75

21640. 8.223372: Medtner—Piano sonatas, op. 27, op. 38, op. 39, op. 56. *Fellegi, piano.*
    • ARG 1-2/92: 75
    • Fa 11-12/91: 390
    - Gr 4/92: 114

21641. 8.223374: Saxophone concertos. Music of Milhaud, Glazunov, Debussy, Ibert, Mussorgsky, and Rahbari. *S. Rahbari, saxophone; Belgian Radio and Television Symphony Orch.; A. Rahbari, cond.*
    + Fa 1-2/92: 418

21642. 8.223376: David—Les brises d'orient; Les minarets. *David Blumenthal, piano.*
    • ARG 7-8/92: 121
    + Fa 5-6/92: 146

21643. 8.223377: Fuchs—Piano sonatas no. 1-2. *D. Blumenthal, piano.*
    + ARG 1-2/93: 98
    + Fa 1-2/93: 151
    + Gr 6/93: 75

21644. 8.223378: Debussy— Arrangements for 2 pianos of works by Saint-Saëns, Schumann, Tchaikovsky, and Wagner. *Blumenthal, Groslot, pianos.*
    • ARG 11-12/93: 243
    + Fa 11-12/93: 213

21645. 8.223379: Tansman—Symphony no. 5; Stèle in memoriam d'Igor Stravinsky; Four movements for orchestra. *Czechoslovak State Phil. Orch. (Kosice); Minsky, cond.*
    + Fa 3-4/93: 310
    • Gr 3/93: 56

21646. 8.223380: Tcherepnin— Symphony no. 4; Romantic overture; Suite for orchestra; Russian dances. *Czecho-Slovak State Phil. Orch., Kosice; Yip, cond.*

    • ARG 1-2/93: 158
    • Fa 11-12/92: 389
    + Gr 10/92: 123

21647. 8.223381: Salieri—Overtures. *Bratislava Radio Symphony Orch.; Dittrich, cond.*
    □ ARG 1-2/94: 147
    + Fa 1-2/94: 300
    • Gr 1/94: 50

21648. 8.223382: Rubinstein—Piano concertos no. 3-4. *Banowetz, piano; Kosice Phil. Orch.; Stankovsky, cond.*
    + ARG 1-2/93: 141
    + Fa 1-2/93: 224

21649. 8.223383: Alkan—Grand duo concertant, op. 21; Sonate de concert, op. 47; Piano trio, op. 30. *Trio Alkan.*
    + Fa 9-10/93: 102
    + Gr 8/93: 46

21650. 8.223384: Korngold—Piano sonatas no. 1-2; Märchenbilder, op. 3; Much ado about nothing, op. 11: excerpts. *Prunyi, piano.*
    + ARG 9-10/93: 144
    • Fa 5-6/93: 239

21651. 8.223385: Korngold—Piano quintet; Violin sonata. *Prunyi, piano; Kiss, violin; Danubius Quartet.*
    • ARG 7-8/93: 110
    + Fa 9-10/93: 201

21652. 8.223389: Villa-Lobos—String quartets no. 1, 8, 13. *Danubius Quartet.*
    + ARG 1-2/93: 163
    + Fa 1-2/93: 263
    + Gr 11/92: 145

21653. 8.223390: Villa-Lobos—String quartets no. 11, 16-17. *Danubius Quartet.*
    + ARG 1-2/93: 163
    + Fa 1-2/93: 263
    + Gr 11/92: 145

21654. 8.223391: Villa-Lobos—String quartets no. 4, 6, 14. *Danubius Quartet.*
    + ARG 5-6/93: 148
    + Fa 5-6/93: 350
    + Gr 1/94: 72

21655. 8.223392: Villa Lobos—String quartets no. 5, 9, 12. *Danubius Quartet.*
    + Fa 3-4/94: 359

21656. 8.223393: Villa Lobos—String quartets no. 3, 15, 10. *Danubius Quartet.*
    + Fa 3-4/94: 359

21657. 8.223394: Villa-Lobos—String quartets no. 2, 7. *Danubius Quartet.*
    + ARG 1-2/95: 197
    • Fa 1-2/95: 297
    + Gr 2/95: 69

21658. 8.223397: Malipiero—Seven inventions; Four inventions; Symphonic fragments from the opera Il finto Arlecchino; Vivaldiana. *Veneto Phil. Orch.; Maag, cond.*

    • ARG 7-8/93: 120
    • Fa 5-6/93: 260
    + Gr 9/93: 54

21659. 8.223399: Waxman—Rebecca. *Czecho-Slovak Radio Orch., Bratislava; Adriano, cond.*
    • ARG 3-4/92: 164

21660. 8.223400: Cui—Suites for orcherstra no. 2, 4; Flibustier: Prelude. *Czecho-Slovak Radio Symphony Orch., Bratislava; Stankovsky, cond.*
    • Fa 3-4/94: 170

21661. 8.223401: Farnon—Portrait of a flirt; How beautiful is night; Melody fair; A la claire fontaine; The peanut polka; In a calm; Gateway to the West; Jumping bean; Pictures in the fire; Little Miss Molly; Colditz march; A star is born; The Westminster waltz; Manhattan playboy; Lake of the Woods; Derby Day; State occasion. *Czechoslovak Radio Orch., Bratislava; Leaper, cond.*
    + ARG 11-12/92: 235
    + Fa 9-10/92: 232
    + Gr 9/92: 66

21662. 8.223402: Wood—Sketch of a dandy; Serenade to youth; Mannin veen; London cameos suite; Rhapsody mylecharane; Joyousness: concert waltz; A brown bird singing; Apollo: overture; The seafarer. *Czechoslovak Radio Orch., Bratislava; Leaper, cond.*
    + ARG 11-12/92: 235
    + Fa 9-10/92: 391
    + Gr 8/92: 42

21663. 8.223403: Virtuoso cello encores. Music of Cassadó, Popper, Bach, Schubert, Shostakovich, Granados, Ravel, Debussy and others. *Kliegel, cello; Havenith, piano.*
    + ARG 5-6/92: 161
    + Fa 5-6/92: 310
    + Gr 9/92: 124

21664. 8.223404: Atterberg—Violin sonata; Autumn ballads; Valse monotone; Rondeau retrospectif; Trio concertante. *Perényi, Kiss, violin; Prunyi, Falvai, piano; Kertész, cello; Sipkay, harp.*
    + ARG 1-2/94: 67
    + Fa 1-2/94: 112
    + Gr 9/94: 70

21665. 8.223405: Atterberg—Piano quintet; Suite no. 1 for piano and strings; Horn sonata. *Prunyi, piano; Kertész, cello; Magyari, horn; New Budapest String Quartet.*
    + ARG 11-12/93: 73
    + Fa 9-10/93: 104
    + Gr 9/93: 70

21666. 8.223409: Ibert—Piano music. *Chang, piano.*
    + Fa 1-2/94: 209

21667. 8.223413: Tomlinson—Little serenade; An English overture;

MARCO POLO

Silverthorn suite; Second suite of English folk dances; Nocturne; Hornpipe; Gaelic lullaby. *Czecho-Slovak Radio Symphony Orch., Bratislava; Tomlinson, cond.*
+ ARG 1-2/93: 160
+ Fa 11-12/92: 392
+ Gr 12/92: 90

21668. 8.223414: SCHMIDT—Quintet for clarinet, strings and piano. *Jánoska, clarinet; Mucha; Lakatos, viola; Slávik, cello; Rusó, piano.*
+ Fa 5-6/92: 239
+ Gr 10/92: 132

21669. 8.223415: SCHMIDT—Clarinet quintet; Kleine Fantasiestücke; Romance; Toccata. *Jánoska, clarinet; Török, violin; Lakatos, viola; Slávik, cello; Rusó, piano.*
+ ARG 1-2/94: 148
+ Fa 1-2/94: 303
+ Gr 7/94: 74

21670. 8.223416: GRECHANINOV—Piano trios no. 1-2. *Šimčisko, violin; Alexander, cello; Rusó, piano.*
• ARG 11-12/93: 112
+ Fa 5-6/93: 214
+ Gr 6/93: 63

21671. 8.223418: *Flemish Romantic music.* Music of Poot, Blockx, Boeck, Mortelmans, Meulemans, and Gilson. *BRT Phil. Orch.; Rahbari, cond.*
+ ARG 11-12/92: 236
+ Fa 9-10/92: 445

21672. 8.223419: GERMAN—Orchestra music. *Czechoslovak Radio Symphony Orch.; Leaper, cond.*
+ ARG 7-8/93: 92
+ Fa 5-6/93: 209

21673. 8.223421: BÜLOW—Piano works and transcriptions. *Blumenthal, piano.*
+ ARG 11-12/93: 90
+ Fa 11-12/93: 202
+ Gr 10/93: 78

21674. 8.223422: SCHREKER—Flammen. *Procter, Theisen, Bollinger, Kruzel; PPP Music Theater; Strobel, cond.*
• ARG 1-2/94: 149
+ Fa 1-2/94: 304
- ON 3/4/95: 41

21675. 8.223423: FUCHS—Cello sonatas no. 1-2; Fantasy piecess. *Dobinsky, cello; Blumenthal, piano.*
+ ARG 11-12/93: 106
+ Fa 9-10/93: 164
+ Gr 11/93: 93

21676. 8.223424: STANCHINSKY—Piano sonatas no. 1-2; Three sketches; Twelve sketches. *Blumenthal, piano.*
+ Fa 1-2/95: 274
+ Gr 11/94: 118

21677. 8.223425: CURZON—The boulevardier; Punchinello; Spanish suite; Dance of an ostracised imp; Saltarello;

Capricante; Galavant; Pasquinade; Simonetta; Cascade; La peineta; Robin Hood suite; Bravada. *Czechoslovak Radio Symphony Orch.; Leaper, cond.*
+ ARG 7-8/93: 79
+ Fa 5-6/93: 190

21678. 8.223430: BERWALD—Piano trios, no. 4; C major; fragments. *Modrian, violin; Kertész, cello; Dráfi, piano.*
+ Fa 9-10/93: 125
+ Gr 10/93: 62

21679. 8.223431: *Clarinet and orchestra.* Music of David, Hummel, Spohr, Späth, Kreutzer, and Stadler. *Klöcker, Heitzler, clarinets; Czechoslovak Radio Symphony Orch.; Schmalfuss, cond.*
+ ARG 7-8/93: 192
+ Fa 5-6/93: 378

21680. 8.223432: SPOHR—Symphonies no. 7-8. *Czechoslovak State Phil. Orch. Kosice; Walter, cond.*
• ARG 9-10/93: 195
+ Fa 5-6/93: 325

21681. 8.223433, 8.223438, 3.223441, 8.223450 (4 separate discs): WALDTEUFEL—The best of Emile Waldteufel, vol. 1-4. *Czechoslovak State Phil. Orch. of Kosice; A. Walter, cond.*
+ ARG 3-4/94: 183
+ Fa 1-2/94: 356
+ Fa 3-4/96: 318 (v.4)
+ Fa 7-8/96: 336 (v.4)
+ Gr 2/94: 57

21682. 8.223435: HELLER—Piano music. *Martin, piano.*
+ ARG 1-2/94: 109
+ Fa 1-2/94: 203

21683. 8.223436: FURTWÄNGLER—Symphony no. 2. *BBC Symphony Orch.; A. Walter, cond.*
• ARG 9-10/93: 122
- Fa 9-10/93: 165 (Fogel)
• Fa 9-10/93: 166 (North)
- Gr 8/93: 28

21684. 8.223439: SPOHR—Symphonies no. 3, 6. *Czechoslovak State Phil. Orch. Kosice; Walter, cond.*
+ ARG 5-6/93: 138
+ Fa 5-6/93: 325
+ Gr 4/93: 62

21685. 8.223442: KETÈLBEY—Orchestra music. *Czecho-Slovak Radio Symphony Orch. Bratislava; Leaper, cond.*
+ Fa 3-4/94: 224
+ Gr 4/94: 48

21686. 8.223444: QUILTER—Orchestral works. *Bratislava Radio Symphony Orch.; Leaper, cond.*
+ ARG 9-10/94: 178
+ Fa 9-10/94: 300
+ Gr 8/94: 52

21687. 8.223445: COATES—The merrymakers overture; London suite;

Cinderella; The selfish giant; London again suite; Calling all workers; The dam busters: march. *Czechoslovak Radio Symphony Orch.; Leaper, cond.*
• ARG 3-4/94: 86
+ Fa 1-2/94: 162
+ Gr 1/94: 42

21688. 8.223446: HOLBROOKE—Ulalume; Bronwen: overture; The bells: prelude; The raven; Byron. *Czechoslovak Radio Symphony Orch., Bratislava; Slovak Phil. Choir; Leaper, cond.*
+ ARG 11-12/93: 127
+ Fa 11-12/93: 274
+ Gr 11/93: 70

21689. 8.223447: BRIAN—Symphonies no. 4, 12. *Vocalists; Czechoslovak Radio Symphony Orch. (Bratislava); Leaper, cond.*
+ ARG 11-12/93: 84
+ Fa 5-6/93: 176
+ Gr 2/93: 39

21690. 8.223448: SCHMITT—La tragédie de Salome. *Fayt, soprano; Rheinland-Pfalz Phil. Orch.; Davin, cond.*
• ARG 1-2/94: 149
• Fa 1-2/94: 303
+ Gr 12/93: 76

21691. 8.223449: HOLMÈS—Andromède; Irlande; Ouverture pour une comédie; Ludus pro patria: Interlude; Pologne. *Rheinland-Pfalz State Phil. Orch.; Friedmann, Davin, conds.*
• Fa 11-12/94: 258 (Rabinowitz)
+ Fa 11-12/94: 259 (D. Johnson)
+ Gr 10/94: 108

21692. 8.223451: WALDTEUFEL—The best of Waldteufel, vol. 5. *Kosice State Phil Orch.; Walter, cond.*
+ ARG 7-8/96: 223
+ Fa 3-4/96: 318
+ Gr 6/96: 62

21693. 8.223452: KEMPFF—Italian suite; Piano sonata; Transcriptions. *Biret, piano.*
+ ARG 11-12/92: 140
+ Fa 11-12/92: 268
+ Gr 5/93: 72

21694. 8.223454: SPOHR—Symphonies no. 2, 9; The seasons. *Kosice State Phil. Orch.; A. Walter, cond.*
+ ARG 11-12/93: 201
+ Fa 1-2/94: 315
+ Gr 2/94: 50

21695. 8.223455: RAFF—Symphony no. 5; Ein feste Burg overture. *Kosice Phil. Orch.; Schneider, cond.*
+ ARG 7-8/94: 155
+ Fa 7-8/94: 208
• Gr 2/95: 52

21696. 8.223456: RUBINSTEIN—Piano concertos no. 1-2. *Banowetz, piano; Kosice State Phil. Orch.; Walter, cond.*

+ Fa 7-8/93: 220
+ Gr 7/93: 50

21697. 8.223457: WELCHER—Haleakala; How Maui snared the sun; Prairie light; Watercolors of Georgia O'Keefe; Clarinet concerto. *Chamberlain, narrator; Jackson, clarinet; Honolulu Symphony; Johanos, cond.*
+ ARG 11-12/93: 219

21698. 8.223458: GIBBS—Songs. *N. Hancock-Child, baritone; R. Hancock-Child, piano.*
• ARG 11-12/93: 107
• Fa 11-12/93: 243
+ Gr 11/93: 127

21699. 8.223460: SULLIVAN—L'Ile enchantée: ballet; Thespis: ballet music. *RTE Concert Orch.; Penny, cond.*
+ ARG 5-6/93: 143
+ Fa 5-6/93: 337
+ ON 7/93: 42

21700. 8.223461: SULLIVAN—Merchant of Venice: incidental music; Henry VIII: incidental music; The sapphire necklace: overture; Overture in C "In memoriam". *RTE Concert Orch.; Penny, cond.*
+ ARG 5-6/93: 143
+ Fa 5-6/93: 337
+ ON 7/93: 42

21701. 8.223462: GUASTAVINO—Music for 2 pianos. *Duo Moreno-Capelli.*
• ARG 11-12/93: 115
+ Fa 11-12/93: 255
+ Gr 5/94: 80

21702. 8.223463: SAUGUET—Symphony no. 1 "Expiatoire". *Moscow Symphony Orch.; Almeida, cond.*
+ ARG 11-12/96: 195
• Fa 11-12/96: 357
+ Fa 1-2/97: 248
• Gr 12/96: 84

21703. 8.223466: HONEGGER—Farinet; Crime et chatiment; Le déserteur; Le grand barrage; L'idée. *Bratislava Radio Orch.; Adriano, cond.*
+ ARG 1-2/94: 110
+ Gr 6/94: 50

21704. 8.223468: LIAPUNOV—Piano works. *Schechter, piano.*
• ARG 11-12/93: 139
+ Fa 11-12/93: 295

21705. 8.223469: MIASKOVSKY—Piano sonatas, vol. 3. *Hegedűs, piano.*
+ ARG 11-12/93: 151
+ Fa 11-12/93: 325
• Gr 10/93: 85

21706. 8.223470—8.223471 (2 separate discs): *Railway music, vol. 1-2.* Music of Lanner, Strausses, Hoyer, Gungl, Lumbye, and others. *Slovak Phil. Orch.; Eichenholz, cond.*
+ ARG 1-2/94: 174

+ Fa 1-2/94: 320
+ Gr 2/94: 57

21707. 8.223473: LAJTHA—Des écrits d'un musicien, op. 1: four pieces; Contes, op. 2; Prélude; Six piano pieces, op. 14; Three berceuses. *Körmendi, piano.*
+ Fa 5-6/93: 242
+ Gr 4/93: 88

21708. 8.223474: FUCHS—Piano sonatas, vol. 2. *Blumenthal, piano.*
+ Fa 1-2/94: 184
+ Gr 2/94: 74

21709. 8.223475: GODOWSKY—Miniatures. *Banowetz, Chan, piano.*
• ARG 1-2/94: 103
+ Fa 1-2/94: 190

21710. 8.223476: TOURNEMIRE—Symphonies no. 1, 5. *Moscow Symphony Orch.; Almeida, cond.*
+ ARG 7-8/95: 212
• Fa 7-8/95: 347
- Gr 7/95: 72

21711. 8.223478: TOURNEMIRE—Symphonies no. 2, 4. *Moscow Symphony Orch.; Almeida, cond.*
+ ARG 7-8/95: 212
• Fa 7-8/95: 347
- Gr 7/95: 72

21712. 8.223479: BRIAN—Jolly miller overture; Violin concerto; Symphony no. 18. *Bisengaliev, violin; BBC Scottish Symphony Orch.; Friend, cond.*
+ ARG 7-8/94: 82
+ Fa 7-8/94: 99
+ Gr 8/94: 44

21713. 8.223480: STEVENS—Dance suite; Piano concerto; Variations. *Roscoe, piano; Irish Symphony Orch.; Leaper, cond.*
+ ARG 11-12/94: 194
+ Fa 1-2/95: 275
+ Gr 11/94: 86

21714. 8.223481: BRIAN—In memoriam; Festal dance; Symphonies no. 17, 32. *National Symphony Orch. of Ireland; Leaper, cond.*
+ Fa 5-6/93: 176
+ Gr 2/93: 39

21715. 8.223482: KUHLAU—Quartets for piano and strings, no. 1-2. *Prunyi, piano; New Budapest String Quartet.*
+ Fa 5-6/93: 241

21716. 8.223484: KOECHLIN—Le livre de la jungle. *Rheinland-Pfalz Phil.; Segerstam, cond.*
ι ARG 1-2/94: 115
+ Fa 1-2/94: 218
+ Gr 6/94: 52

21717. 8.223485: SCOTT—Aubade; Neapolitan rhapsody; Three dances; Suite fantastique; Two passacaglias on Irish themes. *National Symphony of the South*

African Broadcasting Corp.; Marchbank, cond.
- Fa 9-10/94: 336
+ Gr 7/94: 56

21718. 8.223486: L. GLASS—Symphonies no. 5-6. *National Symphony Orch. of the South African Broadcasting Corp.; Marchbank, cond.*
+ ARG 5-6/94: 94
+ Fa 5-6/94: 150

21719. 8.223489: RUBINSTEIN—Piano concerto no. 5; Caprice russe. *Banowetz, piano; Slovak Radio Symphony Orch.; Stankovsky, cond.*
• ARG 11-12/94: 180
+ Fa 1-2/95: 248
+ Gr 2/95: 54

21720. 8.223491: LIAPUNOV—Douze études d'exécution transcendante, op. 11. *Scherbakov, piano.*
+ ARG 11-12/93: 139
+ Fa 11-12/93: 295
+ Gr 4/94: 74

21721. 8.223492: DAVID—Piano trios no. 2-3. *Parkanyi, violin; Perényi, cello; Prunyi, piano.*
+ ARG 1-2/94: 92
+ Fa 1-2/94: 165
+ Gr 5/94: 71

21722. 8.223496: CUI—Twenty-five preludes, op. 64. *Biegel, piano.*
+ Fa 1-2/95: 146
+ Gr 11/94: 116

21723. 8.223497: ARENSKY—Suites no. 1-4 for two pianos. *D. Blumenthal, Groslot, pianos.*
+ Fa 1-2/95: 94

21724. 8.223498: BRUNEAU—Orchestral highlights from operas. *Rhenish Phil. Orch.; Lockhart, cond.*
+ ARG 11-12/94: 85
+ Fa 9-10/94: 160

21725. 8.223499: MIASKOVSKY—Symphonies no. 5, 9. *BBC Phil. Orch.; Downes, cond.*
+ Fa 7-8/94: 182
+ Gr 7/94: 51

21726. 8.223500: ALKAN—Trois études de bravoure, op. 12; Le preux: étude de concert, op. 17; Le chemin de fer, op. 27; Trois grandes études, op. 76. *Martin, piano.*
• ARG 3-4/94: 64
• Fa 1-2/94: 110
• Gr 11/93: 116

21727. 8.223501: ROGER-DUCASSE—Marche française; Nocturne de printemps; Petite suite; Le joli jeu de furet: Scherzo; Orphée: 3 symphonic fragments. *Rheinland-Pfalz State Phil. Orch.; Segerstam, cond.*
+ ARG 3-4/95: 171
+ Fa 1-2/95: 246

MARCO POLO

21728. 8.223502: LACHNER—Symphony no. 5. *Kosice State Phil. Orch.; Robinson, cond.*
- ARG 7-8/94: 122
+ Fa 7-8/94: 160
+ Gr 5/94: 52

21729. 8.223503: RABAUD—Procession nocturne; Marouf: Dances; Suites anglaises, no. 2-3; Divertissement; Eglogue. *Rheinland-Pfalz State Phil.; Segerstam, cond.*
+ ARG 1-2/95: 155
+ Fa 1-2/95: 237
+ Gr 1/95: 52

21730. 8.223504: KOECHLIN—Les heures persanes. *Rheinland-Pfalz State Phil.; Segerstam, cond.*
+ Fa 5-6/94: 176
+ Gr 7/94: 48

21731. 8.223505: DEVREESE—Piano concertos no. 2-4. *Blumenthal, piano; BRT Phil. Orch.; Devreese, cond.*
+ ARG 11-12/93: 100
+ Fa 11-12/93: 216
+ Gr 11/93: 66

21732. 8.223506: RAFF—Symphony no. 7; Concert overture. *Kosice Phil. Orch.; Schneider, cond.*
- ARG 7-8/94: 155
+ Fa 9-10/94: 306
□ Gr 8/94: 52

21733. 8.223507: EMMANUEL—Symphonies no. 1-2; Le poème du Rhône. *Rhenish Phil. Orch.; Lockhart, Nopre, conds.*
- ARG 3-4/94: 93
+ Fa 1-2/94: 177
+ Gr 3/94: 52

21734. 8.223508: IBERT—La ballade de la gaôle de Reading; Trois pièces de ballet; Féerique; Chant de folie; Suite elisabéthaine. *Slovak Phil. Orch. & Chorus; Adriano, cond.*
+ Fa 5-6/94: 171

21735. 8.223510: SPOHR—Violin concertos no. 2, 9. *Edinger, violin; Bratislava Radio Symphony Orch.; Cramer, cond.*
- ARG 1-2/94: 157
+ Fa 1-2/94: 315

21736. 8.223512: BENNETT—Piano music. *Prunyi, piano.*
+ ARG 1-2/94: 78
+ Fa 1-2/94: 130

21737. 8.223513: TOMLINSON—Comedy overture; English folk dances: first suite; Light music suite; Shenandoah; Cumberland Square; Rhapsody and rondo for horn and orchestra; Passepied; Rigadon; Aladdin: dances; A Georgian miniature. *Watkins, horn; Slovak Radio Symphony Orch., Bratislava; Tomlinson, cond.*
+ ARG 3-4/95: 206

+ Fa 3-4/95: 320
+ Gr 3/95: 56

21738. 8.223514: MAYERL—Orchestra music. *Ball, piano; Slovak Radio Symphony Orch., Bratislava; Carpenter, cond.*
+ Fa 1-2/95: 199
+ Gr 12/94: 88

21739. 8.223515: BINGE—Music for orchestra. *Slovak Radio Symphony Orch., Bratislava; Tomlinson, cond.*
+ Fa 1-2/95: 123
+ Gr 11/94:
+ Fa 1-2/95: 123
+ Gr 11/94

21740. 8.223516: COLERIDGE-TAYLOR—Hiawatha overture; Characteristic waltzes; Gipsy suite; Romance of the prairie lillies; Othello suite. *RTE Concert Orch., Dublin; Leaper, cond.*
- ARG 3-4/96: 103
- Fa 3-4/96: 150
+ Gr 1/96: 49

21741. 8.223518: GOODWIN—633 Squadron: Theme; Drake 400: Suite; Puppet serenade; New Zealand suite; Arabian celebration; The Venus waltz; Prisoners of war march; Minuet in blue; The trap: Theme; Girl with a dream; Lancelot and Guinevere: Theme. *New Zealand Symphony Orch.; Goodwin, cond.*
□ ARG 1-2/97: 114
+ Fa 1-2/97: 169
+ Gr 2/97: 52

21742. 8.223522: *British light music miniatures.* Music of Collins, Lubbock, Gibbs, Frankel, Ellis, Benjamin, Docker, Elgar, Dexter, Warner, Jacob, Arne, Vinter, Toye, White, Melachrino, and Richardson. *RTE Concert Orch.; Tomlinson, cond.*
+ ARG 7-8/95: 236
+ Fa 7-8/95: 444
+ Gr 12/95: 98

21743. 8.223524: BOËLLMANN—Piano quartet, op. 10; Piano trio, op. 19. *Prunyi, piano; Bánfalvi, violin; Fejérvári, viola; Botvay, cello.*
+ ARG 1-2/94: 83
+ Fa 11-12/93: 192
+ Fa 1-2/94: 134
□ Gr 11/93: 92

21744. 8.223525: LESCHETIZKY—Piano music. *Ritzen, piano.*
+ ARG 1-2/94: 117
+ Fa 1-2/94: 222
+ Gr 7/94: 80

21745. 8.223526, 8.223578 (2 separate discs): BENNETT—Piano works vol. 2-3. *Prunyi, piano.*
+ ARG 1-2/94: 78
+ Fa 1-2/94: 130
+ Gr 6/94: 88

21746. 8.223527: VILLA-LOBOS—Pequena suite; Bachianas brasileiras no. 2, 5-6 (excerpts); Capriccio, op. 49; Preludio no. 2; Élégie, op. 87; Assobio a jato. *Rust, cello; Apter, piano; Pahud, flute; Edelmann, bassoon.*
+ ARG 3-4/95: 216
+ Fa 3-4/95: 329

21747. 8.223529: RAFF—Symphonies no. 4, 11. *Kosice State Phil. Orch.; Schneider, cond.*
+ ARG 5-6/94: 127
+ Fa 5-6/94: 223
- Gr 2/95: 52

21748. 8.223531: AUBERT—Dryade; Le tombeau de Chateaubriand; Offrande; Feuille d'images; Cinéma. *Rheinland-Pfalz State Phil.; Segerstam, cond.*
- ARG 11-12/94: 63
□ Fa 9-10/94: 116 (Simmons)
- Fa 9-10/94: 118 (Snook)

21749. 8.223532 (2 discs): VICTORY—Ultima rerum. *Kerr, Greevy, Thompson, Opie; Irish National Symphony; Pearce, cond.*
- ARG 1-2/95: 197
+ Fa 1-2/95: 293
+ Gr 6/95: 104

21750. 8.223534: NIN-CULMELL—Tonadas, vol. 1-4. *Cantos, piano.*
+ Fa 5-6/94: 208

21751. 8.223535: HERRMANN—Jane Eyre. *Slovak Radio Symphony Orch.; Adriano, cond.*
+ ARG 3-4/95: 113

21752. 8.223537: HILL—Symphonies no. 3, 7; The lost hunter; The moon's golden horn. *Queensland Symphony Orch.; Lehmann, cond.*
+ ARG 7-8/96: 129
+ Fa 7-8/96: 195
+ Gr 6/96: 48

21753. 8.223539: MOSONYI—Piano concerto; Symphony in D major. *Körmendi, piano; Slovak State Phil. Orch., Kosice; Slovak Radio Symphony Orch, Bratislava; Stankovsky, cond.*
- Fa 11-12/94: 305
+ Gr 3/95: 48

21754. 8.223540: LIATOSHINSKY—Symphonies no. 2-3. *Ukrainian National Symphony Orch.; Kuchar, cond.*
+ ARG 11-12/94: 143
+ Fa 1-2/95: 193
+ Gr 11/94: 80

21755. 8.223541: LIATOSHYNSKYI—Symphonies no. 4-5. *Ukrainian Symphony Orch.; Kuchar, cond.*
+ ARG 3-4/95: 127
+ Gr 1/95: 48

21756. 8.223542: LYATOSHINSKY—Symphony no. 1; Grazhyna. *Ukrainian National Symphony Orch.; Kuchar, cond.*

+ ARG 5-6/95: 130
• Fa 7-8/95: 226
• Gr 4/95: 58

21757. 8.223545: STEVENSON—Passacaglia on DSCH. *Clarke, piano.*
+ ARG 3-4/95: 192
+ Fa 3-4/95: 308
+ Gr 9/95: 84

21758. 8.223546: FURTWÄNGLER—Te Deum; Religious hymn; Schwindet, ihr dunklen Wölbungen; Eleven Lieder. *Pikal, tenor; A. Walter, piano & cond.; Frankfurt a. d. Oder Phil. Orch. & Singakademie.*
• ARG 9-10/95: 147
• Fa 7-8/95: 188
• Gr 12/95: 128

21759. 8.223548: NEPOMUCENO—Piano music. *Guimaraes, piano.*
+ ARG 3-4/95: 150
+ Fa 3-4/95: 245
- Gr 2/95: 74

21760. 8.223549—8.223450 (2 separate discs): CIURLIONIS—Piano works, vol. 1-2. *Rubackyté, piano.*
+ ARG 11-12/94: 94
+ Fa 9-10/94: 168
+ Gr 2/94: 72

21761. 8.223551: VILLA-LOBOS—Discovery of Brazil, suites 1-4. *Blazo, baritone; Slovak Phil. Orch.; Duarte, cond.*
• ARG 7-8/94: 186
• Fa 9-10/94: 365
+ Gr 8/94: 62

21762. 8.223552: VILLA-LOBOS—Rudepoema; Danças africanas; Dança frenética; Dança dos mosquitos. *Slovak Radio Orch.; Duarte, cond.*
• ARG 1-2/95: 198
+ Fa 1-2/95: 296
+ Gr 2/95: 59

21763. 8.223553: GIBBS—Symphonies no. 1, 3. *Irish National Symphony Orch.; Penny, cond.*
+ ARG 3-4/95: 105
+ Fa 5-6/95: 195
+ Gr 5/95: 48

21764. 8.223556: VELASQUEZ—Piano music. *Sverner, piano.*
+ Fa 1-2/95: 292
+ Fa 5-6/95: 366
+ Gr 7/95: 88

21765. 8.223557: MOSONYI—*Piano music, vol. 1.* Hungarian childern's world. *Kassai, piano.*
+ ARG 11-12/94: 159
+ Fa 11-12/94: 305
+ Gr 9/94: 82

21766. 8.223558: MOSONYI—Grand duo; Three colors of burning love; Festival music. LISZT—Missa solemnis (arr.

Mosonyi). *Kassai, Körmendi, pianos.*
+ Gr 12/94: 121

21767. 8.223559: MOSONYI—Piano music. LISZT—Piano music. *Kassai, piano.*
+ ARG 9-10/95: 176
+ Fa 9-10/95: 265

21768. 8.223561: JOSEF STRAUSS—Complete works, vol. 1. *Budapest Strauss Symphony Orch.; A. Walter, cond.*
+ ARG 7-8/95: 205
+ Fa 7-8/95: 331
• Gr 6/95: 58

21769. 8.223562—8.223563 (2 separate discs): JOSEF STRAUSS—The complete orchestral music, vols. 2-3. *Kosice State Phil. Orch.; Walter, cond.*
+ ARG 5-6/96: 205
+ Fa 3-4/96: 293
• Gr 3/96: 54

21770. 8.223576: RUBINSTEIN—Symphony no. 3; Eroica fantasia. *Bratislava Radio Symphony; Stankovsky, cond.*
+ ARG 1-2/95: 163
+ Fa 1-2/95: 248
• Gr 2/95: 54

21771. 8.223577: DONIZETTI—Sinfonias (transcribed from string quartets). *Failoni Chamber Orch.; Oberfrank, cond.*
+ ARG 5-6/94: 88
+ Fa 5-6/94: 136

21772. 8.223592/93 (2 discs): WEBER—Peter Schmoll and his neighbors. *Pfeffer, Basa, Schöpfin, Busching, Schmidt, Porcher; Hagen Phil. Orch.; Markson, cond.*
• Fa 7-8/94: 283
+ Gr 4/94: 109
+ ON 9/94: 58

21773. 8.223594: LACHNER—Symphony no. 8; Ball-suite. *Kosice Phil. Orch.; Robinson, Walter, conds.*
+ ARG 3-4/95: 122
+ Fa 5-6/95: 237
+ Gr 3/95: 46

21774. 8.223595: RESPIGHI—La primavera; Quattro liriche su poesie populari armene. *Valášková, Dvorsky, Haan, Kibovcik, Lednárová, Geriová; Slovak Phil. Chorus; Bratislava Radio Symphony Orch.; Adriano, cond.; chamber ensemble.*
+ Fa 7-8/95: 290
• Gr 5/95: 96

21775. 8.223596: STRAUS—Music of Oscar Straus. *Kincses, soprano; Budapest Strauss Symphony Orch.; A. Walter, cond.*
+ Fa 7-8/94: 252

21776. 8.223597: SPOHR—String quintets no. 1-2. *Danubius Quartet; Papp, viola.*
• ARG 3-4/95: 192
+ Fa 1-2/95: 273

21777. 8.223598: SPOHR—String quintets no. 5-6. *Haydn Quartet, Budapest; Papp, viola.*
• ARG 1-2/96: 178
+ Fa 11-12/95: 384

21778. 8.223599: SPOHR—String quintets vol. 3: no. 3-4. *New Haydn Quartet; Papp, viola.*
+ Fa 5-6/96: 285
+ Gr 5/96: 74

21779. 8.223602—8.223604 (3 separate discs): MALIPIERO—Symphonies no. 1-4, 7; Sinfonie del silenzio e de la morte; Sinfonia del mare; Sinfonia in un tempo; Sinfonia per Antigenida. *Moscow Phil. Symphony Orch.; Almeida, cond.*
+ Fa 7-8/94: 168
+ Gr 4/94: 50

21780. 8.223606: BARGIEL—Character pieces, op. 8; Fantasies, no. 1-2; Suite, op. 31. *D. Blumenthal, piano.*
+ ARG 3-4/95: 70
+ Fa 1-2/95: 106

21781. 8.223609: PONCE—Piano music. *Witten, piano.*
+ ARG 5-6/96: 162
+ Fa 3-4/96: 245
+ Gr 5/96: 90

21782. 8.223617: J. STRAUSS, SR.—Waltzes, quadrilles, galops. *Slovak State Phil. Orch. of Kosice; Eichenholz, cond.*
+ ARG 3-4/95: 193
+ Fa 1-2/95: 276

21783. 8.223627 (2 discs): PFITZNER—Das Herz. *Wenhold, Horn, Cunningham, Johanning; Thuringian Symphony Orch.; Reuter, cond.*
+ Gr 11/94: 148

21784. 8.223629: IPPOLITOV-IVANOV—From songs of Ossian; Armenian rhapsody; Symphonic scherzo; Yarkhmel; Jubilee march; Episode from the life of Schubert. *Slovak Radio Symphony Orch.; Johanos, cond.*
+ ARG 11-12/94: 134
+ Fa 1-2/95: 181
+ Gr 10/94: 110

21785. 8.223630: RAFF—Symphony no. 2; Romeo and Juliet overture; Macbeth overture. *Slovak State Orch. of Kosice; Schneider, cond.*
+ ARG 3-4/95: 164
+ Fa 3-4/95: 269
+ Fa 5-6/95: 302
+ Gr 7/95: 63

21786. 8.223631: MACDOWELL—Woodland sketches; Sea pieces; Fireside tales; New England idyls. *Barbagallo, piano.*
• ARG 1-2/95: 134
+ Fa 9-10/94: 243
+ Gr 4/95: 90

MARCO POLO

21787. 8.223632: MacDowell—Piano music, vol. 2. *Barbagallo, piano.*
+ ARG 5-6/96: 139
+ Fa 11-12/95: 293

21788. 8.223633: MacDowell—Piano music vol. 3. *Barbagallo, piano.*
+ Gr 1/96: 82

21789. 8.223635: Sullivan—Macbeth; King Arthur; Merry wives of Windsor. *MacDonald, mezzo-soprano; Irish Radio Choir & Orch.; Penny, cond.*
+ ARG 1-2/96: 181
+ Fa 3-4/96: 295
+ Gr 1/96: 64

21790. 8.223636: *In memoriam Lili Boulanger.* L. Boulanger—Thème et variations; D'un matin de printemps; Nocturne; Clarières dans le ciel; D'un vieux jardin; D'un jardin clair; Dans l'immense tristesse; Le retour; Pie Jesu. N. Boulanger—Lux aeterna; Two pieces for cello and piano; Le couteau; Vers la vie nouvelle. Naoumoff—In memoriam Lili Boulanger. *Naoumoff, piano & cond.; Charlier, violin; Sabrié, Robert, sopranos; Reinhardt, mezzo- soprano; Pidoux, cello; Marchese, bassoon.*
+ Fa 7-8/94: 87
+ Gr 9/94: 71

21791. 8.223637: Tovey—Elegiac variations; Cello sonata. Bridge—Cello sonata; Mélodie; Scherzo. *Rust, cello; Apter, piano.*
• Fa 7-8/95: 348 (Anderson)
+ Fa 7-8/95: 348 (Jameson)

21792. 8.223638: Raff—Symphony no. 6; Jubilee overture; Dame Kobold overture; Festive march. *Slovak State Phil. Orch., Kosice; Schneider, cond.*
+ ARG 5-6/95: 155
+ Fa 7-8/95: 284

21793. 8.223639: Oswald—Piano music. *Guimaraes, piano.*
+ Fa 9-10/96: 277
• Gr 2/96: 76

21794. 8.223640: Husa—Fresque; Reflections (Symphony no. 2); Music for Prague 1968. *Slovak Radio Symphony Orch.; Kolman, cond.*
+ ARG 7-8/95: 128
+ Fa 3-4/95: 194
+ Gr 5/95: 50

21795. 8.223641: Roger-Ducasse—Prelude d'un ballet; In Marguerite's garden: Interlude; Suite française; Epithalame. *Rheinland-Pfalz State Phil. Orch.; Segerstam, cond.*
+ ARG 3-4/95: 171
+ Fa 1-2/95: 246

21796. 8.223644: Bella—Piano music. *Rusó, piano.*
+ Fa 5-6/95: 139
+ Gr 6/95: 76

21797. 8.223645: Furtwängler—Overture in E♭; Symphony in D: Allegro; Symphony in B minor: Largo. *Kosice Phil.; Walter, cond.*
+ ARG 9-10/95: 146
- Fa 11-12/95: 258
- Gr 7/95: 50

21798. 8.223646: Grechaninov—String quartets no. 2, 4. *Moyzes String Quartet.*
• ARG 1-2/95: 110
+ Fa 1-2/95: 165
+ Gr 10/94: 138

21799. 8.223647: Suppé—Overtures, vol. 1. *Slovak State Phil. Orch.; A. Walter, cond.*
+ ARG 3-4/95: 197
+ Fa 3-4/95: 315

21800. 8.223648: Suppé—Overtures, vol. 2. *Kosice State Phil. Orch.; Walter, cond.*
+ ARG 3-4/95: 197
+ Fa 7-8/95: 335
+ Gr 6/95: 58

21801. 8.223649: Novák—Serenades in F and D major. *Ukrainian Chamber Orch.; Mogrelia, cond.*
+ ARG 3-4/96: 161
+ Fa 5-6/96: 228
• Gr 3/96: 50

21802. 8.223651: F. Devreese—Soundtrack: dances, divertimenti, and preludes. *De Groote, piano.*
+ ARG 9-10/96: 113
+ Fa 1-2/95: 150
+ Gr 1/95: 76

21803. 8.223654: Indy—Médée: suite; Karadec: suite; Souvenirs. *Württemberg State Orch.; Nopre, cond.*
• ARG 11-12/94: 133
• Fa 9-10/94: 220
• Gr 7/95: 59

21804. 8.223655: Le Flem—For the dead; Children's pieces; The great gardener of France; Symphony no. 4. *Rhenish Phil. Orch.; Lockhart, cond.*
• ARG 1-2/95: 131
+ Fa 1-2/95: 186
• Gr 12/94: 86

21805. 8.223656: Blumenfeld—Etudes for piano. *Blumenthal, piano.*
• ARG 1-2/95: 85
+ Fa 3-4/95: 136
+ Gr 12/95: 113

21806. 8.223657: Alkan—Piano music, vol. 1. *Martin, piano.*
• ARG 11-12/94: 60
• Fa 11-12/94: 142 (Rapoport)
• Fa 11-12/94: 144 (Johnson)
+ Gr 4/95: 88

21807. 8.223659: Indy—Tableaux de voyage; Saugefleurie; Fantaisie sur des thèmes populaires français; Etrnager: Prelude; Fervaal: Prelude. *Cousu, oboe; Württemberg Phil. Orch.; Burfin, Nopre,*

conds.
• ARG 1-2/95: 119
+ Fa 1-2/95: 180
• Gr 1/95: 46

21808. 8.223660: Schillings—Kassandra; Das eleusische Fest. S. Wagner—Sehnsucht. C. Harris—Paradise lost; Festival march. *Neubauer, speaker; Thuringian Symphony Orch. Saalfeld-Rudolstadt; K. Bach, cond.*
+ ARG 3-4/95: 176
+ Fa 3-4/95: 220
• Gr 2/95: 44

21809. 8.223663: *Bartók transcriptions of Italian keyboard music of the 17th and 18th centuries.* Music of Rossi, Della Ciaia, Frescobaldi, Zipoli, and Marcello. *Prunyi, piano.*
+ ARG 5-6/95: 81
• Fa 3-4/95: 120 (Rabinowitz)
+ Fa 3-4/95: 120 (Anderson)

21810. 8.223665: Vaughan Williams—Film music. *Irish Radio Orch.; Penny, cond.*
+ ARG 11-12/95: 222
+ Gr 10/95: 76

21811. 8.223667: Lajtha—Suite no. 3; Hortobágy; Symphony no. 7. *Pécs Symphony Orch.; Pasquet, cond.*
+ ARG 3-4/95: 123
+ Fa 3-4/95: 204
• Gr 4/95: 56

21812. 8.223668: Lajtha— Capriccio. *Pécs Symphony Orch.; Pasquet, cond.*
+ ARG 9-10/95: 165
+ Fa 7-8/95: 218

21813. 8.223669: Lajtha—Symphony no. 2; Variations. *Pécs Symphony Orch.; Pasquet, cond.*
+ ARG 9-10/96: 148
+ Fa 5-6/96: 188

21814. 8.223674: Truscott—Suite in G; Elegy; Symphony in E. *National Symphony Orch. of Ireland; Brain, cond.*
+ Fa 7-8/95: 350
+ Gr 2/95: 58

21815. 8.223675: Glière—Shah senem: Overture; Syul'sara: Overture; The bronze horseman: Suite; Heroic march, op. 71. *St. Petersburg State Symphony Orch.; Anichanov, cond.*
• ARG 1-2/96: 113
• Fa 1-2/96: 208

21816. 8.223677: Sullivan—Victoria and merrie England. *Irish Radio Sinfonietta; Penny, cond.*
+ ARG 1-2/96: 181
+ Fa 3-4/96: 295
+ Fi 3/96: 126
+ Gr 6/96: 62

21817. 8.223680: Devreese—Tombelene ballet suite; Violin concerto no. 1; Cello concertino. *Neve, violin; Spanoghe,*

Index to CD and Record Review, 1987 - 1997

MARCO POLO

cello; *Belgian Radio Phil. Orch.;
Devreese, cond.*
+ ARG 1-2/95: 101
+ Fa 1-2/95: 150
+ Gr 11/94: 70

21818. 8.223681: F. Devreese—Film
music. *BRT Phil. Orch.; Devreese, cond.*
+ Gr 11/94: 70

21819. 8.223683: Suppé—Overtures, vol.
3. *Kosice Phil. Orch.; Walter, cond.*
• ARG 1-2/96: 182
+ Gr 12/95: 94

21820. 8.223685: Waldteufel—Waltzes
and polkas, vol. 7. *Kosice State Phil.
Orch.; Walter, cond.*
+ ARG 7-8/96: 223
+ Fa 5-6/96: 313
+ Gr 6/96: 62

21821. 8.223689: Schmitt—Danse
d'Abisag; Habeyssée; Rêves; Symphony
no. 2. *Segerstam, violin; Rheinland-
Pfalz Phil. Orch.; Segerstam, cond.*
+ Fa 3-4/95: 283
+ Fa 7-8/95: 299
+ Gr 3/95: 52

21822. 8.223690: Tansman—Music for
guitar. *Regnier, guitar.*
+ ARG 5-6/95: 184
+ Fa 1-2/95: 288

21823. 8.223691: W. d'Indy—Piano trio
op. 15. V. d'Indy—Quartet no. 3; Piano
quintet in G minor. *Prunyi, piano; New
Budapest String Quartet.*
• ARG 3-4/96: 130
+ Fa 5-6/96: 139

21824. 8.223694: Joyce—Orchestra
music. *RTE Concert Orch., Dublin;
Penny, cond.*
+ ARG 1-2/96: 128
□ Fa 11-12/95: 282
+ Gr 3/96: 46

21825. 8.223695: German—Orchestra
music. *Irish Radio Orch.; Penny, cond.*
+ ARG 11-12/95: 120
+ Fa 3-4/96: 168
+ Gr 11/95: 86

21826. 8.223696: Malipiero—
Symphonies no. 5, 6, 8, 11. *Moscow
Symphony Orch.; Almeida, cond.*
• Fa 5-6/95: 253
• Gr 2/95: 48

21827. 8.223697: Malipiero—Symphony
of the zodiac; Symphonies no. 9, 10.
*Moscow Symphony Orch.; Almeida,
cond.*
• ARG 5-6/95: 135
- Fa 3-4/95: 218
• Fa 5-6/95: 253

21828. 8.223699—8.223700 (2 separate
discs): Ketèlbey—Piano music, vols. 1-2.
Tuck, piano.

+ ARG 3-4/96: 135
+ Fa 3-4/96: 190

21829. 8.223701: Donizetti—Wind
sinfonias, concertos, and concertinos. *I.
Kovács, flute; J. Kiss, oboe; Girgás,
English horn; B. Kovács, clarinet; A.
Kiss, violin; Domonkos, cello; Camerata
Budapest; L. Kovács, cond.*
+ ARG 9-10/95: 136
+ Fa 9-10/95: 193
+ Gr 10/95: 52

21830. 8.223703: Guarnieri—Violin
sonatas no. 4-6. *Larsen, violin;
Müllenbach, piano.*
+ ARG 1-2/95: 111
+ Fa 1-2/95: 167

21831. 8.223704: Koechlin—Au loin; Le
buisson ardent; Sur les flots lointains (2
versions). *Rheinland-Pfalz Phil.;
Segerstam, cond.*
+ ARG 11-12/95: 141
+ Fa 9-10/95: 238
+ Gr 8/95: 76

21832. 8.223705: Smetana—Short
orchestral pieces. *Bratislava Radio
Symphony; Stankovsky, cond.*
• ARG 1-2/95: 182
+ Fa 1-2/95: 272

21833. 8.223706/7 (2 discs): Corghi—
Divara: Wasser und Blut. *Burg, Krieg,
Hildmann; Münster State Orch.; Münster
City Theatre Chorus; Humburg, cond.*
+ Fa 7-8/95: 158
+ Gr 10/95: 131
+ ON 12/23/95: 38

21834. 8.223709: *South African music.*
Music of Wendt, Lissant-Collins,
Moerane, and Fagan. *National Symphony
Orch. of the South African Broadcasting
Corp.; Marchbank, cond.*
• ARG 9-10/95: 248
• Fa 7-8/95: 446

21835. 8.223710: *Latin American
classics: Guatemala, vol. 1.* Castillo—
Sinfonieta; Xibalbá; Guatemala no. 1-2.
Martinez-Sobral—Acuarelas chapinas.
*Moscow Symphony Orch.; Almeida,
cond.*
+ ARG 5-6/95: 199
+ Fa 7-8/95: 150
+ Gr 5/95: 56

21836. 8.223712: Klebe—Piano music.
Matthies, Köhn, pianos.
+ ARG 5-6/96: 130
+ Fa 3-4/96: 191

21837. 8.223713 (2 discs): S. Wagner—
Der Bärenhäuter. *Johanning, Horn,
Waller, Wenhold; Thuringian Symphony
Orch.; Bach, cond.*
+ ARG 1-2/95: 202
- Fa 1-2/95: 309
• Gr 6/95: 114
+ ON 4/15/95: 37

21838. 8.223715: *The American
Indianists.* Music of Cadman, Skilton,
Orem, MacDowell, Gilbert, Loomis,
Strong, Farwell, and Fairchild. *Müller,
piano.*
□ ARG 3-4/95: 243
+ Fa 1-2/95: 357

21839. 8.223716: Berners—Wedding
bouquet; March; Luna Park. *RTE
Chamber Choir & Sinfonietta; Alwyn,
cond.*
+ ARG 9-10/96: 95
- Fa 9-10/96: 153
+ Gr 7/96: 47

21840. 8.223717: Respighi—Lucrezia.
*Remor, Kaluza, Haan, Pasek; Slovak
Radio Orch.; Adriano, cond.*
- ARG 1-2/96: 161
- Fa 11-12/95: 345
• Gr 3/96: 99
+ ON 4/13/96: 54
+ Op 1/96: 72

21841. 8.223718: Rubbra—Cello sonata
op. 60. Moeran—Cello sonata.
Ireland—Cello sonata. *Wallfisch, cello;
York, piano.*
+ ARG 9-10/95: 255
+ Fa 9-10/95: 300
+ Gr 8/95: 96

21842. 8.223721: Holbrooke—The
children of Don: Overture; The birds of
Rhiannon; Dylan: Prelude. *National
Symphony Orch. of Ukraine; Penny,
cond.*
+ ARG 3-4/96: 128
+ Fa 3-4/96: 185
• Gr 12/95: 80

21843. 8.223722: Pizzetti—String
quartets no. 1-2. *Lajtha Quartet.*
+ ARG 5-6/96: 162
+ Fa 5-6/96: 237
• Gr 4/96: 67

21844. 8.223725: Sowerby—Classic
concerto; Medieval poem; Pageant;
Festival musick. *Mulbury, Craighead,
organ; Lilly, soprano; Radcliff, Albach,
trumpets; Hutchinson, Caswell,
trombones; Haskins, timpani; Fairfield
Orch.; Welsh, cond.*
+ ARG 7-8/95: 200
+ Fa 7-8/95: 326 (Snook)
+ Fa 7-8/95: 327 (Anderson)
- Fa 7-8/95: 328 (Ross)

21845. 8.223726: German—Symphony
no. 2; Welsh rhapsody; Valse gracieuse.
*National Symphony Orch. of Ireland;
Penny, cond.*
+ ARG 11-12/95: 120
+ Fa 3-4/96: 168
+ Gr 1/96: 49

21846. 8.223727: Truscott—Trio for
flute, violin, and viola; Clarinet sonata no.
1; Violin sonata; Meditation on themes
from Emmanuel Moór's Suite for four
cellos. *Kovács, flute; Nagy, Eckhardt,*

713

MARCO POLO

violin; *Bársony, viola; Varga, clarinet;*
Lugossy, piano; Domonkos, cello.
+ ARG 5-6/96: 214
+ Fa 7-8/95: 351
+ Gr 6/95: 72

21847. 8.223730: SUPPÉ—Overtures, vol.
4. *Kosice Phil. Orch.; Walter, cond.*
• ARG 1-2/96: 182
+ Fa 3-4/96: 298

21848. 8.223731: BRIAN—Symphonies
no. 20, 25; Variations on an old rhyme.
Ukraine Symphony Orch.; Penny, cond.
+ ARG 7-8/96: 92
+ Fa 7-8/96: 129
+ Gr 6/96: 42

21849. 8.223732: *British light music.*
Music of Addinsell. *Martin, Elms, piano;*
BBC Concert Orch.; Alwyn, cond.
+ ARG 7-8/95: 79
+ Fa 7-8/95: 94
+ Gr 4/95: 47

21850. 8.223736: HOLBROOKE—Piano
quartet no. 1; Symphonic quintet; String
sextet. *Papp, viola; Devich, cello;*
Hegedűs, piano; New Haydn Quartet.
+ Gr 8/96: 66

21851. 8.223740: BOECK—Symphony in
G major; Violin concerto; Dahomeyan
Rhapsody. *Neve, violin; Flanders Phil.*
Orch.; Devreese, cond.
+ ARG 1-2/96: 99
+ Fa 3-4/96: 155

21852. 8.223741: MAES—Symphony no.
2; Viola concerto; Ouverture concertante;
Arabesque and scherzo for flute and
orchestra. *Neve, viola; Vanhove, flute;*
Royal Flanders Phil. Orch.; Oskamp,
cond.
+ ARG 3-4/96: 146
+ Fa 3-4/96: 208
+ Gr 11/95: 88

21853. 8.223742: RESPIGHI—La bella
dormente nel bosco. *Kohutkova,*
Domínguez, Valášková, Haan; Radio
Symphony Orch., Bratislava; Adriano,
cond.
• Fa 5-6/96: 246
+ Gr 7/96: 107
+ ON 4/13/96: 54

21854. 8.223745: BRETÓN—Piano trio;
String quartet. *Oravecz or Eckhart,*
piano; Kiss, violin; Botvay, cello; New
Budapest Quartet.
+ ARG 11-12/95: 98
+ Fa 7-8/95: 137
+ Gr 6/95: 67

21855. 8.223751: CAPLET—Suite persane:
Nihavend; Légende pour orchestre;
Marche triomphale et pompière. DEBUSSY
(ORCH. CAPLET)—Children's corner;
Pagodes; Suite bergamasque: Clair de
lune. *Rheinland-Pfalz Phil. Orch.;*
Segerstam, cond.
• ARG 9-10/95: 131

+ Fa 9-10/95: 185
+ Gr 9/95: 52

21856. 8.223753: MONTSALVATGE—
Concierto breve for piano and orchestra;
Sinfonia de requiem. RODRIGO—
Zarabanda lejana y villancico. *Morales,*
piano; Moncloa, soprano; Madrid
Symphony Orch.; Ros- Marbá, cond.
+ Fa 7-8/95: 249
+ Gr 9/95: 63

21857. 8.223754: STANFORD—Organ
sonatas no. 2-4. *Payne, organ.*
• ARG 9-10/95: 217

21858. 8.223755: *Prix de Rome cantatas.*
RAVEL—Cantatas. DEBUSSY—Le
printemps: chorus. CAPLET—Myrrha:
cantata; Tout est lumière: chorus. *Coste,*
Desnoues, Roi, Duguay, Lapointe, vocal
soloists; Chorus & Orch. of Paris-
Sorbonne; Grimbert, cond.
• ARG 1-2/96: 227
+ Fa 11-12/95: 342
+ Gr 10/95: 105

21859. 8.223756: VITOLS—Dramatic
overture; Fantaisie sur des chants
populaires lettons; Spriditis; Dargakmeni;
Rudens dziesma. *Zarins, violin; Latvian*
National Symphony Orch.; Yablonsky,
cond.
+ ARG 3-4/96: 203
+ Fa 3-4/96: 315

21860. 8.223757: TANSMAN—Concerto for
orchestra; Six études for orchestra;
Capriccio for orchestra. *Moscow*
Symphony Orch.; Almeida, cond.
□ ARG 11-12/96: 222
+ Fa 11-12/96: 393

21861. 8.223765: AURIC—La belle et la
bête. *Axios Chorus; Moscow Symphony*
Orch.; Adriano, cond.
+ ARG 9-10/96: 78
+ Gr 7/96: 100

21862. 8.223768: ROSENTHAL—Les petits
métiers; Trois poèmes de Marie Roustan;
Deux sonnets de Jean Cassou; Trois
pièces liturgiques; Musique de table.
Dubosc, soprano; Orch. Symphonique et
Lyrique de Nancy; Kaltenbach, cond.
+ ARG 3-4/97: 205
+ Fa 3-4/97: 274
+ Gr 6/96: 54

21863. 8.223774: ROPARTZ—Choral
music. *Soloists de la Maîtrise de Radio-*
France; Choeur Regional Vittoria d'Ile
de France; Orchestre Symphonique et
Lyrique de Nancy; Piquemal, cond.
+ ARG 1-2/96: 163
+ Fa 11-12/95: 348

21864. 8.223775: POOT—Symphony no.
6; Pygmalion suite; Symphonic allegro;
Cheerful overture. *Moscow Phil.*
Symphony Orch.; Devreese, cond.
+ ARG 7-8/96: 168
+ Fa 7-8/96: 263

21865. 8.223776: MEULEMANS—Pliny's
fountain; Symphonies no. 2-3; May night.
Moscow Symphony Orch.; Devreese,
cond.
+ ARG 7-8/96: 155
+ Fa 7-8/96: 243

21866. 8.223777/8 (2 discs): S.
WAGNER—Schwarzschwanenreich.
Johanning, Raffeiner, Quandt, Wenhold,
Schmitz, Hartmann, Chireanu, Lukic;
Thuringian Landestheater Rudolstadt;
Thuringian Symphony Orch. Saalfeld-
Rudolstadt; Bach, cond.
+ ARG 1-2/96: 198
• Fa 11-12/95: 423
+ Gr 11/95: 163
• ON 12/9/95: 50

21867. 8.223779: N. TCHEREPNINE—Le
pavillion d'Armide. *Moscow State*
Symphony Orch.; Shek, cond.
□ ARG 3-4/96: 195
+ Fa 3-4/96: 301
• Gr 12/95: 94

21868. 8.223780: BERNERS—Les sirènes
(complete ballet); Caprice peruvien;
Cupid and Psyche ballet suite.
Blennerhassett, alto; RTE Sinfonietta;
Pryce-Jones, cond.
□ Fa 5-6/96: 108
+ Gr 4/96: 42

21869. 8.223781/2 (2 discs):
RUBINSTEIN—The demon. *Lochak,*
Mescheriakova, Serkin, Browner;
National Symphony Orch. of Ireland;
Anisimov, cond.
• ARG 7-8/96: 182
+ Fa 5-6/96: 252
+ Gr 3/96: 102
+ ON 3/30/96: 36

21870. 8.223783: VASILENKO—Chinese
suite; Indian suite. *Moscow Phil.*
Symphony Orch.; Shek, cond.
+ ARG 3-4/96: 197
• Fa 3-4/96: 309
□ Gr 3/96: 56

21871. 8.223785/6 (2 discs): RYELANDT—
Agnus Dei. *Kapelle, Deyck, Cornwell,*
Claessens, MacLeod, vocalists; Audite
Nova; Altra Voce; Royal Flanders Phil.
Orch.; Llewellyn, cond.
+ ARG 3-4/97: 211
+ Fa 11-12/96: 353

21872. 8.223788: Music of Auric,
Honegger, Milhaud, Poulenc, and
Tailleferre. *Ensemble Erwartung;*
Desgaupes, cond.
+ ARG 11-12/96: 165
+ Fa 11-12/96: 485

21873. 8.223792: STANKOVYTCH—
Symphonies no. 1-2, 4. *National*
Symphony Orch. of Ukraine; Kuchar,
cond.
+ ARG 7-8/96: 203
+ Fa 5-6/96: 290

21874. 8.223801: *French ballroom favorites.* Music of Muller, Tavan, Auvray, and others. *Slovak State Radio Orch. of Bratislava; Cohen, cond.*
+ ARG 7-8/96: 235
+ Fa 5-6/96: 313
+ Gr 8/96: 60

21875. 8.223806: Coates—Songs. *Edgar-Wilson, tenor; Asti, piano; Ponder, viola.*
+ ARG 9-10/96: 109
+ Fa 7-8/96: 147
+ Gr 4/96: 86

21876. 8.223809: Gilson—La mer; Mélodies ecossaises; Alvar; Prelude; Symphonic overture. *Moscow Symphony Orch.; Devreese, cond.*
+ ARG 7-8/96: 115
+ Fa 9-10/96: 192

21877. 8.223811: Arensky—String quartets no. 1-2; Piano quintet. *Lajtha Quartet; Prunyi, piano.*
+ ARG 3-4/96: 76
+ Fa 3-4/96: 100

21878. 8.223812: Pizzetti—Piano trio; Violin sonata; Canti. *Rasonyi, violin; Fenyö, cello; Ertüngealp, piano.*
• ARG 5-6/96: 162
+ Fa 3-4/96: 245

21879. 8.223827: Benoît—Flute concerto; Le roi des Aulnes; Piano concerto. *Riet, flute; Devos, piano; Flanders Phil. Orch.; Devreese, cond.*
+ ARG 7-8/96: 81
+ Fa 7-8/96: 110

21880. 8.223832: *African songs.* Music of Van Dijk, Khumalo, and Akpabot. *National Symphony Orch. of the South African Broadcasting Corp.; Cock, cond.*
+ ARG 7-8/96: 236
+ Fa 5-6/96: 367

21881. 8.223833: Fagan—Concert overture; Ilala. Bell—South African symphony. *National Symphony Orch. of the South African Broadcasting Corp.; Cock, Marchbank, conds.*
• ARG 7-8/96: 110
+ Fa 5-6/96: 367

21882. 8.223839: Bella—Quartets; Notturno. *Moyzes Quartet.*
+ ARG 7-8/96: 79
+ Fa 7-8/96: 109

21883. 8.223849: García Abril—Three sonatas for orchestra; Hemeroscopium; Piano concerto. *Gonzalez, piano; Madrid Symphony Orch.; García Asensio, cond.*
+ ARG 5-6/96: 115
+ Fa 3-4/96: 167
+ Gr 6/96: 40

21884. 8.223867: Gerhard—Dos apunts; Soirées de Barcelona; Don Quixote; Dances; Three impromptus. Homs—Piano sonata no. 2. *Maso, piano.*

+ ARG 11-12/96: 126
+ Fa 9-10/96: 191
+ Gr 9/96: 75

21885. 8.223888: May—String quartet in C minor. Fleischmann—Piano quintet. *Vanbrugh Quartet; Tinney, piano.*
+ ARG 11-12/96: 160
+ Fa 11-12/96: 303
+ Gr 12/96: 98

MARCO POLO/DA CAPO

21886. DCCD 8901: Norgård—Symphony no. 3; Twilight. *Danish National Radio Symphony Orch.; Vetö, Latham-Koenig, conds.*
+ Fa 3-4/93: 243

21887. DCCD 9001 (2 discs): Norgård—Gilgamesh; Voyage into the golden screen. *Vocalists; Swedish Radio Symphony Orch.; Vetö, cond.; Danish Radio Symphony Orch.; Knussen, cond.* Reissue.
☐ ARG 7-8/93: 133
+ Fa 7-8/93: 196
+ Gr 1/93: 64

21888. DCCD 9002: Norgård—Remembering child; Between. *Zukerman, viola; Zeuthen, cello; Danish Radio Symphony Orch.; Panula, cond.*
+ ARG 1-2/93: 128
+ Fa 3-4/93: 243
+ Gr 11/92: 94

21889. DCCD 9003 (2 discs): Rasmussen—Solos and shadows; Surrounded by scales. Sorensen—Alman; Adieu; Angels' music. *Arditti Quartet.*
+ Fa 3-4/93: 255
+ Gr 11/92: 142

21890. DCCD 9005: Tarp—Te Deum; Piano concerto; Symphony no. 7; The Battle of Jericho. *Salo, piano; Danish National Radio Symphony Orch. & Choir; Nelson, Schønwandt, Schmidt, conds.*
+ Fa 11-12/93: 412

21891. DCCD 9007: G. Berg—Pastourelle, for flute solo; Cosmogonie, for 2 pianos; Aria, for flute and orchestra. *Rafn, flute; Stenyaard, Kaltoft, pianos; Wiesler, flute; Danish National Radio Symphony Orch.; B. Wagner, cond.*
+ Fa 1-2/93: 112

21892. DCCD 9010 : Gudmundsen-Holmgreen—Symphony-Antiphony. Rasmussen—Symphony in time. *Danish National Radio Symphony Orch.; Segerstam, cond.*
+ Fa 9-10/93: 171

21893. DCCD 9108: Jersild—Orchestra music. *Ellis, harp; Christensen, organ; Vox Danica Choir; Munk, cond.; Aalborg Symphony Orch.; Volmer, cond.*
+ ARG 1-2/94: 112
+ Fa 1-2/94: 211

21894. DCCD 9110: Rosing-Schow—Chamber concerto; Sonata for piano and harpsichord; Trio for flute, viola and harp; Extraction. *Various performers.*
+ Fa 7-8/93: 216

21895. DCCD 9113: Heise—Piano quintet; Cello sonata, Two fantasy pieces for cello and piano. *Kontra Quartet; Malling, piano; Zeuthen, cello.*
+ ARG 1-2/93: 104
+ Fa 11-12/92: 253

21896. DCCD 9115-9116 (2 separate discs): Gade—Piano works, vol. 1-2. *Blyme, piano.*
• ARG 11-12/92: 123
- Fa 9-10/92: 240

21897. DCCD 9117: Gade—Complete piano music, vol. 3. *Blyme, piano.*
+ ARG 11-12/92: 123
• Fa 1-2/93: 152

21898. DCCD 9201, 9004, 9292, 9301 (4 separate discs): Gade—The eight symphonies. *Malling, piano; Collegium Musicum, Copenhagen; Schønwandt, cond.*
+ ARG 7-8/93: 91 (9004)
+ ARG 11-12/94: 113
+ Fa 7-8/93: 139 (9004)
+ Fa 11-12/94: 228
+ Gr 5/94: 50

21899. DCCD 9203: Holmboe—String quartets no. 1, 3-4. *Kontra Quartet.*
+ Gr 6/94: 70

21900. DCCD 9302 (2 discs): Langgaard—String quartets. *Kontra Quartet.*
+ ARG 1-2/96: 131

21901. DCCD 9306: L. Glass—Piano sonatas no. 1-2; Fantasy, op. 35. *Gade, piano.*
+ ARG 1-2/96: 112
+ Fa 1-2/96: 206

21902. DCCD 9307: Weyse—The late piano works. *Jedlickova, piano.*
• ARG 1-2/96: 200
+ Fa 1-2/96: 345

21903. DCCD 9308: Ruders—Violin concerto no. 2; Dramaphonia. *Hirsch, violin; Rosenbaum, piano; Copenhagen Collegium Musicum; Schønwandt, cond.; Lontano; Martinez, cond.*
+ ARG 1-2/96: 165
+ Gr 9/94: 60

21904. DCCD 9310: *Danish golden age piano trios.* Music of Gade, Hartmann, Langgaard, Henriques, and Lange-Muller. *Tre Musici.*
+ ARG 1-2/96: 206

21905. DCCD 9314: Lorentzen—Oboe concerto; Regenbogen. *Hoffmann, oboe; Schuster, trumpet; Aarhus Symphony Orch.; Rasmussen, cond.*

MARCO POLO/DA CAPO

+ ARG 1-2/96: 135
+ Fa 7-8/94: 166

21906. DCCD 9316: Music of Nielsen, Norgard, Nørholm, Gerfors and others. *Moldrup, guitar.*
+ ARG 11-12/95: 250

21907. 8.224001: NIELSEN—Wind quintet. HOLMBOE—Notturno. NORGARD—Whirl's world. ABRAHAMSEN—Walden. *Scandanavian Woodwind Quintet.*
+ ARG 3-4/95: 247

21908. 8.224002: Music of Koppel, Werner, Christiansen, Schultz, and Graugaard. *Danish Wind Octet.*
+ ARG 1-2/95: 233
+ Fa 3-4/95: 391

21909. 8.224003: *Complete chamber music, vol. 1.* BUXTEHUDE—Seven sonatas, op. 1. *Holloway, violin; Linden, viola da gamba; Mortensen, harpsichord.*
+ ARG 9-10/95: 119
+ Fa 7-8/95: 146
+ Gr 1/96: 69

21910. 8.224004: BUXTEHUDE—*Complete chamber music, vol. 2.* Violin sonatas, op. 2. *Holloway, violin; Linden, viola da gamba; Mortensen, harpsichord.*
+ ARG 3-4/96: 99
+ Gr 1/96: 69

21911. 8.224006: WERNER—Twelve tango studies; Tie-break. *Danish Accordion Ensemble; Dyremose, cond.*
+ Fa 11-12/95: 428

21912. 8.224008: RASMUSSEN—Italian concerto for 9 instruments. ROSING-SCHOW—Inner voices. NORDENTOFT—The nervous saurian. HOJSGAARD—Pale landscape. *Capricorn Ensemble.*
+ Fa 11-12/94: 498
+ Fa 3-4/95: 392

21913. 8.224009: THYBO—Mouvement symphonique; Organ concerto no. 2; Aus dem Studenbuch; Sonnengesang; Sumer is icumen in; Contrasti. *Lundkvist, organ; Peterson, trombone; Lange, soprano; Bonnerup, Krogh, organs.*
+ Fa 3-4/95: 319

21914. 8.224011: LANGGAARD—Songs. *Dahl, soprano; Staerk, piano.*
• ARG 1-2/96: 132
+ Fa 1-2/96: 240

21915. 8.224012: WEYSE—Symphonies no. 1-3. *Royal Danish Orch.; Schønwandt, cond.*
• ARG 7-8/95: 227
+ Fa 3-4/95: 345
+ Fa 9-10/95: 368

21916. 8.224013: WEYSE—Symphonies no. 4-5. *Royal Danish Orch.; Schønwandt, cond.·*
• ARG 5-6/96: 221

21917. 8.224014: WEYSE—Symphonies no. 6-7. *Royal Danish Orch.; Schønwandt, cond.*
• ARG 5-6/96: 221

21918. 8.224015: GADE—String quartets. *Copenhagen String Quartet.* Reissue.
+ ARG 3-4/96: 114

21919. 8.224016: KUHLAU—String quartet, op. 122. HORNEMAN—String quartet no. 2. *Copenhagen String Quartet.*
+ ARG 1-2/95: 118
+ Fa 11-12/94: 273

21920. 8.224021/2 (2 discs): J.P.E. HARTMANN—Complete works for violin and piano. *Schneider, violin; Jedlickova, piano.*
+ ARG 1-2/97: 118
+ Fa 11-12/96: 265
+ Gr 6/96: 65

21921. 8.224026: HOLMBOE—String quartets no. 2, 5-6. *Kontra Quartet.*
+ Gr 7/96: 71

21922. 8.224029: Court of King Christian III. *Copenhagen Cornetts and Sackbutts; Ars Nova; Holton, cond.*
+ ARG 7-8/96: 264
• Fa 7-8/96: 373

21923. 8.224031/2 (2 discs): NORGÅRD—Siddharta; Percussion concerto. *Guillaume, Andersen, Kiberg, Haugland; Danish Radio Orch.; Latham-Koenig, cond.*
+ ARG 7-8/96: 165
+ Fa 3-4/96: 240
+ Gr 12/95: 150

21924. 8.224035: O. SCHMIDT—Chamber symphony; Homage to Liszt; Flute concerto; Wind quintet. *Milan, flute; Northern College Chamber Orch.; Schmidt, cond.; Copenhagen Wind Quintet.*
+ ARG 1-2/97: 164
+ Fa 3-4/97: 284
+ Gr 9/96: 59

21925. 8.224036/7 (2 discs): KUNZEN—Holger Danske. *Nielsen, Bonde-Hansen, Henning-Jensen, Mannov, Reuter, Dam-Jensen, Päevatalu, Rørholm; Danish National Radio Choir & Symphony Orch.; Dausgaard, cond.*
+ ARG 9-10/96: 147
+ Fa 9-10/96: 231
+ Gr 7/96: 104
+ ON 12/28/96: 38
+ Op 9/96: 1116

21926. 8.224039: SORENSEN—Violin concerto "Sterbende Gärten"; The echoing garden. *Bäverstam, soprano; Hill, tenor; Hirsch, violin; Danish National Radio Choir & Symphony Orch.; Segerstam, cond.*
+ Gr 6/96: 60

MARK

21927. MCD 559: DRUCKMAN—Paen; In memoriam Vincent Persichetti. WILSON—Piece of mind. KURKA—Good soldier Schweik: Suite. DIAMOND—Tantivy. *Cincinnati College-Conservatory Wind Symphony; Corporon, cond.*
+ ARG 7-8/90: 130

21928. MCD 587: MUSSORGSKY—Pictures at an exhibition. RAVEL—Pavane. TOMASI—Holy Week at Cuzco. *DiMartino, trumpet; Robinson, organ.*
+ ARG 5-6/94: 115

21929. MCD 877: Music of Stamp, Tcherepnin, Tippett, Grainger, Weinstein, and Skalkottas. *CCM Wind Symphony; Corporon, cond.*
+ ARG 7-8/92: 276

21930. MCD 1067: Music of Scheidt, Koetsier, Albinoni, Zaninelli, Peuerl, Renwick, Sclater, Farnaby and Gershwin. *Sonus Brass.*
+ ARG 1-2/93: 176

21931. MCD 1115: MUCZYNSKI—Quintet. REICHA—Quintet, op. 100, no. 6. BACH-GRAHAM—Italian concerto: allegro; allegro molto. HIDAS—Quintet no. 2. GALIMANY-PLESNICAR—Panama. WIEDOEFT-GRAHAM—Saxophobia. *Northwind Quintet.*
• Fa 5-6/94: 335

21932. MCD 1116: PERSICHETTI—Masquerade. GILLINGHAM—Serenade "Songs of the night." GILMORE—Five folksongs. ZAPPA—Envelopes; Dog breath variations. SCHMITT—Dionysiaques. *Paré, soprano; University of Cincinnati College-Conservatory of Music Wind Ensemble; Corporon, cond.*
+ ARG 3-4/93: 178
+ Fa 5-6/93: 278

21933. MCD 1302: Music of Erb, Hodkinson, Harbison, Bassett, and Schuller. *Lawrence University Wind Ensemble; Levy, cond.*
+ ARG 5-6/96: 244

21934. MCD 1524: REYNOLDS—Music for horn. *Gaboury-Sly, horn; Moriarty, piano; Johnson, vibraphone.*
+ ARG 7-8/96: 180

21935. MCD 1701: *Aerodynamics.* Music of Telemann, Tcherepnin, Broughton, Gillingham, and others. *Sinder, tuba; Gaboury-Sly, horn; Moriarty, piano; Michigan State Wind Symphony; Whitwell, cond.*
+ ARG 5-6/96: 241

21936. MCD 1800: Music of Kamen, Bach, Wilson, Danner, Forte, Lockhart-Seitz, Johnston, Davis, James, Foster, Hancock, and Corea. *Tennessee Tech*

Tuba Ensemble; Morris, cond.
+ ARG 3-4/96: 237

21937. MCD 1862: HOLSINGER—
*Complete works, vol. 2. Band music.
Concordia University Wind Symphony;
Fischer, cond.*
• ARG 5-6/96: 127

21938. MCD 1875: Music of Barber,
Puccini, Praetorius, Mahler, and Teike.
*University of Houston Wind Ensemble;
Green, cond.*
+ ARG 5-6/96: 244

21939. MCD 1924: HINDEMITH—Horn
sonata; Alto horn sonata. COOKE—
Nocturnes; Rondo. HEIDEN—Horn sonata.
*Gaboury-Sly, horn; Buggs, mezzo-
soprano; Moriarty, piano.*
+ ARG 7-8/96: 133

21940. MCD 1967 (2 discs): Music of
Britten, Hanson, Debussy, Somers,
Lundvik, and others. *Trenton State
College Wind Ensemble; Silvester, cond.*
+ ARG 5-6/96: 245

21941. MCD 1982: Music of Forte,
Welcher, George, Corwell, and others.
Symphonia; Morris, cond.
+ ARG 11-12/96: 255

21942. MCD 2197: Music of Verdi,
Wagner, Adams, and Stravinsky.
University of Houston Wind Ensemble.
• ARG 1-2/97: 216

MARLBORO

21943. MRSCD-18: SCHUBERT—Octet, D.
803. *Scott, clarinet; Jolley, horn; Heller,
bassoon; Genualdi, Galimir, violins;
Tenenbom, viola; Wiley, cello; Lloyd,
double bass.*
+ Fa 11-12/88: 270

MARQUIS

21944. RVCD 107: *Sweet was the song.*
Music of Praetorius, Walther, Bach,
Attey, Luboff, Willan, Gabrieli, Vaughan
Williams, Carney, Korte, Pinkham.
*Robbin, mezzo-soprano; Mowatt, harp;
Vancouver Chamber Choir; Washburn,
cond.*
+ ARG 11-12/92: 266

21945. ERAD 113: Songs by Schubert,
Brahms, Honegger, Warlock, and others.
*Robbin, mezzo-soprano; McMahon,
piano.*
+ Gr 7/94: 106

21946. ERAD 123: MENDELSSOHN—Piano
concertos no. 1-2; Capriccio brillant.
*Kuertl, piano; London Phil. Orch.;
Freeman, cond.*
• ARG 9-10/90: 87

21947. ERAD 127: BRITTEN—Songs.
*McMillan, baritone; Greer, piano;
Hammer, violin; McBeth, organ; St.*

*James' Cathedral Choir, Toronto; Bryan,
cond.*
+ ARG 5-6/90: 36

21948. RVCD 133: BRITTEN—Choral
music. GIBBS—The song of shadows.
RUTTER—The Lord bless and keep you.
BYRD—Non nobis, Domine. PURCELL—
Sound the trumpet. *Toronto Children's
Chorus; Bartle, cond.; Henderson, piano;
Preston, organ; Loman, harp; Houlo,
percussion; Howard, oboe; Wolfe,
trumpet.*
+ ARG 9-10/92: 88

21949. RVCD 135: *Dancing day.* Music
of Rutter, Cable, Henderson, Telfer,
Bissell, Debussy, Archer, and Willan.
*Toronto Children's Chorus; Bartle,
cond.; Henderson, piano; Loman, harp;
Valdepeñas, clarinet; Dorsey, oboe;
Hetherington, cello.*
+ ARG 11-12/92: 269

21950. RVCD 137: *Danzas y canciones.*
Music of Morel, Bustamente, Lauro,
Falla, Pipo, Brouwer, and Sainz de la
Maza. *Gauk, guitar.*
+ ARG 11-12/92: 239

21951. RVCD 141: Trios by Beethoven,
Czerny, Kuhlau, and Hummel. *Chinook
Trio.*
+ ARG 5-6/94: 173

21952. RVCD 147: Music of
Castelnuovo-Tedesco, Kleynjans,
Stravinsky, Miyagi, Nagasawa, Bozza,
and Rodrigo. *Hoeppner, flute; Gauk,
guitar.*
+ ARG 9-10/94: 233

21953. RVCD 149: MACMILLAN—Celtic
mass for the sea. *Thompson, Rockwell,
Loughhead, Dephilippo; Halifax
Camerata Singers; Celtic Ensemble and
String Orch.; Macmillan, cond.*
• ARG 7-8/94: 127

21954. RVCD 151: SCHUBERT—
Schwanengesang; songs. *McMillan,
baritone; Natochenny, piano.*
- ARG 7-8/94: 166

21955. RVCD 157: REINECKE—Trio;
Nocturne. SCHUMANN—Adagio and
allegro. GOUNOD—Mélodies. *Sommervile,
horn; Mason, oboe; Sharon, piano.*
+ ARG 5-6/95: 158

21956. RVCD 161: *The parlor grand.*
Music of Beethoven, Mendelssohn,
Henselt, Rubinstein, and others.
Silverman, piano.
+ ARG 11-12/95: 256

21957. RVCD 163: D. SCARLATTI—
Sonatas arr. for guitar. *Gauk, guitar.*
+ ARG 3-4/96: 175

21958. RVCD 171: AXELROD—Songs.
*Parks, soprano; Horton, Ford-Livene,
tenors; Mackenzie, Bernstein, basses;*

Orch.; Beltrami, cond.
- ARG 7-8/96: 66

21959. RVCD 177: *Histoire du tango.*
Music of Piazzolla, Machado, Murillo,
Bobri, and others. *Hoeppner, flute; Gauk,
guitar.*
+ ARG 11-12/96: 247

21960. RVCD 179: IVES—Violin sonata
no. 2. CORIGLIANO—Violin sonata. Music
of Copland and Guarnieri. *Schwarz,
violin; Weiser, piano.*
+ ARG 11-12/96: 257

21961. RVCD 181: Bach meets Cape
Breton. *Puirt a Baroque.*
+ ARG 7-8/96: 236

21962. RVCD 1901: BEETHOVEN—Piano
sonatas no. 30-32. *Silverman, piano.*
+ ARG 7-8/92: 95
• Fa 11-12/91: 264, 285

MASTERSOUND

21963. DFCDI-018: CHOPIN—Etudes no.
1-24. *Zarankin, piano.*
• ARG 11-12/92: 103

21964. DFCDI-024: *The young Glenn
Gould (1947-1953).* Music of Berg,
Shostakovich, Taneev, Prokofiev,
Mozart, and Bach. *Gould, piano.*
- ARG 1-2/94: 199

21965. DFCDI-031: STRAUSS—Cello
sonata. RACHMANINOFF—Cello sonata.
Boeckheler, cello; Starr, piano.
+ ARG 3-4/95: 194

21966. DFCDI-034: SCHUMANN—
Papillons; Symphonic etudes;
Kinderszenen. *Marino, piano.*
+ ARG 9-10/96: 198

21967. DFCDI-212: Songs of Handel,
Mahler, Dvořák, Reger, Paladilhe,
Strauss, Schubert, Schumann, Sauguet,
Niles, Brockway, Dougherty, and
Massenet. *Forrester, alto; Davis, piano;
Harnoy, cello.*
• ARG 1-2/92: 174

21968. DFCDI-221: DAVIDSON—Minute
passacaglia; Plaisanteries; No. 5; Mystery
rag; Signor Grinderino; Stolen music;
Between the lines. *Davidson, Eells,
piano; Goethe, flute; Sullivan, saxophone.*
□ ARG 1-2/97: 245

MAYA RECORDINGS

21969. MCD 9302: TELEMANN—Fantasies
for solo violin. *Homburger, violin.*
+ Gr 8/94: 77

MBS

21971. 24: ALKAN—Concerto for solo
piano, op. 39, no. 8-10; Chants, bk. 5, op.
70. *McCallum, piano.*
+ Fa 11-12/92: 174

MCA

21972. MCAD-10055: Mozart—Piano quintet, K. 452. Gershwin—Lullaby. Foss—Saxophone quartet. Blake—Jassamine Lane. Blake and Guarneri—Eubie dubie. *Amherst Saxophone Quartet.*
+ ARG 3-4/91: 160
+ Fa 11-12/90: 460

21973. MCAD-10056: Castelnuovo-Tedesco—Platero and I: Excerpts; Quintet for guitar and strings; Tonadilla for guitar on the name of Andrés Segovia. *Segovia, guitar; Strings of the Quintetto Chigiano .*
+ Fa 3-4/91: 175

21974. MCAD-10100: Tchaikovsky—Symphony no. 6; Romeo and Juliet. *Royal Phil. Orch.; Koizumi, cond.*
+ ARG 5-6/91: 118
● Fa 3-4/91: 405

21975. MCAD2-10102: The Play of Daniel; The Play of Herod. *New York Pro Musica; Greenberg, cond.* Reissues.
+ ARG 11-12/91: 196
+ Fa 11-12/91: 544

21976. MCAD-10280: Bernstein—Fancy free: Selections; On the town: Selections. *Various performers; Bernstein, cond.* Recorded 1944-45.
+ Fa 3-4/92: 155

21977. MCAD-10281: *The Segovia collection, vol. 9.* Music of Grieg, Mendelssohn, Schubert, Haydn, Paganini, Brahms, Chopin, Schumann, Franck, Giuliani, Falla, Scriabin, Debussy. *Segovia, guitar.*
+ ARG 1-2/92: 155

21978. MCAD-10328,10393,10429 (3 separate discs): Liszt—Hungarian rhapsodies; Spanish rhapsody; Consolations no. 1-6. *Farnadi, piano.* Reissue.
● ARG 3-4/92: 89
+ ARG 7-8/92: 164 (10429)
● Fa 3-4/92: 229

21979. MCAD-10515 (3 discs): Handel—Judas Maccabeus. *Arroyo, Bumbry, McCollum, Watts; University of Utah Chorus; Utah Symphony Orch.; Abravanel, cond.* Reissue.
+ ARG 5-6/92: 69

21980. MCAD2-11010 (2 discs): Sullivan—Ruddygore. *New Sadler's Wells Opera; Phipps, cond.*
+ Fa 3-4/88: 109
+ Gr 9/88: 490
+ NYT 5/1/88: H28

21981. MCAD2-11011 (2 discs): Mahler—Symphony no. 2. *Valente, soprano; Forrester, contralto; Ardwyn Singers; BBC Welsh Chorus; Cardiff Polyphonic Choir; London Symphony Orch; Kaplan, cond.*
+ ARG 11-12/88: 54
+ Au 2/89: 128
+ Fa 1-2/89: 195
+ Gr 1/89: 1154
● SR 3/89: 124
● St 4/89: 199

21982. MCAD2-11012 (2 discs): Sullivan—H.M.S. Pinafore. *Ritchie, Ormiston, Gillett, Grace, Lawlor; New Sadler's Wells Opera Orch.; Phipps, cond.* Includes alternative versions of some pieces.
+ Fa 7-8/88: 168
+ Gr 5/88: 1644
- Op 5/88: 633

21983. MCAD-25160: Brahms—Symphony no. 2; Tragic overture. *Hallé Orch.; Skrowaczewski, cond.* Issued also as LP: MCA 25160.
● Fa 1-2/88: 100

21984. MCAD-25161: Chopin—Preludes, op. 28; Piano sonata no. 2. *Shelley, piano.*
+ Fa 3-4/88: 96

21985. MCAD-25162: Mozart—Serenade, K. 525; Serenade, K. 239. Elgar—Serenade, op. 20. Grieg—Holberg suite. *Serenata of London.*
- Fa 1-2/88: 179
+ Gr 11/87: 733

21986. MCAD-25164: *The romance of the flute and harp* Music of Fauré, Parish Alvars, Debussy, Hasselmans, Godefroid, Thomas, Doppler, Bizet, Saint-Saëns, Mendelssohn, and Godard. *Owen, harp; Davies, flute.*
● Fa 1-2/90: 404

21987. MCAD-25171: Tchaikovsky—Symphony no. 4; Marche slave. *London Symphony Orch.; Rozhdestvensky, cond.*
+ Fa 5-6/88: 224

21988. MCAD-25175: Tchaikovsky—Symphony no. 6; The storm: Overture. *London Symphony Orch.; Rozhdestvensky, cond.*
+ Fa 7-8/88: 265
+ Gr 1/88: 1090

21989. MCAD-25177: *Guitar classics from Spain.* Music of Tarrega, Granados, Albéniz, Torroba, Rodrigo, and Anon. *Kayath, guitar.*
+ Fa 7-8/88: 315
+ Gr 5/88: 1627

21990. MCAD-25187: Rimsky-Korsakov—Scheherazade. *London Symphony Orch.; Mauceri, cond.*
+ ARG 11-12/88: 74
+ Fa 7-8/88: 233
+ Gr 5/88: 1607
+ SR 9/88: 114

21991. MCAD-25188: Brahms—Symphony no. 1; Academic festival overture. *Hallé Orch.; Skrowaczewski, cond.*

+ ARG 11-12/88: 23
● Fa 7-8/88: 135
+ Gr 3/88: 1306

21992. MCAD-25189: Monteverdi—Soprano duets and solos. *Kirkby, Tubb, sopranos; Consort of Musicke; Rooley, cond.*
+ ARG 1-2/89: 69
+ Fa 7-8/88: 202
+ Gr 4/88: 1488

21993. MCAD-25191: Palestrina—Missa Papae Marcelli; Stabat Mater. *Pro Cantione Antiqua; Brown, cond.*
● ARG 9-10/88: 72
- Au 1/89: 174
+ Fa 9-10/88: 222 (2 reviews)
+ Gr 11/87: 801

21994. MCAD-25193: Beethoven—Piano trio no. 6; Variations on Ich bin der Schneider Kakadu, op. 121a. *Kalichstein-Laredo-Robinson Trio.*
+ ARG 11-12/88: 17
+ Fa 7-8/88: 123
+ Gr 1/88: 1096

21995. MCAD-25201: Bach—Harpsichord concertos no. 1, 4-6. *Bolton, harpsichord & cond.; St. James's Baroque Players.*
+ Da 5/89: 88
● Fa 9-10/88: 88
+ Gr 11/87: 723

21996. MCAD-25202: Chopin—Piano music. *Ogdon, piano.*
● ARG 11-12/88: 27

21997. MCAD-25203: Rodrigo—Concierto de Aranjuez. Arnold—Guitar concerto, op. 67. *Conn, Michael; Orch. of St. John's Smith Square; Lubbock, cond.*
● ARG 11-12/88: 75
+ Fa 9-10/88: 240

21998. MCAD-25207: Tchaikovsky—Nutcracker: Suite; Swan Lake: Suite; Sleeping beauty: Suite. *London Symphony Orch.; Williams, cond.*
● Fa 5-6/89: 335
+ Gr 7/88: 170

21999. MCAD-25208: Holst—Planets. *London Voices; London Symphony Orch.; Hickox, cond.*
● ARG 1-2/89: 58
- Fa 11-12/88: 202
+ Gr 5/88: 1595

22000. MCAD-25213: *Great Baroque arias.* Music of Handel, Bach, Purcell, Vivaldi, and Weldon. *Fisher, soprano; Bowman, countertenor; Ainsley, tenor; George, bass; King's Consort; King, cond.*
+ ARG 1-2/89: 119
+ Fa 11-12/88: 325
+ Gr 8/88: 326

22001. MCAD-25214: Brahms—Clarinet quintet. Dvořák—String quartet no. 12.

Puddy, clarinet; Delmé String Quartet.
+ ARG 1-2/89: 37

22002. MCAD-25216: TCHAIKOVSKY—
Piano concerto no. 1; String quartet no. 1:
Andante cantabile. *Lill, piano; London
Symphony Orch.; Judd, cond.*
- ARG 5-6/89: 95
• Fa 9-10/89: 339
• Gr 11/88: 789

22003. MCAD-25228: MOZART—Piano
concertos no. 21, 24. *Shelley, piano &
cond.; City of London Sinfonia.*
+ DA 3/89: 55
+ Fa 3-4/89: 220 (2 reviews)

22004. MCAD-25229: MOZART—Horn
concertos (complete); Rondo in E♭, K.
371. *Watkins, horn; City of London
Sinfonia; Hickox, cond.*
• Fa 3-4/89: 218

22005. MCAD-25230: BRAHMS—
Symphony no. 4; Hungarian dances no. 1,
3, 10. *Hallé Orch.; Skrowaczewski, cond.*
+ ARG 5-6/89: 32
+ Fa 5-6/89: 148
+ Gr 9/88: 408

22006. MCAD-25231: FAURÉ—Requiem;
Messe basse; Tantum ergo; Maria, mater
gratiae. *Escott, boy soprano; Wilson-
Johnson, baritone; Westminster
Cathedral Choir; City of London
Sinfonia; Hill, cond.*
+ ARG 9-10/89: 54
+ Fa 5-6/89: 193
+ Gr 10/88: 654

22007. MCAD-25232: BEETHOVEN—Piano
concertos no. 1-2. *Ortiz, piano; City of
London Sinfonia; Hickox, cond.*
+ ARG 5-6/89: 19
- Fa 5-6/89: 122

22008. MCAD-25234: SCHUMANN—
Papillons, op. 2; Kinderszenen, op. 15;
Carnaval, op. 9. *Ortiz, piano.*
- ARG 11-12/90: 112
• Fa 5-6/89: 315
+ Gr 10/88: 649

22009. MCAD-25235: *An evening of
lieder: Felicity Lott sings Schubert.*
SCHUBERT—Songs. *Lott, soprano;
Johnson, piano.*
+ ARG 5-6/89: 83
+ Fa 5-6/89: 306
+ Gr 10/88: 664
+ NYT 6/4/89: H24
+ SR 5/89: 123
+ St 3/89: 173

22010. MCAD-25237: BEETHOVEN—
Symphony no. 3; Coriolan overture.
London Symphony Orch.; Morris, cond.
• ARG 11-12/90: 37
- Fa 5-6/89: 130
+ Gr 12/88: 988
- NYT 1/8/89: H27

22011. MCAD-25855: BACH—
Harpsichord concertos no. 2-3, 7. *Bolton,
harpsichord & cond.; St. James's
Baroque Players.*
+ ARG 9-10/89: 18
- Fa 5-6/89: 104
+ Gr 1/89: 1138

22012. MCAD-25856: MUSSORGSKY—
Pictures at an exhibition (arr. Ravel).
RAVEL—Boléro. *London Symphony
Orch.; Williams, cond.*
• ARG 11-12/89: 84
+ Fa 7-8/89: 205
• Gr 4/89: 1587

22013. MCAD-25858: BEETHOVEN—
Symphony no. 6; Egmont: Overture.
London Symphony Orch.; Morris, cond.
- ARG 11-12/89: 37
• Fa 5-6/89: 132
- Gr 5/88: 1717

22014. MCAD-25867: SCHUBERT—Piano
quintet, D. 667; Hirt auf dem Felsen. *Lott,
soprano; Collins, clarinet; Brown, piano;
Nash Ensemble .*
+ ARG 3-4/90: 102
+ Fa 7-8/89: 238

22015. MCAD-25868: RACHMANINOFF—
Piano concerto no. 2; Rhapsody on a
theme of Paganini. *Golub, piano; London
Symphony Orch.; Morris, cond.*
+ ARG 11-12/89: 100
- Fa 9-10/89: 291
• Gr 6/89: 43

22016. MCAD-25869: ELGAR—Enigma
variations; Pomp and circumstance
marches (complete); Imperial march, op.
32; Coronation march, op. 65. *London
Symphony Orch.; Tuckwell, cond.*
+ ARG 7-8/89: 43
• Fa 7-8/89: 142
• Gr 4/89: 1578

22017. MCAD-25870: BEETHOVEN—Piano
concerto no. 5; Piano sonata no. 21.
*Ortiz, piano; City of London Sinfonia;
Hickox, cond.*
- ARG 7-8/89: 19
- Fa 9-10/89: 132

22018. MCAD-25874: *Great music from
great occasions at Westminster Abbey.*
Music of Vaughan Williams, S.S.
Wesley, Parry, Stanford, Widor, Alcock,
Walton, Grant & Ross, McKie, Hilton,
Bliss, and Anon. *Simcock, organ; London
Brass; Westminster Abbey Choir; Neary,
organ & cond.*
+ DA 1/90: 63
+ Fa 1-2/90: 372

22019. MCAD-25875: MOZART—Clarinet
quintet; Oboe quartet. *Puddy, clarinet;
Boyd, oboe; Gabrieli Quartet.*
• ARG 11-12/90: 85

22020. MCAD-25876: BEETHOVEN—
String quartet no. 10. SCHUBERT—String
quartet no. 13. *Brodsky Quartet.*

- ARG 3-4/90: 101
+ Fa 11-12/89: 131

22021. MCAD-25877: *Great opera
choruses.* Music of Bizet, Verdi, Gounod,
and Borodin . *London Symphony Chorus
& Orch.; Hickox, cond.*
+ ARG 1-2/90: 127
- Fa 11-12/89: 447

22022. MCAD-25878: BEETHOVEN—
Concerto for piano, violin, and cello, op.
56. BOCCHERINI—Cello concerto no. 3.
*Trio Zingara; English Chamber Orch;
Heath, cond.*
- ARG 3-4/90: 20
• Fa 1-2/90: 115
+ Gr 6/89: 24

22023. MCAD-25879: DEBUSSY—Mer;
Nocturnes for orchestra; Prelude à
l'après-midi d'un faune. *London
Symphony Orch.; Frühbeck de Burgos,
cond.*
- ARG 1-2/90 43 m.f.
+ Fa 1-2/90: 160
+ Gr 6/89: 33

22024. MCAD-25880: HAYDN—
Symphonies no. 92, 104. *English
Sinfonia; Groves, cond.*
+ ARG 3-4/90: 60
- Fa 1-2/90: 201 (no. 92)
+ Fa 1-2/90: 201 (no. 104)
+ Gr 6/89: 34

22025. MCAD-25881: BEETHOVEN—
Symphonies no. 7-8. *London Symphony
Orch.; Morris, cond.*
+ ARG 3-4/90: 26
- Fa 1-2/90: 122
+ Gr 2/90: 1455

22026. MCAD-25882: STRAVINSKY—
Firebird. DUKAS—Sorcerer's apprentice.
*National Youth Orch. of Great Britain;
Seaman, cond.*
• Fa 1-2/90: 318

22027. MCAD-25883: MOZART—
Symphonies no. 35, 41. *Orch. of St.
John's Smith Square; Gilmour, cond.*
+ DA 7/90: 60
• Fa 1-2/90: 247

22028. MCAD-25884: SIBELIUS—Swan of
Tuonela; Symphony no. 2. *London
Symphony Orch.; Mackerras, cond.*
+ ARG 5-6/90: 111
+ Fa 5-6/90: 298
+ Gr 1/90: 1338

22029. MCAD-25885: Music of Fauré,
Elgar, Delius, Ravel, Warlock,
Butterworth, and Satie. *English Sinfonia;
Groves, cond.*
• ARG 3-4/90: 50
□ Fa 5-6/90: 390
- Gr 1/90: 1340

22030. MCAD-25886: BEETHOVEN—
Symphony no. 9. *Hargan, Jones, Rendall,
Howell; London Symphony Chorus &*

MCA

Orch.; Morris, cond.
+ ARG 3-4/90: 26
- Fa 3-4/90: 142
• Gr 11/89: 882
+ NYT 4/8/90: H29

22031. MCAD-25887: Music of Rimsky-Korsakov, Albéniz, Falla, Ravel, and Granados. *London Symphony Orch.; Frühbeck de Burgos, cond.*
- ARG 5-6/90: 134
+ Fa 3-4/90: 395

22032. MCAD-25888: Beethoven— Symphonies no. 1-2. *London Symphony Orch.; Morris, cond.*
• ARG 7-8/90: 24
- Fa 7-8/90: 92
• Gr 2/90: 1455

22033. MCAD-25889: Dvořák— Serenade for strings in E major; Romance for violin in F major. Wagner—Siegfried Idyll. *Laredo, violin & cond.; Scottish Chamber Orch.*
- ARG 5-6/90: 48
• Fa 7-8/90: 133
+ Gr 4/90: 1777
• NYT 9/2/90: H22

22034. MCAD-25890: Liszt—Douze grandes études. *Weber, piano.*
+ ARG 7-8/90: 66
+ Fa 9-10/90: 275
• Gr 1/90: 1350

22035. MCAD-25891: *Music for two pianos.* Music of Milhaud, Benjamin, Bach, Dvořák, Arensky, Stravinsky, Khachaturian, Walton, and Brahms. *Ogdon, Lucas, pianos.*
+ ARG 7-8/90: 147
+ Fa 7-8/90: 353
- Gr 2/90: 1483

22036. MCAD-25892: Elgar—Falstaff; Introduction and allegro for strings. Bach—Fantasy and fugue in C minor (arr. Elgar). *National Youth Orch. of Great Britain; Seaman, cond.*
+ ARG 7-8/90: 46
+ Fa 7-8/90: 140
+ Gr 5/90: 1972

22037. MCAD-25894: Schubert— Schöne Müllerin. *Thompson, tenor; Vignoles, piano.*
- Fa 7-8/90: 252
+ Gr 11/89: 952

22038. MCAD-25895: Schubert— Symphonies no. 4, 6. *Orch. of St. John's Smith Square; Gilmour, cond.*
• ARG 9-10/90: 114
- Fa 9-10/90: 377
• Gr 5/90: 1985

22039. MCAD-25896: *A tapestry of English cathedral music.* Music of Aston, Byrd, Britten, Gibbons, Mundy, Howells, Harris, Tomkins, Andrews, and Gray. *Worcester Cathedral Choir; Hunt, cond.; Partington, organ.*

• ARG 11-12/90: 165
• Fa 9-10/90: 467
• Gr 9/90: 599

22040. MCAD-25898: Canteloube— Songs of the Auvergne: Selections. *Rozario, soprano; Philharmonia Orch.; Pritchard, cond.*
- ARG 1-2/91: 40
- Fa 1-2/91: 174
- Gr 10/90: 798

22041. MCAD-25899: Schubert—String quartets no. 9, 14. *New World String Quartet.*
• ARG 1-2/91: 87
+ Fa 11-12/90: 343
• Gr 1/91: 1385

22042. MCAD-25903: Mozart—Nozze di Figaro: Overture; Sinfonia concertante, K. 297b; Finta giardiniera: Overture; Symphony no. 25. *English Sinfonia; Groves, cond.*
+ ARG 7-8/91: 96
+ Fa 1-2/91: 254
- Gr 11/90: 985

22043. MCAD-25963: *Latin guitar: classic favorites performed by Marcelo Kayath.* Music of Ponce, Piazzolla, Barrios, Lauro, Brouwer, Pernambuco, Reys, and Villa-Lobos. *Kayath, guitar.*
+ Fa 9-10/87: 374
+ Gr 9/87: 454

22044. MCAD-25964: Orff— Carmina Burana. *Walmsley-Clark, Graham-Hall, Maxwell; Southend Boys' Choir; London Symphony Chorus & Orch.; Hickox, cond.*
+ Fa 9-10/87: 260
+ Gr 7/87: 212
- Opus 10/87: 58

22045. MCAD-25965: Mozart—Clarinet concerto; Concerto for flute and harp. *Campbell, clarinet; Davies, flute; Masters, harp; City of London Sinfonia; Hickox, cond.*
+ Fa 11-12/87: 177
+ Gr 8/87: 296
• NYT 11/8/87: H29

22046. MCAD-25966: *Great coloratura solos.* Music of Arne, Handel, Mozart, Benedict, Proch, Milhaud, Aliabev, and Glière. *Hoch, soprano; Hong Kong Phil.; Schermerhorn, cond.*
+ Fa 9-10/87: 354
+ Gr 11/87: 738
+ Ov 12/87: 36

22047. MCAD-25967: *The Vienna of Johann Strauss.* Music of J. Strauss, Jr., J. Strauss, Sr., and Josef Strauss. *London Symphony Orch.; Georgiadis, cond.*
• Fa 9-10/87: 311
• Gr 9/87: 490

22048. MCAD-25968: Wagner—Opera overtures and preludes. *London Symphony Orch.; Tuckwell, cond.*

• Fa 9-10/87: 345
+ Gr 9/87: 420

22049. MCAD-25969: *Impressions of France.* Music of Debussy, Chabrier, Satie, Fauré, Ibert, Poulenc, Milhaud, and Ravel. *Ortiz, piano.*
+ DA 6/88: 80
+ Fa 9-10/87: 369
+ Gr 6/87: 81

22050. MLD-32100: Tchaikovsky— Symphony no. 3; Francesca da Rimini. *USSR Symphony Orch.; Svetlanov, cond.*
- Fa 3-4/90: 318

22051. MCL-32102: Brahms—Piano concerto no. 1. *Douglas, piano; USSR Academic Symphony Orch.; Sinaisky, cond.*
- Fa 3-4/90: 153

22052. MLD-32103: Scriabin— Symphony no. 2. *USSR Radio and Television Large Symphony Orch.; Fedoseyev, cond.*
- Fa 3-4/90: 293

22053. MLD-32104: Kravchenko—Fair; Blue Hussars. S. Slonimsky—Quiet flows the Don. Shchedrin—Choruses to Voznesensky. Falik—Severyanin's poesie. *Glinka Choir; Chernushenko, cond.*
+ Fa 3-4/90: 355

22054. MLD-32105: Lyapunov—Solemn overture in C major; Zelazova Woda; Hashish. *USSR Academic Symphony Orch.; Svetlanov, cond.*
• Fa 3-4/90: 212

22055. MLD-32106: Shostakovich— Piano quintet, op. 57; String quartets no. 7, 14. *Nasedkin, piano; Shostakovich Quartet; Borodin Quartet.*
- Fa 3-4/90: 296

22056. MLD-32107: Scriabin—Piano sonatas no. 3-4; 5 preludes, op 74; Etude, op. 2, no. 1. Schumann—Nachtstücke. *Gilels, piano.*
+ ARG 7-8/90: 106
+ Fa 5-6/90: 292

22057. MLD-32108: Prokofiev— Symphonies no. 1, 7. *USSR State Symphony Orch.; Svetlanov, cond.; USSR Radio and Television Symphony Orch.; Rozhdestvensky, cond.*
- ARG 5-6/90: 126
+ Fa 5-6/90: 253

22058. MLD-32110: Mozart— Symphony no. 29. Rossini—Sonata for strings no. 3. Mendelssohn—String symphony no. 10. *Lithuanian Chamber Orch.; Sondeckis, cond.*
+ ARG 7-8/90: 126
+ Fa 5-6/90: 235

22059. MLD-32112: Tchaikovsky— Symphony no. 1. *USSR State Symphony*

Orch.; Svetlanov, cond.
- ● ARG 5-6/90: 120
- + Fa 5-6/90: 311

22060. MLD-32113: GUBAIDULINA AND DENISOV—March. DENISOV—Painting for orchestra. SCHNITTKE—Inspector's tale. *USSR Ministry of Culture Symphony Orch.; Rozhdestvensky, cond.*
- + ARG 11-12/90: 108
- + Fa 11-12/90: 339

22061. MLD-32114: SHOSTAKOVICH— Symphony no. 7. *USSR State Symphony Orch.; Svetlanov, cond.*
- + ARG 5-6/90: 108
- - Fa 7-8/90: 272

22062. MLD-32115: BRUCKNER— Symphony no. 4 (1874 version). *USSR Ministry of Culture Symphony Orch.; Rozhdestvensky, cond.*
- + ARG 7-8/90: 36
- + Fa 7-8/90: 113

22063. MLD2-32116 (2 discs): PROKOFIEV—Romeo and Juliet. *USSR State Symphony Orch.; Žiuraitis, cond.*
- - ARG 7-8/90: 86
- ● Fa 7-8/90: 228

22064. MLD-32118: SHAPORIN—How long shall the kite fly. *USSR State Chorus; Svetlanov, cond.*
- + ARG 7-8/90: 107
- + Fa 7-8/90: 267

22065. MLD2-32119 (2 discs): TCHAIKOVSKY—Swan Lake. *USSR Radio and Television Large Symphony Orch.; Rozhdestvensky, cond.*
- + ARG 1-2/91: 115
- ● Fa 11-12/90: 376

22066. MLD-32120: RIMSKY-KORSAKOV—Scheherazade. *Novosibirsk Phil. Symphony Orch.; Katz, cond.*
- + ARG 9-10/90: 104
- ● Fa 7-8/90: 237

22067. MLD-32122: MUSSORGSKY— Pictures at an exhibition. PROKOFIEV— Tales of the old grandmother. *Merzhanov, piano.*
- ● ARG 7-8/90: 72
- ● Fa 7-8/90: 215

22068. MLD-32124: *Vladimir Spivakov and friends.* Music of Ravel, Messiaen, Shostakovich, Bartók, Bloch, Gershwin, Schubert, and Prokofiev. *Spivakov, violin; Bechterev, piano; Kopelman, violin; Shebalin, Bashmet, violas; Berlinsky, cello; Mikhailov, clarinet.*
- ● Fa 9-10/90: 482

22069. MLD-32126: RACHMANINOFF— Piano concerto no. 2; Rhapsody on a theme of Paganini. *Eresko, piano; USSR State Symphony Orch.; Lazarev, cond.; Dorensky, piano; USSR Ministry of Culture Symphony Orch.; Dmitriev, cond.*
- + ARG 7-8/90: 88

- - Fa 11-12/90: 324 (Concerto)
- + Fa 11-12/90: 324 (Rhapsody)

22070. MLD-32127: *Soviet songs and choruses.* Music of Lyatoshyn'sky, Glinka, Tchaikovsky, Shebalin, Koval, Sviridov, and Rachmaninoff. *Lyatoshinsky Chamber Choir of Kiev; Ikonnik, cond.; USSR Radio and Television Large Chorus; Ptitsa, cond.*
- + ARG 11-12/90: 168
- + Fa 9-10/90: 467

22071. MLD-32128: SHOSTAKOVICH— Symphony no. 5. *USSR Ministry of Culture Symphony Orch.; Rozhdestvensky, cond.*
- + ARG 11-12/90: 356

22072. MLD-32129: Piano music of Schumann, Chopin, and Liszt. *Kissin, piano.*
- ● ARG 11-12/90: 158
- + Fa 11-12/90: 432

22073. MCAD-32130: MENDELSSOHN— Symphony no. 4. ROSSINI—William Tell: Overture. *USSR State Symphony Orch.; Svetlanov, cond.*
- + Fa 1-2/91: 241

22074. MCAD-32131: *To Leonid Kogan's memory.* Music of Gagnidze, Ekimovsky, and Ryabov. *Igolinsky, Kravchenko, Zhuk, violins; Sergeeva, piano & harpsichord.*
- + ARG 1-2/91: 140
- + Fa 1-2/91: 388

22075. MCAD-42067: *The legendary Andres Segovia.* RODRIGO—Fantasia para un gentilhombre. PONCE—Concierto del sur. MORENO TORROBA—Castles of Spain. *Segovia, guitar; Symphony of the Air; Jorda, cond.*
- + Fa 1-2/88: 81

22076. MCAD-42068: BACH—Guitar music. *Segovia, guitar.*
- ● Fa 1-2/88: 80
- + HF 2/88: 60

22077. MCAD-42069: *My favorite works.* Music of Albéniz, Torroba, Sor, Tarrega, Turina, and Castelnuovo-Tedesco. *Segovia, guitar.*
- + ARG 11-12/89: 152
- + DA 6/88: 70
- + Fa 7-8/88: 314
- + HF 2/89: 50

22078. MCAD-42071: *The Segovia collection, vol. 5.* Music of Milan, Narváez, Sanz, Sor, Torroba, Granodos, Esplá, Cassadó, Mompou, and Esteban. *Segovia, guitar.*
- + ARG 11-12/89: 52
- + Fa 9-10/89: 419

22079. MCAD-42072: PONCE—Sonata romantica; Sonata classica; Sonata mexicana; Cancion; Cancion y paisage.

Segovia, guitar.
- + ARG 3-4/90: 258

22080. MCAD-42073: *Guitar etudes.* Music of Novado, Sor, Segovia, Giuliani, Coste, and Tarrega. *Segovia, guitar.*
- + ARG 9-10/90: 142
- + Fa 11-12/90: 445

22081. MCAD-42211: *The Decca masters, vol. 1.* Music of Tchaikovsky, Chopin, Schumann, Krein, Prokofiev, Debussy, Valle, Grasse, Saint-Saëns, Aguirre, Burleigh, Godowsky, Dvořák, Ravel, Shostakovich, Gluck, Rimsky-Korsakov, and Castelnuovo-Tedesco. *Heifetz, violin; Bay, Kaye, pianos.*
- + ARG 3-4/89: 118
- + Fa 1-2/89: 334
- + St 6/89: 226

22082. MCAD-42212: *The Decca masters, vol. 2.* Music of Gershwin, Foster, Gardner, Bennett, Herbert, Benjamin, Dyer, White, Weill, Berlin, Godard, Lohr, and Anon. *Heifetz, violin; Bay, Kaye, pianos.*
- + ARG 3-4/89: 118
- + Fa 1-2/89: 335
- + St 6/89: 226

22083. MCAD-42318: ELLINGTON—New world a'coming; Harlem; Golden broom and the green apple. *Ellington, piano; Cincinnati Symphony Orch.; Kunzel, cond.*
- + Fa 3-4/90: 179

22084. MCAD-42337: MAHLER— Symphony no. 4. *Seefried, soprano; Vienna Phil. Orch.; Walter, cond.* Recorded live 1950.
- + Fa 11-12/90: 263

22085. MCAD-5843: VIVALDI—Four seasons. *Laredo, violin & cond.; Scottish Chamber Orch.* Issued also as LP: MCA 5844.
- + Fa 3-4/87: 234
- ● SR 11/87: 202

22086. MCAD-5845: MOZART— Symphony no. 40. SCHUBERT—Symphony no. 5. *Orch. of St. John's Smith Square; Lubbock, cond.* Issued also as LP: MCA 5846.
- ● Fa 3-4/87: 133
- ● HF 11-87: 78
- + Ov 6/87: 41

22087. MCAD-5846: HAYDN— Symphonies no. 44, 49. *Orch. of St. John's Smith Square; Lubbock, cond.* Issued also as LP; MCA 5846.
- ● Fa 3-4/87: 133
- ● HF 11/87: 78
- ● Ov 11/87: 41

22088. MCAD-5847: *Renaissance masterpieces.* ALLEGRI—Miserere. TALLIS—Spem in alium; Lamentations of Jeremiah the Prophet. *Pro Cantione Antiqua; Brown, cond.* Issued also as LP:

MCA

MCA 5848.
 • Fa 3-4/87: 262

22089. MCAD-5849: Mendelssohn—
Symphony no. 4; Hebrides overture; Son
and stranger: Overture; Fair Melusina:
Overture. *Bern Symphony Orch.; Maag,
cond.* Issued also as LP: MCA 5848.
 • Fa 3-4/87: 160

22090. MCAD-5850: *Masterpieces for
organ.* Music of Bach, Franck,
Meyerbeer, Guilmant, Saint-Saëns,
Brahms, Liszt, and Vierne. *Hill, organ.*
 + Fa 3-4/87: 265

22091. MCAD-5851: Tchaikovsky—1812
overture; Marche slave; Romeo and
Juliet. *London Symphony Orch.;
Ahronovitch, cond.* Issued also as LP:
MCA 5851.
 • Fa 5-6/87: 204

22092. MCAD-5852: Handel—Messiah:
excerpts. *Loft, Finnie, Winslade, Herford;
Scottish Phil. Singers; Scottish Chamber
Orch.; Malcolm, cond.* Issued also as LP:
MCA 5852.
 • Fa 3-4/87: 126

22093. MCAD-5853: *Russian
spectacular.* Music of Khachaturian,
Prokofiev, Shostakovich, Borodin,
Glinka, and Mussorgsky. *London
Symphony Orch.; Ahronovitch, cond.*
 - Fa 3-4/87: 277
 + Ov 10/87: 42

22094. MCAD-5854: Vivaldi—
Concertos for 2, 3, and 4 violins. *Laredo,
violin & cond.; Scottish Chamber Orch.*
 + Fa 3-4/87: 233

22095. MCAD-5933: Saint-Saëns—
Symphony no. 3. *Bern Symphony Orch.;
Maag, cond.*
 + Fa 7-8/87: 175
 + Gr 4/87: 1415

22096. MCAD-5934: Bruch—Violin
concerto no. 1. Mendelssohn—Violin
concerto in E minor. *Laredo, violin &
cond.; Scottish Chamber Orch.*
 • Fa 7-8/87: 79
 + Gr 1/87: 1010

22097. MCAD-5954: Schubert—
Symphonies no. 3, 8. *City of London
Sinfonia; Hickox, cond.*
 + Fa 7-8/87: 180
 + Gr 4/87: 1416

22098. MCAD-5955: Music of Bizet,
Fauré, Debussy, and Ravel. *London
Brass.*
 + Fa 7-8/87: 238

22099. MCAD-5956: Bach—
Brandenburg concertos no. 1-3. *English
Chamber Orch.; Ledger, cond.*
 + Fa 7-8/87: 50
 + Gr 1/87: 1009

22100. MCAD-5957: Bach—
Brandenburg concertos no. 4-6. *English
Chamber Orch.; Ledger, cond.*
 + Fa 7-8/87: 50
 + Gr 5/87: 30

22101. MCAD-6186: Handel—Water
music: Suite; Music for the royal
fireworks; Amaryllis suite (arr.
Beecham). *Royal Phil. Orch.; Menuhin,
cond.* Issued also as LP: 6186.
 • Fa 3-4/87: 127
 + Gr 6/86: 52
 + NYT 6/28/87: H21
 + SR 10/87: 136

22102. MCAD-6187: Walton—
Belshazzar's feast; Henry V: Suite.
*Luxon, baritone; Brighton Festival
Chorus; Royal Phil. Orch.; Previn, cond.*
Issued also as LP: MCA 6187.
 + DA 5/87: 61
 + Fa 3-4/87: 244
 + Gr 6/86: 85
 + HF 5/87: 61
 + NYT 6/28/87: H21
 • NYT 8/30/87: H21
 + Opus 6/87: 54
 + Ov 9/87: 42
 + SR 3/87: 105

22103. MCAD-6199: Fauré—Requiem.
Bernstein—Chichester psalms. *Jones,
Roberts, vocalists; Birch, organ; London
Symphony Orch.; Hickox, cond.*
 + Fa 9-10/87: 199
 + Gr 1/87: 1051
 + Opus 8/87: 38
 + SR 11/87: 184

22104. MCAD-6202: Tippett—A child of
our time. *Armstrong, Palmer, Langridge,
Shirley-Quirk; Brighton Festival Chorus;
Royal Phil. Orch.; Previn, cond.* Issued
also as LP: MCA 6202.
 + Fa 7-8/87: 197
 • Gr 1/87: 1055
 + NYT 6/28/87: H21
 • Opus 8/87: 53
 + SR 7/87: 97

22105. MCAD-6204: Prokofiev—Piano
concerto no. 3. Liszt—Piano concerto no.
2. *Vakeralis, piano; Royal Phil. Orch.;
Rowicki, cond.*
 + Au 1/88: 156
 + Fa 11-12/87: 198
 + Gr 1/87: 1014
 + SR 10/87: 127

22106. MCAD-6215: Sullivan—Mikado:
Excerpts. *Bottone, Idle, van Allan,
Angas; English National Opera Chorus
& Orch.; Robinson, cond.*
 + Fa 11-12/87: 142
 • Gr 3/87: 1334

22107. MCAD-6218: Menotti—Amahl
and the night visitors. *Rainbird,
Haywood, Watson, Maxwell, Dobson;
Royal Opera House Covent Garden;
Syrus, cond.*
 + ARG 11-12/88: 60

 + Fa 3-4/88: 145
 + Gr 7/88: 197
 + Op 4/88: 507

22108. MCAD-6226: Gershwin—Cuban
overture; Rhapsody in blue; The man I
love; Love walked in; Porgy and Bess
fantasy (arr. Grainger); Embraceable you.
R. Contiguglia, J. Contiguglia, pianos.
 + Fa 7-8/88: 171

22109. MCAD-6229: Gershwin—
Concerto in F; An American in Paris.
*Vakarelis, piano; Royal Phil. Orch.;
Lewis, cond.*
 • Fa 7-8/88: 167
 + Gr 2/88: 1182

22110. MCAD-6231: Handel—Orchestra
music. *Royal Phil. Orch.; Menuhin, cond.*
 + ARG 5-6/89: 53
 • DA 1/89: 39
 + Fa 11-12/88: 198
 • Gr 7/88: 163
 + SR 12/88: 149

22111. MCAD-6260: *Johana Harris, a
living legacy.* Debussy—Piano music.
Harris, piano.
 • ARG 7-8/89: 121
 + Fa 3-4/89: 84

22112. MCAD-6261: *Johana Harris, a
living legacy.* Bach—Piano music.
Harris, piano.
 • ARG 7-8/89: 121
 + Fa 3-4/89: 84

22113. MCAD-6264: *Bach on Sax.*
Bach—Music arranged for saxophone
quartet. *Amherst Saxophone Quartet.*
 + ARG 9-10/89: 22
 + Fa 7-8/89: 78

22114. MCAD-6265: Falla—Piano
music. Albéniz—Piano music. *Laredo,
piano.*
 + ARG 7-8/89: 43
 + Fa 5-6/89: 193
 + MA 9/89: 60
 • SR 7/89: 88

22115. MCAD-6269: Beethoven—
Symphony no. 10 in E♭ (completed by
Cooper). *London Symphony Orch.;
Morris, cond.* Lecture on the completion
included on disc.
 □ ARG 3-4/89: 23
 □ Fa 3-4/89: 106 (2 reviews)
 □ Gr 1/89: 1142
 □ NYT 1/8/89: H27
 □ St 5/89: 158

22116. MCAD-6272: Rachmaninoff—
Symphony no. 2. *London Symphony
Orch.; Rozhdestvensky, cond.*
 + ARG 11-12/89: 102
 - Fa 7-8/89: 217
 + Gr 1/89: 1158
 + SR 6/89: 93

22117. MCAD-6277: Tchaikovsky—
Symphony no. 5; Marche slave. *Royal*

Phil. Orch.; Koizumi, cond.
- ARG 7-8/89: 98
- Fa 7-8/89: 265
- Gr 2/89: 1298

22118. MCAD-6278: BIZET—Carmen: Suite; L'Arlésienne: Suites 1-2. *London Symphony Orch.; Frühbeck de Burgos, cond.*
- ARG 1-2/90: 32
- Fa 7-8/89: 104
+ Gr 1/89: 1145

22119. MCAD-6295: *Tortelier, a celebration.* ELGAR—Cello concerto. TCHAIKOVSKY—Variations on a Rococo theme. DVOŘÁK—Rondo in G minor. *Tortelier, cello; Royal Phil. Orch.; Groves, cond.*
- Fa 11-12/89: 201
+ SR 11/89: 155

22120. MCAD-6325: OFFENBACH—Orphée aux enfers: Excerpts. *Soloists; English National Opera; Elder, cond.* Sung in English.
+ ARG 1-2/90: 89
+ Fa 1-2/90: 255

22121. MCAD-6402: *O baroque: music for three oboes and strings.* Music of Handel, Telemann, and Albinoni. *Lucarelli, Robinson, Klein; oboes; Sefcovic, bassoon; Gould, trumpet; New Brandenburg Collegium; Newman, cond.*
+ ARG 3-4/91: 154
+ Fa 11-12/90: 468

22122. MCAD-6414: ELGAR—Serenade for strings. BRITTEN—Variations on a theme of Frank Bridge. VAUGHAN WILLIAMS—Fantasia on a theme by Thomas Tallis. TIPPETT—Fantasia concertante on a theme of Corelli. *Royal Phil. Orch.; Groves, cond.*
+ Fa 9-10/90: 504
+ Gr 3/90: 1627

22123. MCAD-6466: MUSSORGSKY—Khovanshchina: Prelude. BEETHOVEN—Piano concerto no. 3. RAVEL—Daphnis et Chloé: Suite no. 2. TCHAIKOVSKY—Nutcracker: Waltz of the flowers. *Royal Phil. Orch.; Ashkenazy, piano & cond.*
- ARG 11-12/90: 138
- Fa 11-12/90: 477
- Gr 5/90: 1994
- SR 2/91: 137

22124. MCAD-9803 (2 discs): BEETHOVEN—Diabelli variations; Piano sonatas no. 8, 14, 23. *Barenboim, piano.*
+ ARG 1-2/89: 20

22125. MCAD2-9804 (2 discs): BACH—St. John passion. *Curtin, Alberts, Kmentt, Van Kesteren, Wiener, Guthrie; Vienna Academy Chorus; Vienna State Opera Orch.; Scherchen, cond.*
+ ARG 11-12/88: 10

22126. MCAD-9805 (2 discs): BERLIOZ—Roméo et Juliette.

TCHAIKOVSKY—Romeo and Juliet. *Resnik, Turp, Ward; London Symphony Chorus & Orch.; Monteux, cond.; Vienna State Opera Orch.; Scherchen, cond.*
+ ARG 1-2/89: 33

22127. MCAD-9806 (2 discs): BEETHOVEN—Symphonies no. 5, 9. *Söderström, Resnik, Vickers, Ward; London Bach Choir; London Symphony Orch.; Monteux, cond. Phil. Symphony Orch. of London; Rodzinski, cond.*
+ ARG 1-2/89: 28

22128. MCAD2-9809 (2 discs): BEETHOVEN—Fidelio. *Jurinac, Stader, Peerce, Neidlinger, Ernster; with assisting sololists; Bavarian Opera Chorus & Orch.; Knappertsbusch, cond.*
- ARG 1-2/89: 18
- Fa 11-12/88: 134

22129. MCAD2-9810 (2 discs): BEETHOVEN—Symphonies no. 2, 4, 7; Leonore overture no. 3. *Pittsburgh Symphony Orch.; Steinberg, cond.*
+ ARG 1-2/89: 27
- Fa 11-12/88: 237
- MA 3/89: 54

22130. MCAD2-9812 (2 discs): MOZART—Symphonies no. 16-26. *Phil. Symphony Orch. of London; Leinsdorf, cond.*
+ ARG 1-2/89: 72
- Fa 11-12/88: 237

22131. MCAD2-9813 (2 discs): HOLST—Planets. VAUGHAN-WILLIAMS—Fantasia on Greensleeves; English folk song suite; Fantasia on a theme by Thomas Tallis. ELGAR—Introduction and allegro. BRITTEN—Prelude and fugue, op. 29. *Vienna Academy Chorus; Vienna State Opera Orch.; Boult, cond.; Lausanne Chamber Orch.; Desarzens, cond.*
- ARG 1-2/89: 58
- Fa 11-12/88: 202 m.f.

22132. MCAD2-9814 (2 discs): MOZART—Symphonies no. 27-35. *Phil. Symphony Orch. of London; Leinsdorf, cond.*
- ARG 1-2/89: 72
- Fa 3-4/89: 226

22133. MCAD2-9816 (2 discs): MOZART—Requiem; Regina coeli, K. 118; Ave verum corpus, K. 618; Te Deum, K. 141; Sancta Maria, K. 273. HAYDN—Seven last words of Christ. *Jurinac, West, Loeffler, Guthrie; with assisting soloists; Vienna Academy Chorus; Vienna State Opera Orch.; Scherchen, cond.; Leibowitz, cond.*
+ ARG 5-6/89: 71
- Fa 3-4/89: 225 (Mozart)
+ Fa 3-4/89: 225 (Haydn)

22134. MCAD2-9817 (2 discs): BRAHMS—Symphonies (complete). *Pittsburgh Symphony Orch.; Steinberg, cond.*

+ ARG 3-4/89: 27
+ Fa 3-4/89: 124

22135. MCAD2-9820 (2 discs): STRAVINSKY—L'histoire du soldat. PROKOFIEV—Peter and the wolf (in English and in Spanish). *Douglas, Mitchell, Espstein; Kapp Sinfonietta; Vardi, cond.; Ferrer, speaker; Vienna State Opera Orch.; Goossens, cond.*
- ARG 7-8/89: 95
+ Fa 5-6/89: 330 (Stravinsky)
- Fa 5-6/89: 330 (Prokofiev)

22136. MCAD2-9821 (2 discs): BACH—Mass in B minor. *Alarie, Merriman, Simoneau, Neidlinger; Vienna Academy Chorus; Vienna State Opera Orch.; Scherchen, cond.*
+ Fa 9-10/89: 121

22137. MCAD2-9823 (2 discs): SHOSTAKOVICH—Symphonies no. 1, 5; Piano concertos no. 1-2; Age of gold; Ballet suite. *National Symphony Orch. (Washington, DC); Mitchell, cond.; London Symphony Orch.; Rodzinski, cond.; List, piano; Berlin Opera Orch.; Jochum, cond.; Vienna State Opera Orch.; Desarzens, cond.*
+ ARG 1-2/90: 89
- Fa 11-12/89: 359

22138. MCAD2-9824 (2 discs): GRANADOS—Goyescas, pt. 1; Pelele; Escenas romanticas; Spanish dances. ESPLÁ—Sonata española. RODRIGO—Danzas de España. *Larrocha, piano.*
+ ARG 3-4/90: 54
+ Fa 1-2/90: 189

22139. MCAD2-9825 (2 discs): BRUCKNER—Symphonies no. 7-8. *Pittsburgh Symphony Orch.; Steinberg, cond.; Munich Phil. Orch.; Knappertsbusch, cond.*
+ Fa 1-2/90: 147

22140. MCAD2-9826 (2 discs): DAWSON—Negro folk symphony. BRAHMS—Serenade no. 1, op. 11. *American Symphony Orch.; Symphony of the Air; Stokowski, cond.*
+ ARG 1-2/90: 42
+ Fa 1-2/90: 159

22141. MCAD2-9827 (2 discs) *Bach live at Fillmore East.* Organ music of Bach and Middleschulte. *Fox, organ.*
- Fa 3-4/90: 116

22142. MCAD2-9828 (2 discs): BEETHOVEN—Violin sonatas no. 3, 4, 7-8. BRAHMS—Violin sonata no. 2. MOZART—Violin sonata, K. 481. *Morini, violin; Firkusný, piano.*
+ ARG 5-6/90: 140
+ Fa 5-6/90: 113

22143. MCAD2-9829 (2 discs): TCHAIKOVSKY—Violin concerto; Symphony no. 4; Piano concerto no. 2; Romeo and Juliet; 1812 overture. *Morini,*

MCA

violin; Phil. Symphony Orch. of London; Rodzinski, cond.; Lateiner, piano; Vienna State Opera Orch.; Aliberti, cond.; Vienna State Opera Orch.; Scherchen, cond.
- ARG 9-10/90: 119
+ Fa 11-12/90: 373

22144. MCAD2-9830 (2 discs): *Fret works*. Music of Sor, Moreno Torroba, Turina, Falla, Dowland, and Villa- Lobos. *Bream, guitar & lute*.
+ ARG 9-10/91: 161
+ Fa 11-12/90: 443

22145. MCAD2-9831 (2 discs): BACH—Brandenburg concertos (complete). *Vienna State Opera Orch.; Scherchen, cond.*
- Fa 3-4/91: 175

22146. MCAD2-9833 (2 discs): MAHLER—Symphonies no.1-2. *Philharmonia Orch.; Vienna State Opera Orch.; Scherchen, cond.* Reissues.
+ Fa 11-12/91: 379

22147. MCAD2-9834 (2 discs): *Puccini without words*. Excerpts from: Madama Butterfly, La Bohème, Tosca. *Rome Symphony Orch.; Savino, cond.*
- Fa 11-12/91: 447

22148. MCAD2-9840: BACH—Six partitas, BWV 825-830. *Badura-Skoda, piano*.
+ Fa 9-10/92: 168

MCGILL UNIVERSITY

22149. 85024 (LP): HAMBRAEUS—Livre d'orgue, vol. 3. *Grew, organ*.
+ Fa 7-8/87: 118

22150. 85027 (LP): LANZA—Interferences III. STEVEN—Images, refractions of time and space. LLOYD—Breath baby. SCHRYER—Kindred spirit. *Group of the Electronic Music Studio; Lanza, Schryer, cond.*
+ Fa 7-8/87: 239

MD + G

22151. 301 0494-2: MOZART—Chamber music for winds, vol. 1. *Consortium Classicum*.
+ ARG 5-6/95: 145
- Fa 5-6/95: 269

22152. 301 0495-2: MOZART—Divertimento in E♭ major; Theme and variations on Unser dummer Pobel meint; Octet in B♭. *Consortium Classicum*.
+ ARG 5-6/96: 154
- Fa 1-2/96: 261

22153. 301 0496-2: MOZART—Octet; Sextet, K. 439b, no. 3; Partita. *Consortium Classicum*.
- Fa 11-12/96: 315

22154. 301 0501-2: REICHA—Quintet for flute and strings, op. 105; Quintet for oboe and strings, op. 107. *Consortium Classicum*.
+ Fa 11-12/95: 316

22155. 301 0502-2: REICHA—Quintet for clarinet and strings; Quintet for bassoon and strings. *Consortium Classicum*.
+ ARG 3-4/96: 171
+ Fa 11-12/95: 317

22156. 301 0518-2: CZERNY—Nonet; Grand sérénade concertante, op. 126. *Consortium Classicum*.
+ Fa 9-10/95: 182

22157. 301 0527-2: CARTELLIERI—Clarinet concertos no. 1, 3; Clarinet concerto no. 2: Adagio pastorale. *Klöcker, clarinet; Prague Chamber Orch.*
+ ARG 11-12/96: 109
+ Fa 9-10/96: 174

22158. 301 0594-2: BEETHOVEN—Septet, op. 20; Sextet, op. 81b. *Consortium Classicum*.
- ARG 5-6/96: 81
+ Fa 1-2/96: 142

22159. 301 0595-2: BRAHMS—Horn trio, op. 40; Clarinet trio, op. 114. *Weigle, horn; Klöcker, clarinet; Streicher, violin; Henkel, cello; Tanski, piano*.
- ARG 5-6/96: 93
- Fa 5-6/96: 115

22160. 303 0532-2: P. SCHARWENKA—Piano trios op. 110, 112; Cello sonata. *Trio Parnassus*.
+ ARG 3-4/96: 175
- Fa 9-10/95: 304

22161. 303 0655-2: *Complete piano trios, vol. 1*. BRAHMS—Trio no. 1; Sextet no. 1 (arr. Kirchner). *Trio Parnassus*.
+ Fa 7-8/96: 122

22162. 303 0656-2: BRAHMS—Piano trio no. 2; Sextet, op. 18 (arr. for violin, cello, and piano). *Trio Parnassus*.
+ Fa 5-6/97: 92
- Fa 11-12/96: 208

22163. 303 0657-2: BRAHMS—Piano trios no. 1, 3. *Trio Parnassus*.
+ Fa 1-2/97: 122

22164. 304 0478-2: REINECKE—Wind sextet; Piano quintet; Wind octet. *Ensemble Villa Musica*.
+ ARG 5-6/96: 177
+ Fa 9-10/95: 293

22165. 304 0534-2: SPOHR—Piano quintet no. 2; Septet, op. 147. *Ensemble Villa Musica*.
+ Fa 1-2/95: 273

22166. 304 0535-2: HINDEMITH—Vocal chamber music. *Oelze, soprano; Kallisch, mezzo-soprano; Ensemble Villa Musica*.
+ ARG 7-8/96: 130

22167. 304 0536-2: FAURÉ—Piano quartets no. 1-2. *Ensemble Villa Musica*.
+ ARG 3-4/96: 113
+ Fa 7-8/95: 182

22168. 304 0537-2: HINDEMITH—Trio for viola, heckelphone, and piano, op. 47; Quartet for clarinet, violin, cello, and piano; Sonata for four horns. *Ensemble Villa Musica*.
+ ARG 3-4/96: 128
+ Fa 11-12/95: 277
+ Fa 1-2/96: 227

22169. 304 0545-2: HINDEMITH—Vocal chamber music. *Oelze, soprano; Kallisch, mezzo-soprano; Ensemble Villa Musica*.
+ Fa 7-8/95: 206

22170. 304 0617-2: SCHULHOFF—Chamber music. *Various performers*.
+ ARG 9-10/96: 196
+ Fa 5-6/96: 266

22171. 304 0618-2: KLEIN—Chamber music. *Ensemble Villa Musica*.
+ ARG 7-8/96: 142
+ Fa 5-6/96: 186

22172. 304 0666-2: BARTÓK—Violin sonatas no. 1-2. *Ensemble Villa Musica*.
+ Fa 9-10/96: 142

22173. 304 0695-2: HINDEMITH—Flute sonata; Oboe sonata; Clarinet sonata; English horn sonata. *Ensemble Villa Musica*.
+ ARG 3-4/97: 155
+ Fa 1-2/97: 178

22174. 307 0550-2: BEETHOVEN—String quartet no. 14. SCHUBERT—String quartet no. 12. *New Leipzig String Quartet*.
- Fa 1-2/95: 111
+ Fa 3-4/95: 127

22175. 307 0589-2: WEBERN—Complete works for string quartet. *New Leipzig String Quartet; Zichner, cond.*
- ARG 7-8/96: 224
- Fa 11-12/95: 427

22176. 307 0601-2: SCHUBERT—Complete string quartets, vol. 1. *New Leipzig Quartet*.
+ Fa 1-2/96: 139

22177. 307 0602-2: *Complete string quartets, vol. 2*. SCHUBERT—String quartet no. 13; D. 18; Overture, D. 470 (fragment). *New Leipzig String Quartet*.
+ ARG 9-10/96: 193
+ Fa 7-8/96: 289

22178. 307 0603-2: *Complete string quartets, vol. 3*. SCHUBERT—Quintet, op. post. 163; Overture, D. 8a; Quartet fragment, D. 3. *New Leipzig String Quartet; Sanderling, cello*.
+ Fa 7-8/96: 289

22179. 307 0604-2: SCHUBERT—String quartet no. 14 "Death and the maiden";

Menuett, D. 86; Menuette und Deutsche, D. 89. *Leipziger Streichquartett; Ockert, double bass.*
+ Fa 11-12/96: 364

22180. 308 0067-2: BERTINI—Sextet. HUMMEL—Piano quintet. *Sestetto Classico.* Recorded 1982.
+ ARG 11-12/96: 94

22181. 308 0506-2: BERGER—Piano quintet. *Michaels, piano; Verdi Quartet.*
+ ARG 3-4/95: 73

22182. 308 0506-2: PETERSON-BERGER—Piano quintet, op. 95. *Michaels, piano; Verdi Quartet.*
+ Fa 1-2/95: 119

22183. 309 0503-2: *Concert au gout italien: Chamber music, Paris 1740.* Music of Naudot, Corrette, Leclair, Boismortier, and Mondonville. *Musica Alta Ripa.*
+ Fa 1-2/95: 370

22184. 309 0508-2: RICHTER—Flute concerto in G major; Sonata, op. 4, no. 6; Oboe concerto in F major; Sinfonia in G major; Trio for flute, cello, and harpsichord obbligato. *Musica Alta Ripa.*
+ ARG 5-6/96: 178
+ Fa 1-2/96: 285

22185. 309 0632-2: A. SCARLATTI—Cantatas; Sonatas. D. SCARLATTI—Dopo lungo servire. F. SCARLATTI—Come in un'istante. *Wessel, alto; Musica Alta Ripa.*
• ARG 1-2/97: 163
- Fa 7-8/96: 282

22186. 309 0681-2: BACH—Solo concertos, vol. 1. *Hollmann, Innig, Lohr, Rémy, harpsichords; Musica Alta Ripa.*
+ Fa 11-12/96: 168

22187. 310 0220-2: GRABBE—First book of madrigals. *Consort of Musicke; Rooley, cond.* Reissue.
+ ARG 1-2/97: 115
• Fa 9-10/96: 205

22188. 310 0230-2: SCHÜTZ—Lamenti and concerti. *Musicalische Compagney.* Reissue.
+ ARG 11-12/96: 208
+ Fa 7-8/96: 300

22189. 311 0472—311 0474-2 (3 separate discs): TELEMANN—Tafelmusik. *Camerata of the 18th Century; Hünteler, cond.*
- ARG 11-12/93: 209 (v.1)
+ Fa 7-8/93: 257 (v.1)
+ ARG 1-2/97: 184

22190. 311 0520-2: GRAF—Six quartets for flute, violin, viola, and cello. *Hünteler, flute; Members of the Festetics Quartet.*
+ Fa 7-8/95: 196

22191. 311 0613-2: J.C. BACH—Six quintets for flute, oboe, violin, viola, and bass, op. 11. *Camerata of the 18th Century.*
+ ARG 9-10/96: 80
+ Fa 5-6/96: 68

22192. 311 0630-2: REICHA—Quartets for flute and strings, op. 98. *Hünteler, flute; Kussmaul, violin; Kussmaul, viola; Dieltiens, cello.*
+ ARG 1-2/97: 158
+ Fa 11-12/96: 345

22193. 311 0640-2: VIVALDI—Flute concertos, op. 10. *Hünteler, flute; Camerata of the 18th Century.*
+ Fa 11-12/96: 411

22194. 312 0344-2: REUBKE—Organ sonata; Piano sonata. *Sander, organ; Tanski, piano.*
+ ARG 5-6/96: 178

22195. 312 0483-2: SMETANA—Piano music, vol. 1. *Tanski, piano.*
• ARG 1-2/97: 172
+ Fa 11-12/96: 383

22196. 313 0389-2: SCHUMANN—Davidsbündlertänze. KIRCHNER—Neue Davidsbündlertänze. *Maruko, piano.*
+ ARG 5-6/95: 172
+ Fa 1-2/95: 267

22197. 315 0484-2: BACH (ARR. REGER)—Complete organ arrangements. *Haas, organ.*
+ Fa 1-2/95: 100

22198. 316 0403-2: WIDOR—Organ symphonies no. 5-6. *Oosten, organ.*
+ ARG 7-8/96: 225
+ Fa 5-6/96: 319

22199. 316 0405-2: WIDOR—Symphony no. 8. *Oosten, organ.*
+ ARG 1-2/97: 190
+ Fa 11-12/96: 420

22200. 317 0009-2: MESSIAEN—La nativité du Seigneur. *Innig, organ.* Reissue.
- ARG 11-12/96: 162
+ Fa 9-10/96: 261

22201. 317 0346-2: MESSIAEN—Apparition de l'église éternelle; Diptyque; Le banquet céleste; L'ascension. *Innig, organ.* Reissue.
- ARG 11-12/96: 162
+ Fa 9-10/96: 261

22202. 317 0619-2: SCHUMANN—Etudes in canonic form; Sketches for pedal piano; Fugues on the name of Bach. *Innig, organ.*
+ Fa 7-8/96: 295

22203. 317 0621-2: MESSIAEN—Les corps glorieux; Verset pour la fête de la dédicace. *Innig, organ.* Reissue.
- ARG 9-10/96: 198

- ARG 11-12/96: 162
+ Fa 9-10/96: 261

22204. 319 0538-2: *Organ landscape Jerusalem.* Music of Noordt, Ben-Haim, Blarr, Titelouze, Salomon, Weinberger, Dupré, Tal, Alexander, Mendelssohn, and Reger. *Roloff, organ.*
+ Fa 9-10/95: 396

22205. 319 0552-2: *Orgellandschaft Thüringen.* Music of Pachelbel, J.M. Bach, H. Bach, J.S. Bach, J.C. Bach, J.B. Bach, Walther, Kellner, Krebs, Vogler, Kittel, Fischer, Finck, Liszt, Töpfer, Reger, Keller, and Seifert. *Schönheit, organ.*
+ Fa 11-12/95: 470

22206. 320 0529-2 (2 discs): MUFFAT—Apparatus musico-organisticus. *Ullmann, organ.*
+ ARG 5-6/95: 145

22207. 320 0545-2: BOSSI—Complete organ works, vol. 1. *Mehtonen, organ.*
+ Fa 1-2/95: 127

22208. 321 0085-2: L. MOZART—Complete works for horn and orchestra. *Jeurissen, Höltzel, Lévesque, Ruyter, horns; Concerto Rotterdam; Friesen, cond.*
+ ARG 1-2/97: 143
+ Fa 9-10/96: 268

22209. 324 0091-2: *Trombone quartets.* Music of Bozza, Bruckner, Serocki, Staden, and Sweelinck. *Westphalian Trombone Quartet.* Reissue.
+ ARG 1-2/97: 200
• Fa 11-12/96: 473

22210. 324 0098-2: *St. Hubert's mass: French, Austrian, and Bohemian hunting music for parforce horns.* Music of Cantin, Kozeluch, Anton, Rossini, Schantl, and Anon. *Detmold Horn Soloists; Höltzel, cond.*
+ Fa 1-2/97: 340

22211. 324 0143-2: HÖLTZEL—Horn music. *Detmold Hornists; Höltzel, cond.* Recorded 1983.
+ ARG 5-6/95: 120
+ Fa 1-2/95: 177

22212. 324 0544-2: *Fagottissima nova: virtuoso rarities for two to five bassoons.* Music of Jansen, Rossini, Puccini, Hartley, Sieber, Wolken, Joplin, Ter Voert, Gershwin, and Sousa. *Gürzenich Bassoon Quintet.*
+ Fa 9-10/95: 413

22213. 325 0452-2: MÜTHEL—Concertos and chamber music. *Musica Alta Ripa.*
+ Fa 1-2/95: 217

22214. 325 0531-2 (2 discs): BOHNKE—String quartet, op. 1; Piano trio, op. 5; Cello sonata, op. 7; Violin sonata, op. 13, no. 1; Viola sonata, op. 13, no. 2; Cello

MD + G

sonata, op. 13, no. 3; Ciacona for solo violin, op. 15, no. 2. *Verdi Quartet; Alkan Trio; Klass, violin, viola & piano; Schwarz, cello.*
  + ARG 5-6/96: 85
  + Fa 11-12/95: 214

22215. 329 0588-2: WOYRSCH—Symphony no. 1; Symphonic prologue to Dante's Divina commedia. *Hamburg Symphony Orch.; Gómez Martínez, cond.*
  + Fa 11-12/95: 431

22216. 330 0591-2: BRUCKNER—Symphony no. 3 (arr. for piano 4 hands by Mahler). *Trenkner, Speidel, piano.*
  • ARG 3-4/96: 96
  + Fa 1-2/96: 164

22217. 330 0635-2 (2 discs): BACH—Brandenburg concertos (arr. Reger). *Piano Duo Trenkner-Speidel.*
  + Fa 1-2/97: 82

22218. 331 0592-2: MORANDI—Post communio; Sonata terza; Rondo con imitazione de'campanelli; Pastorale; Post communio. DIANA—Raccolta di composizioni per organo. *Krüger, organ.*
  □ Fa 11-12/95: 313

22219. 332 0081-2: MONTEVERDI—Madrigals. *Kölner Kammerchor; Neumann, cond.* Reissue.
  • Fa 9-10/96: 266

22220. 332 0598-2: SCHUMANN—Missa sacra, op. 147. BRAHMS—Kyrie; Missa Canonica; Fugue. *Kölner Kammerchor; Neumann, cond.*
  • ARG 3-4/96: 180
  • Fa 1-2/96: 305

22221. 333 0614-2 (2 discs): BACH—Sonatas and partitas for violin with piano accompaniment by Robert Schumann. *Schmid, violin; Smirnova, piano.*
  + Fa 5-6/96: 76
  + Fa 7-8/96: 96

22222. 333 0674-2: PAGANINI—Caprices, op. 1, with a piano acc. by Robert Schumann. *Schmid, violin; Smirnova, piano.*
  • ARG 9-10/96: 175
  + Fa 7-8/96: 262

22223. 334 0454-2: NUCIUS—Missa Vestivi i colli; Sacred motets. *Alsfelder Vokalensemble; Helbich, cond.*
  + Fa 9-10/96: 277

22224. 335 0661-2: REICHA—Sinfonia concertante for flute and violin; Overture; Symphony in E♭. *Wuppertal Symphony Orch.; Gülke, cond.*
  • ARG 9-10/96: 187
  + Fa 7-8/96: 272
  + Gr 3/97: 53

22225. 336 0715-2: REGER—Quartet for piano, violin, viola, and cello, op. 113; Serenade for 2 violins and viola, op.

141a. *Tanski, piano; Mannheim String Quartet.*
  • Fa 1-2/97: 234

22226. 603 0533-2: MENDELSSOHN—String quintets no. 1-2. *Berlin String Quintet.*
  + Fa 5-6/95: 261

22227. 603 0553-2: MENDELSSOHN—String quintets. *Berlin String Quintet.*
  + ARG 9-10/96: 164

22228. 603 0557-2: FRANÇAIX—Wind quintets no. 1-2; L'heure du berger. *Kammervereingung Berlin; Zichner, piano.*
  + Fa 5-6/95: 190

22229. 603 0585-2: *Music for bassoon and piano.* Music of Tansman, Koechlin, Mihalovici, Bozza, Bitsch, and Dutilleux. *Jensen, bassoon; Kitagawa, piano.*
  + ARG 3-4/96: 227
  + Fa 11-12/95: 464
  + Fa 1-2/96: 384

22230. 603 0599-2: CAPLET—Quintette; Deux pièces; Improvisations; Suite persane. *Calamus Ensemble.*
  + Fa 1-2/96: 175

22231. 603 0616-2: CARULLI—Duo, op. 134; Variations de Beethoven; Grand duo, op. 86; Trois valses, op. 32; Grand duo, op. 70. *Prunnbauer, guitar; Hill, fortepiano.*
  + ARG 11-12/96: 110
  + Fa 5-6/96: 128

22232. 603 0634-2: *Quattro contra bassi.* Music of Alm, Peña, Telemann, Tabakov, Brumby, Haydn, and Vanherenthals. *Frankfurt Double Bass Quartet.*
  + Fa 1-2/97: 340

22233. 603 0665-2: SCHOECK—Complete string quartets. *Minguet Quartet.*
  + Fa 9-10/96: 314

22234. 604 0590-2: SAINT-SAËNS—Album pour piano, op. 72; Etudes, op. 52, 111. *Lee, piano.*
  + ARG 3-4/96: 175
  + Fa 1-2/96: 178

22235. 605 0553-2: *Il cimento: Italian sonatas for the seventeenth century.* Music of Degli Antonii, Rognoni, Farina, Uccellini, Leoni, Guerrieri, and Lonati. *Hellman, recorders; Hickethier, viola da gamba; Hollmann, harpsichord & organ; Freimuth, chitarrone.*
  - ARG 9-10/96: 242
  + Fa 7-8/96: 370

22236. 605 0559-2 (2 discs): ZELENKA—Trio sonatas, ZWV 181. *Northwest German Chamber Soloists.*
  + Fa 11-12/95: 433

22237. 605 0593-2: MONTEVERDI—Vesperae in Nativitate Sancti Joannis Baptistae; music of Erbach, Viadana,

Bildstein, Bazzino, and Hassler. *Hassler Consort; Raml, cond.*
  + EM 11/96: 714
  + Fa 5-6/96: 212

22238. 605 0610-2: *La guitarra española (1546-1732).* Music of Fuenllana, Mudarra, Sanz, Guerau, and Murcia. *Koch, baroque guitar.*
  + Fa 5-6/96: 347

22239. 605 0647-2: *Luneburg 1647: Sacred concertos.* Music of Ghizzolo, G. Weber, Monteverdi, Werner, and Merula. *Spägele, soprano; Buchin, alto; Pöhl, bass; Ensemble Lanterly.*
  + Fa 1-2/97: 320

22240. 606 0273-2: PACHELBEL—Organ music. *Wachowski, organ.*
  + Fa 1-2/97: 220

22241. 606 0567-2: LISZT—Organ music. *Elekes, organ.*
  + Fa 7-8/96: 225

22242. 610 0562-2: *Concert music for guitar and mandolin orchestra.* Music of C. Stamitz, Eichner, Handel, Gluck, and Brahms. *Feit, oboe; Fidium Concentus; Kreidler, cond.*
  + Fa 5-6/95: 431

22243. 611 0547-2: RACHMANINOFF—Piano sonata no. 2; Daisies; Lilacs; Polka de WR; Vocalise; Transcriptions. *Höricke, piano.*
  + Fa 5-6/95: 300

22244. 612 0558-2: REGER—Suites for solo cello, op. 131c. *Zentgraf, cello.*
  • ARG 9-10/96: 187
  + Fa 5-6/95: 307

22245. 612 0577-2: VIVALDI—Cello sonatas (arr. for string orchestra). *Zentgraf, cello & cond.; Harleshäuser Kammerorch.*
  - Fa 5-6/96: 308

22246. 613 0579-2: SCHOENBERG—Pierrot lunaire; Scherzo for string quartet; Six little piano pieces; Phantasy for violin and piano. J. STRAUSS, JR. (ARR. SCHOENBERG)—Emperor waltz. *Kammer, speaker; Seidel, violin; Schleiermacher, piano; Ensemble Avantgarde; Zender, cond.*
  + ARG 3-4/96: 177
  • Fa 11-12/95: 358

22247. 613 0701-2: CAGE—Music for eight; Five (2 versions); Aria; String quartet in 4 parts. *Ensemble Avantgarde; Kammer, voice; Leipzig String Quartet.*
  + ARG 5-6/97: 96
  + Fa 1-2/97: 132

22248. 614 0660-2: PRAETORIUS—Motets and concertos. *Hassler Consort; Raml, cond.*
  + Fa 1-2/97: 226

22249. 615 0673-2: SCHUMANN—Piano quartet, op. 47. DRAESKE—Quintet for piano, horn, and strings, op. 48. *Mozart Klavierquartett; Langenstein, horn.*
+ ARG 1-2/97: 98
+ Fa 9-10/96: 320

22250. 616 0633-2: *Ave Maria.* Music of Parlow, Rudnick, Schubert, Liszt, Sorg, Mozart, Kahl, M. Haydn, Hiller, Seitz, Lemmens, and Gernsheim. *Berlin Male Chorus "Carl Maria von Weber"; Wiedermann, cond.*
• ARG 11-12/96: 268
+ Fa 7-8/96: 359

22251. 617 0631-2: *Oboe and guitar: French sonatas of the eighteenth century.* Music of Hotteterre, Danican- Philidor, Dieupart, Visée, and Marais. *Schmieder, oboe; Tappert, guitar.*
+ Fa 9-10/96: 404

22252. 618 0651-2: CLEMENTI—Piano music, vol. 1. Sonatas, op. 40: no. 1-3. *Irmer, piano.*
+ Fa 11-12/96: 223

22253. 618 0652-2: CLEMENTI—Piano sonatas, op. 50: no. 1-3. *Irmer, piano.*
+ Fa 11-12/96: 224

22254. 619 0658-2: DEBUSSY—Children's corner (arr. Hekkema); Six épigraphes antiques (arr. Wesly). RAVEL—Le tombeau de Couperin (arr. Hekkema). COUPERIN—Forlane (arr. Wesly). *Calefax Reed Quintet.*
+ Fa 7-8/96: 152

22255. 623 0548-2: *Music from the twenties.* Music of Varèse, Schwitters, Stravinsky, and Hindemith. *Bernhardt, speaker; Ensemble Das Neue Werk Hamburg; Cichewiecz, cond.*
• Fa 5-6/95: 423
+ Fa 7-8/96: 395

22256. 624 0556-2: *Music for bass clarinet.* Music of Schoeck, Messiaen, Genzmer, Celis, and Erdmann. *Rusche, bass clarinet; Hagen, piano; Pintev, Reichel, violins; Oepen, viola; Groth, cello; Berlin Symphony Orch.; Varon, cond.*
+ ARG 9-10/96: 242
+ Fa 7-8/96: 375

22257. 625 0549-2: RŮŽIČKA— Introspezione; Ausgeweidet die Zeit; Cello sonata; Préludes for piano; Stille. *Hamburg String Quartet; Tainton, piano; Lorenz, cello.*
□ Fa 1-2/96: 289

22258. 625 0551 2: BRANDMÜLLER— Concerto for organ and orchestra; Enigma; Und der Mond heftet ins Meer ein langes Horn aus Licht und Tanz. *Brandmüller, organ; Rundfunk-Sinfonieorchester Leipzig; Pommer, cond.; Erdinger, violin; Contra-Trio; Radio Sinfonieorchester Saarbrücken;*

Viotti, cond.
□ Fa 3-4/96: 139

22259. 630 0628-2: OLDFIELD—Tubular bells (arr. Duo Sonare). *Duo Sonare.*
+ ARG 3-4/97: 191
+ Fa 11-12/96: 325

22260. E 1040 (LP): BEETHOVEN—Piano music. *Demus, piano.*
+ Fa 7-8/86: 92

E 1085 see L 3085.

22261. E 1119 (LP): BACH—Guitar suites, BWV 995-996; Prelude, BWV 999; Fugue, BWV 1000. *Evers, guitar.*
□ Fa 7-8/86: 84

22262. L 3081: MONTEVERDI—Vocal and instrumental music. *Instrumental ensemble; Cologne Chamber Choir; Neumann, cond.*
• ARG 11-12/86: 70

22263. L 3085: L. MOZART—Instrumental music. *Jeurissen, Höltzel, Lévesque, Ruyter, horns; Concerto Rotterdam; Friesen, cond.* Issued also as LP: E 1085.
+ Fa 1-2/86: 185

22264. L 3110: HENZE—Royal winter music. *Evers, guitar.*
+ ARG 11-12/92: 134
□ Fa 11-12/92: 254

22265. L 3139: Music of Froberger, Böhm, Bach, C.P.E. Bach, and J.C. Bach. *Iseringhausman, clavichord.*
+ Fa 11-12/90: 439

22266. L 3150: SCHUMANN— Fantasiestücke, op. 12; Humoreske. *Demus, piano.*
□ Fa 5-6/86: 242

22267. L 3153: C.P.E. BACH—Rondos: in C major, D major, A minor; Sonatas: in G major, F major, A major, Wq. 56. *Rémy, fortepiano.*
- Fa 11-12/86: 94

22268. L 3180: BARTÓK—Divertimento for strings. BRITTEN—Variations on a theme by Frank Bridge. *Polish Chamber Orch.; Maksymiuk, cond.*
+ ARG 1-2/89: 16

22269. L 3197: SCHUBERT—Cello sonata, D. 821. MENDELSSOHN—Variations concertantes for cello and piano, op. 17. SCHUMANN—Fantasiestücke for cello and piano, op. 73. *Wick, cello; Sakoda, piano.*
+ ARG 5-6/90: 74
+ Fa 3-4/90: 284

22270. L 3207: ROSSINI—Six quartets for flute, clarinet, horn, and bassoon. *Consortium Classicum.*
+ Fa 11-12/86: 204

22271. L 3220: GRABBE—First book of madrigals. *Consort of Musicke; Rooley,*

cond.
+ Fa 11-12/87: 145

22272. L 3224: BURGMÜLLER—Piano sonata, op. 8. SCHUMANN—Piano sonata no. 1. *Maruko, piano.*
+ Fa 9-10/93: 140

22273. L 3226: *Die Egedacher-Orgel der Stiftskirche Zwettl.* Music of Frescobaldi, Kerrl, Lobrich, Bach, and Mozart. *Ullmann, organ.*
+ Fa 11-12/86: 275

22274. L 3229: SCHÜTZ—Christmas Oratorio; Meine Seele; Sieben Worte. *Musicalische Compagney.*
+ Fa 11-12/87: 222
- Gr 9/87: 470

22275. L 3230: SCHÜTZ—Freue dich; Weib, was weinest du; In lectulo/ Invenerunt; Anima mea/Adjuro vos; Wohl dem der ein tugendsam Weib hat; Ich beschwöre euch; Veni dilecte mi; Haus und Güter erbat man von Eltern. *Musicalische Compagney.*
+ Fa 11-12/87: 222
• Gr 9/87: 470

22276. L 3233: STAHLE—Piano quartet, op. 1. DVORÁK—Piano quartet no. 1. *Mozart Piano Quartet.*
+ Fa 11-12/88: 285

22277. L 3236: ARRIAGA—String quartets no. 1-3. *Voces String Quartet.*
• Fa 5-6/90: 102

22278. L 3241: BACH—Organ music. *Van Tricht, organ.*
+ Fa 7-8/88: 106

22279. L 3244: SPOHR—Songs. *Shirai, soprano; Höll, piano.*
+ Fa 11-12/87: 234

22280. L 3245: BEETHOVEN—Wind sextet, op. 71. HAYDN—Suite for winds, H.II:Es/ 17. MOZART—Serenade for winds, K. 375. *Detmold Wind Sextet.*
+ Fa 7-8/88: 115

22281. L 3246: BOCCHERINI—Rondo in C major. BRÉVAL—Cello sonata, op. 12, no. 5. BEETHOVEN—Twelve variations on a theme from Judas Maccabaeus. HUMMEL—Cello sonata, op. 104. *Ginzel, cello; Richter, piano.*
• Fa 11-12/87: 284

22282. L 3247: ARENSKY—Piano trio no. 1. SMETANA—Piano trio, op. 15. *Parnassus-Trio.*
+ ARG 7-8/88: 9
+ Fa 1-2/88: 70

22283. L 3250: GOLDBERG—Harpsichord concertos: in E♭ major; in D minor. *Döling, harpsichord; Sofia Soloists; Tabakov, cond.*
• Fa 3-4/88: 114

22284. L 3255: REGER—Violin sonata no. 5. PROKOFIEV—Flute sonata, op. 94. REINECKE—Flute sonata, op. 167. *Meisen, flute; Rosenberg, piano.*
• Fa 11-12/87: 207

22285. L 3267: WEBER—Freischütz (arr. Sedlak). *Consortium Classicum.*
+ Fa 7-8/88: 284
+ Gr 3/88: 1322

22286. L 3268: *Orgelwerke, vol. 1.* BUXTEHUDE—Organ music. *Vogel, organ.*
+ Fa 7-8/88: 143

22287. L 3269—3270 (2 separate discs): *Orgelwerke, vol. 2-3.* BUXTEHUDE—Organ music. *Vogel, organ.*
+ Fa 9-10/89: 172

22288. L 3272: DEBUSSY—Piano trio. RAVEL—Piano trio. *Parnassus-Trio.*
• ARG 11-12/88: 30
+ Fa 7-8/88: 151
+ Gr 12/87: 966

22289. L 3276: Music of Bruhns, Bohm, Vivaldi, Krebs, Mozart, and Boely. *Collum, organ.*
• Fa 7-8/88: 313

22290. L 3279: V. LACHNER—Forty-two variations on the C major scale, op. 42. RIES—Forty preludes for piano. *Michaels, piano.*
+ Fa 9-10/88: 180

22291. L 3280: KRENEK—String quartets no. 1-2. *Sonare Quartet.*
+ Fa 7-8/88: 183

22292. L 3281: KRENEK—String quartets, no. 3, 7. *Sonare Quartet.*
+ Fa 1-2/89: 185
□ Gr 1/89: 1176

22293. L 3282: KRENEK—String quartets no. 5, 8. *Sonare Quartet.*
+ Fa 9-10/90: 269

22294. L 3283: KRENEK—String quartets no. 4, 6. *Sonare Quartet.*
+ Fa 5-6/91: 200

22295. L 3284/85 (2 discs): C.P.E. BACH—Flute sonatas, Wq. 123-134. *Hünteler, transverse flute; Bylsma, baroque cello; Ogg, Hammerflügel.*
+ Fa 9-10/88: 85

22296. L 3286: FAURÉ—Cello sonatas no. 1-2; Elegie, op. 24. *Schmid, cello; Herzfeld, piano.*
• ARG 7-8/90: 47
- Fa 7-8/90: 143

22297. L 3287: THUILLE—Sextet for piano and winds, op. 6. POULENC—Sextet for piano and winds. *Davies, piano; Stuttgart Wind Quintet.*
• Fa 11-12/88: 298

22298. L 3291: FRANÇAIX—Wind quintet. HINDEMITH—Kleine Kammermusik, op. 24, no. 2. IBERT—Trois pièces brèves. TAFFANEL—Quintet in G minor. *Syrinx-Quintett.*
+ Fa 7-8/88: 326

22299. L 3292: *Guitarrenmusik des 20. Jahrhunderts.* Music of Falla, Martin, Smith-Brindle, Henze, Britten, Medek, Trojahn, and Brandmüller. *Evers, guitar.*
+ Fa 7-8/88: 315

22300. L 3295: Music of Speer, Hassler, Arcadelt, Dowland, Attaingant, Isaac, Gervaise, Beethoven, Peeters, Maniet, and Dubois. *Westphalian Trombone Quartet.*
+ Fa 11-12/88: 346

22301. L 3297: BACH—Ich will den Kreuzstab gerne tragen, BWV 56; Ich habe genug, BWV 82. *Kamp, bass; Fiori Musicali; Vokalensemble des Forum Alte Musik Bremen; Albert, cond.*
• Fa 9-10/90: 148

22302. L 3298: MOZART—Church sonatas (complete). *Ullmann, organ; Concilium Musicum; Angerer, cond.*
+ Fa 1-2/89: 220

22303. L 3299: BEETHOVEN—Octet, op. 103. KROMMER—Octet partita, op. 57. SCHUBERT—Minuet and finale, D. 72. *Bamberg Symphony Wind Ensemble.*
+ Fa 7-8/89: 89

22304. L 3300: FRANÇAIX—Octet; Clarinet quintet; Divertissement for bassoon and string quartet. *Charis Ensemble.*
+ ARG 11-12/89: 59
+ Fa 7-8/89: 148

22305. L 3301: *17th-century Italian recorder music.* Music of Fontana, Selma y Salaverde, Frescobaldi, Virgiliano, Storace, Rognoni, Turini, and Merula. *Ganassi-Consort, Köln.*
+ Fa 3-4/89: 387

22306. L 3304: TELEMANN—Chamber music. *Hünteler, flute & recorder; Kaiser, Schmidt-Casdorff, flute; Krecher, violin; Wahmhoff, cello; Hollmann, harpsichord.*
• ARG 1-2/90: 98
+ Fa 1-2/90: 326

22307. L 3306: BACH—Violin sonatas no. 1-3 (arr. Bungarten). *Bungarten, guitar.*
+ Fa 1-2/89: 107

22308. L 3307/08 (2 discs): HUMMEL—Piano trios (complete). *Parnassus-Trio.*
+ ARG 11-12/89: 69
+ Fa 9-10/89: 222
+ Gr 6/93: 64

22309. L 3309: FASCH—Wind concertos. *Westermann, Dhont, oboes; Kaiser, flute; McGraw, bassoon.*

+ ARG 7-8/90: 47
+ Fa 9-10/89: 200

22310. L 3310/11 (2 discs): WOLF-FERRARI—Piano trios no. 1-2; Piano quintet, op. 6; String quintet, op. 24. *Munich Piano Trio; Sawallisch, piano; Leopold String Quartet; Ruf, viola.*
+ ARG 7-8/89: 110
• Fa 1-2/89: 297

22311. L 3314: HAYDN—Oboe quartets, H.III:48; H.III:65 (arr. Rosinack). MOZART—Oboe quartet, K. 370. *Consortium Classicum.*
□ Fa 3-4/90: 190

22312. L 3315: HAYDN—Clarinet quartets, no. 1-3 (arr. Gambaro). *Consortium Classicum.*
+ ARG 11-12/90: 146
+ Fa 3-4/90: 190

22313. L 3316: KOZELUCH—Sinfonia francese in A major. MYSLIVEČEK—Sinfonia a quatro voce in E♭; Divertimento in F major. TUMA—Partita in D minor. *Suk Chamber Orch.; Vlach, cond.*
• Fa 3-4/90: 209

22314. L 3317: JANÁČEK—Suite for string orchestra. MARTINŮ—Partita; Serenade no. 2. KALABIS—Diptych for strings, op. 66. *Suk Chamber Orch.; Vlach, cond.*
+ Fa 3-4/90: 204

22315. L 3318: Music of Agricola, Goldberg, Krebs, J.E. Bach, Altnikol, and Müthel. *Hollmann, harpsichord.*
+ ARG 11-12/90: 154
+ Fa 1-2/90: 387

22316. L 3319: *Virtuose Musik für Klarinet und Gitarre.* Music of Donizetti, Pleyel, Neumann, Müller, and Giuliani. *Klöcker, clarinet; Prunnbauer, guitar.*
+ Fa 9-10/90: 492

22317. L 3323: *In imitation of birds.* Music of Hilton, Williams, Simpson, Stanley, Keller, Locke, Vincent, and Arne. *Ganassi-Consort Köln.*
+ Fa 7-8/90: 365

22318. L 3324: *Hornquartette.* Music of Homilius, Molter, Wunderer, F. Strauss, Artôt, Rimsky-Korsakov, Bozza, and Jeurissen. *Detmold Horn Quartet.*
+ Fa 11-12/90: 453

22319. L 3330: Music of Bach, C.P.E. Bach, J.C.F. Bach, J.C.Bach, Mendelssohn, C. Schumann, Reger, Karg-Elert, Gadsch, Walcha, Ohse, Ramin, and E. Richter. *Dorfmüller, organ.*
• Fa 3-4/90: 367

22320. L 3334: SHOSTAKOVICH—Piano trios no. 1-2; Romances, op. 127. *Münchner Klaviertrio; Ablaberdyeva,*

soprano.
+ Fa 7-8/90: 273

22321. L 3335: LORTZING—Ali Pascha von Janina; Don Juan und Faust. *Vocal soloists; Cappella der Nordwestdeutschen Musikakademie Detmold; Cologne Radio Symphony Orch.; Stulen, cond.*
● Fa 7-8/90: 188
□ ON 5/90: 48

22322. L 3336: MOZART—Venti, fulgura, proceliae; Exsultate jubilate. *Hofmann, soprano; Schola Cantorum Basiliensis Orch.; Sigrist, cond.*
● Fa 11-12/90: 297

22323. L 3339: VILLA-LOBOS—Cello concertos no. 1-2. *Schmid, cello; Northwest German Phil. Orch.; Roggen, cond.*
● ARG 11-12/89: 133
+ Fa 9-10/89: 356
□ Gr 11/89: 907 m.f.

22324. L 3343: Music of Richter, Froberger, Pachelbel, Muffat, Schubert, Albrechtsberger, Assmayer, Brahms, Bruckner, Schmidt, and Heiler. *Ullmann, organ.*
+ Fa 1-2/91: 385

22325. L 3344: REUBKE—Piano sonata in B minor; Organ sonata in C minor. *Tanski, piano; Sander, organ.*
+ ARG 11-12/89: 104
+ Fa 7-8/89: 224
+ Gr 11/89: 938

22326. L 3345: *Histoires for piano.* Music of Ibert, Roussel, and Dukas. *Schilde, piano.*
+ Fa 7-8/89: 303

22327. L 3348: Music Seixas and Anon. *Edward Tarr Trumpet Ensemble; Krüger, organ.*
+ ARG 11-12/90: 160
+ Fa 11-12/90: 454

22328. R 3350: REGER—Samtliche orgelwerke, vol. 1. *Haas, organ.*
+ ARG 3-4/90: 92
+ Fa 7-8/89: 221

22329. R 3351: REGER—Samtliche orgelwerke, vol. 2. *Haas, organ.*
+ ARG 3-4/90: 93
+ Fa 7-8/89: 222

22330. R 3352: REGER—Samtliche orgelwerke, vol. 3. *Haas, organ.*
+ Fa 11-12/89: 331

22331. R 3353: REGER—Samtliche orgelwerke, vol. 4. *Haas, organ.*
+ Fa 1-2/90: 274

22332. R 3354—3355 (2 separate discs): REGER—Samtliche orgelwerke, vol. 5-6. *Haas, organ.*
+ Fa 9-10/90: 351

22333. R 3356—3357 (2 separate discs): REGER—Samtliche orgelwerke, vol. 7-8. *Haas, organ.*
● Fa 5-6/91: 260

22334. L 3358, 3360/61 (3 separate discs): REGER—Complete organ music, vol. 9, 11-12. *Haas, organ.*
+ Fa 1-2/93: 216

22335. L 3365: MOZART—Concertone for clarinet and bassoon in B♭ major (arr. Hoffmeister). C.P.E. BACH—Duo for clarinet, bassoon and general bass. DANZI—Sinfonia concertante for clarinet and bassoon in B♭ major. *Klöcker, clarinet; Hartmann, bassoon; Suk Chamber Orch.; Škvor, cond.*
+ ARG 11-12/90: 147
+ Fa 11-12/90: 287

22336. L 3366: *Concertos for clarinet and bassoon.* Music of J.F. Schubert, Tausch, and Winter. *Klöcker, clarinet; Hartmann, bassoon; Carneiro, cello; Normann, double bass; Suk Chamber Orch.; Škvor, cond.*
+ ARG 11-12/90: 147
+ Fa 11-12/90: 287

22337. L 3367: CASELLA—Sonata a tré. BLOCH—Three nocturnes. ARRIEU—Piano trio. *Parnassus-Trio.*
+ Fa 5-6/91: 153

22338. L 3369: *Baletii: Sonaten und Serenaden am Hof zu Kremsier.* Music of Schmelzer, Vejvanovsky, Biber, and Anon. *Trompeten Consort Friedmann Immer; Salzburger Barockensemble.*
● Fa 5-6/91: 378

22339. L 3370: BACH—Flute sonata, BWV 1013. C.P.E. BACH—Flute sonata, Wq. 132. DENISOV—Flute sonata. *Meisen, flute.*
● Fa 5-6/91: 113

22340. L 3371/72 (2 discs): *Lusitanische Orgalmusik.* Works by San Lorenzo, de Conceicao, Torrelhas, de Olague, de Arajo, Seixas, Carreira, Coelho, de Deus, and Braga. *Krüger, organ.*
+ Fa 11-12/91: 551

22341. L 3373/74 (2 discs): MOZART—Complete piano trios. *Parnassus-Trio.*
● Fa 11-12/91: 416

22342. L 3386: BACH—Goldberg variations, BWV 988. *Tricht, organ.*
+ ARG 3-4/93: 53
- Fa 1-2/93: 100

22343. L 3387: *Orgellandschaft Finnland.* Music of Düben, Greve, O. Merikanto, Kuusisto, A. Merikanto, Maasalo, Vitala, Salonen, Sallinen, and Sibelius. *Lehtonen, organ.*
+ ARG 5-6/92: 166
+ Fa 1-2/92: 405

22344. L 3390: SOR—Twenty-four études. *Bungarten, guitar.*
● ARG 1-2/92: 118
● Fa 1-2/92: 334

22345. L 3391: SCHUBERT—Winterreise. *Geraerts, tenor; Rémy, fortepiano.*
- Fa 3-4/92: 316

22346. L 3393: ROSSINI—Overtures (arr. for wind band): L'Italiana in Algeri; Der verlorene Akkord; La gazza ladra; Il barbiere di Siviglia; L'inganno infelice; La scala di seta; Otello; Tancredi; La Cenerentola. *Consortium Classicum.*
+ Fa 3-4/92: 299

22347. L 3394: PROKOFIEV—Overture on Hebrew themes; Quintet for oboe, clarinet, violin, viola and contrabass violin; Romeo and Juliet: suite for winds. *Ensemble Villa Musica.*
+ Fa 5-6/92: 225

22348. L 3395: SAINT-SAËNS—Oboe sonata; Clarinet sonata; Bassoon sonata; Romance for flute and piano; Caprice on Danish and Russian melodies. *Ensemble Villa Musica.*
● Fa 5-6/92: 237

22349. L 3396: *Konzertante Sinfonien.* SALIERI—Concerto for flute and oboe. DANZI—Concerto for flute and clarinet. PLEYEL—Symphonie concertante no. 5. *Württemberg Chamber Orch.; Faerber, Jörg.*
+ ARG 3-4/92: 176
+ Fa 5-6/92: 238

22350. L 3397: *Cello sonatas of 1948.* Sonatas by Miaskovsky (no. 2), Carter and Poulenc. *Wick, cello; Rhee, piano.*
+ ARG 7-8/92: 256
+ Fa 7-8/92: 340

22351. L 3398: SCHENCK—L'echo du Danube, op. 9: no. 1-3, 5. *Berliner Concert.*
+ ARG 7-8/93: 148
+ Fa 3-4/93: 273

22352. L 3399: HANDEL—Cantatas and trio sonatas. *Koslowsky, soprano; Musica Alta Ripa.*
+ Fa 1-2/92: 226

22353. L 3400: MAHLER—Symphony no. 6 (arr. Zemlinsky). *Zenker, Trenkner, piano.*
□ Fa 5-6/92: 194
- St 9/92: 191

22354. L 3401: WIDOR—Organ symphonies no. 1-2. *Oosten, organ.*
+ ARG 3-4/94: 185
+ Fa 1-2/94: 358

22355. L 3402: WIDOR—Organ symphonies no. 3-4. *Oosten, organ.*
- ARG 1-2/93: 168
+ Fa 1-2/93: 271

MD + G

22356. L 3404: WIDOR—Organ symphony no. 7; Symphonie gothique. *Oosten, organ.*
+ Fa 3-4/94: 365

22357. L 3414/15 (2 discs): *Orgellandschaft Siebenbürgen.* Music of Richter, Bella, Dressler, Lassel, Diruta, Greff- Bakfark, Marckfelner, Croner, von Baussern, Irtel, Türk, and Ciortea. *Philippi, Schlandt, organ.*
+ Fa 5-6/93: 381

22358. L 3416: *Romantic wind serenades.* Music of Dvořák, Mendelssohn and Hartmann. *Consortium Classicum.*
+ ARG 9-10/93: 241
- Fa 7-8/93: 313

22359. L 3419/20 (2 discs): RHEINBERGER—Piano trios (Complete). *Parnassus-Trio.*
+ ARG 3-4/93: 128
+ Fa 1-2/93: 221

22360. L 3421/22 (2 discs): HANDEL—Solo sonatas. *Ganassi Consort.*
+ Fa 3-4/92: 208

22361. L 3423: HAYDN—Four duets for 2 cellos. ROSSINI—Duet. *Geringas, Klein, cellos.*
+ ARG 3-4/94: 107
+ Fa 5-6/94: 166

22362. L 3424: BACH—Organ works, vol. 4. *Vogel, organ.*
+ Fa 9-10/92: 167

22363. L 3425—3426 (2 separate discs): BUXTEHUDE—Organ works, vol. 5-6. *Vogel, organ.*
+ ARG 11-12/93: 90
+ Fa 11-12/93: 203

22364. L 3427: BUXTEHUDE—Organ works, vol. 7. *Vogel, organ.*
+ Fa 1-2/94: 155

22365. L 3428: LECLAIR—Trio sonatas op. 4. *Musica Alta Ripa.*
+ Fa 9-10/93: 204

22366. L 3430/31 (2 discs): *Orgellandschaft Mecklenburg.* Music of Buxtehude, Erich, Hasse, Kuntzen, Rost and others. *Rost, organ.*
+ Fa 1-2/93: 297

22367. L 3432: LISZT—Piano music. *Killian, piano.*
• Fa 11-12/92: 279

22368. L 3433: *Music at the Westphalian courts, vol. 1: For the amusement and entertainment of the music lover, the music publisher Johann André.* Music of Sterkel, Pleyel, Haydn, and Vanhal. *See, flute; Kertész, violin; Ligeti, viola; Pertorini, cello; Brunner, Rémy, fortepiano.*
+ Fa 9-10/92: 432

22369. L 3434: J.C. BACH—Symphonies for winds. *Consortium Classicum; Klöcker, cond.*
+ ARG 1-2/93: 69
+ Fa 1-2/93: 97

22370. L 3436: BUSONI—Piano music. BACH (ARR. BUSONI)—Wachet auf, ruft uns die Stimme; Ich ruf zu Dir, Herr; Toccata in D minor, BWV 565. *Tanski, piano.*
- Fa 1-2/93: 123

22371. L 3439: JANÁČEK—Mládí; Violin sonata; Pohádka; Presto for cello and piano; Concertino for piano, clarinet, horn, bassoon, 2 violins, and viola. *Ensemble Villa Musica.*
+ ARG 5-6/94: 104
• Fa 1-2/94: 211

22372. L 3440: HUMMEL—Wind serenades; Oboe conertino. *Consortium Classicum; Klöcker, cond.*
• ARG 9-10/94: 146
+ Fa 1-2/94: 208

22373. L 3442: *Barock on the rocks. A musical cocktail from Bach to the Beatles. Nordwestdeutsche Kammersolisten; other instrumentalists.*
• Fa 5-6/93: 401

22374. L 3443: HARTMANN—Burleske Musik. EISLER—Fourteen ways of describing rain. VOGT—Serenade and tarentella. WALTON—Façade. *Ensemble "Das Neue Werk" Hamburg; Cichewiecz, cond.*
+ Fa 7-8/92: 354

22375. L 3445: MAHLER (ARR. CASELLA)—Symphony no. 7. *Zenker, Trenkner, piano 4-hands.*
- Fa 3-4/93: 212

22376. L 3447: HINDEMITH—Septet; Quintet for clarinet and string quartet, op. 30; Octet. *Rodenhäuser, clarinet; Ensemble Villa Musica.*
+ ARG 11-12/93: 126
+ Fa 11-12/93: 273

22377. L 3448: SPOHR—Quintet for piano and wind instruments, op. 52; Sextet for strings, op. 140. *Ensemble Villa Musica.*
+ ARG 7-8/93: 161
+ Fa 3-4/93: 301

22378. L 3449: MILHAUD—Chamber symphonies no. 1-6; Suite d'après Corrette; Les rêves de Jacob. *Ensemble Villa Musica.*
+ ARG 7-8/93: 127
+ Fa 5-6/93: 266
+ Fa 7-8/93: 184

22379. L 3450: *Contemporary chamber music from southeast Europe.* Music of Kaufmann, Klepper, Wendel, Türk, Acker, and Hölszky. *Various performers.*
+ Fa 9-10/93: 376

22380. L 3451: *Silesian concertos for the twentieth century.* Music of Von Borck, Erdmann, Halaczinsky, and Katzer. *Various performers.*
□ 7-8/93: 302

22381. L 3459: MUFFAT—Armonico tributo. *La Stravaganza Köln.*
+ ARG 9-10/93: 163
+ Fa 7-8/93: 191

22382. L 3460: PLEYEL—Two octets and two sextets for winds. *Consortium Classicum.*
+ ARG 7-8/94: 149
+ Fa 3-4/94: 431

22383. L 3461: BACH—Oboe sonatas. *Schmalfuss, oboe; Döling, harpsichord.*
+ Fa 5-6/94: 99

22384. L 3462: SCHOENBERG—String quartet no. 1. *New Leipzig String Quartet.*
+ Fa 7-8/93: 229

22385. L 3464: BRAHMS—Piano quartet no. 1. WEBER—Trio for flute, cello & piano, op. 63. *Berlin Phil. Ensemble.*
+ Fa 9-10/93: 134

22386. L 3476: *Il violino in San Marco.* Music of Castello, Fontana, Uccellini, and Marini. *Trio Arcangelo Corelli.*
+ Fa 9-10/93: 370

22387. L 3482: LALO—The complete piano trios. *Parnassus-Trio.*
• ARG 3-4/94: 114
+ Fa 1-2/94: 222
• Gr 4/94: 63

22388. L 3486: TELEMANN—Twelve fantasies for flute. *Hünteler, flute.*
+ Fa 1-2/94: 333

22389. L 3487/90 (4 discs): MENDELSSOHN—Organ works (complete). *Innig, organ.*
•
+ ARG 5-6/95: 138 Fa 7-8/94: 177

22390. L 3507: BLACHER—String quartet no. 5. LUTOSŁAWSKI—String quartet. *New Leipzig String Quartet.*
+ ARG 7-8/94: 76
+ Fa 7-8/94: 76

22391. L 3510: BEETHOVEN—Piano trio no. 4; Trio after the Symphony no. 2. *Parnassus-Trio.*
+ Fa 9-10/94: 141

22392. L 3511: *Romantische Orgelmusik.* Music of Rinck, Mendelssohn, Brahms, Rheinberger, Karg-Elert, and Wachowski. *Wachowski, organ.*
• Fa 3-4/94: 403

22393. L 3512: *Weihnächtliche Orgelmusik.* Improvisations and carols. *Wachowski, organ.*
• Fa 3-4/94: 404

22394. L 3514: DRAESEKE—Sonata quasi fantasia, op. 6. LISZT—Mosonyis Grabgeleit; Sonata in B minor. *Tanski, piano.*
- Fa 5-6/94: 137

22395. L 4280 (4 discs): KRENEK—Complete string quartets. *Sonare Quartet.*
+ Fa 9-10/92: 270

22396. L 4340/42 (3 discs): GUILMANT—Organ sonatas (complete). *Oosten, organ.*
+ ARG 9-10/90: 69
+ Fa 1-2/90: 192

MEDICI-WHITEHALL

22397. MQCD 4002: Music of Delius, Elgar, Vaughan Williams, Warlock and Holst. *Medici Quartet; Oxford Orch. da Camera; Vass, cond.*
• Gr 9/94: 68

22398. MQCD 5001/02 (2 discs): HAYDN—String quartets op. 20. *Medici Quartet.*
• Gr 10/94: 140

22399. MQCD 6001: MOZART—Clarinet quintet; String quartet K. 499. *Brymer, clarinet; Medici Quartet.*
+ ARG 1-2/95: 145
• Gr 3/93: 67

22400. MQCD 7001: ELGAR—Violin sonata. Life of Elgar in words and music. *Medici Quartet; Bingham, piano.*
+ Gr 11/92: 137

22401. MQCD 7002: ELGAR—Piano quintet; String quartet. *Bingham, piano; Medici Quartet.*
+ ARG 1-2/95: 103
+ Gr 11/92: 137

22402. MQCD 8001: BRAHMS—Clarinet quintet; Piano quintet. *Medici Quartet; Brymer, clarinet; Lill, piano.*
+ ARG 1-2/95: 145

22403. MQCD 9001: DVOŘÁK—String quartet no. 12. SCHUBERT—String quartet no. 14. *Medici Quartet.*
+ Gr 10/93: 69

22404. MQCD 9002: SCHUBERT—String quintet; String quartet no. 8. *Medici Quartet; Phelps, cello.*
• Gr 10/93: 69

MEGADISC

22405. MDC 7853: GOEYVAERTS—String quartets. *Quatuor Danel.*
+ Fa 9-10/96: 201

22406. MDC 7855: *Piano versions of works by Alexander Knaifel.* KNAIFEL—The scars of a march; Passacaglia; In some exhausted reverie; O heavenly King; Prayer to the Holy Spirit. *Malov, piano; Siegle, sampler; Melentieva,*

soprano.
+ Fa 9-10/96: 230

22407. MDC 7858: USTVOLSKAYA—Trio; Composition no. 2; Symphony no. 4; Piano sonata no. 5. *St. Petersburg Soloists; Malov, cond.*
+ ARG 7-8/96: 217

22408. MDC 7859: DE MEY—Kinok; Unknowness; Violin concerto; Amor constante. *ICTUS; Octors, cond.*
+ ARG 7-8/96: 297

22409. MDC 7863: USTVOLSKAYA—Grand duet for cello and piano; Duet for violin and piano. *Vassiliev, cello; Shustin, violin; Malov, piano.*
+ ARG 9-10/95: 232
+ Fa 9-10/95: 343

22410. MDC 7865: USTVOLSKAYA—Trio for violin, clarinet, and piano; Violin sonata; Octet. *Shustin, violin; Malov, piano; Fedorov, clarinet; St. Petersburg Soloists.*
+ ARG 9-10/95: 232
+ Fa 9-10/95: 343

22411. MDC 7866: DE CLERCK—Quintet for piano and strings; String trio; Spheres; Già. *Daniel String Quartet; Bardèche, piano.*
+ Fa 9-10/95: 188

22412. MDC 7867: USTVOLSKAYA—Preludes 1-12; Composition no. 1-3. *St. Petersburg Soloists; Malov, cond.*
+ ARG 9-10/95: 232
+ Fa 9-10/95: 343

22413. MDC 7869: *Champ d'Action: quincunx.* Music of Logghe, Brewaeys, De Visscher, D'Haene, and Verstockt. *Champ d'Action; Antunes, cond.*
+ Fa 9-10/95: 431

22414. MDC 7872/3 (2 discs): GOEYVAERTS—Litanies no. 1-5. *Damme, piano; Champ d'Action; BRT Phil. Orch.; Vis, cond.; Paal, soprano; Wauters, harpsichord.*
+ Fa 9-10/96: 201

22415. MDC 7876: USTVOLSKAYA—Piano sonatas no. 1-6. *Malov, piano.*
+ ARG 9-10/95: 232
+ Fa 9-10/95: 343

MELODIYA

22416. SUCD 10-00002, 10-00030 (2 separate discs): BORTNIANSKI—Concertos for choir (sung in Church Slavonic), vol. 1-2. *USSR Ministry of Culture Chamber Choir; Poliansky, cond.*
+ Fa 11-12/91: 280

22417. SUCD 10-00003: MOZART—Symphony no. 28; Mass in C, K. 317 "Coronation". *Davtyan, Piatigorskaya, Anton, Fresan; Orfeón Donostiarra; Moscow Virtuosi; Spivakov, cond.*

+ ARG 3-4/92: 113
• Fa 1-2/92: 284

22418. SUCD 10-00004: SHCHEDRIN—The sealed Angel: choral music after N. Leskov for mixed choir a capella and shepherd's pipe. *Moscow Chamber Choir; Minin, cond.*
+ ARG 1-2/92: 111
□ Fa 11-12/91: 483

22419. SUCD 10-00005: TCHAIKOVSKY—Piano sonata in G, op. 37; Children's album, op. 39. *Pletnev, piano.*
+ ARG 7-8/92: 237
+ Fa 11-12/91: 506

22420. SUCD 10-00007: SHCHEDRIN—Stikhira for the millenary of the the the Christianization of Russia. IVAN THE TERRIBLE—Stikhira no. 1 in honor of Pyotr, metropolitan of Moscow and all Russia. *Vocal quartet; USSR Ministry of Culture Symphony Orch.; Rozhdestvensky, cond.*
□ Fa 11-12/91: 483

22421. SUCD 10-00012: RACHMANINOFF—Liturgy of St. John Chrysostom. *Moscow Chamber Choir; Minin, cond.* Reissue.
+ ARG 1-2/92: 96
+ Fa 1-2/92: 301

22422. SUCD 10-00014: TCHAIKOVSKY—Liturgy of St. John Chrysostom, op. 41. *USSR Ministry of Culture Chamber Choir; Poliansky, cond.*
+ ARG 1-2/92: 126
+ Fa 11-12/91: 505

22423. SUCD 10-00015: TCHAIKOVSKY—*Choral works.* To sleep (2 versions); Tis not the cuckoo; The nightingale; Nine liturgical choruses: no. 3, 5, 7; Legend; Without time or season; The golden cloud had slept. *Bogdanov, tenor; USSR Ministry of Culture Chamber Choir & Symphony Orch.; Poliansky, cond.*
+ ARG 3-4/92: 151
+ Fa 1-2/92: 348

22424. SUCD 10-00020: GLAZUNOV—Lady-Soubrette: ballet in one act, op. 61. *USSR State Symphony Orch.; Svetlanov, cond.*
+ ARG 1-2/92: 56
+ Fa 11-12/91: 322

22425. SUCD 10-00021: TANEEV—Symphony no. 4; Oresteia: Entr'acte "The temple of Apollo at Delphi". *USSR State Symphony Orch.; Svetlanov, cond.*
• ARG 1-2/92: 124
- Fa 11 12/91: 501

22426. SUCD 10-00022—10-00028 (7 separate discs + Fa 1-2/92: 220): GLAZUNOV—Symphonies, no. 1-8. *USSR State Symphony Orch.; Svetlanov, cond.*
• ARG 7-8/93: 94

MELODIYA

22427. SUCD 10-00033: Liszt—Festklänge; Hungary; Hamlet. *USSR Ministry of Culture Symphony Orch.; Ermler, cond.*
+ ARG 5-6/92: 80

22428. SUCD 10-00036: Khachaturian—The widow from Valencia: suite; Masquerade: suite. *Moscow Symphony Orch.; Dudarova, cond.*
+ ARG 5-6/92: 76
+ Fa 1-2/92: 245

22429. SUCD 10-00040: Franck—Violin sonata. Debussy—String quartet. *Kopelman, violin; Gurfinkel, piano; Borodin Quartet.* Live recording.
+ Fa 11-12/91: 320

22430. SUCD 10-00041—10-00043 (3 separate discs): Messiaen—Vingt regards sur l'Enfant-Jesus. *Batagov, piano.*
+ Fa 11-12/91: 391

22431. SUCD 10-00048: Tchaikovsky—Twelve pieces of average difficulty; Romance; Waltz-scherzo; Capriccio. *Pletnev, piano.*
+ ARG 1-2/92: 126
+ Fa 1-2/92: 353

22432. SUCD 10-00049: Rachmaninoff—Aleko. *Nesterenko, Fedin, Matorin, Volkova, Kotova; USSR Radio and Television Large Chorus; Moscow Phil. Symphony Orch.; Kitaenko, cond.* Recorded 1987.
+ ARG 1-2/92: 94
+ ON 1/16/93: 32

22433. SUCD 10-00050: Prokofiev—Chout. *USSR Ministry of Culture Symphony Orch.; Rozhdestvensky, cond.*
+ ARG 5-6/92: 108
+ Fa 11-12/91: 441

22434. SUCD 10-00051: Prokofiev—Symphonies no. 3-4. *Moscow Phil. Symphony Orch.; Kitaenko, cond.*
+ ARG 1-2/92: 92

22435. SUCD 10-00052: Prokofiev—Symphonies no. 1-2. *Moscow Phil. Symphony Orch.; Kitaenko, cond.*
+ ARG 5-6/92: 110

22436. SUCD 10-00057: Haydn—The seven last words of Jesus Christ. *Borodin Quartet.* Recorded live 1984.
- Fa 1-2/92: 234

22437. SUCD 10-00060: Denisov—Symphony. *USSR Ministry of Culture Symphony Orch.; Rozhdestvensky, cond.*
+ ARG 1-2/92: 49

22438. SUCD 10-00062: Schnittke—Symphony no. 1. *USSR Ministry of Culture Symphony Orch.; Rozhdestvensky, cond.*
+ ARG 1-2/92: 102
+ Fa 3-4/92: 306

22439. SUCD 10-00063: Schnittke—Symphony no. 2. *Leningrad Phil. Orch.; Rozhdestvensky, cond.*
+ ARG 7-8/92: 213
+ Fa 3-4/92: 306

22440. SUCD 10-00064: Schnittke—Symphony no. 3. *USSR Ministry of Culture Symphony Orch.; Rozhdestvensky, cond.*
+ ARG 1-2/92: 102
+ Fa 3-4/92: 306

22441. SUCD 10-00065: Schnittke—Symphony no. 4. *USSR Ministry of Culture Symphony Orch.; Rozhdestvensky, cond.*
• Fa 3-4/92: 306

22442. SUCD 10-00067: Schnittke—Concerto grosso no. 1; Cello concerto. *Grindenko, Kremer, violins; Moscow Phil. Society Soloists; Bashmet, cond.;Gutman, cello; USSR Ministry of Culture Symphony Orch.; Rozhdestvensky, cond.*
□ ARG 7-8/92: 212
+ Fa 3-4/92: 306

22443. SUCD 10-00068: Schnittke—Concerto grosso no. 2; Viola concerto. *Kagan, violin; Bashmet, viola; Gutman, cello; USSR Ministry of Culture Symphony Orch.; Rozhdestvensky, cond.*
+ ARG 3-4/92: 133
+ Fa 3-4/92: 306

22444. SUCD 10-00073—10-00075 (3 separate discs): Shostakovich—Preludes and fugues for piano, op. 87. *Nikolayeva, piano.* 1987 recording.
+ Fa 11-12/91: 484

22445. SUCD 10-00078: Artyomov—Lamentations; Gurian hymn; Symphony of elegies. *Moscow Phil. Symphony Orch.; Kitaenko, cond.; Lithuanian Chamber Orch.; Sondeckis, cond.*
□ Fa 11-12/91: 238

22446. SUCD 10-00090: Shchedrin—Symphony no. 2 "25 Preludes for orchestra". *USSR Radio and Television Large Symphony Orch.; Rozhdestvensky, cond.*
+ ARG 1-2/92: 111
+ Fa 11-12/91: 483

22447. SUCD 10-00091: Shchedrin—Naughty limericks; Not love alone: suite form the opera; The humpbacked horse: Maiden's round dance; Solemn overture; Chimes. *USSR State Symphony Orch.; Svetlanov, cond.*
+ ARG 1-2/92: 111
+ Fa 11-12/91: 482

22448. SUCD 10-00094: Music of Rachmaninoff, Scriabin, Prokofiev, and Kissin. *Kissin, piano.*
• ARG 11-12/92: 247
+ Fa 9-10/92: 321
+ Gr 4/93: 96

22449. SUCD 10-00095: Shostakovich—Violin sonata, op. 134; Viola sonata, op. 147. *Kagan, violin; Bashmet, viola; Richter, piano.* Recorded live.
+ ARG 1-2/93: 148
+ Fa 9-10/92: 353

22450. SUCD 10-00096: Tchaikovsky—Piano concertos no. 1, 3. *Eresko, piano; Moscow Phil. Symphony Orch.; Dudarova, cond.*
+ ARG 3-4/93: 146
+ Fa 11-12/92: 383

22451. SUCD 10-00097: Mozart—Quartet no. 15. Brahms—Quartet no. 3. *Borodin Quartet.*
+ ARG 1-2/92: 83

22452. SUCD 10-00098: Rachmaninoff—Symphony no. 1; The rock, op. 7. *Moscow Phil. Symphony Orch.; Kitaenko, cond.*
+ Fa 9-10/92: 322

22453. SUCD 10-0010-0: Chopin—Piano concertos. *Kissin, piano; Moscow Phil. Symphony Orch.; Kitaenko, cond.*
+ ARG 7-8/92: 116

22454. SUCD 10-0010-4: Tchaikovsky—Suites no. 3, 4. *USSR State Symphony Orch.; Svetlanov, cond.*
+ ARG 5-6/92: 145

22455. SUCD 10-0010-5: Rachmaninoff—Vespers, op. 37. *Arkhipova, mezzo-soprano; Rumiantsev, tenor; USSR Ministry of Culture Chamber Choir; Poliansky, cond.* Reissue.
+ ARG 1-2/92: 96
• Fa 1-2/92: 301

22456. SUCD 10-0010-6: Artyomov—Requiem. *Sveshnikov Boys Chorus of the Moscow Choral School; Kaunas State Chorus; Moscow Phil. Symphony Orch.; Kitaenko, cond.*
• ARG 1-2/92: 21
+ Fa 11-12/91: 238

22457. SUCD 10-0010-7: Denisov—Colin and Chloé; Death is a long sleep; Cello concerto. *Lee, Terentieva, Dumtzev; Latvian Academic Chorus; USSR Ministry of Culture Symphony Orch.; Sinaisky, cond.; Monighetti, cello; Moscow Chamber Orch.; Kogan, cond.; Georgian, cello; Moscow Phil. Symphony Orch.; Kitaenko, cond.*
□ ARG 1-2/92: 49

22458. SUCD 10-0010-9: Gubaidulina—The Seven last words; Rubaiyat; Vivente-non-vivente. *Tonkha, cello; Lips, bayan; Collegium Musicum Ensemble; Mynbaev, cond.; Yakovenko, baritone; unnamed ensemble; Rozhdestvensky, cond.; Gubaidulina, synthesizer.*
+ ARG 3-4/92: 64

22459. SUCD 10-00111: CHOPIN—
Waltzes. SCHUMANN—Blumenstück;
Toccata. *Bunin, piano.*
  - ARG 3-4/92: 47

22460. SUCD 10-00138: BALAKIREV—
Suite in D minor on four pieces by
Chopin. BORODIN—Prince Igor:
Polovetsian dances. MUSSORGSKY—A
night on Bald Mountain; Two choruses
with orchestra: The destruction of
Sennacherib; Jesus Navinus. *USSR State
Symphony Orch.; USSR TV & Radio
Large Chorus; Moscow Chamber Choir;
Svetlanov, cond.*
  + ARG 1-2/92: 24
  - Fa 11-12/91: 252

22461. SUCD 10-00140: LIADOV—
Fragment from the Apocalypse; From the
days of old; Baba Yaga; The enchanted
lake; Kikimora; Eight Russian folksongs;
Musical snuff-box. NAPRAVNIK—Night
intermezzo from Dubrovsky;
Melancholy. *USSR State Symphony
Orch.; Svetlanov, cond.*
  + ARG 1-2/92: 70

22462. SUCD 10-00143:
RACHMANINOFF—Symphony no. 3; Isle of
the dead; Scherzo. *USSR State Symphony
Orch.; Svetlanov, cond.*
  + ARG 5-6/92: 114

22463. SUCD 10-00144:
RACHMANINOFF—Symphonic dances, op.
45; Aleko: selections; Six choruses for
female voices and piano, op. 15.
*Svetlanov, piano & cond.; USSR State
Symphony Orch.; Female Group of the
USSR Radio and Television Large
Chorus. Reissue.*
  + ARG 1-2/92: 96
  + Fa 1-2/92: 302

22464. SUCD 10-00146:
RACHMANINOFF—Prince Rostislav;
Capriccio on Gypsy themes; Piano music.
*USSR State Symphony Orch.; Svetlanov,
piano & cond. Reissue.*
  + ARG 1-2/92: 94
  + Fa 11-12/91: 279

22465. SUCD 10-00147: TANEEV—
Concert suite for violin and orchestra, op.
28. *Korsakov, violin; USSR State
Symphony Orch.; Svetlanov, cond.*
  + Fa 3-4/93: 309

22466. SUCD 10-00148: ARENSKY—
Suites no. 1, 3; Introduction to the opera
Nal and Damajanti. *USSR State
Symphony Orch.; Svetlanov, cond.*
  + ARG 1-2/92: 20
  + Fa 11-12/91: 237

22467. SUCD 10-00150: ARENSKY—Suite
no. 2; Suite Egyptian nights; Variations
on a theme of Tchaikovsky; Fantasia on
themes of Ryabinin. *Timofeeva, piano;
USSR State Symphony Orch.; Svetlanov,
cond.*

  + ARG 1-2/92: 20
  + Fa 11-12/91: 237

22468. SUCD 10-00151: BALAKIREV—
Symphony no. 1; Overture on three
Russian songs; Russia. *USSR State
Symphony Orch.; Svetlanov, cond.*
  + ARG 1-2/92: 24
  + Fa 11-12/91: 252

22469. SUCD 10-00152: BALAKIREV—
Symphony no. 2; Tamara; In Bohemia.
*USSR State Symphony Orch.; Svetlanov,
cond.*
  + ARG 1-2/92: 24
  + Fa 11-12/91: 252

22470. SUCD 10-00153: BALAKIREV—
King Lear: Incidental music; Suite in B
minor; Overture on themes of the Spanish
March. *USSR State Symphony Orch.;
Svetlanov, cond.*
  + ARG 1-2/92: 24
  + Fa 11-12/91: 252

22471. SUCD 10-00154: BORODIN—
Symphonies no. 1-2. *USSR State
Symphony Orch.; Svetlanov, cond.
Reissue.*
  + ARG 1-2/92: 35
  - Fa 11-12/91: 279

22472. SUCD 10-00155: BORODIN—
Symphony no. 3; Petite suite; In the
steppes of central Asia; Prince Igor:
Overture. *USSR State Symphony Orch.;
Svetlanov, cond.*
  + ARG 1-2/92: 35
  + Fa 1-2/92: 180
  + Gr 5/93: 39

22473. SUCD 10-00156: GLAZUNOV—
Forest, op. 19; Sea, op. 28; Oriental
rhapsody, op. 29. *USSR State Symphony
Orch.; Svetlanov, cond.*
  + ARG 1-2/92: 56
  + Fa 11-12/91: 322

22474. SUCD 10-00157: GLAZUNOV—
From the Middle Ages, op. 79; To the
memory of a hero: elegy, op. 8; Slavonic
festival, op. 26, no. 4; Wedding
procession, op. 21. *USSR State
Symphony Orch.; Svetlanov, cond.*
  + ARG 1-2/92: 56
  + Fa 11-12/91: 322

22475. SUCD 10-00158: GLAZUNOV—
Ballade, op. 78; Solemn overture, op. 73;
Spring, op. 34; Introduction and Salome's
dance, op. 90; Romantic intermezzo, op.
69. *USSR State Symphony Orch.;
Svetlanov, cond.*
  + ARG 1-2/92: 56
  + Fa 11-12/91: 322

22476. SUCD 10-00160: GLAZUNOV—
Ballet suite, op. 52; Characteristic suite,
op. 9. *USSR State Symphony Orch.;
Svetlanov, cond.*
  + ARG 1-2/92: 56
  + Fa 1-2/92: 219

22477. SUCD 10-00161: GLAZUNOV—
Stenka Razin, op. 13; Lyric poem in D♭,
op. 12; Finnish fantasia in C, op. 88;
Mazurka in G, op. 18; Theme with
variations in G minor for strings, op. 97.
*USSR State Symphony Orch.; USSR
Radio and Television Large Symphony
Orch.; Svetlanov, cond.*
  + ARG 1-2/92: 56
  - Fa 1-2/92: 219

22478. SUCD 10-00162: GLAZUNOV—
Concert waltzes nos. 1-2; Chopiniana, op.
46; From darkness to light, op. 53;
Triumphal march, op. 40. *USSR State
Symphony Orch.; Svetlanov, cond.*
  + ARG 1-2/92: 56
  + Fa 1-2/92: 219

22479. SUCD 10-00163: GLAZUNOV—
Two preludes, op. 85; To the memory of
N. Gogol, op. 87; Carnival, op. 45;
Fortune-telling and dance, op. 81; Finnish
sketches, op. 89. *USSR State Symphony
Orch.; Svetlanov, cond.*
  + ARG 1-2/92: 56
  + Fa 1-2/92: 219

22480. SUCD 10-00164: GLAZUNOV—
Overture no. 1 on three Greek themes, op.
3; Overture no. 2 on Greek themes, op. 6.
ARENSKY—Marguerite Gautier, op. 9;
Raphael: Introduction to the musical
scenes; March in C minor "To the
memory of Suvorov". *USSR State
Symphony Orch.; Svetlanov, cond.*
  + ARG 1-2/92: 56
  + Fa 1-2/92: 220

22481. SUCD 10-00166: GLINKA—A life
for the Tsar: Overture and three dances;
Russlan and Ludmila: Overture, Four
dances, Chernomor's march; Andante
cantabile and rondo. *USSR State
Symphony Orch.; Bolshoi Theater Orch.;
Svetlanov, cond. Reissues.*
  + ARG 9-10/92: 109
  + Fa 5-6/92: 163

22482. SUCD 10-00167: GLINKA—
Patriotic song; Prayer; Memory of
friendship; Overture in G minor; Overture
in D. DARGOMYZHKY—Kazachok; Baba
Yaga; Boléro; Chukhon Fantasy. *USSR
State Symphony Orch.; Bolshoi Theater
Orch.; Svetlanov, cond. Reissues.*
  - ARG 7-8/92: 137
  + Fa 5-6/92: 163

22483. SUCD 10-00169: KALINNIKOV—
Suite for orchestra; Cedar and palm;
Bylina. *USSR State Symphony Orch.;
Svetlanov, cond.*
  + ARG 11-12/92: 139
  | Fa 5-6/92: 181

22484. SUCD 10-00170: KALINNIKOV—
Symphony no. 2; Intermezzi no. 1-2;
Serenade for strings. *USSR State
Symphony Orch.; Svetlanov, cond.*
  + ARG 7-8/92: 154
  + Fa 5-6/92: 181

22485. SUCD 10-00171: KALINNIKOV—Symphony no. 1. RIMSKY-KORSAKOV—Boyarina Vera Sheloga: Overture; The maid of Pskov: Overture, Intermezzi, Forest, hunt and storm. *USSR State Symphony Orch.; Svetlanov, cond.* Reissues.
  + ARG 7-8/92: 154
  + Fa 7-8/92: 189

22486. SUCD 10-00172: LIAPUNOV—Symphony no. 1; Russian overture. BALAKIREV—Islamey. *USSR State Symphony Orch.; Svetlanov, cond.*
  • ARG 5-6/92: 79

22487. SUCD 10-00173: LIAPUNOV—Symphony no. 2; Zelazowa Wola. *USSR State Symphony Orch.; Svetlanov, cond.*
  - ARG 5-6/92: 79

22488. SUCD 10-00175: MEDTNER—Piano concerto no. 1; Piano music. *Nikolayeva, piano; USSR Academic Symphony Orch.; Svetlanov, cond & piano.* Reissue.
  + ARG 7-8/92: 175
  + Fa 5-6/92: 196
  • St 5/93: 179

22489. SUCD 10-00176: MEDTNER—Piano concerto no. 2; Piano music. *Shatskes, piano; USSR State Symphony Orch.; Svetlanov, cond. & piano.* Reissue.
  + ARG 7-8/92: 175
  + Fa 5-6/92: 197

22490. SUCD 10-00178: MUSSORGSKY—Sunless songs; Khovanshchina: Introduction (twice); Dance of the Persian girls; The fair at Sorochinsk: Introduction and gopak; Scherzo in Bb; Intermezzo in B minor. *Vishnevskaya, soprano; USSR State Symphony Orch.; Svetlanov, cond.* Recorded live.
  + ARG 9-10/92: 134
  + Fa 7-8/92: 238
  + Gr 9/93: 57

22491. SUCD 10-00179: Waltzes and polonaises by Glazounov, Rubinstein, Rimsky-Korsakov, Mussorgsky, and Tchaikovsky. *USSR State Symphony Orch.; Svetlanov, cond.*
  □ ARG 1-2/92: 14

22492. SUCD 10-00180: RIMSKY-KORSAKOV—Scheherazade; Sadko; Fantasia on Serbian themes. *USSR State Symphony Orch.; Svetlanov, cond.*
  • ARG 7-8/92: 207
  • Fa 7-8/92: 238

22493. SUCD 10-00182: RIMSKY-KORSAKOV—Symphonies no. 1-2. *USSR State Symphony Orch.; Svetlanov, cond.*
  + ARG 1-2/93: 139
  • Fa 1-2/93: 221

22494. SUCD 10-00185: RIMSKY-KORSAKOV—Pan voyevoda: Suite; Snow maiden: Suite; Le coq d'or: Suite;

Dubinushka. *Bolshoi Theater Orch.; USSR State Symphony Orch.; Svetlanov, cond.*
  • ARG 7-8/92: 206
  + Fa 5-6/92: 233

22495. SUCD 10-00188: SCRIABIN—Symphony no. 1. *USSR State Symphony Orch.; Svetlanov, cond.*
  + ARG 3-4/92: 138

22496. SUCD 10-00191: SCRIABIN—Piano concerto. KALINNIKOV—Tsar Boris. *Nasedkin, piano; USSR State Symphony Orch.; Svetlanov, cond.*
  + ARG 7-8/93: 155
  + Fa 1-2/93: 235

22497. SUCD 10-00192: STRAVINSKY—Le sacre du printemps; Jeu de cartes. *USSR State Symphony Orch.; Svetlanov, cond.*
  + Fa 1-2/92: 299

22498. SUCD 10-00194: TCHAIKOVSKY—Symphony no. 2; String serenade. *USSR State Symphony Orch.; Svetlanov, cond.* Reissue.
  • Fa 3-4/92: 344

22499. SUCD 10-00196: TCHAIKOVSKY—Symphony no. 4; Fatum; Capriccio italien. *USSR State Symphony Orch.; Svetlanov, cond.*
  + ARG 5-6/92: 146

22500. SUCD 10-00199: TCHAIKOVSKY—Manfred symphony; Danish overture. *USSR State Symphony Orch.; Svetlanov, cond.*
  + ARG 11-12/92: 220

22501. SUCD 10-00202: TCHAIKOVSKY—Romances. RACHMANINOFF—Romances. *Dolukhanova, mezzo-soprano; Kozel, piano.* Recorded 1948-53.
  + ARG 5-6/92: 144
  + Fa 7-8/92: 308

22502. SUCD 10-00205: PROKOFIEV—Le pas d'acier, op. 41; Russian overture, op. 72; Ode on the end of war, op. 105; Flourish mighty homeland, op. 114 (2nd ed.). *USSR Ministry of Culture Symphony Orch. & Chamber Choir; Rozhdestvensky, cond.* Reissue.
  + ARG 1-2/92: 91
  + Fa 11-12/91: 441

22503. SUCD 10-00206: PROKOFIEV—On the Dnieper, op. 51; Hamlet, op. 77. *Gerasimova, soprano; Safiulin, bass; USSR Ministry of Culture Symphony Orch.; Rozhdesvensky, cond.*
  • ARG 1-2/92: 90
  + Fa 1-2/92: 298

22504. SUCD 10-00209: PROKOFIEV—Piano sonatas no. 8-9. *Petrov, piano.* Reissue.
  + ARG 1-2/92: 91
  + Fa 11-12/91: 445

22505. SUCD 10-00212: BRAHMS—Violin concerto. DVOŘÁK—Violin concerto. *Oistrakh, violin; USSR Radio and Television Large Symphony Orch.; USSR State Symphony Orch.; Kondrashin, cond.*
  + Fa 1-2/92: 183

22506. SUCD 10-00213: RIMSKY-KORSAKOV—Scheherazade; Capriccio espagnol. *USSR Radio and Television Large Symphony Orch.; Fedoseyev, cond.*
  - Fa 1-2/92: 307

22507. SUCD 10-00214: SVIRIDOV—Snow storm; Pushkin's garland. *USSR Radio and Television Large Symphony Orch.; Fedoseyev, cond.; Novosibirsk Chamber Choir; Moscow Chamber Choir; Chamber Ensemble of the USSR Radio and Television Large Symphony Orch.; Minin, cond.*
  □ ARG 7-8/92: 233
  + Fa 1-2/92: 345

22508. SUCD 10-00215: SVIRIDOV—Poem in memory of Sergei Esenin; Five choruses to lyrics by Russian poets. *Maselennikov, tenor; Glinka Choir; Leningrad Phil. Orch.; Temirkanov, cond.*
  + Fa 5-6/92: 262

22509. SUCD 10-00216: SVIRIDOV—Romances and songs to lyrics by Alexander Blok; Cast off Russia. *Obraztsova, mezzo-soprano; Kasrashvili, soprano; Sviridov, piano.*
  + ARG 1-2/92: 124
  + Fa 1-2/92: 345

22510. SUCD 10-00219: BEETHOVEN—Romances for violin and orchestra no. 1-2. GODARD—Violin concerto no. 1: Canzonetta. CHAUSSON—Poème, op. 25. SAINT-SAËNS—Introduction and rondo capriccioso. RAVEL—Tzigane. *Oistrakh, violin; USSR State Symphony Orch.; Kondrashin, cond.* Reissue.
  □ Fa 9-10/92: 430

22511. SUCD 10-00224: HAYDN—Symphonies, no. 102, 104. *Moscow Chamber Orch.; Barshai, cond.* Reissue.
  + Fa 5-6/92: 173

22512. SUCD 10-00229: KIKTA—Ukrainian carols; Frescoes of St. Sophia of Kiev; Beyond the verge of darkness; Christ had a garden. *USSR Radio Orch.*
  □ ARG 11-12/92: 141

22513. SUCD 10-00230: MOZART—Violin concertos no. 5; K. 271a (attr. Mozart). *D. Oistrakh; USSR Radio Symphony Orch.; USSR State Symphony Orch.; Kondrashin, cond.* Recorded 1947-50.
  + Fa 11-12/92: 310

22514. SUCD 10-00232: SVIRIDOV—Music for chamber orchestra; Pathetic

oratorio; Time, forward!: film score. *Various performers.*
□ ARG 7-8/92: 233
+ Fa 5-6/92: 262

22515. SUCD 10-00233: SCRIABIN—Symphony no. 1. SIBELIUS—Karelia suite. *Moscow Radio Large Symphony Orch.; Fedoseyev, cond.*
• Fa 7-8/92: 124

22516. SUCD 10-00234: VAUGHAN WILLIAMS—Symphony no. 1. *USSR Ministry of Culture Symphony Orch.; Rozhdestvensky, cond.* Recorded live.
+ ARG 1-2/93: 161
- Fa 11-12/92: 396
+ St 6/93: 255

22517. SUCD 10-00235: B. TCHAIKOVSKY—Juvenile: orchestral poem; Sinfonietta for strings. *USSR Radio and Television Large Orch.; Fedoseyev, cond.; Petrov, viola d'amore; B. Tchaikovsky, piano.*
□ ARG 3-4/92: 235
+ Fa 1-2/92: 346

22518. SUCD 10-00238: TCHAIKOVSKY—Rococo variations; String sextet "Souvenir de Florence". *Rostropovich, cello; Leningrad Phil. Orch.; Rozhdestvensky, cond.; Borodin Quartet; Genrikh, viola.* Reissue.
+ ARG 5-6/92: 148
+ Fa 3-4/92: 347

22519. SUCD 10-00239: TCHAIKOVSKY—Violin concerto. GLAZUNOV—Violin concerto. *D. Oistrakh, violin; USSR State Symphony Orch.; Kondrashin, cond.* Recorded 1957, 1948.
+ Fa 1-2/93: 252

22520. SUCD 10-00240: SHOSTAKOVICH—Symphony no. 8. *USSR Radio and Television Large Symphony Orch.; Fedoseyev, cond.* Recorded live 1985.
• Fa 1-2/92: 331

22521. SUCD 10-00241: SHOSTAKOVICH—Symphony no. 14. *Vishnevskaya, soprano; Reshetin, bass; Moscow Phil. Symphony Orch. Soloists' Ensemble; Rostropovich, cond.*
+ ARG 5-6/92: 134
+ Fa 5-6/92: 255

22522. SUCD 10-00249: CHOPIN—Etudes op. 10 and 25; Trois nouvelles études. *Skavronsky, piano.*
• ARG 7-8/92: 116
• Fa 5-6/92: 141

22523. SUCD 10-00250: TCHAIKOVSKY—Piano concerto no. 1. BEETHOVEN—Piano sonata no. 23. LISZT—Liebestraume no. 3. *Cliburn, piano; Moscow Phil. Symphony Orch.; Kondrashin, cond.* Recorded live 1958.
+ ARG 11-12/92: 246
+ Fa 9-10/92: 374

22524. SUCD 10-00255: *Andrei Korsakov: Fantasias and pieces for violin.* Music of Ernst, Zimbalist, Wieniawski, Castelnuovo-Tedesco, Waxman and Tchaikovsky. *Korsakov, violin; with orchestral & piano accompaniment.*
+ Fa 5-6/92: 329

22525. SUCD 10-00256: R. STRAUSS—Violin sonata, op. 18. RESPIGHI—Violin sonata in B minor. *Fedotov, violin; Ardakov, piano.*
+ Fa 9-10/92: 329

22526. SUCD 10-00257: SCHUMANN—Adagio und Allegro for horn and orchestra. BRAHMS—Vier Ernste Gesänge. SHOSTAKOVICH—Viola sonata. *Shafran, cello; Ginzberg, piano.*
+ Fa 3-4/92: 317

22527. SUCD 10-00262: Arias and duets from Otello, Cavalleria rusticana, Tosca, and Pagliacci. *Milashkina, soprano; Atlantov, tenor; USSR Radio Orch.; Fedoseyev, cond.; Bolshoi Theater Orch.; Ermler, cond.*
+ ARG 5-6/92: 188

22528. SUCD 10-00264: TCHAIKOVSKY—Romances. *Kasrashvili, soprano; Mogilevskaya, piano.*
- Fa 7-8/92: 308

22529. SUCD 10-00267: BOIKO—Songs and choruses. *Various performers.*
+ ARG 3-4/92: 35

22530. SUCD 10-00270: Georgian sacred music. *Rustavi Ensemble.*
+ Fa 3-4/92: 391

22531. SUCD 10-00274: *Early Russian all-night vigil.* RACHMANINOFF—Vespers, op. 37: excerpts. *Moscow Youth and Students' Chorus; Tevlin, cond.; USSR State Academic Russian Choir; Sveshnikov, cond.*
• Fa 1-2/92: 301

22532. SUCD 10-00275: KOMITAS—Patarag: divine liturgy. *Male Chamber Choir of the Yerevan Opera Theater; Keshishyan, cond.*
+ Fa 7-8/92: 192

22533. SUCD 10-00276: Byzantine music of the 6th-15th centuries; Music of early and Muscovite Russia of the 15th-17th centuries. *Madrigal Ensemble; Yanchenko, cond.*
+ Fa 1-2/92: 397

22534. SUCD 10-00279: *The light of Christ illumneth all men.* Music of Chesnokov, Lvovsky, Rutov, Gretchaninov, Bayanov, Frunza, Rachmaninoff, and Azeyev. *Choir of the Moscow Church, Joy to All Sorrows; Matveyev, cond.*
+ Fa 9-10/92: 407

22535. SUCD 10-00281: *300 years of Russian music.* Music of Vedel, Bortnyansky, Gurliev, Alyabiev, Turchaninov, Pushkin, Rimsky-Korsakov, Balakirev, and Taneyev. *Vivat Chamber Choir; Zhuravlenko, cond.*
- Fa 3-4/93: 357

22536. SUCD 10-00282: *Christ is born: glorify Him!* Ukrainian Christmas hymns and carols. *Dumka Choir; Savchuk, cond.*
+ Fa 3-4/93: 356

22537. SUCD 10-00292: *The moon is shining.* Russian folk songs. *Ossipov Russian Folk Orch.; Kalinin, cond.*
+ Fa 7-8/92: 360

22538. SUCD 10-00298: TCHAIKOVSKY—Songs. MUSSORGSKY—Sunless (arr. Denisov). *Nesterenko, bass; Shenderovich, piano; Ministry of Culture Orch.; Rozhdestvensky, cond.* Recorded 1991, 1984.
+ ARG 1-2/93: 156
• Fa 1-2/93: 204

22539. SUCD 10-00303: Concertos for violin and oboe by Bach, Vivaldi, Telemann and Haydn. *Kurlin, oboe; Stadler, violin; Leningrad Chamber Orch.*
+ Fa 5-6/92: 342

22540. SUCD 10-00304: BOCCHERINI—Sonata in A. HAYDN—Divertimento in D. TORTELIER—Sonata bucephale. KODÁLY—Sonata. SHOSTAKOVICH—Sonata. *Gorokhov, cello; Nikitina, piano.*
+ ARG 3-4/92: 182

22541. SUCD 10-00306: Music of Glinka, Taneyev, Glazunov, Liapunov, Pachelbel, Walther, and Scheidt. *Tsatsorin, organ.*
+ ARG 5-6/92: 168

22542. SUCD 10-00403/05 (3 discs): TCHAIKOVSKY—Swan lake; The seasons. *Russian State Symphony Orch.; Svetlanov, cond.*
+ ARG 9-10/93: 206
+ Fa 11-12/93: 421

22543. SUCD 10-00409/10- (2 discs): TCHAIKOVSKY—Nutcracker; Piano concerto no. 2. *Gilels, piano; Russian State Symphony Orch.; Svetlanov, cond.*
+ ARG 9-10/93: 206
+ Fa 11-12/93: 418

22544. SUCD 10-00411/12 (2 discs): TCHAIKOVSKY—Orchestral excerpts from operas. *USSR State Symphony Orch.; Svetlanov, cond.*
+ ARG 9-10/93: 204
+ Fa 11-12/93: 418

22545. SUCD 10-00438: BERLIOZ—Harold in Italy. SCHNITTKE—Trio sonata. *Bashmet, viola; USSR Radio Symphony Orch.; Fedoseyev, cond.; Moscow*

MELODIYA

Chamber Ensemble; Bashmet cond.
- ARG 1-2/94: 79

22546. SUCD 10-00472: MIASKOVSKY—
Symphony no. 17. *USSR Academic
Symphony Orch.; Svetlanov, cond.*
+ ARG 1-2/93: 122
+ Fa 3-4/93: 224

22547. SUCD 10-00474: MIASKOVSKY—
Symphonies no. 24-25. *Russian State
Symphony Orch.; Svetlanov, cond.*
+ ARG 9-10/93: 155

22548. SUCD 10-00484: BERLIOZ—
Harold in Italy. HINDEMITH—Trauermusik.
*Barshai, viola; Moscow Phil. Orch.; D.
Oistrakh,cond.; Moscow Chamber Orch.;
Barshai, cond.* Reissues.
- ARG 9-10/93: 97

22549. SUCD 10-00491: MIKHEYEVA—
The prophecy of Iakhavi. DENISOV—
Concerto piccolo. GUBAIDULINA—
Misterioso. GRISHIN—Guernica. *Bolshoi
Theater Percussion Ensemble; assisting
musicians.*
□ ARG 7-8/93: 195
+ Fa 5-6/93: 396

22550. SUCD 10-00501: BEETHOVEN—
Serenade for string trio, op. 8; String trio
op. 9, no. 1. *Kagan, violin; Bashmet,
viola; Gutman, cello.*
+ Fa 11-12/92: 194

22551. SUCD 10-00504:
RACHMANINOFF—Trio élégiaque.
SHOSTAKOVICH—Piano trio no. 2.
*Serebryakov, piano; Vaiman, violin;
Rostropovich, cello.*
+ ARG 9-10/93: 227
- Fa 11-12/93: 517

22552. SUCD 10-00505: RUBINSTEIN—
Piano trio no. 3; Three pieces.
*Teplukhina, piano; Bisengaliev, violin;
Semenov, cello.*
+ ARG 3-4/94: 146

22553. SUCD 10-00511: CHOPIN—
Etudes, op. 10, 25. *Ashkenazy, piano.*
Reissue; recorded 1959.
+ ARG 5-6/93: 77
+ Fa 5-6/93: 185

22554. SUCD 10-00540: SCHUBERT—
Sonata for viola and piano, D. 821
"Arpeggione." STRAVINSKY—Mavra:
Russian maiden's song. A.
TCHAIKOVSKY—Concerto for viola and
orchestra. DE BÉRIOT—Scène de ballet,
op. 100. *Bashmet, viola; Muntian, piano;
Moscow Phil. Symphony Orch.; Gergiev,
cond.* Recorded live 1986.
● Fa 3-4/93: 381

22555. SUCD 10-00546: FAURÉ—Piano
quartet no. 1. SAINT-SAËNS—Piano trio in
F. *Kogan, violin; Barshai, viola;
Rostropovich, cello; Gilels, piano.*
Reissues.
+ ARG 7-8/93: 88

22556. SUCD 10-00547: HAYDN—Piano
trio, H. XV, 19. MOZART—Piano trio, K.
564. SCHUMANN—Piano trio, op. 63.
*Gilels, piano; Kogan, violin;
Rostropovich, cello.*
+ ARG 3-4/93: 194
+ Fa 1-2/93: 167

22557. SUCD 10-00548: SCHUMANN—
Concerto for cello and orchestra, op. 129.
DVOŘÁK—Concerto for cello and
orchestra, op. 104. *Rostropovich, cello;
Moscow Phil. Symphony Orch.;
Samosud, cond.; USSR TV and Radio
Large Symphony Orch.; Khaikin, cond.*
● Fa 3-4/93: 281

22558. SUCD 10-00549: PROKOFIEV—
Cello symphony-concerto. SAINT-
SAËNS—Cello concerto no. 1.
*Rostropovich, cello; Leningrad Phil.
Orch.; Sanderling, cond.* Reissue.
+ ARG 1-2/93: 132
+ Fa 1-2/93: 208

22559. SUCD 10-00550: BEETHOVEN—
Trio no. 6 "Archduke." SCHUMANN—
Stücke im Volkston, op. 102: no. 1, 4;
Kinderszenen, op. 15: no. 7. R.
STRAUSS—Op. 9: no. 2 "An einsamer
Quelle." SINDING—Presto. VILLA-
LOBOS—Bachianas brasileiras no. 1:
Prelude. *Rostropovich, cello; Gilels,
piano; Kogan, violin; Yampolsky, piano;
Dedyukhin, piano; Cello Players
Ensemble.* Recorded 1948 53.
+ ARG 3-4/93: 162
+ Fa 1-2/93: 109

22560. SUCD 10-00552: BEETHOVEN—
String trio no. 1. BACH—Suite no. 3 BWV
1068: Aria. HANDEL—Sonata op. 1, no.
13, HWV 371: Larghetto. SCHUBERT—
Impromptu, op. 90, no. 3, D. 899.
CHOPIN—Introduction and polonaise
brillante, op. 31. *Rostropovich, cello;
Kogan, violin; Barshai, viola; USSR State
Symphony Orch.; Anosov, cond.;
Dedyukhin, piano.* Recorded 1949-56.
+ ARG 3-4/93: 162
+ Fa 1-2/93: 109

22561. SUCD 10-00553: PROKOFIEV—
Cello sonata. SHOSTAKOVICH—Cello
sonata. *Rostropovich, cello; Richter,
piano.*
+ ARG 3-4/93: 124
+ Fa 1-2/93: 208

22562. SUCD 10-00566: MEDTNER—
Songs. *Chernykh, soprano; Orfenova,
piano.*
+ ARG 9-10/93: 154
- Fa 7-8/93: 178

22563. SUCD 10-00595: PROKOFIEV—
Ivan the Terrible. *Vocal soloists; Yurlov
Russian Choir; Ostankino Radio
Symphony Orch.; Fedoseyev, cond.*
● ARG 1-2/94: 133

22564. SUCD 10-00598: CHESNOKOV—
Vesper mass, op. 44. *Orthodox

Motherland; Georgievsky, cond.
+ Fa 3-4/93: 143

22565. SUCD 10-00601:
RACHMANINOFF—Vespers, op. 37. *Korkan,
mezzo-soprano; Ognevoi, tenor; State
Russian Choir; Sveshnikov, cond.*
Recorded 1965.
+ ARG 9-10/93: 174
+ Fa 5-6/93: 286

22566. SUCD 10-00654: *Scenes & arias
from opera.* Music of Verdi, Puccini, and
Tchaikovsky. *Vishnevskaya, soprano;
Bolshoi Theater Orch.; Melik-Pashaev,
Khaikin, conds.*
+ ARG 7-8/93: 204
+ Fa 5-6/93: 361
+ ON 10/93: 36

22567. SUCD 10-00656:
RACHMANINOFF—Piano concerto no. 3.
PROKOFIEV—Piano sonata no. 8.
*Mogilevsky, piano; Moscow Phil.
Symphony Orch.; Kondrashin, cond.*
- Fa 7-8/93: 208

22568. SUCD 10-00656:
RACHMANINOFF—Piano concerto no. 3.
PROKOVIEV—Piano sonata no. 8.
*Mogilevsky, piano; Moscow Phil.
Symphony Orch.; Kondrashin, cond.*
Recorded 1964, 1977.
+ ARG 9-10/93: 172

22569. SUCD 10-00657: LISZT (ARR.
BUSONI)—Fantasia and fugue on Ad nos,
ad salutarem undam. RAVEL—Gaspard de
la nuit. PROKOFIEV—Visions fugitives, op.
22: no. 10-11, 14-17. *Mogilevsky, piano.*
- Fa 5-6/93: 248

22570. SUCD 11-00308:
SHOSTAKOVICH—String quartets no, 1, 4-5.
Taneev Quartet.
+ ARG 9-10/92: 162

22571. SUCD 11-00308:
SHOSTAKOVICH—String quartets no. 1, 4, 5.
Taneev Quartet.
+ Fa 3-4/93: 289

22572. SUCD 11-00309:
SHOSTAKOVICH—String quartets no. 6-8.
Taneev Quartet.
+ Fa 3-4/93: 289

22573. SUCD 11-00310:
SHOSTAKOVICH—String quartets no. 2, 10.
Taneev Quartet.
+ Fa 3-4/93: 289

22574. SUCD 11-00311:
SHOSTAKOVICH—String quartets no, 3, 9.
Taneev Quartet.
+ ARG 9-10/92: 162

22575. SUCD 11-00311:
SHOSTAKOVICH—String quartets no. 3, 9.
Taneev Quartet.
+ Fa 3-4/93: 289

22576. SUCD 11-00312:
SHOSTAKOVICH—String quartets no. 11-13.
Taneev Quartet.
+ ARG 9-10/92: 162
+ Fa 7-8/92: 283

22577. SUCD 11-00313:
SHOSTAKOVICH—String quartets no. 14-15.
Taneev Quartet.
+ ARG 9-10/92: 162
+ Fa 7-8/92: 283

22578. 36.4 (LP): LOPES-GRAÇA—
Concertino for piano, strings, brass, and
percussion; Divertimento for winds,
percussion, cellos, and basses; Viola
concertino. *Chaves, viola; Sá e Costa,
piano; Budapest Phil. Orch.; Sándor,
cond.*
- Fa 7-8/89: 172

22579. SUCD 60-00137: Kalinka:
popular Russian songs. *Alexandrov Song
and Dance Ensemble of the Soviet Army;
Alexandrov, Maltsev, conds.*
+ ARG 5-6/93: 177
+ Fa 5-6/93: 237

22580. SUCD 90-00200:
RACHMANINOFF—Concertos for piano and
orchestra no. 2-3. *Kim, piano; USSR
Ministry of Culture Symphony Orch.;
Rozhdestvensky, cond.*
+ Fa 3-4/93: 252

22581. MCD 100: GLAZUNOV—
Symphonies no. 1, 7. *USSR Ministry of
Culture Symphony Orch.;
Rozhdestvensky, cond.*
+ ARG 9-10/90: 66
+ Fa 9-10/90: 243

22582. MCD 109: TCHAIKOVSKY—Suites
no. 1, 4. *USSR State Symphony Orch.;
Svetlanov, cond.*
• ARG 9-10/90: 120

22583. MCD 112: Piano music of
Chopin, Tchaikovsky, and Rachmaninoff.
Richter, piano.
• ARG 7-8/90: 146 (Chopin)
+ ARG 7-8/90: 146 (others)
• Fa 9-10/90: 212

22584. MCD 113: SHOSTAKOVICH—
Symphonies no. 5, 9. *USSR Ministry of
Culture Symphony Orch.;
Rozhdestvensky, cond.*
• Fa 5-6/90: 294 (no. 5)
+ Fa 5-6/90: 294 (no. 9)

22585. MCD 114 (2 discs):
MUSSORGSKY—Sorochinsky fair.
BORODIN—Petite suite (orch. Glazunov).
*Chernykh, Zhakharenko, Mishchevsky,
Voinarovsky; Stanislavsky Theater
Chorus & Orch.; Esipov, cond.; USSR
Radio and Television Symphony Orch.;
Cherkassov, cond.*
+ ARG 5-6/90: 75
+ Fa 5-6/90: 238

22586. MCD 115 (2 discs):
TCHAIKOVSKY—Eugene Onegin.
*Milashkina, Atlantov, Mazurok,
Nesterenko; with assisting soloists;
Bolshoi Theater; Ermler, cond.*
• ARG 9-10/90: 120

22587. MCD 116: RACHMANINOFF—
Symphonic dances; The bells. *Soloists;
Moscow Phil. Symphony Orch.; Kitaenko,
cond.; USSR Radio and Television
Symphony Orch.; Fedoseyev, cond.*
• ARG 9-10/90: 101

22588. MCD 117: MUSSORGSKY—Pictures
at an exhibition; Canoes; Ensign;
Reminiscence of childhood; Children's
playroom; Gorzuf and Ayudaga; Tears;
Seamstress; Impromptu passioné; First
punishment. *Postnikova, piano.*
- ARG 7-8/90: 72

22589. MCD 118: SHOSTAKOVICH—
Symphony no. 7. *USSR State Symphony
Orch.; Rozhdestvensky, cond.*
- ARG 5-6/90: 107

22590. MCD 122: Music of Rameau,
Bizet, Saint-Saëns, Dukas, Debussy, and
Ravel. *Petrov, piano.*
+ Fa 3-4/89: 366

22591. MCD 127: BACH—Keyboard
concertos no. 2-4, 6. *Gavrilov, piano;
chamber orchestra; Nikolayevsky, cond.*
+ ARG 5-6/90: 16
- Fa 7-8/90: 71
• Gr 11/89: 880

22592. MCD 129: LYAPUNOV—Solemn
overture on a Russian theme; Zelazowa
Wola; Hashish; Polonaise. BALAKIREV—
Islamey (orch. Lyapunov). *USSR State
Symphony Orch.; Svetlanov, cond.*
• ARG 9-10/90: 80
- Fa 5-6/90: 206
☐ Gr 7/89: 166

22593. MCD 131: SHOSTAKOVICH—
Symphony no. 10; Hamlet: Suite. *USSR
Ministry of Culture Symphony Orch.;
Rozhdestvensky, cond.; Leningrad
Chamber Orch.; Serov, cond.*
+ Fa 9-10/90: 387

22594. MCD 134: MYASKOVSKY—Violin
concerto in D minor; Symphony no. 22.
*Feigin, violin; USSR Radio and
Television Symphony Orch.; Dmitriev,
cond.; USSR State Symphony Orch.;
Svetlanov, cond.*
+ Fa 9-10/90: 295

22595. MCD 138: TANEEV—String
quintet, op. 14. BORODIN—String quartet
no. 2. *Taneev Quartet; Morozov, cello;
Borodin Quartet.*
+ Fa 7-8/90: 287

22596. MCD 139: TCHAIKOVSKY—
Symphony no. 5; Francesca da Rimini.
USSR Radio and Television Symphony

Orch.; Fedoseyev, Ovchinnikov, cond.
+ Fa 7-8/90: 291

22597. MCD 140: RIMSKY-KORSAKOV—
Piano trio in C minor. SHCHEDRIN—Echo,
for solo violin. *Moscow Trio; Stadler,
violin.*
+ ARG 7-8/90: 91
+ Fa 5-6/90: 267

22598. MCD 142: TCHAIKOVSKY—
Symphony no. 4; Romeo and Juliet.
*USSR Radio and Television Symphony
Orch.; Fedoseyev, Ovchinnikov, cond.*
• Fa 7-8/90: 288

22599. MCD 144: CHOPIN—Récollection
de Paganini. SCHUMANN—Six études
concertantes sur un thème de Paganini.
LISZT—Six grandes études d'après
Paganini. *Petrov, piano.*
+ Fa 3-4/89: 137

22600. MCD 145: RIMSKY-KORSAKOV—
Mozart and Salieri. MUSSORGSKY—The
marriage. *Fedin, Nesterenko, Bolshoi
Theater Orch., Ermler, cond.;
Kolmakova, Podbolotov, Khrulev,
Ribasenko; USSR Ministry of Culture
Symphony Orch.; Rozhdestvensky, cond.*
+ Fa 9-10/90: 354

22601. MCD 146: BACH—Keyboard
partitas no. 1-3. *Nikolayeva, piano.*
+ Fa 9-10/90: 152

22602. MCD 147: A Russian concert, no.
2. GLAZUNOV—Symphony no. 9. LVOV—
Violin concerto in A minor.
KABALEVSKY—Romeo and Juliet. *USSR
Radio and Television Symphony Orch.;
Yudin, cond.; Stadler, violin; Leningrad
Phil. Orch.; Chernushenko, cond.;
Moscow Phil. Symphony Orch.; Kitaenko,
cond.*
☐ ARG 7-8/90: 60
+ Fa 1-2/89: 347
+ Fa 5-6/90: 175

22603. MCD 150: GRIEG—Piano
concerto; Old Norwegian dance with
variations; Overture, In autumn; Two
lyric pieces. *Harald Bratlie, Jens; Oslo
Phil. Orch.; Jansons, cond.*
• Fa 5-6/90: 180 m.f.
• Gr 9/89: 450

22604. MCD 152: SHOSTAKOVICH—
Symphony no. 11. *USSR Ministry of
Culture Symphony Orch.;
Rozhdestvensky, cond.*
+ ARG 5-6/90: 107
- Fa 5-6/90: 294

22605. MCD 153: TCHAIKOVSKY—
Symphony no. 2; Suite no. 2. *USSR
Radio and Television Symphony Orch.;
Fedoseyev, cond.; USSR Academic
Symphony Orch.; Svetlanov, cond.*
• ARG 9-10/90: 120
• Fa 11-12/90: 375

MELODIYA

22606. MCD 156: SHOSTAKOVICH—Symphony no. 4; Suite for jazz band no. 1. *Soloists Ensemble; USSR Ministry of Culture Symphony Orch.; Rozhdestvensky, cond.*
- ARG 5-6/90: 107
+ Fa 5-6/90: 294

22607. MCD 157: TCHAIKOVSKY—Piano trio in A minor. GLAZUNOV—String quartet no. 1. *Leningrad Phil. Trio; Shostakovich Quartet.*
+ ARG 11-12/90: 129
+ Fa 9-10/90: 410

22608. MCD 159: SCRIABIN—Symphony no. 1. *Gorokhovskaya, mezzo-soprano; Pluzhnikov, tenor; Glinka State Academic Chorus of Leningrad; USSR Radio and Television Symphony Orch.; Fedoseyev, cond.*
- Fa 7-8/90: 267

22609. MCD 160 (3 discs): BELLINI—Norma. *Bieshu, Nam, Grigoryan, Seleznev, with assisting soloists; USSR Ministry of Culture Chamber Choir; Bolshoi Theater Orch.; Ermler, cond.*
+ Fa 9-10/90: 181

22610. MCD 161: SHOSTAKOVICH—Symphonies no. 1, 3. *A.A. Yurlov Choir; USSR Ministry of Culture Symphony Orch.; Rozhdestvensky, cond.*
• ARG 7-8/90: 108
+ Fa 5-6/90: 294

22611. MCD 165: GLAZUNOV—Violin concerto in A minor; Piano concerto no. 2; Saxophone concerto. *Stadler, violin; Leningrad Phil.; Ponkin, cond.; Alexeiev, piano; USSR Radio and Television Symphony Orch.; Nikolayevsky, cond.; Mikhailov, saxophone; Soloists Ensemble of the USSR Radio and Television Symphony Orch.; Korniev, cond.*
• Fa 5-6/90: 172
+ Gr 2/90: 1461 m.f.

22612. MCD 169: HAYDN—Symphonies no. 28, 44, 49. *Moscow Chamber Orch.*
+ Fa 5-6/90: 189

22613. MCD 170: *Music of the first October years.* Music of Popov, Mosolov, Zhivotov, and Myaskovsky. *Lee, soprano; Bolshoi Theater Soloists Ensemble; Lazarev, cond.; Moscow Phil. Symphony Orch.; Dudarova, cond.*
+ ARG 9-10/90: 135
+ Fa 5-6/90: 386

22614. MCD 171: HAYDN—Seven last words of Christ. *Shostakovich Quartet.*
+ Fa 7-8/90: 167

22615. MCD 173: GLAZUNOV—String quartets no. 2, 4. *Shostakovich Quartet.*
+ ARG 7-8/90: 54
+ Fa 5-6/90: 173

22616. MCD 174: PURCELL—Fairy Queen suite. TARTINI—Flute concerto in G major.

ROSSINI—String sonata no. 6. BARTÓK—Romanian folk dances. HINDEMITH—Trauermusik. PETROV—Creation of the world suite. *Leningrad Chamber Orch.; Serov, cond.*
+ ARG 7-8/90: 127

22617. MCD 175: BRAHMS—Viola sonatas no. 1-2; Piano trio, op. 114. *Bashmet, viola; Belrinsky, cello; Muntian, piano. Recorded live 1983-84.*
+ ARG 7-8/90: 34
+ Fa 5-6/90: 135

22618. MCD 178: PROKOFIEV—Violin concertos (complete). *Zhuk, violin; Moscow Phil. Symphony Orch.; Kitaenko, cond.*
+ Fa 5-6/90: 248

22619. MCD 180: TCHAIKOVSKY—Violin concerto; Tempest; Voyevoda. *Tretiakov, violin; USSR Radio and Television Symphony Orch.; Fedoseyev, Ovchinnikov, cond.*
• ARG 11-12/90: 125
• DA 9/90: 58
• Fa 9-10: 407

22620. MCD 181: ALYABYEV—Selections. *Voskresensky, piano; Ambarpumyan, violin; Knyasev, cello; Pluzhnikov, tenor; Mishuk, piano; Venyavsky, violin; Grach, violin; USSR Academic Symphony Orch.; Verbitzky, cond.*
+ Fa 5-6/90: 173

22621. MCD 182: SHOSTAKOVICH—Symphony no. 14; King Lear: Excerpts. *Kasrashubili, soprano; Safiulin, bass; USSR Ministry of Culture Symphony Orch.; Rozhdestvensky, cond.; Romanova, mezzo-soprano; Leningrad Chamber Orch.; Serov, cond.*
+ ARG 5-6/90: 109
• Fa 5-6/90: 294

22622. MCD 184: ALYABYEV—Violin sonata in E minor. GLINKA—String quartet no. 2; Valse-fantaisie; Divertissement on themes from Bellini's La sonnambula. *Voskresensky, piano; Ambarpumyan, violin; Leningrad Phil. String Quartet; Shakin, piano; Yakovlev, double bass; Kamishov, piano.*
+ Fa 5-6/90: 173

22623. MCD 187: TCHAIKOVSKY—Symphony no. 3; Solemn march in D major. *USSR Radio and Television Symphony Orch.; Fedoseyev, Ovchinnikov, cond.*
- ARG 7-8/90: 118
• Fa 7-8/90: 288

22624. MCD 194: *Manuscripts of different years.* SHOSTAKOVICH—Selections. *Leningrad Chamber Orch.; Serov, cond.; various orchestras; Rozhdestvensky, cond.; Eisen, bass; Bogdanova, piano.*
+ ARG 5-6/90: 107

+ Fa 1-2/89: 265
+ Fa 5-6/90: 294

22625. MCD 195 (2 discs): TANEEV—Oresteia. *Shimko, Galushkina, Dubrovin, Bokov, Chernobayev; Byelorussian State Opera and Ballet Theater Chorus & Orch.; Kolomizheva, cond.*
+ ARG 9-10/90: 119
• Fa 7-8/90: 386

22626. MCD 200: SHOSTAKOVICH—Symphonies no. 2, 12. *Academic Republican Chorus; USSR Ministry of Culture Symphony Orch.; Rozhdestvensky, cond.*
- ARG 5-6/90: 107
• Fa 5-6/90: 294

22627. MCD 201: SHOSTAKOVICH—Young guards: Suite; October. PROKOFIEV—Festive poem for the 30th anniversary of October 1917. ESHPAY—Lenin is amongst us. *USSR Ministry of Culture Symphony Orch.; Rozhdestvensky, cond.; Moscow Chamber Orch.; Dudarova, cond.; USSR Cinematographic Orch.; Gamburg, cond.; USSR Radio and Television Symphony Chorus & Orch.; Gusman, cond.*
+ ARG 9-10/90: 134
• Fa 11-12/90: 358

22628. MCD 202: GLIÈRE—Red poppy: Excerpts. KNIPPER—Symphony no. 4. *Bolshoi Theater Orch.; Fayer, cond.; Biktomirov, tenor; Shumilov, baritone; Russian Academic Chamber Chorus; Moscow Phil. Symphony Orch.; Dudarova, cond.*
□ ARG 7-8/90: 51
+ Fa 5-6/90: 175

22629. MCD 204: SHEBALIN—Lenin. SHCHEDRIN—Lenin in the people's heart; Worker's Marseillaise; Be brave, friends, do not despair; Hymn to democratic youth. *Various choruses and orchestras; Gauk, Rozhdestvensky, cond.*
+ ARG 11-12/90: 115
• Fa 9-10/90: 386

22630. MCD 205: GADZHIEV—Symphony no. 4. DAVIDENKO—The street is aroused; At the tenth verst; About Lenin. *Yakushev, bass; Leningrad Phil. Orch.; Mansurov, cond.*
□ ARG 11-12/90: 58
- Fa 5-6/90: 168

22631. MCD 210 (2 discs): TCHAIKOVSKY—Swan Lake. *USSR Radio and Television Symphony Orch.; Fedoseyev, cond.*
+ ARG 11-12/90: 127
+ Fa 9-10/90: 409

22632. MCD 212: HONEGGER—Symphony no. 2; Phèdre; Napoléon: Excerpts. *USSR Ministry of Culture Chamber Choir & Symphony Orch.; Rozhdestvensky, cond.*
+ ARG 5-6/90: 60
+ Fa 7-8/90: 176

22633. MCD 215: Prokofiev—
*Maddalena. Ivanova, Martynov,
Yakovenko; Male Group of the State
Chamber Choir; USSR Ministry of
Culture Symphony Orch.;
Rozhdestvensky, cond.* Orchestration
completed by Edward Downes.
+ Fa 5-6/90: 249
+ Op 4/89: 499

22634. MCD 219 (2 discs): Shchedrin—
*Humpbacked horse; Chamber suite.
Moscow Stanislavsky & Nemirovich-
Danchenko Musical Theater Orch.;
Zhemchuzin, cond.; Bolshoi Theater
Violinists Ensemble; Reyentovich, cond.*
+ ARG 5-6/90: 106
+ Fa 5-6/90: 292

22635. MCD 224: Stravinsky—Agon.
Shostakovich—Symphony no. 15.
Wagner—*Lohengrin: Prelude to Act 3.
Leningrad Phil. Orch.; Mravinsky, cond.*
- ARG 5-6/90: 110
+ Fa 7-8/90: 283

22636. MCD 225: Beethoven—
Symphony no. 4. Salmanov—Symphony
no. 4. *Leningrad Phil. Orch.; Mravinsky,
cond.*
+ Fa 5-6/90: 122

22637. MCD 227: Rimsky-Korsakov—
*Dubinushka; Skazka; Coq d'or: Suite;
Capriccio espagnol. USSR Radio and
Television Symphony Orch.; Fedoseyev,
cond.; USSR Academic Symphony Orch.;
Svetlanov, cond.*
+ ARG 5-6/90: 96
+ Fa 5-6/90: 266

22638. MCD 237: Rachmaninoff—
Symphony no. 2. Balakirev—*In Czechia.
Moscow Phil. Symphony Orch.; Kitaenko,
cond.; USSR Academic Symphony Orch.;
Svetlanov, cond.*
• ARG 9-10/90: 101
+ Fa 7-8/90: 231
+ Gr 9/89: 476

22639. MCD 238: Bruckner—Symphony
no. 8 (Haas edition). *USSR Academic
Symphony Orch.; Svetlanov, cond.*
+ ARG 7-8/90: 38
- Fa 5-6/90: 140
• Gr 1/90: 1322

22640. MCD 239: Haydn—Piano sonatas
no. 14, 21-22, 43, 45. *Timofeeva, piano.*
• ARG 7-8/90: 55
+ Fa 7-8/90: 170
• Gr 5/90: 2011

22641. MCD 242: Elgar—Violin
concerto. Britten—Violin concerto.
*Oistrakh, violin; USSR Radio and
Television Symphony Orch.; Zhuk, cond.;
Gutnikov, violin; Leningrad Phil. Orch.;
Dimitriev, cond.*
+ ARG 11-12/90: 38
• Fa 9-10/90: 240

22642. MCD 245 (3 discs): Brahms—
Symphonies (complete). *USSR Academic
Symphony Orch.; Svetlanov, cond.*
- Fa 5-6/90: 136

22643. MCD 246: Rossini—String
sonatas no. 1-5. *Leningrad Chamber
Orch.; Serov, cond.*
□ ARG 5-6/90: 97
+ Gr 12/89: 1143

22644. MCD 247: Rachmaninoff—
Vespers, op. 37. *Glinka Choir;
Chernushenko, cond.*
+ Fa 5-6/90: 261
+ Gr 12/89: 1186

22645. MCD 258: Shostakovich—
Symphonies no. 2, 15; The bedbug: Suite.
*Academic Republican Chorus; USSR
Ministry of Culture Symphony Orch.;
Rozhdestvensky, cond.*
+ Fa 5-6/90: 294

22646. MCD 259: Shchedrin—Piano
music. *Krainev, piano; Leningrad Phil.
Orch.; Dmitriev, cond.; Shchedrin, piano.*
+ ARG 7-8/90: 107
+ DA 11/90: 64
+ Fa 9-10/09: 386

22647. MA 3005: Liszt—Piano music.
Pletnev, piano.
- Fa 9-10/89: 237

22648. MA 3006: Myaskovsky—String
quartets no. 3, 10, 13. *Taneev Quartet.*
+ ARG 1-2/90: 66

22649. MA 3011: Myaskovsky—Violin
concerto; Symphony no. 22. *Feigin,
violin; USSR Radio and Television
Symphony Orch.; Dmitriev, Svetlanov,
cond.*
+ ARG 11-12/89: 80

22650. MA 3012: Brahms—Piano
concerto no. 1. *Douglas, piano; USSR
State Symphony Orch.; Sinaisky, cond.*
+ Fa 7-8/89: 107

22651. MA 3013 (2 discs): Prokofiev—
The gambler. *Avdeeva, Borisova,
Maslennikov, Korolev; with assisting
soloists; Bolshoi Theater; Lazarev, cond.*
+ Fa 9-10/89: 283
+ ON 11/89: 54

22652. MA 3015: Myaskovsky—
Sinfonietta in A minor; Symphony no.
27. *USSR Academic Symphony Orch.;
Verbitzky, Svetlanov, cond.*
+ ARG 11-12/89: 80

22653. MA 3016: Rimsky-Korsakov—
Symphonies no. 1, 3. *USSR Academic
Symphony Orch.; Svetlanov, cond.*
• Fa 9-10/89: 303

22654. MA 3018: Shostakovich—
Symphony no. 8; Satires; Three songs.
*Bogacheva, mezzo-soprano; USSR
Ministry of Culture Symphony Orch.;*

Rozhdestvensky, cond.
• Fa 7-8/89: 248

22655. MA 3019: Myaskovsky—
Symphonies no. 5, 11. *USSR Radio and
Television Symphony Orch.; Ivanov,
cond.; Moscow Phil. Symphony Orch.;
Dudarova, cond.*
+ ARG 11-12/89: 80

22656. MA 3020: Shostakovich—
Symphonies no. 5, 9. *USSR Ministry of
Culture Symphony Orch.;
Rozhdestvensky, cond.*
+ ARG 7-8/90: 108
+ Fa 1-2/90: 304

22657. MA 3023: Bartók—Music for
strings, percussion and celesta.
Sibelius—Symphony no. 7. Wagner—
*Lohengrin: Act 1 prelude; Tannhaüser:
Overture. Leningrad Phil. Orch.;
Mravinsky, cond.*
• Fa 1-2/90: 415 m.f.

22658. MA 3025: Rachmaninoff—Piano
concertos no. 2, 4; Lilacs; Daisies (arr.
for piano). *Eresko, piano; USSR State
Symphony Orch.; Provatorov, cond.*
• ARG 5-6/90: 93

22659. MA 3027: Rimsky-Korsakov—
Coq d'or: Suite; Tsar Saltan: Suite.
Stravinsky—*Firebird: Suite. USSR Radio
and Television Symphony Orch.; Ivanov,
cond.; USSR Academic Symphony Orch.;
Kitaenko, cond.*
• Fa 1-2/90: 279

22660. 74321-17082-2: Tchaikovsky—
Swan Lake. *Russian State Symphony
Orch.; Svetlanov, cond.*
+ ARG 3-4/96: 194

22661. 74321-17083-2: Tchaikovsky—
Piano concertos no. 1-2. *Richter, piano;
Leningrad Phil. Orch.; Mravinsky, cond.;
Gilels, piano; USSR Symphony Orch.;
Svetlanov, cond.* Recorded 1959, 1972.
+ Gr 9/94: 66

22662. 74321-17087-2: Tchaikovsky—
Piano trio. *I. Oistrakh, violin; Altman,
cello; Zertsalova, piano.* Recorded 1984.
• Gr 10/94: 146

22663. 74321-17088-2: Tchaikovsky—
Swan Lake. *USSR State Symphony Orch.;
Svetlanov, cond.*
+ Fa 9-10/95: 338

22664. 74321-17090-2 (2 discs):
Tchaikovsky—Eugene Onegin. *Belov,
Vishnevskaya, Lemeshev, Adyeva;
Bolshoi Theater; Khaikin, cond.*
Recorded 1959.
+ Gr 12/94: 162

22665. 74321-17091-2 (3 discs):
Tchaikovsky—Queen of Spades.
*Atlantov, Milashkina, Levko, Valaitis;
Bolshoi Theater; Ermler, cond.* Reissue.
• Gr 10/94: 203

MELODIYA

22666. 74321-17098-2: Tchaikovsky—
Manfred symphony; Festival overture.
*USSR State Symphony Orch.; Svetlanov,
cond.* Recorded 1970.
+ Gr 12/94: 97

22667. 74321-17099-2: Tchaikovsky—
Orchestra suites no. 1-2. *USSR Symphony
Orch.; Svetlanov, cond.*
• ARG 9-10/95: 228
+ Fa 9-10/95: 337

22668. 74321-17100-2: Tchaikovsky—
Orchestra suites no. 3-4. *USSR Symphony
Orch.; Svetlanov, cond.*
• ARG 9-10/95: 228
+ Fa 9-10/95: 337

22669. 74321-17101-2 (6 discs):
Tchaikovsky—Symphonies and orchestral
works. *USSR State Symphony Orch.;
Svetlanov, cond.* Reissues.
• Gr 12/94: 97

22670. 74321-18290-2 (2 discs):
Tchaikovsky— String quartets no. 1-3;
Souvenir de Florence. *Borodin Quartet;
Talalian, viola; Rostropovich, cello.*
Resisues.
• Gr 10/94: 146

22671. 74321-18540-2: Celestial litanies.
Various performers.
• ARG 9-10/96: 260

22672. 74321-19839—19848-2 (10
separate discs): Shostakovich—
Symphonies (complete). *Moscow Phil.
Orch.; Kondrashin, cond.* Reissues.
+ Gr 11/94: 84

22673. 74321-19849-2 (3 discs):
Shostakovich—Preludes and fugues op.
87. *Nikolayeva, piano.* Recorded 1987.
+ ARG 1-2/95: 172
+ Fa 9-10/95: 324
+ Gr 2/95: 75

22674. 74321-25172-2 (11 discs):
Russian piano school. The great pianists.
Various Russian pianists. Also issued
separately; see ARG.
+ ARG 9-10/95: 293-297
+ Fa 9-10/95: 402

22675. 74321-25173-2: *The great
pianists.* Music of Tchaikovsky, Arensky,
Borodin, Rachmaninoff, Goldenweiser,
and Medtner. *Goldenweiser, piano.*
Recorded 1946-55.
+ Gr 8/95: 105

22676. 74321-25174-2: *The great
pianists.* Music of Mozart, Debussy, and
Prokofiev. *Neuhaus, piano.* Recorded
1946-56.
+ Gr 8/95: 105

22677. 74321-25175-2: *The great
pianists.* Music of Bach and Mozart.
Feinberg, piano. Recorded 1951-3 and
1962.
+ Gr 8/95: 105

22678. 74321-25176-2: *The great
pianists.* Music of Stravinsky, Bartók,
Hindemith, Berg, and Krenek. *Yudina,
piano.* Recorded 1960-2 and 1964.
+ Gr 8/95: 105

22679. 74321-25177-2: *The great
pianists.* Music of Mozart, Schubert,
Schumann, Chopin, Rachmaninoff,
Scriabin, and Prokofiev. *Sofronitsky,
piano.* Recorded 1946, 1953, and 1960.
+ Gr 8/95: 105

22680. 74321-25178-2: *The great
pianists.* Music of Bach, Haydn,
Beethoven, and Chopin. *Richter, piano.*
Recorded 1948, 1960-1 and 1963.
• Gr 8/95: 105

22681. 74321-25179-2: *The great
pianists.* Music of Bach, Beethoven,
Weber, Liszt, and Prokofiev. *Gilels,
piano.* Recorded 1968.
+ Gr 8/95: 105

22682. 74321-25180-2: *The great
pianists.* Music of Liszt. *Berman, piano.*
Recorded 1959 and 1961.
+ Gr 8/95: 105

22683. 74321-25181-2: *The great
pianists.* Music of Tchaikovsky,
Shchedrin, Prokofiev, and Mozart.
Pletnev, piano. Recorded 1978 and 1984.
• Gr 8/95: 105

22684. 74321-25182-2: *The great
pianists.* Music of Rachmaninoff,
Scriabin, Prokofiev, and Kissin. *Kissin,
piano.* Recorded 1984 and 1986.
+ Gr 8/95: 105

22685. 74321-25189-2 (10 separate
discs): *The Mravinsky edition, vol. 1-10.*
Music of Weber, Schubert, Brahms,
Mozart, Sibelius, Mussorgsky,
Stravinsky, Shostakovich, Bruckner,
Tchaikovsky, Prokofiev, Hindemith,
Honegger, Beethoven, Debussy, Bartók,
and Wagner. *Leningrad Phil. Orch.;
Mravinsky, cond.*
• ARG 11-12/95: 236
+ Fa 9-10/95: 415

22686. 74321-29346-2 (3 discs):
Borodin—Prince Igor. *Petrov,
Tugarinova, Atlantov, Eisen; Bolshoi
Theater, Moscow; Ermler, cond.*
Recorded 1969.
• ARG 1-2/97: 78
- Fa 11-12/96: 198
• Gr 10/96: 105
- Op 9/96: 1114

22687. 74321-29347-2 (2 discs):
Shchedrin—Dead souls. *Voroshilo,
Piavko, Avdeyeva, Morozov; Moscow
Chamber Chorus; Bolshoi Theater;
Temirkanov, cond.*
+ ARG 1-2/97: 169
+ Fa 11-12/96: 374
+ Gr 12/96: 146

22688. 74321-29348-2 (3 discs):
Glinka—Ruslan and Ludmilla.
*Nesterenko, Rudenko, Sinyavskaya,
Fomina, Morozov, Maslennikov; Bolshoi
Theater Chorus & Orch.; Simonov, cond.*
+ ARG 1-2/97: 112
• Fa 11-12/96: 254
+ Gr 2/97: 107
+ Op 9/96: 1114

22689. 74321-29349-2 (3 discs):
Mussorgsky—Boris Godunov. *Petrov,
Shulpin, Reshetin, Ivanovsky, Arkhipova,
Grigoryev; Bolshoi Theater; Melik-
Pashaev, cond.* Reissue; recorded 1962.
+ ARG 11-12/96: 167
+ Fa 11-12/96: 319
+ Gr 12/96: 140
+ Op 9/96: 1114

22690. 74321-29350-2 (3 discs):
Prokofiev—War and peace.
*Vishnevskaya, Arkhipova, Petrov,
Maslennikov; Bolshoi Theater; Melik-
Pashaev, cond.* Recorded 1961.
+ ARG 1-2/97: 151
+ Fa 11-12/96: 337
+ Gr 2/97: 109
+ Op 5/97: 617

22691. 74321-29459-2 (10 discs): *The
Mravinsky edition, vol. 11-20.* Music of
Beethoven, Brahms, Bruckner, Strauss,
Goldstein, Shostakovich, Tchaikovsky,
Glazunov, and Rimsky-Korsakov.
*Buyanovsky, horn; Leningrad Phil.
Orch., Mravinsky, cond.*
• ARG 11-12/96: 293
+ Fa 9-10/96: 444
+ Fi 11/96: 126

22692. 74321-29460-2 (10 discs): *Richter
in Moscow.* Music of Bach, Beethoven,
Schubert, and others. *Richter, piano.*
Reissues; Recorded 1950s.
+ ARG 7-8/96: 251
+ Fi 5/96: 127
+ Gr 6/96: 76

22693. 74321-32041-2: Shostakovich—
Symphony no. 5; Age of gold: Polka;
Michurin suite. *USSR Symphony; M.
Shostakovich, cond.* Reissue.
+ ARG 9-10/96: 201

22694. 74321-32042-2: Prokofiev—
Symphonies no. 1, 5. *Moscow Phil.
Orch.; Kitaenko, cond.* Reissue.
+ ARG 7-8/96: 172
• Gr 12/96: 82

22695. 74321-32043-2: Moonlight over
Moscow. *Various choral ensemble.*
Reissues.
+ ARG 7-8/96: 272

22696. 74321-32044-2: Stravinsky—
Petrushka. Petrov—Creation of the
world. Ravel—Daphnis et Chloé: Suite
no. 2. *Leningrad Phil. Orch.;
Temirkanov, cond.*
+ ARG 9-10/96: 210
+ Gr 2/97: 54

22697. 74321-32045-2: Music of Arutiunian, Gliere, Gershwin, Biber, and others. *Dokshitzer, trumpet; with various orchs.*
+ ARG 7-8/96: 258

22698. 74321-33230-2 (10 discs): The Russian piano school, vol. 11-20. *Various pianists.*
+ Fa 1-2/97: 327
+ Gr 8/96: 77

22699. 74321-37878-2: TCHAIKOVSKY— Symphony no. 4; Serenade for strings. *USSR Symphony Orch.; Svetlanov, cond.* Reissue.
+ ARG 1-2/97: 182
• Fa 1-2/97: 291

22700. 74321-37879-2: TCHAIKOVSKY— Symphony no. 5; Capriccio italien. *USSR Symphony Orch.; Svetlanov, cond.*
• ARG 5-6/97: 221
• Fa 1-2/97: 291

22701. 74321-37880-2: TCHAIKOVSKY— Symphony no. 6; Francesca da Rimini. *USSR Symphony Orch.; Svetlanov, cond.*
• ARG 5-6/97: 221
• Fa 1-2/97: 291

22702. 74321-37881-2: TCHAIKOVSKY— Manfred symphony; Romeo and Juliet fantasy-overture. *USSR Symphony Orch.; Svetlanov, cond.* Reissue.
+ ARG 1-2/97: 182
• Fa 1-2/97: 291

22703. 09026-68246-2 (5 discs): *Russian choral music.* Music of the Passion and Choral music; Russian Easter; Music of Tchaikovsky and Rachmaninoff. *Various Russian choruses.*
+ ARG 11-12/95: 265
+ Fa 11-12/95: 450

MELODRAM

22704. MEL 167 (2 LPs): REFICE— Cecilia. *Pedrini, Misciano, Clabassi; Italian Radio and Television Milan Chorus & Symphony Orch.; De Fabritiis, cond.* Recorded live 1955.
- Fa 1-2/87: 162

22705. MEL 169 (3 LPs): HALÉVY—La juive. *Brunin, Rottier, Poncet, Bert, Wierzbicki; with assisting soloists; Ghent Theater Chorus & Orch.; Ledent, cond.* Recorded live 1964.
- Fa 3-4/87: 124

22706. MEL 170 (3 LPs): CHERUBINI—Ali Baba. *Stich-Randall, Kraus, Ganzarolli, Montarsolo; with assisting soloists; Teatro alla Scala; Sanzogno, cond.* Recorded live 1963.
+ Fa 7-8/87: 86

22707. MEL 171 (3 LPs): DONIZETTI— Parisina. *Pobbe, Cioni, Fioravanti, Ventriglia; Teatro comunale (Bologna);*

Rigacci, cond. Recorded live 1964.
- Fa 1-2/87: 97

22708. MEL 463 (3 LPs): ROSSINI— Operatic arias. *Callas, Albanese, Filippeschi, Ziliani, Salvarezza, Raimondi; Teatro Comunale (Florence); Serafin, cond.* Recorded live 1952.
+ ARG 1-2/87: 54 (Callas)
+ Fa 3-4/87: 194 (Callas)

22709. MEL 465 (2 LPs): VERDI—I due Foscari. *Gencer, Picchi, Guelfi, Maddalena; with assisting soloists; Teatro La Fenice; Serafin, cond.* Recorded live 1957.
+ Fa 1-2/87: 200

22710. MEL 468 (3 LPs): BELLINI— Norma. *Gencer, Simionato, Previdi, Zaccaria; with assisting soloists; Teatro alla Scala; Gavazzeni, cond.* Recorded live 1964.
+ Fa 11-12/86: 117

22711. MEL 470 (3 LPs): DONIZETTI— Lucia di Lammermoor. VERDI—Macbeth: Vieni! t'affretta. MEYERBEER—Dinorah: Ombre leggiera. ROSSINI—Semiramide: Bel raggio. MOZART—Entführung aus dem Serail: Martern aller Arten . *Callas, Fernandi, Panerai, Modesti; with assisting soloists; Italian Radio and Television Rome Chorus & Symphony Orch.; Serafin, cond.* Recorded live 1957.
• Fa 11-12/86: 136 (Lucia)
+ Fa 11-12/86: 136 (arias)

22712. MEL 988: PAISIELLO—Gli astrologi immaginari. *Rinaldi, Udovick, Boyer, Montarsolo; Francesco M. Veracini Chamber Orch.; Piccolo coro dei Madrigalisti senesi; Rigacci, cond.*
+ ARG 9-10/93: 167
• ON 7/94: 42

22713. MEL 15001: BELLINI—I puritani: Excerpts. *Tucci, Pavarotti, Protti, Raimondi; with assisting soloists; Teatro Bellini di Catania Chorus and Orch.; Quadri, cond.* Recorded live 1968.
• ARG 1-2/89: 31
- Fa 11-12/88: 142 (Tucci)
+ Fa 11-12/88: 142 (others)

22714. MEL 15003: DONIZETTI—Lucia di Lammermoor: Excerpts; Mad scene. *Gencer, Prandelli, Carta; with assisting soloists; Teatro Verdi, Trieste; De Fabritiis, cond.; Italian Radio and Television Milan Symphony Orch.; Simonetto, cond.* Recorded live 1957, 1958.
• Fa 7-8/89: 132

22715. MEL 16000: BELLINI—Norma: Act 1, scenes 1 and 2. *Callas, Pirazzini, Corelli, Neri; Rome Opera; Santini, cond.* Recorded live 1958.
+ Fa 7-8/90: 96

22716. MEL 16021: Opera arias by Massenet, Puccini, Boito, Giordano,

Donizetti, Verdi, Mascagni, and Meyerbeer. *Corelli, tenor; Monte Carlo Phil. Orch.; Santi, cond.* Recorded live 1970.
- Fa 5-6/91: 335

22717. MEL 16502: *Maria Callas recital, vol. 1.* Music of Rossini, Massenet, Puccini, Verdi, and Bellini. *Callas, soprano; various orchs. & conds.*
- Fa 11-12/86: 137

22718. MEL 16506: *Cesare Siepi recital.* Music of Lully, Schumann, Brahms, Mozart, Ravel, Boito, Verdi, Rossini, Gomes, Halévy, and Gounod. *Siepi, bass; Taubmann, piano; various orchs. & conds.*
• ARG 5-6/88: 85
+ Fa 5-6/88: 243

22719. MEL 16508: Opera arias by Rossini, Verdi, Boito, Puccini, Beethoven, Wagner, Borodin, and Mussorgsky. *Christoff, bass; with assisting soloists; various orcs. & conds.* Recorded live 1964-65.
• Fa 7-8/88: 299

22720. MEL 16509: Opera arias by Donizetti, Verdi, Puccini, Cilea, Meyerbeer, Massenet, Mozart, Beethoven, Wagner, and Borodin. *Taddei, baritone; various orchs. & conds.*
+ Fa 9-10/88: 319

22721. MEL 16512: Music of Bach, Giordano, Donizetti, Mendelssohn, Mozart, Weber, Strauss, Verdi, Puccini, and J. Strauss, Jr. *Yeend, soprano; Lanza, tenor; Hollywood Bowl Orch.; Ormandy, cond.* Recorded live 1947.
+ Fa 11-12/89: 420

22722. MEL 16523: STRAUSS—Vier letzte Lieder. ROSSINI—Stabat Mater. *Grümmer, Ilsovay, Ludwig, Fehn; Berlin Radio Symphony Orch.; Kraus, Richard; Cologne Radio Symphony Orch.; Fricsay, cond.* Recorded live 1970, 1953.
+ Fa 5-6/91: 329 (Strauss)
- Fa 5-6/91: 329 (Rossini)

22723. MEL 17048: PUCCINI—Tabarro (complete and excerpts). *Crader, Greenspon, Domingo, Ludgin, Sills; with assisting soloists; New York City Opera; Rudel, Patanè cond.* Recorded live 1968, 1967.
+ Fa 9-10/89: 288

22724. MEL 18001: MOZART—Violin sonatas no. 32, 21. BEETHOVEN—Violin sonatas no. 3, 10. *Grumiaux, violin; Haskil, piano.* Recorded live 1957.
• Fa 1-2/87: 68
+ Fa 7-8/88: 211

22725. MEL 18003: MOZART—Requiem; Don Giovanni: Or sai chi l'onore; Non mi dir. *Price, Rössl-Majdan, Wunderlich, Berry; Vienna Singverein; Vienna Phil. Orch.; Karajan, cond.* Recorded live

MELODRAM

1960.
+ ARG 5-6/88: 49
• DA 8/88: 44
• Fa 5-6/88: 173

22726. MEL 18004: BEETHOVEN—
Symphony no. 9. *Janowitz, Bumbry,
Thomas, London; Bayreuth Festival;
Böhm, cond. Recorded live 1963.*
- Fa 7-8/88: 122

22727. MEL 18013: MENDELSSOHN—
Symphony no. 4; Violin concerto in E
minor; Fair Melusine overture; String
quintet, op. 87: Adagio; Hebrides
overture. *Heifetz, violin; NBC Symphony
Orch.; Toscanini, cond. Recorded live
1944-54.*
+ ARG 1-2/89: 66
• Fa 1-2/89: 208

22728. MEL 18014: TCHAIKOVSKY—Piano
concerto no. 1; Symphony no. 6.
*Horowitz, piano; NBC Symphony Orch.;
Toscanini, cond. Recorded live 1943,
1954.*
+ ARG 3-4/89: 97
• Fa 3-4/89: 309 m.f.

22729. MEL 18015: BEETHOVEN—Piano
sonata no. 23. BRAHMS—Piano concerto
no. 2. *Ney, piano; Leipzig Gewandhaus
Orch.; Konwitschny, cond.*
- Fa 3-4/89: 97
□ MA 7/89: 52
+ NYT 5/7/89: H27

22730. MEL 18016: SCHUBERT—
Winterreise. *Fischer-Dieskau, baritone;
Klust, piano. Recorded live 1953 .*
• Fa 1-2/89: 260

22731. MEL 18017: SCHUBERT—Songs.
*Fischer-Dieskau, baritone; Billing,
piano. Recorded live 1948.*
+ ARG 3-4/89: 79
+ Fa 3-4/89: 265

22732. MEL 18020: BEETHOVEN—Violin
concerto, op. 61; Romance for violin and
orchestra no. 1; Egmont: Overture;
Symphony no. 3: Finale. *Oistrakh, violin;
Berlin Radio Symphony Orch.;
Abendroth, cond. Recorded live 1950.*
+ Fa 7-8/89: 85

22733. MEL 18021: Opera excerpts from
Bellini's Norma, Boito's Mefistofele, and
Verdi. *Merriman, Peerce, Valentino,
Moscona; Peter Wilhousky Chorus; NBC
Symphony Orch.; Toscanini, cond.
Recorded live 1940-45.*
+ Fa 9-10/89: 146

22734. MEL 18023: BEETHOVEN—Piano
concerto no. 5; Piano sonata no. 17.
BACH—Italian concerto, BWV 971.
*Gieseking, piano; Berlin Radio Symphony
Orch.; Rother, cond.*
+ Fa 11-12/89: 126

22735. MEL 18024: MOZART—Piano
concerto no. 9. SCHUMANN—Piano

concerto, op. 54. *Hess, piano; Perpignan
Festival Orch.; Casals, cond.; New York
Phil.; Mitropoulos, cond.*
+ ARG 11-12/89: 85
+ Fa 11-12/89: 287 m.f.

22736. MEL 18025: CHOPIN—Piano
concerto no. 2; Preludes, op. 28;
Barcarolle, op. 60. *Károlyi, piano; Berlin
Radio Symphony Orch.; Blech, cond.
Recorded live 1950, 1954, and 1960.*
- ARG 11-12/89: 52
+ Fa 1-2/90: 154

22737. MEL 18027: *In recital at
Philharmonic Hall, Lincoln Center, NY
(1967).* Music of Piccini, Schubert,
Strauss, Sibelius, Nielsen, Stenhammar,
Wiklund, Melartin, Puccini, Marchesi,
and Loewe. *Nilsson, soprano; Wustman,
piano. Recorded live 1967.*
+ ARG 1-2/90: 136
+ Fa 1-2/90: 356

22738. MEL 18028: *In recital at Hunter
College, NY, NY.* Music of Wolf,
Debussy, Milhaud, Rosenthal, Berlioz,
and Poulenc. *Crespin, soprano;
Wustman, piano. Recorded live 1967.*
+ ARG 1-2/90: 132
+ Fa 1-2/90: 357

22739. MEL 18029: BACH—Piano
concerto no. 1, BWV 1052. CHOPIN—
Scherzo no. 4, op. 54. DVOŘÁK—Piano
concerto. *Richter, piano; Czech Phil.
Orch.; Talich, Smetáček, cond. Recorded
1954-64.*
+ ARG 1-2/90: 138
+ Fa 1-2/90: 97
+ Fa 3-4/90: 111 m.f.

22740. MEL 18030: BEETHOVEN—Violin
concerto in D major; Symphony no. 1.
*Francescatti, violin; New York Phil.;
Mitropoulos, cond. Recorded live 1956,
1951.*
• Fa 1-2/90: 114

22741. MEL 18033: Music of Weber, J.
Strauss, Jr., Schubert, Lanner, and
Komzak. *Munich Phil. Orch.;
Knappertsbusch, cond.*
• Fa 9-10/90: 504

22742. CDM 18040: BEETHOVEN—Violin
concerto, op. 61. BRAHMS—Concerto for
violin and cello, op. 102. *A. Busch,
violin; H. Busch, cello; New York Phil.;
F. Busch, cond.; French Radio Symphony
Orch.; Kletzki, cond. Recorded live.*
• ARG 9-10/92: 213
+ Fa 9-10/92: 174

22743. MEL 19011: BRAHMS—Symphony
no. 1; Serenade no. 1: 1st movement.
*NBC Symphony Orch.; Toscanini, cond.
Recorded live 1940, 1948.*
+ Fa 1-2/89: 139

22744. MEL 19507: CHERUBINI—Les
deux journées (excerpts). *Hillebrecht,
Wunderlich; Stuttgart Radio Orch. &*

*Chorus; Müller-Kray, cond. Sung in
German; recorded live 1960.*
+ ARG 7-8/92: 115

22745. MEL 25007 (2 discs): WAGNER—
Tristan und Isolde: Excerpts. *Flagstad,
Ursuleac, Svanholm, Hotter; with
assisting soloists; Teatro Colón (Buenos
Aires); Kleiber, cond. Recorded live
1948.*
+ ARG 1-2/90: 104
+ Fa 11-12/89: 406

22746. MEL 26001 (2 discs): VERDI—
Trovatore; Trovatore: Act 4, scene 1.
*Callas, Elmo, Lauri-Volpi, Silveri, Tajo;
with assisting soloists; Teatro di San
Carlo; Paris Opéra; Serafin, cond.
Recorded live 1951, 1958.*
- Fa 3-4/90: 329 (Trovatore)
+ Fa 3-4/90: 329 (Excerpt)

22747. MEL 26002 (2 discs):
GIORDANO—Andrea Chénier. *Callas, Del
Monaco, Protti; with assisting soloists;
Teatro alla Scala; Votto, cond. Recorded
live 1955.*
• Fa 3-4/89: 167

22748. MEL 26003 (2 discs): BELLINI—
La sonnambula. *Callas, Angioletti, Monti,
Zaccaria; with assisting soloists; Teatro
alla Scala; Votto, cond. Recorded live
1957 in Cologne.*
• ARG 1-2/89: 32
+ Fa 1-2/89: 127
• ON 2/18/89: 43

22749. MEL 26004 (2 discs):
DONIZETTI—Lucia di Lammermoor.
*Callas, Di Stefano, Panerai, Zaccaria;
with assisting soloists; Teatro alla Scala
Chorus; Berlin Radio Symphony Orch.;
Karajan, cond. Recorded live 1955.*
+ ARG 1-2/88: 80
+ Fa 11-12/86: 136
+ Fa 5-6/88: 117

22750. MEL 26008 (2 discs): SPONTINI—
La vestale. *Callas, Stignani, Corelli,
Sordello, Rossi-Lemeni; with assisting
soloists; Teatro alla Scala; Votto, cond.*
• ARG 1-2/89: 90 m.f.
• Fa 9-10/88: 268 m.f
• OQ Spring/89: 138

22751. MEL 26009 (2 discs): VERDI—
Aida. *Callas, Simionato, Baum, Weede,
Moscona; with assisting soloists; Palacio
de Bellas Artes, Mexico City; Picco,
cond. Recorded live 1950.*
- Fa 3-4/89: 318

22752. MEL 26012 (2 discs): GLUCK—
Iphigenia in Tauride. DONIZETTI—Lucia di
Lammermoor: Mad scene. *Callas,
Cossotto, Albanese, Dondi, Colzani; with
assisting soloists; Teatro alla Scala;
Sanzogno, cond.*
- ARG 1-2/88: 80
• Fa 1-2/88: 130

22753. MEL 26015 (2 discs): VERDI—
*Aida. Callas, Dominguez, del Monaco,
Taddei, Silva; with assisting soloists;
Palacio de Bellas Artes, Mexico City; De
Fabritiis, cond.* Recorded live 1951.
+ ARG 7-8/88: 65
● Fa 5-6/88: 230

22754. MEL 26016 (2 discs):
CHERUBINI—*Medea. Callas, Berganza,
Vickers, Zaccaria; with assisting soloists;
Dallas Opera; Rescigno, cond.* Recorded
live 1958. Includes rehearsals of arias by
Bellini and Verdi.
+ Fa 11-12/88: 163
+ ON 10/88: 67 m.f.

22755. MEL 26017 (2 discs): VERDI—*Il
trovatore. Callas, Simionato, Baum,
Warren, Moscona; with assisting soloists;
Palacio de Bellas Artes, Mexico City;
Picco, cond.* Recorded live 1950.
+ ARG 5-6/89: 102
+ Fa 3-4/89: 327

22756. MEL 26018 (2 discs): BELLINI—
*Norma. Callas, Simionato, Baum,
Moscona; with assisting soloists; Palacio
de Bellas Artes, Mexico City; Picco,
cond.* Recorded live 1950.
● Fa 3-4/89: 108

22757. MEL 26019 (2 discs): VERDI—
*Traviata; Aida: O feschi valli. Callas,
Valletti, Taddei, Stignani; with assisting
soloists; Palacio de Bellas Artes, Mexico
City; De Fabritiis, cond.; Rome Opera
Orch.; Bellezza, cond.* Recorded live
1951, 1950.
● Fa 3-4/91: 416

22758. MEL 26020 (2 discs): ROSSINI—
*Barbiere di Siviglia. Callas, Alva, Gobbi,
Luise, Rossi-Lemeni, with assisting
soloists; Teatro alla Scala; Giulini, cond.*
Recorded live 1956.
- ARG 1-2/89: 79
- Fa 1-2/89: 249

22759. MEL 26021 (2 discs): VERDI—
Traviata. DONIZETTI—*Lucia di
Lammermoor: Act 1, scene 2. Callas, di
Stefano, Campolonghi; with assisting
soloists; Palacio de Bellas Artes, Mexico
City; Mugnai, Picco, conds.* Recorded
live 1952.
+ Fa 3-4/89: 325

22760. MEL 26022 (2 discs):
CHERUBINI—*Medea. Callas, Barbieri,
Penno, Modesti; with assisting soloists;
Teatro alla Scala; Bernstein, cond.*
Recorded live 1953.
+ Fa 7-8/89: 122

22761. MEL 26023 (2 discs): VERDI—
Rigoletto. PUCCINI—*Tosca: Excerpts.*
BELLINI—*Puritani: Vieni fra queste
braccia. Callas, Di Stefano,
Campolonghi; with assisting soloists;
Palacio de Bellas Artes, Mexico City;
Mugnai, Picco, cond.* Recorded live
1952.

- ARG 1-2/89: 97
- Fa 1-2/89: 284

22762. MEL 26024 (2 discs): ROSSINI—
*Armida; Semiramide: Bel raggio
lusingher; Cenerentola: Nacqui all'
affano; Armida: D'amore al dolce
impero. Callas, Albanese, Filippeschi,
Ziliani, Raimondi; with assisting soloists;
Maggio musicale fiorentino; Serafin,
cond.* Recorded live 1952.
+ Fa 3-4/89: 250 (Callas)
- Fa 3-4/89: 250 (others)
+ OQ Summer/89: 129 (Callas)
- OQ Summer/89: 129 (others)

22763. MEL 26027 (2 discs): BELLINI—*I
puritani. Callas, Di Stefano,
Campolonghi, Silva; with assisting
soloists; Palacio de Bellas Artes, Mexico
City; Picco, cond.* Recorded live 1952.
- ARG 9-10/89: 28
- Fa 9-10/89: 147

22764. MEL 26028 (2 discs): PUCCINI—
Tosca. Duets from operas by Verdi,
Donizetti, Bellini. *Callas, Di Stefano,
Campolonghi; with assisting soloists;
Mexico City Opera; Picco, cond.*
Recorded live 1952.
+ Fa 11-12/89: 323

22765. CDM 26033 (2 discs): PUCCINI—
*Tosca. Callas, Cioni, Gobbi; Paris
Opéra; Rescigno, cond.* Recorded live
1965.
+ Fa 9-10/93: 239
- ON 2/27/93: 32

22766. CDM 26039 (2 discs): VERDI—
*Un ballo in maschera. Callas, Ratti,
Simionato, Di Stefano; Teatro alla Scala;
Gavazzeni, cond.* Recorded 1957.
+ ARG 5-6/94: 207
+ Fa 3-4/94: 352

22767. MEL 26101 (2 discs): WAGNER—
*Fliegende Holländer. Rysanek, Uhl,
London, Greindl; with assisting soloists;
Bayreuth Festival; Sawallisch, cond.*
Recorded live 1959.
+ ARG 7-8/88: 67
- Fa 9-10/88: 297

22768. MEL 26107 (2 discs): WAGNER—
*Rheingold. Malaniuk, Windgassen, Fritz,
S. Björling; with assisting soloists;
Bayreuth Festival; Karajan, cond.*
Recorded live 1951.
+ Fa 5-6/90: 331

22769. MEL 26507 (2 discs): Music of
Donizetti, Bellini, Verdi, Puccini, Mozart,
and Rossini. *Pavarotti, tenor; with
assisting artists; various orchs. & conds.*
Recorded live 1961-67.
● Fa 7-8/88: 296

22770. MEL 26511 (2 discs): Music of
Mozart, Weber, Smetana, Dvořák,
Schumann, Schubert, Brahms, Verdi,
Puccini, and Strauss. *Welitsch, soprano;
with assisting soloists; various orchs. &*

conds. Recorded live 1948-55.
+ Fa 9-10/89: 390

22771. MEL 26515 (2 discs): Music of
Bellini, Donizetti, Meyerbeer, Verdi,
Mozart, Weber, Rossini, Bach, Handel,
Dalayrac, and Bononcini. *Sutherland,
soprano; with assisting soloists, orchs. &
conds.* Recorded live 1955-64.
+ Fa 9-10/90: 450

22772. MEL 26517 (2 discs): Music of
Verdi, Leoncavallo, and Berlioz.
*Bastianini, baritone; with assisting
soloists; various orchs. & conds.*
Recorded live 1958-1964.
+ ARG 1-2/91: 149
+ Fa 1-2/91: 369

22773. MEL 26519 (2 discs): Music of
Verdi, Leoncavallo, Saint-Saëns, and
Wagner. *Vinay, tenor; with assisting
soloists; various choruses, orchs. &
conds.* Recorded live 1950-1970.
+ Fa 5-6/91: 336

22774. MEL 26522 (2 discs): Music of
Smetana, Mozart, Puccini, and
Beethoven. *Dermota, tenor; with
assisting soloists; various orchs. &
conds.* Recorded live 1942-1970.
● Fa 5-6/91: 336

22775. MEL 27003 (2 discs): MOZART—
*Idomeneo. Janowitz, Pavarotti;
Glyndebourne Festival Chorus; London
Phil. Orch.; Pritchard, cond.* Recorded
live 1967.
+ Fa 11-12/87: 183
● ON 10/87: 65

22776. MEL 27006 (2 discs): VERDI—
*Rigoletto. D'Angelo, Kraus, Protti,
Tadeo; with assisting soloists; Teatro
Comunale Verdi di Trieste; Molinari-
Pradelli, cond.* Recorded live 1961.
- Fa 5-6/88: 231

22777. MEL 27007 (2 discs): PUCCINI—
*Bohème; Bohème: Act 1 excerpts. Freni,
Güden, Raimondi, Panerai, Vinco; with
assisting soloists; Vienna State Opera;
Teatro alla Scala; Karajan, cond.*
Recorded live 1963-64.
● ARG 1-2/88: 53
● Fa 1-2/88: 189
+ ON 2/13/88: 42

22778. MEL 27008 (2 discs): VERDI—*Il
trovatore. Tucci, Simionato, Bergonzi,
Cappuccilli, Vinco; with assisting
soloists; Teatro alla Scala; Gavazzeni,
cond.* Recorded live 1965.
● ARG 7-8/88: 67
- Fa 5-6/88: 232

22779. MEL 27009 (2 discs): CILEA—
*Adriana Lecouvreur. Olivero, Simionato,
Corelli, Bastianini; with assisting
soloists; Teatro San Carlo, Naples;
Rossi, cond.* Recorded live 1959.
+ ARG 5-6/88: 23
+ Fa 7-8/88: 146

MELODRAM

22780. MEL 27011 (2 discs): Bellini—La straniera. *Caballé, Zambon, Casoni, Sardinero; American Opera Society; Guadagno, cond.* Recorded 1969.
+ ARG 11-12/94: 73

22781. MEL 27012 (2 discs): Bizet—Carmen. *Simionato, Güden, Gedda, Le Roux; with assisting soloists; Vienna Singverein; Vienna Symphony Orch.; Karajan, cond.* Recorded live 1954.
+ Fa 5-6/88: 87

22782. MEL 27013 (2 discs): Verdi—Alzira. Bellini—I puritani: O amato zio. Donizetti—Anna Bolena: Excerpts. *Zeani, Cecchele, MacNeil, Cava, Rossi-Lemeni; Rome Opera; Capuana, cond.; Italian Radio and Television Turin Symphony Orch.; Vernizzi, cond.* Recorded live 1958, 1967.
+ Fa 7-8/88: 268 (Zeani)
- Fa 7-8/88: 268 (others)

22783. MEL 27014 (2 discs): Verdi—Aroldo; Ernani: Ernani involami; Forza del destino: Pace, pace mio dio. Puccini—Manon Lescaut: In quelle trine morbide; Tosca: Vissi d'arte. *Stella, Penno, Protti; Maggio musicale fiorentino; Serafin, cond.* Recorded live 1953.
• Fa 7-8/88: 269

22784. MEL 27015 (2 discs): Bellini—Il pirata. *Caballé, Labò, Cappuccilli; with assisting soloists; Maggio musicale fiorentino; Ghiglia, cond.* Recorded live 1967.
• Fa 7-8/88: 126

22785. MEL 27016 (2 discs): Verdi—Ernani; Ernani involami; Aida: O patria mia. *Gencer, Del Monaco, Bastianini, Christoff; with assisting soloists; Maggio Fiorentino Orch.; Mitropoulos, cond.* Recorded live 1957.
+ ARG 1-2/89: 95
+ Fa 11-12/88: 301

22786. MEL 27018 (2 discs): Donizetti—La fille du regiment (sung in Italian). Excerpts from operas by Mozart, Massenet, Gounod, Bellini, and Verdi. *Moffo, Gardino, Campora, Fioravanti; with assisting soloists; Italian Radio and Television Milan Chorus & Symphony Orch.; Mannino, cond.* Donizetti recorded 1960.
+ ARG 1-2/89: 46
- Fa 11-12/88: 171 (Campora)
• Fa 11-12/88: 171 (others)
• HPR 3/89: 74

22787. MEL 27019 (2 discs): Verdi—Aida. *Jones, Dourian, Vickers, Shaw, Rouleau; Royal Opera House Covent Garden; Downes, cond.* Recorded live 1968.
• Fa 11-12/88: 299

22788. MEL 27020 (2 discs): Donizetti—La favorita. *Cossotto,*

Aragall, Colzani, Vinco; with assisting soloists; Teatro regio (Turin); Gracis, cond. Recorded live 1968.
• Fa 11-12/88: 170

22789. MEL 27021 (2 discs): Verdi—Giovanna d'Arco; Trovatore: Ah si ben mio; Puccini—Madama Butterfly: Love duet. *Tebaldi, Bergonzi, Panerai, Carteri; with assisting soloists; Italian Radio and Television Milan Chorus & Symphony Orch.; Simonetto, cond.*
+ ARG 1-2/89: 94
+ Fa 11-12/88: 301

22790. MEL 27023 (2 discs): Wagner—Rienzi. *Christiansen, Svanholm, Schoeffler, Berry; with assisting soloists; Vienna Symphony Orch.; Krips, cond.* Recorded live 1960.
• Fa 1-2/89: 292

22791. MEL 27025 (2 discs): Puccini—Tosca; La bohème: Excerpts. Opera excerpts by Catalani, Handel, and Wagner. *Olivero, Misciano, Fioravanti; with assisting soloists; Italian Radio and Television Turin Chorus & Symphony Orch.; Vernizzi, cond.* Recorded live 1960.
+ Fa 11-12/88: 248 (Tosca)
- Fa 11-12/88: 248 (arias)
• ON 12/10/88: 65

22792. MEL 27027 (2 discs): Massenet—Don Quichotte; Cid: Dance music; Phèdre: Overture; Roi de Lahore: Overture. *Berganza, Christoff, Badioli; with assisting soloists; Italian Radio and Television Milan Symphony Orch.; Italian Radio and Television Turin Symphony Orch.; Simonetto, cond.* Sung in Italian. Recorded live 1957, 1958.
+ ARG 3-4/89: 56
+ Fa 5-6/89: 231

22793. MEL 27028 (2 discs): Borodin—Prince Igor. *Kalmus, Dominguez, Infantino, Taddei, Christoff; with assisting soloists; Italian Radio and Television Rome Chorus & Symphony Orch.; La Rosa Parodi, cond.* Recorded live 1964.
+ ARG 3-4/89: 25 (Christoff)
- ARG 3-4/89: 25 (others)
+ Fa 1-2/89: 134

22794. MEL 27030 (2 discs): Donizetti—Marin Faliero. *Roberti, Mori, Meliciani, Ferrin; with assisting soloists; Teatro Donizetti di Bergamo; Camozzo, cond.* Recorded live 1966.
• Fa 3-4/89: 151
- OQ Summer/89: 121

22795. MEL 27031 (2 discs): Puccini—La bohème; La bohème: Excerpts. *Freni, Adami, Pavarotti, Saccomani; with assisting soloists; Teatro comunale dell'opera (Genoa); Wolf-Ferrari, cond.; Teatro municipale, Reggio Emilia; Molinari-Pradelli, cond.* Recorded live

1969, 1961.
• Fa 11-12/89: 322

22796. MEL 27032 (2 discs): Rossini—Elisabetta, Regina d'Inghilterra. *Vitale, Pagliughi, Campora, Pirino; with assisting soloists; Italian Radio and Television Milan Chorus & Symphony Orch.; Simonetto, cond.* Recorded 1953.
- Fa 7-8/89: 228

22797. MEL 27033 (2 discs): Verdi—Stiffelio; Aroldo: Excerpts. *Gulín, Limarilli, Alberti, Stella; with assisting soloists; Teatro Reggio, Parma; Maag, Peter; Maggio Musicale Fiorentino; Serafin, cond.* Recorded live 1968, 1953.
• ARG 9-10/89: 112
• Fa 1-2/90: 331 (Stiffelio)
+ Fa 1-2/90: 331 (Aroldo)

22798. MEL 27034 (2 discs): Bizet—Carmen. *Dunn, Cooper, Domingo, Guarrera; with assisting soloists; Cincinnati Summer Opera; Guadagno, cond.* Recorded live 1968.
+ ARG 7-8/89: 28
- Fa 9-10/89: 152

22799. MEL 27035 (2 discs): Verdi—Il trovatore. *Caballé, Mattiucci, Tucker, Zanasi, Vinco; Maggio Musicale Fiorentino; Schippers, cond.* Recorded live 1968.
• Fa 3-4/89: 326

22800. MEL 27036 (2 discs): Donizetti—Il duca d'Alba; La favorita: Excerpts. *Tosini, Cioni, Quilico, Ganzarolli, Simionato, Raimondi; with assisting soloists; Spoleto Festival; Schippers, cond.; Teatro di San Carlo; Previtali, cond.* Recorded live 1959, 1963.
+ Fa 3-4/89: 147

22801. MEL 27037 (2 discs): Verdi—Vespri siciliani. *Gencer, Limarilli, Guelfi, Rossi-Lemeni; with assisting soloists; Rome Opera; Gavazzeni, cond.* Recorded live 1964.
• Fa 1-2/90: 331

22802. MEL 27039 (2 discs): Bellini—La straniera; Sonnambula: Ah, non credea. *Scotto, Zilio, Cioni, Trimarchi; with assisting soloists; Teatro Massimo of Palermo; Sanzogno, cond.; Sicilian Symphony Orch.; Ziino, cond.* Recorded live 1968, 1961.
+ ARG 9-10/89: 29
• Fa 9-10/89: 148

22803. MEL 27043 (2 discs): Rossini—L'Assedio di Corinto. *Sills, Horne, Bonisolli, Díaz; with assisting soloists; Teatro alla Scala; Schippers, cond.* Recorded live 1969.
□ Fa 7-8/89: 228

22804. MEL 27044 (2 discs): Strauss—Elektra. Wagner—Siegfried: Heil dir, Sonne. *Varnay, Mödl, Hillebrecht, King,*

Wächter; with assisting soloists; Vienna Phil. Orch.; Bayreuth Festival; Karajan, cond. Recorded live 1964, 1951.
- ARG 7-8/89: 94 (Strauss)
+ ARG 7-8/89: 94 (Wagner)
- Fa 7-8/89: 258 (Strauss)
+ Fa 7-8/89: 258 (Wagner)

22805. MEL 27046 (2 discs): MASSENET—Manon. *Freni, Pavarotti, Panerai, Zerbini; with assisting soloists; Teatro alla Scala; Maag, cond.* Sung in Italian. Recorded live 1969.
+ Fa 9-10/89: 249

22806. MEL 27047 (2 discs): VERDI—Il trovatore; La traviata: Excerpts. *Caballé, Baldani, Domingo, Sordello, Bonisolli; with assisting soloists; New Orleans Opera; Andersson, cond. Dallas Civic Opera Orch.; Rescigno, cond.* Recorded live 1968, 1965.
+ Fa 9-10/89: 353
● Fa 7-8/90: 302

22807. MEL 27050 (2 discs): CORNELIUS—Barbier von Bagdad; Songs. *Jurinac, Rössl-Majdan, Schock, Frick, Lemnitz; Vienna Radio Chorus & Orch.; Hollreiser, cond.* Recorded live 1952, 1943, 1944.
● Fa 11-12/89: 182 (Barbier)
+ Fa 11-12/89: 182 (Lieder)

22808. MEL 27051 (2 discs): DONIZETTI—Belisario; Roberto Devereux: Excerpts. *Gencer, Pecile, Grilli, Taddei, Rota; Teatro La Fenice; Gavazzeni, cond. Teatro San Carlo, Naples; Rossi, cond.* Recorded live 1969, 1964.
● ARG 1-2/90: 43
+ Fa 9-10/89: 186

22809. MEL 27052 (2 discs): WAGNER—Das Liebesverbot. *Zadek, Sorell, Dermota, Equiluz, Imhahl, Welter; Austrian Radio Chorus & Orch.; Heger, cond.* Recorded live 1962.
● ARG 1-2/90: 103
● Fa 11-12/89: 403

22810. MEL 27053 (2 discs): BOIELDIEU—Dame Blanche; Overtures. *Spoorenberg, Gedda, Vroons, Hoekman; Hilversum Radio Symphony Orch.; Fournet, cond.; Orch. Sinfonica di Lipsia; Senoyi, cond.* Recorded live 1964, 1965.
+ ARG 1-2/90: 33 (Gedda)
● ARG 1-2/90: 33 (others)
+ Fa 11-12/89: 151

22811. MEL 27055 (2 discs): SPONTINI—Agnes von Hohenstaufen. *Udovick, Dow, Corelli, Guelfi; with assisting soloists; Maggio musicale fiorentino; Gui, cond.* Recorded live 1954.
● Fa 1-2/90: 311
+ ON 11/89: 55

22812. MEL 27056 (2 discs): MOZART—Zauberflöte; Entführung: Excerpts. *Berger, Lemnitz, Rosvænge, Hüsch; with*

assisting soloists; Berlin Phil. Orch.; Beecham, Thomas; Berlin Radio Orch.; Steiner, cond.
+ ARG 1-2/90: 70
+ Fa 11-12/89: 299

22813. MEL 27058: MASSENET—Werther. *Casoni, Ravaglia, Bergonzi, Trimarchi; San Carlo Opera, Naples; De Fabritiis, cond.* Sung in Italian. Recorded live 1969.
+ ARG 3-4/90: 71
● Fa 11-12/89: 272

22814. MEL 27063 (2 discs): VERDI—Traviata; Traviata: Ah, fors' e lui. *Sills, Kraus, Zanasi, Callas, Di Stefano, Tebaldi, Filacuridi; Teatro di San Carlo; Ceccato, cond.; Maggio musicale fiorentino; Gavazzeni, cond.* Recorded live 1970, 1955-1956.
● Fa 5-6/90: 322

22815. MEL 27064 (2 discs): VERDI—Ernani; Ernani: Excerpts. *Kabaivanska, Domingo, Meliciani, Ghiaurov; with assisting soloists; Teatro alla Scala; Votto, cond.* Recorded live 1969.
● Fa 5-6/90: 317

22816. MEL 27065 (2 discs): MASSENET—Werther. *Olivero, Lazzari, Meletti; with assisting soloists; Italian Radio and Television Turin Chorus & Symphony Orch.; Rossi, cond.* Recorded live 1963.
+ ARG 3-4/90: 71
+ Fa 3-4/90: 228

22817. MEL 27066 (2 discs): STRAUSS—Ägyptische Helena. *Rysanek, Kupper, Aldenhoff, Uhde; with assisting soloists; Bavarian State Opera; Keilberth, cond.* Recorded live 1956.
+ ARG 3-4/90: 112
+ Fa 3-4/90: 308

22818. MEL 27068 (2 discs): VERDI—Trovatore; Forza del destino: Pace, pace; Ernani: Ernani, involami. *Stella, Cossotto, Corelli, Bastianini, Vinco; with assisting soloists; Teatro alla Scala; Gavazzeni, cond.; Italian Radio and Television Rome Symphony Orch.; Scaglia, cond.* Recorded live 1962, 1959.
- Fa 5-6/90: 324

22819. MEL 27070 (2 discs): TCHAIKOVSKY—Mazeppa. *Olivero, Radev, Poleri, Bastianini, Christoff; with assisting soloists; Maggio musicale fiorentino; Perlea, cond.* Recorded live 1954.
- ARG 3-4/90: 114
+ Fa 5-6/90: 309

22820. MEL 27071 (2 discs): STRAUSS—Schweigsame Frau. *Güden, Wunderlich, Prey, Hotter; with assisting soloists; Vienna Phil. Orch.; Böhm, cond.* Recorded live 1959.
+ ARG 9-10/90: 116
+ Fa 5-6/90: 304

22821. MEL 27074 (2 discs): ROSSINI—Donna del lago. *Caballé, Hamari, Bonisolli, Bottazzo, Washington; with assisting soloists; Italian Radio and Television Turin Symphony Orch.; Bellugi, cond.* Recorded live 1970.
+ ARG 9-10/90: 107
+ Fa 7-8/90: 240

22822. MEL 27076 (2 discs): BEETHOVEN—Fidelio. *Jurinac, Morrison, Vickers, Hotter, Frick; with assisting soloists; Royal Opera House Covent Garden; Klemperer, cond.* Recorded live 1961.
+ ARG 11-12/90: 27
● Fa 11-12/90: 161

22823. CDM 27081 (2 discs): PUCCINI—Fanciulla del West. *Kirsten, Corelli, Colzani; with assisting soloists; Philadelphia Lyric Opera; Guadagno, cond.* Recorded live 1964.
+ Fa 3-4/91: 329

22824. CDM 27082 (2 discs): MASSENET—Manon. *Angeles, Tagliavini, Poli, Clabassi; with assisting soloists; Rome Opera; Annovazzi, cond.* Recorded live 1957. Sung in Italian.
- Fa 5-6/91: 216

22825. CDM 27086 (2 discs): BEETHOVEN—Fidelio; Ah, perfido. *Rysanek, Blegen, Vickers, Berry, Tozzi, Ludwig; with assisting soloists; San Francisco Opera; Böhm, cond.; Louisville Orch.; Whitney, cond.* Recorded live 1968, 1965.
+ ARG 9-10/91: 43
- Fa 5-6/91: 121 (Fidelio)
+ Fa 5-6/91: 121 (Ah, perfido)

22826. CDM 27087 (2 discs): CHERUBINI—Medea; Medea: six excerpts. *Rysanek, Popp, Lilowa, Prevedi, Ghiuselev; Vienna State Opera; Stein, cond.; Borkh, Wagner, Suthaus; Staatskapelle Berlin; Gui, cond.* Recorded live. Complete opera sung in Italian; excerpts sung in German.
+ ARG 11-12/92: 102
+ Fa 9-10/92: 213

22827. MEL 27090 (2 discs): OFFENBACH—Tales of Hoffmann. *Kónya, Bacquier, Mesplé, Harper; Teatro Colon; Maag, cond.* Recorded live 1970.
● ARG 3-4/92: 115
+ ON 2/15/92: 36

22828. MEL 27099 (2 discs): MERCADANTE—Elisa e Claudio. *Zeani, Lazzari; Naples Opera; Rapalo, cond.* Recorded live.
+ ARG 7-8/92: 176

22829. CDM 27504 (2 discs): MAHLER—Symphony no. 2. BEETHOVEN—Piano concerto no. 3. *Selig, soprano; Zareska, alto; Chorus; Arrau, piano; French National Orch.; Schuricht, cond.*

MELODRAM

Recorded live 1958, 1959.
- Fa 9-10/90: 285

22830. CDM 27505 (2 discs): MOZART—
Zauberflöte. *Köth, Della Casa, Simoneau,
Berry, Hotter, Böhme; with assisting
soloists; Vienna Phil. Orch.; Szell, cond.
Recorded live 1959.*
+ ARG 11-12/90: 87
+ Fa 11-12/90: 290 m.f.

22831. MEL 28012 (2 discs): VERDI—
Requiem. ROSSINI—Stabat Mater. *Price,
Cossotto, Pavarotti, Ghiaurov; other
soloists; Teatro alla Scala; Karajan,
cond.; Italian Radio and Television Rome
Chorus & Symphony Orch.; Giulini,
cond. Recorded live 1967.*
• ARG 1-2/89: 96 (Verdi)
+ ARG 1-2/89: 96 (Rossini)
+ Fa 11-12/88: 304 (Verdi)
• Fa 11-12/88: 304 (Rossini)

22832. MEL 28022 (2 discs): VERDI—
Messa da requiem; Te Deum; Rigoletto:
Act 3. *Milanov, Thorborg, Rosvænge,
Moscona, Ribla, Merriman, Peerce,
Valentino; BBC Choral Society; BBC
Symphony Orch.; Westminster Choir;
NBC Symphony Orch.; Toscanini, cond.
Recorded 1938, 1945, 1943.*
+ Fa 11-12/89: 391

22833. MEL 28026 (2 discs): HANDEL—
Judas Maccabaeus; Messiah: Every
valley; Serses: Excerpts; Giulio Cesare:
Excerpts; Alcina: Excerpts. *Giebel, Pöld,
Wunderlich, Welter; Bavarian Radio
Chorus & Symphony Orch.; Kubelik,
cond.; various orchs. & conds. All
selections sung in German except Alcina.
Recorded live 1962 (Judas).*
+ Fa 1-2/90: 195

22834. MEL 28031 (2 discs):
BEETHOVEN—Symphonies no. 2, 7; Piano
concerto no. 3; Coriolan: Overture;
Consecration of the house: Overture;
String quartet no. 16: Lento and Scherzo;
Fantasy for piano, chorus and orchestra,
op. 80. *Hess, Dorfmann, piano;
Westminster Choir; NBC Symphony
Orch.; Toscanini, cond. Recorded live
1939-47.*
+ ARG 3-4/90: 20
- Fa 5-6/90: 121 m.f.

22835. CDM 28033 (2 discs): RAVEL—
Schéhérazade; Alborada del gracioso.
BERLIOZ—Te Deum; Lélio. DVOŘÁK—
Serenade for strings in E major. *Crespin,
soprano; Luchetti, tenor; Sereni,
baritone; Italian Radio and Television
Rome Chorus & Symphony Orch.;
Alessandro Scarlatti Orch. di Napoli;
Schippers, cond. Recorded live.*
- Fa 7-8/91: 261 (Alborada)
+ Fa 7-8/91: 261 (others)

22836. CDM 28034 (2 discs):
BEETHOVEN—Piano concertos no. 4-5; Ah,
perfido; Violin concerto. *Gilels, piano;
Crespin, soprano; D. Oistrakh, violin;*

*Alessandro Scarlatti Orch. di Napoli;
Pradella, Alpert, cond.; Italian Radio and
Television Milan Symphony Orch.;
Martinotti, cond.; Italian Radio and
Television Rome Symphony Orch.;
Schippers, cond. Recorded live.*
- Fa 5-6/91: 120

22837. MEL 28051: Music of Verdi,
Donizetti, Boito, Rossini, Massenet,
Meyerbeer, and others. *Caballé, soprano;
Corelli, tenor; with orch. accomp.
Recorded 1967-71.*
+ ARG 7-8/93:
+ ON 12/10/94: 52

22838. MEL 29001 (2 discs): J. STRAUSS,
JR.—Die Fledermaus. *Schlemm, Streich,
Anders, Krebs; Berlin Radio Chorus &
Symphony Orch.; Fricsay, cond.
Recorded live 1949.*
+ Fa 11-12/89: 367

22839. MEL 29500 (2 discs):
CIMAROSA—Gli Orazi e i Curiazi.
*Simionato, Vercelli, Spataro; with
assisting soloists; Italian Radio and
Television Milan Chorus & Symphony
Orch.; Giulini, cond. Recorded live 1952.*
+ ARG 3-4/91: 57
- Fa 3-4/91: 188 m.f.

22840. CDM 29501: CHERUBINI—
Pigmalione. *Ligabue, Adani, Carturan,
Borghi; with assisting soloists; Italian
Radio and Television Milan Chorus &
Symphony Orch.; Giulini, cond. Recorded
live 1955.*
- Fa 3-4/91: 186 m.f.

22841. CDM 29502 (2 discs):
PAISIELLO—La molinara. RICCI—Crispino
e la comare: Excerpts. *Sciutti, Misciano,
Bruscantini, Gazzera, Calabrese;
Alessandro Scarlatti Orch. di Napoli;
Caracciolo, cond.; Italian Radio and
Television Milan Symphony Orch.;
Simonetto, cond. Recorded live 1959,
1951.*
• Fa 7-8/91: 244

22842. MEL 29505 (2 discs):
CIMAROSA—Giannina e Bernardone.
*Jurinac, Sciutti, Carlin, Bruscantini; RAI
Milan; Sanzogno, cond.*
+ ARG 5-6/93: 77
+ ON 4/10/93: 43

22843. MEL 36020 (3 discs): VERDI—I
vespri siciliani; Opera excerpts. *Callas,
Kokolios, Mascherini, Christoff; Maggio
musicale fiorentino; Kleiber, cond.
Vespri recorded live 1951.*
+ ARG 3-4/89: 101
+ Fa 3-4/89: 328

22844. CDM 36032 (3 discs): PUCCINI—
Tosca (two performances). PROCH—
Variations for soprano, flute and
orchestra. *Callas, Fillipeschi, Weede;
Palacio de Bellas Artes, Mexico City;
Callas, Poggi, Silveri; Teatro Municipal
de Rio de Janeiro; Mugnai, cond.; RAI*

*Symphony Orch. of Turin; Wolf-Ferrari,
cond. Recorded live 1950, 1951.*
+ Fa 9-10/93: 239

22845. MEL 36067 (3 discs): WAGNER—
Lohengrin. *Varnay, Thomas, Neidlinger,
Crass, Krause; Phil. Chorus of Prague;
Teatro alla Scala Orch.; Sawallisch,
cond. Recorded live 1965.*
• ARG 5-6/90: 129
• Fa 7-8/90: 311

22846. MEL 36102 (3 discs): WAGNER—
Walküre. *Varnay, Mödl, Lorenz, Hotter,
Greindl; with assisting soloists; Bayreuth
Festival; Keilberth, cond. Recorded live
1954.*
• ARG 9-10/95
+ Fa 9-10/88: 300 (Hotter)
- Fa 9-10/88: 300 (remainder)

22847. MEL 36104 (3 discs): WAGNER—
Lohengrin. *Nilsson, Varnay, Windgassen,
Uhde, Adam, Fischer-Dieskau; Bayreuth
Festival; Keilberth, cond. Recorded live
1954.*
+ ARG 1-2/89: 101

22848. MEL 36105 (3 discs): WAGNER—
Tannhäuser. *Brouwenstijn, Wilfert, Vinay,
Fischer-Dieskau, Greindl; with assisting
soloists; Bayreuth Festival; Keilberth,
cond. Recorded live 1954.*
- ARG 1-2/89: 103
• Fa 1-2/89: 292

22849. MEL 37010 (3 discs): VERDI—La
forza del destino. *Gencer, Carturan, Di
Stefano, Protti, Siepi; with assisting
soloists; Teatro alla Scala; Votto, cond.
Recorded live at Cologne in 1957.*
+ ARG 5-6/89: 100
+ Fa 3-4/89: 320 (Gencer)
- Fa 3-4/89: 320 (others)

22850. MEL 37017 (3 discs):
DONIZETTI—Pia de' Tolomei; Maria di
Rohan. *Meneguzzer, Bottion, Alberti,
Ventriglia; with assisting soloists; Teatro
comunale (Bologna); Rigacci, cond.;
Teatro di San Carlo; Previtali, cond.
Recorded live 1967, 1962.*
• Fa 11-12/88: 172
• HPR 3/89: 75

22851. MEL 37022 (3 discs): VERDI—
Don Carlo; Opera arias. *Gencer, Prevedi,
Bruscantini, Ghiaurov, Roni; with
assisting soloists; Rome Opera; Previtali,
cond. Recorded live 1968.*
• ARG 1-2/89: 94
+ Fa 11-12/88: 299 (Gencer,
Bruscantini)
• Fa 11-12/88: 299 (others)

22852. MEL 37024 (3 discs):
MEYERBEER—Roberto il diavolo; Opera
excerpts. *Scotto, Malagù, Merighi,
Christoff; with assisting soloists; Maggio
musicale fiorentino; Italian Radio and
Television Turin Symphony Orch.;
Sanzogno, cond. Recorded live 1968,
1958.*

- ARG 1-2/89: 67
- Fa 11-12/88: 226

22853. MEL 37026 (3 discs): MEYERBEER—Les huguenots. Opera excerpts of Donizetti, Bellini, and Verdi. *Sutherland, Simionato, Cossotto, Corelli, Ganzarolli, Ghiaurov, Tozzi, Teatro alla Scala; Gavazzeni, cond.; various orchs. & conds.* Meyerbeer recorded live 1962.
+ Fa 1-2/89: 209

22854. MEL 37029 (3 discs): WAGNER—Tristan und Isolde. *Flagstad, Klose, Melchior, Schoeffler, Nilsson; with assisting soloists; Royal Opera House Covent Garden; Beecham, cond.* Recorded live 1937.
+ Fa 1-2/89: 293

22855. MEL 37038 (3 discs): VERDI—Don Carlo (four-act version). *Orlandi-Malaspina, Cossotto, Prevedi, Cappuccilli, Ghiaurov, Talvela; with assisting soloists; Teatro alla Scala; Abbado, cond.* Recorded live 1968.
- Fa 5-6/89: 342

22856. MEL 37040: MOZART—Zauberflöte; Symphony no. 40. *Novotná, Rosvænge, Domgraf-Fassbaender, Jerger, Kipnis; with assisting soloists; Vienna Phil. Orch.; NBC Symphony Orch.; Toscanini, cond.* Recorded live 1937, 1953.
□ ARG 5-6/89: 70
+ Fa 5-6/89: 246

22857. MEL 37059 (3 discs): HANDEL—Giulio Cesare; Xerxes: Excerpts. *Popp, Ludwig, Wunderlich, Berry; with assisting soloists; Bavarian Radio Chorus; Munich Phil. Orch.; Leitner, cond.* Recorded live 1966.
- ARG 3-4/90: 55
+ Fa 11-12/89: 227

22858. MEL 37060 (3 discs): BERLIOZ—Les troyens. *Horne, Verrett, Gedda, Massard; with assisting soloists; Italian Radio and Television Rome Chorus & Symphony Orch.; Prêtre, cond.* Recorded live 1969.
+ ARG 1-2/90: 30
+ Fa 1-2/90: 127

22859. MEL 37061 (3 discs): STRAUSS—Liebe der Danae; Liebe der Danae: Excerpts. *Kupper, Gostič, Traxel, Schoeffler, Rysanek; with assisting soloists; Vienna State Opera Chorus; Vienna Phil. Orch.; Krauss, cond.; Bavarian Opera Orch.; Kempe, cond.* Recorded live 1952, 1953.
+ ARG 1-2/90: 93
- Fa 1-2/90: 317

22860. MEL 37072 (3 discs): WAGNER—Tristan und Isolde. *Ligendza, Anderson, Heater, Švorc, Smith; with assisting soloists; Teatro Giuseppe Verdi; Toffolo, cond.* Recorded live 1969.
- Fa 7-8/90: 314

22861. MEL 37073 (3 discs): WAGNER—Tannhäuser. *Rysanek, Nilsson, Lustig, Cordes, Frick; with assisting soloists; Teatro di San Carlo; Böhm, cond.* Recorded live 1956.
- ARG 9-10/90: 130
- Fa 7-8/90: 313

22862. MEL 37075 (3 discs): MOZART—Nozze di Figaro. *Schwarzkopf, Seefried, Jurinac, Panerai; with assisting soloists; Teatro alla Scala; Karajan, cond.* Recorded live 1954.
- Fa 1-2/91: 253

22863. MEL 37077 (2 discs): STRAUSS—Arabella. *Reining, Della Casa, Taubmann, Hotter; Vienna State Opera; Böhm, cond.* Recorded live 1947.
- Fa 7-8/92: 291

22864. CDM 37506: MOZART—Don Giovanni. *Rethberg, Helletsgruber, Borgioli, Pinza, Lazzari; with assisting soloists; Vienna Phil. Orch.; Walter, cond.* Recorded live 1937.
- ARG 9-10/90: 92 m.f.
+ Fa 9-10/90: 306

22865. MEL 46103 (4 discs): WAGNER—Die Meistersinger von Nürnberg. *Grümmer, Windgassen, Greindl, Schmitt-Walter, Adam; with assisting soloists; Bayreuth Festival; Knappertsbusch, cond.* Recorded live 1960.
+ ARG 5-6/89: 104
- Fa 1-2/89: 291

22866. MEL 46106 (4 discs): WAGNER—Siegfried; Götterdämmerung: Excerpts. *Varnay, Siewert, Aldenhoff, Kuen, Björling, Dalberg; with assisting soloists; Bayreuth Festival Orch.; Karajan, Knappertsbusch, conds.* Recorded live 1951, 1957.
- ARG 5-6/90: 131
+ Fa 5-6/90: 331

22867. MEL 47041 (4 discs): WAGNER—Die Meistersinger von Nürnberg; Tannhäuser: Overture and Bacchanale. *Reining, Thorborg, Noort, Nissen; with assisting soloists; Vienna State Opera Chorus; Vienna Phil. Orch.; NBC Symphony Orch.; Toscanini, cond.* Recorded live 1947, 1954.
+ ARG 9-10/89: 114

22868. MEL 47083 (4 discs): WAGNER—Die Meistersinger von Nürnberg. *Seefried, Anday, Dickie, Schoeffler, Kunz, Frick; with assisting soloists; Vienna State Opera; Reiner, cond.* Recorded live 1955.
- Fa 5-6/91: 317

22869. MEL 270101 (2 discs): VERDI—Otello. *Tebaldi, Del Monaco, Warren, Zampieri; Teatro La Scala; Votto, cond.* Recorded 1954.
+ ARG 9-10/93: 214

22870. MEL 370102 (3 discs): VERDI—La forza del destino. *Tebaldi, Corelli, Bastianini, Christoff; Teatro San Carlo; Molinari-Pradelli, cond.*
- ARG 9-10/93: 213
- ON 10/94: 50

22871. MEL 370104 (3 discs): VERDI—Don Carlo. *Cerquetti, Barbieri, LoForese, Bastianini, Siepi; Florence May Festival; Votto, cond.* Recorded 1956.
+ ARG 11-12/93: 274

22872. MEL 270105 (2 discs): STRAUSS—Ariadne auf Naxos. *Rysanek, King, Scovotti, Troyanos; Vienna State Opera; Böhm, cond.* Recorded 1967.
- ARG 11-12/93: 203

22873. MEL 270109 (2 discs): DONIZETTI—Lucrezia Borgia. *Gencer, Troyanos, Carreras, Manuguerra; Dallas Civic Opera; Rescigno, cond.* Recorded 1973.
+ ARG 5-6/94: 87

22874. MEL 270110 (2 discs): AUBER—Le domino noir; Fra diavolo: highlights. *Micheau, Berton, Peyron; Radio France; Gressier, cond.; Noni; Truccato-Pace; RAI Milan; Simonetto, cond.* Recorded 1950, 1952.
+ ARG 5-6/94: 202

MEMOIR

22875. CDMOIR 410: Great voices of the century sing Mozart opera, vol. 2. *Various soloists, orchestras, & conds.*
+ Fa 7-8/93: 190

22876. CDMOIR 411: Sacred songs and arias. *Various vocalists.* Historical reissues.
+ ARG 5-6/92: 178
+ Gr 1/93: 71

22877. CDMOIR 413: SULLIVAN—The very best of Gilbert & Sullivan. *D'Oyly Carte Opera Company.* Recorded 1927-36.
+ ARG 11-12/92: 124

22878. CDMOIR 414: Caruso duets. *Caruso, tenor; with various vocalists.*
+ ARG 3-4/93: 201

22879. CDMOIR 416: *The glory of Spain.* Music of Fuentes, Friere, Chapi, Serrano, Longas, Padilla, Alvarez, Luna, Valverde, LaRosa, Caballero, Gaztambide, Martin y Guerrero, Carreno, Jorda, Yradier, Posadas, Granados, and Falla. *Various singers and acc.*
+ Fa 3-4/93: 346
+ ON 3/27/93: 35

22880. CDMOIR 417: *Great voices of the century: Beniamino Gigli.* Music of Puccini, Giordano, Mascagni, Boito, Verdi, Donizetti, Bizet, Meyerbeer, Flotow, Toselli, Bixio, De Curtis, Denza,

MEMOIR

Di Chiara, and Cottrau. *Gigli, tenor; various orchs. & conds.*
- • Fa 5-6/93: 368
- + Gr 6/93: 110

22881. CDMOIR 418: Music of Donizetti, Handel, Mozart, Bizet, Verdi, Rachmaninoff, Wolf, Foster, Macmurrough, Clay, Crouch, Sanders, Ball, Dufferin, Haynes and Marshall. *McCormack, tenor; Schneider, Moore, Clay, pianos; various orchs. & conds.*
- + Fa 5-6/93: 364

22882. CDMOIR 419: Vienna nights. *Various performers.*
- + ARG 9-10/93: 270
- + ON 9/94: 61

22883. CDMOIR 420: Jewels of Italian song. *Various performers.* Historical reissues.
- + ARG 1-2/94: 205
- + ON 3/5/94: 37

22884. CDMOIR 421: *Richard Tauber: only a rose.* Music of Romberg, Silesu, Friml, Geehl, Straus, J. Strauss, Novello, Schertzinger, Kern, Herbert, Coates, Tauber, Sieczynski, and Lehár. *Tauber, tenor; orch. acc.*
- + ARG 1-2/94: 204
- + Fa 11-12/93: 463

22885. CDMOIR 422: *Great voices of the century sing Tchaikovsky.* TCHAIKOVSKY—Music from Queen of spades, Maid of Orleans, Iolanta, Eugene Onegin; and separate songs. *Various artists.*
- + Fa 5-6/94: 267
- + Gr 6/94: 135

22886. CDMOIR 424: One night of love. Music of Schertzinger, Oakland, Kreisler, Kern, and others. *Moore, soprano.*
- + ARG 3-4/95: 278
- + ON 10/96: 42

22887. CDMOIR 425: Three tenors, vol. 2. *Björling, Gigli, Tauber, tenors.*
- • ARG 1-2/95: 247
- + Gr 12/94: 190

22888. CDMOIR 426: *Great voices of the century: Paul Robeson, vol. 2.* Music of Lewis, Parker, Burleigh, Dunayevski, Trinkaus, DeRose, Spoliansky, Jacobs-Bond, Robinson, Franklin, Wayne, Johnson, Brown, Ellington, Kennedy-Fraser, Schindler, Ansell, Redmond, and Samuels. *Robeson, bass; various orch. and piano acc.* Recorded mostly in the 1930s.
- + Fa 5-6/95: 388

22889. CDMOIR 428: VERDI—Duets from Aida, Trovatore, Ernani, and Forza del destino. *Ponselle, soprano; Martinelli, tenor.* Recorded 1915-28.
- + ARG 7-8/95: 279
- + Fa 9-10/95: 351
- + Gr 7/95: 134

22890. CDMOIR 429: *Charles Kullman serenade.* Music of Marvell, Herbert, Toselli, Di Capua, Grieg, Baddeley, Böhm, Gounod, Bizet, Schubert, Fibich, Mahler, Ravini, Handel, Drdla, Ross, Kunneke, Penn, Sullivan, and Russell. *Kullman, tenor; various orch. acc.*
- + ARG 5-6/96: 277
- • Fa 1-2/96: 363
- + Gr 2/96: 116

22891. CDMOIR 430: *Classic love duets.* Music of Offenbach, Massenet, Meyerbeer, Bellini, Verdi, Puccini, Leoncavallo, Mascagni, and Giordano. *Various vocalists and accs.* Recorded 1927-42.
- + ARG 1-2/96: 248
- + Fa 1-2/96: 366

22892. CDMOIR 431: For you alone. *Crooks, tenor.* Recorded mostly 1930s.
- + ARG 5-6/96: 274

22893. CDMOIR 432: *Great voices of the century: Marian Anderson.* Music of Handel, Giordano, Martini, Schubert, Brahms, Schumann, Sibelius, Saint-Saëns, Verdi, and Anon. *Anderson, contralto; various accs.*
- + Fa 9-10/96: 376
- + ON 8/96: 44

MEMORIA

22894. 991-001: PROKOFIEV Piano sonatas no. 6, 9; Cinderella: pieces for piano. *Richter, piano.* Recorded live 1980-81.
- + Fa 3-4/90: 262
- + Fa 1-2/94: 264

22895. 991-002: PROKOFIEV—Piano music. *Richter, piano.* Recorded live 1981.
- + Fa 1-2/94: 264

22896. 991-006 (2 discs): BRAHMS—Symphonies no. 1-4. *Leningrad Phil. Orch.; Mravinsky, cond.* Recorded 1950-78.
- + Fa 1-2/94: 140
- • Gr 3/94: 44

22897. 991-007: *Glenn Gould in Salzburg.* Music of Sweelinck, Schoenberg, Mozart, and Bach. *Gould, piano.* Recorded live 1959.
- + Fa 1-2/94: 408

22898. 991-009: MOZART—Piano sonatas no. 10, 11, 14; Fantasia, K. 475; Rondo, K. 511. *Backhaus, piano.* Recorded live 1956.
- • Fa 1-2/94: 248

22899. 999-001: *The authorized Vatican recordings.* Music of Beethoven, Schumann, Liszt, Debussy, Ravel, and Chopin. *Michelangeli, piano; Orch. of the RAI, Rome; Freccia, Gavazzeni, conds.* Reissue.
- • Gr 10/95: 102

MEMORIES

22900. DR 3101/03 (3 discs): PICCINNI—La cecchina, ossia, La buona figliuola. *Peters, Morino, Praticò; Orch. Serenissima Pro Arte; Campanella, cond.* Live recording.
- • ARG 11-12/91: 134
- • Fa 11-12/91: 438

22901. DR 3105/05 (2 discs): DONIZETTI—Elisir d'amore. *Scarabelli, Bruscantini, Merritt, Romero; Coro del Teatro Regio di Parma; Orch. Sinfonica dell'Emilia-Romagna "Arturo Toscanini"; Soudant, cond.* Live recording. Reissue.
- • Fa 11-12/91: 312

22902. HR 3107/08 (2 discs): CIMAROSA—Il matrimonio segreto. *Baiano, Cosotti, De Simone, Dara; Orch. Filarmonica Marchigiana; Cavallaro, cond.* Recorded live 1990.
- • Fa 7-8/92: 138

22903. DR 3109: VINCI—Opera arias. *M. Peters, soprano; Solisti dell'Orch. Internazionale d'Italia; Carraro, cond.* Recorded live 1990.
- • ARG 1-2/92: 134
- - Fa 1-2/92: 364

22904. HR 4131: DONIZETTI—Messa da requiem. *Vocal soloists; Symphony & Chorus of RAI Milan; Molinari-Pradelli, cond.* Recorded live 1961.
- + Fa 5-6/92: 148

22905. HR 4154/55 (2 discs): A. SCARLATTI—Griselda. *Freni, Alva, Luchetti, Bruscantini, Panerai, Lavani; Alessandro Scarlatti Chorus; Italian Radio and Television Naples Orch.; Sanzogno, cond.* Recorded live 1970.
- • Fa 9-10/90: 367

22906. HR 4156/57 (2 discs): MOZART—Mitridate. *Zara, Gabry, Cotrubas, Fassbaender, Didusch, Kolk, Baillie; Salzburg Mozarteum Orch.; Hager, cond.* Recorded live 1970.
- • Fa 9-10/90: 309

22907. HR 4159: STRAUSS—Death and transfiguration. PFITZNER—Symphony in C. STRAVINSKY—Firebird: Suite. *Berlin Radio Symphony Orch.; Vienna Phil. Orch.; Berlin Phil. Orch.; Böhm, cond.* Recorded live 1950, 1969, 1968.
- - Fa 9-10/90: 399

22908. HR 4160: BACH—Magnificat; Gottes Zeit ist die allerbeste Zeit, BWV 106. *Marimpietri, Panni, Reynolds, Munteanu, Carmelli, László, Handt, Loomis, Italian Radio and Television Milan Symphony Orch.; Italian Radio and Television Turin Symphony Orch.; Scherchen, cond.* Recorded live 1963, 1958.
- • Fa 9-10/90: 148

22909. HR 4186/87 (2 discs): BELLINI—Il pirata. *Caballé, Labò, Cappuccilli; Orch. & Chorus of Maggio musicale fiorentino; Capuana, cond.* Live recording (1967).
• Fa 9-10/91: 158

22910. HR 4218: MOZART—Piano concerto no. 24. LISZT—Piano sonata. *Richter, piano; Maggio musicale fiorentino Orch.; Muti, cond.*
+ Fa 9-10/91: 282

22911. HR 4251/52 (2 discs): BEETHOVEN—Leonore. *Zadek, Schreier, Dermota, Schoeffler, Rohr; with assisting soloists; Men's Chorus of the Vienna State Opera; Women's Chorus of the Bregenz Festival; Vienna Symphony Orch.; Leitner, cond.* Recorded live 1960.
- ARG 9-10/91: 43
• Fa 7-8/91: 111

22912. HR 4281/82 (2 discs): WAGNER—Der fliegende Holländer. *Teatro alla Scala; Sawallisch, cond.*
- Fa 9-10/91: 386

22913. HR 4283 (2 discs): ROSSINI—La Cenerentola. *Berganza, Alva, Montarsolo, Capecchi; Florence May Festival; Abbado, cond.* Recorded 1971.
• ARG 5-6/95: 161

22914. HR 4285/86 (2 discs): CIMAROSA—Le astuzie femminili. *Sciutti, Alva, Bruscantini, Mattioli, Rota, Calabrese; Chorus & Orch. A. Scarlatti of RAI, Naples; Rossi, cond.* Recorded live.
+ ARG 11-12/92: 106
+ Fa 9-10/92: 216

22915. HR 4300/01 (2 discs): *Sesto Bruscantini: Operatic scenes.* Music of A. Scarlatti, Cimarosa, Mozart, Cherubini, Rossini and Donizetti. *Bruscantini, bass-baritone; with accompaniment.* Recorded live 1957-88.
+ Fa 5-6/92: 298

22916. HR 4305/06 (2 discs): HOFFMANN—Undine. *Streich, Muszely, Rauschkolb, Heistermann, Grumbach, Kohn, Proebstl, Engen, Rosner; Chorus & Orch. of the Bavarian Radio; Koetsier, cond.* Recorded live.
+ ARG 9-10/92: 116
+ Fa 9-10/92: 216
+ ON 2/13/93: 32

22917. HR 4366/67 (2 discs): MOZART—Piano sonatas no. 5, 7; Variations, K. 353; Piano concerto no. 22; Sonata for piano, 4 hands, K. 521. *Richter, piano; Britten, piano & cond.; English Chamber Orch.* Live recordings.
+ Fa 11-12/91: 410

22918. HR 4380/81 (2 discs): STRAUSS—Elektra. *Borkh, Della Casa, Madeira, Lorenz, Böhme; Chorus of the Vienna State Opera; Vienna Phil. Orch.; Mitropoulos, cond.* Recorded live 1957.

+ ARG 1-2/92: 121
• Fa 1-2/92: 340

22919. HR 4386 (2 discs): Scenes from Orfeo, Italiana in Algeri, Tancredi, Cenerentola, Huguenots, Anna Bolena, Trovatore, and Aïda. *Simionato, mezzo-soprano.* Recorded 1956-63.
+ ARG 5-6/92: 190

22920. HR 4394/95 (2 discs): *Great voices: Jon Vickers.* Arias by Verdi, Cherubini, Bizet, Beethoven and Wagner. *Vickers, tenor; with orch. accomp.* Recorded live 1961-70.
+ ARG 1-2/93: 195
+ Fa 1-2/93: 280

22921. HR 4396 (2 discs): Music from Don Giovanni, Ernani, Trovatore, Aida, Verdi Requiem, and Turandot. *L. Price, soprano.* Recorded live 1960-67.
+ ARG 5-6/92: 189

22922. HR 4406/7 (2 discs): VERDI—Otello. *Del Monaco, Tucci, Gobbi; NHK Symphony Orch.; Erede, cond.* Recorded live 1959.
+ Fa 5-6/92: 271

22923. HR 4410: BORODIN—Symphony no. 2. MOZART—Symphony no. 33. *Stuttgart Radio Symphony Orch.; Vienna Symphony Orch.; Kleiber, cond.* Recorded live 1962, 1967.
+ Fa 7-8/92: 124

22924. HR 4417 (2 discs): DONIZETTI—Maria Stuarda. *Caballé, Carreras, Menendez, Mazzieri, Serra; ORTF Paris; Santi, cond.*
+ ARG 9-10/92: 98
• ON 12/5/92: 50

22925. HR 4424/25 (2 discs): *Great voices: Wolfgang Windgassen.* Arias by Beethoven and Wagner. *Windgassen, tenor; with orch. accomp.* Recorded live 1951-66.
+ ARG 1-2/93: 195
+ Fa 1-2/93: 281

22926. HR 4448 (2 discs): DONIZETTI—Caterina Cornaro. *Gencer, Aragall, Bruson, Clabassi; Teatro San Carlo di Napoli; Cillario, cond.* Recorded live 1972.
+ ARG 11-12/92: 112

22927. HR 4458/59 (2 discs): ROSSINI—La gazzetta. *Tuccari, Galli, Casoni, Lazzari, Borriello, Tajo, Monreale, Cava; Chorus of the Teatro San Carlo, Naples; Orch. A. Scarlatti of RAI, Naples; Caracciolo, cond.* Recorded live.
+ ARG 9-10/92: 150
- Fa 9-10/92: 216
+ ON 6/93: 40

22928. HR 4460/61 (2 discs): *Great voices: Leonard Warren.* Music of Rossini, Verdi, Gounod, Bizet, Giordano, Romberg and others. *Warren, baritone;*

with accomp. Recorded 1945-59.
+ Fa 1-2/93: 280

22929. HR 4464: FALLA—Atlantida; El amor brujo. *Simionato, Browne, Halley, Stratas; Teatro alla Scala; Schippers, cond.; Berganza; Orch. National de France; Argenta, cond.* Recorded live 1972.
+ ARG 11-12/92: 118
+ ON 10/93: 34

22930. HR 4466 (2 discs): MARSCHNER—Der Vampyr. *Oeggl, Synek, Skladel, Heppe; Vienna Radio Orch. & Chorus; Tenner, cond.* Recorded live 1951.
- ARG 11-12/92: 155
- Fa 11-12/92: 293
- ON 3/4/95: 40

22931. HR 4472: CILEA—Gloria. *Vocalists; Orch. of RAI, Turin; Labò, cond.* Recorded live, 1969.
• ARG 5-6/93: 77
+ Fa 5-6/93: 186
• ON 9/93: 53

22932. HR 4482: DONIZETTI—Il giovedi grasso. *Vocalists; RTE Symphony Orch.; Atherton, cond.* Recorded live, 1970.
• Fa 5-6/93: 194
+ ON 11/93: 42

22933. HR 4489 (2 discs): SCHUMANN—Faust. *Fischer-Dieskau, Mathis, Howell, Burrows; BBC Symphony Orch.; Boulez, cond.* Live recording 1973.
+ ARG 5-6/93: 134
• ON 6/94: 44

22934. HR 4493/94 (2 discs): BRAHMS—Ein deutsches Requiem, op. 45. MAHLER—Symphony no. 9. *Harper, soprano; Prey, baritone; BBC Symphony Orch.; Boulez, cond.*
- ARG 9-10/93: 102
+ Fa 5-6/93: 173

22935. HR 4500/01 (2 discs): VERDI—Falstaff. *Stabile, Tebaldi; other vocal soloists; Orch. & Chorus of La Scala, Milan; De Sabata, cond.* Recorded live 1951.
+ Fa 11-12/93: 431
• ON 1/8/94: 35

22936. HR 4502 (2 discs): PAISIELLO—Fedra. *Udovick, Tuccari, Lazzari, Cesari; RAI Milan; Questa, cond.*
+ ARG 3-4/94: 130
+ ON 7/94: 42

22937. HR 4519 (2 discs): LEONCAVALLO—Zaza. MASCAGNI—Zanetto. *Vocal soloists; RAI Turin; Silipigni, cond.; RAI Milan; Petralia, cond.*
- ARG 1-2/94: 117

22938. HR 4521 (2 discs): VERDI—Il trovatore. *Caballé, Mattiucci, Tucker, Zanasi, Vinco; Florence Opera; Schippers, cond.* Recorded 1968.
+ ARG 3-4/94: 177

22939. HR 4533/4 (2 discs): VERDI— Otello. *Vickers, Freni, Glossop, Davies, Malagù; Vienna State Opera Chorus; Chamber Choir of the Salzburg Festival; Vienna Phil. Orch.; Karajan, cond.* Recorded 1971.
+ Fa 9-10/94: 362
● ON 8/94: 35

22940. HR 4550: LORTZING—Hans Sachs. *Schmitt-Walter; Sailer; Franconian State Orch.; Loy, cond.*
● ARG 11-12/94: 257

22941. HR 4554/5 (2 discs): MASSENET— Werther. *Gencer, Tagliavini, Borriello, Tavolaccini; Teatro Verdi di Trieste; Cillario, cond.* Recorded live; sung in Italian.
+ Fa 1-2/95: 198

22942. HR 4556: Overtures by Lortzing, Marschner, Hoffmann, Cornelius, and Nicolai. *Various performers.*
+ ARG 3-4/95: 275

22943. HR 4560 (2 discs): Arias from Tannhäuser, Flying Dutchman, Lohengrin, Oberon, and others. *Varnay, soprano.*
+ ARG 1-2/95: 266
+ ON 12/24/94: 33

22944. HR 4566/68 (3 discs): MEYERBEER—Gli ugonotti (Les huguenots). *Pastori, Cavalieri, Gardino, Lauri- Volpi, Taddei, Tozzi, Zaccaria; Chorus & Orch. of RAI, Milan; Serafin, cond.* Sung in Italian; recorded from broadcast, 1956.
- Fa 1-2/95: 205

22945. HR 4576: LEONCAVALLO—I Pagliacci. *Tucker, Sighele, Nurmela, Alberti; Florence May Festival; Muti, cond.* Recorded 1971.
● ARG 5-6/95: 30

22946. HR 4577/78 (2 discs): HANDEL— Rodelinda. *Sutherland, Elkins, Baker, Hallett, Herincx, Kern; Philomusica Orch.; Chandos Choir; Farncombe, cond.* Recorded live 1959.
+ Fa 1-2/95: 170

22947. HR 4579 (2 discs): DONIZETTI—Il Duca d'Alba. *Tosini, Cioni, Quilico; Spoleto Festival; Schippers, cond.* Recorded 1958.
● ARG 3-4/95: 95

22948. HR 4582: BRUCKNER—Symphony no. 5. *Vienna Phil. Orch.; Schuricht, cond.* Recorded 1963.
+ ARG 9-10/95: 117

22949. HR 4588: DONIZETTI—Maria di Rudenz. *Andrew, Jenkins, Du Plessis, Greager, King; orch.; Francis, cond.* Recorded live 1974.
● ARG 1-2/96: 104
+ ON 2/3/96: 36

22950. HR 4591 (2 discs): OFFENBACH— Barbe-Bleue. *Legay, Lenoty, Terrasson, Doniat, Dachary; Orchestre de l' ORTF; Doussard, cond.* Recorded 1967.
+ ARG 1-2/96: 151
+ ON 1/6/96: 39

22951. HR 4601 (2 discs): MASSENET— Sapho. *Andrew, Oliver, Sarti, Hill, Taylor; BBC Symphony Orch.; Keefe, cond.* Recorded 1973.
+ ARG 5-6/96: 149
+ ON 3/16/96: 41

22952. HR 4603: BEETHOVEN—Piano concerto no. 5. MOZART—Fantasia, K. 397. SCHUMANN—Arabesque. *Gilels, piano; Czech Phil. Orch.; Böhm, cond.* Recorded 1971.
+ ARG 5-6/96: 79

MENUET

22953. 160002-2: *Russian masterpieces.* Music of Borodin, Ippolitov-Ivanov, Rimsky-Korsakov, and Shostakovich. *National Phil. Orch.; Gerhardt, cond.*
+ Fa 5-6/89: 418

22954. 160003-2: *A salute to America.* Music of Anderson, Bernstein, Gershwin, Gould, Grainger, and Grofé . *National Phil. Orch.; Gerhardt, Gould, Hammerstein, Richardson, conds.*
+ Fa 5-6/89: 411

22955. 160005-2: *Romantic brass music from Scandanavia.* Music of Ramsöe, Hoffmann, Thorvald Hansen, Lindberg, Jorgensen, and Nielsen. *Royal Danish Brass.*
- Fa 9-10/89: 438

22956. 160006-2: Music of Eyck, Castello, Telemann, Heberle, and Berio. *M. Petri, recorders; D. Petri, cello; H. Petri, spinett.*
- Fa 5-6/89: 402

22957. 160007-2: BACH—Brandenburg concerto no. 5; Suite for orchestra no. 2, BWV 1067. *Gurtner, flute; Kurosaki, violin; Wiener Akademie; Haselböck, cond.*
● Fa 5-6/89: 112

22958. 160008-2: RACHMANINOFF—Piano trio no. 2. *Vienna Schubert Trio.*
+ Fa 5-6/89: 285

22959. 160009-2: CHAUSSON—Piano trio, op. 3. DEBUSSY—Piano trio. *Vienna Schubert Trio.*
● Fa 5-6/89: 163

22960. 160010-2: BACH—Organ music. *Haselböck, organ.*
+ Fa 5-6/89: 107

22961. 160011-2: BACH—Organ music. *Haselböck, organ.*
+ Fa 5-6/89: 107

22962. 160012-2: BIZET—Symphony in C. TCHAIKOVSKY—Francesca da Rimini. *Royal Phil. Orch.; Munch, cond.*
+ Fa 1-2/90: 131

22963. 160014-2: DVOŘÁK—Symphony no. 9. STRAUSS—Don Juan. *Royal Phil. Orch.; Kempe, cond.*
+ ARG 1-2/90: 47
+ Fa 1-2/90: 172

22964. 160015-2: BEETHOVEN—Piano concerto no. 5. *Firkušný, piano; Royal Phil. Orch.; Kempe, cond.*
● ARG 7-8/89: 19
+ Fa 7-8/89: 84

22965. 160016-2: SCHUBERT—Symphony no. 9. *Royal Phil. Orch.; Leibowitz, cond.*
□ Fa 5-6/89: 311 m.f.

22966. 160017-2: BEETHOVEN— Symphonies no. 1, 3. *Royal Phil. Orch.; Leibowitz, cond.*
+ ARG 1-2/90: 26
+ Fa 3-4/90: 140

22967. 160018-2: BEETHOVEN— Symphonies no. 2, 4. *Royal Phil Orch.; Leibowitz, cond.*
+ ARG 1-2/90: 26
+ Fa 3-4/90: 140

22968. 160019-2: BEETHOVEN— Symphonies no. 5-6. *Royal Phil. Orch.; Leibowitz, cond.*
+ ARG 1-2/90: 26
+ Fa 3-4/90: 140

22969. 160020-2: BEETHOVEN— Symphonies no. 7-8. *Royal Phil. Orch.; Leibowitz, cond.*
+ ARG 1-2/90: 26
+ Fa 3-4/90: 140

22970. 160021-2: BEETHOVEN— Symphony no. 9; Egmont: Overture. *Borkh, Stewart, Lewis, Weber; Beecham Choral Society; Royal Phil. Orch.; Leibowitz, cond.*
+ ARG 7-8/89: 25
● Fa 9-10/89: 136

22971. 160022-2: MOZART—Symphony no. 35. HAYDN—Symphony no. 104. *Royal Phil. Orch.; Krips, cond.*
+ ARG 1-2/90: 72
+ Fa 1-2/90: 246

22972. 160023-2: SIBELIUS—Symphony no. 2. *Royal Phil. Orch.; Barbirolli, cond.*
+ Fa 1-2/90: 208

22973. 160027-2: DEBUSSY—Nocturnes: Nuages, Fêtes; Prélude à l'après-midi d'un faune. FRANCK—Psyché et Eros. RAVEL—Daphnis et Chloé: Suite no. 2. *Beecham Choral Society; Royal Phil. Orch.; Prêtre, cond.; London Festival Orch.; Leibowitz, cond.*
+ Fa 5-6/91: 161

22974. 160029-2: Music of Beethoven, Gounod, Halvorsen, Berlioz, Tchaikovsky, Meyerbeer, Chabrier, Elgar, Rimsky-Korsakov, and Sibelius. *London Phil. Orch.; Mackerras, cond.*
• Fa 7-8/89: 324

MEPHISTO

22975. MR 3.2122: Liszt—Venezia e Napoli; Les jeux d'eau à la Villa d'Este; Mephisto waltz no. 1; Piano sonata. *Székely, piano.*
+ Fa 7-8/96: 296

MERCURY

22976. 432 002-2: *Piano recital.* Liszt—Piano concertos no. 1-2; Piano music; Piano music of Schumann, Falla and Guion. *Janis, piano; Moscow Phil. Symphony Orch.; Kondrashin, cond.; Moscow Radio Symphony Orch.; Rozhdestvensky, cond.* Reissues.
+ Gr 9/91: 80

22977. 432 010-2: Schumann—Cello concerto. Lalo—Cello concerto. Saint-Saëns—Cello concerto. *Starker, cello; London Symphony Orch.; Skrowaczewski, Dorati, cond.*
• ARG 7-8/91: 129
+ Fa 7-8/91: 283
+ Gr 4/92: 52

22978. 432 011-2: Schumann—Piano concerto; Arabesque, op. 18. Tchaikovsky—Piano concerto no. 1. *Janis, piano; Minneapolis Symphony Orch.; Skrowaczewski, cond.; London Symphony Orch.; Menges, cond.*
+ ARG 7-8/91: 123
+ Fa 9-10/91: 351

22979. 432 012-2: Stravinsky—Fireworks; Firebird: Tango; Scherzo à la russe; Song of the nightingale. *London Symphony Orch.; Dorati, cond.*
+ ARG 7-8/91: 129
+ Fa 7-8/91: 303
+ Gr 11/91: 102

22980. 432 013-2: Anderson—Selections. *Eastman-Rochester Pops; Fennell, cond.* Reissue.
+ ARG 3-4/93: 48

22981. 432 014-2: Music of Hérold, Auber, Gounod, Saint-Saëns, Bizet, Berlioz, Massenet, and Thomas. *Detroit Symphony Orch.; Paray, cond.*
+ ARG 7-8/91: 142 m.f.
+ Fa 7-8/91: 390

22982. 432 015-2: Enesco—Romanian rhapsody no. 1. Liszt—Hungarian rhapsodies no. 1-6. *London Symphony Orch.; Dorati, cond.* Reissue.
+ ARG 9-10/91: 88
+ Fa 11-12/91: 317

22983. 432 017-2: Bartók—Concerto for orchestra; Dance suite; Two portraits;

Two excerpts from Mikrokosmos (arr. Tibor Serly). *London Symphony Orch.; Philharmonia Hungarica; Dorati, cond.* Reissue.
- ARG 1-2/92: 25
+ Fa 11-12/91: 258

22984. 432 018-2: Beethoven—Piano concertos no. 4-5. *Bachauer, piano; London Symphony Orch.; Dorati, Skrowaczewski, conds.* Reissue.
+ ARG 3-4/92: 26
- Fa 11-12/91: 262

22985. 432 179-2: Paray—Joan of Arc mass. Saint-Saëns—Symphony no. 3. *Yeend, Bible, Lloyd, Sze; Rackham Choir; Dupré, organ; Detroit Symphony Orch.; Paray, cond.* Reissue.
+ ARG 3-4/92: 116
+ Gr 9/92: 86

22986. 432 718-2: Bloch—Concerti grossi no. 1-2; Schelomo. *Miquelle, cello; Eastman-Rochester Orch.; Hanson, cond.* Reissue.
+ ARG 1-2/92: 34
+ Fa 11-12/91: 274

22987. 432 750-2: Tchaikovsky—The nutcracker; Serenade in C for strings. *London Symphony Orch.; Philharmonia Hungarica; Dorati, cond.* Reissues.
• ARG 1-2/92: 126
• Fa 1-2/92: 351
+ Gr 9/92: 94

22988. 432 753-2: Prokofiev—Scythian suite, op. 20; The love for three oranges, op. 33a: suite; Symphony no. 5 in B♭, op. 100. *London Symphony Orch.; Minneapolis Symphony Orch.; Dorati, cond.* Reissue.
- ARG 1-2/92: 93
+ Fa 1-2/92: 299

22989. 432 754-2: Persichetti—Symphony no. 6. Grainger—Lincolnshire posy; Hill song no. 2. Rogers—Three Japanese dances. Hartley—Concerto for 23 winds. Khachaturian—Armenian dances. *Eastman Wind Ensemble; Fennell, cond.*
+ ARG 1-2/92: 165
+ Fa 9-10/92: 311

22990. 432 755-2: Piston—Symphony no. 5. Schuman—New England triptych. Ives—Three places in New England. *Eastman-Rochester Orch.; Hanson, cond.* Reissue.
+ ARG 1-2/92: 144
+ Fa 7-8/92: 219

22991. 432 759-2: Rachmaninoff—Piano concertos no. 2-3; Preludes. *Janis, piano; Minneapolis Symphony Orch.; London Symphony Orch.; Dorati, cond.* Reissues.
+ Gr 9/92: 83

22992. 434 300-2: Sousa—Marches. *Eastman Wind Ensemble; Fennell, cond.*

+ ARG 11-12/92: 207
+ Fa 9-10/92: 360

22993. 434 303-2: Chabrier—España; Suite pastorale; Fête polonaise; Danse slave; Gwendoline overture; Joyeuse marche; Bourrée fantasque. Roussel—Suite in F. *Detroit Symphony Orch.; Paray, cond.* Reissue.
+ ARG 3-4/92: 44

22994. 434 304-2: Respighi—Ancient airs and dances. *Philharmonia Hungarica; Dorati, cond.*
• ARG 9-10/92: 149

22995. 434 305-2: Tchaikovsky—Symphony no. 5; Marche slave; Eugene Onegin: waltz and polonaise. *London Symphony Orch.; Minneapolis Symphony Orch.; Dorati, cond.*
• ARG 11-12/92: 221
+ Fa 9-10/92: 376

22996. 434 306-2: Ravel—Daphnis et Chloé: suite no. 2; Valses nobles et sentimentales; Boléro. Debussy—Nocturnes for orchestra; Petite suite. *Detroit Symphony Orch.; Wayne State University Women's Glee Club; Paray, cond.* Reissue.
+ ARG 9-10/92: 145
+ Fa 9-10/92: 325

22997. 434 307-2: Music of Barber, Piston, Griffes, Bergsma, Kennan and McCauley. *Eastman-Rochester Orch.; Hanson, cond.* Reissue.
+ ARG 11-12/92: 232
• Fa 11-12/92: 462

22998. 434 308-2: Rimsky-Korsakov—Coq d'or suite; Capriccio espagnol; Russian Easter overture. Borodin—Prince Igor: Polovtsian dances. *London Symphony Orch. & Chorus; Dorati, cond.* Reissue.
+ ARG 7-8/92: 206
+ Fa 9-10/92: 330

22999. 434 309-2: Suppé—Overtures: Morning, noon and night in Vienna; Pique Dame; Boccaccio; Light cavalry; Beautiful Galatea; Poet and peasant. Auber—Overtures: The bronze horse; Fra Diavolo; Masaniello (La muette di Portici). *Detroit Symphony Orch.; Paray, cond.* Reissue.
+ ARG 9-10/92: 170

23000. 434 310-2: Thomson—Symphony on a hymn tune. McPhee—Tabuh-Tabuhan. Sessions—The black maskers. *Eastman-Rochester Orch.; Hanson, cond.*
+ ARG 9-10/92: 175
+ Fa 11-12/92: 298

23001. 434 311-2: Franck—Pièce héroïque; Chorales. Widor—Organ symphony no. 6: Allegro; Organ symphony no. 2: Salve Regina. *Dupré, organ.* Reissue.
• ARG 1-2/93: 97

MERCURY

23002. 434 312-2: Dvořák—Symphonies no. 7-8. *London Symphony Orch.; Dorati, cond.*
- ARG 9-10/92: 101

23003. 434 313-2 (3 discs): Delibes—Coppélia; Sylvia. *Minneapolis Symphony Orch.; Dorati, cond.; London Symphony Orch.; Fistoulari, cond.* Reissues.
+ ARG 1-2/93: 90
+ Gr 3/93: 39

23004. 434 317-2: Dvořák—Symphony no. 9. Sibelius—Symphony no. 2. *Detroit Symphony Orch.; Paray, cond.* Reissue.
+ ARG 1-2/93: 93
• Gr 3/93: 39

23005. 434 318-2: Brahms—Violin concerto. Khachaturian—Violin concerto. *Szeryng, violin; London Symphony Orch.; Dorati, cond.* Reissue.
+ Gr 2/93: 38

23006. 434 319-2: Music of Carpenter, Moore, Phillips and Rogers. *Eastman-Rochester Orch.; Hanson, cond.* Reissue.
+ ARG 1-2/93: 172

23007. 434 320-2: Giannini—Symphony no. 3. Gould—West Point symphony. Hovhaness—Symphony no. 4. *Eastman Wind Ensemble; Fennell, Roller, conds.* Reissue.
+ ARG 3-4/93: 178
+ Fa 5-6/93: 229

23008. 434 321-2: Bizet—Patrie; Carmen suite; L'Arlésienne suites. Thomas—Mignonne: Overture; Raymond: Overture. *Detroit Symphony Orch.; Paray, cond.* Reissue.
+ Gr 8/93: 25

23009. 434 323-2: Shostakovich—Symphony no. 5. Khachaturian Gayne: Excerpts. *London Symphony Orch.; Dorati; Minneapolis Symphony Orch.; Skrowaczewski, cond.* Reissues.
- ARG 5-6/93: 99
+ Gr 8/93: 32

23010. 434 325-2: Bartók—Blubeard's castle. Berg—Wozzeck: Three excerpts. *Székely, Szőnyi, Pilarczyk; London Symphony Orch.; Dorati, cond.* Reissue.
+ ARG 5-6/93: 66
+ Gr 7/93: 85

23011. 434 326-2: Brahms—Hungarian dances; Haydn variations. Enesco—Romanian rhapsody no. 1. *London Symphony Orch.; Dorati, cond.* Reissue.
+ Gr 8/93: 25

23012. 434 328-2: Berlioz—Symphonie fantastique; Roman carnival; Corsair; Rakoczy march; Trojan march. *Detroit Symphony Orch.; Paray, cond.* Reissue.
+ ARG 5-6/93: 71
• Gr 9/93: 43
- St 10/93: 263

23013. 434 329-2: Schuller—Studies on themes of Paul Klee. Bloch—Sinfonia breve. Copland—Dance episodes from Rodeo. Gershwin—American in Paris. *Minneapolis Symphony Orch.; Dorati, cond.* Reissue.
+ ARG 11-12/93: 191

23014. 434 330-2: Grainger—Country gardens and 10 other tunes. Coates—The three Elizabeths. *Eastman-Rochester Orch.; Fennell, cond.* Reissue.
• ARG 9-10/93: 126
+ Gr 11/93: 90

23015. 434 331-2: Stravinsky—Rite of spring; Petrushka; Etudes. *Minneapolis Symphony Orch.; London Symphony Orch.; Dorati, cond.* Reissue.
• Gr 3/94: 62

23016. 434 332-2: *Marches and overtures à la française.* Music of Adam, Meyerbeer, Gounod, Saint-Saëns, Boieldieu, Offenbach, and Rossini. *Detroit Symphony Orch.; Paray, cond.* Reissue.
+ ARG 9-10/93: 224
+ Gr 11/93: 90

23017. 434 333-2: Prokofiev—Piano concerto no. 3. Rachmaninoff—Piano concerto no. 1; Piano music of Prokofiev, Mendelssohn, Schumann, and Pinto. *Janis, piano; Moscow Phil. Orch.; Kondrashin, cond.* Reissues.
+ ARG 7-8/94: 150

23018. 434 334-2: Marches by Sousa, Goldman, Ganne, Prokofiev, and others. *Eastman Wind Ensemble; Fennell, cond.* Reissue.
+ ARG 9-10/94: 246

23019. 434 336-2: *Dances of death.* Music of Liszt, Weber, Schmitt, Saint-Saëns, and Strauss. *Detroit Symphony Orch.; Paray, cond.* Reissue.
+ ARG 3-4/95: 229

23020. 434 337-2: Chadwick—Symphonic sketches. MacDowell—Suite no. 1. Peter—Symphony in G. *Eastman-Rochester Orch.; Hanson, cond.* Reissue.
• ARG 1-2/95: 95

23021. 434 338-2: *Vienna waltzes.* Lehar, Kalman, Strauss, Dohnanyi, Waldteufel, and Lanner. *Philharmonia Hungarica; Minneapolis Symphony Orch.; Dorati, cond.* Reissue.
• ARG 3-4/95: 226

23022. 434 339-2: Mendelssohn—Violin concerto. Schumann—Violin concerto; Music of Debussy, Novacek, Brahms, Marroquin, and Rimsky-Korsakov. *Szeryng, violin; London Symphony Orch.; Dorati, cond.*
+ ARG 3-4/95: 138

23023. 434 340-2: Brahms—Piano concerto no. 2; Variations on a theme by Paganini. Beethoven—Piano sonata no. 9. Liszt—Hungarian rhapsody no. 12. *Bachauer, piano; London Symphony Orch.; Skrowaczewski, cond.* Reissue; recorded 1963 and 1965.
• ARG 1-2/95: 87
+ Gr 9/95: 50

23024. 434 341-2: Gershwin—Concerto in F; Rhapsody in blue; Cuban overture. Sousa—Stars and stripes forever. *List, piano; Eastman-Rochester Orch.; Hanson, cond.* Reissue.
+ ARG 7-8/95: 112

23025. 434 342-2: Wagner—Overtures. *London Symphony Orch.; Dorati, cond.*
- ARG 3-4/95: 220

23026. 434 344-2: Sonatas by Boccherini, Vivaldi, Corelli, Locatelli, Velantini, and Bach. *Starker, cello; Sebök, piano.* Reissue.
+ ARG 3-4/95: 234

23027. 434 345-2: Verdi—Overtures. Rossini—Overtures. *London Symphony Orch.; Minneapolis Symphony Orch.; Dorati, cond.* Reissues.
+ ARG 3-4/95: 210

23028. 434 346-2: Mussorgsky—Pictures at an exhibition (piano and orchestral versions). Chopin—Waltz, etude. *Janis, piano; Minneapolis Symphony Orch.; Dorati, cond.* Reissue.
+ ARG 3-4/95: 146
+ Gr 2/96: 54

23029. 434 347-2: *Music for quiet listening.* Music of Nelson, Scianni, Gauldin, Mailman, Sutcliffe, and others. *Eastman-Rochester Orch.; Hanson, cond.* Reissue.
+ ARG 3-4/95: 229

23030. 434 348-2: Strauss—Don Juan; Death and transfiguration; Till Eulenspiegel; Rosenkavalier suite. *Minneapolis Symphony Orch.; Dorati, cond.* Reissues.
- ARG 3-4/95: 194

23031. 434 349-2: Music of Faith, Lecuona, Granados, Benjamin, Liszt, Sibelius, and others. *Eastman-Rochester Pops; Fennell, cond.* Reissues.
• ARG 5-6/95: 198

23032. 434 350-2: Bartók—Violin concerto no. 2; Suite no. 2. *Menuhin, violin; Minneapolis Symphony Orch.; Dorati, cond.* Reissue.
• ARG 11-12/95: 80
+ Gr 11/95: 79

23033. 434 352-2: *Kaleidoscope.* Music of Smetana, Nicolai, Weber, Meyerbeer, Brahms, and others. *London Symphony Orch.; Mackerras, cond.* Recorded 1961.
+ ARG 9-10/95: 245

23034. 434 354-2: SCHUBERT—Symphonies no. 6, 9. *Minnesota Orch.; Skrowaczewski, cond.; London Symphony Orch.; Schmidt-Isserstedt, cond.* Reissues.
- ARG 11-12/95: 198

23035. 434 357-2: BARTÓK—The wooden prince; Music for string, percussion, and celesta. *London Symphony Orch.; Dorati, cond.* Reissue.
• Gr 5/96: 53

23036. 434 360-2: TCHAIKOVSKY—1812 overture; Capriccio italien. BEETHOVEN—Wellington's victory. *Minneapolis Symphony Orch.; University of Minnesota Brass Band; London Symphony Orch.; Dorati, cond.* Reissue; recorded 1958.
+ ARG 3-4/96: 192
+ Fa 3-4/96: 300
+ Fi 3/96: 125
+ Gr 12/95: 74

23037. 434 361-2: *Flamenco!* Music of Granados, Tarrega, Sinopoli, and traditional. *P. Romero, guitar.* Reissue.
+ ARG 7-8/96: 244

23038. 434 362-2: BARTÓK—Miraculous mandarin; Divertimento; Sonata for two pianos and percussion. *Frid, Ponse, pianos; BBC Symphony Orch.; Dorati, cond.* Reissue.
+ ARG 5-6/96: 77

23039. 434 363-2: MENDELSSOHN—Symphonies no. 3-4; Hebrides. *London Symphony Orch.; Dorati, cond.; Minneapolis Symphony Orch.; Skrowaczewski, cond.* Reissues.
• ARG 7-8/96: 152

23040. 434 364-2: *Golden age of harpsichord.* Music of Byrd, Bull, Couperin, Rameau, and others. *Puyana, harpsichord.* Reissue.
+ ARG 7-8/96: 244

23041. 434 365-2 (2 discs): ADAM—Giselle. STRAUSS—Graduation ball. OFFENBACH—Gaîté parisienne. *London Symphony Orch.; Fistoulari; Minneapolis Symphony Orch.; Dorati, cond.* Reissues.
+ ARG 11-12/96: 76

23042. 434 368-2: FRANCK—Symphony. RACHMANINOFF—Symphony no. 2. *Detroit Symphony Orch.; Paray, cond.* Reissue.
+ ARG 11-12/96: 124

23043. 434 369-2: RODRIGO—Concierto Andaluz; Concierto de Aranjuez. VIVALDI—Guitar concertos. *P. Romero, Los Romeros, guitars; San Antonio Symphony Orch.; Alessandro, cond.* Reissues.
+ ARG 11-12/96: 189

MERIDIAN

23044. E 77092 (LP): Guitar music of Aguado, Mertz, Mozart (arr. Sor), Legnani, Coste, and Sor. *Gregory, guitar.*
+ Fa 11-12/86: 276

E 77126 see ECD 84126.

23045. CDE 84019: LISZT—Schubert song transcriptions. *Bingham, piano.*
+ ARG 7-8/92: 165
+ Fa 9-10/88: 255
+ Gr 4/89: 1479

23046. CDE 84022: MOZART—Clarinet concerto. SPOHR—Clarinet concerto no. 4. *King, clarinet; English Chamber Orch.; Francis, cond.*
• Fa 3-4/88: 156
+ Gr 10/88: 606

23047. CDE 84060: LISZT—Organ music. LASSUS—Regina coeli (arr. Liszt). *Sanger, organ.*
- Fa 9-10/88: 184

23048. CDE 84079: MOZART—Divertimento for strings, K. 563 . *Cummings String Trio.*
- ARG 11-12/86: 72
+ Fa 5-6/86: 195
+ Gr 9/86: 406

23049. CDE 84081: BACH—Organ music. *Sanger, organ.*
+ Fa 1-2/87: 61

23050. CDE 84082: ELGAR—String quartet, op. 83; String quintet, op. 84. *Bingham, piano; Medici Quartet.*
• ARG 5-6/92: 54
+ Fa 3-4/86: 105
+ Gr 11/92: 137

23051. CDE 84083: HAYDN—Piano sonatas no. 50, 54-55; Adagio in F major. *Cload, piano.*
+ ARG 1-2/87: 37
• Fa 11-12/86: 152
+ Gr 9/86: 419

23052. CDE 84085: ELGAR—Sonata, op. 28; Vesper voluntaries, op. 14. WESLEY—Choral song and fugue; Andante in E minor. LEMARE—Marche moderne. *Herrick, organ.*
+ ARG 9-10/88: 42
+ Fa 3-4/88: 104

23053. CDE 84087: BÖHM—Harpsichord music. *Wooley, harpsichord.*
+ Fa 1-2/89: 133

23054. CDE 84093: JOSQUIN DES PREZ—Motets, antiphons, sequences. *Choir of New College, Oxford; Higginbottom, cond.*
+ ARG 9-10/92: 200
+ Fa 11-12/86: 156
+ Gr 8/86: 295

23055. CDE 84096: *Brass music from 17th-century Germany.* Music of Scheidt, Schein, Schütz, Braun and Weckmann. *Wistreich, bass; His Majesties Sagbutts and Cornetts; Ross, organ.*
+ ARG 3-4/92: 178
+ Fa 11-12/87: 276
+ Gr 9/87: 477

23056. CDE 84098: BEETHOVEN—Piano quartets, WoO 36: in E♭ major, D major and C major. *Goldstone, piano; Cummings String Trio.*
+ ARG 1-2/88: 11
+ Fa 11-12/87: 102
• Gr 9/87: 427

23057. CDE 84101: LISZT—Etudes d'après Paganini. BRAHMS—Variations on a theme of Paganini. *Ponti, piano.*
• ARG 7-8/92: 164
- Fa 3-4/87: 145
• Gr 1/87: 1043

23058. CDE 84102: SCHUBERT—The last three sonatas. Vol. 1. *Berkowitz, piano.*
+ ARG 1-2/88: 60
- Fa 1-2/88: 206
• Gr 11/87: 784

23059. CDE 84104: SCHUBERT—Piano sonata no. 21. *Berkowitz, piano.*
+ Fa 3-4/88: 191
• Gr 2/88: 1215

23060. CDE 84106: HANDEL—Oboe concertos. *Goodwin, oboe; St. James's Baroque Players; Bolton, cond.*
+ Fa 7-8/86: 147

23061. CDE 84107: MOZART—Serenades, K. 388, K. 375. *Albion Ensemble.*
• ARG 11-12/86: 73
+ Gr 6/86: 70

23062. CDE 84110: BACH—Cantatas: Schweigt stille, plaudert nicht, BWV 211; Mer hahn ein neue Oberkeet, BWV 212. *Dawson, Robertson, Adler; Friends of Apollo.*
+ Fa 1-2/87: 53
+ Gr 10/86: 603

23063. CDE 84112: PURCELL—Sacred music. *New College Choir; Higginbottom, cond.*
+ ARG 5-6/92: 111

23064. CDE 84113: MOZART—Piano sonatas no. 12-13, 15. *Kite, piano.*
+ ARG 3-4/88: 63
• Fa 1-2/88: 181
• Gr 11/87: 783

23065. CDE 84114: RAMEAU—Pièces de clavecin en concerts: Suite no. 1. TELEMANN—Parisian quartets II: Concerto no. 2. LECLAIR—Second musical recreation, op. 8. *Music's Recreation.*
- Fa 9-10/88: 233
- Gr 6/88: 40

MERIDIAN

23066. CDE 84115: Mozart—Piano quintet, K. 452; Piano quartet, K. 478. *Ambache Chamber Ensemble.*
- Fa 11-12/86: 181
- Gr 10/86: 593

23067. CDE 84117: Haydn—String quartets: in E♭ major, op. 0; in D minor, op. 42; in E♭ major, op. 103 (incomplete). *English String Quartet.*
+ Fa 5-6/87: 135
+ Gr 3/87: 1288

23068. CDE 84118: Schubert—Quartet for flute, guitar, viola and cello in G major (after Matiegka). Haydn—Quartet for flute, violin, viola, and continuo, op. 5, no. 4. *Liddell, violin; Silverthorne, viola; Tunnell, cello; Conway, flute; Garcia, guitar.*
+ ARG 5-6/88: 62
+ Fa 3-4/88: 193
+ Gr 4/88: 1470

23069. CDE 84119: Britten—Insect pieces; Suite for harp; Tit for tat; Metamorphoses after Ovid; Folksong arrangements. *Shirley-Quirk, baritone; Watkins, oboe; Ellis, harp; Ledger, piano.*
+ ARG 5-6/88: 20
+ Fa 1-2/88: 101
+ Gr 12/87: 984

23070. CDE 84121: Massenzio—Compline. *St. John's College Choir; Guest, cond.*
+ Fa 3-4/88: 143
+ Gr 4/88: 1487

23071. CDE 84123: Music of Vaughan Williams, Leighton, Howells, Rose, Harris, and Harvey. *New College Choir, Oxford; Higginbottom, cond.*
• Gr 9/92: 158

23072. CDE 84124: Stevens—Cello concerto, op. 18; Symphony of liberation (Symphony no. 1). *Baillie, cello; BBC Phil. Orch.; Downes, cond.*
+ Fa 5-6/87: 200
+ Gr 3/87: 1273

23073. CDE 84126: *Eternal source of light.* Music of Handel, Buxtehude, J.C. Bach, Monn, and J.W. Franck. *Bowman, counter-tenor; King's Consort; King, cond.* Issued also as LP: 77126.
+ Fa 1-2/87: 237

23074. CDE 84128: Tosti—Vocal music. *O'Neill, tenor; Vignoles, piano.*
+ Fa 9-10/88: 284

23075. CDE 84129: Vivaldi—Laudate pueri, RV 601; Nisi Dominus, RV 608. *Dawson, soprano; Robson, countertenor; King's Consort; King, cond.*
+ Fa 11-12/87: 253
+ Gr 9/87: 474

23076. CDE 84131: Mendelssohn—String symphonies no. 4, 9, 12. *Guildhall*

String Ensemble.
• Fa 3-4/87: 160

23077. CDE 84133: Rossini—Petite messe solennelle. *Combattimento; Mason, cond.*
+ Fa 3-4/89: 252
- Gr 12/88: 1046

23078. CDE 84134: Music of Turina, Esplá, Montsalvatge, and Granados. *Pappas, mezzo-soprano; Israel Symphony Orch.; Stern, cond.*
• ARG 3-4/88: 115
• Fa 1-2/88: 246
- Gr 2/88: 1235

23079. CDE 84139: Walton—Piano quartet; String quartet in A minor. *McCabe, piano; English String Quartet.*
+ Fa 3-4/88: 234
+ Gr 10/87: 598
+ HF 6/88: 60

23080. CDE 84140: Organ and choral music of Liszt, Franck, Bach, Walisley, Wesley, and Stanford. *Seal, organ & cond.; Salisbury Cathedral Choir.*
• Fa 3-4/88: 257

23081. CDE 84142: Mozart—Piano quintet, K. 493; Piano trio, K. 542; Violin sonata, K. 301. *Ambache, piano; Ambache Chamber Ensemble.*
- Fa 9-10/88: 214
• Gr 12/88: 1027

23082. CDE 84146: Guitar music of Visée, Sanz, Roncalli, Sor, De Fossa, Paganini, Tarrega, Shand, Gregory, and Woolrich. *Gregory, guitar.*
□ Fa 1-2/89: 333

23083. CDE 84147: *The other Donizetti.* Music of Donizetti, Pasculli, and Liszt. *Polmear, oboe & English horn; Ambache, piano.*
+ Fa 9-10/88: 142

23084. CDE 84152: Mendelssohn—String quartets 4-5. *English String Quartet.*
• ARG 5-6/92: 65
• Fa 7-8/89: 183
• Gr 4/89: 1601

23085. CDE 84153: Fauré—Cantique de Jean Racine; Ave verum; Tantum ergo; Ecce fidelis; Maria, mater gratiae; Messe basse. Duruflé—Four motets on Gregorian themes. Villette—Hymne à la Vierge. Poulenc—Four Christmas motets. Debussy—Trois chansons de Charles d'Orleans. Ravel—Trois chansons. *Clare College Choir, Cambridge; Brown, cond.*
+ ARG 5-6/92: 178

23086. CDE 84154: Beethoven—Piano quartet op. 16; Serenade in D, op. 8. *Ben-Or, piano; Jerusalem String Trio.*
+ ARG 1-2/92: 28

23087. CDE 84157: Handel—Dalla guerra amorosa; Entrée; Air; Menuet; Impertinence; Concerto (Allegro); Allegro; German arias no. 1, 6, 8; Oboe sonata in C minor; Duetto; Tacete, ohimè, tacete; Mi palpita il cor. *Kenny, soprano; Shirley-Quirk, bass; Watkins, oboe; Sanger, organ; Isepp, harpsichord; Fenton, cello; Scully, double bass.*
+ ARG 7-8/92: 142

23088. CDE 84158: Music of Vaughan-Williams, Howells, Warlock, Steptoe, and A. Ridout. *Bowman, counter-tenor; Goodwin, oboe d'amore; Grunberg, violin; Downshire Players of London; Ash, cond.*
+ Fa 7-8/89: 267

23089. CDE 84159: Telemann—Cantatas; Sonata for viola da gamba and continuo. *Baird, soprano; Bowman, countertenor; Music's Recreation.*
• ARG 3-4/92: 204
+ DA 11/89: 76
+ Fa 9-10/89: 344

23090. CDE 84160: Prokofiev—Piano sonata no. 7. Debussy—Pour le piano. Rachmaninoff—Variations on a theme of Corelli, op. 42. *Press, piano.*
- Fa 7-8/89: 216

23091. CDE 84163: Choral music of Allegri, Palestrina, Frescobaldi, Orgas, Quagliati, Agazzari, Antonelli, Landi, and Anerio. *Choir of St. John's College, Cambridge; Guest, cond.*
+ Fa 7-8/89: 298

23092. CDE 84164: Brahms—Clarinet sonatas (complete); Klavierstücke, op. 119. *Eban, clarinet; Coffey, piano.*
- Fa 9-10/89: 159

23093. CDE 84167: *Cabaret songs.* Music of Gershwin, Coward, Wright, Duke, Britten, Ives, Mallory and Dankworth. *Walker, mezzo-soprano; Vignoles, piano.*
+ ARG 3-4/92: 202

23094. CDE 84168: *Choral music from Bristol Cathedral.* Elgar—Choral music. *Bristol Cathedral Choir; Bristol Cathedral Special Choir; Foulkes, baritone; Pinel, organ; Archer, organ & cond.*
• ARG 3-4/90: 47
- Fa 1-2/90: 176
• Gr 10/89: 722
- Gr 12/89: 1184

23095. CDE 84170: With dances and delight. *Estampie.*
+ ARG 5-6/92: 175

23096. CDE 84173: Elgar—Songs. *Brecknock, tenor; Phil. Chamber Choir; Morris, piano.*
• ARG 5-6/92: 56

23097. CDE 84176: VIERNE—Organ symphonies no. 3-4. *Sanger, organ.*
• ARG 11-12/91: 166

23098. CDE 84179: FIBICH—Piano quartet in E minor. DVOŘÁK—Piano quartet no. 2 in E♭. *Ben-Or, piano; Jerusalem String Trio.*
+ ARG 5-6/92: 60

23099. CDE 84182: CLÉRAMBAULT—Cantatas: Orphée; Zéphire et Flor; Léandre et Hero; with Sonata la Magnifique. *Baird, soprano; Music's Recreation.*
• ARG 3-4/92: 204

23100. CDE 84183: DONIZETTI—Songs in the bass clef. *Caddy, bass-baritone; Halstead, natural horn; Comberti, cello; Tan, fortepiano.*
+ ARG 3-4/92: 50

23101. CDE 84189: HANDEL—Occhi miei, che faceste?; Udite il mio consiglio; Quel fior che all'alba ride; Harpsichord suite, HWV 433; Violin sonata, HWV 364b. *Baird, soprano; Dornenburg, viola da gamba; Proud, harpsichord.*
+ Gr 12/91: 111

23102. CDE 84192: VIERNE—Symphonies no. 1, 2. *Sanger, organ.*
- ARG 5-6/92: 152

23103. CDE 84193: MENDELSSOHN—String symphonies no. 6-7; Four pieces, op. 81. *Goldberg Ensemble; Layfield, cond.*
- Gr 3/92: 48

23104. CDE 84200: MENDELSSOHN—Piano trios no. 1-2. SCHUMANN—Fantasiestücke, op. 88. *York Piano Trio.*
• Gr 3/92: 70

23105. CDE 84201: SCHUBERT—Piano sonatas D. 894, 784. *Berkowitz, piano.*
• Gr 4/92: 116

23106. CDE 84207: RAVEL—Gaspard de la nuit; Miroirs; Sonatine; Pavane. *Peebles, piano.*
• ARG 11-12/92: 184

23107. CDE 84208: BACH—Partitas for solo violin: No. 2, BWV 1004; No. 3, BWV 1006; Sonata no. 2 for solo violin, BWV 1003. *Zivoni, violin.*
+ Fa 3-4/93: 112

23108. CDE 84210: HAYDN—Piano sonatas no. 39, 41, 44, 48-49. *Cload, piano.*
• Gr 3/93: 72

23109. CDE 84213: WALTHER—Organ music. *Farr, organ.*
+ EM 11/92: 509
+ Gr 8/92: 55

23110. CDE 84216: BERKELEY—Choral music. *Choir of Clare College,*

Cambridge; *T. Brown, cond.*
• ARG 1-2/93: 78

23111. CDE 84217: HUMMEL—Flute trio; Rondo brillant for piano; Rondo brillant for flute and piano; Cello sonata. *Conway, flute; Tunnell, cello; Croshaw, piano.*
+ ARG 1-2/93: 106

23112. CDE 84220: *Music for St. Stephen's Day.* SHEPPARD—Mass, Be not afraide; Anthem; Motets. SAMPSON—Psallite felices. *The Cardinall's Musick; Carwood, cond.*
+ ARG 11-12/92: 202
+ EM 11/92: 501
+ Gr 12/92: 124

23113. CDE 84221: CHOPIN—Etudes op. 10, 25. *Bingham, piano.*
• Gr 5/93: 71

23114. CDE 84222: HAYDN—Scottish songs; Piano trios no. 19, 21. *Mackey, soprano; English Trio.*
+ ARG 1-2/93: 102

23115. CDE 84223: BRAHMS—Cello sonatas. *Dearnley, cello; Drake, piano.*
• Gr 10/93: 64

23116. CDE 84225: VIVALDI—Estro armonico: no. 1, 6-8, 10-11. *Arcangeli Baroque Strings; Sand, cond.*
+ ARG 1-2/93: 164
+ EM 5/93: 311

23117. CDE 84227/28 (2 discs): BRAHMS—Piano trios; Horn trio. *Stirling, horn; Dussek Piano Trio.*
+ Gr 11/92: 120

23118. CDE 84229: MENDELSSOHN—Violin sonatas. *Zivoni, violin; Goldstone, piano.*
+ Gr 9/93: 81

23119. CDE 84232: BRAHMS—Zigeuner Lieder. DVOŘÁK—Gipsy melodies. *Walker, mezzo-soprano; Silverthorne, viola; Jacobson, Vignoles, pianos.*
• Gr 4/94: 79

23120. CDE 84236: HUMMEL—Chamber music, vol. 2. *Conway, flute; Blume, viola; Croshaw, piano.*
+ Gr 6/93: 64

23121. CDE 84237: Sonatas for piano, 4 hands by Fibich, Goetz, and Moscheles. *Goldstone, Clemmow, piano.*
+ Gr 7/93: 58

23122. CDE 84240: LISZT—Harmonies poétiques et réligieuses. *Tinney, piano.*
+ Gr 7/93: 67

23123. CDE 84243: M. HAYDN—Violin concertos in A, B♭; Divertimento in D; Applausus: Sinfonia. *Shepherd, violin; Parnassus Ensemble.*
- ARG 11-12/93: 25

23124. CDE 84245: STOLL—Piano quartet; Piano sonata; Sonata for 2 pianos; String trio. *Pro Arte Trio; Skinner, Ward, pianos.*
□ ARG 11-12/93: 202
□ Gr 10/94: 144

23125. CDE 84248, 84255 (2 separate discs): PARRY—Piano trios no. 1-3; Piano quartet. *Deakin Piano Trio; Inoue, viola.*
+ Gr 7/94: 72

23126. CDE 84253: BEETHOVEN—Scottish songs; Piano trios no. 1, 3. *Mackay, soprano; English Piano Trio.*
• Gr 4/94: 78

23127. CDE 84256: English Renaissance consort music. *Extempore String Ensemble; Weigand, cond.*
• ARG 1-2/96: 225

23128. CDE 84259: FAURÉ—Violin sonatas; Sicilienne; Berceuse. *Smietana, violin; Blakey, piano.*
• Gr 10/94: 138

23129. CDE 84266: TELEMANN—Fantasies for solo violin. *Sheppard, violin.*
+ Gr 8/94: 77

23130. CDE 84267: MOZART—Divertimentos for 3 basset horns. *Mannheim Ensemble.*
+ ARG 3-4/95: 148

23131. CDE 84268: BRAHMS—Hungarian dances. *Alvanis, piano.*
• Gr 3/95: 70

23132. CDE 84269: SUK—Spring; About friendship; Things lived and dreamed; Humoresque; Little idylls; Love song. *Immelman, piano.*
• ARG 5-6/95: 182
• Gr 1/95: 81

23133. CDE 84271: BYRD—Songs and sonnets. *Concordia.*
+ EM 2/95: 166

23134. CDE 84281: DVOŘÁK—Violin and piano music. *Stanzeleit, violin; Jacobson, piano.*
+ Gr 3/96: 61

23135. CDE 84282: J. ALAIN—Organ music. *Farr, organ.*
+ ARG 9-10/95: 90

23136. CDE 84284: DEBUSSY—Violin sonata. JANÁČEK—Violin sonata. STRAUSS—Violin sonata. *Shapira, violin; Abramovich, piano.*
+ Gr 2/96: 66

23137. CDE 84286: SMYTH—Violin sonata, op. 7; Cello sonata, op. 5; Piano trio in D minor. *Chagall Trio.*
+ Gr 10/95: 88

23138. CDE 84298/9 (2 discs): DELIUS—Violin sonatas no. 1-3; Légende;

MERIDIAN

Romance; Two interludes for a modern baby. *Jones, violin; Miller, piano.*
- Gr 8/95: 92

23139. CDE 84301: Sweet swan of Avon. *Howard, mezzo-soprano; MacDougall, tenor; English Serenata; Woolfenden, cond.*
+ ARG 1-2/96: 226

23140. CDE 84313: R. White—The greatest glory of our muses. *Henry's Eight.*
+ Gr 5/96: 108

23141. DUOCD 89009: *The romantic Englishman.* Glees, catches and part-songs. *Hilliard Ensemble.* Reissue.
+ Gr 12/91: 121

23142. DUOCD 89019/21 (3 discs): BEETHOVEN—Violin sonatas (complete). *Cohen, violin; Rael, piano.*
- Gr 12/92: 93

23143. DUOCD 89023: BEETHOVEN—Piano music. *T. Leonhardt, fortepiano.*
- Gr 2/94: 73

METIER

23144. MSV CD 2008: Music of Tippett, Sackman, Saxton, and Connolly. *Neugarten, piano.*
+ Gr 1/96: 83

23145. MSV CD 2009: Music of Tippett, Saxton, Matthews, and Lambert. *Unwin, piano.*
+ Gr 1/96: 83

23146. MSV CD 92002: DARKE—Rhapsody, op. 4. ALCOCK—Introduction and passacaglia. WILLAN—Introduction, passacaglia, and fugue. JACKSON—Toccata, chorale, and fugue. BROCKLESS—Introduction, passacaglia, and coda. *Johnstone, organ.*
+ Fa 11-12/93: 491

23147. MSV CD 92003: HOWELLS—Piano quartet, op. 21; Phantasy string quartet, op. 25; Rhapsodic quintet for clarinet and strings, op. 31. *Lyric String Quartet; West, piano; Collins, clarinet.*
+ Fa 11-12/93: 278
+ Gr 10/93: 71

23148. MSV CD 92005: MATHIAS—String quartets no. 1-3. *Medea Quartet.*
+ Gr 10/95: 82

METRO

23149. 59601: *Permanent transition.* Music of Bogdanović, Davis, Greif, Domeniconi, and Aguila. *Greif, Bogdanović, York, guitar.*
- ARG 1-2/97: 206

METRONOME

23150. CD 1001: Alleluia nativitas. *Orlando Consort.*
+ ARG 1-2/95: 234

23151. CD 1002: COMPÈRE—Motets and songs. *Orlando Consort.*
+ ARG 9-10/94: 119
- Fa 7-8/94: 117
+ Gr 6/94: 94

23152. CD 1003: *Gregorian chant from Canterbury Cathedral.* Mass and Office of St. Thomas Becket. *Lay Clerks and Choristers of Canterbury Cathedral; Flood, cond.*
- ARG 11-12/94: 242
+ Fa 9-10/94: 411
- Gr 2/94: 99

23153. CD 1004: *Insalata.* Music of Gombert, Flecha, D'India, Monteverdi, Janequin, Infantas, Purcell, Bach, Debussy, Britten, Tippett, R. Williams, Brooks, and Sondheim. *I Fagiolini; Hollingworth, cond.*
+ ARG 1-2/95: 237
- Fa 11-12/94: 458

23154. CD 1005: MATTHEWS—String quartet no. 3, 6; The flaying of Marsyas. *Brindisi Quartet; Daniel, oboe.*
+ ARG 3-4/95: 136
+ Fa 5-6/95: 257
+ Gr 2/95: 65

23155. CD 1006: *O sweet woods: love songs and sonnets of John Donne and Sir Philip Sidney.* Music of Tessier, Dowland, Morley, Coperario, Ferrabosco, Corkine, Hilton, and Anon. *Agnew, tenor; Wilson, lute.*
- ARG 9-10/95: 286
+ Fa 7-8/95: 403
+ Gr 5/96: 96

23156. CD 1007: SCHOENBERG—String quartet no. 2. BERG—String quartet, op. 3. WEBERN—Langsamer Satz; Five movements for string quartet, op. 5. *Shave, Kiernan, violins; Khoroshunin, viola; Tunnell, cello; Oelze, soprano.*
+ ARG 9-10/95: 107
+ Fa 5-6/95: 421
+ Gr 6/95: 67

23157. CD 1008: *Popes and antipopes.* Music of Mayhuet de Joan, Egidius, Philipot de Caserta, Ciconia, Bartolomeo de Bononia, Velut, Tapissier, Antonio de Civitate, Nicolaus Zacharie, Brassart, Dufay, and Anon. *Orlando Consort.*
+ ARG 3-4/96: 243
+ EM 8/96: 516
+ Fa 1-2/96: 379
+ Gr 11/95: 148

23158. CD 1009: DUNSTABLE—Sacred music. *Orlando Consort.*
+ ARG 7-8/96: 105
+ EM 8/96: 516

+ Fa 5-6/96: 143
+ Gr 2/96: 85

23159. CD 1010: DOWLAND—Lute songs. *Agnew, tenor; Wilson, lute.*
- ARG 5-6/96: 105
- Fa 3-4/96: 157
+ Gr 5/96: 96

23160. CD 1012: *All the king's men: Henry VIII and the princes of the renaissance.* Music of Anon., Henry VIII, Cornysh, Fayrfax, Philip van Wilder, Alonso, Anchieta, Mateo da Flecha, De Cabezón, Encina, Vásquez, Mainerio, Josquin, Gombert, Richafort, Ninot Le Petit, and Jean l'Heritier. *I Fagiolini; Concordia.*
+ ARG 11-12/96: 261
+ Fa 11-12/96: 445
+ Gr 3/97: 90

23161. CD 1014: TALLIS—Antiphon and Mass Salve intemerata; Ave Dei patris; Ave rosa sine spinis. *Choristers and Clerks of Canterbury Cathedral; Flood, cond.*
+ ARG 3-4/97: 243
+ Fa 1-2/97: 287
+ Gr 11/96: 156

MFA

23162. 216001: BOUCOURECHLIEV—Archipels no. 1-4; Anarchipel. *Various performers.*
+ ARG 9-10/95: 112

MGA PRODUCTION ALLEGORY

23163. MGA 2002: DVOŘÁK—Serenade, op. 44. BONDON—Symphonie concertante. STRAUSS—Serenade, op. 7. *Morace, piano; Kammermusik de Naples; Pezzullo, cond.*
+ Fa 1-2/94: 173

MGB MUSIQUES SUISSES

23164. CD 6091: CRUMB—Makrokosmos I and II. *Henz-Diémand, piano.*
+ ARG 3-4/95: 91

23165. CD 6103: NORET—Cello concerto; Hymn to silence. *Rostropovich, cello; Kuehner, organ; Collegium Musicum Zürich; Symphony Orch. of Basel; Sacher, cond.*

+
+ ARG 1-2/97: 141 Fa 11-12/96: 324

23166. CD 6105: SUTER—Laudi of St. Francis of Assisi. *Ferrarini, Kasarova, Villa, Rosca; Budapest Symphony Orch.; Ligeti, cond.*
+ ARG 7-8/95: 207

23167. CD 6108: BUSCH—Clarinet sonata; Songs; Saxophone quartet. *Friedli, clarinet; Roth, saxophone; Hirzel, soprano; Dünki, piano; Erato*

Quartet.
+ ARG 5-6/95: 97

23168. CD 6110: Liederbuch of Johannes Heer of Glarus. *Ensemble Ludwig Senfl; Piguet, cond.*
+ ARG 7-8/95: 258

23169. CD 6112 (2 discs): SCHOECK—Venus. *Popp, O'Neal, Lang, Skovhus; Kammerchor Heidelberg; Knabenkantorei Basel; Philharmonische Werkstatt Schweiz; Venzago, cond.*
• ARG 5-6/95: 165
+ Fa 5-6/94: 237
+ Fa 5-6/95: 320
+ Gr 10/94: 199

23170. CD 6114: SOLIVA—La testa di bronzo. *Ruffini, Cossutta, Balmelli, Coviello; Italian Swiss Radio Orch.; Campori, cond.*
• ARG 5-6/95: 180
- ON 2/3/96: 38

23171. CD 6115 (2 discs): HONEGGER—Les aventures du roi Pausole. *Bacquier, Sénéchal, Barbaux, Yakar; Swiss Youth Phil. Orch.; Venzago, cond.*
+ ARG 5-6/95: 120
• Gr 9/94: 112
+ Op 2/94: 249

23172. CD 6116: FRÖHLICH—6 elegies; Pastorale and rondo; Cello sonata. *Zoboli, oboe; Monighetti, cello; Dünki, piano; Lubimov, Hammerflügel.*
+ ARG 9-10/95: 145

23173. CD 6117: SCHOECK—Violin concerto; Horn concerto. *Verhey, violin; BBC Scottish Symphony; Maksymiuk, cond.; Schneider, horn; Geneva Chamber Orch.; T. Fischer, cond.*
+ ARG 9-10/95: 207

23174. CD 6118: Songs by Schoeck, Wehrli, Roth-Dalbert, Huber, Salquin, Nieg, and Tanas. *Matti, mezzo- soprano; Demarmels, piano.*
- ARG 7-8/95: 264

23175. CD 6120: FRANCK—Chorales; Fantasy; Cantabile; Pièce héroïque. *Delor, organ.*
+ ARG 5-6/95: 112

23176. CD 6122: SCHUMANN—Manfred. *Larsson, Jakobi, Davislim, Pursio, Lika, Schweiger, Heimberg, Renn, Russius; Basler Madrigalisten; Philharmonische Werkstatt Schweiz; Venzago, cond.*
• ARG 1-2/96: 170
• Fa 7-8/95: 311
• Gr 10/95: 114
- ON 10/95: 44
+ Op 9/95: 1130

23177. CD 6124: JOSQUIN—Missa Da pacem. Motets by Schütz, Eisler, Brahms, and Resinarius. *Basel Madrigalists.*
+ ARG 9-10/96: 142

23178. CD 6126: LIEBERMANN—Freispruch für Medea. *Pollet, Haugland, Kowalski; Gamelan Orch. Arum Sih; Hamburg State Opera Chorus; Hamburg State Phil. Orch.; Albrecht, cond.* Recorded live 1995.
+ Fa 11-12/96: 286
+ ON 10/96: 39

MILAN

23179. 73138-35619-2: PIAZZOLLA—Sur. *Astor Piazzolla Quintet.*
+ Fa 1-2/93: 207

23180. 73138-35640-2: PIAZZOLLA—Adios Nonino; Three tangos; Concierto de nacar; Tangazo; Concerto for concertina. *Marconi, concertina; Buenos Aires Symphony Orch.; Calderón, cond.*
+ Fa 9-10/93: 234

23181. 73138-35692-2: Gregorian chant: cantate Domino. *Benedictine Nuns of Sainte Marie de Maumont.*
+ ARG 3-4/96: 240
• Gr 2/96: 97

23182. 73138-35702-2: BOLLING—Enchanting Versailles (strictly classical). *Nordmann, harp; Kudo, flute; Pidoux, cello; Franceries, guitar; Tutterot, clarinet; Sigallo, bassoon; Portejoie, saxophone; Lagarde, piano.*
+ ARG 1-2/96: 89
+ Fa 9-10/95: 149

23183. 73138-35703-2: The soul of chant. *Benedictine Monks of Santo Domingo de Silos.*
• ARG 9-10/95: 275
+ Fa 7-8/95: 409

23184. 73138-35746-2: SALAS—Choral music. *Exaudi Choir; Sanchez, cond.*
• ARG 11-12/96: 193
• Gr 2/97: 97

23185. 73138-35759-2: SAKAMOTO—Chamber music. *Nelson, violin; Morelenbaum, cello; Sakamoto, piano.*
+ ARG 1-2/97: 245

23186. 73138-35764-2: Music of Grandjany, Soler, Bach, White, Tournemire, and Handel. *Gillock, organ; Bride, harp.*
• ARG 1-2/97: 207

MINERVA

23187. 17: Titta Ruffo: Songs. *Ruffo, baritone.* Recorded 1912-29.
+ ARG 7-8/96: 295
+ ON 10/96: 41

MINMAX MUSIC

23188. CD 010: DRESHER—Slow fire. *Paul Dresher Ensemble; Eckert, voice.*
□ Fa 11-12/94: 218

MINNESOTA COMPOSERS FORUM

23189. MN 104/05 (2 LPs): *A la carte.* Music of Aubart, Hovda, Vandervelde, Fuentes, Bermann, D.J. Olsen, and Maye. *The Minnesota Artists Ensemble.*
+ Fa 5-6/87: 241

MINNESOTA PUBLIC RADIO

23190. MPR PD 1001: *Pipedreams premieres.* Music of Loher, Bach-Ferguson, Menotti, Daněk, Bolcom, Mason, Simons, Faxon, and Mendelssohn. *Various organists.*
+ ARG 1-2/94: 181
+ Fa 11-12/93: 489

MIRABILIS

23191. MRCD 901: *Liverpool encores.* Music of Susato, Albinoni, Soler, Bach, Boyce, and others. *Tracey, organ.*
+ ARG 1-2/95: 226

23192. MRCD 902: BAIRSTOW—Organ music (complete). *Jackson, organ.*
+ ARG 1-2/95: 72

23193. MRCD 903: *Late Romantic masterworks.* Music of Andriessen, Bridge, Dupré, Howells, Pach, Peeters, Reger, Schmidt, and Willan. *Fletcher, organ.*
+ ARG 11-12/94: 227
+ Gr 11/91: 134

23194. MRCD 904: BACH—Orgelbüchlein. *Marlow, organ.*
+ ARG 1-2/95: 70

23195. MRCD 905: *The grand organ of St. Paul's Cathedral.* Music of Bruhns, Bach, Mendelssohn, Liszt, Brahms, Reger, and Edmundson. *Lucas, organ.*
+ Gr 2/94: 76

MITCH MILLER MUSIC

23196. MMM 14610: GERSHWIN—An American in Paris; Piano concerto in F; Rhapsody in blue. *Golub, piano; London Symphony Orch.; Miller, cond.* Reissue; recorded 1987.
+ Fa 1-2/96: 203

23197. MMM 14620: PAGANINI—Violin concerto no. 1. WIENIAWSKI—Violin concerto no. 2. *Kaplan, violin; London Symphony Orch.; Miller, cond.* Reissue; recorded 1988.
+ ARG 1-2/96: 153
+ Fa 1-2/96: 124

23198. MMM 14630 (2 discs): BACH—The six sonatas and partitas for solo violin. *Kaplan, violin.* Reissue; recorded 1991-92.
+ ARG 1-2/96: 75
+ Fa 1-2/96: 124

MJA PRODUCTIONS

23199. 7192: *Stradivarius and Steinway II.* Music of Kreisler, Bach-Arnstein, Mozart, Sarasate, Handel, Saint- Saëns, Borowski, Granados, and Brandl. *Antonello, violin; Arnstein, piano.*
+ Fa 5-6/93: 394

MK

23200. 417001: TCHAIKOVSKY—Piano trio in A minor. *Timofeeva, piano; Fedotov, violin; Rodin, cello.*
+ ARG 9-10/91: 136
+ Fa 5-6/91: 301

23201. 417029: Music of Vivaldi, Bach, Schumann, Brahms, and Paganini. *Kuleshov, piano.*
+ ARG 11-12/92: 247

23202. 417054: TCHAIKOVSKY— Romances. *Martynov, tenor; Konstantinidi, piano.*
+ ARG 11-12/92: 219

23203. 417056: PROKOFIEV—Maddalena. STRAVINSKY—Mavra. *Vocal soloists; Moscow Reliken Theater; Tikhonov, cond.*
+ ARG 11-12/93: 170

23204. 417057: KIKTA—Revelations. *Russian Ballet Orch.; Provatorov, cond.*
□ ARG 1-2/94: 115

23205. 417072: Music of Vaĭnberg, Stravinsky, Scriabin, Prokofiev, and Medtner. *Gilels, piano.* Recorded 1957, 1968.
+ Gr 4/93: 101

23206. 417087: Piano concertos by Balakirev, Rimsky-Korsakov, and Medtner. *Zhukov, piano; USSR Radio Symphony Orch.; Dmitriev, Rozhdestvensky, conds.*
• ARG 5-6/94: 172
+ Gr 2/94: 37

23207. 417106: MOZART—Piano concerto no. 21. TCHAIKOVSKY—Piano concerto no. 2. *Gilels, piano; USSR State Symphony Orch.; Kondrashin, cond.* Recorded 1959.
• Gr 5/93: 48

23208. 417109 (2 discs): MEDTNER—Violin sonatas no. 1-3; Nocturnes; Canzonas and danzas. *Shirinsky, violin; Galynin, piano.*
• Gr 11/93: 94

23209. 417116: Music of Artiomov, Baley, Silvestrov, and Ives. *Suk, Stutz, piano; Mazurkovich, violin; USSR Ministry of Culture Symphony Orch.; Baley, cond.*
+ ARG 11-12/95: 258

23210. 417124: LOKSHIN—Symphony no. 5; Quintet; Suite on lyrics by Villon.

GRIEG—Songs (orch. Tischenko). *Kerechanin, Levina, sopranos; Martynov, tenor; Pochapsky, bass; Northern Crown Soloists; Katayev, cond.*
+ ARG 11-12/93: 141

23211. 418008: TCHAIKOVSKY—The months (Seasons). *Pletnev, piano.*
+ ARG 11-12/92: 218

23212. 418014: SHOSTAKOVICH—Violin sonata. HAYDN—Piano sonata no. 39. BRAHMS—Violin sonata no. 2. *Kagan, violin; Richter, piano.* Recorded live.
+ ARG 1-2/93: 148

23213. 418023: BACH—Two- and three-part inventions. *Nikolayeva, piano.* Recorded live 1977.
+ ARG 11-12/92: 77

23214. 418024: BACH—Keyboard transcriptions. *Nikolayeva, piano.*
• Gr 9/92: 126

23215. 418028: CHOPIN—Preludes op. 28; op. 45, op. posth. *Joffe, piano.*
• Gr 5/92: 71

23216. 418042/43 (2 2-disc sets): BACH—The well-tempered clavier. *Nikolayeva, piano.* Recorded live 1984.
+ ARG 11-12/92: 77
• Gr 5/92: 68

MMC

23217. 2001: Music of Ellison, Hojnacki, Goldenberg, Ierardi, Kondo, Sladek, Mascari, Naeger, Moyer, Olmstead, and McKinley. *Slovak Radio Symphony Orch.; Black, cond.*
• ARG 3-4/94: 188

23218. 2002: Music of Cooper, Dix, Hartley, McKinley, Wolking, Shea, and Schreiner. *Slovak Radio Symphony Orch.; Black, cond.*
• ARG 3-4/94: 189

23219. 2003: MCKINLEY—Symphony no. 3. LENNON—Symphonic rhapsody; Saxophone concerto. CARBON—Inner voices. *Forger, saxophone; Slovak Radio Symphony Orch.; Black, cond.*
+ ARG 3-4/94: 189

23220. 2004: *Master Musicians Collective Warsaw series, vol. 2.* Music of Stanley, Whitaker, Kelly, McKinley, Hoose, and Giobbi. *Griswold, piano; Warsaw National Phil. Orch.; Warsaw National Chorus; Black, cond.*
+ ARG 1-2/95: 211
+ Fa 9-10/94: 432

23221. 2005: *Golden petals.* Music of Stravinsky, Shaw, Misurell-Mitchell, English, and McKinley. *Nunemaker, clarinet & saxophone.*
+ ARG 7-8/94: 207

23222. 2008: *Robert Black conducts.* Music of McKinley, Gideon, Black, Koykkar, Warshauer, Hampton, and Renz. *Silesian Phil. Orch.; Slovak Radio Symphony Orch.; Black, cond.*
+ ARG 1-2/95: 211
+ Fa 9-10/95: 413

23223. 2009: Music of Kessler, Rendleman, Rahbee, Stango, and others. *Vesterman, Burnett, piano; Slovak Radio Symphony Orch.; Black, Stankovsky, cond.*
+ ARG 9-10/95: 302
• Fa 11-12/95: 506

23224. 2010: *American chamber music.* Music of Nelson, Stewart, Sleeper, Tepper, and Goodman. *Slovak Chamber Choir; Virtuoso Strings; Kendall, cond.; Slovak Radio Symphony Orch.; Satanowski, cond.; New Slovak Quintet.*
□ ARG 11-12/95: 298
+ Fa 11-12/95: 508

23225. 2012: FINNEY—Songs on texts by James Joyce. *Lombard, soprano; Norris, piano.*
+ ARG 3-4/95: 99
• Fa 11-12/95: 255

23226. 2014: STILLER—Compostions. *Orch. 2001; Maelström Percussion Ensemble; Freeman, cond.*
+ ARG 9-10/95: 302
+ Fa 11-12/95: 387

23227. 2015: *MMC new century, vol. 1.* Music of Skupinsky, Kidde, Muncy, Colson, Ziffrin, and Ernst. *Pilgrim, soprano; Solati Trio; Slovak Radio Symphony Orch.; Black, Stankovsky, conds.*
+ ARG 1-2/96: 249
• Fa 11-12/95: 496

23228. 2016: *Modern American classics, vol. 1.* Music of Burwasser, McKinley, Nelson, Brisman, and Erickson. *Camparone, harpsichord; Pierce, piano; Slovak Radio Symphony Orch.; Stankovsky, Režucha, Black, conds.*
+ ARG 9-10/96: 234
+ Fa 1-2/96: 415

23229. 2017: *MMC new century, vol. 2.* Music of Nytch, Elkana, Fugarino, Crowell, Giusto, and Hoose. *Slovak Radio Symphony Orch.; Silesian Phil. Orch.; Black, Stankovsky, conds.*
+ ARG 1-2/96: 249
+ Fa 11-12/95: 501

23230. 2018: *Discovering the New World.* Music of Ballard, McKinley, Sierra, and Rechtman. *Quintet of the Americas; Manhattan School of Music Chamber Sinfonia; Cortese, cond.*
+ ARG 11-12/96: 308
+ Fa 9-10/96: 418

23231. 2019: VIENS—York, Maine: Fin des siècles; Twelve études-tableaux.

Underhill, piano.
+ ARG 5-6/96: 279
+ Fa 1-2/96: 338

23232. 2020: *MMC New century, vol. 3.*
MELLONI—Piano symphony. PERLONGO—
Piano concerto. ROSS—Piano concerto
"Mosaics". *Burnett, Coleman, Mitchell,
piano; Slovak Radio Symphony Orch.;
Stankovsky, Black, conds.*
+ ARG 7-8/96: 298
+ Fa 5-6/96: 208

23233. 2021: *MMC new century, vol. 4.*
PACKALES—I was on the sea. LEVY—
Symphony no. 4. VALI—Seven Persian
folk songs (Set no. 7). *Slovak Radio
Symphony Orch. & Chorus; Stankovsky,
Black, conds.; Kallen, soprano;
Hampton, piano.*
+ ARG 11-12/96: 308
• Fa 9-10/96: 432
+ Fa 11-12/96: 327

23234. 2023: *New century of American
music.* Music of Hawthorne, Poley,
Bullen, Mascari, and Nelson. *Slovak
Radio Symphony; Stankovsky, cond.;
Manhattan Chamber Sinfonietta; Cortese,
cond.*
+ ARG 11-12/96: 242
• Fa 3-4/97: 392

23235. 2027: *Modern American classics,
vol. 2.* Music of George, Griebling,
Bokhour, and Goodman. *Warsaw
National Phil. Orch.; Silesian Phil.
Orch.; Swoboda, cond.*
+ ARG 3-4/97: 303
+ Fa 11-12/96: 482

23236. 2038: HOIBY—Piano concerto no.
2; Violin sonata; Narrative; Schubert
variations. *S. Babin, piano; Slovak Radio
Symphony Orch.; Stankovsky, cond.; D.
Heifetz, violin; Hoiby, piano.*
+ ARG 9-10/96: 139
+ Fa 9-10/96: 218

MNEMOSYNE

23237. MN-9 (LP): VAN SLYCK—
Pantomime; 12 cadenzas; Will-o-the-
wisp; Capriccio no. 3. *N. Van Slyck, T.
Van Slyck, Witten, pianos.*
+ Fa 7-8/88: 266

MOBILE FIDELITY

23238. MFCD 781: FRANCK—Violin
sonata. FAURÉ—Violin sonata no. 1;
Après une rêve. *Delmoni, violin; Vas,
piano.*
+ ARG 11-12/90: 57
+ Fa 9-10/90: 242

23239. MFCD 786: OGERMANN—Preludio
and chant; Elegia; Symphonic dances;
Two-piano music. *Kremer, violin;
Uriarte, Mrongovius, pianos; London
Symphony Orch.; Ogermann, cond.*
□ ARG 7-8/90: 81

23240. MFCD 814: DVOŘÁK—Piano
concerto in G minor. *Firkušný, piano; St.
Louis Symphony Orch.; Susskind, cond.*
+ DA 10/86: 61

23241. MFCD 852: GLAZUNOV—
Symphony no. 2. *USSR Radio and
Television Large Symphony Orch.;
Fedoseyev, cond.*
+ Fa 11-12/87: 143

23242. MFCD 858: RACHMANINOFF—
Symphonic dances; Aleko: Intermezzo.
*USSR Radio and Television Large
Symphony Orch.; Fedoseyev, cond.*
+ ARG 5-6/88: 54
+ DA 6/87: 80
• Fa 9-10/87: 271
• HPR 9/87: 98
• SR 2/88: 193

23243. MFCD 863: MENDELSSOHN—
Symphony no. 4. ROSSINI—William Tell:
Overture. *USSR State Symphony Orch.;
Svetlanov, cond.*
- Fa 11-12/87: 175

23244. MFCD 864: TCHAIKOVSKY—
Romeo and Juliet; Francesca da Rimini.
*USSR Radio and Television Large
Symphony Orch.; Ovchinnikov, cond.*
+ ARG 5-6/88: 68 m.f.
+ Fa 11-12/87: 239
+ HPR 12/87: 101

23245. MFCD 865: HAYDN—Cello
concertos no. 1-2. *Rudin, cello;
Lithuanian Chamber Orch.; Sondeckis,
cond.*
• Fa 11-12/87: 152

23246. MFCD 866: GERSHWIN—Rhapsody
in blue. RACHMANINOFF—Rhapsody on a
theme of Paganini. *Dorensky, piano;
USSR Ministry of Culture Symphony
Orch.; Dmitriev, cond.*
+ ARG 5-6/88: 53
- Fa 11-12/87: 140

23247. MFCD 869: DENISOV—Sun of the
Incas. SCHNITTKE—Three madrigals.
GUBAIDULINA—Concordanza.
MANSURIAN—Tovem. *Lee, soprano;
Soloists Ensemble of the Bolshoi Theater
Orch.; Lazarev, cond.*
+ ARG 7-8/88: 72
+ Fa 3-4/88: 185

23248. MFCD 870: TCHAIKOVSKY—
Hamlet: Incidental music; Almaviva's
couplet from the Barber of Seville; Snow
maiden: Overture. *Raikov, tenor; USSR
Radio and Television Symphony Orch.;
Žiuraitis, Akulov, Gauk, cond.*
+ ARG 1-2/89: 93
+ DA 1/89: 38
• Fa 5-6/89: 335
□ HPR 6/89: 88

23249. MFCD 871: SCHUMANN—
Nachtstücke, op. 23. SCHUBERT—
Moments musicaux, D. 780. *Gilels,
piano.*

+ DA 6/88: 80
+ Fa 5-6/88: 205

23250. MFCD 875: GLAZUNOV—String
quintet, op. 39; String quartet no. 7.
Kovalev, cello; Shostakovich Quartet.
+ DA 6/88: 56
+ Fa 5-6/88: 132
+ HPR 7/88: 90

23251. MFCD 876: *Choral music by
Russian composers.* Music of Glinka,
Tchaikovsky, Shebalin, Koval, Sviridov,
and Rachmaninoff. *USSR Radio and
Television Large Chorus; Ptitsa,
Ermakova, cond.*
+ ARG 5-6/88: 82
+ DA 2/88: 58
+ Fa 3-4/88: 245

23252. MFCD 877: *Songs my mother
taught me.* Music of Kreisler, Brahms,
Valdez, Paradis, Sarasate, Massenet,
Tartini, Smetana, Gluck, Vieuxtemps,
Fauré, Ambrosio, Mendelssohn, and
Dvořák. *Delmoni, violin; Vas, piano.*
+ ARG 7-8/89: 126
+ DA 1/88: 52
• Fa 1-2/88: 268
+ Fa 7-8/89: 308

23253. MFCD 878: ARENSKY—
Symphonies no. 1-2. *USSR State
Symphony Orch.; Svetlanov, cond.*
• ARG 5-6/88: 6
□ Fa 3-4/88: 62
+ NYT 1/3/88: H22

23254. MFCD 882: TCHAIKOVSKY—
Symphony no. 5. *USSR State Symphony
Orch.; Svetlanov, cond.*
• Fa 9-10/88: 281

23255. MFCD 885: RACHMANINOFF—
Symphony no. 2. *Bolshoi Theater Orch.;
Svetlanov, cond.*
+ ARG 5-6/88: 52
• Fa 5-6/88: 187

23256. MFCD 888: PROKOFIEV—
Symphonies no. 1, 3; Violin concerto no.
1. *Oistrakh, violin; USSR Radio and
Television Large Symphony Orch.;
Rozhdestvensky, cond.*
+ Fa 5-6/88: 184

23257. MFCD 891: STRAVINSKY—
L'histoire du soldat: Suite; Septet;
Pribaoutki; Ragtime. *Soloists Ensemble
of the Bolshoi Theater;Lazarev, cond.*
+ Fa 7-8/88: 260
• HPR 9/88: 90

23258. MFCD 892: TCHAIKOVSKY—
Symphony no. 6; Undine. Excerpts.
*Milashkina, Raikov; Opera Chorus;
USSR Radio and Television Operatic and
Symphony Orch.; Akulov, cond.; USSR
State Symphony Orch.; Svetlanov, cond.;
USSR Radio and Television Large
Symphony Orch.; Gauk, cond.*
- ARG 11-12/88: 94

MOBILE FIDELITY

+ DA 11/88: 84
+ Fa 9-10/88: 281

23259. MFCD 893: SHCHEDRIN—The lady with a lapdog. *Bolshoi Theater Orch.; Lazarev, cond.*
+ DA 7/88: 50
+ Fa 7-8/88: 251

23260. MFCD 895: RUBINSTEIN—Piano concerto no. 4; Etude, op. 23. LISZT—Piano music. *Ginzburg, piano; USSR State Symphony Orch.; Chershonsky, cond.*
+ ARG 1-2/89: 82
+ Fa 1-2/89: 252

23261. MFCD 896: KANCHELI—Symphony no. 5; Bright sorrow. *Georgian Radio Orch.; State Chorus & Symphony Orch. of Georgia; Kakhidze, cond.*
+ ARG 11-12/89: 71
+ Fa 9-10/89: 227

23262. MFCD 897: GLAZUNOV—Symphony no. 4; Stenka Razin; Violin concerto, op. 82. *Snitkovsky, violin; USSR Radio and Television Large Symphony Orch.; Rozhdestvensky, cond.; USSR State Academy Orch.; Fedoseyev, cond.*
+ ARG 5-6/89: 52
+ Fa 3-4/89: 168
• HPR 6/89: 76

23263. MFCD 899: KHACHATURIAN—Violin concerto in D minor. SIBELIUS—Violin concerto. *Oistrakh, violin; USSR Radio and Television Symphony Orch.; Khachaturian, Rozhdestvensky, cond.*
+ Fa 7-8/88: 181

23264. MFCD 900: RACHMANINOFF—Isle of the dead; The bells. *Pisarenko, Maslennikov, Yakovenko; Yurlov Russian Choir; USSR State Symphony Orch.; Svetlanov, cond.*
• ARG 1-2/89: 75
+ Fa 1-2/89: 239
• HPR 3/89: 86

23265. MFCD 901 (2 discs): KHACHATURIAN—Gayane. *USSR Radio and Television Large Symphony Orch.; Kakhidze, cond.*
• ARG 11-12/89: 72
+ Fa 7-8/89: 167
• St 9/89: 173

23266. MFCD 903: ARTYOMOV—Gurian hymn; Invocations; Way to Olympus. *Davydova, soprano; Shulgin, violin; Yanchenko, organ; percussion ensemble; Artyomov, cond.; Moscow Phil. Symphony Orch.; Kitaenko, cond.; USSR State Symphony Orch.; Mynbaev, cond.*
• ARG 3-4/89: 12
+ Fa 11-12/88: 112
+ HPR 3/89: 67

23267. MFCD 905: Violin music of Prokofiev, Juozapaitis, Kobekin,

Bobylev, and Schnittke. *Malinin, Melnikov, violins; Pekarsky, cymbals; Bobylev, piano.*
+ ARG 1-2/89: 116
+ Fa 11-12/88: 248

23268. MFCD 907: KHRENNIKOV—Symphony no. 2; Violin concerto no. 1. *USSR Academic Symphony Orch.; Svetlanov, cond.*
• ARG 5-6/89: 57
- Fa 5-6/89: 222
• DA 4/89: 72

23269. MFCD 909: SHOSTAKOVICH—Violin sonata, op. 134. FRANCK—Violin sonata in A major. *Oistrakh, violin; Richter, piano.*
+ ARG 11-12/88: 86
+ Fa 11-12/88: 279

23270. MFCD 914: GLINKA—String quartet no. 2. MYASKOVSKY—String quartet no. 13. TANEYEV—String trio, op. 21. *USSR Radio and Television Quartet.*
+ ARG 3-4/90: 130
• Fa 5-6/90: 173

23271. MFCD 915: SCHNITTKE—String quartet no. 2; Hymns no. 1-3. *Beethoven Quartet; chamber ensemble.*
+ Fa 11-12/90: 339

23272. MFCD 917: DENISOV—Romantic music, for oboe, harp, violin, viola, and cello; Piano trio; String trio; Clarinet quintet. *Various performers.*
+ Fa 7-8/90: 130
+ MA 11/90: 71

23273. MFCD 918: ARTYOMOV—Mattinates no. 1-2; Romantic capriccio; Hymns of sudden wafts no. 1-2; Prelude to sonnets; Moonlight dreams. *Various performers.*
□ ARG 11-12/90: 13
+ Fa 11-12/90: 140

MOBIUS

23274. D 0193 (2 discs): *Beyond Beethoven. Music of Beethoven, Ravel, Brahms, Shostakovich, and Mobius. Mobius.*
+ Fa 11-12/93: 517

MODE

23275. 7 (LP): NUROCK—Natural sound. *Natural Sound Ensemble.*
□ Fa 9-10/88: 221

23276. 8 (LP): STEFFENS—La femme-fleur; Spielstrategian; Pluie de feu; Rose quest; Rituelle Aktionen II; Guernica. *Various instrumental soloists; Northwest German Phil. Orch.; Kulka, cond.*
□ Fa 9-10/88: 269

23277. 14: GITECK—Breathing songs from a turning sky; Thunder, like a white bear dancing; Callin' home coyote. *Duykers, tenor; New Performance*

Group.
+ Fa 1-2/89: 167

23278. 15: Piano music of Cage, Hovhaness, Crumb, Satoh, and Gan-Ru. *Tan, piano.*
+ Fa 5-6/89: 390

23279. 16: SPEACH—Moto; Pensees; Trajet; Sonata; Shattered glass; Telepathy. *Davis, speaker; Schanzer, guitar; Krech, trombone; De Mare, piano; Pugliese, Williams, percussion; Bowery Ensemble; Speach, cond.*
+ Fa 9-10/89: 333

23280. 17: CAGE—Music for four; Thirty pieces for string quartet. *Arditti Quartet.*
+ ARG 1-2/90: 39
+ Fa 11-12/89: 168
+ Gr 12/89: 1152
+ NYT 9/17/89: H34

23281. 20: BRUCE—Eight ghosts; The dream of the other dreamers; The plague. *Electric Phoenix; Runswick, instrumentalist.*
+ ARG 7-8/92: 110

23282. 21: PIMENTA—Rings; Rozart; Structures II; Short waves 1985. *Electronic music.*
+ Fa 11-12/90: 315

23283. 24: CAGE—Five stone wind; Cartridge music. *Kosugi, amp. violin, electronics, bamboo flute; Pugliese, clay pots & tapes; Tudor, electronics.*
+ ARG 11-12/91: 51

23284. 25: *Perkin' at Merkin. Music of Xenakis, Feldman, Vigeland, Cage, Norgard and Mancini. Pugliese, percussion.*
+ ARG 3-4/92: 188

23285. 27 : CAGE—String quartet in four parts; Music for four. *Arditti Quartet.*
+ Gr 12/93: 81

23286. 28/29 (2 discs): CAGE—Roaratorio; Laughtears; Writing for the second time through Finnegans wake. *Cage, Schöning, speakers; Heaney, singer; Malloy, flute; Ennis, uillean pipes; Glackin,violin; P. & M. Mercier, bodhrans.*
□ Gr 10/94: 132

23287. 30: LEBARON—Rana, ritual, and revelations. *New Music Consort; various other performers.*
+ Fa 1-2/95: 185

23288. 31: Haydée Schvartz plays Pärt, Cage, Scelsi, Kagel, Berio, Schumann, Gandini, and Valverde. *Schvartz, piano.*
+ Fa 1-2/95: 357

23289. 32, 37 (2 separate discs): CAGE—Freeman etudes. *Arditti, violin.*
+ Fa 1-2/95: 140

23290. 38/39 (2 discs): CAGE—Europera 3; Europera 4. *Soloists; Long Beach Opera; Culver, cond.*
+ Fa 9-10/95: 162

23291. 33: Music of Partch, Pugliese, Drummond, Rosenblum, and Monk. *Newband.*
□ ARG 11-12/94: 216
+ Fa 1-2/95: 371

23292. 34: *Made in America.* RUSSELL—Complete works. *Essential Music.*
+ Fa 1-2/95: 252
□ Fa 3-4/95: 280

23293. 35: HONEGGER—Christophe Colomb. *Rawson, Garvey, Furnival, Knecht, McCabe; Opera Sacra of Buffalo; Peltz, cond.*
- Fa 1-2/95: 178

23294. 36: CAGE—Europera 5. *Herr, soprano; Burgess, tenor; Mikhashoff, piano; Williams, victrola; Metz, tape.*
+ Fa 1-2/95: 139
+ Fa 9-10/95: 165

23295. 40: OLIVEROS—St. George and the dragon; In memoriam Mr. Whitney. *American Voices; Oliveros, accordion & voice.*
□ Fa 3-4/95: 249

23296. 41: CAGE—*Orchestral works, vol. 1.* 101; Apartment house 1776; Ryoanji. *New England Conservatory Philharmonia; Avant-Garde Ensemble of the New England Conservatory; Drury, cond.*
+ ARG 7-8/95: 268
+ Fa 5-6/95: 161

23297. 43: WOLFF—*Bread and roses.* Piano works 1976-1983. *Pinkas, piano.*
+ ARG 9-10/95: 238
+ Fa 9-10/95: 368 (Silverton)
+ Fa 9-10/95: 369 (Burwasser)

23298. 44: *The number pieces, vol. 1.* CAGE—Four; One; Two. *Flammer, violin & rainsticks; Joste, Alchourroun, piano & rainsticks; Michaut, rainsticks.*
+ ARG 11-12/95: 102
+ Fa 1-2/96: 171 (Silverton)
+ Fa 1-2/96: 174 (Lange)

23299. 45: *New classicism.* RAIČKOVIĆ—Happy overture; Romances for violin and orchestra; Prelude and fugue; Dream quartet; Symphony no. 1. *Frolov, Tan, toy pianos; Ensemble Musica da Camera; Moscow Symphony Orch.; Raičković, cond.*
+ ARG 11-12/96: 307
• Fa 11-12/95: 338

23300. 46: *Sanctuary.* Invocation; Hi Bali, hi; Processional; Sanctuary; Non-stop flight (excerpt). *Various soloists; Deep Listening Band; Women Who Drum.*
+ Fa 1-2/96: 419

23301. 47: *The piano works, vol. 1.* CAGE—Music for two; One; Music walk. *Drury, piano(s) and devices.*
+ Fa 1-2/96: 169 (Carl)
+ Fa 1-2/96: 171 (Silverton)
+ Fa 1-2/96: 174 (Lange)

23302. 48: BERIO—Folk songs; Sequenza 3; Chamber music; O king; Circles. *Schadeberg, soprano; Musicians' Accord; León, Biggs, conds.*
• Fa 5-6/96: 106

23303. 50: CAGE—*Piano works, vol. 2.* Sonatas and interludes. *Vandré, piano.*
+ ARG 9-10/96: 105
+ Fa 9-10/96: 172
+ Gr 2/97: 79

23304. 51: WOOD—Village burial with fire; Spirit festival with lamentations. *Percussive Rotterdam.*
□ ARG 9-10/96: 276
+ Fa 5-6/96: 319

23305. 52: *The art of the curved bow, vol. 1.* Music of Bach and Schnebel. *M. Bach, cello (with curved bow) & voice; Seitz, mezzo-soprano.*
• ARG 9-10/96: 192
• Fa 7-8/96: 374

23306. 53: XENAKIS—Plektó; Eonta; Akanthos; Rebonds "b" and "a"; N'shima. *Rubin, piano; May, soprano; McEwan, percussion; Aks, Lindevald, voices; ST-X Ensemble; Bornstein, cond.*
+ Fa 9-10/96: 362

23307. 672001: SCHUBERT—Piano sonata, D. 784. BRAHMS—Intermezzi, op. 117; Variations and fugue on a theme of Handel, op. 24. *Wührer, piano.*
• Fa 9-10/88: 121

23308. 672007: MUSSORGSKY—Pictures at an exhibition (arr. Ravel). RAVEL—Le tombeau de Couperin. KODÁLY—Dances from Galanta. *French Radio and Television National Orch.; Bour, cond.*
• Fa 11-12/88: 239

MOIDART

23309. MIDCD 001: *The Scottish songbook.* Twenty mono historic vocal selections. *Various vocal soloists.*
+ Fa 11-12/95: 447

23310. MIDCD 004: *The star o' Rabbie Burns.* Twenty-six mono historic vocal selections of songs by Robert Burns. *Various vocal soloists.*
+ Fa 11-12/95: 448

MONTILLA

23311. 75: LECUONA—Rosa la China: highlights. *Pérez, Sai-Vela, Córdoba, Lopez; Madrid Chamber Orch.; Guerrero, cond.* Reissue.
+ ARG 1-2/93: 112

23312. 3011: CHAPI—La tempestad: Highlights. *A. Kraus, F. Kraus, Pérez, Huarte; Orch.; Estela, cond.*
+ ARG 9-10/94: 116

MORALEDA

23313. 32 (2 discs): *Manuel de Falla's circle.* Music of Comellas, Cerda, Giro, Cercos, and others. *Various performers.*
+ ARG 1-2/97: 232

23314. 1094: LISZT—Piano music. *Gevers, piano.*
+ ARG 7-8/96: 147

23315. 1294: DEBUSSY—Violin sonata. PROKOFIEV—Violin sonata no. 2. *Mendoza, violin; Borras, piano.*
• ARG 9-10/96: 112

23316. 49522: TOLDRÀ—String quartet no. 2; Songs; Oracio al maig. *Glinka Quartet; Ricci, mezzo-soprano; Soler, Toldra, Carreta, piano.*
• ARG 7-8/96: 216

23317. 49523: Music of Toldra, Grieg, Sarasate, and Turull. *Leon, violin; Muñiz, piano.*
- ARG 11-12/96: 257

MOSS MUSIC

23318. MCD 10037: RIMSKY-KORSAKOV—Scheherazade. MUSSORGSKY—Khovanshshina: Dance of the Persian slaves. *Rabinovitsj, violin; St. Louis Symphony Orch.; Semkow, Slatkin, cond.*
• Fa 3-4/87: 192

23319. MCD 10040: STRAUSS—Death and transfiguration; Metamorphosen. *Cincinnati Symphony Orch.; Gielen, cond.*
+ Fa 3-4/87: 212
• Opus 8/87: 50

23320. MCD 10041: HANDEL—Water music; Music for the royal fireworks. *Minnesota Orch.; Skrowaczewski, cond.*
• Fa 3-4/87: 127

23321. MCD 10042: BRAHMS—Piano trios no. 1, 3. *Kalichstein, piano; Laredo, violin; Robinson, cello.*
+ DA 2/88: 59
+ Fa 9-10/87: 170

23322. MCD 10046: BACH—Cantatas, BWV 53, 158, 211; Motets: BWV 226, 228. *Monoyios, Love, Oosting, Ostendorf; Amor Artis Chorale; Amor Artis Baroque Orch.; Somary, cond.*
+ DA 9/87: 68
+ Fa 9-10/87: 136

23323. MCD 10049: LISZT—Spanish rhapsody (arr. Busoni); Piano concerto no. 1; Totentanz for piano solo. *Marsh, piano; London Phil. Orch.; Freeman,*

MOSS MUSIC

cond.
+ Fa 11-12/87: 167

23324. MCD 10055: sVAUGHAN WILLIAMS—Serenade to music. ELGAR—Serenade for strings, op. 20. BRITTEN—Serenade for tenor, horn and strings. *Hirst, tenor; other vocalists; New York Virtuosi Chamber Orch.; Klein, cond.*
- Fa 5-6/88: 123 (Vaughan Williams)
+ Fa 5-6/88: 123 (Elgar, Britten)

MOTETTE

23325. 11001: SAINT-SAËNS—Marche héroïque; Prelude and fugue, op. 99; Fantasy, op. 101. PLANYAVSKY—Improvisations on themes from Carnival of the animals. *Planyavsky, organ.*
□ 3-4/88: 181

23326. 11041: SCHUMANN—Sketches, op. 58; Etudes for pedal piano, op. 56; Fugues on the name of BACH, op. 60. *Mechler, organ.*
- ARG 11-12/89: 115
+ Fa 9-10/89: 322

23327. 11061 (2 discs): MESSIAEN—Livre du Saint Sacrement. *Rössler, organ.*
● Fa 9-10/88: 199

23328. 11131: WIDOR—Symphonies no. 4, 6. *Chaisemartin, organ.*
+ ARG 9-10/89. 118
+ Fa 7-8/89: 284
□ Gr 6/89: 66

23329. 11141: WIDOR—Symphonies no. 5, 10. *Roth, organ.*
+ Fa 11-12/88: 312

23330. 11171: LANGLAIS—Te Deum; Hommage à Rameau; Incantation pour un jour de saint. HAKIM—Symphonie en 3 mouvments; Fantasie sur Adeste Fideles. *Hakim, Dufourcet, organ.*
+ ARG 1-2/90: 57
+ Fa 11-12/89: 258

23331. 11191: SCHMIDT—Prelude and fugue in E♭ major; Toccata and fugue in A♭ major; Toccata in C major. *Binder, organ.*
+ ARG 11-12/90: 108
+ Fa 1-2/91: 302

23332. 11221: WIDOR—Symphony no. 1. VIERNE—Sur le Rhin; Etoile su soir; Hymne au soleil. *Chaisemartin, organ.*
+ Fa 11-12/89: 412

23333. 11231: WIDOR—Symphony no. 2. VIERNE—Requiem. *Borisset-Bailer, organ.*
● ARG 11-12/89: 138

23334. 11241: WIDOR—Symphonies no. 3, 7. *Roth, organ.*
+ ARG 7-8/90: 123
+ Fa 5-6/90: 348

23335. 11251: WIDOR—Symphony no. 8. VIERNE—Arabesque. GUILMANT—Marche funèbre et chant séraphique. *Pierre, organ.*
+ ARG 11-12/89: 138
+ Fa 11-12/89: 412

23336. 11271, 11281, 11291 (3 separate discs): MENDELSSOHN—Organ music (complete). *Planyavsky, organ.*
- ARG 7-8/93: 124
+ Gr 10/92: 140 (v.1)

23337. 11381: FRANCK—Pièce in A; Andantinos in G minor, A♭; Fantaisie in C; Offertoire in G minor; Grand pièce symphonique. *Roth, organ.*
- ARG 9-10/92: 106

23338. 11382: FRANCK—Prelude, fugue and variations; Pastorale; Prière; Final; Offertoire on Breton noels; Fantaisie in A. *Roth, organ.*
- ARG 9-10/92: 106

23339. 11501: ELGAR—Organ sonatas no. 1-2; Vesper voluntaries; Cantique; Pomp and circumstance march no. 1. *Fisher, organ.*
● ARG 5-6/92: 53

23340. 11561: GUILMANT—Organ works, vol. 6. *Lombard, organ.*
● ARG 3-4/92: 65

23341. 11611: BACH—Prelude and fugue in D; Concerto in A minor after Vivaldi; Prelude and fugue in C, S. 547; Schübler chorales, S. 645-650; Fantasy and fugue in G minor. *Böhme, organ.*
● ARG 5-6/92: 25

23342. 11621 (2 discs): BACH—Clavierübung III. *Friedrich, organ.*
+ ARG 5-6/92: 18

23343. 11641: New organ in St. Stephen's Vienna. *Planyavsky, organ.*
+ ARG 5-6/93: 166

23344. 11671: DEMESSIEUX—Response for Easter; 12 chorale preludes; Andante; Te Deum. DUPRÉ—Preludes and fugues, op. 7. *Leclerc, organ.*
+ ARG 3-4/93: 73

23345. 11691: LEFÉBURE-WÉLY—Marches, offertories, postludes. *Parker-Smith, organ.*
- ARG 1-2/93: 112

23346. 20211: Music of Purcell, Clarke, Lemmens, Stanley, Guilmant, Kee, Schmidt, and others. *Mainz Cathedral Brass; Schönberger, organ.*
● ARG 5-6/94: 181

23347. 30151: FALLA—Four Spanish pieces; Three-cornered hat: Four dances; Amor brujo. *Herweg, Soga, guitars.*
+ Fa 11-12/90: 222

23348. 40111: DUPRÉ—Symphony in G minor; Deux esquisses; Iste confessor; Fileuse; Symphonic-pasion. *Meldau, organ; Zürich Symphony Orch.; Schweizer, cond.*
+ ARG 5-6/93: 82

23349. 40151: EBEN—Organ concerto. *Meisner, organ; Handel-Festspielorchester Halle; Hempfling, cond.*
● ARG 11-12/92: 117
+ Fa 11-12/92: 229

23350. 40161: PEETERS—Organ concerto; Toccata, fugue and hymn; Aria; Three chorale preludes. *Wisskirchen, Meisner, organ; Youth Symphony of Cologne; Hempfling, cond.*
+ ARG 7-8/94: 149
+ Fa 1-2/94: 256

23351. 50241: DURUFLÉ—Requiem; Scherzo; Suite. *Vocal soloists; Neuwieder Chamber Choir; Lombard, organ; Kämpf, Sorger, conds.*
- ARG 3-4/92: 50

23352. 50251: DUPRÉ—Pieces, op. 27; Vespers of the Holy Virgin. *Choral Scholars of St. Nicholas; Chaisemartin, organ.*
+ Gr 1/96: 80

23353. 50451, 50461 (2 separate discs): Ars Gregoriana, vol. 10, 13. *Various performers.*
+ ARG 9-10/93: 242

23354. 50511: *Gregorian chant.* Credo. *Chant Schola of the Robert-Schumann-Hochschule of Düsseldorf; Hodes, cond.*
+ Fa 1-2/94: 391

MOVE

23355. MD 3031: SCULTHORPE—Piano works. W. STANLEY—Rose Bay quadrilles. *Cooke, Coote, Kouvaras, Chamberlain, Beilharz, Furman, Hannan, Schulthorpe, pianos.*
+ Gr 3/92: 70

MOVIMENTO MUSICA

23356. 012-010 (2 discs): DONIZETTI—Lucia di Lammermoor. *Callas, Di Stefano, Panerai, Zaccaria; with assisting soloists; Teatro alla Scala Chorus; Berlin Radio Symphony Orch.; Karajan, cond. Recorded live 1955.*
+ Fa 11-12/89: 191

23357. 051-001 (2 discs): VERDI—Il Trovatore. *Price, Simionato, Corelli, Bastianini, Zaccaria; with assisting soloists; Vienna State Opera Chorus; Vienna Phil.; Karajan, cond. Recorded live 1962.*
● Fa 1-2/90: 334

23358. 051-004 (3 discs): MOZART—Nozze di Figaro. *Güden, Sciutti, Lear,*

Fischer-Dieskau, Evans; with assisting soloists; Salzburg Festival; Maazel, cond. Recorded live 1963.
+ ARG 5-6/90: 83

23359. 051-005 (3 discs): BACH—St. Matthew passion. *Grümmer, Höffgen, Dermota, Fischer-Dieskau, Edelmann; Wiener Singverein; Wiener Sängerknaben; Vienna Phil. Orch.; Furtwängler, cond.* Recorded live 1954.
- ARG 5-6/90: 20 m.f.
+ Fa 1-2/90: 101 m.f.

23360. 051-008: VERDI—Rigoletto: Act 3; Aida: Overture; Luisa Miller: Overture; Forza del Destino: Overture. *Milanov, Merriman, Peerce, Warren, Moscona; NBC Symphony Orch.; Toscanini, cond.* Recorded live.
+ ARG 1-2/90: 101

23361. 051-012 (3 discs): MOZART—Don Giovanni. *Price, Schwarzkopf, Sciutti, Valletti, Wächter, Berry, Panerai, Zaccaria; Vienna State Opera Chorus; Vienna Phil. Orch.; Karajan, cond.* Recorded live 1960.
+ Fa 1-2/90: 239 (Price)
• Fa 1-2/90: 239 (others)

23362. 051-015: *Liederalbum.* Songs of Schubert, Brahms, and Wolf. *Schwarzkopf, soprano; Reutter, piano.* Recorded live 1962.
+ ARG 1-2/90: 137
+ Fa 11-12/89: 423
+ NYT 2/4/90: H33

23363. 051-017: VERDI—Quatro pezzi sacri. *RIAS Chamber Choir; Berlin Radio Symphony Orch.; Fricsay, cond.* Recorded live 1952.
- Fa 11-12/89: 394

23364. 051-019: SCHUBERT—Winterreise. *Fischer-Dieskau, baritone; Billing, piano.* Recorded live 1948.
+ Fa 11-12/89: 349
+ NYT 2/4/90: H33

23365. 051-020 (2 discs): VERDI—Un ballo in maschera. *Gencer, Gatta, Lazzarini, Bergonzi, Zanasi; with assisting soloists; Teatro comunale (Bologna); De Fabritiis, cond.* Recorded live 1961.
• Fa 1-2/90: 330

23366. 051-022 (2 discs): VERDI—Macbeth. *Callas, Penno, Mascherini, Tajo; with assisting soloists; Teatro alla Scala; De Sabata, cond.* Recorded live 1952.
+ Fa 1-2/90: 330

23367. 051-023: Opera arias of Spontini, Verdi, Bellini, Massenet, and Bizet. *Callas, soprano; North German Radio Symphony Orch.; Rescigno, Prêtre, cond.* Recorded live 1959, 1962.
• Fa 11-12/89: 422

23368. 051-024 (2 discs): BEETHOVEN—Fidelio. *Mödl, Seefried, Dermota, Kmentt, Schoeffler, Weber; with assisting soloists; Vienna State Opera Chorus; Vienna Phil. Orch.; Böhm, cond.* Recorded live 1955.
+ ARG 11-12/89: 34
+ Fa 11-12/89: 128

23369. 051-025: Opera arias of Bellini, Verdi, Rossini, and Puccini. *Callas, Lance, Gobbi; with assisting soloists; Paris Opéra; Sebastian, cond.* Recorded live 1958.
• Fa 11-12/89: 422

23370. 051-026 (2 discs): MOZART—Entführung aus dem Serail. *Pütz, Holm, Wunderlich, Wohlfahrt, Littasy; Vienna State Opera Chorus; Salzburg Mozarteum Orch.; Kertész, cond.* Recorded live 1961.
• ARG 11-12/89: 85
• Fa 11-12/89: 290

23371. 051-027 (2 discs): PUCCINI—La bohème. *Freni, Güden, Raimondi, Panerai, Vinco; with assisting soloists; Vienna State Opera; Karajan, cond.* Recorded live 1963.
• Fa 11-12/89: 322

23372. 051-028 (2 discs): MOZART—Zauberflöte. *Hallstein, Lipp, Gedda, Kunz, Frick; with assisting soloists; Karajan, cond.* Recorded live 1962.
• ARG 1-2/90: 70
• Fa 11-12/89: 299

23373. 051-029: BRAHMS—Symphonies no. 2-3. *Italian Radio and Television Milan Symphony Orch.; Celibidache, cond.*
- Fa 1-2/90: 140

23374. 051-032 (2 discs): BIZET—Pêcheurs de perles. *Malagrini, Kraus, Taddei, Cava; Italian Radio and Television Milan Chorus & Symphony Orch.; La rosa Parodi, cond.* Recorded live 1960.
- Fa 1-2/90: 131

MPI

23375. 21001: BROEDERS—20 poemas de amor y una canción desesperada. *Garza, tenor; Conti, piano.*
+ ARG 11-12/96: 103
• Fa 11-12/96: 211

MPV

23376. MPV-14 (LP): Music of Cavalli, Ibert, Ravel, Hemsi, and others. *Gabbai, soprano; Guarino, piano; Parma Conservatory Orch.; Athens Radio Symphony Orch.; Guarino, cond.*
• Fa 5-6/88: 239 m.f.

23377. MPV-15 (LP): GIULIANI—Six Lieder op. 89; Six cavatinas op. 39; Six ariettas op. 95. *Duo Majeron-Balestra*

(soprano and guitar).
• Fa 5-6/88: 130

MULTISONIC

23378. 31 0036-2: DVOŘÁK—Mass in D, op. 86. KOZELUCH—Missa pastoralis. *Vocal soloists & choruses; Prague Phil. Orch.; Kulínsky, cond.*
+ ARG 7-8/92: 125
+ Fa 5-6/92: 150

23379. 31 0076-2: MOZART—Piano sonatas, no. 8, 15, K. 533. *Richter, piano.* Recorded live 1956.
+ ARG 7-8/92: 193
+ Fa 5-6/92: 211

23380. 31 0091-2: HAYDN—Piano sonata no. 20. BEETHOVEN—Piano sonata no. 23. CHOPIN—Piano sonata no. 2. RAVEL—Valses nobles et sentimentales. *Gilels, piano.* Recorded live.
+ ARG 9-10/92: 115
+ Fa 11-12/92: 447

23381. 31 0095-2: EBEN—Job. *Titterington, organ; Lee, narrator.*
+ ARG 7-8/93: 86
+ Fa 3-4/93: 157

23382. 31 0097-2: EBEN—Laudes; Two choral fantasies; Landscapes of Patmos. *Ahrens, organ; Lenniger, percussion.*
• Fa 3-4/93: 158

23383. 31 0098-2: EBEN—Sunday music; Small choral partita; Chagall windows. *Ahrens, organ; Lodenkemper, trumpet.*
+ ARG 7-8/93: 86
• Fa 3-4/93: 158

23384. 31 0104-2: MENDELSSOHN—Violin concerto in E minor. BEETHOVEN—Concerto for piano, violin, cello and orchestra. *Stern, violin; Prague Symphony Orch.; Rohan, cond.; Oborin, piano; D. Oistrakh, violin; Knushevitsky, cello; USSR State Symphony Orch.; Ivanov, cond.* Recorded live 1966, 1961.
+ Fa 5-6/92: 197

23385. 31 0106-2 (3 discs): BEETHOVEN—Piano concertos. *Gilels, piano; Czech Phil. Orch.; Sanderling, cond.* Recorded live 1958.
+ Fa 9-10/92: 174

23386. 31 0109-2: SCHUBERT—Violin sonata (duo), D. 574. BRAHMS—Violin sonata no. 3. RAVEL—Violin sonata. PROKOFIEV—Melodies for violin and piano, op. 35b. *Oistrakh, violin; F. Bauer, piano.* Recorded live.
+ ARG 11-12/92: 250
+ Fa 9-10/92: 431

23387. 31 0150-2: SUK—Ripening. MARTINŮ—Concerto grosso. ROUSSEL—Bacchus et Ariane: Suite no. 1. *Czech Phil. Orch.; Ančerl, cond.* Reissues.
+ ARG 7-8/93: 164

MULTISONIC

23388. 31 0152-2: SMETANA—Má vlast. *Prague Radio Symphony Orch.; Krombholc, cond.* Recorded 1973.
+ ARG 1-2/93: 153

23389. 31 0154-2: JANÁČEK—Šarka. *Nováková, Jurečka, Kunc, Válka; Brno Radio Orch.; Bakala, cond.*
+ ARG 3-4/96: 257

23390. 31 0159-2: C. STAMITZ—Six trios for flute, violin and continuo, op. 14. *Sonatori Ensemble.*
+ ARG 5-6/93: 140
+ Fa 3-4/93: 302

23391. 31 0183-2: KLUSÁK—Sixth invention; Pasticcio olandese per orchestra; String quartet no. 3 in one movement; Symphony no. 1. *Czech Nonet; Prague Radio Symphony Orch.; Vronsky, cond.; Kyncl Quartet; Film Symphony Orch.; Konicek, cond.*
- Fa 9-10/94: 225

23392. 31 0184-2: JANÁČEK—Taras Bulba; Sinfonietta; The Danube. *Brno Radio Symphony; Prague Radio Symphony; Bakala, cond.* Recorded 1952-54.
• ARG 5-6/94: 205

23393. 31 0186-2: RIMSKY-KORSAKOV—Scheherazade; Capriccio espagnol. *Oistrakh, violin; Bolshoi Theatre Orch.; Moscow Radio Orch.; Anosov, cond.*
• Fa 5-6/94: 229

23394. 31 0187-2: TCHAIKOVSKY—Capriccio italien; The Voyevoda; Romeo and Juliet fantasy-overture; Francesca da Rimini. *USSR State Symphony Orch.; Ivanov, cond.*
• Fa 5-6/94: 262

23395. 31 0188-2: BORODIN—Symphony no. 2. PROKOFIEV—Symphony-concerto for cello and orchestra. *Rostropovich, cello; Moscow Radio Orch.; Golovanov, cond.; Leningrad Phil. Orch.; Sanderling, cond.*
+ Fa 5-6/94: 229

23396. 31 0189-2: PROKOFIEV—Symphony no. 6. STRAVINSKY—Petrushka. *St. Petersburg Phil. Orch.; Mravinsky, cond.* Recorded 1958, 1946.
• Fa 3-4/94: 277

23397. 31 0190-2: LISZT—Totentanz. LISZT-BUSONI—Rhapsodie espagnole. RUBINSTEIN—Piano concerto no. 4. *Serebryakov, piano; State Symphony Orch.; Anosov, cond.; Ginzburg, piano; Moscow Radio Orch.; Shereshevsky, cond.* Recorded 1951-58.
+ Fa 5-6/94: 181

23398. 31 0194-2: VORISEK—Violin sonata, op. 5. JANÁČEK—Violin sonata. MARTINŮ—Intermezzo. SMETANA—From the home country. *Ženatý, violin; Hála,*

piano.
+ Fa 5-6/94: 332

23399. 31 0195-2: *Magdaléna Hajóssyová: song recital.* Music of Fibich, Smetana, Foerster, and Dvořák. *Hajóssyová, soprano; Lapsanský, piano.*
+ Fa 5-6/94: 293

23400. 31 0235-2: LECLAIR—Sonata for 2 violins, op. 3, no. 2. MOZART—Violin sonatas K. 526, 296. CUI—Violin sonata in D major. *El. Gilels, Kogan, violins; Em. Gilels, piano.*
+ Fa 9-10/94: 236

23401. 31 0236-2: RUBINSTEIN—Violin sonata, op. 13. GLINKA—Viola sonata. GRECHANINOV—Cello sonata, op. 113. *Barinova, violin; Goldenweiser, piano; Barshai, viola; Nikolayeva, piano; Knushevitsky, cello; Oborin, piano.*
+ Fa 9-10/94: 237

23402. 31 0237-2: RIMSKY-KORSAKOV—Symphony no. 1. GLAZUNOV—Symphony no. 4. *Leningrad Phil. Orch.; Khaikin, Mravinsky, conds.*
- Fa 9-10/94: 313

23403. 31 0238-2: TCHAIKOVSKY—Concert fantasia, op. 56. SIBELIUS—Violin concerto. *Nikolayeva, piano; State Symphony Orch.; Kondrashin, cond.; Barinova, violin; Moscow Radio Orch.; Orlov, cond.*
• Fa 9-10/94: 237

23404. 31 0239-2: TCHAIKOVSKY—Violin concerto. LALO—Symphonie espagnole. *Melnikov, violin; Moscow State Phil. Orch.; Rozhdestvensky, cond.; Grindenko, violin; State Symphony Orch.; Temirkanov, cond.* Recorded live 1962, 1970.
- Fa 9-10/94: 236

23405. 31 0336-2: MOZART—Piano sonatas no. 8, 15; Adagio and andante; Rondo K. 494. *Richter, piano.* Recorded 1956.
• ARG 9-10/95: 183

23406. 310 077-2: MOZART—Symphony no. 29; Serenade no. 8. *Czech Phil. Orch.; Scherchen, cond.* Recorded 1951.
- ARG 5-6/92: 98
- Gr 1/92: 98

23407. 310 078-2: MOZART—Symphonies no. 33, 38. *Czech Phil. Orch.; Talich, cond.* Recorded live 1954.
+ ARG 5-6/92: 98

23408. 310 106-2 (3 discs): BEETHOVEN—Piano concertos. *Gilels, piano; Czech Phil. Orch.; Sanderling, cond.* Recorded 1958.
• Gr 4/93: 42

23409. 310 152-2: SMETANA—Má vlast. *Prague Radio Symphony Orch.;*

Krombholc, cond.
+ Gr 4/93: 62

23410. 310 181-2: RACHMANINOFF—Piano music. SCRIABIN—Piano music. *Sofronitsky, piano.* Recorded 1946-51.
• Gr 5/94: 83

23411. 310 189-2: PROKOFIEV—Symphony no. 6. STRAVINSKY—Petrushka. *Leningrad Phil. Orch.; Mravinsky, cond.* Recorded 1946.
+ Gr 8/94: 51

23412. 310 200-2: RYBA—Pastoral mass. *Prague Chamber Chorus; New Czech Chamber Orch.; Belohlavek, cond.*
+ ARG 11-12/94: 181

23413. 310 253-2: BORTNIANSKY—Piano sonata no. 2; Quintet for harp and strings; Sinfonia concertante. *Golubovskaya, Dizhur, piano; Erdeli, harp; Barshai, violin; Dobrokhotov, viola da gamba; Berlinsky, cello; Moscow Chamber Orch.*
+ ARG 3-4/95: 78

23414. 310 274-2: RIMSKY-KORSAKOV—Suites from Mlada, Snow maiden, Voyevode, and Maid of Pskov. *Moscow Radio Orch.; Žiuraitis, cond.; Bolshoi Theatre Orch.; Ermler, cond.*
+ ARG 1-2/96: 161

23415. 310 348-2: Wind quartets by Fuchs, Fiala, Vent, and Pichl. *Britvik, clarinet; Legat, bassoon; Trnka, oboe; Secky, horn.*
• ARG 7-8/96: 260

MUSIC AND ARTS

23416. CD-235 (2 discs): MAHLER—Symphony no. 9; Kindertotenlieder. *Anderson, contralto; French National Radio Orch.; London Symphony Orch.; Horenstein, cond.*
+ Fa 11-12/87: 171

23417. CD-242: BEETHOVEN—Symphony no. 9. *Brouwenstijn, Hermes, Haefliger, Wilbrink; Amsterdam Toonkunst Choir; Concertgebouw Orch.; Klemperer, cond.* Recorded live 1956.
• ARG 1-2/87: 86
+ Fa 3-4/87: 78

23418. CD-245: *The virtuoso Liszt.* LISZT—Piano music. *Swann, piano.*
+ Fa 11-12/87: 167
+ Ov 11/87: 42

23419. CD-257: BRUCKNER—Symphony no. 3 (1890 ed.). WAGNER—Götterdämmerung: Siegfried's Rhine journey and Funeral march. *Bavarian State Orch.; Berlin State Opera Orch.; Knappertsbusch, cond.* Reissue.
- ARG 11-12/96: 287
+ Fa 11-12/96: 214

23420. CD-258: BRAHMS—Symphony no. 4. MOZART—Symphony no. 40. *Vienna*

Phil. Orch.; Furtwängler, cond.
Recorded live 1950, 1949.
• Fa 1-2/88: 101

23421. CD-259 (2 discs): BEETHOVEN—
Missa solemnis; Choral fantasy, op. 80.
Milanov, Castagna, Björling, Kipnis;
Dorfmann, piano; Westminster Choir;
NBC Symphony Orch.; Toscanini, cond.
Recorded live 1940, 1939.
+ Fa 9-10/87: 147

23422. CD-260: TCHAIKOVSKY—Manfred;
Romeo and Juliet. *NBC Symphony Orch.;*
Toscanini, cond. Recorded live 1953.
+ Fa 9-10/87: 147

23423. CD-261: CHOPIN—Sixteen
waltzes. *Katin, piano.*
• Fa 7-8/88: 144
+ Gr 10/87: 602

23424. CD-265: BEETHOVEN—Piano trios
no. 4, 6. *Mirecourt Trio.*
- Fa 5-6/88: 83

23425. CD-267: SCHUBERT—Piano music.
Badura-Skoda, piano.
+ ARG 5-6/88: 61
• Fa 5-6/88: 205
• Fa 5-6/96: 260

23426. CD-270: BLOCH—Violin concerto.
DEBUSSY—Fantasie for piano and
orchestra. *Szigeti, violin; Gieseking,*
piano; Concertgebouw Orch.;
Mengelberg, cond. Recorded live 1939,
1938.
+ Fa 7-8/88: 132

23427. CD-273 (2 discs): Music of
Berlioz, Schumann, Wagner, Weber, and
Tchaikovsky. *NBC Symphony Orch.;*
Walter, cond. Recorded live 1939, 1940.
+ ARG 5-6/89: 131
+ Fa 7-8/89: 115

23428. CD-274: FRANCK—Symphony in
D minor; Psyché et Eros; Redemption;
Eolides. *NBC Symphony Orch.;*
Toscanini, cond.
+ Fa 1-2/89: 163

23429. CD-275: MOZART—Piano
concertos no. 14, 20. *Hess, piano; New*
York Phil.; Walter, cond. Recorded live.
+ Fa 3-4/90: 238 (no.14)
• Fa 3-4/90: 238 (no.20)

23430. CD-279: BACH—Art of the fugue.
Hill, harpsichord.
+ ARG 11-12/89: 18
+ ARG 7-8/95: 74
- Fa 3-4/89: 101
+ Fa 7-8/95: 100
+ HPR 6/89: 67

23431. CD-280 (2 discs): MAHLER—
Symphony no. 8. DEBUSSY—Nocturnes.
RAVEL—Rapsodie espagnole. *New York*
Phil.; Gewandhaus Orch.; Stokowski,
cond. Recorded live 1950, 1959.
• ARG 9-10/89: 76

• Fa 9-10/89: 244
+ Fa 9-10/94: 247

23432. CD-283: BRAHMS—Cello sonata
no. 1. GRIEG—Cello sonata, op. 36.
Rostropovich, cello; Richter, piano.
Recorded live 1964.
+ ARG 9-10/89: 34
+ Fa 9-10/89: 158

23433. CD-285: BRAHMS—Piano quintet
in F minor; Intermezzo, op. 119, no. 1.
Gould, piano; Montreal String Quartet.
□ Fa 1-2/90: 141

23434. CD-286: *The art of Josef Gingold.*
Music of Fauré, Dvořák, Kreisler,
Mendelssohn, Chopin, and Chaminade.
Gingold, violin; Robert, Webb, piano.
+ ARG 9-10/89: 55
+ Fa 9-10/89: 424

23435. CD-287: SUK—Symphony no. 1.
DVOŘÁK—Symphonic variations, op. 78.
Philharmonia Hungarica; Israel Pro
Music Orch.; Atlas, cond.
+ ARG 3-4/89: 96
+ Fa 9-10/89: 337

23436. CD-288: MENDELSSOHN—Cello
sonatas no. 1-2; Variations concertantes,
op. 17; Song without words, op. 109.
King, cello; Moeling, piano.
• ARG 11-12/89: 79
+ DA 1/90: 62
+ Fa 9-10/89: 250
+ St 2/90: 191

23437. CD-289 (2 discs): BRAHMS—
Deutsches Requiem; Symphony no. 1.
Lindberg-Torlind, Sönnerstedt;
Stockholm Phil. Chorus & Orch.;
Concertgebouw Orch.; Furtwängler,
cond. Recorded live 1948, 1950.
+ ARG 9-10/89: 154
+ Fa 7-8/89: 110

23438. CD-290 (2 discs): *Fritz Kreisler,*
early recordings. Music of Beethoven,
Brahms, Mendelssohn, Mozart, Bach, and
Schumann. *Kreisler, violin; various*
accompaniments. Recorded 1924-27.
+ ARG 9-10/89: 154
+ Fa 7-8/89: 309
+ Fa 9-10/89: 422
+ Ov 9/89: 58
+ St 1/90: 241

23439. CD-291 (2 discs): MOZART—
Symphony no. 34. WAGNER—Faust
overture. STRAUSS—Don Quixote.
SCHUMANN—Symphony no. 3. DVOŘÁK—
Violin concerto, op. 53. *Fournier, cello;*
Krebbers, violin; Concertgebouw Orch.;
Szell, cond. Recorded live 1964-66.
• ARG 9-10/89: 154
+ Fa 7-8/89: 138

23440. CD-293: BUSONI—Piano sonata,
op. 20a; Elegien. *Wolosoff, piano.*
+ ARG 9-10/89: 39
- Fa 9-10/89: 171
+ Gr 10/89: 699

23441. CD-294: BRAHMS—Piano trios no.
1-2. *Mirecourt Trio.*
+ ARG 11-12/89: 45
• Fa 9-10/89: 165
• St 2/90: 191

23442. CD-295 (2 discs): GLUCK—Orfeo
ed Euridice. PURCELL—Dido and Aeneas:
Excerpts. *Baker, Speiser, Gale, Sinclair;*
with assisting soloists; Leppard, cond.;
Drottningholm Festival Orch.; Britten,
cond.
+ DA 8/90: 48
+ Fa 1-2/90: 185
+ St 8/90: 173

23443. CD-296: BEETHOVEN—Piano
concerto no. 5. HAYDN—Piano concerto,
H.VIII, 2. *Michelangeli, piano; Paris*
Symphony Orch.; Celibidache, cond.;
Brescia Festival Orch.; Orizio, cond.
+ ARG 1-2/90: 138
+ Fa 11-12/89: 127

23444. CD-297: BRAHMS—Piano concerto
no. 1. STRAUSS—Burleske for piano and
orchestra. *Gould, piano; Baltimore*
Symphony Orch.; Adler, cond. Recorded
live 1962.
+ Fa 1-2/90: 135

23445. CD-298: BACH—Brandenburg
concerto no. 5; Violin sonata no. 4.
BEETHOVEN—Violin sonata no. 10.
SCHOENBERG—Fantasy for violin and
piano, op. 47. *Gould, piano; Menuhin,*
violin; Baltimore Chamber Orch.; Adler,
cond.
- ARG 1-2/90: 138
+ Fa 1-2/90: 386

23446. CD-299: MOZART—Violin
concerto, K. 218. TCHAIKOVSKY—Violin
concerto. *Huberman, violin; New York*
Phil.; Walter, cond.; Philadelphia Orch.;
Ormandy, cond. Recorded live 1945,
1946.
- ARG 1-2/90: 138
+ Fa 5-6/90: 226

23447. CD-312: STRAVINSKY—Petrushka
(1911); Sacre du printemps. *Boston*
Symphony Orch.; Monteux, cond.
Recorded 1958, 1957.
+ Fa 3-4/88: 212

23448. CD-372: BACH—Piano music.
GIBBONS—Lachrymae pavanne and
galliard. *Gould, piano.* Recorded live
1956, 1967.
□ Fa 11-12/89: 118

23449. CD-386: BRUCKNER—Symphony
no. 5. *Vienna Phil. Orch.; Klemperer,*
cond.
+ Fa 3-4/95: 149

23450. CD-520: BEETHOVEN—Symphony
no. 3; Grosse Fuge. *Berlin Phil. Orch;*
Vienna Phil. Orch.; Furtwängler, cond.
Recorded live 1952, 1954.
+ Fa 9-10/87: 152

MUSIC AND ARTS

23451. CD-600: Mozart—Piano sonata no. 10. Schubert—Piano sonata, D. 575. Liszt—Piano sonata in B minor. *Richter, piano.* Recorded live 1966.
+ ARG 1-2/90: 138
+ Fa 1-2/90: 244

23452. CD-602 (2 discs): Tchaikovsky—Symphonies no. 4-6. *NBC Symphony Orch.; Cantelli, cond.* Recorded live 1952-54.
+ Fa 5-6/90: 311

23453. CD-603: *Cello America.* Music of Barber, Harris, Cooper, and Reale. *King, cello; Jensen, Harris-Heggie, pianos.*
+ ARG 7-8/90: 131
+ Fa 5-6/90: 379

23454. CD-604: *American piano music of our times.* Music of Carter, Adams, Nancarrow, Bolcom, Sahl, Hemphill, Foss, and Jaggard. *Oppens, piano.*
+ ARG 3-4/90: 138
+ Fa 5-6/90: 373
+ Fa 7-8/90: 350
+ Gr 5/90: 2023
+ St 10/90: 253

23455. CD-605: Scriabin—Piano sonatas no. 1-5. *Berman, piano.*
• ARG 7-8/90: 106
• Da 5/90: 72
+ Fa 5-6/90: 291
• Gr 5/90: 2016

23456. CD-606: Carter—String quartet no. 4. Babbitt—String quartet no. 5. Powell—String quartet 1982. *Composers String Quartet.*
□ ARG 5-6/91: 44
+ Fa 5-6/91: 150

23457. CD-608: Debussy—Études. Fauré—Préludes, op. 103. *Swann, piano.*
- ARG 1-2/90: 44
+ Fa 11-12/90: 209
+ Fa 9-10/91: 196
• Gr 9/90: 573

23458. CD-609: Chopin—Piano music. *Rosen, piano.*
- ARG 1-2/91: 40
• Fa 1-2/91: 179
• Gr 4/91: 1866
• MA 3/91: 75

23459. CD-612: *Walter Gieseking: historic broadcast performance 1944-1950.* Music of Bach, Mozart, Beethoven, Scarlatti, Debussy, and Ravel. *Gieseking, piano.* Recorded live 1944.
+ Fa 9-10/90: 475
+ Fa 7-8/91: 231
+ Gr 11/90: 1072

23460. CD-613: Strauss—Death and transfiguration; Don Quixote. *Feuermann, cello; NBC Symphony Orch.; Toscanini, cond.* Recorded 1938.
+ ARG 9-10/95: 298
+ Fa 7-8/95: 331
• Gr 9/95: 122

23461. CD-614: Berlioz—Harold in Italy; Les Francs-juges: Overture; Romeo and Juliet: Love scene; Damnation de Faust: Rakoczy march. *Primrose, viola; NBC Symphony Orch.; Toscanini, cond.* Recorded live 1939-1947.
+ ARG 7-8/90: 27
+ Fa 5-6/90: 126

23462. CD-615: *Alfred Cortot: rare 78 rpm recordings & test pressings, 1919-1947.* Music of Saint-Saëns, Scriabin, Albéniz, Liszt, and Chopin. *Cortot, piano.*
+ ARG 7-8/90: 143
+ Fa 9-10/90: 476

23463. CD-617: Mozart—Fantasia, K. 396. Beethoven—Piano sonata no. 29. *Gould, piano.* Recorded live 1967.
□ Fa 3-4/90: 242

23464. CD-618 (2 discs): Berlioz—Benvenuto Cellini (Weimar edition). *Carlyle, Veasey, Lewis; BBC Chorus & Symphony Orch.; Dorati, cond.* Recorded live 1964.
- ARG 7-8/90: 50
+ Fa 7-8/90: 97

23465. CD-621: Scriabin—The complete sonatas for piano, vol. 2. *Berman, piano.*
+ Fa 9-10/91: 355
+ Gr 6/91: 68

23466. CD-623: Dvořák—Slavonic dances, op. 72. Smetana—Moldau. Martinů—Three Czech dances. *Moon, Lee, piano four-hands.*
+ ARG 7-8/90: 45 (Martinů)
• ARG 7-8/90: 45 (others)
• Fa 7-8/90: 134

23467. CD-625: Chopin—Piano concerto no. 1. Liszt—Piano concerto no. 2. *Arrau, piano; Cologne Radio Orch.; Klemperer, cond.; New York Phil.; Cantelli, cond.*
+ Fa 11-12/90: 201
• Gr 10/90: 833

23468. CD-626: Brahms—Viola sonatas, op. 120. Franck—Violin sonata in A major (arr. Zaslav). *Zaslov Duo.*
+ ARG 9-10/91: 53
• Fa 7-8/91: 128

23469. CD-627: Schoenberg—Variations for orchestra. Bartók—Sonata for 2 pianos and percussion. Hindemith—Violin concerto. *Gitlis, violin; Southwest German Radio Orch.; Rosbaud, cond.* Recorded live.
• ARG 11-12/92: 197
+ Fa 3-4/91: 358

23470. CD-630: Ives—Piano sonatas no. 1-2. *Jensen, piano.*
+ ARG 1-2/90: 58
+ Fa 11-12/90: 252
• Gr 11/90: 1015

23471. CD-631: Mozart—Symphony no. 35. Tchaikovsky—Nutcracker suite. Wagner—Meistersinger: Prelude to Act 1; Tannhäuser: Overture and Venusberg music. *Royal Phil. Orch.; Beecham, cond.*
+ ARG 9-10/90: 28
+ Fa 11-12/90: 475

23472. CD-632: Mozart—Piano concertos no. 23-24. *Schnabel, piano; New York Phil.; Rodzinski, cond.; Standard Symphony Orch.; Wallenstein, cond.* Recorded live 1945, 1946.
• Fa 11-12/90: 288

23473. CD-635: *Soundscapes.* Harrison—Double concerto for violin and cello with Javanese gamelan. Cowell—Cleistogamy. Reale—Trio for piano and strings. *Mirecourt Trio; Winant, Harrison, gongs; Mills College Gamelan Ensemble.*
+ ARG 7-8/91: 150
+ Fa 7-8/91: 169
□ Gr 11/91: 89

23474. CD-637: Beethoven—Piano concerto no. 5. *Gieseking, piano; Berlin Radio Symphony Orch.; Rother, cond.* Recorded live 1944.
+ Fa 3-4/91: 146
• Gr 4/91: 1914

23475. CD-638: *20th century American violin works in historic recordings.* Music of Bloch, Porter, and Still. *L. Kaufman, violin; Pozzi, Balsam, A. Kaufman, pianos; Kaufman String Quartet; Craft, harp.*
+ ARG 7-8/91: 178
+ Fa 7-8/91: 370

23476. CD-639: Beethoven—Piano concerto no. 5; Variations for piano, op. 34; Piano trio no. 4. *Gould, piano; Schneider, violin; Nelsova, cello; unnamed orchestra; Ančerl, cond.*
• Fa 3-4/91: 146

23477. CD-640 (10 discs): Beethoven—Piano sonatas (complete). *Frank, piano.*
+ Fa 3-4/91: 150

23478. CD-642: Schubert—Piano sonatas, D. 566, D. 960. *Richter, piano.* Recorded live 1964.
- Fa 3-4/91: 365

23479. CD-644: *The art of Gregor Piatigorsky.* Music of Brahms, Shostakovich, Weber, Francoeur, Scriabin, Tchaikovsky, and Chopin. *Piatigorsky, cello; Stewart, Newton, pianos.*
+ ARG 5-6/91: 142
+ Fa 5-6/91: 368

23480. CD-648: Bartók—Sonata for 2 pianos and percussion. Stockhausen—Kontakte. *Simms, Avery, pianos; Davis, Schick, percussion.*

+ ARG 5-6/91: 22
+ Fa 7-8/91: 108

23481. CD-649: *Salute to France.*
HAHN—Le bal de Béatrice d'Este.
MILHAUD—Symphony no. 5. IBERT—
Concerto for cello and winds; Paris.
POULENC—Piano concerto. *Kreger, cello;
Votapek, piano; Harmonie Ensemble New
York; Richman, cond.*
+ ARG 5-6/91: 137
+ ARG 7-8/95: 236
+ Fa 5-6/91: 381
• Gr 7/92: 65
+ MA 7/91: 84

23482. CD-650: SCHOENBERG—Cabaret
songs; Songs, op. 2; Book of the hanging
gardens, op. 15. *Bryn-Julson, soprano;
Oppens, piano.*
• ARG 1-2/93: 144
+ Fa 1-2/92: 315
+ Gr 6/92: 77

23483. CD-651: BEETHOVEN—Symphony
no. 6 (arr. Liszt). MENDELSSOHN—Songs
without words. *Gould, piano.*
+ Fa 7-8/91: 115

23484. CD-653: BEETHOVEN—Symphony
no. 9. *Briem, Höngen, Anders, Watzke;
Bruno Kittel Choir; Berlin Phil. Orch.;
Furtwängler, cond. Recorded live 1942.*
+ ARG 1-2/92: 29
+ Fa 7-8/91: 117

23485. CD-654: BACH—French overture,
BWV 831; Widerstehe doch der Sünde,
BWV 54; Keyboard concertos no. 5, 7;
Fugue, BWV 552: Excerpt. *Gould, piano,
harpsi-piano & organ; Oberlin,
countertenor; CBC Chamber Orch.;
Toronto Symphony Orch.; Golschmann,
cond.; CBC Symphony Orch.;
Goldschmidt, cond. Recorded live 1957-
1969.*
+ Fa 7-8/91: 100

23486. CD-655: SAINT-SAËNS—Piano
concerto no. 2. FRANCK—Symphonic
variations for piano and orchestra.
SCHUMANN—Piano concerto. *Rubinstein,
piano; Philharmonic-Symphony Society;
Mitropoulos, cond.; Montreal Symphony
Orch.; Mehta, cond. Recorded live 1953,
1968.*
+ ARG 7-8/91: 173
+ Fa 7-8/91: 362

23487. CD-656: MAHLER—Symphony no.
4. STRAUSS—Death and transfiguration.
*Seefried, soprano; New York Phil.; NBC
Symphony Orch.; Walter, cond. Recorded
live 1953, 1939.*
+ ARG 7-8/91: 83
+ Fa 7-8/91: 302

23488. CD-657: MUSSORGSKY—Night on
bald mountain (arr. Stokowsky).
WAGNER—Siegfried idyll. FRANCK—
Symphony in D minor. *London
Symphony Orch.; Symphony of the Air;
Hilversum Radio Orch.; Stokowski, cond.*

Recorded live.
• Fa 7-8/91: 393

23489. CD-658: DVOŘÁK—Slavonic
dances; Carnival overture. *Czech Phil.
Orch.; Talich, cond.*
+ ARG 9-10/91: 69
□ Fa 1-2/92: 204

23490. CD-659: GIBBONS—The Lord
Salisbury his pavin and galliard; Italian
ground; Fantasia in C. HAYDN—Piano
sonata no. 52 in E♭. HINDEMITH—Piano
sonata no. 3. *Gould, piano. Radio
broadcast (26 Dec. 1968).*
+ Fa 11-12/91: 546

23491. CD-660: MOZART—Igor Kipnis
plays Mozart on the 1793 fortepiano.
*Kipnis, 1793 Graebner Bros. fortepiano
(Dresden).*
+ ARG 3-4/92: 111
+ Fa 11-12/91: 419

23492. CD-661: *Alexander Kipnis sings
Lieder. Music of Wolf, Brahms, R.
Strauss, Schubert and Schumann. Kipnis,
bass; with accompaniment. Historical
reissues.*
+ ARG 9-10/92: 226
+ Fa 5-6/92: 301
+ ON 12/19/92: 40

23493. CD-662: *Alfred Cortot: historical
recordings.* WEBER—Piano sonata no. 2.
LISZT—Piano sonata in B minor; La
leggierezza; Hungarian rhapsody no. 11.
CHOPIN/LISZT—Spring; The ring. *Cortot,
piano.*
+ Fa 9-10/91: 419

23494. CD-663: BEETHOVEN—Piano
sonata no. 24. C.P.E. BACH—Sonata in A
minor, Wq. 49, no. 1. D. SCARLATTI—
Sonatas in D and G. SCRIABIN—Piano
sonata no. 3. *Gould, piano. Recorded
1968.*
+ Fa 11-12/91: 546

23495. CD-665: BEETHOVEN—Violin
sonatas no. 5, 9-10. MOZART—Violin
sonatas, K. 296; K. 377-380; K. 404
(fragment); K. 481; Duos for violin and
viola, K. 423-424. *Goldberg, violin;
Kraus, piano; Riddle, Hindemith, violas.
Reissues.*
+ Fa 1-2/92: 162

23496. CD-667: LARSSON—Violin
concerto. BARBER—Violin concerto.
VAUGHAN WILLIAMS—Concerto
accademico. *Kaufman, violin; Swedish
Radio Orch.; Frykberg, cond.; Lucerne
Festival Orch.; Goehr, cond.; Winterthur
String Orch.; Dahinden, cond. Reissue.*
• ARG 11-12/91: 26
+ Fa 9-10/91: 251

23497. CD-668: BERG—Violin concerto.
BACH—Violin concerto BWV 1058.
MOZART—Violin concerto no. 3. *Szigeti,
violin; NBC Symphony Orch.;
Mitropoulos, cond. Recorded live 1945,*

1949.
+ Fa 1-2/92: 172

23498. CD-669: *Twentieth century piano
classics.* BARBER—Piano sonata.
MARTIN—8 preludes for piano.
PROKOFIEV—Piano sonata no. 2.
BARTÓK—Piano sonata. *Walsh, piano.*
+ ARG 11-12/91: 192
+ Fa 11-12/91: 549

23499. CD-670 (2 discs): CHERUBINI—
Medea; with arias by Puccini and Cilea.
*Olivero, Prevedi, Sciutti, Zaccaria;
Dallas Symphony Orch.; Rescigno, cond.
Recorded live 1967.*
+ ARG 3-4/92: 45

23500. CD-671 (2 discs): GIORDANO—
Fedora. POULENC—La voix humaine.
*Olivero, Prevedi, Patrick, Cruz-Romo,
Tajo, Zaccaria; Dallas Civic Opera;
Dallas Symphony Orch.; Rescigno, cond.
Recorded live 1969 and 1970.*
+ ARG 3-4/92: 119
• Fa 1-2/92: 218

23501. CD-675: *In memoriam William
Hibbard.* HIBBARD—Parsons' piece;
String quartet; Bass trombone, bass
clarinet, harp; Ménage; Schickstück;
Handwork. *Various performers.*
+ Fa 1-2/92: 237

23502. CD-681: BEETHOVEN—Piano
concerto no. 3. MOZART—Piano concerto
no. 22. *Schnabel, piano; New York Phil.;
Szell, Walter, conds. Recorded live 1945,
1941.*
+ Fa 1-2/92: 158

23503. CD-684: BEETHOVEN—
Symphonies, no. 3, 5. *NBC Symphony
Orch.; New York Phil.; Toscanini, cond.
Recorded 1933, 1939.*
+ Fa 5-6/92: 124

23504. CD-685: *Cello America, vol. 2.*
Works by Foss, Creston, Riegger, Drew,
and Cowell. *King, cello; Jensen, piano.*
+ ARG 3-4/92: 183
+ Fa 3-4/92: 395

23505. CD-686: REALE—Piano trio no. 2.
PERSICHETTI—Parable XXIII. COWELL—
Trio in nine short movements. *Mirecourt
Trio.*
+ ARG 1-2/93: 175
+ Fa 5-6/93: 278

23506. CD-687: HARRISON—Piano trio.
COOPER—Parameta trio. SVOBODA—
Passacaglia and fugue. WHITE—Elegy and
exaltation; Six miniatures for 3 players:
no. 1-5. *Mirecourt Trio.*
+ ARG 1-2/93: 175
+ Fa 9-10/92: 252

23507. CD-690: *Fanfares and fantasy
pieces.* SCHUMANN—Music for clarinet,
viola and piano. *Imai, viola; Wright,
clarinet; Goldsmith, piano. Reissue.*

MUSIC AND ARTS

+ ARG 7-8/92: 222
• Fa 7-8/92: 279

23508. CD-691: *Dvořák and friends.* Dvořák—Serenades for winds, op. 44. Myslivecek—Octet for winds no. 2. Krommer—Partita for winds, op. 45, no. 2. *Harmonie Ensemble, New York; Richman, cond.*
+ ARG 7-8/92: 125
+ Fa 5-6/92: 153
+ Gr 8/92: 31

23509. CD-695: Mahler—Symphony no. 7. *Toronto Symphony Orch.; Scherchen, cond.* Recorded live 1965.
• Fa 7-8/92: 207

23510. CD-697 : Bruckner—Symphony no. 5. *BBC Symphony Orch.; Horenstein, cond.* Recorded live 1971.
- ARG 7-8/92: 112
+ Fa 7-8/92: 131

23511. CD-699: *American piano music of our time, vol. 2.* Music of Nancarrow, Rzewski, Wuorinen, Picker, Harbison and Davis. *Oppens, piano.*
+ ARG 1-2/93: 185
+ Fa 11-12/92: 445

23512. CD-703: Ravel—Boléro; Introduction and allegro; String quartet in F; Pavane pour une infante défunte; La valse. *Lamoureux Orch.; Ravel, Woolf, conds.; International String Quartet; Orch. de l'Association des Concerts Colonne; Pierné, cond.*
• Fa 9-10/92: 323

23513. CD-705 (2 discs): Schubert—Symphony no. 8. Mahler—Symphony no. 4; Songs. *Schwarzkopf, soprano; Vienna Phil. Orch.; Walter, cond.* Recorded 1960.
+ Fa 1-2/93: 232

23514. CD-706: Brahms—Piano trios no. 3; op. posth. *Mirecourt Trio.*
+ ARG 1-2/93: 83
- Fa 1-2/93: 119
• Fa 9-10/93: 135

23515. CD-708: Beethoven—Violin concerto. Bach—Orchestral suite no. 3. *Menuhin, violin; Berlin Phil. Orch.; Furtwängler, cond.* Recorded live 1947-48.
+ Fa 11-12/92: 192

23516. CD-709: Mozart—Sonata in D for 2 pianos, K. 448. Schumann—Bilder aus Osten, op. 66. Debussy—En blanc et noir. Britten—Introduction and rondo alla burlesca, op. 23, no. 1. *Richter, Britten, pianos.* Recorded live.
+ Fa 9-10/92: 353
+ St 4/93: 295

23517. CD-710: Braxton—Eight duets. *Braxton, woodwinds; Wilson, double bass.*
+ Fa 3-4/93: 133

23518. CD-711: Beethoven—Symphonies no. 1, 3. *Vienna Phil. Orch.; Berlin Phil. Orch.; Furtwängler, cond.* Recorded live.
• Fa 9-10/92: 179

23519. CD-712: Tchaikovsky—Symphony no. 5. Wagner—Siegfried Idyll; Der fliegende Holländer: overture. *RAI Orch., Turin; Furtwängler, cond.* Recorded live.
• Fa 9-10/92: 377

23520. CD-713: Hindemith—Concerto for orchestra; Die Harmonie der welt. Stravinsky—Baiser de la fée: Divertimento. *Berlin Phil. Orch.; Furtwängler, cond.* Recorded live 1950-53.
+ Fa 11-12/92: 258

23521. CD-717: Chopin—Piano sonatas no. 2-3; Ballade no. 1; Polonaise no. 6; Fantasie op. 49; Barcarolle op. 60. *Cortot, piano.*
+ Fa 9-10/92: 215

23522. CD-719: Debussy—Nocturnes. Honegger—Movement symphonique no. 3. Ravel—Rapsodie espagnole. Strauss—Metamorphosen. *Berlin Phil. Orch.; Vienna Phil. Orch.; Furtwängler, cond.* Recorded 1947-52.
+ Fa 11-12/92: 457

23523. CD-720 (4 discs): *Joseph Szigeti: a centenary tribute.* Music of Bloch, Martin, Corelli, Tartini, Busoni and Mozart. *Szigeti, violin; with accomp.*
+ Fa 1-2/93: 307

23524. CD-721: Schubert—Grand duo for piano, four hands. Mozart—Sonatina for piano, four hands, K. 521. *Richter, Britten, piano.* Recorded live 1965-66.
+ Fa 11-12/92: 357
+ St 4/93: 295

23525. CD-722: Schubert—Variations, piano, four hands, D. 813; Andante varié, D. 823; Fantasie, D. 940; Moments musicaux, no. 1, 3, 6. *Richter, Britten, piano.* Recorded live 1965-66.
+ Fa 11-12/92: 357
+ St 4/93: 295

23526. CD-723: Liszt—*Grand romantic virtuoso.* Réminiscences de Norma; La leggierezza; Un sospiro; Polonaise no. 2; Bénédiction de Dieu dans la solitude; Réminiscences de Don Juan. *Hamelin, piano.*
+ ARG 11-12/92: 148
+ Fa 11-12/92: 281
+ St 4/93: 295

23527. CD-724: Alkan—Concerto for solo piano. *Hamelin, piano.*
+ ARG 1-2/93: 65
+ Fa 1-2/93: 93
+ Gr 8/93: 56
+ St 4/93: 295

23528. CD-726: Brahms—Variations for piano (Complete). *Boriskin, piano.*
• ARG 11-12/92: 96
- Fa 11-12/92: 211
• St 3/93: 181

23529. CD-727: Mahler—Symphony no. 7. *Philharmonia Orch.; Horenstein, cond.* Recorded live 1969.
+ Fa 11-12/92: 289

23530. CD-729: *Masterpieces of cabaret.* Britten—Four cabaret songs. Schoenberg—Brettl-Lieder. Bolcom—Twelve cabaret songs. *Applebaum, soprano; Hamelin, piano.*
+ ARG 9-10/93: 253
+ Fa 1-2/93: 276
+ St 4/93: 295

23531. CD-730: Bruckner—Symphony no. 9. Wagner—Tristan and Isolde: Prelude and Liebestod. *Berlin Phil. Orch.; Furtwängler, cond.* Recorded live.
+ Fa 1-2/93: 122

23532. CD-733: Beethoven—Symphony no. 9. *Baillie, Ferrier, Nash, Parsons; London Phil. Orch.; Walter, cond.* Recorded 1947.
+ ARG 3-4/93: 190
+ Fa 3-4/93: 123

23533. CD-734: Beethoven—Piano sonatas no. 11, 29; Fantasy op. 77. *Oppens, piano.*
+ ARG 1-2/93: 76
+ Fa 1-2/93: 105

23534. CD-737: *Black piano: a treasury of works for solo piano by Black composers.* Music of Still, Swanson, Dett, Kay, Work, Peterson, Ellington, and Coleridge-Taylor. *Gaylord, piano.*
+ ARG 3-4/93: 172
+ Fa 3-4/93: 376

23535. CD-738: Copland—Piano fantasy; Four piano blues. Reale—Piano sonatas no. 1-2. *Jensen, piano.*
+ Fa 7-8/93: 127

23536. CD-743 (4 discs): *Broadcast recitals from 1949-1951.* Music of Bach, Beethoven, and Schumann. *Gieseking, piano.*
+ Fa 7-8/93: 298

23537. CD-744: Liszt—A Faust symphony. *Mitchinson, tenor; BBC Northern Symphony Orch.; Horenstein, cond.* Recorded live, 1972.
• ARG 7-8/93: 115
+ Fa 5-6/93: 248

23538. CD-746: *Emil Gilels in recital.* Music of Beethoven, Prokofiev, Rachmaninoff, Scriabin, and Bach/Siloti. *Gilels, piano.* Recorded live.
+ Fa 5-6/93: 384

23539. CD-747: *Emil Gilels in concert.* Music of Schumann, Chopin, Debussy,

and Ravel. *Gilels, piano*. Reissue; recorded live 1963.
+ Fa 5-6/93: 384

23540. CD-749: MAHLER—Das Lied von der Erde; 2 Rückert Lieder; Symphony no. 5: Adagietto; Bruno Walter on Mahler. *Thorborg, mezzo-soprano; Kullman, tenor; Vienna Phil. Orch.; Walter, cond.* Recorded live 1936.
+ ARG 11-12/93: 272
+ Fa 5-6/93: 254
+ Gr 12/93: 136

23541. CD-750: MOZART—Concertos for piano and orchestra no. 20, 17 (2nd movement); Piano sonata, K. 533/494. *Schnabel, piano; New York Phil. Orch.; Szell, cond.; New Friends of Music Orch.; Stiedry, cond.* Recorded 1942-44.
+ Fa 5-6/93: 271

23542. CD-751: BRUCKNER—Symphony no. 7. R. STRAUSS—Till Eulenspiegel's lustige Streiche. *Berlin Phil. Orch.; Concertgebouw Orch.; Klemperer, cond.* Recorded 1956 & 1958 .
+ Fa 5-6/93: 182

23543. CD-752: BEETHOVEN—Ah, perfido! FALLA—Nights in the gardens of Spain. JANÁČEK—Sinfonietta. BARTÓK—Concerto for viola and orchestra. *Concertgebouw Orch.; Klemperer, cond.; Brouwenstijn, soprano; Andriessen, piano; Primrose, viola.* Recorded live 1951.
+ ARG 7-8/93: 206
+ Fa 5-6/93: 405

23544. CD-753: BEETHOVEN—Symphonies no. 3, 5. *BBC Symphony Orch.; Toscanini, cond.* Recorded 1945.
• Fa 7-8/93: 107

23545. CD-754: STRAUSS—Ein Heldenleben; Don Juan; Till Eulenspiegel. *NBC Symphony Orch.; Toscanini, cond.* Recorded 1940, 1949.
+ ARG 7-8/93: 212
+ Fa 7-8/93: 251

23546. CD-755: SIBELIUS—Symphony no. 4; Four legends: no. 2, 4; En saga. *NBC Symphony Orch.; Toscanini, cond.*
+ ARG 7-8/93: 212
+ Fa 7-8/93: 245

23547. CD-756: *Contemporary American piano trios*. IMBRIE—Piano trio no. 2. SHIFRIN—Piano trio. HARBISON—Piano trio. POWELL—Piano trio. *Francesco Trio.*
+ ARG 11-12/93: 130
+ Fa 9-10/93: 381

23548. CD-757: Music of Bloch, Reale, Ruggles, and Lipkis. *Jensen, piano.*
• Fa 3-4/94: 139

23549. CD-759: BEETHOVEN—Piano sonatas no. 21, 28. LISZT—Piano sonata. *Gilels, piano.* Recorded 1966.
+ Fa 9-10/93: 118

23550. CD-760: LISZT—Piano sonata; Funérailles; Hungarian fantasy; Piano concerto no. 2. *Richter, piano; Hungarian State Orch.; Ferencsik, cond.* Recorded live.
+ Fa 9-10/93: 207

23551. CD-761: MOZART—Piano concertos no. 22, 27. *Richter, piano; English Chamber Orch.; Britten, cond.* Recorded live 1967, 1965.
+ Fa 9-10/93: 219

23552. CD-762: BERLIOZ—Symphonie fantastique; overtures; music of Chabrier and Coppola. *Paris Symphony Orch.; Monteux, cond.* Recorded 1930s.
+ ARG 9-10/93: 262
+ Fa 11-12/93: 186

23553. CD-763: BOULEZ—Piano sonata no. 3. WUORINEN—Piano sonata no. 2. *Swann, piano.*
+ ARG 1-2/94: 83
+ Fa 1-2/94: 361

23554. CD-764: BRUCKNER—Symphony no. 8. *Vienna Phil. Orch.; Furtwängler, cond.*
+ Fa 9-10/93: 139

23555. CD-765: MUSSORGSKY—Pictures at an exhibition; A night on bald mountain (both orch. Stokowski). SHOSTAKOVICH—Symphony no. 5. *BBC Symphony Orch.; London Symphony Orch.; Stokowski, cond.* Recorded 1964-65.
• ARG 11-12/93: 195
• Fa 9-10/93: 225

23556. CD-766 (2 discs): *Jascha Heifetz in performance*. Music of Mendelssohn, Sibelius, Brahms, Beethoven, and Korngold. *Heifetz, violin; New York Phil.; various conds.*
+ ARG 11-12/93: 268
+ Fa 11-12/93: 505

23557. CD-767: HONEGGER—Orchestra music. *Grand Orch. Symphonique; Honegger, cond.; Orch. Pasdeloup; Rhené-Baton, cond.*
+ ARG 11-12/93: 268
+ Fa 1-2/94: 205
+ Gr 4/94: 120

23558. CD-768: BEETHOVEN—Piano concertos no. 3, 5. *Kempff, piano; Montreal Symphony Orch.; Decker, cond.; Toronto Symphony Orch.; Ozawa, cond.* Recorded live 1966.
- Fa 1-2/94: 121
• Fa 3-4/94: 120

23559. CD-769: RACHMANINOFF—Symphony no. 2. PROKOFIEV—Piano concerto no. 3. *Kapell, piano; New York Phil.; Hollywood Bowl Symphony Orch.; Stokowski, cond.* Recorded 1946-49.
+ ARG 7-8/94: 233
+ Gr 7/94: 128

23560. CD-770: VAUGHAN WILLIAMS—Symphony no. 8. FALLA—El amor brujo. MESSIAEN—Hymn for orchestra. *BBC Symphony Orch.; Frankfurt Radio Symphony; Stokowski, cond.* Recorded 1964.
+ ARG 11-12/93: 224
+ Fa 9-10/93: 315

23561. CD-771: KODÁLY—Háry János suite; Te Deum of Buda Castle. FALLA—Nights in the gardens of Spain. *Kapell, piano; Symphony Orch. of Radio Budapest; American Youth Performs Orch.; New York Phil.; Stokowski, cond.*
+ ARG 11-12/93: 275
+ Fa 9-10/93: 200

23562. CD-773: *Emil Gilels: Carnegie Hall recital 1969*. Music of Beethoven, Medtner, Prokofiev, Ravel, and Chopin. *Gilels, piano.*
- Fa 11-12/93: 496

23563. CD-774: BACH—Sonatas for solo violin no. 1-3. *Szigeti, violin.* Recorded live 1946.
+ Fa 11-12/93: 173

23564. CD-775 (4 discs): *Sviatoslav Richter: concert performances and broadcasts, 1958-1976.* Music of Beethoven, Chopin, Debussy, Mussorgsky, Prokofiev, Rachmaninoff, Schumann, Scriabin, Tchaikovsky, and Wagner. *Richter, piano; Moscow Youth Symphony Orch.; Kondrashin, cond.*
+ Fa 11-12/93: 497

23565. CD-776: *Sviatoslav Richter in Romantic repertoire*. Music of Schumann, Liszt, and Tchaikovsky. *Richter, piano; English Chamber Orch.; Britten, cond.; Czech Phil. Orch.; Ančerl, cond.; Leningrad Phil. Orch.; Mravinsky, cond.*
+ Fa 11-12/93: 497

23566. CD-777 (2 discs): BACH—The 6 English suites, BWV 806-811. *Tilney, harpsichord.*
• ARG 3-4/94: 67
+ Fa 3-4/94: 107
+ Gr 2/94: 73

23567. CD-778: *Leopold Stokowski conducts music of France*. Music of Ibert, Ravel, Debussy, and Milhaud. *French National Radio Orch.; Hessian Radio Orch.; Südwestfunk Orch.; Stokowski, cond.*
+ ARG 11-12/93: 268
+ Fa 11-12/93: 519
+ Gr 2/94: 104

23568. CD-779 (4 discs): Music of Beethoven, Mozart, Schubert, and Brahms. *Hess, piano; Stern, violin; New York Phil.; Kurtz, Stokowski, Walter, conds.; BBC Symphony Orch.; Boult, cond.; American Chamber Orch.; Scholz, cond.* Recorded 1949-60.
+ ARG 11-12/93: 268

MUSIC AND ARTS

• Fa 3-4/94: 120
+ Fa 3-4/94: 406

23569. CD-780 (4 discs): *Willem Mengelberg: public performances 1938-1944.* Music of Tchaikovsky, Dvořák, Beethoven, Debussy, Brahms, Schubert, Bruch, and Wagner. *Concertgebouw Orch.; Mengelberg, cond.*
  • ARG 3-4/94: 228
  • Fa 1-2/94: 424

23570. CD-781: BRUCKNER—Symphony no. 9. WAGNER—Faust overture. *BBC Symphony Orch.; Horenstein, cond.*
  + ARG 1-2/94: 89
  + Fa 1-2/94: 151

23571. CD-784 (2 discs): Music of Beethoven, Haydn, Mahler, Gluck, Prokofiev, and Nielsen. *Anderson, alto; Orch. National de Paris; American Symphony Orch.; Hallé Orch.; Horenstein, cond.* Recorded 1956.
  + ARG 3-4/94: 192
  • Fa 3-4/94: 436

23572. CD-785 (4 discs): MAHLER—Symphonies no. 6, 9. BRUCKNER—Symphony no. 8 (Haas edition). *Stockholm Phil. Orch.; American Symphony Orch.; London Symphony Orch.; Horenstein, cond.*
  - ARG 5-6/94: 109 (Mahler)
  + ARG 5-6/94: 109 (Bruckner)
  • Fa 5-6/94: 184

23573. CD-787: MESSIAEN—L'Ascension. IVES—Orchestral suite no. 2; Unanswered question. BRITTEN—Young persons' guide to the orchestra. BARBER—Adagio. *London Symphony Orch.; Japan Phil. Orch.; Moscow Radio Symphony Orch.; Stokowski, cond.*
  + ARG 7-8/94: 132
  + Fa 5-6/94: 351

23574. CD-788: *Bruno Walter conducts.* Music of Dvořák, Smetana, and Tchaikovsky. *Standard Symphony Orch.; Walter, cond.* Recorded 1942.
  • Fa 5-6/94: 358

23575. CD-789: BEETHOVEN—Symphonies no. 5-6. *Berlin Phil. Orch.; Furtwängler, cond.* Recorded 1947 .
  + Fa 3-4/94: 127

23576. CD-790: BEETHOVEN—Symphony no. 9. *Schwarzkopf, Cavelti, Haefliger, Edelmann; Lucerne Festival Choir; Philharmonia Orch.; Furtwängler, cond.* Recorded live 1954.
  + ARG 1-2/96: 240
  • Fa 3-4/94: 128
  + Fa 1-2/96: 149

23577. CD-792: BEETHOVEN—Symphonies no. 1, 4; Egmont overture. *Berlin Phil. Orch.; Vienna Phil. Orch.; Furtwängler, cond.* Recorded live 1948-1954.

• ARG 5-6/94: 202
+ Fa 5-6/94: 109

23578. CD-793: BEETHOVEN—Symphonies no. 7-8; Leonore overture no. 3. *Stockholm Phil. Orch.; Furtwängler, cond.* Recorded live 1948.
  • Fa 5-6/94: 109

23579. CD-794: WAGNER—Die Meistersinger: prelude; Tannhäuser: overture; Parsifal: Good Friday music; Götterdämmerung: Siegfried's funeral music; Tristan und Isolde: Prelude and Liebestod; Die fliegende Holländer: overture. *Bayreuth Festival Orch.; Berlin Phil. Orch.; Stockholm Phil. Orch.; RAI Orch., Turin; Furtwängler, cond.* Recorded live 1942-1951.
  + ARG 5-6/94: 209
  □ Fa 5-6/94: 280

23580. CD-795: SCHUBERT—Symphony no. 9. WEBER—Der Freischütz: overture. *Berlin Phil. Orch.; Furtwängler, cond.*
  • ARG 5-6/94: 206
  • Fa 5-6/94: 246

23581. CD-796: BRUCKNER—Symphony no. 4. *Vienna Phil. Orch.; Furtwängler, cond.* Recorded live 1951.
  + ARG 5-6/94: 204
  + Fa 5-6/94: 123

23582. CD-797: *Overture: historic transcriptions for classical wind ensemble.* Music of Rossini, Beethoven, Mozart, and Weber. *Harmonie Ensemble, New York; Richman, cond.*
  + Fa 5-6/94: 334
  + Fa 7-8/94: 332

23583. CD-798: Masses by Certon, Wuorinen, and Duruflé; Motets by Tallis, Dunstable, and Victoria. *St. Ignatius of Antioch Choir; Chaney, cond.*
  • ARG 7-8/94: 223
  + Fa 7-8/94: 305

23584. CD-799: SIBELIUS—Violin concerto; En saga (2 performances). *Kulenkampff, violin; Berlin Phil. Orch.; Vienna Phil. Orch.; Furtwängler, cond.*
  - ARG 9-10/94: 266
  + Fa 5-6/94: 251

23585. CD-800: WUORINEN—String trio; Arabia felix; Piano variations; Speculum speculi; Flute variations no. 1-2; Glogauer Liederbuch. *Speculum Musicae; Group for Contemporary Music; Wuorinen, cond.; Blackwood, piano.* Reissue.
  + ARG 7-8/94: 188
  + Fa 7-8/94: 288

23586. CD-801: WUORINEN—Grand bamboula; Chamber concerto; Ringing changes; Violin concerto. *Light Fantastic Players; Sherry, cello; Group for Contemporary Music; Wuorinen, cond.; New Jersey Percussion Ensemble; Zukofsky, violin; Univeristy of Iowa*

Symphony; Dixon, cond. Reissue.
  + ARG 7-8/94: 188
  + Fa 7-8/94: 288

23587. CD-802 (2 discs): *Wilhelm Furtwängler: on tour in Stockholm.* Music of Schubert, J. Strauss, Jr., Haydn, R. Strauss, and Beethoven. *Vienna Phil. Orch.; Furtwängler, cond.* Recorded live 1943 and 1950.
  • Fa 5-6/94: 343

23588. CD-803: LISZT—Piano concertos no. 1, 3; Malédiction; Totentanz. *Lowenthal, piano; Vancouver Symphony Orch.; Comissiona, cond.*
  • ARG 7-8/94: 125
  + Fa 7-8/94: 163

23589. CD-804 (4 discs): BRAHMS—Symphonies no. 1-4; Piano concerto no. 2; Violin concerto; Variations on a theme by Haydn. *Fischer, piano; Vito, violin; Lucerne Festival Orch.; Vienna Phil. Orch.; Berlin Phil. Orch.; Turin Radio Orch.; Furtwängler, cond.* Recorded live 1942-52.
  • Fa 9-10/94: 154

23590. CD-805: BRUCKNER—Symphony no. 6. BRAHMS—Haydn variations; Symphony no. 1: 4th movement. *Berlin Phil. Orch.; Furtwängler, cond.* Recorded 1943-45.
  + ARG 7-8/94: 231
  + Fa 7-8/94: 105

23591. CD-809 (2 discs): TCHAIKOVSKY—Symphonies no. 4-6; Romeo and Juliet; Serenade; Waltz. *Concertgebouw Orch.; Mengelberg, cond.*
  + ARG 9-10/94: 266
  + Fa 9-10/94: 352
  + Gr 10/94: 218

23592. CD-812: RAVEL—Daphnis et Chloé; Shéhérazade. *Angeles, soprano; Concertgebouw Orch.; Toonkunst Koor, Amsterdam; Monteux, cond.* Recorded live 1955, 1953.
  + Fa 1-2/95: 239

23593. CD-813 (2 discs): Concertos by Beethoven, Bach, Brahms, and Mozart. *Szigeti, violin; Orchestra; Walter, cond.; Hallé Orch.; Harty, cond.*
  + ARG 1-2/95: 248

23594. CD-814: BEETHOVEN—Symphony no. 3. STRAUSS—Don Juan. *Vienna Phil. Orch.; Stockholm Phil. Orch.; Furtwängler, cond.*
  - ARG 1-2/95: 250
  + Fa 1-2/95: 116

23595. CD-815: BEETHOVEN—Piano concerto no. 3. SCHUMANN—Piano concerto. *Gieseking, piano; Berlin Radio Orch.; Rother, cond.; Berlin Phil. Orch.; Furtwängler, cond.*
  + ARG 1-2/95: 250
  • Fa 3-4/95: 123

+ Fa 5-6/95: 133
+ Gr 5/95: 124

23596. CD-817: Music of Bach-Busoni, Schumann, Brahms, Ravel, and Chopin. *Michelangeli, piano.* Recorded 1973, 1960.
+ ARG 1-2/95: 227
+ Fa 1-2/95: 356

23597. CD-818: BEETHOVEN—Symphony no. 9. *Berlin Phil. Orch.; Furtwängler, cond.* Recorded 1937.
● ARG 5-6/95: 236

23598. CD-819: BACH—Violin concertos no. 1-2; Concerto for 2 violins, BWV 1043; Concerto for 3 violins, BWV 1064. *Sand, violin & cond.; Blumenstock, Weiss, Grodin, violins; Archangeli Baroque Strings.*
+ ARG 3-4/96: 80
+ Fa 7-8/95: 104

23599. CD-821 (2 discs): Concertos by Mozart, C.P.E. Bach, Handel, and Poulenc. *Landowska, harpsichord; New York Phil.; Rodzinski, Stokowski, conds.* Recorded 1943-49.
● ARG 5-6/95: 246
● Fa 9-10/95: 395

23600. CD-822: BERLIOZ—Symphonie fantastique. MENDELSSOHN—Midsummer night's dream: Overture; Scherzo; Nocturne. *New York Phil.; Walter, cond.* Recorded 1954, 1948.
- Fa 1-2/95: 122

23601. CD-823: BRIDGE—String quartet no. 1. FAURÉ—String quartet. MILHAUD—String quartet no. 7. *Stanford String Quartet.*
+ ARG 3-4/95: 230
+ Fa 1-2/95: 133

23602. CD-825: COUPERIN—Les Nations: L'espagnole; La piémontoise; Les gouts réunis: Concert 13. *Musical Assembly.*
+ ARG 11-12/94: 96
+ Fa 1-2/95: 144

23603. CD-826: SCHUBERT—Symphony no. 9. WEBER—Der Freischütz: Overture. BEETHOVEN—Coriolan overture. *Berlin Phil. Orch.; Furtwängler, cond.* Recorded live 1942-44.
+ Fa 1-2/95: 263

23604. CD-829: STRAUSS—Don Juan; Till Eulenspiegel; Four songs; Death and transfiguration. *Anders, tenor; Berlin Phil. Orch.; Hamburg State Phil. Orch.; Furtwängler, cond.* Recorded 1942-47.
● ARG 1-2/95: 248
+ Fa 1-2/95: 278

23605. CD-830: *The University of Iowa Center for New Music: 25th anniversary.* Music of La Barbara, Hervig, Hibbard, Ziolek, Paredes, and Eckert. *University of Iowa Center for New Music.*

+ ARG 5-6/95: 232
+ Fa 1-2/95: 370

23606. CD-831: *Leopold Stokowski conducts music from Russia, vol. 2.* Music of Prokofiev and Tchaikovsky. *Hilversum Radio Phil. Orch.; Southwest German Radio Orch. of Baden-Baden; Hague Residentie Orch.; Stokowski, cond.*
+ Fa 1-2/95: 377

23607. CD-832: GABURO—Antiphony IV; Enough (not enough). *University of Iowa Symphony Orch.; Iowa City Boys Choir; Girls Choir of Iowa City; Dixon, cond.; Lycenus Concert; Schick, percussion.*
+ ARG 5-6/95: 232
□ Fa 1-2/95: 160

23608. CD-833: BRAHMS—Symphony no. 1. MOZART—Symphony no. 41. *NBC Symphony Orch.; Toscanini, cond.* Recorded 1940 broadcasts.
+ Fa 3-4/95: 141

23609. CD-836: BRUCKNER—Symphony no. 5. *Vienna Phil. Orch.; Klemperer, cond.* Recorded 1968.
● ARG 9-10/95: 117

23610. CD-837 (2 discs): BEETHOVEN—Violin concerto. RAVEL—Tzigane. BRAHMS—Violin concerto. CHAUSSON—Poème. *Neveu, violin; Southwest German Radio Orch., Baden-Baden; Rosbaud, cond.; Philharmonic-Symphony of New York; Munch, cond.; Hague Residentie Orch.; Dorati, cond.* Recorded live 1949.
+ ARG 5-6/95: 238
+ Fa 3-4/95: 124

23611. CD-838: WAGNER—Siegfried Idyll; Parsifal: prelude to act 1; Tristan und Isolde: prelude to act 1; Götterdämmerung: Brünnhilde's immolation; Wesendonck songs. *Flagstad, soprano; Standard Symphony Orch. of Los Angeles; New York Phil.; Walter, cond.* Recorded 1944-1952.
- ARG 5-6/95: 244
● Fa 3-4/95: 334

23612. CD-839: BEETHOVEN—Piano concertos no. 1, 4. *Aeschbacher, piano; Lucerne Festival Orch.; Hansen, piano; Berlin Phil. Orch.; Furtwängler, cond.* Recorded live 1947 and 1943.
- Fa 3-4/95: 122

23613. CD-840: BEETHOVEN—Piano trios op. 70, no. 1; op. 97. MOZART—Piano trio, K. 548. SCHUMANN—Piano trio, op. 63. *Edwin Fischer Trio.* Recorded live 1952-1953.
+ ARG 7-8/95: 272
- Fa 5-6/95: 422
- Fa 7-8/95: 121

23614. CD-841: Music of Dvořák, Sibelius, and Ravel. *All-American Youth Orch.; Stokowski, cond.* Recorded 1940.

- ARG 5-6/95: 239
+ Fa 5-6/95: 434

23615. CD-844: BRAHMS—Piano concerto no. 2; Rehearsal excerpts. *Ogdon, piano; American Symphony Orch.; Stokowski, cond.* Reissue; recorded 1969.
+ Fa 5-6/95: 148

23616. CD-845: Music of Brahms, Bach, Mendelssohn, and R. Strauss. *All-American Youth Symphony Orch.; Stokowski, cond.* Recorded 1940-1941.
+ ARG 5-6/95: 236
● Fa 7-8/95: 447

23617. CD-846: BEETHOVEN—Symphony no. 9; Moonlight sontata: adagio sostenuto (arr.). *Davis, Cathcart, Betts, Loewenthal; Philadelphia Orch. Chorus; Philadelphia Orch.; Stokowski, cond.* Recorded 1934 and 1947.
● ARG 5-6/95: 236
● Fa 7-8/95: 447

23618. CD-850: BACH—Goldberg variations. *Hill, harpsichord.*
+ ARG 9-10/95: 100
● Fa 11-12/95: 186

23619. CD-854: YSAŸE—Sonatas for violin solo, op. 27. *Castleman, violin.* Reissue.
+ Fa 7-8/95: 371

23620. CD-855: SARASATE—Caprice basque; Les adieux; Spanish dances no. 7-8; Zapateado; Malaguena; Carmen; Romanza andalusa; Zigeunerweisen; Faust fantasie. *Castleman, violin; Tauber, Lister-Sink, piano.*
● Fa 7-8/95: 297
● Fa 7-8/96: 280

23621. CD-856: BRUCKNER—Symphony no. 8. *Berlin Phil. Orch.; Knappertsbusch, cond.* Recorded 1951.
+ ARG 5-6/96: 261
+ Fa 7-8/95: 141

23622. CD-857: BEETHOVEN—Symphony no. 5. BRAHMS—Symphony no. 1. *All-American Youth Orch.; Stokowski, cond.* Recorded 1940-1941.
+ Fa 7-8/95: 447

23623. CD-858 (2 discs): SCHUMANN—Piano music. *Cortot, piano.*
+ Fa 7-8/95: 314

23624. CD-859: *Ludwigsburg Festival Recital, 11 April 1953.* Music of Bach, Scarlatti, Beethoven, Schumann, Debussy. *Haskil, piano.*
● Fa 7-8/95: 258

23625. CD-860: MOZART—Violin sonatas, K. 454; K. 304. BEETHOVEN—Violin sonatas no. 3, 10. *Grumiaux, violin; Haskil, piano.* Recorded 1957.
● Fa 7-8/95: 258

MUSIC AND ARTS

23626. CD-861: BRAHMS—Violin concerto, op. 77. BEETHOVEN—Romances for violin and orchestra. BUSONI—Violin concerto, op. 35a. *Busch, violin; Orch. of Basel; Münch, cond.; WOR Radio Orch.; Wallenstein, cond.; Concertgebouw Orch.; Walter, cond. Recorded live 1951, 1942, and 1936.*
+ ARG 9-10/95: 298
+ Fa 7-8/95: 131

23627. CD-862: *American piano music of our time.* Music of Nancarrow, Bolcom, Carter, Sahl, Hemphill, Adams, Foss, Jaggard, Rzewski, Wuorinen, Picker, Harbison, and Davis. *Oppens, piano.*
+ Fa 9-10/95: 403

23628. CD-863: BEETHOVEN—Piano concerto no. 4. MOZART—Piano concerto no. 24. *Haskil, piano; French National Orch.; Cluytens, cond. Recorded live 1955.*
• Fa 9-10/95: 137

23629. CD-864: MOZART—Piano concerto no. 20. HINDEMITH—The four temperaments. *Haskil, piano; Orch. National de France; Hindemith, cond. Recorded live 1947.*
+ Fa 9-10/95: 266

23630. CD-865 (2 discs): SCRIABIN—Piano sonatas no. 1-10. *Berman, piano.* Reissue.
+ Fa 9-10/95: 320

23631. CD-866: WAGNER—Die Walküre: Act 1; Götterdämmerung: Act 3. *Konetzni, Treptow, Rohr, Flagstad, Suthaus, Hermann, Greindl; RAI Orch. & Chorus; Furtwängler, cond. Recorded live 1952.*
• ARG 11-12/95: 288
+ Fa 11-12/95: 422

23632. CD-868: TCHAIKOVSKY—Violin concerto. MENDELSSOHN—Violin concerto. *Elman, violin; New York Phil.; Paray, Mitropoulos, conds. Recorded live 1945 and 1953.*
+ ARG 9-10/95: 298
+ Fa 9-10/95: 335

23633. CD-869 (2 discs): BEETHOVEN—Symphonies no. 3, 5-6. *Berlin Phil. Orch.; Furtwängler, cond.*
+ ARG 9-10/95: 298
- Fa 11-12/95: 209

23634. CD-870: WOLF—Mörike Lieder. *Fischer-Dieskau, baritone; Richter, piano. Recorded live 1973.*
+ Fa 7-8/96: 339

23635. CD-871: CHOPIN—The four ballades; Berceuse, op. 57; Impromptu, op. 36; Etude, op. 25, no. 1; Twenty-four preludes, op. 28. *Cortot, piano.*
+ Fa 9-10/95: 175

23636. CD-872: MOZART—Piano concertos no. 22, 24; Rondo for piano and orchestra, K. 382. *Fischer, piano & cond.; Royal Danish Orch. Recorded live 1954.*
+ Fa 9-10/95: 266

23637. CD-873: SCHUBERT—Winterreise. *Abramowitsch, mezzo-soprano; Barth, fortepiano.*
+ ARG 11-12/95: 198
- Fa 11-12/95: 366 (Kasow)
+ Fa 11-12/95: 366 (Lucano)

23638. CD-874: BACH—Harpsichord suites. *Hill, harpsichord.*
+ ARG 11-12/95: 76
+ Fa 11-12/95: 188 (Robins)
+ Fa 11-12/95: 190 (Evans)

23639. CD-875: *John Cage at Summerstage.* CAGE—Music for three; Eight whiskus; Four. *La Barbara, voice & percussion; Cage, voice and "shocking things"; Winant, percussion; Stein, piano, whistles, voice, and percussion. Recorded live 1992.*
+ ARG 3-4/96: 100
+ Fa 1-2/96: 170 (Carl)
+ Fa 1-2/96: 171 (Silverton)
+ Gr 8/96: 81

23640. CD-876 (2 discs): WAGNER—Der fliegende Holländer. *Weber, Varnay, Windgassen, Schärtel, Traxel, Uhde; Bayreuth Festival; Knappertsbusch, cond. Recorded live 1955.*
+ ARG 5-6/96: 270
• Fa 11-12/95: 417

23641. CD-877 (3 discs): Music of Mozart, Schubert, Bach, Beethoven, Brahms, Schumann, and Busch. *Busch, violin; Serkin, piano. Recorded live 1934-49.*
+ ARG 5-6/96: 261
• Fa 11-12/95: 478

23642. CD-878: SCRIABIN—Piano music. *Richter, piano. Recorded live 1972.*
+ Fa 11-12/95: 373

23643. CD-879: BEETHOVEN—Variations on a waltz by Diabelli; Variations and fugue, op. 35; Variations on an original theme, op. 76. *Richter, piano. Recorded live 1970.*
• Fa 11-12/95: 373

23644. CD-880 (2 discs): BEETHOVEN—Fantasia, op. 77; Piano sonatas no. 7-8, 14-15, 21, 30, 32. *E. Fischer, piano. Recorded live 1948-54.*
• Fa 1-2/96: 137

23645. CD-881: MAHLER—Symphony no. 2. *Vishnevskaya, soprano; Rössl-Majdan, alto; Vienna Phil. Orch.; Klemperer, cond. Recorded 1963.*
- ARG 1-2/96: 135
- Fa 1-2/96: 247

23646. CD-882 (3 discs): MOZART—Die Zauberflöte (complete and excerpts). *Seefried, Lipp, Ludwig, Dermota,*

Schmidt-Walter, Kunz, Greindl; Vienna State Opera Chorus; Vienna Phil. Orch.; Furtwängler, cond. Recorded live 1949 and 1951.
• ARG 7-8/96: 286
+ Fa 5-6/96: 219

23647. CD-885: MAHLER—Symphony no. 2 "Resurrection". *Woodland, soprano; Baker, mezzo-soprano; BBC Chorus; BBC Choral Society; Goldsmith's Choral Union; Harrow Choral Society; London Symphony Orch.; Stokowski, cond. Recorded 1963.*
• ARG 7-8/96: 148
+ Fa 5-6/96: 200

23648. CD-886 (5 discs): BEETHOVEN—Symphonies; Overtures. *Lipp, Boese, Wunderlich, Crass; Philharmonia Orch.; Klemperer, cond. Recorded 1960.*
+ ARG 7-8/96: 78
• Fa 7-8/96: 105
• Fi 12/96: 128

23649. CD-891: CHOPIN—Piano etudes (complete). *Zeyas, piano.* Reissue.
+ ARG 1-2/96: 96
+ Fa 1-2/96: 178

23650. CD-892: *Events dancing: recent compositions.* ESCOT—Missa triste; Mirabilis no. 1; Jubilation. COGAN—Gulf coast bound; Fierce singleness; Events dancing. *Various performers.*
+ ARG 9-10/96: 275
+ Fa 5-6/96: 150

23651. CD-894: BRUCKNER—Symphony no. 7. *Berlin Phil. Orch.; Furtwängler, cond. Recorded live 1951.*
+ ARG 9-10/96: 270
• Fa 7-8/96: 132

23652. CD-895: MOZART—Concerto for two pianos; Piano concerto no. 22. *Badura-Skoda, Bella, pianos; Vienna Phil. Orch.; Furtwängler, cond. Recorded 1948, 1952.*
+ ARG 7-8/96: 286
+ Fa 7-8/96: 247

23653. CD-896: BRUCKNER—Symphony no. 9. HAYDN—Symphony no. 94 "Surprise". *Bavarian State Orch.; Berlin Phil. Orch.; Knappertsbusch, cond. Recorded 1958 and 1950.*
+ ARG 11-12/96: 288
- Fa 7-8/96: 133

23654. CD-897 (2 discs): Music of Bach, Handel, Mozart, and Haydn. *Schneiderhan, violin; Vienna Phil. Orch.; Berlin Phil. Orch.; Berlin Opera Orch.; Knappertsbusch, cond.*
• ARG 9-10/96: 270
• Gr 11/96: 102

23655. CD-898 (4 discs): *Arturo Toscanini conducts French music.* Music of Berlioz, Massenet, Meyerbeer, Bizet, Debussy, Ravel, Franck, and Roger-Ducasse. *New York Phil.; NBC*

Symphony Orch.; Toscanini, cond.
+ Fa 5-6/96: 360

23656. CD-900: WUORINEN—The winter's tale. SCHULLER—Six early songs. CARTER—Frost poems; Voyage; Warble for lilac time. *Bryn-Julson, soprano; Markham, piano.*
+ ARG 9-10/96: 264
+ Fa 7-8/96: 339

23657. CD-901: BRITTEN—The rape of Lucretia: excerpts. *Cross, Pears, Ferrier, Kraus, Donleavy, Brannigan, Ritchie, Pollak; Glyndebourne Opera Orch.; Oppenheim, cond.* Recorded live 1946.
+ ARG 7-8/96: 284
+ Fa 5-6/96: 121

23658. CD-903: Music of Hindemith, Armer, Shifrin, Turok, and Milhaud. *Hampton, cello; Schwartz, piano.*
+ ARG 5-6/96: 234
+ Fa 5-6/96: 343

23659. CD-904: *The art of Guido Cantelli, vol. 1.* Music of Corelli, Geminiani, Vivaldi, Monteverdi, A. Gabrieli, Haydn, Beethoven, Brahms, Tchaikovsky, and Mussorgsky-Ravel. *NBC Symphony Orch.; New York Phil.; Cantelli, cond.*
□ ARG 9-10/96: 270
+ Fa 9-10/96: 435

23660. CD-905: TELEMANN—Violin sonatas. SPOHR—Sonatas concertante. *Kaufman, violin; Hammond, piano; McDonald, harp.* Recorded 1970-72.
+ Fa 5-6/96: 300

23661. CD-907: SCARLATTI—Scarlatti high and low. *Tilney, harpsichord.*
+ ARG 1-2/97: 164
+ EM 11/96: 716
+ Fa 9-10/96: 310

23662. CD-910 (2 discs): BEETHOVEN—Piano sonatas, vol. 1. *Richter, piano.* Recorded live 1959, 1965, 1975.
+ Fa 9-10/96: 147

23663. CD-912: WUORINEN—A winter's tale. DALLAPICCOLA—Machado songs. MESSIAEN—Poèmes pour Mi. *Bryn-Julson, soprano; Markham, piano.*
+ ARG 9-10/96: 263
+ Fa 1-2/97: 304
+ ON 8/96: 44

23664. CD-914 (12 discs): WAGNER—Der Ring des Nibelungen. *Flagstad, Frantz, Hermann, Svanholm, Lorenz; Teatro La Scala; Furtwängler, cond.* Recorded live 1950.
+ ARG 1-2/97. 239
+ Gr 12/96: 151
+ Fa 11-12/96: 416
+ ON 10/96: 44

23665. CD-915: THOW—Songs for the earth and other chamber works. *Friedman, mezzo-soprano; San*

Francisco Contemporary Music Players; Members of the San Francisco Symphony Orch.; The Flute Exchange; Gray, clarinet; Francesco Trio; Rosenak, piano.
+ ARG 11-12/96: 307
□ Fa 9-10/96: 344

23666. CD-917: FARRENC—Piano trio, op. 45. C. SCHUMANN—Piano trio, op. 17. *Streicher Trio.*
- Fa 9-10/96: 183

23667. CD-918: BEETHOVEN—Symphony no. 9. *Vocalists; Concertgebouw Orch.; Mengelberg, cond.* Recorded live 1938.
+ ARG 9-10/96: 274
+ Fa 7-8/96: 398

23668. CD-919: BEETHOVEN—Symphony no. 9. *Berger, Pitzinger, Ludwig, Watzke; Bruno Kittel Choir; Berlin Phil. Orch.; Furtwängler, cond.* Recorded live 1937.
● Fa 1-2/95: 117

23669. CD-926: DVOŘÁK—Octet-serenade, op. 22; Terzetto, op. 74. FOSTER (ARR. DVOŘÁK)—Old folks at home. TRAD.—Go down, Moses. *Harmonie Ensemble New York; Richman, cond.; Woodley, bass-baritone; Burleigh, baritone; Rood, Esaki, violins; Poy, viola.*
+ ARG 3-4/97: 128
+ Fa 11-12/96: 241

23670. CD-928 (2 discs): BERLIOZ—La damnation de Faust. *Crespin, Turp, Roux; London Symphony Orch. & Chorus; Monteux, cond.* Recorded live 1962.
● ARG 1-2/97: 236
+ Fa 11-12/96: 188

23671. CD-934: *Trio America, vol. 3.* COWELL—Scenario for 2 violins, cello, and piano; Wedding anniversary music; Duet for violin and cello; Andante for violin and cello. LUENING—Piano trio no. 1. CHIHARA—Elegy. CRESTON—Piano trio, op. 112. *Mirecourt Trio; Muenzer, violin.*
+ ARG 1-2/97: 197
+ Fa 1-2/97: 344

23672. CD-936: SCHUBERT—Symphony no. 9. WEBER—Euryanthe: Overture. *Vienna Phil. Orch.; Cologne Radio Orch.; Knappertsbusch, cond.* Reissues.
+ ARG 5-6/97: 291
+ Fa 1-2/97: 261

23673. CD-937: CAGE—Sonatas and interludes for prepared piano. *Steinberg, prepared piano.*
+ Fa 1-2/97: 132

23674. CD-941 (4 discs): BRAHMS—Symphonies no. 1-4; Variations on a theme of Haydn; Piano concerto no. 2. *Aeschbacher, piano; North German Radio Orch. of Hamburg; Berlin Phil. Orch.; Vienna Phil. Orch.; Furtwängler, cond.* Recorded live 1943-54.
+ ARG 1-2/97: 239
+ Fa 1-2/97: 119

23675. CD-942 (5 discs): BEETHOVEN—Symphonies; Overtures. *Vienna Phil. Orch; Berlin Phil. Orch.; Furtwängler, cond.* Recorded 1943-1953.
+ ARG 1-2/97: 239
+ Fa 3-4/97: 116

23676. CD-944: BRAHMS—Piano concerto no. 1 (with rehearsal). *Ogdon, piano; American Symphony Orch.; Stokowski, cond.* Reissue.
□ ARG 5-6/95: 92

23677. CD-954 (4 discs): *Wilhelm Furtwängler: The best studio recordings.* Music of Beethoven, Brahms, Wagner, Rossini, Bruckner, Bach, Mozart, Furtwängler, and Tchaikovsky. *Berlin Phil. Orch.; Vienna Phil. Orch.; Furtwängler, cond.*
+ ARG 1-2/97: 233
+ Fa 1-2/97: 351

23678. CD-1010: BEETHOVEN—Symphony no. 3. *Symphony of the Air; Walter, cond.* Recorded 1957.
+ ARG 9-10/94: 266
● Fa 7-8/94: 68

23679. CD-2001: BEETHOVEN—Symphonies no. 6; Leonore overture no. 3. *Berlin Phil. Orch.; Concertgebouw Orch.; Furtwängler, cond.* Recorded live 1944-50.
+ Fa 1-2/94: 126

23680. CD-2002: BEETHOVEN—Symphony no. 9 "Choral". *Schymberg, Tunell, Bäckelin, S. Björling; Stockholm Phil. Orch. & Chorus; Furtwängler, cond.* Recorded 1943.
+ Fa 11-12/93: 182
● Gr 5/94: 128

23681. CD-3007: BEETHOVEN—Symphony no. 9; Coriolan overture. *Bovy, Thorborg, Peerce, Pinza; Schola Cantorum; NBC Symphony Orch.; Toscanini, cond.* Recorded live 1938, 1953.
+ Fa 3-4/89: 105

MUSIC ARTS SOCIETY

23682. 41592: Duets by Dittersdorf, Guillement and Romberg. *Fuller, double bass; Chang, viola; Grainger, bassoon; Hirschl, cello.*
+ ARG 1-2/93: 177

MUSIC MEMORIA

23683. 30182: *Chante en français.* Music of Bizet, Massenet, Gounod, Saint-Saëns, Halevy, Tchaikovsky, Rubinstein, Denza, Caruso, Granier, Planquette, Hardelot, and Fauré. *Caruso, tenor; with assisting soloists; various accs.*
+ Fa 11-12/89: 435

23684. 30184: MASSENET—Opera arias. *Vezzani, tenor; various orch. accs.*
+ Fa 11-12/89: 272

MUSIC MEMORIA

23685. 30185: Arias of Donizetti, Thomas, Meyerbeer, David, Auber, Gounod, Massenet, and Charpentier. *Doria, soprano; various orch. accs.*
☐ Fa 11-12/89: 426 m.f.

23686. 30186 (2 discs): GOUNOD—Faust. *Berthon, Vezzani, Journet; with assisting soloists; Paris Opéra; Busser, cond.*
+ Fa 11-12/89: 218
+ NYT 5/14/89: H34

23687. 30189: Music of Bellini, Saint-Saëns, Boito, Bizet, Massenet, Charpentier, Wagner, Bachelet, Hahn, Messager, Schubert, Strauss, Schumann, and Leroux. *Vallin, soprano; various accs.*
+ Fa 11-12/89; 427

23688. 30190: *King of the French tenors.* Music of Gluck, Cherubini, Gounod, Wagner, Reyer, Delibes, Rabaud, Massenet, Meyerbeer, Verdi, Franck, Bruneau, and Krier . *Thill, tenor; various orch. accs.*
+ Fa 11-12/89: 436

23689. 30192: Music of Rossini, Gounod, Massenet, Mussorgsky, Boito, Mozart, Flégier, Rubinstein, Schubert, and Schumann. *Chaliapin, bass; with assisting soloists; orch. accs.*
+ Fa 11-12/89: 440

23690. 30223 (3 discs): CHARPENTIER—Louise: abridged; Vie du poète; Couronnement de la muse du peuple; Impressions of Italy; Six songs. *Vallin, Thill, Pernet, Féraldy; assisting soloists; unnamed choruses and orchestras; Bigot, Charpentier, cond.*
+ Fa 3-4/90: 164

23691. 30226 (2 discs): VERDI—Aida. *Giannini, Minghini-Cattaneo, Pertile, Inghilleri; with assisting soloists; Teatro alla Scala; Sabajno, cond.* Recorded 1929.
+ Fa 5-6/90: 367

23692. 30373: GOUNOD—Mélodies. *Doria, soprano; Bouget, piano.*
+ Gr 12/91: 111

MUSIC OF THE BAROQUE

21970. MB 106: MOZART—Mass in C minor, K. 427; Ave verum Corpus. *Bedi, Brunssen, Watson, Myers; Chicago's Music of the Baroque; Wikman, cond.*
+ ARG 11-12/91: 112

23693. MB 105-2 (2 discs): MONTEVERDI—Vespers of the Blessed Virgin. *Soloists; Music of the Baroque Chorus & Orch.; Wikman, cond.*
+ Fa 3-4/88: 151
• SR 9/88: 109

23694. MB 106-2: MOZART—Mass, K. 427; Ave verum corpus, K. 618. *Music of the Baroque Chorus & Orch.; Wikman,*

cond.
+ ARG 11-12/91: 112
• Fa 3-4/91: 308

MUSICA CLASSICA

23695. MC 2001/02 (2 discs): BRUCKNER—Symphony no. 5. BRAHMS—Piano concerto no. 2. *Backhaus, piano; Swiss Italian Radio Orch.; Schuricht, cond.* Recorded live.
+ Fa 7-8/90: 113

23696. MC 2003/04 (2 discs): DVOŘÁK—Symphony no. 9. HANDEL—Alcina: Ballet music. MOZART—Symphonies no. 38-39; Serenade, K. 525. SCHUBERT—Symphony no. 8. STRAUSS—Till Eulenspiegel's merry pranks. *Various orchestras; Kleiber, cond.* Recorded live.
+ Fa 7-8/90: 373

MUSICA OSCURA

23697. 070971: *The scyence of lutynge: lost lute works and transcriptions.* Music of Holborne, Galilei, W. Lawes, Locke, and Blow. *Rooley, lute.*
+ ARG 11-12/96: 264
+ Fa 9-10/96: 400

23698. 070972: *In loving memory.* W. LAWES—Psalms, songs, and elegies. H. LAWES—Cease you jolly shepherds. WILSON—O doe not now lament and cry. COBB—Dear Will is dead. IVES—Lament and mourne. JENKINS—Why in this shade of night? HILTON—Bound by the neere conjunction. *Consort of Musicke; Rooley, cond.*
+ ARG 11-12/96: 264
• Fa 9-10/96: 236
+ Gr 3/96: 93

23699. 070973 (2 discs): *Don Quixote.* Music of Purcell, Eccles, Courtville, Pack, Lenton, Tollett, Compton, and Anon. *Kirkby, Tubb, Cornwell, King, Hudd, Thomas, vocalists; various assisting speakers; Consort of Musicke; The City Waites; Purcell Simfony; Rooley, cond.*
+ Fa 9-10/96: 293
+ Gr 10/95: 140

23700. 070974: *King of the low seas.* Arias by Caccini and Pulliaschi. *Thomas, bass; Rooley, chitarrone.* Reissue.
+ ARG 11-12/96: 264
+ Fa 9-10/96: 392

23701. 070976: PALLAVICINO—Madrigals, book 6. *Consort of Musicke; Rooley, cond.*
+ ARG 11-12/96: 264

23702. 070977: *The mantle of Orpheus.* Music of Purcell, Weldon, Eccles, D. Purcell, and Blow. *Kirkby, Tubb, Nichols, Cornwell, King, Grant, Thomas, vocalists; Consort of Musicke; Rooley, cond.*

+ ARG 11-12/96: 264
+ Fa 9-10/96: 293

23703. 070978: GREENE—Songs and keyboard works. *Kirkby, soprano; Weiss, Davies, violins; Kelly, viola; Gough, cello; Mortensen, harpsichord.*
+ ARG 11-12/96: 264
+ Gr 8/95: 109

23704. 070979: *Sound the trumpets from shore to shore.* Music of H. Purcell, D. Purcell, Finger, Leveridge, Topham, Blow, Weldon, Barratt, and Eccles. *Kirkby, Tubb, sopranos; English Trumpet Virtuosi; A. & M. Hoskins, cond.*
+ ARG 11-12/96: 264
+ Fa 9-10/96: 293
+ Gr 10/95: 124

23705. 070980: The dark is my delight. *Consort of Musicke; Rooley, cond.*
+ ARG 11-12/96: 264

23706. 070981/2 (2 discs): WARD—Vocal and instrumental works. *Consort of Musicke, Rooley, cond.*
+ ARG 11-12/96: 264
+ EM 2/95: 169
+ Gr 7/95: 106

23707. 070983: NOTARI—Prime musiche nuove. *Consort of Musicke; Rooley, cond.* Reissue.
+ ARG 11-12/96: 264
+ Gr 8/95: 117

23708. 070984: STRADELLA—L'anime del purgatorio. *Consort of Musicke; Rooley, cond.*
+ ARG 11-12/96: 264

23709. 070985: INDIA—Madrigals, book 1. *Consort of Musicke; Rooley, cond.*
+ ARG 11-12/96: 264

23710. 070986: *The mistress: poems by Abraham Cowley.* Music of Purcell, Blundeville, Reggio, King, Blow, Hall, Turner, and Pigott. *Kirkby, Tubb, Cornwell, King, Grant, vocalists; Consort of Musicke; Rooley, cond.*
+ ARG 11-12/96: 264
☐ Fa 9-10/96: 293
+ Gr 1/95: 95

23711. 070987: *The mad lover.* Music of Blow, Lawes, Boyce, Eccles, Weldon, and others. *Tubb, soprano; Kelly, harp.*
+ ARG 11-12/96: 264
• Gr 9/94: 104

23712. 070988: Arie antiche. *Consort of Musicke; Rooley, cond.*
+ ARG 11-12/96: 264

23713. 070989: 21 settings from Guarini. *Consort of Musicke; Rooley, cond.*
+ ARG 11-12/96: 264

23714. 070990: Tasso settings. *Consort of Musicke; Rooley, cond.*
+ ARG 11-12/96: 264

23715. 070991: RORE—Madrigals, book 5. *Consort of Musicke.*
+ ARG 11-12/96: 264
+ Gr 1/94: 88

23716. 070992: MARENZIO—*Baci soavi e cari.* Madrigals. *Consort of Musicke.*
+ ARG 11-12/96: 264
+ Gr 1/94: 84

23717. 070993: PORTER—Madrigals and ayres. *Consort of Musicke; Rooley, cond.*
+ ARG 11-12/96: 264

23718. 070994: MARINI—Concerto terzo delle musiche da camera, op. 16. *Consort of Musicke; Rooley, cond.*
+ ARG 11-12/96: 264
+ Gr 3/94: 92

23719. 070995: MONTEVERDI—Madrigali erotici e spirituali. *Consort of Musicke; Rooley, cond.*
+ ARG 11-12/96: 264
+ Gr 3/94: 94

MUSICA SVECIAE

23720. MSCD 201: Piae cantiones. Sword dance. *Hortus Musicus, Tallinn; Mustonen, cond.*
• Fa 1-2/94: 387

23721. MSCD 202: *The royal court of the Vasa kings.* Music of Phinot, Hofmann, Vinders, Presten, Kellner, Clemens non Papa, Willaert, Josquin, Lasso, Gombert, and Anon. *Hortus Musicus, Tallinn; Mustonen, cond.*
• ARG 5-6/94: 190
• Fa 1-2/94: 387

23722. MSCD 302: *Music across the Baltic.* Music of Meder, Hahn, Busbetzky, and Anon. *Pilotti, soprano; Hortus Musicus.*
+ Fa 3-4/90: 361

23723. MSCD 405: ROMAN—Concertos. *Wallfisch, violin; Beznosiuk, flute; Robson, oboe; Orch. of the Age of Enlightenment; Halstead, cond.*
+ ARG 7-8/95: 182

23724. MSCD 407: *Gustavian composers.* Music of Uttini, Kraus, Naumann, and Vogler. *National Museum Chamber Orch., Stockholm; Génetay, cond.*
+ ARG 7-8/92: 246
+ Fa 3-4/90: 392

23725. MSCD 412: *Music from the age of liberty.* 18th century Swedish symphonies by Agrell, Hopken, Wesstrom, Johnsen, and others. *National Museum Chamber Orch.; Génetay, cond.*
• ARG 5-6/92: 159

23726. MSCD 413: ROMAN—Jubilate; Wedding music; Funeral music for Fredrik I: selections; Te Deum. *Rydén, Högman, sopranos; Lindskog, tenor;*

Mattei, bass; Eric Ericson's Chamber Choir; Drottningholm Baroque Ensemble; Ericson, cond.
• Fa 1-2/94: 279

23727. MSCD 414: KRAUS—Quartets no. 2, 4-6. *Lysell Quartet.*
+ ARG 11-12/92: 142
+ Fa 3-4/91: 253

23728. MSCD 415: KRAUS—Piano trio in D; Flute quintet; Violin sonatas. *Negro, fortepiano; Schröder, Sparf, violins; Ottesen, cello; Weman, flute; Wieslander, harpsichord.*
+ ARG 3-4/93: 101
+ Fa 5-6/93: 239
• Gr 2/93: 53

23729. MSCD 416: KRAUS—Funeral music for Gustav III. *Högman, Martinpelto, Ahnsjö, Lander; Uppsala University Chamber Choir; Drottningholm Baroque Ensemble; Parkman, cond.*
+ ARG 7-8/89: 51
+ Fa 7-8/89: 168

23730. MSCD 417: ROMAN—Shorter Drottningholm music (Suite in D); Pianto amiche; Invalid music (Suite in G). *P. Nilsson, soprano; National Museum Chamber Orch.; Génetay, cond.*
+ ARG 11-12/92: 188
+ Fa 5-6/93: 296
+ Gr 1/93: 43

23731. MSCD 418: ROMAN—Sinfonias no. 3, 9-11, 15, 22, 24, 30. *Drottningholm Baroque Ensemble; Schröder, cond.*
+ ARG 1-2/91: 101
+ ARG 11-12/92: 188
+ Fa 11-12/90: 332

23732. MSCD 419: KRAUS—Symphonies in C major and C minor; Sinfonia per la chiesa; Olympie: overture; Riksdagmarsch. *Orch. of the Age of Enlightenment; Halstead, cond.*
+ Fa 5-6/93: 239
+ Gr 11/92: 64

23733. MSCD 422 (2 discs): KRAUS—Proserpine. *Eklund-Tarantino, Martinpelto, Ryd, Arvidson; Swedish Chamber Orch.; Tatlow, cond.*
+ ARG 5-6/95: 127

23734. MSCD 424: KRAUS—Overture, Ack hvad behad et hjerta njuter; Arias; For the birthday of the King: excerpts. *Bonney, soprano; Ahnsjö, tenor; Drottningholm Court Theater Orch.; Schuback, cond.*
+ ARG 11-12/92: 142
+ Fa 7-8/91: 189

23735. MSCD 425: EGGERT—String quartet, op. 3. DE RON—String quartet in F minor. WESSTRÖM—String quartet in B♭. *Salomon String Quartet.*
+ ARG 11-12/93: 220
+ Fa 7-8/93: 134

23736. MSCD 512: NORMAN—Symphony no. 2; Concert overture in E♭ major; Antony and Cleopatra: Overture; Andante sostenuto e cantabile in A minor for string orchestra. *Helsingborg Symphony Orch.; Frank, cond.*
• ARG 9-10/90: 96
+ ARG 11-12/92: 174
+ Fa 9-10/90: 321

23737. MSCD 518: NORMAN—Piano quartet; String quartet. *Ivaldi, piano; Lysell Quartet.*
+ ARG 3-4/95: 151

23738. MSCD 519: GEIJER—Twenty-eight songs. *Olsson, mezzo-soprano; Wahlgren, baritone; Schuback, piano.*
+ ARG 5-6/95: 113

23739. MSCD 520: BERWALD—String quartet no. 1; Septet. *Lysell Quartet; Supporting instrumentalists.*
+ ARG 7-8/94: 75

23740. MSCD 521: BERWALD—Piano trios no. 1, 3; Piano quintet. *Lysell, violin; Karlsson, cello; Negro, piano; Berwald Quartet; Lindgren, piano.*
+ ARG 11-12/92: 89
+ Gr 10/93: 62

23741. MSCD 523: BERWALD—Estrella de Soria: Highlights. *Nordin, Dalayman, Smith, Lorentzson; Helsingborg Symphony Orch.; Westerberg, cond.*
• ARG 1-2/95: 84

23742. MSCD 525: NORMAN—Waldlieder; Walda sanger. SÖDERMAN—Digte og Sange. *Ahnsjö, tenor; Nilsson, soprano; Kontarsky, Kilström, piano; Eric Ericson Chamber Choir.*
+ ARG 1-2/93: 129
+ Fa 5-6/91: 243

23743. MSCD 527: CRUSELL—Introduction et air suédois varié; Clarinet concerto, op. 5; Concertante for clarinet, French horn, bassoon, and orchestra. *Rosengren, Stevensson, clarinet; Olsen, horn; Sønstevold, bassoon; Swedish Radio Symphony Orch.; Kamu, cond.*
+ Fa 1-2/94: 163

23744. MSCD 531: BERWALD—Symphonies no. 3-4. *Swedish Radio Symphony Orch.; Salonen, cond.*
+ ARG 9-10/92: 86

23745. MSCD 608: AULIN—Violin sonata. HAQUINIUS—String quartet no. 1. *Enoksson, violin; Kilström, piano; Brio Quartet.*
+ ARG 11-12/92: 131
+ Fa 1-2/90: 87

23746. MSCD 611: OLSSON—Ad Dominum; Credo, for organ; Three preludes and fugues. *Eric Ericson Chamber Choir; Idenstam, organ.*
+ ARG 1-2/93: 129
+ Fa 7-8/90: 217

MUSICA SVECIAE

23747. MSCD 612: Lyrical songs and ballads. *Uppsala University Chamber Choir; Parkman, cond.*
+ ARG 11-12/92: 254

23748. MSCD 612 : Choral music of Peterson-Berger, Stenhammar, and Alfvén. *Uppsala University Chamber Choir; Parkman, cond.*
+ Fa 7-8/89: 298

23749. MSCD 613: Piano music of Peterson-Berger, Sjögren, and Stenhammar. *Widlund, piano.*
+ Fa 7-8/91: 298

23750. MSCD 616: STENHAMMAR—Violin sonata, op. 19. AULIN—Fyra akvareller. KALLSTENIUS—Violin sonata, op. 7. *Sparf, violin; Forsberg, piano.*
+ ARG 5-6/94: 144
+ Fa 1-2/94: 319

23751. MSCD 617: *Swedish ballads.* Music of Soderman, Peterson-Berger, Stenhammar, and Rangstrom. *Wixell, baritone; Stockholm Phil. Orch.; Arnell, cond.*
+ ARG 9-10/92: 209
+ Fa 7-8/93: 199

23752. MSCD 618: AULIN—Master Olof: Suite; Stormy day: Excerpts. ATTERBERG—Oriental suite: Excerpts. *Royal Stockholm Orch.; Klas, cond.*
+ ARG 1-2/90: 15
+ Fa 11-12/89: 494 (2 reviews)

23753. MSCD 619: PETERSON-BERGER—28 Songs. *Bohman, soprano; Lander, baritone; Kilström, piano.*
+ ARG 5-6/95: 113

23754. MSCD 620: ATTERBERG—Symphony no. 5. KALLSTENIUS—A summernight's serenade. LINDBERG—From the great forest. *Stockholm Phil. Orch.; Westerberg, cond.*
+ ARG 1-2/93: 68
+ Fa 11-12/92: 178
+ Gr 8/92: 29

23755. MSCD 621: HALLÉN—Swedish rhapsody no. 2; Isle of the dead; Act 3 final scene from Harald the Viking. *Helsingborg Symphony Orch.; Frank, cond.; Vocal soloists; Swedish Radio Choir; Malmö Symphony Orch.; Rybant, cond.*
+ ARG 7-8/92: 139
+ Fa 9-10/92: 249

23756. MSCD 622: STENHAMMAR—Piano concerto no. 2. AULIN—Violin concerto no. 3. *Erikson, piano; Bergqvist, violin; Swedish Radio Symphony Orch.; Svetlanov, Kamu, conds.*
+ ARG 7-8/94: 176
+ Fa 5-6/93: 331

23757. MSCD 623: STENHAMMAR—Songs. *Otter, mezzo-soprano; Hagegård, baritone; Forsberg, Schuback, pianos.*

+ Fa 9-10/90: 319
+ Gr 7/90: 268
+ NYT 9/2/90: H19

23758. MSCD 626: STENHAMMAR—Serenade in F major; Chitra: Incidental music; Midvinter. *Swedish Radio Chorus & Orch.; Salonen, cond.*
+ ARG 1-2/91: 101
+ Fa 11-12/90: 363
+ Gr 11/90: 1038
+ MA 1/91: 81

23759. MSCD 627: ALFVÉN—Symphony no. 2. *Swedish Radio Orch.; Svetlanov, cond.*
- ARG 11-12/92: 71
• Fa 3-4/90: 104

23760. MSCD 628: *Pianolyrik.* Music of Fryklof, Beckman, Eriksson, Haquinius, and Lundberg. *Achatz, piano.*
+ Fa 1-2/94: 407

23761. MSCD 629: RANGSTRÖM—Sånger. *Svendén, mezzo-soprano; Hagegård, baritone; Schuback, piano.*
+ Fa 1-2/94: 272

23762. MSCD 630: PETERSON-BERGER—Symphony no. 3; Romance for violin and orchestra; Gullebarn's lullabies. *Zetterqvist, violin; Otter, mezzo-soprano; Swedish Radio Symphony Orch.; Köhler, cond.*
+ ARG 1-2/93: 131
+ Fa 7-8/93: 199

MUSICA VIVA

23763. MV 30-1099 (LP): RYBA—Czech Christmas mass. *Münzel, Pegelow, Kruse, Grundheber, Henschen; Hamburg Boy's Choir; St. Nikolai Chamber Orch.; Richter, cond.*
• ARG 9-10/86: 33

23764. MVCD 1026: *Original works and transcriptions.* Music of Godowsky, Strauss, Albéniz, Schubert, and Loeillet. *Hamelin, piano.*
+ Fa 7-8/90: 155

MUSICAIMMAGINE

23765. MR 10001: MASCAGNI—Messa di gloria. *Zennaro, Spagnoli; Ensemble Seicentonovecento; Colusso, cond.*
+ ARG 9-10/93: 153
+ Fa 9-10/93: 211

23766. MR 10003: MONTI—Chamber music with guitar. *Monti, guitar; Ensemble Seicentonovecento; Maccari, cond.*
□ ARG 9-10/94: 164
□ Fa 9-10/94: 260

23767. MR 10006: PATERNOSTER—Inzaffirio. *Pace, soprano; Paternoster, cello; Ensemble Seicentonovecento; Colusso, cond.*
• Fa 9-10/94: 284

23768. MR 10008: Music of Lauro, Broqua and Piazzolla. *Vallini, guitar.*
- ARG 7-8/95: 245

23769. MR 10009/10 (2 discs): TCHAIKOVSKY—Piano trio; Seasons (arr. Gedike). *Tchaikovsky Piano Trio.*
+ ARG 5-6/94: 156
• Fa 3-4/94: 341

23770. MR 10011: TCHAIKOVSKY—Romances. *Vitas, soprano; Bogino, piano.*
• ARG 7-8/95: 210
• Fa 11-12/94: 398

23771. MR 10013: LOMBARDI—Faustimmung: concerto intermedia. *Lombardi, piano; Concari, vocalist; Bennici, cello.*
+ Fa 1-2/96: 245

23772. MR 10014: MANCINI—Concertos for recorder, strings, and continuo. *Fête Rustique.*
+ Fa 7-8/95: 235

23773. MR 10029: CASTELNUOVO-TEDESCO—Escarraman; Aranci in fiore; Tarantella; Passacaglia. DEBUSSY—Minstrels. RAVEL—Pavane. *Felici, guitar.*
+ ARG 7-8/96: 96

23774. MR 10031: Music of Cherubini, Bottesini, Mercadante, Salieri, Boccherini, and Donizetti. *Solisti di Roma.*
- ARG 11-12/96: 243

MUSICAL HERITAGE SOCIETY

23775. MHS 7270 (LP): MOZART—Symphonies no. 25, 28-29. *Northern Sinfonia of England; Chung, cond.*
+ Fa 7-8/86: 193

23776. MHS 7290 (LP): CHOPIN—Preludes, op. 28; op. 45; in A♭, op. posth. *Argerich, piano.*
+ Fa 9-10/86: 128

23777. MHS 7321 (LP): VIVALDI—Concertos. *Taylor, oboe; Vivaldi Chamber Orch.; Boughton, cond.*
+ Fa 11-12/86: 240

23778. MHS 7363 (LP): *Romantic variations.* Music of Schumann, Mendelssohn, Brahms, and Chopin. *Frost, piano.*
+ Fa 3-4/87: 263
+ Opus 4/87: 35

23779. MHS 7369 (LP): NIELSEN—Symphony no. 2; Aladdin: Suite. *Gothenburg Symphony Orch.; Chung, cond.*
• Fa 11-12/86: 190

23780. MHS 7389 (LP): CHOPIN—Piano music. *Argerich, piano.*
+ Fa 11-12/86: 130

23781. MHS 7408 (LP): SCRIABIN—Piano music. *Rutstein, piano.*
- Fa 1-2/89: 264

23782. MHS 7413 (LP): *Four great 20th century piano sonatas.* BARBER—Piano sonata. BERG—Piano sonata. SCRIABIN—Piano sonata no. 7. BARTÓK—Piano sonata. *Cocarelli, Wakabayashi, Barone, Tsachor, piano.*
• Fa 11-12/88: 126

23783. MHS 7420 (LP): SCHUBERT—Piano music. *Goldsmith, piano.*
+ Fa 1-2/87: 177

23784. MHS 7458 (LP): THOMSON—Ballet and film scores as arranged for piano. *Helin, piano.*
+ Fa 5-6/88: 227
+ MA 1/89: 82

23785. MHS 7462 (LP): DVOŘÁK—String quintet, op. 77. DOPPLER—The Woodbird, op. 21. *St. Luke's Chamber Ensemble.*
+ Fa 5-6/87: 111

23786. MHS 7470 (LP): CHOPIN—Piano music. *Gorbaty, piano.*
• Fa 11-12/87: 126

23787. MHS 7484 (LP): BEETHOVEN—Piano sonata no. 17; Piano music. *Goldsmith, piano.*
+ ARG 11-12/87: 17
+ Fa 11-12/87: 99

23788. MHS 7530 (LP): SORABJI—Piano music. *Habermann, piano.*
+ ARG 3-4/88: 81
+ Fa 11-12/87: 230

23789. MHS 7537 (LP): ELGAR—String quartet in E minor. DELIUS—String quartet. *Brodsky Quartet.*
• Fa 5-6/87: 116

23790. MHS 7550 (LP): GOULD—Concerto concertante; Cellos; Pavanne. *Yanagita, violin; Peskanov, piano; Bronx Arts Ensemble.*
+ Fa 3-4/88: 115

23791. MHS 11208: BOCCHERINI—Guitar quintets no. 1-2, 7. *Romero, guitar; Academy of St. Martin-in-the-Fields Chamber Ensemble.*
+ Fa 3-4/88: 86

23792. MHS 11209: VIVALDI—Six concertos. *Hutchins, recorder & flute; Baskin, oboe; I Musici de Montréal; Turovsky, cond.*
+ Fa 3-4/88: 231

23793. MHS 11210: *The Baroque concerto in England.* Music of Boyce, Woodcock, and Anon. *Black, oboe; Bennett, flute; Thames Chamber Orch.; Dobson, cond.*
+ Fa 3-4/88: 267

23794. MHS 11216: TELEMANN—Oboe concertos in E minor, D minor, C minor, F minor. *Vries, oboe; Asperen, harpsichord; Alma Musica Amsterdam.*
+ Fa 3-4/88: 218

23795. MHS 11218 (2 discs): TELEMANN—Suites for 3 oboes, strings, and continuo in D major, G minor, D minor, D major. *Concentus Musicus Wien; Harnoncourt, cond.*
+ Fa 3-4/88: 219

23796. MHS 11219 (2 discs): MOZART—Symphonies no. 21, 31, 35-36; Andante in G major (2nd version for symphony no. 31). *Concertgebouw Orch.; Krips, cond.*
+ ARG 7-8/88: 46 m.f.
• Fa 3-4/88: 165

23797. MHS 415576: POULENC—Concerto for 2 pianos; Sonata for 2 pianos. *Yarbrough, Cowan, pianos.*
- ARG 11-12/93: 168

23798. MHS 419409: BEETHOVEN—Piano quartet op. 16; Early piano quartet in C. *An die Musik.*
+ ARG 1-2/92: 28

23799. MHS 424501: IVES—Violin sonatas. *Stepner, violin; Kirkpatrick, piano.*
+ ARG 11-12/92: 138

23800. MHS 512033: MOZART—Serenades, K. 375, K. 388. *Scottish National Orch. Wind Ensemble; Järvi, cond.*
+ Fa 3-4/88: 154

23801. MHS 512048: MOZART—Missa brevis, K. 258; Missa longa, K. 262. *Shirai, Schiml, Ude, Polster; Leipzig Radio Chorus; Dresden Phil. Orch.; Kegel, cond.*
+ Fa 3-4/88: 162

23802. MHS 512072: CRUSELL—Clarinet concerto no. 2. WEBER—Concertino for clarinet, op. 26. BAERMANN—Adagio for clarinet in D♭ major. ROSSINI—Introduction, theme and variations for clarinet. *Johnson, clarinet; English Chamber Orch.; Groves, cond.*
+ Fa 7-8/88: 319

23803. MHS 512076: *Homage to Arthur Rubinstein, vol. 1.* Music of Falla, Mompou, A. Williams, Cluzeau-Mortet, Aguirre, Guarnieri, Brandao, Ponce, R. Halffter, and Villa-Lobos. *Allen, piano.*
+ ARG 7-8/88: 81
+ Fa 5-6/88: 251

23804. MHS 512077: STRAUSS—Enoch Arden, op. 38. *Rowan, narrator; Hough, piano.*
- Fa 3-4/88: 208

23805. MHS 512078: STRAVINSKY—Baiser de la fée. TCHAIKOVSKY—Sleeping

beauty: Bluebird pas de deux (arr. Stravinsky). *Scottish National Orch.; Järvi, cond.*
+ ARG 3-4/88L 86
+ Fa 3-4/88: 211

23806. MHS 512082: VIVALDI—Concertos and trios. *Lindberg, lute; Sparf, Galli, violins; Ottesen, cello; Petersen, violone; Wieslander, organ; Huggett, viola d'amore; Drottningholm Baroque Ensemble.*
+ Fa 7-8/88: 275

23807. MHS 512087: PROKOFIEV—Pas d'acier, op. 41; Ode to the end of the war, op. 105. *USSR Ministry of Culture Symphony Orch.; Rozhdestvensky, cond.*
+ Fa 3-4/88: 173

23808. MHS 512092: MOZART—Concerto for 2 pianos, K. 365. MENDELSSOHN—Concerto for 2 pianos in E major. *Gavrilov, Shon, pianos; Moscow Chamber Orch.; Kogan, cond.*
- ARG 9-10/88: 61
- Fa 3-4/88: 158
- Fa 11-12/88: 231
+ Fa 9-10/89: 256

23809. MHS 512093: Music of Byrd, Handel, Croft, Arne, J.C. Bach, and Anon. *Pinnock, virginals & harpsichord.*
+ Fa 3-4/88: 61

23810. MHS 512099: BOCCHERINI—Cello concerto, G. 479. VIVALDI—Concerto for 2 cellos, RV 531; Cello concertos, RV 424, 413. *Lamothe, cello; Turovsky, cello & cond.; I Musici de Montréal.*
+ Fa 7-8/88: 132

23811. MHS 512100: VIVALDI—Flute concertos, RV 428, RV 433-435, RV 437, RV 439. *Petri, recorders; Academy of St. Martin-in-the-Fields; Brown, cond.*
+ Fa 7-8/88: 274

23812. MHS 512110: GERSHWIN—An American in Paris. BERNSTEIN—West Side story: Symphonic dances. *San Francisco Symphony Orch.; Ozawa, cond.*
+ Fa 3-4/88: 105

23813. MHS 512121: BIZET—Carmen: Suites no. 1-2; L'Arlésienne: Suites no. 1-2. *London Symphony Orch.; Marriner, cond.*
+ Fa 9-10/88: 113

23814. MHS 512123: TCHAIKOVSKY—Symphony no. 6. *Gewandhaus Orch.; Masur, cond.*
+ Fa 11-12/88: 292

23815. MHS 512124: MUSSORGSKY—Pictures at an exhibition (arr. Ravel). RIMSKY-KORSAKOV—Russian Easter overture. *Vancouver Symphony Orch.; Akiyama, cond.*
+ Fa 9-10/88: 221

MUSICAL HERITAGE SOCIETY

23816. MHS 512134: Piano music of Grieg and Grainger. *Smith, piano.*
+ ARG 9-10/88: 48
+ Fa 7-8/88: 171

23817. MHS 512137: GEMINIANI—Enchanted forest. VIVALDI—Concerto for 2 violins, strings, and continuo, RV 513. *Ritchie, Wilcock, violins; CBC Vancouver Orch.; Gardiner, cond.*
+ Fa 9-10/88: 155

23818. MHS 512160: GOLDMARK—Rustic wedding symphony. *Los Angeles Phil. Orch.; López Cobos, cond.*
• Fa 9-10/88: 159

23819. MHS 512162: MOZART—Zauberflöte: Excerpts (arr. Heidenreich); Entführung aus dem Serail: Excerpts (arr. Wendt). *Amadeus Ensemble; Rudel, cond.*
+ Fa 9-10/88: 213

23820. MHS 512164: JOSQUIN—Missa Hercules Dux Ferrariae; Deploration de Johannes Ockeghem. LA RUE—Missa pro defunctis. *New London Chamber Choir; Wood, cond.*
+ Fa 9-10/88: 175

23821. MHS 512169: POULENC—Piano music. *Boriskin, piano.*
+ Fa 9-10/88: 226

23822. MHS 512190: SUK—Four pieces. YSAŸE—Violin sonata no. 3. SZYMANOWSKI—Mity. JANÁČEK—Violin sonata. *Somach, violin; Lazarus, piano.*
• ARG 9-10/89: 131

23823. MHS 512280: JOSQUIN—Missa de Beata Virgine. FAYRFAX—Maria plena virtute. *Capella Alamire; Urquhart, cond.*
+ ARG 1-2/90: 56
+ Fa 7-8/89: 166

23824. MHS 512283: BEACH—Piano trio. IVES—Piano trio. PARKER—Suite for piano and strings, op. 35. *The Toledo Trio.*
+ ARG 11-12/89: 71
+ Fa 1-2/90: 111

23825. MHS 512302: PROKOFIEV—String quartets no. 1-2. *American String Quartet.*
+ ARG 11-12/89: 96
+ Gr 2/90: 1480

23826. MHS 512312: NAZARETH—Piano music. *Ferman, piano.*
+ ARG 7-8/90: 77
+ DA 10/89: 83
+ Fa 1-2/90: 254

23827. MHS 512318: BRAHMS—Deutsches Requiem. *Price, Ramey; Ambrosian Singers; Royal Phil. Orch.; Previn, cond.*
+ ARG 11-12/89: 43

23828. MHS 512319: PATTERSON—Mass of the sea; Sinfonia for strings. *Mackay,*

soprano; Keyte, bass; Brighton Festival Chorus; Royal Phil. Orch.; Simon, cond.
+ ARG 11-12/89: 93

23829. MHS 512331: CHAUSSON—Piano quartet, op. 30. SAINT-SAËNS—Piano quartet, op. 41. *Ames Piano Quartet.*
+ ARG 3-4/90: 38
+ Fa 11-12/89: 175

23830. MHS 512347: SALIERI—Piano concerto in B♭ major; Concerto for flute and oboe; Sinfonia in B♭ major. *Badura-Skoda, fortepiano; Hoogendoorn, flute; Borgonovo, oboe; Solisti Veneti; Scimone, cond.*
• ARG 1-2/90: 82

23831. MHS 512349: BACH—Harpsichord music. *Cooper, harpsichord.*
+ ARG 1-2/90: 16
+ Fa 1-2/90: 95

23832. MHS 512353: BALDASSARE—Trumpet sonata no. 1. ALBINONI—Trumpet concerto op. 7, no. 3. FRANCESCHINI—Trumpet sonata. TORELLI—Trumpet concerto in D major. VIVALDI—Trumpet concertos P. 44, 75. *Carroll, trumpet; Concerto Rotterdam; Friesen, cond.*
+ ARG 1-2/90: 125
• DA 1/90: 56

23833. MHS 512381: WEILL—Symphony no. 2. GINASTERA—Variaciones concertantes, op. 23. *Bavarian Radio Orch.; Rudel, cond.*
- Fa 3-4/90: 339

23834. MHS 512389: *French music for voice and flute.* Music of Ravel, Caplet, Saint-Saëns, Ibert, Martin, Roussel, and Chaminade. *Beardslee, soprano; Lawrence, flute; Ritt, piano; Emelianoff, cello; Levine, viola.*
+ ARG 7-8/90: 150
+ Fa 7-8/90: 330

23835. MHS 512446: BAKSA—Woodwind octet; Nonet. *Bronx Arts Ensemble.*
+ ARG 7-8/90: 16
+ Fa 5-6/90: 109

23836. MHS 512462: SIBELIUS—Orchestral songs. *Hynninen, baritone; Häggander, soprano; Gothenburg Symphony Orch.; Panula, cond.*
+ ARG 7-8/90: 110

23837. MHS 512492: Bassoon music of Ozi, Spohr, Noel-Gallon, and Berr. *Grossman, Ewell, bassoons.*
+ ARG 7-8/90: 130

23838. MHS 512502: *Latin-American flute and piano.* Music of Gutierrez-Heras, Ponce, Brouwer, Lobato, and Delano. *Hershman, flute; Witten, piano.*
• ARG 1-2/92: 152

23839. MHS 512555: SOONG—Piano music. *Rutman, piano.*

□ Fa 5-6/91: 112
+ Fa 3-4/91: 388
+ St 4/91: 261

23840. MHS 512756: OCKEGHEM—Missa l'Homme armé. JOSQUIN—Missa Malheur me bat. *Capella Alamire; Urquhart, cond.*
+ ARG 3-4/92: 114

23841. MHS 512774: NIN—Rapsodia iberica; 5 Commentaries; Suite espagnole; Chants d'espagne. RESPIGHI—4 Pieces for violin and piano. *Gratovich, violin; Golmon, piano.*
- ARG 1-2/92: 85
+ Fa 11-12/91: 427

23842. MHS 512820: MENDELSSOHN—The complete works for cello and piano. *Kreger, cello; Robbins, piano.*
+ ARG 3-4/92: 101
+ Fa 9-10/91: 270

23843. MHS 512827: *The Rubinstein dedications, vol. 3.* Music of Szymanowski, Tansman, Guarnieri, Dutilleux and Albéniz. *Allen, piano.*
+ ARG 3-4/92: 188

23844. MHS 512927: FOSSA—Guitar quartets 1-3. *Wynberg, guitar; Gabrieli Quartet.* Reissue.
+ ARG 5-6/92: 31

23845. MHS 513008: Music of Albeniz, Grau, Duarte, Llobet, Domeniconi, and Machado. *Regnier, guitar.*
- ARG 7-8/92: 260

23846. MHS 513014: GLAZUNOV—Raymonda excerpts. *Scottish National Orch.; Järvi, cond.*
+ ARG 7-8/92: 134

23847. MHS 513016: C.P.E. BACH—Keyboard works for connoisseurs and amateurs, book 5; Sonata in G minor. *De Silva, fortepiano, harpsichord.*
• EM 8/94: 530
+ ARG 11-12/92: 72

23848. MHS 513043: GRIFFES—Three tone-pictures; Fantasy pieces; Roman sketches; Sonata; Three preludes; De profundis; Legend. *J. Smith, piano.*
+ ARG 7-8/92: 139

23849. MHS 513091: PONCE—Intermezzo; Mexican scherzino; Romance of love; Mexican ballad; Gavotte; Full moon; Mazurka no. 2. CASTRO—Love song; Bluette waltz; Capriccio waltz. *Sandoval, piano.*
+ ARG 5-6/93: 118

23850. MHS 513358: The ultimate music box 2. *Light, Kraehenbuehl, performer-programmers.*
- ARG 1-2/94: 184

23851. MHS 513905: VIVALDI—Oboe concertos no. 1-2, 5-6, 10-13. *Klein,*

oboe; New Brandenburg Collegium; Newman, cond.
+ ARG 1-2/96: 193

23852. MHS 514033: Music of Falla, Gershwin, Stravinsky, and Kreisler. *Lee, violin; Lazarus, piano.*
• ARG 1-2/97: 215

23853. MHS 522054 (2 discs): TCHAIKOVSKY—Nutcracker. *Philharmonia Orch.; Lanchbery, cond.*
+ Fa 9-10/88: 277
+ Gr 8/88: 297

23854. MHS 522080 (2 discs): TELEMANN—Essercizii musici: Selections. *Aulos Ensemble.*
+ Fa 5-6/88: 225

23855. MHS 522154 (2 discs): BACH—Eight sonatas for diverse instruments. *Aulos Ensemble.*
+ Fa 9-10/88: 93

23856. MHS 532622 (2 discs): LANGLAIS—Organ music, vol. 6. *Labounsky, organ.*
+ ARG 11-12/95: 144

23857. MHS 837357 (3 LPs): RIMSKY-KORSAKOV—Orchestra music. *Scottish National Orch.; Järvi, cond.*
+ Fa 11-12/86: 201

23858. MHS 912031 (LP): KHRENNIKOV—Hussar ballad: Suite. *USSR Radio and Television Symphony Orch.; Fedoseyev, cond.*
• ARG 3-4/88: 47
• Fa 1-2/88: 146

23859. MHS 912261: MOSCHELES—Variations on Rule Britannia. DUSSEK—Grand sonata in A major, op. 43. PINTO—Sonata in E♭ minor. *Macdonald, piano.*
+ ARG 7-8/89: 123
+ Fa 1-2/90: 383

MUSICAPHON

23860. 51 331: BRAHMS—Zigeunerlieder, op. 103; Six quartets, op. 31. SCHUMANN—Zigeunerleben, op. 29, no. 3. *Galling, piano; Gächinger Kantorei; Rilling, cond.*
+ ARG 9-10/95: 115
+ Fa 7-8/95: 135

23861. 51 351: BACH—Cantata no. 208. *Donath, Speiser, Jochens, Stämpfli; Bach-Collegium Stuttgart; Rilling, cond.* Reissue.
+ ARG 3-4/96: 79
• Gr 4/96: 84

23862. 51 356 (Reissue): BACH—Cantata no. 213; Harpsichord concerto no. 7. *S. Armstrong, Töpper, Altmeyer, Stämpfli; Gedächtniskirche Choir; Bach Collegium Stuttgart; Rilling, cond.; Malcolm, harpsichord; German Bach Soloists;*

Winschermann, cond. Recorded 1967.
• ARG 7-8/96: 69
+ Fa 11-12/96: 171

23863. 51 357: BACH—Cantata no. 249. *Mathis, Plümacher, Altmeyer, Stämpfli; Bach-Collegium Stuttgart; Rilling, cond.* Reissue.
+ ARG 3-4/96: 79
• Gr 4/96: 84

23864. 56 807: Music of Castello, Marini, Frescobaldi, and others. *Musica Fiorita.*
- ARG 11-12/95: 262

23865. 56 808: BYRD—Songs and ensemble music. *Dawson, soprano; English Consort of Viols.*
+ ARG 7-8/95: 97
• Fa 7-8/95: 147

23866. 56 809: MILHAUD—Marimba concerto; Cortège funèbre; Symphonietta. RADANOVICS—Introversion. *Zivkovic, marimba; Austrian Chamber Orch.; Theis, cond.*
+ ARG 9-10/96: 165

23867. 56 813: *Romantic piano trios.* Music of F. Kiel, F. Koch, and Pfitzner. *Pallas-Trio.*
+ ARG 7-8/95: 135
+ Fa 7-8/95: 437

23868. 56 817: HAYDN—Violin sonata no. 39; Piano trio no. 23; Scottish airs. *Castalian Band.*
+ ARG 3-4/96: 124

23869. 56 952: TCHAIKOVSKY—Voyevoda; Manfred-symphony. *National Phil. Orch. of Minsk; Ponnelle, cond.*
+ ARG 9-10/95: 227
• Fa 9-10/95: 339

23870. 56 953 (2 discs): SHOSTAKOVICH—Symphony no. 5. MAHLER—Symphony no. 10: Adagio. *Minsk Phil. Orch.; Ponnelle, cond.*
+ ARG 1-2/96: 172

23871. 57 601: BUXTEHUDE—Wachet auf; Jesu, meine Freude; Cantate Domino; Lauda Sion salvatorem; Mit Fried und Freud; Befiehl dem Engel. *Westphalian Kantorei; Ehmann, cond.; Kantorei Barmen-Gemarke; Kahlhöfer, cond.; Greifswald Cathedral Choir; Berlin Bach Orch.; Pflugbeil, cond.*
+ ARG 3-4/96: 98

MUSICMASTERS

23872. 7004-2 (2 discs): BRAHMS—Violin sonatas; Viola sonatas. *Shumsky, violin & viola; Hambro, piano.*
+ ARG 9-10/91: 54

23873. 7021-2: HOVHANESS—Symphony no. 2. Lousadzak. HARRISON—Symphony no. 2. *Jarrett, piano; American Composers Orch.; D.R. Davies, cond.*
+ Gr 5/93: 47

23874. 7055-2: COPLAND—Appalachian spring; Nonet for strings; Two pieces for string quartet. *St. Luke's Chamber Ensemble; Davies, cond.; St. Luke's String Quartet.*
+ Fa 1-2/92: 197

23875. 7063-2: CHOPIN—Preludes, op. 28; Nocturnes, op. 62. *Chen, piano.*
• Fa 11-12/92: 217

23876. 7064-2: DVOŘÁK—Piano quartet no. 2. SCHUMANN—Piano quartet. *Los Angeles Piano Quartet.*
+ ARG 9-10/91: 69
+ Fa 9-10/91: 205

23877. 7073-2: HARRISON—Symphony no. 3; Grand duo. *Tecco, violin; Cabrillo Music Festival Orch.; Davies, piano & cond.*
□ ARG 11-12/91: 76
+ Gr 5/95: 48

20097 see 60097-2.

20109 see 60109-2.

23878. 60008-2: *Eliot Fisk performs Latin American guitar music.* Music of Sagreras, Barrios, Lauro, Sojo, Ponce, and Anon. *Fisk, guitar.*
+ ARG 9-10/89: 124
+ Fa 9-10/89: 420

23879. 60054-2: MOZART—Flute quartets, K. 533, K. 309. *Wincenc, flute; Muir String Quartet.*
• Fa 7-8/87: 152

23880. 60059-2: *Two American virtuosi.* Music of Giuliani, Gossec, Ravel, Milhaud, godard, Poulenc, and Bartók. *Wincenc, flute; Fisk, guitar.*
+ ARG 9-10/89: 124
+ Fa 9-10/89: 420

23881. 60072/73-2 (2 discs): *Complete violin music.* Music of Kreisler, Tchaikovsky, Grainger, Schubert, Weber, Haydn, Gluck, Mozart, Brahms, Schumann, Mendelssohn, Albéniz, Granados, and Falla. *Shumsky, violin; Wolfram, piano.*
+ Fa 3-4/88: 132

23882. 60074-2: Trumpet music of Purcell, Stanley, Clarke, Corelli, Baldassare, and Torelli. *Burns, trumpet & cond.; ensemble.*
+ Fa 5-6/89: 404

23883. 60077/78-2 (2 discs): MOZART—Violin sonatas, K. 301-302, 376, 379, 454, 526. *Mann, violin; Bronfman, piano*
+ Fa 11-1/86: 184

23884. 60087-2: SAINT-SAËNS—Symphony no. 3. *Rawsthorne, organ; London Phil. Orch.; Bátiz, cond.*
+ Fa 11-12/86: 205

MUSICMASTERS

23885. 60091/92-2 (2 discs): TELEMANN—Essercizii musici, v. 2. *Aulos Ensemble.*
+ ARG 11-12/89: 129
+ Fa 7-8/89: 266

23886. 60093-2: BACH—Musical offering: Trio sonata; Ricercare à 6; Brandenburg concerto no. 4; Cantata no. 156: Sinfonia; Orchestra suite no. 2 in B minor: Badinerie. *Chamber Music Society of Lincoln Center.*
• Fa 5-6/87: 80

23887. 60096-2: MOZART—Sinfonia concertante, K. 297b. BACH—Concerto for oboe and violin, BWV 1060. VIVALDI—Concerto, RV 556. *Chamber Orch. of Europe; Schneider, cond.*
• Fa 3-4/87: 173 (2 reviews)
• Fa 5-6/87: 80
• Gr 3/87: 1248

23888. 60097-2: Ballet excerpts of Tchaikovsky, Falla, Chopin, Delibes, and Pugni. *Polish Radio National Symphony Orch.; Straszynski, cond.* Issued also as LP: 20097.
- Fa 11-12/87: 292

23889. 60101-2: BRAHMS—Violin concerto. *Brodsky, violin; Polish National Radio Symphony Orch.; Wit, cond.*
• Fa 9-10/87: 167

23890. 60102-2: DVOŘÁK—String quartet no. 11. MENDELSSOHN—Andante and scherzo for string quartet, op. 81. *Mendelssohn String Quartet.*
- Fa 5-6/87: 113

23891. 60103-2: BRAHMS—Clarinet trio, op. 114. WEBER—Clarinet quintet, op. 34. *Goodman, clarinet; Members of the Berkshire Quartet; Pommers, piano.*
+ Fa 5-6/87: 103

23892. 60105-2: *A crazy quilt of American piano music.* Music of Ives, Fine, Copland, Cage, Thomson, Smit, Gottschalk, P. Johnson, Macdowell, Bernstein, Shapero, Gershwin, Talma, Kubik, Barber, and Schuman . *Smit, piano.*
+ Fa 5-6/87: 227

23893. 60108-2: PROKOFIEV—Piano sonata no. 6. SCRIABIN—Piano sonata no. 9. LYAPUNOV—Transcendental etudes, op. 11, no. 1, 10-11. *Hough, piano.*
+ Fa 11-12/90: 318

23894. 60109-2: SHOSTAKOVICH—Two pieces for string octet, op. 11 (arr. for string orch.); Sinfonietta for strings, op. 110. TCHAIKOVSKY—Serenade for strings, op. 48. *Soviet Emigré Orch.; Gosman, cond.* Issued also as LP: 20109.
- Fa 5-6/87: 195

23895. 60110-2: BEETHOVEN—Fidelio (arr. Sedlak). *Amadeus Ensemble; Rudel, cond.*
+ DA 10/87: 74
+ Fa 9-10/87: 250
+ NYT 8/16/87: 31
• Opus 10/87: 56

23896. 60117-2: MOZART—Nozze di Figaro (arr. Wendt). *Amadeus Ensemble; Rudel, cond.*
+ Fa 9-10/87: 250
+ NYT 8/16/87: 31
• Opus 10/87: 56

23897. 60118-2: SORABJI—Prelude, interlude and fugue; Valse-fantaisie; St. Bertrand de Commings. *Habermann, piano.*
+ Fa 5-6/88: 218

23898. 60121/22-2 (2 discs): BEETHOVEN—Violin sonatas (selections). *Mann, violin; Hough, piano.*
- Fa 1-2/88: 87

23899. 60125-2: MOZART—Don Giovanni: Excerpts (arr. Triebensee). *Amadeus Ensemble; Rudel, cond.*
+ Fa 1-2/88: 171

23900. 60128-2: Songs of Wolf, Strauss, Rachmaninoff, Ives, and Weill. *Upshaw, soprano; Garrett, piano.*
• Fa 1-2/89: 303

23901. 60129-2: BRAHMS—Piano sonata no. 3; Scherzo in E♭ minor, op. 4. *Bronfman, piano.*
+ Fa 3-4/88: 89

23902. 60134-2: Opera overtures of Rossini, Spontini, Mozart, and Piccini, arranged for 2 guitars. *Newman and Oltman Guitar Duo.*
+ Fa 5-6/88: 257

23903. 60135-2: *My favorite things: virtuoso encores.* Music of Macdowell, Chopin, Quilter, Dohnányi, Paderewski, Schlöser, Gabrilovich, Rodgers, Woodford-Finden, Friedman, Saint-Saëns, Rosenthal, Godowsky, Levitzki, Palmgren, and Moszkowski. *Hough, Piano.*
+ ARG 7-8/89: 123
+ Fa 5-6/89: 385
+ Gr 1/89: 1191

23904. 60138-2: HALPIN—Molly's Pilgrim: Suite. *Ensemble; Halpin, cond.*
+ Fa 3-4/88: 118

23905. 60139-2: TCHAIKOVSKY—Swan Lake: Suite; Sleeping Beauty: Suite; Nutcracker: Suite. *Royal Phil. Orch.; Bátiz, cond.*
• Fa 3-4/88: 217

23906. 60140-2: GOULD—Concerto concertante; Cellos; Pavanne. *Members of Bronx Arts Ensemble; Gould, cond.*
+ Fa 1-2/89: 170

23907. 60141-2: MOZART—Zauberflöte (arr. Heidenreich); Entführung aus dem Serail (arr. Wendt) . *Amadeus Ensemble; Rudel, cond.*
• ARG 3-4/89: 61
+ Fa 1-2/89: 224

23908. 60143-2: BEETHOVEN—Violin sonatas no. 1, 3. *Mann, violin; Hough, piano.* Recorded live 1985.
+ ARG 3-4/89: 22 m.f.
+ DA 2/89: 53
+ Fa 3-4/89: 97
+ Gr 9/89: 486
+ MA 7/89: 51

23909. 60145-2: BACH—Harpsichord concerto no. 1, BWV 1052; Violin concerto no. 1, BWV 1041; Concerto for oboe and violin, BWV 1060; Concerto for 3 violins, BWV 1064. *Wolinsky, harpsichord; Feeney, Fukuhara, Tanaka, Sato, violins; Taylor, oboe; Orch. of St. Luke's.*
+ ARG 9-10/89: 19
+ Fa 9-10/89: 118

23910. 60146-2: DEBUSSY—Piano trio in G; Intermezzo for cello and piano; Cello sonata in D minor. RAVEL—Violin sonata. *Michigan Chamber Players.*
+ ARG 9-10/89: 45
+ Fa 3-4/89: 143
+ Fa 5-6/89: 173

23911. 60152/53-2: KODÁLY—Duo for violin and cello. SHOSTAKOVICH—Piano trio no. 2. DVOŘÁK—Piano trio no. 4. MOZART—Oboe quartet, K. 370. VIVALDI—Concerto for flute, oboe, violin, and continuo, RV 95. *Various performers.*
□ Fa 11-12/88: 347

23912. 60162-2: COPLAND—Music for the theater; Quiet city; Music for movies; Clarinet concerto. *Gekker, trumpet; Taylor, English horn; Blount, clarinet; Orch. of St. Luke's; Davies, cond.*
+ Fa 1-2/89: 149

23913. 60164-2: WEILL—Violin concerto, op. 12; Kleine Dreigroschenmusik. *Tanaka, violin; Orch. of St. Luke's; Rudel, cond.*
+ ARG 7-8/89: 109
+ Fa 7-8/89: 282

23914. 60169-2: *Eliot Fisk plays guitar fantasies.* Music of Bach, Couperin, C.P.E. Bach, Weiss, Milinaro, Milán, Mudarra, Piccinini, Dowland, Mozart, Sor, Henze, Roussel, Poulenc, and Barrios-Mangoré. *Fisk, guitar.*
+ ARG 1-2/90: 118
+ Fa 9-10/89: 420

23915. 60170-2: *Naumburg presents Christopher Trakas.* Music of Ravel, Petridis, Guastavino, Montsalvatge, Barber, Bolcom, Musto, and C. Berg. *Trakas, baritone; Blier, piano.*

+ ARG 3-4/90: 156
- Fa 3-4/90: 352

23916. 60175-2: Mozart—Symphonies
no. 33-34. *Orch. of the Beethovenhalle,
Bonn; Davies, cond.*
+ ARG 7-8/89: 68
+ DA 10/89: 89
• Fa 7-8/89: 203

23917. 60178-2: Mozart—Clarinet
quintet, K. 581. Weber—Clarinet quintet,
op. 34 . *Neidich, basset clarinet &
clarinet; Mendelssohn String Quartet.*
+ ARG 7-8/89: 108
- Fa 7-8/89: 199

23918. 60179-2: Powell—Die Violine;
Madrigal for solo flute; Strand settings;
Darker; String quartet; Computer prelude;
Nocturne for solo violin. *Powell, piano;
Bettina, soprano; Matsuda, violin;
Sequoia String Quartet.*
+ ARG 9-10/89: 90
+ Fa 11-12/89: 318

23919. 60180-2: Dvořák—Serenade, op.
44; Bagatelles, op. 47 (original version
and orchestrated by D.R. Davies). *Orch.
of the Beethovenhalle, Bonn; Davies,
cond.*
+ ARG 9-10/89: 50
• Fa 7-8/89: 136

23920. 60181-2: Schoenberg—String
quartet no. 1. *Mendelssohn String
Quartet.*
+ ARG 7-8/89: 84
- Fa 7-8/89: 236

23921. 60182-2: Beethoven—Violin
sonatas no. 2, 4-5, 7. *Mann, violin;
Hough, piano.* Recorded live 1985, 1986.
- ARG 1-2/90: 24 (no. 2, 5)
+ ARG 1-2/90: 24 (no. 4, 7)
+ Fa 11-12/89: 137

23922. 60188-2: Purcell—Vocal music.
*Vocalists; New York Ensemble for Early
Music's Grande Bande; Renz, cond.*
+ ARG 1-2/90: 77
• Fa 11-12/89: 325
• SR 11/90: 156

23923. 60195-2: Copland—Duo for flute
and piano. Barber—Mélodies passagéres;
Canzone; Harris—Study for flute and
piano. Beaser—Variations for flute and
piano. *Robison, flute; Hester, piano.*
+ ARG 7-8/90: 136
+ DA 5/90: 60
+ Fa 3-4/90: 375

23924. 60198/99 2 (2 discs): Vivaldi—
Twelve concerti for various instruments.
Soloists; Aulos Ensemble.
+ Fa 1-2/90: 337

23925. 60204-2: Hovhanness—
Symphony no. 2; Lousadzak.
Harrison—Elegiac Symphony. *Jarrett,
piano; American Composers Orch.;
Davies, cond.*

• ARG 11-12/89: 68
+ Fa 11-12/89: 243
+ SR 11/89: 155

23926. 60207-2: Bach—Concertos. *Sato,
Feeney, Fukuhara, violins; Mann, flute;
Wolinsky, harpsichord; Taylor, oboe
d'amore; Orch. of St. Luke's.*
+ Fa 7-8/90: 72
+ NYT 6/24/90: H22

23927. 60210-2: Telemann—Don
Quixote: Suite; Concertos. *Schulman,
viola; Mann, Henze, flute; Taylor, Field,
oboes; Orch. of St. Luke's.*
+ ARG 9-10/90: 122
+ Fa 7-8/90: 292
+ NYT 6/24/90: H22

23928. 60213-2: Haydn—Piano sonatas
no. 31-32, 46, 52. *Nel, piano.*
• ARG 7-8/90: 55
+ Fa 3-4/90: 193

23929. 60214-2: Reger—Variations and
fugue on a theme of J.A. Hiller.
Hindemith—Symphonic metamorphoses
on themes of Weber. *Stuttgart State
Orch.; Davies, cond.*
• Fa 5-6/90: 263

23930. 60218-2: Viola music of Bach,
Britten, and Reger. *Isomura, viola.*
+ Fa 9-10/90: 154

23931. 60220-2: Copland—Violin sonata;
Vitebsk; Piano quartet. *Davies, piano;
Tecco, violin; Harrison, viola; Duckles,
cello.*
+ ARG 5-6/90: 43
+ Fa 7-8/90: 126
+ Gr 9/90: 555

23932. 60233-2: Schubert—Overture in
C minor for string quintet, D. 8; String
quintet, D. 956. *St. Luke's Chamber
Ensemble.*
+ ARG 3-4/90: 102
+ Fa 5-6/90: 283

23933. 60237-2: Falla—Amor brujo:
Dance of terror; Ritual fire dance; Six
Spanish folksongs. Schumann—Adagio
and Allegro, op. 70; Five pieces in folk
style, op. 102 . *Díaz, cello; Sanders,
piano.*
+ Fa 7-8/90: 358

23934. 60238-2: Haydn—Seven last
words of Christ. *Orch. of St. Luke's;
Rudel, cond.*
+ Fa 9-10/90: 260

23935. 60239-2: Bernstein—Chichester
psalms. Davidson—I never saw another
butterfly. *American Boychoir Concert
Choir; American Symphony Orch.;
Litton, cond.*
+ Fa 9-10/90: 185

23936. 60241-2: Harrison—Solstice:
Suite; Ariadne; Summerfield set; Canticle
no. 3. *Chamber ensembles; Davies,*

cond.
+ ARG 11-12/90: 66
+ Fa 9-10/90: 258

23937. 67007-2: Weill—Violin concerto;
Kleine Dreigroschenmusik. *Tanaka,
violin; Orch. of St. Luke's; Rudel, cond.*
+ Gr 2/94: 57

23938. 67045-2: Music of Wolf, Strauss,
Rachmaninoff, Ives, and Weill. *Upshaw,
soprano; Garrett, piano.*
• Gr 1/96: 99

23939. 67069-2: Fauré—Sonata, op. 13.
Boulanger—Nocturne. Ravel—Pièce en
forme de habanera. Poulenc—Sonata.
Robison, flute; Laredo, piano.
+ ARG 7-8/92: 259

23940. 67071-2: Rodrigo—Tonadilla.
Françaix—Divertissement. Petit—
Toccata. Piazzolla—Tango suite.
Brouwer—Micro piezas. Lennon-
McCartney (arr. Brouwer)—Fool on the
hill. *Newman & Oltman Guitar Duo.*
• ARG 7-8/92: 261

23941. 67075-2: *Honor to our soldiers.*
Works by Withers, Albert, Bela,
Damarre, Fredricks, Abt, Hare, Verdi,
Mozart, Holloway, Donizetti and Suppé.
Classical Brass.
+ ARG 11-12/91: 182

23942. 67078-2 (2 discs): Stravinsky—
Oedipus Rex; Symphony in 3
movements; Symphony of psalms; Rite of
spring; Requiem canticles; Apollo pas de
deux; Two fanfares. *Vocal soloists; New
York Choral Artists; Orch. of St. Luke's;
Craft, cond.*
- ARG 7-8/92: 231
• St 4/93: 289

23943. 67079-2: Music of Scarlatti,
Frescobaldi, Locatelli, Petrassi, Fiorillo,
Paganini, Castelnuovo-Tedesco, and
Giuliani. *Fisk, guitar.*
+ ARG 1-2/92: 154
+ Fa 5-6/92: 313

23944. 67080-2: Arias and duets from
Ariodante, Julius Caesar, Idomeneo,
Marriage of Figaro, and Clemenza di
Tito. Pachelbel—Canon. Albinoni—
Adagio. *Troyanos, Valente, vocalists;
New York City Opera; Rudel, cond.*
+ ARG 5-6/92: 190
+ ON 6/93: 43

23945. 67082-2: Gershwin—Rhapsody in
blue; I got rhythm variations; Rialto
ripples; Three preludes; Lullaby; Short
story; Two waltzes; Strike up the band
overture. *I. Davis, piano; Mendelssohn
String Quartet; Castelman, violin;
Hodgkinson, piano; New Palais Royale
Orch.; Peress, cond.* Reissue.
+ ARG 9-10/92: 108

MUSICMASTERS

23946. 67083-2: SAINT-SAËNS—Piano music. *Nel, piano.*
- ARG 9-10/92: 152

23947. 67084-2: HANDEL—Dixit Dominus. VIVALDI—Dixit Dominus. *American Boychoir; Albemarle Consort of Voices; 18th-century Ensemble; J. Litton, cond.*
+ ARG 1-2/93: 100
• ARG 5-6/94: 98

23948. 67085-2 (2 discs): VIVALDI—Twelve violin concertos, vols. 1-2. *Mintz, violin & cond.; Israel Chamber Orch.*
• ARG 9-10/92: 178

23949. 67086-2: STRAVINSKY—Pulcinella suite; Symphony in C; Russian peasant choruses; Russian sacred choruses; Les noces. *Gregg Smith Singers; Orch. of St. Luke's; Craft, cond.*
+ ARG 11-12/92: 215

23950. 67087-2: BEETHOVEN—Violin sonatas no. 1, 9. *P. Frank, violin; C. Frank, piano.*
+ ARG 9-10/93: 94

23951. 67089-2: GLANVILLE-HICKS—Etruscan concerto. HARRISON—Seven pastorales. RILEY—June Buddhas. *Jarrett, piano; Ensemble; Davies, cond.*
+ ARG 1-2/93: 171

23952. 67091-2: HARRISON—Philemon and Baukis; Cornish lancaran; Gending Alexander; Homage to Pacifica; Bubaran Robert. *Various performers.*
□ ARG 11-12/92: 131

23953. 67092-2: PAGANINI—24 caprices (arr.). *Fisk, guitar.*
+ ARG 1-2/93: 130

23954. 67093-2: BACH—Goldberg variations. *Feltsman, piano.*
+ ARG 1-2/93: 71

23955. 67094-2: ANTHEIL—Ballet mécanique; A jazz symphony; Violin sonata no. 2; String Quartet no. 1. *Castleman, violin; Davis, Hodgkinson, pianos; Mendelssohn Quartet; Lawson, pianola; New Palais Royale Orch.; Peress, cond.*
+ ARG 1-2/93: 66
+ Gr 4/94: 38

23956. 67097-2: VIVALDI—Guitar concertos. *Fisk, Hand, guitars; Orch. of St. Luke's.*
+ ARG 11-12/93: 216

23957. 67098-2: BEETHOVEN—Piano sonatas no. 30-32. *Feltsman, piano.*
• ARG 7-8/93: 65
+ Gr 6/94: 81

23958. 67100-2: WEILL—Lost in the stars. *Hopkins, Woodley, Pindell, Clarey; Orch. of St. Luke's; Rudel, cond.*

+ Gr 11/93: 160
+ Op 3/94: 376

23959. 67101-2: COPLAND—Dance panels; Emily Dickinson songs; Short symphony. *Schneiderman, mezzo-soprano; Orch. of St. Luke's; Davies, cond.*
+ ARG 3-4/93: 70

23960. 67102-2: JOPLIN—Rags, drags, etc. *Albright, piano.*
+ ARG 7-8/93: 107

23961. 67103-2: STRAVINSKY—Perséphone; Zvezdoliki; Symphonies of wind instruments; Concertino for 12 instruments; Octet. *Jacob, narrator; Aler, tenor; Gregg Smith Singers; Newark Boys Choir; Orch. of St. Luke's; Craft, cond.*
+ ARG 7-8/93: 163

23962. 67104-2: GERSHWIN—Rhapsody in blue; American in Paris; Porgy and Bess: Selections. *Atlantic Brass Quintet.*
+ ARG 9-10/93: 124

23963. 67105-2 (2 discs): BACH—Well-tempered Clavier, book 1. *Feltsman, piano.*
• ARG 5-6/94: 64

23964. 67109-2: MOZART—String quartets no. 4, 16, 22. *American String Quartet.*
- ARG 7-8/94: 142

23965. 67110-2: STRAVINSKY—Complete works, vol. 5. *Soloists; Orch. of St. Luke's; Craft, cond.*
+ ARG 5-6/94: 150
+ Gr 9/94: 64

23966. 67113-2: STRAVINSKY—Greeting prelude; Dumbarton oaks; Instrumental miniatures; Circus polka; Scherzo à la russe; Scènes de ballet; Agon; Variations. *Gregg Smith Singers; Orch. of St. Luke's; Craft, cond.*
+ ARG 1-2/94: 160
+ Gr 6/94: 64

23967. 67119-2: Baroque Christmas. *Baird, soprano; Aulos Ensemble.*
□ ARG 11-12/94: 249

23968. 67120-2: VIVALDI—Anna Maria violin concertos. *Mintz, violin; Israel Chamber Orch.*
- ARG 9-10/94: 218
+ Gr 10/94: 128

23969. 67121-2: BEETHOVEN—Symphony no. 3; Coriolanus. *Beethovenhalle Orch.; Davies, cond.*
+ ARG 7-8/94: 68

23970. 67122-2: BARBER—Piano sonata; Nocturne; Ballade; Interlude I (Adagio for Jeanne); Excursions. *Browning, piano.*
• ARG 3-4/94: 69

23971. 67123-2: BEETHOVEN—Septet; Sextet. *Old Fairfield Academy Orch.; Crawford, cond.*
+ ARG 7-8/95: 84

23972. 67124-2: CHOPIN—Piano music. *Licad, piano.*
- ARG 11-12/95: 106
+ Gr 10/95: 93

23973. 67126-2: BRAHMS—Handel variations; Waltzes, op. 39; Fantasies, op. 116. *Dichter, piano.*
• ARG 9-10/94: 111

23974. 67127-2: *Latin American guitar.* Music of Sagreras, Barrios, Lauro, Sojo, and Ponce. *Fisk, guitar.* Reissue.
+ ARG 3-4/94: 204

23975. 67128-2: Music of Scarlatti, Bach, and Froberger. *Fisk, guitar.* Reissue.
• ARG 3-4/94: 204

23976. 67130-2: *Baroque guitar.* Music of Frescobaldi, Bach, and Scarlatti. *Fisk, guitar.* Reissue.
• ARG 3-4/94: 204

23977. 67131-2 (2 discs): STRAVINSKY—The rake's progress . *West, Garrison, Cheek, White; Orch. of St. Luke's; Craft, cond.*
- ARG 1-2/95: 186
• Gr 3/95: 102

23978. 67132-2: BACH—Keyboard concertos. *Feltsman, piano; Orch. of St. Luke's.*
+ ARG 5-6/95: 72

23979. 67133-2: ROCHBERG—Caprice variations. *Fisk, guitar.*
+ ARG 9-10/94: 183

23980. 67140-2: JOHNSON—Orchestra music. *Stifelman, piano; Concordia Orch.; Alsop, cond.*
+ ARG 11-12/94: 136

23981. 67141-2: MOZART—Symphonies no. 25, 40; Eine kleine Nachtmusik. *Virtuosi di Praga; Rudel, cond.*
• ARG 11-12/94: 163

23982. 67142-2: MUSSORGSKY—Pictures at an exhibition. LISZT—Hungarian rhapsody no. 2. BIZET—Carmen suite. *Atlantic Brass Quintet.*
• ARG 11-12/94: 160

23983. 67145-2: *Laments and dances.* Music of Black, Britten, Bagdanovic, Bursen, Copland, and others. *Newman & Oltman Guitar Duo; Turtle Island String Quartet; Rogers, vocals, dulcimer; Ungar, fiddle.*
+ ARG 5-6/95: 209

23984. 67146-2: SCARLATTI—Sonatas. *Browning, piano.*
+ ARG 5-6/95: 164

23985. 67149-2: MOZART—Piano
concertos no. 9, 23. *Browning, piano;
Orch. of St. Luke's; Rudel, cond.*
+ ARG 5-6/96: 153

23986. 67150-2: Music of Berio,
Scarlatti, Paganini, and Mendelssohn.
Fisk, guitar.
+ ARG 1-2/96: 213

23987. 67151-2: Music of Paganini,
Sagreras, Barrios, Scarlatti, Vivaldi,
Beaser, Mudarra, Locatelli, Bach, Weiss,
Frescobaldi, and Soler. *Fisk, guitar.*
+ ARG 1-2/96: 213

23988. 67152-2: STRAVINSKY—*The
composer, vol. 7.* Histoire du soldat:
Suite; Pribaoutki; Cat's lullabies;
Monumentum pro Gesualdo; Mass;
Canticum sacrum. *Gregg Smith Singers;
Orch. of St. Luke's; Craft, cond.*
+ ARG 11-12/95: 214
+ Gr 10/95: 115

23989. 67154-2: SCHUMANN—
Davidsbündlertänze. Music of Chopin
and Liszt. *Rosen, piano.*
+ ARG 9-10/95: 268

23990. 67155-2: VIVALDI—Concertos.
*Mintz, violin & cond.; Israel Chamber
Orch.*
- ARG 5-6/96: 216

23991. 67159-2: McPHEE—Symphony
no. 2; Piano concerto; Nocturne; Balinese
ceremonial music. *Drury, Takagi, pianos;
Brooklyn Phil. Symphony Orch.; Davies,
cond.*
+ ARG 9-10/96: 161

23992. 67162-2 (2 discs): BACH—Well-
tempered clavier, book 2. *Feltsman,
piano.*
• ARG 9-10/96: 86

23993. 67165-2: BRAHMS—Violin
sonatas. *Mann, violin; Hough, piano.*
• ARG 9-10/96: 100

MUSIDISC

23994. 202012 (2 discs): HÉROLD—Le pré
aux clercs; Le muletier. *Soloists; Radio-
Lyrique Orch.; Benedetti, cond.; Orch.
Lyrique de l'ORTF; Marty, cond.*
Recorded live 1959 & 1968.
+ Fa 3-4/93: 188

MUSIKSTRASSE

23995. 2103: Music of Vivaldi, Mozart,
Amoroso, and others. *Rome Guitar Trio.*
• ARG 9-10/95: 261

MUSIQUE EN WALLONIE

23996. 8801: MICHA—Selections.
*Eynden, piano & organ; Reyghere,
soprano; Bogaerts, violin; Boeykens,
Lybert, Uyttrhoeven, clarinets; Murray,
horn; Le Petite Orgue Men's Choir;*

Moor, cond.
+ Fa 7-8/89: 187

23997. 11856: ROGISTER—Symphony for
string quartet and large orchestra in E
minor; Fantasie burlesque on a popular
theme. *Brahms Quartet; Siwy, violin;
RTBF Symphony Orch.; Walter, cond.*
• Fa 3-4/88: 179

23998. 310083: YSAŸE—Piano quintet in
B minor; Nocturne for piano in A minor;
Variations for 2 pianos. *Blumenthal,
piano; Ensemble César Franck.*
+ Fa 1-2/91: 352

23999. 315018: FRANCK—Chorales, no.
1-3. *Lecaudey, organ.*
- Fa 1-2/91: 197

MUZA

24000. PNCD 001: *International Chopin
piano competitions.* CHOPIN—Piano
music. *Oborin, Uninsky, Zak,
Davidovich, piano.*
□ ARG 3-4/91: 55
+ Fa 1-2/91: 177

24001. PNCD 002: CHOPIN—Piano music.
Czerny-Stefańska, Harasiewicz, piano.
□ ARG 3-4/91: 55
+ Fa 1-2/91: 178

24002. PNCD 003: CHOPIN—Piano music.
Pollini, Argerich, piano.
□ ARG 3-4/91: 55
+ Fa 1-2/91: 178

24003. PNCD 004: CHOPIN—Piano music.
Ohlsson, Zimerman, piano.
□ ARG 3-4/91: 55
+ Fa 1-2/91: 178

24004. PNCD 012: CHOPIN—Nine early
polonaises. *Smendzianka, piano.*
• ARG 1-2/90: 41
• Fa 1-2/90: 154

24005. PNCD 013: CHOPIN—Polonaises.
Małcuzyński, piano.
• ARG 1-2/90: 41
• Fa 1-2/90: 154

24006. PNCD 014: CHOPIN—Preludes, op.
28; in C♯ minor; in A♭ major.
Godziszewski, piano.
• ARG 1-2/90: 41
• Fa 1-2/90: 154

24007. PNCD 015: CHOPIN—Nineteen
waltzes. *Grychtolowna, piano.*
• ARG 1-2/90: 41
• Fa 1-2/90: 154

24008. PNCD 016: CHOPIN—Piano
sonatas no. 2-3; Fantasy in F minor, op.
49; Barcarolle, op. 60. *Sosinska, piano.*
+ Fa 1-2/90: 154

24009. PNCD 017: PENDERECKI—St.
Luke's Passion; Threnody to the victims
of Hiroshima; Polymorphy; String quartet

no. 1; Psalm of David. *Woytowitz,
Hiolski, Ladysz, Herdegen; Cracow Phil.
Boys and Mixed Choir; Cracow Phil.
Orch.; Czyz, cond.; LaSalle String
Quartet; National Phil. Choir & Orch.
(Warsaw); Markowski, cond.*
+ ARG 7-8/90: 82
+ Fa 5-6/90: 242

24010. PNCD 018: PENDERECKI—Utrenya,
parts 1-2. *Ambroziak, Szczepańska,
Woytowicz, Ladysz, Lagger; Pioneer
Choir; National Phil. Choir & Orch.
(Warsaw); Markowski, cond.*
+ ARG 7-8/90: 82
+ Fa 5-6/90: 242
+ Gr 6/90: 56

24011. PNCD 019: PENDERECKI—Violin
concerto; Symphony no. 2. *Kulka, violin;
Polish Radio and Television National
Symphony Orch. (Warsaw); Penderecki,
Kasprzyk, cond.*
+ ARG 7-8/90: 82
+ DA 5/90: 74
+ Fa 5-6/90: 242
+ Gr 6/90: 56

24012. PNCD 020: PENDERECKI—Cello
concerto no. 2; Awakening of Jacob;
Paradise lost: Adagietto; Viola concerto.
*Monighetti, cello; Kamasa, viola; Polish
Radio National Symphony Orch.; Wit,
cond.*
+ ARG 7-8/90: 82
+ DA 5/90: 74
+ Fa 5-6/90: 242
+ Gr 6/90: 56

24013. PNCD 021: PENDERECKI—Polish
requiem; Dies irae. *Gadulanka, Rappé,
Grychnik, Zardo, Woytowicz, Ochman,
Ladysz; Cracow Phil. Choir; Polish
National Symphony Orch., Katowice;
Wit, cond.; Cracow Phil. Choir & Orch.;
Czyz, cond.*
+ ARG 7-8/90: 82
+ Fa 5-6/90: 242

24014. PNCD 022: CHOPIN—Piano music.
Małcuzyński, piano.
+ ARG 5-6/90: 41
+ DA 7/90: 60

24015. PNCD 039 (2 discs):
MACIEJEWSKI—Requiem. *Donat, Rappé,
Knetig, Niziołek; National Phil. Chorus
& Orch. (Warsaw); Strugala, cond.*
+ ARG 5-6/90: 64
+ Fa 5-6/90: 208

24016. PNCD 040: LUTOSŁAWSKI—
Lacrimosa; Symphony no. 1; Concerto
for orchestra; Funeral music. *Woytowicz,
soprano; Silesian Phil. Chorus; Polish
Radio and Television National Symphony
Orch. (Warsaw); Lutoslawsky, Krenz,
cond.; National Phil. Orch. (Warsaw);
Rowicki, cond.*
+ ARG 3-4/90: 67
+ Fa 5-6/90: 204
+ NYT 2/18/90: H27

MUZA

24017. PNCD 041: LUTOSŁAWSKI—
Venetian games; Trois poemes d'Henri
Michaux; Symphony no. 2. *Polish Radio
Chorus; Polish Radio and Television
National Symphony Orch. (Warsaw);
Krenz, cond.; National Phil. Orch.
(Warsaw); Rowicki, Lutosławski, cond.*
+ ARG 3-4/90: 67
+ Fa 5-6/90: 204
+ NYT 2/18/90: H27

24018. PNCD 042: LUTOSŁAWSKI—
Postlude I; Paroles tissées; Livre pour
orchestre; Cello concerto. *Devos, tenor;
Jablonski, cello; Polish Radio and
Television National Symphony Orch.
(Warsaw); National Phil. Orch.
(Warsaw); Krenz, Lutosławski, cond.*
+ ARG 3-4/90: 67
+ Fa 5-6/90: 205
+ NYT 2/18/90: H27

24019. PNCD 043: LUTOSŁAWSKI—
Prelude and fugue for 13 solo strings;
Mi-parti; Novelette. *Warsaw National
Chamber Orch.; Polish Radio and
Television National Symphony Orch.
(Warsaw); Lutosławski, cond.; Junge
Deutsche Philharmonie; Holliger, cond.*
+ ARG 3-4/90: 67
+ Fa 5-6/90: 205
+ NYT 2/18/90: H27

24020. PNCD 044: LUTOSŁAWSKI—
Symphony no. 3; Chain I; Chain II; Chain
III. *Jakowicz, violin; Polish Radio and
Television National Symphony Orch.
(Warsaw); Wit, Lutosławski, cond.;
Junge Deutsche Philharmonie; Holliger,
cond.; National Symphony Orch.
(Warsaw); Kord, cond.*
+ ARG 3-4/90: 67
+ Fa 5-6/90: 205
+ NYT 2/18/90: H27

24021. PNCD 045: LUTOSŁAWSKI—
Selections. *Drewnowski, piano; J.
Lukaszczyk, M. Lukaszczyk, pianos;
Lukomska, soprano; Holliger, oboe;
Jablonski, cello; Esztényi, piano; LaSalle
String Quartet; National Symphony Orch.
(Warsaw); Markowski, cond.*
+ ARG 3-4/90: 67
+ Fa 5-6/90: 205
+ NYT 2/18/90: H27

24022. PNCD 050: STRAUSS—Don Juan;
Death and transfiguration; Till
Eulenspiegel's merry pranks. *Polish
Radio and Television National Symphony
Orch. (Warsaw); Wit, cond.*
+ Fa 3-4/91: 395
+ Gr 3/91: 1677

24023. PNCD 052: NOWOWIEJSKI—Organ
symphonies no. 3, 5; Organ concerto no.
2; Christmas in the Ancient Virgin Mary
Church in Krakow. *Erdman, organ.*
+ ARG 11-12/90: 92
□ Fa 1-2/91: 270

24024. PNCD 055: BACH—Goldberg
variations; Chromatic fantasia and fugue

in D minor; Fantasia and fugue in A
minor, BWV 904. *Kawalla, piano.*
• ARG 3-4/91: 26
+ Fa 5-6/91: 108

24025. PNCD 056 (2 discs): CHOPIN—
Mazurkas (complete). *Ekier, piano.*
+ Fa 5-6/91: 155

24026. PNCD 058: HAYDN—Symphonies
no. 73, 82-83. *Symphony Orch. of the
Silesian Phil.; Stryja, cond.*
• ARG 7-8/92: 147
- Fa 5-6/91: 185

24027. PNCD 060: *Polish opera arias.*
Music of Moniuszko, Nowoniejski,
Paderewski, Statkowski and Zelenski.
Various performers.
+ ARG 3-4/92: 203

24028. PNCD 062: SZYMANOWSKI—
Symphonies no. 2, 4; Concert overture in
E major. *Zmudzinski, piano; National
Phil. Orch. (Warsaw); Rowicki, cond.*
□ ARG 1-2/91: 105
+ Fa 9-10/90: 404
+ Gr 7/90: 230

24029. PNCD 063: SZYMANOWSKI—Stabat
Mater; Symphony no. 3; Litany to the
Virgin Mary; Demeter. *Woytowicz,
Szczepańska, Hiolski, Szostek-Radkowa;
Warsaw National Phil. Choir & Orch.;
Rowicki, cond.; Female Choir of the
Polish Radio in Cracow; Polish Radio
and Television National Symphony Orch.
(Warsaw); Wisłocki, cond.*
□ ARG 1-2/91: 105
+ Fa 9-10/90: 404
+ Gr 7/90: 230

24030. PNCD 064: SZYMANOWSKI—Violin
concertos no. 1-2; Violin sonata; King
Roger: Roxana's song (arr. Kochanski) .
*Wiłkomirska, violin; Chmielewski, piano;
National Phil. Orch. (Warsaw); Rowicki,
cond.*
□ ARG 1-2/90: 105
+ Fa 9-10/90: 405
+ Gr 7/90: 230

24031. PNCD 065: SZYMANOWSKI—
Selections. *Wiłkomirska, violin;
Chmielewski, piano; Wilanów Quartet.*
□ ARG 1-2/91: 105
+ Fa 9-10/90: 405
+ Gr 7/90: 230

24032. PNCD 066: SZYMANOWSKI—Étude
in B♭ minor; Masques; Piano sonata no. 2;
Mazurkas, op. 50. Selections.
*Małcuzyński, Stefański, Hesse-Bukowska,
piano.*
□ ARG 1-2/91: 105
+ Fa 9-10/90: 405
+ Gr 7/90: 230

24033. PNCD 067: SZYMANOWSKI—Songs.
*Zylis-Gara, Gadulanka, Bachleda,
Marchwinski, Sulikowski, piano;
Lukomska, soprano.*
□ ARG 1-2/91: 105

+ Fa 9-10/90: 405
+ Gr 7/90: 230

24034. PNCD 068: TCHAIKOVSKY—
Serenade for strings in C major.
KARLOWICZ—Serenade for strings in C
major. SUK—Serenade for strings in E♭
major. *Amadeus Chamber Orch. Posen;
Polish Radio and Television Orch.,
Cracow; Duczmal, cond.*
+ Fa 5-6/91: 298

24035. PNCD 070: BEETHOVEN—String
quartets no. 12, 13. *Wilanów Quartet.*
+ Fa 5-6/91: 124

24036. PNCD 071: BEETHOVEN—String
quartets no. 14, 16. *Wilanów Quartet.*
+ Fa 5-6/91: 124

24037. PNCD 072: BEETHOVEN—String
quartet no. 15; Grosse Fuge, op. 133.
Wilanów Quartet.
+ Fa 5-6/91: 124

24038. PNCD 073: PADEREWSKI—Piano
music. TANSMAN—Piano music.
Kobayashi, Malicki, pianos.
• ARG 5-6/91: 92
+ Fa 3-4/91: 316

24039. PNCD 074: MLYNARSKI—Violin
concerto no. 2; Symphony in F, Polonia.
*Kulka, violin; Warsaw Phil. Orch.; Kord,
cond.*
□ ARG 9-10/92: 132

24040. PNCD 075: PTASZYŃSKA—
Marimba concerto; Songs of despair and
loneliness; Winter's tale. *Abe, marimba;
Cracow Radio Symphony Orch.;
Kawalla, cond.; Podles, mezzo-soprano;
Marchwinski, piano; Polish Chamber
Orch.; Maksymiuk, cond.*
+ ARG 11-12/92: 181

24041. PNCD 078: ELSNER—Passio
Domini nostri Jesu Christi in D minor,
op. 65. *Harasimowicz, Szmyt, Gałka,
Sliwa, Nowacki; Children's Choir of the
E. Mlynarski State School of Music;
Choir and Phil. Orch. of Warsaw; Kord,
cond. Excerpts.*
+ ARG 3-4/92: 54
+ Fa 1-2/92: 208

24042. PNCD 105: PADEREWSKI—Piano
concerto; Polish fantasy. *Radziwonowicz,
piano; Polish Radio Orch.; Wit, cond.*
+ ARG 1-2/92: 87
+ Gr 2/92: 38

24043. PNCD 110: MOZART—Arias from
Mitridate, Apollo et Hyacinthus, Ascanio
in Alba; Ombra felice, K. 255.
*Stefanowicz, counter-tenor; Sinfonia
Varsovia; Teutsch, cond.*
+ ARG 11-12/91: 99

MY RECORD

24044. COL-003: CAGE—Three dances.
WOLFF—Malvina. KAKO—Concerto for

koto and orchestra. *Sawai, Nishi, Kuribayashi, Gunji, kotos; New Japan Phil.; Inoue, cond.*
+ Fa 9-10/95: 163

MYTO

24045. MCD 890.01: SCHUBERT— Fierrabras (abridged). *Kahmann, Plümacher, Wunderlich; with assisting soloists; Radio Bern Choruses; City of Bern Orch.; Müller-Kray, cond.* Recorded live 1959.
• Fa 7-8/90: 248 m.f.

24046. 3MCD 890.02 (3 discs): WAGNER—Lohengrin. *Rysanek, Varnay, Engen, Wächter; Bayreuth Festival; Cluytens, cond.* Recorded live 1958.
• Fa 7-8/90: 311

24047. 2MCD 890.03 (2 discs): VERDI— Traviata; Traviata: Ah fors' e lui; Ballo in maschera: Ma dall'arido stelo. *Callas, Raimondi, Bastianini; with assisting soloists; Teatro alla Scala; Giulini, cond.; various orchs. and conds.* Recorded live 1956, 1955, 1957.
• Fa 5-6/90: 322

24048. MCD 890.05: BEETHOVEN—Piano concerto no. 2. BRAHMS—Piano concerto no. 1. *Solomon, piano; Berlin Phil. Orch.; Cluytens, Jochum, cond.* Recorded live 1956, 1954.
+ Fa 7-8/90: 84

24049. 2MCD 890.06 (2 discs): BELLINI—La sonnambula. *Callas, Valletti, Modesti; with assisting soloists; Teatro alla Scala; Bernstein, cond.* Recorded live 1955.
+ ARG 9-10/91: 45
+ Fa 9-10/90: 182

24050. 2MCD 890.07 (2 discs): MOZART—Die Zauberflöte. *Streich, Schwarzkopf, Gedda, Taddei, Petri; with assisting soloists; Italian Radio and Television Rome Chorus & Symphony Orch.; Karajan, cond.* Sung in Italian. Recorded live 1953.
+ ARG 9-10/90: 93
+ Fa 9-10/90: 306

24051. MCD 890.08: MAHLER—Songs. *Fischer-Dieskau, baritone; Bernstein, piano.* Recorded live 1968.
+ Fa 9-10/90: 284

24052. MCD 890.09: BRAHMS— Symphony no. 1. MOZART—Symphony no. 40. VIVALDI—Concerto grosso in D minor, op. 3, no. 11. *NBC Symphony Orch.; Toscanini, cond.* Recorded live 1937.
- ARG 9-10/90: 38 (Mozart)
+ ARG 9-10/90: 38 (others)
+ Fa 9-10/90: 197

24053. 2MCD 890.10 (2 discs): VERDI— Battaglia di Legnano; Battaglia di Legnano: Excerpts. *Stella, Corelli,*

Bastianini, Di Stefano, Gencer; with assisting soloists; Teatro alla Scala; Gavazzeni, cond.; Teatro Verdi, Trieste; Molinari-Pradelli, cond.* Recorded live 1961, 1963.
- Fa 9-10/90: 416

24054. MCD 890.11: Lieder of Schumann, Schubert, and Beethoven. *Wunderlich, tenor; Giesen, piano.* Recorded live 1966, 1965.
+ ARG 11-12/90: 82
+ Fa 9-10/90: 461

24055. 2MCD 902.14 (2 discs): DONIZETTI—Linda di Chamounix; La favorite: Aria. PUCCINI—Bohème: Aria. VERDI—Traviata: Aria. *Carosio, Corsi, Raimondi, Taddei; with assisting soloists; Italian Radio and Television Milan Chorus & Symphony Orch.; Simonetto, cond.; unnamed orch. & cond.* Linda recorded live 1953.
• Fa 9-10/90: 229

24056. 3MCD 903.18 (3 discs): MEYERBEER—Le prophète. *Horne, Rinaldi, Gedda, El Hage; with assisting soloists; Italian Radio and Television Turin Chorus & Symphony Orch.; Lewis, cond.*
+ ARG 11-12/90: 82
+ Fa 11-12/90: 281

24057. 2MCD 903.19 (2 discs): DONIZETTI—Lucia di Lammermoor; Lucia di Lammermoor: Excerpts. *Callas, Raimondi, Panerai, Zerbini; with assisting soloists; Teatro San Carlo, Naples Chorus & Orch.; Molinari-Pradelli, cond.* Recorded live 1956.
+ Fa 11-12/90: 216

24058. MCD 904.22 (2 discs): JANÁČEK—Jenůfa (complete); Jenůfa: Excerpts. *Hillebrecht, Varnay, Cochran, Cox, Cassilly, Lanigan; with assisting soloists; Bavarian State Opera; Royal Opera House Covent Garden; Kubelik, cond.* Recorded live 1970.
+ Fa 3-4/91: 246

24059. MCD 904.23 (2 discs): DONIZETTI—Lucrezia Borgia; Lucrezia Borgia: Excerpts. *Caballé, Ruta, Raimondi, Flagello, Gencer; with assisting soloists; Teatro alla Scala; Gracis, cond.* Recorded live 1970.
- Fa 3-4/91: 201

24060. MCD 905.24 (2 discs): VERDI—I vespri siciliani (complete); I vespri siciliani: Excerpts. *Scotto, G. Raimondi, Cappuccilli, R. Raimondi, Gencer, Casellato-Lamberti; with assisting soloists; Teatro alla Scala; Gavazzeni, cond.* Recorded live 1970.
• ARG 9-10/91: 143
- Fa 7-8/91: 319

24061. MCD 905.25 (2 discs): VERDI— Requiem; Te Deum. PERGOLESI—Stabat Mater. *Scotto, Horne, Pavarotti,*

Ghiaurov, Janowitz, Forrester; Italian Radio and Television Rome Chorus & Symphony Orch.; Berlin Phil. Orch.; Abbado, Claudio.* Recorded live 1970, 1968.
• Fa 7-8/91: 316

24062. MCD 905.26: MASSENET—Manon: excerpts. *Di Stefano, tenor; with assisting artists.* Sung in Italian or French; from live performances, 1947, 1951.
+ Fa 9-10/91: 268

24063. 2MCD 905.27 (2 discs): TCHAIKOVSKY—Mazeppa. *Bakocevic, Cakarević, Krnetić, Mitić, Čangalović; National Opera, Belgrade; Danon, cond.* Sung in Serbo-Croatian.
• ARG 9-10/91: 133
+ Fa 5-6/91: 297

24064. 2MCD 905.28 (2 discs): MERCADANTE—Reggente. *Chiara, Zilio, Merighi, Montefusco; with assisting soloists; Maggio Musicale Fiorentino Chorus; Angelicum Orch. of Milan; Martinotti, cond.*
• ARG 3-4/91: 91
• Fa 3-4/91: 277

24065. MCD 905.29 (2 discs): HAYDN— Orfeo ed Euridice. BELLINI—Sonnambula: Excerpts. HANDEL—Alcina: 2 arias. *Sutherland, Gedda, Malas, Lazzari, Rouleau; with assisting soloists; Scottish Opera Chorus; Scottish National Orch.; Royal Opera House Covent Garden; Capella Coloniensis; Bonynge, Serafin, Leitner, cond.* Recorded live 1967, 1960, 1959.
• ARG 5-6/91: 64
+ Fa 7-8/91: 171

24066. 2MCD 905.30 (2 discs): ROSSINI—Elisabetta, regina d'Inghilterra (complete); Elisabetta, regina d'Inghilterra (excerpts). *Gencer, Geszty, Grilli, Bottazzo; with assisting soloists; Teatro Massimo di Palermo; Italian Radio and Television Milan Chorus & Symphony Orch.; Sanzogno, Simonetto, cond.* Recorded live 1970, 1953.
• ARG 3-4/91: 108
□ Fa 3-4/91: 341

24067. 2MCD 906.32 (2 discs): MERCADANTE—Giuramento; Giuramento: Excerpts. *Wells, Wolff, Molese, Panerai, Berdini, Pellegrino; with assisting soloists; Juilliard American Opera Center Chorus; Juilliard Orch.; Italian Radio and Television Milan Symphony Orch.; Schippers, Simonetto, cond.* Recorded live 1970, 1951.
• ARG 9-10/91: 99
- Fa 7-8/91: 214 (complete)
+ Fa 7-8/91: 214 (excerpts)

24068. MCD 911.36 (2 discs): CHERUBINI—Medea. PUCCINI—Tosca. Excerpts. *Olivero, Baggiore, Misciano, Oncina; with assisting soloists; Teatro sociale, Mantua; Italian Radio and*

*Television Turin Symphony Orch.;
Zagreb Opera Orch.; Rescigno, Vernizzi,
cond.* Recorded live 1971, 1960, 1964 .
- ARG 9-10/91: 60
+ Fa 7-8/91: 138 (Olivero)
- Fa 7-8/91: 138 (others)

24069. MCD 911.37 (2 discs):
DONIZETTI—Maria Stuarda (complete);
Maria Stuarda: Excerpts. *Caballé,
Verrett, Garaventa, Arié, Gencer,
Tagliavini; with assisting soloists; Teatro
alla Scala; Maggio Musicale Fiorentino;
Cillario, Molinari-Pradelli, cond.*
- ARG 9-10/91: 68
- Fa 7-8/91: 152 (complete)
+ Fa 7-8/91: 152 (excerpts)

24070. MCD 914.43: WAGNER—Walküre:
Act III. *Flagstad, Müller, Brockelmann;
Royal Opera Covent Garden;
Furtwängler, cond.* Recorded live 1937.
+ Fa 5-6/92: 281

24071. 2MCD 915.44 (2 discs): GLUCK—
Iphigenie auf Tauris. SCHUMANN—
Dichterliebe. SCHUBERT—Lieder. *Jurinac,
Wunderlich, Prey, Engen; Bavarian
Radio Orch.; Kubelik, cond.*
+ Fa 1-2/92: 220

24072. 2MCD 916.48 (2 discs): VERDI—
Requiem; La traviata (excerpts).
SCHUBERT—Lieder. *Wunderlich, tenor;
with supporting soloists & orchestra;
Giesen, piano.* Recorded live 1960, 1965.
+ Fa 5-6/92: 274

24073. 2MCD 921.54 (2 discs):
STRAUSS—Arabella. *Ursuleac, Eipperle,
Taubmann, Hermann; Vienna State
Opera; Krauss, cond.* Recorded live
1942.
+ Fa 7-8/92: 291
+ ON 1/30/93: 36

24074. MCD 921.55: *Ivan Kozlovsky
operatic recital.* Arias by Rossini, Verdi,
Puccini, Leoncavallo, Moniuszko and
Wagner. *Kozlovsky, tenor; with
orchestral accompaniment.* Sung in
Russian.
+ ARG 9-10/92: 227
+ Fa 7-8/92: 331

24075. MCD 922.59 (3 discs):
PFITZNER—Palestrina; Palestrina: 2
excerpts. *Wunderlich, Jurinac, Ludwig,
Berry, Weiner, Frick; Chorus & Orch. of
the Vienna State Opera; Heger, cond.;
Lorenz, Schöffler; Vienna Phil. Orch.;
Kempe, cond.* Recorded live.
- Fa 9-10/92: 314

24076. MCD 923.62 (2 discs):
MASSENET—Manon (sung in German).
*Jurinac, Dermota; Neidlinger; North
German Radio Chorus & Orch.;
Schüchter, cond.; Freni, Pavarotti;
Teatro alla Scala; Maag, cond.* Recorded
live 1950, 1969.
+ Fa 11-12/92: 296

24077. MCD 924.64: *Franco Corelli a
Parma.* Excerpts from Norma, Tosca, and
Il trovatore. *Corelli, tenor; with assisting
vocalists and instrumentalists.* Recorded
1961-71.
+ ARG 3-4/93: 184
- Fa 3-4/93: 338

24078. MCD 924.65 (2 discs):
SMETANA—Dalibor (sung in German).
*Spiess, Rysanek, Wächter, Czerwenka;
Vienna Opera; Krips, cond.* Recorded
1969.
- ARG 1-2/93: 151
+ Fa 3-4/93: 298

24079. MCD 924.67: *Giuseppe Di
Stefano a Chicago.* Music of Massenet,
Gounod, Flotow, Puccini, Verdi,
Ponchielli, and Donizetti. *Di Stefano,
tenor; with orch. acc.* Recorded live
1947-1950.
+ ARG 5-6/93: 182
+ Fa 3-4/93: 339

24080. MCD 925.68: *Ivan Kozlovsky
recital number 2.* Music of Gluck,
Offenbach, Delibes, Massenet, and
Planquette. *Kozlovsky, tenor; with orch.
acc.* Sung in Russian.
+ Fa 3-4/93: 339

24081. MCD 925.69 (4 discs):
WAGNER—Die Meistersinger. *Stewart,
Janowitz, Kónya, Crass, Hemsley;
Bavarian Radio Symphony Orch.;
Kubelik, cond.* Recorded live 1967.
+ ARG 5-6/93: 150
+ Fa 3-4/93: 320
+ ON 10/93: 32
+ St 2/93: 199

24082. MCD 925.71 (2 discs): HANDEL—
Messiah; Xerxes (excerpts); Alcina
(excerpts). *Vocal soloists; Stuttgart Phil.
Choir; South German Radio Orch.;
Bavarian Radio Orch.; Cappella
Coloniensis; Mende, Kubelik, Leitner,
conds.* Recorded live 1959 & 1962.
+ ARG 3-4/93: 85
- Fa 3-4/93: 178

24083. MCD 931.72 (2 discs): VERDI—I
due Foscari; Giovanna d'Arco: excerpts.
*Ricciarelli, Scano, Cappuccilli; Coro del
Centro Lirico di Padova; Orch. Sinfonica
di Bari; Zedda, cond.; Ricciarelli, Labò,
Zanasi; Teatro La Fenice; Franci, cond.*
- ARG 9-10/93: 212
+ Fa 7-8/93: 261

24084. MCD 931.75 (2 discs):
WAGNER—Flying Dutchman. *Varnay,
Mill, London, Traxel; Bayreuth Festival;
Keilberth, cond.* Recorded 1956.
+ ARG 9-10/93: 263
- Fa 7-8/93: 267
+ ON 4/2/94: 33

24085. MCD 932.77 (3 discs):
WAGNER—Tannhäuser. *Angeles, Bumbry,
Windgassen; other soloists; Bayreuth
Festival; Sawallisch, cond.*

- Fa 9-10/93: 327
- ON 1/8/94: 34

24086. MCD 932.78: *Fritz Wunderlich in
concert.* Music of Beethoven, Schubert,
and Schumann. *Wunderlich, tenor;
Giesen, piano.* Recorded live 1966.
+ Fa 11-12/93: 461

24087. 2MCD 932.79 (2 discs): VERDI—I
vespri siciliani; La forza del destino: two
arias. *Rosvænge, Schlusnus, Cunitz,
Rohr; Frankfurt Opera; Schröder, cond.*
Recorded 1951; sung in German.
+ ARG 11-12/93: 274
+ Fa 9-10/93: 317

24088. MCD 932.87 (2 discs): BIZET—
Carmen. *Cossotto, Ferraro, Chiara,
Bruson; La Fenice Chorus & Orch.;
Maag, cond.* Sung in Italian; recorded
live 1971.
+ Fa 1-2/94: 132

24089. MCD 933.81 (3 discs):
WAGNER—Die Walküre. *Suthaus, Müller,
Buchner, Herrmann, Klose, Greindl;
Orch. of the Städtische Oper, Berlin;
Fricsay, cond.* Recorded 1951.
- Fa 11-12/93: 444
- Gr 3/94: 120
- ON 4/2/94: 33

24090. MCD 933.82: *Ferruccio
Tagliavini recital, 1941-1950.* Music of
Rossini, Bellini, Donizetti, Flotow, Verdi,
Meyerbeer, Massenet, Mascagni,
Giordano, Puccini, Cilea, and Wolf-
Ferrari. *Tagliavini, tenor; orch. acc.*
+ Fa 11-12/93: 462

24091. MCD 933.83 (2 discs): PUCCINI—
La fanciulla del West. *Olivero, Barioni,
Guelfi, Chorus & Orch. of La Fenice,
Venice; De Fabritiis, cond.* Recorded
1967.
+ ARG 11-12/93: 171
- Fa 11-12/93: 350

24092. MCD 934.85 (3 discs):
WAGNER—Lohengrin. *Anders, Eipperle,
Kronenberg, Braun, Greindl, Ambrosius;
Chorus & Orch. of Cologne Radio;
Kraus, cond.*
- Fa 1-2/94: 346
- ON 4/2/94: 32

24093. MCD 934.86: *Jussi Björling
recital, 1941-1951.* Music of Donizetti,
Verdi, Gounod, Bizet, Massenet,
Meyerbeer, Ponchielli, Giordano,
Mascagni, Leoncavallo, Cilea, and
Puccini. *Björling, tenor; orch. acc.;
Grevillius, Cellini, conds.*
+ Fa 1-2/94: 374

24094. MCD 934.88: *Max Lorenz recital,
1933-1957.* Music of Wagner, Verdi,
Halévy, Leoncavallo, and Berlin. *Lorenz,
tenor; orch. acc.*
- Fa 1-2/94: 369
+ ON 4/2/94: 33

24095. MCD 935.89 (2 discs): VERDI—
Attila. LEONCAVALLO—Pagliacci: Excerpts.
Christoff, Guelfi, Roberti, Limarelli;
Teatro Comunale Florence; Bartoletti,
cond.; Michieli, Sereni, Limarilli; Teatro
La Fenice; Bogo, cond. Recorded 1962,
1958.
- ARG 5-6/94: 162
+ Fa 3-4/94: 351
- ON 2/18/95: 36

24096. MCD 935.91: Music of Mozart,
Rossini, Bellini, Verdi, Donizetti,
Meyerbeer, and others. *Siepi, baritone;*
with accomp.
+ ARG 5-6/94: 218

24097. MCD 941.96: GOUNOD—Faust
(sung in German). *Rosvænge,*
Singenstreu, Rohnen, Ahlersmeyer,
Melchert, Arndt-Ober; Chorus & Orch.
of Radio Berlin; Steiner, cond.
+ Fa 7-8/94: 141

24098. 3MCD 941.97 (3 discs): VERDI—
Don Carlo. *Grouwenstijn, Barbieri,*
Vickers, Gobbi; Royal Opera Covent
Garden; Giulini, cond. Recorded 1958.
+ ARG 7-8/94: 184
+ Fa 7-8/94: 267

24099. MCD 942.99 (2 discs):
DONIZETTI—Lucia di Lammermoor; Opera
arias by others (Muro Lomanto, tenor).
Caspir, Muro Lomanto, Molinari,
Baccaloni; Professori d' Orch. e l' interno
Corpo Corale del Teatro alla Scala di
Milano; Molajoli, cond. Recorded 1933
(or 1928/29).
- Fa 9-10/94: 181

24100. MCD 941.101: Arias by Gounod,
Borodin, Rubinstein, Massenet, Verdi,
Wagner, and others. *London, bass.*
Recorded 1952-55.
+ ARG 9-10/94: 275
+ Fa 9-10/94: 396

24101. MCD 943.103 (2 discs):
LORTZING—Zar und Zimmermann. *Hann,*
Streinz, Buchta, Gripekoven; Stuttgart
Radio Orch. & Chorus; Zimmermann,
cond. Recorded live 1936.
+ Fa 11-12/94: 282

24102. MCD 943.104: STRAUSS—
Capriccio (excerpts); Songs. *Ursuleac,*
Klarwein, Hotter, Kronenberg, Hann;
Bavarian State Opera Orch.; Krauss,
cond. & piano.
+ Fa 11-12/94: 388
+ ON 3/4/95: 40

24103. MCD 943.105; *Renata Tebaldi*
alla Scala: recital 20.5.1974. Music of A.
Scarlatti, Paradisi, Gluck, Pergolesi,
Rossini, Bellini, Verdi, Donizetti,
Beethoven, Puccini, Zandonai, Buzzi-
Peccia, Mascagni, Massenet, Schubert,
and De Curtis. *Tebaldi, soprano; Katz,*
piano.
+ Fa 1-2/95: 320

24104. MCD 944.108: *Franco Corelli a*
Parma II. Excerpts from La forza del
destino, Norma, Il trovatore, and Tosca.
Corelli, tenor; Orch. of the Teatro Regio,
Parma. Recorded live 1967-1971.
- Fa 3-4/95: 354

24105. MCD 944.109 (4 discs):
WAGNER—Die Meistersinger von
Nürnberg. *Hotter, Kupper, Treptow,*
Kusche, Kuen, Michaelis; Bavarian State
Opera Orch.; Jochum, cond. Recorded
1949.
+ Fa 3-4/95: 333
+ ON 6/95: 44

24106. MCD 945.111 (2 discs): VERDI—
Rigoletto; Opera arias by Verdi,
Meyerbeer, Thomas, and Offenbach.
Metternich, Shock, Streich, Hoppe,
Klose; Berlin Radio Orch.; Fricsay,
cond. Recorded 1950.
+ Fa 3-4/95: 328

24107. MCD 945.114 (2 discs):
GIORDANO—Andrea Chénier. Operatic
arias and scenes (Music of Boito, Puccini,
and Verdi). *Marini, Rasa, Galeffi; Teatro*
alla Scala; Molajoli, cond. Recorded
1930.
- ARG 11-12/95: 285
- Fa 3-4/95: 172
+ ON 5/95: 47

24108. MCD 945.118 (2 discs): BIZET—
Carmen. *G. Besanzoni, Pauli, Carbone,*
E. Besanzoni; Teatro alla Scala; Sabajno,
cond. Recorded 1931.
- Fa 5-6/95: 141

24109. MCD 946.117 (2 discs):
STRAUSS—Elektra. WAGNER—Die Walküre
(excerpts); Siegfried (excerpts); Tristan
und Isolde (excerpts). *Schlüter, Höngen,*
Welitsch, Schöffler, Widdop; BBC
Chorus; Royal Phil. Orch.; Beecham,
cond. Recorded 1947.
+ Fa 5-6/95: 355

24110. MCD 951.122: *Leyla Gencer: vol.*
1. Music of Puccini, Tchaikovsky, Verdi,
Catalani, Mozart, Donizetti, Poulenc, and
Rocca. *Gencer, soprano; various orchs.*
and conds. Recorded 1955.
+ Fa 7-8/95: 377

24111. MCD 951.123 (2 discs): VERDI—
Un ballo in maschera; I Lombardi
(excerpts). *Caballé, Carreras, Bruson,*
Baldani, Davia, Foiani; Teatro alla
Scala; Molinari-Pradelli, cond.;
Carreras; Scotto; Teatro Regio, Parma;
Cillario, cond. Recorded live 1975 and
1973.
+ ARG 7-8/95: 215
- Fa 7-8/95: 356
- ON 2/3/96: 36

24112. MCD 954.136 (4 discs):
WAGNER—Parsifal; Die Walküre: Act 1.
Schöffler, Braun, Weber, Treptow, A.
Konetzni, H. Konetzni; Vienna Symphony

Orch.; Moralt, cond. Recorded 1948.
+ Fa 5-6/96: 310

24113. MCD 961.140 (2 discs): VERDI—
Attila. *Ghiaurov, Malaspina, Luchetti,*
Cappuccilli; Teatro La Scala; Patanè
cond. Recorded 1975.
+ ARG 1-2/97: 186

24114. MCD 961.141 (2 discs):
MEYERBEER—Les Huguenots. *Gedda,*
Shane, Tarres, Scovotti; Díaz; Radio
Austriaca; Märzendorfer, cond. Recorded
1971.
+ ARG 1-2/97: 140
+ ON 11/96: 46

24115. MCD 961.142 (2 discs):
JANÁČEK—Jenůfa (sung in Italian).
Bumbry, Olivero, Merolla, Cioni; Teatro
La Scala; Semkow, cond. Recorded 1974.
+ ARG 1-2/97: 124

NAIM AUDIO

24116. CD 003: *Concertos under the*
Dome. Music of Boccherini, Bartók,
Brahms, and Mendelssohn. *Various*
performers.
- Fa 3-4/94: 422

24117. CD 008: DVOŘÁK—String quartet
no. 9. MESSIAEN—Quatuor pour la fin du
temps. *Yeh, clarinet; Beaver, violin;*
Swan, piano; Vermeer Quartet.
- Gr 4/95: 78

NATIONAL TRUST

24118. NTC 001: *Anthea Gifford at*
Coughton Court. Music of C.P.E. Bach,
Buxtehude, Villa-Lobos, Berkeley,
Crosse, and others. *Gifford, guitar.*
+ Gr 12/92: 106

24119. NTC 006: *Voice and harp recital.*
Music of R. Johnson II, Arne, Croft,
Purcell, Parisotti, Gluck, Durante,
Schubert, Meyer, Watkins, Chausson,
Cannon, and Anon. *Rothschild, soprano;*
Watkins, harp.
+ Gr 5/96: 112

NAXOS

24120. 8.550026: MOZART—Serenades:
no. 13 "Eine kleine Nachtmusik," no. 6
"Serenata notturna"; Divertimento no. 10.
Cappella Istropolitana; Sobotka, cond.
+ ARG 1-2/92: 83
- Fa 7-8/88: 209
+ Fa 1-2/92: 282

24121. 8.550030: TCHAIKOVSKY—Romeo
and Juliet overture; Capriccio italien;
1812 overture. *Slovak Phil. Orch.;*
Gunzenhauser, cond.
- Fa 3-4/88: 217

24122. 8.550031: TCHAIKOVSKY—Piano
concerto no. 1; Marche slave. *Toperczer,*
piano; Slovak Phil. Orch.; Režucha,

Gunzenhauser, conds.
- Fa 9-10/88: 275

24123. 8.550040: BRAHMS—Hungarian dances no. 1-21. *Sinfonia Hungarica; Varga, cond.*
+ Fa 1-2/88: 96

24124. 8.550042: MOZART—Symphonies no. 35-36. *Budapest Symphony Orch.; Pál, cond.*
+ ARG 3-4/88: 64
- Fa 1-2/88: 183

24125. 8.550045: BEETHOVEN—Piano sonatas no. 8, 14, 23. *Jandó, piano.*
- Fa 1-2/88: 87

24126. 8.550046: TCHAIKOVSKY—Symphony no. 5. *Slovak Phil. Orch.; Gunzenhauser, cond.*
- Fa 3-4/88: 217

24127. 8.550047/48 (2 discs): BACH—Brandenburg concertos. *Cappella Istropolitana; Warchal, cond.* Available separately.
- Fa 5-6/88: 66
- HPR 7/88: 75 (v.1)

24128. 8.550051: MUSSORGSKY—Pictures at an exhibition; A night on the Bare Mountain. BORODIN—In central Asia; Polovtsian dances. *Slovak Phil. Orch.; Nazareth, cond.*
+ ARG 1-2/92: 81
- Fa 5-6/88: 178
- Fa 1-2/92: 286
+ Gr 7/91: 56

24129. 8.550052: *Romantic piano favourites.* Music of Mozart, Schubert, Weber, Grieg, Dvořák, and others. *Szokolay, piano.*
+ ARG 5-6/88: 82
- Fa 5-6/88: 254

24130. 8.550054: BEETHOVEN—Piano sonatas no. 17, 21, 26. *Jandó, piano.*
+ ARG 7-8/92: 93
- Fa 5-6/88: 81
+ Fa 3-4/92: 151

24131. 8.550055: MENDELSSOHN—Symphony no. 4; Midsummer night's dream: incidental music. *Slovak Phil. Orch.; Bramall, cond.*
+ ARG 5-6/88: 18
- Fa 5-6/88: 165

24132. 8.550056: VIVALDI—The four seasons; Concerto alla rustica. *Nishizaki, violin; Cappella Istropolitana; Gunzenhauser, cond.*
+ ARG 1-2/92: 135
- Fa 5-6/88: 233

24133. 8.550057: SCHUBERT—Piano quintet "Trout"; Piano trio, D. 897 "Notturno". *Ensemble Villa Musica; Hokanson, piano.*
- ARG 3-4/92: 135
+ Fa 3-4/92: 313

24134. 8.550059: HAYDN—Cello concertos no. 1-2. BOCCHERINI—Cello concerto in B♭. *Kanta, cello; Cappella Istropolitana; Breiner, cond.*
- ARG 5-6/92: 71
- Fa 5-6/92: 169

24135. 8.550060: MOZART—Serenade for 13 winds no. 10, K. 361. *Amadeus Wind Ensemble.*
+ Fa 1-2/88: 178

24136. 8.550061: BIZET—L'arlésienne suites 1-2; Carmen suites 1-2. *Slovak Phil. Orch.; Bramall, cond.*
+ ARG 5-6/88: 18
+ Fa 5-6/88: 86

24137. 8.550063: MOZART—Violin concertos no. 3, 5 . *Nishizaki, violin; Cappella Istropolitana; Gunzenhauser, cond.*
- Fa 7-8/88: 205

24138. 8.550065: MOZART—Violin sonatas K. 296, 376, 378 . *Nishizaki, violin; Harden, piano.*
+ ARG 3-4/88: 64
- Fa 1-2/88: 182

24139. 8.550066: BACH—Italian concerto BWV 971; Chromatic fantasy and fugue BWV 903; Capriccio on the departure of a beloved brother BWV 992; Toccata in C minor BWV 911; Fantasia in C minor BWV 906; French suite no. 6 BWV 817. *Banowetz, Duphil, pianos.*
+ ARG 9-10/88: 15
- Fa 5-6/88: 70

24140. 8.550068: BACH—Preludes and fugues in E♭ BWV 552, in D BWV 582; Partita on O Gott du frommer Gott BWV 767; Kommest du nun, Jesu BWV 650; Passacaglia in C minor BWV 582; Toccata and fugue in D minor BWV 565. *Aratore, organ.*
- Fa 1-2/88: 79

24141. 8.550069: HANDEL—Organ concertos no. 13 in F; Op. 4 no. 2, 4-5; Op. 7 no. 1 . *Aratore, organ; Handel Festival Chamber Orch.; Tinge, cond.*
+ ARG 3-4/88: 44
+ Fa 1-2/88: 134

24142. 8.550070: CHOPIN—Etude in C minor op. 10 no. 12; Mazurkas op. 33 no. 2; Op. 24 no. 2; Op. 41 no. 1; Op. 50 no. 2-3; Grande polonaise brillante in E♭ op. 22; Polonaise-fantasie in A♭ op. 61. *Irinsky, piano.*
- Fa 3-4/88: 96

24143. 8.550071: CHOPIN—Piano sonatas no. 2-3; Barcarolle op. 60; Fantasie-Impromptu. op. 66; Berceuse op. 57. *Székely, piano.*
- Fa 7-8/88: 145

24144. 8.550072: BEETHOVEN—Overtures: Fidelio; Creatures of Prometheus; Coriolan; Ruins of Athens; Egmont;

Consecration of the house; Leonore no. 3. *Slovak Phil. Orch.; Gunzenhauser, cond.*
+ ARG 9-10/88: 21
- ARG 1-2/92: 26
- Fa 5-6/88: 80

24145. 8.550076: SCHUMANN—Kinderszenen; Papillons; Carnaval. *Jandó, piano.*
+ ARG 7-8/92: 221
- Fa 5-6/88: 209
- Fa 5-6/92: 250

24146. 8.550078: BACH—Goldberg variations. *Chen, piano.*
- ARG 5-6/88: 10
- Fa 5-6/88: 70
+ Fa 1-2/94: 115

24147. 8.550079: GLAZUNOV—The seasons. TCHAIKOVSKY—Sleeping beauty: excerpts. *CSR Symphony Orch., Bratislava; Lenárd, cond.*
+ Fa 1-2/92: 220

24148. 8.550082: CHOPIN—19 waltzes. *Székely, piano.*
- Fa 7-8/88: 144

24149. 8.550086: *Spanish festival.* Music of Chabrier, Massenet, Elgar, Rimsky-Korsakov, and Glinka. *CSR Symphony Orch.; Clark, cond.*
- ARG 1-2/92: 147
+ Fa 1-2/92: 436

24150. 8.550091: VERDI—Overtures, preludes, ballet music. *CSR Symphony Orch.; Lenárd, cond.*
- ARG 3-4/92: 156
- Fa 11-12/91: 513

24151. 8.550104: MOZART—String quintets no. 2, 4. *Eder Quartet; Fehérvári, viola.*
+ Fa 3-4/96: 234

24152. 8.550105: MOZART—String quartets no. 17, 19. *Moyzes String Quartet.*
+ Fa 9-10/93: 222

24153. 8.550109: HANDEL—Royal fireworks music; Water music. *Cappella Istropolitana; Warchal, cond.*
- Fa 11-12/91: 342

24154. 8.550114: HAYDN—Famous symphonies, vol. 2. No. 83 "Hen"; No. 94 "Surprise"; No. 101 "Clock". *Cappella Istropolitana; Wordsworth, cond.*
- ARG 3-4/92: 74
- Fa 3-4/92: 212 (Hurwitz)
- Fa 3-4/92: 212 (North)

24155. 8.550117: RACHMANINOFF—Piano concerto no. 2; Rhapsody on a theme of Paganini. *Jandó, piano; Budapest Symphony Orch.; Lehel, Németh, conds.* Reissue.
+ Fa 9-10/91: 316

24156. 8.550118: GRIEG—Piano concerto. SCHUMANN—Piano concerto. *Jandó, piano; Budapest Symphony Orch.; Ligeti, cond.*
    + ARG 1-2/92: 125
    + Fa 11-12/91: 455

24157. 8.550119: MOZART—Symphonies, no. 29-30, 38. *Cappella Istropolitana; Wordsworth, cond.*
    + Fa 5-6/92: 212

24158. 8.550122: BEETHOVEN—Piano concertos no. 3-4. *Vladar, piano; Cappella Istropolitana; Wordsworth, cond.*
    + ARG 7-8/92: 91
    • Fa 5-6/92: 122

24159. 8.550123: CHOPIN—Piano concertos no. 1-2. *Székely, piano; Budapest Symphony Orch.; Németh, cond.*
    - Fa 1-2/92: 194

24160. 8.550132: SCHUBERT—Piano trio no. 2; Notturno for piano trio, D. 897. *Stuttgart Piano Trio.*
    + Fa 5-6/92: 248

24161. 8.550140: GRIEG—Peer Gynt: Overture; Suite nos. 1-2; Wedding day at Troldhaugen; 2 lyric pieces, op. 68: No. 4, Evening in the mountain; No. 5, Cradle song; Norwegian bridal procession; Sigurd Jorsalfar: Suite. *CSR State Phil. Orch., Kosice; Gunzenhauser, cond.*
    + Fa 1-2/92: 223

24162. 8.550142: *Hungarian festival.* Music of Kodály, Liszt, Hubay, and Berlioz. *Hungarian State Orch.; Antal, cond.*
    + Fa 3-4/93: 396

24163. 8.550143: DVOŘÁK—Slavonic dances, op. 46 and 72. *Slovak Phil. Orch.; Košler, cond.*
    + ARG 11-12/91: 61
    • Fa 11-12/91: 316

24164. 8.550144: SCHUMANN—Symphonic etudes; Bunte Blätter no. 1-5; Arabesque. *Vladar, piano.*
    • ARG 7-8/92: 93
    + Fa 11/12/92: 365

24165. 8.550150: BEETHOVEN—Piano sonatas, op. 2. *Jandó, piano.*
    + ARG 7-8/92: 93
    + Fa 5-6/92: 123

24166. 8.550151: BEETHOVEN—Piano sonatas no. 30-32. *Jandó, piano.*
    - ARG 1-2/93: 75
    + Fa 1-2/93: 107

24167. 8.550155: FRANCK—Symphony; Prelude, choral and fugue (arr. Pierné). *Flanders Phil.; Neuhold, cond.*
    - ARG 1-2/93: 98

24168. 8.550156: TELEMANN—Viola concerto in G; Suite in A minor; Tafelmusik: Concerto in F for 3 violins; Concerto in E♭ for 2 horns. *Cappella Istropolitana; Edlinger, cond.*
    + ARG 11-12/91: 161
    • Fa 9-10/91: 377

24169. 8.550160: VIVALDI—Twelve concertos, op. 3 "Estro armonico". *Cappella Istropolitana; Kopelman, cond.*
    + ARG 5-6/92: 154
    • Fa 3-4/92: 358

24170. 8.550161: BEETHOVEN—Piano sonatas no. 5-7, 25. *Jandó, piano.*
    - ARG 1-2/93: 75

24171. 8.550162: BEETHOVEN—Piano sonatas no. 9-10, 24, 27-28. *Jandó, piano.*
    - ARG 1-2/93: 75

24172. 8.550166: BEETHOVEN—Piano sonatas no. 12, 16, 18. *Jandó, piano.*
    - ARG 1-2/93: 75
    + Fa 1-2/93: 107

24173. 8.550167: BEETHOVEN—Piano sonatas no. 4, 13, 19-20, 22. *Jandó, piano.*
    - ARG 1-2/93: 75

24174. 8.550173: RAVEL—Daphnis and Chloé: Suite no. 1; Ma mère l'oye; Valses nobles et sentimentales. *CSR Symphony Orch. (Bratislava); Jean, cond.*
    + ARG 1-2/92: 98
    + Fa 11-12/91: 456

24175. 8.550182: STRAUSS—Also sprach Zarathustra; Salome's dance; Rosenkavalier waltzes. *Slovak Phil. Orch.; Košler, cond.*
    + ARG 1-2/92: 120
    - Fa 11-12/91: 494

24176. 8.550184: BACH—Preludes and fugues, BWV 552, 532, 548; Toccata, BWV 532. *Rübsam, organ.*
    + Fa 5-6/92: 117

24177. 8.550185: MOZART—Overtures. *Cappella Istropolitana; Wordsworth, cond.*
    • ARG 7-8/93: 130
    + Fa 9-10/93: 222

24178. 8.550186: MOZART—Symphonies, no. 34-35, 39. *Cappella Istropolitana; Wordsworth, cond.*
    + ARG 1-2/93: 127

24179. 8.550191: TCHAIKOVSKY—Symphony no. 5; Marche slave. *Slovak Phil. Orch.; Gunzenhauser, cond.*
    + ARG 3-4/92: 152
    • Fa 3-4/92: 345

24180. 8.550193: HOLST—The planets; Suite de ballet, op. 10. *Czechoslovak Radio Symphony Orch.; Leaper, cond.*
    + ARG 1-2/92: 65
    + Fa 9-10/91: 240

24181. 8.550194: BACH—Violin concertos no. 1-2, BWV 1041-1042; Concerto for 2 violins, BWV 1043; Sonata for violin and continuo, BWV 1023 (orch. Respighi); Air on the G string (arr. Wilhelmj). *Nishizaki, Jablokov, violins; Cappella Istropolitana; Dohnányi, cond.*
    • Fa 1-2/92: 151

24182. 8.550196: ORFF—Carmina Burana. *Jenisova, Doležal, Kusnjer; CSR Symphony Orch. of Bratislava; Gunzenhauser, cond.*
    + Fa 1-2/92: 291

24183. 8.550197: SIBELIUS—Symphony no. 1, 6. *Slovak Phil. Orch.; Leaper, cond.*
    + ARG 1-2/93: 151

24184. 8.550198: SIBELIUS—Symphonies no. 2, 7. *Slovak Phil. Orch.; Leaper, cond.*
    • Gr 4/92: 79

24185. 8.550199: SIBELIUS—Symphonies no. 3-4. *Slovak Phil. Orch.; Leaper, cond.*
    + Gr 4/92: 79

24186. 8.550200: SIBELIUS—Symphony no. 5; En saga; Belshazzar's feast. *Slovak Phil. Orch.; Leaper, cond.*
    + Gr 4/92: 79

24187. 8.550201: MOZART—Piano concertos no. 13, 20. *Jandó, piano; Concentus Hungaricus; Ligeti, cond.*
    • Fa 3-4/92: 249

24188. 8.550203: MOZART—Piano concertos no. 9, 27. *Jandó, piano; Concentus Hungaricus; Ligeti, cond.*
    + ARG 5-6/92: 95
    + Fa 5-6/92: 201

24189. 8.550205: MOZART—Piano concertos no. 17-18. *Jandó, piano; Concentus Hungaricus; Mátyás, cond.*
    + ARG 5-6/92: 95
    + Fa 5-6/92: 202

24190. 8.550206: MOZART—Concertos for piano and orchestra no. 11, 22. *Jandó, piano; Concentus Hungaricus; Antal, cond.*
    + Fa 5-6/93: 270

24191. 8.550207: MOZART—Concertos for piano and orchestra no. 16, 25. *Jandó, piano; Concentus Hungaricus; Antal, cond.*
    + Fa 5-6/93: 270

24192. 8.550208: MOZART—Concertos for piano and orchestra no. 6, 8, 19. *Jandó, piano; Concentus Hungaricus; Antal, cond.*
    + Fa 5-6/93: 270

24193. 8.550209: MOZART—Concertos for piano and orchestra no. 5, 26 "Coronation". *Jandó, piano; Concentus*

NAXOS

Hungaricus; Antal, cond.
+ Fa 5-6/93: 270

24194. 8.550210: MOZART—Concertos for piano and orchestra no. 7, 10, 15. *Jandó, Várjon, pianos; Concentus Hungaricus; Antal, cond.*
+ Fa 5-6/93: 270

24195. 8.550212: MOZART—Concertos for piano and orchestra no. 1-4. *Jandó, piano; Concentus Hungaricus; Hegyi, cond.*
+ Fa 5-6/93: 270

24196. 8.550213: BRAHMS—Ein deutsches Requiem. *Gauci, Tumagian; Slovak Phil. Chorus; Bratislava Radio Symphony Orch.; Rahbari, cond.*
- Gr 5/94: 89

24197. 8.550220: RODRIGO—Concierto de Aranjuez. GRANADOS—Zapateado; Spanish dances, no. 2, 6, 8, 11. ALBÉNIZ—Zambra granadina; Asturias. FALLA—Aragonesa. *Garcia, guitar; Czecho-Slovak State Phil. Orch.; Breiner, cond.*
- Fa 11-12/91: 556

24198. 8.550226: *Brazilian portrait.* Works by Bonfa, Jobim, Savio, Pernambuco, Villa-Lobos, Almeida, Baden- Powell and Machado. *Garcia, guitar.*
+ Fa 3-4/92: 399

24199. 8.550230: *Battle music.* Music by Beethoven, Liszt; Ippolitov-Ivanov, Rimsky-Korsakov, Volkman, Tchaikovsky. *CSR Symphony Orch., Bratislava; Lenárd, cond.*
● ARG 11-12/91: 175
+ Fa 11-12/91: 571

24200. 8.550232: BEETHOVEN—Piano concertos no. 2, 5 "Emperor". *Vladar, piano; Cappella Istropolitana; Wordsworth, cond.*
- Fa 1-2/92: 158

24201. 8.550234: BEETHOVEN—Piano sonatas no. 11, 29. *Jandó, piano.*
- ARG 1-2/93: 75

24202. 8.550235: MOZART—Requiem. *Hajóssyová, Horská, Kundlak, Mikulaš, vocalists; Slovak Phil. Orch. & Chorus; Košler, cond.*
● ARG 7-8/92: 97
+ Fa 5-6/92: 208

24203. 8.550236: ROSSINI—Overtures. *Zagreb Festival Orch.; Halász, cond.*
● Fa 11-12/91: 461

24204. 8.550238: BORODIN—Symphonies no. 1-3. *Czecho-Slovak Radio Symphony Orch.; Gunzenhauser, cond.*
+ Fa 9-10/93: 131
● Gr 8/91: 53

24205. 8.550239: SCHUBERT—Moments musicaux; Pieces, D. 946. *Jandó, piano.*
+ ARG 1-2/94: 150

24206. 8.550241: VERDI—Choruses from Nabucco, La traviata, Don Carlo, La battaglia di Legnano, Il trovatore, Ernani, Otello, Macbeth, La forza del destino, and Aïda. *Slovak Phil. Chorus; Slovak Radio Symphony Orch., Bratislava, Dohnányi, cond.*
+ ARG 7-8/92: 242
+ Fa 3-4/92: 353

24207. 8.550244/45 (2 discs): BACH—Orchestral suites; arrangements by Stokowski, J. Dvořák and Bantock. *Cappella Istropolitana; J. Dvořák, cond.*
+ ARG 1-2/93: 71

24208. 8.550246/47 (2 discs): TCHAIKOVSKY—Swan lake. *Czecho-Slovak Radio Symphony Orch.; Lenárd, cond.*
+ Gr 12/91: 80

24209. 8.550250: STRAUSS—Don Juan; Death and transfiguration; Till Eulenspiegel. *Slovak Phil. Orch.; Košler, cond.*
● Fa 1-2/92: 340

24210. 8.550253: DEBUSSY—Suite bergamasque; La plus que lente; Images; Arabesques; Selected preludes. *Körmendi, piano.*
+ ARG 9-10/93: 112

24211. 8.550254: RAVEL—Sonatine; Le tombeau de Couperin; Menuet antique; Gaspard de la nuit. *Körmendi, piano.*
● Fa 5-6/92: 230

24212. 8.550255: BEETHOVEN—*Piano sonatas, vol. 10.* Sonatas no. 15; WoO 47, no. 1-3; WoO 51; Sonatinas Anh. 5, no. 1-2 . *Jandó, piano.*
+ Fa 5-6/93: 156

24213. 8.550257: CHOPIN—Nocturnes. *Falvai, piano.*
+ ARG 7-8/93: 76

24214. 8.550260: SCHUBERT—Impromptus (Complete). *Jandó, piano.*
+ Fa 5-6/92: 242

24215. 8.550262: DEBUSSY—Prélude à l'après-midi d'un faune; Nocturnes; La mer. *BRT Phil. Orch.; Rahbari, cond.*
+ ARG 1-2/92: 48
- Fa 11-12/91: 309
● Fa 1-2/92: 199

24216. 8.550264: MOZART—Symphonies, no. 27, 33, 36. *Cappella Istropolitana; Wordsworth, cond.*
+ ARG 1-2/93: 127

24217. 8.550266—8.550267 (2 separate discs): DVOŘÁK—Symphonies no. 1-2; Legends. *Slovak Phil. Orch.; Gunzenhauser, cond.*

+ ARG 3-4/93: 75
+ Gr 6/92: 40

24218. 8.550268: DVOŘÁK—Symphonies no. 3, 6. *Slovak Phil. Orch.; Gunzenhauser, cond.*
+ ARG 5-6/92: 51
+ Fa 5-6/92: 152
+ Gr 11/91: 84

24219. 8.550269: DVOŘÁK—Symphonies no. 4, 8. *Slovak Phil. Orch.; Gunzenhauser, cond.*
+ Gr 11/91: 84

24220. 8.550270: DVOŘÁK—Symphonies no. 5, 7. *Slovak Phil. Orch.; Gunzenhauser, cond.*
+ ARG 1-2/92: 51
● Fa 1-2/92: 205
+ Gr 11/91: 84

24221. 8.550271: DVOŘÁK—Symphony no. 9; Symphonic variations, op. 78. *Slovak Phil. Orch.; Gunzenhauser, cond.*
+ Fa 3-4/92: 189
+ Gr 11/91: 84

24222. 8.550276: DEBUSSY—Violin sonata. SAINT-SAËNS—Violin sonata no. 1. RAVEL—Violin sonata. POULENC—Violin sonata. *Kang, violin; Devoyon, piano.*
● Fa 5-6/92: 326

24223. 8.550278: BRAHMS—Symphony no. 1; Haydn variations. *BRT Phil. Orch.; Rahbari, cond.*
+ Fa 9-10/91: 178

24224. 8.550279: BRAHMS—Symphony no. 2; Serenade no. 2. *BRT Phil. Orch.; Rahbari, cond.*
+ ARG 1-2/93: 82
● Gr 9/91: 60

24225. 8.550280: BRAHMS—Symphony no. 3; Serenade no. 1. *BRT Phil. Orch.; Rahbari, cond.*
+ ARG 1-2/93: 82
+ Gr 1/92: 52

24226. 8.550281: BRAHMS—Symphony no. 4; Tragic overture, op. 81; Academic Festival Overture, op. 80. *BRT Phil. Orch.; Rahbari, cond.*
- Fa 1-2/92: 186

24227. 8.550285: BEETHOVEN—Violin sonatas no. 4, 10; Variations on Mozart's Se vuol ballare. *Nishizaki, violin; Jandó, piano.*
+ Fa 9-10/94: 267

24228. 8.550286: BEETHOVEN—Sonatas for violin and piano no. 6-8. *Nishizaki, violin; Jandó, piano.*
● ARG 3-4/93: 57
+ Fa 3-4/93: 121

24229. 8.550295: GERSHWIN—Piano concerto in F; Rhapsody in blue; An American in Paris. *Selby, piano; CSR Symphony Orch., Bratislava; Slovak Phil.*

Orch.; Hayman, cond.
+ ARG 1-2/92: 55
+ Fa 1-2/92: 216

24230. 8.550296: Music of Paganini, Mendelssohn, and Schubert. *Garcia, guitar.*
• ARG 1-2/94: 130

24231. 8.550314—8.550315 (2 separate discs): HAYDN—String quartets, op. 76. *Kodály Quartet.*
+ ARG 11-12/92: 77 (v.1)
+ Fa 11-12/91: 343 (v.1)
+ Fa 1-2/92: 233 (v.2)

24232. 8.550324/25 (2 discs): TCHAIKOVSKY—The nutcracker. GLAZUNOV—Chopiniana. *Czecho-Slovak Radio Symphony Orch., Bratislava; Lenárd, cond.*
• Gr 9/91: 76

24233. 8.550326: SHOSTAKOVICH—Symphony no. 10. *BRT Phil. Orch.; Rahbari, cond.*
- ARG 5-6/92: 134
• Fa 11/12/92: 372

24234. 8.550327: ENESCO—Romanian rhapsodies no. 1, 2. DVOŘÁK—Slavonic rhapsody no. 3. LISZT—Hungarian rhapsody no. 2. RAVEL—Rapsodie espagnole. *Slovak Phil. Orch.; Jean, Košler, conds.; Hungarian State Orch.; Antal, cond.*
• ARG 5-6/92: 159
+ Fa 5-6/92: 345

24235. 8.550328: *Russian fireworks.* Music of Ippolitov-Ivanov, Liadov, Kabalevsky, Mussorgsky, Rubinstein, and Halvorsen. *Slovak Phil. Orch.; Hayman, Jean, Gunzenhauser, Halász, conds.*
• Fa 1-2/92: 429

24236. 8.550329: SIBELIUS—Violin concerto. SVENDSEN—Romance. SINDING—Légende. HALVORSEN—Danses norvégiennes; Air norvégien. *Kang, violin; Bratislava Radio Orch.; Leaper, cond.*
• ARG 7-8/92: 227

24237. 8.550330: *Romantic music for strings.* GRIEG—Two melodies, op. 53; Two Norwegian airs, op. 63; Two elegiac pieces, op. 34; Erotik. SIBELIUS—Romance, op. 42; Andante festivo; Canzonetta, op. 62a; Rakastava. *Cappella Istropolitana; Leaper, cond.*
+ Fa 5-6/92: 346

24238. 8.550331: *English string festival.* Music of Elgar, Parry, Dowland, and Bridge. *Cappella Istropolitana; Leaper, cond.*
+ ARG 9-10/94: 223
• Fa 9-10/94: 187

24239. 8.550333: MOZART—Serenade no. 7 "Haffner"; March in D, K. 249.

Nishizaki, violin; Cappella Istropolitana; Wildner, cond.
+ ARG 1-2/92: 83
• Fa 1-2/92: 281

24240. 8.550336: J. STRAUSS JR.—Famous waltzes, polkas, marches, and overtures, vol. 1. *Czecho-Slovak State Phil. Orch.; Sieghart, Lenárd, Walter, conds.; Polish State Phil. Orch.; O. Dohnányi, Wildner, conds.*
+ Fa 1-2/92: 337

24241. 8.550341: GERSHWIN—Preludes for piano; Songs: Fascinatin' rhythm; Somebody loves me; Lisa; The man I love; I've got rhythm; Strike up the band. COREA—Children's songs. *Bates, piano.*
+ Fa 9-10/91: 223

24242. 8.550343: Arias from Rigoletto, Aida, Carmen, Faust, Werther, Le Villi, Tosca, Turandot, Manon Lescaut, Madama Butterfly. LARA—Granada. DE CURTIS—Sorrento. DI CAPUA—O sole mio. *Dvorský, tenor; Bratislava Radio Orch.; Lenárd, cond. Recorded live.*
- ARG 1-2/92: 174
- Gr 5/92: 117

24243. 8.550345: MOZART—Bassoon concerto; Oboe concerto, K. 314; Clarinet concerto. *Turnovsky, bassoon; Gabriel, oboe; Ottensamer, clarinet; Vienna Mozart Academy; Wildner, cond.*
+ ARG 5-6/92: 93
+ Fa 5-6/92: 202

24244. 8.550346: HAYDN—The seven last words of Jesus Christ; String quartet, op. 103. *Kodály Quartet.*
+ Fa 1-2/92: 234

24245. 8.550347: RACHMANINOFF—Études-tableaux, op. 33, 39. *Biret, piano.*
+ ARG 3-4/93: 126
+ Fa 3-4/93: 253
+ St 7/93: 175

24246. 8.550348: RACHMANINOFF—Preludes, op. 23; Morceaux de fantaisie, op. 3. *Biret, piano.*
• ARG 9-10/94: 179
+ Fa 9-10/94: 304
• Gr 3/92: 87

24247. 8.550349: RACHMANINOFF—Piano sonata no. 2; Variations on a theme by Corelli; Moments musicaux. *Biret, piano.*
+ ARG 3-4/94: 139
+ Fa 1-2/94: 270

24248. 8.550350: BRAHMS—Variations on a theme by Schumann; Variations and fugue on a theme by Handel; Variations on a theme by Paganini. *Biret, piano.*
+ ARG 5-6/94: 79
+ Fa 1-2/94: 143

24249. 8.550351: BRAHMS—Piano sonatas no. 1-2. *Biret, piano.*
+ ARG 3-4/93: 63
+ Gr 5/92: 71

24250. 8.550352: BRAHMS—Piano sonata, no. 3; Ballades, op. 10. *Biret, piano.*
+ Gr 12/92: 101

24251. 8.550354: BRAHMS—Scherzo, op. 4; Intermezzi, op. 117; Pieces, op. 118-119. *Biret, piano.*
+ Gr 5/92: 71

24252. 8.550355: BRAHMS—Waltzes, op. 39; Hungarian dances no. 1-10. *Biret, piano.*
□ ARG 11-12/94: 84
+ Fa 1-2/95: 129
+ Gr 10/94: 155

24253. 8.550356—8.550357 (2 separate discs): CHOPIN—Nocturnes, vol. 1-2. *Biret, piano.*
• Gr 7/93: 65

24254. 8.550358: CHOPIN—Complete mazurkas, vol. 1. *Biret, piano.*
+ ARG 7-8/92: 117
• Fa 5-6/92: 140

24255. 8.550361: CHOPIN—Polonaises (posth.); Andante spianato and grand polonaise. *Biret, piano.*
+ ARG 3-4/94: 84

24256. 8.550364: CHOPIN—Etudes op. 10 and 25. *Biret, piano.*
+ ARG 7-8/92: 117
• Fa 5-6/92: 140

24257. 8.550367: CHOPIN—Rondos, mazurkas, variations. *Biret, Sauer, pianos.*
+ ARG 1-2/94: 91
+ Gr 5/93: 70

24258. 8.550368: CHOPIN—Piano concerto no. 1; Fantasy on Polish airs; Andante spianato and grande polonaise brillante. *Biret, piano; Czecho-Slovak State Phil. Orch., Kosice; Stankovsky, cond.*
+ Gr 4/92: 45

24259. 8.550369: CHOPIN—Piano concerto no. 2; La ci darem variations; Krakowiak. *Biret, piano; Kosice State Phil. Orch.; Stankovsky, cond.*
+ ARG 5-6/92: 45
+ Gr 4/92: 45

24260. 8.550370: *Majestic marches.* Music of Wagner, Saint-Saëns, Ippolitov-Ivanovv, Meyerbeer, Tchaikovsky, Hanssen, Rimsky-Korsakov, Suppé, Léhar, Newman, Halvorsen, Delibes, Prokofiev and Mendelssohn. *Slovak Phil. Orch.; Hayman, cond.*
- ARG 5-6/92: 159
- Fa 3-4/92: 432

24261. 8.550378: WEBER—Concertos, no. 1-2; Concertino in E♭; Grand duo concertant. *Ottensamer, clarinet; Czecho-Slovak State Phil. Orch., Kosice; Wildner, cond.*

NAXOS

- Fa 1-2/92: 373
• Gr 7/91: 73

24262. 8.550380: PROKOFIEV—Romeo and Juliet: Excerpts. *Czecho-Slovak State Phil. Orch.; Mogrelia, cond.*
+ Gr 9/91: 69

24263. 8.550381: PROKOFIEV—Orchestral suites from Lt. Kijé, Love for three oranges, Romeo and Juliet, and Cinderella. *Czecho-Slovak State Phil. Orch.; Mogrelia, cond.*
+ Gr 9/91: 69

24264. 8.550382: HAYDN—Symphonies no. 45, 48, 102. *Cappella Istropolitana; Wordsworth, cond.*
+ ARG 1-2/93: 102
+ Gr 9/91: 62

24265. 8.550383: MOZART—Arias. *Dickie, tenor; Cappella Istropolitana; Wildner, cond.*
• Fa 1-2/92: 270
• Gr 12/91: 133

24266. 8.550387: HAYDN—Symphonies no. 85, 92, 103. *Cappella Istropolitana; Wordsworth, cond.*
+ ARG 1-2/93: 102

24267. 8.550389: SCHUBERT—Octets, D. 803, 72. *Budapest Schubert Ensemble.*
+ Gr 8/93: 50

24268. 8.550390: MOZART—Clarinet quintet; Violin sonata, K. 380 (arr. clarinet). *Kovács, Balogh, clarinets; Danubius Quartet.*
+ Gr 2/94: 65

24269. 8.550391: BRAHMS—Clarinet trio; Clarinet quintet. *Balogh, clarinet; Jandó, piano; Onczay, cello; Danubius Quartet.*
- ARG 1-2/94: 84
• Gr 9/93: 71

24270. 8.550394: HAYDN—String quartets op. 71. *Kodály Quartet.*
+ ARG 5-6/92: 72
• Fa 5-6/92: 170

24271. 8.550395: HAYDN—String quartets, op. 54. *Kodály Quartet.*
+ ARG 7-8/92: 146

24272. 8.550396: HAYDN—String quartets op. 74. *Kodály Quartet.*
+ ARG 5-6/92: 72
+ ARG 7-8/92: 146
• Fa 5-6/92: 170

24273. 8.550397: HAYDN—String quartets, op. 55. *Kodály Quartet.*
+ ARG 7-8/92: 146
+ Fa 11-12/92: 250

24274. 8.550399: HAYDN—String quartets H. II, 6; H. III, 6-8. *Kodály Quartet.*
+ ARG 5-6/94: 100
+ Fa 1-2/94: 199

24275. 8.550401: SCHUMANN—Kreisleriana; Waldszenen; Blumenstück. *P. Gulda, piano.*
+ ARG 7-8/93: 155
+ Fa 9-10/93: 281
• Gr 4/93: 96

24276. 8.550403: CORELLI—Concerti grossi op. 6. *Cappella Istropolitana; Krček, cond.*
+ Fa 5-6/92: 143

24277. 8.550404: TCHAIKOVSKY—Serenade in C for strings; Souvenir de Florence. *Vienna Chamber Orch.; Entremont, cond.*
• ARG 1-2/92: 127
• Fa 1-2/92: 350
+ Gr 10/91: 114

24278. 8.550406: BRAHMS—Piano quintet. SCHUMANN—Piano quintet. *Jandó, piano; Kodály Quartet.*
+ ARG 7-8/92: 106
+ Fa 11-12/92: 364

24279. 8.550411: JANÁČEK—Lachian dances; Sinfonietta; Taras Bulba. *Bratislava Radio Orch.; Lenárd, cond.*
+ ARG 5-6/92: 75
- Gr 3/92: 47

24280. 8.550412: MOZART—German dances, K. 586, 600, 602, 605. *Cappella Istropolitana; Wildner, cond.*
+ ARG 3-4/93: 117

24281. 8.550414: MOZART—Violin concertos no. 1-2; Rondo in B♭; Piano concerto no. 21: Andante (arr.). *Nishizaki, violin; Cappella Istropolitana; Wildner, cond.*
+ ARG 1-2/93: 126

24282. 8.550415—8.550416 (2 separate discs): HANDEL—Keyboard works. *Cuckston, harpsichord.*
- ARG 9-10/93: 129
• Fa 7-8/93: 147
- Gr 2/92: 60

24283. 8.550417: FRANCK—Violin sonata. GRIEG—Sonata no. 3; Lyric pieces (arr. Godar). *Nishizaki, violin; Jandó, piano.*
• ARG 9-10/92: 107

24284. 8.550418: MOZART—Violin concertos no. 3, 5; Adagio in E; Rondo in C. *Nishizaki, violin; Cappella Istropolitana; Wildner, cond.*
+ ARG 1-2/93: 126

24285. 8.550419: SUK—Serenade for strings. DVOŘÁK—Serenade for strings. *Cappella Istropolitana; Krček, cond.*
+ Fa 3-4/92: 341

24286. 8.550420: SCHUBERT—Violin sonatinas; Fantasy in C. *Kang, violin; Devoyon, piano.*
+ ARG 5-6/93: 130

24287. 8.550423: BACH—Piano concertos BWV 1052-1054. *Chang, piano; Camerata Cassovia; Stankovsky, cond.*
• ARG 1-2/94: 69

24288. 8.550424: RAVEL—Rapsodie espagnole; Pavane; La valse; Daphnis et Chloé: Suite no. 2. *Bratislava Radio Orch.; Jean, cond.*
• ARG 9-10/94: 180
+ Fa 9-10/94: 307

24289. 8.550427: SHOSTAKOVICH—Symphonies no. 5, 9. *Belgian Radio and Television Symphony Orch.; Rahbari, cond.*
• ARG 11-12/92: 202
+ Fa 1-2/93: 240
+ Gr 3/92: 55

24290. 8.550428/30 (3 discs): BACH—Christmas oratorio. *Kertesi, Németh, Mukk, Tóth; Hungarian Radio Chorus; Budapest Failoni Chamber Orch.; Oberfrank, cond.*
• Gr 4/93: 102

24291. 8.550431: BACH—Cantatas no. 199, 202, 209. *F. Wagner, soprano; Cappella Istropolitana; Brembeck, cond.*
+ Gr 9/92: 140

24292. 8.550432: REICHA—Wind quintets, op. 88, no. 2; op. 100, no. 5. *Michael Thompson Wind Quintet.*
+ ARG 1-2/96: 160
+ Fa 9-10/95: 291

24293. 8.550433: BEETHOVEN—Eleven Viennese dances, WoO 17; Twelve contredances, WoO 14; Twelve German dances, WoO 8; Twelve minuets, WoO 18. *Cappella Istropolitana; O. Dohnányi, cond.*
+ Fa 1-2/94: 122

24294. 8.550435: MOZART—Opera arias and duets. *Various performers.*
- Gr 12/91: 133

24295. 8.550436: BRAHMS—String sextets no. 1-2. *Stuttgart String Sextet.*
+ Fa 5-6/92: 128
• Gr 3/92: 64

24296. 8.550437: MOZART—Quartet for oboe, violin, viola, and cello, K. 370; Quintet for horn, violin, 2 violas, and cello, K. 407; Ein musikalischer Spass. *Kodály Quartet; Kiss, oboe; Keveházi, horn.*
+ Fa 9-10/94: 269

24297. 8.550438: MOZART—Flute quartets. *Gérard, flute; Ensemble Villa Musica.*
+ Fa 1-2/94: 245
+ Gr 10/91: 129

24298. 8.550439: MOZART—Piano trios no. 1-2; Violin sonata K. 378 (all arr. for clarinet(s)). *Kovács, Balogh, clarinets; Konrád, viola; Jandó, piano; Danubius*

Quartet.
+ Fa 9-10/94: 269
• Gr 2/94: 65

24299. 8.550441: BRAHMS—Horn trio. DUVERNOY—Horn trio. HERZOGENBERG—Horn trio. *Keveházi, clarinet; Jandó, piano; Hegyi, violin.*
+ ARG 9-10/94: 110
+ Fa 9-10/94: 156

24300. 8.550445—8.550446 (2 separate discs): MOZART—Piano sonatas no. 8, 10, K. 533; no. 9, 12, 15, 16. *Jandó, piano.*
+ ARG 7-8/92: 194
• Fa 11-12/92: 313

24301. 8.550449: MOZART—Piano sonatas, vol. 5. *Jandó, piano.*
+ ARG 9-10/94: 168
• Fa 9-10/94: 266

24302. 8.550450: GRIEG—Lyric pieces (selections). *Szokolay, piano.*
+ ARG 3-4/94: 102
+ Fa 1-2/94: 193

24303. 8.550451: BARTÓK—Piano music. *Szokolay, piano.*
+ ARG 9-10/94: 98
+ Fa 9-10/94: 136

24304. 8.550452: CLEMENTI—Piano sonatas. *Szokolay, piano.*
+ Fa 11-12/95: 237 (Anderson)
+ Fa 11-12/95: 238 (Kagan)
+ Gr 9/95: 83

24305. 8.550459: *Czech horn concertos.* Music of Fiala, Pokorny and Rossetti. *Z. & B. Tylšar, horns; Capella Istropolitana; Vajnar, cond.*
+ ARG 11-12/92: 241
+ Fa 11-12/92: 441
+ Gr 3/93: 58

24306. 8.550460—8.550461 (2 separate discs): COUPERIN—Harpsichord music. *Cuckston, harpsichord.*
- ARG 3-4/93: 71

24307. 8.550463, 8.550465 (2 separate discs): RAMEAU—Harpsichord music. *Cuckston, harpsichord.*
- ARG 3-4/93: 71

24308. 8.550466: RACHMANINOFF—Preludes, op. 32. KREISLER-RACHMANINOFF—Liebesleid; Liebesfreud. *Biret, piano.*
+ Fa 11-12/92: 326
• Gr 3/92: 87

24309. 8.550467: ARENSKY—Piano trio no. 1. TCHAIKOVSKY—Piano trio. *Stamper, violin; Jackson, cello; Vo. Ashkenazy, piano.*
+ Fa 1-2/94: 112
- Gr 7/93: 57

24310. 8.550469: REGER—Bach variations. SCHUMANN—Humoreske. *Harden, piano.*

+ ARG 7-8/92: 205
+ Fa 11/12/92: 364

24311. 8.550471: SCHUMANN—Symphonies, no. 2, 4. *Kosice State Phil. Orch.; Wildner, cond.*
- Gr 5/92: 48

24312. 8.550472: STRAVINSKY—Rite of spring; Jeu de carts. *Belgian Radio and TV Phil. Orch. Brussels; Rahbari, cond.*
• Gr 8/93: 40

24313. 8.550474: BEETHOVEN—Bagatelles, op. 33, 119, 129. *Jandó, piano.*
+ ARG 9-10/93: 91
+ Fa 9-10/93: 115
+ Gr 8/92: 53

24314. 8.550475: SCHUBERT—Piano sonatas D. 958, 960. *Jandó, piano.*
+ ARG 9-10/93: 184

24315. 8.550476: SCHUBERT—Songs. *Takács, mezzo-soprano; Jandó, piano.*
• ARG 9-10/93: 186
• Gr 3/93: 82

24316. 8.550478: BEETHOVEN—Cello sonatas no. 3-5. *Onczay, cello; Jandó, piano.*
+ ARG 7-8/92: 92
+ Fa 11-12/92: 195

24317. 8.550479: BEETHOVEN—Sonatas for cello and piano, op. 5; Variations on "See the conqu'ring hero comes"; Variations on Ein Mädchen oder Weibchen; Variations on Bei Männern, welche Liebe fühlen. *Onczay, cello; Jandó, piano.*
+ ARG 7-8/93: 64
• Fa 7-8/93: 106

24318. 8.550480: *Romantic French music for guitar and orchestra.* Music of Debussy, Fauré, and Satie. *Garcia, guitar; CSFR State Phil. Orch., Kosice; Breiner, cond.*
- Fa 9-10/94: 416

24319. 8.550485: SCHUMANN—Symphonies no. 1, 3. *Belgian Radio Phil.; Rahbari, cond.*
• ARG 5-6/95: 173

24320. 8.550486: RIMSKY-KORSAKOV—Suites from Coq d'or, Snow maiden, and Mlada. *Bratislava Radio Orch.; Johanos, cond.*
+ ARG 9-10/94: 183
+ Fa 9-10/94: 312
• Gr 9/92: 84

24321. 8.550488: TCHAIKOVSKY—Symphonies no. 2, 4. *Polish Radio Symphony Orch.; Leaper, cond.*
+ ARG 9-10/94: 210
+ Gr 5/93: 52

24322. 8.550489: ELGAR—Violin concerto; Cockaigne overture. *Kang,*

violin; Polish National Radio Symphony Orch.; Leaper, cond.
+ Gr 4/92: 48

24323. 8.550490/92 (3 discs): TCHAIKOVSKY—Sleeping beauty. *Czechoslovak State Phil. Orch. of Kosice; Mogrelia, cond.*
+ Fa 7-8/93: 256
+ Gr 4/93: 64

24324. 8.550493: SCHUMANN—Davidsbündlertänze; Fantasiestücke, op. 12. *Frith, piano .*
+ Gr 3/93: 75

24325. 8.550494: LALO—Symphonie espagnole. RAVEL—Tzigane. SAINT-SAËNS—Havanaise. SARASATE—Zigeunerweisen. *Bisengaliev, violin; Polish National Radio Symphony Orch.; Wildner, cond.*
+ Gr 12/93: 71

24326. 8.550495: MOZART—Coronation mass; Vespers, K. 339; Laudate Dominum; Sub tuum presidium; Ave verum corpus; Exsultate jubilate. *Coles, Mauro, Dickie, Martin; Kosice Teacher's Choir; Camerata Cassovia; Wildner, cond.*
- Gr 5/93: 88

24327. 8.550499: PROKOFIEV—Peter and the wolf. BRITTEN—Young person's guide to the orchestra. SAINT- SAËNS—Carnival of the animals. *Nicholas, narrator; Bratislava Radio Symphony Orch.; Lenárd, cond.*
- ARG 1-2/93: 172

24328. 8.550500: TCHAIKOVSKY—Marche slave; Capriccio italien; Romeo and Juliet. *Royal Philh. Orch.; Leaper, cond.*
+ Fa 11-12/92: 384

24329. 8.550503: DVOŘÁK—Concerto in B minor for cello and orchestra, op. 104. ELGAR—Concerto in E minor for cello and orchestra, op. 85. *Kliegel, cello; Royal Phil. Orch.; Halász, cond.*
+ Fa 3-4/93: 155
+ Gr 9/92: 65

24330. 8.550505: DEBUSSY—Images; Le martyre de Saint Sébastien; Marche écossaise sur un thème populaire; Berceuse héroïque. *BRT Phil. Orch.; Rahbari, cond.*
+ ARG 3-4/94: 89
+ Fa 1-2/94: 166
• Gr 11/93: 66

24331. 8.550506: BRAHMS—Piano concerto no. 2. SCHUMANN—Introduction and allegro appassionato, op. 92. *Jandó, piano; BRT Phil. Orch.; Rahbari, cond.*
+ ARG 9-10/94: 107
• Fa 9-10/94: 151
• Gr 9/93: 43

24332. 8.550508: CHOPIN—Ballades; Nouvelles études; Fantaisie; other. *Biret,*

NAXOS

piano.
+ Gr 5/93: 70

24333. 8.550509: BRAHMS—Variations; Studies. *Biret, piano.*
+ Gr 8/94: 75

24334. 8.550510: LISZT—Piano music. *Jandó, piano.*
• Fa 11-12/94: 280

24335. 8.550511: BEETHOVEN—Quintet for piano and winds. MOZART—Quintet for piano and winds; Adagio and rondo, K. 617. *Kovács, flute; Kiss, oboe; Kovács, clarinet; Keveházi, horn; Vajda, bassoon; Konrád, viola; Koó, cello; Jandó, piano.*
+ Gr 4/93: 74

24336. 8.550512: MOZART—Church sonatas. *Sebestyen, organ; Ferenc Erkel Chamber Orch.*
+ ARG 5-6/94: 117
+ Gr 3/93: 64

24337. 8.550514: MOZART—Organ music. *Sebestyén, organ.*
+ ARG 7-8/92: 186

24338. 8.550518: TCHAIKOVSKY—Symphony no. 3; The tempest. *Polish National Radio Symphony Orch.; Wit, cond.*
- Gr 2/94: 54

24339. 8.550519: TCHAIKOVSKY—Rococo variations; Nocturne; Pezzo capriccioso. BRUCH—Kol nidrei. BLOCH—Schelomo. *Kliegel, cello; Irish National Symphony Orch.; Markson, cond.*
• ARG 1-2/95: 219
+ Fa 5-6/95: 360
• Gr 11/94: 67

24340. 8.550522: MAHLER—Symphony no. 1. *Polish National Radio Symphony Orch. (Katowice); Halász, cond.*
• ARG 5-6/95: 135
+ Fa 5-6/95: 252
• Gr 4/95: 60

24341. 8.550523 (2 discs): MAHLER—Symphony no. 2. *Lisowska, soprano; Rappé, alto; Cracow Radio Choir; Polish Radio Symphony Orch.; Wit, cond.*
• ARG 9-10/94: 157
• Fa 9-10/94: 246
- Gr 3/94: 56

24342. 8.550525 (2 discs): MAHLER—Symphonies no. 3, 10 (Adagio only). *Podles, mezzo-soprano; Cracow Phil. Choir; Polish Radio Symphony Orch.; Wit, cond.*
+ ARG 5-6/96: 142

24343. 8.550525/26 (2 discs): MAHLER—Symphony no. 3; Symphony no. 4: Adagio. *Podles, alto; Cracow Phil. Choir; Cracow Boys' Choir; Polish National Symphony Orch.; Wit, cond.*
+ Fa 3-4/96: 210

24344. 8.550527: MAHLER—Symphony no. 4. *Russell, soprano; Polish Radio Orch.; Wit, cond.*
+ ARG 5-6/94: 108

24345. 8.550528: MAHLER—Symphony no. 5. *Polish Radio National Symphony Orch.; Wit, cond.*
+ ARG 5-6/93: 104
+ Fa 3-4/93: 212
• Gr 1/93: 40

24346. 8.550529/30 (2 discs): MAHLER—Symphony no. 6. *Polish National Radio Symphony Orch.; Wit, cond.*
- Gr 3/94: 56

24347. 8.550531: MAHLER—Symphony no. 7. *Katowice Radio Orch.; Halász, cond.*
• ARG 11-12/95: 150
• Fa 11-12/95: 295
- Gr 10/95: 58

24348. 8.550535/36 (2 discs): MAHLER—Symphony no. 9. *Polish National Radio Symphony Orch.; Halász, cond.*
+ ARG 11-12/95: 153
- Fa 11-12/95: 299
• Gr 7/94: 50

24349. 8.550539: RESPIGHI—Pines of Rome; Fountains of Rome; Roman festivals . *Royal Phil. Orch; Bátiz, cond.*
• ARG 1-2/94: 138
+ Gr 8/92: 38

24350. 8.550543: MOZART—String quartets, vol. 4. Quartet K. 465; Divertimenti K. 136-38. *Eder Quartet.*
+ Gr 9/93: 81

24351. 8.550544: MOZART—String quartets, vol. 5. Quartets K. 589, 160, 168-69. *Eder Quartet.*
+ Gr 9/93: 81

24352. 8.550545: MOZART—String quartets, vol. 6. Quartets no. 12, 13, 21. *Eder Quartet.*
+ Fa 5-6/95: 269
+ Gr 2/95: 68

24353. 8.550546: MOZART—String quartets, vol. 7. Quartets no. 10, 11, 15. *Eder Quartet.*
+ ARG 7-8/95: 160
+ Fa 5-6/95: 269
+ Gr 2/95: 68

24354. 8.550547: MOZART—String quartets, vol. 8. Quartets no. 20, 23; Adagio and fugue, K. 546. *Eder Quartet.*
+ Fa 5-6/95: 269
+ Gr 4/95: 84

24355. 8.550548—8.550550 (3 separate discs): LISZT—Années de pèlerinage. *Jandó, piano.*
+ ARG 5-6/93: 101 (v.2-3)

24356. 8.550551—8.550552 (2 separate discs): BOCCHERINI—Guitar quintets G.

445-450. *Tokos, guitar; Danubius Quartet.*
+ Gr 10/92: 124

24357. 8.550555: SCHUBERT—Allegro in A minor; Marches caractéristiques; Divertissement à la hongroise. *Jandó, Prunyi, pianos.*
+ ARG 9-10/93: 184
+ Gr 12/92: 97

24358. 8.550556: Oboe concertos by C.P.E. Bach and Marcello. *Kiss, oboe; Ferenc Erkel Chamber Orch.*
+ Gr 6/93: 37

24359. 8.550558: BEETHOVEN—String quartets no. 1-2. *Kodály Quartet.*
+ ARG 1-2/94: 75
+ Fa 1-2/94: 123
• Gr 9/93: 71

24360. 8.550559: BEETHOVEN—String quartets no. 3-4. *Kodály Quartet.*
+ ARG 5-6/96: 81
• Gr 3/96: 60

24361. 8.550565: PROKOFIEV—Piano concertos no. 2, 5. *Paik, piano; Polish National Radio Symphony Orch.; Wit, cond.*
+ ARG 7-8/93: 137
+ Fa 7-8/93: 202
• Gr 11/92: 97

24362. 8.550566: PROKOFIEV—Piano concertos no. 1, 3-4. *Paik, piano; Polish National Radio Symphony Orch.; Wit, cond.*
+ ARG 11-12/93: 170
+ Fa 7-8/93: 202
• Gr 11/92: 97

24363. 8.550572: *Lamentations.* Music of R. White, Tallis, Palestrina, Lassus, and E. de Brito. *Oxford Camerata; Summerly, cond.*
• ARG 11-12/94: 244
+ Fa 9-10/94: 232

24364. 8.550573: PALESTRINA—Missa Papae Marcelli; Missa Aeterna Christi munera. *Oxford Camerata; Summerly, cond.*
+ ARG 11-12/94: 167
• Fa 9-10/94: 232
+ Gr 12/92: 123

24365. 8.550574: BYRD—Mass for 4 voices; Mass for 5 voices; Infelix ego. *Oxford Camerata; Summerly, cond.*
+ Fa 9-10/94: 232

24366. 8.550575: VICTORIA—Masses: O magnum mysterium; O quam gloriosum; Ave Maria; Ardens est cor meum. LOBO—Versa ist in luctum. *Oxford Camerata; Summerly, cond.*
+ ARG 3-4/94: 177
+ Fa 9-10/94: 232

24367. 8.550576: TALLIS—Mass for four voices; Motets. *Oxford Camerata;*

Summerly, cond.
+ ARG 9-10/94: 207
+ Fa 9-10/94: 232
• Gr 11/94: 138

24368. 8.550577: GRIEG—Lyric pieces, vol. 2. *Szokolay, piano.*
+ Gr 6/93: 75

24369. 8.550581: Music of Guilmant, Vierne, Charpentier, Langlais, and others. *Lindley, organ.*
+ Gr 3/93: 79

24370. 8.550582: Music of Lang, Howells, Elgar, Vaughan Williams, and others. *Green, organ.*
+ Gr 3/93: 79

24371. 8.550583: RACHMANINOFF—Symphonic dances; Isle of the dead. *Royal Phil. Orch.; Bátiz, cond.*
+ ARG 7-8/93: 139
+ Fa 9-10/93: 243

24372. 8.550585/86 (2 discs): BACH—Mass in B minor. *Wagner, Koppelstetter, Schäfer, Elbert; Cappella Istropolitana; Brembeck, cond.*
• Gr 1/93: 55

24373. 8.550590: SCHUBERT—String quartet no. 14; Quartettsatz. *Kodály Quartet.*
+ ARG 7-8/93: 151
+ Fa 7-8/93: 232

24374. 8.550591: SCHUBERT—String quartets no. 10, 13. *Kodály Quartet.*
+ ARG 9-10/95: 208
• Gr 8/95: 96

24375. 8.550592—8.550694 (3 separate discs): BACH—Partitas. *Rübsam, piano.*
- ARG 5-6/94: 64

24376. 8.550598: DVOŘÁK—Symphonic poems: The midday witch; The wood dove; Golden spinning wheel. *Polish National Radio Symphony Orch.; Gunzenhauser, cond.*
+ ARG 9-10/94: 127
+ Fa 9-10/94: 186
- Gr 5/94: 50

24377. 8.550599: SCHUMANN—Works for oboe and piano. *Kiss, oboe; Jandó, piano.*
+ Fa 7-8/93: 265

24378. 8.550600: DVOŘÁK—Overtures: Carnival; Othello; In nature's realm; My home; Vanda. *BBC Phil. Orch.; Gunzenhauser, cond.*
+ ARG 9-10/94: 127
+ Fa 9-10/94: 186
• Gr 10/93; 44

24379. 8.550601: LAWES—Sett a 4 in G minor; Consort setts a 5: in C; in A minor; Royal consorts no. 1, 6; Three pieces for 2 lutes; Divisions on a pavan in G minor. *Heringman, Miller, lute & theorbo; Roberts, organ; Rose Consort of*

Viols.
+ ARG 9-10/96: 150
+ EM 2/97: 150
+ Fa 7-8/96: 216

24380. 8.550602: TOMKINS—Consort music for viols and voices; Keyboard music. *Roberts, harpsichord & organ; Bryan, harpsichord; Rose Consort of Viols; Red Byrd.*
+ ARG 11-12/95: 220
• Fa 11-12/95: 405

24381. 8.550603: GIBBONS—Consort and keyboard music; Songs and anthems. *Bonner, soprano; Roberts, keyboards; Red Byrd; Rose Consort.*
+ ARG 3-4/95: 104
+ EM 8/96: 517
+ Gr 2/95: 84

24382. 8.550604: BYRD—Consort and keyboard music. *Rose Consort; Red Byrd.*
+ ARG 1-2/95: 93
+ Gr 6/95: 67

24383. 8.550605: *Favorite soprano arias.* Music of Bellini, Puccini, Verdi, and Donizetti. *Orgonasova, soprano; Czechoslovak Radio Orch. of Bratislava; Humburg, cond.*
+ Fa 5-6/93: 362
+ Gr 2/93: 78
+ ON 4/2/94: 33

24384. 8.550606: Arias from Don Carlo, La forza del destino, La Wally, Manon Lescaut, Tosca, and others. *Gauci, soprano; Belgian Radio Orch.; Rahbari, cond.*
+ ARG 7-8/93: 204
+ Fa 9-10/93: 338
• Gr 11/92: 195

24385. 8.550608: SCHUMANN—Overtures: Manfred; Genoveva; Julius Caesar; The bride of Messina; Hermann and Dorothea; Faust; Overture, scherzo and finale. *Polish Radio Symphony Orch.; Wildner, cond.*
• ARG 3-4/94: 153
• Fa 9-10/94: 333

24386. 8.550609: MOZART—Cassations K. 63, 99-100. *Salzburg Chamber Orch.; Nerat, cond.*
+ Gr 4/93: 56

24387. 8.550610: DVOŘÁK—Slavonic rhapsodies; Rhapsody in A minor. *Slovak Phil. Orch.; Košler, Pešek, conds.* Reissue.
+ ARG 11-12/93: 102

24388. 8.550611—8.550613 (3 separate discs): MOZART—Variations for piano (complete). *Nicolosi, piano.*
+ ARG 7-8/94: 144
• Gr 9/94: 82

24389. 8.550615: Music of Borrono, Cara, Josquin, Milano, and Tromboncino.

Rumsey, voice & instruments.
+ ARG 7-8/95: 257

24390. 8.550621—8.550622 (2 separate discs): ROSSINI—String sonatas. *Budapest Rossini Ensemble.*
• Gr 5/93: 50

24391. 8.550623: SHOSTAKOVICH—Symphonies no. 1, 3. *Bratislava Radio Symphony Orch.; Slovák, cond.*
- Gr 11/93: 78

24392. 8.550624: SHOSTAKOVICH—Symphonies no. 2, 15. *Bratislava Radio Symphony Orch.; Slovák, cond.*
- Gr 11/93: 78

24393. 8.550625: SHOSTAKOVICH—Symphony no. 4. *Czecho-Slovak Radio Symphony Orch., Bratislava; Slovák, cond.*
• Fa 3-4/94: 321
- Gr 11/93: 78

24394. 8.550626: SHOSTAKOVICH—Symphonies no. 6, 12. *Bratislava Radio Symphony Orch.; Slovák, cond.*
- Gr 11/93: 78

24395. 8.550627: SHOSTAKOVICH—Symphony no. 7. *Bratislava Radio Symphony Orch.; Slovák, cond.*
- Gr 11/93: 78

24396. 8.550628: SHOSTAKOVICH—Symphony no. 8. *Czecho-Slovak Radio Symphony Orch., Bratislava; Slovák, cond.*
• Fa 3-4/94: 321
- Gr 11/93: 78

24397. 8.550630: SHOSTAKOVICH—Symphony no. 13. *Mikuláš, bass; Slovak Phil. Chorus; Czecho-Slovak Radio Symphony Orch., Bratislava; Slovák, cond.*
• Fa 3-4/94: 321
- Gr 11/93: 78

24398. 8.550631: SHOSTAKOVICH—Symphony no. 14. *Bratislava Radio Symphony Orch.; Slovák, cond.*
- Gr 11/93: 78

24399. 8.550632: SHOSTAKOVICH—Symphonies no. 5, 9. *Bratislava Radio Symphony Orch.; Slovák, cond.*
- Gr 11/93: 78

24400. 8.550633: SHOSTAKOVICH—Symphony no. 10. *Bratislava Radio Symphony Orch.; Slovák, cond.*
- Gr 11/93: 78

24401. 8.550634: ELGAR—Symphony no. 1. *BBC Phil. Orch.; Hurst, cond.*
• ARG 7-8/94: 100
• Gr 2/94: 40

24402. 8.550635: ELGAR—Symphony no. 2. *BBC Phil. Orch.; Downes, cond.*
+ Gr 6/94: 48

NAXOS

24403. 8.550641: BACH—Cantatas: Schweigt stille, plaudert nicht, BWV 211 "Coffee cantata"; Mer hahn ein neue Oberkeet, BWV 212 "Peasant cantata". *Kertesi, Mukk, Gáti; Failoni Chamber Orch., Budapest; Antal, cond.*
- ARG 9-10/93: 86
- Fa 7-8/93: 92
- Gr 3/93: 80

24404. 8.550642: BACH—Cantatas: Ein feste Burg ist unser Gott, BWV 80; Herz und Mund und Tat und Leben, BWV 147. *Kertesi, Németh, Mukk, Gáti; Hungarian Radio Chorus; Failoni Chamber Orch., Budapest; Antal, cond.*
- ARG 9-10/93: 86
- Fa 7-8/93: 92
+ Gr 12/92: 113

24405. 8.550644: TCHAIKOVSKY—Suites for orchestra no. 1-2. *Irish Symphony Orch.; Sanderling, cond.*
+ ARG 11-12/94: 199
+ Fa 11-12/94: 400

24406. 8.550649: PAGANINI—Violin concertos no. 1-2. *Kaler, violin; Polish Radio Symphony Orch.; Gunzenhauser, cond.*
+ ARG 5-6/94: 119
+ Gr 12/93: 74

24407. 8.550651, 8.550653 (2 separate discs): BACH—Trio sonatas; Preludes and fugues. *Rübsam, organ.*
- Gr 5/94: 78

24408. 8.550654: SCHUBERT—Arpeggione sonata. SCHUMANN—Fantasiestücke; Stücke im Volkston; Adagio und Allegro. *Kliegel, cello; Merscher, piano.*
+ Gr 7/93: 62

24409. 8.550655: MENDELSSOHN—Cello sonatas; Variations concertantes; Song without words, op. 109. *Kliegel, cello; Merscher, piano.*
+ Gr 7/94: 72

24410. 8.550656: BRAHMS—Cello sonatas no. 1-2. *Kliegel, cello; Merscher, piano.*
+ Gr 12/93: 81

24411. 8.550657: HAYDN—*Piano sonatas, vol. 1.* Sonatas no. 49-52. *Jandó, piano.*
+ ARG 1-2/95: 113
- Fa 11-12/94: 252
+ Gr 6/94: 81

24412. 8.550658: SCHUBERT—Trout quintet; Adagio and rondo. *Kodály Quartet; Jandó, piano.*
+ ARG 11-12/93: 189
+ Fa 9-10/93: 269
+ Gr 4/93: 81

24413. 8.550660/61 (2 discs): PURCELL—The fairy queen. *Amps, Parker, Atherton, Davidson, Newton; Scholars Baroque Ensemble; Van Asch, cond.*
+ ARG 11-12/94: 169
+ Fa 11-12/94: 345

+ Gr 7/94: 119
+ ON 12/10/94: 52

24414. 8.550662/63 (2 discs): MONTEVERDI—Vespers of the Blessed Virgin (1610). *Scholars Baroque Ensemble.*
- ARG 5-6/96: 151
+ Fa 3-4/96: 228

24415. 8.550664/65 (2 discs): BACH—St. John Passion. *Scholars Baroque Ensemble; Van Asch, cond.*
- ARG 11-12/95: 74
- Fa 3-4/95: 115
- Gr 5/95: 89

24416. 8.550666: RACHMANINOFF—Piano concerto no. 3; Prince Rostislav. *Glemser, piano; National Symphony Orch. of Ireland; Maksymiuk, cond.*
- ARG 5-6/95: 153
- Fa 3-4/95: 266

24417. 8.550667/68 (2 discs): HANDEL—Messiah. *Amps, Parker, Jellard, Davidson, Doveton, Bowen, Peacock; Scholars Baroque Ensemble; Van Asch, bass & cond.*
- Fa 3-4/93: 177
+ Gr 4/93: 107

24418. 8.550673—8.550674 (2 separate discs): HAYDN—String quartets op. 64. *Kodály Quartet.*
+ Gr 1/94: 66

24419. 8.550676: BEETHOVEN—Piano variations. *Jandó, piano.*
- Fa 11-12/94: 167
+ Gr 9/93: 85

24420. 8.550679: BACH—Two and three-part inventions. *Sebestyén, harpsichord.*
+ Gr 6/94: 80

24421. 8.550681: MENDELSSOHN—Piano concertos no. 1-2; Capriccio brillant; Rondo brillant. *Frith, piano; Kosice State Phil. Orch.; Stankovsky, cond.*
- Fa 11-12/94: 296
+ Gr 4/94: 50

24422. 8.550682: LÔBO—Missa pro defunctis à 8. CARDOSO—Missa pro defunctis. *Schola Cantorum of Oxford; Summerly, cond.*
- Fa 7-8/94: 112

24423. 8.550683: RAVEL—Piano works, vol. 1. *Thiollier, piano.*
+ ARG 3-4/95: 165
- Fa 3-4/95: 272
- Gr 2/95: 74

24424. 8.550684: Duets and arias by Donizetti, Leoncavallo, Mascagni, Ponchielli, and Verdi. *Mauro, soprano; Aragall, tenor; Tumagian, baritone; Bratislava Radio Symphony Orch.; Rahbari, cond.* Reissues.
- Gr 12/94: 172

24425. 8.550687: JENKINS—*All in a garden green.* Consort music. *Rose Consort of Viols.*
+ EM 8/94: 516
+ Gr 8/94: 68

24426. 8.550688: SPOHR—Clarinet concertos no. 1, 3; Potpourri, op. 80. *Ottensamer, clarinet; Slovak State Phil., Kosice; Slovak Radio Symphony Orch., Bratislava; Wildner, cond.*
+ ARG 7-8/95: 201
+ Fa 3-4/95: 302
- Gr 7/95: 71

24427. 8.550689: SPOHR—Clarinet concertos no. 2, 4; Fantasia and variations on a theme of Danzi. *Ottensamer, clarinet; Bratislava Radio Symphony Orch.; Wildner, cond.*
+ ARG 7-8/95: 201
+ Fa 7-8/95: 329
- Gr 7/95: 71

24428. 8.550690, 8.550759 (2 separate discs): PAGANINI—Music for violin and guitar. *St. John, violin; Wynberg, guitar.*
- ARG 1-2/95: 149
+ Gr 12/94: 122

24429. 8.550692—8.550694 (3 separate discs): BACH—Partitas; Short pieces. *Rübsam, piano.*
- Gr 8/94: 74

24430. 8.550696: SATIE—Piano music, vol. 1. *Körmendi, piano.*
+ ARG 5-6/94: 135
- Gr 11/93: 119

24431. 8.550697: SATIE—Piano music, vol. 2. *Körmendi, piano.*
+ Gr 7/94: 82

24432. 8.550698: SATIE—Piano music, vol. 3. *Körmendi, piano.*
+ Fa 1-2/95: 254

24433. 8.550699: SATIE—Piano music, vol. 4. *Körmendi, Eckhardt, piano.*
+ ARG 11-12/95: 190
+ Fa 5-6/95: 317
- Gr 6/95: 83

24434. 8.550700: HANDEL—Recorder sonatas, op. 1: no. 2, 4, 7, 11; in D minor; Trio sonata in F. *Czidra, recorder; Harsányi, recorder & bassoon; Pertis, clavichord; Kelemen, cello.*
+ ARG 3-4/94: 106

24435. 8.550701—8.550702 (2 separate discs): HAYDN—String quartets op. 20. *Kodály Quartet.*
+ ARG 7-8/95: 122
+ Fa 7-8/95: 202
- Gr 6/94: 70 (702)

24436. 8.550703—8.550704 (2 separate discs): BACH—The art of fugue. *Rübsam, organ.*
- ARG 9-10/94: 93

- Fa 7-8/94: 44
+ Gr 1/94: 74

24437. 8.550705: *Early Iberian organ music.* Music of Anon., Cabezón, Carreira, Castillo, Peraza, Heredia, Coelho, Arauxo, Bruna, and Cabanilles. *Parkins, organ.*
+ Fa 9-10/94: 417

24438. 8.550708: BACH—Toccatas. *Rübsam, piano.*
- Gr 8/94: 74

24439. 8.550709: BACH—Italian concerto; Chromatic fantasy and fugue, BWV 903; French suites no. 1-2. *Rübsam, piano.*
- Fa 3-4/95: 111
- Gr 10/94: 154

24440. 8.550710: BACH—French suites no. 3-6. *Rübsam, piano.*
+ Fa 3-4/95: 111
- Gr 10/94: 154

24441. 8.550711: Gregorian chants from the Proper of the Mass. *Nova Schola Gregoriana; Turco, cond.*
+ ARG 5-6/94: 192
+ Fa 7-8/94: 308

24442. 8.550712: Seasons of the year. *In Dulci Jubilo; Turco, cond.*
+ ARG 5-6/94: 192
+ Fa 7-8/94: 308

24443. 8.550713: HAYDN—Piano concertos no. 4, 7, 9 11. *Chang, piano; Camerata Cassovia; Stankovsky, cond.*
+ ARG 5-6/94: 99

24444. 8.550715: SCHUMANN—Piano sonata no. 2; Piano music. *Glemser, piano.*
+ ARG 11-12/94: 189
+ Fa 1-2/95: 268
+ Gr 10/94: 164

24445. 8.550716: TCHAIKOVSKY—Symphony no. 5; The storm. *Polish National Radio Symphony Orch.; Wit, cond.*
• Gr 7/94: 62

24446. 8.550717: PAGANINI—Caprices, op. 1. *Kaler, violin.*
+ ARG 5-6/94: 119
• Gr 10/93: 85

24447. 8.550718: *Early English organ music, vol. 1.* Music of Farnaby, Anon., Purcell, Boyce, Gibbons, Croft, Walond, and Blow. *Payne, organ.*
+ Fa 9-10/94: 417

24448. 8.550721: HAYDN—Symphonies no. 26, 35, 49. *Northern Chamber Orch.; Ward, cond.*
• Gr 1/94: 47

24449. 8.550722: HAYDN—Symphonies, vol. 7. No. 6-8. *Northern Chamber Orch.; Ward, cond.*

+ ARG 11-12/94: 128
+ Fa 11-12/94: 253
+ Gr 11/94: 76

24450. 8.550723: HAYDN—Symphonies, vol. 8. Symphonies, no. 23-24, 61. *Northern Chamber Orch.; Ward, cond.*
+ ARG 11-12/94: 128
+ Fa 11-12/94: 254

24451. 8.550724: HAYDN—Symphonies no. 22, 29, 60. *Northern Chamber Orch.; Ward, cond.*
• ARG 7-8/95: 123
• Fa 7-8/95: 204
+ Gr 6/95: 44

24452. 8.550726: RIMSKY-KORSAKOV—Scheherazade; Tale of Tsar Sultan: Suite. *Philharmonia Orch.; Bátiz, cond.*
+ Gr 6/94: 58

24453. 8.550728: TCHAIKOVSKY—Suites for orchestra no. 3-4. *Irish Symphony Orch.; Sanderling, cond.*
• ARG 11-12/94: 199
+ Fa 1-2/95: 289
+ Gr 10/94: 124

24454. 8.550729: CASTELNUOVO-TEDESCO—Guitar concerto no. 1. RODRIGO—Concierto de Aranjuez. VILLA-LOBOS—Guitar concerto. *Kraft, guitar; Northern Chamber Orch.; Ward, cond.*
• Gr 4/94: 42

24455. 8.550730: SCHUBERT—Piano sonatas D. 784, 894. *Jandó, piano.*
+ Gr 6/93: 75

24456. 8.550732: HAYDN—String quartets op. 2, no. 4, 6; op. 42. *Kodály Quartet.*
• Gr 6/94: 70

24457. 8.550733: VAUGHAN WILLIAMS—Symphonies, no. 3, 6. *Bournemouth Sinfonietta; Bakels, cond.*
• ARG 1-2/95: 195
• Fa 1-2/95: 311
• Gr 12/94: 100

24458. 8.550734: VAUGHAN WILLIAMS—Symphony no. 2; The wasps. *Bournemouth Symphony Orch.; Bakels, cond.*
• ARG 11-12/94: 205
+ Fa 11-12/94: 407
• Gr 6/94: 66

24459. 8.550739: ALBINONI—Oboe concertos, op. 9, no. 2-3, 5, 8-9, 11. *Camden, Girdwood, oboes; London Virtuosi; Georgiadis, cond.*
+ Fa 9-10/94: 112
+ Gr 3/94: 40

24460. 8.550741: *Romantic music for flute and harp.* Music of Bizet, Massenet, Durand, Debussy, Ravel, Gluck, and others. *Bálint, flute; Mercz, harp.*
• Gr 12/94: 122

24461. 8.550742: GESUALDO—19 sacrae cantiones à 5. *Oxford Camerata; Summerly, cond.*
+ Fa 9-10/94: 232

24462. 8.550743: NIELSEN—Symphonies no. 4-5. *Irish Symphony Orch.; Leaper, cond.*
- ARG 1-2/95: 146
- Fa 5-6/95: 276
+ Fa 3-4/96: 238
• Gr 10/94: 114

24463. 8.550744: WIENIAWSKI—Violin and piano music. *Bisengaliev, violin; Lenehan, piano.*
• ARG 1-2/95: 204
+ Gr 10/94: 149

24464. 8.550745: GOLDMARK—Rustic wedding symphony; Overtures. *National Symphony of Ireland; Gunzenhauser, cond.*
• ARG 9-10/95: 150
+ Fa 11-12/95: 262
+ Fa 1-2/96: 210
+ Gr 12/95: 80

24465. 8.550746—8.550747 (2 separate discs): BRAHMS—Piano trios. *Vienna Trio.*
+ ARG 1-2/95: 90
+ Fa 1-2/95: 131
• Gr 9/94: 71 (747)
• Gr 10/94: 132 (746)

24466. 8.550749: BARTÓK—Violin sonatas; Contrasts. *Pauk, violin; Jandó, piano; Berkes, clarinet.*
+ ARG 1-2/95: 74
+ Fa 1-2/95: 107
+ Gr 9/94: 71

24467. 8.550750: MARAIS—Viol music. SAINT-COLOMBE—Viol music. *Spectre de la Rose.*
+ ARG 5-6/94: 110
+ Gr 2/94: 62

24468. 8.550752: SAINT-SAËNS—Introduction and Rondo capriccioso, op. 28; Romance, op. 48; Caprice andalous, op. 122; Morceau de concert, op. 62; Violin concerto no. 3. *Kang, violin; Polish National Radio Symphony Orch.; Wit, cond.*
+ ARG 1-2/95: 164
• Fa 11-12/94: 361
+ Gr 10/94: 118

24469. 8.550753: RAVEL—Piano concertos. FALLA—Nights in the gardens of Spain. *Thiollier, piano; Polish Radio Orch.; Wit, cond.*
+ ARG 3-4/95: 164
+ Fa 5-6/95: 306
+ Gr 3/95: 52

24470. 8.550754: INDY—Symphony on a French mountain air. FAURÉ—Ballade. FRANCK—Symphonic variations. *Thiollier, piano; Irish National Symphony Orch.; Almeida, cond.*
+ ARG 11-12/94: 133

+ Fa 1-2/95: 159
+ Gr 1/95: 44

24471. 8.550755 (2 discs): ADAM—
Giselle. *Slovak Radio Symphony Orch. of
Bratislava; Mogrelia, cond.*
- ● ARG 5-6/95: 67
+ Fa 7-8/95: 93
+ Gr 4/95: 46

24472. 8.550757: HAYDN—Symphonies,
no. 30, 55, 63. *Northern Chamber Orch.;
Ward, cond.*
- - ARG 3-4/95: 112
+ Fa 5-6/95: 209
+ Gr 5/95: 48

24473. 8.550758: DVOŘÁK—Violin
concerto; Romance. GLAZUNOV—Violin
concerto. *Kaler, violin; Polish National
Radio Symphony Orch.; Kolchinsky,
cond.*
- + Gr 4/95: 52

24474. 8.550760: FOSSA—Trios
concertants for guitar, violin, and cello,
op. 18: no. 1-3. *Wynberg, guitar; Beaver,
violin; Epperson, cello.*
- + Fa 3-4/95: 169
+ Gr 3/95: 62

24475. 8.550765: FAURÉ—Requiem;
Messe basse; Cantique de Jean Racine.
VIERNE—Andantino. SÉVERAC—Tantum
ergo. *Oxford Schola Cantorum; Oxford
Camerata; Summerly, cond.*
- - ARG 3-4/95: 99
+ Gr 9/94: 88

24476. 8.550766: PERGOLESI—Stabat
Mater; Cantata: Orfeo. *Faulkner,
soprano; Gonda, alto; Camerata
Budapest; Halász, cond.*
- ● ARG 11-12/95: 171
- - Fa 11-12/95: 328
- ● Gr 9/95: 94

24477. 8.550768: HAYDN—Symphonies
no. 53, 86-87. *Nicolaus Esterházy
Sinfonia; Drahos, cond.*
- ● Gr 11/94: 76

24478. 8.550769: HAYDN—Symphonies,
vol. 12. No. 69, 89, 91. *Nicolaus
Esterházy Sinfonia, Budapest; Drahos,
cond.*
- + Fa 11-12/94: 253

24479. 8.550770: HAYDN—Symphonies
no. 64, 84, 90. *Nicolaus Esterházy
Sinfonia; Drahos, cond.*
- ● Gr 3/95: 46

24480. 8.550771: BARTÓK—Piano
concertos no. 1-3. *Jandó, piano;
Budapest Symphony Orch.; A. Ligeti,
cond.*
- + ARG 7-8/95: 79
- ● Fa 3-4/95: 118
- - Fa 5-6/95: 131
+ Gr 2/95: 40

24481. 8.550773: *English organ music,
vol. 2.* Music of Elgar, Parry, Howells,
Whitlock, Vaughan Williams, and
Sumsion. *Hunt, organ.*
- ● ARG 5-6/94: 178
- ● Fa 9-10/94: 418

24482. 8.550780: HAYDN—Symphonies
no. 97, 98. *Nicolaus Esterházy Sinfonia,
Budapest; Drahos, cond.*
- + ARG 3-4/95: 113
- ● Fa 3-4/95: 188
- ● Gr 3/95: 46

24483. 8.550781: Russian folk songs.
*Patriarchal Choir, Moscow; Rybakova,
cond.*
- + Fa 5-6/95: 396

24484. 8.550782: TCHAIKOVSKY—
Francesca da Rimini; Symphony no. 6.
*Polish National Radio Symphony Orch.;
Wit, cond.*
- ● Gr 9/94: 66

24485. 8.550783—8.550784 (2 separate
discs): SCHUMANN—Piano music. *Jandó,
piano.*
- + Gr 4/94: 74

24486. 8.550785: *Le grand tango.* Music
of Tagell, Falla, Rachmaninoff,
Tchaikovsky, and others. *Kliegel, cello;
Glemser, piano.*
- + ARG 1-2/95: 219
- ● Fa 1-2/95: 346
+ Gr 1/95: 71

24487. 8.550786—8.550787 (2 separate
discs): HAYDN—String quartets, op. 9.
Kodály Quartet.
- + ARG 5-6/95: 117
+ Fa 3-4/95: 186
- ● Gr 11/94: 100

24488. 8.550788—8.550789 (2 separate
discs): HAYDN—String quartets, op. 33.
Kodály Quartet.
- + ARG 7-8/95: 122
+ Fa 5-6/95: 206
- ● Gr 6/95: 68

24489. 8.550792: BALAKIREV—Symphony
no. 1; Tamara; Islamey. *Russian State
Symphony Orch.; Golovchin, cond.*
- + ARG 11-12/94: 68
+ Fa 11-12/94: 161
- ● Gr 10/94: 99

24490. 8.550793: BALAKIREV—Symphony
no. 2; Russia. *Russian State Symphony
Orch.; Golovchin, cond.*
- ● ARG 11-12/94: 68
- ● Fa 3-4/95: 117
- ● Gr 9/94: 45

24491. 8.550794/5 (2 discs): FAURÉ—
Nocturnes. *Martin, piano.*
- + Gr 7/94: 80

24492. 8.550797: HAYDN—Symphonies
no. 72, 93, 95. *Nicolaus Esterházy
Sinfonia; Drahos, cond.*

- ● ARG 11-12/95: 134
+ Fa 9-10/95: 223
+ Gr 12/95: 80

24493. 8.550800: KHACHATURIAN—Gayne:
Suites no. 1-3. *St. Petersburg State
Symphony Orch.; Anichanov, cond.*
- ● ARG 1-2/95: 125

24494. 8.550801: KHACHATURIAN—
Spartacus: Suites no. 1-3. *St. Petersburg
State Symphony Orch.; Anichanov, cond.*
- - ARG 7-8/96: 142
+ Fa 5-6/96: 184

24495. 8.550811: RIMSKY-KORSAKOV—
Symphonies no. 1-2. *St. Petersburg State
Symphony Orch.; Anichanov, cond.*
- + ARG 3-4/95: 170
+ Fa 3-4/95: 276

24496. 8.550812: RIMSKY-KORSAKOV—
Symphony no. 3; Sinfonietta on Russian
themes. *St. Petersburg Symphony Orch.;
Anichanov, cond.*
- ● ARG 3-4/95: 170

24497. 8.550820: TCHAIKOVSKY—Piano
concerto no. 2; Concert fantasy. *Glemser,
piano; Polish Radio Symphony Orch.;
Wit, cond.*
- + ARG 1-2/97: 180
+ Fa 3-4/97: 319
+ Gr 4/97: 65

24498. 8.550822: GÓRECKI—Symphony
no. 3; Pieces in olden style. *Kilanowicz,
soprano; Polish Radio Symphony Orch.,
Katowice; Wit, cond.*
- + ARG 11-12/94: 118
+ Fa 11-12/94: 239
+ Gr 10/94: 106

24499. 8.550823: *English string music.*
BRITTEN—Variations on a theme of Frank
Bridge. HOLST—St. Paul's suite.
DELIUS—Aquarelles. VAUGHAN
WILLIAMS—Variants of Dives and
Lazarus. WARLOCK—Capriol suite.
Bournemouth Sinfonietta; Studt, cond.
- + ARG 1-2/95: 208
+ Fa 11-12/94: 502
+ Gr 10/94: 128

24500. 8.550824: BRAHMS—Organ music.
Parkins, organ.
- - ARG 11-12/94: 81
+ Gr 12/94: 125

24501. 8.550825: NIELSEN—Symphonies
no. 2-3. *National Symphony Orch. of
Ireland; Leaper, cond.*
- - ARG 5-6/96: 159
+ Fa 3-4/96: 238
- ● Gr 11/95: 89

24502. 8.550826: NIELSEN—Symphonies
no. 1, 6. *National Symphony Orch. of
Ireland; Leaper, cond.*
- - ARG 5-6/96: 159
+ Fa 3-4/96: 238
+ Gr 12/95: 86

24503. 8.550829 (2 discs): MESSIAEN—Vingt regards sur l'enfant Jésus. *Austbö, piano.*
  + ARG 5-6/95: 139
  + Gr 12/94: 127

24504. 8.550832/4 (3 discs): BACH—St. Matthew passion. *Mukk, Gáti, Verebics, Kiss; Hungarian State Phil. Orch.; Oberfrank, cond.*
  + Gr 8/94: 86

24505. 8.550836: LASSUS—Missa Bell amfitrit' altera. PALESTRINA—Motet and Missa Hodie Christus natus est; Stabat mater. *Schola Cantorum of Oxford; Summerly, cond.*
  + Fa 9-10/94: 232
  • Gr 6/94: 94

24506. 8.550837: HUMMEL—Piano concertos no. 2-3. *Chang, piano; Budapest Chamber Orch.; Pál, cond.* Reissue.
  + ARG 9-10/96: 141
  • Fa 11-12/96: 274

24507. 8.550838: *Latin American classics, vol. 1.* Music of Moncayo, Revueltas, Ponce, Villanueva, Villa-Lobos, Ginastera, Rosas, R. Halffter, Chávez, and Galindo. *Festival Orch. of Mexico; Bátiz, cond.*
  + ARG 5-6/95: 198
  + Fa 3-4/95: 397

24508. 8.550842: LASSUS—Missa Entre vous filles; Missa Susanne un jour; Infelix ego. *Oxford Camerata; Summerly, cond.*
  + ARG 3-4/95: 124
  + Fa 9-10/94: 232
  + Gr 8/94: 90

24509. 8.550843: *Renaissance masterpieces.* Music of Ockeghem, Morales, Rogier, Palestrina, and others. *Oxford Camerata; Summerly, cond.*
  + ARG 1-2/95: 236
  + EM 2/95: 166
  + Fa 1-2/95: 342
  • Gr 3/95: 98

24510. 8.550844: HAYDN—*Piano sonatas, vol. 2.* Sonatas no. 27-32. *Jandó, piano.*
  + ARG 1-2/95: 113
  + Fa 11-12/94: 252

24511. 8.550845: HAYDN—*Piano sonatas, vol. 3.* Sonatas no. 34, 40-48; Variations in F minor. *Jandó, piano.*
  + Fa 11-12/94: 252
  + Gr 8/94: 76

24512. 8.550846: SCHUBERT—Piano sonatas D. 664, D. 537; Wanderer fantasy. *Jandó, piano.*
  + ARG 3-4/95: 180
  + Gr 3/95: 76

24513. 8.550849: SCHUMANN—Albumblätter, op. 124; Impromptus on a theme of Clara Wieck; Six intermezzos,

op. 4; Drei Romanzen, op. 28. *Várjon, piano.*
  + ARG 9-10/95: 211
  + Gr 6/95: 84

24514. 8.550850: BORODIN—String quartets. *Haydn Quartet.*
  + ARG 3-4/95: 77
  + Fa 5-6/95: 145

24515. 8.550858: GLIÈRE—Symphony no. 3. *Czech Radio Symphony Orch.; Johanos, cond.* Reissue.
  + ARG 9-10/94: 133
  + Gr 2/94: 42

24516. 8.550859: VIVALDI—Oboe concertos RV 452-454, 534-536. *Schilli, Jonas, oboes; Kósa, harpsichord; Failoni Chamber Orch.; Morandi, cond.*
  + Fa 11-12/94: 413

24517. 8.550860: VIVALDI—Oboe concertos RV 455, 447, 463, 457, 451, 461. *Schilli, oboe; Failoni Chamber Orch.; Morandi, cond.*
  + Fa 11-12/94: 414

24518. 8.550861—8.550863 (3 separate discs): MENDELSSOHN—String quartets (complete). *Aurora String Quartet.*
  + Fa 11-12/94: 154
  + Fa 11-12/94: 289
  • Gr 10/94: 142 (862)
  • Gr 12/94: 121 (861, 863)

24519. 8.550864: GRIEG—Peer Gynt suites; Orchestra music. *BBC Scottish Orch.; Maksymiuk, cond.*
  - ARG 11-12/94: 122
  • Gr 10/94: 106

24520. 8.550865: C. STAMITZ—Cello concertos. *Benda, cello; Prague Chamber Orch.*
  • ARG 11-12/94: 194
  + Fa 11-12/94: 386

24521. 8.550868: BARTÓK—Sonata for solo violin, Sz. 117; Forty-four duos for 2 violins. *Pauk, Sawa, violins.*
  + ARG 7-8/96: 72
  + Fa 5-6/96: 92
  + Gr 5/96: 72

24522. 8.550870: SCHUMANN—Violin sonatas; FAE sonata: Intermezzo. *Kaler, violin; Slutsky, piano.*
  + ARG 11-12/94: 189
  + Fa 11-12/94: 375
  + Gr 9/94: 76

24523. 8.550871: MOZART—Symphonies no. 1-5. *Northern Chamber Orch.; Ward, cond.*
  + Fa 11-12/95: 319
  + Gr 12/95: 86

24524. 8.550872: MOZART—Symphonies no. 6-10. *Northern Chamber Orch.; Ward, cond.*
  + Fa 3-4/96: 236

24525. 8.550873: MOZART—Symphonies no. 11-14. *Northern Chamber Orch.; Ward, cond.*
  + Fa 11-12/95: 319
  • Gr 9/95: 63

24526. 8.550874: MOZART—Symphonies no. 15-18. *Northern Chamber Orch.; Ward, cond.*
  + Fa 3-4/96: 236
  + Gr 12/95: 86

24527. 8.550875: MOZART—Symphonies no. 19-20, 37. *Northern Chamber Orch.; Ward, cond.*
  • Gr 5/96: 60

24528. 8.550876: MOZART—Symphonies no. 21-24, 26. *Northern Chamber Orch.; Ward, cond.*
  • ARG 5-6/96: 157
  + Fa 3-4/96: 236
  + Gr 1/96: 58

24529. 8.550877: *Italian concerti grossi.* Music of Sammartini, Albinoni, Vivaldi, Locatelli, and others. *Cappella Istropolitana; Krček, cond.*
  + Gr 3/95: 58

24530. 8.550878: GRIEG—Piano sonata; Cello sonata; Intermezzo. *Birkeland, cello; Gimse, piano.*
  + Gr 11/94: 100

24531. 8.550879: GRIEG—String quartets no. 1-2. JOHANSEN—String quartet op. 35. *Oslo String Quartet.*
  + Gr 10/94: 138

24532. 8.550880: French chansons. *Scholars of London.*
  + ARG 3-4/95: 249
  + EM 8/95: 518
  + Gr 2/95: 91

24533. 8.550881—8.550884 (4 separate discs): GRIEG—Piano music, vol. 1-4. *Steen-Nøkleberg, piano, clavichord, organ, & harmonium.*
  • ARG 5-6/96: 118
  • Fa 3-4/96: 173
  + Gr 3/96: 69

24534. 8.550885: DEBUSSY—Children's corner. SCHUMANN—Kinderszenen. TCHAIKOVSKY—Album for the young. *Biret, piano.*
  • Fa 11-12/94: 212
  + Gr 10/94: 158

24535. 8.550886: BARTÓK—Piano quintet; Rhapsodies; Andante. *Pauk, violin; Jandó, piano; Kodály Quartet.*
  + ARG 11-12/95: 80
  + Fa 11-12/95: 201
  + Gr 10/95: 80

24536. 8.550896: DVOŘÁK—Piano concerto; The water goblin. *Jandó, piano; Katowice Radio Orch.; Wit, cond.*
  + ARG 11-12/94: 105

NAXOS

● Fa 1-2/95: 152
+ Gr 12/94: 80

24537. 8.550898: GLIÈRE—Symphony no. 1; The sirens. *Slovak State Phil. Orch.; Gunzenhauser, cond.* Reissue.
+ Fa 5-6/96: 156
+ Gr 10/95: 56

24538. 8.550899: GLIÈRE—Symphony no. 2; The Zaporozhy Cossacks. *Bratislava Radio Symphony Orch.; Clark, cond.*
+ Fa 5-6/96: 156
● Gr 10/95: 56

24539. 8.550900: *Wedding celebrations.* Music of Schrammel, Offenbach, Strauss, Pazaelller, and others. *Budapest Strauss Ensemble; Bogár, cond.*
+ ARG 3-4/95: 233

24540. 8.550901, 8.550927 (2 separate discs): BACH—Organ music. *Rübsam, organ.*
- ARG 1-2/95: 70

24541. 8.550904: SWEELINCK—Organ music. *Christie, organ.*
+ ARG 1-2/95: 189
+ Gr 2/95: 76

24542. 8.550906: FAURÉ—Violin sonatas; Berceuse; Romance; Andante. *Kang, violin; Devoyon, piano.*
● Gr 3/96: 61

24543. 8.550907—8.550910 (4 separate discs): VIVALDI—Cello concertos (complete). *Wallfisch, Harvey, cellos; City of London Sinfonia; Kraemer, harpsichord, organ & cond.*
+ ARG 11-12/95: 224
+ Fa 9-10/95: 353
+ Gr 1/96: 65

24544. 8.550922: L. COUPERIN—Harpsichord music. *Cummings, harpsichord.*
● ARG 1-2/95: 98
+ EM 5/95: 335
+ Fa 1-2/95: 146
+ Gr 3/95: 71

24545. 8.550923: SCHUMANN—Symphonies no. 2, 4. *Polish National Radio Symphony Orch.; Wit, cond.*
- ARG 5-6/95: 173
- Fa 7-8/95: 315
+ Gr 3/95: 54

24546. 8.550928: WEBER—Symphonies no. 1-2; Turandot (excerpts); Silvana (excerpts); Die drei Pintos: entr'acte. *Queensland Phil. Orch.; Georgiadis, cond.*
+ ARG 3-4/95: 222
● Fa 3-4/95: 343
● Gr 2/95: 60

24547. 8.550929—8.550930 (2 separate discs): BACH—Clavierübung III. *Rübsam, organ.*

- Fa 9-10/96: 133
● Gr 12/94: 124

24548. 8.550931: SMETANA—Ma vlast. *Polish Radio Orch.; Wit, cond.*
● ARG 5-6/95: 179
+ Gr 4/95: 72

24549. 8.550932: REGER—Piano music. *Martin, piano.*
+ ARG 11-12/95: 184
+ Fa 11-12/95: 344
+ Gr 10/95: 98

24550. 8.550933: MAHLER—Das Lied von der Erde. *Donose, mezzo-soprano; Harper, tenor; National Symphony Orch. of Ireland; Halász, cond.*
+ ARG 5-6/96: 139
● Fa 3-4/96: 210
+ Gr 11/95: 137

24551. 8.550934: *French piano trios, vol. 1.* DEBUSSY—Piano trio. RAVEL—Piano trio. SCHMITT—Très lent, for piano trio. *Joachim Trio.*
+ ARG 1-2/96: 159
● Fa 11-12/95: 343
+ Gr 8/95: 92

24552. 8.550935: SAINT-SAËNS—Piano trios no. 1-2. *Joachim Trio.*
- ARG 9-10/95: 205
+ Fa 9-10/95: 303
+ Gr 12/95: 108

24553. 8.550936. BACH—Organ concertos; Trio sonatas. *Rübsam, organ.*
- Gr 12/94: 125

24554. 8.550937: TYE—Missa Euge bone; Peccavimus; Omnes gentes. MUNDY—Kyrie; Magnificat. *Oxford Camerata; Summerly, cond.*
+ ARG 7-8/95: 213
+ Fa 3-4/95: 323
+ Gr 2/95: 88

24555. 8.550938: SCHUMANN—Cello concerto. BRAHMS—Double concerto for violin and cello. *Kliegel, cello; Kaler, violin; National Symphony Orch. of Ireland; Constantine, cond.*
+ ARG 11-12/95: 201
+ Fa 11-12/95: 370
+ Gr 10/95: 48

24556. 8.550939: MENDELSSOHN—Piano works, vol. 1. *Frith, piano.*
+ ARG 11-12/95: 159
+ Fa 9-10/95: 259
+ Gr 11/95: 124

24557. 8.550940: MENDELSSOHN—Piano works, vol. 2. *Frith, piano.*
● ARG 7-8/95: 152
□ Fa 7-8/96: 239
+ Gr 5/96: 89

24558. 8.550946—8.550947 (2 separate discs): BEETHOVEN—Piano trios vol. 1-2. *Stuttgart Piano Trio.*

+ Fa 11-12/94: 164
+ Gr 7/94: 70

24559. 8.550948—8.550949 (2 separate discs): BEETHOVEN—Piano trios, vol. 3-4. *Stuttgart Piano Trio.*
+ ARG 1-2/95: 82
+ Fa 11-12/94: 164
● Gr 12/94: 117 (v.3)

24560. 8.550952: Gregorian chant for Good Friday: In passione et morte Domini. *Nova Schola Gregoriana; Turco, cond.*
+ ARG 11-12/94: 242
+ Fa 7-8/94: 308

24561. 8.550955: *Organ showpieces from St. Paul's Cathedral.* Music of Dubois, Franck, Gigout, Langlais, Reger, and others. *Lucas, organ.*
+ Gr 11/94: 121

24562. 8.550956: BRUCKNER—Motets. *Morley, organ; Norman, Wills, Cheetham, Lane, Saunders, vocalists; Choir of St. Bride's Church; Jones, cond.*
+ ARG 11-12/95: 100
+ Fa 9-10/95: 155
+ Gr 7/95: 94

24563. 8.550957: MENDELSSOHN—Symphonies no. 1, 5. *National Symphony Orch. of Ireland; Seifried, cond.*
● Gr 2/96: 50

24564. 8.550958: BRAHMS—Piano transcriptions. *Biret, piano.*
+ Fa 1-2/95: 129
+ Gr 5/95: 79

24565. 8.550959: WEBER—Piano concertos no. 1-2; Konzertstück; Polacca brillante. *Frith, piano; Irish Sinfonietta; O'Duinn, cond.*
+ ARG 5-6/96: 220
- Fa 7-8/96: 336
+ Gr 2/96: 63

24566. 8.550960: BACH—Two-part inventions, BWV 772-786; Three-part sinfonias, BWV 787-801. *Rübsam, piano.*
- Fa 11-12/95: 182

24567. 8.550966—8.550967 (2 separate discs): MENDELSSOHN—Piano quartets no. 1-3; String sextet. *Bartholdy Piano Quartet; Darzins, viola; Wagner, double bass.*
- ARG 11-12/94: 155
+ ARG 5-6/95: 139
● Fa 11-12/94: 300
● Fa 5-6/95: 261
+ Gr 10/94: 140

24568. 8.550968/9 (2 discs): PROKOFIEV—Cinderella: Suites no. 1-3; Scythian suite; On the Dnieper: Suite. *Ukrainian State Symphony Orch.; Kuchar, cond.*
+ ARG 1-2/97: 150
+ Fa 1-2/97: 226
● Gr 4/95: 66

24569. 8.550970/1 (2 discs): BACH—
Well-tempered clavier, book 2. *Jandó,
piano.*
   + ARG 3-4/95: 70
   + Gr 1/96: 78

24570. 8.550972: SHOSTAKOVICH—*String
quartets, vol. 1.* No. 4, 6-7. *Eder Quartet.*
   + ARG 1-2/95: 176
   + Fa 1-2/95: 268

24571. 8.550973: *String quartets, vol. 2.*
SHOSTAKOVICH—String quartets no. 1, 8-9.
Eder Quartet.
   + Fa 7-8/95: 320
   • Gr 10/95: 88

24572. 8.550974: SHOSTAKOVICH—String
quartets no. 3, 5. *Eder Quartet.*
   + ARG 5-6/96: 193

24573. 8.550979: *20th-century string
music.* BARTÓK—Divertimento.
BRITTEN—Simple symphony.
STRAVINSKY—Concerto in D. WALTON—
Henry V. Passacaglia. *Bournemouth
Sinfonietta; Studt, cond.*
   + ARG 1-2/95: 208
   + Gr 10/94: 128

24574. 8.550988—8.550990, 8.553006 (4
separate discs): WEBER—Piano music,
vol. 1-4. *Paley, piano.*
   • ARG 7-8/95: 224
   • Fa 3-4/95: 341
   • Gr 2/95: 76

24575. 8.550996: MOZART—
Divertimentos no. 2, 15. *Cappella
Istropolitana; Nerat, cond.*
   + ARG 5-6/96: 154
   + Gr 6/95: 53

24576. 8.550998: HILDEGARDE OF
BINGEN—Heavenly revelations. *Oxford
Camerata; Summerly, cond.*
   + ARG 3-4/96: 126
   + Fa 11-12/95: 276
   + Gr 9/95: 88

24577. 8.550999: BERLIOZ—Overtures:
Benvenuto Cellini; Waverley; Béatrice et
Bénédict; Le Roi Lear; Le carnaval
romain; Rob Roy; Le corsaire. *San
Diego Symphony Orch.; Talmi, cond.*
   + ARG 3-4/95: 74
   + Fa 3-4/95: 131

24578. 8.553001: DELIUS—Paris:
Nocturne; Brigg Fair; Eventyr; Irmelin:
Prelude; La calinda. *New Zealand
Symphony Orch.; Fredman, cond.*
   + Fa 3-4/96: 156
   • Gr 10/95: 52

24579. 8.553002: ALBINONI—Oboe
concertos, vol. 2. *Camden, Alty, oboes;
London Virtuosi; Georgiadis, cond.*
   + ARG 7-8/96: 65
   + Fa 5-6/96: 63
   + Gr 9/96: 48

24580. 8.553005: DVOŘÁK—A hero's
song; Czech suite; Hussite overture;
Festival march. *Polish National Radio
Symphony Orch.; Wit, cond.*
   + ARG 7-8/95: 107
   • Fa 7-8/95: 178
   + Gr 8/95: 70

24581. 8.553007: *19th century guitar
favorites.* Music of Aguado, Sor, and
Tárrega. *Kraft, guitar.*
   + Gr 1/95: 81

24582. 8.553008: RAVEL—Piano works,
vol. 2. *Thiollier, piano.*
   - ARG 5-6/95: 157
   - Fa 5-6/95: 306
   • Gr 7/95: 86

24583. 8.553009/10; 8.553080 (3
separate discs): CHABRIER—Piano works,
vol. 1-3. *Rabol, piano; Dugas, 2nd piano.*
   - ARG 5-6/95: 98
   • Fa 3-4/95: 153
   • Gr 2/95: 71

24584. 8.553012—8.553013 (2 separate
discs): BACH—English suites. *Rübsam,
piano.*
   - Fa 7-8/96: 89

24585. 8.553016: SZYMANOWSKI—Piano
works, vol. 1. *Roscoe, piano.*
   + ARG 3-4/96: 191
   • Fa 11-12/95: 395 (Corelonis)
   + Fa 11-12/95: 396 (Anderson)
   + Gr 9/95: 85

24586. 8.553017: TCHAIKOVSKY—Romeo
and Juliet fantasy-overture; The tempest
symphonic fantasia; Hamlet fantasy
overture. *Royal Phil. Orch.; Polish
National Radio Symphony Orch.; Leaper,
Wit, conds.*
   + ARG 5-6/95: 185
   + Fa 5-6/95: 359

24587. 8.553018: VERDI—Overtures, vol.
1. *Hungarian State Opera Orch.;
Morandi, cond.*
   + ARG 3-4/95: 210
   • Fa 3-4/95: 327

24588. 8.553021: PROKOFIEV—Piano
sonatas no. 2, 7, 8. *Glemser, piano.*
   + ARG 3-4/95: 158
   + Fa 3-4/95: 255 (Rabinowitz)
   + Fa 3-4/95: 259 (Gerber)

24589. 8.553025: *Psalms of the French
Reformation.* Music of Goudimel,
L'Estocart, and Sweelinck. *Claude
Goudimel Ensemble; Morel, cond.*
   - ARG 3-4/96: 246
   • Gr 6/95: 106

24590. 8.553026: BRAHMS—The 21
Hungarian dances (arr. Joachim for violin
and piano). JOACHIM—Andantino in A
minor; Romance in B♭ major.
Bisengaliev, violin; Lenehan, piano.
   + ARG 7-8/96: 88

   + Fa 5-6/96: 113
   • Gr 3/96: 61

24591. 8.553027: BIZET—Symphony in
C; Jeux d'enfants; La jolie fille de Perth:
scènes bohémiènnes. *New Zealand
Symphony Orch.; Johanos, cond.*
   + ARG 5-6/95: 90
   + Fa 7-8/95: 125

24592. 8.553030: *Operatic duets for
tenor and baritone.* Music of Rossini,
Bizet, Donizetti, and Verdi. *Lotrič, tenor;
Morozov, baritone; Bratislava Radio
Orch.; Wildner, cond.*
   - ARG 7-8/95: 267
   - Fa 5-6/95: 389
   + Gr 2/95: 106

24593. 8.553031/32 (2 discs): BACH—
Orgelbüchlein. *Rübsam, organ.*
   • ARG 5-6/95: 75

24594. 8.553033: BACH—Organ works.
Rübsam, organ.
   + Gr 10/95: 92

24595. 8.553034: BERLIOZ—Harold en
Italie; Les Francs-juges overture; Rêverie
et caprice. *Rolani, viola; Gruppman,
violin; San Diego Symphony Orch.;
Talmi, cond.*
   + ARG 1-2/97: 72
   + Fa 3-4/97: 123

24596. 8.553035: ALBINONI—Oboe
concertos, vol. 3. *Camden, Alty, oboes;
London Virtuosi; Georgiadis, cond.*
   + ARG 7-8/96: 65
   + Fa 5-6/96: 63
   + Gr 9/96: 48

24597. 8.553036: Spirituals. *Conrad,
mezzo-soprano; Page, piano; New
England Symphonic Ensemble; Hopkins,
cond.*
   + ARG 11-12/95: 267

24598. 8.553037: GRANADOS—Spanish
dances; Poetic scenes. *Kraft, guitar;
Razumovsky Sinfonia; Breiner, cond.*
   + ARG 11-12/95: 126
   + Gr 2/96: 46

24599. 8.553038: SHCHEDRIN—Carmen
ballet; Orchestra concerto no. 1 "Naughty
limericks". *Ukrainian National
Symphony Orch.; Kuchar, cond.*
   + ARG 5-6/95: 174
   + Fa 5-6/95: 341

24600. 8.553047—8.553048 (2 separate
discs): RAMEAU—Complete harpsichord
music. *Rowland, harpsichord.*
   + ARG 7-8/95: 178
   • Fa 5-6/95: 304 (Disc 1)
   + Fa 9-10/95: 287 (Disc 2)

24601. 8.553050: NIELSEN—Wind quintet,
op. 43. FERNSTROM—Wind quintet, op. 59.
KVANDAL—Wind quintet, op. 34; Three
hymn tunes, op. 23b. *Oslo Wind
Ensemble.*

□ ARG 3-4/95: 246
+ Fa 3-4/95: 245
+ Gr 3/95: 69

24602. 8.553051—8.553052 (2 separate discs): BERWALD—Symphonies; Piano concerto; Estrella de Soria overture. *Sivelöv, piano; Helsingborg Symphony Orch.; Kamu, cond.*
  ● ARG 7-8/96: 82
  + Fa 7-8/96: 112
  + Fi 10/96: 149
  ● Gr 6/96: 41

24603. 8.553054: PROKOFIEV—Symphonies no. 3, 7. *Ukrainian State Symphony Orch.; Kuchar, cond.*
  ● ARG 3-4/96: 167
  + Fa 3-4/96: 250
  ● Gr 10/95: 64

24604. 8.553056: PROKOFIEV—Symphony no. 5; The year 1941. *National Symphony Orch. of the Ukraine; Kuchar, cond.*
  ● ARG 9-10/96: 182
  ● Fa 9-10/96: 291
  ● Gr 7/96: 60

24605. 8.553063: *Piano works, vol. 1.* TCHAIKOVSKY—Piano sonata, op. 37; Six morceaux, op. 51. *Yablonskaya, piano.*
  + ARG 11-12/95: 218
  + Fa 9-10/95: 336
  ● Gr 10/95: 101

24606. 8.553069: PROKOFIEV—Symphony no. 6; Waltz suite. *Ukrainian State Symphony Orch.; Kuchar, cond.*
  ● ARG 3-4/96: 167
  + Fa 3-4/96: 250
  + Gr 1/96: 59

24607. 8.553076: DANZI—Wind quintets op. 56; Sextet for 2 clarinets, 2 horns, and 2 bassoons. *Michael Thompson Wind Quintet.*
  + ARG 3-4/96: 105
  + Fa 3-4/96: 152
  + Gr 11/95: 105

24608. 8.553078: HINDEMITH—Symphony Mathis der Maler; Nobilissima visione; Symphonic metamorphosis on themes of Carl Maria von Weber. *New Zealand Symphony Orch.; Decker, cond.*
  + ARG 7-8/95: 124
  ● Fa 7-8/95: 206
  ● Gr 6/95: 46

24609. 8.553079: REGER—Variations and fugue on a theme by Mozart; Variations and fugue on a merry theme by J.A. Hiller. *New Zealand Symphony Orch.; Decker, cond.*
  + ARG 9-10/95: 201
  - Fa 9-10/95: 290
  + Gr 7/95: 64

24610. 8.553081: MARAIS—Viol music for the Sun King. *Spectre de la Rose.*
  + ARG 9-10/96: 159
  + Fa 7-8/96: 234

24611. 8.553082: SCHUMANN—Symphonies no. 1, 3. *Polish National Radio Symphony Orch.; Wit, cond.*
  + ARG 1-2/97: 168
  + Fa 1-2/97: 265
  ● Gr 11/96: 98

24612. 8.553083: J.C. BACH—Sinfonias, vol. 1. *Camerata Budapest; Gmür, cond.*
  ● ARG 11-12/95: 68
  ● Fa 11-12/95: 176
  + Fi 10/96: 148
  ● Gr 7/95: 43

24613. 8.553084: J.C. BACH—*Sinfonias, vol. 2.* Symphonies, op. 6. *Camerata Budapest; Gmür, cond.*
  ● ARG 9-10/96: 95
  ● Fa 7-8/95: 99
  + Fi 10/96: 148
  ● Gr 7/95: 43

24614. 8.553085: J.C. BACH—*Sinfonias, vol. 3.* Symphonies, op. 9; Sinfonia concertante, T. 284-4. *Camerata Budapest; Gmür, cond.*
  ● ARG 9-10/95: 95
  ● Fa 7-8/95: 99
  + Fi 10/96: 148
  ● Gr 7/95: 43

24615. 8.553087: DUFAY—Missa L'homme armé; Supremum est mortalibus. Gregorian chant. *Oxford Camerata; Summerly, cond.*
  + ARG 11-12/95: 114
  + Fa 11-12/95: 241
  ● Gr 10/95: 107

24616. 8.553089: VERDI—Opera overtures, vol. 2. *Hungarian State Opera Orch.; Morandi, cond.*
  + ARG 3-4/95: 210

24617. 8.553090: BEETHOVEN—Septet, op. 20; Quintet, H. 19; Sextet, op. 81b. *Various performers.*
  + ARG 1-2/96: 83
  + Fa 11-12/95: 205
  + Gr 11/95: 130

24618. 8.553093: SCHUBERT—Symphonies no. 1-2. *Failoni Chamber Orch.; Halász, cond.*
  + ARG 3-4/95: 181
  + Fa 5-6/95: 330
  ● Gr 8/95: 81

24619. 8.553094: SCHUBERT—Symphonies no. 3, 6. *Failoni Chamber Orch.; Halász, cond.*
  + Fa 5-6/95: 330
  ● Gr 8/95: 81

24620. 8.553095: SCHUBERT—Symphony no. 4; Symphony in C major (orch. by Joachim from the Grand duo sonatas, D. 812). *Failoni Chamber Orch.; Halász, cond.*
  ● ARG 7-8/95: 189
  + Fa 7-8/95: 304
  ● Gr 8/95: 81

24621. 8.553096: SCHUBERT—Symphony no. 9. *Failoni Chamber Orch.; Halász, cond.*
  ● ARG 7-8/95: 189
  + Fa 7-8/95: 305
  ● Gr 8/95: 81

24622. 8.553097: BACH—Selections from the W.F. Bach notebook; Five little preludes, BWV 939-943. *Rübsam, piano.*
  + Fa 9-10/95: 129

24623. 8.553103: MOZART—String quintets, K. 174, 515. *Eder Quartet; Fehérvári, viola.*
  + ARG 7-8/95: 159
  - Fa 3-4/95: 242
  + Gr 4/95: 84

24624. 8.553104: MOZART—*String quintets, vol. 2.* No. 2, 4. *Eder Quartet; Fehérvári, viola.*
  + ARG 9-10/96: 172
  + Gr 1/96: 72

24625. 8.553106: *Scandinavian string music.* Music of Grieg, Svendsen, Nielsen, and Wiren. *Bournemouth Sinfonietta; Studt, cond.*
  + ARG 11-12/95: 239
  + Fa 11-12/95: 503

24626. 8.553107: BRITTEN—Sinfonia da requiem; Peter Grimes: four sea interludes and passacaglia; An American overture. *New Zealand Symphony Orch.; Fredman, cond.*
  ● ARG 11-12/95: 99
  + Fa 9-10/95: 155
  ● Gr 10/95: 51

24627. 8.553110—8.553111 (2 separate discs): MOZART—Violin sonatas. *Nishizaki, violin; Jandó, piano.*
  + ARG 7-8/96: 163
  ● Fa 5-6/96: 224
  ● Gr 2/96: 68

24628. 8.553113: SCHUBERT—Lieder. *Russell, soprano; Hill, piano; Campbell, clarinet.*
  + ARG 1-2/97: 165
  + Fa 11-12/96: 363
  - Gr 8/96: 87

24629. 8.553115: *Swedish orchestra favorites.* Music of Soderman, Stenhammar, Larsson, Peterson-Berger, Wirén, and Alfvén. *Helsingborg Symphony Orch.; Kamu, cond.*
  ● ARG 3-4/96: 221
  + Fa 3-4/96: 391

24630. 8.553122: WEBER—Clarinet quintet; Introduction, theme, and variations for clarinet and string quartet; Grand duo concertante for clarinet and piano; Variations on a theme from Silvana. *Berkes, clarinet; Auer Quartet; Jandó, piano.*
  + ARG 11-12/95: 232
  + Fa 11-12/95: 427
  - Fa 3-4/96: 319

24631. 8.553123: Russian chant for vespers. *Novospassky Monastery Choir.*
+ Fa 11-12/95: 460

24632. 8.553124—8.553125 (2 separate discs): MASSENET—Hérodiade: Ballet music; Suites no. 1-7. *New Zealand Symphony Orch.; Ossonce, cond.*
+ ARG 11-12/95: 155
• Fa 11-12/95: 300 (Anderson)
+ Fa 11-12/95: 300 (McColley)
+ Gr 9/95: 60

24633. 8.553126: SHOSTAKOVICH—Piano concertos no. 1-2; Festive overture; The age of gold: Suite. *Houstoun, piano; Taber, trumpet; New Zealand Symphony Orch.; Lyndon-Gee, cond.*
• ARG 5-6/96: 191
• Fa 3-4/96: 284
• Gr 2/96: 59

24634. 8.553127: HAYDN—Piano sonatas, vol. 4. *Jandó, piano.*
+ Fa 5-6/95: 206
+ Gr 6/95: 76

24635. 8.553128: HAYDN—Piano sonatas, vol. 5. *Jandó, piano.*
+ Fa 5-6/95: 206
+ Gr 7/95: 85

24636. 8.553129: PURCELL—Funeral music; Anthems. *Oxford Camerata; Summerly, cond.*
• ARG 7-8/95: 173
+ Gr 2/95: 89

24637. 8.553130: GIBBONS—Sacred music. *Oxford Camerata; Summerly, cond.*
• ARG 9-10/96: 124
+ Fa 11-12/96: 251
+ Gr 8/96: 84

24638. 8.553131: Chominciamento di gioia. *Ensemble Unicorn.*
+ ARG 7-8/95: 256
+ Fa 11-12/95: 166
+ Gr 8/95: 98

24639. 8.553132: On the way to Bethlehem. Music of the medieval pilgrim. *Ensemble Oni Wytars; Ensemble Unicorn.*
- ARG 11-12/96: 258
• Fa 9-10/96: 389

24640. 8.553133: ALFONSO EL SABIO—Cantigas de Santa Maria. *Ensemble Unicorn.*
• ARG 3-4/96: 75
+ Fa 11-12/95: 166

24641. 8.553134—8.553135 (2 separate discs). BACH—Chorale preludes, vol. 1-2. *Rübsam, organ.*
- Gr 4/96: 73

24642. 8.553136: PROKOFIEV—String quartets no. 1-2; Cello sonata. *Aurora String Quartet; Grebanier, cello;*

Guggenheim, piano.
• Gr 6/95: 71

24643. 8.553141: PAGANINI—Centone di sonate, vol. 1. *Hammer, violin; Kraft, guitar.*
+ ARG 7-8/95: 165
+ Fa 7-8/95: 266
+ Gr 5/95: 70

24644. 8.553142: PAGANINI—Centone di sonate, vol. 2. *Hammer, violin; Kraft, guitar.*
+ Fa 11-12/95: 327
+ Gr 2/96: 68

24645. 8.553146: HAYDN—String quartets, op. 77, no. 1-2. *Kodály Quartet.*
+ Fa 3-4/96: 180
+ Gr 10/95: 82

24646. 8.553154: Russian favorites. *Red Army Chorus & Band; Fedorov, cond.*
+ ARG 11-12/96: 271
+ Fa 9-10/96: 388

24647. 8.553158: SCRIABIN—Piano sonatas, vol. 1. *Glemser, piano.*
+ ARG 5-6/97: 202
• Fa 1-2/97: 268
+ Gr 8/96: 76

24648. 8.553159: CHOPIN—Music for cello and piano. *Kliegel, cello; Glemser, piano.*
• ARG 1-2/97: 89
+ Fa 1-2/97: 136
+ Gr 11/96: 105

24649. 8.553161: MENDELSSOHN—String symphonies no. 1-6. *Northern Chamber Orch.; Ward, cond.*
+ ARG 5-6/96: 150
+ Fa 7-8/96: 240
+ Gr 12/96: 80

24650. 8.553164: SPOHR—Piano trios no. 3, 5. *Hartley Piano Trio.*
• ARG 3-4/96: 187
+ Fa 3-4/96: 290
+ Gr 1/96: 77

24651. 8.553173: CHARPENTIER—Messe des morts, H. 7; Litanies à la Vierge, H. 89; Confitebor, H. 220; Nisi Dominus, H. 160; Élévation, H. 251; Laudate pueri Dominum, H. 203. *Le Concert Spirituel; Niquet, cond.*
+ ARG 7-8/95: 101
+ Fa 7-8/95: 156
+ Gr 6/95: 87

24652. 8.553174: CHARPENTIER—Vespres à la Vierge. *Le Concert Spirituel; Niquet, cond.*
+ Gr 3/96: 80

24653. 8.553176: POULENC—Stabat mater; Gloria; Litanies à la vierge noire. *Borst, soprano; Lebrun, organ; Choeur Régional Vittoria d'Île-de-France; Orchestre de la Cité; Piquemal, cond.*
• Gr 10/95: 108

24654. 8.553178: KROMMER—Clarinet concerto, op. 36; Concertos for two clarinets, op. 35, 91. *Berkes, Takashima, clarinets; Nicolaus Esterházy Sinfonia.*
+ ARG 9-10/95: 164
+ Fa 11-12/95: 288
+ Gr 8/95: 76

24655. 8.553181: STRAVINSKY—Pulcinella; Danses concertantes. *James, Bostridge, Herford, vocalists; Bournemouth Sinfonietta; Sanderling, cond.*
+ ARG 5-6/96: 206
• Fa 5-6/96: 292
+ Gr 5/96: 66

24656. 8.553183: BRITTEN—Choral music. *Kanga, harp; Wells, piano; New London Children's Choir; Corp, cond.*
+ ARG 11-12/96: 102

24657. 8.553184/5 (2 discs): PROKOFIEV—Romeo and Juliet. *National Symphony Orch. of Ukraine; Mogrelia, cond.*
+ ARG 5-6/96: 165
• Fa 7-8/96: 265
+ Gr 7/96: 60

24658. 8.553190: LANGLAIS—Suite medievale; Apocalypse meditations. *Mathieu, organ.*
+ ARG 5-6/96: 134

24659. 8.553192: Ego sum resurrectio. *Aurora Surgit Women's Schola; Randon, cond.*
• ARG 7-8/96: 261
+ Fa 5-6/96: 338

24660. 8.553193: BACH—Sonatas no. 1-3 for unaccompanied violin (arr. for guitar). *Goluses, guitar.*
• ARG 1-2/96: 75
+ Fa 11-12/95: 187
• Gr 12/95: 112

24661. 8.553194: STAMITZ—Symphonies, vol. 1. *New Zealand Chamber Orch.; Armstrong, cond.*
+ ARG 7-8/96: 203
+ Fa 7-8/96: 313

24662. 8.553195: BERLIOZ—Romeo and Juliet; The Trojans at Carthage: Prelude; Royal hunt and storm. *San Diego Master Chorale; San Diego Symphony Orch.; Talmi, cond.*
+ ARG 11-12/95: 88
- Fa 11-12/95: 211
• Gr 11/95: 80

24663. 8.553196: DURUFLÉ—Requiem; Motets; Prelude and fugue on ALAIN; Scherzo; Notre Père. *Lebrun, organ; Ensemble vocal Michel Piquemal; Orch. de la Cité.*
+ ARG 7-8/96: 106
+ Gr 11/95: 131

24664. 8.553197: DURUFLÉ—Mass, Cum jubilo/Suite; Prelude, adagio and choral

variations. *Ensemble Michel Piquemal; Orchestre de la Cité; Piquemal, cond.; Lebrun, organ.*
- ARG 3-4/96: 107
+ Gr 11/95: 131

24665. 8.553204: VIVALDI—Concertos for 2 horns, RV 538, 539; Concerto for 2 flutes, RV 533; Concerto for 2 trumpets, RV 537; Concerto for 2 oboes and 2 clarinets, RV 560; Concerto for oboe and bassoon, RV 545. *City of London Sinfonia; Kraemer, harpsichord & cond.*
+ ARG 11-12/95: 225
+ Fa 9-10/95: 353
+ Gr 1/96: 65

24666. 8.553205: SPOHR—Piano trios no. 2, 4. *Hartley Piano Trio.*
- ARG 3-4/96: 187
+ Fa 3-4/96: 290

24667. 8.553206: SPOHR—Piano trio no. 1; Piano quintet. *Handy, violin; Outram, viola; Hartley Piano Trio.*
- ARG 5-6/96: 203
+ Fa 5-6/96: 285

24668. 8.553207: RESPIGHI—Piano concerto; Toccata for piano and orchestra; Fantasia slava for piano and orchestra. *Scherbakov, piano; Slovak Radio Symphony Orch., Bratislava; Griffiths, cond.*
- ARG 1-2/96: 160
+ Fa 11-12/95: 344
+ Gr 11/95: 90

24669. 8.553209: WEELKES—Anthems. *Oxford Camerata; Summerly, cond.; Cooper, organ.*
- ARG 9-10/96: 124
+ Fa 11-12/96: 251
+ Gr 7/96: 94

24670. 8.553213: STAMITZ—Orchestral trios, vol. 1. *New Zealand Chamber Orch.; Armstrong, cond.*
+ ARG 7-8/96: 203
+ Fa 7-8/96: 313

24671. 8.553214/5 (2 separate discs): *Early French organ music, vol. 1-2.* Music of Marchand, Compère, Japart, G. Corrette, Grigny, Titelouze, Jullien, Lebègue, Roberday, Du Mont, L. Couperin, Attaignant, Raison, Gigault, D'Anglebert, and Anon. *Payne, organ.*
- Gr 10/95: 102

24672. 8.553266: BEETHOVEN—Piano concertos no. 4-5. *Vladar, piano; Cappella Istropolitana; Wordsworth, cond.*
+ ARG 7-8/96: 73

24673. 8.553267: GRIEG—Piano concerto. LISZT—Piano concerto no. 1. MENDELSSOHN—Piano concerto no. 2. *Jandó, piano; Budapest Symphony Orch.; A. Ligeti, cond.; Banowetz, piano; CSR Symphony Orch. Bratislava; O. Dohnányi, cond.; Frith, piano; Slovak*

State Phil. Orch. Kosice; Stankovsky, cond. Reissue.
- Fa 7-8/96: 181

24674. 8.553289: C.P.E. BACH—Sinfonias, Wq. 183, no. 1-4. W.F. BACH—Sinfonia in F major. *Salzburg Chamber Phil. Orch.; Lee, cond.*
+ ARG 7-8/96: 67
+ Fa 5-6/96: 66
+ Gr 4/96: 40

24675. 8.553290: DEBUSSY—Piano works, vol. 1. *Thiollier, piano.*
+ ARG 3-4/96: 106
- Fa 3-4/96: 156
+ Gr 1/96: 79

24676. 8.553291: DEBUSSY—Piano works, vol. 2. *Thiollier, piano.*
- Fa 7-8/96: 153
- Gr 4/96: 74

24677. 8.553298: C.P.E. BACH—Cello concertos. *Hugh, cello; Bournemouth Sinfonietta; Studt, cond.*
+ Gr 8/96: 40

24678. 8.553301: CARULLI—Guitar sonatas, op. 21, no. 1-3; Op. 5. *Savino, guitar.*
+ ARG 11-12/96: 110
+ Fa 7-8/96: 142

24679. 8.553302: SOR—Guitar duets. *Kubica, Berkel, guitars.*
+ ARG 11-12/96: 213

24680. 8.553303: KUHLAU—Flute quintets, op. 51. *Rafn, flute; Sjögren, violin; Rasmussen, Andersen; violas; Johnasen, cello.*
- ARG 1-2/96: 131
+ Fa 11-12/95: 288
+ Gr 10/95: 82

24681. 8.553304: LISZT—A Faust symphony. *Molnár, tenor; Hungarian State Choir; Orch. of the Ferenc Liszt Academy; Ligeti, cond.*
+ ARG 3-4/96: 145
- Fa 3-4/96: 203
+ Gr 10/95: 58

24682. 8.553310: *Portuguese polyphony.* Music of Cardoso, Lobo, Magalhaes, Fonseca, Trosylho, and Escobar. *Ars Nova; Holton, cond.*
+ ARG 5-6/96: 249
+ EM 5/96: 354
+ Fa 1-2/97: 321
+ Gr 3/96: 91

24683. 8.553311: LASSUS—Lagrime di San Pietro. *Ars Nova; Holton, cond.*
+ ARG 3-4/96: 142
- Fa 3-4/96: 199
+ Gr 1/96: 90

24684. 8.553318: *Lamenti barocchi, vol. 1.* Music of Monteverdi, Sances, Rossi, Strozzi, and Anon. *San Petronio Cappella Musicale; Vartolo, cond.*

- EM 5/96: 358
- Gr 3/96: 92

24685. 8.553319: *Lamenti barocchi, vol. 2.* Music of Monteverdi, Bassani, L. Rossi, Fontana, Strozzi, Marcello, and Anon. *Cappella Musicale of San Petronio; Vartolo, cond.*
+ ARG 1-2/97: 217
+ Fa 1-2/97: 208

24686. 8.553321: PERTI—Lamentations. *Cappella Musicale di S. Petronio di Bologna; Vartolo, cond.*
+ Fa 9-10/96: 286

24687. 8.553322: MONTEVERDI—Ballo delle ingrate; Combattimento di Tancredi e Clorinda. *Cappella Musicale of San Petronio; Vartolo, cond.*
- ARG 3-4/97: 182
+ Fa 1-2/97: 208

24688. 8.553325: *A royal songbook: Spanish music from the time of Columbus.* Music of Anon., Escobar, Anchieta, Garcimunos, Mudarra, Fernandes, Gabriel, Ockeghem, Encina, Ponce, Roman, Ortiz, Luchas, Torre, and Vilches. *McGreevy, soprano; Heringman, vihuela, lute & guitar; Musica Antiqua of London; Thorby, cond.*
+ ARG 11-12/96: 262
+ Fa 9-10/96: 393

24689. 8.553333: Sonatas by Hartmann, Frohlich, Weyse, and Kuhlau. *Andreasen, flute; Øland, piano.*
□ ARG 3-4/96: 229

24690. 8.553338/9 (2 discs): DELIBES—Sylvia. SAINT-SAËNS—Fête populaire. *Razumovsky Sinfonia; Mogrelia, cond.*
- ARG 1-2/97: 94
+ Fa 11-12/96: 230
+ Gr 6/96: 44

24691. 8.553340: SOR—Grand sonata, op. 22; Divertissement, op. 23; Eight small pieces, op. 24; Grand sonata, op. 25. *Holzman, guitar.*
+ ARG 1-2/97: 173
+ Fa 9-10/96: 330
+ Gr 8/96: 77

24692. 8.553342: SOR—Fantasy, op. 58; Elegiac fantasy; Twenty-five progressive studies. *Goluses, guitar.*
+ ARG 1-2/97: 173
+ Fa 11-12/96: 384
+ Gr 8/96: 77

24693. 8.553352: *Tugend und Untugend (Virtue and vice): German secular songs and instrumental music from the time of Luther.* Music of Isaac, Obrecht, Senfl, Hofhaimer, Finck, Ammerbach, Bruck, Küpfer, Meyer, Rhaw, and from the Glogauer Liederbuch. *Convivium Musicum Gothenburgense; Ensemble Villanella; Burger, cond.*
- ARG 5-6/96: 248

• Fa 3-4/96: 353
+ Gr 1/96: 97

24694. 8.553353: BOULEZ—Piano sonatas
no. 1-3. *Biret, piano.*
+ ARG 1-2/96: 90
• Fa 3-4/96: 225
+ Gr 11/95: 122

24695. 8.553354: SOR—Guitar music.
Teicholz, guitar.
• ARG 1-2/97: 173
+ Fa 1-2/97: 275
+ Gr 3/97: 76

24696. 8.553356 (2 discs): DELIBES—
Coppélia; La source (excerpts).
*Bratislava Radio Symphony Orch.;
Mogrelia, cond.*
+ ARG 5-6/96: 103
+ Fa 7-8/96: 154
+ Gr 6/96: 44

24697. 8.553367: J.C. BACH—*Sinfonias,
vol. 4.* Symphonies, op. 18. *Failoni
Chamber Orch.; Gmür, cond.*
+ ARG 5-6/96: 70
• Fa 7-8/96: 82
+ Fi 10/96: 148
• Gr 7/96: 46

24698. 8.553368/9 (2 discs):
DITTERSDORF—Six symphonies after
Ovid's Metamorphoses. *Failoni Orch.;
Gmür, cond.*
• Gr 7/96: 48

24699. 8.553371: DVOŘÁK—String
quartets no. 12-13. *Vlach Quartet.*
+ Fa 5-6/96: 146
+ Gr 4/96: 64

24700. 8.553372: DVOŘÁK—String
quartets no. 8, 11. *Vlach Quartet.*
+ ARG 11-12/96: 117
+ Fa 11-12/96: 241
+ Gr 9/96: 69

24701. 8.553386: STRAVINSKY—Sonata for
two pianos; Concerto for two pianos; Le
sacre du printemps. *Frith, Hill, pianos.*
• ARG 11-12/96: 218
- Fa 11-12/96: 388
+ Fa 1-2/97: 284
• Gr 9/96: 72

24702. 8.553391—8.553393 (3 separate
discs): GRIEG—*Piano music, vol. 5-7.*
Norwegian melodies, no. 1-152. *Steen-
Nøkleberg, piano, clavichord, organ, &
harmonium.*
• ARG 5-6/96: 118
+ Fa 5-6/96: 160
+ Gr 5/96: 81

24703. 8.553394—8.553396 (3 separate
discs)· GRIEG— *Piano music, vol. 8-10.*
Lyric pieces. *Steen-Nøkleberg, piano.*
• ARG 5-6/96: 118
+ Fa 7-8/96: 182
+ Gr 5/96: 81

24704. 8.553397—8.553398 (2 separate
discs): GRIEG—*Piano music, vol. 11-12.*
Orchestral transcriptions. *Steen-
Nøkleberg, piano.*
• ARG 5-6/96: 118 (v.11)
+ Fa 7-8/96: 183 (v.11)
+ Fa 9-10/96: 207 (v.12)
+ Gr 8/96: 74

24705. 8.553398: GRIEG—Piano music,
vol. 12-14. *Steen-Nøkleberg, piano.*
+ Fa 9-10/96: 207
+ Gr 8/96: 74

24706. 8.553402: WALTON—Symphony
no. 2; Viola concerto; Johannesburg
Festival overture. *Tomter, viola; English
Northern Philharmonia; Daniel, cond.*
+ ARG 11-12/96: 234
+ Fa 9-10/96: 354
+ Gr 5/96: 68

24707. 8.553406: ARNOLD—Symphonies
no. 1-2. *Irish National Orch.; Penny,
cond.*
+ ARG 7-8/96: 66
+ Fa 7-8/96: 78
+ Gr 5/96: 52

24708. 8.553407: FORQUERAY—
Harpsichord suites no. 1, 3, 5.
Beauséjour, harpsichord.
• ARG 3-4/96: 113
+ Fa 3-4/96: 166
+ Gr 1/96: 80

24709. 8.553408—8.553409 (2 separate
discs): BENDA—Sinfonias. *Prague
Chamber Orch.; C. Benda, cond.*
+ ARG 7-8/96: 79
+ Fa 5-6/96: 106

24710. 8.553410: BRICCIALDI—Wind
quintet, op. 124. CAMBINI—Wind quintets
no. 1-3. *Avalon Wind Quintet.*
+ Fa 9-10/96: 162

24711. 8.553411: KABALEVSKY—Suites
from Romeo and Juliet, The Comedians,
and Colas Breugnon. *Moscow Phil.
Symphony Orch.; Jelvakov, cond.*
• ARG 1-2/97: 125
+ Fa 3-4/97: 201

24712. 8.553412: VERACINI—Overtures
no. 1-4, 6. *Accademia I Filarmonici;
Martini, cond.*
+ ARG 5-6/96: 215
+ Fa 5-6/96: 304

24713. 8.553414: BOISMORTIER—Flute
sonatas, op. 91. *American Baroque.*
+ ARG 11-12/96: 95
+ Fa 9-10/96: 157

24714. 8.553417: KALINNIKOV
Symphonies no. 1-2. *Ukrainian State
Symphony Orch.; Kuchar, cond.*
+ ARG 3-4/96: 133
+ Fa 5-6/96: 181

24715. 8.553431: BEETHOVEN—Overtures,
vol. 2. *Nicolaus Esterhazy Sinfonia;*

Drahos, cond.
+ ARG 5-6/96: 81
+ Fa 9-10/96: 147

24716. 8.553434: ALKAN—Piano music.
Martin, Ringeissen, piano.
+ ARG 5-6/96: 68
• Fa 7-8/96: 74

24717. 8.553443: MILHAUD—Saudades do
Brazil; La muse ménagère (à
M.M.M.M.); L'album de Madame
Bovary. *Tharaud, piano; M. Milhaud,
narrator.*
+ ARG 7-8/96: 156
+ Fa 5-6/96: 211
+ Gr 5/96: 89

24718. 8.553444: PURCELL—Te Deum;
The noise of foreign wars; Raise, raise
the voice; Sonata in D major for trumpet
and strings; Jubilate Deo. *Bern, Bisatt,
Robson, Purefoy, Honeyman, Guthrie,
vocalists; Staff, natural trumpet; Orch. &
Chorus of the Golden Age; Glenton,
cond.*
• ARG 11-12/96: 180
• Fa 9-10/96: 295
+ Gr 7/96: 90

24719. 8.553445: LOCATELLI—Concerti
grossi, op. 1, no. 1-6. *Cappella
Istropolitana; Krček, cond.*
- Fa 11-12/96: 290

24720. 8.553458: DUFAY—Chansons.
*Landauer, counter-tenor; Ensemble
Unicorn; Posch, cond.*
+ ARG 1-2/97: 99
+ Fa 11-12/96: 237
• Gr 9/96: 86

24721. 8.553459: MARTINŮ—Chamber
music with flute. *Feinstein Ensemble.*
• Gr 4/96: 67

24722. 8.553460: BLISS—Colour
symphony; Adam Zero. *English Northern
Philharmonia; Jones, cond.*
+ ARG 1-2/97: 76
+ Fa 3-4/97: 126
• Fi 3/97: 114
+ Gr 10/96: 50

24723. 8.553462: SOLER—Harpsichord
sonatas, vol. 1. *Rowland, harpsichord.*
+ ARG 11-12/96: 213
+ Fa 11-12/96: 384
□ Gr 1/97: 81

24724. 8.553469: PARRY—Symphony no.
2; Symphonic variations; Overture to an
unwritten tragedy. *Scottish National
Orch.; Penny, cond.*
+ ARG 1-2/97: 148
+ Gr 10/96: 58

24725. 8.553473: HUMMEL—Complete
flute sonatas; Trio. *Daoust, flute; Picard,
piano; Dolin, cello.*
• ARG 1-2/97: 122
+ Fa 1-2/97: 150
+ Gr 12/96: 98

NAXOS

24726. 8.553474: BEETHOVEN—
Symphonies no. 1, 6. *Nicolaus Esterházy
Sinfonia; Drahos, cond.*
- ● ARG 11-12/96: 92
- ● Fa 9-10/96: 149
- - Gr 9/96: 48

24727. 8.553475: BEETHOVEN—
Symphonies no. 3, 8. *Nicolaus Esterházy
Sinfonia; Drahos, cond.*
- + ARG 1-2/97: 70
- ● Fa 1-2/97: 105
- ● Gr 9/96: 49

24728. 8.553495: FEENEY—Cinderella:
ballet suite. MULDOWNEY—The Brontes:
ballet suite. DAVIS—A Christmas carol:
ballet suite. *Northern Ballet Theatre
Orch.; Pryce-Jones, cond.*
- + ARG 11-12/97: 241
- ● Fa 11-12/96: 229
- + Gr 3/96: 44

24729. 8.553496/7 (2 discs): GLIÈRE—
The red poppy. *St. Petersburg State
Symphony Orch.; Anichanov, cond.*
- + ARG 9-10/96: 126
- + Fa 9-10/96: 196

24730. 8.553498: KROMMER—Partitas for
winds op. 57, 71, 78; Marches, op. 31.
*Budapest Wind Ensemble; Berkes,
clarinet & cond.*
- + Gr 8/96: 66

24731. 8.553502: Ambrosian chant. *Dulci
Jubilo; Turco, cond.*
- + Fa 9-10/96: 394
- + Fa 11-12/96: 443

24732. 8.553503/4 (2 discs):
GLAZUNOV—Raymonda. *Moscow Phil.
Symphony Orch.; Anisimov, cond.*
- + ARG 9-10/96: 126
- + Fa 9-10/96: 195
- + Gr 8/96: 46

24733. 8.553520/1 (2 discs): MERULO—
Missa apostolorum; Toccata secondo 1
tono; Magnificat 2 tono. *Muñoz, organ;
Grégor vocal group; Andreo, cond.*
- + Fa 7-8/96: 241

24734. 8.553524: VIERNE—Organ
symphonies no. 3, 6. *Mathieu, organ.*
- + ARG 11-12/96: 228
- + Fa 11-12/96: 411
- + Gr 9/96: 62

24735. 8.553526: ARNOLD—Dances.
*Queensland Symphony Orch.; Penny,
cond.*
- + ARG 11-12/96: 78
- + Fa 1-2/97: 76
- + Gr 10/96: 47

24736. 8.553531: *The art of baroque
trumpet, vol. 1.* Music of Torelli, Purcell,
Handel, Telemann, and others. *Eklund,
trumpet; Drottningholm Baroque
Ensemble; Sparf, cond.*
- + ARG 11-12/96: 255
- + Gr 11/96: 102

24737. 8.553537: GLAZUNOV—Orchestra
music. *Moscow Phil. Symphony Orch.;
Krimets, cond.*
- + ARG 9-10/96: 125
- ● Fa 11-12/96: 253
- ● Gr 10/96: 54

24738. 8.553540: ARNOLD—Symphony
no. 9. *National Symphony Orch. of
Ireland; Penny, cond.*
- + ARG 9-10/96: 77
- + Fa 9-10/96: 126
- + Fi 4/97: 105
- + Gr 5/96: 53

24739. 8.553557: GUBAIDULINA—Seven
last words; Silenzio; In croce. *Kliegel,
cello; Moser, bayan; Rabus, violin;
Camerata Transsylvanica; Selmeczi,
cond.*
- + ARG 7-8/96: 121
- + Fa 7-8/96: 184
- + Gr 6/96: 46

24740. 8.553575: GLAZUNOV—The King
of the Jews. *Moscow Phil. Symphony
Orch. & Chorus; Golovchin, cond.*
- ● ARG 1-2/97: 111
- - Fa 3-4/97: 179
- ● Gr 4/97: 54

24741. 8.553634: FAURÉ—Barcarolles;
Ballade. *Volondat, piano.*
- + Fa 1-2/97: 163
- - Gr 11/96: 120

24742. 8.553636: BENEVOLI—Missa
azzolina; Dixit Dominus; Laetatus sum;
Miserere; Magnificat. *Le Concert
Spirituel; Niquet, cond.*
- + ARG 1-2/97: 72
- + Fa 1-2/97: 108
- + Gr 1/97: 84

24743. 8.553661: SIBELIUS—Kyllikki;
Pieces, op. 75, 85; Characteristic
impressions, op. 103; Impromptus, op. 5;
Finlandia (arr. Sibelius). *Lauriala, piano.*
- + ARG 11-12/96: 212
- + Fa 11-12/96: 381
- + Fa 1-2/97: 274

24744. 8.553718: BRIDGE—Music for
string quartet. *Maggini Quartet.*
- + ARG 11-12/96: 101
- + Fi 4/97: 105

24745. 8.660001/2 (2 discs): PUCCINI—
Tosca. *Miricioiu, Lamberti; Slovak Phil.
Chorus; Czecho-Slovak Radio Phil.
Orch., Bratislava; Rahbari, cond.*
- + Fa 11-12/92: 324
- ● Gr 10/91: 188

24746. 8.660003/4 (2 discs): PUCCINI—La
bohème. *Orgonasova, Welch, Gonzales,
Previati; Slovak Phil. Chorus; Bratislava
Radio Orch.; Humburg, cond.*
- ● ARG 7-8/92: 201
- + Fa 11-12/92: 324
- ● ON 9/92: 48

24747. 8.660013 (2 discs): VERDI—
Rigoletto. *Tumagian, Ferrarini, Ramiro;
Bratislava Radio Orch.; Rahbari, cond.*
- ● ARG 9-10/92: 177
- + Fa 11-12/92: 397
- ● Gr 3/92: 117

24748. 8.660015/16 (2 discs): PUCCINI—
Madama Butterfly. *Gauci, Boschkova,
Ramiro, Tichy; Slovak Phil. Chorus;
Czecho-Slovak Radio Orch., Bratislava;
Rahbari, cond.*
- + Fa 11-12/92: 324
- ● Gr 5/92: 113

24749. 8.660017/18 (2 discs): J. STRAUSS,
JR.—Die Fledermaus. *Fontana,
Karwautz, Dickie, Hopferweiser;
Bratislava Radio Symphony Orch.;
Wildner, cond.*
- - Gr 1/94: 97

24750. 8.660019/20 (2 discs): PUCCINI—
Manon Lescaut. *Gauci, Kaludov,
Sardinero, Rosca, George, Gijzegem;
Jaak Gregor Choir; BRT Phil. Chorus &
Orch.; Rahbari, cond.*
- ● Fa 7-8/94: 202
- + Gr 12/92: 139

24751. 8.660021: LEONCAVALLO—
Pagliacci. *Martinucci, Gauci, Tumagian;
Bratislava Radio Symphony Orch.;
Rahbari, cond.*
- ● Gr 4/93: 118

24752. 8.660022: MASCAGNI—Cavalleria
rusticana. *Evstatieva, Aragall, Tumagian,
Mauro; Bratislava Radio Symphony
Orch.; Rahbari, cond.*
- - Gr 3/93: 99

24753. 8.660023 (2 discs): VERDI—Il
trovatore. *Frusoni, Longhi, Servile;
Hungarian State Opera; Humburg, cond.*
- ● ARG 1-2/97: 188
- - Fa 1-2/97: 297
- + Gr 3/96: 103

24754. 8.660025/6 (2 discs): WAGNER—
Der fliegende Holländer. *Muff, Haubold,
Knodt, Seiffert; Austrian Radio
Symphony; Steinberg, cond.*
- + Fa 9-10/94: 373
- + Gr 9/93: 113
- ● ON 9/94: 58
- + Op 7/94: 889

24755. 8.660027/29 (3 discs): ROSSINI—Il
barbiere di Siviglia. *Servile, Ganassi,
Vargas, Romero, De Grandis, Kertesi;
Hungarian Radio Chorus; Failoni
Chamber Orch. of Budapest; Humburg,
cond.*
- ● ARG 9-10/94: 184
- + Fa 7-8/94: 218
- + Gr 3/94: 105
- + Op 10/94: 1234

24756. 8.660030 (2 discs): MOZART—
Magic flute. *Lippert, Norrberg-Schulz,
Rydl, Kwon; Failoni Chamber Orch.;
Hálasz, cond.*

+ ARG 11-12/94: 161
• Fa 11-12/94: 313
+ Gr 7/94: 111
+ ON 1/21/95: 37

24757. 8.660033/4 (2 discs): VERDI—Aïda. *Dragoni, Johannsson, Dever, Rucker, Ellero D'Artegna, Ferrari; National Symphony Orch. of Ireland; Saccani, cond.*
- ARG 3-4/96: 199
- Fa 3-4/96: 310
• Fi 4/96: 127
• Gr 10/95: 142
• ON 11/95: 46
+ Op 12/95: 1495

24758. 8.660037/8 (2 discs): ROSSINI—Tancredi. *Podles, Jo, Olsen, Spagnoli; Capella Brugensis; Collegium Instrumentale Brugense; Zedda, cond.*
+ ARG 11-12/95: 188
+ Fa 11-12/95: 352
+ Gr 11/95: 156
+ ON 1/20/96: 34
+ Op 9/96: 1063

24759. 8.660040/1 (2 discs): MOZART—Ascanio in Alba. *Chance, Feldman, Mannion, Milner, Windsor; Choeur de l' Université de Paris-Sorbonne; Concerto Armonica, Budapest; Grimbert, cond. Reissue.*
+ ARG 3-4/96: 158
• Fa 3-4/96: 230
+ Gr 12/95: 148

24760. 8.990011: ANDERSON—The waltzing cat: the music of Leroy Anderson. *Richard Hayman and his Symphony Orch.*
• Fa 11-12/91: 236
+ Fa 3-4/93: 101

NCD

24761. 0191: GOOSSENS—Five impressions of a holiday. BELL—Innua; Monashee. *Music Mosaic.*
+ Fa 11-12/92: 247

24762. 4915: BIBALO—String quartet. NORDHEIM—String quartet no. 1. *Norwegian String Quartet .*
+ Fa 5-6/88: 85

24763. 4918: JANSON—Interlude; String quartet; Wings; Cradle song . *Faukstad, accordion; Rosseland, soprano; Norwegian String Quartet; Royal Phil. Orch.; Grex Vocalis Choir; instrumental ensemble; Eggen, Janson, conds.*
+ Fa 7-8/88: 180

24764. 4919: KVAM—Querela pacis; Vibrations; Opening. *Grex Vocalis Choir; Academic Choir; Caecilia Choir; Oslo Phil. Orch.; Zealand Symphony Orch. of Denmark; Norwegian Youth Symphony Orch.; Vänskä, Vetö, Andersen, conds.*
• Fa 9-10/88: 179

NEUMA

24765. CD 450-71: *New music series, vol. 1.* Music of Xenakis, Mabry, Risset, Scelsi, Korde, and others. *Black, double bass; Houwe, alto recorder; Sluchin, trombone; Culbertson, tuba; Holy Cross Chamber Players; Wada, cond.*
+ Fa 11-12/89: 482
+ NYT 10/1/89: H32

24766. CD 450-72: *New music series, vol. 2.* Music of Reynolds, Scelsi, Berio, Barney, and others . *Stout, marimba; Supové, piano; Lawrence, harp; Bastian, guitar; Hass, harpsichord; Artaud, flute; Heller, soprano.*
+ Fa 7-8/90: 378

24767. CD 450-73: *Electro acoustic music, vol. 1.* Music of Lansky, Risset, Dodge, Warner, and Saariaho. *Tegzes, soprano; Richards, clarinet; Karttunen, cello; Electronic music.*
+ Fa 1-2/91: 412

24768. CD 450-74: *Electro acoustic music: Classics.* Music of Varèse, Babbitt, Reynolds, and Xenakis. *Bettina, soprano; Sollberger, flute; Electronic music.*
+ Fa 5-6/91: 388

24769. CD 450-75: *Neuma: Electro acoustic music II.* Music of Shapiro, Berger, Dashow, Duesenberry and Child. *Electric Phoenix.*
+ ARG 7-8/92: 258
+ Fa 5-6/92: 334

24770. CD 450-76: CARTER—Night fantasies. CAGE—Etudes australes, book 1. *Drury, piano.*
+ ARG 7-8/92: 114
+ Fa 7-8/92: 136

24771. CD 450-77: *Contemporary flute music.* Music of Mefano, Varèse, Korde, Mabry, and Cage. *Artaud, flutes; François, percussion.*
+ Fa 9-10/92: 418

24772. CD 450-78: REYNOLDS—Personae; Vanity of words; Variation. *Négyésy, violin; SONOR; Steiger, cond.; Larson, baritone; Karis, piano.*
+ Fa 11-12/92: 333

24773. CD 450-80: *The contemporary saxophone.* Music of Shrude, Babbitt, Wuorinen, and Subotnik. *Sampen, saxophones; Shrude, piano.*
+ Fa 5-6/93: 386

24774. CD 450-81: CARTER—Riconoscenza. SOLLBERGER—Riding on the wind II, III, IV. ESCOT—Visione. IMBRIE—Short story. CARL—Time/ Memory/Shadow. DELIO—Contrecoup. *Lieberman, violin; Sollberger, flute; New Events Ensemble; Amper, piano; Extension Works; University of New*

Mexico Chamber Ensemble.
+ Fa 9-10/93: 382

24775. CD 450-82: BARTÓK—The 44 duos for 2 violins. *Négesy, Nykter, violins.*
• Fa 1-2/94: 119

24776. CD 450-83: *Urban cabaret.* Music of Schoenberg and Eisler. *Tegzes, soprano; Burleson, piano.*
+ Fa 5-6/94: 290

24777. CD 450-84: *Great American guitar solo.* Music of Curtis-Smith, Currier, Bolcom, Korde, and Johanson. *Tanenbaum, guitar.*
+ ARG 9-10/94: 233
+ Fa 5-6/94: 318

24778. CD 450-85: KORDE—Rasa; Tenderness of cranes. *Tegzes, soprano; DeMart, flute.*
+ ARG 11-12/94: 139
+ Fa 11-12/94: 272

24779. CD 450-86: XENAKIS—Aïs; Gendy 3; Taurhiphanie; Thalleïn. *Larson, baritone; Schick, percussion; La Jolla Symphony Orch.; Nee, cond.; SONOR Ensemble; Steiger, cond.*
+ Fa 5-6/96: 322

24780. CD 450-87: *Electo-acoustic music III.* Music of Saariaho, Karpen, Nelson, Dusman, Fuller, and Risset. *Various performers; with electronics.*
+ ARG 1-2/95: 222
+ Fa 1-2/95: 382

24781. CD 450-88: *The now and present flute.* Music of Perle, Talma, Krieger, Carter, Boulez, Korde, Jaffe, and Martirano. *Spencer, flute; Hall, piano.*
+ ARG 3-4/95: 236
+ Fa 3-4/95: 373

24782. CD 450-89: Music of Berio, Fussell, Cogan, Babbitt, and Stumpf. *Heller, soprano; Stumpf, piano.*
+ ARG 9-10/95: 302

24783. CD 450-90: DASHOW—Morfologie; Punti di vista no. 2; Reconstructions. DELIO—Anti-paysage; Of; Though; So again; Of again. *Maur, trumpet; Sprecher, piano; Bova, harp; Fonville, flute; Karis, piano; Schick, percussion; Linder, piano.*
+ Fa 5-6/96: 134

24784. CD 450-91 (2 discs): REYNOLDS—The Paris pieces. *Ensemble InterContemporain; with additional musicians.*
+ Fa 11-12/96: 346

NEW ALBION

24785. NA 006 CD: LENTZ—O-Ke-Wa; Missa Umbrarum; Postludium; Lascaux. *Various performers.*
□ Fa 5-6/92: 185

24786. NA 015 CD: HARRISON—La koro sutra; Varied trio; Suite for violin and American gamelan. *Abel, violin; Steinberg, piano; Winant, percussion; University of California, Berkeley Chorus & Chamber Chorus; American Gamelan; Brett, Bergamo, conds.*
+ ARG 7-8/88: 26
+ DA 11/88: 66
+ Fa 7-8/88: 174
+ MA 9/88: 59
+ Ov 8/88: 15

24787. NA 016 CD: SATOH—Mantra; Stabat Mater. *Satoh, voice & electronics; Thorngren, soprano; Pro Arte Chorale; George, cond.*
□ Fa 3-4/89: 258
+ HF 4/89: 73
+ MA 5/89: 84

24788. NA 018 CD: FELDMAN—Three voices. *La Barbara, soprano.*
+ DA 10/89: 78
+ Fa 7-8/89: 146
+ MA 9/89: 59

24789. NA 019 CD: *Contemporary chamber works.* Music of Jarvinen, Steiger, Torke, Stockhausen, Carter and Andriessen. *California EAR Unit.*
+ ARG 11-12/90: 143
+ Fa 5-6/90: 386
□ Gr 9/91: 97
+ MA 11/90: 82

24790. NA 021 CD: *Ars magis subtiliter: Secular music of the Chantilly codex.* Music of Symonis, Susay, Molins, Goschalch, Solage, and others. *Ensemble P.A.N.*
● ARG 11-12/89: 166
+ DA 11/89: 80
+ Fa 9-10/89: 403
+ Fa 3-4/90: 359

24791. NA 022 CD: Music of Oliveros, Dempster, and Pantaiotis. *Dempster, trombone, garden hose, didjeridu, conch shell & voice; Oliveros, accordion & voice; Panaiotis, pipes & voice.*
□ Fa 11-12/89: 309
+ NYT 10/29/89

24792. NA 024 CD: HYKES—Windhorse riders. *Hykes, voice, tanpura; Chemirani, zarb; Ahmed, tabla; Barret, voice.*
□ ARG 3-4/90: 63
□ Fa 3-4/90: 201

24793. NA 025 CD: STOCKHAUSEN—Mantra. *Mikashoff, Bevan, pianos; Ørsted, electronics.*
□ Fa 11-12/90: 363
+ Gr 1/91: 1385

24794. NA 026 CD: SCOTT—Minerva's web; The tears of Niobe. *Colorado College New Music Ensemble.*
+ ARG 7-8/90: 106
+ DA 10/90: 78
+ Fa 7-8/90: 265

24795. NA 027 CD: CURRAN—Electric rags II. *Rova Saxophone Quartet; Curran, electronics.*
+ Fa 11-12/90: 207

24796. NA 029 CD: *Arawi: the doctrine of cycles.* Music of Suárez, Garcia, Pozadas, Monroy, and López. *Members of the Contemporary Orch. of Native Instruments of ARAWI, the Bolivian Workshop of Popular Culture.*
+ Fa 1-2/91: 411
+ MA 3/91: 91

24797. NA 030 CD: LANSKY—Smalltalk; Guy's harp; Late August; Not so heavy metal. *DeRosa, harmonica; Mackey, piano; Lansky, computers.*
- Fa 1-2/91: 227

24798. NA 031 CD: Norwegian folksongs. *Bråten-Berg, alto; Anker, soprano.*
+ Fa 9-10/91: 406

24799. NA 032 CD: *Acoustic counterpoint.* Music of Tippett, Reich, Davies, Sierra, and Takemitsu. *Tanenbaum, guitar; Shanghai String Quartet.*
● Fa 3-4/91: 485

24800. NA 033 CD: KOMITAS—Divine liturgy. *Choir of St. Gayané Cathedral.*
+ ARG 3-4/91: 79
+ Fa 3-4/91: 251

24801. NA 035 CD: CAGE—Singing through: A flower; Mirakus; Eight whiskus; The wonderful widow of eighteen springs; Nowth upon nacht; Sonnekus; Je te veux; La diva de l'empire; Tendrement; Forever and sunsmall; Songbooks: Solo for voice 52, 67; Music for 2 (by one). *La Barbara, voice; Stein, piano; Winant, percussion.*
+ Fa 3-4/91: 173
+ Gr 9/91: 109

24802. NA 036 CD: *Set of five.* CAGE—Nocturne. COWELL—Set of five. HOVHANESS—Invocations to Vahakn. SATOH—Toki no mon. HARRISON—Varied trio. *Abel-Steinberg-Winant Trio.*
+ Fa 9-10/91: 430

24803. NA 037 CD: CAGE—The perilous night; Four walls. *Tan, prepared piano; La Barbara, soprano.*
+ Fa 7-8/91: 133

24804. NA 038 CD: Island of St. Hylarion, music of Cyprus, 1513-22. *Project Ars Nova Ensemble.*
+ EM 5/94: 337
+ Gr 4/93: 114

24805. NA 039 CD: FELDMAN—Rothko Chapel; Why patterns? *UC Berkeley Chamber Chorus; Brett, cond.; California EAR Unit.*
+ ARG 3-4/92: 56

+ Fa 3-4/92: 190
+ Gr 10/92: 127

24806. NA 040 CD: MARSHALL—Alcatraz. *Marshall, piano, synthesizers; Bengston, photography.*
□ Gr 8/92: 54

24807. NA 042 CD: M. HARRISON—From ancient worlds. *M. Harrison, piano.*
+ Fa 9-10/92: 253
□ Gr 10/92: 140

24808. NA 043 CD: DODGE—Any resemblance is purely coincidental; Speech songs; The waves; Viola elegy. *Caruso, tenor; Feinberg, piano; C. Dodge, voice; La Barbara, soprano; B. Dodge, viola.*
+ Fa 11-12/92: 226

24809. NA 044 CD: *Deep listening band.* Balloon payment; Metalorgy; Seven-up; The ready-made boomerang; Phantom; CCCC; Geocentric. *Dempster, trombone; Oliveros, accordion; P. & T. Eckert, voices; W.O. Smith, clarinet.*
● Fa 5-6/92: 338

24810. NA 045 CD: MESSIAEN—Visions de l'Amen. *Niemann, Tilles, pianos.*
+ Fa 11-12/92: 304
- Gr 11/92: 141

24811. NA 047 CD: MOWITZ—A la mémoire d'un ami; Darkening; Shimmering.
□ Fa 3-4/93: 234

24812. NA 048 CD: CICONIA—Sacred and secular vocal music. *Ensemble P.A.N.*
+ ARG 1-2/93: 88
+ EM 5/94: 337
+ Fa 1-2/93: 132
● Gr 5/93: 82

24813. NA 049 CD: STONE—Banteay Srey; Mom's; Gadberry's; Shing Kee; Chao Nue. *Stone, computer electronics.*
□ Fa 3-4/93: 305

24814. NA 050 CD: BRAXTON—Composition no. 165. *University of Illinois Creative Music Orch.; Braxton, cond.*
□ Fa 3-4/93: 133

24815. NA 051 CD: *Memorias tropicales.* Music of Tello, Alvarez, Sierra, and Garrido-Lecca. *Cuarteto Latinoamericano.*
+ ARG 3-4/93: 160
+ Fa 3-4/93: 386

24816. NA 052 CD: GARLAND—Walk in beauty; Sone de flor; Jornada del muerto. *Takahashi, piano; Abel- Steinberg-Winant Trio.*
+ Fa 9-10/93: 166

24817. NA 053 CD: DRESHER—Double ikat; Dark blue circumstance; Channels passing; Night songs. *Various*

instrumentalists; New Performance Group of the Cornish Institute; Strauss, cond.
+ Fa 11-12/93: 221

24818. NA 054 CD: GITECK—Om shanti; Tapasya; Leningrad spring; Home (revisited). *Various performers.*
● ARG 3-4/93: 81
● Fa 3-4/93: 166

24819. NA 055 CD: HARRISON—Harp suite; Serenade; Perilous chapel; Fugue; Song Quetzalcoatl; May rain. *Duykers, tenor; Tanenbaum, guitar; Steinberg, piano; Winant, percussion; San Francisco Contemporary Music Players; Mosko, cond.; Percussion Ensemble.*
+ Fa 9-10/93: 174
□ Gr 2/94: 62

24820. NA 056 CD: SATOH—Ruika; Toward the night; Homa. *String Ensemble Endless; Uzuka, cond.; Kanda, cello; Sato, soprano.*
+ Fa 9-10/93: 261

24821. NA 057 CD: HYKES—True to the times (How to be?). *Hykes, electronics, voice; Biffin, dobro; Lewis, tabla; Caillat, zarb, daff.*
+ Fa 11-12/93: 278

24822. NA 058 CD: GUASTAVINO—Las puertas de la Mañana; Cuatro canciones argentinas; Cuatro canciones coloniales; Siete canciones. *Espaillat, tenor; Zinger, piano.*
+ Fa 1-2/94: 193
+ Gr 1/94: 82

24823. NA 059 CD: WHELDEN—Twin rows; Prelude and divisions on She's so heavy; Fanfare; Quartet after Abel; Galax. ABEL—Gamba quartet; Adagio-Allegro moderato. *Whelden, viola da gamba; American Baroque.*
+ Fa 1-2/94: 358

24824. NA 060 CD: LEWIS—Journey to Still Water Pond; Night lights; Beaming contrasts; Little trio; Through the mountain. *Tanenbaum, guitar; Winant, percussion; McKenzie, flute; Granger, cello; Shapiro, piano; Alexander String Quartet.*
+ Fa 1-2/94: 224

24825. NA 062 CD: REVUELTAS—String quartets no. 1-4. *Quartetto Latinoamericano.*
+ Fa 3-4/94: 290
+ Gr 6/94: 76

24826. NA 063 CD: RZEWSKI—The people united will never be defeated!; Quilapayun. *Drury, piano.*
+ ARG 11-12/95: 189
+ Fa 11-12/94: 360

24827. NA 064 CD: RILEY—Imbas forasnai (Chanting the light of foresight). OCHS AND ADAMS—The chord of war.

Rova Saxophone Quartet.
● Fa 9-10/94: 310

24828. NA 065 CD: PIAZZOLLA—Guitar music. *Tanenbaum, guitar.*
+ Fa 9-10/94: 286

24829. NA 066 CD: BUDD—She is a phantom. *Budd, voice & piano; Zeitgeist.*
+ Fa 11-12/94: 194

24830. NA 067 CD: CURRAN—Crystal psalms. *Various performers.*
□ Fa 1-2/95: 147

24831. NA 068 CD: MACHAUT—Remede de fortune. *Ensemble P.A.N.*
+ Fa 11-12/94: 284
● Gr 10/94: 174

24832. NA 069 CD: SATOH—Sun/moon. *Nakamura, shakuhachi; Miyashita, koto.*
+ Fa 3-4/95: 281

24833. NA 070 CD: CAGE—Bacchanale; In a landscape; Daughters of the Lonesome Isle; The seasons; Suite for toy piano; Ophelia; In the name of the holocaust; Music for piano no. 2. *M. L. Tan, piano.*
+ Fa 1-2/95: 137
+ Fa 3-4/95: 151
+ Gr 7/95: 84

24834. NA 071 CD: RILEY—In C. *New Music Theatre; Life on the Water; Riley, Rush, conds.*
+ Gr 11/95: 90

24835. NA 074 CD: CAGE—Souvenir. PÄRT—Annum per annum; Pari intervallo; Mein Weg hat Gipfel und Wellentäler; Trivium I-III. SCELSI—In nomine lucis. *Moosmann, organ.*
+ Gr 2/96: 73

24836. NA 075 CD: KYR—Threefold vision; Songs of the shining wind; Unseen rain. *Ensemble Project Ars Nova; Back Bay Chorale; Taylor, cond.*
+ ARG 3-4/96: 268

24837. NA 076 CD: *Underground overlays from the Cistern Chapel.* DEMPSTER—Conch calling; Morning light; Didjerilayover; Secret currents; Melodic communion; Shell shock; Cloud landings. *Dempster, trombone, conch, didjeridu; Escobedo, Kirby, conch, 9 trombones; Sykes, Tebetan cymbals.*
+ ARG 3-4/96: 268

24838. NA 079 CD: LEWIS—Violin concerto; Where the heart is pure; Delicate sky; Sun music. *Friedman, mezzo- soprano; Hulsmann, violin; Sutherland, piano; Tichman, violin; Geem, percussion; Berkeley Symphony Orch.; Pilot, cond.*
□ ARG 9-10/96: 275

24839. NA 081 CD: KIEVMAN— Symphony no. 2(42). *Polish Radio*

Symphony Orch.; Gier, cond.
□ ARG 9-10/96: 275

24840. NA 083 CD: KERNIS—100 greatest dance hits; Mozart en route; Superstar etude; Nocturne; America(n) (day) dreams. *Tannenbaum, guitar; Chester Quartet; O'Riley, piano; Lundy, soprano; Barber, mezzo-soprano; Chamber Ensembles; Barrett, cond.*
□ ARG 9-10/96: 275

24841. NA 084 CD: SCOTT—Vikings of the sunrise; Fantasy on the Polynesian star path navigators. *Bowed Piano Ensemble.*
+ ARG 11-12/96: 307

24842. NA 086 CD: MARTIN—Etudes; Violin concerto; Maria triptychon. *Canin, violin & cond.; Ganz, soprano; New Century Chamber Orch.; Berkeley Symphony Orch.*
+ ARG 1-2/97: 136
+ Fi 11/96: 124
● Gr 1/97: 65

NEW MILLENIUM

24843. 61596: WAYNE—Symphony no. 4 "Funk". *State Phil. Orch. of Brno; Svárovsky, cond.*
+ ARG 1-2/97: 245
+ Fa 1-2/97: 301

NEW TONE

24844. 6716: ROUSE—Copperhead; Hope chest; Ranger; Soul menu; Leading the machine. *Mikel Rouse Broken Consort.*
● ARG 3-4/94: 146

24845. 6730: *Century XXI: USA 1.* Music of Stone, Neill, Rouse, Gann, and Collins. *Electronic music.*
+ Fa 11-12/95: 509

NEW WORLD

24846. NW 288/89-2 (2 discs): THOMSON—Mother of us all. *Dunn, Atherton, Booth; Santa Fe Opera Orch.; Leppard, cond.*
+ ARG 9-10/90: 125
+ Fa 7-8/90: 293
+ Gr 7/90: 276
+ MA 1/90: 82

24847. NW 309-2: BARBER—Essay no. 3 op. 47. CORIGLIANO—Clarinet concerto. *Drucker, clarinet; New York Phil.; Mehta, cond.*
+ Fa 1-2/88: 82
+ Gr 5/88: 1578

24848. NW 321-2: Music of Mason, Porter, Carpenter, and Hadley. *Albany Symphony Orch.; Hegyi, cond.*
+ Fa 1-2/88: 274

24849. NW 322/24-2 (2 discs): BARBER—Antony and Cleopatra (revised version). *Hinds, Bunnell, Grayson, Wells,*

NEW WORLD

Halfvarson; Westminster Choir; Spoleto Festival Orch.; Badea, cond.
+ Fa 9-10/88: 95

24850. NW 325-2: LIEBERSON—Piano concerto. *P. Serkin, piano; Boston Symphony Orch.; Ozawa, cond.*
+ Fa 1-2/88: 152

24851. NW 326-2: CRUMB—A haunted landscape. SCHUMAN—Three colloquies for horn and orchestra. *Myers, horn; New York Phil.; Weisberg, Mehta, conds.*
+ Fa 1-2/88: 109

24852. NW 328/29-2 (2 discs): CARPENTER—Collected piano works. *Oldham, piano.*
+ Fa 1-2/88: 106
+ Gr 7/88: 180

24853. NW 332-2: LOEFFLER—The death of Tintagliles; Five Irish fantasies. *Hansen, viola d'amore; Rosenshein, tenor; Indianapolis Symphony Orch.; Nelson, cond.*
+ Fa 1-2/88: 154

24854. NW 334-2: Music of Piston, Schuller, Copland, H. Aitken, and Schoenfield. *Davidovici, violin; De Groote, Schoenfield, pianos.* Issued also as LP: NW 334-1.
• ARG 3-4/88: 108
+ Fa 9-10/87: 377
+ Gr 11/87: 772

24855. NW 335-1 (LP): ROCHBERG—Oboe concerto. DRUCKMAN—Prism. *Robinson, oboe; New York Phil.; Mehta, cond.*
+ Fa 3-4/87: 192
• Ov 6/87: 40

24856. NW 339-2: CHADWICK—Symphony no. 2. PARKER—A northern ballad. *Albany Symphony Orch.; Hegyi, cond.* Issued also as LP: NW 339-1.
+ Fa 7-8/87: 83
• Gr 9/87: 404
+ HF 1/88: 60
+ Opus 10/87: 48
+ Ov 12/87: 38

24857. NW 342-2: PERLE—Pantomime, interlude and fugue; Fantasy-variations; Six new etudes; Suite in C; Short sonata. *Boriskin, piano.* Issued also as LP: NW 342-1.
+ Fa 7-8/87: 158
+ HF 10/87: 67

24858. NW 344-1 (LP): Music of Stravinsky, Wolpe, and P. Lieberson. *P. Serkin, piano.*
+ ARG 5-6/87: 73
+ Fa 3-4/87: 215
+ Gr 4/87: 1432
+ HF 7/87: 70

24859. NW 345-2: SESSIONS—Symphonies no. 4-5; Rhapsody. *Columbus Symphony Orch.; Badea, cond.*

Issued also as LP: NW 345-1.
+ ARG 11-12/87: 71
+ Fa 9-10/87: 294 (reviewed by S.W.E.)
+ Fa 9-10/87: 294 (reviewed by P.R.)
+ Gr 10/87: 584
+ HF 4/88: 77
+ NYT 8/2/87: H28
+ Opus 12/87: 39
+ Ov 2/88: 42

24860. NW 346-2: BABBITT—Piano concerto; The head of the bed. *Feinberg, piano; Bettina, soprano; Parnassus; American Composers Orch.; Wuorinen, Korf, conds.* Issued also as LP: NW 346-1.
+ ARG 11-12/87: 10
+ Fa 9-10/87: 132
+ Gr 12/87: 939
+ Ov 1/88: 19

24861. NW 347-2: CARTER—Piano concerto; Variations for orchestra. *Oppens, piano; Cincinnati Symphony Orch.; Gielen, cond.* Issued also as LP: NW 347-1.
+ Au 9/87: 118
+ Fa 3-4/87: 95
+ Gr 4/87: 1410
+ HF 5/87: 65
• Ov 3/87: 32
+ SR 3/87: 100

24862. NW 348-1 (LP): SCHUMAN—Symphony no. 7. BALADA—Steel symphony. *Pittsburgh Symphony Orch.; Maazel, cond.*
+ Fa 7-8/87: 180
□ HF 8/87: 69
+ NYT 4/12/87: H24
+ Opus 8/87: 49
+ Ov 1/88: 19
+ SR 9/87: 118

24863. NW 350-2: PAINE—Symphony no. 2. *New York Phil.; Mehta, cond.*
+ ARG 3-4/88: 67
+ Fa 3-4/88: 166
+ Gr 5/88: 1602
+ HPR 7/88: 85
+ SR 2/88: 192

24864. NW 353-2: ROREM—String symphony; Sunday morning; Eagles. *Atlanta Symphony Orch.; Shaw, Lane, conds.* Issued also as LP: NW 353-1.
+ ARG 11-12/88: 75
+ Au 1/89: 168
- Fa 11-12/88: 261
+ HF 1/89: 70
+ MA 3/89: 79
+ SR 12/88: 152
+ St 3/89: 170

24865. NW 354-2: BOLCOM—Twelve new etudes. WOLPE—Battle pieces. *Hamelin, piano.* Issued also as LP: NW 354-1.
+ Fa 9-10/88: 116
+ HF 2/89: 59
+ SR 10/88: 117

24866. NW 355-2: SHAPEY—Kroslish sonata; Concertante for trumpet & 10 players no. 1. SILVERMAN—Restless winds; Speaking alone; Passing fancies. *Krosnick, cello; Kalish, piano; Anderson, trumpet; Shostac, flute; University of Chicago Contemporary Chamber Players; Aspen Music Festival Contemporary Ensemble; Shapey, Mosko, conds.*
+ ARG 7-8/88: 56
+ Fa 3-4/88: 200

24867. NW 356-2: BOLCOM—Session no. 1; Symphony no. 4. *Morris, mezzo-soprano; St. Louis Symphony Orch.; Slatkin, cond.*
+ ARG 11-12/88: 19
+ Au 1/89: 170
+ Fa 7-8/88: 132
• Gr 10/88: 588
+ HF 2/89: 59

24868. NW 357-2: CRUMB—An idyll for the misbegotten; Vox balaenae; Madrigals bk. 1-4. *De Gaetani, soprano; Mueller, flute; Gottlieb, Herman, Payson, percussion; Sherry, cello; Gemmell, piano; University of Pensylvania Chamber Players; Wernick, cond.*
+ ARG 7-8/88: 19
+ Fa 3-4/88: 99
+ Gr 9/88: 460
+ HF 4/88: 73

24869. NW 359 2: PERLE—Wind quintets no. 1-4. *Dorian Wind Quintet.*
+ ARG 1-2/89: 75
+ Fa 7-8/88: 218
□ Gr 10/88: 633

24870. NW 360-2: BERGER—Violin and piano duo no. 1; Woodwind quartet; Cello and piano duo; Oboe and clarinet duo; Trio for guitar, violin and piano. *Smirnoff, violin; Krosnick, cello; Lanini, oboe; Stewart, clarinet; Starobin, guitar; Members of the Boehm Quintette; Kalish, piano; Oldfather, cond.*
+ Au 3/89: 114
+ Fa 1-2/89: 129
+ MA 4/89: 55

24871. NW 363-2: PAULUS—Violin concerto; Concertante; Symphony for strings. *Preucil, violin; Atlanta Symphony Orch.; Shaw, Levi, conds.*
+ Fa 11-12/90: 309
+ MA 1/91: 78

24872. NW 364-2: BABBITT—Sextet; The joy of more sextets. *Schulte, violin; Feinberg, piano.* Issued also as LP: NW 364-1.
+ Fa 11-12/88: 115
- MA 3/89: 51

24873. NW 365-2: SOWERBY—Piano trio in C#; Piano trio (1952). *La Musica Gioiosa Trio.*
+ ARG 9-10/90: 115
+ Fa 9-10/90: 393

24874. NW 366-2: HARRISON—Piano concerto; Suite for violin, piano & small orchestra. *Jarrett, piano; Stoltzman, violin; Japan Phil. Orch.; Ensemble; Otomo, Hughes, conds.*
+ ARG 5-6/89: 56
+ Fa 7-8/89: 157
+ HF 3/89: 56
+ MA 5/89: 63
+ Ov 4/89: 60
+ SR 7/89: 92

24875. NW 367-2: DETT—Magnolia suite; In the bottoms; Eight Bible vignettes. *Oldham, piano.* Issued also as LP: NW 367-1.
+ ARG 5-6/89: 40
+ Fa 5-6/89: 175
+ Gr 9/89: 509
+ HF 7/89: 65

24876. NW 368-2: SCHUMAN—In praise of Shahn. COPLAND—Connotations. SESSIONS—The black maskers: Suite. *Juilliard Orch.; Mueller, Ehrling, Zukofsky, conds.* Issued also as LP: NW 368-1.
+ Fa 3-4/89: 268
+ MA 7/89: 68
+ SR 5/89: 125

24877. NW 369-2: *William Sharp, baritone, winner of the 1987 Carnegie Hall International American Music Competition for Vocalists.* Music of Thomson, Hundley, Hoiby, Klein, Bowles, and Musto. *Sharp, baritone; Blier, piano.*
+ ARG 9-10/89: 136
+ Fa 11-12/89: 437
+ NYT 7/23/89: H28

24878. NW 370-2: PERSICHETTI—Symphony no. 5; Piano concerto. *Taub, piano; Philadelphia Orch.; Muti, Dutoit, conds.*
+ Fa 11-12/90: 309
+ Gr 3/91: 1672
• MA 3/91: 84

24879. NW 371-2: MENNIN—Symphonies no. 8-9; Folk overture. *Columbus Symphony Orch.; Badea, cond.*
+ ARG 1-2/90: 64
+ Fa 11-12/89: 279
+ MA 11/89: 56
• NYT 8/20/89: H29

24880. NW 372-2: ZWILICH—Concerto grosso 1985; Symbolon; Concerto for trumpet and 5 players; Double quartet for strings. *Smith, trumpet; New York Phil.; New York Phil. Ensembles; Mehta, Zwilich, conds.*
□ ARG 1-2/90: 109
+ DA 4/90: 51
+ Fa 11-12/89: 419
+ MA 11/89: 65
+ NYT 8/20/89: H29

24881. NW 373-2: SHAPERO—Symphony for classical orchestra; Nine-minute overture. *Los Angeles Phil. Orch.;*

Previn, cond. Issued also as LP: NW 373-1.
+ ARG 3-4/89: 82
+ Fa 3-4/89: 274
+ MA 7/89: 68
+ Ov 9/89: 51

24882. NW 374-2: PAINE—Symphony no. 1; As you like it overture. *New York Phil.; Mehta, cond.*
+ ARG 3-4/90: 85
+ Fa 3-4/90: 254
+ St 11/90: 213

24883. NW 375-2: FOSS—Renaissance concerto for flute; Salomon Rossi suite; Orpheus and Eurydice. *Wincenc, flute; Menuhin, Michell, violins; Brooklyn Phil. Symphony Orch.; Foss, cond.*
+ ARG 9-10/89: 55
+ Fa 9-10/89: 204
+ Gr 10/89: 657
+ MA 1/90: 67
+ NYT 8/20/89: H29
+ SR 8/89: 87

24884. NW 376-2: SOWERBY—Piano sonata; Suite for piano; Passacaglia. *Quillman, piano.* Issued also as LP: NW 376-1.
+ ARG 7-8/89: 94
• Fa 5-6/89: 325
+ MA 11/89: 62

24885. NW 377-2: Music of Bolcom, Shapey, Wright, and Druckman. *American Brass Quintet.*
+ ARG 1-2/90: 116
+ Fa 1-2/90: 409
+ MA 1/90: 73

24886. NW 378-2: IVES—Piano sonata no. 2. WRIGHT—Piano sonata. *Hamelin, piano.*
+ ARG 9-10/89: 65
+ Fa 9-10/89: 224
+ Gr 9/89: 509
+ MA 1/90: 70

24887. NW 379-2: Music of Sierra, Campos Parsi, and Lifchitz. *Bronx Arts Ensemble.*
+ ARG 1-2/90: 90
+ Fa 9-10/89: 331
+ MA 1/90: 70

24888. NW 380-2: Music of Del Tredici, Perle, and Thorne. *Boriskin, piano.*
+ ARG 11-12/89: 161
+ Fa 11-12/89: 188
+ MA 1/90: 66

24889. NW 381-2: DRUCKMAN—Chiaroscuro. SCHWANTNER—Aftertones of infinity. ALBERT—Into eclipse. *Lakes, tenor; Juilliard Orch.; Foss, Slatkin, Schwarz, conds.*
+ ARG 3-4/90: 129
□ Fa 3-4/90: 172
+ NYT 12/10/89: H33

24890. NW 382-2: Percussion works by Cage, Harrison, Rouse, Bazelon,

Verplanck, Kurtz. *Lower, violin; Continuum Percussion Quartet.*
+ ARG 3-4/90: 140
+ Fa 3-4/90: 382

24891. NW 383-2: KORF—Symphony no. 2. DAVIDOVSKY—Divertimento. WRIGHT—Night scenes. *Sherry, cello; Riverside Symphony; Rothman, cond.*
+ ARG 11-12/90: 142
+ Fa 9-10/90: 269
+ MA 3/91: 76

24892. NW 384-2: Music of Hiller, Pearson, Hartley, Piokowski, Oritz, and Chobanian. *Buffalo Guitar Quartet.*
+ ARG 7-8/90: 138
+ Fa 9-10/90: 496

24893. NW 386-2: WUORINEN—Violin sonata; String quartet no. 3; Fast fantasy. *Hudson, Zeavin, violins; Martin, viola; Sherry, cello; Ohlsson, piano; Wuorinen, cond.*
+ Fa 11-12/90: 309

24894. 80203-2: *Sound forms for piano.* Music of Cowell, Johnston, and Nancarrow. *Miller, piano.* Reissue.
+ ARG 5-6/95: 232
+ Fa 5-6/95: 413

24895. 80208-2: HEINRICH—Ornithological combat of kings. GOTTSCHALK—Night in the tropics (arr.). *A. & J. Paratore, pianos; Syracuse Symphony Orch.; Keene, cond.* Reissue.
+ ARG 1-2/93: 103
+ Fa 1-2/93: 168

24896. 80210-2: MARTIRANO—Mass. MARTINO—Seven pious pieces. *Ineluctable Modality; John Oliver Chorale; London, Oliver, conds.*
□ ARG 3-4/94: 120
+ Fa 3-4/94: 241

24897. 80219-2: THOMPSON—Americana. CARTER—To music. SHIFRIN—The odes of shang. *University of Michigan Chamber Choir; University of Michigan Symphony Orch.; Hilbish, cond.* Reissue.
• ARG 1-2/97: 219
+ Fa 11-12/96: 404

24898. 80220-2: *Angels' visits and other vocal gems of Victorian America.* Thirteen Victorian secular and religious songs and hymns. *Battle, soprano; R. Taylor, mezzo-soprano; Crook, tenor; Murcell, baritone; Harmoneion Singers; Skrobacs, piano.* Reissue.
+ ARG 1-2/94: 187
+ Fa 11-12/93: 473
+ Gr 2/94: 91

24899. 80221-2: *I wants to be a actor lady.* Sixteen early musical comedy hits. *Cincinnati's University Singers; Cincinnati's University Theater Orch.; Rivers, cond.* Reissue.
+ Fa 11-12/93: 473
+ Gr 4/94: 110

NEW WORLD

24900. 80228-2: Music of Carpenter, Gilbert, Weiss and Powell. *Carno, piano; Los Angeles Phil. Orch.; Simmons, Foster, conds.* Reissue.
+ ARG 1-2/93: 172
+ Fa 1-2/93: 315

24901. 80243-2: *But yesterday is not today: The American art song, 1927-1972.* Music of Barber, Bowles, Chanler, Citkowitz, Copland, Duke, Helps, and Sessions. *Beardslee, soprano; Helps, piano; Gramm, baritone; Hassard, piano.* Reissue.
+ ARG 3-4/97: 296
+ Fa 1-2/97: 307

24902. 80255-2: *Make a joyful noise: mainstreams and backwaters of American psalmody.* Music of Belcher, Billings, Munson, Kyes, Kimball, Swan, Read, Strong, Holden, King, Wetmore, Bull, and Anon. *Oregon State University Choir; Jeffers, cond.* Reissue.
+ Fa 11-12/96: 440

24903. 80257-2: *The Wind demon and other nineteenth-century piano music.* Music of Warren, Bristow, Grofe, Hoffman, Hopkins, Heinrich, Gottschalk, Fry, Bartlett, and Mason. *Davis, piano.* Reissue.
+ Fa 1-2/96: 394

24904. 80262-2 (2 discs): PAINE—Mass in D. *Balthrop, Blackett, Cole, Cheek; St. Louis Symphony Orch. & Chorus; Schuller, cond.* Reissue.
+ ARG 3-4/92: 116
+ Fa 3-4/92: 280

24905. 80266-2: *The golden age of the American march.* Music of Adams, Carter, Sousa, Weldon, Fillmore, and others. *Goldman Band; Goldman, Cox, conds.*
+ ARG 9-10/91: 157
+ Fa 9-10/91: 443

24906. 80276-2: *Music of the American revolution: the birth of liberty.* Music of Billings, Wood, and Anon. *Continental Harmony Singers; Bruce, Pyle, conds.; American Fife Ensemble; Milnes, baritone; Spong, harpsichord; McCoy, tenor; Richman, harpsichord; Liberty Tree Wind Players.* Reissue.
+ Fa 11-12/96: 439

24907. 80280-2: *Fugues, fantasia, and variations.* Music of Buck, Thayer, Parker, Paine, and Whiting. *Morris, organ.* Reissue.
+ ARG 9-10/95: 263
+ Fa 1-2/95: 355

24908. 80293-2: *Come and trip it: Instrumental dance music 1780s-1920s. Federal Music Society; Dick Hyman & his dance orch.; Gerard Schwarz & his dance orch.* Reissue.
• Fa 11-12/94: 500

24909. 80299-2: *Music of the Federal era.* Music of Holyoke, Taylor, Carr, Gilfer, and others. *Federal Music Society; Baldon, cond.* Reissue.
• ARG 1-2/95: 216
+ Fa 1-2/95: 369

24910. 80309-2: CORIGLIANO—Clarinet concerto. BARBER—Third essay for orchestra. *Drucker, clarinet; New York Phil.; Mehta, cond.* Reissue.
+ Fa 9-10/94: 173

24911. 80313-2: *Cadenzas and variations.* Music of Copland, Glass, Ornstein, and Wernick. *Fulkerson, violin; Shannon, Feinberg, piano.* Reissue.
+ Fa 3-4/96: 370
+ Gr 2/96: 66

24912. 80316-2: PERSICHETTI—Winter cantata; Mass, op. 84; Love. *Barnes, marimba; Schultz, flute; Mendelssohn Club of Philadelphia; Brooks, cond.* Reissue.
+ ARG 3-4/94: 133
+ Fa 1-2/94: 259

24913. 80331-2: WILSON—Sinfonia. HARBISON—Symphony no. 1. *Boston Symphony Orch.; Ozawa, cond.* Reissue.
+ ARG 1-2/93: 168
+ Fa 1-2/93: 273

24914. 80389-2: USSACHEVSKY—No exit suite; Line of apogee. *Electronic music.*
+ ARG 3-4/91: 133
□ Fa 1-2/91: 337
+ MA 5/91: 87

24915. 80391-2: HARBISON—Four songs of solitude. CAGE—Six melodies for violin and keyboard. WYNER—Concert duo for violin and piano. HARTKE—Oh them rats is mean in my kitchen. *Makarski, Copes, violins; McMunn, piano.*
+ ARG 7-8/91: 179
+ Fa 7-8/91: 363
+ HPR v.8, no.3/91: 75

24916. 80392-2: RANDS—Le tambourin suites; Canti dell'eclisse; Ceremonial III. *Paul, bass; Philadelphia Orch.; Muti, Schwarz, conds.*
□ ARG 7-8/94: 157
+ Fa 1-2/94: 271

24917. 80393-2: *A Miriam Gideon retrospective.* GIDEON—Steeds of darkness; Suite for clarinet and piano; The shooting starres attend thee; Eclogue for flute and piano; Böhmischer Krystall; Creature to creature; Leise zieht durch mein Gemüt; Locking; Vergiftet sind meine Lieder; Mixco; To music; Poet to poet; She weeps over Rahoon; The too-late born; Four epitaphs. *Schadeberg, Clark, soprano; Cassolas, tenor; Sharp, baritone; Berkowitz, clarinet; Spencer, flute; Rodgers, Oei, pianos; various ensemble.*

□ ARG 5-6/91: 59
+ Fa 1-2/91: 200

24918. 80394-2: SOWERBY—Forsaken of man. *Hall, Vorrasi; William Ferris Chorale; Weisflog, cond.*
+ ARG 3-4/91: 122
+ Fa 7-8/91: 296

24919. 80395-2: HARBISON—Flight into Egypt; Natural world; Concerto for double brass choir and orchestra. *Anderson, soprano; Felty, mezzo-soprano; Sylvan, baritone; Cantata Singers & Ensemble; Los Angeles Phil. New Music Group; Los Angeles Phil. Orch.; Hoose, Harbison, Previn, conds.*
+ Fa 5-6/91: 183

24920. 80396-2: PERSICHETTI—Night dances. BABBITT—Relata no. 1. DIAMOND—Symphony no. 5. *Juilliard Orch.; De Preist, Zukofsky, Keene, conds.*
+ Fa 3-4/91: 321
+ Gr 7/91: 39

24921. 80399-2: STILL—Suite for violin and piano; Songs or separation; Incantation and dance; Here's one; Summerland; Citadel; Song for the lonely; Out of silence; Ennaga; Lift every voice and sing. *Videmus.*
+ ARG 3-4/91: 124
+ Fa 3-4/81: 391

24922. 80401-2: REYNOLDS—Whispers out of time; Transfigured wind no. 2. *Fonville, flute; San Diego Symphony Ensemble; Sollberger, cond.*
□ ARG 7-8/91: 114
+ Fa 5-6/91: 262

24923. 80402-2: SHAPERO—Piano sonatas no. 1-3; I. FINE—Music for piano. RUGGLES—Evocations. MENOTTI—Ricercare & toccata on a theme from The old maid & the thief. *Boriskin, piano.*
+ ARG 7-8/92: 265
+ Fa 3-4/92: 405

24924. 80403-2: *Flutes.* SCHWANTNER—A Play of shadows; Fantasy for flute and orchestra; Black anemonies. SCHOENFELD—Klezmer rondos; Ufaratsta; Achar Sha'alti. BEASER—Song of the bells; The old men admiring themselvs in the water. *Robison, Wilson, Wincenc, flutes.*
+ ARG 11-12/91: 184
+ Fa 11-12/91: 560

24925. 80404-2: HARBISON—Viola concerto. LADERMAN—Concerto for double orchestra. *Laredo, viola; New Jersey Symphony Orch.; Wolff, cond.*
□ ARG 7-8/92: 143
+ Fa 3-4/92: 209

24926. 80405-2: *Pulse.* CAGE—Second construction; Third construction. CAGE AND HARRISON—Double music. COWELL—Pulse. SOLLBERGER—The two and the one.

FOSS—Percussion quartet. *New Music Consort; Heldrich, Shapiro, conds.* Reissue.
+ Fa 11-12/91: 566

24927. 80407-2: SHENG—H'un; In memoriam 1966-76; The stream flows; 3 Chinese love songs; My song. *Various performers.*
+ ARG 3-4/92: 139
+ Fa 3-4/92: 323
+ Gr 9/92: 152

24928. 80409-2: EHRLICH—Emergency peace; Dusk; The painter; The tucked sleeve of a one-armed boy; Unison; Double dance; Circle the heart; Charlie the parker; Tribute. *Ehrlich, woodwinds; The Dark Woods Ensemble.*
+ Fa 9-10/91: 209

24929. 80412-2: *Aequalis.* UNG—Spiral. DAVIDOVSKY—Synchronism, no. 6. STEIGER—Trio in memoriam. GIDEON— Cello sonata. BRODY—Commedia. *Bronstein, piano; Mohr, cello; Parola, percussion.*
+ ARG 3-4/92: 176
+ Fa 11-12/91: 569

24930. 80413-2: ROSEMAN—Double quintet for woodwinds and brass. POWELL—Woodwind quintet. BRESNICK— Just time. SHAPEY—Movements. *New York Woodwind Quartet; with the American Brass Quintet.*
+ Fa 11-12/91: 569

24931. 80414-2: TSONTAKIS—String quartets no. 3-4. *American String Quartet.*
□ ARG 3-4/92: 154
+ Fa 3-4/92: 351

24932. 80415-2: ERB—Concerto for brass and orchestra; Concerto for cello and orchestra; Ritual observances. *Harrell, cello; St. Louis Symphony Orch.; Slatkin, cond.*
+ ARG 3-4/93: 78
+ Fa 3-4/93: 160

24933. 80416-2: ROREM—Winter pages; Bright music. *Various performers.*
+ ARG 7-8/92: 208
+ Fa 7-8/92: 259
+ Gr 10/92: 132

24934. 80417-2: PORTER—Fifty million Frenchmen. *Vocal soloists; Orch. New England; Haile, cond.*
+ Fa 3-4/92: 283
+ ON 1/30/93: 38

24935. 80422-2: KOLB—Millefoglie; Extremes; Chromatic fantasy; Solitaire. *Various performers.*
+ Fa 7-8/92: 191

24936. 80423-2: Music of Wilson, Anderson, Fox and Baker. *Videmus; Taylor, cond.*
+ Fa 11-12/92: 452

24937. 80424-2: PAINE—Piano music. *Oldham, piano.*
• ARG 9-10/93: 167
+ Fa 9-10/93: 231 (North)
• Fa 9-10/93: 231 (Johnson)

24938. 80425-2: EKIZIAN—Octoéchos, for double string quartet and soprano. KARCHIN—Songs of John Keats, for soprano and 6 instruments; Capriccio for violin and seven instruments. *Cawelti, soprano; Hudson, violin; Group for Contemporary Music; Sollberger, cond.*
+ ARG 11-12/92: 117
+ Fa 9-10/92: 230

24939. 80426-2: DANIELPOUR—Piano sonata. BERNSTEIN—Thirteen anniversaries. SMALDONE— Transformational études. LIEBERMANN— Gargoyles, op. 29. *Boriskin, piano.*
+ Fa 3-4/93: 374

24940. 80428-2: SURINACH—Doppio concerto; Flamenco cyclothemia; Concerto for string orchestra; Quartet for piano and strings. *Bronx Arts Ensemble; Zinger, cond.*
+ ARG 11-12/93: 204
+ Fa 7-8/93: 254

24941. 80429-2: THOMSON—Nine portraits; Parson Weems and the cherry tree; Five 2-part inventions; Seventeen portraits. *Helin, piano.*
+ ARG 11-12/93: 211
+ Fa 7-8/93: 259

24942. 80430-2: *American works for Balinese gamelan orchestra.* Music of Ziporyn, Ziporyn/Windha, Tenzer, and Vitale. *Sekar Jaya Gamelan Orch.; other instrumentalists.*
□ ARG 3-4/94: 204
+ Fa 11-12/93: 513

24943. 80431-2: REYNOLDS— Electroacoustic music: The Ivanov suite; Versions/Stages. *Various performers.*
+ Fa 11-12/93: 363

24944. 80432-2: JOHNSTON—Septet; Three Chinese lyrics; Gambit; Five fragments; Trio for clarinet, violin, and cello; Ponder nothing. *Yassky, clarinet & cond.; Ohrenstein, soprano; Kalm, baritone; Music Amici.*
□ ARG 3-4/94: 111
+ Fa 1-2/94: 212

24945. 80434-2: LEWIS—Changing with the times; Chicago dadagram; So you say; The view from skates in Berkeley; Airplane; Epilogue. *Lewis, trombone; other musicians.*
+ ARG 3-4/94: 115

24946. 80439-2: YORK—Three native songs; My heart is different; Reminiscence 2; Songs from the Levertov scores; Music for strings; Two songs on a poem of Tung Po. *Various*

performers.
+ Fa 11-12/93: 453

24947. 80440-2: CHASALOW—Winding up; Fast forward; Over the edge; The fury of rainstorms; Hanging in the balance; The furies; String quartet no. 1. *Schneider, horn; Knowles, Jarvinen, percussion; Spencer, flute; Schadeberg, soprano; Sherry, cello; Speculum Musicae String Quartet.*
+ ARG 7-8/94: 90
+ Fa 5-6/94: 128

24948. 80441-2: IMBRIE—Dream sequence; Five Roethke songs; Three piece suite; Campion songs; To a traveler. *Soloists; Parnassus; Korf, cond.*
+ ARG 7-8/95: 129
+ Fa 5-6/95: 224

24949. 80442-2: BALADA—Torquemada; Concerto for piano, winds, and percussion; Sonata for ten winds; Transparencies of Chopin's first ballade. *Carnegie Mellon Contemporary Ensemble; Carnegie Mellon Concert Choir; Page, cond.; Carnegie Mellon Concert Winds; Strange, cond.; American Brass Quintet; De Bonaventura, piano.*
+ ARG 7-8/94: 65
+ Fa 3-4/94: 113

24950. 80443-2: SESSIONS—Piano concerto. THORNE—Piano concerto no. 3. *Taub, Oppens, pianos; Westchester Symphony Orch.; Dunkel, cond.*
+ ARG 11-12/94: 189
+ Fa 11-12/94: 378

24951. 80444-2: LEWIS—Invenzione; Diptychon; Kantaten; Symphony no. 4. *Constable, piano; Philharmonia Orch.; London Sinfonietta; Lewis, cond.*
□ ARG 7-8/94: 123
+ Fa 7-8/94: 162

24952. 80445-2: ROREM—Piano concerto (left hand); Eleven studies for 11 players. *Graffman, piano; Curtis Symphony Orch.; Previn, cond.*
+ ARG 7-8/94: 160
+ Fa 7-8/94: 216
+ Gr 2/95: 54

24953. 80447-2: ASIA—Symphonies no. 2-3. *Phoenix Symphony Orch.; Sedares, cond.*
+ ARG 7-8/94: 61
+ Fa 5-6/94: 96

24954. 80448-2: FENNELLY—On civil disobedience; In wildness is the preservation of the world; String quartet; Sonata seria; Empirical rag. *Polish Radio National Symphony Orch.; Suben, cond.; Czechoslovak Radio Symphony Orch. of Prague; Fischer, cond.; Audubon Quartet; Cobb, Fennelly, pianos.*
+ Fa 9-10/94: 189

24955. 80453-2: *Fifty years of American music, 1919-1969.* COWELL—Quartet

NEW WORLD

euphometric. SHEPHERD—Triptych. HARRIS—String quartet no. 2. SCHULLER—String quartet no. 2. IMBRIE—String quartet no. 4. *Emerson String Quartet.* Reissue.
   + ARG 3-4/94: 197
   + Fa 3-4/94: 428

24956. 80454-2 (2 discs): WEISGALL—Six characters in search of an author. *Futral, Byrne, Anderson, Orth; Lyric Opera Center for American Artists; Lyric Opera Orch.; Schaenen, cond.*
   ● ARG 7-8/95: 225
   ● Fa 3-4/95: 344
   + Gr 3/96: 102
   + ON 1/7/95: 36

24957. 80455-2: TILLIS—Freedom. *Tillis, soprano saxophone; Lark String Quartet; University of Massachusetts Chorale; Du Bois, cond.; Stark, soprano; Humphrey, tenor; Shank, piano.*
   + ARG 3-4/97: 304
   + Fa 11-12/96: 404

24958. 80456-2: *None but the lonely flute.* Music of Babbitt, Feldman, Mosko, Alexander, and Cage. *Stone, flute; Duke-Kirkpatrick, cello; Mowrey, piano; Jarvinen, percussion.*
   + ARG 7-8/95: 268
   + Fa 5-6/95: 406

24959. 80457-2: ERB—And then toward the end; Cenotaph (for EV); Woody; Symphony for winds; Drawing down the moon. *Dempster, trombone; Powell, clarinet; Gippo, flute; Brundage, percussion; University Circle Wind Ensemble; Ciepluch, cond.*
   + ARG 3-4/95: 98

24960. 80459-2: J. L. ADAMS—Earth and the great weather. *Various musicians; John Luther Adams, conductor.*
   + ARG 7-8/95: 69
   □ Fa 5-6/95: 113

24961. 80460-2: ASHLEY—Superior seven; Tract. *Held, flute; Buckner, baritone.*
   + ARG 9-10/96: 275
   ● Fa 5-6/96: 66

24962. 80461-2: HARTKE—The king of the sun; Night rubrics; Sonata-variations. *Dunsmuir Piano Quartet; Schwartz, cello; Copes, violin; Bonn, piano.*
   + ARG 11-12/95: 298
   + Fa 9-10/95: 219

24963. 80462-2: ROCHBERG—Music for the Magic Theater; Octet. *New York Chamber Ensemble; Radcliffe, cond.*
   + ARG 1-2/95: 162
   + Fa 1-2/95: 245

24964. 80463-2: *An old song resung.* Music of Farwell, Cadman, Ives, and Griffes. *Parker, baritone; Huckaby, Baldwin, piano.* Reissues.

   + ARG 1-2/96: 235
   ● Fa 11-12/95: 441

24965. 80464-2: FOOTE—Violin music. *Lawrence, violin; Larsen, piano.*
   + ARG 1-2/96: 110
   + Fa 3-4/96: 166

24966. 80466-2: BABBITT—Philomel; Phonemena (2 versions); Post-partitions; Reflections. *Beardslee, Webber, sopranos; Kuderna, Miller, pianos.* Reissue.
   + ARG 9-10/95: 94
   + Fa 9-10/95: 118

24967. 80469-2: ABRAMS—Textures 95; The prism 3; Hypdepth; Tribute to Julius Hemphill and Don Pullen; One one, two views; 11 over 4; Ensemble song. *Abrams, keyboards, percussion, voice; with assisting musicians.*
   + Fa 3-4/96: 96

24968. 80470-2: TOWER—Night fields; Snow dreams; Black topaz; Très lent; Stepping stones. *Muir String Quartet; Wincenc, flute; Isbin, guitar; Flax, clarinet; Spencer, flute; Haas, Moore, percussion; Gosling, piano; Powell, trombone; Gekker, trumpet; Emelianoff, cello; Tower, piano; Niemann, Tilles, pianos.*
   + ARG 11-12/95: 298
   + Fa 7-8/95: 349

24969. 80475-2: Music of Rorem, Hoiby, Chanler, Dello Joio, Evett, Bacon, Niles, and Fine. *Parker, baritone; Huckaby, Baldwin, piano.* Reissue.
   + ARG 1-2/96: 235
   + Fa 3-4/96: 337

24970. 80477-2: LONDON—In Heinrich's shoes; Auricles apertures ventricles; Sonnet haiku. *Cleveland Chamber Symphony; Gregg Smith Singers; Trio Bariano.*
   + ARG 7-8/96: 298
   + Fa 5-6/96: 194

24971. 80479/88-2 (10 discs): MORRIS—Testament: a conduction collection. *ROVA PreEchoes Ensemble; Süleyman Erguner Ensemble; Maarten Altena Ensemble.*
   + Fa 5-6/96: 214

24972. 80489-2: ROREM—English horn concerto. PERSICHETTI—English horn concerto. HODKINSON—The edge of the olde one. *Stacy, English horn; Rochester Phil. Orch.; Palmer, cond.; New York String Orch.; Persichetti, cond.; Eastman Musica Nova; Phillips, cond.*
   + ARG 3-4/96: 234
   + Fa 9-10/95: 273

24973. 80491-2: HYLA—We speak Etruscan; Pre-pulse suspended; String quartets no. 2-3; Piano concerto no. 2. *Berne, baritone saxophone; Smith, bass clarinet; Speculum Musicae; Palma,*

Purvis, conds.; Karis, piano; Lydian String Quartet.
   + ARG 9-10/96: 275
   + Fa 7-8/96: 202

24974. 80492-2: SCHULLER—Of reminiscences and reflections; The past is in the present; Organ concerto. *Diaz, organ; North German Radio Orch.; Schuller, cond.; Calgary Phil. Orch.; Bernardi, cond.*
   + ARG 11-12/95: 298
   + Fa 9-10/95: 315

24975. 80493-2: HUSA—Violin sonata; Piano sonata no. 2; Moravian songs. *Oliveira, violin; Martin, soprano; Oui, Basquin, Rodgers, pianos.*
   + ARG 7-8/96: 136
   + Fa 7-8/96: 202

24976. 80494-2: Music of Rzewski, Liebman, Ewazen, and Dlugoszewski. *Taylor, bass trombone; with assisting musicians.*
   + ARG 9-10/96: 248
   + Fa 9-10/96: 420

24977. 80497-2: KUREK—String quartet no. 2; Sonata for viola and harp; Matisse impressions; Harp concerto. *Blair String Quartet; Kochanowski, viola; Falcao, harp; Blair Woodwind Quintet; Helton, piano; orch.; Schermerhorn, cond.*
   + ARG 11-12/96: 307
   + Fa 9-10/96: 235

24978. 80498-2: BALADA—Maria Sabina; Escenas barrascosas; Guernica. *Dunham, Hardy, Cortés, vocalists; University of Louisville Chorus; Louisville Orch.; Mester, cond.; Shackleton-Williams, Balach, Walley, vocalists; Carnegie Mellon Concert Choir; Izquierdo, cond.* Reissue.
   □ ARG 5-6/96: 76
   + Fa 5-6/96: 80

24979. 80499-2: MOR. POWELL—Red white and black blues; Old man; Ophans; Suite changes; Outlaws; Loneliness; Transitions. *Various performers.*
   + ARG 9-10/96: 275
   + Fa 1-2/97: 225

24980. 80502-2: SCARMOLIN—Symphonies no. 1-3. *Slovak Radio Symphony Orch.; Polish Radio Symphony Orch.; Suben, cond.*
   ● ARG 7-8/96: 183
   ● Fa 7-8/96: 283
   + Gr 8/96: 54

24981. 80505-2: SURINACH—Ritmo jondo; Three Spanish songs and dances; Three songs of Spain; Three Berber songs; Tientos; Three songs; Hollywood carnival. *Rosales, soprano; Zinger, piano & cond.; Bronx Arts Ensemble.*
   + ARG 3-4/97: 241
   □ Fa 1-2/97: 285
   + Gr 4/97: 65

NEW YORK PHILOMUSICA RECORDS

24982. NYPM 10023-1-2: MOZART—String quintet no. 4, K. 516,; Masonic funeral music, K. 477; Piano concerto no. 17. *Soloists; New York Philomusica.*
+ Fa 1-2/93: 162

NEWPORT CLASSIC

24983. NCD 60007: BEETHOVEN—Piano concerto no. 3. MOZART—Fantasy in C minor K. 475. *Newman, fortepiano; Philomusica Orch.; Simon, cond.*
+ ARG 5-6/88: 12
+ MA 9/88: 76
+ Ov 6/88: 36

24984. NCD 60008: BEACH—Grand mass in E♭ op. 5. *Bunse, Schramm, Rogers, Gould; Michael May Festival Chorus; Beckwith, organ; Emmanuel, harp; May, cond.*
+ Fa 11-12/89: 124
• NYT 9/3/89: H22

24985. NCD 60017: POULENC—Organ concerto in G minor. FALLA—Harpsichord concerto. NEWMAN—Concertino for piano. *Newman, keyboards; Pennsylvania Sinfonia; Birney, cond.*
• ARG 1-2/88: 52

24986. NCD 60021: PRAETORIUS—Eight chorale settings. *Baird, Bleeke, Becker, Pauley; Barrows, organ; New York Cornet and Sackbut Ensemble; Peck, cond.*
+ ARG 5-6/90: 89

24987. NCD 60023: BACH—Harpsichord concertos no. 1, 5; Concerto for 2 harpsichords no. 1-2. *A. Newman, M. Newman, harpsichords; Brandenburg Collegium Orch.*
+ ARG 5-6/88: 8

24988. NCD 60024: BACH—Goldberg variations. *Newman, harpsichord.*
+ ARG 5-6/88: 8
+ DA 9/88: 63

24989. NCD 60027: BEETHOVEN—Piano concerto no. 5; Egmont overture. *Newman, fortepiano; Philomusica Antiqua; Simon, cond.*
+ ARG 1-2/88: 11
+ DA 12/88: 62
+ MA 9/88: 76
+ Ov 6/88: 36

24990. NCD 60028: LISZT—Songs. *Aler, tenor; Blumenthal, piano.*
+ ARG 7-8/88: 35
+ MA 9/88: 60
+ Ov 6/89: 58
+ SR 7/88: 102

24991. NCD 60031: BEETHOVEN—Piano concerto no. 1; Choral fantasy. *Newman, piano; Philomusica Chorus & Orch.; Simon, cond.*
+ ARG 5-6/88: 12
+ DA 10/88: 60
+ MA 9/88: 76
+ Ov 6/88: 36

24992. NCD 60032: NEWMAN—Quintet; Flute quartet; Variations and toccata; Introduction and toccata. *Mills, Wana, pianos; Waldman, violin; Bacchus, flute; Laurentian String Quartet; Flute Force.*
+ ARG 5-6/89: 73
• Fa 3-4/89: 231
□ MA 7/89: 77

24993. NCD 60033: Music of Wolf, Puccini, Turina, Gershwin, Kern, Baber, and Dvořák. *Manhattan String Quartet.*
+ ARG 9-10/88: 115

24994. NCD 60034: SCHUMANN—Piano concerto; Piano music. *Lorango, piano; New Brandenburg Collegium; Newman, cond.*
- ARG 11-12/91: 145

24995. NCD 60035 (2 discs): BIBER—Mystery sonatas. *Johnson, violin; O'Sullivan, cello; Milnes, harpsichord, organ.*
+ ARG 11-12/88: 18
+ Gr 10/91: 122
+ St 6/89: 210

24996. NCD 60037: Violin sonatas by Franck, Fauré, and Poulenc. *Somach, violin; Salerno, piano.*
• ARG 11-12/88: 35
+ SR 11/88: 133

24997. NCD 60038: Music of Percell, Green (arr. Boyce), Clarke, and Stanley. *Carroll, Curnow, trumpets; Bernhardt, percussion; Neil, organ.*
+ Fa 5-6/89: 404

24998. NCD 60040: BEETHOVEN—Piano sonatas no. 8, 13-14, 21, 23. *Newman, fortepiano.*
- Fa 3-4/89: 96
+ SR 10/89: 140

24999. NCD 60041: COUPERIN—Two organ masses. *Newman, organ.*
+ ARG 3-4/89: 30
+ Fa 1-2/89: 150
- Ov 6/89: 64
+ SR 7/89: 92

25000. NCD 60043: HANDEL—Della guerra amorosa; Mi palpita il cor; Spande ancor il mio dispetto; Pastorella vagha bella; Concerto grosso in G minor op. 2 no. 8. *Baird, soprano; Ostendorf, bass-baritone; Aurora.*
+ ARG 7-8/89: 47

25001. NCD 60044: *Time pieces.* Music of Haydn, Hummel, Mozart, and Kuhlau. *Zukerman, flute; Newman, piano & organ.*
+ Fa 9-10/89: 429

25002. NCD 60045 (2 discs): HANDEL—Acis and Galatea. *Baird, Dooley, Hirst, Oosting, Ostendorf; Amor Artis Orch.; Somary, cond.*
• ARG 1-2/89: 54
- Fa 3-4/89: 174
+ ON 5/89: 48
+ SR 4/89: 88

25003. NCD 60047: HANDEL—The eight great suites for harpsichord. *Newman, harpsichord.*
+ Fa 9-10/92: 250

25004. NCD 60048: Music of Lauer, Wilson, Gideon, and Newman. *Mills, piano.*
+ Fa 3-4/89: 366

25005. NCD 60050: *Romantic masterworks for organ.* Music of Widor, Gigout, Mulet, Reubke, Liszt, and Vierne. *Newman, organ.*
- ARG 5-6/89: 116
• Fa 3-4/89: 374
+ SR 10/89: 152

25006. NCD 60051: *Vertigo: harpsichord music of 18th century France.* Music of Royer and F. Couperin. *Kroll, harpsichord.*
• ARG 9-10/89: 127

25007. NCD 60053: CHOPIN—Ballades (complete); Fantasie in F minor op. 49. *Rose, piano.*
- ARG 11-12/89: 52
+ DA 9/89: 60
• Fa 9-10/89: 176

25008. NCD 60060—60061 (2 separate discs): FRANCK—Complete organ works. *Newman, organ.*
• ARG 11-12/89: 60
+ Fa 9-10/89: 204

25009. NCD 60063: DEBUSSY—Pour le piano; La soirée dans Grenade; Reflêts dans l'eau; Preludes bk. 1: Le vent dans la plaine; Villes; Les collines d'Anacapri; La fille aux cheveux de lin; Ce qu'a vu le vent d'ouest; La sérénade interrompue; La cathédrale engloutie; Minstrels. *Lipson-Gruzen, piano.*
+ Fa 3-4/90: 169

25010. NCD 60068: CHOPIN—Piano sonatas no. 1-3. *Rose, piano.*
- ARG 7-8/92: 118

25011. NCD 60074: DVOŘÁK—Piano trios no. 1-2. *Raphael Trio.*
+ ARG 11-12/89: 58
+ SR 2/90: 154

25012. NCD 60080: SCARLATTI—Harpsichord sonatas. *Newman, harpsichord.*
+ ARG 9-10/90: 113
+ HPR v.8, no. 1: 75

25013. NCD 60081: BEETHOVEN—Piano concertos no. 2, 4. *Newman, fortepiano;*

NEWPORT CLASSIC

Philomusica Antiqua; Simon, cond.
  - ARG 7-8/89: 18

25014. NCD 60088: *Michael Ponti live at the Newport Music Festival.* Music of Medtner, Rachmaninoff, Moscheles, Blumenfeld, and others. *Ponti, piano.* Recorded live 1988.
  + ARG 11-12/89: 162
  • Fa 7-8/89: 178

25015. NCD 60092: PROKOFIEV—Piano sonatas no. 1-5 (both versions of no. 5). *Nissman, piano.*
  + ARG 11-12/89: 96
  + Fa 9-10: 89: 285

25016. NCD 60092—60094 (3 separate discs): PROKOFIEV—Piano sonatas, vol. 1-3. *Nissman, piano.*
  • Gr 6/91: 67

25017. NCD 60093: PROKOFIEV—Piano sonatas no. 6-8. *Nissman, piano.*
  + ARG 1-2/90: 76
  + DA 10/89: 75
  • Fa 11-12/89: 320

25018. NCD 60097: BEETHOVEN—Violin sonatas no. 5, 9. *Johnson, violin; Newman, fortepiano.*
  + ARG 9-10/91: 44
  + Fa 11-12/91: 265

25019. NCD 60098: WEILL—Concerto for violin and wind orchestra; Kiddush; Kleine Dreigroschenmusik. *Waldman, violin; Hirst, tenor; Amor Artis Chamber Orch. & Choir; Somary, cond.*
  + ARG 11-12/90: 136
  + Gr 12/91: 84

25020. NCD 60103: SCHÜTZ—Fili mi Absalom; St. Matthew passion. *Hirst, Ostendorf; New York Cornet & Sackbut Ensemble; Amor Artis Chorale; Somary, cond.*
  + ARG 7-8/90: 105
  • HPR v.8, no.1: 79

25021. NCD 60110: SAINT-SAËNS—Songs and duets. *Aler, tenor; Ostendorf, bass; Van Buskirk, piano.*
  + ARG 9-10/90: 110

25022. NCD 60111: SCHUBERT—Violin sonatinas. *Lieberman, violin; Kroll, fortepiano.*
  + ARG 5-6/92: 124

25023. NCD 60117: TELEMANN—Pimpinone. *Baird, Ostendorf; St. Luke's Baroque Orch.; Palmer, cond.*
  + Gr 1/92: 94
  + ON 5/93: 53

25024. NCD 60125 (2 discs): HANDEL—Siroe. *Fortunato, Baird, Ostendorf, Rickards; Brewer Chamber Orch.; Palmer, cond.*
  + ARG 9-10/91: 79
  • Gr 5/92: 106
  + ON 8/91: 37

25025. NCD 60130: FIELD—Nocturnes (Complete). *M. Rose, fortepiano.*
  • Fa 11-12/92: 235

25026. NCD 60133: WAGNER—Eine sonata für das Album von Frau M. W.; Grosse Sonata in A; Fantasia in F♯ minor; Albumblatt für Betty Schott. *Lorango, piano.*
  + Fa 1-2/92: 368

25027. NCD 60134: VAUGHAN WILLIAMS—A sea symphony. *Choral Guild of Atlanta; Belgian Youth Orch.; Noll, cond.*
  - ARG 5-6/92: 150

25028. NCD 60140: NEWMAN—Concerto for viola, strings, piano, and timpani; Adagio and rondo for piano and orchestra; Sinfonia; On fallen heroes. *Dexter, viola; Lewis, piano; Fertitta, organ; New York Arts Orch.; Newman, cond.*
  + ARG 11-12/92: 173

25029. NPD 85503: GOLDMARK—Rustic wedding symphony; Im Frühling: overture. *Polish National Radio Symphony Orch.; Bartos, cond.*
  + Fa 1-2/92: 221

25030. NPD 85506: FELDMAN—For Samuel Beckett. *San Francisco Contemporary Music Players; Mosko, cond.*
  + ARG 7-8/92: 130

25031. NPD 85507: Satires, ballads, and bop. *Western Wind.*
  - ARG 7-8/92: 279

25032. NPD 85510: GINASTERA—Piano sonatas nos. 1-3; Danzas Argentinas, op. 2; Tres piezas, op. 6; Malambo, op. 7; Twelve American preludes, op. 12; Suite de danzas criollas, op. 15; Rondo sobre temas infantiles argentinos, op. 19. *Nissman, piano.*
  + Fa 1-2/92: 217

25033. NPD 85511: GINASTERA—Pampeanas no. 1-2; Dos canciones; Tres danzas; Piano quintet; Cello sonata. *Nissman, piano; González, violin; Natola-Ginastera, cello; Laurentian String Quartet.*
  + ARG 7-8/92: 133
  + Fa 7-8/92: 162

25034. NPD 85512: *Never sing before breakfast.* Wind quintets by Mackey, Wood, Sierra, Wolfe, Balcomb, Druckman, and Mamlok. *Quintet of the Americas.*
  + Fa 1-2/92: 422

25035. NPD 85513: NIETZSCHE—Piano music. *Young, Keene, pianos.*
  ☐ ARG 11-12/92: 174
  • Gr 12/92: 105

25036. NPD 85514: *The treble boys.* Music of Couperin, Vaughan Williams, Dering, Piccolo, Marcello, Copland, Fauré, Handel, Hadley, Purcell, Campion, Britten, Lindley and Humperdinck. *Huffman, Dyck, trebles; Whitemore, Piccolo, keyboards; Camus, cello.*
  + ARG 3-4/92: 200

25037. NPD 85515 (2 discs): HANDEL—Joshua. *Baird, Fortunato, Aler, Ostendorf; Palmer Singers; Brewer Chamber Orch.; Palmer, cond.*
  + ARG 11-12/91: 74
  + Gr 7/91: 99
  + ON 8/91: 37

25038. NPD 85516: *Listen to the mocking bird.* Forty-six marches, quick steps, polkas, overtures and medleys. *Chestnut Brass Company.*
  - ARG 1-2/92: 150

25039. NPD 85517: *Jewels from the court of imperial Russia.* Music of Taneev, Glinka, Rimsky-Korsakov, and Liadov. *Waldman, violin; Polish Radio Symphony Orch.; Somary, cond.*
  + ARG 3-4/94: 193

25040. NPD 85518: VILLA-LOBOS—Quintet in choros form; Choros no. 1-4, 7; New York skyline; Trio for oboe, clarinet and bassoon; Fugue on a popular Brazilian theme; Three typical Brazilian songs. *Quintet of the Americas; Sine Nomine Singers.*
  + ARG 7-8/92: 242

25041. NPD 85519: VERDERY—Some towns and cities. *Verdery, guitar; with assisting instrumentalists.*
  + ARG 7-8/92: 241

25042. NPD 85520: TCHAIKOVSKY—Piano concerto no. 2. PROKOFIEV—Piano concerto no. 1. *Boriskin, piano; Polish National Radio Symphony Orch.; Bartos, cond.*
  + ARG 5-6/92: 144
  + Fa 1-2/92: 349

25043. NPD 85521: TCHEREPNIN—Bagatelles; Message; Voeux; Five concert etudes; Songs without words; Piano sonata no. 2. *Braden, piano.*
  + ARG 3-4/92: 153

25044. NPD 85525: PADEREWSKI—Piano concerto; Fantaisie polonaise. *Tirino, piano; Polish National Radio Symphony Orch.; Bartos, cond.*
  + ARG 7-8/92: 197
  + Fa 3-4/92: 278

25045. NPD 85526: *Between the keys: microtonal masterpieces of the twentieth century.* Music of Ives, Wyschnegradsky, Partch, and Cage. *American Festival of Microtonal Music Ensemble.*
  ☐ Fa 9-10/92: 442

25046. NPD 85528: *The modern marimba.* Music of Druckman, Thomas, Bazelon, Wesley-Smith and Bennett. *Moersch, marimba.*
+ ARG 7-8/92: 262
+ Fa 5-6/92: 315

25047. NPD 85530: Bach—Arias. *Baird, soprano; Newbold, flute; O'Sullivan, cello; Mattax, harpsichord.*
2 ARG 9-10/94: 93

25048. NPD 85531: Ibert—Elizabethan suite; Flute concerto; Paris; Capriccio. *E. Zukerman, flute; Manhattan Chamber Orch.; Clark, cond.*
+ ARG 3-4/93: 96

25049. NPD 85534: Lullaby and good night. *Huffman, boy soprano; Piccolo, piano.*
+ ARG 7-8/93: 204

25050. NPD 85535: Nietzsche—A sylvester night; 16 songs; Manfred meditation. *Eanet, violin; Aler, tenor; Young, Coote, pianos.*
+ ARG 7-8/94: 145

25051. NPD 85538: Liszt—Piano sonata; Paganini etudes; Spanish rhapsody. *Nissman, piano.*
● ARG 7-8/93: 116

25052. NPD 85540 (2 discs): Handel and Bononcini—Muzio Scevola. *Baird, Mills, Matthews, Urrey, Ostendorf; Brewer Baroque Chamber Orch.; Palmer, cond.*
● ARG 1-2/93: 101
● Gr 3/93: 94
+ ON 6/93: 41

25053. NPD 85543: Luening—Orchestra music. *Astrup, soprano; Manhattan Chamber Orch.; Clark, cond.*
+ ARG 9-10/95: 169

25054. NPD 85546: Amram—Amercan dance suite; Red River Valley variations; Travels; Songs for America. *Baker, flute; Gekker, trumpet; Courtney, bass; Manhattan Chamber Orch.; Clark, cond.*
+ ARG 11-12/93: 72

25055. NPD 85549: Soldier—The apostles of John Brown; Duo sonata. *Vocalists; Seaton, violin; Clark, cond; Seaton-Friedlander Duo.*
+ ARG 11-12/93: 199

25056. NPD 85551: Music of Sarasate, Paganini, Wieniawski, Chopin, Tchaikovsky, and others. *Fodor, violin.*
● ARG 5-6/94: 187

25057. NPD 85553: Chambers—Ten grand. *Ten pianists; Chambers, cond. Recorded live.*
☐ ARG 11-12/95: 104

25058. NPD 85558 (2 discs): A. Scarlatti—Agar et Ismaele esiliati. *Baird, Harris, Mills, Ostendorf; Brewer*

Baroque Chamber Orch.; Palmer, cond.
+ ARG 9-10/94: 190
+ Gr 7/94: 119
+ ON 7/94: 41

25059. NPD 85568: Handel—Arias. *Baird, soprano; Brewer Chamber Orch.; Palmer, cond.*
● ARG 9-10/94: 138

25060. NPD 85570: Wilder—Carl Sandberg suite; Flute air; Slow dance; Saxophone suite no. 2; Oboe air; Theme and variations; Bassoon air; Wind serenade. *Zukerman, flute; Louie, saxophone; Lucarelli, oboe; Pasmanick, bassoon; Manhattan Chamber Orch.; Clark, cond.*
+ ARG 9-10/95: 236

25061. NPD 85575 (2 discs): Handel—Sosarme. *Baird, Fortunato, Minter, Aler; Amor Artis Orch.; Somary, cond.*
+ ARG 1-2/95: 112
● Gr 12/94: 154

25062. NPD 85582: Bach—Tenor arias with flute. *Gordon, tenor; Newbold, flute; Bethlehem Bach Festival Orch.; Funfgeld, cond.*
+ ARG 9-10/95: 95

25063. NPD 85585: Moore—The devil and Daniel Webster. *Stephens, Guyer, Steele, Woods; Kansas City Lyric Opera; Patterson, cond.*
● ARG 9-10/96: 166
+ ON 10/96: 39

25064. NPD 85591: Tchaikovsky—Piano sonata op. 37. Rubinstein—Etudes, op. 23. *Estrin, piano.*
- ARG 11-12/95: 218

25065. NPD 85594: Rorem—A childhood miracle; Three sisters who are not sisters. *Various performers.*
+ ARG 11-12/95: 185
+ Gr 10/95: 142
+ ON 11/95: 44

25066. NPD 85595: Haydn—La cantarina; Symphony no. 1. Hoffmann—Flute concerto. *Harris, Garrison, Fortunato; Newbold, flute; Palmer Chamber Orch.; Palmer, cond.*
+ ARG 9-10/95: 152
● ON 1/20/96: 33

25067. NPD 85596: Still—Orchestral music and songs. *Astrup, soprano; Manhattan Chamber Orch.; Clark, cond.*
● ARG 11-12/95: 210

25068. NPD 85601: Amram—Violin concerto; Honor song; Bassoon concerto. *Castleman, violin; Rosen, cello; Pasmanick, bassoon; Manhattan Chamber Orch.; Clark, cond.*
+ ARG 1-2/96: 70

25069. NPD 85603: Palestrina—Choral music. Lasso—Choral music. *Amor Artis*

Chorale; Somary, cond.
● ARG 11-12/95: 169

25070. NPD 85605 (2 discs): Rorem—Miss Julie. *Fried, Torre, Sarris; Manhattan School of Music Opera Theater; Gilbert, cond.*
+ ARG 1-2/96: 163
+ Gr 5/96: 120
● ON 11/95: 44

25071. NPD 85606: Harrison—An old time tune for Merce Cunningham's 75th birthday; Three waltzes; Triphony; Suite; Sonatas 3, 5-6; Saraband; Prelude; Tandy's tango. *Boriskin, piano.*
+ ARG 3-4/96: 268

25072. NPD 85612: Herschell—Oboe concertos; Symphony no. 4. Haydn—Symphony no. 23. *Woodhams, oboe; Mozart Orch.; Jerome, cond.*
+ ARG 5-6/96: 125

25073. NPD 85616 (2 discs): Cage—Freeman etudes. *Négyésy, violin.*
● ARG 1-2/96: 95

25074. NPD 85620 (3 discs): Handel—Berenice. *Baird, Fortunato, Lane, Minter; Brewer Chamber Orch.; Palmer, cond.*
+ ARG 5-6/96: 119
+ Gr 4/96: 111
● ON 7/96: 47

NEXUS

25075. 10251: *The best of Nexus.* Music of Nexus, G.H. Green/Becker, G.H. Green/Cahn, Cahn, J. Green/Becker, Birney/Nexus, and Cage. *Nexus.*
+ Fa 5-6/93: 397

25076. 10262: *Nexus now.* Music of Wyre, Cahn, Becker, Takemitsu, and Engelman. *Nexus.*
● Fa 5-6/93: 394

25077. 10273: Green—Novelty music. *Becker, xylophone; Nexus Percussion Ensemble.*
+ Fa 5-6/93: 215

25078. 10284: *Ragtime concert.* Music of G.H. Green, J. Green, C. Johnson, Arndt, Green, Cahn. *Becker, xylophone; Nexus. Reissue.*
+ Fa 5-6/93: 394

25079. 10295: Origins. *Nexus.*
● Fa 5-6/93: 394

25080. 10306: The story of percussion in the orchestra. *Nexus; Rochester Phil. Orch.; Cahn, cond.; Moyers, narrator.*
- Fa 5-6/93: 401

25081. 10317: Wyre—Connexus. Cahn—Kebjar-Bali; The birds; Voices. *Nexus; Rochester Phil. Orch.; Bay, cond.*
+ ARG 9-10/95: 302

25082. 10328: BECKER—Prisoners of the image factory; Noodrem; Mudra; Turning point; There is a time. *Becker, percussion & electronics.*
  + ARG 1-2/96: 249

NICKSON RECORDS

25083. NN-1004: *Popular concert favorite and encores.* Music of Prokofiev, Glière, Milhaud, Chabrier, Ravel and others. *Minneapolis Symphony Orch.; Mitropoulos, cond.* Reissues.
  • Fa 1-2/93: 312

25084. NN-1005: Music of Franck, Mozart, Gould, Siegmeister, and Mendelssohn. *Minneapolis Symphony Orch.; Mitropoulos, cond.* Recorded 1940-47.
  • Fa 3-4/94: 441

25085. NN-1006: *Dimitri Mitropoulos, document six.* Music of Beethoven and Rachmaninoff. *Minneapolis Symphony Orch.; Mitropoulos, cond.*
  • Fa 1-2/95: 376

25086. NN-1008/9 (2 discs): *Dmitri Mitropoulos centennial issue, documents 8 and 9.* Music of Lalo, Chausson, Chopin, Weber, Schumann, and Rossini. *Minneapolis Symphony Orch.; Robin Hood Dell Orch.; NBC Symphony Orch.; Mitropoulos, cond.* Recorded 1940-1946.
  + Fa 3-4/96: 386

NIGHTINGALE CLASSICS

25087. NC 070560-2 (2 discs): BELLINI—Beatrice di Tenda. *Gruberová, Bernardini, Morozov; Austrian Radio Symphony Orch.; Steinberg, cond.* Recorded live.
  • Gr 2/93: 74

25088. NC 070561-2 (3 discs): DONIZETTI—Linda di Chamounix. *Gruberová, Bernardini, Melander, Kim; Swedish Radio Symphony Orch.; Haider, cond.* Recorded 1993.
  + Gr 9/94: 109

25089. NC 070562-2 (3 discs): BELLINI—I puritani. *Gruberová, Lavender, Kim, Artegna; Munich Radio Orch.; Luisi, cond.* Recorded live 1993.
  + ARG 1-2/97: 71
  • Gr 12/94: 150

25090. NC 070563-2 (2 discs): DONIZETTI—Roberto Devereux. *Gruberova, Ziegler, Bernardini, Kim; Strasbourg Orch.; Haider, cond.*
  • ARG 1-2/97: 97
  + Gr 5/95: 110

25091. NC 070566-2 (2 discs): DONIZETTI—La fille du regiment. *Gruberova, Walt, Laghezza, Foureade; Munich Radio Orch.; Panni, cond.*
  • ARG 1-2/97: 97
  + Gr 9/96: 103

25092. NC 070760-2: STRAUSS—Songs. *Winbergh, tenor; Haider, piano.*
  • ARG 1-2/97: 177

25093. NC 070960-2: SCHUBERT—Winterreise. *Weikl, baritone; Deutsch, piano.*
  - ARG 1-2/97: 166
  + Gr 5/95: 98

25094. NC 071260-2: STRAUSS—Songs from his youth. *Margiono, soprano; Weikl, baritone; Vladar, horn; Haider, piano.*
  + ARG 1-2/97: 176

25095. NC 080560-2 (2 discs): BELLINI—Beatrice di Tenda. *Gruberova, Kasarova, Bernardini, Morozov; Austrian Radio Orch.; Steinberg, cond.* Recorded 1992.
  • ARG 1-2/97: 71

25096. NC 161864-2: STRAUSS—Ein Heldenleben (original ending); Four last songs. *Borowska, soprano; Tokyo Phil. Orch.; Cracow Radio Orch.; Haider, cond.*
  + ARG 1-2/97: 174

NIMBUS

25097. NI 1415: G. BENJAMIN—Piano sonata. *Benjamin, piano.*
  • ARG 1-2/92: 31
  + Fa 1-2/92: 171

25098. NI 1432: BENJAMIN—Sudden time. *London Phil. Orch.; Benjamin, cond.*
  + Gr 11/94: 66

25099. NI 1779 (3 discs): SCHUBERT—Piano sonatas. *Deyanova, piano.*
  - Fa 11-12/96: 366

25100. NI 1787 (6 discs): CHOPIN—Piano music. *Perlemuter, piano.*
  + Fa 11-12/93: 208

25101. NI 1791 (4 discs): MOZART—Symphonies no. 40-41; Serenade no. 6; Eine kleine Nachtmusik; Horn concertos, nos. 1-4; Clarinet concerto. *Hanover Band; Goodman, cond.*
  + Fa 9-10/91: 299

25102. NI 1793 (8 discs): *Shura Cherkassky.* Music of Beethoven, Brahms, Chasins, Chopin, Franck, Grieg, Liszt, Rachmaninoff, Schumann and others. *Cherkassky, piano.* Reissues.
  + ARG 1-2/92: 160
  + Fa 3-4/92: 403

25103. NI 4513: *Nativitas.* American Christmas carols. *Kansas City Chorale; Bruffy, cond.*
  + Fa 11-12/95: 449

25104. NI 5003: BEETHOVEN—Piano concerto no. 1; Symphony no. 1. *Verney, fortepiano; Hanover Band.*
  + Fa 11-12/86: 110
  + SR 1/87: 142

25105. NI 5005: RAVEL—Miroirs; Jeux d'eau; Pavane pour une infante défante; Gaspard de la nuit. *Perlemuter, piano.*
  + Fa 1-2/87: 161

25106. NI 5007: BEETHOVEN—Symphony no. 5; Egmont overture; Creatures of Prometheus overture. *Hanover Band.*
  • Fa 11-12/86: 110
  + NYT 12/28/86: H21

25107. NI 5009: MOZART—Violin concertos no. 4-5. *Shumsky, violin; Scottish Chamber Orch.; Tortelier, cond.*
  • Fa 11-12/86: 178

25108. NI 5011: RAVEL—Sonatine; Valse nobles et sentimentales; Le tombeau de Couperin; Prélude; A la manière de Borodin; A la manière de Chabrier; Menuet antique; Menuet sur le nom d'Haydn. *Perlemuter, piano.*
  + Fa 1-2/87: 161

25109. NI 5014: GOTTSCHALK—Souvenirs d'Andalousie; Le banjo; Grande scherzo; Pasquinade; Berceuse; Tournament galop; Mazurka; The Union; The last hope; Scherzo romantique; Le Mancenillier; The dying poet. *Marks, piano.*
  + Fa 11-12/85: 170
  - Fa 5-6/92: 164
  + St 12/92: 239

25110. NI 5017: *Man, the measure of all things: trumpet music from the Italian Baroque.* Music of Monteverdi, Torelli, Albinoni, Vivaldi, Purcell, and others. *Wallace, trumpet; Philharmonia Orch.; Warren-Green, cond.*
  + ARG 9-10/86: 93
  + Fa 5-6/86: 315

25111. NI 5018: *The golden echo: concertos for horns.* Music of Vivaldi, Rosetti, L. Mozart, and Haydn (attrib.). *Thompson, Watkins, horns; Philharmonia Orch.; Warren-Green, cond.*
  + ARG 9-10/86: 95
  + Fa 5-6/86: 315

25112. NI 5019: VAUGHAN WILLIAMS—Fantasia on a theme of Tallis; Oboe concerto; Concerto grosso; Fantasia on Greensleeves; Five variants of Dives and Lazarus. *Bourgue, oboe; English String Orch.; Boughton, cond.*
  + ARG 5-6/86: 82
  + DA 12/86: 78
  + Fa 11-12/86: 230
  + SR 2/87: 180

25113. NI 5022: SCHUBERT—Schwanengesang; Fischerwiese; Im Frühling; Meeres Stille; Gruppe aus dem Tartarus; Der Jüngling am Bache; An Silvia; Du bist die Ruh. *Gehrman, bass; Walker, piano.*
  - Fa 11-12/86: 212

25114. NI 5023: SCHUBERT—Die schöne Müllerin. *Gehrman, bass; Walker, piano.*

Sung in English.
- Fa 11-12/86: 212
• Fa 1-2/92: 318

25115. NI 5024: Music of Schumann, Brahms, and Schubert. *Gehrman, bass; Walker, piano.*
- Fa 11-12/86: 212

25116. NI 5025: Britten—Variations on a theme by Frank Bridge; Simple symphony; Lachrymae; Prelude and fugue for string orchestra op. 29. *Best, viola; English String Orch.; Boughton, cond.*
+ ARG 5-6/86: 65
+ DA 12/86: 78
+ Fa 5-6/86: 124
+ SR 2/87: 246

25117. NI 5026: Scriabin—Preludes, op. 11. Shostakovich—Preludes, op. 24. *Deyanova, piano.*
+ ARG 3-4/86: 69
+ DA 12/86: 78
+ Fa 5-6/86: 246

25118. NI 5027: Song cycles by Menasce, Chabrier, Honegger, Roussel, Satie and Poulenc. *Cuénod, tenor; Parsons, piano.*
+ Fa 5-6/86: 235

25119. NI 5030: *The art of Youra Guller: a legendary pianist.* Music of Bach (arr. Liszt), Albéniz, L. Couperin, Rameau, and others. *Guller, piano.*
+ Fa 11-12/86: 267
• Opus 8/87: 41

25120. NI 5031: Beethoven—Piano concerto no. 3; Symphony no. 2. *Verney, piano; Hanover Band.*
• Fa 11-12/86: 110
+ SR 1/87: 142

25121. NI 5032: Music of Holst, Albinoni, Warlock, Pachelbel, Grieg, and Barber. *English String Orch.; Boughton, cond.*
• Fa 11-12/86: 286

25122. NI 5033: Music of Vaughan Williams, Butterworth, Hely-Hutchinson, and Howells. *Gehrman, bass; Farmer, piano.*
+ Fa 7-8/88: 317

25123. NI 5034: Beethoven—Piano sonatas no. 8, 14, 23 . *Smith, piano.*
• Fa 11-12/86: 106

25124. NI 5035: Haydn—Cello concertos no. 1-2. Boccherini—Cello concerto no. 2. *Michejew, cello; English String Orch.; Boughton, cond.*
+ Fa 1-2/87: 120

25125. NI 5038: Chopin—Piano sonatas no. 2-3. *Perlemuter, piano.*
• Fa 3-4/87: 98

25126. NI 5039: Ysaÿe—Six violin sonatas, op. 27. *Shumsky, violin.*
+ Fa 11-12/86: 251

25127. NI 5041 (2 discs): Mendelssohn—Midsummer night's dream. *James, Howarth, sopranos; Scottish Chamber Orch.; Laredo, cond.*
• ARG 1-2/93: 120

25128. NI 5041/42 (2 discs): Mendelssohn—Midsummer night's dream (complete incidental music in context of an abridged version of Shakespeare's play). *James, Howarth, sopranos; Scottish Phil. Singers; Scottish Chamber Orch.; Laredo, cond.*
+ Fa 11-12/86: 174
• Opus 2/87: 42

25129. NI 5043: Music of Schubert, Schumann, Chopin, and J. Strauss, Jr. (arr. Godowsky). *Cherkassky, piano.*
• Fa 1-2/87: 174
+ NYT 3/1/87: H24
+ Opus 4/87: 29

25130. NI 5044: Chopin—Piano sonata no. 3; Mazurkas op. 33 no. 4, op. 63 no. 3; Nocturnes op. 27 no. 2, op. 62 no. 2, op. 72 no. 1; Andante spianato and grand polonaise op. 22. *Cherkassky, piano.*
+ Fa 3-4/87: 100
+ NYT 3/1/87: H26
+ Opus 4/87: 29
• Ov 5/87: 38

25131. NI 5045 (LP): Liszt—Sonata in B minor; Hungarian rhapsody no. 2. Stravinsky—Three movements from Petrouchka. *Cherkassky, piano.*
+ ARG 11-12/87: 42
+ DA 2/87: 67
- Fa 3-4/87: 149
+ NYT 3/1/87: H24
• Ov 8/87: 20

25132. NI 5048/49 (2 discs): Schubert—String quartets no. 13-15. *Chilingirian String Quartet.*
• Fa 7-8/87: 178

25133. NI 5051: Beethoven—Piano sonatas no. 2, 24, 28. *Roberts, piano.*
• Fa 7-8/87: 64

25134. NI 5052: Beethoven—Piano sonatas no. 3, 19, 21. *Roberts, piano.*
+ ARG 3-4/87: 17
+ Fa 11-12/87: 98

25135. NI 5053: Beethoven—Piano sonatas no. 4, 10, 26. *Roberts, piano.*
+ ARG 3-4/87: 17
+ Fa 11-12/87: 98

25136. NI 5054: Beethoven—Piano sonatas no. 5-7. *Roberts, piano.*
+ ARG 3-4/87: 17
• Fa 11-12/87: 99

25137. NI 5055: Beethoven—Piano sonatas no. 11, 20, 15. *Roberts, piano.*

+ ARG 3-4/87: 17
• Fa 11-12/87: 99

25138. NI 5056: Beethoven—Piano sonatas no. 17-18, 25. *Roberts, piano.*
+ Fa 7-8/88: 117

25139. NI 5057: Beethoven—Piano sonatas no. 13, 29. *Roberts, piano.*
+ ARG 1-2/89: 20
+ Fa 9-10/88: 104

25140. NI 5058: Beethoven—Piano sonatas no. 9, 16, 30. *Roberts, piano.*
+ Fa 1-2/89: 117
+ Ov 7/89: 54

25141. NI 5059: Beethoven—Piano sonatas no. 12, 14. *Roberts, piano.*
+ Fa 1-2/89: 118
+ Ov 7/89: 54

25142. NI 5060: Beethoven—Piano sonatas no. 8, 27, 32. *Roberts, piano.*
• Fa 1-2/89: 118
+ Ov 7/89: 54

25143. NI 5061: Beethoven—Piano sonatas no. 31-32. *Guller, piano.*
+ Fa 7-8/87: 65

25144. NI 5063: Stravinsky—L'histoire du soldat. *Lee, narrator; Scottish Chamber Orch.; Friend, cond.*
+ Fa 3-4/87: 215
+ NYT 7/19/87: H25

25145. NI 5064: Chopin—Preludes op. 28; Fantasy in F minor op. 49; Prelude in C# minor op. 45; Berceuse op. 57. *Perlemuter, piano.*
+ Fa 3-4/87: 98
+ NYT 3/1/87: H26
+ Ov 8/87: 20

25146. NI 5065: *Trumpet concertos and fanfares.* Music of Neruda, Hummel, F. D. Weber, C. M. Weber, Diabelli, and others. *Wallace, Wilbraham, trumpets; Wallace Collection; Philharmonia Orch.; Warren-Green, cond.*
+ Fa 3-4/87: 271

25147. NI 5066: Sullivan—Overtures: Di ballo; Yeomen of the guard; Princess Ida; Pirates of Penzance; Pinafore; The sorcerer; Ruddigore; The gondoliers; Patience; Iolanthe. *Scottish Chamber Orch.; Faris, cond.*
+ DA 6/87: 80
+ Fa 3-4/87: 218

25148. NI 5068: Music of Butterworth, Parry, and Bridge. *English String Orch.; Boughton, cond.*
+ ARG Fall/87: 59
+ DA 9/87: 63
+ Fa 7-8/87: 81
+ Ov 3/88: 33

25149. NI 5071: Mendelssohn—Six preludes and fugues op. 35; Prelude and fugue in E minor; Three preludes and 3

NIMBUS

studies op. 104; Study in F minor. *Jones, piano.*
- • ARG 3-4/88: 55
- + Fa 1-2/88: 159 m.f.

25150. NI 5072: MENDELSSOHN—Variations serieuses op. 54; Three fantasies or caprices op. 16; Variations in E♭ op. 82, in B♭ op. 83; Fantasy in F# minor op. 28; Fantasy on The last rose of summer op. 15. *Jones, piano.*
- • ARG 3-4/88: 55
- + Fa 1-2/88: 159 m.f.

25151. NI 5073: MENDELSSOHN—Songs without words, bk. 1-5. *Jones, piano.*
- + Fa 7-8/88: 200

25152. NI 5074: MENDELSSOHN—Songs without words: selections; Seven characteristic pieces; Gondellied in A; Albumblatt in E minor. *Jones, piano.*
- + Fa 9-10/88: 197

25153. NI 5075: BENJAMIN—At first light; A mind of winter; Ringed by the flat horizon. *Walmsley-Clark, soprano; London Symphony Orch.; Benjamin, cond.*
- + Fa 7-8/87: 67
- + SR 9/87: 111

25154. NI 5076: RAVEL—String quartet. STRAUSS—Capriccio: Introduction for string sextet. *Medici Quartet.*
- • DA 12/87: 17
- - Fa 11-12/87: 207

25155. NI 5077: SHOSTAKOVICH—String quartet no. 8. DEBUSSY—String quartet. *Medici Quartet.*
- + ARG 3-4/87: 79
- - Fa 9-10/87: 297
- - NYT 8/23/87: H25

25156. NI 5078: ROSSINI—Overtures: William Tell; L'italiana in Algeri; Il signor Bruschino; La Cenerentola; Tancredi; Il barbiere di Siviglia; La scala di seta; Semiramide. *Scottish Chamber Orch.; Laredo, cond.*
- + Fa 9-10/87: 279

25157. NI 5079: *Trumpet music.* Music of Fantini, Vivaldi, Alberti, A. Scarlatti, Caldara, and others. *Wallace, trumpet; Philharmonia Orch.; Wright, cond.*
- + ARG 3-4/88: 107
- + DA 7/88: 60
- + Fa 11-12/87: 289

25158. NI 5080: Music of Bach, Debussy, and Chopin. *Perlemuter, piano.*
- • ARG 3-4/88: 110
- + Fa 11-12/87: 87

25159. NI 5081: ALFONSO EL SABIO—Twenty cantigas. *Martin Best Ensemble.*
- + Fa 9-10/87: 130

25160. NI 5086: BARTÓK—Music for strings, percussion & celesta; Divertimento for strings. *English String*

Orch.; Menuhin, cond.
- - ARG 3-4/88: 15
- • Fa 1-2/88: 82

25161. NI 5087: STRAVINSKY—Firebird suite; The rite of spring. *London Symphony Orch.; Rozhdestvensky, cond.*
- • ARG 3-4/88: 84
- + Fa 9-10/87: 313
- + SR 12/87: 150

25162. NI 5088: STRAVINSKY—Petrouchka (1911); Symphony in 3 movements. *London Symphony Orch.; Rozhdestvensky, cond.*
- • ARG 3-4/88: 84
- + Fa 9-10/87: 313
- + HF 4/88: 77
- + SR 12/87: 150

25163. NI 5089: ALKAN—Thirteen prayers op. 64; Little preludes on the 8 modes of plainchant; Impromptu on the Lutheran chorale A mighty fortress is our God. *Bowyer, organ.*
- + ARG 1-2/90: 14
- + Fa 9-10/89: 114
- + NYT 8/6/89: H26

25164. NI 5090: Music of Franck, Grieg, Messiaen, and Rachmaninoff. *Cherkassky, piano.*
- + ARG 3-4/88: 110
- + Fa 3-4/88: 252 m.f.

25165. NI 5091: Music of Chopin, Schubert, Bernstein, and Pabst. *Cherkassky, piano.*
- ▢ Fa 9-10/88: 329

25166. NI 5094: RACHMANINOFF—Preludes op. 3 no. 2; op. 23; op. 32. *Deyanova, piano.*
- • ARG 9-10/88: 74
- • Fa 5-6/88: 187
- • Ov 8/88: 21

25167. NI 5095: CHOPIN—Etudes op. 10; op. 25; Trois nouvelles études. *Perlemuter, piano.*
- - ARG 9-10/88: 34
- + Fa 1-2/88: 107

25168. NI 5096: HAYDN—Symphonies no. 100, 104. *Hanover Band; Goodman, cond.*
- + Fa 11-12/88: 198
- • HF 4/89: 67
- + Ov 2/89: 49

25169. NI 5097: STRAVINSKY—Apollo. TIPPETT—Concerto for double string orchestra. *English String Orch.; Boughton, cond.*
- + ARG 11-12/88: 91
- + Fa 9-10/88: 273
- + MA 7/88: 86
- + Ov 10/88: 44

25170. NI 5099: BEETHOVEN—Symphony no. 6; Consecration of the house overture. *Hanover Band; Goodman, cond.*

- - ARG 9-10/88: 26
- + Fa 7-8/88: 120

25171. NI 5100: PALESTRINA—Missa Dum complerentur; Super flumina Babylonis; Exsultate Deo; Sicut cervus; O bone Jesu; Dum complerentur. *Christ Church Cathedral Choir; Darlington, cond.*
- + Fa 9-10/88: 222
- + Gr 11/88: 842
- • HF 11/88: 78
- + HPR 3/89: 63
- + St 1/89: 217

25172. NI 5101: FINZI—Love's labours lost suite; Clarinet concerto op. 31; Prelude for string orchestra op. 25; Romance for string orchestra op. 11. *Hacker, clarinet; English String Orch.; Boughton, cond.*
- + ARG 7-8/88: 24
- + Fa 5-6/88: 127
- + NYT 4/17/88: H36

25173. NI 5104: MOZART—Horn concertos (complete); Concerto fragment, K. 494a. *Halstead, natural horn; Hanover Band; Goodman, cond.*
- + ARG 9-10/88: 65
- • Fa 5-6/88: 142
- + Gr 8/88: 289
- + MA 11/88: 60
- + NYT 4/7/88: H38

25174. NI 5105: HAYDN—Symphonies no. 101, 103. *Austro-Hungarian Haydn Orch.; Fischer, cond.*
- + ARG 1-2/88: 34
- + DA 4/88: 56
- - Fa 1-2/88: 141

25175. NI 5106: ROSSINI—Operatic arias. *Giménez, tenor; Scottish Phil. Singers; Scottish Chamber Orch.; Veltri, cond.*
- • ARG 7-8/88: 51
- + Fa 5-6/88: 193
- + Gr 8/88: 337
- + NYT 6/12/88: H32
- + ON 8/88: 42
- • Op 3/88: 378
- + Ov 5/88: 40

25176. NI 5107: *Argentinian songs.* Music of Guastavino, Jurafsky, Buchardo, and Ginastera. *Giménez, tenor; Walker, piano.*
- + ARG 11-12/88: 111
- + Fa 9-10/88: 312

25177. NI 5108: SCHUMANN—Symphonic etudes op. 13; Kreisleriana op. 16. *Perlemuter, piano.*
- - ARG 11-12/88: 81
- • Fa 9-10/88: 257

25178. NI 5109: BEETHOVEN—Missa solemnis. *Hirsti, Watkinson, Murgatroyd, George; Oslo Cathedral Choir; Hanover Band; Kvam, cond.*
- - ARG 3-4/89: 20
- • DA 11/88: 66
- • DA 1/89: 48
- - Fa 9-10/89: 99

+ Gr 8/88: 321
• MA 5/89: 52

25179. NI 5112: MENDELSSOHN—Piano
concertos no. 1-2; Hebrides overture op.
26. *Kalichstein, piano; Scottish Chamber
Orch.; Laredo, cond.*
• ARG 1-2/89: 65
+ Fa 9-10/88: 196
- Gr 3/89: 1448

25180. NI 5113: JANÁČEK—String quartet
no. 1-2. *Medici Quartet.*
+ ARG 1-2/88: 41
- Fa 9-10/88: 174

25181. NI 5114: FRANCK—Piano quintet
in F minor. FAURÉ—String quartet in E
minor op. 121. *Bingham, piano; Medici
Quartet.*
- Fa 9-10/88: 152
+ Gr 3/89: 1448

25182. NI 5115: LISZT—Opera
paraphrases and transcriptions: Polonaise
from Eugene Onegin by Tchaikovsky;
Miserere from Il trovatore by Verdi;
Sarabande and chaconne from Almira by
Handel; Fantasy on two motifs from
Nozze di Figaro by Mozart; Liebestod
from Tristan und Isolde by Wagner.
Marks, piano.
• ARG 1-2/89: 62
- Fa 9-10/88: 185

25183. NI 5117: HOLST—The planets;
The perfect fool: ballet music.
Philharmonia Orch.; Boughton, cond.
+ ARG 1-2/89: 58
+ Fa 9-10/88: 171
- HF 12/88: 65
+ SR 9/88: 107

25184. NI 5120: *Popular operatic
overtures.* Music of J. Strauss, Jr, Suppé,
Smetana, Weber, Herold, and others.
Philharmonia Orch.; Boughton, cond.
- ARG 5-6/89: 109
+ DA 4/89: 69
+ Fa 3-4/89: 392

25185. NI 5121: *Virtuoso trumpet
concertos.* Music of Biber, Molter, Fasch,
M. Haydn, L. Mozart, and Mozart
(attrib.). *Wallace, trumpet; Wallace
Collection; Philharmonia Orch.; Wright,
cond.*
+ Fa 3-4/89: 113
+ Gr 4/89: 1597

25186. NI 5122: BEETHOVEN—Symphony
no. 3; Coriolan overture. *Hanover Band;
Goodman, cond.*
+ Fa 1-2/89
• St 1/89: 207

25187. NI 5123: *Arias for soprano and
trumpet.* Music of Handel, A. Scarlatti,
Albinoni, Reutter, Predieri, and Bach.
*Field, soprano; Wallace, trumpet;
Philharmonia Orch.; Wright, cond.*
+ Fa 11-12/88: 313

+ HPR 6/89: 77
+ MA 1/89: 85

25188. NI 5125: WEELKES—Alleluia; I
heard a voice; Give ear, O Lord; Evening
service; Hosanna to the Son of David;
When David heard; O Lord, grant the
King; Give the King thy judgement;
Gloria in excelsis Deo; Ninth Service.
*Christ Church Cathedral Choir;
Darlington, cond.*
+ ARG 9-10/89: 117
+ Fa 1-2/89: 296
• Gr 3/89: 1484
+ St 1/89: 229

25189. NI 5126: HAYDN—Symphonies
no. 94-95. L. MOZART—Toy symphony.
Hanover Band; Goodman, cond.
+ Fa 11-12/88: 198
- HF 4/89: 67
+ Ov 2/89: 49

25190. NI 5128: RIMSKY-KORSAKOV—
Scheherazade; Russian Easter overture.
Philharmonia Orch.; Boughton, cond.
- ARG 1-2/89: 77
+ Fa 1-2/89: 247
• HPR 6/89: 84
• MA 3/89: 79
• St 1/89: 223

25191. NI 5130: BEETHOVEN—
Symphonies no. 4, 8; King Stephen
overture; Ruins of Athens overture.
Hanover Band; Goodman, cond.
+ DA 3/89: 50
+ Fa 1-2/89: 121
+ HPR 3/89: 69
+ St 1/89: 207

25192. NI 5131: SMETANA—String
quartets no. 1-2. *Medici Quartet.*
+ ARG 1-2/89: 89
- Fa 1-2/89: 271
• Gr 12/88: 1028
+ HPR 6/89: 87
• St 6/89: 219

25193. NI 5132: *Soirées musicales.*
ROSSINI—La regata veneziana; Il
rimprovero; L'orgia; La partenza; La
serenata; La pastorella dell'Alpi; La
pesca; La gita in gondola; La danza; La
promessa; L'invito; I marinari. *Anderson,
Bouleyn, Giménez, Corbelli; Walker,
piano.*
+ ARG 1-2/89: 81
+ Fa 1-2/89: 250
• Gr 12/88: 1046
• HPR 6/89: 85
• MA 1/89: 79
• Op 12/88: 1464
+ SR 4/89: 89
- St 6/89: 215

25194. NI 5133: BEETHOVEN—Piano
sonatas no. 23, 26; Variations and fugue
on a theme from Prometheus op. 35.
Perlemuter, piano.
• ARG 7-8/89: 22
+ Fa 11-12/89: 135

25195. NI 5134: BEETHOVEN—Symphony
no. 9. *Harrhy, Bailey, Murgatroyd,
George; Oslo Cathedral Choir; Hanover
Band; Goodman, cond.*
+ ARG 7-8/89: 24
+ DA 8/89: 68
• Fa 3-4/89: 103
• HF 4/89: 61
• MA 5/89: 52
+ St 6/89: 209

25196. NI 5135: HAYDN—Symphonies
no. 96, 102. *Austro-Hungarian Haydn
Orch.; Fischer, cond.*
+ Au 6/89: 143
• Fa 1-2/89: 181

25197. NI 5136: ELGAR—Pomp and
circumstance marches op. 39; Wand of
youth suite no. 2; Three Bavarian dances.
English String Orch.; Boughton, cond.
+ Fa 1-2/89: 162

25198. NI 5138/39 (2 discs): *Beethoven
and the Philharmonic.* Music of
Cherubini, Weber, Sacchini, Neukomm,
Beethoven, and others. *Halstead, horn;
Kite, fortepiano; Harrhy, soprano;
Bailey, mezzo-soprano; Murgatroyd,
tenor; George, baritone; Oslo Cathedral
Choir; Hanover Band; Goodman, cond.*
• DA 5/89: 78
+ Fa 3-4/89: 391
+ Ov 9/89: 60
+ St 6/89: 209

25199. NI 5140: SHOSTAKOVICH—Two
pieces for string octet op. 11; Two pieces
for string quartet. MENDELSSOHN—Octet
for strings in E♭ op. 20. *Medici and
Alberni String Quartets.*
- ARG 3-4/89: 57
- Fa 3-4/89: 276
• Gr 1/89: 1176
• St 6/89: 214

25200. NI 5141: MENDELSSOHN—
Symphonies for strings no. 1-6. *English
String Orch.; Boughton, cond.*
+ ARG 9-10/89: 80
+ Fa 3-4/89: 210
+ Gr 3/89: 1428
+ Ov 4/89: 61
- St 5/89: 163

25201. NI 5142: MENDELSSOHN—
Symphonies for strings no. 7-8, 10.
English String Orch.; Boughton, cond.
+ ARG 9-10/89: 80
+ Fa 3-4/89: 210
+ Gr 3/89: 1428
+ Ov 4/89: 61
- St 5/89: 163

25202. NI 5143: MENDELSSOHN—
Symphonies for strings no. 9, 11-12.
English String Orch.; Boughton, cond.
+ ARG 9-10/89: 80
+ Fa 3-4/89: 210
+ Gr 3/89: 1428
+ Ov 4/89: 61
- St 5/89: 163

25203. NI 5144/48 (5 discs):
BEETHOVEN—Symphonies (complete).
Harrhy, Bailey, Murgatroyd, George;
Oslo Cathedral Choir; Hanover Band;
Huggett, Goodman, conds.
- - Fa 4-5/89: 129
- • Gr 1/89: 1138
- - NYT 1/8/89: H27
- • SR 5/89: 126

25204. NI 5149: BEETHOVEN—Symphony
no. 7; Fidelio overture; Leonore overture
no. 2. *Hanover Band; Goodman, conds.*
- + ARG 7-8/89: 24
- • Fa 5-6/89: 132
- + St 6/89: 209

25205. NI 5150: LASSUS—Missa Qual
donna; Tristis est anima mea; Exaltabo te
Domine; De profundis; Missa
Venatorum. RORE—Qual donna. *Christ*
Church Cathedral Choir; Darlington,
cond.
- + ARG 7-8/89: 52
- + Fa 5-6/89: 223
- + Gr 4/89: 1622

25206. NI 5151: SCHOENBERG—Verklärte
Nacht. STRAUSS—Metamorphosen.
English String Orch.; Boughton, cond.
- • ARG 5-6/89: 92
- • Fa 5-6/89: 303
- + Gr 4/89: 1588

25207. NI 5154: WEBER—Euryanthe
overture; Oberon overture; Der Freischütz
overture; Ruler of the spirits overture;
Abu Hassan overture; Peter Schmoll
overture; Invitation to the dance (arr.
Berlioz). *Hanover Band; Goodman, cond.*
- - ARG 7-8/89: 109
- + Fa 9-10/89: 376
- - Gr 6/89: 47

25208. NI 5155: *Rule Britannia.* Music of
Clarke, Purcell, Handel, Stanley, Eccles
and others. *Wallace, trumpet; Wallace*
Collection; Barham, tenor; Leeds
Festival Chorus; Boughton, cond.
- + ARG 9-10/89: 129
- + Fa 7-8/89: 315

25209. NI 5156: SHOSTAKOVICH—Piano
quintet in G minor op. 57.
MENDELSSOHN—String quartet no. 2.
Medici Quartet; Bingham, piano.
- + ARG 11-12/89: 119
- + Fa 7-8/89: 248
- + Gr 5/89: 1745

25210. NI 5157: BEETHOVEN—Quintet for
piano and winds in Eb op. 16. MOZART—
Quintet for piano and winds, K. 452.
Perlemuter, piano; Albion Ensemble.
- + ARG 9-10/89: 25
- + Fa 7-8/89: 88
- • Gr 7/89: 194

25211. NI 5158: MENDELSSOHN—
Symphony no. 4; Piano concerto no. 1;
Violin concerto op. 64. *Kite, fortepiano;*
Hudson, violin; Hanover Band;
Goodman, cond.

- • ARG 9-10/89: 80 (Piano)
- - ARG 9-10/89: 80 (Symphony;
  Violin)
- • DA 11/89: 80
- + Fa 9-10/89: 253 (Symphony;
  Piano)
- • Fa 9-10/89: 253 (Violin concerto)
- □ Gr 6/89: 40
- + MA 3/90: 78

25212. NI 5159: HAYDN—Symphonies
no. 94, 100; Sinfonia concertante in Bb
for violin, cello, oboe, basson and
orchestra. *Austro-Hungarian Haydn*
Orch.; Fischer, cond.
- + ARG 9-10/89: 62 m.f.
- - Fa 9-10/89: 217
- + Gr 12/89: 1130

25213. NI 5160: DEBUSSY—Images
oubliées; Valse romantique; Rêverie;
Danse; Suite bergamasque; Nocturne;
Ballade; Mazurka; Deux arabesques;
Danse bohèmienne; Pour le piano. *Jones,*
piano.
- • ARG 7-8/89: 36
- + DA 12/89: 92
- + Fa 7-8/89: 128

25214. NI 5161: DEBUSSY—Images sets
1-2; Estampes; Masques; D'un cahier
d'esquisses; L'isle joyeuse; Children's
corner; Morceau de concours; Le petit
nègre. *Jones, piano.*
- - Fa 9-10/89: 185
- + Gr 7/89: 205
- + St 4/90: 197

25215. NI 5162: DEBUSSY—Preludes.
Jones, piano.
- • ARG 11-12/89: 53
- - Fa 11-12/89: 186
- + St 4/90: 197

25216. NI 5163: DEBUSSY—Jeux;
Khamma; La boîte à joujoux. *Jones,*
piano.
- • Fa 1-2/90: 161 m.f.
- + Gr 2/90: 1489
- + St 4/90: 197

25217. NI 5164: DEBUSSY—Etudes bk. 1-
2; Six épigraphes antiques; Hommage à
Haydn; Berceuse héroïque; Elégie; Page
d'album. *Jones, piano.*
- • Fa 3-4/90: 169
- + St 5/90: 183

25218. NI 5165: FAURÉ—Theme and
variations in C# minor; Nocturnes no. 1,
6-7, 12-13; Impromptus no. 2, 5;
Barcarolle no. 5 op. 66. *Perlemuter,*
piano.
- + ARG 9-10/89: 54
- + Fa 9-10/89: 201
- + Gr 5/89: 1751

25219. NI 5166: VAUGHAM WILLIAMS—
Oxford elegy; Flos campi; Te Deum; O
clap your hands; The old 100th psalm
tune. *May, speaker; Best, viola; Christ*
Church Cathedral Choir; English String
Orch.; Darlington, cond.

- + ARG 9-10/89: 111
- + Fa 9-10/89: 349

25220. NI 5167: G. BENJAMIN—Antara.
BOULEZ—Dérive; Mémoriale. HARVEY—
Song offerings. *Walmsley-Clark,*
soprano; Bell, flute; London Sinfonietta;
Benjamin, cond.
- + ARG 1-2/90: 29
- + Fa 1-2/90: 125
- + Gr 10/89: 646

25221. NI 5169: SIBELIUS—Pelléas et
Mélisande suite; Romance in C; Andante
festivo; Valse triste; Suite champêtre;
Rakastava; Suite mignonne . *English*
String Orch.; Boughton, cond.
- • ARG 9-10/89: 105
- + Fa 9-10/89: 330
- + Gr 8/89: 311
- • SR 9/89: 154

25222. NI 5170: SCHUMANN—Carnaval;
Papillons; Phantasiestücke. *Ascoli, piano.*
- + ARG 11-12/90: 112
- - Fa 11-12/89: 351
- + Gr 7/89: 210

25223. NI 5171: GRIEG—Four psalms op.
74. MENDELSSOHN—Three psalms op. 78.
Hagegård, baritone; Oslo Cathedral
Choir; Kvam, cond.
- + ARG 9-10/89: 57
- + Fa 11-12/89: 222
- + Gr 7/89: 215

25224. NI 5172: SCHUBERT—Symphonies
no. 3, 5; Overture in C, D. 591. *Hanover*
Band; Goodman, cond.
- + ARG 1-2/90: 85
- • Fa 9-10/89: 318
- + Gr 7/89: 184

25225. NI 5173: BEETHOVEN—String
quartets op. 18 no. 1-3. *Medici Quartet.*
- + ARG 7-8/90: 22
- + Fa 11-12/89: 130
- + Gr 8/89: 324

25226. NI 5174: BELLMAN—Fredman's
epistles no. 2, 52, 54, 71, 80, 82;
Fredman's songs no. 14, 16, 31-32, 38,
56, 64; Cradle song. *Best, tenor & guitar*
.
- + ARG 11-12/89: 40
- + Fa 11-12/89: 145
- + St 2/90: 187 m.f.

25227. NI 5175: Music of Berlioz,
Gossec, Jadin, Cherubini, and others.
Leeds Festival Chorus; Wallace
Collection; Wallace, cond.
- □ ARG 9-10/89: 31
- • DA 12/89: 68
- + Fa 11-12/89: 146
- + Gr 7/89: 191

25228. NI 5176: PROKOFIEV—Visions
fugitives op. 22; Tales of the old
grandmother. SCRIABIN—Three pieces op.
2; Etudes op. 8 no. 2, 4, 8-9, 11-12; Two
poems op. 32; Etudes op. 42 no. 2-4, 7;
Pieces op. 52; Poème languide; Piano

sonata no. 5 op. 53; Etudes op. 65 no. 2-3. *Deyanova, piano.*
- • ARG 11-12/89: 117
- - Fa 11-12/89: 319
- • St 3/90: 195

25229. NI 5177: *The guitar of Stepan Rak.* RAK—Sonata mongoliana; Czech fairy tales; Elegy; Voces de profundis; Variations on a theme by John W. Duarte; Tango. *Rak, guitar.*
- + ARG 1-2/90: 77
- + Fa 11-12/89: 326

25230. NI 5178: Music of Franck, Mendelssohn, Schubert, and Fauré. *Smith, Sellick, pianos.*
- + ARG 9-10/89: 128
- + Fa 1-2/89: 382
- • Gr 9/89: 498
- + St 3/90: 195

25231. NI 5179: HAYDN—Symphonies no. 22, 24, 45. *Austro-Hungarian Haydn Orch.; Fischer, cond.*
- • Fa 11-12/89: 238
- + Gr 12/89: 1130

25232. NI 5180: WEBER—Symphonies no. 1-2; Concertino for horn in E. *Halstead, natural horn; Hanover Band; Goodman, cond.*
- + ARG 11-12/89: 137
- + Fa 11-12/89: 411
- + MA 9/90: 91
- + St 5/90: 189

25233. NI 5181: SCHUMANN—Piano sonata no. 3; Phantasie in C op. 17. *Marks, piano.*
- - Fa 11-12/89: 356
- • Gr 9/89: 511

25234. NI 5184/85 (2 discs): MÉHUL—Symphonies (complete); La chasse du jeune Henri overture; Le trésor supposé overture. *Gulbenkian Orch.; Swierczewski, cond.*
- + ARG 9-10/89: 78
- + Fa 11-12/89: 274
- + Gr 7/89: 178
- + St 2/90: 197

25235. NI 5186: BEETHOVEN—String quartets op. 18 no. 4-6. *Medici Quartet.*
- + ARG 7-8/90: 22
- + Fa 11-12/89: 130

25236. NI 5187: MUSSORGSKY—Pictures at an exhibition. SCRIABIN—Piano sonata no. 9. BALAKIREV—Piano sonata in B minor. *Smith, piano.*
- + ARG 11-12/89: 82
- + Fa 9-10/89: 269
- + Gr 8/89: 340
- • NYT 5/14/89: H34
- • St 5/90: 189

25237. NI 5188: *Venetian oboe concertos.* Music of Albinoni, Marcello, Vivaldi, and Cimarosa. *Anderson, oboe; Philharmonia Orch.; Wright, cond.*

- + ARG 1-2/90: 119
- • Fa 11-12/89: 399

25238. NI 5189: TELEMANN—Overture in D; Concertos for 3 trumpets, timpani, 2 oboes in D; for trumpet, 2 oboes in D; for trumpet in D; for 2 trumpets in Eb; Sinfonia for trumpet, 3 trombones, recorder, viola da gamba, oboe in F; Suite for trumpet in D. *Wallace, trumpet; English String Orch.; Boughton, cond.*
- + Fa 11-12/89: 381

25239. NI 5190: HAYDN—Horn concerto no. 1; Symphony no. 31. M. HAYDN—Horn concerto no. 1. *Halstead, natural horn; Hanover Band; Goodman, cond.*
- + ARG 1-2/90: 52
- + Fa 1-2/90: 198
- + Gr 11/89: 897

25240. NI 5191: VAUGHAN WILLIAMS—Phantasy quintet; String quartets no. 1-2. *Medici Quartet; Rowland-Jones, viola.*
- + ARG 7-8/90: 120
- + Fa 3-4/90: 325
- + Gr 12/89: 1160

25241. NI 5192: PROKOFIEV—Peter and the wolf; Symphony no. 1; Violin concerto no. 1. *Lee, narrator; Kun, violin; English String Orch.; Menuhin, cond.*
- + ARG 1-2/90: 76 (Peter)
- • ARG 1-2/90: 76 (others)
- + Fa 1-2/90: 265
- • Gr 11/89: 902
- + NYT 11/26/89: H32

25242. NI 5193: BEETHOVEN—Variations on a waltz by Diabelli. *Roberts, piano.*
- • ARG 3-4/90: 27
- • Fa 1-2/90: 124
- • Gr 1/90: 1349
- - MA 3/90: 91

25243. NI 5194: TCHAIKOVSKY—Symphony no. 5. KODÁLY—Háry János suite. *London Symphony Orch.; Frühbeck de Burgos, cond.*
- - ARG 3-4/90: 115
- + Fa 5-6/90: 312
- + Gr 7/90: 233

25244. NI 5197: MARTIN—Mass for double chorus a capella. POULENC—Mass in G; Salve Regina. *Christ Church Cathedral Choir; Darlington, cond.*
- + Fa 5-6/90: 211
- + Gr 12/89: 1185
- + St 10/90: 237

25245. NI 5198: SCHUBERT—Symphonies no. 1, 4. *Hanover Band; Goodman, cond.*
- • ARG 1-2/90: 85
- + Gr 7/90: 227
- + HPR v.8, no.1: 77
- - St 12/90: 225

25246. NI 5199: HAYDN—Symphonies no. 27, 97-98. *Austro-Hungarian Haydn Orch.; Fischer, cond.*
- + ARG 1-2/90: 54

- • Fa 3-4/90: 196
- + Gr 5/90: 1976
- • St 11/90: 207

25247. NI 5200/04 (5 discs): HAYDN—Symphonies no. 93-104. *Austro-Hungarian Haydn Orch.; Fischer, cond.*
- + ARG 9-10/90: 74
- • Fa 11-12/89: 239
- + Gr 12/89: 1130
- + NYT 3/4/90: H31

25248. NI 5205: BEETHOVEN—Coriolan; Ruins of Athens; King Stephen; Leonore no. 2; Fidelio; Egmont; Creatures of Prometheus; Consecration of the house. *Hanover Band; Goodman, Huggett, conds.*
- + ARG 7-8/90: 20
- - Fa 3-4/90: 134

25249. NI 5206: ELGAR—Cockaigne overture; Enigma variations; Froissart overture. *English Symphony Orch.; Boughton, cond.*
- • ARG 5-6/90: 50
- • Fa 3-4/90: 177
- • Gr 12/89: 1129
- • St 8/90: 173

25250. NI 5207: BEETHOVEN—String quintet in C op. 29; String quartet no. 7. *Medici Quartet; Rowland-Jones, viola.*
- • ARG 7-8/90: 22 (Quartet)
- + ARG 7-8/90: 22 (Quintet)
- + Fa 5-6/90: 116
- + Gr 3/90: 627

25251. NI 5208: VAUGHAN WILLIAMS—Wasps overture; The lark ascending. DELIUS—Florida suite; Summer evening. *Bochmann, violin; English Symphony Orch.; Boughton, cond.*
- + ARG 5-6/90: 123
- + DA 3/90: 72
- + Fa 5-6/90: 317
- + Gr 2/90: 1461
- + NY 4/8/90: H29

25252. NI 5209: CHOPIN—Ballades (complete); Polonaise in F# minor; Polonaise-fantasie in Ab. *Perlemuter, piano.*
- • ARG 3-4/90: 39
- + Fa 7-8/90: 121
- + Gr 4/90: 1833

25253. NI 5210/13 (4 discs): *The spirit of England.* Music of Bridge, Britten, Butterworth, Delius, Elgar, and others. *Hacker, clarinet; Bourgue, oboe; Bochmann, violin; English String Orch.; English Symphony Orch.; Boughton, cond.*
- + Fa 5-6/90: 388
- + NYT 4/8/90: H29

25254. NI 5214: Songs of Fauré, Gounod, Ravel, and others. *Gehrman, bass; Walker, piano.*
- • Fa 1-2/91: 372

25255. NI 5215: SCHUMANN—Kinderszenen; Davidsbündlertänze. *Levy, piano.*
+ Fa 9-10/90: 211

25256. NI 5216: HAYDN—Symphonies no. 93, 95; March for the Royal Society of Musicians. *Austro-Hungarian Haydn Orch.; Fischer, cond.*
+ ARG 9-10/90: 75
• Fa 7-8/90: 169
+ Gr 5/90: 1976
• St 11/90: 207

25257. NI 5217: TIPPETT—Midsummer marriage: Ritual dances; Sosostri's aria; Praeludium for brass, bells and percussion; Suite for the birthday of Prince Charles. *Cullis, soprano; McDonald, mezzo-soprano; Hodgson, alto; Curtis, tenor; Best, bass; Opera North Chorus; English Northern Philharmonia; Tippett, cond.*
+ ARG 7-8/90: 120
• Fa 7-8/90: 294
+ Gr 4/90: 1805
+ MA 11/90: 812
+ NYT 6/24/90: H30
+ SR 11/90: 172

25258. NI 5218: TAVERNER—Missa Mater Christi; O Wilhelme pastor bone; Mater Christi sanctissima. *Christ Church Cathedral Choir (Oxford); Darlington, cond.*
+ ARG 11-12/90: 124
+ Fa 7-8/90: 287
+ Gr 4/90: 1854

25259. NI 5219: SCHUMANN—Album für die Jugend. *Levy, piano.*
• ARG 7-8/90: 104
• Fa 7-8/90: 263
• Gr 4/90: 1836

25260. NI 5220: GRAINGER—*Dished up for piano, vol. 1.* Handel in the Strand; Bridal lullaby; English waltz; Mock Morris; Toa nordic princess; In a nutshell; Peace; Saxon; twi-play; Andante con moto; Children's march; The immovable do; Sailor's song; Colonial song; Walking tune; Harvest hymn; In Dahomey. *Jones, piano.*
+ ARG 7-8/90: 52
+ NYT 4/1/90: H34
+ St 1/91: 255

25261. NI 5222: SCHUBERT—Symphony no. 9. *Hanover Band; Goodman, cond.*
+ ARG 7-8/90: 103
• DA 9/90: 56
+ Gr 4/90: 1788
- HPR v.8, no.1: 77
- MA 9/90: 86
- St 7/91: 183

25262. NI 5223: CHOPIN—Etudes. *Smith, piano.*
• ARG 7-8/90: 38 m.f.
+ Gr 12/90: 1235

25263. NI 5224: *Operatic arias.* BELLINI—Puritani: A una fonte; A te o cara; La sonnambula: Tutto e sciolto. DONIZETTI—La faborite: Spirto gentil; Una vergine; La fille du régiment: Ah! mes amis; Elisir d'amore: Una furtiva lagrima; Don Pasquale: Cerchero lontano terra; Com'é gentil; Lucia di Lammermoor: Fra poco a me ricovero. *Giménez, tenor; Scottish Phil. Singers; Scottish Chamber Orch.; Veltri, cond.*
+ ARG 5-6/90: 45
- DA 10/90: 80
+ Fa 7-8/90: 337
+ Gr 5/90: 2042
• NYT 9/2/90: H19
• St 8/90: 171

25264. NI 5225: BEETHOVEN—String quartets no. 8-9. *Medici Quartet.*
• ARG 7-8/90: 22
+ Fa 7-8/90: 89
- Gr 5/90: 1999

25265. NI 5226: Music of Liszt, Schubert (arr. Liszt), and Schumann (arr. Liszt). *Marks, piano.*
+ ARG 7-8/90: 64
- Fa 7-8/90: 184

25266. NI 5228: MOZART—Symphony no. 40; Clarinet concerto in A K. 622; Serenade in G K. 525. *Lawson, basset clarinet; Hanover Band; Goodman, cond.*
+ ARG 9-10/90: 96
+ DA 12/90: 98
+ Fa 9-10/90: 316
- Gr 7/90: 218
• St 1/91: 260

25267. NI 5229: BARTÓK—Concerto for orchestra; Miraculous mandarin: Suite. *Hungarian State Orch.; Fischer, cond.*
• ARG 11-12/90: 24
+ Fa 1-2/91: 145
• Gr 6/90: 41

25268. NI 5230: HAYDN—Symphonies no. 99, 104. *Austro-Hungarian Haydn Orch.; Fischer, cond.*
• ARG 9-10/90: 76 (no. 99)
+ ARG 9-10/90: 76 (no. 104)
• Fa 11-12/90: 246

25269. NI 5231: DEBUSSY—Cinq poèmes de Baudelaire; Nuit d'étoiles; Fleur des blés; Romance; Dans le jardin; Les angélus; L'ombre des arbres; Mandolin; Le son du cor s'afflige; L'echelonnement des haies; Trois poèmes de Stéphane Mallarmé. *Cuénod, tenor; Isepp, piano.*
+ ARG 1-2/91: 45
+ Fa 11-12/90: 212
+ Gr 6/90: 94

25270. NI 5234: BRITTEN—Les illuminations; Serenade; Nocturne. *Hadley, tenor; Halstead, horn; English String Orch.; Boughton, cond.*
- Fa 9-10/91: 179

25271. NI 5235: STRAUSS—Don Juan; Death and transfiguration; Till

Eulenspiegel's merry pranks; Der Rosenkavalier: Waltz sequence no. 1. *BBC Welsh Symphony Orch.; Otaka, cond.*
+ Fa 11-12/90: 367
• Gr 9/90: 544

25272. NI 5236: *Venetian brass music.* Music of G. Gabrieli, A. Gabrieli, Viadana, and Frescobaldi. *Wallace, trumpet; Wallace Collection; Wright, cond.*
+ Fa 11-12/90: 229

25273. NI 5237: BYRD—Mass for 5 voices with the gradualia; Propers for the Feast of all saints; Laudibus in sanctis; Laudate pueri Dominum; Laudate Dominum. *Christ Church Cathedral Choir; Darlington, cond.*
+ Fa 11-12/90: 196
+ Fa 9-10/91: 184

25274. NI 5239: RAK—Six early dances; Romance Ontario; Spanish suite; Balalaika; Era of rock and roll; Happy birthday John; Auld lang syne. *Rak, guitar.*
□ ARG 11-12/90: 100
□ Gr 10/90: 789

25275. NI 5240: HAYDN—Symphonies no. 6-8. *Austro-Hungarian Haydn Orch.; Fischer, cond.*
+ ARG 11-12/90: 68
+ DA 3/91: 43
+ Fa 1-2/91: 215
+ Gr 9/90: 514

25276. NI 5241: MOZART—Requiem. *Janowitz, Bernheimer, Hill, Thomas; Hanover Chorus & Band; Goodman, cond.*
+ ARG 11-12/90: 89
+ Fa 11-12/90: 295
+ Gr 7/90: 261
+ MA 3/91: 83
• SR 2/91: 134

25277. NI 5242: BEETHOVEN—String quartets no. 10-11. *Medici Quartet.*
- ARG 1-2/91: 28
+ Fa 1-2/91: 149
• Gr 9/90: 554

25278. NI 5243: MATHIAS—I will celbrate; O how amiable; Rex gloriae; Canzonetta for organ; Missa Aedis Christi; Jesus College service; A grace; Ave Rex; As truly as God is our Father; Let the people praise thee, o God. *Lawford, organ; Christ Church Cathedral Choir, Oxford; Darlington, cond.*
+ ARG 3-4/91: 88
• Fa 1-2/91: 235
+ Gr 9/91: 590

25279. NI 5246: COPLAND—Rodeo: Four dance episodes; Quiet city; Nonet for strings; Appalachian spring; Fanfare for the common man. *Wallace, trumpet; Taylor, English horn; English Symphony*

Orch.; Boughton, cond.
+ ARG 1-2/91: 41
+ Fa 1-2/91: 181
+ Gr 10/91: 734

25280. NI 5247: *Images: Impressions: Music for flute and harp.* Music of Alwyn, Debussy, Persichetti, Nielsen, Payne, and others. *Hall, flute; Bennett, harp.*
+ ARG 1-2/91: 135
+ DA 4/91: 60
+ Fa 1-2/90: 393

25281. NI 5248: SOLER—Sonatas for harpsichord. *Rowland, harpsichord.* Reissue.
+ ARG 11-12/91: 148
- Fa 11-12/91: 488

25282. NI 5249: CHOPIN—Ballades no. 1-4; Nocturne in C# minor; Berceuse in D♭; Tarentelle in A♭; Andante spianato and grande polonaise in E♭. *Ascoli, piano.*
• Fa 1-2/91: 177
+ Gr 9/90: 573

25283. NI 5250: SCHUMANN— Waldszenen; Nachtstücke; Gesänge der Frühe. *Levy, piano.*
+ ARG 11-12/90: 113
- Fa 1-2/91: 314
• Gr 10/90: 795

25284. NI 5252: SCHUBERT—Symphonies no. 2, 6. *Hanover Band; Goodman, cond.*
• ARG 1-2/91: 93
• Fa 1-2/91: 310

25285. NI 5253: SCHUBERT—Die schöne Müllerin. *Gehrman, bass; Walker, piano.* Recorded 1972.
- Fa 1-2/92: 320

25286. NI 5254: BEETHOVEN—String quartet no. 13; Grosse Fuge. *Medici Quartet.*
- ARG 1-2/91: 28
+ Fa 1-2/91: 149

25287. NI 5256: SCHUMANN—Carnaval; Faschingsschwank aus Wien; Arabesque. *Levy, piano.*
• ARG 7-8/91: 123
- Fa 5-6/91: 283

25288. NI 5258: HAYDN—Violin concertos in C and G; Symphony no. 25. *Kuchl, violin; Austro-Hungarian Haydn Orch.; Fischer, cond.*
+ ARG 11-12/91: 77
+ Fa 11-12/91: 343

25289. NI 5259: MOZART—Symphony no. 41; Piano concerto no. 20; Serenade in D, K. 239. *Kite, fortepiano; Hanover Band; Goodman, cond.*
• Fa 3-4/91: 308

25290. NI 5260: MATHIAS—Symphonies no. 1-2. *BBC Welsh Symphony Orch.; Mathias, cond.*

+ ARG 1-2/91: 88
+ Fa 1-2/91: 236
+ Gr 12/90: 1211

25291. NI 5261: The Last of the Troubadours. *Martin Best Medieval Ensemble.* Reissue.
+ ARG 11-12/91: 195
+ Fa 11-12/91: 543

25292. NI 5262: BRAHMS—Organ works (complete). *Bowyer, organ.*
• ARG 3-4/91: 44
- Fa 1-2/91: 161
+ Gr 11/90: 1009

25293. NI 5264: WALDTEUFEL—Skaters' waltz; Bonne bouche polka; España waltz; Joyeux Paris polka; Béobile pizzicato; Pomone waltz; Grande vitesse galop; Amour et printemps waltz; L'estudiantina waltz; Les grenadiers waltz; Minuit polka; Roses de Noël waltz; Prestissimo galop. *Gulbenkian Orch.; Swierczewski, cond.*
+ ARG 5-6/91: 125
+ Fa 5-6/91: 319

25294. NI 5265: HAYDN—Symphonies no. 1, 2, 4, 5, & 10. *Austro-Hungarian Haydn Orch.; Fischer, cond.*
+ ARG 11-12/91: 79
+ Fa 9-10/91: 232

25295. NI 5266: TIPPETT—Crown of the year; Dance; Clarion air; The weeping babe; Plebs Angelica; bony at morn; Music; Child of our time: Five negro spirituals. *Medici Quartet; Anderson, oboe; Lawson, clarinet; Ashton, trumpet; Hamburger, percussion; Jones, piano; Christ Church Cathedral Choir; Darlington, cond.*
+ ARG 3-4/91: 133
+ Fa 3-4/91: 407
• Gr 1/91: 1401

25296. NI 5267: COPLAND—Rodeo: Four dance episodes; Four piano blues; Piano variations; Old American songs (arr. Marks). *Marks, piano.*
• ARG 3-4/91: 58
+ Fa 3-4/91: 191
+ St 8/91: 195

25297. NI 5269: HAYDN—Symphonies no. 88, 90, 92. *Austro-Hungarian Haydn Orch.; Fischer, cond.*
+ ARG 11-12/91: 80
• Fa 11-12/91: 345

25298. NI 5270 (4 discs): SCHUBERT—Symphonies (complete). *Hanover Band; Goodman, cond.*
• ARG 3-4/91: 114
+ Fa 3-4/91: 366 m.f.
• Gr 3/91: 1673

25299. NI 5274: SCHUBERT—Symphony no. 8; Rosamunde: incidental music. *Hanover Band; Goodman, cond.*
- Fa 9-10/91: 349

25300. NI 5275: KODÁLY—Cello sonata. BRIDGE—Cello sonata. *Michejew, cello; Jones, piano.*
- ARG 5-6/91: 71
+ Fa 5-6/91: 198

25301. NI 5277: SIBELIUS—Violin concerto. KHACHATURIAN—Violin concerto. *Hu Kun, violin; Royal Phil. Orch.; Menuhin, cond.*
- ARG 9-10/91: 129
+ Fa 9-10/91: 359

25302. NI 5278: VIVALDI—Glorias, RV 588, RV 589. *Kwella, Priday, Wyn-Rogers, Carwood; Christ Church Cathedral Choir; Hanover Band; Darlington, cond.*
+ ARG 9-10/91: 144

25303. NI 5279: BEETHOVEN—String quartets no. 12, 14. *Medici Quartet.*
+ ARG 5-6/91: 28
+ Fa 5-6/91: 124

25304. NI 5280: BACH—Organ works, vol. 1. *Bowyer, organ.*
• ARG 11-12/92: 76
+ Fa 9-10/92: 166
+ Gr 10/92: 136

25305. NI 5281: Resolana: fourteen songs from Argentina. *Falù, baritone & guitar.*
• Fa 5-6/91: 261

25306. NI 5282: SCHUBERT—Winterreise. *Gehrman, bass; Walker, piano.*
□ Fa 5-6/91: 280

25307. NI 5283: WEILL—Symphonies no. 1-2; Kleine Dreigroschenmusik. *Gulbenkian Orch.; Swierczewski, cond.*
- ARG 7-8/91: 135
+ Fa 7-8/91: 186
+ NYT 4/28/91: H30

25308. NI 5284: KODÁLY—Háry János suite; Dances of Galanta; Variations on a Hungarian folksong (The peacock). *Hungarian State Orch.; Fischer, cond.*
• ARG 5-6/91: 71
• Fa 7-8/91: 186
• MA 7/91: 76

25309. NI 5285: BEETHOVEN—String quartets no. 15-16. *Medici Quartet.*
- ARG 1-2/92: 28
+ Fa 7-8/91: 114
- St 7/92: 177

25310. NI 5286: *Dished up for piano, vol. 5.* GRAINGER—Piano music. BRAHMS—Paganini variation no. 12. BYRD—Air and variations on The carman's whistle. DELIUS—A dance rhapsody. GERSHWIN—Embraceable you. *Jones, Martin, McMahon, pianos.*
+ Fa 9-10/91: 223

25311. NI 5287: BYRD—Mass for four voices, with Propers and motets for the Feast of Corpus Christi. *Christ Church*

NIMBUS

Cathedral Choir; Darlington, cond.
+ ARG 9-10/91: 56
+ EM 11/91: 667

25312. NI 5288: PEÑA—Misa flamenca.
Flamenco singers, guitars & percussion;
Academy of St. Martin-in-the- Fields
Chorus; Heltay, cond.
+ ARG 11-12/91: 131
+ Fa 7-8/91: 246 (2 reviews)

25313. NI 5289: BACH—Organ works,
vol. 2. *Bowyer, organ.*
+ Fa 3-4/93: 111
● Gr 3/93: 68

25314. NI 5290: BACH—Organ works,
vol. 3. *Bowyer, organ.*
+ Fa 7-8/93: 97
+ Gr 6/93: 72

25315. NI 5291: CHOPIN—Piano concerto
no. 1. WEBER—Konzertstück, op. 79.
Kite, fortepiano; Hanover Band;
Goodman, cond.
- ARG 3-4/92: 46
+ Fa 3-4/92: 178

25316. NI 5292: RACHMANINOFF—
Variations on a theme of Corelli, op. 42;
Moments musicaux, op. 16;
Transcriptions: Lilacs, Daisies, Kreisler:
Liebesleid, Liebesfreud. *Jones, piano.*
Reissue.
+ Fa 11-12/91: 452

25317. NI 5293: SCHUBERT—Impromptus:
op. 90, no. 3; op. 142, no. 1-4; Moments
musicaux, op. 94. *Deyanova, piano.*
+ ARG 11-12/91: 142
+ Fa 11-12/91: 471

25318. NI 5294: BLISS—A colour
symphony; Metamorphic variations. *BBC*
Welsh Symphony Orch.; Wordsworth,
cond.
+ ARG 1-2/92: 33
● Fa 11-12/91: 274

25319. NI 5295: BRITTEN—Young
person's guide to the orchestra; Four sea
interludes from Peter Grimes; Courtly
dances from Gloriana; Suite on English
folk tunes. *English Symphony Orch.;*
Boughton, cond.
- ARG 1-2/92: 39
+ Fa 3-4/92: 166
● St 1/93: 269

25320. NI 5296: PARRY—Symphony no.
1; From death to life. *English Symphony*
Orch.; Boughton, cond.
- ARG 1-2/92: 87
+ Fa 11-12/91: 433
+ Gr 5/92: 44

25321. NI 5297: CHOPIN—Scherzi and
impromptus. *Deyanova, piano.*
□ ARG 11-12/91: 54
● Fa 11-12/91: 299

25322. NI 5299: SCHUMANN—Fantasy, op.
17. LISZT—Sonata in B minor.

Perlemuter, piano.
- ARG 3-4/92: 137
+ Fa 3-4/92: 318

25323. NI 5300: MOZART—Arias.
Giménez; Royal Opera House;
Wordsworth, cond.
+ ARG 11-12/91: 100
● Fa 1-2/92: 270
+ Op 11/91: 1371

25324. NI 5301: TIPPETT—Concerto for
violin, viola, cello and orchestra; Piano
concerto. *Kovacic, violin; Caussé, viola;*
Baillie, cello; Tirimo, piano; BBC Phil.
Orch.; Tippett, cond.
+ ARG 7-8/92: 238
+ Fa 3-4/92: 348
● St 3/93: 189

25325. NI 5302: BYRD—Mass for three
voices; Propers for the 3rd mass and
office of Christmas. *Cathedral Choir of*
Christ Church, Oxford; Darlington, cond.
+ EM 8/92: 501
+ Fa 3-4/92: 168

25326. NI 5303: OFFENBACH—Music from
the operettas. *Gulbenkian Orch.;*
Swierczewski, cond.
+ ARG 3-4/92: 115
+ Fa 3-4/92: 277

25327. NI 5304: BRAHMS—*Complete*
piano music, vol. 1. Sonata no. 1;
Ballades, op. 10; Handel variations, op.
24. *Jones, piano.*
- ARG 7-8/92: 106
+ Fa 3-4/92: 161
- St 9/92: 187

25328. NI 5306: PROKOFIEV-ROMEO AND
JULIET, OP. 64: EXCERPTS. TCHAIKOVSKY—
Romeo and Juliet: fantasy- overture. *BBC*
Welsh Symphony Orch.; Otaka, cond.
● Fa 11-12/91: 443

25329. NI 5308: SHOSTAKOVICH—Piano
concertos no. 1-2; Chamber symphony,
op. 110a. *Jones, piano; English*
Symphony Orch.; Boughton, cond.
- ARG 5-6/92: 133
- Fa 3-4/92: 323

25330. NI 5309: BARTÓK—Romanian folk
dances; Dance suite; Hungarian pictures;
Two pictures; Romanian dance.
Hungarian State Orch.; Fischer, cond.
+ ARG 1-2/92: 25
+ Fa 1-2/92: 158

25331. NI 5310: *Celebration.* Twenty-six
fanfares, carols, and readings. *BBC Welsh*
Chorus; Thomas, cond; Welsh Guard
Trumpeters; Williams, organ; A. Jones,
reader.
+ ARG 11-12/92: 264

25332. NI 5311: RACHMANINOFF—
Symphony no. 1; Four études-tableaux,
op. 39. *BBC Welsh Symphony Orch.;*
Otaka, cond.
+ Fa 7-8/93: 209

25333. NI 5312: HAYDN—String quartets
op. 77; op. 103. *Franz Schubert Quartet.*
+ ARG 9-10/93: 132
+ Fa 9-10/93: 176
+ Gr 7/93: 60

25334. NI 5313: SCHUBERT—String
quintet. *Brandis Quartet; Yang, cello.*
+ Fa 9-10/93: 269
+ Gr 6/93: 70

25335. NI 5316: IVES—Unanswered
question; Central park in the dark; Robert
Browning overture; Three places in New
England. *Gulbenkian Orch.;*
Swierczewski, cond.
+ ARG 11-12/92: 138
● Fa 11-12/92: 265
+ St 4/93: 285

25336. NI 5318: MENDELSSOHN—
Symphony no. 3; Hebrides overture;
Calm sea and prosperous voyage
overture. *Hanover Band; Goodman,*
cond.
● ARG 5-6/92: 85
● Fa 5-6/92: 198

25337. NI 5321: HAYDN—Symphonies
no. 9, 12-13, 40. *Austro-Hungarian*
Haydn Orch.; Fischer, cond.
+ ARG 3-4/92: 71
+ Fa 9-10/92: 255

25338. NI 5322: RACHMANINOFF—
Symphony no. 2; Vocalise. *BBC Welsh*
Symphony Orch., Okata, cond.
- ARG 5-6/92: 114
● Fa 5-6/92: 228
● Gr 5/92: 44
● St 12/92: 245

25339. NI 5324: GOTTSCHALK—Piano
music for four hands. *Marks, Barrett,*
piano.
+ ARG 7-8/92: 137
- Fa 5-6/92: 164
● St 12/92: 239

25340. NI 5325: BACH—Violin concertos;
Concerto for two violins; Concerto for
violin and oboe. *Shumsky, Tunnell,*
violins; Miller, oboe; Scottish Chamber
Orch. Reissue.
+ ARG 5-6/92: 20
+ Fa 5-6/92: 116
+ Gr 9/92: 41

25341. NI 5326: Music of Moszkowski,
Friedman, Hofmann, Sibelius, Ferrata,
Sinding, Albeniz, Strauss, Schubert,
Liadov, Levitzki, Sauer, Kreisler, Busoni,
Bortkiewicz, and Scott. *Jones, piano.*
+ ARG 7-8/92: 267

25342. NI 5327: Wind music of Ibert,
Françaix, Auric, Honegger and Milhaud.
Pro Arte Wind Quintet. Reissue.
+ Fa 1-2/93: 311
+ Gr 1/93: 47

25343. NI 5328: *Taverner to Tavener.*
Music of Taverner, Henry VII, Gibbons,

Greene, Walton and others. *Christ Church Cathedral Choir, Oxford; Darlington, cond.*
- Gr 10/92: 167

25344. NI 5329: Barber—Violin concerto. Bernstein—Serenade for violin and orchestra. *Kun, violin; English String Orch.; Boughton, cond.*
+ ARG 7-8/92: 87
+ Fa 7-8/92: 110
- Gr 6/92: 38

25345. NI 5330: Strauss—Oboe concerto. Françaix—Horloge de flore. Martinů—Oboe concerto. *Anderson, oboe; Philharmonia Orch.; Wright, cond.*
+ ARG 11-12/92: 212
- Fa 11-12/92: 380
+ Gr 12/92: 77

25346. NI 5331: Haydn—Symphonies no. 14-17. *Austro-Hungarian Haydn Orch.; Fischer, cond.*
+ Fa 9-10/92: 256
- Gr 11/92: 62

25347. NI 5333: Bartók—Violin concertos no. 1-2. *Hetzel, violin; Hungarian State Orch.; Fischer, cond.*
- Gr 7/93: 34

25348. NI 5335: *The sound of St. John's.* Music of Langlais, Orr, Tippett, Howells, and Hoddinott. *St. John's College Choir, Cambridge; Guest, cond.*
- Gr 10/92: 172

25349. NI 5337: *Le maître de la mélodie.* Music of Roussel, De Manziarly, Poulenc, Caplet, Auric, Milhaud, and Chabrier. *Cuénod, tenor; Parsons, piano.*
+ ARG 11-12/92: 259
+ Fa 9-10/92: 400

25350. NI 5338: *Os Ingênuos play choros from Brazil.* Music of Do Bandolim, Nazareth, Pixinguinha, Azevedo, Ratinho, Da Violabastos, De Abreu, De Barros, Silveira/Sales, and Ximbinho. *Os Ingênuos; with assisting instrumentalists.*
+ Fa 3-4/93: 383

25351. NI 5340: Ravel—Ma mère l'oye. Beethoven—Piano sonata no. 21 "Waldstein." Chopin—Scherzo no. 3. Mendelssohn—Variations sérieuses. *Perlemuter, Farmer, piano.*
+ Fa 9-10/92: 323

25352. NI 5341: Haydn—Symphonies no. 89, 91; La vera costanza overture. *Austro-Hungarian Haydn Orch.; Fischer, cond.*
- Gr 1/94: 47

25353. NI 5342: John Amis: Aiscellany. *Amis, speaker, whistler and singer; with friends.*
- Fa 11-12/92: 423

25354. NI 5343: Mathias—Helios; Oboe concerto; Requiescat; Symphony no. 3.

Cowley, oboe; BBC Welsh Symphony Orch.; Llewellyn, cond.
+ Fa 1-2/93: 192
+ Gr 11/92: 89

25355. NI 5344: Rachmaninoff—Symphony no. 3; The isle of the dead. *BBC Welsh Symphony Orch.; Otaka, cond.*
+ ARG 3-4/93: 126
+ Fa 3-4/93: 254
+ Gr 4/93: 56

25356. NI 5345: Boyce—Symphonies. *English String Orch.; Boughton, cond.*
- ARG 7-8/94: 78
- Fa 7-8/94: 90

25357. NI 5347: *Orchestral favorites, vol. 2.* Music of Respighi, Arensky, Tchaikovsky, Wirén, Walton, and Ireland. *English String Orch.; Boughton, cond.*
+ ARG 3-4/93: 157
+ Fa 3-4/93: 397

25358. NI 5348: Rachmaninoff—Piano concerto no. 3; Piano sonata no. 2. *Lill, piano; BBC Welsh Symphony Orch.; Otaka, cond.*
- ARG 9-10/94: 179
+ Fa 9-10/94: 302
+ Gr 10/94: 116

25359. NI 5349: Brahms—Piano concerto no. 1. Dohnányi—Variations on a nursery song. *Anderson, piano; Hungarian State Symphony Orch.; Fischer, cond.*
- ARG 9-10/95: 113
+ Fa 7-8/95: 129
+ Gr 3/95: 38

25360. NI 5350: *Dear old Erin's isle.* Irish traditional music from America. *Various performers.*
+ Fa 3-4/93: 388

25361. NI 5351: Mozart—String quartets no. 21-22. *Franz Schubert Quartet.*
+ ARG 7-8/94: 142

25362. NI 5352: Paco del Gastor, flamenco de la frontera. *Gastor, guitar; with assisting instrumentalists.*
+ ARG 5-6/93: 163
- Fa 3-4/93: 384

25363. NI 5353: Beethoven—String quartets no. 4-6. *Brandis Quartet.*
- ARG 1-2/95: 77
+ Fa 11-12/94: 164
- Gr 9/94: 71

25364. NI 5357: Hoddinott—Passagio; The heaventree of stars; Doubles; Star children. *Kun, violin; Cowley, oboe; Armstrong, harpsichord; BBC Welsh Symphony Orch.; Otaka, cond.*
+ ARG 7-8/93: 101
+ Fa 7-8/93: 154
+ Gr 7/93: 40

25365. NI 5358: *The virtuoso violin.* Music of Vecsey, Moszkowski, Sarasate, Chopin, Herbert, Albéniz, Elgar, Dinicu, Paganini, Hubay, Brahms, Kroll, Beethoven, and Bazzini. *Kang, violin; Rahkonen, piano.*
+ Fa 11-12/93: 506
- Gr 9/93: 82

25366. NI 5360: Taverner—Music for our Lady and the Divine Office. *Christ Church Cathedral Choir of Oxford; Darlington, cond.*
+ Fa 11-12/93: 413
+ Gr 10/93: 100

25367. NI 5361: Schumann—Six fugues on B-A-C-H. Reubke—Sonata on the 94th psalm. *Bowyer, organ.*
+ Fa 11-12/93: 388
+ Gr 2/94: 76

25368. NI 5362/63 (2 discs): Bartók—The wooden prince: suite, op. 13; Two portraits, op. 5; Music for strings, percussion, and celesta; Divertimento for string orchestra. *Hungarian State Orch.; Fischer, cond.; Hetzel, violin.*
- Fa 11-12/93: 176
- Gr 7/93: 34

25369. NI 5364: Walton—Choral music. *Christ Church Cathedral Choir, Oxford; Darlington, cond.*
+ Gr 3/94: 97

25370. NI 5366: *An English suite.* Bridge—String-orchestra music. Parry—English suite. Finzi—Eclogue for piano and strings. *Jones, piano; English String Orch.; Boughton, cond.*
+ ARG 11-12/93: 85
- Fa 11-12/93: 521
- Fa 1-2/94: 182
- Gr 8/93: 26

25371. NI 5367: Matthias—Organ music. *Scott, organ.*
+ Fa 11-12/93: 314
+ Gr 6/93: 76

25372. NI 5369: Hoddinott—Piano sonatas no. 1-5. *Jones, piano.*
+ Gr 12/93: 89

25373. NI 5370: Hoddinott—Piano sonatas no. 6-10. *Jones, piano.*
+ ARG 7-8/95: 125
+ Fa 9-10/95: 225
+ Gr 5/95: 83

25374. NI 5377: Bach—Organ music, vol. 4. *Bowyer, organ.*
+ Gr 2/94: 73

25375. NI 5379: Janáček—String quartets no. 1-2. Fauré—String quartet, op. 121. *Medici Quartet. Reissue.*
+ ARG 7-8/94: 118
- Fa 5-6/94: 172

25376. NI 5380: Tchaikovsky—String quartets no. 1, 3. *Franz Schubert Quartet.*

NIMBUS

+ ARG 5-6/94: 155
+ Fa 3-4/94: 336
+ Fa 11-12/94: 397
• Gr 4/94: 66

25377. NI 5381: Mozart—String quartets no. 19, 23. *Franz Schubert Quartet.*
+ ARG 7-8/94: 142
+ Fa 11-12/94: 315
+ Gr 6/94: 76

25378. NI 5382: Beethoven—String quartets no. 9, 11. *Brandis Quartet.*
+ ARG 9-10/94: 99
+ Fa 11-12/94: 164
+ Gr 6/94: 68

25379. NI 5390: Tippett—The blue guitar. Britten—Nocturnal after Dowland. Bennett—Five impromptus. Walton—Five bagatelles. Berkeley—Sonatina, op. 52, no. 1. *Ogden, guitar.*
+ ARG 9-10/95: 261
+ Fa 9-10/95: 392
• Gr 6/95: 84

25380. NI 5392: M. Haydn—Flute concertos; Symphony no. 25. J. Haydn—Symphony no. 22. *Nagy, flute; Austro-Hungarian Haydn Orch.; Fischer, cond.* Partial reissue.
+ Gr 8/93: 31

25381. NI 5394: Palestrina—Missa O sacrum convivium; O sacrum convivium; coenantibus illis; Magnificat sexti toni à 6. Morales—O sacrum convivium. *Christ Church Cathedral Choir, Oxford; Darlington, cond.*
+ ARG 9-10/94: 171
+ Fa 5-6/94: 212

25382. NI 5395: *Arie antiche: the first voice.* Music of Caldara, Giordani, Gluck, Handel, Monteverdi, Paisiello, Pergolesi, and Vivaldi. *Gherman, voice; Farmer, piano.*
• ARG 5-6/94: 196

25383. NI 5399: Tchaikovsky—String quartet no. 2; Souvenir de Florence. *Franz Schubert Quartet; Flieder, viola; Schulz, cello.*
+ ARG 9-10/94: 210
+ Fa 9-10/94: 351

25384. NI 5400: Bach—Organ works, vol. 5. *Bowyer, organ.*
- ARG 9-10/94: 95
• Fa 9-10/94: 128

25385. NI 5403: J.C. Bach—Sinfonias, op. 18. *English String Symphony; Boughton, cond.*
- ARG 9-10/94: 92
+ Fa 11-12/94: 147
• Gr 9/94: 45

25386. NI 5405/06 (2 discs): Szymanowski—Complete piano music, vol. 1. *M. Jones, piano.*
+ ARG 1-2/95: 190
+ Fa 11-12/94: 394

+ Fa 1-2/95: 285
+ Gr 9/94: 84

25387. NI 5407: Haydn—Symphonies no. 3, 11, 18, 20. *Austro-Hungarian Haydn Orch.; Fischer, cond.*
+ Fa 1-2/95: 173

25388. NI 5408: Langlais—Organ music. *Bowyer, organ.*
• ARG 1-2/95: 129
+ Fa 1-2/95: 184
+ Gr 1/95: 78

25389. NI 5410: Hindemith—String quartet no. 3. Schulhoff—String quartet no. 1. Weill—String quartet no. 2. *Brandis Quartet.*
+ Fa 5-6/95: 217
+ Gr 3/95: 64

25390. NI 5411: Hindemith—Organ sonatas no. 1-3. Schoenberg—Variations on a recitative; Organ sonata: 2 fragments. Pepping—Three fugues on B-A-C-H. *Bowyer, organ.*
+ Fa 5-6/95: 218
+ Gr 1/95: 76

25391. NI 5414: *Advent carols from St. John's.* Music of Lloyd, Ord, Guest, Brahms, Howells, Maconchy, Mendelssohn, Britten, Hadley, Holst, Warlock, and Anon. *Choir of St. John's College, Cambridge; Robinson, cond.*
+ Fa 9-10/95: 382

25392. NI 5419/20 (2 discs): Haydn—Paris symphonies. *Austro-Hungarian Haydn Orch.; Fischer, cond.*
+ Fa 5-6/95: 210
+ Gr 3/95: 46

25393. NI 5422: Brahms—Piano sonata no. 3. Liszt—Après une lecture de Dante. Schumann—Toccata, op. 7. *Anderson, piano.*
• ARG 1-2/96: 92
+ Fa 11-12/95: 218
+ Gr 7/95: 84

25394. NI 5423: Bach—Organ music, vol. 6. *Bowyer, organ.*
- ARG 11-12/95: 73
+ Fa 9-10/95: 128
+ Gr 7/95: 82

25395. NI 5424: Bretan—Golem; Arald. *Sandru, Daróczy, Voineag, Agache, Zanku, vocalists; Phil. Orch. Moldava, Iasi; Mandeal, cond.*
+ ARG 1-2/96: 93
+ Fa 11-12/95: 220
+ Gr 10/95: 131
+ ON 2/3/96: 37
+ Op 1/96: 122

25396. NI 5426/30 (5 discs): Haydn—Symphonies no. 1-20. *Austro-Hungarian Haydn Orch.; Fischer, cond.*
+ Fa 1-2/96: 223

25397. NI 5432: Rachmaninoff—Vespers. *Fryer, mezzo-soprano; Butterfield, tenor; Philharmonia Chorus; Hill, cond.*
• Gr 12/95: 131

25398. NI 5433: Mozart—String quartets no. 14, 18. *Franz Schubert Quartet.*
+ ARG 11-12/95: 165
+ Fa 1-2/96: 139

25399. NI 5434: Victoria—Motet and Missa Dum complerentur; Missa Simile est regnum caelorum. *Christ Church Cathedral Choir, Oxford; Darlington, cond.*
• ARG 3-4/96: 202
+ Fa 11-12/95: 413

25400. NI 5435/36 (2 discs): Szymanowski—Complete piano music, vol. 2. *Jones, piano.*
+ ARG 3-4/96: 191
+ Fa 11-12/95: 396
+ Fa 1-2/96: 317

25401. NI 5438: Schubert—String quartets no. 13-14. *Brandis Quartet.*
- ARG 3-4/96: 177
+ Fa 3-4/96: 277
+ Gr 12/95: 108

25402. NI 5439: Rachmaninoff—Études-tableaux, op. 33 and 39. *Lill, piano.*
- ARG 3-4/96: 169
• Fa 1-2/96: 277
+ Gr 9/95: 84

25403. NI 5440: *Oxford church anthems.* Music of Wood, Gibbons, Howells, Schubert, Bruckner, Handel, Harris, Leighton, Rutter, Stanford, Eccard, Purcell, Byrd, Bach, Victoria, Morley, João IV, and Gardiner. *Christ Church Cathedral Choir, Oxford; Darlington, cond.*
+ ARG 3-4/96: 246
+ Fa 1-2/96: 374

25404. NI 5441: *Santa Fe suite and other twentieth-century harp classics.* Music of Mathias, Fauré, Tournier, Hindemith, Roussel, Tailleferre, Arnold, and Britten. *Bennett, harp.*
+ Fa 3-4/96: 362

25405. NI 5443: Schubert—Four-hand piano music. *Walker, Farmer, piano.*
+ ARG 5-6/96: 187
+ Fa 3-4/96: 277

25406. NI 5445: *Forgotten Provence: Music-making in the south of France, 1150-1550.* Sequences from St. Martial; Motets at Montepellier; Troubadour songs; Caroles. Bornelh—Reis glorios. *Martin Best Consort.*
• ARG 5-6/96: 247
• Fa 3-4/96: 346
+ Gr 3/96: 92

25407. NI 5446: Scriabin—Mazurkas, op. 3, 25, 40. *Deyanova, piano.*
+ Fa 3-4/96: 282

25408. NI 5449: *Fern Hill*. Music of Corigliano, Barber, Belmont, Spencer, and Mulholland. *Kansas City Chorale; Fern Hill Orch.; Bruffy, cond.*
+ ARG 3-4/96: 239
+ Fa 3-4/96: 339

25409. NI 5454: *Hear, o Heav'ns*. Chapel Royal anthems by Purcell, Blow, Locke and Humfrey. *Christ Church Cathedral Choir, Oxford; Darlington, cond.*
+ ARG 5-6/96: 251
+ Fa 5-6/96: 335
+ Gr 2/96: 97

25410. NI 5455 (2 discs): Mozart—String quartets no. 15-17, 20. *Franz Schubert Quartet.*
• ARG 5-6/96: 155
+ Gr 3/96: 64

25411. NI 5457 (2 discs): Bach—Orgelbüchlein. *Bowyer, organ; Fynske Chamber Choir; Joensen, cond.*
+ ARG 7-8/96: 70
+ Fa 7-8/96: 94
• Gr 4/96: 72

25412. NI 5459/60 (2 discs): Hindemith—Music for one and two pianos. *Roberts, Strong, pianos.*
□ ARG 1-2/97: 121
• Fa 11-12/96: 270
• Gr 11/96: 108

25413. NI 5461: Beethoven—Septet. Hindemith—Octet. *Berlin Phil. Octet.*
• Gr 4/96: 61

25414. NI 5463: Bretan—The evening star. *Croitoru, Voineag, Pojar, Szabó; Transylvania Phil. Orch.; Hary, cond.*
+ ARG 7-8/96: 91
• Fa 7-8/96: 126
+ Gr 8/96: 92
• ON 5/96: 59

25415. NI 5465: Beethoven—String quartet no. 13; Grosse Fuge. *Brandis Quartet.*
+ Fa 7-8/96: 101
+ Gr 4/96: 60

25416. NI 5466: Hoddinott—Quodlibet on Welsh nursery tunes; Chorales, variants, and fanfares; Ritornelli no. 2. Mathias—Summer dances; Soundings. *Fine Arts Brass Ensemble; Bowyer, organ.*
+ ARG 9-10/96: 138
+ Fa 7-8/96: 201
+ Gr 5/96: 74

25417. NI 5467: Schmidt—String quartets. *Franz Schubert Quartet.*
+ ARG 9-10/96: 191
+ Gr 6/96: 68

25418. NI 5468: Gade—Tre tonestykker, op. 22. Syberg—Präludium, intermezzo, and fugato. Norgård—Partita concertante, op. 23. Nielsen—Commotio. *Bowyer, organ.*

+ Fa 9-10/96: 405
+ Gr 7/96: 81

25419. NI 5470: *The origin of the species: virtuoso Victorian brass music from Cyfarthfa Castle, Wales*. Music of Verdi, Paganini, Sullivan, Levy, Montgomery, Sainton-Dolby, Mozart-Méhul, Bawden, J. Parry, Hérold, and Wagner-Sonntag. *Wallace, cornet; Wallace Collection; Wright, cond.*
- ARG 9-10/96: 239
+ Fa 9-10/96: 426

25420. NI 5471: Maw—Sonata notturno; Life studies. *Wallfisch, cello; English String Orch.; Boughton, cond.*
+ Fa 9-10/96: 257
+ Gr 8/96: 50

25421. NI 5472: Dvořák—Piano trios no. 1, 4. *Vienna Trio.*
+ ARG 9-10/96: 116

25422. NI 5473: Brahms—Viola sonata, op. 120, no. 1. Dvořák—Sonatina for viola and piano, op. 100. Hindemith—Trauermusik for viola and piano; Duett for viola and cello; Viola sonata, op. 11, no. 4. *Strehle, viola; Wisnewska, piano; Boettcher, cello.*
+ Fa 11-12/96: 205
+ Gr 9/96: 65

25423. NI 5478: Rachmaninoff—Piano concerto no. 4; Variations on a theme of Corelli; Rhapsody on a theme of Paganini. *Lill, piano; BBC National Orch. of Wales; Otaka, cond.*
- ARG 11-12/96: 183
+ Fa 9-10/96: 296
+ Gr 8/96: 52

25424. NI 5479: Music of Haydn, Mozart, Danzi, Farkas, and Takács. *Vienna Quintet.*
+ Fa 11-12/96: 477
+ Gr 3/97: 71

25425. NI 5480: Sheppard—English and Latin church music. *Christ Church Cathedral Choir, Oxford; Darlington, cond.*
• ARG 11-12/96: 209
+ Fa 11-12/96: 375
+ Gr 9/96: 92

25426. NI 5484: Liszt—Rhapsodie espagnole; Concert etudes; Jeux d'eau; Legends; Mephisto waltz; Sonetto di Petrarca. *Anderson, piano.*
+ ARG 9-10/96: 153
• Fa 11-12/96: 289
+ Gr 10/96: 81

25427. NI 5485: Schubert—The piano duets, vol. 2. *Walker, Farmer, pianos.*
+ Fa 11-12/96: 361

25428. NI 7007: *Meditations for a quiet night*. Music of Mendelssohn, Vaughan Williams, Pachelbel, Warlock, Barber, Elgar, Sibelius, Copland and Parry.

English String Orch.; English Symphony Orch.; Boughton, cond. Reissues.
+ Fa 7-8/92: 360

25429. NI 7011: *The art of Paco Peña*. Music of Peña, Montoya, Ramirez, Ricardo, Falü, and Lauro. *Peña, guitar; other artists.* Reissue.
+ ARG 5-6/94: 176
+ Fa 5-6/94: 318

25430. NI 7012: *Vivaldi concerti and Baroque trumpet music*. Music of Albinoni, Vivaldi, A. Scarlatti, Torelli, Corelli, Purcell, and Alberti. *Wallace, Miller, trumpets; Philharmonia Orch.; Warren-Green, Wright, conds.* Reissue.
+ Fa 7-8/94: 273

25431. NI 7013: Vaughan Williams—The lark ascending; Tallis fantasia; Greensleeves; Dives and Lazarus; Oboe concerto; Wasps. *English String Orch.; Boughton, cond.*
• ARG 7-8/94: 183
• Fa 9-10/94: 360

25432. NI 7015: Elgar—Enigma variations; Pomp and circumstance no. 1; Cockaigne; Introduction and allegro; Elegy; Sospiri. *English Symphony Orch.; Boughton, cond.*
+ Fa 9-10/94: 187

25433. NI 7016: Concertos by Haydn, Neruda, Hummel and Fasch. *Wallace, trumpet; Philharmonia Orch.; Warren-Green, cond.* Reissues.
+ ARG 11-12/94: 237
+ Fa 11-12/94: 494
+ Gr 2/95: 60

25434. NI 7017: Britten—Young person's guide to the orchestra; Peter Grimes: Four sea interludes; Variations on a theme of Frank Bridge; Simple symphony. *English Symphony Orch.; Boughton, cond.* Reissue.
+ Fa 1-2/95: 134

25435. NI 7023: Mozart—Eine kleine Nachtmusik; Horn concerto no. 4; Clarinet concerto (played on basset horn). *Halstead, natural horn; Lawson, basset clarinet; Hanover Band; Goodman, cond.*
+ Fa 9-10/95: 268

25436. NI 7026: Tippett—Concerto for double string orchestra; Little music for strings; Fantasia concertante on a theme of Corelli; A child of our time; Evening canticles. *English String Orch.; Boughton, cond.; Christ Church Cathedral Choir, Oxford; Darlington, cond., Choir of St. John's College, Cambridge; Guest, cond.* Reissue.
+ Fa 1-2/96: 326

25437. NI 7027: Concertos by Cimarosa, Albinoni, Marcello, and Vivaldi. *Anderson, oboe; Philharmonia Orch.; Wright, cond.* Reissue.

+ ARG 1-2/96: 215
• Fa 1-2/96: 414

25438. NI 7029: ELGAR—Orchestra music. *English Symphony Orch.; Boughton, cond.*
+ Fa 7-8/96: 165

25439. NI 7701: CHOPIN—Andante spianato and grande polonaise brillante; Piano sonata no. 3. LISZT—Piano sonata; Hungarian rhapsody no. 2. *Cherkassky, piano.*
• Fa 5-6/94: 129

25440. NI 7702: DEBUSSY—Piano works. *M. Jones, piano.*
- Fa 7-8/94: 121

25441. NI 7703: GRAINGER—Piano favorites. *M. Jones, Martin, McMahon, pianos.* Reissue.
+ Fa 9-10/94: 197

25442. NI 7704: MENDELSSOHN—Songs without words (selections). *M. Jones, piano.* Reissues.
+ ARG 11-12/94: 155
+ Fa 11-12/94: 298

25443. NI 7705: SCHUMANN—Symphonic etudes; Kreisleriana. FRANCK—Prelude, chorale, and fugue. *Cherkassky, piano.* Reissues.
+ Fa 5-6/95: 335
+ Gr 3/95: 72

25444. NI 7706: MUSSORGSKY—Pictures at an exhibition. RACHMANINOFF—Variations on a theme of Corelli. BRAHMS—Variations on a theme of Paganini. *Cherkassky, piano.*
• Fa 7-8/95: 261

25445. NI 7707: BEETHOVEN—Piano sonatas no. 8, 14, 21, 26. *Roberts, piano.* Reissue.
+ Fa 11-12/95: 207

25446. NI 7708: *Art of the encore.* Music of Chopin, Liszt, and Schubert. *Cherkassky, piano.*
+ ARG 5-6/96: 239
• Fa 1-2/96: 391

25447. NI 7709: BEETHOVEN—Piano sonatas no. 30-32. *Roberts, piano.* Reissue.
+ Fa 1-2/96: 145
+ Gr 11/95: 120

25448. NI 7710: BEETHOVEN—Diabelli variations; Variations with fugue, op. 35 "Eroica". *Roberts, piano.*
• Fa 7-8/96: 106

25449. NI 7711: *Christmas organ music.* Music of Liszt, Bach, Daquin, Blake, Brahms, Pachelbel, Guilmant, Carter, W.S. Lloyd Webber, J.M. Bach, Willcocks, Purvis, Rutter, Corelli, Sumsion, Walch, and Handel. *Bowyer, organ.*
- Fa 11-12/96: 460

25450. NI 7712: *For weddings.* Music of Wagner, Bach, Handel, Mendelssohn, Charpentier, Boëllman, Clarke, Wright, Stanley, Vaughan Williams, Walton, Purcell, Gounod, and Widor. *Bowyer, organ.*
+ Fa 9-10/96: 406

25451. NI 7713/14 (2 discs): RAVEL—Piano music. *Perlemuter, piano.* Reissue.
+ ARG 9-10/96: 187
+ Fa 9-10/96: 301

25452. NI 7715: YSAŸE—Solo violin sonatas. *Shumsky, violin.* Reissue.
+ ARG 1-2/97: 191
+ Gr 10/96: 88

25453. NI 7806: Music of Gounod, Auber, Rossini, Meyerbeer, Bellini, and others. *Galli-Curci, soprano; various orchs. & conds.* Recorded 1917-30.
+ ARG 9-10/90: 155
+ Fa 7-8/90: 323
+ Gr 5/90: 2081

25454. NI 7807: *Gigli, vol. 1.* Music of Ponchielli, Cannio, Boito, Puccini, Donizetti, and others. *Gigli, tenor; various orchs. & conds.*
+ ARG 9-10/90: 158
+ Fa 7-8/90: 335
+ Gr 5/90: 2069

25455. NI 7808: Music of Donizetti, Rossini, Bellini, Eckert, Thomas, and others. *Tetrazzini, soprano; unnamed orchs. & conds.*
+ Fa 9-10/90: 446

25456. NI 7810: Music of Thomas, Verdi, Ponchielli, Donizetti, Rossini, and others. *Ruffo, baritone; various orchs. & conds.*
+ Fa 11-12/90: 418
+ Gr 11/90: 1079

25457. NI 7811: Music of Donizetti, Arditi, Becker, Meyerbeer, Wagner, and others. *Schumann-Heink, alto; various orchs. & conds.*
+ Fa 11-12/90: 414
+ Gr 2/91: 1580

25458. NI 7813: Music of Mascagni, Verdi, Donizetti, Leoncavallo, Massenet, and others. *Schipa, tenor; various orchs. & conds.* Recorded 1913-37.
+ ARG 3-4/91: 173 m.f.
+ Fa 3-4/91: 453

25459. NI 7814: Music of Mascagni, Buzzi-Peccia, Verdi, Pergolesi, Giordano, and others. *Muzio, soprano; various orchs. & conds.*
+ ARG 3-4/91: 173 m.f.
+ Fa 3-4/91: 439
+ Gr 4/91: 1920

25460. NI 7815: Music of Verdi, De Leva, Rossini, Donizetti, Romilli, and others. *De Luca, baritone; orchs. & conds.* Recorded 1907-30.
+ ARG 5-6/91: 162
+ Fa 5-6/91: 339

25461. NI 7816: Music of Wagner, Leoncavallo, Meyerbeer, and Verdi. *Melchior, tenor; various orchs. & conds.*
+ ARG 5-6/91: 163
+ Fa 5-6/91: 334

25462. NI 7817: *Gigli, vol. 2.* Music of Donizetti, Puccini, Verdi, Thomas, Bizet, and others. *Gigli, tenor; various orchs. & conds.* Recorded 1925-40.
+ ARG 5-6/91: 161
+ Fa 5-6/91: 333

25463. NI 7821: Music of Rossini, Mozart, Rimsky-Korsakov, Puccini, Verdi, and others. *Norena, soprano; various orchs. & conds.* Recorded 1930-37.
+ ARG 9-10/91: 184 m.f.
+ Fa 7-8/91: 336

25464. NI 7822: MOZART—Great singers in Mozart. *Various performers.*
+ ARG 11-12/91: 100
+ Fa 11-12/91: 420
+ ON 2/1/92: 36

25465. NI 7823/24 (2 discs): *Feodor Chaliapin.* Songs and arias by Mussorgsky, Rubinstein, Malashkin, Brahms, Verdi, Rimsky-Korsakov, and others. *Chaliapin, bass; various pianists, orchs., & conds.* Recorded 1911-36.
+ ARG 11-12/91: 202
+ Fa 11-12/91: 533

25466. NI 7825: *Tibbett in opera.* Arias by Leoncavallo, Bizet, Puccini, Verdi, Rossini, Giordano, and Wagner. *Tibbett, baritone.* Recorded 1926-39.
+ ARG 11-12/91: 208
+ Fa 11-12/91: 530

25467. NI 7827/28 (2 discs): MOZART—Die Zauberflöte. *Lemnitz, Berger, Rosvænge, Strienz, Hüsch; Berlin Phil. Orch.; Beecham, cond.* Recorded 1937.
□ ARG 3-4/92: 215
+ Fa 3-4/92: 272
- ON 6/92: 48

25468. NI 7829: G. CHARPENTIER—Louise (abridged). *Vallin, Thill, Pernet, ; Chorus and orchestra; Bigot, cond.* Recorded 1935.
+ Fa 3-4/92: 172
+ ON 5/92: 53

25469. NI 7830: *Opera arias.* Music of R. Strauss, Wagner, Kienzl, Smetana, Puccini, Korngold, Verdi, Mozart, Tchaikovsky, Bizet, Lortzing, and Offenbach. *Tauber, tenor; with acc.* Recorded 1919-1928.
+ ARG 3-4/93: 200

+ Fa 9-10/92: 397
+ Gr 12/92: 153

25470. NI 7831: *Mattia Battistini.* Music of Massenet, Thomas, Donizetti, Verdi, Tchaikovsky and others. *Battistini, baritone; with piano & orchestral accompaniment.* Recorded 1902-03.
+ ARG 5-6/92: 183
+ Fa 7-8/92: 296
+ Gr 10/92: 207

25471. NI 7832: *Maria Ivogün.* Songs and arias by Bishop, Handel, Donizetti, Rossini, Verdi, Chopin, Meyerbeer and others. *Ivogün, soprano; with orchestral accompaniment.*
- Fa 7-8/92: 328
+ Gr 8/92: 76

25472. NI 7833: *Lotte Schöne and Richard Tauber in operetta.* Music of Lehár, Suppé, Berté, J. Strauss, Jr., Kálman, Millöcker, Zeller, and Nessler. *Schöne, soprano; Tauber, tenor; with acc.*
+ Fa 9-10/92: 397
+ Gr 12/92: 153
+ ON 3/13/93: 35

25473. NI 7834: *Caruso in ensemble, 1906-1918.* Music of Verdi, Puccini, Donizetti, and Flotow. *Caruso, tenor; various singers and acc.*
- Fa 9-10/92: 401

25474. NI 7835: *Jussi Björling: the first ten years.* Music of Verdi, Puccini, Leoncavallo, Mascagni, Atterberg, Rimsky-Korsakov, Massenet, Rossini and others. *Björling, tenor; with orchestral accomp.*
+ Fa 11-12/92: 420

25475. NI 7836/37 (2 discs): *Conchita Supervia.* Music of Rossini, Thomas, Saint-Saëns, Delibes, Falla, Baldomir, Serrano, Yradier, Valverde, and Bizet. *Supervia, mezzo-soprano; orch. acc.; Marshall, piano.*
+ ARG 3-4/93: 200
+ Fa 3-4/93: 337
+ Gr 3/93: 115

25476. NI 7838: *John Charles Thomas: an American classic.* Music of Strickland, Malotte, Newman-Charles, Kilmer-Rasbach, M. Foster, Wood-Wolfe, Samuels-Whitcup-Powell, Cassel/Mana-Zucca, Guion, Kern, Wolf, Lady John Scott, C. Scott, Moore-Gatty, J. Strauss Jr., Scollard-Speaks, Straus, and Sullivan. *Thomas, baritone; various acc.*
+ Fa 3-4/93: 343
+ ON 6/93: 43

25477. NI 7840/41 (2 discs): *The era of Adelina Patti.* Historical anthology of vocal recordings dating from 1902- 28. *Various performers.*
• ARG 9-10/93: 268
+ Fa 7-8/93: 283

+ Gr 7/93: 100
+ ON 3/19/94: 32

25478. NI 7842: *Jussi Björling, vol. 2.* Music of Beethoven, Schubert, R. Strauss, Sibelius, Alfvén, Eklöf, Sjöberg, Tosti, Puccini, Verdi, Flotow, Gounod, Bizet, Offenbach, J. Strauss, Jr., and Millöcker. *Björling, tenor; Schymberg, soprano; Ebert, piano; orchestra; Grevillius, cond.*
+ ARG 7-8/93: 216
+ Fa 7-8/93: 279
+ Gr 10/93: 145

25479. NI 7845: *Giacomo Lauri-Volpi.* Music of Bellini, Boito, Massenet, Puccini, Mascagni, Leoncavallo, Verdi, Meyerbeer, Gomes, Offenbach, Bizet, Gounod, and Giordano. *Lauri-Volpi, tenor; orch. acc.* Reissues; recorded 1922-42.
+ Fa 11-12/93: 461
+ Gr 7/93: 98

25480. NI 7846: *Rosa Ponselle, vol. 2.* Music of Puccini, Verdi, Mascagni, Herbert, Rimsky-Korsakov, Halévy, Wagner, Tosti, Massenet, Bach-Gounod, and Charles. *Ponselle, soprano; various orchs. & conds.; Romani, piano.*
+ Fa 11-12/93: 456
+ Gr 10/93: 145

25481. NI 7847: *Kirsten Flagstad: arias.* Music of Wagner, Beethoven, and Weber. *Flagstad, soprano; various orchs.*
+ Fa 11-12/93: 457
+ Gr 7/93: 100
+ ON 3/19/94: 32

25482. NI 7852: Amelita Galli-Curci, vol. 2. *Galli-Curci, soprano; with piano & orch. accomp.*
+ ARG 5-6/94: 215
+ Fa 3-4/94: 372
+ Gr 8/94: 124

25483. NI 7854: *McCormack in song. McCormack, tenor; various orch. & piano accs.*
+ Fa 5-6/94: 296

25484. NI 7855: *Great singers in New York: the age of Caruso.* Music of Mascagni, Ponchielli, Verdi, Donizetti, Mozart, Rossini, Gounod, Puccini, Leoncavallo, Thomas, Wagner, Flotow, Gluck, and Bemberg. *Various singers and accs.*
+ ARG 5-6/94: 218
+ Fa 5-6/94: 303

25485. NI 7856: *Legendary tenors. Various performers.*
+ ARG 7-8/94: 237
+ Fa 7-8/94: 295
+ Gr 9/94: 139

25486. NI 7857: Arias by Mozart, Wolf-Ferrari, and Puccini. *Farrar, soprano.* Recorded 1908-13.

+ ARG 9-10/94: 276
+ Fa 9-10/94: 385
+ Gr 10/94: 225

25487. NI 7858: *Great singers at La Scala.* Music of Verdi, Rossini, Meyerbeer, Mascagni, Donizetti, Puccini, Ponchielli, Bizet, and Gounod. *Various singers and acc.* Recorded 1903-1924.
+ Fa 11-12/94: 453

25488. NI 7859: *Caruso, Farrar, Journet: highlights from Faust and French opera.* Music of Massenet, Thomas, Bizet, and Gounod. *Farrar, Caruso, Ancona, Scotti, Journet, vocalists; with orch. acc.*
+ Fa 11-12/94: 430
+ Gr 10/94: 225

25489. NI 7860: *Eames and Plançon.* Music of Bizet, Gounod, Mozart, Wagner, Schubert, Meyerbeer, Berlioz, Thomas, Rossini, and Bellini. *Eames, soprano; Plançon, bass; various accs.*
+ Fa 1-2/95: 334
+ Fa 3-4/95: 349
+ Gr 1/95: 114

25490. NI 7861: *The spirit of Christmas past.* Twenty historical electric and acoustic recordings. *Various vocalists and acc.*
+ Fa 9-10/95: 379

25491. NI 7862/63 (2 discs): PUCCINI—La bohème. Gigli, Albanese, Poli, Menotti, Baronti; Teatro alla Scala; Berrettoni, cond. Recorded 1938.
+ ARG 11-12/95: 286
+ Fa 5-6/95: 296
+ Gr 3/95: 122

25492. NI 7864: *More legendary voices.* Music of Lake, Handel, Leoncavallo, Korngold, Giordano, Bizet, Lehár, Mozart, Zeller, Massenet, Saint-Saëns, Boïto, Wagner, and Bellini. *Vocalists: McCormack, Jeritza, Gigli, Tauber, E. Schumann, Chaliapin, Supervia, Muzio, Melchior, Ferrier, Callas; various acc.* Recorded 1911-1949.
+ Fa 5-6/95: 393

25493. NI 7865: *Great singers at the Maryinsky Theatre.* Twenty-two acoustic historic recordings. *Various singers and accs.*
+ ARG 5-6/95: 252
+ Fa 7-8/95: 391
+ Gr 3/95: 124

25494. NI 7866: *Caruso in opera, vol. 2.* Music of Flotow, Verdi, Donizetti, Mascagni, Puccini, Meyerbeer, Bizet, Leoncavallo, Giordano, Gounod, Tchaikovsky, and Rubinstein. *Caruso, tenor; various orch. acc.* Recorded 1905-20.
+ Fa 5-6/95: 384
+ Gr 7/95: 132

NIMBUS

25495. NI 7867: *Legendary baritones.*
Music of Massenet, Tosti, Verdi, Puccini,
Wagner, Marschner, Lortzing, Rossini,
Giordano, and Leoncavallo. *Various
baritones and acc.*
+ Fa 9-10/95: 377

25496. NI 7868: *McCormack and
Kreisler in recital.* Twenty acoustic
historic vocal and instrumental
recordings. *McCormack, tenor; Kreisler,
violin; various acc.*
+ Fa 9-10/95: 377

25497. NI 7869: *Great singers at the
Gran Teatro de Liceo.* Music of Bizet,
Verdi, Thomas, Wagner, Arrieta,
Meyerbeer, Bellini, Rossini, Donizetti,
and Mascheroni. *Various singers and
acc.*
+ Fa 11-12/95: 444
+ ON 2/3/96: 37

25498. NI 7870: *Schipa in song.* Music of
Scarlatti, Pergolesi (i.e., Legrenzio
Ciampi), Handel, Gluck, Donaudy, Liszt,
Sibella, Palomero, Barrera, Blasco,
Arniches, Oteo, Ponce, Palacios, Perez,
Anton, Guaracha, Falla, Badet, and
Rimsky-Korsakov. *Schipa, tenor; various
accs.*
+ ARG 1-2/96: 247
+ Fa 1-2/96: 363

25499. NI 7871: *Flagstad in song.* Music
of Beethoven, Strauss, Alnaes, Grieg,
Bridge, Dvořák, Scott, Rogers, and
Charles. *Flagstad, soprano; McArthur,
piano.* Recorded 1935-40.
+ ARG 5-6/96: 274
+ Fa 1-2/96: 363
+ Gr 12/95: 176
+ ON 8/96: 45

25500. NI 7872: *Farrar in French opera.*
Music of Massenet, Thomas, Gounod,
Offenbach, and Bizet. *Farrar, soprano;
Martinelli, tenor; Amato, baritone; Orch.
of Teatro alla Scala; Toscanini, cond.*
Recorded 1908 and 1914-15.
+ Fa 1-2/96: 352
+ Gr 1/96: 118
+ ON 5/96: 59

25501. NI 7873: *Lehmann in opera, vol.
1: 1916-21.* Music of Weber, Mozart,
Nicolai, Thomas, Wagner, and
Tchaikovsky. *Lehmann, soprano; various
orch. acc.*
+ ARG 11-12/96: 300
+ Fa 7-8/96: 343
+ Gr 10/96: 112

25502. NI 7874: *Gigli in song.* Music of
De Curtis, di Capua, Toselli, Denza, and
others. *Gigli, tenor; with orch. acc.*
+ Fa 5-6/96: 328

25503. NI 7875: Music of Verdi,
Donizetti, Halévy, Bellini, Gounod,
Puccini, Mozart, Meyerbeer, and
Thomas. *Pinza, bass; various orch. accs.*

+ Fa 7-8/96: 355
+ Gr 6/96: 116

25504. NI 7876: *Great singers in
Moscow.* Music of Rubinstein,
Tchaikovsky, Rimsky-Korsakov, Glinka,
Mussorgsky, Verdi, Wagner, Goldmark,
Massenet, Gounod, and Bizet. *Various
singers and accs.*
+ ARG 11-12/96: 306
+ Fa 9-10/96: 383
+ ON 1/11/97: 41

25505. NI 7877: *Antonina Nezhdanova in
opera and song.* Music of Gounod,
Wagner, Rossini, Bellini, Verdi, Grieg,
Meyerbeer, Glinka, Alyabiev, Arensky,
Taubert, Tosti, Delibes, Pototsky,
Chemberdzhi, Kochetov, Serrano,
Glazunov, and Valverde. *Nezhdanova,
soprano; various accs.*
+ ARG 11-12/96: 302
+ Fa 9-10/96: 372
+ ON 1/11/97: 41

25506. NI 7878: *Ponselle, vol. 3.* Music
of Verdi, Rossini, Meyerbeer, Puccini,
Leoncavallo, Di Capua, Tosti, Bland, and
Foster. *Ponselle, soprano; various accs.*
Recorded 1920-26, 1939.
+ Fa 11-12/96: 425
+ ON 1/11/97: 41

25507. NI 8801: *The grand piano era:
from Duo-Art reproducing piano rolls.*
Music of Chopin, Friedman, Liszt,
Schumann, and others. *Bauer, Busoni,
Friedman, Grainger, Hofmann, and
others, piano.*
● Fa 5-6/96: 351

25508. NI 8802: *The Polish virtuoso:
from Duo-Art reproducing piano rolls.*
Music of Friedman, Hofmann,
Paderewski, and others. *Friedman,
Hofmann, Paderewski, piano.*
● Fa 5-6/96: 351
+ Gr 12/95: 174

25509. NI 8803: CHOPIN—Piano music.
*Hofmann, piano (from Duo-Art
reproducing piano rolls).*
● Fa 5-6/96: 351

25510. NI 8804: SCHUMANN—Piano
sonatas no. 1-2; Toccata, op. 7;
Symphonic etudes, op. 13. *Bauer,
Grainger, pianos.*
+ Fa 9-10/96: 241

25511. NI 8805: LISZT—Don Juan
fantasia; Hungarian rhapsody no. 14;
Paganini etude no. 3; Paraphrase on
Wagner's Tannhäuser Overture.
CHOPIN—Nocturnes, op. 62, no. 1; op. 37,
no. 1; Polonaise, op. 71, no. 2; Waltz, op.
64, no. 1; Ballade no. 4. *Friedman, piano.*
+ Fa 9-10/96: 241

25512. NI 8806: BRAHMS—The Aeolian
Duo-Art piano rolls. *Rubinstein, Bauer,
Hess, Backhaus, Friedberg, Fischer,
piano rolls on Duo-Art reproducing

piano.*
+ Fa 11-12/96: 204

25513. NI 8807: DEBUSSY—The Aeolian
Duo-Art piano rolls. *Rubinstein,
Copeland, Grainger, Schmitz, Lortat,
Paderewski, Hess, Albert, piano rolls on
Duo-Art reproducing piano.*
+ Fa 11-12/96: 204

NIXA

25514. NIXCD 1002: BRAHMS—
Symphonies (complete); Academic
festival overture; Tragic overture;
Variations on a theme by Haydn; Alto
rhapsody. *Sinclair, alto; Croydon Phil.
Choir, male voices; London Phil. Orch.;
Boult, cond.*
● ARG 5-6/89: 28
● Fa 7-8/89: 113
+ Gr 5/89: 121 (conductor)
● Gr 5/89: 121 (orchestra)

25515. NIXCD 1005 (2 discs):
SCHUMANN—Symphonies (complete).
Philharmonia Orch.; Boult, cond.
- Fa 11-12/89: 357

25516. NIXCD 6001: VAUGHAN
WILLIAMS—Symphonies no. 2, 8. *Hallé
Orch.; Barbirolli, cond.*
+ Fa 3-4/89: 316

25517. NIXCD 6002: ELGAR—Symphony
no. 1; Introduction and allegro. *Hallé
Orch.; Barbirolli, cond.*
+ Fa 3-4/89: 317
+ Gr 1/89: 1150

25518. NIXCD 6003: *English music.*
Music of Delius, Butterworth, Elgar, and
Bax. *Fischer, soprano; Walters,
baritone; Hallé Orch.; Barbirolli, cond.*
+ Fa 5-6/89: 174

25519. NIXCD 6004: Music of Corelli,
Pergolesi, Cimarosa, Albinoni, and
others. *Rothwell, oboe; Hallé Orch.;
Barbirolli, cond.*
+ Fa 3-4/89: 382

25520. NIXCD 6005: PUCCINI—Manon
Lescaut: Tu, tu amore; La bohème: Che
gelida manina to the end of Act 1; Tosca:
E lucevan le stella; O dolce mani;
Madama butterfly: Viene la sera.
*Lafayette, soprano; Lewis, tenor; Hallé
Orch.; Barbirolli, cond.*
● Fa 3-4/89: 242
+ Gr 3/89: 1492

25521. NIXCD 6011: ELGAR—Symphony
no. 2. *London Phil. Orch.; Boult, cond.*
● ARG 11-12/89: 58
+ Fa 9-10/89: 198
+ Gr 5/89: 1729

25522. NIXCD 6012: WALTON—
Symphony no. 1; Belshazzar's feast.
*Noble, baritone; London Phil. Choir &
Orch.; Boult, cond.*

• Fa 5-6/89: 359
+ Gr 2/89: 1300

25523. NIXCD 6013: BRITTEN—Peter Grimes: Four sea interludes & passacaglia. HOLST—The planets. *London Phil. Orch.; Boult, cond.*
- Fa 11-12/89: 159

25524. NIXCD 6021: RIMSKY-KORSAKOV—Symphony no. 2; Russian Easter overture; Capriccio espagnol. *London Symphony Orch.; Scherchen, cond.*
+ Fa 9-10/89: 303
• Gr 3/89: 1437

25525. NIXCD 6022: TCHAIKOVSKY—Romeo and Juliet; Marche slave; Capriccio italien; 1812 overture . *London Symphony Orch.; Band of H.M. Irish Guards; Scherchen, cond.*
+ Fa 9-10/89: 121
+ Gr 4/89: 1592

NIXA CLASSICS

25526. NIXC 1: VERDI—Opera arias. *Vaness, soprano; British Concert Orch.; Renton, cond.*
• Fa 1-2/89: 283
+ Gr 3/88: 1334

NKF

25527. NKFCD 50002-2: GRIEG—Symphonic dances op. 64; Holberg suite op. 40; Old Norwegian melody op. 51. *Oslo Phil. Orch.; Jansons, cond.*
+ ARG 3-4/89: 41
• Fa 3-4/89: 172

25528. NKFCD 50003-2: GRIEG—Piano concerto op. 16; In autumn; Two elegiac melodies; Two Norwegian melodies; Two melodies for string orchestra. *Bratlie, piano; Oslo Phil. Orch.; Jansons, cond.*
+ ARG 3-4/89: 39
+ Fa 3-4/89: 172

25529. NKFCD 50004-2: GRIEG—Violin sonatas (complete). *Tellefsen, violin; Knardahl, piano.*
+ ARG 3-4/89: 40
+ Fa 3-4/89: 170

25530. NKFCD 50005-2: GRIEG—Cello sonata op. 36; Twenty-five Norwegian folk songs and dance pieces for piano. *Kvalbein, cello; Bratlie, Baekkelund, pianos.*
+ ARG 3-4/89: 40
+ Fa 3-4/89: 170
⊓ HPR 6/89: 77

25531. NKFCD 50006-2: GRIEG—String quartets (complete). *Norwegian String Quartet.*
+ ARG 3-4/89: 40
+ Fa 3-4/89: 170

25532. NKFCD 50008-2: BULL—Fantasy and variations on a theme by Bellini; Violin concerto in E minor: Adagio; Adagio Religioso; Polaca guerriera; Visit to a summer farm; In lonely hours. *Tellefsen, violin; Bergen Symphony Orch.; Andersen, cond.*
+ ARG 3-4/89: 28
+ Fa 3-4/89: 126

25533. NKFCD 50009-2: SVENDSEN—Norwegian rhapsodies no. 1-4; Zorahayda; Norwegian artists' carnival. *Bergen Symphony Orch.; Andersen, cond.*
□ ARG 3-4/89: 97
• Fa 3-4/89: 302

25534. NKFCD 50010-2: SVENDSEN—Violin concerto in A op. 6; Symphony no. 1. *Tellefsen, violin; Oslo Phil. Orch.; Andersen, Caridis, conds.*
• ARG 3-4/89: 96
• Fa 3-4/89: 302

25535. NKFCD 50011-2: SVENDSEN—Symphony no. 2; Grand polonaise op. 12; Carnival in Paris op. 9; Romance for violin and orchestra in G op. 26. *Hansen, violin; Oslo Phil. Orch.; Fjeldstad, cond.*
• ARG 3-4/89: 96
• Fa 3-4/89: 303

25536. NKFCD 50012-2: SVENDSEN—String octet in A op. 3; String quintet in C op. 5. *Hindar Quartet; with assisting instrumentalists.*
+ ARG 3-4/89: 97
• Fa 3-4/89: 303

25537. NKFCD 50013-2: HALVORSEN—Norwegian rhapsodies no. 1-2; Norwegian festival overture; Entry of the Boyars; Bergensiana; Andante religioso; Wedding march. HANDEL (ARR. HALVORSEN)—Passacaglia for violin and viola. *Bergen Symphony Orch.; Andersen, cond.; Barratt-Due, violin; Chung, violin & viola.*
+ ARG 3-4/89: 42
+ Fa 3-4/89: 173

25538. NKFCD 50014-2: HALVORSEN—Symphony no. 2; Scenes from Norwegian fairytales; Air norvégien; Norwegian dances no. 1-3; Veslemoy's song. *Tonnesen, violin; Oslo Phil. Orch.; Andersen, cond.*
+ ARG 3-4/89: 42
□ Fa 3-4/89: 173

25539. NKFCD 50015-2: SINDING—Serenades for 2 violins and piano no. 1-2. *Barratt-Due, Chung, violins; Knardahl, piano.*
+ ARG 3-4/89: 89
+ Fa 3-4/89: 282

25540. NKFCD 50016-2: SINDING—Piano concerto, op. 6; Symphony no. 1. *Knardahl, piano; Oslo Phil. Orch.; Fjeldstad, cond.*

+ ARG 3-4/89: 88
+ Fa 3-4/89: 282

25541. NKFCD 50017-2: SINDING—Piano pieces op. 32 no. 1, 3; op. 33 no. 4. 6; op. 34 no. 1, 4-5; op. 44 no. 2-4, 12; Piano sonata in B minor; Variations for 2 pianos in E♭ minor op. 2. *Baekkelund, Levine, pianos.*
+ ARG 3-4/89: 88
+ Fa 3-4/89: 283

25542. NKFCD 50018-2: KJERULF—Piano pieces; Songs for male choir. *Kayser, piano; Nowegian Students' Choir; Grythe, cond.*
+ ARG 3-4/89: 50
+ Fa 3-4/89: 186

25543. NKFCD 50019-2: BACKER-GRONDAHL—Thirteen piano pieces; Seventeen songs. *Frisell, soprano; Glaser, piano.*
+ ARG 4/88: 18
+ Fa 3-4/89: 84

25544. NKFCD 50020-2: HOLTER—Violin concerto, op. 22; Symphony, op. 3. *Wenk-Wolff, violin; Royal Phil. Orch.; Dreier, cond.*
□ ARG 3-4/89: 47
• Fa 3-4/89: 186

25545. NKFCD 50021-2: ELLING—Violin concerto; Quartet in D. *Tellefsen, violin; Oslo Phil. Orch.; Jansons, cond.; Norwegian Quartet.*
+ ARG 1-2/92: 52

25546. NKFCD 50022-2: ARNOLD—Piano fantasy; Six German songs; Rondo for soprano and piano; String quartet no. 1. *Steen-Nøkleberg, piano; Mantor, soprano; Norwegian Quartet.*
+ ARG 11-12/91: 20

25547. NKFCD 50023-2: CLEVE—Piano music; Violin sonata. *Braaten, piano; Tonnesen, violin.*
+ ARG 5-6/93: 78

25548. NKFCD 50024-2: OLSEN—Little suite for piano and string orchestra. Piano music by seven Norwegian women composers: Music of I.B. Lund, B. Holmsen, H.M. Hansen, M.B. Nathan, S. Lund, B. Lund, A.S. Lindeman. *Bratlie, piano; Norwegian Radio Orch.; Eggen, cond.*
+ ARG 3-4/92: 174
+ Fa 1-2/92: 289

25549. NKFCD 50026-2: BORGSTROM—Hamlet; A thought. *Bergen Phil. Orch.; Andersen, cond.*
+ ARG 11-12/92: 93
+ Fa 11-12/92: 205

25550. NKFCD 50027-2: HOLTER—String quartet, op. 1; String quartet, op. 18. *Norwegian String Quartet.*
+ ARG 11-12/93: 128

NKF

+ Fa 11-12/93: 277
+ Gr 11/93: 93

25551. NKFCD 50028-2: GRIEG—Norwegian dances; Lyric suite; Lyrical pieces; Funeral march. *Oslo Phil. Orch.; Jansons, cond.*
+ ARG 5-6/94: 96
+ Fa 3-4/94: 199

25552. NKFCD 50029-2: GRIEG—Ballade in G minor; Piano sonata; Norwegian peasant dances (*Slätter*). *Riefling, piano.*
• ARG 3-4/94: 102
+ Fa 5-6/94: 154
+ Gr 10/94: 158

25553. NKFCD 50031-2: Songs of Norway. *Trondheim Male Choir; Giske, cond.*
• ARG 1-2/97: 219

25554. NKFCD 50033-2: HALVORSEN—Orchestra music. *Norwegian Radio Orch.; Rasilainen, cond.*
□ ARG 11-12/96: 135

NM

25555. 92050: DIEPENBROCK—Songs, vol. 1. *Alexander, Nes, Prégardien, Holl; Jansen, piano.*
• ARG 7-8/96: 104

NMBQ

25556. 001: Music of Plog, Moore, and Stevens. *New Mexico Brass Quintet.*
+ ARG 9-10/96: 239

NMC

25557. NMCD 002: Music of Finnissy, Newman, Skempton, and Weir. *Finnissy, piano.*
□ ARG 11-12/93: 241

25558. NMCD 003: *Mary Wiegold's songbook.* Music of Dowland, Weir, Matthews, Bainbridge, Skempton, Birtwistle and others. *Wiegold, soprano; Composers Ensemble; Muldowney, cond.*
+ ARG 9-10/93: 256
+ Gr 4/92: 150

25559. NMCD 004: DILLON—East 11th St. NY 10003; La femme invisible; Windows and canopies. *Music Projects London; Bernas, cond.*
+ Gr 9/92: 106

25560. NMCD 005: SKEMPTON—Lento. *BBC Symphony Orch.; Wigglesworth, cond.* CD single.
+ ARG 11-12/93: 198
□ Gr 6/93: 55

25561. NMCD 006: CASHIAN—String quartet no. 1. BUTLER—Songs and dances from a Haunted Place. NICHOLLS—String quartet. *Bingham String Quartet.*
+ Gr 11/92: 120

25562. NMCD 007: LUMSDAINE—Aria for Edward John Eyre; What shall I sing? *Manning, Wiegold, sopranos; Baddely, Rye, narrators; Gemini; Howarth, cond.*
+ Gr 6/93: 87

25563. NMCD 008: HOLT—Era madrugada; Canciones; Shadow realm; Sparrow night. *Kimm, mezzo-soprano; Hulse, oboe; Nash Ensemble; Friend, cond.*
+ Gr 5/93: 64

25564. NMCD 009: BIRTWISTLE—Melencolia I; Ritual fragment; Meridian. *Van Kampen, cello; Pay, clarinet; Thompson, horn; King, mezzo-soprano; London Sinfonietta; Knussen, cond.*
+ ARG 11-12/93: 80
+ Fa 3-4/94: 136
+ Gr 8/93: 68

25565. NMCD 010: PANUFNIK—Cello concerto. *Rostropovich, cello; London Symphony Orch.; Wolff, cond.*
+ ARG 11-12/93: 163
+ ARG 7-8/95: 166
+ Fa 3-4/94: 267
+ Gr 8/93: 34

25566. NMCD 011: LUTYENS—Vocal and chamber works. *Manning, soprano; Jane's Minstrels; Montgomery, cond.*
+ Gr 10/93: 92

25567. NMCD 013: GUY—After the rain. *City of London Sinfonia; Hickox, cond.*
□ ARG 7-8/94: 109
+ Gr 1/94: 47

25568. NMCD 015: HOLLOWAY—Concerto for orchestra no. 2. *BBC Symphony Orch.; Knussen, cond.*
+ ARG 7-8/94: 114
+ Gr 5/94: 52

25569. NMCD 016: SWAYNE—Cry. *BBC Singers; Poole, cond.* Reissue.
+ Gr 10/94: 184

25570. NMCD 017: SMALLEY—Pulses. *BBC Symphony Orch.; Bernas, cond.*
+ ARG 11-12/94: 192

25571. NMCD 021: D. MATTHEWS—Piano sonata. POWERS—The memory room. *Howard, piano.*
+ Gr 3/95: 74

25572. NMCD 022: BARRY—Chamber music. *Kawai, piano; Nua Nós; Mheadhra, cond.*
+ Gr 4/95: 77

25573. NMCD 023: GOEHR—Piano concerto; Symphony in one movement. *P. Serkin, piano; London Sinfonietta; Knussen, cond.; BBC Scottish Symphony Orch.; Bernas, cond.*
+ Gr 8/95: 70

25574. NMCD 024: TURNAGE—On all fours; Lament for a hanging man;

Sarabande; Release. *Kimm, mezzo-soprano; Robertson, saxophone; Van Kampen, cello; Brown, piano; Nash Ensemble; Knussen, cond.*
+ Gr 9/95: 68

25575. NMCD 025: *Contemporary vocal works.* Music of Weir, P.P. Nash, Connolly, Bauld, Elias, Payne, and A. Gilbert. *Manning, soprano; Jane's Minstrels; Montgomery, cond.*
+ Gr 10/95: 123

25576. NMCD 026: LAMBERT—Tread softly; Slide; Meditations; Toccata; Family affairs; String quartet no. 2. *Aarons, trumpet; Ramirez, guitar; Albion Guitar Quartet; Bingham Quartet; Sounds Positive; Sutton-Anderson, cond.*
+ Gr 3/96: 64

25577. NMCD 027: SACKMAN—Hawthorn. *BBC Symphony Orch.; A. Davis, cond.*
+ Gr 7/96: 62

25578. NMCD 028: SAWER—Byrnan Wood. *BBC Symphony Orch.; A. Davis, cond.*
+ Gr 2/96: 58

25579. NMCD 034: NORMAN—Chamber music with tape. *R. Norman, voice; Cooper, clarinet; K. Norman, tape.*
+ Gr 8/96: 67

NOMOS

25580. CD 9.1012111: Music of Rosenfeld, Grüger, Dinescu, Berio, Janárceková, Malfatti and Kupferman. *Ascher, mezzo-soprano solo.*
+ Fa 11-12/92: 417

NONESUCH

25581. 71249-2: CARTER—String quartets no. 1-2. *The Composers String Quartet.*
+ Fa 5-6/89: 156

25582. 71281-2: WEILL—Kleine Dreigroschenmusik. MILHAUD—La creation du monde. *Contemporary Chamber Ensemble; Weisberg, cond.*
+ Fa 5-6/88: 238

25583. 71309-2: SCHOENBERG—Three piano pieces op. 11; Six little piano pieces op. 19; Five piano pieces op. 23; Suite for piano op. 25; Piano pieces op. 33a and b. *Jacobs, piano.*
+ Fa 5-6/89: 303

25584. 71316-2: MILHAUD—Saudades do Brazil; Trois rag-caprices; Le printemps. *Bolcom, piano.*
+ Fa 5-6/89: 237

25585. 71325-2: IVES—Songs. *De Gaetani, mezzo-soprano; Kalish, piano.*
+ Fa 5-6/89: 205

25586. 71364-2: Schumann—Songs and duets. *De Gaetani, mezzo-soprano; Guinn, baritone; Kalish, piano.* Reissue.
+ ARG 5-6/92: 130
+ Fa 7-8/92: 278

25587. 71450-1 (LP): Chopin—Mazurkas, waltzes, and other works. *Laredo, piano.*
+ ARG 3-4/88: 28
+ Au 1/88: 158
• Fa 1-2/88: 107
+ SR 5/88: 112

25588. 73030-2 (2 discs): Bach—Sonatas and partitas for solo violin (complete). *Luca, violin.*
+ Fa 3-4/91: 139

25589. 73031-2 (2 discs): Debussy—Preludes for piano bk. 1-2. *Jacobs, piano.*
+ Fa 7-8/88: 150
+ HF 11/88: 78

25590. 78028-2: Schubert—Piano sonata D. 959; Impromptu in E♭ minor D. 946 no. 1. *Goode, piano.*
+ Fa 5-6/89: 309

25591. 78338-2: Gershwin—Pardon my English. *Katt, Walker, Nicastro, Cullum; chorus & orch.; Stern, cond.*
• Fa 11-12/94: 232

25592. 79014-2: Schumann—Humoreske op. 20; Fantasia in C op. 17. *Goode, piano.*
+ ARG 3-4/91: 117
+ Fa 1-2/91: 163

25593. 79064-2: Schubert—Piano sonata in C minor D. 958; Ländler D. 790 . *Goode, piano.*
+ Fa 3-4/90: 130

25594. 79068-2: Brahms—String quintets no. 1-2. *Boston Symphony Chamber Players.*
+ Fa 5-6/88: 94

25595. 79123-1 (LP): *Robin is to the greenwood gone.* Music of Bacheler, Cutting, Johnson, De Countie, and others. *O'Dette, lute.*
+ Fa 11-12/87: 282

25596. 79125-2: *Olympia's lament.* Monteverdi—Quel sguardo sdegnosetto; Ohimè ch'io cado; Lamento d'Olimpia; Voglio di vita uscir; Maladetta sià l'aspetto. India—Diana; Amico, hai vinto; Piangono al pianger mio; Lamento d'Olimpia; Torna il sereno Zefiro; Sfere fermate. *Kirkby, soprano; Rooley, chitarrone.*
+ Fa 5-6/89: 238

25597. 79131-2: Weill—Songs. *Stratas, soprano, New York Chamber Symphony; Schwarz, cond.* Issued also as LP: 79131-1.
• DA 7/87: 60
- Fa 1-2/87: 220
+ Fa 1-2/87: 220

+ Gr 4/87: 1466
• HF 6/87: 67
+ NYT 11/20/86: H23
+ Opus 4/87: 53
+ Ov 6/87: 44
- SR 3/87: 108

25598. 79132-2: *A Bach recital.* Prelude and fugue BWV 894; Toccata BWV 914; Chromatic fantasy and fugue BWV 903; Capriccio BWV 992; Prelude, fugue, and allegro BWV 998; Fantasy BWV 906; Musical offering: Ricercare a 3 in C minor. *Gibbons, harpsichord.* Issued also as LP: 79132-1.
+ Fa 9-10/87: 141
+ Fa 11-12/87: 91
- HPR 9/87: 76
+ Opus 2/88: 37

25599. 79135-1 (2 LPs): *A Balanchine album.* Music of Fauré, Hindemith, Stravinsky, and Tchaikovsky. *New York City Ballet Orch.; Irving, cond.* Most works revised for ballet performance.
• Fa 1-2/87: 262
- Ov 5/87: 43

25600. 79138-1 (LP): Reich—Sextet; Six marimbas. *Ensembles; Reich, cond.*
+ Au 5/87: 95
+ Fa 1-2/87: 164
+ HF 6/87: 65
+ Opus 4/87: 46
+ Ov 5/87: 40
+ SR 3/87: 105

25601. 79143-1 (LP): Schwantner—Sparrows; Distant runes and incantations; A sudden rainbow. *Shelton, soprano; Oppens, piano; St. Louis Symphony Orch.; Slatkin, cond.*
+ ARG 1-2/88: 60
+ Fa 11-12/87: 223
+ NYT 11/15/87: H30
+ Opus 4/88: 47

25602. 79144-1 (LP): Adams—The chairman dances; Christian zeal and activity; Tromba lontana; Short ride in a fast machine; Common tone in simple time. *San Francisco Symphony Orch.; Waart, cond.*
+ Fa 7-8/87: 45
+ Fa 9-10/87: 128
+ Fa 11-12/87: 78
+ Ov 10/87: 38
+ SR 11/87: 190

25603. 79145-2: Schoenberg—Concerto for string quartet and orchestra (after Handel's concerto grosso op. 6 no. 7). Strauss—Divertimento after Couperin, op. 86. *American String Quartet; New York Chamber Symphony; Schwarz, cond.*
+ ARG 5-6/88: 67
+ Fa 3-4/88: 188

25604. 79146-2: *Live in Prague.* Music of Korte, Suk, and Smetana. *Moravec, piano.* Issued also as LP: 79146-1.
+ Fa 9-10/87: 226

+ HPR 12/87: 89
+ SR 12/87: 154

25605. 79147-1 (LP): Paulus—Symphony in 3 movements. Larsen—Symphony: Water music. *Minnesota Orch.; Marriner, cond.*
+ Fa 11-12/87: 194
+ NYT 11/15/87: H30
+ Opus 4/88: 47

25606. 79150-2: Music of Varèse, Colgrass, Saperstein, Cowell, and Wuorinen. *New Jersey Percussion Ensemble; Wuorinen, DesRoches, conds.*
• Fa 1-2/88: 273

25607. 79152-1 (LP): Beethoven—Cello sonatas no. 1-2. *Bylsma, cello; Bilson, fortepiano.*
• ARG 1-2/88: 12
+ DA 12/87: 76
+ Fa 9-10/87: 150
+ HPR 12/87: 78

25608. 79153-2: Albert—Into eclipse; Flower of the mountain. *Gordon, tenor; Shelton, soprano; 20th Century Consort; New York Chamber Symphony; Kendall, Schwarz, conds.* Issued also as LP: 79153-1.
+ ARG 7-8/88: 9
+ Fa 5-6/88: 65
+ HPR 4/88: 71

25609. 79154-2: Brahms—Acht Klavierstücke op. 76; Fantasies op. 116; Vier Klavierstücke op. 119. *Goode, piano.*
+ Fa 9-10/87: 167
+ HPR 12/87: 82
+ NYT 9/27/87: H27
+ SR 4/87: 152

25610. 79155-2 (2 discs): Mozart—Violin sonatas K. 296, 376-380. *Luca, violin; Bilson, fortepiano.* Issued also as 2 LPs: 79155-1.
+ ARG 5-6/88: 50
• Fa 11-12/87: 187
+ Fa 3-4/88: 163
+ HF 6/88: 69
+ HPR 4/88: 85

25611. 79156-1 (LP): Blow—Welcome every guest; Rise mighty monarch; Horace to Lydia; If mighty wealth; The self-baniched; Musicke's the cordial; A ground; The bud; Sappho to the goddess of love; Horace to his lute; Arms he delights in; Employed all the day. *Consort of Musicke; Rooley, cond.*
+ Fa 1-2/88: 94
+ HF 6/88: 61

25612. 79160-2: Music of Mozart, Chopin, Debussy, and Beethoven. *Horszowski, piano.* Issued also as LP: 79160-1.
+ Fa 9-10/87: 368
+ HPR 12/87: 92
+ NYT 9/27/87: H27
+ NYT 12/6/87: H29

NONESUCH

+ Opus 12/87: 36
+ SR 9/87: 90

25613. 79163-2: *White man sleeps.* Music of Volans, Ives, Hassell, Lee, Coleman, Johnson, and Bartók. *Kronos Quartet.*
   + ARG 7-8/88: 77
   + Fa 11-12/87: 290
   + Gr 11/87: 771
   + HF 4/88: 78
   □ HPR 12/87: 103
   + MA 5/88: 62
   + Opus 2/88: 43

25614. 79168-2: COPLAND—Sextet for clarinet, piano, and string quartet; Piano variations; Piano quartet. *Boston Symphony Chamber Players.*
   + ARG 7-8/88: 18
   + Fa 3-4/88: 97
   + HPR 4/88: 76
   + NYT 2/7/88: H32
   + SR 7/88: 102

25615. 79169-2: REICH—Come out; Piano phase; Clapping music; It's gonna rain. *Double Edge, piano; Hartenberger, Reich, clapping hands.*
   + ARG 7-8/88: 50
   + Fa 1-2/88: 199
   + HF 2/88: 64
   + MA 5/88: 61

25616. 79170-2: REICH—Drumming. *Steve Reich and musicians.*
   + Au 2/88: 120
   + Fa 1-2/88: 199
   + HF 2/88: 64
   - MA 5/88: 61

25617. 79172-2: ZORN—Spillane; Two-lane highway; Forbidden fruit. *Ensembles; Zorn, cond; Collins, guitar; Kronos Quartet; Marclay, turntables; Hiromi, voice.*
   + Fa 3-4/88: 237

25618. 79174-2: PIAZZOLLA—Concerto for bandoneon and chamber orchestra; Three tangos for bandoneon and chamber orchestra. *Piazzolla, bandoneon; Orch. of St. Luke's; Schifrin, cond.*
   + Fa 9-10/88: 224

25619. 79175-2: FINE—Notturno for strings and harp; Partita for wind quintet; String quartet; Hour-glass; Serious song. *New York Woodwind Quintet; Lydian String Quartet; Cantata Singers; New York Chamber Symphony of the 92nd Street Y; Los Angeles Chamber Orch.; Schwarz, cond.* Issued also as LP: 79175-1. LP lacks Serious song.
   + ARG 3-4/90: 51
   + Fa 3-4/89: 163
   + HF 5/89: 62
   + NYT 4/30/89: H30

25620. 79176-2: REICH—Different trains; Electronic counterpoint. *Kronos Quartet; electronic sounds; Metheny, guitar.*
   - ARG 3-4/90: 93
   + Fa 9-10/89: 298

+ Gr 6/89: 61
+ MA 9/89: 65
+ SR 9/89: 152
+ St 9/89: 175

25621. 79177-2 (3 discs): ADAMS—Nixon in China. *Sylvan, Opatz, Maddalena, Hammons, Duykers; Orch. of St. Luke's; Waart, cond.* Issued also as 3 LPs: 79177-1.
   + ARG 7-8/88: 8
   + DA 9/88: 62
   + Fa 7-8/88: 92
   + Gr 10/88: 670
   + HF 12/88: 63
   + MA 9/88: 78
   + ON 7/88: 42
   □ Op 9/88: 1142
   + SR 10/88: 128

25622. 79178-2: *Songs of America on home, love, nature, and death.* Music of Foster, Carter, Crawford-Seeger, Cadman, and others. *De Gaetani, mezzo-soprano; Kalish, piano.* Issued also as LP: 79178-1.
   + ARG 3-4/89: 122
   + Fa 3-4/89: 351
   + HF 3/89: 52
   + MA 7/89: 85
   + NYT 1/29/89: H27
   + ON 7/89: 35
   + Ov 1/89: 44

25623. 79179-2: Music of Nobre, Gismonti, Assad, Tiso, Pascual, and Gnatalli. *S. & O. Assad, guitars.*
   + ARG 5-6/89: 115
   + Fa 1-2/89: 332

25624. 79180-2: ALFONSO EL SABIO—Cantigas: Quen a Virgen; Connoscudamente; Tota cousa; Gran dereit; A Virgen mui gloriosa; Codax Las Huelgas. *Ensemble Alcatraz.*
   + ARG 3-4/89: 118
   + Fa 1-2/89: 319
   + SR 1/89: 132

25625. 79181-2: *Winter was hard.* Music of Sallinen, Riley, Pärt, Webern, Zorn, and others. *Kronos Quartet.*
   + ARG 7-8/89: 124
   + Fa 3-4/89: 386
   + MA 9/89: 79
   + NYT 1/22/89: H23

25626. 79185-2: WUORINEN—Piano concerto no. 3; Golden dance. *Ohlsson, piano; San Francisco Symphony Orch.; Blomstedt, cond.*
   + Fa 5-6/89: 362
   + HF 7/89: 62

25627. 79187-2: Music of Barber, Menotti, Harbison, and Stravinsky. *Upshaw, soprano; Orch. of St. Luke's; Zinman, cond.*
   + ARG 11-12/89: 32
   + DA 9/89: 78
   + Fa 3-4/91: 445
   + Gr 9/89: 544
   + MA 1/90: 75

+ ON 7/89: 35
+ SR 9/89: 152

25628. 79188-2: KIRCHNER—Concerto for violin, cello, 10 winds and percussion; Piano trio; Five pieces for piano; Music for twelve. *Lowe, violin; Eskin, cello; Kalish, piano; Boston Symphony Chamber Players; Kirchner, piano & cond.*
   □ ARG 7-8/90: 62
   + Fa 5-6/90: 199
   + MA 9/90: 80

25629. 79189-2: HARBISON—Words from Paterson; Simple daylight; Piano quintet. *Upshaw, soprano; Sylvan, baritone; Kalish, piano; Boston Symphony Chamber Players.*
   + ARG 11-12/93: 122
   + Fa 9-10/93: 173
   + Gr 12/93: 82

25630. 79192-2: GLASS—Powaqqatsi. *Various artists; Reisman, cond.*
   □ Fa 9-10/88: 158
   □ HF 1/89: 69

25631. 79200-2 (2 discs): BACH—Well tempered clavier, bk. 2. *Aldwell, piano.*
   + ARG 1-2/90: 17
   ● Fa 1-2/90: 107

25632. 79202-2: Music of Mozart, Chopin, and Schumann. *Horszowski, piano.*
   + ARG 3-4/89: 117
   + Fa 5-6/89: 252
   + SR 3/89: 122

25633. 79203-2: *Guitarra portuguesa.* PAREDES—Variations in D; Cançao verdes anos; Divertimento; Romance no. 1; Danças Portuguesas no. 2; Valsa; Fantasia no. 2; Variations on a folk dance; Mudar de Vida (Tema); Mudar de vida (Musica de Fundo); António Marinheiro; Cançao; Melodia no. 1. *Paredes, guitar.*
   □ ARG 3-4/90: 86

25634. 79211-2 (2 discs): BEETHOVEN—Piano sonatas no. 28-32. *Goode, piano.*
   + ARG 11-12/89: 36
   + DA 11/89: 82
   + Fa 9-10/89: 135
   + Gr 8/89: 503
   + NYT 7/9/89: H30
   + SR 10/89: 110
   + St 2/90: 186

25635. 79212-2: BEETHOVEN—Piano sonatas no. 16-18. *Goode, piano.*
   + ARG 3-4/90: 24
   + ARG 7-8/93: 64
   + Fa 3-4/90: 130

25636. 79213-2: BEETHOVEN—Piano sonatas no. 5-7. *Goode, piano.*
   + ARG 3-4/92: 31
   ● Gr 4/92: 109

25637. 79217-2: RILEY—Salome dances for peace. *Kronos Quartet.*
+ ARG 3-4/90: 95
+ DA 3/90: 64
+ Fa 3-4/90: 275
+ MA 7/90: 83
+ SR 2/90: 156

25638. 79218-2: ADAMS—The wound-dresser; Fearful symmetries. *Sylvan, baritone; Orch. of St. Luke's; Adams, cond.*
+ ARG 3-4/90: 14
+ Fa 3-4/90: 102
+ Gr 6/90: 88
+ MA 9/90: 72

25639. 79219-2: ADAMS—Chamber symphony; Grand pianola music. *London Sinfonietta; Adams, cond.*
+ ARG 3-4/95: 64
+ Gr 3/95: 36

25640. 79220-2: REICH—Four sections; Music for mallet instruments, voices and organ. *London Symphony Orch,; Thomas, cond.; Steve Reich and Musicians.*
+ ARG 7-8/91: 113
+ Gr 6/91: 50

25641. 79227-2: MARSHALL—Three penitential visions; Hidden voices. *Rowe, soprano; Marshall, voice, tape, piano, & synthesizer.*
+ Fa 9-10/90: 288

25642. 79228-2: PANUFNIK—Symphony no. 3; Arbor cosmia. *Concertgebouw Orch.; New York Chamber Symphony; Panufnik, cond.*
+ ARG 7-8/90: 81
+ Fa 11-12/90: 306
+ Gr 5/91: 2017
+ NYT 8/5/90: H26

25643. 79229-2: KRAFT—Contextures II: Final beast; Interplay; Of ceremonies, pageants and celebrations. *Rawcliffe, soprano; Mack, tenor; Samples, cello; Pasadena Boys Choir; New Albion Ensemble; Los Angeles Phil. Orch.; Alabama Symphony Orch.; Utah Symphony Orch.; Previn, Polivnick, Wilkins, conds.*
+ Fa 1-2/90: 209
+ NYT 12/10/89: H33

25644. 79230-2: ROUSE—Symphony no. 1; Phantasmata. *Baltimore Symphony Orch.; Zinman, cond.*
+ Fa 1-2/90: 209
+ NYT 12/10/89: H33

25645. 79231-2: SINGLETON—Shadows; After fallen crumbs; A yellow rose petal. *Atlanta Symphony Orch.; Shaw, Lane, conds.*
+ Fa 1-2/90: 209
+ NYT 12/10/89: H33

25646. 79232-2: Music of Bach, Chopin, and Beethoven. *Horszowski, piano.*

+ ARG 7-8/90: 144
+ DA 3/91: 44
• Fa 11-12/90: 147

25647. 79233-2: CHOPIN—Nocturnes. *Moravec, piano. Reissue.*
+ ARG 3-4/92: 46

25648. 79234-2: SHOSTAKOVICH—Preludes op. 34; Piano sonata no. 2. *Viardo, piano.*
+ ARG 3-4/91: 120
• Fa 3-4/91: 384
• Gr 10/91: 144
+ SR 6/91: 97

25649. 79236-2: BEETHOVEN—Cello sonatas no. 3-5. *Bylsma, cello; Bilson, fortepiano.*
+ Gr 4/92: 93

25650. 79237-2: SCHOENBERG—Pierrot lunaire; Book of the hanging gardens. *De Gaetani, mezzo-soprano; Contemporary Chamber Ensemble; Weisberg, cond.; Kalish, piano.*
• ARG 11-12/91: 141
+ Fa 1-2/91: 303
+ MA 5/91: 90

25651. 79242-2: Music of Crumb, Tallis, Marta, Ives (arr. Geist), and Shostakovich. *Kronos Quartet.*
+ ARG 1-2/91: 131
+ Fa 11-12/90: 457
+ Gr 4/91: 1862
+ MA 3/91: 92

25652. 79245-2: TOWER—Silver ladders; Island prelude; Music for cello and orchestra; Sequoia. *Bowman, oboe; Harrell, cello; St. Louis Symphony Orch.; Slatkin, cond.*
+ ARG 1-2/91: 336
+ Fa 1-2/91: 336
+ MA 3/91: 90

25653. 79246-2: PICKER—Symphony no. 2; String quartet no. 1. *Mitchell, soprano; Houston Symphony Orch.; Comissiona, cond.; Mendelssohn String Quartet.*
+ ARG 1-2/91: 74
+ Fa 1-2/91: 275

25654. 79248-2: CARTER—The minotaur; Two songs; Piano sonata. *De Gaetani, mezzo-soprano; Kalish, Jacobs, pianos; New York Chamber Symphony of the 92nd Street Y; Schwarz, cond.*
+ Fa 7-8/91: 134
+ MA 7/91: 71

25655. 79249-2: Music of Ives, Marchall, Feldman, Adams, and Diamond. *Upshaw, soprano; Crossley, piano; Orch. of St. Luke's; Adams, cond.*
+ ARG 11-12/91: 177
+ Fa 7-8/91: 394
+ Gr 7/91: 73
+ HPR v.8, no.3/91: 65
+ MA 7/91: 94
+ SR 7/91: 84

25656. 79251-2: ANDRIESSEN—De Staat. *Schönberg-Ensemble; Leeuw, cond.*
+ ARG 7-8/92: 83

25657. 79253-2: VOLANS—Hunting; Gathering. *Kronos Quartet.*
+ Fa 7-8/91: 325

25658. 79255-2: LUTOSŁAWSKI—String quartet. *Kronos Quartet.*
+ Fa 7-8/91: 194

25659. 79257-2: GÓRECKI—Already it is dusk (Quartet I); Lerchenmusik; Recitatives and ariosos. *Kronos Quartet; Collins, clarinet; Van Kampen, cello; Constable, piano.*
+ ARG 11-12/91: 68
+ Fa 1-2/92: 222

25660. 79259-2: *Beloved that pilgrammage.* CHANLER—Eight epitaphs. BARBER—Hermit songs. COPLAND—Twelve poems of Emily Dickinson. *Sylvan, baritone; Breitman, piano.*
+ ARG 11-12/91: 208
+ Gr 12/91: 106
+ ON 8/91: 37

25661. 79261-2: *Mieczyslaw Horszowski: a portrait.* Music of Mozart, Chopin, Debussy, Beethoven, Bach, and Schumann. *Horszowski, piano.*
+ Gr 12/93: 91

25662. 79262-2: *The girl with orange lips.* FALLA—Psyché. RAVEL—Trois poèmes de Stéphane Mallarmé. STRAVINSKY—Three poems of Konstantin Balmont; Three Japanese poems. KIM—Where grief slumbers. DELAGE—Quatre poèmes hindous. *Upshaw, soprano; with chamber ensemble.*
+ ARG 1-2/92: 176
+ Gr 11/91: 151

25663. 79263-2: SCHUBERT—Songs. WOLF—Songs; Spanisches Liederbuch. *De Gaetani, mezzo-soprano; Kalish, piano. Reissue.*
• ARG 7-8/92: 218
+ Fa 7-8/92: 278

25664. 79264-2: BACH—French suite no. 6. SCHUMANN—Papillons. CHOPIN—Piano music. *Horszowski, piano.*
• ARG 7-8/92: 267
+ Fa 7-8/92: 104
+ Gr 12/93: 91
+ St 10/92: 275

25665. 79265-2: A Baroque Christmas. *Boston Camerata; Cohen, cond.*
+ ARG 11-12/92: 270

25666. 79271-2: SCHUBERT—Piano sonatas D. 845, D. 850. *Goode, piano.*
+ ARG 7-8/93: 153
+ Fa 7-8/93: 234

25667. 79275-2: Pieces of Africa. *Kronos Quartet; with assisting artists.*
• ARG 7-8/92: 252

NONESUCH

+ Fa 7-8/92: 353
• Gr 11/92: 146
+ St 7/92: 187

25668. 79281-2 (2 discs): ADAMS—The death of Klinghoffer. *Vocalists; London Opera Chorus; Orch. of the Opéra de Lyon; Nagano, cond.*
+ ARG 5-6/93: 58
+ Fa 3-4/93: 99
+ Gr 3/93: 92
+ ON 2/27/93: 32
+ Op 4/93: 487

25669. 79282-2: GÓRECKI—Symphony of sorrowful songs. *Upshaw, soprano; London Sinfonietta; Zinman, cond.*
+ ARG 7-8/92: 136
+ Fa 9-10/92: 247
+ Gr 4/93: 44
+ St 6/93: 251

25670. 79283-2: RACHMANINOFF—Corelli variations. MEDTNER—Piano sonatas. *Viardo, piano.*
+ ARG 11-12/94: 172
• Gr 4/96: 76

25671. 79285-2: Burton Lane Songbook vol. 2. *Feinstein, baritone; Lane, piano.*
+ Gr 8/94: 100

25672. 79286-2: GLASS—Hydrogen jukebox. *Ginsberg, narrator; Wincenc, flute; Sterman, Peck, saxophones; Glass, Goldray, pianos.*
+ Gr 1/94: 82

25673. 79287-2: GERSHWIN—Gershwin plays Gershwin: the piano rolls. *Gershwin, Milne, piano rolls.*
+ ARG 5-6/94: 204
+ Fa 5-6/94: 149
+ Gr 4/94: 70

25674. 79289-2 (2 discs): ASHLEY—Improvement (Don leaves Linda). *Humbert, Buckner, La Barbara, S. Ashley, Klein, Neuburg, vocalists; R. Ashley, narrator & electronics; Hamilton, Erbe, electronics.*
+ Fa 5-6/93: 137
+ ON 5/93: 52

25675. 79290-2: KANCHELI—Symphonies 4-5. *Georgian National Orch.; Kakhidze, cond.*
+ ARG 1-2/93: 109

25676. 79291-2: ANDRIESSEN—De tijd. *Schönberg-Ensemble; Percussion Group the Hague; Netherlands Chamber Choir; Leeuw, cond.*
+ ARG 11-12/93: 73
+ Fa 11-12/93: 165
+ Gr 3/94: 86

25677. 79292-2: Music of Scarlatti, Rameau, Couperin, and Bach. *S. & O. Assad, guitars.*
+ ARG 11-12/93: 234
+ Gr 10/93: 74

25678. 79293-2: SCHUBERT—Die schöne Müllerin. *Sylvan, baritone; Breitman, piano.*
+ ARG 5-6/93: 130
• Gr 3/93: 86

25679. 79294-2: TCHAIKOVSKY—Nutcracker: Excerpts. *New York City Ballet Orch.; Zinman, cond.*
• ARG 5-6/94: 154

25680. 79295-2: REICH—Tehillim; Three movements for orchestra. *Schoenberg Ensemble; Percussion Group The Hague; Leeuw, cond.; London Symphony Orch.; Thomas, cond.*
+ ARG 3-4/95: 166

25681. 79310-2: *Short stories.* Music of Sharp, Dixon, Oswald, Zorn, Cowell, Gubaidulina, and others. *Kronos Quartet.*
□ ARG 7-8/93: 189
+ Gr 8/93: 55
+ St 6/93: 259

25682. 79311-2: ADAMS—Hoodoo zephyr. *J. Adams, keyboards & electronics.*
□ ARG 3-4/94: 63
+ Fa 3-4/94: 98
+ Gr 4/94: 68

25683. 79317-2: *Goethe-Lieder.* Music of Schumann, Schubert, Wolf, and Mozart. *Upshaw, soprano; Goode, piano.*
+ ARG 9-10/94: 264
+ Gr 8/94: 100

25684. 79318-2: LISZT—At Wagner's grave. BERG—Quartet, op. 3. WEBERN—Five pieces, op. 5. *Kronos Quartet; Takahashi, piano; DeCray, harp.*
+ ARG 3-4/94: 196
+ Gr 1/94: 65

25685. 79319-2: GÓRECKI—String quartets no. 1-2. *Kronos Quartet.*
+ ARG 11-12/93: 111
+ Fa 11-12/93: 246
+ Gr 4/93: 44

25686. 79320-2: FELDMAN—Piano and string quartet. *Takahashi, piano; Kronos Quartet.*
□ ARG 3-4/94: 94
+ Fa 3-4/94: 184
+ Gr 2/94: 61

25687. 79323-2 (3 discs): GLASS—Einstein on the beach. *Philip Glass Ensemble; Riesman, cond. New performance.*
+ ARG 3-4/94: 100
+ Fa 3-4/94: 192
+ Gr 1/94: 91

25688. 79327-2 (2 discs): REICH—The cave. *Rowe, Beckenstein, sopranos; Bassi, tenor; Munday, baritone; Steve Reich Ensemble; Reich, cond.*
• ARG 5-6/96: 176
+ Gr 3/96: 99

+ ON 2/17/96: 40
□ Op 4/96: 473

25689. 79328-2 (10 discs): BEETHOVEN—Piano sonatas (complete). *Goode, piano.*
+ ARG 3-4/94: 72
+ Gr 3/94: 77

25690. 79329-2: GLASS—Anima mundi. *Vocalists; orch.; Riesman, cond.*
+ Gr 1/94: 82

25691. 79330-2: *Experiment.* Music of Hupfeld, Kern, Menken, Sondheim, Bernstein, and others. *Patinkin, tenor; Orch.; Stern, cond.*
+ Gr 11/94: 159

25692. 79332-2: OSTERTAG—All the rage. *Kronos Quartet.*
+ Fa 5-6/94: 211

25693. 79335-2: STRAVINSKY—Les noces; Russian wedding songs. *Pokrovsky Ensemble; Pokrovsky, cond.*
+ ARG 9-10/94: 204
+ Gr 9/94: 93

25694. 79338-2: GERSHWIN—Pardon my English. *Katt, Cullum, Walker, Nicastro; chorus & orch.; Stern, cond.*
+ Gr 11/94: 144
+ ON 4/1/95: 44
• Op 10/94: 1240

25695. 79341-2: BACH (ARR. SITKOVETSKY)—Goldberg variations. *New European Strings Chamber Orch.; Sitkovetsky, cond.*
+ ARG 11-12/95: 77
+ Fa 9-10/95: 124
+ Fi 4/96: 129
+ Gr 9/95: 48

25696. 79342-2: ANDRIESSEN—De stijl; M is for man, music, Mozart. *Schoenberg Ensemble; Asko Ensemble; Leeuw., cond; Vollharding Orch.; Hempel, cond.*
+ ARG 1-2/95: 64
+ Fa 1-2/95: 94
+ Gr 2/95: 78

25697. 79343-2: STRAVINSKY—Selections from Histoire du soldat, Petrushka, and Apollo. *O'Riley, piano.*
+ ARG 11-12/94: 196
+ Gr 5/95: 87

25698. 79345-2: *I wish it so.* Show tunes by Bernstein, Blitzstein, Sondheim, and Weill. *Upshaw, soprano; Ensemble; Stern, cond.*
+ ARG 1-2/95: 245
+ Gr 12/94: 166

25699. 79346-2: *Night prayers.* Music of Gubaidulina, Golijov, Kancheli, and others. *Kronos Quartet; Throat Singers of Tuva; Upshaw, soprano; Gasparian, duduk; Alexandrovich, cantor.*
+ ARG 7-8/95: 268

25700. 79347-2: GLASS—Beauty and the beast. *Feltry, Purnhagen, Kuether, Martinez; Philip Glass Ensemble; Riesman, cond.*
- • ARG 11-12/95: 122
- + Gr 7/96: 100

25701. 79348-2: GÓRECKI—Miserere; Amen; Euntes ibant et flebant; My Vistula, grey Vistula; Broad waters. *Chicago Symphony Chorus; Lyric Opera Chorus; Lira Chamber Chorus; Nelson, cond.*
- + ARG 3-4/95: 107
- + Fa 5-6/95: 198
- + Gr 3/95: 85

25702. 79356-2: GLASS—String quartets no. 2-5. *Kronos Quartet.*
- + ARG 7-8/95: 114

25703. 79360-2: ADAMS—Violin concerto; Shaker loops. *Kremer, violin; London Symphony Orch.; Nagano, cond.; Orch. of St. Luke's; Adams, cond.*
- • ARG 9-10/96: 73
- + Fa 9-10/96: 121
- + Fi 3/97: 115
- + Gr 6/96: 40

25704. 79361-2: GERSHWIN—Oh, Kay! *Upshaw, Ollmann, Arkin, Cassidy, Westenberg, Larsen, Logan, Lucci, Weaver; chorus; Orch. of St. Luke's; Stern, cond.*
- + Gr 8/95: 125
- + ON 8/95: 37

25705. 79362-2: GORECKI—Kleines Requiem für eine Polka; Harpsichord concerto; Good night. *Upshaw, soprano; Chojnacka, harpsichord; London Sinfonietta; Zinman, Stenz, conds.*
- + ARG 11-12/95: 126
- + Gr 9/95: 55

25706. 79364-2: *White moon: songs to Morpheus.* Music of Warlock, Handel, Monteverdi, Schwantner, and others. *Upshaw, soprano.*
- + ARG 7-8/96: 281
- • Fi 7-8/96: 138
- + Gr 1/96: 99
- + ON 8/96: 43

25707. 79370-2: *Gershwin piano rolls, vol. 2.* Music of Gershwin, Frey, Conrad, and others. *Gershwin, piano roll.*
- □ Gr 4/96: 74

25708. 79371-2: *L'horizon chimérique.* FAURÉ—Songs. *Sylvan, baritone; Breitman, piano; Lydian String Quartet.*
- + ARG 11-12/96: 121
- + Fa 9-10/96: 184
- • Fi 10/96: 153

25709. 79372-2: *Howl USA.* Music of Daugherty, Partch, Johnson, and Hyla. *Kronos Quartet; Johnston, voice; Ginsberg, narrator.*
- + ARG 11-12/96: 307
- □ Gr 11/96: 112

25710. 79392-2: *Oscar and Steve.* Music of Rodgers, Hammerstein, Romberg, Sondheim, and others. *Patinkin, baritone; Blazer, soprano; Orch.; Stern, cond.*
- • Gr 4/96: 122

25711. 79394-2 (2 discs): *Released 1985-95.* Music of Maraire, Piazzolla, Barber, and others. *Kronos Quartet.* Reissues.
- + Gr 2/96: 70

25712. 79414-2: RODGERS—Rodgers and Hammerstein songs. *Hersch, piano.*
- - ARG 11-12/96: 189

NORD-DISC

25713. NORD 2024: BUECHNER—Erlkönig. *Royal Scottish Orch.; Verineau, cond.*
- + ARG 1-2/93: 85
- + Fa 11-12/92: 214
- + Fa 3-4/93: 137

25714. NORD 2026 (2 discs): BUECHNER—Elizabeth (Immensee): ballet in 3 acts; The old Swedes church: tone poem. *Anthony, soprano; McLean, tenor; Nürnberger Symphoniker; Schmöhe, cond.*
- + ARG 5-6/93: 76
- + Fa 3-4/93: 137

25715. NORD 2028: BUECHNER—The American Civil War: symphonic trilogy. *Scottish National Orch.; Varineau, cond.*
- + ARG 11-12/93: 89
- + Fa 11-12/93: 202
- + Fa 7-8/94: 106

25716. NORD 2030: BUECHNER—Essay 1; Old Swedes church; Erlkönig: Suite no. 1; American Civil War: Blue and the gray; Flight of the American eagle. *Scottish National Orch.; Varineau, cond.; Nürnberger Symphoniker; Schmöhe, cond.*
- □ Fa 7-8/94: 107

25717. NORD 2032: BUECHNER—Phantomgreen: Suite no. 2; Elizabeth: Pas de deux; Suite no. 2; Suite no. 3; Erlkönig: Suite no. 2. *Anthony, soprano; McLean, tenor; Scottish National Orch.; Varineau, cond.; Nürnberger Symphoniker; Schmöhe, cond.*
- + Fa 7-8/94: 107

25718. NORD 2034: BUECHNER—The liberty bell. *Scottish National Orch.; Scottish National Chorus; Mantle, cond.*
- + ARG 9-10/95: 119
- + Fa 7-8/95: 142

NORTH ARKANSAS SYMPHONY ORCHESTRA

25719. NASO 1001 (LP): STILL—Symphony no. 3; Romance for saxphone and piano; Folk suite no. 4 for flute, clarinet, cello, and piano; Three rhythmic spirituals. *Garrison, flute; Umiker,*

saxophone & clarinet; Tollefson, piano; Magill, cello; North Arkansas Symphony Orch.; University of Arkansas Schola Cantorum; Woods, Groh, conds.
- + Fa 3-4/89: 285

NORTH SOUTH

25720. N/S R 1001: *Contemporary romantics.* Music of Appledorn, Schiffman, Quilling, Mazurek, Pizer and Lifchitz. *Lifchitz, piano.*
- + ARG 1-2/93: 185
- □ Fa 1-2/93: 299

25721. N/S R 1002: *American debuts.* Music of Blank, Zifrin, Stewart, Mason, Ovens and Franco. *Lifchitz, piano.*
- + ARG 1-2/93: 185
- + Fa 1-2/93: 301

25722. N/S R 1003: RANDS—In the receding mist. DE LA VEGA—Testimonial. CORDERO—Dodecaconcerto. SAYLOR—See you in the morning. *Ketchum, soprano; Beavon, mezzo-soprano; North-South Consonance Ensemble; Lifchitz, cond.*
- + ARG 7-8/95: 268
- + Fa 1-2/95: 380

25723. N/S R 1004: LIFCHITZ—Of bondage and freedom. PLESKOW—Two arabesques. GREENBERG—La vida es sueño; This man was your brother. C. DVOŘÁK—Amandla Mandela! *Vardaman, Rosales, sopranos; Swygert, narrator; North-South Consonance Ensemble; Lifchitz, cond.*
- + ARG 7-8/95: 241
- + Fa 1-2/95: 380

25724. N/S R 1005: *Music at the crossroads: New American chamber music.* Music of Diemer, Rudajev, Ziffrin, Brings, and Toensing. *North-South Consonance Ensemble; Lifchitz, piano & cond.*
- + ARG 7-8/95: 268
- + Fa 1-2/95: 372

25725. N/S R 1006: *Clarinet fantasy: music from the Americas.* Music of Rokeach, Graetzer, Mazurek, Bell, Enriquez, and Quilling. *Goldsmith, clarinet; Lifchitz, piano; Schenk, soprano.*
- □ ARG 1-2/95: 222
- + Fa 1-2/95: 346

25726. N/S R 1007: *New American romantics.* Music of Van Appledorn, Pleskow, Bell, Toutant, Rovics, and Quilling. *Lifchitz, Bell, piano.*
- □ Fa 7-8/96: 382

25727. N/S R 1008: MAVES—Piano sonatas no. 1-4. *Lifchitz, piano.*
- • Fa 7-8/96: 236

25728. N/S R 1009: SCHIFFMAN—Spectrum, My Ladye Jane's booke. *Perry-Camp, piano.*

+ ARG 11-12/96: 307
+ Fa 7-8/96: 284

25729. N/S R 1010: *Mexico: 100 years of piano music.* Music of Castro, Ponce, Chavez, Moncayo, Moncada, Galindo, Halffter, Renart, Enriquez, and Lavista. *Lifchitz, piano.*
+ ARG 11-12/96: 252
+ Fa 7-8/96: 381

NORTH STAR

25730. NS 024: *Christmas remembered.* Chamber versions of familiar holiday tunes. *Stillman, piano & arr.*
+ ARG 11-12/92: 263

25731. NS 027: *Orientale.* Music of Popper, Debussy, Elgar, Martinů, Granados, Falla, Tchaikovsky and others. *Rosen, cello; Stevenson, piano; with Delmoni, violin.*
+ ARG 5-6/92: 161
+ Fa 11-12/92: 435

25732. NS 034: Music of Mozart, Rung, Sor, Haydn, Brahms, Scheidler, Beethoven, Burgmuller, and J. Strauss. *Mair-Davis Duo (mandolin & guitar); Arm, violin; Rylands, cello; Thomas, flute.*
+ ARG 7-8/92: 260

25733. NS 052: *Seasons remembered, vol. 2.* Music of Gluck, Niles, Vivaldi, Bach, Chaminade, Schumann, Scarlatti, Chopin, Massenet, Mozart, Beethoven, Haydn, and Handel. *Stillman, piano; other instrumentalists.*
+ ARG 3-4/94: 195

NORTHEASTERN

25734. NR 212-CD: R. CLARKE—Viola sonata; Prelude, allegro and pastorale for viola and clarinet; Two pieces for viola and cello; Passacaglia on an old English tune for viola and piano. *McCarty, viola; Babcock, cello; Hadcock, clarinet; Eskin, piano.*
+ ARG 7-8/90: 39
+ Fa 5-6/90: 151

25735. NR 219-CD: PAINE—Violin sonata op. 24; Romanza and humoreske for cello and piano; Larghetto and humoreske for piano and strings op. 32. *Silverstein, violin; J. Eskin, cello; V. Eskin, piano.*
+ Fa 1-2/87: 152
+ HF 4/87: 68
+ MA 5/87: 61
+ SR 6/87: 109

25736. NR 223-CD: BEACH—Les reves de Colombine; Variations on Balkan themes. FOOTE—Five poems after Omar Khayyam; Zweite suite. *Eskin, piano.*
● ARG 9-10/88: 43
+ Fa 5-6/88: 78

25737. NR 226-CD: IVES—The celestial country. LOEFFLER—Psalm 137. *John Oliver Chorale & Orch.*
+ ARG 5-6/88: 38
- Fa 5-6/88: 146 (Ives)
+ Fa 5-6/88: 146 (Loeffler)

25738. NR 228-CD: *Youthful rapture.* GRAINGER—Chamber music. *Members of Collage.*
+ Fa 9-10/87: 208

25739. NR 229 (LP): *Christmas antiphonies.* Music of Schütz, Praetorius, Bax, Scheidt, and Pinkham. *John Oliver Chorale; Oliver, cond.*
+ ARG 11-12/86: 49

25740. NR 230-CD: HARBISON—Mirabai songs; Variations. *R. Harbison, violin; Satz, clarinet; Oppens, piano; Felty, mezzo-soprano; Collage New Music Ensemble; J. Harbison, cond.*
+ Fa 9-10/87: 214
● Ov 2/88: 40

25741. NR 231-CD: *Harp songs and interludes.* Music of Ravel, Fauré, Ginastera, Ibert, Nielsen, and others. *Fortunato, mezzo-soprano; Miron, harp; Melisande Trio.*
● Fa 3-4/87: 248

25742. NR 232-CD: PISTON—Piano sonata; Piano quintet; Improvisation; Passacaglia. *Hokanson, piano; Portland String Quartet.*
● Fa 7-8/89: 212 (Hokanson)
+ Fa 7-8/89: 212 (Portland)
+ Fa 11-12/89: 318
+ SR 4/89: 88

25743. NR 233-CD: SCHUBERT—Piano sonata D. 157, 279; Adagio D. 178; Fantasy D. 2e; Andante D. 29; Menuet in C♯ minor and Trio in E major, D. 600, 610; Ten variations in F major on an original theme D. 156. *Hokanson, piano.*
+ Fa 5-6/87: 192
+ SR 5/87: 116

25744. NR 234-CD: CHADWICK—String quartet no. 1-2. *Portland String Quartet.*
+ ARG 5-6/89: 37
+ Fa 5-6/89: 161
+ Ov 4/89: 59

25745. NR 235-CD: CHADWICK—String quartet no. 3; Piano quintet. *Portland String Quartet; Eskin, piano.*
+ ARG 5-6/89: 37
+ Fa 5-6/89: 161
+ Ov 4/89: 59

25746. NR 236-CD: CHADWICK—String quartets no. 4-5. *Portland String Quartet.*
+ ARG 5-6/89: 37
+ Fa 5-6/89: 161
+ Ov 4/89: 59

25747. NR 237-CD: *A Jenny Lind Recital with James Winn.* Music of Haydn, Bellini, Mozart, Rossini, Henselt, and others. *Parcells, soprano; Honeysucker, baritone; Winn, piano.*
+ ARG 3-4/90: 147
● Fa 3-4/90: 342

25748. NR 238-CD: Music of Debussy, N. Boulanger, Auric, Ravel (arr. Fischer), and others. *Fischer Duo (N. Fischer, cello; J.K. Fischer, piano).*
+ Fa 3-4/90: 372
● Gr 9/91: 97

25749. NR 239-CD: READ—Passacaglia and fugue in D minor; Chorale-Fantasia on Good King Wenceslas; Elegiac aria; Sinfonia da chiesa; And there appeared unto them tongues as of fire; Suite for organ. *Atlantic Brass Quintet; Raver, organ.*
● ARG 5-6/90: 94
+ DA 3/90: 68
+ Fa 5-6/90: 262

25750. NR 240-CD: *Portraits and self-portraits.* THOMSON—Chamber music. *Tommasini, piano; Leventhal, violin; Smith, flute; Cohen, oboe; Haroutunian, bassoon; Miller, cello.*
+ Fa 9-10/90: 413

25751. NR 241-CD: *Choral tapestries: an anthology of contemporary American choral music.* Music of Spencer, Iannaccone, Corigliano, Bassett, and Pinkham. *Gurt, Amolsch, piano; Emily Lowe Singers; Lowe, cond.*
+ ARG 11-12/91: 200
+ Fa 11-12/91: 536

25752. NR 242-CD: SMALL—25 preludes, a musical odyssey. Phoenix; 25 preludes; Trio for flute, cello and piano; Sonata no. 4; Fugue; A game of go. *Nanzetta, flute; Morera, bassoon; Harth, violin; Wolters, cello; Small, Hoffmann, piano.*
□ ARG 7-8/91: 126
+ Fa 11-12/91: 486

25753. NR 243-CD: BRAHMS—Clarinet trio; Clarinet quintet. *Boston Chamber Music Society.*
+ ARG 9-10/91: 54
+ Fa 11-12/91: 286

25754. NR 244-CD: BRAHMS—Piano trio no. 1; Piano quartet no. 2. *Boston Chamber Music Society.*
+ ARG 9-10/91: 52
+ Fa 11-12/91: 286

25755. NR 245-CD: SHOSTAKOVICH—Piano trio no. 2; Cello sonata. *Boston Chamber Music Society.*
+ ARG 3-4/95: 188

25756. NR 246-CD: KOYKKAR—Expressed in units; Circumstance; Modus operandum; Continuum; Impulse; A three-point perspective. *Present Music; Stalheim, cond.; Oakwood Chamber Players; Smith, cond.; Welbourne, piano.*
+ ARG 7-8/93: 111
+ Fa 1-2/93: 175

25757. NR 247-CD : *Alleluia! Sacred choral music in New England.* Music of Thompson, Holyoke, Chadwick, Paine, Beach, Parker, Woodman, Near, Ives, Mechem, Beaudrot and Rorem. *Harvard University Choir; Somerville, cond.; Granert, organ.*
+ ARG 11-12/92: 256
+ Fa 11-12/92: 426

25758. NR 248-CD: *Silenced voices.* SCHULHOFF—String quartet no. 1; Concertino; Flute sonata. KAPRALOVA—Preludia suite. KLEIN—Duo. *Hawthorne String Quartet; Smith, flute; Eskin, Pinkas, piano; Barker, bass.*
+ ARG 7-8/93: 190
+ Fa 9-10/93: 278
+ Gr 5/93: 64

25759. NR 249-CD: TCHAIKOVSKY—Souvenir de Florence. SCHOENBERG—Verklärte Nacht. *Boston Chamber Music Society.*
+ ARG 3-4/95: 202

25760. NR 250-CD: THOMSON—Vocal works. *Armstrong, Fortunato, Kelley, Kirby, Sylvan, Ripley, vocalists; Smith, percussion; Tommasini, piano.*
+ ARG 3-4/95: 205
+ Fa 1-2/96: 324

25761. NR 252-CD: BURLEIGH—Songs and spirituals. *Moses, bass; Sears, piano.*
+ ARG 9-10/96: 105

25762. NR 253-CD: G. READ—Sonata da chiesa for piano, op. 61; String quartet no. 1; Sonoric fantasia no. 1; Five aphorisms, op. 150. *Holt, piano; Boston Composers String Quartet; Horris, harp; Harbach, harpsichord; Berthiaume, celesta; Packer, violin; Karp, piano.*
• ARG 9-10/95: 199
+ Fa 11-12/96: 342

25763. NR 254-CD: INCE—Waves of Talya; Hammer music; Cross scintillations; Night passage. *Present Music; Stalheim, cond.*
+ ARG 7-8/95: 268

25764. NR 256-CD: RACHMANINOFF—Vespers. *Russian Chamber Chorus; Voskreseniye Choir; Roudenko, cond.*
+ ARG 3-4/96: 170

25765. NR 257-CD: LAMB—Rags. *Eskin, piano.*
+ ARG 5-6/96: 134

25766. NR 9001-CD: PISTON—String quartets no. 1-3. *Portland String Quartet.*
+ Fa 7-8/89: 212

25767. NR 9002-CD: PISTON—String quartets no. 4-5; Flute quintet. *Dwyer, flute; Portland String Quartet.*
+ Fa 7-8/89: 212

25768. NR 9003-CD: *Women in ragtime.* Music of Davis, Aufderheide, Dobyns,

Niebergall, Cozad, Zaimont and others. *Eskin, piano.*
+ ARG 3-4/93: 171

25769. NR 9004-CD: *Dark garden.* BEACH—Songs, violin pieces, and piano music. *Fortunato, mezzo-soprano; Silverstein, violin; Eskin, piano.*
+ Fa 5-6/89: 122
+ ON 5/89: 49

NORVARD

25770. 1 (2 discs): BACH—Partitas no. 1-6. *Norton, piano.*
+ Fa 11-12/96: 174

NORWAY IN MUSIC

25771. CDN 31000: VALEN—Symphonies no. 1, 4. *Bergen Symphony Orch.; Ceccato, cond.*
• Fa 11-12/87: 243

25772. CDN 31001: VALEN—Symphonies no. 2, 3. *Bergen Symphony Orch.; Ceccato, cond.*
• Fa 11-12/87: 243

25773. CDN 31003: JENSEN—Passacaglia; Partita sinfonica; Violin sonata. *Nilsson, violin; Bratlie, piano; Oslo Phil. Orch.; Ruud, cond.*
□ ARG 3-4/89: 48
□ Fa 3-4/89: 194

25774. CDN 31008: TVEITT—Hundred folktunes from Hardanger: Suite no. 1; Harp concerto no. 2; Nykken. *Kniejski, harp; Royal Phil. Orch.; Dreier, cond.*
□ ARG 7-8/90: 120
+ Fa 3-4/90: 323 (2 reviews)

NORWAY MUSIC

25775. ALBCD 004: *Cikada duo.* Music of Wallin, Hegdal, Sandstrom, and Balke. *Karlsson, piano and synthesizer; Rabben, percussion.*
• Fa 9-10/93: 378

25776. ALBCD 005: *Cikada.* Music of Murail, Kruse, Nilsson, Lindberg, and Hegdal. *Cikada; Eggen, cond.; Torgersen, mezzo-soprano.*
• Fa 9-10/93: 378

25777. HCD 2902: NYSTEDT—Symphony for strings; Concertino for clarinet, English horn, and strings; Concerto grosso for 3 trumpets and strings. *Minsk Chamber Orch.; Mynbaev, cond.*
+ ARG 11-12/93: 162
+ Fa 11-12/93: 337

25778. GRCD 4055: BEETHOVEN—Violin concerto, op. 61. BRUCH—Violin concerto no. 1. *Tellefsen, violin; London Phil. Orch.; Handley, cond.*
• ARG 7-8/95: 82
+ Fa 5-6/95: 134

NORWEGIAN COMPOSERS

25779. NC 4905 (LP): Music of Braein, Brustad, Mortenson, and Baden. *Gulbransen, flute; Berlin Symphony Orch.; Andersen, cond.*
+ Fa 5-6/87: 233

25780. NCD 4910: NORDHEIM—Wirklicher Wald; Aurora. *Dorow, soprano; Kvalbein, cello; Bergen Cathedral Choir; Bergen Symphony Orch.; Andersen, cond.; Electric Phoenix.*
+ Fa 7-8/87: 157

25781. NC 4912 (LP): HAGERUP BULL—Symphony no. 5; Air solennel; Sonata con spirito op. 40. *Stanese, viola; Trio Ravel; Royal Phil. Orch.; Dreier, cond.*
+ Fa 5-6/87: 125

25782. NCD 4913: SAEVERUD—Symphony no. 9; Rondo amoroso op. 14 no. 7; Galdreslatten op. 20; Kjempeviseslatten op. 22a no. 5. *Royal Phil. Orch.; Dreier, cond.*
+ ARG Fall/87: 48
+ Fa 5-6/87: 182 (2 reviews)
+ NYT 10/4/87: H37

25783. NCD 4916: KOLBERG—Aria in aria, for orchestra; For the time being, for vocal quartet. *Royal Phil. Orch.; Eggen, cond.; Electric Phoenix .*
+ Fa 11-12/87: 160

NOTES

25784. 11007: BEETHOVEN—Piano trios no. 5, 9; Cello sonata no. 5. *Casals, cello; Goldberg, violin; Serkin, Horszowski, piano.*
+ ARG 3-4/93: 188

25785. 11011: SCHUBERT—Variations on a theme of Anselm Huttenbrenner; Piano sonatas, D. 958, 566. *Richter, piano.*
+ Fa 5-6/93: 317

25786. 21001: ROSSINI—L'inganno felice. *Gundari, Jacopucci, Montarsolo, Tadeo; Orch. of RAI, Naples; Franci, cond.*
+ Gr 5/93: 105

NOVADISC

25787. ND-0191-CD: *A Choral flourish.* Music of Vaughan Williams, Stanford, Raminsh, Leighton, Barber, Debussy, Kodály, and Halley. *Exultate Chamber Singers; Tuttle, cond.; McDonald, piano & organ.*
+ Fa 11-12/91: 535

25788. ND-0193-CD: *Popov and Vona, duo pianists.* Music of Debussy, Southam, and Rachmaninoff.
• Fa 7-8/94: 317

25789. ND-0293-CD: *Dance of the white Indian: piano music of South America.* Music of Villa-Lobos, Peres, and

NOVALIS

Guarneri. *Peres, piano.*
+ ARG 3-4/95: 243
+ Fa 7-8/94: 318

NOVALIS

25790. 150 002-2: Schubert—Piano trio in B♭ D. 898; Adagio in E♭ D. 897. *Oppitz, piano; Sitkovetsky, violin; Geringas, cello.*
+ DA 9/86: 46
+ Fa 3-4/87: 201
• Gr 6/87: 71

25791. 150 003-2: Schubert—Piano trio in E♭ D. 929; Trio in B♭ (in one movement). *Oppitz, piano; Sitkovetsky, violin; Geringas, cello.*
+ DA 9/86: 46
+ Fa 3-4/87: 201
• Gr 6/87: 71

25792. 150 004-2: *Baroque festival.* Music of Manfredini, Bach, Pachelbel (arr. Giazotto), Handel and Purcell. *Camerata Bern; Füri, cond.*
+ ARG 1-2/87: 79
• Fa 1-2/87: 255
- NR 7/86: 9

25793. 150 005-2: Bach—Prelude and fugue BWV 552; Partita on O Gott du frommer Gott BWV 767; Fantasia and fugue BWV 542; Nun komm, der Heiden Heiland BWV 659; Wachet auf ruft uns die Stimme BWV 645; Ich ruf zu dir BWV 639; Toccata and fugue BWV 565. *Koopman, organ.*
- Fa 9-10/87: 141

25794. 150 006-2: Mozart—Quintet for horn, violin, 2 violas and bass in E♭ K. 407; Quartet for horn, violin, viola and cello in F K. 370; Clarinet quintet in A K. 581. *Neunecker, horn; Miyamoto, oboe; Wehle, clarinet; Mannheim String Quartet.*
+ Fa 9-10/87: 253

25795. 150 007-2: Mozart—Violin concertos no. 4-5. *Sitkovetsky, violin; English Chamber Orch.*
• Fa 9-10/87: 248
• Gr 10/87: 742

25796. 150 008-2: Beethoven—Piano trio op. 97; Variations on Ich bin der Schneider Kakadu. *Oppitz, piano; Sitkovetsky, violin; Geringas, cello.*
+ Fa 9-10/87: 155
• Gr 8/87: 315

25797. 150 010-2: Mozart—Lieder. *Mathis, soprano; Engel, piano.*
• Fa 9-10/87: 250
• Gr 9/87: 466

25798. 150 011-2: Dvořák—Serenade for string orchestra op. 22; Sextet in A for 2 violins, 2 violas, and 2 cellos op. 48. *Camerata Bern.*
• Fa 9-10/87: 194
+ Gr 9/87: 405

25799. 150 026-2: Schubert—Lieder. *Mathis, soprano; Weber, clarinet; Engel, piano.*
+ ARG 11-12/89: 111
• Fa 11-12/89: 345
+ Gr 2/90: 1510

25800. 150 027-2: Mozart—Serenade no. 7; Symphony no. 32. *Bavarian Radio Orch.; Davis, cond.*
+ ARG 11-12/89: 89
+ Fa 5-6/89: 250
+ Gr 11/88: 783

25801. 150 028-2: Bach—Sei Lob und Ehr dem höchsten Gut BWV 117; Lobet Gott in seinem Reichen BWV 11; Ich habe genug BWV 82. *Cuccaro, Georg, Kraus, Schmidt, Fischer-Dieskau; Gächinger Kantorei; Württemberg Chamber Orch.; Rilling, cond.*
□ ARG 5-6/89: 11
+ Fa 5-6/89: 103
• Gr 1/89: 1191

25802. 150 029-2: Bach—Ich lebe, meine Herze, zu deinem Ergotzen BWV 145; Jauchzet Gott in allen Landen BWV 51; Wachet auf, ruft uns die Stimme BWV 140; Ich will den Kreuzstab gerne tragen BWV 56. *Cuccaro, Georg, Kraus, Schmidt, Augér, Baldin, Huttenlocher, Fischer-Dieskau; Gächinger Kantorei; Württemberg Chamber Orch.; Bach-Collegium Stuttgart; Rilling, cond.*
⊓ ARG 5-6/89: 11
+ Fa 5-6/89: 103
• Gr 1/89: 1191
+ HPR 6/89: 67

25803. 150 030-2: Mozart—Horn concertos (complete). *Neunecker, horn; Camerata Bern; Füri, cond.*
- ARG 5-6/89: 11
+ DA 4/89: 70
• Fa 5-6/89: 240
• Gr 11/88: 783

25804. 150 031-2: Stalder—Symphony no. 5; Flute concerto in B♭. Reindl—Sinfonia concertante in D. *Bennett, flute; English Chamber Orch.; Griffiths, cond.*
+ Fa 5-6/89: 326

25805. 150 032-2: *Romantische Chormusik.* Music of Schumann, Brahms, Schubert, Mendelssohn, and others . *Monteverdi Choir Hamburg; Jürgens, cond.*
+ ARG 9-10/89: 134

25806. 150 033-2: Mahler—Symphony no. 1. *Bavarian Radio Orch.; Davis, cond.*
+ ARG 5-6/89: 61
- Fa 5-6/89: 227
+ Gr 1/89: 1154

25807. 150 034-2: Bach—Concertos for harpsichord no. 1-2, 4-5. *Gilbert, harpsichord; English Chamber Orch.*
+ ARG 5-6/89: 13

+ Fa 5-6/89: 104
• HPR 6/89: 68

25808. 150 035-2: Bach—Brandenburg concertos (complete). *Wiener Akademie; Haselböck, cond.*
• ARG 9-10/89: 18
+ Fa 9-10/89: 117
- Gr 1/90: 1319

25809. 150 036-2: Bach—Toccata and fugue BWV 538; Partita on Sei gegrüsset, Jesu gütig BWV 768; Fantasia BWV 572; Trio sonata no. 6 BWV 530; Vater unser in Himmelreich BWV 682; Jesus Christus, unser Heiland BWV 688; Prelude and fugue BWV 543. *Koopman, organ.*
+ Fa 7-8/89: 79
- Gr 11/89: 933

25810. 150 037-2: Bach—Cello suites (complete). *Nyffenegger, cello.*
• ARG 9-10/89: 23
• Fa 7-8/89: 77

25811. 150 038-2: Widor—Symphonies no. 9-10. *Kaunzinger, organ.*
• ARG 11-12/89: 139
• Fa 11-12/89: 412

25812. 150 040-2: Mozart—Divertimentos no. 10, 15. *Camerata Bern; Füri, cond.*
• Fa 11-12/89: 288
+ Gr 3/90: 1614

25813. 150 041-2: Mozart—Overtures: Don Giovanni; La clemenza di Tito; Mitridate; La betulia liberata; Idomeneo; Lucio Silla; Bastien et BAstienne; La finta semplice; Schauspieldirektor; Nozze di Figaro; Cosi fan tutte; Zauberflöte. *English Chamber Orch.; Hager, cond.*
+ ARG 11-12/89: 86
• Fa 11-12/89: 292

25814. 150 042-2: Mozart—Piano sonatas no. 13-14; Fantasy in C minor K. 475; Rondo in A minor K. 511. *Oppitz, piano.*
+ Fa 11-12/89: 296

25815. 150 043-2: Mozart—Oboe concertos K. 313-314; Sinfonia concertante for winds K. 297b. *Indermühle, oboe; English Chamber Orch.; Hager, cond.*
- ARG 5-6/90: 77
+ Fa 1-2/90: 235
• Gr 4/90: 1785

25816. 150 044-2: Music of Weber, Mozart, Schubert, and Gluck. *English Chamber Orch.; Judd, cond.*
+ Fa 3-4/90: 397
+ Gr 3/90: 1622

25817. 150 045-2: Haydn—Symphonies no. 30, 73, 94. *Vienna Academy; Haselböck, cond.*
+ ARG 3-4/90: 59

• Fa 3-4/90: 193
• Gr 4/90: 1781

25818. 150 046-2: SCHUMANN—Fantasy in C op. 17; Davidsbündlertänze. *Bach, piano.*
+ Fa 9-10/90: 378
+ Gr 11/90: 1015

25819. 150 047-2: HAYDN—Trios for 2 flutes and cello H. IV: 1-3; Trios for flute, cello and piano H. XV: 15-16. *A. & C. Nicolet, flutes; Filippini, cello; Canino, piano.*
+ Fa 5-6/90: 191

25820. 150 048-2: BUXTEHUDE—Organ works. *Koopman, organ.*
• ARG 5-6/90: 38
+ Fa 5-6/90: 143

25821. 150 049-2: VIVALDI—Violin concertos op. 8 no. 1-4; Concertos for 4 violins RV 580; Concertos for 3 violins RV 551. *Füri, violin & cond.; Camerata Bern.*
- ARG 5-6/90: 128
+ DA 7/90: 60
+ Fa 5-6/90: 330
+ Gr 9/90: 546

25822. 150 052-2: BACH—Organ works . *Koopman, organ.*
- Fa 11-12/90: 149

25823. 150 053-2: MOZART—Symphonies no. 17, 35, 41. *English Chamber Orch.; Hager, cond.*
• ARG 7-8/90: 76
• Gr 4/91: 1836

25824. 150 054-2: MOZART—Fantasias K. 594, 608; Andante in F, K. 616; Overture in C, K. 399; Gigue K. 574; Adagio in C, K. 536: Fugues K. 153-154, 401 . *Haselböck, organ. Recorded 1990.*
+ Fa 1-2/91: 255
+ Gr 10/91: 140

25825. 150 055-2: MOZART—Symphonies no. 27, 29-30. *Vienna Academy Symphony; Haselböck, cond.*
+ Fa 9-10/90: 314

25826. 150 056-2: BRAHMS—Piano sextets op. 18, 36 (arr. Kirchner). *Rabinovitch, piano; Hirschhorn, violin; Geringas, cello.*
+ ARG 9-10/90: 52
+ Fa 9-10/90: 200

25827. 150 057-2: TCHAIKOVSKY—Serenade for strings in C; Suite in G. *English Chamber Orch.; Judd, cond.*
• Fa 11-12/90: 375
+ Gr 10/91: 114

25828. 150 058-2: SCHUBERT—String quartets no. 13-14. *Melos Quartet.*
• ARG 7-8/90: 96
- Fa 9-10/90: 371

25829. 150 060-2 (5 discs): MOZART—Symphonies no. 32, 35, 41; Concerto for flute and harp; Horn concertos no. 1, 3; Violin concertos no. 3-4; Serenades no. 9, 13; German dances; Contredances. *Various soloists, ensembles & conductors.*
• ARG 1-2/91: 263
+ HPR v.8, no.2/91: 72

25830. 150 061-2: Clarinet concertos of Mozart, Süssmayr, and Eybler. *Klöcker, clarinet; English Chamber Orch.*
+ Fa 3-4/91: 285

25831. 150 062-2: VIVALDI—Flute concertos RV 428, 433, 439, 440; Oboe concertos RV 454, 461 . *Rachine, flute; Indermühle, oboe; English Chamber Orch.; Preston, cond.*
+ Fa 3-4/91: 418

25832. 150 063-2: BEETHOVEN—Piano sonatas no. 4, 17; Bagatelles op. 126. *A. Bach, piano.*
+ Fa 1-2/91: 149

25833. 150 064-2: MOZART—Schuldigkeit des ersten Gebots; Ave verum corpus; Vespers, K. 339: Laudate Fominum; Exsultate jubilate; Inter natos mulierum; Mass, K. 427: Laudamus te; Mass, K. 275: Denedictus; Regina Coeli, K. 276. *Mathis, soprano; Tallis Chamber Choir; English Chamber Orch.; Klee, cond.*
+ Fa 11-12/90: 296

25834. 150 065-2: WEBER—Trio for flute, cello, and piano in G minor; Flute sonatas op. 10 no. 1-6. *Nicolet, flute; Filippini, cello; Canino, piano.*
+ ARG 1-2/91: 124
+ Fa 3-4/91: 427

25835. 150 066-2: BACH—Organ works, vol. 5. *Koopman, organ.*
• ARG 9-10/91: 39
+ Fa 9-10/91: 147

25836. 150 068-2: MOZART—Mass in C K. 317; Grabmusik K. 42; Church sonatas K. 67, 244, 329. *Wiens, Fink, Hollweg, Hampson, Summereder; Concentus Vocalis; Vienna Academy; Haselböck, cond.*
+ ARG 5-6/91: 88
+ Fa 5-6/91: 234

25837. 150 069-2: LISZT—Prelude and fugue on BACH; Evocation à la Chapelle Sixtin; Variations on Weinen, Klagen, Sorgen, Zagen; Fantasy and fugue on Ad nos, ad salutarem undam. *Kaunzinger, organ.*
- Fa 11-12/90: 258

25838. 150 070-2: SCHOECK—Serenade op. 1; Violin concerto in B♭. *Hoelscher, violin; English Chamber Orch.; Griffiths, cond.*
+ ARG 5-6/91: 101
+ Fa 5-6/91: 274
+ Gr 7/91: 62

25839. 150 071-2: BRUCKNER—Organ music. *Horn, organ.*
- ARG 9-10/91: 55
+ Fa 5-6/91: 144

25840. 150 073-2: WIDOR—Organ symphonies no. 1-2. *Kaunzinger, organ.*
+ ARG 1-2/92: 140

25841. 150 076-2: MENDELSSOHN—Symphony no. 4; Midsummer night's dream: excerpts. *English Chamber Orch.; Hager, cond.*
+ Fa 5-6/92: 198

25842. 150 077-2: BACH—Concertos, BWV 1053, 1059, 1055; Sinfonias, BWV 12, 21; Easter Oratorio: Adagio. *Indermühle, oboe & oboe d' amore; English Chamber Orch.; Preston, cond.*
+ Fa 5-6/92: 116

25843. 150 079-2: BORODIN—Symphony no. 2; Prince Igor overture and Polovtsian dances; In the steppes of central Asia. *Moscow Radio Orch.; Fedoseyev, cond.*
+ ARG 5-6/92: 33
+ Fa 7-8/92: 124

25844. 150 080-2: VIVALDI—Concertos. *Camerata Bern; Füri, violin; Wiener Akademie; Haselböck, organ; Ensemble instrumental de Grenoble; Redel, cond.*
• ARG 5-6/92: 153

25845. 150 081-2: MOZART—Masonic music. *Prégardien, Wildhaber, Hornik, Schneyder; Chorus Viennensis; Vienna Academy Orch.; Haselböck, cond.*
• Gr 10/93: 94

25846. 150 082-2: BOCCHERINI—Flute quintets. KRAUS—Flute quintet in D. *Nicolet, flute; Athenaeum Enesco Quartet of Paris.*
+ ARG 11-12/92: 91
+ Fa 9-10/92: 195

25847. 150 083-2: GEMINIANI—Concerti grossi op. 3. *Camerata Bern; Füri, cond.*
+ ARG 11-12/92: 123
+ Fa 11-12/92: 242
+ Gr 1/93: 40

25848. 150 085-2: WIDOR—Symphonies no. 3-4. *Kaunzinger, organ.*
• ARG 3-4/93: 156

25849. 150 086-2: HAYDN—Symphonies no. 6-8. *Wiener Akademie; Haselböck, cond.*
+ ARG 3-4/93: 89

25850. 150 087-2: MOZART—Missa solemnis, K. 337; Splendente te, K. Anh. 121. Includes music ot Albrechtsberger, Martini, M. Haydn, Salieri, Linek, and Gregorian chant. *Hugo Distler Chor; Vienna Academy; Haselböck, cond.*
+ Fa 3-4/93: 238

25851. 150 088-2: BACH—Orchestral suite no. 2; Flute concertos, BWV 1042,

NOVALIS

1055, 1056; Non sa, che sia dolore: Sinfonia. *Racine, flute; English Chamber Orch.; Preston, cond.*
- ● ARG 5-6/93: 61

25852. 150 089-2 (2 discs): FUX—La deposizione dalla Croce di Gesù Cristo Salvator Nostro. *Vocalists; Wiener Akademie; Haselböck, cond.*
- ● ARG 9-10/93: 123
- ● Fa 5-6/93: 206

25853. 150 091-2: SCHUBERT—Symphonies no. 5, 8; Rosamunde: Entractes. *Wiener Akademie; Haselböck, cond.*
- - ARG 9-10/93: 187
- ● Fa 7-8/93: 236

25854. 150 092-2: TARTINI—Violin concertos D. 45, 56, 86. *Füri, violin & cond.; Camerata Bern.*
- + Fa 9-10/93: 306

25855. 150 093-2: WEBER—Clarinet concertos; Concertino. *Klöcker, clarinet; Bratislava Radio Orch.; Tamayo, cond.*
- ● ARG 1-2/94: 170
- + Fa 11-12/93: 448

25856. 150 094-2: KERLL—Works for organ. *Haselböck, organ.*
- + Fa 11-12/93: 283

25857. 150 095-2: HAYDN—Masses no. 4, 7; Salve Regina. *Hugo Distler Choir; Wiener Akademie; Haselböck, cond.*
- + ARG 5-6/94: 99
- + Fa 3-4/94: 212

25858. 150 099-2: FRITZ—Symphony no. 1; Violin concerto. SCHERRER—Symphony no. 5. *Lohmann, violin; English Chamber Orch.; Griffiths, cond.*
- + ARG 9-10/94: 191
- ● Fa 7-8/94: 136

25859. 150 100-2: WEBER—Oboe concertino; Romanza siciliana; Romanze appassionata; Divertimento; Andante and Hungarian rondo; Horn concertino. *Consortium Classicum; Bratislava Radio Symphony; Tamayo, cond.*
- + ARG 7-8/94: 187

25860. 150 101-2: BEETHOVEN—Piano sonatas no. 21, 23. *Nikolayeva, piano.*
- - ARG 9-10/94: 100

25861. 150 102-2: HANDEL—Royal fireworks music; Concerti a due cori. *English Chamber Orch.; Mackerras, cond.*
- - ARG 11-12/94: 125

25862. 150 103-2: C.P.E. BACH—Oboe concertos, H. 466, 468, 431. *Indermühle, oboe & cond.; English Chamber Orch.*
- + Fa 5-6/95: 121

25863. 150 106-2: SCHOECK—Orchestral songs; Sommernacht. *Berg, baritone; Hering, tenor; English Chamber Orch.;*

Griffiths, cond.
- + ARG 3-4/95: 178
- + Fa 5-6/95: 320

25864. 150 107-2: HAYDN—Symphonies no. 101-102. *Wiener Akademie; Haselböck, cond.*
- + Fa 5-6/95: 212

25865. 150 108-2: HANDEL—Overtures and marches. *English Chamber Orch.; Mackerras, cond.*
- + ARG 11-12/95: 130
- + Fa 9-10/95: 219

25866. 150 109-2: MOZART—Serenade no. 9; Marches, K. 335 no. 1-2; A musical joke. *Vienna Academy; Haselböck, cond.*
- + Fa 11-12/95: 318

25867. 150 112-2 (2 discs): SUPPÉ—Requiem. *Hartelius, Gohl, Bünten, Widmer; Zürich Concert Choir; Zürich Chamber Orch.; Stoutz, cond.*
- - ARG 7-8/95: 206
- ● Fa 7-8/95: 335

25868. 150 113-2: MOZART—Flute concerto no. 2; Sinfonia concertante for flute, oboe, horn, bassoon, and orchestra, K. 297b. WEBER—Concertino for horn and orchestra, op. 45. *Gurtner, flute; McDonald, horn; Vienna Academy; Haselböck, cond.*
- + Fa 3-4/96: 231

25869. 150 115-2: TELEMANN—Concertos. *Wiener Akademie; Haselböck, cond.*
- ● Fa 7-8/95: 343

25870. 150 117-2: *Melodie in F. Music of Falla, Fauré, Granados, Sarasate, and others. Demenga, cello; Wyss, piano.*
- + ARG 5-6/96: 232

25871. 150 118-2: HINDEMITH—Mathis der Maler symphony; Four temperaments; Amor und Psyche. *Canino, piano; Basel Symphony Orch.; Mackerras, cond.*
- + ARG 5-6/96: 126

25872. 150 120-2: HANDEL—Sonatas for flute and continuo. *Gurtner, flute; Máté, cello; Haselböck, harpsichord & organ.*
- ● Fa 9-10/96: 210

25873. 150 122-2: J. STRAUSS, JR.—Orchestra music. *Johann Strauss Chamber Orch. of Vienna; Wildner, cond.*
- - Fa 7-8/96: 314

25874. 150 126-2: TELEMANN—Oboe concertos. *Indermühle, oboe, oboe d'amore & cond.; English Chamber Orch.*
- + ARG 9-10/96: 218
- + Fa 11-12/96: 400

25875. 150 127-2: *Viennese salon music. Music of Suppé, Ziehrer, Lanner, Lehár,*

Ivanovici, Dostal, Kálmán, Fučík, and Waldteufel. *Johann Strauss Chamber Orch.; Wildner, cond.*
- - Fa 11-12/96: 485

25876. 150 128-2 (2 discs): CORELLI—12 sonate a violino e violone o cimbalo, op. 5. *Trio Veracini.*
- + ARG 3-4/97: 118
- + Fa 1-2/97: 141

NOVELBOND

25877. NOVELBOND 1: JAMES—The scarlet letter: sketches from the opera. *Tierney, Anderson; Philharmonia Orch.; Greenwood, cond.*
- ● Gr 10/92: 175

NOVELLO

25878. NVLCD 104: JOSEPHS—Doubles for 2 pianos; Fourteen studies for piano. *Hendrickx, Kende, Solomon, pianos.*
- + Fa 3-4/90: 205

25879. NVLCD 108: MUSGRAVE—Mary Queen of Scots. *Putnam, Garrison, Busse, Gardner; Virginia Opera Association Chorus & Orch.; Mark, cond.*
- + Fa 7-8/90: 213
- + Gr 3/90: 1684
- + Op 5/90: 494

NOVISSE

25880. UC9201: MASLANKA—Symphony no. 3. PENN—A cornfield in July and The river. *Maher, baritone; University of Connecticut Symphonic Wind Ensemble; Green, cond.*
- + Fa 11-12/93: 313

NUOVA ERA

25881. 108: Music of Rota, Casella, Respighi, Dallapiccola, and Malipiero. *Various performers.* Reissues.
- + ARG 11-12/94: 215

25882. 110: *Hidden gems of Italian nineteenth century opera. Music of Salieri, Mercadante, Bellini, Donizetti, Rossini, and Leoncavallo. Various singers & orch. accs.*
- + ARG 7-8/95: 267
- ● Fa 7-8/95: 392

25883. 2201: BRAHMS—Violin concerto, op. 77. WAGNER—Götterdämmerung: Immolation scene. BEETHOVEN—Creatures of Prometheus: Overture. *Morini, violin; Flagstad, soprano; New York Phil.; Walter, cond.* Recorded live 1952-53.
- + ARG 5-6/89: 131
- + Fa 5-6/89: 412

25884. 2204: PROKOFIEV—Symphony no. 5. DEBUSSY—La mer. *Italian Radio and Television Milan Symphony Orch.; Celibidache, cond.* Recorded live 1960.
- - Fa 5-6/89: 275

25885. 2205: BRUCKNER—Symphony no. 4. *Vienna Phil. Orch.; Knappertsbusch, cond.* Recorded live 1960.
- Fa 5-6/89: 152

25886. 2209: MOZART—Requiem. *Della Casa, Malaniuk, Dermota, Siepi; Vienna State Opera Chorus; Vienna Phil. Orch.; Walter, cond.* Recorded live 1956.
+ ARG 7-8/89: 66
- Fa 7-8/89: 200

25887. 2210: SIBELIUS—Symphony no. 1. STRAUSS—Death and transfiguration. *New York Phil.; Vienna Phil. Orch.; De Sabata, cond.* Recorded live 1950 & 1953.
• Fa 11-12/89: 164

25888. 2215/16 (2 discs): GLUCK—Orfeo ed Euridice. *Simionato, Jurinac, Sciutti; Vienna State Opera Chorus; Vienna Phil. Orch.; Karajan, cond.* Recorded live 1959.
- Fa 11-12/89: 217

25889. 2217: STRAUSS—Death and transfiguration; Vier letzte Lieder; Till Eulenspiegel. *Janowitz, soprano; RAI Turin Symphony; Italian Radio and Television Rome Symphony Orch.; Stuttgart Symphony Orch.; Celibidache, cond.* Recorded live 1962, 1969.
- Fa 11-12/89: 164

25890. 2218: Music of Ravel, Debussy, Galuppi, and Scarlatti. *Michelangeli, piano.*
+ Fa 9-10/89: 417

25891. 2219: RAVEL—Boléro; La valse; Ma mère l'oye: Suite. GHEDINI—Marinaresca e baccanale. *New York Phil.; Vienna Phil. Orch.; De Sabata, cond.* Recorded live 1950, 1953.
• ARG 9-10/89: 154
+ Fa 7-8/89: 218

25892. 2220/21 (2 discs): VERDI—Falstaff. *Tebaldi, Noni, Elmo, Valletti, Stabile, Silveri; Teatro alla Scala Chorus & Orch.; De Sabata, cond.* Recorded live 1951.
- ARG 7-8/89: 102
- Fa 11-12/89: 390

25893. 2222 (2 discs): VERDI—Nabucco. *Suliotis, Raimondi, Guelfi, Ghiaurov; Teatro alla Scala; Gavazzeni, cond.* Recorded live 1966.
+ Fa 5-6/89: 344

25894. 2224: MAHLER—Das Lied von der Erde. *Ludwig, mezzo-soprano; Kmentt, tenor; Vienna Symphony Orch.; Kleiber, cond.* Recorded live 1967.
□ ARG 7-8/89: 59 m.f.
- Fa 7-8/89: 173

25895. 2225: BRUCKNER—Symphony no. 9. *New York Phil.; Walter, cond.* Recorded live 1953.

• ARG 9-10/89: 154
- Fa 7-8/89: 119

25896. 2226: BRAHMS—Symphony no. 2; Concerto for violin and cello op. 102. *Corigliano, violin; Rose, cello; New York Phil.; Walter, cond.* Recorded live 1951.
+ Fa 7-8/89: 115

25897. 2235: BEETHOVEN—Symphony no. 7; Coriolan overture; Leonore overture no. 3. *Berlin Phil. Orch.; Vienna Phil. Orch.; Karajan, cond.* Recorded live 1960, 1968.
- Fa 5-6/90: 120 m.f.
+ HPR Fall/90: 54

25898. 2236/37 (2 discs): CHERUBINI—Lodoïska. *Ligabue, Prandelli, Monachesi, Bruscantini; Italian Radio and Television Rome Chorus & Symphony Orch.; De Fabritiis, cond.* Recorded live 1965.
+ ARG 9-10/89: 41
+ Fa 11-12/89: 177

25899. 2249: BEETHOVEN—Symphony no. 9. *Güden, Höngen, Majkut, Frick; Vienna State Opera Chorus; Vienna Phil. Orch.; Walter, cond.* Recorded live 1955.
- ARG 9-10/89: 38
- Fa 9-10/89: 136

25900. 2250: ROSSINI—Stabat Mater. *Gencer, Casoni, Alva, Robinson; Bavarian Radio Chorus & Orch.; Rossi, cond.* Recorded live 1967.
• Fa 9-10/89: 309

25901. 2251/52 (2 discs): BRUCKNER—Symphony no. 8. STRAUSS—Vier letzte Lieder. *Schwarzkopf, soprano; Vienna Phil. Orch.; Berlin Phil. Orch.; Karajan, cond.* Recorded live 1964-65.
- ARG 11-12/89: 76
- Fa 11-12/89: 164

25902. 2253/54 (2 discs): CIMAROSA—Chi dell'altrui si veste presto si spoglia. SCARLATTI—La dirindina. *Bonifaccio, Mariconda, Zilio, Bonisolli, Bruscantini; Alessandro Scarlatti Orch. di Napoli; Muti, cond.* Recorded live 1968.
• ARG 9-10/89: 44 (Cimarosa)
+ ARG 9-10/89: 44 (Scarlatti)
• Fa 9-10/89: 182

25903. 2256/58 (3 discs): ROSSINI—Semiramide. *Sutherland, Sinclair, Garaventa, Petri; Italian Radio and Television Rome Chorus & Symphony Orch.; Bonynge, cond.* Recorded live 1968.
- ARG 9-10/89: 98
+ Fa 9-10/89: 308
+ NYT 8/27/89: H25

25904. 2259/61 (3 discs): MOZART—Symphonies no. 25, 29, 35, 38-40; Overtures to Le nozze di Figaro and Die Zauberflöte; Piano concerto no. 20. *Hess, piano; various orchs.; Walter, cond.*

Recorded live.
+ ARG 11-12/89: 90

25905. 2262/63 (2 discs): BEETHOVEN—Missa solemnis in D. HANDEL—Concerto grosso in B minor op. 6, no. 12. *Price, Ludwig, Gedda, Zaccaria; Vienna Singverein; Vienna Phil. Orch.; Karajan, cond.* Recorded live 1959.
+ Fa 9-10/89: 133 m.f.

25906. 2264/65 (2 discs): Music of Bellini, Donizetti, Meyerbeer, Flotow, and others. *Bergonzi, tenor; various orchs. & conds.* Recorded live 1951, 1969.
+ ARG 9-10/89: 142
+ Fa 9-10/89: 391

25907. 2266/67 (2 discs): Music of Cherubini, Bellini, Donizetti, and Verdi. *Gencer, soprano; various orchs. & conds.*
□ ARG 9-10/89: 145
+ Fa 9-10/89: 386
+ NYT 5/14/89: H34

25908. 2271/72 (2 discs): PAISIELLO—Fedra. *Udovick, Tuccari, Lazzari, Cesari; Italian Radio and Television Milan Chorus & Symphony Orch.; Questa, cond.*
+ Fa 11-12/89: 310
• Gr 9/89: 537
+ NYT 8/27/89: H25

25909. 2278/79 (2 discs): VERDI—I due Foscari. *Vitale, Bergonzi, Guelfi; Italian Radio and Television Milan Chorus & Symphony Orch.; Giulini, cond.* Recorded 1951.
• Fa 11-12/89: 389 m.f.
+ NYT 8/27/89: H25

25910. 2280/81 (2 discs): VERDI—Il trovatore. *Caballé, Mattiucci, Tucker, Zanasi; Florence May Festival Chorus & Orch.; Schippers, cond.* Recorded live 1968.
- Fa 9-10/89: 353
+ Gr 10/89: 751
+ NYT 8/27/89: H25

25911. 2282/83 (2 discs): Music of Bach, Beethoven, Brahms, and Strauss. *Berlin Phil. Orch.; Karajan, cond.* Recorded live 1967.
□ ARG 11-12/89: 143
+ Fa 9-10/89: 441

25912. 2284/85 (2 discs): VERDI—Stiffelio. *Gulín, Limarilli, Alberti; Teatro regio (Parma) Chorus & Orch.; Maag, cond.* Recorded live 1968.
• Fa 11-12/89: 395

25913. 2288/90 (3 discs): STRAUSS—Frau ohne Schatten. *Rysanek, Ludwig, Hoffman, Thomas, Berry; Vienna State Opera Chorus & Orch.; Karajan, cond.* Recorded live 1964. Drastically cut and rearranged.

NUOVA ERA

+ ARG 11-12/89: 124
● Fa 11-12/89: 371

25914. 2291: Music of Sibelius, J. Strauss, Jr., Prokofiev, and others. *Italian Radio and Television Milan Symphony Orch.; Italian Radio and Television Turin Symphony Orch.; Vienna Phil. Orch.; Celibidache, cond.* Recorded live 1952, 1960.
+ Fa 11-12/89: 495

25915. 2292/93 (2 discs): Music of Mozart, Cherubini, Rossini, Donizetti, and others. *Kraus, tenor; various orchs. & conds.*
● ARG 11-12/89: 169
+ Fa 11-12/89: 434

25916. 2294/95 (2 discs): Music of Verdi, Catalani, Puccini, and Giordano. *Tebaldi, soprano; various orchs. & conds.* Recorded live 1951-61.
+ Fa 11-12/89: 427

25917. 2296: Mozart—Symphony no. 33. Strauss—Aus Italien. *Philharmonia Orch.; Italian Radio and Television Milan Symphony Orch.; Kleiber, Muti, conds.* Recorded live 1967-68.
+ Fa 11-12/89: 298

25918. 2301/02 (2 discs): Music of Tchaikovsky, Bizet, Stravinsky, and Prokofiev. *Berlin Phil. Orch.; Celibidache, cond.* Recorded live 1948, 1960.
● Fa 11-12/89: 495 (Tchaikovsky)
+ Fa 11-12/89: 495 (others)

25919. 2303: Brahms—Symphony no. 4. Bruckner—Te Deum. *Güden, Zadek, Majkut, Frick; Vienna State Opera Chorus; Vienna Phil. Orch.; New York Phil.; Walter, cond.* Recorded live 1951, 1955.
+ ARG 11-12/89: 45 (Brahms)
- ARG 11-12/89: 45 (Bruckner)
- Fa 11-12/89: 156 (Brahms)
+ Fa 11-12/89: 156 (Bruckner)

25920. 2304: Brahms—Symphony no. 1. Berlioz—Roman Carnival overture; Roméo and Juliette: Queen Mab scherzo. *Florence May Festival Orch.; Bernstein, cond.* Recorded live 1967.
● Fa 11-12/89: 155

25921. 2311: Debussy—Preludes bk. 2. *Richter, piano.* Recorded live 1968.
- ARG 1-2/90: 43
□ Fa 11-12/89: 187 m.f.

25922. 2312/13 (2 discs): Bach—Brandenburg concertos . *Berlin Phil. Orch.; Karajan, cond.* Recorded live 1968.
● Fa 3-4/90: 108

25923. 2314/15 (2 discs): Mahler—Symphony no. 2. *Cebotari, Anday; Vienna State Opera Chorus; Vienna Phil.*

Orch.; Walter, cond. Recorded live 1948.
+ Fa 3-4/90: 219

25924. 2316/17 (2 discs): Leoncavallo—Zaza. Mascagni—Zanetto. *Petrella, Campora, Turtura; Italian Radio and Television Milan Chorus & Symphony Orch.; Silipigni, Petralia, conds.* Recorded live 1969.
● ARG 3-4/90: 65
+ Fa 3-4/90: 211 m.f.
● Gr 3/90: 1683
+ ON 1/6/90: 35

25925. 2319: Music of Verdi, Berlioz, Stravinsky, Puccini, Brahms, and Strauss. *Tebaldi, soprano; various orchs.; De Sabata, cond.* Recorded live 1947-1953.
- Fa 3-4/90: 394

25926. 2320: Mozart—Piano sonata no. 7; Variations on La belle françois, K. 353. Mendelssohn—Variations sérieuses, op. 54. *Richter, piano.* Recorded live 1968, 1965.
□ Fa 3-4/90: 129 m.f.

25927. 2324/25 (2 discs): Puccini—Fanciulla del West. *Olivero, Limarilli, Puglisi; Giuseppe Verdi Theater of Trieste; Basile, cond.* Recorded live.
● Fa 3-4/90: 263

25928. 2326: Mahler—Symphony no. 5. *BBC Symphony Orch.; Boulez, cond.* Recorded live 1968.
⊔ Fa 3-4/90: 221

25929. 2327/29 (3 discs): Music of Handel, Gluck, Mozart, Rossini, Verdi, and others. *Schipa, tenor; various accs.*
+ ARG 1-2/90: 136
+ Fa 1-2/90: 361
● ON 2/17/90: 39

25930. 2330/32 (3 discs): Mozart—Don Giovanni. *Janowitz, Zylis-Gara, Freni, Kraus, Ghiaurov, Panerai; Salzburg Festival; Karajan, cond.*
● ARG 5-6/90: 83

25931. 2333/34 (2 discs): Bellini—Beatrice di Tenda. *Gencer, Sgourda, Oncina, Zanasi; Teatro La Fenice; Gui, cond.* Recorded live 1964.
+ ARG 1-2/90: 28
+ Fa 1-2/90: 125

25932. 2335: Prokofiev—Violin concerto no. 1. Sivelius—Violin concerto. *Gulli, Haendel, violins; A. Scarlatti Orch. di Napoli; Italian Radio and Television Milan Symphony Orch.; Celibidache, cond.*
- Fa 3-4/90: 261

25933. 2336/37 (2 discs): Mascagni—Guglielmo Ratcliff. *Mattioli, Ferraro, Ciminelli; Italian Radio and Television Rome Chorus & Symphony Orch.; Parodi, cond.* Recorded live 1963.
+ ARG 5-6/90: 72
● Fa 3-4/90: 224

+ Gr 2/90: 1520
+ ON 1/6/90: 35

25934. 2342/44 (3 discs): Bellini—I puritani. *Freni, Pavarotti, Bruscantini, Giaiotti; with assisting soloists; Italian Radio and Television Rome Chorus & Symphony Orch.; Muti, cond.* Recorded live 1970.
+ ARG 1-2/90: 29
+ Fa 3-4/90: 134

25935. 2361/62 (2 discs): Cherubini—Ali Baba. *Stich-Randall, Kraus, Ganzarolli, Montarsolo; Teatro alla Scala; Sanzogno, cond.* Recorded live 1963.
+ ARG 3-4/90: 38
+ Gr 4/90: 1862

25936. 2367: Music of Vivaldi, Spontini, Verdi, Wagner, Catalani, and others. *Favero, soprano; Di Stefano, tenor; various orchs.; Guarnieri, cond.* Recorded live 1940, 1947.
+ Fa 5-6/90: 395
+ Gr 6/90: 122

25937. 2368/69 (2 discs): Music of Bellini, Verdi, Bizet, Puccini, and others. *Del Monaco, tenor; various orchs. & conds.* Recorded live 1951, 1959.
+ Fa 5-6/90: 360

25938. 2370/72 (3 discs): Music of Beethoven, Bruckner, Schuman, and Strauss. *Vienna Phil. Orch.; Knappertsbusch, cond.* Recorded live 1962.
+ Fa 7-8/90: 375

25939. 2375/76 (2 discs): Verdi—I lombardi alla prima crociata. *Scotto, Pavarotti, Raimondi; Rome Opera; Gavazzeni, cond.* Recorded live 1969.
+ Fa 5-6/90: 318

25940. 3106: Grétry—Denys le Tyran. *De Simone, Di Segni, Franceschetto, Donzelli, Chorus & Orch. Internationale d'Italia; Vizioli, cond.*
● ARG 11-12/91: 70

25941. 6304: Wagner—Die Meistersinger: Preludes to Acts 1 & 3; Tristan und Isolde: Prelude & Liebestod; Götterdämmerung: Final scene. *Ludwig, mezzo-soprano; North German Radio Orch.; Knappertsbusch, cond.* Recorded live 1962.
- ARG 7-8/88: 89
+ Fa 9-10/88: 297

25942. 6307/09 (3 discs): Wagner—Tannhäuser. *Brouwenstijn, Ludwig, Beirer, Wächter, Frick; Vienna State Opera Chorus & Orch.; Karajan, cond.* Recorded live 1963.
+ ARG 9-10/88: 94
- Fa 9-10/88: 298
● ON 4/9/88: 48

25943. 6316: Beethoven—Symphony no. 5. Brahms—Violin concerto op. 77.

Milstein, violin; New York Phil.; De Sabata, cond. Recorded live 1950.
+ Fa 9-10/88: 109
+ MA 11/88: 52

25944. 6318/19 (2 discs): PUCCINI—Turandot. *Nilsson, Vishnevskaya, Corelli, Zaccaria; Teatro alla Scala; Gavazzeni, cond. Recorded live 1964.*
+ ARG 9-10/88: 73
• Fa 9-10/88: 230

25945. 6320/21 (2 discs): DONIZETTI—Lucia di Lammermoor. *Scotto, Raimondi, Guelfi, Ferrin; Teatro alla Scala Chorus & Orch.; Abbado, cond. Recorded live 1967.*
+ ARG 7-8/88: 21
+ Fa 9-10/88: 140

25946. 6326: MOZART—Symphonies no. 25, 29; Serenade K. 525; Maurerische Trauermusik K. 477. *New York Phil.; French National Orch.; Walter, cond. Recorded live 1956.*
- Fa 9-10/88: 218

25947. 6327: SCHUMANN—Symphonies no. 2. TCHAIKOVSKY—Romeo and Juliet, overture-fantasia. *Italian Radio and Television Rome Symphony Orch.; Italian Radio and Television Turin Symphony Orch.; Celibidache, cond. Recorded live 1960-61.*
• ARG 1-2/89: 126
+ Fa 9-10/88: 258 (Symphony)
• Fa 9-10/88: 258 (Romeo)

25948. 6329/30 (2 discs): VERDI—Luisa Miller. *Caballé, Tucker, Milnes, Tozzi, Flagello; Metropolitan Opera Chorus & Orch.; Schippers, cond. Recorded live 1968.*
• Fa 9-10/88: 286

25949. 6339: MOZART—Piano concerto no. 22; Sonata for piano 4-hands K. 521. *Richter, piano; English Chamber Orch.; Britten, cond. & piano. Recorded live 1966.*
• ARG 11-12/88: 65
+ Fa 1-2/89: 221

25950. 6340: MOZART—Piano sonata no. 5. WEBER—Piano sonata no. 3. LISZT—Piano sonata. *Richter, piano.*
+ ARG 1-2/89: 62 (Liszt)
• ARG 1-2/89: 62 (others)
+ Fa 1-2/89: 221

25951. 6345: ROSSINI—Overtures to Barbiere di Siviglia, Guillaume Tell, Signor Bruschino, and Semiramide; Passa a sei. VERDI—Overtures to La forza del destino, Luisa Miller, and Aida. *NBC Symphony Orch.; Toscanini, cond. Recorded live 1940-1954.*
+ Fa 5-6/89: 293 m.f.

25952. 6346/47 (2 discs): VERDI—Requiem. *Tebaldi, Rankin, Prandelli, Rossi-Lemeni; Teatro alla Scala; De Sabata, cond. Recorded live 1951.*
+ ARG 3-4/89: 102
+ Fa 3-4/89: 322
+ ON 2/4/89: 42

25953. 6348/49 (2 discs): Music of Haydn, Mendelssohn, Debussy, and Busoni. *Purchel, piano; Borries, violin; Berlin Phil. Orch.; Celibidache, cond. Recorded live 1948-50, 1953.*
+ Fa 5-6/89: 415

25954. 6350: FRANCK—Symphony in D minor. DUKAS—Sorcerer's apprentice. *New York Phil.; De Sabata, cond. Recorded live 1950.*
+ Fa 5-6/89: 197

25955. 6351/53 (3 discs): MUSSORGSKY—Boris Godunov. *Jurinac, Maslennikov, Stolze, Ghiaurov, Diakov, Borg; Salzburg Festival; Karajan, cond. Recorded live 1966.*
- ARG 5-6/89: 67
- Fa 5-6/89: 257

25956. 6378/79 (2 discs): DONIZETTI—Imelda de' Lambertazzi. *Sovilla, D'Auria, Martin; Radio svizzera italiana Chorus & Orch.; Andreae, cond. Recorded live 1989.*
+ Fa 1-2/90: 165
• ON 2/17/90: 39

25957. 6701 (2 discs): DONIZETTI—Alina. *Dessì, Blake, Coni; Gruppo Giovanile della Cooperativa Artisti del Coro; Orch. Arturo Toscanini del Teatro Regio di Parma; Allemandi, cond. 6701: number duplicated by manufacturer.*
+ ARG 5-6/89: 41
+ Fa 1-2/89: 153
• Gr 1/89: 1202
+ ON 11/88: 64
• OQ Spring/89: 156

25958. 6701: VIVALDI—Concertos for strings: RV 118, 129, 133, 145, 150, 151, 154, 565, 578. *Marano, Rebellato, Fontanella, violins; Guidolin, cello; Haydn Philharmonia; Rojatti, cond. 6701: number duplicated by manufacturer.*
+ Fa 9-10/88: 293

25959. 6702: SCHUBERT—Piano trio no. 2; Sonata movement D. 28. *Trio di Trieste.*
• Fa 7-8/88: 249
+ HPR 12/88: 83

25960. 6703: BRAHMS—Piano sonatas no. 1-2. *Mezzena, piano.*
- Fa 9-10/88: 120

25961. 6705: PENDERECKI—Violin concerto. SHOSTAKOVICH—Symphony no. 6. *Accardo, violin, Youth Orch. of Italy; Penderecki, cond.*
+ ARG 11-12/88: 67 (Concerto)
- ARG 11-12/88: 67 (Symphony)
+ Fa 11-12/88: 245 (Concerto)
- Fa 11-12/88: 245 (Symphony)
+ Gr 11-12/88: 784 (Concerto)
- Gr 11-12/88: 784 (Symphony)

25962. 6706: STRAUSS—Eine Alpensinfonie. *European Community Youth Orch.; Judd, cond. Recorded live.*
• Gr 11/91: 102

25963. 6707: MOZART—Requiem. *Pütz, Hamari, Gritschnik, Schramm; Italian Radio and Television Turin Chorus & Symphony Orch.; Celibidache, cond.*
• ARG 1-2/89: 71
□ Fa 9-10/88: 216

25964. 6709 (2 discs): MAHLER—Symphony no. 9. WAGNER—Tristan und Isolde: Prelude to Act 1. *Vienna Phil. Orch.; Klemperer, cond. Recorded live 1968.*
+ ARG 9-10/88: 60
- Fa 9-10/88: 194

25965. 6711: MOZART—Violin sonatas no. 25, 30, 40. *Accardo, violin; Canino, piano.*
+ ARG 7-8/89: 67
+ Fa 5-6/89: 253

25966. 6712: MOZART—Violin sonatas no. 24, 29, 42. *Accardo, violin; Canino, piano.*
+ Fa 5-6/89: 253

25967. 6713 (2 discs): DONIZETTI—Anna Bolena. *Gencer, Simionato, Bertocci, Clabassi; Italian Radio and Television Milan Chorus & Orch.; Gavazzeni, cond.*
• Fa 3-4/89: 147

25968. 6714 (2 discs): MAHLER—Symphony no. 2. *Harper, Baker; Bavarian Radio Chorus & Orch.; Klemperer, cond. Recorded live 1965.*
+ Fa 11-12/88: 218 m.f.

25969. 6715 (2 discs): DONIZETTI—Don Pasquale. *Serra, Bertolo, Corbelli, Dara, Pasella; Teatro Regio di Torino Chorus & Orch.; Campanella, cond.*
• ARG 1-2/89: 46
• Fa 1-2/89: 155
• Gr 5/89: 1777
- ON 11/88: 64 (Serra)
+ ON 11/88: 64 (others)
- OQ Spring/89: 141

25970. 6722: HSIEN—Yellow River concerto. WANG—Yunnan scenes. *Caramella, piano; Beijing Broadcasting Symphony Orch.; Fang, cond.*
+ ARG 3-4/89: 109
+ Fa 3-4/89: 344

25971. 6725 (2 discs): DONIZETTI—L'elisir d'amore. *Scarabelli, Briscik, Merritt, Romero, Bruscantini; Teatro regio (Parma) Chorus; Emilia-romagna Arturo Toscanini Symphony Orch.; Soudant, cond. Recorded live 1988.*
• ARG 5-6/89: 42
• Fa 5-6/89: 177
• Gr 10/91: 184
- ON 4/15/89: 42

NUOVA ERA

25972. 6726: CIMAROSA—Overtures to Italiana in Londra, I due supposti conti, and Li due baroni di Roccazzurra. PAISIELLO—Overtures to Barbiere di Siviglia, Le zingare in fiera, and Nina o La pazza per amore. ROSSINI—Overtures to Cambiale di matrimonio and La scala di seta. *Haydn Philharmonia; Rojatti, cond.*
- ARG 5-6/89: 109
+ Fa 5-6/89: 417

25973. 6728: BEETHOVEN—Septet in E♭, op. 20. *CARME.*
+ ARG 7-8/89: 21
- Fa 7-8/89: 88

25974. 6731: VIVALDI—Concertos RV 98, 101, 103, 105, 107; Sonata for recorder and bassoon BWV 86. *Il Giardino Armonico Ensemble.*
+ Fa 5-6/89: 348
+ HPR 6/89: 89

25975. 6732/33 (2 discs): DONIZETTI—Maria di Rohan. *Nicolesco, Morino, Coni; Coro Filarmonico Slovacco di Bratislava; Internazionale d'Italia Opera Orch.; De Bernart, cond.*
+ ARG 9-10/89: 48
+ Fa 7-8/89: 132
+ Gr 10/91: 184

25976. 6741: DUFAY—Missa Se la face ay pale; Chansons and motets by Dufay, Lasso, Senfl and Isaac. *Chiaroscuro; Rogers, cond.*
+ Fa 5-6/92: 150

25977. 6742: MOZART—Violin sonatas no. 27, 40; Variations on a French song K. 359-60. *Accardo, violin; Canino, piano.*
- ARG 1-2/90: 71
+ Fa 9-10/89: 266
□ Gr 10/89: 691

25978. 6743: MOZART—Violin sonatas no. 26, 28, 35, and K. 403. *Accardo, violin; Canino, piano.*
+ Fa 9-10/89: 266
□ Gr 10/89: 691

25979. 6744/45 (2 discs): BACH—Art of the fugue. *Borciani, Pegreffi, violins; Poggi, viola; Simoncini, cello.*
- ARG 11-12/89: 16
+ Fa 7-8/89: 70

25980. 6749: SCHUMANN—Davidsbundlertänze op. 6; Phantasiestücke op. 111; Gesänge der Frühe op. 133; Klavierstücke op. 32. *Demus, piano.*
+ ARG 11-12/89: 116
• Fa 7-8/89: 244 m.f.

25981. 6750: SCHUMANN—Carnaval op. 9; Albumblätter op. 134; Canon für Alexis; Arabeske op. 18. *Demus, piano.*
+ ARG 11-12/89: 116
• Fa 7-8/89: 244 m.f.

25982. 6751: SCHUMANN—Piano sonata no. 1; Impromptus op. 5; Intermezzi op. 4. *Demus, piano.*
+ ARG 11-12/89: 116
• Fa 7-8/89: 244

25983. 6752/53 (2 discs): DONIZETTI—Gianni di Parigi. *Serra, Zilio, Morino, Romero; Italian Radio and Television Milan Chorus & Symphony Orch.; Cillario, cond. Recorded live 1988.*
• ARG 9-10/89: 47
• Fa 7-8/89: 131
+ Gr 10/91: 184

25984. 6755/56 (2 discs): MOZART—Piano sonatas, 4 hands (complete); Andante con cinque variazioni, K. 501. *Pasotrino, Pang, pianos.*
- Fa 7-8/89: 204

25985. 6760/62 (3 discs): ROSSINI—Barbiere di Siviglia. *Serra, Blake, Pola, Dara, Montarsolo; Teatro regio (Turin); Campanella, cond. Recorded live 1987.*
• ARG 9-10/89: 96
• Fa 9-10/89: 307
+ MA 1/90: 71
+ NYT 8/27/89: H25
+ ON 7/89: 34
+ Op 1/90: 70

25986. 6764/65 (2 discs): BELLINI—La sonnambula. *Devia, Cononici, Verducci; Coro Citta di Como; Orch. Sinfonica di Piacenza; Viotti, cond. Recorded live 1988.*
+ ARG 9-10/89: 29
- Fa 9-10/89: 147
+ NYT 8/27/89: H25
• ON 9/89: 50
• Op 1/90: 71

25987. 6768: SCHUMANN—Kinderszenen; Romances; Fughettas op. 126; Etudes after Paganini op. 10. *Demus, piano.*
+ ARG 11-12/89: 116

25988. 6769: SCHUMANN—Fantasy, op. 17; Fantasiestücke op. 12 and supplement; Etudes after Paganini, op. 3. *Demus, piano.*
+ ARG 11-12/89: 116

25989. 6770: SCHUMANN—Symphonic etudes with posthumous variations; Nachtstücke; Skizzen for pedal piano op. 58; Blumenstück. *Demus, piano.*
+ ARG 11-12/89: 116

25990. 6771: SCHUMANN—Kreisleriana; Three sonatas for the young op. 118. *Demus, piano.*
+ ARG 11-12/89: 116
• Fa 11-12/89: 354
+ Gr 9/89: 511

25991. 6772: SCHUMANN—Album für die Jugend. *Demus, piano.*
• Fa 11-12/89: 354
+ Gr 9/89: 511

25992. 6774—6775, 6801 (3 separate discs): MOZART—String quintets. *Accardo, Batjer, violins; Hoffman, Phelps, violas, Filippini, cello.*
• ARG 11-12/91: 116 (v.1-2)
+ Fa 9-10/91: 291 (v.1-2)
• Fa 11-12/91: 404
+ Gr 6/91: 59 (v.1-2)

25993. 6776/77 (2 discs): DONIZETTI—Poliuto. *Connell, Martinùcci, Bruson; Rome Opera Chorus & Orch.; Latham-Koenig, cond.*
• ARG 1-2/90: 44
- Fa 9-10/89: 190
- Gr 10/89: 738
• NYT 8/27/89: H25

25994. 6778/79 (2 discs): DONIZETTI—Imelda de' Lambertazzi. *Sovilla, Martin, D'Auria, Tenzi, Sarti; Chorus & Orch. of Swiss-Italian Radio and Television; Andreae, cond. Recorded live 1989.*
• Gr 10/91: 184

25995. 6782: SCHUMANN—Waldscenen; Geistervariation über den letzten Gedanken; Piano sonata no. 3; Hasche Mann; Mit Gott . *Demus, piano.*
• Fa 1-2/90: 303

25996. 6783: MOZART—Violin sonatas no. 35-36, 43. *Accardo, violin; Canino, piano.*
- ARG 1-2/90: 71
+ Fa 1-2/90: 244

25997. 6784: MOZART—Violin sonatas no. 32-33, 37; K. 372, 404. *Accardo, violin; Canino, piano.*
+ Fa 1-2/90: 245

25998. 6786/87 (2 discs): PUCCINI—Turandot. *Dimitrova, Gasdia, Martinùcci, Scandiuzzi; Teatro comunale dell' opera (Genoa) Chorus & Orch.; Oren, cond.*
- Fa 9-10/89: 288
- Gr 11/89: 971
• NYT 8/27/89: H25
• ON 9/89: 50

25999. 6789: Music of Corelli, Barsanti, Geminiani, and Veracini. *Ensemble Il Giardino armonico.*
+ DA 6/90: 62
+ Fa 1-2/90: 403

26000. 6790: SCHUMANN—Humoreske; Faschingsschwank aus Wien; Toccata; Album für die Jugend: Supplement. *Demus, piano.*
• Fa 1-2/90: 303

26001. 6791/92 (2 discs): DONIZETTI—La fille du régiment. *Serra, Matteuzzi, Dara; Teatro comunale (Bologna) Chorus & Orch.; Campanella, cond.*
+ ARG 1-2/90: 44
+ Fa 11-12/89: 190
• Gr 10/91: 184
+ Op 2/90: 256

26002. 6794/96 (3 discs): Donizetti—Lucia di Lammermoor. *Mazzola, Morino, Caroli, Rinaudo; Teatro di San Carlo, Naples Chorus & Orch.; De Bernart, cond.* Recorded live 1989.
 • Fa 11-12/90: 216

26003. 6799: Frescobaldi—Toccate, libro II; Aria detta La Frescobalda. *Ghielmi, organ & harpsichord.*
 + Fa 3-4/90: 181

26004. 6800: Schumann—Novelletten; Studies for pedal piano. *Demus, piano.*
 + Fa 7-8/90: 289

26005. 6802: Mozart—Clarinet quintet, K. 581; Horn quintet, K. 407; Oboe quartet, K. 370. *Various performers.*
 • Gr 9/91: 60

26006. 6804: Bach—Goldberg variations. *Demus, piano.*
 • ARG 3-4/90: 18
 • Fa 3-4/90: 112
 • Fa 3-4/90: 113

26007. 6809: Falla—El amor brujo (1st version); Seven popular Spanish songs; Serenata; Serenata Andaluza. *Senn, mezzo-soprano; Bodini, piano; Carme Ensemble; Izquierdo, cond.*
 + ARG 3-4/90: 49
 + Gr 5/90: 2028

26008. 6819: Cherubini—Il Giulio Sabino overture; Faniska overture; Lodoiska overture; Elisa overture; Concert overture. *Bacau Phil. Symphony Orch.; Frontalini, cond.*
 + Fa 5-6/90: 148
 + Gr 5/90: 1971

26009. 6820: Donizetti—Don Pasquale: Quel guardo il cavaliere; Fille du regiment: Excerpts; Gianni di Parigi; Ah, quanto e qual kiletto; Ho simulato assai. Rossini—Barbiere di Siviglia: Una voce poco fa; Contro un cor. *Serra, soprano; Matteuzzi, Blake, tenors; various orchs. & conds.*
 • Fa 5-6/90: 355
 • Gr 4/90: 1866
 + Op 8/90: 1011

26010. 6821: Indian music. Music of Strong, Troyer, Loomis, Farwell, MacDowell, and Cadman. *Müller, piano.*
 + Fa 5-6/90: 375

26011. 6823/24 (2 discs): Donizetti—La favorita. *Tabiadon, Morino, Coni, Ruffini, Farruggia; Slovak Phil. Chorus; Italian International Opera Orch.; Luisi, cond.* Sung in Italian; recorded live 1989.
 • Gr 10/91: 184

26012. 6833: Fauré—Masques et beragmasques; Dolly suite. Ravel—Le tombeau de Couperin; Pavane. *Cannes-Provence-Côte d'Azur Orch.; Bender, cond.*
 • ARG 3-4/90: 50

26013. 6842/44 (3 discs): Bellini—I puritani. *Devia, Matteuzzi, Rovertson, Washington; Teatro Massimo Bellini, Catania Chorus & Orch.; Bonynge, cond.* Recorded live 1989.
 - Fa 11-12/90: 172 (Devia)
 • Fa 11-12/90: 172 (others)
 • Gr 10/91: 183

26014. 6860: Schubert—Songs. *Janowitz, soprano; Spencer, piano.*
 + Fa 9-10/90: 370

26015. 6861: Beethoven—String quartet no. 13 (with Grosse Fuge). *Pražák Quartet.*
 + Fa 3-4/92: 148
 • Gr 10/91: 121

26016. 6862: Beethoven—String quartet no. 15. *Pražák Quartet.*
 + Fa 3-4/92: 148
 • Gr 10/91: 121

26017. 6863/64 (2 discs): Handel—Giulio Cesare. *Orciani, Dupuy, Pierotti, Ligi, Anselmi; Orch. Pro Arte Bassano; Panni, cond.* Recorded live 1989.
 - Fa 9-10/90: 252

26018. 6866: Tchaikovsky—Souvenir de Florence, op. 70; String quartet no. 1. *Accardo, Batjer, violins; Hoffman, Gazeau, violas; Hoffman, Filippini, cellos.*
 + Gr 6/91: 63

26019. 6867: Cherubini—Harpsichord sonatas no. 1-6. *Alvini, harpsichord.*
 + Fa 9-10/90: 208

26020. 6868: Arca—Il carillon del jesuita. *De Simone, Di Segni, Romano; Orch. internazionale d'Italia opera; Coro Ars Pulcherrima Artium; Vizioli, cond.*
 + Fa 9-10/90: 137

26021. 6870: Beethoven—String quintet. Mendelssohn—String quintet no. 2. *Accardo, Batjer, violins; Hoffman, Gazeau, violas; Hoffman, cello.*
 + ARG 7-8/91: 30
 + Fa 7-8/91: 114
 • Gr 6/91: 56

26022. 6872/73 (2 discs): Paisiello—Nina. *Bolgan, Bernardini, Musinu; Teatro Massimo Bellini, Catania; Bonynge, cond.* Recorded live 1989.
 • Gr 9/91: 129

26023. 6881: Stuppner—Ecstasy and nirvana. *Strings of the Gustav Mahler Jugendorch.; Stuppner, cond.*
 + Fa 9-10/90: 403

26024. 6888/89 (2 discs): Salieri—La locandiera. *Ruffini, Petroni, Guarnera, Sarti; Symphony Orch. of Emilia Romagna A. Toscanini; Luisi, cond.* Recorded live 1989.
 • Fa 5-6/91: 271

26025. 6893: Reger—Variations and fugue on a theme of Telemann, op. 134. *Zanini, piano.*
 • ARG 1-2/92: 98
 + Fa 11-12/91: 458

26026. 6897/98 (2 discs): Beethoven—Piano sonatas no. 28-32. *Ciccolini, piano.*
 • ARG 3-4/90: 24
 + Fa 3-4/90: 131
 • Gr 3/90: 1639

26027. 6900: Veracini—Violin sonatas op. 1 no. 12; op. 2 no. 5-6. *Mangiocavallo, violin; Menconi, harpsichord; Ronco, cello.*
 + Fa 9-10/90: 414

26028. 6902, 6926, 6949 (3 separate discs): Mozart—Violin concertos. *Batjer, violin; Hoffman, viola; Accardo, violin & cond.; Prague Chamber Orch.*
 - ARG 11-12/91: 104 (6926)
 • Gr 6/91: 46

26029. 6903: Schumann—Noveletten; Kinderszenen. *Zanini, piano.*
 + Fa 3-4/92: 318

26030. 6906 (2 discs): Mahler—Symphonies no. 9; no. 10: Adagio. *Gustav Mahler Jugendorchester; European Community Youth Orch.; Judd, cond.*
 - ARG 9-10/91: 92
 - Fa 7-8/91: 199

26031. 6928/29 (2 discs): Carvalho—Testoride argonauta. *Magnus, Hennecke, Åkerlund, Meeuwsen, Rayam; Clemencic Consort; Clemencic, cond.* Recorded live 1990.
 • ARG 9-10/91: 57
 • Fa 5-6/91: 150

26032. 6930/31 (2 discs): Fux—Dafne in Lauro. *Sluis, Åkerlund, Lesne, Klietmann; Clemencic Consort; Clemencic, cond.*
 • ARG 9-10/91: 74
 + Fa 5-6/91: 171
 + ON 7/94: 41

26033. 6932/33 (2 discs): Vivaldi—L'Olimpiade. *Ensemble vocal la cappella; Clemencic Consort; Clemencic, cond.*
 + Fa 9-10/91: 383

26034. 6934/35 (2 discs): Keiser—Croesus. *Grigorova, Sluis, Åkerlund, Mildenhall, Klietmann; Ensemble Vocal La Cappella; Clemencic Consort; Clemencic, cond.*
 + ARG 9-10/91: 84
 + Fa 5-6/91: 194
 • ON 7/94: 41

26035. 6936: Torrejon y Velasco—La púrpura de la rosa. *Ensemble vocal la cappella; Clemencic Consort, Clemencic, cond.*
 • ARG 9-10/91: 138
 - Fa 9-10/91: 378

NUOVA ERA

26036. 6937: Vivaldi—Concertos for strings and continuo RV 109, RV 120, RV 126, RV 129, RV 134, RV 143, RV 151, RV 155; Sinfonia, RV 131. *Budapest Strings; Bánfalvi, violin & cond.*
- ● ARG 9-10/91: 145
- ● Fa 11-12/91: 517

26037. 6938: *Works for violin and orchestra, vol. 3.* Mozart—Violin concerto no. 5; Adagio, K. 261; Rondo K. 269; Rondo, K. 373. *Accardo, violin & cond.; Prague Chamber Orch.*
- ● Fa 3-4/92: 252

26038. 6939: Bonporti—Concertini e serenate, op. 12. *Mangiocavallo, violin; Ronco, cello; Mencoboni, harpsichord.*
- + ARG 11-12/91: 42

26039. 6944/45 (2 discs): Bizet—Les pecheurs de perles. *Ruffini, Morino, Praticò, Abumradi; Slovak Phil. Chorus; Orch. internazionale d'Italia opera; Piantini, cond.*
- - Fa 9-10/91: 167
- ● Gr 10/91: 183

26040. 6971/73 (3 discs): Mercadante—Il bravo. *Di Domenico, Tabiadon, Perry; Orch. internazionale d'Italia opera; Aprea, cond.*
- ● ARG 9-10/91: 98
- + Fa 9-10/91: 271

26041. 6982/83 (2 discs): Bellini—Zaira. *Ricciarelli, Alaimo, Vargas, Papadjakou; Orch. & Chorus of the Teatro massimo Bellini; Olmi, cond.*
- + ARG 1-2/92: 30
- + Fa 9-10/91: 159
- + Gr 7/91: 107
- + Op 10/91: 1240

26042. 6994/95 (2 discs): Paisiello—Don Chisciotte. *Peters, Zilio, Barbacini, Franceschetto; Teatro dell'Opera (Rome); Morandi, cond.* Recorded live 1990.
- ● ARG 1-2/92: 87
- ● Fa 11-12/91: 431
- ● Gr 4/92: 159

26043. 6998: Malipiero—Grottesco; Cello concerto; Ricercari; Dialogue, no. 1. *Palm, cello; Festival Orch. di Villa Marigola; Garbarino, cond.*
- + ARG 11-12/91: 92
- ● Fa 11-12/91: 385

26044. 7000: Bonporti—Ten concerti a quattro, op. 11, no. 4-6, 8-9. *I Virtuosi dell'Accademia.*
- + Fa 3-4/92: 158

26045. 7006: Monteverdi—Fourth book of Madrigals. *Solisti del madrigale.*
- - Fa 7-8/92: 221

26046. 7009: Melani—All'armi; Quai bellici acenti. A. Scarlatti—Su le sponde del Tebro. Stradella—3 Sinfonias.

Anon.—Concerto, op. 4, no. 7. *Gambarini, soprano; Cassone, trumpet; Ensemble "pian & forte".*
- + ARG 11-12/91: 179

26047. 7012/13 (2 discs): Renaissance and Baroque music in Lombardy, 1500-1650. *Zambon, countertenor; Gaifa, tenor; with instrumental ensemble.*
- + Fa 3-4/92: 394

26048. 7016: Reger—Suites for solo cello, op. 131c. *Signorini, cello.*
- + ARG 1-2/92: 98
- + Fa 11-12/91: 458

26049. 7017—7019 (3 separate discs): Mozart—String quartets no. 14-19. *Pražák Quartet.*
- ● Fa 11-12/91: 402
- ● Gr 11/91: 116 (as set 6829/31)

26050. 7019: Stanley—Organ concertos, op. 2. *Frigé, organ; Ensemble "pian & forte".*
- + ARG 5-6/92: 138
- ● Fa 3-4/92: 329

26051. 7020/21 (2 discs): Bellini—I Capuleti e i Montecchi. *Ricciarelli, Montague, Raffanti, Salvadori; Teatro La Fenice; Campanella, cond.* Recorded live 1991.
- - ARG 3-4/92: 32
- + Fa 3-4/92: 152
- + Gr 3/92: 110
- ● ON 2/27/93: 33

26052. 7022: G. Sammartini—Four sonatas for flute and continuo. Zuccari—Flute sonata. Fioroni—Flute sonata. *Carbotta, flute; Cognazzo, harpsichord.*
- - Fa 3-4/92: 302

26053. 7023: *Jugend Album.* Music of Tchaikovsky, Prokofiev and Shostakovich. *Müller, piano.*
- - Fa 3-4/92: 403

26054. 7026: *Italian flute concertos.* Music of Boccherini, Cambini, Martini, and Piccini. *Ancillotti, flute & cond; Symphonia Perusina.*
- + Fa 3-4/92: 396

26055. 7030: *Agonia di Cristo.* Sances—Stabat mater. Frescobaldi—Maddalena alla croce. Jommelli—Agonia di Cristo. *Concerto Ensemble; Gini, cond.*
- + ARG 3-4/92: 79
- + Fa 3-4/92: 391

26056. 7033/34 (2 discs): Handel—Suites de pièces pour le clavecin (1720). *Alvini, harpsichord.*
- ● ARG 5-6/92: 70
- + Fa 3-4/92: 208

26057. 7036: Mertz—Guitar music. *Lambiase, Viti, guitars.*
- ● ARG 1-2/93: 178

26058. 7040: Vivaldi—Concertos for strings and continuo, vol. 2. *Budapest Strings; Bánfalvi, cond.*
- ● Fa 3-4/92: 357

26059. 7041: *Canzoni, fantasie e sonate.* Music of Frescobaldi, Selma, Fontana, and Castello. *Tripla Concordia.*
- + ARG 1-2/92: 167
- + Fa 1-2/92: 398

26060. 7042: *The joyful organist.* Music of Storace, Spagnolo, Vivaldi, Taglietti, Krebs, D. Scarlatti, Pugliani, Gherardeschi and Ives. *Frigé, organ.*
- ● ARG 5-6/92: 167
- + Fa 5-6/92: 318

26061. 7043: Paisiello—La serva padrona. *Banks, Ricci; Orch. da Camera di Milano; Vaglieri, cond.*
- ● ARG 3-4/92: 116
- ● Fa 3-4/92: 281
- - Gr 2/93: 75
- - ON 5/93: 53

26062. 7044: Beethoven—String quartet no. 14; String quartet op. 130: Finale. *Pražák Quartet.*
- + Fa 3-4/92: 148

26063. 7045: Donizetti—Rita. *Scarabelli, Ballo, Corbelli; Orch. da Camera Siciliana; Amendola, cond.* Recorded live 1991.
- + ARG 5-6/92: 47
- + Fa 3-4/92: 185
- + ON 3/28/92: 40

26064. 7048: Lanzetti—Cello sonatas, op. 1, no. 5-9, 11, 12. *Ronco, Veggetti, Petech, cellos; Held, continuo.*
- + ARG 9-10/92: 123

26065. 7053: *Gagliarde, canzone e voluntaries per tromba e organo.* Music of Trabaci, Cima, Pietra-Grua, Byrd, Greene, and Stanley. *Cassone, trumpet; Frigé, organ.*
- + Fa 9-10/92: 428

26066. 7057: Martin—Preludes. Martinů—Sketches; Les papillons et paradisiers. *Flückiger, piano.*
- + ARG 7-8/92: 171

26067. 7058: Ferrero—Piano concerto; Parodia; Ostinato; Canzoni d'amore. *Cherici, soprano; Caramella, piano; Prague Chamber Orch.; Ferrero, cond.*
- + ARG 7-8/92: 130

26068. 7059: Cambini—Piano concertos in B♭ and G; Sinfonia concertante for flute & 2 violins. *Redondi, piano; Milan Chamber Orch.; Vaglieri, cond.*
- + ARG 11-12/92: 101

26069. 7060/61 (2 discs): Menotti—Goya. *Daner, Guzman, Hernandez, Bender, Senator, Wentzel; Westminster Choir; Spoleto Festival Orch.; Mercurio, cond.* Recorded live.

• ARG 11-12/92: 160
+ Fa 9-10/92: 289
+ ON 12/19/92: 38
+ St 2/93: 195

26070. 7063: ROTA—Symphony on a love song; Concerto soirée. *Lupo, piano; Sicilian Symphony Orch.; De Bernart, cond.*
+ ARG 1-2/93: 140

26071. 7065: PURCELL—Arias. HANDEL—Arias. *Cotterill, soprano; Frigé, harpsichord; Ensemble "pian & forte".*
• Fa 9-10/92: 319

26072. 7067: TELEMANN—Trios and quartets for recorder, oboe, violin and continuo. *Tripla Concordia.*
+ ARG 9-10/93: 209

26073. 7069/70 (2 discs): ROSSINI—Aureliano in Palmira. *Di Cesare, Mazzola, D'Intino, Marani; Teatro del Giglio, Lucca; Zani, cond.* Recorded live 1991.
• ARG 11-12/92: 190
+ Fa 11-12/92: 341

26074. 7071: *Les délices: French music for viols and recorders from 1639 to 1713.* Music of Du Mont, Moulinié, Morel, Hotteterre, and Marais. *Isabella D'Este.*
+ Fa 1-2/94: 388

26075. 7075: HINDEMITH—Kammermusik no. 3, op. 36, no. 2; Sonata for solo cello, op. 25; Kleine Kammermusik, op. 24, no. 2. *Signorini, cello; Soloisti dell'Academia Musicale Napoletana; Trinca, cond.; Quintetto Scarlatti.*
+ ARG 11-12/92: 135
+ Fa 9-10/92: 261

26076. 7076/77 (2 discs): BELLINI—Bianca e Fernando. *Shin, Kunde; other soloists; Teatro Massimo Bellini; Licata, cond.* Recorded live 1991.
+ ARG 1-2/94: 77
+ Fa 11-12/93: 184
+ Gr 2/94: 92
+ ON 12/10/94: 50

26077. 7090 (2 discs): TOSTI—Songs. *Bruson, baritone; Cognazzo, piano.*
- ARG 9-10/93: 209

26078. 7100/01 (2 discs): ROSSINI—Six sonatas for strings; Prelude, theme and variations for horn and piano. DONIZETTI—Larghetto, theme and variations for violin and piano. *Haydn Phil. Soloists; Rojatti, cond.; Baroncini, horn; Belli, violin; Terekiev, piano.*
+ ARG 7-8/92: 208
+ Fa 7-8/92: 262

26079. 7102: CARULLI—Introduction, theme, and variations; Four andantes; Les adieux; Three sonatas, op. 56; Waltzes from op. 101. *Baschiera, guitar.*
+ ARG 9-10/92: 94

26080. 7103 (3 discs): MONTEVERDI—Il ritorno d'Ulisse in patria. *Banditelli, Villanueva, Calvi, Laurens, Tucker, Palmieri, Fagotto; Sonatori de la Gioiosa Marca; Curtis, cond.*
+ ARG 9-10/92: 133

26081. 7106/07 (2 discs): ROUSSEAU—Le devin du village. MOZART—Bastien und Bastienne. *Kirchner, Choy, Müller de Vries; Gottardo Tomat Chorus of Spilimberg; Alpe Adria Ensemble; Clemencic, cond.*
+ Fa 9-10/92: 337

26082. 7109: DALLAPICCOLA—Piccolo concerto per Muriel Couvreaux; Liriche greche; Tartiniana seconda. *Morrison, soprano; Rizzi, violin; Canino, piano; Dallapiccola Ensemble; Suvini, cond.*
+ ARG 11-12/92: 109
+ Fa 3-4/93: 148
+ Gr 3/94: 46

26083. 7113: VIVALDI—Sinfonias and concertos for strings, vol. 3. *Budapest Strings; Bánfalvi, cond.*
+ Fa 11-12/92: 399

26084. 7114: PICCININI—Lute book 1. *Beier, archlute.*
+ ARG 11-12/92: 178

26085. 7117: A. SCARLATTI—Cantata natalizia: Abramo, il tuo sembiante. *Vocalists; Alessandro Stradella Consort; Velardi, cond.*
+ Fa 5-6/93: 310

26086. 7118: MONTEVERDI—Litaniae della Beate Vergine (1650); Mass for four voices; Magnificat. *Le Istitutioni harmoniche; Longhini, cond.*
+ ARG 3-4/93: 115

26087. 7122: MENOTTI—The telephone; Ricercare and toccata on a theme from The old maid and the thief; Canti della lontananza. *Banks, soprano; Ricci, baritone; Costanzo, piano; Milan Chamber Orch.; Vaglieri, cond.*
- ARG 3-4/93: 111

26088. 7130: MILHAUD—Fantaisie pastorale; Suite provençale; Carnaval d'Aix; Concertino d'hiver. *Carmella, piano; Douay, trombone; Cannes-Provence-Côte d'Azur Orch.; Bender, cond.*
• ARG 3-4/93: 112

26089. 7131: FRESCOBALDI—Canzoni da sonar, vol. 1. *Tripla Concordia.*
+ ARG 5-6/94: 93

26090. 7132/33 (2 discs): ROSSINI—La pietra del paragone. *Müller-Molinari, Barbacini, Scaltriti, Rumetz; Orch. Camerata Musicale; Desderi, cond.*
+ ARG 3-4/93: 130
• Fa 3-4/93: 264
• Gr 5/93: 104
• ON 2/27/93: 33

26091. 7134: TELEMANN—Fantasies for harpsichord. *Frigé, harpsichord.*
+ ARG 3-4/93: 147
• Fa 9-10/93: 311

26092. 7135: TELEMANN—Six concertos for flute and harpsichord. *Balassa, flute; Ensemble Pian e Forte.*
+ Fa 11-12/93: 424

26093. 7140 (3 discs): ROSSINI—Le siège de Corinthe. *Serra, Lippi, Raffanti, Comencini; Genoa Opera; Olmi, cond.* Recorded live 1992.
• ARG 1-2/94: 143

26094. 7140/42 (3 discs): ROSSINI—Le siège de Corinthe. *Serra, Lippi, other vocalists; Teatro "Carlo Felice"; Olmi, cond.*
• Fa 5-6/93: 301
+ Gr 5/93: 106
• ON 10/93: 32

26095. 7143/44 (2 discs): CASELLA—Serenata for small orchestra; Concerto for cello and orchestra; L'adieu à la vie; Pupazzetti; Concerto for strings, piano and timpani. *Palm, cello; Zürcher, mezzo-soprano; Barbareschi, Ragni, pianos; Festival Orch. di Villa Marigola; Garbarino, cond.*
• ARG 3-4/93: 68
• Fa 3-4/93: 140

26096. 7147: PORPORA—Chamber symphonies, op. 2. *Artifizii Musicali; Delvaux, harpsichord.*
+ ARG 5-6/93: 119

26097. 7148: RUBINSTEIN—Violin sonatas no. 1-2. *Lazari, violin; Gibellato, piano.*
• ARG 9-10/93: 181
+ Fa 9-10/93: 259

26098. 7150: MALIPIERO—Preludi autunnali; Maschere che passano; Barlumi; Poemetti lunari. *Terekiev, piano.*
+ ARG 11-12/93: 144
+ Fa 11-12/93: 307

26099. 7151: GHERARDELLO DA FIRENZE—Madrigali, cacce, ballate. *Ensemble Modo antiquo; Sardelli, Hoffmann, conds.*
- Fa 11-12/93: 242

26100. 7152: STANLEY—Harpsichord concertos, op. 10. *Frigé, harpsichord; Ensemble "Pian e Forte".*
+ ARG 5-6/94: 144
• Fa 1-2/94: 318

26101. 7154/55 (2 discs): BELLINI—Adelson e Salvini. *Williams, Nafé, Previati, Rizzi, Coviello; other soloists; Teatro Bellini; Licata, cond.* Recorded live 1991.
• ARG 1-2/94: 76
+ Fa 11-12/93: 184
• Gr 2/94: 92

NUOVA ERA

26102. 7156: RESPIGHI—Unpublished works for piano. *Palumbo, piano.*
+ ARG 11-12/93: 177
+ Fa 11-12/93: 361
+ Gr 10/93: 85

26103. 7157 (2 discs): GRÉTRY—Richard, Coeur de Lion. *Zingerle, Edelmann; Bolzano Conservatory Orch.; Neri, cond.* Recorded live 1990.
• ARG 1-2/94: 103
- Fa 1-2/94: 190
• ON 3/5/94: 36

26104. 7160: BOCCHERINI—Quintets for piano and strings no. 1-3. *Caramella, piano; Zagreb Quartet.*
+ ARG 3-4/94: 79
• Fa 1-2/94: 133

26105. 7161: BUSONI—Music for piano duo. *Giarmanà, Lucchetti, piano duo.*
• Fa 11-12/94: 194

26106. 7162: A. SCARLATTI—Clori mia, clori bella; Filli che esprime la sua fede a Fileno; Ardo e ver per te d'amore; Tu sei quella che al nome sembri giusta; Concerto in A minor; La follia variations. *Piccollo, soprano; Balconi, alto; Bagliano, recorder; Collegium Pro Musica; Curtis, cond.*
+ ARG 3-4/94: 147

26107. 7163: VISÉE—Music for lute or theorbo. *Ensemble Barocco Italiano.*
• ARG 9-10/94: 217

26108. 7165: MONTEVERDI—Madrigals, book 6. *I Solisti del Madrigale; Acciai, cond.*
• Fa 11-12/94: 304

26109. 7168: RACHMANINOFF—Chopin and Corelli variations. *Nicolosi, piano.*
• ARG 7-8/94: 155
• Fa 11-12/94: 351

26110. 7169, 7175 (2 separate discs): CARULLI—Guitar duos. *Saracino, guitar; Palumbo, fortepiano.*
- ARG 11-12/94: 89

26111. 7176: HASSE—Trio sonatas, op. 2. *Artifizii Musicali.*
+ Fa 11-12/94: 250

26112. 7177: *Il cimbalo cromatico napoletano.* Music of Macque, L. Rossi, Trabaci, Mayone, Del Buono, Salvatore, Strozzi, and M. Rossi. *Curtis, harpsichord.*
+ ARG 7-8/95: 246
+ EM 11/95: 713
+ Fa 3-4/95: 368

26113. 7178: LEONCAVALLO—Songs. *Tenzi, tenor; Negri, piano.*
• ARG 11-12/94: 142

26114. 7179 (2 discs): MERCADANTE—Il giuramento. *De Liso, Olmeda, Morino, Barrard; Nantes Opera; Carella, cond.*

Recorded 1993.
• ARG 1-2/95: 139
+ Fa 1-2/95: 202

26115. 7181: LECLAIR—Deuxième récréation de musique. COUPERIN—La françoise. *La Quatrième Chambre.*
+ ARG 1-2/95: 131
+ EM 2/95: 172
+ Fa 1-2/95: 186

26116. 7182: E. RESPIGHI—Canzoni spagnole; Liriche dai Rubaiyat; Berceuse bretonne; Je n'ai rien. O. RESPIGHI—Liriche; Ballata alla luna; Voici Noël; Il pleut, gentil berger; Canzone sarda; Le funtanelle. *Cisternino, soprano; Palumbo, piano.*
+ ARG 5-6/95: 159
• Fa 3-4/95: 273

26117. 7184: *Milanese instrumental canzoni of the 17th century.* Music of Cima, Borgo, Pellegrini, and Anon. *Cassone, natural trumpet; Frigé, organ, harpsichord; Frigerio, cello.*
+ ARG 3-4/95: 251
+ Fa 1-2/95: 344

26118. 7185: ROTA—Cinque pezzi. CASELLA—Barcarola e scherzo; Siciliano e burlesca. CORTESE—Introduzione e allegro; Melodia. PILATI—Sonata. *Carbotta, flute; Cognazzo, piano.*
+ ARG 3-4/95: 236
• Fa 1-2/95: 348

26119. 7186: GIARDINI—Trios, op. 18. NOFERI—Solos, op. 3. *Dandolo, guitar; Ensemble Pian e Forte.*
+ ARG 5-6/95: 113

26120. 7187: BELLINI—Zaira: highlights. *Ricciarelli, Papadjakou, Vargas, Alaimo; Teatro Massimo "Bellini" di Catania; Olmi, cond.* Reissue; recorded live 1990.
• Fa 1-2/95: 118

26121. 7188—7189 (2 separate discs): ROSSINI (ARR. CARULLI)—Overtures. *Saracino, guitar; Palumbo, fortepiano.*
- ARG 3-4/95: 87
+ Fa 1-2/95: 247

26122. 7191: CILEA—Cello sonata. RESPIGHI—Adagio and variations. CASELLA—Cello sonata. *Signorini, cello; Nicolosi, piano.*
+ ARG 1-2/95: 220
+ Fa 1-2/95: 144

26123. 7193: KRAKAMP—Characteristic pieces for flute and piano: L'amore, op. 72; Un'estate all'Ardenza, op. 107- 116. *Carbotta, flute; Cognazzo, piano.*
+ ARG 5-6/95: 126
+ Fa 5-6/95: 235

26124. 7194: GIULIANI—Chamber works with guitar. *Roselli, guitar; Ensemble Urs Mächler.*
+ ARG 7-8/95: 114
+ Fa 5-6/95: 197

26125. 7196: CARULLI—Guitar and piano music. *Saracino, guitar; Palumbo, fortepiano.*
+ Fa 7-8/95: 149

26126. 7197: BOISMORTIER—Flute sonatas, op. 19. *Ensemble Barocco Italiano.*
- Fa 7-8/95: 128

26127. 7200/01 (2 discs): MARINUZZI—Jacquerie. *Solman, Salvadori, Galgani, Surais; Teatro Bellini, Catania; Licata, cond.*
+ ARG 7-8/95: 152
+ Fa 7-8/95: 236

26128. 7202: SATIE—Piano music. *Masala, piano.*
• ARG 11-12/95: 190
- Fa 7-8/95: 298

26129. 7203: DIABELLI—Sonata, op. 102; Eleven easy pieces; Rode variations; Divertimentos, op. 56. *Saracino, guitar; Palumbo, fortepiano.*
- ARG 3-4/96: 107

26130. 7204: MENDELSSOHN—Four-hand piano music. *Modugno, Spinelli, piano.*
• ARG 5-6/96: 149

26131. 7211: *Hommage à Sax: XIX century original works for saxophones.* Music of Savari, Singelée, Rio, Mohr, and Jonas. *Quartetto di Sassofoni Accademia; Delangle, soprano saxophone.*
+ ARG 9-10/95: 269
+ Fa 7-8/95: 434

26132. 7212: ROSSINI—Four beggars; Four appetizers. *Caramella, piano.*
• ARG 11-12/95: 187

26133. 7213 (2 discs): VIVALDI—Farnace. *Solustri, Pierotti, Lazzarini, Bolgan, Anselmi; Graz Symphony Orch.; Carraro, cond.*
• ARG 3-4/96: 204
• ON 2/17/96: 41

26134. 7215 (2 discs): BELLINI—La sonnambula. *Ciofi, Morino, Furlanetto, Mosca; Valle d'Istria Festival; Carella, cond.* Recorded 1994.
+ ARG 5-6/96: 82

26135. 7221 (2 discs): LEO—Amor vuol sofferenza. *Fallot, Donadini, Laurenza, Mosca; Naples Scarlatti Orch.; Moles, cond.* Recorded 1994.
+ ARG 7-8/96: 145

26136. 7224: MONTEVERDI—Ballo delle ingrate. *Ensemble; Razzi, cond.*
+ ARG 7-8/96: 157

26137. 7226: MOSCHELES—Etudes, op. 70; Allegro di bravura, op. 51. *Brigandi, piano.*
- ARG 7-8/96: 157

26138. 7229: HAYDN—Violin sonatas, vol. 1. *Baraldi, violin; Palumbo, piano.*
- ● ARG 9-10/96: 135

26139. 7232: GLINKA—Piano music. *Bertoldi, piano.*
- + ARG 3-4/96: 234

26140. 7238: Music of Myers, Dyens, Barrios, Ponce, Lauro, Albeniz, and Villa-Lobos. *Martucci, guitar.*
- + ARG 3-4/96: 230

26141. 7239: LEGNANI—Caprices, op. 20. *Saracino, guitar.*
- - ARG 3-4/96: 143

26142. 7249: A. FINZI—Chamber music. *Erasmus Quartet; Heger, piano; Crescini, soprano.*
- ● ARG 9-10/96: 118

26143. 7252: FUCHS—Clarinet quintet. KORNAUTH—Clarinet quintet. *Scarponi Quintet.*
- + ARG 1-2/97: 107

26144. 7253 (2 discs): CHERUBINI—Mcdée. *Tamar, Lombardo, Courtis, Ciofi; International Orch. of Italian Opera; Fournillier, cond.* Recorded 1995.
- + ARG 1-2/97: 87
- - ON 1/25/97: 43
- - Op 1/97: 69

26145. 7255: Music of Takemitsu, Martin, Chavez, Villa-Lobos, Britten, and Ehrlich. *Seroussi, guitar.*
- ● ARG 1-2/97: 205

26146. 90001: VERDI—Requiem. *Caniglia, Stignani, Gigli, Pinza; Rome Opera Chorus & Orch.; Serafin, cond.* Recorded live 1939.
- ● Fa 9-10/90: 421

26147. 90002/3 (2 discs): PUCCINI—Turandot. *Cigna, Olivero, Merli, Neroni; EIAR Turin Chorus & Orch.; Franco, cond.*
- + Fa 9-10/90: 340

26148. 90004: BEEHOVEN—Symphony no. 4. TCHAIKOVSKY—Piano concerto no. 1. *Solomon, piano; Hallé Orch.; Harty, cond.*
- + Fa 9-10/90: 178 m.f.

26149. 90034/41 (8 discs): BEETHOVEN—Piano sonatas (complete). *Schnabel, piano.*
- + Fa 9-10/90: 174

26150. 90213 (2 discs): VERDI—Il trovatore (complete); Il trovatore: Excerpts. *Callas, Stignani, Penno, Tagliabue, Modesti, Baum, Warren; Teatro alla Scala; Mexico City Opera; Votto, Picco, conds.*
- + Fa 9-10/90: 424

O.M. RECORDS

26151. OM 80100: TOURNIER—Images; Suites, no. 1-4. DEBUSSY—The girl with the flaxen hair. SOULAGE—Choral. SCHMIDT—Etude. *Cassat, harp.*
- + ARG 11-12/89: 130
- + Fa 11-12/91: 511

26152. OM 80102: TCHAIKOVSKY—Symphony no. 5. *Mineria Symphony Orch.; Herrera de la Fuente, cond.*
- - ARG 1-2/90: 97

26153. OM 80103: RACHMANINOFF—Rhapsody on a theme by Paganini. TCHAIKOVSKY—Piano concerto no. 1. *Osorio, piano; Mineria Symphony Orch.; Herrera de la Fuente, cond.*
- - ARG 11-12/89: 101

26154. OM 80107: RIMSKY-KORSAKOV—Capriccio espagnol. MUSSORGSKY (ORCH. RAVEL)—Pictures at an exhibition. TCHAIKOVSKY—1812 overture. *State of Mexico Symphony Orch.; Diazmuñoz, cond.*
- + ARG 1-2/92: 81
- - Fa 3-4/92: 295

26155. OM 80133: TCHAIKOVSKY—Symphony no. 4. *Orquestra Sinfónica de Xalapa; Herrera de la Fuente, cond.*
- + Fa 11-12/91: 508

26156. OM 80134: FALLA—The three-cornered hat: Suite no. 2; La vida breve: Interlude and dance; Nights in the gardens of Spain. *Osorio, piano; Xalapa Symphony Orch.; Herrera de la Fuente, cond.*
- + Fa 9-10/91: 213

26157. OM 80135: MONCAYO—Huapango. REVUELTAS—Ocho x radio; Sensemaya. BLAS GALINDO—Sones de mariachi. HALFFTER—Don lindo de Almeria. CHAVEZ—Sinfonia india. *Orquesta Sinfonica de Xalapa; Orquesta Sinfonica de Mineria; Herrera de la Fuente, cond.*
- + ARG 11-12/91: 177
- + Fa 9-10/91: 445

26158. OM 80175: *The art of Carlos Prieto.* RACHMANINOFF—Vocalise. BOCCHERINI—Sonata in A. FAURÉ—Elegy. TCHAIKOVSKY—Pezzo capriccioso. MARTINŮ—Cello sonata no. 2. BACH—Cello suite no. 6. *Prieto, cello; Stevenson, piano.*
- + Fa 9-10/91: 257

26159. OM 80176: SHOSTAKOVICH—Cello concerto no. 1; Cello sonata, op. 40. SAINT-SAËNS—Cello concerto no. 1. *Prieto, cello; Stevenson, piano; Orquesta Sinfonica de Xalapa; Orquesta Sinfonica de Mineria; Herrera de la Fuente, cond.*
- + Fa 9-10/91: 357

26160. OM 80177: *Ancient ayres and dances.* Music of Blondel de Nesle,

Ventadour, Machaut, Gervais, Cabézon, Daquin, Couperin and Pachelbel. *Schlomovitz, harp.*
- ● Fa 3-4/92: 400

26161. OM 80236: DVOŘÁK—Symphony no. 9. TCHAIKOVSKY—Symphony no. 2. *Orquestra Sinfónica de Mineria; Herrera de la Fuente, cond.*
- + Fa 11-12/91: 508

26162. OM 80264: *Reflections.* Music of Rachmaninoff, Mendelssohn, Bach, Schubert, Debussy, Granados, Fauré, Schumann, Chopin, and Scarlatti. *Block, piano.*
- + ARG 1-2/92: 160
- + Fa 9-10/91: 189

26163. OM 80325: ORFF—Carmina Burana. *Choir & Orch. of the Sinfonica Mineria; Herrera de la Fuente, cond.*
- + ARG 11-12/91: 129
- + Fa 11-12/91: 429

26164. OM 80326: REGER—Variations and fugue on an original theme, op. 73; Benedictus; Fantasie and fugue on Wachet auf, ruf uns die Stimme, op. 52, no. 2. *Joyce, organ.*
- + ARG 3-4/92: 125
- + Fa 9-10/91: 322

26165. OM 80500: TCHAIKOVSKY—Symphony no. 5; Romeo and Juliet. *Mineria Symphony Orch.; Herrera de la Fuente, cond.*
- + ARG 1-2/92: 129

26166. OM 80501: *España.* ALBÉNIZ—España. FALLA—Four Spanish pieces. GRANADOS—Spanish dances: no. 1-2, 4-6, 10, 12; Escenas poeticas. *Block, piano.*
- + Fa 11-12/91: 548

26167. OM 80502: CHOPIN—Piano music, vol. 1. *Block, piano.*
- + ARG 7-8/91: 46
- + Fa 9-10/91: 189

26168. OM 80504: LISZT—Piano music. *Block, piano.*
- + ARG 3-4/92: 87
- + Fa 11-12/91: 369

26169. OM 80506: GERSHWIN—Piano concerto; Rhapsody in blue; "I got rhythm" variations. JOEL—Root beer rag. *Syme, piano; Orquestra Sinfónica de Mineria; Herrera de la Fuente, cond.*
- + Fa 3-4/92: 193

26170. OM 80508: SCHUMANN—Romance, op. 28, no. 2; Warum?; Arabesque; Album for the young; Waldszenen; Kinderszenen; Bunte Blätter; Morning song, op. 133, no. 1. *Block, piano.*
- + ARG 7-8/92: 222

26171. OM 80515: FRANCK—Pastorale; Prelude, choral and fugue; Prelude, aria

O.M. RECORDS

and finale. *Block, piano.*
- ARG 7-8/92: 132

26172. OM 80516: BEETHOVEN—Piano sonatas no. 10, 17, 27. *Block, piano.*
• ARG 1-2/92: 29
• Fa 11-12/91: 264

26173. OM 80585: BACH—Six organ preludes and fugues (transcribed by Liszt). *Block, piano.*
• Fa 3-4/92: 137

O.O. DISCS

26174. 1: CELLI—Organic oboe. *Celli, oboe, English horn, voice, kazoo, other instruments.*
+ Fa 11-12/95: 233

26175. 2: CELLI AND KIM—No world improvisations; Types of Asia; Dasreng; Mukhanization; Komukha; Duo improvisation. *Celli, English horn without reeds, mukha veena, breath-controlled synthesizer; Kim, komungo, changgo.*
+ Fa 7-8/95: 153

26176. 4: CELLI AND KIM—No world (trio) improvisations; Triple AAA; April one; Baccalau trio; My friend; Valentine ashes. *Celli, English horn without reeds, piri, breath-controlled synthesizer, oboe; Kim, komungo; Planck, didgeridoo; Hirsch, voice; Curran, synthesizer; Thiam, African percussion; Goldstein, violin.*
+ Fa 7-8/95: 153

26177. 6: GARCÍA—Choral music. *Gregg Smith Singers; Smith, cond.*
• Fa 9-10/95: 205

26178. 8: ROLNICK—ElectriCity; Wondrous love; Blowing; Ever-livin' rhythm. *Lewis, trombone; Dick, flute; Gottlieb, percussion; New York Music Ensemble; Bouchard, cond.*
□ Fa 9-10/95: 295

26179. 11: SMITH—Tunnels; Notebook; Family portraits; Here and there. *Goldstein, percusson; Harkins, trumpet; Hoffmann, piano; Turetsky, double bass; Fonville, flute; Moore, piano; Savage, shortwave radio; Yoken, piano interior.*
+ Fa 9-10/95: 325

26180. 13: Hocus-opus. *First Avenue; with various soloists.*
+ Fa 1-2/96: 420

26181. 14: *Black: state of the bass.* Music of Zvonar-Black, Cage, Sellars, Garcia, Knoles-Black, and Dresher. *Black, double bass, electric bass guitar, electronic basses; Williams, snare drum.*
+ Fa 7-8/95: 415

26182. 15: *A decade: Zeitgeist plays Rzewski.* RZEWSKI—Wails; Spots; The lost melody; Crusoe. *Zeitgeist.*

+ ARG 3-4/95: 263
+ Fa 9-10/95: 302

26183. 17: *Outcome inevitable.* Music of Ashley, Vierk, Hovda, and Ho. *Relâche Ensemble; Ho, saxophone.*
+ ARG 3-4/95: 263
+ Fa 1-2/96: 422

26184. 18: *Act of finding.* Music of Harris, Hamilton, Arnold, and Buckner. *Arnold, processed guitar.*
+ ARG 11-12/95: 298
+ Fa 11-12/95: 509

26185. 19: On second thoughts; Machine for making sense. *Machine for Making Sense.*
• Fa 7-8/95: 449

26186. 20: Banter. *Bailey, guitar; Bendian, percussion.*
+ Fa 1-2/96: 416

26187. 21: MANN—Chris Mann and the impediments: 80 tracks for shuffle play. *Mann, Connors, Marsh, Rue, musicians.*
□ Fa 11-12/95: 299

26188. 22: CELLI—Video ears, music eyes: Music of Joseph Celli. *Kim, komungo; Johnson, percussion; Grupo de Musica Folklorica del Peru; Krieger, saxophones; Goldstein, violin.*
+ ARG 7-8/96: 298
+ Fa 1-2/96: 177

26189. 23: FIRST—The good book's (accurate) jail of escape dust coordinates, part 2. *Sullivan, oboe; Jepperson, clarinet; Wiesner, violin; Trosclair, trumpet; Kaplinsky, synthesizer; Henderson, guitars; Sparke, percussion; First, guitars & electronics.*
□ ARG 7-8/96: 298
□ Fa 3-4/96: 164

26190. 24: KIM—Nong rock; Tchong; Yoeum; Piri quartet. *Various performers.*
□ ARG 9-10/96: 275
+ Fa 5-6/96: 184

26191. 25: K. FIELD—Subterranea. *Field, saxophones, sticks, bottles, juice cans, bamboo flute, drums, clapping; with assisting musicians.*
□ Fa 11-12/96: 245

OAKTON RECORDINGS

26192. ORCD 0001: *Come on and hear!* BERLIN—Early songs. *Sears, voice; Conner, piano.*
• Fa 1-2/95: 120

OCCUPANT

26193. WCSQ (LP): *Textures and colors.* CRESTON—Suite for saxophone quartet. BRUNO—Salutations, fugue, and finale; Texture and colors. DALE—Lullabye for Teddy (arr. Bruno). *West Coast*

Saxophone Quartet.
- Fa 9-10/86: 133

OCEAN

26194. OR 101: ALONSO-CRESPO—Overtures and dances from operas. GALBRAITH—Piano concerto no. 1. *Zitterbart, piano; Cincinnati Chamber Orch.; Alonso-Crespo, Lockhart, cond.*
• ARG 3-4/97: 138
+ Fa 1-2/97: 72

ODE

26195. 1327: *The lyric trumpet.* Music of Enesco, Starer, Bloch, Ravel, Debussy, and others . *Friedman, trumpet; with assisting musicians.*
- ARG 7-8/90: 147

26196. 1446: LISZT—Piano music. *Albulescu, piano.*
• ARG 5-6/96: 137

OISEAU-LYRE

26197. 414 277-2: *Virtuoso recorder music.* Music of Palestrina, Frescobaldi, Merula, Locke, Byrd, and others. *Amsterdam Loeki Stardust Quartet.*
+ DA 8/86: 60
+ Fa 7-8/86: 281
+ Gr 8/86: 284

26198. 417 126-2 (2 discs): HANDEL—Athalia. *Sutherland, Kirkby, Jones, Bowman, Rolfe Johnson, Thomas; New College, Oxford Choir; Academy of Ancient Music; Hogwood, cond.* Issued also as 2 LPs: 417 126-1.
+ ARG Fall/87: 19
+ Fa 7-8/87: 120
+ Gr 11/86: 736
+ Gr 2/87: 1169
+ NYT 4/19/87: H26
+ ON 10/87: 64
+ Op 1/87: 61
• Opus 10/87: 54
+ Ov 4/87: 34
+ SR 6/87: 112

26199. 417 234-2: MOZART—Symphonies K. 16a, 167a. *Hogwood, harpsichord; Academy of Ancient Music.*
+ Fa 7-8/87: 152
+ Gr 2/87: 1130

26200. 417 235-2: BEETHOVEN—Symphony no. 3. *Academy of Ancient Music; Hogwood, cond.* Issued also as LP: 417 235-1.
+ Fa 3-4/87: 77
+ Gr 11/86: 705
• Opus 10/87: 31
+ SR 3/87: 99

26201. 417 249-2: MOZART—Serenades no. 11-12. *Amadeus Winds.*
+ Fa 7-8/87: 153
+ Gr 2/87: 1150

26202. 417 250-2: Bach—Cantatas BWV 80, 147. *Bryden, Minter, Thomas, Opalach; Bach Ensemble; Rifkin, cond.* Issued also as LP: 417 250-1.
+ DA 2/88: 52
+ Fa 11-12/87: 85
+ Gr 2/87: 1163
+ Opus 12/87: 31

26203. 417 323-2: Bach—Gottes Zeit ist die allerbeste Zeit, BWV 106; Aus der Tiefen rufe ich, Herr, zu dir, BWV 131. *Monoyios, Rickards, Brownless, Opalach; Bach Ensemble; Rifkin, cond.*
• Fa 9-10/88: 86
+ Gr 12/87: 983
+ HF 3/89: 52

26204. 417 502-2 (2 discs): Vivaldi—La Stravaganza, op. 4. *Huggett, violin; Academy of Ancient Music; Hogwood, cond.*
+ Fa 9-10/87: 344
+ Gr 3/87: 1274
• HF 2/88: 65

26205. 417 610-2: Haydn—Trumpet concerto H. VIIe: 1; Organ concerto H. XVIII: 1; Horn concerto H. VIId: 3. *Immer, keyed trumpet; Brown, natural horn; Hogwood, chamber organ, harpsichord & cond.; Academy of Ancient Music.*
+ DA 11/88: 78
• Fa 7-8/88: 174
+ Gr 1/88: 1076

26206. 417 615-2: Beethoven—Symphonies no. 4-5. *Academy of Ancient Music; Hogwood, cond.*
+ ARG 9-10/88: 25
- Fa 1-2/88: 88
• Gr 11/87: 724

26207. 417 616-2: Bach—Wachet auf, ruft uns die Stimme, BWV 140; Jauchzet Gott in allen Landen, BWV 51. *Baird, Minter, Thomas, Opalach; Bach Ensemble; Rifkin, cond.*
+ Fa 9-10/88: 86
+ Gr 11/87: 795
• HF 3/89: 52
• MA 11/88: 50

26208. 417 621-2: Bach—Cantatas: Schweigt stille, plaudert nicht, BWV 211; Mer hahn en neue Oberkeet, BWV 212. *Kirkby, Covey-Crump, Thomas; Academy of Ancient Music; Hogwood, cond.* Issued also as LP: 417 621-1.
+ Fa 11-12/87: 86
+ Gr 6/87: 82
+ MA 5/88: 59
+ SR 2/88: 191

26209. 417 622-2: Mozart—Concerto for flute and harp; Andante for flute and orchestra K. 315; Bassoon concerto; Flute concerto no. 1. *Beznosiuk, flute; Kelly, harp; Bond, bassoon; Academy of Ancient Music; Hogwood, cond.*
+ Fa 11-12/87: 230

+ Gr 5/88: 1601
+ HF 3/89: 58

26210. 417 824-2: Bach—Orchestra suites BWV 1066-69. *Beznosiuk, flute; Academy of Ancient Music; Hogwood, cond.*
+ ARG 11-12/89: 22
+ Fa 7-8/89: 78
+ Gr 1/89: 1138

26211. 421 060-2: Vivaldi—Cello sonatas op. 14. *Coin, cello; Hogwood, harpsichord; Zweista, continuo cello; Ferre, guitar; Finucane, archlute.*
+ Fa 9-10/89: 358
+ Gr 4/89: 1605

26212. 421 132-2 (2 discs): Handel—La resurrezione. *Kirkby, Kwella, Watkinson, Partridge, Thomas; Academy of Ancient Music; Hogwood, cond.*
+ ARG 9-10/88: 48

26213. 421 333-2: Mozart—Le nozze di Figaro. *Augér, Bonney, Nafé, Hagegård, Salomaa, Feller; Drottningholm Court Theater Chorus & Orch.; Östman, cond.* Includes all alternate versions of arias & ensembles.
+ ARG 3-4/89: 60
+ DA 9/89: 77
+ Fa 5-6/89: 246
+ Gr 12/88: 1058
+ MA 5/89: 81
+ ON 12/10/88: 64
+ Op 2/89: 198
- OQ Summer/89: 107
+ Ov 2/89: 50
+ SR 5/89: 119
+ St 4/89: 201

26214. 421 366-2 (2 discs): Vivaldi—Concerti grossi op. 9. *Standage, Mackintosh, violins; Academy of Ancient Music; Hogwood, cond.*
+ Fa 9-10/89: 357
+ Gr 4/89: 1597

26215. 421 372-2: Vivaldi—Cello concertos RV 401, 412-413, 416, 418, 424. *Coin, cello; Academy of Ancient Music; Hogwood, cond.*
+ Fa 1-2/90: 336
+ Gr 8/89: 319
+ MA 3/90: 87

26216. 421 408-2 (3 discs): Beethoven—Piano concertos (complete). *Lubin, fortepiano; Academy of Ancient Music; Hogwood, cond.*
• ARG 3-4/89: 19
+ DA 12/88: 62
+ Fa 11-12/88: 131
+ Gr 6/88: 1578
+ MA 9/88: 76
+ MA 5/89: 70
+ SR 9/88: 108

26217. 421 416-2: Beethoven—Symphony no. 6; Coriolan overture; Egmont overture. *Academy of Ancient Music; Hogwood, cond.*

• Fa 5-6/89: 132
• Gr 1/89: 1142
+ HF 4/89: 61
- NYT 1/8/89: H27

26218. 421 424-2: Bach—Weichet nur, betrübte Schatten, BWV 202; Non sa che sia dolore, BWV 209. *Baird, soprano; Bach Ensemble; Rifkin, cond.*
+ Fa 7-8/89: 71
+ Gr 2/89: 1319

26219. 421 429-2: Mozart—Clarinet quintet K. 581; Oboe quartet K. 370; Horn quintet K. 407. *Pay, basset clarinet; Hammer, oboe; Thompson, horn; Academy of Ancient Music Chamber Ensemble.*
+ Fa 5-6/89: 249
+ Gr 12/88: 1027
- SR 10/89: 144

26220. 421 437-2: Mozart—Serenade no. 10. *Amadeus Winds; Hogwood, cond.*
+ Fa 9-10/89: 262
+ Gr 4/89: 1587

26221. 421 442-2: Vivaldi—Violin concerto, RV 208. Ernst—Violin concerto op. 1, no. 1. Telemann—Violin concerto in G minor. Bach—Violin concerto in D minor (from BWV 1052, 1052a, 146, 188). *Ritchie, violin; Bach Ensemble; Rifkin, cond.*
+ DA 10/89: 98
+ Fa 11-12/89: 109
+ Gr 2/89: 1302
+ MA 3/90: 87

26222. 421 500-2: Bach—Concerto for oboe and violin, BWV 1060; Concertos for 2 harpsichords, BWV 1060, 1062; Concerto for 2 violins, BWV 1043. *Hammer, oboe; Mackintosh, Schröder, Hirons, violins; Rousset, harpsichord; Academy of Ancient Music; Hogwood, harpsichord & cond.*
+ DA 10/89: 98
+ Fa 11-12/89: 109
+ Gr 9/89: 448
+ SR 11/89: 154

26223. 421 653-2: Dowland—1st book of songs. *Consort of Musicke; Rooley, cond.*
+ ARG 3-4/90: 43
+ Gr 10/89: 721

26224. 421 729-2: Handel—Concerto grosso no. 3; Movement published by Walsh 2d movement of op. 3 no. 6. *Handel and Haydn Society; Hogwood, cond.*
+ Fa 11-12/89: 225
+ Gr 6/89: 34
+ SR 12/89: 150

26225. 421 782-2: Bach—Jesu, der du meine Seele BWV 78; Was Gott tut, das ist wohlgetan BWV 99; Liebster gott, wenn wird ich sterben BWV 8. *Baird, Fast, Kelley, Opalach; Bach Ensemble; Rifkin, cond.*
+ Fa 1-2/90: 93

OISEAU-LYRE

+ Gr 10/89: 715
+ SR 1/90: 134

26226. 425 114-2 (2 discs): Music for Holy Week in proportional rhythm. *Schola Antiqua; Blackley, cond.*
+ Fa 3-4/90: 358

26227. 425 117-2: Carmina Burana v. 3-4. *New London Consort; Pickett, cond.*
+ Fa 7-8/90: 345
+ Gr 3/90: 1676

26228. 425 496-2: HAYDN—Berenice, che fai; Son pietosa, son bonina; Arianna a Naxos; Solo e pensoso; Miseri noi, misera partia. *Augér, soprano; Handel and Haydn Society; Hogwood, cond.*
+ Fa 11-12/90: 244
+ Gr 9/90: 589

26229. 425 517-2: BEETHOVEN—Synphony no. 9. *Augér, Robbin, Johnson, Reinhart; London Symphony Chorus; Academy of Ancient Music; Hogwood, cond.*
+ ARG 3-4/90: 27
• DA 6/90: 60
• Fa 3-4/90: 142
• Gr 11/89: 882
+ SR 3/90: 93
- St 5/90: 178

26230. 425 519-2: SCHUBERT—Octet D. 803. *Academy of Ancient Music Chamber Ensemble.*
+ Fa 11-12/90: 342

26231. 425 528-2: MOZART—Mass in C minor K. 417. *Augér, Dawson, Ainsley, Thomas; Winchester College Quiristers; Academy of Ancient Music; Hogwood, cond.*
+ Fa 11-12/90: 292
+ Gr 7/90: 261
+ MA 5/91: 91

26232. 425 610-2: *The sylvain and oceanic delights of Posilipo.* Music of Giramo, Della Marra, Lambardi, Trabaci, Arpa, Spiardo and others. *New London Consort; Pickett, cond.*
+ Gr 4/92: 145

26233. 425 692-2: PERGOLESI—Stabat Mater; Salve Regina in C minor. *Kirkby, soprano; Bowman, countertenor; Academy of Ancient Music; Hogwood, cond.*
+ Fa 7-8/90: 221
+ Gr 2/90: 1509
+ MA 9/90: 84

26234. 425 695-2: BEETHOVEN—Symphonies no. 7-8. *Academy of Ancient Music; Hogwood, cond.*
• Fa 5-6/90: 124
□ Gr 2/90: 1456
- St 8/90: 171

26235. 425 819-2: MOZART—Wind divertimentos: No. 8 in F, K. 213; No. 9 in B♭; K. 240; No. 12 in E♭, K. 252

(240a); No. 13 in F, K. 253; No. 14 in B♭, K. 270. *Amadeus Winds.*
+ ARG 11-12/91: 109
+ Gr 5/92: 65

26236. 425 822-2: BACH—Cantatas 56, 82 & 158. *Opalach, Monahan, Stevens, Hite; Bach Ensemble; Rifkin, cond.*
+ EM 2/92: 187
+ Fa 11-12/91: 244
+ Gr 9/91: 106

26237. 425 823-2 (2 discs): MONTEVERDI—Vespro della Beata Vergine. *New London Consort; Pickett, cond.*
+ Fa 7-8/91: 221
+ Gr 3/91: 1709
• MA 7/91: 79
+ St 9/91: 207

26238. 425 834-2: Trumpet music by Biber and Schmelzer. *New London Consort; Pickett, leader.*
+ Fa 11-12/91: 565
+ Gr 9/91: 83

26239. 425 836-2: BEETHOVEN—Piano sonatas no. 8, 14, 17. *Lubin, piano.*
+ ARG 7-8/92: 94
+ Fa 5-6/92: 124

26240. 425 886-2 (2 discs): RAMEAU—Harpsichord music. *Rousset, harpsichord.*
+ EM 8/92: 513
+ Fa 1-2/94: 271
+ Gr 12/91: 105

26241. 425 889-2: DOWLAND—Second booke of songs (1600). *Kirkby, soprano; Skinner, alto; Hill, tenor; Thomas, bass; Consort of Musicke; Rooley.* Reissue.
+ Gr 8/91: 65

26242. 425 890-2: L. COUPERIN—Suites no. 1-3. *Hogwood, harpsichord.*
+ Gr 10/91: 138

26243. 425 891-2: *Venice preserv'd.* Music of A. and G. Gabrieli. Cavalli, Cima, Grandi, Legrenzi, Marini, Monteverdi and Spiridion. *Kirkby, Nelson, sopranos; Rogers, tenor; Academy of Ancient Music; Hogwood, cond.* Reissue.
+ Gr 8/91: 72

26244. 425 892-2: *The lady musick.* Lute songs by Bartlet, Campion, Dowland, Edwards, Morley, Pilkington, Danyel and R. Jones. *Kirkby, soprano; Consort of Musicke; Rooley.* Reissue.
+ Gr 8/91: 72

26245. 425 943-2 (3 discs): MOZART—Don Giovanni. *Augér, Jones, Bonney, Meel, Hagegård, Cachemaille, Terfel, Sigmundsson; Drottningholm Court Theatre Chorus & Orch.; Östman, cond.*
• ARG 3-4/91: 94
+ DA 5/91: 71
• Fa 5-6/91: 230
+ Gr 12/90: 1264

• MA 7/91: 80
- NYT 2/3/91: H24
• ON 3/30/91: 33
• Op 12/90: 1454

26246. 430 082-2 (3 discs): HAYDN—Symphonies, vol. 4. *Academy of Ancient Music; Hogwood, cond.*
+ Fa 11-12/91: 348

26247. 430 245-2: MENDELSSOHN—Music for cello and piano (complete). *Coin, cello; Cohen, fortepiano.*
• Gr 2/93: 54

26248. 430 246-2: *Italian recorder music.* Music of Battiferri, Cima, Conforti, Frescobaldi, Guami, Merula, Palestrina, and Trabaci. *Amsterdam Loeki Stardust Quartet.*
+ Gr 2/92: 59

26249. 430 283-2: COUPERIN—Trois leçons de ténèbres; Victoria! Christo resurgenti. *Kirkby, Nelson, sopranos; Ryan, viola da gamba; Hogwood, organ.* Reissue.
+ Gr 12/91: 108

26250. 430 284-2: DOWLAND—The third booke of songs (1603). *The Consort of Musicke; Rooley, cond.* Reissue.
+ Gr 11/91: 139

26251. 430 339-2 (2 discs): MOZART—Die Entführung aus dem Serail. *Dawson, Hirsti, Heilmann, Kannen; Academy of Ancient Music; Hogwood, cond.*
+ Fa 3-4/92: 256
+ Gr 11/91: 152
+ ON 9/92: 48
+ Op 1/92: 122

26252. 430 484-2 (3 discs): BYRD—My Ladye Nevells booke. *Hogwood, harpsichord, virginal, organ.* Reissue.
+ Gr 11/93: 117

26253. 430 538-2 (2 discs): HANDEL (ARR. MOZART)—Acis und Galatea. *Dawson, Ainsley, Van der Meel, George; Handel and Haydn Society; Hogwood, cond.*
+ ARG 11-12/92: 128
+ EM 2/93: 163
+ Fa 11-12/92: 247
+ Gr 7/92: 86

26254. 430 845-2 (3 discs): HANDEL—Orlando. *Bowman, Augér, Kirkby, Thomas; Academy of Ancient Music; Hogwood, cond.*
+ EM 5/92: 363
+ Gr 8/91: 85
+ ON 1/2/93: 36
+ Op 9/91: 1112
+ St 10/92: 263

26255. 433 012-2 (3 discs): HAYDN—Symphonies, vol. 5: No. 35, 38, 39, 41, 58, 59, 65. *Academy of Ancient Music; Hogwood, cond.*
+ ARG 11-12/92: 132

+ Fa 1-2/93: 164
+ Gr 4/92: 50

26256. 433 035-2 (2 discs): Mozart—Violin concertos no. 1-5; Rondo in B♭; Adagio in E; Rondo in C. *Standage, violin; Academy of Ancient Music; Hogwood, cond.*
+ ARG 7-8/92: 182

26257. 433 043-2: Telemann—Suite in A minor; Concerto in C; Concerto for recorder and viola da gamba. *Pickett,recorder & cond.; Levy, viola da gamba; New London Consort.*
+ ARG 5-6/93: 147
+ Gr 11/92: 100

26258. 433 044-2: Beethoven—Septet. Weber—Clarinet quintet. *Academy of Ancient Music Chamber Ensemble.*
+ Gr 7/94: 70

26259. 433 045-2 (2 discs): Mozart—Violin concertos (Complete). *Standage, violin; Academy of Ancient Music; Hogwood, cond.*
+ Gr 4/92: 68

26260. 433 052-2: Vivaldi—Cello concertos and sonatas. *Coin, cello; Academy of Ancient Music; Hogwood, cond.*
+ Gr 1/92: 64

26261. 433 053-2: Bach—Concertos for three harpsichords, BWV 1063-1064; Concerto for four harpsichords, BWV 1065; Concerto for three violins, BWV 1063 (arr. Hogwood). Vivaldi—Concerto for four violins, op. 3, no. 10. *Soloists; Academy of Ancient Music; Hogwood, cond.*
+ EM 2/93: 155
+ Fa 7-8/92: 104
+ Gr 3/92: 37

26262. 433 054-2: Bach—Italian concerto; Overture in the French style; Duettos BWV 802-805; Chromatic fantasy and fugue. *Rousset, harpsichord.*
+ EM 2/93: 155
+ Gr 5/92: 68

26263. 433 148-2: *The pilgrimage to Santiago.* Music from the Codex de Las Huelgas, the Codex Calixtinus, and the Escorial manuscript of the Cantigas de Santa Maria (Alfonso el Sabio). *New London Consort; Pickett, cond.*
+ ARG 9-10/92: 197
+ EM 11/92: 683
+ Fa 11-12/92: 432
+ Gr 7/92: 96

26264. 433 186-2: Llibre Vermell. *New London Consort; Pickett, cond.*
+ ARG 5-6/93: 173
+ Fa 3-4/93: 360
+ Gr 12/92: 129

26265. 433 187-2: *Mad songs.* Music of Purcell, Eccles, Weldon, Finger and

Blow. *Bott, soprano; Roblou, keyboards; Levy, bassviol; Pleeth, cello; Chateauneuf, guitar; Finucane, archlute.*
+ ARG 7-8/93: 200
+ EM 11/93: 645
+ Gr 2/93: 72

26266. 433 189-2: C.P.E. Bach—Three quartets, H. 537-39; Fantasia, H. 291. *McGegan, flute; Mackintosh, violin; Pleeth, cello; Hogwood, fortepiano.* Reissue.
+ Gr 9/92: 102

26267. 433 190-2: Purcell—Sonatas in four parts. *Mackintosh, Huggett, violins; Coin, viola da gamba; Hogwood, spinet, organ.* Reissue.
+ Gr 3/93: 67

26268. 433 191-2: Locke—The tempest; Musick for His Majesty's sackbutts and cornetts. Purcell—Abdelazar. *Vocal soloists; Michael Laird Cornett and Sackbut Ensemble; Academy of Ancient Music; Hogwood, cond.* Reissues.
• Gr 4/94: 83

26269. 433 194-2: The feast of fools. *New London Consort; Pickett, cond.*
+ ARG 11-12/93: 246
• Fa 7-8/93: 288
• EM 8/93: 489
+ Gr 6/93: 81

26270. 433 198-2: Vivaldi—Cantatas and concertos. *Bott, soprano; Pickett, recorder; Finucane, lute, mandolin; London Consort.*
+ ARG 5-6/93: 149
+ Gr 1/93: 44

26271. 433 328-2: Mozart—Piano sonatas K. 545, 570; Rondos K. 485, 511; Minuet, K. 355; Fantasy K. 475; Gigue; Andante. *Schiff, piano.*
• EM 2/93: 161
• Gr 5/92: 76

26272. 433 545-2 (2 discs): Monteverdi—L'Orfeo. *Ainsley, Gooding, Bott; New London Consort; Pickett, cond.*
+ ARG 5-6/93: 112
+ Fa 7-8/93: 185
+ Gr 2/93: 75
+ ON 7/94: 42

26273. 433 661-2 (3 discs): Haydn—Symphonies, vol. 3. *Academy of Ancient Music; Hogwood, cond.*
• ARG 3-4/93: 90
+ Gr 6/93: 44

26274. 433 674-2: Vivaldi—Oboe concertos. *Hammer, De Bruine, oboes; Academy of Ancient Music; Hogwood, cond.*
+ EM 11/93: 655
+ Fa 9-10/93: 320
+ Gr 7/93: 56

26275. 433 848-2: Schubert—Trout quintet; Songs. *Ainsley, tenor; Lubin,*

fortepiano; Academy of Ancient Music Chamber Ensemble.
+ ARG 1-2/94: 151
+ Fa 1-2/94: 306
+ Gr 9/93: 82

26276. 435 592-2 (3 discs): Haydn—Symphonies, vol. 2. *Academy of Ancient Music; Hogwood, cond.*
+ ARG 9-10/93: 133

26277. 436 127-2: Royer—Pièces de clavecin, 1746. *Rousset, harpsichord.*
+ ARG 5-6/94: 134
+ Fa 1-2/94: 297
+ Gr 9/93: 92

26278. 436 131-2: Susato—Danserye: Excerpts. *New London Consort; Pickett, cond.*
+ ARG 9-10/94: 205
+ Gr 1/94: 59

26279. 436 132-2: *Emma Kirkby sings Mrs. Arne.* Music of Handel, Arne, and Lampe. *Kirkby, soprano; Academy of Ancient Music; Hogwood, cond.*
• ARG 11-12/93: 252
+ Fa 9-10/93: 341
+ EM 11/93: 649
+ Gr 7/93: 82

26280. 436 155-2: *A concorde of sweete sounde.* Music of Parson, Tallis, Carver, Aston, Byrd, White, and others. *Amsterdam Loeki Stardust Quartet.*
+ Gr 2/94: 68

26281. 436 172-2: Vivaldi—Concertos op. 11. *Ritchie, violin; De Bruine, oboe; Academy of Ancient Music; Hogwood, cond.*
+ ARG 5-6/94: 166
+ Gr 4/94: 58

26282. 436 185-2: *Musique pour le chambre du Roy.* Music of Couperin, Montéclair, Fourqueray, Marais, and Leclair. *Nelson, soprano; Huggett, violin; Coin, viola da gamba; Academy of Anceint Music; Hogwood, cond.* Reissue.
+ Gr 10/94: 152

26283. 436 191-2 (2 discs): Locatelli—Flute sonata op. 2. *Preston, flute; Pleeth, cello; Hogwood, harpsichord.* Reissue.
+ Gr 6/93: 69

26284. 436 194-2 (2 discs): Ockeghem—Complete secular music. *Medieval Ensemble of London.* Reissue.
+ Gr 9/93: 101

26285. 436 428-2 (3 discs): Haydn—Symphonies, vol. 1. *Academy of Ancient Music; Hogwood, cond.*
+ Gr 4/94: 46

26286. 436 460-2: Biber—Requiem in F minor; Instrumental music. *Bott, Bonner, Robson, Ainsley; New London Consort; Pickett, cond.*
+ Gr 6/94: 93

26287. 436 585-2: MOZART—Coronation mass; Vesperae solennes de confessore, K. 339. *Kirkby, Robbin, Ainsley, George; Westminster Cathedral Choir; Academy of Ancient Music; Hogwood, cond.*
+ ARG 9-10/93: 161
+ Fa 9-10/93: 220
+ Gr 4/93: 110

26288. 436 718-2: *Trionfi!* Carnival songs and dances from 16th-century Florence. *Bott, Robson, King, George; New London Consort; Pickett, cond.*
+ Gr 7/94: 105

26289. 436 761-2: BOYCE—Eight symphonies. *Academy of Ancient Music; Hogwood, cond.*
+ ARG 5-6/94: 71
+ Fa 5-6/94: 119
+ Gr 4/94: 40

26290. 436 845-2 (3 discs): HANDEL—Concerti grossi op. 6. *Handel and Haydn Society Orch.; Hogwood, cond.*
• ARG 1-2/94: 107
+ Fa 1-2/94: 195
+ Gr 8/93: 28

26291. 436 859-2: ARNE—Overtures. *Academy of Ancient Music; Hogwood, cond. Reissue.*
+ Gr 11/93: 64

26292. 436 860-2: GABRIELI—Symphoniae sacrae, book 2. *Kirkby, Covey-Crump, Elliott, Thomas; Taverner Choir; Taverner Consort; Parrott, cond. Reissue.*
+ Gr 12/93: 99

26293. 436 861-2: *Duetti da camera.* Music of Fontei, Frescobaldi, Grandi, Monteverdi, Notari, and others. *Kirkby, Nelson, sopranos; Consort of Musicke; Rooley, cond. Reissue.*
+ Gr 8/94: 100

26294. 436 862-2: MORLEY—Ayres and madrigals. *Consort of Musicke; Rooley, cond. Reissue.*
+ Gr 4/94: 87

26295. 436 867-2: VIVALDI—Bassoon concertos. *Bond, bassoon; Academy of Ancient Music; Hogwood, cond.*
+ Gr 4/95: 74

26296. 436 905-2: Baroque recorder concertos. *Amsterdam Loeki Stardust Quartet; Academy of Ancient Music; Hogwood, cond.*
+ ARG 1-2/95: 236
+ Gr 7/94: 66

26297. 436 992-2: PURCELL—Dido and Aeneas. *Bott, Ainsley, Kirkby, Thomas; Academy of Ancient Music; Hogwood, cond.*
+ ARG 9-10/95: 195
+ Gr 7/94: 116
+ ON 10/95: 47

26298. 436 993-2: BOCCHERINI—Symphonies G. 506, 512, 519. *Academy of Ancient Music; Hogwood, cond.*
+ Gr 2/95: 41

26299. 440 085-2 (2 discs): MOZART—Die Zauberflöte. *Bonney, Jo, Streit, Cachemaille, Sigmundsson; Drottningholm Court Theater; Östman, cond.*
+ ARG 9-10/94: 166
+ Fa 9-10/94: 270
+ Gr 2/94: 93
+ ON 1/21/95: 37

26300. 440 207-2: *Capriccio di flauti.* Music of Merulo, Johnson, Byrd, Bach, Sweelinck, Frescobaldi, and others. *Amsterdam Loeki Stardust Quartet. Reissue.*
+ Gr 10/94: 152

26301. 440 217-2 (2 discs): BACH—Partitas. *Rousset, harpsichord.*
+ ARG 9-10/94: 95
+ Gr 9/93: 84

26302. 440 220-2: BLOW—Venus and Adonis. *Bott, Robson, King, George; New London Consort; Pickett, cond.*
+ Gr 7/94: 109

26303. 440 222-2 (3 discs): HAYDN—Symphonies, vol. 6. No. 26, 42-44, 48-49. *Academy of Ancient Music; Hogwood, cond.*
+ ARG 1-2/95: 114
• Gr 11/94: 73

26304. 440 637-2: MONTEVERDI—Il combattimento di Tancredi e Clorinda; Il ballo delle ingrate; Tirsi e Clori. *Bott, Bonner, King, Ainsley, George; New London Consort; Pickett, cond.*
+ Gr 6/95: 93

26305. 440 649-2: Music for two keyboard instruments by J.S., W.F., C.P.E., and J.C. Bach. *Hogwood, Rousset, keyboards.*
+ ARG 9-10/96: 82
+ Fa 11-12/96: 170
+ Gr 8/96: 68

26306. 440 675-2 (2 discs): BACH—Brandenburg concertos. *New London Consort; Pickett, cond.*
+ ARG 5-6/95: 71
+ Gr 1/95: 40

26307. 443 179-2: SCARLATTI—Sonatas. *Tilney, harpsichord.*
• Gr 10/94: 163

26308. 443 183-2: HANDEL—Alceste; Comus. *Kirkby, Nelson, Elliott, Thomas; Academy of Ancient Music; Hogwood, cond. Reissues.*
+ Gr 11/94: 130

26309. 443 196-2: SCHUBERT—Violin sonatas. MENDELSSOHN—Violin sonata op. 4. *Schröder, violin; Hogwood, fortepiano.*

Reissues.
+ Gr 9/94: 76

26310. 443 216-2: MOZART—Horn concertos no. 1-4; Rondos for horn and orchestra, K. 371, 514. *Halstead, horn; Academy of Ancient Music; Hogwood, cond.*
+ Gr 8/95: 78

26311. 443 326-2: BACH—Concertos for harpsichord and strings no. 2, 4, 7; Concerto no. 1 for violin, strings, and continuo. *Rousset, harpsichord; Schröder, violin; Academy of Ancient Music; Hogwood, cond.*
+ ARG 3-4/96: 80
- Fa 3-4/96: 110
+ Gr 10/95: 47

26312. 443 328-2: MOZART—Piano concertos 9, 12. *Levin, fortepiano; Academy of Ancient Music; Hogwood, cond.*
+ ARG 1-2/95: 145
+ Gr 7/94: 52

26313. 443 329-2: LE ROUX—Pièces de clavessin. *Rousset, harpsichord.*
+ Gr 7/95: 85

26314. 443 669-2: *Sweeter than roses.* Songs by Purcell, Locke, Blow, Draghi, and others. *Bott, soprano; Thorby, recorder; Robson, oboe; Beznosiuk, Podger, violins; Chateauneuf, theorbo, guitar; Egarr, harpsichord; Levy, bass viol.*
+ Gr 4/96: 106

26315. 443 777-2 (3 discs): HAYDN—Symphonies, vol. 7. Symphonies no. 45-47, 51-52, 64. *Academy of Ancient Music; Hogwood, cond.*
• ARG 1-2/97: 119
• Fa 11-12/96: 268
+ Gr 10/96: 54

26316. 444 131-2 (2 discs): MOZART—La clemenza di Tito. *Heilmann, Bartoli, Jones, Bonney, Montague, Cachemaille; Academy of Ancient Music; Hogwood, cond.*
+ ARG 9-10/95: 178
- Fa 7-8/95: 252
+ Gr 3/95: 101
+ ON 12/23/95: 36
• Op 5/95: 618

26317. 444 336-2: LOCKE—Psyche. *Bott, Robson, King, Agnew; New London Consort; Pickett, cond.*
+ Gr 2/96: 101

26318. 444 339-2: PURCELL—The Indian queen. *Ainsley, Kirkby, Thomas, Finley, Williams, Bott, Crabtree, Podger, Berridge, Parker; Academy of Ancient Music; Hogwood, cond.*
+ ARG 5-6/96: 171
+ Fa 3-4/96: 253
+ Fi 5/96: 135
+ Gr 1/96: 105

26319. 444 449-2: PURCELL—Sonatas of three parts. *Beznosiuk, Podger, violins; Coin, bass viol; Hogwood, chamber organ.*
+ ARG 3-4/96: 168
+ Fa 3-4/96: 254
+ Gr 4/96: 67

26320. 444 571-2: MOZART—Piano concertos no. 11, 13; Rondo, K. 386. *Levin, piano; Academy of Ancient Music; Hogwood, cond.*
+ ARG 1-2/96: 148
+ Gr 9/95: 63

26321. 444 620-2: PURCELL—Theater music. *Kirkby, Bowman, Bott; Academy of Ancient Music; Hogwood, cond.* Reissues.
+ ARG 11-12/95: 180

26322. 444 866-2: BACH—Goldberg variations. *Rousset, harpsichord.*
• ARG 9-10/96: 86
+ Gr 11/95: 119

26323. 448 559-2: Sinners and saints. *New London Consort; Pickett, cond.*
+ Fa 11-12/96: 448

26324. 425 819-2: MOZART—Divertimenti, K. 213, 240, 252, 253, 270. *Amadeus Winds.*
+ Gr 5/92: 65

OLYMPIA

26325. OCD 100: GLAZUNOV—Symphonies no. 1, 7. *USSR Ministry of Culture Symphony Orch.; Rozhdestvensky, cond.*
+ Fa 11-12/87: 143
+ Gr 8/87: 277

26326. OCD 101: GLAZUNOV—Symphonies no. 4-5. *USSR Ministry of Culture Symphony Orch.; Rozhdestvensky, cond.*
+ Fa 11-12/87: 143
+ Gr 8/87: 277

26327. OCD 102: SCHUMANN—Cello concerto op. 129 (orch. Shostakovich). BRAHMS—Violin concerto. *Lusanov, cello; Tretiakov, violin; USSR Ministry of Culture Symphony Orch.; Rozhdestvensky, Fedoseyev, conds.*
+ Fa 9-10/87: 293 (Schumann)
• Fa 9-10/87: 293 (Brahms)
+ Gr 8/87: 277

26328. OCD 105: MIASKOVSKY—Serenade op. 32 no. 1; Sinfonietta op. 32 no. 2; Symphony no. 19 op. 46. *USSR Ministry of Culture Symphony Orch.; USSR Academic Symphony Orch.; USSR Ministry of Defense Orch.; Verbitzky, Mihkailov, conds.*
+ Fa 11-12/87: 175
+ Gr 7/87: 184

26329. OCD 107: *A Russian concert.* ARENSKY—Egyptian nights; Piano

concerto in F. IPPOLITOV- IVANOV—Caucasian sketches: Suite no. 1. *Cherkassov, piano; USSR Radio Orch.; Demchenko, Alexeev, Fedoseyev, conds.*
+ Fa 9-10/87: 131
+ Gr 8/87: 277

26330. OCD 108: SHCHEDRIN—Carmen ballet (after Bizet); Frescoes of Dionysus. *Moscow Virtuosi Chamber Orch.; Armenian Chamber Ensemble; Percussion ensemble; Bolshoi Theatre Soloists ensemble; Spivakov, Lazarev, conds.*
+ Fa 9-10/87: 296
+ Gr 8/87: 277

26331. OCD 109: TCHAIKOVSKY—Suites for orchestra no. 1, 4. *USSR Academic Symphony Orch.; Svetlanov, cond.*
+ Fa 9-10/87: 324
+ Gr 8/87: 277

26332. OCD 111: SHOSTAKOVICH—Symphonies no. 6, 12. *USSR Ministry of Culture Symphony Orch.; Rozhdestvensky, cond.*
+ Fa 9-10/87: 297

26333. OCD 113: SHOSTAKOVICH—Symphonies no. 5, 9. *USSR Ministry of Culture Symphony Orch.; Rozhdestvensky, cond.*
+ Fa 9-10/87: 297

26334. OCD 117: MUSSORGSKY—Pictures at an exhibition; On the southern coast of Crimea; Ensign; Reminiscence of childhood; Children's playroom; Crimea: Gorzuf and Ayudage; Tears; Seamstress; Impromptu passione; First punishment. *Postnikova, piano.*
+ Fa 9-10/87: 258

26335. OCD 123: TISHCHENKO—Violin concerto no. 2 op. 84. *Stadler, violin; Leningrad Phil. Orch.; Sinaisky, cond.*
+ Fa 7-8/89: 266
+ Gr 12/88: 1014

26336. OCD 128: TANEYEV—String quartets no. 8-9. *Taneev Quartet.*
+ Fa 1-2/89: 276

26337. OCD 145: RIMSKY-KORSAKOV—Mozart and Salieri. MUSSORGSKY—The marriage (orch. Rozhdestvensky). *Fedin, Nesterenko; Bolshoi Theater Orch.; Ermler, cond.; Vocalists; USSR Ministry of Culture Symphony Orch.; Rozhdestvensky, cond.*
+ Gr 9/93: 113

26338. OCD 153: TCHAIKOVSKY—Symphony no. 2; Suite for orchestra no. 2 op. 53. *USSR Radio Symphony Orch.; USSR Academic Symphony Orch.; Fedoseyev, Svetlanov, conds.*
• Fa 9-10/87: 324

26339. OCD 164: MENDELSSOHN—Symphony no. 1. J.C. BACH—Sinfonia, op. 18, no. 3. POULENC—Sinfonietta.

Israel Sinfonietta; Rohan, cond.
+ Fa 7-8/90: 198

26340. OCD 186: CHOPIN—Ballade no. 4 op. 52; Mazurkas in A minor, Ab, F# minor op. 59; Piano sonata no. 3; Barcarolle op. 60; Polonaise-fantaisie, op. 61. *Katin, piano.*
+ Fa 3-4/89: 135

26341. OCD 188: SCHUBERT—Piano sonatas D. 537, 960. *Katin, piano.*
• ARG 9-10/92: 155

26342. OCD 189: Music of Bach, Haydn, Beethoven, Debussy, and Liszt. *Katin, piano.*
+ ARG 3-4/90: 138
+ Fa 11-12/89: 451

26343. OCD 190: RACHMANINOFF—Piano concertos no. 1-2. PROKOFIEV—Piano concerto no. 1. *Lympany, piano; Philharmonia Orch.; Malko, Susskind, conds.*
• Fa 3-4/89: 243

26344. OCD 191: PROKOFIEV—Piano concerto no. 3. RACHMANINOFF—Piano concerto no. 3. *Lympany, piano; Philharmonia Orch.; New Symphony Orch. (London); Susskind, Colins, conds.*
+ ARG 11-12/89: 98
• Fa 9-10/89: 280

26345. OCD 192: TCHAIKOVSKY—Piano sonata in G; Months. *Katin, piano.*
+ Fa 11-12/90: 375

26346. OCD 193: CHOPIN—Variations brillantes, op. 12; Mazurkas, op. 24; Ballade no. 3 op. 47; Piano sonata no. 2; Andante spianato and grand polonaise in Eb op. 22. *Katin, piano.*
• ARG 9-10/89: 42
• Fa 9-10/89: 179

26347. OCD 197: GRIEG—Ballade op. 24; Songs arr. for piano no. 41 no. 1, 3, 5; op. 52 no. 3-4; Piano sonata in E minor op. 7; Lyric pieces op. 54 no. 3-4; op. 65 no. 6; op. 71 no. 4. *Katin, piano.*
+ Fa 3-4/89: 170
+ Gr 7/89: 182

26348. OCD 198: Music of C.P.E. Bach, Mozart, Mendelssohn, Brahms, and Liszt. *Petrov, piano.*
+ ARG 9-10/89: 34
+ Fa 11-12/89: 453

26349. OCD 199: LISZT—Consolations; Après une lecture du dante; Liebesträume; Polonaises no. 1-2. *Katin, piano.*
• Fa 3-4/89: 202
+ Gr 11/88: 822

26350. OCD 213: TISHCHENKO—Symphony no. 5. *USSR Ministry of Culture Symphony Orch.; Rozhdestvensky, cond.*

OLYMPIA

- ARG 9-10/90: 126
● Fa 7-8/90: 295

26351. OCD 214: MYASKOVSKY—Piano sonatas no. 1-3, 6. *McLachlan, piano.*
+ ARG 11-12/89: 80

26352. OCD 217: MYASKOVSKY—Piano sonatas no. 4-5; Sonatine op. 57; Prelude op. 58. *McLachlan, piano.*
+ ARG 11-12/89: 80

26353. OCD 230: MOZART—Piano sonatas no. 10-11, 14; Fantasie in C minor K. 475. *Katin, piano.*
● ARG 3-4/90: 81
+ Fa 9-10/89: 264
● Fa 1-2/91: 257
+ Gr 7/89: 209

26354. OCD 231: MOZART—Piano sonatas no. 8-9, 12, 15 . *Katin, piano.*
● ARG 3-4/90: 81
+ Fa 9-10/89: 264
● Fa 1-2/91: 257
+ Gr 7/89: 209

26355. OCD 232: MOZART—Piano sonatas no. 1-2, 4, 7. *Katin, piano.*
+ ARG 3-4/90: 81
+ Fa 1-2/90: 244
● Fa 1-2/91: 257
● Gr 5/90: 2014

26356. OCD 233: MOZART—Piano sonatas no. 6, 16, Sonata in F, K. 533/494. *Katin, piano.*
+ ARG 3-4/90: 81
+ Fa 5-6/90: 231
● Fa 1-2/91: 257
● Gr 5/90: 2014

26357. OCD 234: MOZART—Piano sonatas no. 3, 5, 13, 17. *Katin, piano.*
● Fa 5-6/90: 233
● Fa 1-2/91: 257
● Gr 5/90: 2014

26358. OCD 235: GRIEG—Piano concerto. LITOLFF—Concerto symphonique no. 4: Scherzo. TCHAIKOVSKY—Piano concerto no. 1. *Katin, piano; London Phil. Orch.; London Symphony Orch.; Davis, Kundell, conds.*
+ Fa 1-2/90: 190
- Gr 11/89: 894

26359. OCD 236: KHACHATURIAN—Piano concerto in Db. SAINT-SAËNS—Piano concerto no. 1. *Lympany, piano; London Phil. Orch.; Fistoulari, Martinon, conds.*
□ ARG 11-12/89: 108
+ Fa 1-2/90: 207
+ Gr 9/90: 454

26360. OCD 251: SCARLATTI—Sonatas. *Booth, harpsichord.*
+ Gr 3/95: 74

26361. OCD 254 (2 discs): CHOPIN—Nocturnes (complete); Fantasie-impromptu in C# minor; Impromptus no.

1-3. *Katin, piano.*
+ ARG 3-4/90: 39
+ DA 7/90: 60
+ Fa 9-10/90: 210

26362. OCD 255: PROKOFIEV—Piano sonatas no. 1, 4, 5, 9-10. *McLachlan, piano.*
+ ARG 3-4/90: 88
- Fa 3-4/90: 262
+ Gr 3/90: 1645

26363. OCD 256: PROKOFIEV—Piano sonatas no. 2, 7-8. *McLachlan, piano.*
● ARG 7-8/90: 86
● Fa 5-6/90: 252
+ Gr 3/90: 1645

26364. OCD 257: PROKOFIEV—Piano sonatas no. 3, 5 (original version), 6; Sonatine no. 1; 4 pieces op. 4. *McLachlan, piano.*
● ARG 7-8/90: 86
● Fa 5-6/90: 252
● Gr 3/90: 1645

26365. OCD 263: BRAHMS—Fantasias, op. 116; Intermezzi, op. 117; Rhapsodies, op. 79; Handel variations. *Katin, piano.*
+ ARG 7-8/91: 39
- Fa 9-10/91: 174
+ Gr 5/91: 2038

26366. OCD 264: Music of F.G. Scott, Center, and R. Stevenson. *McLachlan, piano.*
□ ARG 3-4/91: 159
● Fa 3-4/91: 380

26367. OCD 265: LISZT—Années de pèleringage: Première année: Harmonies poétiques et religieuses: Funérailles. *Stephenson, piano.*
● Fa 3-4/91: 256

26368. OCD 266: KABALEVSKY—Twenty-four preludes, op. 38; Piano sonatina in C, op. 13, no. 1; Piano sonata no. 3, op. 46. *McLachlan, piano.*
+ ARG 11-12/92: 139
+ Fa 9-10/92: 268
● Gr 4/93: 87

26369. OCD 267: KABALEVSKY—Piano works, vol. 2. *McLachlan, piano.*
+ Gr 5/93: 72

26370. OCD 268: KABALEVSKY—Symphonies no. 1-2. *Szeged Phil. Orch.; Acél, cond.*
● ARG 3-4/93: 99
● Fa 1-2/93: 172
● Gr 10/92: 63

26371. OCD 269: KABALEVSKY—Piano concertos no. 2-4. *Petrov, Gilels, Popov, piano; Moscow Phil. Orch.; USSR Large Radio and TV Symphony Orch.; Kitaenko, Kabalevsky, conds.*
+ Gr 12/92: 81

26372. OCD 277: LISZT—Années de pèlerinage: 2me année, Italie;

Transcendental etudes: Harmonies du soir. *Stephenson, piano.*
● Gr 11/94: 116

26373. OCD 284: KHANIN—Five smallest orgasms; A certain concerto; Middle symphony. *Vocal soloists; St. Petersburg Chamber Orch.; Martynov, cond.*
□ ARG 11-12/92: 140

26374. OCD 286: SCHUBERT—Piano sonatas D. 575, 626; Moments musicaux no. 1, 3, 6. *Richter, piano.* Recorded live 1979.
+ Gr 10/92: 157

26375. OCD 287: CHOPIN—Preludes no. 2, 4-11, 13, 21, 23. SCHUMANN—Novellettes no. 2, 4, 8; Fantasy pieces op. 12, no. 5, 7. *Richter, piano.* Reissue.
● ARG 1-2/93: 87
+ Gr 10/92: 157

26376. OCD 288: SCHUBERT—Piano sonatas D. 664, D. 784; Impromptus D. 899, no. 2, 4. *Richter, piano.* Recorded 1979.
+ ARG 1-2/93: 146
+ Gr 10/92: 157

26377. OCD 289 (2 discs): CHOPIN—Waltzes; Polonaises. *Katin, piano.*
- ARG 11-12/95: 108
● Gr 1/95: 73

26378. OCD 290 (2 discs): KABALEVSKY—Requiem, op. 72; Symphony no. 4. *Vocalists; Moscow Symphony Orch.; Leningrad Phil. Orch.; Kabalevsky, cond.*
+ ARG 9-10/93: 142
+ Fa 5-6/93: 236
+ Gr 1/93: 55

26379. OCD 291 (2 discs): KABALEVSKY—Colas Breugnon. *Boldin, Isakova, Kayevchenko, Maksimenko; Stanislavsky and Nemirovich-Dantchenko Theater; Zhemchuzin, cond.* Recorded 1973.
+ Gr 5/93: 103

26380. OCD 292: KABALEVSKY—Cello concertos no. 1-2; Improvisation; Rondo. *Tarasova, cello; Symphony of Russia; Dudarova, cond.; Likhopoi, cello; Kuritskaya, piano.*
- ARG 9-10/94: 148
● Gr 6/94: 50

26381. OCD 293: KABALEVSKY—String quartets no. 1-2. *Glazunov Quartet.*
+ Gr 7/94: 72

26382. OCD 294: KABALEVSKY—Cello sonata; Major-minor studies; In memory of Prokofiev; Four pieces; Preludes and fugues. *Tarasova, cello; Ploezhaev, MacLachan, piano.*
- ARG 1-2/95: 124

26383. OCD 300: SZABELSKI—Toccata; Etude; Concerto grosso; Aphorisms 9;

Preludes; Flute concerto; Symphony no. 5. *Bronkowski, flute; Polish Radio National Symphony Orch.; National Phil. Choir & Orch.; Krenz, Markowski, conds.*
+ Fa 3-4/89: 305

26384. OCD 301: HACZEWSKI—Symphony in D major. BOHDANOWICZ—Symphony in D major. GOLABEK—Symphonies no. 1-3. *Poznán Chamber Phil. Orch.; Satanowski, cond.*
+ ARG 9-10/89: 121
+ Fa 3-4/89: 396

26385. OCD 302: PADERWESKI—Piano sonata in E♭ minor op. 21; Piano concerto in A minor op. 17. *Stefański, Hesse-Bukowska, pianos; Polish Radio National Symphony Orch. (Katowice); Krenz, cond.*
+ ARG 7-8/89: 71
+ Fa 3-4/89: 234

26386. OCD 303 (2 discs): SZYMANOWSKI—King Roger; Harnasie. *Rumowska, Nikodem, Hiolski, Bachleda; National Opera House, Warsaw Chorus & Orch.; Mierzejewski, Wodiczko, conds.*
+ Fa 11-12/89: 378

26387. OCD 304: KARLOWICZ—Violin concerto in A; Symphony in E minor op. 7. *Kulka, violin; National Phil. Orch. (Warsaw); Pomeranian Symphony Orch. of Bydgoszcz; Rowicki, Wodiczko, conds.*
• Fa 3-4/89: 194

26388. OCD 305: PADERWESKI—Polish fantasy; Symphony in B minor op. 24. *Smendzianka, piano; Natioanl Phil. Orch. (Warsaw); Pomeranian Symphony Orch. of Bydgoszcz; Wisłocki, Wodiczko, conds.*
+ ARG 7-8/89: 72
+ Fa 3-4/89: 233

26389. OCD 306: RÓZYCKI—Ballad for piano and orchestra; Stanczyk; Anhelli; Pan Twardowski: Excerpts. *Hesse-Bukowska, piano; Polish Radio and Television National Symphony Orch. (Katowice); Poznan Phil. Orch.; Warsaw State Opera House Orch.; Krenz, Satanowski, Górzyński, conds.*
+ ARG 7-8/89: 82
□ Fa 1-2/90: 284 m.f.

26390. OCD 307: KARLOWICZ—Eternal songs; Stanislaw and Anna Oswiecim; An episode during a masquerade. *Warsaw National Symphony Orch.; Wisłocki, cond.*
□ ARG 7-8/89: 50
+ Fa 7-8/89: 166

26391. OCD 308: KILAR—Ezodus; Mount Koscielec 1909; Prelude and Christmas carol; Angelus. *Ambroziak, soprano; Polish Radio and Television National Choir; Polish Radio and Television National Symphony Orch. (Katowice); National Phil. Orch. (Warsaw); Rowicki, cond.*

□ ARG 9-10/89: 68
+ Fa 7-8/89: 167

26392. OCD 309: WIENIAWSKI—Violin concerto no. 2; Polonaise in D, in A; Scherzo-tarantelle; Capriccio-valse in E; Eight etudes-caprices. *Wiłkomirska, Kulka, Jakowicz, Grabarczyk, violins; Marchwinski, Borucińska, pianos; National Phil. Orch. (Warsaw); Rowicki, cond.*
+ ARG 9-10/89: 118
+ Gr 10/89: 680

26393. OCD 310: BACEWICZ—String quartet no. 4, 7; Piano quintet no. 1. *Grazyna Bacewicz Warsaw String Quartet; Warsaw Piano Quintet.*
□ ARG 11-12/89: 14
+ Fa 1-2/90: 88

26394. OCD 311: BACEWICZ—Divertimento for strings; Pensieri notturni; Concerto for orchestra; Viola concerto; Concerto for 2 pianos. *Kamasa, viola; Maksymiuk, Witkowski, pianos; National Phil. Chamber Orch. (Warsaw); National Phil. Orch. (Warsaw); Teutsch, Rowicki, Wisłocki, conds.*
□ ARG 11-12/89: 14
+ Fa 1-2/90: 88

26395. OCD 312: BAIRD—Epiphany music; Elegeia; Four love sonnets; Concerto lugubre for viola; Symphony no. 3. *Hiolski, baritone; Kamasa, viola; various orchs. & conds.*
+ Fa 11-12/89: 121

26396. OCD 313: GÓRECKI—Symphony no. 3; Three pieces in old style; Amen. *Woytowicz, soprano; Polish National Radio Symphony Orch.; Katlewicz, cond.; Warsaw National Phil. Chamber Orch.; Teutsch, cond.; Poznan Boys' Choir; Kurczewski, cond.* Reissues.
+ ARG 7-8/89: 46
+ Fa 7-8/89: 153
+ Gr 4/93: 44

26397. OCD 314: *Organ music from Poland.* Music of Freyer, Moniuszko, Selenski, Rogoski, and others. *Raczkowski, Grubich, organs.*
• Fa 7-8/89: 307

26398. OCD 315: WAŃSKI—Symphony in D, in G. PIETROWSKI—Symphony in D. *Poznán Chamber Phil. Orch.; Stankowsky, cond.*
+ ARG 9-10/89: 121
• Fa 9-10/89: 443

26399. OCD 316: *Twentieth century piano music from Poland.* Music of Lutosławski, Rudzinski, Malawski, Serocki, and others. *Dutkiewicz, Osinska, pianos.*
- Fa 11-12/89: 450

26400. OCD 318: Music of Ravel, Honegger, Debussy, and Messenet. *National Phil. Orch. (Warsaw);*

Satanowski, cond.
• ARG 3-4/90: 91
+ Fa 11-12/89: 493
• Gr 8/89: 320

26401. OCD 319: ZWIERCHOWSKI—Requiem. KOBIERKOWICZ—Ego mater pulchrae dilectionis. *Arion Choir; Musiquae Antiquae Collegium Varsoviense & Madrigalists Choirs; Pomeranian Phil. Orch.; Warsaw Chamber Orch.; Chwedczuk, Dobrzański, conds.*
• Fa 3-4/89: 347

26402. OCD 321: ZIELEŃSKI—Two fantasias; Four offertories; Magnificat; Eight communiones. *Various ensembles.*
+ Fa 7-8/89: 284

26403. OCD 323: *The Polish violin.* Music of Meyer, Lutosławski, Rudzinski, Twardowski, and others. *Lasocki, violin; Bozek-Musialska, piano; Polish Radio National Symphony Orch.; Stryja, cond.*
+ Fa 9-10/89: 423

26404. OCD 324: *Polish percussion music.* Music of Serocki, Penherski, Ptaszyńska, Rudzinski, and others. *Warsaw Percussion Group; Rutkowski, percussion; Mazurek, harp; Pronko, voice; Lukasiewicz, accordion.*
+ Fa 11-12/89: 483

26405. OCD 325: KURPIŃSKI—Henry IV at the hunt: Excerpts; Two huts: Overture; Jadwiga, Queen of Poland: Overture; Clarinet concerto in B♭. *Kurkiewicz, clarinet; Malczewski, Spychalski, Werlinski, Michonski; Łód Opera House Chorus & Orch.; Warsaw Phil. Orch.; Bydgoszcz Phil. Orch.; Latoszewski, Wisłocki, Chwedczuk, conds.*
+ ARG 3-4/91: 79
• Fa 1-2/91: 223

26406. OCD 326: BAIRD—Psychodrama; Tomorrow. *Szostek-Radkowa, Artysz, Pawlak, vocalists; Ostrowski, narrator; Poznan Phil. Orch.; Polish Radio and Television National Symphony Orch. (Warsaw); Czajkowski, Michniewski, conds.*
+ Fa 5-6/91: 116

26407. OCD 327: MALAWSKI—Overture. TURSKI—Violin concerto; Symphony no. 2. *Polish Radio and Television National Symphony Orch. (Warsaw); Warsaw Phil. Symphony Orch.; Wisłocki, Markowski, conds.*
+ Fa 5-6/91: 116

26408. OCD 328: SZYMANOWSKI—String quartets no. 1-2. LUTOSŁAWSKI—String quartet. PENDERECKI—String quartet no. 2. *Varsovia String Quartet.*
+ Au 5/90: 68
+ Fa 11-12/89: 379
+ Gr 6/89: 56

OLYMPIA

26409. OCD 329: PENDERECKI—
Symphony no. 2. BRUZDOWICZ—Double-
bass concerto; Violin concerto. *Grillo,
double bass; Jakowicz, violin; Polish
National Symphony Orch.; Artur
Rubinstein State Phil. Orch.; Kasprzyk,
Markowski, conds.*
  + ARG 11-12/89: 93
  + Au 7/90: 80
  + DA 4/90: 51
  + Fa 11-12/89: 312

26410. OCD 330: BEETHOVEN—Piano
sonatas no. 1, 9, 23, 27. *Fischer, piano.*
  • ARG 11-12/89: 35
  • Fa 11-12/89: 132
  + Gr 12/89: 1163

26411. OCD 331: BEETHOVEN—Piano
sonatas no. 2, 14, 16. *Fischer, piano.*
  • ARG 11-12/89: 35
  • Fa 11-12/89: 132
  + Gr 12/89: 1163

26412. OCD 332: BEETHOVEN—Piano
sonatas no. 3, 10, 21. *Fischer, piano.*
  - Fa 5-6/90: 118

26413. OCD 333: BEETHOVEN—Piano
sonatas no. 4, 13, 24, 26. *Fischer, piano.*
  - Fa 5-6/90: 118

26414. OCD 334—339 (6 separate discs):
Sviatoslav Richter, vol. 4-9. Music of
Beethoven, Rachmaninoff, Chopin,
Tchaikovsky, Schubert, and Schumann.
Richter, piano. Recorded 1970-1983.
  + ARG 5-6/94: 184 (v.6-9)
  + Gr 1/94: 78 (v.4-7)
  + Gr 4/94: 76 (v.8-9)

26415. OCD 341: Music of Bach,
Wassenaer, and Muffat. *Combattimento
Consort Amsterdam.*
  + Fa 11-12/90: 477
  + Gr 12/90: 1223

26416. OCD 342: Music of Fux, Biber,
Muffat, Telemann, and Zelenka.
Combattimento Consort Amsterdam.
  + Fa 11-12/90: 477
  + Gr 12/90: 1223

26417. OCD 343: Music of Lutosławski,
Gorecki, and Prokofiev. *Camerata
Vistula.*
  + Fa 5-6/91: 116

26418. OCD 344: SZYMANOWSKI—
Masques; Mazurkas. *Domanska, piano.*
  + Gr 1/96: 82

26419. OCD 350: Music of Prokofiev,
Mozart, Liszt, and Schubert. *Joselson,
piano.* Recorded live 1986.
  + ARG 3-4/90: 138
  - Fa 1-2/90: 380

26420. OCD 351: FALLA—Nights in the
gardens of Spain. ORBON—Partita no. 4.
*Joselson, piano; Frankfurt Radio
Symphony Orch.; Mata, cond.*
  + Fa 1-2/90: 179

26421. OCD 352: Music of Liszt,
Debussy, Ravel, and Gershwin. *Amato,
piano.*
  + Fa 3-4/91: 476

26422. OCD 353: MACDOWELL—Piano
concertos no. 1-2. *Amato, piano; London
Phil. Orch.; Freeman, cond.*
  + Fa 7-8/91: 196

26423. OCD 354: DUTILLEUX—Piano
sonata. BALAKIREV—Piano sonata in B♭
minor. *Amato, piano.*
  • Fa 3-4/91: 204

26424. OCD 355: PROKOFIEV—Violin
sonatas no. 1-2. JANÁČEK—Violin sonata.
Hardy, violin; Devos, piano.
  • Gr 6/92: 58

26425. OCD 356: SCHUMANN—Violin
sonatas. C. SCHUMANN—Romances op. 22.
Hardy, violin; Tsachor, piano.
  + ARG 7-8/93: 155

26426. OCD 360: *Music for two pianos
and piano duet.* RAVEL—Introduction et
allegro; Rapsodie espagnole; Suites
auriculaires: Entre cloches; Ma mère
l'oye; L'eventail de Jeanne: Fanfare;
Shéhérazade overture; Frontispiece; La
valse. *Thorson, Thurber, Gardner,
pianos.*
  + DA 12/90: 107
  + Fa 9-10/90: 222

26427. OCD 362: DVOŘÁK—Slavonic
dances (complete). *Thorson, Thurber,
pianos.*
  + ARG 9-10/90: 62
  - Fa 9-10/90: 235

26428. OCD 380: *18th-century Polish
symphonies.* Music of Orlowski,
Dankowski, Engel, Namieyski,
Pawlowski. *Warsaw Chamber Orch.;
Sewen, cond.*
  + Gr 8/94: 65

26429. OCD 383: ZAREBSKI—Piano
quintet. TANSMAN—Suite-divertissement.
TWARDOWSKI—Piano trio. *Witkowski,
piano; Marczyk, Bojarski, violins;
Marczyk, viola; Krzymiński, cello.*
  + ARG 5-6/93: 154

26430. OCD 385: GÓRECKI—*The essential
Górecki.* Epitafium; Scontri; Genesis II;
Canti strumentali; Refrain; Old Polish
music. *Polish National Phil. Choir;
Polish National Symphony Orch,
Katowice; Krenz, cond.; Polish National
Phil. Orch, Warsaw; Markowski, cond.*
Reissues.
  + Gr 4/93: 44

26431. OCD 386: MONIUSZKO—Overtures.
*Polish National Radio Symphony Orch.,
Katowice; Fitelberg, Krenz, conds.;
National Phil. Orch., Warsaw; Rowicki,
cond.* Recorded 1952/64.
  + ARG 9-10/93: 156
  + Gr 8/93: 34

26432. OCD 387: BACEWICZ—String
quartet no. 3, 5; Piano quintet no. 2.
*Wilanow Quartet; Warsaw Piano
Quintet.*
  + Gr 8/93: 46

26433. OCD 388: BAIRD—Voices fom
afar; Goethe-Briefe; Scene; Canzona.
Various performers.
  + Gr 9/93: 95

26434. OCD 389: NOSKOWSKI—The
Steppe; Elegiac polonaise; The Morskie
Oko Lake in the Tatras. LIPINSKI—Violin
concerto no. 2; Caprice no. 20.
KARLOWICZ—Music to the white dove.
*Ivanov, violin; Polish National Symphony
Orch.; Rowicki, Wisłocki, conds.;
Warsaw Strings; Sewen, cond.* Reissues.
  + ARG 11-12/93: 161

26435. OCD 392: BACEWICZ—Violin
sonata no. 4; Piano sonata no. 2;
Concerto for string orchestra; Violin
concerto no. 7. *Stratkiewicz, Janowski,
violin; Utrecht, Zimerman, pianos; Polish
Chamber Orch.; Maksymiuk, cond.;
Warsaw Phil. Orch.; Markowski, cond.*
Recorded 1968-77.
  + Gr 12/93: 61

26436. OCD 393 (2 discs): JARZEBSKI—
Complete works. *Cappella Arcis
Varsoviensis; Sewen, cond.*
  • ARG 11-12/93: 133

26437. OCD 395: MONIUSZKO—Mass;
Motets. *Polish Radio Choir of Wroclaw;
Kajdasz, cond.*
  + ARG 1-2/94: 125

26438. OCD 398: PADEREWSKI—Piano
concerto. MELCER—Piano concerto no. 1.
*Paleczny, piano; Katowice Radio
Symphony Orch.; Ponti, piano; Warsaw
Phil. Orch.; Strugala, cond.*
  • ARG 5-6/94: 118
  + Gr 7/94: 51

26439. OCD 400: MARSH—Symphonies
1, 3-4, 6. *Chichester Concert; Graham-
Jones, cond.*
  + ARG 3-4/90: 70
  + Fa 3-4/90: 223
  + Gr 2/90: 1464

26440. OCD 402: CONSTANTINESCU—The
nativity. *Petrescu, Kessler, Teodorian,
Bömches; Bucharest George Enescu
Choir & Phil. Orch.; Basarab, cond.*
  + ARG 11-12/92: 107
  + Fa 9-10/90: 216

26441. OCD 404: M. HAYDN—
Symphonies in E♭, B♭, D, D, B♭;
Pastorello in C. *Oradea Phil. Symphony
Orch.; Acél, cond.*
  • ARG 11-12/90: 69
  + Fa 11-12/90: 247
  + Gr 10/90: 740

26442. OCD 405: DITTERSDORF—
Symphonies in C, D; Flute concerto in E

minor; Double bass concerto in E.
*Costea, flute; Thomasz, double bass;
Oradea Phil. Chamber Orch.; Cluj-
Napoca Phil. Orch.; Arad Phil. Orch.;
Acél, Cristescu, Boboc, conds.*
+ Fa 11-12/90: 215

26443. OCD 406: M. HAYDN—Violin
concerto in B♭; Concerto for clarinet,
harpsichord, and viola. *Ille, violin; Botár,
harpsichord; Thurzo, viola; Popa,
clarinet; Oradea Phil. Orch.; Quodlibet
Musicum Chamber Orch.; Acél, cond.*
• ARG 11-12/90: 69
+ Fa 11-12/90: 147
+ Gr 10/90: 740

26444. OCD 407: M. HAYDN—
Symphonies in C major, D major, D
minor. *Oradea Phil. Symphony Orch.;
Acél, Ratiu, conds.*
• ARG 11-12/90: 69
+ Fa 11-12/90: 247
+ Gr 10/90: 740

26445. OCD 408: *Romanian rhapsody.*
Music of Flechtenmachter, Caudella,
Stephanescu, Muresianu, and others.
*Romanian Radio and Television
Symphony Orch.; Cluj-Napoca Phil.
Orch.; Arad Phil. Orch.; Litvin, Simon,
Ráu, conds.*
+ ARG 7-8/91: 143
• Fa 5-6/91: 385

26446. OCD 409: VIERU—Concerto for
violin and cello; Symphony no. 5. *Kagan,
violin; Gutman, cello; Romanian Radio
and Television Chorus & Symphony
Orch.; Vieru, Baci, conds.*
+ ARG 7-8/91: 133
+ Fa 5-6/91: 314 m.f.

26447. OCD 410: NICULESCU—
Concertante symphony no. 3. MARBÉ—
Concerto for Daniel Kientzy and
saxophones. VIERU—Narration no. 2.
*Kientzy, saxophone; Romanian Radio and
Television Symphony Orch.; Ploiesti Phil.
Orch.; Timisoara Phil. Orch.; Conta,
Andreescu, Georgescu, conds.*
+ ARG 7-8/91: 174
+ Fa 5-6/91: 373

26448. OCD 411: CONSTANTINESCU—
Symphony no. 1; Piano concerto.
*Gheorghiu, piano; Iasi Moldova Phil.
Orch.; Cluj-Napoca Phil. Orch.; Baciu,
Simon, conds.*
+ Fa 5-6/91: 158

26449. OCD 412: ENESCO—Piano
quartets no. 1-2. *Voces String Quartet;
Piedemonte, piano.*
+ ARG 9-10/92: 102

26450. OCD 413: ENESCO—Quartets no.
1-2. *Voces String Quartet.*
+ ARG 9-10/92: 102
+ Gr 6/92: 58

26451. OCD 414: ENESCO—Piano suites
no. 1-3. *Ienei, piano.*
+ ARG 9-10/92: 102

26452. OCD 415: CONSTANTINESCU—
Ballad of the outlaw; Concerto for
strings; Byzantine variations; Harp
concerto. *Soloists; Romanian Radio
Orch.; Conta, cond.*
• ARG 11-12/92: 106

26453. OCD 416: TARANU—Symphony
no. 2. BENTOIU—Symphony no. 5.
NICOLESCU—Symphony no. 2. *Various
performers.* Reissue.
• ARG 9-10/92: 187

26454. OCD 417: TODUTA—Four
tablatures for lute by Bakfark.
CONSTANTINESCU—Violin concerto.
NICHIFOR—Symphony no. 4. *Various
performers.* Reissue.
• ARG 9-10/92: 187

26455. OCD 418: Clarinet concertos by
Krommer, Molter, Rossini, and Stroe.
Various performers.
+ Gr 9/92: 98

26456. OCD 419: VIERU—Symphony no.
3 "An earthquake symphony"; Taragot;
Joseph and his brothers. *Romanian Radio
Symphony Orch.; Bacs, cond.; Virtuosi of
Bucharest Ensemble; Andreescu, cond.;
Omnia Ensemble; Soare, cond.*
+ ARG 7-8/93: 175
+ Fa 5-6/93: 348

26457. OCD 424: KANCHELI—
Symphonies no. 1, 7; Epilogue; Liturgy.
*Belongonov, viola; Moscow State
Symphony Orch.; Glushchenko, cond.*
+ Gr 4/93: 52

26458. OCD 427: MILHAUD—Saudades do
Brasil. NAZARETH—Tangos. *Bratke, piano.*
+ Gr 8/93: 59

26459. OCD 428: HAYDN—Violin
concertos. *Kussmaul, violin; Amsterdam
Bach Soloists.*
+ ARG 1-2/94: 109
+ Gr 6/94: 48

26460. OCD 430: DUSSEK—Piano
sonatas. *Govier, piano.*
• EM 8/94: 531
+ Gr 9/93: 89

26461. OCD 431: BERG—Piano sonata.
WEBERN—Variations, op. 27. KRENEK—
Piano sonatas no. 2-4. *Bratke, piano.*
+ Gr 4/94: 70

26462. OCD 434: PICHL—Symphonies;
Symphonie concertante. *Oradea Phil.
Orch.; Rimbu, cond.*
• Gr 5/94: 58

26463. OCD 435: M. HAYDN—
Symphonies no. 12, 32, 43-44. *Oradea.
Phil. Orch.; Rimbu, cond.*
+ Gr 4/94: 48

26464. OCD 436: SCHUMANN—Allegro,
op. 8; Noveletten; Fantasiestücke, op.
111; Gesänge der Frühe. *Brautigam,
piano.*
+ Gr 6/94: 88

26465. OCD 437: BACH—Sonata BWV
964; Concerto BWV 976; Suite BWV
997; Chromatic fantasy and fugue;
Chaconne. *Booth, harpsichord.*
+ Gr 10/94: 154

26466. OCD 438: SHCHEDRIN—Preludes
and fugues; Preludes. *McLachlan, piano.*
+ ARG 3-4/95: 184
• Gr 3/95: 76

26467. OCD 439—440 (2 separate discs):
TCHEREPNIN—Piano concertos no. 1-6.
*McLachlan, piano; Chetham's Symphony
Orch.; Clayton, cond.*
+ ARG 1-2/95: 193 (439)
+ Gr 11/94: 88 (439)
+ ARG 3-4/96: 194 (440)
+ Gr 12/95: 94 (440)

26468. OCD 441—443 (3 separate discs):
ENESCO—Orchestral works, vol. 1-3.
*Romanian National Radio Orch.;
Andreescu, cond.*
+ ARG 1-2/95: 104 (v.1)
+ Gr 11/94: 70

26469. OCD 442: ENESCO—Symphony
no. 2; Romanian rhapsodies. *Romanian
Radio Orch.; Andreescu, cond.*
+ ARG 1-2/95: 104

26470. OCD 444: ENESCO—Suite no. 1;
Symphonie concertante; Two
intermezzos. *Cazacu, violin; Romanian
Radio Orch.; Andreescu, cond.*
+ ARG 1-2/96: 108
+ Gr 6/95: 44

26471. OCD 445: ENESCU—String octet;
Wind decet. *Various performers.*
+ Gr 11/95: 105

26472. OCD 447: GRECHANINOV—The
liturgy of St. John Chrysostom, no. 1.
*Cantus Sacred Music Ensemble;
Arshavskaya, Shcheglov, conds.*
+ Gr 6/95: 89

26473. OCD 449: VIERU—Symphonies
no. 2, 4; Psalm. *Bucharest National
Radio Orch.; Budapest Radio Chamber
Orch.; Bacs, cond.; Cluj-Napoca Phil.
Orch.; Simon, cond.*
+ Gr 4/95: 74

26474. OCD 450: FESCH—Violin
concertos. *Nikolitch, violin; Auvergne
Orch.; Beek, cond.*
+ Gr 7/96: 50

26475. OCD 452: MILHAUD—Symphony
no. 3 "Te Deum"; Les cloches; Saudades
do Brasil. *Russian State Symphonic
Cappella; Rozhdestvensky, cond.*
+ Gr 6/96: 50

OLYMPIA

26476. OCD 453: PROKOFIEV—Pieces from Romeo and Juliet, Cinderella, and Love for three oranges. *Joselson, piano.*
+ Gr 10/92: 144

26477. OCD 454: BAX—Music for viola and piano. *Crabtree, viola; Matthews, piano.*
+ ARG 5-6/95: 81

26478. OCD 455: VILLA-LOBOS—Piano music. *Bratke, piano.*
+ Gr 2/95: 76

26479. OCD 456: CUI—Kaleidoscope; Violin sonata. *Sheppard, violin; Shorr, piano.*
+ Gr 12/95: 103

26480. OCD 457: PIJPER—String quartets. *Schoenberg Quartet.*
+ ARG 3-4/95: 156
+ Gr 2/95: 68

26481. OCD 458: ROUSSEL—Piano trio; Violin sonata no. 1; Divertissement. *Various performers.*
+ ARG 5-6/95: 162

26482. OCD 459: ROUSSEL—Chamber music, vol. 2. *Maessen, soprano; Verhey, flute; Roerade, oboe; Lange, bassoon; Kantorow, violin; Waardenburg, harp; Goudswaard, guitar; Regteren Altena, double bass; Röling, piano; Schoenberg Quartet.*
+ ARG 9-10/95: 204
+ Gr 9/95: 77

26483. OCD 460: ROUSSEL—Chamber music, vol. 3. *Various perfomers.*
+ Gr 11/95: 110

26484. OCD 461: BUSONI—Piano music. BACH—Piano music (trans. Busoni). *Stephenson, piano.*
+ Gr 11/94: 112

26485. OCD 471: VAINBERG—Symphonies no. 6, 10. *Moscow School Boys Choir; Moscow Phil. Orch.; Kondrashin, cond.*
• ARG 1-2/95: 195

26486. OCD 472: VAINBERG—Symphonies no. 7, 12. *Moscow Chamber Orch.; Barshai, cond.; USSR Television and Radio Symphony Orch.; M. Shostakovich, cond.* Recorded 1967, 1979.
+ Gr 11/94: 90

26487. OCD 473: VAINBERG—The golden key: suites no. 1-3; 4 (excerpts). *Bolshoi Theatre Orch.; Ermler, cond.*
+ ARG 9-10/95: 233
+ Gr 5/95: 64

26488. OCD 474: VAINBERG—Piano quintet; String quartet no. 12. *Borodin Quartet; Vainberg, cond.* Recorded 1973, 1976.
+ Gr 4/95: 86

26489. OCD 477: SILVESTROV—Symphony no. 2; Meditatsiya; Serenade. *Hudiyakov, flute; Sokolov, piano; Dunayev, Smirnov, percussion; Musica Viva Chamber Orch.; Rudin, Alexeiev, conds.*
+ Gr 7/96: 64

26490. OCD 478: CAMILLERI—Piano music, vol. 1. *McLachlan, piano.*
+ Gr 8/96: 72

26491. OCD 479: SCHUBERT—Piano music. *Lisney, piano.*
+ Gr 2/96: 76

26492. OCD 480: GRECHANINOV—Liturgy of St. John Chrysostom, no. 4. *Cantus Sacred Music Ensemble; Arshavskaya, cond.*
+ Gr 9/95: 88

26493. OCD 482: CHESNOKOV—Choral music. *Cantus Sacred Music Ensemble; Arshavskaya, cond.*
+ Gr 1/96: 85

26494. OCD 483: PALIASHVILI—Liturgy of St. John Chrysostom. *Cantus Sacred Music Ensemble; Arshavskaya, cond.*
+ Gr 5/96: 102

26495. OCD 489: Piano music from Malta. *McLachlan, piano.*
+ Gr 8/96: 72

26496. OCD 491: KARAEV—Ballet suites. *Moscow Radio and Television Symphony Orch.; Abdullayev, cond.*
+ Gr 12/95: 82

26497. OCD 494: PINTO—Piano sonatas. *Fukuda, piano.*
□ Gr 4/96: 76

26498. OCD 495: ENESCO—Suites no. 2-3; Andantino. *Romanian Radio Orch.; Andreescu, cond.*
+ ARG 1-2/96: 108
+ Gr 11/95: 84

26499. OCD 496: ENESCU—Vox maris; Study symphony no. 1; Violin ballade. *Anghelescu, violin; Hagy, tenor; Romanian Radio Orch.; Andreescu, cond.*
+ ARG 5-6/96: 109
• Gr 8/96: 46

26500. OCD 504: *400 years of Dutch music, vol. 5.* WAGENAAR—Cyrano de Bergerac: overture. VERMEULEN—Symphony no. 3; Thrène et Péan. RUYNEMAN—Hieroglyphen. PIJPER—Piano concerto. ANDRIESSEN—Kuhnau variations. *Hague Phil. Orch.; Leitner, cond.*
□ ARG 11-12/91: 176

26501. OCD 505: *Dutch music, vol. 6.* VERMEULEN—Symphony no. 4. VAN BAAREN—Septet. VAN DER HORST—Chorus II, La nuit. KETTING—Due canzoni. DE LEEUW—Mouvements rétrogrades. *Ifúsági*

Müverszyüttes Choir; Hague Phil. Orch.; Medveczky, Vonk, Bour, conds.
+ ARG 7-8/92: 249

26502. OCD 506: *400 years of Dutch music, vol. 7.* Music of Escher, Janssen, Loevendie and Laman. *Various performers.*
□ ARG 1-2/93: 173

26503. OCD 507: *400 years of Dutch music, vol. 8.* Music of Andriessen, Diepenbrock, Gilse, and Badings. *Hague Phil. Orch.; Spanjaard, cond.*
+ ARG 11-12/93: 72

26504. OCD 510: MIASKOVSKY—Symphony no. 6. *Symphony Orch. of Russia; Anima Moscow Chamber Choir; Dudarova, cond.*
+ ARG 7-8/93: 125
• Fa 3-4/93: 224
• Gr 11/92: 90

26505. OCD 511: KALINNIKOV—Symphonies no. 1-2. *Rousse Symphony Orch.; Dudarova, cond.*
- Gr 5/93: 47

26506. OCD 513: LYADOV—Orchestra music. *Rousse Symphony Orch.; Dudarova, cond.*
+ Gr 6/93: 50

26507. OCD 516: ARTIOMOV—Tristia; In mcmorium; Symphony; Way to Olympus; Violin sonata no. 4; Piano sonata no. 2; Concerto for string orchestra; Violin concerto no. 7. *Krysa, violin; Moscow Phil. Orch.; Kitaenko, cond.; USSR Symphony Orch.; Mynbaev, cond.*
+ ARG 7-8/94: 60

26508. OCD 519: LIAPUNOV—Symphony no. 1; Ballada. *Moscow State Symphony Orch.; Glushchenko, cond.*
+ Gr 11/93: 70

26509. OCD 520: SVIRIDOV—Choral music. *Yurlov State Choir; Ostankino Radio Symphony Orch.; Fedoseyev, cond.*
+ ARG 5-6/94: 152

26510. OCD 521: TCHAIKOVSKY—String quartets no. 1-2; Five early pieces. *Shostakovich Quartet.*
+ ARG 9-10/93: 205

26511. OCD 522: GRECHANINOV—String quartet no. 1. TCHAIKOVKSY—String quartet no. 3; Adagio molto in E♭. *Shostakovich Quartet.*
+ Fa 5-6/93: 214
+ Gr 6/93: 63

26512. OCD 523: GLINKA—Sextet. TCHAIKOVSKY—Quartet movement; Souvenir de Florence. *Belotsvetov, viola; Kovalyov, cello; Gabdullin, double bass; Nasyedkin, piano; Shostakovich Quartet.*
• Gr 7/93: 58

26513. OCD 525—526 (2 separate discs): GLAZUNOV—String quartets no. 3, 5-7. *Shostakovich Quartet.*
+ ARG 1-2/94: 102
+ Gr 8/93: 48 (526)

26514. OCD 528: MIASKOVSKY— Serenade; Sinfonietta; Lyric concertino; Salutory overture. *Moscow New Opera Orch.; Samoilov, cond.*
• ARG 9-10/94: 163
+ Gr 7/94: 52

26515. OCD 529: GLINKA—Septet; Serenade on Anna Bolena; Divertimento on La sonnambula; Sextet. *Soloists of the Russian National Symphony Orch.*
+ ARG 11-12/94: 117
□ Gr 7/94: 71

26516. OCD 530: MIASKOVSKY—Cello sonatas; Cello concerto. *Tarasova, cello; Polezhaev, piano; Moscow New Opera Orch.; Samoilov, cond.*
- ARG 3-4/95: 145
+ Gr 12/94: 90

26517. OCD 531—535 (5 separate discs): SHOSTAKOVICH—Complete string quartets. *Shostakovich Quartet.*
+ ARG 3-4/95: 186
+ Gr 9/94: 78

26518. OCD 538: BORODIN—String quartets no. 1-2. *Shostakovich Quartet.*
• ARG 11-12/94: 80

26519. OCD 540: SVIRIDOV—Piano trio; St. Petersburg songs; Music for chamber orchestra. *Musica Viva; Rudin, cond.*
+ ARG 11-12/95: 216
• Gr 1/96: 65

26520. OCD 541: SVIRIDOV—Choral music. *Moscow New Choir; Rastvorova, cond.*
• ARG 11-12/95: 215
+ Gr 9/95: 96

26521. OCD 542: GLAZUNOV—String quintet; Suite, op. 135; Elegy, op. 105. *Shostakovich Quartet.*
+ ARG 11-12/95: 123
• Gr 11/95: 106

26522. OCD 543: TANEEV—String quartets no. 1-3. *Talan Quartet.*
• ARG 9-10/95: 226
+ Gr 10/95: 90

26523. OCD 547: TISHCHENKO—String quartets no. 1, 4. *Glazunov Quartet.*
+ Gr 7/96: 71

26524. OCD 551: SMOLSKY—Overture; Dulcimer concerto no. 1; Cello concerto; Symphony no. 6; Violin concerto. *Gladkov, dulcimer; Vsaveriyev, cello; Gorelic, violin; Bělorussian Radio Orch.; Raisky, Leonov, conds.*
+ ARG 1-2/93: 173

26525. OCD 552: GLEBOV—Symphony no. 5; Five fantastic dances; The Little Prince suite. *Bělorussian Radio Orch.; Raisky, cond.*
+ ARG 1-2/93: 173
• Gr 10/92: 61

26526. OCD 553: SOLTAN—Symphony no. 2; Symphonic poem; Melody and chorale; Cello concerto. *Soltan, piano; Ksaveriyev, cello; Bělorussian Radio Orch.; Raisky, cond.*
+ ARG 1-2/93: 173

26527. OCD 561—564 (4 separate discs): BEETHOVEN—Piano sonatas, vol. 1-4. *Nikolayeva, piano.* Recorded 1983.
+ Gr 1/95: 73

26528. OCD 565—570 (6 discs): BEETHOVEN—The complete piano sonatas, vol. 5-10. *Nikolayeva, piano.*
• ARG 9-10/95: 103 (v.7-8)
+ Gr 6/95: 75

26529. OCD 574: SHOSTAKOVICH—Piano sonatas no. 1-2; Five preludes; Preludes, op. 34. *Stone, piano.*
• Gr 6/96: 72

26530. OCD 575: *Russian collective works.* Friday polka; Variations; Birthday; Quartet on B-la-F. *Shostakovich Quartet.*
+ ARG 3-4/96: 225

26531. OCD 576: POPOV—Symphonies no. 1-2. *Moscow State Symphony Orch.; USSR Radio Symphony Orch.; Provatorov, cond.*
+ ARG 7-8/96: 169
+ Gr 2/96: 54

26532. OCD 577: SHEBALIN—Symphonies no. 1, 3. *USSR Radio Symphony Orch.; Ermler, Gergiev, conds.*
+ Gr 4/96: 54

26533. OCD 578 (2 discs): AMIROV—The Arabian nights; Symphony for strings; Shur. *Bolshoi Theater Orch.; Rzaev, cond.; Azerbajian Symphony Orch.; Rozhdestvensky, cond.; Moscow Radio Symphony Orch.; Abdullayev, cond.*
+ Gr 8/96: 40

26534. OCD 588: POPOV—Symphony no. 6 "Festive"; Chamber symphony, op. 2. *USSR Radio Symphony Orch.; Chivzhel, cond.; Moscow Chamber Ensemble; Korneyev, cond.*
+ Gr 7/96: 58

26535. OCD 606: SCHNITTKE—Film music. *USSR Cinematography Symphony; E. Khachaturian, cond.*
□ ARG 5-6/95: 165

26536. OCD 608: KANCHELI—Film music. *Georgia Symphony Orch.; Kakhidze, cond.; Cinematography Orch.; Skripka, cond.*
□ ARG 11-12/95: 141

26537. OCD 769: GORECKI— Lerchenmusik. LUTOSŁAWSKI—Dance preludes (1954 chamber orch. version). PROKOFIEV—Overture on Hebrew themes, op. 34. *Camerata Vistula.*
+ Gr 11/91: 86

OMEGA

26538. OCD 1001: *Elly Ameling sings Schubert at Tanglewood.* SCHUBERT— Songs. *Ameling, soprano; Jansen, piano.* Recorded live 1987.
+ ARG 7-8/89: 86
- Fa 5-6/89: 304
+ Gr 8/89: 356
+ NYT 5/14/89: H31

26539. OCD 1003: MOZART—Piano concertos no. 9, 23. *Meyer, piano; Norwegian Chamber Orch.; Brown, cond.*
• ARG 7-8/89: 65
• Fa 5-6/89: 241
+ Gr 8/89: 306
• NYT 5/14/89: H31

26540. OCD 1004: MOZART—Serenade no. 13; Symphony no. 29; Divertimentos K. 136, 138 . *Norwegian Chamber Orch.; Brown, cond.*
- ARG 7-8/89: 68
+ Fa 7-8/89: 202
+ Gr 8/89: 306
+ NYT 5/14/89: H31

26541. OCD 1005: SCHUBERT— Symphonies no. 5-6. *Australian Chamber Orch.; Mackerras, cond.*
• ARG 7-8/89: 87
• Fa 5-6/89: 309
• Gr 9/89: 476
+ NYT 5/14/89: H31

26542. OCD 1006: TELEMANN—Suites for flute and strings in A minor; for strings in G (Don Quichotte); Concerto for flute, violin, cello, and strings in A. *Milan, flute; Potter, cello; Friedman, violin & cond.; Camerata of St. James.*
+ ARG 5-6/89: 97
- Fa 5-6/89: 338
+ Gr 8/89: 314
+ NYT 5/14/89: H31

26543. OCD 1007: RESPIGHI—Ancient airs and dances suites 1-3; The birds. *Australian Chamber Orch.; Gee, cond.*
• ARG 7-8/89: 79
+ Fa 7-8/89: 263
+ Gr 8/89: 308
+ NYT 5/14/89: H31

26544. OCD 1008/9 (2 discs): BACH— Brandenburg concertos. *Academy of St. James; Pini, cond.*
+ Fa 7-8/92: 101

26545. OCD 1010: TCHAIKOVSKY— Serenade for strings op. 48; Souvenir de Florence op. 70. *Australian Chamber Orch.; Pini, cond.*
+ ARG 5-6/89: 95

OMEGA

+ Fa 7-8/89: 263
• Gr 8/89: 314
+ NYT 5/14/89: H31

26546. OCD 1011: STRAVINSKY—
Pulcinella. STRAUSS—Le bourgeois
gentilhomme suite. *Cullen, Edmonds,
Dickinson, vocals; Australian Chamber
Orch.; Gee, cond.*
+ ARG 11-12/89: 126
• Fa 7-8/89: 259
+ Gr 7/89: 186
+ NYT 5/14/89: H31

26547. OCD 1012: *Virtuoso Vivaldi.*
VIVALDI—Concertos RV 428, 495, 532,
537, 565; Sinfonia RV 149. *Camerata of
St. Andrew; Friedman, violin & cond.*
+ ARG 7-8/89: 104
+ Fa 5-6/89: 348
+ NYT 5/14/89: H31

26548. OCD 1013: VIVALDI—The four
seasons. BACH—Concerto for violin,
oboe, strings, and continuo, BWV 1060.
CORELLI—Concerto grosso, op. 6, no. 8.
*Waldman, violin; Brewer, oboe; Amor
Artis Orch. of New York; Somary, cond.*
+ DA 2/90: 58
• Fa 1-2/90: 337

26549. OCD 1016: PERGOLESI—La serva
padrona. VIVALDI—Flute concerto, RV
440. *Baird, soprano; Ostendorf, bass;
Berardi, flute; Philomel Baroque
Chamber Orch.; Palmer, cond.*
• ARG 11-12/91: 132
+ Fa 9-10/91: 310

26550. OCD 3001: JOPLIN—Rags.
Bolcom, piano.
+ ARG 3-4/92: 79

26551. OCD 3010: The Yiddish art song
(22 songs). *Lishner, bass; Weiner, piano.*
Reissue.
+ ARG 9-10/92: 206

26552. OCD 3016: Brasileirinho.
*Robison, flute; Lumbambo, Nasciento,
Silverman, guitars; Brandao,
cavanquinho; Baptista, percussion.*
+ ARG 9-10/93: 232

26553. OCD 3020: VIVALDI—Four
seasons. *Saint-Denis, flute; Rechtman,
computer.*
- ARG 1-2/94: 169

26554. OCD 5005—5006 (2 separate
discs): *Parlour favorites.* Songs by
Foster, Glover, Leslie, Watson, Molloy,
Harris, Harrison, and others. *Luxon,
bass-baritone; Willison, piano; Delmé
String Quartet; Davis, piano.*
+ ARG 9-10/91: 175
+ Fa 11-12/91: 531

ONDINE

26555. ODE 703-2: MERIKANTO—
Concerto for violin, clarinet, horn &
string sextet; Nonet; Viimeiselle; Seven

works for male choir. *Kagan, violin;
Brunner, clarinet; Jolley, ensembles;
Polytech Choir; Söderblom, Länsiö,
conds.*
+ Fa 7-8/89: 184

26556. ODE 704-2 (2 discs):
RAUTAVAARA—Thomas. *Rautawaara,
Lindroos, Hynninen; Savonlinna Opera
Festival Chorus; Joensuu City Orch.;
Haapasalo, cond.*
+ Fa 9-10/88: 233

26557. ODE 709-2: GRIEG—String
quartet op. 27. SCHUBERT—String quartet
no. 13. *Jean Sibelius Quartet.*
+ Fa 11-12/88: 254

26558. ODE 710-2: RAUTAVAARA—
Fiddlers op. 1; Icons, op. 6; Piano sonatas
no. 1-2; Etudes op. 42. *Tateno, piano.*
+ Fa 11-12/88: 253

26559. ODE 713-2: NORDGREN—String
quartets no. 4-5. *Kokkola Quartet.*
• Fa 11-12/88: 242

26560. ODE 714-2 (2 discs):
MADETOJA—Juha. *Lokka, Erkkilä,
Hynninen; Finnish Radio Youth Choir;
Finnish Radio Symphony Orch.; Jalas,
cond.* Recorded 1977.
+ Fa 11-12/88: 217
+ Gr 11/92: 184
+ ON 11/88: 65

26561. ODE 716-2: PROKOFIEV—Piano
sonatas no. 7-9. *Raekallio, piano.*
+ ARG 7-8/89: 85
+ Fa 7-8/89: 216

26562. ODE 717-2: Music of Strauss,
Sibelius, Schumann, and Rautio. *Rousi,
cello; Lagerspetz, piano.*
• ARG 11-12/89: 125
+ Fa 11-12/89: 374

26563. ODE 718-2: SCHUBERT—Piano
sonata in B♭ D. 960; 16 Deutsche Tänze
D. 783. *Gothóni, piano.*
- Fa 1-2/90: 297

26564. ODE 719-2: SCHUBERT—Die
schöne Müllerin. *Hynninen, baritone;
Gothóni, piano.*
• ARG 7-8/89: 85
- Fa 7-8/89: 239
+ MA 9/89: 76

26565. ODE 720-2: SIBELIUS—Two
pieces op. 2; Two pieces op. 77; Four
pieces op. 78; Six pieces op. 79; Sonatina
for violin and piano op. 80. *Arai, violin;
Heinonen, piano.*
+ ARG 9-10/89: 106
• Fa 7-8/89: 250

26566. ODE 721-2: Music of Angelbert,
Morel, Couperin, Boismotier, and
Leclair. *Les Goûts-Réünis.*
+ ARG 1-2/90: 117
+ Fa 11-12/89: 480

26567. ODE 723-2: DEBUSSY—Preludes
bk. 1. RAVEL—Sonatine; Jeux d'eau.
Viitasalo, piano.
+ Fa 7-8/89: 127

26568. ODE 724-2: MELARTIN—Three
pieces; The melancholy garden; Noll me
tangere; The silent forest; On high;
Fantasia apocaliptica. *Tateno, piano.*
+ Fa 7-8/89: 181

26569. ODE 725-2: SCHUBERT—
Winterreise. *Hynninen, baritone;
Gothóni, piano.*
+ Fa 9-10/89: 318

26570. ODE 726-2: ENGLUND—Violin
sonata. HEININEN—Violin sonata.
Saarikettu, violin; Viitasalo, piano.
+ ARG 7-8/90: 47
+ Fa 11-12/89: 204

26571. ODE 727-2: CRUSELL—Clarinet
quartets no. 1-3. *Kriikku, clarinet;
Members of Avanti Quartet.*
+ ARG 11-12/89: 53
+ Fa 11-12/89: 148
+ Gr 12/89: 1152

26572. ODE 728-2: SIBELIUS—Songs.
Auvinen, soprano; Djupsjöbacka, piano.
- ARG 3-4/90: 110
+ Au 12/89: 148
+ Fa 11-12/89: 362
+ NYT 8/20/89: H32

26573. ODE 729-2: PROKOFIEV—Piano
sonatas no. 1-3; Visions fugitives op. 22 .
Raekallio, piano.
+ ARG 11-12/90: 98
+ Fa 5-6/90: 252
+ Gr 5/90: 2014

26574. ODE 730-2: Music of Brouwer,
Donatoni, Koskelin, and Ginastera.
Korhonen, guitar.
+ ARG 7-8/90: 138
+ Fa 5-6/90: 379
+ Gr 8/90: 395

26575. ODE 731-2: Music of
Leoncavallo, Verdi, Tchaikovsky, and
Mozart. *Hynninen, baritone; Estonian
State Symphony Orch.; Klas, cond.*
• ARG 5-6/90: 148
• Fa 3-4/90: 354
+ Gr 4/90: 1871

26576. ODE 732-2: HAYDN—Piano
concertos H. XVIII:11; H. XVIII:F2. L.
HOFMANN (ATTRIB.)—Piano concerto in F.
Gothóni, piano; Finlandia Sinfonietta.
- Fa 5-6/90: 185

26577. ODE 733-2: TCHAIKOVSKY—
Souvenir d'un lieu cher; Sérénade
mélancolique; Valse-scherzo;
Humoresque; Andante funebre e doloroso
ma con moto. *Kagan, violin; Lovanov,
piano.*
+ Fa 5-6/90: 312

26578. ODE 734-2: SCHUBERT—Piano sonata in A minor D. 845; Fantasy in C D. 760 . *Gothóni, piano.*
- Fa 11-12/90: 345
- Gr 4/91: 1870

26579. ODE 735-2: Music of Corelli (arr. Geminiani), Vivaldi, and Farina. *Grindenko, violin; Moscow Chamber Academy.*
+ Fa 9-10/90: 217

26580. ODE 736-2: *Flauto dolce-flauto traverso.* Music of Loeillet, Handel, Boismortier, Quantz, and Telemann. *Sibelius Academy Baroque Ensemble.*
+ Fa 3-4/90: 389

26581. ODE 737-2: NORDGREN— Symphony for strings; Hate-love, for cello and strings; Transe-Choral, for strings. *Ylönen, cello; Ostrobothnian Chamber Orch.; Kangas, cond.*
+ Fa 1-2/91: 269

26582. ODE 738-2: SCHUMANN— Dichterliebe. BRAHMS—Vier ernste Gesänge. *Hynninen, baritone; Gothóni, piano.*
- ARG 1-2/91: 95 (Schumann)
+ ARG 1-2/91: 95 (Brahms)
+ Fa 11-12/90: 350
- Gr 10/90: 798
- NYT 1/31/91: H29

26583. ODE 739-2: Music of Heininen, Hakola, Kurtág, and Koskinen. *Avanti Quartet.*
+ Fa 9-10/90: 494

26584. ODE 740-2: RAUTAVAARA— Symphonies no. 1-3. *Leipzig Radio Symphony Orch.; Pommer, cond.*
+ ARG 11-12/90: 101
+ Fa 9-10/90: 349

26585. ODE 741-2: MENDELSSOHN— Symphonies no. 1; Youth symphony in D. *Queensland Phil. Orch.; Kuchar, cond.*
- ARG 9-10/90: 89
+ Fa 9-10/90: 294

26586. ODE 743-2: *Toki!* Music of Hämeenniemi, Heininen, Linjama, Kortekangas, and others. *Polytech Choir; Länsiö, cond.*
+ Fa 1-2/91: 377

26587. ODE 744-2: SHOSTAKOVICH—Piano trio no. 2 op. 67; Piano quintet op. 57. *Tchaikovsky Piano Trio; Kuhmo Chamber Soloists.*
- ARG 11-12/90: 117
+ Fa 11-12/90: 357

26588. ODE 745-2: SERMILÄ—Quatro rilievi; Contours; A Prague thoroughfare; Love-charm songs. *Komsi, soprano; Avanti Chamber Orch.; Pohjola, cond.*
- Fa 3-4/91: 381

26589. ODE 746-2: SCHUBERT—Violin sonatas (complete); Duo for violin and piano D. 574. *Chumachenko, violin; Gothóni, piano.*
+ ARG 11-12/91: 143
+ Fa 3-4/91: 366
+ Gr 7/91: 79

26590. ODE 747-2: RAUTAVAARA— Symphonies nos. 4-5; Cantus arcticus. *Leipzig Radio Symphony Orch.; Pommer, cond.*
□ ARG 7-8/91: 110
+ Fa 9-10/91: 320

26591. ODE 748-2: CHOPIN—Cello sonata. RACHMANINOFF—Cello sonata. *Rousi, cello; Lagerspetz, piano.*
+ ARG 3-4/92: 47
+ Fa 5-6/91: 156

26592. ODE 749-2: KORTEKANGAS— Grand Hotel; Memoria. *Saarinen, mezzo-soprano; Tiilikainen, baritone; Laurikainen, speaker; Ferchen, percussion; Children's voices; Finnish Chamber Choir; Tapiola Choir; Avanti Chamber Orch.; Pohjola, Söderström, conds.*
□ Fa 7-8/91: 188

26593. ODE 750-2 (2 discs): RAUTAVAARA—Vincent. *Rautavaara, Saarinen, Henkari, Hynninen, Putkonen; Finnish National Opera Chorus & Orch.; Manchurov, cond.*
+ Fa 5-6/91: 258

26594. ODE 751-2: ENGLUND— Symphonies no. 1-2. *Estonian State Symphony Orch.; Lilje, cond.*
- Fa 5-6/91: 166
+ Gr 8/92: 32

26595. ODE 752-2: *Sevilla.* Music of Tárrega, Torroba, and Albéniz. *Korhonen, guitar.*
+ Fa 9-10/91: 420

26596. ODE 753-2: MUSSORGSKY— Pictures at an exhibition. JANÁČEK—On an overgrown path. STRAVINSKY—Three movements from the Firebird. *Gothóni, piano.*
+ Fa 9-10/91: 302

26597. ODE 754-2: SIBELIUS—Cantatas. Oma maa, op. 92; Snöfrid; op. 29; Impromptu, op. 19; Vainön virsi, op. 110; Laulu Lemminkäiselle, op. 31, no. 1; Maan virsi, op. 95; Finlandia. *Finnish National Opera Orch. & Chorus; Klas, cond.*
+ ARG 9-10/91: 129
+ Fa 9-10/91: 358

26598. ODE 755-2: BRAHMS—Die schöne Magelone, op. 33. *Hynninen, baritone; Gothóni, piano.*
+ ARG 9-10/91: 53
- Fa 9-10/91: 177

26599. ODE 756-2: SIBELIUS—Complete works for violin and piano, vol. 2. *Arai, violin; Heinonen, piano.*
+ ARG 11-12/91: 147
- Fa 11-12/91: 486

26600. ODE 757-2: RAUTAVAARA—Piano concertos no. 1-2. *Gothóni, piano; Leipzig Radio Symphony; Pommer, cond.; Bavarian Radio Orch.; Saraste, cond.*
+ ARG 3-4/92: 123
+ Fa 11-12/91: 452

26601. ODE 759-2: SZYMANOWSKI— Complete works for violin and piano. *Koshkinen, violin; Lagerspetz, piano.*
+ ARG 11-12/91: 157
+ Fa 11-12/91: 500

26602. ODE 760-2: ZEMLINSKY—Trio for clarinet, cello and piano, op. 3. BRUCH—8 Pieces for clarinet, viola and piano, op. 83. *Kriikku, clarinet; Hirvikangas, viola; Rousi, cello; Satukangas, piano.*
- ARG 1-2/92: 142
+ Fa 11-12/91: 524

26603. ODE 761-2: PROKOFIEV—Piano sonatas no. 4-6. *Raekallio, piano.*
+ ARG 7-8/92: 200
+ Fa 11-12/91: 445
+ Gr 2/92: 63

26604. ODE 762-2: PROKOFIEV— Symphony no. 2; Summer night, op. 123; Autumn, op. 8. *Tampere Phil. Orch.; Grin, cond.*
+ ARG 11-12/91: 136
+ Fa 11-12/91: 441

26605. ODE 763-2: SCHUBERT—Adagio and rondo in F, D. 487; Trout quintet. *Gothóni, piano; Chumachenko, violin; Lysy, viola; Melhorn, cello; Laine, double bass.*
+ Fa 1-2/92: 317

26606. ODE 765-2: AHO—Symphonies no. 5, 7. *Leipzig Radio Symphony Orch.; Pommer, cond.*
+ Fa 11-12/91: 235

26607. ODE 766-2: *Folk into classic.* Music of Nordgren, Grieg, Lutosławski, Eller, and Tsintsadze. *Ostrobothnian Chamber Orch.; Kangas, cond.*
+ ARG 3-4/92: 170
+ Fa 1-2/92: 424

26608. ODE 767-2: *Hommage à Sibelius.* Works by Sibelius, Musgrave, Englund, Yuasa, Tüür, Picker, Josephs, Constant and Ruders. *Helsinki Phil. Orch.; Comissiona, cond.*
- ARG 7-8/92: 248
+ Fa 3-4/92: 424
+ Gr 4/92: 90

26609. ODE 768-2: *Dilbèr: Coloratura arias.* Works by Bellini, Verdi, Meyerbeer, Delibes, Donizetti, R. Strauss, and J. Strauss, Jr. *Dilbèr,*

ONDINE

soprano; Estonia Theater Orch.; Klas, cond.
  + ARG 5-6/92: 186
  + Fa 3-4/92: 368
  + Gr 9/92: 164
  + ON 3/14/92: 34

26610. ODE 769-2: PROKOFIEV—Waltz suite, op. 110; Pushkin waltzes; A summer day. *Tampere Phil. Orch.; Grin, cond.*
  - ARG 5-6/92: 110
  + Fa 3-4/92: 289

26611. ODE 770-2: PONCE—Sonatina meridional; Thème varié et final; Sonata III; Variations on La folia. *Korhonen, guitar.*
  + ARG 9-10/92: 142
  + Fa 5-6/92: 223
  + Gr 7/92: 78

26612. ODE 771-2: WEILL—Kleine Dreigroschenmusik; Concerto for violin and wind orchestra; Vom Tod im Wald. *Wächter, violin; Möwes, bass; Leipzig Radio Symphony Orch.; Pommer, cond.*
  + ARG 7-8/92: 243
  • Fa 5-6/92: 286
  + Gr 8/92: 42

26613. ODE 772-2: KILPINEN—Spielmannslieder; Lieder um den Tod; Lakeus; Von Zwehl songs. *Hynninen, baritone; Gothóni, piano.*
  + ARG 7-8/92: 156
  + Fa 5-6/92: 183
  + Gr 11/92: 168

26614. ODE 773-2: SIBELIUS—String quartets in A minor and D minor. *Jean Sibelius Quartet.*
  + Fa 5-6/92: 256
  + Gr 8/92: 47

26615. ODE 774-2: BERGMAN—Concertino da camera; Triumf att finnas till; Lament and incantation; Silence and eruptions. *Various performers.*
  + ARG 7-8/92: 98
  + Fa 5-6/92: 126

26616. ODE 775-2: SHOSTAKOVICH—Symphony no. 8. *Helsinki Phil. Orch.; De Preist, cond.*
  - Fa 7-8/92: 283
  • Gr 10/92: 119

26617. ODE 776-2 (2 discs): TUBIN—Barbara von Tisenhusen. *Raamat, Kollo, Puura, Millberg; Estonia Opera Co.; Lilje, cond.*
  + ARG 9-10/92: 176
  + Fa 7-8/92: 314
  + Gr 4/93: 120
  + ON 4/15/95: 36
  • Op 8/92: 997

26618. ODE 777-2: LISZT—Six etudes after Paganini. FRIEDMAN—Studies on a theme of Paganini. BRAHMS—Paganini variations. *Raekallio, piano.*
  + ARG 7-8/92: 108

  + Fa 7-8/92: 201
  + Gr 8/92: 54

26619. ODE 778-2: DEBUSSY—Rhapsody for clarinet. TIENSUU—Clarinet concerto "Puro." KAIPANEN—Clarinet concerto "Carpe diem!". *Kriikku, clarinet; Finnish Radio Symphony Orch.; Avanti Chamber Orch.; Saraste, cond.*
  + Fa 9-10/92: 222
  + Gr 10/92: 58

26620. ODE 779-2: BRITTEN—Songs from the Chinese; Nocturnal; Five folksongs. BERKELEY—Theme and variations; Sonatina; Songs of the half-light. *Partridge, tenor; Savijoki, guitar.*
  + ARG 11-12/92: 98
  + Fa 11-12/92: 211
  + Gr 1/93: 47

26621. ODE 780-2 (3 discs): SALLINEN—Kullervo. *Saarinen, Jakobsson, Hynninen, Salminen; Finnish National Opera; Söderblom, cond.*
  + ARG 7-8/92: 210
  + Fa 7-8/92: 266
  + Gr 8/92: 71
  + ON 6/92: 49
  + Op 8/93: 1004

26622. ODE 781-2: PIAZZOLLA—Histoire du tango; Cinco piezas; Six etudes tanguistiques. *Helasvuo, flute; Savijoki, guitar.*
  + ARG 3-4/93: 123
  + Gr 12/92: 97

26623. ODE 782-2: TCHAIKOVSKY—Seasons (arr. A. Gauk); Hamlet; Four entr'actes. *Tampere Philh. Orch.; Grin, cond.*
  + ARG 11-12/92: 218
  • Fa 11-12/92: 385

26624. ODE 783-2 (2 discs): TUBIN—The parson of Reigi; Requiem for fallen soldiers. *Vocal soloists; Estonia Opera; Mägi, cond.; Estonian National Male Choir; Klas, cond.*
  + ARG 1-2/93: 160
  + Fa 11-12/92: 392
  + Gr 1/93: 64

26625. ODE 784-2: LINDBERG—Kinetics; Marea; Joy. *Bavarian Radio Orch.; Avanti Chamber Orch.; Saraste, cond.*
  + Fa 3-4/93: 205

26626. ODE 786-2: *Dreams.* Music of Bergman, Johansson, Sallinen, Rautavaara, and Kortekangas. *Tapiola Chamber Choir & Sinfonietta; Pohjola, cond.*
  + Fa 3-4/93: 356

26627. ODE 788-2: FRANCK—Solo de concert for piano and string quintet; Quintet in F minor for piano and string quartet. *Kuhmo Chamber Soloists.*
  + ARG 7-8/93: 90
  + Fa 3-4/93: 164

26628. ODE 789-2: ENESCO—Sonatas for violin and piano no. 2-3. *Csaba, violin; Satukangas, piano.*
  • Fa 3-4/93: 159

26629. ODE 790-2: RAITIO—Fantasia poetica; Fantasia estatica; The swans; The column fountain; Antigone. *Finnish Radio Symphony Orch.; Saraste, cond.*
  + ARG 7-8/93: 140
  + Fa 5-6/93: 287

26630. ODE 791-2: SAARIAHO—Maa. *Various instrumentalists; Tuomela, cond.*
  + Fa 5-6/93: 307

26631. ODE 792-2: KAIPANEN—Stärnenatten. MERILÄINEN—Metamorfora per 7. KLAMI—Rag-time and blues. NIELSEN—Serenata in vano. R. STRAUSS-HASENÖHRL—Till Eulenspiegel: einmal anders! *Mattila, soprano; Lahti Chamber Ensemble; Vänskä, cond.*
  + ARG 7-8/93: 108
  + Fa 3-4/93: 205
  + Gr 8/93: 78

26632. ODE 794-2 (2 discs): BERGMAN—The singing tree. *Lindroos, Hellekant, Hannula, Salomaa; Finnish National Opera; Söderblom, cond.*
  □ ARG 7-8/93: 66
  + Fa 9-10/93: 125
  + Gr 5/93: 103
  + ON 5/93: 52
  + Op 8/93: 1004

26633. ODE 796-2: *Verbum.* Music of Länsiö, Kortekangas, Kyllönen, Saariaho, and Heiniö. *Tapiola Chamber Choir; Söderström, cond.*
  + ARG 9-10/93: 252
  • Fa 7-8/93: 286

26634. ODE 797-2: SCHUBERT—Piano sonatas D. 840, D. 537. *Gothóni, piano.*
  + ARG 9-10/93: 184
  + Fa 7-8/93: 235
  + Gr 1/95: 81

26635. ODE 798-2: *Opera arias.* Music of Bizet, Verdi, Giordano, Puccini, and Leoncavallo. *Sirkiä, tenor; Slovak Radio Symphony Orch.; Lehtinen, cond.*
  - Fa 7-8/93: 281
  - ON 2/5/94: 39

26636. ODE 799-2: MELARTIN—Symphonies no. 5-6. *Tampere Phil. Orch.; Grin, cond.*
  + ARG 1-2/94: 122
  + Fa 11-12/93: 318

26637. ODE 800-2: SCHNITTKE—Violin sonatas no. 1-2; Suite in the old style. *Lubotsky, violin; Gothóni, piano.*
  + Gr 4/94: 64

26638. ODE 801-2: HAYDN—Symphonies no. 92 "Oxford"; no. 99. *Finnish Chamber Orch.; Berglund, cond.*
  - ARG 11-12/93: 124
  + Fa 11-12/93: 271

26639. ODE 802-2: IBERT—Flute concerto. JOLIVET—Flute concerto; Suite en concert. NIELSEN—Flute concerto. *Alanko, flute; Finnish Radio Symphony Orch.; Saraste, cond.; Avanti Chamber Orch.; Pulakka, cond.*
  + Gr 11/93: 70

26640. ODE 803-2: Jorma Hynninen: evergreen love songs. *Hynninen, baritone; Sarmanto, piano.*
  + Fa 11-12/93: 469

26641. ODE 804-2: SAARIAHO—Du cristal ... à la fumée; Nymphea. *Los Angeles Phil. Orch.; Salonen, cond.; Alanko, flute; Karttunen, cello; Kronos Quartet.*
  + Fa 9-10/93: 260
  + Gr 10/93: 50

26642. ODE 805-2: SIBELIUS—Complete works for mixed chorus a cappella. *Jubilate Choir; Riska, cond.*
  + ARG 3-4/94: 158
  + Fa 1-2/94: 314

26643. ODE 806-2: BARTÓK—Sonata for 2 pianos and percussion. BERGMAN—Borealis. STRAVINSKY—Sonata for 2 pianos. *Raekallio, Lagerspetz, pianos; Ferchen, Erkkilä, percussion.*
  + ARG 3-4/94: 71
  + Fa 1-2/94: 120

26644. ODE 807-2: PROKOFIEV—Violin sonatas no. 1-2; Solo violin sonata; Five melodies. *Grubert, violin; Raekallio, piano.*
  • ARG 5-6/94: 124

26645. ODE 808-2: Chamber music of Maros, Kaipainen, Svensson, Maerilainen, Bergman, and Saariaho. *Cluster Ensemble.*
  + ARG 5-6/94: 173

26646. ODE 810-2: MENDELSSOHN—Concerto for violin, piano, and string orchestra. HAYDN—Concerto for violin, piano, and string orchestra. *Csaba, violin; Gothóni, piano; Virtuosi di Kuhmo.*
  + Fa 3-4/95: 228
  + Gr 1/95: 44

26647. ODE 813-2: SIBELIUS—The tempest (complete version). *Groop, Vilijankainen, Hynninen, Silvasti, Tiilikainen; Finnish Radio Symphony Orch.; Opera Festival Chorus; Saraste, cond.*
  + Fa 11-12/94: 384

26648. ODE 815-2: *Invitation to the dance.* Music of Weber, Gimenez, Klami, Ziehrer, J. Strauss, and others. *Finnish Opera Orch.*
  • ARG 7-8/94: 199

26649. ODE 817-2: SHOSTAKOVICH—Symphony no. 5; Chamber symphony op. 110a. *Helsinki Phil. Orch.; De Preist, cond.*

  • ARG 1-2/95: 179
  • Gr 12/94: 94

26650. ODE 818-2: RUBINSTEIN—Piano concerto no. 4. MOSZKOWSKI—Piano concerto. *Raekallio, piano; Tampere Phil. Orch.; Grin, cond.*
  - ARG 11-12/94: 179
  • Fa 11-12/94: 358
  • Gr 2/95: 54

26651. ODE 819-2: RAUTAVAARA—Symphony no. 6; Cello concerto. *Ylönen, cello; Helsinki Phil. Orch.; Pommer, cond.*
  + ARG 11-12/94: 172
  + Fa 11-12/94: 351

26652. ODE 820-2: MENDELSSOHN—Concert pieces. WEBER—Clarinet quintet; Grand duo concertant. *Kriikku, clarinet; New Helsinki Quartet; Linkola, basset horn; Satukangas, piano.*
  + ARG 3-4/95: 139

26653. ODE 821-2: RAUTAVAARA—Music for chamber orchestra. *Ostrobothnian Chamber Orch.; Kangas, cond.*
  + ARG 5-6/95: 156
  + Fa 7-8/95: 286

26654. ODE 822-2: MELARTIN—Symphonies no. 2, 4. *Tampere Phil. Orch.; Grin, cond.*
  + ARG 3-4/95: 137
  + Fa 3-4/95: 227
  + Gr 12/94: 88

26655. ODE 823-2: SIBELIUS—Songs with orchestra. *Hynninen, baritone; Tampere Phil. Orch.; Segerstam, cond.*
  + ARG 11-12/94: 190

26656. ODE 824-2: *Scandinavian rhapsody.* Music of Sinding, Bull, Svendsen, Grieg, Alfvén, Nielsen, Lumbye, Melartin, Aaltoila, Kaski, Merikanto, Järnefelt, and Sibelius. *Palola, violin; Höylä, cello; Helsinki Phil. Orch.; Segerstam, cond.*
  + ARG 3-4/95: 226
  + Fa 3-4/95: 399

26657. ODE 825-2: BRITTEN—Piano concerto, op. 23; Soirées musicales; Matinées musicales. *Gothóni, piano; Helsingborg Symphony Orch.; Kamu, cond.*
  + ARG 3-4/95: 82
  + Fa 3-4/95: 143
  + Gr 1/95: 42

26658. ODE 826-2: SIBELIUS—*Early chamber music, vol. 1.* Violin sonata; Suite for string trio; String trio; Quartet for piano, 2 violins, and cello. *Kovacic, Söderblom, Quarta, Miori, violins; Angervo, viola; Gustafsson, Rousi, cellos; Lagerspetz, Novikov, pianos.*
  + ARG 7-8/95: 196
  + Fa 7-8/95: 322
  + Gr 6/95: 71

26659. ODE 827-2: SZYMANOWSKI—Cello sonata, op. 9. KODÁLY—Cello sonata, op. 4. SCHNITTKE—Cello sonata. *Gustafsson, cello; Kärkkäinen, piano.*
  + ARG 7-8/95: 184
  + Fa 7-8/95: 337

26660. ODE 829-2: KANCHELI—Symphonies no. 1, 4-5. *Helsinki Phil. Orch.; De Preist, cond.*
  + ARG 1-2/96: 128
  + Fa 11-12/95: 286
  + Gr 7/96: 52

26661. ODE 830-2: SIBELIUS—Works for string orchestra. *Csaba, violin & cond.; Virtuosi di Kuhmo.*
  • ARG 5-6/95: 178
  + Fa 5-6/95: 344

26662. ODE 831-2: SALLINEN—String quartets no. 1-5. *Jean Sibelius Quartet.*
  + ARG 11-12/95: 189
  + Fa 9-10/95: 303
  + Gr 12/95: 108

26663. ODE 832-2: GOTHÓNI—Der Ochs und sein Hirte. *Isokoski, soprano; Hynninen, baritone; Söderblom, violin; Angervo, viola; Gustafsson, Ylönen, cellos; Kärkkäinen, piano; Gothóni, cond.*
  + ARG 7-8/95: 116
  + Fa 7-8/95: 195
  + Gr 9/95: 88

26664. ODE 833-2: ENGLUND—Symphonies no. 3, 7. *Tampere Phil. Orch.; Rasilainen, cond.*
  + ARG 11-12/95: 115
  + Fa 11-12/95: 180

26665. ODE 834-2: *A night at the opera.* Music of Busoni, Gluck, Horowitz, Liszt, and Wagner. *Raekallio, piano.*
  • ARG 7-8/95: 250
  + Fa 7-8/95: 426

26666. ODE 835-2: HÄMEENNIEMI—Symphonies no. 1-2; Violin concerto. *H. Segerstam, violin; Finnish Radio Symphony Orch.; Saraste, cond.*
  + ARG 9-10/95: 302
  + Fa 7-8/95: 196

26667. ODE 836-2: RAUTAVAARA—Complete works for string orchestra, vol. 2. *Ostrobothnian Chamber Orch.; Kangas, cond.*
  + ARG 5-6/96: 172
  + Fa 1-2/96: 282
  + Fa 3-4/96: 256

26668. ODE 837-2: *Works for guitar, vol. 1.* VILLA-LOBOS—Introduction to choros; Guitar concerto; Twelve etudes. *Korhonen, guitar; Finnish Radio Symphony Orch.; Oramo, cond.*
  + Fa 11-12/95: 223
  • Gr 2/96: 60

26669. ODE 838-2: VILLA-LOBOS—Five preludes for guitar; Sextuor mystique;

ONDINE

Distribuçáo de flôres; Serestas: Modinha; Bachianas brasileiras no. 5: Aria; Suite populaire brésilienne; Choros no. 1. *Korhonen, guitar; Freund, soprano; Mansnerus, flute; Valjakka, oboe; Lehtonen, saxophone; Laivuori, celesta; Kuusimäki, harp.*
+ Fa 7-8/96: 334
• Gr 8/96: 68

26670. ODE 839-2: TAKEMITSU—Works for flute and guitar. *Helasvuo, flute; Savijoki, guitar; Palviainen, lute; Ferchen, percussion.*
+ Fa 7-8/95: 339

26671. ODE 840-2: STRAUSS—Piano quartet, op. 13. MAHLER (COMPLETED SCHNITTKE)—Piano quartet in A minor. *Gothóni, piano; Lubotsky, violin; Hirvikangas, viola; Rousi, cello.*
+ ARG 9-10/95: 222
+ Fa 9-10/95: 328

26672. ODE 841-2: MELARTIN— Symphonies no. 1, 3. *Tampere Phil. Orch.; Grin, cond.*
+ ARG 3-4/96: 153
+ Fa 11-12/95: 302

26673. ODE 842-2: RAUTAVAARA— Sammon ryöstö (The myth of the Sampo). *Nyman, tenor; Tiilikainen, baritone; Suhonen, bass-baritone; P. Hyökki, Rautavaara, narrator; Helsinki University Chorus; M. Hyökki, cond.*
+ Fa 11-12/95: 340
+ Gr 12/95: 131

26674. ODE 843-2: BRAHMS—Piano quartets no. 1, 3. *Gothóni, piano; Csaba, violin; Hilvikangas, viola; Helmerson, cello.*
+ ARG 1-2/97: 80
+ Gr 10/96: 71

26675. ODE 844-2: SALLINEN—Songs of life and death; The iron age. *Hynninen, baritone; Paupen, soprano; East Helsinki Music Institute Choir; Opera Festival Chorus; Helsinki Phil. Orch.; Kamu, cond.*
+ ARG 5-6/96: 182
+ Fa 1-2/96: 290
+ Gr 12/95: 132

26676. ODE 845-2: SHOSTAKOVICH— Symphony no. 14; Adagio and allegretto. *Haverinen, soprano; Salomaa, bass; Tapiola Sinfonietta; Swensen, cond.*
+ ARG 7-8/96: 198
+ Fa 7-8/96: 305
+ Gr 4/96: 54

26677. ODE 846-2: SHOSTAKOVICH— Symphonies no. 9, 12. *Helsinki Phil. Orch.; De Preist, cond.*
+ ARG 11-12/96: 210
• Gr 2/97: 58

26678. ODE 847-2: SIBELIUS—Piano music. *Gothóni, piano.*

+ ARG 1-2/96: 175
+ Fa 5-6/96: 279

26679. ODE 850-2: SIBELIUS—Early chamber music, vol. 2. *Kuusisto, violin; Kerppo, Lagerspetz, piano; Jean Sibelius Quartet.*
+ ARG 5-6/96: 199
+ Fa 1-2/96: 307
+ Fa 5-6/96: 277

26680. ODE 851-2: RAUTAVAARA—Choral works. *Finnish Radio Chamber Choir; Söderström, cond.*
+ ARG 7-8/96: 176
+ Fa 7-8/96: 270
+ Gr 6/96: 85

26681. ODE 852-2: SIBELIUS—Four legends from the Kalevala; Tapiola. *Helsinki Phil. Orch.; Segerstam, cond.*
+ ARG 11-12/96: 212
• Fa 11-12/96: 381
• Fi 11/96: 124
+ Gr 7/96: 64

26682. ODE 854-2: KLAMI—Symphony no. 1; King Lear overture. *Tampere Phil. Orch.; Ollila, cond.*
+ ARG 7-8/96: 142
+ Fa 5-6/96: 185
+ Gr 3/96: 46

26683. ODE 855-2: KAIPAINEN— Symphony no. 2; Oboe concerto; Sisyphus dreams. *Jahren, oboe; Finnish Radio Symphony Orch.; Oramo, cond.*
+ ARG 7-8/96: 140
+ Fa 5-6/96: 180
+ Gr 3/96: 46

26684. ODE 856-2: SIBELIUS—Songs. *Mattila, soprano; Ranta, piano.*
• ARG 9-10/96: 204
• Fa 5-6/96: 280
• Gr 4/96: 96
+ ON 8/96: 42

26685. ODE 858-2: KLAMI—Symphony no. 2; Symphonie enfantine. *Tampere Phil. Orch.; Ollila, cond.*
+ ARG 1-2/97: 127
+ Fa 11-12/96: 279
+ Gr 9/96: 54

26686. ODE 859-2: KLAMI—The adventures of Lemminkäinen on the Island of Saari; The cobblers on the heath overture; Karelian rhapsody; Karelian market place; In the belly of Vilpunen. *Lindroos, baritone; Polytech Male Choir; Finnish Radio Orch.; Oramo, cond.*
+ ARG 3-4/96: 137
+ Fa 11-12/95: 287

26687. ODE 861-2: PROKOFIEV—Sinfonia concertante for cello and orchestra. A. MERIKANTO—Cello concerto no. 2. *Gustafsson, cello; Finnish Radio Symphony Orch.; Oramo, cond.*
+ ARG 1-2/96: 142
+ Fa 11-12/95: 333
+ Fi 4/96: 124

26688. ODE 863-2: *Finnish orchestral favourites.* Music of Kaski, Melartin, Sibelius, Raitio, Rautavaara, and Klami. *Various Finnish orchs. & conds.* Reissue.
+ Fa 11-12/95: 500

26689. ODE 865-2 : *Society of Finnish Composers.* Music of Merilainen, Heino, Jokinen, and Kokkonen. *Avanti!*
+ ARG 9-10/96: 235

26690. ODE 866-2 : *Society of Finnish Composers.* Music of Puumala, Kortekangas, Koskinen, Tuomela, and others. *Avanti!*
+ ARG 9-10/96: 235

26691. ODE 867-2: Music of Heininen, Rautavaara, Vuori, and Berman. *Finnish Radio Symphony; Saraste, Salonen, Segerstam, conds.*
+ ARG 9-10/96: 233

26692. ODE 868-2: KURTÁG—Kafka fragments. *Komsi, soprano; Oramo, violin.*
+ Fa 1-2/97: 189
+ Gr 11/96: 153

26693. ODE 869-2: RAUTAVAARA—Angel of light; Annunciations. *Jussila, organ; Helsinki Phil.; Segerstam, cond.*
+ ARG 9-10/96: 186
+ Gr 6/96: 54

26694. ODE 870-2: HEINIÖ—Hermes; In G. *Ostrobothnian Chamber Orch.; Kangas, cond.; Lagerspetz, piano; Nylund, soprano; Rantamäki, cello.*
□ ARG 3-4/97: 154
+ Fa 11-12/96: 269

26695. ODE 871-2: SIBELIUS—Karelia suite; En Saga; Pohjola's daughter; Valse triste; Finlandia. *Tampere Phil. Orch.; Ollila, cond.*
+ ARG 1-2/97: 172
+ Fa 1-2/97: 273

26696. ODE 872-2 (2 discs): A. MERIKANTO—Juha. *Hynninen, Saarinen, Sirkiä, Nisula, Wirkkala, Lehtinen; Tapiola Chamber Choir; Finnish Chamber Singers; Finnish Radio Orch.; Saraste, cond.*
+ ARG 11-12/96: 162
+ Fa 11-12/96: 306
+ Gr 8/96: 93

26697. ODE 873-2: NORDGREN—Violin concerto no. 4; Cronaca. *Storgårds, violin & cond.; Wegelius Chamber Orch.*
+ ARG 1-2/97: 147
+ Fa 1-2/97: 218
+ Gr 5/97: 64

26698. ODE 874-2: Memoria Sancti Henrici. *Cetus Noster; Köyhät Ritarit.*
+ Fa 9-10/96: 395

26699. ODE 877-2: SEGERSTAM— Symphony no. 18; Epitaph no. 6; Impressions of Nordic nature no. 4;

Flowerbouquette no. 43E. *H. Segerstam, violin; P. Segerstam, cello; Danish National Radio Symphony Orch.; Malmö Symphony Orch.; Finnish Radio Symphony Orch.; L. Segerstam, cond.*
+ ARG 1-2/97: 168
+ Fa 11-12/96: 373

26700. ODE 878-2: SIBELIUS—Violin concerto, op. 47; Karelia suite; Belshazzar's feast: suite. *Kuusisto, violin; Helsinki Phil. Orch.; Segerstam, cond.*
+ ARG 11-12/96: 211
• Fa 9-10/96: 325
+ Gr 5/96: 64

ONE-ELEVEN

26701. URS-50050, 50060, 50080 (3 separate discs): Ricci: The making of a legend, vol. 1-3. *Ricci, violin; with orchestral & piano accompaniment.* Principally reissues.
+ Fa 5-6/92: 330

26702. URS-50090: *The great violinist series: Kreisler, Prihoda.* Music of Bizet, Hubbell, Krakauer, Paderewski, Dawes, Logan, Winternitz, Granados, Tartini, Dvořák, and Sarasate. *Kreisler, Prihoda, violins; various acc.*
+ Fa 5-6/93: 387

26703. URS-50100: *The great violinist series: Ysaÿe, Prihoda, Ricci.* Music of Vieuxtemps, Fauré, Wagner, Dvořák, Ysaÿe, Schubert, Kreisler, Wieniawski, Chabrier, Brahms, Smetana, Mattheson, and Rachmaninoff. *Ysaÿe, Prihoda, Ricci, violins; piano acc.*
+ Fa 5-6/93: 388

26704. URS-50110: *Ricci: the making of a legend, vol. 4.* Music of Bach, Paganini, Dont, Wieniawski, and Paganini. *Ricci, violin; other instrumentalists.*
+ Fa 5-6/93: 388

26705. URS-50140: *The great violinist series: Milstein, Oistrakh.* Music of Goldmark, Mozart, and Bach. *Milstein, Oistrakh, violins; New York Phil. Orch.; Walter, Mitropoulos, conds.*
+ Fa 5-6/93: 388

26706. URS-90010: CHOPIN—Nocturnes. *Ricci, violin; Wilhelmsen, piano.*
+ ARG 3-4/94: 84

26707. URS-90033 (2 discs): SIBELIUS—Violin and piano pieces, op. 2, 78, 79, 80, 81, 102, 106, 115, 115. BACH—Solo violin sonata no. 3. HINDEMITH—Solo violin sonata. YSAŸE—Solo violin sonata no. 3. PAGANINI—Duo merveille; Variations on God save the queen. *Ricci, violin; Rabinoff, piano.* Recorded live 1978.
+ ARG 5-6/92: 136

26708. URS-91020: GINASTERA—Violin concerto. PAGANINI—Violin concerto no.

1. *Ricci, violin; Orquesta de las Americas; Herrera de la Fuente, cond.*
+ ARG 3-4/92: 62
+ Fa 1-2/92: 156

26709. URS-91030: BARTÓK—Violin concerto no. 2. PAGANINI—Violin concerto no. 4. *Ricci, violin; New Hungarian Phil.; Hlask, cond.; Virtuosi d'Assisi; Mordini, cond.*
+ Fa 1-2/92: 156

26710. URS-91040: MOZART—Violin concerto no. 3. LALO—Symphonie espagnole. *Ricci, violin; Budapest Chamber Ensemble; Stassevitch, cond.; RFO Symphony Orch.; Hoffman, cond.*
+ Fa 1-2/92: 156

26711. URS-92010: *Ricci and colleagues in concert.* Music of Shostakovich, Schubert, Spohr and Wieniawski. *Ricci, violin; other instrumentalists.*
+ Fa 5-6/93: 388

26712. URS-92020: BEETHOVEN—Violin sonata no. 1. BARTÓK—Sonata for solo violin. PAGANINI—Caprices for solo violin, op. 1, no. 13-24; Caprice in E "Adieu". *Ricci, violin; Constantino, piano.* Recorded live.
- Fa 11-12/93: 179
+ Fa 3-4/94: 417

26713. URS-92030: CORELLI—Sonatas for violin and continuo, op. 5, no. 8-12. BACH—Partita no. 2 for solo violin, BWV 1004. *Ricci, violin; Keyes, harpsichord; Nesbitt, viola da gamba.*
+ Fa 5-6/93: 188

26714. URS-92033 (2 discs): *Ricci: for the love of the violin: celebrating six decades on stage.* Music of Bach, Bartók, Hindemith, Prokofiev, Paganini, Kreisler, and Tarrega. *Ricci, violin.* Recorded live.
+ ARG 3-4/94: 219
+ Fa 11-12/93: 503

26715. URS-93010—93040 (4 separate discs): Ricci: portrait of an artist, vol. 1-4. *Ricci, violin; assisting instrumentalists.*
+ ARG 3-4/94: 219
+ Fa 11-12/93: 501

26716. URS-93050: *Ricci—Portrait of an artist, vol. 5.* Music of Tartini, Beethoven, R. Strauss, and Ysaÿe. *Ricci, violin; Gilliam, Rados, piano.* Recorded live.
+ Fa 3-4/94: 417

26717. URS-93060: *Ricci—Portrait of an artist, vol. 6.* Music of Flury, Bach, Ysaÿe, Wieniawski, Sarasate, Bartók, and Chopin. *Ricci, violin; Humphries, Davies, violin; Brown, Wilhelmsen, piano.* Recorded live.
+ ARG 3-4/94: 219
+ Fa 3-4/94: 417

26718. URS-93070: PAGANINI—Homage to Paganini . *Ricci, violin; Cardi, guitar.*

+ ARG 5-6/94: 119
+ Fa 3-4/94: 265

ONGAKU

26719. 024-101: *Cohler on clarinet.* Music of Brahms, Weber, Bärmann, and Sargon. *Cohler, clarinet; Gordon, piano.*
+ ARG 9-10/93: 232
+ Fa 7-8/93: 29
+ Gr 11/94: 1042

26720. 024-102: Music of Brahms, Poulenc, Schumann, Milhaud, and Stravinsky. *Cohler, clarinet; Hodgkinson, piano.*
+ ARG 7-8/94: 206
+ Fa 7-8/94: 310
+ Gr 11/94: 104

26721. 024-103: Music of Ysaÿe, Hindemith, Prokofiev, Martinon, and Barkauskas. *Kaler, violin.*
+ ARG 3-4/96: 238
+ Fa 7-8/96: 385
+ Fi 4/96: 131

26722. 024-104: KHUDOYAN—Sonatas for 1 and 2 cellos. CRUMB—Sonata. HINDEMITH—Sonata. *Bagratuni, Khoma, cellos.*
- ARG 5-6/96: 232
+ Fa 7-8/96: 386

26723. 024-105: *The clarinet alone.* Music of Martino, Wellesz, Messiaen, Von Koch, W.O. Smith, Persichetti, W. Osborne, and Paganini. *Cohler, clarinet.*
+ ARG 5-6/96: 234
+ Fa 7-8/96: 386

26724. 024-106: Music of Ravel, Debussy, Fauré, and Satie. *Okada, piano.*
- ARG 5-6/96: 240
+ Fa 7-8/96: 379

26725. 024-107: BACH—Goldberg variations. *Schepkin, piano.*
+ ARG 3-4/96: 84
+ Fa 7-8/96: 90

ONYX

26726. CD 101/103 (3 discs): FIELD—Piano concertos (complete). *O'Conor, piano; New Irish Chamber Orch.; Fürst, cond.*
• ARG 3-4/91: 64
+ Fa 3-4/91: 211

26727. CD 104: LISZT—Transcriptions of works by Liszt, Bach, Beethoven, Chopin, Schumann and Wagner. *Wild, piano.*
+ Fa 3-4/92: 230

OPAL

26728. 832 (LP): *Complete published recordings.* Music of Berlioz, Boccherini, Chopin, Gluck, Mendelssohn, and Schumann. *Planté, piano.*

OPAL

□ ARG 1-2/88: 77
+ Fa 1-2/88: 260

26729. CD 9810 : ELGAR—Dream of
Gerontius: Excerpts. *Balfour, Wilson,
Heyner; Royal Choral Society; Royal
Albert Hall Orch.; Elgar, cond.* Recorded
1927.
　+ ARG 3-4/90: 47
　+ Fa 5-6/90: 163

26730. CD 9823: *Alessandro Moreschi:
The complete recordings.* Music of
Aldega, Pratesi, Tosti, Meluzzi, Stehle,
Mozart, Rossini, Liebach, Terziani, Bach,
Capocci, Vittoria, Palestrina, Calzanera,
and Anon. *Moreschi, castrato; Choir of
the Sistine Chapel.*
　□ ARG 1-2/88: 77
　+ Fa 1-2/88: 244

26731. CD 9836: *His complete published
piano solos.* Music of Scarlatti, Handel,
Chopin, Mendelssohn, Liszt, Weber,
Massenet, Chabrier, Pugno, Saint-Saëns,
and Bizet. *Pugno, piano; Gay, alto.*
　+ Fa 1-2/90: 385

26732. CD 9840: Music of Chopin, Raff,
Schumann, and Liszt. *De Pachmann,
piano.*
　+ ARG 11-12/89: 161
　+ Fa 7-8/89: 124

26733. CD 9843 (2 discs): WAGNER—
Parsifal: Excerpts; Siegfried Idyll. *Pistor,
Hofmann, Brongeest; various orchs. &
conds.*
　+ Fa 1-2/90: 342
　+ Gr 4/90: 1886
　+ NYT 11/12/89: H34

26734. CD 9844: *Song recital.* Music of
Vaughan Williams, Quilter, White, Peel,
and others. *Elwes, tenor; Kiddle, piano;
London String Quartet.*
　+ ARG 9-10/90: 147
　+ Fa 9-10/90: 463

26735. CD 9848: Chime again, beautiful
bells: The historic countertenor. *Eight
countertenors; with various
accompaniments.*
　• ARG 3-4/92: 217
　□ Fa 3-4/92: 383

26736. CD 9851: Joseph Joachim: the
complete recordings (1903); Pablo de
Sarasate: the complete recordings (1904);
Eugène Ysaÿe: a selection of his
recordings (1912). *Joachim, Sarasate,
Ysaÿe, violin; with piano accomp.*
　+ Fa 11-12/92: 449

26737. CD 9852: *Maria Barrientos:
Fonotipia recordings 1905-06; Columbia
Electrical Recordings 1928.* Music of
Handel, Mozart, Auber, Bellini,
Meyerbeer, Thomas, Delibes, Grieg,
Caballero, Chapi, Hernandez, and Falla.
*Barrientos, soprano; Falla, piano; other
unidentified pianists.*
　• Fa 3-4/93: 336

OPEN LOOP

26738. 007: *Vintage flora.* Music of
Maurice, Lunde, Schumann, Husa and
Creston. *Klock, alto saxophone; Shank,
piano.*
　+ ARG 7-8/92: 270
　+ Fa 5-6/92: 324

26739. 018: Music of Ricker, Yasinitzky,
Koch, Young, and others. *Banaszak,
saxophone; Casey, piano.*
　□ ARG 5-6/96: 279

26740. 019: Music of Hartley, Debussy,
Vivaldi, Weiner, and others. *Mauk,
saxophone; Covert, piano.*
　+ ARG 5-6/96: 279

26741. 021: *Chant corse.* Music of
Tansman, Ben-Haim, Bozza, Telemann,
Hartley, Tomasi, and Macchia. *Klock,
saxophone; Shank, piano.*
　+ ARG 5-6/96: 234

OPEN SKY

26742. OSR 5500 (LP): KOSINS—The
walrus and the carpenter; The owl and the
pussy cat; The land where dreams are
made; The happy prince . *Swit, J. & K.
Carradine, narrators; chorus; chamber
ensemble.*
　+ Fa 5-6/87: 146

OPEN SPACE

26743. 1: BORETZ—My chart chines
high... RANDALL—Such words as it were
vain to close. *Rothenberg, Randall,
piano.*
　□ ARG 11-12/93: 81

26744. 2 (4 discs): BORETZ—One. *Boretz,
piano.*
　□ ARG 11-12/93: 81

OPENING DAY

26745. ODR 9301: *Opening day.* Music
of Tiefenbach, Schafer, Irvine, and
Forsyth. *Laughton, trumpet, flugelhorn,
& cornet; Humphreys, soprano & Celtic
harp; Tiefenbach, organ & piano.*
　• Fa 11-12/96: 424

26746. ODR 9302: SCHUBERT—
Schwanengesang; other songs. *Lichti,
bass-baritone; Fialkowska, piano.*
　+ ARG 3-4/96: 178
　• Fa 7-8/96: 291

26747. ODR 9303: *Baroque banquet.*
Music of Susato, Franceschini, Bach,
Handel, Scarlatti, Telemann, and Clarke.
*Laughton, trumpet & cornetto; O'Meara,
organ; Humphreys, soprano; Lichti,
bass-baritone; Campion, percussion.*
　- Fa 7-8/96: 390

26748. ODR 9305: SZYMANOWSKI—Piano
music. *Fialkowska, piano.*

　+ ARG 9-10/96: 213
　+ Fa 7-8/96: 320

OPERA RARA

26749. ORC 1 (3 discs): DONIZETTI—Ugo,
conti di Parigi. *Jones, Harrhy, Kenny,
Arthur; Philharmonia Orch.; Francis,
cond.* Reissue.
　+ ARG 11-12/94: 102

26750. ORC 2 (2 discs): OFFENBACH—
Christopher Columbus. *Arthur; other
vocalists; Geoffrey Mitchell Choir;
London Mozart Players; Francis, cond.*
Reissue.
　+ ARG 11-12/94: 165
　+ Fa 7-8/93: 197
　+ Gr 4/93: 119

26751. ORC 3 (2 discs): DONIZETTI—
Gabriella di Vergy. *Andrew, Du Plessis,
Arthur Tomlinson; Royal Phil. Orch.;
Francis, cond.* Reissue.
　+ ARG 11-12/94: 102
　+ Fa 3-4/94: 175
　• Gr 9/94: 111

26752. ORC 4: DONIZETTI—Ne m'oubliez
pas; Arias. *Elkins, Oliver, Du Plessis;
Philharmonia Orch.; Judd, cond.*
Reissue.
　+ ARG 9-10/94: 123
　+ ARG 11-12/94: 102
　+ Fa 9-10/94: 182
　+ Gr 9/94: 111
　+ Op 6/94: 762

26753. ORC 5 (3 discs): MEYERBEER—
Dinorah. *Cook, Oliver, Jones, Du Plessis,
Hill Smith, Earle, Caley; Geoffrey
Mitchell Choir; Philharmonia Orch.;
Judd, cond.* Reissue.
　+ ARG 11-12/94: 157
　+ Fa 1-2/94: 239
　• Gr 4/94: 98

26754. ORC 6 (3 discs): DONIZETTI—
Maria Padilla. *Vocal soloists; Geoffrey
Mitchell Choir; London Symphony Orch.;
Francis, cond.*
　+ ARG 11-12/94: 102
　+ Fa 1-2/93: 143
　+ Gr 2/93: 74
　+ Op 11/92: 1371

26755. ORC 7 (2 discs): OFFENBACH—
Robinson Crusoe. *Brecknock, Kenny,
Browne; other soloists; Geoffrey Mitchell
Choir; Royal Phil. Orch.; Francis, cond.*
　+ ARG 11-12/94: 165
　+ Fa 9-10/94: 280
　+ Gr 8/94: 104

26756. ORC 8 (3 discs): DONIZETTI—
Emilia di Liverpool; L'Eremitaggio di
Liverpool. *Kenny, Bruscantini, Merritt,
Dolton; Geoffrey Mitchell Choir;
Philharmonia Orch.; Parry, cond.* Also
issued as LPs: OR 8.
　+ ARG 11-12/94: 102
　+ Fa 11-12/91: 312
　+ Fa 3-4/89: 148 (LP)

+ Gr 6/88: 72 (LP)
+ ON 6/89: 46 (LP)
+ Op 9/88: 1142 (LP)
+ OQ Winter/88-89: 137 (LP)

26757. OR 9 (2 discs): DONIZETTI—
L'assedio di Calais. *Focile, Jones,
Harrhy, Plessis; Geoffrey Mitchell Choir;
Philharmonia Orch.; Parry, cond.*
+ ARG 11-12/94: 102
+ Fa 9-10/89: 187
+ Gr 7/89: 230
+ ON 2/17/90: 38
+ Op 8/89: 1017

26758. ORC 10 (4 discs): MEYERBEER—Il
crociato in Egitto. *Kenny, Montague,
Jones, Ford, Platt; Geoffrey Mitchell
Choir; Royal Phil. Orch.; Perry, cond.*
+ ARG 11-12/94: 156
+ Fa 11-12/92: 204
+ Gr 9/92: 161
+ ON 10/92: 45
+ Op 10/92: 1258

26759. ORC 11 (3 discs): MAYR—Medea
in Corinto. *Eaglen, Kenny, Miles, Ford;
Philharmonia Orch.; Parry, cond.*
Recorded 1993.
+ ARG 9-10/94: 160
+ Gr 11/94: 145
+ ON 4/15/95: 35
+ Op 9/94: 1130

26760. ORC 12 (3 discs): MERCADANTE—
Orazi e Curiazio. *Miricioiu, Jerome,
Michaels-Moore, Miles; Geoffrey
Mitchell Choir; Philharmonia Orch.;
Parry, cond.*
+ ARG 1-2/96: 142
+ Gr 12/95: 144

26761. ORC 103 (3 discs): *A hundred
years of Italian opera: 1810-1820.* Music
of Pucitta, Generali, Mosca, Manfroce,
Mayr, Garcia, Pacini, Pavesi, Coccia,
Morlacchi, Meyerbeer, Weber, Winter,
Donizetti, Mercadante and Carafa. *Vocal
soloists; Philharmonia Orch.; Parry,
cond.*
+ ARG 11-12/95: 274
+ Fa 11-12/92: 411

26762. ORC 104 (3 discs): *100 years of
Italian opera: 1820-30.* Music of
Balducci, Bellini, Coccia, Mayr, and
others. *Various performers.*
+ ARG 11-12/95: 274
+ Gr 8/95: 130

26763. ORC 201: Arias by Nicolini,
Meyerbeer, Donizetti, Coccia, Portogallo
and Carafa. *Kenny, soprano;
Philharmonia Orch.; Parry, cond.*
+ ARG 11-12/94: 251
+ Op 1/95: 123

OPERA TRES

26764. 1002: SECO—Piano music.
Narejos, piano.
+ ARG 9-10/95: 212

26765. 1003 (2 discs): TARREGA—Guitar
music (complete). *Russell, guitar.*
+ ARG 1-2/96: 185

26766. 1006: Music of Praetorius,
Dowland, Frescobaldi, Weiss, and Bach.
Girollet, guitar.
• ARG 11-12/95: 250

26767. 1007: Music of Sor, Giuliani,
Tarrega, and Mertz. *Marcotulli, guitar.*
+ ARG 11-12/95: 209

26768. 1008 (2 discs): SOR—Guitar duets.
Ros, Ferrer, guitars.
+ ARG 11-12/95: 209

26769. 1010: Guitar sonatas by Espla,
Brouwer, Bardwell, and Ginastera.
Rodes, guitar.
+ ARG 1-2/96: 214

26770. 1011: VIVALDI—Lute concertos.
*Marcotulli, guitar; Orch. Internazionale
d'Italia; Serenelli, cond.*
+ ARG 11-12/95: 225

26771. 1012: FERNÁNDEZ ALVEZ—Guitar
music. *Estarellas, guitar.*
• ARG 9-10/95: 92

26772. 1013 (2 discs): MORENO
TORROBA—Guitar music. *Escarpa,
Trapaga, Viloria, Blanco, guitars.*
+ ARG 1-2/96: 145

26773. 1015: Music of Pujol, Llobet, and
Mompou. *Socias, guitar.*
+ ARG 9-10/95: 260

26774. 1016: Music of Falla, Santorsola,
Gangi, and Civitareale. *Tordini, Prats,
guitars.*
• ARG 1-2/96: 214

26775. 1018: KLEYNJANS—Guitar music.
*Kleynjans, Chagnot, Fernández; Antares
Quartet.*
• ARG 7-8/96: 143

26776. 1019: BARRIOS—Guitar music.
Estarellas, guitar.
□ ARG 11-12/96: 87

OPHELIA

26777. OP 67103: POULENC—Sonata for
violin and piano. SAUGUET—Sonate
crepusculaire. *Perez, violin; Vakarelis,
piano.*
+ Fa 7-8/87: 161

26778. OP 67104: MENDELSSOHN—Three
caprices op. 33; Andante, Op. 16 no. 3;
Andante and variations op. 82; Piano
sonata op. 105. *Leconte, piano.*
- Fa 9-10/88: 197

26779. OP 67105: BRAHMS—Piano
quartet no. 1 op. 25. *Gothóni, piano;
Munich String Trio.*
+ Fa 5-6/88: 92

26780. OP 67106: HAYDN—Great organ
mass; Missa Sancti Nicolai. *Soloists; St.
Augustin Church, Vienna Choir & Orch.*
• ARG 9-10/88: 51
+ Fa 9-10/88: 165

26781. OP 67107: BRAHMS—Piano
quartet no. 2 op. 26. *Gothóni, piano;
Munich String Trio.*
+ Fa 9-10/88: 119

26782. OP 67108: SCHUBERT—Mass no. 4
D. 324; Deutsche Messe D. 872.
MOZART—Vesperae Solennes de
Confessore, K. 339: Laudate Dominum;
Ave verum corpus K. 618. *St. Augustin
Church, Vienna Choir & Orch.; Wolf,
cond.*
+ Fa 1-2/89: 258

OPUS

26783. 9150 0969: GIULIANI—Guitar
concerto op. 30. RODRIGO—Concierto de
Aranjuez. *Zsapka, guitar; Slovak
Chamber Orch.; Warchal, cond.*
• Fa 11-12/88: 188

26784. 9150 1457: SAINT-SAËNS—
Carnival of the animals. POULENC—
Concerto for 2 pianos in D minor.
*Toperczer, Lapsanský, pianos; Slovak
Phil. Orch.; Režucha, Košler, conds.*
- Fa 11-12/88: 265

26785. 9150 1991—9150 1993 (3
separate discs): HAYDN—Symphonies no.
82-87. *Slovak Phil. Orch.; Pešek, cond.*
• Fa 5-6/89: 216

26786. 9150 1996/97 (2 discs):
DVOŘÁK—The water goblin; The midday
witch; The golden spinning wheel; The
wild dove; A hero's song; Symphonic
variations op. 78. *Slovak Phil. Orch.;
Košler, cond.*
• Fa 3-4/89: 155
+ HF 1/89: 68

26787. 9151 1096: HAYDN—Sinfonia
concertante H. 1: 105. PLEYEL—Sinfonia
concertante no. 5. *Slovak Chamber
Orch.; Warchal, cond.*
+ ARG 5-6/90: 88
+ Fa 7-8/90: 167

26788. 9151 1358: VIVALDI—Flute
concertos op. 10. *Stivín, recorders;
Slovak Chamber Orch.; Warchal, cond.*
• Fa 11-12/88: 308

26789. 9151 1437: ZMESKAL—String
quartets in G, in G minor. *Trávniček
Quartet.*
+ Fa 1-2/91: 356

26790. 9151 2116/17 (2 discs): Music of
Pachelbel, Zimmermann, Valeri, Stanley,
and others. *Klinda, organ; Slovak
Chamber Orch.; Warchal, cond.*
• Fa 3-4/91: 483

OPUS

26791. 9156 0931/32 (2 discs): Puccini—La bohème. *Kincses, Haljaková, Dvorský, Konsulov; National Theater Opera House Chorus; Bratislava Radio Symphony Orch.; Lenárd, cond.*
- Fa 9-10/88: 227 m.f.
• On 8/88: 42

26792. 9350 1364: Gershwin—Piano concerto in F. Addinsell—Warsaw concerto. *Cattarino, piano; Slovak Phil. Orch.; Režucha, cond.*
• Fa 11-12/88: 187

26793. 9350 1618: C.P.E. Bach—Harpsichord concertos Wq. 31, 33. *Cattarino, harpsichord; Slovak Chamber Orch.; Warchal, cond.*
+ ARG 1-2/92: 21
+ Fa 3-4/89: 66

26794. 9350 1668/69 (2 discs): Bach—Orchestra suites. *Slovak Chamber Orch.; Warchal, cond.*
+ Fa 9-10/88: 85

26795. 9350 1684: Saint-Saëns—Piano concerto no. 2. Françaix—Concertino for piano and orchestra. Roussel—Piano concerto, op. 36. *Čápová, piano; Slovak Phil. Orch.; Režucha, Frešo, conds.*
- Fa 9-10/88: 242

26796. 9350 1710: Trumpet concertos by Albinoni, Baldassare, Molter and Torelli. *Touvron, trumpet; Slovak Chamber Orch.; Warchal, cond.*
+ Gr 9/91: 76

26797. 9350 1773: Britten—Simple symphony. Janáček—Suite for strings. Suchon—Serenade for strings, op. 5. *Slovak Chamber Orch.; Warchal, cond.*
+ Fa 9-10/88: 122

26798. 9350 1774: Cello concertos of Vivaldi, Tartini, and Boccherini (arr. Grutzmacher). *Podhoránský, cello; Slovak Chamber Orch.; Warchal, cond.*
+ Fa 9-10/88: 294

26799. 9350 1812: Music of Stamitz, F. Benda, and F.X. Richter. *Slovak Chamber Orch.; Warchal, cond.*
+ Fa 9-10/88: 269

26800. 9350 1844: Respighi—Trittico botticelliano. Martinů—Sinfonia La jolla. *Singerová, piano; State Chamber Orch. of Žilina; Valta, cond.*
+ ARG 1-2/91: 81
• Fa 1-2/91: 288 (Respighi)
+ Fa 1-2/91: 288 (Martinů)
+ Gr 8/90: 368

26801. 9350 1845: Trumpet concertos of Böhme, Molter, Ponchielli, and Perry. *Ghitalla, trumpet & flugelhorn; Slovak Phil. Orch.; Cappella Istropolitana; Perry, cond.*
+ ARG 9-10/88: 113
• Fa 11-12/88: 344

26802. 9350 1851-4 (4 discs): Schmidt—Symphonies no. 1-4. *Bratislava Symphony Orch.; Rajter, cond.*
+ ARG 11-12/88: 77
• Fa 3-4/88: 183
- Fa 9-10/88: 245
+ Gr 2/88: 1199

26803. 9350 1885: Corrette—Organ concertos op. 26. *Michalko, organ; Warchal, violin & cond.; Slovak Chamber Orch.*
+ ARG 7-8/90: 41
• Fa 7-8/90: 126

26804. 9350 1977/78 (2 discs): Corelli—Concerto grossi op.6. *Warchal, violin & cond.; Tedla, violin; Alexander, cello; Slovak Chamber Orch.*
+ Fa 11-12/88: 166

26805. 9350 2000: Music of Ernst, Sarasate, Zimbalist, and Wieniawski. *Han-Gorski, violin; Slovak Phil. Orch.; Szostak, Režucha, conds.*
+ ARG 9-10/90: 146

26806. 9350 2004: Haydn—Cello concertos H. VIIb: 1-2. *Noras, cello; Slovak Chamber Orch.; Warchal, cond.*
+ Fa 1-2/89: 176

26807. 9350 2012: Cikker—Slovak suite; Memories; Variations on a Slovak folk song. *Bratislava Radio Symphony Orch.; Lenárd, cond.*
□ ARG 1-2/90: 41
+ Fa 1-2/91: 180
+ Gr 4/91: 1824

26808. 9350 2050: Music of Ibert, Griffes, Nielsen, and Perry. *Bryan, flute; Bratislava Radio Symphony Orch.; Chen, cond.*
+ Fa 1-2/91: 394

26809. 9350 2114: Nielsen—Czech and Danish folk melodies; At the grave of a young artist. J.P.E. Hartmann—Character pieces, no. 1-3. Hamerik—Symphony no. 6. *Slovak Chamber Orch.; Warchal, cond.*
+ ARG 1-2/91: 129
+ Fa 1-2/91: 400

26810. 9351 1458: *Famous guitar compositions.* Music of Ponce, Lauro, Savio, Villa-Lobos, Falla, and others. *Zsapka, guitar.*
+ Fa 1-2/89: 340

26811. 9351 1720: Hindemith—Horn sonata; Waldhorn sonata; Sonata for 4 horns. *Z. & B. Tylšar, Divoký, Havlik, horns; Toperczer, piano.*
+ Fa 9-10/88: 168

26812. 9351 1755: Janáček—String quartets (complete). *Trávniček Quartet.*
+ Fa 3-4/89: 193

26813. 9351 1758: Bach—Flute sonatas BWV 1030-1032, 1034-1035. *Jurkovic,*

flute; Růžičková, harpsichord; Alexander, cello.
• Fa 11-12/88: 122

26814. 9351 1908: Bartók—Sonata for 2 pianos & percussion; Piano concerto no. 3. *Toperczer, Lapsanský, pianos; Mazáček, Svoboda, percussion; Slovak Phil. Orch.; Slatkin, cond.*
- Fa 9-10/88: 96

26815. 9351 1960: Dvořák—Slavonic dances op. 46, 72. *Toperczer, Lapsanský, pianos.*
• Fa 9-10/88: 145

26816. 9351 2020: Messiaen—Organ music. *Klinda, organ.*
- Fa 3-4/89: 212
- Gr 6/89: 65

26817. 9351 2025: Shostakovich—String quartets no. 3, 8. *Moyzes String Quartet.*
+ Fa 3-4/91: 385

26818. 9351 2034: Gluck—Trio sonatas no. 1-8. *Šimčisko, Plaskurová, violins; Alexander, cello; Dobiásaová, harpsichord.*
- Fa 1-2/91: 202
+ Gr 10/91: 124

26819. 9351 2035: Debussy—String quartet. Ravel—String quartet. *Trávniček Quartet.*
• ARG 9-10/90: 60
• DA 2/91: 60
+ Fa 9-10/90: 224 (Debussy)
• Fa 9-10/90: 224 (Ravel)

26820. 9351 2049: Dvořák—String quartets no. 10, 12. *Trávniček Quartet.*
+ ARG 9-10/90: 62
+ DA 1/91: 78
+ Fa 9-10/90: 232

26821. 9351 2063: *Bonjour, monsieur.* Music of Piazzolla, Almeida, Martincek, Ravel, and others. *Szapková- Sebestová, flute; Zsapka, guitar.*
+ ARG 11-12/90: 150

26822. 9351 2130: Franck—Choral no. 2; Pastorale; Pièce héroïque; Prélude, fugue et variations; Cantabile. *Michalko, organ.*
- Fa 7-8/90: 145
• Gr 6/90: 83

26823. 9352 1719: Patzelt—Castor et Pollux. Speer—Musicalisch Türkischer Eulen-Spiegel: Excerpts. *Zajíčková, Saparova, Oswald, Mikulaš; Musica Aeterna; Baxa, cond.*
+ Fa 3-4/91: 320

26824. 9352 1795: Capricornus—Opus musicum: Excerpts. *Prague Madrigal Singers; Janys, cond.*
• Fa 9-10/88: 125

26825. 9352 1816: Music of Schumann, Brahms, and Strauss. *Hajóssyová,*

soprano; Lapsanský, piano.
- Fa 11-12/88: 274

26826. 9352 1830: SUCHON—Nox et solitudo; Ad astra; Look into the unknown; Three songs on poems by Valek, Stillcha and Smrek. *Hajóssyová, soprano; Blahušiaková, mezzo-soprano; Dvorský, tenor; Kopčák, bass; various orchs. and conds.*
+ Fa 1-2/91: 329

26827. 9352 1887: MAHLER—Frühlingsmorgen; Phantasie; Starke Einbildungskraft; Scheiden und Meiden; Selbstgefühl; Liebst du um Schönheit; Blicke mir nicht in die Lieder; Um Mitternacht. A. MAHLER—Laue Sommernacht; Ich wandle unter Blumen; Anstrum; Hymne; Ekstase; Der Erkennende; Lobgesang; Hymne an die Nacht. *Hajóssyová, soprano; Lapsanský, piano.*
- Fa 1-2/91: 232
• Gr 8/90: 400

26828. 9356 1860: Music of Mussorgsky, Borodin, Glinka, Tchaikovsky, and others. *Kopčák, bass; Brno Janáček Opera Chorus; Brno State Phil. Orch.; Vronsky, cond.*
• Fa 1-2/89: 314

26829. 9356 1928/29 (2 discs): BELLINI—La sonnambula. *Valášková, Antilocova, Kundlak, Mikulaš; Slovak Phil. Choir; Bratislava Symphony Orch.; Lenárd, cond.*
• Fa 1-2/89: 127
• ON 2/18/89: 43
• OQ Summer/89: 33

26830. 9356 2023: Music of Mozart, Donizetti, Verdi, Tchaikovsky, and others. *Mikulaš, bass; Slovak Phil. Choir; Radio Bratislava Symphony Orch.; Frešo, cond.*
+ Fa 11-12/88: 324

OPUS 111

26831. OPS 30-62: D. CASTELLO—Sonate concertate in stil moderno (1621, 1629). *Europa Galante.*
• Fa 7-8/95: 149

26832. OPS 30-66: A. SCARLATTI—Lamentazioni per la Settimana Santa. *Rime, Lins, sopranos; Parlement de Musique; Gester, cond.*
+ Gr 8/93: 72

26833. OPS 30-67: ROMBERG—Das Lied von der Glocke. *Schlick, Georg, Lang, Lika, Mertens; Chorus Musicus Köln; Das Neue Orch.; Spering, cond.*
• Gr 7/93: 81

26834. OPS 30-68: Codex Las Huelgas. *Discantus; B. Lesne, cond.*
+ Fa 5-6/94: 307
+ Gr 8/93: 77

26835. OPS 30-69: BROSSARD—Elevation and motets; Dialogus. *Rime, Fouchécourt, Honeyman, Deletré; Parlement de Musique; Gester, cond.*
• Gr 9/93: 97

26836. OPS 30-70: ROSSINI—Péchés de vieillesse, books 2-3. *Vocalists; Chorus Musicus Köln; Spering, cond. & harmonium.*
+ Gr 7/93: 81

26837. OPS 30-72/73 (2 discs) BACH—St. Matthew passion (arr. Mendelssohn). *Kazimierczuk, Browner, Jochens, Schäfer, Lika; Chorus Musicus; Neue Orch.; Spering, cond.*
+ Gr 9/93: 94

26838. OPS 30-75/76 (2 discs): A. SCARLATTI—Cain overo il primo omicidio. *Concerto Italiano; Europa Galante; Biondi, cond.*
• Fa 7-8/95: 298

26839. OPS 30-77: SCHUMANN—Violin sonatas no. 1-2. C. SCHUMANN — Romances for violin and piano. *Biondi, violin; Ilio, piano.*
• Fa 7-8/95: 314

26840. OPS 30-78: *Chant mystique byzantin.* The divine liturgy of St. John Chrysostom. *Greek Byzantine Choir; Angelopoulos, cond.*
+ Fa 7-8/95: 410

26841. OPS 30-79: BORTNYANSKY—Te Deum; 17th century Russian liturgical chant. *Moscow Patriarchal Choir; Grindenko, cond.*
+ Fa 7-8/95: 410
+ Gr 4/94: 79

26842. OPS 30-80: HASSE—Requiem in C; Miserere. *Reyghere, Hase, Honeyman, Snellings; Il Fondamento Orch. & Chorus; Dombrecht, cond.*
+ Gr 11/93: 128

26843. OPS 30-81: MONTEVERDI—Madrigals, book 4. *Concerto Italiano; Alessandrini, cond.*
- ARG 1-2/94: 125
+ Fa 1-2/94: 241
+ Gr 12/93: 106

26844. OPS 30-82: BOCCHERINI—String quintets. *L'Europa Galante.*
+ Fa 7-8/95: 126

26845. OPS 30-83: CHOPIN—Piano sonata no. 2; Etudes, op. 25. *Sokolov, piano.*
+ Gr 1/94: 75

26846. OPS 30-84: BACH—Goldberg variations. *Hantaï, harpsichord.*
+ Fa 9-10/94: 126
+ Gr 4/94: 69

26847. OPS 30-86: VIVALDI—Violin concertos RV 133, 281, 286, 407, 511, 531, 541. *Europa galante; Biondi, violin*

& cond.
+ ARG 1-2/94: 170
+ Fa 1-2/94: 344
+ Gr 6/94: 66

26848. OPS 30-88: PERGOLESI—Salve Reginas. LEO—Salve Regina. GALLO—Trio sonatas. *Schlick, soprano; Europa Galante; Biondi, cond.*
+ Fa 5-6/95: 285
+ Gr 4/94: 87

26849. OPS 30-89: LE SUEUR—Oratorios for the coronation of the sovereign princes of Christendom. *Chorus Musicus; Neue Orch.; Spering, cond.*
+ ARG 1-2/94: 117
+ Fa 1-2/94: 223
- Gr 10/94: 174

26850. OPS 30-93: *L'ultime Liszt.* LISZT—Piano music. *Pochtar, piano.*
- ARG 1-2/94: 119
+ Fa 1-2/94: 227

26851. OPS 30-94: LASSUS—Villanelle, moresche e altre canzone. *Concerto Italiano; Alessandrini, cond.*
+ ARG 7-8/95: 139
+ Fa 7-8/95: 221
+ Gr 10/95: 108

26852. OPS 30-95: *The poet-violinist.* Music of Biber, Tartini, Benda, Fiorillo, Rode, and Prokofiev. *Biondi, violin.*
+ Fa 5-6/95: 419

26853. OPS 30-96: A. SCARLATTI—Il trionfo della grazia. *Piccollo, Bertini, Banditelli, Europa Galante; Biondi, cond.*
+ Fa 5-6/95: 317
• Gr 10/94: 184

26854. OPS 30-97: *Panikhida.* Orthodox requiem. *Russian Patriarchate Choir; Grindenko, cond.*
+ Fa 7-8/95: 410

26855. OPS 30-98: MENDELSSOHN—Symphony no. 2. *Isokoski, Bach, Lang; Cologne Chorus Musicus; Neue Orchester; Spering, cond.*
+ Fa 5-6/95: 263
+ Gr 9/94: 56

26856. OPS 30-99: CAPRICORNUS—Theatrum musicum (excerpts); Scelta musicale (excerpts); Leider des Leyden: O Traurigkeit. ROSENMÜLLER—Also hat Gott die Welt geliebet. BRIEGEL—Singet dem Herrn ein neues Lied. *La Palement de Musique; Gester, cond.*
+ Fa 5-6/95: 164

26857. OPS 30-100: HASSE—Solo motets and Marian antiphons. *Zanetti, soprano; Lane, alto; Le Parlement de Musique; Gester, cond.*
+ Fa 7-8/95: 200
• Gr 1/95: 84

26858. OPS 30-101: CICONIA—Vocal and instrumental works. *Alla Francesca;*

Ensemble Alta.
- ARG 1-2/95: 96
+ Fa 5-6/95: 175
- Gr 9/94: 87

26859. OPS 30-102: *Campus stellae.*
Saint-Martial de Limoges and Santiago
de Compostela. *Discantus; Lesne, cond.*
+ ARG 1-2/95: 233
+ Fa 5-6/95: 397
+ Gr 7/95: 109

26860. OPS 30-103: Brahms—Piano
sonata no. 3; Ballades, op. 10. *Sokolov,
piano.* Recorded live 1993.
+ ARG 5-6/95: 93
+ Fa 5-6/95: 149
+ Gr 3/95: 71

26861. OPS 30-104: Locatelli—Concerti
grossi; Sinfonia. *Europa Galante; Biondi,
cond.*
+ ARG 7-8/95: 145
+ Fa 9-10/95: 250
● Gr 1/96: 54

26862. OPS 30-105 (2 discs):
Frescobaldi—Arie musicale (1630):
primo e secondo libro (complete).
Concerto Italiano; Alessandrini, cond.
+ Fa 5-6/95: 192

26863. OPS 30-109: Ohana—Avoaha;
Lys de Madrigaux. *Choeur contemporain
d'Aix-en-Provence; Ensemble vocal
Musicatreize; Hayrabedian, cond.*
+ Fa 5-6/95: 281

26864. OPS 30-110: *Romantic choral
music from Russia.* Music of
Tchesnokov, Tchaikovsky, Gretchaninov,
Tcherepnin, Popov-Platonov, Tolstyakov,
Strokin, Kalinnikov, and Martynov.
*Russian Patriarchate Choir; Grindenko,
cond.*
+ ARG 5-6/95: 225
+ Fa 7-8/95: 400

26865. OPS 30-111: Monteverdi—
Madrigals, book 2. *Concerto Italiano;
Alessandrini, cond.*
+ ARG 7-8/95: 157
+ EM 5/96: 358
+ Fa 5-6/95: 265
+ Gr 8/95: 117

26866. OPS 30-112: *Landini and his
contemporaries.* Music of Landini,
Giovanni da Firenze, Magister
Guglielmus, Lorenzo Masi, Donato da
Firenze, Gherardello de Florentia, and
Anon. *Micrologus Ensemble.*
+ ARG 7-8/95: 256
● EM 2/96: 177
+ Fa 5-6/95: 402

26867. OPS 30-113/115 (3 discs):
Handel—Poro, rè dell'Indie. *Banditelli,
Bertini, Fink, Naglia, Lesne,
Abbondanza; Europa Galante; Biondi,
cond.*
● ARG 7-8/95: 120
● EM 8/96: 523

+ Fa 5-6/95: 202
● Gr 11/94: 145
+ ON 9/95: 55

26868. OPS 30-116: Cherubini—
Requiem in C minor; Marche funèbre; In
paradisum. *Chorus Musicus Köln; Das
Neue Orch.; Spering, cond.*
● Fa 5-6/95: 171
+ Gr 2/95: 83

26869. OPS 30-117: Marenzio—
Madrigals for four voices, book 1.
Concerto Italiano; Alessandrini, cond.
+ Fa 5-6/95: 256
+ Gr 10/94: 174

26870. OPS 30-118: *150 anni di musica
italiana (1550-1700). Vol. 1: cembalo.*
Music of Valente, Facoli, De Maque,
Mayone, Trabaci, Picchi, Del Buono,
Frescobaldi, Lambardo, Merula, M.
Rossi, Salvatore, B. Storace, G. Strozzi,
Stradella, and A. Scarlatti. *Alessandrini,
harpsichord.*
+ Fa 5-6/95: 403
+ Gr 4/95: 94

26871. OPS 30-119: *150 years of Italian
music, vol. 2: organ.* Music of A.
Gabrieli, Merulo, Luzzaschi, G. Gabrieli,
Macque, Pasquini, Trabaci, Frescobaldi,
Merula, Salvatore, Strozzi, Picchi, and
Storace. *Alessandrini, organ.*
+ Fa 9-10/95: 385

26872. OPS 30-120: *Russian medieval
chant.* The divine liturgy of St. John
Chrysostom. *Russian Patriarchate
Choir; Grindenko, cond.*
+ Fa 7-8/95: 410

26873. OPS 30-121: Haydn—English and
Scottish songs. *Lawson, soprano;
Tverskaya, fortepiano; Podger, violin;
Kogan, cello.*
+ Fa 7-8/95: 202
+ Gr 5/95: 92

26874. OPS 30-122: *Lucente stella.*
Music of Machaut, Shinohara, and Anon.
*Hamon, recorders; Wright, Yammine,
assisting musicians.*
+ Fa 3-4/96: 379

26875. OPS 30-123: Rossini—Petite
messe solenelle. *Parès-Reyna, Sippola,
Dewald, Lika, vocalists; Chorus Musicus
Köln; Verdin, harmonium; Kalvelage,
piano; Spering, cond.*
+ Fa 7-8/95: 294
● Gr 6/95: 95

26876. OPS 30-125: *150 years of Italian
music (1550-1700), vol. 3: organ and
harpsichord.* Music of Pasquini, Fasolo,
B. Storace, Merula, Soncino, Frescobaldi,
G. Strozzi, Picchi, M. Rossi, Salvatore,
and Banchieri. *Alessandrini, organ &
harpsichord.*
+ Fa 3-4/96: 349

26877. OPS 30-126: Schubert—Violin
sonatas, D. 384, 385, 408, 574. *Biondi,
violin; Tverskaya, fortepiano.*
+ Fa 1-2/96: 299
+ Gr 10/95: 88

26878. OPS 30-127/28 (2 discs): Bach—
Violin sonatas, BWV 1014-19. *Biondi,
violin; Alessandrini, harpsichord.*
+ ARG 11-12/96: 85
- Fa 9-10/96: 137
+ Gr 7/96: 69

26879. OPS 30-129: A. Scarlatti—
Humanità e Lucifero. Corelli—Trio
sonatas. *Bertini, Crispi; Europa Galante;
Biondi, cond.*
+ ARG 5-6/96: 183
● EM 8/96: 520
+ Fa 5-6/96: 256
+ Gr 3/96: 90

26880. OPS 30-130: *The Barcelona
mass, The song of the sibyl.* Music of
Alfonso el Sabio and Anon. *Obsidienne
vocal ensemble; Bonnardot, cond.*
● ARG 11-12/96: 263
+ Fa 7-8/96: 363
+ Gr 9/96: 84

26881. OPS 30-131: Llibre Vermell de
Montserrat. *Alla Francesca.*
+ Fa 7-8/95: 408
+ Gr 12/95: 124

26882. OPS 30-132: Meyerbeer—Songs.
Cherubini—Songs. *Feldman, Poleri,
sopranos; Meijer, mezzo-soprano;
Ragon, tenor; Chambers, baritone;
Hoeprich, clarinet; Murgier, cello;
Weiss, fortepiano.*
● Fa 1-2/96: 256
● Gr 1/96: 85
● ON 5/96: 59

26883. OPS 30-133: Frescobaldi—Primo
libro dei madrigali. *Concerto Italiano;
Alessandrini, cond.*
+ ARG 7-8/96: 113
+ Fa 5-6/96: 154
+ Gr 4/96: 88

26884. OPS 30-134: *Ave Eva: Twelfth
and thirteenth century songs of
womanhood.* Music of Gautier de Coincy,
Codax, Alfonso el Sabio, Robert de
Reims, Beatriz de Dia, Adam de la Halle,
and Anon. *Lesne, mezzo-soprano, harp &
percussion.*
+ Fa 3-4/96: 342
+ Gr 5/96: 112

26885. OPS 30-135/36 (2 discs):
Mendelssohn—Paulus. *Isokoski, Georg,
Trost, Lika; Chorus Musicus Köln; Das
Neue Orchester; Spering, cond.*
+ ARG 3-4/96: 154
● Fa 1-2/96: 253
● Gr 11/95: 141

26886. OPS 30-137: Banchieri—
Madrigal comedies. Striggio—Madrigal
comedies. *Concerto Italiano;*

Alessandrini, cond.
- ARG 1-2/96: 77
+ Fa 3-4/96: 113
+ Gr 3/96: 79

26887. OPS 30-138: VERACINI—Sonate accademiche a violino solo e basso. *Biondi, violin; Naddeo, cello; Alessandrini, harpsichord; Monteilhet, theorbo.*
+ ARG 9-10/95: 234
+ Fa 9-10/95: 345
+ Gr 9/95: 78

26888. OPS 30-139: SCHUBERT—Piano sonata D. 959; Moments musicaux, D. 780. *Tverskaya, fortepiano.*
- Fa 5-6/96: 264
- Fi 10/96: 151
+ Gr 3/96: 73

26889. OPS 30-141: D'amor cantando. *Ensemble Micrologus.*
+ ARG 9-10/96: 254
+ Fa 7-8/96: 363

26890. OPS 30-142: Dança amorosa. *Modo Antiquo instrumental ensemble.*
- ARG 9-10/96: 253
+ Fa 7-8/96: 363

26891. OPS 30-143: Eya Mater. *Discantus vocal ensemble; Lesne, cond.*
+ EM 2/97: 146
+ Fa 7-8/96: 368
+ Gr 5/96: 112

26892. OPS 30-145: Russian Easter liturgy. *Russian Patriarchate Choir; Grindenko, cond.*
+ Fa 7-8/96: 373

26893. OPS 30-146: GAUTIER DE COINCY—Les miracles de Nostre-Dame. *Alla Francesca.*
+ ARG 9-10/96: 123
+ Fa 7-8/96: 170
+ Gr 5/96: 99

26894. OPS 30-147: CORELLI—Concerti grossi, op. 6, no. 1-6. *Europa galante; Biondi, cond.*
+ ARG 11-12/96: 114
+ Fa 9-10/96: 178
- Gr 9/96: 50

26895. OPS 30-149: MARCELLO—*La stravaganza.* Airs and duos. *Bertini, soprano; Cavina, alto; La Venexiana.*
+ ARG 5-6/97: 155
+ Fa 11-12/96: 295
+ Gr 1/97: 75

26896. OPS 30-150: MONTEVERDI—Musica sacra. *Concerto Italiano; Alessandrini, cond.*
- ARG 11-12/96: 167
+ Fa 11-12/96: 311
+ Gr 7/96: 90

26897. OPS 30-151: PUGNANI—Overtures in eight parts: no. 2, 4-6. *Academia Montis Regalis; Mangiacavallo, cond.*

+ ARG 3-4/97: 199
+ Fa 11-12/96: 340
+ Gr 10/96: 58

26898. OPS 30-152: *Per la nascita der verbo.* Music of Caresana, Giaccio, and Storace. *Cappella della Pietà de' Turchini; Florio, cond.*
+ Fa 11-12/96: 450

26899. OPS 30-154: VIVALDI—Dresden sonatas; Violin sonatas; Saraband in C major. *Biondi, violin; Alessandrini, harpsichord; Naddeo, cello.*
+ Fa 11-12/96: 413
+ Gr 12/96: 102

26900. OPS 30-155: CORELLI—Concerti grossi, vol. 2. No. 7-12. *Europa Galante; Biondi, cond.*
+ ARG 3-4/97: 118
+ Fa 11-12/96: 225
- Gr 9/96: 50

26901. OPS 30-157: *Songs of the world.* Music of Anon., Rubin, Hassler, Morley, Passereau, Lasso, Obrecht, Dargomyzhski, Schumann, Werner, Brahms, Ruizaznar, Erdmann, and Mellnäs. *Vesna Children's Choir, Moscow; Ponomarev, cond.*
+ Fa 11-12/96: 436 (Lucano)
+ Fa 11-12/96: 437 (Baumann)

26902. OPS 30-161: Divine liturgy for the Feast of St. Peter and St. Paul. *Russian Patriarchate Choir; Grindenko, cond.*
+ ARG 1-2/97: 222
+ Fa 1-2/97: 292
+ Gr 1/97: 97

26903. OPS 30-164: Songs of old Russia. *Moscow Men's Chorus; Grindenko, cond.*
+ Fa 11-12/96: 437
+ Gr 3/97: 88

26904. OPS 30-165: SHOSTAKOVICH—Symphony no. 14; Chamber symphony, op. 110a. *Bernard, soprano; Peintre, baritone; Musicatreize; Hayrabedian, cond.*
- Fa 11-12/96: 378
- Gr 12/96: 84

26905. OPS 30-861: VIVALDI—Concertos for strings. *Europa Galante; Biondi, cond.*
- Fa 11-12/96: 412

26906. OPS 30-9001: GOTTSCHALK—Le bananier; Ojos criollos; Bamboula; Pasquinade; La savane; Souvenir de Porto Rico; Morte!! CERVANTES—Dances and portraits. SAUMELL—Four country dances. RABOI—Hommage. *Rabol, piano.*
- Fa 11-12/91: 326

26907. OPS 30-9002: GUASTAVINO—Classiques des Amériques, vol. 2: songs. *Parès-Reyna, soprano; Rabol, piano.*
+ Fa 11-12/91: 331

26908. OPS 30-9003: MOZART—Harpsichord concertos, K. 107; Violin sonatas K. 26, 29, 31; Minuets, K. 1-5; Klavierstück, K. 33b. *Hantaï, harpsichord; Fernandez, violin; Le Concert Français.*
+ Fa 11-12/91: 395

26909. OPS 30-9004: VIVALDI—Concertos for violin, RV 761, RV 202; for strings and continuo, RV 129, RV 517; for violin and cello, RV 547; Sonata, RV 130; Sinfonia, RV 169. *Europa galante; Biondi, violin & cond.*
+ Fa 11-12/91: 518
+ Gr 9/91: 76

26910. OPS 30-9005: CHARPENTIER—Quatuor anni tempestates, H. 335-338; Psaumes de David, H. 174, 179, 231. *Le Parlement de musique.*
- Fa 11-12/91: 297
+ Gr 9/91: 110

26911. OPS 30-9006: CHOPIN—Preludes, op. 28. *Sokolov, piano.*
- Fa 11-12/91: 302

26912. OPS 30-90/91 (2 discs): TRAETTA—Buovo d'Antona. *Crook, Trogu-Röhrich, Balconi; Teatro La Fenice; Curtis, cond.* Recorded 1993.
+ ARG 11-12/94: 203
+ Fa 5-6/95: 363
- Gr 4/94: 102
- ON 1/21/95: 37

26913. OPS 37-9101: CHOPIN—Mazurkas. *Olejniczak, piano.*
+ Fa 11-12/91: 300

26914. OPS 38-9102: CHOPIN—Polonaises. *Olejniczak, piano.*
- Fa 11-12/91: 301

26915. OPS 40-9104: SCRIABIN—Piano sonatas no. 3, 9. PROKOFIEV—Piano sonata no. 8. RACHMANINOFF—Prelude, op. 23, no. 4. *Sokolov, piano.*
- Fa 5-6/92: 253

26916. OPS 41-9105: BOCCHERINI—String trios, op. 47. *Europa galante.*
+ Fa 11-12/91: 279
+ Gr 5/92: 62

26917. OPS 42-9106: BEETHOVEN—Diabelli variations. *Sokolov, piano.* Live recording.
- Fa 11-12/91: 270

26918. OPS 43-9107: CHOPIN—La note bleue: original soundtrack. *Olejniczak, piano; Ensemble Mosaiques; Coin, cond.*
- Fa 11-12/91: 301

26919. OPS 45-9109/10 (2 discs): HANDEL—Ode auf St. Caecilia; Acis und Galatea (arr. Mozart). *Vocal solosits; Chorus Musicus Köln; Das Neue Orch.; Spering, cond.*
- ARG 3-4/92: 67

- Fa 1-2/92: 227
- Gr 6/92: 74

26920. OPS 47-9111: Hotteterre—Third suite from Second book. Monteclair—Pan and Syrinx. Couperin—VIe concert; XIVe concert. Marais—Sixth suite from Third book. *Le Parlement de musique.*
+ Fa 1-2/92: 425

26921. OPS 49-9209: *Classics of the Americas: vol. 3, Paraguay.* Music of Barrios. *Castro Balbi, guitar.*
+ Fa 5-6/93: 379

26922. OPS 50-9114: Gottschalk—Piano works. *Rabol, piano.*
+ ARG 1-2/92: 59
• Fa 1-2/92: 223
- Gr 4/92: 113

26923. OPS 54-9118: Corelli—Sonatas after op. 6: no. 4, 12; Concerti grossi, op. 6: no. 3, 8, 10. *Concert Français.*
+ Fa 3-4/92: 179

26924. OPS 55-9119: Charpentier—Office de ténèbres. *Parlement de musique; Gester, cond.*
+ ARG 3-4/93: 69
+ Fa 3-4/93: 142
+ Gr 9/92: 142

26925. OPS 56-9120: Vivaldi—Four seasons; Two concertos. *Europa galante; Biondi, violin & cond.*
+ Fa 3-4/92: 358
+ Gr 4/92: 86

26926. OPS 57-9203: Tchaikovsky—Serenade for strings; Legend; Invocation to sleep. Arensky—Variations on a theme of Tchaikovsky. *Bělorussian Chamber Orch.; Poliansky, cond.; Russian Phil. Choir; Russian Philharmonia.*
• Fa 1-2/93: 254

26927. OPS 58-9204: *Music at Pavlovsky Station: birth of the Russian orchestra.* Music of Dargomyzhsky, Tchaikovsky, Labitsky, Alabiev, Glinka, Rubinstein, and J. Strauss, Jr. *Petershof Orch.; Korkhin, cond.*
- Fa 1-2/93: 314

26928. OPS 59-9205: Tartini—Sonatas for violin and continuo. *Biondi, violin; Naddeo, cello; Alessandrini, harpsichord; Monteilhet, theorbo.*
+ Fa 3-4/94: 332
+ Fa 7-8/95: 340

26929. OPS 61-9207/8 (2 discs): Haydn—Applausus. *Vocal soloists; Haydn Vocal Ensemble; Picardy Regional Orch.; Fourmillier, cond.*
+ ARG 1-2/94: 107
+ Fa 1-2/93: 162
• Gr 4/93: 107
+ ON 1/30/93: 37

26930. OPS 93-9103: Clérambault—Secular cantatas: Léandre et Héro;

Piramé et Tisbé; l'Ile de Délos; Apollon et Doris. *Poulenard, soprano; Ragon, tenor; Ensemble Amalia.*
• Fa 11-12/91: 303
• Gr 10/91: 154

OPUS 3

26931. CD 7915: Music of Bach, Telemann, Frescobaldi, and Cimarosa. *Stockholm Guitar Quartet.*
+ ARG 9-10/95: 261

26932. CD 8015: Music of Bach, Villa-Lobos, Turina, and Weiss. *Riis, guitar.*
• ARG 5-6/96: 236

26933. CD 8801: Mozart—Clarinet concerto. Larsson—Concertino. De Frumerie—Concertino. Crusell—Aria. *Fageus, basset clarinet, clarinet; Häggander, soprano; Stockholm Phil. Orch.; Klas, cond.*
+ ARG 11-12/95: 162

26934. CD 8901: Tournemire—Organ music. *Torén, organ.*
+ Gr 1/92: 79

26935. CD 9001: Music of Mendelssohn, Brahms, and Debussy. *Stockholm Guitar Quartet.*
+ ARG 9-10/95: 261

26936. CD 19304: *Viriditas per Omnibus.* Music of Kraus, Agrell, Alfven, Aulin, and others. *Omnibus Wind Ensemble.*
+ ARG 9-10/95: 274

26937. CD 19501: Music of Saint-Saëns, Korling, Alfven, Badings, Reichel, Hoeberg, Lindberg, Trad., and Krol. *Hermansson, horn; Larsson, organ.*
- ARG 3-4/96: 233

26938. CD 19504: Beethoven—Symphonies no. 1-2. *Stockholm Sinfonietta; Kamu, cond.*
• Gr 7/96: 47

OPUS ONE

26939. 118 (LP): Van de Vate—Nine preludes for piano. Strunk—Quartet no. 4 for flute, clarinet, cello, and piano. Lifchitz—Transformations no. 1 for cello; Yellow ribbons no. 2 for violin, clarinet, and piano. *Lifchitz, piano & cond.; members of the North-South Consonance Ensemble.*
+ Fa 5-6/87: 205

26940. 124 (LP): Hollister—String quartet no. 1. Campanelli—Piano sonata no. 1; Duo, Nocturnus II. *Hampshire Quartet; ; Shames, Gurt, pianos; Jellinek, cello.*
• ARG 1-2/88: 37

26941. 127 (LP): Wolpe—An die Armee der Künstler. Wallach—Of honey and vinegar. D. Handel—Poems of our climate; Rondeaux with oboe. *Bailey,*

Sheryl, soprano; Ganz, mezzo-soprano; Weimer, Nel, Vassiliades, pianos; Watson, flute; Bloom, oboe; Delay, guitar & piano; Griffen, cello; Percussion Group; Samuel, cond.*
+ ARG 3-4/90: 128

26942. 130 (LP): Wilson—Line drawings for clarinets; Gnomics for flute, oboe and clarinet; Dithyramb for oboe and clarinet; Serenade for clarinet, viola and bass. *Krakauer, Guy, clarinets; Ogle, flute; Wolfgang, oboe; Davidson, viola; Masuzzo, bass.*
+ ARG 1-2/88: 100

26943. 138 (LP): Miller—Seven sides of a crystal; Beyound the wheel; Going home. Daugherty—Snap; Blue like an orange; Bounce I; Mxyzptlk; Celestrial hoops IV. *Various soloists & ensembles.*
+ ARG 1-2/90: 67

26944. 139 (LP): King—String quartet no. 3. Johnson—String quartet no. 2. *Crescent Quartet; Tremont String Quartet.*
□ ARG 11-12/88: 42

26945. 143 (LP): Callaway—Paraphrases. Harris—Music after Rimbaud. Moryl—The golden phoenix. *Thompson, organ; Roxbury Chamber Players; Manhattan String Quartet.*
+ ARG 3-4/90: 129

26946. 146: Ornstein—Nocturne for clarinet and piano. Lundborg—Ghost sonatine. Dellaira—Maud. Levine—Tapestry. Ziffrin—Sono. *Various performers.*
+ ARG 1-2/90: 113
+ DA 5/90: 74

26947. 147: *Music from Texas Tech University.* Van Appledorn—Sonatine; Four duos; Liquid gold. Glazer—Concerto for flute and concert band. *Follows, cello; Schoenfeld, viola; Chiles, piano; Underwood, saxophone; Stoune, flute; Inoue Chamber Ensemble; Texas Tech University Symphony Band; Sudduth, cond.*
+ ARG 1-2/90: 99

26948. 148: Hendrick—Allegro. Shawn—Suite, Bacewicz—Quartet. Davidson—Dark child sings. Tansman—2 Movements. *Bennington Cello Quartet.*
+ ARG 11-12/91: 183

26949. 150: Rosner—String quartet no. 4. Swack—String quartet no. 4. Trimble—String quartet no. 1. *Alorian Quartet; Sierra Quartet; Ondine Quartet.*
+ ARG 1-2/91: 130
+ Fa 5-6/91: 268

26950. 151: Schubel—Superscherzo; Christmas treat; String quartet no. 3; Miraplex; Everybody's favorite rag; Scherzo. *Moore, cello; Thomas, harpsichord; Alorian Quartet; Violette,*

piano; Janáček Phil. Orch. Ostrava; Subin, cond.
+ ARG 5-6/96: 279

26951. 153: JACOBS—Electro-acoustic music. *Davis, viola; Jacobs, piano; Leach, trumpet.*
+ ARG 1-2/92: 65

26952. 156: *New music for orchestra.* Music of Retzel, Couper, Blank, Bassett, B. Anderson, and Matsuo. *Slovak Radio Symphony Orch., Bratislava; Janáček Phil. Orch. Ostrava; Suben, cond.; Hamilton College Orch.; Matsuo, cond.*
• Fa 9-10/96: 436

26953. 158: FLEISCHER—Lamentaion; The gown of nigh; In the mountains if Armenia; The clock wants to sleep; Girl-butterfly-girl; Scenes of Israel. *Modus Vivendi; Rinat National Choir.*
+ ARG 7-8/93: 89

26954. 160: Music of Misurell-Mitchell, Brooke, Pelosi, Singer, and Nelson. *Various performers.*
+ ARG 7-8/95: 268

26955. 161: BASSETT—Illuminations; Arias. BEVLANDER—A letter from Nathaniel Giles; Synthecisms 2-3. *Collaborative Arts Ensemble; Brown, cond.*
+ ARG 11-12/96: 87

26956. 162: *The sonorous landscape.* Music of Boziwick, Appledorn, and Holmes. *Various performers.*
□ ARG 7-8/94: 204
+ Fa 3-4/94: 427

26957. 166: GRYC—Chamber music. *Various performers.*
+ ARG 7-8/95: 268

26958. 167: WHITE—Introit; Illusions; Ritual and dance; Music of the open road; Music for violin and piano; But God's own descent. *Toth, cello; Burrichter, tenor; Lower, violin; Sharpe, Oberlin Percussion Ensemble; Rosen, cond.; Florida Musica Nova; University of Florida Choir and Wind Ensemble; Waybright, cond.*
+ ARG 5-6/95: 232

26959. 169: MOORE—Modes. WEBER—Eight etudes. LIEBERMANN—Soliloquy. APPLEDORN—Atmospheres; Rhapsody; Sonic mutation. BARBER—Songs of destiny. JOHNSON—Invention no. 2. *Meaux Quartet; Weber, piano; Kernier, flute; Texas Tech Trombone Ensemble; Deahl, cond.; Streider, trumpet; Barber, harp; Vonn Pried, mezzo-soprano; Davidson, viola.*
+ ARG 3-4/96: 268

26960. 1098: *New American works.* Music of Liptak, Wagner, Willey, Lindenfeld, and Caltabiano. *Society for*

New Music; Caltabiano, cond.
+ ARG 3-4/95: 263

ORAGNO PHON

26961. 90018 (LP): Music of Bach, Schoeder, Selby, and Mendelssohn. *Mardirosian, organ.*
+ Fa 9-10/87: 372

ORATA

26962. ORA BYZ 002/3: *The masterpieces of ancient pagan music, vol. 3.* Music of Chrysaphes, Koukouzeles, Aliatis, Koronis, and others. *Vocal group; OP & PO Orch.; Halaris, cond.*
+ Fa 11-12/90: 425

ORFEO

26963. C 005 822 H: EGK—Peer Gynt. *Sharp, Lövaas, Hopf, Hermann; Bavarian Radio Chorus; Munich Radio Orch.; Walberg, cond.*
+ ARG 3-4/90: 47
+ Fa 1-2/90: 173
+ Gr 10/89: 743
+ ON 3/31/90: 31

26964. C 008 101 A: BRAHMS—Serenades no. 1-2. *Vienna Symphony Orch.; Bertini, cond.*
• ARG 5-6/90: 34
• Fa 5-6/90: 135
+ Gr 6/90: 43

26965. C 011 101 A: SCHUBERT—Lazarus. *Mathis, Wulkopf, Schwarz, Hollweg, Laubenthal, Prey; Radio Stuttgart Chorus & Symphony Orch.; Chmura, cond.*
+ Fa 3-4/88: 191

26966. C 013 821 A: RAVEL—Piano concertos in G & D (left hand). *Paik, piano; Stuttgart Radio Symphony Orch.; Bertini, cond.*
+ ARG 3-4/92: 124
+ Fa 3-4/92: 293
- Gr 5/92: 44

26967. C 018 821 A: BÖHM—Compositions for flute. *Various performers.* Recorded live.
+ Fa 3-4/92: 157

26968. C 020 821 A: BRAHMS—Piano sonata no. 3; Klavierstücke op. 119. *Oppitz, Gerhard.*
+ Fa 3-4/90: 155 m.f.

26969. C 023 822 H (2 discs): LEONCAVALLO—La bohème. *Popp, Milcheva, Bonisolli, Weikl; Bavarian Radio Chorus & Orch.; Wallberg, cond.*
• ARG 11-12/88: 43
• Fa 11-12/88: 213
• Gr 8/88: 331

26970. C 043 831 A: SCHUBERT—Fantasie in C, D. 760: Piano sonata in A minor D. 784; Fragments for piano D. 348, 900. *Maisenberg, piano.*

+ Fa 3-4/89: 266
• Gr 1/89: 1189

26971. C 053 851 A: TCHAIKOVSKY—Lieder. *Varady, soprano; Reimann, piano.*
+ ARG 9-10/89: 110
+ Fa 7-8/89: 264
• Gr 8/89: 359

26972. C 054 831 A: MEYERBEER—Gli amori di Teolinda. *Varady, soprano; Fadle, clarinet; Berlin Radio Symphony Orch.; Albrecht, cond.* Reissue.
+ Gr 10/92: 164
+ Op 1/93: 124

26973. C 055 832 I: MOZART—Zaide. *Blegen, Hollweg, Moser, Schöne, Holl; Salzburg Mozarteum Orch.; Hager, cond.*
+ Fa 1-2/91: 263
• Gr 5/91: 2061

26974. C 070 833 D (3 discs): BRAHMS—Symphonies (complete). *Bavarian Radio Orch.; Kubelik, cond.*
+ ARG 11-12/89: 44
- Fa 9-10/89: 164

26975. C 085 843 F (3 discs): MOZART—La finta semplice. *Donath, Ihloff, Berganza, Rolfe Johnson, Moser, Holl, Lloyd; Mozarteum Orch. Salzburg; Hager, cond.*
+ ARG 9-10/89: 84
+ Fa 9-10/89: 259
+ Gr 8/89: 365
+ Op 10/89: 1269

26976. C 097 841 A: ZELTER—Ausgewählte Lieder. *Fischer-Dieskau, baritone; Reimann, piano.* Issued also as LP: S 097 841 A.
+ Fa 5-6/87: 219

26977. C 102 842 H (2 discs): EINEM—Dantons Tod. *Laki, Mayr, Hollweg, Adam; ORF Chorus & Orch.; Zagrosek, cond.*
+ ARG 7-8/90: 46
+ Fa 1-2/90: 175
+ Gr 1/90: 1369

26978. C 112 851 A: HINDEMITH—Requiem for those we love. *Fassbaender, Fischer-Dieskau, vocalists; Vienna State Opera Chorus; Vienna Symphony Orch.; Sawallisch, cond.* Issued also as LP: S 112 851 A.
• ARG 1-2/88: 36
- Fa 9-10/87: 220
• Gr 7/87: 211
+ ON 3/12/88: 42
• Opus 12/87: 34

26979. C 115 841 A: SMETANA—Má vlast. *Bavarian Radio Orch.; Kubelik, cond.*
- ARG 11-12/90: 118
- Fa 9-10/90: 391

26980. C 116 842 H (2 discs): BRAHMS—Die schöne Magelone. *A. Prey, narrator; H. Prey, baritone; Deutsch, piano.*

ORFEO

+ Fa 7-8/87: 73 (Singing)
- Fa 7-8/87: 73 (Narrator)

26981. S 118 843 F (3 LPs): GLUCK—
Paride ed Elena. *Cotrubas, Greenberg, Fontana, Bonisolli; Arnold Schoenberg & ORF Choruses; Orch. of the Austrian Radio; Zagrosek, cond.*
  • Fa 3-4/87: 118
  + Gr 3/87: 1325
  + ON 3/14/87: 50
  - Op 5/87: 544
  + OQ Spring/87: 149

26982. C 124 862 H (2 discs): SUDER—
Kleider machen leute. *Coburn, Klare, König, Probst; Bavarian Radio Chorus; Bamberg Symphony Orch.; Mund, cond.*
  + ARG 9-10/92: 160
  + Fa 7-8/92: 299
  + Gr 5/92: 116

26983. S 124 863 F (3 LPs): SUDER—
Kleider machen Leute. *Coburn, König, Morgan, Probst; Bavarian Radio Chorus; Bamberg Symphony Orch.; Mund, cond.*
  + Fa 3-4/87: 217
  + Gr 6/87: 103
  • ON 5/87: 59
  + Op 3/87: 344

26984. S 125 846 G (6 LPs): LISZT—
Organ music (complete). *Haselböck, organ.*
  + Fa 7-8/87: 135

26985. C 126 901 A: *Die Berliner play salon music.* Music of E. Strauss, Gounod, J. Strauss, Jr., Tchaikovsky, Leoncavallo, Fučík, Gilbert, Ketelbey, Lincke, Schmalstich, Fetrás, and Lehár. *Die Berliner.*
  + Fa 7-8/93: 309

26986. C 129 881 A: SPOHR—Sonata concertante for flute & harp op. 113; Sonata for flute & harp WoO. 23, op. 115; Larghetto in G; Fantasy on themes by Danzi & Vogler, Op. 118. *Norman, harp; Adorján, flute.*
  + Fa 1-2/89: 272

26987. C 131 851 A: *Harmonies du soir: Virtuose Celloromantik.* Music of Offenbach, Françaix, Popper, Schubert, Wagner, and others. *Thomas-Mifune, cello; Munich Chamber Orch.; Stadlmair, cond.* Issued also as LP: S 131 851 A.
  + Fa 1-2/87: 149
  + Fa 1-2/88: 267

26988. C 133 852 H (2 discs): HANDEL—
Acis and Galatea (arr. Mozart). *Mathis, Rolfe Johnson, Cambill, Lloyd; Austrian Radio Chorus & Orch.; Schreier, cond.* Issued also as 2 LPs: S 133 852 H.
  + ARG 5-6/87: 28
  + Fa 7-8/87: 119
  + Fa 9-10/88: 161
  + Gr 4/87: 1445
  + ON 5/89: 48

- Opus 8/87: 41
+ Ov 9/87: 39

26989. C 135 872 H (2 discs): GLUCK—
La corona; La danza. *Słowakiewicz, Gorzynska, Juranek, Nowicka, Ignatowicz, Myrlak, vocalists; Warsaw Chamber Opera; Bugaj, cond.*
  • Fa 3-4/88: 113
  • Gr 3/88: 1340

26990. C 137 862 H (2 discs): SPONTINI—Olympie. *Varady, Toczyska, Tagliavini, Fischer-Dieskau, Fortune; RIAS Chamber Choir; Berlin Radio Symphony Orch.; Albrecht, cond.* Issued also as 3 LPs: S 137 863 F.
  - Fa 9-10/87: 304 (LP)
  • Fa 1-2/88: 214
  • Gr 11/87: 818
  • On 12/19/87: 43
  • Op 12/87: 1414
  • OQ Winter/87-88: 138

26991. C 139 861 A: *Englische Virginalisten.* Music of Bull, Byrd, Croft, Morley, Munday, and others. *Růžičková, harpsichord.*
  • Fa 11-12/89: 455
  + Gr 10/89: 708

26992. C 140 101 A: *Salzburg Festival live 1957-1965: vol. 1.* SCHUBERT—Lieder. *Fischer-Dieskau, baritone; Moore, piano.* Recorded live at Salzburg, 1957.
  + Fa 3-4/87: 198
  + HF 6/87: 61

26993. C 140 201 A: *Salzburg Festival live 1957-1965: vol. 2.* BRAHMS—Lieder. *Fischer-Dieskau, baritone; Moore, piano.* Recorded live at Salzburg, 1958.
  + Fa 3-4/87: 199
  + HF 6/87: 61

26994. C 140 301 A: *Salzburg Festival live 1957-1965: vol. 3.* SCHUMANN—Kerner Lieder op. 35; Liederkreis op. 39. *Fischer-Dieskau, baritone; Moore, piano.* Recorded live at Salzburg, 1959.
  + Fa 3-4/87: 199
  + HF 6/87: 61

26995. C 140 401 A: *Salzburg Festival live 1957-1965: vol. 4.* WOLF—Lieder. *Fischer-Dieskau, baritone; Moore, piano.* Recorded live at Salzburg, 1961.
  + Fa 3-4/87: 199
  + HF 6/87: 61

26996. C 140 501 A: *Salzburg Festival live 1957-1965: vol. 5.* BEETHOVEN—Lieder. *Fischer-Dieskau, baritone; Moore, piano.* Recorded live at Salzburg, 1965.
  + Fa 3-4/87: 199
  + HF 6/87: 61

26997. S 140 855 R (5 LPs): Lieder recitals. *Fischer-Dieskau, baritone; Moore, piano.* Salzburg Festivals, 1957-1965.

+ Fa 7-8/86: 267
+ Gr 9/86: 433

26998. C 141 861 A: MOZART—Clarinet quintet K. 581. CRUSELL—Clarinet quartet no. 2. *Leister, clarinet; Pražák Quartet.*
  + ARG 1-2/88: 48
  - Fa 9-10/87: 253 (Mozart)
  + Fa 9-10/87: 253 (Crusell)
  + Gr 7/87: 192

26999. C 143 862 H (2 discs): SCHMIDT—Das Buch mit sieben Siegeln. *Greenberg, Watkinson, Moser, Schreier, Holl, Rydl; Vienna State Opera Concert Choir; Austrian Radio Symphony Orch.; Zagrosek, cond.* Issued also as 2 LPs: S 143 862 H.
  + ARG 5-6/88: 58
  - Fa 3-4/88: 182
  + Gr 2/88: 1231

27000. C 144 851 A: SCARLATTI—Harpsichord sonatas K. 8, 12, 29, 84, 113, 159, 384, 388, 406, 420, 519. *Růžičková, harpsichord.*
  + Fa 5-6/88: 202

27001. C 145 851 A: BRUCKNER—Symphony no. 1 (Linz version). *Bavarian State Orch.; Sawallisch, cond.* Issued also as LP: S 145 851 A.
  + Fa 1-2/87: 79
  + Fa 3-4/87: 92

27002. C 146 852 H (2 discs): BACH—Cello suites BWV 1007-1012. *Beger, cello.* Issued also as 3 LPs: S 146 852 H.
  • ARG 11-12/89: 28
  + Fa 9-10/86: 95
  + Fa 11-12/89: 117

27003. S 147 861 B (LP): FUČÍK—Entrance of the gladiators; Winterstorms; Mississippi River march; Tales of the Danube; Attila; Dream ideal; Triglav; Marinarella. *Czech Phil. Orch.; Neumann, cond.*
  + Fa 3-4/87: 114

27004. S 148 852 H (2 LPs): GLAZUNOV—Symphonies no. 2, 4, 7; Concert waltz no. 1. *Bamberg Symphony Orch.; Järvi, cond.*
  + Fa 1-2/87: 112
  + Gr 10/86: 575

27005. C 150 852 H (2 discs): HAYDN—Die Schöpfung. *Marchall, Popp, Cole, Howell, Weikl; Bavarian Radio Choir & Orch.; Kubelik, cond.*
  + Fa 7-8/88: 175
  - Gr 5/88: 1630

27006. S 151 862 H (2 LPs): F. BENDA—Flute concertos no. 1-4. *Adorján, flute; Ars Rediviva Ensemble; Munclinger, cond.*
  + Fa 5-6/87: 93
  + Gr 6/87: 36

27007. S 152 861 A (LP): MOZART—Divertimentos K. 213, 240, 252-53, 270.

Winds of the Berlin Phil. Orch.
+ ARG 11-12/87: 57
+ Fa 5-6/87: 163

27008. S 153 861 A (LP): *Lieder der Romantik.* Music of Neukomm, Kreutzer, Donizetti, Reissiger, and others . *Fischer-Dieskau, baritone; Klöcker, clarinet; Wallendorf, horn; Höll, piano.*
- Fa 1-2/87: 238
+ Gr 6/87: 93

27009. C 155 871 A: SPOHR—Notturno for winds and janissary music op. 34; Nonet for strings and winds op. 31. *Consortium Classicum; Klöcker, cond.*
+ Fa 9-10/87: 303
+ Gr 9/87: 434

27010. S 156 861 A (LP): HINDEMITH—Lieder. *Fischer-Dieskau, baritone; Reimann, piano.*
+ ARG 1-2/88: 35
• Fa 1-2/88: 142
+ Gr 2/88: 1225
+ ON 3/12/88: 42
+ Opus 4/88: 36

27011. S 157 872 H (2 LPs): GLAZUNOV—Symphonies no. 3, 6; Concert waltz no. 2 op. 51; Poeme lyrique op. 12. *Bamberg Symphony Orch.; Järvi, cond.*
+ Fa 11-12/87: 143

27012. C 158 871 A: HAYDN—Organ concertos H. XVIII, 2; XVIII, 7-8. *Haselböck, organ; Divertimento Salzburg.*
+ Fa 3-4/88: 124

27013. C 159 871 A: SCHUBERT—Lieder. *Lipovsek, mezzo-soprano; Parsons, piano.*
+ ARG 3-4/89: 79
+ Fa 1-2/89: 257
+ Gr 11/88: 846

27014. C 160 851 A: BRUCKNER—Symphony no. 9. *Bavarian State Orch.; Sawallisch, cond.*
• Fa 5-6/88: 99
• Gr 7/88: 160

27015. C 161 871 A: Overtures by Wagner, Verdi, Mozart, Beethoven, and Brahms. *Bavarian State Orch.; Sawallisch, cond.*
- Fa 5-6/88: 271

27016. C 162 871 A: ZIMMERMANN—Die weisse Rose. *Fontana, Harder; Instrumental ensemble; Zimmermann, cond.*
+ ARG 5-6/89: 106
+ Fa 9-10/88: 303
+ Gr 9/88: 464
+ MA 1/89: 84

27017. C 163 881 A: MOZART—Divertimentos K. 166, 186, and K. Anh. 226-27. *Winds of Berlin Phil. Orch.*
+ Fa 9-10/88: 210

27018. C 164 881 A: MARTIN—Die Weise von Liebe und Tod des Cornets Christoph Rilke. *Lipovsek, alto; Austrian Radio Symphony Orch.; Zagrosek, cond.*
+ ARG 3-4/89: 55
+ Fa 1-2/90: 220

27019. C 165 881 A: RICHTER—Symphonies in G, in C, in B minor. KOHOUT—Symphony in F minor. *Slovak Chamber Orch.; Warchal, cond.*
+ Fa 1-2/89: 245

27020. C 166 881 A: Music of Bach, Ewald, Arnold, Roblee, Monti, and others. *Munich Brass.*
+ Fa 11-12/89: 484
+ Gr 8/89: 339

27021. C 167 881 A: KREUTZER—Grand septet op. 62. BRUCH—Septet, op. posth. *Consortium Classicum.*
+ ARG 5-6/89: 57
+ Fa 1-2/89: 185

27022. C 168 881 A: PFITZNER—Palestrina: Preludes; Das Kätchen von Heilbronn Overture; Die Rose vom Liebesgarten: Blütenwunder; Trauermarsch. *Bavarian Radio Orch.; Sawallisch, cond.*
+ ARG 3-4/89: 69
+ Fa 9-10/88: 223

27023. C 169 882 H (2 discs): STRAUSS—Arabella. *Varady, Donath, Dallapozza, Fischer-Dieskau, Berry; Bavarian State Opera Chorus; Bavarian State Orch.; Sawallisch, cond.*
+ ARG 3-4/89: 90
+ Fa 1-2/89: 274
+ Gr 1/89: 1210
+ ON 3/4/89: 43

27024. C 171 881 A: *Opera arias.* Music of Rossini, Mozart, Mercadante, Donizetti, and others. *Baltsa, mezzo-soprano; Munich Radio Orch.; Wallberg, cond.*
• Fa 5-6/89: 369

27025. C 172 881 A: DONIZETTI—Messa da requiem. *Studer, Müller-Molinari, Baldin, Rootering, Bogart; Bamberg Symphony Chorus & Orch.; Gómez Martínez, cond.*
+ ARG 7-8/89: 39
• Fa 7-8/89: 133
+ Gr 8/89: 349

27026. C 174 881 A: BIZET—Djamileh. *Popp, Bonisolli, LaFont; Bavarian Radio Chorus; Munich Radio Orch.; Gardelli, cond.*
+ Fa 3-4/90: 149

27027. C 176 891 A: Music of Wolf, Mahler, Schreker, and Strauss. *Lipovsek, mezzo-soprano; Werba, piano.*
+ ARG 9-10/89: 147
+ Fa 11-12/89: 429

27028. C 178 891 A: GLUCK—Le cinesi. *Erickson, Milcheva, Schiml, Moser; Munich Radio Orch.; Gardelli, cond.*
+ ARG 3-4/90: 54
+ Fa 1-2/90: 195
• Gr 1/90: 1369

27029. C 179 891 A: *Beruhmte Opernarien.* Music of Gluck, Handel, Mozart, Verdi, Bizet, and others. *Lipovsek, mezzo-soprano; Munich Radio Orch.; Patanè cond.*
• ARG 3-4/90: 150
• Au 6/90: 114
• Fa 3-4/90: 348
+ Gr 6/90: 113

27030. C 180 891 A: *Galakonzert aus Prag.* Music of Blodek, Dvořák, Fibich, Janacek, Kovarovic, and others. *Czech Phil. Orch.; Neumann, cond.*
+ ARG 11-12/90: 140
+ Gr 9/90: 616

27031. C 182 891 A: ARCHDUKE RUDOLPH OF AUSTRIA—Septet in E minor. J.M. WEBER—Septet in E. *Consortium Classicum.*
• Fa 1-2/90: 85 (Rudolph)
+ Fa 1-2/90: 85 (Weber)

27032. C 184 891 A: BIZET—Roma; Symphony no. 1. *Munich Radio Orch.; Gardelli, cond.*
- ARG 9-10/89: 32
- Fa 9-10/89: 153
• Gr 1/90: 1321

27033. C 185 891 A: *Lieder nach Gedichten von Eichendorff.* Music of Mendelsohn, Schumann, Pfitzner, Walter, and others. *Fischer-Dieskau, baritone; Sawallisch, piano.* Recorded live 1975.
+ ARG 5-6/90: 147
+ Fa 1-2/90: 366
+ Gr 1/90: 1365
+ NYT 2/4/90: H33

27034. C 186 951 A: *Verdi heroines, vol. 1.* VERDI—Opera arias. *Varady, soprano; Bavarian State Orch.; Fischer- Dieskau, cond.*
+ ARG 1-2/96: 190
• Fa 1-2/96: 337
+ Gr 1/96: 107
+ ON 10/96: 44

27035. C 187 891 A: WEBER—Grand duo concertante for clarinet & piano; Seven variations for clarinet & piano on a theme from Silvana; Trio for flute, cello, and piano in G minor. *Brunner, clarinet; Adorján, flute; Pergamenschikow, cello; Oppitz, Gililov, pianos.*
□ ARG 11-12/90: 136
+ Fa 11-12/90: 403

27036. C 188 891 A: MOZART—Serenade K. 361; Adagio for 2 clarinets and 3 bassethorns K. 411; Adagio for clarinet and 3 bassethorns K. Anh. 94. *Berlin Phil. Orch. Winds.*

ORFEO

+ ARG 3-4/90: 80
+ Au 4/90: 103
● Fa 3-4/90: 245

27037. C 189 891 A: *Musik aus Spanien und Lateinamerika für zwei Gitarren.* Music of Rodrigo, Falla, Albéniz, Lauro, Granados, and Piazolla. *Feybli, Erni, guitars.*
+ ARG 11-12/90: 152
□ Fa 9-10/90: 481

27038. C 194 901 A: ZEMLINSKY—String quartet no. 2. SCHOENBERG—String quartet in D. *Artis Quartet Vienna.*
+ ARG 5-6/91: 130
+ Fa 11-12/90: 408
● Gr 7/90: 241

27039. C 195 892 H (2 discs): VERDI—Requiem. BRUCKNER—Te Deum. *Cunitz, Högen, Ludwig, Greindl, Kupper, Siewert, Fehenberger, Borg; Bavarian Radio Chorus & Symphony Orch.; Jochum, cond.* Recorded live 1950, 1954.
+ ARG 9-10/90: 164
● Fa 7-8/90: 305
+ MA 9/90: 89

27040. C 196 891 A: HAYDN—Symphony no. 88. RAVEL—Rapsodie espagnole. STRAUSS—Symphonia domestica. *Bavarian Radio Orch.; Krauss, cond.* Recorded live 1953.
● ARG 9-10/90: 164
+ Fa 7-8/90: 374

27041. C 197 891 A: HINDEMITH—Symphony in B♭ for concert band; Theme with 4 variations. BERG—Chamber concerto. *Marschner, violin; Haskil, Seemann, pianos; Bavarian Radio Orch.; Hindemith, cond.* Recorded live 1961.
+ Fa 7-8/90: 283

27042. C 198 891 A: STRAVINSKY—Apollon musagète; Jeu de cartes. *Bavarian Radio Orch.; Stravinsky, cond.* Recorded live 1957.
+ ARG 9-10/90: 164
+ Fa 7-8/90: 283

27043. C 199 891 A: Music of Hindemith, Einem, Roussel, and Ravel. *Bavarian Radio Orch.; Ormandy, cond.* Recorded live 1959.
+ ARG 9-10/90: 164
+ Fa 7-8/90: 375

27044. C 200 891 A: BARTÓK—Piano concerto no. 3. TCHAIKOVSKY—Symphony no. 6. *Fischer, piano; Bavarian Radio Orch.; Fricsay, cond.* Recorded live 1960.
+ ARG 9-10/90: 164
+ Fa 7-8/90: 82

27045. C 201 891 A: BACH—Orchestra suite no. 3. BRAHMS—Symphony no. 4. *Bavarian Radio Orch.; Klemperer, cond.* Recorded live 1957.
- ARG 9-10/90: 164
● Fa 7-8/90: 76

27046. C 202 891 A: HONEGGER—Symphony no. 3. BRAHMS—Symphony no. 3. *Bavarian Radio Orch.; Ansermet, cond.*
+ Fa 7-8/90: 176

27047. C 203 891 A: BRUCKNER—Symphony no. 8. *Bavarian Radio Orch.; Kubelik, cond.* Recorded live 1963.
- ARG 9-10/90: 164
● Fa 7-8/90: 117

27048. C 204 891 A: SCHOENBERG—Violin concerto. PROKOFIEV—Symphony no. 5. *Krasner, violin; Bavarian Radio Orch.; Mitropoulos, cond.* Recorded live.
+ ARG 9-10/90: 164
+ Fa 7-8/90: 283

27049. C 205 891 A: MOZART—Mass in C minor K. 427. *Seefried, Kupper, Fehenberger, Borg; Bavarian Radio Chorus & Symphony Orch.; Jochum, cond.* Recorded live 1956.
- ARG 9-10/90: 164
+ Fa 7-8/90: 210

27050. C 206 891 A: HAYDN—Symphony no. 99. MOZART—Symphonies no. 25, 38. *Bavarian Radio Orch.; Kubelik, cond.* Recorded live 1981-1983.
+ ARG 7-8/90: 506
+ Fa 7-8/90: 170
+ NYT 6/24/90: H25

27051. C 207 891 A: BEETHOVEN—Symphony no. 9. *Donath, Fassbaender, Laubenthal, Sotin; Bavarian Radio Chorus & Symphony Orch.; Kubelik, cond.* Recorded live 1982.
● ARG 7-8/90: 56
+ Fa 7-8/90: 93

27052. C 208 891 A: BRUCKNER—Symphony no. 7. *Bavarian Radio Orch.; Davis, cond.* Recorded live 1987.
+ ARG 7-8/90: 36
● Fa 7-8/90: 116

27053. C 209 901 A: REGER—Der Einsiedler; Hymnus der Lieve; Requiem; An die Hoffnung. *Fischer-Dieskau, baritone; St. Michaelis Choir, Hamburg; Monteverdi Choir, Hamburg; Hamburg Phil. Orch.; Albrecht, cond.*
● ARG 7-8/91: 113
+ Fa 1-2/91: 286
+ Gr 2/91: 1546

27054. C 210 901 A: BRAHMS—Violin sonata no. 1 (arr. Klengel). DVOŘÁK VIOLIN SONATINA OP.100 (ARR. PERGAMENSCHIKOW). WEBER VIOLIN SONATA OP. 10B (ARR. PERGAMENSCHIKOW). *PERGAMENSCHIKOW, CELLO; GILILOV, PIANO.*
● Fa 11-12/91: 284

27055. C 212 901 A: REIMANN—Unrevealed, for baritone and string quartet; Shine and dark, for baritone and piano. *Fischer-Dieskau, baritone; Cherubini Quartet; Reimann, piano.*

+ Fa 1-2/91: 286
□ Gr 10/91: 170

27056. C 213 901 A: Music of Meyerbeer, Bärmann, Spohr, and Busoni. *Klöcker, clarinet; Philharmonia Quartet Berlin; Consortium Classicum.*
+ ARG 11-12/90: 146
+ Fa 11-12/90: 462

27057. C 214 902 H (2 discs): GAZZANIGA—Don Giovanni. *Coburn, Kaufmann, Kinzel, Steinsky, Aler, Scharinger; Bavarian Radio Chorus; Munich Radio Orch.; Soltesz, cond.*
+ ARG 5-6/91: 58
+ Fa 3-4/91: 215
+ Gr 4/91: 1898
+ MA 5/91: 74
+ ON 3/30/91: 32

27058. C 216 901 A: BERG—String quartet, op. 3; Lyric suite for string quartet. WEIGL—String quartet no. 3. *Artis Quartet Vienna.*
+ ARG 9/10/91: 46
+ Fa 11-12/91: 271

27059. C 218 911 A: MOZART—Notturni, K. 346, K. 436-439, K. 549; Divertimenti, K. 439, no. 2, 4; Adagio, K. 410; Divertimento "Le nozze di Figaro" for 2 clarinets and basset horn (arr. anon.). *Vocal soloists; Winds of the Berlin Phil.*
+ Fa 11-12/91: 400

27060. C 219 911 A: WOLF—Orchestral songs. *Fischer-Dieskau, baritone; Munich Radio Orch.; Soltesz, cond.* Recorded 1990.
● ARG 9-10/92: 183
+ Fa 7-8/92: 325
+ Gr 10/92: 168

27061. C 220 901 A: WOLF—Italienisches Liederbuch. *Seefried, soprano; Fischer-Dieskau, baritone; Werba, piano.* Recorded live 1958.
- ARG 1-2/91: 125 (Seefried)
+ ARG 1-2/91: 125 (Fischer-Dieskau)
● Fa 1-2/91: 351
- Gr 12/90: 1255
+ MA 5/91: 61

27062. C 221 901 A: HAYDN—Cello concerto in C; Symphony no. 104. *Boettcher, cello; Camerata Academica Salzburg; Fischer-Dieskau, cond.*
+ Fa 1-2/91: 213 (Concerto)
● Fa 1-2/91 213 (Symphony)

27063. C 223 911 A: *Fagotto concertante.* Music of Mozart, M. Haydn, Villa-Lobos, Françaix, and Gershwin. *Turković, bassoon; Stuttgart Chamber Orch.; Sieghart, cond.*
+ ARG 3-4/92: 181
● Fa 1-2/92: 418

27064. C 230 901 A: HAYDN—Symphony no. 93. PROKOFIEV—Symphony no. 5.

Vienna Symphony Orch.; Szell, cond.
Recorded live 1954.
- Fa 5-6/91: 186

27065. C 231 901 A: Bruckner—
Symphony no. 5. *Vienna Symphony
Orch.; Karajan, cond.* Recorded live
1954.
+ Fa 5-6/91: 145
- Gr 3/91: 1662

27066. C 235 901 A: Music of Haydn,
Schubert, Einem, and Bruckner. *Vienna
Symphony Orch.; Matacic, cond.*
Recorded live 1983-84.
+ ARG 5-6/91: 134
+ Fa 5-6/91: 186 (Haydn)
• Fa 5-6/91: 186 (others)

27067. C 239 911 A: Mozart—
Divertimento, K. 137; Andante and five
variations, K. 501; Adagio and allegro, K.
594; Orgelstück in F minor, K. 608;
Andante in F for organ, K. 616. Prinz—
Zauberflötiana. *Vienna Flautists.*
• Fa 9-10/91: 285

27068. C 240 912 H (2 discs): Spohr—
Jessonda. *Varady, Behle, Moser, Haage,
Fischer-Dieskau, Moll, bass; Chor der
Hamburgischen Staatsoper;
Philharmonisches Staatsorch. Hamburg;
Albrecht, cond.*
+ ARG 1-2/92: 118
+ Fa 11-12/91: 489
+ Gr 11/91: 161
+ ON 1/4/92: 39

27069. C 241 911 A: Bruckner—
Symphony no. 5. *Bavarian State Orch.;
Sawallisch, cond.*
+ ARG 7-8/92: 113
+ Fa 7-8/92: 131

27070. C 242 912 H (2 discs): Gluck—
Les pèlerins de Mecque, ou, La rencontre
imprévue. *Gambill, Kaufmann, Rodde,
Rootering; Munich Radio Orch.; Hager,
cond.*
+ ARG 1-2/92: 58
• Fa 3-4/92: 196
+ Gr 12/92: 135
+ ON 11/92: 46

27071. C 243 913 F (3 discs): Mozart—
Così fan tutte. *Antonacci, Bacelli,
Cherici, Decker, Dohmen, Bruscantini;
Orch. Filarmonica Marchigiana; Kuhn,
cond.* Live recording 1990.
• ARG 11-12/91: 108
+ Fa 9-10/91: 283
+ ON 12-21/91: 42

27072. C 243 931 F (3 discs): Mozart—
Così fan tutte. *Antonacci, Bacelli,
Decker, Dohmen; Orch. filarmonica
marchigiana; Kuhn, cond.* Recorded live.
+ Gr 10/92: 176
- Op 5/93: 616

27073. C 245 921 A: Reichardt—
Selected songs. *Fischer-Dieskau,
baritone; Graf, harp.*

+ ARG 9-10/92: 148
• Fa 9-10/92: 327

27074. C 246 922 I (2 discs): Haydn—
Notturni. *Wiener Concert-Verein.*
+ ARG 11-12/92: 132
+ Fa 9-10/92: 254

27075. C 248 921 A: Mozart—Songs.
Strauss—Songs. *Varady, soprano;
Bashkirova, piano.*
+ ARG 3-4/93: 119
+ Gr 5/93: 88

27076. C 249 921 A: Roslavets—Cello
sonata; Meditation. Prokofiev—Cello
sonata, op. 119; Ballade, op. 15;
Cinderella, op. 97 bis: Adagio.
Pergamenshikov, cello; Gililov, piano.
+ ARG 11-12/92: 190
+ Fa 9-10/92: 336

27077. C 251 912 H (2 discs): Vivaldi—
Cello sonatas, "op. 14"; Cello sonatas,
RV 44, RV 39, RV 42; In A (attrib.).
Berger, cello; Bleicher, organ.
+ ARG 3-4/92: 159
+ Fa 1-2/92: 367
+ Gr 8/92: 48

27078. C 252 931 A: Hummel—Trio for
flute, cello & piano, op. 78; Cello sonata,
op. 104; Piano sonata, op. 81. *Adorján,
flute; Pergamenshikov, cello; Gililov,
piano.*
+ ARG 9-10/93: 140
+ Fa 9-10/93: 190

27079. C 253 931 A: Haydn—
Symphonies no. 47, 62, 75. *Stuttgart
Chamber Orch.; Sieghart, cond.*
+ ARG 7-8/94: 112
• Fa 7-8/94: 153

27080. C 254 921 A: Kraus—Symphony
in C minor; Symphonie funèbre; Violin
concerto. *Peinemann, violin; Stuttgart
Chamber Orch.; Sieghart, cond.*
• ARG 11-12/92: 142
+ Fa 7-8/92: 194
+ Gr 11/92: 64

27081. C 255 912 H: Orff—Die
Bernauerin. *Ostermayer, Lippert, Popp,
Laubenthal; Munich Radio Orch.;
Eichhorn, cond.*
+ ARG 9-10/92: 140
• Fa 7-8/92: 240
+ ON 1/2/93: 36
+ St 3/93: 185

27082. C 256 922 H (2 discs):
Spontini—La vestale. *Plowright,
soprano; Pasino, mezzo-soprano; other
vocalists; Munich Radio Orch.; Kuhn,
cond.*
• ARG 5-6/93: 139
+ Fa 5-6/93: 327
+ Gr 7/93: 89
• Op 8/93: 1002

27083. C 257 921 A: Killmayer—
Yolimba, or The frontiers of magic.

*Venuti, Prégardien, Titus; Munich Radio
Orch.; Schneider, cond.*
+ ARG 3-4/93: 101
+ Fa 3-4/93: 201
+ Gr 5/93: 104

27084. C 259 921 A: Dvořák—The
specter's bride. *Ághová, Protchka,
Kusnjer; Hamburg State Phil. Orch.;
Albrecht, cond.*
+ ARG 3-4/93: 72
• Fa 5-6/93: 197
• Gr 7/93: 74

27085. C 260 931 A: Mozart—Così fan
tutte: selections; The abduction from the
seraglio: selections. *Winds of the Berlin
Phil. Orch.*
+ Fa 7-8/93: 188

27086. C 261 921 A: *Famous opera
arias.* Music of Rossini, Verdi, Mozart,
Jommelli, Marcello-Respighi, and
Puccini. *Dragoni, soprano; Munich
Radio Orch.; Kuhn, cond.*
• ARG 5-6/93: 179
+ Fa 5-6/93: 362

27087. C 262 932 H (2 discs): Haydn—
L'anima del filosofo. *Donath, Swensen,
Quasthoff; Bavarian Radio Orch.; Hager,
cond.*
+ ARG 1-2/95: 112
• Fa 1-2/95: 170
+ Gr 9/95: 101
• ON 12/10/94: 52

27088. A 264 921 C: Strauss—Ein
Heldenleben. Schubert—Symphony no.
2. *Bavarian Radio Symphony Orch.;
Böhm, cond.* Recorded 1973.
+ ARG 5-6/94: 146

27089. C 265 921 A: Brahms—
Symphony no. 2. Vaughan Williams—
Symphony no. 6. *Bavarian Radio Orch.;
Barbirolli, cond.* Recorded 1970.
+ ARG 5-6/94: 78

27090. C 267 921 B : Haydn—Sinfonia
concertante. Strauss—Don Quixote.
*Kalmus, oboe; Keller, bassoon; Koeckert,
Schmid, violins; Nothas, Tortelier, cellos;
Bavarian Radio Symphony Orch.;
Kempe, cond.* Recorded 1966.
+ Gr 2/94: 40

27091. C 273 922 I (2 discs): Pfitzner—
Urworte Orphisch; Von deutscher Seele;
Das dunkle Reich. *Ebers, Kupper,
sopranos; Pitzinger, alto; Ludwig, tenor;
Hotter, baritone; Bavarian Radio Chorus
& Symphony Orch.; Jochum, cond.*
Recorded live 1952 and 1955.
+ Fa 7-8/94: 200

27092. C 280 291 A: Rossini—Sonate a
quattro (arr. for flutes): no. 1-3, 6. *Vienna
Flautists.*
+ Fa 3-4/93: 266

27093. C 281 931 A: Pfitzner—Piano
quintet; Piano sextet. *Consortium*

ORFEO

Classicum.
- ARG 5-6/94: 122
+ Fa 3-4/94: 272

27094. C 282 921 A: REICHA—Octet, op. 96. BLANC—Septet, op. 40. *Consortium Classicum.*
+ ARG 7-8/93: 142
+ Fa 5-6/93: 292

27095. C 283 921 A: JANÁČEK—Suite for strings; Idyll for strings; Adagio. *Munich Phil. Chamber Orch.; Helmrath, cond.*
+ Fa 1-2/93: 171

27096. C 285 931 A: PENDERECKI—Violin concerto; Cello concerto no. 2. *Edinger, violin; Pergamenschikow, cello; Bamberg Symphony Orch.; Penderecki, cond.*
+ ARG 3-4/94: 131
+ Fa 3-4/94: 269

27097. C 286 961 A: HAAS—Chamber music. *Stuttgart Wind Quintet; Dürmüller, tenor; Hölszky-Wiedemann, violin; Davies, piano.*
+ ARG 9-10/96: 129

27098. C 287 921 A: SCHMIDT—Quintet for piano (left hand), 2 violins, viola and cello; Quintet for piano (left hand), clarinet, violin, viola and cello. *Keuschnig, piano; Ottensamer, clarinet; Hell, Wächter, violins; Pecha, viola; Iberer, Wallisch, cellos.*
+ ARG 7-8/93: 149
+ Fa 5-6/93: 311

27099. C 288 921 A: BEETHOVEN—Egmont overture and incidental music, op. 84; Leonore overture no. 2, op. 72. *Ziesak, soprano; Tukur, speaker; Hamburg State Phil. Orch.; Albrecht, cond.* Recorded live.
- ARG 7-8/93: 62
+ Fa 5-6/93: 149

27100. C 289 932 H (2 discs): SCHUMANN—Genoveva. *Faulkner, Lewis, Titus, Behle; Hamburg State Opera Chorus; Hamburg State Phil. Orch.; Albrecht, cond.*
- ARG 3-4/94: 152
+ Fa 1-2/94: 310
+ Gr 1/94: 97
+ ON 6/94: 44

27101. C 290 931 A: SCHACHT—Clarinet concertos in D and B♭; Concertos for 2 and 3 clarinets. *Klöcker, Link, Wandel, clarinets; Bamberg Symphony Orch.; Stadlmair, cond.*
+ ARG 1-2/94: 148
+ Fa 11-12/93: 373

27102. C 291 931 A: *Soirée dansante.* Music of J. Strauss Sr. and Jr., E. Strauss, and Josef Strauss. *Johann Strauss Ensemble of the Vienna Symphony Orch.; Wildner, cond.*
- ARG 9-10/93: 196
+ Fa 7-8/93: 249

27103. C 297 921 B: *Goethe Lieder.* Songs by Mozart, Beethoven, Schubert, Schumann, and Wolf. *Seefried, soprano; Werba, piano.*
+ Gr 9/93: 106

27104. C 302 921 B: MOZART—Eine kleine Nachtmusik. TCHAIKOVSKY—Symphony no. 5. *Vienna Phil. Orch.; Oistrakh, cond.* Recorded 1972.
+ Gr 6/93: 50

27105. C 304 921 A: TAKTAKISHVILI—Concerto no. 2 for violin and orchestra. NASIDZE—Concerto for violin, cello, and orchestra. GABUNIYA—Sinfonia gioconda. TSINTSADZE—Phantasy for violin and orchestra. *Issakadze, cello; Issakadze, violin & cond.; Georgian Chamber Orch.*
+ ARG 3-4/93: 159
+ Fa 3-4/93: 396

27106. C 305 931 A: Julie Kaufmann: songs by Schoenberg, Strauss, and Debussy. *Kaufmann, soprano; Gage, piano.*
+ ARG 1-2/94: 191
+ Fa 11-12/93: 456
+ Gr 2/94: 78

27107. C 306 931 A: GERSHWIN—Rhapsody in brass. *Munich Brass; other instrumentalists.*
+ ARG 11-12/93: 107
- Fa 11-12/93: 241

27108. C 307 921 A: TCHAIKOVSKY—Souvenir de Florence; Souvenir d'un lieu cher. *Georgian Chamber Orch.; Issakadze, cond.*
+ ARG 9-10/93: 205

27109. C 308 921 A: MENDELSSOHN—Piano trios no. 1-2. *Stuttgart Piano Trio.*
- Fa 7-8/93: 180

27110. C 309 931 A: BIZET—Mélodies. *Jänicke, mezzo-soprano; Hans, piano.*
+ ARG 1-2/94: 81
+ Fa 11-12/93: 189

27111. C 310 941 A: HAYDN—Divertimenti; Organ concertos. *Divertimento Salzburg.*
- ARG 7-8/94: 111
- Fa 7-8/94: 152

27112. C 311 931 A: VIVALDI—Four concertos, op. 8 "The four seasons" (arr. for flutes). *The Vienna Flautists.*
+ Fa 5-6/94: 276

27113. C 312 941 A: WAGNER—Cantatas and overtures. *Bamberg Symphony Orch. & Chorus; Rickenbacher, cond.*
□ ARG 1-2/95: 199
+ Fa 1-2/95: 303
□ ON 4/15/95: 34

27114. C 313 101—313 102 A (2 separate discs): HAYDN—String quartets op. 20. *Kocian Quartet.*

+ ARG 9-10/94: 142
- Fa 9-10/94: 206

27115. C 314 941 A: *Clarinet quintets.* Music of Mendelssohn, A. Romberg, Weber, and Meyerbeer. *Klöcker, clarinet; Consortium Classicum.*
+ ARG 5-6/95: 206
+ Fa 3-4/95: 372

27116. C 315 931 B: BEETHOVEN—String quartets no. 7, 14. *Schneiderhan String Quartet.*
+ Fa 5-6/94: 106

27117. C 317 931 A: SCHUBERT—String quartet no. 15. BARTÓK—String quartet no. 3. *Végh Quartet.*
+ Fa 9-10/93: 268

27118. C 318 931 A: MENDELSSOHN—String quartet no. 1. SCHUMANN—String quartet no. 2. SMETANA—String quartet no. 1. *Koeckert Quartet.*
+ Fa 7-8/94: 178

27119. C 319 931 B: HAYDN—String quartet op. 74. no. 1. SCHUBERT—Quartettsatz. REGER—String quartet op. 121. *Koeckert Quartet.*
- Fa 3-4/94: 212

27120. C 320 941 A: VANHAL—Symphonies in C major, G minor, E minor, and D minor. *Munich Phil. Chamber Orch.; Helmrath, cond.*
+ ARG 3-4/95: 208
+ Fa 3-4/95: 323

27121. C 322 941 A: BOCCHERINI—Six quartets for clarinet, flute, horn, and bassoon. *Consortium Classicum.*
- ARG 9-10/94: 105
+ Fa 7-8/94: 79

27122. C 323 941 A: PUCCINI—Opera arias. *Varady, soprano; Berlin Radio Symphony Orch.; Votti, cond.*
+ ARG 3-4/95: 158
- Fa 11-12/94: 332
+ Gr 5/95: 111

27123. C 324 941 A: VANHAL—Stabat Mater; Symphony in D major. *Melnik, soprano; Benackova, alto; Prague Chamber Chorus; Prague Chamber Orch.; Neumann, cond.*
+ ARG 3-4/95: 209
+ Fa 3-4/95: 323

27124. C 326 931 A: BERNSTEIN—Piano trio; Clarinet sonata; Three meditations from Mass for cello and piano; Anniversaries; Touches. *New Munich Piano Trio.*
+ ARG 3-4/94: 76
+ Fa 3-4/94: 133

27125. C 327 951 A: BRUCKNER—Motets; Choral-Mess in F major. *Mašková, Zbytovska, Nachazel, Uherek, vocal soloists; Prague Chamber Choir; Novotný, Seiler, Votava, trombones;*

Kšica, organ; Pancik, cond.
+ Fa 3-4/96: 140

27126. C 328 931 B: Liebermann—
Penelope. *Goltz, Rothenberger, Schock,
Lorenz, Baylé, Böhme; Vienna State
Opera Chorus; Vienna Phil. Orch.; Szell,
cond. Recorded 1954.*
+ ARG 3-4/94: 234
+ Fa 1-2/94: 225

27127. C 329 931 B: Brahms—
Symphony no. 3; Tragic overture. *Vienna
Phil. Orch.; Knappertsbusch, cond.
Recorded live 1955.*
• Fa 1-2/94: 140

27128. C 330 931 A: Mozart—Piano
concerto no. 16; Symphony no. 36; Ch'io
mi scordi di te; March, K. 408. *Anda,
piano; Ludwig, mezzo-soprano;
Mozarteum Orch.; Paumgartner, cond.*
+ Fa 1-2/94: 243

27129. C 331 931 A: Music of Brahms,
Mahler, Strauss, Pfitzner, and Berg.
*Ludwig, mezzo-soprano; Werba, piano.
Recorded 1960s.*
+ ARG 1-2/94: 192
+ Fa 1-2/94: 367
+ Gr 7/94: 106

27130. C 332 931 A: Schubert—Piano
sonata D. 784; Moments musicaux.
Liszt—Sonata. *Gilels, piano. Recorded
1970.*
• Gr 7/94: 82

27131. C 332 931 B: Schubert—Piano
sonata D. 784; Moments musicaux.
Liszt—Piano sonata. *Gilels, piano.
Recorded 1970.*
+ ARG 3-4/94: 149
• Fa 3-4/94: 310

27132. C 333 931 B: Mahler—Lieder
aus Des Knaben Wunderhorn; Encores.
*Fischer-Dieskau, baritone; Sawallisch,
piano. Recorded live 1976.*
+ Fa 1-2/94: 229
+ Gr 6/94: 98

27133. C 334 931 B: Schubert—Lieder.
*Fischer-Dieskau, baritone; Richter,
piano. Recorded live 1977.*
+ Fa 1-2/94: 305
+ Gr 2/94: 88

27134. C 335 931 B: Opera highlights,
1956-1985. *Fischer-Dieskau, baritone;
with orch.*
• Fa 1-2/94: 305

27135. C 336 931 B: *Orchesterlieder.*
Mahler—Lieder eines fahrenden
Gesellen; Fünf Lieder nach Gedichten
von Friedrich Rückert. Schumann—
Szenen aus Goethe's Faust. Martin—
Sechs Monologe aus Hugo
Hofmannstahl's Jedermann. *Fischer-
Dieskau, baritone; Vienna Phil. Orch.;
Furtwängler, Mehta, Sawallisch, conds.;
Austrian Radio Symphony Orch.; Zender,*

cond.
+ Fa 1-2/94: 229

27136. C 337 941 A: Schulhoff—
Symphony no. 2. Haas—Study for string
orchestra. Klein—Partita for strings.
Ullmann—Symphony no. 2. *Czech Phil.
Orch.; Albrecht, cond.*
+ ARG 1-2/95: 209
• Fa 11-12/94: 372

27137. C 338 941 A: Pergolesi—Missa
romana; Salve Regina in F minor.
Durante—Magnificat. *Prague Chamber
Choir; Stuttgart Chamber Orch.;
Sieghart, cond.*
+ ARG 7-8/95: 167
+ Fa 5-6/95: 284

27138. C 340 941 A: Rachmaninoff—
Songs and romances. *Pusar, soprano;
Hans, piano.*
+ ARG 9-10/94: 180
+ Fa 9-10/94: 305

27139. C 341 941 A: *Duets for organ.*
Music of Clarke, Konstanz, Marchand,
Albrechtsberger, Beethoven, Bachmann,
Mozart, Wesley, Schubert, and Stanley.
Bleicher, Hospach-Martini, organs.
• Fa 9-10/94: 416

27140. C 342 932 I (2 discs): Strauss—
Salome. *Borkh, Hotter, Lorenz, Barth;
Bavarian State Orch.; Keilberth, cond.
Recorded 1951.*
+ ARG 5-6/94: 207
• Fa 3-4/94: 326
• Gr 9/94: 139

27141. C 343 932 I (2 discs): Egk—Die
Verlobung in San Domingo. *Lear, Bence,
Wunderlich, Nöcker, Bavarian State
Orch.; Egk, cond. Recorded 1963.*
+ ARG 7-8/94: 99
+ Fa 3-4/94: 179
+ Gr 9/94: 111

27142. C 344 932 A (2 discs): Verdi—La
traviata. *Stratas, Wunderlich, Prey;
Bavarian State Orch.; Patanè cond.
Recorded 1965.*
+ ARG 5-6/95: 189

27143. C 344 932 I (2 discs): Verdi—La
traviata. *Stratas, Wunderlich, Prey;
Bavarian State Opera; Patanè, cond.
Recorded 1965.*
+ Fa 3-4/94: 356

27144. C 345 953 D: Wagner—Das
Liebesverbot. *Prey, Fassler, Schunk,
Lenz, Engen, Haas, Coburn, Kuhn,
Grumbach, Seibel, Sabell; Chorus of the
Bavarian State Opera; Bavarian State
Orch.; Sawallisch, cond. Recorded live
1983.*
+ ARG 1-2/96: 195
+ Fa 1-2/96: 339
+ ON 12/23/95: 37

27145. C 346 953 D (3 discs):
Wagner—Rienzi. *Kollo, Studer,*

*Rootering, Janssen, Brinkmann, Helm,
Orth, Engen, Anhorn; Chorus of the
Bavarian State Opera; Bavarian Radio
Orch.; Sawallisch, cond. Recorded live
1983.*
+ ARG 1-2/96: 197
• Fa 1-2/96: 340
• Gr 5/96: 120
• ON 12/23/95: 37

27146. C 347 941 A: Fauré—Mélodies.
Schmiege, mezzo-soprano; Sulzen, piano.
• ARG 5-6/95: 110
+ Fa 3-4/95: 168

27147. C 348 951 A: Bruckner—String
quartet (arr. for string orchestra).
Schoenberg—Verklärte Nacht. *Bamberg
Symphony Orch.; Zagrosek, cond.*
• ARG 9-10/95: 117
+ Fa 9-10/95: 156
+ Gr 11/95: 80

27148. C 349 951 A: *Beau soir.* Music
of Saint-Saëns, Debussy, Ravel, Ibert,
and Fauré. *Pergamenschikow, cello;
Gililov, piano.*
+ ARG 11-12/95: 247

27149. C 350 951 A: Fibich—Toman and
the wood nymph; The tempest;
Symphony no. 3. *Czech Phil. Orch.;
Albrecht, cond.*
- ARG 5-6/96: 112
+ Fa 1-2/96: 198

27150. C 351 943 D (3 discs): Handel—
Julius Caesar. *Berry, Popp, Ludwig,
Wunderlich; Bavarian Radio Chorus;
Munich Phil. Orch.; Leitner, cond.
Recorded live 1965.*
+ Fa 9-10/94: 201
+ Gr 3/95: 100

27151. C 352 952 H (2 discs): Spohr—
Piano trios no. 1-5. *New Munich Piano
Trio.*
• ARG 5-6/96: 203
• Fa 5-6/96: 285

27152. C 353 951 A: Vanhal—Mass in
E♭. *Filová, M. Benackova, Dürmüller,
Sulženko; Prague Chamber Choir;
Virtuosi di Praga; Neumann, cond.*
+ ARG 7-8/96: 217
- Fa 7-8/96: 330

27153. C 354 942 I (2 discs): Janáček—
The excursions of Mr. Broucek (sung in
German). *Fehenberger, Lipp,
Wunderlich, Böhme, Engen; Bavarian
State Opera Chorus; Bavarian State
Orch.; Keilberth, cond. Recorded live
1959.*
+ ARG 3-4/95: 271
+ Fa 3-4/95: 195
• Gr 2/95: 101
+ ON 1/20/96: 32

27154. C 355 943 D (3 discs):
Wagner—Tristan und Isolde. *Treptow,
Frantz, Braun, Schöffler, Peter, Klose,
Kuen, Bender; Bavarian State Opera;*

ORFEO

Knappertsbusch, cond. Recorded 1950.
- Fa 3-4/95: 334
+ Gr 5/95: 133
+ ON 4/15/95: 34

27155. C 356 944 L (4 discs): WAGNER—Götterdämmerung. *Aldenhoff, Uhde, Frick, Kraus, Nilsson, Rysanek, Malaniuk, Sommerschuh, Lindermeier, Michaelis, Barth, Töpper, Schech; Bavarian State Opera; Knappertsbusch, cond.* Recorded live 1955.
+ ARG 3-4/95: 274
+ Fa 3-4/95: 332
- ON 4/15/95: 34

27156. C 357 942 I (2 discs): MOZART—Così fan tutte. *Seefried, Hermann, Otto, Dermota, Kunz, Schöffler; Chorus of the Vienna State Opera; Vienna Phil. Orch.; Böhm, cond.* Recorded live 1954.
- Fa 1-2/95: 209
- Gr 2/95: 102

27157. C 358 941 B: BEETHOVEN—String quartet no. 12. MOZART—String quartet no. 19. *Amadeus String Quartet.* Recorded live, Salzburg Festival, 1956.
+ Fa 1-2/95: 111
+ Gr 10/95: 81

27158. C 359 941 A: *Karl Böhm at the Salzburg Festival.* Music of Brahms, Mozart, and Schubert. *Schneiderhan, violin; Mainardi, cello; Vienna Phil. Orch.; Böhm, cond.*
+ Fa 1-2/95: 378

27159. C 360 941 B: BACH—Cello suites no. 1-3. *Mainardi, cello.* Recorded live, Salzburg Festival, 1957.
- Fa 1-2/95: 102

27160. C 361 941 B : HAYDN—String quartet, op. 77, no. 2. BEETHOVEN—String quartet no. 3. DEBUSSY—String quartet. *Végh Quartet.*
+ Fa 1-2/95: 111

27161. C 362 941 B: MOZART—Les petits riens: ballet music; Flute concerto no. 1; Concert arias: Voi avete un cor fedele; Ah, lo previdi; Symphony no. 31. *Schulz, flute; Popp, soprano; Salzburg Mozarteum Orch.; Hager, cond.* Recorded live, Salzburg Festival, 1979.
+ Fa 1-2/95: 212

27162. C 363 941 B: Songs by Prokofiev, Kodály, Mahler, Brahms, Mozart, and others. *Popp, soprano; Parsons, piano.* Recorded 1981.
+ ARG 1-2/95: 244
+ Fa 1-2/95: 314
+ Gr 6/95: 106

27163. C 364 941 B: SCHOECK—Penthesilea. *Dernesch, Adam, Marsh, Lipovsek; Austrian Radio Orch.; Albrecht, cond.* Recorded 1982.
+ ARG 1-2/95: 167
+ Fa 1-2/95: 255
+ Gr 3/95: 102

27164. C 365 941 B: Arias from Le nozze di Figaro, Iphigénie in Aulis, Ariadne, Fidelio, and others. *Ludwig, mezzo-soprano; Vienna Phil. Orch.; Böhm, cond.* Recorded 1955-74.
+ ARG 1-2/95: 242
+ Fa 1-2/95: 323

27165. C 366 951 A: ULLMANN—Don Quixote dances a fandango; The lay of the love and death of Cornet Christoph Rilke; Piano concerto. *Pluhar, narratore; Ardasev, piano; Czech Phil. Orch.; Albrecht, cond.*
+ ARG 5-6/96: 214
+ Fa 5-6/96: 303

27166. C 367 942 A (2 discs): DEBUSSY—Pelléas et Mélisande. *Donath, Gedda, Fischer-Dieskau; Bavarian Radio Orch.; Kubelik, cond.* Recorded 1971.
- ARG 1-2/95: 99
- Fa 1-2/95: 149
+ ON 4/1/95: 42

27167. C 368 951 A: J. LANNER—Orchestra music. A.J. LANNER—D'ersten Gedanken. *Johann Strauss Ensemble of the Vienna Phil.; Wildner, cond.*
+ ARG 11-12/95: 144
+ Fa 9-10/95: 246

27168. C 369 961 A: BRAHMS—Lieder and duets. *Kaufmann, soprano; Schmiege, mezzo-soprano; Sulzen, piano.*
+ ARG 11-12/96: 100
+ Fa 11-12/96: 203

27169. C 370 942 B (2 discs): BEETHOVEN—Missa solemnis. *Donath, Fassbaender, Schreier, Shirley-Quirk; Bavarian Radio Symphony Orch.; Kubelik, cond.* Recorded 1977.
+ ARG 1-2/95: 77
- Fa 1-2/95: 110

27170. C 372 941 A: SUDER—Chamber symphony; Symphonic music. *Lehrndorfer, organ; Bamberg Symphony Orch.; Mund, cond.*
- Fa 7-8/95: 334

27171. C 373 951 A: KRENEK—Lieder. *Schäfer, soprano; Bauni, piano.*
+ ARG 9-10/95: 163
+ Fa 11-12/95: 407
+ Gr 2/96: 89

27172. C 374 951 A: C. KREUTZER—Lieder. *Schreier, tenor; Hans, piano.*
+ ARG 9-10/95: 163
+ Fa 9-10/95: 240

27173. C 375 941 A: FURTWÄNGLER—Symphony no. 2. *Vienna Phil. Orch.; Furtwängler, cond.* Recorded 1953.
- ARG 3-4/95: 270
+ Gr 4/95: 52

27174. C 376 941 A: STRAUSS—Horn concerto no. 2. MOZART—Symphony no. 41; Eine kleine Nachtmusik. *Freiberg, horn; Vienna Phil. Orch.; Böhm, cond.*

Recorded live 1944 (Concerto).
- ARG 3-4/96: 259

27175. C 376 941 B: MOZART—Symphony no. 41; Eine kleine Nachtmusik. R. STRAUSS—Horn concerto no. 2. *Freiberg, horn; Vienna Phil. Orch.; Böhm, cond.* Recorded live 1943 (Mozart) and 1944 (Strauss).
+ Fa 3-4/95: 243

27176. C 377 941 A: PETTERSSON—Symphony no. 8. *Hamburg State Phil. Orch.; Albrecht, cond.*
+ ARG 5-6/95: 148
+ Fa 3-4/95: 251

27177. C 378 951 A: BEETHOVEN—Irish, Welsh, and Scottish songs. *Kaufmann, soprano; New Munich Piano Trio.*
+ ARG 9-10/95: 103
- Fa 9-10/95: 138

27178. C 380 952 H (2 discs): ULLMANN—Lieder. *Schäfer, soprano; Himmelheber, mezzo-soprano; Windmüller, baritone; Bauni, piano.*
+ ARG 11-12/95: 221
+ Fa 11-12/95: 407
+ Gr 5/96: 108

27179. C 381 953 F (3 discs): JOMMELLI—Didone abbandonata. *Röschmann, Borst, Kendall, Bach, Taylor, Raunig; Stuttgart Chamber Orch.; Bernius, cond.*
+ ARG 5-6/96: 129
+ Fa 5-6/96: 178
+ Gr 9/96: 104
- ON 3/16/96: 40

27180. C 382 951 A: LACHNER—Septet; Nonet. *Consortium Classicum.*
- ARG 11-12/95: 143
+ Fa 1-2/96: 240

27181. C 384 951 A: JANÁČEK—Osud. *Ághová, Beňačková, Straka, vocal soloists; Prague Chamber Chorus; Czech Phil. Orch.; Albrecht, cond.* Recorded live.
- Fa 3-4/96: 187
- Gr 7/96: 104
+ ON 1/20/96: 32

27182. C 386 961 A: HAAS—Wind quintet, op. 10; Piano suite, op. 13; Suite for oboe and piano, op. 17; Vyvolená. *Stuttgart Wind Quintet; Davies, piano; Dürmüller, tenor; Hölszky-Wiedemann, violin.*
+ Fa 11-12/96: 261

27183. C 387 961 A: MASSENET—Thérèse. *Baltsa, Araiza, Fortune, Luccardi, Sinimberghi, Michalopoulos; Orch. e Coro Sinfonica di Roma della RAI; Albrecht, cond.* Recorded live 1981.
- ARG 3-4/97: 176
- Fa 1-2/97: 205
+ ON 12/14/96: 52

27184. C 389 951 B: *Goethe-Lieder.* Music of Anna Amalia von Sachsen-Weimar, Reichardt, Zelter, Beethoven, Schubert, Schumann, Brahms, Strauss, Schoeck, Reger, Busoni, and Wolf. *Fischer-Dieskau, baritone; Engel, piano.* Recorded 1970.
   + ARG 11-12/95: 269
   + Fa 11-12/95: 441
   + Gr 3/96: 92

27185. C 390 951 A: *Richard Dehmel songs.* Music of Szymanowski, Reger, Zemlinsky, Pfitzner, and others. *Fischer-Dieskau, baritone; Reimann, piano.* Recorded live 1985.
   - ARG 7-8/96: 278
   + Fa 7-8/96: 354

27186. C 391 952 B (2 discs): GLUCK—Orfeo ed Euridice. *Fischer-Dieskau, Söderström, Pütz; Kölner Rundfunkchor; Cappella Coloniensis; Leitner, cond.* Recorded live 1964.
   + ARG 1-2/96: 114
   + Fa 1-2/96: 209
   - Gr 4/96: 111

27187. C 392 952 I (2 discs): MOZART—Die Entführung aus dem Serail. *Rothenberger, Grist, Wunderlich, Unger, Corena; Vienna State Opera Chorus; Vienna Phil. Orch.; Mehta, cond.* Recorded live 1965.
   + ARG 1-2/96: 145
   • Fa 1-2/96: 258
   + ON 12/23/95: 36

27188. C 393 952 B (2 discs): EINEM—Der Prozess. *Lorenz, Poell, Della Casa, Berry; Vienna State Opera Chorus; Vienna Phil. Orch.; Böhm, cond.* Recorded live 1953.
   + ARG 1-2/96: 194
   + Fa 1-2/96: 193
   + ON 12/23/95: 38

27189. C 394 101 B: MOZART—Arias, vol. 1: 1922-1942. *Various artists.*
   + ARG 1-2/96: 146

27190. C 394 201 B: MOZART—Arias, vol. 2: 1949-1960. *Various artists.*
   + ARG 1-2/96: 146

27191. C 394 301 B: MOZART—Arias, vol. 3: 1961-1982. *Various artists.*
   + ARG 1-2/96: 146

27192. C 394 401 B: MOZART—Arias, vol. 4: 1956-1970. *Various artists.*
   + ARG 1-2/96: 146

27193. C 394 501 B: MOZART—Arias, vol. 5: 1972-1983. *Various artists.*
   + ARG 1-2/96: 146

27194. C 395 951 B: DVOŘÁK—Violin concerto; Symphony no. 9. SMETANA—The bartered bride: Overture. *Suk, violin; Czech Phil. Orch.; Ančerl, cond.* Recorded live 1963.
   + ARG 1-2/96: 105

   + Fa 1-2/96: 192
   + Gr 4/96: 44

27195. C 396 951 B: MOZART—Requiem; Grabmusik, K. 42; Kirchensonate, K. 67. *Seebach-Ziegler, Stader, Braun-Fernwald, Gallos, Mayr, Wiener; Salzburger Domchor; Orchester des Dom-Musik-Vereins; Mozarteum-Orchester Salzburg; Messner, cond.* Recorded live 1931, 1952.
   - ARG 3-4/96: 258
   - Fa 1-2/96: 263

27196. C 397 591 B: MOZART—Great mass in C minor, K. 427. *Stader, Cahnbley, Maran, Raninger; Salzburg Mozarteum Choir & Orch.; Paumgartner, cond.* Recorded 1958.
   • Fa 1-2/96: 261

27197. C 398 951 B: *1960 Salzburg recital.* Music of Schumann and Brahms. *Seefried, soprano; Werba, piano.* Recorded live 1960.
   + ARG 1-2/96: 236
   + Fa 1-2/96: 355
   + Gr 3/96: 90

27198. C 399 951 B: *1979 Salzburg Festival.* Music of Dvořák, Beethoven, and Strauss. *Schreier, tenor; Werba, piano.* Recorded live.
   • Fa 1-2/96: 364

27199. C 400 951 B: BACH—Sonatas and partitas. PAGANINI—Caprice in A minor. *Milstein, violin.* Reissue; recorded 1957.
   + Fa 1-2/96: 123

27200. C 401 951 B: SCHUMANN—Fantasy, op. 17. SCHUBERT—Piano sonata, D. 960. *Curzon, piano.* Recorded live 1974.
   + ARG 3-4/96: 178
   + Fa 1-2/96: 296
   + Gr 4/96: 76

27201. C 402 951 B: BEETHOVEN—String quartet no. 6. MOZART—String quartet no. 1. RAVEL—String quartet. *Schneiderhan String Quartet.* Recorded 1949-50.
   + Fa 1-2/96: 138

27202. C 404 962 H (2 discs): DVOŘÁK—Armida. *Borowska, Ochman, Fortune, Kriz, Podskalský, Daniluk; Prague Chamber Choir; Czech Phil. Orch.; Albrecht, cond.* Recorded live 1995.
   + ARG 3-4/97: 130
   • Fa 1-2/97: 156
   + ON 2/22/97: 41

27203. C 406 961 A: FURTWÄNGLER—Symphony no. 3. *Bavarian State Orch.; Sawallisch, cond.* Recorded live 1980.
   + ARG 11-12/96: 125
   • Gr 9/96: 52

27204. C 407 952 I (2 discs): ORFF—Antigonae. *Goltz, Uhde, Haefliger, Böhme, Barth; Bavarian State Opera;*

Solti, cond.
   + ARG 1-2/96: 152

27205. C 408 955 R (5 discs): *Grosse Mozartsänger 1922-1983.* MOZART—Opera and concert arias. *Various artists.*
   + Fa 1-2/96: 259

27206. C 411 951 A: WEBERN—Lieder. *Hesse, mezzo-soprano; Bätzner, piano; Barainsky, soprano; Bauni, piano; Gecer, soprano; Israel, piano; Doufexis, mezzo-soprano; Söler, piano.*
   + Fa 5-6/96: 316

27207. C 412 961 A: REIMANN—Nightpiece; Eingedunkelt; Entsorgt; Lady Lazarus; Wir, die wie der strandhafer Wahren. *Schäfer, Hesse, Quasthoff, Barainsky, vocalists; Bauni, piano.*
   + Fa 9-10/96: 303

27208. C 414 961 A: *Verdi heroines, vol. 2.* Music from Macbeth, Don Carlo, Aïda, and Otello. *Varady, soprano; Bavarian State Orch.; Fischer-Dieskau, cond.*
   + ARG 11-12/96: 227
   + Fa 11-12/96: 410
   + ON 10/96: 44

27209. C 423 962 I (2 discs): STRAUSS—Feuersnot. *Cordes, Cunitz; Bavarian State Opera; Kempe, cond.* Recorded 1958.
   • Fa 1-2/97: 278

27210. C 424 962 I (2 discs): STRAUSS—Die ägyptische Helena. *Rysanek, Kupper, Aldenhoff, Malaniuk; Bavarian State Opera; Keilberth, cond.* Recorded 1956.
   + ARG 1-2/97: 173
   + Fa 1-2/97: 278

27211. C 425 963 D (3 discs): STRAUSS—Der Rosenkavalier. *Watson, Töpper, Köth, Böhme; Bavarian State Opera; Keilberth, cond.* Recorded 1965.
   + ARG 1-2/97: 175
   • Fa 1-2/97: 278

27212. C 428 962 I (2 discs): GLUCK—Iphigenie in Aulis (sung in German). *Berry, Borkh, Ludwig, King, Edelmann; Vienna Staatsoper Chorus; Salzburg Festival Chamber Chorus; Vienna Phil. Orch.; Böhm, cond.* Recorded 1962.
   + ARG 1-2/97: 113
   • Fa 11-12/96: 256

27213. C 429 962 I (2 discs): LIEBERMANN—Die Schule der Frauen. *Rothenberger, Ludwig, Gedda, Berry, Böhme; Vienna Phil. Orch.; Szell, cond.* Recorded 1957.
   + ARG 1-2/97: 129
   + Fa 11-12/96: 286
   + ON 11/96: 44

27214. C 430 961 B: MOZART—Symphony no. 25; Requiem. *Della Casa, Malaniuk, Dermota, Siepi, vocalists; Choir of the Vienna State Opera; Vienna Phil. Orch.; Walter, cond.* Recorded

ORFEO

1956.
- Fa 11-12/96: 318
+ Gr 10/96: 95

27215. C 431 962 I (2 discs): Music of
Bach, Brahms, Chopin, Richard Rodney
Bennett, and Liszt. *Cherkassky, piano.*
Recorded live 1968.
- Fa 11-12/96: 464

27216. C 432 961 A: *Fritz Wunderlich:
1965 Salzburg recital.* Music of
Beethoven, Schubert, Schumann, and
Schubert. *Wunderlich, tenor; Giesen,
piano.* Recorded live 1965.
+ Fa 11-12/96: 428

ORGANUM RECORDS

27217. OR 871.011: Music of Liszt,
Rheinberger, and Reubke. *Söregi-
Wunderlich, violin; Wunderlich, organ.*
+ Fa 9-10/88: 183

27218. OR 871.012: Music of Widor,
Ritter, Rheinberger, and Vierne.
*Wunderlich, organ; Söregi-Wunderlich,
violin.*
+ Fa 11-12/89: 460

27219. OR 881.010: BACH—Goldberg
variations. *Wunderlich, harpsichord.*
- Fa 11-12/88: 119

ORIGINALS

27220. SH 837: BRUCKNER—Symphony
no. 8. *NDR Symphony Orch.; Schuricht,
cond.* Recorded live 1955.
+ Fa 7-8/95: 141

ORION

27221. 7802: CASTELNUOVO-TEDESCO—
Sonata for cello and harp; Sonatina for
flute and guitar; Piano music. *Stutch,
cello; Chertok, harp; Bolotowsky, flute;
Karpienia, guitar; McFrederick, piano.*
Recorded 1979.
- ARG 1-2/97: 86

27222. 7804: KOECHLIN—Piano music;
Pieces for clarinet and piano. *Sharon,
piano; Ciompi, clarinet.* Recorded 1979,
1981.
+ ARG 1-2/97: 127

27223. 7805: The art of Steven Staryk.
*Staryk, violin; Niwa, Boucher, piano;
London Festival Orch.; Gamley, cond.*
Reissue.
- ARG 1-2/97: 216

27224. 7806: COLERIDGE-TAYLOR—Negro
melodies. *Walker, piano.* Reissue.
+ ARG 11-12/96: 113

27225. 7807: REINAGLE—Piano sonatas.
Glickman, piano.
+ ARG 11-12/96: 187

27226. 7812: WÖLFL—Piano sonatas;
Grand duo. *Pleshakov, piano; Hampton,*

cello. Recorded 1969.
+ ARG 11-12/96: 237

27227. 7813: BLOCH—Cello suite; Baal
shem; Violin sonata no. 2. *G. Rejto, cello;
Davis, violin; Bafler, Harper, piano.*
Reissue.
- ARG 11-12/96: 94

27228. 7814: RUST—Piano sonatas.
ASIOLI—Sonata in G. *Pleshakov, piano.*
- ARG 11-12/96: 192

27229. 7816: The art of Laurindo
Almeida. *Almeida, guitar.* Reissues.
- ARG 9-10/96: 243

27230. 7817: BACH—Guitar
arrangements. *Almeida, guitar.* Reissues.
- ARG 11-12/96: 81

27231. 7820: LALO—Violin sonata.
INDY—Violin sonata. DUKAS—Rameau
variations. *Temianka, violin; Dominguez,
Pleshakov, piano.* Reissue.
- ARG 11-12/96: 149

27232. 85490 (LP): SCHONTHAL—
Fragments from a woman's diary; In
homage of... *Steigerwalt, piano.*
+ Fa 7-8/88: 244

27233. 86498 (LP): TORKANOWSKY—Piano
quartet. HUSA—Variations for piano and
string trio. *New England Piano Quartette.*
+ ARG 3-4/88: 89
+ Fa 1-2/88: 223

ORNAMENTI

27234. FE 002: Arias by Rossini, Bellini,
Donizetti, and Verdi. *A. Negri, soprano;
with orch. accomp.*
- ARG 9-10/94: 261

27235. FE 101 (2 discs): BOITO—
Mefistofele. *Ghiaurov, Tebaldi, Suliotis,
Kraus; Lyric Opera of Chicago;
Sanzogno, cond.* Recorded live 1965.
- Fa 9-10/94: 150

27236. FE 103/4 (2 discs): VERDI—Un
ballo in maschera. *Caballé, Domingo,
MacNeil, Chookasian, Paniagua; Teatro
Liceo, Barcelona; Patanè cond.* Recorded
live 1973.
- Fa 9-10/94: 361

27237. FE 105: Arias by Rossini,
Mercadante, Pacini, Meyerbeer,
Malibran, and Colbran. *A. Negri,
soprano; with orch. accomp.* Recorded
live 1993.
- ARG 9-10/94: 262

27238. FE 106: *Soprano assoluto: the
versatile prima donna.* Music of Verdi,
Cherubini, Thomas, Puccini, Bellini, and
Mozart. *Callas, Deutekom, Gencer,
Negri, sopranos; orch. acc.*
- Fa 9-10/94: 388

27239. FE 107 (2 discs): BELLINI—I
puritani. *Maliponte, Kraus, Cappuccilli,
Raimondi; Chorus & Orch. of Teatro
Bellini di Catania; Gavazzeni, cond.*
Recorded live 1972.
- Fa 9-10/94: 143
+ ON 9/94: 60

27240. FE 108 (2 discs): DELIBES—
Lakmé. *Welting, Kraus, Plishka; Dallas
Civic Opera; Rescigno, cond.* Recorded
1980.
+ ARG 11-12/94: 99
+ ON 9/94: 60

27241. FE 109: *Maria Callas, intimate
portrait.* Music of Puccini, Verdi, Bellini,
Wagner, Bizet, Massenet, and Beethoven.
Callas, soprano; various acc. Recorded
1935-1974.
+ Fa 9-10/94: 391

27242. FE 110 (2 discs): VERDI—Don
Carlo. *Caballé, Bumbry, Aragall, Bruson,
Estes; orch. & chorus; Fulton, cond.*
- Fa 11-12/94: 407
- ON 10/94: 53

27243. FE 112 (2 discs): PUCCINI—
Madama Butterfly. *Angeles, Lanigan,
Evans; Orch. of the Royal Opera House,
Covent Garden; Kempe, cond.* Recorded
live 1957.
- Fa 11-12/94: 332
- ON /94: 53

27244. FE 115: *Caballé in recital.* Music
of Schubert, R. Strauss, Debussy,
Granados, Rodrigo, Gálvez, Toldrá, and
Anon. *Caballé, soprano; Rossi, piano.*
+ Fa 7-8/95: 376

OSF

27245. 49003: FAURÉ—Orchestral suites:
Dolly, Masques et bergamasques, Pelléas
et Mélisande, Shylock. *Orch.
symphonique français; Petitgirard, cond.*
+ ARG 3-4/93: 79

27246. 49008/09 (2 discs): HONEGGER—
Jeanne d'Arc au bûcher. *Soloists; Orch.
symphonique français; Petitgirard, cond.*
+ ARG 3-4/93: 94
+ Fa 3-4/93: 192

27247. 49013: PETITGIRARD—Le
marathon: Suite; Euphonia; Le
legendaire. *Dumay, violin; Orch.s;
Petitgirard, cond.*
+ ARG 11-12/93: 165
+ Fa 9-10/93: 234

OTTAVO

27248. OTRC 18924: MEIJ—Symphony
no. 1; Lord of the rings. BILIK—
Symphony for band. *Royal Dutch
Military Band; Kuijpers, cond.*
+ ARG 11-12/90: 144

27249. OTRC 28922: SAINT-SAËNS—Trio
no. 1 for piano and strings. RAVEL—Trio

for piano and strings in A minor.
Martin—Trio on popular Irish melodies.
Guarneri Trio.
+ Fa 3-4/91: 354

27250. OTRC 29134 (2 discs):
Brahms—Trios for violin, cello and
piano, no. 1-3; Trio for clarinet, cello and
piano, op. 114; Trio for horn, violin and
piano, op. 40. *Guarneri Trio; Pieterson,
clarinet; Slagter, horn.*
+ Fa 5-6/93: 176
+ Gr 11/92: 120

27251. OTRC 38607: Janáček—On an
overgrown path; In the mist; Piano
sonata. *Röling, piano.*
+ Fa 9-10/88: 173
• Gr 8/88: 319

27252. OTRC 38611: Liszt—Piano
sonata in B minor; Hungarian rhapsody
no. 12; Funérailles. *Grubert, piano.*
- Fa 1-2/90: 214

27253. OTRC 38616: Shostakovich—
Piano sonata no. 2; Preludes and fugues
op. 87 no. 1-2, 4, 15, 19. *Berman, piano.*
+ Fa 1-2/90: 304
+ Gr 10/89: 707

27254. OTRC 39027: Brahms—Fantasy
pieces, op. 116. Schumann—
Davidsbündlertänze; Abegg variations.
Cooper, piano.
+ ARG 11-12/92: 200
+ Gr 5/92: 68

27255. OTRC 39029: Music of De Meij,
Kozjevnikov, Absil, and Nixon. *Dutch
Royal Military Band; Kuijpers, cond.*
• ARG 9-10/95: 254

27256. OTRC 48503: Bach—Kunst der
Fuge. *Amsterdam Bach Soloists.*
□ Fa 1-2/90: 92
+ Gr 8/89: 323

27257. OTRC 48609: Music of Bach,
Scheidt, Scarlatti, Pachelbel, and others.
Netherlands Brass Quintet.
□ Fa 9-10/88: 338

27258. OTRC 48710: Music of Falla,
Albéniz, Rodrigo, and Granados.
Groningen Guitar Duo.
+ Fa 9-10/88: 332
+ Fa 1-2/90: 397

27259. OTRC 49135: Music of Satie,
Debussy, Jolivet and Ravel. *Groningen
Guitar Duo.*
+ ARG 1-2/93: 179

27260. OTRC 58714: Schubert—Piano
sonatas D. 840, 959; Eleven écossaises D.
781. *Cooper, piano.*
+ Fa 1-2/90: 297

27261. OTRC 58920: Bernstein—
Jeremiah symphony; Age of anxiety. *Nes,
mezzo-soprano; Ortiz, piano; Arnhem*

Phil. Orch.; Shapirra, cond.
+ ARG 11-12/90: 34

27262. OTRC 68608: Schubert—Piano
sonatas D. 784, 790, 894. *Cooper, piano.*
+ Fa 7-8/88: 246
+ Fa 1-2/90: 297
+ Gr 4/88: 1480

27263. OTRC 68819: Brahms—String
quartets no. 2-3. *Orlando Quartet.*
+ Fa 11-12/90: 182
+ Gr 6/90: 67

27264. OTRC 69028: Dvořák—String
quartet no. 12, "American." Smetana—
String quartet no. 1 "From my life".
Orlando Quartet.
• Gr 3/92: 69

27265. OTRC 69031: Janáček—Mladi.
Reicha—Andantes and adagio.
Foerster—Wind quintet. *Fodor Quintet;
Sparnaay, bass clarinet.*
+ ARG 9-10/93: 141

27266. OTRC 69449: Enescu—
Symphonie concertante; Suite no. 2.
*Hoogeveen, cello; Philharmonia
Moldova; Lascae, cond.*
• ARG 5-6/96: 109

27267. OTRC 78923: Schubert—Piano
sonata, D. 958; Impromptus, D. 899;
German dances, D. 783. *Cooper, piano.*
+ ARG 1-2/92: 106
+ Gr 2/92: 64

27268. OTRC 78926: Schubert—Piano
sonatas in B♭, A minor, D. 784. *Grubert,
piano.*
• ARG 9-10/92: 155
+ Gr 7/92: 81

27269. OTRC 79238: Mahler—Des
Knaben Wunderhorn. *Nes, contralto;
Bröcheler, bass; Arnhem Phil. Orch.;
Benzi, cond.*
+ Gr 2/94: 82

27270. OTRC 88505: Brahms—Songs.
*Nes, mezzo-soprano; Mendelssohn, viola;
Blerk, piano.*
+ DA 11/89: 86
- Fa 1-2/90: 138

27271. OTRC 88817: Schubert—Piano
sonata D. 845; Impromptus D. 935.
Cooper, piano.
+ ARG 7-8/90: 98
+ Fa 7-8/90: 253
+ Gr 2/90: 1495

27272. OTRC 89241: Schumann—
Frauenliebe und Leben. Wolf—Songs.
Dvořák—Gypsy songs. *Nes, mezzo-
soprano; Vignoles, piano.*
• ARG 11-12/94: 253

27273. OTRC 98402: Brahms—Vier
ernste Gesänge; Choral preludes op. post.
122 no. 7-8. Mahler—Symphony no. 1:
Blumine movement; Rückertlieder. *Holl,*

bass; Nes, mezzo-soprano; Het Gelders
Orkest; Talmi, cond.*
• ARG 5-6/90: 65
• Fa 9-10/88: 118

27274. OTRC 109033: Fauré—*Late
piano works.* Barcarolles no. 9-12, 16;
Impromptu no. 5; Nocturnes no. 10-13;
Preludes, op. 103. *Röling, piano.*
• Gr 9/92: 129

27275. OTRC 118818: Music of Lawes,
Giuliani, Bach, Petit, Veldhuis, and
Piazzola. *Groningen Guitar Duo.*
+ ARG 11-12/90: 151

27276. OTRC 128612: Brahms—Songs.
Van der Meer, baritone; Jansen, piano.
• ARG 1-2/90: 33
• Fa 1-2/90: 138

27277. OTRC 128715: Schubert—
Moments musicaux D. 780; Piano sonata
D. 850. *Cooper, piano.*
+ ARG 1-2/90: 84
+ Fa 1-2/90: 297

27278. OTRC 128925: Sor—Fantasies,
op. 34, 41, 54, 63; Trois duos, op. 55.
Groningen Guitar Duo.
+ ARG 9-10/92: 166

OTTER BAY

27279. 102—103 (2 separate discs):
Robert Minden Ensemble. *Robert Minden
Ensemble.*
+ ARG 5-6/95: 220

OUR MUSICAL PAST

27280. OMP 104: MacDowell—Hamlet
and Ophelia; Lancelot and Elaine; Lamia;
Two fragments after the song of Roland;
The Saracens, The lovely Alda. *Royal
Phil. Orch.; Krueger, cond.*
+ ARG 7-8/88: 36
+ Fa 5-6/88: 156

27281. OMP 105: Beach—Symphony in
E minor op. 32. Foote—Four character
pieces after the Rubaiyat. *Royal Phil.
Orch.; Krueger, cond.*
□ ARG 5-6/89: 17
+ Fa 1-2/89: 111 (2 reviews)

27282. OMP 106: Still—Afro-American
symphony. Hadley—Salome. *Royal Phil.
Orch.; Krueger, cond.*
• Fa 7-8/90: 113
+ Fa 11-12/89: 364

27283. OMP 107: Chadwick—Symphony
no. 3; Sinfonietta in D. *Royal Phil. Orch.;
Krueger, cond.*
+ Fa 3-4/91: 181

OWL

27284. 31 (LP): Eakin—Frames.
Parmelee, piano.
+ Fa 7-8/88: 161

OWL

27285. 32 (LP): J.L. ADAMS—Forest without leaves. *Arctic Chamber Choir & Orch.; McGilvray, cond.*
　☐ Fa 1-2/89: 97
　• St 2/89: 149

27286. 34: MACBRIDE—Nocturnes de la ventana. SHORE—July remembrances. MCKINLEY—Concerto for flute and strings. *Hoffmeister, tenor; Podenski, soprano; Stallman, flute; Prism Orch.; Black, cond.*
　☐ ARG 7-8/90: 149
　+ Fa 7-8/93: 171

27287. 35: GOOSSEN—Garland; Casterbridge Fair (excerpts). BARBER—Three songs, op. 45. VERCOE—Herstory III. *Mabry, mezzo-soprano; Wade, Platt, piano.*
　- ARG 7-8/92: 282
　+ Fa 7-8/93: 141

OZ MUSIC

27288. OZM 1001: SMALLEY—Piano concerto; Symphony. *Smalley, piano; West Australian Symphony Orch.; Sydney Symphony Orch.; Masson, Thomas, conds.*
　+ Fa 9-10/88: 266

PALADINO

27289. CD 002 : ZIMMERMANN—Oboe concerto. MADERNA—Oboe concerto no. 3. BON—Oboe concerto. *Koten, oboe; Dutch Radio Chamber Orch.; Bour, cond.; Dutch Radio Phil. Orch.; Nagano, cond.*
　+ Fa 3-4/91: 492

PALLADIO

27290. 4104: TCHAIKOVSKY—Symphony no. 4. LISZT—Les preludes. *New York Phil.; Mitropoulos, cond.* Recorded 1940, 1957.
　- ARG 9-10/93: 257

27291. 4131: CHOPIN—Twelve mazurkas; Three waltzes; Polonaise, op. 53; Nocturne, op. 9, no. 2; Étude, op. 25, no. 3. SCRIABIN—Five études from op. 8; Fantasia, op. 28; Two poems, op. 32. *Sofronitsky, piano.*
　• Fa 5-6/94: 130

27292. 4133 (2 discs): MAHLER—Symphony no. 7; Symphony no. 10: Adagio. *Vienna State Opera Orch.; Scherchen, cond.*
　+ ARG 1-2/95: 135

PAN

27293. 510 049 (2 discs): GUILMANT—Organ sonatas no. 1, 6; Short pieces. *Hauser, organ.*
　+ ARG 1-2/96: 118

27294. 510 053: HONEGGER—Symphony no. 3; Chant de joie; Horace victorieux.

Basel Symphony Orch.; Sacher, cond.
　+ ARG 3-4/95: 116
　+ Fa 1-2/95: 179

27295. 510 058: GINASTERA—Harp concerto. PIAZZOLLA—Tangazo variations. VILLA-LOBOS—Bachiana brasileiras no. 5. MILHAUD—Saudades do Brasil. *Holliger, harp; Sutter, soprano; Basel Serenata; Schläfli, cond.*
　• ARG 3-4/95: 105

27296. 510 059: Music of Poulenc, Debussy, Saint-Saëns, Français, and Milhaud. *D. Ashkenazy, clarinet; Lang, piano.*
　• Gr 4/96: 70

27297. 510 061: *Brazilian songs.* Music of Villa-Lobos, Mignone, Trindade, Telles, Leal, Lago, Moneiro, Nazareth, Guimaraes, Marcellino, and Anon. *Silva, countertenor; Costayas, guitar.*
　+ ARG 3-4/95: 261
　+ Fa 1-2/95: 331

27298. 510 063: MOSER—Doric rhapsody; Spielmusik; Three women's choruses; Cello concerto no. 2; The 33rd psalm; Passacaglia for cellos; Three mixed choruses; Olympic hymn. *Pachlatko, organ; other soloists; English Chamber Orch.; Judd, cond.; Tallis Chamber Choir; Kleiner Konzertchor Basel; Polus, cond.*
　☐ Fa 1-2/95: 207

27299. 510 066: D'ALBERT—Symphony in F, op. 4; Cello concerto. *Meneses, cello; Basel Symphony Orch.; Zollman, cond.*
　• ARG 5-6/95: 68
　• Fa 1-2/95: 92

27300. 510 067: KROMMER—Sinfonia concertante, op. 70; Clarinet concerto, op. 36. *D. Ashkenazy, clarinet; Kutluer, flute; Schatz, violin; Northern Sinfonia of England; Griffiths, cond.*
　+ ARG 3-4/95: 122
　+ Fa 1-2/95: 183

27301. 510 068: LOCKE—Suites for recorder and continuo. *Ensemble Aspecte.*
　+ ARG 5-6/95: 133
　+ Fa 5-6/95: 244

27302. 510 070: MENDELSSOHN—Piano sextet; Clarinet sonata; Four songs without words; Concert pieces for clarinet and basset horn. *Kolly, piano; Ashkenazy, clarinet; Furniss, basset horn; Friedrich, violin; Anderes, Burkhalter, viola; Riniker, cello; Burkard, double bass.*
　+ ARG 3-4/96: 155

27303. 510 075: POPPER—Cello concerto no. 2; Im Walde; Hungarian rhapsody; Papillon; Tarantelle; Elf's dance. *Meneses, cello; Basel Symphony Orch.; Zollman, cond.*
　+ ARG 11-12/95: 171

27304. 510 076: Four-hand piano music by Debussy and Koechlin. *Soos, Haag, piano.*
　+ ARG 5-6/96: 103

27305. 510 077: BRUNETTI—Stabat mater. GREGORIAN CHANT—Four Mass propers. *Ensemble Turicum.*
　• ARG 9-10/95: 118
　+ Fa 7-8/95: 142

27306. 510 078: SAINT-SAËNS—Symphony no. 2; La foi; Phaeton; Ouverture de fête. *Basel Symphony; Zollman, cond.*
　+ ARG 1-2/96: 166

27307. 510 079: SCRIABIN—Piano concerto; Piano sonatas no. 4-5; Preludes; Etudes. *Kolly, piano; Basel Symphony Orch.; Jordan, cond.*
　+ ARG 5-6/96: 190

27308. 510 080: *Cançao do amor.* Music of Piazzolla, Villa-Lobos, Ravel, Gnattali, Abreu, Guimares, and others. *Ziegler, flute; Erni, guitar.*
　+ ARG 5-6/95: 209

27309. 510 084: GLAZUNOV—Piano concertos no. 1-2; Carnival overture. *Kolly, piano; Slovak Radio Symphony Orch.; Griffiths, cond.*
　+ ARG 1-2/97: 109
　+ Fa 1-2/97: 167

27310. 510 085: FARRENC—Trio for clarinet, cello, and piano, op. 44. INDY—Trio for clarinet, cello, and piano, op. 29. *Leroy-Trio.*
　• ARG 9-10/95: 140
　• Fa 7-8/95: 182

27311. 510 086: ALBÉNIZ—Guitar music. GRANADOS—Guitar music. *Erni, guitar.*
　• ARG 9-10/95: 260
　+ Fa 7-8/95: 96

27312. 510 087: Music of Arter, Nickerson, Dinescu, Lehmann, Marti, and Holliger. *Arter, oboe.*
　+ ARG 3-4/96: 233

27313. 510 088: Concertos by Lebrun, Holzbauer, Winter, and Eichner. *Meier, oboe; Northern Sinfonia Orch.; Griffiths, cond.*
　+ ARG 9-10/96: 245

27314. 510 091: SCHUMANN—Impromptus on a theme by Clara Schumann; Piano sonata no. 3; Romances, op. 28. C. SCHUMANN—Romances, op. 11. *Mazzola, piano.*
　+ Fa 1-2/97: 264

27315. 510 535: *The story of Babar: an orchestral concert for children.* Music of Poulenc, Bernstein, Anderson, and Tchaikovsky. *Preuss, narrator; Basel Symphony Orch.; Griffiths, cond.*
　+ Fa 7-8/95: 441

PAN VERLAG VLEUGELS

27316. 0120-342 (2 LPs): HAYDN—Die Feuersbrunst. *Fuchs, Weber, Boesch; Niederösterreichisches Kammerorchester; Ortner, cond.* Recorded live 1979.
  • Fa 9-10/86: 161

27317. OV 3092 (LP): *Musik aus Renaissance und Barock.* Music of Morley, Dowland, Arbeau, Piccinini, Phalèse, Susato, Molinaro, Attaingnant, Scarlatti, Bach, Handel, Frescobaldi, and Anon. *Würzburg Guitar Trio.*
  + Fa 1-2/87: 196

27318. OV 30106 (LP): *Duette für Holzbläser.* TELEMANN—Duets for recorders, bassoon, flute, and oboe. *Musica Poetica.*
  - Fa 1-2/87: 196

27319. OV 30107 (LP): HEILMANN—Organ sonata; Invocation; Partita on Christ ist erstanden; Meditation on BACH. *Kratzenstein, organ.*
  + Fa 7-8/86: 153

27320. OV 65006 (2 LPs): HEILMANN—Von der Weisheit Gottes. *Soloists; choruses; instrumental ensembles; Haupt, cond.*
  □ Fa 7-8/86: 153

PANTHEON

27321. 0981: HINDEMITH—Trauermusik. MARTINŮ—Rhapsody concerto. MARTIN—Ballade. HOLST—Lyric movement. *Golani, viola; M.I.T. Symphony Orch.; Epstein, cond.*
  • Fa 11-12/88: 200
  - HF 10/88: 73

27322. D 1032X: SCRIABIN—Poème de l'extase; Piano concerto in F♯ minor. *Houston Symphony Orch.; Stokowski, cond.; Ruskin, piano; M.I.T. Symphony Orch.; Epstein, cond.*
  - Fa 5-6/88: 212

27323. D 14104: HANSON—Piano concerto. COPLAND—Piano concerto. BARBER—Piano concerto. *List, Ruskin, piano; M.I.T. Symphony Orch.; Epstein, cond.*
  • Fa 5-6/89: 210
  + Gr 11/88: 772 m.f.

27324. FCD 97707: CARULLI—Deux aires russes variés, op. 110; Serenades, op. 96. *Albéniz Guitar Duo.*
  + Fa 1-2/89: 144

PANTON

27325. 80 0242-2: REICHA—Te Deum. *Boháčová, Lindauer, Prusa, vocalists; Vaculka, organ; Kühn Chorus; Prague Symphony Orch.; Smetáček, cond.* Reissue.
  + ARG 3-4/96: 172

27326. 81 0706-2: DVOŘÁK—Cello concerto in B minor. *Fukačová, cello; Prague Symphony Orch.; Bělohlávek, cond.*
  + Fa 11-12/90: 218

27327. 81 0750-2: BACH—Musical offering. *Popelka, organ.*
  - Fa 9-10/90: 151

27328. 81 0758-2: REICHA—Der neue Psalm. *Hajóssyová, Barová, Schmidt, Prusa; Czech Phil. Chorus; Dvořák Chamber Orch.; Mátl, cond.*
  • ARG 11-12/90: 104
  + Fa 9-10/90: 352

27329. 81 0855-2: DVOŘÁK—Violin concerto in A minor; Romance for violin and orchestra in F minor; Mazurek for violin and orchestra in E minor. *Hudeček, violin; Czech Phil. Orch.; Bělohlávek, cond.*
  + Fa 11-12/90: 219

27330. 81 0884-2: *Genus 1.* COPLAND—Clarinet concerto. MARIN—Disco gramofonico. MILHAUD—Scaramouche. STRAVINSKY—Ebony concerto. BERNSTEIN—Prelude, fugue and riffs. *Hlaváč, clarinet & saxophone; Müllerová, harp; Klánský, piano; Barock Jazz Quintet; Solist Band; Altrichter, cond.; Suk Chamber Orch.; Bogunia, cond.*
  + Fa 11-12/90: 465

27331. 81 0891-2: SCHUMANN—Abegg variations; Papillons; Davidsbündlertänze; Toccata. *Novotná, piano.*
  + Fa 9-10/90: 378

27332. 81 0966-2: HALVELKA—Poggii fiorentini. *Šulcová, Barová, Doležal, Novák; Czech Phil. Orch.; Neumann, cond.*
  + ARG 3-4/93: 87

27333. 81 1011-2: *Czech classical string quartets.* Music of Mysliveček, Richter, Kramar, and Ryba. *Martinů String Quartet.*
  + ARG 9-10/93: 229
  + Fa 7-8/93: 307

27334. 81 1014-2: KABELÁC—Cello sonata, op. 9. HANUS—Sonata-rhapsody for cello and piano, op. 9. *Veis, cello; Veisová, piano.*
  + Fa 11-12/93: 280

27335. 81 1024-2: A. KRAFT—Cello concertos. N. KRAFT—Polonaise. *Hošek, cello; Prague Symphony Orch.; Hrnčíř, cond.*
  • ARG 7-8/96: 144

27336. 81 1100-2: DVOŘÁK—Water goblin; Midday witch; Wild dove. *Czech Phil. Orch.; Talich, cond.* Recorded 1954.

  + ARG 3-4/93: 192
  + Fa 1-2/93: 144

27337. 81 1101-2: SUK—Asrael. *Bavarian Radio Symphony Orch.; Kubelik, cond.* Recorded 1981.
  + Gr 1/94: 59

27338. 81 1102-2: SUK—Ripening. KABELAČ—Symphony no. 5. *Domanínská, soprano; Czech Phil. Orch.; Czech Women's Chorus; Ančerl, cond.*
  + ARG 3-4/96: 214

27339. 81 1105-2: JANÁČEK—Sinfonietta; Taras Bulba; Amarus. *Moravian Chorus; Brno Radio Orch.; Bakala, cond.*
  + ARG 3-4/96: 256

27340. 81 1122-2: MARTINŮ—Symphony no. 6; Parables. *Prague Radio Symphony Orch.; Munch, cond.; Czech Phil. Orch.; Rozhdestvensky, cond.* Recorded 1967.
  + ARG 11-12/94: 153

27341. 81 1141-2: EBEN—Vox calmantis; Organ concerto no. 2; Missa cum populo. *Kšica, organ; Czech Phil. Orch. & Chorus; Neumann, Pešek, conds.*
  + ARG 7-8/93: 85

27342. 81 1142-2: SLAVICKY—Sinfonietta no. 4; Psalms. *Šulcová, soprano; Peller, narrator; Rabas, organ; Prague Symphony Orch.; Belohlavek, cond.; Losova, Pecková, Vele, vocalists; Hora, organ; Kühn Chorus; Kühn, cond.*
  + ARG 1-2/96: 176

27343. 81 1144-2: FISER—Double; Lament for the ruined town of Ur; Istanu; Sonata for chorus, piano, and orchestra. *Various vocalists & instrumentalists; Czech Phil. Orch.; Smetáček, cond.; Prague Radio Orch.; Pešek, cond.*
  + Fa 1-2/96: 198

27344. 81 1180-2: CALDARA—Missa ex F. ARBESSER—Stabat mater. PRUSTMANN—Miserere. *Prague Chamber Chorus; Musica Bohemica; Krček, cond.*
  □ ARG 9-10/93: 106
  + Fa 7-8/93: 122

27345. 81 1234-2: ZELENKA—Ouverture a 7 concertanti in F major; Sinfonia a 8 concertanti in A minor; Hypocondria a 7 concertanti in A major. *Suk Chamber Orch.; Vajnar, cond.*
  • ARG 1-2/96: 202

27346. 81 1235-2: ZELENKA—Concerto a 8 in G major; Capriccios. *Suk Chamber Orch.; Vajnar, cond.*
  + ARG 1-2/96: 201

27347. 81 1241-2: DVOŘÁK—Arias. *Randová, mezzo-soprano; Czech Phil. Orch.; Košler, cond.*
  • ARG 3-4/96: 108

27348. 81 1257-2: KORTE—Piano sonata; Wonderful circus; Philosophical dialogs;

PANTON

Concerto grosso. *Moravec, piano; Film Symphony Orch.; Beflin, cond.; Czechoslovak Army Central Band; Kudelásek, cond.; Ishikawa, violin; Korte, piano; Czech Phil. Orch.; Belohlavek, cond.*
+ ARG 3-4/96: 139

27349. 81 1264-2: KUBELIK—Orphikon; Cantata without words; Inventions and interludes. *Kühn Children's Chorus; Bavarian Radio Symphony Orch.; Kubelik, cond.*
+ Gr 2/95: 46

27350. 81 1269-2: MARTINŮ—Slovak folk song variations; Rossini variations; Ariette; Nocturne; Pastorals. *Ericsson, cello; Maly, piano.*
+ ARG 1-2/96: 140

27351. 81 1306-2: Music of Vaughan Williams, Hindemith, and Forsyth. *Maly, viola; Prague Symphony Orch.; Prague Radio Chorus.*
+ ARG 3-4/96: 238

27352. 81 1336-2: DVOŘÁK—Piano quartets. *Martinů Piano Quartet.*
+ ARG 7-8/96: 107

27353. 81 1338-2: BÁCHOREK—Lidice; Stereophonietta; Hukvald poem. *Sololists, narrators, choruses; Ostrava Janáček Phil.; Prague Symphony Orch.; Trhlík, cond.*
+ ARG 5-6/96: 75

27354. 81 1366-2: BORKOVEC—The star; Symphony no. 3; Symphonietta no. 2. *Czech Phil. Orch.; Košler, cond.* Reissue.
+ ARG 5-6/96: 86

27355. 81 1368-2: Music of Albinoni, Hummel, Tomasi, and others. *Halíř, trumpet; Cerny, organ; Wiesner, piano.*
• ARG 7-8/96: 257

27356. 81 1373-2: ŘEZÁČ—Angel on the rubbish-heap. LOUDOVA—Chorale. MARTINŮ—Symphony no. 6. *Prague Symphony Orch.; Slovák, cond.*
+ ARG 5-6/96: 178

27357. 81 1374-2: SCHNITTKE—Requiem. TCHAIKOVSKY—Piano concerto no. 1. *Toperczer, piano; Kuhn Mixed Chorus; Prague Symphony Orch.; Belohlavek, cond.*
- ARG 5-6/96: 183

27358. 81 1393-2: JANÁČEK—Capriccio; Concertino; Sonata. *Wiesner, piano; Ensemble; Svárovský, cond.*
+ ARG 7-8/96: 138

27359. 81 1401-2: MONTE—Missa Cara la vita mia; Motets; Requiem. *Pavel Kühn Chamber Soloists; Symposium Musicum; Kühn, cond.*
+ ARG 7-8/96: 103

27360. 81 1417-2: MARTINŮ—The amazing fly; The butterfly that stamped: suite; Echec au Roi. *Barová, soprano; Brno State Phil. Orch.; Nosek, cond.*
+ ARG 9-10/96: 160

27361. 81 1425-2: FIBICH—Piano quartet; Piano quintet. *Kvapil, piano; Suk Quartet.*
+ ARG 7-8/96: 111

27362. 81 1427-2: SUK—Trio; Elegy. SMETANA—Trio. *Dvořák Trio.*
+ ARG 9-10/96: 212

27363. 81 1430-2: 17th and 18th century Czech dances. *Musica Bohemica; Krček, cond.*
+ ARG 9-10/96: 260

PAPE

27364. OD 1003 (3 LPs): BACH—Trio sonatas, BWV 525-530. *Gross, organ.*
+ Fa 9-10/86: 97

PARACLETE

27365. S 827/8 (2 discs): The Church sings her saints, vol. 1-2. *Monks of St. Peter's Abbey, Solesmes; Claire, cond.*
+ Fa 5-6/93: 376

27366. S 831: ANONYMOUS—Gregorian chant: Maundy Thursday. *St. Pierre de Solesmes Abbey Choir; Claire, cond.*
+ Fa 7-8/90: 344

27367. S 832: ANONYMOUS—Gregorian chant: Christmas, the night office, Vigils. *St. Pierre de Solesmes Abbey Choir; Claire, cond.*
+ Fa 5-6/91: 347

27368. S 833: *Christ in Gethsemane.* Gregorian chant. *Monks of St. Peter's Abbey, Solesmes; Claire, dir.*
+ Fa 5-6/92: 305

27369. S 834: *Gregorian chant.* Tenebrae of Good Friday. *Monks of St. Peter's Abbey, Solesmes; Claire, cond.*
+ Fa 1-2/94: 391

27370. S 835: Gregorian chant rediscovered. *Monks of Solesmes; Gajard, cond.*
+ ARG 9-10/95: 275
+ Fa 11-12/95: 458

PARTRIDGE

27371. 1115-2: *20th century works for solo guitar.* Music of Berkeley, Arrigo, Takemitsu, Martin, Petrassi, Bennett, and Britten. *Wolf, guitar.*
• ARG 7-8/90: 137

27372. 1116-2: RACHMANINOFF—Five fantasy pieces, op. 3. DEBUSSY—Suite bergamasque; Rêverie. *Kooiker, piano.*
- Fa 9-10/90: 345

27373. 1117-2: F. BURGMÜLLER—25 études faciles et progressives, op. 100. *Franssen, piano.*
+ Fa 9-10/90: 204

27374. 1118-2: Music of Purcell, Rossini, Dvořák, and Grieg. *Arion Ensemble; Lascae, cond.*
+ Fa 9-10/90: 501

27375. 1122-2: HAYDN—Piano sonatas no. 4, 7-11; Twelve short pieces. *Kooiker, piano.*
+ Fa 5-6/91: 184

27376. 1124-2: BEETHOVEN—String quartet no. 13 (arr. Broussard). LISZT—Angelus; Am Grabe Richard Wagners. *String Ensemble La Primavera; Broussard, cond.*
- Fa 11-12/91: 262

27377. 1125-2: SCHUMANN—Märchenerzählung, op. 132. MOZART—Trio for clarinet, viola, and piano, K. 498. BRUCH—Pieces for clarinet, viola, and piano, op. 83, no. 2-8. *Speranza Trio.*
- Fa 7-8/90: 263

27378. 1126-2: TCHAIKOVSKY—Souvenir d'un lieu cher (arr. Lascae). PROKOFIEV—Visions fugitives, op. 22, no. 1- 6, 8-16 (arr. Barshai). BARTÓK—Divertimento for strings. *Beths, violin; Arion Ensemble; Lascae, cond.*
+ ARG 5-6/91: 138
- Fa 11-12/90: 375

27379. 1127-2: PROKOFIEV—Piano sonata no. 6. SHOSTAKOVICH—Preludes, op. 34. *Soifertis-Lukjanenko, piano.*
• Fa 11-12/90: 318

27380. 1128-2: Music of Franck, Mendelssohn, Brahms, Schubert, and Granados, arranged for 2 guitars. *Netherlands Guitar Duo.*
- ARG 3-4/91: 150
+ Fa 11-12/90: 444
+ Fa 1-2/91: 386

27381. 1129—1131-2 (3 separate discs): C. SCHUMANN—Complete works for piano. *Beenhouwer, piano.*
+ ARG 1-2/92: 108 (v.1)
+ Fa 5-6/91: 280 (v.1)
+ Fa 11-12/91: 476 (v.2)
+ Fa 3-4/92: 316 (v.3)

27382. 1132-2: Schubertiade. SCHUBERT—Vocal and piano music. *Aalbers, soprano; Hoogland, fortepiano; Brink, clarinet.*
- Fa 7-8/91: 280

27383. 1133-2: BRAHMS—Vocal quartets. *Ensemble Ottovoci; Schul, piano; Broussard, cond.*
• ARG 1-2/92: 36
+ Fa 11-12/91: 284

27384. 1134-2: *The double bass.* MÍSEK—Sonatas for double bass and

piano no. 1-2. SKORZENY—Sonatinas for double bass and piano no. 1-2. *Duo Bassanova.*
+ ARG 7-8/92: 179
+ Fa 5-6/92: 309

27385. 1136-2: BRAHMS—Piano trio in A, op. posth. SCHUMNN—Piano trio no. 2. *Leonardo Trio.*
• Fa 5-6/92: 131

27386. 1138-2: STRAVINSKY—Complete works for string quartet. SZYMANOWSKI—Complete works for string quartet. *Silesian Quartet.*
+ ARG 7-8/93: 165
+ Fa 3-4/93: 306

27387. 9293-2 (3 discs): C. SCHUMANN—Piano music. *Beenhouwer, piano.*
+ Gr 1/93: 50

PAULA

27388. 12: GADE—Novelettes for strings no. 1-2. *Aarhus Chamber Orch.; Larsen, cond.*
+ Fa 9-10/88: 154

27389. 18: NIELSEN—Orchestral pieces. *Southern Jutland Symphony Orch.; Frandsen, cond.*
• ARG 9-10/96: 174

27390. 36: OLSEN—Serenade, op. 14; Trio no. 2; String quartet no. 2; Concertino, op. 73. *Elbæk, Larsen, violins; Skovlund, viola; Winslow, cello; Bevan, piano.*
+ ARG 7-8/90: 81

27391. 37: RUDERS—Four compositions. ABRAHAMSEN—Winternacht; Walden. *London Sinfonietta; Knussen, cond.*
+ Fa 7-8/90: 242

27392. 43: WEISS—Lute sonata in D major; Partita grande in C minor for lute. *Mangor, lute.*
+ Fa 9-10/88: 302

27393. 46 (2 discs): RACHMANINOFF—Music for pianos. *Thorson, Thurber, Gardiner, pianos.*
+ Fa 9-10/88: 232
+ Gr 10/88: 634

27394. 51: RAVEL—Music for pianos. *Thorson, Thurber, Gardiner, pianos.*
+ Fa 9-10/88: 235
+ Gr 10/88: 634

27395. 52: ZEMLINSKY—Trio for piano, clarinet and cello, op. 3. BRAHMS—Trio for piano, clarinet and cello, op. 114. *The Danish Trio.*
• Fa 11 12/88: 313

27396. 54: *Virtuoso overtures: guitar duets arranged by Mauro Giuliani.* Music of Giuliani, Mozart, Rossini, Spontini, and Bellini. *Kämmerling, Christensen, guitars.*
+ Fa 1-2/89: 144

27397. 55: NIELSEN—Commotio; Twenty-nine little preludes for organ, op. 51; Two preludes for organ. *Spang-Hanssen, organ.*
• Fa 9-10/88: 221

27398. 56: NIELSEN—Songs. *Klint, bass; Bevan, piano.*
• ARG 7-8/90: 79
+ ARG 11-12/96: 172
+ Fa 7-8/90: 216

27399. 57: GUDMUNDSEN-HOLMGREEN—Mirror pieces. HOJSGAARD—Phantasy pieces. RUDERS—Tattoo for three. LORENTZEN—Mambo. *Schou, clarinet; Winslow, cello; Bevan, piano.*
+ Fa 7-8/90: 364

27400. 58: Music of Ibert, Milhaud, Taffanel, Ravel, Villa-Lobos, and Bozza. *Scandanavian Wind Quintet.*
+ Fa 7-8/90: 368

27401. 59: Music of Llobet and Tarrega. *Christensen, guitar.*
+ ARG 1-2/90: 118
+ Fa 9-10/89: 419
+ Fa 11-12/89: 215

27402. 60: Guitar music of Maderna, Halffter, and Borup-Jorgensen. *Kämmerling, guitar.*
+ ARG 1-2/90: 118
+ Fa 11-12/89: 464

27403. 62: Music of Ewald, Poulenc, Almila, Horovitz, Dubois, King, Arban, Moller, and Anon. *Aarhus Brass Quintet.*
+ Fa 7-8/90: 368

27404. 76: ROVSING OLSEN—Piano music. *Bevan, piano.*
+ ARG 1-2/97: 161

PAVANE

27405. ADW 7029: BACH—The well-tempered clavier, book 1: Prelude and fugues no. 5, 13, 24; Italian concerto, BWV 971. *Egorov, piano.* Recorded 1975.
• ARG 5-6/94: 66
• Fa 5-6/94: 102

27406. ADW 7071/2 (2 discs): BEETHOVEN—Piano sonatas no. 8, 14, 22, 23, 29, 31. *Pueyo, piano.*
+ ARG 5-6/95: 85
- Fa 5-6/95: 135

27407. ADW 7090: *Harp recital.* BACH—Italian concerto. PESCETTI—Sonata in C minor; Sonata in D. M. ALBÉNIZ—Sonata in D. ROUSSEL—Impromptu. SALZEDO—Variations sur un thème dans le style ancien. SPOHR—Fantaisie pour harpe, op. 35. CASELLA—Sonata per arpa. *Mildonian, harp.*
+ ARG 5-6/92: 165
+ Fa 1-2/92: 407

27408. ADW 7110: FIELD—Nocturnes. *Mamou, piano.*
+ Gr 8/93: 59

27409. ADW 7124/5 (2 discs): *Romantic cello sonatas.* Music of Franck, Brahms, Chopin, and Servais. *Baert, cello; Bémant, piano.*
+ Fa 3-4/95: 370

27410. ADW 7158: ROSSINI—Il Signor Bruschino. *Mahler, Wolanski, Słowakiewicz, Myrlak; Warsaw Chamber Opera Orch.; Kaspszyk, cond.* Reissue.
+ Gr 5/93: 105

27411. ADW 7173: CHOPIN—Four ballades; Andante spianato and Grande polonaise. *Yassa, piano.* Reissue; recorded 1984.
+ Gr 10/95: 93

27412. ADW 7192: MOMPOU—Piano music. *Ayats, piano.*
• ARG 7-8/94: 134

27413. ADW 7197: KABALEVSKY—Flute concerto. IBERT—Pièces pour flûte seule. MARTIN—Ballade. KENNAN—Night soliloquy. LIPSKY—Three images for flute and jazz ensemble. *A. Duchemin, flute; M. Duchemin, piano; Ensemble de jazz Helmut Lipsky; Orch. Métropolitain du Grand-Montréal; Bélanger, Jean, cond.*
+ ARG 7-8/90: 136
- Fa 3-4/90 375

27414. ADW 7199 : PROKOFIEV—Piano sonata no. 2; Sonatine pastoral, op. 59, no. 3; Ten pieces from Cinderella, op. 97. *Yassa, piano.*
+ ARG 1-2/90: 76
+ Fa 11-12/89: 319

27415. ADW 7200: SCHUMANN—Bunte Blätter; Piano sonata, op. 11. *Pirmez, piano.*
• Fa 11-12/89: 350

27416. ADW 7201: TRAZEGNIES—Six divertissements for harpsichord. *Parys, harpsichord.*
+ ARG 5-6/90: 122
+ Fa 11-12/89: 384

27417. ADW 7202: HAYDN—Trios for flute, cello, and piano, H.XV:15-17; Variations for piano in F minor, H.XVII:6. *Kudo, flute; Williencourt, cello; Mamou, piano.*
+ Fa 3-4/90: 197

27418. ADW 7206: HAYDN—Piano sonatas no. 31, 33, 38. *Rappe, piano.*
+ Fa 7-8/90: 168

27419. ADW 7207: BACH—Musical offering: Trio sonata in C minor; Trio sonatas, BWV 1020, BWV 525. *Horigome, violin; Tanguy, flute; Willmyns, harpsichord.*
• Fa 5-6/90: 109

PAVANE

27420. ADW 7215: *Harp recital.* Music of Fauré, Debussy, Liszt, Paganini, Glinka, Godefroid, Tournier, Hasselmans, and Posse. *Mildonian, harp.*
+ ARG 11-12/90: 153

27421. ADW 7216: Mozart—Oboe quartet, K. 370. Stamitz—Oboe quartet, op. 8, no. 4. Giardini—Oboe quartet, op. 25. Vanhal—Oboe quartet, op. 7, no. 1. *Stringwood Quartet.*
+ Fa 9-10/90: 494

27422. ADW 7217: Markevitch—Variations, fugue and envoy on a theme by Handel; Stefan the poet. Galais—Meditation on the death of a painter. *Fujii, piano; Depetris, flute; Galais, harp.*
+ Fa 11-12/90: 266

27423. ADW 7218: Bruzdowicz—String quartets no. 1-2. Zarebski—Piano quintet. *Varsovia String Quartet; Malicki, piano.*
+ Fa 11-12/90: 195 (2 reviews)

27424. ADW 7219: Szymanowski—Piano sonata no. 1; Masques. *Trzeciak, piano.*
● ARG 3-4/91: 138
- Fa 11-12/90: 369

27425. ADW 7220: Mozart—Violin sonata, K. 377. Schubert—Sonata for arpeggione, D. 821 (arr. for viola). Tartini—Violin sonata in G minor. *M. Bezverkhny, violin & viola; O. Bezverkhny, piano.*
- Fa 11-12/90: 300

27426. ADW 7223: *Original arias for soprano, trumpet and organ.* Music of Stachowicz, Melani, A. Scarlatti, Pucell, and aldrovandini. *Callataÿ, soprano; Roelant, trumpet; Landeghem, organ.*
+ ARG 11-12/91: 179
+ Fa 11-12/91: 525

27427. ADW 7225: Music of J.S. and C.P.E. Bach, Effendi, Haydn, Delius, Françaix and others. *Pinar, harpsichord.*
+ Fa 7-8/92: 346

27428. ADW 7227: Pinchart—Organ music. *Pinchart, organ.*
+ ARG 7-8/91: 163
□ Fa 5-6/91: 361

27429. ADW 7228: Mozart—Flute quartets, K. 285, 285a, 285b, 298. *Depetris, flute; Trio Euterpe.*
- Fa 7-8/91: 233
+ MA 11/91: 53

27430. ADW 7230: Beethoven—Bagatelles. *De Spiegeleir, piano.*
- ARG 7-8/91: 30
● Fa 5-6/91: 119

27431. ADW 7231: Mozart—Violin sonatas, K. 296, K. 301, K. 378, K. 30, K. 454. *Rubenstein, violin; Ouziel, piano.*
● Fa 1-2/92: 284

27432. ADW 7232: Mozart—Piano sonatas no. 5, 12; Fantasia, K. 397; Variations on La belle française; Adagio in B minor. *Leconte, piano.*
- Fa 7-8/91: 237

27433. ADW 7233: Cherubini—Six sonatas for cembalo. *Parys, harpsichord.*
+ Fa 1-2/92: 193

27434. ADW 7234: *Airs d'operas.* Music of Mozart, Verdi, Puccini, Rossini, Mussorgsky, Massenet, G. Charpentier, Debussy, Berlioz, Gounod, Bizet, and Offenbach. *Bastin, bass; various orchestras & conductors.*
● Fa 7-8/91: 346

27435. ADW 7235: Loeillet—Sonatas for oboe and harpsichord, op. 3. *Vandeville, oboe; Delfosse, harpsichord.*
+ Fa 9-10/91: 257

27436. ADW 7236/37 (2 discs): Mozart—Apollo et Hyacinthus. *Schäfer, tenor; Soloists of the Tölzer Knabenchor; Ensemble baroque de Nice; Schmidt-Gaden, cond.*
+ ARG 11-12/91: 98
● Fa 9-10/91: 276
● Gr 11/91: 157

27437. ADW 7238: *Iberic impressionist piano works.* Music of Carneyo, Falla, Vasconcelos, Fernandes, Costa and Pires. *Gouveia, piano.*
+ Fa 3-4/92: 406

27438. ADW 7239: Chant grégorien. *Poisblaud, soloist.*
+ Fa 11-12/91: 541

27439. ADW 7241: Music of Bach, Mozart, Clementi, Schubert, Chopin, Brahms, and Taneyev. *Rudenko, piano.*
● ARG 7-8/92: 269
+ Fa 11/12/92: 444

27440. ADW 7242: Jongen—Mass, op. 130. Franck—Prière. Van Nuffel—Cantica ad laudes vespertinas: 2 motets. Peeters—Entrata festiva. *Hughes, organ; Brussels Choral Society; Brass Ensemble Luc Capouillez; Cunningham, cond.*
+ ARG 1-2/92: 66
● Fa 1-2/92: 396

27441. ADW 7243: Mendelssohn—Caprices, op. 33; Andante, Scherzo, op. 16; Andante and variations, op. 82. *Leconte, piano.*
- ARG 5-6/93: 109

27442. ADW 7244/5 (2 discs): Mozart—Complete piano duets. *Orit & Dalia Ouziel, pianos.*
+ ARG 7-8/92: 192
● Gr 1/93: 46

27443. ADW 7251: Chopin—Piano sonata no. 3. Mozart—Piano sonata no. 14. Schubert—Piano sonata, D. 64. *Melnikov, piano.*

+ ARG 3-4/92: 192
+ Fa 1-2/92: 403

27444. ADW 7254: Van Herenthals—Varium et mutabile; Entre ether e terre. Bottesini—Capriccio de bravoura. Joplin—Bethena; The entertainer; Magnetic rag; The ragtime dance; Two negro spirituals. Alt—Suite romantique. Prokofiev—Scherzo humoristique. *Brussels Double Bass Quartet.*
+ ARG 7-8/92: 253

27445. ADW 7255: Bach—Partita no. 2 for solo violin: Chaconne (arr. Raff, Brahms, Busoni). Handel—Chaconne with 21 variations. Liszt—Sarabande and chaconne on themes from Handel's Almira. *Akl, piano.*
● ARG 3-4/92: 188
● Fa 3-4/92: 138

27446. ADW 7257: Mozart—Concertos for 2 pianos and orchestra, K. 365; Concerto for 3 pianos and orchestra, K. 242 (arr. by Mozart for 2 pianos). *O. & D. Ouziel, pianos; Orch. de Chambre de Wallonie; Octors, cond.*
● Fa 7-8/94: 191

27447. ADW 7258: The synthesizer through all ages: from Bach to Satie. *Nicolai, synthesizers.*
+ Fa 3-4/92: 410

27448. ADW 7259: Schumann—Fantasiestücke, op. 12; Humoreske, op. 20. *Carbonel, piano.*
+ ARG 7-8/92: 221
● Fa 7-8/92: 280

27449. ADW 7260: Mozart—Sonatas for flute and harpsichord, K. 10-15. *Depetris, flute; Raibaldi, harpsichord.*
+ Fa 3-4/92: 266

27450. ADW 7264: Chopin—Piano music. *Moguilevsky, piano.*
+ ARG 7-8/92: 117

27451. ADW 7266: Bruzdowicz—Solo violin sonata; Five epigrams. Bacewicz—Solo violin sonata no. 2. Prokofiev—Solo violin sonata. *Szreder, violin.*
+ ARG 7-8/92: 84
+ Fa 5-6/92: 326

27452. ADW 7267: Negro spirituals. *Thompson, soprano; Miller, piano; Iepers Chamber Choir; Coutigny, cond.*
+ ARG 11-12/92: 262

27453. ADW 7270: Pour ung plaisir. *Unidentified performers.*
+ ARG 1-2/93: 189

27454. ADW 7272: Tchaikovsky—Seasons. *Avaliani, piano.*
- ARG 1-2/93: 156

27455. ADW 7273: *Tactus plays Gershwin.* Gershwin—Arrangements for

string quartet. *Tactus String Quartet.*
+ Fa 3-4/93: 165

27456. ADW 7275: LISZT—Paraphrases
and transcriptions. *Du Plessis, piano.*
+ Fa 3-4/93: 210
• Gr 7/93: 66

27457. ADW 7277: Music of Schumann,
Ravel, Prokofiev and Gluck. *Mogilevsky,
piano.*
+ ARG 7-8/93: 196

27458. ADW 7280: LEKEU—Sonata for
violin and piano. SZYMANOWSKI—Mythes:
La fontaine d'Aréthuse. SUK—Ballade,
op. 17: Quasi ballata; Appassionato.
DEBUSSY—Sonata for violin and piano.
Morton, violin; Presland, piano.
+ Fa 5-6/93: 392

27459. ADW 7282: BOCCHERINI—Quartets
for 2 harpsichords no. 1-6. GRÉTRY—
Sonatas for 2 harpsichords no. 1- 2.
Parys, Mol, harpsichords.
+ Fa 1-2/94: 133

27460. ADW 7283: PADEREWSKI—Sonata
for violin and piano, op. 13.
SZYMANOWSKI—Sonata for violin and
piano, op. 9. LUTOSŁAWSKI—Partita for
violin and piano. *Szreder, violin; Strobel,
piano.*
+ ARG 5-6/93: 118
+ Fa 7-8/93: 198

27461. ADW 7284: BACH—Flute sonatas
BWV 1020, 1030-31, 1039; Partita,
BWV 1013, Prelude and fugue, BWV
539. *Depetris flute; Langlamet, harp.*
• ARG 5-6/93: 61

27462. ADW 7285: RACHMANINOFF—
Piano music. *Akl, piano.*
+ ARG 7-8/93: 139

27463. ADW 7287: *Across three
continents: twentieth-century music for
piano.* Music of Gershwin, Ginastera,
Bruzdowicz, and Piston. *Honigberg,
piano; BRT Chamber Orch.; Terby, cond.*
• ARG 7-8/94: 215
+ Fa 7-8/93: 299

27464. ADW 7290: JONGHE—A
composer's testimony: back to emotion.
Various performers.
+ ARG 11-12/93: 99
• Fa 9-10/93: 151

27465. ADW 7291: CHOPIN—Rondos;
Piano sonata no. 1. *Trzeciak, piano.*
• ARG 11-12/93: 94

27466. ADW 7292/93 (2 discs): FAURÉ—
Violin sonatas no. 1-2; Berceuse, op. 16;
Andante, op. 75. FRANCK—Violin sonata.
LEKEU—Violin sonata. *Bobesco, violin;
Genty, piano.* Reissue.
- ARG 11-12/93: 105
- Fa 11-12/93: 236

27467. ADW 7295: BRAHMS—Horn trio.
BEETHOVEN—Horn sonata. CHERUBINI—
Horn sonata, no. 2. SCHUMANN—Adagio
and allegro. *Trio Aglae.*
• ARG 3-4/94: 206
• Fa 3-4/94: 425

27468. ADW 7296: GRIEG—Holberg
suite; Elegiac melodies. SIBELIUS—
Rakastava; Andante festivo; Romance;
Impromptu. *Musiciens de l'Art Nouveau;
France, cond.*
+ Fa 3-4/94: 198

27469. ADW 7298: Music of Gragnani,
Giuliani, Paganini, and Legnani.
Depetris, flute; Polidori, guitar.
+ Fa 3-4/94: 397

27470. ADW 7299: Qilian Chen sings
Chinese songs. *Chen, soprano; Wittek,
piano.*
+ Fa 1-2/94: 366

27471. ADW 7300: GRANADOS—
Tonadillas escritas en estilo antiguo.
FALLA—Seven Spanish folk songs.
MONTSALVATGE—Canciones negras.
Castellanza, soprano; Du Plessis, piano.
- Fa 3-4/94: 371

27472. ADW 7301: SCHUBERT—Die
schöne Müllerin. *Baert, baritone;
Stantcheva, piano.*
• ARG 5-6/94: 138
• Fa 3-4/94: 308

27473. ADW 7302: LESUR—Symphonie
de danses; Nocturne; Variations; Stèle à
la mémoire d'une jeune fille; Sérénade.
*Penot, oboe; du Plessis, piano; Chapron,
flute; Orch. Bernard Calmel; Calmel,
cond.*
• ARG 7-8/94: 123
+ Fa 5-6/94: 178

27474. ADW 7303: BRAHMS—Quartet for
piano and strings, op. 25. JANÁČEK—
Lachian dances. J. STRAUSS, JR.—
Schnell-polka, op. 332. *Jeune
Philharmonie; Hirsch, cond.*
+ Fa 7-8/94: 93

27475. ADW 7308: Duets by Halvorsen-
Handel, Rolla, and Glière. *Raudales,
violin; Goetham, viola.*
+ ARG 7-8/94: 219
+ Fa 7-8/94: 146

27476. ADW 7310: Music of Mores,
Powell, Tirao, Rodriguez, Cardose,
Piazzolla, Ramos, and others. *Tirao,
Lukowski, guitars.*
• ARG 9-10/94: 236

27477. ADW 7312: CHOPIN—Etudes op.
10; Piano sonata no. 3. *Berzins, piano.*
+ ARG 11-12/94: 93
- Fa 11-12/94: 199

27478. ADW 7313: SCHUMANN—
Carnaval; Abegg variations. BRAHMS—
Intermezzi, op. 117; Rhapsodies, op. 79.

Mamou, piano.
• ARG 3-4/95: 181
+ Fa 1-2/95: 267

27479. ADW 7314: OLEY—Organ works.
Mol, organ.
• Fa 11-12/94: 322

27480. ADW 7315: BRAHMS—Organ
music. *Golebiowski, organ.*
+ ARG 11-12/94: 81
+ Fa 11-12/94: 185

27481. ADW 7316: BUSONI—Variations
and fugue on Chopin's C-minor prelude,
op. 22; Six études, op. 16; Étude in the
form of variations, op. 17. *Blumenthal,
piano.* Reissue.
+ Fa 5-6/95: 160

27482. ADW 7317: JOPLIN—Rags and
waltzes. *Blumenthal, piano.*
• ARG 11-12/95: 140

27483. ADW 7318: LISZT—Fantasy and
fugue on Ad nos, ad salutarem undam.
REUBKE—Sonata in C minor.
Golebiowski, organ.
+ ARG 7-8/95: 142
• Fa 1-2/95: 191

27484. ADW 7322: NIETSCHZE—Piano
music. SCRIABIN—Piano sonata no. 1;
Etude, op. 42, no. 5. WAGNER—Overture
to Tannhäuser (arr. Liszt). *Akl, piano.*
• ARG 11-12/95: 168

27485. ADW 7323: WOLF—Mörike
Lieder: selections. *Bryant, soprano;
Blumenthal, piano.* Reissue.
+ ARG 3-4/96: 211
+ Fa 3-4/96: 320

27486. ADW 7324: JOSQUIN—Missa
Faizant regretz; Early Russian
monophony and polyphony. *Russki
Partes; Juravlenko, cond.*
• ARG 7-8/95: 134

27487. ADW 7326: D. SCARLATTI—
Sonatas. *Benoit, piano.*
+ Fa 9-10/95: 304

27488. ADW 7328: RIVIER—Symphonies
no. 3-4, 8. *Orch. Bernard Calmel;
Calmel, cond.*
• ARG 5-6/95: 160
+ Fa 7-8/95: 293

27489. ADW 7330: WYGANOWSKI—Pieces
for violin, 2 violins, violin and piano. *M.
Bezverkhny, Morton, violins; O.
Bezverkhny, piano.*
+ ARG 5-6/95: 194
+ Fa 7-8/95: 370

27490. ADW 7332: DEBUSSY—Piano
music. LISZT—Piano music. *De
Spiegeleir, piano.*
- Gr 10/95: 94

27491. ADW 7334: BRUCH—Stücke, op.
83. SCHUMANN—Märchenerzählungen.

PAVANE

Lethiec, clarinet; Mendelssohn, viola; Mamou, piano.
+ Gr 2/96: 65

27492. ADW 7335: Music of Fauré, Ravel, Vellones, Ibert, and others. *Bastin, baritone; Driessche, piano.* Partial reissues.
+ ARG 9-10/96: 262

27493. ADW 7338: BON—Sonatas, op. 2. *Parys, harpsichord.*
• ARG 3-4/96: 93

27494. ADW 7353: *Argentine piano music.* Music of Pignoni, Piazzolla, Guastavino, Castro, Ginastera, and Lopez Buchardo. *Goimard, piano.*
- ARG 5-6/96: 240

27495. ADW 7355: BRUZDOWICZ—Chamber music. ANTHEIL—Chamber music. *Szreder, violin; Strobel, piano; Strahl, cello.*
+ ARG 9-10/96: 104

27496. ADW 7357: BONNAL—Organ music. *Lecaudey, organ.*
+ ARG 7-8/96: 85

PEARL

27497. GEMM 289 (LP): Opera arias of Donizetti, Rossini, Verdi, Leoncavallo, Mascagni, and Giordano. *Martinelli, tenor; with assisting soloists; various orchs. and conds.*
+ Fa 1-2/88: 248

27498. GEMM 300 (LP): Piano music of Chopin, Schumann, Brahms, Henselt, Rubinstein, Granados, and J. Strauss, Jr. *Moiseiwitsch, piano.*
• Fa 3-4/87: 99

27499. GEMM 305 (LP): *Tenors of Wales.* Music of Handel, Meyerbeer, Sullivan, Spross, Bizet, Elgar, Clay, White, Purcell, Parry, and Anon. *Williams, Beddoe, T. Davies, B. Davies, Glynne, Jones, tenor.*
+ Fa 1-2/88: 252

SHE 564 see SHE 9564.

27500. SHE 582: BRIDGE—Christmas rose. *Eathorne, James, Davies, Herford, Wilson-Johnson; Chelsea Opera Group; Williams, cond.*
+ ARG 11-12/90: 38
+ Fa 5-6/90: 138

27501. SHE 593 (LP): BRITTEN—Choral music. BRIDGE—Choral music. *Mattinson, baritone; Trinity College Choir (Cambridge); Marlow, cond.*
+ ARG 1-2/88: 9
+ Fa 7-8/87: 78

SHE 601 see SHE 9601.

27502. CLA 1000 (9 LPs): Pupils of Clara Schumann. *Davies, Eibenschütz,*

De Lara, piano.
+ ARG 5-6/87: 76
+ Fa 11-12/86: 272
+ NR 9/86: 25

27503. GEMM 3191: TCHAIKOVSKY—Capriccio italien; Romeo and Juliet; Song without words; Symphony no. 4. WEBER—Oberon overture. BRUCKNER—Symphony no. 4. SMETANA—Bartered bride overture. *Philadelphia Orch.; Stokowski, cond.; NBC Symphony Orch.; Walter, cond.* Recorded 1929-30, 1939-40.
+ ARG 3-4/95: 266

27504. GEMM 7042: Tauber in operetta. *Tauber, tenor.* Recorded 1920s-30s.
+ ARG 1-2/95: 266

27505. GEMM 7073: Spirituals; Music of Foster, Giordano, and Martini. *Anderson, contralto.* Recorded 1927-43.
+ ARG 5-6/96: 272

27506. GEMM 9010: *Giacomo Lauri-Volpi.* Music of Cilèa, Puccini, Mascagni, Giordano, Bellini, Offenbach, Meyerbeer, Gounod, Bizet, Gomez, Ponchielli, and Verdi. *Lauri-Volpi, tenor; various acc.* Reissues; recorded 1920-42.
+ ARG 1-2/94: 203
+ Fa 11-12/93: 468

27507. GEMM 9011: Music of Bach, Beethoven, Chopin, Liszt, Falla, and Scriabin. *Gieseking, piano; Hessian Radio Orch.; Schröder, cond.* Partial reissues; recorded 1924-51.
+ ARG 1-2/94: 199

27508. GEMM 9012: BERLIOZ—Symphonie fantastique; overtures; music of Chabrier and Coppola. *Paris Symphony Orch.; Monteux, cond.* Recorded 1930s.
+ ARG 9-10/93: 262
+ Fa 9-10/93: 385

27509. GEMM 9013: Music of Chopin and Schumann; Arrangements. *Grainger, piano.*
+ ARG 11-12/93: 276

27510. GEMM 9016: Music of Gluck, Berlioz, Gounod, Thomas, Massenet, Mozart, Bellini, and others. *Battistini, baritone.*
+ ARG 7-8/95: 276
+ ON 9/95: 56

27511. GEMM 9017: Arias by Donizetti, Puccini, Massenet, Gounod, and others. *Schipa, baritone.* Reissues; recorded 1913-42.
+ ARG 1-2/94: 204
+ Fa 1-2/94: 373

27512. GEMM 9018: *Willem Mengelberg and the Concertgebouw Orchestra: the complete Columbia recordings, vol. 1.* Music of Bach, J.C. Bach, Cherubini, Beethoven, Weber, Mendelssohn,

Berlioz, and Liszt. *Concertgebouw Orch.; Mengelberg, cond.*
+ ARG 9-10/93: 257
+ Fa 5-6/93: 411

27513. GEMM 9019: Music of Byrd, Purcell, Rameau, Couperin, Daquin, Scarlatti, and others. *Landowska, harpsichord.* Recorded 1928-54.
+ ARG 11-12/93: 275

27514. GEMM 9020: STRAVINSKY—Petrushka: Suite; Apollo pas de deux; Song of the Volga boatman; Capriccio. MUSSORGSKY—Pictures at an exhibition. *Sanromá, piano; Boston Symphony Orch.; Koussevitzky, cond.* Recorded 1928-30.
+ ARG 7-8/93: 213
+ ARG 9-10/93: 257
+ Gr 6/93: 108

27515. GEMM 9022: Eileen Joyce, piano. *Joyce, piano.*
+ ARG 11-12/93: 276

27516. GEMM 9023: Music of Ravel, Paganini, Debussy, Bazzini, Mendelssohn, and others. *Heifetz, violin; with piano accomp.* Recorded 1925-37.
+ ARG 9-10/93: 265

27517. GEMM 9024: GERMAN—Selections. *Various performers.*
+ ARG 9-10/93: 257

27518. GEMM 9025 (2 discs): SULLIVAN—The Mikado; The sorcerer: Excerpts. *D'Oyly Carte Opera Company.* Recorded 1926, 1933.
+ Fa 9-10/93: 304

27519. GEMM 9026: BEETHOVEN—Violin sonatas no. 5, 10. MOZART—Violin sonata K. 481. *Szigeti, violin; Schnabel, piano.* Recorded 1948.
+ ARG 11-12/93: 268
+ Fa 11-12/93: 180

27520. GEMM 9027: *Victor Maurel: the complete recordings.* 20 acoustic vocal recordings. *Maurel, baritone; piano acc.*
+ ARG 1-2/94: 203
+ Fa 9-10/93: 345

27521. GEMM 9029: *Leff Pouishnov.* Music of Schubert, Albéniz, Chopin, Liszt, Paderewski, Debussy, Rachmaninoff, Pouishnov, and Grainger. *Pouishnov, piano.*
+ ARG 1-2/94: 199
- Fa 11-12/93: 496

27522. GEMM 9030 (2 discs): Enrico Caruso: electrical recreations. *Caruso, tenor; with new accomps.*
+ ARG 1-2/94: 200

27523. GEMM 9031: LIADOV—Eight Russian folk songs. STRAVINSKY—Petrushka (1911 version); The firebird: suite (1919 version); Pastorale; Fireworks, op. 4. *Philadelphia Orch.;*

Stokowski, cond. Reissue.
+ ARG 11-12/93: 268
+ Fa 11-12/93: 295

27524. GEMM 9032: Arias and songs by Handel, Mozart, Rossini, Donizetti, Verdi, and others. *Hempel, soprano; with orch. & piano accomp.* Reissues.
+ ARG 1-2/94: 202

27525. GEMM 9033: Beniamino Gigli, 1925-1935. *Gigli, tenor; with orch. & piano accomp.*
+ ARG 1-2/94: 201

27526. GEMM 9035: Ruby Helder: the girl tenor. *Helder, tenor; with accomp.* Reissues; recorded 1908-21.
+ ARG 1-2/94: 201

27527. GEMM 9036: The great Armenian baritone Pavel Lisitsian. *Lisitsian, baritone; with piano & orch. accomp.* Recorded 1948-61.
+ Fa 3-4/94: 385

27528. GEMM 9037: SCHUBERT—Symphony no. 8. MENDELSSOHN—Symphony no. 4. SCHUMANN—Symphony no. 1. *Boston Symphony Orch.; Koussevitzky, cond.*
• ARG 9-10/95: 298

27529. GEMM 9038: *Gieseking retrospective, vol. 3.* Music of Mozart, Brahms, Chopin, Casella, and Ravel. *Gieseking, piano.*
+ ARG 5-6/94: 211
• Gr 3/94: 120

27530. GEMM 9041: Songs by Beethoven, Schubert, Strauss, and Sibelius. *Björling, tenor; with piano accomp.*
+ ARG 1-2/94: 200

27531. GEMM 9042—9043 (2 separate discs): Jussi Björling, vol. 2-3. *Björling, tenor; with accomp.*
+ ARG 5-6/94: 213

27532. GEMM 9044: SHOSTAKOVICH—Prelude no. 14; Symphonies no. 1, 5, 7. *NBC Symphony Orch.; Philadelphia Orch.; Stokowski, cond.*
+ ARG 3-4/94: 228
+ Gr 1/94: 106

27533. GEMM 9045: MOZART—Sinfonia concertante, K. 364. H. CASADESUS—Viola concerto. BRAHMS—Viola sonata, op. 120, no. 2. *Primrose, viola; Spalding, violin; Moore, piano; New Friends of Music Orch.; Stiedry, Goehr, conds.*
+ Fa 1-2/94: 247

27534. GEMM 9049: WAGNER—Arias. *Flagstad, soprano; Melchior, tenor; with acc.*
+ ARG 3-4/94: 236
+ ON 9/94: 61

27535. GEMM 9055 (2 discs): Povla Frijsh. *Frijsh, soprano.*
+ ARG 11-12/95: 292

27536. GEMM 9063 (3 discs): BEETHOVEN—Piano concertos (complete); Piano pieces. *Schnabel, piano; London Phil. Orch.; Sargent, cond.*
+ ARG 3-4/94: 231
+ Fa 3-4/94: 119

27537. GEMM 9064 : HAYDN—Symphonies no. 93, 99, 104. *London Phil. Orch.; Beecham, cond.*
• ARG 5-6/94: 200

27538. GEMM 9065: Music of Berlioz, Franck, Debussy, and Offenbach. *London Phil. Orch.; Beecham, cond.*
• ARG 7-8/94: 229
+ Gr 7/94: 128

27539. GEMM 9066 (2 discs): SCHOENBERG—Gurrelieder. SCRIABIN—Poem of ecstasy; Prometheus. *Vocal soloists; Philadelphia Orch.; Stokowski, cond.* Recorded live 1932.
+ ARG 3-4/94: 228
+ Fa 3-4/94: 304

27540. GEMM 9067: Arias and songs 1903-1929. *Garden, soprano; with accomp.*
• ARG 5-6/94: 216
+ Op 8/94: 1001

27541. GEMM 9068: MILLÖCKER—The Dubarry. FALL—Madame Pompadour. *Ahlers, Alpar, Nash, Laye, Oldham; with original orch. accomp.*
+ ARG 5-6/94: 205
• ON 3/19/94: 30

27542. GEMM 9070 (3 discs): *Mengelberg and the Concertgebouw, complete rcordings, vol. 2.* Music of Suppé, Tchaikovsky, Bizet, Mahler, Ravel, Beethoven, Wagner, and Mendelssohn. *Concertgebouw Orch.; Mengelberg, cond.*
+ ARG 3-4/94: 228
+ Fa 5-6/94: 344

27543. GEMM 9071 (3 discs): Fernando de Lucia: Operatic recordings 1902-1921. *De Lucia, tenor; with piano & orch. accomp.*
• ARG 5-6/94: 214
+ Fa 3-4/94: 382

27544. GEMM 9072 (2 discs): *Claudia Muzio: a selection of her finest Edison recordings, including unpublished items.* Music of Verdi, Tchaikovsky, Gomes, Giordano, Sodero, Bachelet, Catalani, Leoncavallo, and others. *Muzio, soprano; orch. acc.; Sodero, cond.*
+ ARG 5-6/94: 216
+ Fa 5-6/94: 289

27545. GEMM 9076 (2 discs): WAGNER—Ring des Nibelungen: Excerpts. *Philadelphia Orch.; Stokowski,*

cond. Recorded 1927-39.
• ARG 7-8/94: 229
• Fa 7-8/94: 277

27546. GEMM 9077: Music of Dvořák, Bruch, Haydn, Popper, Saint-Saëns, Sarasate, and others. *Feuermann, cello; with accomp.*
+ ARG 7-8/94: 234

27547. GEMM 9078: *Egon Petri, vol. 3.* Music of Brahms, Busoni, Bach, Schubert, Chopin, and Liszt. *Petri, piano.*
• ARG 7-8/94: 234

27548. GEMM 9079: My song to you. *Kiepura, tenor.*
+ ARG 9-10/94: 275
+ ON 5/94: 51

27549. CDS 9083 (2 discs): BEETHOVEN—Solo piano music, vol. 1. *Schnabel, piano.*
+ Fa 9-10/94: 139

27550. GEMM 9083, 9099, 9123, 9139, 9142 (11 discs total): BEETHOVEN—Complete piano sonatas. *Schnabel, piano.* Recorded 1932-39.
• ARG 5-6/95: 239
+ Gr 11/94: 184

27551. GEMM 9084: *Lollipops.* Music of Rossini, Respighi, and Mendelssohn. *London Phil. Orch.; Beecham, cond.*
+ ARG 1-2/95: 257

27552. GEMM 9088: Arias by Gounod, Flotow, Verdi, Mozart, Thomas, Massenet, Bizet, Leoncavallo, and Paladilhe. *Ruffo, baritone.*
+ ARG 3-4/96: 265

27553. GEMM 9090: Music of Ravel, Satie, Debussy, and Fauré. *Various orchs.; Koussevitzky, cond.*
+ ARG 7-8/94: 234

27554. GEMM 9091: Arias form Barber of Seville, Favorita, Don Pasquale, Traviata, Carmen, and others. *Borgioli, tenor.*
+ ARG 5-6/95: 248

27555. GEMM 9093: *Richard Crooks, vol. 1.* Music of Handel, Schubert, Foster, Herbert, Verdi, and others. *Crooks, tenor.*
+ ARG 11-12/94: 260

27556. GEMM 9094: *Lollipops.* Music of Wagner, Grieg, Dvořák, Weber, Suppé, and Mozart. *London Phil. Orch.; Beecham, cond.*
+ ARG 1-2/95: 257

27558. GEMM 9098 (2 discs): BACH—Transcriptions for orchestra. *Philadelphia Orch.; Stokowski, cond.*
+ ARG 11-12/94: 255

27559. GEMM 9101: *Great virtuosi of the golden age, vol. 1.* Music of Vieuxtemps, Wieniawski, Mendelssohn,

PEARL

Schubert, Sarasate, Beethoven, Brahms, and Bach. *Ysaÿe, Elman, Sarasate, Powell, Joachim, violin; unnamed pianists.*
 □ ARG 5-6/89: 120
 + Fa 3-4/89: 380

27560. GEMM 9102: *Great virtuosi of the golden age, vol. 2.* Music of Paganini, Sarasate, Wieniawski, Fibich, Mendelssohn, Handel, Raff, Brahms, Bach, Chopin, and Bazzini. *Thibaud, Hall, Kreisler, Drdla, Vecsey, violin; unnamed pianists.*
 + Fa 3-4/89: 377

27561. GEMM 9103: Music of Mozart, Scarlatti, Paradies, Beethoven, Granados, and others. *Iturbi, piano.*
 + ARG 11-12/94: 260

27562. GEMM 9104: Arias by Rossini, Bellini, Donizetti, Verdi, Gounod, Bizet, Meyerbeer, Ponchielli, and Leoncavallo. *Amato, baritone.*
 + ARG 3-4/96: 265

27563. GEMM 9106: Arias from Boris Godunov, Carmen, Huguenots, Manon, and others. *Smirnov, tenor.* Recorded 1912-24.
 ● ARG 1-2/95: 266

27564. GEMM 9108 (2 discs): Music of Chopin, Liszt, Bach, Haydn, Mozart, Beethoven, and Schubert. *Horszowski, piano.* Recorded live 1940-1979.
 + ARG 1-2/95: 258

27565. GEMM 9109: *Paderewski, vol. 3.* Music of Schumann, Mendelssohn, Brahms, Rubinstein, Debussy, and Strauss-Tausig. *Paderewski, piano.*
 + ARG 3-4/95: 276

27566. GEMM 9114: Music of Mozart, Bach, Scarlatti, Field, Chopin, Beethoven, and Bach. *Hess, piano; Concertgebouw Orch.; Beinum, cond.* Recorded 1950s.
 + ARG 3-4/95: 276

27567. GEMM 9116: *Love me forever.* Music of Berlin, Edwards, Nin, Bizet, and others. *Moore, soprano.* Recorded 1925-42.
 + ARG 1-2/95: 265

27568. GEMM 9117: Arias from Sonnambula, Rigoletto, Traviata, Lucia di Lammermoor, and others. *Pareto, soprano; Longas, piano.* Recorded 1907-26.
 ● ARG 7-8/95: 278

27569. GEMM 9118: Mozart—Flute concertos; Flute and harp concerto. *Moyse, flute; Laskine, harp; with orch. accomp.* Recorded 1930s.
 ● ARG 3-4/95: 271

27570. GEMM 9119: Schumann—Dichterliebe; Frauenlieben und Leben;

Liederkreis, op. 39. *Hüsch, baritone; Lehmann, soprano; Schorr, bass.* Recorded 1928, 1928, 1937-38.
 + ARG 3-4/95: 273
 ● Gr 11/94: 184

27571. GEMM 9121 (2 discs): Wagner—Meistersinger: Act III; Rarities. *Nissen, Kremer, Ralf, Teschemacher; Dresden State Opera; Böhm, cond.* Recorded 1938.
 + ARG 1-2/95: 256
 + ON 12/24/94: 32

27572. GEMM 9122: 20 great basses. *Various.* Historical recordings.
 + ARG 11-12/95: 297

27573. GEMM 9124: Great harpsichord virtuosos, vol. 1. *Various performers.* Recorded 1924-39.
 + ARG 11-12/95: 289

27574. GEMM 9127: Arias from Nabucco, Ernani, Simon Boccanegra, Gioconda, and others. *Mardones, bass.*
 + ARG 5-6/95: 249

27575. GEMM 9128: *Casals: the bow and the baton.* Music of Beethoven, Brahms, Vivaldi, Bach, Tartini, and others. *Casals, cello & cond.* Recorded 1929.
 + ARG 5-6/95: 245

27576. GEMM 9130: 20 great sopranos. *Various.* Historical recordings.
 + ARG 11-12/95: 297

27577. GEMM 9132: *Brailowsky: early discs.* Music of Scarlatti, Weber, Schubert, Mendelssohn, Chopin, Schumann, and others. *Brailowsky, piano.* Recorded 1928-34.
 + ARG 5-6/95: 245
 ● Gr 2/95: 115

27578. GEMM 9133: Ida Presti and Luise Walker. *Presti, Walker, guitar.* Historical recordings.
 + ARG 11-12/95: 289

27579. GEMM 9134: Music of Debussy, Duparc, Berlioz, and Fauré. *Teyte, soprano; Cortot, Moore, piano; London Symphony Orch.; Howard, cond.*
 + ARG 3-4/96: 265
 + Gr 11/95: 188
 + ON 5/96: 61

27580. GEMM 9135: Music of Brahms, Mendelssohn, Schumann, Liszt, Wagner, and others. *Moiseiwitsch, piano.* Recorded 1925-41.
 + ARG 5-6/95: 246

27581. GEMM 9137 (7 discs): Wagner—Ring des Nibelungen: Excerpts. *Various performers.* Recorded 1927-32.
 + ARG 5-6/95: 243
 + Gr 4/95: 143
 + ON 4/15/95: 34

27582. GEMM 9138 (2 discs): Mozart—Piano concertos no. 9, 11, 13-14, 19; Sonata no. 15. *Horszowski, piano; Musica Aeterna Orch.; Waldman, cond.* Recorded 1962-72.
 + ARG 5-6/95: 240
 + Gr 3/95: 50

27583. GEMM 9140: Songs by Nielsen, Reesen, Agerby, and Heise. *Schiøtz, tenor.* Recorded 1938-41.
 + ARG 3-4/95: 272
 + ON 4/1/95: 43

27584. GEMM 9141 (2 discs): Schubert—String quartets no. 8, 14-15; Fantasy in C; Trio in E♭. *A. Busch, violin; H. Busch, cello; R. Serkin, piano; Busch Quartet.*
 + ARG 9-10/95: 298

27585. GEMM 9145: Arias by Mozart Wagner, Tchaikovsky, Nessler, Verdi, and others. *Tauber, tenor.*
 + ARG 7-8/95: 279
 ● ON 10/96: 43

27586. GEMM 9147: Music of Beethoven, Chopin, Moszkowski, Liszt, Falla, and others. *Hambourg, piano.* Recorded 1909-33.
 ● ARG 7-8/95: 275

27587. GEMM 9148—9149 (2 separate discs): The recorded viola, vol. 1-2. *Various performers.* Recorded 1934-42.
 + ARG 11-12/95: 290

27588. GEMM 9152 (2 discs): Gregorian chants: 1930 recordings. *St. Pierre de Solesmes; Gajard, cond.*
 + ARG 9-10/95: 275
 + Fa 11-12/95: 457

27589. GEMM 9153 (2 discs): Mozart—Piano concertos no. 17-18, 20, 22; Fantasy, K. 475. *Horszowski, piano; Musica Aeterna; Waldman, cond.* Recorded 1962, 1966.
 + ARG 9-10/95: 179

27590. GEMM 9154: Music of Bach, Mozart, Schubert, Berlioz, and Borodin. *Concertgebouw Orch.; Mengelberg, cond.*
 + ARG 1-2/96: 240
 + Gr 3/96: 108

27591. GEMM 9155: Arias by Wagner, Mozart, Gounod, and others. *Strienz, bass.* Recorded 1926-40.
 + ARG 11-12/95: 295

27592. GEMM 9158: Songs and operetta arias. *Printemps, soprano.* Recorded 1920-40.
 + ARG 11-12/95: 294

27593. GEMM 9161: French songs and arias. *Clément, tenor.*
 + ARG 11-12/95: 292
 + Gr 8/95: 138
 + Op 8/95: 1006

27594. GEMM 9162: VERDI—Requiem. *Caniglia, Stignani, Gigli, Pinza; Rome Opera; Serafin, cond.* Recorded 1939.
+ ARG 11-12/95: 287

27595. GEMM 9163: Music of Tchaikovsky, Mendelssohn, Schumann, Brahms, and others. *Sapellnikoff, piano.* Historical recordings.
+ ARG 11-12/95: 290

27596. GEMM 9164 (2 discs): HANDEL—Concerti grossi op. 6. *Boyd Neel Orch.; Neel, cond.*
• ARG 9-10/95: 298

27597. GEMM 9165: Spanish songs and zarzuela. *Supervia, mezzo-soprano.*
+ ARG 11-12/95: 296

27598. GEMM 9166: BARTÓK—Piano music. *Bartók, piano.* Recorded 1929-42.
+ ARG 3-4/96: 254
+ Gr 6/96: 106

27599. GEMM 9167 (2 discs): Music of Brahms, Saint-Saëns, Prokofiev, Vieuxtemps, Wieniawski, Sarasate, and Walton. *Heifetz, violin; Boston Symphony Orch.; Koussevitzky, cond.; London Symphony Orch.; Barbirolli, cond.; Cincinnati Symphony Orch.; Goossens, cond.*
□ ARG 5-6/96: 261
□ Fi 3/96: 130

27600. GEMM 9168: Arias from La bohème, Marta, Manon, Faust, and others. *Bonci, tenor.* Recorded 1912-13.
+ ARG 11-12/95: 291

27601. GEMM 9169: GLUCK—Orphée. *Raveau, Féraldy, Delille; Paris Symphony Orch.; Tomasi, cond.*
+ ARG 11-12/95: 285
+ Gr 12/95: 176
+ ON 9/95: 55

27602. GEMM 9170: BRAHMS—Piano concerto no. 2. SCHUBERT—Wanderer fantasy. BEETHOVEN—Variations on Nel cor più. *Ney, piano; Berlin Phil. Orch.; Fiedler, cond.* Recorded 1937-41.
+ ARG 5-6/96: 272
+ Gr 3/96: 109

27603. GEMM 9171: Opera arias and songs. *Kurz, soprano.* Recorded 1907-24.
+ ARG 3-4/96: 263

27604. GEMM 9174: SAINT-SAËNS—Violin sonata no. 1; Cello sonatas. PHILIPP—Black swans. *Philipp, piano; Pascal, violin; Bazelaire, cello.* Recorded mid-1930s.
+ ARG 1-2/96: 246

27605. GEMM 9175: Music of Bizet, Gounod, Verdi, Puccini, and others. *Nash, tenor.*
+ ARG 5-6/96: 278
+ Gr 11/95: 190

27606. GEMM 9178: Arias. *Stracciari, baritone.*
• ARG 3-4/96: 265
+ ON 10/96: 43

27607. GEMM 9179: Music of Vivaldi, Corelli, H. Casadesus, Handel, Mozart, Schubert, Liszt, and Grieg. *Maynor, soprano; Harvard Glee Club; Radcliffe Choral Society; Boston Symphony Orch.; Koussevitzky, cond.*
+ ARG 3-4/96: 260
+ Gr 2/96: 114

27608. GEMM 9181: Opera arias. *Sammarco, baritone.* Recorded 1902-1910.
• ARG 11-12/96: 303

27609. GEMM 9182: Music of Rossini, Massenet, Mozart, and others. *Chaliapin, bass.* Recorded 1922-35.
+ ARG 5-6/96: 273

27610. GEMM 9185 (2 discs): HAYDN—Symphonies no. 94, 102. MOZART—Symphonies no. 29, 34. BEETHOVEN—Symphonies no. 2, 8. *Boston Symphony Orch.; Koussevitzky, cond.*
+ ARG 5-6/96: 261
+ Gr 2/96: 114

27611. GEMM 9186: Music of Mozart, Verdi, Gounod, Offenbach, and others. *Korjus, soprano.* Recorded 1934-36.
+ ARG 5-6/96: 276
+ Gr 8/96: 103

27612. GEMM 9187: Arias and songs. *Lilli Lehmann, soprano.* Recorded 1906-07.
- ARG 5-6/96: 277
• Gr 3/96: 112

27613. GEMM 9188 (2 discs): The final recordings (1941-42). *McCormack, tenor.*
+ ARG 3-4/96: 264
+ Gr 2/96: 115

27614. GEMM 9189 (2 discs): WEILL—From Berlin to Broadway. *Various performers.*
+ ARG 5-6/96: 271
+ Fi 6/96: 134
+ Op 5/96: 604

27615. GEMM 9190: WAGNER—Duets from Lohengrin, Parsifal, Tristan, and Götterdämmerung. *Flagstad, soprano; Melchior, tenor; McArthur, cond.*
+ ARG 7-8/96: 296

27616. GEMM 9192 (2 discs): Music of Beethoven, Chopin, Mussorgsky, Schumann, and Palmgren. *Moiseiwitsch, piano.* Recorded 1961.
+ ARG 7-8/96: 292

27617. GEMM 9193 (2 discs): Music of Brahms, Bach, Mendelssohn, Liszt and others. *Freund, piano.* Recorded 1950s.
+ ARG 11-12/96: 295

27618. GEMM 9194: BEETHOVEN—Piano concerto no. 2. RACHMANINOFF—Paganini rhapsody. SCHUBERT—Songs. CHOPIN—Piano music. *Kapell, piano; NBC Symphony Orch.; Golschmann, cond.; New York Phil.; Rodzinski, cond.; Stader, soprano.*
+ ARG 7-8/96: 291
+ Fi 6/96: 130

27619. GEMM 9195: Arias and songs by Donizetti, Rossini, Verdi, Thomas, and others. *Dal Monte, soprano.* Recorded 1920s.
+ ARG 7-8/96: 292

27620. GEMM 9197: Arias from Oberon, Lohengrin, Ballo in maschera, Turandot, and others. *Németh, soprano.*
• ARG 11-12/96: 301
• Gr 6/96: 117

27621. GEMM 9210: Arias from Norma, La vestale, Ernani, Aida, and others. *Ponselle, soprano.*
+ ARG 11-12/96: 302

27622. GEMM 9211: Vocal music of Mendelssohn, Handel, Schubert, Brahms, and Anon. *Lough, boy soprano; Thalben-Ball, organ & piano.*
+ ARG 11-12/89: 170
+ Fa 11-12/89: 424

27623. GEMM 9215: Music of Puccini, Moniuszko, Boito, Verdi, and others. *Kruszeinicka, soprano.* Recorded 1902-1928.
+ ARG 11-12/96: 299

27624. GEMM 9218: BEETHOVEN—Piano concerto no. 5; Piano sonatas no. 8, 23. *E. Fischer, piano; Staatskapelle Dresden; Böhm, cond.* Recorded 1935, 1938.
+ ARG 11-12/96: 284

27625. GEMM 9219: Arias by Verdi, Bellini, Donizetti, Gounod, and others. *Boninsegna, soprano.*
+ ARG 1-2/97: 242

27626. GEMM 9234 (2 discs): Music of Strauss, Wagner, Schumann, and others. *Lehmann, soprano.* Recorded 1927-1935.
+ ARG 1-2/97: 242

27627. GEMM 9235 (2 discs): LISZT—Hungarian rhapsodies no. 1-15; Au bord d'une source. BACH—Concertos (arr. Busoni). *Borowski, piano.*
+ ARG 1-2/97: 241

27628. GEMM 9236: MOZART—Piano concertos no. 21, 27; Piano sonata no. 17. *Gieseking, piano; New York Phil.; Cantelli, cond.; Lausanne Chamber Orch.; Desarzens, cond.*
+ ARG 1-2/97: 237

27629. GEMM 9237: BRAHMS—Symphonies no. 3-4. *Boston Symphony Orch.; Koussevitzky, cond.* Recorded

PEARL

1930-40s.
• ARG 11-12/96: 285

27630. GEMM 9239: *The recordings (1899-1913).* Music of Eckert, Delibes, Donizetti, Massé, Smith, David, Thomas, Yaw, Auber, Paer, and Meyerbeer. *Yaw, soprano; various accs.*
☐ ARG 3-4/90: 158
+ Fa 11-12/89: 428

27631. GEMM 9245: *Musicraft solo recordings, vol. 2.* Music of Couperin, Scarlatti, Purcell, Morely, and Gibbons. *Kirkpatrick, harpsichord.* Recorded 1933-38.
+ ARG 1-2/97: 241
+ Gr 11/96: 126

27632. GEMM 9254: *The rarest recordings.* Music of Bach, Mozart, Schubert, Berlioz, and Borodin. *Concertgebouw Orch.; Mengelberg, cond.*
+ Fa 7-8/95: 445

27633. GEMM 9307: *The best of Lawrence Tibbett.* Msic of Loewe, Bizet, Offenbach, Rossini, Gershwin, Foster, Lehmann, Goetze, Mussorgsky, Tchaikovsky, Dvořák, and Anon. *Tibbett, baritone; various accs.* Recorded 1927-1935.
+ ARG 5-6/89: 129
+ Fa 5-6/89: 375

27634. GEMM 9308: Music of Bellini, Donizetti, Verdi, Mozart, Auber, David, Meyerbeer, Bizet, Delibes, Massenet, Chopin, Rimsky-Korsakov, and Valverde. *Galli-Curci, soprano; various orchs. & conds.*
+ Fa 11-12/88: 317
+ Gr 2/89: 1348

27635. GEMM 9309: Music of Verdi, Meyerbeer, Puccini, Leoncavallo, Tosti, and Di Capua. *Caruso, tenor; with assisting soloists; various orchs. & conds.*
+ Fa 11-12/88: 318
+ Gr 5/89: 1794
+ Op 10/88: 1257

27636. GEMM 9311: *Poulenc d'après Poulenc.* POULENC—Selections. *Peignot, Croiza, soprano; Lamorlette, oboe; Dherin, bassoon; Poulenc, piano; Orch. de Concerts Straram; Straram, cond.*
+ ARG 1-2/89: 126
+ Fa 1-2/89: 230
☐ Gr 10/88: 644
+ MA 1/89: 64
+ St 4/89: 207

27637. GEMM 9312: Music of Mozart, Gounod, Arditi, Moore, Bach, Bishop, Rothchild, Patti, Hook, Lotti, Foster, Crouch, Tosti, Bellini, Yradier, Thomas, and Anon. *Patti, soprano; Ronald, Barili, piano.* Recorded 1905-1906.
+ ARG 9-10/89: 150
+ Fa 9-10/89: 387

27638. GEMM 9314: Music of Glinka, Serov, Mussorgsky, Archangelsky, Rossini, Mozart, Bellini, Boito, Gounod, and Massenet. *Chaliapin, bass; various orchs. & conds.*
+ ARG 9-10/88: 119
+ Fa 9-10/88: 311

27639. GEMM 9315: *Kreisler & McCormack.* Music of Braga, Leroux, Godard, Schubert, Bach, Macagni, Moskowski, De Curtis, Meyer-Helmund, Bohm, Raff, Offenbach, Kramer, Johnson, Rachmaninoff, Strauss, Larchet, and Anon. *McCormack, tenor; Kreisler, violin; various pianists.*
+ ARG 9-10/88: 120
+ Fa 9-10/88: 315

27640. GEMM 9316: Music of Bizet, Meyerbeer, Verdi, Thomas, Boito, Ponchielli, Puccini, Toselli, Mario, Cottrau, Donaudy, Di Capua, and De Crescenzo. *Gigli, tenor; with assisting soloists; various orchs. & conds.*
+ ARG 1-2/89: 120
+ Fa 11-12/88: 317
+ Gr 9/88: 484
+ MA 5/89: 69
+ Op 10/88: 1257

27641. GEMM 9318: Music of Bach, Handel, Giordani, Martini, Schubert, Schumann, Brahms, Verdi, Tchaikovsky, Saint-Saëns, and Anon. *Anderson, contralto; various accs.* Recorded 1929, 1937.
+ ARG 3-4/89: 121
+ Fa 5-6/89: 371

27642. GEMM 9319: *Arias and songs 1926-31.* Music of Handel, Mozart, Rossini, Donizetti, Meyerbeer, Gounod, Thomas, Verdi, Leoncavallo, Puccini, Balfe, Wallace, Sullivan, and Carey. *Nash, tenor; with assisting soloists; various orchs. & conds.*
+ ARG 9-10/89: 149
+ Fa 1-2/90: 363
+ Gr 8/89: 373

27643. GEMM 9322: Music of Handel, Rossini, Donizetti, Verdi, Flotow, Delibes, Thomas, Massenet, Leoncavallo, Liszt, Padilla, Arona, Martini, and Barthelmy . *Schipa, tenor; various orchs. & conds.*
+ ARG 1-2/89: 122
+ Fa 1-2/89: 309
+ Gr 2/89: 1348
+ MA 5/89: 69
+ ON 11/88: 65

27644. GEMM 9323: CHOPIN—Piano music. *Paderewski, piano.* Recorded 1912, 1937.
+ ARG 3-4/89: 117
+ Fa 3-4/89: 136

27645. GEMM 9324: *Fritz Kreisler plays encores.* Music of Mendelssohn, Tchaikovsky, Dvořák, Massenet, Bizet, Kreisler, Lehár, Godowsky, Falla,

Debussy, and Albéniz. *Kreisler, Fritz; various pianists.*
+ Fa 1-2/89: 337
+ HF 12/88: 62

27646. GEMM 9326: *Maggie Teyte in concert.* Music of Massenet, Mozart, Offenbach, Puccini, Tchaikovsky, Debussy, Giordini, Hageman, Messager, Russell, and Anon. *Teyte, soprano; with assisting soloists; various accs.*
+ ARG 9-10/89: 150
+ Fa 9-10/89: 389

27647. GEMM 9327: *The vocal prime of Richard Tauber.* Music of Mozart, Lortzing, J, Strauss, Jr., Albert, Wagner, Offenbach, Rossini, Verdi, Bizet, Puccini, Grieg, Tosti, and Liszt. *Tauber, tenor; with assisting soloists; various accs.*
+ ARG 1-2/89: 123
+ Fa 1-2/89: 311
+ HPR 6/89: 92
+ MA 5/89: 69
+ ON 11/88: 65

27648. GEMM 9329: STRAVINSKY Rite of spring; Petrushka. *Grand Symphony Orch.; Monteux, Stravinsky, cond.* Recorded 1929, 1928.
+ Fa 5-6/89: 331

27649. GEMM 9330: BEETHOVEN—Violin sonatas, op. 12, no. 1-3. *Kreisler, violin; Rupp, piano.*
+ Fa 5-6/89: 399

27650. GEMM 9331: WAGNER—Götterdämmerung: Excerpts; Tristan und Isolde: Excerpts; Parsifal: Excerpts. *Leider, soprano; with assisting artists.*
+ ARG 1-2/90: 102
+ Fa 11-12/89: 401
+ Gr 11/89: 1012

27651. GEMM 9332: TCHAIKOVSKY—Violin concerto. LALO—Symphonie espagnole. VIEUXTEMPS—Polonaise. MENDELSSOHN—Violin concerto in E minor, Movements 2-3. BRUCH—Kol nidrei. *Huberman, violin; various orchs. & conds.* Recorded 1923-31.
+ Fa 3-4/89: 378

27652. GEMM 9334: STRAVINSKY—Rite of spring; Firebird: Suite. *Paris Symphony Orch.; Stravinsky, cond.*
+ ARG 1-2/90: 138
+ Fa 11-12/89: 375

27653. GEMM 9335 : *Count John McCormack, vol. 1: Italian opera.* Music of Donizetti, Rossini, Verdi, Puccini, Boito, and Ponchielli. *McCormack, tenor; various orchs. & conds.*
+ ARG 5-6/89: 127
+ Fa 3-4/89: 356

27654. GEMM 9337: *The tenors, vol. 1.* Music of Mozart, Rossini, Thomas, Wagner, Verdi, Grieg, and Anon. *Jadlowker, Tauber, Senius, Melchior, Walter, Slezak, Urlus, Clement, Vaquet,*

Dalmorès, Ansseau, Franz, tenors; various accs.
+ ARG 3-4/89: 125
+ Fa 3-4/89: 357

27655. GEMM 9339: Music of Chopin, J. Strauss, Jr., and Rosenthal. *Rosenthal, piano; unnamed orch.; Weissman, cond.* Recorded 1928-31.
+ ARG 1-2/89: 126
+ Fa 1-2/89: 147

27656. GEMM 9340: WAGNER—Die Meistersinger: Excerpts. *Marherr, Hutt, Schorr, Schützendorf, List; Berlin State Opera; Blech, cond.* Recorded live 1928.
+ ARG 1-2/90: 138
+ Fa 9-10/89: 359

27657. GEMM 9341: BACH—Violin concertos no. 1-2. MOZART—Violin concerto no 3. *Huberman, violin; Vienna Phil. Orch.; Dobrowen, cond.*
+ ARG 7-8/89: 14
+ Fa 7-8/89: 309
+ Gr 8/89: 373

27658. GEMM 9342: VAUGHAN WILLIAMS— Serenade to music; Te Deum in F; Dona nobis pacem. *Soloists; BBC Chorus & Symphony Orch.; Wood, Vaughan Williams, cond.; Coronation Chorus & Orch.; Flynn, Henderson, cond.*
+ ARG 3-4/90: 159
+ Fa 1-2/90: 328
+ Gr 12/89: 1230

27659. GEMM 9343 : *Lieder and art song.* Music of Lotti, Schubert, Mendelssohn, Brahms, Wolf, Parry, Fauré, and Elgar. *McCormack, tenor; Schneider, piano.* Recorded 1923-32.
+ Fa 7-8/89: 291

27660. GEMM 9344: *The great tenors, vol. 2.* Music of Handel, Mozart, Rossini, Thomas, Tchaikovsky, Wagner, Verdi, Leoncavallo, Puccini, Barthelemy, and Crescenzo. *Anselmi, Caruso, Bonci, de Lucia, Martinelli, Tomagno, Albani, Zenatello, Taccani, Schipa, tenors; various accs.*
+ ARG 9-10/89: 138
+ Fa 7-8/89: 292

27661. GEMM 9345: BEETHOVEN—Violin concerto in D major. BRAHMS—Violin concerto. *Szigeti, violin; British Symphony Orch.; Walter, cond.; Hallé Orch.; Harty, cond.* Recorded 1932, 1928.
+ ARG 7-8/90: 153
+ Fa 7-8/90: 87

27662. GEMM 9347: Music of Chopin, Bach, Beethoven, Liszt, Busoni, and Mozart. *Busoni, Petri, piano; Minneapolis Symphony Orch.; Mitropoulos, cond.*
□ ARG 3-4/90: 15
+ Fa 1-2/90: 150
+ Gr 4/90: 1881

27663. GEMM 9348: DEBUSSY—Flute sonata; Sonata for viola and harp; Violin sonata; Danses sacré et profane; Rhapsody for saxophone and orchestra. *Moyse, flute; Ginot, viola; Laskine, harp; Marechal, cello; Casadesus, Cortot, piano; Thibaud, violin; Viard, saxophone; Symphony Orch.; Coppola, cond.*
+ ARG 3-4/90: 159
+ Fa 1-2/90: 162

27664. GEMM 9349: DVOŘÁK—Cello concerto, op. 104. BOCCHERINI—Cello concerto in B♭ major. BRUCH—Kol nidrei. *Casals, cello; Czech Phil. Orch.; Szell, cond.; London Symphony Orch.; Ronald, cond.*
+ ARG 1-2/90: 138
+ Fa 9-10/89: 191
+ Gr 5/89: 1722

27665. GEMM 9350: VERDI—Trovatore: Excerpts. *Ponselle, Milanov, Homer, Martinelli, de Luca, Stracciari, Pinza; various choruses, orchs., & conds.*
+ ARG 5-6/89: 128
+ Fa 3-4/89: 355

27666. GEMM 9351: *Giovanni Martinelli.* Music of Verdi, Donizetti, Rossini, Leoncavallo, and Giordano. *Martinelli, Ponselle, De Luca, Pinza, Journet, Mardones; various orchs. & conds.*
+ ARG 5-6/89: 128
+ Fa 3-4/89: 355

27667. GEMM 9353: *Arias and songs 1907-1926.* Music of Lotti, Mozart, Handel, Thomas, Lalo, Wagner, Verdi, Puccini, Dvořák, Mendelssohn, and Anon. *Melba, soprano; with assisting soloists; various accs.*
+ ARG 9-10/89: 148
+ Fa 11-12/89: 428

27668. GEMM 9354: BEETHOVEN—Violin sonatas no. 4-6. *Kreisler, violin; Rupp, piano.*
+ ARG 11-12/89: 37
+ Fa 11-12/89: 137

27669. GEMM 9358: BEETHOVEN— Concerto for piano trio and orchestra, op. 56; Piano sonata no. 29 (orch. Weingartner). *Odnoposoff, violin; Auber, cello; Morales, piano; Vienna Phil. Orch.; Royal Phil. Orch.; Weingartner, cond.*
+ ARG 1-2/90: 24
• Fa 9-10/89: 132

27670. GEMM 9361: *Enrico Caruso, vol. 2.* Music of Donizetti, Verdi, Boito, Ponchielli, Goldmark, Flotow, Gounod, Halévy, Massenet, Bizet, Leoncavallo, Costa, and Anon. *Caruso, tenor; with assisting soloists; various accs.*
+ ARG 9-10/89: 144
+ Fa 9-10/89: 394

27671. GEMM 9362: MENDELSSOHN— Violin concerto in E minor. BEETHOVEN— Violin concerto in D major. BRAHMS— Violin concerto. PAGANINI—Violin concerto no. 1. *Kreisler, violin; various orchs. & conds.*
• ARG 11-12/89: 163
+ Fa 11-12/89: 467

27672. GEMM 9363: *Pablo Casals plays Brahms.* BRAHMS—Concerto for violin and cello, op. 102; Cello sonata no. 2. BOCCHERINI—Cello sonata no. 6; Adagio and Allegro. HAYDN—Minuet in C major. *Casals, cello; Thibaud, violin; various pianists; Casals Orch.; Cortot, cond.*
+ ARG 1-2/90: 138
+ Fa 11-12/89: 153
+ NYT 6/25/89: H28

27673. GEMM 9364: *Tito Schipa, vol. 2.* Music of Pergolesi, Mozart, Bellini, Donizetti, Verdi, Puccini, Thomas, Massenet, Donaudy, Costa, Huarte, Tosti, Nutile, and Anon. *Schipa, tenor; with assisting soloists, orchs., & conds.*
+ ARG 1-2/90: 136 m.f.
+ Fa 11-12/89: 433

27674. GEMM 9365 (2 discs): STRAUSS—Rosenkavalier: Abridged; Ägyptische Helena: Excerpts; Breit über mein haupt; Morgen. *Lehmann, Schumann, Olczewska, Mayr, Hutt; Strauss, piano; Vienna Phil. Orch.; Heger, cond.; Berlin State Opera Orch.; Busch, cond.*
+ ARG 11-12/89: 125
+ Fa 11-12/89: 372
+ Gr 3/90; 1706 m.f.
+ St 4/90: 207

27675. GEMM 9366: STRAUSS—Don Juan; Till Eulenspiegel's merry pranks; Bourgeois gentilhomme; Suite. *Berlin State Opera Orch; Strauss, cond.*
+ ARG 3-4/90: 159
+ Fa 1-2/90: 176 m.f.
+ Gr 5/90: 2082

27676. GEMM 9367: Music of Donizetti, Verdi, Ponchielli, Bizet, Rimsky-Korsakov, Buzzi-Peccia, Denza, Seismit-Doda, De Curtis, and Nutile. *Gigli, tenor; with assisting soloists; various orchs. & conds.*
+ ARG 3-4/90: 151
+ Fa 1-2/90: 362
+ Gr 5/90: 2069

27677. GEMM 9369 (2 discs): MOZART—Don Giovanni. *Souez, Helletsgruber, Mildmay, Pataky, Brownlee; Glyndebourne Chorus & Orch.; Busch, cond.*
+ ARG 1-2/90: 68
+ Fa 11-12/89: 289 m.f.

27678. GEMM 9370: *Richard Tauber sings Lieder.* Music of Schubert, Schumann, and Anon. *Tauber, tenor; Spoliansky, Kahn, piano.*
+ Fa 11-12/89: 432

PEARL

27679. GEMM 9371 (2 discs): Mozart—Zauberflöte. *Berger, Lemnitz, Rosvænge, Hursch, Strienz; with assisting soloists; Berlin Phil. Orch.; Beecham, cond.*
+ ARG 1-2/90: 70 m.f.
+ Fa 11-12/89: 299 m.f.

27680. GEMM 9372: Beethoven— Symphony no. 9. *Leonard, Sonnenberg, Transky, Guttman; Bruno Kittel Choir; Berlin State Opera Orch.; Fried, cond.* Recorded 1927.
+ ARG 11-12/89: 38
+ Fa 11-12/89: 142

27681. GEMM 9373 (3 discs): *The great recordings 1926-36.* Music of Mendelssohn, Verdi, Haydn, Mozart, Dukas, Gluck, Beethoven, Wagner, Brahms, and Rossini. *New York Phil.; Toscanini, cond.*
+ ARG 3-4/90: 159
+ Gr 3/90: 1700

27682. GEMM 9374: Verdi—Requiem. *Fanelli, Minghini-Cattaneo, Giudice, Pinza; Teatro alla Scala; Sabajno, cond.*
• Fa 1-2/90: 331

27683. GEMM 9375 (2 discs): Mozart—Nozze di Figaro. *Rautawaara, Mildmay, Helletsgruber, Henderson, Domgraf-Fassbaender; Glyndebourne Festival Chorus & Orch.; Busch, cond.*
+ ARG 3-4/90: 78
• Fa 1-2/90: 241 m.f.
+ St 7/90: 175 m.f.

27684. GEMM 9378: Beethoven— Diabelli variations. *Schnabel, piano.*
• ARG 11-12/90: 32
+ Fa 1-2/90: 124

27685. GEMM 9379: Music of Strauss, Handel, Reger, Marx, Josef Strauss, Zeller, Heuberger, Ziehrer, Schubert, Benatsky, and Sieczynski. *Schumann, soprano; various orchs. & conds.*
+ ARG 11-12/90: 177
+ Fa 7-8/90: 326

27686. GEMM 9380: *Favourite choral music.* Music of Handel, Haydn, Mendelssohn, Sullivan, Elgar, Parry, and Anon. *Various choruses and orchestras; Sargent, cond.*
+ ARG 3-4/90: 159
+ Fa 1-2/90: 371

27687. GEMM 9381: *Tauber sings Lieder.* Music of Martini, Schubert, Schumann, Mendelssohn, Loewe, Wolf, Rubinstein, Grieg, and Liszt. *Tauber, tenor; unnamed orchs. & conds.*
+ ARG 3-4/90: 157
+ Fa 3-4/90: 350
+ Gr 4/90: 1885
+ Gr 7/90: 245

27688. GEMM 9383: *Julius Patzak sings opera and operetta.* Music of Donizetti, Verdi, Puccini, Thomas, Massenet, Tchaikovsky, Offenbach, Flotow, Nocolai, Smetana, Suppé, J. Strauss, Jr., Millocker, and Anon. *Patzak, tenor; various orchs. & conds.*
+ ARG 3-4/90: 154
+ Fa 3-4/90: 349
+ Gr 3/90: 1709

27689. GEMM 9385: *Ballades.* Brahms—Piano music. *Backhaus, piano.*
+ ARG 5-6/90: 35
+ Fa 3-4/90: 153
+ Gr 3/90: 1700

27690. GEMM 9387: Beethoven—Violin concerto; Romance for violin and orchestra no. 2. Mozart—Violin concerto no. 5. *Wolfsthal, violin; Berlin Phil. Orch.; Gurlitt, cond.; Staatskapelle Berlin; Weissman, cond.*
+ ARG 5-6/90: 22
+ Fa 5-6/90: 112

27691. GEMM 9388: Music of Tchaikovsky, Bach, Ysaÿe, Mendelssohn, Chopin, and Sarasate. *Elman, violin; Gool, Hollister, pianos; London Symphony Orch.; Barbirolli, cond.*
+ ARG 5-6/90: 140
+ Fa 5-6/90: 113

27692. GEMM 9394: *Operatic arias & duets.* Music of Boieldieu, Mozart, Puccini, Bizet, Verdi, Beethoven, and Weber. *Rosvænge, tenor; with assisting soloists; various orchs. & conds.*
+ ARG 5-6/90: 151
+ Fa 5-6/90: 358 m.f.
+ Gr 5/90: 2079

27693. GEMM 9395: Beethoven—Violin sonatas no. 8-9. *Kreisler, violin; Rupp, piano.*
+ Fa 7-8/90: 90
• Gr 9/90: 618

27694. GEMM 9398: Music of Haydn, Mozart, Weber, Beethoven, Mendelssohn, Wagner, Schubert, Wolf, and Strauss. *Schorr, baritone; with assisting soloists; various orchs. & conds.*
+ ARG 7-8/90: 152
• Fa 7-8/90: 338

27695. GEMM 9399: Brahms—Piano concerto no. 2. Bach—Concerto for 2 pianos, BWV 1061. *A. & K. Schnabel, pianos; BBC Symphony; London Symphony Orch.; Boult, cond.*
+ ARG 7-8/90: 153
- Fa 7-8/90: 105

27696. GEMM 9400: Beethoven—Violin sonatas no. 7, 10. *Kreisler, violin; Rupp, piano.*
+ Fa 7-8/90: 90

27697. GEMM 9401: Music of Tartini, Pergolesi, Nardini, Vitali, Bach, Vivaldi, Chopin, Liszt, Smetana, and Paganini. *Milstein violin; Mittman, piano.*

• ARG 7-8/90: 153
+ Fa 7-8/90: 357

27698. GEMM 9403: Liszt—Piano concertos no. 1-2; Ricordanza; Consolation no. 3; Valse oubliée no. 1: Gnomenreigen; Campanella. *Sauer, piano; Paris Conservatory Orch.; Weingartner, cond.*
+ ARG 7-8/90: 64
+ ARG 7-8/90: 153
+ Fa 7-8/90: 186

27699. GEMM 9404: Glazunov— Seasons; Symphony no. 7. *Orch.; Glazunov, cond.; USSR Radio and Television Symphony Orch.; Golovanov, cond.*
+ ARG 7-8/90: 153 (Seasons)
• ARG 7-8/90: 153 (Symphony)
+ Fa 7-8/90: 152

27700. GEMM 9405: Music of Brahms, Donizetti, Saint-Saëns, Sibelius, and Anon. *Anderson, alto; various accs.*
+ Fa 7-8/90: 332 m.f.

27701. GEMM 9406 (3 discs): Mozart—Così fan tutte. *Souez, Helletsgruber, Eisinger, Nash, Domgraf-Fassbaender, Brownlee; Glydebourne Festival Orch.; Busch, cond.*
+ ARG 9-10/90: 92
+ Fa 7-8/90: 205 m.f.

27702. GEMM 9407: Beethoven— Symphony no. 9; Eleven Viennese dances. *Helletsgruber, Anday, Maikl, Mayr; Vienna State Opera Chorus; Vienna Phil. Orch.; London Phil. Orch.; Weingartner, cond.* Recorded 1935.
+ ARG 7-8/90: 26
+ Fa 7-8/90: 94

27703. GEMM 9409: Music of Puccini, J. Strauss, Jr., Godard, Jensen, Eulenberg, and Werner. *Lehmann, soprano; Kiepura, Tauber, tenor; various orchs. & conds.*
+ ARG 11-12/90: 176
+ Fa 9-10/90: 443

27704. GEMM 9410: Music of Offenbach, Wagner, Albert, Strauss, Giordano, Lehár, Meyer-Helmund, and Ketelbey . *Lehmann, Heidersbach, sopranos; various orchs. & conds.*
+ ARG 11-12/90: 176
+ Fa 9-10/90: 443

27705. GEMM 9412: *Opera arias.* Music of Meyerbeer, Verdi, Ponchielli, Puccini, Wagner, Gounod, Massenet, Tosti, and Woodford-Finden. *Piccaver, tenor; with assisting soloists; various accs.*
+ Fa 9-10/90: 463

27706. GEMM 9413: Mahler—Lied von der Erde; Ich bin der Welt abhanden gekommen; Symphony no. 5: Adagietto. *Thorborg, alto; Kullman, tenor; Vienna Phil. Orch.; Walter, cond.*

• ARG 9-10/90: 164
+ Fa 9-10/90: 286

27707. GEMM 9414: RACHMANINOFF—
Symphony no. 3; Isle of the dead;
Vocalise. *Philadelphia Orch.;
Rachmaninoff, cond.*
+ ARG 9-10/90: 164
+ Fa 9-10/90: 347

27708. GEMM 9415: *Opera arias and
songs.* Music of Mozart, Rossini,
Donizetti, Verdi, Delibes, Gounod,
Offenbach, Saint-Saëns, Proch, Bishop,
Dell'Acqua, and J. Strauss, Jr. *Pons,
soprano; various orchs. & conds.*
+ Fa 9-10/90: 448

27709. GEMM 9448: WAGNER—Music
from Tannhäuser and Parsifal.
Philadelphia Orch.; Stokowski, cond.
+ Fa 7-8/94: 277

27710. GEMM 9461: CHOPIN—Etudes.
Binns, piano.
+ ARG 7-8/96: 100
+ Gr 1/96: 79

27711. GEMM 9468: VAUGHAN
WILLIAMS—Hugh the Drover. *Davies,
Lewis, Anderson, Dawson; Orch.;
Sargent, cond.* Recorded 1925.
+ ARG 5-6/95: 188

27712. GEMM 9474: Music of Handel,
Bach, J.C. Bach, Mozart, Beethoven,
Mendelssohn, Meyerbeer, Wagner,
Humperdinck, and Saint-Saëns. *New York
Phil.; Mendelberg, cond.*
+ Fa 5-6/91: 384

27713. GEMM 9486: WAGNER—Music
from Die Meistersinger, Lohengrin, and
Tristan; Three Wesendonck Lieder.
*Traubel, soprano; Philadelphia Orch.;
Stokowski, cond.*
+ Fa 7-8/94: 277

27714. GEMM 9496: ELGAR—Violin
concerto; Sonata. *Sammons, violin; New
Queen's Hall Orch.; Wood, cond.;
Murdoch, piano.* Recorded 1935.
+ ARG 11-12/91: 63

27715. SHE 9510: WARLOCK—Vocal
music. *Griffett, tenor; Murdoch, English
horn; Ryan, flute; Haffner String Quartet.*
+ ARG 3-4/88: 97
+ Fa 1-2/88: 237
+ Gr 12/87: 990

27716. SHE 9537: WAGNER—Walküre:
Excerpts from Acts 2 and 3. *Leider,
Ljungberg, Leisner, Schorr; Berlin State
Opera Orch.; Blech, cond.; London
Symphony Orch.; Barbirolli, cond.*
Recorded 1927, 1932.
+ Fa 9-10/89: 370

27717. SHE 9538: GLAZUNOV—Piano
sonatas no. 1-2; Grand concert waltz, op.
41. *Howard, piano.*

+ ARG 3-4/88: 37
+ Fa 3-4/88: 112

27718. SHE 9564: FOULDS—String
quartets no. 9-10; Three aquarelles, op.
32; Lento quieto. *Endellion String
Quartet.* Issued also as LP: SHE 564.
+ Fa 1-2/88: 120

27719. SHE 9590: *Song recital.* Music of
Arne, Handel, Bishop, Gounod, Bizet,
and Satie. *Masterson, soprano; Adeney,
flute; Vignoles, piano.*
+ Fa 3-4/90: 341

27720. SHE 9601: BRIDGE—Oration;
Enter spring. *Baillie, cello; Cologne
Radio Symphony Orch.; Carewe, cond.*
Issued also as LP: SHE 601.
• Fa 3-4/88: 205
+ Gr 11/87: 730
+ Ov 4/88: 37

27721. SHE 9602: ELGAR—Carillon;
Polonia; Voix dans le désert; Drapeau
belge; Fringes of the fleet. *Pasco,
narrator; Cahill, soprano; Kenyon,
Godward, Theogald, Watson, baritones;
Rutland Sinfonia; Collett, cond.*
+ Fa 5-6/88: 124
• Gr 5/88: 1628

27722. SHE 9603: MENDELSSOHN—String
quartets no. 3, 5. *Roth String Quartet.*
+ Fa 5-6/88: 164
• Gr 5/88: 1616

27723. SHE 9608: *Romantic songs for
tenor and guitar.* Music of Schubert,
Giuliani, and Spohr. *Partridge, tenor;
Lindberg, guitar.*
+ ARG 3-4/90: 146
• Fa 1-2/90: 362
+ Gr 10/89: 737

27724. SHE 9609: Guitar music of
Tippett, Pijol, Villa-Lobos, Delerue,
Giorginakis, and Fampas. *Kotzia, guitar.*
+ ARG 7-8/89: 115
+ Fa 7-8/89: 308
+ Gr 6/89: 69

27725. SHE 9610: BRIDGE—Piano trio no.
2; Cello sonata; Spring song. *Yajima,
violin; Blake, cello; Prutsman, Palmer,
piano.*
+ ARG 9-10/89: 36
+ Fa 9-10/89: 127
+ Gr 9/89: 491

27726. SHE 9611: GRAINGER—Piano
music for four hands, vol. 1. *Thwaites,
Lavender, pianos.*
+ Fa 1-2/90: 188
+ Gr 10/89: 691

27727. SIIE 9623: GRAINGER—Piano
music for four hands, vol. 2. *Thwaites,
Lavender, piano.*
+ ARG 11-12/92: 127
+ Gr 1/94: 66

27728. SHE 9624: LIAPUNOV—
Transcendental studies, op. 11. *Binns,
piano.*
+ ARG 7-8/92: 163
- Gr 5/92: 75

27729. SHE 9628: MEDTNER—Piano
sonatas op. 27, op. 53, no. 2, op. 56;
Skazki, op. 26. *Binns, piano.*
+ ARG 1-2/93: 120
• Fa 11-12/92: 298

27730. SHE 9631: GRAINGER—Piano
music for four hands, vol. 3. *Thwaites,
Lavender, piano.*
+ ARG 3-4/94: 101
+ Gr 1/94: 66

27731. SHE 9636: SULLIVAN—Ballads. *R.
Conrad, bass.*
+ ARG 5-6/95: 182
+ Gr 2/95: 90

27732. SHE 9639: *The Tarrega dynasty.*
Music of Arcas, Tarrega, Llobet, and
Pujol. *Parsons, guitar.*
- ARG 5-6/96: 236

27733. GEMM 9850: Music of Bach,
Schubert, Chopin, Schumann, Brahms,
and others. *Grünfeld, piano.* Recorded
1899-1914.   + ARG 9-10/93: 264

27734. GEMM 9855 (2 discs): Arias and
songs by Rubinstein, Rimsky-Korsakov,
Mussorgsky, and others. *Koshetz,
soprano; with orch. & piano accomp.*
+ ARG 1-2/94: 203
+ Fa 3-4/94: 367

27735. GEMM 9857: Music of Chopin,
Gluck, Scarlatti, Schumann, and others.
Planté, Viñes, piano. Recorded 1928,
1930, 1936. + ARG 1-2/95: 260

27736. GEMM 9860: Music of Liszt,
Beethoven, Brahms, Chopin, Debussy,
and others. *Samaroff, piano.* Recorded
1920-30.   + ARG 1-2/97: 241

27737. GEMM 9909 (6 discs): *Pupils of
Clara Schumann.* Music of Schumann,
Brahms, Beethoven and Scarlatti. *Davies,
De Lara, Ferber, Brahms, Eibenschütz,
pianos.*
+ Fa 3-4/92: 407

27738. GEMM 9910 (2 discs):
WAGNER—Der fliegende Holländer.
*Lawrence, Destal, Kipnis; Teatro Colón,
Buenos Aires; Busch, cond.* Recorded
live 1936.
+ Fa 5-6/92: 275
+ ON 12/19/92: 40

27739. GEMM 9912: *Vanni Marcoux.*
Music of Fevrier, Massenet, Laparra,
Thomas, Mussorgsky, Debussy, Berlioz,
Schumann, Duparc and Martini.
*Marcoux, bass-baritone; with orchestral
and piano accomp.*
+ Fa 11-12/92: 421
+ ON 4/10/93: 42

PEARL

27740. GEMM 9917: GAY-PEPUSCH-AUSTIN—The beggar's opera. *Various performers.* Recorded 1940.
+ ARG 1-2/92: 178
+ Fa 5-6/92: 160

27741. GEMM 9919: SCHUMANN—Dichterliebe. FAURÉ—Songs. DUPARC—Songs. *Panzéra, baritone; Cortot, Panzéra-Baillot, piano.*
+ ARG 3-4/93: 199
+ Gr 3/93: 112
+ ON 4/10/93: 42

27742. GEMM 9920 (2 discs): Music of Verstovsky, Glinka, Dargomizhsky, Serov, and Borodin. *Chaliapin, bass.* Recorded 1898-1936.   + ARG 5-6/92: 185 + ON 10/93: 36

27743. GEMM 9921: Music of Malashki, Rimsky-Korsakov, Rubinstein, Tchaikovsky, Liapounov, Rachmaninoff, and Grechaninoff. *Chaliapin, bass.* Reissue. + ARG 5-6/92: 185 + ON 10/93: 36

27744. GEMM 9934: *Dame Isobel Baillie.* Music of Purcell, Bach, Handel, Mozart, Schubert, Mendelssohn, Offenbach and Arditi. *Baillie, soprano; with accompaniment.*
+ Fa 5-6/92: 292

27745. GEMM 9939: Josef Hassid, Ida Haendel: the 1940 recordings. *Hassid, Haendel, violin; with piano accompaniment.*
● ARG 9-10/92: 217
+ Fa 7-8/92: 352
+ Gr 10/92: 198

27746. GEMM 9941: WAGNER—Tannhäuser. *Müller, Jost-Arden, Pilinszky; Chorus & Bayreuth Festival, 1930; Elmendorff, cond.*
● Fa 3-4/93: 325

27747. GEMM 9944: WAGNER—Die Meistersinger: selections. *Schorr, baritone; various assisting artists.* Historical reissue.
+ Fa 9-10/92: 382
+ ON 2/5/94: 38

27748. GEMM 9947: *Georges Thill.* Music of Bach, Wagner, Rinsky-Korsakov, Verdi, Puccini, Bizet, Massenet, Berlioz, Gounod and Fauré. *Thill, tenor; with various accomps.*
+ Fa 11-12/92: 419
+ ON 4/10/93: 42

27749. GEMM 9950: *Louise Homer.* Music of Gluck, Meyerbeer, Saint-Saëns, Homer, Handel, Schubert, Watson, Gounod, Delibes, Walthew, Adams, Claribel, Tchaikovsky, and Bohm. *Homer, alto; orch. acc.*
+ Fa 3-4/93: 337

27750. GEMM 9956: *Joseph Hislop.* Music of Gounod, Donizetti, Verdi, Wagner, Massenet, Puccini, Mascagni and others. *Hislop, tenor; with various accomps.*
● ARG 3-4/93: 198
+ Fa 11-12/92: 418
+ Gr 1/93: 71

27751. GEMM 9958: *Pinza: early Italian songs; Mozart arias and duets, with Elisabeth Rethberg.* Music of Monteverdi, Handel, Legrenzi, Scarlatti, Cavalli, Torelli, Paisiello, Giordani, Falconieri, Sarti, Buononcini, and Mozart. *Pinza, bass; Rethberg, soprano; various acc.*
+ Fa 3-4/93: 345

27752. GEMM 9963: Music of Chopin, Liszt, Debussy, Schubert, and others. *Rosenthal, piano.* Recorded 1922-36.
       + ARG 7-8/93: 216 + Gr 9/93: 125

27753. GEMM 9964 (2 discs): *Rosa Ponselle: The Columbia acoustic recordings.* Music of Bellini, Mascagni, Leoncavallo, Tosti, Rimsky-Korsakov, Rossini, Meyerbeer, Ponchielli, and others. *Ponselle, soprano; with orchestral accomp.*
+ ARG 9-10/93: 269
+ Fa 11-12/92: 414

27754. GEMM 9965: COLERIDGE-TAYLOR—Othello suite; Four characteristic waltzes; Petite suite de concert; The forest of wild thyme: Incidental music. *Various performers.* Reissues.
+ Fa 11-12/92: 220

27755. GEMM 9967: Music of Mozart, Donizetti, Rossini, Verdi, Berlioz, and others. *De Luca, baritone; with orch. acc.*
+ ARG 3-4/93: 197

27756. GEMM 9969: *Unknown Supervia.* Music of De Grignon, Longás, Mompou, Manen, Alvárez, Morera, Godes and others. *Supervia, soprano; with various accomps.*
+ Fa 1-2/93: 278

27757. GEMM 9970: English songs. *McCormack, tenor; with piano accomp.*
+ ARG 9-10/93: 267

27758. GEMM 9972 (2 discs): *The pupils of Liszt.* Music of Grieg, Beethoven, Liszt, Chopin, Mendelssohn and others. *Greef, Weiss, Ansorge, Lamond, Rosenthal, Vianna da Mota, Friedheim, Sauer, d'Albert, piano.*
+ Fa 1-2/93: 304

27759. GEMM 9974: *Arthur de Greef, vol. 1.* Music of Saint-Saëns, Grieg, Schumann, Chopin, Prokofiev, Gretry, Raff, and Liszt. *Greef, piano; New Symphony Orch.; Ronald, cond.* Recorded 1918-31.   + ARG 7-8/93: 214 + Fa 7-8/93: 301

27760. GEMM 9975: Conchita Supervia, vol. 1. *Supervia, mezzo-soprano; various acc.*
+ ARG 9-10/93: 269
+ Fa 9-10/93: 342

27761. GEMM 9976: Arias and songs. *Kiepura, tenor; with orch. and piano acc.*
+ ARG 3-4/93: 198
+ Fa 7-8/93: 285
+ ON 12/25/93: 33

27762. GEMM 9977: Concert ballads. *John Charles Thomas, baritone.*
□ ARG 3-4/93: 201
+ ON 6/93: 43

27763. GEMM 9978: Music of Purcell, Scarlatti, Boyce, Chopin, Mendelssohn, Liszt, and others. *Scharrer, piano.*
+ ARG 3-4/93: 195

27764. GEMM 9979 (2 discs): *Horszowski: a centenary celebration.* Music of C.P.E. Bach, Mozart, Schubert, Chopin, Beethoven, and Bach. *Horszowski, piano.* Recorded 1958-83. + ARG 3-4/93: 195 <\@> Fa 5-6/93: 381 + Gr 12/93: 91

27765. GEMM 9980: *Boninsegna.* 19 acoustic vocal recordings. *Boninsegna, soprano; various acc.*
+ Fa 9-10/93: 345

27766. GEMM 9981/3—9984/6 (2 3-disc sets): The recorded cello: the history of cello on record. *Various performers.*
+ ARG 3-4/93: 194
+ Fa 1-2/93: 291

27767. GEMM 9987 (2 discs): GOUNOD—Faust. *Montfort, Vezzani, Journet; Paris Opéra; Busser, cond.* Recorded 1930.
+ ARG 9-10/93: 262
- Gr 9/93: 126
+ Op 7/93: 876

27768. GEMM 9991: SULLIVAN—*The art of the Savoyard.* 29 historic early acoustic recordings of Gilbert and Sullivan arias and related musical comedy selections. *Various performers.*
+ ARG 7-8/93: 213
+ Fa 5-6/93: 336

27769. GEMM 9993: Music of Liszt, Paganini, Beethoven, Chopin, and others. *Friedheim, Siloti, Sauer, piano.*
+ ARG 3-4/93: 195
● Gr 8/93: 89

27770. GEMM99997/99, 9001/03, 9004/06, 9007/09, 9111 (5 3-disc sets): Singers of Imperial Russia. *Various artists.*
+ ARG 3-4/93: 201
+ ARG 11-12/96: 306 (v.5)
+ Fa 3-4/93: 350
+ Fa 7-8/93: 282 (v.4)
+ Gr 6/93: 111

PERFORMANCE RECORDINGS

27771. PR-7-CD: MUSSORGSKY—Pictures at an exhibition. *Boyk, piano.*
- Fa 9-10/91: 303
+ Gr 1/92: 79

PERETUA

27772. PR 7006: RACHMANINOFF—Rhapsody on a theme of Paganini. PROKOFIEV—Piano concerto no. 3. *Joselson, piano; Philharmonia Hungarica; Rozsnyai, cond.*
+ ARG 11-12/86: 75
+ Fa 1-2/87: 158

27773. PR 7010 (LP): STRAVINSKY—Pulcinella: Suite. RESPIGHI—The birds. *English Chamber Orch.; McRae, cond.*
• Fa 1-2/87: 190
+ Opus 12/86: 46

PG

27774. PCD 7464: LISZT—Totentanz; Hungarian fantasy for piano and orchestra. *Clidat, piano; Hague Residentie Orch.; Norrington, cond.*
- Fa 1-2/88: 153

PGM

27775. 101: *Ricercar: keyboard music in Germany before Bach.* Music of Froberger, Böhm, and Kuhnau. *Black, harpsichord.*
• ARG 5-6/96: 237
+ EM 11/95: 714
• Fa 11-12/95: 467
+ Fa 1-2/96: 387

27776. 102: BUXTEHUDE—Sacred cantatas. *Matthews, Heimes, Rickards, Russell, Alston, vocalists; Chamber Choir of St. Peter's in the Great Valley; Sarum Consort; Johnson, cond.*
+ ARG 3-4/96: 98
• Fa 11-12/95: 230
+ Fa 1-2/96: 168
• Fi 3/96: 124

PHAEDRA

27777. 92007 (2 discs): STERNEFELD—Symphonies no. 1-2; Orchestra music. *Belgian Radio Symphony; Sternefeld, Minsky, conds.*
+ ARG 9-10/96: 207

PHILIPS

27778. DMA 074 (LP): KOPPEL—Variations on a Jewish folk dance. ROVSING-OLSEN—String trio, op. 85. WEIS—String trio. THYBO—String trio. *Copenhagen Chamber Trio.*
+ Fa 11-12/86: 281

27779. PHCD 104: BRITTEN—Scottish ballad, op. 26. MARTINŮ—Concerto for 2 pianos; Fantasy for 2 pianos; Three

Czech dances. *Pierce, Jonas, pianos; Luxembourg Radio Symphony Orch.; Stratta, cond.*
+ Fa 11-12/89: 160 m.f.

27780. 314 522 933: *From Holland with love: waltzes I've saved for you.* Music of Rieu, J. Strauss, Jr., Josef Strauss, Karas, Shostakovich, Kálmán, Lehár, Benatzky-Stolz-Gilbert, Sieczynski, Wunsch, and Gruber. *Rieu, violin & cond.; Johann Strauss Orch.*
- Fa 9-10/96: 440

27781. 411 463-2: SCHUBERT—Die Winterreise. *Fischer-Dieskau, baritone; Brendel, piano.* Issued also as LP: 411 463-1.
• Fa 5-6/87: 190
+ Gr 12/86: 920
+ Opus 4/87: 49

27782. 412 121-2: MOZART—String quartets no. 21-22. *Orlando Quartet.*
+ Fa 11-12/86: 180
+ Gr 3/86: 1169
+ Gr 7/86: 188

27783. 412 233-2: *Eighteenth century bel canto.* Music of Giordani, Vivaldi, Paisello, Heinichen, Handel, Gluck, Pergolesi, Mozart, and Purcell . *Ameling, soprano; Gewandhaus Orch.; Masur, cond.* Issued also as LP: 412 233-1.   + Fa 1-2/87: 277 + Gr 7/86: 204 + Gr 10/86: 622 + Ov 5/87: 42

27784. 412 620-2 (2 discs): SCHUBERT—Piano trios no. 1-2; Notturno in E♭, op. posth. 149; Sonata, D. 28. *Beaux Arts Trio.* Issued also as LP: 412 620-1.
+ DA 6/87: 92
• Fa 9-10/86: 226
• Gr 5-86: 1328
+ Gr 7/86: 188
• NYT 12/7/86: H28
+ SR 11/86: 174 (no. 1)
• SR 11/86: 174 (no. 2)

27785. 412 624-2: VIVALDI—Guitar concertos. *Los Romeros, guitars; Academy of St. Martin-in-the-Fields; Brown, cond.*
+ DA 9/86: 38
+ Fa 5-6/86: 272
+ NR 5/86: 10

27786. 412 628-2: *Soirée française.* Music of Debussy, Franck, Gounod, Poulenc, Canteloube, Roussel, Messiaen, Chausson, Fauré, Caplet, Honneger, Bizet, Duparc, and Satie. *Ameling, soprano; Jansen, piano.*
+ Fa 7-8/87: 210
+ Gr 3/87: 1321
+ Opus 12/87: 31
+ Ov 2/88: 43
+ SR 7/87: 106

27787. 412 723-2: BEETHOVEN—Piano sonatas no. 24, 29. *Brendel, piano.*
+ Fa 11-12/86: 107

+ Gr 4/86: 1301
+ Gr 7/86: 191

27788. 412 724-2: LISZT—Hungarian rhapsodies no. 1-6. *Gewandhaus Orch.; Masur, cond.*
+ Fa 1-2/87: 137
• Gr 8/86: 268

27789. 412 725-2: MOZART—Serenade no. 9; Two marches, K. 335. *Academy of St. Martin-in-the-Fields; Mariner, cond.*
+ Fa 3-4/86: 195

27790. 412 726-2: MOZART—Serenade no. 10. *Academy of St. Martin-in-the-Fields; Marriner, cond.* Issued also as LP: 412 726-1.
+ Fa 9-10/87: 255
+ Gr 5/87: 1554
+ SR 12/87: 148

27791. 412 727-2: SIBELIUS—Karelia suite; Swan of Tuonela. GRIEG—Holberg suite; Two lyric pieces; Evening in the mountains; At the cradle. *Academy of St. Martin-in-the-Fields; Marriner, cond.*
+ Fa 5-6/86: 249
+ NR 5/86: 2

27792. 412 732-2: RACHMANINOFF—Cello sonata, op. 19; Vocalise, op. 34, no. 14. SIBELIUS—Malinconia. DVOŘÁK—Polonaise in A major. *Schiff, cello; Leonskaja, piano.*
+ Fa 7-8/87: 165
+ Gr 11/87: 728

27793. 412 735-2: BRUCKNER—Symphony no. 4. *Vienna Phil. Orch.; Haitink, cond.*
+ Fa 1-2/87: 80
+ Gr 7/86: 159
• Gr 9/86: 372

27794. 412 741-2: MOZART—Piano sonatas no. 7-9. *Uchida, piano.* Issued also as LP: 412 741-1.
+ Fa 11-12/86: 183
+ Gr 4/86: 1302
+ Gr 7/86: 193
+ NR 10/86: 31

27795. 412 742-2: PROKOFIEV—Piano music. SCRIABIN—Piano music. *Davidovich, piano.*
• Fa 5-6/87: 175
- Gr 3/87: 1300
+ NYT 9/13/87: H42
• Ov 11/87 42

27796. 412 788-2: BEETHOVEN—Piano concertos no. 3-4. *Brendel, piano; Chicago Symphony Orch.; Levine, cond.*
+ Fa 5-6/86: 98

27797. 412 790-2 (2 discs): BACH—Brandenburg concertos. *Soloists; I Musici.*
+ DA 6/86: 50
• Fa 3-4/86: 108
• Gr 10/85: 498
• Gr 1/86: 913

PHILIPS

+ NR 3/86: 3
• Opus 6/86: 36

27798. 412 794-2 (4 discs): BACH—
Well-tempered clavier, BWV 846-93.
Gulda, piano. Issued also as LP: 412
794-1.
   + Fa 9-10/86: 97
   + Gr 2/86: 1050

27799. 412 856-2 (10 discs): MOZART—
Piano concertos (complete). *Brendel,
Cooper, piano; Academy of St. Martin-
in-the-Fields; Marriner, cond.*
   + Fa 9-10/86: 190
   + Gr 4/86: 1274

27800. 412 881-2: RACHMANINOFF—Piano
concertos no. 1-2. *Kocsis, piano; San
Francisco Symphony Orch.; Waart, cond.*
   • ARG 11-12/86: 75
   + Fa 7-8/86: 204
   + Gr 5/86: 1414
   + Ov 10/86: 44

27801. 414 822-2 (6 discs): BEETHOVEN—
Symphonies (complete); Egmont:
Overture. *Popp, Watkinson, Schreier,
Holl; Netherlands Radio Chorus;
Concertgebouw Orch.; Haitink, cond.*
   + ARG 1-2/89: 22
   • Fa 1-2/89: 119
   + Gr 6/88: 22
   • NYT 1/8/89: H27
   • SR 1/89: 128
   • St 4/89: 185

27802. 416 126-2 (2 discs): SCHUMANN—
Symphonies (complete). *Concertgebouw
Orch.; Haitink, cond.*
   - Fa 3-4/86: 228
   • Gr 3/86: 1158

27803. 416 137-2: MASCAGNI—Cavalleria
rusticana. *Obraztsova, Domingo, Bruson;
with assisting soloists; Teatro alla Scala;
Prêtre, cond.*
   - Fa 7-8/86: 174
   • Gr 11/85: 677
   • Gr 2/86: 1070
   + Nr 5/86: 14
   + ON 10/86: 80
   + Op 2/86: 183
   - Opus 8/86: 43

27804. 416 144-2: BEETHOVEN—Piano
concerto no. 4; Thirty-two variations in C
minor, WoO 80. *Arrau, piano; Dresden
State Orch.; C. Davis, cond.* Issued also
as LP: 416 144-1.
   + ARG 5-6/88: 12
   + DA 2/88: 59
   - Fa 11-12/87: 95
   + Gr 5/87: 1544
   + HF 4/88: 70
   + Ov 4/88: 36
   + SR 12/87: 136

27805. 416 145-2: BEETHOVEN—Piano
sonatas no. 21, 30; Andante favori, WoO
57. *Arrau, piano.*
   • Fa 1-2/87: 67 (op.53)
   + Fa 1-2/87: 67 (others)

+ Gr 6/86: 73
+ NR 2/87: 28

27806. 416 146-2: BEETHOVEN—Piano
sonatas no. 13, 23, 26. *Arrau, piano.*
Issued also as LP: 416 146-1.
   - Fa 9-10/87: 151
   + Gr 2/87: 1153

27807. 416 148-2 (2 discs): GLUCK—
Iphigénie en Tauride. *Montague, Aler,
Allen, Massis; Monteverdi Choir; Lyon
Opera Orch.; Gardiner, cond.* Issued also
as 2 LPs: 416 148-1.
   - Fa 3-4/87: 116
   + Gr 6/86: 89
   + NYT 4/19/87: H23
   + ON 3/14/87: 50
   + Op 3/87: 295
   • Opus 10/87: 54
   • OQ Spring/87: 128 (2 reviews)
   + Ov 11/87: 39

27808. 416 155-2: MOZART—Symphonies
no. 35, 38. *Staatskapelle Dresden; C.
Davis, cond.*
   + DA 12/90: 92
   + Fa 11-12/90: 303
   + MA 1/91: 77
   + SR 10/90: 114
   + St 1/91: 260

27809. 416 156-2: STRAUSS—Alpine
symphony. *Concertgebouw Orch.;
Haitink, cond.*
   + Fa 1-2/87: 187
   + Gr 4/86: 1292
   + Gr 7/86: 175
   + HF 3/87: 63
   + MA 5/87: 62
   + NR 2/87: 4
   + NYT 12/28/86: H14
   + Opus 8/87: 50
   + Ov 6/87: 43

27810. 416 157-2: FRANCK—Violin sonata
in A major. SAINT-SAËNS—Violin sonata
in D minor. *Zukerman, violin; Neikrug,
piano.*
   + Fa 1-2/87: 109
   • Gr 6/86: 69
   + HF 5/87: 61

27811. 416 159-2: Music of Wagner,
Rheinberger, Gigout, Vierne, and
Boellmann. *Chorzempa, organ.*
   • DA 12/86: 66
   + Fa 9-10/86: 290
   - Gr 6/86: 77

27812. 416 204-2: BEETHOVEN—
Symphonies no. 7, 8. *Concertgebouw
Orch.; Mengelberg, cond.*
   + HF 12/86: 77
   • Gr 4/86: 1266

27813. 416 205-2: BEETHOVEN—
Symphony no. 9. *Sluys, Luger, Tulder,
Ravelli; Amsterdam Toonkunst Chorus;
Royal Oratorio Society; Concertgebouw
Orch.; Mengelberg, cond.*
   + HF 12/86: 77
   - Gr 4/86: 1266

27814. 416 211-2: MAHLER—Symphony
no. 4. *Vincent, vocalist; Concertgebouw
Orch.; Mengelberg, cond.*
   + HF 12/86: 77
   + Gr 4/86: 1266

27815. 416 214-2: FRANCK—Symphony in
D minor. STRAUSS—Don Juan.
*Concertgebouw Orch.; Mengelberg,
cond.*
   + HF 12/86: 77
   + Gr 4/86: 1271

27816. 416 283-2: BERLIOZ—Requiem;
Symphonie funèbre et triomphale. *Dowd,
tenor; London Symphony Chorus &
Orch.; C. Davis, cond.*
   + HF 12/86: 83
   + Gr 4/86: 1306

27817. 416 289-2 (2 discs): SCHUBERT—
Winterreise; Piano sonata, D. 840.
Schreier, tenor; Richter, piano.
   + Fa 7-8/86: 227
   + Gr 3/86: 1190

27818. 416 295-2: BEETHOVEN—Diabelli
variations. *Arrau, piano.* Issued also as
LP: 416 295-1.
   • DA 12/87: 78
   + Fa 9-10/87: 156
   + Gr 5/87: 1579
   • Gr 6/87: 66
   + Ov 4/88: 36

27819. 416 296-2: MUSSORGSKY—Pictures
at an exhibition (orch. Ravel). RAVEL—La
valse. *Vienna Phil. Orch.; Previn, cond.*
Recorded live 1985. Issued also as LP:
416 296-1.
   - ARG 1-2/87: 49
   • Fa 1-2/87: 152
   + Gr 7/86: 170
   - HF 4/87: 60
   + NR 2/87: 1
   + Opus 8/87: 175

27820. 416 297-2: DVOŘÁK—Piano trio
no. 4. MENDELSSOHN—Piano trio no. 1.
Beaux Arts Trio. Issued also as LP: 416
297-1.
   - Fa 11-12/87: 136
   • Gr 5/87: 1572
   + SR 11/87: 183

27821. 416 298-2: STRAUSS—Songs.
Norman, soprano; Parsons, piano. Issued
also as LP: 416 298-1.
   + Fa 3-4/87: 213
   • Gr 8/86: 296
   + Ov 8/87: 22

27822. 416 306-2: SCHOENBERG—
Verklärte Nacht (sextet version); String
trio, op. 45; Phantasy for violin and
piano, op. 47. *Schoenberg Ensemble.*
   + Fa 5-6/87: 188
   + Gr 1/87: 1037
   + NYT 8/23/87: H21
   + SR 8/87: 89

27823. 416 352-2: SCHUMANN—
Dichterliebe; Liederkreis, op. 39.

Fischer-Dieskau, baritone; Brendel, piano. Issued also as LP: 416 352-1.
- • Fa 5-6/87: 190
- • Gr 9/86: 429
- - Opus 6/87: 31

27824. 416 355-2: Vivaldi—Bassoon concertos. *Thunemann, bassoon; I Musici.* Issued also as LP: 416 355-1.
- + Fa 5-6/87: 212
- + Gr 9/86: 392
- + HF 6/87: 67

27825. 416 356-2: Rota—Concerto for strings. Respighi—Ancient airs and dances for lute: Suite no. 3. Barber—Adagio for strings. Elgar—Serenade for string orchestra in E minor. *I Musici.*
- + DA 4/87: 53
- + Fa 5-6/87: 242
- + Gr 1/87: 1031

27826. 416 358-2: Haydn—Mass no. 9 (Nelson). *Hendricks, Lipovsek, Araiza, Meven; Bavarian Radio Choir & Symphony Orch.; C. Davis, cond.* Issued also as LP: 416 358-1 .
- + Fa 5-6/87: 133
- • Gr 1/87: 1052

27827. 416 359-2: Concertos for flute and oboe by Salieri, Cimarosa, and Stamitz. *Nicolet, flute; Holliger, oboe; Academy of St. Martin-in-the-Fields; Sillito, cond.*
- + Fa 11-12/86: 205
- + Gr 6/86: 50
- + SR 12/86: 144

27828. 416 361-2: *Pops in love.* Music of Fauré, Debussy, Albinoni, Saint-Saëns, Satie, Tchaikovsky, Ravel, Pachelbel, and Vaughan Williams. *Boston Pops Orch.; Williams, cond.*
- + DA 10/87: 82
- + Fa 9-10/87: 391

27829. 416 364-2: Mozart—Concertos for 2 pianos, K. 242, K. 365. *Brendel, Cooper, pianos; Academy of St. Martin-in-the-Fields; Marriner, cond.* Issued also as LP: 416 364-1.
- + ARG 11-12/86: 72

27830. 416 365-2: Haydn—Piano sonatas, H.XVI: 52, H.XVI: 37; Andante con variazioni, H.XVII: 6. *Brendel, piano.*
- + Fa 7-8/87: 64
- + Gr 12/86: 907
- + HF 6/87: 62
- + Ov 9/87: 42

27831. 416 369-2: *Recorder sonatas.* Music of Bach, Schickhardt, Telemann, Handel, and Frederick the Great. *Petri, recorder; Malcolm, harpsichord.*
- + Fa 7-8/87: 232
- + Gr 3/87: 1292
- + SR 1/88: 166

27832. 416 378-2: Bartók—Concerto for 2 pianos, percussion, and orchestra. Kodály—Dances of Galanta. *Freire,*

Argerich, pianos; Labordus, Pustjens, percussion; Concertgebouw Orch.; Zinman, cond.
- • Fa 5-6/87: 84
- + Gr 12/86: 858 (Bartók)
- - Gr 12/86: 858 (Kodály)
- + HF 8/87: 60
- + Ov 8/87: 19

27833. 416 380-2: Glière—Horn concerto, op. 91. Saint-Saëns—Morceau de concert, op. 94. Chabrier—Larghetto, op. posth. Dukas—Villanelle. *Baumann, horn; Gewandhaus Orch.; Masur, cond.*
- + ARG 3-4/88: 106
- + ARG 7-8/93: 95
- + Fa 11-12/87: 287
- + Gr 8/87: 309
- + Gr 5/93: 54
- + Ov 3/88: 35

27834. 416 381-2: Mozart—Piano concertos no. 20-21. *Uchida, piano; English Chamber Orch.; Tate, cond.* Issued also as LP: 416 381-1.
- + DA 7/87: 61
- • Fa 5-6/87: 161
- + Gr 7/86: 167
- + Ov 7/87: 33

27835. 416 382-2: Glinka—Ruslan and Lyudmilla: Overture. Tchaikovsky—Romeo and Juliet. Smetana—Moldau. Mussorgsky—Night on Bald Mountain. *Los Angeles Phil. Orch.; Previn, cond.* Issued also as LP: 416 382-1.
- + ARG 3-4/88: 105
- • Fa 11-12/87: 294
- • Gr 6/87: 59

27836. 416 384-2: Guitar music of Albéniz, Tarrega, Torroba, and Romero. *Romero, guitar.*
- + Fa 3-4/88: 259
- + Gr 9/87: 453
- + Ov 11/88: 41

27837. 416 385-2: Beethoven—Symphony no. 6; Consecration of the house overture. *Academy of St. Martin-in-the-Fields; Marriner, cond.* Issued also as LP: 416 385-1.
- • Fa 9-10/87: 153
- • Gr 1/87: 1009
- • SR 1/88: 151

27838. 416 386-2: Music of Mozart, Pachelbel, and L. Mozart. *Academy of St. Martin-in-the-Fields; Marriner, cond.*
- + Fa 1-2/88: 179
- + Gr 11/87: 744

27839. 416 387-2: Lutosławski—Symphony no. 3; Espaces du sommeil. *Fischer-Dieskau, baritone; Berlin Phil. Orch.; Lutosławski, cond.*
- + Fa 7-8/87: 139
- + Gr 1/87: 1017
- + Gr 6/87: 45
- + SR 7/87: 98

27840. 416 389-2: Bach—Violin concerto no. 2; Concerto for 2 violins,

BWV 1043. Vivaldi—Violin concerto, RV 199; Concerto for 2 violins, RV 522. *Zukerman, Midori, violins; St. Paul Chamber Orch.; Zukerman, cond.* Issued also as LP: 416 389-1.
- + Au 5/87: 89
- + Fa 3-4/87: 63
- + Gr 12/86: 858
- + Ov 9/87: 38

27841. 416 390-2 (4 discs): Wagner—Parsifal. *Dalis, Thomas, London, Hotter, Neidlinger; with assisting soloists; Bayreuth Festival; Knappertsbusch, cond.*
- + Gr 6/86: 90
- + HF 12/86: 83

27842. 416 410-2: Bach—Italian concerto, BWV 971; French overture, BWV 831; Four duets, BWV 831. *Steuerman, piano.*
- + Fa 1-2/87: 58
- - Gr 6/86: 73
- + Ov 5/87: 38
- • SR 2/87: 175

27843. 416 412-1 (2 LPs): Bach—Violin concertos. *Accardo, Batjer, violins; Chamber Orch. of Europe; Accardo, cond.*
- + Gr 2/87: 1115

27844. 416 413-2: Bach—Violin concertos. *Accardo, Batjer, violins; Chamber Orch. of Europe; Accardo, cond.*
- + Fa 7-8/87: 50
- + Gr 5/87: 30

27845. 416 415-2 (2 discs): Bach—Mass in B minor. *Marshall, Baker, Tear, Ramey; Chorus & Academy of St. Martin-in-the-Fields; Marriner, cond.*
- + Fa 9-10/86: 92

27846. 416 418-2: Beethoven—Violin concerto in D major; Romances no. 1-2. *Szeryng, violin; Concertgebouw Orch.; Haitink, cond.*
- • Fa 9-10/86: 100
- + Gr 7/86: 158

27847. 416 438-2: Brahms—Violin concerto. Mendelssohn—Violin concerto in E minor. *Szeryng, violin; Concertgebouw Orch.; Haitink, cond.*
- + Fa 3-4/88: 87

27848. 416 443-2: Chopin—Piano concerto no. 2. Falla—Nights in the gardens of Spain. *Haskil, piano; Orch. des Concerts Lamoureux; Markevitch, cond.*
- + Fa 11-12/86: 129

27849. 416 463-2 (2 discs): Liszt—Hungarian rhapsodies (complete). *Dichter, piano.*
- - ARG 3-4/88: 49

27850. 416 490-2: Mozart—Symphonies no. 31, 35. *Orch. of the 18th Century;*

PHILIPS

Brüggen, cond. Issued also as LP: 416 490-1.
+ Fa 5-6/87: 166
+ Gr 12/86: 875
+ Gr 3/87: 1266
+ Opus 12/87: 45
+ Ov 6/87: 41

27851. 416 497-2: SCHUBERT—Octet, D. 803. *Academy of St. Martin-in-the-Fields Chamber Ensemble.*
+ Fa 11-12/86: 211
+ Ov 12/86: 44

27852. 416 613-2: LOCATELLI—Flute sonatas op. 2, no. 2, 6-7, 10. *Hazelzet, flute; Koopman, harpsichord; Van der Meer, cello.*
- Fa 9-10/87: 231
+ Gr 2/87: 1149

27853. 416 614-2: CORELLI—Trio sonatas. *Huggett, Bury, violins; Linden, cello; Smith, theorbo; Koopman, harpsichord & organ.*
+ Fa 1-2/89: 149
+ Gr 7/88: 174

27854. 416 615-2: C.P.E. BACH—Harpsichord concertos and quartets . *Hazelzet, flute; Peeters, viola; Van der Meer, cello; Amsterdam Baroque Orch.; Koopman, harpsichord & cond.*
+ Fa 3-4/89: 66
+ Gr 1/89: 1202

27855. 416 616-2 (2 discs): BACH—Partitas, BWV 825-30. *Steuerman, piano.* Issued also as 2 LPs: 416 616-1.
● Fa 5-6/87: 81
+ Gr 2/87: 1153

27856. 416 624-2: DVOŘÁK—Slavonic dances, op. 72, no. 9-16; Slavonic rhapsody no. 2. *Gewandhaus Orch.; Masur, cond.*
+ Fa 5-6/87: 112

27857. 416 627-2: SPOHR—Die letzten Dinge. *Shirai, Lipovsek, Protschka, Hölle; South German Radio Chorus & Symphony Orch.; Kuhn, cond.*
+ Fa 11-12/87: 233
+ Gr 2/87: 1149
+ Opus 2/88: 47

27858. 416 648-2: MOZART—Piano sonatas no. 8, 10. *Arrau, piano.* Issued also as LP: 416 648-1.
● DA 9/87: 62
- Fa 5-6/87: 166
● Gr 2/87: 1159
- NR 4/87: 32

27859. 416 649-2: LISZT—Via crucis. *Netherlands Chamber Choir; Leeuw, cond.* Issued also as LP: 416 649-1.
+ Fa 11-12/86: 162
+ Gr 9/86: 426
+ Opus 12/86: 39
+ St 12/86: 112

27860. 416 660-2: BERLIOZ—Te Deum. *Tagliavini, vocalist; Wandsworth School Boys' Choir; London Symphony Chorus & Orch.; C. Davis, cond.*
● Fa 9-10/88: 112
● Gr 4/88: 1484
+ HF 10/88: 73

27861. 416 807-2: WAGNER—Wesendonck Lieder. BERLIOZ—Nuits d'été. *Baltsa, mezzo-soprano; London Symphony Orch.; Tate, cond.* Issued also as LP: 416 807-1.
- Fa 5-6/87: 217
- Gr 9/86: 604
● Ov 11/87: 38
● SR 10/87: 149

27862. 416 813-2: ELGAR—Enigma variations; Pomp and circumstance marches, op. 39. *Royal Phil. Orch.; Previn, cond.*
● Fa 1-2/88: 118
+ Gr 8/87: 744
- HF 3/88: 59

27863. 416 815-2: *Concerti da caccia.* Music of L. Mozart, Mouret, and Fasch. *Baumann, Vlatkovic, Brown, Hill, horns; Les Trompes de France; Academy of St. Martin-in-the-Fields; Brown, violin & cond.*
+ DA 2/88: 62
+ Fa 1-2/88: 167
+ Gr 11/87: 734
● Ov 3/88: 35

27864. 416 816-2: *Works for horn and piano.* Music of Beethoven, Czerny, Rossini, Kruft, and Strauss. *Baumann, horn; Hokanson, piano.*
+ Fa 1-2/88: 167
+ Gr 11/87: 771
● Ov 3/88: 35

27865. 416 817-2: LUTOSŁAWSKI—Cello concerto; Dance preludes; Concerto for oboe, harp, and chamber orchestra. *Schiff, cello; H. Holliger, oboe; U. Holliger, harp; Brunner, clarinet; Bavarian Radio Orch.; Lutosławski, cond.*
+ Fa 11-12/87: 169
+ Gr 9/87: 473
+ Opus 2/88: 44
+ SR 11/87: 188

27866. 416 818-2: VERDI—Opera arias. *Estes, bass-baritone; Philharmonia Orch.; Delogu, cond.*
- ARG 9-10/89: 144
- Gr 12/88: 1065
- ON 9/89: 51

27867. 416 819-2: Music of J. Strauss, Jr., J. Strauss, Sr., and Josef Strauss. *Vienna Volksoper Orch.; Bauer- Theussl, cond.*
● Fa 9-10/87: 311

27868. 416 820-2: BEETHOVEN—Piano sonatas no. 4, 7. *Arrau, piano.*
+ ARG 9-10/88: 23
● Fa 5-6/88: 81 m.f.

+ Gr 2/88: 1212
+ NYT 4/17/88: H35

27869. 416 821-2: TCHAIKOVSKY—Violin concerto. SIBELIUS—Violin concerto. *Mullova, violin; Boston Symphony Orch.; Ozawa, cond.* Issued also as LP: 416 821-1.
+ Fa 9-10/87: 322
+ Gr 1/87: 1025 (Sibelius)
● Gr 1/87: 1025 (Tchaikovsky)
+ Gr 5/87: 1558 (Sibelius)
● Gr 5/87: 1558 (Tchaikovsky)
+ NR 4/87: 14
+ Ov 12/87: 43
+ SR 7/87: 103

27870. 416 831-2 (3 discs): BARTÓK—Piano concertos no. 1-3; Music for strings, percussion, and celesta; Rhapsody for piano and orchestra; Scherzo for piano and orchestra. *Kocsis, piano; Budapest Festival Orch.; Fischer, cond.*
+ Fa 5-6/88: 76
+ Gr 1/88: 1072
+ Ov 8/88: 16
+ SR 6/88: 112

27871. 416 838-2: BRAHMS—Piano trios (complete). *Beaux Arts Trio.*
+ ARG 11-12/88: 24
+ DA 7/88: 54
● Fa 5-6/88: 97
+ Gr 1/88: 1101

27872. 416 841-2: SAINT-SAËNS—Carnival of the animals. RIDOUT—Ferdinand; Little sad sound. MESCHWITZ—Tier-Gebete. *Argerich, Freire, pianos; Kremer, violin; Posch, double bass.*
+ Fa 11-12/88: 265
+ MA 3/89: 80
+ SR 12/88: 160

27873. 416 842-2 (4 discs): WAGNER—Parsifal. *Meier, Hofmann, Mazura, Estes, Salminen, Sotin; with assisting soloists; Bayreuth Festival; Levine, cond.* Recorded live 1985. Issued also as 5 LPs: 416 812-1.
+ ARG 5-6/88: 72
● Fa 5-6/88: 236
● Gr 2/88: 1243
- NYT 11/22/87: H27
● ON 7/88: 42
+ Op 6/88: 754
● Opus 4/88: 19
+ Ov 10/88: 47 (conducting)
- Ov 10/88: 47 (singing)
+ SR 5/88: 113

27874. 416 949-2 (2 discs): BERLIOZ—L'enfance du Christ. *Baker, Tappy, Allen, Bastin; John Alldis Choir; London Symphony Orch.; C. Davis, cond.*
+ Fa 3-4/88: 79
+ Gr 1/88: 1108

27875. 416 952-2 (2 discs): BERLIOZ—Béatrice et Bénédict. *Baker, Eda-Pierre, Tear, Bastin; with assisting soloists; John Alldis Choir; London Symphony Orch.;*

C. Davis, cond.
- Fa 1-2/88: 92
+ Gr 9/87: 478

27876. 416 955-2 (3 discs): Berlioz—
Benvenuto Cellini. *Eda-Pierre, Gedda,
Cuénod, Massard, Bastin, Soyer; with
assisting soloists; Royal Opera House
Covent Garden; C. Davis, cond.*
+ Fa 3-4/89: 110
+ Gr 1/89: 1202
+ Op 12/88: 1463

27877. 416 960-2: Berlioz—Cléopâtre;
Herminie; La belle voyageuse; La
chasseur danois; La captive; Le jeune
pâtre breton; Zaïde. *Baker, Armstrong,
Veasey, Patterson, Shirley-Quirk;
London Symphony Orch.; C. Davis, cond.*
- Fa 3-4/89: 109
+ Gr 9/88: 459

27878. 416 961-2: Berlioz—Nuits d'été;
Lélio. *Armstrong, Veasey, Patterson,
Shirley-Quirk, Carreras, Allen; John
Alldis Choir; London Symphony Orch.;
C. Davis, cond.*
- Fa 3-4/89: 109
+ Gr 9/88: 459

27879. 416 962-2 (2 discs): Berlioz—
Roméo et Juliette. *Kern, Tear, Shirley-
Quirk; John Alldis Choir; London
Symphony Chorus & Orch.; C. Davis,
cond.*
+ Fa 9-10/88: 112
+ Gr 6/88: 56

27880. 416 985-2: Stravinsky—
Symphony in 3 movements; Symphony in
C. *Bavarian Radio Orch.; C. Davis,
cond.*
+ Fa 11-12/87: 237
- Gr 5/87: 1558
- NYT 1/10/88: H27

27881. 420 069-2: Shostakovich—
Symphony no. 5. *Berlin Phil. Orch.;
Bychkov, cond.*
- Fa 7-8/87: 183
+ Gr 3/87: 1270
+ Gr 6/87: 52
- HF 7/87: 65
- Ov 12/87: 41
+ SR 9/87: 87

27882. 420 070-2: Music of Verdi,
Massenet, Puccini, Cilea, and
Tchaikovsky. *Araiza, tenor; English
Chamber Orch.; Zedda, cond.*
- Fa 1-2/88: 247
+ Gr 6/87: 104
- ON 1/16/88: 44
- Op 2/88: 200
- Opus 2/88. 37

27883. 420 071-2: Brahms—Piano
concerto no. 1. *Brendel, piano; Berlin
Phil. Orch.; Abbado, cond.*
+ Fa 5-6/88: 91
+ Gr 11/87: 729
+ SR 5/88: 111

27884. 420 080-2: Mahler—Symphony
no. 1. *Concertgebouw Orch.; Haitink,
cond.*
+ Fa 3-4/88: 138
- Gr 1/88: 1076

27885. 420 081-2: Grieg—Peer Gynt:
Suites no. 1-2; Four Norwegian dances;
Old Norwegian romance. *Philharmonia
Orch.; English Chamber Orch.; Leppard,
cond.*
+ ARG 1-2/88: 26
- Gr 12/87: 944 (Gynt)
+ Gr 12/87: 944 (others)

27886. 420 084-2: Music of Haydn,
Mozart, and Rossini. *Von Stade, mezzo-
soprano; Lausanne Chamber Orch.;
Dorati, cond.; Rotterdam Phil. Orch.;
Waart, cond.*
+ Fa 9-10/88: 324

27887. 420 085-2: *The last night of the
proms.* Music of Elgar, Berlioz, Wagner,
Mendelssohn, Wood, Handel, Arne, and
Parry. *Norman, soprano; BBC Chorus,
Choral Society, & Symphony Orch.; C.
Davis, cond.*
+ Fa 3-4/88: 268

27888. 420 088-2: Beethoven—Piano
sonatas no. 17-18. *Haskil, piano.*
- Fa 3-4/88: 75
+ Gr 2/88: 1212

27889. 420 097-2 (2 discs): Mozart—La
clemenza di Tito. *Baker, Minton, Von
Stade, Popp, Burrows, Lloyd; Royal
Opera House Covent Garden; C. Davis,
cond.*
+ Fa 1-2/88: 169
+ Gr 9/88: 481

27890. 420 106-2 (2 discs):
Mendelssohn—Elias. *Ameling,
Burmeister, Schreier, Adam; Leipzig
Radio Chorus; Gewandhaus Orch.;
Sawallisch, cond.*
+ DA 6/88: 69
+ Fa 7-8/88: 199
+ Gr 2/88: 1225

27891. 420 109-2 (2 discs): Rossini—
Mosè in Egitto. *Anderson, Raimondi,
Nimsgern; Philharmonia Orch.; Scimone,
cond. Reissue.*
- ARG 3-4/93: 130
+ Gr 12/92: 140
+ OQ summer 93: 221

27892. 420 113-2 (2 discs): Mahler—
Symphony no. 3; Das klagende Lied.
*Forrester, Harper, Procter, Hollweg;
Netherlands Radio Women's Chorus;
Boy's Chorus of St. Willibrord Church;
Netherlands Radio Chorus;
Concertgebouw Orch.; Haitink, cond.*
+ Fa 9-10/88: 193
+ Gr 11/88: 780

27893. 420 122-2 (3 discs): Wagner—
Tannhäuser. *Silja, Bumbry, Windgassen,
Wächter, Greindl; with assisting soloists;*

Bayreuth Festival; Sawallisch, cond.
+ Fa 1-2/88: 235
+ Gr 8/87: 337
- OQ Winter 1987/88: 130

27894. 420 130-2 (3 discs): Mozart—
Idomeneo. *Tinsley, Rinaldi, Shirley,
Davies, Tear; with assisting soloists;
BBC Chorus & Symphony Orch.; C.
Davis, cond.*
+ Fa 3-4/88: 159
+ Gr 2/88: 1240

27895. 420 142-2 (2 discs):
Tchaikovsky—Symphonies no. 4-6.
Concertgebouw Orch.; Haitink, cond.
+ Fa 7-8/88: 265

27896. 420 153-2: Beethoven—Piano
sonatas no. 3, 8. *Arrau, piano.* Issued also
as LP: 420 153-1.
+ ARG 9-10/88: 23
+ DA 5/88: 57
- Fa 3-4/88: 71
+ Gr 11/87: 777
+ HPR 7/88: 76
- NYT 4/17/88: H35
- Ov 4/88: 36

27897. 420 154-2: Beethoven—Piano
sonatas no. 5, 32. *Arrau, piano.*
+ ARG 3-4/89: 21
+ Fa 1-2/89: 117

27898. 420 155-2: Music of Walton,
Villa-Lobos, Falla, Satie, Delius,
Rachmaninoff, Vaughan Williams,
Canteloube, Barber, and Britten. *Mattila,
soprano; Academy of St. Martin-in-the-
Fields; Marriner, cond.*
- Fa 7-8/88: 331
+ Gr 2/88: 1202

27899. 420 156-2: Mussorgsky—Pictures
at an exhibition. Liszt—Piano music.
Brendel, piano.
- ARG 11-12/88: 63 (Liszt)
- ARG 11-12/88: 63 (Mussorgsky)
+ Fa 9-10/88: 219
+ Gr 1/88: 1107
+ SR 11/88: 144

27900. 420 157-2: Bartók—Sonata for 2
pianos and percussion. Stravinsky—
Concerto for 2 pianos. Britten—
Introduction and rondo alla Burlesca;
Mazurka elegiaca. *Richter, Lobanov,
pianos; Barkov, Snegirev, percussion.*
- Fa 3-4/89: 90
- Gr 8/88: 306
- MA 5/89: 52

27901. 420 158-2: Brahms—Piano
quartet no. 2. *Richter, piano; members of
the Borodin String Quartet.*
- Fa 7-8/88: 134
+ Gr 10/87: 594

27902. 420 159-2: Bizet—Jeux d'enfants.
Fauré—Dolly suite, op. 56. Ravel—Ma
mère l'oye. *K. & M. Labèque, pianos.*
+ Fa 1-2/88: 94
+ Gr 11/87: 759

PHILIPS

27903. 420 160-2: STRAUSS—
Metamorphosen; Sonatina for winds no.
1. *Vienna Phil. Orch.; Previn, cond.*
+ ARG 11-12/88: 90
+ Fa 9-10/88: 272 (Metamorphosis)
● Fa 9-10/88: 272 (Sonatina)
+ Gr 4/88: 1462
+ HF 10/88: 73
+ SR 9/88: 94

27904. 420 161-2: MENDELSSOHN—A
midsummer night's dream. *Lind,
soprano; Cairns, mezzo-soprano; Vienna
Youth Choir; Vienna Phil. Orch.; Previn,
cond.*
● ARG 3-4/87: 54
● Fa 11-12/87: 175
+ Gr 6/87: 45
+ SR 11/87: 190

27905. 420 162-2: HAYDN—Missa in
honerem B. V. Mariae (Great organ);
Missa brevis Sancti Joannis de Deo
(Little); Gloria (arr. M. Haydn).
*Orieschnig, Nigl, Schwendinger, Jelosits,
Scharinger; Vienna Choir Boys; Chorus
Viennensis; Vienna Symphony Orch.;
Harrer, cond.*
+ Fa 3-4/88: 125
+ Gr 2/88: 1219
- ON 4/9/88: 48

27906. 420 163-2: MOZART—Bastien und
Bastienne; Zufriedenheit; Komm, liebe
Zither . *Orieschnig, Nigl, Busch; Vienna
Symphony; Harrer, cond.; Wurdinger,
mandolin.*
● Fa 3-4/88: 154
+ Gr 11/87: 814
+ Ov 10/88: 46

27907. 420 164-2 (3 discs): GOUNOD—
Faust. *Te Kanawa, Coburn, Lipovsek,
Araiza, Schmidt, Nesterenko; Bavarian
Radio Chorus & Orch.; C. Davis, cond.*
● Fa 9-10/87: 206
+ Gr 5/87: 1500 (conducting)
● Gr 5/87: 1500 (singing)
● ON 9/87: 66
- Op 5/87: 585
- Opus 6/87: 45
- OQ Winter 87-88: 140
+ SR 10/87: 134

27908. 420 168-2: Music of Beethoven,
Schubert, and Dvořák. *Zukerman, violin
& cond.; St. Paul Chamber Orch.*
+ Fa 5-6/88: 80
+ Gr 11/88: 754

27909. 420 169-2: LISZT—Années de
pèlerinage: Italie. *Brendel, piano.*
+ DA 1/89: 37
+ Fa 9-10/88: 182

27910. 420 172-2: PROKOFIEV—
Symphonies no. 1, 5. *Los Angeles Phil.
Orch.; Previn, cond.*
+ Fa 5-6/88: 184
+ Gr 11/87: 744
+ SR 5/88: 113

27911. 420 174-2: LISZT—Années de
pèlerinage: 3rd year. *Kocsis, piano.*
+ Fa 1-2/89: 192
+ Gr 1/88: 1107
+ SR 6/89: 118

27912. 420 175-2: RACHMANINOFF—Piano
trios no. 1-2. *Beaux Arts Trio.* Issued also
as LP: 420 175-1.
+ ARG 5-6/88: 55
□ Fa 1-2/88: 195
● Gr 10/87: 598

27913. 420 176-2: BACH—Piano music.
Steuerman, piano. Issued also as LP: 420
176-1.
+ ARG 3-4/88: 14
+ Fa 11-12/87: 91
● Gr 7/87: 198

27914. 420 177-2: HOLST—The planets.
Boston Pops Orch.; Williams, cond.
● Fa 9-10/88: 170
● Gr 5/88: 1595
+ SR 9/88: 107

27915. 420 179-2: MOZART—Oboe
concerto, K. 313; Ma che vi fece, K. 368;
Ah se in ciel, K. 538. FERLENDIS—Oboe
concerto no. 1. *Holliger, oboe; Academy
of St. Martin-in-the-Fields; Sillito, cond.*
+ Fa 7-8/88: 204
+ Gr 5/88: 1590

27916. 420 181-2: MOZART—
Divertimentos, K. 251, K. 137, K. 113.
*Academy of St. Martin-in-the-Fields
Chamber Ensemble.*
● Fa 3-4/88: 158
+ Gr 11/87: 766

27917. 420 182-2: MOZART—Piano
quintet, K. 452. BEETHOVEN—Piano
quintet, op. 16. *Brendel, piano; Holliger,
oboe; Brunner, clarinet; Baumann, horn;
Thunemann, bassoon.* Issued also as LP:
420 182-2.
+ ARG 3-4/88: 16
+ Fa 1-2/88: 176
● Gr 8/87: 310

27918. 420 183-2: MOZART—Serenades
for winds no. 11-12. *Holliger, Pellerin,
oboes; Brunner, Schmid, clarinets;
Thunemann, Wilkie, bassoons; Baumann,
Vlatkovic, horns.*
● ARG 1-2/89: 72
+ Fa 11-12/88: 235
● Gr 5/88: 1616

27919. 420 184-2: *Opera arias.* Music of
Verdi, Mozart, Boito, Handel, Bellini,
Rossini, and Montemezzi. *Ramey, bass;
Ambrosian Opera Chorus; Philharmonia
Orch.; Renzetti, cond.*
+ ARG 5-6/88: 84
+ Fa 5-6/88: 241
+ Gr 11/87: 821
● ON 2/27/88: 43
+ Op 2/88: 200
+ Ov 5/88: 46

27920. 420 185-2: MOZART—Piano
sonatas no. 6, 16; Rondo, K. 485. *Uchida,
piano.* Issued also as LP: 420 185-1.
+ DA 5/88: 42
+ Fa 1-2/88: 180
+ Gr 7/88: 204

27921. 420 189-2: *Concerti per oboe.*
Music of Marcello, Sammartini,
Albinoni, Lotti, and Cimarosa (arr.
Benjamin). *Holliger, oboe & oboe
d'amore; I Musici.*
+ Fa 9-10/88: 334
+ Gr 4/88: 1465

27922. 420 190-2 (3 discs): HALÉVY—La
juive. *Varady, Anderson, Carreras,
Gonzales, Furlanetto; with assisting
soloists; Ambrosian Opera Chorus;
Philharmonia Orch.; Almeida, cond.*
● ARG 9-10/90: 69
● DA 7/90: 52
● Fa 5-6/90: 183
+ Gr 11/89: 965
+ MA 11/90: 75
+ ON 3/3/90: 30
● Op 3/90: 381

27923. 420 198-2: SAINT-SAËNS—Violin
concerto no. 3. VIEUXTEMPS—Violin
concerto no. 5. YSAŸE—Violin sonata no.
5. *Keulen, violin; London Symphony
Orch.; C. Davis, cond.*
+ ARG 3-4/89: 75
+ Fa 11-12/88: 266
+ Gr 7/88: 168

27924. 420 200-2: BACH—Keyboard
concertos no. 1, 5, 7. *Steuerman, piano;
Chamber Orch. of Europe; Judd, cond.*
+ Fa 9-10/88: 88
● Gr 5/88: 1577
● MA 3/89: 51

27925. 420 201-2: MOZART—Serenades
no. 3, 6; March in D major, K. 237.
*Academy of St. Martin-in-the-Fields;
Marriner, cond.*
+ Fa 7-8/88: 209
+ Gr 5/88: 1601

27926. 420 202-2: LISZT—Années de
pèlerinage: Suisse. WAGNER—Tristan und
Isolde: Liebestod (arr. Liszt). *Brendel,
piano.*
+ ARG 11-12/88: 45
+ Fa 9-10/88: 182

27927. 420 203-2: *Trumpet concertos.*
Music of Haydn, Hummel, Hertel, and
Stamitz. *Hardenberger, trumpet;
Academy of St. Martin-in-the-Fields;
Marriner, Neville.*
● ARG 9-10/88: 113
+ DA 11/88: 78
+ Fa 7-8/88: 175
+ Gr 12/87: 960
+ SR 9/88: 109

27928. 420 210-2: MOZART—Mass in C
minor, K. 427. *McNair, Montague, Rolfe
Johnson, Hauptmann; Monteverdi Choir;
English Baroque Soloists; Gardiner,*

cond.
+ Fa 1-2/89: 215
+ Fa 3-4/89: 224
+ Gr 5/88: 1630
+ HPR 3/89: 83
+ SR 1/89: 129

27929. 420 211-2: MENDELSSOHN—
Symphonies no. 3-4. *London Phil. Orch.;
Bychkov, cond.*
• ARG 7-8/88: 42
+ Fa 7-8/88: 200
• Gr 12/87: 944
- HF 3/89: 57
+ SR 7/88: 82

27930. 420 212-2: MENDELSSOHN—Paulus.
*Janowitz, Lang, Blochwitz, Adam;
Leipzig Radio Chorus; Gewandhaus
Orch.; Masur, cond.*
+ Fa 7-8/88: 199
+ Gr 2/88: 1226
+ SR 6/88: 142

27931. 420 216-2: VIVALDI—Four
seasons. Concerto for violin, 2 oboes, 2
recorders, bassoon, strings, and continuo,
RV 577. *Mullova, violin; Chamber Orch.
of Europe; Abbado, cond.*
+ Fa 7-8/88: 275
+ Gr 1/88: 1095

27932. 420 217-2: HAYDN—Songs.
Ameling, soprano; Demus, piano.
+ Fa 5-6/88: 141
+ Gr 9/88: 465

27933. 420 231-2: BEETHOVEN—Concerto
for piano trio and orchestra, op. 56; Piano
trio op. 11. *Beaux Arts Trio; London
Phil. Orch.; Haitink, cond.*
• Fa 7-8/88: 113

27934. 420 234-2 (2 discs): MAHLER—
Symphony no. 2; Des Knaben
Wunderhorn. *Ameling, Heynis, Norman,
Shirley-Quirk; Netherlands Radio
Chorus; Concertgebouw Orch.; Haitink,
cond.*
• Fa 3-4/89: 203 (Symphony)
+ Fa 3-4/89: 203 (Knaben)
• Gr 7/88: 163

27935. 420 237-2 (2 discs):
TCHAIKOVSKY—Nutcracker; Eugene
Onegin: Waltz and Polonaise. *Berlin Phil.
Orch.; Bychkov, cond.*
+ ARG 3-4/88: 86
+ Gr 9/87: 419
+ Ov 12/87: 43

27936. 420 240-2: RAMEAU—Les
boréades: Suite; Dardanus: Suite. *Orch.
of the 18th Century; Brüggen, cond.*
+ Fa 1-2/88: 197
+ Gr 5/87: 1557

27937. 420 241-2: MOZART—Symphony
no. 41; Clemenza di Tito: Overture. *Orch.
of the 18th Century; Brüggen, cond.*
+ Fa 5-6/88: 176
+ HPR 7/88: 85

27938. 420 242-2: MOZART—Clarinet
concerto; Clarinet quintet, K. 581.
*Hoeprich, basset clarinet; Dael, Stuurop,
violins; Have, viola; Möller, cello; Orch.
of the 18th Century; Brüggen, cond.*
+ Fa 1-2/89: 179
• Gr 6/88: 30
- MA 7/89: 61
+ SR 7/89: 94

27939. 420 243-2: TELEMANN—Recorder
music. HEBERLE—Recorder concerto in G
major. *Petri, recorders; St. Paul
Chamber Orch.; Zukerman, violin, viola,
& cond.*
+ DA 12/88: 68
+ Fa 9-10/88: 282
• Gr 5/88: 1595
+ MA 11/88: 88

27940. 420 245-2: VILLA-LOBOS—Etude
no. 1 in E minor; Five preludes; Suite
populaire bresilienne. BUSTAMANTE—
Misionera. BARRIOS MANGORÉ—Limosna.
Romero, guitar.
• ARG 1-2/89: 100
+ Fa 9-10/88: 290
+ Gr 1/88: 1102

27941. 420 246-2: Vocal music of J.
Strauss, Jr., Josef Strauss, and Arditi.
*Lind, soprano; Vienna Volksoper Chorus
and Orch.; Bauer-Theussl, cond.* Issued
also as LP: 420 246-1.   - Fa 1-2/
88: 243 - ON 2/13/88: 43

27942. 420 375-2 (3 discs):
TCHAIKOVSKY—Queen of spades.
*Milashkina, Levko, Atlantov, Valaitis,
Fedoseyev; with assisting soloists;
Bolshoi Theater; Ermler, cond.*
- Fa 7-8/88: 264
• Gr 3/88: 1342

27943. 420 385-2: BOCCHERINI—Guitar
quintets no. 4-6. *Romero, guitar;
Academy of St. Martin-in-the-Fields
Chamber Ensemble .*
+ Fa 3-4/88: 86

27944. 420 392-2: DEBUSSY—Images for
orchestra; Martyre de Saint Sebastien:
Excerpts. *London Symphony Orch.;
Monteux, cond.*
+ Fa 1-2/88: 110

27945. 420 393-420 394-2 (2 separate
discs): DEBUSSY—Piano music. *Arrau,
piano.*
+ Fa 7-8/88: 150
- Gr 12/87: 978

27946. 420 396-2: DVOŘÁK—String
quartet no. 12. MENDELSSOHN—String
quartet no. 1. *Orlando Quartet.*
+ Fa 3-4/88: 144
• Gr 11/87: 760

27947. 420 400-2: MENDELSSOHN—String
octet, op. 20; String quintet, op. 87.
*Academy of St. Martin-in-the-Fields
Chamber Ensemble.*

+ Fa 3-4/88: 143
+ Gr 11/87: 765

27948. 420 468-2 (3 discs): ROSSINI—La
Cenerentola. *Baltsa, Araiza, Alaimo,
Raimondi; with assisting soloists;
Ambrosian Opera Chorus; Academy of
St. Martin-in-the-Fields; Marriner, cond.*
+ ARG 3-4/89: 74
• DA 7/89: 46
• Fa 3-4/89: 251
+ Gr 11/88: 862
+ NYT 3/12/89: H29
+ ON 2/4/89: 42
+ Op 11/88: 1335
+ SR 2/89: 146
+ St 4/89: 207

27949. 420 472-2: SATIE—Four ogives;
Three gymnopédies; Three sarabandes.
Leeuw, piano.
• Fa 7-8/89: 233
- Gr 5/89: 1751

27950. 420 482-2: VIVALDI—Four
seasons; Concerto for violin, 2 oboes, 2
horns, timpani, strings, and continuo in D
major, RV 562a. *Academy of St. Martin-
in-the-Fields; Brown, violin & cond.;
Marriner, cond.*
+ Fa 3-4/88: 232
- Gr 11/87: 753

27951. 420 483-2: PROKOFIEV—Romeo
and Juliet: Suite no. 2. Excerpts.
TCHAIKOVSKY—Nutcracker. Excerpts.
Leningrad Phil. Orch.; Mravinsky, cond.
Recorded live 1981.
+ Fa 1-2/89: 233
+ Gr 8/88: 293

27952. 420 485-2: RESPIGHI—Ancient airs
and dances: Suite no. 3; Gli uccelli.
ROSSINI—Boutique fantasque (arr.
Respighi). *Academy of St. Martin-in-
the-Fields; Marriner, cond.*
+ Fa 9-10/88: 238
+ Gr 6/88: 55

27953. 420 538-2: BEETHOVEN—
Symphony no. 3 (with rehearsal
sequence). *Concertgebouw Orch.;
Monteux, cond.*
+ ARG 1-2/89: 27
• Gr 3/89: 1413

27954. 420 540-2: BEETHOVEN—
Symphonies no. 5, 7. *Concertgebouw
Orch.; Haitink, cond.*
• ARG 7-8/88: 13
• Fa 5-6/88: 83
+ Gr 10/87: 574

27955. 420 543-2 (2 discs): MAHLER—
Symphonies no. 8, 10: Adagio. *Cotrubas,
Harper, Bork, Finnilä, Dieleman,
Cochran, Prey, Sotin; various choruses;
Concertgebouw Orch.; Haitink, cond.*
+ Fa 7-8/88: 195
+ Gr 4/88: 1452

27956. 420 607-2 (2 discs): SMETANA—
Ma vlast. DVOŘÁK—In nature's realm

PHILIPS

overture. *Concertgebouw Orch.; Dorati, cond.*
- ARG 9-10/88: 85
+ DA 10/88: 70
• Fa 7-8/88: 253
• Gr 12/87: 942

27957. 420 648-2: VIVALDI—Choral music. *Marshall, Lott, Murray, Finnilä; John Alldis Choir; English Chamber Orch.; Negri, cond.*
+ Fa 7-8/88: 276
+ Gr 5/88: 1637

27958. 420 688-2: HAYDN—Symphonies no. 82-83. *Concertgebouw Orch.; C. Davis, cond.*
+ Fa 7-8/88: 177
+ Gr 2/88: 1185

27959. 420 711-2: MOZART—Serenades no. 10-11. *Netherlands Wind Ensemble; Waart, cond.*
+ Fa 5-6/88: 174
+ HF 5/88: 52

27960. 420 713-2: ORFF—Carmina Burana. *Casapietra, Hiestermann, Stryczek; Dresden Boys' Choir; Leipzig Radio Chorus & Symphony Orch.; Kegel, cond.*
+ Fa 5-6/88: 180

27961. 420 740-2 (6 discs): BUSONI—Major piano works. *Madge, piano.*
+ ARG 5-6/88: 21
• Fa 5-6/88: 100
+ Gr 4/88: 1477
+ Ov 7/88: 38
+ SR 7/88: 100

27962. 420 775-2: FAURÉ—Songs. *Souzay, baritone; Baldwin, piano.*
+ Fa 11-12/89: 205
+ Gr 11/88: 836
+ MA 3/89: 61

27963. 420 781-2: TIPPETT—Concerto for string trio and orchestra; Concerto for orchestra. *Pauk, violin; Imai, viola; Kirschbaum, cello; London Symphony Orch.; C. Davis, cond.*
+ Gr 3/89: 1438
+ MA 11/89: 63

27964. 420 782-2: MOZART—Piano concertos no. 9, 23; Rondo, K. 386. *Haskil, piano; Vienna Symphony Orch.; Sacher, Paumgartner, piano.*
+ Fa 1-2/89: 212
+ Gr 9/88: 416

27965. 420 790-2: HAYDN—Piano trios H. XV:28-31. *Beaux Arts Trio.*
+ Fa 9-10/88: 168

27966. 420 791-2: SCHUMANN—Piano quartet, op. 47; Piano quintet, op. 44. *Beaux Arts Trio; Rhodes, viola; Bettelheim, violin.*
+ Fa 9-10/88: 256

27967. 420 792-2 (3 discs): TCHAIKOVSKY—Sleeping Beauty. *Concertgebouw Orch.; Dorati, cond.*
+ Fa 9-10/88: 277

27968. 420 796-2: WEBERN—Music for string quartet. *Quartetto Italiano.*
+ Fa 9-10/88: 301
+ SR 3/89: 181

27969. 420 803-2: DVOŘÁK—String quartet no. 12. SMETANA—String quartet no. 1. *Guarneri Quartet.*
+ Fa 7-8/88: 158
+ Gr 2/88: 1209
+ SR 6/88: 135

27970. 420 805-2: BRUCKNER—Symphony no. 7. *Concertgebouw Orch.; Haitink, cond.*
+ ARG 11-12/88: 26

27971. 420 822-2: STRAVINSKY—Concerto for 2 pianos; Three movements from Petrushka; Five easy pieces; Three easy pieces. *K. & M. Labèque, pianos.*
• Fa 7-8/88: 260
+ Gr 1/88: 1101

27972. 420 823-2: MOZART—Piano concertos no. 20, 24. *Gibbons, fortepiano; Orch. of the 18th Century; Brüggen, cond.*
+ DA 8/88: 36
+ Fa 7-8/88: 204
+ Gr 5/88: 1596

27973. 420 824-2 (2 discs): MAHLER—Symphony no. 2. *Te Kanawa, soprano; Horne, mezzo-soprano; Tanglewood Festival Chorus; Boston Symphony Orch.; Ozawa, cond.*
• ARG 11-12/88: 52
- Fa 7-8/88: 194
• Gr 12/87: 944
+ SR 7/88: 102

27974. 420 882-2: BEETHOVEN—Piano concertos no. 1-2. *Brendel, piano; London Phil. Orch.; Haitink, cond.*
+ ARG 1-2/89: 17

27975. 420 923-2: HAYDN—Cello concertos, H. VIIb:1-2. *Schiff, cello; Academy of St. Martin-in-the-Fields; Marriner, cond.*
+ ARG 5-6/89: 54
+ Fa 1-2/89: 175
+ Gr 11/88: 776
+ HPR 3/89: 77

27976. 420 924-2: MOZART—Divertimento in D major, K. 131; Cassation in B♭ major, K. 99. *Academy of St. Martin-in-the-Fields; Marriner, cond.*
+ Fa 9-10/88: 209
+ Gr 4/88: 1454

27977. 420 925-2: TCHAIKOVSKY—Symphony no. 6. *Concertgebouw Orch.; Bychkov, cond.*
+ ARG 11-12/88: 93
+ Fa 9-10/88: 281

- Gr 1/88: 1090
• HPR 12/88: 86

27978. 420 926-2: BEETHOVEN—String quartets no. 12, 16. *Guarneri Quartet.*
• Fa 11-12/88: 135
+ Gr 5/88: 1612

27979. 420 932-2 (2 discs): BRUCH—Symphonies (complete); Swedish dances, op. 68. *Gewandhaus Orch.; Masur, cond.*
• ARG 9-10/89: 38
• Fa 9-10/89: 166
+ NYT 9/3/89: H19

27980. 420 934-2: PROKOFIEV—Symphony no. 6; Scythian suite. *Los Angeles Phil. Orch.; Previn, cond.*
+ Fa 3-4/89: 240
• Gr 5/88: 1607
+ SR 2/89: 166

27981. 420 935-2: SHOSTAKOVICH—Symphony no. 11. *Berlin Phil. Orch.; Bychkov, cond.* <\@> ARG 7-8/89: 91 + Fa 5-6/89: 321 <\@> Gr 11/88: 786

27982. 420 936-2: MAHLER—Symphony no. 1. *Berlin Phil. Orch.; Haitink, cond.*
• ARG 3-4/89: 53
+ DA 6/89: 87
- Fa 3-4/89: 202
+ Gr 10/88: 605
• HF 6/89: 68
+ St 5/89: 162

27983. 420 937-2: MOZART—Symphonies, no. 31, 34; Minuet, K. 409. *English Baroque Soloists; Gardiner, cond.*
+ Fa 3-4/89: 227
+ Gr 7/88: 164

27984. 420 938-2: *Baroque concertos.* Music of Telemann, Corelli, Albinoni, Bach, and Loeillet. *Zamfir, panpipes; Black, oboe; García, violin; English Chamber Orch.; Judd, cond.*
+ Fa 11-12/88: 342
• Gr 5/88: 1611

27985. 420 939-2: Harpsichord music of F., L. and A. Couperin. *Leonhardt, harpsichord.*
+ Fa 3-4/89: 131
+ Gr 7/89: 182
+ HF 7/89: 68
+ SR 3/89: 120

27986. 420 943-2: PAGANINI—Violin concerto no. 1. TCHAIKOVSKY—Serenade mélancolique, op. 26; Valse-scherzo, op. 34. *Midori; London Symphony Orch.; Slatkin, cond.*
+ ARG 3-4/89: 67
+ DA 1/89: 38
+ Fa 1-2/89: 227
• Gr 8/88: 290
+ HPR 6/89: 83

27987. 420 944-2: STRAUSS—Violin sonata, op. 18. PROKOFIEV—Violin sonata no. 2. *Zukerman, violin; Neikrug, piano.*

+ Fa 7-8/89: 259
- Gr 6/89: 61

27988. 420 945-2: *Encore.* Music of Wieniawski, Tchaikovsky, Milhaud, Saint-Saëns, Fauré, Falla, Granados, Kreisler, Paganini, Mainardi, Schmidt, Prokofiev, Glière, and Joplin. *Schiff, cello; Sanders, piano.*
+ Fa 3-4/90: 373

27989. 420 946-2: Music of Walton, Delius, Grainger, Vaughan Williams, Davies, Williams, and Anon. *Boston Pops Orch.; Williams, cond.*
+ Fa 9-10/89: 443

27990. 420 948-2: BACH—Violin partita no. 1, BWV 1002. BARTÓK—Sonata for solo violin. PAGANINI—Introduction and variations on Nel cor più non mi sento. *Mullova, violin.*
+ DA 4/89: 56
+ Fa 3-4/89: 81
+ Gr 9/89: 444
● SR 4/89: 92

27991. 420 949-2: CHOPIN—Piano sonatas no. 2-3. *Uchida, piano.*
● Fa 3-4/90: 167
+ NYT 5/27/90: H19

27992. 420 950-2: MOZART—Entführung aus dem Serail: Traurigkeit; Martern aller Arten; Mitridate: Lungi da te; Don Giovanni: Or sai chi l'onore; Ch'io mi scordi di te, K. 505; Misera, dove son, K. 369. *Te Kanawa, soprano; Uchida, piano; Lloyd, horn; English Chamber Orch.; Tate, cond.*
+ Fa 3-4/89: 215
+ Gr 10/88: 658

27993. 420 951-2: MOZART—Piano concertos no. 26-27. *Uchida, piano; English Chamber Orch.; Tate, cond.*
+ Fa 3-4/89: 221
+ Gr 11/88: 783
+ NYT 2/19/89: H32

27994. 420 953-2: STRAVINSKY—Violin and piano music. *Keulen, violin; Mustonen, piano.*
+ ARG 5-6/90: 117
+ Fa 11-12/89: 376
+ Gr 8/89: 332
+ MA 3/90: 84

27995. 420 954-2: TELEMANN—Trumpet concertos. *Hardenberger, Laird, Houghton, trumpets; Nicklin, Miller, oboes; Academy of St. Martin-in-the-Fields; Brown, cond.*
+ Fa 3-4/89: 313
+ Gr 8/88: 298

27996. 420 955-2: RAMÍREZ—Misa criolla; Navidad in verano; Navidad nuestra. *Carreras, tenor; Coral Salvé de Laredo; Sociedad Coral de Bilbao; Ocejo; Sanchez, cond.*
+ Fa 3-4/89: 244
+ Gr 11/88: 846

27997. 422 022-2: HAYDN—Symphonies no. 90, 93. *Orch. of the 18th Century; Brüggen, cond.*
+ DA 5/89: 82
+ Fa 1-2/89: 179
+ Gr 5/88: 1590
+ SR 7/89: 92
● St 2/89: 155

27998. 422 031-2: TCHAIKOVSKY— Serenade for strings, op. 48. DVOŘÁK— Serenade for strings, op. 22. *Bavarian Radio Orch.; C. Davis, cond.*
+ ARG 3-4/89: 98
+ Fa 5-6/89: 335
+ Gr 5/88: 1590

27999. 422 038-2 (6 discs): CHOPIN— Piano music. *Arrau, piano.*
+ Fa 5-6/89: 164

28000. 422 048-2: *Lieder.* Music of Handel, Schumann, Schubert, Brahms, Strauss, and Anon. *Norman, soprano; Parsons, piano.* Recorded live 1987.
- Fa 1-2/89: 301 + Gr 8/88: 329 + NYT 6/4/89: II24 + Ov 5/89: 52 + SR 1/89: 101 + St 3/89: 185

28001. 422 049-2: PROKOFIEV—Romeo and Juliet: Excerpts. *Gewandhaus Orch.; Masur, cond.*
+ DA 8/89: 56
- Fa 7-8/89: 215
● Gr 12/88: 1007
+ SR 8/89: 92

28002. 422 050-2: Music of J. Strauss, Sr., Waldteufel, Weber, J. Strauss, Jr., Brahms, Josef Strauss, Delibes, and Smetana. *Academy of St. Martin-in-the-Fields; Marriner, cond.*
+ Fa 5-6/89: 420

28003. 422 052-2: BEETHOVEN— Symphony no. 3. *Orch. of the 18th Century; Brüggen, cond.*
● Fa 3-4/89: 102
+ Gr 11/88: 306
+ NYT 1/8/89: H27

28004. 422 053-2 (2 discs): HANDEL— Alexander's feast; Concerto grosso in C major. *Brown, Watkinson, Stafford, Robson, Varcoe; Monteverdi Choir; English Baroque Soloists; Gardiner, cond.*
+ Fa 5-6/89: 208
+ Gr 11/88: 838
+ NYT 2/19/89: H29
+ Ov 8/89: 53
+ SR 6/89: 117

28005. 422 056-2: MOZART—Piano sonatas no. 2, 9; Rondo, K. 485. *Arrau, piano.*
● Fa 1-2/90: 243
□ Gr 1/90: 1350
+ NYT 11/12/89: H30

28006. 422 057-2: OFFENBACH—Overtures and ballet music. *Philharmonia Orch.; Almeida, cond.*

● Fa 5-6/89: 262
+ Gr 10/88: 611
+ MA 5/89: 81

28007. 422 058-2: VIERNE—Symphony no. 1; Organ music. *Chorzempa, organ.*
● Fa 3-4/89: 329
+ Gr 12/88: 1036

28008. 422 059-2: BEETHOVEN—String quartet no. 13; Grosse Fuge. *Guarneri Quartet.*
+ ARG 7-8/89: 20
+ MA 3/90: 69

28009. 422 060-2: LISZT—Piano music. *Arrau, piano.*
- Fa 5-6/91: 205
● Gr 2/91: 1537
● MA 7/91: 77
+ SR 4/91: 100

28010. 422 061-2: BACH—Flute sonatas, BWV 1031, 1033; Flute partita, BWV 1013; Suite for harp, BWV 1006a; Sonata for flute, harp, and cello, BWV 1020. *Grafenauer, flute; Graf, harp; Geringas, cello.*
+ DA 9/89: 70
● Fa 5-6/89: 109
● Gr 11/88: 795
- HPR 6/89: 68

28011. 422 062-2: SCHUBERT—Piano sonata in B♭ major, D. 960; Fantasia, D. 760. *Brendel, piano.*
+ Fa 7-8/90: 254
+ Gr 1/90: 1352
+ SR 11/90: 172

28012. 422 063-2: SCHUBERT—Piano sonatas, D. 784, D. 850. *Brendel, piano.*
+ ARG 9-10/89: 102
+ Fa 1-2/90: 297
+ St 1/90: 235

28013. 422 065-2: VIVALDI—Four seasons; Concerto for 4 violins; Concerto for 3 violins. *I Solisti Settimane Internazionali di Napoli; Accardo, violin & cond.*
+ ARG 11-12/89: 134
● Fa 5-6/89: 349
+ Gr 12/88: 1016
● MA 11/89: 64

28014. 422 066-2: BEETHOVEN—Piano concertos no. 1-2. *Arrau, piano; Staatskapelle Dresden; C. Davis, cond.*
+ ARG 1-2/89: 17
+ Gr 7/88: 152

28015. 422 067-2: BEETHOVEN—Piano sonatas no. 17, 31. *Arrau, piano.*
- Fa 9-10/91: 157
● Gr 4/91: 1866

28016. 422 068-2: SCRIABIN—Piano sonatas no. 3-5; Deux poèmes, op. 32; Poème tragique, op. 34; Deux poèmes, op. 44; Deux morceaux, op. 57. *Steuerman, piano.*
- Fa 1-2/92: 329

PHILIPS

28017. 422 071-2: Beethoven—
Symphonies no. 5, 8. *Academy of St.
Martin-in-the-Fields; Marriner, cond.*
- Fa 7-8/89: 96
- Gr 3/89: 1414

28018. 422 072-2: Mahler—Symphony
no. 4. *Te Kanawa, soprano; Boston
Symphony Orch.; Ozawa, cond.*
- DA 10/89: 68
- Fa 3-4/89: 204
- + Gr 11/88: 776

28019. 422 073-2: *Opera arias.* Music of
Mozart, Weber, Rossini, Gounod, and
Dvořák . *Mattila, soprano; Philharmonia
Orch.; Pritchard, cond.*
- ARG 7-8/89: 128
- Fa 7-8/89: 286
- Gr 1/89: 1211
- MA 1/90: 73
- - NYT 7/30/89: H25
- + ON 9/89: 51
- + Op 6/89: 756

28020. 422 074-2: *Vespri di S. Giovanni
Battista.* Music of Monteverdi, G.
Gabrieli, Grandi, Castello, Bazzino, and
Anon. *Soloists; Monteverdi Amsterdam
Ensemble; Netherlands Chamber Choir;
Leonhardt, cond.; Chorus Viennensis;
Dopf, cond.*
- + Fa 9-10/90: 298
- + MA 7/90: 77

28021. 422 075-2: Schubert—Piano
sonata in A minor, D. 845; Klavierstücke,
D. 946. *Brendel, piano.*
- ARG 7-8/90: 98
- + Fa 3-4/90: 285
- + Gr 10/89: 704
- + HPR Fall/90: 68

28022. 422 076-2: Schubert—Piano
sonata in C minor, D. 958; Moments
musicaux, D. 780. *Brendel, piano.*
- - ARG 9-10/89: 101
- + DA 5/90: 72
- + Fa 1-2/90: 297
- + MA 11/89: 157
- + St 1/90: 235

28023. 422 079-2 (3 discs): Mozart—
Piano trios, K. 254, 442, 496, 502, 542,
548, 564. *Beaux Arts Trio.*
- + Fa 3-4/89: 228
- + Gr 11/88: 803

28024. 422 082-2 (2 discs): Strauss—
Ariadne auf Naxos. *Norman, Gruberová,
Varady, Frey, Fischer-Dieskau, Bär; with
assisting soloists; Gewandhaus Orch.;
Masur, cond.*
- + Fa 3-4/89: 289
- + Gr 11/88: 862
- NYT 3/19/89: H28
- + ON 3/4/89: 42
- + Ov 4/89: 65
- + SR 3/89: 119
- + St 6/89: 221

28025. 422 088-2 (2 discs): Bach—St.
John passion. *Alexander, Lipovsek,*

*Schreier, Bär, Holl; Leipzig Radio
Chorus; Staatskapelle Dresden; Schreier,
cond.*
- + ARG 9-10/89: 21
- Fa 7-8/89: 73
- Gr 12/88: 1040

28026. 422 128-2: Beethoven—Piano
concerto no. 3; Piano sonata no. 6. *Arrau,
piano; Staatskapelle Dresden; C. Davis,
cond.*
- ARG 9-10/89: 24
- + Fa 11-12/89: 125
- + Gr 6/89: 24

28027. 422 147-2: Mozart—Piano sonata
no. 6; Piano sonata in F major, K. 533/
494. *Arrau, piano.*
- + ARG 9-10/89: 86
- Fa 7-8/89: 202
- + Gr 12/88: 1030

28028. 422 212-2: Vivaldi—Concerti per
strumenti diversi. *I Musici.*
- + ARG 3-4/90: 120
- + Fa 11-12/89: 401

28029. 422 229-2: Schubert—Piano
sonata in A major, D. 959; Hungarian
melody, D. 817; Sixteen German dances,
D. 783; Allegretto, D. 915. *Brendel,
piano.*
- + ARG 9/89: 73
- + Fa 1-2/90: 297
- + NYT 4/2/89: H30
- + St 1/90: 235

28030. 422 235-2: *Jessye Norman live.*
Music of Haydn, Handel, Mahler, Berg,
Strauss, Ravel, and Anon. *Norman,
soprano; Parsons, piano.*
- + ARG 7-8/89: 128
- + Fa 7-8/89: 287
- + Gr 6/89: 78

28031. 422 237-2: Schubert—
Impromptus, D. 899, D. 935. *Brendel,
piano.*
- + ARG 7-8/90: 99
- + DA 5/90: 72
- + Fa 7-8/90: 253
- + Gr 10/89: 704
- + SR 4/90: 96

28032. 422 240-2: Haydn—Symphonies
no. 101, 103. *Orch. of the 18th Century;
Brüggen, cond.*
- + Fa 11-12/89: 238
- + Gr 1/89: 1153

28033. 422 250-2: Bach—Violin
concertos no. 1-2; Concerto for 2 violins,
BWV 1043; Orchestra suite no. 3, BWV
1068: Air. *Szeryng, Hasson, violins;
Academy of St. Martin-in-the-Fields;
Marriner, cond.*
- + Fa 1-2/89: 106

28034. 422 264-2: Mozart—Missa
brevis, K. 65; Missa brevis, K. 140;
Missa in honorem S. Smae Trinitatis, K.
167. *Donath, Markert, Heilmann,
Schmidt; Leipzig Radio Chorus &*

Symphony Orch.;Kegel, cond.
- + ARG 7-8/89: 66

28035. 422 328-2: Bach—Trio sonatas.
*Holliger, oboe & oboe d'amore;
Zimmermann, viola; Jaccottet,
harpsichord; Demenga, cello.*
- + Fa 11-12/89: 115

28036. 422 329-2: Mahler—Symphony
no. 1. *Boston Symphony Orch.; Ozawa,
cond.*
- ARG 9-10/90: 84
- - Fa 5-6/90: 209
- + St 7/90: 171

28037. 422 330-2: Mozart—Horn
concertos (complete); Concert rondo, K.
371. *Damm, horn; Academy of St.
Martin-in-the-Fields; Marriner, cond.*
- + ARG 1-2/90: 67
- + Fa 11-12/89: 287
- + Gr 4/89: 1587
- + SR 12/89: 156

28038. 422 331-2: Mozart—Piano
concertos no. 24-25. *Uchida, piano;
English Chamber Orch.; Tate, cond.*
- + ARG 7-8/90: 74
- + Fa 9-10/90: 301

28039. 422 332-2: Paganini—Violin
concerto no. 1. Vieuxtemps—Violin
concerto no. 5. *Mullova, violin; Academy
of St. Martin-in-the-Fields; Marriner,
cond.*
- + ARG 5-6/90: 87
- + Fa 5-6/90: 240
- + Gr 10/89: 671

28040. 422 333-2: *On wings of song.*
Music of Mendelssohn, Beethoven,
Schubert, Schumann, Loewe, Brahms,
Strauss, Massenet, Hahn, Ravel, Chopin,
Tosti, Tchaikovsky, Barber, Yamada, and
Anon. *Ameling, soprano; Jansen, piano.*
- - Fa 11-12/89: 420

28041. 422 334-2: Brahms—Symphony
no. 2; Academic festival overture.
Philadelphia Orch.; Muti, cond.
- + ARG 9-10/90: 52
- DA 5/91: 69
- + Fa 9-10/90: 198
- + Gr 3/90: 1597
- - MA 1/91: 71

28042. 422 337-2: Brahms—Symphony
no. 4; Tragic overture. *Philadelphia
Orch.; Muti, cond.*
- + ARG 1-2/90: 36
- + DA 12/89: 66
- Fa 11-12/89: 156
- + Gr 6/89: 25

28043. 422 338-2: Mozart—Serenade, K.
361. *Orch. of the 18th Century members;
Brüggen, cond.*
- + Fa 11-12/89: 295
- + Gr 4/89: 1587
- + NYT 9/17/89: H34

28044. 422 339-2: MOZART—Flute and harp concerto, K. 299; Flute concerto no. 1; Andante for flute and orchestra, K. 315. *Grafenauer, flute; Graf, harp; Academy of St. Martin-in-the-Fields; Marriner, cond.*
- • Fa 11-12/89: 286
- + Gr 7/89: 180
- + SR 11/89: 156

28045. 422 340-2: SCHUBERT—Piano sonatas, D. 894, D. 840. *Brendel, piano.*
- + ARG 7-8/90: 99
- + DA 5/90: 72
- + Fa 7-8/90: 253
- + Gr 10/89: 704
- + SR 4/90: 96

28046. 422 341-2: BEETHOVEN—String quartets no. 10, 14. *Guarneri Quartet.*
- + Fa 5-6/90: 116
- • Gr 1/90: 1342

28047. 422 342-2 (2 discs): BRUCKNER—Symphony no. 5; Te Deum. *Mattila, Mentzer, Cole, Holl; Bavarian Radio Chorus; Vienna Phil. Orch.; Haitink, cond.*
- • ARG 9-10/90: 53 (Symphony)
- + ARG 9-10/90: 53 (Te Deum)
- • Fa 7-8/90: 113
- + Gr 11/89: 888
- • MA 3/91: 74

28048. 422 343-2: GRIEG—Peer Gynt. *Wiens, soprano; with assisting speakers; Leipzig Radio Chorus; Gewandhaus Kinderchor; Gewandhaus Orch.; Masur, cond.*
- • ARG 11-12/89: 63
- + Fa 11-12/89: 221
- • Gr 7/89: 176

28049. 422 345-2: BRITTEN—Cello sonata in C. PROKOFIEV—Ballade. SHOSTAKOVICH—Cello sonata. *Lloyd Webber, cello; McCabe, piano.*
- + ARG 7-8/90: 132
- • Gr 10/89: 682

28050. 422 346-2: HAYDN—Horn concertos no. 1-2; Concerto for 2 horns in E♭ major. POKORNY—Horn concerto in D major. *Baumann, Brown, horns; Academy of St. Martin-in-the-Fields; Brown, cond.*
- • ARG 5-6/90: 58
- + Fa 1-2/90: 198

28051. 422 347-2: REGER—Variations and fugue on a theme by Mozart. HINDEMITH—Symphonic metamorphoses on themes by Weber. *Bavarian Radio Orch.; C. Davis, cond.*
- - ARG 3-4/91: 107
- + Fa 1-2/91: 286
- + Gr 9/90: 514

28052. 422 348-2: MOZART—Piano concertos no. 18-19. *Uchida, piano; English Chamber Orch.; Tate, cond.*
- + ARG 7-8/90: 74
- • DA 9/90: 57

- + Fa 9-10/90: 301
- • Gr 7/90: 217

28053. 422 349-2: *Clavichord recital.* Music of Ritter, Bach, W.F. Bach, and C.P.E. Bach. *Leonhardt, clavichord.*
- + ARG 3-4/91: 149
- + Fa 11-12/90: 439
- + Gr 8/90: 392

28054. 422 350-2: FAURÉ—Piano quartet no. 1; Piano trio in D minor. *Beaux Arts Trio; Kashkashian, viola.*
- - ARG 11-12/90: 54
- - Fa 11-12/90: 223
- + SR 11/90: 164

28055. 422 351-2 (3 discs): HANDEL—Jephtha. *Dawson, Otter, Chance, Robson, Varcoe, Monteverdi Choir; English Baroque Soloists; Gardiner, cond.*
- • Fa 11-12/89: 225
- + Gr 6/89: 73
- + ON 1/20/90: 31
- • SR 9/89: 145

28056. 422 355-2: MAHLER—Symphony no. 5. *Berlin Phil. Orch.; Haitink, cond.*
- + ARG 5-6/90: 68
- + DA 5/90: 56
- - Fa 3-4/90: 220
- • Gr 7/90: 178
- + St 6/90: 201

28057. 422 356-2: MOZART—Mass in C major, K. 66; Missa brevis in G major, K. 49. *Mathis, Lang, Heilmann, Rootering; Leipzig Radio Chorus & Symphony Orch.; Kegel, cond.*
- + Fa 1-2/90: 241
- • Gr 8/89: 355

28058. 422 357-2: STRAUSS—Also sprach Zarathustra; Don Juan. *Philharmonia Orch.; Concertgebouw Orch.; Bychkov, cond.*
- + ARG 7-8/91: 128
- - Fa 9-10/91: 364
- - Gr 5/91: 2022

28059. 422 358-2: BRUCKNER—Mass in F minor no. 3. *Mattila, Lipovsek, Moser, Moll; Bavarian Radio Chorus & Symphony Orch.; C. Davis, cond.*
- • ARG 7-8/90: 36
- • Fa 7-8/90: 112
- • ST 12/90: 215

28060. 422 359-2: MOZART—Piano concertos no. 13-14. *Uchida, piano; English Chamber Orch.; Tate, cond.*
- + ARG 7-8/90: 75
- + Fa 11-12/89: 287
- • Gr 2/89: 1286

28061. 422 360-2: MOZART—Schuldigkeit des ersten Gebots; Grabmusik, K. 42; Kommet her, ihr frechen Sünder, K. 146. *Marshall, Murray, Nielsen, Blochwitz, Baldin, Varcoe; South German Radio Chorus & Symphony Orch.; Marriner, cond.*
- + Fa 5-6/90: 229

28062. 422 363-2: ORFF—Carmina Burana. *Gruberová, Aler, Hampson; Knabenchor der Staats und Domchores Berlin; Shinyukai Choir; Berlin Phil. Orch.; Ozawa, cond.*
- - ARG 1-2/90: 73
- • DA 2/90: 61
- + Fa 11-12/89: 309
- + Gr 7/89: 219
- + SR 10/89: 145
- + St 1/90: 231

28063. 422 364-2: SHOSTAKOVICH—Violin concerto no. 1. PROKOFIEV—Violin concerto no. 2. *Mullova, violin; Royal Phil. Orch.; Previn, cond.*
- + ARG 1-2/90: 75
- + DA 11/89: 64
- + Fa 11-12/89: 359
- + Gr 6/89: 43
- + MA 5/90: 76
- + NYT 9/24/89: H27
- + SR 11/89: 123

28064. 422 366-2 (3 discs): BIZET—Carmen. *Norman, Freni, Shicoff, Estes; with assisting soloists; Children of the Choir School; Radio France Chorus; French National Orch.; Ozawa, cond.*
- - ARG 3-4/90: 31
- • DA 2/90: 56
- ☐ Fa 1-2/90: 129
- • Gr 8/89: 360
- • MA 3/90: 69
- - NYT 1/14/90: H29
- • ON 12/9/89: 58
- - Op 8/89: 1018
- - SR 1/90: 129
- - St 3/90: 185

28065. 422 370-2 (3 discs): HANDEL—Concerti grossi, op. 6. *I Musici.*
- • Fa 7-8/90: 163
- + Gr 2/90: 1461

28066. 422 374-2 (3 discs): OFFENBACH—The tales of Hoffmann. *Lind, Studer, Araiza, Ramey; Dresden State Orch.; Tate, cond.*
- + ARG 3-4/93: 120
- • Fa 3-4/93: 245
- • Gr 11/92: 183
- + ON 2/13/93: 32
- • St 9/93: 183

28067. 422 378-2: *Jessye Norman: Salzburg recital.* Songs by Beethoven, Wolf, and Debussy. *Norman, soprano; Levine, piano.*
- • ARG 5-6/92: 188
- • Fa 3-4/92: 373
- + Gr 11/91: 148

28068. 422 380-2: LISZT—Piano concertos no. 1-2. DOHNÁNYI—Variations on a nursery song. *Kocsis, piano; Budapest Festival Orch.; Fischer, cond.*
- • ARG 7-8/90: 65
- + Au 11/90: 133
- • Fa 7-8/90: 185
- • Gr 1/90: 1325
- + NYT 4/1/90: H34

PHILIPS

28069. 422 381-2 (3 discs): MOZART—
Così fan tutte. *Mattila, Otter, Szmytka,
Araiza, Allen, Dam; Ambrosian Opera
Chorus; Academy of St. Martin-in-the-
Fields; Marriner, cond.*
+ ARG 11-12/91: 107
+ Fa 5-6/91: 228
+ Gr 11/90: 1051
+ MA 5/91: 80
• NYT 2/3/91: H24
• ON 9/91: 38
+ Op 4/91: 475
+ SR 3/91: 93

28070. 422 386-2: VIVALDI—Concertos,
op. 8, no. 7-12. *Agostini, violin; Pellerin,
oboe; I Musici.*
+ Fa 3-4/91: 420
+ Gr 2/91: 1522

28071. 422 387-2: DVOŘÁK—Cello
concerto, op. 104; Russalka: Polonaise;
Carnival overture. *Lloyd Webber, cello;
Czech Phil. Orch.; Neumann, cond.*
+ ARG 1-2/90: 46
+ Fa 11-12/89: 194
• Gr 5/89: 1722

28072. 422 388-2: BEETHOVEN—String
quartets no. 11, 15. *Guarneri Quartet.*
+ Fa 9-10/90: 173
• Gr 7/90: 236
+ St 2/91: 193

28073. 422 389-2: MOZART—Symphony
no. 39. BEETHOVEN—Symphony no. 2.
*Orch. of the 18th Century; Brüggen,
cond.*
+ ARG 11-12/90: 92
+ Fa 3-4/90: 248

28074. 422 390-2: MOZART—Clarinet
concerto; Sonata for bassoon and cello,
K. 292; Bassoon concerto, K. 191.
*Leister, clarinet; Thunemann, bassoon;
Orton, cello; Academy of St. Martin-in-
the-Fields; Marriner, cond.*
+ ARG 7-8/90: 73
• Fa 5-6/90: 224
+ Gr 3/90: 1613

28075. 422 391-2 (4 discs): ROSSINI—
Guillaume Tell. *Studer, Merritt,
Zancanaro, Surian, Roni; with assisting
soloists; Teatro alla Scala; Muti, cond.*
Sung in Italian; recorded live 1988.
• ARG 9-10/90: 108
+ Fa 9-10/90: 355
+ ON 5/90: 48
+ Op 3/90: 384
+ SR 8/90: 92
• St 1/91: 263 m.f.

28076. 422 397-2: *Coloratura arias.*
Music of Gounod, Thomas, Meyerbeer,
Delibes, Donizetti, Verdi, Bellini. *Lind,
soprano; Bavarian Radio Chorus &
Orch.; Wallberg, cond.*
- Fa 5-6/90: 353
- Gr 12/89: 1212

28077. 422 398-2: MOZART—Symphonies
no. 36, 40. *Staatskapelle Dresden; C.*

Davis, cond.
+ ARG 11-12/90: 91
+ DA 12/90: 92
• Fa 9-10/90: 314
+ Gr 3/90: 1614

28078. 422 399-2: STRAUSS—Aus Italien;
Don Juan. *Berlin Phil. Orch.; Muti, cond.*
• Fa 3-4/91: 394
+ Gr 9/90: 542 (Aus Italien)
- Gr 9/90: 542 (Don Juan)

28079. 422 400-2: TCHAIKOVSKY—Piano
trio in A minor. *Beaux Arts Trio.*
+ ARG 3-4/90: 115
+ Fa 1-2/90: 325
+ Gr 12/89: 1159
+ SR 1/90: 132

28080. 422 403-2: HOLST—The planets.
*Berlin Radio Women's Chorus; Berlin
Phil. Orch.; C. Davis, cond.*
• Fa 7-8/90: 175
+ NYT 4/1/90: H34

28081. 422 404-2: DEBUSSY—Piano
music. *Kocsis, piano.*
• Fa 11-12/90: 211
+ Gr 2/90: 1489

28082. 422 405-2: MOZART—Piano
sonatas no. 1, 3. *Arrau, piano.*
- ARG 7-8/91: 95
- Fa 1-2/91: 257
• Gr 9/90: 557
+ MA 3/91: 84

28083. 422 406-2 (2 discs): ROSSINI—Le
comte Ory. *Jo, Montague, Aler, Quilico,
Cachemaille; with assisting solists; Lyon
Opera; Gardiner, cond.*
+ ARG 5-6/90: 97
+ Fa 5-6/90: 270
+ Gr 10/89: 744
+ MA 3/90: 82
+ ON 3/31/90: 30
+ Op 12/89: 1505
+ SR 5/90: 108
+ St 1/91: 263

28084. 422 410-2: *German opera
choruses.* Music of Weber, Nicolai,
Mozart, Beethoven, and Wagner. *Leipzig
Radio Chorus; Staatskapelle Dresden;
Varviso, cond.*
+ ARG 11-12/90: 168
+ Fa 9-10/90: 466
+ Gr 4/90: 1871

28085. 422 412-2: DEBUSSY—Études for
piano. *Uchida, piano.*
+ ARG 1-2/91: 44
+ DA 1/91: 71
+ Fa 11-12/90: 209
+ Gr 7/90: 245
+ MA 1/90: 70
+ NYT 5/27/90: H19

28086. 422 413-2: MOZART—Serenade
no. 9; Marches, K. 335. *Soloists;
Camerata Salzburg; Végh, cond.*
+ Fa 9-10/90: 311
+ Gr 4/90: 1782

28087. 422 414-2: SCHUMANN—Cello
concerto; Adagio and allegro; Fantasy
pieces; Pieces in folk style. *Schiff, cello;
Berlin Phil. Orch.; Haitink, cond.*
+ ARG 11-12/93: 192
• Gr 6/93: 54

28088. 422 415-2: STRAVINSKY—
Petrouchka (original version); Scènes de
ballet. *Berlin Phil. Orch.; Haitink, cond.*
+ ARG 1-2/92: 123
• Fa 1-2/92: 341
+ Gr 10/91: 113

28089. 422 416-2: BEETHOVEN—Diabelli
variations, op. 120 . *Richter, piano.*
+ Fa 5-6/90: 124
+ SR 7/89: 89

28090. 422 419-2: MOZART—Symphonies
no. 32, 35-36. *English Baroque Soloists;
Gardiner, cond.*
- ARG 5-6/90: 85
+ Fa 5-6/90: 235

28091. 422 420-2 (2 discs): VERDI—I
Lombardi alla prima crociata. *Deutekom,
Domingo, Raimondi; with assisting
soloists; Ambrosian Singers; Royal Phil.
Orch.; Gardelli, cond.*
+ Fa 5-6/90: 318
+ Gr 11/89: 979

28092. 422 429-2 (2 discs): VERDI—Un
giorno di regno. *Norman, Cossotto,
Carreras, Wixell, Ganzarolli, Sardinero;
Ambrosian Singers; Royal Phil. Orch.;
Gardelli, cond.*
+ Fa 5-6/90: 318
+ Gr 12/89: 1210

28093. 422 432-2 (2 discs): VERDI—
Stiffelio. *Sass, Carreras, Manuguerra,
Ganzarolli; with assisting soloists;
Austrian Radio Chorus & Symphony
Orch.; Gardelli, cond.*
+ Fa 5-6/90: 321
+ Gr 3/90: 1689

28094. 422 442-2: SHOSTAKOVICH—
Symphony no. 8. *Leningrad Phil. Orch.;
Mravinsky, cond.*
• ARG 11-12/89: 120
+ ARG 5-6/90: 109
+ DA 4/90: 57
+ Fa 11-12/89: 359
• St 4/90: 203

28095. 422 458-2: MOZART—Piano
concertos no. 11-12. *Uchida, piano;
English Chamber Orch.; Tate, cond.*
+ Fa 5-6/91: 223
+ Gr 1/91: 1375

28096. 422 508-2 (4 discs): MOZART—
Philips Mozart edition, vol. 8. Violin
concertos (7); Rondos; Concertone;
Sinfonia concertante; Violin and piano
concerto in D, K. 315f. *Szeryng, violin;
Philharmonia Orch.; Gibson, cond.;
Academy of St. Martin-in-the-Fields;
Brown, cond. Reissues.*

+ ARG 11-12/91: 105
+ Gr 6/91: 46

28097. 422 509-2 (5 discs): Mozart—
Philips Mozart edition, vol. 9. Works for
wind instruments and orchestra. *Soloists;
Academy of St. Martin-in-the-Fields;
Marriner, cond.* Reissues.
- ARG 11-12/91: 105
+ Gr 7/91: 52

28098. 422 510-2 (3 discs): Mozart—
Philips Mozart edition, vol. 10. Flute
quartets; Oboe quartet; Clarinet quintet;
Horn quintet; Sonata for bassoon and
cello; Miscellaneous movements and
fragments. *Various performers.* Reissues.
+ ARG 11-12/91: 117
+ Gr 9/91: 90

28099. 422 511-2 (3 discs): Mozart—
Philips Mozart edition, vol. 11. String
quintets. *Grumiaux, Gérecz, violins;
Janzer, Lesueur, violas; Czako, cello.*
Reissues.
+ Gr 9/91: 90

28100. 422 512-2 (8 discs): Mozart—
Philips Mozart edition, vol. 12. String
quartets. *Quartetto Italiano.* Reissues.
+ Gr 8/91: 60

28101. 422 514-2 (5 discs): Mozart—
Philips Mozart edition, vol. 14. Piano
quintet, quartets, trios, etc. *Various
performers.* Reissues.
+ Gr 9/91: 92

28102. 422 515-2 (7 discs): Mozart—
Philips Mozart edition, vol. 15. Sonatas
for keyboard and violin. *Grumiaux, Van
Keulen, Poulet, violin; Brautigam, Verlet,
Klien, harpsichord, piano.* Reissues.
• Gr 9/91: 91

28103. 422 516-2 (2 discs): *Complete
edition, vol. 16.* Mozart—Music for two
pianos and piano duet. *Haebler,
Hoffmann, Demus, Badura-Skoda,
pianos.*
+ Gr 11/91: 121

28104. 422 517-2 (5 discs): Mozart—
Philips Mozart edition, vol. 17. Piano
sonatas. *Uchida, piano.*
+ Gr 9/91: 102

28105. 422 518-2 (5 discs): *Complete
edition, vol. 18.* Mozart—Piano
variations, rondos, etc. *Haebler, Uchida,
pianos; Koopman, harpsichord.*
+ Gr 10/91: 140

28106. 422 521-2 (2 discs): *Complete
edition, vol. 21.* Mozart—Organ sonatas
and solos. *Chorzempa, organ; Deutsche
Bachsolisten; Winschermann, cond.*
Reissues.
+ Gr 12/91: 100

28107. 422 522-2 (5 discs): Mozart—
Philips Mozart edition, vol. 22. Oratorios,
cantatas and Masonic music. *Various*

performers. Some reissues.
+ Gr 4/92: 133

28108. 422 526-2 (2 discs): *Complete
edition, vol. 26.* Mozart—Apollo et
Hyacinthus. *Mathis, Augér, Rolfe
Johnson; Salzburg Chamber Choir;
Mozarteum Orch.; Hager, cond.*
• Gr 11/91: 157

28109. 422 527-2: Mozart—*Philips
Mozart edition, vol. 27.* Bastien und
Bastienne; Two Lieder. *Nigl, Orieschnig,
Busch; Vienna Symphony Orch.; Harrer,
cond.* Reissue.
+ Gr 5/92: 110

28110. 422 528-2 (2 discs): *Complete
edition, v. 28.* Mozart—La finta
semplice. *Hendricks, Blochwitz, Schmidt;
C.P.E. Bach Chamber Orch.; Schreier,
cond.*
+ Gr 11/91: 152

28111. 422 529-2 (3 discs): Mozart—
Philips Mozart edition, vol. 29. Mitridate,
rè di Ponto. *Hollweg, Augér, Gruberová,
Baltsa, Cotrubas, Kübler, Weidinger;
Mozarteum Orch.; Hager, cond.*
+ Gr 2/92: 77

28112. 422 530-2 (3 discs): *Complete
edition, vol. 30.* Mozart—Ascanio in
Alba. *Baltsa, Mathis, Augér, Schreier;
Salzburg Chamber Choir; Mozarteum
Orch.; Hager, cond.* Reissue.
• Gr 1/92: 92

28113. 422 531-2 (2 discs): *Complete
edition, vol. 31.* Mozart—Il sogno di
Scipione. *Popp, Gruberová, Mathis,
Moser, Schreier; Salzburg Chamber
Choir; Mozarteum Orch.; Hager, cond.*
Reissue.
+ Gr 1/92: 92

28114. 422 532-2 (3 discs): Mozart—
Philips Mozart edition, vol. 32. Lucio
Silla. *Schreier, Augér, Varady, Donath,
Mathis, Krenn; Salzburg Radio Chorus;
Salzburg Mozarteum Chorus & Orch.;
Hager, cond.*
• Gr 2/92: 77

28115. 422 533-2 (3 discs): Mozart—
Philips Mozart edition, vol. 33. La finta
giardiniera. *Conwell, Sukis, Di Cesare,
T. Moser; Salzburg Mozarteum Orch.;
Hager, cond.* Reissue.
• Gr 5/92: 109

28116. 422 534-2 (3 discs): Mozart—
Philips Mozart edition, vol. 34. Die
Gärtnerin aus Liebe. *Donath, Norman,
Unger, Hollweg; North German Radio
Orch.; Schmidt-Isserstedt, cond.* Reissue.
• Gr 5/92: 109

28117. 422 535-2 (2 discs): *Complete
edition, vol. 35.* Mozart—Il rè pastore.
*McNair, Blasi, Hadley, Ahnsjö; Academy
of St. Martin-in-the-Fields; Marriner,*

cond.
+ Gr 12/91: 133

28118. 422 536-2 (2 discs): Mozart—
Philips Mozart edition, vol. 36. Zaide;
Schauspieldirektor. *Various performers.*
Reissues.
• Gr 4/92: 159

28119. 422 537-2 (3 discs): *Complete
edition, vol. 37.* Mozart—Idomeneo.
*Araiza, Mentzer, Hendricks, Alexander;
Bavarian Radio Orch. & Chorus; C.
Davis, cond.*
+ Fa 5-6/92: 206
• Gr 12/91: 130

28120. 422 538-2 (2 discs): Mozart—
Philips Mozart edition, vol. 38. Die
Entführung aus dem Serail. *Eda-Pierre,
Burrowes, Burrows, Tear, Lloyd;
Academy of St. Martin-in-the-Fields;
Marriner, cond.* Reissue.
• Gr 4/92: 160

28121. 422 539-2: Mozart—*Philips
Mozart edition, vol. 39.* L'Oca del Cairo;
Lo sposo deluso. *Fischer-Dieskau,
Wiens, Schreier, D. Johnson; C.P.E.
Bach Chamber Orch.; Schreier, cond.;
Palmer, Cotrubas, Tear, Rolfe Johnson;
London Symphony Orch.; C. Davis, cond.*
Part reissue.
• Gr 5/92: 110

28122. 422 540-2 (3 discs): *Complete
edition, vol. 40.* Mozart—Le nozze di
Figaro. *Freni, Norman, Ganzarolli,
Wixell; Royal Opera Covent Garden; C.
Davis, cond.* Reissue.
• Gr 1/92: 91

28123. 422 541-2 (3 discs): Mozart—
Complete edition, vol. 41. Don Giovanni.
*Wixell, Arroyo, Te Kanawa, Ganzarolli;
Royal Opera Covent Garden; C. Davis,
cond.* Reissue.
+ Fa 7-8/92: 229
+ Gr 1/92: 91

28124. 422 542-2 (3 discs): *Complete
edition, vol. 42.* Mozart—Così fan tutte.
*Caballé, Baker, Cotrubas, Ganzarolli,
Van Allan; Royal Opera Covent Garden;
C. Davis, cond.* Reissue.
• Gr 1/92: 91

28125. 422 543-2 (3 discs): Mozart—
Philips Mozart edition, vol. 43. Die
Zauberflöte. *M. Price, Serra, Schreier,
Melbye, Moll; Staatskapelle Dresden; C.
Davis, cond.* Reissue.
+ Gr 4/92: 160

28126. 422 544-2 (? discs): *Complete
edition, vol. 44.* Mozart—La clemenza di
Tito. *Baker, Minton, Von Stade, Popp,
Burrows; Royal Opera Covent Garden;
C. Davis, cond.* Reissue.
+ ARG 7-8/92: 180
+ Gr 4/92: 160

28127. 422 545-2 (3 discs): *Complete edition, vol. 45.* MOZART—Rarities and surprises. *Academy of St. Martin-in- the-Fields; Marriner, cond.; Netherlands Wind Ensemble.*
+ Gr 12/91: 93

28128. 422 574-2: STRAUSS—Elektra. *Behrens, Secunde, Ludwig, Ulfung, Hynninen; with assisting soloists; Tanglewood Festival Chorus; Boston Symphony Orch.; Ozawa, cond.*
+ ARG 11-12/89: 123
+ DA 10/89: 73
• Fa 11-12/89: 369
+ HPR v.7, no.1/90: 89
- MA 3/90: 85
+ ON 8/89: 31
• Op 4/89: 498
+ OQ Spring/90: 240

28129. 422 579-2: BACH—Violin concertos BWV 1041, 1042; Concerto for 2 violins, BWV 1043. *Agostini, Pérez, violins; I Musici.*
+ Gr 10/91: 81

28130. 422 592-2: MOZART—Quintet for piano and winds, K. 452; Concerto for piano and orchestra no. 17. *Uchida, piano; Black, oboe; King, clarinet; Lloyd, horn; O'Neill, bassoon; English Chamber Orch.; Tate, cond.*
+ Fa 5-6/93: 273
• Gr 4/93: 81

28131. 422 843-2: ROSSINI—Ballet music from operas. *Monte Carlo Opera Orch.; Almeida, cond.*
+ Fa 11-12/89: 386

28132. 422 844-2: DONIZETTI—Ballet music from operas. *Philharmonia Orch.; Almeida, cond.*
+ Fa 11-12/89: 386

28133. 422 845-2: TCHAIKOVSKY—Ballet music from operas; Caprices of Oxana. *Royal Opera House Covent Garden Orch.; C. Davis, cond.*
+ Fa 11-12/89: 387

28134. 422 847-2 (2 discs): VERDI—Ballet music from operas. *Monte Carlo National Opera Orch.; London Symphony Orch.; Almeida, cond.*
+ Fa 11-12/89: 386

28135. 422 893-2 (2 discs): *The Jessye Norman collection.* Music of Schubert, Adams, Franck, Gounod, Mozart, Purcell, Strauss, Berlioz, Duparc, Satie, Poulenc, and Wagner. *Norman, soprano; various accs.*
- Fa 11-12/89: 421

28136. 422 996-2: BORODIN—Symphonies no. 1-2. *Rotterdam Phil. Orch.; Gergiev, cond.*
• Gr 8/91: 53

28137. 426 075-2: BACH—Violin concertos BWV 1041, 1042; Concerto for 2 violins, BWV 1043; Concerto for violin and oboe, BWV 1060. *Driehuys, oboe; Michelucci, Ayo, violins; I Musici.* Reissue.
- Gr 10/91: 81

28138. 426 104-2: BARTÓK—Violin concerto no. 2. *Székely, violin; Concertgebouw Orch.; Mengelberg, cond.* World premiere performance, March 23, 1939.
+ Fa 9-10/90: 163

28139. 426 108-2: MAHLER—Symphony no. 4. *Vincent, soprano; Concertgebouw Orch.; Mengelberg, cond.* Recorded live 1939.
+ Fa 9-10/90: 163

28140. 426 118-2 (2 discs): VERDI—Il Corsaro. *Norman, Caballé, Carreras, Mastromei; Ambrosian Singers; Philharmonia Orch.; Gardelli, cond.* Reissue.
• ARG 9-10/91: 140

28141. 426 144-2: *Mysteries of the macabre.* Music of Hansen, Enescu, Hindemith, Schmitt, and Ligeti. *Hardenberger, trumpet; Pöntinen, piano.*
+ ARG 11-12/90: 159
+ Fa 9-10/90: 487
+ Gr 1/90: 1349

28142. 426 145-2 (4 discs): BACH—Orchestral music. *Adeney, flute; Grumiaux, Garcia, violins; English Chamber Orch.; Leppard, cond.* Reissue.
• Gr 10/91: 81

28143. 426 169-2: HAYDN—Symphonies no. 86, 88. *Orch. of the 18th Century; Brüggen, cond.*
+ Fa 5-6/90: 189
+ Gr 12/89: 1129

28144. 426 199-2 (2 discs): BERLIOZ—La damnation de Faust. *Otter, Myers, Lafont; Edinburgh Festival Chorus; Lyon Opera Orch.; Gardiner, cond.* Recorded live 1987.
- Fa 7-8/90: 98
+ Gr 3/90: 1654
+ NYT 4/29/90: H31
• Op 8/90: 1010

28145. 426 231-2: MOZART—Symphony no. 38; Nozze di Figaro: Overture. *Orch. of the 18th Century; Brüggen, cond.*
+ Fa 9-10/90: 315
+ Gr 2/90: 1467
• SR 10/90: 114

28146. 426 232-2: BEETHOVEN—Diabelli variations. *Brendel, piano.*
+ Fa 11-12/90: 171
+ Gr 8/90: 390

28147. 426 233-2 (2 discs): DONIZETTI—Maria Stuarda. *Gruberová, Baltsa, Araiza, Alaimo; Bavarian Radio Chorus & Symphony Orch.; Patanè cond.*
+ ARG 11-12/90: 48

+ Fa 9-10/90: 231
+ Gr 4/90: 1862
+ ON 10/90: 48
+ SR 9/90: 120

28148. 426 236-2: MOZART—Symphonies no. 28-29, 34. *Staatskapelle Dresden; C. Davis, cond.*
+ Fa 1-2/91: 260 (no. 28)
• Fa 1-2/91: 260 (others)

28149. 426 237-2: *Deutsche Volkslieder.* Music of Brahms, Prokofiev, and Schumann. *Schreier, tenor; Sawallisch, piano.* Recorded live 1984.   + Fa 9-10/90: 461

28150. 426 238-2 (2 discs): BACH—Mass in B minor. *Smith, Chance, Van der Meel, Kamp; Netherlands Chamber Choir; Orch. of the 18th Century; Brüggen, cond.* Recorded live 1989.
• Fa 9-10/90: 149
+ Gr 2/90: 1496

28151. 426 239-2: BEETHOVEN—Symphony no. 7; Wellington's victory. *Academy of St. Martin-in-the-Fields; Marriner, cond.*
- Fa 3-4/91: 155 (Symphony)
+ Fa 3-4/91: 155 (Wellington)
• Gr 1/91: 1369
- St 6/91: 235

28152. 426 240-2: MOZART—String quartets no. 14-15. *Guarneri Quartet.*
+ ARG 1-2/91: 70
+ Fa 11-12/90: 293
• Gr 10/90: 760

28153. 426 241-2: MOZART—Concerto for 2 pianos, K. 365; Concerto for 3 pianos, K. 242. *K. & Labèque, pianos; Berlin Phil. Orch.; Bychkov, piano & cond.*
- ARG 3-4/91: 93
+ DA 2/91: 60
+ Fa 3-4/91: 288
• Gr 9/90: 524

28154. 426 243-2 (2 discs): SAINT-SAËNS—Samson et Dalila. *Baltsa, Carreras, Summers, Estes, Burchuladze; Chor und Symphonie-Orch. des Bayerischen Rundfunks; Davis, cond.*
+ ARG 9-10/91: 117
+ Fa 9-10/91: 332
- ON 7/91: 34

28155. 426 249-2 (2 discs): MAHLER—Symphony no. 7; Kindertotenlieder. *Norman, soprano; Boston Symphony Orch.; Ozawa, cond.*
• ARG 7-8/91: 83
- Fa 7-8/91: 199 (Symphony)
• Fa 7-8/91: 199 (Songs)
- St 8/91: 82 (Symphony)
+ St 8/91: 82 (Songs)

28156. 426 252-2: BEETHOVEN—Symphony no. 9. *Mattila, Otter, Araiza, Ramey; Academy of St. Martin-in-the-Fields Chorus & Orch.; Marriner, cond.*
• ARG 11-12/90: 31

+ Fa 11-12/90: 170
• Gr 6/90: 42

28157. 426 253-2: BRAHMS—Symphony no. 3; Alto rhapsody. *Norman, mezzo-soprano; Choral Arts Society of Philadelphia; Philadelphia Orch.; Muti, cond.*
- Fa 5-6/91: 140
• Gr 1/91: 1370
- MA 7/91: 69
+ SR 2/91: 131

28158. 426 254-2: STRAVINSKY—Divertimento (arr. Dushkin). RAVEL—Violin sonata. PROKOFIEV—Violin sonata no. 2. *Mullova, violin; Canino, piano.*
+ ARG 11-12/91: 155
+ DA 11/90: 58
+ Fa 11-12/90: 367
+ Gr 8/90: 388
• MA 8/91: 81

28159. 426 255-2: DEBUSSY—Prélude à l'après-midi d'un faune. DUKAS—Sorcerer's apprentice. IBERT—Escales. RAVEL—Daphnis et Chloé: Suite no. 2. *Los Angeles Phil. Orch.; Previn, cond.*
+ ARG 1-2/91: 128
+ Fa 11-12/90: 474
• Gr 9/90: 554

28160. 426 256-2: BEETHOVEN—Piano sonatas no. 12, 15, 19-20. *Arrau, piano.*
- ARG 1-2/93: 75

28161. 426 257-2 (2 discs): MAHLER—Symphony no. 6; Lieder eines fahrenden Gesellen. *Norman, mezzo-soprano; Berlin Phil. Orch.; Haitink, cond.*
• ARG 9-10/91: 90
+ Fa 9-10/91: 262
+ Gr 4/91: 1832

28162. 426 260-2: RAVEL—Daphnis et Chloé. *Boston Symphony Orch.; Haitink, cond.*
+ ARG 11-12/90: 101
+ DA 10/90: 74
+ Fa 11-12/90: 325
• Gr 8/90: 376
- MA 11/90: 78

28163. 426 261-2: SCHOENBERG—Erwartung; Brettl-Lieder. *Norman, soprano; Metropolitan Opera Orch.; Levine, piano & cond.*
+ ARG 3-4/94: 147
+ Fa 1-2/94: 304
+ Gr 9/93: 102
• ON 11/93: 43

28164. 426 262-2: STRAUSS—Don Quixote; Romance in F for cello and orchestra; Till Eulenspiegel. *Schiff, cello; Gewandhausorch. Leipzig, Masur, cond.*
+ ARG 11-12/91: 151
+ Fa 11-12/91: 495
• Gr 7/91: 62

28165. 426 263-2: Guitar music of Carulli, Molino, and Mozart. *Romero, guitar; Academy of St. Martin-in-the-*

Fields; Brown, cond.
+ ARG 3-4/93: 163
• Fa 1-2/91: 175
+ Gr 9/90: 554

28166. 426 264-2: DVOŘÁK—Slavonic dances. *K. & M. Labèque, piano.*
+ ARG 5-6/93: 83
• Gr 12/92: 94

28167. 426 265-2 (3 discs): HANDEL—Saul. *Brown, Dawson, Ragin, Miles, Ainsley; Monteverdi Choir; English Baroque Soloists; Gardiner, cond.*
+ ARG 3-4/92: 68
+ EM 8/92: 518
+ Fa 3-4/92: 207
+ Gr 8/91: 65
+ ON 9/93: 52
+ St 10/92: 263

28168. 426 269-2: SCHUBERT—Symphony no. 9. *Gewandhaus Orch.; Masur, cond.*
• ARG 1-2/92: 107
• Fa 1-2/92: 322
- Gr 10/91: 109

28169. 426 270-2: *Opera duets.* Music of Donizetti, Delibes, Gounod, Verdi, and Massenet. *Lind, soprano; Araiza, tenor; Zürich Opera Orch.; Weikert, cond.*
• ARG 3-4/91: 175
- Fa 3-4/91: 441
- Gr 10/90: 820 (Lind)
+ Gr 10/90: 820 (Araiza)

28170. 426 271-2: WAGNER—Overtures & preludes: Flying Dutchman; Lohengrin; Meistersinger; Tannhäuser, Tristan & Isolde (w/ Liebestod). *Berlin Phil. Orch.; Ozawa.*
- ARG 9-10/91: 146

28171. 426 272-2: MOZART—Variations, K. 573. MENDELSSOHN—Variations sérieuses. LISZT—Variations on Weinen, Klagen, Sorgen, Zagen. BRAHMS—Theme with variations (arrangement of 2nd movement of the String sextet op. 18). *Brendel, piano.*
+ ARG 1-2/92: 161
+ Fa 9-10/91: 417

28172. 426 273-2: MOZART—Mass in C minor, K. 427. *Hendricks, Coburn, Blochwitz, Schmidt; Leipzig Radio Chorus; Staatskapelle Dresden; Schreier, cond.*
• ARG 3-4/91: 95
+ Fa 1-2/91: 254
+ Gr 8/90: 403
+ MA 5/91: 81
• St 4/91: 259

28173. 426 274-2: MOZART—Opera arias. *Schreier, tenor & cond.; Staatskapelle Dresden.* Several arias are in alternate versions.
• Fa 3-4/91: 284
+ Gr 10/90: 815

28174. 426 275-2: MOZART—Coronation mass; Vespers, K. 339; Ave verum

corpus. *Mathis, Rappé, Blochwitz, Quasthoff; Leipzig Radio Chorus; Staatskapelle Dresden; Schreier, cond.*
- Gr 2/94: 84

28175. 426 276-2 (2 discs): MOZART—Zauberflöte. *Studer, Te Kanawa, Araiza, Bär, Dam, Ramey; with assisting soloists; Ambrosian Opera Chorus; Academy of St. Martin-in-the-Fields; Marriner, cond.*
+ DA 2/91: 56
+ Fa 3-4/91: 293
+ Gr 11/90: 1050
+ MA 5/91: 80
• NYT 2/3/91: H24
• ON 2/2/91: 32
- Op 10/90: 1262

28176. 426 280-2: VIVALDI—Violin concertos, op. 4 "La stravaganza". *Agostini, violin; I Musici.*
• Gr 10/91: 117

28177. 426 283-2: MOZART—Symphonies no. 38-39. *English Baroque Soloists; Gardiner, cond.*
+ ARG 7-8/91: 97
+ Fa 7-8/91: 239
+ Gr 2/91: 1510
+ SR 3/91: 94

28178. 426 284-2: POULENC—Concerto for 2 pianos; Sonata for piano 4-hands; Capriccio (d'après le bal masqué); L'embarquement pour Cythère; Élégie. MILHAUD—Scaramouche. *K. & L. Labèque, pianos; Boston Symphony Orch.; Ozawa, cond.*
+ ARG 3-4/92: 119
+ Fa 1-2/92: 295
• Gr 8/91: 55

28179. 426 286-2: GRIEG—String quartet, op. 27. SIBELIUS—String quartet, op. 56 "Voces intimae". *Guarneri Quartet.*
+ ARG 1-2/92: 60
+ Fa 11-12/91: 330
- Gr 9/91: 87

28180. 426 290-2 (5 discs): BEETHOVEN—Symphonies (complete). *Gewandhaus Orch.; Masur, cond.* Reissues.
+ Gr 5/93: 38

28181. 426 297-2: BEETHOVEN—Piano sonatas no. 11, 18. *Arrau, piano.*
- ARG 7-8/91: 32
+ Fa 1-2/91: 151

28182. 426 298-2: BRAHMS—Serenade no. 1. WAGNER—Siegfried Idyll. *Academy of St. Martin-in-the-Fields Chamber Ensemble.*
+ ARG 5-6/92: 36
+ Fa 1-2/92: 185
+ Gr 9/91: 83

28183. 426 301-2: *Hunting music.* Music of Zwierzna, Schneider, Corrette, Chalmel, Sombrun, Rossini, and Pont. *Baumann, horn & cond.; Folkwang Horn Ensemble; German Natural Horn*

PHILIPS

Soloists; Kläsener, organ.
+ Fa 11-12/91: 263

28184. 426 302-2: MAHLER—Symphony no. 9; Symphony no. 10: Adagio. *Boston Symphony Orch.; Ozawa, cond.*
• ARG 7-8/92: 169
• Fa 7-8/92: 208
- Gr 1/92: 55

28185. 426 305-2: MOZART—Piano concertos no. 15-16. *Uchida, piano; English Chamber Orch.; Tate, cond.*
+ ARG 11-12/91: 102
+ Fa 9-10/91: 279
+ Gr 6/91: 49

28186. 426 306-2: PROKOFIEV—Sinfonia concertante for cello; Symphony no. 7. *Schiff, cello; Los Angeles Phil. Orch.; Previn, cond.*
- Fa 5-6/91: 251

28187. 426 307-2: Choral music by Handel, Mozart, Schubert, Herbeck and R. Strauss. *Cencic, boy soprano; Vienna Boys' Choir; Harrer, cond.*
- ARG 11-12/91: 200

28188. 426 308-2 (2 discs): BEETHOVEN—Fidelio. *Norman, Coburn, Goldberg, Wlaschiha, Moll; with assisting soloists; Dresden State Opera Chorus; Staatskapelle Dresden; Haitink, cond.*
• ARG 9-10/91: 42
+ Fa 7-8/91: 111
+ Gr 1/91: 1404
+ ON 5/91: 48
+ Op 1/91: 121
+ SR 7/91: 58

28189. 426 311-2: *Trumpet concertos.* Works by Richter, L. Mozart, M. Haydn, Hertel and Molter. *Hardenberger, trumpet; London Phil. Orch.; Howarth.*
+ ARG 9-10/91: 267
+ Gr 3/91: 1681

28190. 426 312-2: ROSSINI—Stabat Mater. *Vaness, Bartoli, Araiza, Furlanetto; Bavarian Radio Chorus & Symphony Orch.; Bychkov, cond.*
+ ARG 7-8/91: 117
+ Fa 7-8/91: 269
+ Gr 3/91: 1710

28191. 426 314-2: BEETHOVEN—Piano sonatas op. 14, 90, 101. *Arrau, piano.*
+ Gr 3/93: 71

28192. 426 315-2: MOZART—Symphonies no. 40-41. *English Baroque Soloists; Gardiner, cond.*
+ Gr 11/92: 94

28193. 426 317-2: STRAVINSKY—The firebird; Scherzo à la Russe. *Berlin Phil. Orch.; Haitink, cond.*
+ ARG 7-8/92: 230
+ Fa 7-8/92: 298
• Gr 12/91: 79

28194. 426 318-2: MERCADANTE—Flute concerto in E minor. MOZART—Flute concerto no. 2. STAMITZ—Flute concerto in G major. *Grafenauer, flute; Academy of St. Martin-in-the-Fields; Marriner, cond.*
+ Gr 11/91: 90

28195. 426 319-2 (2 discs): WEBER—Der Freischütz. *Mattila, Araiza, Wlaschiha, Lorenz; Leipzig Radio Chorus; Staatskapelle Dresden; Davis, cond.*
+ ARG 1-2/92: 139
• Fa 1-2/92: 374
+ Gr 7/91: 114
- ON 12/7/91: 54
- Op 9/91: 1115

28196. 426 352-2: *Harpsichord recital.* Music of L. Couperin, Purcell, Kuhnau, Bach, Scarlatti, Royer, Boismortier, Février, and Rameau. *Leonhardt, harpsichord.*
+ ARG 1-2/91: 136
• Fa 9-10/90: 219
+ Gr 4/90: 1845

28197. 426 388-2: MOZART—March, K. 189; Serenade, K. 185; March, K. 62; Serenade, K. 100. *Sillito, violin; Nicklin, oboe; Academy of St. Martin-in-the-Fields; Marriner, cond.*
+ Fa 9-10/90: 307
+ Gr 7/90: 217

28198. 426 392-2: MOZART—Quartets no. 16-17. *Guarneri Quartet.*
+ ARG 11-12/92: 170
• Gr 9/92: 111

28199. 426 404-2: GERSHWIN—Rhapsody in blue; An American in Paris; Suites from Porgy and Bess and Girl crazy. *Dichter, piano; Boston Pops Orch.; Williams, cond.*
• Gr 9/91: 61

28200. 426 437-2: TCHAIKOVSKY—Francesca da Rimini. MUSSORGSKY—Pictures at an exhibition (orch. Ravel). *London Phil. Orch.; Gergiev, cond.*
- ARG 1-2/91: 68
• Fa 1-2/91: 333
• Gr 9/90: 531
+ SR 12/90: 130

28201. 426 439-2: BRAHMS—Ballades, op. 10. WEBER—Sonata in A♭, op. 39. *Brendel, piano.*
- ARG 11-12/91: 42
+ Fa 9-10/91: 171
+ Gr 6/91: 64

28202. 426 440-2: Mozart—Horn quintet; Horn concerto no. 3: Movt. 2. HAYDN—Divertimento a tre. BEETHOVEN—Sextet. REICHA—Horn quintet. *Baumann, Dshambasov, horns; Gewandhaus Quartet.*
• ARG 11-12/93: 156
+ Gr 9/93: 69

28203. 426 462-2 (2 discs): BACH—Orchestral music. *Kremer, Szeryng, Hasson, violins; Academy of St. Martin-in-the-Fields; Marriner, cond.; Holliger, oboe.* Reissue.
+ Gr 10/91: 81

28204. 426 487-2: BEETHOVEN—Egmont: Overture; Symphony no. 5; Wellington's victory. *Augmented Canadian Brass; Tintner, cond.*
- Fa 5-6/91: 121
+ Gr 11/90: 973

28205. 426 669-2: *Twentieth-century music for strings.* MARTIN—Etudes. HINDEMITH—Trauermusik. ROUSSEL—Sinfonietta. NIELSEN—Little suite. BARTÓK—Romanian folkdances. BRITTEN—Simple symphony. *I Musici.*
+ Gr 7/91: 73

28206. 426 714-2: PURCELL—Fantasias. RAMEAU—Castor et Pollux: Suite. *Orch. of the 18th Century; Brüggen, cond.*
+ ARG 9-10/91: 110
+ Fa 5-6/91: 255

28207. 426 715-2: MOZART—Violin concertos no. 3, 5. *Keulen, violin; Concertgebouw Chamber Orch.*
+ Fa 9-10/91: 294
• Gr 5/91: 2012

28208. 426 721-2: MOZART—Arias from Entführung, Zauberflöte, Idomeneo, Nozze di Figaro, Don Giovanni, La clemenza di Tito, and Così fan tutte. *Studer, soprano; Academy of St. Martin-in-the-Fields; Marriner, cond.*
+ ARG 11-12/91: 99
+ Fa 9-10/91: 277
+ Gr 5/91: 2060
+ ON 1/4/92: 39
+ Op 11/91: 1371

28209. 426 740-2: *Arias.* Music of Tchaikovsky and Verdi. *Hvorostovsky, baritone; Rotterdam Phil. Orch.; Gergiev, cond.*
• ARG 11-12/90: 174
• Fa 11-12/90: 419
+ Gr 7/90: 279
• MA 1/91: 83
+ NYT 7/29/90: H23
+ ON 9/90: 46
• Op 9/90: 1139
+ SR 10/90: 109
• St 6/91: 253

28210. 426 782-2: BEETHOVEN—Symphonies no. 1, 5. *Gewandhaus Orch.; Masur, cond.*
- ARG 1-2/90: 30
• ARG 3-4/94: 73
• Fa 11-12/90: 168
+ Gr 7/90: 207
• MA 5/91: 69
+ SR 1/91: 97

28211. 426 846-2: BEETHOVEN—Symphonies no. 7-8. *Orch. of the 18th Century; Brüggen, cond.*

+ DA 5/91: 69
□ Fa 7-8/91: 116
● Gr 2/91: 1498
● MA 7/91: 66

28212. 426 847-2: VIVALDI—Violin concertos, op. 8, no. 1-4; RV 253; RV 180. *Agostini, violin; I Musici.*
+ ARG 3-4/91: 137
+ Fa 11-12/90: 390
+ Gr 9/90: 546
● SR 11/90: 105

28213. 426 863-2: NIETSCHZE—Songs and piano music. *Fischer-Dieskau, baritone; Reimann, Budde, piano.*
+ Gr 3/96: 82

28214. 426 925-2 (19 discs): VIVALDI— The Edition. Concertos: op. 1-12. *Various performers.* Reissues.
+ Gr 7/91: 72

28215. 426 955-2 (2 discs): VIVALDI— Juditha triumphans. *Ameling, Finnilä, Burmeister, Hamari; Berlin Radio Ensemble; Berlin Chamber Orch.; Negri, cond.* Reissue.
+ Gr 4/92: 139

28216. 429 299-2: BRAHMS—Symphony no. 1; Variations on a theme by Haydn. *Philadelphia Orch.; Muti, cond.*
● Fa 5-6/91: 139
● Gr 4/91: 1823
● SR 2/91: 131

28217. 430 420-2 (3 discs): HAYDN—Il mondo della luna. *Trimarchi, Alva, Von Stade, Augér, Mathis, Valentini- Terrani, Rolfe Johnson; Lausanne Chamber Orch.; Dorati, cond.* Reissue.
+ Fa 11-12/93: 266
+ Gr 6/93: 99

28218. 432 061-2 (9 discs): HAYDN— Complete piano trios. *Beaux Arts Trio.*
+ Fa 7-8/92: 180
+ Gr 7/92: 70

28219. 432 075-2: BIRTWISTLE—Endless parade. BLAKE WATKINS—Trumpet concerto. DAVIES—Trumpet concerto. *Hardenberger, trumpet, Patrick, vibraphone; BBC Phil. Orch.; Howarth, cond.*
+ ARG 7-8/92: 272
+ Fa 3-4/92: 411
+ Gr 6/91: 46

28220. 432 076-2: MOZART—String quartets no. 18-19. *Guarneri Quartet.*
● Gr 11/92: 142

28221. 432 077-2: MENDELSSOHN—Violin concertos in E minor, op. 64; in D minor. *Mullova, violin; Academy of St. Martin-in-the-Fields; Marriner, cond.*
+ ARG 11-12/91: 96
+ Fa 9-10/91: 269
+ Gr 5/91: 2010

28222. 432 079-2: SHOSTAKOVICH—Piano trio no. 2; Piano quintet, op. 57. *Beaux Arts Trio; Drucker, violin; Dutton, viola.*
● ARG 1-2/92: 114
+ Fa 11-12/91: 485
- Gr 8/91: 60

28223. 432 080-2: *French opera arias.* Works by Bizet, Gounod, Rossini, Meyerbeer, Offenbach, Thomas, and Massenet. *Ramey, bass; London Phil. Orch.; Rudel, cond.*
+ ARG 1-2/92: 175
+ Fa 3-4/92: 389
+ Gr 12/91: 141

28224. 432 081-2: WEBER—Bassoon concerto; Andante e rondo ungarese. HUMMEL—Bassoon concerto. *Thunemann, bassoon; Academy of St. Martin-in-the-Fields; Marriner, cond.*
+ ARG 3-4/92: 164
+ Fa 11-12/91: 520
+ Gr 5/91: 2009

28225. 432 082-2: MOZART—Piano concertos no. 5-6; Rondo, K. 382. *Uchida, piano; English Chamber Orch.; Tate, cond.*
+ ARG 5-6/92: 94
+ Fa 5-6/92: 201
+ Gr 1/92: 59

28226. 432 083-2: PROKOFIEV— Symphony no. 5; The meeting of the Volga and the Don. *Philadelphia Orch.; Muti, cond.*
+ ARG 1-2/92: 92
● Fa 3-4/92: 289
● Gr 7/91: 58

28227. 432 084-2: SAINT-SAËNS—Cello concerto no. 1; Allegro appassionato, op. 43. FAURÉ—Elégie. INDY—Lied. HONEGGER—Cello concerto. *Lloyd Webber, cello; English Chamber Orch.; Tortelier, cond.*
- ARG 11-12/91: 183
+ Fa 11-12/91: 465
+ Gr 6/91: 55

28228. 432 086-2: MOZART—Piano concertos no. 8-9. *Uchida, piano; English Chamber Orch.; Tate, cond.*
+ ARG 1-2/93: 125
+ Fa 11-12/92: 309
+ Gr 7/92: 58
+ St 8/93: 184

28229. 432 087-2: MOZART—Requiem, K. 626. *McNair, Watkinson, Araiza, Lloyd; Academy & Chorus of St. Martin-in-the-Fields; Marriner, cond.*
+ ARG 11-12/91: 118
+ Fa 9-10/91: 292
+ Gr 12/91: 114

28230. 432 088-2: VIVALDI—Sacred music for solo voices & orchestra, vol. 1. *Marshall, soprano; Kowalski, alto; Concertgebouw Chamber Orch.; Negri, cond.*

+ Fa 9-10/91: 385
+ Gr 10/91: 178

28231. 432 089-2: Gregorian chant. *Choralschola of the Vienna Hofburgkapelle; Dopf, cond.*
- ARG 11-12/91: 196
+ Fa 11-12/91: 541

28232. 432 090-2: SHOSTAKOVICH— Symphony no. 8. *Berlin Phil. Orch.; Bychkov, cond.*
+ ARG 9-10/93: 192
+ Fa 9-10/93: 288
● Gr 5/93: 51

28233. 432 091-2: VIVALDI—Sacred vocal music, vol 2. Laudate pueri Dominum, RV 600; Stabat mater, RV 621; Deus tuorum militum, RV 612; Sanctorum meritis, RV 620. *Marshall, soprano; Kowalski, alto; Meel, tenor; Constable, Ogg, organs; Concertgebouw Chamber Orch.; Negri, cond.*
+ Gr 2/92: 72

28234. 432 092-2: BACH—Virtuoso orchestral transcription (Stokowski, Webern, Schoenberg et al. *Tanglewood Festival Chorus; Boston Symphony Orch.; Ozawa, cond.*
● Gr 7/92: 51

28235. 432 093-2: *Theme and variations II.* SCHUMANN—Symphonic etudes. BEETHOVEN—Variations, op. 34; Variations on "Rule Britannia"; Variations on "Nel cor più non mi sento". *Brendel, piano.*
+ ARG 1-2/92: 161
+ Fa 3-4/92: 402
+ Gr 3/92: 75

28236. 432 094-2: BRAHMS—Symphony no. 2; Tragic overture. *Boston Symphony Orch.; Haitink, cond.*
+ ARG 3-4/93: 64
- Fa 3-4/93: 132
+ Gr 10/92: 55

28237. 432 095-2: BRUCH—Concerto for two pianos. MENDELSSOHN—Concerto for two pianos in E. *K. & M. Labèque, pianos; Philharmonia Orch.; Bychkov, cond.*
+ Gr 7/93: 36

28238. 432 096-2: FRANCK—Symphony in D minor. BIZET—Symphony no. 1 in C. *Orch. de Paris; Bychkov, cond.*
● ARG 11-12/92: 120
+ Fa 9-10/92: 238

28239. 432 100-2: MOZART—Violin concertos, no. 1 2, 4. *Keulen, violin & cond.; Concertgebouw Chamber Orch.*
● Gr 5/93: 50

28240. 432 101-2: RACHMANINOFF— Symphony no. 2. *Orch. de Paris; Bychkov, cond.*
- ARG 9-10/91: 111

PHILIPS

+ Fa 11-12/91: 451
+ Gr 9/91: 69

28241. 432 102-2: *La paloma: Spanish and Latin American favourites.* Music of J. Sagreras, Barrios Mangoré, S. Iradier, Villa-Lobos, Ponce, Romero, Lauro, L. Brouwer, G. Gomez, J. Guimaraes, and Matos Rodriguez. *P. Romero, guitar.*
+ Gr 3/92: 88

28242. 432 103-2: *Harp recital.* Caplet—Divertissements. Debussy—Deux arabesques. Fauré—Une châtelaine en sa tour; Impromptu. Ravel—Impromptu. Tailleferre—Sonata. Tournier—Au matin. *Graf, harp.*
+ Gr 11/91: 134

28243. 432 104-2: Vivaldi—Sacred music for solo voices and orchestra, vol. 3. *Marshal, Kowalski, Van der Meel, Scharinger, Anton; Concertgebouw Chamber Orch.; Negri, cond.*
+ Fa 3-4/92: 359
+ Gr 4/92: 139

28244. 432 105-2: Mascagni—Cavalleria rusticana. *Norman, Senn, Giacomini, Hvorostovsky; Orch. de Paris; Bychkov, cond.*
● ARG 3-4/92: 99
+ Fa 3-4/92: 239
● Gr 12/91: 129
+ ON 5/92: 52
- St 4/92: 271

28245. 432 108-2: Schubert—String quintet. *Guarneri Quartet; Greenhouse, cello.*
+ Gr 10/93: 72

28246. 432 110-2: Handel—Israel in Egypt; Coronation anthems: Zadok the priest; The king shall rejoice. *Vocal soloists; Monteverdi Choir; English Baroque Soloists; Gardiner, cond.*
+ Fa 3-4/96: 175
● Gr 11/95: 132
+ ON 7/96: 48

28247. 432 114-2: Purcell—Dido and Aeneas; Ode for St. Cecilia's Day. *Watkinson, Holton, Mosley, Chance; Monteverdi Choir; English Baroque Soloists; Gardiner, cond.*
+ ARG 7-8/94: 152
+ Fa 7-8/94: 205
● Fa 11-12/94: 340
+ Gr 3/94: 101

28248. 432 115-2 (2 discs): Albinoni—Concertos, op. 7; 2 concertos from op. 5. *Holliger, Bourgue, oboes; I Musici.*
+ Gr 1/93: 37

28249. 432 118-2: Torelli—Concerti grossi op. 8: Selections. *Sirbu, Pérez, violins; I Musici.*
+ Gr 1/94: 60

28250. 432 119-2: *Russian romances.* Song by Rachmaninoff and Tchaikovsky.

Hvorostovsky, baritone; Boshnikovich, piano.
+ ARG 9-10/91: 182
+ Fa 9-10/91: 408
+ Gr 10/91: 181

28251. 432 121-2: Brahms—Symphony no. 1; Hungarian dances no. 1, 3, 10. *Saito Kinen Orch.; Ozawa, cond.*
● ARG 5-6/92: 37
+ Fa 3-4/92: 163
● Gr 2/92: 34

28252. 432 123-2: Mendelssohn—Symphony no. 4 "Italian." Schubert—Symphony no. 5. *Orch. of the 18th Cent.; Brüggen, cond.*
+ Fa 3-4/92: 245
+ Gr 12/91: 75

28253. 432 124-2: Vivaldi—Bassoon concertos, RV 471, 481, 493, 496, 500, 504. *Thunemann, bassoon; I Musici.*
+ ARG 11-12/92: 227
+ Fa 7-8/92: 321

28254. 432 125-2: Mendelssohn—Trio no. 2 in G minor for piano, violin, and cello, op. 66. Smetana—Trio in G minor for piano, violin, and cello, op. 15. *Beaux Arts Trio.*
+ Fa 9-10/92: 288
+ Gr 6/92: 58

28255. 432 126-2: Bartók—Concerto for orchestra; Divertimento for string orchestra. *Academy of St. Martin-in-the-Fields; Marriner, cond.*
- Fa 3-4/92: 140
● Gr 12/91: 63
● St 11/92: 215

28256. 432 127-2: Beethoven—Piano sonatas no. 1, 5, 8, 17. *Kocsis, piano.*
● ARG 7-8/92: 94
● Fa 5-6/92: 123
+ Gr 3/92: 76
● St 11/92: 217

28257. 432 128-2: Frescobaldi—Harpsichord music. *Leonhardt, harpsichord.*
+ Gr 5/92: 72

28258. 432 129-2 (3 discs): Mozart—Don Giovanni. *Sweet, Mattila, Allen, Alaimo; Ambrosian Opera Chorus; Academy of St. Martin-in-the-Fields; Marriner, cond.*
● ARG 5-6/92: 96
● Fa 3-4/92: 254
● Gr 1/92: 91
+ ON 4/11/92: 46
+ Op 4/92: 487

28259. 432 132-2: Rossini—Messa di Gloria. *Jo, Murray, Araiza, Ramey; Academy of St. Martin-in-the-Fields; Marriner, cond.*
+ ARG 9-10/93: 179
+ Fa 7-8/93: 218
+ Gr 12/92: 123

28260. 432 133-2: Respighi—Pini di Roma; Fontane di Roma; Feste Romane. *Academy of St. Martin-in-the-Fields; Marriner, cond.*
- ARG 5-6/92: 117
- Fa 5-6/92: 232
+ Gr 4/92: 75

28261. 432 138-2: Chédeville—Sonatas op. 13. *Grafenauer, flute; Baumann, cello; Stoll, double bass; Engelhard, harpsichord & organ.*
● Gr 10/92: 124

28262. 432 139-2: Haydn—Symphonies, no. 99, 102. *Academy of St. Martin-in-the-Fields; Marriner, cond.*
● Gr 6/92: 43

28263. 432 140-2: Brahms—Ein deutsches Requiem. *Margiono, soprano; Gilfry, baritone; Monteverdi Choir; Orch. Révolutionnaire et Romantique; Gardiner, cond.*
+ ARG 11-12/91: 44
- Fa 11-12/91: 281
+ Gr 4/91: 1881

28264. 432 141-2: Mahler—Symphony no. 5. *Boston Symphony Orch.; Ozawa, cond.*
● ARG 11-12/92: 153
● Fa 9-10/92: 281
● Gr 10/92: 63

28265. 432 142-2: Franck—Quintet in F minor for piano and strings. Liszt—Harmonies poètiques et religieuses; Pensées des morts; Andante lagrimoso; Ave Maria, S. 182. *Richter, piano; Borodin Quartet.*
+ ARG 3-4/92: 58
+ Fa 1-2/92: 214
+ Gr 11/91: 115

28266. 432 145-2: Stravinsky—Petrushka (1947 vers.); Fairy's kiss: Divertimento. *Orch. de Paris; Bychkov, cond.*
● ARG 5-6/92: 142
+ Fa 5-6/92: 261
+ Gr 7/92: 61

28267. 432 146-2: Weber—Clarinet concertos no. 1-2; Clarinet concertino. *A. Marriner, clarinet; Academy of St. Martin-in-the-Fields; N. Marriner, cond.*
+ ARG 9-10/92: 181
● Fa 9-10/92: 389
+ Gr 9/92: 46

28268. 432 147-2 (3 discs): Mussorgsky—Khovanshchina. *Minjelkiev, Galusin, Steblianko, Ohotnikov, Alexeev; Kirov Opera; Gergiev, cond.*
+ ARG 1-2/93: 124
+ Gr 6/92: 84
● ON 9/92: 48
+ Op 1/93: 121

28269. 432 151-2: Berlioz—Symphonie fantastique. *Vienna Phil. Orch.; C. Davis,*

cond.
- ● ARG 9-10/92: 84
- + Fa 7-8/92: 120
- + Gr 5/92: 32
- + St 9/92: 187

28270. 432 152-2: BRAHMS—*Choral music.* Liebeslieder waltzes, op. 52; Songs, op. 17, 42, 104; Quartets, op. 92. *Monteverdi Choir; with assisting instrumentalists; Gardiner, cond.*
- + ARG 11-12/92: 93
- + Fa 11-12/92: 205
- + Gr 8/92: 56
- + St 5/93: 175

28271. 432 153-2 (2 discs): STRAUSS— Salome. *Norman, Morris, Leech; Staatskapelle Dresden; Ozawa, cond.*
- + ARG 1-2/95: 185
- + Gr 10/94: 200
- ● ON 12/24/94: 32
- ● Op 11/94: 1353

28272. 432 157-2 (2 discs): J. STRAUSS, JR.—Die Fledermaus. *Te Kanawa, Fassbaender, Gruberová, Brendel, Krause; Vienna Phil. Orch.; Previn, cond.*
- + ARG 5-6/92: 139
- + Fa 5-6/92: 259
- + Op 3/92: 374
- + St 2/93: 199

28273. 432 161-2: BACH—Cantatas: Zerreisset, zersprenget, zerstrummert die Gruft, BWV 205 "Der zufriedengestellte Äolus"; Tönet, ihr Pauken! Erschallet, Trompeten! BWV 214. *Sluis, Jacobs, Prégardien, Thomas; Orch. & Choir of the Age of Enlightenment; Leonhardt, cond.*
- + EM 5/93: 319
- + Fa 7-8/93: 92
- + Gr 12/92: 113

28274. 432 162-2 (2 discs): MAHLER— Symphony no. 3. *Nes, contralto; Tölzer Knabenchor; Ernst-Senff Chor; Berlin Phil. Orch.; Haitink.*
- + ARG 3-4/94: 118
- ● Fa 1-2/94: 230
- + Gr 4/92: 65

28275. 432 165-2 (2 discs): SCHUMANN— Piano trios. *Beaux Arts Trio.*
- + Gr 8/93: 54

28276. 432 166-2: PROKOFIEV—Romeo and Juliet. *Kirov Orch.; Gergiev, cond.*
- + ARG 5-6/92: 109
- ● Fa 5-6/92: 226
- ● Gr 12/91: 76
- + St 7/92: 247

28277. 432 170-2: MUSSORGSKY—Pictures at an exhibition; Night on Bald Mountain. *Philadelphia Orch.; Muti, cond.*
- ● ARG 9-10/92: 134

28278. 432 173-2: BEETHOVEN—Piano sonatas no. 1-2, 16, 22, 24-25. *Arrau,*

piano. Reissues.
- ● Gr 7/95: 83

28279. 432 176-2: TAKEMITSU— November steps; Eclipse; Viola concerto. *Yokoyama, shakuhachi; Tsuruta, biwa; Imai, viola; Saito Kinen Orch.; Ozawa, cond.*
- + Fa 1-2/93: 251
- + Gr 8/92: 41

28280. 432 177-2: MOZART—Symphonies no. 28, 36. *Orch. of the 18th Century; Brüggen, cond.*
- + ARG 11-12/91: 123
- + Fa 11-12/91: 415
- ● Gr 12/91: 76

28281. 432 252-2: *Musical jokes.* Music of Prof. Bor, L. Mozart, Thomas, Kreisler, Pärt, Cage, and others. *Various performers.*
- + ARG 3-4/93: 177

28282. 432 286-2 (4 discs): HAYDN— London symphonies. *Concertgebouw Orch.; Davis, cond.* Reissues.
- + Fa 5-6/92: 172
- + Gr 7/92: 57

28283. 432 301-2 (11 discs): BEETHOVEN—Piano sonatas (complete). *Arrau, piano.* Reissues.
- + ARG 3-4/92: 30
- + Gr 1/92: 73

28284. 432 302-2 (3 discs): BRAHMS— Piano sonatas, op. 2, 5; Scherzo, op. 4; Ballades, op. 10; Handel variations; Paganini variations. *Arrau, piano.* Reissues.
- + ARG 3-4/92: 36
- ● Gr 12/91: 100

28285. 432 303-2 (6 discs): CHOPIN— Piano music. *Arrau, piano.*
- + ARG 7-8/92: 116

28286. 432 304-2: DEBUSSY—Piano works. *Arrau, piano.*
- + Gr 2/92: 60

28287. 432 306-2 (7 discs): MOZART— Piano works. *Arrau, piano.*
- ● Gr 3/92: 80

28288. 432 307-2 (3 discs): SCHUBERT— Piano sonatas in A, B♭, C minor; Impromptus, D. 899; Allegretto in C minor. *Arrau, piano.* Reissue.
- + ARG 9-10/92: 155
- + Gr 5/92: 76

28289. 432 308-2 (7 discs): SCHUMANN— Piano music. *Arrau, piano.*
- + ARG 7-8/92: 220

28290. 432 381-2 (5 discs): BEETHOVEN— Piano trios. *Beaux Arts Trio.*
- + Gr 3/92: 63

28291. 432 413-2 (2 discs): HAYDN— L'infideltà delusa. *Mathis, Hendricks,*

Ahnsjö, Baldin, Devlin; Lausanne Chamber Orch.; Dorati, cond. Reissue.
- + Fa 11-12/93: 265
- + Gr 6/93: 99

28292. 432 416-2 (3 discs): HAYDN— L'incontro improvviso. *Ahnsjö, Zoghby, Marshall, D. Jones; other soloists; Lausanne Chamber Orch.; Dorati, cond.* Reissue.
- + Fa 11-12/93: 266
- + Gr 6/93: 99

28293. 432 424-2 (2 discs): HAYDN—La vera costanza. *Norman, Donath, Ahnsjö, Ganzarolli, Trimarchi, Lövaas, Rolfe Johnson; Lausanne Chamber Orch.; Dorati, cond.* Reissue.
- + Fa 11-12/93: 266
- + Gr 6/93: 99

28294. 432 427-2 (2 discs): HAYDN— L'isola disabitata. *Lerer, Zoghby, Alva, Bruson; Lausanne Chamber Orch.; Dorati, cond.* Reissue.
- + Fa 11-12/93: 266
- + Gr 6/93: 99

28295. 432 430-2 (3 discs): HAYDN—La fideltà premiata. *Valentini-Terrani, Landy, Von Stade, Titus, Cotrubas, Alva, Mazzieri, Lövaas; Chorus of the Radio Suisse romande; Lausanne Chamber Orch.; Dorati, cond.* Reissue.
- + Fa 11-12/93: 266
- + Gr 6/93: 99

28296. 432 434-2 (3 discs): HAYDN— Orlando paladino. *Augér, Ameling, Killebrew, Shirley, Ahnsjö, Luxon, Trimarchi, Mazzieri, Carelli; Lausanne Chamber Orch.; Dorati, cond.* Reissue.
- + Fa 11-12/93: 266
- + Gr 6/93: 99

28297. 432 438-2 (2 discs): HAYDN— Armida. *Norman, Ahnsjö, Burrowes, Ramey, Leggate, Rolfe Johnson; Lausanne Chamber Orch.; Dorati, cond.* Reissue.
- + Fa 11-12/93: 266
- + Gr 6/93: 100

28298. 432 453-2 (2 discs): ROSSINI— Elisabetta, regina d'Inghilterra. *Caballé, Carreras, Masterson, Benelli; London Symphony Orch.; Masini, cond.* Reissue.
- ● ARG 3-4/93: 130
- + Gr 12/92: 140
- + OQ summer 93: 179

28299. 432 456-2 (2 discs): ROSSINI— Otello. *Von Stade, Carreras, Pastine, Ramey; Philharmonia Orch.; López Cobos, cond.* Reissue.
- ● ARG 3-4/93: 130
- + Gr 12/92: 140
- ● OQ summer 93: 201

28300. 432 486-2: VERDI—Thirty-one tenor arias. *Bergonzi, tenor; Santi, Gardelli, conds.*
- + ARG 5-6/92: 151

PHILIPS

28301. 432 546-2: Amazing grace. *Norman, soprano; Baldwin, Parsons, piano; Bowers-Broadbent, organ; Ambrosian Singers; Royal Phil. Orch.; Gibson, Patterson, conds.*
+ ARG 1-2/92: 174

28302. 432 573-2 (4 discs): WAGNER— Die Meistersinger von Nurnberg. *Soloists; Bayreuth Festival Chorus & Orch.; Varviso, cond.* Reissue; recorded live 1974.
+ Gr 11/91: 162
+ Op 1/92: 122

28303. 432 578-2: BRITTEN—Peter Grimes. *Vickers, Harper, Summers, Robinson, Allen; Covent Garden; Davis, cond.*
• ARG 1-2/92: 38
+ Gr 11/91: 152

28304. 432 730-2: TAKEMITSU—Litany; Pause interrompue; Piano distance; For away; Les yeux clos I & II; Rain tree sketch. *Ogano, piano.*
+ ARG 1-2/93: 155
+ Fa 1-2/93: 251
• Gr 11/92: 162

28305. 432 760-2: BACH/BUSONI—Nun komm der Heiden Heiland. HAYDN— Sonatas no. 20, 44. BEETHOVEN—Sonata no. 31. *Brendel, piano.*
+ ARG 3-4/93: 169
+ Gr 11/92: 165
• St 8/93: 193

28306. 432 821-2: Music from the time of Christopher Columbus. *Musica Reservata; Beckett, cond.* Reissue.
+ Gr 7/92: 95

28307. 432 889-2: José Carreras sings songs of Falla and Verdi. *Carreras, tenor; English Chamber Orch.; Berio, cond.*
+ Fa 7-8/92: 156
• Gr 1/92: 84

28308. 432 964-2: BEETHOVEN— Symphonies no. 4, 6. *Orch. of the 18th Century; Brüggen, cond.*
- ARG 9-10/92: 79
• Fa 9-10/92: 181
+ Gr 6/92: 38

28309. 432 968-2: RAMEAU—Les paladins: Suite. *Orch. of the Age of Enlightenment; Leonhardt, cond.*
+ ARG 9-10/92: 145
• EM 5/94: 354
+ Fa 9-10/92: 322
+ Gr 9/92: 84

28310. 432 969-2 (2 discs): BACH— Orchestral suites. *Carl Philipp Emanuel Bach Chamber Orch.; Schreier, cond.*
+ Fa 1-2/93: 98
• Gr 8/92: 30

28311. 432 972-2 (2 discs): BACH—Mass in B minor. *Augér, Murray, Lipovsek,*

Schreier, Scharinger; Staatskapelle Dresden; Rundfunkchor Leipzig; Schreier, cond.
- Fa 1-2/93: 100
- Gr 6/92: 73

28312. 432 975-2: BRAHMS—Piano concerto no. 2. *Brendel, piano; Berlin Phil. Orch.; Haitink, cond.*
• ARG 11-12/92: 93
+ Gr 6/92: 39

28313. 432 977-2: MOZART—Symphonies no. 30-33. *Staatskapelle Dresden; Davis, cond.*
• Fa 7-8/93: 190

28314. 432 980-2 (2 discs): BEETHOVEN— String quartets, op. 59. *Guarneri Quartet.* Reissue.
- ARG 3-4/96: 89
• Fa 1-2/96: 138

28315. 432 983-2: JANÁČEK—Glagolitic mass; Taras Bulba. *Hrubá-Freiberger, Lang, Mitchinson, Adam; Prague Radio Chorus; Leipzig Gewandhaus Orch.; Masur, cond.*
• Gr 9/93: 98

28316. 432 984-2 (2 discs): MENDELSSOHN—Elijah. *Kenny, Otter, Rolfe Johnson, Allen; Academy of St. Martin-in- the-Fields; Marriner, cond.*
• ARG 1-2/93: 120
• Fa 3-4/93: 219
+ Gr 10/92: 164

28317. 432 987-2: SCHUBERT—Piano sonata D. 894; Moments musicaux. *Arrau, piano.*
- ARG 5-6/93: 129
+ Gr 11/92: 161
• St 9/93: 185

28318. 432 989-2: MOZART—Mitsuko Uchida live in concert. *Uchida, piano.*
+ Gr 4/93: 88

28319. 432 992-2: PROKOFIEV— Symphonies no. 1, 3. *Philadelphia Orch.; Muti, cond.*
• ARG 7-8/93: 138
• Fa 7-8/93: 205
+ Gr 2/93: 47
• St 10/93: 275

28320. 432 993-2: POULENC—Les biches. MILHAUD—Le boeuf sur le toit. HONEGGER—Pacific 231. *Orch. de Paris; Bychkov, cond.*
+ Gr 3/94: 60

28321. 432 994-2: BEETHOVEN— Symphonies no. 2, 7. *Gewandhaus Orch.; Masur, cond.*
+ ARG 3-4/94: 74
• Fa 3-4/94: 126

28322. 432 995-2: BEETHOVEN— Symphony no. 9. *McNair, Nes, Heilmann, Weikl; Leipzig Radio Chorus; Gewandhaus Orch. Leipzig; Masur,*

cond.
• ARG 3-4/94: 74
• Fa 3-4/94: 129

28323. 432 996-2: DVOŘÁK—Symphony no. 9; In Nature's realm. *Vienna Phil. Orch.; Ozawa, cond.*
+ ARG 1-2/93: 92

28324. 432 997-2: MOZART—Serenade no. 7 "Haffner"; March in D, K. 249. *Orch. of the 18th Century; Brüggen, cond.*
+ Fa 7-8/93: 190
• Gr 3/93: 48

28325. 433 070-2: PROKOFIEV—Alexander Nevsky; Cinderella suite no. 1. *Lipovsek, alto; Orch. de Paris; Choir of the Orch. de Paris; Bychkov, cond.*
+ Fa 9-10/94: 290
• Gr 5/94: 58

28326. 434 016-2 (3 discs): ROSSINI— Overtures (complete). *Academy of St. Martin-in-the-Fields; Marriner, cond.*
+ ARG 9-10/92: 151
+ Gr 10/92: 116

28327. 434 029-2: BEETHOVEN— Symphonies no. 1-2. *Orch. of the 18th Century; Brüggen, cond.* Reissues.
+ ARG 5-6/93: 68
+ Fa 5-6/93: 157

28328. 434 031-2—434 041-2 (10 separate discs): *Lockenhaus collection, vol. 1-10.* Music of Anon., Haydn, Messiaen, Casals, Mozart, Schubert, Beethoven, Schumann, Mendelssohn, Brahms, Schulhoff, Prokofiev, Lourié, Stravinsky, Schnittke, and Gubaidulina. *Various performers.*
+ ARG 5-6/93: 147
+ Fa 5-6/93: 407

28329. 434 053-2 (15 discs): MAHLER— Symphonies (complete). *Concertgebouw Orch.; Haitink, cond.* Reissues.
• Gr 12/92: 82

28330. 434 071-2: FAURÉ—Piano quartet no. 1. SAINT-SAËNS—Piano trio no. 1. *Beaux Arts Trio; Dutton, viola.*
+ ARG 1-2/94: 99

28331. 434 072-2: KORNGOLD—Piano trio. ZEMLINSKY—Piano trio in D minor. *Beaux Arts Trio.*
+ ARG 9-10/94: 150
+ Gr 6/94: 73

28332. 434 074-2: Music of Martini, Clarke, Albinoni, Bach, Loeillet, Gounod and Telemann. *Hardenberger, trumpet; Preston, organ.*
+ ARG 1-2/93: 187
- Gr 12/92: 98

28333. 434 075-2: BACH—Violin partitas. *Mullova, violin.*
• ARG 9-10/94: 95
+ Gr 6/94: 80

28334. 434 076-2: BRITTEN—Six metamorphoses after Ovid; Temporal variations; Phantasy; Insect pieces. MOZART—Oboe quartet. *Holliger, oboe; Zehetmair, violin; Zimmermann, viola; Demenga, cello.*
+ Gr 12/94: 117

28335. 434 077-2: HAYDN—Symphonies no. 99, 102. *Orch. of the 18th Century; Brüggen, cond.*
+ ARG 5-6/93: 93
+ Fa 5-6/93: 220
+ St 9/93: 178

28336. 434 078-2: LISZT—Piano sonata; Funérailles; Nuages gris; Klavierstück in F♯; En rêve; Richard Wagner: Venezia. *Brendel, piano.*
● ARG 5-6/93: 101
+ Fa 5-6/93: 249
+ St 8/93: 193

28337. 434 080-2: Dark eyes. *Hvorostovsky, baritone; Ossipov State Russian Folk Orch.; Kalinin, cond.*
+ ARG 3-4/93: 185
+ Gr 11/92: 178

28338. 434 083-2: BACH—Schemelli Lierderbuch: Excerpts; Organ mass: Excerpts. *Schreier, tenor; Linden, cello; Koopman, organ.*
+ Gr 4/93: 104

28339. 434 084-2: J.S. BACH—Violin sonatas BWV 1014-15, 1019. C.P.E. BACH—Violin sonata H. 514. *Mullova, violin; Canino, piano.*
- Fa 1-2/94: 117
- Gr 7/93: 57

28340. 434 087-2: BEETHOVEN— Symphony no. 5; Egmont overture; Coriolan overture. *Orch. of the 18th Century; Brüggen, cond.*
+ ARG 5-6/93: 68
+ Fa 5-6/93: 160
+ Gr 12/92: 74

28341. 434 089-2: BRAHMS—Symphonies no. 2-3. *Saito Kinen Orch.; Ozawa, cond.*
● ARG 5-6/94: 78
● Fa 3-4/94: 148
● Gr 10/93: 44

28342. 434 093-2 (2 discs): GLUCK— Orfeo ed Euridice. *Ragin, McNair, Sieden; Monteverdi Choir; English Baroque Soloists; Gardiner, cond.*
+ ARG 11-12/94: 117
+ Fa 9-10/94: 194
+ Gr 2/94: 93

28343. 434 096-2: HAYDN—Symphonies no. 100 "Military"; 104 "London". *Orch. of the 18th Century; Brüggen, cond.*
+ ARG 7-8/93: 100
+ Fa 7-8/93: 152
+ Gr 6/93: 47
+ St 9/93: 178

28344. 434 097-2 (3 discs): PROKOFIEV— War and peace. *Gergalov, Prokina, Volkova, Kanunnikova; Kirov Theater; Gergiev, cond.*
+ ARG 3-4/94: 136
- Fa 3-4/94: 278
● Gr 6/93: 102
+ ON 5/94: 48
+ Op 10/93: 1255

28345. 434 101-2: SCHUBERT— Impromptus, D. 935; Piano pieces, D. 946. *Arrau, piano.*
- ARG 11-12/93: 188
● Gr 8/93: 60

28346. 434 102-2: *The heroic bel canto tenor.* Arias by Donizetti and Rossini. *Merritt, tenor; Münchner Rundfunkorchester; Fiore, cond.*
+ ARG 1-2/96: 233
● Fa 1-2/96: 359
● Gr 9/94: 120
+ ON 11/95: 49

28347. 434 104-2: BARTÓK—Works for piano solo, vol. 1. *Kocsis, piano.*
+ ARG 7-8/93: 61
+ Fa 7-8/93: 100
+ Gr 1/94: 75

28348. 434 105-2: HONEGGER—Concerto da camera; Petite suite; Antigonoae. MARTIN—Three danses; Petite complainte; Pièce brève. MARTINŮ—Oboe concerto. *Nicolet, flute; H. Holliger, oboe; U. Holliger, harp; Constable, piano; Academy of St. Martin-in-the-Fields; Marriner, cond.*
+ Fa 7-8/94: 170
+ Gr 9/93: 50

28349. 434 106-2: MIASKOVSKY—Cello concerto. TCHAIKOVSKY—Variations on a rococo theme; Nocturne in D. SHOSTAKOVICH—Limpid stream: Adagio. *Lloyd Webber, cello; London Symphony Orch.; M. Shostakovich, cond.*
+ ARG 11-12/93: 232
● Fa 11-12/92: 306
+ Gr 5/92: 38
+ St 2/93: 195

28350. 434 107-2: MOZART—Symphonies no. 36, 40. *Vienna Phil. Orch.; Muti, cond.*
● Gr 3/94: 58

28351. 434 108-2: TCHAIKOVSKY— Serenade for strings. WOLF—Italian serenade. BARBER—Adagio for strings. ELGAR—Introduction and allegro. *Berlin Phil. Orch.; Bychkov, cond.*
● Gr 3/94: 66

28352. 434 114-2: ZIMMERMANN—Oboe concerto; Trumpet concerto; Canto di speranza; Cello concerto. *Holliger, oboe; Hardenberger, trumpet; Schiff, cello; South-West German Radio Symphony Orch.; Gielen, cond.*
+ Gr 11/93: 85

28353. 434 115-2 (3 discs): BEETHOVEN— String quartets, op. 18. *Guarneri Quartet.* Reissue.
+ ARG 3-4/96: 88
● Fa 1-2/96: 138
● Gr 9/95: 73

28354. 434 120-2: BEETHOVEN— Symphony no. 3; Egmont overture. *Staatskapelle Dresden; C. Davis, cond.*
+ Gr 3/93: 34

28355. 434 122-2: HANDEL—Water music. *English Baroque Soloists; Gardiner, cond.*
+ ARG 9-10/93: 129
+ Fa 11-12/93: 262
+ Gr 5/93: 44

28356. 434 123-2: MAHLER—Symphony no. 4. *McNair, soprano; Berlin Phil. Orch.; Haitink, cond.*
● ARG 7-8/94: 128
+ Fa 7-8/94: 168
● Gr 2/94: 44

28357. 434 124-2: Cello sonatas by Geminiani and Vivaldi. *Schiff, cello; Koopman, harpsichord, organ; Linden, cello.*
● Gr 6/93: 63

28358. 434 128-2 (2 discs): ROSSINI—Il turco in Italia. *Alaimo, Jo, Giménez, Fissore, other vocalists; Academy of St. Martin-in-the-Fields; Marriner, cond.*
+ ARG 5-6/93: 125
+ Fa 5-6/93: 302
+ Gr 12/92: 142
+ ON 6/93: 40
+ Op 12/92: 1498

28359. 434 131-2: LEONCAVALLO— Pagliacci. *Pavarotti, Dessì, Pons; Philadelphia Orch.; Muti, cond.*
● Gr 4/93: 116
+ Op 6/93: 741

28360. 434 147-2: STRAVINSKY— Petrushka; Rite of spring. *London Phil. Orch.; Haitink, cond.* Reissues.
+ Gr 8/92: 41

28361. 434 163-2: LISZT—Piano concertos no. 1-2. BEETHOVEN—Cello sonata op. 5, no. 2. *Richter, piano; Rostropovich, cello; London Symphony Orch.; Kondrashin, cond.* Reissues.
+ Gr 9/92: 72

28362. 434 165-2: BACH—Motets. *Netherlands Chamber Choir; Koopman, cond.*
+ Gr 5/93: 76

28363. 434 166-2: PROKOFIEV—Cello concerto. KHACHATURIAN—Cello concerto. *Walevska, cello; Monte Carlo Opera Orch.; Inbal, cond.* Reissue.
+ ARG 1-2/93: 132

28364. 434 167-2: MOZART—Violin concerto no. 1. STRAVINSKY—Violin

PHILIPS

concerto. *D. Oistrakh, violin; Lamoureux Orch.; Haitink, cond.* Reissues.
+ ARG 3-4/93: 117

28365. 434 172-2: SHOSTAKOVICH—The execution of Stepan Razin; Symphony no. 12. *Vogel, bass; Leipzig Radio Symphony; Kegel, cond.; Leipzig Gewandhaus Orch.; Durjan, cond.* Reissues.
+ Gr 3/93: 52

28366. 434 252-2: Lockenhaus encores! *Various artists.*
+ ARG 5-6/93: 157
+ Fa 5-6/93: 408
+ St 10/93: 281

28367. 434 276-2: *Red, white and brass.* Music of Purcell, Meacham, Cohan, Wright, Sousa, Berlin and Foster. *Canadian Brass; Brass of the Boston Symphony & New York Phil.; Foss, cond.*
+ ARG 3-4/92: 179

28368. 434 402-2: BERLIOZ—Symphonie fantastique. *Orch. révolutionnaire et romantique; Gardiner, cond.*
+ ARG 9-10/93: 98
+ Fa 11-12/93: 185
+ Gr 6/93: 38

28369. 434 421-2 (2 discs): WAGNER—Das Rheingold. *McIntyre, Egel, Jerusalem; other soloists; Bayreuth Festival; Boulez, cond.*
+ Fa 9-10/93: 325

28370. 434 422-2 (3 discs): WAGNER—Die Walküre. *Hofmann, Salminen, McIntyre; other soloists; Bayreuth Festival; Boulez, cond.*
+ Fa 9-10/93: 325

28371. 434 423-2 (3 discs): WAGNER—Siegfried. *Jung, Zednik, McIntyre; other soloists; Bayreuth Festival; Boulez, cond.*
+ Fa 9-10/93: 326

28372. 434 424-2 (4 discs): WAGNER—Götterdämmerung. *Jung, Mazura, Hübner; other soloists;Bayreuth Festival; Boulez, cond.*
+ Fa 9-10/93: 326

28373. 434 595-2 (2 discs): PUCCINI—. Tosca. *Vaness, Giacomini, Zancanaro; Philadelphia Orch.; Muti, cond.*
• Fa 3-4/94: 280
+ Gr 9/93: 110
• ON 3/19/94: 30
• Op 1/94: 121

28374. 434 626-2: DEBUSSY—Suite bergamasque; La plus que lent; Valse romantique; Sarabande. *Arrau, piano.*
- ARG 7-8/93: 80

28375. 434 663-2: MOZART—Piano sonatas no. 4, 18; Fantasy, K. 475; Rondo, K. 511. *Brendel, piano.*
+ ARG 11-12/92: 171
+ Gr 8/92: 55

28376. 434 695-2 (2 discs): HANDEL—Messiah. *McNair, Otter, Chance, Hadley, Lloyd; Academy & Chorus of St. Martin-in-the-Fields; Marriner, cond.*
- ARG 9-10/93: 128
- Fa 5-6/93: 218
- Gr 2/93: 68

28377. 434 781-2 (2 discs): ALBERT—Tiefland. *Schoeffler, Czerwenka, Wächter, Brouwenstijn; Vienna Symphony; Moralt, cond.* Reissue.
+ Gr 3/93: 92

28378. 434 784-2 (2 discs): GLUCK—Orphée et Eurydice. *Simoneau, Danco; Roger Blanchard Vocal Ensemble; Lamoureux Orch.; Rosbaud, cond.* Recorded 1956.
+ Gr 5/93: 103

28379. 434 799-2: MOZART—Mass, K. 317; Vesperae solennes de confessore; Ave verum corpus. *Pennicchi, Patriasz, Vandersteene, Draijer; Netherlands Chamber Choir; Orch. of the Eighteenth Century; Brüggen, cond.*
+ Gr 6/95: 95

28380. 434 904-2: BACH—Partitas no. 1-3, 5. *Arrau, piano.*
- Gr 8/93: 56

28381. 434 905-2 (2 discs): BACH—St. John passion. *Stumphius, Bowman, Prégardien, Van der Meel, Kooy; Netherlands Chamber Choir; Orch. of the 18th Century; Brüggen, cond.*
• ARG 11-12/93: 77
+ EM 2/94: 161
+ Gr 5/93: 76

28382. 434 909-2 (3 discs): MAHLER—Symphonies no. 3, 6. *Norman, soprano; Tanglewood Festival Chorus; American Boychoir; Boston Symphony Orch.; Ozawa, cond.* Reissues.
• Gr 3/95: 46

28383. 434 912-2: *Bel canto arias.* Music of Rossini, Donizetti, and Bellini. *Hvorostovsky, baritone; Philharmonia Orch.; Marin, cond.*
+ ARG 11-12/94: 250
+ Gr 9/94: 120

28384. 434 914-2: DVOŘÁK—Cello concerto in B minor; Silent woods; Rondo; Slavonic dance no. 8. *Schiff, cello; Vienna Phil. Orch.; Previn, cond.*
+ Gr 9/93: 56

28385. 434 915-2: HAYDN—Symphonies no. 92, 96. *Vienna Phil. Orch.; Previn, cond.*
• Gr 11/93: 70

28386. 434 916-2: SULLIVAN—Overtures. *Academy of St. Martin-in-the-Fields; Marriner, cond.*
+ Fa 9-10/93: 305

28387. 434 917-2: *Cello song.* Music of Villa-Lobos, Bach, Scriabin, Rachmaninoff, Chopin, and others. *Lloyd Webber, cello; Lenehan, piano.*
+ Gr 10/93: 72

28388. 434 918-2: BACH—Brandenburg concertos; Concerto for flute, violin, and harpsichord; Concerto for three violins, BWV 1064. *Grafenauer, flute; Rosenbusch, Eschenburg, Schergaut, viiolins; Preston, harpsichord; Carl Philipp Emanuel Bach Chamber Orch.; Schreier, cond.*
- Gr 4/94: 39

28389. 434 920-2: HANDEL—Silete venti; Laudate pueri Dominum. MOZART—Exsultate, jubilate. *McNair, soprano; Monteverdi Choir; English Baroque Soloists; Gardiner, cond.*
+ ARG 3-4/94: 106
+ Fa 3-4/94: 207
• Gr 2/94: 79

28390. 434 921-2: HAYDN—Symphonies no. 97-98. *Orch. of the 18th Century; Brüggen, cond.*
- Fa 9-10/94: 209
+ Gr 9/94: 52

28391. 434 922-2 (3 discs): TCHAIKOVSKY—Sleeping beauty. *Kirov Orch.; Gergiev, cond.*
• ARG 9-10/93: 206
+ Gr 7/93: 54

28392. 434 926-2: Arias and songs by Martini, Caldara, Scarlatti, Handel, Mercadante, and others. *Carreras, tenor; English Chamber Orch.; Sutej, cond.*
+ ARG 1-2/94: 189
- Gr 6/93: 94

28393. 434 930-2: TCHAIKOVSKY—Sleeping beauty: Excerpts. *Kirov Orch.; Gergiev, cond.*
- ARG 3-4/95: 202

28394. 434 986-2: *Duetti amorosi.* Music of Verdi, Rossini, Donizetti, and Puccini. *Caballé, soprano; Carreras, tenor; with orch. acc.* Reissues.
• ARG 3-4/93: 183

28395. 434 990-2: DVOŘÁK—Symphony no. 8; The noon witch. *Vienna Phil. Orch.; Ozawa, cond.*
• ARG 7-8/94: 98
• Fa 7-8/94: 129
• Gr 4/94: 44

28396. 434 991-2: BRAHMS—Symphony no. 4; Haydn variations. *Boston Symphony Orch.; Haitink, cond.*
+ ARG 3-4/95: 82
+ Gr 9/94: 48

28397. 434 992-2: *The sorceress (film soundtrack).* HANDEL—Songs and arias. *Te Kanawa, soprano; Academy of Ancient Music; Hogwood, cond.*

+ ARG 5-6/95: 116
+ Gr 8/94: 102

28398. 434 993-2: Violin sonatas by Biber, Schmelzer, and Walther. *Dael, violin; Möller, cello; Asperen, harpsichord.*
+ Gr 8/93: 55

28399. 434 995-2: VIVALDI—Chamber concertos. *Ensemble Philidor.*
+ Gr 9/93: 64

28400. 434 996-2: BACH—Sonatas for flute and continuo; Partita, BWV 997. *Grafenauer, flute; Baumann, cello; Engelhard, harpsichord.*
• Gr 4/94: 60

28401. 434 997-2 (2 discs): MAHLER— Symphony no. 7; Symphony no. 10: Adagio. *Berlin Phil. Orch.; Haitink, cond.*
• ARG 11-12/95: 151
- Fa 11-12/95: 295
• Gr 5/95: 52

28402. 438 005-2: BEETHOVEN—Triple concerto; Choral fantasy. *Beaux Arts Trio; Pressler, piano; Chorus of Leipzig Radio; Gewandhaus Orch.; Masur, cond.*
• Fa 9-10/94: 138
+ Gr 6/94: 43

28403. 438 006-2: SCHUBERT—Symphony no. 9. *Orch. of the 18th Century; Brüggen, cond.*
+ Gr 1/94: 54

28404. 438 008-2: DUTILLEUX— Symphony no. 2; Timbres; Espace; La nuit étoilée; Métaboles. *Orch. de Paris; Bychkov, cond.*
+ ARG 9-10/94: 126
• Fa 5-6/95: 184
+ Gr 5/94: 50

28405. 438 013-2 (2 discs): HUMPERDINCK—Hänsel und Gretel. *Murray, Gruberova, Grundheber, Jones; Dresden State Opera; C. Davis, cond.*
+ ARG 11-12/94: 132
• Fa 3-4/94: 219
+ Gr 10/93: 113
+ ON 6/94: 44
+ Op 12/93: 1495

28406. 438 016-2: RODRIGO—Concierto de Aranjuez; Fantasia para un gentilhombre; Guitar music. *Romero, guitar; Academy of St. Martin-in-the-Fields; Marriner, cond.*
+ ARG 5-6/95: 161
+ Gr 8/94: 56

28407. 438 017-2: SPOHR—Nonet; Octet; Waltz. *Academy of St. Martin-in-the-Fields Chamber Ensemble.*
+ Gr 11/95: 116

28408. 438 132-2: LEONCAVALLO—I pagliacci. *Pavarotti, Dessì, Pons; Philadelphia Orch.; Muti, cond.*

- ARG 9-10/93: 147
• Fa 9-10/93: 204
- ON 10/93: 36

28409. 438 134-2: BEETHOVEN—Piano sonatas op. 31. *Brendel, piano.*
+ Gr 7/93: 64

28410. 438 135-2: TAKEMITSU—Choral music. *Shin-yu Kai Choir; Sekiya, cond.*
+ ARG 3-4/95: 199
+ Gr 8/94: 96

28411. 438 137-2: MOZART—Eine kleine Nachtmusik; Divertimento, K. 136, TCHAIKOVSKY—Serenade for strings. *Saito Kinen Orch.; Ozawa, cond.*
+ Gr 9/94: 58

28412. 438 138-2 (2 discs): SULLIVAN— Yeomen of the guard. *Lloyd, Streit, Dean, Allen; Academy of St. Martin-in- the-Fields; Marriner, cond.*
• Fa 3-4/94: 330
+ Gr 11/93: 160
• ON 6/94: 45
+ Op 12/93: 1496

28413. 438 141-2 (3 discs): TCHAIKOVSKY—The Queen of spades. *Grigoryan, Gulegina, Arkhipova, Putilin; Kirov Theater; Gergiev, cond.*
• Fa 3-4/94: 337
• Gr 10/93: 118
+ ON 4/16/94: 36
+ Op 12/93: 1494

28414. 438 145-2: GEMINIANI—Concerti grossi op. 3. *I Musici.*
• Gr 8/94: 67

28415. 438 149-2: FAURÉ—Requiem. DEBUSSY—Chansons de Charles d'Orléans. RAVEL—Chansons. SAINT-SAËNS—Choral music. *Bott, soprano; Cachemaille, baritone; Vatin, piano; Salisbury Cathedral Boys Choir; Monteverdi Choir; Orch. Révolutionnaire et Romantique; Gardiner, cond.*
+ Gr 9/94: 88

28416. 438 150-2: GLASS—Low symphony. *Brooklyn Phil. Symphony Orch.; Davies, cond.*
□ ARG 7-8/93: 93
□ Gr 5/93: 43

28417. 438 153-2: *Fantasias, pavans, and galliards.* Music of Byrd, Johnson, Philips, Morley, Bull, Dowland, Farnaby, Gibbons, and Tomkins. *Leonhardt, harpsichord & virginal.*
+ Gr 7/94: 84

28418. 438 158-2: BEETHOVEN— Symphony no. 9. *Dawson, Nes, Rolfe Johnson, Schulte; Gulbenkian Choir; Orch. of the 18th Century; Brüggen, cond.*
+ EM 11/94: 704
• Fa 3-4/94: 128
• Gr 10/93: 32

28419. 438 209-2: RAVEL—Rapsodie espagnole; Pavane; Daphnis et Chloé: Suite no. 2; Valse; Boléro. *Orch. de Paris; Bychkov, cond.*
+ ARG 7-8/94: 158
+ Fa 7-8/94: 210
• Gr 12/94: 93

28420. 438 211-2 (2 discs): ROSSINI—La donna del lago. *Anderson, Dupuy, Blake, Merritt; Teatro La Scala; Muti, cond.* Recorded live 1992.
+ Gr 2/95: 104

28421. 438 235-2 (2 discs): TCHAIKOVSKY—Eugene Onegin. *Hvorostovsky, Focile, Shicoff, Borodina, Anisimov; St. Petersburg Chamber Choir; Orch. de Paris; Bychkov, cond.*
+ ARG 7-8/94: 180
+ Fa 5-6/94: 263
+ Gr 12/93: 120
+ Op 3/94: 375
+ ON 4/16/94: 36

28422. 438 238-2 (2 discs): VERDI—La traviata. *Te Kanawa, Kraus, Hvorostovsky; Maggio Musicale Florence; Mehta, cond .*
• ARG 3-4/94: 176
- Fa 3-4/94: 355
- Gr 12/93: 120
• Op 12/93: 1495

28423. 438 277-2: BEETHOVEN— Symphony no. 3. *Concertgebouw Orch.; Kondrashin, cond.* Reissue.
+ Gr 9/93: 68

28424. 438 278-2: BRAHMS—Symphony no. 1. MENDELSSOHN—Symphony no. 4. *Concertgebouw Orch.; Kondrashin, cond.* Reissue.
+ Gr 9/93: 68

28425. 438 279-2: BRAHMS—Symphony no. 2. SIBELIUS—Symphony no. 5. *Concertgebouw Orch.; Kondrashin, cond.* Reissue.
+ Gr 9/93: 68

28426. 438 280-2: BORODIN—Symphony no. 2. STRAVINSKY—Petrushka. *Concertgebouw Orch.; Kondrashin, cond.* Reissue.
+ Fa 7-8/94: 84
+ Gr 9/93: 68

28427. 438 281-2: RAVEL—Daphnis et Chloé. CASELLA—Paganiniana. *Concertgebouw Orch.; Kondrashin, cond.* Reissue.
+ Gr 9/93: 68

28428. 438 282-2: RAVEL—Rapsodie espagnole; La valse; Concerto for piano, left hand; Tzigane. GERSHWIN—An American in Paris. *Wayenberg, piano; Krebbers, violin; Concertgebouw Orch.; Kondrashin, cond.* Reissue.
• Gr 9/93: 68

PHILIPS

28429. 438 283-2: Nielsen—Symphony no. 5. Shostakovich—Symphony no. 6. *Concertgebouw Orch.; Kondrashin, cond.* Reissue.
- Gr 9/93: 68

28430. 438 284-2: Prokofiev—Symphony no. 3. Shostakovich—Symphony no. 9. *Concertgebouw Orch.; Kondrashin, cond.* Reissue.
+ Fa 7-8/94: 84
+ Gr 9/93: 68

28431. 438 301-2: Beethoven—Symphonies no. 6, 8. *Academy of St. Martin-in-the-Fields; Marriner, cond.* Reissues.
• Gr 7/93: 35

28432. 438 303-2: Tchaikovsky—Symphony no. 4. Glinka—Ruslan and Ludmilla: Overture. *Pittsburgh Symphony Orch.; Los Angeles Phil.; Previn, cond.* Reissues.
• Gr 7/93: 65

28433. 438 307-2: Berlioz—Carnaval romain; Nuits d'été; Roméo et Juliette: Love scene, Queen Mab scherzo; Béatrice et Bénédict: Overture. *Armstrong, Veasey, Patterson, Shirley-Quirk; London Symphony Orch.; C. Davis, cond.* Reissues.
+ Gr 7/93: 68

28434. 438 310-2 (3 discs): Tchaikovsky—Symphonies, no. 5-6; Orchestra music. *Concertgebouw Orch.; Lamoureux Orch.; Kempen, cond.* Recorded 1954-58.
• Gr 1/94: 60

28435. 438 323-2 (2 discs): Mozart—Works for violin and orchestra; Sinfonia concertante. *Grumiaux, violin; Pelliccia, viola; London Symphony Orch.; C. Davis, cond.; Philharmonia Orch.; Leppard, cond.* Reissues.
+ Gr 9/93: 57

28436. 438 329-2 (2 discs): Tchaikovsky—Piano concertos; Andante and finale; Concert fantasia. *W. Haas, piano; Monte Carlo National Opera Orch.; Inbal, cond.* Reissues.
+ Gr 9/93: 63

28437. 438 335-2 (2 discs): Tchaikovsky—Symphonies no. 4-6. *London Symphony Orch.; Markevitch, cond.* Reissues.
+ Gr 2/94: 54

28438. 438 344-2 (2 discs): Vivaldi—Concertos op. 8. *Ayo, violin; I Musici.* Reissue.
• Gr 9/93: 64

28439. 438 347-2 (2 discs): Dvořák—Symphonies no. 7, 9; Symphonic variations. *Concertgebouw Orch.; London Symphony Orch.; C. Davis, cond.*

Reissues.
+ Gr 8/93: 27

28440. 438 350-2 (2 discs): Stravinsky—Rite of spring; Firebird; Petrushka; Apollo. *London Phil. Orch.; Haitink, cond.; London Symphony Orch.; Markevitch, cond.* Reissues.
• Gr 1/94: 56

28441. 438 353-2 (2 discs): Ravel—Piano concertos; Piano music. *W. Haas, piano; Monte-Carlo National Opera Orch.; Galliera, cond.* Reissue.
• Gr 10/94: 160

28442. 438 356-2 (2 discs): Handel—Messiah. *Harper, Watts, Wakefield, Shirley-Quirk; London Symphony Chorus & Orch.; C. Davis, cond.* Reissue.
+ Gr 8/93: 70

28443. 438 358-2 (2 discs): Puccini—Tosca. *Caballé, Carreras, Ramey; Royal Opera House Covent Garden; C. Davis, cond.* Reissue.
+ Gr 8/93: 82

28444. 438 362-2 (2 discs): Beethoven—Missa solemnis; Mass in C, op. 86. *Tomowa-Sintow, Eda-Pierre, Payne, Tear, Lloyd, Moll; London Symphony Orch.; C. Davis, cond.* Reissues.
+ Gr 8/93: 66

28445. 438 365-2 (2 discs): Brahms—Piano trios; Horn trio; Clarinet trio. *Beaux Arts Trio; Pieterson, clarinet; Grumiaux, violin; Orval, horn; Sebök, piano.* Reissues.
+ Gr 8/93: 46

28446. 438 368-2 (2 discs): Mendelssohn—Elijah (sung in German). *Ameling, Burmeister, Schreier, Adam; Leipzig Radio Chorus; Gewandhaus Orch.; Sawallisch, cond.* Reissue.
+ Gr 8/93: 70

28447. 438 371-2 (2 discs): Liszt—Hungarian rhapsodies (complete). *Campanella, piano.* Reissue.
• Gr 8/93: 59

28448. 438 374-2 (2 discs): Beethoven—Piano sonatas no. 27-32. *Brendel, piano.* Reissues.
+ Gr 8/93: 56

28449. 438 380-2 (2 discs): Grieg—Piano concerto; Peer Gynt: Suites no. 1-2; Other orchestra music; Lyric pieces. *Kovacevich, Kocsis, pianos; English Chamber Orch.; Philharmonia Orch.; Leppard, cond.; BBC Symphony Orch.; C. Davis, cond.* Reissues.
+ Gr 8/93: 28

28450. 438 392-2: *Gabrieli for brass.* Music of G. and A. Gabrieli, Schütz, Lassus, and Monteverdi. *Canadian Brass; New York Phil.; Philadelphia Orch.; Iseler, cond.*

+ Fa 9-10/94: 192
- Gr 7/94: 71

28451. 438 472-2: Beethoven—Piano sonatas no. 21, 22, 28; Andante favori. *Brendel, piano.*
+ ARG 3-4/94: 73
+ Gr 11/93: 116

28452. 438 480-2 (2 discs): Mozart—Piano sonatas. *Richter, piano.* Reissues.
• ARG 11-12/94: 234

28453. 438 483-2 (2 discs): Schubert—Piano sonatas. *Richter, piano.* Reissues.
+ ARG 11-12/94: 234

28454. 438 486-2 (2 discs): Beethoven—Piano sonatas no. 19-20, 22-23, 30-32. *Richter, piano.* Reissues.
+ ARG 11-12/94: 234

28455. 438 493-2: New Year's concert 1993. *Vienna Phil. Orch.; Muti, cond.*
+ Gr 3/93: 58

28456. 438 511-2 (4 discs): Schubert—Lieder. *Souzay, baritone; Baldwin, piano.* Recorded 1962-68.
+ Gr 11/93: 130

28457. 438 516-2 (3 discs): Music of Debussy, Schubert, Lekeu, Kreisler, Tartini, Corelli, and others. *Grumiaux, violin; Castiglione, piano.* Recorded 1950s.
+ Gr 11/93: 113

28458. 438 520-2 (3 discs): Beethoven—Piano trios no. 3-4, 6; Cello sonatas no. 1-2, 4. *Végh, violin; Casals, cello; Engel, Horszowski, Kempff, piano.* Recorded 1959-61.
+ Gr 3/94: 68

28459. 438 524-2 (3 discs): *Concertgebouw Orchestra: the early years.* Music of Beethoven, Strauss, Mozart, Tchaikovsky, and Schubert. *Various conductors.*
+ Gr 2/94: 58

28460. 438 528-2 (4 discs): Schubert—Songs. *Ameling, soprano; Baldwin, Jansen, pianos.* Reissues.
+ Gr 4/94: 92

28461. 438 533-2 (2 discs): Beethoven—Symphonies no. 3, 7-9; Consecration of the house. *Berlin Phil. Orch.; Kempen, cond.* Recorded 1953-55.
+ Gr 3/94: 39

28462. 438 613-2 (3 discs): Bach—Piano music. *Richter, piano.* Reissues.
+ ARG 11-12/94: 234
+ Gr 8/94: 79

28463. 438 617-2 (2 discs): Beethoven—Piano sonatas no. 9, 11-12, 27. Haydn—Piano sonata no. 24, 52. Weber—Piano sonata no. 3. *Richter, piano.* Reissues.
• ARG 11-12/94: 235

28464. 438 620-2 (3 discs): CHOPIN—Piano music. LISZT—Piano music. *Richter, piano.* Reissues.
- ● ARG 11-12/94: 235

28465. 438 624-2 (2 discs): BEETHOVEN—Piano sonatas no. 18, 28; Piano music; Archduke trio; Quintet for piano and winds. *Richter, piano.* Reissues.
- ● ARG 11-12/94: 235

28466. 438 627-2 (2 discs): SCRIABIN—Piano music. PROKOFIEV—Piano music. SHOSTOKOVICH—Preludes and fugues: Selections. *Richter, piano.* Reissues.
- + ARG 11-12/94: 235

28467. 438 663-2: *American classics.* GERSHWIN—An American in Paris. ELLINGTON—Harlem. BERNSTEIN—West side story: Symphonic dances. ADAMS—The Chairman dances. *Hollywood Bowl Orch.; Mauceri, cond.*
- ● Gr 1/94: 62

28468. 438 664-2 (2 discs): STRAUSS—Salome. *Wegner, Metternich, Szemere, Milinkovic; Vienna Symphony Orch.; Moralt, cond.* Recorded 1954.
- + Gr 5/94: 112

28469. 438 667-2 (2 discs): SCHOENBERG—Moses und Aron. *Reich, Devos, Mann, Csapó; Austrian Radio Symphony Orch.; Gielen, cond.* Reissue.
- + Gr 4/94: 100

28470. 438 670-2 (3 discs): MOZART—Marriage of Figaro. *Berry, Streich, Schoeffler, Jurinac; Vienna Symphony Orch.; Böhm, cond.* Recorded 1956.
- ● Gr 10/94: 192

28471. 438 674-2 (3 discs): MOZART—Don Giovanni. *London, Zadek, Jurinac, Berry; Vienna Symphony Orch.; Moralt, cond.* Recorded 1955.
- ● Gr 10/94: 192

28472. 438 678-2 (3 discs): MOZART—Cosí fan tutte. *Stich-Randall, Malaniuk, Kmentt, Berry; Vienna Symphony Orch.; Moralt, cond.* Recorded 1956.
- ● Gr 10/94: 192

28473. 438 685-2: *The great waltz.* Music of Tiomkin, Bennett, R. Strauss, Herrmann, Loewe, Prokofiev, Sondheim, Bernstein, Rozsa, Waxman, Steiner, Korngold, and Ravel. *Hollywood Bowl Symphony Orch.; Mauceri, cond.*
- - ARG 3-4/94: 196
- + Gr 6/94: 67

28474. 438 703-2 (2 discs): SCHUBERT—Piano sonatas D. 958-960; Impromptus, D. 946. *Brendel, piano.* Reissues.
- + Gr 5/94: 87

28475. 438 706-2 (2 discs): BEETHOVEN—Overtures, minuets, dances. *Gewandhaus Orch.; Masur, cond.; Academy of St. Martin-in-the-Fields; Marriner, cond.*

Reissues.
- + Gr 5/94: 47

28476. 438 715-2 (2 discs): HAYDN—The seasons. *Mathis, Jerusalem, Fischer-Dieskau, Academy of St. Martin-in-the-Fields; Marriner, cond.* Reissue.
- + Gr 6/94: 94

28477. 438 733-2 (2 discs): STRAUSS—Wind music; Oboe concerto. *Holliger, oboe; Netherlands Wind Ensemble; New Philharmonia Orch.; Waart, cond.* Reissues.
- + Gr 7/94: 62

28478. 438 736-2 (2 discs): BACH—Sonatas and partitas for solo violin. *Grumiaux, violin.* Reissue.
- + Gr 2/94: 72

28479. 438 742-2 (2 discs): DEBUSSY—Orchestra music. *Concertgebouw Orch.; Haitink, Beinum, conds.* Reissues.
- + Gr 3/94: 46

28480. 438 751—438 754 2 (2 2-disc sets): LISZT—Complete symphonic poems. *London Phil. Orch.; Haitink, cond.* Reissues.
- + Gr 10/94: 110

28481. 438 760-2 (2 discs): BRAHMS—Ein deutsches Requiem; Choral music. *Lipp, Heynis, Crass; Vienna Singverein; Vienna Symphony Orch.; Sawallisch, cond.* Reissues.
- ● Gr 5/94: 89

28482. 438 800-2 (2 discs): MOZART—Masses K. 317, K. 427; Requiem. *Vocal soloists; John Alldis Choir; London Symphony Orch.; BBC Symphony Orch.; Davis, cond.* Reissues.
- + Gr 3/94: 94

28483. 438 806-2 (2 discs): AVISON—Concerti grossi after Scarlatti. *Academy of St. Martin-in-the-Fields; Marriner, cond.* Reissue.
- + Gr 8/94: 40

28484. 438 812-2 (2 discs): BARTÓK—Piano concertos; Violin concerto no. 2; Concerto for orchestra. *Kovacevich, piano; BBC Symphony Orch.; C. Davis, cond.; Szeryng, violin; Concertgebouw Orch.; Haitink, cond.* Reissues.
- ● Gr 2/94: 37

28485. 438 863-2: BEETHOVEN—Piano sonatas no. 12-14, 19. *Brendel, piano.*
- ● Gr 12/94: 125

28486. 438 864-2: RACHMANINOFF—Symphony no. 2. *Kirov Orch.; Gergiev, cond.*
- ● Gr 8/94: 52

28487. 438 865-2: STRAVINSKY—Oedipus Rex. *Schreier, Norman, Terfel; Shinyukai Male Choir; Saito Kinen Orch.; Ozawa, cond.*

- - ARG 7-8/94: 178
- + Fa 7-8/94: 254
- ● Gr 3/94: 107
- ● Op 7/94: 890

28488. 438 866-2: *Spring music.* Music of Rorem, Baker, and Rochberg. *Beaux Arts Trio.*
- + Fa 9-10/94: 429
- □ Gr 8/94: 66

28489. 438 868-2: MOZART—Clarinet concerto. SPOHR—Clarinet concerto no. 1. WEBER—Clarinet concerto no. 2. *Ottensamer, clarinet; Vienna Phil. Orch.; C. Davis, cond.*
- + ARG 1-2/95: 146

28490. 438 872-2: MUSSORGSKY—Songs and dances of death; Arias. *Hvorostovsky, baritone; Kirov Orch.; Gergiev, cond.*
- ● ARG 9-10/94: 260
- + Gr 5/94: 116
- + ON 4/16/94: 36

28491. 438 873-2 (2 discs): BACH—Magnificat; Masses, BWV 233-236. *Bonney, Remmert, Trost, Bär; RIAS Chamber Choir; CPE Bach Chamber Orch.; Schreier, cond.*
- ● Gr 2/95: 82

28492. 438 874-2 (14 discs): MAHLER—Symphonies. *Boston Symphony Orch.; Ozawa, cond.* Reissues.
- ● Gr 1/96: 54

28493. 438 876-2: VIVALDI—Concertos for strings. *I Musici.*
- + Gr 5/94: 64

28494. 438 905-2: *Van Cliburn Ninth International Piano Competition 1993 gold medal winner: Simone Pedroni.* Music of Mussorgsky, Rachmaninoff, and Hindemith. *Pedroni, piano.*
- - ARG 3-4/94: 213
- ● Fa 1-2/94: 408
- + Gr 4/94: 76

28495. 438 906-2: *Van Cliburn Ninth International Piano Competition 1993 silver medalist Valery Kuleshov and bronze medalist Christopher Taylor.* Music of Liszt, D. Scarlatti, Gould, Messiaen, and Boulez. *Kuleshov, Taylor, piano.*
- + ARG 3-4/94: 213
- ● Fa 1-2/94: 408
- + Gr 4/94: 76

28496. 438 932-2: SCHUBERT—Lieder. *Blochwitz, tenor; Jansen, piano.*
- + Gr 3/95: 95

28497. 438 933-2: STRAUSS—Serenade, op. 7; Suite in B♭, op. 4; Sonatina no. 2 "Fröhliche Werkstatt". *Wind soloists of the Chamber Orch. of Europe; Holliger, cond.*
- + Gr 9/95: 68

PHILIPS

28498. 438 934-2: HAYDN—Symphonies no. 102, 104. *Vienna Phil. Orch.; Previn, cond.*
- Gr 12/94: 82

28499. 438 935-2 (2 discs): MAHLER—Symphony no. 2. *McNair, soprano; Nes, contralto; Ernst Senff Choir; Berlin Phil. Orch.; Haitink, cond.*
- ARG 3-4/95: 132
- Gr 11/94: 80

28500. 438 938-2: *España*. Music of Falla, Lecuona, Albéniz, and Infante. *K. & M. Labèque, pianos.*
+ ARG 11-12/95: 255
+ Gr 9/94: 78

28501. 438 939-2: BERLIOZ—Symphonie fantastique; Roman carnival overture. *Orch. de Paris; Bychkov, cond.*
+ ARG 7-8/94: 74
- Fa 7-8/94: 75
+ Gr 11/94: 66

28502. 438 941-2: RIMSKY-KORSAKOV—Scheherazade; Russian Easter overture. *Vienna Phil. Orch.; Ozawa, cond.*
- ARG 3-4/95: 170
- Gr 6/94: 58

28503. 438 946-2: RAMEAU—Les indes galantes: Suite. *Orch. of the 18th Century; Brüggen, cond.*
+ Gr 8/94: 52

28504. 438 948-2 (3 discs): BEETHOVEN—Piano trios. *Beaux Arts Trio.* Reissues.
+ Gr 11/94: 97

28505. 438 952-2: *Album de musique, offert par G. Rossini à Mademoiselle Louise Carlier*. Music of Bazzini, Bellini, Bertin, Berton, Cherubini, and others. *Danco, soprano; Orel, mezzo-soprano; Molinari-Pradelli, piano.* Recorded 1960.
+ Gr 9/94: 107

28506. 438 959-2 (3 discs): *Magda Tagliaferro (1893-1986).* Music of Liszt, Chopin, Weber, Saint-Saëns, Granados, Villa-Lobos, Brahms, Schubert, and Schumann. *Tagliaferro, piano; Orch. des Concerts Lamoureux; Fournet, cond.*
+ Fa 5-6/95: 414

28507. 438 964-2 (4 discs): Songs by Bizet, Chabrier, Duparc, Fauré, Franck, and others. *Souzay, baritone; Baldwin, piano.* Reissues.
+ Gr 3/95: 98

28508. 438 973-2 (2 discs): STRAVINSKY—Apollon musagète; Suites for small orchestra; Norwegian moods; Circus polka; Histoire du soldat; Symphony of psalms. *Russian State Academic Choir; London Symphony Orch.; Markevitch, cond.* Reissues.
+ Gr 2/95: 58

28509. 438 998-2: BRAHMS—Violin concerto, op. 77. *Mullova, violin; Berlin Phil. Orch.; Abbado, cond.* Recorded live 1992.
+ Fa 7-8/95: 131
+ Gr 11/94: 67

28510. 438 999-2: MOZART—Mass in C minor, K. 427; Ave verum corpus. *Te Kanawa, Otter, Rolfe Johnson, Lloyd; Academy of St. Martin-in-the-Fields; Marriner, cond.*
+ Gr 12/94: 143

28511. 442 011-2: *White nights: romantic Russian showpieces.* Music of Glinka, Khachaturian, Borodin, Liadov, and Tchaikovsky. *Kirov Orch.; Gergiev, cond.*
- ARG 7-8/94: 200
- Gr 4/94: 58

28512. 442 012-2: *Toward the sea III.* Music of Honegger, Denisov, Takemitsu, Britten, and Debussy. *Nicolet, flute; Imai, viola; Yoshino, harp.*
+ Gr 12/94: 122

28513. 442 013-2: TCHAIKOVSKY—Romances. *Borodina, mezzo-soprano; Gergieva, piano.*
+ ARG 3-4/95: 201
+ Gr 6/94: 102

28514. 442 015-2: MADERNA—Oboe concertos no. 1-3. *Holliger, oboe; Cologne Radio Symphony Orch.; Bertini, cond.*
+ Gr 9/94: 54

28515. 442 016-2: BARTÓK—Piano music, vol. 2. *Kocsis, piano.*
+ Gr 11/94: 111

28516. 442 050-2 (10 discs): MAHLER—Symphonies (complete). *Concertgebouw Orch.; Haitink, cond.* Reissues.
- Gr 11/94: 80

28517. 442 061-2 (6 discs): TCHAIKOVSKY—Symphonies and orchestral works. *Concertgebouw Orch.; Haitink, cond.* Reissues.
- Gr 10/94: 126

28518. 442 068-2 (4 discs): BRAHMS—Complete orchestral music. *Concertgebouw Orch.; Haitink, cond.* Reissues.
+ Gr 9/94: 50

28519. 442 073-2 (5 discs): BEETHOVEN—Complete symphonies. *Concertgebouw Orch.; Haitink, cond.* Reissue.
- Gr 9/94: 46

28520. 442 079-2 (2 discs): SCHUMANN—Symphonies; Overtures. *Concertgebouw Orch.; Haitink, cond.* Reissues.
- Gr 7/94: 54

28521. 442 082-2 (3 discs): CHARPENTIER—Louise. *Monmart, Laroze, Musy, Michel; Paris Opéra-Comique; Fournet, cond.* Recorded 1956.
+ Gr 9/94: 109
+ Op 1/95: 122

28522. 442 086-2 (3 discs): STRAUSS—Der Rosenkavalier. *Lear, Von Stade, Bastin, Welting; Rotterdam Phil. Orch.; Waart, cond.* Reissue.
- Gr 12/94: 160

28523. 442 090-2 (2 discs): DONIZETTI—Don Pasquale. *Capecchi, Rizzoli, Munteanu, Valdengo; Teatro San Carlo Naples; Molinari-Pradelli, cond.* Recorded 1956.
- Gr 10/94: 188

28524. 442 093-2 (2 discs): DONIZETTI—Linda di Chamounix. *Stella, Valletti, Capecchi, Taddei; Teatro San Carlo Naples; Serafin, cond.* Recorded 1960.
- Gr 9/94: 109

28525. 442 096-2 (3 discs): HANDEL—Ariodante. *Baker, Mathis, Burrowes, Bowman; English Chamber Orch.; Leppard, cond.* Reissue.
- Gr 12/94: 154

28526. 442 100-2 (2 discs): ROSSINI—Mosé. *Rossi-Lemeni, Lazzari, Taddei, Filippeschi; Teatro San Carlo, Naples; Serafin, cond.* Recorded 1957.
- Gr 3/95: 102

28527. 442 106-2 (2 discs): PUCCINI—La bohème; Gianni Schicchi. *Stella, Poggi, Capecchi, Rizzoli; Teatro San Carlo Naples; Molinari-Pradelli, cond.* Recorded 1957, 1956.
- Gr 12/95: 150

28528. 442 117-2: SCHUBERT—Symphonies no. 6, 8. *Orch. of the Eighteenth Century; Brüggen, cond.*
- Gr 8/95: 81

28529. 442 119-2: BACH—Easter oratorio; Cantata no. 11. *Frimmer, Popken, Prégardien, Wilson-Johnson; Choir & Orch. of the Age of Enlightenment; Leonhardt, cond.*
- Gr 10/94: 166

28530. 442 120-2: BRAHMS—Symphony no. 3; Alto rhapsody. *Nes, alto; Tanglewood Festival Chorus; Boston Symphony Orch.; Haitink, cond.*
+ ARG 7-8/95: 93
- Fa 9-10/95: 154
- Gr 3/95: 40

28531. 442 121-2: SCHUMANN—Symphonies no. 1, 4. *Vienna Phil. Orch.; Muti, cond.*
+ Gr 1/95: 56

28532. 442 123-2: BEETHOVEN—Piano trio no. 7 "Archduke". BRAHMS—Piano trio no. 1. *Previn, piano; Mullova, violin; Schiff, cello.*
+ ARG 1-2/96: 85
+ Fa 1-2/96: 138
+ Gr 8/95: 91

28533. 442 124-2: BEETHOVEN—Piano sonatas, op. 2. *Brendel, piano.*
+ Fa 7-8/95: 117
+ Gr 7/95: 83

28534. 442 125-2: DVOŘÁK—Slavonic dances. *Vienna Phil. Orch.; Previn, cond.*
+ Gr 10/94: 104

28535. 442 126-2: MOZART—Symphonies no. 31, 41. *Vienna Phil. Orch.; Muti, cond.*
● Gr 7/95: 62

28536. 442 127-2: ARENSKY—Piano trios no. 1-2. *Beaux Arts Trio.*
+ ARG 9-10/95: 92
+ Gr 6/95: 66

28537. 442 128-2: BIZET—Arlésienne: Suites no. 1-2; Carmen: Suites no. 1-2. *Orch. de Paris; Bychkov, cond.*
● Gr 12/94: 75

28538. 442 129-2: *Sure thing.* The Jerome Kern songbook. *McNair, soprano; Previn, piano; Finck, double bass.*
● Gr 12/94: 172

28539. 442 130-2: MENDELSSOHN—Symphonies, no. 3-4. *Academy of St. Martin-in-the-Fields; Marriner, cond.*
+ Gr 10/94: 112

28540. 442 131-2: *Baroque trumpet concertos.* Music of Vivaldi, Corelli, Albinoni, Torelli, A. Marcello, Viviani, Franceschini, and Baldassare. *Hardenberger, trumpet; I Musici.*
+ Gr 5/95: 65

28541. 442 133-2: Music of Gershwin, Loesser, Lloyd Webber, Rodgers, Sondheim, Sullivan, Styne, Ellington, and Willson. *Canadian Brass.*
+ ARG 1-2/96: 208

28542. 442 134-2 (2 discs): BERLIOZ—Roméo et Juliette. *Borodina, Moser, Miles, vocalists; Bavarian Radio Chorus; Vienna Phil. Orch.; C. Davis, cond.*
- ARG 1-2/97: 73
● Fa 1-2/97: 109
+ Gr 10/96: 90

28543. 442 137-2: BERLIOZ—Messe solennelle. *Brown, Viala, Cachemaille, Monteverdi Choir; Orch. Révolutionnaire et Romantique; Gardiner, cond.*
● ARG 7-8/94: 73
+ Fa 7-8/94: 74
+ Gr 4/94: 79
+ ON 6/94: 44

28544. 442 138-2 (3 discs): RIMSKY-KORSAKOV—Sadko. *Galusin, Tsidipova, Tarassova, Alexashkin, Dyadkova; Kirov Chorus & Orch.; Gergiev, cond.*
+ ARG 7-8/95: 180
+ Fa 7-8/95: 292
● Gr 1/95: 98

● ON 8/95: 35
+ Op 2/95: 246

28545. 442 142-2 (2 discs): VERDI—Requiem; Sacred pieces. *Orgonasova, Otter, Canonici, Miles; Monteverdi Choir; Orch. révolutionnaire et romantique; Gardiner, cond.*
+ ARG 7-8/95: 216
+ Fa 9-10/95: 347
+ Gr 4/95: 111

28546. 442 145-2: VIVALDI—Violin concertos, RV 199, 234, 270-271, 277, 581. *Sirbu, violin; I Musici.*
+ Gr 7/95: 72

28547. 442 146-2: BARTÓK—For children. *Kocsis, piano.*
+ Gr 6/95: 74

28548. 442 148-2: MOZART—Flute concertos; Andante; Concerto for flute and harp. *Hünteler, flute; Storck, harp; Orch. of the 18th Century; Brüggen, cond.*
+ Gr 8/96: 52

28549. 442 149-2: BRAHMS—Clarinet quintet, op. 115. MOZART—Clarinet quintet, K. 581. *Wright, clarinet; Boston Symphony Chamber Players.*
+ ARG 7-8/96: 161
+ Fa 5-6/96: 115
+ Gr 9/94: 72

28550. 442 150-2: *Noches en España.* Music of Tarrega, Sor, Albéniz, Granados, Mudarra, and others. *P. Romero, guitar.*
+ Gr 4/95: 94

28551. 442 152-2: ELGAR—Symphony no. 2; Cockaigne. *London Symphony Orch.; Previn, cond.*
● Gr 3/95: 44

28552. 442 154-2: ROLLA—Music for viola and orchestra. *Paris, viola; I Musici.*
+ Gr 11/95: 90

28553. 442 260-2 (2 discs): PUCCINI—La bohème. *Ricciarelli, Carreras, Putnam, Wixwll; Royal Opera House Covent Garden; C. Davis, cond.* Reissue.
● Gr 10/94: 197

28554. 442 281-2 (2 discs): STRAUSS—Also sprach Zarathustra; Ein Heldenleben; Don Juan; Death and transfiguration; Till Eulenspiegel; Rosenkavalier suites. *Concertgebouw Orch.; Haitink, Jochum, conds.* Reissue.
+ ARG 1-2/96: 180

28555. 442 284-2 (3 discs): BARTÓK—Complete string quartets. *Novák Quartet.* Reissue.
+ Gr 10/94: 130

28556. 442 344-2: RACHMANINOFF—Vespers. *Borodina, mezzo-soprano;*

Mostowoy, tenor; St. Petersburg Chamber Choir; Korniev, cond.
+ Gr 11/94: 137
+ ON 4/1/95: 44

28557. 442 360-2: SCHUBERT—Winterreise. *Schreier, tenor; Richter, piano.* Reissue.
● Gr 9/94: 92

28558. 442 389-2: SIBELIUS—Symphony no. 2; Finlandia; Valse triste; Swan of Tuonela. *Boston Symphony Orch.; C. Davis, cond.* Reissue.
+ Gr 9/94: 62

28559. 442 399-2: PROKOFIEV—Symphonies, no. 1, 5. *Los Angeles Phil. Orch.; Previn, cond.* Reissue.
+ Gr 9/94: 58

28560. 442 411-2: GÓRECKI—Symphony no. 3 "Symphony of sorrowful songs". *Kozlowska, soprano; Warsaw Phil. Orch.; Kord, cond.*
+ Fa 3-4/95: 175
● Gr 1/95: 44

28561. 442 424-2: BEETHOVEN—Symphony no. 5. SCHUBERT—Symphony no. 8. *Saito Kinen Orch.; Ozawa, cond.*
- Gr 7/95: 44

28562. 442 425-2: *Hollywood nightmares.* Music of Savino, Steiner, Stravinsky, Williams, Herrmann, and others. *Hollywood Bowl Symphony Orch.; Mauceri, cond.*
+ Gr 1/95: 64

28563. 442 426-2: *Cradle song.* Music of Schumann, Schubert, Quilter, Rutter, and others. *Lloyd Webber, cello; Lenehan, Chowhan, Bennett, piano.*
● ARG 7-8/96: 241
+ Gr 1/96: 77

28564. 442 427-2: VAUGHAN WILLIAMS—The wasps: overture; Fantasia on a theme by Thomas Tallis; In the Fen Country; Variations for orchestra; Norfolk Rhapsody no. 1; Five variants of Dives and Lazarus. *Academy of St. Martin-in-the-Fields; Marriner, cond.*
+ ARG 11-12/95: 223
+ Fa 9-10/95: 345
● Gr 6/95: 60

28565. 442 459-2: Music of Franck, Debussy, Wagner, Chopin, Liszt, and others. *Richter, piano.* Reissues.
+ ARG 11-12/94: 236

28566. 442 460-2: SCHUBERT—Schwanengesang; Songs. *Holzmair, baritone; Cooper, piano.*
● Fa 1-2/96: 304
+ Gr 11/94: 137

28567. 442 530-2: *English idylls.* Music of Vaughan Williams, Elgar, Delius, Grainger, Dyson, and others. *Lloyd Webber, cello; Academy of St. Martin-*

PHILIPS

in-the-Fields; Marriner, cond.
+ ARG 7-8/95: 238
+ Gr 12/94: 107

28568. 442 531-2: GUBAIDULINA—Jetzt immer Schnee; Perception. *Kleindienst, soprano; Lorenz, baritone; Netherlands Chamber Choir; Schoenberg Ensemble; Leeuw, cond.*
+ Gr 4/95: 98

28569. 442 532-2: USTVOLSKAYA—Compostitions no. 1-3. *Schoenberg Ensemble; Leeuw, cond.*
+ Gr 4/95: 74

28570. 442 533-2: GÓRECKI—Kleines Requiem für eine Polka; Lerchenmusik. *Schoenberg-Ensemble; Leeuw, cond.*
+ ARG 7-8/96: 120
+ Fa 7-8/96: 177
+ Gr 5/96: 58

28571. 442 534-2: JANÁČEK—Choral music. *Netherlands Chamber Choir; Schoenberg Ensemble; Leeuw, cond.*
+ Gr 12/95: 128

28572. 442 535-2: MARTIN—Der Cornet. *Nes, contralto; Nieuw Sinfonietta Amsterdam; Leeuw, cond.*
+ Gr 11/95: 141

28573. 442 536-2: *Russian romances, vol. 2.* Music of Tchaikovsky, Borodin, Rimsky-Korsakov, and Rachmaninoff. *Hvorostovsky, baritone; Arkadiev, piano.*
+ ARG 3-4/96: 253
+ Fa 5-6/96: 332
• Gr 2/95: 91

28574. 442 537-2 (3 discs): BORODIN—Prince Igor. *Kit, Gorchakova, Grigoryan, Ognovienko, Minjelkiev, Borodina, Seleznev, Pluzhnikov; Kirov Chorus & Orch.; Gergiev, cond.*
+ ARG 9-10/95: 112
+ Fa 9-10/95: 149
+ Gr 4/95: 119
+ ON 9/95: 55
+ Op 7/95: 871

28575. 442 542-2: RAVEL—Mother Goose; La valse; Pavane; Rapsodie espagnole; Bolero. *London Symphony Orch.; Monteux, cond.* Reissue.
+ ARG 1-2/96: 159

28576. 442 543-2: SCHUBERT—Impromptus; Allegretto; Eccosaise; Ungarische Melodie. *Brendel, piano.* Reissues.
+ Gr 1/96: 82

28577. 442 544-2 (5 discs): *Pierre Monteux: the early years.* Music of Beethoven, Schubert, Tchaikovsky, Brahms, Ravel, and Debussy. *Concertgebouw Orch.; London Symphony Orch.; Monteux, cond.* Recorded 1962-65.
+ Gr 12/94: 104

28578. 442 577-2 (2 discs): BEETHOVEN—Piano concertos no. 1-4; Romances. *Kovacevich, piano; Grumiaux, violin; BBC Symphony Orch.; Davis, cond.; Concertgebouw Orch.; Haitink, cond.* Reissue.
+ Gr 8/95: 67

28579. 442 580-2 (2 discs): BEETHOVEN—Piano concerto no. 5; Concerto for violin, cello, piano, and orchestra; Violin concerto; Piano concerto, WoO 4. *Szeryng, Krebbers, violins; Starker, cello; Kovacevich, Arrau, Grychtolowna, piano; London Symphony Orch.; Davis, cond.; New Philharmonia Orch.; Inbal, cond.; Concertgebouw Orch.; Haitink, cond.; Folkwang Chamber Orch.; Dressel, cond.* Reissue.
• Gr 8/95: 67

28580. 442 586-2 (2 discs): TCHAIKOVSKY—Symphonic poems. *Concertgebouw Orch.; Philharmonia Orch.; Haitink, cond.; Frankfurt Radio Symphony Orch.; Inbal, cond.* Reissues.
+ ARG 3-4/95: 200

28581. 442 600-2: Arias and songs by Verdi, Puccini, Leoncavallo, Rossini, and others. *Carreras, tenor.* Reissues.
• ARG 11-12/95: 266

28582. 442 603-2: Music of Richard Rodgers. *Andrews, soprano; London Musicians Orch.; Fraser, cond.*
+ Gr 1/95: 100

28583. 442 604-2 (5 discs): MOZART—Symphonies no. 29, 31-38, 39-41. *English Baroque Soloists; Gardiner, cond.* Reissues.
+ Gr 3/95: 50

28584. 442 640-2: WAGNER—Die Walküre: Act 1. *King, Rysanek, Nienstedt; Bayreuth Festival Orch.; Böhm, cond.* Reissue; recorded live 1967.
+ Gr 7/95: 118

28585. 442 645-2: STRAUSS—Also sprach Zarathustra; Ein Heldenleben. *Boston Symphony Orch.; Ozawa, cond.*
• ARG 1-2/96: 180

28586. 442 648-2: MOZART—Piano concertos no. 23-24. *Uchida, piano; English Chamber Orch.; Tate, cond.* Reissue.
+ Gr 7/95: 60

28587. 442 650-2: MUSSORGSKY—Pictures at an exhibition (piano and orchestral versions). *Brendel, piano; Vienna Phil. Orch.; Previn, cond.* Reissue.
+ Gr 2/96: 54

28588. 442 653-2: SCHUMANN—Kreisleriana; Fantasy in C major; Piano sonata no. 2. *Orozco, Varsi, pianos.* Recorded 1969 and 1976.
• ARG 1-2/96: 170

28589. 442 659-2: HAYDN—Piano sonatas no. 35-39. *Haebler, fortepiano.* Reissue.
+ ARG 1-2/96: 122

28590. 442 661-2: MENDELSSOHN—Violin concerto; Symphony no. 3; Hebrides overture. *Szeryng, violin; Concertgebouw Orch.; London Phil. Orch.; Haitink, cond.* Reissue.
• ARG 1-2/96: 141

28591. 442 685-2 (12 discs): *Clara Haskil: the legacy.* Music of Beethoven, Mozart, Schumann, Scarlatti, and Ravel. *Haskil, piano; in part with orchestra.* Reissues.
• Gr 11/95: 129

28592. 442 727-2 (2 discs): *The Concertgebouw recordings.* Music of Beethoven, Mendelssohn, Mozart, Schubert, and Sibelius. *Concertgebouw Orch.; Szell, cond.* Reissues.
+ Gr 11/95: 101

28593. 442 730-2: BRUCKNER—Symphony no. 8. *Concertgebouw Orch.; Beinum, cond.* Recorded 1956.
+ Gr 3/96: 42

28594. 442 731-2: BRUCKNER—Symphony no. 9. *Concertgebouw Orch.; Beinum, cond.* Recorded 1956.
+ Gr 3/96: 42

28595. 442 744-2: STRAUSS—Songs. WOLF—Italienisches Liederbuch. *Ameling, soprano; Souzay, baritone; Baldwin, piano.* Reissue.
+ Gr 10/95: 119

28596. 442 774-2: BEETHOVEN—Piano sonatas no. 8-11. *Brendel, piano.*
+ ARG 9-10/95: 103
+ Fa 9-10/95: 139

28597. 442 775-2: TCHAIKOVSKY—Capriccio italien; Marche slav; Eugene Onegin: Polonaise and waltz. MUSSORGSKY—Boris Godunov: Coronation scene. LIADOV—Enchanted lake. *Kirov Opera; Gergiev, cond.*
- ARG 7-8/95: 209
+ Gr 7/95: 72

28598. 442 776-2: RACHMANINOFF—Liturgy of St. John Chrysostom. *St. Petersburg Chamber Choir; Korniev, cond.*
+ ARG 9-10/96: 184
+ Fa 9-10/96: 297
+ Gr 6/95: 97

28599. 442 777-2: SCHUMANN—Kreisleriana; Carnaval. *Uchida, piano.*
- ARG 7-8/95: 191
• Fa 7-8/95: 310
+ Gr 5/95: 84

28600. 442 778-2: TCHAIKOVSKY—Capriccio italien; Swan lake (selections); Sleeping beauty (selections); Slavonic march. SCRIABIN—Fantasy in A minor. K.

& M. Labèque, pianos.
+ Fa 7-8/96: 321
+ Gr 12/95: 110

28601. 442 779-2: BACH—Cantatas no.
211, 213. *Bonney, Popken, Prégardien,
Wilson-Johnson; Orch. & Choir of the
Age of Enlightenment; Leonhardt, cond.*
+ Gr 7/95: 92

28602. 442 780-2: *Songs of desire.* Music
of Rimsky-Korsakov, Borodin,
Mussorgsky, Balakirev, and Cui.
*Borodina, mezzo-soprano; Gergieva,
piano.*
+ ARG 11-12/95: 266
+ Gr 8/95: 123

28603. 442 781-2: Music of Gimenez,
Boccherini, Romero, Falla, and others.
Los Romeros.
+ ARG 11-12/95: 251

28604. 442 783-2: BARTÓK—Concerto for
orchestra; The miraculous mandarin.
*Boston Symphony Orch.; Tanglewood
Festival Chorus; Ozawa, cond.* Recorded
live.
• ARG 11-12/95: 79
• Fa 11-12/95: 195
• Gr 8/95: 66

28605. 442 785-2: *The incomparable
Alfredo Kraus.* Music of Offenbach,
Cilea, Donizetti, Gounod, Meyerbeer,
Delibes, and Strauss. *Kraus, tenor; Welsh
National Opera; Rizzi, cond.*
• ARG 9-10/95: 289
• Fa 1-2/96: 362
+ Fa 3-4/96: 336
+ Gr 8/95: 130

28606. 442 787-2: BEETHOVEN—Piano
sonatas no. 23-25, 27. *Brendel, piano.*
+ ARG 1-2/96: 84
+ Fa 1-2/96: 145
• Gr 11/95: 120

28607. 442 795-2: SKALKOTTAS—Quartets
for piano and winds no. 1-2; Concertino
for oboe and piano; Sonata concertante
for bassoon and piano; Concertino for
trumpet and piano. *Holliger, oboe;
Thunemann, bassoon; Hardenberger,
trumpet; Canino, piano.*
+ Gr 10/95: 88

28608. 442 796-2 (2 discs):
TCHAIKOVSKY—Iolanta. *Gorchakova,
Grigoryan, Hvorostovsky, Alexashkin,
Putilin; Kirov Opera; Gergiev, cond.*
+ ARG 9-10/96: 215
• Fa 9-10/96: 341
+ Gr 7/96: 109

28609. 442 902-2 (2 discs): BERLIOZ—
Symphonic fantastique; Overtures;
Harold in Italy. *Imai, viola; London
Symphony Orch.; Davis, cond.* Reissues.
+ Gr 10/94: 100

28610. 446 001-2: SCHUBERT—Trout
quintet. MOZART—Piano quartet no. 1.

*Zehetmair, violin; Zimmermann, viola;
Duven, cello; Riegelbauer, double bass;
Brendel, piano.*
+ Fa 5-6/96: 262
+ Fi 5/96: 134
+ Gr 1/96: 72

28611. 446 002-2: Music of Lagoya,
Granados, Albéniz, Villa-Lobos, Sanz,
Carcassi, Tárrega, and Marcello. *Lagoya,
guitar; Academy of St. Martin-in-the-
Fields; Sillito, cond.*
+ Fa 9-10/96: 438
• Gr 10/96: 68

28612. 446 047-2 (14 discs): WAGNER—
Ring des Nibelungen. *Adam, Windgassen,
Neidlinger, Nilsson; Bayreuth Festival;
Böhm, cond.* Recorded 1966-67.
• Gr 10/94: 204

28613. 446 062-2: SHOSTAKOVICH—
Symphony no. 8. *Kirov Orch., St.
Petersburg; Gergiev, cond.*
• ARG 11-12/96: 210
• Fa 9-10/96: 323
• Gr 8/95: 82

28614. 446 064-2: *The healing harp.*
Music of Spohr, Rosetti, Debussy,
Prokofiev, Casella, Damase, Renié,
Tournier, and Fauré. *Yoshino, harp.*
+ Fa 7-8/96: 376
+ Gr 2/96: 80

28615. 446 066-2: VIVALDI—Bassoon
concertos, RV 472, 482, 484, 492, 494,
495, 499. *Thunemann, bassoon; I
Musici.*
+ Gr 2/96: 63

28616. 446 067-2 (6 discs): BEETHOVEN—
Symphonies; Overtures. *Staatskapelle
Dresden; C. Davis, cond.*
+ Gr 12/95: 73

28617. 446 073-2 (2 discs): HAYDN—Die
Schöpfung. *Orgonasova, Rodgers,
Ainsley, Schulte, Vollestad; Gulbenkian
Foundation Chorus; Orch. of the
Eighteenth Century; Brüggen, cond.*
• Gr 5/96: 99

28618. 446 078-2 (2 discs): PROKOFIEV—
The fiery angel. *Gorchakova, Leiferkus,
Markova-Mikhailenko, Pluzhnikov,
Alexashkin, Ognovienko; Kirov Orch. &
Chorus; Gergiev, cond.* Recorded live
1993.
+ ARG 5-6/96: 164
• Fa 3-4/96: 246
+ Gr 1/96: 103
+ ON 2/17/96: 40

28619. 446 081-2: *The echoing air.*
PURCELL—Songs with orchestra. *McNair,
soprano; Academy of Ancient Music;
Hogwood, cond.*
+ ARG 9-10/95: 195
+ Gr 9/95: 94
+ ON 10/95: 47

28620. 446 082-2: BEETHOVEN—Piano
concertos no. 3-4. *Uchida, piano; Royal
Concertgebouw Orch.; Sanderling, cond.*
• ARG 11-12/96: 88
• Fa 11-12/96: 180
• Gr 5/96: 54

28621. 446 084-2: FAURÉ—Requiem, op.
48; Pavane, op. 50. KOECHLIN—Choral sur
le nom de Fauré. SCHMITT—In memoriam,
op. 72: No. 2, Scherzo sur le nom de
Gabriel Fauré. RAVEL—Pavane pour une
infante défunte. *McNair, soprano; Allen,
baritone; Chorus & Academy of St.
Martin-in-the-Fields; Marriner, cond.*
- ARG 5-6/96: 111
+ Fa 5-6/96: 151
+ Gr 1/96: 88

28622. 446 085-2: SCHOENBERG—
Verklärte Nacht. STRAUSS—Capriccio:
Finale. STRAVINSKY—Apollo. *Saito Kinen
Orch.; Ozawa, cond.*
• Gr 6/96: 56

28623. 446 086-2: SCHUMANN—
Dichterliebe; Liederkreis; Heine-Lieder.
Holzmair, baritone; Cooper, piano.
+ ARG 1-2/96: 169
+ Fa 1-2/96: 304
+ Gr 9/95: 95
+ ON 8/96: 43

28624. 446 091-2: JANÁČEK—Violin
sonata. PROKOFIEV—Violin sonata no. 1.
DEBUSSY—Violin sonata. *Mullova, violin;
Anderszewski, piano.*
+ ARG 7-8/96: 170
+ Fa 5-6/96: 177
+ Fi 4/96: 131
• Gr 1/96: 70

28625. 446 092-2: ARRIAGA—String
quartets no. 1-3. *Guarneri Quartet.*
• Gr 7/96: 68

28626. 446 093-2: BEETHOVEN—Piano
sonatas no. 26, 29. *Brendel, piano.*
+ ARG 11-12/96: 91
• Fa 11-12/96: 186
+ Gr 8/96: 71

28627. 446 094-2: BERIO—Canticum
novissimi testamenti no. 2; Sinfonia.
*London Sinfonietta Voices; Rascher
Saxophone Quartet; Electric Phoenix;
Orch. de Paris; Bychkov, cond.*
• Gr 7/96: 84

28628. 446 097-2 (2 discs): ROSSINI—
Petite messe solennelle; Messa di Milano.
*Focile, Mentzer, Giménez, Alaimo;
Academy of St. Martin-in-the-Fields;
Marriner, cond.*
• Gr 1/96: 91

28629. 446 100-2: SCHUBERT—
Symphonies no. 2-3, 5. *Orch. of the 18th
Century; Brüggen, cond.*
• Gr 7/96: 62

28630. 446 131-2: TCHAIKOVSKY—Violin
concerto, op. 35. SIBELIUS—Violin

PHILIPS

concerto, op. 47. *Josefowicz, violin; Academy of St. Martin-in-the-Fields; Marriner, cond.*
+ Fa 1-2/96: 320
+ Gr 1/96: 64

28631. 446 157, 446 170-2 (2 2-disc sets): SIBELIUS—Symphonies (complete); Tone poems; Violin concerto. *Boston Symphony Orch.; Davis, cond.* Reissues.
+ ARG 11-12/95: 206

28632. 446 166-2 (2 discs): TCHAIKOVSKY—Sleeping beauty. *Concertgebouw Orch.; Dorati, cond.* Reissue.
• ARG 11-12/95: 219

28633. 446 169-2 (2 discs): VIVALDI—Estro armonica. *Michelucci, violin; I Musici.* Reissue.
+ ARG 11-12/95: 226

28634. 446 172-2 (2 discs): BRAHMS—Quintets (complete). *W. Haas, piano; Berlin Phil. Octet.* Reissue.
+ ARG 11-12/95: 94

28635. 446 192-2: GRIEG—Piano concerto; Piano sonata, op. 7. SCHUMANN—Piano concerto. *Kovacevich, Kocsis, pianos; BBC Symphony Orch.; C. Davis, cond.* Reissue.
+ Gr 6/96: 46

28636. 446 195-2: MAHLER—Symphony no. 8. *Cotrubas, Harper, Bork, Finnilä, Dieleman, Cochran, Prey, Sotin; chorus; Concertgebouw Orch.; Haitink, cond.* Reissue.
+ ARG 1-2/96: 136
• Gr 1/96: 56

28637. 446 199-2 (2 discs): RACHMANINOFF—Works for piano and orchestra. *Kocsis, piano; San Francisco Symphony Orch.; Waart, cond.* Reissue.
+ Gr 7/96: 62

28638. 446 200-2: LISZT—Piano concertos; Sonata. *Richter, piano; London Symphony Orch.; Kondrashin, cond.* Reissues.
+ Gr 11/95: 88

28639. 446 202-2: BERLIOZ—Symphonie fantastique; Roméo et Juliette: Love scene; Queen Mab scherzo. *Concertgebouw Orch.; London Symphony Orch.; C. Davis, cond.* Reissue.
+ Gr 6/96: 42

28640. 446 220-2: RACHMANINOFF—Piano sonata no. 2 (original version); Piano pieces. *Kocsis, piano.*
+ Gr 2/96: 76

28641. 446 328-2 (2 discs): PENDERECKI—Die Teufeln von Loudun. *Troyanos, Hiolski, Ladysz, Sotin; Hamburg State Opera; Janowski, cond.*

Reissue.
+ Gr 6/96: 95

28642. 446 331-2 (2 discs): TIPPETT—The knot garden; A child of our time. *Minton, Gomez, Barstow, Tear, Norman, Baker, Cassilly, Shirley-Quirk; BBC Singers; BBC Choral Society; Orch. of the Royal Opera House, Covent Garden; BBC Symphony Orch.; C. Davis, cond.* Reissue; recorded 1974-75.
+ Gr 9/95: 109

28643. 446 332-2: VIVALDI—Tito Manlio. *Marshall, Hamari, Finnilä, Trimarchi, Ahnsjö; Berlin Radio Chorus; Berlin Chamber Orch.; Negri, cond.* Reissue; recorded 1978.
+ Gr 7/96: 109
+ Op 4/97: 491

28644. 446 337-2 (3 discs): WAGNER—Lohengrin. *Thomas, Silja, Varnay, Vinay; Bayreuth Festival; Sawallisch, cond.* Recorded 1962.
• Gr 12/95: 164

28645. 446 366-2: BARTÓK—Piano concertos no. 1-3. *Kocsis, piano; Budapest Festival Orch.; Fischer, cond.* Reissues.
+ Gr 12/95: 72

28646. 446 368-2 (4 discs): BARTÓK—Piano music. *Kocsis, piano.*
+ Fa 1-2/96: 131
+ Fi 3/96: 113

28647. 446 405-2: Verdi and Tchaikovsky arias. *Gorchakova, soprano; Kirov Orch.; Gergiev, cond.*
+ ARG 9-10/96: 265
+ Fa 9-10/96: 371
+ Gr 3/96: 102
+ Op 4/96: 476

28648. 446 406-2: BERLIN—Heat wave. Patti Lupone sings Irving Berlin. *Lupone, vocalist; Hollywood Bowl Orch.; Mauceri, cond.*
+ Gr 11/95: 154

28649. 446 407-2: SCHUBERT—Winterreise. *Holzmair, baritone; Cooper, piano.*
+ ARG 7-8/96: 189
+ Fa 7-8/96: 293
+ Gr 5/96: 102
+ ON 8/96: 43

28650. 446 452-2 (2 discs): HAYDN—Keyboard concertos. *Koopman, keyboards; Musica Antiqua Amsterdam; Amsterdam Baroque Orch.*
• ARG 9-10/96: 132

28651. 446 472-2: BARTÓK—Rhapsody; Scherzo. DOHNÁNYI—Variations on a nursery theme. *Kocsis, piano; Budapest Festival Orch.; Fischer, cond.* Reissues.
+ Gr 4/96: 40

28652. 446 527-2, 446 530-2 (2 discs each): DVOŘÁK—Symphonies (complete); Hussites; My home. *London Symphony Orch.; Rowicki, cond.* Recorded 1960s.
• ARG 7-8/96: 107

28653. 446 554-2 (2 discs): LISZT—Piano music. *Dichter, piano.* Reissues.
+ ARG 9-10/96: 154

28654. 446 580-2: BRUCKNER—Symphony no. 7. *Concertgebouw Orch.; Haitink, cond.* Reissue.
+ Gr 6/96: 42

28655. 446 624-2: BEETHOVEN—Piano sonatas no. 4, 15, 20. *Brendel, piano.*
+ Gr 2/96: 73

28656. 446 657-2: GRAINGER—Danny boy: songs and dancing ballads. *Monteverdi Choir; English Country Gardiner Orch.; Gardiner, cond.*
+ ARG 11-12/96: 130
+ Fa 9-10/96: 206
+ Fa 11-12/96: 257
+ Fi 10/96: 151
+ Gr 4/96: 93

28657. 446 666-2: SVIRIDOV—Russia cast adrift. RACHMANINOFF—Nine songs. *Hvorostovsky, baritone; Arkadiev, piano.*
+ ARG 11-12/96: 219
+ Fa 11-12/96: 390
+ Fi 10/96: 153
+ Gr 8/96: 87
• ON 8/96: 43

28658. 446 669-2 (2 discs): VERDI—Ernani. *Lamberti, Sass, Miller, Kováts; Hungarian State Opera; Gardelli, cond.* Reissue.
+ Gr 8/96: 95

28659. 446 672-2: SATIE—Sarabandes; Gymnopédies; Gnossiennes; Ogives; Petite ouverture. *Leeuw, piano.*
• ARG 1-2/97: 163
• Fa 11-12/96: 356
+ Gr 2/96: 76

28660. 446 673-2: RACHMANINOFF—Piano concerto no. 3. TCHAIKOVSKY—Piano concerto no. 1. *Argerich, piano; Berlin Radio Orch.; Chailly, cond.; Bavarian Radio Orch.; Kondrashin, cond.* Recorded live 1982 (Rachmaninoff).
+ ARG 1-2/96: 156
+ Gr 8/95: 80

28661. 446 675-2: BACH—Violin concertos no. 1-2; Concerto for violin, and oboe. *Mullova, violin; Leleux, oboe; Mullova Ensemble.*
+ ARG 1-2/97: 63
• Fa 11-12/96: 169
• Gr 8/96: 41

28662. 446 676-2: BERLIOZ—Harold en Italie; Tristia: Méditation religieuse; La mort d'Ophélie; Marche funèbre pour la dernière scène d'Hamlet. *Caussé, viola; Monteverdi Choir; Orch. Révolutionnaire*

et Romantique; Gardiner, cond.
- ARG 1-2/97: 72
- Fa 11-12/96: 189
+ Gr 8/96: 42

28663. 446 683-2: SCHOENBERG—
Chamber symphonies no. 1-2; Piano
concerto. *Brendel, piano; Southwest
German Radio Orch. Baden-Baden;
Gielen, cond.*
+ ARG 1-2/97: 164
+ Fa 1-2/97: 251
- Gr 9/96: 60

28664. 446 714-2: SCHUMANN—
Symphonies no. 2-3. *Vienna Phil. Orch.;
Muti, cond.*
- Gr 8/96: 56

28665. 446 818-2: ARLEN—Come rain or
come shine: the Harold Arlen songbook.
*McNair, vocals; Previn, piano; Finck,
double bass.*
- Fa 11-12/96: 161
- Fi 10/96: 153

28666. 446 920-2 (25 discs): *The art of
Alfred Brendel.* Music of Haydn, Mozart,
Beethoven, Schubert, Liszt, Brahms, and
Schumann. *Brendel, piano.* Reissues.
+ Gr 2/96: 80

28667. 452 253-2 (2 discs):
TCHAIKOVSKY—Orchestra suites.
Philharmonia Orch.; Dorati, cond.
Reissue.
+ ARG 1-2/97: 182

28668. 454 032, 454 035, 454 038-2 (3
2-disc sets): BEETHOVEN—Symphonies;
Choral fantasy; Overtures. *Gewandhaus
Orch.; Masur, cond.; London Phil.
Orch.; Haitink, cond.* Reissues.
+ ARG 1-2/97: 70

28669. 454 011-2 (2 discs): BACH—
Violin sonatas. *Grumiaux, violin;
Jaccottet, harpsichord; Mermoud, cello.*
Reissue.
- ARG 1-2/97: 65

28670. 454 014-2 (2 discs): MAHLER—
Das Lied von der Erde;
Kindertotenlieder; Lieder eines fahrenden
Gesellen; Des Knaben Wunderhorn.
*Baker, King, Prey, Norman, Shirley-
Quirk; Concertgebouw Orch.; Haitink,
cond.* Reissues.
+ ARG 11-12/96: 155

28671. 454 017-2 (2 discs): BRAHMS—
Piano quartets; Trio in A. *Beaux Arts
Trio; Trampler, viola.* Reissues.
+ ARG 11-12/96: 99

28672. 454 020-2 (2 discs): WAGNER—
Der Ring des Nibelungen: Highlights.
*Nilsson, Rysanek, Windgassen, King,
Adam; Bayreuth Festival; Böhm, cond.*
Recorded 1967.
+ ARG 11-12/96: 231

28673. 454 143-2: ZAWINUL—Stories of
the Danube. *Zawinul, keyboards, vocals;
Chatterjee, guitar, vocals; Öçal, oud,
percussion, vocals; Tuncboyaci,
percussion, vocals; Czech State Phil.
Orch.; Richter, cond.*
- Fa 11-12/96: 424

28674. 314528922-2: McCARTNEY-
AUBUT-MARTIN—Variations concertantes.
BENJAMIN—Hymn to the child;
Reminiscences. BARKER—Double-march.
LACOMBE—Le Capitaine Bonhomme.
RUFF—Le pirate Maboule; Sol et gobelet;
Grujot et delicat; Monsieur Surprise.
AUBUT—Children of Sarajevo. *Aubut,
guitar; Marchand, Moisan, woodwinds;
Claudel String Quartet.*
- Fa 5-6/96: 208

PHOENIX

28675. PHCD 101: MENOTTI—Sebastian.
LUENING—Lyric scene; Legend. *Øien,
flute; Larsen, oboe; London Symphony
Orch.; Oslo Phil. Orch.; Serebrier, cond.*
+ ARG 11-12/90: 80
+ Fa 11-12/89: 281

28676. PHCD 102: ARNOLD—Four
Scottish dances; Symphony no. 3.
London Phil. Orch.; Arnold, cond.
□ Fa 11-12/89: 102

28677. PHCD 103: MOORE—Devil and
Daniel Webster. *Winters, Blankenship;
Festival Choir & Orch.; Aliberti, cond.*
- ARG 11-12/90: 83
+ Fa 11-12/89: 285

28678. PHCD 104: BRITTEN—Scottish
ballad. MARTINŮ—Concerto for two
pianos and orchestra; Fantasie for two
pianos; Three Czech dances. *Pierce,
Jonas, pianos; Luxembourg Radio
Symphony Orch.; Stratta, cond.*
- Fa 11-12/91: 289

28679. PHCD 105: BARBER—Piano
sonata. CUMMING—Twenty-four preludes.
Browning, piano.
+ Fa 11-12/89: 122

28680. PHCD 106: FINE—Symphony
1962; Toccata concertante; Serious song.
*Boston Symphony Orch.; Fine, Leinsdorf,
cond.*
+ ARG 11-12/90: 55
+ Fa 7-8/90: 144

28681. PHCD 107: MENNIN—Symphony
no. 4. GINASTERA—Milena. *Curtin,
sorano; Camerata Singers and Symphony
Orch.; Denver Symphony Orch.; Kaplan,
Priestman, cond.*
+ ARG 11-12/90: 80
+ Fa 7-8/90: 200

28682. PHCD 108: ROREM—Poems of
love and the rain; Four madrigals; From
an unknown past. *Wolff, mezzo-soprano;
Rorem, piano; Modern Madrigal Quartet.*
+ ARG 1-2/91: 83

+ DA 1/91: 70
+ Fa 7-8/90: 238

28683. PHCD 109: JANÁČEK—Capriccio;
Concertino; Youth; Nursery rhymes for
mixed voices and chamber ensemble.
*Somer, piano; Caramoor Festival Orch.;
Rudel, cond.*
+ ARG 7-8/90: 60

28684. PHCD 110: GINASTERA—Piano
sonata no. 1; Piano concerto no. 1.
*Somer, piano; Vienna Phil. Orch.;
Maerzendorfer, cond.*
+ ARG 7-8/90: 50
- Fa 7-8/90: 150

28685. PHCD 111: BARBER—Souvenirs:
ballet suite; Canzonetta for oboe and
strings. BRITTEN—Les illuminations;
Young Apollo. *Girdwood, oboe; Farley,
soprano; Evans, piano; London
Symphony Orch.; Scottish Chamber
Orch.; Serebrier, cond.*
+ Fa 11-12/91: 253

28686. PHCD 112: YARDUMIAN—
Armenian suite; Symphony no. 2.
*Chookasian, alto; Utah Symphony Orch.;
Kojian, cond.*
+ ARG 3-4/91: 139
+ Fa 3-4/91: 434
+ HPR v.8, no.2: 80

28687. PHCD 113: HUSA—String quartets
no. 2-3; Evocations of Slovakia, for
clarinet, viola, and cello. *Fine Arts
Quartet; Long Island Chamber Ensemble.*
+ Fa 3-4/91: 244

28688. PHCD 114: SCRIABIN—Preludes,
op. 11, op. 74; Poem, op. 32, no. 1.
Laredo, piano.
+ Fa 3-4/91: 381

28689. PHCD 115: *Gerard Schwarz
performs new music for trumpet.* Music
of Brant, Carter, Moryl, Whittenberg, and
Wolpe. *Schwarz, Ranger, Rosenzweig,
trumpets; instrumental ensemble; Brant,
cond.*
+ Fa 3-4/91: 493

28690. PHCD 116: ROREM—War scenes;
Five songs to poems by Walt Whitman;
Four dialogues for 2 voices and 2 pianos.
Various performers.
+ ARG 3-4/92: 128
+ Fa 3-4/92: 297

28691. PHCD 117: KHACHATURIAN—Piano
concerto. PROKOFIEV—Piano concerto no.
1. SHOSTAKOVICH—Piano concerto no. 2.
*Pierce, piano; Berlin Radio Symphony
Orch.; Slovenian Radio Symphony Orch.;
Freeman, cond.*
- Fa 1-2/92: 245

28692. PHCD 118: HARRISON—Pacifika
rondo; Four pieces for harp; Two pieces
for psaltery; Music for violin with various
instruments. *Oakland Youth Orch.;
Hughes, cond.; Boughton, violin;*

PHOENIX

Bellows, harp; Harrison, psalteries.
+ ARG 7-8/92: 145
+ Fa 1-2/92: 231

28693. PHCD 119: GRAINGER—
Lincolnshire posy and other works for
concert band. BRITTEN—Simple
symphony. WARLOCK—Capriol suite.
*UCLA Wind Ensemble; Westbrook,
cond.; Rome Chamber Orch.; Flagello,
cond.*
+ Fa 1-2/92: 223

28694. PHCD 120: MAYER—Two pastels;
Andante for strings. SKROWACZEWSKI—
Concerto for English horn and orchestra.
*Stacey, English horn; Minnesota Orch.;
Skrowaczewski, cond.* Reissue.
+ ARG 3-4/92: 141
+ Fa 1-2/92: 262

28695. PHCD 121: SCHOENBERG—
Concerto for string quartet and orchestra;
Trio for strings, op. 45. *Lenox Quartet;
London Symphony Orch.; Farberman,
cond.*
• Fa 3-4/93: 273

28696. PHCD 122: LADERMAN—Concerto
for orchestra. BRITTEN—Diversions on a
theme, op. 21. *Fleisher, piano; Baltimore
Symphony Orch.; Comissiona, cond.*
Reissue.
• ARG 7-8/93: 74
• Fa 3-4/93: 202

28697. PHCD 123: ROREM—Day music;
Night music. *J. Laredo, Carlyss, violins;
R. Laredo, Schein, piano.* Reissue;
recorded 1973-74.
+ Fa 3-4/93: 260
+ Gr 9/94: 76

28698. PHCD 124: RESPIGHI—Toccata for
piano and orchestra. CASELLA—Partita for
piano and orchestra. RACHMANINOFF—
Rhapsody on a theme of Paganini. *Pierce,
piano; Symphony Orch. of RTV Slovenia;
Nanut, cond.*
+ Fa 3-4/93: 257

28699. PHCD 125: FLAGELLO—
Contemplazioni di Michelangelo;
Lautrec; Capriccio for cello and
orchestra; Remembrance; She walks in
beauty. *Soloists; Orch. Sinfonica di
Roma; Flagello, cond.*
• Fa 3-4/93: 161

28700. PHCD 126: ROREM—Ariel;
Gloria; King Midas. *Curtin, Vanni,
Walker, Stewart, vocalists; Rabbai,
clarinet; Edwards, Rorem, Schein, piano.*
Reissues.
+ ARG 11-12/96: 190

28701. PHCD 127: BRANT—Kingdom
come; Machinations. *Brant, various
instruments; Oakland Symphony Orch.;
Samuel, cond.; Oakland Youth Orch.;
Hughes, cond.* Reissues.
+ ARG 1-2/97: 83

28702. PHCD 128: HUSA—Divertimento;
Fantasies; The Trojan women: Excerpts.
*Orch. de Paris; Brno State Orch.; Husa,
cond.*
+ ARG 11-12/96: 147

28703. PHCD 129: ARGENTO—To be sung
on the water. BRITTEN—Michelangelo
sonnets; Abraham and Isaac. *Stewart,
tenor; Shade, soprano; Russo, clarinet;
Katz, Hassard, piano.* Reissues.
+ ARG 11-12/96: 78

28704. PHCD 505: DONIZETTI—Caterina
Cornaro; Arias by Donizetti, Bellini,
Rossini, and Verdi. *Caballé, Aragall,
Meloni, Edwards, Howell; Radio France
Orch.; Masini, cond.* Recorded live
1973-74.
+ ARG 1-2/96: 103

28705. PHCD 506: VERDI—Jerusalem
(sung in Italian); I due Foscari (excerpts).
*Gencer, Aragall, Guelfi; Teatro La
Fenice; Gavazzeni, Serafin, conds.*
Recorded live 1963, 1957.
• ARG 1-2/96: 191

28706. PHCD 904: LALO—Songs. *Zylis-
Gara, soprano; Ivaldi, piano.*
+ ARG 3-4/96: 141

PHONO SUECIA

28707. PSCD 12: PETTERSSON—
Symphony no. 14. *Stockholm Phil. Orch.;
Comissiona, cond.*
□ Fa 3-4/87: 181

28708. PSCD 21: LINDGREN—Fragments
of a circle; Bowijaw; Shadowes that in
darknesse dwell; Guggi-guggi. *Various
performers.*
+ Fa 9-10/93: 205

28709. PSCD 22: MELLNÄS—Nocturnes;
Rendez-vous; L'infinito; Transparence.
*Höglind, mezzo-soprano; Stevensson,
clarinet; Sparnaay, bass clarinet;
Sonanza Ensemble; Risberg, cond.;
Swedish Radio Chorus; Ericson, cond.;
Swedish Radio Symphony Orch.;
Westerberg, cond.*
□ Fa 7-8/89: 181

28710. PSCD 23: MAROS—Symphonies
no. 1, 3; Four songs from Gitanjali;
Saxophone concerto. *Various performers.*
+ Fa 9-10/93: 210

28711. PSCD 24: BÖRTZ—Selections.
*Maros, soprano; Scholz, Persson, pianos;
Lundkvist, organ; Stockholm Phil. Orch.;
Wolff, cond.; Stockholm Chamber Choir;
Ericson, cond.*
+ Fa 1-2/89: 134

28712. PSCD 25: Hägerstens Motettkör.
Music of Sandström, Jennefelt, Sagvik,
Tykesson, and Förare. *Hägersten Motet
Choir; Mänsson, cond.; Tykesson, organ.*
+ Fa 9-10/93: 348

28713. PSCD 27: RÓZMANN—Images of
the dream of death. *Electronic music.*
□ Fa 9-10/92: 338

28714. PSCD 31 (2 discs): *Organo con
forza.* Music of Ericsson, Hanson, Ligeti,
Scott, Lützow-Holm, Morthenson,
Sandström, Mellnäs, Feiler, and Ungvary.
Ericsson, organ.
□ Fa 3-4/89: 370

28715. PSCD 35: LIDHOLM—Laudi; Canto
LXXXI. WERLE—Canzone 126 di
Petrarca, op. 6; Trees. *Stockholm
Chamber Choir; Swedish Radio Chorus;
Ericson, cond.*
+ Fa 1-2/89: 190

28716. PSCD 35, 38, 44 (3 separate
discs): *Swedish contemporary vocal
music, vol. 1-3.* Music of Lidholm, Werle,
Bäck, Edlund, Mellnäs, Maros, J.
Sandström, Hillborg, Eliasson, Jennefelt,
and S.D. Sandström. *Stockholm Chamber
Choir; Swedish Radio Choir; Eric
Ericson Chamber Choir; Ericson, cond.*
+ Fa 9-10/92: 409

28717. PSCD 49: HOLEWA—String trio;
Piano concerto; Concertinos VIII-IX;
Duettinos I-II. *Various performers.*
Reissue.
+ Fa 11-12/92: 261

28718. PSCD 52: HILLBORG—Music of
Hillborg. *Various performers.*
+ Fa 3-4/93: 190

28719. PSCD 53: NILSSON—Ariel; Five
orchestral pieces for piano; Cadenze;
Concerto per organo ed orchestra.
*Jahren, oboe; Tapiola Sinfonietta;
Engeset, cond.; Pöntinen, piano;
KammarensembleN; Krook, cond.;
Lundkvist, organ; Stockholm Phil. Orch.;
Willén, cond.*
+ Fa 11-12/94: 322

28720. PSCD 55: KOCH—Nordic
capriccio; Two Scandinavian dances;
Saxophone concerto; Swedish dance
rhapsody; Characters, for violin and
piano. *Swedish Radio Symphony Orch.;
Munich Phil. Orch.; Westerberg, cond.;
Rascher, saxophone; Röhn, violin;
Hindart, piano.*
+ Fa 9-10/92: 269

28721. PSCD 57: *KammarensembleN:
the Swedish ensemble for new music.*
Music of Eliasson, Strindberg,
Hambraeus, Valkare, and Ekstrom.
KammarensembleN; Krook, cond.
+ Fa 3-4/93: 388

28722. PSCD 58 (3 discs): *Föreningen
svenska tonsättare (The Society of
Swedish Composers), 1918-1993.*
Anthology of the works of 29 Swedish
composers issued for the 75th
anniversary of the Society. *Various
Swedish orchs. & soloists.*
+ Fa 11-12/94: 506

28723. PSCD 62: *Möte med musik.* Music of Bjork, Magnell, Brandquist, Bjorkman, Johansson, Unge/Mansfield, Lundblad, Hambe, Andersson, Steijen, Thornquist, Ramquist, Goransson, Hansson, Gerthel, and Kullenberg. *Various performers.*
  + Fa 9-10/93: 393

28724. PSCD 66: BERGLUND—The universe within. *Berglund, performer.*
  - Fa 1-2/94: 131

28725. PSCD 68: JENNEFELT—Dichterliebe I-X; Music by a mountain; Music to a cathedral-builder; Warning to the rich. *Swedish Radio Choir; Chamber Choir of the Royal University College of Music in Stockholm; Sjökvist, cond.; Fredriksson, baritone; Swedish Radio Symphony Orch.; Koivula, cond.; Sonanza; Risberg, cond.*
  + Fa 11-12/94: 266

28726. PSCD 71: BERGLUND—The saga of the Nordic gods. *Berglund, performer.*
  - Fa 1-2/94: 131

28727. PSCD 73: GEFORS—Christina-scencr; En obol; Whales weep not!; L'invitation au voyage. *Soloists; Swedish Radio Symphony Orch.; Swedish Radio Choir; Willén, cond.*
  + Fa 1-2/95: 161

28728. PSCD 75: FAHLSTRÖM—Animations. *Ericsson, organ; Norbotten Big Band; Fahlström, cond.*
  □ Fa 11-12/94: 224

28729. PSCD 76: JOHANSON—Symphonie chez nous (Symphony no. 10); Trio for clarinet, cello, and piano; String quartet no. 7. *Gothenburg Symphony Orch.; Sundkvist, cond.; Kingstedt, clarinet; Lavotha, cello; Wallin, piano; Saga Quartet.*
  + Fa 5-6/95: 228

PHONOGRAPHE

28730. 5006 (2 discs): PUCCINI—Manon Lescaut. *Zamboni, Merli, Conati, Teatro La Scala; Molajoli, cond.* Recorded 1930.
  + ARG 11-12/95: 286
  - ON 9/95: 57

28731. 5013 (2 discs): BIZET—Carmen. *Buades, Pertile, Franci, Alfani; Teatro La Scala; Molajoli, cond.* Recorded 1933.
  + ARG 11-12/95: 284
  ● ON 9/95: 57

28732. 5020 (2 discs): J. STRAUSS, JR.—Gypsy baron. *Patzak, Preger, Zadek, Loose; Vienna Phil. Orch.; Krauss, cond.* Recorded 1950.
  ● ARG 7-8/95: 272
  + ON 8/95: 36

28733. 5035: *Celebrated Italian singers perform Italian songs.* Music of Tosti, Donaudy, Zardo, Cardillo, Arditi, Rossini, Denza, Scarlatti, Arona, Olivieri, Cottrau, Capua, Rotoli, Giordano, Masini, and Bixio. *Various vocalists.*
  ● ARG 3-4/96: 267

28734. 5039 (2 discs): Music of Mozart, Rossini, Verdi, Wagner, Brahms, Gounod, and Schubert. *Kipnis, bass.* Recorded 1927-42.
  + ARG 5-6/96: 275

PIANISSIME

28735. MAG 2018 (LP): Piano music of Albéniz, Longas, Granados, Turina, and Falla. *Gahnassia, piano.*
  + Fa 7-8/86: 276

28736. MAG 2022 (LP): LISZT—Music for 2 pianos and piano 4 hands. *Goldina, Loumbrozo, pianos.*
  ● ARG 3-4/87: 50
  + Fa 11-12/87: 165

28737. MAG 2025: RAVEL—Daphnis et Chloé: Suite no. 2 (arr. Garban-Millow); Rhapsodie espagnole; La valse (arr. Millow). *Job, Millow, pianos.*
  + Fa 7-8/87: 167

PIANISSIMO

28738. PP 10393: Music of Saint-Saëns, Debussy, Tchaikovsky, Brahms, MacDowell, and Liszt. *C. & A. Cann, pianos.*
  + Gr 5/93: 68

28739. PP 10394: SCRIABIN—Piano sonatas no. 3-5; Etudes, op. 8. *Matsuzawa, piano.*
  + Gr 6/94: 88

28740. PP 10792: CHABRIER—Piano music. *McMahon, piano.*
  ● Fa 11-12/92: 215
  + Gr 8/92: 54

28741. PP 11192: BENJAMIN—Caribbean dances. GRAINGER—Lincolnshire posy; Porgy and Bess fantasy. *Jones, McMahon, pianos.*
  + ARG 9-10/93: 96

28742. PP 20792: WEBER—Piano sonatas no. 1-2. *Jones, piano.* Reissue.
  ● Gr 9/92: 138

PICKWICK

28743. Duet 36: GLAZUNOV—Raymonda. *Bolshoi Theater Orch.; Zhuraitis, cond.*
  ● ARG 11-12/94: 116

28744. PWKS 4141: *Showstoppers.* Music of Bernstein, Boublil, Webber, Herman, Leigh, Sondheim, Bizet/Hammerstein, Schifrin/Koren, and Harnick. *Fisher, tenor; London Symphony Orch.; Weiss, cond.*
  ● Fa 1-2/94: 375

PIERRE VERANY

28745. PV-079812: SOR—Twenty etudes. *Battaglia, guitar.*
  - ARG 9-10/92: 166

28746. PV-087019: RIMSKY-KORSAKOV—Scheherazade. *Loire District Phil. Orch.; Soustrot, cond.*
  ● Fa 9-10/88: 239

28747. PV-087020: BACH—Organ music. *Brosse, organ.*
  ● Fa 9-10/88: 89

28748. PV-730020: BACH—Violin concertos no. 1-2; Concert for 2 violins, BWV 1043; Concerto for oboe and violin, BWV 1060. *Crenne, violin; Arrignon, oboe; Ensemble Instrumental de France; Bride, violin & cond.*
  ● Fa 11-12/89: 109

28749. PV-730046: TELEMANN—Suites and concertos. *Unnamed orch.; Kuentz, cond.*
  ● ARG 3-4/96: 196

28750. PV-730056: French Renaissance dance. *Compagnie Maitre Guillaume; Rousseau, cond.*
  ● ARG 9-10/96: 260

28751. PV-784011: *Organists at the court of the Sun King.* Music of Marchand, Clérambault, Dandrieu and Raison. *Bardon, organ.* Reissue.
  + ARG 3-4/92: 185

28752. PV-784093: CAMPRA—Motets. *Nicolas, soprano; Lasla, viola da gamba; Christie, organ.*
  + Fa 1-2/87: 82
  ● Gr 9/86: 422

28753. PV-785021: BACH—Toccatas and fugues. *Guillou, organ.*
  ● ARG 3-4/92: 20

28754. PV-785094: *Flûte et orgue à Notre-Dame de Paris.* Music of Marcello, Chopin, Vivaldi, Bizet, Corelli, Boehm, Bach, Ravel, Fibich, Fauré, and Miyagi. *Angelloz, flute; Batselaere, organ.*
  ● Fa 1-2/87: 250

28755. PV-786031: CHABRIER—España; Cortège burlesque; Romantic waltzes. INFANTE—Musiques d'Espagne; Andalusian dances. *Corre-Exerjean piano duo.*
  + ARG 3-4/92: 44

28756. PV-786091: LES SIX—Piano duets. *Corre, Exerjean, pianos.*
  + Gr 5/94: 68

28757. PV-786094: *Batailles à Versailles.* Music of Dandrieu, Couperin, Kuhnau, Kerll, Frescobaldi, and Byrd. *Brosse, harpsichord.*
  + Fa 9-10/87: 185

PIERRE VERANY

28758. PV-786101: CAMPRA—Didon; Arion; Hébé; Achille oisif; Daphné. *Nicolas, soprano; Cuiller, violin; Allain-Dupré, flute; Bernfeld, viola da gamba; Chapuis, harpsichord.*
+ Fa 9-10/87: 176

28759. PV-786102: DEBUSSY—String quartet in G minor. RAVEL—String quartet in F major. FAURÉ—String quartet, op. 121. *Quatuor Viotti.*
+ Fa 9-10/87: 188
- Gr 3/87: 1287

28760. PV-786103: Music of Albeniz, Dyens, Dumond, Kleynjans, Sor, Lauro, Mudarra, Tarrega, Pujol, LeRoy, Bach, Villa-Lobos, and Anon. *Dumond, guitar.*
- ARG 1-2/92: 153

28761. PV-786105: BEETHOVEN—Variations for flute and piano, op. 107, no. 3-4, 6-8, 10; Flute sonata, WoO Anh. 4. *Redel, flute; Hokanson, piano.*
+ Fa 11-12/87: 103

28762. PV-786111: CAMPRA—Tancrède (excerpts). *Bona, Dussault, Arapian; Vocal Ensemble of Avignon; Instrumental Ensemble of Provence; Zaffini, cond.*
□ ARG 1-2/92: 41

28763. PV-787022: RAVEL—La valse; Pavane pour une infante défunte; Valses nobles et sentimentales; Miroirs. *Dussaut, piano.*
- Fa 9-10/87: 273

28764. PV-787032: STRAVINSKY—Les noces. OHANA—Cantigas. *Choeur Contemporain; Les Percussions de Strasbourg; instrumental ensemble; Hayrabedian, cond.*
+ ARG 11-12/91: 155
• Fa 11-12/87: 237
+ Gr 10/87: 614

28765. PV-787033: MOZART—Music from Don Giovanni, Così fan tutte, and Die Zauberflöte. *Burgue Wind Ensemble.*
+ Fa 9-10/87: 249

28766. PV-787051: *Le concert des oiseaux à Versailles.* Music of Daquin, Rameau, Dandrieu, Couperin, Duphly, Kerll, Poglietti, Pasquini, and Anon. *Brosse, harpsichord.*
+ Fa 9-10/87: 372
- Gr 11/87: 788

28767. PV-787091: BACH—Organ concertos after Vivaldi and Johann Ernst von Saxe-Weimar. *Brosse, organ.*
+ Fa 3-4/88: 63

28768. PV-787092: Airs and dances of Shakespeare's time. *Elwes, tenor; Stubbs, lute; Musica Antiqua; Mendoze, cond.*
+ Gr 9/93: 106

28769. PV-787093: *Six Venetian concertos.* Music of Vivaldi, Sammartini, and Locatelli. *Mendoze, recorder; Concerto Köln.*
+ Fa 3-4/88: 230

28770. PV-787101: WALDTEUFEL—Galops, waltzes, and polkas. *Slovak Phil. Orch.; Redel, cond.*
+ ARG 3-4/92: 163
• Fa 3-4/88: 233

28771. PV-787102: MOZART—Divertimentos no. 1-3; Serenade no. 6. *Ensemble Instrumental de France; Bride, cond.*
+ Fa 7-8/88: 211

28772. PV-788011: ARUTJUNJAN—Trumpet concerto. HUMMEL—Trumpet concerto. JOLIVET—Trumpet concerto no. 2. *B. Soustrot, trumpet; Loire Phil. Orch.; M. Soustrot, cond.*
• ARG 11-12/88: 106
+ Fa 9-10/88: 335
+ Gr 1/89: 1138

28773. PV-788012: *Bass viol suites.* Music of Marais, Couperin, and Boismortier. *Re, viola da gamba; Kohnen, harpsichord.*
+ ARG 1-2/92: 168
• Fa 9-10/88: 194
• Gr 9/88: 439

28774. PV-788013: VIERNE—Organ symphony no. 1; Hymne au soleil; Clair de lune; Toccata, op. 53. *Houbart, organ.*
+ ARG 1-2/89: 99
+ Fa 9-10/88: 287
+ Gr 12/88: 1036

28775. PV-788051: MONTÉCLAIR—Morte de Didion; IVe. concert; Dépit généroux; Ier. concert; Retour de la paix. *Nicolas, soprano; Pariser Quartet.*
+ Fa 1-2/89: 210

28776. PV-788052: *La vielle à roue baroque.* Music of Chedeville, Baton, and Anon. *Poteur, hurdy-gurdy; Raskin, harpsichord; Gabriel, musette de cour.*
+ Fa 1-2/89: 328

28777. PV-788053: STAMITZ—Quartet in F major for orchestra. ZACH—Sinfonia no. 2. TUMA—Parthia in D minor. MYSLIVEČEK—Sinfonia in E major. *Musici de Praga; Vymer, cond.*
+ Fa 11-12/88: 348

28778. PV-788091: BRAHMS—Twenty-one Hungarian dances. *Budapest MAV Symphony Orch.; Redel, cond.*
- ARG 5-6/89: 26
• Fa 5-6/89: 144

28779. PV-788092: Trumpet music of Lully, Telemann, Corbett, Hertel, Pezel, Clarke, Philidor, and Albinoni. *Caens, trumpet & cond.; La Camerata de Bourgogne.*
+ Fa 5-6/89: 409

28780. PV-788111: POULENC—Choral music. *Provence Vocal Ensemble; Guy, cond.*
+ ARG 5-6/89: 77
• DA 9/89: 72
+ Fa 7-8/89: 214
• Gr 12/89: 1186

28781. PV-789011: Court of Alphonse X the wise. *Compagnie Médiévale.*
+ ARG 5-6/92: 173

28782. PV-789012: HÉROLD—Rondo, op. 7. JADIN—Sonata no. 2. CHARPENTIER—Bergères du Hammeau. ONSLOW—Sonata, op. 7. *Corre, Exerjean, piano.*
+ Fa 9-10/89: 446

28783. PV-789022: CORELLI—Recorder sonatas, op. 5: 7-12. *Ensemble La Serenata.*
+ ARG 5-6/92: 45

28784. PV-789023: Music of Barbella, Latilla, Mancini, Rubino, Porsile, and Anon. *Ensemble Musica Ficta.*
- Fa 1-2/90: 410

28785. PV-789051: MUSSORGSKY—Night on Bald Mountain (arr. Rimsky-Korsakov); Pictures at an exhibition (orch. Ravel). BORODIN—In the steppes of central Asia. *Orch. Philharmonique des Pays de la Loire; Soustrot, cond.*
• Fa 1-2/90: 251

28786. PV-789052: RIMSKY-KORSAKOV—Scheherazade. *Orch. Philharmonique des Pays de la Loire; Soustrot, cond.*
• Fa 1-2/90: 251

28787. PV-789054: Harpsichord music of C.P.E. Bach, M. Albéniz, Soler, Cimarosa, Mozart, Duphly, and Balbastre. *Brosse, harpsichord.*
+ DA 4/90: 62
+ Fa 5-6/90: 157

28788. PV-789091: CHOPIN—Preludes, op. 28; Ballade no. 1; Fantaisie in F minor, op. 49; Scherzo no. 1 in B minor. *Tacchino, piano.*
• Fa 5-6/90: 150
+ SR 2/90: 154

28789. PV-789092: Harpsichord music of L. Couperin, Lebègue, and Couperin. *Brosse, harpsichord.*
+ ARG 5-6/90: 43
+ DA 4/90: 62
• Fa 5-6/90: 157

28790. PV-789094: Harpsichord music of Mouchy, Balbastre, Dussek, and G.F. Couperin. *Brosse, harpsichord.*
+ DA 4/90: 62
• Fa 5-6/90: 157

28791. PV-789101: REICHA—Octet; Clarinet quintet. *Sajot, clarinet; Carl Stamitz Ensemble.*
• ARG 11-12/92: 185

28792. PV-789103: Music of Purcell, Telemann, Albinoni, Tomasi, Landowski, and Handel. *Soustrot, trumpet; Houbart, organ.*
+ Fa 9-10/88: 335

28793. PV-789104: BACH—Organ music. *Brosse, organ.*
+ ARG 9-10/90: 112
- Fa 9-10/90: 151

28794. PV-789105: SATIE—Piano music. *Tacchino, piano.*
+ ARG 7-8/90: 92
+ Fa 5-6/90: 275

28795. PV-790011: SCHUMANN—Symphonies no. 3-4. *Staatsorchester Rheinische Philharmonie; Redel, cond.*
- Fa 9-10/90: 384

28796. PV-790012: BRAHMS—Tragic overture; Symphony no. 4; Academic festival overture. *Philharmonia Hungarica; Redel, cond.*
+ Fa 9-10/90: 199

28797. PV-790013: A. SCARLATTI—Diana e Endimione; Ero e Leandro; Correa nel sen amato. *Nicolas, soprano; Aubin, countertenor; Deeks, Julien-Laferrière, violins; Williams, viola; Verzier, cello; Bothwell, bass viol; Ramin, harpsichord.*
+ ARG 9-10/90: 112
• Fa 9-10/90: 366
• Gr 9/90: 592

28798. PV-790031: GRIGNY—Organ book, pt. 1: Mass. *Bardon, organ.*
+ Fa 11-12/90: 206

28799. PV-790032: *Le piano-forte en France.* Music of J.L. Adam, Méhul, Jadin, Edelmann, Hüllmandel, and Dussek. *Raynaud, piano.*
• Fa 11-12/90: 432

28800. PV-790033: SCHUBERT—Octet, D. 803. *Ensemble Carl Stamitz.*
• Fa 11-12/90: 163
• Gr 11/90: 1000

28801. PV-790041: Music of Saint-Saëns, L. Lefébure-Wély, Blanc, Gouvy, and Pierné. *Corre, Exerjean, pianos.*
+ Fa 11-12/90: 433

28802. PV-790042: Ultreia! A pilgrimage to St. James of Compostela. *Polyphonia Antiqua.*
- ARG 5-6/92: 172

28803. PV-791031: SCHOENBERG—String quartet no. 1. *Manfred Quartet.*
+ Gr 4/94: 64

28804. PV-791042: SCHOBERT—Piano trios. *Concerto rococo.*
+ Gr 6/94: 78

28805. PV-791112: PROKOFIEV—Quartets no. 1, 2. *Manfred Quartet.*
+ ARG 11-12/92: 179

28806. PV-792011: MOLTER—Clarinet concertos no. 1-6. *Veilhan, clarinet; Academie Sainte Cecile, Couvert, cond.*
+ ARG 7-8/92: 179

28807. PV-792021: WEBER—Clarinet quintet; Piano quartet; Introduction, theme and variations. *Sajot, clarinet; Corre, piano; Carl Stamitz Ensemble.*
+ ARG 11-12/92: 230

28808. PV-792031: SCHOBERT—Harpsichord quartets no. 1-3; Sonata in E♭. *Concerto Rococo.*
• ARG 1-2/93: 144
+ Gr 12/92: 97

28809. PV-792032: CHAUSSON—String quartet. FRANCK—Piano quintet. *Athenaeum-Enescu Quartet; Tacchino, piano.*
• Gr 12/92: 94

28810. PV-792051: CHAUSSON—Symphony. FAURÉ—Pelléas et Mélisande; Pénélope: Prélude. *Loire Phil. Orch.; Soustrot, cond.*
• Gr 6/94: 46

28811. PV-792092: JANÁČEK—String quartets no. 1 "Kreutzer sonata," no. 2 "Intimate pages". *Quatuor Manfred.*
• Fa 3-4/93: 197

28812. PV-792111: SOLER—String quintets no. 3-5. *Concerto Rococo.*
+ Gr 4/94: 64

28813. PV-792192: FRANÇAIX—Octet; Clarinet quintet; Bassoon divertissement. *Sajot, clarinet; Wallez, bassoon; Ensemble Carl Stamitz.*
+ ARG 5-6/94: 92

28814. PV-793021: DUPHLY—Pièces de clavecin, book 1. *Raskin, harpsichord.*
+ Gr 3/94: 79

28815. PV-793032: DEMANTIUS—Dances and madrigals. *Amaryllis Consort; Brett, cond.; Musica Antiqua Toulon; Mendoze, cond.*
+ ARG 11-12/93: 99

28816. PV-793101: PEROTIN—Organa and motets. *Mora Vocis.*
- ARG 3-4/94: 132

28817. PV-793105: *L'orientale.* Music of Lagoya, Bach, Granados, Vivaldi, Marcello, and others. *S. Lagoya, guitar; Printemps, keyboard programming.*
- ARG 5-6/94: 176

28818. PV-793121: Music of Weber, Schumann, Hummel, Chausson, Vieuxtemps, Glazunov, and Fauré. *Verney, viola; Le Guay, piano.*
+ ARG 7-8/94: 219

28819. PV-794011: LECLAIR—1er récréation de musique, op. 6; 2me récréation de musique, op. 8. *Les Nièces*

de Rameau.
+ Gr 9/94: 74

28820. PV-794012: MESSIAEN—Quartet for the end of time. *Olivier Messiaen Quartet.*
• Gr 8/94: 68

28821. PV-794023: FRANÇAIX—Cello fantasy; Concert variations; Six pieces; Scuola di celli. *Demarquette, cello; Orch. de Bretagne; Françaix, cond.*
+ ARG 1-2/95: 106

28822. PV-794031: LALO—Piano trios. *Trio Henry.*
+ ARG 11-12/94: 140
+ Gr 8/94: 68

28823. PV-794032: FRESCOBALDI—Harpsichord music. *Stewart, harpsichord.*
+ ARG 11-12/94: 112

28824. PV-794033: VIVALDI—Stabat Mater; Nisi dominus; Flute concertos. *Brett, alto; Musica Antiqua of London; Mendoze, recorder & cond.*
• Gr 10/94: 186

28825. PV-794034: DANDRIEU—Premier livre d'orgue: Mass and vespers for Easter Sunday. GREGORIAN CHANT—Mass and vespers for Easter Sunday. *Paris Gregorian Choir; Tulve, cond.; Brosse, organ.*
+ Gr 6/95: 88

28826. PV-794041: PALESTRINA—Vergine bella; Motets. *Akademia; Lasserre, cond.; Stewart, organ.*
+ Gr 9/94: 91

28827. PV-794043: BALBASTRE—Sonatas op. 3. *Concerto Rococo.*
+ Gr 3/95: 60

28828. PV-794051: A. FORQUERAY—Pièces de viole: Selections (arr.). *Raskin, harpsichord.*
• Gr 2/95: 72

28829. PV-794052: MORLAYE—Music for guitar and lute. *Marincola, lute, guitar.*
+ Gr 2/95: 74

28830. PV-794091: DOWLAND—First booke of songs or ayres. *Elwes, tenor; Spaeter, lute.*
+ Gr 3/95: 82

28831. PV-794092 (2 discs): VIVALDI—Dorilla in tempe. *Kiehr, Elwes, Cantor, Nirouët; Nice Baroque Ensemble; Bezzina, cond.*
+ ARG 5-6/95: 191
• Gr 2/95: 104

28832. PV-794101: SCHUMANN—Romances; Adagio and allegro. KALLIWODA—Salon piece, op. 228. PIXIS—Sonata op. 35. *Capezzali, oboe; Chou, piano.*
+ ARG 7-8/95: 247

PIERRE VERANY

28833. PV-794111: PACHELBEL—
Musicalische Ergötzung. *Les Cyclopes.*
  + Gr 7/95: 80

28834. PV-794114: GRAUPNER—
Overture-suites. *Ensemble Mensa
Sonara; Maillet, cond.*
  • Gr 4/95: 52

28835. PV-795012: ANGLEBERT—Pièces
de clavecin: Suites in G major, G minor,
D minor. *Tramier, harpsichord.*
  + Gr 9/95: 80

28836. PV-795041: SMETANA—String
quartets. *Manfred Quartet.*
  • ARG 9-10/95: 216
  • Gr 12/95: 100

28837. PV-795051: BYRD—Harpsichord
works. GIBBONS—Harpsichord works.
Stewart, harpsichord.
  + Gr 3/96: 69

28838. PV-795101: Romantic cello.
Demarquette, cello; Guy, piano.
  • ARG 5-6/96: 232
  + Gr 4/96: 70

28839. PV-795111: PERGOLESI—La serva
padrona; Olimpiade: Overture.
*Poulenard, Cantor; Nice Baroque
Ensemble; Bezzina, cond.*
  + Gr 4/96: 114

28840. PV-796022: TELEMANN—Overture
"Hamburger Ebb und Fluth"; Overture-
suite in D major; Concerto for 2
recorders, 2 oboes, and strings in A
minor; Concerto for recorder, flute, and
strings in E minor. *Gauthier, flute;
Foulon, viola da gamba; Orch. Musica
Antiqua; Mendoze, recorder & cond.*
  + Gr 7/96: 66

28841. PV-796023: VIVALDI—Concertos
for multiple instruments, RV 555-556,
558-560. *Ensemble Matheus; Spinosi,
violin & cond.*
  + Gr 7/96: 66

PILZ

28842. CD 78004: FURTWÄNGLER—Piano
concerto (Symphonic concerto) in B
minor. *E. Fischer, piano; Berlin Phil.
Orch.; Furtwängler, cond.*
  • Fa 9-10/92: 239

28843. CD 160106: SCARLATTI—Sonatas.
Tomšič, piano.
  • Gr 11/93: 120

28844. 442055-2: MOZART—Don
Giovanni: Overture. SCHUBERT—Marches
caractéristiques. BEETHOVEN—Symphony
no. 5. *Staatskapelle Berlin; Suitner, cond.*
  + ARG 11-12/90: 139
  • Fa 3-4/91: 361

28845. 442058-2: WEBER—Euryanthe:
Overture. MOZART—Symphony no. 38.
Staatskapelle Dresden; Blomstedt, cond.

Recorded live 1973.
  + ARG 11-12/90: 139
  • Fa 3-4/91: 307

28846. 442059-2: BEETHOVEN—
Symphony no. 3. *Staatskapelle Dresden;
Blomstedt, cond.* Recorded live 1973.
  + Fa 3-4/91: 154

28847. 442060-2: SCHUBERT—
Rosamunde: Overture. LISZT—Piano
concerto no. 1. BEETHOVEN—Symphony
no. 8. *Ringeissen, piano; Dresden Phil.
Orch.; Masur, cond.*
  + ARG 11-12/90: 139
  • Fa 3-4/91: 362

28848. 442061-2: BACH—Cantatas BWV
44, 78, 112. *Werner, Schriever, Reiss,
Menzel, Polster; Thomanerchor Leipzig;
Gewandhaus Orch.; Rotzsch, cond.*
  • Fa 3-4/91: 130

28849. 442062-2: Music of Bach,
Messiaen, Ives, and Saint-Saëns.
*Gewandhaus Chamber Ensemble;
Pommer, cond.*
  + ARG 11-12/90: 139

28850. 442064-2: BRAHMS—Symphony
no. 2. MOZART—Symphony no. 40.
*Leipzig Radio Symphony Orch.; Kegel,
cond.*
  • Fa 3-4/91: 167

28851. 442067-2: BEETHOVEN—Piano
concerto no. 2; Symphony no. 7. *Zechlin,
piano; Berlin Radio Symphony Orch.;
Kleinart, cond.*
  • Fa 3-4/91: 362

28852. 442069-2: SCHUBERT—German
mass. HAYDN—Cassation in D major.
BEETHOVEN—Choral fantasy. *Kootz,
piano; Berlin Radio Chorus & Symphony
Orch.; Koch, cond.*
  + ARG 11-12/90: 139

28853. 442072-2: SCHUBERT—Overtures,
D. 470, D. 556, D. 648; Symphonies no.
2, 6. *Berlin Radio Symphony Orch.;
Rögner, cond.*
  • Fa 3-4/91: 361

28854. 442073-2: BEETHOVEN—King
Stephen: Overture. MOZART—Clarinet
concerto. BRAHMS—Serenade no. 2.
*Rumpler, clarinet; Berlin Radio
Symphony Orch.; Rögner, cond.*
  + ARG 11-12/90: 139
  - Fa 3-4/91: 148

28855. 442074-2: HAYDN—Symphony no.
96. MOZART—Symphony, K. 19. BIZET—
Jeux d'enfants. TCHAIKOVSKY—Capriccio
italien. *Berlin Radio Symphony Orch.;
Masur, cond.*
  • Fa 3-4/91: 131

28856. 442075-2: HAYDN—Symphony no.
69. SCHUBERT—Rondo for violin and
strings. MOZART—Divertimento no. 15.
Pietsch, violin; Berlin Radio Symphony

*Orch.; Leipzig Radio Symphony Orch.;
Pommer, cond.*
  + ARG 11-12/90: 139

28857. 442078-2: Music of Katzer,
Herchet, Goldmann, Wolschina and
Voigtländer. *Leipzig Radio Symphony
Orch.; Guhl, cond.; Scholze, organ;
Leipzig Radio Chorus; Weigle, cond.;
Brahms-Trio Weimar; Brauer, piano.*
  + Fa 3-4/91: 508

PISCITELLI

28858. 005: Arias and songs by Verdi,
Puccini, Leoncavallo, and others. *Rigal,
soprano.* Recorded 1952.
  •
  + ARG 7-8/96: 294

PITTSBURGH SYMPHONY
ORCHESTRA

28859. [no number] (4 discs): Pittsburgh
Symphony: 100 years of glory.
*Pittsburgh Symphony Orch.; Reiner,
Steinberg, Previn, Maazel, conds.*
  • ARG 7-8/96: 228

PIZZICATO CLASSIQUE

28860. PIZ 10011: *Accordeon ad-libitum.*
Music of Bach, Rachmaninoff, Ligeti,
Olczak, Constant, Goyone, Tcherenikof,
and Steckar. *Bonnay, accordion.*
  + Fa 11-12/94: 472

PLAT

28861. PLCC-548: BEETHOVEN—String
quartets no. 1, 16. *Musikverein Quartet.*
  • Gr 6/93: 58

PLUM MUSIC

28862. [no number]: *Our pleasure.* Music
of Khachaturian, Gluck, Falla, Debussy,
and others. *Pam Arnstein, violin; Peter
Arnstein, piano.*
  + Fa 5-6/96: 351

PLYMOUTH MUSIC SERIES

28863. PMS 003 (LP): LARSEN—Coming
forth into day. *Russell, Sykes; Bel Canto
Voices; Plymouth Festival Chorus &
Orch.; Brunelle, cond.*
  + Fa 5-6/87: 146

PMP

28864. 7: IBERT—Songs. *Dolorian,
soprano; Cebro, piano.*
  + ARG 1-2/97: 123

PNEUMA

28865. 010: ALFONSO X—Cantigas de
Toledo. *Musica Antigua de Eduardo
Paniagua.*
  • ARG 9-10/95: 91

POINT

28866. 432 966-2: GLASS AND SUSO—Music from the screens. *Goldray, keyboards and cond.; Hudson, violin; Parloff, flute, piccolo; Blustine, clarinet; Grossman, cello; Benincasa, percussion; Suso, instruments and voice.*
☐ ARG 9-10/92: 108
+ Fa 9-10/92: 244

28867. 432 967-2: MORAN—The Manson family. *Pop, Roche, Snell, Lane, McGrath, Greenawalt, Moran, Sortomme.*
☐ ARG 11-12/92: 163
+ ON 8/92: 45

28868. 434 873-2: *In good company.* Music of Gibson, Adams, Jennings, Glass, and Riley. *Gibson, saxophone, keyboard, percussion; Goldray, Young, pianos; Riesman, keyboards; Ruyle, Snyder, percussion.*
+ Gr 6/93: 71

28869. 438 823-2: BRYARS—Jesus' blood never failed me yet. *Waits, singer; Hampton String Quartet; chorus, orch.; Riesman, cond.*
+ Gr 10/93: 44

28870. 446 061-2: BRYARS—The sinking of the Titanic. *Westhaston Boys' Choir; C. Thornton, viola; Z. Bryars, O. Bryars, L. Thornton, cellos; Gavin Bryars Ensemble.*
☐ ARG 9-10/95: 118
+ Gr 2/95: 42

28871. 446 505-2: BRANCA—Symphony no. 9; Freeform. *Camerata Silesia; Polish Radio Symphony Orch.; Borries, cond.*
+ ARG 3-4/96: 268
- Gr 7/96: 48

28872. 454 053-2: JOHNSON—Convertible debts; Rock/paper/scissors. *Scott Johnson Ensemble.*
+ ARG 11-12/96: 307

28873. 454 054-2: WOLFE—Tell me everything; Early that summer; Four Marys; Arsenal of democracy; Steam. *SPIT Orch.; Lark Quartet; Volharding Orch.; Hempel, cond.; Cassatt Quartet; Newband; Lubman, cond.*
+ ARG 1-2/97: 245

28874. PCD 5070 (LP): NØRGÅRD—Symphonies no. 2, 4. *Aarhus Symphony Orch.; Panula, cond.*
• Fa 3-4/87: 178

28875. PCD 5073: *Contemporary Danish accordion music.* Music of Pade, Nørgård, Bentzon, and Schmidt. *Ellegaard, accordion; Danish Radio Symphony Orch.; Schmidt, cond.*
+ Fa 1-2/89: 341
+ Fa 11-12/95: 463

28876. PCD 5075: LISZT—Missa choralis; Salve Regina. *Graaner, Paaske, K. Hansen, M. Hansen, Andersen, Hans Christian; Copenhagen University Choir; Vetö, cond.*
• Fa 9-10/88: 185

28877. PCD 5082: KOPPEL—Suite for piano; Ternio; Quartet for piano and strings; Cantilena. *Koppel, piano; Cantilena Piano Quartet.*
+ Fa 5-6/89: 222
+ Fa 9-10/95: 238

28878. PCD 5083: PADE—Piano concerto. T. NIELSEN—Giardino magico. NORBY—Rolke Lieder. *Zanini, piano; Rørholm, mezzo-soprano; Aalborg Symphony; Erös, cond.*
• ARG 3-4/90: 84

28879. PCD 5084: RUDERS—Corpus cum figuris; Thus saw Saint John; Manhattan abstraction. *Ensemble InterContemporain; Eötvös, cond.; Danish Radio Symphony Orch.; Knussen, Schønwandt, cond.*
+ Fa 5-6/89: 222

28880. PCD 5085: SCHIERBECK—Häxa; Natten; Fêtes galantes: Overture; Chinese flute. *Lange, soprano; South Jutland Symphony Orch.; Schønwandt, cond.*
+ ARG 3-4/56
+ Fa 1-2/89: 255

28881. PCD 5088: MUSSORGSKY—Songs and dances of death. IBERT—Chansons de Don Quichotte. DORUMSGAARD—Dusk in the enchanted wood. *Haugland, bass; Rosenbaum, piano.*
+ Fa 7-8/89: 205

28882. PCD 5089: T. NIELSEN—Selections. *Danish Radio Symphony Orch.; Gardelli, cond.; Malling, Kaltoft, Stengard, piano; Esbjerg Ensemble; Vistesen, cond.; Da Camera Choir; Killberg, cond.*
☐ Fa 11-12/89: 306

28883. PCD 5090: RACHMANINOFF—Piano sonata no. 1. MEDTNER—Sonata romantica, op. 53, no. 1. *Rosenbaum, piano.*
• ARG 3-4/89: 56
• Fa 1-2/89: 240

28884. PCD 5091: *O quan dulcis: choral music from the time of Christian IV.* Music of Pederson, Borchgrevink, H. Nielsen, Tollius, Dowland, Trehou, Schattenburg, and Anon. *Copenhagen University Choir Lille MUKO; Jørgensen, Latham-Koenig, conds.*
+ Fa 3-4/95: 366

28885. PCD 5092: Organ music of Olsson, Bach, and Liszt. *Larsen, organ.*
☐ Fa 11-12/89: 460

28886. PCD 5093: HORNEMAN—Gurre suite. GADE—Summer's day in the

country; Michel Angelo, op. 39; Mariotta: Overture. *Lyngby-Taarbaek Symphony Orch.; Eriksson, cond.*
- ARG 3-4/90: 52
+ Fa 11-12/89: 494
• Fa 11-12/95: 279

28887. PCD 5110: *Romantic choral music.* Music of Dvořák, Rossini, Bruckner, Brahms, and Reger. *Copenhagen University Choir Lille MUKO; Jørgensen, cond.; Christensen, organ.*
+ Fa 3-4/95: 362

28888. PCD 5111: *Ebba Wilton: the Danish nightingale.* Music of Donizetti, Dupuy, Backer-Grondahl, Weyse, Heise, Schubert, Lange-Müller, Bach-Gounod, Handel, Henriques, Flotow, Thomas, Mozart, and Rossini. *Wilton, soprano; various acc.*
+ Fa 9-10/95: 372

28889. PCD 5112: MONTEVERDI—Sestina; Ecco Silvio. MATTHIASSEN—Complete choral songs. *Music Students' Chamber Choir of Aarhus University; Jacobsen, cond.*
+ Fa 3-4/95: 235

28890. PCD 5114: *A recital of seventeenth and eighteenth century organ music.* Music of Buxtehude, Correa de Arauxo, Blow, Clerambault, Purcell, Muffat, Frescobaldi, and Bach. *Hodgson, organ.*
• Fa 9-10/95: 397

28891. PCD 5115: HOLMBOE—Benedic Domino; Speravi in Domino; Laudate Dominum. LA COUR—Three Latin motets; Missa brevis. *Copenhagen University Choir "Lille MUKO"; Jørgensen, cond.*
+ ARG 9-10/95: 157
+ Fa 5-6/95: 219

28892. PCD 5116: CHRISTENSEN—Vinterlys; Vårnatsfugle; Dreamless fragments; Reflets du cristal. ODRIOZOLA—Seven Danish miniatures; Four dances; Psalms. *R. Odriozola, violin; Kristensen, recorder; J. Odriozola, cello.*
• Fa 1-2/96: 235

28893. PCD 5117: BORUP-JORGENSON—Winter pieces; O barn; Raindrop interludes; Two songs; Summer intermezzi; Über die Heide; Epigrams; Ende des Herbstes; Schlusztück; Thalatta! Thalatta! *Skjoldan, piano; Gjerris, mezzo-soprano.*
+ Fa 1-2/96: 235

28894. PCD 5120: Music of Frandsen, Siegel, Nielsen, and Dorge. *Danish Guitar Duo.*
+ ARG 9-10/96: 243

POLAR

28895. POLCD 361: Roman—Drottningholm music: Royal wedding music performed in 1744. *Chamber Orch. of the National Museum, Stockholm; Génetay, cond.*
+ Fa 1-2/87: 167

POLIMUSICA

28896. CD 1000: *Contemporary Spanish piano music.* Music of Alonso, Barce, Cano, Marco, Aracil, Balboa and Stefani. *Quagliata, piano.*
□ Fa 3-4/92: 404

POLTON TWIN

28897. CD PAJ 101: *Music for horn by great romantic composers.* Music of Chopin, Dvořák and Schumann. *Machala, horn; Teicher, piano.*
+ ARG 7-8/92: 261
+ Fa 5-6/92: 315

28898. CD PAJ 119: Music of Hummel, Granados, Beethoven, Debussy, and Fauré. *Machala, horn; Teicher, piano.*
● ARG 11-12/94: 226

POLYDOR

28899. 429 333-2: Weill—Seven deadly sins; Berlin requiem. *May, Schreier, Rotzsch, Leib, Polster, Langridge, Luxon, Rippon; Leipzig Radio Symphony Orch.; Kegel, cond.; London Sinfonietta; Atherton, cond.*
+ Fa 5-6/90: 343

28900. 839 727-2: Weill—Jasager; Violin concerto; Lady in the dark: Dance of the tumblers; Lost in the stars: Gold. *Symonette, Protschka, Vohla, vocalists; Ajemian, violin; Düsseldorf Children's Chorus; Chamber Orch. of Düsseldorf; Köhler, cond.; MGM Wind Orch.; Solomon, cond.; MGM Chamber Orch.; Winograd, cond.*
+ Fa 5-6/90: 343

POLYPHONIA

28901. POL 63014 (LP): Telemann—Double concerto for flute and bassoon in F major. Baird—Suite Colas Breugnon. Bach—Suite no. 5, BWV 1070. *Bartkiewicz, flute; Pluzek, bassoon; Kammerorchester Leopoldinum, Wroclaw; Pijarowski, cond.*
● Fa 11-12/86: 228

28902. POL 63015 (LP): Zieritz—Gypsy concerto for violin. Szymanowski—Symphony no. 3. *Boettcher, violin; Gadulanka, soprano; Filharmonia Pomorska; Bugaj, cond.*
+ Fa 1-2/88: 232

POLYPHONIC

28903. QPRZ 005D: *Premiere: Music for brass ensemble.* Music of Berlin, Boyce, Debussy, Ravel, Rossini and Sparke. *Howard Snell Brass; Snell, cond.*
+ Gr 9/91: 80

POPEMUSIC

28904. PM 1002-2: Shchedrin—Carmen ballet. Shostakovich—The bolt: Suite no. 5. *Young Russia State Symphony Orch.; Gorenstein, cond.*
● ARG 11-12/95: 203
+ Fa 11-12/95: 373 (Fogel)
+ Fa 11-12/95: 374 (Rabinowitz)

28905. PM 1004-2: Beethoven—Piano concerto no. 5; Piano sonata no. 14. *Starkman, piano; Russian Symphony Orch.; Gorenstein, cond.*
+ ARG 3-4/96: 86
+ Fa 1-2/96: 137
+ Fi 9/96: 131

28906. PM 1006-2: Tchaikovsky—Symphony no. 6; Francesca da Rimini. *Russian State Symphony Orch.; Gorenstein, cond.*
● Fa 5-6/96: 297
● Fi 9/96: 131

28907. PM 1007-2: Schnittke (arr. Rozhdestvensky)—Gogol suite. Schnittke—(K)ein Sommernachtstraum. Khrennikov—Love for love. *Russian State Symphony Orch.; Gorenstein, cond.*
+ Fa 9-10/96: 311

POSITIVELY ARMENIAN

28908. PA 106 (LP): Hovhaness—Piano music. *Arzruni, Hovhaness, pianos.*
+ Fa 1-2/88: 144

PRAGA

28909. PR 250 000: Honegger—Cris du monde (sung in Czech); Symphony no. 3. *Tattermuschová, Soukupová, Majtner; Prague Symphony Orch.; Baudo, cond.; Prague Radio Symphony; Klemens, cond.*
+ ARG 1-2/93: 105

28910. PR 250 003: Shostakovich—Symphony no. 10; Suite from The nose. *Jindrak, baritone; Löbl, tenor; Avksentiev, balalaika; Czech Phil. Orch.; Rozhdestvensky, Serov, conds. Recorded live.*
+ ARG 11-12/92: 203
+ Fa 3-4/93: 292

28911. PR 250 004: Kabeláč—Organ music; Symphony no. 8. *Rabas, organ; Strasbourg Percussion; Choirs; Stoll, cond.*
+ ARG 11-12/93: 134
+ Fa 1-2/94: 214

28912. PR 250 007—250 008 (2 separate discs): Milhaud—The Darius Milhaud

centenary, vol. 1-2. *Various performers.* Live recordings 1957-90.
+ ARG 3-4/93: 112
+ Fa 1-2/93: 197

28913. PR 250 009: Shostakovich—Satires to words by S. Chorny; Seven romances to words by Alexander Blok; Suite on verses of Michaelangelo: excerpts. *Šulcová, soprano; Zichová, Leichner, pianos; Leichner, Jr., violin; Duda, cello; Kopčák, bass; Prague Radio Symphony Orch.; Vajnar, cond.*
● Fa 1-2/93: 238

28914. PR 250 011: Lutosławski—Concerto for orchestra. Kalabis—Symphony no. 2. Britten—Cantata misericordium. *Czech Phil. Orch.; Prague Symphony Orch.; Smetáček, cond.; with Löbl, tenor; Jindrák, baritone; Czech Singers' Chorus.* Reissues.
+ Fa 1-2/93: 181

28915. PR 250 012: *The Darius Milhaud centenary, vol. 3. Milhaud in Prague.* Milhaud—Concertino d'hiver; Symphony no. 10; Music for Prague; Cantata, Hommage à Comenius. *Various performers.* Recorded live 1966 & 1970.
+ ARG 3-4/93: 112
+ Fa 3-4/93: 226

28916. PR 250 013: *The Darius Milhaud centenary, vol. 4. The musician of the Rhône.* Milhaud—Cantique du Rhône; Scaramouche; La cheminée du Roi René; Préludes pour orgue no. 3, 7, 8; Symphony no. 8 "Rhodanienne". *Various performers.* Recorded live 1966 & 1987.
+ ARG 3-4/93: 112
+ Fa 3-4/93: 226

28917. PR 250 014: Prokofiev—Chout: suite; Symphony no. 7. *Czech Phil. Orch.; Smetáček, cond.*
+ Fa 3-4/93: 292

28918. PR 250 015: Prokofiev—Piano sonatas no. 2, 6, 9. *Richter, piano.* Recorded live.
+ Fa 3-4/93: 284

28919. PR 250 016: Dvořák—Concerto for piano and orchestra, op. 33; Symphony no. 9. *Richter, piano; Prague Symphony Orch.; Prague Radio Symphony Orch.; Smetáček, cond.*
+ Fa 5-6/93: 195

28920. PR 250 018: Suk—Fantastic scherzo; Symphony, op. 27 "Asrael". *Prague Radio Symphony Orch.; Válek, cond.*
+ ARG 7-8/93: 164
+ Fa 5-6/93: 335

28921. PR 250 021: Beethoven—Concerto no. 5 for piano and orchestra "Emperor"; Symphony no. 4. *Michelangeli, piano; Prague Symphony*

Orch.; Smetáček, cond.; Leningrad Phil. Orch.; Mravinsky, cond.
- Fa 7-8/93: 101
+ Gr 10/93: 43

28922. PR 250 022/23 (2 discs): SMETANA—The two widows. *Jonášová, Machotková, Švejda; Chorus & Symphony Orch. of Radio Prague; Krombholc, cond.* Reissue.
+ ARG 7-8/93: 160
- Fa 7-8/93: 246
+ Gr 6/93: 103

28923. PR 250 024: FRANCK—Sonata for violin and piano; String quartet. *Kremer, violin; Maisenberg, piano; Prague String Quartet.*
● Fa 5-6/93: 205

28924. PR 250 025: MILHAUD—Ballade for piano and orchestra; Fantaisie pastorale; Concerto no. 1 for 2 pianos and orchestra; Concerto for harp and orchestra. *Lejsek, Lejsková, pianos; Brno State Phil. Orch.; Waldhans, cond.; Šperlová, harp; Prague National Theater Orch.; Konvalinka, cond.*
+ ARG 7-8/93: 126
+ Fa 7-8/93: 183

28925. PR 250 036: LISZT—A Dante symphony; Années de pèlerinage. Italie; Sonetto 123 del Petrarca; Après une lecture de Dante. *Mašková, soprano; Langer, piano; Czech Phil. Orch.; Albrecht, cond.* Broadcast 1986.
● Gr 3/94: 54

28926. PR 250 038: BARTÓK—Violin sonatas no. 1-2; For children: Excerpts (arr. Szigeti). *Oistrakh, Kremer, violin; Bauer, Maisenburg, piano.* Recorded 1972, 78, 69.
+ Gr 10/93: 61

28927. PR 250 039: BRAHMS—Ballades, op. 10; Piano pieces, op. 116. WEBER—Piano sonata no. 2. *Gilels, piano.* Recorded 1968-78.
● Gr 9/93: 85

28928. PR 250 040: SHOSTAKOVICH—Symphony no. 8; Overture, op. 115. *Moscow Phil. Symphony Orch.; Kondrashin, cond.* Recorded 1969, 1964.
● Gr 9/93: 60

28929. PR 250 042: CHOPIN—Piano sonatas no. 2-3; Ballade no. 1. *Michelangeli, Magaloff, piano.* Recorded 1957/60.
+ ARG 1-2/94: 196

28930. PR 250 048: GRIEG—Piano concerto; Violin sonata; Psalms, op. 74. *Richter, piano; Moscow Phil. Orch.; Kondrashin, cond.; D. Oistrakh, violin; Oborin, piano; Bělor, baritone; Pavel Kühn Chorus.*
+ ARG 11-12/94: 121

28931. PR 250 050 (2 discs): SMETANA—Dalibor. *Přibyl, Abrahamova, Jindrák, Šounova- Brouková; Prague Radio Orch.; Krombholc, cond.* Recorded 1977.
● ARG 7-8/95: 198
+ ON 8/95: 34

28932. PR 250 053: SHOSTAKOVICH—Symphony no. 10; The bolt: Suite (selections). *Leningrad Phil. Orch.; Mravinsky, cond.; Czech Phil. Orch.; Rozhdestvensky, cond.*
● Gr 9/95: 66

28933. PR 250 056: SCHOENBERG—String quartets no. 2; in D; String trio. *Prazak Quartet; Whittlesey, soprano.*
+ ARG 5-6/95: 167

28934. PR 250 059/60 (2 discs): DVOŘÁK—Saint Ludmila. *Šounova-Brouková, Drobková, Vodička, Vraspir, Švorc; Prague Radio Chorus & Symphony Orch.; Smetáček, cond.* Recorded 1984.
● ARG 5-6/95: 107
● Fa 5-6/95: 183
● Gr 7/95: 96
● ON 1/20/96: 33

28935. PR 250 062: LALO—Symphonie espagnole; Concerto russe. *Poulet, violin; Prague Radio Symphony Orch.; Válek, cond.*
+ Fa 7-8/96: 213

28936. PR 250 069: HAYDN—String quartets op. 76 no. 1-3. *Pražák Quartet.*
● ARG 3-4/96: 122
+ Fa 3-4/96: 180

28937. PR 250 073: STRAVINSKY—Three pieces for string quartet; Concertino for string quartet; Three pieces for clarinet; Suite italienne; Duo concertant for violin and piano; Piano sonata; Élégie for solo violin; Epitaphium. *Zilka, flute; Mareš, Nemec, clarinet; Spivakov, Ishikawa, violin; Doležal, viola; Tokyo String Quartet; Bekhterev, Petrov, Hála, piano; Platilová, harp.*
+ Fa 7-8/96: 319

28938. PR 250 074: BRAHMS—String quartets no. 2-3. *Vlach Quartet.*
+ Fa 7-8/96: 120

28939. PR 250 076: BEETHOVEN—Symphony no. 9. *Beňačková-Čápová, Soukupová, Přibyl, Prusa; Czech Phil. Orch.; Matacic, cond.* Recorded live 1980.
+ ARG 1-2/96: 85
● Fa 11-12/95: 209

28940. PR 250 077: SHOSTAKOVICH—String quartets no. 5-7. *Taneev Quartet.*
□ ARG 7-8/96: 196
● Fa 11-12/96: 376

28941. PR 250 078: DVOŘÁK—String quintet, op. 97; Piano quintet no. 2. *Suk Quartet; Maly, viola; Maxián, piano;*

Ondřícek Quartet. Recorded live 1978, 1947.
● ARG 3-4/96: 255
● Fa 11-12/95: 243

28942. PR 250 082: SCHOENBERG—Erwartung; Five pieces for orchestra, op. 16; Die glückliche Hand. *Pilarczyk, soprano; Švorc, baritone; Prague Phil. Choir; Czech Phil. Orch.; Neumann, Košler, conds.* Recorded live 1967, 1964, and 1981.
● Fa 9-10/96: 315

28943. PR 250 087: SCHUBERT—Octet, D. 803; Eine kleine Trauermusik, D. 79. *Czech Nonet.*
● Fa 3-4/96: 271

28944. PR 250 088: HINDEMITH—String quartets, vol. 1. *Kocian Quartet.*
● Fa 3-4/96: 184

28945. PR 250 089: ROUSSEL—Chamber music. *Various perfomers.*
+ Fa 5-6/96: 248 (Corleonis)
+ Fa 5-6/96: 249 (Wiser)

28946. PR 250 090: SHOSTAKOVICH—Symphony no. 4; Two pieces from Scarlatti for wind orchestra. *USSR Ministry of Culture Symphony Orch.; Winds of the USSR State Symphony Orch.; Rozhdestvensky, cond.*
● Fa 7-8/96: 305

28947. PR 250 091: SCHUBERT—String quartets no. 13-14. *Pražák Quartet.*
● Fa 7-8/96: 289

28948. PR 250 092: ZEMLINSKY—String quartet no. 3; Lyrische Symphonie. *Kocian Quartet; Marková, soprano; Kusnjer, baritone; Prague Radio Symphony Orch.; Válek, cond.* Recorded live 1992.
● ARG 9-10/96: 227
● Fa 7-8/96: 342
● Gr 7/96: 67

28949. PR 250 093 (2 discs): HINDEMITH—String quartets no. 0, 3-5; Flying Dutchman overture; Minimax. *Kocian Quartet.*
- ARG 11-12/96: 145
● Fa 11-12/96: 271
+ Gr 10/96: 71

28950. PR 250 095: MOZART—Divertimento no. 11 "Nannerl-Septett"; Quartet for oboe, violin, viola, and cello, K. 370; Adagio for English horn, violin, viola, and cello, K. 580a; Quintet for horn, 2 violins, viola, and cello, K. 407. *Czech Nonet; Kudelasek, violin; Leixner, cello.*
● Fa 9-10/96: 270
+ Fa 11-12/96: 313

28951. PR 250 096: SCHUMANN—Symphonies no. 1 "Spring", 3 "Rhenish". *Prague Radio Symphony Orch.; Smetáček, cond.; Czech Phil. Orch.;*

PRAGA

Pedrotti, cond. Recorded 1971.
- Fa 9-10/96: 321

28952. PR 250 097: MARTINŮ—String quartet no. 7; Quartet for clarinet, horn, cello, and side-drum; Quartet for oboe, violin, cello, and piano; Mazurka-notturno; Nonet. *Pražák Quartet; Czech Nonet; Mareš, clarinet; Rehor, side drum; Langer, piano; Kutman, violin.*
+ Fa 11-12/96: 298

28953. PR 250 098: MOZART—String quartets no. 17, 19. HAYDN—String quartet, op. 74, no. 3. *Vlach Quartet.*
+ Fa 11-12/96: 316

28954. PR 250 099: BARTÓK—Violin concertos no. 1-2. *Suk, Ishikawa, violins; Czech Phil. Orch.; Pešek, Košler, conds.* Recorded live 1985, 1980.
• Fa 11-12/96: 178

28955. PR 250 100: JANÁČEK—Amarus; Cunning little vixen suite; From the house of the dead suite. *Soukupová, soprano; Přibyl, tenor; Czech Phil. Orch.; Neumann, Jílek, conds.* Recorded 1974, 1988, 1979.
+ ARG 7-8/96: 137
+ Fa 7-8/96: 204

28956. PR 254 002/003 (2 discs): SHOSTAKOVICH—Symphonies, no. 5, 7, 9. *Czech Phil. Orch.; Ančerl, cond.* Recorded 1961-67.
+ ARG 1-2/93: 149
+ Fa 3-4/93: 292
• Gr 5/93: 51

28957. PR 254 004: PROKOFIEV—Concerto for piano and orchestra no. 1; Scythian suite; Symphony no. 1 "Classical"; Seven, they are seven. *Moravec, piano; Kachel, tenor; Prague Phil. Chorus; Czech Phil. Orch.; Ančerl, cond.* Recorded 1960-1966.
+ Fa 5-6/93: 282

28958. PR 254 005: MOZART—Don Giovanni: overture; Ergo interest, an quis; Vesperae solennes de confessore: Laudate dominum; Coronation mass: Agnus Dei; Il re pastore: L'amerò, sarò costante; Concerto for violin and orchestra no. 2; Symphony no. 31. *Seefried, soprano; Schneiderhan, Suk, violins; Prague Phil. Chorus; Czech Phil. Orch.; Ančerl, cond.* Recorded 1966 & 1968.
• Fa 5-6/93: 273

28959. PR 254 006: DVOŘÁK—Violin concerto; Symphony no. 8. *Oistrakh, violin; Prague Radio Symphony Orch.; Czech Phil. Orch.; Ančerl, cond.*
+ Fa 5-6/93: 195

28960. PR 254 007: BEETHOVEN—Symphony no. 5; Violin concerto. *Szeryng, violin; Czech Phil. Orch.; Ančerl, cond.* Recorded 1958 & 1966.
• Fa 7-8/93: 108

28961. PR 254 008: *Edition live Karel Ančerl, vol. 7.* Music of Debussy, Ravel, Poulenc, and Roussel. *Soloists; Brno State Phil. Orch.; Czech Phil. Orch.; Ančerl, cond.* Recorded 1957-64.
+ ARG 9-10/93: 226
+ Fa 5-6/93: 414

28962. PR 254 009/015 (7 discs): BEETHOVEN—The string quartets. *Vlach Quartet; Janáček Quartet.*
+ Fa 5-6/93: 154
+ Gr 4/93: 74

28963. PR 254 016: RAVEL—Sonata (posth.); Habanera; Violin and cello sonata; Violin sonata; Tzigane. *Suk, violin; Navarra, cello; Hála, piano; D. Oistrakh, violin; Bauer, Yampolsky, pianos.* Broadcasts.
+ ARG 9-10/94: 181

28964. PR 254 017: SHOSTAKOVICH—Symphonies no. 6, 12. *Leningrad Phil. Orch.; Mravinsky, cond.* Recorded 1955, 1962.
+ Gr 8/94: 58

28965. PR 254 018: SHOSTAKOVICH—Symphony no. 11. *Leningrad Phil. Orch.; Mravinsky, cond.* Recorded 1967.
+ Gr 8/94: 58

28966. PR 254 019: SCHUBERT—Piano trio no. 1; Piano sonata. MOZART—Variations. *D. Oistrakh, violin; Bauer, Oborin, pianos; Knushevitsky, cello.* Broadcasts, 1961, 1966, 1972.
+ ARG 9-10/94: 195

28967. PR 254 020—254 023 (4 separate discs): BEETHOVEN—Piano sonatas. *Richter, piano.* Recorded 1959/75.
+ ARG 1-2/94: 71
+ Fa 3-4/94: 124

28968. PR 254 025: MOZART—Piano sonatas no. 2, 4, 8. HAYDN—Piano sonata no. 39. *Richter, piano.*
+ Fa 11-12/94: 316

28969. PR 254 026: MOZART—Piano sonatas no. 13, 15; K. 533/494. *Richter, piano.*
+ Fa 11-12/94: 318

28970. PR 254 033: SCHUMANN—Symphonic etudes; Fantasy, op. 17. *Richter, piano.* Broadcasts, 1956, 1959.
• ARG 9-10/94: 242

28971. PR 254 034: RACHMANINOFF—Etudes-tableaux. MUSSORGSKY—Pictures at an exhibition. *Richter, piano.*
• ARG 9-10/94: 242

28972. PR 254 050: MARTINŮ—Symphony no. 6; Memorial to Lidice; Frescoes; Vigil. *Prague Radio Symphony Orch.; Vilek, cond.; Uhlíř, organ.* Recorded 1986.
• ARG 11-12/94: 153

28973. PR 254 059: BRAHMS—Piano sonatas no. 1-2; Variations on a Hungarian song, op. 1. *Richter, piano.* Recorded 1984 and 1988.
• ARG 7-8/96: 253
• Fa 3-4/96: 139

28974. PR 254 060: BEETHOVEN—Rondos, op. 51; Bagatelles, op. 126 no. 1, 4, 6. CHOPIN—Etudes, op. 10 no. 1-3, 12; op. 25 no. 6-7; Four ballades. *Richter, piano.* Recorded live 1960-1986.
+ Fa 5-6/96: 102

28975. PR 254 061: MARTINŮ—Kytice; Symphony no. 3. *Domanínská, Cervená, Havlak, Mráz, vocalists; Czech Phil. Chorus & Orch.; Ančerl, cond.* Reissue.
+ ARG 11-12/96: 158
- Fa 11-12/96: 298

28976. PR 255 000: KABELÁC—Symphony no. 5 "Dramatic"; Hamlet improvisation. *Domanínská, soprano; Czech Phil. Orch.; Ančerl, cond.*
+ Fa 11-12/93: 280

28977. PR 255 002: KALABIS—Symphonies no. 3, 5; Tristium; Bajka (The fable). *Prague Radio Symphony Orch.; Belohlavek, Kout, conds.; Maly, viola; Slovak Chamber Orch.; Warchal, cond.; Pardubice Chamber Phil. Orch.; Škvor, cond.*
+ Fa 11-12/93: 282

28978. PR 255 005: HÁBA—Nonets no. 1, 4; String quartets no. 7-8, 13, 15-16. *Czech Nonet; Suk Quartet.*
+ ARG 11-12/93: 116
+ Fa 9-10/94: 199

28979. PR 255 006: SCHULHOFF—Violin sonata no. 2; Sonata for solo violin; Duo for violin and cello; Partita for piano; String quartet no. 1. *Tomášek, violin; Růžička, piano; Novák, violin; Bernášek, cello; Krajný, piano; Talich Quartet.*
+ ARG 11-12/96: 203
+ Fa 11-12/96: 367

28980. PR 354 001/15 (15 discs): *Richter in Prague.* Music of Haydn, Mozart, Beethoven, Brahms, and others. *Richter, piano.* Recorded 1954-86.
+ ARG 7-8/96: 251
+ Gr 6/96: 76

PREAMBLE

28981. PRCD 1776: *American piano music, vol. 1.* Music of Gershwin, Waxman, Antheil, Copland, Stevens, and Barber. *Parkin, piano.*
+ Fa 3-4/88: 253

28982. PRCD 1786: WHITHORNE—American piano music. *Kozar, piano.*
+ ARG 3-4/92: 167
+ Fa 11-12/91: 521

PREISER

28983. LV 1356 (LP): Music of Bellini, Donizetti, and Verdi. *Gentile, soprano; with assisting soloists; various orchs. & conds.* Recorded 1927-35.
+ Fa 7-8/88: 291

28984. LV 1357 (LP): Music of Mozart, Lortzing, Flotow, Cornelius, Verdi, Tchaikovsky, and Mussorgsky. *Strienz, bass; with assisting soloists; Staatskapelle Berlin; Seidler-Winkler, cond.* Recorded 1935-40.
+ Fa 7-8/88: 300

28985. LV 1358 (LP): Music of Wagner, Verdi, Leoncavallo, Albert, Wolf, Brull, and Frommer. *Ritter, tenor; various orchs. & conds.* Recorded 1923-28.
• Fa 7-8/88: 297

28986. LV 1359 (LP): *Feodor Schaljapin, vol. 3.* Music of Glinka, Dargomizhsky, Mussorgsky, Borodin, Rimsky- Korsakov, Rachmaninoff, and Anon. *Chaliapin, bass; with assisting soloists; various orchs. & conds.* Recorded 1927-31.
+ Fa 7-8/88: 298

28987. LV 1360 (LP): Music of Rossini, Bizet, Saint-Saëns, Humperdinck, and Valverde. *Supervia, mezzo- soprano; with assisting soloists; various orchs. & conds.* Recorded 1927-29.
+ Fa 7-8/88: 298

28988. LV 1372 (LP): Music of Weber, Beethoven, and Wagner. *Flagstad, soprano; various orchs. & conds.*
+ Fa 1-2/90: 355

28989. LV 1373 (LP): Music of Rossini, Verdi, Gounod, Ponchielli, Leoncavallo, Puccini, and Wagner. *Molinari, baritone; with assisting soloists; Teatro alla Scala Orch.; Molajoli, cond.*
+ Fa 1-2/90: 367

28990. LV 1374 (LP): Music of Bellini, Rossini, Verdi, Wagner, Meyerbeer, Bizet, Leoncavallo, Giordano, and Boito. *Merli, tenor; various orchs. & conds.*
+ Fa 1-2/90: 359

28991. LV 1375 (LP): Music of Mascagni, Cilea, Puccini, Rocca, Giordano, Verdi, Boito, and Schubert. *Oltrabella, soprano; with assisting soloists; various orchs. & conds.*
+ Fa 1-2/90: 355

28992. LV 1376 (LP): WOLF—Songs. *Kipnis, bass; various piano accs.*
+ Fa 1-2/90: 368

28993. LV 1377 (LP): Music of Mozart, Gounod, Bizet, Rimsky-Korsakov, Verdi, Leoncavallo, Mascagni, Puccini, Wolf-Ferrari, Chapi, and Yradier. *Bori, soprano; with assisting soloists; various*
orchs. & cond.
+ Fa 1-2/90: 354

28994. LV 1378 (LP): Music of Glinka, Tchaikovsky, Dargomizhsky, Borodin, Mussorgsky, Rubinstein, Rimsky-Korsakov, and Rachmaninoff. *Reizen, bass; various orchs. & conds.*
+ Fa 1-2/90: 369

28995. LV 1380 (LP): Music of Verdi, Puccini, Flotow, Spoliansky, Stolz, and Di Capua. *Kiepura, tenor; various orchs. and conds.*
+ Fa 1-2/90: 363

28996. SPR 3350: BRAHMS—Songs. *Loibl, baritone; Shetler, piano.*
+ Fa 9-10/86: 117

28997. 89001: Music of Bellini, Donizetti, Thomas, Bizet, Verdi, Bishop, and Benedict. *Dal Monte, soprano; various accs.*
+ ARG 3-4/90: 153
+ Fa 3-4/90: 341
+ Gr 2/90: 1540

28998. 89002: Music of Bellini, Donizetti, Verdi, Bizet, Puccini, Meyerbeer, Leoncavallo, Mascagni, and Zandonai. *Fleta, tenor; Austral, Bori, soprano; various orchs. & conds.*
+ Fa 3-4/90: 351
• Gr 2/90: 1542

28999. 89003: Music of Rossini, Donizetti, Verdi, Wagner, Berlioz, Meyerbeer, Massenet, Ponchieli, Leoncavallo, Puccini, and Di Capua. *Stacciari, baritone; various orchs. & conds.*
+ ARG 3-4/90: 155
+ Fa 3-4/90: 352
• Gr 2/90: 1542

29000. 89004: Music of Gluck, Mozart, Beethoven, and Wagner. *Leider, soprano; various orchs. & conds.*
+ ARG 3-4/90: 152
+ Fa 3-4/90: 331
+ Gr 2/90: 1542

29001. 89005: Music of Wagner, Halévy, Meyerbeer, Verdi, and Leoncavallo. *Völker, tenor; various orchs. & conds.*
+ ARG 3-4/90: 158
+ Fa 3-4/90: 331
+ Gr 2/90: 1542

29002. 89006: Music of Marschner, Lortzing, Wagner, Verdi, Bizet, Borodin, Tchaikovsky, and Leoncavallo. *Schlusnus, baritone; with assisting soloists; various orchs. & conds.*
+ ARG 5-6/90: 152
+ Fa 5-6/90: 364
+ Gr 9/90: 626

29003. 89007: Music of Donizetti, Rossini, Verdi, Bizet, Ponchielli, and Puccini. *Pertile, tenor; with assisting soloists; unnamed orchs. & conds.*

+ ARG 3-4/91: 174
+ Fa 3-4/91: 453
+ Gr 9/90: 626

29004. 89008: Music of Bellini, Donizetti, Verdi, Ponchielli, Bizet, and Saint-Saëns. *Minghini-Cattaneo, mezzo-soprano; with assisting soloists; various orchs. & conds.*
+ Fa 5-6/90: 356
+ Gr 6/90: 126

29005. 89009: Music of Verdi, Leoncavallo, and Catalani. *Bechi, baritone; Lauri-Volpi, tenor; Pasero, bass; various orchs & conds.*
+ ARG 3-4/90: 117
- Fa 3-4/90: 351
+ Gr 2/90: 1540

29006. 89010: Music of Rossini, Bellini, Verdi, Meyerbeer, Gounod, Thomas, Ponchielli, and Boito. *Pasero, bass; with assisting soloists; orchestra; Malajoli, cond.*
+ Fa 5-6/90: 366
+ Gr 6/90: 126

29007. 89011: Music of Reyer, Wagner, and Strauss. *Lawrence, soprano; orchestra; Coppola, cond.*
+ ARG 5-6/90: 150
+ Fa 5-6/90: 353
+ Gr 5/90: 2081

29008. 89013: Music of Donizetti, Verdi, Ponchieli, Mascagni, and Puccini. *Arangi-Lombardi, soprano; with assisting soloists; various orchs. & conds.*
+ ARG 5-6/90: 145
+ Fa 5-6/90: 364
+ Gr 10/90: 838

29009. 89014: Music of Gluck, Rossini, Bellini, Donizetti, Verdi, Mascagni, Thomas, and Saint-Saëns. *Stignani, mezzo-soprano; various orchs. & conds.*
+ ARG 11-12/90: 169
+ Fa 7-8/90: 332

29010. 89016: Music of Bellini, Verdi, Gounod, Boito, Catalani, Ponchielli, Cilea, and Puccini. *Cigna, soprano; with assisting soloists; various orchs. & conds.*
+ ARG 5-6/90: 146
+ Fa 5-6/90: 364
+ Gr 11/90: 1080

29011. 89018: Music of Auber, Adam, Weber, Beethoven, Bizet, Verdi, Leoncavallo, Puccini, Glinka, Strauss, and Wille. *Rosvænge, tenor; various orchs. & conds.*
+ ARG 11-12/90: 169
+ Fa 7-8/90: 333
+ Gr 5/90: 2074

29012. 89020: Music of Weber, Auber, Rossini, Halévy, Meyerbeer, Wagner, Verdi, Gounod, and Goldmark. *Slezak, tenor; with assisting soloists; various*

PREISER

orchs. & conds.
+ Fa 7-8/90: 336

29013. 89023: Music of Mozart, Rossini, Bizet, Saint-Saëns, Humperdinck, and Strauss. *Supervia, mezzo-soprano; with assisting soloists; various orchs. & conds.*
+ ARG 3-4/91: 174
+ Fa 3-4/91: 448

29014. 89025: Music of Mozart, Weber, Wagner, and Verdi. *Lemnitz, soprano; various orchs. & conds.*
+ ARG 11-12/90: 170
+ Fa 7-8/90: 326
• Gr 10/90: 847

29015. 89030: Music of Rossini, Bellini, Donizetti, Meyerbeer, Verdi, Boito, Gounod, Delibes, Glinka, and Rubinstein. *Chaliapin, bass; with assisting soloists; various orchs. & conds.*
+ ARG 3-4/91: 174
+ Fa 3-4/91: 459

29016. 89036: Music of Mozart, Rossini, Bellini, Donizetti, Verdi, Founod, Diaz, and Massenet. *De Luca, baritone; with assisting soloists; various orchs. & conds.*
+ ARG 3-4/91: 174
+ Fa 3-4/91: 457

29017. 89040: Music of Rossini, Gounod, Verdi, Mascagni, Leoncavallo, and Giordano. *Galeffi, baritone; with assisting soloists; Teatro alla Scala Orch.; Molajoli, cond.*
+ Fa 5-6/91: 339

29018. 89041: Music of Handel, Haydn, Mozart, Meyerbeer, Rossini, Verdi, Thomas, Bizet, and Puccini. *Norena, soprano; various orchs. & conds.*
+ Fa 3-4/91: 443

29019. 89044: *Dusolina Giannini.* Music of Bellini, Verdi, Puccini, Di Capua, Bizet and Valente. *Giannini, soprano; with orchestral accomp.* Reissues.
+ Fa 11-12/92: 414

29020. 89047: *Xenia Belmas.* Music of Meyerbeer, Verdi, Thomas, Rimsky-Korsakov, Tchaikovsky, Mascagni, Leoncavallo, and Puccini. *Belmas, soprano; unnamed orch.; Domgraf-Fassbaender, Kitschin, conds.* Recorded 1927-1929.
• Fa 1-2/95: 316

29021. 89051: Arias and songs. *Rethberg, soprano.* Recorded 1920-25.
+ ARG 5-6/95: 250

29022. 89054: *Operatic arias.* Music of Mozart, Adam, Donizetti, Verdi, Gounod, Meyerbeer, Offenbach, Delibes, Rimsky-Korsakov and Proch. *Korjus, soprano; with orchestral accomp.* Recorded 1934-38.

+ ARG 3-4/93: 198
+ Fa 11-12/92: 409

29023. 89055: *Cesare Formichi: opera arias and songs.* Music of Verdi, Wagner, Saint-Saëns, Massenet, Giordano, Puccini, Hahn, De Fontenailles, and Brogi. *Formichi, baritone; orch.; Ketelbey, Hamilton, conds.*
+ Fa 1-2/95: 332
+ Gr 11/94: 190

29024. 89057: *Charles Kullman.* Music of Wagner, Verdi, Offenbach, Tchaikovsky, Borodin, Smetana, Strauss and Puccini. *Kullman, tenor; with orchestral accomp.* Recorded 1931-38.
+ Fa 11-12/92: 418

29025. 89058: SCHUBERT—Lieder. *Rehkemper, baritone; with piano acc.* Recorded 1924-28.
+ ARG 3-4/93: 193

29026. 89059: *Mark Reizen.* Music of Glinka, Dargomizhsky, Mussorgsky, Rubinstein, Borodin, Tchaikovsky, Rimsky-Korsakov, and Rachmaninoff. *Reizen, bass; Bolshoi Theater Orch.; Nebolsin, Melik-Pashaev, Samosud, Golovanov, conds.*
+ ARG 9-10/92: 229
+ Fa 9-10/92: 403
+ Gr 12/92: 153

29027. 89060: Music of Donizetti, Verdi, Weber, Cornelius, Thomas, Gounod, Offenbach, Massenet, Tchaikovsky, and Puccini. *Piccaver, tenor; with orch. acc.*
+ ARG 9-10/93: 268
+ Fa 7-8/93: 279
+ Gr 8/93: 93

29028. 89061: *Opera arias.* Music of Verdi, Gounod, Leoncavallo, Rubinstein, Tchaikovsky, Rimsky-Korsakov, and Tchukhadzian. *Lisitsian, baritone; various orchs. & conds.* Recorded 1947-1960.
+ ARG 1-2/95: 264
+ Fa 11-12/94: 444

29029. 89062: Music of Verdi, Giordano, Mascagni, Leoncavallo, and Puccini. *Martinelli, tenor; Metropolitan Opera Orch.; Setti, cond.; Unidentified orchs.; Pasternak, Bourdon, conds.* Recorded 1926-27.
+ Fa 5-6/93: 366
+ ON 12/10/94: 52

29030. 89063: *Rosetta Pampanini.* Arias by Gounod, Catalani, Puccini, Mascagni, Zandonai, Wagner and Verdi. *Pampanini, soprano; with orch. accomp.* Recorded 1927-40.
+ ARG 3-4/93: 199
+ Fa 1-2/93: 274

29031. 89064: *Pasquale Amato.* Music of Rossini, Donizetti, Verdi, Meyerbeer, Puccini, Franchetti, De Curtis, and De

Christofaro. *Amato, baritone; with orch. acc.*
+ ARG 9-10/93: 265
+ Fa 7-8/93: 284
+ ON 2/18/95: 38

29032. 89065: Arias and songs by Mozart, Wagner, Strauss, Puccini, and others. *Reining, soprano; with orch. & piano accomp.* Recorded 1941-43.
+ ARG 1-2/94: 203

29033. 89066: *Arias.* Music of Handel, Rossini, Meyerbeer, Gounod, Massenet, Saint-Saëns, Verdi, Mussorgsky, Tchaikovsky, and Rimsky-Korsakov. *Dolukhanova, mezzo-soprano; USSR Radio Orch.; Kovailov, Gauk, Brohn, conds.*
+ Fa 7-8/93: 277

29034. 89067: Arias by Rossini, Wagner, Verdi, Thomas, Bizet, Rubinstein, and others. *Ivanov, baritone.* Recorded 1945-51.
+ ARG 9-10/93: 266

29035. 89070: *Franz Völker II.* Music of Mozart, Weber, Beethoven, Halévy, Wagner, Verdi, Leoncavallo, Smetana, and d'Albert. *Völker, tenor; orch. acc.*
+ Fa 1-2/94: 371
+ ON 4/2/94: 32

29036. 89073: *Giuseppe de Luca.* Music of Verdi, Gounod, Bizet, Ponchielli, Puccini, and Wolf-Ferrari. *De Luca, baritone; Metropolitan Opera; Setti, Bourdon, conds.*
+ Fa 1-2/94: 379

29037. 89074: *Tancredi Pasero II (1893-1983).* Music of Mozart, Rossini, Bellini, Verdi, Mussorgsky, Gounod, Boito, Porrino, and Beethoven. *Pasero, bass; various acc.* Recorded 1940-1944.
+ Fa 11-12/94: 444
+ Gr 4/95: 145

29038. 89075: Music of Mozart, Flotow, Nicolai, Thomas, Verdi, Smetana, Tchaikovsky, Offenbach, Massenet, Kienzl, and R. Strauss. *Patzak, tenor; various orchs. & conds.* Recorded 1929-37.
+ ARG 5-6/94: 217
+ Fa 5-6/94: 295

29039. 89076: *Josef Herrmann.* Music of Marschner, Weber, Beethoven, Wagner, Verdi, and Leoncavallo. *Herrmann, baritone; orch. acc.; Moralt, Böhm, Seidler-Winkler, Merten, conds.*
+ ARG 3-4/94: 236
+ Fa 1-2/94: 378

29040. 89077: Music of Wagner, Bizet, Puccini, d'Albert, and Strauss. *Ralf, tenor; orch. acc.*
+ ARG 3-4/94: 237
+ Fa 1-2/94: 371
+ ON 12/10/94: 52

29041. 89078: Arias by Meyerbeer, Boito, Gounod, Glinka, Dargomizhky, and others. *Pirogov, bass.*
+ ARG 7-8/94: 236
+ Fa 11-12/94: 444

29042. 89079: Opera arias. *Jeritza, soprano; with acc.*
+ ARG 3-4/94: 236
- Gr 4/94: 127

29043. 89080: Arias by Dargomizhky, Gounod, Rossini, Verdi, Wagner, and Mussorgsky. *Reizen, bass.*
+ ARG 7-8/94: 236

29044. 89082: Arias from Orfeo, Alceste, Il trovatore, Don Carlo, and others. *Klose, contralto.* Recorded 1930s.
+ ARG 5-6/96: 276
+ ON 3/30/96: 38

29045. 89083: Arias and songs by Mozart, Wagner, Strauss, and others. *List, bass.* Recorded 1927-30, 1951.
• ARG 7-8/96: 294
• ON 10/96: 42

29046. 89084: Arias and songs by Gluck, Bizet, Saint-Saëns, Wagner, Schubert, Brahms, and Wolf. *Thorborg, contralto; with acc.* Recorded 1933, 1940.
+ ARG 1-2/96: 247
+ ON 3/30/96: 38

29047. 89086: *Melchior III.* Lauritz Melchior sings selections from Wagner and other composers. *Melchior, tenor; with acc.*
+ ARG 1-2/95: 265
+ Fa 11-12/94: 424

29048. 89087: *Feodor Chaliapin, vol. 2.* Arias from Barber of Seville, Sonnambula, Faust, Rusalka, and others. *Chaliapin, bass.* Recorded 1925-31.
+ ARG 7-8/95: 277

29049. 89092: *Erna Berger, vol. 2.* Music of Mozart, Donizetti, Verdi, Puccini, Strauss, and others. *Berger, soprano.* Recorded 1935-40.
+ ARG 7-8/95: 276

29050. 89094: Arias and duets from Magic flute, Barber of Seville, Lucia di Lammermoor, and others. *Ivogün, soprano; with Erb, tenor.* Recorded 1916-19.
+ ARG 1-2/95: 263

29051. 89098: Arias from Tristan, Walküre, and Götterdämmerung; Songs. *Leider, soprano; Berlin State Orch.; Blech, cond.; Raucheisen, piano.* Recorded 1920s, 1941-42.
+ ARG 7-8/95: 278

29052. 89100: *Mario Sammarco.* Music of Mozart, Donizetti, Verdi, Meyerbeer, Thomas, Ponchielli, Giordano, Leoncavallo, Cilea, Franchetti, Wolf-Ferrari, and Costa. *Sammarco, baritone;*

various accs.
+ Fa 7-8/95: 384

29053. 89106: *Marcel Journet, vol. 2.* Arias and songs by Donizetti, Verdi, Wagner, Godard, and others. *Journet, bass.* Recorded 1916-24.
+ ARG 7-8/96: 293

29054. 89109: Arias by Weber, Wagner, Verdi, Puccini, and Goldmark. *Németh, soprano.*
+ ARG 11-12/96: 301
+ Gr 6/96: 117

29055. 89110: Arias from Don Giovanni, William Tell, Rigoletto, Don Carlos, and others. *Schlusnus, baritone.* Recorded 1921-25.
+ ARG 5-6/96: 278
+ Gr 12/95: 178

29056. 89122: Music of Mozart, Beethoven, Strauss, and others. *Schumann, soprano.*
- ARG 11-12/96: 304
• Gr 7/96: 119

29057. 89126: Arias from Pagliacci, Tosca, Turandot, Aida, and others. *Valente, tenor.*
• ARG 11-12/96: 300

29058. 89129: Arias by Rossini, Verdi, Wagner, Meyerbeer, Giordano, and others. *Molinari, baritone.* Recorded late 1920s.
- ARG 1-2/97: 243
+ Gr 12/96: 152

29059. 89204 (2 discs): Alexander Kipnis sings Brahms and Wolf. *Kipnis, bass; Wolff, piano.* Recorded 1930-1940.
+ ARG 5-6/93: 182
+ Fa 9-10/92: 202
+ ON 12/19/92: 40

29060. 89205 (2 discs): Songs by Beethoven, Brahms, Giordani, Graener, Handel, and others. *Schlusnus, baritone.* Recorded 1930-34.
+ ARG 1-2/94: 204
+ Fa 1-2/94: 376
+ Gr 1/94: 111

29061. 89206 (2 discs): *Heinrich Schlusnus Liederalbum, vol. 2.* Music of Beethoven, Schubert, Loewe, Gretchaninoff, Tchaikovsky, Brahms, Wolf, and R. Strauss. *Schlusnus, baritone; Raucheisen, Peschko, piano.* Recorded 1934-1938.
+ Fa 11-12/94: 442

29062. 89207 (2 discs): The Feodor Chaliapin song book. *Chaliapin, bass; with orch. and piano acc.*
+ ARG 3-4/93: 196
+ Fa 3-4/93: 345
+ Gr 6/93: 110

29063. 89208 (2 discs): Songs by Bach, Beethoven, Brahms, Liszt, Loewe, and

others. *Erb, tenor; Seidler-Winkler, piano.*
+ ARG 1-2/94: 201
+ Fa 1-2/94: 370

29064. 89209 (2 discs): *Helge Rosvaenge, vol. 2.* Music of Meyerbeer, Verdi, Wagner, Flotow, Thomas, Bizet, Offenbach, Massenet, Puccini, Mozart, Weber, Cornelius, Auber, and Künneke. *Rosvænge, tenor; various orchs. & conds.*
+ ARG 5-6/94: 217
+ Fa 5-6/94: 296

29065. 89210 (2 discs): Arias from Xerxes, Orfeo, Trovatore, Carmen, Don Carlos, and others. *Leisner, contralto.* Recorded 1913-39.
• ARG 7-8/95: 278

29066. 89212 (2 discs): Arias and scenes. *Schlusnus, baritone; Berlin State Opera Orch.; various conds.*
+ ARG 11-12/95: 294
+ Fa 7-8/95: 384
+ ON 3/30/96: 38

29067. 89215: Arias by Gounod, Wagner, Verdi, Meyerbeer, and others. *Bohnen, bass.* Recorded 1914-30.
+ ARG 5-6/96: 273

29068. 89216: *Heinrich Schlusnus Liederalbum, vol. 3.* Music of Beethoven, Schubert, Schumann, Brahms, Wolf, R. Strauss, Schillings, Lothar, Vollerthun, Grabert, and Schoeck. *Schlusnus, baritone; Peschko, piano; Orch. der Staatsoper, Berlin; Steeger, cond.*
+ ARG 11-12/95: 294
+ Fa 7-8/95: 385

29069. 89217 (2 discs): Complete electrics, 1928-30. *Piccaver, tenor.*
• ARG 3-4/96: 264
+ Gr 4/96: 136

29070. 89220 (2 discs): Titta Ruffo: early recordings. *Ruffo, baritone.* Recorded 1904-1912.
+ ARG 7-8/96: 295

29071. 89221: Arias by Strauss, Straus, Zeller, Kalman, and others. *Völker, tenor.*
• ARG 11-12/96: 305

29072. 89222 (2 discs): Arias, duets and songs by Verdi, Meyerbeer, Giordano, Leoncavallo, Flotow, and others. *Pattiera, tenor.* Recorded 1916-1928.
+ ARG 1-2/97: 243
• Gr 10/96: 112

29073. 89224 (2 discs): Arias by Mozart, Rossini, Meyerbeer, Puccini, and others. *Schöne, soprano.* Recorded 1922-31.
+ ARG 1-2/97: 243
+ Gr 1/97: 115

29074. 89301 (3 discs): Music of Mozart, Beethoven, Weber, Wagner, Verdi, Puccini, and Strauss. *Leider, soprano;*

PREISER

*with assisting soloists; various orchs. &
conds.*
+ ARG 3-4/91: 174
+ Fa 3-4/91: 444
+ Gr 5/91: 2081

29075. 89303 (3 discs): *Titta Ruffo
edition.* Victor recordings 1912-29. *Ruffo,
baritone; with acc.*
+ ARG 3-4/93: 199
+ Fa 5-6/93: 371
+ Gr 2/93: 82

29076. 89993: *Kyra Vayne, vol. 2: Opera
arias and songs.* Music of Tchaikovsky,
Kotchetov, Gretchaninov, Vasilenko,
Mussorgsky, Szymanowski, Berlioz,
Wagner, Puccini, Provost, Bach-Gounod,
Lehár, and J. Strauss, Jr. *Vayne,
soprano; various accs.*
+ Fa 9-10/96: 369
+ Gr 11/96: 185

29077. 89994: Arias from Rigoletto,
Traviata, Lohengrin, Mefistofele, and
others. *Ciniselli, tenor.*
+ ARG 11-12/96: 300
+ ON 10/96: 40

29078. 89996: *Kyra Vayne: arias and
songs.* Music of Borodin, Verdi, Gluck,
Boito, Tchaikovsky, Spontini, Puccini,
Schubert, Mussorgsky, Gretchaninov, and
Rachmaninoff. *Vayne, soprano; various
accs.*
+ ARG 5-6/95: 251
+ Fa 7-8/95: 376
+ Gr 6/95: 135

29079. 89997: *Franz Völker: Lieder
recital.* Music of Mozart, Schubert,
Schumann, Loewe, Wolf, and Brahms.
*Völker, tenor; Heidenreich, Raucheisen,
Altmann, Steeger, Grossman, piano.*
Recorded 1920s-1940s.
• ARG 3-4/95: 279
+ Fa 1-2/95: 329

29080. 90014: STRAUSS—Krämerspiegel.
SALMHOFER—Heiteres Herbarium. *Patzak,
tenor; Klien, Salmhofer, piano.*
+ Fa 1-2/90: 316

29081. 90015: WAGNER—Die Walküre:
Act 1. *Teschemacher, Lorenz, Böhme;
Sächsische Staatskapelle; Elmendorff,
cond.* Recorded live 1944.
+ Fa 5-6/89: 356
+ St 7/89: 155

29082. 90020: Music of Bellini,
Donizetti, Verdi, Giordano, Cilea, Mario,
Falvo, De Curtis, Tosti, Tagliaferri, Di
Capua, Pennino, and Lama. *Taddei,
baritone; Teatro di San Carlo Orch.;
Gian Stellari's Orch.; Rapolo, cond.*
+ ARG 3-4/90: 156
- Fa 1-2/90: 364

29083. 90021: MOZART—Piano concertos
no. 21, 27; Serenade no. 13. *Gulda,
piano; Vienna Volksopernorchester;*

Swarowsky, cond.
• Fa 3-4/90: 232

29084. 90022: Music of Mozart,
Beethoven, Weber, Donizetti,
Tchaikovsky, and Puccini. *Dermota,
tenor; various orchs. & conds.*
+ Fa 9-10/90: 455

29085. 90028: El Cancionero musical de
Palacio. *Danserye.*
• ARG 1-2/92: 166

29086. 90029: PFITZNER—Orchestral
music. *Strub, violin; Hoelscher, cello;
Hüsch, baritone; Staatskapelle Berlin;
Berlin Phil. Orch.; Pfitzner, piano &
cond.*
+ ARG 7-8/90: 153
+ Fa 7-8/90: 222

29087. 90030: LEONCAVALLO—I pagliacci.
*Scheppan, Rosvænge, Hann, Schmitt-
Walter; Berlin Radio Chorus &
Symphony Orch.; Rother, cond.*
+ Fa 9-10/90: 272

29088. 90035 (3 discs): MOZART—Le
nozze di Figaro. *Teschemacher, Cebotari,
Ahlersmeyer, Schöffler; with assisting
soloists; South German Radio Chorus &
Symphony Orch.; Böhm, cond.* Sung in
German. Recorded live 1938.
- Fa 11-12/90: 291
+ Gr 7/90: 271

29089. 90036 (2 discs): VERDI—
Rigoletto; Don Carlo: Duet; Forza del
destino: Duets. *Berger, Rosvænge,
Schlusnus; with assisting soloists;
Staatskapelle Berlin; Heger, cond.* Sung
in German.
• Fa 11-12/90: 387

29090. 90040 (2 discs): GOUNOD—Faust.
*Teschemacher, Rosvænge, Nissen, Hann;
with assisting soloists; South German
Radio Chorus & Symphony Orch.;
Keilberth, cond.* Sung in German.
Recorded live 1937.
+ Fa 3-4/91: 223

29091. 90042: MASCAGNI—Cavalleria
rusticana. *Arangi Lombardi, Melandri,
Lulli; with assisting soloists; Teatro alla
Scala; Molajoli, cond.*
• Fa 3-4/91: 271

29092. 90043 (3 discs): WAGNER—
Lohengrin; Fliegende Holländer:
Excerpts. *Müller, Klose, Völker,
Prohaska, Hofmann, Grossman, Greindl;
Staatskapelle Berlin; Heger, cond.;
orchestra; Rother, cond.* Recorded live
1942, 1943.
+ Fa 3-4/91: 423

29093. 90048: LOEWE—Songs.
SALMHOFER—Heiteres Herbarium.
Czerwenka, bass; Cerny, piano.
• ARG 5-6/91: 161
• Fa 3-4/91: 158

29094. 90053: MOZART—Mass in C
minor, K. 427; Vesperae solennes de
Confessore: Laudate Dominum. *Lipp,
Ludwig, Dickie, Berry; Vienna Oratorio
Chorus; Pro Musica Orch.; Grossmann,
Horenstein, cond.*
+ ARG 11-12/91: 112
+ Fa 7-8/91: 231

29095. 90055 (2 discs): VERDI—Luisa
Miller; Don Carlo. Excerpts. *Cebotari,
Hopf, Böhme, Hann, Ahlersmeyer; with
assisting soloists; Dresden State Opera
Chorus; Sächsische Staatskapelle;
Elmendorff, cond.; Berlin Radio
Symphony Orch.; Rother, cond.* Sung in
German. Recorded live 1944.
• Fa 3-4/91: 414

29096. 90067: LEOPOLD I—Missa pro
defunctis. WERNER—Requiem in G minor.
*Chorus of the Maria Treu Basilica;
Convivium Musicum Vindobonense;
Kramer, cond.*
• ARG 9-10/91: 86
• Fa 9-10/91: 253

29097. 90073: KRENEK—Reisebuch aus
den österreichischen Alpen, op. 62.
Patzak, tenor; Schmidt, piano.
+ ARG 3-4/92: 82
+ Fa 1-2/92: 248

29098. 90074: PUCCINI—Gianni Schicchi.
*Taddei, Rapisardi, Savio, Corena,
Dubbini; Orch. of Radio Italiana of
Turin; Simonetto, cond.* Mono.; recorded
1949.
+ Fa 1-2/92: 301

29099. 90075 (2 discs): WAGNER—Die
Walküre: Scenes from Act II; Act III
(complete). *Rünger, Rode, Friedrich,
Buschmann; Grosses Orch. des
Reichssenders Königsberg; Brückner,
cond.* Mono.
- Fa 9-10/91: 391

29100. 90080: WAGNER—Lohengrin:
Prelude; Tristan und Isolde: Prelude and
Liebestod; Siegfried: Forest murmurs;
Götterdämmerung: Siegfried's Rhine
journey; Parsifal: Prelude,
Flowermaidens' scene, Good Friday
music, concluding scene. *Berlin State
Opera Orch.; Schillings, cond.* Recorded
1927.
+ Fa 11-12/92: 400

29101. 90102 (2 discs): VERDI—Falstaff;
Aïda: excerpts. *Hotter, bass; with
supporting soloists & orchestras.*
Recorded 1939; sung in German.
• ARG 9-10/92: 221
+ Fa 5-6/92: 270

29102. 90103: BEETHOVEN—Symphony
no. 9. *Helletsgruber, Anday, Maikl,
Mayr; Vienna State Opera Chorus;
Vienna Phil. Orch.; Weingartner, cond.*
Recorded 1935.
+ Fa 11-12/94: 172

29103. 90105 (2 discs): BEETHOVEN—
Fidelio. *Neralić, Schöffler, Ralf, Konetzni,
Alsen, Seefried, Klein; Vienna State
Opera; Böhm, cond.* Recorded live 1944.
- Fa 11-12/94: 167

29104. 90111: BEETHOVEN—Symphonies
no. 6, 8. *Vienna Phil. Orch.; Schalk,
cond.*
+ ARG 9-10/92: 213
+ Fa 9-10/92: 185
+ Gr 11/92: 223

29105. 90112: *Clemens Krauss conducts
the Vienna Philharmonic Orchestra.*
Music of Johann Strauss Jr. and Sr.,
Ziehrer and Haydn (Symphony no. 88).
Vienna Phil. Orch.; Krauss, cond.
Recorded 1929-31.
+ Fa 7-8/92: 290

29106. 90113: BEETHOVEN—Symphonies
no. 3, 8. *Vienna Phil. Orch.;
Weingartner, cond.*
+ ARG 9-10/92: 217
+ Fa 9-10/92: 180
+ Gr 11/92: 223

29107. 90114: BRAHMS—Symphony no.
1. HAYDN—Symphony no. 96. MAHLER—
Symphony no. 5: Adagietto. *Vienna Phil.
Orch.; Walter, cond.* Recorded 1937-38.
- Fa 7-8/92: 127

29108. 90116: *Hans Knappertsbusch
conducts the Vienna Philharmonic
Orchestra.* Music of Johann Strauss Jr.,
Ziehrer, Verdi and Wagner. Recorded
1940-42.
- ARG 9-10/92: 217
+ Fa 7-8/92: 290

29109. 90117: BEETHOVEN—Folksongs;
Mödlinger dances; 12 contradances.
*Loose, soprano; Dieman, baritone;
Weller, violin; Beini, cello; Werba,
piano; Vienna Volksoper Orch.; Angerer,
cond.* Recorded 1964.
- ARG 1-2/96: 84

29110. 90118: BEETHOVEN—Concerto for
violin and orchestra, op. 61. LALO—
Symphonie espagnole, op. 21. J. STRAUSS,
JR.—On the beautiful blue Danube;
Voices of spring. *Huberman, violin;
Vienna Phil. Orch.; Szell, cond.*
+ ARG 7-8/93: 206
- Fa 5-6/93: 153

29111. 90122 (2 discs): BOITO—
Mefistofele. *Neri, Noli, Argine, Poggi;
Chorus and Orch. of La Scala; Capuana,
cond.* Reissue.
- Fa 9-10/92: 195
+ ON 10/94: 50

29112. 90125: *Josef Metternich singt.*
Music of Rossini, Mozart, Marschner,
Meyerbeer, Bizet, Tchaikovsky, Borodin,
Verdi, Ponchielli, Giordano, and Puccini.
Metternich, baritone; orch. acc.
+ Fa 3-4/93: 342

29113. 90133 (3 discs): WAGNER—
Tannhäuser; Die Walküre (excerpts).
*Krauss, Eipperle, Reining, Schmitt-
Walter, Karén; Stuttgart Radio
Symphony; Leonhardt, cond.* Recorded
1937.
+ ARG 3-4/93: 193
- Fa 3-4/93: 328

29114. 90139: New Year's concerts,
1929-1940. *Vienna Phil. Orch.; various
conds.*
+ ARG 3-4/93: 199

29115. 90148: BRUCKNER—Symphony no.
9. *Munich Phil. Orch.; Hausegger, cond.*
Recorded 1938.
+ Fa 1-2/94: 150

29116. 90151: WAGNER—Die Walküre:
act I. *Krauss, Reining, Manowarda;
Stuttgart Radio Orch.; C. Leonhardt,
cond.* Recorded 1938.
- Fa 5-6/93: 352
+ Gr 11/93: 192
- ON 4/15/95: 34

29117. 90152 (2 discs): BIZET—Carmen.
*Höngen, mezzo-soprano; other vocalists;
Dresden State Opera Orch.; Böhm, cond.*
Sung in German; recorded 1942.
+ ARG 7-8/93: 210
+ Fa 5-6/93: 167

29118. 90157: BEETHOVEN—Symphony
no. 6; Leonore overture no. 3. WAGNER—
Siegfried idyll. *Vienna Phil. Orch.;
Walter, cond.* Recorded 1935/36.
+ ARG 1-2/94: 196

29119. 90160: VERDI—La traviata:
Excerpts; Rigoletto: Excerpts. *Cebotari,
Rosvænge, Schlusnus; Berlin State
Opera; Steinkopf, Rother, cond.*
Recorded 1942.
+ Fa 3-4/94: 356

29120. 90164: WAGNER—
Götterdämmerung. *Svanholm, Fuchs,
Koch, Fischer; other soloists; Bayreuth
Festival; Elmendorff, cond.* Recorded
1942.
+ Fa 9-10/93: 320

29121. 90166 (2 discs): MOZART—Don
Giovanni. *Stabile, Czerwenka, Grob-
Prandl, Konetzni, Handt, Pernerstorfer,
Poell, Heusser; Vienna State Opera
Chorus; Vienna Symphony Orch.;
Swarowsky, cond.* Reissue; recorded
1950.
+ Fa 11-12/93: 333
+ ON 2/5/94: 38

29122. 90167: *Virtuoso concertos from
the Biedermeier period.* Music of
Hummel, Krommer, and Kalkbrenner.
*Galling, piano; Stuttgart Phil. Orch.;
Paulmüller, cond.; Glazer, clarinet;
Württemberg Chamber Orch.; Faerber,
cond.; Kann, piano; Hamburg Symphony
Orch.; Beissel, cond.*
- Fa 11-12/93: 491

29123. 90168: WAGNER—Die
Meistersinger: Act II. *Hann, Schirp,
Fügel, Windisch; other soloists; Orch. of
the Berlin Radio; Rother, cond.* Recorded
1942.
+ Fa 9-10/93: 322

29124. 90172: BEETHOVEN—String
quartets no. 9, 11, 14-15. *Busch Quartet.*
Recorded 1933-37.
+ ARG 1-2/94: 196
+ Fa 11-12/93: 178
+ Gr 11/93: 189

29125. 90174 (4 discs): WAGNER—Die
Meistersinger. *Schöffler; other soloists;
Orch. & Chorus of the Bayreuth Festival,
1943; Abendroth, cond.*
+ Fa 1-2/94: 347
+ Gr 2/94: 111

29126. 90175: VERDI—Macbeth; Don
Carlo (excerpts). *Vocal soloists; Vienna
State Opera; Böhm, Baltzer, conds.*
Recorded 1943.
+ ARG 1-2/94: 198
+ Gr 5/94: 132

29127. 90182 (2 discs): WOLF—Der
Corregidor. DVOŘÁK—Der Jakobiner:
Schlaf, Kindelein. *Teschemacher, Fuchs,
Erb, S. Nilsson, Herrmann; Dresden
State Opera Chorus; Dresden State
Orch.; Elmendorff, cond.*
+ Fa 5-6/94: 284

29128. 90185 (2 discs): WOLF—
Italienisches Liederbuch; Italian
serenade. *Lier, soprano; Holl, baritone;
Lutz, piano; Pro Arte Quartet.*
- ARG 7-8/94: 188
+ Fa 11-12/94: 426

29129. 90189: *Hans Knappertsbusch in
London and Switzerland.* Music of
Wagner and Brahms. *Zürich Tonhalle
Orch.; London Phil. Orch.; Orch. de la
Suisse romande; Knappertsbusch, cond.*
Recorded 1947.
+ ARG 5-6/95: 236
+ Fa 5-6/95: 436

29130. 90190: Music of Mozart, Wagner,
Verdi, Schumann, and Brahms.
Schoeffler, baritone.
- ARG 7-8/94: 236
- Fa 11-12/94: 444

29131. 90191: Troubadors and the fourth
Crusade. *Ensemble Lyra Wien.*
- ARG 9-10/94: 249

29132. 90199: BEETHOVEN—Symphony
no. 6. BRAHMS—Variations on a theme by
Haydn. *Vienna Phil. Orch.; Furtwängler,
cond.* Recorded 1943.
- Fa 11-12/94: 171
- Gr 5/95: 124

29133. 90200: Arias from Hans Heiling,
Flying Dutchman, Meistersinger, Aida,
Otello, and others. *Hotter, bass.*
Recorded 1939-43.

PREISER

+ ARG 7-8/95: 277
+ ON 4/13/96: 53

29134. 90201: BEETHOVEN—Symphony no. 3. *Berlin Phil. Orch.; Pfitzner, cond.* Recorded 1929.
+ ARG 5-6/95: 236
• Fa 1-2/95: 116

29135. 90203 (3 discs): MOZART—Die Hochzeit des Figaro. *Hotter, Braun, Beilke, Kunz, Sommerschuh, Fischer, Witt, Neidlinger, Wernigk, Norman, Timm; Vienna State Opera Chorus; Vienna Phil. Orch.; Krauss, cond.* Recorded 1942; sung in German.
• ARG 1-2/95: 254
• Fa 11-12/94: 314

29136. 90205, 90216 (2 and 3 discs): STRAUSS—Conducts his tone poems. *Bavarian State Orch.; Vienna Phil. Orch.; Strauss, cond.*
+ ARG 1-2/95: 248
• Fa 1-2/95: 279

29137. 90208 (2 discs): NICOLAI—Die lustigen Weiber von Windsor. Opera arias and songs of Mozart, Rossini, Cornelius, Puccini, Nicolai, and Schumann. *Strienz, Hann, Windisch, Ludwig, Florian, Heyer, Beilke, Schilp, Hoffmann; Chorus of the Städtische Oper; Berlin Radio Symphony Orch.; Rother, Steinkopf, conds.* Recorded 1943.
+ Fa 1-2/95: 219
+ ON 7/95: 46

29138. 90210 (2 discs): PUCCINI—Tosca; Il tabarro (final portion). *Ranczak, Rosvænge, Hann, Berlin Radio Orch. & Chorus; Ludwig, cond.; Ranczak, Anders, Ahlersmeyer; Stuttgart Radio Orch.; Krauss, cond.* Sung in German. Recorded live 1944, 1938.
- Fa 1-2/95: 231 (Tosca)
+ Fa 1-2/95: 231 (Il tabarro)

29139. 90213: WAGNER—Opera excerpts. *Lorenz, tenor; various assisting artists.*
• Fa 1-2/95: 306
+ ON 4/15/95: 34

29140. 90217 (2 discs): STRAUSS—Ariadne auf Naxos. *Reining, Seefried, Noni, Lorenz; Vienna State Opera; Böhm, cond.* Recorded 1944.
+ ARG 1-2/95: 255
+ Fa 1-2/95: 277
+ Gr 11/94: 153
+ ON 3/4/95: 40

29141. 90221: BEETHOVEN—Symphonies no. 6, 8. *Berlin State Opera Orch.; Berlin Phil. Orch.; Pfitzner, cond.* Recorded 1929.
+ ARG 5-6/96: 262

29142. 90222. STRAUSS—Taillefer; Opera excerpts. *Cebotari, Ludwig, Hotter; Singgemeinschaft Rudolf Lamy; Berlin Radio Symphony Orch.; Rother, cond.* Recorded 1943-44.

+ ARG 5-6/95: 241
• Fa 3-4/95: 312
+ Gr 8/95: 136
+ ON 10/96: 42

29143. 90223: WAGNER—Rienzi: Excerpts. *Lorenz, Klose, Scheppan; Berlin State Opera; Schüler, cond.* Recorded 1941.
+ ARG 5-6/95: 243
+ Fa 9-10/95: 358
☐ ON 4/15/95: 34

29144. 90226: BRUCKNER—Symphony no. 4. *Berlin Phil. Orch.; Knappertsbusch, cond.*
+ ARG 3-4/95: 268
+ Fa 3-4/95: 148

29145. 90227: Arias from Il re pastore, Idomeneo, Marriage of Figaro, Falstaff, Gianni Schicchi, Turandot, and others. *Gueden, soprano.* Recorded 1951-54.
+ ARG 5-6/95: 227

29146. 90228 (2 discs): BACH—St. Matthew passion. *Erb, Hüsch, Lemnitz, Beckmann; Leipzig Thomanerchor; Leipzig Gewandhaus Orch.; Ramin, cond.*
+ Fa 7-8/95: 108

29147. 90229: SCHUBERT—Symphony no. 8. Music of Mozart, Liszt, Smetana, Dvořák, and J. Strauss. *Berlin Phil. Orch.; Berlin State Opera Orch.; E. Kleiber, cond.*
• ARG 5-6/95: 236

29148. 90230 (2 discs): VERDI—Otello. *Ralf, Konetzni, Schöffler, Nikolaidi; Vienna State Opera; Böhm, cond.* Sung in German; recorded 1944.
• ARG 5-6/95: 242

29149. 90232 (2 discs): WAGNER—Der fliegende Holländer. *Berglund, Hofmann, Müller, Amus, Zimmermann; Bayreuth Festival, 1942; Kraus, cond.* Recorded 1942.
+ ARG 5-6/95: 242
+ Fa 3-4/95: 332
+ ON 6/95: 44
• ON 4/15/95: 34

29150. 90234 (4 discs): WAGNER—Die Meistersinger von Nürnberg. *Schöffler, Alsen, Kunz, Krenn, Seider, Klein, Seefried, Schürhoff; Vienna State Opera; Böhm, cond.* Recorded 1944.
+ ARG 7-8/95: 274
+ Fa 7-8/95: 361
+ ON 6/95: 44

29151. 90236: Waltzes and polkas by Strauss, Ziehrer, and Komzak. *Berlin State Opera Orch.; Berlin Symphony Orch.; Vienna Phil. Orch.; Berlin Phil. Orch.; Knappertsbusch, cond.*
+ ARG 5-6/96: 261

29152. 90237 (2 discs): STRAUSS—Daphne. *Reining, Dermota, Alsen,*

Frutschnigg; Vienna State Opera; Böhm, cond. Recorded 1944.
+ ARG 5-6/96: 269
+ Gr 11/95: 190
+ ON 3/30/96: 36

29153. 90239: Spanish music around 1500. *Ensemble Accentus.*
+ ARG 9-10/95: 279

29154. 90258: BEETHOVEN—Symphony no. 2. BRUCKNER—Symphony no. 4: Scherzo. BRAHMS—Symphony no. 3; Hungarian dances no. 1-3. *Vienna Phil. Orch.; Krauss, cond.*
+ ARG 9-10/96: 270

29155. 90266: WAGNER—Götterdämmerung: Excerpts. *Leider, Melchior, Thorborg, List; Royal Opera Covent Garden; Beecham, cond.* Recorded 1936.
+ ARG 11-12/96: 292
+ ON 1/11/97: 42

29156. 90267: WAGNER—Excerpts from Tannhäuser, Tristan, Meistersinger, and Götterdämmerung. *Berlin State Opera Orch.; Schillings, cond.*
• ARG 1-2/97: 233

29157. 90268: Arias from Martha, Rigoletto, Trovatore, Tosca, and others. *Schmidt, tenor.*
+ ARG 11-12/96: 303

29158. 90271: VERDI—Otello: Excerpts. PUCCINI—Tosca: Excerpts. *Rosvænge, tenor; Berlin State Opera Orch.; Berlin Radio Orch.; Steinkopf, cond.* Recorded 1942-43.
+ ARG 11-12/96: 303

29159. 90272: VERDI—Rigoletto: Excerpts (sung in German). GIORDANO—Andrea Chénier. *Rosvænge, tenor; Berlin Radio Orch.; Berlin State Opera Orch.; Heger, Rother, conds.* Recorded 1942-43.
+ ARG 11-12/96: 303

29160. 90273: VERDI—Scenes from Il trovatore and Un ballo in maschera (sung in German). *Rosvænge, tenor; Berlin Radio Orch.; Rother, cond.* Recorded 1942-43.
+ ARG 11-12/96: 303

29161. 90288: SCHUBERT—Winterreise. *Schmitt-Walter, baritone; Leitner, piano.* Recorded 1940-43.
• ARG 11-12/96: 289

29162. 90293: SCHUBERT—Die schöne Müllerin. *Schiøtz, tenor; Moore, piano.* Recorded 1945.
+ ARG 11-12/96: 289
+ Gr 9/96: 121
+ ON 1/11/97: 41

29163. 90294: SCHILLINGS—Hexenlied; Der Pfeifertag; Moloch; Excerpts; Mona Lisa: Excerpts; Songs. *Wullner, Kemp, Mann, Berlin Phil. Orch.; Berlin State*

Opera Orch.; Schillings, cond.
□ ARG 1-2/97: 233

29164. 90299: *Erich Kleiber conducts.* Music of Dvořák, Liszt, Mozart, Schubert, and Smetana. *Berlin Phil. Orch.; Czech Phil. Orch.; Berlin State Opera Orch.; Kleiber, cond.* Recorded 1927-1934.
+ Fa 5-6/95: 433

29165. 90301: LOEWE—Ballads. *Hotter, bass; Raucheisen, piano.* Recorded 1943-45.
+ ARG 1-2/97: 237

29166. 90302: Music of Verdi, Giordano, Mascagni, and others. *Borkh, soprano.* Recorded 1956-58.
• ARG 1-2/97: 224

29167. 90303: SCHUBERT—Symphonies no. 3, 5. MOZART—Symphony no. 41. *Munich Phil. Orch.; Vienna Phil. Orch.; Kabasta, cond.*
• ARG 1-2/97: 233

29168. 90304: BRUCKNER—Symphony no. 4. *Munich Phil. Orch.; Kabasta, cond.*
• ARG 1-2/97: 233

29169. 90308: BRUCKNER—Symphony no. 7. *Munich Phil. Orch.; Kabasta, cond.*
• ARG 1-2/97: 233

29170. 90901/12 (12 discs): HAYDN—The string quartet collection. *Konzerthaus Quartet.*
• Fa 1-2/95: 171

29171. 90922: *The wartime Electrola recordings.* Music of Brahms, Schubert, Mozart, and Bach. *Vienna Phil. Orch.; Böhm, cond.* Recorded 1940-1944.
• ARG 5-6/95: 236
• Fa 5-6/95: 443

29172. 90951: MOZART—Symphonies no. 39-41. *Berlin State Opera Orch.; Vienna Phil. Orch.; Knappertsbusch, cond.* Recorded 1929, 1941.
+ ARG 9-10/93: 257
+ Fa 9-10/93: 224

29173. 90953: *Famous tenors of the 1930s.* Music of Bizet, Puccini, Cilèa, Verdi, Rossini, Bellini, Wagner, Halévy, Boito, Massenet, Glinka, Donizetti, Meyerbeer, Nessler, and Klenau. *Various performers.*
+ Fa 7-8/93: 280

29174. 90976: BEETHOVEN—Symphony no. 3. LISZT—Les preludes. *Berlin Phil. Orch.; Knappertsbusch, cond.*
+ ARG 3-4/94: 228
+ Fa 5-6/94: 110
• Gr 5/94: 128

29175. 93053 (2 discs): HAYDN—Jahreszeiten. *Eipperle, Patzak, Hann; Vienna State Opera Chorus; Vienna Phil.*

Orch.; Krauss, cond.
• Fa 3-4/90: 190

29176. 93063: SCHMIDT—String quartet no. 2; Piano pieces. *Wiener Konzerthaus Quartet; Demus, piano.* Reissue.
□ ARG 9-10/91: 120
+ Fa 9-10/91: 336

29177. 93067: SCHUBERT—Winterreise. *Patzak, tenor; Demus, piano.*
+ Fa 5-6/89: 312

29178. 93071: HAYDN—Seven last words of Christ. *Wiener Konzerthaus Quartet.*
• Fa 7-8/91: 173

29179. 93109: SCHUBERT—String quintet. HAYDN—String quartet, op. 76, no. 1. *Wiener Konzerthaus Quartet.*
+ Fa 3-4/92: 313

29180. 93110: SCHUBERT—Octet in F major, D. 803. *Wlach, clarinet; Freiberg, horn; Öhlberger, bassoon; Hermann, double bass; Wiener Konzerthaus Quartet.*
• Fa 3-4/91: 360

29181. 93111: PFITZNER—Piano quintet, op. 23; Sextet for piano, clarinet, violin, viola, cello, and double bass, op. 55. *W. Kamper, piano; Wlach, clarinet; A. Kamper, Titze, violins; Weis, viola; Kvarda, cello; Hermann, double bass.*
+ Fa 1-2/90: 258

29182. 93128: SCHUBERT—Die schöne Müllerin. *Patzak, tenor; Raucheisen, piano.*
+ ARG 11-12/89: 112
+ Fa 9-10/89: 316
+ Gr 11/89: 952

29183. 93145: SCHUBERT—Songs. Schumann—Dichterliebe. *Hotter, bass-baritone; Altmann, piano.*
+ Fa 5-6/88: 204
+ Gr 7/88: 190

29184. 93211: *Ballads.* LOEWE—Songs. *Wächter, baritone; Dokoupil, piano.*
+ ARG 11-12/89: 75
- Fa 9-10/89: 238

29185. 93256: *Ein Liederabend mit Anton Dermota.* Music of Mozart, Beethoven, Schubert, Schumann, Brahms, Wolf, and Strauss. *A. Dermota, tenor; H. Dermota, piano.*
+ ARG 9-10/90: 152
• Fa 7-8/90: 333

29186. 93261: STRAUSS—Songs. *Dermota, tenor; Konetzni, soprano; Poell, baritone; Strauss, piano.* Recorded 1943.
+ ARG 9-10/89: 108
+ Fa 9-10/89: 334

29187. 93262: STRAUSS—Richard Strauss begleitet. *Reining, Piltti, sopranos; Dermota, tenor; Strauss, piano.*

+ Fa 1-2/92: 341
+ Gr 10/92: 203

29188. 93263 (2 discs): SCHMIDT—Das Buch mit sieben Siegeln. *Kyriaki, Töpper, Dermota, Moser, Korn, Holl; Graz Concert Choir; Lower Austrian Tonkunstler Orch.; Hochstrasser, cond.*
+ Fa 7-8/88: 242
+ ON 3/26/88: 42

29189. 93274: 93274: SCHUBERT—Die schöne Müllerin. *A. Dermota, tenor; H. Dermota, piano.*
+ ARG 1-2/91: 90
• Fa 7-8/90: 252

29190. 93287: SCHUBERT—Winterreise. *A. Dermota, tenor; H. Dermota, piano.*
+ Fa 3-4/91: 370

29191. 93311: PFITZNER—Das dunkle Reich. BRAHMS—Schicksalslied; Nänie. *Patchell, soprano; Holl, baritone; Scholz, organ; Graz Concert Choir; Graz Symphony Orch.; Savaria Symphony; Hochstrasser, cond.*
+ ARG 9-10/89: 89
+ Fa 9-10/89: 278

29192. 93316: SCHUBERT—Songs. *Holl, baritone; Richter, piano.*
+ ARG 9-10/89: 103
- Fa 5-6/89: 306

29193. 93325: SCHUBERT—Mass no. 4; Deutsche Messe, D. 872. MOZART—Vesperae Solennes de confessore, K. 339: Laudate Dominum; Ave verum corpus. *St. Augustin, Vienna Choir & Orch.; Wolf, cond.*
• Fa 3-4/91: 359

29194. 93331: PFITZNER—Songs. *Holl, bass-baritone; Richter, piano.*
+ ARG 9-10/89: 88
+ Fa 7-8/89: 211

29195. 93333: HAYDN—Nelson Mass. *Beretovac, Lipovsek, Moser, Holl; Scholz, organ; St. Augustin, Vienna Choir & Orch.; Wolf, cond.*
+ ARG 5-6/89: 54
+ Fa 5-6/89: 312

29196. 93337: SCHUBERT—Die schöne Müllerin. *Holzmair, baritone; Demus, piano.*
+ Fa 5-6/88: 207

29197. 93345: SCHUBERT—Songs. *Holl, baritone; Richter, piano.*
• Fa 5-6/88: 203

29198. 93347: HAYDN—Missa in honorem Beatissimae Virginis Mariae "Great organ solo mass"; Missa Sancti Nicolai. *Borowska, Poschner, Schmid, Reinprecht, Spitzer, Sramek; Chorus & Orch. of St. Augustin, Vienna; Wolf, cond.* Reissue.
• Fa 11-12/93: 269

PREISER

29199. 93355: Music of Brahms, Reger, and Stephan. *Holl, baritone; Richter, piano.*
  - Fa 11-12/89: 439

29200. 93357: SCHMIDT—Clarinet quintet in A major. *Vienna Chamber Musicians.*
  + Fa 7-8/88: 242

29201. 93368: MENDELSSOHN—Songs. *Holzmair, baritone; Wagner, piano.*
  + ARG 9-10/89: 80
  + Fa 5-6/89: 232
  + Fa 7-8/89: 181
  + Gr 7/91: 100

29202. 93370: BRAHMS—Cello sonata, op. 78. PFITZNER—Cello sonata in F♯ major. *Hornstein, cello; Jakab, piano.*
  • ARG 7-8/90: 33 (Brahms)
  + ARG 7-8/90: 33 (Pfitzner)
  + Fa 7-8/90: 107

29203. 93373: SCHUBERT—Songs. *Holl, baritone; Lutz, piano.*
  + ARG 9-10/89: 103
  + Fa 5-6/89: 306

29204. 93378: DVOŘÁK—Mass in D major. *Schmid, Bernheimer, Reinprecht, Sramek; St. Augustin, Vienna Chorus & Orch.; Wolf, cond.*
  • Fa 5-6/88: 119

29205. 93379: MOZART—String quartet, K. 156; Divertimento no. 7. HAYDN—String quartet, op. 2, no. 5. *Salzburg String Quartet; Harlander, double bass.*
  + Fa 5-6/89: 248

29206. 93382: HOLL—Frühlingsreise. MUSSORGSKY—Sunless. WOLF—Michelangelo Lieder. *Holl, baritone; Jansen, piano.*
  • ARG 9-10/89: 63
  • Fa 5-6/89: 218
  • Fa 7-8/89: 294

29207. 93383: SCHMIDT—Piano quintet in G major; Quintet for clarinet and piano quartet. *Demus, piano; Prinz, clarinet; Kamper, Hink, violins; Stangler, viola; Resel, cello.*
  + ARG 5-6/89: 82
  + Fa 5-6/89: 303
  • Gr 2/89: 1308

29208. 93384: *Tirsi morir volea.* Vocal music by Gabrieli, Zanotti, Gesualdo, Marenzio, Certon, Le Jeune, Gombert, Sermisy, Passeraeu, Josquin, Hassler, Senfl, Morley, Bartlet, Cornyshe, Tomkins and Gibbons. *La Capella.*
  + ARG 11-12/91: 197

29209. 93387: MOZART—Serenade no. 13 (Eine kleine Nachtmusik). HAYDN—String quartet in D minor, H. III:76. BOCCHERINI—String quintet, op. 13, no. 5: Minuet. *Salzburg String Quartet; Harlander, double bass.*
  • Fa 9-10/89: 263

29210. 93393: *Liederabend.* Music of Schubert, Tchaikovsky, Mussorgsky, Borodin, and Holl. *Holl, bass; Maisenberg, piano.*
  + Fa 5-6/91: 342

29211. 93395: SCHMIDT—Variations on a Hussar song; Concertante variations on a theme of Beethoven for piano (left hand) and orchestra. *Adam, piano; Lower Austrian Musicians' Orch.; Eschwe, cond.*
  + ARG 9-10/91: 120
  + Fa 9-10/91: 336

29212. 93400: SCHUBERT—Die schöne Müllerin. *Holl, baritone; Lutz, piano.*
  • Fa 3-4/92: 314

29213. 93401: A. MAHLER—Lieder. SCHOENBERG—Brettl-Lieder. R. STRAUSS—Krämerspiegel. *Zednik, tenor; Leitner, piano.*
  - ARG 7-8/92: 166
  + Fa 5-6/92: 190

29214. 93402: SCHUBERT—Schwanengesang; Herbst; Am Fenster; Der Wanderer an den Mond; Das Zügenglöcklein. *Holl, baritone; Lutz, piano.*
  • ARG 7-8/95: 188
  • Fa 5-6/95: 326

29215. 93403: SCHUMANN—Dichterliebe; Selected songs. *Holl, baritone; Beenhouwer, piano.*
  • ARG 9-10/95: 211
  + Fa 7-8/95: 310

PRELUDIO

29216. PRL 90 665: *Sacred music of the twentieth century.* Music of Poulenc, Penderecki, Gesseney, Britten and Burkhard. *Choeur des XVI; Ducret, cond.; Oberson, organ.*
  + Fa 5-6/92: 304

29217. PHC 1120/21 (2 discs): BACH—Brandenburg concertos. *Zürich Baroque Ensemble; Schuricht, cond.*
  • Fa 5-6/88: 66

29218. PHC 1123: BEETHOVEN—Overtures: Fidelio; Egmont; Coriolan; Leonore no. 3; Consecration of the house. *Vienna Festival Orch.; Krips, cond.*
  + Fa 7-8/88: 115

29219. PHC 1124: BRAHMS—Symphony no. 4; Tragic overture. *Bavarian Radio Orch.; Schuricht, cond.*
  + Fa 5-6/88: 96

29220. PHC 1125: BRAHMS—Piano concerto no. 2. *Magaloff, piano; Hague Phil. Orch.; Otterloo, cond.*
  + ARG 5-6/88: 19
  + Fa 5-6/88: 91

29221. PHC 1126: BRUCKNER—Symphony no. 7. *Hague Phil. Orch.; Schuricht, cond.*
  - Fa 5-6/88: 99

29222. PHC 1127: BRAHMS—Symphony no. 1. *Vienna Festival Orch.; Krips, cond.*
  • Fa 5-6/88: 96

29223. PHC 1128: MENDELSSOHN—Piano trio no. 1. DVOŘÁK—Piano trio no. 4. *Beaux Arts Trio.*
  + Fa 5-6/88: 164

29224. PHC 1129: MOZART—Symphonies no. 35, 39. *North German Radio Symphony Orch.; Monteux, cond.*
  • ARG 5-6/88: 50
  + Fa 5-6/88: 174

29225. PHC 1130: LALO—Cello concerto. SAINT-SAËNS—Cello concerto no. 1. *Fournier, cello; Monte Carlo National Opera Orch.; Conta, cond.*
  • ARG 5-6/88: 38
  + Fa 7-8/88: 184

29226. PHC 1133/34 (2 discs): SCHUBERT—Octet, D. 803. BEETHOVEN—Septet, op. 20. *Pascal Quartet; Lancelot, clarinet; Coursier, horn; Hongne, bassoon.*
  + ARG 9-10/88: 22
  - Fa 5-6/88: 206

29227. PHC 1136: TCHAIKOVSKY—Piano concerto no. 1. CHOPIN—Krakowiak, op. 14. *Magaloff, piano; Hague Phil. Orch.; Otterloo, cond.*
  • Fa 9-10/88: 275

29228. PHC 2112: LISZT—Tasso (arr. Vaucher and Favre); Orpheus (arr. Vaucher and Favre); Mazeppa (arr. Vaucher and Favre). *Vaucher, organ; Favre, piano.*
  - Fa 5-6/88: 156

29229. PHC 2116: Guitar music of Barrios, Villa-Lobos, Martin, and Mersson. *Petrou, guitar.*
  • ARG 5-6/89: 115
  + Fa 5-6/89: 395

29230. PRL 2144: Organ music of Grigny, Bach, and Mozart. *Jacquenod, organ.*
  □ Fa 5-6/91: 356
  + HPR v.8, no.3/91: 74

29231. PRL 2147: MARTIN—Cello concerto; The four elements. *DeCroos, cello; Concertgebouw Orch.; Haitink, cond.*
  + ARG 5-6/90: 70
  + Fa 9-10/91: 264
  + Gr 10/91: 90

29232. PHC 2148: BERG—Violin concerto. PONCE—Violin concerto. PROKOFIEV—Violin concerto no. 2. *Szeryng, violin; Polish Radio and Television National Symphony Orch. (Warsaw); Krenz, cond.* Recorded live

1958.
- ARG 7-8/89: 126
+ Fa 7-8/89: 194

29233. PHC 2149: MOZART—Violin concerto no. 5. VIVALDI—Concerto for 2 violins in D minor. SZYMANOWSKI—Violin concerto no. 1. *D. & I. Oistrakh, violins; USSR State Symphony Orch.; Kondrashin, cond.; National Phil. Orch (Warsaw); Stryja, cond.* Mozart and Szymanowski recorded live 1961.
+ Fa 7-8/89: 194

29234. PRL 2152: MOZART—Complete concert arias. *Alva, tenor; Olejniczak, piano; Silesian Phil. Orch.; Rajski, cond.*
• Fa 5-6/91: 220

29235. PHC 2153/54 (2 discs): ALAIN—Piano music (complete). *Fuchs, piano.*
- Fa 5-6/91: 99
+ Gr 3/92: 75

29236. PRL 2155: DAQUIN—Noëls. DANDRIEU—Noëls. *Capt, oboe, English horn; Meylan, organ, harpsichord.*
- Fa 5-6/92: 146

29237. PRL 2156: LUTOSŁAWSKI—Symphony no. 1. SHOSTAKOVICH—Symphony no. 5. *National Phil. Orch. (Warsaw); Czech Phil. Orch.; Stokowski, cond.* Recorded live 1959, 1961.
• ARG 9-10/91: 88
+ Fa 7-8/91: 195

29238. PRL 2157: BEETHOVEN—Piano concertos no. 1, 3. *Richter, piano; Czech Phil. Orch.; Ančerl, cond.*
+ Fa 11-12/91: 261

29239. PRL 2157 : BEETHOVEN—Piano concertos no. 1, 3. *Richter, piano; Czech Phil. Orch.; Ančerl, cond.* Recorded 1962.
• ARG 7-8/96: 73

29240. PRL 2159: RACHMANINOFF—Trio elégiaque no. 2. ARENSKY—Piano trio no. 1. *Trio Amati.*
+ Fa 11-12/91: 451

29241. PRL 2161: Music of Bach, F. Couperin, Marchand, Böhm, and Buxtehude. *Meylan, organ.*
□ Fa 11-12/91: 550

29242. PRL 2165: CHOPIN—Piano concertos no. 1-2. *Rubinstein, piano; Polish Radio Orch.; Krenz, cond.* Recorded 1966.
+ ARG 7-8/96: 99

29243. SBCD 2600: C. SCHUMANN—Piano music. *Tsachor, piano.*
• ARG 11-12/88: 81
- Fa 1-2/89: 262

29244. PHC 3138: HAYDN—Concertos for lyra, 2 violins, 2 violas, cello, double bass, and 2 horns, no. 2, 4; Organ concerto no. 1. *Ruf, lyra; Lehrndorfer,*

organ; Stuttgart Soloists.
• ARG 9-10/88: 50
• Fa 9-10/88: 164

29245. PHC 3141: MOZART—Requiem. *Lipp, Höngen, Dickie, Weber; unidentified chorus; Vienna Symphony Orch.; Horenstein, cond.*
• ARG 1-2/89: 71
- Fa 9-10/88: 216

29246. PHC 3142: MOZART—Minuets and contradances. *Paul Angerer & His Soloists.*
+ Fa 9-10/88: 210

29247. PHC 3143: MAHLER—Symphony no. 1. *Vienna Symphony Orch.; Horenstein, cond.*
+ Fa 9-10/89: 241

29248. PHC 3145: BRUCKNER—Symphony no. 6. *Vienna Festival Orch.; Swarowsky, cond.*
- Fa 7-8/89: 119

29249. PHC 3146: MOZART—Piano concertos no. 15, 17. *Haebler, piano; Bamberg Symphony Orch.; Vienna Chamber Orch.; Hollreiser, cond.*
+ ARG 9-10/89: 84
- Fa 7-8/89: 193

29250. SBCD 4600: BACH—Violin concertos no. 1-2; Violin concerto, BWV 1056; Violin sonata no. 1. *Lysy, violin; Camerata Lysy Gstaad; Menuhin, violin & cond.*
• Fa 9-10/88: 87

29251. SBCD 5600: MENDELSSOHN—Violin concerto in D minor; Concerto for violin and piano in D minor. *Lysy, violin; Delle-Vigne, piano; Camerata Lysy Gstaad.*
□ Fa 9-10/88: 196

29252. SBCD 6700: LOBO—Mass e credo. *Associação de Canto Coral; Camerata Rio de Janeiro; Morelenbaum, cond.*
• ARG 11-12/88: 26
- Fa 11-12/88: 160

PREMIER

29253. PRCD 1004: ARLEN—Americanegro suite ; Songs from stage and screen. *Kay, soprano; Howard, piano; Premier Gospel Quartet.*
+ Fa 9-10/91: 141

29254. PRCD 1005: BLITZSTEIN—A Blitzstein cabaret. *Williams, soprano; Edwards, tenor; Lehrman, piano.*
+ Fa 9-10/91: 169

29255. PRCD 1006: Music of Piston, Fine, Siegmeister, Persichetti, and Carter. *Boehm Quintette.*
+ Fa 1-2/91: 402

29256. PRCD 1007: BERLIN—Let's go back to the waltz. *Baird, Tate, vocals; Renzi, piano.*
+ Fa 9-10/91: 162

29257. PRCD 1008: BILLINGS—The continental harmonist (Selections). GREGG SMITH—The continental harmonist ballet. *Gregg Smith Singers; Adirondack Chamber Orch.; Smith, cond.* Reissue.
- Fa 11-12/91: 273

29258. PRCD 1009: SCHUMAN—The mighty Casey: excerpts. Barber—A hand of bridge. Blitzstein—The harpies. *Gregg Smith Singers; Long Island Symphonic Choral Assoc.; Adirondack Chamber Orch.; Smith, cond.*
+ Fa 9-10/91: 350

29259. PRCD 1010: SIEGMEISTER—Flute concerto; Sextet for brass and percussion; Theatre set; Clarinet concerto. *Lloyd, flute; London Symphony Orch.; Siegmeister, cond.; Schwarz, trumpet; Brymer, clarinet; Brass Ensemble; Eastman-Rochester Orch.; Hanson, cond.*
+ Fa 7-8/91: 291

29260. PRCD 1011: SOUSA—Concert, theater and parlor songs. *Guyer, soprano; Willson, baritone; Buck, piano.*
+ Fa 9-10/91: 363

29261. PRCD 1012: PERRY—Mark Twain. *Vocal soloists; Unnamed accompaniment; Patterson, cond.*
+ Fa 11-12/91: 436

29262. PRCD 1013: *American piano, vol. 1.* GOULD—Prelude and toccata. NORTH—Streetcar named Desire: Nine piano sequences. DUKE—Piano sonata. SIEGMEISTER—Sunday in Brooklyn: Suite. *Mandel, piano.*
+ Fa 7-8/91: 165

29263. PRCD 1014: FLAGELLO—Electra; Divertimento; Sonata for piano; Prelude, ostinato and fugue; Étude "Homage to Chopin"; Two waltzes; Three episodes. *Pierce, piano; Paul Price Percussion Ensemble.*
+ Fa 9-10/91: 216

29264. PRCD 1017: NORTH—A Streetcar named desire: ballet. ROSENSTOCK—The Legend of John Henry: ballet. *Various performers.*
+ Fa 11-12/91: 427

29265. PRCD 1018: GOTTLIEB—Evening, morn, and noon (sacred music). *Vocal and instrumental soloists; Metropolitan Brass Ensemble; New York Motet Choir; Sturk, cond.*
□ ARG 9-10/92: 111

29266. PRCD 1020: SMITH—Magnificat; Prayer for peace; Variations on a Bach chorale. *Rees, soprano; Gregg Smith Singers; Children's Choir; Adirondack*

PREMIER

Chamber Orch.; Smith, cond.
• Fa 9-10/91: 361

29267. PRCD 1021: *Rags and other riches.* Music of Hampton, Sousa, Matthews, Confrey, Lamb, Ashwander, Morath, P. Johnson, and Ammons & Johnson. *Mandel, piano.*
+ Fa 1-2/94: 410

29268. PRCD 1023: Music of Amram, Fine, Hoiby, Dello Joio, Mayer, Cowell, and McBride. *Boehm Quintet.*
+ ARG 9-10/94: 246
+ Fa 7-8/95: 437

29269. PRCD 1024: *Prairie echoes.* GUION—Piano music. *Rowley, piano.*
+ Fa 1-2/94: 194

29270. PRCD 1025: SAINT-SAËNS—Requiem. SOMARY—A ballad of God and his people. *Hewes, Weld, MacMaster, Watson; Fairfield County Chorale; Horace Mann Glee Club; Amor Artis Gregorian Soloists; Amor Artis Orch.; Somary, cond.*
- Fa 1-2/94: 299

29271. PRCD 1026: *Twentieth century flute.* Music of Ibert, Griffes, Nielsen, and Perry. *Bryan, flute; Czechoslovak Radio Symphony Orch., Bratislava; Chen, cond.*
+ Fa 1-2/94: 396

29272. PRCD 1027: *Trumpet concertos from three centuries.* Music of Böhme, Molter, Ponchielli, and Perry. *Ghitalla, trumpet & flugelhorn; Slovak Phil. Orch.; Capella Istropolitana; Perry, cond.*
• Fa 1-2/94: 414

29273. PRCD 1028: *Ameican piano, vol. 4.* Music of Foster, Herbert, Joplin, Gershwin, Johnson, Beiderbecke, Arlen, Levant, and Ellington. *J. Smith, piano.*
+ ARG 7-8/94: 215
• Fa 1-2/94: 407

29274. PRCD 1029: *American flute, vol. 1.* Music of Antheil, Barber, Porter, Hanson, Thomson, and Sowerby. *Mueller, flute; Waldman, violin; Levine, viola; Tahmizian, piano.*
+ ARG 9-10/94: 232

29275. PRCD 1030: *Songs of humor and satire.* Music of Weill, Ross, Sowash, Fine, Gottlieb, Gershwin, Menotti, Smith, and Ives. *Gregg Smith Singers; Farley, Sherry, Cybriwsky, Holroyd, piano.*
+ Fa 7-8/95: 399

29276. PRCD 1031: A world of folksong. *Gregg Smith Singers; Smith, cond.; Dorothy Shaw Bell Choir; Texas Boys' Choir; Texas Little Symphony.*
⊔ Fa 1-2/94: 385
+ Fa 5-6/94: 306

29277. PRCD 1032: *Twentieth-century French classics.* Music of Indy, Martin,

Duruflé, and Poulenc. *The New Jersey Chamber Music Society.*
+ Fa 5-6/94: 333

29278. PRCD 1033: RIETI—Sinfonia tripartita; Second Avenue waltzes; Trio for violin, cello, and piano; Concerto for 2 pianos and orchestra. *Gold, Fizdale, pianos; NBC Symphony Orch.; Toscanini, cond.; Orch. de la Suisse romande; Ansermet, cond.; Beaux Arts Trio.*
+ Fa 7-8/94: 213

29279. PRCD 1035: ROREM—Hearing; Songs. *Rees, Wheeler, Galloway, Hilley; instrumental ensemble; Rorem, piano; G. Smith, cond.*
+ Fa 5-6/94: 231
+ ON 10/94: 51

29280. PRCD 1036: *South American landscapes.* Music of Franzetti, Ginastera, Guarnieri, Guastavino, Mignone, Piazzolla, and Villa-Lobos. *Franzetti, piano.*
+ Fa 5-6/95: 413

29281. PRCD 1038: *Traditional patterns.* ASHWANDER—Music of Ashwander. *Moore, Bogdan, vocals; Huff, Ashwander, piano.*
+ Fa 7-8/95: 97

29282. PRCD 1039: *Jubilee: organ music, vol. 1.* SOWERBY—Comes autumn time; Fantasy for flute stops; Requiescat in pace; Pageant of autumn; Picardy; Carillon; Bright, blithe, and brisk; Jubilee. *Parris, organ.*
+ Fa 7-8/95: 326 (Snook)
• Fa 7-8/95: 327 (Anderson)

29283. PRCD 1041: BURLEIGH—From the Southland; Songs. *Harris, mezzo-soprano; Creech, Cole, tenor; Woodley, bass; Smith, piano.*
+ ARG 5-6/96: 97
+ Fa 7-8/95: 144

29284. PRCD 1043: *The entertainer.* JOPLIN—Piano music arr. for harpsichord, flute, and oboe. *Trio Bell'Arte.*
• Fa 11-12/95: 282

29285. PRCD 1044: FRANZETTI—Aubade; Oboe concerto; Concertino for bass trombone; Suite for flute and chamber ensemble; Images before dawn; Variations for brass. *Orquesta y Coro de la Ciudad de Buenos Aires; Modus Chamber Ensemble; Franzetti, cond.; Millar Brass Ensemble; Briney, cond.*
• Fa 9-10/95: 205

29286. PRCD 1045: GOULD—Flute concerto. LA MONTAINE—Flute concerto. *Bryan, flute; Slovak Radio Symphony Orch., Bratislava; Chen, cond.*
+ Fa 1-2/96: 213

29287. PRCD 1052: JACOB—Mini concerto; Trio; Quintet; Concertino.

Russo, clarinet; Premier Chamber Orch.; Gilbert, cond.
+ ARG 7-8/96: 137

PREMIUM

29288. 1019: Music of Paine, Foote, Farwell, Chadwick, Beach, Riegger, Carpenter, and Foster. *Salvatore, piano.*
+ ARG 7-8/92: 264

PREZIOSO

29289. CD 800 001: RHEINBERGER—*Complete organ sonatas. No. 1, 8, 20. Eden, Munns, Farrell, organ.*
• ARG 7-8/89: 79
+ Fa 1-2/89: 245

29290. CD 800 002: RHEINBERGER—*Complete organ sonatas. No. 2, 11, 16. Eden, Fisher, Farrell, organ.*
+ Fa 1-2/90: 277

29291. CD 800 003: RHEINBERGER—*Complete organ sonatas. No. 3, 15, 19. Eden, Fisher, Farrell, organ.*
• ARG 3-4/90: 95
+ Fa 3-4/90: 274
+ Gr 6/90: 84

29292. CD 800 004: RHEINBERGER—*Complete organ sonatas. No. 4, 10, 14. Eden, Munns, Farrell, organ.*
• ARG 3-4/90: 95
+ Fa 3-4/90: 274
+ Gr 6/90: 84

29293. CD 800 005: RHEINBERGER—*Complete organ sonatas. No. 5, 9, 17. Eden, Munns, Farrell, organ.*
+ ARG 9-10/90: 104
+ Fa 5-6/90: 265
+ Gr 6/90: 84

29294. CD 800 006: RHEINBERGER—*Complete organ sonatas. No. 6, 13, 18. Munns, Fisher, Farrell, organ.*
+ Fa 1-2/90: 277

29295. CD 800 007: RHEINBERGER—*Complete organ sonatas. No. 7, 12; 6 pieces for organ. Munns, Fisher, Lindley, organ.*
+ ARG 9-10/90: 104
+ Fa 5-6/90: 265
+ Gr 6/90: 84

29296. CD 800 008: RHEINBERGER—*Twelve monologs for organ, op. 162; Suite for violin, cello, and organ, op. 149. Fisher, Lindley, organ; Williams, violin; Green, cello.*
+ Fa 1-2/90: 277

29297. CD 800 009: RHEINBERGER—*Piano sonatas 3-4; Romantic; Toccatina, G minor; Toccata, C minor. Hanselmann, piano.*
+ ARG 11-12/91: 137

29298. CD 800 010: RHEINBERGER—*Four-hand piano music. Hanselmann,*

Hanselmann-Kästli, piano.
+ ARG 3-4/95: 169

29299. CD 800 014: MEDTNER—Piano sonatas. *Hanselmann, piano.*
• ARG 1-2/95: 139

29300. CD 820 201: BOECK—Marche nuptiale; Trois pièces; Allegro con fuoco. TINEL—Improvisata in C major; Organ sonata, op. 29. *Sluys, organ.*
+ ARG 11-12/90: 46
+ Fa 5-6/90: 153

29301. CD 820 202: DUPRÉ—Quartet for organ and strings, op. 52; Trio for organ, violin, and cello, op. 55; Sonata for cello and organ in A minor. *Sluys, organ; with string strio.*
+ ARG 7-8/90: 44

29302. CD 820 203: LEMMENS—Organ music. *Sluys, organ.*
+ ARG 1-2/95: 132

29303. CD 820 204: PEETERS—Organ works. *Sluys, organ.*
+ Gr 9/91: 105

PRIMAVERA

29304. AMP 5030-2: HUMMEL—Trumpet concerto in E major. ENESCO—Legend. KROL—Magnificat variations. HENDERSON—Variation movements. GRUNELIUS—Jeux pour deux. *Bauer, trumpet; Becker, trumpet; Radio Symphony Orch. of Frankfurt; Kitayenko, cond.*
+ Fa 9-10/95: 404

PRIORY

29305. PRCD 189: Music for trumpet and organ of Mathias, L. Mozart, Boyce, Telemann, Gounod, Steel, and Anon. *Perkins, trumpet; Cleobury, organ.*
• Fa 3-4/88: 262
+ Gr 4/88: 1474

29306. PRCD 218: *English choral music.* Music of Sumsion, Sanders, Wesley, Shepherd, Brewer, Howells, and Bax. *Blatchly, organ; Gloucester Cathedral Choir; Sanders, cond.*
+ ARG 3-4/92: 199
+ Fa 7-8/88: 302

29307. PRCD 221: *Graham Barber plays the new Walker organ of Bolton Town Hall.* Music of Mendelssohn, Bach, Grainger, Karg-Elert, Jongen, and Peeters. *Barber, organ.*
+ Fa 7-8/88: 313

29308. PRCD 226: Music of Parry, Bairstow, Whitlock, and Statham. *Barber, organ.*
+ Fa 7-8/88: 313

29309. PRCD 228: *James Lancelot plays the organ of Durham Cathedral.* Music of Reger, Rheinberger, Howells, Mathias,

Mendelssohn, Martin, Alain, and Langlais. *Lancelot, organ.*
• Fa 9 10/88: 330
+ Gr 8/88: 320

29310. PRCD 235: BACH—Eight little preludes and fugues, BWV 553-560. HANDEL—Water music (arr. John). MOZART—Fantasies in F minor, K. 594, K. 608. *John, organ.*
• Fa 1-2/89: 107

29311. PRCD 236: VIERNE—Symphony no. 1. DURUFLÉ—Suite, op. 5. *Walsh, organ.*
+ ARG 1-2/89: 98
+ Fa 1-2/89: 287
+ Gr 12/88: 1036

29312. PRCD 237: Organ music of Guilmant, Karg-Elert, and Dupré. *Watts, organ.*
+ ARG 5-6/89: 117
+ Fa 3-4/89: 372

29313. PRCD 242 (2 discs): MULET—Organ music (complete). *Derrett, organ.*
- Fa 7-8/89: 205
+ Gr 12/89: 1167

29314. PRCD 243: *Germanic choral music.* Music of Hassler, Bruckner, Liszt, and Cornelius. *Exon Singers; Tolley, cond.*
+ ARG 9-10/89: 133
+ Fa 7-8/89: 298
+ Gr 7/89: 26

29315. PRCD 246: Organ music of Giullou, Widor, Parry, and Wills. *Wills, organ.*
+ ARG 7-8/89: 116
+ Fa 7-8/89: 307

29316. PRCD 251: *My beloved spake.* Music of Purcell, Bairstow, Jackson, Townhill, and Leighton. *Choir of St. Mary's Episcopal Cathedral; Orch. of St. Mary's Music School, Edinburgh; Townhill, cond.*
+ ARG 5-6/89: 124
+ Fa 9-10/89: 399

29317. PRCD 257: *Great cathedral anthems.* Music of S.S. Wesley, Bairstow, Stanford, Elgar, Bainton, Walker, and Bullock. *Wright, organ; Choir of Guildford Cathedral; Millington, cond.*
• ARG 9-10/89: 135
• Fa 9-10/89: 398
+ Gr 5/89: 1766

29318. PRCD 260: DUPRÉ—Choral and fugue; Souvenir; Carillon; Légende; Final. DEMESSIEUX—Choral preludes on Gregorian chant themes. *Barber, organ.*
+ Fa 5-6/89: 392

29319. PRCD 261: Organ music of Dupré, Alain, Franck, Duruflé, and Messiaen. *Marshall, organ.*
+ Fa 11-12/89: 458

29320. PRCD 262: MUSSORGSKY—Pictures at an exhibition (arr. John). ALAIN—Trois danses. *John, organ.*
• ARG 7-8/89: 64
+ Fa 9-10/89: 269
+ Gr 4/89: 1606

29321. PRCD 264: BACH—Organ music. REUBKE—Sonata on the 94th Psalm. *John, organ.*
- ARG 11-12/90: 21
+ Gr 4/90: 1833

29322. PRCD 265 : *John Scott Whiteley plays the Müller organ of St. Bavo's Church, Haarlam.* Organ music of Leiding, Bach, Buxtehude, Brahms, and Lübeck. *Whiteley, organ.*
+ Fa 11-12/89: 458
+ Gr 10/89: 708

29323. PRCD 268: *The versatile English organ.* Organ music of Anain, Stanley, Rheinberger, Brewer, Peeters, Buxtehude, Boyle, and Dupré. *Millington, organ.*
+ Fa 1-2/90: 390

29324. PRCD 269: RHEINBERGER—Pastorale-sonata, op. 88; Organ sonatas no. 10, 11. *Barber, organ.*
+ Fa 1-2/90: 390

29325. PRCD 270: *The holy Eucharist.* Music of Howells, Darke, Ireland, Bridge, Bairstow, Harris, and Vaughan Williams. *Trepte, Cousins, organ; Choir of St. Edmundsbury Cathedral; Trepte, cond.*
+ Fa 9-10/89: 398
+ Gr 5/89: 1766

29326. PRCD 272: *Colin Andrews plays the organ of Bordeax Cathedral.* Music of Boellmann, Alain, Vierne, Messiaen, Bonnet, Litaize, and Langlais. *Andrews, organ.*
+ Fa 1-2/90: 390

29327. PRCD 281: Organ music of Gigout, Franck, Guilmant, Saint-Saëns, and Widor. *Walsh, organ.*
+ ARG 9-10/90: 143

29328. PRCD 284: Organ music of Vierne, Dupré, and Cochereau (arr. Briggs). *Briggs, organ.*
+ ARG 1-2/91: 138
+ Fa 11-12/90: 441

29329. PRCD 286: Organ music of Dupré, Franck, Tournemire, and Alain. *Watts, organ.*
+ Fa 11-12/90: 441

29330. PRCD 289: *John Scott Whiteley plays the Marcussen organ of Haderslev Cathedral, Denmark.* Organ music of Eben, Martinů, Dvořák, Janáček, Novak, Bruckner, Beethoven, and Planyavsky. *Whiteley, organ.*
+ Fa 11-12/90: 441

PRIORY

29331. PRCD 291: Bruckner—Ave Maria; Motets. Liszt—Missa choralis. *Worcester Cathedral Choir; Hunt, cond.; Smith, organ.*
+ Fa 9-10/91: 182

29332. PRCD 292: Poulenc—Mass in G major. Milhaud—Deux cités. Finzi—Seven poems of Robert Bridges. Berkeley—Mass for 5 voices. *Michael Brewer Singers; Brewer, cond.*
+ Fa 9-10/90: 468
• Gr 7/90: 271

29333. PRCD 294: Tournemire—Triple choral; Improvisations, vol. 2; Symphonie-choral, op. 69. *Watts, organ.*
+ Fa 3-4/91: 407
• Gr 1/92: 79

29334. PRCD 312: Stanford—Six Biblical songs and anthems; Communion service in C major. *Suter, organ; Chichester Cathedral Choir; Thurlow, cond.*
+ ARG 3-4/91: 123
+ ARG 3-4/92: 142
- Fa 3-4/91: 390
• Gr 4/91: 1890

29335. PRCD 315: Great European organs, vol. 30. *Barber, organ.*
• ARG 11-12/93: 238
+ Gr 11/93: 120

29336. PRCD 319 (2 discs): Vierne—Triptyque, op. 58; Pièces en style libre, op. 31. *Walsh, organ.*
• ARG 11-12/91: 166
+ Gr 3/92: 88

29337. PRCD 324: Jongen—Organ music, vol. 1. *Whiteley, organ.*
+ Gr 7/93: 66

29338. PRCD 326 (3 discs): PRCD 326 (3 discs): Leighton—Organ music (complete). *Townhill, organ.*
- ARG 3-4/96: 144

29339. PRCD 332: *Great European organs, vol. 24.* Music of Bach, Buxtehude, Clérambault, Krebs, and Scheidt. *Wagler, organ.*
+ Gr 10/91: 146

29340. PRCD 335: Music of Hollins, Bridge, Grainger, Whitlock, and Ireland. *King, organ.*
• ARG 1-2/93: 180

29341. PRCD 337: *Psalms of David, vol. 2.* Music of Beale, Boyce, Camidge, Cooper/Walker, Flintoft, H. Smart, Havergal/Walmisley, Howells, Ley, Lloyd, Monk, Noble, Randall/Cooper, S. Wesley, Stainer, Stanford, Stonex, Turle, Wadely, and Whitlock. *Wells Cathedral Choir; Crossland, cond.; Brayne, organ.*
+ ARG 5-6/92: 178
• Gr 10/91: 182

29342. PRCD 341: *Heaven and earth are full of Thy glory.* Music of Harwood, Ireland, Wood, Darke, Oldroyd, and Leighton. *Wakefield Cathedral Choir; Bielby, cond.; Wright, organ.*
+ ARG 11-12/92: 255

29343. PRCD 346: Music of Jackson, Vaughan Williams, Harris, Parry, Bossi, Brahms, and others. *Lancelot, organ.*
- ARG 11-12/94: 228

29344. PRCD 352: *Garlands for the queen.* Music of Bliss, Bax, Tippet, Vaughan Williams, Berkeley, Ireland, Howells, Finzi, Rawsthorne, Rubbra, and Mathias. *Bristol Bach Choir; Jenkins, cond.; Shelton, piano.*
+ Fa 9-10/92: 406

29345. PRCD 365: Bairstow—Choral music. *York Minster Choir; Moore, cond.*
+ Gr 6/93: 81

29346. PRCD 368: Smart—Organ works. *Thomas, organ.*
+ Gr 9/92: 138

29347. PRCD 369: Hakim—Variations; Improvisation; Rubaiyat. Tournemire—Sei fioretti. *Hakim, organ.*
+ ARG 11-12/94: 123

29348. PRCD 370: *Great European organs, vol. 26.* Music of Stanford, Reger, Shostakovich, Schmidt, and Ravanello. *John, organ.*
+ ARG 1-2/93: 180
+ Gr 11/92: 165

29349. PRCD 371: *Great European organs, vol. 28.* Music of Bonnet, Guilmant, Widor, Poellmann, Tournemire and Languetuit. *Patrick, organ.*
+ ARG 5-6/93: 167
+ Gr 5/93: 74

29350. PRCD 373: *Great European organs, vol. 25.* Music of Karg-Elert, F. Jackson, and L. Sowerby. *Barber, organ.*
+ Gr 3/92: 88

29351. PRCD 374: Darke—Organ music. *Rennert, organ.*
+ Gr 1/95: 76

29352. PRCD 377, 384, 414 (3 separate discs): Great European organs vol. 29, 31-32. *Watts, Scott, organ.*
+ Gr 8/94: 78

29353. PRCD 379: Music of Jacob, Alcock, Howells, MacPherson, Harris, Bennett and others. *Walsh, organ.*
+ ARG 3-4/93: 167
+ Gr 11/92: 165

29354. PRCD 383: *Psalms of David, vol. 4.* Music of Barnby, Walmisley, Bairstow, Harris, Rogers, Parratt, Hine, and others. *Lichfield Cathedral Choir; Rees-Williams, cond.; Shepherd, organ.*
+ Gr 4/92: 149

29355. PRCD 387: *Psalms of David, vol. 5.* Music of Stanford, Barnby, Sanders, Parratt, Booth, and others. *Gloucester Cathedral Choir; Sanders, cond.; Lee, organ.*
+ Gr 4/92: 149

29356. PRCD 390 (2 discs): Pott—Christus. *Simcock, organ.*
+ ARG 3-4/93: 124
+ Gr 7/92: 81

29357. PRCD 391: *Great European organs, vol. 27.* Karg-Elert—Partita in E. Jackson—Organ sonata IV. Milhaud—Pastorals. Demessieux—Te Deum. *Barber, organ.*
+ ARG 9-10/92: 194
+ Gr 1/93: 50

29358. PRCD 396: *Norwich Cathedral in 1600.* Music of Morley, Parsley, and Inglott. *Norwich Cathedral Choir; Nicholas, cond.*
+ ARG 5-6/93: 174

29359. PRCD 399: Mayerl—Piano music. *Jacobs, piano.*
+ Fa 3-4/93: 218
• Gr 3/93: 72

29360. PRCD 401: Elgar—Organ sonata no. 1. Bairstow—Sonata. Harris—Sonata in A minor. *Scott, organ.*
+ ARG 11-12/94: 109
+ Gr 8/94: 78

29361. PRCD 406: *Great European organs, vol. 35.* Barie—Three pieces. Dupré—Le tombeau de Titelouze. *Wright, organ.*
+ ARG 11-12/94: 69
+ Gr 10/94: 155

29362. PRCD 409: *Psalms of David, vol. 7.* Music of Goss, Nicholas, Sratham, Archer, and others. *Norwich Cathedral Choir; Nicholas, cond.; Taylor, organ.*
+ Gr 5/93: 98

29363. PRCD 416: *Psalms of David, vol. 6.* Music of Hopkins, Goss, Watson, Garrett, and others. *Guildford Cathedral Choir; Millington, cond.; Morgan, organ.*
+ Gr 5/93: 98

29364. PRCD 422: *Great European organs, vol. 36.* Music of Barié, R. Vierne, Indy, Roussel, Honegger, Dupré, Langlais, and L. Vierne. *Dufourcet, organ.*
+ Gr 6/95: 84

29365. PRCD 427: *Great European organs, vol. 38.* Music of Petrali, Bossi, Galliera, Bettinelli, and Ambrosi. *Benedetti, organ.*
+ Gr 4/95: 94

29366. PRCD 428: Cochereau—Organ music. *Briggs, organ.*
+ ARG 5-6/94: 84

29367. PRCD 435, 454, 429 (3 separate discs): Great cathedral anthems vol. 3-5. *Southwark Cathedral Choir; Wright, cond.; Lincoln Cathedral Choir; Walsh, cond.; Truro Cathedral Choir; Briggs, cond.*
+ Gr 7/94: 106

29368. PRCD 437: STANFORD—Morning and evening services; Benedictus and Agnus Dei. *Durham Cathedral Choir; Lancelot, cond.*
+ Gr 4/94: 92

29369. PRCD 445 (2 discs): STANFORD—Organ sonata; Short preludes and postludes. *Hunter, organ.*
+ ARG 11-12/94: 194
• Gr 9/94: 84

29370. PRCD 446: VIERNE—Organ symphonies no. 2-3. *Walsh, organ.*
• ARG 11-12/94: 207
+ Gr 10/94: 164

29371. PRCD 449: STANFORD—Preludes, op. 163; Characteristic pieces, op. 132. *Jacobs, piano.*
+ Gr 4/96: 81

29372. PRCD 451: PARRY—Shulbrede tunes; Theme and 19 variations; Hands across the centuries. *Jacobs, piano.*
+ Gr 10/95: 98

29373. PRCD 460: *Praise the Lord, o my soul.* Psalms of David, vol. 8. *Ely Cathedral Choir; Trepte, cond.*
+ Gr 12/93: 111

29374. PRCD 461: *Psalms of David vol. 9.* Music of Carter, Ashfield, Stewart, and others. *Rochester Cathedral Choir; Ferguson, cond.*
+ Gr 6/94: 106

29375. PRCD 466: MAYERL—Piano transcriptions, vol. 1. *Parkin, piano.*
+ Gr 1/95: 79

29376. PRCD 467: MAYERL—Piano transcriptions, vol. 2. *Parkin, piano.*
+ Gr 5/95: 83

29377. PRCD 468: MAYERL—Piano transcriptions, vol. 3. *Parkin, piano.*
+ Gr 7/95: 86

29378. PRCD 470: *Te Deum and Jubilate, vol. 2.* Music of Elgar, Stratham, Howells, Moeran, Wesley, Britten, and Glastone. *Norwich Cathedral Choir; Nicholas, cond.*
+ Gr 10/94: 187

29379. PRCD 480: HOWELLS—Psalm-preludes, set 1 2; Rhapsody no. 4. *Cleobury, organ.*
+ Gr 6/95: 79

29380. PRCD 485: *Great European organs, vol. 40.* Music of Eben, Ligeti,

Sokola, Martin, and others. *Scott, organ.*
+ Gr 8/96: 78

29381. PRCD 486: *The psalms of David, vol. 10.* Music of Cooper, Bairstow, South, Gauntlett, Battishill, Hopkins, Boyce, Stanford, Turle, and Walmisley. *York Minster Choir; Moore, cond.; Whiteley, organ.*
+ Gr 5/95: 105

29382. PRCD 487: *Great European organs, vol. 41.* Music of Malengreau, Peeters, Widor, Pierné, and Guillou. *Whiteley, organ.*
+ Gr 2/96: 78

29383. PRCD 491: *Great European organs, vol. 37.* Music of Preston, Daniel Jones, and Langlais. *Watts, organ.*
+ Gr 10/95: 101

29384. PRCD 494: *Magnificat and Nunc dimittis, vol. 1.* Music of Brewer, Sumsion, Wesley, Howells, Lloyd, Aston, and Kelly. *Gloucester Cathedral Choir; Sander, cond.*
+ Gr 4/95: 114

29385. PRCD 495: *Great European organs, vol. 41.* Music of Bach, Bonnal, Langlais, Ferguson, and Dupré. *Sayer, organ.*
+ Gr 4/96: 82

29386. PRCD 505: *Magnificat and Nunc dimittis, vol. 3.* Music of Stanford, S. Watson, G. Ives, Gibbons, Leighton, Howells, and Dyson. *Lichfield Cathedral Choir; Lumsden, cond.; Shepherd, Potts, organ.*
+ Gr 10/95: 124

29387. PRCD 507: *Te Deum and Jubilate, vol. 3.* Music of Stanford, Darke, Lloyd, Sumsion, Ley, and others. *Hereford Cathedral Choir; Massey, cond.; Bowen, organ.*
+ Gr 2/95: 99

29388. PRCD 510: *Great cathedral anthems, vol. 6.* Music of Weelkes, Battishill, Walmisley, Stainer, Mansel Thomas, Stanton, Howells, W. Harris, R. Shephard, and Rubbra. *Llandaff Cathedral Choir; Smith, cond.; Hoeg, organ.*
+ Gr 10/95: 123

29389. PRCD 511: *Magnificat and Nunc dimittis, vol. 2.* Music of Ayleward, Hawes, Holst, Kelway, Naylor, D. Purcell, Smart, Sumsion, Vann, and Weelkes. *Chichester Cathedral Choir; Thurlow, cond.*
+ Gr 5/95: 105

29390. PRCD 514: STANFORD—Services, op. 12, 81. *Durham Cathedral Choir; Lancelot, cond.; Wright, organ.*
+ Gr 6/95: 98

29391. PRCD 527: *Magnificat and Nunc dimittis, vol. 4.* Music of Brewer, Andrews, Howells, Stanford, and others. *Portsmouth Cathedral Choir; Lucas, cond.*
+ Gr 2/96: 95

29392. PRCD 528: *Magnificat and Nunc dimittis, vol. 5.* Music of Harker, Howells, Jackson, Moore, and others. *Bristol Cathedral Choir; Brayne, cond.*
+ Gr 8/96: 91

29393. PRCD 529: *Magnificat and Nunc dimittis, vol. 6.* Music of Walton, Whitlock, Watson, Stewart, Tippett, Heath, Ashfield, Murrill, and Walmisley. *Rochester Cathedral Choir; Sayer, cond.; Whitehead, organ.*
+ Gr 7/96: 94

29394. PRCD 535: *Magnificat and Nunc dimittis, vol. 7.* Music of Sumsion, Darke, Lloyd, Davies, Vann, Dyson, Harwood, Shephard, and Stanford. *Hereford Cathedral Choir; Massey, cond.; Williams, organ.*
+ Gr 7/96: 94

29395. PRCD 539: *Great cathedral anthems, vol. 7.* Music of Goss, Clarke, S.S. Wesley, Mendelssohn, Ouseley, Schubert, and Parry. *Chichester Cathedral Choir; Thurlow, cond.; Thomas, organ.*
+ Gr 5/96: 108

29396. PRCD 545: HAKIM—Saul de Tarse; Vexilla Regis prodeunt; Missa resurrectionis; Le tombeau d'Olivier Messiaen. *Pettersson, Annmo, Lassen, Hedström, vocalists; Merienne, speaker; Hakim, organ; Schola Cantorum Scaniensis, Malmö; Wallin, cond.; Lund Academic Orch. & Choir; Malmberg, cond.*
+ Gr 6/96: 72

29397. PRCD 903: *A European organ tour.* Music of Reger, Bowen, Dupré, Karg-Elert, and Bach. *Barber, Rochester, Marshall, Whiteley, organ.*
☐ Fa 11-12/89: 459

29398. PRCD 904: *Romantic music of yesteryear.* Music of Best, Hopkins, Lefébure-Wely, Guilmant, Boely, Lemmens, Cocker, Smart, Nevin, Hollins, Lemare, Brewer, and Dubois. *Bielby, organ.*
• Fa 11-12/89: 460

29399. PRCD 905: *French organ music.* Music of Langlais, Vierne, and Duruflé. *Richards, soprano; Walsh, organ.*
+ Fa 1-2/90: 390

PRO/AM

29400. MR 1534: MOZART—Piano sonata, 4 hands, K. 497. MENDELSSOHN—Andante and variations, op. 83. BRAHMS—Variations on a theme by Schumann.

PRO ARTE

Weekley, Arganbright, piano 4-hands.
- Fa 11-12/90: 299

PRO ARTE

29401. CDD 233: MOZART—Symphonies no. 40-41. *Collegium Aureum.*
+ DA 6/86: 59

29402. CDD 237: DVOŘÁK—String quartet no. 12; Cypresses. *Cleveland Quartet.*
- Fa 11-12/86: 139
+ SR 11/86: 166

29403. CDD 238: DOHNÁNYI—Serenade for string trio, op. 10; Piano quintet, op. 1. *Snyder, piano; Cleveland Quartet.*
+ Ov 3/87: 34
+ SR 11/86: 164

29404. CDD 239: DOHNÁNYI—Violin sonata, op. 21; Cello sonata, op. 8. *Salaff, violin; Katz, cello; Snyder, piano.*
+ Ov 3/87: 34
+ SR 11/86: 164

29405. CDD 240: DOHNÁNYI—Piano music. *Snyder, piano.*
• Fa 11-12/86: 134
+ Ov 3/87: 34
+ SR 11/86: 164

29406. CDD 245: BEETHOVEN—Symphony no. 9. *Valante, Kopleff, Hadley, Cheek; Atlanta Symphony Chorus & Orch.; Shaw, cond.*
+ DA 4/86: 67

29407. CDD 246: CHOPIN—Piano music. *Serkin, piano.*
• Fa 7-8/87: 88

29408. CDD 247: MOZART—Piano sonatas no. 16-17; Rondos for piano, K. 485, K. 511. *Serkin, piano.*
+ DA 5/87: 67
+ Fa 7-8/87: 64

29409. CDD 251: TCHAIKOVSKY—Waltzes from ballet, opera, and symphony; Serenade for strings: 2nd movement . *Houston Symphony Orch.; Comissiona, cond.*
• Fa 11-12/86: 227

29410. CDD 266: BRAHMS—Piano concerto no. 1. *Serkin, piano; Atlanta Symphony Orch.; Shaw, cond.*
• Fa 7-8/87: 72
+ SR 6/87: 104

29411. CDD 270: BEETHOVEN—Piano sonata no. 29. *Serkin, piano.*
+ DA 5/87: 66
+ Fa 7-8/87: 64

29412. CDD 277: MOZART—Violin concerto no. 5; Piano concerto no. 27. *Serkin, piano; Silverstein, violin & cond.; Rochester Phil. Orch.*
- Fa 11-12/87: 179

29413. CDD 278: Music of Chetham, Copland, Vizzutti/Tyzik, Bernstein, and Haufrecht. *Summit Brass.*
+ ARG 1-2/90: 115

29414. CDD 310: BRAHMS—Variations on a theme by Paganini, op. 35. *Sherman, piano.*
• Fa 7-8/87: 76

29415. CDD 311: CHOPIN—Twenty-four preludes; Barcarolle, op. 60. *Sherman, piano.*
• Fa 7-8/87: 91

29416. CDD 318: *All American brass.* Music of Dukas, Copland, Bernstein, Scott, Strauss, and Reed. *Summit Brass.*
+ ARG 1-2/90: 115

29417. CDD 319: HOLST—The planets. *Women of the Dallas Symphony Chorus; Dallas Symphony Orch.; Mata, cond.*
+ Fa 5-6/88: 144

29418. CDD 320: SIBELIUS—Symphony no. 2. *Dallas Symphony Orch.; Mata, cond.*
+ ARG 5-6/88: 64
• Fa 11-12/87: 230
• HPR 12/87: 99
• SR 10/87: 144

29419. CDD 325: BERLIOZ—Roman carnival overture. STRAUSS—Don Juan. RESPIGHI—Pines of Rome. *Pacific Symphony Orch.; Clark, cond.*
• Fa 11-12/87: 106
• HPR 12/87: 81
+ Opus 4/88: 53

29420. CDD 336: BRAHMS—Piano concerto no. 2. *Serkin, piano; Atlanta Symphony Orch.; Shaw, cond.*
+ DA 10/87: 80
+ Fa 7-8/87: 73

29421. CDD 358: SCHUBERT—Dances for piano. *Serkin, piano.*
+ Fa 11-12/87: 217

29422. CDD 362: BEETHOVEN—Piano sonatas no. 30-32. *Serkin, piano.*
+ Fa 3-4/89: 92

29423. CDD 380: LISZT—Piano music. SCHUBERT—Soirées de Vienne: no. 6 (arr. Liszt). *Sherman, piano.*
- Fa 9-10/88: 186
+ Ov 2/89: 49

29424. CDD 389: DVOŘÁK—Violin concerto in A minor; Serenade for strings, op. 22. *Utah Symphony Orch.; Wilkins, cond.; Silverstein, violin & cond.*
• Fa 11-12/88: 177
+ HPR 3/89: 75
+ SR 12/88: 149

29425. CDD 393: SCHUMANN—Symphonies no. 1, 4. *Houston Symphony Orch.; Comissiona, cond.*

+ Fa 11-12/88: 275
+ HPR 3/89: 89

29426. CDD 394: SCHUMANN—Symphonies no. 2, 3. *Houston Symphony Orch.; Comissiona, cond.*
+ Fa 11-12/88: 275
+ HPR 12/88: 83

29427. CDD 395: C. SCHUMANN—Piano concerto, op. 7; Piano trio, op. 17. *Jochum, piano; Silverstein, violin; Carr, cello; Bamberg Symphony Orch.; Silverstein, cond.*
+ DA 12/88: 82
+ Fa 11-12/88: 273
+ Ov 1/89: 41
+ SR 10/88: 124

29428. CDD 396: *Clara, Robert & Johannes.* Piano music of Schumann, C. Schumann, and Brahms. *Jochum, piano.*
+ DA 12/88: 82
+ Fa 11-12/88: 273

29429. CDD 399: TCHAIKOVSKY—Variations on a rococo theme, op. 33; Nocturne for cello and piano, op. 19, no. 4. HAYDN—Cello concerto no. 1. SAINT-SAËNS—Cello concerto no. 1. *Harnoy, cello; Victoria Symphony Orch.; Freeman, cond.; Bowkun, piano; Toronto Chamber Orch.; Robinson, cond.*
+ DA 9/88: 56
• Fa 11-12/88: 293

29430. CDD 402: Overtures of Suppé, Glinka, Offenbach, Reznicek, J. Strauss, Jr., Saint-Saëns, Beethoven, Rossini, and Berlioz. *Utah Symphony Orch.; Silverstein, cond.*
- Fa 3-4/89: 333
+ HPR 6/89: 87

29431. CDD 403: KODÁLY—Háry János: Suite. PROKOFIEV—Lieutenant Kije: Suite. STRAUSS—Till Eulenspiegel. *Dallas Symphony Orch.; Mata, cond.*
- ARG 1-2/89: 60
• Fa 3-4/89: 196
+ HPR 3/89: 79

29432. CDD 404: BOLLING—Suite for flute and jazz piano no. 1. GERSHWIN—Impromptu in 2 keys; Promenade; Swanee. *Baxtresser, flute; Eric Robertson Trio.*
+ Fa 3-4/89: 119

29433. CDD 405: C.P.E. BACH—Flute concerto, Wq. 22. BACH—Flute sonata, BWV 1030. *Baxtresser, flute; Toronto Chamber Orch.; A. Davis, harpsichord & cond.*
• ARG 9-10/89: 16
+ DA 11/89: 81

29434. CDD 406: Music for flute and piano of Debussy, Bartók, Chopin, Kuhlau, Rachmaninoff, and Barber. *Baxtresser, flute; A. Davis, piano.*
+ ARG 9-10/89: 124
+ DA 11/89: 81

29435. CDD 409: TCHAIKOVSKY—Mazeppa: Cossack dance; Coronation march in D major; Romeo and Juliet; March slave; Overture 1812. *Dallas Symphony Orch.; Mata, cond.*
- ARG 3-4/89: 98
+ Fa 3-4/89: 310

29436. CDD 410: *Vive la France.* Music of Rouget de Lisle, Chabrier, Berlioz, Ravel, Dukas, and Saint-Saëns. *Denver Symphony Orch.; Entremont, cond.*
- ARG 1-2/89: 107
+ DA 8/89: 67
+ Fa 1-2/89: 347
+ HPR 6/89: 92

29437. CDD 442: RACHMANINOFF—Piano concerto no. 3; Preludes, op. 23, no. 1, 7; Preludes, op. 32, no. 5, 12. *Viardo, piano; Dallas Symphony Orch.; Mata, cond.*
+ ARG 11-12/89: 98
• DA 6/89: 88
• Fa 1-2/90: 269
+ MA 1/90: 70
+ SR 8/89: 92

29438. CDD 443: STRAVINSKY—Firebird (1910 version); Fireworks. *Dallas Symphony Orch.; Mata, cond.*
- ARG 11-12/89: 125

29439. CDD 447: BEETHOVEN—Diabelli variations, op. 120. *Serkin, piano.*
• ARG 11-12/89: 40
+ Fa 9-10/89: 145
+ SR 8/89: 86

29440. CDD 448: STRAUSS—Bourgeois gentilhomme. *New York Chamber Symphony & Chorus; Schwarz, cond.*
+ ARG 11-12/89: 122
+ Fa 11-12/89: 368
+ SR 12/89: 123

29441. CDD 453: MUSSORGSKY—Pictures at an exhibition (2 versions, for piano and in Ravel orchestration). *Denver Symphony Orch.; Entremont, piano & cond.*
- ARG 11-12/89: 83

29442. CDD 469: MOZART—Piano quartets in G minor, E♭ major; Fantasia, K. 397. *Members of the Vienna Chamber Orch.; Entremont, piano.*
+ ARG 9-10/90: 96

29443. CDD 470: SCHUBERT—Piano quintet in A major. DVOŘÁK—Piano quintet, op. 81. *Entremont, piano; Members of the Vienna Chamber Orch.*
+ ARG 7-8/90: 97

29444. CDD 477: RACHMANINOFF—Symphonic dances. GRIEG—Symphonic dances. *Dallas Symphony Orch.; Mata, cond.*
- ARG 9-10/90: 101

29445. CDD 479: MAHLER—Symphony no. 2. BEETHOVEN—Consecration of the house overture. *McNair, soprano; Nes, alto; Dallas Symphony Orch & Chorus; Mata, cond.*
• ARG 5-6/90: 66
• DA 3/90: 73
- Fa 7-8/90: 190

29446. CDD 514: GERSHWIN—Cuban overture; Concerto in F; Rhapsody in blue; Lullaby. *Zizzo, piano; George Gershwin Festival Orch.; Charry, cond.*
- ARG 1-2/92: 55

29447. CDS 527: *Fireworks for orchestra.* Music of Copland, Khachaturian, Suppé, Holst, Tchaikovsky, Stravinsky, Mussorgsky, Beethoven, Handel and Dukas. *Various performers.*
• Fa 3-4/92: 424

29448. CDS 542: HOLST—The Planets. *Dallas Symphony Orch.; Mata, cond.* Reissue.
+ Fa 3-4/92: 214

29449. CDS 543: *Roman carnival: The world's great overtures.* Works by Suppé, Glinka, Offenbach, Reznicek, J. Strauss, Jr., Saint-Saëns, Beethoven, Mendelssohn, Rossini and Berlioz. *Utah Symphony Orch.; Silverstein, cond.*
+ Fa 3-4/92: 428

29450. CDD 551: SHOSTAKOVICH—Excerpts from film scores: The gadfly; 5 Days and 5 nights; Hamlet; Tahiti trot; Piano concerto no. 1. *Han, piano; Chicago Sinfonietta; Freeman, cond.*
+ ARG 1-2/92: 113
• Fa 11-12/91: 483

29451. CDD 552: *Ofra Harnoy and friends.* Music of Danzi, Schubert, Puccini, Massenet, Foss, Liszt, Falla, Gershwin, and Lennon. *Harnoy, cello; with assisting instrumentalists.*
- ARG 1-2/92: 151
- Fa 1-2/92: 414

29452. CDS 560: *It's a grand old flag.* Music of Gershwin, Cohan, Greenwood, Foster, Bates, Meachum and Steffe. *Ambrose, theater organ.*
- Fa 5-6/92: 318

29453. CDS 578: MOZART—Symphonies no. 40-41. *Vienna Chamber Orch.; Entremont, cond.*
+ Fa 3-4/92: 270

29454. CDS 579: MOZART—Eine kleine Nachtmusik; Divertimenti: K. 136-138. *Vienna Chamber Orch.; Entremont, cond.*
+ ARG 5-6/92: 97
+ Fa 3-4/92: 266

29455. CDD 580: *Tempest: classic storms.* Music of Britten, Berlioz, Beethoven, Rossini, R. Strauss, J. Strauss, Sibelius and Rimsky-Korsakoff.

Helsinki Phil. Orch.; Comissiona, cond.
+ ARG 3-4/92: 174

29456. CDS 581: ALBÉNIZ-ARBÓS—Iberia suite. FALLA—The three-cornered hat. *Dallas Symphony Orch.; Mata, cond.*
+ Fa 3-4/92: 130
+ Gr 9/92: 65

29457. CDD 584: TCHAIKOVSKY—Waltzes from Swan Lake; Sleeping beauty; Nutcracker; Serenade for strings; Symphony no. 5; Eugene Onegin. *Houston Symphony Orch.; Comissiona, cond.*
• ARG 9-10/92: 174

29458. CDD 587: STRAVINSKY—Firebird; Fireworks. *Dallas Symphony Orch.; Mata, cond.*
• ARG 11-12/92: 213

29459. CDD 588: BEETHOVEN—Violin concerto; Consecration of the house. *Silverstein, violin & cond.; Utah Symphony Orch.*
• ARG 9-10/92: 78

29460. CDS 589: GLIÈRE—Symphony no. 3 "Ilya Murometz". *San Diego Symphony Orch.; Talmi, cond.*
+ Fa 3-4/92: 195
• St 6/92: 241
• Gr 9/92: 66

29461. CDD 593: MOZART—Piano concertos no. 3, 13, 24. *Han, piano; Philharmonia Orch.; Freeman, cond.*
• ARG 11-12/92: 165
+ Fa 5-6/93: 271

29462. CDS 596: STRAVINSKY—Petrushka (1947); Fairy's kiss: Divertimento. *Dallas Symphony Orch.; Mata, cond.*
+ ARG 3-4/92: 147
+ Fa 3-4/92: 340

29463. CDD 597: SULLIVAN—The pirates of Penzance. *D'Oyly Carte Opera Company.* Recorded 1929.
+ ARG 11-12/92: 124

29464. CDD 598: SULLIVAN—HMS Pinafore. *D'Oyly Carte Opera Company.* Recorded 1930.
+ ARG 11-12/92: 124

29465. CDD 259/61 (3 discs): BEETHOVEN—Piano concertos (complete); Bagatelles, op. 119. *Sherman, piano; Czech Phil. Orch.; Neumann, cond.*
• DA 1/88: 50
• Fa 7-8/87: 62

29466. CDG 3164: SAINT-SAËNS—Piano quartet, op. 41. INDY—Piano quartet, op. 7. *Cantilena Chamber Players.*
+ Fa 3-4/89: 257

29467. CDG 3183: COPLAND—Piano music. *Tocco, Foss, piano.*
+ Fa 3-4/89: 140

PRO ARTE

29468. CDG 3301: Taneev—Piano quartet, op. 20. *Cantilena Piano Quartet.*
+ Fa 3-4/89: 306

29469. CDG 3302: Taneev—Concert suite for violin and orchestra, op. 28. *Altenburger, violin; Vienna Symphony Orch.; Ahronovitch, cond.*
+ Fa 3-4/89: 306

29470. CDG 3303: Taneev—Piano trio, op. 22. Tcherepnin—Piano trio, op. 34. *Odeon Trio.*
+ Fa 3-4/89: 306

29471. CDS 3412: Macdowell—Piano concertos no. 1-2; Poème érotique. *Han, piano; Chicago Sinfonietta; Freeman, cond.*
• Fa 5-6/93: 252

29472. CDS 3430: Beethoven—Symphony no. 9. *Valente, Kopleff, Hadley, Cheek; Atlanta Symphony Orch. & Chorus; Shaw, cond.*
+ Fa 5-6/93: 161

29473. CDS 3434: Mozart—Concertos for piano and orchestra no. 11, 15, 23. *Han, piano; Philharmonia Orch.; Freeman, cond.*
+ Fa 5-6/93: 271

29474. CDD 3439: Satie—Piano works. *Spasovski, piano.*
• ARG 11-12/93: 183
- Fa 11-12/93: 372

29475. CDD 3441: Tchaikovsky—Piano concertos no. 1-2. *Han, piano; St. Petersburg Phil. Orch.; Freeman, cond.*
- ARG 11-12/93: 207
+ Fa 11-12/93: 415

29476. CDD 3445: Mozart—Concertos for piano and orchestra no. 1, 21, 25. *Han, piano; Philharmonia Orch.; Freeman, cond.*
• Fa 11-12/93: 331

29477. CDS 3448: Haydn—Piano concertos no. 3-4, 11. *Han, piano; English Chamber Orch.; Freeman, cond.*
+ ARG 3-4/94: 107
+ Fa 3-4/94: 210

29478. CDD 3457: *Three heroes.* Kodály—Hary Janos. Prokofiev—Lt. Kijé. Strauss—Ein Heldenleben. *Dallas Symphony Orch.; Mata, cond.*
+ ARG 5-6/94: 171

29479. CDD 3464: Schumann—Carnaval; Piano concerto. *Robilette, piano; St. Petersburg Phil. Orch.; Freeman, cond.*
• ARG 7-8/94: 168

29480. CDD 3466—3468 (3 separate discs): Beethoven—Piano concertos (complete); Piano sonata no. 21. *Vered, piano; Warsaw Phil. Orch.; Kord, cond.*
+ ARG 5-6/94: 67
- Fa 3-4/94: 119

29481. CDD 3475: Mozart—Concerto for 2 pianos; Sonata, K. 448; Andante and fugue, K. 546; Larghetto and allegro. *Pierce, Jonas, pianos; Slovak Phil.; Freeman, cond.*
• ARG 5-6/95: 143

29482. CDD 3491: Music of Franck, Fauré, Poulenc, and Chopin. *Robilette, piano; Russian State Symphony Orch.; Freeman, cond.*
• ARG 11-12/94: 232
+ Fa 11-12/94: 490

29483. CDS 3507: Mendelssohn—Capriccio brillant; Piano concertos no. 1-2. *Han, piano; Israel Chamber Orch.; Gunzenhauser, cond.*
• ARG 5-6/95: 137
• Fa 7-8/95: 243

PRO MUSICA

29484. PPC 9028: Music of Albertsen, Bonsaksen, Bottcher, Kleiberg, Bjørklund, Johansen, Alterhaug, Sommero, and Nielsen. *Piro, soprano; Lillebjerka, violin; Aune, recorder; Bonaksen, organ; Nidaros Choir; Rustad, cond.*
+ ARG 3-4/94: 222

29485. PPC 9032: Bach—Organ music. *Haga, organ.*
+ Fa 3-4/94: 110

PRO ORGANO

29486. 005: Howells—Organ sonata; Six pieces. *Benjamin, organ.*
• Fa 11-12/88: 204

29487. 7006: Guilmant—Organ music. *Callahan, organ.*
• Fa 5-6/88: 136

29488. 7007: Lemare—Organ music. *Hohman, organ.*
+ Fa 5-6/88: 136

29489. 7023: Eben—Organ music. *Fishell, organ.*
+ ARG 3-4/96: 111

29490. 7025: *The people respond: Amen!* Music of Locklair, Sowerby, Wyton, Ferguson, Howells, Mendelssohn, Duruflé, and Vierne. *Keiser, organ.*
+ ARG 9-10/95: 265
+ Fa 7-8/95: 327

29491. 7031: *What sweeter music: Carols for year round.* Music of Rutter, Mathias, Britten, Holst, Freund, Howells, Abell, Manz, Smedley, and Anon. *Memphis Boy Choir; Memphis Chamber Choir; Ayer, cond.; Belcher, organ.*
+ ARG 11-12/92: 268

29492. 7044: Music of Willan, Batiks, Karg-Elert, Vierne, and Liszt. *Wilkinson, organ.*
+ ARG 5-6/94: 182

29493. 7045: Wagner—Meistersinger overture (arr.). Reubke—Psalm 94. Liszt—Ad nos, ad salutarem undam. *Laubach, organ.*
• ARG 1-2/96: 217

29494. 7054: Music of Buxtehude, Bruhns, and Bach. *Dumschat, organ.*
+ ARG 1-2/96: 216

PRODIGITAL

29495. PRO-VM 1066: Soler—Harpsichord sonatas. *Shapiro, harpsichord.*
+ ARG 7-8/93: 161

29496. PRO-VM 1113: *Tangos and habaneras.* Music of Piazzolla, Amargos, Gonzalez, Ravel, and others. *Gascon, flute; Coll, guitar.*
• ARG 11-12/96: 247

29497. PRO-VM 1229: Turina—Violin sonatas no. 1-2; Poema de una sanluguena. Granados—Violin sonata. *Palomares, violin; Wagemans, piano.*
+ ARG 3-4/94: 175
+ Fa 3-4/94: 349

29498. PRO 1314: Grieg—Violin sonatas no. 1-3. *Palomares, violin; Wagemans, piano.*
• ARG 11-12/95: 126
• Fa 9-10/95: 152

29499. PRO-VM 5162: Mompou—Variations sur un thème de Chopin; Impresiones intimas; Palsajes; Canción y danza no. 6-8. *Wagemans, piano.*
• ARG 7-8/95: 157
• Fa 7-8/95: 249

29500. PRO-VM 5308: *19th century viola music.* Music of Brahms, Joachim, Sitt, and Enesco. *Hatch, viola; Stevens, piano.*
+ ARG 3-4/93: 176
+ Fa 3-4/93: 380

29501. PRO 6215: Brahms—Viola sonatas no. 1-2. *Hatch, viola; Wagemans, piano.*
• ARG 11-12/95: 96
- Fa 9-10/95: 152

29502. PRO-VM 7192: Dohnányi—Cello sonata. Music of Bartók, Kodály, and Hubay. *Cooke, cello; Watkins, piano.*
+ ARG 5-6/96: 232
+ Fa 5-6/96: 342

29503. PRO-VM 9226: Jacob—Concertino; Five pieces; Three songs; Clarinet quintet. *D. Geeting, clarinet; Primes, piano; Beasom, soprano; Stenske, Phelps-Beckstead, violins; Rintoul, viola; J. Geeting, cello.*
+ ARG 7-8/95: 131
+ Fa 7-8/95: 211

PRODUCTIONES FONOGRAFICAS

29504. PFCD 1967: REVUELTAS—La noche de los mayas. MONCAYO—Tierra de temporal. PONCE—Sinfonia ferial. *Phil. Society of Symphony Orch. Concerts; Alvarez, cond.*
+ Fa 1-2/95: 241

PROPHONE

29505. PCD 002: *Bella Madre de' Fiori.* Music of A. Scarlatti, Verdelot, Monteverdi, Grandi, and Merula. *Rydén, soprano; Croton, lute & theorbo; Gäfvert, harpsichord & organ; Akerberg, cello; Wallström, Bergman, violins; Dongois, cornetto.*
● ARG 5-6/96: 257
+ Fa 9-10/93: 339

29506. PCD 007: *Impressions of Latin America.* Music of Piazzolla, Ginastera, Barrios, Lauro, Cortes, and Wye. *Schenck, flute; Haraldsson, guitar; other instrumentalists.*
+ Fa 9-10/93: 375

PROPIANO

29507. 224501: Music of Schumann, Mozart, Scarlatti, Chopin, Scriabin, and Brahms. *Okashiro, piano.*
+ ARG 1-2/96: 171

29508. 224502: Music of Scriabin, Debussy, Takemitsu, and Okashiro. *Okashiro, piano.*
+ ARG 7-8/95: 249

29509. 224503: DEBUSSY—Etudes. BARTÓK—Hungarian peasant songs. *Song, piano.*
● ARG 7-8/95: 104

29510. 224504: Music of Bach-Godowski, Brahms, Fauré, Scriabin, and Chopin. *Block, piano.*
- ARG 3-4/95: 241

29511. 224505: FRANCK—Violin sonata. WALTON—Violin sonata. *Kamei, violin; Okashiro, piano.*
● ARG 5-6/95: 113

29512. 224506: SCARLATTI—Sonatas. *Babayan, piano.*
+ ARG 5-6/96: 183
+ Fa 7-8/96: 282

29513. 224507: CHOPIN—22 mazurkas. *Block, piano.*
+ ARG 5-6/96: 100
● Fa 7-8/96: 146

29514. 224508: HINDEMITH—Ludus tonalis. FAURÉ—Nocturnes no. 4, 7, 13. *Aldwell, piano.*
+ ARG 7-8/96: 131
+ Fa 7-8/96: 196

29515. 224509: *Franck-Liszt organ-piano transcriptions.* BACH—Prelude and fugue, BWV 543. FRANCK—Chorals no. 2-3; Prélude, fugue, et variation, op. 18. *Viardo, piano.*
+ Fa 7-8/96: 167

29516. 224510: SCRIABIN—Études. *Okashiro, piano.*
- ARG 9-10/96: 199
+ Fa 7-8/96: 300

29517. 224511: VIÑAO—Etudes, book 1 (selections); Trio for piano, violin, and cello. *Song, piano; Steinberg, violin; Kitsopoulos, cello.*
+ ARG 11-12/96: 307
+ Fa 7-8/96: 335

PROPRIUS

29518. PRCD 7762: *Cantate domino.* Music of Bossi, Walther, Olsson, Handel, Vogler, Adam, Gruber, Reger, and Berlin. *Oscars Motettkör; Nilsson, cond.; Linder, organ.* Reissue.
- Fa 9-10/93: 350

29519. PRCD 9004: *Aftonpsalm och Julesång.* Music of Adam, Nordqvist, Tegner, Köhler, Schubert, Bach, Gruber, Franck, Dvorak, Grieg, Wolf, and Reger. *Hagegård, baritone; Öhrwall, organ & piano; Adolf Fredriks Bachkör.*
- Fa 9-10/93: 344

29520. PRCD 9008: HANDEL—Arias from Hercules, Giulio Cesare, and Semele. MONTEVERDI—O rosetta, che rosetta; La violetta; Lamento d'Arianna. TELEMANN—Trauer-Music eines kunsterfahrenen Canarienvogels. ROMAN—Swedish mass (1752): Agnus dei. *Otter, mezzo-soprano; Drottningholm Baroque Ensemble.* Reissue.
+ Gr 10/91: 195

29521. PRCD 9009—9015 (7 separate discs): MESSIAEN—Complete works for organ. *Bokström, organ.*
● Fa 9-10/93: 216

29522. PRCD 9040: *Contrasts.* Music of Adolphson, Yeston, C.M. Schönberg, Mahler, Laurinius, Klingo, Ravel, and Ingemann. *Hagegård, baritone; Idenstam, organ.*
- Fa 9-10/93: 345

29523. PRCD 9064: HOLEWA—Preludes; Sonatina; Piano pieces; Suite; Inventions. *Ribbing, piano.*
+ Fa 9-10/93: 187

29524. PRCD 9070/71 (2 discs): BACH—Mass in B minor. *Högman, Groop, Crook, Salomaa; Micaeli Chamber Choir; Drottningholm Baroque Ensemble; Eby, cond.*
+ Fa 9-10/93: 108

29525. PRCD 9076/78 (3 discs): Swedish military marches. *Royal Swedish Army Band.*
+ Fa 9-10/93: 389

29526. PRCD 9085: POULENC—Organ concerto. ALAIN—Suite for organ. LANGLAIS—Organ concerto no. 2. *Johnsen, organ; Royal Orch. Stockholm; Ingebretsen, cond.* Reissue.
● Fa 3-4/94: 274

29527. PRCD 9086: OLSSON—Requiem. *Lindenstrand, Blom, Haugen, Skold; Gustav Vasa Oratorio Choir; Royal Opera Orch.; Ohlson, cond.*
+ Fa 3-4/94: 260

29528. PRCD 9089: *Transcriptions for organ.* Music of Ernst and Vivaldi (trans. Bach), Bach and Roman (trans. Janacek). *Janacek, organ.*
● Fa 3-4/94: 403

29529. PRCD 9093: *Now the green blade riseth.* Hymns and songs from the Swedish Ecumenical Hymnal. *Stockholm Cathedral Choir; Sjökvist, cond.; Johannes Youth Choir; Eby, cond.*
+ Fa 3-4/94: 388

29530. PRCD 9982: ARGENTO—From the diary of Virginia Woolf. WERLE—Chants for dark hours. *Schéle, soprano; with instrumental accomp.*
+ Fa 9-10/93: 103

PROTONE

29531. PRCD 1101: RACHMANINOFF—Preludes: op. 3, no. 2; op. 23; op. 32. *Keene, piano.*
● Fa 1-2/88: 195

29532. PRCD 1102: *Constance Keene plays familiar favorites.* Music of Mendelssohn, Chopin, Liszt, Saint-Saëns, Rachmaninoff, Griffes, Chasins, Gluck, and Weinberger. *Keene, piano.*
+ Fa 3-4/88: 253

29533. PRCD 1103: BACH—Art of fugue. *Los Angeles Saxophone Quartet.*
● Fa 3-4/89: 101

29534. PRCD 1104: Forgotten gems from the Heifetz legacy. *Kloss, violin; Agus, piano.*
+ ARG 9-10/94: 245
● Fa 1-2/94: 416

29535. PRCD 1107: *Caribbean rhythms.* Music of Cervantes, Saumell, and Morel Campos. *Fernández, piano.*
+ Fa 1-2/94: 411

29536. PRCD 1108: *Musical mementos of Jascha Heifetz.* Music of Achron, Albéniz, Bach, Chopin, Debussy, Dinicu, Gershwin, Godowsky, Kreisler, Medtner, Mendelssohn, Rachmaninoff, Ravel, and Schubert. *Agus, piano.*
- Fa 1-2/94: 405

PROTONE

29537. PRCD 1110: Starer—Five preludes for piano. Noon—Three études, op. 69. Siegmeister—Three studies. Prokofiev—Piano sonata no. 6. *Rust, piano.*
+ ARG 3-4/95: 244
+ Fa 11-12/93: 494

29538. PRCD 1111: *An American collage, vol. 1.* Music of Chasins, Schickele, Rob. R. Bennett, Kroll, Piston, Chihara, Erb, and Bond. *Instrumentalists; Chamber Singers of the University of Southern California; Eichenberger, cond.*
+ ARG 7-8/94: 203
• Fa 5-6/94: 335

29539. PRCD 1112: Variations for piano by Handel, Beethoven, Mendelssohn, Schumann, and Rachmaninoff. *Keene, piano.*
+ ARG 7-8/94: 215

29540. NRPR 2202/3 (2 discs): MacDowell—Piano music. *Keene, piano.*
+ ARG 11-12/93: 143
• Fa 11-12/93: 301

29541. NRPR 2204: Liszt—Two legends; Harmonies poétiques et religieuses: Bénédiction de Dieu dans la solitude; Années de pèlerinage, book 3: Après une lecture de Dante. Respighi—Ancient airs and dances; Siciliana; Gagliarda; Three preludes on Gregorian themes. *Raphael, piano.*
+ Fa 11-12/93: 298

29542. NRPR 2205: *Live from Shanghai.* Tchaikovsky—Symphony no. 6. Liu Tingyu—Su-san suite. Bond—Thinking like a mountain. Sousa—Stars and stripes forever. *Shanghai Symphony Orch.; Bond, Xieyang, conds.*
+ ARG 3-4/96: 268
+ Fa 11-12/95: 398

PROUDSOUND

29543. PROUCD 129: *20th-century sacred music.* Music of Martin, Duruflé, Stanford, Górecki, and Byron. *Schola Cantorum Oxford; Summerly, cond.*
+ Gr 4/92: 146

29544. PROUCD 133: Josquin—Déploration sur la mort de Johannes Ockeghem. Obrecht—Salve Regina. Ockeghem—Missa Ecce ancilla Domini; Motets. *Clerks' Group; Wickham, cond.*
+ Gr 10/93: 90

29545. PROUCD 135: Music of Albinoni, Frescobaldi, Fasch, Muffat, Viviani, Telemann, and Mouret. *Freeman-Attwood, trumpet; Simcock, organ.*
+ Gr 5/94: 76

29546. PROUCD 136: Górecki—Euntes ibant et flebant; Totus tuus; Amen. Pärt—Magnificat; Summa. Tavener—

Choral music. *Oxford Pro Musica Singers; Smedley, cond.*
+ Gr 12/94: 137

29547. PROUCD 139: Balakauskas—Like the touch of a sea wave. Barkauskas—Partita. Pärt—Fratres; Spiegel im Spiegel. Schnittke—Violin sonata no. 1. *Mataityté, violin; Zimmermann, piano.*
+ Gr 7/96: 69

PROVIVA

29548. 147: Meyer—Calrinet quintet. Bloch—Music for clarinet and strings; Clarinetto divertente. *Brunner, clarinet; Wilanow Quartet.*
+ ARG 11-12/93: 150

29549. 151: Meyer—String quartets no. 1, 7-8. *Wilanów Quartet.*
+ ARG 11-12/93: 150

29550. 156: Music of Behrend, Walter, Bast, Stahmer, and others. *Behrend, mandolin; DZO Chamber Orch.; Ochi, Behrend, conds.*
□ ARG 11-12/93: 237

29551. 162: Meyer—String quartets no. 4-6. *Wilanow Quartet.*
+ ARG 11-12/93: 150

29552. 164: Music of Stammer, Glynn, Hamari, Blank, and Betz. *Zelinsky, Smeyers, clarinets.*
+ ARG 11-12/93: 233

29553. 165: *Like fire burning.* Music of Kucera, Dinescu, Stahmer, Nickerson, and Jung. *Evers, Weigel, guitars.*
+ ARG 7-8/94: 210

29554. 169: Bloch—Denn dein Licht kommt; Du sollst nicht töten. *Schwarz, organ; Schweigmann, narrator; Gmelin, cello; Schollum, baritone; North German Radio Symphony Orch. & Chorus; H. Neumann, Wit, conds.*
+ ARG 7-8/94: 77

29555. 170: Pfifner—Cambiamenti concertanti; Monologs on peace and war; Componimento; Don Quixote. *Doherty, oboe; Waldner, percussion; Serenata Basel; Schiaefli, cond.; Reinmann, baritone; Burkhard, piano; Hinking, organ; Basel Symphony; Atzmon, cond.*
□ ARG 11-12/93: 166

PRT

29556. CDPCN 9: Music of Tchaikovsky, Glazunov, Blumenfeld, Rubinstein, Stravinsky, Rachmaninoff, Prokofiev, Mussorgsky, and Scriabin. *Cooper, piano.*
• Fa 3-4/88: 254

29557. PVCD 8398: Dohnányi—Piano concerto no. 1. *Vázsonyi, piano; New*

Philharmonia Orch.; Pritchard, cond.
• Fa 7-8/87: 94

PWK

29558. 1141: Ravel—Introduction and allegro. Debussy—Sonata for flute, viola and harp. Roussel—String trio. Caplet—Masque of the red death. *Giles, harp; Jerusalem String Trio.*
+ ARG 9-10/90: 136

PWOA PRODUCTIONS

29559. 011: Koenigsberg—Audiophile computer music. *Koenigsberg, electronics.*
+ Fa 5-6/95: 234

PYRAMID

29560. 13485: Beethoven—Violin sonatas no. 5, 8-9. *N. Gotkovsky, violin; I. Gotkovsky, piano.*
+ ARG 11-12/86: 54
+ Fa 7-8/86: 93

29561. 13486: Bartók—Violin concertos (complete). *Gotkovsky, violin; National Phil. Orch.; Gerhardt, cond.*
+ ARG 7-8/86: 89
+ Fa 7-8/86: 88

29562. 13487: Brahms—Violin sonatas (complete). *N. Gotkovsky, violin; I. Gotkovsky, piano.*
- ARG 9-10/86: 68
+ Fa 7-8/86: 93
+ Gr 4/87: 1424
+ HF 1/87: 74

29563. 13488: Haydn—Piano sonatas (selections). *Gotkovsky, piano.*
+ Fa 3-4/87: 130
- Ov 9/87: 42

29564. 13489: Brahms—String quartet no. 3; Clarinet quintet, op. 115. *Moraguès, clarinet; Talich Quartet.*
+ Fa 9-10/87: 170

29565. 13490/92 (3 discs): Beethoven—Violin sonatas (complete). *N. Gotkovsky, violin; I. Gotkovsky, piano.*
• Fa 3-4/88: 75
• Fa 5-6/89: 127
• HPR 7/88: 76

29566. 13493: Shostakovich—Violin concertos (complete). *Gotkovsky, violin; Bulgarian Radio Symphony; Kazandjiev, cond.*
- ARG 11-12/89: 118 (no. 1)
+ ARG 11-12/89: 118 (no. 2)
+ Fa 3-4/89: 276
- Gr 10/91: 113

29567. 13494: Mussorgsky—The nursery cycle; Songs. *Milcheva, mezzo-soprano; Protich, piano.*
- Fa 1-2/90: 251 (Nursery)
+ Fa 1-2/90: 251 (others)

29568. 13496: STRAVINSKY—Duo concertante. WEBERN— Four pieces for violin and piano, op. 7. SCHOENBERG—Fantasy for violin and piano. PROKOFIEV—Violin sonata no. 2; Sonata for solo violin, op. 115. *N. Gotkovsky, violin; I. Gotkovsky, piano.*
+ Fa 11-12/90: 448
● Gr 9/91: 97

29569. 13497: HINDEMITH—Piano sonata no. 2; Ludus tonalis. *Richter, piano.* Recorded live 1985.
+ Fa 9-10/90: 263

29570. 13498: The Magic of Bulgarian voices. *Georgiev Sisters.*
□ Fa 11-12/91: 539

29571. 13499: BEETHOVEN—Violin concerto. BERG—Violin concerto. *Gotkovsky, violin; Sofia Phil. Orch.; Yampolsky, cond.*
● Fa 1-2/91: 146

29572. 13501 (2 discs): BEETHOVEN—Piano sonatas no. 6-7, 17-18. CHOPIN—Étude in C minor, op. 10, no. 12; Prelude in D♭ major, op. 28, no. 15. *Richter, piano.*
+ Fa 1-2/91: 150
+ Gr 3/91: 1704

29573. 13503: MIASKOVSKY—Piano sonata no. 3. PROKOFIEV—Piano sonata no. 8. SHOSTAKOVICH—Preludes and fugues, op. 87, no. 19, 21-22. *Richter, piano.* Recorded live 1973.
+ Fa 11-12/91: 446
● Gr 10/92: 143

29574. 13504: BARTÓK—Sonata for two pianos and percussion. STRAVINSKY—Rite of spring (arr. for two pianos and percussion). *Linea Ensemble.*
- Fa 5-6/92: 120

29575. 13507: DEBUSSY—Preludes, book 2. CHOPIN—Rondo à la Mazur, op. 5; Ballade no. 1, op. 23. *Richter, piano.* Recorded live 1968.
+ Fa 3-4/93: 152

29576. 13508: Music of Pujol, Piazzolla, Mores, Troilo, Pignoni, and Millet. *Garau, Millet, guitars.*
● ARG 9-10/94: 237

29577. 13509: BARTÓK—Songs. *Csordás, soprano; Krausz, piano.*
+ ARG 11-12/95: 81

29578. 13510: CHOPIN—Preludes, op. 28. SHOSTAKOVICH—Preludes, op. 34. *Krausz, piano.*
● ARG 9-10/95: 126

29579. 13511: GINASTERA—String quartets no. 1-2. *Miami String Quartet.*
+ ARG 9-10/95: 149

QUADRIVIUM

29580. SCA 004: Amor mi fa cantar. *Ensemble Micrologus.*
+ Fa 11-12/93: 480

29581. SCA 012: *La bassa fiamenga.* Music of Bach, Scheidt, Frescobaldi, Langlais, Corrette, and Dupré. *Brizi, organ & harpsichord.*
+ Fa 11-12/93: 489

29582. SCA 014: ALFONSO EL SABIO—Cantigas de Santa Maria. *Ensemble Micrologus; Zosso, vocals.*
+ Fa 11-12/93: 164

29583. SCA 015: Gabriele Mirabassi Electroacoustic Quartetto.
+ Fa 11-12/93: 515

29584. SCA 016: TESSADRELLI—Concatenazione I; E forme e gesti; E apparve una cattedrale di cristallo; Sette speculazioni sulla Melanconia. *Clapasson, piano.*
+ Fa 11-12/93: 425

29585. SCA 018: *Duo Maratti-Trovato.* Music of Bach, Leclair, Reid, Liviabella, Solbiati, Facchinetti, and Anders. *Maratti, flute; Trovato, harp.*
+ Fa 11-12/93: 482

29586. SCA 019: MORLACCHI—Twelve little sonatas for pianoforte; Romanza for strings and guitar; Finaletto for winds and strings; Quoniam tu solus sanctus; Salve Regina. *Ragni, piano; Maccabei, tenor; Rinaldi, baritone; Borgher, horn; I Cantori di Perugia; other instrumentalists.*
+ Fa 11-12/93: 328

29587. SCA 020: BROUWER—Concerto di Toronto; Guitar concerto no. 3. *Angelis, guitar; Symphonia Perusina; Brouwer, cond.*
+ Fa 11-12/93: 199

29588. SCA 021: *La vida de Colin.* Music of Zesso, Patavino, Dalza, Martini, Ambrogio, Oriola, and anon. *Sine Nomine.*
● Fa 11-12/93: 478

29589. SCA 022: *Il gusto italiano.* Music of Bach and Walther. *Brizi, organ.*
+ Fa 11-12/93: 490

29590. SCA 024: SETACCIOLI—Clarinet sonata. MARTUCCI—Piano fantasia. CASTELNUOVO-TEDESCO—Clarinet sonata. *Mirabassi, clarinet; Lisi, piano.*
+ ARG 9-10/94: 230
+ Fa 7-8/94: 239

29591. SCA 025: FUMAGALLI—Trio de bravoure. CANTI—Concerto for flute, oboe, and clarinet. DE MICHELIS—Trio scolastico. CAVALLINI—Terzetto. *Camerata a quattro.*
● Fa 11-12/93: 508

29592. SCA 026: ALBINONI—Sinfonias, op. 2. *Orch. d'Archi Symphonia Perusina; Briccetti, cond.*
+ Fa 11-12/93: 164

29593. SCA 030: FANTINI—Modo per imparare a sonare di tromba tanto di guerra quanto musicalmente in organo, con tromba sordina, col cimbalo, e ogn'altro istrumento. *Conforzi, trumpet; with ensemble.*
+ Fa 11-12/93: 234

29594. SCA 033: TCHAIKOVSKY—Moscow. PROKOFIEV—Alexander Nevsky. *Chistiakova, Kichigin, Svechnikova, vocal soloists; Municipal Theater of Moscow Orch. & Chorus; Kolobov, cond.*
● Fa 1-2/94: 329

29595. SCA 034: PROKOFIEV—Maddalena. RACHMANINOFF—Spring. *Pisarenko, Martynov, Moiseenko, Kichigin; Chorus & Orch. of the Moscow Municipal Theater; Kolobov, cond.* Recorded live.
- Fa 11-12/93: 347

29596. SCA 040: La musica Italiana del XV secolo. *Sine Nomine.*
□ Fa 11-12/93: 478

QUANTUM

29597. QM 6893: SCHUMANN—Piano music. *Hugonnard-Roche, piano.*
- ARG 5-6/89: 86
+ Fa 5-6/89: 313

29598. QM 6896: MOZART—Arias. *Hagen-William, bass-baritone; Sinfonia d'Anvers; Proost, cond.*
- ARG 9-10/89: 85
- Fa 9-10/89: 225

29599. QM 6897: CRAS—Quintet for harp, flute, and string trio; Flute de Pan. *Michel, harp; Prevost, flute & pan pipes; Henry, baritone; Millière, violin; Benatar, viola; Bary, cello.*
+ Fa 5-6/89: 170

29600. QM 6898: *En hommage à Martine Géliot.* Music of Porter, Bax, Lemeland, Leclair, and Debussy. *Géliot, harp; Prevost, flute; Dupouy, viola.*
+ Fa 11-12/92: 439

29601. QM 6899: Stirps Jesse: chant. *Ensemble Venance Fortunat; Deschamps, cond.*
+ ARG 11-12/92: 122
+ Fa 11-12/92: 429

29602. QM 6900: CHOPIN—19 Polish songs. LISZT—6 Polish songs of Chopin. *Choi, soprano; Grasser, piano.*
- ARG 11-12/92: 105

29603. QM 6902: LEMELAND—Violin concerto; Viola concerto; Symphony no. 5 for strings; Elegie in memory of Samuel Barber. *Plasson, violin; Jeandet, viola; Instrumental Ensemble of Grenoble;*

QUANTUM

Tardue, cond.
  □ ARG 11-12/92: 147

29604. QM 6915: DJABADARY—Georgian rhapsody; Piano concerto no. 3; Serpentine threnody; Tbilisiana. *Goraieb, piano; Luxembourg Radio Symphony Orch.; Froment, cond.*
  + ARG 9-10/92: 98
  • Fa 11-12/92: 226

29605. QM 6918: WISSMER—Piano concerto no. 2; Violin concerto no. 2. *Perretti, piano; Devries, violin; Suisse romande Orch.; Wissmer, Appia, conds.*
  + ARG 9-10/92: 183

29606. QM 6939: BACH—Piano music. *Sombart, piano.*
  - Fa 9-10/94: 128

29607. QM 6947: *Musique française.* Music of Satie, Ravel, Franck, Fauré, and Desbriere. *Sombart, piano.*
  • Fa 7-8/94: 318

29608. QMC 122257: Opera fantasies and variations. *Vidal, clarinet; Takishima, piano.*
  + ARG 11-12/95: 247

29609. QMC 122279: Music of Rossini, Farkas, Brouwer, Crell, Confrey, Joplin, Karia, Balada, Funk Pearson, and Bizet. *Versailles Guitar Quartet.*
  • ARG 3-4/96: 232

QUEEN'S UNIVERSITY MUSIC

29610. 9101: *20th-century Canadian chamber music.* CLARKE—Three Shakespearean miniatures; Two soliloquies. CRAWLEY—Stabat Mater. KEANE—Parthenope. BURGE—Still time. ALLIK—Rhapsody. *Windsong; Seiffert, oboe; Tryczynski, cello; Burge, piano; Craig, clarinet.*
  + ARG 9-10/92: 187

29611. 9301: KEANE—Dialogics: works for wind instruments and digital electronic. *Various instrumentalists.*
  + Fa 9-10/93: 194

QUINTANA

29612. QUI 903001: HAYDN—String quartets: op. 77, no. 1-2; op. 103. *Festetics Quartet.*
  + ARG 9-10/91: 82
  • Fa 7-8/91: 172
  • Gr 7/91: 77

29613. QUI 903002/03 (2 discs): HAYDN—String quartets, op. 33; op. 42. *Festetics Quartet.*
  + ARG 3-4/92: 72
  + Fa 1-2/92: 233
  + Gr 8/92: 46

29614. QUI 903005: TCHAIKOVSKY—Serenade for strings. DVOŘÁK—Serenade for strings. GRIEG—Holberg suite. *Franz*

Liszt Chamber Orch.; Rolla, cond.
  • ARG 9-10/91: 134

29615. QUI 903006: Piano music of Mozart, Beethoven, Schumann, Debussy, and Bartók. *Kocsis, piano.*
  - ARG 11-12/91: 191
  - Fa 7-8/91: 358

29616. QUI 903008: MOZART—Wind transcriptions of music from La clemenza di Tito, Die Entführung aus dem Serail, Così fan tutte, Die Zauberflöte, Le nozze di Figaro, and Don Giovanni. *Budapest Wind Ensemble; Berkes, cond.*
  + ARG 11-12/91: 122
  + Fa 9-10/91: 301

29617. QUI 903010: BACH—Weichet nur, betrübte Schatten, BWV 202; Non sa che sia dolore, BWV 209; O holder Tag, BWV 210. *Zádori, soprano; Capella Savaria; Németh, cond.*
  • ARG 9-10/91: 37
  + Fa 7-8/91: 104
  - Gr 7/91: 95

29618. QUI 903011: PERGOLESI—Stabat Mater; Salve Regina in C minor; Salve Regina in A minor. *Zádori, soprano; Ragin, countertenor; Capella Savaria; Németh, cond.*
  + Fa 9-10/91: 311
  • Gr 11/91: 147

29619. QUI 903012: *Songs to my lady.* Music of Morley, Ford, Byrd, Dowland, Hume, Purcell, Ravenscroft, and Anon. *Esswood, countertenor; Jübscher, lute & baroque guitar.*
  • ARG 9-10/91: 173
  + Fa 7-8/91: 345

29620. QUI 903013: MOZART—Symphonies no. 29, 32-33. *Franz Liszt Chamber Orch.; Rampal, cond.*
  + Fa 9-10/91: 298

29621. QUI 903014: MONTEVERDI—Tirsi e Clori; Fifteen madrigals. *Capella Savaria; McGegan, cond.*
  • ARG 5-6/92: 87
  + Fa 11-12/91: 393

29622. QUI 903015: MOZART—Exsultate, jubilate; Grabmusik; Kommet her; Ave verum corpus; Sub tuum praesidium; Regina coeli. *Zádori, soprano; Bach Singers; Vocal Ensemble and Capella Savaria; Németh, cond.*
  + ARG 11-12/91: 109
  + Fa 7-8/91: 229

29623. QUI 903017: DVOŘÁK—Symphony no. 8; Carnival overture. *Budapest Festival Orch.; Fischer, cond.*
  - ARG 1-2/92: 51
  + Fa 1-2/92: 205
  + Gr 11/92: 58

29624. QUI 903018: VIVALDI—Oboe concertos, RV 450, 454, 457; Concerto for oboe and bassoon, RV 545; Concerto

for 2 oboes, RV 535; Recorder concerto, RV 442; Concerto for 2 oboes, 2 violins, and bassoon, RV 557. *Wolf, oboe & recorder; Capella Savaria; Németh, cond.; Brandisz, oboe; Tognon, bassoon; Luisi, Tamás, violins.*
  + Fa 9-10/92: 380

29625. QUI 903020: BEETHOVEN—Quintet for piano and winds, op. 16. MOZART—Quintet for piano and winds, K. 452. *Members of the Budapest Wind Ensemble; Kocsis, piano.*
  - ARG 1-2/92: 28
  + Fa 3-4/92: 149
  - Gr 9/92: 102

29626. QUI 903021: SCHOENBERG—Chamber symphony no. 1 (arr. Schoenberg). BARTÓK—Miraculous mandarin (arr. Bartók). *Kocsis, Hauser, piano.*
  + Fa 5-6/92: 241

29627. QUI 903022: MOZART—Piano concertos no. 8, 13, 25. *Kocsis, piano; Franz Liszt Chamber Orch.; Rolla, cond.*
  + ARG 7-8/92: 181
  • Fa 7-8/92: 225
  • Gr 9/92: 79

29628. QUI 903024: LISZT—Sonata in B minor; Piano music. *Ránki, piano.*
  + ARG 11-12/91: 90
  + Fa 11-12/91: 374
  • Gr 3/92: 80

29629. QUI 903025: SCHUBERT (ARR. MAHLER)—String quartet no. 14 "Death and the maiden"; Quartettsatz. *Franz Liszt Chamber Orch.; Rolla, cond.*
  + Fa 3-4/92: 311
  + Gr 3/92: 52

29630. QUI 903026: C.P.E. BACH—Cello concertos, H. 436, H. 432, H. 439. *Perényi, cello; Franz Liszt Chamber Orch.; Rolla, cond.*
  + ARG 5-6/92: 14
  + Fa 5-6/92: 113
  + Gr 9/92: 40

29631. QUI 903031: Gregorian chant from Aquitaine. *Schola Hungarica; Dobszay, Szendrei, conds.*
  + Fa 3-4/92: 392

29632. QUI 903032: Gregorian chant: from Adam to Abraham. *Schola Hungarica; Dobszay, Szendrei, conds.*
  + Fa 7-8/92: 335

29633. QUI 903037: *Gregorian chant. Christmas eve. Schola Hungarica; Dobszay, Szendrei, conds.*
  + Fa 3-4/93: 358

29634. QUI 903038 : From Abraham to Moses: Gregorian chant. *Schola Hungarica; Dobszay, Szendrei, conds.*
  + Fa 1-2/93: 290

29635. QUI 903040/41 (2 discs): HAYDN—String quartets, op. 64, no. 1-6. *Festetics Quartet.*
+ Fa 1-2/93: 162

29636. QUI 903043 : HAYDN—The seven last words. *Festetics Quartet.*
+ EM 8/92: 521
+ Fa 5-6/92: 170

29637. QUI 903046: LISZT (ARR. P. WOLF)—Hungarian rhapsodies no. 2, 6, 9, 12, 14-15. *Franz Liszt Chamber Orch.; Rolla, cond.*
+ Fa 11-12/92: 279

29638. QUI 903048: MARCELLO—Estro poetico-armonico: Psalms 14, 17. *Vocalists; Capella Savaria; Németh, cond.*
+ ARG 9-10/93: 152
+ Fa 5-6/93: 262

29639. QUI 903049: LISZT—Tasso, lamento e trionfo; Les préludes; Mazeppa; Mephisto waltz no. 1. *Budapest Festival Orch.; Fischer, cond.*
+ ARG 3-4/93: 105
+ Fa 3-4/93: 209

29640. QUI 903051: MOZART—Serenades for winds, no. 10, 12. *Budapest Wind Ensemble; Kocsis, cond.*
• Fa 5-6/92: 208

29641. QUI 903052: BARTÓK—Music for strings, percussion and celesta; Divertimento for strings. *Franz Liszt Chamber Orch.; Rolla, cond.* Reissue.
+ ARG 3-4/93: 54
+ Fa 3-4/93: 116

29642. QUI 903053: TELEMANN—Christmas cantatas. *Zádori, J. Németh, Kállay, Mertens; Capella Savaria; P. Németh, cond.*
+ ARG 11-12/92: 222
+ Fa 5-6/92: 267

29643. QUI 903059: Seventeenth-century Hungarian songs. *Zádori, soprano; Ars Renata; Vagantes.*
+ ARG 7-8/92: 277
+ Fa 7-8/92: 334

29644. QUI 903061: GRAUN—Der Tod Jesu. *Zádori, Fers, Klietmann, Mertens; Kammerchor Cantamus; Capella Savaria; Németh, cond.*
• ARG 7-8/92: 137
+ EM 2/93: 157
+ Fa 7-8/92: 165

29645. QUI 903062: WERNER—Debora. *Banditelli, Hill, Mertens, Klietmann; Ensemble Vocal Savaria; Capella Savaria; Németh, cond.*
• Fa 7-8/94: 286

29646. QUI 903063: VIVALDI—Motets for soprano and orchestra. *Zádori, soprano; Capella Savaria; Németh, cond.*
+ Fa 1-2/93: 265

29647. QUI 903067/68 (2 discs): CILEA—L'Arlesiana. *Spacagna, Zilio, Kelen, B. Anderson; Hungarian State Choir and Orch.; Rosekrans, cond.*
+ Fa 11-12/92: 219
• Gr 12/92: 135
• ON 9/93: 53

29648. QUI 903082: BRAHMS—Piano music. *Ránki, piano.*
+ Fa 1-2/93: 116

RADIOTON

29649. SLPX 12998 (LP): *Lieder recital.* SCHUBERT—Die Winterreise: Selections. WOLF—Italienisches Liederbuch: Selections; 3 Michelangelo Lieder. *Pólgar, bass; Rados, Salgo, Garam, piano.*
• Fa 1-2/89: 315

29650. HCD 31048: *Russian liturgical music.* Music of Rachmaninov, Stravinsky, Kastalsky, Mussorgsky, Glinka, Gretchaninov, Tchaikovsky, Berezovsky, Bortniansky, and Rimsky-Korsakov. *Tomkins Vocal Ensemble.*
+ Fa 1-2/92: 397

29651. SLPX 31084: HAYDN (ARR. KESZLER)—Wind quintet after piano trio H. XV:4. KOSCÁR—Wind quintet no. 3. ROSSINI—Wind quartet no. 6. RÁNKI—Pentaerophonia. *Hungarian Radio Wind Quintet.*
+ Fa 3-4/89: 388

RADIUS MUSIC

29652. 02: DOLAT-SHAHI—When the moon whispers. *Dolat-Shahi, tar.*
+ Fa 11-12/95: 240

29653. no number: DOLAT-SHAHI—Garden of butterflies. *Dolat-Shahi, electronics.*
+ Fa 5-6/95: 181

RAM

29654. 59131: EISENBERG—Improvisations on Lutheran chorales. *Eisenberg, organ.*
+ ARG 11-12/94: 108

29655. 59271: BACH—Coffee cantata; Peasant cantata. *Claus, soprano; Krumbiegel, tenor; Biller, bass; Eisenberg, harpsichord & cond.*
+ ARG 11-12/94: 64

29656. 59306: Music of Bizet, Vivaldi, Horovitz, Mascagni, Gershwin, and others. *Young German Brass Quintet.*
+ ARG 11-12/94: 219

29657. 59307: Music of Tagell, Kodály, Ysaÿe, and Reger. *Feltz, Kerstin, cello.*
+ ARG 11-12/94: 220

RAPTORIA CAAM

29658. RCD 1001: *New raptorial moon.* Music of M. Newman, Walker, Fink, Cox, and Fox. *Amelite Consortium.*
+ Fa 9-10/93: 372

29659. RCD 1002/3: Maria Newman's musical stories, vol. 1-2. *R. Newman, narrator; Viklarbo Chamber Ensemble; Thatcher, spoken voice; M. Newman, violin.*
+ Fa 9-10/93: 372

29660. RCD 1005: SCHICKELE—Quartet. DAHL—Concerto a tre. FREUND—Triomusic. RÓZSA—Introduction and allegro. *Viklarbo Chamber Ensemble.*
+ ARG 9-10/95: 206

29661. RCD 1007: NEWMAN—Maskil; Terpsichore; Colores de Mexico. *Viklarbo Chamber Ensemble.*
□ ARG 7-8/96: 298

RARE RECORDED EDITIONS

29662. SRRE 183 (2 LPs): JOPLIN—Treemonisha. *Stegart, Lowe, Gamage, Watts; Davis, piano.*
- Fa 1-2/87: 130

RAVEN

29663. OAR-180: RHEINBERGER—Organ sonatas no. 2, 6, 8. *Stevens, organ.*
• ARG 11-12/91: 137
+ Fa 5-6/91: 263

29664. OAR-190: *Yankee, come home! Seven historic organs in Newburyport, Mass.* Music of White, Ruhl, Johnson, Ives, Zundel, and others. *Ruhl Metson, organ.*
+ ARG 5-6/91: 146
+ Fa 5-6/91: 361

29665. OAR-200: Music of Rheinberger, Stanley, Sowerby, Raff, Weiner, Reger, Ravanello, Bender and Vieuxtemps. *Murray, violin; Lohuis, organ.*
+ ARG 3-4/92: 186

29666. OAR-210: Organ music of Cook and Bacon. *Metson, organ.*
+ ARG 3-4/93: 166

29667. OAR-220: RHEINBERGER—Organ sonatas no. 16-17, 20. *Stevens, organ.*
+ ARG 5-6/93: 124
+ Fa 5-6/93: 294

29668. OAR-230: Music of Schroeder, Becker, Rheinberger, Foote, Bender, Sowerby, and others. *Murray, violin; Lohuis, organ.*
• ARG 7-8/94: 214

29669. OAR-240: Music of Sowerby, Scheidemann, Bach, Hancock, Distler, and Neswick. *Neswick, organ.*
+ ARG 5-6/94: 180

RAVEN

29670. OAR-250: BACH—Toccata & fugue in F; Partita on Sei gegrusset; Canzona, BWV 588; Prelude & fugue in D, BWV 532; Pastorella in F, BWV 590; Fantasy & fugue in C minor. *Ritchie, organ.*
- ARG 3-4/94: 67

29671. OAR-270: *A Tennessee organ tour.* Music of Duruflé, Guilain, Taylor, Merula, Buxtehude, and others. *Brock, organ.*
+ ARG 7-8/94: 213

29672. OAR-280: Music of Widor, Vierne, Bruhns, Buxtehude, Mendelssohn, and others. *Stevens, organ.*
+ ARG 11-12/94: 229

29673. OAR-300 (2 discs): BACH—Organ music from Leipzig. *Ritchie, organ.*
• ARG 11-12/95: 73

29674. OAR-310: SOWERBY—Comes autumn time; Requiescat in pace; Air with variations; Arioso; Whimsical variations; Sonatina; Dialog; Carillon. *Maycher, organ; Culp, piano; Watkins, organ.*
+ ARG 1-2/96: 178

29675. OAR-340: PARKER—Organ music. *Ahlstrom, organ.*
+ ARG 9-10/96: 176

29676. OAR-350: LISZT—Organ music. SCHEIDE—Organ music. *Scheide, organ.*
+ ARG 7-8/96: 146

29677. OAR-360: *The great organ at Methuen.* Music of Bach, Liszt, Franck, Josephs, and Howard. *Quinn, organ.*
- ARG 11-12/96: 250

RBM

29678. CD 6.3036: *Virtuose Posaunenmusik aus 5 Jahrhunderten.* Music of Speer, Corelli, Beethoven, Bruckner, and others. *Paul Schreckenberger & his Trombone Ensemble.*
+ ARG 1-2/90: 124
+ Fa 11-12/89: 479

29679. CD 6.3087: BACH—Goldberg variations (arr. Rheinberger; rev. Reger). *Lechler, Eisenlohr, pianos.*
+ ARG 1-2/93: 72
+ Fa 11-12/89: 110
+ Fa 11-12/92: 186
• St 3/90: 183

29680. CD 6.3108: MOZART—Rondo in A, K. 464a; String quartet no. 18. DITTERSDORF—String quartet no. 3. *Mannheim Quartet.*
+ Fa 11-12/89: 294

29681. CD 6.3112: *Perles musicales: celebrated pieces for cello and piano.* Music of Popper, R. Strauss, Offenbach, Leoncavallo, Rachmaninoff, Saint-Saëns, Davidoff, Dvorak, Massenet, and Bruch. *Boettcher, cello; Trede-Boettcher, piano.*
• ARG 3-4/90: 133
+ Fa 11-12/89: 472
+ Fa 9-10/93: 356

29682. CD 6.3116: RIES—Piano quintet. MOZART—Piano quartet in E♭; Trio movement in G. *Northwest German Chamber Ensemble.*
+ ARG 1-2/93: 138

29683. CD 6.3119: TCHAIKOVSKY—Variations on a rococo theme. DVOŘÁK—Czech suite; Rondo for cello and orchestra. *Feltz, cello; Kammerorchester Merck; Simane, cond.*
+ Fa 11-12/92: 389

29684. CD 6.3120: Arias from Fidelio, Freischütz, Tannhäuser, Meistersinger, Parsifal, and Götterdämmerung. *Cox, tenor; Mannheim Symphony Orch.; Shipway, cond.*
• ARG 11-12/92: 259

29685. CD 6.3183: HERTEL—Symphony in G. F.L. BENDA—Violin concerto in D. ROSETTI—Symphony in G minor. *Rau, violin; Neubrandenburger Philharmonie; Pfund, cond.*
+ Fa 11-12/92: 257

29686. CD 6.3191: Music of Vivaldi, Sor, Falla, and Albeniz. *Süddeutsches Guitar Duo; Janáček Chamber Orch.; Dejmek, cond.*
+ ARG 1-2/93: 179

29687. 463 182: SIBELIUS—Finlandia; Karelia suite; Valse triste. GRIEG—Peer Gynt: selections. *New Brandenburg Phil. Orch.; Pfund, cond.*
- Fa 5-6/93: 323

29688. 463 186: Music of Mendelssohn, Reger, Dupré, and Vierne. *Kaiser, organ.*
- ARG 5-6/93: 166

29689. 3084 (LP): WEBER—Piano quartet, op. 8. J. C. BACH—Piano quartet, G major. *Northwest German Chamber Ensemble.*
• Fa 11-12/86: 249

29690. 3086 (LP): DANZI—String quartets op. 55, no. 3; op. 29, no. 2; op. 6, no. 5. MOZART—5 four-part fugues arr. from Bach's Well-tempered clavier, bk. 2, K. 405. *Mannheim Quartet.*
+ Fa 9-10/86: 134

RCA

29691. 0185-2-RG: KORNGOLD—Cello concerto; Private lives of Elizabeth and Essex; Prince and the pauper; Anthony Adverse; Sea Wolf; Another dawn; Of human bondage. *Gabarro, cello; National Phil. Orch.; Gerhardt, cond.*
+ ARG 1-2/92: 68

29692. 0370-2-RC (3 discs): VERDI—I vespri siciliani. *Arroyo, Domingo, Milnes, Raimondi; John Alldis Choir; New Philharmonia Orch.; Levine, cond.*
+ Fa 7-8/88: 270
+ Gr 9/88: 483

29693. 0707-2-RG: HERRMANN—*Film music.* Music from Citizen Kane, Beneath the 12-mile reef, Hangover Square, White witch doctor, On dangerous ground. *Te Kanawa, soprano; Achucarro, piano; National Phil. Orch.; Gerhardt, cond.*
+ ARG 1-2/92: 63

29694. 0911-2-RG: RÓZSA—*Spellbound.* Classic film music. *National Phil. Orch.; Gerhardt, cond.*
+ ARG 9-10/91: 117

29695. 1969-2-RG (2 discs): VERDI—Otello. *Rysanek, Vickers, Gobbi; Rome Opera; Serafin, cond.*
+ Fa 3-4/89: 321
+ Gr 11/88: 868
+ Op 1/89: 71

29696. 2046-2-RG (2 discs): GIORDANO—Andrea Chénier. *Scotto, Domingo, Milnes; John Alldis Choir; National Phil. Orch.; Levine, cond.*
+ ARG 11-12/89: 61
• Fa 11-12/89: 213
+ Gr 9/89: 528

29697. CCD 3002: *Musica da camera.* Music of Pennisi, Samori, Scogna, Gentile, La Licata, Ronchetti and Dashow. *Various performers.*
• Fa 7-8/92: 357

29698. CCD 3008: *Musica classica contemporanea.* Music of Ceccarelli, Keberle, Curran, Renna, Scogna, and Laneri. *Keberle, clarinets.*
+ Fa 1-2/94: 394

29699. CCD 3009: MARCOS—Quinteto filarmonico; Memoria deshabitada; Settecento; Cuarto cartas. *Quagliata, piano; Orch. da camera Goffredo Petrassi; Orch. sinfonica Abruzzese; Scogna, cond.*
+ Fa 7-8/93: 175

29700. CCD 3010: STEFANI—Elegia IV; Sonata 1990; Quinteto no. 1 for saxophones and piano; Homage to John Cage/Trio for flute, piano, and cello; Musica a la sombra; Tu, mar desnudo. *Ginastera, cello; Colom, Quagliata, pianos; Italian Saxophone Ensemble; Bongelli, piano; Zurria, flute; Pizzo, piano; Tucker, cello; Symphonia Perusina; Scogna, cond.*
+ Fa 1-2/94: 319

29701. 3969-2-RG (2 discs): PUCCINI—La bohème. *Moffo, Costa, Tucker, Merrill, Tozzi; Rome Opera; Leinsdorf, cond.*
- DA 12/88: 26
+ Fa 3-4/88: 174

+ HF 10/88: 69
+ Op 6/88: 757

29702. 4144-2-RG (2 discs): VERDI—La traviata. *Moffo, Tucker, Merrill; Rome Opera; Previtali, cond.*
+ DA 3/89: 52
+ Fa 5-6/89: 345
+ Op 1/89: 70

29703. 4145-2-RG (2 discs): PUCCINI—Madama Butterfly. *Moffo, Elias, Valletti, Cesari; Rome Opera; Leinsdorf, cond.*
+ Fa 9-10/88: 229
• Gr 9/88: 478
+ Op 10/88: 1255

29704. 4514-2-RG (2 discs): PUCCINI—Tosca. *Milanov, Björling, Warren; Rome Opera; Leinsdorf, cond.*
• Fa 3-4/88: 175
• HF 10/88: 19

29705. 4516-2-RG (2 discs): VERDI—Macbeth. *Rysanek, Bergonzi, Warren; Rome Opera; Leinsdorf, cond.*
+ Fa 3-4/88: 225
+ Gr 9/88: 482
+ HF 10/88: 69

29706. 4586-2-RG (3 discs): MOZART—Die Zauberflöte. *Donat, Cotrubas, Tappy, Boesch, Talvela; Vienna State Opera Chorus; Vienna Phil. Orch.; Levine, cond.*
• Fa 11-12/89: 300
• Gr 10/89: 743
+ Op 12/89: 1508

29707. 5234-2-RG: GERSHWIN—Porgy and Bess: Excerpts. *Price, Bubbles, Warfield, Boatwright; RCA Victor Chorus & Orch.; Henderson, cond.*
+ Fa 5-6/89: 200
+ Gr 4/89: 1632

29708. AGL1-5275 (LP): MOZART—Clarinet concerto; Clarinet quintet, K. 581. *Goodman, clarinet; Budapest String Quartet; Boston Symphony Orch.; Munch, cond.*
+ ARG 5-6/86: 29
• Fa 1-2/86: 190
• Opus 12/86: 32

29709. AGL1-5287 (LP): CHOPIN—Piano concerto no. 1. *Cliburn, piano; Philadelphia Orch.; Ormandy, cond.*
+ Fa 11-12/86: 130

29710. AGL2-5289 (2 LPs): BACH—Brandenburg concertos (complete). *Paillard Chamber Orch.; Paillard, cond.*
+ Fa 9-10/86: 85

29711. AGM1-5296 (LP): BRAHMS—Symphony no. 4. *NBC Symphony Orch.; Toscanini, cond.*
+ Fa 9-10/86: 118 m.f.

29712. AGM1-5298 (LP): BACH—Two-part inventions; Partita no. 2; Fantasia in

C minor . *Landowska, harpsichord.*
• Fa 9-10/86: 89

29713. 5608-1-RC (LP): SHOSTAKOVICH—Symphony no. 5. *St. Louis Symphony Orch.; Slatkin, cond.*
+ Fa 5-6/87: 194
- Gr 3/87: 1270

29714. 09026-56518-2: BRAHMS—Piano concerto no. 2. BEETHOVEN—Piano sonata no. 23. *Richter, piano; Chicago Symphony Orch.; Leinsdorf, cond.* Reissue.
+ ARG 3-4/93: 62
+ Fa 5-6/93: 172

29715. 5664-2-RC: SCHUMANN—Liederkreis, op. 39; Märzveilchen; Muttertraum; Der Soldat; Der Spielmann; Stille Tränen; Der Schätzgraber; Mit Myrten und Rosen; Der Kontrabandiste . *Hagegård, baritone; Schuback, piano.* Issued also as LP: 5664-1-RC.
+ ARG Fall/87: 80
+ Fa 5-6/87: 193
- Opus 6/87: 31
+ SR 11/87: 200

29716. 5666-2-RC: Music of Saint-Saëns, Falla, Franck, and Prokofiev. *Rubinstein, piano; Philadelphia Orch.; Ormandy, Wallenstein, conds.*
+ Fa 1-2/88: 261
+ Gr 10/87: 593
+ MA 9/88: 72

29717. 5672-2-RC: BRAHMS—Piano sonata no. 3; Intermezzo, op. 116, no. 6; Romance, op. 118, no. 5; Ballades, op. 10 . *Rubinstein, piano.*
+ ARG 5-6/88: 20
+ Fa 1-2/88: 261
+ Gr 2/88: 212
+ MA 9/88: 71

29718. 5673-2-RC: FRANCK—Prelude, chorale & fugue; BACH—Chaconne (arr. Busoni); LISZT—Piano sonata. *Rubinstein, piano.*
+ ARG 7-8/89: 118
+ Fa 7-8/88: 312
+ Gr 9/88: 444
+ MA 9/88: 72

29719. 5677-2-RG: BRAHMS—Piano quartets no. 1, 3. *Guarneri Quartet; Rubinstein, piano.*
+ ARG 7-8/89: 118
• Fa 5-6/89: 145
+ Gr 5/89: 1741

29720. 5679-2-RC: Music of Giuliani, Rossini, Cimarosa, Paganini, and Bazzini. *Galway, flute; Yamashita, guitar.*
+ DA 9/87: 89
+ Fa 5-6/87: 232
+ Gr 4/87: 1431
+ NR 4/87: 34

29721. 5708-2-RC: TCHAIKOVSKY—Piano concerto no. 1. *Douglas, piano; London Symphony Orch.; Slatkin, cond.* Issued

also as LP: 5708-1-RC.
+ ARG 3-4/87: 57
- Fa 7-8/87: 193
+ Gr 1/87: 1026
+ NR 4/87: 14
• NYT 8/2/87: H26
- Opus 4/87: 50
+ Ov 2/87: 42
+ SR 3/87: 105

29722. RCD1-5854: BEETHOVEN—Piano concerto no. 5. *Ax, piano; Royal Phil. Orch.; Previn, cond.* Issued also as LP: HRC1-5854.
+ Fa 1-2/87: 65
• Gr 3/87: 1254
- NR 3/87: 7
+ NYT 10/19/86: H25
- Ov 6/87: 39
+ SR 3/87: 99

29723. RCD1-5866: MOZART—Violin concerto no. 1, 2, and 5. *Ughi, violin; Chamber Orch. of Santa Cecilia.* Issued also as LP: HRC1-5866; LP lacks concerto no. 2.
+ ARG 5-6/87: 44
• Fa 1-2/87: 145
• Gr 8/86: 271
• MA 7/87: 60
+ NR 3/87: 6
+ Ov 3/87: 36

29724. 5910-2-RC: *Legendary performances.* Music of Paganini (arr. Kreisler), Beethoven, Dohnányi, and Kreisler . *Kreisler, violin; Philadelphia Orch.; Ormandy, cond.*
+ Fa 7-8/87: 229
+ HF 8/87: 70

29725. 5913-2-RC: *Music of Spain.* Music of Mompou, Rodrigo, Manén, and others. *Yamashita, guitar.*
+ Fa 7-8/87: 227

29726. 5914-1-RC (LP): *Guitar concertos.* Music of Giuliani, Vivaldi, Carulli. *Yamashita, guitar; Janáček Chamber Orch.*
+ Fa 7-8/87: 227 (2 reviews)

29727. 5915-2-RC: CHOPIN—Piano music. *Edelmann, piano.*
• Fa 7-8/87: 90
+ SR 8/87: 76

29728. 5930-2-RC: BEETHOVEN—Piano concertos no. 3, 4 . *Ax, piano; Royal Phil. Orch.; Previn, cond.*
• ARG 5-6/88: 12
• Fa 11-12/87: 94

29729. 5931-2-RC: Music of Mussorgsky, Liszt, and Wagner (arr. Liszt). *Douglas, piano.*
• Fa 9-10/87: 258
+ Gr 5/87: 580
- HF 2/88: 64
+ SR 10/87: 132

29730. 5959-2-RC: *Leonard Slatkin conducts concert classics.* Music of

RCA

Saint-Saëns, Chabrier, Humperdinck, and others. *National Phil. Orch.; Slatkin, cond.*
- • ARG 3-4/88: 104
- • Fa 11-12/87: 293
- • HPR 12/87: 97

29731. 5995-2-RC: WAGNER—Götterdämmerung: Siegfried's Rhine journy & Funeral march; Die Meistersinger: Act III prelude; Dance of the apprentices; Procession of the masters; Tristan and Isolde: Prelude und Liebestod. *Royal Phil. Orch.; Stokowski, cond.*
- • Fa 1-2/88: 233

29732. 5998-2-RC: CHOPIN—Piano music. *Kapell, piano.*
- + ARG 3-4/88: 28
- + Fa 11-12/87: 125
- + NYT 12/6/87: H29

29733. 6180-2-RC (2 discs): VERDI—La traviata. *Caballé, Bergonzi, Milnes; RCA Italiana Opera; Prêtre, cond.*
- • Gr 9/88: 482

29734. 6182-2-RG (2 discs): HANDEL—Giulio Cesare. *Sills, Forrester, Wolff, Treigle; New York City Opera; Rudel, cond.*
- + ARG 1-2/90: 52
- + Op 6/89: 753

29735. 6198-2-RC (3 discs): VERDI —Aida. *Price, Bumbry, Domingo, Milnes, Raimondi; John Alldis Choir; London Symphony Orch.; Leinsdorf, cond.*
- • Fa 7-8/88: 267
- • Gr 8/88: 338
- • Op 11/88: 1388

29736. 6199-2-RG (3 discs): BIZET—Carmen. *Price, Freni, Corelli, Merrill; Vienna State Opera Chorus; Vienna Phil. Orch.; Karajan, cond.*
- - Fa 7-8/88: 130
- + Gr 10/88: 670
- + Op 10/88: 1255

29737. 6210-2-RC (2 discs): BERLIOZ—Requiem; Symphonie fantastique. *Simoneau, tenor: New England Conservatory Chorus; Boston Symphony Orch.; Munch, cond.*
- • ARG 3-4/88: 20
- + Gr 2/88: 1216

29738. 6214-2-RC: BRUCH—Violin concerto no. 1; Scottish fantasy. VIEUXTEMPS—Violin concerto no. 5. *Heifetz, violin; New Symphony Orch.; Sargent, cond.*
- + ARG 3-4/88: 26
- + Fa 1-2/88: 103

29739. 6215-2-RG: SCRIABIN—Piano music. *Horowitz, piano.*
- + ARG 1-2/90: 121
- + Fa 3-4/90: 293
- + St 2/90: 181

29740. 6217-2-RC (2 discs): BACH—Well-tempered clavier, bk.1. *Landowska, harpsichord.*
- + DA 7/88: 56
- • Fa 7-8/88: 110
- + Ov 11/88: 43

29741. 6242-2-RC: BRAHMS—Serenade no. 1. *St. Louis Symphony Orch.: Slatkin, cond.* Issued also as LP: 6242-1- RC .
- + ARG 1-2/88: 16
- - Fa 9-10/87: 168
- • Gr 4/88: 1448

29742. 6254-2-RC: HAYDN—Seven last words of Christ. *Guarneri Quartet.*
- + Fa 1-2/88: 138
- • Gr 4/88: 1470

29743. 6255-2-RC: SCHUMANN—Piano concerto in A minor; Novelettes op. 21 no. 1 and 2. LISZT—Piano concerto no. 1. *Rubinstein, piano; Chicago Symphony Orch.; RCA Symphony Orch.; Giulini, Wallenstein, cond.*
- + Fa 3-4/88: 196
- + Gr 9/88: 412 (Liszt)
- - Gr 9/88: 412 (Schumann)
- + MA 9/88: 71

29744. 6256-2-RC: DVOŘÁK—Piano quartet, op. 87. FAURÉ—Piano quartet no. 1. *Rubinstein, piano; Guarneri Quartet.*
- + Fa 1-2/88: 116
- • MA 9/88: 72

29745. 6257-2-RC: SCHUBERT Fantasia in C; Impromptus no. 3-4; Piano sonata no. 21. *Rubinstein, piano.*
- + Fa 5-6/88: 208
- + MA 9/88: 71

29746. 6258-2-RC: SCHUMANN—Fantasy in C; Kreisleriana. *Rubinstein, piano.*
- + Fa 1-2/88: 209

29747. 6259-2-RC: TCHAIKOVSKY—Piano concerto no.1. GRIEG—Piano concerto. *Rubinstein, piano; Boston Symphony Orch.; Leinsdorf, Wallenstein, conds.*
- + Fa 3-4/88: 215
- + MA 9/88: 72

29748. 6262-2-RG: SCHUMANN—Piano trio no. 1. SCHUBERT—Piano trio no. 1. *Rubinstein, piano; Szeryng, violin; Fournier, cello.*
- + ARG 7-8/89: 118
- + Fa 5-6/89: 318
- + Gr 4/89: 1602

29749. 6263-2-RG: DVOŘÁK—Piano quintet no. 2; String quartet no. 12. *Rubinstein, piano; Guarneri Quartet.*
- + ARG 7-8/89: 118
- + Fa 7-8/89: 158

29750. 6264-2-RG: BRAHMS—Violin sonatas no. 1, 3. BEETHOVEN—Violin sonata no. 8. *Szeryng, violin; Rubinstein, piano.*
- + ARG 7-8/89: 118

- • Fa 5-6/89: 145
- + Gr 4/89: 1598

29751. 6357-2-RC: MOZART—Piano concertos no. 9, 12. *Fou, piano & cond.; Polish Chamber Orch.*
- + ARG 3-4/88: 58
- • Fa 11-12/87: 178

29752. 6359-2-RC: NIELSEN—Flute concerto; Wind quintet; Two Fantasy pieces. *Galway, flute & cond.; Nielsen, oboe; Thomsen, clarinet; Tofte-Hansen, bassoon; Fosdal, horn; Williams, harp; Hawkins, viola; Moll, piano; Danish Radio Symphony Orch.*
- • ARG 3-4/88: 66
- • Fa 11-12/87: 188
- + Gr 2/88: 1194
- + SR 10/87: 138

29753. 6485-2-RG: MENOTTI—Amahl and the night visitors. *Allen, Kuhlman, Lishner, Aiken, McKinley; chorus & orch.; Schippers, cond.*
- + Fa 3-4/88: 145
- + HF 4/88: 68

29754. 6498-2-RC: SCHUMANN—Piano quartet, op. 47; Piano quintet, op. 44. *Ax, piano; Cleveland Quartet.*
- + ARG 3-4/88: 78
- + Fa 1-2/88: 159
- + SR 1/88: 128

29755. 6503-2-RG (2 discs): VERDI—Ernani. *Price, Bergonzi, Sereni, Flagello; RCA Italiana Opera; Schippers, cond.*
- + Fa 5-6/88: 231
- + GR 8/88: 337
- - HF 10/88: 69
- + Op 6/88: 757

29756. 6504-2-RG (2 discs): DONIZETTI—Lucia di Lammermoor. *Moffo, Bergonzi, Sereni, Flagello; RCA Italiana Opera; Prêtre, cond.*
- + Fa 3-4/88: 100
- • GR 9/88: 475
- + HF 10/88: 70

29757. 6505-2-RG (3 discs): ROSSINI—Il barbiere di siviglia. *Peters, Valletti, Merrill, Corena, Tozzi; Metropolitan Opera; Leinsdorf, cond.*
- • Fa 5-6/88: 195
- • Gr 9/88: 478
- + HF 10/88: 69
- + Op 6/88: 757

29758. 6506-2-RG (2 discs): VERDI—Rigoletto. *Moffo, Elias, Kraus, Merrill, Flagello; RCA Italiana Opera; Solti, cond.*
- + Fa 3-4/88: 227
- + Gr 9/88: 482
- • HF 10/88: 69
- + Op 6/88: 757

29759. 6510-2-RG: MASCAGNI—Cavalleria rusticana. *Milanov, Björling, Merrill; Robert Shaw Chorale; RCA Victor Orch.; Cellini, cond.*

+ Fa 3-4/88: 142
+ Gr 8/88: 332
• HF 10/88: 69

29760. 6511-2-RG (3 discs): MOZART—
Die Zauberflöte. *Geszty, Donath,
Schreier, Leib, Adam; Leipzig
Rundfunkchor; Dresden Staatskapelle;
Suitner, cond.*
+ Fa 3-4/88: 160
• Gr 9/88: 476
• HF 10/88: 69

29761. 6519-2-RG: GERSHWIN—Concerto
in F; Rhapsody in blue; American in
Paris; I got rhythm variations. *Wild,
piano; Boston Pops Orch.; Fiedler, cond.*
Reissue.
+ ARG 3-4/92: 62

29762. 6522-2-RG: RAVEL—Boléro;
Rapsodie espagnole; Pavane pour une
infante défunte; Ma mère l'oye: Suite; La
valse. *Boston Symphony Orch.; Munch,
cond.* Reissue.
+ Fa 11-12/91: 453

29763. 6526-2-RG: RODRIGO—Concierto
dc Aranjuez. VILLA-LOBOS—Guitar
concerto; Five preludes; Mazurka- chôro
from Suite populaire brésilienne. *Bream,
guitar.* Reissue.
+ ARG 7-8/92: 259

29764. 6534-2-RG: VERDI—Arias and
duets. *Ricciarelli, soprano; Phil. Orch. of
Rome; Domingo, tenor; Orch. of the
National Academy of Santa Cecilia;
Gavazzeni, cond.*
• Fa 9-10/91: 382

29765. 6546-2-RC: BACH—Brandenburg
concertos no. 2-3, 5-6 (arr. for 3 guitars).
Amsterdam Guitar Trio.
+ Au 7/88: 83
+ Fa 1-2/88: 72

29766. 6567-2-RG: BOLLING—Suite for
flute and jazz piano no. 1; California
suite. *Duran, Fleming, flutes; Holloway,
piano; Walley, bass; Ganley, drums;
Kain, guitar.*
+ Fa 5-6/88: 90

29767. 6597-2-RC: SHOSTAKOVICH—
Symphony no. 10. *St. Louis Symphony
Orch.; Slatkin, cond.*
• Fa 1-2/88: 210
• Gr 7/88: 170

29768. 6602-2-RC: CORIGLIANO—Pied
piper fantasy; Voyage. *Galway, flute;
Eastman Philharmonia; Effron, cond.*
□ ARG 11-12/88: 29
+ DA 5/88: 42
+ Fa 3-4/88: 98
- Gr 10/88: 595
+ Ov 7/88: 34

29769. 6603-2-RC: *Film music.*
SHOSTAKOVICH—The gadfly: suite;
Priogov: suite . *Belgian Radio Symphony
Orch.; Serebrier, cond.*

- ARG 11-12/88: 84
• Fa 5-6/88: 214
• Gr 5/88: 1608

29770. 6642-2-RG (2 discs): DONIZETTI—
Lucrezia Borgia. *Caballé, Verrett, Kraus,
Flagello; RCA Italiana Opera; Perlea,
cond.*
+ ARG 5-6/90: 46
+ Fa 3-4/90: 171
+ Gr 9/90: 605

29771. 6643-2-RG (2 discs): VERDI—Il
trovatore. *Milanov, Barbieri, Björling,
Warren; Robert Shaw Chorale; RCA
Victor Orch.; Cellini, cond.*
+ Fa 9-10/88: 287
+ Gr 8/88: 337
+ Op 10/88: 1255

29772. 6644-2-RG (2 discs): STRAUSS—
Salome. *Caballé, Resnik, Lewis, Milnes;
London Symphony Orch.; Leinsdorf,
cond.*
+ ARG 7-8/90: 40
+ Fa 3-4/90: 310
• Gr 9/90: 611

29773. 6645-2-RG (2 discs): VERDI—Un
ballo in maschera. *Price, Grist, Verrett,
Bergonzi, Merrill; RCA Italiana, chorus
& orch.; Leinsdorf, cond.*
+ Fa 3-4/89: 319
• Gr 11/88: 868
+ Op 1/89: 70

29774. 6646-2-RG (2 discs): VERDI—
Luisa Miller. *Moffo, Verrett, Bergonzi,
MacNeil, Tozzi, Flagello; RCA Italiana
chorus & orch.; Cleva, cond.*
+ DA 3/89: 52
+ Fa 3-4/89: 321
• Gr 10/88: 676
+ Op 1/89: 70

29775. 6652-2-RG (3 discs): VERDI—
Aida. *Milanov, Barbieri, Björling,
Warren, Christoff; Rome Opera; Perlea,
cond.*
+ Fa 7-8/88: 267
+ Op 10/88: 1255

29776. 6656-2-RC: VIVALDI—Concerto
op. 8 no. 1-4 (Four seasons); Flautino
concerto in C. *Petri, recorders;
Malcolm, harpsichord; Guildhall String
Ensemble.*
+ Fa 3-4/88: 231
+ Gr 12/87: 959

29777. 6659-2-RC: RACHMANINOFF—Piano
concertos no. 1, 4; Rhapsody on a theme
of Paganini. *Rachmaninoff, piano;
Philadelphia Orch.; Ormandy, Stokowski,
cond.*
+ DA 11/88: 81
+ Fa 7-8/88: 228
+ MA 11/88: 60

29778. 6673-2-RC: BRAHMS—Piano
quintet, op. 34; Piano music. *Douglas,
piano; Tokyo String Quartet.*
+ DA 6/88: 63

+ Fa 5-6/88: 93
• Gr 12/87: 966
+ HF 10/88: 78
+ Opus 4/88: 49
+ SR 4/88: 98

29779. 6677-2-RG (3 discs): MOZART—
Così fan tutte. *Price, Troyanos, Raskin,
Shirley, Milnes, Flagello; Ambrosian
Opera Chorus; New Philharmonia Orch.;
Leinsdorf, cond.*
+ Fa 9-10/88: 209
- Gr 9/88: 477
+ MA 3/89: 63
• Op 10/88: 1255

29780. 6680-2-RG (3 discs):
SCHUMANN—Piano sonata no. 3;
Humoreske; Fantasiestücke; Nachtstücke
op. 23 no. 3-4. *Horowitz, piano.*
• ARG 1-2/90: 121
+ Fa 11-12/89: 356

29781. 6716-2-RG: BRAHMS—Violin
concerto in D; Variations on a theme by
Haydn; Alto rhapsody. *Szeryng, violin;
Verrett, mezzo-soprano; Men of Temple
University Choirs; London Symphony
Orch.; Philadelphia Orch.; Monteux,
Ormandy, conds.*
+ Fa 5-6/88: 92
• Gr 8/88: 280

29782. 6718-2-RG: *Classics for children.*
Music of Prokofiev, Saint-Saëns, and
Tchaikovsky. *Guiness, narrator; Litwin,
Lipman, pianos; Boston Pops Orch.;
Fiedler, cond.*
+ Fa 7-8/88: 329

29783. 6719-2-RG: DEBUSSY—La mer;
Prélude à l'après-midi d'un faune;
Nocturnes: Nuages and Fêtes; Printemps.
Boston Symphony Orch.; Munch, cond.
+ Fa 5-6/88: 113
• Fa 11-12/91: 308
• Gr 7/88: 160

29784. 6720-2-RG: BERLIOZ—Symphonie
fantastique; Le carnaval romain; Le
corsaire. *Boston Symphony Orch.; Prêtre,
Munch, cond.*
+ DA 8/88: 46
- Fa 7-8/88: 129 (Symphony)
+ Fa 7-8/88: 129 (others)

29785. 6721-2-RG: Music of
Mussorgsky, Borodin, and Prokofiev.
Philadelphia Orch.; Ormandy, cond.
• Fa 5-6/88: 178

29786. 6722-2-RG: STRAUSS—Also
sprach Zarathustra; Vier letze Lieder;
Frau ohne Schatten: Empress' awakening
scene. *Price, soprano; Chicago
Symphony Orch.; New Philharmonia
Orch.; Reiner, Leinsdorf, cond.*
+ DA 8/88: 46
+ Fa 5-6/88: 221
+ Gr 7/88: 170
+ MA 11/88: 83

RCA

29787. 6723-2-RG: Mozart—Andante for flute and orchestra, K. 315; Flute concerto no. 1; Concerto for flute and harp. *Galway, flute; Robles, harp; Lucerne Festival Strings; London Symphony Orch.; Baumgartner, Mata, conds.*
  + Fa 5-6/88: 169

29788. 6724-2-RG: Mozart—Mass in C; Mass in honorem Ssmae Trinitatis; Nocturnes K. 439, 437, 346, 549. *Soloists; Vienna Choir Boys; chorus & orch.; Gillesberger, cond.*
  • Fa 9-10/88: 213

29789. 6725-2-RG: Mozart—Violin concerto no. 3; Concertone for 2 violins, K. 190. L. Mozart—Duets for 2 violins no. 2, 4-5, 8, 11. *Kremer, Grindenko, violins; Viena Symphony Orch.; Kremer, cond.*
  + Fa 7-8/88: 205
  + Gr 8/88: 289

29790. 6772-2-RC: Schumann—Fantasiestücke for clarinet and piano; Three romances for clarinet and piano. Schubert—Clarinet sonatas, D. 384, 385. *Stoltzman, clarinet; Goode, piano.*
  + Fa 1-2/89: 261
  + Ov 9/88: 46

29791. 6773-2-RC: Beethoven—Piano sonatas no. 18, 23. *Edelmann, piano.*
  - Fa 7-8/88: 118
  • SR 6/88: 135

29792. 6777-2-RC: Music of Rimsky-Korsakov, Debussy, and Françaix. *K. & N. Yamashita, guitars .*
  + Fa 5-6/88: 259
  + Ov 10/88: 39

29793. 6778-2-RC: Music of Bach, Brahms, and Mozart. *Heifetz, violin; Piatigorsky, cello; Primrose, viola; various orchs. & conds.*
  + Fa 5-6/88: 70
  • Gr 6/88: 27

6779-2-RG see 60588-2-RG.

6780-2-RG see 60583-2-RG.

6781-2-RG see 60590-2-RG.

6782-2-RG see 60586-2-RG.

29794. 6798-2-RG: Music of Paganini, Mendelssohn, Tarrega, Albeniz, Turina, Torroba, Villa-Lobos, and Llobet. *Bream, guitar.* Reissue.
  + ARG 7-8/92: 259

29795. 6799-2-RG: J. Strauss, Jr.—On the beautiful blue Danube; Vienna blood; Emperor waltz; Treasure waltz; Where the citrons bloom; Morning papers; Artist's life; Tales from the Vienna Woods. *Philadelphia Orch.; Ormandy, cond.*
  - Fa 11-12/88: 289

29796. 6802-2-RG: Copland—Appalachian spring suite; The tender land suite; Billy the kid suite. *Boston Symphony Orch.; Philadelphia Orch.; Copland, Ormandy, conds.*
  + ARG 11-12/91: 54
  + Fa 9-10/88: 135
  + Fa 7-8/91: 141
  + St 3/89: 169

29797. 6805-2-RG: Franck—Symphony in D minor. Indy—Symphony on a French mountain air. Berlioz—Béatrice et Bénédict: Overture. *Henriot-Schweitzer, piano; Chicago Symphony Orch.; Boston Symphony Orch.; Monteux, Munch, conds.*
  + Fa 9-10/88: 152
  + Gr 3/89: 1414

29798. 6806-2-RC: Music of Gould, Grofé, Copland, Bernstein, Gershwin, and Rodgers. *Boston Pops Orch.; Fiedler, cond.*
  + Fa 9-10/88: 343

29799. RCD1-7018: Rimsky-Korsakov—Scheherazade. Debussy—La mer. *Chicago Symphony Orch.; Reiner, cond.*
  + Fa 5-6/88: 192

29800. RCD1-7019: Sibelius—Violin concerto, op. 47. Prokofiev—Violin concerto no. 2. Glazunov—Violin concerto, op. 82. *Heifetz, violin; Chicago Symphony Orch.; Boston Symphony Orch.; RCA Victor Symphony Orch.; Munch, Hendl, conds.*
  + Fa 7-8/88: 252

29801. 7701-2-RC: Nielsen—Symphonies no. 1, 4 . *Royal Danish Orch.; Berglund, cond.*
  + DA 2/89: 48
  + Fa 7-8/88: 212
  + HF 12/88: 68

29802. 7703-2-RC: Mercadante—Flute concertos in D, E minor, and E . *Galway, flute; I Solisti veneti; Scimone, cond.*
  + ARG 1-2/89: 66
  + DA 1/89: 39
  + Fa 11-12/88: 223

29803. 7704—7706-2-RG (3 separate discs): Beethoven—Violin sonatas (complete). *Heifetz, violin; Bay, Smith, piano.*
  + Fa 9-10/88: 106
  + Gr 11/88: 796

29804. 7708-2-RG (2 discs): Bach—Sonatas and partitas for solo violin. *Heifetz, violin.*
  + Fa 9-10/88: 109
  + Gr 9/88: 443

29805. 7709-2-RG: *Showpieces.* Music of Lalo, Sarasate, Chausson, and Saint-Saëns. *Heifetz, violin; RCA Victor Symphony Orch.; Steinberg, Solomon, conds.*
  + Fa 7-8/88: 316

29806. 7710-2-RG: Music of Bach (arr. Busoni), Chopin, and Wagner (arr. Liszt). *Bolet, piano.*
  + Fa 9-10/89: 126

29807. 7718-2-RC: Brouwer—Guitar concerto no. 3. Rodrigo—Fantasia para un gentilhombre. *Bream, guitar; RCA Victor Chamber Orch.; Brouwer, cond.*
  + Fa 7-8/88: 139
  + Gr 8/88: 280

29808. 7719-2-RC: Schickele—String quartet no. 1. Laderman—String quartet no. 6. *Andubon Quartet.*
  + ARG 1-2/89: 83
  + DA 1/89: 53
  + Fa 9-10/88: 245

29809. 7720-2-RC: Beethoven—Piano sonata no. 29; Andante favori. *Douglas, piano.*
  + Fa 9-10/88: 104
  + Gr 6/88: 48
  • MA 9/88: 50
  + SR 10/88: 117

29810. 7725-2-RG: *Selections from The Chopin collection.* Chopin—Piano music. *Rubinstein, piano.*
  + Fa 7-8/88: 144

29811. 7726-2-RV: Gershwin—An American in Paris; Cuban overture; Symphonic picture: Porgy and Bess (arr. Bennett). *Dallas Symphony Orch.; Mata, cond.*
  + Fa 7-8/88: 166

29812. 7727-2-RV: Music of Tchaikovsky, Mussorgsky, Dukas, and Enesco. *Dallas Symphony Orch.; Mata, cond.*
  + Fa 9-10/88: 350

29813. 7728-2-RV: Ravel—Bolero; Alborada del gracioso; Rapsodie espagnole. *Dallas Symphony Orch.; Mata, cond.*
  - Fa 9-10/88: 235 (Bolero)
  + Fa 9-10/88: 235 (others)

29814. 7729-2-RV: Mussorgsky—Pictures at an exhibition (arr. Ravel). Ravel—Valses nobles et sentimentales; La valse. *Dallas Symphony Orch.; Mata, cond.*
  + Fa 7-8/88: 212
  + HF 2/89: 65

29815. 7730-2-RV: Sibelius—Violin concerto, op. 47. Saint-Saëns—Introduction and rondo capriccioso. *Jenson, violin; Philadelphia Orch.; Ormandy, cond.*
  • Fa 9-10/88: 263

29816. 7731-2-RV: Beethoven—Wellington's victory. Tchaikovsky—1812 overture. *Philadelphia Orch.; New Philharmonia Orch.; Ormandy, Buketoff, cond.*
  • Fa 11-12/88: 140

29817. 7734-2-RV: OFFENBACH (ARR. ROSENTHAL)—Gaité parisienne. KHACHATURIAN—Gayane suite. *Boston Pops Orch.; Fiedler, cond.*
- Fa 9-10/88: 221

29818. 7735-2-RV: BERLIOZ—Symphonie fantastique. *Boston Symphony Orch.; Munch, cond.*
+ Fa 9-10/88: 112

29819. 7736-2-RV: BACH—Toccata and fugue in D minor; Fugue in G minor (Little); Jesu, joy of man's desiring; Now thank we all our God; Air for the G-string; Sheep may safely graze; Arioso; Sleepers wake. *Fox, organ.*
□ Fa 9-10/88: 90

29820. 7737-2-RV: SAINT-SAËNS—Symphony no. 3. *Fox, organ; Philadelphia Orch.; Ormandy, cond.*
- Fa 9-10/88: 243

29821. 7738—7739-2-RV (2 separate discs): BACH—Brandenburg concertos. *Festival Strings Lucerne; Baumgartner, cond.*
- Fa 9-10/88: 85

29822. 7740-2-RV: TCHAIKOVSKY—Symphony no. 6. *Philadelphia Orch.; Ormandy, cond.*
- Fa 9-10/88: 281

29823. 7741-2-RV: VIVALDI—Violin concertos RV 253, 271, 180, 551, 565, 523. *Nuovi Virtuosi di Roma.*
+ Fa 9-10/88: 294

29824. 7742-2-RV: J. STRAUSS, JR.—On the beautiful blue Danube; Roses from the south; Emperor waltz; Voices of spring; Morning papers; Tales from the Vienna Woods. *Vienna Symphony Orch.; Berlin Symphony Orch.; Stolz, cond.*
+ Fa 9-10/88: 271

29825. 7743-2-RV: RIMSKY-KORSAKOV—Scheherazade. *Royal Phil. Orch.; Stokowski, cond.*
- Fa 9-10/88: 239

29826. 7744-2-RV: CHOPIN—Waltzes. *Anda, piano.*
- Fa 9-10/88: 128

29827. 7746-2-RC: SCHUBERT—Wanderer fantasie. SCHUMANN—Fantasie, op. 17. *Edelmann, piano.*
- Fa 5-6/89: 311

29828. 7747-2-RC: BEETHOVEN—Symphony no. 6; Egmont overture. *Royal Phil. Orch.; Previn, cond.*
+ ARG 1-2/89: 29
- Fa 9-10/88: 107
- Gr 7/88: 156
+ MA 11/88: 52
- SR 9/88: 107

29829. 7748-2-RC: BEETHOVEN—Symphony no. 7; Coriolan overture;

Creatures of Prometheus overture. *Royal Phil. Orch.; Previn, cond.*
+ Fa 9-10/88: 107
- Gr 7/88: 156
- MA 11/88: 52
- SR 9/88: 132

29830. 7749-2-RC: *The virtuoso recorder.* Music of Telemann, Heberle, Bach, and Kramer. *M. Petri, recorders; H. Petri, harpsichord; D. Petri, cello.*
+ Fa 9-10/88: 334
+ Gr 10/88: 641
+ MA 11/88: 88

29831. 7750-2-RC: SCHUBERT—String quartets no. 9, 13. *Tokyo String Quartet.*
+ Fa 9-10/88: 250
+ Gr 8/88: 312
+ MA 11/88: 62
- SR 12/88: 160

29832. 7752-2-RG: CHOPIN—Horowitz plays Chopin, vol. 1. *Horowitz, piano.*
+ Fa 9-10/90: 176
+ Gr 9/90: 581

29833. 7753-2-RG: CLEMENTI—Sonata quasi concerto in C; Piano sonatas in G minor, F minor, and F# minor; Sonata op. 47 no. 2: Rondo . *Horowitz, piano.*
+ ARG 1-2/90: 121
+ Fa 11-12/89: 179

29834. 7754-2-RG: RACHMANINOFF—Piano sonata no. 2; Moment musicale in E♭ minor; Prelude in G; Polka de V. R.; Piano concerto no. 3 . *Horowitz, piano; RCA Victor Symphony Orch.; Reiner, cond.*
+ ARG 1-2/90: 121
+ Fa 11-12/89: 326

29835. 7755-2-RG: *Encores.* Music of Bizet (arr. Horowitz), Saint-Saëns (arr. Liszt and Horowitz), Mozart, and others . *Horowitz, piano.*
+ Fa 7-8/90: 351
+ Gr 9/90: 581
+ St 10/90: 251

29836. 7756-2-RC: BEETHOVEN—Serenade for flute, violin, and viola, op. 25; Flute sonata in B♭; Serenade for flute and piano, op. 8. *Galway, flute; Swensen, violin; Neubauer, viola; Moll, piano.*
+ DA 9-10/90: 54
+ Fa 7-8/90: 89
- Gr 7/90: 234

29837. 7761-2-RC: *English music for strings.* Music of Holst, Delius, Ireland, Finzi, and others. *Guildhall String Ensemble.*
+ DA 9/88: 47
+ Fa 9-10/88: 341
+ Gr 9/88: 432

29838. 7762-2-RC: Music of Corgliano, Copland, and Bernstein. *Stoltzman, clarinet; London Symphony Orch.; Smith, cond.*
+ ARG 7-8/90: 40

+ Fa 5-6/90: 152
+ SR 7/89: 89

29839. 7763-2-RC: *Film music.* SHOSTAKOVICH—Hamlet; King Lear; Five days and five nights. *Belgian Radio Symphony Orch.; Serebrier, cond.*
+ Fa 11-12/88: 278
+ Gr 10/88: 617

29840. 7764-2-RC: MENDELSSOHN—A midsummer night's dream. *Popp, soprano; Lipovsek, mezzo-soprano; Bamberg Symphony Chorus & Orch.; Flor, cond.*
- Fa 9-10/88: 197
+ Gr 10/88: 606
+ SR 10/88: 118

29841. 7765-2-RC: SIBELIUS—Symphony no. 1; Karelia overture; Suite op. 11; Finlandia. *Finnish Radio Symphony Orch.; Saraste, cond.*
+ ARG 3-4/89: 87
+ Fa 9-10/88: 263
- Gr 11/88: 786

29842. 7766-2-RG: *Rachmaninoff plays Rachmaninoff.* Music of Rachmaninoff, Bach, Mendelssohn, Kreisler, and others. *Rachmaninoff, piano.*
+ ARG 7-8/90: 88
+ Fa 5-6/90: 259 m.f.
+ Gr 5/90: 2082

29843. 7767-2-RG (2 discs): KORNGOLD—Die tote Stadt. *Neblett, Kollo, Luxon, Prey; Bavarian Radio Chorus; Tölz Boys Choir; Munich Radio Orch.; Leinsdorf, cond.*
+ ARG 1-2/90: 57
+ DA 8/90: 33
+ Fa 1-2/90: 209
+ Gr 11/89: 965
+ NYT 9/17/89: H31
+ St 3/90: 189

29844. 7768-2-RG: TCHAIKOVSKY—Piano trio, op. 50. MENDELSSOHN—Piano trio no. 1. *Rubinstein, piano; Heifetz, violin; Piatigorsky, cello.*
+ Fa 5-6/89: 318
+ Gr 9/89: 492

29845. 7770-2-RC: MOZART—String quintets no. 1, 4 . *Guarneri Quartet; Kavafian, Tenenbom, violas.*
+ ARG 1-2/89: 70
- Fa 9-10/88: 214
+ Gr 9/88: 439

29846. 7771-2-RC: MOZART—String quintets no. 2, 5 . *Guarneri Quartet; Kashkashian, Tenenbom, violas.*
+ ARG 1-2/89: 70
- Fa 9-10/88: 214
+ Gr 9/88: 439

29847. 7772-2-RC: MOZART—String quintets no. 3, 6 . *Guarneri Quartet; Kavafian, Kashkashian, 2nd viola.*
+ ARG 1-2/88: 70

RCA

• Fa 11-12/88: 234
• Gr 2/89: 1306

29848. 7774-2-RC: VIVALDI—Cello concertos RV 405, 401, 423, 399, 409; Concerto for 2 horns, RV 538; Largo in D minor. *Harnoy, cello; McKay, bassoon; Toronto Chamber Orch.; Robinson, cond.*
+ ARG 1-2/89: 100
+ Fa 9-10/88: 293
+ Gr 8/88: 302

29849. 7777-2-RC: BEETHOVEN—Violin concerto; Romances for violin no. 1-2. *Swensen, violin; Royal Phil. Orch.; Previn, cond.*
+ ARG 3-4/89: 20
□ Fa 1-2/89: 114
+ Gr 3/89: 1408
• MA 5/89: 55
+ Ov 12/88: 46

29850. 7780-2-RC: BRAHMS—Piano concerto no. 1. *Douglas, piano; London Symphony Orch.; Skrowaczewski, cond.*
- ARG 5-6/89: 26
+ DA 6/89: 92
- Fa 1-2/89: 135
+ Gr 3/89: 1414
+ MA 5/89: 56
+ Ov 1/89: 41
+ SR 2/89: 164
• St 6/89: 213

29851. 7799-2-RG: Music of Bizet, Puccini, and Verdi. *Björling, Albanese, Milanov, Tebaldi, Merrill; Various orchs. & conds.*
+ DA 9/89: 78
+ Fa 3-4/89: 349
+ Gr 2/89: 1342
+ Ov 1/89: 43

29852. 7800-2-RC: Music of Debbussy, Fauré, and Chopin. *Amsterdam Guitar Trio.*
+ DA 5/89: 82
+ Fa 1-2/89: 153

29853. 7801-2-RC: *Fantasies, ayres and dances: Elizabethan and Jacobean consort music.* Music of Morley, Philips, Dowland, Nicholson, Byrd and others. *Julian Bream Consort.*
+ Fa 1-2/89: 321
+ Gr 2/89: 1308

29854. 7804-2-RC (2 discs): TCHAIKOVSKY—Swan Lake. *St. Louis Symphony Orch.; Slatkin, cond.*
- ARG 1-2/90: 96
• DA 6/90: 62
+ Fa 1-2/90: 324
• Gr 12/89: 1144

29855. 7805-2-RC: MARTINŮ—Symphonies no. 5-6. *Berlin Symphony Orch.; Flor, cond.*
+ ARG 9-10/89: 76
• Fa 3-4/89: 204
+ Gr 12/88: 1003

29856. 7807-2-RG: *Leonard Warren on tour in Russia.* Music of Handel, Beethoven, Caccini, Bach, Donaudy, and others. *Warren, baritone; Sektberg, piano.*
• ARG 1-2/90: 130
• Fa 11-12/89: 439

29857. 7808-2-RG: Music of Leoncavallo, Rossini, Verdi, Puccini, Bizet, and others. *Tibbett, baritone; Bampton, soprano; Various orchs. & conds.*
+ ARG 1-2/90: 132
+ Fa 11-12/89: 438
+ Gr 3/90: 1709

29858. 7809-2-RG: Music of Cimara, Sadero, Gounod, Paladilhe, Duparc, and others. *Lehmann, soprano; Balogh, Ulanowsky, piano.*
+ ARG 1-2/90: 130
+ Fa 11-12/89: 430
+ Gr 1/90: 1386
+ ON 2/3/90: 31

29859. 7810-2-RG: Music of Verdi, Rimsky-Korsakov, Fontenailles, Meyerbeer, and others. *Ponselle, soprano; various accs.*
+ ARG 1-2/90: 131
+ Fa 11-12/89: 426
+ Gr 1/90: 1386
+ ON 2/3/90: 31

29860. 7811-2-RG: Music of Giordano, Donizetti, Gounod, Lalo, and others. *Gigli, tenor; various orchs. & conds.*
+ ARG 1-2/91: 146
+ DA 10/90: 80
+ Fa 9-10/90: 457
+ Gr 10/90: 847
+ NYT 10/7/90: H32

29861. 7812-2-RV: BRAHMS—Symphony no. 1 . *Boston Symphony Orch.; Munch, cond.*
+ ARG 11-12/89: 121
+ Fa 3-4/89: 123

29862. 7819-2-RV: WAGNER—Die Walküre: Ride of the Walküres; Magic fire music; Das Rheingold: Invocation of Alberich; Entrance of the Gods into Valhalla; Götterdämmerung: Rhine journey; Funeral music; Immolation scene . *Philadelphia Orch.; Ormandy, cond.*
+ Fa 3-4/89: 334

29863. 7820-2-RV: TCHAIKOVSKY—Symphony no. 5. *Philadelphia Orch.; Ormandy, cond.*
+ Fa 3-4/89: 312

29864. 7822-2-RC: SIBELIUS—Symphony no. 5; En saga; Tapiola. *Finnish Radio Symphony Orch.; Saraste, cond.*
+ ARG 11-12/89: 121
• Fa 3-4/89: 278
+ Gr 6/89: 44
+ SR 3/89: 125

29865. 7823-2-RC: SCHUBERT—Violin sonatas, D. 574, 385; Fantasie for violin and piano, D. 934. *Swensen, violin; Kahane, piano.*
+ ARG 5-6/89: 85
+ Fa 1-2/89: 114
+ Gr 1/89: 1181
+ MA 5/89: 55
+ Ov 12/88: 46

29866. 7825-2-RC: BACH—Well-tempered clavier, bk. 2. *Landowska, harpsichord.*
• Fa 3-4/89: 83
+ Gr 7/89: 205

29867. 7831-2-RG: Music of Canteloube, Villa-Lobos, and Rachmaninoff. *Moffo, soprano; American Symphony Orch.; Stokowski, cond.*
+ ARG 9-10/89: 40
+ Fa 5-6/89: 155

29868. 7834-2-RG: GRIEG—Piano concerto. LISZT—Piano concertos no. 1-2. *Cliburn, piano; Philadelphia Orch.; Ormandy, cond.*
+ ARG 9-10/89: 57
+ DA 11/89: 66
+ Fa 9-10/89: 210
• Gr 8/89: 295
+ MA 9/89: 72
+ Ov 9/89: 58

29869. 7835-2-RG: MESSIAEN—Quartet for the end of time. *Tashi.*
+ ARG 9-10/89: 82
+ Fa 5-6/89: 236
+ Gr 4/89: 1601
+ HF 7/89: 68

29870. 7841-2-RG (2 discs): BACH—Goldberg variations; Chromatic fantasy and fugue; Inventions no. 2, 6, 8; Sinfonias no. 2, 6, 15. *Arrau, piano.* Recorded in 1942, 1945.
+ Fa 5-6/89: 105
+ Gr 7/98: 244
+ NYT 6/25/89: H27
+ Ov 4/89: 59
+ St 7/89: 161

29871. 7843-2-RC: *Two loves: a sequence of poetry and music by William Shakespeare and John Dowland. Bream, lute; Ashcroft, reader.*
+ ARG 3-4/90: 43
+ Fa 1-2/90: 168

29872. 7844-2-RC: PAGANINI—Violin concertos no. 2, 4. *Ughi, violin & cond.; Chamber orch. of Santa Cecilia.*
• Fa 5-6/89: 264
• Ov 4/89: 63

29873. 7845-2-RC: SCHUBERT—Arpeggione sonata, D. 821. PROKOVIEV—Cello sonata, op. 119. *Harnoy, cello; Dussek, piano.*
+ ARG 11-12/89: 111
+ ARG 11-12/90: 110 (Schubert)
• ARG 11-12/90: 110 (Prokofiev)

+ Fa 5-6/89: 307
• Gr 7/89: 200

29874. 7846-2-RC: Music of Oldham, Tippett, Britten, Walton, and others. *Guildhall String Ensemble; Salter, cond.*
+ ARG 11-12/89: 146
+ Fa 5-6/89: 408
+ Gr 5/89: 1741

29875. 7861-2-RC (2 discs): MOZART—Flute concertos no. 1-2; Concerto for flute and harp; Divertimento in D; Rondo and Menuetto (arr. Galway); Serenade no. 13 *. Robles, harp; Galway, flute & cond.; Chamber Orch. of Europe.*
+ Fa 7-8/89: 190
+ Gr 7/89: 180

29876. 7862-2-RC (2 discs): Music of Elgar, Bach (arr. Elgar), and Handel (arr. Elgar). *Kenny, Hodgson, Gillett, Luxon; London Phil. Choir & Orch.; Slatkin, cond.*
• ARG 5-6/89: 46
+ Fa 3-4/89: 158
+ Gr 3/89: 1473

29877. 7869-2-RG: MOZART—Violin concerto no. 5; Violin sonata, K. 378; String quintet, K. 516. *Heifetz, Baker, violin; Primrose, Majewski, viola; Piatigorsky, cello; Smith, piano; unidentified chamber orch.*
- Fa 5-6/90: 226
+ Gr 9/90: 531

29878. 7870-2-RG: BEETHOVEN—Serenade for string trio, no. 5. SPOHR—Violin concerto no. 8; Double quartet in D minor. *Heifetz, Baker, Amoyal, Rosenthal, violins; Primrose, Thomas, Harshman, violas; Piatigorsky, Lesser, cello; RCA Victor Orch.; Solomon, cond.*
- Fa 5-6/90: 117
+ Gr 9/90: 531

29879. 7871-2-RG: Music of Debussy (arr. Hartmann), Respighi, Ravel (arr. Roques), and Martinů. *Heifetz, violin; Bay, Rubinstein, piano; Piatigorsky, cello.*
+ Fa 5-6/90: 117

29880. 7872-2-RG: Music of Castelnuovo-Tedesco, Ferguson, Françaix, and Khachaturian. *Heifetz, violin; Steuber, piano; De Pasquale, viola; Piatigorsky, cello; Los Angeles Phil. Orch.; Wallenstein, cond.*
+ ARG 11-12/90: 161
+ Fa 5-6/90: 117
+ Fr 9/90: 531

29881. 7873-2-RG: *Heifetz collection.* Music of Schubert, Brahms, and Beethoven. *Heifetz, violin; Smith, Lateiner, piano; Schonbach, Primrose, viola; Piatigorsky, cello.*
+ Fa 5-6/90: 117
+ Gr 5/90: 531

29882. 7878-2-RV: BEETHOVEN—Symphony no. 3. *Boston Symphony Orch.; Leinsdorf, cond.*
• Fa 3-4/89: 103

29883. 7884-2-RC: NIELSEN—Symphonies no. 2, 5. *Royal Danish Orch.; Berglund, cond.*
- Fa 3-4/90: 251
+ MA 7/90: 81
+ SR 2/90: 156

29884. 7885-2-RC: VIVALDI—Recorder concertos, RV 441-445; Concerto for recorder and 2 violins, RV 108. *Petri, recorders; I Solisti veneti; Scimone, cond.*
+ DA 6/90: 54
+ Fa 5-6/90: 329
+ Gr 7/90: 233

29885. 7887-2-RC: TCHAIKOVSKY—Grand sonata, op. 37; Romance, op. 51, no. 5; Seasons: May, June, August, September, and October. *Douglas, piano.*
+ Fa 11-12/89: 380

29886. 7889-2-RG: KORNGOLD—String quartets no. 1, 3. *Chilingirian String Quartet.*
+ ARG 1-2/90: 56
+ Fa 11-12/89: 254
+ Gr 12/89: 1152

29887. 7894-2-RC: BEETHOVEN—Symphony no. 5; Fidelio overture; Leonore overture no. 3. *Royal Phil. Orch.; Previn, cond.*
+ ARG 1-2/90: 27
• Fa 1-2/90: 121
• Gr 1/90: 1320
+ SR 1/90: 129

29888. 7895-2-RC: HANDEL—Concerti grossi op. 6, no. 1-4. *Guildhall String Ensemble; Salter, violin & cond.*
+ ARG 5-6/90: 56
• DA 12/89: 84
+ Fa 1-2/90: 195
+ Gr 2/90: 1461
+ SR 3/90: 98

29889. 7896-2-RG (2 discs): GLUCK—Orfeo ed Euridice. *Moffo, Raskin, Verrett; Polyphonic Chorus of Rome; I Virtuosi di Roma; Fasano, cond.*
+ Fa 9-10/90: 244

29890. 7898-2-RC: BERIO—Voci; Requies; Coral. *Chiarappa, violin; Bennici, viola; London Sinfonietta; Berio, cond.*
+ ARG 11-12/91: 30
+ Fa 9-10/91: 160

29891. 7899-2-RG (2 discs): BARBER—Vanessa. *Steber, Elias, Resnik, Gedda, Tozzi; Metropolitan Opera Chorus & Orch.; Mitropoulos, cond.*
+ ARG 11-12/91: 23
+ Fa 1-2/91: 144
+ Gr 7/90: 272

29892. 7901-2-RC: *Rendezvous with Tashi.* Music of Hindemith, Foss, Shulman, and Gershwin. *Tashi; Foss, piano.*
+ ARG 1-2/90: 114
+ Fa 11-12/89: 484
+ Gr 3/90: 1635

29893. 7902-2-RC: RACHMANINOFF—Symphony no. 3; The rock. *Stockholm Phil. Orch.; Berglund, cond.*
- ARG 11-12/89: 102
+ Fa 1-2/90: 271
- Gr 6/89: 43

29894. 7903-2-RC: TELEMANN—Sonatas for 2 recorders no. 1-6. *Petri, Selin, recorders.*
+ Fa 11-12/90: 379
• Gr 4/91: 1861

29895. 7905-2-RC: MENDELSSOHN—Overtures: Wedding of Comacho; Midsummer night's dream; Hebrides; Calm sea and prosperous voyage; Athalia; Ruy Blas. *Bamberg Symphony Orch.; Flor, cond.*
+ ARG 3-4/89: 57
+ Fa 1-2/89: 208
+ Gr 1/89: 1154

29896. 7907-2-RG: HANDEL—Concerti grossi op. 6, no. 5-8. *Guildhall String Ensemble; Salter, violin & cond.*
+ ARG 5-6/90: 56
+ Fa 3-4/90: 186
+ Gr 2/90: 1461

29897. 7911-2-RG: Music of Bach, Handel, Schubert, Schumman, Brahms, and others. *Anderson, alto; various accs.*
+ ARG 1-2/90: 130
+ Fa 11-12/89: 430
• Gr 1/90: 1386
+ ON 2/3/90: 31

29898. 7914-2-RG: Arias and duets by Wagner, Hildach, Trunk, Lembcke, Riego, and Schumann. *Melchior, tenor; Flagstad, Lehmann, sopranos; various orchs. & conds.*
+ ARG 1-2/91: 147
+ Fa 9-10/90: 429
• Gr 10/90: 848

29899. 7915-2-RG: WAGNER—Tristan und Isolde: Liebestod; Lohengrin: Euch lüften; Parsifal: Ich sah das Kind; Die Walküre: Du bist der Lenz; Ho jo to ho; Götterdämmerung: Dawn duet; Immolation scene. *Flagstad, soprano; Melchior, tenor; various orchs. & conds.*
+ ARG 1-2/91: 147
+ DA 10/90: 80
+ Fa 9-10/90: 429
• Gr 10/90: 833

29900. 7916-2-RC: LISZT—Piano concertos (complete); Hungarian fantasy. *Douglas, piano; London Symphony Orch.; Hirokami, cond.*
• DA 4/91: 66
• Fa 9-10/90: 275

• Gr 8/90: 367
+ SR 9/90: 100

29901. 7918-2-RC: SHOSTAKOVICH—Cello concertos no. 1-2. *Gutman, cello; Royal Phil. Orch.; Temirkanov, cond.*
+ ARG 5-6/91: 108
+ DA 8/91: 38
• Fa 3-4/91: 382
• Gr 1/91: 1377

29902. 7919-2-RC: SIBELIUS—Symphony no. 2; Kuolema: Valse triste; Scene with cranes; Night ride and sunrise. *Finnish Radio Symphony Orch.; Saraste, cond.*
• ARG 11-12/90: 117
+ Gr 4/90: 1801

29903. 7920-2-RC: BRAHMS—Serenade no. 2; Variations on a theme of Haydn; Academic festival overture. *St. Louis Symphony Orch.; Slatkin, cond.*
+ ARG 11-12/90: 36
• Fa 9-10/90: 195
+ Gr 8/90: 364 (Serenade)
• Gr 8/90: 364 (Others)

29904. 7921-2-RC: HANDEL—Concerti grossi op. 6, no. 9-12. *Guildhall String Ensemble; Salter, violin & cond.*
+ ARG 5-6/90: 56
+ Fa 3-4/90: 186
+ Gr 4/90: 1781

29905. 7928-2-RC: VIVALDI—Flute concertos, RV 108, 426-426, 429, 438. *Galway, flute; I Solisti veneti; Scimone, cond.*
+ ARG 11-12/90: 133
+ Fa 3-4/90: 331

29906. 7929-2-RC: DVOŘÁK—Symphony no. 9. STRAVINSKY—Firebird suite. *Yamashita, guitar.*
+ Au 2/90: 100
+ DA 9/89: 73
- Fa 7-8/89: 139

29907. 7940-2-RG (2 discs): BERLIOZ—La damnation de faust. DEBUSSY—La damoiselle élue. *Danco, Poleri, Singher, Angeles; Harvard Glee Club; Radcliffe Choral Society; Boston Symphony Orch.; Munch, cond.*
• Fa 5-6/89: 138 (Berlioz)
+ Fa 5-6/89: 138 (Debussy)
• Gr 2/89: 1320
+ Ov 6/89: 61

29908. 7941-2-RG: PROKOFIEV—Piano sonata no. 6. RACHMANINOFF—Piano sonata no. 2; Prelude in D; Etude- tableau in E♭. *Cliburn, piano.*
+ ARG 11-12/89: 101 (Rachmaninoff)
• ARG 11-12/89: 101 (Prokofiev)
+ DA 11/89: 66
+ Fa 9-10/89: 285
+ MA 9/89: 72
+ Ov 9/89: 58

29909. 7942-2-RG: BRAHMS—Piano concerto no. 2; Intermezzos op. 117, no.

1-2; op. 119, no. 1-3. *Cliburn, piano; Chicago Symphony Orch.; Reiner, cond.*
- ARG 11-12/89: 43
+ DA 11/89: 66
• Fa 9-10/89: 155
• Gr 8/89: 295
+ MA 9/89: 72
+ Ov 9/89: 58

29910. 7943-2-RG: BEETHOVEN—Piano concertos no. 4-5. *Cliburn, piano; Chicago Symphony Orch.; Reiner, cond.*
+ ARG 9-10/89: 24
+ DA 11/89: 66
- Fa 9-10/89: 131
+ MA 9/89: 72
+ Ov 9/89: 58

29911. 7945-2-RG: CHOPIN—Piano concerto no. 1. RACHMANINOFF—Rhapsody on a theme of Paganini. *Cliburn, piano; Philadelphia Orch.; Ormandy, cond.*
• ARG 9-10/89: 42
+ DA 11/89: 66
+ Fa 9-10/89: 176
+ Gr 8/89: 295
+ MA 9/89: 72
+ Ov 9/89: 58

29912. 7946-2-RC: *The modern recorder.* Music of Christiansen, Thommessen, O. Buck, Jacob, and others. *M. Petri, recorder; H. Petri, harpsichord; D. Petri, cello.*
+ Fa 5-6/89: 401
+ Gr 5/89: 1746

29913. 7947-2-RC: SHOSTAKOVICH—Concerto for piano, trumpet and strings no. 1; Chamber symphony in C minor; Preludes op. 34. *Kissin, piano; Kan, trumpet; Moscow Virtuosi; Spivakov, cond.*
• ARG 1-2/90: 88
+ DA 1/90: 63
+ Fa 11-12/89: 359
- Gr 12/89: 1143
+ MA 3/90: 74
+ SR 11/89: 157

29914. 7948-2-RC: HAYDN—Piano concerto, H. XVIII, 11; Violin concerto, H. VIIa, 1; Sinfonia concertante, H. I, 105. *Kissin, piano; Spivakov, violin; Milman, cello; Utkin, oboe; Minkowski, bassoon; Moscow Virtuosi.*
+ ARG 3-4/89: 58
+ Fa 11-12/89: 232

29915. 7962-2-RC: SCHUBERT—Arpeggione sonata, D. 821; Violin sonatas, D. 384, 408; Rondo brillant, D. 895. *Swensen, violin; Kahane, piano.*
+ ARG 11-12/90: 110
+ Fa 5-6/89: 308
• Gr 8/89: 332

29916. 7963-2-RG: Music of Rözsa, Korngold and Waxman. *Heifetz, violin; Piatigorsky, cello; Dallas Symphony Orch.; chamber orch.; Los Angeles Phil. Orch.; RCA Victor Symphony; Hendl, Wallenstein, Voorhees, conds.*

+ Fa 3-4/89: 253 (2 reviews)
+ Gr 4/89: 1581
+ MA 5/89: 85

29917. 7964-2-RG: SCHUBERT—String quintet, D. 956; String trio no. 2; Ave Maria. BACH—Sinfonias no. 3-4, 9. *Heifetz, Baker, violin; Primrose, viola; Piatigorsky, Rejto, cellos; Bay, piano.*
+ Fa 3-4/89: 264
+ Gr 4/89: 1602
+ MA 5/89: 85

29918. 7965-2-RG: DVOŘÁK—Piano quintet no. 2. BRAHMS—String sextet, op. 36; Hungarian dances 11, 17, 20. *Lateiner, Smith, pianos; Heifetz, Baker, violins; De Pasquale, Primrose, Majewski, violas; Piatigorsky, Rejto, cellos.*
☐ Fa 3-4/89: 153
+ Gr 7/89: 199
+ MA 5/89: 85

29919. 7966-2-RG: WALTON—Violin concerto in B minor. ELGAR—Violin concerto in B minor. *Heifetz, violin; Philharmonia Orch.; London Symphony Orch.; Walton, Sargent, cond.*
+ Fa 3-4/89: 264 m.f.
+ Gr 3/89: 1512
+ MA 5/89: 85

29920. 7967-2-RG: MOZART—Piano concertos no. 20-21. HAYDN—Variations in F minor. *Rubinstein, piano; orch.; Wallenstein, cond.*
+ ARG 3-4/90: 78

29921. 7969-2-RG: Music of Massenet, Cilea, Rossini, Donizetti, Mozart, and others. *Schipa, tenor; Galli-Curci, soprano; various accs.*
• ARG 1-2/90: 131
+ Fa 11-12/89: 430
+ Gr 12/89: 1235
+ ON 2/17/90: 39

29922. 7971-2-RG (3 discs): VERDI—La forza del destino. *Price, Verrett, Tucker, Merrill, Tozzi, Flagello; RCA Italiana Chorus & Orch.; Schippers, cond.*
+ Fa 5-6/89: 343
+ Gr 12/88: 1062
+ Op 1/89: 70

29923. 7979-2-RC: VIVALDI—Concertos op. 8, no. 1-4 (Four seasons); Concerto for violin and strings in A minor op. 3, no. 6. *Ughi, violin & cond.; I Virtuosi di Santa Cecilia.*
- Fa 7-8/89: 272
+ Gr 3/89: 1438

29924. 7980-2-RC: BRAHMS—Symphony no. 2; Academic festival overture. *Bavarian Radio Orch.; C. Davis, cond.*
• ARG 1-2/90: 36
• Fa 9-10/89: 161
- Gr 9/89: 448

29925. 7981-2-RG (3 discs): BIZET—Carmen. *Stevens, Albanese, Peerce,*

Merrill; Robert Shaw Chorale; RCA Victor Orch.; Reiner, cond.
- • Fa 3-4/89: 113
- - Gr 5/89: 1777
- + Ov 4/89: 68

29926. 7982-2-RC: RACHMANINOFF—Piano concerto no. 2; Etudes-tableaux op. 39. *Kissin, piano; London Symphony Orch.; Gergiev, cond.*
- - ARG 1-2/90: 75
- + DA 10/89: 75
- + Fa 5-6/89: 283
- + Gr 3/89: 1434
- • Ov 3/89: 51
- + SR 4/89: 84
- • St 5/89: 165

29927. 7985-2-RC: STRAVINSKY—Rite of spring; Petrushka (1947 version). *Royal Phil. Orch.; Temirkanov, cond.*
- • ARG 7-8/90: 115
- + Fa 3-4/90: 314
- + Gr 9/90: 544
- • MA 5/90: 83
- - SR 2/90: 158

29928. 7986-2-RC: VILLA-LOBOS—Harmonica concerto; other music for harmonica and orchestra. *Bonfiglio, harmonica; New York Chamber Symphony; Schwarz, cond.*
- • ARG 11-12/89: 133
- + Fa 11-12/89: 398
- + Gr 4/90: 1806

29929. 7987-2-RC: MARTINŮ—Les ritournelles; Fantaisie et toccata; Piano sonata no. 1; Julietta: Act 2 scene 3: Moderato; Etudes and polkas (selections). *Firkušný, piano.*
- + ARG 1-2/90: 62
- + Fa 1-2/90: 221
- + Gr 12/89: 1167
- + NYT 10/15/89: H29
- + SR 12/89: 126

29930. 7988-2-RC: MENDELSSOHN—Piano concertos (complete); Capriccio brillant, op. 22. *Edelmann, piano; Bamberg Symphony Orch.; Flor, cond.*
- - ARG 9-10/90: 87
- • Fa 3-4/90: 231
- • Gr 12/89: 1141
- • SR 2/90: 154

29931. 7989-2-RG: Music of Strauss, Françaix, Satie (arr. Debussy), and Ibert. *De Lancie, oboe; Chamber Orch.; London Symphony Orch.; Wilcox, Previn, conds.*
- • Fa 7-8/91: 300

29932. 7990-2-RC: SCHUBERT—String quartets no. 4, 14. *Tokyo String Quartet.*
- + ARG 1-2/91: 87
- + Fa 11-12/90: 342
- + Gr 1/91: 1385

29933. 7991-2-RC: BACH—Concerto for violin and oboe; Concerto for violin, flute, and harpsichord; Concerto for 2 violins; Concerto for 3 violins. *Spivako,*

violin & cond.; Moscow Virtuosi.
- + DA 6/90: 56
- + Fa 7-8/90: 72

29934. 7992-2-RG: BEETHOVEN—Piano concerto no. 5. TCHAIKOVSKY—Piano concerto no. 1. *Horowitz, piano; RCA Victor Symphony Orch.; NBC Symphony Orch.; Reiner, Toscanini, cond.*
- + Fa 9-10/90: 167
- + Gr 12/90: 1276

29935. 74321-20297-2 (3 discs): SCRIABIN—Symphonies; Tone poems; Piano concerto. *Krainev, Oppitz, pianos; Frankfurt Radio Symphony Orch.; Kitaenko, cond.*
- + Gr 12/95: 91

29936. 09026-23675-2: *Montserrat Caballé: Casta diva.* Songs and arias by Schubert, Strauss, Mompou, Verdi, and others. *Caballé, soprano. Reissues.*
- • ARG 9-10/95: 286

29937. 74321-24217-2: ELGAR—Symphony no. 1; Introduction and allegro; Pomp and circumstance no. 1. *BBC Symphony Orch.; C. Davis, cond.; Boston Pops Orch.; Fiedler, cond.; Boston Symphony Orch.; Munch, cond. Reissues.*
- + Gr 2/96: 46

29938. 74321-24894-2: SCHNITTKE—Concerto grosso no. 1; Viola concerto; Concerto for piano and strings; Monologue; Praeludium in memoriam Dmitri Shostakovich; Suite in the old style. *Kremer, Grindenko, S. Rozhdestvensky, violins; Krainev, Bezrodny, pianos; London Symphony Orch.; Rozhdestvensky, Rostropovich, conds.; Moscow Virtuosi; Spivakov, violin; Moscow Soloists; Bashmet, viola. Reissue.*
- + Gr 5/95: 58

29939. 74321-25283-2 (2 discs): MOZART—Die Entführung aus dem Serail. *Gruberová, Ebel, Araiza, Orth, Bracht, Leipnitz; Bavarian Radio Chorus; Munich Radio Orch.; Wallberg, cond.*
- • Gr 10/95: 140

29940. 74321-25285-2: PUCCINI—Gianni Schicchi. *Panerai, Donath, Seiffert, Baniewicz, Pane, Errante, Kunz, Auer, Federici, Riener, Georg; Bavarian Radio Chorus; Munich Radio Orch.; Patanè, cond.*
- + Gr 6/95: 112

29941. 74321-25286-2 (2 discs): VERDI—Rigoletto. *Weikl, Popp, Aragall, Rootering, Takács; Bavarian Radio Chorus; Munich Radio Orch.; Gardelli, cond. Reissue; recorded 1984.*
- • Gr 10/95: 142

29942. 74321-25287-2 (2 discs): WEBER—Der Freischütz. *Watson, Schock, Schädle, Frick, Nicolai, Böhme, Meisel,*

Lang; Deutsche Oper Berlin; Matacic, cond. Reissue; recorded 1968.
- • Gr 6/95: 116

29943. 74321-27601-2 (14 discs): MAHLER—Symphonies no. 1-9. *Vocal soloists; choruses; Netherlands Radio Phil. Orch.; Waart, cond. Recorded live 1992-1995.*
- • ARG 5-6/96: 140
- • Fa 3-4/96: 209
- • Gr 1/96: 54

29944. 09026-29646-2: Songs and duets by Stolz, Gounod, Bellini, and others. *M. & M. Caballé, sopranos.*
- + ARG 7-8/96: 276
- + Fa 9-10/96: 366

29945. 09026-32046-2: RACHMANINOFF—The bells; Symphonic dances. *Shumskaya, soprano; Dovenman, tenor; Bolshakov, baritone; Russian Republic Capelle; Moscow Phil. Orch.; Kondrashin, cond. Reissues.*
- + ARG 7-8/96: 173
- + Gr 10/96: 58

29946. 74321-32225-2 (2 discs): DEBUSSY—Pelléas et Mélisande. *Dormoy, Command, Bacquier, Soyer, Taillon, Pouradier-Duteil, Tamalet; Burgundian Chorus; Orch. of the Opéra de Lyon; Baudo, cond. Reissue; recorded 1978.*
- + Gr 7/96: 100

29947. 60002-2-RG: BEETHOVEN—Symphonies no. 1, 6. *Chicago Symphony Orch.; Reiner, cond.*
- + Fa 9-10/90: 177 (no. 1)
- • Fa 9-10/90: 177 (no. 6)

29948. 60010-2-RG: RACHMANINOFF—Piano concerto no. 2. TCHAIKOVSKY—Piano concerto no. 1. *Bachauer, Devoyon, piano; Strasbourg Phil. Orch.; Philharmonia Orch.; Lombard, Dutoit, cond.*
- + ARG 11-12/89: 99
- • Fa 9-10/89: 291

29949. 60023-2-RG: *The art of Lily Laskine.* Music of Handel, Boieldieu, Bochsa, and Pierné. *Laskine, harp; various orchs. & conds.*
- + ARG 9-10/89: 127

29950. 60032-2-RC: MOZART—Symphonies no. 36, 40; Nozze di Figaro overture. *Berlin Phil. Orch.; unnamed cond.*
- • ARG 11-12/89: 91
- + Fa 11-12/89: 298
- + Gr 4/89: 900

29951. 60035-2-RG: Music of Weber, Mozart, and Rossini. *Stoltzman, clarinet; Mostly Mozart Festival Orch.; Schneider, cond.*
- + Fa 11-12/89: 410
- + Gr 10/89: 668

RCA

29952. 60036-2-RG: BRAHMS—Clarinet sonatas (complete). *Stoltzman, clarinet; Goode, piano.*
+ ARG 11-12/89: 43
+ Fa 9-10/89: 159
• Gr 9/89: 491

29953. 60046-2-RG: Music of Szymanowski, Falla, and Liszt. *Rubinstein, piano; Los Angeles Phil. Orch.; San Francisco Symphony Orch.; Dallas Symphony Orch.; Wallenstein, Jorda, Dorati, cond.*
+ ARG 7-8/90: 116
+ Fa 3-4/90: 362 (Liszt)
• Fa 3-4/90: 362 (others)

29954. 60047-2-RG: CHOPIN—Preludes, op. 28; Piano sonata no. 2; Berceuse, op. 57; Barcarolle, op. 60 . *Rubinstein, piano.*
+ ARG 5-6/90: 41
+ Fa 3-4/90: 166

29955. 60051-2-RC: PROKOFIEV—Piano concerto no. 3; Visions fugitives, op. 22, no. 10-11, 16-17; Pieces, op. 32, no. 1. KISSIN—Two inventions. *Kissin, piano; Moscow Phil. Symphony Orch.; Chisiakov, cond.*
- ARG 1-2/89: 75
• Fa 9-10/89: 280 m.f.
• NYT 9/24/89: H27
+ SR 10/89: 145

29956. 60058-2-RC: BEETHOVEN—Symphonies no. 2, 4. *North German Radio Symphony Orch.; Wand, cond.*
• ARG 11-12/89: 37
+ Fa 9-10/89: 137
+ Gr 9/89: 447
+ NYT 7/9/89: H30

29957. 60061-2-RC: BRUCKNER—Symphony no. 6. *North German Radio Symphony Orch.; Wand, cond.*
+ Fa 9-10/89: 168
+ SR 9/89: 144

29958. 60066-2-RC: MOZART—Serenade, K. 525; Divertimentos, K. 136-138. *Moscow Virtuosi; Spivakov, cond.*
+ Fa 7-8/90: 211
+ St 4/90: 195

29959. 60068-2-RC: MOZART—German dances; Serenade no. 7. *Greutter, violin; North German Radio Symphony Orch.; Wand, cond.*
+ Fa 1-2/91: 253
• Gr 1/91: 1375

29960. 60071-2-RG (2 discs): CORELLI—Concerti grossi op. 6. *Guildhall String Ensemble; Salter, violin & cond.*
+ Fa 7-8/92: 139
+ Gr 9/92: 46

29961. 60072-2-RC: ELGAR—Symphony no. 2 in E♭; Serenade in E minor. *London Phil. Orch.; Slatkin, cond.*
+ ARG 3-4/90: 49
+ Fa 11-12/89: 203
+ Gr 8/89: 301

• MA 3/90: 72
+ St 5/90: 183

29962. 60073-2-RC: ELGAR—Enigma variations; Froissart overture; Cockaigne overture. *London Phil. Orch.; Slatkin, cond.*
• ARG 3-4/90: 49
+ Fa 11-12/89: 203
+ Gr 8/89: 301
- MA 3/90: 72

29963. 60074-2-RG: Music of Bellini, Verdi, Ponchielli, Mascagni, Puccini, and others. *Milanov, soprano; various accs.*
+ ARG 1-2/91: 146
+ Fa 9-10/90: 449
+ Gr 11/90: 1079

29964. 60075-2-RG (10 discs): BRUCKNER—Symphonies (complete). *Cologne Radio Symphony Orch.; Wand, cond.* Haas edition used for all except no. 3 which is Nowak edition.
+ Fa 1-2/90: 145
□ Gr 2/90: 1457
• NYT 10/29/89: H27

29965. 60085-2-RG (3 discs): BRAHMS—Symphonies (complete). *North German Radio Symphony Orch.; Wand, cond.*
+ ARG 1-2/90: 35
+ Fa 1-2/90: 139
• NYT 10/29/89: H27
+ St 4/90: 193

29966. 60090-2-RC (6 discs): BEETHOVEN—Symphonies (complete). *North German Radio Symphony Orch.; Wand, cond.*
+ ARG 1-2/90: 25
+ Fa 11-12/89: 137
• NYT 10/29/89: H27
+ St 1/90: 223

29967. 60096-2-RG (5 discs): SCHUBERT—Symphonies (complete); Rosamunde: excerpts. *Cologne Radio Symphony Orch.; Wand, cond.*
- ARG 1-2/90: 85
+ Fa 1-2/90: 299
• NYT 10/29/89: H27
+ St 4/90: 193

29968. 60112-2-RC: Music of Schubert, Schumann, Bruch, and Enesco. *Bashmet, viola; Muntian, piano.*
+ ARG 3-4/91: 113
+ DA 11/90: 67
+ Fa 1-2/90: 307
+ Gr 12/90: 1231
+ MA 1/91: 82

29969. 60118-2-RC: BRAHMS—Symphony no. 3; Tragic overture. *Bavarian Radio Orch.; Davis, cond.*
+ Fa 5-6/90: 136
• Gr 5/90: 1971
+ SR 5/90: 106
• St 9/90: 193

29970. 60119-2-RC: Music of Smetana, Liszt, Sibelius, Glinka, and Tchaikovsky.

Berlin Symphony Orch.; Flor, cond.
+ ARG 11-12/90: 138
+ Fa 5-6/90: 394
• Gr 4/90: 1809

29971. 60145-2-RC: SHOSTAKOVICH—Symphony no. 8. *St. Louis Symphony Orch.; Slatkin, cond.*
- ARG 3-4/90: 108
+ Fa 3-4/90: 296
• Gr 4/90: 1801
• St 4/90: 203

29972. 60146-2-RC: FRANCK—Symphony in D minor; Symphonic variations for piano and orchestra. *Firkušný, piano; Royal Phil. Orch.; Flor, cond.*
• Fa 7-8/90: 147
+ MA 1/91: 74

29973. 60147-2-RC: JANÁČEK—Piano sonata; On an overgrown path series 1 and 2; A recollection; In the mist. *Firkušný, piano.*
+ ARG 5-6/91: 69
+ DA 4/91: 58
+ Fa 3-4/91: 238
+ Gr 3/91: 1700
+ MA 7/91: 75
+ St 7/91: 80

29974. 60149-2-RC: COPLAND—Symphony no. 3; Music for a great city. *St. Louis Symphony Orch.; Slatkin, cond.*
+ ARG 5-6/91: 47
+ DA 4/91: 58
+ Fa 3-4/91: 191
+ Gr 2/91: 1500
+ MA 5/91: 72
+ ST 6/91: 241

29975. 60152-2-RG: MOZART—Violin concertos no. 2-3, 5. *Spivakov, violin & cond; Moscow Virtuosi.*
• ARG 7-8/92: 183
+ Fa 7-8/92: 226
+ Gr 9/92: 80

29976. 60154-2-RC: MARTINŮ—Symphonies no. 1-2 . *Berlin Symphony Orch.; Flor, cond.*
+ ARG 1-2/91: 64
+ Fa 11-12/90: 267
+ Gr 11/90: 984
+ MA 3/91: 80
+ SR 11/90: 168

29977. 60155-2-RC: VIVALDI—Concertos for cello, vol. 2. *Harnoy, cello; Toronto Chamber Orch.; Robinson, cond.*
+ ARG 9-10/90: 129
+ DA 4/90: 52
+ Fa 5-6/90: 328
+ Gr 4/90: 1806

29978. 60156-2-RC: STRAVINSKY—Concertos for string orchestra in D; Double canon; Three pieces; Apollon musagète. *Guildhall String Ensemble; Salter, cond.*
+ Fa 9-10/90: 400

29979. 60157-2-RC: SIBELIUS—
Symphony no. 6; Scènes historiques:
Suites 1-2. *Finnish Radio Symphony
Orch.; Saraste, cond.*
- ARG 11/90: 990
• ARG 3-4/91: 121
• Fa 11-12/90: 360

29980. 60170-2-RC: Music of Bartók,
Ives, and Stravinsky. *L. Stoltzman, violin;
R. Stoltzman, clarinet; Goode, piano.*
+ ARG 9-10/90: 129
+ Fa 7-8/90: 83
+ Gr 11/90: 999 (Ives)
• Gr 11/90: 999 (others)
+ NYT 4/15/90: H32

29981. 60172-2-RG (2 discs): VERDI—
Rigoletto. *Peters, Björling, Merrill,
Tozzi; Rome Opera Chorus & Orch.;
Perlea, cond.*
+ Fa 9-10/90: 422

29982. 60173-2-RC: STRAUSS—Don Juan;
Burleske; Serenade, op. 7; Till
Eulenspiegel. *Edelman, piano; Stockholm
Phil. Orch.; Berglund, cond.*
+ ARG 5-6/92: 139
+ Fa 11-12/91: 495
+ Gr 11/91: 102

29983. 60174-2-RC: SCHUBERT—
Symphony no. 9. *St. Louis Symphony
Orch.; Slatkin, cond.*
+ ARG 9/90: 56
+ Fa 7-8/90: 257
• Gr 6/90: 61

29984. 60175-2-RG: BARTÓK—Concerto
for orchestra; Music for strings,
percussion and celesta. *Chicago
Symphony Orch.; Reiner, cond.*
+ ARG 3-4/90: 19
+ DA 1/90: 51
+ Fa 1-2/90: 108

29985. 60176-2-RG: PROKOFIEV—
Alexander Nevsky; Lieutenant Kije suite.
GLINKA—Ruslan and Lyudmilla overture.
*Elias, mezzo-soprano; Chicago
Symphony Chorus & Orch.; Reiner, cond.*
+ ARG 1-2/90: 75
+ DA 1/90: 51
+ Fa 1-2/90: 263

29986. 60178-2-RG: MAHLER—Das Lied
von der Erde. *Forrester, alto; Lewis,
tenor; Chicago Symphony Orch.; Reiner,
cond.*
+ DA 1/90: 51
• Fa 1-2/90: 215
+ Gr 10/91: 166

29987. 60179-2-RG: DEBUSSY—Images
for orchestra: Ibéria. RAVEL—Rapsodie
espagnole; Pavane pour une infante
défunte; Valses nobles et sentimentales;
Alborada del gracioso. *Chicago
Symphony Orch.; Reiner, cond.*
+ DA 1/90: 51
+ Fa 1-2/90: 160

29988. 60180-2-RC: BACH—Violin
sonatas no. 4-6; Violin sonata, BWV
1021. *Swensen, violin; Gibbons,
harpsichord; Anderson, cello.*
+ ARG 5-6/91: 20
+ DA 8/91: 52
• Fa 3-4/91: 140
+ Gr 4/91: 1850

29989. 60195-2-RC: MUSSORGSKY—
Pictures at an exhibition (arr. Ravel);
Songs and dances of death (arr.
Shostakovich); Khovanshchina: prelude
(arr. Rimsky-Korsakov). *Leiferkus,
baritone; Royal Phil. Orch.; Temirkanov,
cond.*
+ Fa 11-12/91: 423
• Gr 3/92: 51

29990. 60198-2-RC: *Romance.* Music of
Debussy, Poulenc, Satie, and Saint-Saëns.
*Stoltzman, clarinet; Vallecillo, piano;
Allen, harp.*
+ ARG 5-6/91: 143
+ Fa 5-6/91: 373
+ Gr 4/92: 106

29991. 60199-2-RC: SCHUBERT—String
quartet no. 15. *Tokyo String Quartet.*
+ ARG 11-12/90: 108
+ Fa 5-6/90: 284
• Gr 4/90: 1826
+ SR 10/90: 120

29992. 60207-2-RC: ALBINONI—Recorder
concertos op. 7, 9 (selections). *Petri,
recorders; I Solisti veneti; Scimone,
cond.*
+ ARG 5-6/91: 14
+ Fa 3-4/91: 128
• Gr 4/91: 1821

29993. 60209-2-RC: MOZART—String
quartets no. 13-14; Adagio and fugue, K.
546. *Pro Arte Quartet.*
+ ARG 11-12/89: 87
- Fa 9-10/89: 261

29994. 60224-2-RC: *Baroque oboe
concertos.* Music of Vivaldi, Handel, A.
Marcello, Bach, and Albinoni. *Messiter,
oboe; Guildhall String Ensemble; Salter,
cond.*
+ Fa 9-10/90: 485
+ Gr 9/90: 553

29995. 60226-2-RC: *Motion picture
music.* SHOSTAKOVICH—Golden mountains
suite; Michurin suite; Fall of Berlin suite.
*Belgian Radio Symphony Chorus &
Orch.; Serebrier, cond.*
• Fa 11-12/90: 358

29996. 60234-2-RC: DVOŘÁK—
Symphony no. 8; Serenade, op. 22. *Royal
Phil. Orch.; Flor, cond.*
- ARG 3-4/91: 63
+ Fa 1-2/91: 192
• Gr 4/91: 1827

29997. 09026-60237-2: GIULIANI—Gran
duetto concertante in A for flute and
guitar, op. 52; Duo concertante in E

minor for violin and guitar, op. 25;
Serenade in A for violin, cello, and
guitar, op. 19. *Yamashita, guitar;
Galway, flute; Swensen, violin; Anderson,
cello.*
+ ARG 11-12/92: 126
+ Fa 9-10/92: 244
+ Gr 12/92: 94

29998. 60244-2-RC: C.P.E. BACH—Flute
concertos in D minor, A major, and G
major . *Galway, flute; Württemberg
Chamber Orch.; Faerber, cond.*
+ Fa 1-2/91: 132

29999. 60247-2-RC: QUANTZ—Flute
concertos in G major, C major, G minor,
and D major . *Galway, flute;
Württemberg Chamber Orch.; Faerber,
cond.*
+ ARG 1-2/92: 94
+ Fa 7-8/91: 256
+ Gr 11/91: 98

30000. 60248-2-RC: MENDELSSOHN—
Symphony no. 2. *Popp, sopranos;
Protschka, tenor; Bamberg Symphony
Chorus & Orch.; Flor, cond.*
+ Fa 11-12/90: 273
• Gr 9/90: 518

30001. 60252-2-RG: BEETHOVEN—
Symphonies no. 1, 3. *NBC Symphony
Orch.; Toscanini, cond.*
• Fa 5-6/91: 126

30002. 60261-2-RG: BEETHOVEN—Violin
concerto in D; Piano concerto no. 3 .
*Heifetz, violin; Rubinstein, piano; NBC
Symphony Orch.; Toscanini, cond.*
• ARG 1-2/90: 28
+ Fa 11-12/90: 160

30003. 60262-2-RG: RESPIGHI—Pines of
Rome; Fountains of Rome; Roman
festivals. *NBC Symphony Orch.;
Toscanini, cond.* Recorded live 1953,
1951, and 1949.
+ ARG 3-4/91: 108
+ Fa 11-12/90: 329
+ Gr 1/91: 1416

30004. 60264-2-RG: WAGNER—Die
Walküre: Act 1 scene 3; Ride of the
Valkyries; Tristan und Isolde: Prelude
and Liebestod; Siegfried Idyll. *Traubel,
Melchior; NBC Symphony Orch.;
Toscanini, cond.*
+ Fa 7-8/91: 326

30005. 60265-2-RG: DEBUSSY—La mer;
Ibéria; Prélude à l'après-midi d'un faune;
Nocturnes: Nuages and Fête. *NBC
Symphony Orch.; Toscanini, cond.*
+ Fa 7 8/91: 146

30006. 09026-60267-2: BEETHOVEN—
Overtures. *NBC Symphony Orch.;
Toscanini, cond.*
+ Fa 9-10/92: 175
• Gr 11/92: 214

RCA

30007. 60268-2-RG: BEETHOVEN—Piano concertos no. 1, 4. *Dorfmann, Serkin, piano; NBC Symphony Orch.; Toscanini, cond.*
- Fa 7-8/92: 112

30008. 60269-2-RG: BEETHOVEN—Symphonies no. 3, 8. *NBC Symphony Orch.; Toscanini, cond.* Recorded 1939.
+ Fa 7-8/92: 117

30009. 09026-60270-2: BEETHOVEN—Symphony no. 5; Septet; Egmont: Overture. *NBC Symphony Orch.; Toscanini, cond.*
+ ARG 9-10/92: 217
+ Fa 9-10/92: 182
+ Gr 11/92: 213

30010. 60271-2-RG: BEETHOVEN—Symphony no. 3 in E♭, op. 55 "Eroica." MOZART—Symphony no. 40 in G minor, K. 550. *NBC Symphony Orch.; Toscanini, cond.* Recorded 1953 and 1950.
+ Fa 1-2/92: 167
+ Gr 10/92: 197

30011. 60272-2-RG (2 discs): BEETHOVEN—Missa solemnis. CHERUBINI—Requiem in C minor. *Marshall, Merriman, Conley, Hines; Robert Shaw Chorale; NBC Symphony Orch.; Toscanini, cond.*
+ ARG 5-6/91: 26
+ Fa 5-6/91: 122
+ Gr 5/91: 1738
+ St 6/91: 259

30012. 60273-2-RG (2 discs): BEETHOVEN—Fidelio. *Bampton, Steber, Peerce, Janssen; NBC Symphony Orch.; Toscanini, cond.* 1944 broadcast recording.
+ ARG 3-4/92: 214
- Fa 3-4/92: 144
+ Gr 10/92: 202

30013. 60274-2-RG: *Arturo Toscanini collection, vol. 34.* Music of Berlioz and Bizet. *NBC Symphony Orch.; Toscanini, cond.*
+ Fa 3-4/93: 395

30014. 60275-2-RG: BERLIOZ—Harold en Italie, op. 16; Roméo et Juliette, op. 17: Excerpts. *NBC Symphony Orch.; Toscanini, cond.*
+ Fa 9-10/92: 213
+ Gr 11/92: 214

30015. 60276-2-RG: VERDI—Rigoletto: Act 3; Lombardi: Act 3 trio. BOITO—Mefistofele: Prologue. *Milanov, Merriman, Peerce, Warren, Moscona, Della Chiesa, Peerce, Moscona; Robert Shaw Chorale; NBC Symphony Orch.; Toscanini, cond.*
+ ARG 5-6/91: 32
+ Fa 3-4/91: 415
+ Gr 6/91: 107
+ St 6/91: 259

30016. 60277-2-RG: BRAHMS—Symphony no. 1; Serenade no. 2. *NBC Symphony Orch.; Toscanini, cond.* Reissue.
- ARG 9-10/92: 218
+ Fa 9-10/92: 183
+ Gr 11/92: 214

30017. 09026-60278-2: CHERUBINI—Symphony in D; Overtures to Ali Baba, Anacréon, and Médée. CIMAROSA—Overtures to Il matrimonio segreto and Il matrimonio per raggiro. *NBC Symphony Orch.; Toscanini, cond.*
+ Fa 1-2/93: 129

30018. 60279-2-RG: DVOŘÁK—Symphony no. 9. KODÁLY—Háry János: Suite. SMETANA—The Moldau. *NBC Symphony Orch.; Toscanini, cond.*
+ Fa 11-12/90: 220
+ Gr 1/91: 1416
- MA 11/90: 73

30019. 60280-2-RG: GLUCK—Orfeo ed Euridice: Act II; Dance of the blessed spirits; Iphigénie en Aulide: Overture. BEETHOVEN—Fidelio: Abscheulicher! Wo eilst du hin? *Merriman, mezzo-soprano; Gibson, Bampton, sopranos; Robert Shaw Chorale; NBC Symphony Orch.; Toscanini, cond.* Reissue.
+ Fa 1-2/93: 155

30020. 60281-2-RG: HAYDN—Symphonies no. 88, 98. *NBC Symphony Orch.; Toscanini, cond.* Recorded 1938.
- Fa 1-2/93: 166

30021. 60282-2-RG: HAYDN—Symphonies no. 99, 101; Sinfonia concertante in B♭ for violin, cello, oboe, bassoon, and orchestra, H. I, 105. *NBC Symphony Orch.; Toscanini, cond.; Mischakoff, violin; Miller, cello; Renzi, oboe; Sharrow, bassoon.*
- ARG 9-10/92: 220
+ Fa 9-10/92: 259
+ Gr 11/92: 213

30022. 09026-60283-2: MENDELSSOHN—A midsummer night's dream: Overture, Incidental music; Octet. *NBC Symphony Orch.; Toscanini, cond.* Reissue.
- Fa 1-2/93: 195

30023. 60284-2-RG: MENDELSSOHN—Symphonies no. 3-4; A midsummer night's dream: Scherzo; Octet in E♭: Scherzo. *NBC Symphony Orch.; Toscanini, cond.*
+ Fa 1-2/92: 265

30024. 09026-60285-2: MOZART—Symphonies no. 39-41. *NBC Symphony Orch.; Toscanini, cond.*
- ARG 9-10/92: 220
- Fa 9-10/92: 303
+ Gr 11/92: 213

30025. 09026-60286-2: MOZART—Marriage of Figaro: Overture; Symphony no. 35; Bassoon concerto; Divertimento

K. 287. *Sharrow, bassoon; NBC Symphony Orch.; Toscanini, cond.* Reissues.
- Fa 1-2/93: 201

30026. 60287-2-RC: *Modern pictures.* Music of Stravinsky, Fortner, Webern and Martin. *North German Radio Symphony Orch.; Wand, cond.*
+ ARG 7-8/92: 170
+ Fa 5-6/92: 342
+ Gr 1/92: 64

30027. 60287-2-RG: MUSSORGSKY—Pictures at an exhibition (arr. Ravel). ELGAR—Enigma variations. *NBC Symphony Orch.; Toscanini, cond.*
- Fa 7-8/91: 241

30028. 60288-2-RG (2 discs): PUCCINI—La bohème. *Albanese, McKnight, Peerce, Valentino, Moscona; NBC Symphony Chorus & Orch.; Toscanini, cond.*
+ DA 1/91: 70
+ Fa 7-8/91: 253
+ Gr 9/91: 152

30029. 60289-2-RG: ROSSINI—Overtures: L'Italiana in Algeri, Il signor Bruschino, Il barbiere di Siviglia, La Cenerentola, La gazza ladra, Le siège de Corinth, Semiramide and Guillaume Tell. *NBC Symphony Orch.; Toscanini, cond.* Recorded 1945-53.
+ Fa 7-8/92: 261

30030. 60290-2-RG: SCHUBERT—Symphonies no. 8-9. *NBC Symphony Orch.; Toscanini, cond.* Recorded 1950 and 1953.
- Fa 1-2/92: 167

30031. 60291-2-RG: SCHUBERT—Symphonies no. 5, 9. *NBC Symphony Orch.; Toscanini, cond.*
- ARG 9-10/92: 220
+ Fa 9-10/92: 346
- Gr 11/92: 213

30032. 09026-60292-2: SCHUMANN—Symphony no. 3; Manfred overture. WEBER—Overtures. *NBC Symphony Orch.; Toscanini, cond.*
+ Fa 1-2/93: 234

30033. 60293-2-RG: SHOSTAKOVICH—Symphony no. 7. *NBC Symphony Orch.; Toscanini, cond.* Recorded 1942.
+ Fa 1-2/92: 331
+ Gr 4/92: 167

30034. 60294-2-RG: SIBELIUS—Symphony no. 2; Finlandia; Pohjola's daughter; Swan of Tuonela. *NBC Symphony Orch.; Toscanini, cond.* Reissue.
- Fa 7-8/92: 286

30035. 60295-2-RG: STRAUSS—Death and transfiguration; Don Quixote. *NBC Symphony Orch.; Toscanini, cond.*
+ Fa 11-12/90: 365
+ Gr 1/91: 1416

30036. 09026-60296-2: R. Strauss—Don Juan; Till Eulenspiegel's merry pranks; Salome: Dance of the 7 veils. Wagner—Götterdämmerung: Dawn and Siegfried's Rhine journey; Siegfried Idyll. *NBC Symphony Orch.; Toscanini, cond.*
    + Fa 9-10/92: 365
    + Gr 11/92: 213

30037. 60298-2-RG: Tchaikovsky—Manfred symphony, op. 58; Romeo and Juliet. *NBC Symphony Orch.; Toscanini, cond.* Recorded 1949 and 1946.
    + Fa 1-2/92: 167

30038. 60301-2-RG (2 discs): Verdi—Ballo in maschera. *Nelli, Peerce, Merrill; Robert Shaw Chorale; NBC Symphony Orch.; Toscanini, cond.* Recorded live 1954.
    • Fa 7-8/91: 314
    + Gr 7/91: 122

30039. 60302-2-RG (2 discs): Verdi—Otello. *Nelli, Vinay, Valdengo; NBC Symphony Orch.; Toscanini, cond.* Recorded 1947.
    + ARG 5-6/92: 151
    + Fa 3-4/92: 353
    + OQ winter 92: 138

30040. 60303-2-RG (2 discs): Verdi—La traviata. *Albanese, Peerce, Merrill; NBC Symphony Orch.; Toscanini, cond.* Recorded 1946.
    • Fa 3-4/92: 356
    • Gr 4/92: 172

30041. 09026-60304-2: Wagner—Götterdämmerung: Excerpts. *Traubel, Melchior, NBC Symphony Orch.; Toscanini, cond.* Reissue.
    + Fa 1-2/93: 268
    • Fa 3-4/93: 323

30042. 60305-2-RG: Wagner—Overtures and preludes from Lohengrin, Meistersinger and Parsifal; Faust overture. *NBC Symphony Orch.; Toscanini, cond.*
    + Fa 7-8/92: 324

30043. 09026-60306-2: Wagner—Music from Tannhäuser, Lohengrin, Tristan und Isolde, and Götterdämmerung. *NBC Symphony Orch.; Toscanini, cond.*
    • Fa 3-4/93: 324

30044. 09026-60307-2: Gershwin—An American in Paris. Sousa—Star and stripes forever; El Capitan. Grofé—Grand Canyon suite. Barber—Adagio for strings. Smith—The star-spangled banner. *NBC Symphony Orch.; Toscanini, cond.* Reissues.
    + Fa 11-12/92: 242
    + Gr 11/92: 214

30045. 60308-2-RG: *Blue Danube waltz.* Music of J. Strauss, Jr, Waldteufel, L. Mozart, Suppé, and others. *NBC Symphony Orch.; Toscanini, cond.*

    • Fa 11-12/90: 364
    + Gr 1/91: 1416

30046. 09026-60309-2: *Music from Italian opera.* Music of Mozart, Donizetti, Rossini, Catalani, Puccini, and Verdi. *NBC Symphony Orch.; Toscanini, cond.* Reissues.
    + Fa 11-12/92: 462
    + Gr 11/92: 214

30047. 09026-60310-2: Overtures by Hérold, Humperdinck, Kabalevsky, Mozart, Rossini, Smetana, Thomas, Verdi, and Weber. *NBC Symphony Orch.; Toscanini, cond.*
    • Fa 1-2/93: 234

30048. 60314-2-RG (4 discs): Music of Debussy, Respighi, Tchaikovsky, Strauss, Schubert, and others. *Philadelphia Orch.; Toscanini, cond.*
    + ARG 3-4/91: 142
    + Fa 3-4/91: 503
    + Gr 6/91: 98
    + St 6/91: 259

30049. 09026-60315-2: *La Scala Orchestra acoustic recordings.* Music of Beethoven, Berlioz, Bizet, Donizetti, Respighi, Massenet, Mendelssohn, Mozart, Pizzetti, and Wolf-Ferrari. *La Scala Orch.; Toscanini, cond.*
    • ARG 9-10/92: 213
    + Fa 9-10/92: 443
    + Gr 11/92: 214

30050. 09026-60319-2: Tchaikovsky—Piano concerto no. 1. Brahms—Piano concerto no. 2. *Horowitz, piano; NBC Symphony Orch.; Toscanini, cond.* Reissue.
    + ARG 3-4/93: 193
    • Gr 9/93: 121

30051. 60320-2-RG: Franck—Symphony in D minor. Saint-Saëns—Symphony no. 3. *NBC Symphony Orch.; Toscanini, cond.* Recorded 1940, 1946, and 1952.
    + Fa 7-8/92: 157

30052. 09026-60321-2: Tchaikovsky—Piano concerto no. 1. Mussorgsky—Pictures at an exhibition. *Horowitz, piano; NBC Symphony Orch.; Toscanini, cond.* Reissue.
    + ARG 3-4/93: 193
    + Gr 9/93: 121

30053. 09026-60322-2: Music of Ravel, Franck, Dukas, Saint-Saëns, Berlioz, and Thomas. *NBC Symphony Orch.; Toscanini, cond.* Reissues.
    + Fa 11-12/92: 462
    + Gr 11/92: 214

30054. 09026-60323-2: Prokofiev—Symphony no. 1. Shostakovich—Symphony no. 1. Glinka—Kamarinskaya. Liadov—Kikimora. Stravinsky—Petrushka: Tableaux 1 and 4. *NBC Symphony Orch.; Toscanini, cond.* Reissues.

    + Fa 11-12/92: 459
    + Gr 11/92: 214

30055. 60324-2-RG (5 discs): Beethoven—Symphonies (complete); Leonore overture no. 3. *Farrell, Merriman, Peerce, Scott; Robert Shaw Chorale; NBC Symphony Orch.; Toscanini, cond.*
    + ARG 9-10/90: 33
    + Fa 7-8/90: 91 m.f.
    + Gr 5/90: 1969
    + St 8/90: 152

30056. 60325-2-RG (4 discs): Brahms—Symphonies (complete); Variations on a theme by Haydn; Academic festival overture; Tragic overture; Concerto for violin and cello; Liebeslieder walzer op. 52; Gesang der Parzen; Hungarian dances no. 1, 17, 20, 21 . *Mischakoff, violin; Miller, cello; Balsam, Kahn, pianos; Robert Shaw Chorale; NBC Symphony Orch.; Toscanini, cond.*
    - ARG 9-10/90: 33
    + Fa 7-8/90: 107
    + Gr 5/90: 1970
    + St 8/90: 152

30057. 60326-2-RG: Verdi—Aida; Falstaff; Requiem; Te deum; Hymn of the nations; Nabucco; Va pensiero; Luisa Millar: Quando le sere al placido. *Various soloists and choirs; NBC Symphony Orch.; Toscanini, cond.*
    • ARG 9-10/90: 36 (Aida)
    • ARG 9-10/90: 36 (others)
    + Fa 7-8/90: 299
    + Gr 5/90: 1969
    + St 8/90: 152

30058. 60329-2-RG (3 discs): *Arturo Toscanini: The New York Philharmonic recordings.* Music of Haydn, Mozart, Beethoven, Mendelssohn, Gluck, Dukas, Brahms, Wagner, Rossini and Verdi. *New York Phil.; Toscanini, cond.*
    + ARG 3-4/92: 216
    + Fa 3-4/92: 430

30059. 60355-2-RC: Castelnuovo-Tedesco—Guitar concertos no. 1-2; Concerto for 2 guitars. *K. Yamashita, N. Yamashita, guitars; London Phil. Orch.; Slatkin, cond.*
    + Fa 11-12/90: 200
    • Gr 12/90: 1202

30060. 60356-2-RG: Beethoven—Piano sonatas no. 8, 14, 23, 26. *Cliburn, piano.*
    + ARG 9-10/90: 48
    + Fa 5-6/90: 119

30061. 60357-2-RG: Brahms—Piano concerto no. 1; Variations and fugue on a theme by Handel, for piano. *Cliburn, piano; Boston Symphony Orch.; Leinsdorf, cond.*
    + ARG 7-8/90: 31
    + Fa 5-6/90: 119

30062. 60358-2-RG: Chopin—Polonaise op. 53; Nocturne op. 62 no. 1; Fantaisie

op. 49; Etudes op. 25 no. 11, op. 10 no. 3; Ballade no. 3; Waltzes op. 64 no. 1-2; Scherzo no. 3; Barcarolle in F#. *Cliburn, piano.*
+ Fa 5-6/90: 149

30063. 60360-2-RC (2 discs): BACH— Orchestral suites (complete). *Carron, flute; Moscow Virtuosi; Spivakov, cond.*
+ ARG 9-10/91: 39
• Fa 5-6/91: 114
+ Gr 5/91: 2003
+ NYT 1/27/91: H28

30064. 60361-2-RC: BRUCKNER— Symphony no. 5. *North German Radio Symphony Orch.; Wand, cond.*
• ARG 5-6/91: 42
+ Fa 1-2/91: 170
+ Gr 3/91: 1662
+ MA 3/91: 74

30065. 60362-2-RC: BEETHOVEN— Symphonies no. 4, 8. *Royal Phil. Orch.; Previn, cond.*
- Fa 9-10/90: 178
- St 1/91: 249

30066. 09026-60363-2: BEETHOVEN— Symphony no. 9. *Alexander, Quivar, Lakes, Plishka; Royal Phil. Orch.; Ambrosian Singers; Previn, cond.*
• ARG 7-8/95: 85
+ Fa 5-6/95: 139
+ Gr 4/95: 48

30067. 60364-2-RC: BRUCKNER— Symphony no. 8. *North German Radio Symphony Orch.; Wand, cond.*
+ ARG 11-12/90: 43
+ DA 10/90: 66
• Fa 7-8/90: 117
+ SR 11/90: 158

30068. 60365-2-RC: BRUCKNER— Symphony no. 9. *North German Radio Symphony Orch.; Wand, cond.*
- ARG 9-10/90: 54
• Fa 7-8/90: 119

30069. 60368-2-RC: TCHAIKOVSKY— Serenade for strings in C. GRIEG— Holberg suite; Norwegian dances. *Moscow Soloists; Bashmet, cond.*
• ARG 5-6/91: 116
+ Fa 1-2/91: 334
+ Gr 3/91: 1677
+ MA 1/91: 82

30070. 60369-2-RC: VIVALDI—Violin concertos, op. 8, no. 1-4 "The seasons"; E minor, RV 278; A minor, RV 357. *Moscow Virtuosi; Spivakov, cond.*
+ Fa 11-12/90: 390
+ Gr 11/91: 105
• SR 11/90: 165

30071. 60370-2-RC: *Modern portraits.* Music of Hartmann, Stravinsky, Penderecki, Schnittke, and Prokofiev. *Kissin, piano; Moscow Virtuosi.*
+ DA 12/90: 100

+ Fa 11-12/90: 465
+ Gr 10/90: 755

30072. 60375-2-RG: BEETHOVEN—Piano sonatas no. 14, 21, 23. *Horowitz, piano.*
+ Fa 9-10/90: 175

30073. 60376-2-RG: CHOPIN—Piano sonata no. 2; Piano music. *Horowitz, piano.*
+ ARG 1-2/92: 43

30074. 60377-2-RG: Music of Prokofiev, Barber, Kabalevsky, Fauré, and Poulenc. *Horowitz, piano.*
+ Fa 1-2/91: 278
+ Gr 7/91: 54

30075. 60378-2-RG: BACH—Brandenburg concertos no. 2, 5; Weichet nur, betrübte Schatten, BWV 202. *Battle, soprano; Ravinia Festival Ensemble; Levine, harpsichord & cond.*
+ ARG 5-6/90: 16
+ Fa 3-4/90: 108

30076. 60379-2-RC: MOZART—Clarinet concerto; Bassoon concerto (arr. for clarinet). *Stoltzman, clarinet; English Chamber Orch.; Schneider, cond.*
+ ARG 5-6/90: 77
+ MA 11/90: 168

30077. 60380-2-RC: ELGAR—Symphony no. 1; In the south. *London Phil. Orch.; Slatkin, cond.*
• ARG 5-6/92: 57
+ Fa 7-8/91: 155
+ Gr 6/91: 38

30078. 60382-2-RC: BRAHMS— Symphony no. 1; Haydn variations. *Bavarian Radio Orch.; C. Davis, cond.*
- ARG 1-2/92: 37
+ Fa 9-10/91: 177
• Gr 8/91: 53

30079. 60383-2-RC: BRAHMS— Symphony no. 4. *Bavarian Radio Orch.; Davis, cond.*
+ ARG 5-6/91: 37
• Fa 3-4/91: 167
- Gr 12/91: 1201
+ MA 5/91: 72
• St 6/91: 239

30080. 60384-2-RG: Music of Puccini, Verdi, Mozart, Cilea, G. Charpentier, and Tchaikovsky. *Albanese, soprano; various orchs. & conds.*
+ ARG 1-2/91: 147
+ Fa 9-10/90: 444

30081. 60387-2-RG: ROSSINI—Overtures to Barbier di Siviglia; Gazza ladra; Cenerentola; Il Signor Bruschino; Scala di seta; Guillaume Tell . *Chicago Symphony Orch.; Reiner, cond.*
+ Fa 9-10/90: 358
+ St 1/91: 263

30082. 60388-2-RG: STRAUSS— Symphonia domestica; Death and

transfiguration. *Chicago Symphony Orch.; RCA Victor Orch.; Reiner, cond.*
+ Fa 9-10/90: 398
+ Gr 12/90: 1276

30083. 09026-60391-2: MENDELSSOHN— Symphonies no. 1, 5. *Bamberg Symphony Orch.; Flor, cond.*
• Fa 5-6/93: 264

30084. 60394-2-RC: STRAVINSKY— Firebird suite (1919 version); Divertimento; Pulcinella suite. *Royal Phil. Orch.; Temirkanov, cond.*
+ ARG 11-12/91: 156
• Fa 7-8/91: 303
• Gr 6/91: 52

30085. 60395-2-RG: CORIGLIANO—Oboe concerto; Three Irish folk song settings; Poem in October. *Lucarelli, oboe; White, tenor; Nyfenger, flute; Rabbai, clarinet; American Symphony Orch.; American String Quartet; Akiyama, cond.; Peress, harpsichord & cond.*
+ Fa 3-4/91: 193
+ Gr 5/91: 2005

30086. 60398-2-RG: STRAUSS—Frau ohne Schatten: Awakening scene; Rosenkavalier: Marschallin's monolog; Guntram: Fas'ich sie bang; Ägyptische Helena: Zweite Brautnacht; Salome: Interlude and final scene; Ariadne auf Naxos: Es gibt ein Reich . *Price, soprano; various orchs. & conds.*
+ Fa 9-10/90: 397
+ Gr 8/90: 408

30087. 09026-60400-2: MOZART—Piano concertos no. 12, 20; Rondo K. 382. *Kissin, piano; Moscow Virtuosi; Spivakov, cond.*
+ ARG 3-4/93: 117
+ Gr 2/93: 47

30088. 60401-2-RC: SIBELIUS— Symphony no. 4; Pohjola's daughter; The bard; The oceanides. *Finnish Radio Symphony Orch.; Saraste, cond.*
• ARG 5-6/91: 110
+ Fa 5-6/91: 285 (Symphony; Pohjola)
- Fa 5-6/91: 285 (Bard; Oceanides)
+ Gr 1/91: 1378
+ HPR v.8, no.2/91: 76
+ MA 5/91: 85

30089. 60404-2-RG: CHOPIN—Piano concerto no. 2; Fantasia on Polish airs; Andante spianato and grand polonaise. *Rubinstein, piano; Philadelphia Orch.; Ormandy, cond.; Symphony of the Air; Wallenstein, cond.*
+ ARG 5-6/91: 44
• Fa 3-4/91: 187

30090. 60406-2-RC: MOZART—Piano quartets K. 478, K. 493. *Rubinstein, piano; Members of the Guarneri Quartet.*
+ ARG 11-12/91: 115
+ Fa 5-6/91: 235

30091. 60407-2-RC: Mozart—Piano sonatas no. 5, 11-13. *Larrocha, piano.*
  + ARG 1-2/90: 71
  + DA 12/90: 107
  + Fa 11-12/90: 299
  + MA 3/91: 84
  + SR 10/90: 114

30092. 60408-2-RC: Granados—Goyescas; El pelete; Allegro de concierto; Danza lenta. *Larrocha, piano.*
  + ARG 5-6/91: 61
  + Fa 5-6/91: 176
  + Gr 2/91: 1533

30093. 60414-2-RG: *A romantic collection.* Music of Liszt, Brahms, Schumann, Tchaikovsky, Granados, and others . *Cliburn, piano.*
  + DA 1/91: 80
  • Fa 1-2/91: 382

30094. 60415-2-RG: Barber—Piano sonata, op. 26. Mozart—Piano sonata no. 10 in C, K. 330. Debussy—La soirée dans Grenade; Étude pour les octaves; La terrasse des audiences du clair de lune; Jardins sous la pluie; Reflets dans l'eau; Feux d'artifice. *Cliburn, piano.* Reissue.
  + Fa 1-2/92: 154

30095. 60417-2-RC: Chopin—Sonatas no. 2, 3. Liszt—Un sospiro; Petrarch sonnet no. 123; Mephisto waltz. *Cliburn, piano.*
  + ARG 7-8/92: 118

30096. 60419-2-RC: Beethoven—Piano concerto no. 3. Brahms—Piano music. *Cliburn, piano; Philadelphia Orch.; Ormandy, cond.*
  + ARG 7-8/92: 91

30097. 60420-2-RC: MacDowell—Piano concerto no. 2; To a wild rose. Schumann—Piano concerto. *Cliburn, piano; Chicago Symphony Orch.; Hendl, Reiner, conds.*
  + Gr 10/91: 86

30098. 60421-2-RC: Castelnuovo-Tedesco—Quintet for guitar and strings, op. 143. Boccherini—Quintets for guitar and strings no. 4, 6. *Yamashita, guitar; Tokyo String Quartet.*
  + ARG 5-6/92: 31
  + Fa 1-2/92: 192
  + Gr 1/92: 69

30099. 60425-2-RC: Tchaikovsky—Symphony no. 5; Tempest. *St. Louis Symphony Orch.; Slatkin, cond.*
  • ARG 3-4/91: 131
  • DA 2/91: 52
  • Fa 3-4/91: 404 (Symphony)
  + Fa 3-4/91: 404 (Tempest)
  • Gr 3/91: 1533
  + MA 5/91: 87
  + SR 3/91: 97

30100. 60427-2-RC: Nielsen—Symphonies no. 3, 6. *Royal Danish Orch.; Berglund, cond.*
  • ARG 11-12/91: 129

  + Fa 11-12/91: 425
  + Gr 4/92: 71

30101. 60428-2-RC: Brahms—Symphony no. 1. *Chicago Symphony Orch.; Wand, cond.*
  • ARG 5-6/91: 36
  • Fa 3-4/91: 166
  + Gr 4/91: 1823
  + SR 5/91: 83
  - St 6/91: 239

30102. 60429-2-RC: *La guitarra romantica.* Music of Tárrega, Malats, Pujol, and Llobet. *Bream, guitar.*
  + Fa 11-12/91: 554
  + Gr 7/92: 82

30103. 09026-60430-2: Vivaldi—Cello sonatas. *Harnoy, Tetel, cellos; Tilney, harpsichord & organ.*
  • ARG 3-4/95: 217

30104. 60431-2-RC: Dvořák—Violin concerto in A minor; Romance for violin and orchestra in F minor; Four romantic pieces for violin and piano. *Ughi, violin; Philharmonia Orch.; Slatkin, piano & cond.*
  + ARG 1-2/92: 51
  + Fa 7-8/91: 153
  + Gr 7/91: 45
  + MA 7/91: 72

30105. 60432-2-RC: Tchaikovsky—Symphony no. 4, op. 36; Fate: symphonic poem, op. 77; The voyevoda: symphonic ballad, op. 78. *St Louis Symphony Orch.; Slatkin, cond.*
  - ARG 1-2/92: 129
  + Fa 7-8/91: 307
  • Gr 7/91: 70

30106. 60433-2-RC: Tchaikovsky—Symphony no. 3; Capriccio italien. *St. Louis Symphony Orch.; Slatkin, cond.*
  • ARG 7-8/92: 237
  • Fa 9-10/92: 376
  + Gr 8/92: 41

30107. 09026-60434-2: Sibelius—Symphony no. 3; Belshazzar's feast; King Christian II suite. *Finnish Radio Orch.; Saraste, cond.*
  • ARG 11-12/92: 206
  + Fa 1-2/93: 242

30108. 60436-2-RC: Dvořák—Piano quintets no. 1-2. *Firkušný, piano; Ridge Quartet.*
  + ARG 7-8/92: 125
  + Fa 7-8/92: 147
  + Gr 7/92: 66

30109. 60437-2-RC: Finzi—5 bagatelles; Clarinet concerto, op. 31, in C minor. Ashmore—Four seasons; Greensleeves. *Stoltzman, clarinet; Guildhall String Ensemble; Salter, cond.*
  + Fa 9-10/91: 215
  + Gr 9/91: 61

30110. 09026-60438-2: Tchaikovsky—Symphony no. 6; Hamlet. *St. Louis Symphony Orch.; Slatkin, cond.*
  + ARG 7-8/93: 168
  + Fa 9-10/93: 310

30111. 60439-2-RC: *Scandanavian suite.* Nielsen—Little suite. Grieg—Holberg suite; Two elegiac melodies; Two melodies, op. 53. Wiren—Serenade. Sibelius—Romance. *Guildhall String Ensemble.*
  - ARG 5-6/92: 160
  + Fa 11-12/91: 570
  + Gr 3/92: 58

30112. 60440-2-RC (3 discs): Mozart—Le nozze di Figaro. *Donath, Varady, Schmiege, Titus, Furlanetto; Bavarian Radio Orch. & Chorus; Davis, cond.*
  + Fa 11-12/91: 401
  • Gr 9/91: 126
  • ON 1/18/92: 36
  + OQ Autumn/91: 185

30113. 60441-2-RC: Handel—Recorder sonatas from op. 1. *Petri, recorder; Jarrett, harpsichord.*
  + ARG 5-6/92: 69
  + Fa 11-12/91: 340

30114. 09026-60442-2: Mozart—Quartets for flute and strings no. 1-4; K. 370. *Galway, flute; Tokyo String Quartet.*
  + ARG 5-6/93: 116
  + Fa 7-8/93: 189
  + Gr 6/93: 69

30115. 60443-2-RC (2 discs): *Carnegie Hall debut concert.* Music of Schumann, Prokofiev, Liszt, and Chopin. *Kissin, piano.*
  + Fa 3-4/91: 479
  + Gr 3/91: 1703
  • HPR v.8, no.3: 77
  + MA 5/91: 89
  • St 9/91: 211

30116. 09026-60444-2: Sibelius—Violin concerto, op. 47; Six humoresques for violin and orchestra, op. 87, 89; Two serenades for violin and orchestra, op. 69. *Swensen, violin; Finnish Radio Symphony Orch.; Saraste, cond.*
  + ARG 11-12/92: 205
  + Fa 9-10/92: 355
  + Gr 1/93: 44

30117. 09026-60445-2: Chopin—Piano music. *Kissin, piano.*
  • ARG 7-8/94: 90
  + Fa 9-10/94: 166
  + Gr 5/94: 79

30118. 60446-2-RC: Schnittke—Trio sonata; Viola concerto. *Moscow Chamber Soloists; Bashmet, viola & cond.; London Symphony Orch.; Rostropovich, cond.*
  + ARG 7-8/92: 214
  + Fa 3-4/92: 304
  + Gr 2/92: 38

30119. 60447-2-RC: MOZART—Violin sonatas K. 8, K. 377, K. 379; Variations in G minor on Hélas, j'ai perdu mon amant K. 360 . *Zukerman, violin; Neikrug, piano.*
+ ARG 11-12/91: 121
+ Fa 7-8/91: 237
+ MA 11/91: 49
+ SR 7/91: 58

30120. 60448-2-RC: SHOSTAKOVICH—Symphony no. 10. *Concertgebouw Orch.; Flor, cond.*
- ARG 5-6/92: 134
- Fa 3-4/92: 325
● Gr 6/92: 48

30121. 60449-2-RG: MUSSORGSKY—Pictures at an exhibition; By the water. TCHAIKOVSKY—Piano concerto no. 1. *Horowitz, piano; NBC Symphony Orch.; Toscanini, cond.*
+ ARG 5-6/91: 85
● Fa 1-2/91: 266

30122. 60451-2-RG: SCHUBERT—Piano sonata D. 960. CZERNY—Variations on La ricordanza. MOZART—Piano sonata no. 12. MENDELSSOHN—Variations sérieuses. *Horowitz, piano.*
+ Fa 9-10/91: 172

30123. 60452-2-RC: SCHUBERT—Five German dances; Symphony no. 5; Five menuets with six trios. *Moscow Virtuosi; Spivakov, cond.*
+ ARG 7-8/92: 219
+ Fa 7-8/92: 274
● Gr 9/92: 89

30124. 09026-60453-2: MOZART—Piano sonatas no. 1, 2, 14; Fantasies, K. 397, K. 475; Rondo, K. 485. *Larrocha, piano.*
+ Fa 3-4/93: 240
● Gr 4/93: 88

30125. 60454-2-RC: MOZART—Piano sonatas no. 7-10. *de Larrocha, piano.*
● ARG 7-8/92: 193
● Fa 9-10/92: 302
● Gr 7/92: 78

30126. 60456-2-RG (3 discs): BEETHOVEN—String quartets op. 18. *Guarneri Quartet.*
+ ARG 5-6/91: 26
+ Fa 1-2/91: 147
● Gr 3/91: 1682

30127. 60457-2-RG (3 discs): BEETHOVEN—String quartets op. 59, 74, 95. *Guarneri Quartet.*
+ Fa 1-2/91: 147
● Gr 3/91: 1682

30128. 60458-2-RG (3 discs): BEETHOVEN—String quartets op. 127, 130, 131, 132, 135; Grosse fugue. *Guarneri Quartet.*
+ ARG 5-6/91: 26
+ Fa 1-2/91: 147
● Gr 3/91: 1682

30129. 60459-2-RG (2 discs): PUCCINI—La rondine. *Moffo, Sciutti, Barioni, Palme, Sereni; RCA Italiana Opera Chorus & Orch.; Molinari-Pradelli, cond.*
+ Fa 9-10/90: 339

30130. 60461-2-RG: Music of Brahms, Beethoven, Haydn, Scarlatti, Bach, and Schumann. *Milstein, violin; Horowitz, piano.*
+ Fa 3-4/91: 481

30131. 60462-2-RC (3 discs): BEETHOVEN— *The middle string quartets.* Quartets op. 59, op. 74, op. 95. *Tokyo String Quartet.*
+ ARG 1-2/92: 27
+ Fa 9-10/91: 153
+ Gr 3/92: 63

30132. 60464-2-RC: SCHNITTKE—Monologue. REGER—Suite in G minor. BRITTEN—Lachrymae. HINDEMITH—Trauermusik. *Bashmet, viola; Moscow Chamber Soloists.*
+ ARG 1-2/92: 163
+ Fa 9-10/91: 441
● Gr 6/91: 55

30133. 60465-2-RC: TCHAIKOVSKY—The nutcracker; Eugene Onegin: Introduction and waltz; Polonaise. *Royal Phil. Orch.; Temirkanov, cond.*
+ ARG 3-4/92: 151
+ Fa 1-2/92: 351

30134. 09026-60466-2: *Modern portraits II.* GUBAIDULINA—Seven last words. SHCHEDRIN—Music for the city of Cöthen. SCHNITTKE—Piano concerto no. 3. *Krainev, piano; Lips, bayan; Milman, cello; Moscow Virtuosi; Spivakov, cond.*
+ Fa 7-8/93: 313
+ Gr 5/93: 44

30135. 09026-60467-2: MOZART—Sinfonia concertante K. 364; Concertone, K. 190. *Spivakov, violin & cond.; Mintz, viola; Garlitski, violin; Moscow Virtuosi.*
● ARG 5-6/93: 116
+ Fa 5-6/93: 275
● Gr 10/93: 46

30136. 60469-2-RG: RAVEL—Daphnis et Chloé. ROUSSEL—Bacchus et Ariane suite no. 2. *Boston Symphony Orch.; Munch, cond.*
+ Fa 7-8/91: 260

30137. 60520-2-RG: *Jussi Björling at Carnegie Hall.* Music of Verdi, Schubert, Beethoven, Brahms, Tchaikovsky, and others. *Björling, tenor; Schauwecker, piano.* Recorded live March 2, 1958.
● Fa 9-10/91: 406

30138. 60521-2-RG: Arias by Mozart, Verdi, Gounod, Bizet, Charpentier, Puccini, Bachelet, and Duparc. *Steber, soprano.*
+ Fa 9-10/91: 402

30139. 60523-2-RG: BRAHMS—Piano concerto no. 2. SCHUBERT—Impromptu, D. 899/3. LISZT—Au bord d'une source; Sonetto no. 104 del Petrarca; Hungarian rhapsody no. 2. *Horowitz, piano; NBC Symphony Orch.; Toscanini, cond.* Reissue.
- ARG 7-8/91: 36
+ Fa 9-10/91: 172

30140. 09026-60556-2: VAUGHAN WILLIAMS—Symphonies no. 5-6. *Philharmonia Orch.; Slatkin, cond.*
+ Fa 11-12/93: 428

30141. 60556-2-RC: VAUGHAN WILLIAMS—Symphonies no. 5-6. *Philharmonia Orch.; Slatkin, cond.*
+ ARG 1-2/92: 132
+ Fa 3-4/92: 352
● Gr 4/92: 85

30142. 60557-2-RC: *Evelyn Glennie: Light in darkness.* Music of Rosauro, Abe, McLeod, Edwards, Miki, Glennie, and Tanaka. *Glennie, marimba; with piano and percussion.*
+ ARG 7-8/92: 262
+ Fa 3-4/92: 168
+ Gr 1/92: 80

30143. 60560-2-RG (2 discs): VERDI—Il trovatore. *Price, Elias, Tucker, Warren, Tozzi; Rome Opera Chorus & Orch.; Basile, cond.* Recorded 1959.
● ARG 9-10/91: 143
● DA 4/91: 64
+ Fa 3-4/91: 417
● Gr 6/91: 91

30144. 60561-2-RC: STRAUSS—Till Eulenspiegel; Don Quixote. *Starker, cello; Bavarian Radio Orch.; Slatkin, cond.*
+ ARG 5-6/92: 140
+ Fa 3-4/92: 336
+ Gr 4/92: 80
● St 1/93: 279

30145. 60562-2-RC: MOZART—Opera arias. *Vaness, soprano; Munich Radio Orch.; Hager, cond.*
+ ARG 1-2/92: 81
+ Fa 1-2/92: 278
- Gr 12/91: 134
+ ON 1/4/92: 39

30146. 09026-60563-2: BACH—Works for violin and harpsichord, vol. 2. *Swensen, violin; Gibbons, harpsichord; Anderson, cello.*
+ Fa 5-6/94: 101

30147. 60567-2-RC (2 discs): Piano concertos of Mozart, Shostakovich, Haydn, Rachmaninoff, and Prokofiev. *Kissin, piano; various orchs. & conds.*
● Fa 1-2/91: 383

30148. 60568-2-RG: RACHMANINOFF—Preludes op. 3, no. 2; op. 23, no. 32. *Weissenberg, piano.*
+ Fa 5-6/91: 257

30149. 60573-2-RG (2 discs): PUCCINI— Manon Lescaut. *Albanese, Björling, Merrill; Teatro dell' Opera (Rome); Perlea, cond.* Recorded 1954.
+ ARG 9-10/91: 110
+ Fa 5-6/91: 254
• Gr 10/91: 190

30150. 09026-60575-2: SIBELIUS— Symphony no. 7; Lemminkäinen suite, op. 22. *Finnish Radio Symphony Orch.; Saraste, cond.*
• ARG 9-10/92: 165
+ Fa 9-10/92: 356
+ Fa 9-10/92: 357
+ Gr 11/92: 100

30151. 60580-2-RG: VAUGHAN WILLIAMS—Sea symphony. *Harper, soprano; Shirley-Quirk, baritone; London Symphony Chorus & Orch.; Previn, cond.*
+ DA 3/91: 42
+ Fa 1-2/91: 338
+ Gr 3/91: 1678

30152. 60581-2-RG: VAUGHAN WILLIAMS—Symphony no. 2; Concerto accademico for violin; Wasps overture. *Buswell, violin; London Symphony Orch.; Previn, cond.*
+ ARG 3-4/91: 134
+ DA 3/91: 42
+ Fa 1-2/91: 338
+ Gr 3/91: 1678

30153. 60583-2-RG: VAUGHAN WILLIAMS—Symphonies no. 3-4. *Harper, soprano; London Symphony Orch.; Previn, cond.* Issued also as 6780-2-RG.
+ ARG 111-12/88: 95 (6780)
+ ARG 3-4/91: 134
+ DA 3/91: 42
• Fa 7-8/88: 267 (6780)
+ Fa 1-2/91: 338
+ Gr 3/91: 1678

30154. 60586-2-RG: VAUGHAN WILLIAMS—Symphony no. 5; Three portraits from The England of Elizabeth; Tuba concerto. *Fletcher, tuba; London Symphony Orch.; Previn, cond.* Issued also as: 6782-2-RG.
+ ARG 3-4/91: 139
+ DA 3/91: 42
+ Fa 3-4/88: 221 (6782)
+ Fa 1-2/91: 338
+ Gr 3/91: 1678

30155. 60588-2-RG: VAUGHAN WILLIAMS—Symphonies no. 6, 9 . *London Symphony Orch.; Previn, cond.* Issued also as 6779-2-RG.
+ DA 3/91: 42
+ Fa 3-4/88: 221 (6779)
+ Fa 1-2/91: 339
+ Gr 3/91: 1678

30156. 60590-2-RG: VAUGHAN WILLIAMS—Symphonies no. 7-8. *Harper, soprano; Richardson, speaker; Ambrosian Singers; London Symphony Orch.; Previn, cond.*

+ DA 3/91: 42
+ Fa 1-2/91: 339
+ Gr 3/91: 1678

30157. 09026-60593-2 (2 discs): MASSENET—Chérubin. *Von Stade, J. Anderson, Upshaw, Ramey; Munich Radio Orch.; P. Steinberg, cond.*
+ ARG 1-2/93: 118
+ Fa 1-2/93: 189
+ Gr 12/92: 138
+ ON 3/13/93: 34

30158. 09026-60597-2 (2 discs): PUCCINI—La fanciulla del West. *Marton, O'Neill, Fondary, Planté, Rootering; Bavarian Radio Chorus; Munich Radio Orch.; Slatkin, cond.*
+ ARG 1-2/93: 133
• Fa 1-2/93: 210
• Gr 11/92: 191
- ON 12/19/92: 38
- Op 12/92: 1500
- St 3/93: 185

30159. 60598-2-RC: SCHUMANN— Fantasiestücke, op. 73. BRAHMS—Cello sonata, op. 78. RACHMANINOFF—Cello sonata. *Starker, cello; Neriki, piano.*
• ARG 5-6/92: 114
+ Fa 3-4/92: 318
+ Gr 4/92: 94

30160. 09026-60599-2: MOZART— Requiem. *Blasi, Lipovsek, Heilmann, Rootering; Bavarian Radio Orch.; C. Davis, cond.*
• Gr 11/92: 173

30161. 60599-2-RC: MOZART—Requiem. *Soloists; Bavarian Radio Orch. & Chorus; C. Davis, cond.*
• Fa 3-4/92: 264

30162. 60600-2-RC: MOZART—Piano concertos no. 12, 20. *Kissin, piano; Moscow Virtuosi; Spivakov, cond.*
+ Fa 1-2/93: 200

30163. 09026-60681-2 (2 discs): BERLIOZ—Roméo et Juliette; Nuits d'été. *Angeles, soprano; Vocal soloists; Boston Symphony Orch.; Munch, cond.* Reissues.
• Gr 4/93: 104

30164. 60681-2-RG (2 discs) BERLIOZ— Romeo et Juliette; Nuits d'été. *Angeles, Roggero, Chabay, Sze; Harvard Glee Club; Radcliffe Choral Society; Boston Symphony Orch.; Munch, cond.* Reissue.
+ ARG 7-8/92: 99
+ Fa 9-10/92: 213

30165. 09026-60682-2: BRAHMS— Symphony no. 2; Tragic overture. SCHUMANN—Genoveva: Overture. *Boston Symphony Orch.; Munch, cond.* Reissue.
+ ARG 9-10/92: 94
+ Fa 9-10/92: 201

30166. 09026-60683-2: CHAUSSON— Symphony in B♭, op. 20; Poème, for violin and orchestra. SAINT-SAËNS—

Introduction and rondo capriccioso, for violin and orchestra. *Boston Symphony Orch.; Munch, cond.; Oistrakh, violin.* Reissue.
+ ARG 9-10/92: 94
+ Fa 9-10/92: 213

30167. 09026-60684-2: DEBUSSY—Le martyre de St. Sebastien; Ibéria. *Kopleff, Akos, altos; Curtin, soprano; New England Conservatory Chorus; Boston Symphony Orch.; Munch, cond. and speaker.* Reissue.
+ ARG 11-12/92: 110
• Fa 9-10/92: 221

30168. 09026-60685-2: HONEGGER— Symphonies no. 2, 5. MILHAUD—La création du monde; Suite provençale. *Boston Symphony Orch.; Munch, cond.* Reissue.
+ ARG 9-10/92: 199
+ Fa 9-10/92: 264

30169. 60696-2-RC: INDY—Symphony on a French mountain air. DEBUSSY— Prelude to the afternoon of a faun; Reverie; Clair de lune. SATIE— Gnossiennes no. 1-3. SAINT-SAËNS—Mon coeur (arr. cello). *Henriot-Schweitzer, piano; Boston Symphony Orch.; Munch, cond.*
+ ARG 7-8/92: 152

30170. 09026-60704-2: Music of Bartók, Brahms, Chaminade, Falla, and Tchaikovsky. *Takezawa, violin; Moll, piano.*
+ Gr 2/93: 63

30171. 60704-2-RC: BARTÓK—Sonata for solo violin. TCHAIKOVSKY—Méditation. Music for violin and piano by Falla, Chaminade and Brahms. *Takezawa, violin; Moll, piano.*
+ ARG 7-8/92: 274
+ Fa 5-6/92: 264

30172. 09026-60705-2 (2 discs): VERDI—Falstaff. *Panerai, Titus, Lopardo, Sweet, Horne; Bavarian Radio Orch.; C. Davis, cond.*
- ARG 1-2/93: 161
• Fa 1-2/93: 259
• Gr 10/92: 183
• ON 1/16/93: 32
• Op 11/92: 1370
• St 7/93: 179

30173. 60709-2-RC: MOZART—Piano sonatas no. 3-4, 6, 15. *Larrocha, piano.*
• ARG 11-12/91: 121
+ Fa 11-12/91: 409
• Gr 10/91: 142

30174. 09026-60713-2: MOZART—Piano quartets no. 1-2. *Previn, piano; Kim, violin; Ohyama, viola; Hoffman, cello.*
• ARG 5-6/94: 116
- Fa 5-6/94: 202

30175. 60714-2-RC: MOZART— Symphonies no. 39, 41. *North German*

RCA

Radio Symphony Orch.; Wand, cond.
+ ARG 7-8/91: 97
+ DA 9/91: 66
+ Fa 7-8/91: 240
+ MA 7/91: 81
+ NYT 5/12/91: H34

30176. 60715-2-RC: Mozart—Symphonies no. 15, 24, 28-29. *Moscow Virtuosi; Spivakov, cond.*
+ Fa 11-12/91: 414
• Gr 11/91: 92

30177. 60717-2-RC: Dvořák—Cello concerto, op. 104. Bartók—Viola concerto. *Starker, cello; St. Louis Symphony Orch.; Slatkin, cond.*
+ ARG 1-2/92: 50
+ Fa 9-10/91: 203
+ Gr 3/92: 43

30178. 60718-2-RC: Bach—Violin concertos (complete); Concerto for 2 violins BWV 1043. *García, violin; Zukerman, violin & cond.; English Chamber Orch.*
+ ARG 5-6/92: 18
+ Fa 7-8/91: 99
• Gr 11/91: 82
• HPR v.8, no.3/91: 66
+ SR 8/91: 91

30179. 09026-60722-2: Haydn—Cello concertos. *Harnoy, cello; Toronto Chamber Orch.; Robinson, cond.*
- ARG 11-12/96: 141

30180. 60723-2-RC: Mozart—Clarinet concerto; Clarinet quintet. *Stoltzman, clarinet; English Chamber Orch.; Tokyo String Quartet.*
+ ARG 5-6/92: 94
• Fa 1-2/92: 270

30181. 09026-60729-2: Haydn—Symphonies no. 88, 95, 101. *Orch.; Reiner, cond. Reissues.*
+ ARG 9-10/93: 134
+ Fa 11-12/93: 271

30182. 60732-2-RC: Barber—Symphony no. 1, op. 9; Piano concerto, op. 38; Souvenirs, op. 28. *Browning, piano; St. Louis Symphony Orch.; Slatkin, piano & cond.*
+ ARG 11-12/91: 26
+ Fa 11-12/91: 253
+ Gr 11/91: 82

30183. 60735-2-RC: Mozart—Duos for violin and viola, K. 423-424. Leclair—Sonata for 2 violins, op. 3, no. 4. *Perlman, violin; Zukerman, violin or viola.*
+ ARG 5-6/92: 96
• Fa 3-4/92: 252
• Gr 12/91: 90

30184. 60737-2-RC: Sondheim—Assassins. *Original cast.*
+ ARG 1-2/92: 177
+ Gr 4/92: 165

+ ON 11/91: 41
+ St 9/92: 198

30185. 60739-2-RC: *Tchaikovsky gala in Leningrad.* Tchaikovsky—Eugene Onegin: Polonaise; Sérénade mélancolique; Valse scherzo; Chansons françaises no. 1, 6; Variations on a rococo theme; Jeanne d'Arc: Adieu, forêts; 1812 overture. *Leningrad Phil. Orch.; Temirkanov, cond.; Perlman, violin; Norman, soprano; Ma, cello.*
• ARG 5-6/92: 148
+ Fa 1-2/92: 347

30186. 60740-2-RC: Mozart—Violin sonatas, K. 454, K. 27, K. 303; Variations, K. 359. *Zukerman, violin; Neikrug, piano.*
+ Fa 11-12/91: 411
+ Gr 12/91: 93

30187. 09026-60742-2: Mozart—Violin sonatas K. 526, 304, 28, 30. *Zukerman, violin; Neikrug, piano.*
+ Fa 9-10/93: 223
- Gr 7/93: 60

30188. 60743-2-RC: Mozart—Violin sonatas, K. 301, 306, 378. *Zukerman, violin; Neikrug, piano.*
+ ARG 3-4/92: 111
+ Fa 3-4/92: 252
+ Gr 4/92: 98

30189. 09026-60744-2: Mozart—Violin sonatas K. 296, 26, 31, 9, 547. *Zukerman, violin; Neikrug, piano.*
• ARG 11-12/94: 163
• Fa 11-12/94: 318
+ Gr 10/94: 144

30190. 60749-2-RC: Bartók—Violin concerto no. 2; Viola concerto, op. posth.; Finale, Allegro molto, with alternate ending, for Violin concerto no. 2. *Zukerman, violin & viola; St. Louis Symphony Orch.; Slatkin, cond.*
+ ARG 3-4/92: 24
+ Fa 1-2/92: 155

30191. 60755-2-RC: Beethoven—Symphony no. 3; Leonore overture no. 3, op. 72a. *North German Radio Symphony Orch.; Wand, cond.*
• ARG 3-4/92: 32
+ Fa 1-2/92: 167
+ Gr 10/91: 74

30192. 60757-2-RC: Bloch—Schelomo. Bruch—Kol Nidrei; Canzone; Adagio on Celtic themes; Ave Maria. *Harnoy, cello; London Phil. Orch.; Mackerras, cond.*
• ARG 3-4/92: 34
+ Fa 11-12/91: 278
+ Gr 12/91: 64

30193. 60758-2-RC: Tchaikovsky—Variations on a Rococo theme; Transcriptions. *Harnoy, cello; London Phil. Orch.; Mackerras, cond.*
+ ARG 5-6/92: 148

+ Fa 7-8/92: 310
• Gr 10/92: 122

30194. 09026-60759-2: Tchaikovsky—Violin concerto. Prokofiev—Violin concerto no. 2. *Takezawa, violin; Moscow Radio Symphony Orch.; Fedoseyev, cond.*
• Gr 12/93: 78

30195. 60759-2-RC: Tchaikovsky—Violin concerto. Prokofiev—Violin concerto no. 2. *Takezawa, violin; Moscow Radio Symphony Orch.; Fedoseyev, cond.*
+ ARG 7-8/92: 236
+ Fa 1-2/92: 349
+ Fa 5-6/92: 264

30196. 09026-60764-2: Music of Ford, Castelnuovo-Tedesco, Carulli, Ruiz-Pipo, Petit, Gurdjieff, and Rodrigo. *Yepes, Monden, guitars.*
+ ARG 3-4/93: 163

30197. 60778-2-RC: *The American album.* Music of Copland, Gould, Sousa, Ives (arr. Schuman), Herbert, and others. *St. Louis Symphony Orch.; Slatkin, cond.*
+ ARG 9-10/91: 152
+ Fa 7-8/91: 390

30198. 60779-2-RC: Prokofiev—Piano sonatas no. 4, 7; Piano music. *Douglas, piano.*
• Fa 3-4/92: 287
+ Gr 3/92: 87

30199. 09026-60781-2: Dvořák—Piano concerto, op. 33. Janáček—Concertino for piano and chamber ensemble; Capriccio for piano left-hand, brass, and flute. *Firkušný, piano; Czech Phil. Orch.; Neumann, cond.*
+ ARG 11-12/92: 114
+ Fa 9-10/92: 226

30200. 60784-2-RC: Bruckner—Symphony no. 4. *NDR Symphony Orch.; Wand, cond.*
+ ARG 1-2/92: 40
+ Fa 9-10/91: 183
• Gr 10/91: 76

30201. 09026-60797-2: Haydn—Violin concertos, H. VIIa, 1; H. VIIa, 4; Symphony no. 22. *Zukerman, violin & cond.; National Arts Centre Orch.*
• ARG 9-10/93: 131
• Fa 7-8/93: 150

30202. 60798-2-RC: Piston—Symphony no. 6; Three New England sketches; The incredible flutist. *St. Louis Symphony Orch.; Slatkin, cond.*
+ ARG 5-6/92: 105
+ Fa 5-6/92: 221
+ Gr 1/92: 60
+ St 3/92: 179

30203. 60811-2-RC: Rossini—Twenty-four songs. *Horne, mezzo-soprano; Katz, piano.*

+ ARG 9-10/92: 151
+ Fa 7-8/92: 263
• Gr 4/92: 133
+ ON 12/5/92: 51

30204. 60812-2-RC: MOZART—Mass, K. 317; Exsultate jubilate; Ave verum corpus. *Kenny, soprano; London Voices; Philharmonia Orch.; Flor, cond.*
• ARG 7-8/92: 185
• Fa 7-8/92: 230

30205. 60813-2-RC: WALTON—Belshazzar's feast; Henry V: two pieces for strings; Partita for orchestra. *Allen, baritone; London Phil. Orch.; Slatkin, cond.*
+ ARG 11-12/92: 228
+ Fa 5-6/92: 284
+ Gr 9/92: 152

30206. 60817-2-RG: SAINT-SAËNS—Symphony no. 3. POULENC—Organ concerto. FRANCK—Le chasseur maudit. *Boston Symphony Orch.; Munch, cond.* Reissue.
+ ARG 3-4/92: 130
+ Fa 11-12/91: 467

30207. 60818-2-RG: Duets from Semiramide, Anna Bolena, Norma, Tales of Hoffmann, Aida, Madama Butterfly, and La gioconda. *Caballé, Verrett, vocalists; Philharmonia Orch.; Guadagno, cond.* Recorded 1969.
+ ARG 5-6/92: 185
+ Gr 5/92: 117

30208. 09026-60823-2: *Czech songs.* Music of Dvořák, Martinů, and Janáček. *Benackova, soprano; Firkušný, piano.*
+ ARG 3-4/94: 226
+ Fa 1-2/94: 366
+ Gr 1/94: 81
+ ON 12/11/93: 47

30209. 60825-2-RC: MOZART—Piano concertos no. 9, 21. *Larrocha, piano; English Chamber Orch.; C. Davis, cond.*
+ Fa 3-4/92: 248
• Gr 1/92: 59

30210. 60826-2-RC: SCHUMANN—Symphony no. 4. SCHUBERT—Symphony no. 8. *North German Radio Orch.; Wand, cond.*
- ARG 7-8/92: 224
+ Gr 5/92: 48

30211. 09026-60848-2: PROKOFIEV—Romeo and Juliet: 10 pieces for piano, op. 75; Piano sonata no. 8. *Edelmann, piano.*
+ Fa 5-6/93: 283

30212. 60855-2-RC: BERG—Lyric suite. VERDI—String quartet. *Vogler Quartet.*
+ ARG 7-8/92: 97
+ Fa 3-4/92: 153
• Gr 12/91: 88

30213. 60856-2-RC: SCHUMANN—Kinderszenen; Papillons; Fantasy, op. 17.

Oppitz, piano.
+ Fa 5-6/92: 251
• Gr 1/92: 79

30214. 60857-2-RC: WOLF—Italienisches Liederbuch. *Ziesak, soprano; Schmidt, baritone; Eisenlohr, Jansen, piano.*
+ ARG 5-6/92: 158
+ Fa 3-4/92: 365
• Gr 12/91: 118

30215. 60858-2-RC: *Classic trumpet.* Concertos by J. Haydn, Hummel, Neruda and M. Haydn. *Touvron, trumpet & cond.; Prague Chamber Orch.*
+ ARG 5-6/92: 169
+ Fa 3-4/92: 411

30216. 09026-60859-2: BRAHMS—Piano sonata no. 1. LISZT—Consolation no. 6; Hungarian rhapsody no. 17; Transcendental etude no. 11; Scherzo and march. *Richter, piano.* Recorded live 1988.
• ARG 1-2/93: 81
+ Fa 11-12/92: 208
+ Gr 4/92: 110

30217. 60865-2-RG (2 discs): LEONCAVALLO—Pagliacci. PUCCINI—Il Tabarro. *Caballé, Price, Domingo, Milnes; John Alldis Choir; London Symphony Orch.; Philharmonia Orch.; Santi, Leinsdorf, conds.* Reissues.
+ ARG 7-8/92: 162
+ Fa 3-4/92: 225
+ Op 8/92: 1000

30218. 09026-60868-2: BRAHMS—Ein deutsches Requiem. *Blasi, soprano; Terfel, bass-baritone; Bavarian Radio Orch. & Chorus; C. Davis, cond.*
• ARG 5-6/94: 74
+ Fa 3-4/94: 145
• Gr 5/93: 81

30219. 60870-2-RG: *Dancin'.* Percussion music with orchestra. *Glennie, percussion; National Phil. Orch.; Wordsworth, cond.*
• Gr 1/92: 80

30220. 09026-60873-2: MOZART—Serenades no. 10, 12. *Bavarian Radio Symphony Orch.; C. Davis, cond.* Recorded live.
+ ARG 1-2/93: 127
• Fa 1-2/93: 202

30221. 09026-60874-2: STRAUSS—Selections from Elektra and Salome. *Borkh, Yeend, Schoeffler; Chicago Lyric Opera Chorus; Chicago Symphony Orch.; Reiner, cond.* Reissues.
+ Gr 5/93: 106

30222. 60887-2-RC: SHOSTAKOVICH—Symphony no. 4. *St. Louis Symphony Orch.; Slatkin, cond.*
+ Fa 5-6/92: 254
• Gr 6/92: 48

30223. 09026-60893-2: MENDELSSOHN—Symphonies no. 3-4. *Bamberg Symphony Orch.; Flor, cond.*
• ARG 9-10/94: 162
• Fa 9-10/94: 255

30224. 60895-2-RC: TURINA—Danzas fantasticas; Sinfonia Sevillana; Procesion del rocio; Ritmos. *Bamberg Symphony Orch.; Almeida, cond.*
+ ARG 9-10/92: 177
+ Fa 11-12/92: 393
+ Gr 7/92: 62

30225. 60897-2-RG: GRIEG—Piano concerto; Ballade; Lyric pieces. *Rubinstein, piano; Philadelphia Orch.; Ormandy, cond.* Reissues.
+ ARG 7-8/92: 290
• Fa 7-8/92: 167

30226. 09026-60898-2 (2 discs): PUCCINI—Turandot. *Marton, Heppner, M. Price; Bavarian Radio Chorus; Munich Radio Orch.; R. Abbado, cond.*
• ARG 3-4/94: 138
- Fa 1-2/94: 267
• Gr 12/93: 115
• ON 1/8/94: 34

30227. 09026-60899-2: DEBUSSY—Ariettes oubliées; Cinq poèmes de Baudelaire; Chansons de Bilitis. RAVEL—Histoires naturelles. *Stutzmann, alto; C. Collard, piano.*
+ ARG 1-2/93: 89
+ Fa 11-12/92: 224
+ Gr 7/92: 86

30228. 09026-60900-2: BACH—Orchestral suite no. 2, BWV 1067; Concerto for flute and orchestra, BWV 1032; Concerto for flute, violin, harpsichord and orchestra, BWV 1044. *Galway, flute; Wolters, violin; Duetschler, harpsichord; Württemberg Chamber Orch.; Faerber, cond.*
• ARG 3-4/93: 53
+ Fa 3-4/93: 113
+ Gr 6/93: 37

30229. 09026-60901-2: BRAHMS—Songs. *M. Price, soprano; Johnson, piano.*
+ ARG 7-8/94: 81
+ Fa 7-8/94: 92
+ Gr 5/94: 89

30230. 09026-60902-2 (2 discs): VERDI—Requiem. *Vaness, Quivar, O'Neill, Colombara; Bavarian Radio Symphony Orch. & Chorus; Davis, cond.*
- ARG 9-10/93: 214
- Fa 7-8/93: 262
• Gr 1/93: 58

30231. 09026-60903-2: BACH—St. John Passion, BWV 245. *Ahnsjö, tenor; Scharinger, bass; Nielsen, soprano; Stutzmann, alto; Swensen, tenor; Quasthoff, bass; Chorgemeinschaft Neubeuern; Bach-Collegium München; Guttenberg, cond.*
+ ARG 11-12/92: 74

• Fa 9-10/92: 169
- Gr 10/92: 158

30232. 09026-60919-2: BACH—
Harpsichord works. *Landowska, harpsichord.* Reissue.
+ Fa 9-10/92: 165
+ Gr 3/93: 111

30233. 60920-2-RG: TCHAIKOVSKY—
Symphony no. 6; Romeo and Juliet. *Boston Symphony Orch.; Koussevitzky, cond.* Reissue.
• Fa 7-8/92: 309

30234. 09026-60922-2: BACH—
Stokowski transcriptions. *Stokowski Orch.; Stokowski, cond.*
• ARG 9-10/92: 213
+ Fa 9-10/92: 170

30235. 09026-60926-2: BEETHOVEN—
Piano trio, op. 97. SCHUBERT—Piano trio no. 1. *Rubinstein, piano; Heifetz, violin; Feuermann, cello.*
+ ARG 9-10/92: 218
• Fa 9-10/92: 187
+ Fa 11-12/92: 504

30236. 09026-60927-2: BRUCH—Violin concerto no. 2. CONUS—Violin concerto. WIENIAWSKI—Violin concerto no. 2. TCHAIKOVSKY—Sérénade mélancolique. *Heifetz, violin; RCA Victor Symphony Orch.; Solomon, cond.; Los Angeles Phil. Orch.; Wallenstein, cond.*
+ ARG 9-10/92: 222
+ Fa 9-10/92: 431

30237. 09026-60929-2 (2 discs): STRAUSS—Ein Heldenleben; Also sprach Zarathustra; Don Quixote; Death and transfiguration; Aus Italien: On the shores of Sorrento. *New York Phil.; Mengelberg, Beecham, conds.; Boston Symphony Orch.; Koussevitzky, cond.; Philadelphia Orch.; Stokowski, cond.; Chicago Symphony Orch.; Stock, cond.* Reissue.
+ ARG 9-10/92: 213
+ Fa 9-10/92: 362
+ Fa 9-10/92: 366
+ Gr 11/92: 222
+ St 10/29: 275

30238. 09026-60930-2: STRAUSS—Also sprach Zarathustra; Le bourgeois gentilhomme: suite; Der Rosenkavalier: waltzes. *Chicago Symphony Orch.; Reiner, cond.* Reissue.
+ ARG 11-12/92: 84
• Fa 9-10/92: 362
+ Gr 12/92: 88

30239. 09026-60940-2: MOZART—
Quintets for 2 violins, 2 violas and cello no. 3-4. *Tokyo String Quartet; Zukerman, viola.*
+ ARG 11-12/93: 157
+ Fa 5-6/93: 274
• Gr 1/93: 46

30240. 09026-60941-2 (2 discs): *Rarities.* Music of Rossini, Donizetti, and Verdi.

Caballé; with orch. acc. Reissues.
+ ARG 11-12/92: 258
+ Fa 3-4/93: 333
+ Gr 11/92: 184

30241. 60942-2-RG: LALO—Symphonie espagnole. BRUCH—Scottish fantasy. *Meyers, violin; Royal Phil. Orch.; López Cobos, cond.*
+ ARG 7-8/92: 111
+ Fa 7-8/92: 197
+ Gr 9/92: 45

30242. 09026-60950-2: *Jugenstil-Lieder.* Music of Berg, Schoenberg, Pfitzner, Schreker, and R. Strauss. *Popp, soprano; Gage, piano.*
+ Fa 9-10/92: 397
+ Gr 4/92: 149

30243. 60950-2-RC: *Jugendstil-Lieder.* Songs by Schoenberg, Berg, Pfitzner, Schreker, and Strauss. *Popp, soprano; Gage, piano.*
+ ARG 1-2/93: 144

30244. 09026-60953-2: LISZT—Concertos for piano and orchestra no. 1-2; Hungarian fantasy for piano and orchestra. *Oppitz, piano; Bamberg Symphony Orch.; R. Abbado, cond.*
+ ARG 9-10/92: 125
+ Fa 9-10/92: 275
• Gr 6/92: 44

30245. 09026-60954-2: LISZT—Variations on Weinen, klagen, sorgen, zagen; Légendes: St. François d'Assise: la prédication aux oiseaux; St. François de Paule marchant sur les flots; Consolations; Ballade no. 2. *Oppitz, piano.*
+ ARG 9-10/92: 125
• Fa 9-10/92: 275
+ Gr 9/92: 135

30246. 60957-2-RC: SIBELIUS—Violin concerto. SCHNITTKE—Concerto grosso no. 1. *Kremer, Grindenko, violins; London Symphony Orch.; Rozhdestvensky, cond.*
+ ARG 11-12/92: 205
- Gr 9/92: 90

30247. 09026-60962-2: BEETHOVEN—
Symphony no. 3; Coriolan overture; Fidelio overture, op. 72b. *Chicago Symphony Orch.; Reiner, cond.*
• ARG 11-12/92: 84
+ Fa 9-10/92: 180
+ Gr 12/92: 73
+ St 1/93: 267

30248. 09026-60963—60964-2 (2 separate discs): RODGERS—Victory at sea; More victory at sea. *Bennett, cond.* Reissue.
+ ARG 11-12/92: 186

30249. 09026-60967-2 (2 discs): BEETHOVEN—Missa solemnis; Choral fantasy. *Orgonasova, soprano; Rappé, mezzo-soprano; Heilmann, tenor;*

Rootering, bass; Oppitz, piano; Bavarian Radio Symphony Orch.; C. Davis, cond.
+ Fa 5-6/94: 105
• Gr 3/94: 88

30250. 09026-60970-2: *Songs and psalms of the divine.* Music of Hancock, R. Strauss, Schütz, A. Scarlatti, Bruckner, Gabrieli, Schoenberg, Tallis, and Thompson. *Futral, soprano; Malafronte, mezzo-soprano; Urrey, tenor; Pauley, bass; Musica Sacra; Westenburg, cond.*
+ ARG 3-4/93: 182
+ Fa 1-2/93: 286
+ Gr 1/93: 58

30251. 09026-60971-2 (2 discs): BACH—The six sonatas and partitas for solo violin, BWV 1001-06. *Ughi, violin.*
+ Fa 7-8/93: 98

30252. 60972-2-RC (3 discs): BEETHOVEN—String quartets no. 12-16; Grosse Fuge. *Tokyo String Quartet.*
+ ARG 7-8/92: 91

30253. 09026-60973-2: Music of Beethoven, Brahms, Chopin, Debussy, Liszt, Mozart, Rachmaninoff, Schubert, Schumann, and Tchaikovsky. *Cliburn, piano.*
+ ARG 11-12/92: 247

30254. 09026-60977-2: SCHUMANN—Carnaval; Waldszenen; Nachtstücke. *Oppitz, piano.*
- ARG 5-6/93: 133
+ Fa 5-6/93: 318
- Gr 5/93: 74

30255. 60978-2-RC: SCHUBERT—Symphony no. 9. *North German Radio Symphony Orch.; Wand, cond.*
+ ARG 7-8/92: 219
+ Fa 5-6/92: 247
+ Gr 1/92: 60

30256. 60983-2-RC: *American portraits.* Music of Copland, Schuman, Sousa, Thomson, Herbert and others. *N. Schwarzkopf, narrator; St. Louis Symphony Orch.; Slatkin, cond.*
+ Fa 5-6/92: 342
• Gr 9/92: 98

30257. 60984-2-RC: PROKOFIEV—Symphony no. 5; Lt. Kijé: Suite. *Leningrad Phil. Orch.; Temirkanov, cond.*
• ARG 11-12/92: 180
+ Fa 7-8/92: 248
- Gr 9/92: 80

30258. 09026-60985-2: RAVEL—Concertos for piano; Valses nobles et sentimentales; Sonatine. *Larrocha, piano; St. Louis Symphony Orch.; Slatkin, cond.*
• ARG 3-4/94: 141
• Fa 3-4/94: 287
• Gr 12/93: 76

30259. 09026-60988-2: SCHUBERT (ARR. MAHLER)—Quartet no. 14 "Death and the maiden." BEETHOVEN (ARR. MAHLER)—Quartet no. 11. *Moscow Chamber Soloists; Bashmet, cond.*
+ ARG 9-10/92: 154
• Fa 9-10/92: 343

30260. 09026-60989-2: MOZART—Piano concertos no. 23-24. *Larrocha, piano; English Chamber Orch,.; C. Davis, cond.*
• Fa 1-2/93: 201
• Gr 3/93: 48

30261. 09026-60990-2: TCHAIKOVSKY—Violin concerto. PROKOFIEV—Violin concerto no. 1. *Spivakov, violin; Royal Phil. Orch.; Temirkanov, cond.*
+ ARG 7-8/93: 167
+ Fa 7-8/93: 255
- Gr 12/93: 78

30262. 09026-60991-2 (4 discs): BEETHOVEN—The sonatas for violin and piano. *Zukerman, violin; Neikrug, piano.*
+ ARG 9-10/92: 78
+ Fa 9-10/92: 177
• Gr 7/92: 66

30263. 09026-60992-2 (3 discs): TCHAIKOVSKY—Queen of spades. *Freni, Forrester, K. Ciesinski, Atlantov, Hvorostovsky; Boston Symphony Orch.; Ozawa, cond.*
+ ARG 1-2/93: 155
• Fa 1-2/93: 253
+ Gr 11/92: 191
+ ON 12/19/92: 38
• Op 11/92: 1369

30264. 09026-60993-2: STRAVINSKY—Le sacre du printemps. GINASTERA—Popul vuh. HAYDN—The creation: representation of chaos. *St. Louis Symphony Orch.; Slatkin, cond.*
• ARG 5-6/93: 141
- Fa 5-6/93: 334
+ Gr 5/93: 44

30265. 09026-61044-2 (2 discs): Eternal Caballé. *Caballé, soprano; with orch. or piano accomp.*
+ ARG 1-2/94: 189
+ Gr 11/92: 195
+ ON 12/10/94: 52

30266. 09026-61153-2: *Francisco Araiza: Romantic tenor.* Songs and arias. *Araiza, tenor; Bavarian Radio Orch.; Weikert, cond.*
• ARG 7-8/93: 202

30267. 09026-61160-2: *The last recital for Israel.* Music of Beethoven, Schumann, Debussy, and Chopin. *Rubinstein, piano.*
+ Fa 5-6/93: 383
+ Gr 3/93: 76
+ St 4/93: 295

30268. 09026-61163-2: *The romantic tenor.* Music of Léhar, Rossini, Bernstein, Chopin, and others. *Araiza,*

tenor; Munich Radio Symphony Orch.; Weikert, cond.
• Gr 3/93: 100

30269. 09026-61164-2: Music of Pergolesi, Galuppi, Picentino, Gianella, and Tartini. *Galway, flute; I Solisti Veneti; Scimone, cond.*
+ Fa 3-4/94: 441
+ Gr 4/94: 52

30270. 09026-61173-2: RIMSKY-KORSAKOV—Scheherazade; Russian Easter overture. *New York Phil.; Temirkanov, cond.*
+ ARG 9-10/93: 177
+ Fa 7-8/93: 216
• Gr 5/93: 50

30271. 09026-61179-2: SCHOENBERG—Pierrot lunaire; Chamber symphony no. 1. *Bryn-Julson, Sprechstimme; Wiesner, flute, piccolo; Diry, clarinet; Stryi, bass clarinet; Rundel, violin; Dickel, viola; Stirling, cello; Kretzschmar, piano; Ensemble Modern; Eötvös, cond.*
+ ARG 11-12/93: 185
+ Fa 11-12/93: 378

30272. 09026-61180-2: NANCARROW—Studies for player piano; Tango; Toccata; Piece no. 2 for small orchestra; Trio; Sarabande and scherzo. *Ensemble Modern; Metzmacher, cond.*
+ ARG 11-12/93: 160
+ Fa 1-2/94: 252
+ Gr 11/93: 74

30273. 09026-61181-2: ZIMMERMANN—Antiphonen; Omnia tempus habent; Présence. *T. Zimmermann, viola; Moffat, soprano; Rundel, violin; Stirling, cello; Kretzschmar, piano; Ensemble Modern; Zender, cond.*
+ ARG 5-6/97: 239
+ Fa 1-2/97: 306
+ Gr 2/97: 62

30274. 09026-61184-2: MAHLER—Songs (orch. Berio). STRAUSS—Songs. *Schmidt, baritone; Berlin Radio Symphony Orch.; Garben, cond.*
+ ARG 9-10/94: 155
- Fa 9-10/94: 244
+ Gr 8/94: 91
+ ON 10/94: 52

30275. 09026-61185-2: BARTÓK—String quartet no. 2, op. 17 "Rasoumovsky." BEETHOVEN—String quartet no. 7, op. 59, no. 1. *Vogler Quartet.*
+ ARG 3-4/93: 55
+ Fa 3-4/93: 116
• Gr 12/92: 93

30276. 09026-61186-2: *Windows.* Music of Eben, Jolivet, Genzmer, Constant, and Langlais. *Touvron, trumpet; Krapp, organ.*
+ ARG 11-12/93: 103
+ Gr 9/93: 82

30277. 09026-61187-2: SCHUMANN—Frauenliebe und Leben; Aus dem Liederbuch eines Malers; Dichterliebe. *Stutzmann, alto; Collard, piano.*
+ ARG 11-12/93: 193
+ Fa 11-12/93: 387
• Gr 8/93: 73

30278. 09026-61190-2: TCHAIKOVSKY—Symphony no. 6 "Pathétique." STRAVINSKY—Pulcinella: suite. *NDR Symphony Orch.; Wand, cond.* Recorded live.
• ARG 5-6/93: 146
+ Fa 3-4/93: 313
• Gr 4/93: 62

30279. 09026-61191-2: *Gala lirica.* Music of Gimenez, Verdi, Serrano, Bizet, Donizetti, Puccini, Massenet, Rossini, Catalani, Sorozabal, and Barbieri. *Various Spanish vocalists.* Recorded live at the inauguration of the Gran Teatro de la Maestranza, Seville, May 10, 1991.
- ARG 9-10/92: 205
- Fa 9-10/92: 404
• ON 3/27/93: 35

30280. 09026-61193-2: VAUGHAN WILLIAMS—Norfolk rhapsody no. 1; Fantasia on a theme by Thomas Tallis; A London symphony. *Philharmonia Orch.; Slatkin, cond.*
+ Fa 11-12/93: 428
• Gr 8/93: 41

30281. 09026-61194-2: VAUGHAN WILLIAMS—A pastoral symphony; Symphony no. 4. *Hohenfeld, soprano; Philharmonia Orch.; Slatkin, cond.*
+ ARG 11-12/93: 213
+ Fa 11-12/93: 428
+ Gr 11/93: 85

30282. 09026-61195-2: VAUGHAN WILLIAMS—Sea songs: quick march; Five variants of Dives and Lazarus; Sinfonia Antartica. *Hohenfeld, soprano; Women of the Philharmonia Chorus; Philharmonia Orch.; Slatkin, cond.*
• ARG 11-12/93: 213
+ Fa 11-12/93: 428

30283. 09026-61196-2: VAUGHAN WILLIAMS—Flourish for glorious John; Symphonies no. 8-9. *Philharmonia Orch.; Slatkin, cond.*
• ARG 11-12/93: 213
+ Fa 11-12/93: 428
+ Gr 8/93: 41

30284. 09026-61197-2: VAUGHAN WILLIAMS—A sea symphony. *Valente, soprano; Allen, baritone; Philharmonia Chorus & Orch.; Slatkin, cond.*
• ARG 1-2/94: 167
+ Fa 11-12/93: 428
• Gr 2/94: 54

30285. 09026-61200-2: MOLTER—Concertos for 2 trumpets, strings and continuo; Concertos in D for trumpet, strings and continuo (selections).

RCA

Messler, Touvron, trumpets; Württemberg Chamber Orch. of Heilbronn; Faerber, cond.
- • ARG 3-4/93: 114
- + Fa 3-4/93: 231
- + Gr 5/93: 48

30286. 09026-61201-2: BRAHMS— Schicksalslied; Alto rhapsody; Nänie; Gesang der Parzen; Marienlieder. *Stutzmann, alto; Bavarian Radio Orch.; C. Davis, cond.*
- • ARG 9-10/93: 99
- + Fa 9-10/93: 131
- • Gr 5/93: 81

30287. 61203-2-RC: BERLIOZ— Symphonie fantastique; Overture: Béatrice et Bénédict. *Royal Phil. Orch.; Temirkanov, cond.*
- - ARG 9-10/92: 84
- + Fa 11-12/92: 200
- • Gr 11/92: 57

30288. 09026-61204-2: *From the offical Barcelona Games ceremony.* Music of Bellini, Massenet, Verdi, Rossini, Leoncavallo, Donizetti, and others. *Caballé, Berganza, Aragall, Carreras, Domingo, Pons; City of Barcelona Symphony Orch.; García Navarro, cond.*
- - Fa 1-2/93: 283
- - Gr 11/92: 196
- • ON 3/27/93: 35

30289. 09026-61205-2: HANDEL—Opera arias. *Stutzmann, alto; Hanover Band; Goodman, cond.*
- + ARG 3-4/94: 84
- + Fa 1-2/93: 159
- + Gr 3/93: 94

30290. 09026-61210-2: Music of Sarasate, Wieniawski, Ravel, Chausson, and others. *E. Friedman, violin; London Symphony Orch.; Sargent, cond; Chicago Symphony Orch.; Hendl, cond.* Reissue.
- + Gr 8/93: 45

30291. 61210-2-RC: Music of Sarasate, Wieniawski, Saint-Saëns, Chausson, Ravel, and Paganini. *E. Friedman, violin; London Symphony Orch.; Sargent, cond.; Chicago Symphony Orch.; Hendl, cond.* Reissue.
- + ARG 11-12/92: 250

30292. 09026-61214-2: Arias from Martha, La clemenza di Tito, Don Giovanni, Fidelio, and others. *Seiffert, tenor; Munich Radio Orch.; Kout, cond.*
- • ARG 1-2/95: 244
- • ON 4/15/95: 35

30293. 09026-61215-2: PERGOLESI— Stabat mater; Salve regina. *Norberg-Schulz, soprano; Stutzmann, contralto; Hanover Band; Goodman, cond.*
- + ARG 3-4/94: 132
- + Gr 1/94: 86

30294. 09026-61219-2: BEETHOVEN— Violin concerto; Violin sonata no. 10.

Zukerman, violin; Los Angeles Phil. Orch.; Mehta, cond.; Neikrug, piano.
- + ARG 3-4/93: 56
- • Fa 1-2/93: 104
- + Gr 11/92: 56

30295. 09026-61220-2: MARTINŮ— Sonatas for cello and piano no. 1-3. *Starker, cello; Firkušný, piano.*
- • ARG 3-4/93: 108
- + Fa 3-4/93: 217

30296. 09026-61221-2: LISZT—Piano sonata in B minor; Nuages gris; Richard Wagner: Venezia; Schlaflos, Frage und Antwort; Elegy no. 2. BERG—Piano sonata, op. 1. WEBERN—Piano variations, op. 27. *Douglas, piano.*
- • ARG 3-4/93: 169
- + Fa 3-4/93: 208
- + Gr 12/92: 108

30297. 09026-61222-2: IVES—Three places in New England; March III with the air "Old Kentucky home"; The unanswered question; Central Park in the dark; Fugue on four keys on "The shining shore"; Symphony no. 3 "The camp meeting". *St. Louis Symphony Orch.; Slatkin, cond.*
- + ARG 3-4/93: 96
- + Fa 3-4/93: 196
- + Gr 4/93: 51

30298. 09026-61225-2: SCHUMANN— Dichterliebe; Romanzen und Balladen, op. 53; Belsatzar; Liederkreis, op. 39. *Quasthoff, baritone; Szidon, piano.*
- + ARG 3-4/94: 152
- + Fa 3-4/94: 314
- • Gr 2/94: 90

30299. 09026-61226-2: BRITTEN— Sinfonia da requiem; Young person's guide to the orchestra; Peter Grimes: four sea interludes. PURCELL—Chaconny. *London Phil. Orch.; Slatkin, cond.*
- + ARG 5-6/94: 80
- + Fa 3-4/94: 151
- + Gr 3/94: 42

30300. 09026-61228-2: BOCCHERINI— Cello concerto in B♭. MYSLIVEČEK—Cello concerto. VIOTTI—Cello concerto. *Harnoy, cello; I Solisti Veneti; Scimone, cond.*
- + ARG 9-10/93 230
- + Fa 7-8/93: 291
- + Gr 8/93: 25

30301. 09026-61234-2 (2 discs): BERLIOZ—L'enfance du Christ; Nuits d'été. *Kopleff, Valletti, Souzay, Tozzi; New England Conservatory Chorus; Boston Symphony Orch.; Munch, cond.; Price, Chicago Symphony Orch.; Reiner, cond.* Reissues.
- + ARG 11-12/92: 87
- • Fa 1-2/93: 113
- • Gr 12/92: 114

30302. 09026-61236-2 (4 discs): Leontyne Price: The prima donna

collection. *L. Price, soprano; with orch. accomp.* Reissues.
- + ARG 1-2/93: 193
- + Fa 1-2/93: 277
- + Gr 12/92: 142

30303. 09026-61245-2: *Ezio Pinza.* Music of Tosti, Puccini, Thomas, Mozart, Gounod, Bellini, Verdi, Monteverdi, Handel, Legrenzi, Scarlatti, Cavalli, Torelli, Paisiello, Giordani, Falconieri, Sarti, Buononcini, Rossini, Mussorgsky, and Weill. *Pinza, bass; Kitzinger, piano; orch. acc.*
- + ARG 7-8/93: 217
- • Fa 7-8/93: 286
- + Gr 9/93: 125
- + ON 10/93: 37

30304. 09026-61246-2: TCHAIKOVSKY— Symphony no. 6; 1812 overture. LISZT— Mephisto waltz. *Chicago Symphony Orch.; Reiner, cond.* Reissue.
- + ARG 7-8/96: 211

30305. 09026-61249-2: *Marches in Hi-fi.* Music of Verdi, Herbert, Sousa, Tchaikovsky, Berlioz, and others. *Boston Pops Orch.; Fiedler, cond.* Reissue.
- + ARG 9-10/93: 223

30306. 09026-61251-2: Music of Bach, Handel, Boyce, Mulet, Purcell, Schumann, and Widor. *Fox, organ.* Reissue.
- + ARG 5-6/93: 155
- • ARG 7-8/93: 195

30307. 09026-61253-2: FOSTER—Songs. *Robert Shaw Chorale.* Reissue.
- + ARG 9-10/93: 121

30308. 09026-61255-2: Music of Sousa, Gould, Bagley, Goldman, Emmett and Meacham. *M. Gould and his symphonic band.* Reissue.
- + ARG 5-6/93: 155
- + ARG 7-8/93: 190

30309. 09026-61260-2 (3 discs): BEETHOVEN—Piano concertos. *Rubinstein, piano; Symphony of the Air; Krips, cond.* Reissues.
- • Gr 4/93: 42

30310. 09026-61261-2: Music of Albeniz, Falla, Granados, and Mompou. *Rubinstein, piano.* Reissues.
- + ARG 3-4/93: 195
- + Gr 9/93: 122

30311. 09026-61263-2: BRAHMS—Piano concerto no. 1; Piano music. *Rubinstein, piano; Chicago Symphony Orch.; Reiner, cond.* Reissues.
- + Gr 2/93: 38

30312. 09026-61264-2: SCHUMANN— Kreisleriana; Fantasy, op. 17. *Rubinstein, piano.* Reissue.
- + Gr 3/93: 75

30313. 09026-61265-2 (10 discs): Sergei Rachmaninoff: the complete recordings, 1919-42. *Rachmaninoff, piano; in part with instrumental and orch. accomp.* Reissues.
+ Fa 1-2/93: 302
+ Gr 3/93: 108

30314. 09026-61266-2 (3 discs): HANDEL—Messiah. *Vyvyan, Sinclair, Vickers, Tozzi; Royal Phil. Chorus & Orch.; Beecham, cond.* Recorded 1959.
+ ARG 11-12/92: 129
+ Fa 11-12/92: 249

30315. 61272-2-RC: *Hark!* Christmas music. *Stoltzman, clarinet; Mitchell, harp; Guildhall String Ensemble; Boys' Choir of Harlem; Kalmen Opperman Clarinet Choir.*
+ ARG 11-12/92: 266

30316. 61273-2-RC: SHOSTAKOVICH—Viola sonata. GLINKA—Viola sonata. ROSLAVETS—Viola sonata. *Bashmet, viola; Muntian, piano.* Recorded live.
+ ARG 1-2/93: 148
+ Fa 3-4/93: 290
+ Gr 3/93: 63

30317. 09026-61274-2: BACH—Three sonatas for flute and harpsichord obbligato, BWV 1030-1032; Three sonatas for flute and continuo, BWV 1033-1035. *Petri, recorder; Jarrett, harpsichord.*
+ ARG 3-4/93: 52
+ Fa 3-4/93: 113
+ Gr 2/93: 52

30318. 09026-61275-2: *Strings! the definitive collection.* Music of Pachelbel, Vivaldi, Hofstetter, Elgar, Purcell, and others. *Guildhall String Ensemble; Salter, cond.*
+ Gr 2/94: 58

30319. 09026-61276-2: BRAHMS—Viola sonatas; Songs with viola. *Horne, mezzo-soprano; Zukerman, viola; Neikrug, Katz, piano.*
• ARG 9-10/94: 108
+ Fa 9-10/94: 153
+ Gr 9/94: 71

30320. 09026-61277-2: *Rebounds.* Music of Milhaud, R.R. Bennett, Rosauro, and Miyoshi. *Glennie, percussion; Scottish Chamber Orch.; Daniel, cond.*
+ ARG 3-4/93: 165
+ Fa 3-4/93: 370
+ Gr 4/93: 73

30321. 61278-2-RC: *Lullabies.* Tradional music of Wales, West Indies, France, Denmark, etc.; music of Canteloube, Bach, Spohr, Brahms, and others. *Horne, mezzo-soprano; with accomp.*
• ARG 1-2/93: 193

30322. 09026-61279-2: SCHUMANN—Piano quintet; Piano concerto. *Larrocha, piano; Tokyo String Quartet; London Symphony Orch.; Davis, cond.*
• ARG 7-8/93: 154
• Fa 7 8/93: 239
+ Gr 5/93: 67

30323. 09026-61280-2: BEETHOVEN—Piano sonatas no. 21, 23, 27. *Douglas, piano.*
- ARG 1-2/94: 73
• Fa 9-10/93: 119
+ Gr 6/94: 81

30324. 09026-61281-2: RACHMANINOFF—Symphony no. 2; Vocalise. *St. Petersburg Phil. Orch.; Temirkanov, cond.*
• ARG 11-12/94: 172
• Fa 11-12/94: 350
• Gr 9/94: 60

30325. 09026-61282-2: SCHUMAN—Symphony no. 10 "American muse;" New England triptych; American festival overture. IVES (ARR. SCHUMAN)—Variations on America. *St. Louis Symphony Orch.; Slatkin, cond.*
+ ARG 9-10/92: 159
+ Fa 9-10/92: 347
+ Gr 5/93: 51
+ St 3/93: 187

30326. 09026-61283-2: FRANCK—Sonata for violin and piano. R. STRAUSS—Sonata for violin and piano, op. 18. *Meyers, violin; De Silva, piano.*
+ Fa 5-6/93: 205

30327. 09026-61284-2 (3 discs): BEETHOVEN—String quartet op. 18; Quartet after op. 14, no. 1; String quintet. *Tokyo String Quartet; Zukerman, viola.*
+ ARG 9-10/93: 93
+ Fa 9-10/93: 117
+ Gr 9/93: 71

30328. 09026-61349-2: BRAHMS—German Requiem. *Battle, Hagegård; Chicago Symphony Orch.; Levine, cond.* Reissue.
+ ARG 5-6/93: 74

30329. 09026-61350-2: PROKOFIEV—Symphonies no. 1, 5. *St. Louis Symphony Orch.; Slatkin, cond.* Reissue.
• ARG 3-4/93: 125
+ ARG 9-10/93: 169
+ Fa 5-6/93: 284
• Gr 3/93: 51

30330. 09026-61354-2: MUSSORGSKY—Night on bald mountain; Orchestral and choral works. *Gal, contralto; London Symphony Orch.; Abbado, cond.* Reissue.
+ ARG 5-6/93: 113
+ Fa 7-8/93: 191
+ Gr 6/93: 51

30331. 09026-61356-2: *Domingo sings Caruso.* Music of Leoncavallo, Donizetti, Massenet, Cilea, Flotow and others. *Domingo, tenor; with orch. acc.* Reissues.
+ ARG 3-4/93: 184

30332. 09026-61357-2: MOZART—Vocal music. *L. Price, soprano; with orch. acc.*
+ Fa 3-4/93: 241
+ Gr 6/93: 87

30333. 09026-61360-2: COPLAND—Clarinet concerto. STRAVINSKY—Ebony concerto. BERNSTEIN—Prelude, fugue and riffs. CORIGLIANO—Clarinet concerto. *Stoltzman, clarinet; London Symphony Orch.; Smith, cond.; Woody Herman's Thundering Herd.* Reissue.
+ ARG 11-12/93: 95

30334. 61367-2-RC: Peace on earth: A Bavarian Christmas. *Various performers.*
• ARG 11-12/92: 264

30335. 09026-61370-2 (2 discs): HINDEMITH—Kammermusiken no. 1-7. *Wiget, piano; Stirling, cello; Rundel, violin; Dickel, viola; Just, viola d'amore; Lücker, organ; Ensemble Modern; Stenz, cond.*
+ ARG 3-4/96: 127
• Fa 3-4/96: 183
• Gr 1/96: 52

30336. 61370-2-RC: *Standing room only.* Excerpts from Phantom of the opera, Les miserables, A chorus line, Guys and dolls, and 15 other musicals. *Hadley, tenor; American Theatre Orch.; Gemignani, cond.*
+ ARG 1-2/93: 192

30337. 61373-2-RC: Sleighride! Classic Christmas favorites. *Various performers.*
+ ARG 11-12/92: 265

30338. 09026-61374-2: BRUCKNER—Symphony no. 3 (1889 version). *Symphony Orch. of the North German Radio, Hamburg; Wand, cond.*
+ ARG 5-6/93: 75
+ Fa 3-4/93: 135
• Gr 3/93: 36

30339. 09026-61377-2 (2 discs): TCHAIKOVSKY—Symphonies no. 4-6. *St. Petersburg Phil. Orch.; Temirkanov, cond.*
- ARG 1-2/93: 157
+ Fa 3-4/93: 313
• Gr 5/93: 52

30340. 09026-61384-2: SCHUMANN—Piano quartets in E♭, op. 47, in C minor, op. posth. *Previn, piano; Kim, violin; Ohyama, viola; Hoffman, cello.*
+ ARG 5-6/93: 135
• Fa 3-4/93: 282
+ Gr 5/93: 68

30341. 09026- 61386-2: DEBUSSY—Violin sonata. RAVEL—Violin sonata. SAINT-SAËNS—Violin sonata no. 1. *Takezawa, violin; De Silva, piano.*
+ Fa 9-10/93: 151
+ Gr 3/94: 71

30342. 09026-61387-2: BRITTEN—String quartet no. 2. BARBER—String quartet, op.

11. TAKEMITSU—A way a lone. *Tokyo String Quartet.*
>   + ARG 3-4/94: 163
>   + Fa 1-2/94: 147
>   + Gr 2/94: 60

30343. 09026-61388-2: PROKOFIEV—Romeo and Juliet (excerpts). *Philharmonia Orch.; Flor, cond.*
>   + ARG 9-10/93: 169
>   + Fa 11-12/93: 348
>   + Gr 10/93: 48

30344. 09026-61389-2: FALLA—Piano music. MONTSALVATGE—Piano music. *Larrocha, piano.*
>   + ARG 11-12/94: 110
>   + Fa 11-12/94: 490
>   + Gr 9/94: 81

30345. 09026-61390-2: BRAHMS—Violin sonatas; Scherzo in C minor. *Spivakov, violin; Rudy, piano.*
>   + ARG 7-8/94: 81
>   - Fa 7-8/94: 96

30346. 09026-61392-2: RAVEL—Boléro; Daphnis et Chloe: Suite no. 2. DEBUSSY—Pour le piano: Sarabande (orch. Ravel). MUSSORGSKY—Pictures at an exhibition (orch. Ravel). *Boston Symphony Orch.; Koussevitzky, cond.* Reissue.
>   + ARG 9-10/93: 257
>   + Fa 9-10/93: 247

30347. 09026-61393-2: BEETHOVEN—Piano concertos no. 4-5. *Schnabel, piano; Chicago Symphony Orch.; Stock, cond.* Recorded 1942.
>   + Fa 9-10/93: 117

30348. 09026-61394-2: STRAVINSKY—Pterushka; Rite of spring. *Philadelphia Orch.; Stokowski, cond.* Recorded 1937, 1929-30.
>   + Fa 9-10/93: 304
>   + Gr 8/93: 89

30349. 09026-61396-2: MOZART—Symphonies no. 40-41. *Chicago Symphony Orch.; Levine, cond.* Reissue.
>   + ARG 11-12/93: 159

30350. 09026-61398-2: BRUCKNER—Symphony no. 7. *North German Radio Symphony Orch.; Wand, cond.*
>   + ARG 11-12/93: 88
>   + Fa 9-10/93: 138
>   - Gr 9/93: 45

30351. 09026-61399-2: BEETHOVEN—Symphonies no. 1, 3. *Boston Symphony Orch.; Munch, cond.* Reissue.
>   + ARG 7-8/93: 66
>   + Fa 9-10/93: 120

30352. 09026-61400-2: BERLIOZ—Overtures. SAINT-SAËNS—Rouet d'Omphale. *Boston Symphony Orch.; Munch, cond.* Reissues.
>   + Gr 11/93: 65

30353. 09026-61401-2: MUSSORGSKY—Pictures at an exhibition. RESPIGHI—Fountains of Rome; Pines of Rome. *Chicago Symphony Orch.; Reiner, cond.* Reissue.
>   - ARG 9-10/93: 157
>   + Fa 11-12/93: 362
>   + Gr 8/93: 34

30354. 09026-61403-2 (2 discs): VERDI—Requiem. *L. Price, Baker, Luchetti, Dam; Chicago Symphony Orch.; Solti, cond.* Reissue.
>   + Gr 9/93: 104

30355. 09026-61411-2: Arias from Rigoletto, Barber of Seville, Lakmé, Dinorah, and others. *Pons, soprano; with accomp.*
>   + ARG 7-8/93: 217
>   + Fa 11-12/93: 459

30356. 09026-61412-2: Arias from Hamlet, Faust, Traviata, La Bohème, Louise and others. *Melba, soprano; with accomp.*
>   + ARG 7-8/93: 216
>   + Fa 11-12/93: 458
>   + Gr 9/93: 125

30357. 09026-61413-2: Music of Verdi, Bellini, Donizetti, Rossini, Thomas, Meyerbeer, and others. *Galli-Curci, soprano.*
>   + ARG 5-6/94: 215

30358. 09026-61415-2: LISZT—Piano music. *Horowitz, piano.* Reissues.
>   • Gr 11/93: 119

30359. 09026-61424-2: TCHAIKOVSKY—Serenade for strings. ELGAR—Introduction and allegro. BARBER—Adagio for strings. *Boston Symphony Orch.; Munch, cond.* Reissue.
>   + ARG 9-10/93: 205
>   + Gr 9/93: 42

30360. 09026-61429-2: IBERT—Divertissement. OFFENBACH—Overtures. *Boston Pops Orch.; Fiedler, cond.* Reissue.
>   + ARG 9-10/93: 223

30361. 09026-61438-2: BRAHMS—String quartet no. 3. SCHUMANN—String quartet no. 1. *Vogler Quartet.*
>   + Fa 11-12/93: 194
>   • Gr 9/93: 71

30362. 09026-61439-2: FAURÉ—Selected mélodies. *Stutzmann, alto; C. Collard, piano.*
>   + ARG 3-4/94: 94
>   • Fa 1-2/94: 178
>   • Gr 1/94: 82

30363. 09026-61442-2: BRAHMS—Piano concerto no. 2; Intermezzos, op. 116, no. 5; op. 117, no. 2; Rhapsody, op. 79, no. 2. *Rubinstein, piano; RCA Victor Symphony Orch.; Krips, cond.* Reissue.

>   + ARG 3-4/94: 212
>   + Gr 10/93: 78

30364. 09026-61443-2: BEETHOVEN—Piano sonatas no. 8, 14, 23, 26. *Rubinstein, piano.* Reissue.
>   + ARG 3-4/94: 212
>   • Gr 10/93: 78

30365. 09026-61444-2: SCHUMANN—Piano concerto; Symphonic etudes; Arabesque. *Rubinstein, piano; RCA Victor Symphony Orch.; Krips, cond.* Reissue.
>   + ARG 3-4/94: 212
>   • Gr 10/93: 78

30366. 09026-61445-2: *Carnegie Hall highlights.* Music of Debussy, Szymanowski, Prokofiev, Villa-Lobos, Schumann, and Albeniz. *Rubinstein, piano.* Reissue.
>   + ARG 3-4/94: 212
>   + Gr 10/93: 78

30367. 09026-61446-2: *Music of France.* Music of Ravel, Poulenc, Fauré, Chabrier, and Debussy. *Rubinstein, piano.* Reissue.
>   + ARG 3-4/94: 212
>   + Gr 10/93: 78

30368. 09026-61447-2: MERCADANTE—Flute concertos. *Galway, flute; Solisti veneti; Scimone, cond.* Reissue.
>   + Gr 4/94: 52

30369. 09026-61450-2: Music of Lawes, Carulli, Sor, Granados, Falla, and others. *Bream, Williams, guitars.* Reissue.
>   + ARG 11-12/93: 235

30370. 09026-61452-2: Music of Carulli, Grandos, Albéniz, Giuliani, Johnson, and others. *Bream, Williams, guitars.* Reissue.
>   + ARG 11-12/93: 235

30371. 09026-61454-2: PROKOFIEV—Violin sonatas no. 1-2; Violin concerto no. 2. *Perlman, violin; Ashkenazy, piano; Boston Symphony Orch.; Leinsdorf, cond.* Reissues.
>   + Gr 9/94: 74

30372. 09026-61457-2: Arias by Gluck, Donizetti, Berlioz, Gounod, Massenet, and others. *Verrett, mezzo-soprano.* Reissues.
>   + ARG 5-6/96: 259

30373. 09026-61458-2: DONIZETTI—Arias. BELLINI—Arias. *Caballé, soprano; Orch.; Cillario, cond.* Reissue.
>   + ARG 7-8/93: 202

30374. 09026-61460-2 (6 discs): VAUGHAN WILLIAMS—9 symphonies; Orchestra music. *Philharmonia Orch.; Slatkin, cond.*
>   + ARG 5-6/94: 159

30375. 09026-61485-2: STRAUSS—Don Quixote. BRAHMS—Double concerto. *Piatigorsky, cello; Milstein, violin; Boston Symphony Orch.; Munch, cond.; Robin Hood Dell Orch. of Philadelphia; Reiner, cond.* Reissues.
  + ARG 9-10/93: 198
  + Fa 9-10/93: 299
  • Gr 10/93: 138

30376. 09026-61495-2: TCHAIKOVSKY—Violin concerto. BRAHMS—Violin concerto. *Heifetz, violin; Chicago Symphony Orch.; Reiner, cond.* Reissues.
  + ARG 5-6/93: 145
  + ARG 5-6/93: 155

30377. 09026-61497-2: Music of Rimsky-Korsakov, Rossini, Tchaikovsky, Chabrier, and Liszt. *Boston Pops Orch.; Fiedler, cond.* Reissue.
  • ARG 9-10/93: 223

30378. 09026-61498-2: DVOŘÁK—Cello concerto. WALTON—Cello concerto. *Piatigorsky, cello; Boston Symphony Orch.; Munch, cond.* Reissue.
  + ARG 5-6/93: 155
  + ARG 7-8/93: 84

30379. 09026-61499-2: *A program of song.* Songs of Fauré, Poulenc, Strauss, and Wolf. *L. Price, soprano; Garvey, piano.* Reissue.
  + Gr 5/93: 97

30380. 09026-61500-2: SAINT-SAËNS—Symphony no. 3. DEBUSSY—La mer. IBERT—Escales. *Zamkochian, organ; Boston Symphony Orch.; Munch, cond.* Reissues.
  + ARG 5-6/93: 155
  + ARG 7-8/93: 147

30381. 09026-61501-2: KAY—Cakewalk; Stars and stripes. GOULD—Interplay: Excerpts. COPLAND—Rodeo: Hoedown. BERNSTEIN—Dances from Fancy free. *Boston Pops Orch.; Fiedler, cond.* Reissue.
  + ARG 7-8/93: 109

30382. 09026-61503-2: *Rhapsodies.* Music of Liszt, Enesco, Smetana, and Wagner. *Symphony of the Air; Stokowski, cond.*
  + ARG 1-2/94: 173
  + Gr 3/94: 66

30383. 09026-61504-2: BARTÓK—Concerto for orchestra; Music for strings, percussion, and celesta; Hungarian sketches. *Chicago Symphony Orch.; Reiner, cond.* Recorded 1955/58.
  + ARG 1-2/94: 70
  + Fa 1-2/94: 118
  + Gr 3/94: 41

30384. 09026-61505-2: COPLAND—Suites from Appalachian spring and Tender Land. GOULD—Fall River legend; Latin-American symphonette: Tango & Guaracha . *Boston Symphony Orch.;*

Copland, cond.; Orch.; Gould, cond. Reissues.
  • ARG 9-10/93: 109

30385. 09026-61508-2 (2 discs): *A salute to American music: The Richard Tucker Music Foundation: Gala XVI.* Music of Menotti, Weill, Thomson, Griffes, Foster, Bernstein, Copland, Bolcom, Moore, Blitzstein, Gershwin, Stravinsky, Levy, Barber, Floyd, Porter, Ellington, Rodgers, and Berlin. *Various performers.*
  + ARG 5-6/93: 177
  + Fa 3-4/93: 349

30386. 09026-61509-2: Salute to American music. *Vocal soloists; Metropolitan Opera Orch.; Conlon, cond.*
  + Gr 6/93: 93

30387. 09026-61511-2 (4 discs): BRAHMS—Symphonies, Haydn variations; Overtures. *Bavarian Radio Orch.; C. Davis, cond.* Reissues.
  • ARG 9-10/93: 104

30388. 09026-61520-2 (2 discs): MESSIAEN—Turangalîla symphony; Un sourire. LUTOSŁAWSKI—Concerto for orchestra. *Muraro, piano; Hartmann-Claveric, ondes Martenot; Orch. Philharmonique de Radio France; Janowski, cond.*
  • ARG 3-4/94: 123
  • Fa 1-2/94: 237
  • Gr 11/93: 70

30389. 09026-61534-2: BEETHOVEN—Piano concerto no. 1. CHOPIN—Etudes, op. 10: selections. *Richter, piano; Schleswig-Holstein Festival Orch.; Eschenbach, cond.* Recorded 1988.
  • ARG 7-8/94: 66
  • Fa 7-8/94: 61
  - Gr 9/94: 46

30390. 09026-61541-2: Music of Gabrieli, Banchieri, Clarke, Susato, Speer, Scheidt, and others. *English Chamber Orch. Brass; Fraser, cond.*
  • ARG 11-12/93: 106

30391. 09026-61547-2: *Farewell to Salzburg: Christa Ludwig.* Songs of Schumann, Mahler, Brahms, and Strauss. *Ludwig, mezzo-soprano; Spencer, piano.*
  + ARG 1-2/94: 191
  + Fa 11-12/93: 460
  + Gr 10/93: 106

30392. 09026-61548-2: RACHMANINOFF—Piano concerto no. 3. *Kissin, piano; Boston Symphony Orch.; Ozawa, cond.* Recorded live.
  - ARG 9-10/93: 172
  - Fa 11-12/93: 353
  • Gr 8/93: 36

30393. 09026-61561-2: BEETHOVEN—Violin sonatas no. 5, 9. *Zukerman, violin; Neikrug, piano.* Reissue.
  • Gr 3/94: 68

30394. 09026-61562-2: BRAHMS—Cello sonatas. SCHUMANN—Adagio and allegro. *Starker, cello; Buchbinder, piano.*
  + ARG 1-2/95: 89
  + Gr 11/94: 98

30395. 09026-61563-2: TCHAIKOVSKY—Symphony no. 6; Romeo and Juliet. *Boston Symphony Orch.; Munch, cond.* Reissue.
  + ARG 7-8/93: 169
  • Gr 8/93: 41

30396. 09026-61564-2: RACHMANINOFF—Piano concerto no. 3. *Horowitz, piano; New York Phil.; Ormandy, cond.* Recorded 1978.
  • ARG 9-10/93: 172
  • Fa 9-10/93: 242

30397. 09026-61568—61569-2 (3, 4 discs): GRIEG—Piano music vol. 1-2. *Oppitz, piano.*
  + ARG 3-4/94: 102
  + Fa 3-4/94: 199
  • Gr 4/94: 73

30398. 09026-61574-2: CAGE—Sixteen dances for soloists and company of three. *Ensemble Modern; Metzmacher, cond.*
  + ARG 7-8/95: 98
  + Fa 9-10/95: 161
  + Fa 9-10/95: 162
  □ Gr 4/95: 78

30399. 09026-61578-2 (2 discs): VIVALDI—Cello concertos. *Harnoy, cello; I. Oistrakh, violin; Toronto Chamber Orch.; Robinson, cond.*
  + ARG 3-4/94: 178
  + Fa 3-4/94: 360
  + Gr 1/94: 60

30400. 09026-61580-2 (6 discs): RCA/Met: 100 singers, 100 years. *Various performers.*
  + ARG 3-4/94: 237
  + Gr 4/94: 109

30401. 09026-61581-2: BERNSTEIN—Songfest; In memoriam Nathalie Koussevitzky; Symphony no. 1 "Jeremiah". *Vocal soloists; St. Louis Symphony Orch.; Slatkin, cond.; Slatkin, piano; Merriman, mezzo-soprano; St. Louis Symphony Orch.; Bernstein, cond.* Symphony recorded 1945.
  + ARG 11-12/93: 79
  + Fa 11-12/93: 186
  + Gr 6/94: 91

30402. 09026-61582-2: BACH—Violin concertos; Oboe concerto; Oboe d'amore concerto. *Spivakov, violin & cond.; Utkin, oboe; Moscow Virtuosi.*
  • ARG 3-4/94: 66

30403. 09026-61583-2 (28 discs): The Julian Bream edition. *Bream, lute, guitar; with accompanying artists.* Reissues.
  + Gr 8/93: 64

30404. 09026-61612-2: Elgar—Violin concerto; Introduction and allegro. *Takezawa, violin; Bavarian Radio Symphony Orch.; C. Davis, cond.*
- ARG 7-8/94: 99
- Fa 7-8/94: 132
+ Gr 3/94: 51

30405. 09026-61614-2: Schubert—Piano sonata D. 850. Liszt—Piano sonata. *Gilels, piano.* Reissue.
+ ARG 1-2/94: 152
+ Gr 4/94: 73

30406. 09026-61616-2: Pablo Casals: Early recordings, 1925-28. *Casals, cello.*
+ ARG 3-4/95: 266

30407. 09026-61618-2: Brahms—Piano concerto no. 1; Ballades, op. 10, no. 1-4. *Oppitz, piano; Bavarian Radio Symphony Orch.; C. Davis, cond.*
- ARG 5-6/94: 73
- Fa 5-6/94: 119

30408. 09026-61619-2: Brahms—Piano concerto no. 2; Eight piano pieces, op. 76. *Oppitz, piano; Bavarian Radio Symphony Orch.; C. Davis, cond.*
- Fa 5-6/94: 119

30409. 09026-61620-2 (2 discs): Brahms—Piano concertos no. 1-2; Ballades, op. 10; Pieces, op. 76. *Oppitz, piano; Bavarian Radio Symphony Orch.; C. Davis, cond.*
- Gr 7/94: 41

30410. 09026-61630-2 (2 discs): Grieg—Songs, vol. 1-2. *Hagegård, baritone; W. Jones, piano.*
- ARG 1-2/94: 105
+ Fa 3-4/94: 201
+ Gr 2/94: 79
+ ON 4/2/94: 33

30411. 09026-61631-2 (2 discs): Tchaikovsky—Piano concertos no. 1-3; Concert fantasia. *Douglas, piano; London Symphony Orch.; Philharmonia Orch.; Slatkin, cond.* Part reissue.
- Gr 6/94: 65

30412. 09026-61632-2: Tchaikovsky—Piano concerto no. 1; Concert fantasy for piano and orchestra. *Douglas, piano; London Symphony Orch.; Slatkin, cond.*
+ ARG 5-6/94: 153
- Fa 3-4/94: 333

30413. 09026-61633-2: Tchaikovsky—Piano concertos no. 2-3. *Douglas, piano; London Symphony Orch.; Slatkin, cond.*
+ ARG 5-6/94: 153
- Fa 3-4/94: 333

30414. 09026-61634-2: Duets from Otello, Ballo in maschera, Manon Lescaut, Tosca and Madame Butterfly. *Price, soprano; Domingo, tenor.* Reissues.
- ARG 5-6/96: 260

30415. 09026-61635-2: Mozart—Arias. Mussorgsky—The nusery. Liszt—Petrarch sonnets. *M. Price, soprano; English Chamber Orch.; London Phil. Orch.; Lockhart, cond.* Reissues.
+ ARG 3-4/95: 261
+ Gr 5/95: 111

30416. 09026-61638-2: Caruso duets. *Caruso, tenor.*
+ ARG 1-2/97: 242

30417. 09026-61640-2: Caruso in song. *Caruso, tenor; with piano accomp.*
+ ARG 5-6/94: 214

30418. 09026-61649-2 (11 discs): Fritz Kreisler: the complete RCA recordings. *Kreisler, violin; with assisting musicians.* Reissue.
+ ARG 5-6/96: 261
+ Fa 3-4/96: 371
+ Fi 3/96: 130
+ Gr 5/96: 130

30419. 09026-61650-2: *Leonard Bernstein: the early years II.* Music of Ravel, Bernstein, Copland, and Gershwin. *Bernstein, piano & cond.; Philharmonia Orch.; RCA Victor Orch.*
- ARG 5-6/94: 209
- Fa 5-6/94: 349
- Gr 7/94: 131

30420. 09026-61651-2: Gould—Fall River legend suite; Interplay; Latin American Symphonette; Declaration. *Morton Gould Orch.; National Symphony Orch.; Gould, cond.* Reissues.
+ ARG 5-6/94: 96

30421. 09026-61655-2 (22 discs): Vladimir Horowitz collection. *Horowitz, piano.* Reissues.
+ Gr 7/94: 84

30422. 09026-61656-2: Chopin—Piano concertos no. 1-2; Piano music. *Brailowsky, piano; RCA Symphony Orch.; Steinberg, cond.; Boston Symphony Orch.; Munch, cond.* Reissues.
- ARG 7-8/94: 232

30423. 09026-61657-2: Prokofiev—Symphonies, no. 1, 5; Chout: Finale; Romeo and Juliet: Suite no. 2. *Boston Symphony Orch.; Koussevitzky, cond.* Recorded 1945-47.
+ ARG 3-4/95: 266
+ Gr 4/95: 138

30424. 09026-61666-2: *Pops roundup.* Music of Hayman and Tiomkin; Arrangements. *Boston Pops Orch.; Fiedler, cond.* Reissue.
+ ARG 9-10/93: 223

30425. 09026-61667-2: Copland—Suites from Billy the kid and Rodeo. Grofé—Grand Canyon suite. *Morton Gould Orch.; Gould, cond.* Reissue.
- ARG 9-10/93: 109
+ Gr 2/94: 40

30426. 09026-61672-2: Elgar—Violin concerto. *Zukerman, violin; St. Louis Symphony Orch.; Slatkin, cond.*
+ ARG 1-2/94: 98
- Fa 3-4/94: 180
- Gr 1/94: 44

30427. 09026-61673-2: Orff—Carmina Burana. *McNair, Aler, Hagegard; St. Louis Symphony Orch. & Chorus; Slatkin, cond.*
+ ARG 1-2/95: 148
+ Gr 4/95: 104

30428. 09026-61674-2: Borodin—Symphonies no. 1, 3; Prince Igor: Overture, Polovtsian march. *Russian State Symphony Orch.; Svetlanov, cond.*
- ARG 11-12/93: 82
- Fa 1-2/94: 135
+ Gr 1/94: 41

30429. 09026-61675-2: Bartók—Violin concerto no. 2; Two rhapsodies for violin and orchestra. *Takezawa, violin; London Symphony Orch.; Thomas, cond.*
+ Fa 1-2/94: 118
+ Gr 12/93: 62

30430. 09026-61676-2: Beethoven—Piano concerto no. 1; Piano sonata no. 15. *Larrocha, piano; London Symphony Orch.; Thomas, cond.*
+ ARG 3-4/94: 71
+ Fa 1-2/94: 120
+ Gr 12/93: 62

30431. 09026-61678-2: Saint-Saëns—Music for cello. *Isserlis, cello; Devoyon, piano; London Symphony Orch.; Thomas, cond.*
+ ARG 1-2/94: 145
+ Fa 1-2/94: 298
+ Gr 12/93: 62

30432. 09026-61679-2: Rachmaninoff—Piano concerto no. 2; Preludes. *Douglas, piano; London Symphony Orch.; Thomas, cond.*
- ARG 1-2/94: 135
+ Fa 1-2/94: 268
- Gr 12/93: 62

30433. 09026-61681-2: Schumann—Frauenliebe und Leben. Dvořák—Zigeunermelodien. Mendelssohn—Vocal duets. *Horne, Von Stade, mezzo-sopranos; Katz, piano.*
- ARG 5-6/94: 197
- Fa 3-4/94: 314
+ Gr 3/94: 94

30434. 09026-61682-2 (2 discs): Tchaikovsky—Sleeping Beauty. *St. Louis Symphony Orch.; Slatkin, cond.*
- ARG 1-2/94: 164
- Fa 1-2/94: 331

30435. 09026-61687-2: Jan Peerce sings Hebrew melodies. *Peerce, tenor.*
- ARG 1-2/95: 243

30436. 09026-61688-2: J. STRAUSS JR.—Waltzes and polkas. *Boston Pops; Fiedler, cond.* Reissue.
+ ARG 1-2/95: 184

30437. 09026-61696-2: BRAHMS—Violin concerto; Double concerto. *Spivakov, violin; Kniazev, cello; Royal Phil. Orch.; Temirkanov, cond.*
• ARG 7-8/94: 79
- Fa 7-8/94: 90

30438. 09026-61697-2: BRAHMS—Violin sonatas no. 1-3; Sonatensatz. *Zukerman, violin; Neikrug, piano.*
+ ARG 11-12/96: 100
• Fa 9-10/96: 159
+ Fi 10/96: 149

30439. 09026-61698-2: MOZART—Piano concertos no. 22, 26. *Larrocha, piano; English Chamber Orch.; C. Davis, cond.*
- ARG 9-10/94: 165
+ Fa 9-10/94: 253
• Gr 7/94: 52

30440. 09026-61699-2: COPLAND—The red pony; Our town; The heiress; Music for movies; Prairie journal. *St. Louis Symphony Orch.; Slatkin, cond.*
• ARG 7-8/94: 91
+ Gr 11/94: 69

30441. 09026-61700-2: MENDELSSOHN—Violin concerto. VAUGHAN WILLIAMS—Lark ascending. DVOŘÁK—Romance. MASSENET—Meditation from Thaïs. *Meyers, violin; Philharmonia Orch.; Litton, cond.*
• ARG 7-8/94: 131
• Fa 3-4/94: 248
+ Gr 2/94: 46

30442. 09026-61701-2: SIBELIUS—Violin concerto; Symphony no. 2. *Spivakov, violin; St. Petersburg Phil. Orch.; Temirkanov, cond.*
• ARG 1-2/97: 171
• Fa 11-12/96: 380
• Gr 2/97: 58

30443. 09026-61702-2: BARTÓK—Concerto for orchestra; Miraculous mandarin. *St. Louis Symphony Orch.; Slatkin, cond.*
+ ARG 11-12/94: 70
• Fa 11-12/94: 161
• Gr 9/94: 45

30444. 09026-61705-2: SCHUBERT—Die schöne Müllerin. *Hagegård, baritone; Ax, piano.*
• ARG 11-12/94: 186
+ Gr 2/95: 90

30445. 09026-61728-2: SCHUMANN—Liederkreis, op. 39; Songs. *Stutzmann, alto; C. Collard, piano.*
+ ARG 9-10/94: 197
+ Fa 9-10/94: 332
+ Gr 8/94: 96

30446. 09026-61729-2 (2 discs): SONDHEIM—Putting it together. *Andrews, Collins, Durang, Rupert (original cast).*
+ Gr 7/94: 120

30447. 09026-61778-2 (65 discs in 46 vols.): The Heifetz collection. *Heifetz, violin; with piano and orch. accomp.* Reissues.
+ ARG 5-6/95: 216
+ Gr 11/94: 178

30448. 09026-61789-2: MOZART—Flute and harp concerto; Sonatas K. 296, 376. *Galway, flute; Robles, harp; Moll, piano; London Symphony Orch.; Thomas, cond.*
• ARG 1-2/94: 126
• Fa 1-2/94: 242
+ Gr 12/93: 62

30449. 09026-61790-2: COPLAND—Clarinet concerto. BERNSTEIN—Clarinet sonata; West Side variants. GERSHWIN—Arrangements. *Stoltzman, clarinet; London Symphony Orch.; Thomas, cond.*
+ ARG 11-12/93: 95
- Fa 1-2/94: 394
+ Gr 12/93: 62

30450. 09026-61792-2: WAGNER—Excerpts from Die Meistersinger; Götterdämmerung; Lohengrin; Tannhäuser. HUMPERDINCK—Hansel and Gretel: Dream pantomime. *Chicago Symphony Orch.; Reiner, cond.* Recorded 1950-1959.
• ARG 3-4/94: 182
+ Fa 5-6/94: 280
• Gr 8/94: 62

30451. 09026-61793-2: BRAHMS—Symphony no. 3. MENDELSSOHN—Hebrides overture. SCHUBERT—Symphony no. 5. *Chicago Symphony Orch.; Reiner, cond.* Reissues.
+ ARG 7-8/95: 93
+ Gr 9/95: 50

30452. 09026-61795-2: BEETHOVEN—Symphony no. 9. *Curtin, Kopleff, McCollum, Gramm; Chicago Symphony Orch. & Chorus; Reiner, cond.* Reissue.
• ARG 7-8/94: 70
+ Fa 5-6/94: 111
• Gr 7/94: 40

30453. 09026-61796-2: STRAUSS—Don Quixote; Burleske. *Janigro, cello; Preves, viola; Weicher, violin; Janis, piano; Chicago Symphony Orch.; Reiner, cond.* Reissue.
+ ARG 5-6/94: 146
+ Fa 5-6/94: 257
• Gr 9/94: 64

30454. 09026-61806-2 (2 discs): PUCCINI—Tosca. *Kabaivanska, Pavarotti, Wixell; Chorus & Orch. of the Teatro dell' Opera (Rome); Oren, cond.*
+ ARG 3-4/94: 137
• Fa 1-2/94: 266
- Gr 12/93: 115
• ON 1/8/94: 34

30455. 09026-61809-2: MOZART—String quartets no. 10, 16, 18. *Pro Arte Quartet.*
+ ARG 1-2/94: 127
+ Fa 1-2/94: 246

30456. 09026-61811-2: BRAHMS—Handel variations; Paganini variations; Rhapsodies, op. 79. *Oppitz, piano.* Reissue.
• ARG 9-10/94: 107
• Gr 9/94: 81

30457. 09026-61814-2: JOSQUIN—Chansons and motets. *King's Singers.*
+ ARG 9-10/94: 147
+ Fa 5-6/94: 172

30458. 09026-61815-2: *Carnival in Venice.* Music of Tessarini, Bellini, Albinoni, Tartini, Marcello, Corelli, and Arban. *Touvron, trumpet; I Solisti Veneti; Scimone, cond.*
• ARG 9-10/94: 244
+ Fa 5-6/94: 330

30459. 09026-61816-2: DEBUSSY—String quartet. SHOSTAKOVICH—String quartet no. 11. JANÁČEK—String quartet no. 1. *Vogler Quartet.*
+ ARG 7-8/94: 93
• Fa 9-10/94: 176
+ Gr 7/94: 71

30460. 09026-61818-2: CHOPIN—Cello sonata. FRANCK—Cello sonata. *Harnoy, cello; Katsaris, piano.*
+ ARG 9-10/94: 118
• Fa 9-10/94: 166
• Gr 10/94: 134

30461. 09026-61821-2 (6 discs): TCHAIKOVSKY—Symphonies no. 1-6; Orchestra music. *Royal Phil. Orch.; Temirkanov, cond.*
- ARG 3-4/94: 167 (Vroon)
• ARG 3-4/94: 167 (Hansen)
+ Fa 3-4/94: 339
+ Gr 5/94: 63

30462. 09026-61843-2: *Concert in Villa Wahnfried.* WAGNER—Songs; Piano music. LISZT—Piano music. *Stutzmann, contralto; Oppitz, piano.*
• Gr 2/95: 94

30463. 09026-61846-2: RAVEL—Daphnis et Chloé. *Boston Symphony Orch.; Munch, cond.* Reissue.
+ ARG 1-2/94: 137
+ Fa 1-2/94: 273
+ Gr 3/94: 60

30464. 09026-61847-2: OFFENBACH—Gaité Parisienne. RESPIGHI—La boutique fantasque. *Boston Pops; Fiedler, cond.* Reissue.
+ ARG 1-2/94: 128
+ Fa 1-2/94: 254

30465. 09026-61859-2: MOZART—Piano concertos no. 17, 23. *Rubinstein, piano; Orch.; Wallenstein, cond.; St. Louis Symphony Orch.; Golschmann, cond.*

RCA

Reissues.
+ ARG 9-10/94: 165

30466. 09026-61860-2: Liszt—Piano music. Rubinstein—Barcarolles; Valse-caprice. *Rubinstein, piano.* Reissues.
+ ARG 9-10/94: 153
+ Gr 1/95: 78

30467. 09026-61861-2: Beethoven—Violin sonatas no. 5, 8-9. *Szeryng, violin; Rubinstein, piano.* Reissue.
+ ARG 9-10/94: 100

30468. 09026-61862-2: Brahms—Piano sonata no. 3; Ballades, op. 10. *Rubinstein, piano.* Reissue.
+ ARG 9-10/94: 108
+ Gr 9/94: 81

30469. 09026-61863-2: Saint-Saëns—Piano concerto no. 2. Falla—Nights in the gardens of Spain. Franck—Symphonic variations. *Rubinstein, piano; Philadelphia Orch.; Ormandy, cond.; Symphony of the Air; Wallenstein, cond.* Reissues.
+ ARG 9-10/94: 243
+ Gr 8/94: 65

30470. 09026-61864-2: Schubert—Songs. *Quasthoff, baritone; Spencer, piano.*
• Gr 8/95: 119

30471. 09026-61866-2: Brahms—String quartet no. 2. Schumann—String quartet no. 3. *Vogler Quartet.*
• ARG 7-8/95: 93
+ Fa 5-6/95: 152
+ Gr 7/95: 77

30472. 09026-61876-2: Schumann—Symphony no. 3. Schubert—Symphony no. 3. *NDR Symphony Orch.; Wand, cond.*
• ARG 5-6/94: 142
• Fa 5-6/94: 245
+ Gr 2/94: 50

30473. 09026-61879-2: Grieg—Vocal, piano, and chamber music. *Various performers.*
+ ARG 3-4/94: 232
+ Gr 4/94: 125

30474. 09026-61881-2: Grieg—Holberg suite; Melodies: Dances. *Petri, recorder; English Chamber Orch.; Kamu, cond.; English Chamber Orch. Ensemble; Langford, cond.*
+ Fa 7-8/94: 143

30475. 09026-61885-2: *Here's a howdy do!* Sullivan—Operetta numbers. *King's Singers.*
+ Gr 5/94: 116

30476. 09026-61902-2: Foss—Clarinet concerto. Englund—Clarinet concerto. McKinley—Clarinet concerto no. 2. *Stoltzman, clarinet; Deutsches Symphonie-Orch. Berlin; Foss, cond.*

+ ARG 11-12/96: 246
+ Fa 11-12/96: 245
+ Gr 12/96: 72

30477. 09026-61911-2: Baroque duets. *Philharmonia Virtuosi; Kapp, cond.*
+ Fa 1-2/94: 428

30478. 09026-61924-2 (2 discs): Donizetti—Don Pasquale. *Bruson, Mei, Allen, Lopardo; Chorus of the Bavarian Radio; Munich Radio Orch.; R. Abbado, cond.*
+ ARG 3-4/95: 94
- Fa 1-2/95: 151
+ Gr 12/94: 153
+ ON 1/7/95: 36
+ Op 11/94: 1353

30479. 09026-61926-2: Prokofiev—Alexander Nevsky (complete film score). *Gorokhovskaya, mezzo-soprano; Chorus of St. Petersburg Teleradio Co.; Chamber Chorus of St. Petersburg; St. Petersburg Chorus Capella "LIK"; St. Petersburg Phil. Orch.; Temirkanov, cond.*
+ ARG 5-6/95: 150
+ Fa 7-8/95: 276

30480. 09026-61927-2: Mozart—Posthorn serenade; Bassoon concerto. *Marschall, bassoon; Bavarian Radio Orch.; C. Davis, cond.*
+ ARG 11-12/94: 162
• Fa 11-12/94: 316
+ Gr 9/94: 58

30481. 09026-61930-2: Beethoven—Symphonies no. 5-6. *North German Radio Symphony Orch.; Wand, cond.*
• ARG 7-8/94: 69
+ Fa 5-6/94: 110
+ Gr 5/94: 47

30482. 09026-61931-2 (2 discs): Schumann—Symphonies; Overture, scherzo and finale. *Hanover Band; Goodman, cond.*
+ ARG 1-2/95: 173
+ Fa 3-4/95: 293
+ Gr 3/95: 54

30483. 09026-61934-2: Martinů—Piano concertos no. 2-4. *Firkušný, piano; Czech Phil. Orch.; Pešek, cond.*
+ ARG 3-4/95: 134
+ Gr 4/95: 60

30484. 09026-61936-2: Dreams. *Stoltzman, clarinet; Gomez, double bass; Samuels, percussion; Wall, Douglas, keyboards; Kalmen Opperman Clarinet Choir.*
+ ARG 9-10/94: 231

30485. 09026-61955-2: Koechlin—The jungle book. *Vermillion, mezzo-soprano; Botha, tenor; Lukas, baritone; Berlin Radio Symphony Orch.; Zinman, cond.*
• ARG 9-10/94: 150
+ Fa 9-10/94: 227
+ Gr 6/94: 52

30486. 09026-61956-2: Ravel—Rapsodie espagnole; La valse; Boléro. Debussy—Images. *Boston Symphony Orch.; Munch, cond.* Reissues.
• ARG 7-8/94: 158
+ Gr 12/94: 78

30487. 09026-61957-2: Hovhaness—Symphony no. 2 "Mysterious mountain." Prokofiev—Lieutenant Kijé: Suite. Stravinsky—Divertimento from La baiser de la fée. *Chicago Symphony Orch.; Reiner, cond.*
+ Gr 9/95: 56

30488. 09026-61958-2: Music of Mussorgsky, Tchaikovsky, Borodin, Glinka, and Kabalevsky. *Chicago Symphony Orch.; Reiner, cond.* Reissues.
+ ARG 9-10/94: 222
+ Gr 8/94: 65

30489. 09026-61960-2: Spirituals. *Anderson, contralto; Rupp, Motley, piano.* Reissue.
+ ARG 9-10/94: 257

30490. 09026-61961-2: Beethoven—Piano concerto no. 5. Rachmaninoff—Piano concerto no. 2. *Cliburn, piano; Chicago Symphony Orch.; Reiner, cond.* Reissue.
• ARG 7-8/94: 67

30491. 09026-61963-2: Sibelius—Symphonies no. 3, 5. *London Symphony Orch.; Davis, cond.*
+ ARG 3-4/95: 190
• Fa 3-4/95: 299
+ Gr 3/95: 56

30492. 09026-61964-2: Tchaikovsky—Children's album; Snow maiden; Melodrama; Serenade for strings. *Moscow Virtuosi; Spivakov, cond.*
+ ARG 1-2/95: 191
+ Gr 12/94: 97

30493. 09026-61966-2: Tavener—Eternal memory. Bloch—From Jewish life. *Isserlis, cello; Moscow Virtuosi; Spivakov, cond.*
+ Gr 4/94: 56

30494. 09026-61968-2: Nocturne. Music of Mozart, Beethoven, Mendelssohn, Chopin, Szymanowski, Liszt, Scriabin, Albéniz, Falla, Debussy, Fauré, and Ravel. *Oppitz, piano.*
• Fa 9-10/96: 407

30495. 09026-61969-2: Beethoven—Piano sonatas no. 15, 17, 26. *Oppitz, piano.*
• ARG 7-8/95: 84
• Fa 7-8/95: 117
+ Gr 5/95: 79

30496. 09026-61976-2: Danzi—Flute concerto no. 2; Sinfonia concertante for flute and clarinet; Fantasia on La ci darem la mano. *Galway, flute; Meyer, clarinet; Württemberg Chamber Orch.;*

Faerber, cond.
+ ARG 3-4/95: 91
+ Gr 2/95: 42

30497. 09026-61983-2: BARBER—
Knoxville summer of 1915; Hermit
songs; Scenes from Antony and
Cleopatra. *L. Price, soprano; Barber,
piano; Philharmonia Orch.; Schippers,
cond.* Reissue.
+ ARG 9-10/94: 96
+ Fa 9-10/94: 132
+ Gr 8/94: 87

30498. 09026-62501-2: Music of
Tchaikovsky, Mussorgsky,
Dargomizhsky, Glinka, and others.
Ghiaurov, bass; Dokovska, piano.
+ ARG 1-2/95: 239
+ Gr 1/95: 94

30499. 09026-62504-2: Ben Heppner
sings great tenor arias. *Heppner, tenor;
Munich Radio Orch.; Abbado, cond.*
• ARG 1-2/96: 233
+ Fa 1-2/96: 314
• Fa 1-2/96: 361
+ Gr 11/95: 165
+ ON 2/3/96: 37

30500. 09026-62505-2: BORODIN—
Symphony no. 2; Petite suite. *Russian
State Symphony Orch.; Svetlanov, cond.*
• ARG 7-8/94: 78
+ Fa 7-8/94: 86
• Gr 8/94: 42

30501. 09026-62511-2: ROUSSEL—
Symphonies no. 1-4. *Orch. Phil. de Radio
France; Janowski, cond.*
+ ARG 7-8/96: 181
• Fa 5-6/96: 249
• Gr 6/96: 54

30502. 09026-62512-2: MENDELSSOHN—
Violin concertos in D and E minor.
*Takezawa, violin; Bamberg Symphony
Orch.; Flor, cond.*
- ARG 3-4/95: 138
+ Gr 2/95: 50

30503. 09026-62514-2, 68014-2 (2
separate discs): *Pavarotti: the early
years, vol. 1-2.* Music of Puccini,
Donizetti, Massenet, Bellini, Rossini, and
Verdi. *Pavarotti, tenor; with various
artists.*
+ Gr 10/95: 146
+ ON 10/96: 42

30504. 09026-62520-2: TCHAIKOVSKY—
Seasons; Piano music. *Kong, piano.*
+ ARG 3-4/95: 200

30505. 09026-62521-2: MAHLER—
Symphony no. 4. *Blasi, soprano;
Bavarian Radio Symphony Orch.; C.
Davis, cond.*
+ ARG 7-8/96: 149
• Fa 7-8/96: 232
+ Gr 7/96: 56

30506. 09026-62524-2: *It's peaceful
here.* Music of Rachmaninoff, Kreisler,
Tchaikovsky, Massenet, Elgar, and
others. *Spivakov, violin; Bezrodny, piano.*
- ARG 7-8/95: 254
+ Gr 5/95: 76

30507. 09026-62530-2: Music of
Telemann, Koppel, Krahmer, Vivaldi,
Ibert, and others. *Petri, recorder;
Hannibal, lute, guitar Lars.*
+ ARG 1-2/95: 224

30508. 09026-62532-2: RACHMANINOFF—
Symphony no. 3; Isle of the dead;
Vocalise. *Philadelphia Orch.;
Rachmaninoff, cond.* Recorded 1939,
1929.
+ ARG 7-8/96: 287

30509. 09026-62537-2: TAKEMITSU—
Fantasma/cantos; Water-ways; Waves;
Quatrain II. *Stolzman, clarinet; Tashi;
instrumental soloists; BBC Welsh
Symphony; Otaka, cond.*
+ ARG 1-2/95: 191
+ Fa 1-2/95: 287
+ Gr 1/95: 58

30510. 09026-62538-2 (2 discs):
WEBER—Der Freischütz. *Sweet, Ziesak,
Seiffert, Rydl; German Symphony Berlin;
Janowski, cond.*
+ ARG 3-4/95: 222
+ Gr 1/95: 100
• ON 3/4/95: 40
+ Op 11/94: 1352

30511. 09026-62539-2: GRANADOS—
Songs. *Caballé, soprano; Ferrer, piano.*
Reissue.
+ ARG 11-12/94: 121

30512. 09026-62540-2: BERIO—Recital I
for Cathy; Folk songs; Kurt Weill songs.
*Berberian, soprano; London Sinfonietta;
Juilliard Ensemble; Berio, cond.*
Recorded 1968.
+ ARG 5-6/95: 89
+ Gr 7/95: 93

30513. 09026-62541-2: Pavarotti: the
early years (1964-69), vol. 1. *Pavarotti,
tenor.* Reissues.
+ ARG 9-10/95: 290

30514. 09026-62542-2: CHOPIN—Piano
sonata no. 3; 12 mazurkas. *Kissin, piano.*
• ARG 5-6/95: 100
+ Gr 11/94: 112

30515. 09026-62543-2: *Moonchild's
dream.* Music of Holmboe, Kulesha,
Arnold, Christiansen, and Koppel. *Petri,
recorder; English Chamber Orch.;
Kamu, cond.*
+ ARG 1-2/96: 212
+ Fa 1-2/96: 412
+ Fi 3/96: 126

30516. 09026-62544-2: BERLIOZ—
Requiem. *Cole, tenor; Tanglewood
Festival Chorus; Boston Symphony*

Orch.; Ozawa, cond. Reissue.
+ ARG 3-4/95: 74
+ Fa 5-6/95: 141
• Gr 3/95: 81

30517. 09026-62546-2: *Salut d'amour.*
Music of Falla, Debussy, Elgar, Kreisler,
Rachmaninoff, and others. *Meyers,
violin; Rivers, piano.*
+ ARG 11-12/94: 238
+ Fa 11-12/94: 495
• Gr 4/95: 86

30518. 09026-62547-2: *Divas in song.*
Music of Britten, Schubert, Mendelssohn,
Mahler, Granados, and others. *Horne,
mezzo-soprano; with colleagues.* Concert
recording.
+ ARG 3-4/95: 262
+ Gr 1/95: 95

30519. 09026-62548-2: SHOSTAKOVICH—
Symphony no. 7. *St. Petersburg Phil.
Orch.; Temirkanov, cond.*
• ARG 7-8/96: 197
+ Fa 5-6/96: 277
• Gr 6/96: 56

30520. 09026-62549-2: HAYDN—
Symphonies, no. 94, 98, 104.
Philharmonia Orch.; Slatkin, cond.
+ ARG 11-12/94: 129
+ Fa 1-2/95: 174
+ Gr 2/95: 44

30521. 09026-62552-2: RAVEL—String
quartet; Introduction and allegro.
DEBUSSY—String quartet. *Tokyo String
Quartet; Galway, flute; Stoltzman,
clarinet; Lehwalder, harp.*
+ ARG 5-6/95: 102
+ Fa 7-8/95: 287
• Gr 4/95: 78

30522. 09026-62553-2: MENDELSSOHN—
Music for cello and piano. *Isserlis, cello;
Tan, fortepiano.*
+ ARG 3-4/95: 139
+ Gr 3/95: 66

30523. 09026-62554-2: MOMPOU—Songs
and dances, no. 1-14; Preludes no. 5-7,
11. *Larrocha, piano.*
+ ARG 5-6/95: 141
• Fa 5-6/95: 264
+ Gr 11/94: 116

30524. 09026-62555-2: BACH—Flute
sonatas. *Galway, flute; Moll,
harpsichord; Cunningham, viola da
gamba.*
+ ARG 5-6/95: 73
• Fa 7-8/95: 108
+ Gr 6/95: 66

30525. 09026-62558-2: RIMSKY-
KORSAKOV—Symphony no. 1; Antar.
*Russian State Symphony Orch.;
Svetlanov, cond.*
- ARG 11-12/94: 177
• Fa 1-2/95: 244
+ Gr 11/94: 84

30526. 09026-62568-2: BLITZSTEIN—Symphony "Airborne"; Dusty sun. *Holland, tenor; Scheff, baritone; Shaw, narrator; RCA Victor Chorale; New York City Symphony Orch.; Bernstein, piano & cond.* Recorded 1946.
+ ARG 3-4/95: 269
+ Fa 3-4/95: 135
+ Gr 7/95: 128

30527. 09026-62571-2: Music of Stanley, Handel, Bach, Hindemith, Mozart, and Pachelbel. *Biggs, organ; Hindemith, viola; Fiedler Sinfonietta; Fiedler, cond.* Recorded 1940s.
+ ARG 5-6/95: 236

30528. 09026-62582-2: BERLIOZ—Harold in Italy. INDY—Symphony on a French mountain air. *Primrose, viola; Henriot-Schweitzer, piano; Boston Symphony Orch.; Munch, cond.* Reissues.
+ ARG 3-4/95: 73
+ Gr 5/95: 44

30529. 09026-62585-2: MOZART—Symphonies no. 39-40; Eine kleine Nachtmusik. *Chicago Symphony Orch.; Reiner, cond.* Recorded 1955.
+ ARG 5-6/95: 143

30530. 09026-62586-2: FALLA—El amor brujo; Three-cornered hat: Dances; La vida breve: Excerpts. ALBENIZ—Orchestra music. GRANADOS—Goyescas: Intermezzo. *Price, soprano; Chicago Symphony Orch.; Reiner, cond.* Reissues.
+ ARG 11-12/95: 116

30531. 09026-62587-2: DVOŘÁK—Symphony no. 9; Carnival overture. SMETANA—Bartered bride overture. WEINBERGER—Polka and fugue. *Chicago Symphony Orch.; Reiner, cond.* Reissues.
+ ARG 7-8/95: 110

30532. 09026-62590-2: LISZT—Piano sonata. FRANCK—Prélude, choral et fugue. BACH—Chaconne (arr. Busoni). *Rubinstein, piano.* Reissues.
+ ARG 7-8/95: 143

30533. 09026-62592-2: BRAHMS—Cello sonatas; Intermezzi. *Piatigorsky, cello; Rubinstein, piano.* Reissues.
+ ARG 11-12/95: 95

30534. 09026-62595-2: Opera duets. *Domingo, tenor; Milnes, baritone; Ricciarelli, soprano; orch. acc.* Reissues.
+ ARG 1-2/96: 232

30535. 09026-62596-2: Highlights from the Prima donna collection. *Price, soprano.* Reissues.
• ARG 9-10/95: 291

30536. 09026-62643-2: *The private collection.* Music of Bach, Clementi, Mendelssohn, Chopin, Liszt and Rachmaninoff. *Horowitz, piano.* Recorded live.
+ ARG 1-2/95: 259

30537. 09026-62644-2: *Horowitz: the private collection, vol. 2.* Music of Debussy, Prokofiev, Poulenc, Kabalevsky, and Barber. *Horowitz, piano.* Recorded 1945-49.
+ ARG 1-2/96: 245
+ Fa 1-2/96: 398

30538. 09026-62646-2 (3 discs): WAGNER—Lohengrin. *Rootering, Heppner, Sweet, Leiferkus, Marton, Terfel; Bavarian State Opera; Bavarian Radio Symphony Orch.; Davis, cond.*
• ARG 1-2/96: 196
• Fa 1-2/96: 342
• Gr 11/95: 161
• ON 12/9/95: 46

30539. 09026-62647-2: *The men in my life.* Music of Gershwin, Porter, Rogers, sondheim, Bernstein, and others. *Horne, mezzo-soprano; with Ramey, Hadley, Hampson, and Malas, male vocalists; American Theatre Orch.; Gemignani, cond.*
+ ARG 1-2/95: 241

30540. 09026-62650-2: BRUCKNER—Symphony no. 9. *NDR Symphony Orch.; Wand, cond.*
• ARG 1-2/95: 93
+ Fa 11-12/94: 192
• Gr 11/94: 68

30541. 09026-62651-2: VERDI—Ballet music from Aïda, Don Carlos, Macbeth, Otello, and Les vêpres siciliennes. *Munich Radio Orch.; Abbado, cond.*
• ARG 9-10/96: 221
+ Fa 9-10/96: 346

30542. 09026-62652-2: *Tribute to Vienna.* Music of Beethoven, Schubert, Mahler, Wolf, Strauss, Bernstein, and Brahms. *Ludwig, mezzo-soprano; Spencer, piano.*
+ ARG 5-6/95: 228

30543. 09026-62655-2: BACH—Cantatas no. 54, 82, 170. *Stutzmann, alto; Robson, oboe; Hanover Band; Goodman, organ, violin & cond.*
- ARG 11-12/96: 80
+ Fa 11-12/96: 167
• Gr 11/96: 131

30544. 09026-62661-2: Concertos by L. Mozart, Hummel, and Arutunian. *Sandoval, trumpet; London Symphony Orch.; Haza, cond.*
• ARG 11-12/94: 237

30545. 09026-62666-2: Chill to the chant. *Sequentia; Schola Cantorum Basel.* Reissues.
• ARG 3-4/95: 253

30546. 09026-62681-2: Operetta arias by Friml, Herbert, and Romberg. *Hadley, tenor; American Theatre Orch.; Gemignani, cond.*
- ARG 11-12/94: 250
• Gr 12/95: 164

30547. 09026-62684-2: RIMSKY-KORSAKOV—Symphony no. 3; Overtures; Orchestra music. *Russian State Symphony Orch.; Svetlanov, cond.*
+ ARG 11-12/95: 185
+ Gr 10/95: 66

30548. 09026-62685-2: *Amber waves.* Music of Gershwin, Bernstein, McKinley, Fisher, and others. *Stoltzman, clarinet; Vallecillo, piano.*
+ ARG 7-8/96: 243
+ Fa 9-10/96: 401
+ Gr 9/96: 72

30549. 09026-62687-2 (2 discs): PUCCINI—Turandot. *Nilsson, Tebaldi, Björling, Tozzi; Rome Opera; Leinsdorf, cond.* Recorded 1959.
+ ARG 1-2/97: 154

30550. 09026-62691-2: PROKOFIEV—Piano concerto no. 3. SCHUMANN—Piano concerto. *Cliburn, piano; Chicago Symphony Orch.; Hendl, Reiner, conds.* Reissues.
+ Gr 8/96: 54

30551. 09026-62695-2: BRAHMS—Piano concerto no. 2. RACHMANINOFF—Rhapsody on a theme of Paganini. *Cliburn, piano; Moscow Phil. Orch.; Kondrashin, cond.*
• ARG 1-2/95: 87
• Fa 11-12/94: 183
- Gr 2/95: 41

30552. 09026-62696-2: HAYDN—Symphony no. 6; Sinfonia concertante; Cello concerto no. 2. *Zukerman, violin & cond.; Kirshbaum, cello; Hunt, oboe; O'Neill, bassoon; English Chamber Orch.*
+ ARG 3-4/95: 112
• Gr 1/96: 49

30553. 09026-62697-2: FRANCK—Violin sonata. DEBUSSY—Violin sonata. FAURÉ—Violin sonata no. 1. *Zukerman, violin; Neikrug, piano.*
+ ARG 9-10/95: 141
• Fa 7-8/95: 187
• Gr 5/95: 68

30554. 09026-62698-2 (7 discs): 100 Fiedler favorites. *Boston Pops; Fiedler, cond.* Reissues.
+ ARG 1-2/95: 205

30555. 09026-62699-2: Opera's greatest duets. *Various performers.*
+ ARG 1-2/95: 246

30556. 09026-62710-2: RACHMANINOFF—Aleko: Overture; Paganini rhapsody; Symphonic dances. *Alexeev, piano; St. Petersburg Phil. Orch.; Temirkanov, cond.*
+ ARG 3-4/95: 161
• Fa 5-6/95: 299
• Gr 4/95: 68

30557. 09026-62711-2: *Voyage à Paris.* Music of Poulenc, Satie, Debussy,

Honegger, Ravel, and Messiaen. *Von Stade, mezzo-soprano; Katz, piano.*
+ ARG 7-8/95: 265
+ Fa 7-8/95: 379
+ Gr 4/95: 116

30558. 09026-62712-2: WEBER—Symphonies no. 1-2; Der Freischütz overture. *Philharmonia Orch.; Flor, cond.*
+ ARG 11-12/95: 232
- Fa 11-12/95: 427
• Gr 11/95: 101

30559. 09026-65538-2 (2 discs): WEBER—Der Freischütz. *Sweet, Ziesak, Seiffert, Schmidt, Rydl, Hölle, Matić; Rundfunkchor Berlin; Deutsches Symphonie-Orchester Berlin; Janowski, cond.*
+ Fa 1-2/95: 309

30560. 09026-66163-2: *The romantic tenor. Music of Lehár, Rossini, Bernstein, Grever, Chopin/Kühn, Ponce/Sommerlatte, Leoncavallo, Lennon/McCartney, Di Capua, Tauber, Lara, Martini, and De Curtis. Araiza, tenor; Munich Radio Orch.; Weikert, cond.*
• Fa 5-6/93: 368

30561. 09026-68004-2: BYRD—Motets and anthems. TALLIS—Anthems. *King's Singers.*
+ ARG 7-8/95: 98

30562. 05472-61868-2: Ancient music for a modern age. *Sequentia.* Reissues.
+ ARG 1-2/94: 186

30563. 09026-68006-2: ANTHEIL—Fighting the waves. *Hill, tenor; Mistry, violin; Kreyzschmar, piano; Ensemble Modern; Gruber, cond.*
□ ARG 11-12/96: 77
+ Fa 11-12/96: 160
+ Gr 12/96: 68

30564. 09026-68007-2: Chant of the season. *Choirs of Mount Angel Abbey.*
• ARG 3-4/95: 253

30565. 09026-68008-2: BERLIOZ—Les nuits d'été. RAVEL—Shéhérazade. CHAUSSON—Poème de l'amour et de la mer. *Kasarova, mezzo-soprano; ORF-Symphonieorchester; Steinberg, cond.*
• ARG 11-12/95: 88
• Fa 11-12/95: 210
• Gr 9/95: 87
- ON 2/22/97: 42

30566. 09026-68014-2: Pavarotti: the early years (1964-69), vol. 2. *Pavarotti, tenor.* Reissues.
• ARG 9-10/95: 290

30567. 09026-68025-2: *Eva Mei at midnight.* Songs by Rossini, Bellini, and Donizetti. *Mei, soprano; Bidini, piano.*
• ARG 1-2/96: 233
- Fa 1-2/96: 352
+ Gr 1/96: 85

• ON 10/96: 44
• Op 12/95: 1497

30568. 09026-68027-2: HINDEMITH—Cello concerto. SCHUMANN—Cello concerto. *Starker, cello; Bamberg Symphony Orch.; D.R. Davies, cond.*
+ ARG 11-12/95: 135
+ Fa 1-2/96: 225 (Wiser)
• Fa 1-2/96: 227 (North)
+ Gr 10/95: 58

30569. 09026-68030-2: *The age of bel canto.* Music of Donizetti, Rossini, Flotow, Planquette, Halévy, Thomas, and others. *Hadley, tenor; English Chamber Orch.; Bonynge, cond.*
+ ARG 5-6/96: 255
• Fa 5-6/96: 327
+ Gr 1/96: 107

30570. 09026-68031-2 (6 discs): ORFF—Musica poetica (Schulwerk). *Tölzer Boychoir.*
+ ARG 7-8/95: 164
+ Fa 9-10/95: 271
+ Gr 8/95: 119

30571. 09026-68032-2: MOZART—Symphony no. 40. TCHAIKOVSKY—Symphony no. 5. *North German Radio Symphony Orch.; Wand, cond.*
+ Gr 6/95: 52

30572. 09026-68033-2: BRAHMS—Clarinet quintet, op. 115. WEBER—Clarinet quintet, op. 34. *Stoltzman, clarinet; Tokyo String Quartet.*
+ ARG 9-10/95: 114
+ Fa 9-10/95: 153
• Gr 8/95: 92

30573. 09026-68038-2: BEETHOVEN—String quartets no. 4, 11, 16. *Tokyo String Quartet.* Reissues.
+ ARG 1-2/95: 77

30574. 09026-68043-2: MAHLER (ARR. SCHOENBERG AND RIEHN)—Das Lied von der Erde. *Rigby, mezzo-soprano; Tear, tenor; Premiere Ensemble; Wigglesworth, cond.*
• ARG 7-8/95: 151
• Fa 7-8/95: 230
• Gr 3/95: 88

30575. 09026-68044-2: MOZART—Concerto for 2 pianos, K. 365; Sonata for 2 pianos, K. 448. *Larrocha, piano; Previn, piano & cond.; Orch. of St. Luke's.*
+ Fa 9-10/95: 266
• Gr 10/95: 63

30576. 09026-68045-2: TCHAIKOVSKY—Symphony no. 2; Romeo and Juliet fantasy-overture; 1812 overture. *St. Louis Symphony Orch.; Slatkin, cond.*
+ ARG 1-2/96: 186
• Fa 11-12/95: 397
• Gr 11/95: 94

30577. 09026-68046-2: BRAHMS—Violin concerto. BRUCH—Violin concerto no. 1. *Zukerman, violin; Los Angeles Phil. Orch.; London Phil. Orch.; Mehta, cond.*
- ARG 5-6/96: 88
+ Fa 3-4/96: 136
+ Gr 4/96: 42

30578. 09026-68047-2 (2 discs): BRUCKNER—Symphony no. 8 (Haas ed.). *NDR Sinfonieorchester, Hamburg; Wand, cond.*
• ARG 11-12/95: 100
+ Fa 11-12/95: 226
• Gr 8/95: 67

30579. 09026-68048-2: *The typewriter: Leroy Anderson favorites.* ANDERSON—Orchestra music. *St. Louis Symphony Orch.; Slatkin, cond.*
+ ARG 1-2/96: 70
• Fa 1-2/96: 104
+ Gr 1/96: 48

30580. 09026-68049-2: FAURÉ—Music for cello and piano. *Isserlis, cello; Devoyon, piano.*
+ ARG 7-8/95: 111
+ Fa 9-10/95: 200
+ Gr 8/95: 96

30581. 09026-68052-2 (2 discs): SCHUMANN—Violin sonatas no. 1-2; Phantasiestücke, op. 73; Romances, op. 94; Märchenbilder for viola and piano, op. 113. *Zukerman, violin & viola; Neikrug, piano.*
+ ARG 11-12/95: 202
+ Fa 9-10/95: 318
• Gr 11/95: 116

30582. 09026-68061-2: *Stalin cocktail.* Music of Shostakovich, Pärt, Denisov, and Shchedrin. *Moscow Virtuosi; Spivakov, cond.*
+ ARG 9-10/95: 246
+ Fa 11-12/95: 495
• Gr 12/95: 101

30583. 09026-68062-2: RAVEL—Piano trio. DEBUSSY—Piano trio. *Previn, piano; Rosenfeld, violin; Hoffman, cello.*
• ARG 11-12/95: 183
+ Fa 11-12/95: 343
+ Gr 11/95: 105

30584. 09026-68067-2 (2 discs): ZENDER—Schubert's Die Winterreise: a composed interpretation. *Blochwitz, tenor; Ensemble Modern; Zender, cond.*
• ARG 11-12/95: 198
- Fa 11-12/95: 434
• Fa 1-2/96: 349
+ Gr 9/95: 96
+ ON 8/96: 42

30585. 09026-68069-2 (3 discs): MENDELSSOHN—Twelve string symphonies; Symphonic movement in C minor. *Hanover Band; Goodman, cond.*
• ARG 3-4/96: 155
+ Fa 3-4/96: 223
+ Gr 1/96: 58

RCA

30586. 09026-68076-2: Music of Monteverdi, Gabrieli, Beethoven, Vaughan Williams, and Sousa. *Canadian Brass.*
• ARG 9-10/95: 253

30587. 09026-68079-2: DEBUSSY—La mer. RESPIGHI—The pines of Rome; The fountains of Rome. *Chicago Symphony Orch.; Reiner, cond.* Reissue; recorded 1961.
+ ARG 7-8/95: 179
+ Gr 9/95: 54

30588. 09026-68095-2: Opera's greatest drinking songs. *Various performers.* Reissues.
+ ARG 7-8/95: 267

30589. 09026-68100-2: CORIGLIANO—Tournaments; Fantasia on an ostinato; Elegy; Piano concerto. *Douglas, piano; St. Louis Symphony Orch.; Slatkin, cond.*
+ ARG 7-8/96: 101
+ Fa 7-8/96: 149
+ Gr 11/96: 82

30590. 09026-68111-2: ZEMLINSKY—Lyrische Sinfonie; Six Lieder. *Orgonasova, soprano; Skovhus, baritone; Deutsch, piano; North German Radio Symphony Orch.; Flor, cond.*
+ ARG 1-2/97: 192
• Fa 1-2/97: 306
+ Gr 12/96: 90
+ ON 2/8/97: 40

30591. 09026-68114-2: *The American album.* Music of Piston, Copland, Ives, and Baker. *Meyers, violin; Schub, piano.*
+ ARG 9-10/96: 252
• Fa 9-10/96: 414
+ Gr 8/96: 68

30592. 09026-68116-2: OFFENBACH—Arias and overtures. *Von Stade, mezzo-soprano; Scottish Chamber Orch.; Almeida, cond.*
+ ARG 1-2/96: 151
• Fa 3-4/96: 241
+ Gr 2/96: 105
+ ON 5/96: 58

30593. 09026-68131-2: *Classics for children.* Music of Saint-Saëns, Britten, Grieg, Gounod, and Loesser. *Boston Pops; Fiedler, cond.* Reissue.
+ ARG 9-10/95: 245

30594. 09026-68132-2: *Pops caviar.* Music of Borodin, Rimsky-Korsakov, Khachaturian, and Tchaikovsky. *Boston Pops; Fiedler, cond.* Reissues.
+ ARG 11-12/95: 239

30595. 09026-68139-2: ROSSINI—Overtures. *Hanover Band; Goodman, cond.*
+ ARG 3-4/96: 174
• Fi 4/96: 124
• Gr 1/96: 60

30596. 09026-68148-2: Zarzuela: arias and duets. *Caballé, soprano; Marti, tenor; orch.; Marco, cond.* Reissues.
+ ARG 1-2/96: 230
+ Gr 4/96: 122

30597. 09026-68153-2 (11 discs): The essential Leontyne Price. *Price, soprano.* Reissues.
+ ARG 1-2/97: 228
+ Fa 3-4/97: 349
+ Gr 11/96: 181

30598. 09026-68159-2: HANDEL—Messiah: Excerpts. *Royal Phil Orch.; Beecham, cond.* Reissue.
+ ARG 11-12/96: 138

30599. 09026-68163-2: THOMSON—Four saints in three acts (abridged); The plow that broke the plains. *Soloists, chorus, orchestra, Thomson, cond.; Hollywood Bowl Symphony Orch.; Stokowski, cond.* Recorded 1947, 1945.
+ ARG 7-8/96: 288
+ Fa 5-6/96: 300
ı Fi 4/96: 127
+ ON 5/96: 59

30600. 09026-68164-2 (2 discs): CHOPIN—Piano music. *Brailowsky, piano.*
• ARG 7-8/96: 291
+ Fa 1-2/97: 138

30601. 09026-68165-2 (2 discs): Music of Bach, Saint-Saëns, Liszt, Liapunov, Fauré, Ravel, Debussy, Falla, Beethoven, Schubert, Mendelssohn, Brahms, Rachmaninoff, Bartók, Rimsky-Korsakov, and Scriabin. *Brailowsky, piano; Boston Symphony Orch.; Munch, cond.* Reissues.
+ Fa 1-2/97: 138
• Gr 11/96: 126

30602. 09026-68168-2: RIMSKY-KORSAKOV—Scheherazade. STRAVINSKY—Song of the nightingale. *Chicago Symphony Orch.; Reiner, cond.* Reissue.
+ ARG 7-8/96: 180

30603. 09026-68170-2: STRAUSS—Don Quixote; Don Juan. *Janigro, cello; Chicago Symphony Orch.; Reiner, cond.* Reissues.
- ARG 7-8/96: 206

30604. 09026-68181-2: *French chamber music.* Music of Poulenc, Milhaud, and Saint-Saëns. *Previn, piano; Kavafian, Rosenfeld, violins; Hoffman, viola; Brey, cello; Kulowitsch, double bass; Mann, flute; Taylor, oboe; Shifrin, clarinet; Todd, horn; Stevens, trumpet.*
+ ARG 11-12/95: 246
+ Fa 11-12/95: 484
+ Gr 11/95: 110

30605. 09026-68184-2: GRANADOS—Danzas españolas; Valses poéticos. *Larrocha, piano.*
+ ARG 5-6/96: 118

• Fa 3-4/96: 171
+ Gr 1/96: 80

30606. 09026-68185-2: *Encore!* Music of Anderson, Gershwin, Falla, Elgar, Boccherini, Tchaikovsky, Albéniz, Rossini, Bach, Corelli, Vivaldi, Schubert, Mozart, Sieczynski, Kreisler, Prokofiev, Shostakovich, Bartók, Bock, and Poltoratzsky. *Moscow Virtuosi; Spivakov, violin & cond.*
- ARG 3-4/96: 222
+ Fa 3-4/96: 383

30607. 09026-68186-2: DVOŘÁK—Cello concerto; Silent woods; Rondo; Slavonic dances, op. 46: no. 3, 8; Polonaise. *Harnoy, cello; Dussek, piano; Prague Symphony Orch.; Mackerras, cond.*
• ARG 3-4/96: 109
- Fa 5-6/96: 144
• Fi 4/96: 123
• Gr 4/96: 44

30608. 09026-68187-2: MOZART—Rare arias. *Stutzmann, alto; Moscow Virtuosi; Spivakov, cond.*
+ Fa 3-4/96: 230
+ Gr 3/96: 96

30609. 09026-68188-2: BACH—Italian concerto; Goldberg variations. *P. Serkin, piano.*
- ARG 11-12/96: 86
• Fa 9-10/96: 135
• Fi 11/96: 122
- Gr 9/96: 74

30610. 09026-68189-2: *In real time.* Music of Lieberson, Knussen, Henze, Goehr, Berio, Kirchner, and Takemitsu. *P. Serkin, piano.*
+ ARG 9-10/96: 248
+ Fa 9-10/96: 410

30611. 09026-68190-2: MAHLER—Symphony no. 10 (Mazzetti ed.). *St. Louis Symphony Orch.; Slatkin, cond.*
+ ARG 3-4/96: 149
+ Fa 3-4/96: 212
+ Fi 4/96: 117
• Gr 4/96: 48

30612. 09026-68218-2: SIBELIUS—Symphonies no. 2, 6. *London Symphony Orch.; Davis, cond.*
+ ARG 11-12/95: 206
+ Fa 11-12/95: 378
+ Gr 12/95: 91

30613. 09026-68221-2: STRAUSS—Symphonia domestica; Death and transfiguration. *Bavarian Radio Orch.; Maazel, cond.*
• ARG 11-12/96: 216
+ Fa 11-12/96: 386
+ Gr 11/96: 98

30614. 09026-68225-2: STRAUSS—Also sprach Zarathustra; Der Rosenkavalier: Suite; Don Juan. *Bavarian Radio Symphony Orch.; Maazel, cond.*
+ ARG 1-2/96: 179

- Fa 1-2/96: 310
- Gr 10/95: 71

30615. 09026-68226-2: BEETHOVEN— Piano concertos no. 1, 3. *Oppitz, piano; Leipzig Gewandhaus Orch.; Janowski, cond.*
+ ARG 5-6/96: 79
- Fa 3-4/96: 122
- Gr 3/96: 41

30616. 09026-68239-2: WAGNER— Lohengrin (excerpts). *Rootering, Heppner, Sweet, Leiferkus, Marton, Terfel; Bavarian State Opera Chorus; Bavarian Radio Orch.; C. Davis, cond.* Reissue.
+ Fa 11-12/96: 415

30617. 09026-68244-2: On angels' wings. *Schola Benedictina of Mount Angel Abbey (Oregon); Baumgartner, cond.*
- Fa 11-12/96: 443

30618. 09026-68255-2: *Sermons and devotions.* Music of Górecki, Tormis, Stravinsky, Poole, Tavener, and Bennett. *King's Singers.*
+ ARG 9-10/96: 261
+ Fa 11-12/96: 434
+ Gr 8/96: 91

30619. 09026-68257-2: *Fireworks! Baroque brass favorites.* Music of Purcell, Handel, Clarke, and Tallis. *Canadian Brass.*
+ ARG 1-2/96: 208
+ Fa 1-2/96: 404

30620. 09026-68262-2: SCHUMANN— Fantasy, op. 17. LISZT—Études d'exécution transcendante no. 5, 8, 10-12. *Kissin, piano.*
- ARG 9-10/96: 154
- Fa 7-8/96: 296
+ Gr 5/96: 85

30621. 09026-68268-2: *Remembering the future.* Music by Morel, Bustamente, Fauré-Ravel, Romero, and others. *A. Romero, guitar; & friends.*
- ARG 5-6/96: 236

30622. 09026-68283-2: BARBER—Violin concerto; Cello concerto; Capricorn concerto. *Takezawa, violin; Isserlis, cello; Berg, flute; Bowman, oboe; Slaughter, trumpet; St. Louis Symphony Orch.; Slatkin, cond.*
+ ARG 7-8/96: 71
+ Gr 5/96: 53

30623. 09026-68284-2 (2 discs): BOITO—Mefistofele. *Ramey, La Scola, Crider, Jankovic, Gavazzi; Teatro alla Scala; Muti, cond.* Recorded live 1995.
ARG 1-2/97: 77
+ Fa 1-2/97: 113
- Gr 8/96: 92
- ON 11/96: 44
+ Op 9/96: 1064

30624. 09026-68286-2 (3 discs): BARTÓK—String quartets no. 1-6. JANÁČEK—String quartets no. 1-2. *Tokyo String Quartet.*
+ ARG 9-10/96: 88
+ Fa 5-6/96: 89
+ Fi 6/96: 130
+ Gr 8/96: 62

30625. 09026-68288-2: PROKOFIEV— Romeo and Juliet: scenes. *San Francisco Symphony Orch.; Thomas, cond.*
- ARG 5-6/96: 165
+ Fa 3-4/96: 248
+ Fi 5/96: 123
- Gr 5/96: 63

30626. 09026-68290-2: *Forgotten romance.* GRIEG—Cello sonata. RUBINSTEIN—Cello sonata no. 1. Music of Liszt. *Isserlis, cello; Hough, piano.*
+ ARG 5-6/96: 233
- Fa 5-6/96: 343
+ Gr 4/96: 64

30627. 09026-68291-2: VIVALDI— Concertos. *A. Romero, guitar & cond.; L. Romero, guitar; Blume, viola d'amore; Sillito, violin; Constable, harpsichord; Sheen, bassoon; Academy of St. Martin-in-the-Fields.*
+ ARG 3-4/96: 204
- Fa 3-4/96: 316

30628. 09026-68292-2: COPLAND—Organ symphony; Dance symphony; Short symphony; Variations. *Preston, organ; St. Louis Symphony Orch.; Slatkin, cond.*
+ ARG 9-10/96: 110
- Fa 11-12/96: 225
+ Gr 6/96: 44

30629. 09026-68314-2 (2 discs): SCHUBERT—Symphonies no. 8-9. *Berlin Phil. Orch.; Wand, cond.*
+ ARG 5-6/96: 188
+ Fa 7-8/96: 291
+ Gr 1/96: 62

30630. 09026-68319-2: ROSSINI— Overtures. *Hanover Band; Goodman, cond.*
+ Fa 3-4/96: 263

30631. 09026-68328-2: MACMILLAN— The berserking; Sowetan spring; Britannia; Sinfonietta. *Donohoe, piano; Scottish National Orch.; Stenz, MacMillan, conds.*
+ ARG 11-12/96: 307
+ Gr 7/96: 54

30632. 09026-68344-2 (2 discs): BEETHOVEN—Fidelio; Leonore overture no. 2. *Voigt, Heppner, Kannen, Hölle, Norberg-Schulz, Schade, Quasthoff; Orch. & Chorus of the Bavarian Radio; C. Davis, cond.*
- ARG 1-2/97: 68
- Fa 1-2/97: 100
- Gr 11/96: 161
- ON 12/28/96: 37
+ Op 11/96: 1369

30633. 09026-68349-2 (3 discs): ROSSINI—Tancredi. *Kasarova, Mei, Vargas, Peeters; Chor des Bayerischen Rundfunks; Münchner Rundfunkorchester; R. Abbado, cond.*
+ ARG 3-4/97: 209
+ Fa 1-2/97: 242
+ Gr 12/96: 140
+ ON 12/28/96: 36
+ Op 1/97: 72

30634. 09026-68351-2: WIDOR—Suite for flute and piano. FAURÉ—Flute sonata. DEBUSSY—Arrangements for flute and piano. *Galway, flute; O'Riley, piano.*
+ ARG 7-8/96: 111
+ Fa 5-6/96: 318
+ Gr 8/96: 63

30635. 09026-68378-2: CHOPIN—Piano concertos no. 1-2; Mazurkas, op. 63, no. 2; op. 68, no. 4; Waltz, op. posth. *Kissin, piano; Moscow Phil. Orch.; Kitaenko, cond.* Reissue.
+ ARG 3-4/96: 101
+ Fa 3-4/96: 148
+ Gr 2/96: 46

30636. 09026-68387-2: GÓRECKI— Symphony no. 3 "Symphony of sorrowful songs". *Feis, soprano; Orquesta Filarmónico de Gran Canaria; Leaper, cond.*
+ ARG 7-8/96: 121
+ Fa 5-6/96: 159

30637. 09026-68399-2: MOZART—Piano concertos no. 20, 25. *Larrocha, piano; English Chamber Orch.; Davis, cond.*
- ARG 11-12/96: 168
+ Fa 9-10/96: 269
+ Gr 12/96: 80

30638. 09026-68406-2: MUSSORGSKY— Sunless; Orchestral pieces. *Gerasimova, soprano; Russian State Symphony Orch.; Svetlanov, cond.*
- ARG 9-10/96: 169
+ Fa 11-12/96: 322

30639. 09026-68413-2 (2 discs): SCHNITTKE—Historia von D. Johann Fausten. *Schwarz, Büchner, Fersch, vocalists; Chor der Hamburgischen Staatsoper; Philharmonisches Staatsorchester Hamburg; Albrecht, cond.*
+ ARG 11-12/96: 197
+ Fa 9-10/96: 312
+ Gr 7/96: 107
- ON 1/11/97: 38

30640. 09026-68414-2: *Virtuoso violin.* Music of Gershwin, Kreisler, Dvořák, Godowsky, Tchaikovsky, Massenet, Prokofiev, and Debussy. *Maazel, violin; Weber, piano.*
+ ARG 9-10/96: 251
+ Fa 9-10/96: 414
+ Gr 6/96: 68

30641. 09026-68420-2: OFFENBACH— Concerto militaire; Andante. LALO—Cello

RCA

concerto. *Harnoy, cello; Bournemouth Symphony Orch.; Almeida, cond.*
- ARG 11-12/96: 175
- Fa 1-2/97: 218

30642. 09026-68421-2 (2 discs): *New Year's in Vienna 1996.* Music of J. Strauss, Sr., J. Strauss, Jr., Jos. Strauss, and Ziehrer. *Vienna Phil. Orch.; Maazel, cond.*
- ARG 1-2/97: 193
- Fa 3-4/97: 314
+ Gr 5/96: 68

30643. 09026-68424-2: HAYDN—*London symphonies, vol. 2.* Symphonies no. 96, 102-103. *Philharmonia Orch.; Slatkin, cond.*
+ ARG 11-12/96: 142
+ Fa 9-10/96: 215
- Fi 10/96: 141

30644. 09026-68428-2: RODRIGO—Fantasia para un gentilhombre; Concierto pastoral; Concierto de Aranjuez. *Galway, flute; Yamashita, guitar; Philharmonia Orch.; Mata, cond.; Paillard Chamber Orch.; Paillard, cond.* Reissues.
+ ARG 9-10/96: 189

30645. 09026-68429-2: Arias from Africana, Aida, Carmen, Trovatore, and others. *Björling, tenor; with orch. acc.* Recorded 1951-58.
+ ARG 11-12/96: 273

30646. 09026-68433-2: VIVALDI—Violin concertos RV 187, 195, 197, 204, 209, 234, 364. *Zukerman, violin & cond.; English Chamber Orch.*
+ ARG 11-12/96: 230
- Fa 9-10/96: 351

30647. 09026-68437-2: JANÁČEK—Pohadka (1923 version and supplementary version). SHOSTAKOVICH—Cello sonata, op. 40. PROKOFIEV—Cello sonata, op. 119. *Isserlis, cello; Mustonen, piano.*
+ ARG 9-10/96: 240
+ Fa 9-10/96: 226
+ Gr 5/96: 74

30648. 09026-68440-2 (2 discs): GOUNOD—Roméo et Juliette. *Domingo, Swenson, Graham, Clarke, Ollmann, Vernhes, Miles; Münchner Rundfunkorchester; Slatkin, cond.*
- ARG 9-10/96: 128
- Fa 9-10/96: 204
+ Gr 6/96: 95
+ ON 5/96: 60
- Op 9/96: 1244

30649. 09026-68446-2: VERDI—Arias. *Domingo, tenor.* Reissues.
+ ARG 1-2/97: 186

30650. 09026-68450-2: CORIGLIANO—Of rage and remembrance; Symphony no. 1. *De Young, mezzo-soprano; Choral Arts Society of Washington; National Symphony Orch.; Slatkin, cond.*

+ ARG 3-4/97: 119
+ Fa 1-2/97: 141
+ Gr 1/97: 62

30651. 09026-68452-2: BRUCKNER—Symphony no. 6. *North German Radio Symphony; Wand, cond.* Reissue.
- ARG 11-12/96: 107
+ Fa 1-2/97: 127
- Gr 10/96: 50

30652. 09026-68534-2: *Three legendary tenors.* Music of Verdi, Mozart, Donizetti, Bizet, Puccini, and others. *Caruso, McCormack, Gigli, tenors.*
+ ARG 1-2/97: 244

30653. 09026-68539-2: STRAUSS—Four last songs; Orchestral songs; Der Rosenkavalier: Suite. *Fleming, soprano; Houston Symphony Orch.; Eschenbach, cond.*
+ ARG 3-4/97: 239
+ Fa 1-2/97: 280
+ Gr 3/97: 86

30654. 09026-68595-2: TAKEMITSU—Piano music. *Serkin, piano.*
+ ARG 3-4/97: 242
+ Fa 1-2/97: 287
+ Gr 3/97: 76

30655. 09026-69185-2 (2 discs): Music of Liszt, Liapunov, Ravel, Debussy, and others. *Brailowsky, piano.*
- ARG 7-8/96: 291

30656. 87989-2-RG: *Works for oboe and orchestra.* R. STRAUSS—Oboe concerto. FRANÇAIX—L'horloge de flore. SATIE—Gymnopédie no. 1 (orch. Debussy). IBERT—Symphonie concertante. *De Lancie, oboe; London Symphony Orch.; Previn, cond.* Reissues.
+ Gr 12/91: 86

RCD

30657. 13002: BERLIOZ—Symphonie fantastique (arr. Liszt). *Petrov, piano.*
- ARG 11-12/95: 89

30658. 13003: NIKOLSKY—Liturgy of St. John Chrysostom. *Church of Three Saints Choir, Kharkov; Kurilo, cond.*
+ ARG 11-12/95: 168

30659. 13005: SVIRIDOV—Choral music. *Moscow Chamber Choir; Minin, cond.*
+ ARG 11-12/95: 215

30660. 15008: Music of Bach, Khandoshkin, and Vysotsky. *Starodumov, guitar .*
- ARG 11-12/95: 251

30661. 16001: *Singers of Russia: Ivan Kozlovsky.* Arias by Rachmaninoff, Mussorgsky, Napravnik, Rubinstein, and others. *Kozlovsky, tenor.* Recorded 1947-64.
+ ARG 9-10/95: 289

30662. 16209: BRAHMS—Paganini variations. LISZT—Paganini etudes. *Merzhanov, piano.* Recorded 1951, 1955.
- ARG 7-8/96: 283

30663. 16213: Music of Szymanowski, Tchaikovsky, Kabalevsky, and others. *Grach, violin; Epstein, piano; Moscow State Symphony Orch.; Dudarova, cond.*
+ ARG 9-10/96: 251

30664. 16251: BABAJANYAN—Orchestra music. *Babajanyan, piano; All-Union Orch.; Silatniev, cond.; Armenian Radio Orch.; Mavisakhalyan, cond.*
+ ARG 9-10/96: 79

30665. 29004, 29005, 29007, 29008 (4 separate discs): Orthodox shrine of the Russian North. *Valaam Male Choir; Singing Culture Institute; Ushakov, cond.*
+ ARG 1-2/97: 222

30666. 30001: SCHUBERT—Symphonies no. 1, 4. *Moscow Orch.; Freisitzer, cond.*
- ARG 7-8/96: 188

RCM

30667. 19502: *La cortesia.* LASSUS—Chansons, madrigals, motets, fantasias. *Ensemble de' Medici; Coker, cond.*
+ ARG 1-2/97: 129

30668. 19602: HAYDN—Symphonies no. 43, 48; Lo speziale: Overture. *Los Angeles Mozart Orch.; Carver, cond.*
+ ARG 7-8/96: 128

30669. 19603: MOZART—Symphonies no. 17, 29, 34. *Los Angeles Mozart Orch.; Carver, cond.*
+ ARG 11-12/96: 170

RECIDIVE

30670. REV 89004: HAHN—Cimetière de campagne; Nuit; L'incrédule; Paysage; Si mes vers avaient des ailes; La chere blesseur; Trois jour de vendange; Offrande; Neere; Tyndaris; Pholoe; Phyllis; Le plus beau présent; Mai; Infidélité; Les cygnes; D'une prison; Séraphine; Nocturne. *Miraille, baritone; F. Boulanger, piano.*
- Fa 7-8/90: 161

30671. REV 89007: Music of Martinů, Dohnányi, and Beethoven. *Trio Sibelius.*
+ Fa 5-6/90: 214

RECITAL

30672. KNEWCD 501: GRIEG—Holberg suite; Two elegiac melodies; The wounded heart; The last spring. NIELSEN—Little suite for strings. *Orch. da Camera di Roma; Flagello, cond.*
- Fa 11-12/89: 221

30673. KNEWCD 502: Music of Warlock, Britten, Walton, Chagrin, and Rawsthorne. *Orch. da Camera di Roma;*

Flagello, cond.
+ Fa 11-12/89: 447

30674. KNEWCD 505: STAMITZ—
Clarinet concertos no. 1, 3. TARTINI—
Concertino for clarinet and strings (trans.
Jacob). *Sobol, clarinet; Orch. da
Camera di Roma; Flagello, cond.*
- Fa 11-12/89: 477

30675. KNEWCD 508: *Clarinet
concertos.* Music of Hovhaness, Barber,
Flagello, Diamond, Barlow, and others.
*Sobol, clarinet; Orch. da Camera di
Roma; Flagello, cond.*
• Fa 11-12/89: 243

RECORD COLLECTOR

30676. 3: Arias form Tosca, Fedora,
Puritani, Sonnambula, and others.
Giorgini, tenor.
+ ARG 5-6/95: 248
+ ON 5/95: 47

30677. TRC 5: TOSTI—Songs. *Various
performers.* Recorded 1900-1939.
+ ARG 1-2/96: 244
+ Gr 6/96: 117
+ ON 10/96: 44

30678. 7: Arias from Tosca, Rigoletto,
Manon and others. *Tagliavini, tenor.*
+ ARG 11-12/96: 304

RECORDED TREASURES

30679. CD 1: LISZT—Réminiscences de
Don Juan; Valse à capriccio sur deux
motifs du Lucia et Parisina; Mélodies
hongroises; Adelaide of Beethoven;
Rigoletto, paraphrase de concert;
Réminiscences de Norma; Polonaise no.
2; La campanella. *Busoni, piano.* From
piano rolls.
+ Fa 3-4/90: 213

RECORDS INTERNATIONAL

30680. 7004-2: LACHNER—Symphony no.
1. SPOHR—Symphony no. 2. *Singapore
Symphony Orch.; Hoey, cond.* Issued also
as LP: 7004-1.
+ ARG 11-12/86: 68
• Fa 9/10/86: 176
+ HF 8/87: 61
+ NR 7/86: 8

30681. 7007-2: GOLDMARK—Symphony
no. 2; Overture: Penthesilea op. 35.
Rhenish Phil. Orch.; Halász, cond.
Issued also as LP: 7007-1.
+ ARG 11-12/86: 29
+ Fa 1-2/87: 115
+ NR 4/87: 3

30682. 7008-2: JANÁČEK—The Danube;
Schlick und Jau: Incidental music;
Moravian dance; Suite op. 3. *Slovak Phil.
Orch.; Pešek, cond.* Issued also as LP:
7008-1.
+ ARG 11-12/86: 19

+ Fa 1-2/87: 128
+ NR 4/87: 3

30683. 7009-1 (LP): RIMSKY-KORSAKOV—
Night on Mount Triglav; Pan Voyevoda.
Slovak Phil. Orch.; Režucha, cond.
• ARG Fall/87: 46
- Fa 5-6/87: 178

30684. 7010-2: RESPIGHI—Sinfonia
drammatica. *Slovak Phil. Orch.;
Nazareth, cond.* Issued also as LP: 7010-
1.
+ ARG 1-2/87: 54
+ DA 9/87: 67
• Fa 1-2/87: 164
+ NR 4/87: 3

30685. 7012-2: DELIUS—Paa Vidderne;
Spring morning; Norwegiana suite;
American rhapsody. *Slovak Phil. Orch.;
Hopkins, cond.*
• ARG 3-4/88: 31
+ Fa 11-12/87: 132
• Opus 4/88: 30

RED MARK

30686. 9204: PROTO—Carmen fantasy;
Fantasy; Concerto no. 2. *Rabbath, double
bass; Charleston Symphony Orch.;
Wolfgang Chamber Orch.; Symphonistes
de Paris; Stahl, cond.*
+ ARG 11-12/95: 172

30687. 9209: PROTO—String quartet no.
1; Piano quintet; String trio. *Ensemble
Sans Frontiere.*
+ ARG 1-2/97: 152

REDCLIFFE RECORDINGS

30688. RR 005: BARBER—Piano sonata;
Nocturne. ROUTH—Celebration; Elegy.
Jacob, piano.
+ Fa 11-12/88: 126

30689. RR 006: LUTYENS—Oboe quartet.
RAWSTHORNE—Oboe quartet; Theme and
variations. ROUTH—Oboe quartet; Tragic
interludes. *Redcliffe Ensemble.*
+ Gr 11/92: 138

30690. RR 007: RAINIER—Chamber
music. *Redcliffe Ensemble; Royal
Northern College of Music Wind
Ensemble; Reynish, cond.*
+ Gr 11/92: 142

30691. RR 008: A. BUSH—Instrumental
music. *Various performers.*
+ Gr 4/95: 77

REDWOOD

30692. ES-39 (LP): *Contemporary
Chinese piano music.* Music of Cheng, C.
Wang, L. Wang, and Chu. *Jacob, piano.*
+ Fa 1-2/87: 243

30693. ESCD-45: *Currents.* Music of
Iannaccone, Brant, Pinkham, and Wilson.
Horowitz-Gurt Piano Duo; Leaman,

*saxophone; Michigan Chamber Players;
Dickey; Gonway-Aschbrenner Piano
Duo; Accordo Perfetto.*
+ ARG 7-8/90: 127

REFERENCE RECORDINGS

30694. RR-9CD: *In formation.* Music of
Kechley, Benshoof, Thunes, Beyer,
Dorsey, and others. *Kronos Quartet.*
□ 3-4/91: 145

30695. RR-10CD: CHIHARA—The
tempest: Excerpts. *Performing Arts Orch.
of San Francisco; LeRoux, cond.*
□ ARG 11-12/89: 51
+ Fa 9-10/89: 176

30696. RR-13CD: *Popular masterworks
of the Baroque.* Music of Handel,
Pachelbel, Bach, Purcell, Vivaldi, and
Telemann. *Tafelmusik Chamber Orch.*
+ Fa 11-12/89: 491

30697. RR-22CD: COPLAND—
Appalachian Spring suite (original
version); Eight poems of Emily
Dickinson; An outdoor overture. *Nixon,
soprano; Pacific Symphony Orch.; Clark,
cond.*
+ DA 10/87: 88
• Fa 7-8/87: 92
+ Opus 12/87: 32

30698. RR-23CD: VIVALDI—Sinfonia RV
116; Trio sonata RV 73; Concerto for 2
violins, and strings RV 515. BACH—
Well-tempered clavier bk. 1: Prelude in C
BWV 846; Trio sonata BWV 1037;
Concerto for 2 violins, and strings BWV
1043. *Helicon Ensemble; Fuller, cond.*
+ Fa 1-2/88: 231

30699. RR-25CD: LISZT—Mephisto waltz
no. 1; La campanella; Harmonies du soir;
Feux follets; Piano sonata in B minor.
Nojima, piano. Issued also as LP: RR 25.
+ Fa 5-6/88: 153
+ SR 5/88: 98

30700. RR-27CD: RAMEAU—Suite in A;
Pièces de clavecin: La Dauphine;
Menuets; La Cupis; La Livrie; L'entretien
des Muses; Les Sauvages;
L'enharmonique; Les cyclopes. *Fuller,
harpsichord.*
+ DA 4/89: 72
+ Fa 3-4/89: 131
+ HF 6/89: 70
• SR 6/89: 124
• St 2/89: 163

30701. RR-29CD: Music of Weill,
Bowles, Martinů, and Varèse. *Chicago
Pro Musica.*
• ARG 11-12/89: 144
+ Fa 9-10/89: 437
+ Gr 8/89: 320
+ Ov 9/89: 60

30702. RR-35CD: RAVEL—Miroirs;
Gaspard de la nuit. *Nojima, piano.*
+ ARG 9-10/90: 103

REFERENCE RECORDINGS

+ Fa 11-12/90: 325
+ Fa 1-2/91: 285
+ Gr 10/90: 790
+ SR 11/90: 170
+ St 12/90: 223

30703. RR-38CD: *Fiesta!* Music of Reed, Gould, C. Williams, Nixon, and Perkins (arr. Werle). *Dallas Wind Symphony; Dunn, cond.*
+ ARG 9-10/91: 169
• Fa 7-8/91: 397
+ Fa 7-8/91: 397

30704. RR-39CD: Holst—Suite no. 1 in E♭; A moorside suite; Suite no. 2 in F; Hammersmith: prelude and scherzo. *Dallas Wind Symphony; Dunn, cond.*
• ARG 9-10/91: 169
+ Fa 9-10/91: 240

30705. RR-40CD: Brahms—Clarinet quintet. Weber—Clarinet quintet. *Daniels, clarinet; Composers String Quartet.*
+ ARG 11-12/91: 44
+ Fa 1-2/92: 375
+ Fa 3-4/92: 162
+ Gr 12/91: 90
+ St 10/92: 281

30706. RR-43CD: *Fennell favorites!* Arrangements of music by Bach, Brahms, Halvorsen, MacDowell, Goldmark and Prokofiev, *Dallas Wind Symphony; Fennell, cond.* Recorded live 1991.
+ ARG 5-6/92: 160
+ Fa 3-4/92: 423

30707. RR-47CD: Farnon—Captain Horatio Hornblower suite; A la claire fontaine; State occasion; Lake of the Woods; A promise of spring; Intermezzo for harp and strings; Rhapsody for violin and orchestra. *Cohen, violin; Royal Phil. Orch.; Farnon, Gamley, conds.*
+ ARG 9-10/92: 103
+ Fa 9-10/92: 231
+ Gr 9/92: 66
□ St 12/92: 239

30708. RR-48CD: Arnold—*Overtures.* A Sussex overture; Beckus the dandipratt; The smoke; The fair field; Commonwealth Christmas overture. *London Phil. Orch.; Arnold, cond.*
+ ARG 9-10/92: 75
+ Fa 9-10/92: 163
+ Gr 6/92: 37
• St 12/92: 235

30709. RR-49CD: Thompson—The testament of freedom; Frostiana: 2 excerpts; Alleluia. Hanson—Song of democracy. Nelson—Behold man. Copland—The tender land: The promise of giving; Simple gifts. Bernstein—Candide: Make our garden grow. *Turtle Creek Chorale; Dallas Wind Symphony; Seelig, cond.*
+ ARG 3-4/93: 182
+ Fa 3-4/93: 314

30710. RR-51CD: Bach—Italian concerto; WTC book 2: F minor, D major; French suite no. 6; 6 pieces from the Anna Magdalena notebook. *Fuller, harpsichord.*
• ARG 7-8/93: 58
• Fa 9-10/93: 107

30711. RR-52CD: Giannini—Symphony no. 3. Nelhybel—Trittico. Dello Joio—Variants on a medieval tune. Grieg—Funeral march for Rikard Nordraak. Albéniz-Cailliet—Feast day in Seville. *Dallas Wind Symphony; Fennell, cond.*
+ ARG 11-12/93: 245
+ Fa 9-10/93: 386

30712. RR-55CD: Music of Stravinsky, Babin, Gould, Bernstein, and Shaw. *Yeh, clarinet; DePaul University Wind Ensemble; DeRoche, cond.; DePaul University Jazz Ensemble; Lark, cond.*
+ ARG 3-4/94: 161
+ Fa 3-4/94: 421

30713. RR-57CD: Rutter—Requiem; Five anthems. *Turtle Creek Chorale; Dallas Women's Chorus; instrumental ensemble; Seelig, cond.*
+ ARG 5-6/94: 135
+ Fa 5-6/94: 233

30714. RR-58CD: Music of Karg-Elert, Gigout, Wills, Grainger, Dupré, Nelson, Widor, and Weinberger. *Riedo, organ; Dallas Wind Symphony; Fennell, cond.*
+ ARG 5-6/94: 180
+ Fa 7-8/94: 331

30715. RR-61CD: *Postcards.* Music of Mecham, Sontanga, Chesnakov, Situ, Varner, Schafer, Thompson, Parra, Fauré, Schubert, Toch, Olatunji, Genée, and Wilberg. *Turtle Creek Chorale; Seelig, cond.*
+ Fa 7-8/95: 398

30716. RR-62CD: *Beachcomber: encores for band.* Music of Anderson, Glière, Osser, Abreu, Fillmore, Bernstein, Hamlisch, Richardson, Willson, Ginastera, Grainger, Shostakovich, Cavez, Gould, End, Iwai, Kaneda, and Ward. *Dallas Wind Symphony; Fennell, cond.*
+ Fa 7-8/95: 442

30717. RR-64CD: Chadwick—Symphonic sketches; Melpomene overture; Tam O'Shanter. *Czech State Phil. Orch.; Serebrier, cond.*
• ARG 11-12/95: 103
+ Fa 11-12/95: 233
+ Gr 2/96: 46

30718. RR-65CD: Janáček—Sinfonietta; Lachian dances; Taras Bulba. *Brno State Phil. Orch.; Serebrier, cond.*
+ ARG 11-12/95: 140
- Fa 11-12/95: 281

30719. RR-66CD: Arnold—Band music. *Dallas Wind Symphony; Junkin, cond.*

+ ARG 5-6/96: 69
+ Fa 3-4/96: 100

30720. RR-67CD: *Late romantic male choral music.* Music of Bruckner, Brahms, Schubert, Biebl, Mendelssohn, and Strauss. *Turtle Creek Chorale; Fort Worth Chamber Chorale; Fort Worth Symphony Brass; Seelig, cond.*
• ARG 5-6/96: 253
• Fa 3-4/96: 341

30721. RR-68CD: Mozart—Piano concertos no. 21, 24. *Istomin, piano; Seattle Symphony Orch.; Schwarz, cond.*
• ARG 7-8/96: 158 (Vroon)
+ ARG 7-8/96: 159 (Manildi)

30722. RR-69CD: Beethoven—Piano sonatas no. 14, 21, 31. *Istomin, piano.*
• ARG 7-8/96: 77
- Fa 7-8/96: 103
+ Fi 10/96: 145

30723. RR-70CD: Stravinsky—Rite of spring; Firebird: Suite; Chant du rossignol. *Minnesota Orch.; Oue, cond.*
+ ARG 9-10/96: 211
• Fa 11-12/96: 387

30724. RR-71CD: *Exotic dance from the opera.* Music of Rimsky-Korsakov, Strauss, Tchaikovsky, Mussorgsky, Rabaud, Rubinstein, Dvořák, and Saint-Saëns. *Minnesota Orch.; Oue, cond.*
+ ARG 9-10/96: 229
+ Fa 9-10/96: 430

REGENT

30725. REGCD 101: Poulenc—Mass in G; Four Christmas motets. Langlais—Messe solennelle. *Yates, soprano; Lucas, organ; Regent Chamber Choir; Cele, cond.*
+ Fa 1-2/89: 187
• Gr 10/88: 663

30726. REGCD 107: Lole—Choral music. *St. Mary's Collegiate Church Choir, Warwick; Lole, cond.; Bowyer, organ.*
+ Gr 3/94: 92

REGIS

30727. TRO RTAC 001 (2 discs): Bach—The well-tempered clavier, book 1. *Milà, piano.*
• Fa 7-8/94: 52

30728. TRO RTAC 002: Music of Turina, Guridi, Falla, and Mila. *Milà, piano; Spanish Radio Orch.; Gómez Martínez, cond.*
- ARG 7-8/94: 200
+ Fa 7-8/94: 328

30729. TRO RTAC 003: Beethoven—Concerto for piano, violin, and cello. Hua Yanjun and Wu Zuqiang—Reflections of the moon on the second best fountain. *Milà, piano; León, violin; Corostola,*

cello; Central Phil. Orch. of China; Zongjie, cond.
- Fa 7-8/94: 62

30730. TRO RTAC 004: MOZART—String quintets K. 406, 516. *Berlin String Quintet.*
+ ARG 9-10/94: 167

30731. TRO RTAC 005: MILÀ—Tirant lo Blanc. *London Phil. Orch.; Wright, cond.*
• ARG 7-8/94: 133
+ Fa 7-8/94: 184

30732. TRO RTAC 006: MILÀ—Havaneres; Llunyania; Quatre estudis; Nocturn; Euqitant. *Milà, piano.*
+ Fa 7-8/94: 184

30733. TRO RTAC 007: RAVEL—Piano concerto in G major; Piano concerto in D major for the left hand; Pavane pour une infante défunte. *Milà, piano; Orch. National de l'Opéra de Monte-Carlo; Colombo, cond.* Recorded 1972.
+ Fa 3-4/95: 271

30734. TRO RTAC 010/1-3 (3 discs): SARASATE—Obra completa integral de violi i orquestra. *Croitoru, Navarro, violins; Orquestra Ciudad de Málaga; Bodmer, cond.*
- Fa 7-8/96: 280

RELIEF

30735. CR 911 013: SCHERCHEN—String quartet, op. 1. *Erato Quartet.*
+ Fa 1-2/92: 315

30736. CR 911 026: BORODIN—Petite suite; Scherzo in A♭. LIADOV—Barcarolle in F♯, op. 44; Variations on a Polish folk song, op. 51. PROKOFIEV—Prelude in C, op. 12, no. 7; The love of three oranges, op. 33: March. *Nikolayeva, piano.*
+ Fa 5-6/93: 171

30737. CR 911 027: SCHUMANN—Piano music. *Nikolayeva, piano.*
+ ARG 5-6/93: 134

30738. CR 1825: *Recital, Tokyo 1970.* Music of Brahms, Wolf, Mahler, Dvořák, and Strauss. *Della Casa, soprano; Kobayashi, piano.* Recorded live 1970.
+ ARG 5-6/91: 160
+ Fa 5-6/91: 326

30739. CR 1861: BEETHOVEN—Symphonies no. 1, 4; Fidelio overture. *NBC Symphony Orch.; Toscanini, cond.* Recorded live 1939.
+ Fa 3-4/90: 139

30740. CR 1884: ROSSINI—Overtures to La cenerentola; Guillaume Tell; La gazza ladra; Il Signor Bruschino; Il barbiere di Siviglia; La scala di seta; Semiramide; Guillaume Tell: Passo a sei; Soldiers' dance. *NBC Symphony Orch.; Toscanini, cond.* Recorded live 1938-1951.
+ Fa 3-4/90: 278

30741. CR 1885: BEETHOVEN—Symphony no. 7; Egmont overture; Septet op. 20. *NBC Symphony Orch.; Toscanini, cond.* Recorded live 1939.
+ Fa 3-4/90: 139

30742. CR 1886: Music of Glinka, Kalinnikov, Lyadov, Mussorgsky, and Rubinstein. *NBC Symphony Orch.; Toscanini, cond.*
+ Fa 3-4/90: 390

30743. CR 1887: TCHAIKOVSKY—The tempest; The Voyevoda. PROKOFIEV—Symphony no. 1. BORODIN—Symphony no. 2. *NBC Symphony Orch.; Toscanini, cond.* Broadcast recording.
+ Fa 11-12/91: 267

30744. CR 1888: ELGAR—Introduction and allegro for strings, op. 47; Enigma variations, op. 36. VAUGHAN WILLIAMS—Fantasia on a theme by Thomas Tallis. *NBC Symphony Orch.; Toscanini, cond.* Broadcast recording.
+ Fa 11-12/91: 267

30745. CR 1891: BEETHOVEN—Symphony no. 3; Leonore overtures no. 1-2. *NBC Symphony Orch.; Toscanini, cond.*
+ Fa 11-12/91: 267

30746. CR 1892: BEETHOVEN—Symphonies no. 6, 8. *NBC Symphony Orch.; Toscanini, cond.* Recorded live 1939.
+ ARG 3-4/91: 34
+ Fa 5-6/91: 128

30747. CR 1893: BEETHOVEN—Symphonies no. 9; Fantasy for piano, chorus and orchestra. *Novotná, Thorborg, Peerce, Moscona; Dorfmann, piano; Westminster Choir; NBC Symphony Orch.; Toscanini, cond.*
+ Fa 1-2/91: 153

30748. CR 87021: LISZT—Consolations; Elégies: no. 1-2; Nuages gris; Preludio funèbre; La lugubre gondola (versions 1 & 2); Recueillement; Schlaflos, Frage und Antwort; En reve. *Van Loo, piano.*
• Fa 1-2/89: 192

30749. CR 861003: Music of Vivaldi, Bach, Haydn, De Call, and Kuffner. *Borghese, Frosali, Saldarelli, guitars.*
+ Fa 9-10/89: 422

30750. CR 861005: VILLA-LOBOS—Twelve etudes; Suites populaires no. 1-5; Choro no. 1. *Marcos, guitar.*
+ Fa 9-10/88: 291

30751. CR 861006: BACH—Goldberg variations. *Nikolayeva, piano.*
- Fa 1-2/88: 77
+ Fa 9-10/89: 120

30752. CR 871007: VILLA-LOBOS—Cello sonata no. 2; Four rondos for piano; Five pieces for cello and piano; Capriccio op. 49; Song of the black swan; Elegy in A

minor; Bachiana brasiliera no. 5: Aria; Bachiana brasiliera no. 2: Caipira. *Carneiro, cello; Genuit, piano.*
- Fa 9-10/88: 291

30753. CR 891008: SHOSTAKOVICH—Trio for piano and strings no. 2. TCHAIKOVSKY—Trio for piano and strings in A minor. *Yuval Trio.*
• ARG 3-4/90: 115
- Fa 7-8/90: 273

30754. CR 891009: SAINT-SAËNS—Piano trios no. 1-2. *Yuval Trio.*
+ Fa 11-12/90: 275

30755. CR 911020—911022 (3 separate discs): BEETHOVEN—Piano sonatas no. 26, 28-32; Diabelli variations. *Horszowski, piano.* Recorded 1949-82.
+ Gr 12/93: 91

30756. CR 911023: CHOPIN—Piano concerto no. 1; Piano music. *Horszowski, piano; Vienna State Opera Orch.; Swarowsky, cond.* Recorded 1953-82.
+ Gr 12/93: 91

REM

30757. 10985: BACH—Passacaglia and fugue in C minor BWV 582; Aus tiefer Not BWV 686-687; Tocata, adagio and fugue in C BWV 564; Allein Gott in der Höh sei ehr BWV 662; Partita: Sei gegrüsset, Jesu gutig BWV 768. *Maitre, organ.*
• Fa 11-12/88: 121

30758. 11010: WIDOR—Symphonies no. 4-5. *Caire, organ.*
• Fa 7-8/87: 209

30759. 11036: CHAILLEY—A ma femme; Le pélerin d'Assise; Deux poèmes sur la mort; Sept chansons légères; Melodies diverses; Trois madrigaux galants; Trois noëls polonaise; Thyl de Flandre. *Steyer, Norska, sopranos; Piquemal, baritone; Renault-Rousseau, Bronk-Dzunowska, pianos.*
+ ARG 7-8/88: 17
+ Fa 9-10/88: 126

30760. 11039: SCHUMANN—Intermezzi op. 4; Carnaval; Phantasiestücke op. 111. *Cottet, piano.*
• Fa 11-12/88: 275

30761. 11047 (2 discs): VIERNE—Symphonies no. 1-2, 4 . *Bocher, Arel, Regnaud, organs.*
+ Fa 9-10/88: 288

30762. 11048: VIERNE—Symphonies no. 3, 5-6 . *Reboulot, Proulx, Rochette, organs.*
• Fa 11-12/88: 306

30763. 310990: Music of Anglebert, Caix d'Hervelois, and Balbastre. *Baumont, harpsichord.*
+ Fa 9-10/88: 137

30764. 311030: PAGANINI—Violin concerto no. 1. KHACHATURIAN—Violin concerto in D minor. *Boulier, violin; Monte Carlo Phil. Orch.; Anguelov, cond.*
□ Fa 7-8/89: 208

30765. 311033: LISZT—Via crucis. MALLIÉ—Improvisations on themes by Liszt. *Mallié, organ.*
- Fa 9-10/88: 186

30766. 311043: *L'orgue historique du Palais Princier de Monaco.* Music of Lucchesi, Valeri, Cervellini, Tartini, Galuppi, and others. *Saorgin, organ.*
+ Fa 7-8/89: 306

30767. 311049: DUPARC—L'invitaition au voyage; Sérénade fiorentine; Extase; Chanson triste; La manoir de Rosemonde; Lamento; Au pays ou se fait la guerre; La vague et la cloche; Sérénade; Testament; Phidylé; Romance de mignon; Élégie; Le galop; Soupir; La vie antérieure; La fuit. *Le Roux, baritone; Borst, soprano; Cohen, piano.*
- Fa 9-10/88: 144

30768. 311053: BOELLMANN—Suite gothique; Deuxième suite op. 27; Douze pièces pour grand orgue. *Caire, organ.*
□ Fa 11-12/88: 149 m.f.

30769. 311054: RAVEL—Cinq mélodies greques; Histoires naturelles; Trois poèmes de Stéphane Mallarmé; Chansons madécasses. *Henry, baritone; Pondepeyre, piano; Members of the French National Orch.*
+ Fa 11-12/88: 256

30770. 311058: SHOSTAKOVICH—String quartet no. 1. WEBERN—String quartet. *Verlaine Quartet.*
- ARG 7-8/89: 90
● Fa 7-8/89: 247

30771. 311059: FRANCK—Violin sonata in A. LEKEU—Violin sonata in G. *Boulier, violin; Dedieu-Vidal, piano.*
- ARG 7-8/89: 45
- Fa 7-8/89: 150
● Gr 8/89: 326

30772. 311060: NIGG—String quartet. PHILIPPOT—String quartet no. 2. HERSANT—String quartet no. 1. *Enesco Quartet.*
+ Fa 7-8/89: 207

30773. 311067: LEMMENS—Fanfare; Prière; Organ sonatas no. 1-3. LEFÉBURE-WELY—Sortie in E♭; Offertories in A, B♭, E♭, C minor; March in C; Sorties in B♭, E♭. *Caire, organ.*
+ ARG 7-8/89: 52
□ Fa 7-8/89: 169

30774. 311068: REGER—Fantasia and fugue on Halleluia, Gott zu loben; Introduction, passacaglia and fugue in E minor; Fantasia and fugue in D minor.

Matrone, organ.
□ ARG 7-8/89: 78
+ Fa 7-8/89: 220

30775. 311069: HAHN—Songs. *Le Roux, baritone; Cohen, piano.*
+ ARG 7-8/93: 97
+ Gr 11/91: 139

30776. 311070: Music of Poulenc, Auric, and Honegger. *Carey, baritone; Dedieu-Vidal, piano.*
● Fa 3-4/91: 445
+ Gr 1/90: 1353

30777. 311102 (2 discs): FRANCK—Organ music (complete). *Caire, organ.*
● ARG 9-10/90: 63
+ ARG 1-2/91: 49

30778. 311105: POULENC—Le bal masqué; Le bestiaire; Calligrammes; Poèmes de Ronsard; Cocardes; Tel jour, telle nuit. *Henry, baritone; Pondepeyre, piano; Carl Stamitz Ensemble.*
- Gr 10/91: 169

30779. 311135: SCHUMANN—Six canonic studies, op. 56; Four sketches, op. 58; Six fugues on B-A-C-H, op. 60. *Delvallée, organ.*
- ARG 1-2/92: 110

30780. 311136: HAYDN—Harpsichord concertos in D and G; Concerto for violin and harpsichord. *Sartoretti, harpsichord; Millière, violin; Jean-Louis Petit Chamber Orch.; Petit, cond.*
+ ARG 3-4/92: 70

30781. 311142: Songs by Hahn, Debussy, Poulenc, Honegger, Aubert, Leguerney, Ravel, Beydts, Saint-Saëns, Chailley and Françaix. *Carey, baritone; Dedieu-Vidal, piano.*
● ARG 3-4/92: 202

30782. 311144: *L'immortel.* BACH—Fantasy and fugue in G minor; Preludes and fugues in G and E minor; Trio sonata in C; Toccata and fugue in F. *Mechler, organ.*
+ ARG 1-2/92: 22

30783. 311146: IBERT—Concertino da camera; Cinq pièces en trio; Carignane; Trio; Cello concerto. *Jean-Louis Petit Chamber Orch.*
+ ARG 5-6/92: 74

30784. 311150: ALBÉNIZ—Cantos de España. DEBUSSY—Images I and II. *G. Romero, piano.*
● ARG 3-4/92: 16

30785. 311153: FRANCK—Piano quintet; Prelude, chorale and fugue. *Taddei, piano; Molia, Lenert, violins; Adamopoulos, viola; Boufil, cello.*
- ARG 9-10/92: 106

30786. 311162: WIDOR—Symphony no. 9. BONNET—Versets Ave Maris stella;

Prelude on Salve Regina; Magnificat; Concert variations. *Boucher, organ.*
+ ARG 1-2/93: 168

30787. 311163: SCIORTINO—Kaleidophone; Calamus; Signatures; Sept souffles. *Ensemble Erwartung; Gazeau, violin; Lamberger, clarinet.*
+ Fa 9-10/92: 351

30788. 311167: VIVALDI—Motets for mezzo-soprano and orchestra. *Kobayashi, mezzo-soprano; Orch. de Chambre de Ville d'Avray; Petit, cond.*
- Fa 1-2/93: 265

30789. 311168: WIDOR—Symphonies 1-2. *Caire, organ.*
● ARG 1-2/93: 167

30790. 311175: FAURÉ—Songs. *Le Roux, baritone; Cohen, piano.*
+ ARG 7-8/93: 88
+ Gr 11/92: 168

30791. 311202: Music of Gigout, Vierne, Pierné, Hure, Bonnet, and Tournemire. *Landale, organ.*
+ ARG 5-6/94: 179

30792. 311214: HEROLD—String quartets. *Arnesci Quartet.*
+ ARG 1-2/95: 115

30793. 311215: MUSSORGSKY—Pictures at an exhibition. PROKOFIEV—Peter and the wolf. *Mechler, organ.*
● ARG 9-10/95: 177

30794. 311218: SCHUMANN—Violin sonatas. *Ngoc, violin; Ganz, piano.*
- ARG 11-12/94: 189

30795. 311219: KHACHATURIAN—Piano music. *Schön, piano.*
+ ARG 11-12/94: 139

30796. 311225: FRANÇAIX—Clarinet trio; Le promenade d'un musicologue eclectique; Theme and variations; Habanera de Chabrier; Rhapsodie. *Trio Jean Françaix; Françaix, piano.*
+ ARG 1-2/95: 107

30797. 311252: DUPRÉ—Symphonie-passion; Variations on a noel; Evocation. *Beck, organ.*
- ARG 9-10/95: 138

30798. 311260: PIERNÉ—Violin sonata. TOURNEMIRE—Sonata-poem. FRANCK—Violin sonata. *Robert, violin; Deferne, piano.*
● ARG 5-6/96: 162

30799. 350501: Music of Bartók, Hindemith, Prokofiev, and Martinù. *Pierlot, flute; Pondepeyre, piano.*
+ ARG 1-2/96: 211

RENAISSANCE

30800. ARF-94001: Demars—Am American requiem. *J. Killian, Childs, G. Killian, La France; Arizona State University Choirs; orch.; DeMars, cond.*
● Fa 1-2/96: 187

RENÉ GAILLY

30801. CD 86001: Mompou—Scènes d'enfants; Suburvis; Trois variations; Dialogues; Souvenirs de l'Exposition; Paisajes; Impresiones intimas; Chanson de berceaux. *Huybregts, piano.*
- Fa 1-2/88: 164

30802. CD 86003: Shostakovich—Violin concerto no. 1. Huybrechts—Violin sonata. *Volckaert, violin; BRT Symphony Orch.; Defossez, cond.; Canck, piano.*
+ Fa 9-10/93: 286

30803. CD 86006: Music of Misek, Bottesini, Koussevitzky, Lorenziti, Van Rossum, and Coryn. *Coppieters, double bass; Eeman, piano.*
+ ARG 7-8/94: 207

30804. CD 86007: Music of Krebs, W. F. Bach, Bach, and Handel. *Heyerick, Penson, harpsichords.*
+ Fa 1-2/90: 388

30805. CD 86008: Rossum—Réquisitoire; Eloquences; Sinfonia concertante. *Orval, haron; Groote, piano; Belgian National Orch.; Priestman, Devreese, conds.*
+ ARG 9-10/95: 202

30806. CD 86009: Rossum—Piano music; Miniatures for orchestra. *Rossum, piano; Belgian National Orch.; Vandernoot, cond.*
+ ARG 9-10/95: 202

30807. CD 86012: *Serenades.* Music of Mozart, Elgar, Wolf, and Tchaikovsky. *I Fiamminghi; Werthen, cond.*
+ Fa 9-10/88: 347

30808. CD 86013: Vivaldi—Violin concertos op. 8 no. 1-4 (Four seasons); Concerto for violin, 2 string orchestras RV 583. *Werthen, violin; I Fiamminghi.*
+ Fa 1-2/88: 229

30809. CD 86014: *Unknown lieder.* Schubert—Über allen Zauber Liebe; Auf den Tod einer Nachtigall; Aria di Abramo; L'incanto degli occhi; Psalm XII; Frühlingslied; Mein Freiden; Entzückung an Laura; Sie in jedem Liede; Das war ich; An Chloen; Liebestauch; Lied in der Abwesenheit. *Vandersteene, tenor; Kende, piano.*
+ Fa 1-2/88: 205

30810. CD 87001/2 (2 discs): Ryelandt—Piano sonatas no. 2, 4. 7; Fünf Phantasiestück; En Ardenne; Prelude and fugue; Six preludes op. 62; Three preludes op. 96; Six nocturnes op.

81, 90-91, 93, 97, 126. *Beenhouwer, piano.*
+ Fa 1-2/88: 202

30811. CD 87003: *From J. S. Bach to J. L. Coeck.* Music of Bach, Schubert, Debussy, Lutosławski, Heim, and Coeck. *Walter Boeykens Clarinet Choir; Boeykens, Groslot, conds.* All works arr. for clarinet choir.
+ Fa 1-2/88: 270

30812. CD 87004: Vocht—Flemish Christmas carols; Cantica; Missa in honorem Angelorem; Annual cycle of spiritual songs. *Camerata Ostendia; Duinenkantorij; Muzeschuit; Benoit, cond.*
+ Fa 5-6/90: 154

30813. CD 87006: Hoof—Songs. *Bollen, alto; Vandersteene, tenor; Beenhower, Kende, pianos.*
+ Fa 1-2/88: 224

30814. CD 87007: Alkan—Les mois; Sonatine in A minor; Trois petites fantaisies. *Capelletti, piano.*
+ Fa 3-4/89: 60

30815. CD 87014: Franck—Violin sonata in A. Lekeu—Violin sonata in G. *Kang, violin; Devoyon, piano.*
● Fa 11-12/89: 208

30816. CD 87017: Rojer—Twelve Curacao waltzes. *Martina, Rojer, pianos.*
+ ARG 3-4/89: 73
- Fa 3-4/89: 250

30817. CD 87018: Statius Muller—Antillean dances. *Statius Muller, piano.*
+ ARG 7-8/90: 77
+ Fa 9-10/90: 318

30818. CD 87026 : *Belgian flute concertos.* Music of Fétis, Renoit, and Waelput. *Riet, flute; New Flemish Symphony Orch.; Van den Broeck, cond.*
□ ARG 1-2/95: 223

30819. CD 87031: Schubert—Waltzes and dances. *Nitto, piano.*
+ ARG 5-6/94: 139
+ Fa 7-8/94: 231

30820. CD 87033: Haydn—Cello concertos no. 1-2, 4. *Springuel, cello; I Fiamminghi; Werthen, cond.*
- Fa 1-2/88: 136

30821. CD 87035: Reger—Intermezzo in F minor; Seelenbräutigam; Fantasia and fugue on BACH; Introduction and passacaglia in D minor; Straf mich nicht in deinen Zorn; Jesu meine Zuversicht; Prelude in D minor; Fantasia on Wachet auf. *Kooy, organ.*
+ Fa 3-4/89: 247

30822. CD 87037: Gotkovsky—Concerto for symphonic band; Concerto for saxophone and symphonic band; Poem of

fire. *Leclercq, saxophone; Symphonic Band of the Belgian Guides; Nozy, cond.*
+ Fa 5-6/90: 178

30823. CD 87038: Schubert—Winterreise. *Vandersteene, tenor; Kende, piano.*
+ ARG 5-6/90: 103
+ Fa 5-6/90: 288

30824. CD 87042: *American diversions.* Music of Persichetti, Rorem, Hanson, Carpenter, Daly, Bolcom, Logan, Baker, Gershiwn, and Kroll. *Herbein, piano; Spanoghe, violin.*
● Fa 9-10/89: 413

30825. CD 87044: Ravel—Rapsodie espagnole; Ma mère l'oye; La valse. Debussy—Petite suite; En blanc et noir. *Kende, Hendrickx, pianos.*
- Fa 9-10/90: 222

30826. CD 87045: Schumann—Nachtstücke op. 23; Bunte Blätter op. 99; Fantasiestücke op. 111. *Tamamdjieva, piano.*
● Fa 5-6/89: 314

30827. CD 87046: *International Baroque, 17th century.* Music of Merula, Turini, Castello, Locke, Schmelzer, and others. *Les Ennemis Confus.*
+ ARG 3-4/91: 163
+ Fa 1-2/91: 398

30828. CD 87047: Music of Gilson, Absil, Legley, and Strens. *Symphonic Band of the Belgian Guides; Nozy, cond.*
● Fa 1-2/91: 403

30829. CD 87048: Tchaikovsky—1812 overture; Romeo and Juliet; Capriccio italien; Marche slave. *Symphonic Band of the Belgian Guides; Nozy, cond.*
● Fa 3-4/91: 401

30830. CD 87050: C.P.E. Bach—Organ concertos Wq. 34-35; Double concerto for harpsichord and piano Wq. 47. *Huys, organ & piano; Penson, harpsichord; Collegium Instrumentale Brugense; Peire, cond.*
● Fa 3-4/89: 66

30831. CD 87052: Biarent—Piano quintet in B minor; Prélude moyen age. *Andersen, piano; Arriaga String Quartet.*
+ ARG 3-4/90: 30
+ Fa 1-2/90: 128

30832. CD 87053: Music of C.P.E. Bach, Haydn, and Mozart. *Huys, tangent piano.*
+ Fa 1-2/90: 90

30833. CD 87057: *Belgian works for symphonic band, vol. 2.* Music of Legley, Simonis, Louel and Glorieux. *Symphonic Band of the Belgian Guides; Nozy, cond.; with Groslot, piano.*
+ Fa 11-12/92: 460

RENÉ GAILLY

30834. CD 87058: Gotkovsky—Fanfare; Symphonie de printemps; Symphonie brillante; Chant de la forêt. *Symphonic Band of the Belgian Guides; Vocal Ensemble Ex Tempore; Nozy, cond.*
    + Fa 11-12/92: 247

30835. CD 87059: Nuffel—Psalms; Te Deum. *Malines Cathedral Choir with organ & brass.*
    + ARG 5-6/92: 150

30836. CD 87061: *20th century Belgian clarinet.* Music of Stekke, Lysight, Pousseur, and van Rossum. *Vanspaendonck, clarinet; Anglani, piano.*
    + ARG 9-10/92: 189

30837. CD 87063: De Vocht—Concerto for violin and orchestra. Van Eechaúté—Romantic lullaby. Coryn—Concerto for violin and orchestra. *Raudales, violin & cond.; New Flemish Symphony Orch.*
    + ARG 7-8/93: 183
    + Fa 5-6/93: 191

30838. CD 87066: Jongen—Pièce symphonique. Stravinsky—Piano concerto. Taeye—Les croix de bois. *Mogilevsky, piano; Symphonic Band of the Belgian Guides; Nozy, cond.*
    + ARG 5-6/93: 99

30839. CD 87069: Music of Tarrega, Ponce, Bach, Santorsola, Feldbusch, Lauro Carlevaro, Barrios, and Alfonso. *Alfonso, guitar.*
    - ARG 11-12/93: 234

30840. CD 87073: Handel—Water music. *Prima la Musica; Vermeulen, cond.*
    + ARG 9-10/94: 141

30841. CD 87078: Ives—Piano sonata no. 2; Studies no. 9, 21-23. *Vandewalle, piano; Klinck, violin; Jacobs, flute.*
    + ARG 11-12/96: 148

30842. CD 87079: Stravinsky—Piano music. *Coppens, piano.*
    • ARG 11-12/96: 217

30843. CD 87080: *Composers from west Flanders.* Music of Coryn, Devreese, and Carron. *Raudales, violin; New Flemish Symphony Orch.; Brosse, cond.*
    + ARG 1-2/95: 210

30844. CD 87081: *Belgian works for saxophone.* Music of Waigen, Gilson, Poot, Absil, Cabus, and Carron. *Nozy, saxophones; New Flemish Symphony Orch.; Bollon, cond.*
    + Fa 5-6/95: 440

30845. CD 87082: F. Constant—Concerto for accordion and symphonic band; Fantasia for alto saxophone and symphonic band; Concerto for piano and wind instruments; Concerto for symphonic band. *Guerouet, accordion; Nozy, saxophone; Vanden Eynden, piano;*

Symphonic Band of the Belgian Guides; Nozy, cond.
    + Fa 5-6/95: 177

30846. CD 87085: Chausson—Chamber concerto; Piano quartet. *Ensemble César Franck; Bogaerts, violin; Vanden Eynden, piano.*
    + ARG 5-6/95: 98

30847. CD 87094: *Alto saxophone concertos.* Music of Boutry, De Jonghe, Verbesselt, and Erickson. *Nozy, saxophone; Symphonic Band of the Belgian Guides; Boeykens, cond.*
    + Fa 5-6/95: 440

30848. CD 87095: Music of Martinů, Piazzolla, Cobian, Berenguer, Ginastera, and Geom. *Trio ad Hoc.*
    + ARG 5-6/95: 201

30849. CD 87096: Absil—Brazilian rhapsody; Flemish rhapsody; Fantasia-capriccio; Rites; Bulgarian dances. *Cornil, saxophone; Belgian Guides Band; Nozy, cond.*
    + ARG 9-10/95: 90

30850. CD 87097: Music of Kabalevsky, Falla, Ravel, and Wagenaar. *Muller, piano.*
    + ARG 9-10/95: 267

30851. CD 87098: Prokofiev—Peter and the wolf; Pieces, op. 12; Sonata no. 2. *Cornil, piano.*
    + ARG 5-6/96: 164

30852. CD 87099: Jolivet—Piano music. *Lemmens, piano.*
    + ARG 5-6/96: 129

30853. CD 87102: Resurrexit. *Schola Gregoriana Bruges; Deruwe, cond.*
    + Fa 11-12/95: 460

30854. CD 87105: *Festive overtures.* Music of Shostakovich, Berlioz, Lalo, Mendelssohn, Rossini, Verdi, and Wagner. *Symphonic Band of the Belgian Guides; Nozy, cond.*
    + Fa 3-4/96: 383

30855. CD 87107: *Spanish music.* Music of Granados, Falla, and Brotons. *Symphonic Band of the Belgian Guides; Nozy, cond.; Dieltjens, piano.*
    + Fa 7-8/96: 403

30856. CD 87114: Legley—Violin and piano music. *Spanoghe, violin; Blumenthal, piano.*
    + ARG 11-12/96: 150
    + Fa 1-2/97: 191 (Snook)
    • Fa 1-2/97: 192 (Anderson)

30857. CD 87117: 18th-century Flemish dance music. *Kleine Compagnie; Wylin, cond.*
    + ARG 7-8/96: 235

30858. CD 87118: *Contemporary chamber music.* Music of Mozetich, Berkeley, and Crumb. *Royal Conservatory of Ghent Chamber Music Ensembles.*
    • Fa 11-12/96: 473

30859. CD 87125: M. Haydn—Requiem; Passion aria. Puccini—Crisantemi. *L. Lootens, Salje, B. Loonens, Snellings; Vivente Voce; Capella Vivente; Benoit, cond.*
    • ARG 11-12/96: 140

30860. CD 87505: Music of Ponce, Giuliani (rev. Chiessa), and Rodrigo. *Isaac, Casquero, Zanetti, guitars; Belgian National Orch.; Octors, cond.*
    + ARG 9-10/89: 124
    + Fa 5-6/89: 396

30861. CD 87506: Tchaikovsky—Violin concerto. Paganini—Violin concerto no. 1. *Repin, Suwanai, violins; Belgian National Orch.; Octors, cond. Recorded live 1989.*
    + Fa 11-12/89: 469

30862. CD 87507: Brahms—Violin concerto. Mendelssohn—Violin concerto in E minor. *Bouchkov, Kanno, violins; Belgian National Orch.; Octors, cond. Recorded live 1989.*
    + Fa 11-12/89: 469 (Tchaikovsky)
    • Fa 11-12/89: 469 (Mendelssohn)

30863. CD 87508: *Queen Elizabeth competition, 1989.* Music of Sibelius, Walton, and Laporte. *Mathé, Cho, Bouchkov, violins; Belgian National Orch.; Octors, cond.*
    • Fa 11-12/89: 469

30864. CD 87516: *Queen Elisabeth competition.* Mozart—Violin sonata K. 454. Mendelssohn—Violin sonata in F. Ravel—Violin sonata. *Tseng, Prunaru, Beaver, violin; Lin, Blumenthal, Protopopescu, pianos.*
    • ARG 7-8/94: 220

30865. CD 88007: Liszt—Piano sonata in B minor; Trauervorspiel und Trauermarsch; Après une lecture de Dante; Liebestraum no. 3; Hungarian rhapsody no. 6. *Ritzen, piano.*
    - Fa 5-6/88: 155

30866. CD 88800: Lemmens—Fanfare; Cantabile; Finale. Franck—Pièce héroïque; Trois chorales. *Deriemaeker, organ.*
    + Fa 1-2/88: 151

30867. CD 88802: *Organ of Our Lady's and St. Peter's Church and the Carmelites' Church at Ghent.* Music of Albrechtsberger, Rodriguez, Boely, Fetis, Czerny, and others. *Huys, organ.*
    + Fa 1-2/88: 264

30868. CD 88803: *The Penceler organ at Balen and the Van Peteghem organ at*

Zele. Music of Mareschall, Speth, Pachelbel, and C.P.E. Bach. *Huys, organ.*
+ Fa 11-12/89: 458

30869. CD 88804: *The Cavaille-Coll organ of the Heilig Hart Church at Hasselt.* Music of Lemmens, Franck, Vierne, Saint-Saëns, and others. *Kooy, organ.*
+ Fa 5-6/89: 391

30870. CD 88805: *The organ of the St. Germanus Church in Tienen.* BACH— Organ music. *Hooghe, organ.*
+ Fa 11-12/90: 150

30871. CD 88901: *Carillon of the belfry of Ghent.* Music of Stoop, V. Gheyn, Saint-Saëns, Leblan, Hollander, and others. *J. Hollander, G. Hollander, carillons.*
+ Fa 7-8/89: 305

30872. CD 90001: SCHUBERT— Winterreise. *Moller, baritone; Statius Muller, piano.*
+ ARG 1-2/91: 92
- Fa 11-12/90: 348

30873. CD 90006 (3 discs): *Queen Elisabeth of Belgium International Music Competition: Violin 1993.* Music of Sibelius, Swerts, Janáček, Saint-Saëns, Brahms, Shostakovich, and Tchaikovsky. *Toda, Prunaru, Beaver, Tseng, Prischepenko, violin; Protopopescu, piano; National Orch. of Belgium; Zollman, cond.*
• Fa 1-2/94: 418

30874. CD 92004: *Flemish contemporary recorder.* Music of Geysen, Swerts, Van Landeghem, and Pieters. *Flanders Recorder Quartet.*
+ ARG 3-4/96: 229

30875. CD 92012: Browning my dere. *Verbruggen, recorder; Flanders Recorder Quartet.*
+ ARG 3-4/96: 244

30876. CD 92018: WILFORD—Choral and chamber music. *Ysaÿe Ensemble; Flemish Radio Choir; Nees, cond.*
• ARG 7-8/95: 229

30877. CD 92020: HUYBRECHTS—Sextuor for winds; Trio for flute, viola, and piano; Suite for wind quintet and piano; Wind quintet. *Hendrickx, flute & piccolo; Verpoest, viola; Michiels, piano; Wind Ensemble Quintessens.*
+ ARG 5-6/95: 124
+ Fa 7-8/95: 210

30878. CD 92025: TELEMANN—The death of Jesus. *Anthoni, Saelens, Geyer, vocal soloists; Vocal Ensemble Ex Tempore, Mercure Galant; Heyerick, cond.*
+ ARG 3-4/96: 196

30879. 75 1303: BERLIOZ—Symphonie fantastique. *Hamburg NDR Symphony Orch.; Monteux, cond.* Recorded 1964.
- Fa 7-8/89: 99

30880. 75 1304: Music of Scarlatti, Marcello, Platti, Martini, and others. *Sgrizzi, harpsichord.*
- Fa 7-8/89: 234

30881. RIC 001031: PRAETORIUS— Terpsichore: 18 dances. *Ensemble Musica Aurea; Ensemble Ludi Musici.*
• Fa 9-10/88: 226

30882. RIC 008029: PALESTRINA—Missa Assumpta est Maria; O bone Jesu; Peccantem me quotidie; Ave Maria; Sicut cervus/Sitivit anima mea; O beata et gloriosa trinitas/O vera suma sempiterna trinitas. *La Chapelle royale de Paris; Herreweghe, cond.*
+ Fa 11-12/88: 245

30883. RIC 014024: BOESMANS— Conversions; Violin concerto; Piano concerto. *Pieta, violin; Mercenier, piano; Orch. Phil. de Liège; Bartholomée, cond.*
+ Fa 5-6/89: 143
+ Gr 10/89: 646

30884. RIC 015030: BACH—Fantasie BWV 572; Fugue BWV 579; Fantasie and fugue BWV 537; Concerto BWV 595; Pastorale BWV 590; Fantasia BWV 562; Allabreve BWV 589; Partita on Sei gegrüsset Jesu gutig BWV 769. *Foccroulle, organ.*
+ Fa 3-4/89: 107

30885. RIC 023003: SCHUBERT— Symphony no. 10. *Liège Symphony Orch.; Bartholomée, cond.*
+ ARG 5-6/92: 127

30886. RIC 028064: BROUWER—El decameron negro; Preludio; Fuga; Danza caracteristica; Tres piezas sin titulo; Elogio de la danza; Temas populares cubanos; Estudios sencillos. *Lemaigre, guitar.*
+ ARG 9-10/92: 90

30887. RIC 032013: BACH— Orgelbüchlein BWV 599-644. *Foccroulle, organ.*
+ Fa 3-4/88: 65

30888. RIC 036015: POUSSEUR—Couleurs croisées. J.L. ROBERTS—Aquatilis. *Orch. Phil. de Liège; Bartholomée, cond.*
+ Fa 3-4/88: 172

30889. RIC 037011: CHARPENTIER— Orphée descendant aux enfers; Stances du Cid; Tristes déserts; Ah! qu'on est malheureux; Amour vous avez beau; Rendez-moi mes plaisirs; Auprès du feu; Le bavolet; Epitaphium carpentarii;

Sonata à huit. *Reyghere, M. Ledroit, H. Ledroit, Mey, Bona; Ricercar consort.*
+ Fa 3-4/88: 95

30890. RIC 038014: BACH—Harpsichord concertos BWV 909, 971-975 . *Penson, harpsichord.*
• Fa 7-8/88: 104

30891. RIC 039012: VILLA-LOBOS—Five preludes; Etudes: in C# minor, A minor; Choro typico; Suite populaire bresilienne. *Lemaigre, guitar.*
+ Fa 3-4/88: 229
+ SR 5/88: 116

30892. RIC 041016: BUXTEHUDE—Herr ich lasse; Dialogus inter Christum; Nichts soll uns scheiden; Ich halte es dafur; Ich suchte des Nachts; Das neugeborne Kindelein. *Reyghere, Ledroit, Mey, Egmond; Ricercar consort.*
+ Fa 3-4/88: 91

30893. RIC 042018/19 (2 discs): BACH— Clavierübung bk. 3. *Foccroulle, organ.*
• Fa 7-8/88: 105

30894. RIC 043020: TELEMANN—Parisian quartets: Concerto primo in G, secondo in D; Sonata prima in A, seconda in G minor; Première suite in E minor. *Quatuor Ricercar.*
+ Fa 11-12/88: 295
+ Gr 3/89: 1451
• HF 2/89: 68

30895. RIC 044021: TELEMANN— Recorder concertos: with viola da gamba in A minor, with bassoon in F, with flute in E minor; Suite for recorder, and strings in A minor . *Roos, recorder; Pierlot, basse de viole; Minkowski, bassoon; Beuckels, flute; Ricercar Consort.*
+ Fa 11-12/88: 295

30896. RIC 045022: WALTHER—Scherzi for violin no. 4; Sonata no. 8, 10; Imitatione del Cuccu in G; Hortulus Chelicus for violin no. 8; Passacaglia in D minor no. 12; Suite in F no. 14; Aria in G minor no. 25; Suite in B minor. *Fernandez, violin; Ricercar Consort.*
+ Fa 3-4/89: 340
+ HPR 6/89: 91

30897. RIC 046023: *Deutsche barock Kantaten, 3.* Music of Schein, Tunder, Buxtehude, and others. *Reyghere, Mellon, sopranos; Ricercar consort.*
+ ARG 9-10/89: 133
+ Fa 5-6/89: 380

30898. RIC 048035—048036 (2 separate discs): BRUHNS—Cantatas, vol. 1-2. *Reyghere, Feldman, Bowman, Mey, Honeyman, Egmond; Ricercar consort.*
+ ARG 1-2/90: 38
+ Fa 11-12/89: 165
+ Gr 1/90: 1358
+ MA 5/90: 74

RICERCAR

30899. RIC 048037: BRUHNS—Organ music. *Foccroulle, organ.*
+ ARG 1-2/90: 39
+ Fa 11-12/89: 165
+ Gr 1/90: 1358
+ MA 5/90: 74

30900. RIC 049027: *Sonate e concerti per il corno da caccia.* Music of Vivaldi, Stölzel, Graun, Fasch, Handel, and others. *Maury, horn; Ricercar consort.*
+ Fa 3-4/89: 384

30901. RIC 051043: W.F. BACH—Fugue no. 8; Keyboard sonatas no. 2-3, 7; Arioso con variazioni; Polonaises no. 9-10. *Penson, harpsichord & fortepiano.*
+ Fa 3-4/90: 122

30902. RIC 052034: CHARPENTIER—Magnificat; Messe H. 5; Elévation; Dixit Dominus; Laudate Dominum; Stabat mater. RAISON—Livre d'orgue: Excerpts. *Capella Ricercar.*
+ Fa 5-6/89: 162

30903. RIC 054032: *Motetti et arie a basso solo.* Music of Monteverdi, Carissimi, Frescobaldi, Caccini, and others. *Egmond, bass; Ricercar consort.*
+ Fa 9-10/89: 412
+ Gr 1/90: 1368

30904. RIC 056038: Music of Pohle, Löwe, Farina, and Furchheim. *Ricercar consort.*
+ Fa 1-2/90: 411

30905. RIC 057039: *Flauti diversi.* Music of Schickhardt, Graun, Telemann, C.P.E. Bach, and others. *Ricercar consort.*
+ Fa 5-6/90: 387

30906. RIC 060048: *Deutsche barock Kantaten, 5.* Music of Hammerschmidt, Selle, Schein, Schütz, and others . *Reyghere, Mellon, Visse, Mey, Demaiffe; Capella Ricercar; Ricercar consort.*
• Fa 9-10/90: 498
+ Gr 5/90: 2037

30907. RIC 062026: FRESCOBLDI—Missa sopra la monica; Toccata; 3 canzoni. MARENZIO—Laudate Dominum; Lamentabatur Jacob; Jubilate Deo. *Capella Sancti Michaelis; Nevel, cond.*
+ Fa 11-12/89: 210
+ Gr 11/89: 960

30908. RIC 063033: GRÉTRY—Jugement de Midas: Excerpts. *Sluis, Elwes, Bastin; Chapelle Royale de Paris Chorus; La Petite Bande; Leonhardt, cond.*
+ ARG 1-2/90: 52
+ Fa 11-12/89: 220

30909. RIC 065044: BRAHMS—Clarinet conatas (complete); Clarinet trio op. 114. *Boeykens, clarinet; Dieltiens, cello; Eynden, piano.*
+ Fa 3-4/90: 154

30910. RIS 066045/47 (3 discs): MOZART—La finta giardiniera. *Kozlowska, Poulson, Benelli, Torzewski, Smythe; Théâtre royal de la Monnaie, Orch.; Cambreling, cond.* Recorded live 1989.
+ ARG 9-10/93: 160
• Fa 7-8/90: 209
• Gr 4/90: 1865
• ON 4/14/90: 46

30911. RIC 067050: HAYDN—Divertimenti for 8 voices in G, A minor, G; Divertimento for baryton, 2 horns, viola, and bass . *Ricercar Consort.*
+ ARG 11-12/90: 66
• Fa 11-12/90: 245
+ Gr 9/91: 88

30912. RIC 067124: HAYDN—Divertimenti for baryton octet. *Ricercar consort.*
+ ARG 11-12/94: 126

30913. RIC 068053: DU MONT—Motets à deux voix. *Reyghere, Mellon, Bowman, Mey, Egmond; Ricercar Consort.*
+ ARG 11-12/91: 60

30914. RIC 069049: W.F. BACH—Harpsichord concertos in E minor, F minor; Sinfonia in D minor. *Penson, harpsichord; Ricercar Consort; Chamorro, cond.*
+ ARG 1-2/91: 26
+ Fa 9-10/90: 154
+ Gr 9/90: 507

30915. RIC 072051: Music of Berio, Darasse, Jolas, and Boesmans. *Foccroulle, organ.*
+ Fa 11-12/90: 440

30916. RIC 073052: Music of Harvey, Donatoni, Lindberg, and Dufort. *Kubler, mezzo-soprano; Ensemble Musique Nouvelle; Octors, cond.*
+ Fa 11-12/90: 464

30917. RIC 075057: FRANCK—Harmonium music and other rarities. *Verdin, harmonium; Immerseel, piano.*
+ Fa 1-2/92: 212

30918. RIC 076054: Music of Schütz, Viadana, Buxtehude, Telemann, and De Fesch. *Ledroit, counter-tenor; Fernandez, violin; Pierlot, bass viol; Foccroulle, organ & harpsichord; Meer, cello; Immerseel, organ.*
+ Fa 11-12/90: 417

30919. RIC 077055: *Motets.* J. MICHAEL BACH—Halt was du hast; Fürchtet euch nicht; Sei lieber Tag willkommen; Ich weiss, dass mein Erlöser lebt; Herr, ich warte auf dein Heil; Herr, wenn ich nur dich habe; Unser Leben währet siebenzig Jahr. J. CHRISTOPH BACH—Sei getreu bis in den Tod; Der Mensch, vom Weibe geboren. H. PRAETORIUS—Angelus ad pastores mass. *Ricercar Consort; Nevel, cond.*
+ ARG 5-6/92: 14

30920. RIC 079061: *German Baroque cantatas, vol. 6.* Funeral cantatas: BACH—Cantata no. 106. BOXBERG—Bestelle dein Haus. RIEDEL—Harmonische Freude, frommer Seelen. TELEMANN—Du aber, Daniel gehe hin. *Reyghere, Bowman, Mey, Egmond; Ricercar Consort.*
+ Gr 7/91: 107
+ EM 8/91: 480
+ Fa 5-6/91: 379

30921. RIC 081063: BIBER—Requiem. KERLL—Missa pro defunctis. *Reyghere, Feldman, Bowman, Mey, Honeyman, Egmond; Capella Sancti Michaelis; Ricercar consort; Nevel, cond.*
+ Fa 5-6/91: 133

30922. RIC 087062: Sonatas for horn and piano by Beethoven, Ries and Danzi. *Maury, natural horn; Penson, piano.*
+ ARG 3-4/92: 184

30923. RIC 089125 (2 discs): W.F. BACH—Chamber music. *Various performers.*
• ARG 1-2/96: 76

30924. RIC 900006 (6 discs): BACH—Organ works (Weimar period) on historic organs. *Foccroulle, organ.*
- ARG 5-6/92: 24

30925. RIS 090072/4 (3 discs): MOZART—Lucio Silla. *Rolfe Johnson, Cuberli, Murray, Barbaux, Aruhn, Baasbank; Chorus & Orch. of the Théâtre royal de la Monnaie, Brussels; Cambreling, cond.*
- Gr 2/92: 77

30926. RIC 092001 (2 discs): *Die Familie Bach.* Music of Johann, Johann Michael, Johann Christoph, Johann Sebastian, Carl Philipp Emmanuel, and Wilhelm Friedemann Bach. *Vocal soloists; Capella Sancti Michaelis; Ricercar Consort; Nevel, cond.* Reissues.
+ ARG 11-12/92: 77
+ Fa 11-12/92: 182

30927. RIS 093070/71 (2 discs): VERDI—Simon Boccanegra. *Gustafson, Cupido, Dam, Stone, Pittsinger; Théâtre Royal de la Monnaie, Brussels; Cambreling, cond.* Recorded live 1990.
- Gr 1/92: 96

30928. RIC 092078: BEETHOVEN—Rondino for octet; Trio for 2 oboes and English horn; Sextet; Quintet for oboe, 3 horns and bassoon; Variations on Là ci darem la mano. *Ricercar Academy.*
+ ARG 7-8/92: 92

30929. RIC 093001 (3 discs): Guide des instruments baroques. *Ricercar Consort.*
+ Fa 5-6/94: 342

30930. RIC 903005: *A defense of the bass viol against the ventures of the violin and the pretensions of the violoncello.* Music of Morel Cappus, Marais, and others. *Ricercar consort.*

+ ARG 11-12/94: 221

30931. RIC 904001 (9 discs): LEKEU—Centenary edition. *Various performers.*
+ ARG 5-6/95: 128
+ Fa 3-4/95: 206

30932. RIC 094076: *Seven cantatas.* BUXTEHUDE—O clemens, o mitis, BuxWV 82; An filius non est Dei, BuxWV 6; Mein Herz ist bereit, BuxWV 73; Drei schöne Dinge, BuxWV 19; Quemadmodum desiderat cervus, BuxWV 92; Ich bin eine Blume zu Saron, BuxWV 45; Erbarm dich mein, O Herre Gott, BuxWV s.9. *Reyghere, soprano; Bowman, countertenor; Honeyman, tenor; Egmond, bass; Ricercar Consort.*
+ Fa 9-10/92: 209

30933. RIC 905001 (3 discs): Compendium of Renaissance musical instruments. *Various performers.*
+ ARG 7-8/96: 264
• Fa 7-8/96: 366

30934. RIC 096080: MOZART—Divertimento in E♭ for violin, viola, and cello, K. 563. *Trio Ricercar.*
+ Fa 9-10/92: 300

30935. RIC 098112: *Deutsche Barock Kammermusik, V.* Music of Scheidt, Hentzschel, Posch, Nicolai, Kuhnel, Schenk, and Funck. *Ricercar Consort; Pierlot, cond.*
+ Fa 1-2/94: 389
+ Gr 8/94: 72

30936. RIS 099083: LEKEU—Andromède; Les burgraves: Introduction symphonique. *Bryant, Vandersteene, Huttenlocher, Bastin; Liège Symphony Orch.; Bartholomée, cond.*
+ Gr 10/92: 163

30937. RIC 100084/85 (2 discs): GRÉTRY—Le caravane du Caire. *Poulenard, Reyghere, Ragon, Huttenlocher; Chamber Chorus of Namur; Ricercar Academy; Minkowski, cond.*
+ ARG 9-10/92: 113
+ Fa 7-8/92: 166
+ ON 11/92: 46
+ OQ spring 93: 178

30938. RIC 101095: *Cantatas for alto solo.* Music of Vivaldi, Ziani, Marcello, Tuma, and Monn. *Bowman, countertenor; Ricercar Consort.*
+ Gr 4/93: 114

30939. RIC 102110: TELEMANN—Chamber music with recorder. *Roos, recorder; Ricercar Consort.*
+ ARG 1-2/94: 166
+ Fa 11-12/93: 424

30940. RIC 103086/87 (2 discs): *German Baroque cantatas, vol. 8.* Music of J.S.

Bach, Hoyoul, Hellingk, Lechner, Schütz, Sweelinck, Selle, Schein and others. *Vocal soloists; Capella Sancti Michaelis; Ricercar Consort; Nevel, cond.*
+ Fa 11-12/92: 181

30941. RIS 104091: LEKEU—*La musique de chambre, vol. 1.* Piano quartet (unfinished); Violin sonata. *Domus; Hirschhorn, violin; Vanden Eynden, piano.*
+ Fa 11-12/92: 277
+ Fa 1-2/93: 178

30942. RIC 105081 (3 discs): MOZART—Keyboard music. *Foccroulle, organ; Devos, piano; James, glass harmonica; Penson, harpsichord.*
+ Gr 12/92: 105

30943. RIC 107099: LEKEU—String quartet; Meditation; Adagio. *Camerata Quartet.*
□ ARG 3-4/93: 104

30944. RIS 108094: VIEUXTEMPS—Music for violin and piano. *Koch, violin; Devos, piano.*
• ARG 5-6/93: 148
+ Fa 1-2/93: 263

30945. RIC 109097/98 (2 discs): WECKMANN—The cantatas. *Ricercar Consort; Reyghere, soprano; Bowman, countertenor; Honeyman, tenor; Egmond, bass; Capella St. Michaelis; Nevel, cond.*
+ Fa 3-4/93: 330
+ Gr 4/93: 112

30946. RIC 111082: JANACEK—Sinfonietta; Diary of one who disappeared. BARTÓK—Miraculous mandarin. SCHOENBERG—Pelleas and Melisande. BERG—Three orchestral pieces. *Ardam, mezzo-soprano; Hamilton, tenor; Monnaie Theater Orch.; Cambreling, cond.*
- ARG 7-8/92: 154

30947. RIC 118100: *Le tombeau de Monsieur de Sainte Colombe.* Music of Marais, Du Buisson, Demachy, Sainte-Colombe the younger, and Dautrecourt (Sainte-Colombe). *Pierlot, bass viol; Lislevand, theorbo; Watillon, Zipperling, bass viols.*
+ ARG 9-10/93: 249
+ Fa 5-6/93: 376
+ Gr 2/94: 62

30948. RIC 120109: DU MONT—Cantica sacra: motets. *Ricercar Consort.*
+ ARG 11-12/93: 101
+ Fa 9-10/93: 156

30949. RIC 122107: BOCCHERINI— Cello sonatas G. 8, 10, 13, 17, 565. *Suzuki, cello; Zipperling, cello continuo; Penson, harpsichord.*
+ ARG 9-10/93: 98
• Fa 9-10/93: 129

30950. RIC 123111: Music of Bizet, Berlioz, Rossini, Guillmant, Mustel, and others. *Verdin, harmonium.*
+ ARG 11-12/93: 236

30951. RIC 124113: ABSIL—Guitar music. *Lemaigre, Verba, guitars.*
+ ARG 5-6/94: 62

30952. RIC 126114: ROSSINI—Overtures (transcribed for wind instruments). *Ricercar Academy; Ponseele, cond.*
+ Fa 5-6/94: 334

30953. RIC 127140: PURCELL—Ten sonatas in four parts. *Ricercar Consort.*
• Fa 11-12/95: 336

30954. RIS 131117: ARENSKY—Piano trio no. 1. SMETANA—Piano trio. *Grumiaux Piano Trio.*
+ Gr 11/94: 96

30955. RIC 132116: CHOPIN—Nocturnes. *Devos, piano.*
• ARG 5-6/94: 83
• Fa 5-6/94: 130

30956. RIC 133122/23 (2 discs): BOESMANS—Riegen. *Raymond, Curtis, Ardam, Sacca; other soloists; Orch. Symphonique de la Monnaie; Cambreling, cond.*
+ Fa 5-6/95: 144
+ ON 3/18/95: 36

30957. RIC 134115: BACH—The great toccatas. *Foccroulle, organ.* Reissue.
• ARG 5-6/94: 65
+ Fa 3-4/94: 108

30958. RIC 135119: ARENSKY—Trio in D Minor. SMETANA—Trio. *Arthur Grumiaux Piano Trio.*
+ ARG 5-6/94: 63

30959. RIC 139131: PRAETORIUS—Terpsichore: 36 dances. *Ricercar Consort; Fernandez, Pierlot, conds.; La Fenice; Tubery, cond.*
+ ARG 11-12/95: 172

30960. RIC 147135: *Musiques de salon.* Music of Gobbaerts, Eilenberg, G. Bachmann, Stadeler, H. Hoffmann, Wachs, Burgmein, Gillet, Durand de Grau, J. Wieniawski, Kölling, Van Gael, E. Fischer, and W. Ganz. *Bernier, Penson, piano 4 hands.*
+ Fa 7-8/96: 380

30961. RIC 148130: BARRIOS—Guitar music. *Lemaigre, guitar.*
• ARG 5-6/95: 80

30962. RIC 151145: WILLAERT—Madrigals, chansons, villanelle. *Romanesque; Malfeyt, cond.*
• ARG 9-10/96: 226
+ Fa 11-12/96: 421

30963. RIC 153138: BRAHMS—Liebeslieder waltzes, op. 52; Waltzes, op.

RICERCAR

39; Neue Liebeslieder waltzes, op. 65. *Vanden Eynden, Devos, piano 4 hands; Reyghere, soprano; Deyck, mezzo-soprano; Mey, tenor; Claessens, bass.*
+ ARG 9-10/95: 113
- Fa 9-10/95: 152

30964. RIC 154149: LASSUS—Chansons. Music by Philips, Dalla Casa, and Jarzebski. *Collot, soprano; Ricercar Consort.*
+ ARG 1-2/97: 129
• Fa 1-2/97: 190

30965. RIC 155141: LASSO—Mass, Ad imitationem moduli vinum bonum; Magnificat; Motets. *Chamber Choir of Namur; Ricercar Consort; La Fenice; Phillips, cond.*
+ ARG 3-4/96: 142

30966. RIC 157142: *Dialoghi venetiani.* Music of Castello, Kapsberger, Marini, and Uccellini. *La Fenice.*
+ ARG 5-6/96: 250

30967. RIC 167136: Music of Picchi, Merulo, Luzzaschi, Gabrieli, Frescobaldi, and others. *Henstra, harpsichord.*
+ ARG 1-2/97: 208

RICERCARE IN ECCO

30968. 245692 (2 discs): HANDEL—Sonatas for flute or recorder and continuo. *Roos, flute; Beuckels, recorder; Ricercar Consort.* Reissues.
+ ARG 9-10/96: 132 (as 8004/5)

RICORDI

30969. ACDOCL 202 (2 discs): DONIZETTI—Lucia di Lammermoor. *Scotto, Di Stefano, Bastianini; with assisting soloists; Teatro alla Scala; Sanzogno, cond.*
- Fa 11-12/88: 172

30970. ACDOCL 205 (2 discs): VERDI—Rigoletto. *Scotto, Cossotto, Kraus, Bastianini, Vinco; with assisting soloists; Maggio Musicale Fiorentino Chorus & Orch.; Gavazzeni, cond.*
+ Fa 3-4/89: 323

30971. CRMCD 1002: BUSSOTTI—Le passion selon Sade (concerto extracts); Le bal Mirò: first suite, anthology for orchestra. *Ross, soprano; instrumentalists; Panni, cond.; RAI Symphony Orch., Rome; Zagrosek, cond.*
• Fa 5-6/94: 124

30972. CRMCD 1003: NONO—A Pierre: dell'azzurro silenzio, inquietum; Diario polacco no. 2; Post-prae-ludium per Donau. *Various performers; Cecconi, cond.*
+ Fa 5-6/94: 210

30973. CRMCD 1004: A. CLEMENTI—Capriccio for viola and 24 instruments; Cent sopirs; AEB; Concerto for violin, 40 instruments, and carillons; Fantasia su Giorgio Moench; Intermezzo for fourteen winds and prepared piano. *Various performers.*
+ Fa 5-6/94: 131

30974. CRMCD 1006: CORGHI—Mazapegul. *The New Swingle Singers.*
• Fa 5-6/94: 132

30975. CRMCD 1013: DONATONI—Rima; Ala; Alamari; Spiri; Flag. *Carme; Guida, cond.*
- Fa 5-6/94: 136

30976. CRMCD 1015: SCIARRINO—Vanitas. *Turchetta, mezzo-soprano; Filippini, cello; Pestalozza, piano.*
+ Fa 5-6/94: 250

30977. CRMCD 1017: BERIO—Passaggio; Visage for magnetic tape and voice. *Ross, Berberian, sopranos; Orch. da Camera "Nuova consonanza"; Coro dell'Accademia Filarmonica Romana; Panni, cond.*
+ Fa 5-6/94: 114

30978. RFCD 2001 (2 discs): ROSSINI—L'occasione fa il ladro. *Serra, Giménez, Raftery, Desderi; Orch. Giovanile Italiana; Accardo, cond.* Recorded live.
+ ARG 1-2/94: 143
• Fa 11-12/93: 367
+ ON 1/21/95: 36

30979. RFCD 2002 (2 discs): ROSSINI—Il Signor Bruschino. *Devia, Dara, Rinaldi, Gonzales; RAI Turin; Renzetti, cond.* Recorded 1988.
• ARG 1-2/94: 141
• Fa 1-2/94: 292
- ON 1/21/95: 36

30980. RFCD 2003 (2 discs): ROSSINI—La scala di seta. *Serra, Bartoli, Matteuzzi, Coviello; Bologna Opera; Ferro, cond.* Recorded live 1988.
+ ARG 11-12/93: 180
+ Fa 1-2/94: 288
+ ON 1/21/95: 36
+ Op 10/94: 1233

30981. RFCD 2004 (2 discs): MASCAGNI—Le maschere. *Vocal soloists; Chorus & Orch. of the Teatro Comunale di Bologna; Gelmetti, cond.* Recorded live 1988.
• ARG 11-12/93: 146
+ Fa 11-12/93: 312
• ON 2/4/95: 41

30982. RFCD 2005 (2 discs): DONIZETTI—Elisabetta al castello di Kenilworth. *Devia, Kundlak, Mazzola, Anderson; other soloists; Orch. & Chorus of RAI Milan; Latham-Koenig, cond.* Recorded live 1989.
+ ARG 1-2/94: 95
+ Fa 11-12/93: 218
+ ON 12/11/93: 44
+ Op 10/94: 1235

30983. RFCD 2006: PERGOLESI—La morte di San Giuseppe. *Farruggia, Manca di Nissa, M. Peters, Pace; Orch. Alessandro Scarlatti di Napoli; Panni, cond.*
+ ARG 3-4/94: 131
• Fa 11-12/93: 340
+ ON 7/94: 42

30984. RFCD 2007 (2 discs): MAYR—La rosa bianca e la rosa rossa. *Antonacci, Mazzoni, Anselmi, Canonici, Facini, Serraiocco; Coro Accademia, Milan; Orch. Stabile di Bergamo; Briccetti, cond.* Recorded live 1990.
• ARG 11-12/93: 147
+ Fa 11-12/93: 316
• Gr 12/94: 156
+ ON 4/15/95: 35

30985. RFCD 2008 (3 discs): ROSSINI—Bianca e Falliero. *Ricciarelli, Horne, Merritt, Surian; Pesaro Festival; Renzetti, cond.* Recorded 1986.
• ARG 1-2/94: 141
+ Fa 1-2/94: 287
+ Gr 9/94: 117
+ ON 5/94: 48
+ Op 10/94: 1233

30986. RFCD 2009: TOSTI—Songs. *Focile, soprano; Gallo, baritone; Battaglia, piano.*
+ ARG 1-2/94: 166
+ Fa 1-2/94: 336

30987. RFCD 2010 (2 discs): BELLINI—La straniera. *Aliberti, Bello, Frontali, Mingardo; Trieste Opera; Masini, cond.* Recorded live 1990.
+ ARG 1-2/94: 77
• Fa 1-2/94: 129

30988. RFCD 2011: ROSSINI—La cambiale di matrimonio. *Jeun, Laurenza, Canonici, Dara; Turin Radio Orch.; Renzetti, cond.* Recorded live 1991.
+ ARG 11-12/93: 180
• Fa 1-2/94: 288

30989. RFCD 2012: ROSSINI—Messa di gloria. *Antonacci, Manca di Nissa, Araiza, Gambill, Spagnoli, Pietro; Chorus of the Accademia Nazionale di Santa Cecilia; Accardo, cond.* Recorded live.
+ Fa 1-2/94: 291

30990. RFCD 2014 (2 discs): WOLF-FERRARI—Il campiello. *Mazzucato, Devinu, Benelli; Chorus & Orch. of the Verdi Theater of Trieste; Bareza, cond.* Recorded live 1992.
+ ARG 11-12/93: 222
+ Fa 11-12/93: 452
+ Op 10/94: 1236
+ ON 10/94: 50

30991. RFCD 2015 (3 discs): DONIZETTI—La favorite. *Scalchi, Canonici, Massis, Surian; Chorus & Orch. of RAI, Milan; Renzetti, cond.*
• Fa 1-2/94: 170
• ON 12/11/93: 44

30992. RFCD 2016 (2 discs): FERRERO—Mare nostro. *Felle, Jankovic, Di Segni, Antoniozzi, Serraiocco, Rigosa, Visentin, Sonia; orch. acc.; Masini, cond.*
- ARG 7-8/94: 102
+ Fa 5-6/94: 145
+ ON 2/4/95: 41

30993. RFCD 2017 (2 discs): TCHAIKOVSKY—Iolanta. *Kudriavchenko, Tarastchenko, Seleznev, Morozov, Redkin; Chorus & Orch. of RAI Milan; Delman, cond.*
+ ARG 5-6/94: 154
- Fa 5-6/94: 265
+ ON 4/1/95: 44

30994. RFCD 2018 (3 discs): ROSSINI—Semiramide. *Tamar, Scalchi, Kunde, Pertusi; Teatro Comunale di Bologna; Zedda, cond. Recorded 1992.*
- ARG 5-6/94: 134
- Fa 3-4/94: 293
+ ON 5/94: 48

30995. ARCL 22700: BACH—Flute sonatas, BWV 1020, BWV 1030-35; Partita for solo flute, BWV 1013. *Gazzelloni, flute; Canino, harpsichord.*
+ Fa 11-12/88: 123

RIVO ALTO

30996. CRA 8922: PERGOLESI—Mass in F. *Coro polifonico di Milano; Solisti di Milano; Ephrikian, cond. Reissue.*
- Fa 3-4/94: 270

RIZZOLI

30997. 206 (3 discs): BELLINI—Beatrice di Tenda. *Nicolesco, Toczyska, La Scola, Cappuccilli; Prague Phil. Choir; Monte Carlo Orch.; Zedda, cond.*
+ DA 9/88: 58
- Fa 7-8/88: 124
+ Gr 6/88: 72
+ HPR 9/88: 77
+ ON 5/88: 46
- OQ Win/88: 147
+ SR 7/88: 100

30998. 2003 (LP): Music of Poulenc, Ravel, and Duparc. *Maurice, mezzo-soprano; Baldwin, piano.*
- Fa 7-8/87: 215
+ SR 8/87: 88

30999. 2005: RAVEL—Alcyone; Alyssa. *Nicolesco, Enize, mezzo-soprano; Meens, tenor; Glashof, baritone; Bamberg Symphony Orch.; Soudant, cond.*
+ DA 12/88: 52
□ Fa 5-6/88: 189
- Gr 5/88: 1634
+ HF 10/88: 83
- MA 9/88: 63

RNE

31000. M3/02: Organ music of De Soto, Cabezon, Santa Maria, De Peraza, De Heredia, Del Castillo, Cabanilles, Duron

and Bruna. *Rios, organ.*
- Fa 5-6/92: 317

31001. M3/03: *Piano works by women composers.* Music of L. Boulanger, Prieto, De la Cruz, Escribano, Ozaita, Catalan, Diez, and Bacewicz. *Marin, piano.*
□ Gr 4/93: 96

31002. AME-002: *Musica da camara contemporanea.* Music of Guerrero, Riviere, Pablo, Seco and Ibarrondo. *Grupo Koan; Encinar, cond.*
□ Fa 3-4/92: 420

31003. AME-003: CASTRO—Trattenimenti armonici da camera. *Academia d'Harmonia.*
+ Fa 3-4/92: 184

31004. AME-005: *Musica para violoncello y piano.* Music of Montsalvatge, Granados, Cassadó, Turina, and Nin. *Ramos, cello; Colom, piano.*
- Fa 3-4/92: 395

RODOLPHE

31005. 005: CHERUBINI—Il giocatore. *Bacelli, Gatti; L'Accademia Strumentale Italiana; Bernasconi, cond.*
- Fa 3-4/91: 184

31006. RP 12465/66 (2 LPs): BEETHOVEN—Symphony no. 9. SCHUBERT—Symphony no. 8. *Seefried, Anday, Dermota, Schöffler; Vienna Singakademie Chorus; Vienna Phil. Orch.; Berlin Phil. Orch.; Furtwängler, cond.*
- Fa 11-12/86: 114

RP 12467/68 see RPC 32467/68.

31007. RPC 32399: SCHUBERT—Piano sonata D. 960. *Bärtschi, piano.*
+ Fa 1-2/87: 177
- Gr 2/87: 1160

31008. RPC 32406: TELEMANN—Trio for oboe and viola in C minor; Fantasy for unaccompanied oboe in B minor; Cello sonata in D; Partita for oboe in G; Oboe sonata in E minor. *Musica Viva et Antiqua Ensemble.*
+ Fa 1-2/87: 90
+ Gr 2/87: 1150

31009. RPC 32426/27 (2 discs): DELIBES—Lakmé. *Robin, Richard, Savignol; French Broadcasting System Lyric Chorus & Orch.; Gressier, cond.*
- Fa 1-2/87: 90
- Gr 3/87: 1325

31010. RPC 32431/32 (2 discs): VERDI—La traviata. *Callas, Di Stefano, Campolonghi; Mexico City Opera Chorus & Orch.; Mugnai, cond.*
+ ARG 3-4/88: 92
- Fa 1-2/88: 228

31011. RPC 32445/46 (2 discs): Music of Verdi, Mozart, Fauré, Pizzetti, Wagner, and others. *Crespin, soprano; various orchs. & conds. Recorded live 1964-1970.*
+ Fa 11-12/89: 425

31012. RPC 32459/60 (2 discs): VERDI—Otello. *Tucci, Del Monaco, Gobbi; Tokyo Radio Chorus; Japan Radio Symphony Orch.; Erede, cond.*
- Fa 11-12/86: 236

31013. RPC 32465: BEETHOVEN—Symphony no. 9. *Seefried, Anday, Dermota, Schöffler; Wiener Singakademie Chorus; Vienna Phil. Orch.; Furtwängler, cond.*
- Fa 11-12/86: 114

31014. RPC 32467/68 (2 discs): MOZART—Idomeneo. *Stich-Randall, Tarres, Dowd, MacAlpine; Orch. de l'Association des concerts Colonne; Maag, cond. Issued also as 2 LPs: RP 12467/68. Severely abridged performance recorded live in 1963.*
- Fa 1-2/87: 146
- Gr 3/87: 1326
- Op 12/86: 1388
- OQ Spring/87: 153

31015. RPC 32473: LALO—Guitare; Prière de l'enfant à son réveil; A celle qui part; Chanson de l'alouette; Puisqu'ici bas toute âme; Chanson de Barberine; Chant breton; Aubade; Oh! Quand je dors; Viens!; L'eslave; Humoresque; Marine; La Zuecca; A une fleur; Dieu qui sourit; Souvenir; La Fenaisson; Si j'étais petit oiseau; La pauvre femme; Ballade à la lune; Le rouge-gorge; Laube nait; Tristesse; Chanson à boire. *Zylis-Gara, soprano; Ivaldi, piano.*
+ Fa 9-10/88: 180

31016. RPC 32479: BACH—Cantatas: Weicht nur, betrübt Schatten BWV 202; Ich habe genug BWV 82a; Mein Herz schwimmt im Blut BWV 199. *Zylis-Gara, soprano; Ensemble Instrumental de Basse Normandie; Debart, cond.*
- Fa 9-10/87: 135

31017. RPC 32488/89 (2 discs): MOZART—Entführung aus dem Serail. *Stich-Randall, Prietto, Gedda, Sénéchal, Arié; Paris Conservatory Chorus; Societe des concerts du Conservatoire Orch.; Rosbaud, cond. Recorded live 1954.*
- Fa 11-12/87: 180
+ ON 12/19/87: 42

31018. RPC 32491: BEETHOVEN—Piano sonatas no. 21, 28. LISZT—Piano sonata in B minor. *Gilels, piano.*
+ ARG 7-8/88: 13
- Fa 3-4/88: 71

31019. RPC 32492 (2 discs): ZANDONAI—Francesca da Rimini. *Ligabue, Bondino, Protti; French Radio Chorus; French National Orch.; Santi,*

RODOLPHE

cond.
- ARG 7-8/88: 71
+ Fa 3-4/88: 236
- Op 3/88: 327 m.f.

31020. RPC 32496: *Luciano Pavarotti en public.* Music of Puccini, Mozart, Bellini, and Verdi . *Pavarotti, tenor; various orchs. & conds.* Recorded live 1961-1966.
+ Fa 11-12/88: 321
+ St 4/89: 211

31021. RPC 32497/98 (2 discs): BELLINI—I Capuleti e i Montecchi. *Rinaldi, Aragall, Pavarotti, Monachesi, Zaccaria; Teatro comunale (Bologna) Chorus; Residentie Orch. The Hague; Abbado, cond.* Recorded live 1966.
+ Fa 7-8/88: 125 (m.f.)
+ OQ Win/88: 130

31022. RPC 32499/500 (2 discs): DONIZETTI—Gemma di Vergy. *Caballé, Lima, Sardinero, Pons; Radio France Chorus; French Radio New Philharmonia Orch.; Gatto, cond.* Recorded live 1975.
- Fa 7-8/88: 153
- OQ Aut/88: 137

31023. RPC 32501: *Montserrat Caballé et José Carreras à Paris.* Music of Rossini, Bellini, Charpentier, Massenet, Donizetti, and others. *Caballé, soprano; Carreras, tenor; orch.; Müller, cond.* Recorded live 1979.
+ Fa 11-12/88: 325

31024. RPC 32510: GIULIANI—Integrale delle opere per voce e chitarra. *Brown, soprano; Sebastiani, guitar.*
+ ARG 3-4/89: 36
- Fa 1-2/89: 168

31025. RPC 32513: LOCATELLI—Violin concertos with 24 caprices ad libitum op. 3 no. 1-3. *Conti, violin; Virtuosi dell'Accademia.*
+ Fa 9-10/89: 238
+ Gr 3/90: 1610

31026. RPC 32519/20 (2 discs): WEBER—Der Freischütz. *Grümmer, Streich, Hopf, Böhme, Edelmann; Salzburg Festival; Furtwängler, cond.* Recorded live 1954.
- Fa 5-6/89: 360
+ St 8/89: 187

31027. RPC 32521: WEBER—Four hand piano music (complete). *Marrucci, Galli, pianos.*
+ ARG 9-10/89: 117
- Fa 9-10/89: 377

31028. RPC 32525/26 (2 discs): GRÉTRY—Zémire et Azor. *Masquelin, Garino, Kelly, Voli; Opéra Royal de Wallonie Chorus & Orch.; Curtis, cond.*
- Fa 1-2/90: 189
- Gr 9/89: 533

31029. RPC 32531: LOCATELLI—Violin concertos with 24 caprices ad libitum op. 3 no. 4-6. *Conti, violin; Virtuosi dell'Accademia.*
+ ARG 11-12/89: 75
+ Fa 11-12/89: 268
+ Gr 3/90: 1610

31030. RPC 32539/50 (12 discs): *Teatro alla Scala.* VERDI—Rigoletto; Il trovatore; Aida; Otello; Requiem. LEONCAVALLO—I pagliacci. *Soloists; Teatro alla Scala Chorus & Orch.; Sabajno, cond.* Recorded in the 1930's. Includes 2 discs of arias sung by soloists from La Scala recorded between 1900 & 1955.
+ Fa 5-6/90: 367
+ Gr 10/90: 834

31031. RPC 32553/55 (3 discs): WAGNER—Tristan und Isolde. *Nilsson, Hesse, Vickers, Berry, Rundgren; New Philharmonia Chorus; French Radio and Television National Orch.; Böhm, cond.* Recorded live 1973.
- ARG 5-6/90: 131
+ DA 3/90: 71 m.f.
- Fa 5-6/90: 338
☐ St 4/90: 213

31032. RPC 32561/62 (2 discs): VERDI—Otello. *Martinis, Vinay, Schöffler; Vienna State Opera Chorus; Vienna Phil. orch.; Furtwängler, cond.* Recorded live 1951.
+ Fa 9-10/90: 419

31033. RPC 32563/64 (2 discs): HANDEL—Alcina. *Sutherland, Wunderlich, Monti, Hemsley; Cologne Radio Chorus; Cappella Coloniensis; Leitner, cond.* Recorded live 1959.
+ Fa 7-8/90: 161

31034. RPC 32671/72 (2 discs): SPONTINI—Agnes von Hohenstaufen. *Caballé, Stella, Prevedi, Bruscantini, Guelfi; Italian Radio and Television Rome Chorus & Orch.; Muti, cond.* Recorded live 1970.
+ Fa 7-8/91: 297

31035. RPC 32755: MASCAGNI—Cavalleria rusticana. *Simionato, Loforese, Orazi; Tokyo Radio Chorus; NHK Symphony Orch.; Morelli, cond.*
- Fa 9-10/86: 184

31036. RPA 232551/2 (2 discs): GIORDANO—Andrea Chénier. *Callas, Del Monaco, Protti; Teatro alla Scala Chorus & Orch.; Votto, cond.*
+ Fa 5-6/90: 171

ROMANTIC ROBOT

31037. RR 1941 (2 discs): *Theresienstadt, the music 1941-44.* Music of Klein, Ullmann, Krása and Haas. *Various performers.*
- Gr 8/92: 48
+ Op 6/92: 746

31038. RR 1973: *An American in Prague.* Music of Copland, Ives, Stravinsky, Martinů, Schuman, and Bernstein. *Czech Phil. Orch.; Copland, cond.* Recorded live 1973.
- ARG 11-12/93: 225
+ Fa 9-10/93: 391
+ Gr 6/93: 57

ROMOPHONE

31039. 81001-2 (2 discs): *Emma Eames: the complete Victor recordings (1905-1911).* 47 acoustic vocal recordings and a 1939 radio broadcast interview. *Eames, soprano; with acc.*
+ ARG 7-8/94: 237
+ Fa 9-10/93: 339
+ Gr 11/93: 192
+ Op 10/93: 1258

31040. 81002-2 (2 discs): *Emmy Destinn: the complete Victor recordings 1914-21.* 37 acoustic recordings. *Destinn, soprano; with acc.*
- ARG 7-8/94: 237
+ Fa 9-10/93: 341
+ Gr 11/93: 192
+ Op 10/93: 1258

31041. 81003-2 (2 discs): Amelita Galli-Curci, the complete acoustic recordings, vol. 1 1916-20. *Galli-Curci, soprano; orch. acc.*
+ ARG 7-8/94: 237
+ Fa 11-12/93: 455
+ Gr 3/94: 120

31042. 81004-2: Amelita Galli-Curci: the complete acoustic recordings, vol. 2. *Galli-Curci, soprano; with orch. accomp.* Recorded 1920-24.
+ ARG 7-8/94: 237
+ Fa 3-4/94: 371
+ Gr 8/94: 124

31043. 81005-2 (2 discs): Claudia Muzio: the complete HMV (1911) and Edison (1920-25) recordings. *Muzio, soprano; orch. acc.*
+ ARG 7-8/94: 237
+ Fa 1-2/94: 366
+ Gr 1/94: 109

31044. 81006-2 (2 discs): Rosa Ponselle: the Victor recordings (1923-25). *Ponselle, soprano; various orchs. & conds.*
+ ARG 9-10/94: 276
+ ARG 7-8/94: 237
+ Fa 5-6/94: 294
+ Gr 11/94: 187

31045. 81007-2 (2 discs): Rosa Ponselle, the Victor recordings 1926-29. *Ponselle, soprano; orch. & piano acc.*
+ Fa 11-12/94: 435
+ Gr 11/94: 187

31046. 81008-2: Mary Garden: Complete Victor recordings, 1926-29. *Garden, soprano.* Recorded 1926-29.
- ARG 7-8/94: 237

+ Fa 7-8/94: 291
+ Gr 8/94: 122

31047. 81009-2: *Edith Mason: the complete recordings (1924-28).* Music of Puccini, Gounod, Cadman, Strickland, Flotow, Tosti, Del Riego, Woodforde-Finden, Mendelssohn, G. Charpentier, Nevin, Bland, and Foster. *Mason, soprano; unnamed orch.; Black, cond.*
+ Fa 9-10/94: 386
+ Gr 8/94: 122

31048. 81010-2 (2 discs): Claudia Muzio, the complete Pathé recordings (1917-18). *Muzio, soprano.*
+ ARG 9-10/94: 276
+ Fa 9-10/94: 386

31049. 81011-2 (3 discs): Nellie Melba, the complete Victor recordings 1907-1916. *Melba, soprano.*
+ ARG 1-2/95: 267
+ Fa 1-2/95: 321
+ Gr 5/95: 131
+ ON 10/96: 43

31050. 81012-2 (2 discs): Elisabeth Rethberg, the complete Brunswick recordings 1924-1929. *Rethberg, soprano.*
+ ARG 1-2/95: 267
+ Fa 1-2/95: 319
+ Gr 2/95: 116

31051. 81013-2 (2 discs): Lotte Lehmann: the Victor recordings. *Lehmann, soprano; Balogh, Ulanowsky, pianos; orch.; Reibold, cond.* Recorded 1935-1940.
+ ARG 3-4/95: 277
+ Fa 5-6/95: 382

31052. 81014-2 (2 discs): *Elisabeth Rethberg: The HMV, Parlophone, and Victor recordings, 1927-1934.* Forty-six historic vocal recordings. *Rethberg, soprano; with other vocalists and various accompaniments.*
+ ARG 11-12/95: 294
+ Fa 11-12/95: 436
+ Gr 10/95: 165

31053. 81015-2 (2 discs): Claudia Muzio: the complete Columbia recordings (1934-35). *Muzio, soprano.*
+ ARG 5-6/96: 277
+ Fa 5-6/96: 325
+ Gr 6/96: 114

31054. 81016-2 (2 discs): *Lucrezia Bori: The Victor recordings, 1914-1925.* Forty-six acoustic and electric historic vocal recordings. *Bori, soprano; various accompaniments.*
+ ARG 11-12/95: 291
+ Fa 11-12/95: 437
+ Gr 3/96: 112

31055. 81017-2 (2 discs): *Lucrezia Bori: the Victor recordings (1925-37).* Forty-five historic vocal recordings. *Bori, soprano.*

+ Fa 7-8/96: 344
+ Gr 7/96: 119

31056. 81018-2: Lieder by Mendelssohn, Schumann, and Brahms. *Schumann, soprano; various assisting musicians.*
+ ARG 11-12/95: 295
+ Fa 11-12/95: 437
+ Gr 1/96: 115
+ ON 8/96: 45

31057. 81019-2: Mozart opera and Viennese operetta arias. *Schumann, soprano; various accs.*
+ ARG 7-8/96: 295
+ Fa 1-2/96: 355
• Gr 7/96: 119
+ ON 8/96: 45

31058. 81020-2: Amelita Galli-Curci: the Victor recordings (1925-28). *Galli-Curci, soprano; various accs.*
+ ARG 11-12/96: 298
+ Fa 11-12/96: 426

31059. 81021-2: Amelita Galli-Curci: the Victor recordings (1930). *Galli-Curci, soprano; various accs.*
+ Fa 11-12/96: 426

31060. 82001-2 (2 discs): Pol Plançon: the complete Victor recordings (1903-08). *Plançon, bass; various acc.*
+ ARG 7-8/94: 237
+ Fa 1-2/94: 380

31061. 82002-2: Edmond Clément: the complete Odéon (1905) and Victor (1911-13) recordings. *Clément, tenor; various orchs. & pianists.*
+ ARG 7-8/94: 237
+ Fa 5-6/94: 298

31062. 82003-2 (2 discs): *Beniamino Gigli: the complete Victor recordings, vol. 1 (1921-25).* Thirty-seven historic vocal recordings. *Gigli, tenor; various accs.*
+ ARG 11-12/96: 299
+ Fa 7-8/96: 353
+ Gr 11/96: 175

31063. 82004-2 (2 discs): *Beniamino Gigli: the complete Victor recordings, vol. 2: 1926-28.* Twenty-seven historic vocal recordings. *Gigli, tenor; various orch. accs.*
+ ARG 11-12/96: 299
+ Fa 9-10/96: 376
+ Gr 11/96: 175

31064. 82005-2 (2 discs): Beniamino Gigli: the complete Victor recordings, vol. 3 (1929-32). *Gigli, tenor; various accs.*
+ ARG 11-12/96: 299
+ Fa 11-12/96: 429
+ Gr 11/96: 175
+ ON 10/96: 43

31065. 82006-2 (2 discs): Acoustic and HMV recordings (1910-11). *McCormack, tenor.*
+ ARG 3-4/96: 264

+ Fa 5-6/96: 330
+ Gr 4/96: 132

31066. 89001-2 (2 discs): PUCCINI—Madama Butterfly. *Sheridan, Cecil, Mannarini; Teatro La Scala; Sabajno, cond.* Recorded 1929.
+ Fa 5-6/96: 240

31067. 89002-2 (2 discs): SULLIVAN—H.M.S. Pinafore; The pirates of Penzance. *Lytton, Baker, Goulding, Fancourt; London Symphony Orch.; Light Opera Orch.; Sargent, cond.* Recorded 1929-1930.
+ Fa 9-10/96: 337
+ ON 10/96: 44

RONDOGRAMOFON

31068. RCD 6344: Music of Handel, Scheidt, Bach, Lumbye, Grieg, Bellstedt, and others. *Royal Danish Brass.*
+ ARG 9-10/94: 229

31069. RCD 8319, 8323, 8325, 8327, 8329 (5 separate discs): NIELSEN—The lesser-known Nielsen, vols. 1-5. *Various vocal soloists and pianists.*
+ ARG 5-6/89: 73 (v.1-2)
+ Fa 1-2/96: 269

31070. RCD 8336: MOZART—Serenades no. 11-12; Divertimentos no. 8, 12. *Danish Wind Octet.*
• Fa 1-2/96: 266

31071. RCD 8341: KUHLAU—Piano music. *Trondhjem, piano.*
+ Fa 9-10/95: 241

31072. RCD 8342: GRIEG—Complete works for string orchestra. *Salomon Ensemble; Dausgaard, cond.*
+ Fa 9-10/95: 213

31073. RCD 8343: Music of Telemann, Biber, Purcell, Hume, Marini, Clarke, and Schmelzer. *Violin-Banden.*
+ Fa 11-12/95: 483

31074. RCD 8345: *Trumpet concertos, vol. 3.* Music of Handel, Loeillet, Torelli, Reger, Viviani, Lindberg, Tolar, Albinoni, Wallin, Charpentier, Mouret, Horovitz, Bach, and Giordani. *K. Christensen, Schmidt, trumpets; P.N. Christensen, organ & harpsichord; Moravian-Silesian Chamber Orch.; Vitek, P.N. Christensen, conds.*
+ Fa 9-10/95: 421

31075. RCD 8346: DE MEIJ—Symphony no. 1 "The lord of the rings." BERNSTEIN—Divertimento. *Danish Concert Band; Jensen, cond.*
+ Fa 9-10/95: 189

31076. RCD 8347: Music of Byrd, Boddecker, Eyck, Schop, and others. *Rosenborg Trio.*
+ ARG 9-10/96: 261

RONDOGRAMOFON

31077. RCD 8348: Brahms—Clarinet sonata no. 1. Winding—Fantasies. Reger—Clarinet sonata no. 3. *Aabo, clarinet; Balshem, piano.*
- ARG 7-8/96: 90

31078. RCD 8349: *Trombone concepts.* Music of Rimsky-Korsakov, Simons, Guilmant, McDunn-Christensen, Von Koch, Jacob, Pryor, Bozza, Lohmann, and Saint-Saëns. *Svanberg, trombone; Danish Concert Band; Jensen, cond.*
+ Fa 9-10/95: 427

ROSE

31079. 3: Music of Dowland, Johnson, and Holborne. *Thodey, lute.*
- ARG 7-8/95: 247

ROSENHAUS

31080. 013: Music of Lubeck, Scheidt, Carvalho, Bach, Haydn, and others. *Jones, organ.*
+ ARG 5-6/94: 179

ROUND TOP

31081. RTR 002: Chopin—Piano concerto no. 1. Prokofiev—Piano concerto no. 3. *Dick, piano; Texas Festival Orch.; Ohyama, Verrot, conds.*
• ARG 9-10/93: 109

31082. RTR 003: Welcher—Shiva's drum. Saint-Saëns—Piano concerto no. 2. *Dick, piano; Texas Festival Orch.; Verrot, cond.*
+ ARG 5-6/96: 220

31083. RTR 116/861/3: Music of Mompou, Granados, and Chopin. *Rowley, piano.*
+ Fa 11-12/95: 476

31084. RTR 116/861/4: *Voice of the flute.* Music of Hüe, Copland, Taktakishvili, Foote, and Boehm. *Gedigian, flute; Rowley, piano.*
+ Fa 11-12/95: 464

ROYAL

31085. D 321791: Tchaikovsky—Nutcracker suite; Swan lake suite. *German Phil. Orch.; Scholz, cond.*
• Fa 3-4/88: 217

ROYAL OPERA HOUSE

31086. ROH 006: Delibes—Coppélia. *Orch. of the Royal Opera House, Covent Garden.; Ermler, cond.*
+ Gr 7/93: 36

31087. ROH 007: Adam—Giselle. *Orch. of the Royal Opera House Covent Garden; Ermler, cond.*
+ Gr 4/94: 38

31088. ROH 309/10 (2 discs): Prokofiev—Romeo and Juliet. *Orch. of the Royal Opera House, Covent Garden; Ermler, cond.*
• Gr 11/94: 82

RPO

31089. CDRPO 5002: Barber—Violin concerto. Bruch—Concerto no. 1. *Meyers, violin; Royal Phil. Orch.; Seaman, cond.*
- ARG 11-12/92: 78

31090. CDRPO 5007: Mahler—Symphony no. 4. *Kenny, soprano; Royal Phil. Orch.; Inoue, cond.*
+ ARG 1-2/93: 115

31091. CDRPO 5012: Gershwin—An American in Paris; Concerto in F. *Vakarelis, piano; Royal Phil. Orch.; Lewis, cond.*
- Fa 11-12/93: 241

31092. CDRPO 7004: Tchaikovsky—Symphony no. 6; Romeo and Juliet. *Royal Phil. Orch.; Koizumi, cond.*
+ Gr 6/92: 50

31093. CDRPO 7007: Fauré—Requiem. Bernstein—Chichester psalms. *A. Jones, soprano; S. Roberts, baritone; Birch, organ; London Symphony Chorus; Royal Phil. Orch.; Hickox, cond.*
+ ARG 11-12/92: 118

31094. CDRPO 7008: Tchaikovsky—Symphony no. 4; Capriccio italien. *Royal Phil. Orch.; Koizumi, Kazuhiro.*
+ Gr 4/92: 80

31095. CDRPO 7009: Opera spectacular 2. *Barstow, soprano; A. Davies, tenor; Royal Opera Chorus; Royal Phil. Orch.; Stapleton, cond.*
+ ARG 11-12/92: 257

31096. CDRPO 7011: Mahler—Symphony no. 5. *Royal Phil. Orch.; Inoue, cond.*
+ ARG 11-12/92: 153
+ Fa 1-2/93: 184

31097. CDRPO 7013: Walton—Belshazzar's feast; Henry V suite (arr. Mathieson). *Luxon, baritone; Royal Phil. Orch.; Brighton Festival Chorus; Collegium Musicum of London; Previn, cond.*
• ARG 11-12/92: 228

31098. CDRPO 7016: Berlioz—Symphonie fantastique; Corsaire: overture. *Royal Phil. Orch.; Previn, cond.*
- ARG 9-10/92: 84
• Gr 5/92: 322

31099. CDRPO 7020: Tchaikovsky—Manfred symphony. *Royal Phil. Orch.; Kozumi, cond.*
• ARG 9-10/93: 202
• Fa 5-6/93: 340

31100. CDRPO 7022: Rachmaninoff—Piano concertos no. 2, 4. *Costa, piano; Royal Phil. Orch.; Seaman, cond.*
• Gr 4/94: 54

31101. CDRPO 7023: Ravel—Piano concerto in G. Fauré—Ballade. Franck—Les Djinns; Symphonic variations. *Parham, piano; Royal Phil. Orch.; Casadesus, cond.*
• Gr 7/94: 54

31102. CDRPO 7024: Rachmaninoff—Piano concerto no. 1; Suite for two pianos no. 1. *Costa, Pizarro, pianos; Royal Phil. Orch.; Seaman, cond.*
+ ARG 3-4/95: 160

31103. CDRPO 9005 (2 discs): Mahler—Symphony no. 6. *Royal Phil. Orch.; Inoue, cond.*
+ ARG 1-2/93: 115
+ Fa 1-2/93: 184

RS APPLAUSI

31104. RS951-0170: Strauss—Don Juan; Macbeth; Tod und Verklärung. *Turin Phil. Orch.; Sanderling, cond.*
+ ARG 3-4/97: 239
• Fa 1-2/97: 283

31105. RS953-0186 (2 discs): Mahler—Symphony no. 6. *St. Petersburg Phil. Orch.; Sanderling, cond.*
+ ARG 3-4/97: 173
• Fa 1-2/97: 199 (Tuttle)
• Fa 1-2/97: 200 (Pernick)

31106. RS 6367-10: Liszt—Concerto pathétique for piano and orchestra; Malédiction for piano and string orchestra. Weber (arr. Liszt)—Polonaise brillante for piano and orchestra. *Crismani, piano; Philharmonia Orch.; Sanderling, cond.*
+ Fa 11-12/95: 291

31107. RS 6367-33: Boccherini—Divertimenti. *Boccherini Ensemble.*
+ ARG 11-12/95: 91

RUSSIAN DISC

31108. RD CD 10 001: Music of Prokofiev, Schnittke, K. Khachaturian, and Eshpai. *Ambartsumian, violin; Sheludyakov, piano.*
+ Fa 11-12/96: 467

31109. RD CD 10 002: Shostakovich—Zoya: suite; The young guard: suite. *Bĕlorussian Radio and TV Symphony Orch.; Minsk Chamber Choir; Mnatsakanov, cond.*
+ ARG 11-12/96: 211
• Fa 11-12/96: 379

31110. RD CD 10 003: Dmitriev—Symphony no. 3; Violin concerto; Warsaw fantasy; Vespers (excerpts). *Russian State Symphony Orch.; P. Kagan, cond.; O. Kagan, violin; Moscow*

Phil. Orch.; Glushchenko, cond.;
Igolinsky, violin; Sergeeva, piano;
Choral Art Academy; Popov, cond.
  + Fa 1-2/97: 153

31111. RD CD 10 004: KOLLONTAI—Six
sacred symphonies. *Ensemble Northern*
Crown; Zaydenshir, cond.
  + ARG 5-6/97: 142
  + Fa 1-2/97: 185

31112. RD CD 10 005: MECHEM—The
jayhawk: magic bird overture;
Symphonies no. 1-2. *USSR Radio and*
Television Large Symphony Orch;
Brown, cond.
  • ARG 7-8/93: 123
  • Fa 7-8/93: 177

31113. RD CD 10 007: SHOSTAKOVICH—
Odna. *Bělorussian Radio; Mnatsakanov,*
cond.
  + ARG 1-2/97: 169
  + Fa 3-4/97: 300

31114. RD CD 10 009: SHOSTAKOVICH—
The golden age. *Bolshoi Theater Orch.;*
Simonov, cond.
  - ARG 11-12/96: 209
  • Fa 1-2/97: 269

31115. RD CD 10 010: KHACHATURIAN—
Concerto-rhapsody. CONUS—Violin
concerto. FROLOV—Concert fantasy on
themes from Porgy and Bess. *Korsakov,*
violin; with orch. accomp.
  • ARG 11-12/93: 135
  + Fa 9-10/93: 197

31116. RD CD 10 012: SIBELIUS—Violin
concerto, op. 47. BRUCH—Violin concerto
no. 1. *Grubert, violin; State Symphony*
Orch.; Golovchin, cond.
  • Fa 5-6/95: 134

31117. RD CD 10 013: BRAHMS—
Concerto no. 2 for piano and orchestra,
op. 83. FAURÉ—Ballade in F♯ for piano
and orchestra, op. 19. *Coll, piano;*
Moscow Phil. Symphony Orch.; Sinaisky,
cond.
  • Fa 3-4/93: 127

31118. RD CD 10 014: MEDTNER—Piano
music. *Nikonovich, piano.*
  - ARG 9-10/95: 174
  - Fa 7-8/95: 241 (Wiser)
  + Fa 7-8/95: 242 (Evans)

31119. RD CD 10 015: *Twentieth century*
Russian piano music. Music of
Gubaidulina, Shostakovich, Shchedrin,
and Karayev. *Yurigin-Klevke, piano.*
  • ARG 7-8/95: 117
  + Fa 7-8/95: 428

31120. RD CD 10 016: LAZAREV—Master
and Margarita (eight scenes from the
ballet). *Moldavian Phil. Symphony Orch.;*
Goya, cond.
  + ARG 9-10/95: 166
  + Fa 5-6/95: 239

31121. RD CD 10 020: TCHAIKOVSKY—
Piano concerto no. 1. LISZT—Piano
concerto no. 1. *Kuzmin, piano; Moscow*
Phil. Symphony Orch.; Chistiakov, cond.
  + Fa 9-10/93: 307

31122. RD CD 10 021: *Inferno.* LISZT—
Piano music. *Kuzmin, piano.*
  + Fa 11-12/93: 299
  • Gr 5/94: 80

31123. RD CD 10 022: CHOPIN—Piano
music. *Kuzmin, piano.*
  • ARG 3-4/94: 85
  - Fa 3-4/94: 162

31124. RD CD 10 023: GRIEG—Piano
concerto. BEETHOVEN—Piano concerto no.
5. *Kuzmin, piano; Ostankino Radio*
Orch.; Vedernikov, cond.
  - ARG 1-2/94: 104
  + Fa 1-2/94: 192

31125. RD CD 10 024: SCHUBERT—
Wanderer fantasy; Sonata no. 17.
SCHUBERT-LISZT—Valse-Caprice no. 6;
Soirée de Vienne. *Kuzmin, piano.*
  • ARG 7-8/94: 216
  - Fa 5-6/94: 242

31126. RD CD 10 025: RACHMANINOFF—
Piano sonata no. 2; Moments musicaux
no. 2-3; Étude tableau, op. 39, no. 9;
Preludes, op. 13, no. 5, 10; Daisies; Polka
de W.R.; Rhapsody on a theme of
Paganini. *Kuzmin, piano; Russian State*
Symphony Orch.; Golovchin, cond.
  + Fa 5-6/95: 301

31127. RD CD 10 026: *Encores.* Music
of Schulz-Evler, Scarlatti, Shchedrin,
Busoni, Schumann, Scriabin, Debussy,
Balakirev, Moszkowski, and M.
Rosenthal. *Kuzmin, piano.*
  + ARG 9-10/96: 247
  • Fa 9-10/96: 410

31128. RD CD 10 030 (2 discs):
SHCHEDRIN—Anna Karenina. *Korolev,*
tenor; Lebedeva, soprano; Bolshoi
Theater Orch.; Simonov, cond.
  + ARG 7-8/95: 195
  + Fa 3-4/95: 294
  + Gr 7/96: 62

31129. RD CD 10 031: SHOSTAKOVICH—
Piano quintet. SCHNITTKE—Piano quintet.
Orbelian, piano; Moscow Quartet.
  • ARG 7-8/94: 172
  + Fa 7-8/94: 243

31130. RD CD 10 032: Bassoon
concertos by Danzi, Vivaldi, and
Hummel. *Popov, bassoon; USSR*
Symphony Chamber Orch.
  + ARG 1-2/95: 217
  + Fa 1-2/95: 180

31131. RD CD 10 033: SHOSTAKOVICH—
The lady and the hooligan; Ballet suite
no. 2. *Minsk Symphony Orch.;*
Mnatsakanov, cond.

  + ARG 9-10/95: 212
  • Fa 9-10/95: 323

31132. RD CD 10 034: *Romances.*
Music of Glinka, Dargomyzhsky,
Tchaikovsky, and Rachmaninoff.
Davtyan, soprano; Yurigin-Klevke, piano.
  + ARG 7-8/96: 277
  • Fa 1-2/96: 354

31133. RD CD 10 035: *Three centuries of*
the Russian viola, vol. 1. GLINKA—Viola
sonata in D minor. RUBINSTEIN—Viola
sonata, op. 49. *Stepchenko, viola; Abolitz,*
piano.
  • ARG 9-10/96: 190
  + Fa 9-10/96: 197

31134. RD CD 10 037: GLIÈRE—The
bronze horseman: suite; Zaporozhy
cossacks. *Ural Phil. Orch.; Liss, cond.*
  + ARG 11-12/95: 123
  • Fa 11-12/95: 262

31135. RD CD 10 038: RUBINSTEIN—
Cello sonatas. *Vasilieva, cello; Muntyan,*
Shchmitov, piano.
  • ARG 1-2/97: 161
  + Fa 3-4/97: 279

31136. RD CD 10 039: GLAZUNOV—
Serenades no. 1-2; Violin concerto, op.
62; Symphony no. 4. *Aharonian, violin;*
Russian State Symphony Orch.;
Gorenstein, cond.
  + Fa 3-4/96: 170

31137. RD CD 10 041: RUBINSTEIN—
Piano trios no. 1, 3. *Romantic Trio.*
  - ARG 9-10/95: 205
  + Fa 9-10/95: 301

31138. RD CD 10 043: KASTALSKY—
Brotherly prayer for the dead.
Belobragina, Aleshchenkova, Vladimirov;
Radio Large Choir; USSR Symphony
Orch.; Svetlanov, cond.
  - ARG 11-12/96: 149
  • Fa 9-10/96: 229

31139. RD CD 10 044: TANEYEV—
Cantata no. 2 "After reading a psalm".
Kozlova, Kotova, Antonov, Belokrynkin,
vocalists; Yurlov State Choir; USSR
Symphony Orch.; Svetlanov, cond.
  + ARG 11-12/95: 216
  • Fa 9-10/95: 334

31140. RD CD 10 045: MEDTNER—Piano
music. *Svetlanov, piano.*
  • ARG 3-4/96: 152
  + Fa 9-10/95: 259

31141. RD CD 10 046: RACHMANINOFF—
Trio no. 2 "Trio élégiaque". *Svetlanov,*
piano; Kogan, violin; Luzanov, cello.
  - ARG 1-2/96: 158
  + Fa 9-10/95: 285

31142. RD CD 10 047: RACHMANINOFF—
Cello sonata, op. 19; Moments musicaux,
op. 16, no. 3, 5; Morceaux de fantasie,
op. 1, no. 1, 3; Vocalise, op. 34, no. 14

RUSSIAN DISC

(arr. piano). *Luzanov, cello; Svetlanov, piano.*
+ Fa 11-12/95: 337

31143. RD CD 10 050: SHCHEDRIN—The seagull. *Bolshoi Theater Orch.; Lazarev, cond.*
+ ARG 1-2/96: 171
+ Fa 9-10/95: 321

31144. RD CD 10 051: RIMSKY-KORSAKOV—Complete romances, vol. 1. *Kovalova, Tarassova, Pluzhnikov, Slavny, Okhotnikov, vocalists; Serov, piano.*
+ ARG 11-12/96: 189
+ Fa 11-12/96: 347

31145. RD CD 10 401: GLINKA—Piano trio. RACHMANINOFF—Piano trio no. 1. SHOSTAKOVICH—Piano trio no. 2. *Romantic Trio.*
+ ARG 11-12/96: 127

31146. RD CD 10 900: PROKOFIEV—Symphony no. 6. SCRIABIN—Poem of ecstasy. LIADOV—Baba Yaga. *Leningrad Phil. Orch.; Mravinsky, cond. Recorded live 1959.*
• Fa 1-2/95: 229

31147. RD CD 10 901: Music of Mozart, Beethoven, Lyadov, and Glazunov. *Leningrad Phil. Orch.; Mravinsky, cond. Recorded 1972-73.*
+ ARG 3-4/95: 228
• Fa 1-2/95: 378

31148. RD CD 10 902: LIATOSHINSKY—Symphony no. 3. LIADOV—Enchanted lake; Baba-Yaga. SHOSTAKOVICH—Festive overture. *Leningrad Phil. Orch.; Mravinsky, cond.*
+ ARG 11-12/94: 143
+ Fa 11-12/94: 279

31149. RD CD 10 903: WEBER—Euryanthe overture. SCHUBERT—Symphony no. 8. TCHAIKOVSKY—Symphony no. 4. *Leningrad Phil. Orch.; Mravinsky, cond.*
• Fa 3-4/95: 341

31150. RD CD 10 905: BRAHMS—Symphony no. 3. MUSSORGSKY—Dawn over the Moscow River. TCHAIKOVSKY—Symphony no. 5; Nutcracker suite. *Leningrad Phil. Orch.; Mravinsky, cond. Recorded 1971-83.*
• ARG 3-4/95: 228
+ Fa 1-2/95: 289

31151. RD CD 10 907: BRAHMS—Symphony no. 4. WEBER—Oberon overture. SIBELIUS—The swan of Tuonela. *Leningrad Phil. Orch.; Mravinsky, cond.*
• Fa 7-8/95: 133

31152. RD CD 10 908: TCHAIKOVSKY—Symphony no. 5. STRAVINSKY—Apollo. *Leningrad Phil. Orch.; Mravinsky, cond.*
• ARG 11-12/95: 236
+ Fa 9-10/95: 338

31153. RD CD 10 909: MOZART—Symphony no. 33; Horn concerto no. 3; Sinfonia concertante for oboe, clarinet, bassoon, horn, and strings. *Buyanovsky, horn; Nikonchuk, oboe; Krasavin, clarinet; Yeremin, bassoon; Leningrad Phil. Orch.; Mravinsky, cond. Recorded live 1961 (Symphony).*
• Fa 1-2/96: 267

31154. RD CD 10 910: SHOSTAKOVICH—Symphonies no. 5-6. *Leningrad Phil. Orch.; Mravinsky, cond. Recorded live 1964, 1972.*
+ Fa 11-12/95: 375
+ Fa 11-12/96: 377

31155. RD CD 10 914: TCHAIKOVSKY—Symphony no. 5. DAVIDOV—Cello concerto no. 2. *Shafran, cello; Leningrad Phil. Orch.; Mravinsky, cond. Recorded 1949.*
• ARG 11-12/96: 291
+ Fa 11-12/96: 399

31156. RD CD 10 917: SHOSTAKOVICH—Symphony no. 8. *Leningrad Phil. Orch.; Mravinsky, cond.*
+ Fa 11-12/96: 377
+ Gr 2/97: 58

31157. RD CD 11 001: SCHUBERT—Fantasy, D. 760 "Wanderer." SCHUMANN—Piano sonata no. 1. BRAHMS—Fantasien, op. 118: no. 3-4. *Feltsman, piano.*
+ Fa 5-6/93: 314

31158. RD CD 11 002: HINDEMITH—Cello concerto. BLOCH—Schelomo. HAYDN—Cello concerto in D. *Rostropovich, cello; USSR Radio and Television Symphony Orch.; Ahronovitch, cond.*
- Fa 5-6/93: 221

31159. RD CD 11 003: SHOSTAKOVICH—Poems of Aleksandr Blok. MUSSORGSKY—Songs. STRAVINSKY—Spring; Russian song from Mavra. *Vishnevskaya, soprano; Rostropovich, piano; Kagan, violin; Mogilevskaya, piano. Recorded live 1973.*
+ ARG 11-12/93: 194
+ Fa 9-10/93: 337

31160. RD CD 11 004: SCRIABIN—Symphonic poem, op. posth.; Fantasy in A minor for 2 pianos (arr. Zinger). NEMTIN—Universe: Prefatory act. *USSR Radio Symphony Orch.; Demchenko, cond.; Lubimov, Zhukov, pianos; Moscow Radio Chamber Orch.; Yurovsky, cond.; Moscow Phil. Orch.; Yurlov Russian Choir; Kondrashin, cond.*
- Fa 11-12/93: 393

31161. RD CD 11 005: KHACHATURIAN—Symphony no. 1; Masquerade: suite. *USSR Radio and Television Symphony Orch.; Gauk, Khachaturian, conds. Recorded 1959.*
+ ARG 3-4/94: 112
+ Fa 11-12/93: 284

31162. RD CD 11 006: VAÏNBERG—Symphony no. 5; Trumpet concerto. *Dokshitser, trumpet; Moscow Phil. Orch.; Kondrashin, Zhuraitis, conds.*
• ARG 1-2/94: 167
+ Fa 1-2/94: 340
+ Gr 2/94: 54

31163. RD CD 11 007: MIASKOVSKY—Symphonies no. 1, 19. *USSR Ministry of Culture Symphony Orch.; Rozhdestvensky, cond.; Russian State Brass Orch.; Sergeyev, cond.*
• ARG 1-2/94: 124
+ Fa 1-2/94: 251
+ Gr 3/94: 58

31164. RD CD 11 008: TANEEV—Symphonies no. 2, 4. *USSR Radio Symphony Orch.; Fedoseyev, cond.; Novosibirsk Phil. Orch.; Katz, cond.*
• ARG 1-2/94: 163
+ Fa 1-2/94: 327

31165. RD CD 11 009: STRAUSS—Don Quixote. VILLA-LOBOS—Bachianas brasileiras no. 1. *Rostropovich, cello; Moscow Phil. Orch.; Kondrashin, cond.*
+ Fa 1-2/94: 321

31166. RC CD 11 010: VAÏNBERG—Symphony no. 12; Flute concerto, op. 75. *Moscow Radio Symphony Orch.; M. Shostakovich, cond.; Korneyev, flute; Moscow Chamber Orch.; Barshai, cond.*
+ ARG 7-8/94: 182
+ Fa 5-6/94: 270

31167. RD CD 11 011: SUK—Asrael symphony. *USSR State Symphony Orch.; Svetlanov, cond.*
+ ARG 1-2/94: 162
- Fa 3-4/94: 330
+ Gr 1/94: 59

31168. RD CD 11 012: KHACHATURIAN—Violin concerto; Piano concerto. *Oistrakh, violin; Petrov, piano; USSR Radio and Television Large Symphony Orch.; USSR State Symphony Orch.; Khachaturian, cond. Recorded 1965-77.*
• Fa 1-2/94: 216

31169. RD CD 11 013: MIASKOVSKY—String quartets no. 1, 4. *Taneev Quartet.*
+ ARG 11-12/96: 164
+ Fa 5-6/94: 196
+ Fa 7-8/94: 181
+ Gr 12/96: 100

31170. RD CD 11 014: KHACHATURIAN—Concerto-rhapsody for cello and orchestra; Concerto-rhapsody for piano and orchestra; Spartacus: Excerpts; Ode to joy. *Rostropovich, cello; Petrov, piano; USSR Radio and Television Large Symphony Orch.; Khachaturian, cond. Recorded 1973.*
+ ARG 7-8/94: 120
+ Fa 3-4/94: 225

31171. RD CD 11 016: RACHMANINOFF—Vespers. *Glinka Choir; Chernushenko,*

cond.
- ARG 3-4/94: 140
+ Fa 3-4/94: 286

31172. RD CD 11 017, 11 019 (2 separate discs): MEDTNER—Violin sonatas no. 1-3; Piano quintet. *Labko, violin; Svetlanov, piano; Borodin Quartet.*
• Fa 3-4/94: 246

31173. RD CD 11 018: KHACHATURIAN—Symphony no. 2; Gayne: Excerpts. *USSR State Symphony Orch.; Khachaturian, cond.* Recorded 1977.
+ ARG 5-6/94: 104
+ Fa 3-4/94: 225

31174. RD CD 11 020: BOIKO—Symphony no. 3; Gutsul rhapsody; Volga rhapsody; Carapathian rhapsody; Gypsy rhapsody; Festival procession. *Korsakov, violin; Sakharov, piano; USSR State Symphony Orch.; Svetlanov, cond.*
• ARG 7-8/94: 78
+ Fa 5-6/94: 118

31175. RD CD 11 021: DARGOMYZHSKY—Romances. CUI—Romances. *Sharonova, soprano; Yurigin-Klevke, piano.*
+ Fa 11-12/94: 211

31176. RD CD 11 022 (2 discs): PROKOFIEV—The tale of the stone flower. *Bolshoi Theater Orch.; Rozhdestvensky, cond.*
• Fa 7-8/94: 201

31177. RD CD 11 023: SHOSTAKOVICH—Symphony no. 5. SALMANOV—Symphony no. 2. *Leningrad Phil. Orch.; Mravinsky, cond.*
• ARG 3-4/94: 146
+ Fa 3-4/94: 322

31178. RD CD 11 024: GLAZUNOV—Piano concerto no. 1; Mazurka-Oberek. LIAPUNOV—Piano concerto no. 2. *Nasedkin, Grindenko, piano; USSR Radio Symphony Orch.; iuraitis, cond.; Bakhchiev, piano; Moscow Radio Symphony; Khaikin, cond.*
+ ARG 7-8/94: 104
• Fa 7-8/94: 140

31179. RD CD 11 025: SHOSTAKOVICH—Violin concertos no. 1-2. *Kogan, Oistrakh, violin; Moscow Phil. Orch.; Kondrashin, cond.*
• Fa 3-4/94: 320

31180. RD CD 11 026: VAINBERG—Cello sonatas no. 1-2. B. TCHAIKOVSKY—Cello sonata. *Vasilieva, cello; Vaĭnberg, B. Tchaikovsky, pianos.*
• Fa 9-10/94: 360

31181. RD CD 11 029 (2 discs): KHACHATURIAN—Gayne. *USSR Radio and TV Large Orch.; Kakhidze, cond.*
• ARG 1-2/95: 125
• Fa 11-12/94: 269

31182. RD CD 11 030: *Russian songs.* Music of Tariverdiev, Shchedrin, and Gavrilin. *Dolukhanova, mezzo- soprano; Svetlanova, piano.* Recorded 1971.
+ ARG 3-4/94: 164
+ Fa 1-2/94: 368

31183. RD CD 11 031: MIASKOVSKY—String quartets no. 2, 6, 10. *Taneev Quartet.*
+ ARG 11-12/96: 164
• Fa 11-12/96: 308
+ Gr 12/96: 100

31184. RD CD 11 032: MIASKOVSKY—String quartets no. 3, 5. *Taneev Quartet.*
+ ARG 11-12/96: 164
• Fa 11-12/96: 308
+ Gr 12/96: 100

31185. RD CD 11 033: MIASKOVSKY—String quartets no. 7-8. *Taneev Quartet.*
+ ARG 11-12/96: 164
+ Fa 1-2/97: 207
+ Gr 12/96: 100

31186. RD CD 11 034: MIASKOVSKY—String quartets no. 9, 11. *Taneev Quartet.*
+ ARG 11-12/96: 164
+ ARG 5-6/97: 160
+ Fa 1-2/97: 207
+ Gr 12/96: 100

31187. RD CD 11 035: MIASKOVSKY—String quartets no. 12-13. *Taneev Quartet.*
+ Fa 1-2/97: 208

31188. RD CD 11 040: TCHAIKOVSKY—Liturgy of St. John Chrysostom. *Leningrad Glinka Choir; Chernushenko, cond.*
+ ARG 11-12/94: 197
+ Fa 11-12/94: 396

31189. RD CD 11 041: BEETHOVEN—Piano concertos no. 1, 3. *Richter, piano; Moscow Phil. Orch.; Kondrashin, cond.*
+ Fa 7-8/94: 61
• Gr 9/94: 46

31190. RD CD 11 042: SVETLANOV—Symphony no. 1; Poem for violin and orchestra in memory of David Oistrakh. *I. Oistrakh, violin; USSR State Symphony Orch.; Svetlanov, cond.*
• ARG 7-8/94: 180
+ Fa 5-6/94: 259

31191. RD CD 11 043: SVETLANOV—The red guelder-rose; Eight preludes "Symphonic reflections"; Piano concerto. *Svetlanov, piano; USSR Symphony Orch.; Svetlanov, cond.; USSR Radio and Television Large Symphony Orch.; M. Shostakovich, cond.*
+ Fa 9-10/94: 348

31192. RD CD 11 044: SVETLANOV—Three Russian songs; Orchestra music. *Bobrineva, soprano; USSR Symphony Orch.; Svetlanov, cond.*

+ ARG 11-12/94: 197
+ Fa 11-12/94: 393

31193. RD CD 11 045: BOIKO—Symphony no. 2; Vyatka songs; Peter's chimes. *Vedernikov, bass; USSR Symphony Orch.; Svetlanov, cond.*
+ ARG 1-2/95: 86
+ Fa 1-2/95: 127

31194. RD CD 11 046: SOLIN—Concert pieces for symphony orchestra. ZHIGANOV—Symphonic songs. KULIEV—Violin concerto in A minor. *Lubotsky, violin; Moscow Phil. Orch.; USSR Radio and TV Large Symphony Orch.; Temirkanov, cond.*
+ ARG 5-6/95: 180
+ Fa 1-2/95: 273

31195. RD CD 11 048: SHOSTAKOVICH—Song of the forests; The sun shines over the motherland. *Ivanovsky, tenor; Petrov, bass; Moscow Phil. Orch.; Yurlov, cond.; Yurlov Choir; USSR Symphony Orch.; Ivanov, cond.* Recorded 1970, 1961.
+ ARG 9-10/94: 198
• Fa 11-12/94: 381

31196. RD CD 11 050: PASARDANIAN—Symphonies no. 1-2. *Kadinskaya, soprano; Moscow Radio Orch.; USSR Symphony Orch.; Svetlanov, cond.*
+ ARG 1-2/95: 152
+ Fa 11-12/94: 325

31197. RC CD 11 051: ESHPAI—Symphonies no. 4-5. *USSR Radio and TV Large Symphony Orch.; USSR Symphony Orch.; Fedoseyev, cond.*
+ ARG 5-6/95: 110
• Fa 3-4/95: 167

31198. RD CD 11 052: BLUMENFELD—Symphony in C minor. BANSHCHIKOV—Duodecimet. SHEBALIN—Violin concertino. *USSR State Symphony Orch.; Golovchin, cond.; Laebsky, cello; Shulgin, violin; Ensemble of the USSR Symphony Orch.; Sinaisky, Provatorov, conds.*
+ ARG 7-8/95: 237
• Fa 5-6/95: 143

31199. RC CD 11 054: ESHPAI—Viola concerto; Violin concerto no. 2; Piano concerto no. 2; Concerto grosso. *Bashmet, viola; USSR Symphony Orch.; Glushchenko, Svetlanov, conds.; Grach, violin; Kraniev, piano; Moscow Phil. Orch.; Kitayenko, cond.; Maksimenko, trumpet; Azarkin, double bass; Meshchaninov, piano; Stepanov, vibraphone.*
+ ARG 5-6/95: 110
• Fa 3-4/95: 167

31200. RD CD 11 055: LIATOSHINSKY—Symphony no. 1; Ukranian overture; Poem of reunification. *Ukrainian National Symphony Orch.; Gnedash, cond.*

+ ARG 11-12/94: 143
• Fa 1-2/95: 193

31201. RD CD 11 056: SCRIABIN—Symphony no. 1; The poem of ecstasy. *USSR State Symphony Orch.; USSR Radio Chorus; Svetlanov, cond.; Gaponova, mezzo-soprano; Salynikov, tenor.* Recorded live.
+ ARG 5-6/93: 135
• Fa 3-4/93: 284
• Gr 9/93: 60

31202. RD CD 11 057: SCRIABIN—Symphony no. 2; Rêverie. *USSR State Symphony Orch.; Svetlanov, cond.* Recorded live.
+ ARG 5-6/93: 135
• Fa 3-4/93: 284

31203. RD CD 11 058: SCRIABIN—Symphony no. 3 "The divine poem"; Prometheus. *USSR State Symphony Orch.; Svetlanov, cond.; Richter, piano.* Recorded live.
+ ARG 5-6/93: 135
• Fa 3-4/93: 284

31204. RD CD 11 059: LIATOSHINSKY—Symphony no. 2; Slavic piano concerto. *Ukrainian National Symphony Orch.; Glushchenko, cond.; Rzhanov, piano; Ukrainian Radio Symphony Orch.; Gnedash, cond.*
• ARG 11-12/94: 143
+ Fa 1-2/95: 193

31205. RD CD 11 060: LIATOSHINSKY—Symphony no. 3; Romeo and Juliet suite. *Ukrainian National Symphony Orch.; Ukrainian Radio and TV Symphony Orch.; Turchak, Gnedash, conds.*
+ ARG 3-4/95: 127
+ Fa 1-2/95: 193
+ Gr 7/95: 59

31206. RD CD 11 061: RUBINSTEIN—Viola sonata; Quintet for piano and winds. *Various performers.*
• ARG 1-2/95: 163
- Fa 1-2/95: 248

31207. RD CD 11 062: LIATOSHINSKY—Symphony no. 4; On the banks of the Vistula; Lyric poem. *Ukrainian National Symphony Orch.; Blazhkov, cond.; Ukrainian Radio and TV Symphony Orch.; Sirenko, Glushchenko, conds.*
+ ARG 3-4/95: 127
• Fa 1-2/95: 193

31208. RD CD 11 063: B. TCHAIKOVKSY—Symphony no. 2. KHACHATURIAN—Ode in memory of Lenin; Song- poem for violin and piano; Gayaneh: Sabre dance. *Kogan, violin; Walter, Mytnik, piano; Moscow Phil. Orch.; Kondrashin, cond.; Bolshoi Theatre Orch.; Khachaturian, cond.*
+ ARG 5-6/95: 185
+ Fa 1-2/95: 288

31209. RD CD 11 064: SHOSTAKOVICH—The new Babylon suite; The golden hills suite. *Stepanov, Hawaiian guitar; Golub, organ; Moscow Phil. Orch.; USSR Ministry of Culture Symphony Orch.; Rozhdestvensky, cond.*
+ ARG 5-6/95: 176
+ Fa 3-4/95: 297
• Gr 6/95: 58

31210. RD CD 11 067: KARAYEV—Seven beauties: ballet suite; In the path of thunder: ballet suite. *Ostankino Radio and Television Symphony Orch.; Abdullayev, cond.*
+ Fa 7-8/93: 161

31211. RD CD 11 078: TCHAIKOVSKY—Complete romances, vol. 1. *Krasnaya, soprano; Fedorovtsev, piano.*
• ARG 1-2/95: 192
• Fa 9-10/94: 352

31212. RD CD 11 087: SHOSTAKOVICH—String quartet no. 8; Elegie. BEETHOVEN—Grosse Fuge. *Borodin Quartet.*
- Fa 7-8/93: 243
- Gr 10/93: 72

31213. RD CD 11 101: LALO—Cello concerto. SAINT-SAËNS—Cello concerto no. 1. HONEGGER—Cello concerto. *Rostropovich, cello; USSR State Symphony Orch.; Dubrovsky, cond.* Recorded 1964.
• Fa 3-4/94: 229

31214. RD CD 11 103: PROKOFIEV—Sinfonia concertante; Cello concertino. *Rostropovich, cello; USSR State Symphony Orch.; USSR Radio and Television Symphony Orch.; Rozhdestvensky, cond.* Recorded live 1964.
+ ARG 11-12/93: 169
+ Fa 9-10/93: 237

31215. RD CD 11 104: ELGAR—Cello concerto. RESPIGHI—Adagio con variazione. MILHAUD—Cello concerto no. 1. *Rostropovich, cello; Moscow Phil. Orch.; USSR Radio and Television Large Symphony Orch.; Rozhdestvensky, cond.* Recorded live 1964.
+ ARG 7-8/94: 205
+ Fa 5-6/94: 142
+ Gr 7/94: 42

31216. RD CD 11 106: SCHUMANN—Concerto for cello and orchestra, op. 129. SHOSTAKOVICH—Concerto no. 1 for cello and orchestra. *Rostropovich, cello; USSR State Symphony Orch.; Moscow Phil. Symphony Orch.; Oistrakh, cond.* Recorded live, 1965 & 1969.
- Fa 3-4/93: 281
+ Gr 7/94: 58

31217. RD CD 11 108: SAUGUET—Mélodie concertante for cello and orch. BRITTEN—Cello symphony. *Rostropovich, cello; Moscow Phil. Symphony Orch.; Sauguet, Britten, conds.* Recorded live

1964.
+ ARG 11-12/93: 184
+ Fa 7-8/93: 225

31218. RD CD 11 109: SHOSTAKOVICH—Cello concertos no. 1-2. *Rostropovich, cello; USSR State Symphony Orch.; Svetlanov, cond.* Recorded 1966-67.
• Fa 7-8/93: 242 (North)
+ Fa 7-8/93: 242 (Brown)
+ Gr 7/94: 58

31219. RD CD 11 110: KHRENNIKOV—Cello concerto. VLASOV—Cello concerto; Improvisation. TCHAIKOVSKY—Pezzo capriccioso. *Rostropovich, cello; USSR Radio and Television Symphony Orch.; Rozhdestvensky, cond.* Recorded 1964.
+ ARG 1-2/94: 177
+ Fa 1-2/94: 217

31220. RD CD 11 111: VAÏNBERG—Cello concerto. KNIPPER—Concerto-monologue for cello, wind ensemble, and timpani. LEVITIN—Cello concertino. *Rostropovich, cello; Moscow Phil. Orch.; Rozhdestvensky, cond.; USSR Symphony Orch.; Kondrashin, cond.* Recorded live 1964.
+ ARG 1-2/94: 177
+ Fa 11-12/93: 426

31221. RD CD 11 113: *Cello concertos.* Music of Vivaldi, Tartini, C.P.E. Bach, and Casadesus. *Rostropovich, cello; Moscow Chamber Orch.; Barshai, cond.* Recorded live 1963.
+ ARG 9-10/93: 230
+ Fa 9-10/93: 355

31222. RD CD 11 114: BRAHMS—Concerto for violin, cello, and orchestra. DVOŘÁK—Cello concerto no. 2. *Gutnikov, violin; Rostropovich, cello; USSR State Symphony Orch.; Khaikin, cond.* Recorded 1963.
• Fa 7-8/93: 115
+ Gr 5/94: 48

31223. RD CD 11 115: BABADJANIAN—Cello concerto. B. TCHAIKOVSKY—Cello concerto. *Rostropovich, cello; Moscow Phil. Symphony Orch.; Kondrashin, cond.*
+ ARG 11-12/93: 206
+ Fa 7-8/93: 86

31224. RD CD 11 129: SHCHEDRIN—Concertos for piano and orchestra no. 1-3. *Shchedrin, Petrov, piano; USSR State Symphony Orch.; Svetlanov, cond.*
+ Fa 7-8/93: 241

31225. RD CD 11 155: KALINNIKOV—Symphony no. 2. GLAZUNOV—The seasons (abridged). *Leningrad Phil. Orch.; Mravinsky, cond.*
• Fa 7-8/94: 158

31226. RD CD 11 157: SHOSTAKOVICH—Symphony no. 11. *Leningrad Phil. Orch.; Mravinsky, cond.* Recorded live 1957.
+ ARG 9-10/93: 193

- Fa 9-10/93: 288
+ Gr 1/94: 54

31227. RD CD 11 158: BRAHMS—Piano concerto no. 2. *Richter, piano; Leningrad Phil. Orch.; Mravinsky, cond.* Recorded 1961.
    - ARG 9-10/93: 99
    • Fa 7-8/93: 114
    • Gr 2/94: 38

31228. RD CD 11 159: BEETHOVEN— Symphony no. 6. DEBUSSY—La mer; Rhapsody no. 1 for clarinet and orchestra. *Krasavin, clarinet; Leningrad Phil. Orch.; Mravinsky, cond.* Recorded live 1962.
    + Fa 1-2/94: 127

31229. RD CD 11 160: TCHAIKOVSKY— Francesca da Rimini. STRAVINSKY—Le baiser de la fée. *Leningrad Phil. Orch.; Mravinsky, cond.* Recorded live 1983.
    • ARG 1-2/94: 160
    + Fa 11-12/93: 417

31230. RD CD 11 162 : KLYUZNER— Symphony no. 2. STRAVINSKY—Petrushka. *Leningrad Phil. Orch.; Mravinsky, cond.*
    + ARG 1-2/95: 126
    + Fa 1-2/95: 280

31231. RD CD 11 163: HAYDN— Symphonies no. 88, 104. R. STRAUSS— Horn concerto no. 1. *Buyanovsky, horn; Leningrad Phil. Orch.; Mravinsky, cond.* Recorded live 1964-67.
    + Fa 11-12/94: 255

31232. RD CD 11 165: PROKOFIEV— Symphony no. 5. GLAZUNOV—Symphony no. 5. *Leningrad Phil. Orch.; Mravinsky, cond.* Recorded live.
    + ARG 7-8/93: 138
    • Fa 7-8/93: 205

31233. RD CD 11 166: WAGNER— Orchestral concert. *Leningrad Phil. Orch.; Mravinsky, cond.*
    - Fa 1-2/94: 350
    + Gr 3/94: 64

31234. RD CD 11 167: BACH—Suite no. 2. BARTÓK—Music for strings, percussion, and celesta. DEBUSSY—Nocturnes. *Leningrad Phil. Orch.; Mravinsky, cond.*
    • ARG 1-2/95: 206
    + Fa 1-2/95: 107

31235. RD CD 11 170: TCHAIKOVSKY— Piano concerto no. 1; Piano sonata, op. 80. *Gilels, piano; Leningrad Phil. Orch.; Mravinsky, cond.*
    • ARG 3-4/94: 165
    • Fa 1-2/94: 328
    • Gr 4/94: 58

31236. RD CD 11 172: RACHMANINOFF— Symphony no. 3; Concerto no. 2 for piano and orchestra. *Son, piano; Moscow Phil. Symphony Orch.; Ermler, cond.*
    + Fa 7-8/93: 210

31237. RD CD 11 180: PROKOFIEV— Romeo and Juliet suite no. 2. SHOSTAKOVICH—Symphony no. 5. *Leningrad Phil. Orch.; Mravinsky, cond.*
    • Fa 9-10/94: 292
    - Gr 7/95: 62

31238. RD CD 11 188: SHOSTAKOVICH— Symphonies no. 1, 5. *USSR State Symphony Orch.; Svetlanov, cond.; Moscow Phil. Symphony Orch.; Kitaenko, cond.*
    + ARG 9-10/93: 191
    + Fa 7-8/93: 244
    • Gr 1/94: 54

31239. RD CD 11 190: SHOSTAKOVICH— Symphony no. 4. *Bolshoi Theater Orch.; Rozhdestvensky, cond.* Recorded live 1981.
    • ARG 11-12/93: 195
    • Fa 9-10/93: 288
    + Gr 1/94: 54

31240. RD CD 11 191: SHOSTAKOVICH— Symphony no. 13. *Gromadsky, bass; Moscow Phil. Symphony Orch.; Kondrashin, cond.* Recorded live 1962.
    + ARG 9-10/93: 193
    + ARG 11-12/93: 196
    + Fa 9-10/93: 288
    + Gr 3/94: 60

31241. RD CD 11 192: SHOSTAKOVICH— Symphonies no. 9, 14. *USSR State Symphony Orch.; D. Oistrakh, cond.; Vishnevskaya, soprano; Reshetin, bass; Moscow Chamber Orch.; Barshai, cond.* Recorded live 1969.
    + ARG 9-10/93: 193
    + Fa 9-10/93: 288
    + Gr 1/94: 54

31242. RD CD 11 195: SHOSTAKOVICH— Symphonies no. 2, 10. *Leningrad Phil. Choir & Orch.; Blazhkov, Temirkanov, conds.*
    • ARG 3-4/94: 156
    + Fa 11-12/93: 394
    • Gr 1/94: 54

31243. RD CD 11 208: Music of Beethoven, Chopin, and Debussy. *Ashkenazy, piano.* Recorded live 1963.
    + ARG 11-12/93: 240
    • Gr 5/94: 79

31244. RD CD 11 337: RUBINSTEIN— Piano works. *Bakhchiev, piano.*
    • ARG 3-4/95: 175
    • Fa 11-12/94: 359

31245. RD CD 11 341 : PROKOFIEV— Songs. STRAVINSKY—Songs. *Dolukhanova, mezzo-soprano.*
    + ARG 9-10/94: 174

31246. RD CD 11 342: *Romances.* Music of Tchaikovsky, Rachmaninoff, Scriabin, and Medtner. *Z. Dolukhanova, mezzo-soprano; Kozel, A. Dolukhanian, Svetlanova, piano.*

31247. RD CD 11 355: STRAVINSKY— Symphony in 3 movements; The firebird: suite (1945 version). *USSR State Symphony Orch.; Golovchin, cond.*
    + Fa 9-10/94: 348

31248. RD CD 11 356: RUBINSTEIN— Symphony no. 2; Feramors. *Russian State Symphony Orch.; Golovchin, cond.*
    • ARG 7-8/94: 162
    • Fa 7-8/94: 225
    • Gr 10/94: 118

31249. RC CD 11 357: RUBINSTEIN— Symphony no. 4. *Russian State Symphony Orch.; Golovchin, cond.*
    • ARG 1-2/95: 163
    + Fa 1-2/95: 248
    • Gr 6/95: 54

31250. RD CD 11 358: GLIÈRE— Symphony no. 3 "Ilya Murometz". *USSR State Symphony Orch.; Golovchin, cond.*
    + ARG 1-2/95: 108
    - Fa 11-12/94: 237

31251. RD CD 11 360: RUBINSTEIN— Piano concertos no. 2, 4. *Paley, piano; Russian State Symphony Orch.; Golovchin, cond.*
    - ARG 7-8/94: 162
    • Fa 7-8/94: 225
    - Gr 2/95: 54

31252. RC CD 11 372: TCHAIKOVSKY— Songs. RACHMANINOFF—Songs. SVIRIDOV—Approaching Izhory. *Nesterenko, bass; Shenderovich, piano.*
    + ARG 11-12/94: 198
    + Fa 11-12/94: 399

31253. RD CD 11 382: LEVINA—Piano concerto no. 2; Poem for viola and piano. MARKOVNA—Symphony in D minor. *Petrushansky, piano; Moscow Symphony Orch.; Dudarova, cond.; Kalacheva, viola; Bakhchiev, piano; USSR Symphony Orch.; Koch, cond.*
    + Fa 1-2/95: 188

31254. RD CD 11 397: RUBINSTEIN—Don Quixote; Ivan IV. *USSR State Symphony Orch.; Golovchin, cond.*
    + Fa 9-10/94: 316
    + Gr 9/95: 65

31255. RD CD 15 001: PROKOFIEV—Piano music. *Sofronitsky, piano.*
    - Fa 11-12/93: 349

31256. RD CD 15 002: TCHAIKOVSKY— Violin concerto; Variations on a rococo theme; Romeo and Juliet: duet for soprano and tenor, after the fantasy-overture. *Oistrakh, violin; Knushevitsky, cello; Lavrova, soprano; Lemeshev, tenor; All-Union Radio Orch.; Gauk, Samosud, conds.*
    + ARG 11-12/93: 273
    + Fa 11-12/93: 416

RUSSIAN DISC

31257. RD CD 15 003: TCHAIKOVSKY—Francesca da Rimini; Serenade for strings; Capriccio italien. *Leningrad Phil. Orch.; Mravinsky, cond.*
+ ARG 11-12/93: 273
+ Fa 11-12/93: 417

31258. RD CD 15 004: SCRIABIN—Piano concerto; Piano music. *Neuhaus, piano; All-Union Radio Orch.; Golovanov, cond.* Recorded 1946.
+ ARG 5-6/94: 206
• Fa 11-12/93: 391

31259. RD CD 15 005: SHOSTAKOVICH—Cello sonata; Piano concertos no. 1-2. *Shostakovich, piano; Rostropovich, cello; Moscow Radio Symphony Orch.; Gauk, cond.; Moscow Phil. Orch.; Samosud, cond.* Recorded live 1957-58.
+ ARG 1-2/94: 154
• Fa 1-2/94: 313
+ Gr 2/95: 58

31260. RD CD 15 007: CHOPIN—Piano concerto no. 1; Polonaise-fantaisie, op. 61; Barcarolle, op. 60; Nocturne, op. 62, no. 2; Impromptu, op. 51. *Neuhaus, piano; All-Union Radio Orch.; Gauk, cond.*
- Fa 5-6/94: 130

31261. RD CD 15 008: MIASKOVSKY—Symphony no. 6. *USSR State Symphony Orch.; Kondrashin, cond.*
+ ARG 7-8/94: 133
+ Fa 7-8/94: 183
+ Gr 10/94: 112

31262. RD CD 15 009: KHACHATURIAN—Violin concerto. GLAZUNOV—Violin concerto. *J. Sitkovetsky, violin; Moscow Youth Orch.; Kondrashin, cond.; Romanian Radio Orch.; Niyazi, cond.* Recorded 1954, 1952.
+ Fa 11-12/94: 269

31263. RD CD 15 010: BEETHOVEN—Variations on a waltz by Diabelli; Variations on an original theme, op. 35. *Yudina, piano.*
• Fa 11-12/94: 172

31264. RD CD 15 013 (4 discs): BACH—The well-tempered clavier. *Feinberg, piano.*
+ ARG 7-8/95: 79
+ Fa 11-12/94: 156

31265. RD CD 15 015: *Zara Dolukhanova.* Music of Shostakovich, Shaporin, Ippolitov-Ivanov, and Kabalevsky. *Dolukhanova, mezzo-soprano; D. Shostakovich, Kozel, Svetlanova, pianos.*
+ Fa 9-10/94: 393

31266. RD CD 15 021: Romances by Rachmaninoff and Tchaikovsky. *Lisitsian, baritone; various pianists.* Recorded 1930s-60s.
+ ARG 1-2/96: 246
+ Fa 11-12/95: 442

31267. RD CD 15 022: *Great Russian artists: Pavel Lisitsian.* Music of Glinka, Dargomizhsky, Cui, Balakirev, Arensky, Rimsky-Korsakov, Schubert, Schumann, Liszt, Grieg, Saint-Saëns, and Ravel. *Lisitsian, baritone; various accs.*
+ ARG 3-4/95: 278
+ Fa 1-2/95: 333

31268. RD CD 15 023: *Opera arias.* Music of Tchaikovsky, Prokofiev, Mussorgsky, Rimsky-Korsakov, Meyerbeer, Saint-Saëns, Verdi, Mozart, and Rossini. *Dolukhanova, mezzo-soprano; Moscow Phil. Orch.; Stolarov, cond.* Recorded live 1954.
+ Fa 9-10/95: 374

31269. RD CD 15 025: GLIÈRE—Symphony no. 3. *USSR Radio Symphony Orch.; Rakhlin, cond.* Recorded 1974.
+ ARG 7-8/96: 117
• Fa 9-10/96: 196

31270. RD CD 15 100: SHOSTAKOVICH—Symphony no. 11 "The year 1905". *Moscow Radio Symphony Orch.; Stokowski, cond.* Recorded live 1958.
+ ARG 9-10/96: 201
+ Fa 9-10/96: 324

31271. RD CD 16 002: Music of Verdi, Wagner, Liszt, Tchaikovsky, and others. *Kozlovsky, tenor.*
+ ARG 7-8/96: 293

31272. RD CD 26 601: PETROV—Russia of bells; Violin concerto; Creation of the world. *Stadler, violin; Glinka School Boys Choir; Leningrad State Academic Symphony; Ensemble of Bell Music; Temirkanov, cond.* Reissue.
• ARG 3-4/96: 165

SAGA

31273. SCD 9012: Songs by Vaughan Williams, Ireland, Head, Gibbs, Dunhill, and others. *Baker, mezzo-soprano; Isepp, piano.* Reissue.
+ ARG 1-2/92: 172
+ Gr 3/92: 109

31274. SCD 9032: Music of Sanseverino, Stefani, Sanz, Guerau, Murcia, Granata, and others. *Tyler, guitars.*
+ ARG 1-2/93: 179

31275. SCD 9034: Songs by Bizet, Berlioz, and Debussy. *Gomez, soprano; Constable, piano.* Reissue.
+ ARG 3-4/93: 185

31276. SCD 9039: *The Renaissance virtuosi.* Music of Anon., Vallet, Borrono, Corbetta, Rore/Terzi, Allison, Bernia, Kapsberger, Piccinini, Ferrabosco, Castello, and Dowland. *Tyler, lute, baroque guitar, mandora.*
+ ARG 11-12/92: 254

31277. SCD 9047: BEETHOVEN—Symphony no. 7. *Leningrad Phil. Orch.;*

Mravinsky, cond. Recorded 195-.
+ ARG 11-12/92: 83

SAGA CLASSICS

31278. EC 3336-2: *A recital of English songs.* Music of Purcell, Humfrey, Butterworth, and Moeran. *Shirley-Quirk, baritone; Isepp, violin, harpsichord & piano; Liddell, violin; Gauntlett, cello.* Recorded 1966.
+ ARG 1-2/97: 230

31279. EC 3339-2: *Songs of travel.* Music of Vaughan Williams, Ireland, Stanford, Warlock, and others. *Shirley-Quirk, baritone.* Recorded 1963.
+ ARG 1-2/97: 230

31280. EC 3343-2 (3 discs): HANDEL—Messiah. *Harper, Watts, Robertson, Stalman, Woods, Downes; London Phil. Choir & Orch.; Jackson, cond.* Reissue; recorded 1961.
• Fa 7-8/95: 198

31281. EC 3347-2: DEBUSSY—Preludes, book 2. *Rév, piano.* Recorded 1977.
• Gr 4/95: 89

31282. EC 3349-2: *The virtuoso recorder.* Music of Vivaldi, Marcello, Bononcini, Barsanti, Matteis, and Corelli. *Pickett, recorder; Pleeth, cello; Roblou, harpsichord.* Reissue.
• Fa 3-4/95: 386

31283. EC 3350-2: *Renaissance virtuosos.* Music of Vallet, Borrono, Corbetta, Rore, and others. *Tyler, lute.* Reissue.
+ ARG 11-12/94: 224

31284. EC 3352-2: *Popular music from the time of Queen Elizabeth I.* Music of Johnson, Cornysh, Dowland, Byrd, Morley, Bull, Campion, and Anon. *Camerata of London.*
- Fa 5-6/95: 401

31285. EC 3353-2: *Music of England.* Music of Butterworth, Delius, Gurney, Holst, Elgar, and Vaughan Williams. *Baker, Shirley-Quirk, Case, vocalists; Isepp, Ibbott, Tunnard, piano; Bournemouth Symphony Orch.; Groves, cond.* Reissues.
• Fa 11-12/94: 511

31286. EC 3354-2: *Elizabethan ayres and dances.* Music of Campion, Holborne, Daniel, and Rosseter. *Bowman, countertenor; Spencer, lute.*
+ Fa 5-6/95: 400

31287. EC 3356-2: *The early guitar.* Music of Sanseverino, Stefani, Sanz, Guerau, Bach, and others. *Tyler, guitar.* Reissue.
+ ARG 11-12/94: 224

31288. EC 3357-2: Music for Henry VIII. *Hilliard Ensemble; New London Consort.*

Reissue.
+ ARG 5-6/92: 171 (as Saga 9003)
+ ARG 3-4/95: 250
+ Fa 1-2/95: 342

31289. EC 3361-2: *Janet Baker: Lieder recital.* Music of Schumann, Schubert, and Brahms. *Baker, mezzo-soprano; Isepp, piano.* Reissue.
+ ARG 5-6/92: 183 (as Saga 9001)
+ Fa 1-2/95: 324
+ Gr 3/92: 109 (as Saga 9001)

31290. EC 3362-2: CHOPIN—Nocturne, op. 9, no. 3; Ballade no. 2. LISZT—Mephisto waltz no. 1. HAYDN—Piano sonata no. 33. *Ashkenazy, Richter, piano.* Reissues.
+ Fa 1-2/95: 143

31291. EC 3363-2: WIDOR—Symphonies no. 5; No. 8: prelude; No. 6: Allegro. *Sanger, organ.*
• Fa 3-4/95: 346

31292. EC 3365-2: *Music of merchants and monarchs.* Music of Newsidler, Foscarini, Robison, Melli, Calvi, and others. *Tyler, lute.* Reissue.
+ ARG 11-12/94: 224

31293. EC 3366-2: SHOSTAKOVICH—Symphony no. 10. *Leningrad Symphony Orch.; Mravinsky, cond.* Recorded 1954.
+ ARG 1-2/95: 180
+ Fa 11-12/94: 383
+ ARG 5-6/92: 177 (as Saga 9018)

31294. EC 3367-2: Kings and courtiers. *Simpson, mezzo-soprano; Camerata of London.* Reissue.
+ ARG 5-6/92: 177 (as Saga 9018)
+ ARG 11-12/94: 241

31295. EC 3369-2: SATIE—Piano music. *McCabe, piano.*
+ ARG 1-2/93: 143 (as Saga SCD 9041)

31296. EC 3374-2: FRANCK—Fantasy in A; Cantabile in B; Pièce héroïque; 8 pieces from L'Organiste. *Cochereau, organ.*
- ARG 11-12/91: 66 (as Saga 9019)

31297. EC 3376-2: DEBUSSY—Images I & II; Images (1894), 1, 3; Pour le piano; Danse bohémienne; Arabesques; Ballade; Nocturne; Mazurka. *Rév, piano.*
• ARG 3-4/92: 49 (as Saga 9020)

31298. EC 3379-2: BOYCE—Anthems and voluntaries. *Ely Cathedral Choir; Wills, cond.*
+ ARG 5-6/92: 33 (as Saga 9006)

31299. EC 3382-2: BEETHOVEN—Symphony no. 7. *Leningrad Phil. Orch.; Mravinsky, cond.* Probably recorded 1958.
• Fa 3-4/95: 130

31300. EC 3384-2: *Virtuoso Spanish guitar music.* Music of Turina and Rodrigo. *Hill, guitar.* Reissue.
• Fa 3-4/95: 375

31301. EC 3385-2: BRITTEN—Choral music. PURCELL—Choral music. *New College Choir, Oxford; Lumsden, cond.*
+ ARG 9-10/94: 111

31302. EC 3388—3389-2 (2 separate discs): CHOPIN—Nocturnes (complete). *Fiorentino, piano.*
• ARG 9-10/94: 117
+ Fa 9-10/94: 165

31303. EC 3397—3398-2 (2 separate discs): FAURÉ—Piano music, vol. 1-2. *Ferber, piano.* Recorded 1974.
+ Fa 11-12/94: 225

SAIN

31304. SCDC 2013: WILLIAMS—Songs. *Terfel, bass-baritone; Parry, piano.*
+ Gr 8/93: 74

31305. SCDC 2070: Music of Dvořák, Bernstein, Puccini, Bizet, Britten, and others. *Bullock, soprano; A. Davies, tenor; Parri, piano.*
+ Gr 11/95: 165

31306. SCDC 2085: Music of Puccini, Bizet, Lewis, Giordano, and others. *A. Davies, tenor; Bullock, soprano; Parri, piano.*
+ Gr 11/95: 165

31307. SCDC 4035: SCHUBERT—Schwanengesang. *Terfel, bass-baritone; Martineau, piano.*
+ Gr 5/92: 96

SALABERT

31308. CMCD 5606: CONSTANT—Concerto for violin and 12 instruments. TANGUY—Concerto for violin and 12 winds; Concerto for flute and 16 instruments. *Milosi, violin; Artaud, flute; Orchestre de Caen; Bardon, cond.*
- Fa 11-12/94: 202

31309. CYP 5611: LANDOWSKI—Leçons de ténèbre; Adagio cantabile. *Calos, soprano; Harasteanu, bass; Chorus of Timisoara; Philharmonie de Timisoara; Georgescu, cond.*
+ Fa 11-12/94: 274

31310. SCD 8801: Music of Miereanu, Levinas, Murail, Lefebvre, and others. *Froger, soprano; Ensemble de l'Itinéraire; Mechkat, cond.*
☐ Fa 3-4/91: 501

31311. SCD 8802: FRANÇOIS—Un regard oblique; Deuxième récit; Sonnet; Reflets II; Tulles écoutes; Les chemins de la nuit. *Artaud, François, flutes; Alsina, Méfano, pianos; Carmelli, bass; Meunier, cello;*

Ensemble 2e2m; Méfano, cond.
+ Fa 3-4/91: 212

31312. SCD 8803: MIEREANU—Kammerkonzert; Désordre dérisoire; Aquarius; Sursum corda triplum; Musique élémentaire de concert. *Kientzy, saxophones; Jarsky, soprano; Méfano, Bou, pianos; Ensemble 2e2m; Méfano, cond.*
+ Fa 3-4/91: 280

31313. SCD 8804: SINGIER—Blocs en crac de bric et de broc; Bouts rimes burines; Figures en phases éparses, emphases, épures. HUREL—Diamants imaginaires, diamant lunaire; Pour l'image. *Arrignon, clarinet; instrumental ensemble; Spanjaard, cond.*
+ Fa 3-4/91: 387

31314. SCD 8901: MALEC—Attacca; Week-end; Lumina; Gam(m)es. *Geoffroy, percussion; Ensemble 2e2m; Malec, cond. & electronics; Ljubljana Radio & Television Orch.; Hubad, cond.*
+ Fa 3-4/91: 266

31315. SCD 8902: MURAIL—Gondwana; Désintégrations; Time and again. *French National Orch.; Ensemble de l'Itinéraire; Orch. of the Beethoven Hall at Bonn; Prin, Rickenbacher, conds.*
+ Fa 1-2/91: 264

31316. SCD 8903: LEFEBVRE—Océan de terre; Valée; Orégon; Berzweigungen; Mosella. *Ensemble 2e 2m; Méfano, cond.*
☐ Fa 3-4/91: 255

31317. SCD 8904/05 (2 discs): SCELSI—String quartets (complete); String trio; Khoom. *Arditti Quartet; Hirayama, soprano; Lloyd, horn; Omar, percussion; Brizzi, cond.*
+ Fa 1-2/91: 299 (2 reviews)
+ Fa 1-2/96: 292
+ Gr 9/90: 562
+ MA 7/91: 85

31318. SCD 8906: XENAKIS—Oresteia. *Sakkas, baritone; Gualda, percussion; University of Strasbourg Choir; Ensemble Vocal d'Anjou; Ensemble de Basse-Normandie; Debart, cond.*
+ Fa 7-8/91: 329
+ Fa 1-2/96: 348

31319. SCD 9001: REVERDY—Scenic railway; Sept enluminures; Figure; Meteores; Kaleidoscope. *Gottlieb, piano; Roullier, flute; Spieth, harpsichord; Ensemble InterContemporain; Ensemble Accroche Note; Ensemble Ars Nova; Pennetier, Constant, conds.*
+ Fa 3-4/91: 340

31320. SCD 9002: Music of Jarrell, Devillers, and Durieux. *Ensemble Forum; Foster, cond.*
• Fa 5-6/91: 192

SALABERT

31321. SCD 9101: MADERNA—Satyricon. *Sperry, Tomicich, Oliveri, Vargas; Divertimento Ensemble; Gorli, cond.*
+ ARG 11-12/95: 148
+ Fa 9-10/95: 252
□ Gr 9/93: 110

31322. SCD 9401: CONSTANT—Chamber music. *Various performers.*
+ ARG 9-10/95: 127

31323. SCD 9402: LEVINAS—Préfixes; Arsis et Thésis; Froissements d'ailes; Voûtes; Rebonds; Trois études pour piano; La cloche fêlée. *Ensemble Itinéraire; Louvier, cond.; Artaud, flute; Les Percussions de Strasbourg; Orchestre Philharmonique de Radio-France; Mechkat, cond.; Neveu, piano; Orchestre National de France; Rophé, cond.*
□ Fa 11-12/94: 279

31324. SCD 9404: JANSEN—String quartets no. 1-2. DELAISTIER—String quartet. *Quatuor Musique Vivante.*
+ Fa 7-8/95: 213

31325. SCD 9408: TANGUY—Océan, N.Y. Fantasie; Solo for cello; Azur C; Towards; Alloys; Azur B; Wadi; Avénement de la ligne. *Guy, piano & organ; Linal, cello; Nessi, flute; Geoffrey, percussion; Dutrieu, clarinet.*
□ Fa 7-8/95: 339

31326. SCD 9410: GAUSSIN—Irisation-rituel; Arcane; Camaïeux. *Jarsky, soprano; Artaud, flute; Gottlieb, piano; Nouvel Orch. Philharmonique; Eötvös, cond.; Ensemble of Electronic Instruments of L'Itinéraire; Prin, cond.*
+ Fa 9-10/95: 206

31327. SCD 9411: *Percussions.* Music of Miroglio, Dufourt, Féron, Korelis, Jolas, and Giraud. *Miroglio, percussion.*
● Fa 7-8/95: 248

31328. SCD 9501: MIEREANU—Symphony no. 1 "Un temps sans mémoire"; Voyage d'hiver II; Miroirs célestes; Rosenzeit. *Orch. Philharmonique de Radio-France; Bilger, Prin, conds.; Orch. Philharmonique de Lorraine; Pennetier, cond.*
+ Fa 9-10/95: 263

31329. SCD 9502: KOJOUKHAROV—Cendrillon: opera in 3 acts and 9 scenes. *Children of the Junior Opera Workshop, Montpellier-Nimes; Montpellier Opera Orch.; Kojoukharov, cond.*
+ Fa 5-6/96: 187

SANCTUS

31330. SCSH 001: *Elena Gerhardt, Povla Frijsh, Lotte Lehmann: great voices of the century.* Music of Brahms, Schubert, Wolf, Koechlin, Georges, Tchaikovsky, Grieg, Fauré, Kricka, Cui, and Bach. *Gerhardt, Frijsh, Lehmann,*

sopranos; various accs.
+ Fa 7-8/96: 344
+ ON 8/96: 45

31331. SCSH 002/3 (2 discs): GRAZIANI—Six sonatas for cello and continuo, op. 3. *Meneses, cello; Lanzelotte, harpsichord; Tavares, cello continuo.*
+ Fa 7-8/96: 180

SAYDISC

31332. CD SDL 385: *The musical life of Samuel Pepys.* Music of Locke, Reggio, Carissimi, Pepys, Goodgroome, and others. *Wistreich, speaker & bass; Jeffrey, theorbo & baroque guitar; other instrumentalists.*
+ ARG 5-6/91: 154
+ Fa 5-6/91: 351

31333. CD-SDL 386: *Baroque guitar quartets.* HANDEL—Concerto grosso, op. 3, no. 1. BACH—Passacaglia and fugue, BWV 582. CORELLI—Sonata da camera, op. 2, no. 6; Sonata da chiesa, op. 3, no. 1. PURCELL—The fairy queen: suite no. 1. VIVALDI—Concerto for two mandolins and strings in G major, RV 532. *English Guitar Quartet.*
+ ARG 5-6/91: 151
+ Fa 5-6/91: 363
+ Gr 11/91: 125

31334. CD-SDL 395: *Raisins and almonds.* Jewish songs from the Ashkenazi and Sephardic traditions. *Skeaping, soprano; The Burning Bush.*
+ Gr 8/92: 64

31335. CD-SDL 399: Music of Albeniz, Soler, Falla, Milan, and Granados. *English Guitar Quartet.*
● ARG 9-10/93: 234

31336. CD-SDL 400: English national songs. *Potter, tenor; Skeaping, mezzo-soprano; Broadside Band.*
+ ARG 7-8/93: 199
+ EM 11/93: 645
+ Gr 6/93: 97

31337. CD-SDL 409: Songs and dances from Shakespeare. *Roberts, soprano; Potter, tenor; Broadside Band; Barlow, cond.*
+ ARG 9-10/95: 284

SCALEN DISC ARIANE

31338. ARI 136: TREMBLAY—Vêpres de la Vierge. *Vaillancourt, soprano; Lyon Orch. Chorus; Ensemble of Young Quebeçois Instrumentalists; Tremblay, cond.*
+ Fa 9-10/88: 284

SCARLET

31339. IS-88802: SPIEGEL—Unseen worlds. *Spiegel, performer.*
+ ARG 7-8/92: 228

SCHWANN

31340. VMS 1043 (LP): PLEYEL—Oboe quartets op. 25 no. 1; op. 28 no. 1-3. *Feit Concertino.*
+ Fa 5-6/86: 205
+ NR 5/86: 12

31341. VMS 1047 (LP): RACHMANINOFF—Preludes op. 23 no. 1-2, 4, 7; op. 32 no. 10-12. REGER—Romanze; Silhouetten op. 53 no. 3, 6; Intermezzi op. 45 no. 1, 3, 5; Träume am Kamin op. 143 no. 12. *Falkner, piano.*
+ Fa 5-6/86: 215
+ NR 6/86: 20

31342. VMS 1053 (LP): BLOCH—Violin sonata no. 2; Baal Shem suite; Abodah; Melodie. *Epstein, violin; Canck, piano.*
+ Fa 1-2/89: 131

31343. VMS 1054 (LP): DOHNÁNYI—String quartets no. 1-2. *Artis Quartet Vienna.*
+ Fa 3-4/87: 107

AMS 1605 see CD 11605.

VMS 1623 see CD 11623.

VMS 1642 see CD 11642.

31344. VMS 1071 (LP): SCHOENBERG—String quartet no. 1, op. 7. *Schönberg Quartet.*
+ Fa 3-4/87: 198

AMS 2115 see CD 11101.

31345. CD 11003: Trumpet concertos by Hummel, Gros, and Hertel. *Basch, trumpet; Karcher, Vetter, oboes; Ventulett, Roscher, bassoons; Orpheus Chamber Orch.*
● Fa 1-2/88: 144

31346. CD 11060: *Virtuoso viola concertos.* Viola concertos of M. Haydn, H. Casadesus (attrib. to J.C. Bach), and C. Stamitz . *Christ, viola; Trimborn, harpsichord; Cologne Chamber Orch.; Müller-Brühl, cond.*
+ Fa 7-8/88: 178

31347. CD 11088: MENDELSSOHN—Concertos for 2 pianos: in E; in A♭. *A. & J. Paratore, pianos; RIAS Sinfonietta; Lajovic, cond.*
+ Fa 11-12/86: 174

31348. CD 11091: REZNICEK—Symphonies no. 3-4. *Philharmonia Hungarica; Wright, cond.*
+ ARG 11-12/86: 77
+ Fa 9-10/86: 213
+ Opus 4/87: 46

31349. CD 11101: MOZART—Piano concertos: K. 414, K. 449. *Entremont, piano & cond.; Vienna Chamber Orch.* Issued also as LP: AMS 2115.

• ARG 9-10/86: 79
• Fa 9-10/86: 192

31350. CD 11111: Music of
Mendelssohn, Cramer, and Barmann.
*Klöcker, clarinet; Wandel, clarinet &
basset horn; Southwest German Radio
Symphony Orch.; Tamayo, cond.*
  + ARG 9-10/88: 61
  + Fa 5-6/88: 163

31351. CD 11117: STRAUSS—Symphony
in D minor. GRIEG—Symphony in C
minor. *Bavarian Radio Symphony Orch.;
Rickenbacher, cond.*
  + Fa 3-4/88: 210

31352. CD 11119: TISHCHENKO—Concerto
for cello, 17 wind instruments,
percussion, and organ. GLAZUNOV—
Concerto ballata for cello, op. 108;
Melodie, op. 20, no. 1; Serenade
espagnole for cello and orchestra op. 20
no. 2. *Pergamenschikow, cello; Bavarian
Radio Symphony Orch.; Shallon, cond.*
  + ARG 5-6/88: 31
  + Fa 3-4/88: 186

31353. CD 11403: MOZART—String
quartets K. 465, 589. *Kolisch Quartet.*
  + Fa 1-2/88: 174

31354. CD 11602: ZEMLINSKY—Lyric
symphony; Six songs on texts of
Maeterlinck op. 13. *Söderström,
Duesing; Berlin Radio Symphony Orch.;
Klee, cond.*
  + Fa 9-10/86: 263

31355. CD 11605: REGER—Symphonic
prologue for a tragedy op. 108; Two
romances for violin and orchestra op. 50.
*Maile, violin; Berlin Radio Symphony
Orch.; Albrecht, Lajovic, conds.* Issued
also as LP: AMS 1605.
  + ARG 1-2/87: 53
  + Fa 7-8/86: 211

31356. CD 11608: Music of Blodek,
Demersseman, Fürstenau, Doppler, and
Ciardi. *Sebon, flute; Berlin Radio
Symphony Orch.; Lajovic, conds.*
  + Fa 3-4/87: 269

31357. CD 11615: GORECKI—Three
pieces in olden style; Symphony no. 3 for
soprano and orchestra, op. 26.
*Woytowicz, soprano; Warsaw Chamber
Orch.; Berlin Radio Symphony Orch.;
Teutsch, Kamirski, conds.*
  + ARG 5-6/88: 32
  + DA 1/88: 56
  + Fa 9-10/87: 205

31358. CD 11618: SCHREKER—Chamber
symphony; Prelude to a drama; Valse
lent, Der ferne Klang: Nachtstuck. *Berlin
Radio Symphony Orch.; Gielen,
Rickenbacher, conds.*
  + ARG 5-6/88: 60
  + DA 1/88: 56
  + Fa 9-10/87: 285

  + Fa 11-12/87: 215
  + MA 1/88: 63

31359. CD 11623: STEPHAN—
Liebeszauber; Music for orchestra; Music
for violin and orchestra. *Fischer-
Dieskau, baritone; Maile, violin; Berlin
Radio Symphony Orch.; Zender, cond.*
Issued also as LP: VMS 1623.
  + Fa 7-8/86: 232
  + Gr 7/86: 172

31360. CD 11637: MAHLER—Totenfeier;
Suite (arr. from Bach suites). *Berlin
Radio Symphony Orch.; López Cobos,
cond.*
  • ARG 3-4/89: 45

31361. CD 11641 (2 discs): WOLF—Der
Corregidor. *Donath, Soffel, Hollweg,
Fischer-Dieskau; RIAS Chamber Choir;
Berlin Radio Symphony Orch.; Albrecht,
cond.* Issued also as 2 LPs: VMS 1641.
  + ARG 5-6/88: 74
  + DA 12/87: 74
  + Fa 11-12/87: 256
  + Gr 8/87: 337
  • Opus 12/87: 50

31362. CD 11642: BOTTESINI—Grand duo
concertante for double bass, violin and
orchestra in A; Grande concerto for 2
double basses and orchestra; Gran duetto
for double bass and viola no. 2; Duo
concertant for double bass and cello.
*Güttler, Stoll, double basses; Sebestyén,
violin & viola; Ostertag, cello; Berlin
Radio Symphony Orch.; Bamert, cond.*
  + ARG 5-6/88: 19
  + Fa 3-4/88: 86

31363. CD 11644: TCHAIKOVSKY—Piano
concerto no. 1 (original version). *Berman,
piano; Berlin Radio Symphony Orch.;
Temirkanov, cond.*
  - Fa 3-4/88: 213
  • Gr 8/88: 297
  + SR 4/88: 108

31364. CD 11734: *Virtuoso concertos for
viola.* HINDEMITH—Kammermusik no. 4-5;
Konzertmusik op. 48; Der
Schwanendreher. *Schmid, viola;
Bavarian Radio Symphony Orch.; Heger,
Kubelik, conds.*
  • Fa 11-12/88: 200

31365. CD 11855: FRANCK—Ce qu'on
entend sur la montagne; Eight short
pieces for small orchestra (orch. by
Busser). *Orch. Symphonique de la RTBF;
Priestman, Walter, conds.*
  + ARG 9-10/88: 44
  + Fa 3-4/88: 104

31366. CD 11857: GRESNICK—Le baisé
donné et rendu. *Reyghere, Raoult, Van
Dyck, Demaiffe; Orch. Symphonique de
la RTBF; Walter, cond.*
  + ARG 9-10/88: 48
  + Fa 3-4/88: 116

31367. VMS 1621 (LP): *Romantic
clarinet concertos.* Music of Lindpainter,
Danzi, Reissiger, and Kalliwoda.
*Klöcker, clarinet; Berlin Radio Symphony
Orch.; López Cobos, cond.*
  + Fa 3-4/87: 270

31368. VMS 2105 (LP): AVISON—
Concerti grossi after Domenico Scarlatti
no. 7-9, 11. *Ensemble Berlin.*
  - Fa 9-10/86: 84

31369. VMS 2106 (LP): SHOSTAKOVICH—
Symphony no. 6. RIMSKY-KORSAKOV—
Legend of the invisible city of Kitezh:
Suite. *Saar Radio Symphony Orch.;
Chung, cond.*
  + Fa 3-4/87: 204
  • Gr 6/87: 52
  + NR 3/87: 3

31370. VMS 2113 (LP): Trumpet
concertos by Haydn, Reutter, Telemann,
and L. Mozart. *Basch, trumpet; Bamberg
Symphony Orch.; Andreae, cond.*
  • Fa 1-2/87: 120
  + Fa 1-2/87: 252

31371. AMS 3545 (LP): DEMANTIUS—St.
John passion. SCHEIN—Was betrübst du
dich; Zion spricht; Ist nicht Ephraim;
Seihe, nach Trost war mir sehr bange.
Alsfeld Vocal Ensemble; Helbich, cond.
  + Fa 3-4/86: 153

31372. AMS 3558 (LP): GOUNOD—Messe
solennelle de Ste. Cécile. *Fukuda,
soprano; Lenz, tenor; Pleis, bass;
Wittmann, organ; St. Michael's Church,
Munich Chorus & Orch.; Schloter, cond.*
  • Fa 9-10/87: 208

31373. MM 4001 (LP): Music of Mozart,
Beethoven, Rossini, Flotow, Maillart, and
others. *Various orchs.; Zemlinsky, cond.*
  • Fa 5-6/87: 245

31374. VMS 4528 (3 LPs): SCHOECK—
Massimilla Doni. *Mathis, Protschka,
Lindsley, Hermann; Cologne Radio
Choir; Cologne Radio Symphony Orch.;
Albrecht, cond.*
  + Fa 5-6/87: 187
  + Gr 6/87: 102

31375. CD 310 004: HENZE—
Kammermusik 1958. *Jenkins, tenor;
Walker, guitar; Scharoun-Ensemble
Berlin; Jones, cond.*
  + Fa 11-12/88: 199
  + Gr 1/89: 1196

31376. CD 310 017: HUMMEL—Sonata op.
52, 92; Nocturne, Theme and variations
op. 99. *Tal, Groethuysen, pianos.*
  + Fa 11-12/88: 206

31377. CD 311 004: F.X. MOZART—Piano
concertos no. 1-2. *Hellwig, piano;
Cologne Radio Symphony Orch.; Bader,
cond.*
  + ARG 9-10/88: 63

SCHWANN

+ Fa 11-12/88: 228
□ Ov 12/88: 51

31378. CD 311 006: Haydn—Concertos for lira for Ferdinand IV, H. VII: 1-5. *Ensemble Wolfgang von Karajan; Berlin Instrumental Soloists.*
+ ARG 11-12/88: 38
+ Fa 11-12/88: 198

31379. CD 311 015: Messiaen—Chronochromie; L'ascension. *Bavarian Radio Symphony Orch.; Rickenbacher, cond.*
● ARG 11-12/88: 62
● Fa 9-10/88: 199

31380. CD 315 000—315 002 (3 separate discs): Vierne—Organ symphonies (complete). *Kaunzinger, organ.*
+ ARG 1-2/89: 98
+ Fa 9-10/88: 288

31381. CD 96100: Bach—Ich will den Kreuzstab gerne tragen; Ich habe genug; Der Friede sei mit dir. *Loibl, baritone; Munchner Vokalensemble; Munich Chamber Orch.; Stadlmair, cond.*
- Fa 9-10/86: 86

SDG

31382. CD 503: *Berkey meets Horowitz on the 503.* Berkey—Piano derivations; American perspective; Voice from the earth. *J. Berkey, piano; Low, cello; A. Berkey, soprano; Galante, clarinet.*
- Fa 11-12/94: 175

31383. CD 941: *Arvo the magnificat.* Music of Chilcott, Berkey, Palestrina, Söderman, Pärt, and Raminsch. *Soli Deo Gloria Cantorum; Berkey, cond.*
+ ARG 5-6/95: 222
- Fa 3-4/95: 363

SECOND HEARING

31384. GS 9006: Liszt—Années de pèlerinage: Suisse. *Villa, piano.*
+ DA 4/86: 47
+ Fa 1-2/86: 165

31385. GS 9007: Beethoven—Piano sonatas no. 3, 20, 23, 26. *Laredo, piano.*
● Fa 11-12/86: 109
● Fa 7-8/88: 116

31386. GS 9009: Music of Handel, Kodály, Mozart, and Ravel. *Laredo, violin; Robinson, cello.*
+ Fa 9-10/86: 295
+ Ov 10/86: 45
+ SR 10/86: 100

31387. BS 9014: Scriabin—Piano sonatas no. 3-5, 7; Poème op. 32 no. 1; Album leaf op. 45 no. 1; Mazurka in E minor op. 25 no. 3. *Villa, piano.*
+ Fa 9-10/86: 229 (2 reviews)

SEFEL

31388. SE/CD 5023: Brahms—Concerto for violin, and cello, op. 102; Tragic overture. *Verhey, violin; Starker, cello; Amsterdam Phil. Orch.; Joó, cond.*
- Fa 9-10/86: 115

SEM GRAMOPHONE

31389. DS 0034: Byung-Ki—Forest; Spring; Pomegranate house; Fall; Kara town; Chimhyang-moo. *Byung-Ki, kayagum; Hyeran, changgu.*
+ Fa 9-10/95: 163

31390. DS 0039: Debussy—Violin sonata. Bartók—Rhapsody no. 2 for violin and piano. Prokofiev—Violin sonata no. 1. *Lee, violin; Suits, piano.*
+ Fa 1-2/94: 179

SERAPHIM

31391. 6145 (3 LPs): Mozart—Don Giovanni. *Grümmer, Schwarzkopf, Berger, Dermota, Siepi, Edelmann, Berry; Vienna Phil. Orch.; Furtwängler, cond.* Recorded live 1954.
+ Fa 7-8/86: 187
+ Gr 5/86: 1455
● ON 8-86: 48
+ Op 10/86: 1168

31392. 6149 (2 LPs): Schubert—Songs. *Schumann, soprano; Kell, clarinet; various pianists.* Recorded live 1927-49.
+ Fa 7-8/86: 223
+ Gr 3/86: 1190

31393. 6153 (7 LPs): Complete recordings of Mattia Battistini. *Battistini, baritone; various accs.*
+ Fa 11-12/86: 259
+ Gr 7/86: 205
+ ON 9/86: 69
+ Op 11/86: 1278

31394. 6156 (3 LPs): Beethoven—Symphonies no. 1, 4, 6-7; Leonore overture no. 1; Creatures of Prometheus overture. *BBC Symphony Orch.; Toscanini, cond.*
+ Fa 5-6/87: 90
+ Gr 2/87: 1116

31395. 6159 (2 LPs): Music of Tchaikovsky, Wieniawski, Glazunov, Vieuxtemps, and others. *Heifetz, violin; London Phil. Orch.; London Symphony Orch.; Barbirolli, cond.* Recorded 1934-37.
+ Fa 7-8/88: 316

31396. 69018: Beethoven—Piano concertos no. 3, 5. *Firkušný, piano; Philharmonia Orch.; Susskind, cond.; Pittsburgh Symphony Orch.; Steinberg, cond.* Recorded 1959-60.
+ ARG 5-6/96: 79

31397. 69019: Beethoven—Piano sonatas no. 8-10, 13-14. *Gieseking, piano.*

Reissue.
+ ARG 3-4/96: 90

31398. 69021: Borodin—Symphony no. 2; Polovtsian dances; Prince Igor overture. Ippolitov-Ivanov—In the steppes of central Asia. Mussorgsky—Night on Bald Mountain; Dance of the Persian slaves. *Vienna Phil. Orch.; Kubelik, cond.; Pittsburgh Symphony Orch.; Steinberg, cond.; Philharmonia Orch.; Karajan, Cluytens, Silvestri, conds.* Reissues.
+ ARG 1-2/96: 90

31399. 69022: Elgar—Enigma variations; Pomp and circumstance marches; Cockaigne overture. *London Symphony Orch.; London Phil. Orch.; Boult, cond.; Philharmonia Orch.; Barbirolli, cond.* Reissue.
+ ARG 3-4/96: 112

31400. 69026: Brahms—Symphony no. 1. Haydn—Symphony no. 94. *Pittsburgh Symphony Orch.; Steinberg, cond.* Reissue; recorded 1958-1959.
● ARG 3-4/96: 95

31401. 69028: Music of Beethoven, Brahms, Chopin, Debussy, Ravel, Dvořák, Liszt, Mozart, Rachmaninoff, Rubinstein, Satie, and Schumann. *Lympany, piano.* Reissue.
+ ARG 1-2/96: 219

31402. 69029: Rachmaninoff—Symphony no. 2; Piano concerto no. 2. *Pennario, piano; Los Angeles Phil.; Wallenstein, Leinsdorf, conds.* Reissue.
● ARG 1-2/96: 156

31403. 69030: Rimsky-Korsakov—Scheherazade; Russian Easter overture; Capriccio espagnol. *London Phil. Orch.; Litton, cond.; Concert Arts Orch.; Leinsdorf, cond.; Hollywood Bowl Symphony Orch.; Slatkin, cond.* Reissue.
● ARG 3-4/96: 173

31404. 69031: Schubert—Symphony no. 8; Rosamunde ballet music; Marche militaire. Mendelssohn—Midsummer night's dream: Excerpts; Ruy Blas overture. *Berlin Phil. Orch.; Karajan, cond.; Philharmonia Orch.; Kurtz, cond.; Hollywood Bowl Symphony Orch.; F. Slatkin, cond.; London Symphony Orch.; Previn, cond.* Reissues.
● ARG 5-6/96: 188

31405. 69032: Sibelius—Symphony no. 2; Finlandia; Karelia suite; Swan of Tuonela. *Philharmonia Orch.; Kletzki, cond.; Vienna Phil. Orch.; Sargent, cond.* Recorded 1959, 1962.
+ ARG 3-4/96: 184

31406. 69033: Tchaikovsky—1812 overture; Romeo and Juliet; Francesca da Rimini; Marche slav. *Hollywood Bowl Symphony Orch.; F. Slatkin, cond.; Philharmonia Orch.; Markevitch, Giulini,*

conds.; Pittsburgh Symphony Orch.; Steinberg, cond. Reissues.
• ARG 7-8/96: 209

31407. 69034: TCHAIKOVSKY—Piano concerto no. 1; Symphony no. 6. *Pennario, piano; Los Angeles Phil.; Leinsdorf, cond.* Reissue.
+ ARG 1-2/96: 156

31408. 69035: TCHAIKOVSKY—Violin concerto. BRAHMS—Violin concerto. *Milstein, violin; Pittsburgh Symphony Orch.; Steinberg, cond.; Philharmonia Orch.; Fistoulari, cond.* Reissue.
+ ARG 3-4/96: 192

31409. 69037: WAGNER—Overtures to Tristan und Isolde; Parsifal; Die Meistersinger (Prelude to Act 3); Lohengrin; Tannhäuser; Liebestod from Tristan und Isolde; Good Friday music from Parsifal. *Vienna Phil. Orch.; Kempe, cond.; Philharmonia Orch.; Boult, cond.* Reissue.
+ ARG 3-4/96: 206

31410. 69038: LISZT—Les préludes; Hungarian rhapsodies no. 2, 3, 14; Mazeppa; Racoczy march; Hungarian battle march. *Hollywood Bowl Symphony; Rózsa, cond.; Leipzig Gewandhaus Orch.; Masur, cond.; London Phil. Orch.; Philharmonia Hungarica; Boskovsky, cond.* Reissues.
• ARG 5-6/96: 138

31411. 69131 (2 discs): RIMSKY-KORSAKOV—Scheherazade. BORODIN—Polovtsian dances. STRAVINSKY—Firebird. PROKOFIEV—Piano concerto no. 3. *Weissenberg, piano; Chicago Symphony Orch; Orch. de Paris; Ozawa, cond.* Reissues.
• ARG 7-8/96: 230

31412. 69134: SIBELIUS—Symphonies no. 2, 5; Finlandia; En saga; Swan of Tuonela; Karelia suite; Pohjola's daughter. *Sinfonia of London; Hannikainen, cond.; Vienna Phil. Orch.; BBC Symphony Orch.; Sargent, cond.* Reissues.
+ ARG 7-8/96: 198

SEVEN SEAS

31413. KICC 96: CIURLIONIS—Piano miniatures. *Radvilaite, Kontrimas, Maceina, Vainiunaite, Juozopenaite, Dvarionaite, pianos.*
+ ARG 1-2/96: 97

31414. KICC 147-148 (2 separate discs): LIPATTI—Orchestral and chamber music. *Various performers.*
+ ARG 11-12/95: 145

31415. KICC 2072: MOZART—Symphonies no. 25, 29, and 35. *New York Phil.; Walter, cond.* Recorded live 1953, 1956.
+ Fa 3-4/91: 305

31416. KICC 2073: MOZART—Symphonies no. 38-39, and 40. *New York Phil.; Berlin Phil. Orch.; Walter, cond.* Recorded live 1950, 1954, 1956.
+ Fa 3-4/91: 305

31417. KICC 2074: MOZART—Piano concerto K. 466; Divertimento K. 287; Minuets K. 568-599; German dances K. 605. *NBC Symphony Orch.; Walter, piano & cond.* Recorded live 1939-40.
+ Fa 3-4/91: 305

31418. KICC 2075: MAHLER—Das Lied von der Erde. *Nikolaidi, contralto; Svanholm, tenor; New York Phil.; Walter, cond.* Recorded live 1953.
+ Fa 5-6/91: 209

31419. KICC 2076: MUSSORGSKY—Pictures at an exhibition (orch. Stokowski); Night on bald mountain. SHOSTAKOVICH—Symphony no. 5. *BBC Symphony Orch.; London Symphony Orch.; Stokowski, cond.* Recorded live 1963, 1964.
+ Fa 3-4/91: 311

31420. KICC 2077: MAHLER—Symphony no. 7. *Toronto Symphony Orch.; Scherchen, cond.* Recorded live 1965.
+ Fa 3-4/91: 264

31421. KICC 2078: BRUCKNER—Symphony no. 5. *Vienna Phil. Orch.; Klemperer, cond.* Recorded live 1968.
• Fa 5-6/91: 146

31422. KICC 2080: BEETHOVEN—Symphony no. 5. MOZART—Oboe concerto, K. 314. WEBER—Symphony no. 1. *Cologne Radio Symphony Orch.; Kleiber, cond.* Recorded live 1955, 1956.
+ Fa 3-4/91: 506

31423. KICC 2081: RAVEL—Daphnis et Chloé; Schéhérazade. *Angeles, soprano; Concertgebouw Orch.; Monteux, cond.* Recorded live 1955, 1963.
• Fa 3-4/91: 335

31424. KICC 2155: BRAHMS—Piano concerto no. 2; Haydn variations on a theme by Haydn. *Aeschbacher, piano; Berlin Phil. Orch.; Furtwängler, cond.* Broadcast recordings (Dec. 1943).
- Fa 11-12/91: 281

31425. KICC 6191 (8 discs): SCHUBERT—Four-hand piano music (complete). *S. & K. Kodama, piano.*
+ ARG 5-6/96: 186

SHEFFIELD LAB

31426. CD-28 : GERSHWIN—I got rhythm variations; Rhapsody in blue; Promenade; Lullaby; Porgy and Bess: Summertime; Three preludes; Two waltzes; Rialto ripples; Impromptu in 2 keys. *Mayorga, piano; Moscow Phil. Orch.; Kitaenko, cond.*
• ARG 3-4/89: 36

+ Fa 5-6/89: 200
+ St 5/89: 159

31427. SLS-503: BRIDGE—Quartet no. 4. BEETHOVEN—Quartet no. 10. *Ciompi Quartet.*
- ARG 5-6/92: 39
+ Fa 1-2/92: 187

31428. SLS-504: Music of Bach, Giuliani, Legnani, Carulli, Albeniz, Turina, Sainz de la Maza. *Newman, Oltman, guitars; Sequoia String Quartet.*
- ARG 1-2/92: 153

31429. SLS-506: MOZART—Serenade no. 11. GRIEG—Four lyric pieces. HUSA—Concerto. *Chicago Symphony Winds; Moscow Phil. Symphony Winds.*
+ ARG 5-6/93: 171

31430. SLS-10039: STRAUSS—Violin sonata. DVOŘÁK—Romantic pieces; Sonatina. *Steinhardt, violin; Mayorga, piano.*
+ ARG 11-12/95: 213

31431. 10043-2-G: *The Sheffield-Leinsdorf sessions, vol. 1.* Music of Prokofiev, Debussy, and Wagner. *Los Angeles Phil. Orch.; Leinsdorf, cond.* Recorded 1977.
+ ARG 9-10/95: 193
• Fa 9-10/95: 424

31432. SLS-10044: GERSHWIN—Rhapsody in blue; Piano music. *Mayorga, piano; Moscow Phil. Orch.; Kitaenko, cond.*
• ARG 11-12/95: 122

31433. 10052-2-G: *The Sheffield-Leinsdorf sessions, vol. 2.* Music of Stravinsky and Wagner. *Los Angeles Phil. Orch.; Leinsdorf, cond.* Recorded 1977.
• Fa 9-10/95: 424

31434. SLS-10054: SCHUBERT—Piano music, four hands. *Duo Schnabel.*
+ ARG 11-12/95: 195
+ Fa 3-4/96: 271

SIERRA

31435. 5001: MATHIAS—Zodiac trio. HAGEN—Harp trio (1989). KIBBE—Trio, op. 99. BONDON—Le soleil multicolore. *Debussy Trio.*
+ ARG 11-12/93: 231

31436. 5002: DEBUSSY—Sonata for flute, viola and harp. RAVEL—Sonatine (arr. Salzedo). MENDOZA—Trio music 5/90. *Debussy Trio.*
• ARG 3-4/93: 72

31437. 5004: Trio sonatas by Leclair, Telemann, Locatelli, and Graun. *Debussy Trio.*
• ARG 1-2/95: 216

SIGLA

31438. 600 208 (3 discs): VILLA-LOBOS—Bachianas brasileiras (complete). *Brazil Symphony Orch.; Karabtchevsky, cond.*
- ARG 3-4/89: 103
- Fa 3-4/89: 330
+ SR 4/89: 87

SIGNUM

31439. SIGX 03-00: MOZART—Clarinet quartets op. 79 (arr. of K. 378, K. 380, K.496). *Buer, clarinet; Raphael Trio.*
+ Fa 11-12/86: 187

31440. SIGX 06-00: MOZART—Quintet for piano, oboe, clarinet, horn, and bassoon, K. 452. BEETHOVEN—Quintet for piano, oboe, clarinet, horn, and bassoon, op. 16. *Eschenbach, piano; Leek, oboe; Moog, clarinet; Scott, horn; Freund, bassoon.* Reissue.
+ Fa 5-6/94: 204
- Gr 10/92: 131

31441. SIGX 07-00: Music of Balbastre, Bergamo, Liszt, Ives, and Buck. *Szathmáry, organ.*
- ARG 5-6/94: 181

31442. SIG 009-00 (LP): SCRIABIN—Piano sonata no. 2 op. 19. KABALEVSKY—Piano sonata no. 3 op. 46; Twenty- four preludes op. 38 no. 6. *Zaritskaya, piano.*
+ Fa 11-12/87: 225

31443. SIGX 10-00: *Blumenlieder.* Music of Loewe, Schumann, Milhaud, Strauss, Wolf, and others. *Shirai, soprano; Höll, piano.*
+ Fa 9-10/88: 318
+ Gr 5/92: 100

31444. SIGX 10-56: SCHUBERT—Arpeggione sonata. MERTZ—Guitar duos . *Folkwang Guitar Duo.*
+ ARG 5-6/95: 210

31445. SIGX 10-64: Cello sonatas by Pfitzner, Strauss, and Hindemith. *Henkel, cello; Pludermacher, piano.*
+ ARG 7-8/96: 241

31446. SIGX 10-66: LALO—Symphony; Scherzo; Piano concerto; Romance-serenade. *Gross, piano; Toschmakov, violin; Frankfurt (Oder) Symphony Orch.; Athinäos, cond.*
- ARG 5-6/96: 133
+ Fa 7-8/96: 212

31447. SIGX 10-68: Music of Bogdanović, Aubert, Brindle, and others. *Gruber & Maklar Duo (guitars).*
+ ARG 9-10/96: 243

31448. SIGX 10-69: *Music of the silence.* Music of Jolivet, Lohrmann, Alain, and Schnebel. *Nunc Ensemble for New Music; Valentin, cond.*
□ ARG 7-8/96: 271

31449. SIGX 18-00: STRAUSS—Suite for winds op. 13; Serenade for winds op. 7; Duet-Concertino for clarinet, bassoon, and string orchestra. *Moog, clarinet; Freund, bassoon; Chamber Soloists of the Rheinland-Pfalz State Phil.; Concertino Filarmonico; Segerstam, cond.*
- Fa 9-10/88: 272

31450. SIGX 19-00: VILLA-LOBOS—Chôros no. 7; Quintette en forme de chôros; Chôros no. 2; Two chôros for violin and cello; Fantasie concertante. *Chamber Soloists of the Rhineland-Pfalz State Phil.*
+ ARG 7-8/90: 121
+ Fa 7-8/90: 307
+ MA 11/90: 81

31451. SIGX 20-00: RYBA—Bohemian shepherds' mass. *Münzel, Pegelow, Kruse, Grundheber; Hamburg Boys Choir; Chamber Orch. St. Nikolai; Richter, cond.*
- ARG 11-12/90: 107
+ Fa 3-4/90: 279
+ Fa 3-4/94: 299

31452. SIGX 21-00: *Magic French flute.* FRANCK—Violin sonata in A major (arr. for flute). POULENC—Flute sonata. DUTILLEUX—Flute sonatine. *Gérard, flute; Killian, piano.*
- ARG 7-8/90: 50
+ ARG 5-6/94: 175

31453. SIGX 22-00: *Rarities for double bass.* Music of Hoffmeister, Findeisen, Sperger, and Bottesini. *Dzwiza, double bass; Rüssmann, violin; Fukai, viola; Seiler, cello; Koster, horn; Pollet, soprano; Dutilly, piano.*
+ ARG 5-6/94: 175
+ Fa 5-6/94: 314

31454. SIGX 24-00: WEBER—Trio for flute, cello and piano; Flute sonatas, op. 10 no. 2, 5-6. *Gérard, flute; Lechler, piano; Schmidt, cello.*
- Fa 3-4/94: 264

31455. SIGX 26-00: REGER—Organ music. *Wunderlich, organ.*
+ ARG 5-6/94: 129

31456. SIGX 38-00: REGER—Viola suites, op. 131. HINDEMITH—Solo viola sonata. *Fukai, viola.*
- ARG 5-6/94: 130

31457. SIGX 39-00: L. BOULANGER—Songs. *Ott, soprano; Lemaire, piano; Quartetto di Lugano; Antonini, cond.*
- ARG 3-4/94: 79
+ Fa 3-4/94: 142

31458. SIGX 40-00: BLACHER—Symphony; Violin concerto; Poem for large orchestra. *K. Blacher, violin; Frankfurt an der Oder Phil. Orch.; Athinäos, cond.*
+ ARG 3-4/94: 78

+ ARG 7-8/94: 76
+ Fa 3-4/94: 137

31459. SIGX 41-00: Music of Paganini, Ponce, Brouwer, and Villa-Lobos. *Hoppstock, guitar.* Reissue.
+ ARG 9-10/94: 235

31460. SIGX 42-00: Music of Bach, Froberger, and Buxtehude. *Hoppstock, guitar.* Reissue.
- ARG 9-10/94: 235

31461. SIGX 43-00: Music of Granados, Ponce, Castelnuovo-Tedesco, Brouwer, and Piazzolla. *Gruber, Maklar, guitars.*
+ ARG 9-10/94: 237

31462. SIGX 44-00: DVOŘÁK—Terzetto. KODÁLY—Serenade. TANEEV—String trio. BRIDGE—Rhapsody. *Japan String Trio.*
+ Fa 3-4/94: 177

31463. SIGX 45-00: Music of Bottesini, Vanhal, and Bock. *Stoll, Dzwiza, double basses; Mehne, violin; Solothurski, viola; Langenstein, Stobart, horns.*
+ ARG 5-6/94: 175

31464. SIGX 46-00: Music of Beethoven, M. Haydn, Romberg, Rossini, and Sperger. *Fukai, viola; Stoppel, cello; Dzwiza, double bass.*
+ ARG 5-6/94: 175

31465. SIGX 48-00: CHOPIN—Cello sonata. BRAHMS—Cello sonata no. 2. *Schmidt, cello; Lechler, piano.*
- Fa 3-4/94: 164

31466. SIGX 49-00: Music of Praetorius, Gibbons, Bach, Robinson, Dowland, and Visée. *Folkwang Guitar Duo.*
+ ARG 9-10/94: 235

31467. SIGX 50-00: RHEINBERGER—Wallenstein; Sieben Raben overture. *Frankfurt an der Oder Phil. Orch.; Athinäos, cond.*
- ARG 9-10/94: 181
+ Fa 9-10/94: 309

31468. SIGX 52-00: *One woman tango.* Music of Strobl, Kupperman, Gruger, Malfatti, Berio, and Janarcekova. *Ascher, mezzo-soprano & percussion.*
- Fa 7-8/95: 380

31469. SIGX 53-00: Music of Michel, Blacher, Koetsier, Clarke, and Bolling. *Trio Troppo Piano.*
+ ARG 9-10/95: 254
+ Fa 7-8/95: 439

31470. SIGX 54-00: LEKEU—Piano trio. JONGEN—Pieces for piano trio. *Clara Wieck Trio.*
+ ARG 1-2/95: 131

31471. SIGX 55-00: BACH—Trio sonata, BWV 529; French suite no. 2; Suite, BWV 1006a; Sonata, BWV 1020. VISÉE—Suite in C minor. VIVALDI—

Sonata. *Zipperling, cello, cello piccolo, viola da gamba; Hoppstock, guitar.*
+ ARG 5-6/95: 73

31472. SIGX 57-00: EINEM—Symphonic scenes; Tanz-Rondo; Vienna symphony. *Frankfurt an der Oder Phil. Orch.; Athinäos, cond.*
+ ARG 5-6/95: 108
+ Fa 3-4/95: 331

31473. SIGX 60-00: RHEINBERGER—Overture to Shakespeare's The taming of the shrew; The vally of the Espingo; Fantasy, op. 79; Overture to Schiller's Demetrius; Hymn to music; Academic overture. *Phil. Orch. of Frankfurt (Oder); Chorus of St. Hedwigs Cathedral Berlin; Athinäos, cond.*
- ARG 7-8/95: 179
• Fa 7-8/95: 291

31474. SIGX 65-00: DESSAU—Symphony no. 1; Mozart adaptation; The voices. *Lukic, soprano; Göbel, piano; Frankfurt (Oder) State Orch.; Athinäos, cond.*
• ARG 1-2/96: 101

31475. SIGX 73-00: BLACHER—Songs. *Wosnitsa, Richter, sopranos; Köler, baritone; Göbel, piano.*
□ ARG 1-2/97: 75

SILVA

31476. 1011: *British film music.* Music of Vaughan Williams, Easdale, Schurmann, and Bliss. *Philharmonia Orch.; Alwyn, cond.*
+ ARG 11-12/92: 234

31477. 1023: Music of Handel, Orff, Massenet, Weill, Puccini, Flotow, and others. *Garrett, soprano; Philharmonia Orch.; Boulton, cond.*
+ ARG 9-10/93: 254

SILVA CLASSICS

31478. SILVAD 3002: Jerome Kern collection. *Parkin, piano.*
+ Gr 3/95: 72

31479. SILKD 6001: *Lament.* Music of Stravinsky, Alvarez, Matthews, Szmanski, and others. *Fernandez, soprano; Costello, singer; Brodsky Quartet; Monks, cello; Scully, double bass.*
+ Gr 10/94: 150

31480. SILKCD 6004: *Simple gifts.* Music of Handel, Delibes, Boyce, Massenet, Cilea, Gounod, and others. *Garrett, soprano; Royal Phil. Orch.; Robinson, cond.*
+ Gr 4/95: 128

31481. SILKCD 6005: Arias from Fedora, Elisir d'amore, Traviata, Magic flute, and others. *Beltran, tenor; Royal Phil. Orch.; Stapleton, cond.*

- ARG 11-12/96: 272
• Op 1/96: 122

31482. SILKCD 6007: COWARD—Ballet music: The grand tour; London morning. *City of Prague Phil. Orch.; White, cond.*
+ Fa 3-4/96: 151
+ Fi 3/96: 126

31483. SILKCD 6008: *Soprano in red.* Music of Romberg, J. Strauss, Jr., Offenbach, Novello, Chabrier, Lehár, Coward, Heuberger, and Sullivan. *Garrett, soprano; Royal Phil. Concert Orch.; Holmes, cond.*
• Fa 3-4/96: 324
+ Gr 2/96: 107
+ Op 4/96: 477

31484. SILKCD 6009: Songs from Spain, Chile, Sweden, and Italy. *Beltran, tenor; Royal Phil. Orch.; Stapleton, cond.*
+ ARG 11-12/96: 272

31485. SILKCD 6010: *Meeting point.* Music of Heath, Wilson, Torke, McGlynn, and Nyman. *McChrystal, saxophone; London Musici; Stevenson, cond.*
+ ARG 1-2/97: 204
+ Fa 9-10/96: 448
+ Gr 6/96: 62

31486. SILKCD 6011: RÓZSA—Cello concerto. SCHURMANN—The gardens of exile. *P. Rejto, cello; Pécs Symphony Orch.; Williams, cond.*
+ ARG 11-12/96: 191
+ Fa 11-12/96: 352
+ Gr 9/96: 59

31487. SILKCD 6012: MOZART—String quartet no. 17 "The hunt"; Adagio and fugue, K. 546. HAYDN—String quartet, op. 54, no. 2. *Brodsky Quartet.*
• Fa 1-2/97: 214
• Gr 11/96: 106

SILVA SCREEN

31488. SONGCD 906 : COPLAND—Piano music. *Parkin, piano.*
+ Gr 8/93: 58

SIMAX

31489. PSC 1007: MARCHAND—Harpsichord works: Book 1 in D minor; Book 2 in G minor. *Haugsand, harpsichord.*
• Fa 1-2/89: 110
+ HF 5/89: 70
• St 7/89: 168

31490. PSC 1008: *Hommage!* Music of Kucera, Hvoslef, Duarte, Castérède, and Brouwer. *Olsen, guitar.*
+ ARG 3-4/89: 113

31491. PSC 1010: *Romantic flute and harp.* Music of C.P.E. Bach, Rossini, Chopin, Nielsen, Ibert, Jongen, Fauré, Sønstevold, Debussy, Ravel, and Saint-

Saëns. *Øien, flute; Sønstevold, harp.* Reissue.
+ Fa 5-6/93: 380

31492. PSC 1011: GRIEG—Six poems by Ibsen op. 25; Poems by Krag op. 60; Haugtussa op. 67. *Andersen, soprano; Bratlie, piano.*
+ ARG 3-4/88: 40
- Fa 1-2/88: 133

31493. PSC 1014: SHOSTAKOVICH—Trios for piano and strings no. 1-2; Three fantastic dances op. 5. *Bratlie, piano; Oslo Trio.*
+ ARG 1-2/88: 61
+ Fa 11-12/87: 227

31494. PSC 1018: Music of Mozart, Schubert (arr.), and Cahuzac. *Bonden, clarinet; Tomter, viola; Smebye, piano.*
+ ARG 11-12/89: 91

31495. PSC 1019: Music of Falla, Montsalvatge, Dvořák, and Ravel. *Thallaug, mezzo; Knardahl, piano; Bye, flute; Kvalbein, cello.*
• Fa 3-4/87: 247

31496. PS 1020 (LP): PAGANINI—Twenty-four caprices for solo violin. *Milanova, violin.*
• Fa 9-10/87: 261

31497. PSC 1021: BRAHMS—Piano sonata no. 1; Fantasies op. 116; Intermezzi op. 117 . *Knardahl, piano.*
+ Fa 9-10/87: 169

31498. PSC 1022: Music of Mozart, Carlstedt, and Britten. *Zubicky, oboe; Tonnesen, violin; Tomter, viola; Mørk, cello.*
+ ARG 1-2/88: 49
+ Fa 11-12/87: 184

31499. PSC 1023: Music of Nordheim, Crumb, Lidholm, and Kodály. *Mørk, cello.*
+ ARG 7-8/88: 82
• Fa 1-2/88: 266

31500. PSC 1024: BACH—Viola da gamba sonatas. *Dreyfus, viola da gamba; Haugsand, harpsichord.*
+ Fa 3-4/87: 66

31501. PSC 1026: Music of Hindemith, Schoenberg, and Mortensen. *Veselka, violin; Dratvová, piano.*
+ Fa 1-2/91: 218

31502. PSC 1027: GRIEG—Four hymns; Two religous choirs; Album for male voices op. 30. *Bjørkøy, baritone; Malmö Chamber Choir; Stenlund, cond.*
+ Fa 1-2/88: 133

31503. PSC 1029: BRAHMS—Cello sonatas (complete); Songs (arr. for cello): Liebestreu; Wiegenlied; Minnelied; Feldeinsamkeit; Sapphische Ode; Wie melodien zieht es mir; Immer leiser wird

mein Schlummer. *Mørk, cello; Lagerspetz, piano.*
+ ARG 5-6/89: 27
• Fa 3-4/89: 120
+ Gr 8/89: 324

31504. PSC 1030: BACH—English suite no. 1; French suite no. 5; Cantata BWV 29: Sinfonia (arr. Kempff); Chromatic fantasy & fugue BWV 903; Suite in F minor (fragment); Sarabande & gigue BWV 823. *Riefling, piano.*
+ ARG 1-2/88: 13
+ Fa 1-2/88: 77

31505. PSC 1031: Music of Duarte, Kvandal, Bibalo, and Britten. *Olsen, guitar.*
• ARG 11-12/88: 104
+ Fa 9-10/88: 332
+ Gr 9/88: 454

31506. PSC 1032: BACH—Italian concerto; Partita in B minor BWV 831; Sonata in D minor BWV 964 (after BWV 1003); Adagio in G BWV 968 (after BWV 1005). *Haugsand, harpsichord.*
• ARG 3-4/89: 17
• Fa 9-10/88: 88
+ Gr 9/88: 44

31507. PSC 1033: *Nordic contemporary songs.* Music of Valen, Morad Johansen, Nyström, De Frumerie, and Rautavaara. *Maeland, soprano; Hjelseth, piano.*
+ ARG 3-4/89: 119
+ Fa 1-2/89: 280

31508. PSC 1034: *Contemporary church music from Scandinavia.* Music of Nystedt, Hovland, Kverno, Holmboe, and Hambraeus. *Nordstoga, organ; Oslo Cathedral Choir; Kvam, cond.*
+ Fa 7-8/88: 302

31509. PSC 1035: Music of Britten, Mozart, and Tchaikovsky. *Norwegian Chamber Orch.; Brown, cond.*
+ ARG 11-12/89: 146
+ Fa 5-6/89: 152
+ Gr 1/89: 1146
+ HPR 6/89: 81

31510. PSC 1036: PROKOFIEV—Piano sonata no. 6. SHOSTAKOVICH—Piano sonata no. 2 op. 64. *Plagge, piano.*
+ ARG 11-12/89: 97
+ Fa 9-10/89: 285 (Prokofiev)
• Fa 9-10/89: 285 (Shostakovich)
• Gr 10/89: 707

31511. PSC 1037: MOZART—Serenade no. 12. KVANDAL—Nonets for winds & double bass: op. 54, 57. *Norwegian Wind Ensemble.*
+ ARG 3-4/89: 51
+ Fa 3-4/89: 226
+ Gr 7/89: 200

31512. PSC 1038: BACH—Nun komm der Heiden Heiland, BWV 659-661; Canonic variations on Vom Himmel hoch, BWV 769; Schübler Chorale preludes, BWV

645-650; Preludes & fuges, BWV 541, 547; Pastorale, BWV 590. *Haga, organ.*
• Fa 1-2/89: 106

31513. PSC 1039: Music of Ore, Stockhausen, Dallapiccola, Mainardi, and others. *Ianke, double bass.*
+ ARG 7-8/90: 133
+ Fa 3-4/90: 373

31514. PSC 1040: GRIEG—Slatter op. 72. *Buen, Hardanger fiddle; Steen-Nøkleberg, piano.*
+ ARG 9-10/89: 57
+ Fa 7-8/89: 155

31515. PSC 1044/45 (2 discs): BACH—Well-tempered clavier book 1. *Riefling, piano.*
+ ARG 7-8/89: 13
+ DA 11/89: 64
+ Fa 7-8/89: 70

31516. PSC 1046/47 (2 discs): BACH—Well-tempered clavier book 2. *Riefling, piano.*
+ ARG 7-8/89: 13
+ Fa 7-8/89: 70

31517. PSC 1048: BEETHOVEN—Piano sonatas no. 18, 32. *Riefling, piano.*
+ ARG 7-8/89: 13

31518. PSC 1049: Music of A. Marcello, Scarlatti (arr. Bryan), and Albinoni. *Hoff, oboe; English Chamber Orch.; Watson, cond.*
+ ARG 7-8/90: 140
+ Fa 3-4/90: 376
+ Gr 2/90: 1471

31519. PSC 1050: VIERNE—Organ symphonies no. 1, 4. *Boysen, organ.*
+ ARG 11-12/94: 206
+ Fa 1-2/95: 191

31520. PSC 1051: *Liederkreis.* SCHUMANN—Liederkreis op. 24; Zwei venetianische Lieder op. 25. WOLF—Songs. *Vollestad, baritone; Hjelseth, piano.*
• ARG 1-2/90: 107
+ Fa 11-12/89: 436
+ Gr 11/89: 956

31521. PSC 1052: *Contemporary music for soprano and cello.* Music of Wilson, Sommerfeldt, Fontyn, Gershwin, and others. *Dorow, soprano; Kvalbein, cello.*
+ Fa 3-4/90: 348
+ Gr 4/90: 1858

31522. PSC 1053: MARAIS—Suites for viola da gamba and harpsichord in E minor, in B minor, Les folies d'Espagne, from Pièces de violes, livre 2. *Dreyfus, viola da gamba; Haugsand, harpsichord.*
+ ARG 5-6/90: 70
+ Fa 3-4/90: 222

31523. PSC 1055: SCRIABIN—Piano sonatas no. 1, 4-5, 7, 9. *Austbö, piano.*

+ Fa 7-8/90: 266
+ Gr 5/90: 2016

31524. PSC 1056: SCRIABIN—Piano sonatas no. 2-3, 6, 8, 10. *Austbö, piano.*
- Fa 7-8/91: 286
+ HPR v.8, no. 3/91: 83

31525. PSC 1057: Music of Deslandres, Grovlez, Saint-Saëns, Dutilleux, and Poulenc. *Zubicky, oboe; Hirvonen, piano; Hanniscal, bassoon.*
+ ARG 7-8/90: 140
+ Fa 3-4/90: 376

31526. PSC 1058: FRANCK—Violin sonata. CHAUSSON—Piece, op. 39. DEBUSSY—Cello sonata. POULENC—Cello sonata. *Mørk, cello; Austbo, piano.*
+ Fa 1-2/92: 408

31527. PSC 1059: BRAHMS—Rhapsodies op. 79; Variations and fugue on a theme by Handel; Klavierstücke op. 118. *Knardahl, piano.*
+ Fa 9-10/90: 194

31528. PSC 1060: PROKOFIEV—Piano concerto no. 3; Symphony no. 7. *Andsnes, piano; Bergen Symphony Orch.; Ruud, cond.*
+ Fa 1-2/91: 277

31529. PSC 1062: HALVORSEN—Symphonies no. 2-3. *Trondheim Symphony Orch.; Ruud, cond.*
+ ARG 3-4/91: 73
+ Fa 3-4/91: 229

31530. PSC 1064: Music of Strauss, Martinů, and Françaix. *Zubicky, oboe; Scottish Chamber Orch.; Saraste, cond.*
+ Fa 1-2/91: 324

31531. PSC 1065: *Norwegian contemporary percussion music.* Music of Hegdal, Kruse, Sommerfeldt, Samkopf, Christensen. *Various performers.*
□ Fa 3-4/92: 168

31532. PSC 1066: MOZART—Piano sonatas, no. 1-5. *Glaser, piano.*
+ Fa 9-10/91: 296

31533. PSC 1067: *Children's corner.* Music of Grovlez, Severac, Ibert and Debussy. *Katin, piano.*
+ ARG 5-6/92: 168
+ Fa 3-4/92: 403
+ Gr 7/93: 68

31534. PSC 1068: Music of Rachmaninoff, Metner, and Balakirev. *Hill, piano.*
• Fa 1-2/91: 281

31535. PSC 1069: MENDELSSOHN—Piano trios no. 1-2. *Grieg Trio.*
- ARG 9-10/92: 130
+ Fa 7-8/92: 218

31536. PSC 1070: Saeverud—*Saeverud amoroso.* Piano pieces. *Kayser, piano.*
+ ARG 7-8/92: 209
+ Fa 9-10/91: 330

31537. PSC 1071: Schubert—Lieder. *Vollestad, baritone; Hjelseth, piano.*
• ARG 5-6/92: 125
+ Fa 3-4/92: 310
+ Gr 9/92: 152

31538. PSC 1072: Franck—Trois chorales; Grand pièce symphonique. *Nordstoga, organ.*
+ ARG 7-8/93: 90
+ Fa 7-8/93: 138

31539. PSC 1073: Widor—Symphonies no. 5-6. *Nordstoda, organ.*
+ ARG 7-8/93: 180
+ Fa 7-8/93: 138

31540. PSC 1074: Music of Hindemith, Arutyunian, Plagge, Berg, Ives, and Andresen. *Arctic Brass.*
+ ARG 3-4/94: 199
+ Fa 5-6/94: 337

31541. PSC 1076: Grieg—Songs with orchestra. *Vollestad, baritone; Lithuanian National Symphony Orch.; Mikkelsen, cond.*
+ Fa 1-2/95: 166

31542. PSC 1078: Haydn—Cello concertos in C and D. *Mørk, cello; Norwegian Chamber Orch.; Brown, cond.*
+ ARG 11-12/92: 131
+ Gr 8/92: 32

31543. PSC 1079: *Music from nineteenth-century Vienna for guitar and fortepiano.* Music of Giuliani, Hummel, Diabelli, and Beethoven. *Stenstadvold, guitar; Blewett, fortepiano.*
+ Fa 7-8/93: 295

31544. PSC 1080: Sonstevold—Wind quintets no. 1-2; Duet for flute and oboe; Rose in a paper twist. *E. Sønstevold, harp; Stockholm Phil. Wind Quintet.*
+ ARG 3-4/95: 192
+ Fa 3-4/95: 302

31545. PSC 1081: Schubert—Sonata for violin and piano, D. 384. Smetana—From my homeland. Bloch—Baal shem: Nigun. Grieg—Sonata no. 2 for violin and piano. Svendsen—Romance, op. 26. *Thorsen, violin; Larsen, piano.*
+ Fa 3-4/93: 382

31546. PSC 1082: *Piano recital.* Music of Albéniz, Barber, Liszt, and Gershwin. *Knardahl, piano.*
• ARG 1-2/97: 211
+ Fa 11-12/96: 463

31547. PSC 1084: *Songs and dances.* Music of Dyens, Sainz de la Maza, Piazolla, Koshkin, Duarte and others. *Olsen, guitar.*

- ARG 11-12/92: 239
+ Fa 7-8/92: 345

31548. PSC 1085: Svendsen—Norwegian rhapsodies no. 1-4. Halvorsen—Norwegian rhapsodies no. 1-2. *Trondheim Symphony Orch.; Ruud, cond.*
+ ARG 11-12/92: 217
+ Fa 7-8/92: 302

31549. PSC 1086: Bach—Partitas. *Haugsand, harpsichord.*
+ ARG 1-2/95: 70
+ Fa 3-4/95: 113
• Gr 1/95: 72

31550. PSC 1087: Saeverud—Violin concerto; Romanza for violin and orchestra; Small duets for violins; Elegie. *T. Saeverud, Dalsgaard, violins; Sonder Jutland Orch.; Andersen, cond.*
+ ARG 7-8/94: 164
+ Fa 3-4/94: 299

31551. PSC 1088: Music of Lindberg, Hovhaness, Eben, and Sommerfeldt. *Kvebæk, trumpet; Nordstoga, organ.*
+ ARG 3-4/94: 215
• Fa 3-4/94: 414

31552. PSC 1089: Grieg—Songs. *Vollestad, baritone; Hjelseth, piano.*
+ ARG 9-10/93: 128
+ Fa 7-8/93: 145
+ Fa 9-10/93: 170

31553. PSC 1090: Weill—Concerto for violin, wind instruments and percussion, op. 12. Berg—Chamber concerto for piano, violin and 13 wind instruments. *Aadland, violin; Smebye, piano; Norwegian Wind Ensemble; Ruud, cond.*
+ ARG 7-8/93: 180
• Fa 5-6/93: 356
+ Gr 8/93: 42

31554. PSC 1091: Grieg—Symphony in C minor; Symphonic dances. *Lithuanian State Phil. Symphony Orch.; Mikkelsen, cond.*
• Gr 5/93: 44

31555. PSC 1093: Handel—Recorder sonatas. *Thorsen, recorder; Sveen, harpsichord & organ; Odriozola, cello.*
+ Fa 3-4/95: 181

31556. PSC 1094: Ibert—Trois pièces brèves. Reicha—Wind quintet, op. 88, no. 2. Arnold—Three shanties. Klughardt—Wind quintet, op. 79. Saeverud—Wind quintet no. 2. *Bergen Wind Quintet.*
+ ARG 11-12/93: 245
+ Fa 9-10/93: 376

31557. PSC 1095: Rameau—Pièces de clavecin en concerts. *Mackintosh, violin; Dreyfus, viola da gamba; Haugsand, harpsichord.*
+ ARG 1-2/95: 159
+ Fa 5-6/95: 305
+ Gr 6/94: 76

31558. PSC 1096: *Classical accordion.* Music of Stravinsky, Holmboe, Lorentzen, Mossenmark, and others. *Draugsvoll, Crabb, accordion.*
+ ARG 1-2/95: 217

31559. PSC 1097: Svendsen—Octet, op. 3; Romance for violin and orchestra; I fjol gjaett'e gjeitinn; Swedish folk tunes, op. 27; Icelandic folk tunes, op. 30. Schumann (arr. Svendsen)—Abendlied. *Kraggerud, violin; Risor Festival Strings; Tomter, cond.*
+ ARG 3-4/95: 198
+ Fa 3-4/95: 316

31560. PSC 1101: *Oystein Baadsvik, tuba.* Music of Hindemith, Madsen, Sivelöv, Craft, and Gaathaug. *Baadsvik, tuba; Sivelöv, piano; Swedish Brass Quintet.*
+ ARG 7-8/94: 219
+ Fa 5-6/94: 329

31561. PSC 1102: Grieg—Norwegian folk songs, op. 66 (selections); Norwegian peasant dances, op. 72 (selections). *Botnen, piano; Hamre, Hardanger fiddle; Horvei, singer.*
+ ARG 1-2/94: 106
+ Fa 11-12/93: 250

31562. PSC 1103: Bibalo—Piano "solo" in the evening; Miniatures; Four Balkan dances; Trois hommages; Toccata; Piano sonatas no. 1-2. *Brunsvik, piano.*
+ Fa 9-10/96: 154

31563. PSC 1105: Valen—Piano pieces, op. 22; Variations, op. 23; Gavotte and musette, op. 24; Intermezzo, op. 36. Thoresen—Four variations in memoriam Fartein Valen; Arise!; Solspill/Sun glitter; Stages of the inner dialog. *Torgersen, piano.*
+ Fa 3-4/96: 308

31564. PSC 1107: Grieg—Piano concerto; Lyric pieces. *Knardahl, piano; Lithuanian National Symphony Orch.; Mikkelsen, cond.*
• ARG 1-2/96: 118
+ Fa 11-12/95: 265

31565. PSC 1109: Tchaikovsky—Symphony no. 5. *Ukrainian National Symphony Orch.; Mikkelsen, cond.*
+ ARG 3-4/95: 203
+ Fa 3-4/95: 319

31566. PSC 1110: Alnæs—Songs. *Arensen, soprano; Eriksen, piano.*
+ ARG 11-12/94: 61

31567. PSC 1114: Nystedt—String quartets no. 2-4; No. 5 (third movement only). *Oslo String Quartet.*
+ ARG 11-12/95: 169
+ Fa 11-12/95: 325
+ Fa 1-2/96: 272

31568. PSC 1115: *Quasi una sonata: a variety of twentieth century violin music.*

SIMAX

Music of Szymanowski, Penderecki, Hvoslef, and Schnittke. *Jung, violin; Smebye, piano.*
+ ARG 3-4/96: 238
+ Fa 11-12/95: 478

31569. PSC 1116 (3 discs): SAEVERUD—The complete piano music. *Rottingen, piano.*
+ Fa 11-12/96: 355

31570. PSC 1118: Music of Dutilleux, Jolivet, Messiaen, Martinů, and Mortensen. *Øien, flute; Botnen, piano.*
• ARG 9-10/95: 259

31571. PSC 1119: L'HOYER—Music for 2 guitars. *Stenstadvold, Haug, guitars.*
+ ARG 5-6/95: 130
+ Fa 5-6/95: 241

31572. PSC 1120: GRIEG—Songs. DELIUS—Songs. GRAINGER—Songs. *Aambo, mezzo-soprano; Johnson, piano.*
• ARG 7-8/96: 273
+ Fa 5-6/96: 160

31573. PSC 1121: TVEITT—Two-part inventions, op. 1; Piano sonata no. 29; Danse du dieu soleil. *Bohnen, piano.*
+ Fa 1-2/96: 331

31574. PSC 1128: NIELSEN—String quartets no. 1-2. *Vertavo String Quartet.*
+ ARG 7-8/96: 164
+ Fa 5-6/96: 226

31575. PSC 1133: *Edvard Grieg in Hardanger.* GRIEG—Piano music. *Botnen, Bratlie, piano.*
+ ARG 1-2/97: 116
+ Fa 11-12/96: 258

31576. PSC 1805: TVEITT—Piano concerto no. 3; Piano sonata no. 29; Aeolean harp; Sillages phospherescants. *Tveitt, piano; Bergen Phil. Orch.; Wolff, cond.* Reissues.
+ ARG 3-4/95: 274
+ Fa 3-4/95: 322

31577. PSC 1809: GRIEG—The piano music in historic interpretations. *Various pianists.*
+ ARG 7-8/93: 210
+ Fa 5-6/93: 216
+ Gr 6/93: 108

31578. PSC 1810 (3 discs): GRIEG—The vocal music in historic interpretations. *Various performers.* Recorded 1888-1924.
+ ARG 3-4/94: 233
+ Fa 11-12/93: 254
+ Gr 4/94: 125

31579. PSC 1821 (3 discs): *Kirsten Flagstad, vol. 1.* The early recordings, 1914-1941. *Flagstad, soprano; various accs.* Recorded 1914-41.
+ ARG 5-6/96: 274
+ Fa 1-2/96: 353

+ Gr 12/95: 176
+ ON 8/96: 45

31580. PSC 2131 (2 discs): BRÆIN—Anne Pedersdotter. *Ekeberg, Carlsen, Hanssen, Sandve; Norwegian Opera; Andersson, cond.*
+ ARG 5-6/94: 72

31581. PSC 3101 (2 discs): VALEN—Symphonies no. 1-4. *Bergen Phil. Orch.; Ceccato, cond.* Reissues.
+ Fa 5-6/93: 343
+ Gr 8/93: 41

31582. PSC 3105: HALL—Verlaine suite; Julius Caesar suite; Suite for wind quintet; Four tosseriers; Little dance suite for winds. *Kringleborn, soprano; Bergen Wind Quintet; Norwegian Broadcasting Orch.; Eggen, cond.*
□ ARG 1-2/91: 53
+ Fa 1-2/91: 205

31583. PSC 3106: KLEVEN—Lotusland; Sleeping forest; Violin sonata. *Böhn, violin; Braaten, piano; Norwegian Broadcasting Orch.; Eggen, cond.*
- Fa 5-6/91: 197 (Sonata)
+ Fa 5-6/91: 197 (others)

31584. PSC 3107: JORDAN—Fever poems; Holberg silhouettes; Toward the peaks; No birds sing; Spring song; Young Aslaug; Morning; Thirteen years old; Lullaby; Concerto piccolo for piano in F. *Maurstad, speaker; Lövaas, soprano; Bratlie, piano; Bergen Symphony Orch.; Andersen, cond.*
+ Fa 5-6/91: 192

31585. PSC 3109 (2 discs): JENSEN—Heimferd. *Bolstad, Gilhuus, Stabell, Vollestad; Trondheim Symphony Orch.; Ruud, cond.*
+ ARG 11-12/94: 135
+ Fa 11-12/94: 262
+ ON 4/15/95: 36

31586. PSC 3111: GROVEN—Piano concerto; Symphony no. 2. *Plagge, piano; Trondheim Symphony Orch.; Rund, cond.*
+ ARG 7-8/94: 108
+ Fa 5-6/94: 155

31587. PSC 3115: VALEN—Pastorale; Le cimetière marin; Sonetto di Michelangelo; Nenia; Cantico di ringraziamento; La isla de las calmas; Ode to solitude; Ave Maria; Zwei chinesische Gedichte; Darest thou now, o soul; Die dunkle Nacht der Seele. *Dorow, soprano; Oslo Phil. Orch.; Caridis, cond.*
+ ARG 7-8/93: 172
• Fa 7-8/93: 260
+ Gr 6/93: 56

31588. PSC 3116: VALEN—Violin concerto; Epithalamion; An die Hoffnung; Piano concerto; Piano trio; Serenade for 5 wind instruments. *Various*

performers.
+ Fa 11-12/95: 408

31589. PSC 3117: BRAEIN—Overture; Capriccio for piano and orchestra; Concertino for flute; Serenade; The merry musicians; Seawards. *Various performers.* Reissue.
+ ARG 5-6/94: 73
+ Fa 3-4/94: 143

31590. PSC 3118: JENSEN—Theme and variations; Symphony in D minor; Japanese spring. *Langebo, soprano; Oslo Phil. Orch.; Grüner-Hegge, Fjeldstad, conds.* Reissues.
+ ARG 5-6/94: 103

31591. PSC 3119: JOHANSEN—Pan; Symphonic variations and fugue; Scenes from Nordland; Two portraits from the Middle Ages; From Gudbrandsdalen; Prillar-Guri. *Bratlie, piano; Bergen Phil. Orch.; Andersen, cond.*
+ Fa 11-12/95: 312

31592. PSC 3120: KIELLAND—Sinfonia no. 1; Villarkorn. *Knardahl, piano; Royal Phil. Orch.; Keilland, cond.*
+ ARG 7-8/94: 121

SINE QUA NON

31593. 39820212 (2 discs): PUCCINI—La fanciulla del West. *Jones, Murgu, Otelli, Ombuena; Frankfurt Radio Symphony Orch.; Viotti, cond.*
• Gr 1/94: 96

SIPARIO

31594. 27: BRAHMS—Clarinet sonatas; Clarinet trio. *Tirincanti, clarinet; Boni, cello; Deoriti, piano.*
- ARG 7-8/94: 81

31595. 28: PLEYEL—Quintet for flute, oboe and strings; Flute quartet; String sextet. *Ensemble Urs Mächler.*
• ARG 1-2/95: 153

SKARBO

31596. SK 1933: LANGLAIS—Organ music (with Gregorian chants). *Michel, mezzo-soprano; Kauffmann, organ; Schola St. Gregory, Mans.*
+ ARG 11-12/94: 141

31597. SK 3891: *Suite de danses pour piano.* Music of Roussel, Rameau, Ravel, and Bartók. *Ferey, piano.*
+ Fa 11-12/93: 492

31598. SK 3901: LEMELAND—Duo variations for viola and guitar; Fantasia for clarinet and guitar; Ys; Hommage à Albert Roussel; Variations; Musique nocturne for wind quintet; Scansions for solo oboe; Five pieces for solo clarinet. *Herrera, guitar; Dupouy, viola; Fontaine, clarinet; Casier, oboe; Paris Wind Quintet.*

+ ARG 3-4/94: 115
+ Fa 11-12/93: 293

31599. SK 3911: HARSANYI—The story of the little tailor. PROKOFIEV—Peter and the wolf. *Guiot, narrator; Orch. Symphonique du Mans; Gendille, cond.* Narrations in French.
+ Fa 11-12/93: 263

31600. SK 3913: LEMELAND—L'automne et ses envols d'étourneaux; L'hiver qui vient; American epitaph; Concertino grosso; Hommage à Jean Rivier. *Instrumental soloists; Ensemble Instrumental de Grenoble; Tardue, cond.*
+ ARG 3-4/94: 115
+ Fa 11-12/93: 293

31601. SK 3921: FAURÉ—Allegro symphonique. FRANCK—Variations symphoniques. MESSAGER—Symphony in A. *Ferey, piano; Orch. Symphonique du Mans; Gendille, cond.*
• ARG 3-4/94: 123
+ Fa 11-12/93: 235, 324

31602. SK 3922: LEMELAND—Concerto funèbre; Violin concertos no. 1-2. *Nicolas, violin; Orch. de Chambre National de Toulouse; Plasson, cond.*
+ ARG 3-4/94: 115
+ Fa 11-12/93: 293

31603. SK 3924: KOECHLIN—In search of Charles Koechlin: some noteworthy archive recordings. *Various performers.*
+ Fa 11-12/93: 286

31604. SK 3925: CHAMOUARD—Opalescence. MESSIAEN—Diptyque; Le banquet celeste; Apparition de l'eglise eternelle; Les enfants de dieu; Dieu parmi nous. *Imbert, organ.*
+ ARG 3-4/94: 84

31605. SK 3932: KOECHLIN—Ballade; The old house in the country; Preludes. *Ferey, piano.*
+ ARG 1-2/95: 127

31606. SK 3954: CHAMOUARD—Symphony no. 2; Halabja; The veils of silence. *Lamprecht, mezzo-soprano; Bayonne-Cote Basque Orch.; Delcroix, cond.*
+ ARG 11-12/95: 105

31607. SK 4941: CRAS—Music for violin and piano. *Nicolas, violin; Ferey, piano.*
+ ARG 1-2/97: 93

31608. SK 4952: LADMIRAULT—Violin sonata; Cello sonata; Clarinet sonata. *Daugareil, violin; Chiffoleau, cello; Lancelot, clarinet; Plantard, piano.*
+ ARG 9-10/95: 164

SKYLARK

31609. 8501: HAYDN—Piano sonatas no. 33, 53, 55-56. *Coop, piano.*
• ARG 7-8/90: 55

31610. 8801: MOZART—Fantasies K. 397, 457; Rondos K. 485, 511; Variations K. 455; Minuet K. 355; Gigue, K. 574; Piano sonata K. 282. *Coop, piano.*
+ ARG 3-4/90: 79
+ MA 9/90: 92

31611. 8802: BEETHOVEN—Variations for piano (Eroica); Piano sonata no. 30, 32. *Coop, piano.*
+ ARG 5-6/90: 26
+ MA 9/90: 92

SMITHSONIAN COLLECTION

31612. ND 033: GOTTSCHALK—Deuxième banjo; Solitude; La brise; Souvenir de la Havane; Le chant du Martyr; Manchega; La savane; Union. *Orkis, piano.*
• ARG 3-4/89: 38
+ Au 4/89: 128
+ Fa 1-2/89: 168
+ Fa 1-2/89: 169

31613. ND 034: SMETANA—Piano trio op. 15. DVOŘÁK—Piano trio no. 4 op. 90. *Castle Trio.*
+ ARG 5-6/89: 44
+ Fa 1-2/89: 271

31614. ND 035: CORELLI—Trio sonatas op. 3. *Smithsonian Chamber Players.*
+ ARG 9-10/89: 44
+ Fa 9-10/89: 184
+ SR 12/89: 148

31615. ND 036: BEETHOVEN—Piano trios no. 4-5. *Castle Trio.*
+ ARG 3-4/90: 27
+ Fa 9-10/89: 144

31616. RD 041: *The art of Roland Hayes: art songs, African-American spirituals.* Music of Quilter, Handel, Dowland, Schumann, Schubert, and others. *Hayes, tenor; Boardman, piano.*
+ ARG 7-8/90: 152
+ DA 10/90: 80
+ Fa 7-8/90: 334
+ NYT 4/15/90: H29
+ St 7/90: 179

31617. ND 0321-0324 (6 discs): *Early years through the Eroica.* BEETHOVEN—Symphonies no. 1-3; String quartet op. 18; Cello sonatas op. 5 no. 1-2. *Slowik, Kenneth; Weaver, fortepiano; Smithson String Quartet; Smithsonian Chamber Orch.; Schröder, cond.*
+ Fa 1-2/89: 121
+ HF 4/89: 61
• NYT 1/8/89: H27
+ St 8/89: 173

31618. ND 0381 (2 discs): BACH—St. John passion. *Thomas, Weaver, Ripley; Smithsonian Chamber Chorus & Players; Slowik, cond.*
+ Fa 7-8/90: 74

31619. ND 0382: BACH—Violin sonata and partitas. *Schröder, violin.*
+ Fa 7-8/90: 75

31620. ND 0383: BACH—Concerto in D minor BWV 974; Italian concerto BWV 971; Partita in B minor BWV 831. *Weaver, harpsichord.*
+ Fa 7-8/90: 71

SNEDEKER

31621. [no number]: *Musique de salon: 19th-century French music for horn and piano.* Music of Dauprat, Saint-Saëns, Gallay, Panseron, Bordogni, and Rossi. *Snedeker, natural horn; Willbanks, fortepiano; Seraphinoff, bass horn.*
+ ARG 1-2/97: 209

SOLARIS

31622. 10913: MEYERS—Meditation no. 5; Je vous chante; Elegiac melodies. BIBALO—Piano sonata no. 2; Solo violin sonata; Invenzione evolutiva. *Brunsvik, piano; Sponberg, violin; Zeppezauer, double bass.*
+ ARG 9-10/94: 163

SOLSTICE

31623. SOCD 10: LISZT—Mephisto waltzes no. 1-4; Bagatelle sans tonalité; Mephisto polka; Valses oubliées no. 1-4. *Setrak, piano.*
• Fa 3-4/87: 150

31624. SOCD 14: LANGLAIS—Salve Regina mass; Psalm 3; Chorales with trumpet; Motets. *Various boychoirs; Roger Delmotte Brass Ensemble; Paris Trombone Quartet.*
□ ARG 7-8/92: 161

31625. SOCD 17: BARIÉ—Organ music (complete). *Jehan, organ.*
+ Fa 9-10/95: 134

31626. SOCD 18: Piano sonatas of Dutilleux, Auric, and Jolivet. *Girod, piano.*
+ ARG 7-8/89: 10
+ ARG 7-8/89: 122
+ Fa 5-6/89: 180

31627. SOCD 34: GEMINIANI—Cello sonata op. 5. *Simpson, cello; Giardelli, continuo cello; Spieth, harpsichord.*
+ Fa 5-6/90: 168

31628. SOL 41 (LP): VIERNE—Messe solennelle op. 16; Sur le Rhin op. 54 no. 5; Tantum ergo op. 2; Ave verum op. 15; Ave Maria op. 3; Marche triomphale pour le centenaire de Napoleon op. 46. *Boys Choirs of Chartres Cathedral; St.e Chapelle and Ste. Marie d'Antony; Bardot, cond.*
+ Fa 11-12/86: 239

31629. SOL 45 (LP): ANONYMOUS—Codex Calixtinus. *Ensemble Venance Fortunat; Deschamps, cond.*
+ Fa 11-12/86: 264

SOLSTICE

31630. SOCD 47: SOLER—Harpsichord sonatas. *Spieth, harpsichord.*
+ Fa 3-4/87: 209

31631. SOCD 49—50 (2 separate discs): BACH—Partitas. *Stigliani, piano.*
• Fa 3-4/88: 66

31632. SOCD 51: SWEELINCK—Ballo del granduca; Engelsche fortuyn; Fantasia chromatica; Malle sijmen; Mein junges Leben hat ein End'; More palatino; Onder een linde groen; Pavana lachrimeae; Praeludium-Toccata in A minor; Ricercar; Toccatas. *Spieth, harpsichord.*
+ ARG 5-6/92: 143
+ Fa 3-4/88: 66

31633. SOCD 52: PIERNÉ—Piano concerto in C minor; Fantaisie-ballet for piano and orchestra; Bouton d'or: Suite de ballet; Ramuntcho: Suite no. 1. *Raës, piano; Jeune Orch. Symphonique de Douai; Vachey, cond.*
- ARG 11-12/88: 67
+ Fa 3-4/88: 171 m.f.

31634. SOCD 53: Music of Handel, Duvernoy, Labarre, Thomas, Hasselmans, and Andres. *Cagnon, horn; Cochereau, harp.*
• ARG 11-12/88: 105
+ Fa 9-10/88: 338 m.f.

31635. SOCD 54: ROSSI—Fifteen airs. *Ledroit, countertenor.*
+ Fa 5-6/89: 291

31636. SOCD 55: SCHUMANN—Piano concerto in A minor; Kinderszenen. RAVEL—Piano concerto in G. *Lefébure, piano; French Radio Phil. Orch.; Paray, cond.*
- ARG 3-4/92: 124
• Fa 5-6/89: 313 (Schumann)
+ Fa 5-6/89: 313 (Ravel)

31637. SOCD 56: BACH—Organ music. *Amade, organ.*
• Fa 7-8/89: 72

31638. SOCD 64: MENDELSSOHN—Organ sonatas no. 1-6, op. 65. *Amade, organ.*
- Fa 9-10/90: 293

31639. SOCD 65: BACH—Toccata in D BWV 912; Chromatic fantasy and fugue BWV 903; Partita no. 1 BWV 825; Preludes and fuges BWV 503 (trans. Liszt), 853; Chorales BWV 615 (trans. Busoni), 639; Jesu bleibet meine Freude BWV 147; Siciliene from BWV 596 (trans. Lefebure) . *Lefébure, piano.*
• Fa 3-4/88: 66

31640. SOCD 67: GRASSI—Prelude for string orchestra; Contrastes for clarinet and percussion; Three ésquisses for solo oboe; Pièce symphonique . *Ghiro, clarinet; Perez, percussion; Ognibene, oboe; Orch. de Chambre de Montéclair; Orch. symphonique des jeunes Arpege;*

Hui, Cochereau, conds.
+ Fa 11-12/90: 240

31641. SOCD 82: WEBER—Grand duo concertant, op. 48; Seven variations, op. 33; Clarinet quintet, op. 37; Introduction, theme, and variations, op. posth. *Faucomprez, clarinet; Raës, piano; Quartet Lalo.*
• Fa 7-8/94: 282

31642. SOLCD 83: SCRIABIN—Études (complete). J. SCRIABIN—Four preludes. *Setrak, piano.*
+ Fa 5-6/93: 320

31643. SOCD 84: RAVEL—Gaspard de la nuit. TCHAIKOVSKY—Theme and variations, op. 19. BABADJANIAN—Danse Vagarchabad; Élégie; Poème. STRAVINSKY—Tango. KHACHATURIAN—Toccata. *Mamikonian, piano.*
+ Fa 3-4/93: 371

31644. SOCD 85: COUPERIN—1st, 18th and 27th ordres. *Spieth, harpsichord.*
• Fa 3-4/93: 147

31645. SOLCD 86: LANGLAIS—Organ works. *Houbart, organ.*
□ Fa 5-6/93: 245

31646. SOCD 87/93 (7 discs): VILLA-LOBOS—The works for piano. *Schic, piano.* Reissue.
+ Fa 3-4/93: 318

31647. SOCD 94/96 (3 discs): *Pierre Cochereau: l'organiste de Notre-Dame.* Music of Bach, Franck, Messiaen, Dupré, De Lisle, and Cochereau. *Cochereau, organ.*
• Fa 3-4/93: 366

31648. SOCD 97: *En concert.* Music of Bach, Barber, Arnold, Boyce, Jevtic, Gershwin, and Waller. *Atlantic Brass Quintet.* Recorded live.
+ Fa 3-4/93: 389

31649. SOCD 98/99 (2 discs): SAUGUET—Les caprices de Marianne. *Esposito, Kolassi, Sénéchal, Maurane, Rondeleux; Orch. Radio-Lyrique; Rosenthal, cond.*
+ Fa 5-6/94: 234
+ Op 4/94: 502

31650. SOCD 100: WALDTEUFEL—Waltzes. *A. Sorel, piano.*
+ Fa 3-4/93: 329

31651. SOLCD 103: Voix de la Méditerranée médiévale. *Duo Wayal.*
+ Fa 7-8/93: 290

31652. SOCD 114: GERSHWIN—Piano music. *Schic, piano.*
- Fa 1-2/95: 163

31653. SOCD 115: WALDTEUFEL—Valses inédites. *Sorel, piano.*
• Fa 7-8/95: 364

31654. SOCD 116: *The great Cavaillé-Coll organ of the Basilica of St. Denis.* Music of Boëly, Saint-Saëns, Alkan, Chauvet, Franck, and Lefébure-Wély. *Pincemaille, organ.*
+ Fa 1-2/95: 353

31655. SOCD 119: CHAILLEY—A due violini; Rejoindre les étoiles; Solmisation. FASCE—Le monastre de la montagne de jade. *Ensemble Instrumental de la Mayenne; Gaugain, cond.*
□ Fa 1-2/95: 142

31656. SOCD 120: PHILIPPOT—Composition no. 2; Carrés magiques; Composition; Composition no. 4; Concerto pour violon, alt, et orchestre. *Schic, piano; Lautman, harp; Orch. de Chambre de l' O.R.T.F.; Girard, cond.; Ensemble Instrumental du Nouvel Orch. Philharmonique de Radio France; Vinogradov, cond.; Orch. National de la R.T.F.; Scherchen, cond.; Orch. Philharmonique de Radio France; Soudant, cond.; Bernède, violin; Laléouse, viola; Nouvel Orch. Philharmonique de Radio France; Chais, cond.*
□ Fa 7-8/95: 274

31657. SOCD 122/3 (2 discs): RAVEL—Piano music. *N'Kaoua, piano.*
+ Fa 7-8/95: 287

31658. SOCD 911/8 (8 discs): VIERNE—Complete organ works. *Cochereau, Baker, organs; Maîtrise de Notre-Dame de Paris; Coeurs de la Cathédrale; Revert, cond.*
+ Fa 1-2/95: 294
• Gr 2/96: 78

SOMM RECORDINGS

31659. SOMMCDPR 201: JANÁČEK—Male-voice choruses; Nursery rhymes. *Moravian Teachers' Choir; Tučapský, cond.; Czech Phil. Orch. & Chorus; Kühn, cond.* Reissue.
+ Gr 2/96: 88

31660. SOMMCD 205: TUČAPSKÝ—The sacrifice; Five lenten motets; Lauds; The seven sorrows. *Foulkes, baritone; Tulacek, violin; Hunt, organ; Bath Camerata; Perrin, cond.*
+ Gr 7/96: 91

SONATA

31661. 96080 (LP): Music of Barrios, Bach, Sainz de la Maza, and Britten. *Klee, guitar.*
+ Fa 11-12/86: 277

31662. 96082 (LP): Music of Rodrigo, Torroba, Falla, Sainz de la Maza, and others. *Klee, guitar.*
+ Fa 11-12/86: 277

31663. 96085 (LP): PONCE—Twenty-four guitar preludes; Tropics; Alborada;

Preludium; Mazurka; Rondino; Vespertina. *Klee, guitar.*
+ Fa 1-2/87: 157

SONG

31664. CD 903: *Diva! a soprano at the movies.* Music of Catalani, Delibes, Mozart, Gounod, Puccini, Dvořák, Canteloube, Rossini, Bizet/Hammerstein II, Offenbach, and Forrest/Wright. *Garrett, soprano; Philharmonia Orch.; Greenwood, cond.*
+ Gr 11/91: 165
+ Op 11/91: 1372

SONG LION PRODUCTIONS

31665. SLCD4-01 (4 discs): The greatest songs ever written, vol. 1. *White, tenor; various accs.*
+ Fa 7-8/96: 350

SONGBIRD

31666. AEACD 1401: Jewels of the Sephardim. *Pomerantz, voice, dulcimer; Higginson, recorders; Maund, percussion.*
+ Fa 7-8/94: 309
+ Fa 1-2/95: 343

31667. AEACD 1405: Wings of time. *Pomerantz, voice, dulcimer; Higginson, recorder, psaltery; Kammen, vielle, rebec; Maund, percussion.*
+ Fa 7-8/94: 309
+ Fa 1-2/95: 343

SONORA

31668. SACD 101: GUZMAN—Ambrosio. *Herrera, Lopez, Gorra, Sosa; La Camerata; García, cond.*
• ARG 5-6/93: 89
+ St 4/93: 281

31669. SO 22561 CD: LISZT—Inna Heifetz plays Liszt. *Heifetz, piano.*
• ARG 11-12/93: 140
+ Fa 11-12/93: 299
+ Fa 7-8/95: 426

31670. SO 22562 CD: Music of Tchaikovsky, Rachmaninoff, and Prokofiev. *I. Heifetz, piano.*
+ Fa 7-8/95: 425

31671. SO 22563 CD: TCHAIKOVSKY—Children's album. PROKOFIEV—Music for children. SHOSTAKOVICH—Dances of the dolls. *I. Heifetz, piano.*
• Fa 5-6/95: 357

31672. SO 22564 CD: *Concerto!* BACH—Two-piano concerto, BWV 1060; Piano concerto, BWV 1052; Italian concerto, BWV 971. *Heifetz, Zusman, pianos; Russian Chamber Orch.; Blank, cond.*
• ARG 7-8/95: 76
- Fa 5-6/95: 124

31673. SO 22565 CD: *The maiden's wish.* Music of Chopin-Liszt, Liszt, Tchaikovsky, Scriabin, Rachmaninoff, and Prokofiev. *I. Heifetz, piano.*
+ Fa 5-6/95: 411

31674. SO 22566 CD: *The revisionist's tale.* Music of Schnittke, Shostakovich, Glière, and Borodin. *Zusman, Heifetz, pianos.*
+ ARG 7-8/96: 255
+ Fa 1-2/96: 396

31675. SO 22567 CD: *Magic of the Russian flute.* Music of Gubaidulina, Denisov, Vasilenko, Sinisalo, Nagovitzin, and Taktakishvili. *L. Mironovich, flute; E. Mironovich, piano.*
+ Fa 9-10/95: 390

31676. SO 22569 CD: HAYDN—Piano sonatas no. 30, 34, 52-53. *Heifetz, piano.*
• Fa 1-2/97: 175

31677. SO 22570 CD: *The monogram.* RYABICHIKOVA—Piano music. *Ryabichikova, piano.*
+ ARG 7-8/96: 298
+ Fa 1-2/96: 289

31678. SO 22571 CD: *Gutzul watercolors: Ukrainian music of the twentieth century.* Music of Shamo, Stepovoy, Lyatoshinsky, and Silvestrov. *Ryabichikova, piano.*
• ARG 3-4/96: 234
+ Fa 1-2/96: 397

31679. SO 22572 CD: PROKOFIEV—Cello sonata, op. 119. SHOSTAKOVICH—Cello sonata, op. 40. RACHMANINOFF—Vocalise; Oh stay, my love, forsake me not!; A dream; When silent night doth hold me; So many hours, so many fancies. *Yablonsky, cello; Yablonskaya, piano.*
+ Fa 11-12/96: 336

31680. SO 22573 CD: *Simplicity.* Music for oboe and guitar by Moriarty, Ibert, Pilss, Coste, Cimarosa, and Couperin. *D'Amore Duo.*
+ ARG 5-6/96: 237
+ Fa 5-6/96: 349

31681. SO 53001 CD: *Elegie.* Music of Tchaikovsky, Taneev, Rachmaninoff, and Arensky. *Ricercata de Paris; Brussilovsky, cond.*
+ ARG 7-8/96: 235

31682. SO 53002 CD: GLINKA—Sextet; Divertissement; Serenade. *Various performers.*
+ ARG 11-12/95: 124
+ Fa 1-2/96: 208

SONORIS

31683. SCD 5150: BRAHMS—Sonatas for violin and piano no. 1-3. *Almond, violin; Wolfram, piano.*
+ ARG 3-4/93: 64
• Fa 3-4/93: 131

SONPACT

31684. SPT 91001: SAUGUET—Sonatine aux bois; Sonate crèpesculaire; Wind trio; Golden suite. *Cassen, oboe; Rosbach, piano; Lefevre, violin; Desmarais, piano; Trio d'Anches Deols; Quintette de Cuivres Paul Dukas.*
+ ARG 3-4/93: 133
+ Fa 1-2/93: 226

31685. SPT 92002: GLUCK—Orfeo ed Euridice. *Vocal soloists; Chorus & Chamber Orch. of Aix-en-Provence; Lamarca, cond.*
+ Fa 1-2/93: 155
• ON 5/93: 40

31686. SPT 92003: Music of Rachmaninoff, Scriabin, Medtner, and Kabalevsky. *Pleshakov, piano.*
- Fa 1-2/93: 304

31687. SPT 92004: MILHAUD—Les songes; Le bal martiniquais; Suite concertante; Concertino d'automne; Fantasie pastorale; Scaramouche. *Pleshakov, Winther, pianos; Almeida, cond.*
- Fa 5-6/93: 266

31688. SPT 92005: *Noëls romantiques.* Music of Franck, Boëllmann, Gigout, and Guilmant. *Gueit, organ.*
+ ARG 11-12/94: 228
+ Fa 3-4/94: 187

31689. SPT 92006: POULENC—Histoire de Babar. *Renucci, narrator; Le Sage, piano.*
+ Fa 3-4/94: 275

31690. SPT 93007: BOIELDIEU—Le Calife de Bagdad. *Mayo, Michelini, Cheriez, Dale; Camerata de Provence; Almeida, cond.*
• ARG 9-10/93: 98
+ Fa 9-10/93: 130
+ Gr 9/94: 108
• ON 7/93: 43

31691. SPT 93008: SAUGUET—Mélodies. *Brechbüller, baritone; Antonicelli, Masquelin, sopranos; Mortagne, tenor; Abramovitz, piano.*
+ ARG 5-6/94: 135
- Fa 5-6/94: 235

31692. SPT 93009: TOMASI—Chants de l'île de Corse; Noëls de Nicolas Saboly; Messe de la Nativité. *Maîtrise Gabriel Fauré; Farré-Fizio, cond.*
+ Fa 3-4/94: 347

31693. SPT 94010: CAPLET—Le miroir de Jésus: mystères du rosaire. *Allouche, mezzo-soprano; Gabriel Fauré Choir; Orchestre Regional de Cannes Provence Alpes Côte d'Azur; Bender, cond.*
+ ARG 1-2/95: 94
+ Fa 11-12/94: 195

SONPACT

31694. SPT 94011: *Music for oboe.* Music of Poulenc, Saint-Saëns, Britten, Dutilleux, and Hindemith. *F. Meyer, oboe; Le Sage, piano.*
 + Fa 5-6/95: 404

31695. SPT 94012: AURIC—Trio for oboe, clarinet, and bassoon. CONSTANT—Trio for oboe, clarinet, and bassoon. FRANÇAIX—Divertissement. JACOB—Trio for oboe, clarinet, and bassoon. *Auric Wind Trio.*
 + ARG 5-6/95: 219
 + Fa 5-6/95: 428

31696. SPT 94013: BERLIOZ—Les nuits d'été. REYER—Mélodies. *Pruett, tenor; Fabre, piano.*
 • Fa 9-10/95: 143

31697. SPT 95014: Fratris solis. *Aubin, vocals.*
 • Fa 11-12/95: 455

31698. SPT 96017: SAUGUET—Sonatine for flute and piano; Ballade for cello and piano; Les jeux de l'amour et du hasard; Suite for clarinet and piano; Sonatine bucolique. *Tachibana, flute; Takeda, piano; Sook-Jung Lee, cello; Sun-Jung Lee, piano; Lanoë, Holleville, pianos; Perrier, clarinet; Henrich, piano; Vadrot, saxophone; Garnier, piano.*
 + Fa 1-2/97: 247

SONUS LUXQUE

31699. 103: *The Angelucci collection.* Oboe solos from the orchestral repertory. *Angelucci, oboe; Minneapolis Symphony Orch.; Minnesota Orch.; various conds.*
 + Fa 5-6/95: 408

31700. 105: TOURNEMIRE—L'orgue mystique: Christmas; Fifth Sunday after Pentecost; All Saints; Trinity. *Kassling, Peterson, Handford, Eschbach, organ.*
 + ARG 5-6/95: 186
 + Fa 5-6/95: 362

SONY CLASSICAL

31701. SMK 64468: MOZART—Violin concertos 3-4; Eine kleine Nachtmusik. *Francescatti, violin; unnamed orch.; Walter, cond.* Reissue.
 + ARG 11-12/95: 162

31702. SM2K 27622 (2 discs): SIBELIUS—Symphonies no. 4-7. *New York Phil.; Bernstein, cond.* Reissues.
 + ARG 1-2/94: 156

31703. MDK 35207: Kol nidre service. *Tucker, tenor; Garnett, organ; Irving, narrator.*
 + ARG 11-12/93: 254

31704. SM2K 35902 (2 discs): BELLINI—Norma. *Scotto, Troyanos, Giacomini, Plishka, Crook, Murray; Ambrosian Opera Chorus; National Phil. Orch.;*

Levine, cond. Reissue.
 + Gr 10/95: 129

31705. S2K 39073 (3 discs): ROSSINI—Tancredi. *Horne, Palacio, Cuberli; Teatro La Fenice; Weikert, cond.* Recorded live 1983.
 + ARG 3-4/93: 131
 + OQ summer 93: 168

31706. SK 42450: ADAM—Giselle: Excerpts. *London Symphony Orch.; Thomas, cond.*
 + ARG 5-6/92: 10
 + Fa 5-6/92: 112
 + Gr 3/92: 37

31707. S2K 44504 (2 discs): SCHUBERT—Violin sonatas D. 384-85, 408; Violin and piano duo D. 574; Fantasie for violin and piano D. 934; Rondo for violin and piano D. 895 . *Stern, violin; Barenboim, piano.*
 + ARG 11-12/90: 111
 + Fa 9-10/90: 373
 + Gr 10/90: 769

31708. SK 44552: *Music for flute and harp.* Music of Rossini, Saint-Saëns, Spohr, Fauré, and others. *Rampal, flute; Nordmann, harp.*
 + DA 4/91: 58
 + Fa 11-12/90: 451
 + Gr 10/90: 775

31709. SK 44568: Music of Mozart, Telemann, J.C. Bach, and Reicha. *Rampal, flute; Stern, violin; Rostropovich, cello; Spaeter, lute.*
 + ARG 11-12/90: 144
 + Fa 9-10/90: 495
 + Gr 9/90: 566

31710. S3K 44878 (3 discs): BORODIN—Prince Igor. *Evstatieva, Miltcheva, Kaludov, Martinovich, Ghiuselev, Ghiaurov; Sofia National Opera Chorus; Sofia Festival Orch.; Tchakarov, cond.*
 + ARG 9-10/90: 51
 + DA 8/90: 30
 + Fa 1-2/91: 157
 + Gr 12/90: 1215
 • MA 1/91: 70
 • ON 10/90: 42
 • Op 6/90: 749
 + St 9/90: 189

31711. SK 44913: MOZART—Violin concertos no. 2, 7; Rondo for violin and orchestra in C. *Lin, violin; English Chamber Orch.; Leppard, cond.*
 + ARG 1-2/91: 69
 + Fa 1-2/91: 246
 • Gr 12/90: 1215
 + MA 5/91: 79
 + SR 3/91: 94

31712. SK 44914: HAYDN—Seven last words of Christ. *Valente, De Gaetani, Humphrey, Paul; Juilliard String Quartet.*
 • Fa 1-2/91: 214
 - Gr 10/91: 126
 + St 4/91: 255

31713. SK 44915: MOZART—Concerto no. 10 for 2 pianos, K. 365; Concerto no. 7 for 3 pianos, K. 242 "Lodron" (arr. for 2 pianos and orchestra); Fantasia in F minor for musical clock, K. 608 (arr. for 2 pianos); Andante and variations for piano 4-hands, K. 501. *Perahia, Lupu, pianos.*
 • ARG 1-2/92: 82
 + Fa 1-2/92: 274
 + Gr 10/91: 93
 + St 8/93: 184

31714. SK 44922: CHOPIN—Piano concertos (complete). *Perahia, piano; Israel Phil. Orch.; Mehta, cond.*
 + ARG 9-10/90: 57
 + DA 10/90: 72
 + Fa 9-10/90: 209
 + Gr 6/90: 44
 + NYT 5/27/90: H19
 + SR 12/90: 127

31715. SK 44935: MAHLER—Des Knaben Wunderhorn; Lieder eines fahrenden Gesellen. *Fischer-Dieskau, baritone; Berlin Phil. Orch.; Barenboim, cond.*
 - ARG 9-10/90: 83
 + Gr 5/90: 2031

31716. SK 44939: IVES—Symphony no. 1; Hymns; Symphony no. 4. *Chicago Symphony Orch.; Members of the Chicago Symphony Chorus; Thomas, cond.*
 + ARG 7-8/91: 69
 + Fa 9-10/91: 242
 + Gr 2/91: 1509

31717. S2K 44983 (2 discs): BOITO—Mefistofele. *Ramey, Domingo, Marton; Hungarian State Opera; Patanè, cond.*
 • ARG 11-12/91: 40
 • Gr 4/91: 1894
 + ON 8/91: 36
 + OQ summer/91: 151

31718. SBK 45500: MAHLER—Das Lied von der Erde. *Miller, mezzo-soprano; Haefliger, tenor; New York Phil.; Walter, cond.*
 • Gr 10/91: 166

31719. SK 45577: MOZART—Requiem. *Dawson, Nes, Lewis, Estes; Philharmonia Chorus & Orch.; Giulini, cond.*
 - ARG 11-12/90: 89
 - Fa 11-12/90: 295
 - Gr 8/90: 400
 - MA 3/91: 83
 - SR 2/91: 134

31720. SB2K 45675 (2 discs): MENDELSSOHN—Music for piano(s) and orchestra. *Serkin, Entremont, Gold, Fizdale, piano; Philadelphia Orch.; Ormandy, cond.*
 + Gr 10/91: 90

31721. SK 45683: *Italian opera composer's songs.* Music of Rossini, Donizetti, Bellini, and Verdi. *Carreras,*

tenor; Katz, piano.
- ARG 11-12/90: 173
+ Fa 1-2/91: 365
- Gr 9/90: 599
- HPR v.7 Winter/90: 65
- MA 3/91: 91
- St 5/91: 181

31722. S3K 45720 (3 discs): TCHAIKOVSKY—Queen of Spades. *Evstatieva, Dilova, Ochman, Mazurok; Bulgarian National Choir; Sofia Festival Orch.; Tchakarov, cond.*
+ ARG 5-6/91: 116
• Fa 3-4/91: 402
+ Gr 12/90: 1271
• ON 1/91: 43
+ Op 5/91: 598

31723. SK 45742: SCHUMANN—Carnaval; Papillons; Toccata. *Licad, piano.*
+ ARG 1-2/91: 94
+ Fa 1-2/91: 312
+ Gr 1/91: 1390
+ MA 3/91: 87

31724. SK 45748: BARTÓK—Concerto for orchestra; Miraculous mandarin suite. *Berlin Phil. Orch.; Mehta, cond.*
• ARG 11-12/90: 24
+ DA 9/90: 46
- Fa 9-10/90: 163
• Gr 6/90: 41
• MA 11/90: 69

31725. SK 45749: WAGNER—Parsifal: Prelude and Good Friday spell; Rienzi: Overture; Tannhäuser: Overture and Bacchanale. *New York Phil.; Mehta, cond.*
+ ARG 1-2/93: 165
- Fa 11-12/92: 401

31726. S2K 45754 (2 discs): MAHLER—Symphony no. 8. *Sweet, Coburn, Quivar, Fassbaender, Leech, Nimsgern, Estes; Vienna State Opera Chorus; Vienna Phil. Orch.; Maazel, cond.*
• ARG 1-2/91: 63
• Fa 11-12/90: 264
- Gr 9/90: 518

31727. SK 45756: TCHAIKOVSKY—Piano concertos no. 1, 3. *Feltsman, piano; National Symphony Orch.; Rostropovich, cond.*
• ARG 7-8/91: 130
+ Fa 1-2/91: 332
+ Gr 1/91: 1380

31728. S3K 45763 (3 discs): MUSSORGSKY—Boris Godunov. *Ghiaurov, Frank, Ghiuselev, Svetlev; Sofia National Opera; Tchakarov, cond.*
• ARG 5-6/92: 89
• Fa 5-6/92: 214
• Gr 4/92: 159
+ ON 4/11/92: 46
+ Op 2/92: 247
+ St 11/92: 225

31729. SK 45796: STRAVINSKY—Sacre du printemps; Symphony in three

movements. *Philharmonia Orch.; Salonen, cond.*
+ ARG 1-2/91: 104
• Fa 1-2/91: 327
+ Gr 11/90: 995
• MA 1/91: 82

31730. SK 45797: STRAVINSKY—Capriccio for piano and orchestra; Symphonies of wind instruments; Piano concerto; Movements for piano and orchestra. *Crossley, piano; London Sinfonietta; Salonen, cond.*
+ ARG 1-2/91: 104
+ Fa 1-2/91: 327
+ Gr 10/90: 747
+ MA 1/91: 82

31731. SK 45800: STRAUSS—An Alpine symphony; Horn concerto no. 1. *Seifert, horn; Berlin Phil. Orch.; Mehta, cond.*
+ ARG 9-10/90: 117
• DA 12/90: 94
+ Fa 9-10/90: 395
+ Gr 8/90: 382
• NYT 10/21/90: H36
+ SR 10/90: 118

31732. SK 45818: *The last recording.* Music of Haydn, Chopin, Liszt, and Wagner (arr. Liszt) . *Horowitz, piano.*
+ ARG 9-10/90: 144
+ DA 7/90: 40
+ Fa 9-10/90: 176
+ Gr 8/90: 395
+ SR 8/90: 73

31733. SK 45819: BRAHMS—Violin sonatas (complete). *Perlman, violin; Barenboim, piano. Recorded live 1989.*
• ARG 11-12/91: 45
+ DA 3/91: 46
• Fa 3-4/91: 165
• Gr 12/90: 1227

31734. S2K 45820 (2 discs): BRAHMS—String sextets; Theme and variations for piano (arr. from op. 18). *Stern, Lin, violins; Laredo, Tree, violas; Ma, Robinson, cellos; Ax, piano.*
• ARG 11-12/92: 94
+ Fa 11-12/92: 208
+ Gr 9/92: 105

31735. SK 45830: BEETHOVEN—Piano concerto no. 1; Symphony no. 7. *Barenboim, piano & cond.; Berlin Phil. Orch. Recorded live 1989.*
- ARG 11-12/90: 26
+ DA 7/90: 44
- Fa 9-10/90: 166
• Gr 4/90: 1770

31736. S3K 45831: MUSSORGSKY—Khovanshchina (ed. and orch. by Shostakovich). *Miltcheva, Gadjev, Ghiaurov, Ghiuselev; Sofia National Opera & Orch.; Tchakarov, cond.*
+ DA 1/91: 76
• Fa 3-4/91: 309
+ Gr 10/90: 816
+ HPR v. 8 no. 2: 73

31737. SK 45835: BARTÓK—Piano concertos (complete). *Sándor, piano; Hungarian State Orch.; Fischer, cond.*
• Fa 7-8/91: 106
+ MA 7/91: 64

31738. SK 45836: *Return to Russia.* Music of Tchaikovsky, J. Strauss Jr., Grieg, Paganini, Prokofiev, Gershwin, and Sousa. *National Symphony Orch. of Washington; Rostropovich, cond.*
+ ARG 1-2/92: 130
+ Fa 1-2/92: 434
+ Gr 9/91: 79

31739. SMK 45837: BARTÓK—Miraculous mandarin; Four pieces; Three village scenes. *New York Phil.; Boulez, cond. Reissue.*
- ARG 7-8/92: 89
+ Fa 5-6/92: 119

31740. S3K 45840 (3 discs): ROSSINI—La gazza ladra. *Ricciarelli, Nissa, Matteuzzi, Furlanetto, Ramey; Prague Phil. Choir; Italian Radio and Television Turin Symphony Orch.; Gelmetti, cond. Recorded live 1989.*
+ ARG 5-6/91: 98
+ Fa 3-4/91: 342
+ Gr 10/90: 816
• ON 1/5/91: 34

31741. SK 45841: MAHLER—Das klagende Lied. *Hoffman, Lear, Söderström, sopranos; Burrows, Haefliger, tenors; Nienstedt, baritone; London Symphony Orch.; Boulez, cond.*
+ ARG 11-12/92: 151
+ Fa 5-6/92: 191

31742. SM3K 45842 (3 discs): RAVEL—Orchestral works. *New York Phil.; Cleveland Orch.; Boulez, cond. Reissues.*
+ ARG 9-10/91: 113
• Gr 2/91: 1513

31743. SK 45843: STRAVINSKY—Firebird suite; Pulcinella suite; Scherzo fantastique; Suite 1 and 2 for small orchestra. *New York Phil.; Ensemble InterContemporain; Boulez, cond.*
+ ARG 5-6/92: 142

31744. SM3K 45845 (3 discs): WEBERN—Complete works, ops. 1-31. *London Symphony Orch.; Boulez, cond.; Juilliard String Quartet. Reissue.*
• ARG 11-12/91: 169
+ Fa 9-10/91: 394
• Gr 6/91: 55

31745. S2K 45846 (2 discs): BRAHMS—Piano quartets no. 1-3. *Ax, piano; Stern, violin; Laredo, viola; Ma, cello.*
+ ARG 3-4/91: 45
+ Fa 5-6/91: 135
+ Gr 3/91: 1682

31746. S2K 45847 (2 discs): PUCCINI—Tosca. *Marton, Carreras, Pons, Tajo; Hungarian State Radio and Television Chorus; Hungarian State Orch.; Thomas,*

SONY CLASSICAL

cond.
- ARG 5-6/91: 94
- Fa 3-4/91: 331
+ Gr 10/90: 819
- HPR v.8 no.2: 74
- ON 1/5/91: 35
- Op 11/90: 1375
+ St 7/91: 181

31747. SK 45855: MOZART—Bastien und Bastienne; Un moto di gioia; Nozze di Figaro: Deh vieni, non tardr; Misero O sogno; Menre ti lascio. *Gruberová, Cole, Pólgar; Franz Liszt Chamber Orch.; Leppard, cond.*
+ ARG 5-6/91: 86
+ DA 3/91: 46
- Fa 3-4/91: 285
- Gr 1/91: 1409
- Op 1/91: 119

31748. S2K 45858 (2 discs): BACH—Works for lute in original keys and tunings. *Kirchhof, lute.*
- ARG 11-12/91: 24
- EM 8/91: 482
+ Gr 3/91: 1695

31749. SK 45859: BACH—Motets. *Stuttgart Chamber Choir; Stuttgart Baroque Orch.; Bernius, cond.*
- ARG 9-10/91: 38
+ Gr 2/91: 1542

31750. SK 45860: *La Dissection d'un Homme armé.* Six masses atter a Burgundian song. *Huelgas Ensemble; Nevel, cond.*
+ ARG 9-10/91: 170
+ Gr 6/91: 82

31751. SK 45862: BERIO—Ritorno degli snovidenia; Chemins II (su Sequenza VI); Chemins IV (su Sequenza VII); Corale (su Sequenza VIII); Points on the curve to find. *Ensemble InterContemporain; Boulez, cond.*
+ ARG 11-12/91: 30
+ Fa 9-10/91: 160

31752. S2K 45864 (2 discs): BRUCKNER—Symphonies no. 8, 0. *Israel Phil. Orch.; Mehta, cond.*
+ ARG 1-2/93: 84
- Fa 1-2/93: 120
- Gr 3/93: 35

31753. SK 45867: VIVALDI—Concertos for flute, violin, and strings RV 509, 512, 514, 516-17, 524. *Rampal, flute; Stern, violin; Franz Liszt Chamber Orch.; Rolla, cond.*
+ ARG 7-8/91: 133
+ Fa 7-8/91: 322
+ HPR v.8, no.3/91: 88
+ SR 6/91: 97

31754. SK 45868: RAMEAU—Pièces de clavecin en concert. *Rampal, flute; Stern, violin; Ritter, harpsichord.*
+ ARG 11-12/90: 100
- Fa 1-2/91: 282

31755. SK 45870: SCHOENBERG—Pelleas und Melisande. SIBELIUS—Pelléas et Mélisande: Excerpts. FAURÉ—Pelléas et Mélisande. *Israel Phil. Orch.; Mehta, cond.*
+ ARG 5-6/91: 102 (Schoenberg)
- ARG 5-6/91: 102 (others)
+ DA 8/91: 38
- Fa 3-4/91: 357
+ Gr 1/91: 1372

31756. SMK 45901: SCHUBERT—String quintet in C; Hirt auf dem Felsen. *Frank, Galimir, Tenenbom, Wiley, Lichten; Valente, soprano; Wright, clarinet; Serkin, piano.*
+ ARG 11-12/90: 109
- MA 7/91: 59
+ NYT 8/26/90: H23

31757. SK 45930: *Concertos for two flutes.* MOZART—Concertone in C major, K. 190. CIMAROSA—Concerto in G major. VIVALDI—Concerto in C major, RV 533. A. STAMITZ—Concerto in G major. *Kudo, flute; Mozarteum Orch.; Rampal, flute & cond.*
+ ARG 9-10/91: 160
- Fa 7-8/91: 371
+ Gr 2/92: 43

31758. SK 45931: *Yevgevy Kissin in Tokyo.* Music of Rachmaninoff, Prokofiev, Liszt, Chopin, and others. *Kissin, piano.*
- ARG 3-4/91: 158
+ Fa 1-2/91: 380
+ Gr 11/90: 1016
+ MA 5/91: 89
- St 4/91: 263

31759. SK 45932: BRAHMS—Serenade no. 1; Tragic overture; Academic festival overture. *London Symphony Orch.; Thomas, cond.*
+ ARG 1-2/91: 36
+ Fa 3-4/91: 164
+ Gr 1/91: 1371

31760. SK 45933: BRAHMS—Piano sonata no. 3; Intermezzi op. 117. *Ax, piano.*
+ ARG 1-2/91: 37
+ Fa 1-2/91: 163
+ Gr 12/90: 1016
+ MA 5/91: 89
- St 4/91: 263

31761. SK 45935: MUSSORGSKY—Pictures at an exhibition (orch. Ravel). STRAVINSKY—Firebird suite (1919 version). *Berlin Phil. Orch.; Royal Concertgebouw Orch.; Giulini, cond.*
- ARG 3-4/91: 92
+ Fa 3-4/91: 310
+ Gr 12/90: 1215

31762. SK 45936: CZERNY—Piano music for four hands. *Tal, Groethuysen, pianos.*
+ ARG 7-8/91: 50
+ Fa 9-10/91: 194
+ Gr 5/91: 2030

31763. SK 45937: BACH—The art of fugue. *Juilliard String Quartet.*
+ ARG 9-10/92: 76
+ Gr 6/92: 55
- St 9/92: 186

31764. SK 45939: TCHAIKOVSKY—Symphony no. 3 "Polish"; 1812 overture. *Chicago Symphony Orch.; Abbado, cond.*
+ ARG 5-6/92: 145
+ Fa 11/12/92: 386
- Gr 3/92: 56

31765. SK 45941: BARTÓK—Violin concertos no. 1-2. *Midori, violin; Berlin Phil. Orch.; Metha, cond.*
+ ARG 9-10/91: 40
+ DA 4/91: 69
- Fa 3-4/91: 144
+ Gr 2/91: 1498
+ MA 3/91: 68

31766. SK 45942: *In morte di Madonna Laura: madrigal cycle after texts of Petrarch.* Compositions by Hoste da Reggio, Mauro de' Servi, Pisano, Cimello, Rossetti, Donato, Tudino, Rota, and Vicentino. *Huelgas Ensemble; Nevel, cond.*
+ ARG 11-12/91: 198
□ Fa 11-12/91: 542

31767. SK 45943: SCHÜTZ—Christmas oratorio; Easter oratorio. *Stuttgart Chamber Choir; Musica Fiata; Stuttgart Baroque Orch.; Bernius, cond.*
+ ARG 11-12/91: 146
+ Gr 3/91: 1713

31768. SK 45946: *In natali Domini.* Medieval Christmas songs. *Niederaltaich Scholars; Ruhland, cond.*
+ EM 11/92: 683
+ Fa 5-6/92: 306

31769. SM3K 45952 (3 discs): *The Issac Stern collection: the early concerto recordings, vol. 1.* Concertos of Bach, Vivaldi, Haydn, Mozart, and others. *Stern, Oistrakh, violins; Rose, cello; various orchs. & conds.*
+ ARG 1-2/91: 141
+ Fa 1-2/91: 389
+ Gr 12/90: 1220
+ HPR v.8 no.1/91: 81

31770. SM3K 45956 (3 discs): *The Issac Stern collection: the early concerto recordings, vol. 2.* Concertos of Lalo, Bruch, Sarasate, Sibelius, and others. *Stern, violin; various orchs. & conds.*
+ ARG 1-2/91: 141
+ Fa 1-2/91: 389
+ Gr 12/90: 1220
+ HPR v.8 v.1/91: 81

31771. SK 45964: ROSSINI—*Agnes Baltsa sings Rossini.* Arias from Italiana in Algeri, Barbiere di Siviglia, Maometto II, Tancredi, Cenerentola, Semiramide, and Donna del lago. *Baltsa, contralto; Konzertvereinigung Wiener Staatsopernchor; Wiener Symphoniker;*

Marin, cond.
- ARG 11-12/91: 139
+ Fa 11-12/91: 462
+ Gr 9/91: 130
+ ON 2/29/92: 35

31772. SK 45965: STRAVINSKY—
Pulcinella; Ragtime for 11 instruments;
Renard; Octet for winds. *Kenny, Aler,
Robson, Tomlinson; London Sinfonietta;
Salonen, cond.*
+ ARG 3-4/92: 147
+ Fa 1-2/92: 342
+ Gr 1/92: 89
+ St 12/92: 245

31773. SK 45968: BEETHOVEN—
Symphony no. 5. BEN-HAIM—Molto
calmo e cantabile. RAVEL—La valse.
*Israel Phil. Orch.; Berlin Phil. Orch.;
Mehta, cond.* Recorded live 1990.
- ARG 7-8/92: 96
• Gr 12/91: 86

31774. SK 45970: STRAUSS—Also sprach
Zarathustra; Don Juan. *London Symphony
Orch.; Thomas, cond.*
+ ARG 1-2/92: 120
• Fa 11-12/91: 497
+ Gr 9/91: 73

31775. SK 45972: HAYDN—Symphonies
no. 22, 78, 82. *Stockholm Chamber
Orch.; Salonen, cond.*
+ ARG 9-10/91: 81
+ Fa 9-10/91: 232
- Gr 9/91: 62

31776. S3K 45973 (3 discs): VERDI—
Aida. *Millo, Domingo, Zajick, Morris,
Ramey; Metropolitan Opera Orch. &
Chorus; Levine, cond.*
• ARG 9-10/91: 139
+ Fa 9-10/91: 380
+ Gr 5/91: 2062
+ ON 7/91: 34
+ St 2/92: 197

31777. SM4K 45989 (4 discs):
NIELSEN—Symphonies (complete); Flute
concerto; Clarinet concerto; Maskerade:
Overture 7 Act 2 prelude; Helios
overture; Pan and Syrinx; Rhapsodic
overture. *Baker, flute; Drucker, clarinet;
Guldbaek, soprano; Moller, baritone;
New York Phil. Orch.; Royal Danish
Orch.; Philadelphia Orch.; Bernstein,
Ormandy, conds.*
+ ARG 3-4/91: 98
+ Fa 5-6/91: 241

31778. SK 45996: NIELSEN—Wind
quintet. TAFFANEL—Wind quintet.
Ensemble Wien-Berlin.
+ ARG 7-8/91: 98
+ Fa 7-8/91: 242
• Gr 1/91: 1376

31779. SK 45999: BERG—Chamber
concerto for piano, violin and 13 winds.
BRAHMS—Concerto for violin and cello.
*Stern, violin; Serkin, piano; Ma, cello;
London Symphony Orch.; Chicago

Symphony Orch.; Abbado, cond.
- ARG 7-8/91: 35 (Brahms)
+ ARG 7-8/91: 35 (Berg)
- Fa 7-8/91: 119

31780. SMK 46246: BEETHOVEN—
Symphony no. 4. SCHUBERT—Symphony
no. 5. *Marlboro Festival Orch.; Casals,
cond.*
+ ARG 3-4/91: 32
• Fa 1-2/91: 152
• MA 7/91: 56 (Beethoven)
+ MA 7/91: 57 (Schubert)
+ St 3/91: 193

31781. SMK 46247: BEETHOVEN—
Symphony no. 2; Egmont overture.
BRAHMS—Variations on a theme by
Haydn. *Marlboro Festival Orch.; Casals,
cond.*
+ ARG 3-4/91: 32
• Fa 1-2/91: 152
+ MA 7/91: 57
+ St 3/91: 193

31782. SMK 46248: MOZART—Serenade
no. 10 K. 361; Sonata for bassoon and
cello K. 292. *Marlboro Festival, Moyse,
flute; Heller, bassoon; Ma, cello.*
+ ARG 1-2/91: 132
+ Fa 1-2/91: 256
+ MA 7/91: 57

31783. SMK 46249: BRAHMS—String
sextet no. 2; Horn trio. *Carmirelli, Toth,
violins; Naegele, Levine, violas; Arico,
Reichenberger, cellos; Bloom, horn;
Tree, violin; Serkin, piano.*
+ ARG 1-2/91: 36
• Fa 1-2/91: 163
- MA 7/91: 57 (Sextet)
+ MA 7/91: 57 (Trio)

31784. SMK 46250: BARBER—Summer
music. NIELSEN—Wind quintet.
HINDEMITH—Octet. *Marlboro Festival.*
+ ARG 1-2/91: 132
+ DA 4/98: 61
+ Fa 1-2/91: 256

31785. SMK 46251: MENDELSSOHN—
Symphony no. 4; Octet for strings.
*Laredo, Schneider, Steinhardt, Dalley,
violins; Tree, Rhodes, violas; Parnas,
Soyer, cellos; Marlboro Festival Orch.;
Casals, cond.*
+ ARG 5-6/91: 80
+ Fa 3-4/91: 275
+ MA 7/91: 59

31786. SMK 46252: SCHUBERT—Piano
quintet D. 667. MOZART—Clarinet quintet
K. 581. *Serkin, piano; Wright, Laredo,
Schneider, Cohen, violins; Naegele,
Rhodes, violas; Parnas, cello; Levine,
double bass.*
+ ARG 3-4/91: 113
+ DA 12/90: 88
+ Fa 3-4/91: 360
+ MA 7/91: 59

31787. SMK 46253—46254 (2 separate
discs): BACH—Brandenburg concertos no.

1-3; Suite for orchestra no. 1. *Marlboro
Festival Orch.; Casals, cond.*
+ Fa 3-4/91: 130
• MA 7/91: 59

31788. SMK 46255: MOZART—Concertos
for 2 pianos K. 365; Piano concerto no.
12 K. 414; Piano trio K. 502 . *R. & P.
Serkin, pianos; Laredo, violin; Foley,
cello; Marlboro Festival Orch.;
Schneider, cond.*
+ DA 5/91: 72
+ Fa 3-4/91: 288
• Gr 5/91: 2009

31789. SK 46279: *Glenn Gould conducts
& plays Wagner.* WAGNER—Siegfried
Idyll; Die Meistersinger: Prelude;
Götterdämmerung: Dawn and Siegfried's
Rhine journey.
+ ARG 9-10/91: 146
+ Fa 9-10/91: 388
+ Gr 4/91: 1873

31790. SX22K 46290 (22 discs):
STRAVINSKY— The Complete edition.
*Various performers; Stravinsky, Craft,
conds.* Reissues.
+ ARG 11-12/91: 153
+ Gr 7/91: 68

31791. SBK 46332: HAYDN—Symphonies
no. 92, 94, 96. *Cleveland Orch.; Szell,
cond.* Reissues.
+ ARG 3-4/92: 774

31792. SBK 46334: TCHAIKOVSKY—
Symphony no. 4; Marche slave; 1812
overture. *Philadelphia Orch.; Ormandy,
cond.*
+ ARG 3-4/92: 152

31793. SBK 46335: BRAHMS—Violin
concerto; Double concerto. *Stern, violin;
Rose, cello; Philadelphia Orch.;
Ormandy, cond.* Reissues.
+ ARG 3-4/92: 35

31794. SBK 46343: SCHUBERT—Trout
quintet; String quartet no. 14. *Budapest
String Quartet; Horszowski, piano;
Juilliard String Quartet.* Reissues.
+ ARG 3-4/92: 135

31795. SK 46348: BRUMEL—Missa Et
ecce terrae motus; Dies irae. *Huelgas
Ensemble; Nevel, cond.*
+ ARG 9-10/91: 56
+ Gr 5/19: 2051

31796. SK 46352: GLASS—Itaipu; The
canyon. *Atlanta Symphony Orch. &
Chorus; Shaw, cond.*
+ Fa 11-12/93: 245
• Gr 11/93: 128

31797. S3K 46429 (3 discs):
CHARPENTIER—Louise. *Cotrubas,
Domingo, Bacquier, Sénéchal;
Ambrosian Opera Chorus; Philharmonia
Orch.; Prêtre, cond.* Reissue.
+ Gr 6/91: 87

SONY CLASSICAL

31798. S2K 46433 (2 discs): Rossini—La Cenerentola. *Valentini Terrani, Araiza, Trimarchi, Dara; West German Radio Choir; Cappella Coloniensis; Ferro, cond. Reissue.*
+ Gr 6/91: 88

31799. SK 46437: *The Aldeburgh recital. Music of Beethoven, Schumann, Liszt, and Rachmaninoff. Perahia, piano.*
+ ARG 7-8/91: 173
+ Fa 7-8/91: 361
+ MA 7/91: 93
+ SR 6/91: 74

31800. SK 46440: Ives—Symphonies no. 2-3. *Concertgebouw Orch.; Thomas, cond.*
+ DA 5/91: 72
+ Fa 5-6/91: 192
• Gr 5/91: 2009

31801. SK 46481: Mussorgsky—Pictures at an exhibition. Stravinsky—Three movements from Petrouchtka. Tchaikovsky—Dumka in C minor. *Bronfman, piano.*
+ ARG 5-6/92: 92
+ Fa 5-6/92: 215
+ Gr 1/92: 79

31802. SK 46482: Telemann—Scherzo no. 1; Trietto no. 3. Kuhlau—Trio. Bach—Gamba sonata no. 3. Mozart—Magic flute (excerpts). Doppler—Hungarian duettino. *Rampal, Kudo, flutes; Ritter, piano & harpsichord.*
+ ARG 1-2/92: 152
+ Fa 9-10/91: 426
+ Gr 2/92: 59

31803. SK 46483: Mozart—String quintets no. 4-5. *Artis Quartet Vienna.*
• ARG 11-12/91: 116
- Fa 9-10/91: 288
• Gr 7/91: 78

31804. SK 46485: Mozart—Piano concertos no. 21, 27. *Perahia, piano; Chamber Orch. of Europe.*
+ ARG 1-2/92: 82
+ Fa 11-12/91: 396
• Gr 8/91: 56

31805. SK 46486: Prokofiev—Cello sonata. Rachmaninoff—Cello sonata. *Ma, cello; Ax, piano.*
• ARG 5-6/92: 109
- Fa 3-4/92: 287

31806. S3K 46487 (3 discs): Glinka—A life for the Tsar (Ivan Susanin). *Pendachanska, Toczyska, Merritt, Popov, Martinovich, Georgiev; Sofia National Opera Chorus; Sofia Festival Orch.; Tchakarov, cond.*
+ ARG 11-12/91: 67
+ Fa 11-12/91: 323
+ Gr 9/91: 122
- ON 1/4/92: 38
- Op 10/91: 1240

31807. SK 46491: Verdi—Four sacred pieces. Vivaldi—Credo in E minor, RV 591. *Sweet, soprano; Ernst-Senff- Chor; Berlin Phil. Orch.; Giulini, cond.*
- ARG 3-4/92: 156
- Fa 1-2/92: 361
• Gr 10/91: 177

31808. SK 46492: Bach—Auf, schmetternde Töne der muntern Trompeten: Cantata BWV 207a; Schleicht, spielende Wellen: Cantata BWV 206. *Ziesak, Chance, Prégardien, Kooy; Kammerchor Stuttgart; Concerto Köln; Bernius, Frieder, cond.*
+ Fa 11-12/91: 248
+ Gr 9/91: 106

31809. SK 46493: Mozart—Missa longa in C, K. 262; Internatos mulierum, K. 72; Te Deum, K. 141; Venite populi, K. 260; Regina coeli. K. 276; Ave verum corpus, K. 618. *Tölzer Knabenchor; European Baroque Soloists; Schmidt-Gaden, cond.*
+ Fa 11-12/91: 406

31810. SK 46494: Mozart—Divertimenti for 2 horns and strings, K. 247, K. 334. *Archibudelli.*
+ ARG 3-4/92: 110
+ Fa 3-4/92: 253

31811. SK 46497: Mozart—Divertimento for string trio, K. 563. Mozart-Bach—Adagios and fugues, string trio, no. 1 3, 6. *Archibudelli.*
+ ARG 3-4/92: 110
+ Fa 3-4/92: 253

31812. SK 46499: Sibelius—Symphonies no. 4-5. *Pittsburgh Symphony Orch.; Maazel, cond.*
+ ARG 1-2/92: 115
• Fa 3-4/92: 327
• Gr 8/91: 57
• St 10/92: 271

31813. SK 46500: Nielsen—Symphonies no. 3, 6. *P. Nilsson, soprano; Persson, baritone; Swedish Radio Symphony Orch.; Salonen, cond.*
• ARG 3-4/92: 113
+ Fa 1-2/92: 287
• Gr 10/91: 96

31814. SM3K 46511 (3 discs): Mozart—Symphonies no. 35-36, 38-41. *Columbia Symphony Orch.; Walter, cond. Reissues.*
+ Fa 3-4/92: 269

31815. SM3K 46515 (3 discs): Mozart—Symphonies no. 28, 33, 35, 39-41; Serenades no. 9, 13; Exsultate, jubilate; Nozze di Figaro: Overture. *Raskin, soprano; Cleveland Orch.; Szell, cond. Reissues.*
+ Fa 3-4/92: 268

31816. SM3K 46527 (3 discs): Mozart—String quintets; Piano quartet, K. 478; Eine kleine Nachtmusik. *Budapest String Quartet; with asissting*

artists. Reissues.
+ Fa 3-4/92: 262

31817. SBK 46532: Beethoven—Symphonies no. 1, 6; Egmont: Overture, op. 84. *Cleveland Orch.; Szell, cond. Reissue.*
+ ARG 1-2/92: 143 (Bauman)
+ ARG 1-2/92: 30 (Linkowski)
• Fa 1-2/92: 165

31818. SBK 46533: Beethoven—Symphony no. 9; Fidelio: Overture, op. 72. *Vocal soloists; Cleveland Orch.; Szell, cond. Reissue.*
+ ARG 1-2/92: 30
+ ARG 1-2/92: 143
+ Fa 1-2/92: 170

31819. SBK 46534: Brahms—Symphony no. 1; Haydn variations; Hungarian dances no. 17-21. *Cleveland Orch.; Szell, cond.; Philadelphia Orch.; Ormandy, cond. Reissues.*
+ ARG 1-2/92: 143

31820. SBK 46536: Mendelssohn—Symphonies nos. 3, 4; Hebrides overture. *Cleveland Orch.; Szell, cond.; Bavarian Radio Orch.; A. Davis, cond.*
+ ARG 1-2/92: 143

31821. SBK 46538: Tchaikovsky—Symphony no. 5; Serenade for strings. *Philadelphia Orch.; Ormandy, cond. Reissues.*
+ ARG 3-4/92: 152

31822. SBK 46541: Rachmaninoff—Piano concertos 1, 4; Paganini rhapsody. *Entremont, piano; Philadelphia Orch.; Ormandy, cond. Reissues.*
+ ARG 1-2/92: 95

31823. SBK 46542: Mendelssohn—Piano concertos; Violin concerto. *Serkin, piano; Stern, violin; Philadelphia Orch.; Ormandy, cond. Reissues.*
+ ARG 1-2/92: 76

31824. SBK 46550: Chopin—Les sylphides. Delibes—Sylvia and Coppelia suites. Tchaikovsky—Nutcracker suite. *Philadelphia Orch.; Ormandy, cond. Reissues.*
+ ARG 1-2/92: 44

31825. SBK 46551: Bach—Toccata and fugue in D minor; Passacaglia and fugue; Pastorale; Preludes and fugues in G minor, A minor, B minor, and C. *Biggs, organ. Reissue; recorded 1960-71.*
+ ARG 7-8/92: 86

31826. S3K 46552 (3 discs): Mozart—String quartets no. 14-19. *Artis Quartet Vienna.*
• ARG 7-8/92: 187
• Fa 11-12/91: 402

31827. SK 46556: Vivaldi—Guitar concertos. *Williams, Verdery, guitars; Blume, viola d'amore; Franz Liszt*

Chamber Orch.; Rolla, cond.
+ ARG 9-10/92: 192
• Fa 11-12/91: 518
+ Gr 11/91: 105

31828. SM3K 46559 (3 discs): *Copland collection, vol. 1.* Copland conducts Copland: Orchestral and ballet works, 1936-48. *Various orchestras; Copland, cond.* Reissues.
+ Gr 7/91: 42

31829. S2K 46592 (2 discs): Tchaikovsky—Swan lake. *London Symphony Orch.; Thomas, cond.*
• ARG 1-2/92: 127
+ Fa 1-2/92: 350
+ Gr 4/92: 80

31830. SK 46631: Mozart—Grand sestetto concertant (after K. 364); Duos for violin and viola no. 1-2. *L'Archibudelli.*
+ ARG 11-12/91: 116
+ Fa 11-12/91: 411
+ Gr 4/92: 100

31831. SK 46667: Stravinsky—Apollo; Concerto in D for strings; Cantata. *Kenny, Aler; London Sinfonietta Chorus; London Sinfonietta; Stockholm Chamber Orch.; Salonen, cond.*
+ ARG 5-6/92: 141
+ Fa 1-2/92: 342
• Gr 10/91: 114
+ St 12/92: 245

31832. SK 46668: *Nordic festival.* Works by Alfvén, Sibelius, Grieg, Leifs, Nielsen and Jarnefelt. *Swedish Radio Symphony; Salonen, cond.*
+ ARG 11-12/91: 177
+ Fa 1-2/92: 428
• Gr 11/91: 106

31833. SK 46669: Schubert—String quintet; Rondo for violin and string quartet, D. 438. *Beths, Rautenberg, Gatwood, violins; Dann, viola; Slowik, Bylsma, cellos.*
+ ARG 11-12/91: 143
+ Fa 11-12/91: 472
• Gr 9/91: 92

31834. SK 46670: Dvořák—Symphony no. 8 in G. Ravel—Ma mere l'oye suite. *Concertgebouw Orch.; Giulini, cond.*
+ ARG 11-12/91: 63
+ Fa 1-2/92: 205
+ Gr 10/91: 78

31835. SK 46671: Mozart—Mass in C minor, K. 427. *Bonney, Augér, Blochwitz, Holl; Rundfunkchor Berlin; Berlin Phil. Orch.; Abbado, cond.*
+ ARG 3-4/92: 109
+ Fa 1-2/92: 278
+ Gr 10/91: 169
+ ON 1/18/92: 36
• St 12/92: 241

31836. SK 46672: *Baroque duet.* Music of Handel, A. Scarlatti, Predieri,

Stradella, and Bach. *Battle, soprano; Marsalis, trumpet; Newman, harpsichord & organ; Orch. of St. Luke's; Nelson, cond.*
+ ARG 9-10/92: 202
+ Fa 9-10/92: 393
+ Gr 8/92: 63

31837. SMK 46680: Tchaikovsky—Symphony no. 5; The snow maiden (selections). *St. Petersburg Phil. Orch.; Dmitriev, cond.*
- ARG 1-2/96: 187
• Fa 1-2/96: 321

31838. SMK 46683: Arnell—Punch and the child. Berners—The triumph of Neptune. Delius—Paris. *Grooters, baritone; Royal Phil. Orch.; Philadelphia Orch.; Beecham, cond.* Recorded 1951-56.
+ Gr 11/94: 62

31839. SMK 46684: Elgar—Enigma variations; Pomp and circumstance. *Philharmonia Orch.; A. Davis, cond.* Reissue.
• Gr 9/94: 54

31840. SK 46690: Schubert—Piano sonatas D. 958-959. *Swartzentruber, piano.*
+ Gr 4/94: 74

31841. SK 46691: *The first Plácido Domingo International Voice Competition gala concert.* Music of Meyerbeer, Bellini, Catalani, Gounod, Massenet, Donizetti, Verdi, Penella, Sorozabal, Mozart, and Puccini. *Arteta, Mula- Tchako, Stemme, sopranos; Domingo, tenor; Yuon, bass; Orchestre de l'Opéra de Paris-Bastille; Kohn, cond.*
+ ARG 1-2/95: 247
• Fa 11-12/94: 451
+ Gr 6/94: 116

31842. SK 46693: Gazzaniga—Don Giovanni, ossia, Il convitato di pietra. *Johnson, Serra, Szmytka, Furlanetto; Stuttgart Chamber Choir; Tafelmusik Baroque Orch.; Weil, cond.*
• ARG 7-8/92: 132
+ EM 11/92: 695
+ Fa 3-4/92: 191
• Gr 1/92: 92
+ ON 4/11/92: 47

31843. SK 46694: *1994 New Year's concert.* Music of Lanner and the Strausses. *Vienna Phil. Orch.; Maazel, cond.*
+ ARG 9-10/94: 222
• Fa 9-10/94: 345
+ Gr 7/94: 66

31844. SK 46695: Mozart—Overtures: Idomeneo; Entführung; Schauspieldirektor; Nozze di Figaro; Don Giovanni; Così fan tutte; Clemenza di Tito; Zauberflöte; Eine kleine Nachtmusik. *Tafelmusik; Weil, cond.*
+ ARG 3-4/92: 109

+ Fa 3-4/92: 260
+ Gr 5/92: 43

31845. SK 46696: Mozart—German dances, K. 509, K. 536-37, K. 571, K. 586. *Tafelmusik; Weil, cond.*
+ ARG 3-4/92: 110
+ Fa 3-4/92: 260
+ Gr 5/92: 40

31846. SK 46697: Schubert—Symphonies no. 5-6. *Classical Band; Weil, cond.*
- ARG 5-6/92: 126
• EM 5/93: 324
• Fa 3-4/92: 315

31847. SK 46699: Flecha—Ensaladas. *Huelgas Ensemble; Nevel, cond.*
+ ARG 3-4/92: 57
+ Fa 5-6/92: 160
+ Gr 9/92: 142

31848. SK 46700: Mozart—Piano sonata no. 5, 11; Rondo, K. 485; Adagio, K. 540; Variations, K. 573. *Vladar, piano.*
+ ARG 11-12/91: 121
- Fa 9-10/91: 296
+ Gr 6/91: 67

31849. SMK 46701: *Leonard Bernstein: A tribute.* Music of Bernstein, Gershwin, Mahler, and Ives. *Bogart, alto; Camerata Singers; Columbia Symphony Orch.; New York Phil. Orch.; Bernstein, cond.*
+ ARG 7-8/91: 34
+ Fa 5-6/91: 386

31850. SK 46702: Mozart—3 Marches, K. 445; K. 248; K. 290; 12 Duos for horns, K. 487, no. 2, 5, 8, 10; Quintet in E♭ for horn and strings, K. 407; A musical joke (Sextet in F), K. 522; 2 divertimento fragments: in F, K. 288; in D, K. 246b. *L'Archibudelli.*
+ ARG 11-12/91: 116
+ Fa 11-12/91: 407
+ Gr 12/91: 93

31851. S2K 46717 (2 discs): Strauss—Salome. *Marton, Zednik, Fassbaender, Weikl; Berlin Phil. Orch.; Mehta, cond.*
• ARG 1-2/92: 122
• Fa 3-4/92: 334
• Gr 10/91: 190
• ON 2/1/92: 36
+ Op 1/92: 120
• OQ spring 93: 170
+ St 5/92: 199

31852. SK 46720: Takemitsu—To the edge of dream; Folios for guitar; Toward the sea; Twelve songs for guitar: Excerpts; Vers, l'arc-en-ciel, Palma. *Williams, guitar; London Sinfonietta; Salonen, cond.*
+ ARG 9-10/92: 192
+ Fa 7-8/92: 303
+ Gr 1/92: 63

31853. SMK 46727: Barber—Vocal music. *Various artists.* Reissues; recorded

SONY CLASSICAL

1950-68.
+ Gr 10/91: 152

31854. SM4K 46738 (4 discs):
BEETHOVEN—The complete piano trios.
Istomin, piano; Stern, violin; Rose, cello.
Reissue.
+ ARG 11-12/91: 30
• Fa 11-12/91: 268

31855. SK 46742: *Midori live at
Carnegie Hall.* BEETHOVEN—Violin sonata
no. 8. R. STRAUSS—Violin sonata, op. 18.
CHOPIN—Nocturne in C♯ minor, op. posth.
ERNST—Variations on an Irish air: The
last rose of summer. DEBUSSY—Beau soir.
RAVEL—Tzigane. *Midori, violin;
McDonald, piano.*
+ ARG 1-2/92: 164
+ Fa 9-10/91: 423

31856. SM2K 46743 (2 discs): *Concert of
the century.* BEETHOVEN—Leonore
overture no. 3. TCHAIKOVSKY—Piano trio:
Pezzo elegiaco; Pater noster.
RACHMANINOFF—Cello sonata: Andante.
SCHUMANN—Dichterliebe, op. 48. BACH—
Concerto for 2 violins. HANDEL—
Messiah: Hallelujah chorus. *Fischer-
Dieskau, baritone; Stern, Menuhin,
violins; Rostropovich, cello; Horowitz,
piano; Oratorio Society; Woodside,
cond.; members of the New York Phil.;
Bernstein, cond.* Reissue.
• Fa 9-10/91: 445
- Gr 11/91: 106

31857. SK 46747: *I love a parade.*
Marches by Sousa, Williams, Arlen,
Willson; Allen, Bauduc and Haggart,
Alford, Gershwin, and F. Wagner. *Boston
Pops Orch.; Williams, cond.*
+ ARG 11-12/91: 175
+ Fa 11-12/91: 573

31858. SK 46748: MOZART—Piano
sonatas, K. 332, K. 333, K. 457; Fantasia,
K. 475. *Haefliger, piano.*
+ ARG 7-8/92: 194
• Fa 3-4/92: 268
+ Gr 9/92: 135

31859. SM3K 47154 (3 discs):
BERNSTEIN—On the town dance episodes;
Candide overture; West Side story
dances; On the waterfront suite; Fance
free ballet; Trouble in Tahiti; Facsimile.
Bernstein, cond. Reissues.
+ ARG 5-6/92: 30
+ Gr 5/92: 105

31860. SM3K 47158 (3 discs):
BERNSTEIN—Mass; Dybbuk. *Titus;
Norman Scribner Choir; Berkshire Boy
Choir; D. Johnson, baritone; Ostendorf,
bass; Bernstein, cond.* Reissue.
+ ARG 7-8/92: 99
+ Gr 5/92: 80

31861. SM3K 47162 (3 discs):
BERNSTEIN—Symphony no. 1 "Jeremiah";
Symphony no. 2 "Age of anxiety";
Symphony no. 3 "Kaddish"; Chichester

psalms; Serenade; Prelude, fugue and
riffs. *Tourel, mezzo-soprano; Entremont,
piano; Camerata Singers; Francescatti,
violin; Goodman, clarinet; New York
Phil.; Bernstein, cond.* Reissue.
+ ARG 7-8/92: 99
+ Gr 3/92: 39

31862. S2MK 47166 (3 discs): *Bernstein
at the piano.* Music of Mozart,
Beethoven, Shostakovich, Gershwin,
Ravel and Schumann. *L. Bernstein,
piano; with accompanying orchestras or
instrumentalists.* Reissues.
+ ARG 3-4/92: 189
+ Gr 3/92: 58

31863. S2K 47170 (2 discs): MAHLER—
Des Knaben Wunderhorn; Lieder und
Gesänge aus der Jugendzeit; Rückert
Lieder; Lieder eines fahrenden Gesellen.
*Ludwig, alto; Berry, bass; Fischer-
Dieskau, baritone; Bernstein, piano.*
Reissue.
+ ARG 3-4/92: 92
+ Gr 3/92: 103

31864. SK 47178: WAGNER—Tannhäuser:
orchestral excerpts. *Pittsburgh Symphony
Orch.; Maazel, cond.*
+ ARG 3-4/92: 163
+ Fa 3-4/92: 362
• Gr 4/92: 86

31865. SK 47179: TCHAIKOVSKY—1812
overture; Marche slave; Romeo and
Juliet; The tempest. *Chicago Symphony
Orch.; Abbado, cond.* Reissues.
• ARG 3-4/92: 152
• Fa 3-4/92: 343
• Gr 10/91: 114

31866. SK 47180: FRANCK—Prélude,
choral et fugue. LISZT—Mephisto waltz,
no. 1; Sonetto 104 del Petrarca; Two
concert studies; Rhapsodie espagnole.
Perahia, piano.
+ ARG 3-4/92: 58
• Fa 3-4/92: 191
+ Gr 10/91: 139
+ St 11/92: 233

31867. SK 47181: BRAHMS—Piano sonata
no. 3; Rhapsody, op. 119, no. 4;
Capriccio, op. 76, no. 2; Intermezzo, op.
118, no. 6; Rhapsody, op. 79, no. 2.
Perahia, piano.
+ ARG 3-4/92: 37
+ Fa 3-4/92: 164
+ Gr 10/91: 138
• St 11/92: 233

31868. SK 47182: JANÁČEK—Glagolitic
mass; Sinfonietta. *Beňačková, Palmer,
Lakes, Kotcherga; London Symphony
Orch. & Chorus; Thomas, cond.*
+ ARG 3-4/93: 97
+ Fa 11-12/92: 266 (Hurwitz)
- Fa 11-12/92: 267 (Wiser)
• Gr 9/92: 146

31869. SK 47183: RACHMANINOFF—Piano
concertos no. 2-3. *Bronfman, piano;*

Philharmonia Orch.; Salonen, cond.
• ARG 7-8/92: 202
• Fa 9-10/92: 320
• Gr 9/92: 83

31870. SK 47184: *Glenn Gould the
composer.* GOULD—Lieberson madrigal;
String quartet op. 1; Two pieces for
piano; Sonata for bassoon and piano;
Piano sonata (unfinished); So you want to
write a fugue? *Varous performers.*
• ARG 3-4/93: 82
+ Fa 3-4/93: 170
• Gr 11/92: 138

31871. SK 47187: *Souvenir aus Wien.*
Music of Johann Strauss Jr. and Sr.,
August and Josef Lanner, and Schubert.
Ensemble Wien.
+ Fa 7-8/92: 290
+ Gr 9/92: 120

31872. SK 47188: RAVEL—Concerto for
piano and orchestra "For the left hand."
PROKOFIEV—Concerto no. 4 for piano (left
hand) and orchestra. BRITTEN—Diversions
for piano (left hand) and orchestra.
*Fleisher, piano; Boston Symphony Orch.;
Ozawa, cond.*
+ ARG 5-6/93: 123
+ ARG 7-8/93: 74
+ Fa 5-6/93: 288
+ Gr 4/93: 43

31873. S2K 47189 (2 discs): PUCCINI—La
fanciulla del West. *Zampieri, Domingo,
Pons; Chorus & Orch. of La Scala,
Milan; Maazel, cond.*
- ARG 9-10/92: 143
• Fa 9-10/92: 316
• Gr 6/92: 85
• ON 7/92: 38
• Op 9/92: 1127
- St 5/93: 181

31874. SK 47192: MOZART—Arias from
Le nozze di Figaro; Don Giovanni; Cosí
fan tutte; Die Zauberflöte. *Furlanetto,
bass-baritone; Vienna Symphony Orch.;
Marin, cond.*
+ ARG 5-6/92: 92
+ Fa 5-6/92: 201
+ Gr 3/92: 113
+ ON 3/14/92: 35
+ Op 8/92: 1000

31875. SK 47193: *On the twentieth
century.* Music of Ravel, Honegger,
Tomasi, Stevens, Poulenc, Enesco,
Bernstein, Bozza, and Hindemith.
Marsalis, trumpet; Stillman, piano.
+ ARG 3-4/94: 216
• Gr 5/94: 76

31876. SK 47195: BRAHMS—Serenade no.
2; Haydn variations; Hungarian dances,
no. 1, 3, 10, 17-21. *London Symphony
Orch.; Thomas, cond.*
+ ARG 5-6/92: 36
+ Fa 5-6/92: 128
• Gr 4/92: 45

31877. SK 47196: BRAHMS—Piano sonata no. 1; Four ballades, op. 10. *Vladar, piano.*
- ● ARG 7-8/92: 106
- + Fa 5-6/92: 129
- ● Gr 3/92: 76
- + St 11/92: 223

31878. SK 47197: STRAUSS—Suites from Der Rosenkavalier, Intermezzo, Die Frau ohne Schatten, and Die Liebe der Danae. *Berlin Phil. Orch.; Mehta, cond.*
- + ARG 9-10/93: 199
- + Fa 9-10/93: 300
- ● Gr 7/93: 54

31879. SK 47198: *Live in Osaka.* Music of Bach, Holst, Schwantner, Grainger, Ives, Shostakovich, Rimsky- Korsakov, Mamiya, and Sousa. *Eastman Wind Ensemble; Hunsberger, cond.*
- ● Fa 9-10/92: 441

31880. SK 47199: DVOŘÁK—From the Bohemian forest. RUBINSTEIN—Six characteristic pieces, op. 50. RACHMANINOFF—Six pieces, op. 11. *Tal, Groethuysen, piano, 4 hands.*
- + ARG 11-12/92: 115
- ● Fa 11-12/92: 227
- + Gr 11/92: 137

31881. SM3K 47207 (3 discs): MOZART—Piano concertos no. 10, 12, 14, 17, 19, 20, 27; Rondo, K. 382; Rondo, K. 511. *R. Serkin, piano; various orchestras & conds.* Reissues.
- + Fa 5-6/92: 203

31882. SM2K 47219 (2 discs): MOZART—Six quartets dedicated to Haydn. *Budapest String Quartet.* Reissue.
- + Fa 3-4/92: 262

31883. SM4K 47222 (4 discs): MOZART—Piano sonatas (complete). *Kraus, piano.* Reissue.
- + Fa 3-4/92: 267

31884. SK 47228: *Italian flute concertos.* ROMANO—Concerto in G major. CECERE—Concerto in A major. ALBERTI—Concerto in F major "Con sordini." SAMMARTINI—Concerto in G major. *Rampal, flute; I Solisti Veneti; Scimone, cond.*
- + Gr 2/92: 43

31885. S2K 47229 (2 discs): CARTER—The 4 String quartets; Duo for violin and piano. *Juilliard String Quartet; Oldfather, piano.*
- + ARG 3-4/92: 43
- + Fa 3-4/92: 170
- + Gr 4/92: 94
- + St 8/92: 183

31886. SK 47230: MOZART—Divertimento, K. 334; String quintet, K. 577; Andante for mechanical organ, K. 616; Adagio and rondo, K. 617. *Rampal, flute; Trio Pasquier.*
- - ARG 11-12/91: 108

- + Fa 11-12/91: 399
- + Gr 11/91: 121

31887. SM2K 47232 (2 discs): COPLAND—*Early orchestral works, 1922-1935.* Dance symphony; Two pieces for string orchestra; Symphony for organ and orchestra; Music for the theatre; Piano concerto; Symphonic ode; Short symphony; Statements. *London Symphony Orch.; Copland, cond.; New York Phil.; Bernstein, cond.; Copland, piano.* Reissues.
- + ARG 1-2/92: 46
- + Fa 1-2/92: 197

31888. SM2K 47236 (2 discs): COPLAND—*Orchestral works, 1948-1971.* The red pony; Preamble for a solemn occasion; Orchestral variations; Dance panels; Connotations; Down a country lane; Music for a great city; Inscape; Three Latin-American sketches. *New Philharmonia Orch.; Copland, cond.; New York Phil.; Bernstein, cond.* Reissues.
- + ARG 3-4/92: 48
- + Fa 1-2/92: 197

31889. MDK 47253: The Noël Coward album. *Coward, performer; Carl Hayes and his orch.; orch. cond. by Matz.*
- + Fa 1-2/92: 395

31890. S2K 47260 (2 discs): MOZART—Symphonies after serenades, K. 100, K. 203, K. 250, K. 185, K. 204, K. 320. *Tafelmusik; Weil, cond.*
- + Fa 3-4/92: 260
- + Gr 12/92: 85

31891. SK 47264: MOZART—Symphonies no. 40, 41. *Berlin Phil. Orch.; Giulini, cond.*
- + ARG 7-8/92: 99
- + Fa 5-6/92: 212
- + Gr 3/92: 48

31892. SM3K 47265 (3 discs): DEBUSSY—Pelléas et Mélisande. *Shirley, Söderström, MacIntyre, Ward; Royal Opera Covent Garden; Boulez, cond.* Reissue.
- + Gr 4/92: 153

31893. SM3K 47269 (3 discs): *Rudolf Serkin: The legendary concerto recordings, 1950-1956.* BEETHOVEN—Concerto no. 5. BRAHMS—Concerto no. 2. MOZART—Concertos no. 21, 25. SCHUMANN—Concerto, op. 54. R. STRAUSS—Burleske. *Serkin, piano; Philadelphia Orch.; Ormandy, cond.; Columbia Symphony Orch.; Schneider, Szell, conds.* Reissues.
- + ARG 3-4/92: 192
- + Fa 1-2/92: 404

31894. S2K 47290 (2 discs): CHERUBINI—Lodoïska. *Devia, Lombardo, Moser, Shimell; Teatro alla Scala; Muti, cond.* Recorded live 1991.
- ● ARG 3-4/92: 45

- + Fa 3-4/92: 173
- + Gr 10/91: 183
- ● ON 12/7/91: 54
- + OQ spring 93: 199

31895. SMK 47294: MOZART—Symphonies no. 35, 40-41. *Marlboro Festival Orch.; Casals, cond.* Reissue.
- + ARG 11-12/91: 119
- + Fa 11-12/91: 415

31896. SMK 47295: MOZART—Eine kleine Nachtmusik; Serenades no. 11-12. *Marlboro Festival Orch.; Casals, cond.* Reissue.
- + ARG 11-12/91: 119
- + Fa 11-12/91: 407

31897. SMK 47296: BEETHOVEN—Trio for piano, clarinet and cello, op. 11; Quintet for piano and winds, op. 16; Variations for piano trio, op. 121a. *Various performers; with Serkin, piano.* Reissue.
- + ARG 3-4/92: 30
- ● Fa 11-12/91: 268

31898. SMK 47297: SCHUBERT—Symphony no. 8. SCHUMANN—Symphony no. 2. *Marlboro Festival Orch.; Casals, cond.* Reissue.
- + ARG 1-2/92: 107
- ● Fa 11-12/91: 476

31899. SMK 47298: BOCCHERINI—Guitar quintets G449, G541; String quintet, G308. *Instrumentalists; Starobin, guitar.* Reissue.
- ● ARG 5-6/92: 31
- + Fa 11-12/91: 278
- + Gr 9/92: 104

31900. SMK 47510: BARTÓK—Concerto for orchestra; Music for strings, percussion, and celesta. *New York Phil.; Bernstein, cond.* Reissue.
- + ARG 11-12/92: 78

31901. SMK 47511 (2 discs): BARTÓK—Piano concertos no. 2-3; Violin concerto and rhapsodies; Two-piano concerto. *Entremont, piano; Stern, violin; New York Phil.; Bernstein, cond.*
- ● ARG 11-12/92: 78

31902. SMK 47514—47521 (7 separate discs): BEETHOVEN—9 symphonies; Violin concerto; Piano concertos no. 3, 5; Overtures: Consecration of the house; Coriolan; Egmont; Fidelio; Leonore no. 3. *Serkin, piano; Stern, violin; New York Phil.; Bernstein, cond.*
- ● ARG 11-12/92: 82

31903. SMK 47519: MOZART—Piano concerto no. 25. BEETHOVEN—Piano concerto no. 1. *Bernstein, piano & cond.; Israel Phil. Orch.*
- + ARG 11-12/92: 166

31904. SM2K 47522 (2 discs): BEETHOVEN—Missa solemnis; Choral fantasy. HAYDN—Mass no. 12. *Vocal soloists; R. Serkin, piano; New York Phil.*

SONY CLASSICAL

Orch.; London Symphony Orch.;
Bernstein, cond. Reissues.
+ ARG 1-2/93: 73

31905. SMK 47525: BERLIOZ—
Symphonie fantastique; Benvenuto
Cellini overture; Roman carnival
overture; Rákóczy march. *New York*
Phil.; Bernstein, cond. Reissue.
+ ARG 11-12/92: 88
+ Fa 1-2/93: 113

31906. SM2K 47526 (2 discs):
BERLIOZ—Requiem; La mort de
Cléopâtre; Roméo et Juliette: Excerpts.
Burrows, tenor; Radio France Choirs;
Orch. National de France; Tourel,
mezzo-soprano; New York Phil. Orch.;
Bernstein, cond. Reissue.
+ ARG 11-12/92: 87

31907. SMK 47529: BERNSTEIN—West
Side story dances; Candide overture.
GERSHWIN—An American in Paris;
Rhapsody in blue. *New York Phil. Orch.;*
Bernstein, cond. Reissues.
+ ARG 1-2/93: 78

31908. SMK 47530: BERNSTEIN—On the
town dances; Fancy free; On the
waterfront suite. *New York Phil. Orch.;*
Bernstein, cond. Reissues.
+ ARG 1-2/93: 78

31909. SMK 47531: BIZET—Carmen
suites; Arlésienne suites. *New York Phil.;*
Bernstein, cond. Reissues.
+ ARG 1-2/93: 79

31910. SMK 47532: BIZET—Symphony.
OFFENBACH—Gaité parisienne; Orpheus in
the underworld overture. *New York Phil.;*
Bernstein, cond. Reissues.
+ ARG 1-2/93: 79

31911. SMK 47533: BLOCH—Sacred
service. FOSS—Song of songs. BEN-
HAIM—Sweet psalmist of Israel. *Vocal*
soloists; Chorus; New York Phil.;
Bernstein, cond. Reissues.
+ ARG 1-2/93: 79
+ Fa 5-6/93: 169

31912. SMK 47536: BRAHMS—Symphony
no. 1; Serenade no. 2. *New York Phil.;*
Bernstein, cond. Reissues.
+ ARG 1-2/93: 82

31913. SMK 47537: BRAHMS—
Symphonies, no. 2-3. *New York Phil.;*
Bernstein, cond. Reissues.
+ ARG 1-2/93: 82

31914. SMK 47538: BRAHMS—Symphony
no. 4; Academic festival overture; Tragic
overture. *New York Phil.; Bernstein,*
cond. Reissues.
+ ARG 1-2/93: 82

31915. SMK 47539: BRAHMS—Piano
concerto no. 2; Haydn variations. *Watts,*
piano; New York Phil.; Bernstein, cond.

Reissues.
- ARG 1-2/93: 80

31916. SMK 47540: BRAHMS—Violin
concerto. SIBELIUS—Violin concerto.
Francescatti, violin; New York Phil.;
Bernstein, cond. Reissues.
+ ARG 1-2/93: 80

31917. SMK 47541: *Royal edition.*
BRITTEN—Purcell variations; Peter Grimes
sea interludes and passacaglia; Suite on
English folk tunes. *New York Phil.;*
Bernstein, cond.
• ARG 11-12/92: 98

31918. SMK 47542: BRUCKNER—
Symphony no. 9. *New York Phil.;*
Bernstein, cond. Reissue.
• ARG 11-12/92: 99
• Fa 1-2/93: 121

31919. SMK 47543: COPLAND—
Appalachian spring; Rodeo: four dance
episodes; Billy the Kid: orchestral suite;
Fanfare for the common man. *New York*
Phil.; Bernstein, cond. Reissue.
+ Fa 3-4/93: 147
+ Gr 5/93: 56

31920. SMK 47544: Music of Copland,
Grofe, Guarnieri, Revueltas, and others.
New York Phil.; Bernstein, cond. Reissue.
+ Gr 5/93: 56

31921. SMK 47545: DEBUSSY—Images
pour orchestre; Rhapsody no. 1 for
clarinet and orchestra. RAVEL—Ma Mère
l'Oye; Pavane pour une infante défunte.
New York Phil.; Bernstein, cond.
+ Fa 3-4/93: 150
• Gr 5/93: 56

31922. SMK 47546: DEBUSSY—La mer;
Prélude à l'après-midi d'un faune; Jeux;
Nocturnes: Nuages ; Fêtes. *New York*
Phil.; Bernstein, cond. Reissues.
+ Fa 3-4/93: 150
• Gr 5/93: 56

31923. SMK 47547: DVOŘÁK—Symphony
no. 9; Carnival overture; Slavonic dances.
SMETANA—Moldau. *New York Phil.;*
Bernstein, cond. Reissue.
• Gr 5/93: 56

31924. SMK 47548: FRANCK—
Symphony. CHAUSSON—Poème. FAURÉ—
Ballade. RAVEL—Tzigane. *Casadesus,*
piano; Francescatti, violin; New York
Phil.; Bernstein, cond. Reissues.
+ Gr 5/93: 56

31925. SMK 47549: GRIEG—Peer Gynt:
Suites 1-2; Norwegian dances; Lyric
suite: March of the dwarves. SIBELIUS—
Finlandia; Valse triste; Swan of Tuonela.
New York Phil.; Bernstein, cond.
Reissues.
• Gr 5/93: 56

31926. SM2K 47550 (2 discs): HAYDN—
The six "Paris" symphonies. *New York*

Phil.; Bernstein, cond.
+ ARG 3-4/93: 91
+ Fa 3-4/93: 185
+ Gr 5/93: 56

31927. SM3K 47553 (3 discs): HAYDN—
Symphonies no. 93-99. *New York Phil.*
Orch.; Bernstein, cond.
+ ARG 3-4/93: 91
• Gr 5/93: 56

31928. SM2K 47557 (2 discs): *Five*
"London" symphonies. HAYDN—
Symphonies no. 100 "Military," no. 101
"The clock," 102, 103 "Drum roll," 104
"London". *New York Phil.; Bernstein,*
cond.
+ ARG 3-4/93: 91
• Fa 3-4/93: 185
• Gr 5/93: 56

31929. SM2K 47560 (2 discs): HAYDN—
The creation; Mass no. 14
"Harmoniemesse". *Soloists; New York*
Phil.; Bernstein, cond.
• ARG 3-4/93: 88
• Fa 3-4/93: 185
+ Gr 5/93: 56

31930. SM2K 47563 (2 discs): HAYDN—
Missa in tempore belli; Missa in angustiis
"Nelson mass"; Symphony no. 88.
Soloists; New York Phil.; Bernstein,
cond. Reissue.
• ARG 5-6/93: 91
+ Fa 3-4/93: 181
+ Gr 5/93: 56

31931. SMK 47566: HINDEMITH—
Symphony in E♭; Symphonic
metamorphoses on themes of Carl Maria
von Weber; Concert music for strings and
brass, op. 50. *New York Phil. Orch.;*
Bernstein, cond. Reissue.
+ ARG 5-6/93: 95
+ Fa 5-6/93: 222
+ Gr 5/93: 56

31932. SMK 47567: HOLST—Planets.
BARBER—Adagio for strings. ELGAR—
Pomp and circumstance no. 1. *New York*
Phil.; Bernstein, cond. Reissues.
• Gr 5/93: 56

31933. SMK 47568: IVES—Symphonies
no. 2-3. *New York Phil.; Bernstein, cond.*
Reissues.
• Gr 5/93: 56

31934. SMK 47569: JANÁČEK—Slavonic
mass. POULENC—Gloria. *Westminster*
Choir; New York Phil.; Bernstein, cond.
Reissues.
+ ARG 5-6/93: 98
• Gr 5/93: 56

31935. SMK 47570: LISZT—Faust
symphony. *Bressler, tenor; New York*
Phil.; Bernstein, cond. Reissue.
+ ARG 5-6/93: 102
+ Gr 5/93: 56

31936. SMK 47571: LISZT—Piano concerto no. 1. RACHMANINOFF—Rhapsody on a theme of Paganini. RAVEL—Piano concerto in G. *Watts, Graffman, Bernstein, piano; New York Phil.; Bernstein, cond.* Reissues.
+ Gr 5/93: 56

31937. SMK 47572: Music of Liszt, Enescu, and Brahms. *New York Phil.; Bernstein, cond.* Reissues.
● Gr 5/93: 56

31938. SM2K 47573 (2 discs): MAHLER—Symphonies no. 1-2. *New York Phil.; London Symphony Orch.; Bernstein, cond.* Reissues.
+ Gr 5/93: 56

31939. SM2K 47576 (2 discs): MAHLER—Symphony no. 3. *New York Phil.; Bernstein, cond.* Reissue.
+ Gr 5/93: 56

31940. SMK 47579: MAHLER— Symphony no. 4. *Grist, soprano; New York Phil.; Bernstein, cond.* Reissue.
+ Gr 5/93: 56

31941. SMK 47580: MAHLER— Symphony no. 5. *New York Phil.; Bernstein, cond.* Reissue.
+ Gr 5/93: 56

31942. SM3K 47581 (3 discs): MAHLER—Symphonies no. 6, 8. *New York Phil.; Bernstein, cond.* Reissues.
+ Gr 5/93: 56

31943. SM3K 47585 (3 discs): MAHLER—Symphonies no. 7, 9, 10: Adagio. *New York Phil.; Bernstein, cond.* Reissues.
+ Gr 5/93: 56

31944. SMK 47591: MENDELSSOHN— Symphonies no. 3, 5; Ruy Blas; War march of the priests. *New York Phil.; Bernstein, cond.* Reissues.
● Gr 8/93: 32

31945. SMK 47592: MENDELSSOHN— Symphony no. 4; Violin concerto; Hebrides. *Zukerman, violin; New York Phil.; Bernstein, cond.* Reissues.
● Gr 8/93: 32

31946. SMK 47597: NIELSEN— Symphonies no. 2, 4. *New York Phil.; Bernstein, cond.* Reissues.
- Gr 7/93: 46

31947. SMK 47598: NIELSEN— Symphonies no. 3, 5. *New York Phil.; Bernstein, cond.* Reissues.
+ Gr 7/93: 46

31948. SMK 47599: NIELSEN—Flute concerto; Clarinet concerto. HINDEMITH— Violin concerto. *Baker, flute; Drucker, clarinet; Stern, violin; New York Phil.; Bernstein, cond.* Reissues.
+ Gr 7/93: 46

31949. SMK 47600: *Music from famous opera.* Music of Borodin, Gounod, Ponchielli, Rimsky-Korsakov, Saint-Saëns, and Verdi. *New York Phil.; Bernstein, cond .* Reissues.
● Gr 9/93: 68

31950. SMK 47601: *Opera overtures.* Music of Mozart, Nicolai, Reznicek, Strauss, Weber, and Smetana. *New York Phil.; Bernstein, cond .* Reissues.
+ Gr 9/93: 68

31951. SMK 47602: PROKOFIEV— Symphonies no. 1, 5. *New York Phil.; Bernstein, cond.*
- Fa 11-12/93: 349
● Gr 7/93:
- Fa 11-12/93: 349
● Gr 7/93

31952. SMK 47603: RAVEL—Bolero; La valse; Alborada del gracioso; Daphnis et Chloé: Suite no. 2; Rapsodie espagnole. *French National Orch.; New York Phil.; Bernstein, cond.* Reissues.
● Gr 7/93: 49

31953. SMK 47604: RAVEL—Daphnis et Chloé; Shéhérazade. *Horne, mezzo-soprano; French National Orch.; New York Phil.; Bernstein, cond.* Reissues.
● Gr 7/93: 49

31954. SMK 47606: ROSSINI—Overtures. SUPPÉ—Overtures. *New York Phil.; Bernstein, cond.* Reissue.
+ ARG 11-12/93: 181

31955. SMK 47608: SAINT-SAËNS— Symphony no. 3; Piano concerto no. 4; Introduction and rondo capriccioso. *Raver, organ; Casadesus, piano; Francescatti, violin; New York Phil.; Bernstein, cond.* Reissue.
+ ARG 11-12/93: 182

31956. SMK 47609: SCHUMANN—Cello concerto; Genoveva overture. SCHUBERT—Symphony no. 5; Der Teufels Lustschloss overture. *Rose, cello; New York Phil.; Bernstein, cond.* Reissues.
+ ARG 11-12/93: 192
+ Gr 9/93: 58

31957. SMK 47611—47612 (2 separate discs): SCHUMANN—Symphonies . *New York Phil.; Bernstein, cond.* Reissues.
+ ARG 11-12/93: 192
+ Gr 9/93: 58

31958. SMK 47614: SHOSTAKOVICH— Symphonies, no. 1, 6. *New York Phil.; Bernstein, cond.* Reissue.
+ ARG 1-2/94: 154
● Gr 6/94: 60

31959. SMK 47615: SHOSTAKOVICH— Symphonies no. 5, 9. *New York Phil.; Bernstein, cond.* Reissue.
+ ARG 3-4/94: 156
● Gr 6/94: 60

31960. SMK 47616: SHOSTAKOVICH— Symphony no. 7. *New York Phil.; Bernstein, cond.*
+ ARG 3-4/94: 156
● Gr 6/94: 60

31961. SMK 47617: SHOSTAKOVICH— Symphony no. 14. *Kubiak, soprano; Bushkin, bass; New York Phil.; Bernstein, cond.* Reissue.
+ ARG 3-4/94: 157
● Gr 6/94: 60

31962. SMK 47618: SHOSTAKOVICH— Piano concertos no. 1-2. POULENC—2-piano concerto. *Previn, Bernstein, Gold, Fizdale, pianos; New York Phil.; Bernstein, cond.*
+ ARG 3-4/94: 155
● Gr 6/94: 62

31963. SM2K 47619 (2 discs): SIBELIUS—Symphonies no. 1-3. *New York Phil.; Bernstein, cond.* Reissues.
+ ARG 1-2/94: 156

31964. SMK 47625: STRAUSS—Don Quixote; Festival prelude; Dance of the seven veils. *Munroe, cello; New York Phil.; Bernstein, cond.* Reissue.
+ ARG 1-2/94: 159
● Gr 9/94: 64

31965. SMK 47626: STRAUSS—Also sprach Zarathustra; Till Eulenspiegel; Don Juan. *New York Phil.; Bernstein, cond.*
● ARG 3-4/94: 160

31966. SMK 47627: J. STRAUSS, JR.— Orchestral music. *New York Phil.; Bernstein, cond.*
+ ARG 3-4/94: 159

31967. SMK 47628: STRAVINSKY— Symphony of psalms; Piano concerto; Pucinella suite. *Lipkin, piano; English Bach Festival Chorus; London Symphony Orch.; New York Phil.; Bernstein, cond.* Reissue.
● ARG 5-6/94: 150
+ Gr 11/94: 88

31968. SMK 47629: STRAVINSKY—Rite of spring; Petrushka. *New York Phil.; Bernstein, cond.* Reissue.
+ ARG 5-6/94: 149

31969. SMK 47630: TCHAIKOVSKY—Piano concerto no. 1. RACHMANINOFF—Piano concerto no. 2. *Watts, Graffman, piano; New York Phil.; Bernstein, cond.* Reissues.
+ ARG 5-6/94: 153

31970. SMK 47631: TCHAIKOVSKY— Symphonies no. 1-2. *New York Phil.; Bernstein, cond.*
+ ARG 3-4/94: 170

31971. SMK 47632: TCHAIKOVSKY— Symphony no. 3. *New York Phil.;*

SONY CLASSICAL

Bernstein, cond.
+ ARG 3-4/94: 170

31972. SMK 47633: TCHAIKOVSKY—
Symphony no. 4; Francesca da Rimini.
New York Phil.; Bernstein, cond.
+ ARG 3-4/94: 170

31973. SMK 47634: TCHAIKOVSKY—
Symphony no. 5; 1812 overture; Marche
slave. *New York Phil.; Bernstein, cond.*
+ ARG 3-4/94: 170

31974. SMK 47635: TCHAIKOVSKY—
Symphony no. 6; Hamlet. *New York
Phil.; Bernstein, cond.*
+ ARG 3-4/94: 171

31975. SMK 47636: TCHAIKOVSKY—
Nutcracker suite; Swan Lake excerpts.
New York Phil.; Bernstein, cond.
● ARG 3-4/94: 166

31976. SMK 47637: TCHAIKOVSKY—
Violin concerto; Serenade for strings.
*Stern, violin; New York Phil.; Bernstein,
cond.*
● ARG 3-4/94: 165

31977. SMK 47638: VAUGHAN
WILLIAMS—Symphony no. 4; Tallis
fantasia; Greensleeves; Serenade to
music. *New York Phil.; Bernstein, cond.*
Reissues.
ı ARG 5-6/94: 162
+ Gr 7/94: 66

31978. SM2K 47639 (2 discs): VERDI—
Requiem. *Arroyo, Veasey, Domingo,
Raimondi; London Symphony Orch. &
Chorus; Bernstein, cond.* Reissue.
● ARG 5-6/94: 164

31979. SMK 47642: VIVALDI—Four
seasons; Concertos. *Corigliano, violin;
Gomberg, oboe; Wummer, flute; New
York Phil.; Bernstein, cond.* Reissues.
+ ARG 5-6/94: 165

31980. SMK 47643: WAGNER—Overtures.
New York Phil.; Bernstein, cond.
+ ARG 3-4/94: 180

31981. SMK 47644: WAGNER—Selections
from Tannhäuser, Tristan und Isolde,
Götterdämmerung; Wesendonck Lieder.
*Farrell, soprano; New York Phil.;
Bernstein, cond.* Reissues.
● ARG 5-6/94: 165

31982. SMK 47646: BRUCKNER—
Symphony no. 7. *Vienna Phil. Orch.;
Szell, cond.* Reissue.
● ARG 1-2/95: 92
- Gr 1/95: 42

31983. SBK 47651: BEETHOVEN—
Symphonies, no. 2, 5. *Cleveland Orch.;
Szell, cond.* Reissues.
+ ARG 7-8/92: 90
+ Fa 5-6/92: 124

31984. SBK 47653: BRUCKNER—
Symphony no. 4. *Philadelphia Orch.;
Ormandy, cond.* Reissue.
+ ARG 3-4/92: 38

31985. SBK 47658: BEETHOVEN—Piano
concertos no. 1, 3. *Fleisher, piano;
Cleveland Orch.; Szell, cond.* Reissues.
+ ARG 7-8/92: 90
+ Fa 5-6/92: 121

31986. SBK 47666: BEETHOVEN—Piano
sonatas no. 8, 29; Fantasy, op. 77. *R.
Serkin, piano.* Reissues.
+ ARG 11-12/92: 82
+ Fa 11-12/92: 195

31987. SBK 47667: SCHUBERT—Wanderer
fantasy; Piano sonata, D. 664;
Impromptus, D. 899. *Fleisher, Freire,
piano.* Reissues.
● ARG 11-12/92: 199
+ Fa 11-12/92: 358

31988. SK 47671: REGER—Six
burlesques; Introduction and passacaglia;
Twelve waltz caprices; Variations and
fugue on a theme by Mozart. *Tal,
Groethuysen, piano, 4 hands.*
+ ARG 7-8/92: 204
+ Fa 7-8/92: 255
+ Gr 6/92: 60

31989. SK 47672: MOZART—Divertimenti
K. 136-138; Twelve German dances.
LANNER—Die Mozartisten. *Ensemble
Wien.*
● Fa 7-8/92: 228
- Gr 5/92: 38

31990. SBK 47682: *Songs and waltzes
from Vienna.* Music of J. Strauss, Dostal,
Arnold, Mendelssohn, and others.
*Lehmann, soprano; Ulanowsky, piano;
Walter, cond.*
+ ARG 5-6/92: 188

31991. MPK 47687: BEETHOVEN—String
quartets no. 7, 13. *Busch Quartet.*
Monaural.
+ Fa 5-6/93: 155

31992. SK 47690: SCHOENBERG—
Verklärte Nacht; String trio, op. 45.
*Juilliard String Quartet; Trampler, viola;
Ma, cello.*
+ ARG 7-8/93: 151
+ Fa 5-6/93: 313
+ Gr 5/93: 67
+ St 10/93: 277

31993. SK 47693: MOZART—Sinfonia
concertante, K. 364; Concertone for two
violins, K. 190. *Lin, violin; Laredo,
violin & viola; English Chamber Orch.;
Leppard, cond.*
+ ARG 5-6/92: 98
● Fa 5-6/92: 204
● Gr 6/92: 47

31994. SK 47964: WEISS—Lute sonatas.
Kirchhof, lute.
+ ARG 11-12/95: 233

31995. SK 48030: RACHMANINOFF—Piano
concerto no. 2. TCHAIKOVSKY—Piano
concerto no. 1. *Nakamura, piano; USSR
Academic Symphony Orch.; Svetlanov,
cond.*
- ARG 5-6/92: 144
+ Fa 5-6/92: 227
● Gr 9/92: 83

31996. SK 48031: MOZART—Violin
concertos no. 3-4. *Horigome, violin;
Camerata Academica Salzburg; Végh,
cond.*
+ ARG 5-6/92: 95
+ Fa 5-6/92: 204
● Gr 4/92: 68

31997. SK 48032: MOZART—Oboe
concertos K. 313-314; Andante, K. 315.
*Miyamoto, oboe; English Chamber
Orch.; Garcia, cond.*
+ Fa 7-8/92: 225
+ Gr 9/92: 80

31998. SK 48035: SCHUMANN—Clarinet
sonatas no. 1-2 (orig. violin); Three
romances for clarinet and piano, op. 94.
Neidich, clarinet; Hokanson, piano.
+ ARG 7-8/92: 223
+ Fa 7-8/92: 280
- Gr 9/92: 118

31999. SK 48036: SCHUMANN—
Davidsbündlertänze; Waldszenen;
Fantasiestücke. *Haefliger, piano.*
+ ARG 11-12/92: 200
+ Fa 11-12/92: 363
+ Gr 10/92: 153

32000. SK 48037: BRUCKNER—Mass no. 2
in E minor (version of 1882); Motets:
Locus iste; Virga Jesse; Christus factus
est pro nobis; Ave Maria. *Kammerchor
Stuttgart; Bernius, cond.; Deutsche
Bläserphilharmonie.*
● ARG 9-10/92: 91
+ Fa 9-10/92: 205
+ Gr 8/92: 56

32001. SK 48039: PRAETORIUS—Sacred
music. *Huelgas Ensemble; Nevel, cond.*
+ ARG 11-12/92: 178
+ EM 2/93: 141
+ Fa 9-10/92: 315

32002. SX2K 48040: GLUCK—Orfeo ed
Euridice. *Chance, Argenta; Kammerchor
Stuttgart; Tafelmusik; Bernius, cond.*
+ ARG 11-12/92: 126
● Fa 11-12/92: 244
+ Gr 8/92: 69
+ ON 6/93: 40
● Op 6/92: 744

32003. S2K 48042 (2 discs): SCHÜTZ—
Psalmen Davids. *Kammerchor Stuttgart;
Musica fiata; Bernius, cond.*
+ EM 8/93: 495
+ Fa 9-10/93: 284

32004. SK 48043: GEMINIANI—Six
concerti grossi, op. 2; Concerti grossi in
C and G minor. *Lamon, violin and cond.;*

Tafelmusik.
+ Fa 9-10/92: 242
+ Gr 11/92: 61

32005. SK 48044: VIVALDI—Concertos for strings and continuo, RV 117, 143, 134, 159; Cello concertos, RV 418, 413; Concerto for violin and cello, RV 547; Concerto for 2 violins and 2 cellos, RV 575; Concerto for 4 violins, RV 549. *Lamon, violin & cond.; Tafelmusik; Bylsma, Mahler, cellos; Rémillard, Marvin, Roberts, violins.*
+ ARG 9-10/92: 179
+ Fa 9-10/92: 380
+ Gr 9/92: 97

32006. SK 48045: Flute concertos by K. Stamitz, Richter, J. Stamitz, and Haydn. *Kuijken, flute; Tafelmusik; Lamon, cond.*
+ Gr 7/93: 56

32007. SK 48046: BRAHMS—Handel variations; Six pieces op. 118; Rhapsodies, op. 79. *Ax, piano.*
+ ARG 11-12/92: 96
• Fa 11-12/92: 211
• Gr 10/92: 136

32008. S2K 48047 (2 discs): BACH— Cello suites. *Bylsma, cello.*
+ EM 5/93: 318
+ Gr 1/93: 49

32009. SK 48051: *Salon music of the nineteenth century.* Music of Genin, Boehm, Kalliwoda, Demersseman, and Demersseman-Berthélemy. *Schulz, flute; Schellenberger, oboe & English horn; Koenen, piano.*
+ ARG 3-4/93: 161
+ Fa 3-4/93: 390

32010. SK 48052: *Twentieth-century wind music.* Music of Françaix, Barber, Berio, Eder, and Ligeti. *Ensemble Wien-Berlin.*
+ ARG 3-4/93: 178
+ Fa 3-4/93: 392
+ Gr 11/92: 146

32011. S2K 48053 (2 discs): MOZART— Die Entführung aus dem Serail. *Studer, Szmytka, Streit, Gambill, Missenhardt; Vienna Symphony Orch.; Weil, cond.*
• Gr 5/92: 110
+ ON 1/21/95: 38

32012. SK 48056: TCHAIKOVSKY— Symphony no. 1; Nutcracker suite. *Chicago Symphony Orch.; Abbado, cond.*
• ARG 1-2/93: 156
+ Fa 11-12/92: 386

32013. SK 48057: STRAVINSKY—Oedipus Rex. *Otter, Cole, Estes, Sotin; Swedish Radio Chorus; Eric Ericson Chamber Choir; Swedish Radio Symphony Orch.; Salonen, cond.*
+ ARG 11-12/92: 215
+ Fa 11-12/92: 381
+ Gr 7/92: 109
• ON 10/92: 44

32014. SK 48058: BEETHOVEN—String quartets, op. 18, no. 1; op. 132. *Artis Quartet Vienna.*
- ARG 1-2/93: 74
+ Fa 11-12/92: 193

32015. SK 48059: WEBERN—String quartets: (1905), op. 28; Music for string quartet: Slow movement, Rondo, Five movements, Six bagatelles. *Artis Quartet Vienna.*
+ ARG 11-12/92: 230
+ Fa 11-12/92: 406
+ Gr 7/92: 69

32016. SK 48060: BEETHOVEN—Diabelli variations. *Vladar, piano.*
- ARG 7-8/92: 93
+ Fa 7-8/92: 120
+ Gr 4/92: 110
+ St 10/92: 259

32017. SK 48061: HAYDN—"London" trios no. 1-4; Duet no. 4 for 2 flutes; "Echo" for two flutes, eH. II, 39). *Rampal, Schulz, flutes; Audin, bassoon.*
+ Fa 1-2/93: 167
+ Gr 3/93: 63

32018. SK 48062: Music of C.P.E. Bach, Mozart, Bach, Britten, and Handel. *C.P.E. Bach Chamber Orch.; Haenchen, cond.*
+ Fa 11-12/92: 464

32019. SK 48063: MOZART—Symphonies no. 28-29, 35 "Haffner". *Berlin Phil. Orch.; Abbado, cond.*
+ ARG 7-8/92: 194
• Fa 7-8/92: 237
+ Gr 3/92: 51

32020. SK 48064: MOZART—Sinfonia concertante K. 297b; Symphony no. 39. *Instrumental soloists; Berlin Phil. Orch.; Giulini, cond.*
+ ARG 1-2/93: 127
+ Fa 1-2/93: 203

32021. SK 48065: *Italia mia.* Music of Verdelot, Alberti, Fiamengo, Rore, Dentice, Fontanelli, Villani, Nenna, and Anon. *Huelgas Ensemble; Nevel, cond.*
• EM 2/93: 136
+ Fa 9-10/92: 411

32022. SK 48066: FAURÉ—Quartets for piano, violin, viola and cello no. 1-2. *Ax, piano; Stern, violin; Laredo, viola; Ma, cello.*
+ ARG 1-2/94: 99
+ Fa 5-6/93: 200
+ Gr 9/93: 77

32023. SK 48067: SIBELIUS—Four legends; En saga. *Los Angeles Phil. Orch.; Salonen, cond.*
+ ARG 1-2/93: 150
• Fa 1-2/93: 241
• Gr 8/92: 40

32024. SK 48068: *The lute in dance and dream: Three centuries of lute*

masterpieces. Music of Anon., Mudarra, Godard, Reis, Hassler, Mertel, Dowland, Kapsberger, Ballard, E. Gaultier, Mouton/Dubut, Weiss, Falkenhagen, and Durant. *Kirchhof, lutes.*
+ ARG 3-4/93: 163
+ EM 5/93: 313
+ Fa 9-10/92: 420
+ Gr 11/92: 165

32025. S2K 48070 (2 discs): VERDI—Il trovatore. *Millo, Domingo, Chernov, Zajick; Metropolitan Opera; Levine, cond.*
+ ARG 9-10/94: 216
+ Fa 9-10/94: 364
+ Gr 6/94: 114
+ ON 8/94: 34

32026. S2K 48073 (2 discs): VERDI— Luisa Miller. *Millo, Quivar, Domingo, Rootering; Metropolitan Opera; Levine, cond.*
+ ARG 1-2/93: 162
+ Fa 1-2/93: 261
• Gr 9/92: 162
+ ON 12/19/92: 39
• Op 10/92: 1258
• St 4/93: 293

32027. S2K 48077 (2 discs): SCHOENBERG—Gurrelieder. *Marton, Quivar, Lakes, Cheek; New York Choral Artists; New York Phil.; Mehta, cond.*
+ ARG 7-8/93: 150
• Fa 7-8/93: 228
• Gr 4/93: 111
• ON 10/93: 43

32028. SK 48080: FORQUERAY—Suites in D and G minor. COUPERIN—La superbe, ou La forqueray. DUPHLY—La forqueray. *Leonhardt, harpsichord.*
+ EM 5/93: 317
• Fa 9-10/92: 234
+ Gr 10/92: 140

32029. SK 48081: Music of Bach, Blumenfeld, Saint-Saëns, Scriabin, Saxton, and others. *Fleisher, piano (left hand).*
+ ARG 11-12/93: 241
+ Fa 1-2/94: 411
+ Gr 10/93: 86

32030. S2K 48082 (2 discs): Mozart no end and the Paradise Band. *Gulda, piano; with guests; Munich Phil. Orch.; Paradise Band.*
- Gr 4/92: 66

32031. S2K 48083: TCHAIKOVSKY— Nutcracker. *Klassische Philharmonie Telekom Bonn; Beissel, cond.*
• Gr 3/93: 55

32032. SK 48093: *Discovered treasures.* Music of Scarlatti, Bach, Clementi, Chopin, Medtner, Scriabin, and Liszt. *Horowitz, piano.*
+ ARG 3-4/93: 173
+ Fa 3-4/93: 375

SONY CLASSICAL

+ Gr 11/92: 162
+ St 3/93: 191

32033. MDK 48094: *Three sopranos sing Puccini favorites.* PUCCINI—Arias from Bohème, Tosca, Manon Lescaut, Turandot, Gianni Schicchi, Suor Angelica, and La rondine. *Marton, Scotto, Te Kanawa, sopranos.*
+ ARG 5-6/92: 110

32034. SK 48132: SCHUBERT—Symphonies no. 8 "Unfinished," 9 "Great". *Classical Band; Weil, cond.*
• ARG 9-10/92: 158
- Fa 9-10/92: 346
• Gr 9/92: 86

32035. SMK 48155: *Souvenirs.* Music of Giordano, Verdi, Puccini, Rodgers, Bellini, Schubert, Donizetti, Ribas, Brahms, and others. *Carreras, Caballé; with acc.*
• ARG 11-12/92: 258

32036. SMK 48164: J. STRAUSS, JR.—Blue Danube; Wiener Blut; Vienna woods; Voices of spring; Roses from the south; 1001 nights; Wine, women and song; Annen; Tritsch-tratsch; Pizzicato; New pizzicato; Donner und Blitz; Auf der Jagd. *Philadelphia Orch.; Ormandy, cond.*
+ ARG 11-12/92: 211

32037. SMK 48171: Music of Mendelssohn, Schubert and Schumann. *F. Sellheim, cello; E. Sellheim, piano.* Reissues. + Gr 10/92: 131

32038. SK 48190: BEETHOVEN—Trios for violin, viola and cello, op. 9, no. 1-3. *L'Achibudelli.*
+ ARG 9-10/92: 81
+ Fa 9-10/92: 187
+ Gr 9/92: 102

32039. SK 48191: BRAHMS—Sonatas for cello and piano: no. 1-2; Sonata no. 3 for violin and piano, op. 108 (arr. cello and piano). *Ma, cello; Ax, piano.*
+ ARG 3-4/93: 63
+ Fa 3-4/93: 129
+ Gr 11/92: 120

32040. SK 48193: VERDI—String quartet. SIBELIUS—String quartet in D minor. *Juilliard String Quartet.* Recorded 1989, 1990.
+ ARG 1-2/93: 163
• Fa 1-2/93: 262
• Gr 10/92: 132

32041. SK 48195: *Febus avant!* Music at the court of Gaston Febus. *Huelgas Ensemble; Nevel, cond.*
+ EM 8/93: 489
• Fa 9-10/93: 352
+ Gr 2/93: 72

32042. SK14K 48198 (14 discs): MAHLER—Symphonies (complete). *Vienna Phil. Orch.; Maazel, cond.*

Reissues.
• Gr 11/92: 64

32043. SK 48231: DEBUSSY—Jeux; La boite à joujoux; Prélude à l'après midi d'un faune. *London Symphony Orch.; Thomas, cond.*
• ARG 1-2/93: 90
• Fa 1-2/93: 140
+ Gr 11/92: 57

32044. SK 48233: MOZART—Piano sonatas no. 8, 11; K. 533/494. *Perahia, piano.*
+ ARG 7-8/93: 131
+ Fa 3-4/93: 240
+ Gr 12/92: 102

32045. SK 48236: BEETHOVEN—Symphonies no. 1, 7. *La Scala Phil. Orch.; Giulini, cond.*
+ ARG 3-4/93: 58
- Fa 3-4/93: 122
- Gr 11/92: 56

32046. SK 48237: SCHUBERT—Winterreise. *Fischer-Dieskau, baritone; Perahia, piano.*
• Fa 7-8/93: 238
- Gr 1/93: 56

32047. SK 48238: BEETHOVEN—Symphonies no. 2, 8. *La Scala Phil. Orch.; Giulini, cond.*
- ARG 3-4/94: 74
- Fa 1-2/94: 125
• Gr 3/94: 42

32048. SK 48239: PROKOFIEV—Symphonies no. 1, 5. *London Symphony Orch.; Thomas, cond.*
+ ARG 3-4/93: 125
• Fa 5-6/93: 283
• Gr 3/93: 51

32049. SK 48240: DEBUSSY—Le martyre de Saint Sebastien. *Caron, narrator; McNair, Stutzmann, Murray, vocalists; London Symphony Orch.; Thomas, cond.*
+ ARG 9-10/93: 112
+ Fa 9-10/93: 149
+ Gr 3/93: 80
• Op 6/93: 742

32050. SK 48241: SCHNITTKE—Cello concerto no. 2; In memoriam. *Rostropovich, cello; London Symphony Orch.; Ozawa, cond.*
+ ARG 11-12/92: 195
+ Gr 7/92: 61

32051. SK 48242: STRAUSS—Four last songs; Songs. *Gruberova, Mattila, Popp, sopranos; London Symphony Orch.; Thomas, cond.*
• ARG 1-2/95: 184
• Gr 11/94: 138
+ ON 4/15/95: 37

32052. SK 48249: GOMBERT—Music from the court of Charles V. *Huelgas Ensemble; Nevel, cond.*
+ EM 5/93: 297

+ Fa 7-8/94: 141
+ Gr 4/93: 107

32053. SK 48250: *Airs de cour.* Music of Anon., Francisque, Ballard, Guedron, Bataille, Boesset, Moulinié, Grand Rue, Richard, and Boyer. *Vallin, soprano; Egmond, baritone; Kirchhof, lute.*
+ EM 5/93: 312
+ Fa 9-10/93: 351

32054. SK 48251: VIVALDI—Concertos, op. 8, no. 1-4 "The four seasons"; Sinfonia, RV 169 "Al santo sepolcro"; Concerto for 4 violins, cello, strings, and continuo, RV 580. *Tafelmusik; Lamon, violin & cond.*
+ ARG 5-6/93: 149
+ Fa 3-4/93: 319

32055. SK 48252: BARBER—Adagio for strings. JANÁČEK—String quartet no. 1 (arr. Tognetti). WALTON—Sonata for strings. *Australian Chamber Orch.; Tognetti, cond.*
+ Gr 8/92: 30

32056. SBK 48263: BARTÓK—Concerto for orchestra; Miraculous mandarin: Suite; Two pictures. *Philadelphia Orch.; Ormandy, cond.* Reissues.
• Gr 5/93: 38

32057. SBK 48269—48270 (2 separate discs): SCHUMANN—Symphonies. *Bavarian Radio Orch.; Kubelik, cond.* Reissues.
• Gr 7/93: 52

32058. SMK 48272: STRAUSS—Ein Heldenleben; Don Juan; Till Eulenspiegel. *Philadelphia Orch.; Ormandy, cond.; Cleveland Orch.; Szell, cond.* Reissues.
+ Gr 5/93: 51

32059. SMK 48274: BRUCH—Violin concerto no. 1. LALO—Symphonie espagnole. VIEUXTEMPS—Violin concerto no. 5. *Zukerman, violin; Los Angeles Phil. Orch.; Mehta, cond.; London Symphony Orch.; Mackerras, cond.* Reissues.
• ARG 7-8/93: 75

32060. SBK 48279: OFFENBACH—Gaîté parisienne: excerpts. RACHMANINOFF—Symphonic dances, op. 45. SMETANA—The bartered bride: 3 dances. *Philadelphia Orch.; Ormandy, cond.; Cleveland Orch.; Szell, cond.* Reissue.
+ ARG 7-8/93: 140
+ Fa 7-8/93: 197
+ Gr 6/93: 52

32061. SBK 48280: BACH—Magnificat, BWV 243. VIVALDI—Beatus vir, RV 598; Gloria, RV 589. *Vocalists; Gächinger Kantorei Stuttgart; Bach-Collegium Stuttgart; Rilling, cond.; Ensemble Vocal Raphaël Passaquet; Grand Écurie et la Chambre du Roy; Malgoire, cond.*
• Fa 7-8/93: 264

32062. SMK 48282: VIVALDI—Stabat Mater; Dixit Dominus. A. SCARLATTI—Stabat Mater. *BBC Singers; Poole, cond.; English Bach Festival; Malgoire, cond.* Reissues.
+ ARG 9-10/93: 217

32063. SBK 48287: SCHUBERT—Die schöne Müllerin. *Haefliger, tenor; Werba, piano.* Reissue.
• ARG 7-8/93: 152
+ Fa 7-8/93: 232

32064. MDK 48296: BACH—Choruses. HANDEL—Choruses. *Mormon Tabernacle Choir; Philadelphia Orch.; Ormandy, cond.* Reissues.
+ ARG 1-2/93: 70

32065. MDK 48304: *A passover seder festival.* SECUNDA—Passover seder festival. SECUNDA, ZILBERTS—Five Hebrew prayers. *Tucker, tenor.*
+ ARG 9-10/92: 209

32066. SK 48307: GADE—Octet. MENDELSSOHN—Octet. *Archibudelli; Smithsonian Chamber Players.*
- Gr 3/93: 60

32067. SK 48370: HAYDN—Symphonies no. 41-43. *Tafelmusik; Weil, cond.*
+ Gr 4/93: 47

32068. SK 48371: HAYDN—Symphonies no. 44, 51-52. *Tafelmusik; Weil, cond.*
+ Gr 4/93: 47

32069. SMK 48372: SHOSTAKOVICH—Chamber symphony. HINDEMITH—Funeral music. HAYDN—Symphony no. 49. *Jakubovsky, viola; St. Petersburg Camerata; Sondeckis, cond.*
+ ARG 5-6/95: 177

32070. SK 48373: SAINT-SAËNS—Concerto no. 3 for violin and orchestra, op. 61. WIENIAWSKI—Concerto no. 2 for violin and orchestra, op. 22. *Rachlin, violin; Israel Phil. Orch.; Mehta, cond.* Recorded live.
+ ARG 3-4/93: 132
+ Fa 3-4/93: 269
+ Gr 12/92: 86

32071. SK 48376: Strauss family: 1992 New Year's concert. *Vienna Phil. Orch.; Kleiber, cond.*
+ ARG 11-12/92: 210
+ Fa 9-10/92: 361
+ Gr 4/92: 90
+ St 11/92: 233

32072. SK 48380: MAHLER—Symphony no. 4. *Hendricks, soprano; Los Angeles Phil. Orch.; Salonen, cond.*
+ ARG 3-4/93: 107
+ Fa 5-6/93: 257
+ Gr 8/92: 36

32073. SK 48381: *Encore!* Music of Bach, Bartók, Berio, Bernstein, Brahms,

and others. *K. & M. Labèque, pianos.*
+ ARG 5-6/94: 184

32074. SK 48382: PROKOFIEV—Cello symphony-concerto. TCHAIKOVSKY—Rococo variations; Andante cantabile. *Ma, cello; Pittsburgh Symphony Orch.; Maazel, cond.*
+ ARG 1-2/93: 132
- Fa 3-4/93: 251
+ Gr 11/92: 97

32075. SK 48383: HAYDN—Piano concertos, H. XVIII, 3; H. XVIII, 4; H. XVIII, 11. *Ax, piano & cond.; Franz Liszt Chamber Orch.*
+ ARG 7-8/93: 98
+ Fa 5-6/93: 219
+ Gr 5/93: 44

32076. SK 48385: MOZART—Symphonies no. 25, 31; Posthorn symphony; Masonic funeral music. *Berlin Phil. Orch.; Abbado, cond.*
+ ARG 5-6/95: 144
+ Gr 5/95: 56

32077. SK 48386: SCHUBERT—Music for violin and string orchestra. *Guggenberger, violin; Ensemble Wien.*
+ Fa 7-8/93: 237

32078. S2K 48387 (2 discs): PROKOFIEV—Ivan the terrible (Michael Lankester version); Alexander Nevsky. *Plummer, narrator; Sinyavskaya, mezzo-soprano; Leiferkus, baritone; New London Children's Choir; Zajick, mezzo-soprano; London Symphony Orch. & Chorus; Rostropovich, cond.*
• ARG 7-8/93: 136
• Fa 7-8/93: 203
+ Gr 4/93: 110
+ ON 1/22/94: 41

32079. S2K 48391 (2 discs): WEISS—Lute works, vol. 1-2. *Kirchhof, theorbo, lute.*
+ EM 5/93: 312
+ Fa 9-10/93: 331

32080. SB5K 48396 (5 discs): BEETHOVEN—The nine symphonies; Overtures: Egmont; Fidelio; King Stephen. *Cleveland Orch.; Szell, cond.*
• Fa 3-4/93: 121

32081. SB2K 48397 (3 discs): BEETHOVEN—The five concertos for piano and orchestra; Concerto in C for piano, violin, cello and orchestra, op. 56. *Fleisher, Istomin, piano; Stern, violin; Rose, cello; Cleveland Orch.; Szell, cond.; Philadelphia Orch.; Ormandy, cond.* Reissue.
⊔ Fa 3-4/93: 118

32082. SMK 48399: ROSSINI—Favourite Rossini Opera arias. *Various performers.*
+ Fa 9-10/93: 257

32083. SK 48400: Music of Granados, Rodrigo, Llobet, and Albeniz. *Williams,*

guitar; *London Symphony Orch.; Daniel, cond.*
+ ARG 5-6/93: 164

32084. SM2K 48456 (2 discs): SCHOENBERG—Moses and Aaron; Chamber symphony no. 2. *Cassilly, Angas, Reich; BBC Singers; Ensemble InterContemporain; BBC Symphony Orch.; Boulez, cond.* Reissues.
+ ARG 11-12/93: 185
+ Gr 12/93: 106

32085. SM2K 48459 (2 discs): SCHOENBERG—Gurrelieder; Songs, op. 22. *Napier, Minton, Thomas, Bowen, Nimsgern; BBC Singers; BBC Choral Society; London Phil. Choir; BBC Symphony Orch.; Boulez, cond.* Reissues.
+ ARG 11-12/93: 185
• Gr 12/93: 106

32086. SMK 48462: SCHOENBERG—Die Jakobsleiter (fragment); Chamber symphony no. 1; Accompaniment to a cinematographic scene. *Nimsgern, Mesplé, Wenkel, Rolfe Johnson, Bowen, Partridge, Shirley-Quirk, Hudson; BBC Singers; BBC Symphony Orch.; Members of the Ensemble InterContemporain; Boulez, cond.* Reissue.
+ ARG 11-12/93: 185
+ Fa 11-12/93: 375
+ Gr 12/93: 106

32087. SMK 48463: SCHOENBERG—Serenade; Pieces, op. 16; Ode to Napoleon. *Shirley-Quirk, Wilson-Johnson, baritones; Ensemble Intercontemporain; BBC Symphony Orch.; Boulez, cond.* Reissues.
+ ARG 11-12/93: 185
+ Gr 12/93: 106

32088. SMK 48464: SCHOENBERG—Die Glückliche Hand; Variations; Verklärte Nacht (orch.). *Nimsgern, bass- baritone; BBC Singers; BBC Symphony Orch.; New York Phil.; Boulez, cond.* Reissues.
+ ARG 11-12/93: 185
+ Gr 12/93: 106

32089. SMK 48465: SCHOENBERG—Suite; Verklärte Nacht (sextet); Pieces. *Ensemble InterContemporain; Boulez, cond.* Reissues.
+ ARG 11-12/93: 185
+ Gr 12/93: 106

32090. SMK 48466: SCHOENBERG—Erwartung; Pierrot Lunaire; Song of the wood-dove. *Martin, Norman, sopranos; Ensemble InterContemporain; BBC Symphony Orch., Boulez, cond.* Reissues.
+ ARG 11-12/93: 185
• Gr 12/93: 106

32091. SM5K 48467 (5 discs): RACHMANINOFF—Complete solo piano music. *Laredo, piano.* Reissues.
• Gr 3/94: 80

SONY CLASSICAL

32092. SMK 48468—48472 (5 separate discs): RACHMANINOFF—Piano music (complete). *Laredo, piano.* Reissues.
- ARG 1-2/94: 136

32093. S2K 48474 (2 discs): PUCCINI—Manon Lescaut. *Rautio, Dvorsk}, Quilico, Roni; Teatro alla Scala; Maazel, cond.*
- ARG 11-12/93: 172
+ Fa 9-10/93: 238
- Gr 7/93: 88
- ON 9/93: 53
- Op 5/93: 616

32094. SK 48480: *Iberia.* Music of Granados, Rodrigo, Llobet, and Albéniz. *Williams, guitar; London Symphony Orch; Daniel, cond.*
+ Fa 1-2/93: 296
+ Gr 7/92: 82

32095. SK 48483: CHOPIN—Piano sonatas no. 1-3. *Katsaris, piano.*
- ARG 3-4/93: 69
+ Fa 3-4/93: 144
+ Gr 6/93: 72
- St 9/93: 181

32096. SK 48484: LISZT—Piano sonata; Vallée d'Obermann. VERDI-LISZT—Aïda: danza sacra e duetto finale; Rigoletto: paraphrase du concert. *Ax, piano.*
- ARG 11-12/93: 140
+ Fa 11-12/93: 298
- Gr 11/93: 117

32097. SK 48494: MENDELSSOHN—Trio no. 2 for violin, cello and piano (arr. piano duet); Andante and variations, op. 83a; Andante and allegro brillant, op. 92. MENDELSSOHN HENSEL—Three pieces for piano, four-hands. *Tal, Groethuysen, piano.*
+ Fa 5-6/93: 264
+ Gr 6/93: 69

32098. SMK 48984: MOZART—Piano concertos no. 14, 27; Ch'io mi scordi di te? *Horszowski, Istomin, piano; Tourel, mezzo-soprano; Casals Festival Orch.; Casals, cond.*
+ ARG 9-10/94: 272
□ Fa 7-8/94: 190

32099. AK 52424: RÓZSA—King of kings. *Rózsa, cond.* Reissue.
+ ARG 9-10/92: 152

32100. SK 52483: PROKOFIEV—Piano concertos no. 1, 3, 5. *Bronfman, piano; Israel Phil. Orch.; Mehta, cond.*
- ARG 1-2/94: 133
- Fa 1-2/94: 261
+ Gr 12/93: 74

32101. SK 52484: PROKOFIEV—Piano sonatas no. 1, 4, 6. *Bronfman, piano.*
+ Gr 11/94: 118

32102. SK 52485: *Waltzes, polkas, galoppe.* Music of Lanner, J. Strauss Sr., and Josef Strauss. *Ensemble Wien.*

- ARG 7-8/93: 184
+ Fa 7-8/93: 249

32103. S2K 52486 (2 discs): VERDI—La traviata. *Fabbricini, Alagna, Coni; Teatro La Scala; Muti, cond.*
+ ARG 1-2/94: 169
+ Fa 3-4/94: 357
+ Gr 10/93: 118
+ ON 12/25/93: 33
- Op 11/93: 1366

32104. SK 52489: VERDI—Operatic ballet music. *Metropolitan Opera Orch.; Levine, cond.*
- ARG 5-6/94: 162
+ Fa 5-6/94: 272
- Gr 6/94: 66

32105. SK 52490: BRAHMS—Songs. *Lipovsek, mezzo-soprano; Spencer, piano; Geringas, cello.*
+ ARG 11-12/93: 82
+ Gr 9/93: 94

32106. SK 52491: GROFÉ—Grand Canyon suite. HERBERT—Hero and Leander; Favorites. *Pittsburgh Symphony Orch.; Maazel, cond.*
+ ARG 9-10/94: 137
+ Fa 9-10/94: 198

32107. S2K 52492 (2 discs): GLUCK—Iphigénie en Tauride. *Vaness, Surian, Allen, Winbergh; La Scala Theater Orch. & Chorus; Muti, cond.*
+ ARG 3-4/94: 100
+ Fa 1-2/94: 188
+ Gr 10/93: 113

32108. S2K 52495 (2 discs): SCHNITTKE—Life with an idiot. *Ringholz, Haskin, Duesing; Netherlands Opera; Rostropovich, cond.* Recorded live 1992.
+ ARG 7-8/93: 150
+ Fa 7-8/93: 227
+ Gr 4/93: 119
+ ON 7/93: 43
+ St 7/93: 177

32109. SK 52499: *Gulda non-stop.* Music of Gulda, Mozart, Debussy, Chopin, Schubert, J. Strauss, Jr., and trad. *Gulda, piano.* Recorded live.   <\@> Fa 7-8/93: 297

32110. S3K 52500 (3 discs): VERDI—Don Carlo. *Millo, Chernov, Sylvester, Furlanetto, Ramey; Metropolitan Opera; Levine, cond.*
+ ARG 9-10/93: 211
+ Fa 9-10/93: 316
+ Gr 4/93: 120

32111. SK 52524: ROSSINI—Quartets for flute, clarinet, horn and bassoon. *Ensemble Wien-Berlin.*
+ Fa 7-8/93: 219
+ Gr 11/93: 96

32112. SMK 52526: MOZART—Violin concertos no. 2-3, 5. *Francescatti, violin; Zürich Chamber Orch.; Stoutz, cond;*

Columbia Symphony Orch.; Walter, cond. Reissues.
+ Gr 4/93: 55

32113. MPK 52527: *Masterworks portrait.* Music of Debussy, Fauré, Satie, and Casadesus. *R. & G. Casadesus, pianos.* Reissues.   + Fa 7-8/93: 301 + Gr 4/93: 82

32114. MP2K 52531 (2 discs): BEETHOVEN—Six string quartets, op. 18. *Budapest String Quartet.*
- Fa 7-8/93: 105

32115. MPK 52534: BEETHOVEN—Sonatas for violin and piano no. 4, 6-8. *Francescatti, violin; Casadesus, piano.* Reissue; recorded 1961.
+ Fa 7-8/93: 106
+ Gr 4/93: 74

32116. MPK 52535: BRAHMS—Violin concerto; Piano trio no. 2. *Szigeti, violin; Philadelphia Orch.; Ormandy, cond.; Hess, piano; Casals, cello.* Recorded 1947 & 1952.
+ Fa 7-8/93: 115

32117. MPK 52536: BEETHOVEN—Violin concerto; Violin sonata no. 5. *Szigeti, violin; Phil. Symphony Orch. of New York; Walter, cond.; Horszowski, piano.*
+ ARG 7-8/93: 209
+ Fa 7-8/93: 102

32118. MPK 52537: BUSONI—Sonata no. 2 for violin and piano; Concerto for violin and orchestra. *Szigeti, violin; Horszowski, piano; Little Orch. Society; Scherman, cond.*
+ Fa 7-8/93: 118

32119. SK 52551: *Mozartiana.* Music of Mozart, Gelinek, Liszt, Czerny, Beethoven, Thalberg, and Katsaris. *Katsaris, piano.*
+ ARG 5-6/93: 168
+ Fa 5-6/93: 386
+ Gr 6/93: 77

32120. SK 52553: HANDEL—Six concerti grossi, op. 3. *Lamon, violin & cond.; Tafelmusik.*
+ ARG 11-12/93: 117
+ EM 11/93: 649
+ Fa 11-12/93: 259
+ Gr 7/93: 39

32121. SK 52554: DUTILLEUX—String quartet "Ainsi la nuit." DEBUSSY—String quartet. RAVEL—String quartet. *Juilliard String Quartet.*
+ ARG 5-6/94: 86
+ Fa 5-6/94: 140
- Gr 3/94: 71

32122. SK 52563: SIBELIUS—Kullervo. *Rørholm, soprano; Hynninen, baritone; Los Angeles Phil. Orch.; Salonen, cond.*
+ ARG 11-12/93: 196
+ Fa 9-10/93: 291
+ Gr 7/93: 53

32123. SK 52564: *Opera fantasies.*
Music of Liszt, Borne, Pasculli,
Kroepsch, Horvath, and Czadek. *Vladar,
piano; Ensemble Wien-Berlin.*
+ ARG 1-2/94: 183
+ Fa 11-12/93: 495

32124. SK 52565: STRAUSS—*New Year's
Eve concert.* Don Juan; Burleske; Til
Eulenspiegel; Rosenkavalier: Final trio.
*Fleming, Battle, Von Stade, Schmidt,
vocalists; Argerich, piano; Berlin Phil.
Orch.; Abbado, cond.* Recorded 1992.
- Gr 7/93: 54

32125. SK 52566: SIBELIUS—
Symphonies, no. 1, 7. *Pittsburgh
Symphony Orch.; Maazel, cond.*
+ ARG 7-8/93: 158
+ Fa 9-10/93: 292
● Gr 7/93: 54

32126. SK 52567: SCHUMANN—Piano
concerto; Piano music of Schubert,
Schumann, and Grieg. *Kissin, piano;
Vienna Phil. Orch.; Giulini, cond.*
+ ARG 1 2/94: 153
+ Fa 9-10/93: 281
● Gr 6/93: 54

32127. SK 52568: *Encore!* Music of
Kreisler, Sarasate, Paganini, Bacewicz,
Elgar, Shostakovich, Dvořák, Prokofiev,
Tchaikovsky, Szymanowski, Gluck,
Fauré, Scriabin, Bartók, and Ysaÿe.
Midori, violin; McDonald, piano.
+ Fa 5-6/93: 387
+ Gr 6/93: 70

32128. MPK 52569: *Recital.* Music of
Corelli, Beethoven, Ravel, Hindemith,
Debussy, Lalo, and Tchaikovsky. *Szigeti,
violin; various piano acc.*
+ Fa 7-8/93: 304

32129. SK 52570: *Concert for planet
Earth.* Music of Serrano, Sorozabal,
Meyerbeer, Jobim, Marsalis, Paganini,
Puccini, Saint-Saëns, Gardel, Bernstein,
and Barroso. *Soloists; Orch. of the
Municipal Theatre of Rio de Janeiro;
DeMain, cond.*
+ Fa 5-6/93: 415

32130. S2K 52579 (2 discs): MAHLER—
Symphony no. 3; Symphony no. 10:
Adagio. *Quivar, mezzo-soprano;
choruses; Israel Phil. Orch.; Mehta,
cond.*
● ARG 11-12/93: 143
+ Fa 11-12/93: 305

32131. SK 52582: SCHUBERT—String
quartets no. 2, 14. *Artis String Quartet.*
+ ARG 9-10/93: 184
+ Fa 9-10/93: 268
+ Gr 6/93: 70

32132. SK 52583: DEBUSSY—Preludes,
book 1; Images, sets 1-2. *Crossley, piano.*
+ ARG 9-10/93: 112
● Fa 9-10/93: 150
● Gr 4/93: 87

32133. SMK 52589: Music of Byrd,
Gibbons, and Sweelinck. *Gould, piano.*
Reissues.
+ Gr 11/93: 120

32134. SMK 52594: BACH—Goldberg
variations; Two fugues. *Gould, piano.*
Reissue.
+ ARG 3-4/93: 53
+ Gr 4/93: 84

32135. SMK 52596: BACH—Inventions
and sinfonias. *Gould, piano.* Reissue.
+ ARG 9-10/93: 86
+ Gr 6/93: 72

32136. SM2K 52597 (2 discs): BACH—
Partitas, Preludes, fugues, and fughettas.
Gould, piano. Reissues.
+ ARG 7-8/94: 63
+ Gr 11/94: 110

32137. SM2K 52600 (2 discs): BACH—
Well-tempered clavier, bk. 1. *Gould,
piano.* Reissue.
+ Gr 11/94: 110

32138. SM2K 52603 (2 discs): BACH—
Well-tempered clavier, book 2. *Gould,
piano.* Reissue.
+ ARG 7-8/94: 63
+ Gr 11/94: 110

32139. SM2K 52606 (2 discs): BACH—
English suites. *Gould, piano.* Reissue.
+ ARG 7-8/95: 76
+ Gr 4/96: 73

32140. SM2K 52609 (2 discs): BACH—
French suites; French overture. *Gould,
piano.* Reissue.
+ ARG 7-8/95: 76
+ Gr 7/95: 82

32141. SMK 52612 (2 discs): BACH—
Toccatas. *Gould, piano.* Reissue.
+ ARG 9-10/94: 240
+ Gr 9/94: 80

32142. SM2K 52615 (2 discs): BACH—
Violin sonatas; Viola da gamba sonatas.
Laredo, violin; Rose, cello; Gould, piano.
Reissue.
+ ARG 7-8/95: 76

32143. SM2K 52622 (2 discs): CHOPIN—
Piano sonata no. 3. MENDELSSOHN—5
Songs without words. SCRIABIN—Piano
sonatas no. 3, 5; Preludes; Album leaf.
PROKOFIEV—Piano sonata no. 7; Vision
fugitive no. 2. *Gould, piano.* Reissues.
+ ARG 11-12/95: 108
● Gr 4/96: 82

32144. SM2K 52623 (2 discs): HAYDN—
Sonatas no. 42, 48-52. *Gould, piano.*
Reissue.
+ ARG 9-10/94: 240
+ Gr 1/95: 76

32145. SM2K 52627 (4 discs):
MOZART—Piano sonatas (complete);

Fantasies. *Gould, piano.* Reissues.
● ARG 7-8/95: 159

32146. SM3K 52632 (3 discs):
BEETHOVEN—Piano concertos. *Gould,
piano; Columbia Symphony Orch.; New
York Phil.; American Symphony Orch.;
Golschmann, Bernstein, Stokowski,
conds.* Reissues.
+ Gr 4/93: 42

32147. SMK 52636: BEETHOVEN—
Symphonies no. 5-6 (1st mvt.). *Gould,
piano.* Reissue.
+ Gr 12/92: 101

32148. SMK 52637: BEETHOVEN—
Symphony no. 6 (arr. Liszt). *Gould,
piano.* Reissue.
- ARG 9-10/93: 94
+ Gr 6/93: 72

32149. SM3K 52638, 52642 (2 3-discs
sets): BEETHOVEN—Sonatas. *Gould, piano.*
Reissues.
+ ARG 9-10/94: 240

32150. SMK 52645: BEETHOVEN—Piano
sonatas no. 24, 29. *Gould, piano.*
Recorded 1970.
● ARG 1-2/94: 73
+ Gr 10/93: 77

32151. SMK 52646: BEETHOVEN—Piano
music. *Gould, piano.* Reissues.
+ Gr 4/93: 84

32152. SMK 52650: WAGNER—Siegfried
idyll; Meistersinger prelude; Dawn and
Siegfried's Rhine jouney. *Gould, piano.*
Reissue.
+ ARG 9-10/94: 240

32153. SM2K 52651 (2 discs):
BRAHMS—Ballades, op. 10; Rhapsodies,
op. 79; 10 intermezzi. *Gould, piano.*
Reissues.
+ ARG 9-10/93: 100

32154. SMK 52654: GRIEG—Piano
sonata. BIZET—Nocturne; Variations
chromatiques. SIBELIUS—Sonatinas;
Kyllikki, op. 41. *Gould, piano.* Reissues.
+ Gr 3/93: 79

32155. SMK 52657 (2 discs): STRAUSS—
Lieder and piano works. *Schwarzkopf,
soprano; Gould, piano.* Reissues.
+ Gr 3/93: 86

32156. SMK 52661: Music of Berg,
Krenek, Webern, Debussy, and Ravel.
Gould, piano. Reissues (Berg, Krenek).
+ ARG 11-12/95: 254

32157. SM2K 52664 (2 discs):
SCHOENBERG—Piano music; Piano
concerto; Phantasy; Ode to Napoleon;
Pierrot Lunaire. *Gould, piano; BBC
Symphony Orch.; Craft, cond.; Baker,
violin; Juilliard String Quartet, Rideout,
speaker.* Reissues.

SONY CLASSICAL

+ ARG 7-8/95: 186
+ Gr 4/95: 90

32158. SM2K 52667 (2 discs): SCHOENBERG—Songs. *Faull, soprano; Vanni, mezzo-soprano; Opthof, Gramm, basses; Gould, piano . Reissues.*
+ ARG 11-12/95: 193

32159. SMK 52670: HINDEMITH—Piano sonatas no. 1-3. *Gould, piano. Reissue.*
+ ARG 9-10/93: 136
+ Gr 6/93: 72

32160. SMK 52671: HINDEMITH—Sonatas for wind instruments and piano. *Johnson, trumpet; Jones, horn; Smith, trombone; Torchinsky, tuba; Gould, piano. Reissues.*
+ Gr 3/93: 63

32161. SM2K 52674 (2 discs): HINDEMITH—Marienleben. STRAUSS—Songs. KRENEK—Wanderlied. *Roslak, Rideout, Marshall, vocalists; Gould, piano. Reissues.*
+ ARG 11-12/95: 135

32162. SK 52677: Music of Morawetz, Anhalt, Hétu, Pentland, and Valen. *Gould, piano. Reissue.* + ARG 3-4/93: 172 + Gr 3/93: 79

32163. SM2K 52685: BACH—Goldberg variations; 3-part inventions. *Gould, piano. Recorded live 1959, 1957.*
+ Gr 11/94: 110

32164. SMK 52687: BEETHOVEN—Piano concerto no. 5. STRAUSS—Burleske. *Gould, piano; Toronto Symphony; Ancerl, Golschmann, conds. From 1970, 1967 television broadcasts.*
● ARG 1-2/96: 82
- Gr 4/96: 82

32165. SMK 52688: BACH—Violin sonata no. 4. BEETHOVEN—Violin sonata no. 10. SCHOENBERG—Phantasy, op. 47. *Menuhin, violin; Gould, piano. Recorded 1965.*
+ Gr 10/93: 61

32166. SK 53104: SCHUBERT—Goethe-Lieder. *Fassbaender, mezzo-soprano; Garben, piano.*
+ ARG 11-12/93: 190
+ Fa 9-10/93: 266

32167. SK 53105: VIVALDI—Four seasons; Flute concertos RV 430, 541, 783. *Rampal, flute; Franz Liszt Chamber Orch.; Rolla, cond.*
+ Fa 11-12/93: 437

32168. SK 53106: Music of Handel, Purcell, Rameau, Roussel, Martinů, and others. *Battle, soprano; Rampal, flute; Garrett, Ritter, piano; Lutzke, cello; Newman, harpsichord.*
+ ARG 5-6/94: 194
● Gr 9/94: 107

32169. SK 53107: BRAHMS—Violin sonatas no. 1-3; Scherzo. *Stern, violin;*

Bronfman, piano.
+ ARG 5-6/94: 77
● Fa 3-4/94: 146
+ Gr 3/94: 69

32170. SK 53108: SCHUBERT—Impromptus for piano. *Haefliger, piano.*
+ ARG 9-10/93: 183
+ Fa 9-10/93: 267

32171. SK 53109: WAGNER—Siegfried idyll. MENDELSSOHN—String symphony no. 10. WEBER—Symphony no. 1. WOLF—Italian serenade. *CPE Bach Chamber Orch.; Haenchen, cond.*
● ARG 9-10/93: 219
+ Fa 9-10/93: 390
+ Gr 8/93: 45

32172. SK 53110: GOUVY—Four-hand piano music. *Tal, Groethuysen, piano.*
+ ARG 9-10/93: 125
+ Fa 11-12/93: 247
+ Gr 10/93: 70

32173. SK 53111: DEBUSSY—Complete works for solo piano, vol. 2. *Crossley, piano.*
- ARG 11-12/93: 98
+ Fa 11-12/93: 213
+ Gr 9/93: 86

32174. SK 53112: CHOPIN—Piano trio; Polonaise brillante; Cello sonata. *Frank, violin; Ma, cello; Ax, Osinska, piano.*
+ ARG 3-4/95: 88
+ Gr 6/95: 67

32175. SK 53114: BÖHM—Keyboard music. *Leonhardt, harpsichord & clavichord.*
+ ARG 11-12/93: 81
+ Fa 11-12/93: 193
+ Fa 7-8/94: 83
+ Gr 9/93: 85

32176. SK 53115: REBELO—Vesper psalms and lamentations. *Huelgas Ensemble; Nevel, cond.*
+ ARG 11-12/93: 176
+ EM 2/94: 160
+ Fa 11-12/93: 359

32177. SK 53116: FESTA—Sacred and secular vocal works. *Huelgas Ensemble; P. Nevel, cond.*
+ Gr 11/94: 130

32178. SK 53117: *The art of the motet in the 17th century: Austria, Bohemia, Bavaria.* Music of Mayr, Mazak, Rittler, Endres, Schmelzer, Aufschnaiter, Fux, Bernardi, Stadlmayr, Dolar, Poglietti, Biber, and Hofer. *Niederaltaicher Scholaren; Ruhland, cond.*
● EM 2/94: 159
+ Fa 11-12/93: 480
- Gr 10/93: 105

32179. SK 53118: REICHA—String quintets no. 1-3. *L'Archibudelli.*
+ ARG 11-12/93: 176
+ EM 2/94: 162

+ Fa 11-12/93: 360
+ Gr 10/93: 72

32180. SK 53119: GLUCK—Don Juan; Semiramis. *Tafelmusik; Weil, cond.*
+ ARG 11-12/93: 111
+ Fa 11-12/93: 245
+ Gr 10/93: 46

32181. SK 53120: HAYDN—Piano trios no. 42-45. *Beths, violin; Bylsma, cello; Levin, fortepiano.*
+ ARG 11-12/93: 125
+ EM 2/94: 162
+ Gr 6/94: 69

32182. SK 53121: BOCCHERINI—Cello concertos no. 3, 11; Overture (Sinfonia) in D, op. 43; Octet (Notturno), op. 38, no. 4; Sinfonia, G. 519. *Bylsma, cello; Tafelmusik; Lamon, cond.*
+ ARG 11-12/93: 80
+ Fa 11-12/93: 192
+ Gr 7/93: 35

32183. SK 53126: BERNSTEIN—Clarinet sonata. KIRCHNER—Triptych. GERSHWIN—Preludes. IVES—Piano trio. *Chang, Lefkowitz, violins; Ma, cello; Kahane, Kalish, piano.*
+ ARG 1-2/94: 176
+ Fa 1-2/94: 392
+ Gr 4/94: 66

32184. SB2K 53246 (2 discs): CHOPIN—Mazurkas. *Fou, piano. Reissue.*
- Gr 11/93: 117

32185. SB2K 53249 (2 discs): CHOPIN—Nocturnes. *Fou, piano. Reissue.*
● Gr 11/93: 117

32186. SM2K 53252 (2 discs): VERDI—Requiem. ROSSINI—Stabat mater. *Vocal soloists; Philadelphia Orch.; Ormandy, cond.; New York Phil.; Bernstein, cond. Reissues.*
+ ARG 9-10/93: 214

32187. SMK 53255: BERLIOZ—Harold in Italy; Damnation of Faust: Excerpts; Les Troyens: Excerpts. *De Pasquale, viola; Philadelphia Orch.; Ormandy, Munch, cond; Orch. de Paris; Barenboim, cond. Reissues.*
+ ARG 9-10/94: 102
+ Gr 8/94: 41

32188. SMK 53256: DEBUSSY—La mer; Nocturnes; Prélude à l'après-midi d'un faune; Danse. *Philadelphia Orch.; Ormandy, cond. Reissue.*
+ ARG 1-2/94: 94

32189. SMK 53257: GRIEG—Orchestra music. *Philharmonia Orch.; A. Davis, cond.; Philadelphia Orch.; Ormandy, cond.*
+ ARG 7-8/94: 107

32190. SBK 53258: HINDEMITH—Mathis der Maler symphony; Symphonic metamorphoses. WALTON—Hindemith

variations. *Cleveland Orch.; Szell, cond.; Philadelphia Orch.; Ormandy, cond.* Reissues.
    + ARG 7-8/94: 113
    • Gr 4/94: 48

32191. SMK 53260: PROKOFIEV—Symphonies no. 1, 5. *Philadelphia Orch.; Ormandy, cond.* Reissues.
    + ARG 7-8/94: 151

32192. SBK 53261: SHOSTAKOVICH—Symphony no. 5. PROKOFIEV—Love for three oranges: Suite. *Philadelphia Orch.; Ormandy, cond.* Reissues.
    + ARG 7-8/94: 172

32193. SK 53265: VIVALDI—Violin concertos. *Zweden, violin; Combattimento Consort Amsterdam; Vriend, cond.*
    + Gr 8/93: 42

32194. S2K 53266 (2 discs): *Christmas concertos.* Music of Heinichen, Molter, Handel, Telemann, Bach, Manfredini, and others. *C.P.E. Bach Chamber Orch.; Haenchen, cond.*
    + Fa 3-4/94: 440

32195. SK 53267: STRAUSS—Ein Heldenleben; Horn concerto no. 2. *Hauptmann, horn; Berlin Phil. Orch.; Mehta, cond.*
    + ARG 9-10/95: 221

32196. SK 53268: SIBELIUS—Symphonies no. 2, 6. *Pittsburgh Symphony Orch.; Maazel, cond.*
    + ARG 5-6/96: 199
    • Fa 3-4/96: 288
    • Gr 3/96: 52

32197. SK 53269: TCHAIKOVSKY—Piano trio, op. 50. ARENSKY—Piano trio no. 1. *Bronfman, piano; Lin, violin; Hoffman, cello.*
    + ARG 11-12/94: 200
    • Fa 9-10/94: 354
    + Gr 9/94: 70

32198. SK 53271: SCHNITTKE—Quasi una sonata; Piano sonata no. 2; Piano trio. *Lubotsky, violin; Schnittke, piano; English Chamber Orch.; Rostropovich, cello & cond.*
    + ARG 7-8/94: 165
    + Gr 4/94: 94

32199. SK 53272: SIBELIUS—Violin concerto; Serenade; En saga. *Rachlin, violin; Pittsburgh Symphony Orch.; Maazel, cond.*
    + ARG 7-8/94: 174
    • Fa 7-8/94: 245
    + Gr 6/94: 62

32200. SK 53273: PROKOFIEV—Piano sonatas no. 2-3, 5. *Bronfman, piano.*
    • Fa 5-6/96: 239

32201. SK 53274: STRAVINSKY—Petrushka (revised version); Orpheus.

Philharmonia Orch.; Salonen, cond.
    + ARG 5-6/94: 147
    • Fa 3-4/94: 326
    • Gr 2/94: 52

32202. SK 53275: STRAVINSKY—Symphony of psalms; Symphony in C; Symphony in 3 movements. *London Symphony Orch. & Chorus; Thomas, cond.*
    + ARG 5-6/94: 147
    • Fa 9-10/94: 347
    + Gr 7/94: 58

32203. SK 53276: NIELSEN—Flute concerto; Clarinet concerto; Rhapsody overture; Saul and David: excerpts. *Flemström, flute; Rosengren, clarinet; Swedish Radio Symphony Orch.; Salonen, cond.*
    + ARG 7-8/94: 144
    + Fa 5-6/94: 206
    • Gr 4/94: 52

32204. SK 53277: MOZART—Serenade no. 9; Divertimenti K. 251; Marches, K. 335. *Berlin Phil. Orch.; Abbado, cond.*
    - ARG 3-4/94: 126
    + Fa 3-4/94: 255
    + Gr 3/94: 58

32205. SK 53278: WOLF—Goethe and Mörike Lieder. *Ziesak, soprano; Eisenlohr, piano.*
    + ARG 3-4/94: 186
    • Gr 3/94: 97

32206. SX4K 53279 (4 discs): BRAHMS—Symphonies no. 1-4; Variations on a theme by Haydn; Tragic overture. *Philharmonia Orch.; Mehta, cond.*
    • ARG 9-10/94: 109
    + Fa 7-8/94: 98

32207. SK 53280: BUSONI—Turandot suite. CASELLA—Paganiniana. MARTUCCI—Notturno; Novelletta; Giga. *La Scala Phil. Orch.; Muti, cond.*
    + ARG 3-4/94: 82
    + Fa 3-4/94: 158
    + Gr 4/94: 42

32208. SK 53281: DEBUSSY—Complete piano works, vol. 3. *Crossley, piano.*
    • Fa 1-2/94: 166
    • Gr 2/94: 74

32209. SK 53282: DVOŘÁK—String quartet no. 14. SMETANA—String quartet no. 1. *Artis Quartet Vienna.*
    • ARG 3-4/94: 92
    + Fa 3-4/94: 177

32210. SK 53284: DEBUSSY—Images for orchestra. ELGAR—Variations on an original theme. *Berlin Phil. Orch.; Levine, cond.*
    + ARG 9-10/95: 132
    + Fa 7-8/95: 164
    + Gr 2/95: 42

32211. SK 53285: BRAHMS—Hungarian dances; Waltzes. *Tal, Groethuysen,*

piano.
    + ARG 5-6/94: 74
    + Fa 7-8/94: 90
    + Gr 4/94: 61

32212. S3K 53286 (3 discs): MOZART—Marriage of Figaro. *Mattila, McLaughlin, Gallo, Pertusi; Florence May Festival; Mehta, cond.*
    • ARG 9-10/94: 166
    • Fa 9-10/94: 264
    • Gr 6/94: 114
    • ON 1/21/95: 38
    • Op 5/94: 634

32213. SK 53287: BEETHOVEN—Violin concerto; Romances for violin and orchestra no. 1-2. *Accardo, violin; La Scala Phil. Orch.; Giulini, cond.*
    - ARG 5-6/95: 82
    • Fa 3-4/95: 123
    + Gr 1/95: 41

32214. SK 53288: OFFENBACH—Overtures. *Vienna Symphony Orch.; Weil, cond.*
    - ARG 1-2/94: 129
    + Fa 3-4/94: 260
    • Gr 1/94: 48

32215. SK 53289: SCHOENBERG—Piano concerto. LISZT—Piano concertos no. 1-2. *Ax, piano; Philharmonia Orch.; Salonen, cond.*
    + ARG 7-8/94: 166
    • Fa 5-6/94: 240
    + Gr 12/93: 71

32216. SK 53290: KURTÁG—Messages of the late Miss R.V. Troussova; Quasi una fantasia; Scenes from a novel. *Hardy, soprano; Kretzschmar, piano; Whittlesey, soprano; Fábián, cimbalom; Tacke, violin; Fichter, double bass; Ensemble Modern; Eötvös, cond.*
    + ARG 3-4/94: 114
    + Fa 1-2/94: 220
    + Gr 12/93: 100

32217. SK 53296: Excerpts from South Pacific, Poliuto, Andrea Chénier, Fedora, Tosca, Turandot; Catalan songs. *Carreras, tenor; with accomp.* Reissues.
    + ARG 7-8/93: 203

32218. S2K 53336 (2 discs): ROSSINI—Il viaggio a Reims. *Vocal soloists; Berlin Radio Chorus; Berlin Phil. Orch.; Abbado, cond.*
    • ARG 3-4/94: 145
    • Fa 1-2/94: 293
    + Gr 12/93: 116
    • ON 12/24/94: 33

32219. SK 53339: SCHUMANN—Piano quartet. BEETHOVEN—Piano quartet. *Stern, violin; Laredo, viola; Ma, cello; Ax, piano.*
    + ARG 11-12/94: 188
    + Fa 11-12/94: 168
    + Gr 10/94: 131

SONY CLASSICAL

32220. SK 53341: Codex Las Huelgas. *Huelgas Ensemble; Nevel, cond.*
+ ARG 5-6/94: 188
+ Fa 5-6/94: 307

32221. SK 53355: CHOPIN—Preludes; Bolero and other pieces. *Katsaris, piano.*
• ARG 11-12/93: 93
+ Fa 11-12/93: 208
• Gr 10/93: 80

32222. SK 53357: SCHNITTKE—Canon; Sonata for violin and chamber orchestra; Congratulatory rondo; Piano quintet. *Lubotsky, violin; Schnittke, piano; Bauer-Wirth, harpsichord; Batiashvili, violin; Orch.-Akademie Hamburg; Lampson, cond.*
+ ARG 7-8/94: 165

32223. SK 53359: *The Seville concert.* Music of Albéniz, Bach, Scarlatti, Barrios, Koshkin, Yocoh, and Rodrigo. *Williams, guitar; Seville Symphony Orch.; Buenagu, cond.*
+ ARG 7-8/94: 210
+ Gr 1/94: 62

32224. SK 53360: NONO—Il canto sospeso. MAHLER—Kindertotenlieder; Ich bin der Welt abhanden gekommen. *Vocal soloists; Berlin Phil. Orch.; Abbado, cond.; Lipovsek, mezzo-soprano; Rundfunkchor Berlin.*
+ ARG 11-12/93: 161
+ Fa 11-12/93: 336
+ Gr 10/93: 99

32225. SK 53361: SCULTHORPE—Nourlangie; From Kakadu; Into the dreaming. WESTLAKE—Antarctica. *Williams, guitar; London Symphony Orch.; Daniel, cond.; Australian Chamber Orch.; Hickox, cond.*
+ ARG 7-8/95: 194
+ Gr 5/95: 58

32226. SK 53362: BOCCHERINI—Cello sonatas; Fugues for two cellos. *Bylsma, Slowik, cellos.*
+ ARG 3-4/94: 79
+ EM 5/95: 341
+ Fa 3-4/94: 141
+ Gr 3/94: 69

32227. SK 53363: MONTEVERDI—Selva morale et spirituale: Selections. PICCHI—Canzoni. *Capella Ducale; Musica fiata; Wilson, cond.*
+ ARG 5-6/94: 114
+ Fa 3-4/94: 251
+ Gr 7/94: 105

32228. SK 53364: SCHUBERT—Piano sonatas, D. 537, 850. *Levin, fortepiano.*
+ ARG 11-12/95: 195
• Fa 11-12/95: 362
+ Fa 1-2/96: 296

32229. SK 53365: Music of Biber, Stradella, Vivaldi, Albinoni, Telemann, and Handel. *Steele-Perkins, trumpet; Tafelmusik; Lamon, cond.*

+ ARG 11-12/94: 78
+ Gr 4/95: 74

32230. SK 53366: MOZART—Clarinet quintet; Clarinet quartet after K. 378; Clarinet trio. *Neidich, clarinet, basset clarinet; L'Archibudelli; Levin, fortepiano.*
+ ARG 5-6/94: 116
+ Fa 3-4/94: 254
+ Gr 5/94: 74

32231. SK 53367: BEETHOVEN—Octet, op. 103; other wind music. *Mozzafiato; Neidich, cond.*
• Fa 9-10/94: 265
+ Gr 8/94: 67

32232. SK 53368: HAYDN—Small religious choral works. *Vallin, Monoyios, sopranos; Tölzer Knabenchor; L'Archibudelli; Tafelmusik; Weil, cond.*
+ ARG 11-12/94: 126
• Fa 9-10/94: 206
+ Gr 9/94: 88

32233. SK 53369: MOZART—Horn concertos; Rondo, K. 371. *Koster, horn; Tafelmusik; Weil, cond.*
+ ARG 7-8/94: 139
• Fa 5-6/94: 202
+ Gr 2/94: 48

32234. SK 53370: SPOHR—Double quartet in D minor; Sextet in C; Quintet in G. *Archibudelli; Smithsonian Chamber Players.*
+ ARG 5-6/94: 143
• EM 5/95: 341
+ Fa 7-8/94: 249
+ Gr 4/94: 64

32235. SK 53371: *North German organ music.* Music of Lorentz, Strungk, Morhardt, Weckmann, Schildt, and others. *Leonhardt, organ.*
+ Gr 10/94: 164

32236. SK 53373: LASSUS—Lagrime di San Pietro. *Huelgas Ensemble; Nevel, cond.*
+ ARG 5-6/94: 105
+ Fa 3-4/94: 229
• Gr 8/94: 90

32237. SX13K 53456 (13 discs): *Sony Horowitz edition.* Music of Chopin, Schumann, Schubert, Beethoven, Mozart, Rachmaninoff, Bach, Busoni, Debussy, Scarlatti, Scriabin, Medtner, Haydn, Liszt, Mendelssohn, and Moszkowski. *Horowitz, piano.*
+ ARG 3-4/94: 210
+ Gr 7/94: 84

32238. SMK 53474: *Salzburg recital, 1959.* BACH—Goldberg variations. MOZART—Keyboard sonata, K. 330/300h. SCHOENBERG—Suite, op. 25. SWEELINCK—Fantasia. *Gould, piano.* Recorded live.
+ Gr 9/95: 80

32239. SK 53507: VERDI—Don Carlo: Highlights. *Millo, Zajick, Chernov, Furlanetto; Metropolitan Opera; Levine, cond.*
+ ARG 11-12/94: 206

32240. SBK 53509: SIBELIUS—Symphonies no. 2, 7. *Philadelphia Orch.; Ormandy, cond.* Reissues.
+ Gr 9/94: 62

32241. SBK 53515 (Reissues): CHOPIN—Piano music. *Fou, piano.*
• Gr 12/94: 125

32242. SBK 53517: BEETHOVEN—Missa solemnis. *Arroyo, Forrester, Lewis, Siepi; Philadelphia Orch.; Ormandy, cond.*
- Gr 10/94: 167

32243. SM2K 53519 (2 discs): BRUCKNER—Symphonies no. 3, 8. *Cleveland Orch.; Szell, cond.* Reissues.
+ ARG 1-2/95: 92
• Gr 1/95: 42

32244. SM2K 53531 (2 discs): BEETHOVEN—Piano sonatas no. 27-32. *Rosen, piano.* Reissue.
+ ARG 1-2/95: 78
+ Gr 11/94: 111

32245. SK 53627: STRAUSS—Ein Heldenleben; Horn concerto no. 2. *Hauptmann, horn; Berlin Phil. Orch.; Mehta, cond.*
• Fa 11-12/95: 391

32246. SK 53635: HAYDN—Piano sonatas no. 32, 34, 44, 49. *Ax, piano.*
+ ARG 3-4/95: 112
+ Gr 7/95: 84

32247. SK 53899: Gregorian chant. *Chant Schola of the Niederaltaicher Scholaren; Ruhland, cond.*
+ ARG 9-10/94: 247
+ Fa 7-8/94: 305

32248. SK 53959: BERG—Three fragments from Wozzeck; Three pieces for orchestra, op. 6; Lulu-Suite. *Fleming, soprano; Metropolitan Opera Orch.; Levine, cond.*
+ ARG 7-8/96: 81
+ Fa 5-6/96: 106
• Gr 6/96: 41

32249. SK 53960: GUBAIDULINA—Chaconne; Sonata; Musical toys; Piano concerto. *Haefliger, piano; Hannover Radio Orch.; Klee, cond.*
□ ARG 7-8/95: 117
+ Gr 5/95: 83

32250. SK 53961: BEETHOVEN—String trio op. 3, no. 1; Serenade, op. 8. *L'Archibudelli.*
+ ARG 3-4/94: 75
• Fa 3-4/94: 122
• Gr 5/94: 71

32251. SK 53963: SCHMELZER—Sonatas; Balletti francesi; Ciaconna. *Tafelmusik.*
+ ARG 5-6/94: 136
+ Fa 5-6/94: 236

32252. S2K 53964 (2 discs): C.P.E. BACH—Complete flute sonatas. *Kuijken, transverse flute; Asperen, harpsichord.*
+ Fa 3-4/94: 102
+ Gr 5/94: 70

32253. SK 53965: MOZART—Harmonie music on the Marriage of Figaro. ROSSINI—Harmonie music. *Mozzafiato; Neidich, clarinet.*
• Gr 3/94: 74

32254. SK 53967 (2 discs): CHOPIN—Polonaises; Andante spianato; Funeral march. *Katsaris, piano.*
• ARG 11-12/94: 94
• Fa 11-12/94: 200
• Gr 6/95: 75

32255. SK 53968: *Agnes Baltsa and José Carreras: opera duets.* Music of Massenet, Mascagni, Verdi, Bellini, and Bizet. *Baltsa, mezzo-soprano; Carreras, tenor; London Symphony Orch.; Domingo, cond.*
- ARG 7-8/94: 228
- Fa 5-6/94: 301
• ON 2/3/96: 37

32256. SK 53969: PROKOFIEV—Violin concertos no. 1-2. STRAVINSKY—Violin concerto. *Lin, violin; Los Angeles Phil. Orch.; Salonen, cond.*
• ARG 5-6/95: 151
+ Fa 3-4/95: 256
+ Gr 3/95: 52

32257. SK 53971: SCHUBERT—Symphony no. 9. *Bavarian Radio Orch.; Giulini, cond.*
- ARG 7-8/95: 190
+ Gr 8/95: 80

32258. SK 53972: MOZART—Violin sonatas. *Stern, violin; Bronfman, piano.*
+ ARG 11-12/94: 163
+ Fa 9-10/94: 267
+ Gr 9/94: 74

32259. SK 53973: DEBUSSY—Piano works, vol. 4. *Crossley, piano.*
• Fa 7-8/94: 121
+ Gr 6/94: 81

32260. SK 53974: BEETHOVEN—Symphony no. 6; Coriolan; Egmont. *La Scala Phil. Orch.; Giulini, cond.*
• ARG 7-8/94: 69
- Fa 7-8/94: 68
+ Gr 5/94: 47

32261. SK 53975: Choral works by Brahms, Reger, Rihm, and Strauss. *Leipzig Radio Chorus; Berlin Phil. Orch.; Abbado, cond.*
+ Gr 3/95: 82

32262. SK 53976: The court of King Janus at Nicosia. *Huelgas Ensemble; Nevel, cond.*
+ ARG 9-10/94: 248
+ Fa 9-10/94: 411
- Gr 11/94: 142

32263. SK 53977: Psalms and canticles, 1400-1600. *Niederaltaicher Scholaren; Ruhland, cond.*
+ ARG 11-12/94: 242

32264. SK 53978: *Prometheus.* BEETHOVEN—Creatures of Prometheus. LISZT—Prometheus. SCRIABIN—Prometheus. NONO—Promoteo: Suite. *Vocal soloists; Berlin Phil. Orch.; Abbado, cond .*
+ Gr 1/95: 62

32265. SK 53980: FRANCHOMME—Chamber music. *Bylsma, cello; Orkis, fortepiano; L'Archibudelli; Smithsonian Chamber Players.*
+ ARG 5-6/95: 111
+ Gr 4/95: 80

32266. SK 53981: PURCELL—Anthems. *Cordier, Elwes, Kooy, Kamp, vocal soloists; Tölzer Boys Choir; instrumental ensemble; Leonhardt, cond.*
+ ARG 11-12/95: 173
• Gr 11/95: 142

32267. SK 53982: SCHUBERT—String quartet no. 10; String trio, D. 471 (incomplete); String trio, D. 581 (second version). *L'Archibudelli.*
+ EM 5/95: 345
+ Fa 11-12/94: 370

32268. SK 53984: SCHUBERT—Mass no. 6; Deutsche Messe. *Preyer, Weinhoppel, Hering, Kamp; Wiener Sängerkanben; Orch. of the Age of Enlightenment; Weil, cond.*
+ ARG 9-10/94: 193
- Fa 9-10/94: 325
+ Gr 8/94: 92

32269. SK 53985: HAYDN—Symphonies, no. 50, 64-65. *Tafelmusik; Weil, cond.*
+ ARG 11-12/94: 128
+ Fa 11-12/94: 254
+ Gr 11/94: 76

32270. SK 53986: HAYDN—Symphonies, no. 45-47. *Tafelmusik; Weil, cond.*
+ ARG 11-12/94: 128
+ Fa 11-12/94: 254
+ Gr 11/94: 76

32271. SK 53987: M. HAYDN—String quintets. *L'Archibudelli.*
+ EM 5/95: 341
+ Fa 9-10/94: 209
+ Gr 8/94: 67

32272. SK 54290: BRAHMS—Lieder. *Lipovsek, mezzo-soprano; Spencer, piano; Geringas, cello.*
• Fa 1-2/94: 137

32273. SK 54787: BACH—Organ music. *Antonini, organ.*
• Gr 10/94: 154

32274. SK 57485: DUPRÉ—Symphonie-passion. *Castagnet, organ.*
• Gr 11/94: 116

32275. SK 57486: COUPERIN—Messe pour les couvents. *Demoiselles de Saint-Cyr; Mandrin, cond.*
+ Gr 8/94: 76

32276. SK 57488: DURUFLÉ—Complete organ music. *Lecaudey, piano.*
• Gr 7/94: 79

32277. SK 57489: GUILAIN—Pièces d'orgue pour le magnificat. MARCHAND—Pièces choisies pour l'orgue, 1re livre. *Espinasse, organ.*
+ Gr 7/94: 80

32278. SK 57490: SCHUMANN—Organ music. *Latry, piano.*
+ Gr 10/94: 164

32279. SK 57497: *The London concert.* Concertos by Haydn, L. Mozart, Fasch, and Hummel. *Marsalis, trumpet; English Chamber Orch.; Leppard, cond.*
• Gr 5/95: 64

32280. SK 57499: BEETHOVEN—Clarinet trio. BRAHMS—Clarinet trio. MOZART—Clarinet trio. *Stoltzman, clarinet; Ma, cello; Ax, piano.*
+ ARG 1-2/96: 85
+ Fa 1-2/96: 138
+ Gr 1/96: 68

32281. SMK 57650: RACHMANINOFF—Symphony no. 2; The rock. *Academic Symphony Orch. of the St. Petersburg Philharmonia; Dmitriev, cond.*
- ARG 5-6/95: 155
• Fa 5-6/95: 301
+ Gr 2/95: 52

32282. SK 57653: Russian arias and folk songs. *Sotkilava, tenor.*
• ARG 5-6/95: 230

32283. SM2K 57654 (2 discs): TCHAIKOVSKY—String quartets no. 1-3; in B♭, op. post.; Movements for string quartet. *St. Petersburg String Quartet.*
+ ARG 3-4/95: 201
+ Fa 3-4/95: 317
• Gr 1/95: 68

32284. SMK 57660: RACHMANINOFF—Symphonic dances; Vocalise. STRAVINSKY—Jeu de cartes. *Lee, soprano; Novosibirsk Phil. Orch.; Kaz, cond.*
• ARG 5-6/95: 154
• Fa 5-6/95: 301
• Gr 2/95: 52

32285. SK 57960: ZEMLINSKY—Posthumous songs. *Ziesak, soprano; Vermillion, mezzo-soprano; Blochwitz, tenor; Schmidt, baritone; Garben, piano.*

SONY CLASSICAL

+ ARG 1-2/96: 202
+ Fa 9-10/95: 369
+ Gr 6/95: 104

32286. SK 57961: *Yo-Yo Ma: The New York album.* Music of Albert, Bartók, and Bloch. *Ma, cello, alto violin; Baltimore Symphony Orch.; Zinman, cond.*
+ ARG 3-4/95: 235
+ Fa 1-2/95: 345
+ Gr 3/95: 58

32287. SX2K 57965 (2 discs): HAYDN—The creation. *Monoyios, Hering, Kamp; Tölzer Knabenchor; Tafelmusik; Weil, cond.*
● ARG 11-12/95: 133
+ Fa 11-12/95: 269
+ Gr 2/95: 84
+ ON 11/95: 47

32288. SK 57968: WEBER—Quintet for clarinet and strings, op. 34. HUMMEL—Quartet for clarinet and strings. REICHA—Quintet for clarinet and strings. *Neidich, clarinet; L'Archibudelli.*
+ ARG 11-12/95: 232
+ Fa 11-12/95: 316
+ Gr 9/95: 74

32289. SK 57969: WOLF—Eichendorff Lieder. KORNGOLD—Eichendorff Lieder. *Skovhus, baritone; Deutsch, piano.*
+ ARG 7-8/95: 229
+ Gr 1/95: 86

32290. SK 57971: LIEBERSON—King Gesar. *Ebrahim, narrator; Ma, cello; Serkin, piano; Adorján, flute & piccolo; Marshall, clarinet & bass clarinet; Purvis, horn; Taylor, trombone; Hüge, percussion; Lieberson, cond.*
+ ARG 3-4/97: 166
+ Fa 1-2/97: 193

32291. SK 57972: SCHUMANN—Songs. *Lipovsek, mezzo-soprano; Johnson, piano.*
+ ARG 11-12/95: 202
+ Gr 8/95: 120
+ ON 8/96: 43

32292. SK 57973: BRAHMS—Serenade no. 1. ELGAR—In the south. *La Scala Phil. Orch.; Muti, cond.*
● ARG 11-12/94: 82
+ Fa 1-2/95: 130
● Gr 1/95: 42

32293. SK 57974: LANNER—Dance music. *Ensemble Wien.*
+ ARG 7-8/95: 139

32294. SK 58497: Concertos by Haydn, L. Mozart, Fasch, and Hummel. *Marsalis, trumpet; English Chamber Orch.; Leppard, cond.*
+ ARG 5-6/95: 215

32295. SK 58914: FRANCK—Prelude, fugue et variations; Prelude, chorale et fugue; Danse lente; Prelude, aria et final; Chorale no. 3. *Crossley, piano.*

● ARG 5-6/95: 112
+ Gr 2/95: 74

32296. SK 58918: PLA—Flute concertos; Double concerto; Trio sonatas. *Rampal, flute & cond.; Arimany, flute; Pertis, harpsichord; Franz Liszt Chamber Orch.*
- ARG 9-10/95: 192

32297. SK 58919: BOIELDIEU—Harp concerto. PARISH ALVARS—Harp concerto. VIOTTI—Violin concerto no. 19: 2nd movement. *Nordmann, harp; Franz Liszt Chamber Orch.; Rampal, cond.*
+ ARG 7-8/95: 246
+ Gr 10/95: 48

32298. SK 58920: BIBER—Harmonia artificioso-ariosa. *Tafelmusik; Lamon, cond.*
+ ARG 7-8/95: 88
+ EM 5/95: 336
● Gr 5/95: 67

32299. SK 58921: BEETHOVEN—Symphonies no. 4-5. *La Scala Phil. Orch.; Giulini, cond.*
● Fa 3-4/96: 130
- Fi 3/96: 129
● Gr 11/95: 79

32300. SMK 58927: ELGAR—Violin concerto; In the south. *Zukerman, violin; London Phil. Orch.; Barenboim, cond.* Reissue.
- Gr 1/94: 44

32301. SMK 58934: DELIUS—Over the hills and far away; North country sketches; Eventyr; Koanga. *Royal Phil. Orch.; Beecham, cond.* Recorded 1951-53.
+ Gr 11/94: 62

32302. SK 58944: SMETANA—Má vlast. *Israel Phil. Orch.; Mehta, cond.*
- ARG 1-2/95: 181
● Fa 1-2/95: 271
● Gr 4/95: 72

32303. SK 58945: LIGETI—Cello concerto; Piano concerto; Chamber concerto. *Perényi, cello; Wiget, piano; Ensemble Modern; Eötvös, cond.*
+ ARG 7-8/94: 124
+ Gr 6/94: 52

32304. SX2K 58946 (2 discs): DVOŘÁK—Symphonies, no. 7, 9. *Concertgebouw Orch.; Giulini, cond .*
- ARG 11-12/94: 107
● Fa 11-12/94: 222
● Gr 11/94: 70

32305. SK 58949: STRAVINSKY—Le baiser de la fée. BARTÓK—Deux images. *Orch. Filarmonica della Scala; Muti, cond.*
+ ARG 9-10/95: 223
+ Fa 7-8/95: 332
+ Gr 9/95: 49

32306. SK 58950: MOZART—Serenade, K. 361/370 "Gran partita". *Berlin Phil.*

Orch. Wind Ensemble; Mehta, cond.
+ ARG 9-10/95: 183
+ Fa 11-12/95: 319
+ Gr 9/95: 64

32307. SK 58952: DEBUSSY—Nocturnes; Le martyre de Saint Sébastien: symphonic fragments; La damoiselle élue. *Upshaw, soprano; Rasmussen, mezzo-soprano; Women of the Los Angeles Master Chorale; Los Angeles Phil. Orch.; Salonen, cond.*
+ ARG 11-12/94: 98
+ Fa 9-10/94: 175
+ Gr 12/94: 78

32308. SK 58954: SCHUMANN—Piano quintet, op. 44. BRAHMS—Piano quintet, op. 34. *Vladar, piano; Artis String Quartet.*
● ARG 3-4/95: 80
+ Fa 1-2/95: 131
● Gr 10/94: 132

32309. S2K 58955 (2 discs): SCHUBERT—Music for two pianos. *Tal, Groethuysen, pianos.*
+ ARG 11-12/94: 185
+ Fa 11-12/94: 370
+ Gr 9/94: 76

32310. SK 58958: FRANCK—Symphony; Symphonic variations. *Crossley, piano; Vienna Phil. Orch.; Giulini, cond.*
- ARG 3-4/95: 102
Fa 5-6/95: 191
● Gr 3/95: 44

32311. S2K 58961 (2 discs): VERDI—Falstaff. *J. Pons, Frontali, Dessì, O'Flynn, Vargas, Manca di Nissa; Teatro alla Scala; Muti, cond.*
+ ARG 3-4/95: 211
+ Fa 3-4/95: 326
● Gr 11/94: 156
+ ON 12/10/94: 50
+ Op 12/94: 1430

32312. SK 58966: PROKOFIEV—Piano concertos no. 2, 4; Overture on Hebrew themes. *Bronfman, piano; Israel Phil. Orch.; Mehta, cond.; Feidman, clarinet; Juilliard String Quartet.*
- ARG 3-4/95: 157
● Fa 3-4/95: 255
+ Gr 5/95: 57

32313. SK 58967: BRUCH—Scottish fantasy. SIBELIUS—Violin concerto. *Midori, violin; Israel Phil. Orch.; Mehta, cond.*
+ ARG 1-2/95: 91
+ Fa 3-4/95: 299
+ Gr 2/95: 41

32314. S3K 58968: ROSSINI—Armida. *Fleming, Kaasch, Kunde, Francis, Bosi, Zennaro, Fowler, Zadvorny, D'Arcangelo; Teatro Comunale, Bologna; Gatti, cond.* Recorded live.
+ ARG 3-4/95: 172
● Fa 3-4/95: 277
● Gr 3/95: 102

+ ON 1/21/95: 36
+ Op 12/94: 1429

32315. SK 58971; RHEINBERGER—Nonet.
LACHNER—Nonet. *Ensemble Wien-Berlin.*
+ ARG 7-8/94: 158
+ Fa 7-8/94: 159

32316. SK 58972: HENZE—Requiem: nine
sacred concertos for piano solo, trumpet
concertante, and chamber orchestra.
*Wiget, piano; Hardenberger, trumpet;
Ensemble Modern; Metzmacher, cond.*
+ Fa 3-4/95: 189
+ Gr 11/94: 76

32317. SK 58974: BEETHOVEN—
Symphony no. 3. *La Scala Phil. Orch.;
Giulini, cond.*
+ ARG 5-6/95: 87
• Gr 4/95: 48

32318. SMK 58976: TCHAIKOVSKY—
Serenade for string orchestra, op. 48; The
snow maiden: Melodrama; Andante
cantabile for string orchestra; Elegy for
string orchestra. ARENSKY—Variations on
a theme of Tchaikovsky. *St. Petersburg
Camerata; Sondeckis, cond.*
- ARG 1-2/96: 186
+ Fa 1-2/96: 321

32319. S3K 58977 (3 discs):
MUSSORGSKY—Boris Godunov.
*Kotcherga, Ramey, Larin, Lipovsek;
Berlin Phil. Orch.; Abbado, cond.*
+ ARG 7-8/94: 135
+ Fa 9-10/94: 217
+ Gr 5/94: 108
• Op 7/94: 889

32320. SMK 58982: BACH—Violin
concerto in A minor; Piano concerto in F
minor; Violin, oboe concerto;
Brandenburg concerto no. 5. *Stern,
Szigeti, violins; Haskil, Istomin, pianos;
Tabuteau, oboe; Wummer, flute; Casals
Festival Orch.; Casals, cond.* Recorded
1950.
• ARG 9-10/94: 272
• Gr 5/94: 66

32321. SMK 58983: MOZART—Violin
concerto no. 5; Sinfonia concertante.
*Stern, Morini, violins; Primrose, viola;
Perpignan Festival Orch.; Casals, cond.*
+ ARG 9-10/94: 272
• Gr 5/94: 66

32322. SMK 58984: MOZART—Piano
concertos no. 14, 27. *Istomin,
Horszowski, piano; Perpignan Festival
Orch.; Casals, cond.* Recorded 1951.
• Gr 5/94: 66

32323. SMK 58985 (2 discs):
BEETHOVEN—Cello sonatas; Variations.
Casals, cello; Serkin, piano.
• ARG 9-10/94: 272
• Gr 5/94: 66

32324. SMK 58988—58991 (4 separate
discs): BEETHOVEN—Piano trios

(complete) SCHUBERT—Piano trios.
*Istomin, piano; Schneider, violin; Casals,
cello.* Reissues.
• ARG 9-10/94: 101
+ Gr 5/94: 66

32325. SMK 58992: SCHUBERT—String
quintet, D. 956; Symphony no. 5. *Stern,
Schneider, violins; Katims, viola; Casals,
Tortelier, cellos; Casals Festival Orch.;
Casals, cond.*
+ ARG 9-10/94: 272
+ Fa 7-8/94: 232
+ Gr 5/94: 66

32326. SMK 58993: SCHUMANN—Cello
concerto; Trio in D minor; Pieces in folk
style. *Casals, cello; Horszowski, Mannes,
piano; Schneider, violin; Casals Festival
Orch.; Ormandy, cond.*
- ARG 9-10/94: 272
• Gr 5/94: 66

32327. SMK 58994: BRAHMS—String
sextet no. 1; Piano trio no. 1. *Stern,
Schneider, violins; Katims, Thomas,
violas; Casals, Foley, cellos; Hess,
piano.*
+ ARG 9-10/94: 272
+ Gr 5/94: 66

32328. SK 61963: SIBELIUS—Symphony
no. 3; The swan of Tuonela; Karelia
suite; Valse triste; Finlandia. *Pittsburgh
Symphony Orch.; Maazel, cond.*
• ARG 11-12/96: 213
+ Fa 11-12/96: 382

32329. SK 61964: SCHUBERT—Trout
quintet; Arpeggione sonata; Die Forelle.
*Bonney, soprano; Frank, violin; Young,
viola; Ma, cello; Meyer, double bass; Ax,
piano.*
+ Fa 5-6/96: 262
+ Fi 5/96: 134
• Gr 4/96: 68

32330. SK 61970: SCHUBERT—String
quartet no. 14 (arr. Mahler). MAHLER—
Adagietto. *Mito Chamber Orch.*
• ARG 7-8/96: 186
• Fa 7-8/96: 290

32331. SMK 61980: Around the world.
Mormon Tabernacle Choir. Reissues.
+ ARG 5-6/96: 254

32332. SMK 61981: March favorites and
college songs. *Mormon Tabernacle
Choir.* Reissues.
- ARG 5-6/96: 254

32333. SK 61995: ZIMMERMANN—
Requiem für einen jungen Dichter.
*Orsanic, Johnson; Choirs; South-West
German Radio Symphony Orch.; Gielen,
cond.*
+ Gr 12/95: 134

32334. SK 62006: EINHORN—Voices of
light. *Vocal soloists; Anonymous 4;
Netherlands Radio Phil. Orch.;
Netherlands Radio Choir; Mercurio,*

cond.
+ ARG 5-6/96: 108
+ Fa 3-4/96: 163
+ Gr 6/96: 81
+ ON 2/17/96: 40

32335. SK 62014: J. STRAUSS, JR.—
Orchestra music. *Slovak Phil. Orch.;
Lenárd, cond.*
• ARG 11-12/96: 214

32336. SMK 62019—62022 (4 separate
discs): SCHOENBERG—Compositions.
Various performers. Reissues.
• Gr 8/96: 56

32337. SK 62036: *Virtuoso piano
transcriptions.* Music of Chopin, Handel,
Rachmaninoff, Tchaikovsky, and others.
Wild, piano.
+ Fa 5-6/96: 352
+ Gr 12/95: 119

32338. SK 62254: *Bang On a Can all-
stars.* Music of Lang, Gosfield, Ziporyn,
Vierk, Didkovsky, Rzewski, and Pascoal.
*Beiser, cello; Black, double bass; Moore,
keyboards; Schick, percussion; Stewart,
electric guitar; Ziporyn, clarinet.*
+ ARG 11-12/96: 307
+ Fa 9-10/96: 427
+ Gr 10/96: 76

32339. SK 62256: Tears of Lisbon.
Huelgas Ensemble; Nevel, cond.
Recorded live 1995.
+ ARG 3-4/97: 290
+ Fa 11-12/96: 449

32340. MH2K 62334 (2 discs): *The 1903
grand opera series.* Fifty-seven historic
vocal recordings made from 1903-07.
Various performers.
+ ARG 5-6/97: 301
+ Fa 1-2/97: 316
+ Gr 4/97: 105
+ ON 1/11/97: 40

32341. MHK 62337: *Eugène Ysaÿe,
violinist and conductor: the complete
violin recordings.* Music of Brahms,
Chabrier, Dvořák, Fauré, Kreisler, and
others. *Ysaÿe, violin & cond.; DeCreus,
piano; Cincinanti Symphony Orch.*
+ Fa 1-2/97: 338

32342. MHK 62338: LISZT—Hungarian
rhapsodies no. 8-11, 13; Piano concerto
no. 1; Fantasia on Hungarian folk themes.
*Arrau, piano; Philadelphia Orch.;
Ormandy, cond.* Reissue.
+ ARG 1-2/97: 131
+ Fa 1-2/97: 195

32343. MHK 62343: SHOSTAKOVICH—
Symphony no. 6. KODÁLY—Galánta
dances. WEINER—Divertimento no. 1.
BARTÓK—Two Hungarian sketches.
GLINKA—Kamarinskaya. *Pittsburgh
Symphony Orch.; Reiner, cond.* Reissue.
+ ARG 5-6/97: 285
+ Fa 1-2/97: 270

SONY CLASSICAL

32344. SMK 62345 (2 discs): BACH—Brandenburg concerto no. 5; Chorale preludes; Organ music. Music of J.C., W.F., and C.P.E. Bach. Transcribed for orchestra. *Philadelphia Orch.; Ormandy, Stokowski, cond.* Reissues.
+ ARG 1-2/97: 61

32345. MH2K 62349 (2 discs): SCHUMANN—Symphonies no. 1-4; Manfred: Overture. *Cleveland Orch.; Szell, cond.* Reissue.
+ ARG 3-4/97: 223
+ Fa 1-2/97: 266
+ Gr 2/97: 56

32346. SMK 62353: GABRIELI—Antiphonal brass. *Brass of Philadelphia Orch., Cleveland Orch., Chicago Symphony Orch.* Reissue.
+ ARG 11-12/96: 126
+ Fa 1-2/97: 166

32347. MHK 62355: *Bidú Sayao: Opera arias and Brazilian folk songs.* Music of Villa-Lobos, Gounod, Massenet, Hahn, Duparc, Debussy, Ravel, Koechlin, Moret, and Braga. *Sayao, soprano; various orch. acc.* Reissue.
+ ARG 5-6/97: 299
+ Fa 1-2/97: 309
+ Gr 5/97: 121
+ ON 1/11/97: 41

32348. MHK 62356: *Eleanor Steber: Arias and songs.* Music of Berlioz, Bach, Handel, Haydn, and Mendelssohn. *Steber, soprano; Columbia Symphony Orch.; Mitropoulos, Morel, Rudolf, conds.*
+ ARG 5-6/97: 300
+ Fa 1-2/97: 310
+ Gr 3/97: 90
+ ON 1/11/97: 41

32349. SK 62372: SCHUMANN—Dichterliebe; Liederkreis, op. 24 C. SCHUMANN—Selected songs. *Skovhus, baritone; Deutsch, piano.*
• ARG 11-12/96: 206
+ Fa 11-12/96: 370
+ Gr 10/96: 96

32350. SMK 62401: COPLAND—Orchestra music. *Various performers.* Reissues.
• ARG 9-10/96: 111

32351. SMK 62402: GROFÉ—Grand Canyon suite. GERSHWIN—An American in Paris; Porgy and Bess: symphonic picture. *Philadelphia Orch.; Ormandy, cond.* Reissues.
+ ARG 9-10/96: 129

32352. SMK 62403: WAGNER—Overtures. *Cleveland Orch.; Szell, cond.; Philadelphia Orch.; Ormandy, cond.* Reissues.
+ ARG 9-10/96: 225

32353. SM2K 62406 (2 discs): BORODIN—Symphonies; Orchestra music. *Toronto Symphony Orch.; A. Davis,*

cond.; New York Phil.; Bernstein, cond.; St. Petersburg Camerata; Sondeckis, cond. Reissues.
+ ARG 9-10/96: 98
+ Gr 10/96: 50

32354. SM2K 62409 (2 discs): SHOSTAKOVICH—Symphonies no. 4, 10. *Philadelphia Orch.; Ormandy, cond.* Reissues.
+ ARG 9-10/96: 200

32355. SMK 62415: CHOPIN—Preludes; Ballades. *Freire, Entremont, piano.* Reissues.
+ ARG 9-10/96: 108

32356. SMK 62422: SCHUBERT—Songs. *Raskin, soprano; Schick, piano; Te Kanawa, soprano; Amner, piano.* Reissues.
+ ARG 9-10/96: 195

32357. SMK 62424: MOZART—Flute concertos; Clarinet concerto. *E. Zukerman, flute; English Chamber Orch.; P. Zukerman, cond.; Marcellus, clarinet; Cleveland Orch.; Szell, cond.* Reissues.
• ARG 9-10/96: 169

32358. SMK 62425: Music of Paganini, Scarlatti, Villa-Lobos, and Giuliani. *Williams, guitar.* Reissue.
+ ARG 1-2/97: 206

32359. SMK 62426: GABRIELI—Sacred music. *Biggs, organ; Gregg Smith Singers; Edward Tarr Brass Ensemble; Gabrieli Consort; Negri, cond.* Reissue.
• ARG 9-10/96: 122

32360. SK 62605: CHOPIN—Etudes. *Yokoyama, piano.*
• ARG 1-2/97: 87

32361. SK 62625: LARA—Songs. *Domingo, tenor; VVC Symphony Orch.; Silveti, cond.*
+ ARG 11-12/96: 150

32362. SK 62627: *Spirit of Spain.* Music of Albéniz, Mudarra, Falla, Tarrega, Villa-Lobos, Sagreras, Moreno- Torroba, Corea-Grigoryan, and Turina. *Grigoryan, guitar.*
• ARG 1-2/97: 205
+ Fa 11-12/96: 453

32363. SK 62634: BEETHOVEN—Symphony no. 9. *Eaglen, Meier, Heppner, Terfel, vocalists; Eric Ericsson Choir; Eric Ericson Chamber Choir; Berlin Phil. Orch.; Abbado, cond.*
+ ARG 3-4/97: 91
+ Fa 1-2/97: 106
• Gr 1/97: 55

32364. SMK 62637: Music of Rimsky-Korsakov, Glière, Balakirev, Mussorgsky, Kabalevsky, and others. *Philadelphia Orch.; Ormandy, cond.* Reissues.
• ARG 1-2/97: 194

32365. SMK 62642: SHOSTAKOVICH—Symphony no. 1; Festive overture; Ballet suites no. 1-2. *Philadelphia Orch.; Ormandy, cond.; Orch.; Kostelanetz, cond.* Reissues.
+ ARG 1-2/97: 170

32366. SMK 62645: VAUGHAN WILLIAMS—Tallis fantasia; The lark ascending; Greensleeves. DELIUS—Brigg fair; Dance rhapsody no. 2; First cuckoo in spring; Summer garden. *Philadelphia Orch.; Ormandy, cond.* Reissues.
+ ARG 11-12/96: 226

32367. SMK 62646: Arias and cantatas by A. Scarlatti, Mozart, and Handel. *Blegen, soprano; Mostly Mozart Festival Orch.; Zukerman, cond.* Reissue.
+ ARG 1-2/97: 143

32368. SMK 62652: MOZART—Oboe concerto; Bassoon concerto. STRAUSS—Oboe concerto. WEBER—Hungarian rondo. *De Lancie, John, oboe; Garfield, bassoon; Philadelphia Orch.; Ormandy, cond.; Black, oboe; English Chamber Orch.; Barenboim, cond.* Reissues.
+ ARG 1-2/97: 144

32369. SMK 62653: ROSSINI—Overtures. *Various performers.* Reissues.
• ARG 1-2/97: 160

32370. SMK 62654 : SCARLATTI—Harpsichord sonatas. *Newman, harpsichord.* Reissue.
+ ARG 1-2/97: 163

32371. SMK 62686: BEETHOVEN—Piano concerto no. 2. BACH—Piano concerto no. 1. *Gould, piano; Leningrad Conservatory Orch.; Slovák, cond.* Recorded 1957.
+ ARG 7-8/94: 67

32372. SK 64091: IPPOLITOV-IVANOV—Liturgy of St. John Chrysostom; Vespers. *Lege Artis Chamber Choir; Abalyan, cond.*
+ ARG 5-6/95: 124

32373. SMK 64092: RACHMANINOFF—Liturgy of St. John Chrysostom; Choir concerto. *Lege Artis Chamber Choir; Abalyan, cond.*
+ ARG 3-4/96: 169
+ Fa 3-4/96: 255
• Gr 6/95: 97

32374. SMK 64097: BORODIN—String quartets no. 1-2. *St. Petersburg Quartet.*
• ARG 11-12/95: 91
+ Fa 11-12/95: 215

32375. SM2K 64100 (2 discs): BARTÓK—Music for strings, percussion, and celesta; The wooden prince; Dance suite. SCRIABIN—Poem of ecstasy. *BBC Symphony Orch.; New York Phil.; Boulez, cond.* Reissues.
+ ARG 9-10/95: 240
• Gr 9/95: 49

32376. SM3K 64103 (3 discs): BERLIOZ—Symphonie fantastique; Lélio; Les nuits d'été; Overtures; others. *Minton, soprano; Mitchinson, Burrows, tenors; Shirley-Quirk, baritone; London Symphony Orch.; BBC Symphony Orch.; New York Phil.; Boulez, cond.* Reissues.
+ ARG 7-8/95: 87
+ Gr 3/95: 38

32377. SMK 64107: RAVEL—Songs with orchestra. ROUSSEL—Symphony no. 3. *Gomez, Norman, sopranos; Dam, baritone; BBC Symphony Orch.; New York Phil.; Boulez, cond.* Reissues.
+ ARG 7-8/95: 178
• Gr 5/95: 57

32378. SMK 64108: WAGNER—Overtures. *New York Phil.; Boulez, cond.* Reissues.
+ ARG 7-8/95: 178
• Gr 7/95: 72

32379. SMK 64109: STRAVINSKY—Petrushka; Rite of spring. *New York Phil.; Cleveland Orch.; Boulez, cond.* Reissues.
+ ARG 7-8/95: 178
+ Gr 5/95: 60

32380. SMK 64110: BARTÓK—Duke Bluebeard's castle. *Nimsgern, Troyanos; BBC Symphony Orch.; Boulez, cond.* Reissue; recorded 1976.
+ ARG 3-4/96: 85
+ Gr 3/95: 100

32381. SK 64133: GLASS—The essential Philip Glass. *Various performers.* Reissues.
+ Gr 1/94: 47

32382. SMK 64239: BACH—Organ music. *Danby, organ.*
+ Gr 5/95: 78

32383. SMK 64241: CHOPIN—Piano concertos no. 1-2. *Nakamura, Licad, piano; London Symphony Orch.; Fistoulari, cond.; London Phil. Orch.; Previn, cond.* Reissues.
+ Gr 7/95: 46

32384. SMK 64251: MOZART—Piano concertos no. 20, 25; Rondo, K. 382. *Vladar, piano; Academy of St. Martin-in-the-Fields; Marriner, cond.*
• Gr 3/95: 50

32385. SM3K 64263 (3 discs): MOZART—Don Giovanni. *Siepi, Grümmer, Simoneau, Corena; Vienna State Opera; Mitropoulos, cond.* Recorded 1956.
+ ARG 1-2/95: 252
+ Fa 1-2/95: 210
+ Gr 11/94: 146
• ON 12/24/94: 32

32386. SK 64301: BEETHOVEN—British folk songs. *Woods, Watkinson, Protschka, Salter, vocalists; Altenburger, violin; Berger, cello; Deutsch, piano.*

+ ARG 3-4/96: 91
+ Gr 12/95: 125

32387. SK 64302: DANZI—Clarinet sonata. MENDELSSOHN—Clarinet sonata. WEBER—Grand duo concertant. *Neidich, clarinet; Levin, fortepiano.*
+ ARG 7-8/95: 243
+ Gr 9/95: 74

32388. SK 64303: DVOŘÁK—Symphony no. 8; The noon witch. *Berlin Phil. Orch.; Abbado, cond.*
+ ARG 5-6/95: 106
+ Gr 2/95: 42

32389. SK 64305: HANDL—Opus musicum (excerpts); Sancta Maria Mass. *Huelgas Ensemble; Nevel, cond.*
+ ARG 3-4/96: 114
+ Fa 5-6/96: 155

32390. SK 64306: MOZART—Serenade, K. 375; Sextet, K. Anh. 183. PLEYEL—Sextet for 2 clarinets, 2 horns, 2 bassoons, and double bass. *Mozzafiato.*
+ ARG 5-6/96: 157
• Fa 3-4/96: 234
+ Gr 9/95: 76

32391. SK 64307: DOTZAUER—Chamber music. *L'Archibudelli; Smithsonian Chamber Players.*
+ ARG 11-12/95: 113
+ Gr 3/95: 62

32392. SK 64308: ONSLOW—String quintets. *L'Archibudelli; Smithsonian Chamber Players.*
+ ARG 9-10/95: 186
+ Gr 6/96: 68

32393. SK 64309: MOZART—Violin sonatas, K. 302, 303, 305, 376, 380. *Stern, violin; Bronfman, piano.*
+ ARG 1-2/96: 149
+ Gr 11/95: 108

32394. SK 64396: *The great Paraguayan.* BARRIOS—Guitar music. *Williams, guitar.*
+ ARG 1-2/96: 77
+ Fa 1-2/96: 130
+ Gr 9/95: 81

32395. SK 64397: BEETHOVEN—Piano sonatas no. 1-3. *Perahia, piano.*
+ ARG 11-12/95: 83
+ Fa 9-10/95: 139
+ Gr 8/95: 101

32396. SK 64399: CHOPIN—Ballades; Piano music. *Perahia, piano.*
+ ARG 9-10/95: 125
+ Fa 7-8/95: 157
+ Gr 12/94: 126

32397. SK 64400: HINDEMITH—Kleine Kammermusik, op. 24, no. 2; Flute sonata; Bassoon sonata; Horn sonata; English horn sonata. *Ensemble Wien-Berlin.*

+ ARG 1-2/97: 121
+ Fa 11-12/96: 270

32398. SK 64446: TAVENER—Akathist of Thanksgiving. *Bowman, Wilson, altos; Westminster Abbey Choir; BBC Singers; BBC Symphony Orch.; Neary, cond.*
+ ARG 5-6/95: 232
+ Gr 9/94: 93

32399. SMK 64448: SCHUMANN—Symphony no. 3. BEETHOVEN—Overtures: Egmont; Leonore no. 2. *New York Phil.; Columbia Symphony Orch.; Walter, cond.* Recorded 1949, 1954, and 1960.
+ Fa 1-2/97: 267

32400. SMK 64459: BEETHOVEN—Violin concerto. MENDELSSOHN—Violin concerto. *Szigeti, Milstein, violin; New York Phil.; Walter, cond.*
• ARG 9-10/95: 298

32401. SMK 64465: BEETHOVEN—Symphonies no. 4-5, 7, 9: rehearsals. *Walter, cond.*
• ARG 11-12/95: 85

32402. SMK 64466: STRAUSS—Don Juan; Death and transfiguration. BARBER—Symphony no. 1. DVOŘÁK—Slavonic dance no. 1. *New York Phil.; Walter, cond.* Recorded 1952.
• ARG 11-12/95: 287

32403. SMK 64467: J. STRAUSS, JR.—Waltzes. BRAHMS—Hungarian dances. SMETANA—The Moldau. *New York Phil.; Walter, cond.*
+ ARG 11-12/95: 211

32404. SMK 64469: BRAHMS—German Requiem; Alto rhapsody. *Seefried, soprano; London, baritone; Westminster Choir; New York Phil.; Walter, cond.* Reissue.
+ ARG 11-12/95: 95

32405. SM3K 64470—64472 (3 separate discs): BRAHMS—Symphonies; Overtures; Haydn variations. *Columbia Symphony Orch.; Walter, cond.* Recorded 1960.
+ ARG 5-6/96: 92
+ Fi 6/96: 129

32406. SMK 64473: MOZART—Symphonies no. 25, 28-29, 35. *Columbia Symphony Orch.; New York Phil.; Walter, cond.* Reissues.
+ ARG 5-6/96: 158

32407. SM2K 64474 (2 discs): MOZART—Symphonies no. 36 (with rehearsal), 38. *New York Phil.; Walter, cond.* Reissues.
+ ARG 5-6/96: 158

32408. SM2K 64477: MOZART—Symphonies no. 39-41. *New York Phil.; Walter, cond.* Reissues.
+ ARG 5-6/96: 158

SONY CLASSICAL

32409. SMK 64478: Schubert—Symphony no. 9; Rosamunde suite. *Columbia Symphony Orch.; Walter, cond.* Recorded 1955, 1959.
  • ARG 5-6/96: 189

32410. SMK 64479: Brahms—Double concerto. Beethoven—Triple concerto. *Francescatti, violin; Fournier, cello; Corigliano, violin; Rose, cello; Hendl, piano; New York Phil.; Walter, cond.* Reissues.
  • ARG 5-6/96: 89

32411. SMK 64480: Mozart—Requiem. Bruckner—Te Deum. *Seefried, Tourel, Simoneau, Warfield; Westminster Choir; New York Phil.; Walter, cond.* Reissues.
  + ARG 5-6/96: 156

32412. SMK 64481: Bruckner—Symphony no. 4. *Columbia Symphony Orch.; Walter, cond.* Reissue.
  - ARG 11-12/96: 106

32413. SMK 64482: Bruckner—Symphony no. 7. *Columbia Symphony Orch.; Walter, cond.* Reissue.
  + ARG 11-12/96: 106

32414. SMK 64483: Bruckner—Symphony no. 9. *Columbia Symphony Orch.; Walter, cond.* Reissue.
  • ARG 11-12/96: 106

32415. SMK 64484: Dvořák—Symphonies no. 8-9. *Columbia Symphony Orch.; Walter, cond.* Reissues.
  + ARG 11-12/96: 119

32416. SMK 64485: Haydn—Symphonies no. 88, 100, 102. *New York Phil.; Walter, cond.* Reissues.
  + ARG 11-12/96: 142
  • Fi 10/96: 141

32417. SMK 64486: Haydn—Symphony no. 96. Mozart—Overtures; Masonic funeral music; Dances. *New York Phil.; Walter, cond.* Recorded 1955-56.
  • ARG 11-12/96: 289

32418. SMK 64488: Schumann—Symphony no. 3. Beethoven—Overtures. *New York Phil.; Walter, cond.* Recorded 1941, 1954.
  + ARG 11-12/96: 207

32419. SMK 64489: Beethoven—Piano concerto no. 5. Schumann—Piano concerto. *Serkin, Istomin, pianos; New York Phil.; Columbia Symphony Orch.; Walter, cond.* Recorded 1941, 1960.
  + ARG 11-12/96: 284
  + Fa 11-12/96: 181

32420. SM3K 64490 (3 discs): Beethoven—Piano sonatas no. 1, 6, 12-13, 16, 21, 30-32. *Serkin, piano.* Partly reissues.
  + ARG 1-2/95: 78
  + Fa 1-2/95: 113

32421. SM2K 64501 (2 discs): *Isaac Stern, vol. 8.* Music of Lalo, Saint-Saëns, Chausson, Fauré, Ravel, Sarasate, Waxman, and Debussy. *Stern, violin; orch. acc.*
  + ARG 1-2/96: 223

32422. SMK 64502: Bartók—Violin concertos. *Stern, violin; Philadelphia Orch.; Ormandy, cond.; New York Phil.; Bernstein, cond.* Reissues.
  + ARG 1-2/96: 78

32423. SMK 64504: Berg—Violin concerto; Chamber concerto. *Stern, violin; New York Phil.; Bernstein, cond.; P. Serkin, piano; London Symphony Orch.; Abbado, cond.* Reissue.
  + ARG 1-2/96: 87

32424. SMK 64505: Rochberg—Violin concerto. Stravinsky—Violin concerto. *Stern, violin; Pittsburgh Symphony Orch.; Previn, cond.; Orchestra; Stravinsky, cond.* Reissues.
  + ARG 11-12/95: 185
  + Fa 1-2/96: 315

32425. SMK 64506: Barber—Violin concerto. Davies—Violin concerto. *Stern, violin; New York Phil.; Bernstein, cond.; Royal Phil. Orch.; Previn, cond.* Reissues.
  + ARG 11-12/95: 78
  + Fa 1-2/96: 315

32426. SMK 64507: Hindemith—Violin concerto. Penderecki—Violin concerto no. 1. *Stern, violin; New York Phil.; Bernstein, cond.; Minnesota Orch.; Skrowaczewski, cond.* Reissue.
  + ARG 1-2/96: 124
  + Fa 1-2/96: 315

32427. SMK 64508: Bernstein—Serenade. Dutilleux—Violin concerto. *Stern, violin; Symphony of the Air; Bernstein, cond.; Orchestre National de France; Maazel, cond.* Reissue.
  + ARG 1-2/96: 87
  + Fa 1-2/96: 315

32428. SK 64509: Bach—Trio sonatas, BWV 1038, 1079. J.C. Bach—Trio sonata. Telemann—Quartet. *Stern, violin; Rampal, flute; Ritter, harpsichord; Spaeter, lute; Rostropovich, Parnas, cello.*
  • ARG 5-6/96: 75

32429. SM3K 64524 (3 discs): Beethoven—Violin sonatas (complete). *Stern, violin; Istomin, piano.* Reissue.
  - ARG 9-10/96: 92

32430. SMK 64531: Brahms—Violin sonatas. *Stern, violin; Zakin, piano.* Reissue.
  • ARG 9-10/96: 100

32431. SMK 64534: Prokofiev—Violin sonatas. *Stern, violin; Zakin, piano.*

Reissue.
  + ARG 9-10/96: 182

32432. SMK 64535: Bartók—Violin sonatas no. 1-2. Webern—Pieces, op. 7. *Stern, violin; Zakin, Rosen, piano.* Reissue.
  • ARG 11-12/96: 87

32433. SMK 64537: Encores with orchestra. *Stern, violin.* Reissues.
  + ARG 5-6/96: 242

32434. SK 64538: Haydn—Piano sonatas no. 45, 62. Schubert—Piano sonata, D. 784; Military march, D. 733, no. 1 (arr. Tausig). *Kissin, piano.*
  + ARG 1-2/96: 121
  • Fa 1-2/96: 296
  + Fi 3/96: 127
  + Gr 9/95: 83

32435. SK 64542: *Lambarena: Bach to Africa.* Music of Bach and traditional Gabonese music. *Traditional music ensembles from Gabon; Gubitsch, cond.*
  + ARG 3-4/96: 250
  □ Fa 3-4/96: 378

32436. S2K 64573 (2 discs): J. Strauss, Jr.—Die Fledermaus (in English). *Arthars, Grummet, Fieldsend, Mahsoori; D'Oyly Carte Opera; Edwards, cond.*
  + Gr 1/96: 106

32437. SK 64582: Martucci—La canzone dei ricordi; Piano concerto no. 2. *Bruno, piano; Freni, soprano; Orch. Filarmonica della Scala; Muti, cond.*
  + ARG 11-12/96: 159
  + Fa 9-10/96: 253

32438. SK 64584: Shostakovich—String quartets no. 1-2, 4. *St. Petersburg Quartet.*
  + ARG 5-6/96: 193

32439. SK 64586: *Songs of the cherubim.* Music of Tchesnokov, Grechaninov, Arkhangelsky, Stravinsky, Penderecki, and Smirnov. *Chamber Choir "Lege Artis"; Abalyan, cond.*
  + ARG 7-8/96: 270
  + Fa 5-6/96: 335

32440. SK 64600: *Paper music.* Music of Mozart, Vivaldi, Fauré, Boccherini, and others. *McFerrin, vocalist & cond.; St. Paul Symphony Orch.*
  - ARG 11-12/95: 239
  • Fa 11-12/95: 302

32441. SK 66169: Purcell—Theatre music. *Tafelmusik; Lamon, cond.*
  + ARG 11-12/95: 180
  + Gr 2/96: 56

32442. SMK 66171: Gay—Beggar's opera. *Waters, Gilmore, Cuka, Carter; 1968 London Cast; Rhoden, cond.* Reissue.
  + Gr 10/94: 189

32443. SMK 66176: SLADE—Salad days.
Original cast. Recorded 1955.
  + Gr 11/94: 148

32444. SK 66240: MOZART—Flute
quartets. *Grafenauer, flute; Kremer,
violin; V. Hagen, viola; C. Hagen, cello.*
  + ARG 5-6/96: 156
  + Gr 6/96: 66

32445. SK 66243: PURCELL—Funeral
music for Queen Mary. *Westminster
Abbey Choir; New London Consort;
Neary, cond.*
  + ARG 7-8/95: 173
  + Gr 3/95: 89
  + ON 10/95: 47

32446. SK 66244: *In Gabriel's garden.*
Music of Mouret, J. Clarke, Torelli,
Purcell, Dandrieu, Charpentier, Stanley,
and Bach. *Marsalis, trumpet; English
Chamber Orch.; Newman, cond.*
  • ARG 9-10/96: 249
  • Fa 9-10/96: 437
  + Fa 11-12/96: 487
  + Gr 11/96: 102

32447. SK 66251: BRUCKNER—String
quintet; Intermezzo; Rondo; String
quartet. *L'Archibudelli.*
  + ARG 11-12/95: 100
  + Gr 3/95: 61

32448. SK 66253: HAYDN—Symphonies
no. 88-90. *Tafelmusik; Weil, cond.*
  + ARG 11-12/95: 134
  + Fa 11-12/95: 272
  + Fi 5/96: 130
  + Gr 10/95: 58

32449. S2K 66254: *The feast of San
Rocco, Venice 1608.* Music of G.
Gabrieli, Grandi, Cima, Barbarino,
Monteverdi, and Castaldi. *La Capella
Ducale; Musica Fiata Köln; Wilson,
cond.*
  • ARG 3-4/96: 244
  • EM 5/96: 356
  + Fa 3-4/96: 345
  + Gr 6/96: 90

32450. SK 66255: SCHUBERT—Mass no. 6.
*Schmidlinger, Lenzer, Hering,
Azesberger, Kamp; Wiener
Sängerknaben; Chorus Viennensis; Orch.
of the Age of Enlightenment; Weil, cond.*
  • ARG 5-6/96: 185
  - Fa 1-2/96: 296
  + Gr 8/95: 120

32451. S2K 66256 (2 discs): SCHUBERT—
Piano music for four hands, vol. 2. *Tal,
Groethuysen, piano.*
  + Fa 3-4/96: 272
  + Gr 4/96: 68

32452. SK 66259: MOZART—String
quintets no. 3-4. *L'Archibudelli.*
  - ARG 11-12/95: 166
  + Fa 1-2/96: 139
  + Gr 9/95: 76

32453. SK 66260: HAYDN—Missa Sancti
Bernardi de Offida; Mare Clausum;
Motetto Insanae et vanae curae; Motetti
de Venerabili Sacramento. *Hering, tenor;
Kamp, bass; Tölzer Knabenchor;
Tafelmusik; Weil, cond.*
  + ARG 3-4/96: 121
  + EM 5/96: 359
  + Fa 3-4/96: 179
  + Gr 7/96: 88

32454. SK 66261: *Utopia triumphans.*
Music of Tallis, Porta, Josquin,
Ockeghem, Manchicourt, G. Gabrieli,
and Striggio. *Huelgas Ensemble; Nevel,
cond.*
  + ARG 5-6/96: 208
  • EM 11/96: 709
  + Fa 3-4/96: 354
  + Gr 4/96: 104

32455. SK 66262: Music of
Scheidemann, Schildt, Boehm, Bruhns,
and Bach. *Leonhardt, organ.*
  + ARG 7-8/96: 246
  + Fa 7-8/96: 376

32456. SK 66263: ADRIAENSSEN—Pratum
musicum. *Vallin, Cavina, Egmond,
vocalists; Liuto Concertato; Kirchhof,
cond.*
  + ARG 5-6/96: 68
  • Fa 3-4/96: 96
  • Gr 8/96: 80

32457. SK 66265: BACH—Violin
concertos. *Lamon, Melsted, Greenberg,
violins; Tafelmusik.*
  • ARG 3-4/96: 80
  • Fa 3-4/96: 110
  + Gr 2/96: 43

32458. SK 66267: *From the court of
Frederick the Great.* Music of F. Benda,
J.G. Graun, Kirnberger, Frederick the
Great, C.H. Graun, Quantz, and Müthel.
*B. Kuijken, flute; W. Kuijken, cello;
Asperen, harpsichord.*
  + Fa 7-8/96: 391

32459. SK 66270: MOZART—Serenade no.
7; March, K. 249. *Stern, violin; Franz
Liszt Chamber Orch.; Rampal, cond.*
  • ARG 11-12/95: 166
  - Fa 11-12/95: 318

32460. SK 66271: VIVALDI—Oboe
concertos. *Schellenberger, oboe & cond.;
Franz Liszt Chamber Orch.*
  + Fa 3-4/96: 316

32461. SK 66272: BACH—Italian
concerto; Toccata in G; Vivaldi
transcriptions. *Katsaris, piano.*
  • ARG 7-8/96: 69
  + Fa 7-8/96: 90
  - Gr 1/96: 79

32462. S2K 66273 (2 discs): GOMES—Il
guarany. *Tian, Villarroel, Domingo,
Alvarez; Beethovenhalle Orch.;
Neschling, cond.*
  + ARG 7-8/96: 119

+ Fa 7-8/96: 173 (Johnson)
+ Fa 7-8/96: 175 (Miller)
+ Gr 5/96: 119
+ ON 6/96: 43
• Op 5/96: 552

32463. SK 66276: TCHAIKOVSKY—
Symphony no. 5. MUSSORGSKY—Songs
and dances of death. *Kotcherga, bass;
Berlin Phil. Orch.; Abbado, cond.*
  • ARG 7-8/95: 210
  + Gr 3/95: 52

32464. SBK 66278: Gregorian chant, vol.
2. *Schola Cantorum of Amsterdam;
Gerven, cond.*
  + Fa 11-12/95: 451

32465. SK 66279: ROTA—La strada:
suite; Concerto for strings; The leopard:
dances. *Orch. Filarmonica della Scala;
Muti, cond.*
  □ ARG 9-10/95: 203
  + Fa 9-10/95: 298
  + Gr 8/95: 80

32466. SK 66280: LUTOSŁAWSKI—
Symphonies, no. 3-4; Les espaces du
sommeil. *Shirley-Quirk, baritone; Los
Angeles Phil.; Salonen, cond.* Partial
reissues.
  + ARG 1-2/95: 133
  + Fa 3-4/95: 215
  • Gr 11/94: 78

32467. SK 66284: PENDERECKI—
Sinfonietta; Clarinet quartet; Violin
sonata; Benedicamus Domino; Song of
Cherubim; Lacrimosa; Flute concerto.
*Instrumentalists; Warsaw National Phil.
Choir; Sinfonia Varsovia; Wojnarowski,
Penderecki, conds.*
  • Gr 1/96: 72

32468. S2K 66285 (2 discs): BRAHMS—
String quartets no. 1-3; Clarinet quintet,
op. 115. *Juilliard String Quartet;
Neidich, clarinet.*
  - ARG 11-12/95: 93 (French)
  + ARG 11-12/95: 93 (Rawson)
  + Fa 11-12/95: 216
  • Gr 9/95: 74

32469. SK 66288: *Portuguese cançoes,
vilancicos, and motets.* Music of Lésbio,
Machado, Pinheiro, Fernandes, Lusitano,
Tavares, Madre de Deus, and Anon.
Huelgas Ensemble; Nevel, cond.
  + ARG 3-4/96: 242
  + EM 5/96: 354
  + Fa 1-2/96: 377

32470. S2K 66289 (2 discs): BACH—
Brandenburg concertos. *Tafelmusik;
Lumon, cond.*
  + ARG 3-4/96: 79
  + EM 5/95: 336
  + Fa 3-4/96: 105
  + Gr 4/95: 47

32471. SK 66295—66296 (2 separate
discs): HAYDN—Symphonies no. 82-87.
Tafelmusik; Weil, cond.

SONY CLASSICAL

+ ARG 11-12/95: 134
+ Fa 11-12/95: 271
+ Gr 7/95: 50

32472. S2K 66308 (2 discs): SCHUMANN—Scenes from Goethe's Faust. *Terfel, Mattila, Rootering, Bonney, Wottrich, Vermillion, Poschner, Graham, Blochwitz, Peeters; Tölzer Knabenchor; Swedish Radio Chorus; Berlin Phil. Orch.; Abbado, cond.*
+ ARG 7-8/95: 191
+ Fa 7-8/95: 311
+ Gr 5/95: 98
+ ON 10/95: 44

32473. S2K 66314 (2 discs): VERDI—Rigoletto. *Bruson, Rost, Alagna, Pentcheva, Kavrakos; Teatro alla Scala; Muti, cond.* Recorded live 1994.
• ARG 3-4/96: 200
• Fa 1-2/96: 334 (Lucano)
• Fa 1-2/96: 334 (Camner)
• Gr 12/95: 163
- ON 12/9/95: 48

32474. SM2K 66345 (2 discs): COPLAND—Piano music (complete). *Smit, piano.* Reissue.
+ ARG 1-2/95: 96

32475. SK 66351: MENDELSSOHN—Piano trios. *Wanderer Trio.*
+ Gr 11/95: 108

32476. S2K 66354 (2 discs): BACH—Mass in B minor. *Ziesak, Alexander, Nes, Lewis, Wilson-Johnson; Bavarian Radio Symphony Orch. & Chorus; Giulini, cond.*
• Gr 3/95: 81

32477. S3K 66357: SPONTINI—La vestale. *Moore, Huffstodt, Graves; Teatro alla Scala; Muti, cond.*
• ARG 5-6/96: 204
• Fa 3-4/96: 292
• Gr 12/95: 159
• ON 2/3/96: 36

32478. SMK 66363: TSINTSADZE—Miniatures; String quartet no. 6. NASIDZE—String quartet no. 5. *Georgian State Quartet.*
+ ARG 3-4/96: 197

32479. SMK 66471: BACH—Violin concertos; Concertos for violin and oboe. *Stern, Perlman, violin; Gomberg, oboe; English Chamber Orch.; Schneider, cond.; New York Phil.; Mehta, cond.* Reissues.
• ARG 11-12/95: 71

32480. SMK 66472 (2 discs): VIVALDI—Four seasons; Concertos for 2 and 3 violins. STAMITZ—Sinfonia concertante for violin and viola. *Stern, Zukerman, Perlman, Oistrakh, violins; Rampal, flute; orch. acc.*
• ARG 1-2/96: 193

32481. SM3K 66475 (3 discs): MOZART—Violin concertos; Adagio, K. 261; Rondo, K. 373; Concertone, K. 190; Sinfonia concertante, K. 364. *Stern, violin; Zukerman, viola; orchestras; Szell, Schneider, Barenboim, conds.* Reissues.
• ARG 11-12/95: 162

32482. SK 66482: SKEMPTON—Well, well, Cornelius. *Tilbury, piano.*
□ ARG 9-10/96: 275
+ Fa 7-8/96: 310

32483. SK 66483: *Industry.* Music of Wolfe, Andriessen, Lang, and Gordon. *Bang on a Can All-Stars.*
□ ARG 9-10/95: 251
+ Gr 2/96: 70

32484. S2K 66563 (2 discs): VIVES—Doña Francisquita. *Domingo, Arteta, Mirabel, Portal; Coro Titular del Gran Teatro de Córdoba; Orquesta Sinfónica de Sevilla; Rondalla del Real Centro Filarmónico de Córdoba; Roa, cond.*
+ ARG 5-6/95: 192
+ Fa 5-6/95: 373
+ Gr 4/95: 126
+ ON 8/95: 37
+ Op 3/95: 364

32485. SK 66567: PROKOFIEV—Violin concerto no. 1. TCHAIKOVSKY—Violin concerto. *Rachlin, violin; Moscow Radio Symphony Orch.; Fedoseyev, cond.* Recorded live.
• ARG 11-12/95: 217
+ Fa 11-12/95: 333
+ Gr 8/95: 78

32486. SMK 66569: MOZART—Eine kleine Nachtmusik; Divertimento no. 11; Symphony no. 29. *Perpignan Festival Orch.; Casals, cond.*
• ARG 9-10/95: 298

32487. SMK 66570: MOZART—Piano concertos no. 20, 22. *Lefébure, R. Serkin, piano; Perpignan Festival Orch.; Casals, cond.*
• ARG 9-10/95: 298

32488. SMK 66571: BRAHMS—Piano trio no. 2. MENDELSSOHN—Piano trio no. 1. *Szigeti, violin; Hess, Horszowski, piano; Schneider, Casals, cello.*
+ ARG 9-10/95: 298

32489. SMK 66572: BACH—Cello sonatas; Brandenburg concerto no. 4. *Casals, cello & cond.; Baumgartner, piano; Prades Festival Orch.* Recorded 1950.
+ ARG 7-8/95: 272

32490. SMK 66573: *Encores.* Music of Bach, Handel, Popper, Schumann, and others. *Casals, cello.*
+ ARG 7-8/95: 242

32491. SMK 66590: KANCHELI—Symphonies no. 6-7. *Tblisi Symphony Orch.; Kakhidze, cond.*
+ ARG 11-12/95: 141
+ Fa 9-10/95: 235
• Gr 5/95: 52

32492. SMK 66591: SHOSTAKOVICH—Symphony no. 13. *Baikov, bass; Estonia National Male Voice Choir; St. Petersburg Camerata; Lithuanian Chamber Orch.; Sondeckis, cond.*
+ ARG 9-10/96: 202
- Fa 7-8/96: 305
• Gr 7/95: 71

32493. SK 66592: SHOSTAKOVICH—String quartets no. 3, 5, 7. *St. Petersburg Quartet.*
+ ARG 11-12/95: 204

32494. SK 66605: SMITH—Fifteen wild Decembers. *N.W. Smith, singer; G. Smith, keyboards.*
+ Gr 11/95: 144

32495. SK 66613: TAVENER—The lamb; Innocence; The tyger; Annunciation; Two hymns to the Mother of God; Little requiem for Father Malachy Lynch; Song for Athene. *A. Neary, cello; Fullbrook, bells; Baker, organ; Westminster Abbey Choir; English Chamber Orch.; M. Neary, cond.*
+ ARG 5-6/96: 209
□ Fa 3-4/96: 299
+ Gr 12/95: 132

32496. SK 66614: *Millennium of music.* Music of Tye, Cornysh, Whyte, Gibbons, Purcell, Blow, Handel, Turle, McKie, Howells, D. Guest, Hurford, and Grier. *Westminster Abbey Choir; Neary, cond.*
+ ARG 3-4/96: 247
+ Fa 1-2/96: 374
+ Gr 12/95: 141

32497. SK 66615: *Miserere.* Music of Allegri, Bai, Lotti, Gesualdo, G. Gabrieli, Monteverdi, John IV, and Gregorian chant. *Baker, organ; Jeffrey, theorbo; Westminster Abbey Choir & Consort; Neary, cond.*
+ EM 11/96: 709
+ Fa 7-8/96: 370
+ Gr 7/96: 98

32498. SM2K 66616 (2 discs): OFFENBACH—Orphée aux enfers (in English). *Fieldsend, Hegarty, Patterson, Suart; D'Oyly Carte Opera; Edwards, cond.*
+ Gr 2/95: 102

32499. SK 66711: LOEWE—My fair lady (original film cast). *Nixon, Harrison, Hyde-White, Holloway, Cooper, Shirley; orch.; Previn, cond.* Reissue.
+ Gr 5/95: 111

32500. SK 66718: BARTÓK—Piano concertos no. 1-3. *Bronfman, piano; Los Angeles Phil. Orch.; Salonen, cond.*
+ ARG 5-6/96: 76

+ Fa 5-6/96: 82
• Gr 5/96: 53

32501. SK 66720: SCHUBERT—String quartets no. 10, 13; Quartettsatz. *Artis Quartet Vienna.*
+ Fa 5-6/96: 260

32502. SK 66823: Alilo: ancient Georgian chorales. *Rustavi Choir; Erkomaishvili, cond.*
+ ARG 7-8/96: 267
+ Fa 7-8/96: 361

32503. SK 66824: *A new heaven.* KORNDORF—Hymns no. 2-3. *Bott, soprano; BBC Symphony Orch.; Lazarev, cond.*
+ ARG 9-10/96: 145
□ Fa 7-8/96: 209
+ Gr 6/96: 48

32504. SK 66825: SILVESTROV—Symphony no. 5; Postludium. *Deutsches Symphonie-Orch. Berlin; Robertson, cond.; Lubimov, piano.*
⊓ ARG 9-10/96: 204
+ Fa 9-10/96: 328
□ Fi 11/96: 126
+ Gr 10/96: 65

32505. SK 66826: BERG—Songs. *Norman, soprano; Schein, piano; London Symphony Orch.; Boulez, cond.*
• ARG 9-10/95: 107
+ Gr 3/95: 81

32506. SMK 66827: DVOŘÁK—Violin concerto; Romance. MENDELSSOHN—Violin concerto. *Stern, violin; Philadelphia Orch.; Ormandy, cond. Reissues.*
+ ARG 9-10/95: 139

32507. SMK 66829: SIBELIUS—Violin concerto. TCHAIKOVSKY—Violin concerto. *Stern, violin; Philadelphia Orch.; Ormandy, cond. Reissues.*
- ARG 9-10/95: 215

32508. SMK 66830: BRUCH—Violin concerto no. 1. WIENIAWSKI—Violin concerto no. 2. TCHAIKOVSKY—Serenade mélancolique; Méditation. *Stern, violin; Philadelphia Orch.; Ormandy, cond. Reissues.*
+ ARG 9-10/95: 116

32509. SK 66832: DEBUSSY—La mer; Prélude à l'après-midi d'un faune. RAVEL—Ma mère l'oye; Pavane pour une infante défunte. *Concertgebouw Orch.; Giulini, cond.*
+ ARG 1-2/96: 100
- Fa 11-12/95: 341
+ Gr 11/95: 82

32510. SK 66833: SCHUBERT—Symphonies no. 4, 8. *Bavarian Radio Orch.; Giulini, cond.*
- ARG 7-8/96: 188
• Fa 9-10/96: 319
• Gr 12/96: 84

32511. SK 66835: SCHUBERT—Schwanengesang; Fünf Lieder. *Skovhus, baritone; Deutsch, piano.*
+ ARG 11-12/95: 197
+ Fa 11-12/95: 360
• Gr 10/95: 113
+ ON 8/96: 43

32512. S2K 66836 (2 discs): GOLDSCHMIDT—Beatrice Cenci; Four songs. *Alexander, Jones, Wottrich, Díaz, Rose; Rundfunkchor Berlin; Deutsches Symphonie-Orchester Berlin; Zagrosek, cond.; Vermillion, mezzo-soprano; Goldschmidt, piano.*
+ ARG 1-2/96: 115
+ Fa 1-2/96: 211
+ Gr 7/95: 113
+ ON 1/20/96: 33
+ Op 3/96: 346

32513. SK 66839: POULENC—Violin sonata (rev. 1949). RAVEL—Sonate posthume for violin and piano; Violin sonata; Tzigane; Berceuse sur le nom de Gabriel Fauré. DEBUSSY—Violin sonata. *Lin, violin; Crossley, piano.*
• ARG 9-10/96: 180
• Fa 9-10/96: 289
+ Gr 7/96: 70

32514. SK 66840: JANÁČEK—String quartets. BERG—Lyric suite. *Juilliard String Quartet.*
• ARG 9-10/96: 142
• Gr 12/96: 95

32515. S2K 66847 (2 discs): MASSENET—Hérodiade. *Fleming, Zajick, Domingo, Pons, Cox; San Francisco Opera; Gergiev, cond. Recorded live.*
+ ARG 5-6/96: 148
• Fa 5-6/96: 204 (North)
• Fa 5-6/96: 205 (Kasow)
• Gr 2/96: 102
• ON 6/96: 58
- Op 2/96: 188

32516. S2K 66850: SCHREKER—Irrelohe. *DeVol, Randová, Pabst, Zednik, Pederson; Singverein der Gesellschaft der Musikfreunde; Vienna Symphony Orch.; Gülke, cond. Recorded live 1989.*
+ ARG 5-6/96: 185
• Fa 3-4/96: 270
+ Gr 12/95: 157
+ ON 3/2/96: 38
+ Op 2/96: 192

32517. SK 66858: MUSSORGSKY—The nursery; Sunless; Songs and dances of death; Hebrew song; The song of the flea; Hopak. *Lipovsek, mezzo-soprano; Johnson, piano.*
+ ARG 1-2/97: 142
+ Fa 11-12/96: 321
+ Gr 9/96: 90
• ON 1/11/97: 42

32518. SK 66859: MOZART—Symphonies no. 23, 36; Sinfonia concertante, K. 364. *Kussmaul, violin; Christ, viola; Berlin Phil. Orch.; Abbado, cond.*

32519. SK 66860: *New Year's concert 1995.* Music of the Strauss family and Lanner. *Vienna Phil. Orch.; Mehta, cond.*
+ ARG 7-8/95: 204
+ Gr 5/95: 64

32520. SK 66924: Archaica: modern Georgian choral music. *Gori Women's Choir; Mosidze, cond.*
+ ARG 7-8/96: 267
+ Fa 9-10/96: 387

32521. SM2K 66941 (2 discs): BEETHOVEN—Violin concerto; Triple concerto. BRAHMS—Violin concerto; Double concerto. *Stern, violin; Rose, cello; Istomin, piano; New York Phil.; Barenboim, Mehta, conds.; Philadelphia Orch.; Ormandy, cond. Reissues.*
• ARG 11-12/95: 82

32522. SK 67172: Table songs. *Rustavi Choir; Erkomaishvili, cond.*
+ Fa 5-6/96: 336

32523. SK 67173: DVOŘÁK—Cello concerto, op. 104. HERBERT—Cello concerto no. 2. *Ma, cello; New York Phil.; Masur, cond.*
+ ARG 5-6/96: 106
+ Fa 5-6/96: 145
+ Fi 4/96: 123
+ Gr 4/96: 44

32524. SMK 67175: HAYDN—Symphonies no. 93, 95, 97. *Cleveland Orch.; Szell, cond.*
+ ARG 9-10/95: 154

32525. SBK 67176: ELGAR—Symphony no. 2; Serenade; Elegy. *London Phil. Orch.; English Chamber Orch.; Barenboim, cond. Reissue.*
• ARG 1-2/96: 106

32526. SMK 67177: MOZART—Symphonies concertantes. *Soloists; Cleveland Orch.; Szell, cond.; Philadelphia Orch.; Ormandy, cond. Reissues.*
+ ARG 11-12/95: 167

32527. SMK 67178: MOZART—Piano concertos no. 21, 26; Variations K. 265. *Casadesus, Previn, piano; Cleveland Orch.; Szell, cond. Reissue.*
• ARG 9-10/95: 180

32528. SMK 67179: BACH—Concertos for two and three pianos. *R. J. & G. Casadesus, piano; Zürich Chamber Orch.; Stoutz, cond.; Philadelphia Orch.; Ormandy, cond. Reissues.*
• ARG 1-2/96: 73

32529. SBK 67180: VERDI—Arias from Battaglia di Legnano, Nabucco, Vespri, Otello, Traviata, Lombardi, Rigoletto,

SONY CLASSICAL

and Forza del destino. *Scotto, soprano; London Phil. Orch.; Gavazzeni, cond.; Cotrubas, soprano; Philharmonia Orch.; Pritchard, cond.* Reissues.
+ ARG 1-2/96: 190

32530. SBK 67181: BEETHOVEN—Diabelli variations; Piano sonata no. 21. *Varsano, Nakamura, pianos.*
• ARG 1-2/96: 86

32531. SK 67189: LUTOSŁAWSKI—Chantefleurs et chantefables; Fanfare for Los Angeles Philharmonic; Piano concerto; Symphony no. 2. *Upshaw, soprano; Crossley, piano; Los Angeles Phil. Orch.; Salonen, cond.*
+ ARG 9-10/96: 155
+ Fa 7-8/96: 229
+ Gr 6/96: 48

32532. S2K 68240 (2 discs): SCHUBERT—Piano music for four hands, vol. 3. *Tal, Groethuysen, piano.*
+ ARG 11-12/96: 201
+ Fa 11-12/96: 364
+ Gr 11/96: 110

32533. SK 68245: KELLER—Carmina humana. *G. Ruhland, bass; Krems, baritone; instrumentalists; Niederaltaicher Scholaren; Singer Pur; Münchener Percussionensemble; K. Ruhland, cond.*
+ ARG 7-8/96: 141
+ Fa 3-4/96: 190

32534. SK 68249: BRAHMS—Cello sonatas. SCHUMANN—Five pieces in folk style. *Bylsma, cello; Orkis, piano.*
• ARG 1-2/96: 91
+ Fa 3-4/96: 138
• Gr 1/96: 69

32535. SK 68250: BEETHOVEN—Piano concertos no. 1-2. *Immerseel, fortepiano; Tafelmusik; Weil, cond.*
+ ARG 1-2/97: 66
• Fa 11-12/96: 179
• Gr 2/97: 45

32536. SK 68252: BRAHMS—String sextets. *L'Archibudelli.*
- ARG 1-2/97: 81
• Gr 12/96: 95

32537. SK 68255: HAYDN—Missa in tempore belli "Paukenmesse"; Salve Regina, H. XXIIIb, 2; Motetto O coelitum beati. *Monoyios, Groop, Hering, Kamp, vocalists; Lancaster, organ; Tölzer Knabenchor; Tafelmusik; Weil, cond.*
+ ARG 3-4/97: 151
+ Fa 1-2/97: 173
• Gr 11/96: 151

32538. SK 68257: HANDEL—Water music; Pastor fido: Suite. *Tafelmusik; Lamon, cond.*
+ ARG 7-8/96: 124
+ Fa 7-8/96: 187

+ Fi 7-8/96: 133
+ Gr 7/96: 50

32539. SK 68258: PIPELARE—Missa L'homme armé; Chansons; Motets. *Huelgas Ensemble; Nevel, cond.*
+ ARG 11-12/96: 179
+ Fa 9-10/96: 288
+ Gr 10/96: 96

32540. SK 68260: HANDEL—The great harpsichord works. Passacaille, HWV 430; Suites no. 2, 5, 8-9; Chaconne, HWV 435. *Asperen, harpsichord.*
• ARG 11-12/96: 138
+ Fa 9-10/96: 209
• Gr 11/96: 123

32541. SK 68265: BACH—Cantatas no. 27, 34, 41. *Pohl, Sapara, Ritter, Will, Schäfer, Kamp; Tölzer Knabenchor; Tölzer Baroque Orch.; Leonhardt, cond.*
+ Fa 11-12/96: 167
• Gr 1/97: 84

32542. SX4K 68275 (4 discs): BARTÓK—Piano music. *Sándor, piano.* Recorded 1993-94.
+ ARG 1-2/96: 80
+ Fa 1-2/96: 131
+ Fi 3/96: 113
+ Gr 11/95: 119

32543. SK 68323: DALLAPICCOLA—Il prigioniero; Canti di prigionia. *Bryn-Julson, Hynninen, Haskin, vocal soloists; Swedish Radio Symphony Orch.; Swedish Radio Choir; Eric Ericson Chamber Choir; Salonen, cond.*
+ ARG 5-6/96: 101
+ Fa 3-4/96: 151
+ Gr 3/96: 96
+ ON 2/3/96: 38

32544. SM2K 68327 (2 discs): DEBUSSY—Orchestra works. *Philharmonia Orch.; Cleveland Orch.; Boulez, cond.* Reissues.
+ ARG 5-6/96: 102
+ Fi 5/96: 124

32545. SMK 68330: WAGNER—Wesendonck songs; Das Liebesmahl der Apostel. *Minton, mezzo-soprano; Westminster Choir; London Symphony Orch.; New York Phil.; Boulez, cond.* Reissue.
+ ARG 5-6/96: 219
• Gr 7/96: 89

32546. SMK 68331: BERG—Chamber concerto; Orchestra pieces, op. 6; Violin concerto. *Gawriloff, violin; Barenboim, piano; BBC Symphony Orch.; Zukerman, violin; London Symphony Orch.; Boulez, cond.* Reissues.
+ ARG 5-6/96: 83

32547. SMK 68332: MESSIAEN—Et exspecto resurrectionem mortuorum; Couleurs de la cité céleste. STRAVINSKY—Symphonies of wind instruments. *Loriod, piano; Strasbourg Percussion Ensemble;*

Domaine Musicale Orch.; New York Phil.; Boulez, cond. Reissues.
+ ARG 7-8/96: 153
• Gr 7/96: 47

32548. SMK 68333: FALLA—Three-cornered hat; Harpsichord concerto. DUKAS—La peri. *Kipnis, harpsichord; New York Phil. Orch.; Boulez, cond.* Reissue.
+ ARG 3-4/96: 112

32549. SMK 68334: CARTER—Symphony of 3 orchestras. VARÈSE—Déserts; Ecuatorial; Hyperprism. *New York Phil.; French Radio Choirs; Ensemble InterContemporain; Boulez, cond.* Reissues.
+ ARG 7-8/96: 95
+ Gr 7/96: 47

32550. SMK 68335: BOULEZ—Pli selon pli; Livre pour cordes. *Lukomska, soprano; BBC Symphony Orch.; New Philharmonia Orch.; Boulez, cond.* Reissue.
+ Gr 7/96: 47

32551. SK 68337: HARVEY—Concerto antico. GRAY—Guitar concerto. *Williams, guitar; London Symphony Orch.; Daniel, cond.*
+ ARG 11-12/96: 140
+ Fa 7-8/96: 191
+ Gr 10/96: 54

32552. SK 68339: Ev'ry time we say goodbye. Music of Barber, Foster, Griffes, Gershwin, Bowles, and Porter. *Ramey, bass; Jones, piano.*
• ARG 3-4/97: 301
• Fa 1-2/97: 316
+ Gr 2/97: 104
• ON 1/11/97: 40

32553. SMK 68345: SCHUMANN—Davidsbündlertänze; Carnaval; Papillons. *Rosen, Casadesus, piano.* Reissues.
+ ARG 11-12/95: 201

32554. SK 68368: GOLDENTHAL—Fire water paper: a Vietnam oratorio. *Ma, cello; Panagulias, Maddalena, vocalists; Pacific Chorale; Ngan-Khoi Vietnamese Children's Chorus; Pacific Symphony Orch.; St. Clair, cond.*
+ ARG 11-12/96: 308
+ Fa 7-8/96: 172
+ Gr 6/96: 81

32555. SM2K 68442 (2 discs): SCHMIDT—Das Buch mit sieben Siegeln. *Dermota, Berry, Güden, Malaniuk, Wunderlich, vocal soloists; Forrer, organ; Singverein der Gesellschaft der Musikfreunde; Vienna Phil. Orch.; Mitropoulos, cond.* Recorded 1959.
+ ARG 5-6/96: 268
+ Fa 3-4/96: 269
+ Gr 3/96: 90
+ ON 4/13/96: 52

32556. SKM 68445: MOZART—Piano concerto no. 9; Symphony no. 41. *Firkušný, piano; Amsterdam Concertgebouw Orch.; Szell, cond.* Recorded 1958.
+ ARG 3-4/96: 259
+ Fa 3-4/96: 232
• Gr 2/96: 52

32557. SMK 68446: MOZART— Symphony no. 35; Violin concerto no. 5. HAYDN—Symphony no. 92. *Morini, violin; Orchestre de l'ORTF; Szell, cond.* Recorded live 1959.
• ARG 3-4/96: 259
• Fa 5-6/96: 225
+ Gr 2/96: 52

32558. SKM 68447: BEETHOVEN— Symphony no. 3; Egmont: Overture. *Czech Phil. Orch.; Szell, cond.* Recorded 1963.
+ ARG 3-4/96: 259
- Fa 3-4/96: 130
• Gr 3/96: 41

32559. SMK 68448: BRUCKNER— Symphony no. 3 (1888/89 version, ed. Nowak). *Staatskapelle Dresden; Szell, cond.* Recorded live 1965.
• ARG 3-4/96: 259
+ Fa 3-4/96: 141
- Gr 3/96: 41

32560. SK 68468: VERDI—Overtures and preludes. *Phil. Orch. of La Scala; Muti, cond.*
• ARG 3-4/96: 200
• Fa 3-4/96: 311

32561. SK 68473: *So many stars.* Music of Ovalle, Montsalvatge, Dvořák, Villa-Lobos, Obrados, Barroso, Mendes, and Anon. *Battle, soprano; instrumental ensemble.*
• Fa 1-2/96: 356

32562. SMK 68476: BRAHMS—String quintets. *Juilliard Quartet; Trampler, viola.* Reissue.
• ARG 11-12/96: 99
+ Gr 12/96: 95

32563. SK 68488: GERSHWIN—Rhapsody in blue; I got rhythm variations. JOHNSON—Yamekraw. *Roberts, piano; Orch. of St. Luke's; Lincoln Center Jazz Orch.; Sadin, cond.*
- ARG 11-12/96: 127
• Fa 11-12/96: 250
- Fi 9/96: 126

32564. S2K 69258 (2 discs): PUCCINI— Madama Butterfly. *Huang, Troxell, Cowan, Liang, Fan; Orch. de Paris; Chorus of Radio France; Conlon, cond.*
• ARG 9-10/96: 183
+ Fa 9-10/96: 291
+ ON 8/96: 45

32565. SK 69284: BRAHMS—Piano sonata no. 2; Fantasies, op. 116; Pieces, op. 118. *Ax, piano.*

` + ARG 5-6/96: 90
+ Fa 7-8/96: 120
• Gr 6/96: 71

32566. SK 69290: SCHUBERT—Mass no. 6. *Ziesak, Nes, Lippert, Bünten, Schmidt, vocalists; Bavarian Radio Symphony Orch. & Chorus; Giulini, cond.*
• ARG 11-12/96: 200
+ Fa 11-12/96: 363
- Gr 2/97: 98

SOTHEBY'S

32567. 2: CHOPIN—Piano music. *Kogosowski, piano.*
- ARG 11-12/92: 104

SOUND

32568. 3441: RAVEL—Daphnis et Chloé suites no. 1-2; La valse; Boléro; Alborada del gracioso. *Czech Phil. Chorus & Orch.; Baudo, cond.*
+ Fa 7-8/87: 167

32569. 3444: BARTÓK—Forty-four duos for 2 violins. *Gertler, Suk, violins.*
+ ARG 5-6/87: 45
+ ARG 11-12/87: 13
+ Fa 5-6/87: 85

32570. 3446: PADEREWSKI—Piano concerto in A minor. *Paleczny, piano; Polish Radio National Symphony Orch.; Maksymiuk, cond.*
+ Fa 5-6/87: 172

32571. 3459: *Works for harp and orchestra.* Music of Caplet, Debussy, and Ravel. *Klintcharova, harp; Philharmonia Bulgarica; Tabakov, cond.*
- Fa 9-10/87: 179

SOUND-STAR-TON

32572. SST 30208: SHOSTAKOVICH—Cello sonata. BRITTEN—Cello sonata. *Remenikova, cello; Braginsky, piano.*
+ Fa 11-12/92: 368

32573. SST 31109: SHOSTAKOVICH— Preludes op. 34; Piano sonata no. 2. *Braginsky, piano.*
+ Fa 11-12/92: 368

SOUNDBOARD RECORDS

32574. SBCD 921: C.P.E. BACH— Keyboard sonatas, H. 25, 29-41, 51. *Booth, harpsichord.*
+ EM 8/93: 502
+ Gr 8/93: 56

SOUNDPRINTS

32575. SP 9301: *Pressure points.* Music of Mott, Celona, Degazio, and Tenney. *Sound Pressure.*
+ Fa 3-4/94: 419

32576. SP 9302: *The devil's staircase: composers and chaos.* Electronic music by Degazio, Cimaga, Celona, Del Buono, Foster, and Free.
+ Fa 3-4/94: 420

SOUNDSPELLS PRODUCTIONS

32577. CD 101: KUPFERMAN—A little ivory concerto; Piano quintet. *Hayami, piano; Hudson Valley Phil. String Quartet; Hudson Valley Wind Quintet; Laurentian String Quartet.*
+ ARG 5-6/89: 58
+ Fa 7-8/88: 183
+ MA 11/88: 59

32578. CD 102: KUPFERMAN—Triple play; Soundspells fantasy; Clarinet quartet; Five flings; Four double features. *S. & N. Drucker, clarinets; Abram, Hayami, pianos; Laurentian String Quartet.*
+ ARG 5-6/89: 58

32579. CD 103: KUPFERMAN—Images of Chagall; Summer music; Sound phantoms no. 7. *Cygnus Ensemble; Mauk, soprano saxophone; Stout, percussion; Bronx Arts Ensemble; Kupferman, cond.*
+ Fa 5-6/91: 200

32580. CD 104: KUPFERMAN—Jazz symphony; Challenger. *Lithuanian National Phil.; Domarkas, cond.*
• Fa 11-12/91: 364 (Silverton)
+ Fa 11-12/91: 364 (Snook)

32581. CD 105: KUPFERMAN—Aristo variations; Night voices; Dark Orpheus; Blue sonata. *Varga, cello; Rosenak, piano; Anderson, guitar.*
+ ARG 3-4/93: 102
• Fa 11-12/92: 272

32582. CD 106: BACH—Sonatas for flute and obbligato harpsichord, BWV 1030-32; Sonatas for flute and continuo, BWV 1034-35. *Baron, flute; Ranck, harpsichord; Eddy, cello.*
- ARG 3-4/93: 52
- Fa 11-12/92: 187

32583. CD 107: KUPFERMAN—The proscenium (...on the demise of Gertrude). *Hardgrave, soprano; Music in the Mountains Festival Chamber Players; Kupferman, cond.*
□ ARG 7-8/94: 122
+ Fa 3-4/94: 227

32584. CD 108: KUPFERMAN—Bassoon quintet; Clarinet quintet; O Harlequin. *Bronx Arts Ensemble; Music in the Mountains Quartet.*
+ ARG 1-2/95: 128
□ Fa 3-4/95: 203
+ Fa 5-6/95: 236

32585. CD 109: KUPFERMAN—Ice cream concerto; Flavors of the stars. *Atril 5.*
+ ARG 9-10/95: 302
+ Fa 5-6/95: 236

SOUNDSPELLS PRODUCTIONS

32586. CD 110: KUPFERMAN—The Moor's concerto; Wings of the highest tower. *Hayami, piano; Moscow Symphony Orch.; Krimets, cond.*
+ ARG 7-8/95: 139
+ Fa 5-6/95: 236

32587. CD 111: KUPFERMAN—Orchestral music, vol. 1. *Wells, cello; Japan Phil. Orch.; Watanabe, cond.; Hartt Jazz Ensemble; Mattran, cond.* Reissues.
+ ARG 3-4/96: 140
+ Fa 3-4/96: 196

32588. CD 112: KUPFERMAN—Orchestral music, vol. 2. *New Philharmonia Orch.; Farberman, cond.; Stuttgart Phil. Orch. Prisma Chamber Players of Copenhagen; Royal Phil. Orch.; Freeman, cond.; De Gaetani, mezzo-soprano; Roseman, oboe; Speigelman, electric harpsichord.* Reissues.
+ ARG 3-4/96: 140
+ Fa 3-4/96: 196

32589. CD 113: *Orchestral music, vol. 3.* KUPFERMAN—Guitar concerto; Banners. *Limón, guitar; Orquesta de Baja California; García Barrios, cond.*
• Fa 7-8/96: 210

32590. CD 114: KUPFERMAN—Hexagon skies; Infinities projections. *Limón, guitar; Orquesta de Baja California; García Barrios, cond.*
+ Fa 1-2/97: 189

32591. CD 115: KUPFERMAN—Piano music. *Vassiliades, piano.*
□ ARG 9-10/96: 148
+ Fa 7-8/96: 210

32592. CD 116: CORY—Images. *New York Camerata; Polish Radio National Symphony Orch.; Suben, cond.; Fulkerson, violin; Finckel, cello; Oldfather, piano.*
+ ARG 3-4/97: 120
+ Fa 1-2/97: 146

SOUTHERN CROSS

32593. SCCD 1021: *Australian percussion music, vol. 1.* Music of Westlake, Wesley-Smith, Sculthorpe, and Edwards. *Askill, percussion.*
+ Fa 3-4/89: 385

SPARTACUS

32594. 21001: *Colonial sacred music.* Music of Hernandez, Franco, Lienas, Sumaya, and Lopez y Capillas. *Mexico City Cathedral Choir; Lopez Nava, cond.*
- ARG 3-4/95: 251

32595. 21004: Mexican romantics. *Mexico City Phil. Orch.; Herrera de la Fuente, cond.*
+ ARG 3-4/95: 226

32596. 21005: REVUELTAS—Homenaje a Federico Garcia Lorca; Sensemaya;

Janitzio; La noche de los mayas. CHÁVEZ—Toccata. MONCAYO—Bosques. *Mexico City Phil. Orch.; Herrera de la Fuente, cond.*
+ ARG 3-4/95: 167
+ Fa 1-2/95: 240

32597. 21006: Music of Halffter, Lavalle, Kuri-Aldana, Duran, Jimemez-Mabarek, and Sandi. *Mexico City Phil. Orch.; Herrera de la Fuente, cond.*
+ ARG 3-4/95: 226

32598. 21007: REVUELTAS—La noche de los Mayas. MONCAYO—Huapango. GALINDO—Sones de mariachi. ROSAS—Sobre las Olas. VILLANEUVA—Vals poetico; La bamba. *Mexico City Phil. Orch.; Herrera de la Fuente, cond.*
+ ARG 3-4/95: 167

32599. 21008: PONCE—Music for cello and piano. *Cedillo, cello; Olechovsky, piano.*
• ARG 5-6/95: 149

32600. 21017: ROSAS—Piano music. *Stankovitch, piano.*
□ ARG 11-12/95: 186

32601. 21031: BERNAL JIMENEZ—3 cartas de Mexico; Angelus; Noche en Morelia; El chueco. *Carlos Chávez Symphony Orch.; Lozano, cond.*
• ARG 1-2/96: 127

32602. 21032: JIMENEZ MABAREK—Orchestra music. *Carlos Chavez Symphony Orch.; Lozano, cond.*
- ARG 11-12/95: 148

32603. 21033: *Musica latinoamericana de concierto.* Music of Ginastera, Márquez, Fariñas, Bernstein, Cupido, and Enriquez. *Orquesta Sinfonica Carlos Chávez; Lozano, cond.*
• ARG 1-2/96: 206
• Fa 11-12/95: 498

SPECTRUM

32604. SR 312 (LP): *Songs of Spanish masters.* Music of Mompou, Falla, and Turina. *Stark, soprano; Garvey, piano.*
+ ARG 1-2/87: 81

32605. SR 320 (LP): Music of Grigny, Bach, Pachelbel, Scheidt, and others. *Butler, organ.*
+ Fa 11-12/87: 281

32606. SR 321 (LP): HOIBY—At the round earth's imagined corners; Magnificat and Numc Dimittis; Hear us, o hear us Lord; Hymn to the new age; The offering; Let this mind be in you; Inherit the Kingdom; Ascension, Holy sonnet no. 7. *Choir of Trinity Church, New York City; Simms, King, conds.*
• AO 8/88: 29
- Fa 1-2/88: 142

32607. SR 322 (LP): *Piano theatre.* Music of Gershwin, Antheil, Fennimore, Satie, Poulenc, and others. *Verbit, piano.*
+ Fa 7-8/87: 223

ST. LOUIS SYMPHONY ORCHESTRA

32608. LSC 51201—LSC 51206 (6 discs): *The Slatkin years.* Music of Adams, Bach, Baker, Beethoven, Borodin, Debussy, Dukas, Dvořák, Erb, Haydn, Herold, Husa, Ives, Mahler, Mendelssohn, Mussorgsky, Schubert, Schwantner, Tower, Vaughan Williams, and Villa-Lobos. *Hohenfeld, Popp, Valente, sopranos; McGuire, baritone; Aller, cello; Isbin, guitar; St. Louis Symphony Orch. & Chorus; Slatkin, cond.*
+ ARG 1-2/96: 203
+ Fi 3/96: 118

STANDING ROOM ONLY

32609. SRO-501-2 (2 discs): VERDI—La traviata; Il trovatore: Act 3, scene 3; Luisa Miller: Excerpts. *Ricciarelli, Carreras, Zancanaro, Ricciarelli, Carreras; unidentified chorus, orchs & conds.; Bartoletti, cond.*
• Fa 7-8/90: 306

32610. SRO-502-2 (2 discs): BIZET—Pêcheurs de perles. Arias by Pergolesi, Cimarosa, Rossini, Bellini, Donizetti, and Puccini. *Devia, Kraus, Sardinero, Foiani; Bilbao Opera Chorus & Orch.; Rivoli, cond.* Recorded live 1982 (Bizet).
- ARG 7-8/89: 28
- Fa 7-8/89: 104

32611. SRO-505-2 (2 discs): MASCAGNI—Iris. *Petrella, Di Stefano, Meletti, Christoff; with assisting soloists; Rome Opera Chorus & Orch.; Gavazzeni, cond.* Recorded live 1956.
+ ARG 9-10/89: 77

32612. SRO-506-2 (2 discs): PUCCINI—Fanciulla del West. *Frazzoni, Corelli, Gobbi, Zaccaria; Teatro alla Scala; Votto, cond.* Recorded live 1956.
+ ARG 9-10/89: 90 m.f.

32613. SRO-507-2 (2 discs): GOUNOD—Roméo et Juliette. *Wise, Carreras, Rydl; Barcelona Opera Chorus & Orch.; Delacôte, cond.* Recorded live 1983.
• ARG 9-10/89: 56

32614. SRO-509-2 (2 discs): ROSSINI—Semiramide. *Caballé, Horne, Araiza, Ramey; with assisting soloists; Aix-en-Provence Festival Chorus & Orch.; Lopez-Cobos, cond.* Recorded live 1980.
+ ARG 9-10/89: 97

32615. SRO-510-2 (2 discs): DONIZETTI—Roberto Devereux. *Caballé, Marsee, Carreras, Sardinero; with assisting soloists; Aix-en-Provence Festival Chorus & Orch.; Rudel, cond.*

Recorded live 1977.
+ ARG 9-10/89: 49

32616. SRO-511-2 (2 discs): PUCCINI—
Tosca. *Milanov, Corelli, Guelfi; with
assisting soloists; Royal Opera House
Covent Garden; Gibson, cond.* Recorded
live 1957.
+ ARG 9-10/89: 90

32617. SRO-512-2 (2 discs): BELLINI—I
puritani. *Freni, Pavarotti, Bruscantini,
Giaiotti; with assisting soloists; Italian
Radio and Television Rome Chorus &
Symphony Orch.; Muti, cond.* Recorded
live 1970.
+ ARG 9-10/89: 29 m.f.

32618. SRO-513-2 (2 discs):
DONIZETTI—Fille du regiment. *Freni,
Ganzarolli; with assisting soloists;
Teatro La Fenice; Sanzogno, cond.* Sung
in Italian. Recorded live 1975.
+ ARG 9-10/89: 49

32619. SRO-515-1: LEONCAVALLO—I
pagliacci. *Micheluzzi, Corelli, Gobbi,
Puglisi; with assisting soloists; unnamed
chorus & orch.; Simonetto, cond.*
Recorded live 1954.
+ ARG 9-10/89: 69

32620. SRO-801-2 (2 discs):
DONIZETTI—Lucrezia Borgia; Roberto
Devereux: excerpts. *Caballé, Berbié,
Vanzo, Paskalis, Chookasian unnamed
chorus & orch.; Perlea, Cillario, conds.*
Recorded live 1965.
+ Fa 1-2/91: 189

32621. SRO-802-3 (3 discs): *Toscanini at
La Scala.* Mucic of Rossini, Verdi,
Puccini, and Boito. *Favero, Tebaldi,
Nelli, Simionato, Prandelli, Stabile, Siepi,
Pasero; Teatro alla Scala Chorus &
Orch.; Toscanini, cond.* Recorded live
1946, 1948.
+ ARG 9-10/90: 38
+ Fa 11-12/90: 473 m.f.

SRO-803-2 see **Foyer**   CF
2028.

32622. SRO-804-2 (2 discs): VERDI—Un
ballo in maschera. *Cerquetti, Stignani,
Poggi, Bastianini; Teatro Comunale,
Florence Chorus & Orch.; Tieri, cond.*
Recorded live 1957.
+ Fa 11-12/90: 381

32623. SRO-805-1: *Gina Cigna: a
ninetieth birthday celebration.* Music of
Gounod, Verdi, Ponchielli, Giordano,
Bellini, and others. *Cigna, soprano;
various orchs. & conds.*
+ ARG 9-10/90: 153
+ Fa 1-2/91: 357
+ Gr 11/90: 1080

32624. SRO-806-1: MASCAGNI—
Cavalleria rusticana. *Arangi Lombardi,
Melandri, Lulli; unnamed chorus; Milan*

Symphony Orch.; Molajoli, cond.
- Fa 11-12/90: 170

32625. SRO-807-1: VERDI—Forza del
destino: Abridged. *Barbato, Gigli,
Mascherini, Neri; Teatro Municipal, Rio
de Janeiro Chorus & Orch.; Votto, cond.*
• ARG 9-10/90: 158
- Fa 11-12/90: 383

32626. SRO-808-1: WAGNER—Der
fliegende Holländer: Abridged. *Flagstad,
Jarred, Lorenz, Jansen; Royal Opera
House Covent Garden Chorus & Orch.;
Reiner, cond.*
+ ARG 11-12/90: 138 (Flagstad)
• ARG 11-12/90: 138 (others)
• Fa 1-2/91: 347

32627. SRO-809-2 (2 discs):
DONIZETTI—Lucia di Lammermoor.
*Deutekom, Carreras, Fioravanti, Cava;
unnamed chorus & orchs.; Gatto, cond.*
Recorded live 1975.
• Fa 1-2/91: 189

32628. SRO-810-2 (2 discs): VERDI—La
traviata. GOUNOD—Faust: Excerpts.
*Tebaldi, Prandelli, Filippeschi, Panerai,
Tajo; Italian Radio and Television Milan
Chorus & Symphony Orch.; Teatro San
Carlo, Naples Chorus & Orch.; Giulini,
Patanè, conds.* Recorded live 1951, 1952.
• Fa 1-2/91: 341

32629. SRO-811-3 (3 discs): GOUNOD—
Faust. MASSENET—Manon: Duets. *Scotto,
Kraus, Saccomani, Ghiaurov; unnamed
choruses & orchs.; Ethuin, cond.*
Recorded live 1973.
+ ARG 11-12/90: 62 (Faust)
- ARG 11-12/90: 62 (Manon)
+ Fa 11-12/90: 238

32630. SRO-813-2 (2 discs): MOZART—
Don Giovanni. *Stich-Randall, Caballé,
Kmentt, Wächter, Kunz; Teatro San
Carlos, Lisbon Chorus & Orch.; Gielen,
cond.* Recorded live 1960.
+ Fa 3-4/91: 291

32631. SRO-815-1: *Magda Olivero in
recital.* Music of Donaudy, Tosti, Hahn,
Respighi, Puccini, and others. *Olivero,
soprano; Davis, Ohlsson, Schneider,
piano.* Recorded live.
• ARG 5-6/91: 164
- Fa 5-6/91: 327

32632. SRO-816-2 (2 discs):
DONIZETTI—La favorita. MASCAGNI—
Caballeria rusticana: Tu qui Santuzza.
*Simionato, Di Stefano, Mascherini, Siepi;
Mexico City Opera Chorus & Orch.;
Teatro Alla Scala Orch.; Cellini, Votto,
conds.* Recorded live 1949, 1955.
+ ARG 9-10/91: 67 m.f.
• Fa 7-8/91: 151

32633. SRO-817-1: *New York farewell
recital, 1962.* Music of Schubert, A.
Scarlatti, Handel, Donizetti, and others.
Schipa, tenor; Amato, piano. Recorded

live 1962.
☐ Fa 7-8/91: 341

32634. SRO-819-1: ROSSINI—Barbiere di
Siviglia: excerpts. *Resemba, De Lucia,
Novelli, Schottler; unnamed chorus &
orch.; Sassano, cond.* Recorded live
1918.
+ ARG 3-4/91: 177
☐ Fa 7-8/91: 341

32635. SRO-820-2 (2 discs): PUCCINI—
Tosca (complete); Tosca: excerpts.
*Callas, Filippeschi, Weede, Di Stefano;
Mexico City Opera Chorus & Orch.;
Mugnai, Picco, conds.* Recorded live
1950, 1952.
+ Fa 7-8/91: 255

32636. SRO-821-2 (2 discs): PUCCINI—La
bohème. GIORDANO—Andrea Chénier.
*Tebaldi, Candida, Corelli, Guarrera,
Hines, Bastianini; Vienna State Opera
Chorus & Orch.; unnamed chorus &
orch.; Matacic; Guadagno, conds.*
Recorded live 1960, 1969.
+ ARG 9-10/109
- Fa 7-8/91: 254

32637. SRO-822-1: *Scenes and arias.*
Music of Bellini, Berlioz, Wagner, Verdi,
Strauss, and others. *Horne, mezzo-
soprano; various orchs. & conds.*
Recorded live 1966-1979.
+ Fa 7-8/91: 339

32638. SRO-823-1: Music of Verdi,
Puccini, Halévy, and Erkel. *Tókódy,
soprano; various orchs. & conds.*
Recorded live 1981-1990.
- Fa 7-8/91: 337

32639. SRO-824-2 (2 discs): BOITO—
Mefistofele. *Ghiaurov, Tebaldi,
Bergonzi; American Opera Society;
Gardelli, cond.* Recorded 1966.
+ ARG 11-12/91: 40
+ ON 8/91: 36

32640. SRO-825-2: PUCCINI—Madama
Butterfly (excerpts). VERDI—Otello:
Willow song and Ave Maria. *Tebaldi,
soprano; Chorus and Orch. of Teatro San
Carlo, Naples; Questa, Adler, conds.*
Live performances 1956-1958.
+ Fa 9-10/91: 315

32641. SRO-839-2 (2 discs): ALFANO—
Risurrezione. PUCCINI—Turandot: Final
scene (compl. Alfano). *Olivero,
Gismondo, Boyer; RAI Turin;
Boncompagni, cond.; Kelm, West; chorus
& orch.; Keene, cond.*
+ Gr 10/93: 110

STAR OF INDIANA PRODUCTIONS

32642. 488779469-2: *Brass theater II.*
Music of Stravinsky, Miki, Britten,
Barber, Mussorgsky, Bartók, Harline, and
Sousa. *Canadian Brass; Star of Indiana;
Cramer, Schermerhorn, conds.*
+ Fa 11-12/96: 472

STARKLAND

32643. ST-201: DOCKSTADER—Water music; Two moons of quartermass; Quartermass. *Dockstader, tape recorder.*
+ Fa 5-6/93: 192

32644. ST-202: DOCKSTADER—Traveling music; Luna Park; Apocalypse; Drone; Four telemetry tapes. *Dockstader, electronics.*
□ ARG 1-2/94: 95
+ Fa 11-12/93: 217

32645. ST-204: DRESHER—Underground; Other fire; Mirrors; Casa Vecchia. *Dresher, electronics; Black, electric bass & electronics; Ensemble 9; Morimoto, cond.*
+ ARG 7-8/96: 298
+ Fa 1-2/96: 190

START

32646. SCD 13: Music of Vivaldi, Schubert, and Haydn. *Parikian, Hanson, García, Philps, violins; Cohen, cello; English Chamber Orch.; Menuhin, cond.*
• Fa 1-2/89: 287

STEEPLECHASE

32647. 32018: RACHMANINOFF—Cello sonata in G minor. SHOSTAKOVICH—Cello sonata in D minor. *Bengtsson, cello; Kavtaradze, piano.*
• Fa 9-10/89: 292

32648. 32023: BACH—Goldberg variations. *Mortensen, harpsichord.*
+ Fa 11-12/89: 111

STEFANOTIS

32649. 249001: HANDEL—Suite in B♭ (1733); Chaconne in G; Sonata in G; Fantasy in C; Menuets I & II in F; Fugues I-VI. *Grémy-Chauliac, harpsichord.*
+ Fa 9-10/87: 213

32650. 249606: BRAHMS—Variations on a theme by Schumann op. 9; Variations on a theme by Paganini op. 35. *Fernier, piano.*
- Fa 1-2/87: 78

STEREOPHILE

32651. STPH 003-2: BRAHMS—Piano sonata no. 3; Intermezzi, op. 117. *Silverman, piano.*
• ARG 1-2/92: 36
• Fa 11-12/91: 284

32652. STPH 007-2: *Festival.* COPLAND—Appalachian spring. KOHJIBA—Transmigration of the soul. MILHAUD—Creation du monde. *Santa Fe Chamber Music Festival; Ohyama, cond.*
• ARG 7-8/96: 237

STERLING

32653. CDS 1004-2: STENHAMMAR—Piano concerto no. 1; Late summer nights. *Mannheimer, piano; Gothenburg Symphony Orch.; Dutoit, cond.*
+ ARG 5-6/90: 113
+ Fa 7-8/93: 248
+ Gr 7/90: 230

32654. CDS 1005-2: LINDBLAD—Symphony no. 2. ÖLANDER—Symphony in E♭ major. *Gävleborg Symphony Orch.; Liljefors, cond.; Västerås Symphony Orch.; Damgaard, cond.* Lindblad recorded live 1977.
+ ARG 11-12/96: 152
+ Fa 11-12/96: 288

32655. CDS 1009-2: *Overtures for the Royal Theater.* Music of Norman, Randel, Soderman, Berwald, Kraus, and others. *Stockholm Opera Orch.; Westerberg, cond.; St. Petersberg Hermitage Orch.; Liljefors, cond.*
+ ARG 7-8/96: 235
• Fa 7-8/96: 402

32656. CDS 1010-2: ATTERBERG—Symphonies no. 1, 4. *Swedish Radio Symphony; Westerberg, cond.; Norköpping Symphony Orch.; Frykberg, cond.* Reissues; issued also as LP: S 1010.
+ ARG 9-10/93: 85
+ Fa 7-8/87: 48 (LP)

32657. CDS 1011-2: *Strindberg in music.* AULIN MÄSTER OLAF. RANGSTRÖM—Dithyramb. *Örebro Symphony Orch.; Nilson, cond.*
+ ARG 9-10/93: 85
+ Fa 9-10/88: 84
+ Fa 7-8/93: 310

32658. CDS 1013-2: LINDBERG—Requiem; Choral pieces; Florenz and Blanzflor. *Vocal soloists; Englebreit Church Choirs; Stockholm College of Music Orch.; Swedish Radio Symphony Orch.; Kyhle, Westerberg, conds.*
- ARG 7-8/94: 125

32659. CDS 1015-2: LINDBERG—Symphony in F; Fiddler Per, he fiddled; Three impressions of travel (suite no. 2). *Örebro Symphony Orch.; Westerberg, cond.*
• ARG 5-6/95: 131
+ Fa 5-6/95: 242

32660. CDS 1016-2: ANDRÉE—Fritiof: Suite; Symphony no. 2. *Stockholm Phil. Orch.; Sjökvist, cond.*
• ARG 1-2/96: 70
• Fa 1-2/96: 104

32661. CDS 1017-2: LILJEFORS—Piano concerto; Symphony. *Mannheimer, piano; Gävleborg Symphony Orch.; M. Liljefors, cond.*
• ARG 5-6/96: 136
□ Fa 3-4/96: 202

32662. CDS 1018-2: *Romantic Danish overtures.* Music of Du Puy, Weyse, Kuhlau, Hartmann, Heise, and Horneman. *Royal Danish Orch.; Hye-Knudsen, cond.* Reissue.
+ ARG 11-12/96: 240
+ Fa 11-12/96: 478

STILNOVO

32663. SN 8801: Music of Carissimi, Marazzoli, Rossi, and Tenaglia. *Anfuso, soprano; Waterhouse, chitarrone.*
□ Fa 3-4/91: 446

32664. SN 8802: *Il canto alla corte d'Isabella d'Este.* Music of Tromboncino, Milanese, Cara, Scotti, and others. *Anfuso, soprano; Waterhouse, lute.*
□ Fa 3-4/91: 447

32665. SN 8804: PERI—Madrigali (1609). *Anfuso, soprano; Clerici, harpsichord.*
□ Fa 3-4/91: 447

32666. SN 8805: VIVALDI—In furore jusiddimae irae; Nulla in mundo pax sincera; Canta in prato, ride in monte; O qui coeli terraeque serenitas. *Anfuso, soprano; Concerto Strumentale Italiano.*
□ Fa 3-4/91: 447

32667. SN 8806 (2 discs): Music of Bellini, Beethoven, Catalani, Paganini, and Giuliani. *Anfuso, soprano; Marcante, fortepiano.*
□ Fa 3-4/91: 447

STOMP OFF

32668. 1246: Rags by Huff, Jewell, Alford, Pryor, Fillmore, King, and Goodman. *University of Wisconsin, Eau-Claire Symphony Band; George, Goodman, conds.*
+ ARG 3-4/93: 161

STRADIVARI CLASSICS

32669. SCD 6027: *Organ masterpieces.* Music of Handel, Bach, Mozart, Franck, Widor, and Liszt. *Schnorr, organ.*
+ ARG 9-10/88: 102
- Fa 7-8/88: 313

32670. SCD 6028: Music of Kabalevsky, Mendelssohn, and Ravel. *Milenković, violin; Ljubljana Symphony Orch.; Nanut, cond.*
- ARG 3-4/89: 49
- MA 5/89: 78

32671. SCD 6030: DVOŘÁK—Symphony no. 9; Carnival overture op. 92. GLINKA—Ruslan and Lyudmila overture. *Slovenian Phil. Orch.; Ljubljana Symphony Orch.; Horvat, Nanut, conds.*
• Fa 7-8/88: 160

32672. SCD 6036: MOZART—Piano concertos no. 12, 23. *Israel Chamber*

Orch.; Vardi, piano & cond.
- ARG 5-6/89: 69

32673. SCD 6038: Enesco—Romanian rhapsodies no. 1-2; Romanian poem. *Romanian Radio Orch.; Conta, cond.*
+ ARG 9-10/90: 63

32674. SCD 6041: Sibelius—Symphony no. 2; Finlandia. *Ljubljana Symphony Orch.; Nanut, Munih, conds.*
• ARG 7-8/92: 227

32675. SCD 6044: Shostakovich— Symphony no. 7. *Ljubljana Symphony Orch.; Nanut, cond.*
• ARG 3-4/89: 89
- Fa 1-2/89: 265

32676. SCD 6051: Chopin—Piano concerto no. 1. Mozart—Piano concerto no. 26. *Tomšič, piano; Ljubljana Symphony Orch.; Nanut, Munih, cond.*
• ARG 1-2/90: 41

32677. SCD 6056: Dvořák—Symphony no. 8. Smetana—Moldau. *Ljubljana Symphony Orch.; Nanut, cond.*
+ ARG 9-10/89: 51

32678. SCD 6059: Bruckner— Symphony no. 8 . *Ljubljana Symphony Orch.; Nanut, cond.*
• ARG 1-2/90: 38

32679. SCD 6068: Prokofiev—Piano concerto no. 3. Bartók—Piano concerto no. 3. *Krajný, piano; Czech Phil. Orch.; Belohlavek, cond.*
+ ARG 11-12/90: 97

32680. SCD 6071: *Piano masterpieces.* Music of Bach, Mozart, Beethoven and Chopin. *Krieger, piano.*
+ Fa 5-6/92: 321

32681. SCD 6073: Tchaikovsky— Symphony no. 4; Capriccio italien. *Ljubljana Symphony Orch.; Nanut, cond.*
• ARG 1-2/90: 97

32682. SCD 6090: Strauss—Don Quixote; Burleske. *Despalj, cello; Olevsky, piano; Janáček Phil. Orch.; Burkh, cond.*
• ARG 11-12/90: 121

32683. SCD 6097: Brahms—Viola sonatas no. 1-2; Intermezzo op. 116 no. 4, op. 118 no. 1; Capriccio op. 76 no. 2 . *Imai, viola; Goldsmith, piano.*
+ ARG 7-8/90: 34

32684. SCD 6300: Music of Suppé, Dvořák, Berlioz, Mendelssohn, Beethoven, and others. *Ljubljana Symphony Orch.; Nanut, Munih, conds.*
• Fa 1-2/89: 347

32685. SCD 6301: Music of Mozart, Weber, Rossini, Beethoven, and others. *Ljubljana Symphony Orch.; Nanut,*

Munih, conds.
• Fa 1-2/89: 347 m.f.

32686. SCD 8000: Gershwin—Concerto in F (trans. Castagnetta); Three preludes; Rhapsody in blue (trans. Gershwin). *Kreiger, piano.*
+ Fa 9-10/88: 155
+ SR 7/88: 102
+ St 10/88: 165

32687. SCD 8003: Ben-Haim— Symphony no. 2; Concerto for strings op. 40. *Royal Phil. Orch.; Alwyn, cond.*
+ Fa 9-10/89: 148

32688. SCD 8004: Liburn—Symphony no. 2; Aotearoa overture; Diversions for string orchestra. *New Zealand Symphony Orch.; Heenan, Hopkins, conds.*
+ Fa 11-12/89: 264

32689. SCD 8007: Mussorgsky—Pictures at an exhibition; Night on bald mountain. *Prague Symphony Orch.; Belohlavek, cond.*
- ARG 11-12/89: 83

32690. SCD 8011: Vaughan Williams— The lark ascending; Charterhouse suite; Violin concerto in D minor; Fantasia on a theme by Thomas Tallis. *Schiff, violin; Israel Phil. Orch.; Israel Chamber Orch.; Atlas, cond.*
- ARG 11-12/89: 130
+ Fa 11-12/89: 385
+ Gr 3/90: 1622

32691. SCD 8012: Barber—Overture to The school for scandal; Music for a scene from Shelley; Essay no. 1; Adagio for strings; Symphony no. 2. *New Zealand Symphony Orch.; Schenck, cond.*
+ ARG 7-8/89: 16
□ Au 5/90: 70
+ DA 8/89: 64
+ Gr 8/89: 294
+ MA 7/89: 68

32692. SCD 8013: Respighi—Three Botticelli pictures; The birds; Ancient airs and dances: Suite no. 3. *New Zealand Symphony Orch.; Schenck, cond.*
• ARG 5-6/90: 95

STRADIVARIUS

32693. STR 10001: Beethoven— Symphonies no. 4-5. *Boston Symphony Orch.; NBC Symphony Orch.; Monteux, Cantelli, conds. Recorded live 1954, 1963.*
+ Fa 3-4/89: 103

32694. STR 10002: Beethoven—Piano concertos no. 4-5. *Backhaus, piano; Vienna Phil. Orch.; Stuttgart Radio Orch.; Knappertsbusch, Keilberth, conds. Recorded live 1954, 1962.*
• ARG 3-4/89: 20
• Fa 3-4/89: 93

32695. STR 10003: Beethoven— Symphony no. 9. *Lipp, Boese, Wunderlich, Crass; Vienna Singverein; Philharmonia Orch.; Klemperer, cond. Recorded live 1960.*
+ Fa 3-4/89: 104

32696. STR 10004: Mozart— Symphonies no. 1, 39, 41. *Zürich Tonhalle Orch.; Colgone Radio Symphony; Italian Radio and Television Milan Symphony Orch.; Ackermann, Kleiber, Celibidache, conds. Recorded live 1956, 1960.*
- Fa 7-8/89: 203 (no. 41)
+ Fa 7-8/89: 203 (others)

32697. STR 10005: Mozart—Piano concerto no. 25; Violin concerto no. 5. *Ciani, piano; Oistrakh, violin; Italian Radio and Television Naples Symphony Orch.; Leningrad Phil. Orch.; Barbirolli, Mravinsky, cond. Recorded live 1968, 1956.*
+ Fa 7-8/89: 194

32698. STR 10006: Mozart—Requiem; Exsultate jubilate. *Raskin, Kopleff, Haefliger, Paul, Seefried; Cleveland Chorus & Orch.; New York Phil. Orch.; Szell, Walter, conds. Recorded live 1968, 1953.*
+ Fa 7-8/89: 200
+ Fa 7-8/89: 201

32699. STR 10007: Brahms—Symphony no. 1; Tragic overture; Alto rhapsody. *Lipton, mezzo-soprano; Westminster Choir; New York Phil. Orch.; NBC Symphony Orch.; Cantelli, cond. Recorded live 1952, 1951, 1956.*
+ Fa 7-8/89: 114

32700. STR 10008: Schoenberg—Moses und Aron: La vocazione di Mosè. Nono—Il canto sospeso. Maderna— Hyperion (excerpts). *Orch. e Coro Radio Amburgo; Hollweg, Bornemann, Lenz; Orch. e Coro di Radio Colonia; Gazzelloni, flute; Dorow, soprano; Orch. e Coro della RAI di Roma; Rosbaud, Maderna, conds. Recorded 1966, 1954.*
+ Fa 9-10/91: 259
+ Fa 11-12/93: 302

32701. STR 10010: Mahler—Symphony no. 1; Lieder eines fahrenden Gesellen. *Zareska, mezzo-soprano; Italian Radio and Television Turin Symphony Orch.; French National Orch.; Markevitch, Schuricht, conds.*
- Fa 9-10/89: 241

32702. STR 10011: Mahler—Lied von der Erde. *Hoffman, Melchert; Southwest German Radio Symphony Orch.; Rosbaud, cond.*
+ ARG 11-12/89: 78
+ Fa 9-10/89: 242

32703. STR 10012: Mahler—Symphony no. 9. *Cleveland Orch.; Szell, cond. Recorded live 1968.*

STRADIVARIUS

+ ARG 3-4/90: 69 m.f.
• Fa 3-4/90: 221

32704. STR 10013: SCHUBERT—Stabat mater D. 383. BRAHMS—Concerto for violin and cello. *László, Traxel, Pezzetti; Grumiaux, violin; Janigro, cello; Italian Radio and Television Milan Chorus & Symphony Orch.; Scherchen, Monteux, conds.* Recorded live 1966 & 1962.
+ ARG 7-8/90: 32
- Fa 3-4/90: 285

32705. STR 10017: Music of Berio, Posseur, and Cage. *Berberian, soprano; Italian Radio and Television Rome Symphony Orch.; Teatro La Fenice Orch.; Berio, cond.* Recorded live 1967-1969.
+ ARG 3-4/90: 150
• Fa 3-4/90: 345 m.f.

32706. STR 10018: BRAHMS—Piano trio no. 1, op. 87; String sextet op. 18 . *Menuhin, Gérecz, violins; Tuttle, Wallfisch, violas; Casals, Foley, cellos; Istomin, piano.* Recorded live 1955.
• Fa 3-4/90: 159

32707. STR 10019: SCHUMANN—Piano trio no. 3. MOZART—Piano quartet no. 2. BEETHOVEN—Variations for cello and piano on Ein Mädchen oder Weibchen. *Végh, Menuhin, violins; Wallfisch, viola; Casals, cello; Serkin, Horszowski, pianos.* Recorded live 1956, 1954.
- Fa 3-4/90: 159 (Schumann)
+ Fa 3-4/90: 159 (Mozart, Beethoven)

32708. STR 10020: BRAHMS—Piano trios no. 1, 3. BEETHOVEN—Violin sonata no. 1. *Menuhin, Grumiaux, violins; Casals, cello; Istomin, Kapell, pianos.* Recorded live 1955, 1953.
• Fa 3-4/90: 159

32709. STR 10021: MADERNA—Violin concerto; Oboe concerto no. 2; Quadrivium for 4 percussionists and orchestra. *Various performers.* Recorded live 1968, 1969.
□ Fa 3-4/90: 218 m.f.

32710. STR 10022: HINDEMITH—Concerto for winds, harp, and orchestra. CASTIGLIONI—Sequenze per orchestra. RAVEL—Valses nobles et sentimentales. SCHOENBERG—Moses und Aron: Act 2, scene 3. *Soloists; Italian Radio and Television Rome Symphony Orch.; Hamburg Radio Chorus & Orch.; Rosbaud, cond.* Recorded live.
• Fa 5-6/90: 392

32711. STR 10023: BERG—Chamber concerto for piano and violin. SCHOENBERG—Chamber symphony no. 1; Friede auf Erden. WEBERN—Passacaglia for orchestra. *Jacobs, piano; Marschner, violin; Radio Cologne Chorus & Orch.; Scherchen, cond.* Recorded live 1958, 1959.

+ ARG 7-8/90: 94 (Berg)
• ARG 7-8/90: (others)
+ Fa 5-6/90: 279

32712. STR 10024/26 (3 discs): Music of Mozart, Schumann, Ravel, Brahms, Prokofiev, and others. *Richter, piano; various orchs. & conds.* Recorded live.
+ Fa 9-10/90: 477

32713. STR 10027: SCHOENBERG—Five orchestral pieces. WEBERN—Symphony, op. 21; Variations, op. 30. BERG—Sieben frühe Lieder. *Lear, soprano; London Symphony Orch.; Boulez, cond.* Recorded live 1969.
+ Fa 7-8/90: 248 m.f.

32714. STR 10028: BOULEZ—Improvisations sur Mallarmé; Le marteau sans maître; Figures, doubles, prisms. *Rogner, soprano; Henius, alto; Bergmann, piano; Italian Radio and Television Rome Symphony Orch.; Residentie Orch. The Hague; Boulez, Maderna, conds.*
+ Fa 7-8/90: 104

32715. STR 10030/31 (2 discs): BERG—Lulu. *Steingruber, Zareska, Ruesche, Rehfuss; Italian Radio and Television Rome Symphony Orch.; Maderna, cond.* Recorded live 1959.
+ Fa 9-10/90: 184 m.f.

32716. STR 10034: DALLAPICCOLA—Il prigioniero; Cinque canti; Preghiere. *Pilarczyk, Krebs, Wächter; Bavarian Radio Chorus & Orch.; Teatro La Fenice Orch.; Basiola, Scherchen, conds.* Recorded live 1956, 1964.
+ ARG 1-2/91: 43
• Fa 1-2/91: 185
+ Fa 3-4/93: 148

32717. STR 10035: PROKOFIEV—Alexander Nevsky. SHOSTAKOVICH—Symphony no. 10. *Companez, alto; Italian Radio and Television Rome Chorus & Symphony Orch.; Rodzinski, cond.* Recorded live 1958, 1955.
- ARG 1-2/91: 76
□ Fa 11-12/90: 317 m.f.

32718. STR 10036: MAHLER—Symphony no. 1. *Southwest German Radio Orch.; Rosbaud, cond.*
- ARG 3-4/91: 85
+ Fa 3-4/91: 262

32719. STR 10037/38 (2 discs): Music of Tchaikovsky, Scarlatti, Moszkowski, Schuman, and others. *Horowitz, piano; Hollywood Bowl Symphony Orch.; New York Phil. Orch.; Steinberg, Toscanini, conds.*
- Fa 3-4/91: 477

32720. STR 10054: SCHOENBERG—Von Heute auf Morgen. *Schmidt, Olsen, László, Schachtschneider; Residentie Orch.; Rosbaud, cond.* Recorded live

1958.
• Fa 11-12/92: 357

32721. STR 10060 (2 discs): ORFF—Antigonae. *Fischer, Uhde, Haefliger, Greindl; Vienna Phil. Orch.; Fricsay, cond.* Recorded at world premier 1949.
+ Fa 11-12/92: 318

32722. STR 10061: MADERNA—Satyricon; Ages. *Neill, Brown, Sperry; NOS Radio Orch., Hilversum; RAI Radio and Television, Milan Orch. & Chorus; Maderna, cond.*
+ Fa 7-8/93: 171

32723. STR 10062: RAVEL—L'heure espagnole. *Danco, Hamel, Cameron, Giraudeau, Vessières; BBC Symphony Orch.; Maderna, cond.* Recorded 1960.
+ Fa 1-2/94: 274

32724. STR 10063: DALLAPICCOLA—Ulisse. *Saedén, baritone; other soloists; Deutsche Oper, Berlin; Maazel, cond.* Recorded live 1968.
• ARG 7-8/95: 104
+ Fa 11-12/93: 212

32725. STR 10064: BERG—Wozzeck: Three pieces. DALLAPICCOLA—Two pieces for orchestra. HARTMANN—Symphony no. 6. *Kupper, soprano; Symphony Orch. of the Bavarian Radio; Kleiber, cond.*
+ ARG 3-4/93: 191
+ Fa 1-2/93: 112

32726. STR 10066: PETRASSI— Corodi morti; Noche oscura; Salmo IX. *Orch.s and choruses; Petrassi, Maderna, conds.* Recorded 1952, 1962.
+ Fa 1-2/93: 206

32727. STR 10067 (2 discs): EINEM—Dantons Tod. *Schöffler, Cebotari, Patzak, Witt, Weber, Alsen; Vienna State Opera Chorus; Vienna Phil. Orch.; Fricsay, cond.* Recorded live 1947.
• Fa 1-2/94: 174

32728. STR 13597-99 (3 discs): MOZART—Cosi fan tutte; Divertimento no. 15. *Schwarzkopf, Merriman, Sciutti, Alva, Panerai, Calabrese; Teatro alla Scala Chorus & Orch.; New York Phil. Orch.; Cantelli, cond.* Recorded live 1956, 1954.
+ ARG 9-10/88: 67
+ Fa 11-12/88: 233
• ON 1/7/89: 43

32729. STR 13602: Music of Bach, Scarlatti, Beethoven, Schumann, and others. *Haskil, piano.*
• Fa 3-4/89: 83

32730. STR 13603: HINDEMITH—Theme and variations. MOZART—Concerto for 2 pianos K. 365; Piano sonata no. 10. *Haskil, Anda, pianos; French Radio and Television National Orch.; Camerata Academica Salzburg; Hindemith, Paumgartner, conds.* Recorded live.
+ Fa 3-4/89: 184

32731. STR 13606/07 (2 discs): CAVALLI—*La calisto. Mantovani, Piscitelli, Bandera, Piccoli; Sonatori de la Gioiosa Marca; Moretti, cond.*
+ Fa 11-12/89: 170

32732. STR 13608: MALIPIERO—Pause di silenzio. WEBERN—Six pieces, op. 6. DALLAPICCOLA—Partita. *Rizzoli, soprano; Italian Radio and Television Turin Symphony Orch.; Maderna, Celibidache, conds.*
• Fa 9-10/89: 245

32733. STR 13610: SAINT-SAËNS—Piano concerto no. 4. RODRIGO—Concierto de Aranjuez. BRITTEN—Peter Grimes: Four sea interludes. BELLINI—Sinfonia in E♭. *Casadesus, piano; Yepes, guitar; Italian Radio and Television Turin Symphony Orch.; Muti, cond.* Recorded live 1968.
• Fa 9-10/89: 444

32734. STR 13611: PROKOFIEV—Piano concerto no. 3. BEETHOVEN—Piano concerto no. 5. *Pollini, piano; Italian Radio and Television Turin Symphony Orch.; Italian Radio and Television Rome Symphony Orch.; Albert, Abbado, conds.* Recorded live 1967.
+ Fa 9-10/89: 280

32735. STR 13612: BACH—Cello suites no. 3, 5, 6. *Rostropovich, cello.*
• Fa 5-6/90: 109

32736. STR 13613: SCRIABIN—Symphony no. 3. PROKOFIEV—Symphony no. 5. *Italian Radio and Television Rome Symphony Orch.; Rodzinski, cond.*
• Fa 3-4/90: 294 (Scriabin)
+ Fa 3-4/90: 294 (Prokofiev)

32737. STR 13614: BARTÓK—Concerto for orchestra. BRAHMS—Symphony no. 1. *Boston Symphony Orch.; Koussevitzky, cond.* Recorded live 1944, 1945.
☐ Fa 3-4/90: 123 m.f.

32738. STR 13615/16 (2 discs): SCHOENBERG—Moses und Aron. *Melchert, Greindl; Deutsche Oper Berlin Chorus & Orch.; Scherchen, cond.* Recorded live 1966.
• ARG 7-8/90: 94
- Fa 5-6/90: 279

32739. STR 13617: BACH—Magnificat. VIVALDI—Gloria. *Maimpietri, Panni, Reynolds, Munteanu, Carmelli; Italian Radio and Television Milan Chorus & Symphony Orch.; Scherchen, cond.* Recorded live 1963.
• Fa 3-4/91: 265

32740. STR 33301: VIVALDI (ARR. ROUSSEAU)—The four seasons. HANDEL—Water music: suite; Music for the royal fireworks. *Ferrarini, flute; Fontana, harpsichord.*
+ Fa 7-8/93: 263

32741. STR 33304: CARTER—Woodwind quintet; Eight etudes and a fantasy. DONATONI—Blow. KURTÁG—Wind quintet. LIGETI—Ten pieces for wind quintet. *Arnold Quintet.*
+ Fa 7-8/92: 358

32742. STR 33306: DEVIENNE—Sonatas for flute and harpsichord, no. 1-4. *Ferrarini, flute; Fontana, harpsichord.*
+ Fa 1-2/93: 141

32743. STR 33308: CROCE—Triaca musicale. PELEGRINI—Canzon L'arcangiola; Canzon La mariana; Canzon La barbarina. *Collegio vocale e strumentale Euterpe; Negri, cond.*
+ Fa 7-8/93: 129

32744. STR 33312: CASELLA—Serenata for clarinet, bassoon, trumpet, violin, and cello. PIZZETTI—Trio for violin, cello, and piano. ROTA—Trio for flute, violin, and piano. *Ex Novo Ensemble.*
+ ARG 3-4/94: 198
+ Fa 1-2/94: 157

32745. STR 33313: BEETHOVEN—Piano sonata op. 106 "Hammerklavier". *Richter, piano.* Recorded live 1976.
+ Fa 7-8/92: 115

32746. STR 33314: Tablatures for lute. *Lonardi, lute.*
+ ARG 9-10/94: 238

32747. STR 33315: DONATONI—For Grilly; Lied; Lumen; Ash; Arpège; L'ultima sera. *Gruppo Musica Insieme di Cremona; Molino, cond.*
+ ARG 3-4/94: 90
+ Fa 1-2/94: 169

32748. STR 33316: GALUPPI—Concerti a quattro. *Quartetto Aglaia.*
+ ARG 9-10/94: 132

32749. STR 33318: BONPORTI—Inventions op. 10, no. 1-5. *Aglaia Ensemble; Barbagelata, violin.*
+ ARG 1-2/94: 83
+ Fa 1-2/94: 134

32750. STR 33323: BACH—Sonatas, BWV 963, 964, 966; Capriccio, BWV 993; Four duets, BWV 802-5; Italian concerto. *Richter, piano.* Recorded 1991.
+ Fa 7-8/92: 115

32751. STR 33324: GÓRECKI—Symphony no. 2; Beatus vir. *Soós, soprano; Altorjay, baritone; Bartók Chorus; Fricsay Symphony Orch.; Pál, cond.*
+ Gr 7/94: 44

32752. STR 33325: WILLAERT—Madrigali di Verdelot. *Il Desiderio.*
+ ARG 9-10/95: 237

32753. STR 33330: MADERNA—Divertimento; Quartet; Honeyreves; Aulodia per Lothar; Widmung; Serenata per un satellite; Dialodia. *Ex Novo*

Ensemble.
+ ARG 7-8/95: 148

32754. STR 33333: BACH—English suites no. 1, 3. *Richter, piano.*
+ ARG 3-4/93: 173
+ Fa 1-2/93: 101

32755. STR 33334: BACH—English suites no. 4, 6. *Richter, piano.* Recorded live 1991.
+ Fa 7-8/93: 94

32756. STR 33339: CAVALIERI—Rappresentazione di anima et di corpo. *Bertagnolli, Mattei; Istituzioni Harmoniche; Longhini, cond.*
+ ARG 9-10/94: 15

32757. STR 33343: HAYDN—Piano sonata no. 33; Andante con variazioni in F minor. MOZART—Fantasia, K. 475; Piano sonata no. 14. *Richter, piano.* Recorded live 1991-92.
• Fa 1-2/94: 201

32758. STR 33347: PETRASSI—Sonata da camera; Beatitudines; Grand septuor; Sestina d'autunno. *Hollmann, harpsichord; Kiefer, baritone; Tedesco, clarinet; Compania; Molino, cond.*
+ ARG 1-2/95: 153

32759. STR 33380: Music of Banchieri, Byrd, Frescobaldi and others. *La Rovattina.*
• ARG 11-12/95: 262

32760. STR 33384: DEMESSIEUX—Etudes; Meditations. *Ciampi, organ.*
+ ARG 9-10/95: 133

32761. STR 33389: GALUPPI—Keyboard music. *Bonizzoni, harpsichord, organ.*
+ ARG 11-12/95: 119

STRINGS IN THE MOUNTAINS

32762. 921: LALO—Piano trio no. 1. DVOŘÁK—Dumky trio. *Eroica Trio.*
• ARG 7-8/93: 111

STUDIO CLASSIQUE

32763. CD-SC 100 300 (3 discs): HANDEL—Serse. *Teal, Cole, Atkinson, Terzian, Schumann-Halley, Anderson, Allen; Amadeus Chamber Orch.; Duczmal, cond.*
- ARG 3-4/90: 57
- Fa 1-2/90: 194
- ON 5/90: 48
- Op 6/90: 750

32764. CD-SC 100 303 (3 discs): HANDEL—Alessandro. *Atkinson, Watson, Terzian, Price, Poole; Sinfonia Varsovia; Nowakowski, cond.*
- ARG 3-4/90: 57
+ Fa 1-2/90: 193
• ON 5/90: 48
- Op 6/90: 750

STUDIO SM

32765. 12-1634: *Salve Regina.* Gregorian chant. *Monks of Citeaux, Timadeuc, and Sept-Fons Abbeys.*
+ ARG 11-12/94: 242

32766. 12-2002 (2 discs): A voyage through the Gregorian era. *Various performers.*
● ARG 11-12/94: 242

32767. 12-2080: SWEELINCK—Organ music. SCHEIDT—Organ music. *Heurtematte, organ.*
+ ARG 9-10/94: 205

32768. 12-2114: *Organ at St. Sulpice.* Music of Franck, Boellmann, Mendelssohn, Reger, and others. *Choplin, organ.*
+ ARG 1-2/95: 225

32769. 12-2160 (2 discs): LEHÁR—Merry widow (sung in French). *Stich-Randall, Jacquin, Guy, Legay; Orch. de l' ORTF; Sibort, cond.* Recorded 1970.
+ ARG 5-6/96: 265
● Fa 7-8/96: 219

32770. 12 2161: ALAIN—Organ music. *Mantoux, organ.*
+ ARG 7-8/94: 60

32771. 12-2175: BERNART DE VENTADORN—Songs. *Le Vot, vocalist.*
- ARG 11-12/94: 76

32772. 12-2222: *Viennese operettas.* Music of Lehár and J. Strauss, Jr. *Stutzmann, Vanzo, Dachary, Dran, Legay, vocalists; Orch. & Chorus of the French Radio and Television; Sibert, cond.*
● Fa 7-8/96: 220

32773. 12-2239: Misericordia Domini. *Choir of Monks of the Abbey of Ligugé.*
+ Fa 5-6/95: 402

32774. 12-2240: *Notre Dame de France.* Songs of pilgrimage for the Holy Virgin. *Les Petits Chanteurs de Touraine.*
● Fa 7-8/95: 409

32775. 12-2262: *Viennese music.* Music of Lehár, Hellmesberger, J. Strauss, Sr., and J. Strauss, Jr. *Fontanarosa, violin; Lyric Orch. of the French Radio and Television; Sibert, cond.*
- Fa 7-8/96: 220

32776. 12-2300: MUSSORGSKY—Pictures at an exhibition. *Genvrin, organ.*
+ ARG 9-10/95: 177

32777. 12-2307: Music of Telemann, Krebs, Sweelinck, and Balbastre. *Isoir, organ; Giboreau, oboe.* Recorded 1971.
+ ARG 5-6/95: 212

32778. 12-2327 (3 discs): ROSSINI—Complete unpublished sacred choral

works. *Vocal soloists; Choirs ; Czech Phil. Orch.; Brizio, cond.*
+ ARG 3-4/95: 173
+ Fa 5-6/95: 312
● Gr 1/95: 89
+ ON 1/20/96: 34

32779. 12-2389: PAISIELLO—Music for Napoleon Bonaparte's chapel. *Vocal soloists; Czech Radio Choirs; Prague Symphony Orch.; Brizio, cond.*
- ARG 7-8/95: 166
- Fa 7-8/95: 267
● Gr 11/95: 142

32780. 12-2460: *Mélodies sacrées.* Music of Bach-Gounod, Saint-Saëns, Franck, Caplet, Adam, and others. *Ivery, mezzo-soprano; Parmentier, piano.*
● Fa 5-6/96: 326

32781. 12-2515 (2 discs): LISZT—Via crucis. A. SCARLATTI—Responsori per la settimana santa (Venerdi). *Zamballi, Alberghini, Mazzanti, Choeur polyphonique Fabio de Bologne; Manduchi, cond.; Mazzucato, tenor & cond.; Caristi, Serno, Scavazza, vocalists; Choeur polyphonique Città di Rovigo.*
- Fa 7-8/96: 226

32782. D 2460: *Mélodies sacrées.* Music of Vidal, Gounod, Beethoven, Franck, and others. *Ivery, mezzo-soprano; Parmentier, piano.*
● ARG 7-8/96: 279 (as Opus 3 [no number])

32783. D 2473: *The Malta manuscripts.* Music of Carissimi, Monteverdi, and Rubino. *New College Choir, Oxford; London Bach Consort; Higginbottom, cond.*
+ ARG 5-6/96: 249

32784. D 2482: *Musique sacrée française du XXème siècle pour choeur d' hommes a cappella.* Music of M. Godard, Milhaud, Poulenc, Caplet, Schmitt, and Dumas. *Ensemble Vocal Phonandre; Grégoire, cond.*
+ Fa 7-8/96: 360

32785. D 2484: DONIZETTI—Unpublished sacred music, vol. 1. *Cola, Calzolari, Deffai, Bencivenga, Cristoforo, Salvati, Macedonia, vocalists; Chorus of the Czech Radio; Prague Symphony Orch.; Brizio, cond.*
● Fa 5-6/96: 139

32786. D 2490: *Répons.* Monks of the Abbey of Ligugé; Godard, tuba & serpent.
- Fa 7-8/96: 365

32787. D 2499: *Ubi caritas.* Monks of the Abbey of Timadeuc.
+ Fa 7-8/96: 365

32788. D 2514: APRIKIAN—The birth of David of Sassoun. *Chanoyan, Karakaya,*

Arapian, vocalists; Chorale Sipan-Komitas; Petits Chanteurs of the Tebrotzassere School; Orch. Bell' Arte; Aprikian, cond.
● ARG 9-10/96: 77
+ Fa 9-10/96: 125

32789. D 2517: GENERALI—Unpublished sacred music. *Vocal soloists; Chorus & Orch. of the Czech Radio; Brizio, cond.*
- ARG 11-12/96: 126
- Fa 11-12/96: 249

32790. D 2518: MOZART—Vesperae solennes de Dominica; Misericordias Domini; Kyries, K. 322, 341. *Camerata Academica Salzburg; Hinreiner, cond.* Reissue; recorded 1965.
● Fa 7-8/96: 249

32791. D 2522: INGHELBRECHT—Requiem; Vézelay. *Eda-Pierre, Corazza, Kruysen, Demigny, vocalists; Baudry- Godard, organ; Choeurs et Orch. de l' ORTF; Fournet, cond.*
+ Fa 11-12/96: 275

32792. D 2527: TELEMANN—Der getreue Music-Meister: selections; Essercizi musici: Sonata in A minor for cello and continuo. *Parrot, oboe; Allard, bassoon; Péclard, cello; Siegel, harpsichord.* Reissue.
● Fa 9-10/96: 343

32793. D 2543: *Sainteté russe. St. Nicholas Choir; Spassky, cond.*
□ Fa 1-2/97: 292

32794. D 2544: *Trombone et orgue.* Music of Bach, Dandrieu, M. Franck, Handel, Loeillet, Petzold, Purcell, and Stanley. *Schnorhk, trombone; Athanasiàdes, organ.*
- Fa 11-12/96: 467

SUB ROSA

32795. SUB CD018-41: FELDMAN—Piece for four pianos; Intermission VI; Piano four hands; Two pieces for two pianos; Two pianos; Five pianos. *Le Bureau des Pianistes.*
+ Fa 11-12/92: 232

SUGO

32796. 9308: Music of Debussy, Beethoven, Bach, Schubert, Bolling, and others. *Ware-Patterson Duo (flute & guitar).*
+ ARG 1-2/94: 179

32797. 9515: Piano serenade. *Postolovskaya, piano.*
+ ARG 1-2/96: 220

SUMMIT

32798. DCD 107: Music of Mozart, Grieg, Kreisler, Rachmaninoff (arr. Kreisler), and Smetana. *S. Weiss, violin;*

trombone; Johnson, organ; Pearl, piano.
+ ARG 7-8/94: 217

32830. DCD 149: Persichetti—Pastoral. Barber—Summer music I. Fine—Partita. Carter—Quintet. Berger—Quartet in C. Barrows—March. *Lieurance Woodwind Quintet.*
+ Fa 5-6/94: 335

32831. DCD 151: Beethoven—Trio for clarinet, cello, and piano, op. 11. Zemlinsky—Trio for clarinet, cello, and piano, op. 3. Chan—Among friends. *Amici.*
+ ARG 7-8/94: 71
+ Fa 5-6/94: 111

32832. DCD 153: Music of Pierce, Bitsch, Arnold, Arutunian, Plog, George, and others. *Jackson, trumpet; Moss, piano.*
+ ARG 7-8/94: 218

32833. DCD 154: *Walter Cosand, pianist.* Music of Cohen, Aschaffenburg, Rorem, and Matthews.
+ Fa 7-8/94: 319

32834. DCD 157: Saint-Saëns—Chamber music. *Banff Camerata.*
+ ARG 1-2/95: 165

32835. DCD 160: Orchestral excerpts for oboe. *Mack, oboe.*
+ ARG 3-4/95: 240

32836. DCD 161: Orchestral excerpts for clarinet. *Combs, clarinet.*
+ ARG 1-2/95: 221

32837. DCD 163: Music of McBeth, Plog, Demars, Mahler, Penderecki, and others. *Perantoni, tuba; Arizona State Symphonic Band; Strange, cond; St. Louis Brass Quintet; Selheim, piano.*
+ ARG 1-2/95: 231

32838. DCD 164: Brass quintets by Reynolds and Stevens. *Wisconsin Brass Quintet.*
+ ARG 1-2/95: 218

32839. DCD 165: Baker—Washington Square. *London Symphony Orch.; Crum, cond.* Reissue.
+ ARG 1-2/95: 72

32840. DCD 167: Castelnuovo-Tedesco—Goya capriccios. *Afshar, guitar.*
+ ARG 11-12/94: 89

32841. DCD 168: Messiaen—Quartet for the end of time. Chan—I think that I shall never see. *Amici.*
+ ARG 9-10/96: 165

32842. DCD 170: Wilder—Horn and piano music. *Bacon, horn; Moll, piano.*
+ ARG 7-8/95: 228

32843. DCD 171: Music of Ewazen, Tomasi, Holst, Shostakovich, Ives, and Copland. *Summit Brass.*
+ ARG 9-10/95: 253

32844. DCD 172: Music of Bernstein, Copland, Gershwin, and Gould. *Combs, clarinet; Opland, double bass; Sobol, piano.*
+ ARG 9-10/95: 256

32845. DCD 176: Music of Gallay, Heiden, Faust, Françaix, and Hill. *Farkas, horn.*
• ARG 11-12/95: 252

32846. DCD 177: Music of Mendez, Monterede, Anderson, Monti, and others. *Mendez, cornet.* Recorded 1940s-50s.
+ ARG 11-12/95: 290

32847. DCD 180: Mendelssohn—Symphony no. 4; Violin concerto; Midsummer night's dream scherzo. *Grabiec, violin; American Sinfonietta; Palmer, cond.*
+ ARG 7-8/96: 152

32848. DCD 181: 16th century dances, ayres, canzonas, madrigals, and sonatas. *American Brass Quintet.*
+ ARG 11-12/95: 247

32849. DCD 182: Baker—Summit concerto; Flight of Aphrodite; Through the lion's gate. *Hickman, trumpet; Davis, violin; Pro Musica Chamber Orch.; Russell, cond.; Sinfonia of London; Dunn, cond.*
+ ARG 3-4/96: 268

32850. DCD 185: Trumpet vocalise. *R. Mase, trumpet; D. Mase, piano.*
+ ARG 7-8/96: 257

32851. DCD 1001: Have yourself a merry little Christmas. *The Hollywood Trombones.*
+ Fa 9-10/91: 435

32852. DCD 1002: Castelnuovo-Tedesco—Platero and I; Guitar music. *Doyle, narrator; Koonce, guitar.*
• ARG 1-2/96: 95

SUNRISE

32853. 8501: Ma—Bamboo flute concerto; The peacock flies southwest. *Chen, bamboo flute; Mitsuhashi, hsiao; Yomiuri Nippon Symphony Orch.; Mu Sashi No University Chorus; Hsu, cond.*
+ Fa 1-2/96: 246

32854. 8503: Koh—Formosan dance; Confucian temple rites. *NHK Symphony Orch.; Chen, cond.*
+ Fa 1-2/96: 236

32855. 8507: Pan—Red chamber dream; Romance capriccio; The countryside path; The gardenside joys of drinking alone. *Pan, p'i p'a; Taipei Municipal*

Chinese Classical Orch.; Chen, cond.
• Fa 1-2/96: 307

32856. 8516: *The poetic violin of Nai-Yuan Hu.* Music of Sarasate, Ravel, Saint-Saëns, and Chausson. *Hu, violin; Royal Phil. Orch.; Chen, cond.*
+ ARG 9-10/89: 131
• Fa 1-2/96: 401

32857. 8532: Markov—Violin concerto; Formosa suite; Porgy rhapsody. *Markov, violin; New Russia Orch.; Lü, cond.*
+ Fa 1-2/96: 248

SUONI E COLORI

32858. AB 31001: Bach—Sonatas no. 1-2 for solo violin; Partita no. 1 for solo violin. *Brussilovsky, violin.*
• Fa 5-6/96: 74

32859. AB 31004: Franck—Violin sonata in A major. Strauss—Violin sonata, op. 18. *Brussilovsky, violin; Lazko, piano.*
+ Fa 5-6/96: 74

32860. SC 53003: Glinka—String quartet no. 1 (finished Chirinsky); String quartet no. 2. *Anton Quartet.*
+ ARG 7-8/96: 118
+ Fa 5-6/96: 157

SUPRAPHON

32861. 10 0206-2: Dvořák—Biblical songs; Gypsy songs; Evening songs; Love songs. *Soukupová, alto; Moravec, piano; Jindrák, baritone; Holeček, piano; Blachut, tenor; Pohlreich, piano.*
+ ARG 5-6/96: 108

32862. 10 1271-2: Vivaldi—Concertos for two violins. *Suk, violin; Vlček, violin & cond.; Virtuosi di Praga.*
+ ARG 1-2/93: 164

32863. 10 1481-2: Janáček—In the mist; Piano sonata "1.X.1905"; On an overgrown path, 1st series. *Páleníček, piano.* Reissue.
+ Fa 11-12/91: 358
• Gr 3/92: 79

32864. 10 1566-2 (2 discs): Honegger—Symphonies, no. 1-5; Pacific 231; Mouvement symphonique no. 3; The tempest; Prelude. *Czech Phil. Orch.; Baudo, cond.* Reissues.
- ARG 1-2/93: 106

32865. 10 1948-2: Prokofiev—Alexander Nevsky. Stravinsky—Rite of spring. *Soukupová, mezzo-soprano; Czech Phil. Orch.; Ančerl, cond.* Reissues.
+ ARG 1-2/93: 131

32866. 10 2751-2 (2 discs): Janáček—Jenůfa. *Benackova, Kniplová, Přibyl, Krejčík; Brno Opera; Jílek, cond.* Reissue.
• ARG 1-2/93: 108

+ Fa 1-2/93: 170
● Gr 4/93: 115

32867. 10 2941-2 (2 discs): JANÁČEK—From the house of the dead. *Novák, Jirglová, Přibyl, Striska, Berman, ídek; Czech Phil. Chorus & Orch.; Neumann, cond.*
● Fa 9-10/94: 222
+ Gr 9/94: 115

32868. 10 3393-2: MARTINŮ—Double concerto for 2 string orchestras, piano, and timpani; Frescoes of Piero della Francesca. *Prague Radio Symphony Orch.; Mackerras, cond.*
+ ARG 5-6/90: 71
+ Fa 5-6/90: 213

32869. 10 3400-2: JANÁČEK—Sinfonietta; Taras Bulba. *Czech Phil. Orch.; Neumann, cond.*
+ Fa 9-10/90: 266

32870. 10 3511-2 (3 discs): SMETANA—The bartered bride. *Beňačková-Čápová, Dvorský, Novák, Kopp, Jindrak; Czech Phil. Orch.; Košler, cond.* Reissue.
+ ARG 1-2/92: 117
+ Gr 10/91: 190

32871. 10 3561/62-2 (2 discs): DVOŘÁK—Stabat Mater. *Beňačková, Wenkel, Dvorský, Rootering; Czech Phil. Chorus & Orch.; Sawallisch, cond.*
+ Fa 11-12/90: 219

32872. 10 3575-2: JANÁČEK—Glagolitic mass. *Söderström, Drobkova, Livora, Novák, Hora; Czech Phil. Chorus & Orch.; Mackerras, cond.*
+ Fa 9-10/90: 266

32873. 10 3611-2 (2 discs): MARTINŮ—Greek passion. *Field, Mitchinson, Davies, Tomlinson, Moses; Czech Phil. Chorus; Kühn Children's Choir; Brno State Phil. Orch.; Mackerras, cond.*
+ Fa 7-8/90: 192
+ NYT 6/10/90: H24

32874. 10 3615-2: BACH—Violin concertos no. 1-2; Concerto for 2 violins. *Suk, Kosina, violins; Suk Chamber Orch.; Vlach, cond.* Reissue.
● Fa 1-2/92: 151

10 3624-2 see CO 72890.

32875. 10 3633-2: RAVEL—Boléro; Daphnis et Chloé suites no. 1-2. *Czech Phil. Orch.; Kühn Mixed Chorus; Pešek, cond.*
+ Fa 1-2/91: 285

32876. 10 3641/43-2 (3 discs): DVOŘÁK—Rusalka. *Beňačková-Čápová, Drobková, Soukupová, Ochman, Novák; Czech Phil. Orch. & Chorus; Neumann, cond.* Reissue.
+ Fa 1-2/92: 203

32877. 10 3868-2: VOŘÍŠEK—Symphony in D; Variations de bravoure; Introduction et rondeau brillant. *Krajný, piano; Prague Chamber Orch.; Parik, cond.*
+ ARG 11-12/90: 134
+ Fa 7-8/90: 310

32878. 10 4093-2: DVOŘÁK—Moravian duets op. 20, 32, 38; Two supplemental Moravian duets: Na tej nasej strese; Zivot vojensky. *Bogunia, piano; Kühn Mixed Chorus; Kühn, cond.*
- Fa 3-4/91: 204

32879. 10 4110-2: DEBUSSY—String quartet. RAVEL—String quartet. *Talich String Quartet.*
● Fa 7-8/90: 129

32880. 10 4115-2: DVOŘÁK—Piano quintets no. 1-2. *Panenka, piano; Smetana Quartet.*
● ARG 3-4/91: 62 (no. 1)
- ARG 3-4/91: 62 (no. 2)
+ Fa 3-4/91: 205

32881. 10 4127-2: BACH—Concerto for violin and oboe, BWV 1060. VIVALDI—Violin concerto, RV 230; Concerto for violin and oboe, RV 576. A. MARCELLO—Oboe concerto. *Suk, violin; Adamus, oboe; Suk Chamber Orch.; Vlach, cond.*
● Fa 1-2/91: 196

32882. 10 4136-2: DVOŘÁK—Serenade for string orchestra, op. 22. SUK—Serenade for string orchestra, op. 6. *Suk Chamber Orch.; Suk, cond.*
+ Fa 5-6/93: 335

32883. 10 4140-2: MARTINŮ—The parables; Estampes; Overture; Rhapsody. *Czech Phil. Orch.; Bělohlávek, cond.*
+ ARG 3-4/91: 88
+ Fa 3-4/91: 269
+ Gr 4/91: 44

32884. 10 4149-2: SCRIABIN—The poem of ecstasy; Reverie; Piano concerto, op. 20. *Ohlsson, piano; Czech Phil. Orch.; Pešek, cond.*
+ Fa 7-8/90: 266
● Fa 9-10/96: 193

32885. 10 4241-2 (2 discs): DVOŘÁK—Requiem, op. 89. *Beňačková-Čápová, Fassbaender, Moser, Rootering; Czech Phil. Chorus & Orch.; Sawallisch, cond.*
+ Fa 9-10/91: 206

32886. 10 4395-2: MARTINŮ—Ariane. *Lindsey, Philips, Novák; Czech Phil. Orch.; V. Neumann, cond.*
+ ARG 1-2/93: 116
+ Fa 11-12/92: 293
+ Gr 12/92: 120

32887. 10 8258-2 (2 discs): HÁBA—Mother. *Spisar, Urbanová, Borsky, Zikmundová, Kočí; Prague National Theater Chorus & Orch.; Maly, cond.*

Reissue.
+ ARG 11-12/93: 116
● Fa 11-12/93: 258
+ Gr 1/94: 93
+ ON 12/11/93: 44

32888. 10 8351-2 (2 discs): JANÁČEK—The Makropulos case. *Prylova, ídek, Vonasek, Kočí; Prague National Opera; Gregor, cond.* Recorded 1966.
+ ARG 7-8/95: 132
+ Gr 5/95: 110

32889. 11 0006-2 (3 discs): MYSLIVEČEK—Il Bellerofonte. *Lindsley, Mayo, Laki, Giménez, Czech Phil. Chorus; Prague Chamber Orch.; Peskó, cond.*
+ ARG 5-6/92: 101
+ Fa 5-6/92: 216
+ Gr 3/92: 114

32890. 11 0013-2 (2 discs): DVOŘÁK—Rusalka. *Subrtova, Ovcacikova, Mikoval, ídek, Haken; Prague National Theatre; Chalabala, cond.* Reissue; recorded 1961.
+ ARG 3-4/96: 110
+ Gr 1/96: 103
+ ON 1/20/96: 34

32891. 11 0018-2: HÁBA—Complete nonets. *Czech Nonet.* Reissues.
+ ARG 3-4/96: 118
+ Fa 3-4/96: 173
+ Gr 9/96: 69

32892. 11 0022-2: JANÁČEK—Diary of one who disappeared. *Gedda, tenor; Soukupová, alto; Prague Radio Women's Chorus; Blachut, tenor; Stepanova, alto; Czech Singers' Womens' Chorus; Páleníček, piano.*
+ ARG 3-4/96: 130
+ Gr 2/96: 89

32893. 11 0035-2: KOPELENT—Canto degli Augei. KABELAČ—Symphony no. 3. FISER—Concerto for 2 pianos and orchestra. *Osten, soprano; Veselá, organ; Ohlsson, Maxián, piano; Czech Phil. Orch.; Pešek, cond.*
+ ARG 3-4/96: 138
+ Fa 1-2/96: 198

32894. 11 0042-2 (2 discs): BACH—Clavier-Übung pt. 3. *Růžičková, harpsichord; Veselá, organ.*
● Fa 5-6/91: 107

32895. 11 0048-2: BRAHMS—Serenade no. 2. STRAUSS—Serenade. *Prague Chamber Orch.; Smetáček, cond.* Recorded 1986.
- ARG 5-6/94: 75

32896. 11 0076-2 (6 discs): Music of Smetana, Janáček, Jaroch, Dvořák, Suk, Novák, Mozart, and Beethoven. *Smetana Quartet.* Reissue.
+ Fa 3-4/96: 161

32897. 11 0081-2: DVOŘÁK—Slavonic dances (complete). *Czech Phil. Orch.;*

SUPRAPHON

Neumann, cond.
+ Fa 7-8/90: 132

32898. 11 0082-2: SMETANA—Má vlast. *Czech Phil. Orch.; Smetáček, cond.*
+ ARG 5-6/90: 111
+ Fa 5-6/90: 299

32899. 11 0086-2 (2 discs): SCHUMANN—Das Paradies und die Peri. *Mattila, Pitti, Gjevang, Schreckenbach, Lewis, Kundlak, Bröcheler; Czech Phil. Chorus & Orch.; Albrecht, cond.*
+ ARG 3-4/91: 118
+ Fa 11-12/90: 350
+ Gr 11/90: 1033
+ MA 5/91: 84

32900. 11 0087/88-2 (2 discs): BACH—The art of the fugue; A musical offering. *Ars Rediviva; Munclinger, cond.*
+ ARG 3-4/96: 78

32901. 11 0092-2: BRIXI—Missa integra in D minor; Opus patheticum de septem doloribus beatae Mariae Virginis. *Verebics, Borchers, Weir, Gebhardt; Kühn Mixed Chorus; Prague Chamber Orch.; Rilling, cond.*
+ ARG 11-12/90: 40
+ Fa 11-12/90: 190

32902. 11 0096-2: *Twentieth-century flute sonatas.* Music of Poulenc, Hindemith, Prokofiev, and Martinů. *Válek, flute; Hála, piano.*
+ Fa 3-4/96: 359

32903. 11 0097-2: Music of Krommer, Masek, Druzecky, and Mysliveček. *Collegium Musicum Pragense.*
+ ARG 3-4/94: 219
+ Fa 3-4/94: 431

32904. 11 0098-2: MARTINŮ—Serenades no. 1-5. *Prague Chamber Orch.; Vlček, cond.*
• Fa 11-12/90: 267

32905. 11 0099-2: MARTINŮ—Violin sonatas no. 2-3; Five madrigal stanzas for violin and piano. *Suk, violin; Hála, piano.*
+ ARG 7-8/90: 69
+ Fa 7-8/90: 136
+ Gr 8/90: 388

32906. 11 0107-2: MARTINŮ—Harpsichord concerto; Oboe concerto; Concertino for cello with piano, wind, and percussion accompaniment. *Růžičková, harpsichord; Krejčí, oboe; Vectomov, cello; Topinka, piano; Czech Phil. Chamber Orch.; Czech Phil. Orch.; Neumann, Škvor, conds.*
+ ARG 7-8/94: 129
+ Fa 5-6/94: 187

32907. 11 0109-2: VIVALDI—Bassoon concertos RV 472, 481, 484, 497, 501. *Herman, bassoon; Slovak Chamber Orch.; Warchal, cond.*
• ARG 5-6/90: 127
+ Fa 7-8/90: 309

32908. 11 0111-2: Music for violin and orchestra by Chausson, Sarasate, Rimsky-Korsakov, Tchaikovsky, and Saint-Saëns. *Pavlík, violin; Dvořák Chamber Orch.; Válek, cond.*
+ Gr 4/92: 89

32909. 11 0116-2: SUK—Epilog. *Jehličková, Kusnjer, Galla; Czech Phil. Chorus & Orch.; Neumann, cond.*
+ ARG 7-8/90: 115
+ Fa 5-6/90: 306

32910. 11 0119-2: BRAHMS—Symphony no. 4; Academic festival overture. *Czech Phil. Orch.; Bělohlávek, cond.*
+ Fa 11-12/90: 183

32911. 11 0122-2: TELEMANN—Oboe concertos. *Verner, oboe; Suk Chamber Orch.; Vlach, cond.*
+ Fa 1-2/92: 354

32912. 11 0132-2: HONEGGER—Le roi David. *Eda-Pierre, Senn, Raffalli, Mesguich, Gaillard; Kühn Children's Chorus; Czech Phil. Chorus & Orch.; Baudo, cond.*
+ ARG 7-8/90: 58
• Fa 7-8/90: 176

32913. 11 0133-2: Music of Verdi, Giordano, Mascagni, Puccini, and others. *Beňačková, soprano; Czech Phil. Orch.; Gregor, cond.*
+ ARG 9-10/90: 151
• Fa 7-8/90: 327

32914. 11 0166-2: PUNTO—Horn concertos no. 5-7, 10 . *Klánská, horn; Prague Chamber Orch.; Vajnar, cond.*
+ Fa 9-10/90: 341

32915. 11 0180-2: SMETANA—Festive symphony. MARTINŮ—Oboe concerto. MOZART—Sinfonia concertante for winds. *Séquardt, oboe; Pivoda, flute; Mihule, oboe; Tylšar, horn; Herman, bassoon; Czech Phil. Orch.; Košler, Neumann, Pešek, cond.*
- ARG 1-2/96: 176
+ Fa 1-2/96: 309

32916. 11 0206-2: DVOŘÁK—Biblical songs; Gypsy songs; Evening songs; Love songs. *Soukupová, alto; Moravec, piano; Jindrák, baritone; Holeček, piano; Blachut, tenor; Pohlreich, piano.*
• Fa 3-4/96: 158

32917. 11 0268-2: TCHAIKOVSKY—Piano concerto no. 1. PROKOFIEV—Piano concerto no. 1. *Richter, piano; Czech Phil. Orch.; Prague Symphony Orch.; Ančerl, cond.* Reissues.
+ ARG 7-8/93: 166

32918. 11 0269-2: CHAUSSON—Concerto for violin, piano and string quartet in D major. FAURÉ—Violin sonata no. 2. *Suk, violin; Hála, piano; Suk Quartet.*
+ Fa 9-10/90: 207

32919. 11 0271-2: MOZART—Piano concertos no. 23, 25. *Moravec, piano; Czech Chamber Orch.; Czech Phil. Orch.; Vlach, cond.*
+ Fa 11-12/90: 287

32920. 11 0273-2: STRAVINSKY—Petrushka; Les noces. *Soloists; Czech Phil. Chorus & Orch.; Ančerl, cond.*
+ ARG 7-8/90: 115

32921. 11 0274-2: Music of Dvořák, Smetana, Suk, Novák, and Janáček. *Various Czech orchs. and conds.*
+ Fa 11-12/90: 478

32922. 11 0278-2: SUK—Asrael. *Czech Phil. Orch.; Neumann, cond.*
+ ARG 5-6/90: 118
+ Fa 5-6/90: 306

32923. 11 0281-2: BACH—Concerto for 2 violins, BWV 1043. VIVALDI—Seasons. *Suk, Kosina, violins; Prague Chamber Orch.; Hlaváček, cond.; Suk Chamber Orch.; Vlach, cond.*
+ Fa 5-6/90: 330
• Gr 11/91: 105

32924. 11 0282-2: JANÁČEK—Sinfonietta; Taras Bulva; Lachian dances. *Brno State Phil. Orch.; Jílek, cond.*
• Fa 5-6/90: 194 (reviewed by Rabinowitz)
- Fa 5-6/90: 194 (reviewed by Wiser)
• Gr 8/90: 366
+ NYT 6/10/90: H24

32925. 11 0290-2: DVOŘÁK—Symphony no. 9; Serenade for string orchestra, op. 22. *Czech Phil. Orch.; Prague Soloists' Ensemble; Talich, cond.*
+ ARG 11-12/90: 53
+ Fa 1-2/91: 192

32926. 11 0291-2: RESPIGHI—Pines of Rome; Fountains of Rome; Roman festivals. *Czech Phil. Orch.; Pedrotti, cond.*
• Fa 5-6/90: 264

32927. 11 0304-2: MYSLIVEČEK—Sinfonias in B; in G; in F; in F; in B; in G. *Prague Chamber Orch.*
+ Fa 5-6/90: 239

32928. 11 0308-2: RACHMANINOFF—Moments musicaux. LISZT—Rigoletto and Trovatore paraphrases; Funerailles. TCHAIKOVSKY—Theme and variations, op. 19, no. 6. *Ardasev, piano.*
• ARG 7-8/92: 202

32929. 11 0330-2: RYBA—Sixteen pastorellas. *Vernerova, Doležal, Jindrák, Vinický, Haderer; Kühn Children's Chorus; Dvorak Chamber Orch.; Chvála, cond.*
+ ARG 1-2/92: 100

32930. 11 0332-2: REICHA—Requiem. *Hrubá-Freiberger, Barová, Doležal,*

Vele; Czech Phil. Chorus; Dvořák Chamber Orch.; Mátl, cond.
- ARG 3-4/91: 107
+ Fa 1-2/91: 387

32931. 11 0347-2: *European danserye and ayres.* Music of Phalese, Gastoldi, Praetorius, Susato, and Anon. *Rozmberk Ensemble; Pok, cond.*
+ Fa 11-12/94: 470

32932. 11 0359-2: BACH—Chromatic fantasia and fugue. MOZART—Piano sonata no. 13. SCHUMANN—Kinderszenen. *Moravec, piano.*
+ Fa 5-6/91: 107

32933. 11 0365-2: SCHUBERT—String quintet, D. 965. *Kocian Quartet; Veis, cello.*
- ARG 5-6/91: 103
- Fa 3-4/91: 361

32934. 11 0366-2: SCHUBERT—Four impromptus D. 899, 935. *Klánský, piano.*
- Fa 1-2/91: 305

32935. 11 0367-2: SCHUMANN—Piano quintet op. 44; Piano quartet op. 47. *Panenka, piano; Smetana Quartet; Panocha Quartet members.*
- ARG 9-10/91: 124 (Quintet)
+ ARG 9-10/91 124 (Quartet)
+ Fa 7-8/91: 284

32936. 11 0369-2: *Guitar works and arrangements.* Music of Tarrega, Malats, Bach (arr. Tarrega), Mendelssohn (arr. Tarrega), and others. *Brabec, guitar.*
+ ARG 3-4/91: 129
- Fa 1-2/91: 331

32937. 11 0373-2: MARTINŮ—Sinfonietta giocosa for piano and small orchestra; Divertimento for piano left- hand and orchestra. *Panenka, piano; Prague Chamber Orch.; Gregor, cond.*
- ARG 1-2/90: 64
+ Fa 11-12/90: 267
+ MA 3/91: 80

32938. 11 0374-2: MARTINŮ—Piano concerto no. 2; Rhapsody-concerto for viola. *Páleníček, piano; Suk, viola; Czech Phil. Orch.; Neumann, cond.*
+ ARG 11-12/90: 77 (Rhapsody)
- ARG 11-12/90: 77 (Concerto)
+ Fa 11-12/90: 267
- Gr 11/90: 984
+ MA 3/91: 80

32939. 11 0377-2: SMETANA—Má vlast: Vltava; From Bohemia's woods and fields; Bartered bride overture; Polka and furiant; Dance of the comedians; Festive symphony: Scherzo; Libuše: Prelude. *Prague Symphony Orch.; Bělohlávek, cond.*
+ ARG 9-10/91: 130
- Fa 7-8/91: 294

32940. 11 0378-2 (2 discs): DVOŘÁK—Slavonic rhapsodies; My home overture;

The hero's song; Symphonic variations; Scherzo capriccioso. *Czech Phil. Orch.; Gregor, cond.*
+ ARG 11-12/91: 61
- Gr 12/91: 66

32941. 11 0380-2: MARTINŮ—The butterfly that stamped. *Prague Symphony Orch.; Belohlavek, cond.*
+ ARG 7-8/95: 153
+ Gr 9/95: 94

32942. 11 0381-2: MARTINŮ—Concerto grosso; Three ricercari; Sinfonia concertante for 2 orchestras. *Czech Phil. Orch.; Bělohlávek, cond.*
+ ARG 3-4/92: 98
+ Fa 3-4/92: 239

32943. 11 0382-2 (3 discs): MARTINŮ—Symphonies (complete); Fantaisies symphoniques. *Czech Phil. Orch.; Neumann, cond.* Reissues.
+ ARG 9-10/91: 94
+ Fa 5-6/91: 212
- Gr 1/92: 56

32944. 11 0388-2: BERLIOZ—Overtures: Benvenuto Cellini; Rob Roy; King Lear; Le corsaire. *Brno State Phil. Orch.; Vronsky, cond.*
- ARG 9-10/91: 47
+ Gr 10/91: 75

32945. 11 0389-2: BERLIOZ—La mort de Cléopâtre; Symphonie funèbre et triomphale. *Vejzovic, mezzo-soprano; Czech Phil. Orch.; Eschenbach, cond.*
- Gr 5/92: 31

32946. 11 0391-2: RIMSKY-KORSAKOV—Scheherazade. *Suk, violin; Czech Phil. Orch.; Rahbari, cond.*
- ARG 1-2/91: 82
+ Fa 11-12/90: 332

32947. 11 0392-2: MOZART—Divertimenti K. 334, K. 137. *Suk Chamber Orch.; Vlach, cond.*
- ARG 5-6/91: 89
+ Fa 1-2/91: 250

32948. 11 0394-2: BRAHMS—Symphony no. 1. *Czech Phil. Orch.; Bělohlávek, cond.*
- Fa 5-6/91: 138

32949. 11 0395-2: ZEMLINSKY—Lyric symphony. *Armstrong, soprano; Kusnjer, baritone; Czech Phil. Orch.; Gregor, cond.*
+ ARG 3-4/92: 169
- Gr 10/91: 118

32950. 11 0396-2: DEBUSSY—La mer; Images for orchestra. *Czech Phil. Orch.; Pešek, cond.*
+ Fa 1-2/92: 199
- Gr 2/92: 35

32951. 11 0402-2: Music of Frescobaldi, Bach, Dowland, Mudarra, Losy, Sanz, Tárrega, Giuliani, Tesař, Villa-Lobos,

Pipó, Vivaldi, and Coste. *Filipová, guitar.*
- ARG 11-12/92: 239

32952. 11 0404-2: MESSIAEN—Trois petites liturgies; Cinq rechants. *Y. Loriod, piano; J. Loriod, ondes Martenot; Bambini di Praga; Pavel Kühn Female Chorus; Prague Symphony Orch.; Kulínský, cond.; Kühn Chamber Soloists; Kühn, cond.*
+ ARG 9-10/93: 154

32953. 11 0419-2: *Famous opera marches.* Music of Verdi, Mozart, Gounod, Wagner, and Meyerbeer. *Prague Castle Guard Band; Horák, Hanzai, conds.*
+ ARG 1-2/94: 175

32954. 11 0526-2: DVOŘÁK—Symphonic poems and concert overtures. *Czech Phil. Orch.; Gregor, cond.*
- Gr 10/91: 78

32955. 11 0557-2 (2 discs): HONEGGER—Jeanne d'Arc au bûcher; Une cantate de Noël. *Vocal soloists; Czech Phil. Orch.; Prague Symphony Orch.; Baudo, cond.* Reissues.
+ ARG 9-10/92: 117
+ Fa 5-6/92: 174
- Gr 2/92: 67

32956. 11 0559-2 (2 discs): DVOŘÁK—Symphonies no. 7-9. *Czech Phil. Orch.; Neumann, cond.* Reissues.
+ Fa 1-2/91: 192
- Gr 12/91: 65

32957. 11 0564-2: EBEN—Sunday music; Laudes; Hommage à Dietrich Buxtehude. *Klugarová, organ.*
+ ARG 7-8/92: 127
- Fa 7-8/92: 153

32958. 11 0572-2: Music of Beethoven, Weber (arr. Berlioz), Berlioz, Liszt, and Strauss. *Czech Phil. Orch.; Ančerl, cond.*
+ ARG 9-10/90: 135

32959. 11 0579-2: DITTERSDORF—Six symphonies after Ovid's Metamorphoses. *Prague Chamber Orch.; Gregor, cond.*
+ ARG 11-12/91: 59

32960. 11 0581-2: DVOŘÁK—String quartets no. 10, 12. *Panocha Quartet.*
+ ARG 7-8/91: 53
+ Fa 7-8/91: 154

32961. 11 0582-2: BEETHOVEN—Romance for violin and orchestra no. 1; Violin sonata, op. 12, no. 1. MOZART—Violin concerto K. 216. *D. Oistrakh, violin; Yampolsky, piano; Czech Phil. Orch.; Ančerl, cond.* Reissue.
+ Fa 1-2/91: 247
+ Gr 12/91: 63

32962. 11 0600-2: SCHUBERT— Mass in A♭ D. 678. *Terner, Röhr-Bach, Doležal, Slowioczek; Prague Radio Chorus &*

SUPRAPHON

Symphony Orch.; Válek, cond.
+ ARG 9-10/91: 122
- Fa 7-8/91: 281

32963. 11 0601-2: Dvořák—Violin
concerto. Suk—Fantasy for violin and
orchestra in G minor. *Suk, violin; Czech
Phil. Orch.; Ančerl, cond.*
+ Fa 9-10/90: 232

32964. 11 0605-2: Dvořák—In nature's
realm; Carnival; Othello; My home;
Hustiská. *Czech Phil. Orch.; Ančerl,
cond.*
+ Fa 9-10/90: 235

32965. 11 0608-2: Vivaldi—Concertos
RV 445, 535, 484, 545, 107, 88 . *Ars
Rediviva; Munclinger, cond.*
+ Fa 9-10/90: 427

32966. 11 0610-2: Mozart—Piano
concertos no. 21, 24. *Badura-Skoda,
piano; Prague Chamber Orch.*
• ARG 5-6/90: 80

32967. 11 0613-2: Franck—Symphony in
D minor; Chasseur maudit; Les djinns.
*Maxián, piano; Czech Phil. Orch.;
Barbirolli, Fournet, conds.*
+ Fa 7-8/90: 147

32968. 11 0616-2: Mendelssohn—
Midsummer night's dream: Excerpts.
Grieg—Peer Gynt: Suites no. 1-2. *Prague
Symphony Orch.; Smetáček, cond.*
• Fa 9-10/90: 291

32969. 11 0618-2: *The best of Caruso.*
Music of De Capua, Handel, Meyerbeer,
Flotow, Bizet, and others. *Caruso, tenor;
various orchs. & conds.*
+ Fa 5-6/90: 363

32970. 11 0620-2: Pergolesi—Stabat
Mater. Palestrina—Stabat Mater. *Czech
Phil. Chorus; Prague Chamber Orch.;
Bruni, Veselka, conds.*
+ Fa 5-6/90: 246

32971. 11 0621-2: Mozart—Don
Giovanni: Overture; Bella mia fiamma,
K. 528; Clarinet concerto; Symphony no.
38. *Jonášová, soprano; Mareš, clarinet;
Prague Chamber Orch.; Prague
Chamber Soloists; Chamber Harmony
Players; Prague Radio Symphony Orch.;
Pešek, Lukáš, conds.*
+ Fa 7-8/90: 206

32972. 11 0622-2: *Greetings from Russia.*
Music of Glinka, Balakirev, Borodin,
Tchaikovsky, and Rimsky- Korsakov.
*Czech Phil. Orch.; Prague Symphony
Orch.; Brno State Orch.; Belohlavek,
Smetáček, Danon, conds.*
+ ARG 5-6/90: 133

32973. 11 0623-2: Mendelssohn—
Symphonies no. 4-5; Hebrides overture .
Czech Phil. Orch.; Delogu, cond.
+ Fa 9-10/90: 295

32974. 11 0624-2: *Little pearls of Czech
classics.* Music of Fučík, Dvořák,
Nedbal, Fibich, Smetana, and others.
Czech Phil. Orch.; Neumann, cond.
+ Fa 5-6/90: 391

32975. 11 0626-2: Bach—Toccata and
fugue BWV 565; Prelude and fugue
BWV 546, 548, 549; Herzlich tut mich
verlangen BWV 727; Wir glauben all an
einen Gott BWV 681; Vater unser in
Himmelreich BWV 683; Canonic
variations BWV 769. *Reinberger, organ.*
- Fa 5-6/90: 105

32976. 11 0627-2: Dvořák—Symphony
no. 8. Smetana—Má vlast: Moldau; From
Bohemia's woods and fields. *Czech Phil.
Orch.; Talich, cond.*
+ ARG 5-6/90: 49
+ Fa 7-8/90: 135

32977. 11 0629-2: Dvořák—Symphony
no. 9; Scherzo capriccioso. *Czech Phil.
Orch.; Neumann, cond.*
- Fa 5-6/90: 161

32978. 11 0630-2: Chopin—Preludes
(complete); Ballade no. 4. *Moravec,
piano.*
+ Fa 9-10/90: 212

32979. 11 0631-2: Dvořák—Cello
concertos no. 1-2 (no. 1 orch.
Burghauser). *Sádlo, cello; Czech Phil.
Orch.; Neumann, cond.*
• ARG 5-6/90: 48
+ Fa 5-6/90: 158

32980. 11 0632-2: Bartók—Violin
concertos no. 1-2. *Gertler, violin; Brno
State Phil. Orch.; Czech Phil. Orch.;
Ferencsik, Ančerl, conds.*
+ ARG 5-6/90: 22
+ Fa 5-6/90: 111

32981. 11 0633-2: Music of J. Stamitz,
Brixi, and Linek. *Veselá, organ; Dvořák
Chamber Orch.; Bohuslav Martinů
Chamber Orch.; Válek, Jílek, conds.*
+ ARG 5-6/90: 113
- Fa 5-6/90: 301

32982. 11 0634-2: Haydn—String
quartets op. 33 no. 1-4. *Panocha Quartet.*
+ Fa 5-6/90: 186

32983. 11 0636-2: Mozart—Flute
concerto K. 313; Oboe concerto in C;
Bassoon concerto K. 191. *Válek, flute;
Mihule, oboe; Herman, bassoon; Czech
Phil. Orch.; Neumann, cond.*
• ARG 5-6/90: 79
• Fa 5-6/90: 225

32984. 11 0637-2: Dufay—Missa Ave
Regina caelorum; Missa Ecce ancilla
Domini. *Prague Madrigal Singers;
Venhoda, cond.*
• Fa 5-6/90: 156

32985. 11 0638-2: Beethoven—Octet op.
103; Sextet op. 71; Quintet for piano and

winds op. 16. *Jílek, piano; Czech Phil.
Wind Ensemble.*
+ Fa 5-6/90: 115

32986. 11 0639-2: Bruch—Violin
concerto no. 1. Mendelssohn—Violin
concerto in E minor. Berlioz—Rêverie et
caprice. *Suk, violin; Czech Phil. Orch.;
Prague Symphony Orch.; Ančerl,
Smetáček, conds.*
+ Fa 5-6/90: 139

32987. 11 0642-2: Bach—Violin
concertos BWV 1041-1042; Concerto for
2 violins, BWV 1043; Concerto for violin
and oboe, BWV 1060. *Suk, Jácek,
violins; Adamus, oboe; Prague Symphony
Orch.; Suk, Chamber Orch.; Smetáček,
Vlach, conds.*
+ ARG 11-12/90: 16
• Fa 9-10/90: 146

32988. 11 0644-2: Brahms—String
quartets no. 1-2. *Janáček Quartet.*
- ARG 7-8/90: 33
• Fa 7-8/90: 106

32989. 11 0647-2: Dvořák—Slavonic
dances. *Czech Phil. Orch.; Talich, cond.*
+ ARG 11-12/90: 51

32990. 11 0648-2: Mendelssohn—String
octet; Piano trio no. 1. *Smetana Quartet;
Janáček Quartet; Suk Trio.*
+ ARG 5-6/90: 74
+ Fa 5-6/90: 219

32991. 11 0649-2: Dvořák—Serenade for
strings; Czech suite. *Prague Chamber
Orch.*
• Fa 5-6/90: 159

32992. 11 0653-2: Britten—Violin
concerto; Simple symphony. Vaughan
Williams—Concerto accademico.
*Grumlikova, violin; Prague Symphony
Orch.; Maag, cond.*
+ ARG 7-8/92: 109

32993. 11 0657-2: Fibich—Symphonies
no. 2-3. *Brno State Phil. Orch.;
Waldhans, Belohlavek, conds.*
□ ARG 7-8/92: 131

32994. 11 0658-2: Debussy—Images;
Danses sacrée et profane; Prélude à
l'après-midi d'un faune; Jeux. *Patras,
harp; Czech Phil. Orch.; Baudo, cond.*
+ ARG 9-10/92: 96

32995. 11 0659-2: Stravinsky—The rite
of spring; Firebird suite. *Czech Phil.
Orch.; Ančerl, Delogu, conds.*
• ARG 11-12/92: 216

32996. 11 0664-2: Dvořák—Small
orchestral pieces; 8 waltzes, op. 54;
Prague waltzes; Festival march; Polka;
Polonaise. Suk—Fantastic scherzo.
*Prague Symphony Orch.; Belohlavek,
cond.*
□ ARG 5-6/92: 50

32997. 11 0667-2: Honegger—Symphonies no. 3, 5; Pastorale d'été; Chant de joie; Pacific 231. *Czech Phil. Orch.; Baudo, cond.* Reissue.
+ ARG 9-10/92: 120

32998. 11 0669-2: Smetana—Má vlast. *Czech Phil. Orch.; Ančerl, cond.* Recorded 1963.
+ ARG 1-2/93: 152
+ Fa 1-2/93: 243

32999. 11 0672-2: Stravinsky—L'histoire du soldat: suite; Octet for winds; Symphonies of wind instruments; Piano rag-music; Ragtime for 11 instruments; Ebony concerto. *Prague Chamber Harmony; Pešek, cond.; Novotný, piano; Karel Krautgartner Orch.; Krautgartner, cond.* Reissue; recorded 1962-68.
+ Fa 5-6/93: 334

33000. 11 0674-2: Bloch—Schelomo; Concerto for violin and orchestra; Hebrew suite for violin and orchestra. *Navarra, cello; Czech Phil. Orch.; Ančerl, cond.; Bress, violin; Prague Symphony Orch.; Rohan, cond.* Reissue.
+ ARG 7-8/93: 69
+ Fa 5-6/93: 170

33001. 11 0675-2: Dvořák—Concerto for piano and orchestra, op. 33; Symphony no. 7. *Moravec, piano; Czech Phil. Orch.; Belohlavek, Neumann, conds.*
+ Fa 5-6/93: 195
• Gr 8/93: 26

33002. 11 0676-2: Shostakovich—Symphony no. 5; Cello concerto no. 1. *Sádlo, cello; Czech Phil. Orch.; Ančerl, cond.* Reissues.
+ ARG 7-8/93: 157
+ Gr 8/93: 38

33003. 11 0678-2: Beethoven—Symphony no. 3; Concerto no. 2 for piano and orchestra. *Czech Phil. Orch.; Kletzki, cond.; Panenka, piano; Prague Symphony Orch.; Smetáček, cond.*
+ Fa 7-8/93: 107

33004. 11 0679-2: Handl—Motets, Mass. *Prague Madrigal Singers; Venhoda, cond.; Vienna Musica Antiqua; Clemencic, cond.* Reissue.
+ ARG 9-10/93: 130

33005. 11 0680-2: Beethoven—Symphonies no. 2, 8. *Czech Phil. Orch.; Kletzki, cond.*
+ Fa 7-8/93: 107

33006. 11 0681-2: Roussel—Symphony no. 3; Bacchus et Ariane: Suite no. 2; Spider's feast. *Brno State Phil. Orch.; Neumann, cond.; Prague Symphony Orch.; Smetáček, cond.* Reissues.
+ Gr 5/93: 50

33007. 11 0682-2: Novák—Slovak suite; Eternal longing; In the Tatras. *Czech

Phil. Orch.; Brno State Phil. Orch.; Sejna, cond. Reissues.
+ ARG 5-6/93: 117
+ Fa 9-10/93: 228
+ Gr 6/93: 51

33008. 11 0683-2: Respighi—Trittico botticelliano; Gli uccelli; La boutique fantasque: ballet suite after Rossini. *Prague Chamber Orch.; Škvor, cond.; Czech Phil. Orch.; Pedrotti, cond.*
+ Fa 5-6/93: 293

33009. 11 0684-2: Poulenc—Aubade. Ravel—Piano concertos. *Krajný, piano; Prague Chamber Orch.; Prague Symphony Orch.; Bělohlávek, cond.* Reissues.
• Gr 8/93: 36

33010. 11 0701-2: Dvořák—Violin concerto. Suk—Fantasy for violin and orchestra. *Suk, violin; Czech Phil. Orch.; Neumann, cond.*
+ ARG 11-12/90: 50
+ Fa 5-6/90: 159
+ NYT 6/10/90: H24

33011. 11 0702-2: Martinů—Violin concertos no. 1-2. *Suk, violin; Czech Phil. Orch.; Neumann, cond.*
+ ARG 5-6/90: 71
+ Fa 5-6/90: 214
+ NYT 6/10/90: H24

33012. 11 0703-2: Dvořák—Violin sonata; Sonatina for violin in G; Four romantic pieces, op. 75. *Suk, violin; Holeček, piano.*
+ ARG 7-8/90: 45
+ Fa 5-6/90: 160
+ NYT 6/10/90: H24

33013. 11 0704-2: Smetana—Piano trio in G minor. Dvořák—Piano trio no. 4. *Suk Trio.*
+ ARG 5-6/90: 111
+ Fa 5-6/90: 160

33014. 11 0705-2: Janáček—Violin sonata. Foerster—Sonata quasi fantasia. Novák—Violin sonata in D minor. *Suk, violin; Panenka, pinao.*
+ Fa 5-6/90: 160
+ NYT 6/10/90: H24

33015. 11 0706-2: Bartók—Violin concerto no. 1. Berg—Violin concerto. *Suk, violin; Czech Phil. Orch.; Ferencsik, Neumann, conds.*
• Fa 7-8/90: 83

33016. 11 0707-2: Beethoven—Concerto for violin, cello, and piano; Piano trio no. 6. *Suk Trio; Czech Phil. Orch.; Masur, cond.*
+ ARG 7-8/90: 18
+ Fa 7-8/90: 87

33017. 11 0708-2: Berlioz—Harold en Italie; Rêverie et caprice. *Suk, violin & viola; Czech Phil. Orch.; Prague Symphony Orch.; Fischer-Dieskau,*

Smetáček, conds.
+ ARG 7-8/90: 26
• Fa 7-8/90: 99

33018. 11 0709-2: Beethoven—Violin sonatas no. 5, 9. *Suk, violin; Panenka, piano.*
+ Fa 7-8/90: 87

33019. 11 0710-2: Franck—Violin sonata. Respighi—Violin sonata. Poulenc—Violin sonata. *Suk, violin; Panenka, Hála, piano.*
+ ARG 7-8/90: 49
+ Fa 7-8/90: 146

33020. 11 0711-2: Smetana—Má vlast. *Czech Phil. Orch.; Neumann, cond.*
• Fa 5-6/91: 287

33021. 11 0713-2: Dvořák—Symphonies no. 7-8. *Czech Phil. Orch.; Neumann, cond.* Reissues.
+ Gr 12/91: 65

33022. 11 0714-2: Dvořák—Symphony no. 9. *Czech Phil. Orch.; Neumann, cond.* Reissue.
• Gr 12/91: 65

33023. 11 0715-2: Suk—Asrael symphony. *Czech Phil. Orch.; Neumann, cond.*
• Gr 9/91: 74

33024. 11 0716-2: Suk—Ripening. Dvořák—Symphonic variations. *Czech Phil. Orch.; Neumann, cond.*
+ Fa 7-8/91: 304

33025. 11 0717-2: Janáček—Violin concerto: "The wandering of a soul"; Sinfonietta; Taras Bulba: rhapsody for orchestra. *Suk, violin; Czech Phil. Orch.; Neumann, cond.*
+ Fa 7-8/91: 181
+ Gr 6/91: 43

33026. 11 0718-2: Martinů—Symphonies no. 3, 6; Inventions. *Leichner, piano; Czech Phil. Orch.; Neumann, cond.*
+ Fa 5-6/91: 212

33027. 11 0719-2: Beethoven—Symphony no. 5; Piano concerto no. 3. *Moravec, piano; Czech Phil. Orch.; Neumann, cond.*
- Fa 5-6/91: 127 (Symphony)
+ Fa 5-6/91: 127 (Concerto)

33028. 11 0720-2: Beethoven—Symphonies no. 7-8. *Czech Phil. Orch.; Neumann, cond.*
• Fa 5-6/91: 127

33029. 11 0721-2: Mahler—Symphonies no. 1; 10: Adagio. *Czech Phil. Orch.; Neumann, cond.*
• Fa 7-8/91: 197

SUPRAPHON

33030. 11 0722-2: Mahler—Symphony no. 5. *Czech Phil. Orch.; Neumann, cond.*
+ Fa 7-8/91: 197

33031. 11 0724-2: Music of Suppé, Offenbach, and J. Strauss, Jr. *Czech Phil. Orch.; Neumann, cond.*
+ ARG 9-10/91: 153
- Fa 5-6/91: 380

33032. 11 0725-2: *Tribute to Václav Neumann.* Music of Komzák, Popisil, Procházka, Fučík, and others. *Czech Phil. Orch.; Neumann, cond.*
+ Fa 5-6/91: 380

33033. 11 0749-2: Bizet—Symphony in C; Jeux d'enfants; Patrie. *Czech Phil. Orch.; Košler, cond.*
- ARG 1-2/91: 32 (Patrie)
+ ARG 1-2/91: 32 (others)
• Fa 1-2/91: 156

33034. 11 0751-2: Martinů—Mount of three lights; The prophecy of Isaiah; Hymn to St. James. *Hora, organ; Prague Symphony Orch.; Kühn, cond.*
+ ARG 11-12/92: 156
• Gr 12/92: 120

33035. 11 0752-2 (2 discs): Martinů—Špalíček; Romance of the dandelions; Primrose. *Vocal soloists; Brno State Phil. Orch.; Jílek, cond.*
+ Gr 4/93: 110

33036. 11 0755-2: Music of Dauprat, Gallay, and Rossini. *Czech Phil. Orch. Horn Section.*
• Fa 11-12/90: 208

33037. 11 0756-2: Vanhal—Symphonies in A, in G minor, in D. *Prague Chamber Orch.; Vlček, cond.*
• ARG 3-4/91: 134
- Fa 1-2/91: 338

33038. 11 0760-2: Music of Artophaeus, Vanura, and Černohorský. *Prague Radio Chorus; Dvořák Chamber Orch.; Hercl, cond.*
+ Fa 7-8/91: 351

33039. 11 0767-2: Martinů—The opening of the wells; The legend of the smoke from potato fires; Mikes of the mountains. *Vocal soloists; instrumentalists; Kühn Mixed Chorus; Kühn, cond.*
+ ARG 11-12/93: 145
+ Fa 11-12/93: 311
+ Gr 5/94: 96

33040. 11 0768-2: Janáček—Concertino for piano and chamber ensemble; Capriccio for piano left hand and chamber ensemble; Nonsense rhymes. *Páleníček, piano; Czech Phil. Orch. & Chorus; Veselka, cond.* Reissues.
+ Fa 5-6/92: 180
• Gr 3/92: 44

33041. 11 0769-2: Music of Reicha, Rosetti, L. Mozart, and Haydn (attrib.). *Z. Tylšar, B. Tylšar, horns; Dvořák Chamber Orch.; Altrichter, cond.*
+ ARG 3-4/91: 152
+ Fa 11-12/90: 453

33042. 11 0780-2: B.D. Weber—Four sextets in F for horns. Mechura—Horn quartet in E♭. *Czech Phil. Orch. Horn Section.*
+ ARG 3-4/91: 152
+ Fa 1-2/91: 349

33043. 11 0816-2: Zelenka—Missa in D, Z. 13; Responsoria pro hebdomada sancta, Z. 55: Nos. 10-11, 13-15; Sub tuum praesidium, Z. 157. *Czech Phil. Orch. & Chorus; Bělohlávek, Mátl, conds.*
+ Fa 1-2/92: 379
• Gr 5/92: 99

33044. 11 0936-2: Laub—Polonaise in G; Romance. Ondricek—Valse triste; Nocturne; Scherzo capriccioso. Sevcik—Two Bohemian dances. Kubelik—Nocturne; Minuet in the old style. Kocian—Serenade in G; Humoresque; Springtime song. Prihoda—Waltz in A. *Snútil, violin; Hála, piano.*
+ ARG 7-8/92: 275

33045. 11 0938-2: Mendelssohn—Cello sonatas no. 1-2; Variations concertantes; Songs without words, op. 109. *Veis, cello; Tirimo, piano.*
• ARG 5-6/93: 110

33046. 11 0942-2: Schubert—String quartets no. 12, 15. *Panocha Quartet.*
+ ARG 3-4/94: 148
+ Fa 3-4/94: 306

33047. 11 0951-2: Dittersdorf—Double bass concerto no. 1; Sinfonia concertante in D for viola, double bass, and orchestra; Viola concerto in F. *Maly, viola; Posta, double bass; Dvořák Chamber Orch.; Vajnar, cond.*
+ ARG 9-10/94: 122
• Fa 7-8/94: 122

33048. 11 0952-2: Tchaikovsky—Piano concerto no. 1; Piano music. *Ardasev, piano; Czech Phil. Orch.; Belohlavek, cond.*
+ ARG 7-8/92: 236

33049. 11 0957-2: Smetana—Má vlast. *Czech Phil. Orch.; Bělohlávek, cond.*
• Gr 3/93: 54

33050. 11 0960-2: Dvořák—Symphony no. 9 "From the New World;" Carnival. *Czech Phil. Orch.; Belohlavek, cond.*
+ Gr 2/92: 35

33051. 11 0967-2: Brahms—Symphony no. 2; Haydn variations. *Czech Phil. Orch.; Bělohlávek, cond.*
+ ARG 5-6/93: 75

33052. 11 0969-2 (2 discs): Tchaikovsky—Orchestral suites. *Prague Symphony Orch.; Bělohlávek, cond.*
+ ARG 1-2/94: 164
+ Fa 1-2/94: 332

33053. 11 0971-2: Saint-Saëns—Symphony no. 3; Suite algérienne. *Hora, organ; Prague Radio Symphony Orch.; Válek, cond.*
• ARG 3-4/92: 131
+ Fa 5-6/92: 237
+ Gr 4/92: 75

33054. 11 0992-2: Martinů—Cello sonatas no. 1-3. *Chuchro, cello; Hála, piano.* Reissue.
- ARG 11-12/93: 146
• Fa 9-10/93: 211

33055. 11 0994-2 (3 discs): Martinů—String quartets (complete). *Panocha Quartet.* Recorded 1979-82.
+ ARG 3-4/95: 134
• Gr 9/95: 76

33056. 11 0997-2: Martinů—Parables; Frescoes of Piero della Francesca; Fantaisies symphoniques (Symphony no. 6). *Czech Phil. Orch.; Ančerl, cond.*
+ ARG 7-8/92: 172

33057. 11 0999-2: Mozart—Clarinet quintet, K. 581; Oboe quartet, K. 370; Horn quintet, K. 407. *Zahradník, clarinet; Krejčí, oboe; Langweil, horn; Panocha String Quartet.*
+ Fa 1-2/92: 280
- Gr 1/92: 70

33058. 11 1001-2: F. Benda—Harpsichord concertos. *Hála, harpsichord, with string quintet.*
□ ARG 7-8/92: 97

33059. 11 1002-2: Schumann—Cello concerto, op. 129. Bloch—Schelomo. Respighi—Adagio and variations for cello and orchestra. *Navarra, cello; Czech Phil. Orch.; Ančerl, cond.* Reissue.
+ Fa 1-2/92: 323

33060. 11 1003-2 (2 discs): Dvořák—Symphonies 1-3. *Czech Phil. Orch.; Neumann, cond.*
- ARG 5-6/92: 51

33061. 11 1005-2 (2 discs): Dvořák—Symphonies no. 4-6. *Czech Phil. Orch.; Neumann, cond.*
• Gr 3/92: 43

33062. 11 1090-2: Martinů—Magic nights; Nipponari; The spectre's bride. *Soloists; Kühn Chorus; Prague Symphony Orch.; Belohlavek, cond.*
+ ARG 5-6/94: 111

33063. 11 1101-2: Dvořák—Slavonic dances (complete). *Czech Phil. Orch.; Sejna, cond.*
+ Fa 7-8/90: 132

33064. 11 1102-2: TCHAIKOVSKY—Symphony no. 4; Francesca da Rimini. *Czech Phil. Orch.; Brno State Phil. Orch.; Slovák, Danon, conds.*
+ Fa 7-8/90: 291

33065. 11 1103-2: BERLIOZ—Symphonie fantastique; King Lear overture. *Czech Phil. Orch.; Prague Symphony Orch.; Zecchi, Smetáček, conds.*
- ARG 7-8/90: 27
• Gr 12/90: 1198

33066. 11 1104-2: BEETHOVEN—Symphonies no. 2, 4. *Czech Phil. Orch.; Ferencsik, cond.*
+ ARG 7-8/90: 24

33067. 11 1106-2: DVOŘÁK—Symphony no. 7; Water goblin. *Czech Phil. Orch.; Košler, Chalabala, conds.*
• ARG 7-8/90: 46
- Fa 7-8/90: 139

33068. 11 1107-2: RIMSKY-KORSAKOV—Legend of the invisible city of Kitezh: Suite; Le coq d'or: Suite; Antar. *Prague Symphony Orch.; Brno State Phil. Orch.; Smetáček, Bělohlávek, conds.*
- ARG 7-8/90: 91

33069. 11 1108-2: TCHAIKOVSKY—Piano concerto no. 1. RACHMANINOFF—Piano concerto no. 1. *Kameníková, piano; Brno State Phil. Orch.; Pinkas, cond.*
• ARG 7-8/90: 116

33070. 11 1111-2: BEETHOVEN—Symphony no. 3; Choral fantasy. *Panenka, piano; Czech Phil. Orch.; Prague Radio Symphony Chorus & Orch.; Matacic, Smetáček, conds.*
• Fa 9-10/90: 178

33071. 11 1112-2: LISZT—Orpheus; Prometheus; Tasso. WAGNER—Siegfried Idyll. *Prague Radio Symphony Orch.; Czech Phil. Orch.; Macura, Košler, conds.*
+ ARG 7-8/90: 65 (Liszt)
• ARG 7-8/90: 65 (Wagner)

33072. 11 1113-2: DVOŘÁK—Piano concerto in G minor; Humoresques op. 101. *Kvapil, piano; Brno State Phil. Orch.; Jílek, cond.*
+ Fa 7-8/90 132

33073. 11 1114-2: SCHUBERT—Konzertstück in D major, K. 345; Polonaise in B♭ major, D. 580. SCHUMANN—Violin concerto in D minor, op. posth.; Fantasie in C major, op. 131. *Snítil, violin; Prague Symphony Orch.; Hlaváček, Hrnčíř, conds.*
+ ARG 7-8/90: 104
• Gr 10/91: 110

33074. 11 1115-2: SMETANA—Bartered bride: Overture, Polka, Furiant; Six polkas; Five Czech dances; Festive symphony: Scherzo. *Prague National Theatre Chorus & Orch.; Brno State*

Phil. Orch.; Czech Phil. Orch.; Chalabala, Jílek, Sejna, conds.
+ ARG 7-8/90: 112
+ Fa 7-8/90: 276

33075. 11 1116-2: INDY—Mort de Wallenstein; Istar. BERLIOZ—Le corsaire overture; Benenuto Cellini overture. *Prague Symphony Orch.; Fekete, cond.*
• ARG 7-8/90: 59
+ Fa 7-8/90: 131

33076. 11 1117-2: *Jazz-inspired piano music.* Music of Debussy, Satie, Auric, Gershwin, Hindemith, and others. *Toperczer, Vrána, Leichner, Marcol, Mikula, pianos.*
+ Fa 7-8/90: 351

33077. 11 1118-2: BEETHOVEN—Overtures: Leonore no. 3; Egmont; Coriolan; Ruins of Athens; King Stephan; Ah! perfido. *Děpoltová, soprano; Czech Phil. Orch.; Bajnar, cond.*
• Fa 7-8/90: 88

33078. 11 1119-2: HAYDN—Violin concertos no. 1, 4, 9 (attrib.). *Matousek, violin; Prague Chamber Orch.; Hlaváček, cond.*
• ARG 7-8/90: 54
+ Fa 7-8/90: 164

33079. 11 1166-2 (2 discs): MOZART—Opera overtures; Idomeneo ballet music. *Prague Chamber Orch.; Vlček, Vovotny, conds.*
+ ARG 11-12/92: 168

33080. 11 1174-2: BEETHOVEN—Symphony no. 9. *Beňačková, Gjevang, G. Neumann, Korn; Czech Phil. Orch. & Chorus; V. Neumann, cond. Recorded live.*
- Gr 4/92: 44

33081. 11 1195-2: MOSCHELES—Piano concerto in G minor; Bonbonnière musicale; Flute and oboe concerto. *Klánský, piano; Válek, flute; Mihule, oboe; Dvorak Chamber Orch.; Parik, cond.*
+ ARG 11-12/91: 97

33082. 11 1208-2: SMETANA—Má vlast. *Czech Phil. Orch.; Kubelik, cond. Recorded live 1991.*
+ ARG 11-12/93: 199
+ Fa 7-8/91: 293

33083. 11 1242-2: DVOŘÁK—Symphony no. 9; Overtures: My home; In nature's realm. *Czech Phil. Orch.; Ančerl, cond. Reissue.*
+ ARG 11-12/92: 116
◻ Fa 7 8/92: 145

33084. 11 1259-2 (3 discs): DVOŘÁK—Dimitri. *Vodička, Drobková, Hajóssyová, Ághová, Mikulaš, Kusnjer; Czech Phil. Orch.; Albrecht, cond.*
+ ARG 11-12/92: 114
+ Gr 3/93: 93

33085. 11 1263-2: TESAŘ—Guitar music. *Zelenka, Tesař, guitars; Urbanek, harpsichord; Kubin Quartet.*
◻ ARG 11-12/93: 210

33086. 11 1264-2: DANZI—Wind quintets, op. 56; op. 68. *Academia Wind Quintet.*
+ ARG 9-10/94: 121
+ Fa 5-6/94: 132

33087. 11 1265-2: VIVALDI—Recorder concertos RV 440-445. *Stivín, recorders; Virtuosi di Praga; Vlček, cond.*
+ Fa 1-2/94: 344

33088. 11 1268-2: SIBELIUS—Symphony no. 2; Karelia suite; Valse triste. *Prague Radio Symphony; Válek, cond.*
• ARG 5-6/96: 199

33089. 11 1269-2: DEBUSSY (ARR. CONSTANT)—Pelléas et Mélisande symphonie. SIBELIUS—Pelléas et Mélisande: Suite, op. 46. *Czech Phil. Orch.; Baudo, cond.*
+ ARG 3-4/93: 72
+ Fa 1-2/93: 139

33090. 11 1270-2: SPOHR—Nonet. BERWALD—Septet. *Czech Nonet.*
+ ARG 9-10/94: 202

33091. 11 1272-2: BRAHMS—Symphony no. 3; Tragic overture. *Czech Phil. Orch.; Belohlavek, cond.*
+ ARG 7-8/92: 107

33092. 11 1274-2: BRAHMS—Piano concerto no. 1; Intermezzo, op. 118, no. 2. *Moravec, piano; Czech Phil. Orch.; Bělohlávek, cond.*
+ ARG 7-8/92: 104
+ Fa 7-8/92: 125

33093. 11 1276-2 (3 discs): SMETANA—Libuše. *Beňačková, Děpoltová, Soukupová, Marian; Prague National Theater; Košler, cond. Reissue.*
+ ARG 7-8/94: 175
+ Gr 4/94: 100
+ ON 9/94: 60

33094. 11 1293-2: The oldest collections of Czech folk songs. *Vraspir, tenor; Chlomková, mezzo-soprano; Miháilková, soprano; Krček, baritone & cond.; Musica Bohemica.*
+ Fa 3-4/93: 354

33095. 11 1303-2: MENDELSSOHN—Piano trios. *New Prague Trio.*
+ ARG 1-2/94: 123

33096. 11 1308-2: F. BENDA—Flute concerto in E minor; Flute sonata. C. STAMITZ—Flute concerto in G. *Rampal, flute; Prague Chamber Orch.; Munclinger, Neumann, conds.; Svihlíková, harpsichord.*
+ ARG 7-8/92: 96

33097. 11 1313-2 (2 discs): MARTINŮ—Piano concertos no. 1-5; Concertino for

SUPRAPHON

piano and orchestra. *Leichner, piano; Czech Phil. Orch.; Belohlavek, cond.*
  + ARG 7-8/94: 129
  + Fa 5-6/94: 187

33098. 11 1327-2: DvoŘÁK—Cello concerto in B minor; Othello: overture; The noon witch: symphonic poem. *Rostropovich, cello; Czech Phil. Orch.; Talich, cond.* Reissue.
  + ARG 5-6/92: 49
  + Fa 5-6/92: 151

33099. 11 1332-2: WRANITZKY— Symphonies in C, op. 11; in D, op. 36. *Dvořák Chamber Orch.; Gregor, cond.*
  + Fa 7-8/94: 274

33100. 11 1333-2: VORISEK—Violin sonata, op. 5; Rondo for violin and piano, op. 8; Variations for cello and piano, op. 9. *Pavlík, violin; Jerie, cello; Klánský, piano.*
  + Fa 7-8/92: 321

33101. 11 1354-2: JANÁČEK—String quartets no. 1 "Kreutzer sonata," no. 2 "Intimate pages"; Mládí (Youth suite). *Talich Quartet; Prague Wind Quintet.*
  + Fa 3-4/93: 197

33102. 11 1408-2, 11 0362-2 (2 separate discs): HAYDN—String quartets, op. 76. *Panocha Quartet.*
  + ARG 5-6/94: 100
  + Fa 1-2/94: 199
  + Fa 11-12/90: 293 (0362)

33103. 11 1409-2: Trumpet concertos by Hummel, Goedicke, Arutyunian, and Tomasi. *Freeman, trumpet; Prague Radio Symphony Orch.; Válek, cond.*
  + ARG 3-4/94: 215

33104. 11 1413-2: NEDBAL—Selections from the ballets Anderson, and, From tale to tale. *Dvořák Chamber Orch.; Homolka, cond.*
  + Fa 3-4/94: 257
  + Fa 5-6/94: 205

33105. 11 1414-2: NEDBAL—Princess Hyacinth; The tale of Honza. *Dvořák Chamber Orch.; Homolka, cond.*
  + Fa 7-8/94: 195

33106. 11 1415-2: MARTINŮ—Echec au roi; The revolt. *Kachlíková, alto; Prague Symphony Orch.; Bělohlávek, cond.*
  + ARG 1-2/94: 121
  + Fa 1-2/94: 232
  + Gr 5/94: 96

33107. 11 1416-2: *Baroque music from Kromeriz.* Music of Schmelzer, Ebner, Bruckner, Flixius, and Lamb. *Musica Antiqua Praha; Klikar, cond.*
  + ARG 9-10/92: 202

33108. 11 1418-2: Music of Rudnev, Koshkin, Ancelin, Brobrowicz, Kramskoi, Tesař, and Ruiz-Pipo.

Mikulka, guitar.
  + ARG 1-2/93: 179

33109. 11 1421-2: SCHUMANN— Waldszenen; Fantasiestücke, op. 12; Märsche, op. 76. SHOSTAKOVICH—Preludes and fugues, op. 87, no. 2-3, 6-7, 18. *Richter, piano.* Recorded live 1956.
  + ARG 3-4/94: 153
  + Fa 3-4/94: 317

33110. 11 1424-2: K. STAMITZ—Clarinet concerto in E♭; Horn concerto in E♭. A. STAMITZ—Concerto for two flutes. *Zahradník, clarinet; Z. Tylšar, horn; Válek, Pivoda, flutes; Prague Chamber Orch.; Vajnar, cond.*
  + ARG 3-4/93: 139

33111. 11 1430-2: DvoŘÁK—Mass in D; Ave Maria; Hymnus ad laudes in festo Sanctae trinitatis; Ave maris stella; O sanctissima dulcis virgo Maria. *Romanová, Barová, Kopp, Vele, Drobková, Novák, vocal soloists; Kšica, organ; Czech Phil. Chorus; Mátl, cond.*
  - Fa 1-2/94: 173

33112. 11 1432-2: BRAHMS—Sonatas for viola and piano, op. 120. SCHUMANN— Märchenbilder, op. 113. *Suk, viola; Panenka, piano.*
  + ARG 3-4/93: 64
  + Fa 3-4/93: 131

33113. 11 1438-2: EBEN—The Prague Te Deum 1989; Missa Adventus et Quadragesima; Vesperae in Festo Nativitas; The song of Ruth; Two invocations on the St. Wenceslas chorale for trombone and organ. *Czech Phil. Chorus; Mátl, cond.; Mašková, soprano; Bělor, baritone; Busova, mezzo-soprano; Prague Trumpeters; Eben, Kšica, organ; Votava, trombone; Kalfus, organ.*
  + Fa 7-8/94: 131

33114. 11 1445-2: REICHA—Trios for horns and bassoon, BEETHOVEN—Wind sextet; Quintet. *Various performers.*
  + ARG 3-4/93: 128
  + Gr 3/93: 60

33115. 11 1446-2: REICHA—Trios for horns. *Z. Tylšar, B. Tylšar, Divoký, horns.*
  + ARG 3-4/93: 128

33116. 11 1456-2: DvoŘÁK—*Chamber music, vol. 6.* String quartets no. 8-9. *Panocha Quartet.*
  + ARG 7-8/95: 108
  + Fa 7-8/95: 176

33117. 11 1457-2: DvoŘÁK—String quartet no. 10; Cypresses. *Panocha Quartet.*
  + ARG 7-8/94: 97
  + Fa 11-12/94: 264

33118. 11 1459-2: DvoŘÁK—String quartets no. 13-14. *Panocha Quartet.* Reissue.

  + ARG 1-2/93: 92
  + Fa 11-12/92: 228

33119. 11 1461-2: DvoŘÁK—String quintet; String sextet; Intermezzo. *Panocha Quartet; Kluson, viola; Kanka, cello; Netjek, double bass.*
  + ARG 9-10/93: 116
  + Fa 7-8/93: 133
  + Gr 5/94: 73

33120. 11 1464-2: DvoŘÁK—Piano quartets no. 1-2. *Hála, piano; Suk, violin; Kodousek, viola; Chuchro, cello.* Reissue.
  + ARG 1-2/93: 92
  + Fa 11-12/92: 228

33121. 11 1465-2: DvoŘÁK—Piano quintets no. 1-2. *Panenka, piano; Panocha Quartet.*
  • ARG 1-2/95: 102
  + Fa 11-12/94: 264

33122. 11 1466-2: DvoŘÁK—Violin sonatas; Sonatina; Romantic pieces; Nocturne; Ballade. *Suk, violin; Hála, piano.*
  + ARG 5-6/96: 108
  + Fa 7-8/96: 159

33123. 11 1469-2: DvoŘÁK—Sextet, op. 48; Quintet, op. 97. *Smetana Quartet; Suk, viola; Chuchro, cello.*
  + ARG 1-2/93: 97
  + Fa 11-12/93: 224
  + Gr 9/93: 71
  + Gr 10/93: 69

33124. 11 1472-2: Music of Balbastre, Boellmann, Franck, Vierne, and Messiaen. *Heřmanová, organ.*
  • ARG 3-4/93: 166

33125. 11 1476-2: RAVEL—Piano music. *Krajný, piano.*
  • ARG 1-2/94: 137
  • Fa 1-2/94: 274

33126. 11 1484-2: HAYDN—The seven last words of Christ. *Panocha Quartet.*
  + Fa 11-12/93: 269

33127. 11 1489-2: BACH—Chromatic fantasia and fugue, BWV 903; French suite no. 5; English suite no. 3; Toccata in C minor, BWV 911. *Růžičková, harpsichord.*
  + Fa 11-12/94: 150

33128. 11 1491-2: *Jarmila Novotná: Czech songs and arias.* Music of Masaryk, Kovarovic, Smetana, Dvořák, Fibich, and Stelibsky. *Novotná, soprano; with orch. and piano acc.* Recorded 1926-56.
  + Fa 1-2/93: 275

33129. 11 1492-2 (2 discs): FIBICH—The bride of Messina. *Márová, Zítek, ídek, Beňačková-Čápová; Prague National Theater; Jílek, cond.* Recorded 1975.
  + ARG 9-10/94: 131
  + Gr 12/94: 153

+ ON 1/20/96: 33
+ Op 12/94: 1477

33130. 11 1494-2: HANDEL—Organ concertos, op. 4, 7. *Tuma, organ; Virtuosi di Praga; Vlček, cond.*
• Fa 9-10/94: 201

33131. 11 1508-2: Dances for orchestra by SMETANA, JANÁČEK, AND DVOŘÁK. *PRAGUE SYMPHONY ORCH.; ALTRICHTER, COND.*
- Fa 3-4/94: 324
+ Fa 5-6/94: 142

33132. 11 1514-2: SMETANA—String quartets. *Panocha Quartet.*
• ARG 9-10/95: 216

33133. 11 1515-2: SMETANA—Piano trio, op. 15; Fantasy on a Bohemian song; From my homeland: 2 duos for violin and piano. *Guarneri Trio Prague.* Reissue.
+ ARG 3-4/95: 191
+ Fa 1-2/95: 272

33134. 11 1518-2: BACH—Concertos by Vivaldi. *Růžičková, harpsichord.*
+ Fa 9-10/93: 106

33135. 11 1519-2: LISZT—Piano sonata; Rhapsodie espagnole; Valse oubliée; Waldesrauschen; Gnomenreigen; La leggierezza; Sonetto 123 del Petrarca. *Ardasev, piano.*
+ ARG 1-2/93: 113
+ Fa 11-12/92: 282

33136. 11 1520-2: JANÁČEK—Lachian dances; Suite for strings; Idyll for strings. *Brno State Phil. Orch.; Jílek, cond.*
+ Fa 11-12/93: 279

33137. 11 1521-2: JANÁČEK—Orchestral works, vol. 2. *Brno State Phil. Orch.; Jílek, cond.*
• ARG 11-12/93: 132
• Fa 9-10/93: 192

33138. 11 1522-2: JANÁČEK—Sinfonietta; The Danube; Concerto for violin and orchestra "Wandering of a little soul"; Schluck und Jau: incidental music. *Brno State Phil. Orch.; Jílek, cond.; Dvořáková, soprano; enatý, violin.*
• ARG 7-8/93: 107
- Fa 5-6/93: 234
+ Gr 9/93: 52

33139. 11 1523—11 1524-2 (2 separate discs): MOZART—Divertimenti no. 10, 15. *Z. & B. Tylšar, horns; Stamitz Quartet.*
+ ARG 5-6/93: 115

33140. 11 1525-2: MOZART—Divertimento no. 17, K. 334. *Z. & B. Tylšar, horns; Stamitz Quartet.*
+ Fa 9-10/92: 300

33141. 11 1528-2: KOZELUH—String quartets, op. 33. *Stamitz String Quartet.*
+ ARG 11-12/93: 136
+ Fa 11-12/93: 288

33142. 11 1529-2: KOZELUH—String quartets, op. 32. *Stamitz String Quartet.*
+ Fa 11-12/93: 288

33143. 11 1531—1533-2 (3 separate discs): SUK—Chamber music. *Suk Trio; Suk Quartet; Talich, viola; Štěpán, piano.*
+ ARG 1-2/94: 161
+ Fa 1-2/94: 325

33144. 11 1544-2: DVOŘÁK—Cello concerto; Silent woods; Rondo. *May, cello; Czech Phil. Orch.; Neumann, cond.* Reissue.
+ ARG 5-6/94: 89

33145. 11 1545-2: CHOPIN—Piano sonata no. 2; Preludes; Mazurkas, op. 17. *J. Simon, piano.*
• ARG 7-8/93: 77

33146. 11 1561-2: DVOŘÁK—Piano trio, op. 90 "Dumky." SMETANA—Piano trio, op. 15. *Guarneri Trio Prague.*
+ ARG 3-4/93: 76
+ Fa 1-2/93: 145

33147. 11 1563-2: RODRIGO—Concierto de Aranjuez; Fantasia para un gentilhombre. *Brabec, guitar; Prague Chamber Orch.*
+ Fa 9-10/92: 332

33148. 11 1564-2 (2 discs): BRAHMS—Cello sonatas no. 1-2; Violin sonata no. 1. SCHUMANN—Phantasiestücke op. 73; Adagio und Allegro, op. 70; Funf Stücke im Volkston, op. 102. *Veis, cello; Panenka, piano.*
- Fa 1-2/94: 138

33149. 11 1573-2: KRUMPHOLZ—Six harp sonatas, op. 13, 14. *Müllerová, harp.*
+ Fa 3-4/93: 202

33150. 11 1596-2: KROMMER—Clarinet concerto, op. 36; Concerto for 2 clarinets, op. 35, 91. *Mareš, Hlaváč, clarinets; Prague Chamber Orch.; Pešek, cond.*
+ Fa 11-12/93: 290

33151. 11 1597-2: F. BENDA—Flute sonatas. J. BENDA—Flute sonata. *Kröper, flute; Gillitzer, harpsichord, fortepiano; Fritzsch, cello.*
+ Fa 9-10/93: 122

33152. 11 1598-2: ČERNOHORSKÝ—Religious works and organ works. *Czech Madrigal Singers; Czech Phil. Chorus; Gioia della Musica; Thuri, cond.*
+ Fa 7-8/94: 113

33153. 11 1800-2 (2 discs): DVOŘÁK—The devil and Kate. *Šulcová, Barová, Novák, Brno Janáček Opera Chorus & Orch.; Pinkas, cond.* Reissue.
+ ARG 9-10/94: 127
+ Fa 7-8/94: 128
+ Gr 9/94: 109

33154. 11 1802-2 (2 discs): MARTINŮ—Hry o Marii (The miracle of Our Lady).

Vocal soloists; Prague Radio Chorus; Prague Symphony Orch.; Belohlavek, cond.
+ ARG 11-12/93: 143
• Fa 11-12/93: 310
• Gr 1/94: 93
• ON 12/11/93: 44

33155. 11 1804-2 (2 discs): SMETANA—The Brandenburgers in Bohemia. *Sbrtová, Fidlerová, Soukupová, Vich; Prague National Theater; Tichy, cond.* Reissue.
+ ARG 7-8/94: 175
+ Gr 5/94: 111
+ ON 4/15/95: 35
+ Op 12/94: 1477

33156. 11 1806-2 (2 discs): BACH—The six sonatas and partitas for solo violin. *Novotný, violin.*
+ Fa 5-6/94: 101

33157. 11 1808-2: MENDELSSOHN—Violin concertos in E minor & D minor. *enatý, violin; Prague Symphony Orch.; Altrichter, cond.*
• Fa 9-10/93: 214

33158. 11 1810-2: DVOŘÁK—Symphony no. 9. JANÁČEK—The cunning little vixen: Suite. *Prague Symphony Orch.; Altrichter, cond.*
+ Fa 11-12/93: 227

33159. 11 1811-2: REGER—Hiller variations. ZEMLINSKY—Maeterlinck songs. *Fassbender, mezzo-soprano; Czech Phil. Orch.; Neumann, cond.*
+ ARG 9-10/93: 175
+ Fa 7-8/93: 275
+ Gr 7/93: 49

33160. 11 1814-2: MILHAUD—Concerto no. 2 for violin and orchestra; Sonata no. 2 for violin and piano. ENESCO—Sonata no. 3 for violin and piano. *Gertler, violin; Andersen, piano; Prague Symphony Orch.; Smetáček, cond.* Reissue.
+ ARG 7-8/93: 126
+ Fa 5-6/93: 265

33161. 11 1816-2: *Italian music of the early Baroque.* Music of Uccellini, Donati, Turini, Merulo, Picchi, Mariani, Tarditi, Arrigoni, Cima, Rossi, and Capuana. *Musica Antiqua Praha; Klikar, cond.*
+ ARG 9-10/93: 250
+ EM 2/94: 153
+ Fa 7-8/93: 308

33162. 11 1821-2: DVOŘÁK—Mass in D; Biblical songs no. 1-5; Te Deum. *Vocal soloists; Czech Phil. Chorus; Prague Symphony Orch.; Smetáček, cond.* Reissue.
+ ARG 3-4/95: 96

33163. 11 1822-2: FOERSTER—Symphony no. 4 "Easter"; Springtime and desire. *Prague Symphony Orch.; Smetáček, cond.* Reissue.

+ ARG 3-4/95: 100
+ Fa 11-12/94: 225

33164. 11 1823-2: FIBICH—Comenius overture; Toman and the wood nymph; Fall of Arkona overture; Zaboj, Slavoj, and Ludek. *Prague Symphony Orch.; Válek, cond.*
+ ARG 7-8/95: 111

33165. 11 1824-2: MARTINŮ—Epic of Gilgamesh. *Machotková, Zahradníček, Zítek, Prusa; Czech Phil. Orch.; Bělohlávek, cond.*
+ ARG 11-12/94: 152

33166. 11 1825-2: SUK—Praga; Dramatic overture; St. Wenceslas meditation; Legend of the dead victors; Towards a new life. *Prague Symphony Orch.; Altrichter, cond.*
+ ARG 7-8/94: 178

33167. 11 1826-2 (6 discs): OSTRČIL—Symphony in A; Sinfonietta. *Prague Symphony Orch.; Belohlavek, cond.*
+ ARG 7-8/95: 164

33168. 11 1828-2: FRANCK—Cello sonata. DEBUSSY—Cello sonata. JANÁČEK—Fairytale for cello and piano. *Bárta, cello; Lapsanský, piano.*
- Fa 1-2/94: 182

33169. 11 1830-2: BRAHMS—Symphony no. 1. DVOŘÁK—Overtures. *Czech Phil. Orch.; Albrecht, cond.*
● ARG 11-12/93: 84
● Gr 6/93: 38

33170. 11 1832-2 (2 discs): BRAHMS—Piano concerto no. 1; Violin concerto. *L. Berman, piano; P. Berman, violin; Prague Symphony Orch.; Altrichter, cond.*
● Fa 9-10/93: 132
- Gr 10/93: 44

33171. 11 1837-2: *Menuhin conducts Czech music.* Music of Smetana, Saint-Saëns, Martinů, and Dvořák. *Michell, violin; Gorokhov, cello; Mulligan, piano; Brno State Phil. Orch.; Menuhin, cond.*
+ Fa 11-12/93: 520

33172. 11 1840-2: SCHUMANN—Cello concerto. BLOCH—Schelomo. RESPIGHI—Adagio con variazioni. *Navarra, cello; Czech Phil. Orch.; Ančerl, cond.* Reissues.
+ ARG 9-10/95: 255

33173. 11 1844-2: BRAHMS—Piano sonata no. 2; Variations on a theme by Paganini; Six waltzes, op. 39. *Simon, piano.*
- ARG 5-6/94: 76
● Fa 5-6/94: 121

33174. 11 1845-2: Music of Mussorgsky, Debussy, and Granados. *Jackman-Zacek Guitar Duo.*
- ARG 1-2/94: 178

33175. 11 1846-2: *Famous opera arias.* Music of Verdi, Leoncavallo, Mascagni, Wagner, and Dvořák. *Randová, mezzosoprano; Brno State Phil. Orch.; Lenárd, cond.*
- Fa 5-6/94: 294

33176. 11 1850-2: MENDELSSOHN—Violin sonatas no. 1-3. *enatý, violin; Hála, piano.*
+ ARG 7-8/94: 132
+ Fa 7-8/94: 175

33177. 11 1851-2: *Eva Urbanová: celeste Aida: famous opera arias.* Music of Verdi, Puccini, Bellini, and Mozart. *Urbanová, soprano; Prague Symphony Orch.; Belohlavek, cond.*
+ Fa 9-10/94: 390

33178. 11 1852-2: Music of Bach, Weiss, Fasch, and Handel. *Brabec, guitar; Virtuosi di Praga; Vlček, cond.*
+ ARG 7-8/94: 209

33179. 11 1855-2: *Homenaje a Andrés Segovia.* Music of Albéniz, Turina, Torroba, Rodrigo, Falla, and Pujol. *Zelenka, guitar.*
● ARG 7-8/94: 209
- Fa 5-6/94: 317

33180. 11 1862-2: FRESCOBALDI—Fiori musicali. *Novenko, organ.*
+ ARG 3-4/94: 97

33181. 11 1865-2 (3 discs): HÁBA—Alois Hába centenary. *Various performers.*
+ Fa 9-10/94: 199

33182. 11 1868-2: *Due virtuosi.* Music of Leclair, Viotti, Spohr, and De Bériot. *Hůla, Kotmel, violins.*
+ Fa 7-8/94: 323

33183. 11 1870-2: SCHULHOFF—Jazz-inspired piano works. *Víšek, piano.*
+ Fa 11-12/94: 372

33184. 11 1871-2: *Mannheim flute concertos, vol. 2.* J. STAMITZ—Flute concertos. FILS—Flute concerto. *J. Válek, flute; Hála, harpsichord; Dvořák Chamber Orch.; V. Válek, cond.*
+ ARG 7-8/95: 202

33185. 11 1872-2: RICHTER—Flute concertos in E minor; in D major. K. STAMITZ—Flute concertos in D major; in G major. *J. Válek, flute; Dvořák Chamber Orch.; V. Válek, cond.*
+ Fa 3-4/95: 275

33186. 11 1873-2: NOVÁK—Lady Godiva; South Bohemian suite; De profundis. *Brno State Phil. Orch.; Vogel, cond.*
● Fa 7-8/95: 264

33187. 11 1874-2 (3 discs): SUK—Chamber works, vol. 1-3. *Various performers.* Reissues.
+ Gr 2/94: 66

33188. 11 1878-2: The unknown Janáček. *Various artists.*
+ ARG 5-6/95: 125
+ Fa 3-4/95: 198
+ Gr 3/95: 86

33189. 11 1896-2: SMETANA—Má vlast. *Czech Phil. Orch.; Talich, cond.* Recorded 1954.
+ ARG 11-12/93: 199
+ Fa 9-10/93: 294
+ Gr 1/94: 56

33190. 11 1897-2: DVOŘÁK—Slavonic dances op. 46, 72. *Czech Phil. Orch.; Talich, cond.* Recorded 1950.
+ ARG 9-10/93: 262
+ Fa 9-10/93: 159

33191. 11 1898-2: DVOŘÁK—Symphony no. 8; Overtures: In nature's realm; Carnival; Otello. *Czech Phil. Orch.; Talich, cond.*
+ Fa 9-10/94: 185

33192. 11 1899-2: DVOŘÁK—Symphony no. 9. SUK—Serenade in E♭ for string orchestra, op. 6. *Czech Phil. Orch.; Talich, cond.* Reissue.
+ Fa 11-12/93: 225

33193. 11 1900-2: DVOŘÁK—Symphonic poems: The water goblin; The noon witch; The golden spinning wheel; The wild dove. *Czech Phil. Orch.; Talich, cond.*
ⱶ Fa 9-10/94: 185

33194. 11 1902-2 (2 discs): DVOŘÁK—Stabat mater. SUK—Asrael. *Tikalová, Krásová, Blachut, Kalas; Czech Phil. Orch.; Talich, cond.* Recorded 1953-54.
+ ARG 1-2/94: 162
+ Gr 12/93: 99

33195. 11 1904-2: SUK—Ripening; A fairy tale. *Czech Phil. Orch.; Talich, cond.* Recorded 1956, 1949.
+ ARG 1-2/95: 256

33196. 11 1905-2: JANÁČEK—Taras Bulba; The cunning little vixen: suite. NOVÁK—Moravian-Slovak suite for small orchestra, op. 32. *Czech Phil. Orch.; Talich, cond.* Reissue.
+ ARG 1-2/94: 197
+ Fa 11-12/93: 225
+ Gr 1/94: 48

33197. 11 1908-2: TCHAIKOVSKY—Symphony no. 6. MOZART—Symphony no. 39. *Czech Phil. Orch.; Talich, cond.*
+ Fa 1-2/94: 332
+ Gr 4/94: 120

33198. 11 1914-2: SMETANA—Festive symphony; Festive overture. DVOŘÁK—Cunning peasant overture. ŠKROUP—Tinker overture. *Czech Phil. Orch.; Sejna, cond.* Reissues.
+ ARG 7-8/96: 202

33199. 11 1915-2: DVOŘÁK—In nature's realm; Scherzo capriccioso. SMETANA—Richard III; Wallenstein's camp; Hakon Jarl. *Czech Phil. Orch.; Sejna, cond.*
+ ARG 3-4/96: 111

33200. 11 1916-2: DVOŘÁK—Slavonic dances. *Czech Phil. Orch.; Sejna, cond.* Reissue; recorded 1959.
+ ARG 3-4/96: 109
+ Fi 4/96: 120

33201. 11 1917-2: DVOŘÁK—Symphony no. 5; Slavonic rhapsodies. *Czech Phil. Orch.; Sejna, cond.* Reissue.
+ ARG 3-4/96: 111

33202. 11 1918-2: DVOŘÁK—Symphonies no. 6-7. *Czech Phil. Orch.; Sejna, cond.* Reissue.
+ ARG 3-4/96: 111

33203. 11 1920-2: FIBICH—Symphony no. 1; At twilight; Romance of spring. *Tikalová, soprano; Kalas, bass; Czech Phil. Orch.; Sejna, cond.* Mono.
+ ARG 5-6/96: 112

33204. 11 1921-2: FIBICH—Symphonies no. 2-3. *Czech Phil. Orch.; Sejna, cond.* Mono.
+ ARG 5-6/96: 112

33205. 11 1922-2: NOVÁK—In the Tatras; Eternal longing. FIBICH—The water goblin; Christmas day. *Czech Phil. Orch.; Sejna, cond.* Reissues.
+ ARG 7-8/96: 165

33206. 11 1923-2: SUK—A summer tale; Meditation on St. Wenceslas. DVOŘÁK—Hussites overtures. *Czech Phil. Orch.; Sejna, cond.* Reissues.
+ ARG 7-8/96: 208

33207. 11 1925-2: SMETANA—Má vlast. *Czech Phil. Orch.; Ančerl, cond.* Recorded 1963.
+ ARG 5-6/94: 141
• Gr 7/94: 60

33208. 11 1926-2: DVOŘÁK—Symphony no. 6; My home; Hussites; Carnival. *Czech Phil. Orch.; Ančerl, cond.* Recorded 1961-66.
- ARG 7-8/94: 98

33209. 11 1930-2: KABELÁČ—The mystery of time; Hamlet improvisation. JANÁČEK—Glagolitic mass. *Domanínská, Soukupová, Blachut, Haken, vocalists; Vodrážka, organ; Czech Phil. Chorus & Orch.; Ančerl, cond.*
+ ARG 9-10/94: 146
• Fa 11-12/94: 267
• Gr 12/94: 140

33210. 11 1931-2: MARTINŮ—Symphony no. 5; Memorial to Lidice; Les fresques de Piero della Francesca; The parables. *Czech Phil. Orch.; Ančerl, cond.* Recorded 1955-59.
+ ARG 7-8/93: 121

• Fa 3-4/93: 217
+ Gr 3/93: 58

33211. 11 1933-2 (2 discs): VYCPÁLEK—Czech requiem; Cantata of the last things of man. *Vocal soloists; Czech Phil. Orch.; Ančerl, cond.* Reissues.
+ ARG 3-4/93: 154
+ Gr 7/93: 82

33212. 11 1937-2: BEETHOVEN—Symphonies no. 1, 5; Leonore overture no. 3. *Czech Phil. Orch.; Ančerl, cond.* Reissue.
• ARG 3-4/96: 214

33213. 11 1938-2: BERLIOZ—Roman carnival overture. LISZT—Les préludes. STRAUSS—Till Eulenspiegel. WEBER—Invitation to the dance. GLINKA—Ruslan and Ludmilla overture. BORODIN—In the steppes of central Asia. TCHAIKOVSKY—1812 overture. *Czech Phil. Orch.; Ančerl, cond.* Reissue.
+ ARG 3-4/96: 214

33214. 11 1939-2: BRUCH—Violin concerto no. 1. MENDELSSOHN—Violin concerto. BERG—Violin concerto. *Suk, violin; Czech Phil. Orch.; Ančerl, cond.*
+ ARG 1-2/96: 95

33215. 11 1941-2: BRAHMS—Symphony no. 1; Tragic overture. *Czech Phil. Orch.; Ančerl, cond.* Reissue.
• ARG 3-4/96: 95

33216. 11 1943-2: MUSSORGSKY—Pictures at an exhibition; Night on Bald mountain. RIMSKY-KORSAKOV—Capriccio espagnol. TCHAIKOVSKY—Capriccio italien. *Czech Phil. Orch.; Ančerl, cond.* Reissues.
+ ARG 7-8/94: 136

33217. 11 1944-2: TCHAIKOVSKY—Piano concerto no. 1. PROKOFIEV—Piano concerto no. 2. *Richter, Baloghová, piano; Czech Phil. Orch.; Ančerl, cond.*
- ARG 7-8/94: 233
+ Fa 5-6/94: 262

33218. 11 1945-2: STRAVINSKY—Petrushka. PROKOFIEV—Peter and the wolf. BRITTEN—Young person's guide to the orchestra. *Schilling, speaker; Czech Phil. Orch.; Ančerl, cond.* Reissue.
□ ARG 3-4/93: 144
+ Gr 3/93: 58

33219. 11 1947-2: STRAVINSKY—Oedipus Rex; Symphony of psalms. *ídek, Soukupová, Berman; Czech Phil. Orch.; Ančerl, cond.* Reissues.
+ ARG 3-4/93: 144
+ Gr 3/93: 58
+ ON 11/93: 44

33220. 11 1949-2: PROKOFIEV—Romeo and Juliet excerpts; Symphony no. 1. *Czech Phil. Orch.; Ančerl, cond.* Recorded 1959.
+ ARG 11-12/92: 179

33221. 11 1950-2: PROKOFIEV—Symphony concertante. SHOSTAKOVICH—Cello concerto no. 1. *Navarra, Sádlo, cello; Czech Phil. Orch.; Ančerl, cond.* Recorded 1965, 1968.
+ ARG 7-8/96: 172

33222. 11 1952-2: SHOSTAKOVICH—Symphony no. 7. *Czech Phil. Orch.; Ančerl, cond.* Recorded 1957.
+ ARG 1-2/93: 149

33223. 11 1953-2: MAHLER—Symphony no. 1. *Czech Phil. Orch.; Ančerl, cond.* Reissue.
+ ARG 3-4/96: 214

33224. 11 1954-2: MAHLER—Symphony no. 9. *Czech Phil. Orch.; Ančerl, cond.* Reissue.
+ ARG 3-4/96: 214

33225. 11 1955-2: HARTMANN—Concerto funèbre. HINDEMITH—Violin concerto; Cello concerto. *Gertler, violin; Tortelier, cello; Czech Phil. Orch.; Ančerl, cond.* Recorded 1955, 1968.
+ ARG 11-12/95: 131
+ Fa 7-8/94: 152

33226. 11 1956-2: BARTÓK—Violin concerto no. 2; Viola concerto. *Gertler, violin; Karlovsky, viola; Czech Phil. Orch.; Ančerl, cond.* Reissue.
+ ARG 11-12/95: 80

33227. 11 1961-2: DVOŘÁK—Symphony no. 9; Te Deum, op. 103. *Beňačková-Čápová, soprano; Souček, baritone; Czech Phil. Orch. & Chorus; Neumann, cond.*
• Fa 5-6/93: 197

33228. 11 1962-2 (2 discs): SUK—Ripening; Asrael symphony; Epilogue. *Soloists; Czech Phil. Orch.; Neumann, cond.* Reissue.
• ARG 3-4/95: 196

33229. 11 1964-2: SUK—Symphony no. 1. OSTRČIL—Calvary. *Czech Phil. Orch.; Neumann, cond.*
+ ARG 3-4/95: 196

33230. 11 1967-2: MARTINŮ—Symphonies no. 3-4. *Czech Phil. Orch.; Neumann, cond.* Reissue.
+ Gr 12/95: 84

33231. 11 1969-2: MARTINŮ—Violin concertos; Viola concerto. *Suk, violin, viola; Czech Phil. Orch.; Neumann, cond.*
+ ARG 7-8/95: 153
+ Gr 11/95: 89

33232. 11 1982-2: DVOŘÁK—The specter's bride. NOVÁK—The storm. *Tikalová, Tauberová, Blachut, Mráz, Jedenáctík, Veverka; Czech Phil. Orch. & Chorus; Krombholc, cond.*
+ ARG 7-8/95: 109
+ Fa 7-8/95: 179

SUPRAPHON

33233. 11 1984-2: Suk—A summer tale; Praga. *Czech Phil. Orch.; Pešek, cond.* Reissues.
+ ARG 7-8/95: 206
+ Gr 8/95: 86

33234. 11 1985-2: Roussel—Evocations; The spider's feast. *Czech Phil. Orch.; Košler, cond.*
+ ARG 9-10/95: 203

33235. 11 1987-2: Dvořák—Symphony no. 9; Carnival overture; Symphonic variations. *Czech Phil. Orch.; Belohlavek, cond.*
+ ARG 1-2/95: 102

33236. 11 1992-2: Brahms—Serenades. *Czech Phil. Orch.; Belohlavek, cond.*
+ ARG 9-10/95: 114

33237. 11 2031-2: Bach—Violin concertos no. 1-2; Concertos for 2 violins, BWV 1043, 1060. *Hudeček, violin; Sitkovetsky, violin & cond.; Virtuosi di Praga.*
● Fa 7-8/96: 88

33238. 11 2121-2: Vivaldi—Cello concertos RV 421, 424, 422, 404, 418; Concerto for 2 cellos, strings, and continuo, RV 531; Concerto for violin, cello, strings, and continuo, RV 547. *Kanka, cello; Remes, violin; Prague Chamber Orch.*
+ Fa 9-10/94: 366

33239. 11 2122-2 (2 discs): Smetana— The two widows. *Šormová, Machotková, Zahradníček, Horáček, Šounová, Švehla; Prague National Theater Chorus & Orch.; Jílek, cond.* Reissue.
+ ARG 11-12/94: 192
+ Fa 9-10/94: 342
+ Gr 10/94: 200

33240. 11 2136-2 (12 discs): The complete Destinn. *Destinn, soprano; orch. acc.* Historical acoustic recordings.
+ ARG 1-2/95: 260
+ Fa 11-12/94: 433
+ Gr 12/94: 186

33241. 11 2137-2: Palestrina—Missa Papae Marcelli; Missa Hodie Christus natus est; Stabat mater. *Czech Phil. Chorus; Veselka, cond.* Reissue.
+ Fa 9-10/94: 283

33242. 11 2138-2: Tomášek—Missa solemnis, op. 81. Vranicky—Mass in E♭ major. *Jonášová, Mrázová, Doležal, Novák; Kühn Mixed Chorus; Prague Chamber Orch.; Kühn, cond.* Recorded 1986.
+ ARG 3-4/96: 196
+ Fa 11-12/95: 404

33243. 11 2139-2: Mendelssohn—Piano trio no. 1. Brahms—Piano trio op. 8 (second version). *Guarneri Trio Prague.*
● ARG 1-2/95: 90
+ Fa 11-12/94: 300

33244. 11 2140-2: Martinů—Comedy on the bridge; Alexandre. *Brno Janáček Chamber Orch.; Jílek, cond.* Recorded 1973, 1982.
+ ARG 1-2/95: 137

33245. 11 2141-2 (2 discs): Dvořák— Saint Ludmila. *Zikmundová, Soukupová, Blachut, Krejčík, Novák; Czech Phil. Chorus; Prague Symphony Orch.; Smetáček, cond.*
+ ARG 5-6/95: 107
+ Fa 3-4/95: 165

33246. 11 2148-2: *Musica Antiqua Citolibensis.* Music of Galina, K.B. Kopriva, Debefe, V.C. Kopriva, J.J. Kopriva, and Lokaj. *Soloists; Prague Symphony Orch.; Prague Chamber Orch.; Prague Radio Chorus; Stárek, Vajnar, conds.*
+ ARG 1-2/95: 236
● Fa 11-12/94: 510

33247. 11 2153-2 (2 discs): Janáček— The excursions of Mr. Broucek. *Přibyl, Jonášová, Švejda, Marsik, Novák; Czech Phil. Orch.; Chorus; Jílek, cond.* Reissue.
+ ARG 7-8/95: 132
+ Fa 3-4/95: 195
+ Gr 2/95: 101
+ ON 4/15/95: 35
+ ON 1/20/96: 32

33248. 11 2155-2: Mozart—Freimaurer Kantaten und Lieder. *Doležal, tenor; Prague Phil. Chorus; Prague Chamber Orch.; Kühn, cond.; Kšica, piano; Pokorný, piano.*
● ARG 5-6/95: 141
● Fa 3-4/95: 238

33249. 11 2156-2: Schnittke—Cello sonata. Rachmaninoff—Cello sonata. Pärt—Fratres. *Bárta, cello; Lapsanský, piano.*
+ ARG 7-8/95: 184

33250. 11 2159-2: Lassus—Psalmi poenitentiales no. 1, 5, 7. *Czech Phil. Chorus; Veselka, cond.* Reissue.
+ ARG 3-4/95: 125
+ Fa 3-4/95: 205

33251. 11 2164-2: Schulhoff—Piano concertos no. 1-2. *Simon, piano; Prague Radio Symphony Orch.; Válek, cond.*
+ ARG 11-12/95: 199
+ Fa 11-12/95: 367
● Gr 8/95: 82

33252. 11 2166-2: Schulhoff—Chamber works, vol. 1. String quartets. *Kocian Quartet.*
+ ARG 11-12/95: 199
+ Fa 11-12/95: 367
+ Gr 8/95: 97

33253. 11 2167-2: Schulhoff— Divertimento; Sextet; Duo. *Kocian Quartet.*
+ ARG 11-12/95: 199

33254. 11 2168-2: Schulhoff—Chamber works, vol. 3. *enatý, violin; Hála, piano.*
+ ARG 5-6/95: 170
+ Fa 3-4/95: 292

33255. 11 2169-2: Schulhoff—*Chamber works, vol. 4.* Cello sonata; Flute sonata; Hot sonata. *Bárta, sello; Foltýn, flute; Koutník, saxophone; Čech, Víšek, piano.*
+ ARG 11-12/95: 199
+ Fa 1-2/96: 301

33256. 11 2170-2: Schulhoff—Chamber works, vol. 5. *Foltýn, flute; Perina, viola; Kumpera, double bass; Novák Trio; Fait, contrabassoon; Kusnjer, baritone; Víšek, piano; Stone, diseuse.*
+ ARG 5-6/96: 189
+ Fa 1-2/96: 301

33257. 11 2175-2: Zelenka—Four psalms. *Vocal soloists; Prague Madrigal Singers & Orch.; Baxa, cond.*
+ ARG 7-8/95: 233
+ Fa 5-6/95: 381

33258. 11 2176-2: *From the time of Rudolf II.* Music of Monte, Orologio, Turini, and others. *Duodena Cantitans; Capella Rudolphina; Michael Consort; Daněk, cond.*
● ARG 9-10/95: 285

33259. 11 2177-2 (2 discs): Smetana— The secret. *Zitek, Horáček, Soukupová, Sounova; Prague National Theater; Košler, cond.* Recorded 1982.
● ARG 9-10/95: 216
+ Fa 11-12/95: 380
+ ON 8/95: 34

33260. 11 2180-2 (2 discs): Smetana— The kiss. *Děpoltová, Márová, Vodička, Zítek, Haken; Brno Janáček Opera; Vajnar, cond.* Reissue.
+ ARG 5-6/95: 179
- Fa 3-4/95: 301
+ Gr 9/95: 106
+ ON 8/95: 34

33261. 11 2182-2: *Court music of the 17th and 18th centuries for wind ensemble.* Music of Philidor, Morin, Lully, Müller, Druzecky, and Fiala. *Ensemble Philidor; Baude-Delhommais, cond.*
+ ARG 1-2/95: 233
● Fa 11-12/94: 471

33262. 11 2185-2 (2 discs): Smetana— Dalibor. *Kniplová, Svobodová-Janků, Přibyl, Jindrák, Švorc, Horáček; Prague National Theater Chorus & Orch.; Krombholc, cond.* Reissue.
+ Fa 9-10/94: 342

33263. 11 2187-2: Schulhoff—*Chamber works, vol. 2.* Divertimento for string quartet; String sextet; Duo for violin and cello. *Kocian Quartet; Talich, viola; Rattay, cello.*
+ Fa 11-12/95: 367

33264. 11 2188-2: BROD—Chamber works. *Kusnjer, baritone; Kachlíková, soprano; Kůda, piano; Stamic Quartet.*
- ARG 5-6/96: 94
+ Fa 11-12/95: 221

33265. 11 2190-2 (2 discs): DVOŘÁK—The Jacobin. *Prusa, Sitek, Tucek; Brno Phil. Orch.; Pinkas, cond.* Reissue.
+ ARG 1-2/95: 101
• Fa 11-12/94: 220
+ Gr 12/94: 153
+ ON 4/15/95: 35

33266. 11 2192-2 (2 discs): MÍČA—L'origine di Jaromeriz in Moravia. *Nowak, Cassidy, Geister, Equiluz, Dearing, Lebeda, Pospisil, Saturová; Le Monde Classique, Wien; Neumann, cond.*
+ ARG 11-12/95: 160
• Fa 7-8/95: 245
+ ON 1/20/96: 33

33267. 11 2195-2: Wind trios by Mozart, Dussek, Devienne, Druzecky, and Krommer. *Novák Trio.*
□ ARG 3-4/95: 246

33268. 11 2201-2 (2 discs): SMETANA—The devil's wall. *Subrtova, Domanínská, ídek, Bednar, Berman, Mráz; Prague National Theater; Chalabala, cond.* Reissue.
+ ARG 11-12/95: 207
+ Fa 11-12/95: 380
+ Gr 11/95: 158

33269. 11 2203-2: TROJAN—Prince Bajaja: Suite; The emperor's nightingale: Suite; Czech and Slovak folk songs. *Hudeček, violin; Drešer, accordion; Brabec, guitar.*
+ ARG 5-6/96: 213
+ Fa 1-2/96: 329

33270. 11 2213-2: Musica in tempore Caroli IV. *Symposium Musicum; Prague Madrigal Singers; Venhoda, cond.*
+ ARG 1-2/96: 226
+ Fa 11-12/95: 459

33271. 11 2214-2 (2 discs): JANÁČEK—Moravian folk poetry; Hukvaldy folk poetry; Silesian songs. *Pecková, mezzo-soprano; Kusnjer, baritone; Lapsanský, piano.*
+ ARG 3-4/96: 130
+ Gr 11/95: 132

33272. 11 2217-2: MOZART—Opera arias. *Pecková, mezzo-soprano; Prague Chamber Orch.; Belohlavek, cond.*
- ARG 11-12/95: 162
• Fa 11-12/95: 315

33273. 11 2233-2: SUK—Spring; Suite; Summer moods; About mother. *Štěpán, piano.*
+ ARG 5-6/95: 182

33274. 11 2239-2: Music of Smetana, Dvořák, Janáček, Tchaikovsky, Prokofiev, Verdi, and others. *Benackova,*

soprano; Czech Phil. Orch.; Neumann, Gregor, conds. Recorded 1981.
+ ARG 7-8/95: 261

33275. 11 2941-2 (2 discs): JANÁČEK—From the house of the dead. *Přibyl, ídek, Souček, Novák; Czech Phil. Orch.; Neumann, cond.* Recorded 1979.
+ ARG 11-12/94: 135
+ Gr 9/94: 115

33276. 11 3029-2: BRIXI—Organ concertos no. 2, 4-5. *Hora, organ; Prague Chamber Orch.; Vajnar, cond.* Reissue.
• Fa 1-2/92: 189
+ Gr 9/92: 45

33277. 11 3183-2: SMETANA—Dreams. SUK—Spring. NOVÁK—My May. *Ardasev, piano.*
+ ARG 7-8/96: 201

33278. 11 3200-2 (2 discs): SMETANA—Libuše. *Urbanová, Vele, Kriz, Podskalský, Cervinka; Prague National Theater; O. Dohnanyi, cond.*
+ ARG 7-8/96: 199
+ Fa 7-8/96: 311
• Gr 4/96: 118
+ ON 12/28/96: 38

33279. 11 3471-2 (2 discs): JANÁČEK—Cunning little vixen. *Hajóssyová, Beňačková, Nowak; Czech Phil. Orch.; Neumann, cond.* Reissue.
• ARG 3-4/93: 97
• Gr 4/93: 115

33280. 11 3619-2: MOZART—Horn concertos; Rondo, K. 371. *Tylšar, horn; Prague Chamber Orch.; Vlček, cond.*
+ ARG 7-8/92: 180

33281. 11 3640-2: SUK—Ripening. *Women's Chorus; Czech Phil. Orch.; V. Neumann, cond.*
• ARG 11-12/92: 217

33282. 11 3907-2: *Compositions with two French horns.* Music of Beethoven, Barsanti, Handel, and Mozart. *Z. & B. Tylšar, horns; Dvořák Chamber Orch.; Pešek, cond.*
+ ARG 9-10/92: 193

33283. 11 4424-2 : MOZART—Piano quartet, K. 478. *Firkušný, piano; Panocha Quartet.*
+ ARG 11-12/95: 165

33284. 11 8016-2 (2 discs): JANÁČEK—Katya Kabanova. *Tikalová, Vich, Komancová, Blachut; Prague National Theater; Krombholc, cond.* Reissue.
• ARG 11-12/93: 131
+ Gr 11/93: 150

33285. 11 8176-2 (3 discs): MARTINŮ—Julietta. *Tauberová, ídek; National Theater Prague; Krombholc, cond.* Recorded 1964.
+ ARG 5-6/93: 108

+ Gr 6/93: 102
+ ON 12/11/93: 44

33286. 11 9101-2: DVOŘÁK—Cello concerto; Piano concerto. *Rostropovich, cello; Maxián, piano; Czech Phil. Orch.; Talich, cond.*
+ ARG 1-2/94: 196

33287. SU 0001-2: DVOŘÁK—Slavonic dances, op. 46, 72. *I. & A. Ardasev, piano, 4 hands.*
+ ARG 3-4/96: 109
+ Fa 11-12/95: 243

33288. SU 0002-2: F. BENDA—Violin concerto in D major. PICHL—Violin concerto, op. 3, no. 1. A. VRANICKY—Violin concerto in C major. *Demeterová, violin; Prague Chamber Orch.; Lajčík, cond.*
+ Fa 11-12/95: 506
+ Fa 7-8/96: 110

33289. SU 0003-2: Bohemorum sancti. *Schola Gregoriana Pragensis; Eben, cond.*
+ ARG 5-6/96: 245
+ Fa 11-12/95: 459

33290. SU 0005-2: STRAUSS—An Alpine symphony. *Czech Phil. Orch.; Košler, cond.*
+ ARG 3-4/96: 188
+ Fa 1-2/96: 310
- Gr 12/95: 94

33291. SU 0006-2: Music of Brahms, Lyadov, Tanc, and Milhaud. *Sözüar, piano.*
+ Fa 11-12/95: 472

33292. SU 0009-2: ZELENKA—Concertos and suites. *Collegium 1704; Leferriere, cond.*
+ ARG 7-8/96: 227
+ Fa 7-8/96: 341

33293. SU 0010-2: HAAS—Study for string orchestra; Overture for radio; Psalm 29. SCHOENBERG—Verklärte Nacht. *Soloists; New Czech Chamber Orch.; Prague Chamber Orch.; Belohlavek, cond.*
+ ARG 3-4/96: 176
+ Fa 11-12/95: 265

33294. SU 0011-2: *Agnus Dei.* Music of Barber, Poulenc, Slavicky, Novák, Strauss, and Bach. *Prague Phil. Chorus; Kühn, cond.*
+ ARG 3-4/96: 248
• Fa 11-12/95: 448

33295. SU 0013-2: HANDEL—Water music suite no. 1; Music for the royal fireworks; Concerto grosso in G, op. 6 no. 1. *Ars Rediviva; Prague Chamber Soloists; Munclinger, Fischer, conds.*
• Fa 1-2/89: 174

33296. SU 0016-2: MYSLIVEČEK—Violin concertos. *Ishikawa, violin; Dvořák*

Chamber Orch.; Pešek, cond.
+ ARG 3-4/96: 161
+ Fa 11-12/95: 322

33297. SU 0017-2: Mozart—Quintet for
clarinet and strings, K. 581. Krommer—
Quintet for clarinet and strings, op. 92.
*Mareš, basset clarinet & clarinet; Stamitz
Quartet.*
+ ARG 3-4/96: 140
+ Fa 11-12/95: 316

33298. SU 0019-2 (2 discs): Dvořák—
The cunning peasant. *Sobehartova,
Děpoltová, Veselá, Kundlak, Vodička,
Zítek, Berman, Prusa; Prague Radio
Symphony Orch.; Vajnar, cond.*
• ARG 5-6/96: 107
• Fa 11-12/95: 242
• Gr 2/96: 100
• ON 1/20/96: 34
+ Op 5/96: 601

33299. SU 0031-2: Suk—Piano music.
Štěpán, piano.
+ ARG 5-6/96: 207

33300. SU 0032-2: Suk—Fantasy-
polonaise; Humoresque in C major;
Moods; Pieces, op. 12; Village serenade.
Štěpán, piano.
+ Fa 11-12/96: 390

33301. SU 0033-2: Blodek—In the well.
*Márová, Šounová, Kocián, Berman, vocal
soloists; Kuhn Mixed Choir; Prague
National Theatre Orch.; Stych, cond.*
Recorded 1981.
+ ARG 5-6/96: 85
+ Fa 1-2/96: 155
• Gr 5/96: 115

33302. SU 0036-2 (2 discs): Fibich—
Šarka. *Děpoltová, Randová, Přibyl, Zítek;
Brno Janáček Chorus; Brno State Phil.
Orch.; Stych, cond.* Reissue.
• Fa 9-10/96: 185
+ Gr 2/97: 107

33303. SU 0038-2: Castelnuovo-
Tedesco—Guitar concertos, op. 99; Op.
160. *Zelenka, guitar; Prague Chamber
Orch.*
• ARG 11-12/96: 110
+ Fa 7-8/96: 143

33304. SU 0040-2 (2 discs): Smetana—
The bartered bride. *Tikalová, ídek, Kovář,
Haken; Prague National Theater;
Chalabala, cond.* Recorded 1959.
+ ARG 5-6/96: 201
+ Fa 5-6/96: 283

33305. SU 0045-2: Janáček—Osud.
*Hajóssyová, Palivčová, Přibyl; Brno
Janáček Opera; Jílek, cond.* Reissue;
recorded 1976.
• ARG 3-4/96: 131
+ Fa 11-12/95: 242
+ Gr 1/96: 103
• ON 1/20/96: 32

33306. SU 0049-2: Duets by Mozart,
Stamitz, Spohr, Rolla, and Halvorsen.
Kotmel, violin; Peruska, viola.
+ ARG 5-6/96: 243

33307. SU 0051-2: Reicha—Clarinet
quintets. *Mareš, clarinet; Stamitz
Quartet.*
+ ARG 7-8/96: 179
+ Fa 7-8/96: 272
+ Fa 9-10/96: 302

33308. SU 0052-2: Zelenka—Requiem,
ZWV 48; Miserere (Psalm 50), ZWV 57.
*Pelarová, Hlavenková, Kožená, Ricter,
Pospisil; Ensemble Baroque 1994; Czech
Chamber Choir; Válek, cond.*
• ARG 3-4/96: 214
• Fa 11-12/95: 433
• Gr 12/95: 134

33309. SU 0064-2: Brahms—Secular
unacc. part-songs. *Prague Phil. Chorus;
Kühn, cond.*
• ARG 5-6/96: 91

33310. SU 0076-2 (6 discs): String
quartets by Beethoven, Dvořák, Suk,
Novak, Janáček, Jaroch, Mozart, and
Smetana. *Smetana Quartet.* Reissues.
+ ARG 5-6/96: 229

33311. SU 0077-2 (2 discs): Smetana—
Dalibor. *Urbanová, Marková, Vodička,
Kopp; Prague National Theater; Košler,
cond.*
+ ARG 7-8/96: 199
• Fa 5-6/96: 283
+ Gr 12/95: 159
+ ON 12/28/96: 38

33312. SU 0080-2: Smetana—Dreams;
Sketches, op. 4-5; Czech dances;
Macbeth. *Rauch, piano.* Reissue.
• ARG 5-6/96: 201

33313. SU 0091-2 (4 discs): Prokofiev—
The seven symphonies. *Czech Phil.
Orch.; Košler, cond.* Reissues; recorded
1976-82.
+ ARG 9-10/96: 182
• Fa 7-8/96: 266

33314. SU 0160-2: Shostakovich—
Symphony no. 13. *Mikulaš, bass; Prague
Symphony Orch.; M. Shostakovich, cond.*
• ARG 5-6/96: 196
+ Fa 5-6/96: 277
• Gr 4/96: 53

33315. SU 0162-2: Beethoven—String
quartet no. 11. Smetana—String quartet
no. 2. Dvořák—Two waltzes, op. 54, no.
1, 4. *Skampa String Quartet.*
+ ARG 9-10/96: 90
+ Fa 1-2/96: 142

33316. SU 0179-2: Dvořák—String
quartet no. 12. Smetana—String quartet
no. 1. *Panocha Quartet.*
+ Gr 2/96: 66

33317. SU 0181-2: Eben—Job. *Thon,
organ; Yegar, narrator.*
+ Fa 7-8/96: 162

33318. SU 0188-2: Fibich—Moods, op.
41, no. 1-44. *Lapsanský, piano.*
• Fa 11-12/96: 245

33319. SU 0189-2: Fibich—Impressions,
part 1: no. 45-85. *Lapsanský, piano.*
+ ARG 1-2/97: 106
+ Fa 1-2/97: 164

33320. SU 0192-2: *Mirabile mysterium.*
Music of Luython, Gallus, De Monte,
Pinello, Zangius, Regnart, and Anon.
*Duodena Cantitans; Daněk, cond.;
Capella Rudolphina.*
+ Fa 11-12/96: 449

33321. SU 0194-2: Rosa mystica. *Schola
Gregoriana Pragensis; Eben, cond.*
+ Fa 9-10/96: 396

33322. SU 0198-2: Smetana—Tone
poems. *Czech Phil. Orch.; Neumann,
cond.; Prague Symphony Orch.; Válek,
Belohlavek, conds.* Reissues.
+ ARG 7-8/96: 201
+ Fa 7-8/96: 159

33323. SU 0199-2: Dvořák—The water
goblin; Midday witch; Golden spinning
wheel; Wild dove. *Czech Phil. Orch.;
Neumann, cond.*
• ARG 7-8/96: 108
+ Fa 7-8/96: 159

33324. SU 0215-2: Janáček—String
quartets no. 1-2. *Panocha Quartet.*
+ Fa 11-12/96: 276
• Gr 11/96: 108

33325. SU 0216-2: Tchaikovsky—Violin
concerto. Prokofiev—Romeo and Juliet:
ballet suites no. 1-2. *Hudeček, violin;
Czech Phil. Orch.; Oistrakh, cond.*
Recorded live 1972.
+ ARG 1-2/97: 181
+ Fa 1-2/97: 157

33326. CO 1018: Janáček—Cunning little
vixen: Suite; Fate: Suite; From the house
of the dead: Suite. *Czech Phil. Orch.;
Jílek, cond.*
+ Fa 1-2/87: 128
+ MA 7/87: 60

33327. CO 1030: Suk—A summer tale.
Czech Phil. Orch.; Pešek, cond.
+ ARG 3-4/87: 55
• Fa 5-6/87: 203
+ HF 11/87: 92

33328. CO 1041: Janáček—Sinfonietta;
Taras Bulba. *Czech Phil. Orch.;
Neumann, cond.*
+ ARG 3-4/87: 25
+ Fa 1-2/87: 128
+ NR 4/87: 5

33329. CO 1056: Martinů—Double
concerto for 2 string orchestras, piano &

timpani; Les fresques de Piero della Francesca. *Růžička, piano; Bouse, timpani; Prague Radio Symphony Orch.; Mackerras, cond.*
+ Fa 1-2/87: 141
+ HF 3/87: 68
+ SR 2/87: 178

33330. CO 1074: *Concertos for violin and oboe.* Music of Bach, Vivaldi, and A. Marcello. *Suk, violin; Adamus, oboe; Suk Chamber Orch.; Vlach, cond.*
• Fa 1-2/87: 54
+ HF 5/87: 61
+ NR 3/87: 8

33331. CO 1090: Honegger—Une cantate de Noël. Poulenc—Stabat Mater. *Zítek, baritone; Beňačková, soprano; Kühn Children's Chorus; Czech Phil. Chorus & Orch.; Pešek, cond.*
• Fa 5-6/87: 140 (Honegger)
+ Fa 5-6/87: 140 (Poulenc)

33332. CO 1091: Fibich—Symphony no. 1; The tempest. *Brno State Phil. Orch.; Vronsky, cond.*
+ DA 9/87: 66
+ Fa 5-6/87: 118

33333. 1111 3195 (LP): *The singing Grancino of Frantisek Posta.* Music of Chopin, Beethoven, Bach, Kuchynka, Saint-Saëns, and others. *Posta, double bass & violone; Hála, piano; Patras, harp; Pitter, theorbo; Mach, double bass.*
+ Fa 5-6/87: 231

33334. CO 1130: Janáček—String quartets no. 1-2. *Smetana Quartet.* Recorded 1979.
+ ARG Fall/87: 43
+ Fa 5-6/87: 111
+ NR 3/87: 8

33335. CO 1150: Janáček—The Danube; Idyll for strings. *Jonášová, soprano; Novák, viola; Janáček Phil. Orch., Ostrava; Trhlík, cond.*
+ ARG Fall/87: 25
• Fa 7-8/87: 132

33336. CO 1152: Dvořák—Cello concerto op. 104. Martinů—Sonata de camera for cello and orchestra. *May, cello; Czech Phil. Orch.; Neumann, cond.*
+ Fa 7-8/87: 96
+ SR 11/87: 183

33337. CO 1326: Moscheles—Piano concerto no. 3; Bonbonnière musicale; Concerto for flute and oboe. *Klánský, piano; Válek, flute; Mihule, oboe; Dvořák Chamber Orch.; Parik, cond.*
+ ARG 11-12/87: 55
+ Fa 7-8/87: 146

33338. CO 1332: Mozart—Clarinet quintet K. 581; Horn quintet K. 407. *Zahradník, clarinet; Langweil, horn; Panocha String Quartet.*
• Fa 7-8/87: 149

33339. CO 1372: Suk—Serenade for string orchestra op. 6; Under the apple tree. *Děpoltová, soprano; Czech Phil. Orch.; Pešek, cond.*
+ ARG Fall/87: 56
+ ARG 11-12/87: 76
+ Fa 9-10/87: 317

33340. SU 1458-2: Dvořák—String quartets no. 11-12; Quartet movement, B. 120. *Panocha Quartet.*
+ ARG 1-2/97: 101
+ Fa 1-2/97: 159

33341. CO 1475: *Compositions with two French horns.* Music of Beethoven, Barsanti, Handel, and Mozart. *Z. & B. Tylšar, French horns; Dvořák Chamber Orch.; Pešek, cond.*
+ Fa 9-10/87: 383
+ NYT 11/8/87: H31

33342. CO 1519: Music of Satie, Poulenc, and Milhaud. *Czech Phil. Orch.; Válek, cond.*
• Fa 3-4/88: 181

33343. CO 1521: Chausson—Concerto for violin, piano and string quartet in D, op. 21. *Suk, violin; Hála, piano; Suk Quartet.*
+ ARG 1-2/88: 20
- Fa 1-2/88: 107

33344. CO 1592: Beethoven—Piano concerto no. 1; Piano sonata no. 14. *Kameníková, piano; Prague Chamber Orch.*
+ DA 3/88: 55
• Fa 11-12/87: 94

33345. CO 1668: Schmidt—Symphony no. 3. *Slovak Phil. Orch.; Pešek, cond.*
+ ARG 3-4/88: 74
- Fa 3-4/88: 182
+ Gr 2/88: 1199
+ Opus 2/88: 46

33346. CO 1669: Martinů—Half time; La bagarre; Intermezzo; Thunderbolt P-47; The rock. *Brno State Phil. Orch.; Vronsky, cond.*
+ ARG 1-2/88: 45
+ Fa 1-2/88: 157
+ Gr 4/88: 1454

33347. CO 1743: Novák—South Bohemian suite, op. 64; Slovak suite op. 32. *Czech Phil. Orch.; Vajnar, cond.*
+ ARG 7-8/88: 47
+ Fa 7-8/88: 214

33348. CO 1744: Bruckner—String quintet in F major. *Kocian Quartet; Maly, viola.*
• ARG 7-8/88: 16
+ Fa 7-8/88: 141
- Gr 4/88: 1469

33349. CO 1746/48 (3 discs): Fibich—Šarka. *Děpoltová, Randová, Přibyl, Zítek; Brno, Janacek Opera; Brno State Phil. Orch.; Stych, cond.*

+ ARG 7-8/88: 23
• Fa 7-8/88: 162
+ Gr 10/88: 670

33350. CO 1787: Vorisek—Symphony in D; Variations for Bravoure op. 14; Introduction et rondeau brilliant op. 22. *Krajný, piano; Prague Chamber Orch.; Parik, cond.*
+ Fa 7-8/88: 277

33351. CO 1788: Dvořák—Serenade for string orchestra op. 22. Suk—Serenade for string orchestra op. 6. *Suk Chamber Orch.; Suk, cond.*
- ARG 11-12/88: 32
• Fa 3-4/88: 102

33352. CO 1853: Dussek—Piano sonata op. 77; Rondo; 12 Etudes mélodiques op. 16: no. 3, 5, 11. *Panenka, fortepiano.*
+ ARG 9-10/88: 39
+ Fa 7-8/88: 157

33353. CO 1854: *Famous encores.* Music of Handel, Telemann, Rossini, Mendelssohn, and others. *Prague Chamber Orch.; Vlček, cond.*
• Fa 7-8/88: 330

33354. SU 1870-2: Schulhoff—Pittoresques; Partita; Jazz etudes; Hot music; Suite dansante in jazz. *Víšek, piano.*
+ ARG 11-12/96: 203

33355. SU 1909-2: Tchaikovsky—Symphony no. 6. Dvořák—Carnival overture. Novák—In the Tatras. *Czech Phil. Orch.; Stupka, cond.* Recorded 1959-65.
+ ARG 11-12/96: 291

33356. SU 1911-2: Smetana—Richard III; Wallenstein's camp; Hakon Jarl. Suk—Meditation on the old Czech chorale Saint Wenceslas; Legend of the dead victors; Towards a new life. *Czech Phil. Orch.; Kubelik, cond.*
+ ARG 11-12/96: 292
+ Fa 9-10/96: 329

33357. SU 1912-2: Foerster—Symphony no. 4 "Easter eve". *Czech Phil. Orch.; Kubelik, cond.*
+ ARG 11-12/96: 292
+ Fa 9-10/96: 187

33358. SU 1913-2: Smetana—Ma vlast. *Czech Phil. Orch.; Sejna, cond.* Recorded 1950.
+ ARG 11-12/96: 290
+ Gr 8/96: 100

33359. SU 1924-2: Martinů—Double concerto; Symphony no. 3. Dvořák—Suite in A. *Panenka, piano; Hejduk, timpani; Czech Phil. Orch.; Sejna, cond.* Reissues.
+ ARG 9-10/96: 161

33360. SU 1928-2: Dvořák—Violin concerto; Romance. Suk—Fantasy. *Suk,*

SUPRAPHON

violin; Czech Phil. Orch.; Ančerl, cond.
+ ARG 1-2/96: 104

33361. CO 1969: A. Reicha—Piano concerto in E♭. J. Reicha—Viola concerto op. 2, no. 1. *Kvapil, piano; Spelina, viola; Brno State Phil. Orch.; Vronsky, cond.*
+ ARG 9-10/88: 75
+ Fa 7-8/88: 233

33362. CO 1970: *Operatic recital.* Music of Giordano, Puccini, and Verdi. *Beňačková, soprano; Czech Phil. Orch.; Gregor, cond.*
• ARG 7-8/88: 84
+ Fa 7-8/88: 288

33363. SU 1988-2: Martinů—Piano concerto no. 2; Ricercari; Estampe; Parables. *Firkušný, piano; Czech Phil. Orch.; Belohlavek, cond.*
+ ARG 9-10/96: 161

33364. SU 1989/91-2 (3 discs): Brahms—Orchestra music. *Czech Phil. Orch.; Belohlavek, cond.* Reissue.
• Gr 7/96: 48

33365. CO 2047: Scriabin—Symphony no. 4; Reverie; Piano concerto. *Ohlsson, piano; Czech Phil. Orch.; Pešek, cond.*
+ Fa 9-10/89: 324

33366. CO 2048: Prokofiev—Romeo and Juliet: Suites no. 1-2. *Czech Phil. Orch.; Válek, cond.*
- ARG 7-8/88: 46
+ Fa 9-10/88: 227

33367. CO 2049: Martinů—Piano quintet no. 2; Three madrigals for violin and viola. *Páleníček, piano; Smetana Quartet; Novák, violin; Skampa, viola.*
+ ARG 7-8/88: 40
+ Fa 9-10/88: 195

33368. CO 2059: Dussek—Piano concertos in D major; in E♭ major. *Novotný, piano; Pardubice State Chamber Orch.; Pešek, cond.*
- ARG 9-10/88: 39
+ Fa 11-12/88: 176

33369. CO 2113: *Horn compositions.* Music of Weber, F. Strauss, Saint-Saëns, and Schumann. *Tylšar, horn; Czech Phil. Orch.; Neumann, cond.*
+ ARG 11-12/88: 105
+ Fa 9-10/88: 168

33370. CO 2143: Dvořák—Symphony no. 1. *Czech Phil. Orch.; Neumann, cond.*
+ ARG 11-12/88: 33
+ Fa 9-10/88: 145
+ HPR 12/88: 77

33371. SU 2160-2: Schulhoff—Symphonies no. 1-2. *Prague Radio Symphony Orch.; Válek, cond.*
+ ARG 9-10/96: 196

33372. SU 2161-2: Schulhoff—Symphonies no. 3, 5. *Prague Radio*

Symphony Orch.; Válek, cond.
• ARG 9-10/96: 196
+ Gr 10/96: 62

33373. CO 2196/97 (2 discs): Dvořák—Water goblin; The midday witch; The golden spinning wheel; The wild dove; A hero's song. *Czech Phil. Orch.; Gregor, cond.*
• ARG 3-4/89: 32
• Fa 3-4/89: 155
+ HF 1/89: 68
+ HPR 3/89: 75

33374. CO 2198: Novák—Nikotina, op. 59. *Brno Madrigal Singers; Brno State Phil. Orch.; Jílek, cond.*
+ ARG 7-8/89: 69
• Fa 5-6/89: 259
+ HF 7/89: 62
+ HPR 3/89: 84

33375. CO 2202: Dussek—Harp concerto op. 15. Krumpholz—Harp concerto no. 5. *Platilová, harp; I Musici di Praga; Eliska, Hrnčíř, conds.*
+ ARG 3-4/89: 33
+ Fa 1-2/89: 158

33376. CO 2253: Dvořák—Symphony no. 2. *Czech Phil. Orch.; Neumann, cond.*
- ARG 1-2/89: 49
• Fa 3-4/89: 155

33377. CO 2254: Dvořák—Serenade in D minor op. 44; Terzetto for 2 violins and viola in C, op. 74. *Collegium Musicum Pragense; Members of the Panocha Quartet; Vajnar, cond.*
+ ARG 3-4/89: 32
+ Fa 1-2/89: 160

33378. CO 2255: Reicha—Woodwind quintets op. 88: no. 2, 6; op. 91: no. 7. *Academia Wind Quintet.*
- Fa 1-2/89: 244

33379. CO 2300: Lalo—Piano trio op. 26. Chopin—Piano trio op. 8. *New Prague Trio.*
+ ARG 3-4/89: 51
+ Fa 1-2/89: 186

33380. CO 2304: Brahms—Symphony no. 1. *Czech Phil. Orch.; Bělohlávek, cond.*
• ARG 5-6/89: 29
+ Fa 5-6/89: 148

33381. CO 2305: Martinů—Serenades no. 1-5. *Prague Chamber Orch.*
+ ARG 1-2/89: 64
- Fa 1-2/89: 205

33382. CO 2306: Vivaldi—Mandolin concertos RV 425, 532; Viola d'amore concerto RV 540; Concerto for lute and 2 violins RV 93. *Brabec, Myslivacek, guitars; Maly, viola; Prague Chamber Orch.; Vlček, cond.*
+ ARG 1-2/89: 101
+ Fa 1-2/89: 289

33383. SU 3001-2 (2 discs): Foerster—Eva. *Děpoltová, Márová, Barová, Vodička, Souček, Petr; Prague Radio Chorus & Symphony Orch.; Vajnar, cond.*
+ ARG 11-12/96: 122
• Fa 9-10/96: 187
+ Gr 10/96: 105
+ ON 12/28/96: 38

33384. SU 3005-2: Shostakovich—Violin concerto no. 1. Sibelius—Violin concerto. Beethoven—Violin romance no. 2. *Kogan, violin; Moscow Phil. Orch.; Kondrashin, cond.; Sitkovetsky, D. Oistrakh, violin; Czech Phil. Orch.; Anosov, Ančerl, conds.* Recorded 1953-1964.
+ ARG 9-10/96: 200

33385. SU 3009-2: *Wind trios.* Music of Haydn, Triebensee, Vent, Beethoven, Vranicky. *Novák Trio (oboe, clarinet, bassoon).*
+ ARG 9-10/96: 253
+ Fa 9-10/96: 430

33386. SU 3014-2: Bruch—Eight pieces for clarinet, viola, and piano, op. 83. Mozart—Trio for piano, clarinet, and viola, K. 498. *Peterková, clarinet; Suk, viola; Hála, piano.*
+ ARG 11-12/96: 104
+ Fa 9-10/96: 167
+ Gr 2/97: 69

33387. SU 3015-2: *The young Bach: organ music and influences of the early years.* Music of Böhm, Pachelbel, Buxtehude, and Bach. *Hollick, organ.*
+ ARG 11-12/96: 249
+ Fa 7-8/96: 95

33388. SU 3016-2: *Songs of winter nights.* Music of Novák, Foerster, Fibich, and Janáček. *Lapsanský, piano.*
+ Fa 11-12/96: 461

33389. SU 3017-2: Grandi—Motets. *Musica Antiqua Prague; Klikar, cond.*
+ ARG 9-10/96: 129

33390. SU 3018-2: Mozart (arr. Wendt)—Don Giovanni; Abduction from the Seraglio. *Philidor Ensemble; Baude-Delhommais, cond.*
• ARG 9-10/96: 172
• Fa 7-8/96: 248

33391. SU 3020-2: Kabelač—Symphony no. 4 "Camerata"; Euphemias mysterion; Reflections; Do not retreat!; Six cradle songs. *Various performers.*
+ ARG 9-10/96: 143
□ Fa 9-10/96: 226

33392. SU 3023-2: Vivaldi—Concertos, RV 108, 540, 542, 554, 558. *Prague Chamber Orch.; Janáček Chamber Orch.; Delogu, cond.; Hudeček, violin; Brabec, guitar; Stívin, recorder.*
+ Fa 9-10/96: 350

33393. SU 3024-2: REICHA—Piano trios no. 1-3. *Guarneri Trio Prague.*
+ ARG 1-2/97: 158
+ Fa 1-2/97: 235

33394. SU 3026-2: MARTINŮ—Symphony no. 6. MAHLER—Lieder eines fahrenden Gesellen. *Kusnjer, baritone; Czech Phil. Orch.; Belohlavek, cond.*
+ ARG 11-12/96: 159
• Fa 9-10/96: 248

33395. SU 3027-2: *Gabriela Benackova in Prague.* Music of Caccini, Mozart, Strauss, Schneider-Trnavsky, Dvořák, and Verdi. *Beňačková-Čápová, soprano; Schneider, piano.* Recorded live 1995.
- ARG 11-12/96: 272
• Fa 9-10/96: 373
• Gr 10/96: 102

33396. SU 3029-2: TELEMANN—Recorder music. *Stivín, Klement, recorders; Válek, flute; Prague Chamber Orch.; Munclinger, cond.* Reissue.
- Fa 11-12/96: 401

33397. SU 3030-2: MAHLER—Lieder eines fahrenden Gesellen; Kindertotenlieder; Symphony no. 5: Adagietto; Fünf Lieder nach Gedichten von Friedrich Rückert. *Pecková, mezzo-soprano; Prague Phil. Chamber Orch.; Belohlavek, cond.*
+ ARG 11-12/96: 155
• Fa 9-10/96: 247
+ Fi 11/96: 125
• Gr 6/96: 85

33398. SU 3039-2: TELEMANN—Suite in A minor; Concertos for 1 and 2 recorders; Fantasies. *Stivín, Klement, recorders; Prague Chamber Orch.; Munclinger, cond.* Part reissue.
+ ARG 1-2/97: 185

33399. SU 3041-2: FOERSTER—Cyrano de Bergerac; Shakespeare suite. *Czech Phil. Orch.; Prague Symphony Orch.; Smetáček, cond.* Reissue.
+ ARG 11-12/96: 122
□ Fa 1-2/97: 164

33400. SU 3049-2: NOVÁK—Signorina Gioventù; Eternal longing. *Brno State Phil. Orch.; Jílek, cond.* Reissue.
• ARG 11-12/96: 174

33401. SU 3050-2: NOVÁK—Nikotina; Toman and the wood nymph. *Brno Madrigal Singers; Brno State Phil. Orch.; Jílek, cond.* Reissue.
+ ARG 11-12/96: 174

33402. SU 3053-2: MOZART—Sinfonia concertante for winds and orchestra, K. Anh. 9; Bassoon concerto. *Hanták, oboe; Kopecký, clarinet; Stefek, horn; Vacek, Bidlo, bassoons; Czech Phil. Orch.; Prague Symphony Orch.; Smetáček, cond.*
+ Fa 11-12/96: 317

33403. SU 3056-2: DVOŘÁK—Tone poems. *Czech Phil. Orch.; Chalabala, cond.* Reissue.
• ARG 1-2/97: 102

33404. SU 3058-2: MARTINŮ—Works inspired by jazz and sport. *Dlouhy, clarinet; Formáček, bassoon; Junek, trumpet; Belcik, violin; Sádlo, cello; Rauch, piano; Prague Symphony Orch.; Vostřák, cond.; Panenka, piano; Prague Wind Quintet; Brno State Phil. Orch.; Vronsky, cond.*
+ Fa 11-12/96: 300

33405. SU 3059-2: BERLIOZ—Symphonie fantastique. *Czech Phil. Orch.; Košler, cond.*
• Fa 9-10/96: 152

33406. SU 3067-2: DVOŘÁK—Piano concerto (arr. by Vilém Kurz, and original version). *Moravec, piano; Czech Phil. Orch.; Belohlavek, cond.; Kvapil, piano; Brno State Phil. Orch.; Jílek, cond.* Reissue.
+ ARG 1-2/97: 101
+ Fa 11-12/96: 239

33407. SU 3071-2 (2 discs): JANÁČEK—The cunning little vixen. *Tattermuschová, Zikmundová, Márová, Kroupa; Prague National Theater; Gregor, cond.* Recorded 1970.
+ ARG 1-2/97: 123
+ Fa 1-2/97: 181
• Gr 1/97: 99

33408. SU 3076-2: MOZART—Piano concertos no. 14, 23, 25. *Moravec, piano; Czech Chamber Orch.; Czech Phil. Orch.; Vlach, cond.* Reissue.
+ ARG 1-2/97: 145
+ Fa 1-2/97: 211

33409. SU 3084-2: *If music be the food of love: songs and recipes prepared by Neil Jenkins and Jan Zacek.* Music of Handel, Beethoven, Schubert, Weber, Novák, and Britten. *Jenkins, tenor; Zacek, guitar.*
+ ARG 9-10/96: 267
- Fa 7-8/96: 352

33410. SU 3091-2: DVOŘÁK—The specter's bride. *Urbanová, Ludha, Kusnjer, vocalists; Prague Phil. Choir; Prague Symphony Orch.; Belohlavek, cond.* Recorded live 1995.
+ ARG 1-2/97: 102
+ Fa 11-12/96: 242
+ Gr 12/96: 139

33411. SU 3097-2: *Vivaldi and his time.* Music by Vivaldi, Bach, and Lotti. *Musica Concertiva.*
+ Fa 11-12/96: 414

33412. SU 3157-2: DVOŘÁK—Serenade for strings. SUK—Serenade. *Prague Chamber Phil.; Belohlavek, cond.*
• ARG 1-2/97: 101
• Fa 3-4/97: 165
+ Gr 4/97: 54

33413. SU 3160-2: ORFF—Carmina Burana. *Kloubová, Doležal, Kusnjer, vocalists; Prague Symphony Orch.; Kühn Mixed Choir; Prague Boys' Choir; Delogu, cond.* Recorded live 1995.
+ Fa 11-12/96: 326

33414. SU 3176-2: BACH—Organ mass, BWV 669-689. *Tuma, organ.*
+ Fa 1-2/97: 90

33415. SU 3178-2: DVOŘÁK—American suite. SHOSTAKOVICH—Violin concerto no. 2. *Kotmel, violin; Czech Phil. Orch.; Altrichter, cond.*
• ARG 11-12/96: 118
+ Fa 1-2/97: 157

33416. SU 3180-2: *Dagmar Pecková and Ivan Kusnjer: Live in Prague.* Arias and duets by Rossini, Mozart, Tchaikovsky, Smetana, Donizetti, Massenet, Berlioz, and Thomas. *Pecková, mezzo-soprano; Kusnjer, baritone; Prague National Theatre Orch.; Stych, cond.* Recorded 1996.
+ ARG 1-2/97: 232
• Fa 1-2/97: 312

33417. SU 3182-2: *Song of love.* Music of Novák, Suk, and Smetana. *Ardasev, piano.*
+ Fa 7-8/96: 382

33418. SU 3186-2: Arias by Dvořák, Smetana, Tchaikovsky, Adam, and others. *Haken, bass.*
+ ARG 1-2/97: 231

33419. SU 3187-2: DVOŘÁK—Violin concerto; Romance, op. 11; Mazurek, op. 49. *Hudeček, violin; Czech Phil. Orch.; Belohlavek, cond.* Reissue.
+ ARG 1-2/97: 101
+ Fa 1-2/97: 157

33420. SU 3189-2: *Ivo ídek: Operatic recital.* Arias by Smetana, Fibich, Dvořák, Janáček, and Martinů. *ídek, tenor; Prague National Theatre Orch.; various conds.*
+ ARG 1-2/97: 231
+ Fa 1-2/97: 314

33421. SU 3196-2: SCHULHOFF—Songs. *Cerné, soprano; Kůda, piano.*
+ ARG 11-12/96: 204
+ Gr 12/96: 128

33422. SU 3197-2: FIBICH—Spring; The romance of spring; At twilight; A night at Karlstein. *Šormová, soprano; Prusa, bass; Prague Radio Symphony Orch. & Chorus; Vajnar, cond.* Reissue.
+ ARG 7-8/96: 111
+ Fa 7-8/96: 159

33423. SU 3209-2 (2 discs): MYSLIVEČEK—Abramo ed Isacco. *Doležal, Korovina, Kim, Czaková, Luchianez, Kusnjer; Kühn Mixed Chorus; Sinfonietta Praha; Parik, cond.*

SUPRAPHON

• ARG 9-10/96: 172
+ Fa 7-8/96: 255

33424. SU 3243-2: Prokofiev—Cello sonata. Stravinsky—Suite italienne. Shostakovich—Cello sonata. *Gorokhov, cello; Melnikov, piano.*
+ ARG 1-2/97: 201
+ Fa 1-2/97: 227

33425. 38C37 7230: Dvořák—Te Deum; Psalm 149; Hymnus. *Soloists; Prague Phil. Chorus; Czech Phil. Orch.; Neumann, cond.*
+ ARG Fall/87: 13
+ Fa 7-8/87: 102

33426. 38C37 7244: Berlioz—Harold in Italy. *Maly, viola; Czech Phil. Orch.; Jílek, cond.*
• ARG 11-12/87: 28
- Fa 9-10/87: 157

33427. 60C37 7307/08 (2 discs): Mahler—Symphony no. 8. *Beňačková, Nielsen, Šounová, Soukupová, Márová, Moser, Schone, Novák; Prague Phil. Chorus; Czech Radio Chorus; Kühn's Children's Chorus; Czech Phil. Orch.; Neumann, cond.*
- Fa 7-8/87: 140

33428. 90C37 7309/11 (3 discs): Smetana—The bartered bride. *Beňačková, Dvorský, Kopp, Novák; Czech Phil. Chorus & Orch.; Košler, cond.*
+ ARG 11-12/86: 80
+ Gr 4/86: 1306
+ NR 3/87: 9

33429. 60C37 7340/41 (2 discs): Mahler—Symphony no. 9. *Czech Phil. Orch.; Neumann, cond.*
• ARG 11-12/87: 50
• Fa 7-8/87: 140

33430. 33C37 7377: Dvořák—Symphony no. 5. *Czech Phil. Orch.; Neumann, cond.*
• ARG 11-12/87: 29
+ Fa 7-8/87: 100

33431. 60C37 7378/79 (2 discs): Dvořák—Stabat Mater. *Beňačková, Wenkel, Dvorský, Rootering; Czech Phil. Chorus & Orch.; Sawallisch, cond.*
• ARG 11-12/87: 28
+ Fa 9-10/87: 194

33432. 60C37 7427/28 (2 discs): Dvořák—Requiem. *Beňačková, Gabriela, Fassbaender, Rootering; Czech Phil. Chorus & Orch.; Sawallisch, cond.*
+ Fa 7-8/87: 98

33433. 33C37 7448: Janáček—Glagolitic mass. *Söderström, Drobková, Livora, Novák; Prague Phil. Chorus & Orch.; Mackerras, cond.*
+ ARG 3-4/87: 25 m.f.
+ Fa 1-2/87: 129

33434. 38C37 7491: Dvořák—Slavonic dances op. 46, 72. *Czech Phil. Orch.; Neumann, cond.*
+ ARG 11-12/87: 26
+ Fa 7-8/87: 97

33435. 33C37 7509: Suk—Praga op. 26; A fairy tale, op. 16. *Czech Phil. Orch.; Pešek, cond.*
+ ARG Fall/87: 56
+ ARG 11-12/87: 76
+ Fa 9-10/87: 317

33436. 33C37 7540: Suk—Symphony in E op. 14; Fantasy in G minor op. 24. *Suk, violin; Czech Phil. Orch.; Neumann, cond.*
+ ARG 11-12/87: 76
+ Fa 9-10/87: 317

33437. 33C37 7565: Dvořák—String quartets no. 12, 14. *Panocha Quartet.*
+ ARG 5-6/87: 22
+ Fa 1-2/87: 101
• NR 2/87: 16

33438. 33C37 7571: Haydn—Violin concerto no. 4. Vanhal—Violin concerto. *Suk, violin; Suk Chamber Orch.; Vlach, cond.*
+ ARG 11-12/87: 37
• Fa 9-10/87: 216

33439. 33C37 7602: Dvořák—Piano quartets no. 1-2. *Suk Trio; Kodousek, viola.*
+ ARG 3-4/87: 18
+ Fa 1-2/87: 102
+ NR 3/87: 8

33440. 33C37 7668: Dvořák—Symphony no. 3. *Czech Phil. Orch.; Neumann, cond.*
+ ARG 11-12/87: 28
+ Fa 9-10/87: 195

33441. 33C37 7702: Dvořák—Symphony no. 9. *Czech Phil. Orch.; Neumann, cond.*
+ ARG 3-4/87: 20
+ Fa 1-2/87: 103
+ MA 5/87: 58

33442. 33C37 7703: Dvořák—Symphony no. 8. *Czech Phil. Orch.; Neumann, cond.*
• ARG 3-4/87: 20
+ DA 7/87: 84
+ Fa 1-2/87: 103
+ MA 5/87: 58

33443. 33C37 7705: Dvořák—Symphony no. 6. *Czech Phil. Orch.; Neumann, cond.*
• ARG 11-12/87: 29
• Fa 7-8/87: 100

33444. 33C37 7831: Ravel—Boléro; Daphnis et Chloé: Suites no. 1-2. *Kühn Mixed Chorus; Czech Phil. Orch.; Pešek, cond.*
+ Fa 1-2/87: 86
+ NR 3/87: 4

33445. 33C37 7910: Dvořák—String quartets no. 10, 13. *Panocha Quartet.*
+ DA 5/87: 62

+ Fa 5-6/87: 111
+ NR 3/87: 8

33446. 32C37 7922: Dvořák—Festival march; Polonase in E major; Polka in B major; Prague waltzes; Waltzes, op. 54 (arr. Burghauser). *Prague Symphony Orch.; Bělohlávek, cond.*
+ ARG 11-12/87: 27
+ Fa 7-8/87: 97

33447. 33C37 7955: Suk—Ripening, op. 34. *Women of the Czech Phil. Chorus; Czech Phil. Orch.; Neumann, cond.*
+ ARG Fall/87: 56
+ ARG 11-12/87: 76
+ Fa 9-10/87: 317

33448. DC-8023: Mozart—Serenade in D, K. 250; Deutsche Tänze K. 510: no. 1-4, 6-7. *Suk, violin; Prague Chamber Orch.; Hlaváček, cond.*
+ ARG 5-6/89: 72

33449. DC-8024: Mozart—Symphonie concertante for violin and viola, K. 364; Duo for violin and viola, K. 424. *Suk, violin; Skampa, viola; Czech Phil. Orch.; Redel, cond.*
+ ARG 5-6/89: 72

33450. DC-8026: Beethoven—Piano concertos no. 4-5. *Panenka, piano; Prague Symphony Orch.; Smetáček, cond.*
+ ARG 5-6/89: 20

33451. DC-8029: Brahms—Concerto for violin and cello in A minor; Tragic overture. Schumann—Cello concerto. *Suk, violin; Navarra, cello; Czech Phil. Orch.; Ančerl, cond.*
- ARG 5-6/89: 26

33452. DC-8031: Dvořák—Symphony no. 9; Carnival overture. Smetana—Moldau. *Czech Phil. Orch.; Neumann, cond.*
+ ARG 11-12/89: 56

33453. DC-8032: Dvořák—Cello concertos (complete). *Sádlo, Chuchro, cellos; Czech Phil. Orch.; Neumann, cond.*
+ ARG 11-12/89: 56

33454. DC-8033: Suk—Fantasy in G minor; Ballad; Four pieces. *Suk, violin; Panenka, piano; Czech Phil. Orch.; Ančerl, cond.*
+ ARG 5-6/89: 93

33455. DC-8034: Tchaikovsky—Violin concerto. Sibelius—Violin concerto. *Ishikawa, violin; Czech Phil. Orch.; Brno State Phil. Orch.; Košler, Bělohlávek, conds.*
+ ARG 5-6/89: 70

33456. DC-8035: Franck—Symphony in D minor; Le chasseur maudit; Les djinns. *Czech Phil. Orch.; Barbirolli, Fournet,*

conds.
- ARG 5-6/89: 51

33457. DC-8037: JANÁČEK—Slavonic mass; Taras Bulba. *Soloists; Czech Phil. Chorus & Orch.; Ančerl, cond.*
+ ARG 5-6/89: 56

33458. DC-8038: BARTÓK—Concerto for orchestra. JANÁČEK—Sinfonietta. *Czech Phil. Orch.; Ančerl, cond.*
+ ARG 9-10/89: 23

33459. DC-8040: Music of J. Strauss, Suppé, and Offenbach. *Czech Phil. Orch.; Neumann, cond.*
- ARG 5-6/89: 110

33460. DC-8041: MAHLER—Symphony no. 1. *Czech Phil. Orch.; Neumann, cond.*
● ARG 7-8/89: 58

33461. DC-8043: BEETHOVEN—Symphony no. 5. SCHUBERT—Symphony no. 8. *Czech Phil. Orch.; Neumann, cond.*
● ARG 7-8/89: 24

33462. DC-8045: HAYDN—Symphonies no. 94, 100-101. *Prague Chamber Orch.*
● ARG 7-8/89: 49

33463. DC-8046: DVOŘÁK—Slavonic dances. *Czech Phil. Orch.; Sejna, cond.*
+ ARG 7-8/89: 40

33464. DC-8047: MOZART—Piano concerto no. 25; Fantasia in C minor. *Moravec, piano; Czech Phil. Orch.; Vlach, cond.*
+ ARG 5-6/89: 69

33465. DC-8048: DVOŘÁK—String quartet no. 12. SCHUBERT—String quartet no. 14. *Prague Quartet.*
+ ARG 7-8/89: 42

33466. DC-8050: BEETHOVEN—Violin sonatas no. 5, 9. *Suk, violin; Panenka, piano.* Also issued as Supraphon 11 0709-2.
+ ARG 5-6/89: 22
+ ARG 7-8/90: 24

33467. DC-8051: DVOŘÁK—Symphony no. 8; In nature's realm overture. SMETANA—From Bohemia's woods and fields. *Czech Phil. Orch.; Neumann, cond.*
+ ARG 11-12/89: 56

33468. DC-8052: BEETHOVEN—Symphony no. 3; Leonore overture no. 3. *Czech Phil. Orch.; Matacic, Ančerl, conds.*
+ ARG 5-6/89: 21

33469. DC-8053: TCHAIKOVSKY—Symphony no. 5. RIMSKY-KORSAKOV—Capriccio espagnol. *Czech Phil. Orch.; Matacic, Ančerl, conds.*
+ ARG 7-8/89: 98

33470. DC-8054: Music of Lalo, Ravel, and Sarasate. *Haendel, violin; Holeček, piano; Czech Phil. Orch.; Ančerl, cond.*
- ARG 5-6/89: 58

33471. DC-8055: RIMSKY-KORSAKOV—Scheherazade. BORODIN—Prince Igor: Polovtsian dances. *Belcik, violin; Czech Phil. Chorus & Orch.; Danon, Smetáček, conds.*
+ ARG 7-8/89: 81

33472. DC-8056: DVOŘÁK—The water goblin; The midday witch; The golden spinning wheel. *Czech Phil. Orch.; Neumann, cond.*
● ARG 5-6/89: 44

33473. DC-8057: HANDEL—Water music suite no. 1; Royal fireworks music. BACH—Easter oratorio: Adagio in B minor; Non sa che sia dolore: Sinfonia. *Ars Rediviva; Munclinger, flute & cond.*
+ ARG 7-8/89: 16

33474. DC-8058: MOZART—Piano concertos no. 21, 24. *Prague Chamber orch.; Badura-Skoda, piano & cond.*
+ ARG 5-6/89: 69

33475. DC-8059: BRUCH—Violin concerto no. 1. MENDELSSOHN—Violin concerto in E minor. *Suk, violin; Czech Phil. Orch.; Ančerl, cond.*
+ ARG 5-6/89: 33

33476. DC-8060: CHOPIN—Preludes (complete). *Moravec, piano.*
+ ARG 7-8/89: 35

33477. DC-8061: TCHAIKOVSKY—Symphony no. 6; Capriccio italien. *Czech Phil. Orch.; Matacic, Ančerl, conds.*
+ ARG 7-8/89: 98

33478. DC-8062: BIZET—L'Arlésienne: Suites no. 1-2. CHABRIER—España. DUKAS—Sorcerer's apprentice. *Prague Symphony Orch.; Czech Phil. Orch.; Smetáček, Almeida, conds.*
+ ARG 5-6/89: 110

33479. DC-8063: MUSSORGSKY—Pictures at an exhibition; Night on Bald Mountain. RAVEL—Bolero. *Czech Phil. Orch.; Ančerl, Baudo, conds.*
+ ARG 7-8/89: 64

33480. DC-8064: *Small Czech musical gems.* Music of Smetana, Fibich, Dvořák, Foerster, Nedbal, and others. *Prague Symphony Orch.; Smetáček, cond.*
● ARG 5-6/89: 110

33481. DC-8065: DEBUSSY—Prelude à l'après-midi d'un faune; Jeux; Images; Danses sacré et profane. *Patras, harp; Czech Phil. Orch.; Baudo, cond.*
● ARG 7-8/89: 37

33482. DC-8066: BACH—Orchestral suites no. 2-3; Concerto for violin and harpsichord in A minor. *Válek, flute;*

Snítil, violin; Hála, harpsichord; Ars Rediviva; Munclinger, cond.
+ ARG 7-8/89: 16

33483. DC-8067: MOZART—Violin concertos no. 3, 5. *Ishikawa, violin; Dvořák Chamber Orch.; Pešek, cond.*
+ ARG 5-6/89: 70

33484. DC-8068: MOZART—Piano concertos no. 14, 23. *Moravec, piano; Dvořák Chamber Orch.; Vlach, cond.*
- ARG 7-8/89: 65

33485. DC-8069: DVOŘÁK—Violin concerto; Piano concerto. *Suk, violin; Kvapil, piano; Czech Phil. Orch.; Brno State Phil. Orch.; Neumann, Jílek, conds.*
+ ARG 5-6/89: 43 (Violin)
● ARG 5-6/89: 43 (Piano)

33486. DC-8070: Music of Mozart, Brahms, and Debussy. *Gilels, piano.* Recorded live 1973.
● ARG 5-6/89: 118

33487. CO 72435: BERLIOZ—Cléopâtre; Symphony funèbre et triomphale. *Vejzovic, mezzo-soprano; Czech Phil. Orch.; Eschenbach, cond.*
+ ARG 3-4/89: 24
- Fa 3-4/89: 111

33488. CO 72437: NOVÁK—Piano quintet op. 12; String quartet no. 1. *Štěpán, piano; Suk Quartet.*
+ ARG 7-8/89: 69
+ Fa 5-6/89: 259

33489. CO 72438: VRANICKY—Aphrodite symphony. TOMÁŠEK—Symphony in D major. *Dvořák Chamber Orch.; Válek, cond.*
+ ARG 3-4/89: 104
+ Fa 5-6/89: 351

33490. CO 72509: MARTINŮ—The parables; Estampes; Overture; The rhapsody. *Czech Phil. Orch.; Bělohlávek, cond.*
+ ARG 5-6/89: 63
+ Fa 3-4/89: 204

33491. CO 72511: VEJVANOVSKY—Serenada; Sonata venatoria in D; Sonata secunda à 6; Sonata vespertina à 8; Sonata à 4, à 5; Serenade in C. *Kejmar, Šedivý, trumpets; Hora, harpsichord & organ; Prague Chamber Orch.; Pešek, cond.*
+ ARG 3-4/89: 101
+ Fa 5-6/89: 341

33492. CO 72542: BRAHMS—Symphony no. 4; Academic festival overture. *Czech Phil. Orch.; Bělohlávek, cond.*
● ARG 5-6/89: 28
+ Fa 5-6/89: 148

33493. CO 72543: ROUSSEL—Violin sonata no. 1. MILHAUD—Violin sonata no. 2. RAVEL—Violin sonata in G major. *Snítil, viola; Hála, piano.*

SUPRAPHON

- ARG 11-12/89: 107
- Fa 9-10/89: 309

33494. CO 72544: ROSETTI—Horn concertos no. 2, 6. *Langweil, horn; Prague Symphony Orch.; Pešek, cond.*
+ Fa 5-6/89: 295

33495. CO 72586: SMETANA—Má vlast. *Czech Phil. Orch.; Bělohlávek, cond.*
+ ARG 7-8/89: 92
+ Fa 9-10/89: 331

33496. CO 72645: MARTINŮ—Czech rhapsody. *Kusnjer, baritone; Kühn Mixed Chorus; Prague Symphony Orch.; Bělohlávek, cond.*
+ ARG 5-6/89: 63
□ Fa 5-6/89: 229

33497. CO 72647: BRUCKNER—Symphony no. 7; Overture in G minor. *Czech Phil. Orch.; Pešek, cond.*
+ Fa 7-8/89: 119
+ HF 7/89: 56

33498. CO 72721/22 (2 discs): *Bach family.* Music of J.S. Bach, W.F. Bach, C.P.E. Bach, J. Christoph Bach, and J. Christian Bach. *Ars Rediviva.*
+ ARG 7-8/89: 10
• Fa 5-6/89: 117

33499. CO 72723: *Czech pastoral partitas.* Music of Masek, Havel, Fiala, Pichl, and others. *Prague Collegium Musicum; Vajnar, cond.*
+ Fa 5-6/89: 410

33500. CO 72746 (3 discs): SMETANA—The secret; Viola. *Soukupová, Šounová, Vodička, Zítek; Prague National Theater Chorus & Orch.; Košler, cond.*
+ ARG 5-6/89: 90

33501. CO 72887: FOERSTER—From Shakespeare; Springtime and desire. *Prague Symphony Orch.; Smetáček, cond.*
+ ARG 11-12/89: 59
+ Fa 7-8/89: 148

33502. CO 72888: NOVÁK—Piano trio, op. 27. SUK—Piano trio, op. 2. FIBICH—Piano trio, F minor. *New Prague Trio.*
• ARG 7-8/89: 69
+ Fa 7-8/89: 207

33503. CO 72890: FIALA—Oboe concerto. KROMMER—Oboe concerto, op. 52. ZACH—Oboe concerto. *Krejčí, oboe; Prague Chamber Orch.; Vajnar, cond.*
+ Fa 7-8/89: 147
+ Fa 1-2/91: 196 (as 10 3624-2)

33504. CO 73079: NOVÁK—Signorina Gioventù. *Brno State Phil. Orch.; Jílek, cond.*
+ ARG 7-8/89: 69
+ Fa 9-10/89: 194

33505. CO 73080: LISZT—Réminiscences de Don Juan; Hussitenlied;

Réminiscences from I puritani. SCHUBERT (ARR. LISZT)—Ständchen; Ave Maria; Der Lindenbuam. *Panenka, piano.*
+ Fa 9-10/89: 236

33506. CO 73081: REICHA—Clarinet quintet op. 89; Horn quintet op. 106. *Zahradník, clarinet; Klánská, horn; Zalud, double bass; Panocha String Quartet.*
+ ARG 9-10/89: 93
+ DA 11/89: 82
+ Fa 7-8/89: 223

33507. CO 73150: BACH—Concertos BWV 1059/35, 1059/156, 1055. *Mihule, oboe; Sláma, viola da gamba; Kimel, oboe d'amore; Ars Rediviva; Munclinger, cond.*
+ Fa 9-10/89: 118

33508. CO 73151: *Czech organ music of the baroque and classicist eras.* Music of Seger, Kuchar, and Zach. *Hora, organ.*
□ Fa 9-10/89: 326

33509. CO 76246: DVOŘÁK—Moravian duets (complete); Na tej nasej strese; Zivot vojensky. *Kühn Mixed Chorus; Bogunia, piano; Kühn, cond.*
+ Fa 5-6/89: 183

SUPRAPHON GEMS

33510. 2 SUP 0001: MOZART—Piano concertos K. 449, 491; Rondo for piano and orchestra K. 382. *Moravec, Štěpán, pianos; Czech Chamber Orch.; Czech Phil. Orch.; Neumann, cond.*
+ Fa 1-2/89: 213

33511. 2 SUP 0002: SIBELIUS—Violin concerto op. 47. BRUCH—Violin concerto no. 1 op. 26. *Ishikawa, violin; Brno State Phil. Orch.; Bělohlávek, cond.*
• Fa 1-2/89: 267
+ Gr 9/88: 423

33512. 2 SUP 0003: DVOŘÁK—Symphony no. 9; Symphonic variations op. 78. *Czech Phil. Orch.; Neumann, cond.*
• Fa 1-2/89: 161

33513. 2 SUP 0004: TCHAIKOVSKY—Violin concerto; Variations on a rococo theme. *Ishikawa, violin; Apolin, cello; Philharmonia Orch.; Prague Symphony Orch.; Košler, Smetáček, conds.*
• Fa 1-2/89: 267 m.f.

33514. 2 SUP 0005: MOZART—Horn concertos no. 1-4; Adagio and fugue in C minor K. 546. *Petr, horn; Musici di Praga; Czech Chamber Orch.; Hlaváček, Vlach, conds.*
• Fa 1-2/89: 215

33515. 2 SUP 0006: MOZART—Serenade no. 7. *Suk, violin; Prague Chamber Orch.; Hlaváček, cond.*
• Fa 1-2/89: 220

33516. 2 SUP 0007: CHOPIN—Nocturnes op. 9, 15, 27, 32. *Štěpán, piano.*
• Fa 1-2/89: 147

33517. 2 SUP 0008: TCHAIKOVSKY—Symphony no. 6; Capriccio italien. *Czech Phil. Orch.; Prague Symphony Orch.; Matacic, Bělohlávek, conds.*
+ Fa 3-4/89: 312
+ Gr 4/88: 1462

33518. 2 SUP 0009: DVOŘÁK—Cello concerto no. 1; Polonaise for cello and piano in A major; The golden spinning wheel. *Sádlo, cello; Holeček, piano; Czech Phil. Orch.; Neumann, cond.*
• Fa 1-2/89: 159
+ MA 1/89: 68

33519. 2 SUP 0010: MENDELSSOHN—Symphonies no. 4-5. *Czech Phil. Orch.; Delogu, cond.*
+ Fa 1-2/89: 207

33520. 2 SUP 0011: TCHAIKOVSKY—Piano concerto no. 1. RACHMANINOFF—Piano concerto no. 2. *Kameníková, Pokorná, pianos; Brno State Phil. Orch.; Pinkas, Waldhans, conds.*
• Fa 3-4/89: 309

33521. 2 SUP 0012: SCHUMANN—Piano concerto in A minor. LISZT—Piano concertos no. 1-2. *Moravec, Kameníková, pianos; Czech Phil. Orch.; Brno State Phil. Orch.; Neumann, Bělohlávek, conds.*
+ Fa 1-2/89: 260
+ MA 1/89: 68

33522. 2 SUP 0014: BRAHMS—Symphony no. 4; Variations on a theme by Paganini. *Kliicik, piano; Czech Phil. Orch.; Fischer-Dieskau, cond.*
+ Fa 1-2/89: 139

33523. 2 SUP 0015: RIMSKY-KORSAKOV—Scheherazade; Russian Easter overture. *Czech Phil. Orch.; Brno State Phil. Orch.; Danon, cond.*
+ Fa 1-2/89: 247

33524. 2 SUP 0016: HAYDN—Symphonies no. 93-95. *Prague Chamber Orch.*
+ Fa 1-2/89: 180
+ MA 1/89: 68

33525. 2 SUP 0017: BEETHOVEN—Piano concerto no. 5; Concerto for violin, cello, and piano op. 56. *Panenka, piano; Suk, violin; Chuchro, cello; Prague Symphony Orch.; Czech Phil. Orch.; Smetáček, Masur, conds.*
• Fa 3-4/89: 94

33526. 2 SUP 0019: SIBELIUS—Symphony no. 5 op. 82; Swan of Tuonela. GRIEG—Peer Gynt suites no. 1-2. *Czech Phil. Orch.; Prague Symphony Orch.; Delogu, Smetáček, conds.*
• Fa 1-2/89: 269
+ MA 1/89: 68

33527. 2 SUP 0020: MAHLER—Symphony no. 2. *Beňačková, soprano; Randová, alto; Prague Phil. Chorus & Orch.; Neumann, cond.*
- Fa 1-2/89: 197
• MA 1/89: 68

33528. 2 SUP 0021: MAHLER—Symphony no. 5. *Czech Phil. Orch.; Neumann, cond.*
- Fa 1-2/89: 197

33529. 2 SUP 0022: CHOPIN—Nocturnes op. 37, 48, 55, 62, 72. *Štěpán, piano.*
• Fa 1-2/89: 148

33530. 2 SUP 0023: DEBUSSY—Prélude à l'après-midi d'un faune; Rhapsodie for clarinet and orchestra no. 1; Jeux; Images for orchestra. *Boutard, clarinet; Czech Phil. Orch.; Baudo, cond.*
+ Fa 1-2/89: 151
+ MA 1/89: 68

33531. 2 SUP 0029: MOZART—Piano concertos no. 19, 27. *Štěpán, piano; Musici di Praga; Hlaváček, cond.*
- Fa 1-2/89: 212
+ Gr 12/88: 1007

33532. 2 SUP 0030: BACH—Toccatas BWV 911-916. *Růžičková, harpsichord.*
• Fa 1-2/89: 109

33533. 2 SUP 0034: HAYDN—Symphonies no. 96-98. *Prague Chamber Orch.*
+ Fa 1-2/89: 180
• Gr 2/89: 1282

33534. 2 SUP 0035: MAHLER—Symphony no. 4. *Hajóssyová, soprano; Czech Phil. Orch.; Neumann, cond.*
- Fa 1-2/89: 197

33535. 2 SUP 0036: MOZART—Serenades no. 10-11; Divertimento no. 6. *Czech Phil. Wind Ensemble; Cerny, cond.*
• Fa 1-2/89: 214

SWEDISH SOCIETY DISCOFIL

33536. SKCD 1: BOLDEMANN—Piano concerto; Sechs kleine Liebeslieder; Morgenstern Sanger. *Faringer, soprano; Achatz, piano; Stockholm Phil. Orch.; Totsuka, cond.*
+ Fa 9-10/89: 153

33537. SCD 1001: ALFVÉN—Symphony no. 1; Legend of the Skerries. *Swedish Radio Orch.; Westerberg, cond.*
+ Fa 7-8/87: 46

33538. SCD 1002: PETTERSSON—Symphony no. 7. *Stockholm Phil. Orch.; Dorati, cond.*
□ Fa 7-8/87: 160

33539. SCD 1003: ALFVÉN—Swedish rhapsody no. 1; The mountain king, op. 37; The prodigal son; Festive music. *Stockholm Phil. Orch.; Royal Opera Orch. (Stockholm); Westerberg, Alfvén,*

conds.
+ Fa 7-8/87: 46

33540. SCD 1004: LARSSON—Violin concerto; En vintersaga: Incidental music; Concertino for violin and string orchestra. *Berlin, violin; Stockholm Phil. Orch.; Westerberg, cond.*
+ Fa 7-8/87: 133

33541. SCD 1005: ALFVÉN—Symphony no. 2. *Stockholm Phil. Orch.; Segerstam, cond.*
+ Fa 7-8/87: 46

33542. SCD 1006: ATTERBERG—Symphony no. 2; Suite for violin, viola and strings no. 3. *Saulesco, violin; Roehr, viola; Swedish Radio Symphony Orch.; Westerberg, cond.*
+ Fa 7-8/87: 49

33543. SCD 1007: *Romantic Scandanavia.* Music of Grieg, Gulberg, Sibelius, Peterson-Berger, and others. *Örebro Chamber Orch.; Hedwall, cond.*
+ Fa 11-12/89: 496

33544. SCD 1008: ALFVÉN—Symphony no. 3; Swedish rhapsody no. 3. *Stockholm Phil. Orch.; Grevillius, Westerberg, conds.*
+ Fa 3-4/88: 60

33545. SCD 1011: LINDBERG—Seven Dalecarlian paintings; Four tunes. *Wickman, clarinet; Lindberg, piano, organ; Socken Trio; Fresk Quartet; Swedish Radio Symphony Orch.; Lindberg, cond.*
□ Fa 11-12/87: 162

33546. SCD 1014: STENHAMMAR—Symphony no. 2. *Stockholm Phil. Orch.; Mann, cond.*
+ Fa 5-6/88: 219

33547. SCD 1015: NYSTROM—Symphony no. 3; Sinfonia concertante for cello and orchestra. *Söderström, soprano; Bengtsson, cello; Swedish Radio Orch.; Westerberg, cond.*
+ Fa 1-2/88: 185

33548. SCD 1016: STENHAMMAR—Serenade op. 31; Stjärnaga, Sverige; Flickan kom ifran sin älsklingns möte; Flickan knyter i Johannesnatten; I skogen; der far ett skep. *Gedda, tenor; Söderström, soprano; Meyer, mezzo-soprano; Eyron, piano; Stockholm Phil. Orch.; Kubelik, Grevillius, conds.*
+ Fa 5-6/88: 219

33549. SCD 1019: ROMAN—Drottningholmsmusiken; Sinfonias for strings in D, in E minor, in B♭; Trio for 2 violins in F; Concerto for violin and strings in D minor. *Phil. Chamber Ensemble; Stockholm Chamber Soloists; Drottningholm Chamber Orch.; Berlin, violin & cond.; Westerberg, cond.*
+ Fa 7-8/88: 233

33550. SCD 1020: LARSSON—God in disguise; Pastoral suite; Concerto for double bass and string orchestra; Orchestral variations. *Ekborg, narrator; Söderström, Sæden, vocalists; Ossoinak, double bass; Martin Lidstam Choir; Swedish Radio Orch.; Stockholm Phil. Orch.; Phil. Chamber Ensemble; Westerberg, Ehrling, conds.*
+ Fa 7-8/88: 184

33551. SCD 1022: DE FRUMERIE—Pastoral suite; Three songs with orchestra; Two songs; Three songs; Chaconne op. 8; Piano trio no. 2. *Meyer, mezzo-soprano; Söderström, soprano; Marelius, flute; Berlin, violin; Olofsson, cello; Eyron, De Frumerie, Sellergren, piano; Swedish Radio Symphony Orch.; Stockholm Phil. Orch.; Westerberg, Ehrling, conds.*
+ Fa 1-2/89: 164

33552. SCD 1023: KARKOFF—Seven pezzi, for orchestra; Six Chinese impressions, for soprano and 4 instruments; Vision; Six serious songs; Three songs; Symphony no. 4. *Dorow, soprano; Meyer, mezzo-soprano; ensemble; Swedish Radio Symphony Orch.; Stockholm Phil. Orch.; Westerberg, Bell, Ehrling, conds.*
+ Fa 3-4/89: 198

33553. SCD 1024: KOCH—Lapland metamorphoses; Impulsi triology; Oxberg variations. *Stockholm Phil. Orch.; Westerberg, cond.*
+ Fa 3-4/89: 198

33554. SCD 1027: LIDHOLM—Poesis per orchestra; Rites; Ritornello. *Stockholm Phil. Orch.; London Symphony Orch.; Blomstedt, Ehrling, Schmidt-Isserstedt, conds.*
+ Fa 3-4/89: 198

33555. SCD 1030: GRIEG—Piano concerto in A minor op. 16; Ballade in G minor op. 24; Wedding day in Troldhaugen op. 65 no. 6; Nocturne in C, op. 54 no. 4; Gangar, op. 54 no. 2; Summer bird, op. 43, no. 4. *Waldeland, piano; Danish Radio Orch.; Westerberg, cond.*
+ Fa 7-8/89: 154

33556. SCD 1032: STENHAMMAR—Sensommarnätter; String quartet no. 3; Two sentimental romances, op. 28. *Lysell, violin; Negro, Waldeland, piano; Borodin String Quartet.*
+ Fa 7-8/89: 254 (Sensommarnätter)
• Fa 7-8/89: 254 (others)

33557. SCD 1033: PETTERSSON—Six songs; Twenty-four barefoot songs. *Rödin, mezzo-soprano; Sæden, baritone; Ostman, piano.*
+ Fa 7-8/89: 210

33558. SCD 1034: Music of Agrell, Linde, Carlstedt, Börtz, and Larsson.

SWEDISH SOCIETY DISCOFIL

Trogé, trombone; Örebro Chamber Orch.; Nilson, Hedwall, conds.
  • Fa 9-10/89: 442

33559. SCD 1035: WIRÉN—Serenade for strings; Sinfonietta in C; Symphony no. 4; Music for string orchestra. *Stockholm Phil. Orch.; Swedish Radio Symphony Orch.; Orebro Chamber Orch.; Westerberg, Ehrling, Hedwall, conds.*
  + ARG 7-8/89: 110

33560. SCD 1036: ALFVÉN—Swedish rhapsody no. 2; En bat med blommor; Pictures from the Skerries; Song of the waves; Champagnevien; Sveriges flagga; Herdsman's song; Skogen sover; Du är stilla ro; Som stärman uppa himmelen sa klar; I stilla timmar. *Saedén, baritone; Göransson, soprano; Höjer, piano; Berlin Symphony Orch.; Swedish Radio Orch.; Kempekören; Siljian Choir; Rybrant, Alfvén, Westerberg, conds.*
  + ARG 7-8/89: 9
  ☐ Fa 7-8/89: 67

33561. SCD 1037: BLOMDAHL—Sisyphos; Chamber concerto for piano, woodwinds and percussion; Symphony no. 3; Trio for clarinet, cello and piano. *Janson, clarinet; Bengtsson, cello; Baekkelund, Leygraf, pianos; Stockholm Royal Orch.; London Symphony Orch.; Stockholm Phil. Orch.; Kojian, Ehrling, conds.*
  + ARG 9-10/89: 33

33562. SCD 1038: EKLUND—Music for orchestra; Fantasia for cello and string orchestra; String quartet no. 3; Small talk. *Norrköpingskvartetten; Marelius, flute; Westlund, clarinet; Olofsson, cello; Swedish Radio Symphony Orch.; Westerberg, Damgaard, conds.*
  + Fa 9-10/89: 196

33563. SCD 1039: NYSTROEM—Songs by the sea; The merchant of Venice: Theatre suite no. 4; Soul and landscape; The midsummer dream. *Rautawaara, soprano; Meyer, mezzo-soprano; Ahnsjö, tenor; Eyron, Schuback, pianos; Stockholm Radio Orch.; Mann, cond.*
  - Fa 7-8/89: 208

33564. SCD 1040: RANGSTRÖM—Miss Julie: Ballet; Legends from Lake Mälaren; Advent; Summer skies: Three excerpts; Divertimento elegaico; King Erik's songs; Villemo, villemo; Notturno. *Söderström, soprano; Meyer, mezzo-soprano; Saedén, baritone; Roos, Eyron, pianos; Stockholm Royal Orch.; Kojian, Westerberg, conds.*
  ☐ ARG 7-8/89: 77
  - Fa 7-8/89: 218

33565. SCD 1041: *Music of a royal family: The Bernadottes of Sweden.* Music of Oscar I, Queen Josephine, Princess Therese, Princess Eugenie, and Prince Gustav. *Various performers.*
  + ARG 1-2/92: 172

33566. SCD 1043: *Women composers.* Music of Szymanowska, F. Mendelssohn, C. Schumann, Andrée, and others. *Funseth, piano.*
  - Fa 9-10/89: 418

33567. SCD 1048: *Romanza.* Music of Sibelius, Stenhammar, Nielsen, and Grieg. *Svanberg, piano.*
  + Fa 9-10/93: 364

33568. SCD 1049: Music of Grieg, Alfven, Rangstrom, Linde, De Frumerie, Petersen-Berger, Weyse, Lange- Muller, Heise, Nielsen, Kjertulf, Thrane, Backer-Grondahl, Dorumsgaard, Kuuia, Merikanto, Hannikainen, Kilpinen, and Sibelius. *Faringer, soprano; Nowels-Stenhoim, piano.*
  • ARG 3-4/96: 253

33569. SCD 1050: *Where love reigns.* Music of Orff, Werle, Kokkonen, Martinaitis, Penderecki, Welin, Nystroem, and Fissinger. *Pro Musica Chamber Choir; Yvgwe, cond.*
  + ARG 3-4/96: 249
  + Fa 9-10/93: 349

33570. SCD 1053: TCHAIKOVSKY—Piano sonatas: in C major, op. posth.; in G major, op. 37. *Negro, piano.*
  + ARG 11-12/96: 223
  • Fa 11-12/96: 398

33571. SCD 1055· Scandanavian choral music. *Göteborg Chamber Choir; Eriksson, cond.*
  + ARG 3-4/96: 249

33572. SCD 1060/1 (2 discs): ROMAN—Complete music for harpsichord. *Nordenfeld, harpsichord.* Reissue.
  - ARG 11-12/96: 190
  • Fa 11-12/96: 349

33573. SCD 1070: SATIE—The complete piano music, vol. 1: Le gymnopédiste. *Höjer, piano.*
  + Fa 11-12/96: 356

33574. SCD 1076: Music about Mary Stuart by Carissimi, Schumann, and Donizetti. *Nordin, soprano; supporting soloists; Stockholm Opera; Guidarini, cond.*
  + ARG 9-10/96: 106
  • Op 8/96: 988

33575. SCD 1078: *The Swedish tenors.* Music of Alfvén, Körling, Sibelius, Peterson-Berger, Norlén, Merikanto, Stenhammar, Beethoven, Sjöberg, Althén, and Bach-Gounod. *Björling, tenor; Royal Orch. of Stockholm; Grevillius, cond.; Gedda, tenor; Stockholm Phil. Orch.; Grevillius, cond.; Winbergh, tenor; Stockholm Ensemble; Liljefors, cond.*
  • Fa 11-12/96: 429

33576. SCD 1080: HAGG—Complete organ music. *Gustafsson, organ.*
  + ARG 11-12/96: 134

33577. SLT 33273 (LP): Music of Rossini, Meyerbeer, Ponchielli, and Flotow. *Soffel, mezzo-soprano; Royal Swedish Chamber Orch.; Liljefors, cond.*
  - Fa 9-10/87: 356

33578. SLT 33275/76 (2 LPs): *Jussi Björling memorial concert.* Music of Grieg, Donizetti, Verdi, Wagner, Bizet, and others. *Various vocalists; Stockholms Ensemblens Symphony Orch.; Liljefors, cond.* Recorded live 1985.
  + Fa 9-10/87: 359
  + HF 1/88: 64 (reviewed by B.Z.)
  - HF 1/88: 64 (reviewed by D.H.)

SYMPHONIA

33579. SY92D17 (2 discs): A. SCARLATTI—Lamentazioni per la Settimana Santa. *Miatello, soprano; Fagotto, tenor; Aurora Ensemble.*
  • Gr 10/93: 100

33580. 91505: Villancicos and oraciones in 17th-century Latin America. *Ensemble Elyma; Garrido, cond.*
  + ARG 11-12/93: 250

SYMPOSIUM

33581. 1036: SCHUBERT—Die schöne Müllerin. *Norton-Welsh, baritone; Kirkwood, fortepiano.*
  ☐ ARG 1-2/89: 86

33582. 1037: *Virtuoso variations for piano duet.* Music of Alkan, Beethoven, Franck, Schubert, and others. *Goldstone, Clemmow, piano 4-hands.*
  + Fa 7-8/89: 390

33583. 1039: HORDER—Forty songs. *Soutter, soprano; Allanson, Murray, baritones; Betteridge, Kirkwood, pianos.*
  + Fa 3-4/89: 189

33584. 1042: *Die Kroll-Jahre.* Music of Beethoven, Wagner, Ravel, Debussy, and others. *Berlin State Opera Orch.; Klemperer, cond.*
  + Fa 5-6/89: 416 m.f.
  + Gr 2/89: 1346

33585. 1043: Music of Weber, Bach, Mozart, Schubert, Rossini, and others. *Berlin Phil. Orch.; Furtwängler, cond.* Recorded 1926-1935.
  + Fa 5-6/89: 419

33586. 1045: *Eugène Ysaÿe.* Music of Wagner, Chabrier, Schumann, Ysaÿe, Fauré, and others. *Ysaÿe, violin & cond.; Decreus, piano; Cincinnati Symphony Orch.*
  + Fa 3-4/89: 381

33587. 1046: Music of Albert, Beethoven, Brahms, Chopin, Liszt, and

others. *Albert, piano & cond.; Pistor, tenor; Staatskapelle Berlin; Berlin Radio Orch.; Seidler-Winkler, cond.*
☐ Fa 9-10/89: 113

33588. 1057: ALKAN—Trois andantes romantiques; L'offrande; Trois études de bravoure; Coeur; Barcarolle. *Rivard, piano.*
- Fa 1-2/90: 85

33589. 1059: ALKAN—Large preludes op. 66 no. 1, 9, 11; Little preludes on the 8 modes of plainchant; Pieces in the religious style op. 72 no. 1-5, 7, 9-11. *King, organ.*
• Fa 9-10/89: 114

33590. 1064: *Lieder recital.* Songs by Schubert and Wolf. *Hammond-Stroud, baritone; Kirkwood, piano.*
• ARG 5-6/90: 148
• Fa 1-2/91: 306
• Gr 1/90: 1363

33591. 1070: *Enrico Caruso: Greatest operatic recordings.* Music of Donizetti, Puccini, Giordano, Verdi, Leoncavallo, Meyerbeer, Massenet, Halévy, Bizet, Franchetti and Ponchielli. *Caruso, tenor; with accompaniment.*
- Fa 5-6/92: 293

33592. 1074: *An album of Victorian song, vol. 1.* Music of Hatton, Loder, Balfe, Bennett, Pearson, and others. *Allanson, baritone; Betteridge, piano.*
- Fa 1-2/91: 371

33593. 1078: Music of Beethoven, Berlioz, Gluck, Mahler, Schubert, and others. *New York Phil.; Concertgebouw Orch.; Mengelberg, cond.* Recorded 1923-1938.
• ARG 9-10/90: 164 m.f.
+ Fa 1-2/91: 406

33594. 1087/88 (2 discs): *Artur Nikisch: The complete orchestral recordings.* Music of Beethoven. Berlioz, Mozart, Liszt and Weber. *Berlin Phil. Orch.; London Symphony Orch.; Nikisch, cond.* Recorded 1913-21.
+ ARG 9-10/92: 213
• Fa 5-6/92: 343

33595. 1091: *Franz Liszt's British Isles tour, 1840-41.* LISZT—Marche héroïque; Grand galop chromatique; Transcriptions and paraphrases of works by Schubert, Rossini, Donizetti and Bellini. *Wakefield, Losemore, pianos.*
+ Fa 3-4/92: 228

33596. 1092: BRAHMS—Handel variations; Andante, ma moderato; Paganini variations. *Petrushansky, piano.*
- Fa 9-10/91: 171

33597. 1093: The Harold Wayne collections, vol. 7. *Garden, Albani, Saville, Mrs. Henry J. Wood, Palliser,*

O'Mara, Bispham, Santley, vocalists. 25 historic acoustic recordings.
+ Fa 9-10/91: 412

33598. 1098/99 (2 discs): SCHUBERT—Winterreise; Aufenthalt; Die Stadt; Der Doppelgänger; Rastlose Liebe; Sei mir Gegrüsst; An die Leier; Du bist die Ruh'; Erlkönig. MUSSORGSKY—Songs and dances of death. *Rothmüller, baritone; Gyr, piano.*
+ ARG 7-8/91: 122
+ Fa 7-8/91: 345

33599. 1101: *Harold Wayne collection, vol. 9.* Acoustic recordings by Felia Litvinne (with Alfred Cortot) and Victor Maurel. Recorded 1902-3.
☐ Fa 3-4/92: 370
+ Gr 10/92: 204

33600. 1103: *Renée Doria.* Arias by Rossini, Herold, Meyerbeer, David, Gounod, Massenet, Rimsky-Korsakov, and Saint-Saëns. *Doria, soprano; various accompaniments.*
+ Fa 3-4/92: 369

33601. 1107: SCHOENBERG—Complete piano music. *Wolpe, piano.*
• Fa 3-4/92: 308
- Gr 10/92: 154

33602. 1125: Music of Messager, Massenet, Thomas, Chabrier, Meyerbeer, and others. *Frugère, baritone; with orch. and piano accomp.*
+ ARG 3-4/93: 197
+ Gr 6/93: 111

33603. 1131: Salon pieces. *Quiroga, violin.* Reissues.
+ ARG 11-12/96: 298

33604. 1136: *Opera in Chicago, vol. 1.* Music of Mendelssohn, Cadman, Del Riego, Strickland, Tosti, and others. *Mason, Garden, sopranos.*
+ ARG 9-10/93: 270
+ Gr 8/93: 90

33605. 1137: Music of Borodin, Mussorgsky, Tchaikovsky, Rimsky-Korsakov, and others. *Koshetz, soprano; Dougherty, piano.*
+ ARG 9-10/93: 266

33606. 1149: *Historic acoustic vocal recordings.* Music of Rossini, Bellini, Donizetti, Verdi, Gounod, Bizet, Mascagni, Massenet, Puccini, and Giordano. *De Lucia, tenor; various accs.* Recorded 1903-08.
+ Fa 7-8/95: 382
+ Gr 1/95: 114

33607. 1159: QUILTER—Songs. *Benton, baritone; Lowe, piano.*
+ ARG 9-10/94: 178

33608. 1170: *Harold Wayne collection, vol. 20.* Music by Donizetti, Verdi, Thomas, Bizet, Massenet, and others.

Anselmi, tenor. Recorded 1907-10.
+ ARG 3-4/95: 277
+ Gr 7/95: 134

33609. 1172: Harold Wayne Collection, vol. 21. *Various performers.*
+ ARG 5-6/94: 218
+ Gr 12/94: 190

33610. 1175: *Ave Maria.* Music of Bruch, Bruckner, Cherubini, Coates, Franck, Gounod, and others. *Segal, soprano; Bowyer, organ; Dudakoff, violin; Keogh, harp.*
- ARG 9-10/94: 263

33611. 1180: WALTON—Façade. WATSON—Dick Whittington and his cat. GORB—Hymns uproarious. *Luxon, baritone; Amit, soprano; Belmont Ensemble; Gilbert-Dyson, cond.*
+ ARG 1-2/95: 203

33612. 1183: *24 aspects of an amorous nature.* Music of Ireland, Bridge, Quilter, Finzi, and others. *Jeffes, tenor; Woodcock, piano.*
+ ARG 11-12/95: 271

33613. 1184: QUILTER—Songs, vol. 2. *Benton, bass; Lowe, Kirkland, piano.*
- ARG 11-12/95: 182

33614. 1189: Arturo Toscanini: early records. *Teatro La Scala Orch.; New York Phil.; Toscanini, cond.*
+ ARG 1-2/97: 233

33615. 1197: *Harold Wayne collection, vol. 27.* Arias from Don Giovanni, Dinorah, Hamlet, Ernani, and others. *Luca, baritone.*
+ ARG 11-12/96: 298

33616. 2200: *Harold Wayne collection, vol. 8.* The London Reds. *Plançon, Rooy, Scotti, Adams, Calvé, Renaud, vocalists.* Historical reissue.
+ ARG 5-6/92: 181

SYRINX

33617. CSR 90101: *La belle époque de la flûte.* Music of Mouquet, Saint-Saëns, Ravel, Demaré, Donizetti, Moscheles and Fauré. *Grauwels, flute; BRT Symphony Orch; Vandernoot, cond.*
+ Fa 7-8/92: 342

33618. CSR 91101: *Glass music from Mozart's time.* Music of Mozart, Naumann, Schmittbauer, Vanhal, Reichardt, Haydn and Beethoven. *James, glass harmonica; Grauwels, flute; Hauwe, oboe; Salzburg Soloists; Leskowitz, cond.*
+ Fa 7-8/92: 344

33619. CSR 91102: UY—Paix sur les champs; Les quatre éléments; Athirsatha; Concerto for bass trombone; Concertante for clarinet. *Instrumental soloists; BRT Symphony Orch.; Vandernoot, cond.*

SYRINX

+ ARG 7-8/92: 240
+ Fa 7-8/92: 316

33620. CSR 91103: *Piazzolla ... Shankar.* Music of Piazzolla, Ginastera, Villa-Lobos, Pla, Garcia Lorca, Bartók and Shankar. *Grauwels, flute; Storms, guitar; Michiels, percussion; Bhattacharya, tabla.*
+ Fa 7-8/92: 343

33621. CSR 92101: sDEVIENNE—Flute concertos no. 2, 7; Symphonie concertante for flute and bassoon. *Grauwels, flute; Walloon Chamber Orch.; Labadie, cond.*
□ ARG 9-10/92: 98
+ Fa 11-12/92: 225

33622. CSR 92102: DROUET—Études célèbres pour la flûte; Fantasy for flute and harp. *Grauwels, flute; Michel, harp.*
+ Fa 7-8/93: 132

33623. CSR 93102: *Le rossignol de l'opéra: French music of the belle époque.* Music of Delibes, Donjon, Génin, Godard, Gaubert, Berlioz, Ropartz, and Gounod. *Grauwels, flute; Callataÿ, soprano; Arimany, flute; Lavoisier, harp; Orch. de Chambre de Waterloo; Waterlot, cond.*
+ Fa 5-6/94: 315

33624. CSR 93104. MOZART— Oboe quartet, K. 370; Adagio for English horn and strings, K. 580a; Oboe quintet, K. 406. *Hauwe, oboe & English horn; Salzburger Solisten; Leskowitz, cond.*
● Fa 7-8/95: 255

33625. CSR 93105: SCHUBERT—Music for flute. *Grauwels, flute; Blumenthal, piano; Storms, guitar; Matison, viola; Drobinsky, cello.*
+ ARG 5-6/94: 137
+ Fa 5-6/94: 242

33626. CSR 94101: *This is not Mozart.* Music of Traeg, Beethoven, Sor, Spohr, and Glinka. *Grauwels, flute; Bressler, violin; Springuel, viola; Herbert, harp; Storms, guitar.*
+ ARG 1-2/95: 215
+ Fa 11-12/94: 501

33627. CSR 94102: Music of Handel, Rossini, Mozart, Bizet, R. Strauss, and Massenet. *Hoffman, mezzo-soprano; New Polish Phil. Orch.; Kowalski, cond.*
● ARG 1-2/95: 241
● Fa 11-12/94: 439

33628. CSR 94103: GLORIEUX—Gallery; Offley encores; Nocturne in Kiev; Divertimento. *Grauwels, flute; Koch, piano; Kiev Chamber Orch.; Glorieux, cond.*
+ ARG 9-10/95: 149
+ Fa 7-8/95: 191

33629. CSR 94106: Music of Villa-Lobos, Brouwer, Lauro, Barrios, Sojo,

Cardoso, and Guimaraes. *Storms, guitar; Strange, maracas; Martins, cavaquinho.*
+ ARG 3-4/96: 230

33630. CSR 94107: WEBER—Grand duo concertant, op. 48. DEBUSSY—Première rhapsodie. BENJAMIN—Le tombeau de Ravel. POULENC—Clarinet sonata. *Roeck, clarinet; Michiels, piano.*
+ ARG 5-6/95: 89
+ Fa 5-6/95: 405

TACET

33631. 5: SCHUBERT—String quartet no. 15; Quartettsatz. *Auryn String Quartet.*
+ Fa 9-10/93: 268

33632. 8: *Unter Donner und Blitz: Coburg New Year's concert I.* Music of the Strausses, and Lanner. *Alt-Wiener Strauss-Ensemble; Kulling, cond.*
+ Fa 9-10/93: 298

33633. 10: BACH—Partitas for solo violin. *Paul, violin.*
+ Fa 9-10/93: 109

33634. 13 (2 discs): BACH—The art of the fugue, BWV 1080. *Koroliov, Hadzigeorgieva, pianos.*
+ ARG 3-4/94: 64
+ Fa 11-12/93: 168

33635. 14: ROSSINI—Petite messe solenelle. *Verebics, Franz, Sacca, Escobar; Kammerensemble des Figuralchors Stuttgart; Moesus, cond.*
+ ARG 1-2/94: 142
+ Fa 9-10/93: 255

33636. 15: BRITTEN—String quartets no. 2-3. *Auryn String Quartet.*
● ARG 1-2/94: 88
+ Fa 9-10/93: 137

33637. 16: MOZART—Lieder. *Verebics, soprano; Végvári, piano.*
● ARG 1-2/94: 128
+ Fa 9-10/93: 222

33638. 17: *The condenser microphone.* Music of Haydn, J. Strauss II, Beethoven, Rossini, Bach, Keril, C.P.E. Bach, Mozart, Schubert, Wolf, Mendelssohn, and Rodgers. *Various performers.*
□ Fa 9-10/93: 392

33639. 18: *Sturm und Drang.* Music of C.P.E. Bach, Schaffrath, Kleinknecht, W.F. Bach, and Beethoven. Readings of literary works by Goethe, Schubart, Schiller, and Beethoven. *Münchner Rokoko Solisten; Traupe, speaker.*
+ Fa 9-10/95: 407

33640. 21: *Beau soir: the virtuoso viola.* Music of Debussy, Vieuxtemps, Paganini, Delius, Kreisler, Bach, Hubay, and Ravel. *Lindemann, viola; Herzfeld, piano.*
+ ARG 1-2/94: 183
+ Fa 9-10/93: 369

33641. 25: TCHAIKOVSKY—The seasons. *Koroliov, piano.*
+ Fa 1-2/96: 320

33642. 26: MENDELSSOHN—Piano trios no. 1-2. *Trio Opus 8.*
● Fa 9-10/93: 216

33643. 30: *Zwischen Barock und Rokoko.* Music of Krebs, Homilius, W.F. Bach, Kittel, and C.P.E. Bach. *Wegele, organ.*
+ ARG 3-4/94: 208
+ Fa 9-10/93: 361

33644. 31: HAYDN—String quartets op. 71. *Auryn String Quartet.*
● ARG 3-4/94: 107
+ Fa 9-10/93: 177

33645. 32: PROKOFIEV—Piano music. *Koroliov, piano.*
+ ARG 1-2/94: 134
+ Fa 9-10/93: 236
+ Fa 1-2/96: 275

33646. 33: MOZART—Symphony no. 25. HAYDN—Symphony no. 39. VANHAL—Symphony in G minor. *Saxon Chamber Orch. of Leipzig; Moesus, cond.*
+ ARG 11-12/93: 158

33647. 34: Music of Blacher, Debussy, Stravinsky, Scriabin, Berg, and Stockhausen. *Zitterbart, piano.*
+ Fa 11-12/96: 463

33648. 36: *What about this, Mr. Paganini: violins of Amati, Guadagnini, A. Guarneri, Horvath, Stradivari, Vuillaume.* Music of Bach, Veracini, Kreisler, Dvořák, Paganini, and Webern. *Gawriloff, violin; Ratner, piano.*
+ Fa 11-12/96: 468

33649. 37: TCHAIKOVSKY—Piano trio, op. 50. *Trio Opus 8.*
+ Fa 1-2/96: 322

33650. 42: MERTZ—Works for 2 guitars. *Duo Favori (Barbara Gräsle & Frank Armbruster, guitars).*
+ ARG 3-4/96: 156
+ Fa 1-2/96: 256

33651. 46: SCHUBERT—Piano sonata, D. 960; Moments musicaux. *Koroliov, piano.*
+ Fa 3-4/96: 273

TACTUS

33652. TC 510001: G. GABRIELI—Organ music. A. GABRIELI—Organ music. *Tagliavini, Tamminga, organ.*
□ Fa 7-8/92: 160

33653. TC 520001: *San Filippo Neri Oratorio.* Music of Arascione, Razzi, and Palestrina. *Progetto Musica; Monaco, cond.*
- ARG 11-12/95: 262

33654. TC 520002: *Cantar alla pavana.* 16th-century canzoni, frottole, and madrigals. *Consort Veneto; Toffano, cond.*
● ARG 1-2/97: 218

33655. TC 521601: PALESTRINA—Madrigals, book 1. *Concerto Italiano; Alessandrini, cond.*
+ ARG 9-10/94: 171

33656. TC 531301: MAINERIO—Balli, book 1. *Veneto Consort; Toffano, cond.*
● ARG 9-10/94: 158

33657. TC 540001: Musica nova (1540). *Tamminga, organ.*
+ ARG 9-10/96: 245

33658. TC 551801: ROTA—Missa Resurrectio Christi; Motets by Perti, Trombetti, and Barbieri. *Cappella musicale di San Petronio; Vartolo, cond.*
● ARG 3-4/94: 221
+ Fa 3-4/94: 297

33659. TC 561304: MONTEVERDI—Sacred music. G. GABRIELI—Four intonazioni. A. GABRIELI—Two intonazioni. *Ensemble concerto; Gini, cond.*
+ Fa 11-12/92: 306

33660. TC 571801: ROSSI—Book 3. *Il Ruggiero; Marcante, cond.*
- ARG 7-8/95: 182

33661. TC 580401: TC 580401: INDIA—Madrigali, arie e balletti. *Ensemble Elyma; Garrido, cond.*
+ Fa 11-12/92: 265

33662. TC 580690 (2 discs): FRESCOBALDI—Fiori musicali. *Vartolo, organ; Female voices of the Cappella Musicale di San Petronio; Nova Schola Gregoriana.*
+ ARG 11-12/92: 121
● Fa 7-8/91: 160
+ Fa 9-10/92: 238
- Gr 1/91: 1389

33663. TC 580691: FRESCOBALDI—Capricci no. 1-12. *Vartolo, harpsichord.*
● Fa 9-10/92: 238

33664. TC 600001: *Canti nel chiostro.* Music from bolognese nunneries 1580-1680. *Cappella Artemisia; Smith, cond.*
+ ARG 7-8/95: 258

33665. TC 600002: MELLI—Lute songs. *Torelli, voice & lute.*
● ARG 11-12/96: 161

33666. TC 630301: COLONNA—Nisi Dominus; Motets; Lamentaions. *Ensemble Arte-Musica; Cera, cond.*
+ ARG 1-2/97: 90

33667. TC 650001: *San Petronio in Bologna.* Music of Franceschini, Torelli, and Gabrielli. *Cappella Musicale of San Petronio; Tölz Boychoir; Avignon Vocal Ensemble; Vartolo, cond.*
+ ARG 3-4/94: 221

33668. TC 660002: A. SCARLATTI—Andate, o miei sospiri; Per un momento solo; Lascia più di tormentarmi; Lontan dalla sua Clori. BONONCINI—Cieco nume, tiranno spietato; Ah, non avesse, no, permesso il fato; Vidi in cimento due vaghi amori; Che tirannia di stelle. *Miatello, soprano; Morini, Fossà, continuo.*
+ ARG 9-10/92: 153
+ Fa 11-12/92: 351

33669. TC 661601: PERTI—Gesù al sepolcro. *Capella musicale di S. Petronio; Vartolo, cond.*
+ ARG 3-4/93: 122
+ Fa 11-12/92: 320

33670. TC 661901: A. SCARLATTI—Cantatas and duets. *Miatello, soprano; Cavina, alto; Fagotto, tenor; Scoppola, flute; Pandolfo, viola da gamba; Sensi, double bass; Alessandrini, harpsichord.*
+ Fa 5-6/93: 310

33671. TC 661903—661904 (2 separate discs): A. SCARLATTI—Motets, op. 2. *Il Ruggiero; Marcante, cond.*
- ARG 11-12/96: 195

33672. TC 680401: DURANTE—Twelve duets for soprano and alto. *Ensemble concerto.*
+ ARG 9-10/93: 115
+ Fa 9-10/93: 157

33673. TC 672203: VIVALDI—Oboe sonatas. *Pollastri, oboe; Vivaldi Consort.*
● ARG 11-12/95: 229

33674. TC 672205: VIVALDI—Concertos RV 88, 94, 99, 101, 103, 107. *Nuovo Quintetto Venice.*
+ ARG 5-6/96: 216

33675. TC 672222/3 (2 discs): VIVALDI—Violin sonatas, op. 2. *I Filarmonici.*
+ Fa 9-10/95: 357

33676. TC 670101/2 (2 discs): ALBINONI—Twelve violin concertos, op. 5. *Trentin, violin & cond.; Le Cameriste.*
+ Fa 11-12/95: 164

33677. TC 672228: VIVALDI—Violin sonatas, op. 5. *I Filarmonici.*
● ARG 5-6/96: 218

33678. TC 672232—672233 (2 separate discs): VIVALDI—Concertos, op. 8. *Pagliani, violin; Pollastri, oboe; I Filarmonici; Martini, cond.*
● ARG 9-10/96: 223

33679. TC 682602: ZIPOLI—Sonate d'intavolatura per cimbalo, part 2. *Vartolo, harpsichord.*
+ Fa 9-10/92: 392

33680. TC 711601: PERGOLESI—Cantatas. *Rossi, soprano; Ensemble Concerto; Gini, cond.*
+ ARG 11-12/93: 164

33681. TC 740202: BOCCHERINI—Sonata a tre (1781). *Galimathias Musicum.*
+ Fa 9-10/93: 129

33682. TC 740203: BOCCHERINI—Quintets for piano and strings no. 1, 5, 6. *Galimathias Musicum.*
+ ARG 3-4/94: 79
+ Fa 1-2/94: 133

33683. TC 740301: CAMBINI—Flute quintets; Oboe quintets. *Accademia Classica.*
● ARG 3-4/95: 87

33684. TC 751901: SALIERI—Overtures; Scherzos; Divertimentos. *Quartetto Amati; Pollastri, oboe.*
● ARG 5-6/95: 163

33685. TC 40012201: *Musica del XV secolo in Italia.* Music of Brassart, Arnold de Lantins, Johannes de Lymburgia, J. Pullois, Pierre Fontaine, Domenico da Piacenza, and Anon. *Ensemble Ars Italica.*
● Fa 11-12/91: 542

33686. TC 53012001: *Firenze 1539.* Music of Corteccia, Festa, Rampollini, Masacone, and Moschini. *Centro di Musica Antica of Geneva; Studio di Musica Renascimentale of Palermo; Schola Jacopo da Bologna; Garrido, cond.*
+ Fa 11-12/90: 429

33687. TC 53030501: CAVALIERI—Nine lamentations of Jeremiah the Prophet; Nine responsories. *I Madrigalisti del Centro di Musica Antica di Padova; Picotti, cond.*
+ ARG 9-10/91: 58
+ Fa 3-4/91: 178
+ Gr 1/91: 1394

33688. TC 56012001: *Musica al tempo del Guido Reni: Sonate, canzoni et madrigali diminuiti.* Music of Frescobaldi, Palestrina, Marini, Selma, and others. *Cadelo, soprano; Gaifa, Manno, tenors; Ensemble Concerto; Gini, cond.*
+ ARG 3-4/90: 142
+ Fa 1-2/90: 410

33689. TC 56031101: MONTEVERDI—Tempo la cetra; Quel sguardo; Interrote; Bel pastor; Con che soavita; Et e pur dunque; Combattimento di Tancredi e Clorinda. *Cadelo, soprano; Gaifa, Manno, tenors; Ensemble concerto; Gini, cond.*
+ ARG 3-4/90: 142
+ Fa 1-2/90: 231

33690. TC 56031102: MONTEVERDI—Se i languidi; Il ballo della ingrate; Il lamento

TACTUS

della Ninfa; Se pur destina. *Ensemble Concerto; Gini, cond.*
   • ARG 11-12/90: 83
   + Fa 9-10/90: 297

33691. TC 56031103: MONTEVERDI—Madrigals, book 7. *Ensemble Concerto; Capella Mauriziana; Gini, cond.*
   + Fa 9-10/90: 297

33692. TC 56130303: MONTEVERDI—Madrigals on Texts of Tasso. *Concerto Italiano; Alessandrini, cond.*
   + ARG 5-6/92: 87
   + Fa 11-12/91: 393

33693. TC 58060701: FRESCOBALDI—Toccata e partite d'intavolatura di cimbalo bk. 1: Toccatas 1-8. *Vartolo, harpsichord.*
   • ARG 3-4/90: 142
   - Fa 1-2/90: 181

33694. TC 63030701/2 (2 discs): COLONNA—Dixit à 9; Beatus vir à 9; Laudate pueri à 8; Laudate Dominum à 8; Magnificat à 8. *Soloists; Tölz Boys Choir; Cappella Musicale di San Petronio Chorus & Orch.; Vartolo, cond.*
   • Fa 9-10/90: 215

33695. TC 65030101: CORELLI—Sonata a tre, v. 1. *Ensemble Aurora.*
   + ARG 3-4/90: 142
   + Fa 1-2/90: 157

33696. TC 65030102: CORELLI—Trio sonatas: op. 1 no. 5, 11-12; op. 2 no. 7, 10; op. 3 no. 4; op. 4 no. 1, 4. *Gatti, violin & cond.; Ensemble Aurora.*
   + Fa 11-12/90: 205

33697. TC 66030601: COUPERIN—Concertos royaux, 1722: Troisième concert; Les goûts-réunis ou Nouveaux concerts, 1724: Neuvième concert intitulé; Il ritratto dell'amore; Quatorzième concert. *Rufa, flute; Randolfo, viola da gamba; Alessandrini, harpsichord.*
   + Fa 11-12/90: 205

33698. TC 67012001: A. SCARLATTI—Bella Madrede' fiori. BONONCINI—Il lamento d'Olimpia; Care luci del mio bene. *Ensemble Aurora.*
   + Fa 11-12/90: 468
   + Gr 4/91: 1881

33699. TC 67200101: VIVALDI—Concertos RV 124, RV 154, RV 302, RV 367, RV 522, RV 578 . *Concerto Italiano; Alessandrini, harpsichord & cond.*
   • ARG 3-4/90: 142
   + Fa 1-2/90: 336

33700. TC 68021901: BACH—Sonatas for viola da gamba BWV 1027-29; Italian concerto BWV 971. *Gini, viola da gamba; Alvini, harpsichord.*
   - Fa 5-6/91: 113
   + Gr 1/91: 1382

33701. TC 71020501: C.P.E. BACH—Viola da gamba sonatas. *Pandolfo, viola da gamba; Alessandrini, harpsichord.*
   + ARG 9-10/91: 35
   + Fa 9-10/91: 143
   + Gr 12/91: 88

33702. TC 74021201: BOCCHERINI—Sonatas for fortepiano with accompaniment of a violin op. 5. *Angeleri, fortepiano; Gatti, violin.*
   + Fa 11-12/90: 177

TAHRA

33703. TAH 101: MAHLER—Symphony no. 3; no. 10: Adagio. *Cervená, alto; Rundfunk Sinfonieorchester Leipzig; Scherchen, cond.* Recorded live 1960.
   + Fa 9-10/93: 120

33704. TAH 102 (2 discs): *L'art de Hermann Abendroth, vol. 1: 1927-41.* Music of Beethoven, Brahms, Handel, Mozart, and Vivaldi. *Leipzig Radio Orch.; Berlin Phil. Orch.; London Symphony Orch.; Cologne Chamber Orch.; Abendroth, cond.*
   • ARG 5-6/94: 200
   • Fa 5-6/94: 348
   • Gr 9/94: 133

33705. TAH 103/5 (3 discs): *Musique et litterature.* Music of Schumann, Beethoven, Mendelssohn, Grieg, and Bizet. *Narrators; Leipzig Radio Symphony Orch.; Scherchen, cond.* Recorded 1960.
   • Fa 3-4/94: 438

33706. TAH 106/7 (2 discs): *Hermann Abendroth, Gewandhauskapellmeister (1934-45).* Music of Bach, Brahms, Handel, Haydn, Mozart, Schubert, and Schumann. *Gewandhaus Orch.; Abendroth, cond.*
   • ARG 5-6/94: 200
   • Fa 5-6/94: 348
   + Gr 9/94: 133

33707. TAH 110/11 (2 discs): MAHLER—Symphony no. 6; Symphony no. 8 (1st mvt.); Kindertotenlieder. *Cervená, alto; Leipzig Radio Symphony; Berlin Opera Orch.; Scherchen, cond.* Recorded live 1960, 1951, 1960.
   - ARG 11-12/94: 152
   + Fa 11-12/94: 289

33708. TAH 113: MOZART—Les petits riens (excerpts); Flute and harp concerto; Eine kleine Nachtmusik. *Hurlimann, harp; Urfer, flute; Winterthur Municipal Orch.; Radio-Beromünster Studio Orch.; Vienna State Opera Orch.; Scherchen, cond.* Recorded 1941, 1951, 1948.
   - Fa 1-2/95: 213

33709. TAH 114/15 (2 discs): BRUCKNER—Symphonies no. 7-8. *Berliner Rundfunk-Sinfonieorchester; Rundfunk-Sinfonieorchester Leipzig; Abendroth, cond.* Recorded 1949 and 1956.

   • ARG 9-10/96: 270
   + ARG 11-12/96: 287
   + Fa 1-2/96: 165
   + Fa 7-8/96: 133

33710. TAH 116: DVOŘÁK—Cello concerto, op. 104. BRAHMS—Symphony no. 3. *Fournier, cello; Orch. della Radio Svizzera Italiana; Scherchen, cond.* Recorded live 1962.
   + Fa 1-2/95: 213

33711. TAH 117—119 (3 separate discs): *Karel Ančerl edition, vol. 1-3.* Music of Haydn, Schubert, Dvořák, Rimsky-Korsakov, and Prokofiev. *Berlin Radio Symphony Orch.; Gewandhaus Orch.; Ančerl, cond.*
   + ARG 7-8/96: 289
   + Gr 11/95: 102

33712. TAH 120: MAHLER—Symphony no. 8. *Matheis, Ilitsch, Anday, Milinkovic, Majkut, Weiner, Oeggl; Vienna Singakademie; Vienna Kammerchor; Vienna Sängerknaben; Vienna Symphony Orch.; Scherchen, cond.* Recorded live 1951.
   • ARG 5-6/96: 267
   • Fa 1-2/96: 247

33713. TAH 121/3 (3 discs): *Karel Ančerl edition, vol. 1.* Music of Beethoven, Mendelssohn, Mozart, Smetana, and Schumann. *Toronto Symphony Orch ; Ančerl, cond.* Recorded live 1968-72.
   + ARG 3-4/96: 214
   • Fa 1-2/96: 408
   • Gr 3/96: 58

33714. TAH 124/5 (2 discs): *Karel Ančerl edition, vol. 2.* Music of Haydn, Franck, Dvořák, and Prokofiev. *Concertgebouw Orch., Amsterdam; Ančerl, cond.* Recorded live 1969-70.
   + ARG 3-4/96: 214
   + Fa 1-2/96: 408
   • Gr 3/96: 58

33715. TAH 126 (3 discs): BEETHOVEN—Orchestra music. *Italian-Swiss Radio Orch.; South German Radio Orch.; Toronto Symphony; Scherchen, cond.*
   + ARG 1-2/96: 240
   + Fa 3-4/96: 129

33716. TAH 129/31 (3 discs): BEETHOVEN—Symphonies no. 3, 9; Violin concerto; Romance no. 1; Coriolan overture; Egmont overture. *Oistrakh, violin; Berlin Radio Symphony Orch.; Czech Phil. Orch.; Leipzig Radio Symphony Orch.; Abendroth, cond.* Recorded 1951-54.
   - ARG 1-2/96: 240
   • Fa 1-2/96: 148

33717. TAH 132/5 (4 discs): *L'art de Hans Knappertsbusch.* Music of Wagner, Bruckner, and Beethoven. *Ludwig, mezzo-soprano; Badura-Skoda, Foldes, piano; NDR Hamburg Orch.;*

Knappertsbusch, cond. Recorded 1960-63.
+ ARG 5-6/96: 261
+ Fa 1-2/96: 410

33718. TAH 136 (2 discs): DVOŘÁK—Piano concerto; Symphony no. 7; Cello concerto; Slavonic dances, op. 72. *Maxián, piano; Rostropovich, cello; Hessian Radio Orch.; Toronto Symphony Orch.; Czech Phil. Orch.; Ančerl, cond.*
+ ARG 3-4/96: 214
+ Gr 3/96: 58

33719. TAH 138: STRAUSS—Don Juan; Death and transfiguration; Till Eulenspiegel's merry pranks. *Leipzig Radio Symphony Orch.; Abendroth, cond.*
+ ARG 9-10/96: 270
+ Fa 7-8/96: 315

33720. TAH 139/40 (2 discs): *Hermann Abendroth, vol. 1.* Music of Gluck, Haydn, Mendelssohn, Mozart, Schubert, and Weber. *Berlin Phil. Orch.; Leipzig Radio Orch.; Berlin Radio Orch.; Bavarian State Orch.; Abendroth, cond.*
+ ARG 9-10/96: 270
• Fa 7-8/96: 316

33721. TAH 141/2 (2 discs): *Hermann Abendroth, vol. 2.* Music of Brahms, Kalinnikov, Schumann, and J. Strauss, Jr. *Leipzig Radio Orch.; Berlin Radio Orch.; Bavarian State Orch.; Abendroth, cond.*
+ ARG 9-10/96: 270
• Fa 7-8/96: 316

33722. TAH 143 (2 discs): BERLIOZ—Les Troyens: Acts 3-5. *Mandikian, Giraudeau, Collard, Depraz; Paris Conservatory Orch.; Scherchen, cond.* Recorded 1952.
• ARG 7-8/96: 283
+ Fa 7-8/96: 111

33723. TAH 147 (4 discs): MAHLER—Symphonies no. 3, 6 (abridged), 8 "Symphony of a thousand": first movement; 10: first movement; Kindertotenlieder. *Cervená, Meinl-Weise, Ekkehard, Müller, Prenzlow, Reinhold, Rehm, Heyer-Krämer, vocalists; Rundfunk-Symphonieorchester Leipzig; Berlin Staatskapelle; Berlin Staatsoper Chorus; Scherchen, cond.* Reissue; recorded live 1951 and 1960.
+ Fa 9-10/96: 249

33724. TAH 148 (7 discs): *Karel Ančerl and the Czech Philharmonic.* Music of Mozart, Brahms, Smetana, Sibelius, and others. *Czech Phil. Orch.; Ančerl, cond.*
+ ARG 7-8/96: 289

33725. TAH 154: MOZART—Concerto for flute and harp; Symphonies no. 40-41. *Laskine, harp; Bourdin, flute; Champs-Elysées Orch.; Scherchen, cond.* Recorded 1953.
+ ARG 7-8/96: 287
• Fa 7-8/96: 247

33726. TAH 162 (9 discs): BRUCKNER—Symphonics no. 1-9. *Concertgebouw Orch.; E. Jochum, cond.; RIAS Orch.; Stuttgart Radio Orch.; Linz Bruckner Orch.; G.-L. Jochum, cond.* Recorded 1944-1984.
• ARG 11-12/96: 286
+ Fi 6/96: 127

33727. TAH 175/8 (4 discs): *Pierre Monteux in Amsterdam.* Music of Berlioz, Brahms, Sibelius, and Stravinsky. *Concertgebouw Orch.; Monteux, cond.*
• ARG 1-2/97: 233
+ Fa 11-12/96: 489
+ Fi 10/96: 139

33728. TAH 185/9 (5 discs): *Hommage à Hermann Scherchen, vol. 1.* Music of Bach, Schoenberg, Bartók, Beethoven, Berlioz, Kalinnikov, Krenek, Prokofiev, and Verdi. *Various ensembles; Scherchen, cond.*
+ ARG 1-2/97: 233
+ Fa 11-12/96: 478

33729. FURT 1001: BRAHMS—Symphony no. 1; Variations on a theme by Haydn. *North German Radio Orch.; Furtwängler, cond.* Recorded live 1951.
+ Fa 5-6/95: 150
+ Gr 3/95: 118

33730. FURT 1003: BEETHOVEN—Symphony no. 9. *Schwarzkopf, Cavelti, Haefliger, Edelmann; Lucerne Festival Chorus; Philharmonia Orch.; Furtwängler, cond.* Recorded 1954.
+ ARG 9-10/96: 273

33731. FURT 1006: BRAHMS—Piano concerto no. 2; Symphony no. 1, finale. *Aeschbacher, piano; Berlin Phil. Orch.; Furtwängler, cond.* Recorded live 1943, 1945.
+ Fa 5-6/95: 147

33732. TAH 1008: BACH—Art of fugue. *CBC Toronto Chamber Orch.; Scherchen, cond.* Recorded 1965.
+ ARG 7-8/96: 68

33733. FURT 1012/3 (2 discs): BRAHMS—Symphony no. 1; Variations on a theme by Haydn. BEETHOVEN—Leonore overture no. 3; Symphony no. 1; String quartet no. 13: Cavatina. *Concertgebouw Orch. of Amsterdam; Vienna Phil. Orch.; Berlin Phil. Orch.; Furtwängler, cond.*
□ ARG 9-10/96: 270
• Fa 5-6/96: 114

TALENT

33734. DPM 2910 04: MOZART—Sonatas for piano K. 439b (complete). *Miyazawa, piano.*
+ Fa 1-2/90: 245

33735. DPM 2910 05: SCHUBERT—Violin sonatas no. 1-3. *Bobesco, violin; Miyazawa, piano.*
+ Fa 1-2/90: 293

33736. DPM 2910 08: WEBER—Clarinet concertos: no. 1-2; Concertino for clarinet. *Boeykens, clarinet; Bulgarian National Broadcast Symphony Orch.; Antwerp Phil. Orch.; Kazandzhiev, Bloomfield, conds.*
+ Fa 1-2/90: 346
- Fa 5-6/95: 377

33737. DPM 2910 09: WEBER—Clarinet quintet; Variations for clarinet and piano op. 33; Introduction, theme & variations for clarinet and string quartet; Grand duo concertante for clarinet and piano. *Boeykens, clarinet; Via Nova String Quartet; Groslot, piano.*
+ Fa 1-2/90: 346
- Fa 5-6/95: 377

33738. DPM 2910 10: ANONYMOUS—Gregorian chant: Laudes Mariae. *Schola Gregoriana of the Bruges Cathedral; Deruwe, cond.*
- Fa 1-2/90: 372

33739. DOM 2910 11: SHOSTAKOVICH—Cello concertos no. 1-2. *Spanoghe, cello; Sofia Soloists; Tabakov, cond.*
• Fa 7-8/94: 240

33740. DOM 2910 13: VIOTTI—Violin concertos no. 22-23. *Bobesco, violin; Staatliche Philharmonie Rheinland-Pfalz; Redel, cond.*
• Fa 9-10/94: 365

33741. DOM 2910 14: *French sonatas for cello and piano, vol. 1.* Biarent—Cello sonata. Chausson—PIECE. MAGNARD—CELLO SONATA. DROBINSKY, ANDERSEN, CELLOS; RABINOVITCH, COND.
+ ARG 7-8/94: 206
+ Fa 9-10/94: 413

33742. DOM 2910 15 (2 discs): CHERUBINI—Sonatas for keyboard, no. 1-6. *Andersen, fortepiano & piano.*
• ARG 7-8/95: 101
• Fa 7-8/95: 156

33743. DOM 2910 16: PLEYEL—Six duets for 2 violins, op. 24. *Bobesco, Rubenstein, violins.*
• Fa 9-10/94: 365

33744. DOM 2910 19: NAZARETH—Piano music. *Ferman, piano.*
+ Fa 3-4/95: 244

33745. DOM 2910 25: CASSADO—Solo cello suite; Cello sonata; Sonata nello stilo antico spagnuolo; Danse; Lamento; Requiebos. *Spanoghe, cello; Groote, piano.*
+ ARG 7-8/94: 89

33746. DOM 2910 30: TCHAIKOVSKY—Works for violin and piano. *Nagata, violin; Elena Gilels, piano.*
• Fa 7-8/94: 262

33747. DOM 2910 35: Cello sonatas by Jongen, Vierne, and Tournemire.

TALENT

Spanoghe, cello; Groote, piano.
+ ARG 9-10/96: 240

33748. DOM 2910 36: PLEYEL—Clarinet concerto in B♭; Flute concertos in C and G. *Lethiec, clarinet; Jensen, flute; South Jutland Symphony Orch.; Wallez, cond.*
• Fa 7-8/94: 201

33749. DOM 2910 37: Clarinet quintets by Hummel, Vanhal, and Kreutzer. *Lethiec, clarinet; New Pasquier Trio.*
+ ARG 1-2/96: 210

33750. DOM 2910 41: PIAZZOLLA—Tango clásicó. *Vigne, piano.*
+ Fa 7-8/95: 275

33751. DOM 2910 50: GOSSEC—Flute quartets. *Nicolet, flute; R. Pasquier, violin; B. Pasquier, viola; Pidoux, cello.*
+ ARG 9-10/96: 128

TALENTS

33752. 15244: BACH—Well-tempered clavier, book 1: no. 13-18. Mozart—Rondo in A minor. Beethoven—Piano sonata no. 24. *Neuhaus, piano.* Recorded 1950-52.
+ ARG 11-12/96: 297

33753. 16007: Russian songs. *Obraztsova, mezzo-soprano; Russian Folk Instruments Academic Orch.; Nekrasov, cond.*
+ ARG 7-8/96: 279

33754. 16203: BOCCHERINI—Cello concerto. SCHUMANN—Cello concerto. TCHAIKOVSKY—Rococo variations. *Shakhovskaya, cello; Moscow Symphony Orch.; Kondrashin, cond.; Moscow Chamber Orch.; Markiz, cond.*
• ARG 1-2/97: 201

TALL POPPIES

33755. TP 001: Piano music for children by Bach, Mozart, Tchaikovsky, Schubert, Prokofiev, and others. *Tozer, piano.*
• Gr 12/92: 108

33756. TP 002: Music of Vine, Wesley-Smith, Westlake, Whitehead, and Isaacs. *Australia Ensemble.*
+ Gr 7/92: 74

33757. TP 003: Music of Ibert, Fauré, Ravel, Gossec, Coste, and others. *Taylor, flute; Kain, guitar.*
+ Gr 9/92: 122

33758. TP 011: SCHUBERT—String quintet; Der Hirt auf dem Felsen. *Bates, soprano; Australia Ensemble.*
+ Gr 7/92: 73

33759. TP 023: SCHUMANN—Liederkreis, op. 24, op. 39; Dichterliebe. *English, tenor; Smalley, piano.*
- ARG 9-10/96: 197

33760. TP 025: CAGE—Twenty sonatas and interludes; Music for Marcel Duchamp; The wonderful widow of Eighteen Springs. *English, tenor; Butterley, prepared piano.*
+ Gr 10/94: 157

33761. TP 029: MOZART—Flute quartets. *Australia Ensemble.*
+ Gr 7/94: 72

33762. TP 032: PROKOFIEV—Cello sonata. CARTER—Cello sonata. *Pereira, cello; Moore, piano.*
+ ARG 5-6/96: 166

33763. TP 035: LENTZ—Caeli enarrant no. 4-5. *Lentz, Booth, violins; Wicks, viola; Morrison, cello; Marie, piano.*
- ARG 3-4/95: 126

33764. TP 037: *Notations.* Music of Henderson, Butterley, Boulez, Dench, and others. *McCallum, piano.*
+ ARG 5-6/95: 214

33765. TP 039: *Windows in time.* Music of Xenakis, Bright, Dean, Smith, Cresswell, and Rue. *AustraLYSIS; Stanhope, cond.*
+ ARG 5-6/96: 279

33766. TP 040: *Stroke.* Music of Smetanin, Ford, Brophy, Yu, and others. *Moore, piano.*
+ ARG 7-8/96: 297

33767. TP 042: Concertos by Haydn, Foerster, Telemann, Teyber, and others. *McDonald, horn; Academy of Melbourne; Kelly, cond.*
+ ARG 7-8/96: 244

33768. TP 047: WESTLAKE—Chamber music. *Various performers.*
+ ARG 9-10/94: 220

33769. TP 051: EDWARDS—Flower songs; Etymalong; Ecstatic dance; Tower of remoteness; Ulpitta; Prelude and dragonfly dance; Kumari; Marimba dances. *Various performers.*
+ ARG 7-8/96: 298

33770. TP 053: FORD—The art of puffing; Sacred places; Pastoral; Whispers. *Duo Contemporain; English, tenor; Griffith University Ensemble; Savage, Ford, conds.; Tasmanian Symphony Chamber Players; Delpratt, soprano.*
□ ARG 1-2/97: 245

33771. TP 054: JOSQUIN—Missa Pange lingua; Motets. *Sydney Chamber Choir; Routley, cond.*
+ ARG 3-4/95: 119

33772. TP 055: ALKAN—Etudes in all the major keys, op. 35. *McCallum, piano.*
+ ARG 5-6/95: 69
+ Fa 5-6/95: 116

33773. TP 056: *Souvenir.* Music of Bridge, Martinů, Suk, Reger, Kreisler, and others. *Wood, violin; Bollard, piano.*
+ ARG 5-6/96: 243

33774. TP 058: Music of Williamson, Kerry, Humble, Sculthorpe, Smalley, and Parker. *Munro, piano.*
+ ARG 3-4/95: 243

33775. TP 060: Australian piano music, vol. 6. *Smalley, piano.*
• ARG 5-6/96: 241

33776. TP 064: *The green CD.* Environmentally friendly Australian choral music. *Song Co. and Friends; Peelman, cond.*
• ARG 11-12/96: 271

33777. TP 065: SCHULTZ—Dead songs; Sea change; Stick dance II; Mephisto. *Schindler, soprano; Perihelion; Roberts, cond.*
+ ARG 1-2/97: 245

33778. TP 066: JANÁČEK—Sonata; In the mist; On an overgrown path. *Moose, piano.*
• ARG 7-8/96: 138

33779. TP 068: LEMMONE—The flute music. *Curtis, flute; Miller, piano.*
+ ARG 5-6/96: 135

33780. TP 071: *Awakening.* Music of Granville-Hicks, Gifford, Conyngham, Fowler, Koehne, and Sculthorpe. *McGuire, harp.*
+ ARG 1-2/97: 208

TE DEUM

33781. 004: *In quires and places where they sing.* Music of Gibbons, Eccard, Schütz, Tallis, Palestrina, Handl, and Byrd. *Te Deum Singers; Birney-Smith, cond.*
+ ARG 3-4/95: 254

TELARC

DG-10126 see CD-80126.

DG-10128 see CD-80128.

DG-10137 see CD-80137.

DG-10139 see CD-80139.

DG-10333 see CD-80133.

33782. CD-38294: OFFENBACH—Gaité parisienne (arr. Rosenthal); Les belles américaines; Geneviève de Brabant: Galop. IBERT—Divertissement. *Cincinnati Pops Orch.; Kunzel, cond.*
+ Fa 9-10/92: 307
+ Gr 11/92: 94

33783. CD-80046: CHAUSSON—Concerto for violin, piano and string quartet, op. 21. *Maazel, violin; Margalit, piano;*

Cleveland Orch. String Quartet. Reissue.
- Fa 11-12/91: 298

33784. CD-80110: SCHUBERT—Symphony
no. 9. *Cleveland Orch.; Dohnányi, cond.*
Issued also as LP: DG-10110.
   • ARG 3-4/86: 66
   + Fa 1-2/86: 211
   + Ov 11/86: 44

33785. CD-80112: *American piano
classics.* Music of Anderson, Gershwin,
Gottschalk-Kay, Bowman, Joplin, and
Gould. *Goodyear, Tritt, Lockhart, piano;
Cincinnati Pops Orch.; Kunzel, cond.*
   + ARG 7-8/93: 183
   + Fa 5-6/93: 385

33786. CD-80115: *Orchestral
spectaculars.* Music of Rimsky-
Korsakov, Dukas, Weinberger, Saint-
Saëns, and Liszt. *Cincinnati Pops Orch.;
Kunzel, cond.* Issued also as LP: DG-
80115.
   - ARG 1-2/86: 73
   + Fa 1-2/86: 280

33787. CD-80116: *William Tell and other
favorite overtures.* Music of Suppé,
Auber, Hérold, Reznicek, and others.
Cincinnati Pops Orch.; Kunzel, cond.
   • ARG 9-10/86: 94
   - Fa 7-8/86: 287
   - HF 9/86: 72

33788. CD-80117: COPLAND—A Lincoln
portrait; Old American songs: Set 1; An
outdoor overture; John Henry, a railroad
ballad for orchestra; The Tender Land:
The promise of living; Ceremonial
fanfare; Jubilee variations. *Hepburn,
narrator; Milnes, baritone; Cincinnati
Pops Orch.; Kunzel, cond.*
   - Fa 7-8/87: 92
   + Gr 10/87: 579
   + HF 11/87: 80

33789. CD-80119: *Choral masterworks.*
Music of Bach, Beethoven, Belrioz,
Brahms, Duruflé, and others. *Atlanta
Symphony Chorus & Orch.; Shaw, cond.*
Issued also as LP: DG-10119.
   + Fa 3-4/86: 276
   + Opus 12/86: 44

33790. CD-80120: BEETHOVEN—
Symphony no. 9. *Vaness, Taylor,
Jerusalem, Lloyd; Cleveland Chorus &
Orch.; Dohnányi, cond.*
   • ARG 7-8/86: 59
   + Fa 7-8/86: 96
   + Gr 2/86: 1025
   • HF 9/86: 71
   + NR 5/86: 1
   • NYT 5/4/86: H28
   • Ov 10/86: 42
   + SR 9/86: 118

33791. CD-80122: *Pomp and pizazz.*
Music of Williams, Suk, Elgar, Ireland,
and others. *Cincinnati Pops Orch.;
Kunzel, cond.*

   + Fa 7-8/87: 242
   + NR 4/87: 8

33792. CD-80124: TCHAIKOVSKY—Piano
concerto no. 1. PROKOFIEV—Piano
concerto no. 3. *Parker, piano; Royal Phil.
Orch.; Previn, cond.*
   + DA 5/87: 67
   • Fa 11-12/86: 226 (Tchaikovsky)
   + Fa 11-12/86: 226 (Prokofiev)
   • Gr 12/86: 868
   + HF 3/87: 63
   + NR 1/87: 8
   + Opus 4/87: 50
   • Ov 2/87: 42
   - SR 12/86: 136

33793. CD-80125: WALTON—Symphony
no. 1; Crown imperial; Orb and sceptre.
Royal Phil. Orch.; Previn, cond.
   - Fa 9-10/87: 347
   + Gr 8/87: 309
   + HPR 12/87: 103
   + MA 5/88: 62
   - Opus 2/88: 52
   + SR 10/87: 149

33794. CD-80126: PROKOFIEV—Peter and
the wolf. BRITTEN—Young person's guide
to the orchestra; Gloriana: Courtly
dances. *Royal Phil. Orch.; Previn,
narrator & cond.* Issued also as LP: DG-
10126.
   + ARG Fall/87: 43
   • DA 3/87: 69
   + Fa 3-4/87: 182
   + Gr 5/87: 1557
   + NR 4/87: 10

33795. CD-80127: BACH—Organ music.
Murray, organ.
   • ARG 9-10/86: 64
   + Fa 7-8/86: 81

33796. CD-80128: MOZART—Requiem.
*Augér, Ziegler, Hadley, Krause; Atlanta
Symphony Chorus & Orch.; Shaw, cond.*
Issued also as LP: DG-10128.
   + ARG 5-6/87: 43
   • Fa 3-4/87: 169
   • Gr 5/87: 1585
   • Opus 6/87: 44
   + Ov 7/87: 34

33797. CD-80129: *The Stokowski sound.*
Music of Bach, Boccherini, Debussy,
Beethoven, and others. *Cincinnati Pops
Orch.; Kunzel, cond.*
   + ARG 5-6/87: 67
   + Fa 1-2/87: 255
   + HF 3/87: 70
   + NR 4/87: 8
   + NYT 12/28/86: H14

33798. CD-80130: TCHAIKOVSKY—
Symphony no. 6: Eugen Onegin:
Polonaise. *Cleveland Orch.; Dohnányi,
cond.*
   • ARG 11-12/87: 77
   + Fa 7-8/87: 195
   + Gr 10/87: 590

33799. CD-80131: RIMSKY-KORSAKOV—
Symphony no. 2. TCHAIKOVSKY—
Symphony no. 2. *Pittsburgh Symphony
Orch.; Maazel, cond.*
   • ARG 3-4/87: 57
   + DA 4/87: 56
   • Fa 1-2/87: 166
   • HF 6/87: 66
   + Opus 6/87: 60

33800. CD-80132: HINDEMITH—A
requiem for those we love. *De Gaetani,
Stone; Atlanta Symphony Chorus &
Orch.; Shaw, cond.*
   + ARG 11-12/87: 38
   + Fa 7-8/87: 128
   + Gr 7/87: 211
   + Opus 12/87: 34
   + SR 1/88: 156

33801. CD-80133: HOLST—Planets.
*Women of the Brighton Festival Chorus;
Royal Phil. Orch.; Previn, cond.* Issued
also as LP: DG-10333.
   • Fa 1-2/87: 125
   + Gr 12/86: 868
   • NR 2/87: 5
   + NYT 12/28/86: H14
   + Opus 4/87: 37

33802. CD-80135: FAURÉ—Requiem.
DURUFLÉ—Requiem. *Blegen, Morris,
vocalists; Atlanta Symphony Chorus &
Orch.; Shaw, cond.*
   + ARG 3-4/88: 35
   + Fa 9-10/87: 200
   - Gr 10/87: 608
   + HF 11/87: 80

33803. CD-80136: DUPRÉ—Symphony
for organ, op. 25. RHEINBERGER—Organ
concerto no. 1. *Murray, organ; Royal
Phil. Orch.; Ling, cond.*
   + ARG 11-12/88: 66
   + Fa 5-6/88: 118
   + Gr 6/87: 43

33804. CD-80137 (2 discs):
TCHAIKOVSKY—Nutcracker (complete);
Queen of spades: Duet of Daphnis and
Chloe. *London Symphony Orch.;
Mackerras, cond.* Issued also as 2 LPs:
DG-10137.
   + ARG 1-2/87: 65
   + DA 12/86: 40
   • Fa 3-4/87: 220
   + Gr 5/87: 1563
   + NR 4/87: 9
   + SR 2/87: 182

33805. CD-80138: VAUGHAN WILLIAMS—
Symphony no. 2; The lark ascending.
*Griffiths, violin; Royal Phil. Orch.;
Previn, cond.*
   + ARG Fall/87: 59
   + Fa 7-8/87: 199
   + Gr 7/87: 187
   • HF 7/87: 68
   + NR 4/87: 1
   + NYT 6/28/87: H21
   + SR 9/87: 114

TELARC

33806. CD-80139: Mozart—Symphonies no. 40-41. *Prague Chamber Orch.; Mackerras, cond.* Issued aslo as LP: DG-10139.
+ ARG Fall/87: 41
- Fa 5-6/87: 167
+ Gr 5/87: 1557
+ Opus 12/87: 44
+ Ov 6/87: 41
+ SR 5/87: 114

33807. CD-80142: Mendelssohn—String quartet no. 1; String octet op. 20. *Cleveland Quartet; Meliora String Quartet.*
• ARG 1-2/88: 46
- Fa 1-2/88: 159
• Gr 1/88: 1101 (m.f.)
+ HF 2/88: 60

33808. CD-80143: Prokofiev—Alexander Nevsky, op. 78: Lieutenant Kije suite, op. 60. *Cairns, mezzo-soprano; Los Angeles Phil. Orch.; Previn, cond.*
+ ARG 3-4/88: 67
+ Au 1/88: 152
+ DA 6/88: 54
+ Fa 1-2/88: 188
• Gr 2/88: 1231
+ HF 2/88: 64

33809. CD-80145: Beethoven—Symphony no. 6; Leonore overture no. 3. *Cleveland Orch.; Dohnányi, cond.*
+ Fa 9-10/87: 154
• Gr 11/87: 729
- HPR 12/87: 80
+ SR 10/87: 127

33810. CD-80147: Chopin—Piano sonata no. 2 op. 35; Polonaise in A op. 40 no. 1; Ballade in A♭, op. 47; Etudes op. 10 no. 3, no. 12; Waltzes no 1-2; Nocturnes op. 9 no. 2; Op. 27 no. 2; Scherzo in B♭ minor op. 31 . *Parker, piano.*
• ARG 3-4/89: 29
+ DA 5/89: 78
+ Fa 1-2/89: 147
• Gr 1/89: 1183
+ HPR 3/89: 74
+ Ov 1/89: 42
• St 1/89: 209

33811. CD-80148: Mozart—Symphony no. 36, 38. *Prague Chamber Orch.; Mackerras, cond.*
- Fa 9-10/87: 257
+ Gr 10/87: 583
+ Opus 12/87: 44

33812. CD-80149: Falla—The three-cornered hat; Homenajes; La vida breve: Interlude and dance. *Quivar, mezzo-soprano; Cincinnati Symphony Orch.; López-Cobos, cond.*
+ ARG 5-6/88: 28
+ Fa 9-10/87: 198
+ Gr 11/87: 734
+ HF 11/87: 80
+ HPR 12/87: 85
+ NYT 8/2/88: H28
+ Opus 10/87: 52
+ SR 11/87: 194

33813. CD-80150 (2 discs): Beethoven—Missa solemnis op. 123. Mozart—Mass in C minor K. 427. *McNair, Taylor, Aler, Krause, Wiens, Ziegler, Aler, Stone; Atlanta Symphony Chorus & Orch.; Shaw, cond.*
+ ARG 3-4/89: 20
+ DA 1/89: 48
+ Fa 9-10/88: 99
+ Gr 11/88: 835 (Beethoven)
• Gr 11/88: 835 (Mozart)
• Ov 1/89: 39 (Beethoven)
+ Ov 1/89: 39 (Mozart)
• SR 8/88: 91 (Beethoven)
+ SR 8/88: 91 (Mozart)
+ St 11/88: 163

33814. CD-80151: Tchaikovsky—Sleeping beauty: Suite; Swan lake: Suite. *Royal Phil. Orch.; Mackerras, cond.*
• ARG 1-2/88: 66
+ Fa 3-4/88: 217
• Gr 2/88: 1200

33815. CD-80152 (2 discs): Verdi—Requiem; Aida: Chorus; Don Carlo: Chorus; Macbeth: Chorus; Nabucco: Chorus; Otello: Chorus. *Dunn, Curry, Hadley, Plishka; Atlanta Symphony Chorus & Orch.; Shaw, cond.*
+ ARG 3-4/88: 94
+ Fa 3-4/88: 226
+ Gr 3/88: 1339
+ MA 9/88: 80
+ NYT 12/20/87: H29
+ Ov 5/88: 42

33816. CD-80154: Wagner—Orchestra highlights from Das Rheingold, Die Walküre, Siegfried, and Götterdämmerung. *Berlin Phil. Orch.; Maazel, cond.*
- ARG 7-8/88: 68
+ DA 9/88: 54
• Fa 9-10/88: 298
□ Gr 10/88: 618
• HF 1/89: 71
• MA 11/88: 85
- St 9/88: 159

33817. CD-80155: Brahms—Symphony no. 4; Academic festival overture. *Royal Phil. Orch.; Previn, cond.*
+ ARG 3-4/88: 25
- Fa 3-4/88: 89
+ Gr 3/88: 1308
• HPR 4/88: 75

33818. CD-80156: Haydn—Symphonies no. 31, 45. *St. Luke's Baroque Orch.; Mackerras, cond.*
+ ARG 11-12/89: 67
+ DA 9/89: 78
+ Fa 9-10/89: 217
+ Gr 3/90: 1604
+ SR 10/89: 144

33819. CD-80157 (2 discs): Britten—War requiem. *Haywood, Rolfe Johnson, Luxon; Atlanta Symphony Chorus & Orch.; Shaw, cond.*
• ARG 11-12/89: 48
+ Au 2/90: 104

• DA 12/89: 68
+ Fa 11-12/89: 160
+ Gr 11/89: 946
+ NYT 11/12/89: H34
+ SR 11/89: 154
+ St 3/90: 187

33820. CD-80158: Vaughan Williams—Symphony no. 5 in D; Fantasia on a theme of Thomas Tallis. *Royal Phil. Orch.; Previn, cond.*
+ ARG 7-8/89: 102
+ DA 1/90: 54
+ Fa 7-8/89: 268
+ Gr 5/89: 1738
+ MA 9/89: 77

33821. CD-80160: Beethoven—Piano sonatas no. 17, 21, 26. *O'Conor, piano.*
• ARG 3-4/88: 17
- Fa 3-4/88: 72
+ Gr 5/88: 1620
+ HPR 4/88: 72

33822. CD-80163: Beethoven—Symphonies no. 5, 7. *Cleveland Orch.; Dohnanyi, cond.*
+ ARG 7-8/88: 13
+ DA 8/88: 41
+ Fa 7-8/88: 118
• Gr 9/88: 408
+ HPR 12/88: 73
+ MA 7/88: 52

33823. CD-80164: Berlioz—La Marseillaise and other Berlioz favorites. *McNair, Leech; Boys from the Choir of St. Michael and All Angels; Boys from Choir of St. David's Episcopal Church; Baltimore Symphony Chorus & Orch.; Zinman, cond.*
+ ARG 11-12/88: 17
• Au 12/88: 170
• Fa 11-12/88: 145
• Gr 12/88: 993
+ HF 12/88: 58
+ HPR 3/89: 70

33824. CD-80165: Mozart—Symphonies no. 25, 28-29. *Prague Chamber Orch.; Mackerras, cond.*
+ ARG 11-12/88: 66
+ Au 12/88: 170
+ Fa 9-10/88: 217
+ Gr 9/88: 418
+ HPR 12/88: 84

33825. CD-80166: Gershwin—Rhapsody in blue; Concerto for piano in F; I got rhythm variations; Rialto ripples. *Tritt, piano; Cincinnati Jazz Orch.; Cincinnati Pops Orch.; Kunzel, cond.*
+ DA 7/88: 61
+ Fa 7-8/88: 167
+ Gr 9/88: 42
+ HPR 12/88: 78

33826. CD-80167: Strauss—Also sprach Zarathustra; Tod und Verklärung. *Vienna Phil. Orch.; Previn, cond.*
+ ARG 11-12/88: 90
+ Fa 9-10/88: 271
+ Gr 10/88: 618

33827. CD-80171: RAVEL—Alborada del gracioso; Rapsodie espagnole; Valses nobles et sentimentales; La valse; Boléro. *Cincinnati Symphony Orch.; López-Cobos, cond.*
- • ARG 11-12/88: 72
- • Au 4/89: 130
- + DA 11/88: 66
- + Fa 11-12/88: 255
- • Gr 12/88: 1008
- • St 2/89: 165

33828. CD-80172: RACHMANINOFF—Vespers op. 37. *Dent, tenor; Robert Shaw Festival Singers; Shaw, cond.*
- + DA 12/90: 86
- + Fa 9-10/90: 348
- • Gr 10/90: 807
- - MA 1/91: 78

33829. CD-80173: DVOŘÁK—Symphony no. 7; My home. *Los Angeles Phil. Orch.; Previn, cond.*
- + ARG 3-4/89: 32
- + Fa 5-6/89: 184
- • Gr 4/89: 1578
- - HPR 6/89: 75
- + Ov 9/89: 512
- + SR 6/89: 116
- + St 9/89: 179

33830. CD-80174: BARTÓK—Concerto for orchestra. JANÁČEK—Sinfonietta. *Los Angeles Phil. Orch.; Previn, cond.*
- + ARG 5-6/89: 16
- + Fa 5-6/89: 120
- - Gr 3/89: 1407
- + HPR 3/89: 68
- • Ov 9/89: 51
- + SR 5/89: 119

33831. CD-80176: BRAHMS—Alto rhapsody; Gesang der Parzen; Nänie; Schicksalslied. *Horne, mezzo-soprano; Atlanta Symphony Chorus & Orch.; Shaw, cond.*
- • ARG 5-6/89: 26
- + Fa 3-4/89: 119
- • Gr 3/89: 1470 (Rhapsody)
- + Gr 3/89: 1470 (others)
- + HPR 3/89: 72
- + NYT 6/4/89: H24

33832. CD-80178: BORODIN—String quartet no. 2. SMETANA—String quartet no. 1. *Cleveland Quartet.*
- + ARG 9-10/89: 33
- • Fa 9-10/89: 154
- • Gr 10/89: 684
- + MA 11/89: 52

33833. CD-80179: *The young Bach.* BACH—Preludes and fugues BWV 531, 535, 539, 567, 572, 578, 588, 592, 751. *Murray, organ.*
- + ARG 3-4/89: 58
- + Fa 5-6/89: 108

33834. CD-80180: STRAUSS—Ein Heldenleben; Vier letzte Lieder. *Augér, soprano; Vienna Phil. Orch.; Previn, cond.*
- - ARG 7-8/89: 95

- Fa 9-10/89: 335
- Gr 8/89: 312
- • SR 9/89: 156

33835. CD-80181: WALTON—Belshazzar's feast. BERNSTEIN—Chichester psalms; Missa brevis. *Stone, baritone; Ragin, male alto; Atlanta Symphony Chorus & Orch.; Shaw, cond.*
- + ARG 3-4/90: 123
- + Fa 5-6/90: 339
- • Gr 3/90: 1654
- + MA 7/90: 85 (Walton)
- • MA 7/90: 85 (Bernstein)
- • St 1/91: 267

33836. CD-80182: SCHUMANN—Symphonies no. 2-3. *Baltimore Symphony Orch.; Zinman, cond.*
- - ARG 7-8/91: 124
- - Fa 7-8/91: 285
- • Gr 6/91: 51
- + HPR v.8, no.2/91: 68
- + MA 7/91: 88

33837. CD-80184: MENDELSSOHN—Die erste Walpurgisnacht; Symphony no. 3. *Cairns, Garrison, Krause, Wells; Cleveland Orch. & Chorus; Dohnányi, cond.*
- + ARG 3-4/89: 58
- + Fa 3-4/89: 211
- • Gr 3/89: 1431
- + HPR 6/89: 80
- + SR 2/89: 164
- • St 7/89: 169

33838. CD-80185: BEETHOVEN—Piano sonatas no. 15-16, 18. *O'Conor, piano.*
- • ARG 7-8/89: 22
- + DA 1/90: 46
- • Fa 1-2/90: 119
- + HPR v.7, no.1/90: 69
- + St 6/90: 192

33839. CD-80186: MOZART—Symphonies: no. 24, 26-27, 30. *Prague Chamber Orch.; Mackerras, cond.*
- + ARG 7-8/89: 67
- + Fa 5-6/89: 255
- • St 7/89: 171

33840. CD-80187: BEETHOVEN—Symphonies no. 1-2. *Cleveland Orch.; Dohnányi, cond.*
- - ARG 7-8/89: 22
- • Fa 9-10/89: 137
- • Gr 6/89: 24

33841. CD-80188: BRUCKNER—Symphony no. 7. *Cincinnati Symphony Orch.; López Cobos, cond.*
- + ARG 11-12/89: 49
- • DA 2/90: 52
- - Fa 11-12/89: 163
- - Gr 2/90: 1458
- • SR 11/89: 154

33842. CD-80190: MOZART—Symphonies no. 31, 33-34. *Prague Chamber Orch.; Mackerras, cond.*
- + ARG 3-4/90: 83
- + DA 12/89: 84

+ Fa 1-2/90: 246
+ Gr 3/90: 1613
- St 6/90: 203

33843. CD-80192: ELGAR—Cockaigne overture; Enigma variations; Serenade for strings in E minor. *Baltimore Symphony Orch.; Zinman, cond.*
- • ARG 5-6/90: 50
- + DA 2/90: 64
- • Fa 3-4/90: 177
- + Gr 10/90: 739
- + St 8/90: 173

33844. CD-80193: TCHAIKOVSKY—Piano concerto no. 1. RACHMANINOFF—Rhapsody on a theme of Paganini. *Gutiérrez, piano; Baltimore Symphony Orch.; Zinman, cond.*
- - Fa 11-12/90: 373
- • Gr 10/90: 744

33845. CD-80194: BACH—Magnificat. VIVALDI—Gloria. *Upshaw, Jensen, Simpson, Gordon, Stone; Atlanta Symphony Chorus & Orch.; Shaw, cond.*
- • ARG 11-12/89: 135
- + Fa 9-10/89: 120

33846. CD-80195: HINDEMITH—Symphony Mathis der Maler; Nobilissima visione; Symphonic metamorphosis on themes of Carl Maria von Weber. *Atlanta Symphony Orch.; Levi, cond.*
- • ARG 5-6/90: 59
- + Fa 5-6/90: 193
- • Gr 7/90: 212
- + St 7/90: 171

33847. CD-80197: BRAHMS—Piano concerto no. 2; Variations on a theme by Haydn. *Gutiérrez, piano; Royal Phil. Orch.; Previn, cond.*
- + ARG 7-8/89: 29
- • Fa 7-8/89: 107
- - Gr 7/89: 171
- + SR 6/89: 115
- - St 9/89: 179

33848. CD-80198: BEETHOVEN—Symphonies no. 4, 8. *Cleveland Orch.; Dohnányi, cond.*
- - ARG 7-8/89: 22
- • Fa 9-10/89: 137
- - Gr 6/89: 24

33849. CD-80199: FIELD—Fifteen nocturnes. *O'Conor, piano.*
- + ARG 7-8/90: 48
- + DA 4/90: 52
- • Fa 7-8/90: 143
- • Gr 5/90: 2011
- + NYT 6/17/90: H23
- + St 1/91: 253

33850. CD-80200 (5 discs): CD-80200 (5 discs): BEETHOVEN—Symphonies (complete); Leonore overture no. 3. *Vaness, Taylor, Jerusalem, Lloyd; Cleveland Chorus & Orch.; Dohnányi, cond.*

TELARC

• ARG 3-4/90: 25
- Fa 3-4/90: 137

33851. CD-80201: COPLAND—Symphony no. 3; Music for the theater. *Atlanta Symphony Orch.; Levi, cond.*
+ ARG 1-2/90: 40
+ DA 5/90: 58
+ Fa 1-2/90: 156
• Gr 1/90: 1322
+ NYT 12/10/89: H33
• St 3/90: 187

33852. CD-80203: MOZART—Symphonies no. 32, 35, 39. *Prague Chamber Orch.; Mackerras, cond.*
• ARG 1-2/91: 71
+ Au 12/90: 138
• Fa 1-2/91: 259
+ Gr 4/91: 1836

33853. CD-80204: Music of Gabrieli, Isaac, Banchieri, and Diaz. *Empire Brass; with assisting performers.*
+ ARG 7-8/89: 114
+ Fa 7-8/89: 152
+ Gr 10/89: 695
+ SR 11/89: 162
+ St 9/89: 171

33854. CD-80205: BAX—Quintet for oboe and strings. BLISS—Quintet for oboe and strings. BRITTEN—Phantasy quartet for oboe and string trio. *Woods, oboe; Audubon String Quartet.*
+ ARG 1-2/90: 21
+ Fa 9-10/89: 127
+ Gr 10/89: 682

33855. CD-80206: DVOŘÁK—Symphony no. 8; Scherzo capriccioso; Notturno for strings. *Los Angeles Phil. Orch.; Previn, cond.*
- ARG 1-2/90: 47
• Fa 3-4/90: 175
+ Gr 1/90: 1326
+ SR 3/90: 96
+ St 6/90: 197

33856. CD-80207: BUSONI—Piano concerto. *Ohlsson, piano; Cleveland Orch. & Men's Chorus; Dohnányi, cond.*
• ARG 3-4/90: 37
+ DA 3/90: 72
+ Fa 3-4/90: 162
+ Gr 4/90: 1772
+ SR 2/90: 153

33857. CD-80208: RIMSKY-KORSAKOV—Scheherazade; Capriccio espagnol. *Hulsmann, Gaehler, violins; London Symphony Orch.; Mackerras, cond.*
• ARG 1-2/91: 82
• DA 11/90: 56
+ Fa 1-2/91: 289
+ Gr 10/90: 744

33858. CD-80209: *Renaissance madrigals.* Music of Rore, Wert, Monteverdi, A. Scarlatti, and Stradella. *Quink Vocal Quintet.*
+ ARG 11-12/89: 168

• DA 11/89: 84
+ Fa 11-12/89: 450

33859. CD-80211: STRAUSS—An Alpine symphony. *Vienna Phil. Orch.; Previn, cond.*
+ ARG 9-10/90: 117
+ DA 12/90: 94
+ Fa 9-10/90: 395
+ Gr 9/90: 542
• NYT 10/21/90: H36
+ SR 10/90: 118

33860. CD-80212: SCHUBERT—Masses no. 2, 6. *Upshaw, Valente, Simpson, Gordon, Humphrey, Siebert, Stone, Myers; Atlanta Symphony Chorus & Orch.; Shaw, cond.*
+ ARG 5-6/90: 102
+ Fa 7-8/90: 251
• Gr 9/90: 592

33861. CD-80213: *A touch of romance.* Music of Sanz, Barrios, C. Romero, Albéniz, and others. *Romero, guitar.*
+ DA 10/89: 84
+ Fa 11-12/89: 215
+ Gr 4/90: 1845

33862. CD-80214: BEETHOVEN—Piano sonatas no. 1-3. *O'Conor, piano.*
+ ARG 11-12/90: 97
+ DA 2/90: 50
- Fa 3-4/90: 131
+ Gr 9/90: 566

33863. CD-80215: SHOSTAKOVICH —Symphonies no. 5, 9. *Atlanta Symphony Orch.; Levi, cond.*
• ARG 7-8/90: 109
- Fa 7-8/90: 271
+ Gr 6/90: 62
• NYT 5/27/90: H22

33864. CD-80216: GRANADOS—Danzas españolas (complete). *A. & C. Romero, guitars.*
+ Fa 5-6/91: 176
+ Gr 6/91: 59

33865. CD-80217: MOZART—Symphonies no. 19-23. *Prague Chamber Orch.; Mackerras, cond.*
+ ARG 7-8/90: 77
+ Fa 9-10/90: 313
+ Gr 9/90: 524

33866. CD-80218: *Music for organ, brass, and percussion.* Music of Gigout, Dupré, Poulenc, Monteverdi, Telemann, and others. *Murray, organ; Empire Brass.*
+ ARG 11-12/90: 157
+ Fa 7-8/90: 372

33867. CD-80219: MOZART—Piano concertos no. 21, 27. *O'Conor, piano; Scottish Chamber Orch.; Mackerras, cond.*
- ARG 7-8/90: 74
• Fa 9-10/90: 302
• Gr 9/90: 524

33868. CD-80224: BIZET—Carmen suite; L'Arlésienne suite no. 1; Symphony in C. *Cincinnati Symphony Orch.; López-Cobos, cond.*
+ ARG 7-8/90: 29 (Carmen)
- ARG 7-8/90: 29 (others)
• Fa 9-10/90: 187
+ Gr 11/90: 974

33869. CD-80225: SCHUBERT—Piano quintet D. 667; String quartet D. 804. *Cleveland Quartet; O'Conor, piano; Van Demark, double bass.*
+ ARG 3-4/91: 113 (Quartet)
• ARG 3-4/91: 113 (Quintet)
+ Fa 5-6/91: 275
+ MA 5/91: 83

33870. CD-80227: BACH—Brandenburg concerto no. 2; Suite no. 2 for flute and strings, BWV 1067. L. MOZART—Concerto for trumpet and orchestra. TELEMANN—Concerto for trumpet and orchestra. *Smedvig, trumpet; Scottish Chamber Orch.; Ling, cond.*
+ ARG 3-4/94: 216
+ Fa 3-4/94: 104

33871. CD-80228: TCHAIKOVSKY—Symphony no. 4; Romeo and Juliet. *Baltimore Symphony Orch.; Zinman, cond.*
- ARG 9-10/90: 121 m.f.
+ DA 1/91: 72
• Gr 4/91: 1846

33872. CD-80229: BEETHOVEN—String quartets no. 6-7. *Cleveland Quartet.*
• ARG 7-8/93: 64
+ Fa 5-6/93: 154
+ Gr 5/93: 60

33873. CD-80230: SCHUMANN—Symphonies no. 1, 4. *Baltimore Symphony Orch.; Zinman, cond.*
• ARG 11-12/90: 113
+ Fa 9-10/90: 383
+ Gr 10/90: 747 (no. 1)
• Gr 10/90: 747 (no. 4)

33874. CD-80232: *Trumpet concertos.* Music of Haydn, Tartini, Hummel, Torelli, and Bellini. *Smedvig, trumpet; Scottish Chamber Orch.; Ling, cond.*
+ ARG 9-10/90: 145
+ DA 8/90: 36
+ Gr 8/90: 387

33875. CD-80233 (2 discs): BACH—Mass in B minor. *McNair, Ziegler, Simpson, Aler, Stone, Paul; Atlanta Symphony Chamber Chorus & Orch.; Shaw, cond.*
+ ARG 3-4/91: 20
+ Fa 3-4/91: 135
• Gr 4/91: 1878
+ HPR v.8, no.1: 62

33876. CD-80234: FRANCK—Fantasy in A, in C; Cantabile; Pièce héroïique; Prélude, fugue and variation; Prière; Final: Pastorale; Grande pie'ce symphonique; Trois chorals. *Murray, organ.*

+ ARG 9-10/90: 63
+ Fa 7-8/90: 145
+ Gr 7/90: 246

33877. CD-80236: POULENC—Mass in G; Quatre petites prières de St. François; Quatre motets de pénitence; Quatre motets de Noël. *Carter, soprano; Cock, tenor; Robert Shaw Festival Singers; Shaw, cond.*
+ ARG 11-12/90: 97
+ Fa 3-4/91: 325
+ Gr 10/90: 807
+ MA 3/91: 85

33878. CD-80238: DVOŘÁK—Symphony no. 9; Carnival overture. *Los Angeles Phil. Orch.; Previn, cond.*
+ ARG 3-4/91: 63
• DA 1/91: 74
• Fa 3-4/91: 206
• Gr 4/91: 1827

33879. CD-80242: MOZART—Symphonies no. 14-17. *Prague Chamber Orch.; Mackerras, cond.*
+ ARG 1-2/91: 71
+ Fa 1-2/91: 259
• Gr 4/91: 1835

33880. CD-80246: SIBELIUS—Symphonies no. 1, 5. *Atlanta Symphony Orch.; Levi, cond.*
• ARG 3-4/91: 121
+ Fa 3-4/91: 386
• Gr 7/91: 62
• MA 5/91: 85

33881. CD-80247: FRANCK—Symphony in D minor; Le chasseur maudit. *Cincinnati Symphony Orch.; López-Cobos, cond.*
+ ARG 3-4/91: 67
• Fa 3-4/91: 213
• Gr 3/91: 1667

33882. CD-80248: BEETHOVEN—Mass in C; Elegaic song op. 118; Calm sea, prosperous voyage op. 112. *Schellenberg, Simpson, Humphrey, Myers; Atlanta Symphony Chorus & Orch.; Shaw, cond.*
+ ARG 5-6/91: 24
+ Fa 5-6/91: 122
• Gr 2/91: 1542
+ MA 7/91: 66

33883. CD-80249: *Braggin' in brass.* 14 tunes by Duke Ellington, Fats Waller, Jelly Roll Morton, Cole Porter and others. *Empire Brass.*
+ ARG 9-10/91: 159

33884. CD-80250: BARBER—Overture to the School for scandal; Adagio for strings; Essay for orchestra no. 1-2; Knoxville, summer of 1915; Medea's dance of vengeance. *McNair, soprano; Atlanta Symphony Orch.; Levi, cond.*
+ ARG 7-8/92: 88
+ Fa 7-8/92: 111
+ Gr 5/92: 31
+ St 6/93: 247

33885. CD-80252: BRAHMS—Piano concerto no. 1; Tragic overture. *Gutiérrez, piano; Royal Phil. Orch.; Previn, cond.*
• ARG 7-8/91: 36
- Fa 7-8/91: 125
+ SR 8/91: 82

33886. CD-80253: HANDEL—Twelve concerti grossi, op. 6: no. 1-6. *Boston Baroque; Pearlman, cond.*
+ ARG 11-12/92: 128
• Fa 9-10/92: 250
+ Gr 10/92: 61

33887. CD-80254: VERDI—Quattro pezzi sacri. STRAVINSKY—Symphony of psalms. *Atlanta Symphony Orch. & Chorus; Shaw, cond.; Carter, soprano.*
+ ARG 11-12/91: 165
+ Fa 9-10/91: 382
+ Gr 10/91: 177

33888. CD-80255: *The Willis organ at Salisburg Cathedral.* Music of Jackson, Cook, Duruflé, Schumann, Brahms, and others. *Murray, cond.*
+ ARG 3-4/91: 156
+ Fa 5-6/91: 357
+ HPR v.8, no.3/91: 79

33889. CD-80256: MOZART—Symphonies no. 1, 4-7; K. 19a; K. 45b. *Prague Chamber Orch.; Mackerras, cond.*
+ ARG 11-12/91: 123
+ Fa 11-12/91: 413
+ Gr 11/91: 92

33890. CD-80257: *Royal brass.* Music of Mouret, Holborne, Palestrina, Priuli, and others. *Empire Brass.*
• ARG 5-6/91: 139
+ Fa 5-6/91: 375

33891. CD-80258: WAGNER—Die Walküre, Act I. *Dunn, König; Pittsburgh Symphony Orch.; Maazel, cond.*
- ARG 9-10/91: 147
- Fa 9-10/91: 390
- Gr 7/91: 113
• ON 7/91: 34

33892. CD-80259: RACHMANINOFF—Piano concertos no. 2-3. *Gutiérrez, piano; Pittsburgh Symphony Orch.; Maazel, cond.*
• ARG 5-6/92: 112
+ Fa 3-4/92: 291
• St 11/92: 225

33893. CD-80260: PUCCINI—*Pops plays Puccini: Puccini without words.* Selections from Gianni Schicci, Tosca, Turandot, Madama Butterfly, Manon Lescaut, and La bohème. *Cincinnati Pops Orch.; Kunzel, cond.*
- ARG 9-10/91: 110
+ Fa 9-10/91: 316

33894. CD-80261: BEETHOVEN—Piano sonatas, vol. 6. *O'Conor, piano.*
+ Fa 9-10/91: 157
• Gr 11/92: 150

33895. CD-80262: STRAUSS—Don Juan; Don Quixote. *Bartolomey, cello; Vienna Phil.; Previn, cond.*
+ ARG 11-12/91: 151
• Fa 11-12/91: 495
+ Gr 10/91: 113

33896. CD-80263: Down on the farm. *Cincinnati Pops Orch.; Kunzel, cond.*
+ ARG 1-2/92: 146

33897. CD-80264: BRUCKNER—Symphony no. 6. *Cincinnati Symphony Orch.; López Cobos, cond.*
+ ARG 11-12/91: 48
+ Fa 11-12/91: 290

33898. CD-80265: SMETANA—Má vlast. *Milwaukee Symphony Orch.; Macal, cond.*
+ ARG 1-2/93: 152
• Fa 9-10/92: 358
+ Gr 9/92: 90
+ St 10/92: 273

33899. CD-80266: STRAVINSKY—Rite of spring; Pulcinella suite. *Atlanta Symphony Orch.; Levi, cond.*
+ ARG 1-2/93: 154
+ Fa 1-2/93: 251
• Gr 12/92: 89
- St 4/93: 289

33900. CD-80267 (2 discs): MAHLER—Symphony no. 8. *Soloists and choruses; Atlanta Symphony Orch.; Shaw, cond.*
• ARG 7-8/92: 169
• Fa 3-4/92: 233 (Pernick)
+ Fa 3-4/92: 235 (Hurwitz)
- Gr 1/92: 56
• St 8/92: 185

33901. CD-80268: BEETHOVEN—String quartets no. 8-9. *Cleveland Quartet.*
+ ARG 3-4/94: 71
+ Fa 3-4/94: 122
• Gr 2/94: 61

33902. CD-80269: MAHLER—Lieder eines fahrenden Gesellen; Kindertotenlieder; Rückert Lieder. *Schmidt, baritone; Cincinnati Symphony Orch.; López Cobos, cond.*
• ARG 3-4/92: 93
+ Fa 3-4/92: 235
+ Gr 5/92: 88

33903. CD-80270: STRAVINSKY—Petrouchka (1947 version); Firebird: Suite (1919 version); Fireworks, op. 4. *Baltimore Symphony Orch.; Zinman, cond.*
- ARG 1-2/92: 123
+ Fa 11-12/91: 498
• Gr 11/91: 102

33904. CD-80271: BERLIOZ—Symphonie fantastique; Roman carnival overture; Les francs-juges overture. *Baltimore Symphony Orch.; Zinman, cond.*
• ARG 9-10/91: 47
• Fa 9-10/91: 164
• Gr 11/91: 83

TELARC

33905. CD-80272: Mozart—Symphonies no. 8-9, 11; K. 73i; K. 73m; K. 73n. *Prague Chamber Orch.; Mackerras, cond.*
+ ARG 11-12/91: 123
+ Fa 11-12/91: 413

33906. CD-80273: Mozart—Symphonies no. 10, 12-13; K. 111b; K. 75. *Prague Chamber Orch.; Mackerras, cond.*
+ ARG 11-12/91: 123
+ Fa 11-12/91: 413

33907. CD-80274: Saint-Saëns—Symphony no. 3; Phaéton. *Murray, organ; Royal Phil. Orch.; Badea, cond.*
● ARG 3-4/92: 130
+ Fa 1-2/92: 313
● Gr 12/91: 79
+ St 10/92: 267

33908. CD-80275: Folk songs of the world. *Woerden, De Wit, Pronk, Berne, De Koning, vocalists.*
+ ARG 9-10/91: 175
- Fa 9-10/91: 411

33909. CD-80276: Willson—The music man. *Noble, Brett, Severinson; Indiana Univ. Singing Hoosiers; Cincinnati Pops Orch.; Kunzel, cond.*
+ Fa 1-2/92: 378

33910. CD-80278: Rodgers and Hammerstein—Songbook for orchestra. Orchestral arrangements from Oklahoma!, Carousel, State fair, South Pacific, The King and I, Cinderella, Flower drum song and The sound of music. *Cincinnati Pops Orch.; Kunzel, cond.*
+ Fa 5-6/92: 234

33911. CD-80279: Handel—Water music. *Orch. of St. Luke's; Mackerras, cond.*
+ ARG 1-2/92: 62
+ Fa 1-2/92: 230
+ Gr 1/92: 52

33912. CD-80280: Chopin—Polonaise, op. 53; Andante spianato and grand polonaise, op. 22; Introduction and variations, op. 12; 4 Mazurkas, op. 6; Contredanse, Tarantelle, op. 43; Sonata no. 3, op. 58. *Frager, piano.*
+ ARG 7-8/91: 46
+ Fa 7-8/91: 139
+ Gr 6/91: 64

33913. CD-80282: Haydn—Symphonies no. 100, 103. *Orch. of St. Luke's; Mackerras, cond.*
+ ARG 3-4/92: 75
+ Fa 3-4/92: 213

33914. CD-80283: Dvořák—String quartets no. 12, 14. *Cleveland Quartet.*
+ ARG 3-4/92: 52
+ Fa 3-4/92: 188
- Gr 3/92: 69 ·
- St 9/92: 189

33915. CD-80284: Sullivan—The Mikado. *McLaughlin, Palmer, Rolfe Johnson, Adams; Welsh National Opera; Mackerras, cond.*
+ ARG 11-12/92: 124
+ Fa 7-8/92: 301
+ Gr 5/92: 120
● ON 9/92: 53
● Op 8/92: 999
+ St 7/92: 239

33916. CD-80285: Mozart—Piano concertos no. 19, 23; Rondo, K. 386. *O'Conor, piano; Scottish Chamber Orch.; Mackerras, cond.*
- ARG 7-8/91: 92
+ Fa 9-10/91: 282
+ Gr 11/91: 97

33917. CD-80286: Bach—Bach at St. Bavo's. *Murray, organ.*
- ARG 7-8/92: 86
+ Fa 7-8/92: 109
- Gr 10/92: 136

33918. CD-80287: Janáček—Glagolitic mass. Dvořák—Te Deum, op. 103. *Brewer, Simpson, Dent, Roloff; Atlanta Symphony Orch. & Chorus; Shaw, cond.*
● ARG 7-8/91: 71
+ Fa 9-10/91: 244
+ Gr 7/91: 100

33919. CD-80288: Bach—Guitar arrangements. *A. Romero, guitar.*
- ARG 9-10/93: 87
+ Fa 11-12/93: 173

33920. CD-80289: Prokofiev—Symphonies no. 1, 5. *Atlanta Symphony Orch.; Levi, cond.*
- ARG 3-4/92: 120
+ Fa 11-12/91: 447
+ Gr 10/91: 100

33921. CD-80290: Field—Piano sonatas (complete); Nocturnes no. 3, 7, 17. *O'Conor, piano.*
+ Fa 11-12/92: 235
+ Gr 11/92: 150

33922. CD-80291: Shostakovich—Symphony no. 8. *Atlanta Symphony Orch.; Levi, cond.*
+ ARG 7-8/94: 174
● Fa 9-10/94: 338
● Gr 7/94: 56

33923. CD-80293: Beethoven—Piano sonatas vol. 7. *O'Conor, piano.*
+ ARG 1-2/93: 75
● Fa 1-2/93: 106
● Gr 5/93: 70

33924. CD-80295: Schickele—PDQ Bach: WTWP classical talkity-talk radio. *Schickele, announcer.*
+ Fa 1-2/92: 153
□ St 5/92: 191

33925. CD-80296: Mussorgsky—Pictures at an exhibition; A night on Bald Mountain; Khovanshchina: introduction.

Atlanta Symphony Orch.; Levi, cond.
+ ARG 5-6/92: 91
● Fa 1-2/92: 286
+ Gr 4/92: 68

33926. CD-80297: Mozart—String quartets no. 14-15. *Cleveland Quartet.*
● ARG 7-8/92: 187
+ Fa 7-8/92: 233
+ Gr 9/92: 111
+ St 11/92: 223

33927. CD-80298 (2 discs): Haydn—The creation. *Upshaw, Murphey, Humphrey, Cheek, McGuire; Atlanta Symphony Orch.; Shaw, cond.*
● ARG 3-4/93: 88
● Gr 12/92: 119
● ON 1/30/93: 37

33928. CD-80299: Bruckner—Symphony no. 9. *Cincinnati Symphony Orch.; López Cobos, cond.*
● ARG 11-12/92: 99
● Fa 11-12/92: 213

33929. CD-80301: Music of Albeniz, Debussy, Falla, Turina, Ravel, and others. *Empire Brass.*
+ ARG 7-8/92: 255

33930. CD-80302 (2 discs): Mozart—Die Zauberflöte. *Hendricks, Anderson, Hadley, Allen, Lloyd; Scottish Chamber Orch.; Mackerras, cond.*
+ ARG 3-4/92: 108
● Fa 3-4/92: 272
● Gr 12/91: 129
+ ON 1/18/92: 36
+ St 8/92: 185

33931. CD-80303: *Empire Brass on Broadway.* 16 show tunes. *Empire Brass.*
+ ARG 11-12/92: 238

33932. CD-80305: *On the edge.* Music of Khachaturian, Saint-Saëns, Bizet, Shostakovich, Ippolitov-Ivanov, Fauré, Enesco, Prokofiev, Janáček, Glière, Stravinsky, Bernstein, Copland, and Offenbach. *Empire Brass.*
+ ARG 7-8/93: 190
+ Fa 7-8/93: 306

33933. CD-80306: Mozart—Concertos for piano and orchestra no. 17, 24. *O'Conor, piano; Scottish Chamber Orch.; Mackerras, cond.*
- ARG 9-10/92: 135
● Fa 9-10/92: 296
● Gr 10/92: 114

33934. CD-80307: Schickele—Music for an awful lot of winds and percussion. *Turtle Mountain Naval Base Tactical Wind Ensemble; Graham, cond.; Tennessee Bassoon Quartet; McGill, bassoon; Bishop, tuba.*
- ARG 3-4/93: 54
+ Fa 1-2/93: 102

33935. CD-80308: Mozart—Concertos for piano and orchestra no. 20, 22.

O'Conor, piano; Scottish Chamber Orch.; Mackerras, cond.
- ARG 7-8/93: 130
- Fa 7-8/93: 187
+ Gr 11/93: 72

33936. CD-80309: RESPIGHI—Ancient airs and dances, suites, no. 1-3; Trittico Botticelliano. *Lausanne Chamber Orch.; López Cobos, cond.*
- Fa 7-8/92: 256
+ Gr 9/92: 84

33937. CD-80310: ELGAR—Symphony no. 1; Pomp and circumstances no. 1-2. *Baltimore Symphony Orch.; Zinman, cond.*
+ ARG 1-2/93: 94
+ Fa 11-12/92: 230
- Gr 11/92: 258

33938. CD-80311: HAYDN—Symphonies no. 101, 104. *Orch. of St. Luke's; Mackerras, cond.*
+ ARG 1-2/93: 103
- Fa 11-12/92: 252
+ Gr 2/93: 43

33939. CD-80312: RACHMANINOFF— Symphony no. 2; Vocalise. *Baltimore Symphony Orch.; Zinman, cond.*
- ARG 9-10/92: 144
+ Fa 11-12/92: 328
+ Gr 10/92: 114
+ St 8/93: 189

33940. CD-80313: *Piano classics: popular works for solo piano.* Music of Beethoven, Raff, Chopin, Grieg, MacDowell, Sibelius, Mendelssohn, Rachmaninoff, Scriabin, Satie, Schumann, Brahms, Mozart, and Debussy. *O'Conor, piano.*
+ Fa 3-4/93: 378

33941. CD-80314: *Ein Straussfest II.* Music of J. Strauss Sr. and Jr., Josef Strauss, and Eduard Strauss. *Cincinnati Pops Orch. & Chorale; Kunzel, cond.*
- ARG 9-10/93: 197
+ Fa 7-8/93: 249
+ Gr 7/93: 91

33942. CD-80317: FALLA—La vida breve. *Nafé, Ordoñez, Notare, Keen; May Festival Chorus; Cincinnati Symphony Orch.; López Cobos, cond.*
- ARG 1-2/93: 95
- Fa 1-2/93: 147
+ ON 10/93: 34
+ Op 1/93: 124

33943. CD-80318: MENDELSSOHN—A midsummer night's dream: overture; incidental music (selections); Symphony no. 4 "Italian". *Atlanta Symphony Orch.; Levi, cond.*
- ARG 5-6/93: 109
- Fa 3-4/93: 221
- Gr 5/93: 48

33944. CD-80320: SIBELIUS—Karelia suite; En saga; Pohjola's daughter; The

swan of Tuonela; Finlandia. *Atlanta Symphony Orch.; Levi, cond.*
- ARG 7-8/93: 158
+ Fa 7-8/93: 244
+ Gr 6/93: 55
+ St 10/93: 279

33945. CD-80322 (2 discs): HANDEL— Messiah. *Clift, soprano; Robbin, mezzo-soprano; Fowler, tenor; Ledbetter, bass; Boston Baroque Orch. & Chorus; Pearlman, cond.*
- ARG 3-4/93: 85
- Fa 1-2/93: 159
- Gr 12/92: 119
- St 1/93: 273

33946. CD-80323: BACH-CARLOS— Switched-on Bach 2000. *Carlos, electronics.*
+ ARG 1-2/93: 72

33947. CD-80325: *Amazing grace.* American hymns and spirtuals. *Robert Shaw Festival Singers; Shaw, cond.*
+ ARG 3-4/94: 223

33948. CD-80326: BRAHMS—Liebeslieder waltzes; Neue Liebeslieder waltzes; Seven evening songs. *Robert Shaw Festival Singers; Mackenzie, Wustman, pianos; Shaw, cond.*
+ ARG 9-10/93: 100
+ Fa 9-10/93: 133
+ Gr 11/93: 123

33949. CD-80328: *English madrigals.* Music of Morley, Pilkington, Tomkins, Bateson, Byrd, Farmer, Wilbye, and Weelkes. *Quink Vocal Ensemble.*
+ ARG 9-10/93: 248
+ Fa 7-8/93: 289

33950. CD-80329: VIERNE—Organ symphonies no. 1, 3. *Murray, organ.*
+ ARG 3-4/94: 177
+ Fa 1-2/94: 343
+ Gr 5/94: 87

33951. CD-80331: RACHMANINOFF— Symphony no. 3; Symphonic dances, op. 45. *Baltimore Symphony Orch.; Zinman, cond.*
+ ARG 3-4/95: 162
- Fa 3-4/95: 268
+ Gr 1/95: 54

33952. CD-80332: MOZART— Arrangements for brass. *Empire Brass.*
+ ARG 1-2/94: 127
- Fa 1-2/94: 249

33953. CD-80333: Operatic choruses by Handel, Purcell, Mussorgsky, Bizet, Beethoven, and others. *Atlanta Symphony Orch. & Chorus; Shaw, cond.*
- ARG 9-10/94: 257
- Fa 9-10/94: 399

33954. CD-80334: ROSSINI—Overtures. *Atlanta Symphony Orch.; Levi, cond.*
- ARG 11-12/94: 177

+ Fa 11-12/94: 358
+ Gr 11/94: 84

33955. CD-80335: BEETHOVEN—Piano sonatas no. 27-29. *O'Conor, piano.*
- ARG 9-10/93: 94
- Fa 9-10/93: 119
+ Gr 8/93: 56

33956. CD-80337: SCHUBERT— Impromptus, D. 899, D. 935; Waltzes, D. 145. *O'Conor, piano.*
- ARG 3-4/94: 148
- Fa 3-4/94: 305
- Gr 3/94: 83

33957. CD-80338: *The fantastic Stokowksi transcriptions.* Music of Bach, Boccherini, Beethoven, Debussy, Albeniz, Rachmaninoff, Mussorgsky, and Brahms. *Cincinnati Pops Orch.; Kunzel, cond.*
- ARG 3-4/94: 195
+ Fa 5-6/94: 102

33958. CD-80340: SCHUBERT—Songs for male chorus. *Robert Shaw Chamber Singers; Shaw, cond.*
+ ARG 7-8/94: 166
+ Fa 5-6/94: 241
- Gr 6/94: 100

33959. CD-80341: *Ceremonial music for trumpet and symphonic organ.* Music of Charpentier, Purcell, Mouret, Von Paradis, Handel, Vaughan Williams, Bach-Gounod, Bach, Schubert, Clarke, Saint-Luc, Martini, Hovhaness, and Mendelssohn. *Smedvig, trumpet; Hackleman, horn; Murray, organ.*
+ Fa 9-10/93: 368

33960. CD-80343: BRUCKNER— Symphony no. 8. *Cincinnati Symphony Orch.; López Cobos, cond.*
+ ARG 3-4/94: 81
+ Fa 3-4/94: 155

33961. CD-80345: MOZART—Magic flute; Highlights. *Hendricks, Hadley, Allen, Anderson, Lloyd; Scottish Chamber Orch.; Mackerras, cond.*
+ ARG 7-8/93: 130

33962. CD-80346: BRAHMS—String quartets op. 51. *Cleveland Quartet.*
+ ARG 1-2/95: 88
- Fa 1-2/95: 131
+ Gr 2/95: 64

33963. CD-80347: GLAZUNOV—The seasons; Scènes de ballet. *Minnesota Orch.; Waart, cond.*
+ ARG 11-12/93: 110
- Fa 1-2/94: 187
+ Gr 12/93: 67

33964. CD-80349: BRAHMS—Serenade no. 1, op. 11; Variations on a theme by Haydn. *Atlanta Symphony Orch.; Levi, cond.*
+ ARG 11-12/93: 83

TELARC

+ Fa 11-12/93: 195
• Gr 11/93: 65

33965. CD-80350: PROKOFIEV—Sneaky Pete and the wolf. SAINT-SAËNS—Carnival of the animals. *Schickele, narrator; Markham, Broadway, pianos; Atlanta Symphony Orch.; Levi, cond.*
• ARG 1-2/94: 134
• Fa 1-2/94: 263

33966. CD-80351: BEETHOVEN—String quartets no. 10-11. *Cleveland Quartet.*
+ ARG 11-12/94: 71
+ Fa 11-12/94: 164
• Gr 10/94: 131

33967. CD-80352: RAVEL—Daphnis et Chloé; Pavane pour une infante défunte. *Atlanta Symphony Orch.; Levi, cond.*
• ARG 5-6/94: 129
• Fa 3-4/94: 288
• Gr 3/94: 60

33968. CD- 80353: SULLIVAN—Pirates of Penzance. *Adams, Ainsley, Stuart, Evans; Welsh National Opera; Mackerras, cond.*
+ Gr 11/93: 160
• Fa 3-4/94: 330
+ ON 6/94: 45

33969. CD-80354, 80368 (2 separate discs): BACH—Brandenburg concertos. *Boston Baroque; Perlman, cond.*
• ARG 11-12/93: 74 (80354)
+ EM 2/95: 171 (80368)
+ Fa 9-10/93: 105 (80354)
• Fa 1-2/95: 98 (80368)
+ Gr 2/96: 43

33970. CD-80355: Passage: 138 BC-AD 1611. *Empire Brass.*
• ARG 1-2/95: 217
+ Fa 3-4/95: 390

33971. CD-80356: RESPIGHI—Church windows; Brazilian impressions; Roman festivals. *Cincinnati Symphony Orch.; López Cobos, cond.*
+ ARG 5-6/94: 130
+ Fa 7-8/94: 212
+ Gr 7/94: 54

33972. CD-80357: Movie music by Nyman, Grainger, Williams, Debussy, Grusin, and others. *Chertok, piano.*
• ARG 11-12/94: 231

33973. CD-80359: MOZART—Serenade no. 10 (Gran partita). *Members of the Orch. of St. Luke's; Mackerras, cond.*
+ Fa 9-10/94: 265
+ Gr 8/94: 51

33974. CD-80360: MOZART—Così fan tutte. *Lott, Hadley, McLaughlin, Corbelli, Focile, Cachemaille; Edinburgh Festival Chorus; Scottish Chamber Orch.; Mackerras, cond.*
+ ARG 7-8/94: 140
+ Fa 5-6/94: 200
+ Gr 4/94: 98
+ ON 9/94: 58

33975. CD-80361: *Scintillation.* Music of Ravel, Debussy, Salzedo, Grandjany, and Gershwin. *Kondonassis, harp; with assisting instrumentalists.*
+ ARG 11-12/93: 236
+ Fa 9-10/93: 359

33976. CD-80362: POULENC—Stabat Mater. SZYMANOWSKI—Stabat Mater. Gregorian chant—Stabat Mater. *Atlanta Symphony Orch. & Chorus; Shaw, cond.*
+ ARG 3-4/95: 198
+ Fa 3-4/95: 253
• Gr 5/95: 96

33977. CD-80363: BEETHOVEN—Piano sonatas, no. 4, 11, 13. *O'Conor, piano.*
• Fa 9-10/94: 140
+ Gr 8/94: 74

33978. CD-80364: VERDI—Verdi without words (arr. Kunzel and Beck). *Cincinnati Pops Orch.; Kunzel, cond.*
□ Fa 7-8/95: 357

33979. CD-80366: *Puttin' on the Ritz: the great Hollywood musicals.* Music of Schwartz, Berlin, Arlen, Warren, Brown, Rodgers, Prince, Conrad, Gershwin, Porter, Kern, and Rainger. *Vocal soloists; Indiana University Singing Hoosiers; Cincinnati Pops Orch.; Kunzel, cond.*
• Fa 1-2/96: 370

33980. CD-80367: MOZART—Horn concertos; Rondo. FLANDERS AND SWANN—Ill wind. *Ruske, horn; Suart, voice; Scottish Chamber Orch.; Mackerras, cond.*
+ ARG 1-2/95: 144
+ Gr 10/94: 114

33981. CD-80369: SCHUBERT—Piano sonata, D. 959; Moments musicaux, op. 94. *O'Conor, piano.*
• Fa 1-2/96: 298
+ Gr 10/95: 98

33982. CD-80370: FIELD—Piano concertos no. 2-3. *O'Conor, piano; Scottish Chamber Orch.; Mackerras, cond.*
+ ARG 9-10/94: 131
+ Fa 9-10/94: 190
+ Gr 8/94: 46

33983. CD-80371: STRAUSS—Salome: Dance of the seven veils; Der Rosenkavalier: Suite; Burleske for piano and orchestra; Festival prelude for organ and orchestra. *Kahane, piano; Chertok, organ; Cincinnati Symphony Orch.; López-Cobos, cond.*
+ ARG 9-10/95: 221
+ Fa 11-12/95: 393
• Gr 12/95: 92

33984. CD-80372: SCHOENBERG—Verklärte Nacht; Pelleas und Melisande. *Atlanta Symphony Orch.; Levi, cond.*
- ARG 5-6/95: 168
• Fa 3-4/95: 287
• Gr 3/95: 54

33985. CD-80373: BARRIOS MANGORÉ—Guitar music. *Russell, guitar.*
+ ARG 1-2/96: 77
+ Fa 7-8/95: 112
+ Gr 1/96: 79

33986. CD-80374: SULLIVAN—H.M.S. Pinafore. *Suart, Allen, Schrade, Evans, Palmer, Adams, Van Allan; Welsh National Opera; Mackerras, cond.*
• ARG 5-6/95: 114
+ Fa 3-4/95: 171
+ Gr 1/95: 98
• ON 8/95: 37

33987. CD-80376: P.D.Q. BACH—Concerto for 2 pianos vs. orchestra; Trio (sic) sonata; Musical sacrifice. SCHICKELE—Chaconne à son goût. *Various performers.*
• ARG 5-6/95: 79
+ Fa 1-2/95: 103

33988. CD-80377: *Songs of angels.* Christmas hymns and carols. *Robert Shaw Chamber Singers; Shaw, cond.*
+ Fa 11-12/95: 449

33989. CD-80378: *Russian sketches.* Music of Glinka, Ippolitov-Ivanov, Rimsky-Korsakov, and Tchaikovsky. *Baltimore Symphony Orch.; Zinman, cond.*
• ARG 1-2/96: 205
• Fa 11-12/95: 504
• Gr 12/95: 78

33990. CD 80379: WAGNER—Orchestral works from operas. *Cincinnati Symphony Orch.; López-Cobos, cond.*
+ ARG 3-4/95: 220
- Fa 1-2/95: 303

33991. CD-80380: *King's court and celtic fair.* Music of Susato, Byrd, Praetorius, Caccini, Macleod, Scarlatti, Purcell, Rameau, Newton, Beethoven, and Anon. *Empire Brass Quintet.*
□ ARG 9-10/96: 238
• Fa 9-10/96: 425

33992. CD-80382: BEETHOVEN—String quartets no. 1-3. *Cleveland Quartet.*
+ ARG 9-10/95: 101
+ Fa 9-10/95: 138
• Gr 8/95: 91

33993. CD-80384: *Invisible cities.* Music of Leeuw, Manneke, Kertens, and others. *Quink Vocal Ensemble.*
+ ARG 7-8/96: 273
+ Fa 7-8/96: 358
+ Gr 10/96: 100

33994. CD-80385: BACH—Bach at Zwolle. *Murray, organ.*
+ ARG 11-12/96: 82
• Fa 11-12/96: 175
• Gr 5/97: 84

33995. CD-80386: TCHAIKOVSKY—Piano concerto no. 1. SAINT-SAËNS—Piano concerto no. 2. *Watts, piano; Atlanta*

Symphony Orch.; Levi, cond.
+ ARG 11-12/95: 216
+ Fa 11-12/95: 396
• Gr 10/95: 66

33996. CD-80387: PÄRT—Fratres (6 versions); Cantus in memory of Benjamin Britten; Summa; Festina lente. *Mannings, violin; Lavoisier, harp; Springuel, cello; Gleizes, piano; I Fiamminghi; Werthen, cond.*
+ ARG 9-10/95: 189
+ Fa 5-6/95: 283
+ Gr 6/95: 53

33997. CD-80388 (3 discs): MOZART—Le nozze di Figaro. *Vaness, Focile, Mentzer, Corbelli, Miles, Murphy, Davies, Antoniozzi; Scottish Chamber Orch.; Mackerras, cond.*
+ ARG 11-12/95: 164
+ Fa 11-12/95: 314
+ Gr 8/95: 126
+ ON 9/95: 57

33998. 2CD-80389 (2 discs): MENDELSSOHN—Elijah (sung in English). *Bonney, Schellenberg, Quivar, Simpson, Hadley, Clement, Hampson, Paul, Bartelme; Atlanta Symphony Chorus & Orch.; Shaw, cond.*
+ ARG 3-4/96: 154
• Fa 1-2/96: 251 (Greene)
+ Fa 1-2/96: 251 (Lucano)
• Gr 1/96: 90

33999. CD-80390: SCHICKELE—Short tempered clavier; Little pickle book; Sonata da circo; Three chorale-based piecelets. *O'Riley, piano; James, theater organ; Robinson, Schickele, steam calliope; Schickele, organ.*
+ ARG 3-4/96: 85
+ Fa 1-2/96: 129

34000. CD-80391: *Autumn songs.* Music of Bach, Daquin, Debussy, Durand, Gershwin, Grieg, Liszt, Mendelssohn, Mozart, Rachmaninoff, Rimsky-Korsakov, Rubinstein, Schumann, Strauss, and Tchaikovsky. *O'Conor, piano.*
• ARG 1-2/96: 220
+ Fa 11-12/95: 472

34001. CD-80392: HOVHANESS—Symphony no. 6; Concerto no. 7 for orchestra; Alleluia and fugue; Prelude and quadruple fugue; Tzaikerk; Prayer of St. Gregory. *Wiame, trumpet; I Fiamminghi; Werthen, cond.*
+ ARG 1-2/96: 126
+ Fa 1-2/96: 231

34002. CD-80393: VILLA-LOBOS—Bachianas brasileiras no. 2, 4, 8. *Cincinnati Symphony Orch.; Lopez-Cobos, cond.*
+ ARG 1-2/96: 192
+ Fa 3-4/96: 313
+ Fi 4/96: 120
+ Gr 2/96: 60

34003. CD-80394: MAHLER—Symphony no. 5. *Atlanta Symphony Orch.; Levi, cond.*
+ ARG 5-6/96: 143
- Fa 3-4/96: 212
• Gr 3/96: 48

34004. CD-80395: LEHÁR—The Czarevitch (in English). *Gustafson, Hadley, Itami, Atkinson; English Chamber Orch.; Bonynge, cond.*
+ ARG 9-10/96: 151
+ Fa 11-12/96: 284
+ Gr 1/97: 99
• ON 12/14/96: 52

34005. CD-80397: *The power and the majesty.* Essential choral classics. *Robert Shaw Festival Singers; Atlanta Symphony Orch. & Chorus; Shaw, cond.* Reissues.
- ARG 5-6/95: 223

34006. CD-80398: PAGANINI—Caprices, op. 1. *Ehnes, violin.*
+ ARG 9-10/96: 175
• Fa 9-10/96: 280
+ Gr 9/96: 79

34007. CD-80402: *Viennese violin: The romantic music of Lehár, Kreisler, and Strauss.* Music of Lehár, Heuberger, Poldini, Gärtner, Kreisler, J. Strauss, Jr., and Sieczynski. *McDuffie, violin; Cincinnati Pops Orch.; Kunzel, cond.*
- ARG 1-2/97: 215
+ Fa 1-2/97: 337
+ Gr 12/96: 92

34008. CD-80403: *A new Baroque: Pachelbel's Canon and other Baroque favorites.* Music of Handel, Scarlatti, Pachelbel, and Bach. *Kondonassis, harp.*
+ ARG 5-6/95: 210
+ Fa 3-4/95: 376

34009. CD-80404 (2 discs): SULLIVAN—The yeomen of the guard; Trial by jury. *Mellor, Suart, Palmer, Adams, Stephens, Hoare, Evans, Banks; Welsh National Opera; Mackerras, cond.*
- Fa 3-4/96: 297
+ Gr 2/96: 105

34010. CD-80406: *Evocation of the spirit.* Music of Górecki, Pärt, Martin, Barber, and Schoenberg. *Shaw Festival Singers; Shaw, cond.*
+ ARG 7-8/95: 260
+ Fa 9-10/95: 382

34011. CD-80407: Divine sopranos. *Various performers.* Reissues.
+ ARG 9-10/94: 263

34012. CD-80408: *Appear and inspire.* Music of Britten, Debussy, Ravel, Poulenc, Badings, and Argento. *Robert Shaw Festival Singers; Shaw, cond.; Mackenzie, piano.*
+ Fa 7-8/96: 357

34013. CD-80409: *American voices: the African-American Composers' Project.*

Music of Childs, Baker, and Banfield. *Akron Symphony Orch.; Balter, cond.*
+ Fa 3-4/96: 382
+ Fi 7-8/96: 132

34014. CD-80410: MOZART—Requiem. *Ziesak, Maultsby, Croft, Arnold; Boston Baroque; Pearlman, cond.*
• ARG 1-2/96: 148
+ Fa 1-2/96: 263
• Fi 3/96: 127
• Gr 11/95: 142

34015. CD-80411: *The artistry of Fernando de la Mora.* Music of Gounod, Verdi, Puccini, Cilea, Bizet, Donizetti, Ponchielli, Massenet, and Giordano. *Mora, tenor; Orch. of the Welsh National Opera; Mackerras, cond.*
• ARG 1-2/96: 234
+ Fa 1-2/96: 361
+ Gr 1/96: 107

34016. CD-80414: BEETHOVEN—String quartets, op. 18, no. 4-5. *Cleveland Quartet.*
- ARG 3-4/96: 90
+ Fa 3-4/96: 126
• Gr 3/96: 60

34017. CD-80415: CORIGLIANO—String quartet. HAYDN—String quartet, op. 76, no. 5. *Cleveland Quartet.*
+ ARG 11-12/96: 307
+ Fa 11-12/96: 226

34018. CD-80417: GÓRECKI—Three pieces in the old style; Kleines Requiem für eine Polka; Good night. *Szmytka, soprano; Gleizes, piano; Edmund-Davies, alto flute; Righarts, percussion; I Fiamminghi; Werthen, cond.*
• ARG 11-12/96: 130
+ Fa 9-10/96: 203
+ Gr 9/96: 54

34019. CD-80418: *Sky music: music for harp.* Music of Salzedo, Fauré, Debussy, Hovhaness, and Rorem. *Kondonassis, harp.*
+ ARG 5-6/97: 254
+ Fa 11-12/96: 454

34020. CD-80419: LEHÁR—Land des Lächelns (in English). *Gustafson, Hadley, Itami, Atkinson; English Chamber Orch.; Bonynge, cond.*
+ ARG 9-10/96: 151
+ Fa 11-12/96: 284
+ Gr 1/97: 99
• ON 12/14/96: 52

34021. CD-80420 (3 discs): MOZART—Don Giovanni. *Skovhus, Brewer, Lott, Focile, Hadley, Corbelli, Chiummo; Scottish Chamber Orch. & Chorus; Mackerras, cond.*
• ARG 1-2/97: 145
• Fa 1-2/97: 213
+ Gr 11/96: 161
• ON 11/96: 46
• Op 12/96: 1444

TELARC

34022. CD-80423: BEETHOVEN—
Bagatelles (complete). *O'Conor, piano.*
+ ARG 7-8/96: 73
• Gr 11/96: 119

34023. CD-80429: MACDOWELL—Piano
concerto no. 2. LISZT—Piano concertos
no. 1-2. *Watts, piano; Dallas Symphony
Orch.; Litton, cond.*
+ ARG 9-10/96: 156
+ Fa 9-10/96: 246
+ Fi 10/96: 151
• Gr 7/96: 56

34024. CD-80430: BRUBECK—To hope! a
celebration: a mass in the revised Roman
ritual. *Brubeck, piano; Militello,
saxophone; Six, bass; Jones, drums;
Cathedral Choral Society & Orch.; Duke
Ellington School of the Arts Show Choir;
Gloyd, cond.*
+ ARG 1-2/97: 85
+ Fa 11-12/96: 212

34025. CD-80432: *Richard Leech: From
the heart: Italian arias and Neapolitan
songs.* Music of Puccini, Donizetti, Verdi,
Cilea, Tosti, De Curtis, Di Capua, and
Leoncavallo. *Leech, tenor; London
Symphony Orch.; Fiore, cond.*
• ARG 3-4/97: 299
• Fa 1-2/97: 315
+ Gr 2/97: 117
+ ON 1/11/97: 40

34026. CD-80448: Angeli. *Ensemble
PAN; Tapestry ensemble.*
• ARG 11-12/96: 258
+ Fa 9-10/96: 394

34027. CD-80637: MOZART—Horn
concertos; Concerto rondo for horn and
orchestra; Fragment for horn and
orchestra. FLANDERS AND SWANN—Ill wind.
*Ruske, horn; Stuart, baritone; Scottish
Chamber Orch.; Mackerras, cond.*
+ Fa 9-10/94: 261

34028. CD-82001: SHOSTAKOVICH—
Symphony no. 5. STRAVINSKY—The rite of
spring. *Cleveland Orch.; Maazel, cond.*
Reissue.
• ARG 1-2/94: 155
+ Fa 11-12/93: 396

34029. CD-82005: WAGNER—Overtures.
Minnesota Orch.; Marriner, cond.
Reissue.
• Gr 2/94: 57

34030. CD-82006: BRAHMS—Symphony
no. 4; Academic festival overture. *Royal
Phil. Orch.; Previn, cond.* Reissue.
• Gr 1/94: 42

34031. CD-82007: DVOŘÁK—Symphony
no. 9. *St. Louis Symphony Orch.; Slatkin,
cond.* Reissue.
• ARG 7-8/94: 98
+ Fa 7-8/94: 130

34032. CD-82018: DVOŘÁK—
Symphonies, no. 7-8. *Los Angeles Phil.*

Orch.; Previn, cond. Reissue.
+ ARG 11-12/94: 107
+ Fa 1-2/95: 152

TELDEC

6.35656 see 8.35656.

6.35687 see 8.35687.

6.43259 see 8.43259.

34033. 8.35283 (2 discs): BACH—
Cantatas, vol. 12. *Vienna Choir Boys;
Hannover Boys Choir; Concentus
Musicus Wien; Leonhardt Consort;
Harnoncourt, Leonhardt, conds.*
• Fa 1-2/88: 73
+ Gr 1/88: 1107

34034. 8.35284 (2 discs): BACH—
Cantatas, vol. 13. *Vienna Choir Boys;
Concentus Musicus Wien; Harnoncourt,
cond.*
□ Fa 1-2/88: 73
+ Gr 1/88: 1107

34035. 8.35304 (2 discs): BACH—
Cantatas, vol. 14. *Hannover Boys Choir;
Leonhardt Consort; Leonhardt, cond.*
+ Fa 7-8/88: 103
+ Gr 11/88: 830

34036. 8.35654 (2 discs): BACH—
Cantatas, vol. 36. *Tölz Boys Choir;
Collegium Vocale; Concentus Musicus
Wien; Leonhardt Consort; Harnoncourt,
Leonhardt, conds.*
+ Fa 11-12/87: 82

34037. 8.35656 (2 discs): BACH—
Cantatas, vol. 37. *Tölz Boys Choir;
Concentus Musicus Wien; Harnoncourt,
cond.* Issued also as 2 LPs: 6.35656.
+ Fa 9-10/86: 86
+ Gr 4/86: 1305
+ Opus 8/86: 33

34038. 8.35657 (2 discs): BACH—
Cantatas, vol. 38. *Tölz Boys Choir;
Collegium Vocale; Leonhardt Consort;
Concentus Musicus Wien; Leonhardt,
Harnoncourt, conds.*
+ Fa 11-12/87: 82
+ Gr 4/87: 1436

34039. 8.35658 (2 discs): BACH—
Cantatas, vol. 39. *Tölz Boys Choir;
Collegium Vocale; Leonhardt Consort;
Concentus Musicus Wien; Leonhardt,
Harnoncourt, conds.*
+ Fa 11-12/87: 83
+ Gr 9/87: 457

34040. 8.35659 (2 discs): BACH—
Cantatas, vol. 40. *Knaben Chor
Hannover; Tölz Boys Choir; Collegium
Vocale; Leonhardt Consort; Concentus
Musicus Wien; Leonhardt, Harnoncourt,
conds.*
+ Fa 1-2/88: 73
+ Gr 1/88: 1107

34041. 8.35687 (2 discs): HANDEL—Saul.
*Varady, Gale, Esswood, Rolfe Johnson,
Fischer-Dieskau; Vienna State Opera
Chorus; Concentus Musicus, Wien;
Harnoncourt, cond.* Issued also as 2 LPs:
6.35687.
+ Fa 9-10/86: 155
• Gr 8/86: 292

34042. 8.35710 (2 discs): MONTEVERDI—
Vespro della Beata Vergine. *Marshall,
Palmer, Langridge, Equiluz, Hampson,
Korn; Arnold Schönberg Choir; Tölz
Boys Choir; Choralschola der Wiener
Hofburgkapelle; Concentus Musicus
Wien; Harnoncourt, cond.*
+ Fa 1-2/88: 166
• Gr 9/87: 466

34043. 8.35722 (2 discs): HAYDN—Die
Schöpfung. *Gruberová, Protschka, Holl;
Arnold Schönberg Choir; Vienna
Symphony Orch.; Harnoncourt, cond.*
- Fa 7-8/87: 123
+ Gr 4/87: 1445

34044. 8.35741 (2 discs): HAYDN—Die
Jahreszeiten. *Blasi, Protschka, Holl;
Arnold Schönberg Choir; Vienna
Symphony Orch.; Harnoncourt, cond.*
• ARG 9-10/88: 52
+ DA 3/88: 624
• Fa 1-2/88: 138
+ Gr 2/88: 1220

34045. 8.35755 (2 discs): BACH—
Cantatas, vol. 41. *Hannover Boys Choir;
Tölz Boys Choir; Collegium Vocale;
Leonhardt Consort; Concentus Musicus
Wien; Leonhardt, Harnoncourt, conds.*
+ Fa 5-6/88: 67

34046. 8.35762 (2 discs): J. STRAUSS,
JR.—Die Fledermaus. *Gruberová,
Bonney, Lipovsek, Hollweg, Protschka,
Boesch; Netherlands Opera Chorus;
Concertgebouw Orch.; Harnoncourt,
cond.* Dialogue omitted, most reviewers
take exception to the added narration.
- ARG 7-8/88: 57
+ DA 9/88: 52
• Fa 7-8/88: 255
+ Gr 5/88: 1643
+ Op 6/88: 755

34047. 8.35785: BRUCKNER—Symphony
no. 5; no. 9: Finale (reconstructed by
Samale & Mazzuca). *Frankfurt Radio
Symphony Orch.; Inbal, cond.*
+ ARG 9-10/88: 30
• Fa 7-8/88: 141

34048. 8.35838: SMETANA—Má vlast;
Bartered bride: Overture; Dances.
*Frankfurt Radio Symphony Orch.; Inbal,
cond.* Issued also as 2 LPs: 244 183-2.
+ ARG 1-2/90: 91
+ DA 2/90: 55
- Fa 9-10/89: 333
• Gr 10/89: 672
+ SR 9/89: 156

34049. 8.41286: BEETHOVEN—Mass in C op. 86. *Kuhse, Burmeister, Schreier, Adam; Leipzig Radio Choir; Leipzig Gewandhaus Orch.; Kegel, cond.*
+ Fa 3-4/88: 70
+ Gr 10/88: 649

34050. 8.42917: HAYDN—Violin concerto in C, H. VIIa:1. M. HAYDN—Violin concerto in B♭. *Zehetmair, violin & cond.; Franz Liszt Chamber Orch.*
+ Fa 3-4/88: 124

34051. 8.43044: BACH—Harpsichord concertos no. 2-5. *Leonhardt, harpsichord & cond.; Leonhardt Consort.*
+ Fa 9-10/86: 91

34052. 8.43105: DVOŘÁK—String quartet no. 10. Verdi—String quartet in E minor. *Vermeer Quartet.*
+ Fa 11-12/89: 196

34053. 8.43115: BRAHMS—String quartets no. 1-2. *Alban Berg Quartet.*
+ Fa 1-2/90: 141

34054. 8.43202: SCHUBERT—Piano sonata in B♭, D. 960. BEETHOVEN—Piano sonata no. 12, op. 26. *Katsaris, piano.*
• Fa 9-10/86: 224
• Gr 6/86: 74

34055. 8.43203: BACH—Wachet auf, ruft uns die Stimme BWV 140; Herz und Mund und Tat und Leben BWV 147. *Tölz Boys Choir; Concentus Musicus Wien; Harnoncourt, cond.*
+ Fa 3-4/88: 62

34056. 8.43208: BACH—Harpsichord concertos no. 1, 3, 5-6. *Katsaris, harpsichord; Franz Liszt Chamber Orch.; Rolla, cond.*
+ Fa 9-10/86: 88
+ Gr 9/86: 366

34057. 8.43241: SIBELIUS—Violin concerto; Finlandia; Swan of Tuonela; Karelia overture. *Zehetmair, violin; Leipzig Gewandhaus Orch.; Masur, cond.*
- Fa 1-2/88: 211
• Fa 1-2/90: 307

34058. 8.43259: BRUCKNER—Symphony no. 7. *Frankfurt Radio Symphony Orch.; Inbal, cond.* Issued also as LP: 6.43259.
• Fa 9-10/86: 123
• Gr 8/86: 264

34059. 8.43300: BERLIOZ—Symphonie fantastique. *Vienna Phil. Orch.; Prêtre, cond.*
- Fa 9-10/86: 110

34060. 8.43302: BRUCKNER—Symphony no. 9 (Linz version). *Frankfurt Radio Symphony Orch.; Inbal, cond.*
• Fa 1-2/88: 103
+ Gr 8/87: 287

34061. 8.43336: SALIERI—Prima la musica, poi le parole (abridged). Mozart—Der Schauspieldirektor. *Alexander, Hamari, Hampson, Holl, Nador, Laki, Hampson, Kamp; Concertgebouw Orch.; Harnoncourt, cond.*
+ Fa 9-10/87: 281
+ Fa 1-2/88: 177
+ Gr 10/87: 625
+ ON 4/9/88: 49
+ SR 2/88: 196

34062. 8.43339: TCHAIKOVSKY—Symphony no. 4. *Gewandhaus Orch.; Masur, cond.*
- ARG 9-10/88: 88
+ Fa 5-6/88: 244
+ Gr 2/88: 1200
+ HPR 1/24/88: H25

34063. 8.43340: TCHAIKOVSKY—Symphony no. 6. *Gewandhaus Orch.; Masur, cond.*
• Fa 6-7/87: 195
- Gr 9/87: 419

34064. 8.43419: BEETHOVEN (ARR. LISZT)—Symphonies no. 4, 8. *Katsaris, piano.*
- Fa 1-2/88: 89
+ Gr 8/87: 322

34065. 8.43479: BRAHMS—Symphony no. 1. *Cleveland Orch.; Dohnányi, cond.*
+ DA 6/88: 58
• Fa 1-2/88: 99
+ Gr 7/87: 178

34066. 8.43535: MOZART—Mass in C, K. 317; Vesperae solennes de confessore, K. 339. *Rodgers, Magnus, Protschka, Pólgar; Arnold Schönberg Choir; Choralschola der Wiener Hofburgkapelle; Concentus Musicus Wien; Harnoncourt, cond.*
+ ARG 9-10/88: 69
+ Fa 1-2/88: 173
+ Gr 7/88: 190
+ SR 5/88: 113

34067. 8.43619: BRUCKNER—Symphony no. 1 (Linz version). *Frankfurt Radio Symphony Orch.; Inbal, cond.*
• ARG 9-10/88: 30
• Fa 1-2/88: 103
+ SR 3/88: 97

34068. 8.43626—8.43627 (2 separate discs): BACH—Brandenburg concertos. *Concentus Musicus Wien; Harnoncourt, cond.*
• Fa 1-2/88: 71
+ Gr 8/87: 278

34069. 8.43628: HANDEL—Organ concertos op. 4 no. 1-2, op. 7 no. 1-2. *Chamber orch.; Richter, organ & cond.*
+ Fa 1-2/88: 135
- Gr 8/87: 278

34070. 8.43629: HAYDN—Horn concerto no. 1. DANZI—Horn concerto in E major.

ROSETTI —Horn concerto in D minor. *Baumann, horn; Concerto Amsterdam; Schröder, cond.*
+ Fa 1-2/88: 167
+ Gr 8/87: 278

34071. 8.43630: VIVALDI—Concertos RV Anh. 17, RV 130, 169, 208, 424, 461. *Schröder, violin & cond.; Concerto Amsterdam.*
+ Fa 1-2/88: 231
+ Gr 8/87: 278

34072. 8.43631: BACH—Schweigt stille, plaudert nicht BWV 211; Mer hahn en neue Oberkeet BWV 212. *Hansmann, Equiluz, Egmond; Concentus Musicus Wien; Harnoncourt, cond.*
+ Fa 1-2/88: 73
+ Gr 8/87: 278

34073. 8.43632: BACH—Goldberg variations BWV 988. *Leonhardt, harpsichord.*
+ Fa 1-2/88: 71
+ Gr 8/87: 278

34074. 8.43633—8.54634 (2 separate discs): BACH—Orchestral suites. *Stastny, flute; Concentus Musicus Wien; Harnoncourt, cond.*
• Fa 1-2/88: 71-72
+ Gr 8/87: 278

34075. 8.43635: MONTEVERDI—Lettera amorosa; Con che soavità; Lamento d'Arianna; L'Orfeo: Mira, Orfeo; L'incoronazione di Poppea: 3 excerpts. *Berberian, soprano; Concentus Musicus Wien; Harnoncourt, cond.*
+ Fa 1-2/88: 166
• Gr 8/87: 278

34076. 8.43673: MOZART—Serenade no. 6; Bassoon concerto; Notturno for orchestra K. 286. L. Mozart—Trumpet concerto in D. *Turković, bassoon; Immer, trumpet; Concentus Musicus Wien; Harnoncourt, cond.*
+ DA 5/88: 53
+ Fa 1-2/88: 179

34077. 8.43675: TCHAIKOVSKY—Symphony no. 5. *Leipzig Gewandhaus Orch.; Masur, cond.*
+ Fa 9-10/89: 343
• Gr 2/89: 1298

34078. 8.43677: BEETHOVEN—String quartet no. 14. *Vermeer String Quartet.*
+ DA 6/88: 60
+ Fa 1-2/88: 86
+ Gr 2/88: 1204

34079. 8.43678: BRAHMS—Symphony no. 4. *Cleveland Orch.; Dohnányi, cond.*
+ Fa 1-2/88: 99
+ Gr 1/88: 1074
+ SR 1/88: 152

34080. 8.43681: MENDELSSOHN—Piano concertos no. 1-2; Capriccio brillant in B minor for piano and orchestra op. 22.

TELDEC

Katsaris Cyprien; Leipzig Gewandhaus Orch.; Masur, cond.
- • ARG 1-2/89: 65
- + Fa 9-10/88: 199
- • Gr 6/88: 30

34081. 8.43682: SCHUBERT—Piano trio no. 1; Notturno for piano and strings D. 897. *Haydn Trio.*
- - Fa 5-6/88: 206

34082. 8.43683: SCHUBERT—Piano trio no. 2; Sonata movement for piano and strings D. 28. *Haydn Trio.*
- - Fa 3-4/88: 194

34083. 8.43686: VILLA-LOBOS—A próle do bébé, book 1: Banquinha; Moreninha; Caboclinha; Mulatinha; Neginha; A pobreshiha; O polichinello; Bruxa; Bachianas brasileiras no. 4: Preludio; As trés marias; Rudepoema. *Freire, piano.*
- + Fa 1-2/88: 229
- + Gr 12/87: 983

34084. 8.43687: BRAHMS—Ballades, op. 10; Klavierstücke, op. 76. *Frantz, piano.*
- • Fa 1-2/88: 96

34085. 8.43745: BACH—Cantatas, vol. 15. *Tölz Boys Choir; Concentus Musicus Wien; Harnoncourt, cond.*
- + Fa 7-8/88: 103
- + Gr 11/88: 830

34086. 8.43749: SCHUMANN—Violin sonatas no. 1-2; Märchenbilder for viola. *Zehetmair, violin & viola; Katsaris, piano.*
- + ARG 7-8/88: 55
- • Fa 3-4/88: 199
- + Gr 3/88: 1322

34087. 8.43752: HAYDN—Symphonies no. 103-104. *Concertgebouw Orch.; Harnoncourt, cond.*
- + Fa 1-2/88: 141
- + Gr 2/88: 1185

34088. 8.43753: LOEWE—Lieder and Balladen. *Fischer-Dieskau, baritone; Höll, piano.*
- • Fa 1-2/88: 154
- + Opus 4/88: 38

34089. 8.43754: *Mélodies der Belle Epoch.* Music of Gounod, Franck, Saint-Saëns, Bizet, Massenet, and others. *Fischer-Dieskau, baritone; Höll, piano.*
- + DA 2/88: 52
- + Fa 3-4/88: 242
- + Gr 9/88: 472
- - Opus 4/88: 32

34090. 8.43765: SCHUMANN—Violin concerto in D minor; Piano concerto in A minor, op. 54. *Kulenkampff, violin; Michelangeli, piano; Berlin Phil. Orch.; La Scala Orch.; Schmidt-Isserstedt, Pedrotti, conds.*
- • Fa 3-4/88: 197
- + Fa 5-6/88: 210 (Piano concerto)
- - Fa 5-6/88: 210 (Violin concerto)

34091. 8.43770: HANDEL—Organ concertos op. 4 no. 3-4, op. 7, no. 3-4. *Chamber orch.; Richter, organ & cond.*
- + Fa 1-2/88: 135

34092. 8.43771: BACH—Art of the fugue BWV 1080. *Tachezi, organ.*
- + Fa 1-2/88: 71

34093. 8.43772: BACH—Sonatas for viola da gamba and harpsichord BWV 1027-29; Trio sonata for 2 flutes BWV 1039. *N. Harnoncourt, viola da gamba; Tachezi, harpsichord; Brüggen, Stastny, flutes.*
- • Fa 1-2/88: 71

34094. 8.43773: TELEMANN—Recorder concerto in F; Concerto for 4 violins in G; Concerto for 3 oboes in B♭; Suite for horn and strings in F. *Concentus Musicus Wien; Harnoncourt, cond.*
- + Fa 1-2/88: 221

34095. 8.43774: FRESCOBALDI—Primo libro di toccate: Toccata nona and decima; Cento partite sopra passacagli; Partite 14 sopra L'aria della romanesca; Secundo libro di Toccate: Canzona terza; Toccata nona; Capriccio sopra la bassa Flamenga; Canzon terza detta La crivelli. *Asperen, harpsichord.*
- + Fa 1-2/88: 122

34096. 8.43776: TELEMANN—Tafelmusik: Overtures. *Concerto Amsterdam; Brüggen, cond.*
- + Fa 1-2/88: 222

34097. 8.43777: *Blockfloten-Konzerte.* Music of Vivaldi, Sammartini, Telemann, and Naudot. *Brüggen, recorder; Concentus Musicus Wien; Harnoncourt, Brüggen, conds.*
- + Fa 1-2/88: 267

34098. 8.43778: PURCELL—Rejoice in the Lord alway; Blow up the trumpet in Zion; O God, Thou art my God; Chaconne, Z. 730; O God, Thou hast cast us out; My heart is inditing; Remember not, Lord, our offenses. *Bowman, Rogers, Egmond; King's College Choir (Cambridge); Leonhardt Consort; Willcocks, Leonhardt, conds.*
- + Fa 1-2/88: 193

34099. 8.43779: BIBER—Sonatas, Ballettae, and Battalia. *Concentus Musicus Wien; Harnoncourt, cond.*
- + Fa 1-2/88: 93

34100. 8.43921: DVOŘÁK—Piano trio no. 3. BRAHMS—Piano trio no. 3. *Trio Fontenay.*
- + ARG 11-12/88: 33
- + DA 11/88: 62
- - Fa 7-8/88: 161
- • Gr 9/88: 434
- + Ov 8/88: 17

34101. 8.43922: PAGANINI—Caprices op. 1. *Paetsch, violin.*

- • Fa 5-6/88: 180
- • Gr 7/88: 182

34102. 8.43927: HANDEL—Giulio Cesare: Excerpts. *Alexander, Popp, Lipovsek, Murray, Esswood; Arnold- Schoenberg Choir; Concentus Musicus Wien; Harnoncourt, cond.*
- - Fa 7-8/88: 172

34103. 8.44005: BRAHMS—Symphony no. 2; Variations on the St. Antoni chorale op. 56a. *Cleveland Orch.; Dohnányi, cond.*
- • ARG 11-12/88: 23
- + Fa 7-8/88: 136
- • Gr 7/88: 156

34104. 8.44006: BEETHOVEN—Symphonies no. 1-2 (arr. Liszt). *Katsaris, piano.*
- + Fa 9-10/89: 145

34105. 8.44007: HANDEL—Organ concertos op. 4 no. 5-6, op. 7 no. 5-6. *Chamber orch.; Richter, organ & cond.*
- • Fa 7-8/88: 172

34106. 8.44010: Music of Buonamente, Schmelzer, Bruckner, Ferro, and others. *Musicalische Compagney.*
- + ARG 9-10/88: 108
- + Fa 7-8/88: 314

34107. 8.44011: *Fiori concertati.* Music of Castello, Falconieri, and Kapsberger. *Musicalische Compagney.*
- + ARG 9-10/88: 108
- + Fa 7-8/88: 325

34108. 8.44013: LASSUS—Prophetiae Sibyllarum; Sieben Moresken. *Münchener Vokalsolisten; Münchener Flötenconsort; Hirsch, cond.*
- + Fa 7-8/88: 185
- + Gr 9/88: 466

34109. 8.44014: BACH—Concertos BWV 1041-43, 1056. *A. Harnoncourt, Pfeiffer, violins; Schaeftlein, oboe; Concentus Musicus Wien; N. Harnoncourt, cond.*
- + Fa 7-8/88: 104

34110. 8.44092: EISLER—Lieder. *Fischer-Dieskau, baritone; Reimann, piano.*
- + Fa 5-6/89: 186
- + Gr 7/89: 215

34111. 8.44134: BRAHMS—Symphony no. 3; Tragic overture. *Cleveland Orch.; Dohnányi, cond.* Issued also as LP: 243 711-2.
- + ARG 11-12/89: 45
- + Fa 9-10/89: 161
- + Gr 12/88: 993

34112. 8.44136: *Tea for two.* Music of Henze, Bartók, Praetorius, Schubert, and others. *London Brass.*
- + Fa 9-10/89: 435

8.44143 see 244 197-2.

34113. 8.44145: Dvořák—String quartet no. 12. Mendelssohn—String quartet no. 2. *Vermeer Quartet.*
+ Fa 11-12/89: 196

34114. 8.44198: Brahms—Piano trio no. 2. Dvořák—Piano trio no. 1. *Trio Fontenay.* Issued also as LP: 244 177-2.
+ ARG 9-10/89: 35
- Fa 1-2/90: 141
+ Gr 2/90: 1479

34115. 8.44251: Bruckner—Symphony no. 6. *Frankfurt Radio Symphony Orch.; Inbal, cond.* Issued also as LP: 244 182-2.
+ ARG 11-12/89: 49
● Fa 9-10/89: 168
- Gr 7/89: 71
● SR 9/89: 144

34116. 8.44253: Chopin—Piano sonata no. 3; Fantasy in F minor op. 49. Scriabin—Fantasy op. 28; Piano sonata no. 2. *Leonskaja, piano.*
+ Fa 9-10/89: 179
+ Gr 11/89: 942

34117. 8.44255: Brahms—Piano sonata no. 2; Variations in D minor from the String sextet no. 1; Rhapsodies op. 79 no. 1-2. *Katsaris, piano.*
+ Fa 9-10/89: 160
+ Gr 7/89: 205

34118. 8.44258: Schubert—Octet in F, D. 803. *Berliner Solisten.* Issued also as LP: 244 195-2.
+ ARG 1-2/90: 85
+ Fa 11-12/89: 346
+ Gr 9/89: 497

34119. 8.48262 (2 discs): *Benny Goodman plays classics.* Music of Brahms, Beethoven, and Weber. *Goodman, clarinet; Berkshire String Quartet; Pommers, piano.*
+ Fa 9-10/89: 430

34120. 8.48272 (2 discs): Brahms—Ein deutsches Requiem. *Price, Ramey; Ambrosian Singers; Royal Phil. Orch.; Previn, cond.*
- Fa 7-8/87: 74
+ Gr 6/87: 88

34121. 242 630-2 (2 discs): Bach—Cantatas, vol. 35. *Tölz Boys Choir; Hannover Boys Choir; Collegium Vocale; Concentus Musicus Wien; Leonhardt Consort; Harnoncourt, Leonhardt, conds.*
+ Fa 9-10/90: 140

34122. 242 716-2 (2 discs): Mozart—Die Zauberflöte. *Gruberová, Bonney, Blochwitz, Scharinger, Hampson, Salminen; Zürich Opera House Chorus & Orch.; Harnoncourt, cond.* Dialogue replaced by narrator.
- Fa 5-16/89: 244

34123. 242 738-2 (2 discs): Bach—Cantatas, vol. 42. *Hannover Boys Choir; Tölz Boys Choir; Collegium Vocale; Concentus Musicus Wien; Leonhardt, Harnoncourt, conds.*
+ Fa 9-10/90: 140

34124. 243 463-2: Mendelssohn—Symphonies no. 3-4. *Leipzig Gewandhaus Orch.; Masur, cond.*
● Fa 5-6/89: 233
+ Gr 11/88: 780

34125. 243 673-2: Schumann—Piano sonata no. 1. Brahms—Piano sonata no. 2. *Leonskaja, piano.*
+ Fa 5-6/89: 316

243 711-2 see 8.44134.

34126. 243 718-2: Bruckner—Symphony no. 2. *Frankfurt Radio Symphony Orch.; Inbal, cond.*
+ ARG 7-8/89: 32

34127. 243 722-2: Brahms—Symphony no. 2; Tragic overture. *Concertgebouw Orch.; Mengelberg, cond.*
● ARG 5-6/89: 31
+ Gr 9/89: 554

34128. 243 724-2: Brahms—Symphony no. 4. Strauss—Don Juan. *Concertgebouw Orch.; Mengelberg, cond.*
● ARG 5-6/89: 31
+ Gr 9/89: 554

244 177-2 see 8.44198.

34129. 244 178-2: Mendelssohn—Symphony no. 2. *Bonney, Wiens, Schreier; Leipzig Radio Choir; Leipzig Gewandhaus Orch.; Masur, cond.*
- ARG 3-4/90: 74
+ Fa 3-4/90: 233
+ Gr 4/90: 1782
+ St 5/90: 187

34130. 244 179-2 (2 discs): Bach—Cantatas, vol. 43. *Tölz Boys Choir; Hannover Boys Choir; Concentus Musicus Wien; Leonhardt Consort; Harnoncourt, Leonhardt, conds.*
+ Fa 9-10/90: 141

244 182-2 see 8.44251.

244 183-2 see 8.35838.

34131. 244 184-2 (3 discs): Mozart—Don Giovanni. *Gruberová, Alexander, Bonney, Blochwitz, Hampson, Pólgar, Scharinger, Holl; Netherlands Opera Chorus; Royal Concertgebouw Orch.; Harnoncourt, cond.*
+ ARG 11-12/90: 86
+ Fa 7-8/90: 207 (conductor)
● Fa 7-8/90: 207 (singers)
+ Gr 3/90: 1683

+ MA 11/90: 77
+ NYT 4/1/90: H33
● ON 12/22/90: 37
+ Op 3/90: 382
● SR 6/90: 111
+ St 11/90: 209

34132. 244 189-2: Schubert—Fantasia in C, D. 760; Piano sonata in G, D. 894. *Leonskaja, piano.*
● Fa 3-4/90: 283
● Gr 1/90: 1352

34133. 244 191-2: Mozart—Piano sonata K. 309, 457; Fantasies K. 396-397, 475. *Katasaris, piano.*
- ARG 7-8/90: 76
+ DA 4/90: 58
+ Fa 3-4/90: 246
- St 7/90: 175

244 195-2 see 8.44258.

34134. 244 196-2: Haydn—Piano concerto no. 11; Mondo della luna: Overture; Sinfonia concertante for violin, cello, oboe, and bassoon in B♭. *Tachezi, piano; Höbarth, violin; Coin, cello; Reichenberger, oboe; Turkovic, bassoon; Concentus Musicus Wien; Harnoncourt, cond.*
● ARG 11-12/89: 65
- Fa 9-10/89: 216
+ Gr 4/90: 1782

34135. 244 197-2: Villa-Lobos—Guitar music (complete). *Lendle, guitar.* Issued also as LP: 8.44143.
● ARG 11-12/89: 65
+ Fa 9-10/89: 357

34136. 244 918-2 (2 discs): Bach—Well-tempered clavier bk. 1. *Wilson, harpsichord.*
+ Fa 3-4/90: 113
+ Gr 4/90: 1830

34137. 244 919-2: Shostakovich—String quartets no. 7-9. *Brodsky Quartet.*
+ ARG 11-12/90: 115
● Fa 11-12/90: 355
+ Gr 5/90: 2004
+ SR 3/91: 97

34138. 244 920-2: Mussorgsky—Pictures at an exhibition; Night on Bald Mountain (both arr. Ravel). *Cleveland Orch.; Dohnányi, cond.*
- ARG 11-12/89: 82
● Fa 1-2/90: 252
● Gr 6/89: 40

34139. 244 923-2: *Lieder aus Des knaben Wanderhorn* Music of Mendelssohn, Mahler, Schumann, Brahms, and others. *Hampson, baritone; Parsons, piano.*
+ ARG 9-10/90: 159
+ Fa 7-8/90: 339
+ Gr 10/90: 812
+ MA 11/90: 77
+ SR 6/90: 84

TELDEC

34140. 244 924-2: BRAHMS—Piano trio no. 1. IVES—Piano trio. *Trio Fontenay.*
   + ARG 9-10/90: 52
   • Fa 9-10/90: 200
   + Gr 4/90: 1813
   + MA 1/91: 72

34141. 244 926-2: MOZART—Sonata for 2 pianos K. 448. SCHUBERT—Fantasy for piano 4-hands D. 940. *G. & S. Pekinel, pianos.*
   • Fa 11-12/90: 300
   • Gr 4/90: 1826

34142. 244 929-2: BEETHOVEN—String quartets no. 10-11. *Vermeer Quartet.*
   • ARG 9-10/90: 48
   • Fa 9-10/90: 173 (no. 10)
   • Fa 9-10/90: 173 (no. 11)
   • Gr 7/90: 234

34143. 244 972-2 (4 discs): BRAHMS—Symphonies (complete); Variations on a theme by Haydn; Tragic overture. *Cleveland Orch.; Dohnányi, cond.*
   • ARG 3-4/90: 33
   + Fa 3-4/90: 155

34144. 246 007-2: *Romantic journey.* Music of Tchaikovsky (arr. Harvey), Brahms (arr. Purser), Schubert (arr. Harvey), and others. *London Brass.*
   + ARG 5-6/90: 135
   + Fa 3-4/90: 389
   + St 8/90: 177

34145. 246 008-2: RACHMANINOFF—Symphony no. 2. *Philharmonia Orch.; Sanderling, cond.*
   + ARG 7-8/90: 89
   - Fa 3-4/90: 269
   - St 7/90: 177

34146. 246 103-2 (2 discs): *8th van Cliburn International Piano Competition, 1989: "The Winners".* Music of Beethoven, Schuman, Chopin, Liszt, and others. *Sultanov, Cocarelli, Lupo, pianos.*
   + ARG 7-8/90: 143
   □ Fa 3-4/90: 364
   + SR 5/90: 112

34147. 0630-10329-2 (2 discs): MOZART—Flute concertos; Flute and harp concerto. HAYDN—Flute concerto. GLUCK—Dance of the blassed spirits. *Nicolet, flute; Munich Bach Orch.; Richter, cond.* Reissues.
   • ARG 9-10/96: 169
   • Gr 5/96: 68

34148. 0630-10788-2: Concertos by Telemann, Neruda, Marcello, and Bach. *Nakariakov, trumpet; St. Paul Chamber Orch.; Wolff, cond.*
   + ARG 9-10/96: 249
   • Gr 9/96: 62

34149. 0630-10904-2: TCHAIKOVSKY—Symphony no. 5; 1812 overture. *Chicago Symphony Orch.; Barenboim, cond.* Recorded live.

   • ARG 9-10/96: 217
   + Fa 9-10/96: 342
   + Gr 8/96: 59

34150. 0630-11084-2: SCHUBERT—Piano sonata D. 845; Impromptus, D. 946. *Staier, fortepiano.*
   + Gr 7/96: 78

34151. 0630-11427-2: BACH—Cantata no. 4; Flute sonatas no. 1-2. *Engen, bass; Nicolet, flute; Munich Bach Choir; Munich State Opera Orch.; Richter, cond.* Recorded 1959 and 1963.
   • Gr 5/96: 68

34152. 0630-12319-2: HANDEL—Ode for St. Cecilia's day. *Palmer, Rolfe Johnson; Stockholm Bach Choir; Concentus Musicus Wien; Harnoncourt, cond.* Reissue.
   • ARG 7-8/96: 124

34153. 0630-12323-2 (2 discs): TELEMANN—Pimpinone; Concertos by Tessarini, Albinoni, and Vivaldi. *Spreckelsen, Nimsgern; Florilegium Musicum; Hirsch, cond.* Reissues.
   + ARG 9-10/96: 219
   • Gr 9/96: 114

34154. 0630-12372-2 (2 discs): PUCCINI—Tosca. *Malfitano, Domingo, Raimondi, Prestia, Gatti, Buffoli; Chorus & Orch. of RAI, Rome; Mehta, cond.*
   • ARG 1-2/97: 153
   • Fa 11-12/96: 339
   • Gr 3/97: 95
   + ON 11/96: 46

34155. 0630-12465-2: CHARPENTIER—Te Deum; Missa Assumpta est Maria. *St. James's Singers; St. James's Baroque Players; Bolton, cond.*
   - ARG 7-8/96: 98
   + Gr 9/96: 85

34156. 0630-12601-2: SCARLATTI—Keyboard sonatas. *Staier, harpsichord.*
   + Gr 7/96: 78

34157. 0630-12672-2 (3 discs): BIZET—Carmen. *Larmore, Moser, Gheorghiu, Ramey; Bavarian State Orch.; Bavarian State Opera Chorus; Sinopoli, cond.*
   - ARG 1-2/97: 75
   + Fa 1-2/97: 110
   • Gr 10/96: 04
   • ON 11/96: 44

34158. 0630-13132-2: Lost in the stars. *Chanticleer; Don Haas Trio; Orch.; Stratta, cond.*
   • ARG 11-12/96: 270

34159. 0630-13161-2: SIBELIUS—Violin concerto. NIELSEN—Violin concerto. *Vengerov, violin; Chicago Symphony Orch.; Barenboim, cond.*
   + ARG 1-2/97: 171
   + Fa 1-2/97: 272
   • Gr 9/96: 56

34160. 0630-15549-2: Music of Bizet, Gluck, Handel, Mozart, and others. *Larmore, mezzo-soprano.*
   + ARG 1-2/97: 228

34161. 2292-42494-2 (2 discs): MONTEVERDI—Orfeo. *Kozma, Hansmann, Villisech, Egmond; Munich Capella Antiqua; Concentus Musicus Wien; Harnoncourt, cond.* Reissue.
   + ARG 11-12/93: 152

34162. 2292-42496-2 (3 discs): MONTEVERDI—Il ritorno d'Ulisse in patria. *Lerer, Eliasson, Hansmann, Egmond; Junge Kantorei; Concentus Musicus Wien; Harnoncourt, cond.* Reissue.
   + ARG 11-12/93: 152

34163. 2292-42510-2 (3 discs): RAMEAU—Castor et Pollux. *Vandersteene, Souzay; other vocalists; Stockholm Kammerkören; Concentus Musicus Wien; Harnoncourt, cond.* Reissue.
   • ARG 11-12/93: 174
   + Fa 11-12/93: 355

34164. 2292-42547-2 (4 discs): MONTEVERDI—L'incoronazione di Poppea. *Donath, Söderström, Berberian, Esswood; Concentus Musicus Wien; Harnoncourt, cond.* Reissue.
   + ARG 11-12/93: 152

34165. 2292-42567-2: HANDEL—Bclshazzar. *Palmer, soprano; Lehane, contralto; Esswood, alto; Tear, Sunnegardh, tenors; Bilt, Sandlund, basses; Stockholm Chamber Choir; Vienna Concentus Musicus; Harnoncourt, cond.* Reissue.
   + Gr 10/91: 162

34166. 2292-44180-2: MOZART—Mass in C minor, K. 139; Exsultate jubilate. *Bonney, Rappé, Protschka, Hagegård; Arnold Schönberg Chor; Concentus Musicus Wien; Harnoncourt, cond.*
   + Fa 3-4/91: 294
   + Gr 2/91: 1546

34167. 2292-44193-2 (2 discs): BACH—Cantatas, vol. 44. *Tölz Boys Choir; Hannover Boys Choir; Collegium Vocale; Concentus Musicus Wien; Leonhardt Consort; Harnoncourt, Leonhardt, conds.*
   + Fa 9-10/90: 141
   + Gr 5/90: 2024

34168. 2292-44194-2 (2 discs): BACH—Cantatas, vol. 45. *Tölz Boys Choir; Hannover Boys Choir; Collegium Vocale; Concentus Musicus Wien; Leonhardt Consort; Harnoncourt, Leonhardt, conds.*
   + Fa 9-10/90: 141
   + Gr 5/90: 2024

34169. 2292-44198-2: HAYDN—Symphonies no. 45, 60. *Concentus Musicus Wien; Harnoncourt, cond.*

+ ARG 3-4/92: 74
+ Fa 11-12/91: 344

34170. 2292-44633-2: TELEMANN—Ino.
HANDEL—Apollo e Dafne. *Alexander,
soprano; Hampson, baritone; Concentus
musicus Wien; Harnoncourt, cond.*
+ ARG 11-12/91: 161
+ Fa 11-12/91: 334
+ Gr 4/91: 1890

34171. 2292-44809-2: MOZART—Eine
kleine Nachtmusik; Divertimento no. 11;
Musical joke. *Concentus Musicus Wien;
Harnoncourt, cond.*
- ARG 11-12/90: 87
- Gr 6/90: 50

34172. 2292-44921-2: BEETHOVEN—
Symphony no. 5 (arr. Liszt); Eroica
variations op. 35. *Katsaris, piano.*
● Fa 9-10/90: 179
● Gr 8/90: 390
● MA 1/91: 70

34173. 2292-44922-2 (2 discs):
STRAUSS—Lieder. *Gruberova, soprano;
Haider, piano.*
- Fa 11-12/91: 496
+ Gr 6/91: 77
+ ON 12-7/91: 54

34174. 2292-44928-2 (2 discs):
MOZART—Lucio Silla. *Gruberová,
Upshaw, Kenny, Bartoli, Schreier;
Arnold Schoenberg Chorus; Concentus
Musicus Wien; Harnoncourt, cond.*
Recorded live 1989.
+ ARG 11-12/91: 110
+ Fa 7-8/91: 223
● Gr 3/91: 1721
+ MA 9/91: 48

34175. 2292-44931-2: Music of Ravel,
Infante, and Granados (arr. Barlett &
Robertston). *G. & S. Pekinel, pianos.*
● Fa 3-4/91: 337

34176. 2292-44932-2: STRAVINSKY—
Firebird; Scherzo fantastique.
Philharmonia Orch.; Inbal, cond.
- ARG 1-2/91: 104
- Fa 9-10/90: 400
+ Gr 7/90: 230

34177. 2292-44933-2: MENDELSSOHN—
Symphonies no. 1, 5. *Leipzig
Gewandhaus Orch.; Masur, cond.*
+ ARG 9-10/91: 104
+ Fa 9-10/90: 294 m.f.
+ Gr 6/90: 50
● MA 3/91: 80
+ SR 9/90: 124

34178. 2292-44934-2 (2 discs): BACH—
Well-tempered clavier bk. 2. *Wilson,
harpsichord.*
+ ARG 1-2/91: 24
+ DA 4/91: 68
+ Fa 9-10/90: 154
+ Gr 6/90: 79

34179. 2292-44935-2: SCHUMANN—Fünf
frühe Lieder; Kerner-Lieder op. 35; Fünf
Lieder op. 40; Sängers Trost; Trost im
Gesang. *Hampson, baritone; Parsons,
piano.*
+ ARG 1-2/91: 96
+ Fa 1-2/91: 313
● Gr 4/91: 1889
+ MA 3/91: 88

34180. 2292-44936-2: BRAHMS—Piano
concerto no. 2. *Katsaris, piano;
Philharmonia Orch.; Inbal, cond.*
- ARG 11-12/90: 36
+ DA 12/90: 90
+ Fa 11-12/90: 181
● Gr 8/90: 363
● MA 1/90: 70

34181. 2292-44937-2: FAURÉ—Trio.
RAVEL—Trio. DEBUSSY—Trio. *Fontenay
Trio.*
+ ARG 9-10/92: 103
+ Fa 11-12/92: 330
● Gr 7/92: 69

34182. 2292-44938-2: STRAVINSKY—Sacre
du printemps; Quatre études pour
orchestre; Scherzo à la russe.
Philharmonia Orch.; Inbal, cond.
- ARG 5-6/91: 113
- Fa 3-4/91: 399
+ SR 6/91: 97

34183. 2292-44939-2: TCHAIKOVSKY—
Symphony no. 1; Francesca da Rimini.
Gewandhaus Orch.; Masur, cond.
● ARG 11-12/90: 128
+ Fa 11-12/90: 376 (Symphony)
+ Fa 11-12/90: 376 (Francesca)
● Gr 6/90: 63
● MA 3/91: 88

34184. 2292-44941-2: MUSSORGSKY (ORCH.
GORTCHAKOV)—Pictures at an exhibition.
PROKOFIEV—Symphony no. 1. *London
Phil. Orch.; Masur, cond.*
+ ARG 5-6/92: 90
● Fa 3-4/92: 274
+ Gr 11/91: 97

34185. 2292-44942-2: CHOPIN—Preludes
op. 28. SCHUMANN—Symphonic etudes.
Grützman, piano.
- Fa 5-6/91: 156
+ Gr 4/91: 1866

34186. 2292-44943-2: TCHAIKOVSKY—
Symphony no. 2; Romeo and Juliet.
*Gewandhausorchester Leipzig; Masur,
cond.*
● ARG 9-10/91: 134
+ Fa 9-10/91: 371
+ Gr 5/91: 2022

34187. 2292-44944-2: BRAHMS—Violin
concerto; Academic festival overture.
*Zehetmair, violin; Cleveland Orch.;
Dohnányi, cond.*
- ARG 9-10/91: 51
+ DA 8/91: 41
● Fa 3-4/91: 163
● Gr 2/91: 1499

34188. 2292-44945-2: RAVEL—Alborada
del gracioso; La valse; Daphnis et Chloé:
suite no. 2; Boléro. *Cleveland Orch. &
Chorus; Dohnányi, cond.*
+ ARG 9-10/92: 146
● Fa 9-10/92: 323
+ Gr 4/92: 72

34189. 2292-44946-2: MENDELSSOHN—
Lieder. *Bonney, soprano; Parsons, piano.*
● ARG 7-8/93: 124
+ Fa 7-8/93: 179
+ Gr 2/93: 70

34190. 2292-44947-2: MENDELSSOHN—
Piano trios no. 1-2. *Trio Fontenay.*
+ ARG 11-12/90: 115
● Fa 1-2/91: 241
+ Gr 9/90: 558
+ MA 1/91: 72

34191. 2292-44948-2: LISZT—Piano
sonata in B minor; Petrach sonatas; Après
une lecture du Dante. *Leonskaja, piano.*
- ARG 11-12/90: 74
+ DA 8/90: 46
● Fa 11-12/90: 258
● Gr 7/90: 251

34192. 2292-46009-2: SHOSTAKOVICH—
String quartets no. 1, 3-4. *Brodsky
Quartet.*
+ ARG 11-12/90: 115
● Fa 11-12/90: 354
+ Gr 6/90: 75

34193. 2292-46010-2: TCHAIKOVSKY—
Piano concerto no. 1; Violin concerto.
*Berezovsky, piano; Suwanai, violin;
Moscow Phil. Orch.; Kitaenko, cond.*
Recorded live 1990.
● ARG 7-8/91: 131
● Fa 3-4/91: 401
- Fa 7-8/91: 306
● Gr 1/91: 1380 (Piano)
+ Gr 1/91: 1380 (Violin)

34194. 2292-46011-2: RACHMANINOFF—
Piano sonata no. 2. PROKOFIEV—Piano
sonata no. 7. SCRIABIN—Piano sonata no.
5. *Sultanov, piano.*
+ ARG 1-2/94: 183
● Fa 1-2/94: 270
● Gr 8/93: 59

34195. 2292-46013-2: *Christmas
concertos.* Music of Corelli, Vivaldi,
Torelli, Antonacci, Pez and Manfredini.
Giardino Armonico; Antonini, cond.
● ARG 11-12/92: 266
- Fa 3-4/92: 422

34196. 2292-46014-2 (3 discs):
MOZART—Complete piano duets. *G. & S.
Pekinel, piano(s).*
+ ARG 7-8/92: 192
+ Fa 7-8/92: 231
+ Gr 6/92: 58

34197. 2292-46015-2: *Brodsky unlimited:
a compilation of favorite encores.* Music
of Shostakovich, Falla, Gershwin,
Copland, Brubeck, Prokofiev, Debussy

TELDEC

and others. *Brodsky Quartet.*
- ARG 9-10/92: 188
+ Fa 7-8/92: 359
+ Gr 4/92: 106

34198. 2292-46016-2 (2 discs): BEETHOVEN—String quartets op. 59. *Vermeer Quartet.*
+ ARG 3-4/91: 30
+ Fa 3-4/91: 149
• Gr 3/91: 1682
• MA 3/91: 68
+ SR 2/91: 131

34199. 2292-46017-2: SHOSTAKOVICH—String quartet no. 15. BEETHOVEN—String quartet no. 16. *Brodsky Quartet.*
+ ARG 3-4/90: 107
• Gr 4/90: 1818

34200. 2292-46018-2: HAYDN—Symphonies no. 6-8. *Concentus Musicus Wien; Harnoncourt, cond.*
• Gr 7/91: 46

34201. 2292-46019-2: BERG—Chamber concerto. SCHOENBERG—Chamber symphony no. 1. *Zehetmair, violin; Maisenberg, piano; Chamber Orch. of Europe; Holliger, cond.*
+ ARG 3-4/91: 111
+ Fa 3-4/91: 155
+ Gr 2/91: 1498
+ MA 5/91: 82
+ SR 4/91: 85

34202. 2292-46151-2: BACH—Was mir behagt, BWV 208; Mer hahn en neue Oberkeet, BWV 212. *Blasi, Kenny, Equiluz, Holl; Arnold Schönberg Choir; Concentus Musicus Wien; Harnoncourt, cond.*
+ ARG 3-4/91: 18
+ Fa 1-2/91: 137

34203. 2292-46152-2: MAHLER—Symphony no. 5. *New York Phil. Orch.; Mehta, cond.*
• ARG 11-12/90: 76
• Fa 9-10/90: 285
• Gr 8/90: 368
+ MA 1/91: 76

34204. 2292-46154-2 (3 discs): SCHUMANN—Dichterliebe; Liederkreis, op. 39, op. 24; Myrthen: selections; Songs. *Schreier, tenor; Eschenbach, piano.*
+ ARG 1-2/92: 109
+ Fa 11-12/91: 479
+ Gr 6/91: 74

34205. 2292-46155-2: SAINT-SAËNS—Le carnaval des animaux. POULENC—Concerto for two pianos. *Güher & Süher Pekinel, pianos; Orch. Philharmonique de Radio France; Janowski, cond.*
- ARG 9-10/91: 106
• Fa 9-10/91: 312

34206. 2292-46249-2: MOZART—Clarinet quintet K. 581. BRAHMS—Clarinet quintet op. 115. *Berliner Solisten.*
• ARG 3-4/91: 96

+ Fa 1-2/91: 261
+ Gr 9/90: 555

34207. 2292-46276-2: MAHLER—Das Lied von der Erde. *Fassbaender, mezzo-soprano; Moser, tenor; Katsaris, piano.*
+ ARG 9-10/90: 82
• Fa 9-10/90: 284
+ Gr 6/90: 97
+ SR 9/90: 121
• St 3/91: 199

34208. 2292-46281-2: TCHAIKOVSKY—Piano concerto no. 1. RACHMANINOFF—Piano concerto no. 2. *Sultanov, piano; London Symphony Orch.; Shostakovich, cond.*
• ARG 7-8/90: 116
• DA 10/90: 75
• Fa 9-10/90: 406
• Gr 7/90: 218
+ MA 9/90: 84
+ SR 8/90: 94

34209. 2292-46313-2: HAYDN—Symphonies no. 85-86. *St. Paul Chamber Orch.; Wolff, cond.*
+ ARG 11-12/91: 80
+ Fa 11-12/91: 345
+ Gr 9/91: 62

34210. 2292-46314-2: COPLAND—Appalachian spring (original version); Music for the theater; Three Latin American sketches; Quiet city. *St. Paul Chamber Orch.; Wolff, cond.*
+ ARG 11-12/91: 54
+ ARG 1-2/92: 45
+ Fa 11-12/91: 304
+ Gr 7/91: 41

34211. 2292-46315-2: DVOŘÁK—Serenades: for strings, op. 22; for winds, op. 44. *St. Paul Chamber Orch.; Wolff, cond.*
• ARG 3-4/92: 52
+ Fa 3-4/92: 189
• Gr 12/91: 65

34212. 2292-46316-2: HOLST—The planets. *New York Choral Artists; New York Phil. Orch.; Mehta, cond.*
+ ARG 5-6/91: 67
+ Fa 3-4/91: 242
• Gr 12/90: 1208

34213. 2292-46317-2: SIBELIUS—Symphony no. 2; Finlandia. *New York Phil. Orch.; Mehta, cond.*
- ARG 11-12/90: 118
+ Fa 11-12/90: 359
• Gr 1/91: 1378
+ MA 5/91: 85

34214. 2292-46318-2: GERSHWIN—Selections from Porgy and Bess; An American in Paris; Cuban overture. *Alexander, Baker; New York Choral Artists; New York Phil.; Mehta, cond.*
- ARG 11-12/91: 66
- Fa 11-12/91: 321
• Gr 6/91: 39

34215. 2292-46319-2: BORODIN—String quartet no. 2. TCHAIKOVSKY—String quartet no. 3. *Brodsky Quartet.*
• ARG 9-10/91: 49
- Gr 9/91: 83

34216. 2292-46322-2: TCHAIKOVSKY—Symphony no. 3; Mazeppa: Gopek; Festival coronation march. *Gewandhaus Orch.; Masur, cond.*
- ARG 5-6/92: 145
+ Fa 5-6/92: 265
• Gr 3/92: 56

34217. 2292-46323-2: MENDELSSOHN—A midsummer night's dream: incidental music, op. 21, 61. *Wiens, soprano; Oertel, mezzo-soprano; Eberle, narrator; Leipzig Radio Chorus; Lepizig Gewandhaus Orch.; Masur, cond.*
+ ARG 9-10/92: 129
+ Fa 9-10/92: 287
+ Gr 5/92: 37

34218. 2292-46327-2: STRAVINSKY—Petrushka (1911); Scherzo à la Russe; Circus polka; Fireworks. *Philharmonia Orch.; Inbal, cond.*
• ARG 3-4/92: 147
• Fa 3-4/92: 339
• Gr 10/91: 113

34219. 2292-46328-2: DVOŘÁK—Violin concerto; Romance, op. 11. *Zehetmair, violin; Philharmonia Orch.; Inbal, cond.*
• ARG 5-6/91: 49
• Fa 11-12/91: 313
+ Gr 7/91: 46

34220. 2292-46329-2: *Live Berlin 90: Waldbühnenkonzert.* Music of Wagner, Liszt, Dvořák, Moniuszko, Enesco, Mozart, Glinka, and Lincke. *Berlin Phil. Orch.; Barenboim, cond.*
+ ARG 3-4/92: 171
• Fa 1-2/92: 433
+ Gr 9/91: 79

34221. 2292-46330-2: BRUCKNER—Symphony no. 0 in D minor. *Radio-Sinfonie-Orch. Frankfurt; Inbal, cond.*
+ ARG 7-8/91: 42
• Fa 9-10/91: 182
- Gr 3/91: 1660

34222. 2292-46331-2: HAYDN—Symphonies no. 98-99. *Concertgebouw Orch.; Harnoncourt, cond.*
+ Fa 11-12/91: 347

34223. 2292-46334-2 (3 discs): MOZART—Lieder. *Bonney, soprano; Parsons, piano.*
+ ARG 9-10/92: 137
+ Fa 7-8/92: 230
• Gr 1/92: 86

34224. 2292-46336-2: WAGNER—Tannhäuser: highlights. *Te Kanawa, Kollo, Hagegård, Meier; Ambrosian Singers; Philharmonia Orch.; Janowski, cond.* Soundtrack for film Meeting Venus.

• ARG 3-4/92: 163
+ Gr 12/91: 145
+ ON 3/28/92: 40

34225. 2292-46337-2 (3 discs):
BEETHOVEN—String quartets, op. 18.
Vermeer Quartet.
    + ARG 5-6/92: 29
    + Fa 5-6/92: 122

34226. 2292-46340-2: MOZART—Violin
concertos no. 2-3, 5. *Zehetmair, violin &
cond.; Philharmonia Orch.*
    + ARG 11-12/91: 105
    + Fa 11-12/91: 314
    + Gr 9/91: 66

34227. 2292-46419-2: SCARLATTI—
Sonatas. *Wilson, harpsichord.*
    - ARG 9-10/93: 182
    - Gr 5/93: 74

34228. 2292-46420-2: STRAVINSKY—Rite
of spring; Symphony in 3 movements.
New York Phil.; Mehta, cond.
    • ARG 3-4/92: 148
    - Fa 3-4/92: 341
    - Gr 12/91: 80

34229. 2292-46439-2 (2 discs):
MOZART—Piano trios (complete).
Fontenay Trio.
    + ARG 7-8/92: 99
    • Gr 11/91: 121

34230. 2292-46441-2: BEETHOVEN—Triple
concerto; Piano trio op. 70, no. 1. *Trio
Fontenay; Philharmonia Orch.; Inbal,
cond.*
    + ARG 3-4/92: 27
    + Fa 3-4/92: 143
    • Gr 10/91: 75

34231. 2292-46442-2: *Modern times with
the London Brass.* Music of Tippett,
Takemitsu, Xenakis, Britten, Crosse,
Rouders, Ruggles, and Lutosławski.
London Brass; Hind, piano.
    + ARG 7-8/91: 152
    + Fa 9-10/91: 439

34232. 2292-46444-2: *I got rhythm:
songs from the shows.* Music of
Gershwin, Porter, Rogers, Kern and
Warren. *London Brass; Nightengale,
cond.*
    + ARG 7-8/92: 254
    - Fa 7-8/92: 356

34233. 2292-46446-2: SCHUMANN—
Symphonies no. 2-3. *London Phil. Orch.;
Masur, cond.*
    + ARG 5-6/92: 132
    • Fa 5-6/92: 252
    + Gr 12/91: 79

34234. 2292-46447-2 (2 discs):
HANDEL—Theodora. *Alexander,
Kowalski, Nes, Blochwitz, Scharinger;
Arnold Schönberg-Chor; Concentus
Musicus Wien; Harnoncourt, cond.*
    + ARG 11-12/91: 75

+ Fa 11-12/91: 340
+ Gr 8/91: 66

34235. 2292-46448-2: BEETHOVEN—
Romances. MOZART—Rondos in B♭, C;
Adagio in E. SCHUBERT—Konzertstück,
Polonaise; Rondo. *Zehetmair, violin &
cond.; Deutsche Kammerphilharmonie;
Philharmonia Orch.*
    + ARG 1-2/93: 188
    + Gr 9/92: 41

34236. 2292-46449-2: BERG—Concerto
for violin and orchestra. JANÁČEK—
Concerto for violin and orchestra.
HARTMANN—Concerto funèbre for violin
and strings. *Zehetmair, violin & cond.;
Deutsche Kammerphilharmonie;
Philharmonia Orch.; Holliger, cond.*
    + ARG 5-6/93: 70
    - Fa 5-6/93: 164
    + Gr 3/93: 34

34237. 2292-46450-2 (2 discs):
BRAHMS—Piano sonatas (complete);
Variations on a theme of Paganini.
Leonskaja, piano.
    + Fa 5-6/91: 137

34238. 2292-46451-2: DVOŘÁK—Piano
trios no. 2, 4. *Trio Fontenay.*
    + ARG 5-6/92: 52
    + Fa 5-6/92: 153

34239. 2292-46452-2 (5 discs):
BEETHOVEN—Complete symphonies.
*Chamber Orch. of Europe; Harnoncourt,
cond.*
    + ARG 3-4/92: 31
    + Fa 1-2/92: 164
    + Gr 11/91: 83
    + St 4/92: 262

34240. 2292-46458-2: HAYDN—Seven
last words of Christ on the cross. *Nielsen,
Hintermeier, Rolfe Johnson, Holl; Arnold
Schoenberg Choir; Concentus Musicus
Wien; Harnoncourt, cond.*
    + ARG 3-4/93: 89
    + Fa 11-12/92: 250
    + Gr 5/92: 87

34241. 2292-46459-2: BRAHMS—Piano
concerto no. 1. *Leonskaja, piano;
Philharmonia Orch.; Inbal, cond.*
    • ARG 7-8/92: 105
    • Fa 7-8/92: 125

34242. 2292-46460-2: DVOŘÁK—
Symphony no. 7; The water goblin.
Philharmonia Orch.; Inbal, cond.
    + ARG 9-10/92: 101
    + Fa 7-8/92: 152

34243. 2292-46463-2: CHOPIN—Scherzos,
no. 1-4; Polonaise, op. 53; Ballade no. 4;
Andante spianato and grande polonaise.
Sultanov, piano.
    • ARG 11-12/92: 104
    - Fa 11-12/92: 218
    + Gr 7/92: 77
    - St 6/93: 251

34244. 2292-46467-2: BEETHOVEN—
Septet, op. 20. MOZART—Horn quintet.
Berliner Solisten.
    + ARG 5-6/92: 29
    + Fa 7-8/92: 119
    + Gr 3/92: 64

34245. 2292-46468-2: DVOŘÁK—
Symphony no. 9; Wood dove.
Philharmonia Orch.; Inbal, cond.
    + ARG 3-4/91: 63
    • Fa 3-4/91: 206
    • Gr 4/91: 1827
    • St 9/91: 205

34246. 2292-46469-2: MOZART—Missa
solemnis, K. 66; Vesperae de Dominica,
K. 321. *Bonney, Margiono, Magnus,
Heilmann, Cachemaille; Arnold
Schoenberg Choir; Concentus Musicus
Wien; Harnoncourt, cond.*
    + Fa 3-4/92: 259

34247. 2292-46471-2: MOZART—
Serenade in B♭, K. 361. *Soloists of the
Chamber Orch. of Europe.*
    + ARG 3-4/91: 96
    + Fa 3-4/91: 299
    + Gr 3/91: 1671

34248. 2292-46472-2: MOZART—
Divertimenti for winds (complete). *Wind
soloists of the Chamber Orch. of Europe.*
    + ARG 3-4/92: 106
    + Fa 5-6/92: 210

34249. 9031-71381-2 (3 discs):
MOZART—Così fan tutte. *Margiono,
Ziegler, Cachemaille, Hampson;
Concertgebouw Orch.; Harnoncourt,
cond.*
    + ARG 7-8/92: 183
    • Fa 7-8/92: 227
    + Gr 11/91: 156
    + ON 5/92: 52
    + Op 12/91: 1495

34250. 9031-71702-2 (6 discs):
SHOSTAKOVICH—String quartets
(complete). *Brodsky Quartet.* Reissues.
    • ARG 9-10/91: 126
    + Gr 6/92: 60

34251. 9031-72024-2 (4 discs):
MOZART—Piano concertos no. 20-27.
*Barenboim, piano & cond.; Berlin Phil.
Orch.*
    • ARG 11-12/91: 103
    - Fa 11-12/91: 397
    + Gr 4/91: 1833

34252. 9031-72140-2: BRUCKNER—
Symphony no. 9. *Berlin Phil. Orch.;
Barenboim, cond.*
    + ARG 1-2/92: 38
    • Fa 1-2/92: 190
    + Gr 10/91: 76

34253. 9031-72168-2: IVES—Lieder.
MACDOWELL—Lieder. GRIFFES—Lieder.
Hampson, baritone; Guzelimian, piano.
    + ARG 5-6/92: 187

TELDEC

+ Fa 5-6/92: 178
+ Gr 4/92: 140

34254. 9031-72289-2: Mozart—
Symphony no. 27; March, K. 215;
Serenade, K. 204. *Concentus Musicus
Wien; Harnoncourt, cond.*
    + ARG 9-10/92: 138
    • Fa 7-8/92: 236
    + Gr 5/92: 38

34255. 9031-72296-2: Tchaikovsky—
Piano concerto no. 2; Piano sonata no. 1.
*Leonskaja, piano; Gewandhaus Orch.;
Masur, cond.*
    • ARG 9-10/92: 172
    + Fa 9-10/92: 375
    • Gr 9/92: 94

34256. 9031-72297-2 (2 discs):
Chopin—Nocturnes. *Leonskaja, piano.*
    • ARG 7-8/93: 76
    + Fa 5-6/93: 185
    • Gr 7/93: 65

34257. 9031-72300-2: Bruckner—
Symphony in F minor "School
symphony". *Frankfurt Radio Symphony
Orch.; Inbal, cond.*
    + ARG 9-10/92: 91
    + Fa 9-10/92: 206
    + Gr 6/92: 39

34258. 9031-72301-2: Wolf—
Italienisches Liederbuch. *Bonney,
soprano; Hagegård, baritone; Parsons,
piano.*
    + ARG 11-12/94: 213
    + Fa 11-12/94: 426
    + Gr 7/94: 102

34259. 9031-72302-2: Mozart—Concert
arias. *Gruberova, soprano; Chamber
Orch. of Europe; Harnoncourt, cond.*
Recorded live 1991.
    + ARG 11-12/92: 164
    + Fa 11-12/92: 308
    • Gr 5/92: 90
    + ON 3/27/93: 34

34260. 9031-72304-2: Mozart—Credo
mass; Litaniae de venerabili altaris
sacramento. *Blasi, Magnus, Walt, Miles;
Arnold Schoenberg Choir; Concentus
Musicus Wien, Harnoncourt, cond.*
    + ARG 9-10/93: 161
    + Gr 6/93: 87

34261. 9031-72305-2: Dvořák—
Symphony no. 8; The golden spinning
wheel. *Philharmonia Orch.; Inbal, cond.*
    + Gr 11/92: 58

34262. 9031-72306-2 (2 discs):
Donizetti—Lucia di Lammermoor.
*Gruberova, Shicoff, Agache, Miles;
London Symphony Orch.; Bonynge, cond.*
    + ARG 7-8/93: 81
    + Fa 3-4/93: 153
    + Gr 11/92: 183

34263. 9031-72308-2: Mendelssohn—
Symphonies no. 3-4. *Chamber Orch. of
Europe; Harnoncourt, cond.*
    • ARG 9-10/92: 130
    • Fa 11-12/92: 303
    + Gr 5/92: 37

34264. 9031-72309-2 (3 discs):
Mozart—La finta giardiniera.
*Gruberova, Margiono, Moser, Heilmann;
Concentus Musicus Wien; Harnoncourt,
cond.*
    + ARG 9-10/93: 160
    • Gr 3/93: 100
    + ON 11/93: 42
    + Op 3/93: 372

34265. 9031-72479-2 (4 discs):
Mozart—*Sacred music.* Great mass in C
minor, K. 427; Mass in C, K. 317
"Coronation"; Vesperae solemnes de
confessore, K. 339; Missa solemnis in C
minor, K. 138; Exsultate, jubilate, K. 165;
Requiem, K. 626. *Vienna State Opera
Chorus; Arnold Schönberg-Chor;
Concentus Musicus Wien; Harnoncourt;
cond.* Reissues.
    • ARG 11-12/91: 118
    • Fa 11-12/91: 406

34266. 9031-72480-2 (4 discs):
Mozart—*Late string quartets.* Quartets
no. 14-23. *Alban Berg Quartet.* Reissues.
    + ARG 11-12/91: 114
    + Fa 11-12/91: 416

34267. 9031-72482-2 (10 discs):
Mozart—Piano concertos (complete).
*Engel piano; Mozarteum Orch.; Hager,
cond.*
    • ARG 11-12/91: 104

34268. 9031-72483-2 (6 discs):
Mozart—Solo piano music. *Engel,
piano.*
    - ARG 1-2/92: 83

34269. 9031-72484-2 (4 discs):
Mozart—Symphonies no. 31-41.
*Concertgebouw Orch.; Harnoncourt,
cond.* Reissues.
    + ARG 11-12/91: 125
    - Fa 11-12/91: 415

34270. 9031-72775-2 (2 discs):
Zimmermann—Die Soldaten. *Munkittrick,
Shade, Vargas, Hoffman; Stuttgart
Opera; Kontarsky, cond.*
    □ ARG 1-2/92: 142
    + Fa 1-2/92: 379
    + Gr 7/91: 114
    • ON 9/91: 38
    + Op 1/92: 121

34271. 9031-73126-2: Britten—The
young person's guide to the orchestra, op.
34; Variations on a theme of Frank
Bridge, op. 10; Peter Grimes: 4 sea
interludes, op. 33a; Passacaglia, op. 33b.
BBC Symphony Orch.; A. Davis, cond.
    + ARG 1-2/92: 38
    + Fa 1-2/92: 189
    + Gr 8/91: 54
    + St 1/93: 269

34272. 9031-73127-2: Vaughan
Williams—Symphony no. 6; Fantasia on
a theme by Thomas Tallis; The lark
ascending. *Little, violin; BBC Symphony
Orch.; A. Davis, cond.*
    • ARG 1-2/92: 132
    + Fa 1-2/92: 359
    + Gr 8/91: 59

34273. 9031-73128-2: Mozart—Piano
concertos no. 9, 17. *Barenboim, piano;
Berlin Phil. Orch.*
    • ARG 11-12/92: 165
    + Gr 11/92: 93

34274. 9031-73129-2: Chopin—Etudes
op. 10 and 25; Trois nouvelles études.
Berezovsky, piano.
    • Fa 5-6/92: 141
    + Gr 4/92: 113

34275. 9031-73130-2: Tchaikovsky—
Manfred symphony. *Gewandhaus Orch.;
Masur, cond.*
    + ARG 9-10/92: 172
    + Fa 9-10/92: 375

34276. 9031-73131-2 (2 discs):
Mendelssohn—Elias. *Donath, Nes,
George, Miles; MDR Chorus, Leipzig;
Israel Phil. Orch.; Masur, cond.*
    + ARG 11-12/93: 149
    + Fa 11-12/93: 320
    + Gr 5/93: 88
    + ON 11/95: 48

34277. 9031-73133-2: Haydn—
Symphonies no. 83, 87. *St. Paul Chamber
Orch.; Wolff, cond.*
    + ARG 11-12/92: 133
    + Fa 11-12/92: 251
    + Fa 1-2/93: 164
    • Gr 10/92: 62

34278. 9031-73134-2: Bartók—
Divertimento; Romanian folk dances.
Kodály—Marosszek and Galanta dances.
St. Paul Chamber Orch.; Wolff, cond.
    + ARG 7-8/94: 65
    + Fa 7-8/94: 58
    + Gr 5/94: 46

34279. 9031-73135-2: Christmas with
Thomas Hampson. *Hampson, baritone;
St. Paul Chamber Orch.; Wolff, cond.*
    + ARG 11-12/92: 267

34280. 9031-73148-2: Haydn—
Symphonies no. 94-95. *Concertgebouw
Orch.; Harnoncourt, cond.*
    • ARG 11-12/91: 79
    + Fa 11-12/91: 347
    + Gr 7/91: 46

34281. 9031-73184-2: Brahms—Piano
sonatas no. 1, 3. *Leonskaja, piano.*
    - Gr 6/92: 64

34282. 9031-73239-2: Messiaen—
Quatuor pour la fin du temps. *Brunner,
clarinet; Trio Fontenay.*
    + ARG 7-8/93: 125

+ Fa 5-6/93: 265
+ Gr 12/92: 97

34283. 9031-73241-2: *Russia sings.*
Choral music of Rachmaninoff,
Tchesnokov and Tchaikovsky. *Glinka
Choir; Tchernushenko, cond.*
+ ARG 7-8/92: 281
- Fa 7-8/92: 333
+ Gr 3/92: 109

34284. 9031-73242-2: ROSSINI—Arias
from Il viaggio a Rheims, Stabat Mater,
La cenerentola, L'Italiana in Algeri and
Semiramide. *Ramey, bass; Welsh
National Opera Orch.; Ferro, cond.*
+ ARG 5-6/92: 119
+ Fa 7-8/92: 260
+ ON 6/93: 44
+ Op 4/92: 489

34285. 9031-73243-2: BRUCKNER—
Symphony no. 7. *New York Phil.; Masur,
cond.*
+ ARG 3-4/92: 39
+ Fa 3-4/92: 167
• Gr 3/92: 40

34286. 9031-73244-2: DVOŘÁK—
Symphony no. 9; Slavonic dances, op. 72,
no. 2, 6, 8. *New York Phil.; Masur, cond.*
+ ARG 7-8/92: 126
+ Fa 7-8/92: 153
+ Gr 6/92: 39

34287. 9031-73257-2 (2 discs):
PROKOFIEV—Piano concertos (complete).
*Krainev, piano; Frankfurt Radio
Symphony Orch.; Kitaenko, cond.*
+ ARG 1-2/94: 133
• Fa 1-2/94: 261
+ Gr 7/93: 46

34288. 9031-73266-2: PAGANINI—Violin
concerto no. 1. SAINT-SAËNS—
Introduction and rondo capriccioso;
Havanaise. WAXMAN—Carmen fantasy.
*Vengerov, violin; Israel Phil. Orch.;
Mehta, cond.*
+ Fa 9-10/92: 308
+ Gr 5/92: 43

34289. 9031-73267-2: VIVALDI—
Concertos with recorder, RV 90, 98, 101,
104, 435, 442. *Antonini, recorder;
Giardino Armonico.*
• Fa 5-6/92: 275
+ Gr 4/92: 86

34290. 9031-73267/69, 74727-2 (4
separate discs): VIVALDI—Chamber
concertos, vol. 1-4. *Giardino armonico;
Antonini, cond.*
- ARG 9-10/93: 216

34291. 9031-73270-2: *Around the world
with the London Brass.* 14 international
folk songs. *London Brass.*
+ ARG 11-12/92: 238
+ Fa 11-12/92: 451

34292. 9031-73271-2: BRUCKNER—
Symphony no. 5. *Berlin Phil. Orch.;*

Barenboim, cond.
• ARG 3-4/93: 66
• Fa 5-6/93: 181
+ Gr 3/93: 39

34293. 9031-73272-2: BRUCKNER—
Symphony no. 4. *Berlin Phil. Orch.;
Barenboim, cond.*
• ARG 1-2/94: 88
+ Fa 3-4/94: 153
+ Gr 3/94: 44

34294. 9031-73278-2: ELGAR—
Symphony no. 1; Pomp and
circumstances marches no. 1, 3-4. *BBC
Symphony Orch.; Davis, cond.*
+ ARG 9-10/92: 101
• Fa 7-8/92: 155
+ Gr 1/92: 51
+ St 3/93: 183

34295. 9031-73279-2: ELGAR—
Cockaigne overture; Introduction and
allegro; Serenade for strings; Enigma
variations. *BBC Symphony Orch.; A.
Davis, cond.*
+ ARG 1-2/93: 93
+ Fa 7-8/92: 154
+ Gr 3/92: 44
+ St 3/93: 183

34296. 9031-73281-2 (3 discs):
BEETHOVEN—Piano trios; Variations. *Trio
Fontenay.*
+ ARG 9-10/94: 101
• Fa 9-10/94: 141
• Gr 3/94: 69

34297. 9031-73282-2: SHOSTAKOVICH—
Piano concertos no. 1-2; Piano sonata no.
2. *Leonskaja, piano; St.Paul Chamber
Orch.; Wolff, cond.*
+ ARG 9-10/93: 190
+ Fa 9-10/93: 286
• Gr 6/93: 54

34298. 9031-73283-2: Duets by
Donizetti, Meyerbeer, Bizet, Verdi,
Puccini, and others. *Hadley, tenor;
Hampson, baritone; Welsh National
Opera Orch.; Rizzi, cond.*
+ ARG 1-2/94: 195
+ Fa 3-4/94: 377
+ Gr 11/93: 165
+ ON 10/94: 51

34299. 9031-73284-2: PROKOFIEV—
Alexander Nevsky; Scythian suite.
*Watkinson, mezzo-soprano; Leipzig
Gewandhaus Orch.; Masur, cond.*
- ARG 7-8/92: 199
• Fa 7-8/92: 248
• Gr 5/92: 95
• St 4/93: 287

34300. 9031-73400-2: HINDEMITH—Octet.
PROKOFIEV—Quintet. *Berlin Soloists;
Bashkirova, piano.*
+ ARG 9-10/93: 168
+ Fa 9-10/93: 185
+ Gr 6/93: 64

34301. 9031-73741-2: *Nessun dorma!
Placido Domingo sings opera arias.*
Music of Mascagni, Leoncavallo, Verdi,
Cilea, Ponchielli. Puccini, Giordano, and
Donizetti. *Domingo, tenor; Orch. der
Deutschen Oper Berlin; Santi, cond.*
Reissue.
+ ARG 1-2/92: 173
+ Fa 11-12/91: 528

34302. 9031-73742-2: LLOYD WEBBER—
The symphonic Lloyd Webber. Orchestral
suites from musicals: Cats; Evita; Aspects
of love; Phantom of the opera. *Royal
Phil. Orch.; Stratta, cond.*
• Fa 11-12/91: 376

34303. 9031-73743-2 (3 discs):
MOZART—*Wind concertos.* Horn
concertos no. 1-4; Oboe concerto, K. 314;
Clarinet concerto; Bassoon concerto;
Flute concertos no. 1-2; Flute and harp
concerto; Andante in G for flute and
orchestra, K. 315. *Baumann, horn;
Schaeftlein, oboe; Klöcker, clarinet;
Turković, bassoon; Schultz, Glass, flute;
Stein, harp; Mozarteum Orch.; Hager,
cond.; Süddeutsches Kammerorchester;
Reinhardt, cond.* Reissue.
- ARG 1-2/92: 84
- Fa 1-2/92: 275

34304. 9031-73797-2: RACHMANINOFF—
Piano concerto no. 3; Preludes, op. 23,
no. 2-3, 6, 9-10. *Berezovsky, piano;
Philharmonia Orch.; Inbal, cond.*
• ARG 11-12/92: 182
• Fa 11-12/92: 327
• Gr 9/92: 83

34305. 9031-74001-2: BEETHOVEN—
Violin sonata no. 9. BRAHMS—Violin
sonata no. 2. *Vengerov, violin;
Markovich, piano.*
+ Fa 9-10/92: 308
+ Gr 5/92: 62

34306. 9031-74002-2: MAHLER—Songs.
*Hampson, baritone; Lutz, piano;
Philharmonia Orch.; Berio, cond.*
+ ARG 9-10/94: 155
+ Fa 9-10/94: 244
• Gr 8/94: 91

34307. 9031-74005-2: HAYDN—
Symphonies no. 82 "The bear," 84. *St.
Paul Chamber Orch.; Wolff, cond.*
+ Fa 3-4/93: 186
+ Gr 4/93: 48

34308. 9031-74006-2: RAVEL—Le
tombeau de Couperin; Pavane pour une
infante défunte; Ma Mère l'oye. DEBUSSY
(ARR. RAVEL)—Danse; Sarabande. *St. Paul
Chamber Orch.; Wolff, cond.*
• ARG 9-10/92: 146
+ Fa 9-10/92: 325
• Gr 10/92: 58

34309. 9031-74007-2: REGER—Mozart
variations. BRAHMS—Haydn variations.
IVES—Variations on America (arr.
Schuman). *New York Phil.; Masur, cond.*

TELDEC

Recorded live.
  + ARG 1-2/93: 135
  + Fa 1-2/93: 218
  • Gr 12/92: 74

34310. 9031-74389-2 (6 discs): TCHAIKOVSKY—The six symphonies; Francesca da Rimini; Romeo and Juliet: overture; Mazeppa: Gopak; Festival coronation march. *Gewandhaus Orch.; Masur, cond.*
  • ARG 9-10/92: 173
  • Fa 9-10/92: 377

34311. 9031-74448-2 (4 discs): WAGNER—Parsifal. *Van Dam, Tomlinson, Jerusalem, Meier; Berlin Phil. Orch.; Barenboim, cond.*
  + ARG 3-4/92: 160
  + Fa 3-4/92: 359
  + ON 2/29/92: 45
  + ON 5/92: 52
  + Op 12/91: 1497
  + St 4/92: 272

34312. 9031-74529-2: SHOSTAKOVICH—Symphony no. 10. *London Symphony Orch.; Rostropovich, cond.*
  - ARG 11-12/92: 203
  • Fa 7-8/92: 284
  - Gr 3/92: 55
  - St 5/93: 183

34313. 9031-74560-2: SHOSTAKOVICH—Symphony no. 15. *London Symphony Orch.; Rostropovich, cond.*
  • ARG 11-12/92: 203
  • Fa 7-8/92: 284 (Brown)
  + Fa 7-8/92: 285 (Hurwitz)
  - Gr 3/92: 55
  - St 5/93: 183

34314. 9031-74717-2: RACHMANINOFF—Suites for two pianos no. 1-2; Symphonic dances. *Argerich, Rabinovitch, pianos.*
  + ARG 11-12/92: 182
  • Fa 11-12/92: 327
  + Gr 9/92: 117

34315. 9031-74719-2: SHOSTAKOVICH—Symphony no. 8. *National Symphony Orch.; Rostropovich, cond.*
  + ARG 1-2/93: 150
  • Fa 1-2/93: 240
  + Gr 10/92: 119

34316. 9031-74726-2: MAHLER—Des Knaben Wunderhorn. *Hampson, baritone; Parsons, piano.*
  + ARG 3-4/94: 118
  + Fa 3-4/94: 237
  • Gr 2/94: 82

34317. 9031-74728-2: MOZART—Symphonies no. 12, 19, 24. *Concentus Musicus Wien; Harnoncourt, cond.*
  + ARG 9-10/93: 163
  • Gr 4/93: 56

34318. 9031-74780-2: BACH—Organ music. *Tachezi, organ.*
  - Fa 1-2/93: 102

34319. 9031-74781-2: CHOPIN—Four ballades; Four scherzos. *Katsaris, piano.*
  + Fa 1-2/93: 131

34320. 9031-74786-2: J. STRAUSS, JR.—Orchestra music. *Concertgebouw Orch.; Harnoncourt, cond.*
  • Fa 1-2/93: 247

34321. 9031-74798-2: Thomas Hampson sings Bach. *Hampson, baritone; supporting soloists; Concentus Musicus Wien; Harnoncourt, cond.*
  + ARG 5-6/92: 16
  • Fa 5-6/92: 118
  + Gr 4/92: 125

34322. 9031-74858-2 (2 discs): MOZART—Symphonies no. 39-41. *Chamber Orch. of Europe; Harnoncourt, cond.*
  + ARG 11-12/92: 172
  + Fa 11-12/92: 314
  + Gr 5/92: 40
  • St 4/93: 287

34323. 9031-74859-2: HAYDN—Symphonies no. 68, 93, 100. *Concertgebouw Orch.; Harnoncourt, cond.*
  + ARG 9-10/93: 133
  + Gr 8/93: 31

34324. 9031-74862-2 (2 discs): BACH—St. John passion. *Rolfe Johnson, Holl, Blasi, Lipovsek, Scharinger; Arnold Schoenberg Choir; Concentus Musicus Wien; Harnoncourt, cond.*
  • ARG 11-12/95: 74
  + EM 8/95: 522
  • Fa 9-10/95: 129

34325. 9031-74863-2: FRANCK—Symphony in D minor; Les éolides. *New York Phil. Orch.; Masur, cond.*
  - ARG 9-10/93: 121
  + Fa 7-8/93: 138
  • Gr 5/93: 43

34326. 9031-74865-2: SCHUBERT—Piano sonatas, D. 664, 959. *Leonskaja, piano.*
  - ARG 1-2/94: 152
  • Fa 1-2/94: 307
  + Gr 10/93: 85

34327. 9031-74868-2: MAHLER—Symphony no. 1; Lieder eines fahrenden Gesellen. *Hagegard, baritone; New York Phil.; Masur, cond.*
  • ARG 5-6/93: 103
  + Fa 1-2/93: 183
  • Gr 12/92: 82

34328. 9031-74871-2 (2 discs): HANDEL—Samson. *Alexander, Blasi, Kowalski, Miles; Arnold Schoenberg Choir; Concentus Musicus Wien; Harnoncourt, cond.*
  + ARG 9-10/94: 139
  - Fa 7-8/94: 150
  • Gr 2/94: 81

34329. 9031-74872-2: BRAHMS—Songs. SCHUMANN—Liederkreis, op. 39. *Fassbaender, mezzo-soprano; Leonskaja, piano.*
  + ARG 3-4/95: 81
  + Gr 10/94: 168

34330. 9031-74881-2: BEETHOVEN—Violin concerto; Romances. *Kremer, violin; Chamber Orch. of Europe; Harnoncourt, cond.; Sacharov, piano.* Recorded live.
  - Fa 11-12/93: 177
  + Gr 12/93: 62

34331. 9031-74882-2: MENDELSSOHN—Ein Sommernachtstraum; Die erste Walpurgisnacht. *Coburn, Magnus-Harnoncourt, Bantzer, Remmert, Heilmann, Hampson, Pape; Arnold Schoenberg Choir; Chamber Orch. of Europe; Harnoncourt, cond.*
  • ARG 5-6/94: 113
  + Fa 5-6/94: 193
  + Gr 2/94: 84
  + ON 6/94: 44

34332. 9031-74884-2 (2 discs): BEETHOVEN—Missa solemnis. *Mei, Lipovsek, Rolfe Johnson, Holl; Arnold Schoenberg Chorus; Chamber Orch. of Europe; Harnoncourt, cond.*
  + ARG 9-10/93: 93
  + Fa 7-8/93: 103
  + Gr 4/93: 104

34333. 9031-74885-2 (2 discs): ROSSINI—Barber of Seville. *Larmore, Giménez, Hagegård, Ramey; Lausanne Chamber Orch.; López Cobos, cond.*
  • ARG 1-2/94: 140
  + Fa 1-2/94: 286
  • Gr 11/93: 158
  + ON 12/25/93: 32
  + Op 11/93: 1366

34334. 9031-74886-2: ORFF—Carmina Burana. *Jo, Kowalski, Skovhus; Southend Boys' Choir; London Phil. Orch.; Mehta, cond.*
  + ARG 7-8/94: 147
  + Fa 3-4/94: 264
  + Gr 2/94: 86

34335. 9031-74888-2: ELGAR—Symphony no. 2; In the south. *BBC Symphony Orch.; A. Davis, cond.*
  + ARG 3-4/93: 77
  • Fa 3-4/93: 158
  + Gr 11/92: 58
  + St 9/93: 183

34336. 9031-75277-2: PORTER—Centennial gala. *Various performers.*
  - Fa 7-8/92: 246

34337. 9031-75710-2: MOZART—Piano concertos no. 20-21. *Barenboim, piano & cond.; Berlin Phil. Orch.*
  + ARG 1-2/93: 125
  + Gr 11/92: 93

34338. 9031-75711-2: Mozart—Piano concertos no. 22-23. *Barenboim, piano & cond.; Berlin Phil. Orch.*
+ ARG 1-2/93: 125
+ Gr 11/92: 93

34339. 9031-75715-2: Mozart—Piano concertos no. 24-25. *Barenboim, piano & cond.; Berlin Phil. Orch.*
+ ARG 9-10/93: 159
• Fa 7-8/93: 187

34340. 9031-75716-2: Mozart—Piano concertos no. 26-27. *Barenboim, piano & cond.; Berlin Phil. Orch.*
+ ARG 9-10/93: 159
• Fa 7-8/93: 187

34341. 9031-75857-2: Chopin—Nineteen waltzes. *Katsaris, piano.*
+ Fa 1-2/93: 131

34342. 9031-75858—75859-2 (2 separate discs): Bach—Brandenburg concertos. *Concentus Musicus Wien; Harnoncourt, cond.* Reissues.
+ Gr 9/92: 40

34343. 9031-75860-2: Mendelssohn—Piano concertos no. 1-2; in A minor with string orchestra. *Katsaris, piano; Leipzig Gewandhaus Orch.; Masur, cond.; Franz Liszt Chamber Orch.; Rolla, cond.* Reissues.
+ Fa 1-2/93: 194

34344. 9031-75864-2: Music of Tárrega, Alard, Albéniz, Rodrigo, Pujol, Sainz de la Maza, Segovia, and Moreno Torroba. *Lendle, guitar.*
• Gr 7/92: 82

34345. 9031-76036-2 (2 discs): Brahms—Piano trios. *Trio Fontenay.* Reissues.
+ ARG 1-2/93: 83
+ Gr 11/92: 120

34346. 9031-76047-2 (4 discs): Wagner—Parsifal. *London, Mill, Weber, Windgassen, Uhde, Mödl; Orch. & Chorus of the Bayreuth Festival 1951; Knappertsbusch, cond.*
+ ARG 11-12/93: 274
+ Fa 11-12/93: 440
+ Gr 8/93: 90
+ ON 10/93: 37

34347. 9031-76138-2 (2 discs): Bach—Sonatas and partitas for solo violin. *Zehetmair, violin.*
+ ARG 11-12/92: 75
• Fa 11-12/92: 188

34348. 9031-76139-2 (3 discs): Bartók—For children; Mikrokosmos. *Ránki, piano.* Reissue.
+ ARG 11-12/92: 79
+ Fa 11-12/92: 191
+ Gr 10/92: 136

34349. 9031-76259-2: Paganini—Caprices op. 1. *Zehetmair, violin.*

+ ARG 3-4/94: 129
ℸ Fa 3-4/94: 265
+ Gr 5/94: 83

34350. 9031-76260-2: Schubert—String quartet no. 14. Crumb—Black angels. *Brodsky Quartet.*
- ARG 11-12/93: 188
+ Fa 11-12/93: 381
+ Gr 9/93: 82

34351. 9031-76261-2: Shostakovich—Symphony no. 4. *National Symphony Orch.; Rostropovich, cond.*
+ ARG 1-2/93: 149
• Fa 3-4/93: 292
+ Gr 11/92: 98

34352. 9031-76262-2: Shostakovich—Symphony no. 11. *National Symphony Orch.; Rostropovich, cond.*
• ARG 1-2/94: 155
+ Fa 1-2/94: 313
- Gr 8/93: 40

34353. 9031-76263-2: Respighi—Roman trilogy. *London Phil. Orch.; Rizzi, cond.*
+ ARG 9-10/93: 176
- Fa 11-12/93: 362
• Gr 9/93: 57

34354. 9031-76348-2 (2 discs): Verdi—La traviata. *Gruberová, Shicoff, Zancanaro; London Symphony Orch.; Rizzi, cond.*
+ ARG 7-8/93: 175
+ Fa 5-6/93: 346
+ Gr 2/93: 76
• Op 11/93: 1368

34355. 9031-76349-2: Beethoven—Sonata no. 5 for violin and piano. Mozart—Sonata for violin and piano, K. 378. Mendelssohn—Sonata for violin and piano. *Vengerov, violin; Golan, Markovich, piano.*
+ Fa 5-6/93: 393
• Gr 3/93: 60

34356. 9031-76350-2: Bartók—Concerto for orchestra; Miraculous mandarin: Suite; Pictures. *Philharmonia Orch.; Wolff, cond.*
• ARG 9-10/94: 97
• Fa 9-10/94: 134
+ Gr 9/94: 45

34357. 9031-76435-2: Bruckner—Symphony no. 7: Adagio. Gluck—Alceste overture. Beethoven—String quartet no. 13, mvt. 5. *Berlin Phil. Orch.; Furtwängler, cond.* Recorded 1940/42.
+ ARG 11-12/93: 268

34358. 9031-76436-2: Beethoven—Symphony no. 2. Schubert—Symphony no. 8 "Unfinished". *Brussels Phil. Orch.; Berlin Phil. Orch.; Kleiber, cond.* Recorded 1935, 1938.
+ ARG 11-12/93: 268
+ Fa 11-12/93: 180

34359. 9031-76438-2: Schubert—Symphony no. 9. Enesco—Romanian rhapsody no. 1. *Vienna Phil. Orch.; Krauss, cond.* Recorded 1950-51.
+ ARG 11-12/93: 268

34360. 9031-76439-2: Schumann—Piano concerto. Grieg—Piano concerto. *Michelangeli, piano; Orch. del Teatro alla Scala di Milano; Pedrotti, Galliera, conds.* Reissues; recorded 1942.
+ ARG 11-12/93: 268
+ Fa 11-12/93: 386

34361. 9031-76440-2: Stravinsky—Jeu de cartes. Hindemith—Symphony Mathis der Maler. *Berlin Phil. Orch.; Stravinsky, Hindemith, conds.* Reissues.
+ ARG 11-12/93: 268
+ Fa 11-12/93: 410

34362. 9031-76441-2: Strauss—Ein Heldenleben; Don Juan. *Concertgebouw Orch.; Mengelberg, cond.* Recorded 1938-41.
+ ARG 11-12/93: 268
+ Fa 11-12/93: 409
+ Gr 12/93: 132

34363. 9031-76442-2: *Bayreuth 1936.* Wagner—Selections from Lohengrin, Die Walküre, and Siegfried. *Völker, Lorenz, Müller, Klose, Prohaska, Manowarda, Zimmermann; Chorus & Orch. of the Bayreuth Festival 1936; Tietjen, cond.*
• ARG 3-4/94: 235
+ Fa 11-12/93: 446
+ Gr 8/93: 90
+ ON 10/93: 37

34364. 9031-76443-2: Beethoven—Violin concerto. Bruch—Violin concerto no. 1. *Kulenkampff, violin; Berlin Phil. Orch.; Keilberth, Schmidt-Isserstedt, conds.* Recorded 1941/36.
+ ARG 11-12/93: 268
+ Gr 11/93: 186

34365. 9031-76444-2: Beethoven—Symphony no. 3. Wagner—Tannhäuser overture. *Berlin Phil. Orch.; Jochum, cond.* Recorded 1937/33.
+ ARG 11-12/93: 268

34366. 9031-76456-2: Tchaikovsky—Romeo and Juliet; Francesca da Rimini; Festival coronation march; Gopak from Mazeppa. *Gewandhaus Orch.; Masur, cond.* Reissue.
- ARG 7-8/93: 167
• Fa 9-10/93: 308
+ Gr 5/93: 52

34367. 9031-76458-2: Dvořák—Piano trios (complete). *Trio Fontenay.* Reissues.
+ ARG 1-2/94: 89
- Fa 9-10/93: 158

34368. 9031-76460-2: Haydn—Symphonies no. 30, 53, 69. *Concentus Musicus Wien; Harnoncourt, cond.*

TELDEC

• ARG 9-10/93: 133
+ Gr 6/93: 44

34369. 9031-76989-2: VIVALDI—Gloria, RV 589. PERGOLESI—Stabat Mater. *McNair, Magnus-Harnoncourt, Mei, sopranos; Lipovsek, alto; Concentus Musicus Wien; Harnoncourt, cond.*
• ARG 1-2/95: 152
+ Fa 7-8/94: 274
• Gr 7/94: 100

34370. 9031-76997-2: Symphonic tango. *Royal Phil. Orch.; Stratta, cond.*
+ Fa 1-2/93: 319
+ Gr 1/93: 68

34371. 9031-77118-2: BRUCKNER—Symphony no. 7. *Berlin Phil. Orch.; Barenboim, cond.*
• ARG 9-10/93: 106
• Fa 9-10/93: 139
• Gr 9/93: 45

34372. 9031-77291-2: BRAHMS—Symphony no. 2; Academic festival overture. *New York Phil. Orch.; Masur, cond.*
• ARG 9-10/93: 104
- Fa 7-8/93: 117
+ Gr 5/93: 40

34373. 9031-77307-2: Kalinka! Traditional songs and arrangements. *Red Star Army Chorus; Bazhalkin, cond*
+ Fa 1-2/93: 285
+ Gr 11/92: 178

34374. 9031-77308-2: Music of Frescobaldi, Marcello, Bach, Handel, Rheinberger, and others. *Rostropovich, cello; Tachezi, organ .*
+ ARG 5-6/94: 181

34375. 9031-77309-2: PROKOFIEV—Symphony no. 1. BIZET—Symphony. HAYDN—Symphony no. 1. *St. Paul Chamber Orch.; Wolff, cond.*
- ARG 3-4/94: 195
+ Fa 3-4/94: 277
• Gr 2/94: 38

34376. 9031-77310-2: COPLAND—Old American songs; Dickinson songs; Billy the Kid: Highlights. *Hampson, baritone; Upshaw, soprano; St. Paul Chamber Orch.; Wolff, cond.*
• ARG 9-10/94: 119
+ Fa 11-12/94: 205

34377. 9031-77311-2: VIVALDI—Cello concerto RV 406. TARTINI—Cello concerto in D major. C.P.E. BACH—Cello concerto H. 436. *Rostropovich, cello; St. Paul Chamber Orch.; Wolff, cond.*
+ ARG 3-4/94: 202
+ Fa 3-4/94: 394
+ Gr 1/94: 40

34378. 9031-77313-2: BEETHOVEN—Symphony no. 5; Egmont overture and incidental music. *McNair, soprano; New York Phil.; Masur, cond.*

+ ARG 3-4/94: 73
• Fa 1-2/94: 125
+ Gr 1/94: 40

34379. 9031-77314-2: SCHOENBERG—Verklärte Nacht (1943 string-orch. version); Begleitmusik zu einer Lichtspielszene; Kammersymphonie no. 2. *Chamber Orch. of Europe; Holliger, cond.*
+ ARG 1-2/95: 168
+ Fa 11-12/94: 368
+ Gr 10/94: 118

34380. 9031-77315-2: HAYDN—Symphonies no. 96-97. *Concertgebouw Orch.; Harnoncourt, cond.*
+ ARG 7-8/94: 112
+ Fa 7-8/94: 153

34381. 9031-77340-2: LISZT—Dante symphony; Dante sonata. *Berlin Phil. Orch.; Barenboim, cond.*
+ ARG 11-12/94: 145
+ Fa 11-12/94: 280
+ Gr 7/94: 50

34382. 9031-77351-2: Music of Bazzini, Bloch, Kreisler, Messiaen, Paganini, Sarasate, Tchaikovsky, and Wieniawski. *Vengerov, violin; Golan, piano.*
+ ARG 7-8/94: 220
+ Gr 4/94: 66

34383. 9031-77476-2: SCHUMANN—Davidsbündlertanze; Piano sonata, op. 22; Toccata, op. 7. *Berezovsky, piano.*
• ARG 11-12/93: 193
+ Fa 11-12/93: 387
+ Gr 8/93: 64

34384. 9301-77547-2: LISZT—Mazeppa; Mephisto waltz no. 1. KODÁLY—Theater overture; Háry János: Suite. *New York Phil.; Masur, cond.*
+ ARG 5-6/96: 131
+ Fa 5-6/96: 191
+ Fi 5/96: 125

34385. 9031-77608-2 (2 discs): PURCELL—Anthems, instrumental music and songs. *Bowman, Rogers, Egmond; King's College Choir, Cambridge; Willcocks, cond.; Leonhardt Consort; Leonhardt, cond.; Brüggen Consort; Brüggen, cond. Reissues.*
+ Gr 9/93: 101

34386. 9031-77611-2 (2 discs): BACH—Brandenburg concertos. *Concentus Musicus Wien; Harnoncourt, cond. Recorded 1967.*
+ Gr 7/93: 33

34387. 9031-77614-2: BACH—Cantatas no. 67, 108, 127. *Fahberg, Benningsen, Pears, Engen; Munich Bach Choir; Munich State Opera Orch.; Richter, cond. Recorded 1958.*
+ Gr 5/93: 76

34388. 9031-77617-2: MARAIS—Pièces en trio. *Quadro Hotteterre. Reissue.*
• Gr 7/93: 33

34389. 9031-77618-2: RAMEAU—Pièces de clavecin en concerts. *Brüggen, flute; S. Kuijken, violin; W. Kuijken, viola da gamba; Leonhardt, harpsichord. Reissue.*
+ Gr 7/93: 33

34390. 9031-77620-2: TELEMANN—Suite in A minor; Concerto for flute and recorder; Viola concerto; Ouverture des Nations. *Various performers. Reissues.*
+ ARG 11-12/93: 210
+ Gr 9/93: 64

34391. 9031-77623-2 (3 discs): C.P.E. BACH—Prussian sonatas; Württemberg sonatas. *Asperen, harpsichord. Reissues.*
+ Gr 7/93: 33

34392. 9031-77624-2: BOCCHERINI—Cello concertos no. 4, 6-8. *Bylsma, cello; Concerto Amsterdam; Schröder, cond. Reissue.*
+ ARG 11-12/93: 80
+ Fa 11-12/93: 192
• Gr 7/93: 35

34393. 9031-77631-2 (2 discs): TELEMANN—Der Tag des Gerichts; Ino. *Landwehr-Herrmann, Alexander, Canne-Meijer, Equiluz, Egmond; Vienna Boys' Choir; Concentus Musicus Wien; Harnoncourt, cond. Reissues.*
+ Gr 7/93: 33

34394. 9031-77705-2: Music of Gershwin, Arensky, Arban, Ravel, Bernstein, and others. *Nakariakov, trumpet; Markovich, piano.*
+ ARG 3-4/94: 216
+ Gr 5/93: 68

34395. 4509-90201-2: TCHAIKOVSKY—1812 overture; Capriccio italien; Marche slave; Swan lake: suite. *Israel Phil. Orch.; Mehta, cond.*
• ARG 11-12/93: 207
• Fa 11-12/93: 417
• Gr 8/93: 41

34396. 4509-90267-2: VERDI—Famous opera choruses. *Orch. & Chorus of the Accademia Nazionale di Santa Cecilia; Rizzi, cond.*
+ ARG 11-12/93: 214
• Fa 11-12/93: 433
+ Gr 8/93: 84

34397. 4509-90422-2 (2 discs): TCHAIKOVSKY—String quartets no. 1-3; Souvenir de Florence. *Borodin Quartet; Yurov, viola; Milman, cello.*
• ARG 5-6/94: 155
+ Fa 3-4/94: 336
+ Gr 1/94: 72

34398. 4509-90494-2: MOZART—Missa solemnis, K. 337; Litaniae de venerabili altaris sacramento, K. 125; Regina coeli, K. 276. *Bonney, Magnus-Harnoncourt,*

Heilmann, Cachemaille; Arnold Schoenberg Choir; Concentus Musicus Wien; Harnoncourt, cond.
+ ARG 11-12/93: 155
+ Fa 11-12/93: 334
+ Gr 8/93: 70

34399. 4509-90674-2: MOZART—Piano concertos no. 18-19; Rondo, K. 382. *Barenboim, piano & cond.; Berlin Phil. Orch.*
• ARG 5-6/95: 142
+ Gr 4/95: 66

34400. 4509-90696-2: SCHUMANN—Piano concerto; Violin concerto. *Argerich, piano; Kremer, violin; Chamber Orch. of Europe; Harnoncourt, cond.* Recorded live.
+ ARG 5-6/95: 171
+ Fa 5-6/95: 332
+ Fa 7-8/95: 308
• Gr 1/95: 56

34401. 4509-90798-2: MONTEVERDI— Tempro la cetra; Il ballo delle ingrate; Tirsi e Clori; Il combattimento di Tancredi e Clorinda. *Tragicomedia; Stubbs, cond.*
+ ARG 11-12/93: 151
+ Fa 11-12/93: 328
+ Gr 10/93: 92

34402. 4509-90799-2: ROSSI—Le canterine romane: Roman cantatas for 2 and 3 sopranos. *Tragicomedia; Stubbs, cond.*
+ ARG 11-12/93: 179
+ Fa 11-12/93: 366
+ Gr 10/93: 99

34403. 4509-90825-2: MOZART—Piano sonatas (arr. Grieg). *Richter, Leonskaja, piano.* Recorded 1993.
• ARG 7-8/96: 162
+ Fa 7-8/96: 252
+ Gr 2/96: 68

34404. 4509-90841-2: *A gift of nature.* Music of Baltazar, Schop, Matteis, Brade, Lawes, Simpson, and others. *Trio Sonnerie; Stubbs, theorbo; Lawrence-King, harp & organ.*
+ ARG 9-10/94: 254
+ Fa 9-10/94: 426
+ Gr 5/94: 76

34405. 4509-90842-2: MOZART— Serenade, K. 203; March, K. 237; Symphony no. 23. *Concentus Musicus Wien; Harnoncourt, cond.*
+ ARG 11-12/94: 162
+ Fa 7-8/94: 193
• Gr 10/94: 112

34406. 4509-90843-2: HAYDN— Symphonies no. 31, 59, 73. *Concentus Musicus Wien; Harnoncourt, cond.*
+ ARG 3-4/95: 113
- Fa 3-4/95: 187
• Gr 4/95: 54

34407. 4509-90844-2: VAUGHAN WILLIAMS—Symphonies, no. 4-5. *BBC Symphony Orch.; A. Davis, cond.*
• ARG 7-8/94: 184
• Fa 7-8/94: 266
- Gr 2/94: 54

34408. 4509-90845-2: DELIUS—Orchestra music. *BBC Symphony Orch.; A. Davis, cond.*
+ ARG 5-6/94: 86
+ Fa 3-4/94: 172
+ Gr 1/94: 44

34409. 4509-90846-2: Concertos by Jolivet, Haydn, Hummel, and Tomasi. *Nakariakov, trumpet; Markovich, piano; Lausanne Chamber Orch.; López Cobos, cond.*
• Gr 10/93: 58

34410. 4509-90847-2: DVOŘÁK— Symphony no. 8. JANÁČEK—Sinfonietta. *New York Phil.; Masur, cond.*
+ ARG 9-10/94: 129
+ Fa 9-10/94: 186
• Gr 12/94: 80

34411. 4509-90848-2: SHOSTAKOVICH— Symphony no. 13. *Leiferkus, bass; Yevtushenko, narrator; New York Phil.; Masur, cond.*
+ ARG 9-10/94: 199
+ Fa 9-10/94: 339
• Gr 10/94: 124

34412. 4509-90849-2: SHOSTAKOVICH— Symphonies no. 1, 9. *National Symphony Orch.; Rostropovich, cond.*
• ARG 11-12/94: 190
• Fa 11-12/94: 382
+ Gr 10/94: 122

34413. 4509-90851-2 (2 discs): VERDI— Rigoletto. *Vaduva, Leech, Agache, Ramey; Welsh National Opera; Rizzi, cond.*
• ARG 5-6/94: 164
- Fa 3-4/94: 355
• Gr 11/93: 160
+ ON 3/5/94: 37
• Op 11/93: 1366

34414. 4509-90852-2: *Ballets.* Music of Falla, Milhaud, Walton, and Martin. *Larmore, mezzo-soprano; St. Paul Chamber Orch.; Wolff, cond.*
+ ARG 1-2/95: 208
+ Fa 11-12/94: 506

34415. 4509-90853-2: SHOSTAKOVICH— Symphonies no. 2-3. *London Voices; London Symphony Orch.; Rostropovich, cond.*
+ ARG 1-2/95: 178
• Fa 11-12/94: 383
+ Gr 10/94: 122

34416. 4509-90854-2: BRAHMS—Schöne Magelone. *Fassbaender, mezzo-soprano; Leonskaja, piano.*
+ ARG 3-4/95: 81
+ Gr 10/94: 168

34417. 4509-90855-2: BERLIOZ— Symphonie fantastique; Overtures: Roman carnival; Béatrice et Bénédict. *London Phil. Orch.; Mehta, cond.*
• ARG 11-12/94: 74
+ Fa 11-12/94: 177
• Gr 4/96: 41

34418. 4509-90856-2: *Gabrieli in Venice.* Music of G. Gabrieli, Viadana, Marini, A. Gabrieli, Massaino, and Frescobaldi. *London Brass; Pickett, cond.*
+ ARG 9-10/94: 229
+ Fa 7-8/94: 137

34419. 4509-90857-2 (2 discs): MOZART—La clemenza di Tito. *Langridge, Popp, Ziesak, Murray; Zürich Opera; Harnoncourt, cond.*
• ARG 7-8/94: 138
+ Fa 7-8/94: 187
+ Gr 5/94: 109
+ Op 6/94: 761

34420. 4509-90858-2: VAUGHAN WILLIAMS—Symphonies no. 2, 8. *BBC Symphony Orch.; A. Davis, cond.*
+ ARG 3-4/95: 210
• Gr 2/95: 59

34421. 4509-90861-2 (3 discs): MOZART—Le nozze di Figaro. *Margiono, Bonney, Lang, Hampson, Scharinger; Chorus of the Netherlands Opera; Royal Concertgebouw Orch.; Harnoncourt, cond.*
+ ARG 3-4/95: 149
- Fa 3-4/95: 239
• Gr 10/94: 192
+ ON 1/21/95: 38

34422. 4509-90864-2: SCHUMANN—Piano trios no. 2-3. *Trio Fontenay.*
+ ARG 3-4/96: 181
• Fa 5-6/96: 115
+ Gr 12/95: 110

34423. 4509-90867-2: SCHUMANN— Symphonies no. 3-4. *Chamber Orch. of Europe; Harnoncourt, cond.*
+ ARG 3-4/95: 182
+ Fa 5-6/95: 337
+ Gr 2/95: 56

34424. 4509-90872-2 (3 discs): GOUNOD—Faust. *Gasdia, Mentzer, Fassbaender, Hadley, Ramey; Welsh National Opera; Rizzi, cond.*
• ARG 11-12/94: 119
+ Fa 11-12/94: 240
+ Gr 7/94: 109

34425. 4509-90873-2: SCHUBERT—Songs. *Bonney, soprano; Parsons, piano; Kam, clarinet.*
+ ARG 5-6/95: 168
+ Gr 3/95: 91

34426. 4509-90875-2: BRUCH—Violin concerto no. 1. MENDELSSOHN—Violin concerto in E minor. *Vengerov, violin; Gewandhaus Orch.; Masur, cond.*
+ ARG 7-8/94: 85

TELDEC

+ Fa 7-8/94: 103
+ Gr 4/94: 40

34427. 4509-90876-2: BEETHOVEN—The creatures of Prometheus. *Chamber Orch. of Europe; Harnoncourt, cond.*
- ARG 7-8/95: 83
+ Fa 7-8/95: 115

34428. 4509-90879-2: DURUFLÉ— Requiem. FAURÉ—Requiem. *Bonney, Larmore, Hampson; Ambrosian Singers; Philharmonia Orch.; Legrand, cond.*
+ ARG 5-6/94: 88
• Fa 7-8/94: 133
+ ON 4/1/95: 43

34429. 4509-90881-2: TCHAIKOVSKY— Violin concerto, op. 35. GLAZUNOV— Violin concerto, op. 82. *Vengerov, violin; Berlin Phil. Orch.; Abbado, cond.*
- ARG -56/96: 210
+ Fa 3-4/96: 300
+ Gr 11/95: 86

34430. 4509-90882-2: MAHLER— Symphony no. 9. *New York Phil.; Masur, cond.*
• ARG 7-8/95: 150
+ Fa 7-8/95: 235
• Gr 5/95: 54

34431. 4509-90888-2: SCHUBERT—Piano sonatas, op. 53; op. posth. 122. *Leonskaja, piano.*
- ARG 7-8/95: 188
+ Fa 5-6/95: 326

34432. 4509-90889-2: BRAHMS—String quartets no. 1, 3. *Borodin Quartet.*
+ ARG 11-12/94: 82
+ Fa 11-12/94: 300
+ Gr 11/94: 98

34433. 4509-90890-2: RACHMANINOFF— Chopin variations; Piano sonata no. 1. *Berezovsky, piano.*
+ ARG 9-10/94: 179
- Fa 9-10/94: 306
+ Gr 7/94: 82

34434. 4509-91002-2: *Music at the court of Mannheim.* Music of J.C. Bach, Holzbauer, J. Stamitz, and Richter. *Concentus Musicus Wien; Harnoncourt, cond. Reissue.*
+ Gr 7/93: 33

34435. 4509-91181-2: *Lettera amorosa.* Music of Monteverdi, Kapsberger, D'India, Piccinini, Caccini, Melli, and L. Rossi. *Laurens, mezzo-soprano; Pianca, theorbo & archlute.*
+ ARG 1-2/94: 186
+ Fa 11-12/93: 479

34436. 4509-91183-2: BACH—Anna Magdalena notebook: Selections. *Tragicomedia; Stubbs, cond.*
+ ARG 11-12/94: 63
+ Fa 11-12/94: 150
• Gr 12/94: 116

34437. 4509-91184-2 (4 discs): SCHUBERT—Symphonies (complete). *Concertgebouw Orch.; Harnoncourt, cond.*
+ ARG 3-4/94: 150
• Fa 3-4/94: 310
+ Gr 12/93: 76

34438. 4509-91185-2 (2 discs): WAGNER—Das Rheingold. *Tomlinson, Brinkmann, Finnie; other soloists; Bayreuth Festival, 1991; Barenboim, cond.*
- ARG 3-4/94: 180
- Fa 1-2/94: 351
+ ON 4/2/94: 32

34439. 4509-91186-2 (4 discs): WAGNER—Die Walküre. *Elming; Secunde; Evans; other soloists; Bayreuth Festival, 1992; Barenboim, cond.*
- ARG 3-4/94: 180
+ Fa 1-2/94: 351
+ ON 4/2/94: 32

34440. 4509-91188-2 (2 discs): HANDEL—Organ concertos, op. 4, 7. *Tachezi, organ; Concentus Musicus Wien; Harnoncourt, cond. Reissues.*
+ ARG 11-12/93: 118
• Gr 10/94: 106

34441. 4509-91191-2: PURCELL—Dido and Aeneas. *D. Jones, Deam, Harvey, Bickley, Jenkin, Mel. Marshall, Ashton, Murgatroyd; St. James's Baroque Singers; Bolton, cond.*
• ARG 11-12/93: 173
+ Fa 11-12/93: 352
• Fa 11-12/93: 341
+ Gr 9/93: 110
+ ON 2/19/94: 33

34442. 4509-91192-2: *Baroque music of Bologna.* Music of Torelli, Franceschini, Jacchini, and Gabrielli. *St. James's Baroque Players; Bolton, cond.*
+ ARG 11-12/93: 211
+ Fa 11-12/93: 478
+ Gr 9/93: 68

34443. 4509-91378-2: MOZART—Sonata for 2 pianos, K. 448; Andante and five variations, K. 501; 4-hand piano sonatas, K. 521; K. 381. *Argerich, Rabinovitch, pianos.*
• ARG 5-6/95: 143
+ Fa 7-8/95: 308
• Gr 1/95: 67

34444. 4509-91445-2: BRUCKNER— Symphony no. 3. *Frankfurt Radio Symphony Orch.; Inbal, cond.*
+ Gr 9/93: 46

34445. 4509-91448-2: SCHUBERT—Octet, D. 803. *Berlin Soloists. Reissue.*
+ Gr 11/93: 96

34446. 4509-91494-2 (9 discs): BEETHOVEN—String quartets (complete). *Vermeer String Quartet.*
+ Fa 9-10/93: 118

34447. 4509-91683-2: VIVALDI—Violin concertos, op. 8, no. 1-6. *Blankestijn, violin; Chamber Orch. of Europe.*
• ARG 9-10/94: 218
• Fa 9-10/94: 367
+ Gr 6/94: 66

34448. 4509-91729-2: RESPIGHI—Trittico Botticelliano; Ancient airs and dances suites 1, 3; Gli uccelli. *Saint Paul Chamber Orch.; Wolff, cond.*
+ ARG 5-6/95: 158
+ Fa 3-4/95: 274
+ Gr 1/95: 54

34449. 4509-91765-2 (60 discs): BACH— Sacred cantatas. *Vocal soloists; Choirs; Leonhardt Consort; Leonhardt, cond.; Concentus Musicus Wien; Harnoncourt, cond. Reissues.*
+ Gr 2/95: 79

34450. 4509-91786-2: Moscow nights. *Red Star Army Chorus; Bazhalkin, cond.*
+ ARG 9-10/93: 253
+ Fa 9-10/93: 348

34451. 4509-91852-2: VIVALDI— Concertos for recorder, oboe, violin and bassoon, RV 94, 107; Concerto for recorder, oboe, violin and bassoon, RV 98; Concerto for recorder, 2 violins and bassoon, RV 104; Concerto for lute, 2 violins, and continuo, RV 93; Concerto for recorder, 2 violins, viola, and continuo, RV 442; Concerto for recorder, 2 violins, and continuo, RV 108; Sonata for 2 violins and continuo, RV 63. *Il Giardino armonico.*
+ Fa 11-12/93: 438
+ Gr 7/94: 66

34452. 4509-91971-2: MONTEVERDI— Madrigali concertati. *Tragicomedia.*
+ ARG 3-4/94: 124
+ Fa 3-4/94: 251
• Gr 1/94: 86

34453. 4509-92058-2: BRAHMS—Choral songs op. 17, 42, 63, 93a, 104. *Arnold Schoenberg Choir; Ortner, cond.*
+ ARG 11-12/94: 81
+ Fa 11-12/94: 182

34454. 4509-92174-2 (2 discs): BACH— Orchestral suites. *Concentus Musicus Wien; Harnoncourt, cond. Reissue.*
+ Gr 2/94: 37

34455. 4509-92175-2 (2 discs): MONTEVERDI—Vespers. *Vienna Boys Choir; Munich Capella Antiqua; Monteverdi Choir, Hamburg; Concentus Musicus Wien; Jürgens, cond. Reissue.*
• ARG 11-12/94: 159

34456. 4509-92176-2 (2 discs): Organ music by J.S., J.L., J.M., J.C., J.B., and J.E. Bach. *Krumbach, organ.*
• ARG 1-2/95: 67
• Gr 1/95: 72

34457. 4509-92180-2: LECLAIR—Violin concertos. NAUDOT—Recorder concerto, op. 17, no. 5. *Concerto Amsterdam; Schröder, violin & cond.; Brüggen, recorder; Concentus Musicus Wien; Harnoncourt, cond.* Reissues.
 • Gr 2/94: 44

34458. 4509-92181-2: MONTEVERDI—Combattimento di Tancredi e Clorinda; Madrigals. *Vocalists; Concentus Musicus Wien; Harnoncourt, cond.* Reissue.
 + Gr 2/94: 84

34459. 4509-92256-2: SHOSTAKOVICH—Violin concerto no. 1. PROKOFIEV—Violin concerto no. 1. *Vengerov, violin; London Symphony Orch.; Rostropovich, cond.*
 + ARG 5-6/95: 175

34460. 4509-92257-2: BRAHMS—Variations on a theme by Haydn; Sonata for 2 pianos, op. 34b; Waltzes, op. 39, no. 1-5. *Argerich, Rabinovitch, pianos.*
 + ARG 5-6/95: 93
 + Fa 7-8/95: 308
 + Gr 1/95: 67

34461. 4509-92373-2: HAYDN—Seven last words of Christ. *Borodin Quartet.*
 + ARG 3-4/95: 111
 + Gr 4/95: 80

34462. 4509-92374-2: ELGAR—The music makers; Dream children; Elegy; Sursum corda; Sospiri; Chanson de matin; Chanson de nuit; Salut d'amour. *Rigby, mezzo-soprano; BBC Symphony Orch. & Chorus; A. Davis, cond.*
 + Gr 2/95: 83

34463. 4509-92425-2: BACH—Piano concertos BWV 1054, 1058. MOZART—Piano concerto no. 25. *Richter, piano; Orch. da camera di Padova e del Veneto; Bashmet, cond.* Recorded 1993.
 • Gr 8/96: 41

34464. 4509-92628-2 (6 discs): HAYDN—Symphonies no. 68, 93-104. *Concertgebouw Orch; Harnoncourt, cond.* Reissues.
 • Gr 4/94: 46

34465. 4509-93025-2: MOZART—Sacred choral works. *Mei, Bonney, Azesberger, Heilmann; Arnold Schoenberg Choir; Concentus Musicus Wien; Harnoncourt, cond.*
 + ARG 11-12/94: 161
 + Fa 11-12/94: 312

34466. 4509-93157-2: Music of Sarro, A. and D. Scarlatti, Durante, and Mancini. *Giardino armonico; Antonini, cond.*
 + ARG 9-10/94: 255
 + Gr 11/94: 109

34467. 4509-93332-2: BRUCKNER—Symphony no. 4 (Haas ed.). *New York Phil.; Masur, cond.*
 + ARG 3-4/95: 84

 • Fa 3-4/95: 147
 • Gr 12/94: 76

34468. 4509-93333-2: *Mexican Baroque.* Choral music of Jerúsalem and Zumaya. *Chanticleer; Jennings, cond.*
 + Gr 12/94: 148

34469. 4509-93348-2: MOZART—Serenade no. 3; Divertimento no. 1. *Concentus Musicus Wien; Harnoncourt, cond.*
 + ARG 7-8/96: 162
 • Gr 9/96: 55

34470. 4509-93671-2: Music of Bach, Chopin, Grieg, Scarlatti, and Tomeoni. *Michelangeli, piano.* Recorded 1942-43.
 + ARG 9-10/94: 274

34471. 4509-93672-2: SCHUMANN—Violin concerto. MENDELSSOHN—Violin concerto. *Kulenkampff, violin; Berlin Phil. Orch.; Schmidt-Isserstedt, cond.* Recorded 1937 (Schumann).
 • ARG 9-10/94: 266
 + Fa 9-10/94: 331
 + Gr 9/94: 134

34472. 4509-93673-2: TCHAIKOVSKY—Symphony no. 6; 1812 overture. *Concertgebouw Orch.; Mengelberg, cond.* Recorded 1941.
 + ARG 9-10/94: 266
 + Fa 9-10/94: 353
 + Gr 10/94: 218

34473. 4509-93674-2 (4 discs): WAGNER—Lohengrin. *Windgassen, Steber, Greindl, Varnay; Bayreuth Festival; Keilberth, cond.* Recorded 1953.
 + ARG 9-10/94: 271
 + Gr 10/94: 223
 • ON 9/94: 60

34474. 4509-93687-2: BACH—Cantatas no. 27, 158, 198. *Hansmann, Watts, Equiluz, Egmond; Monteverdi Choir; Concerto Amsterdam; Jürgens, cond.* Recorded 1967-68.
 + Gr 10/94: 167

34475. 4509-93691-2: *Queen of coloratura, Edita Gruberová.* Music of Mozart, Donizetti, Verdi, and J. Strauss, Jr. *Gruberová, soprano; orch.; Bonynge, Harnoncourt, Rizzi, conds.* Reissues.
 + ARG 1-2/95: 240
 + Fa 11-12/94: 437

34476. 4509-93706-2 (2 discs): Duets by Meyerbeer, Mozart, Verdi, Bizet, Giordano, and others. *Tucker, tenor; Merrill, baritone; Schick, piano.*
 + ARG 9-10/94: 264

34477. 4509-93772-2 (2 discs): TELEMANN—Darmstadt overtures. *Concentus Musicus Wien; Harnoncourt, cond.* Reissue.
 + ARG 9-10/94: 211
 + Gr 12/94: 98

34478. 4509 93805-2: BACH—Arias and choruses. *Various choirs; Concentus Musicus Wien; Harnoncourt, cond.* Reissues.
 • ARG 7-8/94: 62

34479. 4509-93856-2: BORTNIANSKY—Sacred choral works. *Glinka Choir of St. Petersburg; Chernushenko, cond.*
 • ARG 7-8/95: 92
 + Gr 4/95: 97

34480. 4509-94193-2 (4 discs): WAGNER—Siegfried. *Jerusalem, Clark, Tomlinson, Kannen, Kang, Evans, Svendén, Leidland; Bayreuth Festival 1992; Barenboim, cond.* Recorded 1992.
 - ARG 1-2/95: 202
 • Fa 11-12/94: 422
 • Gr 10/94: 204

34481. 4509-94194-2 (4 discs): WAGNER—Götterdämmerung. *Evans, Jerusalem, Kang, Meier; Bayreuth Festival 1991; Barenboim, cond.* Recorded 1992.
 • ARG 1-2/95: 202
 • Fa 11-12/94: 422
 • Gr 10/94: 204

34482. 4509-94458-2: BACH—Organ works, vol. 1. *Koopman, organ.*
 - ARG 11-12/95: 71
 + Gr 8/95: 100

34483. 4509-94459-2: BACH—Organ works, vol. 2. *Amsterdam Baroque Choir; Koopman, organ.*
 + Gr 6/96: 70

34484. 4509-94460-2: BACH—Organ works, vol. 3. Trio sonatas. *Koopman, organ.*
 + ARG 9-10/96: 85
 + Gr 7/96: 74

34485. 4509-94539-2: RAVEL—Piano music. *Berezovsky, piano.*
 • ARG 5-6/95: 157
 + Gr 3/95: 74

34486. 4509-94540-2: SCHNITTKE—Violin concertos no. 2-3; Stille Nacht; Gratulationsrondo. *Kremer, violin; Chamber Orch. of Europe; Eschenbach, cond.*
 + Gr 2/95: 56

34487. 4509-94541-2: HOLST—The planets; Egdon Heath. *BBC Symphony Orch.; A. Davis, cond.*
 • ARG 3-4/95: 115
 • Gr 12/94: 84

34488. 4509-94542-2: TIPPETT—Concerto for double string orchestra; Fantasia concertante on a theme of Corelli; The midsummer marriage: Ritual dances. *BBC Symphony Orch. & Chorus; Davis, cond.*
 + ARG 11-12/96: 225
 + Fa 11-12/96: 405
 + Gr 10/96: 67

TELDEC

34489. 4509-94543-2 (2 discs): SCHUMANN—Symphony no. 4. SCHUBERT—Symphony no. 4. MENDELSSOHN—Fair Melusine. *Berlin Phil. Orch.; Harnoncourt, cond.*
• ARG 7-8/96: 194
+ Fa 9-10/96: 440
+ Gr 5/96: 60

34490. 4509-94544-2: BRAHMS—Piano concerto no. 2. *Leonskaja, piano; Leipzig Gewandhaus Orch.; Masur, cond.* Recorded live 1994.
+ ARG 7-8/95: 92
• Fa 7-8/95: 130
• Gr 7/95: 46

34491. 4509-94545-2: MAHLER— Symphony no. 2. *Gustafson, soprano; Quivar, alto; Prague Phil. Choir; Israel Phil. Orch.; Mehta, cond.*
• ARG 7-8/95: 149
• Fa 7-8/95: 232
- Gr 2/95: 47

34492. 4509-94548-2: STRAVINSKY— Pulcinella; Renard: Suites no. 1-2; Ragtime. *Larmore, Aler, Kelley, Opalach, Cheek, vocalists; St. Paul Chamber Orch.; Wolff, cond.*
+ ARG 5-6/96: 206
+ Fa 5-6/96: 291
+ Gr 5/96: 66

34493. 4509-94549-2 (2 discs): HUMPERDINCK—Hansel und Gretel. *Larmore, Ziesak, Schwarz, Behrens, Weikl; Bavarian Radio Symphony Orch.; Runnicles, cond.*
+ ARG 5-6/95: 123
+ Gr 1/95: 97
• ON 12/23/95: 38
• Op 2/95: 248

34494. 4509-94550-2: VAUGHAN WILLIAMS—Symphony no. 1 "A sea symphony". *Roocroft, soprano; Hampson, baritone; BBC Symphony Orch. & Chorus; Davis, cond.*
• ARG 11-12/95: 223
+ Fa 11-12/95: 409
• Gr 8/95: 88

34495. 4509-94551-2: LOCATELLI— Concerti grossi, op. 1, no. 3, 12; op. 4, no. 10; op. 7, no. 4, 6. *Concerto Köln.*
• ARG 3-4/95: 130
• Gr 2/95: 47

34496. 4509-94552-2: VIVALDI—Cello concertos RV 564, 551, 531, 552, 561, 544. *Coin, cello; Giardino Armonico; Antonini, cond.*
+ ARG 11-12/95: 228
+ Gr 8/95: 88

34497. 4509-94553-2 (2 discs): ROSSINI—La Cenerentola. *Larmore, Giménez, Quilico, Corbelli; Covent Garden Opera; Rizzi, cond.*
+ ARG 7-8/95: 182
+ Fa 9-10/95: 297
• Gr 4/95: 123

+ ON 8/95: 34
+ Op 7/95: 872

34498. 4509-94554-2: *Virtuoso music for trumpet.* Music of Waxman, Arban, Falla, Saint-Saëns, Paganini, Tchaikovsky, Sarasate, Fauré, and Brandt. *Nakariakov, trumpet; Markovich, piano.*
+ ARG 9-10/95: 270
+ Gr 6/95: 72

34499. 4509-94555-2 (2 discs): J. STRAUSS, JR.—The gypsy baron. *Lippert, Coburn, Oelze, Holzmair; Vienna Symphony Orch.; Harnoncourt, cond.*
+ ARG 7-8/95: 205
+ Fa 11-12/95: 389
+ Gr 6/95: 114
+ ON 8/95: 36

34500. 4509-94556-2: BRUCKNER— Symphony no. 6. *Berlin Phil. Orch.; Barenboim, cond.*
+ ARG 5-6/96: 96
+ Fa 5-6/96: 124
• Gr 9/95: 52

34501. 4509-94557-2: SHOSTAKOVICH— Symphony no. 5. *National Symphony Orch.; Rostropovich, cond.*
+ ARG 5-6/96: 195
• Fa 3-4/96: 285
- Gr 11/95: 92

34502. 4509-94558-2: SCHUBERT—Piano trios. *Fontenay Trio.*
+ ARG 9-10/96: 195
+ Gr 2/97: 74

34503. 4509-94560-2 (2 discs): BEETHOVEN—Fidelio. *Margiono, Seiffert, Leiferkus, Pólgar, Bonney, Walt, Skovhus; Arnold Schoenberg Chorus; Chamber Orch. of Europe; Harnoncourt, cond.*
+ ARG 3-4/96: 87
• Fa 3-4/96: 122
+ Gr 10/95: 128
+ ON 11/95: 44
+ Op 10/95: 1240

34504. 4509-94561-2: PALESTRINA— Requiem; Motets. *Chanticleer.*
- ARG 3-4/95: 154
• Gr 2/95: 88

34505. 4509-94564-2: SCHUBERT—String quintet. *Borodin Quartet; Milman, cello.*
+ ARG 1-2/96: 168
+ Gr 4/95: 86

34506. 4509-94565-2: MENDELSSOHN— String symphonies, no. 8-10. *Concerto Köln.*
+ ARG 3-4/95: 141
+ Gr 12/94: 88

34507. 4509-94566-2: VIVALDI—Violin concertos. *Onofri, Grazzi, violins; Il Giardino Armonico; Antonini, cond.*
+ Gr 4/96: 58

34508. 4509-94567-2: BRUCKNER— Symphony no. 8 (ed. Haas, 1939). *Berlin Phil. Orch.; Barenboim, cond.*
+ ARG 5-6/96: 96
+ Fa 5-6/96: 126
+ Gr 2/96: 44

34509. 4509-94568-2 (4 discs): WAGNER—Tristan und Isolde. *Jerusalem, Salminen, Meier, Struckmann, Botha, Lipovsek, Maus, Trekel, Heilmann; Chorus of the Berlin State Opera; Berlin Phil. Orch.; Barenboim, cond.*
• ARG 1-2/96: 198
+ Fa 11-12/95: 420
+ Gr 9/95: 110
• ON 11/95: 44
• Op 9/95: 1128

34510. 4509-94569-2: SALIERI—Piano concertos in C, B♭; STEPAN—Piano concerto in B♭. *Staier, fortepiano; Concerto Köln.*
+ ARG 9-10/95: 206
+ Gr 11/95: 92

34511. 4509-94570-2: SHCHEDRIN—Cello concerto. GAGNEUX—Triptyque. *Rostropovich, cello; London Symphony Orch.; Ozawa, cond.*
+ ARG 7-8/96: 114
+ Fa 5-6/96: 273
+ Fi 9/96: 127
+ Gr 6/96: 46

34512. 4509-94571-2: TCHAIKOVSKY— Waltzes. *New York Phil.; Masur, cond.*
+ ARG 9-10/95: 230

34513. 4509-95029-2: WEILL—Die sieben Todsünden. BERG—Lulu suite. *Réaux, soprano; members of Hudson Shad; New York Phil.; Masur, cond.*
• ARG 3-4/95: 224
• Fa 3-4/95: 343
+ Gr 12/94: 146

34514. 4509-95068-2: PURCELL—Songs of welcome and farewell. *Vocal soloists; Tragicomedia; Stubbs, Headley, conds.* Reissue.
+ ARG 11-12/95: 178
+ ARG 1-2/97: 154
+ Gr 7/95: 101

34515. 4509-95085-2: HAYDN—Stabat Mater, H. XX bis. *Bonney, Magnus-Harnoncourt, Lippert, Miles; Arnold Schoenberg Chorus; Concentus Musicus Wien; Harnoncourt, cond.*
• ARG 3-4/96: 125
+ Fa 11-12/95: 271
• Gr 8/95: 112

34516. 4509-95354-2: *Composers play their own works.* Music of d'Albert, Humperdinck, Grieg, Kienzl, Leoncavallo, Mahler, Saint-Saëns, and Strauss. *Piano rolls.*
- ARG 9-10/94: 272

34517. 4509-95500-2 (4 discs): HANDEL—Concerti grossi, op. 3; op. 6.

Concentus Musicus Wien; Harnoncourt, cond. Reissues.
+ Gr 2/96: 48

34518. 4509-95503-2 (2 discs): BRAHMS—String quartets (complete). DVOŘÁK—String quartet no. 13. *Alban Berg Quartet.* Reissues.
+ Gr 2/95: 64

34519. 4509-95512-2: Arias from Magic flute, Freischütz, Undine, Martha, and others. *Anders, tenor.* Recorded 1935-40.
+ ARG 7-8/95: 275

34520. 4509-95513-2: Waltzes by Strauss, Lanner, and Heuberger. *Berlin Phil. Orch.; E. Kleiber, cond.*
+ ARG 5-6/96: 261

34521. 4509-95515-2: BEETHOVEN—Symphonies no. 5, 8. *Concertgebouw Orch.; Mengelberg, cond.*
+ ARG 1-2/96: 240

34522. 4509-95516-2: WAGNER—Tristan und Isolde: highlights. *Mödl, Blatter, Windgassen; Berlin Opera; Rother, cond.* Recorded 1952-54.
+ ARG 11-12/95: 288
● Gr 5/95: 133

34523. 4509-95517-2 (2 discs): BACH—Mass in B minor. *Hansmann, Iliyama, Watts, Equiluz, Egmond; Vienna Boys' Choir; Chorus Viennensis; Concentus Musicus Wien; Harnoncourt, cond.* Reissue.
+ Gr 4/95: 97

34524. 4509-95518-2: BACH—Concerto for 2 violins, BWV 1043; Violin concertos; Concerto for oboe, violin, and strings, BWV 1060. *A. Harnoncourt, Pfeiffer, violins; Schaeftlein, oboe; Vienna Concentus Musicus; N. Harnoncourt, cond.* Reissue.
● Gr 5/95: 43

34525. 4509-9552-2: VIVALDI—Concertos for violins and cellos. *Il giardino armonico; Antonini, cond.*
+ Fa 9-10/95: 353

34526. 4509-95979-2: MOZART—Thamos, König in Aegypten; Der Schauspieldirektor. *Vocal soloists; Collegium Vocale; Netherlands Chamber Choir; Concertgebouw Orch.; Harnoncourt, cond.*
● Gr 3/95: 101

34527. 4509-95980-2 (2 discs): BACH—Brandenburg concertos, Orchestra suites no. 2-3. *Vienna Concentus Musicus; Harnoncourt, cond.* Reissue.
● Gr 5/95: 43

34528. 4509-95988-2 (2 discs): BOCCHERINI—Six string quartets, op. 32. *Esterházy Quartet.* Reissue.
+ Gr 10/95: 81

34529. 4509-95990-2: MOZART—Coronation mass; Vesperae solennes de confessore. *Rodgers, Magnus, Protschka, Pólgar; Arnold Schoenberg Choir; Concentus Musicus Wien; Harnoncourt, cond.* Reissue.
● Gr 3/96: 82

34530. 4509-95991-2: MOZART—Mass in C minor, K. 427. *Laki, Dénes, Equiluz, Holl; Vienna State Opera Chorus; Concentus Musicus Wien; Harnoncourt, cond.* Reissue.
● Gr 3/96: 82

34531. 4509-95998-2: *The last recital.* Music of Bach, Beethoven, Handel, Liszt, Paganini, Prokofiev, Sarasate, and Tchaikovsky. *Milstein, violin; Pludermacher, piano.* Recorded 1986.
+ Gr 5/95: 76

34532. 4509-96061-2: SOUSA—Marches. *Grenadier Guards; Hills, cond.*
● ARG 11-12/95: 209

34533. 4509-96158-2: VIVALDI—Four seasons; Concertos op. 8, no. 8-9. *Onofri, violin; Grazzi, oboe; Il Giardino armonico.*
+ Gr 1/95: 62

34534. 4509-96200-2: *Three tenors in concert, 1994.* Music of Massenet, Moreno-Torroba, Leoncavallo, Puccini, Verdi, and others. *Carreras, Domingo, Pavarotti; Los Angeles Phil. Orch.; Mehta, cond.*
+ Gr 12/94: 172

34535. 4509-96221-2: Piano music of Franck, Chausson, and Dukas. *Hubeau, piano.*
● Gr 4/96: 82

34536. 4509-96353-2: JERUSALEM—Mass; Motets. ZUMAYA—Motets. *Chanticleer; Jennings, cond.*
+ ARG 11-12/94: 248
+ Fa 11-12/94: 463

34537. 4509-96435-2: STRAUSS—Sinfonia domestica. DUKAS—Sorcerer's apprentice. RAVEL—La valse. *Argerich, Rabinovitch, pianos.*
+ ARG 9-10/96: 210
+ Gr 7/96: 70

34538. 4509-96515-2: *Out of this world.* Music of Sametz, Gibbons, Tallis, Gabrieli, Conte, Strauss, Shearer, and others. *Chanticleer.*
+ ARG 3-4/95: 257

34539. 4509-96516-2: Music of Mussorgsky, Rachmaninoff, Lyadov, Medtner, and Balakirev. *Berezovsky, piano.*
● ARG 9-10/96: 246
+ Gr 7/96: 81

34540. 4509-96517-2: LISZT—Piano concertos no. 1-2; Totentanz. *Berezovsky,*

piano; Philharmonia Orch.; Wolff, cond.
● ARG 5-6/96: 136
+ Fa 3-4/96: 203
+ Gr 1/96: 54

34541. 4509-96532-2: CHOPIN—Polonaises. *Leonskaja, piano.*
+ ARG 7-8/96: 100
● Gr 9/96: 75

34542. 4509-96800-2: *Where shall I fly?* MOZART—Arias. HANDEL—Arias. *Larmore, soprano; Lausanne Chamber Orch.; Lopez Cobos, cond.*
- ARG 1-2/96: 146
+ Fa 3-4/96: 333
+ Gr 12/95: 143
+ ON 2/17/96: 43
● Op 10/95: 1244

34543. 4509-96998-2 (6 separate discs): *Milstein: the last recital.* Music of Beethoven, Bach, Handel, Sarasate and others. *Milstein, violin; Pludermacher, piano.*
+ ARG 9-10/95: 273

34544. 4509-97304-2: NONO—Intolleranza 1960. *Rampy, Koszut, Harries, Schaaf, Probst, Dieken, Hoening, Otto, Wenning; Stuttgart Opera; Kontarsky, cond.* Recorded live 1993.
+ Gr 10/95: 140

34545. 4509-97445-2: SAINT-SAËNS—Carnival of the animals. POULENC—Concerto for two pianos. *S. & G. Pekinel, pianos; French Radio Phil. Orch.; Janowski, cond.*
+ Gr 2/96: 58

34546. 4509-97452-2 (3 discs): BACH—Harpsichord concertos (complete). *Leonhardt, Tachezi, Uittenbosch, Curtis, Müller, harpsichords; Leonhardt Consort; Concentus Musicus Wien; Harnoncourt, cond.* Reissue.
● ARG 9-10/95: 96
● Gr 11/95: 79

34547. 4509-97454-2: VIVALDI—Concertos RV 208, 169, 424, 461, 130, app 17. *Schröder, violin; Möller, cello; Piguet, oboe; Concerto Amsterdam.* Recorded 1978.
- ARG 11-12/95: 226

34548. 4509-97457-2: Songs by Gounod, Franck, Bizet, Massenet, and others. *Fischer-Dieskau, baritone; Höll, piano.* Reissue.
+ Gr 12/95: 135

34549. 4509-97458-2: LOEWE—Lieder. *Fischer-Dieskau, baritone; Höll, piano.* Reissue.
+ Gr 12/95: 135

34550. 4509-97459-2: EISLER—Lieder. *Fischer-Dieskau, baritone; Reimann, piano.* Reissue.
+ Gr 12/95: 135

TELDEC

34551. 4509-97460-2: Reimann—Poems of Michelangelo. Shostakovich—Verses of Michelangelo. *Fischer- Dieskau, baritone; Reimann, piano.* Reissue.
+ Gr 12/95: 135

34552. 4509-97461-2: Brahms—Piano quintet; String quartet no. 2. *Borodin Quartet; Virzaladze, piano.*
+ ARG 9-10/95: 114
+ Gr 5/95: 67

34553. 4509-97463-2: *The Thomas Hampson collection.* Portrait: Music of Bach, Handel, Mozart, Puccini, and others. *Hampson, baritone.* Reissues.
+ ARG 9-10/95: 288

34554. 450997504-2 (2 discs): Handel—Saul. *Fischer-Dieskau, Esswood, Rolfe Johnson, Varady, Gale; Concentus Musicus Wien; Harnoncourt, cond.* Reissue.
• ARG 11-12/95: 131

34555. 4509-97684-2 (2 discs): Purcell—Fairy Queen. *Magnus, McNair, Chance, Dale, Holl; Concentus Musicus Wien; Harnoncourt, cond.*
- ARG 5-6/96: 167
+ Fa 5-6/96: 242
• Gr 2/96: 102

34556. 4509-97758-2 (2 discs): Weber—Der Freischütz. *Holzmair, Orgonasova, Schäfer, Salminen, Wottrich; Berlin Phil. Orch.; Harnoncourt, cond.*
+ ARG 1-2/97: 189
+ Gr 11/96: 173
+ ON 12/28/96: 37
+ Op 10/96: 1243

34557. 4509-97868-2: *Last night of the Proms 1994: 100th season.* Music of Bach, Walton, Miki, Elgar, Massenet, and others. *Terfel, bass-baritone; Glennie, percussion; M. Davis, violin; BBC Symphony Orch. & Chorus; A. Davis, cond.*
• ARG 9-10/95: 245
• Gr 2/95: 94

34558. 4509-97900-2 (3 discs): Handel—Organ concertos. *Chamber Orch.; Richter, organ & cond.* Recorded 1959.
• ARG 7-8/96: 123
+ Gr 5/96: 68

34559. 4509-97901-2 (2 discs): Bach—Organ music. *Richter, organ.* Reissues.
- ARG 7-8/96: 69
• Gr 5/96: 68

34560. 4509-97902-2 (3 discs): Bach—Christmas oratorio. *Owen, Töpper, Günter, Engen; Munich Bach Choir & Orch.; Richter, cond.* Recorded 1958.
• ARG 11-12/96: 80
+ Gr 5/96: 68

34561. 4509-97903-2 (2 discs): Bach—Brandenburg concertos. *Unnamed chamber orch.; Richter, cond.* Recorded 1958.
- ARG 5-6/97: 73
• Gr 5/96: 68

34562. 4509-97904-2 (2 discs): Bach—Goldberg variations; Partitas. *Richter, harpsichord.* Reissues.
• ARG 9-10/96: 86
- Gr 5/96: 68

34563. 4509-97906—97909-2 (4 separate discs): Wagner—Ring highlights. *Vocal soloists; Bayreuth Festival; Barenboim, cond.* Reissues.
+ ARG 11-12/95: 230

34564. 4509-97914-2: Biber—Battalia; Pauern Kirchfahrt; Ballettae; Sonatas. *Concentus Musicus Wien; Harnoncourt, cond.* Recorded 1971.
+ ARG 7-8/96: 83
+ Gr 9/96: 49

34565. 4509-97926-2: Mozart—Requiem. *Stader, Töpper, Kesteren, Kohn; Munich Bach Orch.; Richter, cond.* Reissue.
+ ARG 9-10/96: 172
+ Gr 5/96: 68

34566. 4509-97983-2: Vivaldi—Concertos. *Concentus Musicus Wien; Harnoncourt, cond.* Reissue.
+ ARG 9-10/96: 224

34567. 4509-97984—97985-2 (2 separate discs): Bach—Brandenburg concertos; Orchestral suites no. 2-3. *Concentus Musicus Wien; Harnoncourt, cond.* Reissues.
• ARG 9-10/96: 81

34568. 4509-97987-2: Handel—Water music; Concerti grossi, op. 6: no. 4-5. *Concentus Musicus Wien; Harnoncourt, cond.* Reissue.
• ARG 9-10/96: 132
• Fa 9-10/96: 211

34569. 4509-97994-2: Bach—Goldberg variations. *Leonhardt, harpsichord.* Recorded 1965.
• Gr 3/96: 68

34570. 4509-98143-2: Prokofiev—Violin concerto no. 1. Shostakovich—Violin concerto no. 1. *Vengerov, violin; London Symphony Orch.; Rostropovich, cond.*
+ Gr 2/95: 51

34571. 4509-98256-2: Schoenberg—Verklärte Nacht (string orchestra version); Three piano pieces, op. 11; Five orchestral pieces, op. 16; Six little piano pieces, op. 19; Piano piece, op. 11, no. 2 (arr. Busoni). *Barenboim, piano & cond.; Chicago Symphony Orch.*
+ ARG 11-12/95: 191
+ Fa 9-10/95: 308
+ Gr 8/95: 80

34572. 4509-98320-2: Schumann—Symphonies no. 1-2. *Chamber Orch. of Europe; Harnoncourt, cond.*
+ ARG 11-12/96: 207
• Fa 11-12/96: 369

34573. 4509-98405-2: Bruckner—Symphony no. 3 (1877 version, ed. Nowak). *Concertgebouw Orch.; Harnoncourt, cond.*
• ARG 3-4/96: 96
+ Fa 3-4/96: 142
• Gr 12/95: 76

34574. 4509-98408-2 (2 discs): Verdi—Un ballo in maschera. *Leech, Crider, Chernov, Zaremba, Bayo; Welsh National Opera; Rizzi, cond.*
• ARG 9-10/96: 221
+ Fa 9-10/96: 347
+ Gr 6/96: 96

34575. 4509-98410-2: *Vanitas vanitatum: Rome 1650.* Music of Carissimi, Marazzoli, Landi, and others. *Tragicomedia; Stubbs, cond.*
+ Gr 3/96: 92

34576. 4509-98412-2: Mozart—Piano concertos no. 9, 17. *Staier, fortepiano; Concerto Köln.*
+ ARG 5-6/96: 152
+ Fi 3/97: 112
+ Gr 3/96: 50

34577. 4509-98413-2: Brahms—Ein deutsches Requiem. *McNair, Hagegård; Westminster Symphonic Choir; New York Phil. Orch.; Masur, cond.* Recorded live.
• ARG 5-6/96: 89
• Fa 3-4/96: 137
+ Fi 5/96: 125
+ Gr 2/96: 85

34578. 4509-98418-2 (2 discs): Gluck—Orphée et Eurydice. *Larmore, Upshaw, Hagley; San Francisco Opera; Runnicles, cond.*
+ ARG 11-12/96: 128
+ Fa 9-10/96: 198
• Fi 10/96: 147
+ Gr 7/96: 101
• ON 10/96: 39

34579. 4509-98420-2: Rosetti—Sinfonias. *Concerto Köln.*
+ ARG 1-2/96: 164
+ Fa 1-2/96: 288
+ Gr 12/95: 88

34580. 4509-98423-2: Mahler—Symphony no. 6. *Israel Phil. Orch.; Mehta, cond.*
• ARG 9-10/96: 157 (Chakwin)
+ ARG 9-10/96: 157 (Fox)
+ Fa 9-10/96: 250
• Gr 7/96: 56

34581. 4509-98424-2: Schoenberg—Gurrelieder. *Voigt, Larmore, Moser; Dresden Opera Chorus; Leipzig Radio Chorus; Staatskapelle Dresden; Sinopoli, cond.*

+ Gr 8/96: 87
+ ON 10/96: 38

34582. 4509-98435-2: MENDELSSOHN—
String symphonies no. 1, 4, 6, 7, 12.
Concerto Köln.
+ ARG 9-10/96: 164
+ Gr 7/96: 58

34583. 4509-98800-2: BERLIOZ—
Symphonie fantastique; La marseillaise.
*Domingo, tenor; Chicago Symphony
Chorus & Orch.; Barenboim, cond.*
- ARG 9-10/96: 94
• Fa 9-10/96: 153
• Gr 8/96: 42

34584. 4509-98802-2: LOKUMBE—African
portraits. *Soloists; Chicago Symphony
Orch.; Barenboim, cond.*
• ARG 7-8/96: 125
+ Fa 7-8/96: 188
+ Gr 2/96: 88
+ ON 10/96: 39

34585. 4509-98822—98825 2 (4 separate
discs): *The Thomas Hampson collection.*
Mahler songs; Song collection; Opera
scenes; American composers. *Hampson,
baritone.* Reissues.
+ ARG 9-10/95: 288

34586. 4509-98928-2: MOZART—Sacred
music. *Prégardien, tenor; Hampson,
baritone; Arnold Schoenberg Choir;
Concentus Musicus Wien; Harnoncourt,
cond.*
+ ARG 9-10/95: 182

34587. 4509-99051-2: *András Schiff live
at the Concertgebouw.* BRAHMS—Handel
variations. HANDEL—Suite no. 1.
REGER—Bach variations. *Schiff, piano.*
Recorded 1994.
• ARG 5-6/96: 175
+ Fa 3-4/96: 367
• Gr 11/95: 124

34588. 4509-99175-2: STRAUSS—Elektra.
*Polaski, Meier, Marc, Struckmann,
Botha; Chor der Deutschen Staatsoper
Berlin; Staatskapelle Berlin; Barenboim,
cond.*
• ARG 11-12/96: 215
• Fa 9-10/96: 334
• Fi 10/96: 147
• Gr 7/96: 107
+ Op 7/96: 857

34589. 4509-99176-2: SCHUMANN—
Arabeske, op. 18; Davidsbündlertänze
(1838 ed.); Blumenstück; Symphonische
Etuden (1852 ed.). *Schiff, piano.*
• ARG 3-4/96: 181
+ Fa 3-4/96: 279
+ Gr 11/95: 126

34590. 4509-99203-2: Mysteria:
Gregorian chants. *Chanticleer.*
+ ARG 9-10/95: 275

34591. 4509-99207-2: BEETHOVEN—Piano
concerto no. 1. MOZART—Piano concerto

no. 23. *Huang, piano; New York Phil.;
Masur, cond.*
+ ARG 3-4/96: 86
• Fa 3-4/96: 122
+ Gr 1/96: 48

34592. 4509-99595-2: WAGNER—
Overtures and preludes. *Chicago
Symphony Orch.; Barenboim, cond.*
+ ARG 5-6/96: 218
+ Fa 5-6/96: 308
+ Gr 4/96: 58

34593. 4509-99596-2: CARTER—Partita.
BERIO—Continuo. TAKEMITSU—Visions.
*Chicago Symphony Orch.; Barenboim,
cond.* Recorded live.
• ARG 9-10/95: 121
+ Fa 11-12/95: 232
+ Gr 8/95: 67

34594. 4509-99872-2: C.P.E. BACH—
Symphony in D major, H. 663. J.C.
BACH—Symphony, op. 18, no. 2.
MOZART—Symphony no. 29. *Munich
Bach Orch.; Richter, cond.* Reissue.
- Gr 5/96: 68

34595. 4509-99873-2: BACH—
Harpsichord concerto no. 1; Concertos
for 2-4 harpsichords. *Richter,
harpsichord & cond.; Müller, Aeschbach,
Gurtner, harpsichords; Bachwoche
Ansbach.* Reissues.
• ARG 9-10/96: 86
• Gr 5/96: 68

34596. 4509-99874-2: BACH—Cantatas
no. 67, 108, 127. *Fahberg, Benningsen,
Pears, Engen; Munich Bach Choir;
Munich State Opera Orch.; Richter,
cond.* Recorded 1959-1960.
• Gr 5/96: 68

TER

34597. CDTER2 1185 (2 discs):
WEILL—Street scene. *Ciesinski, Kelly,
Patterson, Van Allan; English National
Opera; Davis, cond.*
+ Fa 5-6/92: 287
+ Gr 11/91: 165
+ Op 11/91: 1370

34598. CDTER 1187 (2 discs):
SULLIVAN—The gondoliers. *New D'Oyly
Carte Opera Company.*
+ ARG 11-12/92: 124
• Gr 5/92: 119
• Op 11/92: 1372

34599. CDTER 1188 (2 discs):
SULLIVAN—Iolanthe. *New D'Oyly Carte
Opera Company; Pryce-Jones, cond.*
+ ARG 11-12/92: 124
• Gr 5/92: 119
+ Op 6/92: 745

34600. CDTER2 1197 (2 discs):
BERNSTEIN—West side story. *Olafimihan,
Manuel, O'Connor, Wanford; National
Symphony Orch.; Edwards, cond.*

+ Fa 3-4/94: 134
+ Gr 2/94: 93

34601. CDTER2 1199 (2 discs): KERN—
Show boat. *Kelly, Howard, Burgess,
White; National Symphony Orch.;
Edwards, cond.*
+ Gr 6/94: 114

34602. CDTER 1224: FLAHERTY—Once
on this island. *Original London cast;
Balcombe, cond.*
+ Gr 6/95: 109

34603. CDTER 1225: SONDHEIM—Merrily
we roll along. *Leister Haymarket
Theatre; Kerryson, cond.*
+ Gr 4/95: 126

34604. CDVIR 8317: *If I loved you.* Love
duets from musicals. *Masterson,
soprano; Allen, baritone; Philharmonia
Orch.; Edwards, cond.*
+ Gr 5/94: 116
+ ON 10/94: 51

TESTAMENT

34605. SBT 1009: STRAUSS—Horn
concerto no. 1; Oboe concerto. WEBER—
Bassoon concerto. *Brain, horn;
Goossens, oboe; Brooke, bassoon;
Philharmonia Orch.; Royal Liverpool
Phil.; Galliera, Sargent, conds.*
+ ARG 3-4/93: 188
+ Gr 10/92: 197

34606. SBT 1011: DEBUSSY—Nocturnes;
Prelude to the afternoon of a faun;
Martyrdom of St. Sebastien; La mer.
Philharmonia Orch.; Cantelli, cond.
Recorded 1954-55.
+ ARG 3-4/93: 192
+ Gr 10/92: 197

34607. SBT 1020: BEETHOVEN—Piano
concertos no. 2, 5. *Schnabel, piano;
Philharmonia Orch.; Dobrowen,
Galliera, conds.* Recorded 1946-47.
+ Fa 1-2/94: 121
+ Gr 3/94: 118

34608. SBT 1021: BEETHOVEN—Piano
concertos no. 3, 4. *Schnabel, piano;
Philharmonia Orch.; Dobrowen, cond.*
Recorded 1946-47.
+ Fa 1-2/94: 121

34609. SBT 1022: SCHUMANN—Adagio
and Allegro for horn and piano; Three
Fantasiestücke for clarinet and piano;
Three romances for oboe and piano.
BEETHOVEN—Trio for clarinet, cello, and
piano; Horn sonata. DUKAS—Villanelle
for horn and piano. *Brain, horn; Kell,
clarinet; Goossens, oboe; Pini, cello;
Moore, Matthews, piano.*
• Fa 1-2/94: 143
+ Gr 12/93: 135

34610. SBT 1023: SCHUMANN—Fantasie,
op. 17; Fantasiestücke, op. 12. BRAHMS—
Variations and fugue on a theme by

TESTAMENT

Handel. *Moiseiwitsch, piano.*
+ Fa 1-2/94: 310
+ Gr 1/94: 108

34611. SBT 1024: BRAHMS—Violin
sonatas no. 1-3. *De Vito, violin; E.
Fischer, Aprea, piano.*
+ Fa 1-2/94: 140
+ Gr 12/93: 136

34612. SBT 1026: *Irmgard Seefried.*
Music of Mozart, Flies, Brahms,
Schubert, and Wolf. *Seefried, soprano;
Moore, Nordberg, Schmidt, piano;
London Mozart Players; Blech, cond.*
+ ARG 5-6/94: 217
• Fa 1-2/94: 364
+ Fa 9-10/94: 384
+ Gr 4/94: 125

34613. SBT 1027: MEDTNER—Piano
concertos no. 2-3; Arabesque op. 7, no. 2;
Skazka op. 26, no. 3. *Medtner, piano;
Philharmonia Orch.; Dobrowen, cond.*
+ Fa 1-2/94: 233
+ Gr 4/94: 120

34614. SBT 1028: MOZART—Violin
concertos no. 3-5. *Goldberg, violin;
Philharmonia Orch.; Susskind, cond.*
Recorded 1951.
+ Fa 3-4/94: 193
+ Gr 4/94: 122

34615. SBT 1029: SAINT-SAËNS—Piano
concerto no. 2. RACHMANINOFF—Piano
concerto no. 3. *Gilels, piano; Orch. de la
Société des Concerts du Conservatoire,
Paris; Cluytens, cond.* Recorded 1954.
• Fa 3-4/94: 301
+ Gr 2/94: 105

34616. SBT 1030: CHOPIN—Piano music.
Solomon, piano. Recorded 1933-46.
+ ARG 9-10/94: 268
+ Fa 3-4/94: 163

34617. SBT 1031: SCHOENBERG—
Verklärte Nacht (sextet). SCHUBERT—
String quintet. *Hollywood String Quartet;
Dinkin, viola; Reher, cello.* Recorded
1950.
+ ARG 9-10/94: 270
+ Fa 3-4/94: 306
+ Gr 4/94: 122

34618. SBT 1032: BEETHOVEN—Violin
concerto, op. 61. SIBELIUS—Violin
concerto, op. 47. *Oistrakh, violin;
Stockholm Festival Orch.; Ehrling, cond.*
• Fa 9-10/94: 138
+ Gr 7/94: 128

34619. SBT 1033: LISZT—Piano concerto
no. 1; Piano music. SAINT-SAËNS—Le
carnaval des animaux: Le cygne (arr.
Godowsky). LIADOV—A musical
snuffbox. *Cherkassky, piano;
Philharmonia Orch.; Fistoulari, cond.*
+ ARG 11-12/94: 257
+ Fa 9-10/94: 239

34620. SBT 1034: *Guido Cantelli
conducts.* Music of Beethoven,
Mendelssohn, and Rossini. *Philharmonia
Orch.; Cantelli, cond.*
+ Fa 9-10/94: 433
+ Gr 11/94: 183

34621. SBT 1035: WAGNER—Music from
Der fliegende Holländer, Tannhäuser, Die
Meistersinger, and Götterdämmerung.
*Choruses; Berlin Phil. Orch.; Kempe,
cond.* Recorded 1956.
+ ARG 11-12/94: 259
+ Fa 9-10/94: 377

34622. SBT 1036: STRAUSS—Ariadne auf
Naxos: Excerpts; Songs with orchestra.
*Della Casa, Otto, Kirchstein, Schock;
Berlin Phil. Orch.; Erede, cond.* Reissues
(1964).
+ Fa 9-10/94: 345
+ Gr 11/94: 153

34623. SBT 1037: MENDELSSOHN—Violin
concerto. BRAHMS—Violin concerto.
*Martzy, violin; Philharmonia Orch.;
Kletzki, cond.* Recorded 1954, 1958.
+ Fa 9-10/94: 252
• Gr 9/94: 133

34624. SBT 1038: BRAHMS—Violin
concerto, op. 77. TCHAIKOVSKY—Violin
concerto, op. 35. *Haendel, violin; London
Symphony Orch.; Celibidache, cond.;
Royal Phil. Orch.; Goossens, cond.*
Reissue.
+ Fa 11-12/94: 184
+ Gr 10/94: 216

34625. SBT 1039: *Opera arias.* Music of
Verdi, Leoncavallo, Puccini, Mascagni,
Giordano, Cilea, Meyerbeer, Flotow,
Bizet, Massenet, and Wagner. *Del
Monaco, tenor; Orch. Sinfonica di
Milano; Quadri, Benintende-Neglia,
conds.* Sung in Italian.
• Fa 11-12/94: 439

34626. SBT 1040: MOZART—Così fan
tutte (excerpts). *Jurinac, Thebom, Noni,
Lewis, Kunz, Borriello; Glyndebourne
Festival Orch.; Philharmonia Orch.;
Busch, Susskind, conds.* Recorded 1950-
51.
+ Fa 11-12/94: 310
+ Gr 6/94: 132

34627. SBT 1041: BRAHMS—Piano
concerto no. 1; Variations and fugue on a
theme by Handel. *Solomon, piano;
Philharmonia Orch.; Kubelik, cond.*
+ Fa 11-12/94: 182
+ Gr 10/94: 216

34628. SBT 1042: BRAHMS—Piano
concerto no. 2; Rhapsody, op. 79, no. 2;
Intermezzo, op. 117, no. 2; Intermezzo,
op. 119, no. 3. *Solomon, piano;
Philharmonia Orch.; Dobrowen, cond.*
+ Fa 11-12/94: 182
+ Gr 10/94: 216

34629. SBT 1043: Andrés Segovia: the
complete 1949 London recordings.
*Segovia, guitar; New London Orch.;
Sherman, cond.*
+ Fa 11-12/94: 479

34630. SBT 1044: RAVEL—L'enfant et les
sortilèges. *Sautereau, Scharley,
Vessières, Michel, Marc'hadour; Chorus
& Orch. of the French National Radio;
Bour, cond.*
+ Fa 5-6/95: 306
+ Gr 2/95: 115
+ Op 7/95: 876

34631. SBT 1045: CHOPIN—Piano
concerto no. 2; Piano sonata no. 3;
Barcarolle, op. 60; Etudes, op. 10, no. 1;
op. 25, no. 3. *Ashkenazy, piano; Warsaw
Phil. Orch.; Górzyński, cond.* Reissue;
originally released late 1950s.
+ Fa 5-6/95: 172

34632. SBT 1046: CHOPIN—Piano music.
LISZT—Transcendental etudes no. 5;
Mephisto waltz no. 1. RACHMANINOFF—
Variations on a theme of Corelli.
PROKOFIEV—Piano sonata no. 7.
Ashkenazy, piano. Reissue; originally
released late 1950s.
+ Fa 5-6/95: 172

34633. SBT 1047: GOLDMARK—Violin
concerto, op. 28. LALO—Symphonie
espagnole. *Milstein, violin; Philharmonia
Orch.; Blech, cond.; St. Louis Symphony
Orch.; Golschmann, cond.* Recorded
1957.
+ ARG 11-12/95: 125
+ Fa 7-8/95: 192
+ Gr 11/95: 180

34634. SBT 1048: BORODIN—Symphony
no. 2. TCHAIKOVSKY—Manfred symphony.
Philharmonia Orch.; Kletzki, cond.
Recorded 1954.
+ Fa 5-6/95: 146
+ Gr 3/95: 118

34635. SBT 1049: SIBELIUS—Symphonies
no. 1, 3. *Philharmonia Orch.; Kletzki,
cond.* Recorded 1955.
+ Fa 5-6/95: 344
+ Gr 4/95: 138

34636. SBT 1050: BRUCKNER—Symphony
no. 4 "Romantic", Loewe/Schalk ed.;
Overture in G minor. *Philharmonia
Orch.; Matacic, cond.* Reissue; recorded
1954.
+ Fa 5-6/95: 156
+ Gr 2/95: 110

34637. SBT 1052: HINDEMITH—String
quartet no. 3. PROKOFIEV—String quartet
no. 2. WALTON—String quartet.
Hollywood String Quartet. Recorded
1951-52.
+ Fa 5-6/95: 216
+ Gr 3/95: 120

34638. SBT 1053: CRESTON—String
quartet. VILLA-LOBOS—String quartet no.

6. RAVEL—Introduction and allegro. DEBUSSY—Danses sacrée et profanc. TURINA—La oración del torero. *Hollywood String Quartet; Stockton, harp; Gleghorn, flute; Lurie, clarinet; Concert Artists Strings; F. Slatkin, cond.* Reissue; recorded 1949-53.
+ ARG 3-4/95: 275
+ Fa 5-6/95: 216
+ Fa 1-2/96: 182
+ Gr 3/95: 120

34639. SBT 1057: BEETHOVEN—Lieder. *Fischer-Dieskau, baritone; Klust, piano.* Recorded 1955.
+ Fa 11-12/95: 202

34640. SBT 1058: *James Johnston: opera and song.* Music of Verdi, Gounod, Bizet, Wagner, Puccini, Leoncavallo, Mascagni, Vaughan Williams, German; English and Irish folk songs. *Johnston, tenor; various orch. acc.* Sung in English; recorded 1947-1951.
+ Fa 5-6/95: 386
+ Gr 4/95: 145
+ Op 6/95: 744

34641. SBT 1059: *Opera, operetta, and song.* Music of Mozart, Lortzing, Zeller, J. Strauss, Jr., Arnold, Pick, Hochmuth and Werner-Zillner, Weill-Arnold, Krakauer, Gruber, Biczko-Kratzl, and Fellner. *Kunz, baritone; orch. acc.* Recorded 1947-1953.
+ Fa 11-12/95: 443
+ Gr 9/95: 128

34642. SBT 1060: Music of Bartók, Ravel, Satie, Busoni, Liadov, Chabrier, and Liszt. *Philharmonia Orch.; Markevitch, cond.*
● Fa 11-12/95: 504
+ Fi 4/96: 118
+ Gr 2/96: 114

34643. SBT 1061: TCHAIKOVSKY—String quartet no. 1. BORODIN—String quartet no. 2. GLAZUNOV—Five novelettes for string quartet. *Hollywood String Quartet.* Recorded 1952.
+ Fa 11-12/95: 215
+ Fa 11-12/96: 396
+ Fi 3/96: 123
+ Gr 8/95: 135

34644. SBT 1062: BORODIN—Prince Igor overture and Polovtsian dances; Symphony no. 3. RIMSKY- KORSAKOV—Ivan the Terrible overture. LIADOV—Russian folksongs. *Philharmonia Orch.; Malko, cond.* Recorded 1953-56.
+ ARG 7-8/96: 86
+ Fa 1/96: 409
+ Fi 4/96: 118

34645. SBT 1064: TCHAIKOVSKY—Piano concerto no. 1. RACHMANINOFF—Piano concerto no. 2; Preludes op. 23, no. 5; op. 32, no. 5. *Anda, piano; Philharmonia Orch.; Galliera, cond.* Recorded 1950s.
+ ARG 7-8/96: 247

+ Fa 11-12/95: 236
+ Gr 10/95: 160

34646. SBT 1065: BARTÓK—For children. *Anda, piano.* Recorded 1950s.
+ ARG 7-8/96: 247
+ Fa 11-12/95: 236
+ Fi 3/96: 127

34647. SBT 1066: CHOPIN—Piano concerto no. 1; Etudes, op. 25; Ballade no. 1. *Anda, piano; Philharmonia Orch.; Galliera, cond.* Recorded 1950s.
+ ARG 7-8/96: 247
+ Fa 11-12/95: 236

34648. SBT 1067: LISZT—Piano sonata; Mephisto waltz no. 1; Etude de concert no. 3; Etude d'après Paganini no. 3. BARTÓK—Sonatina. DELIBES (ARR. DOHNÁNYI)—Coppélia, act 1: Valse lente. *Anda, piano.* Recorded 1950s.
+ ARG 7-8/96: 247
+ Fa 11-12/95: 236
+ Fi 3/96: 127

34649. SBT 1069: SCHUMANN—Carnaval; Études symphoniques; Kreisleriana. *Anda, piano.*
+ Fa 7-8/96: 296

34650. SBT 1070: BEETHOVEN—Piano sonatas no. 7, 14, 28. *Anda, piano.* Recorded 1955 and 1958.
+ ARG 11-12/96: 90
+ Fa 7-8/96: 101
+ Fa 11-12/96: 185

34651. SBT 1071: LISZT—Piano concerto no. 1; Hungarian fantasia. SAINT-SAËNS—Carnival of the animals. *Anda, Siki, piano; Philharmonia Orch.; Ackermann, Markevitch, conds.*
● Fa 7-8/96: 296

34652. SBT 1072: DVOŘÁK—String quartet no. 12. SMETANA—String quartet no. 1. KODÁLY—String quartet no. 2. *Hollywood String Quartet.* Recorded 1959.
+ ARG 7-8/96: 290
+ Fa 3-4/96: 159
+ Fa 11-12/96: 396
+ Fi 3/96: 123
+ Gr 5/96: 130

34653. SBT 1073: *Opera arias and songs.* Music of Gluck, Weber, Verdi, Ponchielli, Tchaikovsky, Massenet, Debussy, Menotti, Gershwin, Arlen, Nordoff, Sargent, Homer, Youmans, Rachmaninoff, and Grieg. *Farrell, soprano; Philharmonia Orch.; Schippers, cond.; Trovillo, piano.* Reissue.
+ Fa 9-10/96: 370
+ Fi 12/96: 135
+ Gr 8/96: 103

34654. SBT 1074: DVOŘÁK—String quartet no. 12; Piano quintet, op. 81. JANÁČEK—String quartet no. 1. *Smetana Quartet; Štěpán, piano.* Recorded 1965-1966.

+ ARG 5-6/96: 96
+ Fa 3-4/96: 161
+ Gr 3/96: 66

34655. SBT 1075: DVOŘÁK—String quartet no. 14; Terzetto. JANÁČEK—String quartet no. 2. *Smetana Quartet.* Recorded 1965-66.
+ ARG 5-6/96: 229
+ Fa 11-12/96: 243
+ Fa 3-4/96: 161
+ Gr 3/96: 66

34656. SBT 1077: SHOSTAKOVICH—Piano quintet, op. 56. FRANCK—Piano quintet. *V. Aller, piano; Hollywood String Quartet.* Reissue.
+ Fa 3-4/96: 159
+ Fa 11-12/96: 376
+ Fi 3/96: 123
+ Gr 5/96: 130

34657. SBT 1078: SHOSTAKOVICH—Symphony no. 10; The age of gold: Ballet suite. *Philharmonia Orch.; Kurtz, cond.* Recorded 1955.
● ARG 3-4/97: 228
+ Fa 1-2/97: 271
+ Gr 2/97: 58

34658. SBT 1079: DVOŘÁK—Symphonies no. 7-8. *Philharmonia Orch.; Kubelik, cond.* Recorded 1948 and 1951.
+ Fa 9-10/96: 182
● Gr 10/96: 52

34659. SBT 1080: *Two renaissance dance bands; Monteverdi's contemporaries.* Music of Susato, Morley, Mainero, Lappi, and Priuli. *Early Music Consort of London; Morley Consort; Munrow, cond.*
+ ARG 9-10/96: 259
+ Fa 9-10/96: 399
+ Gr 9/96: 94

34660. SBT 1081: WOLF—Italian serenade. DOHNÁNYI—String quartet no. 3. SCHUBERT—String quartet no. 14 "Death and the maiden". *Hollywood String Quartet.*
+ Fa 11-12/96: 396

34661. SBT 1084: SCHUMANN—Carnaval. BRAHMS—Piano sonata no. 3. LISZT—La leggierezza; Au bord d'une source; Hungarian rhapsody no. 15. *Solomon, piano.* Recorded 1930, 1932, and 1952.
+ ARG 1-2/97: 212
+ Fa 11-12/96: 368

34662. SBT 1085: HAYDN—String quartet, op. 76, no. 2. MOZART—String quartet no. 17 "Hunting." HUMMEL—String quartet, op. 30, no. 2. *Hollywood String Quartet.* Recorded 1957.
● Fa 11-12/96: 268
+ Gr 8/96: 102

34663. SBT 1087: *The early recordings, 1942-1953.* Music of Handel, Schumann, Brahms, Respighi, Falla, Granados, Guridi, Vives, Nin, Toldra, Turina, Fuste,

TESTAMENT

Valverde, and Anon. *Angeles, soprano; Moore, Newton, piano; Agrupación de Cámara de Barcelona; Ars Musicae de Barcelona.*
+ ARG 1-2/97: 226
+ Fa 9-10/96: 374
• Fi 12/96: 135
+ Gr 8/96: 102

34664. SBT 1088: *Baroque and religious arias.* Music of Mozart, Handel, Bach, and Franck. *Angeles, soprano; various accs.*
+ ARG 1-2/97: 226
+ Fa 11-12/96: 427
• Gr 9/96: 100

34665. SBT 2025 (2 discs): ELGAR—The dream of Gerontius; Cello concerto. *Nash, Ripley, Noble, Walker; Liverpool Phil. Orch.; Tortelier, cello; BBC Symphony Orch.; Sargent, cond.* Recorded 1945.
+ ARG 9-10/94: 130
+ Fa 3-4/94: 181
+ Gr 2/94: 108

34666. SBT 3051 (3 discs): DEBUSSY—Pelléas et Mélisande. *Jansen, Angeles, Souzay, Froumenty; Raymond St. Paul Chorus; French National Radio Orch.; Cluytens, cond.* Recorded 1956.
• Fa 7-8/95: 167
+ Gr 6/95: 134

34667. SBT 3054 (3 discs): BRAHMS—Symphonies no. 1-4; Variations on a theme by Haydn; Tragic overture. *Berlin Phil. Orch.; Kempe, cond.* Recorded 1955-1961.
• Fa 5-6/95: 150
+ Gr 4/95: 48

34668. SBT 3055 (3 discs + 4 discs): HAYDN—String quartets, vol. 1-2. *Pro Arte Quartet.* Recorded 1931-38.
+ Fa 5-6/95: 203
+ Gr 6/95: 130

34669. SBT 3063 (3 discs): BRAHMS—Piano quartets no. 1-3; String quartet no. 2; Piano quintet, op. 34. SCHUMANN—Piano quintet, op. 44. *Hollywood String Quartet; V. Aller, piano.* Recorded 1954-58.
+ Fa 11-12/95: 216
+ Fi 3/96: 123
+ Gr 1/96: 115

34670. SBT 3082 (3 discs): BEETHOVEN—String quartets no. 12-16; Grosse Fuge. *Hollywood String Quartet.* Recorded 1957.
+ ARG 3-4/97: 88
• Fa 1-2/97: 101
+ Gr 1/97: 73

THEOREMA

34671. 121152: MAHLER—Symphony no. 1. *Minneapolis Symphony Orch.; Mitropoulos, cond.* Recorded 1940.
• ARG 3-4/96: 258

34672. 121181: MENDELSSOHN—Songs without words: Selections. *Gieseking, piano.* Recorded 1956.
+ ARG 9-10/95: 174

THESIS

34673. THC 11002: BERLIOZ—Te Deum. *Bardot, tenor; Choeurs de Paris; Orch. de l'Ecole Nationale de Musique de Meudon; Guoinguené, cond.*
+ Fa 7-8/92: 120

34674. THC 11003: MOZART—Great mass in C minor, K. 427. *Pozderec, soprano; Leblanc, alto; Bardot, tenor; Peintre, bass; Orch. Symphonique Altaïr; Maîtrise des Hauts-de-Seine; Bardot, cond.*
• Fa 9-10/92: 298

34675. THC 11004: MOZART—Waisenhaus-Messe. *Maîtrise des Hauts-de-Seine; Orch. symphonique Altaïr; Bardot, cond.*
• Fa 11-12/92: 316

34676. THC 82001: GERSHWIN—Three preludes; Rhapsody in blue; Impromptu in 2 keys; Rialto ripples; Song book; American in Paris. *Thiollier, piano.*
+ Fa 11-12/90: 232

34677. THC 82002: LISZT—Sonetti di Petrarca (1st version); Die Loreley (2nd version); Was Liebe sei? (1st version); Three songs from Wilhelm Tell (1st version); Ich möchte hingehn; Isten veled; Kling leise, mein Lied (1st version); Wie singt der Lerche schon; In Liebeslust; Wieder mocht' ich dir begegnen; An Edlitam. *Brewer, tenor; Thiollier, piano.*
• ARG 9-10/88: 56
• Fa 7-8/88: 190

34678. THC 82003: DONIZETTI—Nuits d'été à Pausilippe; Teresa e Giangaldoni. *Gal, mezzo-soprano; Brewer, tenor; Cohen, piano.*
□ ARG 11-12/88: 31
+ Fa 9-10/90: 231

34679. THC 82004 (2 discs): RACHMANINOFF—Preludes op. 23, 32; Piano sonatas no. 1-2. *Thiollier, piano.*
+ ARG 7-8/90: 88
• Fa 9-10/90: 345

34680. THC 82005 (2 discs): RACHMANINOFF—Piano music. *Thiollier, piano.*
• Fa 9-10/90: 346

34681. THC 82006 (2 discs): RACHMANINOFF—Moments musicaux; Variations on a theme by Chopin; Variations on a theme by Corelli; Four pieces; Fantasy pieces; Pieces op. 10. *Thiollier, piano.*
• Fa 9-10/90: 346

34682. THC 82007 (3 discs): LISZT—Intégrale des mélodies pour ténor.

Brewer, tenor; Thiollier, piano.
- ARG 9-10/90: 81
- Fa 9-10/90: 277

34683. THC 82008: *Horszowski en concert.* Music of Bach, Beethoven, Chopin, Schumann, and others. *Horszowski, piano.*
• ARG 7-8/90: 144
+ Fa 9-10/90: 472
+ NYT 6/17/90: H23

34684. THC 82013: TELEMANN—Fantasies for solo flute (complete). *Gallois, flute.*
+ Fa 9-10/90: 411

34685. THC 82015: *La révolution souriante.* BOIELDIEU—Le calife de Bagdad. DAMASE—La fille mal gardée. *Monestier, Ouaki, Elloir, Plantak, Fokenoy; Ensemble Vocal Patrick Marco; Orch.; Orch. Bernard Thomas; Thomas, cond.*
+ Fa 9-10/90: 191

34686. THC 82017: Music of Enesco, Webern, Schoenberg, and Janáček. *Flammer, violin; Pennetier, piano.*
+ Fa 11-12/90: 448

34687. THC 82018: *Emile Naoumoff live.* Music of Scriabin, Rachmaninoff, Mussorgsky, Stravinsky, and others. *Naoumoff, piano.*
□ Fa 9-10/90: 473

34688. THC 82019: Music of Ravel (arf. Garban), Bizet, Poulenc, and Satie. *Rigutto, Tacchino, piano 4 hands.*
• Fa 9-10/90: 336

34689. THC 82022: PROKOFIEV—Piano sonatas no. 6-7. *Akl, piano.*
- Fa 9-10/90: 337

34690. THC 82023: PROKOFIEV—Piano sonatas no. 8-9. *Akl, piano.*
- Fa 3-4/91: 327
• MA 7/91: 56

34691. THC 82025—82026 (2 2-disc sets): BACH—Well-tempered clavier. *Naoumoff, piano.*
+ Fa 9-10/90: 159

34692. THC 82027: BACH—Italian concerto; Passacaglia in C minor (arr. Naoumoff); Preludes in E minor BWV 533, in A BWV 536, Preludes in G minor (arr. Siloti); Chorale: O Mensch bewein dein Sünde gross; no. 202: Weichet nur betrübte Schatten; Chorale: Nun komm der Heiden Heiland (arr. Busoni); St. Matthew Passion: Betrachte meine Seele; Aus Liebe will mein Heiland sterben; Cantatas: no. 127, 198, 147 (arr. Hess). *Naoumoff, piano.*
+ Fa 9-10/90: 152

34693. THC 82039: *Mieczyslaw Horszowski au Théâtre des Champs-Élysées.* Music of Bach, Beethoven, Schumann, and Chopin. *Horszowski,*

piano.
- ARG 3-4/91: 158
+ Fa 3-4/91: 480

34694. THC 82040: RACHMANINOFF—
Piano concerto no. 2. DEBUSSY—Rêverie;
Valse romantique; La plus que lente;
Danse; Estampes: Soirée dans Grenade;
L'isle joyeuse. *Thiollier, piano; Radio
Television Luxembourg Symphony Orch.;
Bardon, cond.* Recorded live 1989.
- ARG 9-10/90: 100
- Fa 9-10/90: 221

34695. THC 82041: SCHUBERT—
Impromptus D. 899; Moments musicaux
D. 780. *Pennetier, piano.*
+ ARG 3-4/91: 112
+ Fa 3-4/91: 359

34696. THC 82042: RAVEL—Sonatine;
Menuet antique; Valses nobles et
sentimentales; Pavane pour une infante
défunte. MESSIAEN—Etudes de rhythme:
Ile de feu 1-2; Vingt regards sur l'enfant
Jésus: Le baiser de l'enfant Jésus; Regard
de l'esprit de joie. *Kanno, piano.*
- Fa 3-4/91: 337

34697. THC 82043: BEETHOVEN—Piano
sonatas no. 1, 8. BRAHMS—Intermezzi op.
117. *Naoumoff, piano.*
- ARG 7-8/91: 31
- Fa 5-6/91: 126

34698. THC 82045: MOZART—Flute
concertos no. 1-2; Andante for flute &
orchestra K. 315; Rondo for flute &
orchestra K. 184e. *Gallois, flute;
Ensemble instrumental de France;
Krivine, cond.*
+ Fa 5-6/91: 222

34699. THC 82046: *Panorama des
mélodies russes, vol. 1.* Music of Titov,
Glinka, Dargomizhsky, Mussorgsky,
Borodin, and others. *Storojev, bass;
Naoumoff, piano.*
- Fa 9-10/91: 403

34700. THC 82058: FRANCK—Violin
sonata. DEBUSSY—Violin sonata. BONIS—
Violin sonata. *A. Rozhdestvensky, violin;
Constantin, piano.*
- ARG 9-10/94: 132

THOROFON

34701. MTH 203 (LP): *Musik der 20er
Jahre.* Music of Malipiero, Juon,
Schoenberg (arr. Greissle), and Bloch.
Göbel Trio.
+ ARG 9-10/87: 56

34702. MTH 278 (LP): GENZMER—
Concerto for harp and strings; Sonata for
cello and harp; Fantasie for harp.
*Herbert, harp; Berger, cello; Munich
Chamber Orch.; Stadlmair, cond.*
+ ARG 5-6/86: 17

34703. MTH 318 (LP): *Kontra-bass.*
Music of Paganini, Bottesini, and

Genzmer. *Reinke, double bass; Göbel,
piano.*
+ Fa 5-6/87: 231

34704. ETHK 341/44 (4 discs): *Musik
zwischen den Kriegen: eine Berliner
Dokumentation.* Music of Blacher, Borris,
Chemin-Petit, Pfitzner, Schoenberg, and
others. *Various performers.*
+ Fa 9-10/87: 160

34705. CTH 2002: Music of Bruch,
Hiller, and Widor. *Göbel Trio Berlin.*
+ ARG 10/87: 64
+ Fa 5-6/87: 104

34706. CTH 2003: *Drums.* Music of
Liebermann, Lacerdo, Fink, Cowell, and
others. *Würzburger Percussion
Ensemble; Fink, cond.*
+ Fa 9-10/87: 384

34707. CTH 2005: SMETANA—Souvenirs
de Bohème en forme de Polka: op. 12 no.
2, op. 13 no. 1-2; Polka poètique, op. 7
no. 1; Bohemian dances vol. 1 no. 1;
Rêves; Konzertetude op. 17; Sketches op.
5 no. 3. *Schmalfuss, piano.*
+ Fa 5-6/88: 217

34708. CTH 2006: C.P.E. BACH—
Symphony in F, Wq. 182 no. 4; Cembalo
concertos Wq. 33, 31. *Göbel, piano;
Kammerorchester Dall' Arco; Händler,
cond.*
+ Fa 9-10/87: 134

34709. CTH 2007: BOCCHERINI—Cello
concertos G. 476, 478. WAGENSEIL—Cello
concerto in C. *Hochmuth, cello;
Kammerorchester Dall' Arco; Händler,
cond.*
+ Fa 9-10/87: 162

34710. CTH 2008: BEETHOVEN—Piano
sonatas no. 17, 21, 31. *Benz, piano.*
- ARG 11-12/88: 15
- Fa 11-12/88: 138

34711. CTH 2009: BEETHOVEN—Piano
sonatas no. 2, 14, 25, 30. *Benz, piano.*
- ARG 5-6/89: 22
- Fa 9-10/89: 135

34712. CTH 2010: HAYDN—String
quartets op. 64 no. 5, op. 76 no. 3.
Joachim String Quartet.
- ARG 9-10/88: 52
+ Fa 5-6/88: 142

34713. CTH 2011: *Miniaturen.*
SCHUBERT—Piano music. *Kitchin, piano.*
+ ARG 5-6/88: 61
+ Fa 5-6/88: 205

34714. CTH 2012: COPLAND—Vitebsk;
Sextet for clarinet, piano, and strings;
Sonata for violin and piano; Duo for flute
and piano. *Maile, violin; Senn, flute;
Göbel, piano; Göbel-Trio-Berlin; Orch.
Academy of the Berlin Phil. Orch.*
- Fa 1-2/88: 108
- Gr 4/88: 1469

34715. CTH 2013: MARTINŮ—Concerto
for piano trio and string orchestra;
Concertino for piano and string orchestra;
La bagarre. *Göbel-Trio Berlin;
Filharmonia Pomorska; Ukigaya, cond.*
- ARG 7-8/88: 41
+ Fa 5-6/88: 160
+ Gr 5/88: 1595

34716. CTH 2015: HUBER—Cantiones de
circulo gyrante. SCELSI—I presagi. *Osten,
soprano; Mathez-Wüthrich, alto; Kunz,
baritone; Maier, speaker; Collegium
Vocale; Choir of the Köln Bach-Vereins;
Ensemble Köln; Platz, cond.*
+ Fa 5-6/95: 221

34717. CTH 2016: LOUIS FERDINAND,
PRINCE OF PRUSSIA—Larghetto varié op.
11; Piano trio op. 10; Notturno op. 8.
*Göbel-Trio Berlin; Members of the Berlin
Radio Symphony Orch.*
+ ARG 1-2/89: 57

34718. CTH 2017: PENDERECKI—Violin
concerto. *Edinger, violin; Radio
Symphonie Orchester Katowice;
Penderecki, cond.*
- ARG 5-6/88: 51
+ Fa 3-4/88: 169
- Gr 3/88: 1314
+ MA 5/88: 80
+ SR 6/88: 142

34719. CTH 2018: SCHWARZ-SCHILLING—
Violin concerto. BERWALD—Violin
concerto op. 2. *Spierer, violin; Berlin
Radio Symphony Orch.; Schwarz-
Schilling, Chmura, cond.*
+ ARG 5-6/88: 18
+ Fa 5-6/88: 212

34720. CTH 2021: A. TCHEREPNIN—
Rapsodie georgienne; Trio concerto for
violin, cello, and piano; Symphony no. 3.
*Hochmuth, cello; Göbel-Trio Berlin;
Polish Chamber Phil. Orch.; Nürnberger
Symphoniker; Rheinland-Pfalz State
Phil.; Rajski, Mund, Gülke, conds.*
- ARG 7-8/90: 118
□ Fa 5-6/90: 313

34721. CTH 2022: *Die letzten
Klavierkompositionen.* BEETHOVEN—
Grosse Fuge op. 134; Ziemlich lebhaft,
WoO 60; Allegretto, WoO 61; Andante
quasi allegretto, WoO 61a; Waltze, WoO
84-85; Six bagatelles op. 126. *Möller,
piano.*
+ DA 2/89: 53
- Fa 7-8/88: 116

34722. CTH 2023: CHIANG—Formosa
dance; Bagatelles; Three dances, op. 7;
The Peking myriorama, v. 1. *Tsai, piano.*
+ Fa 3-4/89: 133

34723. CTH 2024: HSU—Piano concerto.
KUO—Concertino for piano. MA—Sketch
of the rainy harbor for solo piano. *Tsai,
piano; Polish Chamber Orch.; Rajski,
cond.*

+ ARG 3-4/89: 116
+ Fa 1-2/89: 323

34724. CTH 2026: Music of Behrend, Hartig, Logothetis, Kagel, Heidler, and Spannheimer. *DZO Chamber Orch.; Behrend, cond.*
☐ ARG 9-10/89: 127

34725. CTH 2027: TCHAIKOVSKY—Variations on a rococo theme; Pezzo capriccioso; Nocturne for cello and orchestra; Serenade for strings in C. *Hochmuth, cello; Polnische Kammerphilharmonie; Rajski, cond.*
• Fa 11-12/90: 375

34726. CTH 2028: SCHUMANN—Novellettes, op. 21. *Rösler, piano.*
- ARG 3-4/89: 81

34727. CTH 2029: MOZART—Violin concerto no. 5; Symphony no. 40. *Kostecki, violin; Polish Chamber Phil. Orch.; Rajski, cond.*
• Fa 7-8/89: 193

34728. CTH 2030: SCHUMANN—Phantasiestücke op. 88; Piano trio no. 1 op. 63. *Göbel-Trio Berlin.*
+ ARG 5-6/89: 87
+ Fa 5-6/89: 318
+ Gr 4/89: 1605
+ HPR 6/89: 86

34729. CTH 2031: SCHUMANN—Piano trios no. 2-3. *Göbel-Trio Berlin.*
+ Fa 5-6/89: 318
+ Gr 4/89: 1605

34730. CTH 2033: CORNELIUS—Requiem; Requiem aeternam; Absolve Domine; Three psalms songs after J. S. Bach; Liebe; So weich und warm; Trost in Tränen; Der Tod, das ist die kühle Nacht; An den Sturmwind; Die drei Frühlingstage. *Norddeutsche Figuralchor; Straube, cond.*
+ ARG 1-2/89: 42
+ Fa 11-12/89: 183
+ Gr 4/90: 1849

34731. CTH 2034: *Children's suite: Chinese piano music.* Music of Ding, Jiang, Moy, Lam, Chou, Hsu, Tcherepnin, and Heh. *Tsai, piano.*
+ ARG 11-12/96: 255
• Fa 11-12/96: 462

34732. CTH 2035: SCHEIDT—Organ music (selections). SCHEIDEMANN—Dic nobis Maria; Benedicam. *Eichhorn, organ.*
+ Fa 7-8/89: 234

34733. CTH 2037: VERDI—String quartet. STRAUSS—String quartet. *Joachim Quartet.*
• ARG 1-2/94: 169
+ Fa 1-2/94: 323

34734. CTH 2038: OSTENDORF—Mein Wagner; Creuser pour bien sortir au soleil; Tempus ex machina; William Ratcliff. *Stange, Bidlingmaier, pianos; Sien, Krohn, Grammersdorf, percussion; NDR Symphony Orch.; Stuttgart Radio Symphony Orch.; Wakasugi, Drewanz, conds.*
• Fa 5-6/89: 262

34735. CTH 2040: *Humor im Lied.* Music of Bach, Haydn, Mozart, Telemann, Schubert, and others. *Halem, bass; Göbel, piano.*
+ ARG 1-2/89: 123
+ Fa 1-2/89: 314

34736. CTH 2042: JENKINS—Seventeen fantasias à 4. *Kölner Violen-Consort.*
+ ARG 1-2/92: 66
- Fa 11-12/91: 359

34737. CTH 2043: *The twenties: music between the world wars: a Berlin documentation.* Music of Schreker, Ziertiz, Krenek, Tathaus, Weill, and others. *Various performers.*
+ Fa 5-6/89: 423

34738. CTH 2044: *The thirties: music between the world wars: a Berlin documentation.* Music of Schoenberg, Hindemith, Blacher, Egk, Toch, and others. *Various performers.*
+ Fa 5-6/89: 424

34739. CTH 2045: BUSONI—Violin sonatas no. 1-2. *Edinger, violin; Puchelt, piano.*
+ ARG 9-10/89: 39
• Fa 9-10/89: 171

34740. CTH 2046: KARLOWICZ—Violin concerto, op. 8; Eternal songs, op. 10. *Zienkowski, violin; Filharmonia Pomorska; Ukigaya, cond.*
• ARG 7-8/94: 119
+ Fa 5-6/94: 173

34741. CTH 2047: BACH—Goldberg variations. SWEELINCK—Fantasia on BACH in D minor. *Hussong, accordion.*
- Fa 11-12/89: 110

34742. CTH 2048: BEETHOVEN—Piano sonatas no. 3, 8, 10, 13. *Benz, piano.*
- Fa 3-4/90: 131

34743. CTH 2049: BEETHOVEN—Piano sonatas no. 6, 18, 24, 28. *Benz, piano.*
+ Fa 3-4/91: 151

34744. CTH 2050: Music of Cimarosa, W.F. Bach, Cambini, and Paisiello. *Polish Chamber Phil. Orch.; Rafski, cond.*
+ ARG 11-12/89: 144
+ Fa 7-8/89: 333

34745. CTH 2051: WIDOR—Violin sonata no. 2. D'INDY—Violin sonata, op. 59. *Maile, violin; Göbel, piano.*
+ ARG 3-4/92: 167
+ Fa 11-12/91: 320

34746. CTH 2052: VILLA-LOBOS—Guitar music (complete). *Tröster, guitar.*
+ ARG 9-10/89: 113
+ Fa 7-8/89: 271

34747. CTH 2054: SCHUMANN—Schön ist das Fest des Lenzes; So wahr die Sonne scheinet; Von dem Rosenbusch; Und schläfst du; Dereinst, o Gedanke mein; Alle gingen, Herz, sur Ruh; Dass ihr steht in Liebesglut; Nelken wind ich; Mögen all bösen Zungen. JENNER—Zwolf Quartette. *Marburg Bachchor; Walther-Lindqvist, piano; Wehnert, cond.*
• ARG 9-10/89: 105
• Fa 9-10/89: 320

34748. CTH 2055: WILLIAMS—Sonata in imitation of birds; Trio sonata in C; Sonata in A minor. PEPUSCH—Trio sonatas in F, in G minor; Sonatas no. 1-2; Sonata in D minor. *Musica Poetica.*
- Fa 11-12/90: 405

34749. CTH 2056: SCHUBERT—Winterreise. *C-H. Müller, baritone; H. Müller-Thiemens, piano.*
- ARG 11-12/89: 112
- Fa 11-12/89: 349
• Gr 11/89: 956

34750. CTH 2057: HARTMANN—Concerto funèbre. SZYMANOWSKI—Violin concerto no. 1. *Edinger, violin; Kattowitz Radio Symphony Orch.; Penderecki, cond.*
+ Fa 1-2/90: 197

34751. CTH 2058: BEETHOVEN—Piano sonatas no. 5, 12, 26-27. *Benz, piano.*
+ ARG 1-2/93: 75
• Fa 11-12/92: 195

34752. CTH 2059: BEETHOVEN—Piano sonatas no. 4, 29. *Benz, piano.*
+ ARG 1-2/94: 73
• Fa 5-6/94: 107

34753. CTH 2060: RHEINBERGER—String quintet op. 82; Piano quintet op. 114. *Sonare Quartet; Noda, viola; Göbel, piano.*
+ ARG 9-10/89: 93
☐ Fa 9-10/89: 299

34754. CTH 2061: RHEINBERGER—Piano trio op. 112; Theme and variations for string quartet op. 93; Nonet in E♭ op. 139. *Göbel-Trio Berlin; Sonare Quartet; Bronx Arts Ensemble.*
+ ARG 11-12/89: 105
☐ Fa 9-10/89: 299

34755. CTH 2062: SCHUBERT—Piano sonatas D. 568, 960. *Kitchin, piano.*
- ARG 7-8/90: 101
• Fa 5-6/90: 286
- Fa 9-10/90: 375

34756. CTH 2063: Music of Paliev, Fink, B. Hummel, Cage, Patachich, and others. *Percussion Art Quartett Würzburg.*
+ Fa 9-10/90: 490

34757. CTH 2064: JÖDE—Der kleine Rosengarten: Selections. *Schortemeier, baritone; Behrend, guitar.*
+ ARG 3-4/90: 63

34758. CTH 2066: HEIDER—*Mein Klavier und ich, vol. 2.* Fifteen extras for piano; Musical story for piano and orchestra. *Heider, piano; Bavarian Radio Orch.; Tang, cond.*
□ Fa 11-12/91: 349

34759. CTH 2068: WAGENSEIL—Two sinfonias; Two cello concertos. *Filharmonia Pomorska; Ukigaya, cond.; Hochmuth, cello; Kammerorchester Dall' Arco; Händler, cond.*
• ARG 11-12/96: 231
+ Fa 11-12/96: 415

34760. CTH 2069: VOSS—Noch aber Rauchen die Ruinen der Tage; Violin sonata; Concertino for organ, strings, and kettledrums; Sinfonia humana. *Sumpik, violin; Dallmann, organ; South German Radio Chorus Stuttgart; Southwest German Chamber Orch.; Berlin Radio Symphony Orch.; Dahmen, Schweizer, Wallat, conds.*
+ ARG 9-10/90: 65
+ Fa 9-10/90: 428

34761. CTH 2070: *Siegfried Behrend and friends: virtuoso instrumental concertos.* BEHREND—Serenade for mandolin; Conserere for guitar; Der Sonnengesang, for voice; Figuration III, for accordion; Spanish dance. BUDASHKIN—Concerto for domra. SCHWENK—Divertimento for ocarina; Wilhelmer Konzert. WALTER—Concerto for accordion. *Various soloists; DZO-Kammerorchester; Behrend, cond.*
- ARG 1-2/92: 154
+ Fa 11-12/91: 349

34762. CTH 2071/2 (2 discs): FUX—La fede sacrilega nella morte del precursor S. Giovanni Battista. *Lins, Koslowsky, sopranos; Helling, contralto; Calaminus, tenor; Schwarz, bass; Neuss Capella Piccola; Reuber, cond.*
+ ARG 9-10/90: 65
+ Fa 9-10/90: 242
+ Gr 10/91: 161

34763. CTH 2073: QUANTZ—Trio sonatas in D, in C, in D minor; Flute sonatas in E minor, in G minor. *Musica Poetica.*
- Fa 1-2/91: 280

34764. CTH 2077: RHEINBERGER—Violin sonatas no. 1-2; Theme and variations for piano op. 61. *Maile, violin; Göbel, piano.*
+ ARG 7-8/90: 90
+ Fa 5-6/90: 265

34765. CTH 2078: RHEINBERGER—Sextet op. 191b. WOLF-FERRARI—Chamber symphony op. 8. *Orch. Academy of the Berlin Phil. Orch.; Göbel, piano & cond.*
+ ARG 11-12/90: 106
+ Fa 5-6/90: 265

34766. CTH 2079: FARRENC—Trio for piano, flute, and cello in E minor. RIES — Trio for piano, flute, and cello in E♭ major. MENDELSSOHN—Piano trio no. 1: Andante and scherzo. BRUCH—Three pieces from Op. 83. *Trio Cantabile.*
+ Fa 3-4/91: 494

34767. CTH 2080: *Ein Bass und zwei Gitarren.* CASTELNUOVO-TEDESCO—Well-tempered guitar: Excerpts. GIBRAN—In the garden of the prophet: Excerpts. *Duo Tedesco; Gunsch, reader.*
- Fa 11-12/90: 201

34768. CTH 2081/2 (2 discs): BACH—Mass in B minor. *Blackburn, Jakobi, Groenewold, Prégardien, Müller; North German Figuralchor; Camerata Hannover; Straube, cond.*
- Fa 7-8/91: 100

34769. CTH 2083: *Tears of brass.* HEYDUCK—Solo. SELL—Lexikon. ROELFS—ohne papiere. BURBA—Changes. HESPOS—omziff. KURZ—Plakat(iv). *Burba, trumpet, euphonium & alphorn.*
□ Fa 11-12/91: 349
□ ARG 1-2/92: 149

34770. CTH 2085: *Art of percussion.* Music of Fink, Hashagen, Guinjoan, and Benguerel. *Fink, percussion; various soloists & ensembles.*
+ Fa 9-10/90: 490

34771. CTH 2088: LOUIS FERDINAND, PRINCE OF PRUSSIA—Rondos for piano and orchestra, op. 9, op. 13; Octet, op. 12. *Various performers.*
+ ARG 1-2/92: 73
+ Fa 11-12/91: 376

34772. CTH 2089: Music of Giuliani, Carulli, Coste, Mertz, and Rossini (arr.). *Duo Tedesco (B. & E. Hölzer, guitars).*
• Fa 11-12/90: 201

34773. CTH 2090: Music of Lachner, Rheinberger, Thuille, West, and Gibbs. *Weyer, organ.*
+ ARG 9-10/91: 165
+ Fa 5-6/91: 360

34774. CTH 2091: RHEINBERGER—Improvisation on motives from Die Zauberflöte; Piano sonata no. 2. WOLF-FERRARI—Three impromptus; Six bagatelles. *Göbel, piano.*
+ ARG 1-2/91: 81
• Fa 11-12/90: 329

34775. CTH 2092: Music of Vivaldi, Hoffmann, Gervasio, Leone, Calace, and Munier. *Duo Capriccioso (Weyhofen, mandolin; Tröster, guitar).*
+ ARG 1-2/92: 158
+ Fa 1-2/91: 387

34776. CTH 2094: *Konzert für Arno Schmidt.* HESPOS—Ruhil. HEYN—SMPH. PLATZ—Flötenstücke. KAGEL—Phantasiestück. *Ensemble Köln; Platz,*

cond.; Ascher, mezzo-soprano; Levine, flute; Becker, piano.
□ Fa 1-2/92: 425

34777. CTH 2095: CHOPIN—Preludes op. 28. *Haase, piano.*
- Fa 7-8/91: 140

34778. CTH 2096: *Zigeunerlieder.* BRAHMS—Zigeunerlieder, op. 103. SPOHR—Zigeunerlied. STOLZ—Zigeunerlied. TCHAIKOVSKY—Lied der Zigeunerin, op. 60, no. 7. LISZT—Die drei Zigeuner. SCHUMANN—Zigeunerliedchen. DVOŘÁK—Zigeunermelodien, op. 55. *Theisen, soprano; Kayser, piano.*
- Fa 11-12/91: 527

34779. CTH 2097: *Romantic organ, vol. 1.* Music of Reger, Liszt, Blumenthal, Pierné, and Karg-Elert. *Rost, organ; Reinhold, soprano; Holzhausen, violin.*
+ ARG 5-6/93: 167

34780. CTH 2098: WEISS—Sonatas for lute, op. 23, 30. *Dücker, lute.*
• EM 8/94: 527
+ Fa 5-6/92: 290

34781. CTH 2099: *The magic bassoon.* Works by Mercadante, Tulou, Saint-Saëns, Weber, Hindemith, Yun, Fontyn, and Kaneta. *Tanaka, bassoon; Sumi, piano.*
+ Fa 11-12/91: 563

34782. CTH 2101: RHEINBERGER—Piano trios no. 1, 3. *Göbel-Trio Berlin.*
+ ARG 3-4/92: 126
+ Fa 1-2/92: 305

34783. CTH 2102: RHEINBERGER—String quartets no. 1-2. *Göbel-Trio Berlin.*
+ ARG 5-6/92: 118
+ Fa 1-2/92: 305

34784. CTH 2103: BRAHMS—Rhapsodies, op. 79; Klavierstücke, op. 119; Hungarian dances no. 1-3, 7-11. *D. Kraus, piano.*
+ Fa 1-2/92: 185

34785. CTH 2104: ERDMANN—Concerto for cello and small orchestra; Spektrum, for orchestra; Konzertstück for alto saxophone; Serenità notturna for string orchestra. *Boettcher, cello; Berlin Radio Symphony Orch.; Carewe, Wolf, conds.; Bensmann, saxophone; Pomeranian Phil. Orch.; Ukigaya, cond.*
• ARG 7-8/92: 128
• Fa 11-12/91: 349

34786. CTH 2105: Music of Tomasi, Jolivet, Françaix, Bloch, and Harutunyan. *H. Yoshida, trumpet; J. Yoshida, piano; Filharmonia Polmorska; Ukigaya, cond.*
• ARG 5-6/91: 150
• Fa 3-4/91: 493

34787. CTH 2106: SZYMANOWSKI—Symphonies no. 2, 4. *Czapiewski, piano; Filharmonia Polmorska; Ukigaya, cond.*
• ARG 11-12/91: 157 (no. 2)

THOROFON

+ ARG 11-12/91: 157 (no. 4)
+ Fa 7-8/91: 305

34788. CTH 2107: Britten—Ceremony of carols. Herzogenberg—Mädchenlieder. Eben—Dizionario greco. *Mädchenchor Hannover; Rutt, Schröfel, conds.; Wegner, harp; Schnaus, piano.*
- Fa 11-12/91: 289

34789. CTH 2108: Rheinberger—Piano quartet; Cello sonata; Horn sonata. *Göbel-Trio Berlin; Krug, horn.*
+ ARG 3-4/92: 126

34790. CTH 2109: *Trumpet and piano.* Music of Enesco, Martinů, Hindemith, Koetsier, Erbse, Mihalovici and Français. *H. Yoshida, trumpet; J. Yoshida, piano.*
• ARG 1-2/92: 163
- Fa 11-12/91: 564

34791. CTH 2111: *Sonatas for guitar.* Ponce—Sonata meridional. Berkeley—Sonatina, op. 51. Turina—Sonata, op. 61. Rodrigo—Sonata giocosa. Castelnuovo-Tedesco—Sonata , op. 77. *Tröster, guitar.*
+ ARG 1-2/92: 156
• Fa 11-12/91: 556

34792. CTH 2112: Mauersberger—Piano trio; String quartet. *Apel, piano; Dresden Soloists.*
+ ARG 7-8/94: 130

34793. CTH 2113: *Stick attack.* Music of Cage, Miki, Fink and Rosauro. *Percussion Art Quartett.*
+ Fa 5-6/92: 340

34794. CTH 2114: Messiaen—Eight preludes; Petites esquisses d'oiseaux. *Reinhold, piano.*
- ARG 7-8/92: 177
+ Fa 3-4/92: 246

34795. CTH 2115: Hotteterre—Complete duets. *Ensemble Musica Poetica.*
- Fa 1-2/93: 170

34796. CTH 2116: Reger—String quartet no. 3. *Philharmonia Quartet.*
+ ARG 5-6/92: 116
- Fa 5-6/92: 230

34797. CTH 2117: *Works for violin and orchestra.* Music of A. Becker, Dvořák, Ysaÿe, G. Raphael, and Bach. *Raphael, violin; Nordwestdeutsche Philharmonie; A. Walter, cond.; Rheinisches Kammerorchester; Corazolla, cond.*
+ Fa 5-6/95: 436

34798. CTH 2118: Music for fun. *Pifferari di Santo Spirito.*
+ Fa 3-4/92: 419

34799. CTH 2119: Stockmeier—Andante. Heilmann—Fantasy for cello and organ. Schilling—Sonata lirica. *Blees, cello; Stockmeier, organ.*

+ ARG 7-8/92: 257
+ Fa 7-8/92: 288

34800. CTH 2123: Jiddische Lieder. *Rohland, bass-baritone; various accompaniments.*
+ ARG 1-2/92: 171
+ Fa 11-12/91: 531

34801. CTH 2124: Brahms—Handel variations; Theme and variations in D minor; arrangements. *D. Kraus, piano.*
+ Fa 5-6/92: 131

34802. CTH 2125: Music for mandolin and guitar by Munier, Ambrosius, Sprongl, Baumann and Piazzolla. *Duo Capriccioso.*
+ ARG 7-8/92: 261
+ Fa 7-8/92: 347

34803. CTH 2126: *Komm Trost der Welt.* Music of Wolf, R. Strauss, Reger, and Schoenberg. *Norddeutscher Figuralchor; Straube, cond.*
+ ARG 5-6/93: 175
+ Fa 3-4/93: 355

34804. CTH 2127: Mauersberger—St. Luke passion. *Bassenge, Uhle, Töringscher Akademischer Singkreis; Unger, cond.*
+ ARG 7-8/94: 130

34805. CTH 2128: Honegger—König David (first version). *Dortmund Instrumental Soloists; University of Dortmund Chamber Choir; Gundlach, cond.; Quadflieg, speaker; Frühhaberm, soprano; Grorg, alto; Immer, tenor. Sung in German.*
• ARG 9-10/92: 117
+ Fa 9-10/92: 263

34806. CTH 2130: Lasso—Motets. *Orlando di Lasso Ensemble of Hannover; Bratschke, cond.*
+ ARG 3-4/92: 84
+ Fa 3-4/92: 225

34807. CTH 2131: Franz—Fifty songs to lyrics by Heinrich Heine. *Köhler, baritone; Göbel, piano.*
+ ARG 11-12/92: 120
+ Fa 11-12/92: 237

34808. CTH 2132: Lachner—Nonet; Piano quintet no. 2. *Orch. Akademie of the Berlin Phil. Orch.*
+ ARG 5-6/94: 105
• Fa 3-4/94: 228
+ Fa 7-8/95: 218

34809. CTH 2134: Schubert—String trio. Villa-Lobos—String trio. *Gasteig-Trio München.*
+ Fa 7-8/93: 237

34810. CTH 2135: *Französische Impressionen: works for flute, cello, and piano.* Music of Damase, Goossens, Pierné, and Manziarly. *Trio Cantabile.*
+ Fa 3-4/93: 392

34811. CTH 2137: Schwarz-Schilling—Quintet for piano and winds; String quartet; String trio; Study on B-A-C- H. *Consortium Classicum; Mannheim Quartet; Reger Trio.*
+ ARG 11-12/92: 201
+ Fa 11-12/92: 366

34812. CTH 2138: Beethoven—*Piano sonatas, vol. 7. No. 9, 11, 15, 19. Benz, piano.*
• Fa 3-4/95: 128

34813. CTH 2141: Szymanowski—String quartet no. 2. Bartók—String quartet no. 2. Ravel—String quartet. *Philharmonia Quartet.*
• ARG 7-8/93: 165

34814. CTH 2144: Hensel—Lyric pieces. *Sternlicht, piano.*
• Fa 1-2/93: 193

34815. CTH 2145: Erdmann—Music for string orchestra; Musica multicolore; Concertino for piano and orchestra; Nuances for chamber orchestra; Concertino for flute and orchestra. *Thüringen-Philharmonie Suhl; Wolf, Koch, conds.; Lohmer, piano; Ensemble Slavko Osterc, Ljubljana; J. Ukigaya, flute; Pomeranian Phil. Orch.; T. Ukigaya.*
+ Fa 9-10/92: 230

34816. CTH 2146: *Carneval di mandoline.* Music of Strack, Konietzny, Vivaldi, Baumann, Behrend, and Tober-Vogt. *Tröster-Weyhofen, mandolin; Bavarian Youth Orch. of Plucked Instruments; Vogt, cond.*
+ Fa 5-6/93: 380

34817. CTH 2147: *Modern piano trios.* Music of Kagel, Blacher, and Erbse. *Göbel-Trio Berlin.*
+ ARG 1-2/93: 174
+ Fa 9-10/92: 439

34818. CTH 2148: Louis Ferdinand, Prince of Prussia—Trios for piano, violin and cello, op. 2-3. *Göbel-Trio Berlin.*
+ ARG 11-12/92: 150
+ Fa 9-10/92: 278

34819. CTH 2149: Rachmaninoff—Piano trios no. 1-2. *Göbel-Trio Berlin.*
+ ARG 11-12/92: 183

34820. CTH 2151: Jírovec—Divertissement, op. 50. Kozeluh—Sonata, op. 34, no. 2. Dussek—Sonata, op. 65. *Trio Cantabile.*
• Fa 1-2/94: 212

34821. CTH 2152: Schumann—Davidsbündlertänze. Ravel—Gaspard de la nuit. *M. Zimmermann, piano.*
+ Fa 1-2/93: 233

34822. CTH 2153: Korn—Beckmesser Variations; Symphony no. 3; Exorcism of a Liszt fragment. *Thüringen-*

Philharmonie Suhl; Koch, cond.
☐ Fa 11-12/92: 269

34823. CTH 2157: RHEINBERGER—
Improvisations on motifs from The magic
flute; Piano sonata no. 2; Variations, op.
61. *Göbel, piano.* Reissue.
+ ARG 5-6/94: 132
+ Fa 3-4/94: 291

34824. CTH 2159: HINDEMITH—Clarinet
concerto. BUSONI—Clarinet concertino,
op. 48. WEBER—Clarinet concerto no. 1.
*Isobe, clarinet; Pomeranian Phil. Orch.;
Ukigaya, cond.*
+ ARG 9-10/93: 135
+ Fa 7-8/93: 153

34825. BCTH 2161/6 (6 discs):
RHEINBERGER—The chamber music.
*Sonare Quartet; Camerata Quartet;
Göbel Trio Berlin; Bronx Arts Ensemble;
Maile, violin; Ruge, cello; Krug, horn;
Göbel, piano; Wind players of the Berlin
Phil. Orch.*
+ ARG 1-2/94: 138
+ Fa 11-12/93: 365

34826. CTH 2167: BLACHER—Piano
concertos no. 1-3. *Göbel, piano;
Bavarian Radio Orch.; Alberoth, cond.;
Pomorska Phil. Orch.; Ukigaya, cond.*
+ ARG 1-2/93: 79
+ Fa 1-2/93: 114

34827. CTH 2168: RÜFER—Bilder zum
Hören [electronic music]. *Rüfer, with
students .*
☐ Fa 7-8/93: 221

34828. CTH 2169: FINK—Toccatina;
Ostinati machina; Batu Ferringhi; Top-
Kapi; Picture; Marcha del Tambor;
Images; Vibracussion; Ritmo; conga
Brasil. *Polyrhythmia Ensemble.*
+ ARG 7-8/93: 89

34829. CTH 2170: PLATZ—Dunkles
Haus. *Ensemble Marstall.*
+ Fa 1-2/97: 224

34830. CTH 2171: RODRIGO—Concierto
de Aranjuez. TORROBA—Concierto de
Castila. CASTELNUOVO- TEDESCO—
Serenade, op. 118. *Tröster, guitar;
Warsaw Phil. Orch.; Przybylski, cond.*
+ ARG 1-2/94: 139
+ Fa 1-2/94: 397

34831. CTH 2174: *Kaleidoskop.* Music of
Caplet, Rossini, Holst, Distler, Koerppen,
and Rutt. *Pieweck, soprano; Schnaus,
piano; Mädchenchor Hannover; Rutt,
Schröfel, conds.*
+ Fa 3-4/94: 388

34832. CTH 2175: ROSENMÜLLER—
Laudate pueri; Sonata no. 4; Missa
brevis; Sonata no. 3. *University Chamber
Choir of Dortmund; Gundlach, cond.*
+ ARG 9-10/93: 178
+ Fa 5-6/93: 297

34833. CTH 2176: BRAHMS—Fantasies,
op. 116; Sixteen waltzes, op. 39; Scherzo,
op. 4. *Kraus, piano.*
• Fa 7-8/93: 116

34834. CTH 2185: DISTLER—
Choralpassion. *Jochens, Kooy, Miehlke;
Chamber Chorus of Dortmund
University; Gundlach, cond.*
+ ARG 7-8/94: 95
+ Fa 5-6/94: 135

34835. CTH 2186: *Chopin und seine Zeit.*
Music of Chopin, Hiller, Meyerbeer,
Gutmann, F. David, and Heller. *Kröger,
piano.*
+ ARG 1-2/95: 227
- Fa 11-12/94: 201

34836. CTH 2190: Music of Yun,
Schnebel, Bussotti, and Cage. *Nolte, flute.*
+ ARG 7-8/94: 207

34837. CTH 2193: *Romantische Orgeln
III.* Music of Sokulski, Medins,
Telemann, Roguski, Sosnowski,
Nowowiejski, Surzynski, Glazunov,
Gulbins, Moniusko, Kalnins, and Süda.
Rost, organ.
☐ Fa 11-12/94: 487

34838. CTH 2194: *Interlude: French
music for flute, violin, and harp.* Music of
Goossens, Tournier, Moyse, Berthomieu,
and Ibert. *H.-J. Wegner, violin; M.
Honegger, violin; E. Wegner, harp.*
+ Fa 3-4/95: 387

34839. CTH 2195: CHOPIN—Études, op.
10 and 25; Trois nouvelles études. *Haase,
piano.*
+ ARG 9-10/94: 117
• Fa 7-8/94: 113

34840. CTH 2196: BAUMANN—Chamber
music. *Residenz-Quintet; Solera,
saxophone; Quellmelz, percussion;
Wollenweber, oboe; Sirotek, English
horn.*
+ Fa 7-8/94: 60

34841. CTH 2197: SCHUMANN—Poetic
miniatures. *Kraus, piano.*
• ARG 5-6/94: 140
• Fa 5-6/94: 249

34842. CTH 2198: *Le vertige des
profondeurs.* Music of Sell, Holszky,
Askin, H.W. Erdman, Hespos, Burba,
and Newman. *Liebermann, soprano;
other musicians.*
☐ Fa 11-12/94: 223

34843. CTH 2199: Music of Telemann,
Vivaldi, Turina, Granados, Arnold, and
others. *Berlin Guitar Ensemble.*
+ ARG 7-8/94: 211

34844. CTH 2201/2 (2 discs): *Siegfried
Behrend in memoriam.* Music of
Behrend, Newsidler, Piaf, Dowland,
Carulli, Hindemith, Poulenc, Giuliani,
Ponce, Bussotti, Logothetis, and Hartig.

Behrend, guitar; other artists.
- ARG 7-8/94: 209
• Fa 5-6/94: 319

34845. CTH 2204: *Duo capricciosio, vol.
3.* Music of Piccone, Hoffmann, Di Pisa,
Calace, Miguel, Pisl, and Gnattali. *G.
Tröster, mandolin; M. Tröster, guitar.*
+ ARG 3-4/95: 238
+ Fa 1-2/95: 350

34846. CTH 2205: *Terremoto con
variazioni.* Music of Legnani, Regondi,
Carulli, and Giuliani. *Tröster, guitar;
Brodzinska-Behrend, speaker.*
+ ARG 5-6/95: 210
+ Fa 1-2/95: 350

34847. CTH 2206: BLACHER—
Divertimento for trumpet, trombone, and
piano; String quartet no. 2; Divertimento
for 4 woodwinds; Octet for clarinet, horn,
bassoon, and string quartet; Sonata for 2
cellos; Duo for flute and piano. *Various
performers.*
+ Fa 1-2/95: 124

34848. CTH 2207: PLEYEL—Piano trios
no. 1-3. *Göbel Trio.*
+ ARG 1-2/95: 153
+ Fa 1-2/95: 228

34849. CTH 2209: LASSUS—Motets,
madrigals, chansons, lieder. *Orlando di
Lasso Ensemble Hannover; Bläser-
Collegium Leipzig; La Gamba Freiburg;
Bratschke, cond.*
+ ARG 1-2/95: 130
+ Fa 11-12/94: 275

34850. CTH 2210: STAHMER—I can fly;
Dreamscape; Commentaries; Rotations;
Grabstele für Erich Arendt; Die
Landschaft in meiner Stimme. *A. & W.
Schneider, percussion; Levine, flute;
White, didgeridoo; Eblenkamp,
percussion; Ars Nova Ensemble
Nürnberg; Heider, cond.; Zelinsky,
Smeyers, clarinets; Nies, voice.*
☐ Fa 1-2/97: 276

34851. CTH 2211: *The romantic
mandolin.* CALACE—Preludes no. 1-3, 5,
10-12, 14-15; Gran preludio, op. 175.
Tröster, mandolin.
+ ARG 9-10/95: 120
+ Fa 7-8/95: 422

34852. CTH 2212: *Guitar quartets, vol.
1.* Music of Angulo, Duarte, and B.
Hummel. *Tröster, guitar; Saxon String
Quartet.*
+ ARG 11-12/95: 252
+ Fa 11-12/95: 482

34853. CTH 2213: ERDMANN—Music for
plectral ensemble. *Landezupforchester
Berlin; Betton, cond.*
☐ ARG 11-12/94: 110
☐ Fa 11-12/94: 223

34854. CTH 2214: MOZART—String
quartet no. 14. SCHUBERT—String quartet

THOROFON

no. 13. *Philharmonia Quartet Berlin.*
+ Fa 1-2/96: 139

34855. CTH 2215: DISTLER—Totentanz, op. 12, no. 2; Motette, op. 12, no. 6; Organ partita, op. 8, no. 2. *Quadflieg, Krämer, Ostermann, Uter, speakers; University of Dortmund Chamber Choir; Gundlach, cond.; Innig, organ.*
• Fa 5-6/95: 180

34856. CTH 2216: BRAHMS—Violin sonata no. 3. PROKOFIEV—Violin sonata no. 2. TCHAIKOVSKY—Meditation, op. 42, no. 1. PAGANINI—Moto perpetuo. *Prischepenko, violin; Fock, piano.*
+ Fa 1-2/95: 130

34857. CTH 2217: DEBUSSY—Three chansons to texts by Charles d'Orléans. RAVEL—Three chansons. POULENC—Choral music. *Norddeutscher Figuralchor; Straube, cond.*
+ ARG 11-12/95: 263
+ Fa 9-10/95: 187

34858. CTH 2220: RŮŽIČKA—Tallis: das Gesegnete, das Verfluchte; Annäherung und Stille; Etym; Torso. *Various performrs.*
+ Fa 3-4/96: 266

34859. CTH 2231: DISTLER—Mörike-Chorliederbuch, op. 19: extracts. *Chamber Choir of the Hochschule der Künste Berlin; Grube, cond.*
• Fa 3-4/95: 162

34860. CTH 2233: B. HUMMEL—Percussion music. *Sadlo & Ensemble.*
+ Fa 9-10/95: 233

34861. CTH 2235: JENTZSCH—Improvisation; ...und ihr Schatten; Paysages SM; Paysages FLbV; Paysages PC. *Chojnacka, harpsichord; Sparnaay, bass clarinet; Inda, tuba; Schicker, bass flute; Pilch, percussion.*
+ Fa 5-6/95: 227

34862. CTH 2236: CHOPIN—Piano concerto no. 1. RAVEL—Piano concerto in G major. *Triendl, piano; Polish National Radio Symphony Orch.; Ukigaya, cond.*
+ Fa 5-6/95: 171

34863. CTH 2237: HINDEMITH—Das Marienleben. *Lenz-Kuhn, soprano; Kaiser, piano.*
+ Fa 5-6/95: 216

34864. CTH 2240: SCHUMANN—Symphonic etudes. SCHOENBERG—Klavierstücke, op. 11. RIHM—Klavierstücke no. 5. *Werz, piano.*
+ Fa 5-6/95: 335

34865. CTH 2243: Music of Boccherini, Mercadante, Donizetti, Rossini, Ciardi, and Rota. *H.J. Wegner, flute; E. Wegner, harp.*
+ Fa 3-4/96: 356

34866. CTH 2245: MAUERSBERGER—Geistliche Sommermusik. *J. Unger, organ; Thüringer Akademische Singkreis; W. Unger, cond.*
□ Fa 5-6/96: 207

34867. CTH 2246: *Le copain.* PILSL—Music of Pilsl. *Hiemenz, guitar; Duo Capriccioso; S. Pilsl, guitar; Geller, voice; Gerter, accordion; Terasawa, flute; Tappert, guitar; Rotenbek-Trio; Geiss, cello.*
+ Fa 5-6/95: 291

34868. CTH 2247: WIDOR—Symphony no. 4. REGER—Benedictus. LISZT—Prelude and fugue on B-A-C-H. GUILMANT—Organ sonata no. 4. *Rost, organ.*
• ARG 9-10/96: 226
- Fa 9-10/96: 406

34869. CTH 2248: BRUCH—Eight pieces for clarinet, cello, and piano, op. 83. DELANOFF—Trio for piano, clarinet, and cello. *Budapester Klaviertrio.*
+ ARG 9-10/95: 116
+ Fa 7-8/95: 139

34870. CTH 2249: FERGUSON—Octet no. 4. FRANÇAIX—Octuor. *Ensemble Acht.*
+ ARG 7-8/95: 111
+ Fa 5-6/95: 187

34871. CTH 2250: DU MAGE—Suite du premier ton. BACH—Prelude and fugue, BWV 544; Allein Gott in der Höh sei Ehr, BWV 662. FRANCK—Choral in A minor. WIDOR—Symphonie romane: Choral; Symphony no. 6: Allegro. *Brandstetter, organ.*
+ ARG 11-12/95: 253
• Fa 9-10/95: 397

34872. CTH 2256: BAUMANN—Variations on a theme of Franz Schubert; String quartet in C major; Strophes; Autumn music; Transformations of a Baroque theme. *Cello X 12 Ensemble; Polásek, cond.; Munich Phil. Orch.; Ruge, Schmidhuber, cellos; Grobholz, violin; Stiehler, viola; Klug, cello; Berlin Violin Phil. Ensemble; Dinca, cond.*
+ ARG 11-12/95: 81
+ Fa 11-12/95: 201

34873. CTH 2257: *Allusions in moonlight: a Japanese lieder recital.* Music of Taki, Yamada, Hirai, Ishiketa, Nakata, Moroi, Hirota, Narita, Takata, and Nobutoki. *Ohno, tenor; Kobayashi, piano.*
• Fa 11-12/96: 428

34874. CTH 2259: *Frauentöne, vol. 1.* Music of Müller-Hermann, M. Bach, and Dickenson-Auner. *Mährische Phil. Orch.; Müssauer, cond.*
• ARG 11-12/95: 244
• Fa 9-10/95: 418

34875. CTH 2260: FUCHS—Symphony no. 3; Des Meeres und der Liebe Wellen

overture; Andante grazioso and capriccio. *Mährische Philharmonie; Müssauer, cond.*
• ARG 9-10/95: 145
• Fa 11-12/95: 257

34876. CTH 2261: MARTIN—Mass for double choir; Ariel songs; Passacaglia, organ. *Smidt, organ; North German Figural Choir; Straube, cond.*
+ ARG 9-10/96: 159
+ Fa 11-12/96: 297

34877. CTH 2262: DOMHARDT—Violin concerto. MÜLLER—Concerto for piano and chamber orchestra. STENDEL—Inventionen. *Wächter, violin; Kontarsky, piano; Thüringen-Philharmonie Suhl; Domhardt, Müller, Koch, conds.*
□ Fa 9-10/95: 192

34878. CTH 2263: J.C.F. BACH—Motet, Wachet auf, ruft uns der Stimme; Sinfonia. BACH—Cantata, Wachet auf, ruft uns die Stimme. *Zumbült, Kobow, Frank; Knabenchor Hannover; Barockorchester L'Arco; Hennig, cond.*
• Fa 1-2/96: 114

34879. CTH 2264: MOZART—String quartet no. 14. SHOSTAKOVICH—String quartet no. 3. *Phil. Quartett Berlin.*
+ Fa 7-8/95: 255

34880. CTH 2265: ZELENKA—Missa Sanctissimae trinitatis. *Frimmer, Graf, Brutscher, Richter; Marburg Baroque Ensemble; Marburg Bach Choir; Wehnert, cond.*
+ ARG 3-4/96: 213
+ Fa 11-12/96: 433

34881. CTH 2266: DURANTE—Beatus vir à 4; Magnificat in A minor; Laudate pueri; Magnificat in C minor; Beatus vir à 5; Miserere. *Cappella Durante; Durante Chamber Orch.; Boymann, cond.*
+ ARG 9-10/95: 139
+ Fa 7-8/95: 174

34882. CTH 2269: ERDMANN—Saxophone concerto; Saxophonata; Resonanzen; Akzente; Persiflagen; Fantasia colorata; Konzertstücke for alto saxophone and small orchestra. *Bensmann, saxophone; Thüringen Philharmonie Suhl; Loch, cond.; Berlin Saxophone Quartet; Rische, piano; Metropol Saxophone Quartet; Filharmonia Pomorska; Ukigaya, cond.*
+ Fa 1-2/97: 162

34883. CTH 2270: BAUR—Symphonic metamorphoses on Gesualdo; Romeo and Juliet; Music with Schumann; Concerto romano. *Winter, oboe; Cologne Radio Symphony Orch.; Barshai, cond.; Stuttgart Radio Symphony Orch.; Müller-Kray, cond.; Bavarian Radio Symphony Orch.; Bamberg Symphony Orch.; Schneidt, cond.*
+ Fa 3-4/96: 121

TIMPANI

34917. 1C 1021: Le Flem—Symphony no. 1; Fantasy for piano and orchestra; Le magicienne de la mer; Two interludes. *Girod, piano; Orch. de Bretagne; Schnitzler, cond.*
+ Fa 9-10/94: 238

34918. 1C 1022: Milhaud—Alissa; Trois poèmes de Lucile de Chateaubriand; D'un cahier inédit d'Eugénie de Guérin; Deux poèmes de Coventry Patmore. *Katz, mezzo-soprano; Cyferstein, piano.*
● ARG 7-8/95: 156
+ Fa 5-6/95: 264

34919. 1C 1025: Cras—Mélodies. *Estourelle, soprano; Peintre, baritone; Jacquon, piano; Syrinx, panpipes; Phillips, violin; Lenert, viola; Demarquette, cello.*
+ ARG 9-10/95: 129
● Fa 7-8/95: 161

34920. 1C 1027: Jolivet—Symphony for strings; Yin-yang; Adagio; La flèche du temps; Andante. *Orch. du Pays de Savoie; Foster, cond.*
+ ARG 7-8/95: 133
+ Fa 7-8/95: 214

34921. 1C 1029: Furtwängler—Violin sonata no. 1. *Kang, violin; Kerdoncuff, piano.*
+ ARG 1-2/96: 110
+ Fa 1-2/96: 202

34922. 1C 1030: Emmanuel—Les mélodies. *Katz, mezzo-soprano; Girod, piano; Lefebvre, flute; Peintre, baritone; Philips, violin; Demarquette, cello.*
● ARG 7-8/96: 109
+ Fa 5-6/96: 148

34923. 1C 1033: Cras—Danze; Paysages; Poèmes intimes. *Jacquon, piano.*
+ ARG 11-12/96: 114
+ Fa 11-12/96: 227

34924. 1C 1034: Ropartz—Petite symphonie; Pastorale; Sons des cloches; Serenade champêtre; Divertimento. *Orch. de Bretagne; Verrot, cond.*
● ARG 11-12/96: 190

34925. 1C 1035: Honegger—Impératrice aux rochers; Amphion. *Lallouette, baritone; Manzoni, narrator; Timisoara Phil. Orch.; Antonioli, cond.*
● ARG 9-10/96: 141
+ Fa 11-12/96: 272

34926. 1C 1284: Sacre—Preludes; Serenades no. 1-2; Chansons enfantines; Variations. *Eidi, piano.*
+ ARG 5-6/96: 180

34927. 2C 2019 (2 discs): Vierne—Chamber music (complete). *Phillips Quartet; Kerdoncuff, Gardon, piano; Galpérine, violin; Carracilly, alto; Chiffoleau, cello; Moreaux, oboe; Zanlonghi, harp.*

+ ARG 3-4/95: 214
+ Fa 7-8/94: 271

34928. 2C 2023 (2 discs): Vierne—Piano music. *Gardon, piano.*
+ Fa 11-12/95: 414

34929. 2C 2028 (2 discs): Chausson—Les mélodies. *Balleys, mezzo-soprano; Gardeil, baritone; Piau, soprano; Eidi, piano; Quatuor Ludwig.*
● ARG 11-12/95: 105
+ Fa 11-12/95: 235

34930. 4C 4017 (4 discs): Franck—Recordings 1923-1942. *Various performers.* Historic reissues.
+ Fa 11-12/93: 238

34931. 4C 4024 (4 discs): *L'Orchestre des Concerts Lamoureux: Albert Wolff: un panorama de musique symphonique française: Polydor recordings 1929-1933.* Music of Méhul, Berlioz, Lalo, Saint-Saëns, G. Charpentier, Roussel, Dupont, d'Indy, Franck, Rameau, Chabrier, Debussy, Rabaud, Dukas, Schmitt, Laparra, and Ravel. *Lamoureux Orch.; Wolff, cond.* Recorded 1929-1933.
+ ARG 3-4/95: 266
+ Fa 3-4/95: 395

TITANIC

34932. Ti-35: *Eighteenth century recorder sonatas.* Music of Telemann, Loeillet, La Barre, Bach, and Corelli. *Verbruggen, recorder; Gibbons, harpsichord; Mahler, cello.*
+ Fa 3-4/89: 314

34933. Ti-151: Bach—Kunst der Fuge. *Bagger, Cleverdon, harpsichords.*
● Fa 5-6/91: 104

34934. Ti-152: Soler—Six concertos for 2 keyboard instruments. *Brauchli, clavichord, & organ; Elizondo, clavichord, organ, & harpsichord.*
- Fa 11-12/87: 230
● Gr 11/87: 771

34935. Ti-153: *The Iberian organ, vol. 1.* Works by de Heredia, Bruna, Elias, Rodriguez, de Alberto, de Larranaga, de Echeverria, and de Bidaurre. *Elizondo, organ.*
+ Fa 11-12/91: 551

34936. Ti-154: Mozart—String quartets no. 14, 17. *The Classical Quartet.*
● ARG 1-2/88: 50
+ Au 12/87: 144
+ Fa 11-12/87: 185

34937. Ti-155: Grainger—Piano music. *Coxe, piano.*
+ ARG Fall/87: 19
+ Fa 11-12/87: 146
+ Gr 11/87: 778
+ HF 11/87: 90
+ MA 11/87: 60
+ NYT 6/28/87: H28

34938. Ti-156: Haydn—Piano sonatas H. XVI: 19, 39, 48, 60; Variations on Gott erhalte. *Odiaga, fortepiano.*
+ Fa 1-2/88: 139

34939. Ti-158: Bach—Organ music. *Ritchie, organ.*
● ARG 1-2/88: 8
● Fa 11-12/87: 88
+ SR 12/87: 141

34940. Ti-160: Haydn—Piano sonatas H. XVI: 40-42, 51-52; Andante con variazione in F minor H. XVI: 6. *Odiaga, fortepiano.*
+ Fa 5-6/88: 141

34941. Ti-161: *A potpourri of 19th-century salon music on period instruments.* Music of Meyerbeer, Giuliani, Hummel, Gossec, Sor, and others. *Boland, flute; Dowdall, guitar.*
+ Fa 7-8/88: 317

34942. Ti-162: Bach—Prelude and fugue BWV 532, 544; Concerto in D minor BWV 596; Trio sonata no. 1 BWV 525; Nun komm der Heiden Heiland BWV 659; In dulci jubilo BWV 729; BWV 751; Wie schön leuchtet der Morgenstern BWV 739; Vom Himmel hoch BWV 738. *Johnson, organ.*
+ Fa 3-4/89: 81
+ Ov 2/89: 45

34943. Ti-163: Brahms—Violin concerto op. 77. Lipinski—Violin concerto op. 21. *Totenberg, violin; Polish National Radio Orch.; Wit, cond.*
+ ARG 11-12/88: 44
□ Fa 11-12/88: 150

34944. Ti-164: Bach—Prelude and fugue BWV 547-48; Allein Gott BWV 664; Pastorale BWV 590; Passacaglia and fugue BWV 582. Franck—Prelude, fugue, and variation op. 18. *Johnson, organ.*
+ Fa 9-10/89: 121

34945. Ti-166: Haydn—Six easy variations H. XVII: 5; Piano sonatas H. XVI: 20, 44-46. *Odiaga, fortepiano.*
+ ARG 3-4/90: 59
+ Fa 11-12/89: 233

34946. Ti-167: Beethoven—Piano sonatas no. 15, 21; Bagatelles op. 126. *Carlin, fortepiano.*
- ARG 5-6/90: 26
- Fa 11-12/89: 133

34947. Ti-168: *Three hundred years of French glory.* Music of Tournemire, Couperin, Daquin, Alain, and others. *Spillman, organ.*
● ARG 11-12/89: 159
□ Fa 11-12/89: 458

34948. Ti-171: Bach—Sei gegrüsset, Jesu gütig, BWV 768; Fugue, BWV 539; Canonic variations on Von Himmel hoch da komm' ich her, BWV 769; Trio

sonata, BWV 527, 529; Toccata and fugue, BWV 566. *Joyce, organ.*
+ Fa 3-4/91: 136

34949. Ti-174: BRAHMS—Zigeunerlieder. SCHUMANN—Minnespiel. MASSENET—Chansons des bois d'amarante. L. BOULANGER—Renouveau. *American VocalArts Quintet.*
+ ARG 7-8/90: 150
+ Fa 7-8/90: 341

34950. Ti-175: *New music for organ and percussion.* LOCKLAIR—Constellations. ALBRIGHT—Enigma syncopations. BEADELL—Arcotor. ROBERTS—Five for organ and marimba. BOLCOM—Black host. *Ritchie, organ; Rometo, percussion; Bailey, flute; White, double bass.*
• ARG 11-12/90: 156
+ Fa 11-12/90: 459 (2 reviews)

34951. Ti-176: *Four new American organs by Bedient.* Music of Buxtehude, Sweelinck, Bach, Zipoli, Fischer, and others. *Ritchie, organ.*
+ Fa 11-12/90: 442

34952. Ti-177: Music of Dornel, Quantz, Cima, Castello, Turini, and others. *Ensemble Arion.*
+ Fa 7-8/90: 366

34953. Ti-179: *An American masterpiece: the C. B. Fisk organ.* Music of Guilain, Franck, Vierne, Bach, Mendelssohn, and Widor. *Johnson, organ.*
- ARG 11-12/90: 155
• Fa 9-10/90: 479

34954. Ti-181: *From the heartland: two Nordlie organs in South Dakota.* Music of Buxtehude, Brahms, Bruhns, Woodman, Bach, and Heiller. *Sykes, organ.*
+ Fa 1-2/93: 296

34955. Ti-182: Music of Rossini, Mozart, Giuliani, Kuhlau, and Donizetti. *Boland, flute; Dowdall, guitar.*
• ARG 3-4/93: 163
- Fa 1-2/93: 295

34956. Ti-183: *Music for viola da gamba.* DEMACHY—Suite no. 5 in D minor; Suite no. 8 in A. SCHAFFRATH—Duet in D minor for 2 violas da gamba. ABEL—Suite in D minor for bass viol. MOZART—Duo in B♭ for 2 violas da gamba, K. 292. *Jeppeson, Hershey, violas da gamba.*
+ ARG 1-2/92: 168
+ Fa 11-12/91: 559

34957. Ti-185: *Eighteenth century music for two keyboard instruments.* Music of Krebs, Schaffrath, Blanco, Olivares, and J. C. Bach. *Brauchli, harpsichord & clavichord; Elizondo, organ & harpsichord.*
+ ARG 1-2/91: 137
+ Fa 11-12/90: 434
- Fa 5-6/91: 356

34958. Ti-186: C.P.E. BACH—Fantasia Wq. 67; Keyboard sonatas Wq. 48, 50, 63; Twelve variations on the Folies d'Espagne Wq. 118; Farewell to my Silbermann clavichord Wq. 66. *Brauchli, clavichord.*
+ Fa 3-4/91: 129

34959. Ti-187: *17th and 18th century music of the Spanish and Portuguese.* Music of Cabanilles, Correa de Arauxo, Jiménez, Cabezón, Aguilera de Heredia, and Bruna. *Joyce, organ.*
+ Fa 11-12/91: 552

34960. Ti-188: *The organ at La Valenciana.* Music of Braga, Santa Maria, Cabezon, De Soto, Bruna, De Araujo, Correa de Arauxo, De Heredia, Conceiçao, Cabanilles, Aguilera, Soler, and San Lorenzo. *Joyce, organ.*
+ ARG 11-12/92: 243
+ Fa 9-10/92: 421

34961. Ti-189: *Bridges of song.* Music of the Spanish Jews of Morocco. *Voice of the Turtle; Wachs, cond.*
+ ARG 11-12/91: 197

34962. Ti-191: *Romantic music for flute and guitar.* Works by Doppler, Coste, Giuliani, Diabelli, Godard, Fauré. *Sindelar, flute; Schilling, guitar.*
- Fa 11-12/91: 561

34963. Ti-192: CORELLI—Concerto grosso, op. 6 no. 8. CALDARA—Sinfonias no. 4, 12. HANDEL—Concerto grosso, op. 6 no. 3. HAYDN—Symphony no. 47. *Aston Magna; Hsu, cond.*
• Fa 7-8/91: 382

34964. Ti-194: SCARLATTI—Keyboard sonatas K. 11, 29, 32, 44, 113, 132, 146, 162, 209, 366, 380, 435, 513, 2011. *Di Bonaventura, piano.*
+ Fa 7-8/91: 274

34965. Ti-195: RACHMANINOFF—Preludes op. 32. *Di Bonaventura, piano.*
• ARG 7-8/91: 110
• Fa 7-8/91: 257

34966. Ti-196: *The 1794 Giovanni Bruna organ of Magnano.* Music of Paumann, Heredia, Araujo, Chaumont, A. Scharlatti, and others. *Brauchli, organ.*
• Fa 7-8/91: 364

34967. Ti-198: SCHUBERT—Piano sonatas D. 537, 894; Moments musicaux, D. 780: no. 1-2, 5. *Carlin, fortepiano.*
+ Fa 9-10/92: 344

34968. Ti-199: FLYNN—Fantasy etudes. BALEY—Figments. SHAPEY—Four etudes. BLANK—Toccatina and mixtures. *Gratovich, violin.*
+ Fa 11-12/92: 236

34969. Ti-200: DURUFLÉ—Complete organ works. *Spillman, organ.* Reissue.

+ ARG 9-10/92: 100
+ Fa 9-10/92: 225

34970. Ti-201: *The organs of Guanajunato, Mexico.* Music of De Gamarra, Soler, De Oxinaga and Ledesma. *Elizondo, organ.*
+ Fa 5-6/92: 318

34971. Ti-202: *Motets.* BUSNOIS—Noel; In hydraulis; Regina caeli; Victimae paschali laudes. JOSQUIN DES PREZ—Inviolata, integra et casta es; Ave maris stella/Descendi in hortum meum; Ecce tu pulchra es. GOMBERT—Tota pulchra es; Sancta Maria; Hortus conclusus. *Capella Alamire; Urquhart, cond.*
+ ARG 9-10/92: 200
+ Fa 9-10/92: 207

34972. Ti-203: Balkan vistas, Spanish dreams. *Voice of the Turtle.*
+ ARG 5-6/92: 174
+ Fa 5-6/92: 305

34973. Ti-204: MESSIAEN—L'Ascension. CLÉRAMBAULT—Suites. DURUFLÉ—Suite, op. 5. *Spillman, organ.*
- Fa 1-2/93: 296

34974. Ti-205: *A diversity of riches: multi-ethnic organ music by twentieth-century American composers.* Music of Kerr, Fax, Persichetti, Berlinski, Guthrie, Simpson, and Hampton. *Spillman, organ.*
+ Fa 3-4/93: 369

34975. Ti-207: *Bernard Lagacé at the C.B. Fisk organ, Wellesley College.* Music of Scheidt, Scheidemann, Froberger, Tunder, and Buxtehude.
+ Fa 11-12/93: 488

34976. Ti-208: CHOPIN—Piano sonata no. 3; Scherzo no. 4; Polonaise-fantaisie, op. 61; Barcarolle, op. 60. *Di Bonaventura, piano.*
- Fa 7-8/94: 113

34977. Ti-210: SCHUBERT—Piano sonata D. 960. SCHUMANN—Kreisleriana. *Vosgerchian, piano.*
• Fa 9-10/93: 270

34978. Ti-212: Music of Berlioz, Gounod, Thomas, Franck, Delibes, and others. *O'Keefe, soprano; Schilling, guitar.*
+ ARG 1-2/94: 193

34979. Ti-213: WEISS—Lute works from the Dresden manuscripts. *Stone, baroque lute.*
+ ARG 1-2/94: 170
+ Fa 11-12/93: 450

34980. Ti-214: *Sonatas for fortepiano.* Music of Marianne von Martinez, Marianna von Auenbrugger, and Haydn. *Jakuc, piano.*
+ Fa 11-12/93: 484

34981. Ti-215: Musical traditions of the Sephardim. *Canto Antiguo.*
+ Fa 7-8/94: 309

34982. Ti-216: *Poetic license: transcriptions for flute and piano.* Music of Debussy, Mozart, Handel, and Brahms. *Pollet, flute; Vogt, piano.*
+ Fa 7-8/95: 417

34983. Ti-217: LOVENSTEIN—Blake songs. *Various performers.*
- ARG 3-4/95: 131
+ Fa 5-6/95: 245

34984. Ti-218: MERTZ—Guitar music. *Anderson, guitar.*
+ ARG 1-2/95: 140

34985. Ti-219: *The virtuoso double bass.* Music of Vanhal, Haydn, Mannl, and Sperger. *Musicians of the Old Post Road; Sinclair, double bass.*
+ ARG 9-10/95: 257
+ Fa 9-10/95: 389

34986. Ti-220: ALKAN—Symphony op. 39. BEETHOVEN—Piano sonata no. 31. LISZT—Mephisto waltz no. 2. *Salman, piano.*
+ ARG 11-12/94: 236

34987. Ti-221: BACH—Das Orgelbüchlein. *Somerville, organ.*
+ Fa 7-8/95: 107

34988. Ti-223: *Under Aegean moons.* Music of the Spanish Jews of Rhodes and Salonika. *Voice of the Turtle.*
+ Fa 3-4/95: 367

34989. Ti-224: ROSSINI—Zelmira (arr. Sedlak). *Harmonie; Traphagan, cond.*
+ ARG 5-6/96: 179
+ Fa 5-6/96: 248

34990. Ti-225: BYRD—*The passinge mesures.* Keyboard pieces. *Nicholson, double virginal & organ.*
- ARG 11-12/95: 101
- Fa 11-12/95: 231

34991. Ti-226: *Elgar and Co.* Music of Elgar, Roger-Ducasse, Whitlock, and Bourgeois. *Maki, organ.*
+ ARG 1-2/96: 106
● Fa 9-10/95: 398

34992. Ti-227: THALBERG—Piano music. *Hominick, piano.*
● Fa 9-10/95: 341

34993. Ti-228: *The merry company: music for Baroque basssoon and friends.* Music of Guillemant, Boismortier, Frescobaldi, Bertoli, and others. *Bedford, bassoon; Fitch, harpsichord & organ; Robbins, cello; Epple, flute; Maiben, violin.*
● Fa 5-6/96: 341

34994. Ti-229: COUPERIN—L'art de toucher le clavecin (selections).

RAMEAU—Pièces de clavecin: Les cyclopes; Nouvelles suites de pièces de clavecin (selections). *Sykes, harpsichord.*
● Fa 5-6/96: 133

34995. Ti-230: *A neurosurgeon's art.* Music of Rachmaninoff, Chopin, Scarlatti, Granados, Ravel, and others. *Miller, piano.*
+ Fa 5-6/96: 353

34996. Ti-232: *Renaissance dances and improvisations.* Improvisations and music of Caroso, Negri, Phalese, Rognoni, Della Casa, and Gervaise. *Renaissonics.*
+ Fa 1-2/97: 319

34997. Ti-233: POGLIETTI—Rossignolo. *Lindorff, harpsichord.*
+ ARG 3-4/97: 197
+ Fa 11-12/96: 333

34998. Ti-313: WEISS—Lute sonatas no. 45, 46, 49, 52. *Stone, lute.*
+ Fa 5-6/95: 377

TLP RECORDS

34999. TLPC-35001: OFFENBACH—Ile de Tulipatan. *Soloists; Jupille Saint-Amand Choral Royal Circle; Liege Soloists; Koch, cond.*
□ Fa 9/10/87: 260

TOCCATA

35000. FCD 383642: BACH—Goldberg variations. *Tracey, harpsichord.*
- Fa 9-10/88: 88

TOMATO

35001. 70390: PARTCH—Revelation in the Courthouse Park. *Costallos, Durham, Babatunde, vocalists; Partch Musicians; Mitchell, cond.*
+ ARG 9-10/92: 141

35002. 2696172: CAGE—Three constructions; A flower; Forever and sunsmall. *Clayton, voice; Donald Knack Percussion Ensemble.*
+ Fa 9-10/90: 206

35003. 2696392: BACH—Orchestral suite no. 3: Air (arr. Prado); Toccata and fugue in D minor (arr. Busoni); Choral preludes: I call on thee, Lord; Awake, the voice commands; Partitas for unaccompanied violin no. 2: Chaconne; Organ preludes: in G minor, in E minor (arr. Siloti); Jesu, joy of man's desiring (arr. Hess). *Martins, piano.*
- Fa 9-10/90: 146

35004. 2696422: BACH—Anna Magdalena Bach notebook: Selections; Little preludes, BWV 924-930, 939-942, 999; Italian concerto. *Martins, piano.*
- Fa 9-10/90: 146

35005. 2696442: BACH—Goldberg variations. *Martins, piano.*
- Fa 9-10/90: 146

35006. 2696452: BACH—Partitas, BWV 825-830. *Martins, piano.*
- Fa 9-10/90: 146

35007. 2696462: BACH—French suites, BWV 812-817; Overture in the French style. *Martins, piano.*
- ARG 1-2/91: 22
- Fa 9-10/90: 146

35008. 2696472: BACH—Two-part inventions (complete); Three-part inventions (complete). *Martins, piano.*
- Fa 9-10/90: 146

35009. 2696482: BACH—Well-tempered clavier bk. 1: Preludes. CHOPIN—Preludes, op. 28. *Martins, piano.*
- Fa 9-10/90: 147

35010. 2696552 (2 discs): PARTCH—Revelation in the courthouse park. *Costallos, Durham, Babatunde; Orch. of Partch Instruments and Marching Band; Mitchell, cond.*
+ Fa 9-10/90: 328 (2 reviews)

35011. 2699132 (4 discs): BACH—Well-tempered clavier. *Martins, piano.*
- Fa 9-10/90: 146

TONMEISTER UMKAPELL

35012. 89: Music of Liszt, Martino, Debussy, and Scriabin. *Paik, piano.*
- DA 4/91: 69
+ Fa 3-4/91: 472

TOPAZ

35013. TLSCD 1242: Music of Dinicu (arr. Heifetz), Perlman, Bartók (arr. Székely), Hovhaness, and others. *Rosenthal, violin; Bergman, piano.*
+ Fa 7-8/89: 310

TOSCANINI SOCIETY

35014. 100 (2 discs): Music of Scarlatti, Boccherini, Cherubini, Bazzini, and others. *NBC Symphony Orch.; Toscanini, cond.*
+ ARG 9-10/96: 270

TOWERHILL

35015. CD-900103: MOZART—Piano sonatas no. 3, 11, 14; Variations on a minuet of Duport K. 573. *Richner, piano.*
● Fa 11-12/88: 235

TOWN HALL

35016. 29: Music of Beethoven, Chopin, Brahms, and Bach-Busoni. *Cosma, piano.*
● ARG 7-8/96: 248

35017. 35: SCHUBERT—Variations D. 603; Grand duo. *Schnabel Piano Duo.*
- ARG 7-8/94: 168

35018. 43: SCHUMANN—Carnaval; Fantasy in C; Presto passionato; Waldszenen; Abschied. *Rowland, piano.*
- ARG 7-8/95: 191
- Fa 3-4/96: 280

35019. 44: *Cantares for soprano and guitar.* Music of Pisador, Valderrabano, Milan, Handel, Gerhard, Ponce, Sandoval, and Moreno. *Bartos, soprano; Nestor, guitar.*
+ Fa 9-10/96: 373

35020. 45: *Fiddle-de-bop.* Music of Schoenfield, Foss, Steinhardt, Copland, White, Bolcom, Kroll, Stravinsky, Gardner, Still, and Mayorga. *Rosenthal, violin; Mayorga, piano; Levine, bass.*
+ ARG 11-12/96: 256
+ Fa 9-10/96: 423

TR RECORDS

35021. TRC 115 (LP): Music of S. Stravinsky, Hauer, Norman, Hindemith, and others. *M. Elgart, Yates, guitars.*
+ Fa 9-10/87: 374

TRADITIONS MONASTIQUES

35022. CD 12: Gregorian chant: Easter. *Monks of St. Joseph de Clairval, Flavigny.*
- Fa 9-10/96: 392

35023. CD 26: Gregorian chant: Time after Christmas. *Monks of St. Joseph de Clairval, Flavigny.*
- Fa 9-10/96: 392

35024. CD 493: Gregorian chant: Pentecost. *Monks of St. Joseph de Clairval, Flavigny.*
- Fa 9-10/96: 392

TRAVELLING

35025. K 1506: AURIC—Le testament d'Orphée; Orphée; La belle et la bête; Aigle à deux têtes. *Various performers.*
□ ARG 9-10/96: 78

TRAX CLASSIQUE

35026. TRXCD 110: SHOSTAKOVICH—Chamber symphony in C minor op. 110a; Symphony for strings op. 118a. *Phoenix Chamber Orch.; Bigg, cond.*
+ Fa 11-12/87: 227

35027. TRXCD 112 (2 discs): WAGNER—Das Rheingold; Entry of the gods; Die Walkure: Ride of the valkyries; Wotan's farewell; Magic fire music; Parsifal: Act 3 prelude; Good Friday spell; Siegfried Idyll; Huldigungsmarsch; Tannhäuser: Entry of the guests; Lohengrin: Act I prelude; Tristan und Isolde: Prelude and Liebestod. *Various*

orchs.; Wagner, cond.*
- Fa 1-2/88: 234

35028. TRXCD 114: LLOYD—Symphony no. 10. JOSEPHS—Concerto for brass op. 88. *London Collegiate Brass; Stobart, cond.*
+ Fa 11-12/87: 169

TREMULA

35029. TREM 101-2: LEIGH—Piano music and songs. *Nash, soprano; Hewitt, Douglas, Mountford, Down, pianos.*
+ ARG 11-12/93: 139
+ Gr 9/92: 146

35030. TREM 102-2: RUBBRA—String quartet no. 2. TATE—String quartet in F. WISHART—String quartet no. 3. *English String Quartet.*
- ARG 11-12/93: 181
+ Fa 11-12/93: 198
+ Gr 12/93: 84

TREVAK

35031. TREC-0-005: MUFFAT—Componimenti musicali per il cembalo, vol. 1. *Rusó, harpsichord.*
- Fa 11-12/92: 316

35032. TREC-4-0001: MATTHESON—Die wohlklingende Fingersprache: fugues 1-12; Suite movements. *Rusó, harpsichord.*
+ Fa 11-12/91: 389

35033. TREC-4-0002: SPERGER—Trios for violin, flute or oboe, with viola and cello. *Various performers.*
+ Fa 11-12/91: 488

35034. TREC-4-0003: ZIMMERMANN—Six sonatas for harpsichord and violin, op. 2. *Kucharsky, violin; Rusó, harpsichord.*
- Fa 7-8/92: 326

35035. TREC-4-0004: *Tabulatura Vietrois saeculi XVII.* Selected dances, organ preambulas and scared songs. *Musa antiqua Sloveniae; Rusó, cond.*
- Fa 7-8/92: 338

35036. TREC-4-0006: SPERGER—Three symphonies for strings. *Musica Aeterna Bratislava; Zajíček, cond.*
+ Fa 11-12/92: 375

TRING INTERNATIONAL

35037. TRP 001: BEETHOVEN—Symphony no. 6; Egmont: Overture. *Royal Phil. Orch.; Ermler, cond.*
- Gr 5/94: 47

35038. TRP 007: HOLST—The planets; St. Paul's suite. *Royal Phil. Orch.; Handley, cond.*
+ Gr 7/94: 46

35039. TRP 010: DVOŘÁK—Symphony no. 9; Carnival; Scherzo capriccioso.

Royal Phil. Orch.; Järvi, cond.
+ Gr 3/95: 42

35040. TRP 020: MENDELSSOHN—Symphonies no. 3-4. *Royal Phil. Orch.; S. Sanderling, cond.*
- ARG 5-6/96: 150

35041. TRP 022: BEETHOVEN—Symphony no. 5. SCHUBERT—Symphony no. 8. *Royal Phil. Orch.; Gibault, cond.*
- Gr 7/95: 44

35042. TRP 023: TCHAIKOVSKY—Piano concerto no. 1; The seasons (selections). *O'Hora, piano; Royal Phil. Orch.; Judd, cond.*
+ Gr 10/95: 75

35043. TRP 024: GRIEG—Piano concerto; Lyric pieces. *O'Hora, piano; Royal Phil. Orch.; Judd, cond.*
+ Gr 6/95: 44

35044. TRP 026: BEETHOVEN—Symphony no. 3; Fidelio overture. *Royal Phil. Orch.; Herbig, cond.*
- Gr 6/95: 43

35045. TRP 027: BEETHOVEN—Piano sonatas no. 8, 14, 17. *Ortiz, piano.*
+ Gr 10/95: 92

35046. TRP 031: VAUGHAN WILLIAMS—Orchestra music. *Royal Phil. Orch.; Seaman, cond.*
- Gr 2/96: 60

35047. TRP 032: SHOSTAKOVICH—Festive overture; Symphony no. 5. *Royal Phil. Orch.; Mackerras, cond.*
+ Gr 9/95: 66

35048. TRP 033: BEETHOVEN—Symphonies no. 1, 7. *Royal Phil. Orch.; Wordsworth, cond.*
- Gr 8/95: 67

35049. TRP 036: DELIUS—Orchestra music. *Royal Phil. Orch.; Seaman, cond.*
- Gr 9/95: 54

35050. TRP 037: *English string music.* Music of Elgar, Delius, Warlock, Holst, Walton, and Purcell. *Royal Phil. Orch.; Wordsworth, cond.*
+ ARG 5-6/96: 226

35051. TRP 039: BEETHOVEN—Symphonies no. 2, 8. *Royal Phil. Orch.; Lockhart, cond.*
+ Gr 11/95: 79

35052. TRP 040: COPLAND—Fanfare for the common man; Billy the Kid: Suite; El salón Mexico: Rodeo: Hoe-down; Appalachian spring: suite. *Royal Phil. Orch.; Ellis, cond.*
- Gr 12/95: 76

35053. TRP 043: MOZART—Piano concertos no. 21, 23. *O'Hora, piano;*

Royal Phil. Orch.; Carney, cond.
- Gr 1/96: 58

35054. TRP 045: MOZART—Piano concertos no. 20, 27. *Monetti, piano; Royal Phil. Orch.; Bolton, cond.*
- Gr 2/96: 52

35055. TRP 046: PROKOFIEV—Peter and the wolf. BIZET—Jeux d'enfants. SAINT-SAËNS—Carnival of the animals. *Gielgud, narrator; Royal Phil. Orch.; Licata, cond.*
+ Gr 11/95: 90

35056. TRP 048: TAVENER—The protecting veil; Thrinos; Eternal memory. *Wallfisch, cello; Royal Phil. Orch.; Brown, cond.*
+ ARG 7-8/96: 209
+ Gr 1/96: 65

35057. TRP 069: SATIE—Trois gymnopédies; Six gnossiennes; Cinq nocturnes; Trois embryons desséchés; Trois avant-dernières pensées; Valse-ballet; Fantaisie-valse; Je te veux. *O'Hora, piano.*
+ Gr 7/96: 78

TRIPLE LETTER BRAND

35058. 1409 (LP): Music of Ewazen, Lieman, Wuorinen, and Rzewski. *Taylor, bass trombone; various ensembles.*
+ Fa 7-8/87: 236

TRITONUS

35059. 5002: BRAHMS—Piano quintet. SCHUBERT—Piano sonata, D. 959. *Natochenny, piano; Penderecki Quartet.*
+ ARG 5-6/93: 74
+ Fa 7-8/93: 247

TRITTICO

35060. TCMA 27103: BEETHOVEN—Violin concerto. TCHAIKOVSKY—Violin concerto. *Vanessa-Mae, violin; London Symphony Orch.; Bakels, cond.*
+ Gr 11/92: 56

TROLD

35061. 03: GRIEG—Piano concerto op. 16; Solveig's song op. 55 no. 4; Morning mood op. 46 no. 1; Symphonic dance op. 64 no. 2; Last spring op. 34 no. 2. *Kayser, piano; Bergen Symphony Orch.; Andersen, cond.*
+ Fa 1-2/88: 131

TROLL

35062. DA-535: GRIEG—Piano sonata op. 7; Ballade op. 24; Lyric pieces op. 43 no. 1. *Schechter, piano.*
+ Fa 11-12/88: 194 m.f.

TRONIA DISC

35063. TRD 0190: DOLDEN—Threshold of deafening silence. *Electronic music.*
☐ Fa 3-4/91: 199

TROUBADISC

35064. TRO-CD 03 (2 discs): SMYTH—Violin sonata; String quintet; Cello sonata; String quartet. *Kupsa, violin; Verner, cello; Dutilly, piano; Fanny Mendelssohn Quartet.*
+ Fa 7-8/93: 88
+ Gr 7/94: 74

35065. TRO-CD 04: BACEWICZ—String quartets no. 4, 6-7. *Fanny Mendelssohn Quartet.*
+ Fa 7-8/93: 88

35066. TRO-CD 01405: SMYTH—Four songs for mezzo-soprano and chamber ensemble; Three songs for mezzo-soprano and piano; Double concerto for violin, horn and piano. *Paulsen, mezzo-soprano; Ethel Smyth Ensemble; Schmeller, cond.; Gassenhuber, piano; Eggebrecht-Kupsa, violin; Draxinger, horn; Dutilly, piano.*
+ Fa 7-8/93: 88
+ Gr 7/94: 74

35067. TRO-CD 01406: TAILLEFERRE—Chamber music. *Fanny Mendelssohn Quartet.*
+ Fa 9-10/93: 305

35068. TRO-CD 01407: N. BOULANGER—Songs and chamber music. *Paulsen, mezzo-soprano; Gassenhuber, piano; Kupsa, cello.*
+ Fa 1-2/94: 135

35069. TRO-CD 01408: HENSEL—Piano quartet in A♭; String quartet in E♭; Piano trio in D minor. *Mickisch, piano; Fanny Mendelssohn Quartet.*
- Fa 7-8/93: 179 (as 02)
+ Fa 9-10/94: 256

35070. TRO-CD 01409: MILHAUD—String quartets no. 1-2; Quatre poèmes de Léo Latil; Trois poèmes de Jean Cocteau. *Sonntag, soprano; Jansen, piano; Fanny Mendelssohn Quartet.*
- Fa 3-4/95: 231
+ Gr 5/95: 70

35071. TRO-CD 01410: MILHAUD—String quartets no. 3-5; Machines agricoles; Catalogue des fleurs. *Fanny Mendelssohn Quartet; Sonntag, soprano; Horowitz, cond.; Nolte, flute; Marshall, clarinet; Wiegel, bassoon; Eggebrecht, violin; Berg, viola; Kupsa, cello; György, double bass.*
- Fa 9-10/95: 264
+ Gr 6/96: 66

35072. TRO-CD 01411: MILHAUD—Quatre poèmes de Paul Claudel; Les soirées de Pétrograde; Poème du Journal

intime de Léo Latil; String quartets no. 6-8. *Koningsberger, baritone; Jansen, piano; Fanny Mendelssohn Quartet.*
- Fa 5-6/96: 210

35073. TRO-CD 01412: BLISS—String quartets no. 1-2. *Fanny Mendelssohn Quartet.*
- ARG 1-2/97: 77
- Fa 11-12/96: 195

TUDOR

35074. 701: MOZART—Flute quartets K. 285, 285a, 285b, 298. *Nicolet, flute; Munich String Trio.*
+ ARG 5-6/91: 88
- Fa 5-6/91: 235

35075. 702: STAMITZ—Concerto in G major for 2 flutes. ROSSINI—Introduction and variations for clarinet and orchestra. DANZI—Concertante for flute, clarinet, and orchestra in B♭ major. *A. & C. Nicolet, flutes; Brunner, clarinet; Württemberg Chamber Orch.; Faerber, cond.*
+ Fa 5-6/91: 289

35076. 703: MOZART—Piano concertos no. 8-9. *Dubourg, piano; Munich Chamber Orch.; Stadlmair, cond.*
- Fa 9-10/86: 191
- Fa 9-10/88: 208

35077. 705: PFITZNER—Six studies, op. 51; Aus dem Notenbuch des Elfjährigen; Liebesmelodie; Five piano pieces op. 47. *Schuchter, piano.*
+ Fa 1-2/91: 275
+ Gr 6/90: 83

35078. 706: LECLAIR—Deuxième récréation de musique op. 8; Flute sonata op. 9 no. 7; Sonata en trio op. 2 no. 8. *A. & C. Nicolet, flutes; Jaccottet, harpsichord; Mermound, viola da gamba.*
+ Fa 9-10/88: 181

35079. 707: SCARLATTI—Le quattro stagioni. *Lövaas, Marheineke, Bollen, Hopfner; Münchener Vokalsolisten; Munich Chamber Orch.; Hirsch, cond.* Issued also as LP: 73014.
☐ Fa 7-8/86: 221
- Fa 11-12/88: 269

35080. 709 (2 discs): VIVALDI—Cello sonata op. 14; Cello sonatas RV 39, 42, 44. *Starck, cello; Ahlgrimm, harpsichord; Frey, continuo cello.*
+ Fa 1-2/91: 347

35081. 710: DUPHLY—Harpsichord works, book 2. *Kiss, harpsichord.*
- Fa 11-12/87: 135

35082. 711: REGER—Clarinet sonatas op. 49 no. 1-2; Romanze in G for clarinet and piano. *Brunner, clarinet; Oppitz, piano.*
+ Fa 9-10/87: 274 m.f.

35083. 712: L. Mozart—Sinfonia in D major. Salulini—Dulcimer concerto. Jommelli—Sinfonia for dulcimer, strings, and continuo. *Schickhaus, dulcimer; Munich Chamber Orch.; Stadlmair, cond.*
+ Fa 9-10/87: 388
+ Fa 11-12/88: 228

35084. 713: Beethoven—Trio for piano, clarinet and cello op. 11; Duos for clarinet and bassoon WoO 27. *Leonskaja, piano; Brunner, clarinet; Boettcher, cello; Thunemann, bassoon.*
• Fa 9-10/87: 155

35085. 714: Anonymous—Gregorian chant. *Fribourg Cathedral Choir; Kaelin, cond.*
- Fa 1-2/90: 372

35086. 715: Music of Purcell, Frescobaldi, Haydn, Mozart, and others. *Athanasiàdes, organ.*
- Fa 11-12/88: 337

35087. 716: *Glockeninspirierte Klaviermusik.* Music of Borodin, Liszt, Schmitt, Debussy, Rachmaninoff, and others. *Schalker, piano.*
+ Fa 9-10/88: 328

35088. 717: Schoenberg—Chamber symphony no. 1 (arr. Webern). Zemlinsky—Trio for piano, clarinet and cello op. 3. *Adorján, flute; Brunner, clarinet; Sitkovetsky, violin; Geringas, cello; Oppitz, piano.*
+ Fa 9-10/88: 247

35089. 718: Danzi—Concertino for clarinet, bassoon, and orchestra op. 47; Fantasy on La ci darem la mano for clarinet and orchestra. C. Stamitz—Clarinet concerto no. 3; Concerto for clarinet, and bassoon in B♭. *Brunner, clarinet; Thunemann, bassoon; Munich Chamber Orch.; Stadlmair, cond.*
+ Fa 5-6/89: 240

35090. 719: *Musik der Renaissance.* Music of Josquin, Isaac, Senfl, Praetorius, and others. *Vienna Recorder Ensemble.*
- Fa 5-6/89: 381

35091. 720: Chopin—Scherzos (complete); Ballades no. 1-2; Prelude op. 28 no. 15; Fantasy op. 49; Barcarolle op. 60. *Cherkassky, piano.*
- ARG 3-4/91: 57
+ Fa 1-2/91: 177

35092. 721: Weber—Flute sonata no. 2. Franck—Violin sonata in A (arr. for flute). *Nicolet, flute; Berman, piano.*
+ ARG 3-4/91: 67
+ Fa 5-6/91: 321

35093. 723: Beethoven—Romances for violin (complete). Mozart—Violin concerto no. 5. *Ashkenasi, violin; Zürich Chamber Orch.; Stoutz, cond.*
+ Fa 5-6/89: 124

35094. 724: Reger—Quintet for clarinet and strings op. 146; Clarinet sonata op. 107; Album leaf for clarinet and piano in E♭; Tarantella for clarinet and piano in G minor. *Brunner, clarinet; Wilanów Quartet; Oppitz, piano.*
• ARG 3-4/90: 93
• Fa 5-6/90: 263
+ Gr 5/90: 2003

35095. 725: Music of Buxtehude, Bach, Mozart, Franck, and Athanasiàdes. *Athanasiàdes, organ.*
□ Fa 5-6/91: 357

35096. 726 (2 discs): Scriabin—Piano sonatas (complete). *Dubourg, piano.*
- ARG 3-4/89: 82
+ Fa 9-10/91: 354

35097. 727: Music of Prokofiev (arr. Bruner), Lobanov, and Shostakovich (arr. Bruner). *Brunner, clarinet; Adorján, flute; Lobanov, Levin, pianos.*
• Fa 5-6/91: 252

35098. 728: Music of Giampieri, Cimarosa, Rossini, Donizetti, and Mercadante. *Brunner, clarinet; Munich Chamber Orch.; Stadlmair, cond.*
+ ARG 3-4/91: 148
+ Fa 1-2/91: 395

35099. 729: Devienne—Flute concertos no. 9, 12, in G (op. posth.). *Adorján, flute; Munich Chamber Orch.; Stadlmair, cond.*
+ Fa 11-12/93: 216

35100. 730: Mercadante—Flute quartets in A minor, in C, in E minor, in A. *Adorján, flute; Münchner Streichtrio.*
+ ARG 5-6/91: 84
+ Fa 1-2/91: 242
+ Gr 6/90: 71

35101. 731/34 (4 discs): Debussy—Piano music (complete). *Boguet, piano.*
• Fa 1-2/91: 185

35102. 735: Music of Vivaldi, B. Marcello, Carissimi, and Mancini. *Quadro Saltero; Schickhaus, dulcimer.*
• ARG 11-12/89: 168
- Fa 1-2/90: 408
+ Fa 7-8/91: 378

35103. 736: Music of Conti, Chiesa, Monza, and Beretti. *K. Schickhaus, dulcimer; J. Schickhaus, harpsichord.*
+ Fa 7-8/91: 378

35104. 737: L. Mozart—Musical sleighride; Cassation in G major "Toy symphony"; Symphony in D major; Sinfonia da caccia "Hunting symphony". *Münchener Kammerorchester; Stadlmair, cond.*
• Fa 1-2/97: 209

35105. 738: Anon.—Sonatas: V in E minor; VIII in D major; IX in F major; Divertimento in B minor. *Schickhaus,*

dulcimer.
+ Fa 1-2/92: 146

35106. 739: C. Stamitz—Clarinet concertos no. 1, 7, 8, 11. *Brunner, clarinet; Munich Chamber Orch.; Stadlmair, cond.*
+ Fa 11-12/93: 407

35107. 740: C. Stamitz—Clarinet concertos no. 6, 10; Concerto for violin, clarinet, and orchestra; Concerto for clarinet, bassoon, and orchestra. *Brunner, clarinet; Chumachenko, violin; Thunemann, bassoon; Münchner Kammerorchester; Stadlmair, cond.*
+ Fa 3-4/95: 306

35108. 741/43 (3 discs): Schubert—*Complete piano works, vol. 1.* Sonatas D. 459/459a, 625, 845, 840; Sonata fragment D. 571; Scherzo D. 570; Huttenbrenner variations D. 576; Fantasy D. 605a; Hungarian melody D. 817; 12 noble waltzes D. 969; Adagio D. 178; German dances K. 783; Moments musicaux D. 780; Ecossaises D. 145; Waltz D. 844 . *Schuchter, piano.*
• ARG 11-12/89: 113
• Fa 9-10/89: 315

35109. 744/46 (3 discs): Schubert—*Complete piano works, vol. 2.* Sonatas D. 279, 537, 567, 575, 664; Piano pieces D. 604; Impromptus D. 935; German dances D. 974; Ecossaises D. 781; Allegretto D. 915; scherzo D. 593/II; Diabelli variation D. 718; Fantasy D. 2e; March D. 606; Sentimental waltzes D. 779; Impromptus D. 899. *Schuchter, piano.*
• ARG 11-12/89: 113
- Fa 9-10/89: 316

35110. 747/49 (3 discs): Schubert—*Complete piano works, vol. 3.* Variation D. 156; Sonatas D. 157, 784, 949, 958; Ecossaises with German dance D. 722, 783; Piano pieces D. 946; Fantasy with Andante D. 29, 605; Fantasy D. 760; Adagio D. 612. *Schuchter, piano.*
• ARG 11-12/89: 113
+ Fa 11-12/89: 347

35111. 750/52 (3 discs): Schubert—*Complete piano works, vol. 4.* Sonatas D. 557, 568: Minuet, 850, 894, 960; Sonata in E minor with rondo in E minor D. 506/566; Erste Waltzer D. 365 no. 1-2; Cotillon D. 976; Scherzo D. 593 no. 1; Allegretto D. 900; Galopp and 8 ecossaises D. 735; Twelve German dances D. 790. *Schuchter, piano.*
• ARG 11-12/89: 113
+ Fa 11-12/89: 347

35112. 753: Du Phly—Pièces de clavecin, books III and IV. *Kiss, harpsichord.*
+ Fa 1-2/92: 203

35113. 754: M. Haydn—Missa S. Leopoldi; Vespers. Mozart—Andante, K. 616. Haydn—Five pieces for flute- clock.

TUDOR

Zürich Boys Choir; Capella Concertante; Aarburg, cond.
- Fa 3-4/93: 187

35114. 755: Reger—Serenades for flute, violin, and viola no. 1-2; Romance for flute and piano; Allegretto grazioso for flute and piano; Suite for flute and piano, op. 103a. *Adorján, flute; Chumachenko, violin; Lysy, viola; Kontarsky, piano.*
+ Fa 3-4/95: 273

35115. 756: *Hungarian fantasy.* Music of Andersen, Bartók, Farkas, Dohnányi, Doppler, Kocsár, Terschak, and W. Popp. *Adorján, flute; Ivaldi, piano.*
+ Fa 3-4/93: 362
- Fa 11-12/93: 483

35116. 757: Krommer—Sinfonia concertante, op. 80. Schnyder von Wartensee—Concerto for 2 clarinets and orchestra. *Graf, flute; Stadler, Friedli, clarinets; Wicky, violin; Ensemble Capriccio Zürich.*
+ Fa 5-6/93: 240

35117. 760: Janáček—In the mist; Piano sonata; On an overgrown path, series 1 and 2; In the mist: 4th movement (1st version). *Mishory, piano.*
+ Fa 1-2/92: 242

35118. 761 (2 discs): Brahms—Die schöne Magelone. *Holzmair, baritone; Quadflieg, speaker; Wyss, piano.*
• Fa 1-2/88: 98
+ Fa 3-4/91: 164
• Gr 5/92: 80

35119. 762: Schubert—Lieder. *Holzmair, baritone; Wyss, piano.*
+ Fa 3-4/92: 311
+ Gr 12/91: 118

35120. 763: Mercadante—Chamber music for flutes. *Adorján, Nicolet, Henkel, flutes; Liu, harp; Edelmann, bassoon; Salewski, English horn; Berger, cello.*
+ Fa 1-2/97: 150

35121. 764: Schubert—Lieder. *Holzmair, baritone; Wyss, piano.*
• Fa 11-12/93: 379
+ Gr 1/93: 56

35122. 765: Devienne—Flute concertos no. 4-7. *Adorján, flute; Munich Chamber Orch.; Stadlmair, cond.*
+ Fa 1-2/97: 150

35123. 766: Comme-ci, comme-ça: hommage à Georges Boulanger. *Original Salon-Ensemble Prima-Carezza.*
+ Fa 1-2/92: 423

35124. 767: *Pastorale con salterio.* Music of Eberlin, Rathgeber, Corelli, Vivaldi, Noëlli, and Gruber. *Schichkaus, hammered dulcimer; Ensemble Pantaleon.*
• Fa 11-12/93: 515

35125. 768: J.C. Bach—Sinfonias for winds no. 1-6. *Swiss Wind Soloists.*
• Fa 11-12/93: 168

35126. 769: Scarlatti—Sonatas. *Francesch, piano.* Reissue.
+ Fa 11-12/93: 372

35127. 771: Brahms—Horn trio, op. 40. Koechlin—Quatre petites pièces. Banks—Horntrio. *Tuckwell, horn; Langbein, violin; Jones, piano.*
+ Fa 3-4/92: 165

35128. 774: *Variations.* Music of Schubert, Silcher, Beethoven, Chopin, and Gieseking. *Adorján, flute; Kontarsky, piano.* Recorded 1991.
+ Fa 3-4/95: 373

35129. 775: C. Stamitz—Clarinet concertos no. 2-5. *Brunner, clarinet; Munich Chamber Orch.; Stadlmair, cond.*
+ ARG 11-12/94: 193

35130. 776: Mozart—Serenade no. 13 "Eine kleine Nachtmusik"; Quartet no. 1 for flute and strings; Concertone for 2 violins, oboe, cello, and orchestra. *Füri, violin; Camerata Bern; Turpie, violin; Pellerin, oboe; Demenga, cello; Nicolet, flute; Munich String Trio.*
• Fa 11-12/93: 336

35131. 777: Ravel—Piano music. *Francesch, piano.*
• ARG 7-8/94: 157

35132. 781: Ravel—Selected piano works. *Francesch, piano.*
- Fa 3-4/95: 272

35133. 784: Raff—Symphony no. 8; Ode to spring. *Aronsky, piano; Basel Radio Symphony Orch.; Lehel, Meier, conds.* Reissue.
• Fa 1-2/97: 233

35134. 785: Raff—Symphony no. 9 "In summer"; Piano concerto, op. 185. *Aronsky, piano; Basel Radio Symphony Orch.; Auberson, Bamert, conds.*
• Fa 3-4/95: 269

35135. 786: Raff—Symphony no. 10 (Autumn); Eine feste Burg overture. *Basel Radio Symphony Orch.; Travis, Steinberg, conds.*
+ ARG 3-4/94: 140

35136. 787: Raff—Symphony no. 11; Sinfonietta. *Basel Radio Symphony; Venzago, Joho, conds.*
+ ARG 5-6/94: 127

35137. 788: C. Schumann—Concerto for piano and orchestra, op. 7; Trio for violin, cello, and piano, op. 17; Three romances for violin and piano, op. 22. *Jochum, piano; Bamberger Symphoniker; Silverstein, violin & cond.; Carr, cello.*
• Fa 3-4/93: 279

35138. 791: Schubert—Goethe songs. *Holzmair, baritone; Wyss, piano.*
+ ARG 11-12/94: 187

35139. 792: Reinecke—Flute sonata "Undine"; Ballade for flute and piano; Suite for flute and piano "Vom der Wiege bis zum Grabe"; Sonatinas no. 1-3 for flute and piano. *Adorján, flute; Ivaldi, piano.*
+ Fa 1-2/97: 236

35140. 796: Brahms—Piano trios no. 1-2. *Trio Novanta.*
+ Fa 1-2/96: 160

35141. 797: Brahms—Piano trios no. 1 (1st version, 1854); no. 3. *Trio Novanta.*
+ Fa 5-6/95: 152

35142. 798: Mozart—Trio for clarinet, viola, and piano, K. 498. Reinecke—Trio for clarinet, viola, and piano, op. 264; Flute sonata, op. 167. *Leister, clarinet; Schiller, viola; Francesch, piano; Adorján, flute; Ivaldi, piano.* Recorded 1987 and 1991.
+ ARG 3-4/95: 150
+ Fa 3-4/95: 244

35143. 799: Danzi—Potpourris for clarinet and orchestra no. 1-3; Concertino for clarinet, bassoon, and orchestra, op. 47; Concertante for flute, clarinet, and orchestra, op. 41. *Brunner, clarinet; Thunemann, bassoon; Nicolet, flute; Munich Chamber Orch.; Stadlmair, cond.; Wurttemburg Chamber Orch.; Faerber, cond.*
+ Fa 5-6/95: 178

35144. 7001: Krommer—Partitas for winds and double bass, op. 57, 67, 69, 79. *Zürich Wind Octet.*
+ Fa 1-2/97: 187

35145. 7003: Janáček—Zdenka variations; In memoriam; Music for exercises with clubs; Reminiscence; Violin sonata; Romance; Dumka; Fairy tale; Presto; March of the blue-breasts. *Mishory, piano; Gawriloff, violin; Yang, cello; Adorján, piccolo.*
• Fa 1-2/97: 180

35146. 7004: K. Stamitz—Clarinet concertos no. 6, 10; Clarinet and violin concerto; Clarinet and bassoon concerto. *Brunner, clarinet; Thunemann, bassoon; Chumachenko, violin; Munich Chamber Orch.; Stadlmair, cond.*
+ ARG 3-4/96: 187

35147. 7008: J. Stamitz—Clarinet concerto in B♭ major. Hoffmeister—Clarinet concerto no. 2. Pokorny—Clarinet concertos no. 1-2. *Brunner, clarinet; Munchener Kammerorchester; Stadlmair, cond.*
+ Fa 1-2/97: 277

35148. 7011—7012 (2 separate discs): Mozart—The complete piano works, vol.

1-2. *Schuchter, piano.*
• Fa 1-2/97: 215

35149. 7021: VIOTTI—Three quartets for flute and strings, op. 22. *Petrucci, flute; Kodály Quartet.*
+ Fa 1-2/97: 298

35150. 7022: KROMMER—Quartets no. 1-2 for oboe, violin, viola, and cello. FIALA—Quartets no. 1-2 for oboe, violin, viola, and cello. *Fuchs, oboe; Novák Trio.*
+ Fa 1-2/97: 188

73014 see 707.

35151. 73036 (LP): MOZART—Mass in C major K. 317; Exsultate jubilate; Ave verum corpus. *Schlick, Bardot, D'Hollander; Chorale & Orch. Paul Kuentz; Kuentz, cond.*
- Fa 7-8/86: 190

TURNIPSEED

35152. 11: *Dancing on glass.* Music of Weigl, Ganucheau, and Battiste. *Various performers.*
+ ARG 11-12/96: 307

TUTL

35153. 5: BLAK—Two string quartets; The Queen of Bohmen for violin; Nadn for violin and guitar; Elinborg for quartet; Ariettes for cello. *Moyzes String Quartet; Zsapka, guitar.*
+ ARG 11-12/92: 90

35154. 6: Music of Petersen, Rasmussen, Blak, Debess, and Meitl. *Boreas Wind Quintet.*
+ ARG 7-8/94: 221

TUXEDO

35155. 1026: HUMMEL—Mandolin concerto; Violin sonata; Partita. *Bauer-Slais, mandolin; Topolsy, violin; Kann, piano; Collegium Musicum Prague; Vienna Pro Musica; Hladky, cond.* Reissue.
□ ARG 7-8/96: 135

35156. 1051: MOZART—Requiem. *Lipp, Höngen, Dickie, Weber; Academy Chamber Choir; Vienna Symphony Orch.; Horenstein, cond.*
+ ARG 11-12/92: 167

35157. 1054: HUMPERDINCK—Sleeping beauty suite; King's children suite; Handel and Gretel suite. *Vienna State Opera Orch.; Swarowsky, cond.*
+ ARG 11-12/92: 137
- ARG 7-8/96: 135

35158. 1061: HINDEMITH—Requiem. *Höngen, Braun; Vienna Symphony Orch. & Chorus; Hindemith, cond.* Recorded 1956.
+ ARG 7-8/96: 133

35159. 5032: *Sousa and American marches.* Music of Sousa, Sweet, Lighten, Klohr, Seitz, J.F. Wagner, Teike, and Beethoven. *West Point Military Band; Donally, cond.*
- Fa 9-10/96: 448

TZADIK

35160. 7012: PARTCH—Lyrics of Li Po. *Kalm, voice; Mook, tenor violin.*
• ARG 9-10/96: 176

ULTRAPHON

35161. 11 1337-2: *Emmy Destinn.* Music of Mozart, Weber, Wagner, Gounod, Bizet, Thomas, Smetana, Tchaikovsky, Verdi, Ponchielli, Leoncavallo, Mascagni, Puccini, and Strauss. *Destinn, soprano; orch. acc.* Recorded 1906-16.
+ Fa 1-2/94: 363
+ Gr 5/94: 136

UMMUS

35162. UMM 103: PRÉVOST—Sonates and improvisations. *Turovsky, cello; J.-E. Vaillancourt, piano; Landsman, violin; P. Vaillancourt, soprano; Baril, piano; Puchhammer-Sédillot, viola.*
+ Fa 9-10/94: 289

35163. UMM 106: *Nouvelle Ensemble Moderne: forum 91.* Music of Cherney, Oña, and Gervasoni. *La Nouvel Ensemble Moderne; Vaillancourt, cond.*
+ Fa 5-6/94: 332

35164. UMM 304: *A tre violini.* Music of G. Gabrieli, Marini, Fontana, Uccellini, Schmelzer, Purcell, Dornel, Boismortier, Telemann, and Pachelbel. *Ensemble Da Sonar.*
+ Fa 5-6/94: 339

UNICAL

35165. 9102: Trios by Archer, C. Schumann, Storace, and Shostakovich. *Hertz Trio.*
• ARG 5-6/94: 174

35166. 9501: Sonatas by Archer, Barber, Copland, and Jordan. *Foreman, piano.*
• ARG 7-8/96: 249

UNICORN-KANCHANA

35167. UK CD 2035: GRIEG—Lyric pieces: Book VIII, op. 65; Book IX, op. 68; Book X, op. 71. *Katin, piano.*
- Fa 9-10/91: 225
+ Gr 2/91: 1534

35168. UK CD 2036: BRAHMS—Symphony no. 2; Serenade no. 2. *Danish Radio Symphony Orch.; Horenstein, cond.* Recorded live 1972.
+ Gr 9/91: 60

35169. UK CD 2039: GOEHR—Metamorphosis/Dance, op. 36; Romanza, op. 24. *Welsh, cello; Royal Liverpool Phil. Orch.; Atherton, cond.* Reissue.
+ Gr 7/91: 46

35170. UK CD 2043: WOOD—Violin concerto; Cello concerto. *Parikian, violin; Welsh, cello; Royal Liverpool Phil. Orch.; Atherton, cond.*
+ Fa 9-10/91: 400

35171. UK CD 2044: *Renaissance and baroque realizations.* Music of Purcell, Bach, Dunstable; Three early Scottish motets. Kinloch his fantassie. *Fires of London; Davies, cond.* Reissue.
+ Fa 1-2/92: 262

35172. UK CD 2045: *Virtuoso French organ music.* BOELLMANN—Suite gothique. GUILMANT—Cantilène pastorale; March on Lift up your heads. SAINT-SAËNS—Improvisation no. 7. GIGOUT—Toccata; Scherzo; Grand choeur dialogué. *Bate, organ.*
• Fa 9-10/91: 419

35173. UK CD 2046: BARBER—Symphony no. 1; Essays 1 and 2; Night flight. *London Symphony Orch.; Measham, cond.* Reissue.
• ARG 3-4/92: 24
- Fa 7-8/92: 111

35174. UK CD 2047: GRIEG—Holberg suite; Elegiac melodies. NIELSEN—Little suite. SIBELIUS—Rakastava. *Little Orch. of London; Jones, cond.* Reissue.
• Gr 9/92: 100

35175. UK CD 2048: WIENIAWSKI—Virtuoso showpieces. *Ricci, violin; Gruenberg, piano.* Reissue.
+ Gr 6/92: 63

35176. UK CD 2049 : BULLER—Proença. The theatre of memory. *Walker, mezzo-soprano; BBC Symphony Orch.; Elder, cond.*
+ Gr 11/92: 168

35177. UK CD 2050/52 (3 discs): HERRMANN—Wuthering Heights. *Beaton, Bell, Kitchiner; Pro Arte Orch.; Herrmann, cond.* Reissue.
□ ARG 11-12/92: 135
- Fa 11-12/92: 256
+ Gr 8/93: 80

35178. UK CD 2056: GRIEG—Olav Trygvason; Landkjenning; Peer Gynt choral scenes. *Oslo Phil. Chorus; London Symphony Orch.; Dreier, cond.*
□ ARG 7-8/92: 137

35179. UK CD 2057: L. JOHNSON—Symphony "Synthesis"; The wind in the willows; Three paintings by Lautrec; Royal tour suite. *Various ensembles; Johnson, cond.*
+ ARG 7-8/93: 107
+ Fa 1-2/93: 171

35180. UK CD 2059: Music of Chavez, Galindo, Moncayo, and Halffter. *National Symphony Orch. of Mexico; Klein, cond.* Reissue.
+ ARG 9-10/93: 226

35181. UK CD 2060: BRITTEN—Early chamber music. *Wickens, oboe; Constable, piano; Gabireli Quartet; Essex, viola.* Reissues.
+ Gr 6/93: 58

35182. UK CD 2061: HERRMANN—Moby Dick: cantata; For the fallen. *Amis, tenor; Kelly, baritone; Aeolian Singers; London Phil. Orch.; Herrmann, cond.* Reissue.
+ ARG 9-10/93: 135
+ Fa 11-12/93: 272

35183. UK CD 2062: VAUGHAN WILLIAMS—On Wenlock Edge. IRELAND—Overlanders suite; Epic march. *English, tenor; West Australian Symphony Orch.; Measham, cond.*
+ ARG 9-10/93: 210

35184. UK CD 2063: HERRMANN— Symphony no. 1; The fantasticks. *Dickinson, Humphreys, Rippon, Amis; National Phil. Orch.; Herrmann, cond.* Reissues.
+ ARG 11-12/94: 130
+ Gr 1/94: 48

35185. UK CD 2065: HERRMANN—Film music. *London Phil. Orch.; Hermann, cond.*
+ ARG 9-10/94: 144
+ ARG 11-12/94: 130

35186. UKCD 2066: MIASKOVSKY— Symphony no. 21. KABALEVSKY— Symphony no. 2. SHOSTAKOVICH—Hamlet (excerpts). *New Philharmonia Orch.; Measham, cond.; National Phil. Orch.; Herrmann, cond.* Reissues.
+ ARG 11-12/94: 158
• Fa 7-8/95: 244
+ Gr 2/95: 46

35187. UK CD 2067: BACH—Violin concertos. *Ricci, violin & cond.; City of London Ensemble.* Reissue.
+ Fa 7-8/95: 104
+ Gr 10/94: 98

35188. UK CD 2068: DAVIES—Vesalii icones; The bairns of Brugh; Runes from a holy land. *Fires of London; Davies, cond.* Reissue.
□ Fa 7-8/95: 239
+ Gr 2/95: 48

35189. UK CD 2069: HERRMANN— Quintet for clarinet and strings (Souvenirs de voyage); String quartet (Echoes). *Hill, clarinet; Ariel Quartet; Amici Quartet.* Reissue.
+ Fa 11-12/95: 276
+ Gr 5/95: 70

35190. UK CD 2070: *French romantic organ music.* Music of Tournemire,

Hakim, Alain, Langlais, Franck, and Duruflé. *Bertram, organ.*
+ Fa 7-8/95: 423

35191. UK CD 2071: *The Delius collection, vol. 1.* DELIUS—Orchestral and piano works. *Parkin, piano; Ambrosian Singers; Royal Phil. Orch.; Fenby, Del Mar, conds.* Reissue.
+ Fa 11-12/95: 239
+ Gr 8/95: 68

35192. UK CD 2072: *The Delius collection, vol. 2.* DELIUS—Irmelin prelude; A song of summer; A late lark; Concertos. *Holmes, violin; Fowke, piano; Rolfe Johnson, tenor; Royal Phil. Orch.; Fenby, Del Mar, Handley, conds.* Reissue.
+ ARG 11-12/95: 111
+ Fa 11-12/95: 239
+ Gr 8/95: 68

35193. UK CD 2073: *The Delius collection, vol. 3.* DELIUS—The walk to the Paradise garden; Songs of sunset; Idyll; La Calinda. *Lott, soprano; Walker, mezzo-soprano; Allen, baritone; Ambrosian Singers; Royal Phil. Orch.; Fenby, Del Mar, conds.* Reissue.
+ Fa 11-12/95: 239
+ Gr 8/95: 68

35194. UK CD 2074: *The Delius collection, vol. 4.* DELIUS—Violin sonatas; Cello sonata. *Lloyd Webber, cello; Holmes, violin; Fenby, piano.* Reissue.
+ ARG 11-12/95: 112
+ Fa 11-12/95: 239
+ Gr 8/95: 92

35195. UK CD 2075: DELIUS—The Delius collection, vol. 5. *Lott, Walker, Rolfe Johnson, vocal soloists; Royal Phil. Orch.; Fenby, cond.*
+ Fa 3-4/96: 156
+ Gr 4/96: 85

35196. UK CD 2076: DELIUS—The Delius collection, vol. 6. *Holmes, violin; Allen, baritone; Ambrosian Singers; Royal Phil. Orch.; Fenby, Handley, Del Mar, conds.*
+ Fa 3-4/96: 156
+ Gr 4/96: 85

35197. UK CD 2077: DELIUS—The Delius collection, vol. 7. *Holmes, violin; Lloyd Webber, cello; Allen, baritone; Ambrosian Singers; Royal Phil. Orch.; Fenby, Handley, Del Mar, conds.*
+ Fa 3-4/96: 156
+ Gr 4/96: 85

35198. UK CD 2078: ENESCO—Marot songs. ROUSSEL—Songs. DEBUSSY— Songs. *Walker, mezzo-soprano; Vignoles, piano.* Reissue.
+ ARG 11-12/96: 275

35199. DKP CD 7147/8 (2 discs): CHOPIN—Twenty-one nocturnes; Fantasie-impromptu, op. posth. 66;

Barcarolle, op. 60. *Stott, piano.*
+ Fa 9-10/95: 176

35200. DKP CD 9054: NIELSEN— Springtime in Funen; Aladdin suite. *Nielsen, soprano; Binzer, tenor; Kunt, baritone; Lille Muko Choir; Odense Symphony Orch.; Vetö, cond.* Reissue.
+ ARG 11-12/96: 172

35201. DKP CD 9084: BEETHOVEN— Diabelli variations. *Hill, piano.*
+ Fa 11-12/91: 269
+ Gr 11/91: 127

35202. DKP CD 9092: GRIEG—Quartet. SCHUMANN—Quartet no. 3. *English String Quartet.*
• ARG 5-6/92: 65
+ Gr 3/92: 69

35203. DKP CD 9097: STEVENS—Theme and variations for string quartet, op. 11; String quartet no. 2, op. 34; Lyric suite for string trio, op. 30. *Delmé String Quartet.*
+ ARG 11-12/91: 149
+ Fa 9-10/91: 364
+ Gr 6/91: 63

35204. DKP CD 9098: WESLEY— Symphonies no. 3-6. *Milton Keynes Chamber Orch.; Wetton, cond.*
+ ARG 9-10/91: 149
• Fa 9-10/91: 397
+ Gr 10/91: 118

35205. DKP CD 9102: GOEHR—A musical offering (J.S.B. 1985); Behold the sun; Lyric pieces; Sinfonia. *London Sinfonietta; Knussen, cond.; Thames, soprano.*
+ Fa 11-12/91: 325
+ Gr 11/91: 89

35206. DKP CD 9104—9105 (2 separate discs): *From Stanley to Wesley, vol. 4-5.* Works by Dupuis, Greene, Handel, Roseingrave, Stanley, Wesley, Burney, Keeble and Walond. *Bate, organ.*
+ EM 2/92: 188 (v. 1-6)
+ Gr 7/91: 91

35207. DKP CD 9106: *From Stanley to Wesley, vol. 6.* Music of Boyce, Handel, Heron, Hook, Russell, Stanley, Stubley, and S. Wesley. *Bate, organ.*
+ EM 2/92: 188
+ Gr 11/91: 134

35208. DKP CD 9107: MOZART—Oboe quartet K. 370; Quintet, K. 406; Divertimento no. 11. *Watkins, oboe; Amadeus Ensemble.*
+ Fa 9-10/91: 290
+ Gr 9/91: 91

35209. DKP CD 9108: DELIUS—Paris; Life's dance; Piano concerto; Dance rhapsody no. 1. *Fowke, piano; Royal Phil. Orch.; Del Mar, cond.*
+ ARG 5-6/92: 46
+ Gr 3/92: 40

35210. DKP CD 9109: PURCELL—Hail! Bright Cecilia. CALDARA—Laudate pueri Dominum. *Fiori Musicali Choir and Orch.; Rapson, cond.*
+ Fa 11-12/91: 447
+ Gr 10/91: 170

35211. DKP CD 9110: KUHLAU— Elverhoj overture; Concertino for two horns, op. 45; Piano concerto, op. 7. *Ponti, piano; Odense Symphony Orch.; Maga, cond.*
+ ARG 9-10/91: 85
+ Fa 11-12/91: 362
+ Gr 9/91: 65

35212. DKP CD 9111: IVES—Songs, vol. 1. *Herford, baritone; Bowman, piano.*
+ ARG 5-6/92: 74
- Fa 1-2/92: 241
+ Gr 9/91: 113

35213. DKP CD 9112: IVES—Songs, vol. 2. *Herford, baritone; Bowman, piano.*
• Gr 3/92: 103

35214. DKP CD 9113: BUTTERWORTH— Six songs from A Shropshire lad. VAUGHAN WILLIAMS—The house of life; Linden Lea; In the spring. *B. Cook, baritone; Benson, piano.*
- ARG 5-6/92: 42

35215. DKP CD 9114: RUDERS—Violin concerto no. 1; Clarinet concerto; Drama trilogy for cello and orchestra. *Hirsch, violin; Thomsen, clarinet; Zeuthen, cello; Odense Symphony Orch.; Vetö, cond.*
+ Fa 5-6/92: 235
+ Gr 4/92: 75

35216. DKP CD 9115: DVOŘÁK— Cypresses; Biblical songs. *Langridge, tenor; Kvapil, piano.*
+ ARG 3-4/92: 51
+ Fa 3-4/92: 187

35217. DKP CD 9116: ELGAR—Part songs. VAUGHAN WILLIAMS—Festival Te Deum in F; Mass in G minor. *Holst Singers; Wetton, cond.*
- ARG 5-6/92: 56
+ Gr 4/92: 125

35218. DKP CD 9117 : MENDELSSOHN— Symphonies no. 1, 5. *Milton Keynes Chamber Orch.; Wetton, cond.*
+ Gr 2/93: 44

35219. DKP CD 9118: BEETHOVEN— Variations on Ich bin der Schneider Kakadu; Allegretto, WoO 39; Piano trio, op. 38. *Raphael Trio.*
+ Gr 4/92: 93

35220. DKP CD 9119, 9124 (2 separate discs): D. SCARLATTI—Late cantatas, vol. 2-3. *Eckersley, soprano; Fiori Musicali; Rapson, cond.*
- Fa 11-12/92: 354
+ Gr 5/92: 96
+ Gr 9/92: 151

35221. DKP CD 9120: MAHLER—Songs (orch. Matthews). *Gomez, soprano; Bournemouth Sinfonietta; Carewe, cond.*
+ ARG 7-8/93: 122

35222. DKP CD 9121: Music of Arnold, Bowen, Britten, Dring, Rubbra, and Vaughan Williams. *Polmear, oboe, English horn; Ambache, piano.*
+ Gr 9/92: 124

35223. DKP CD 9122/3 (2 discs): MESSIAEN—Vingt regards sur l'Enfant-Jésus. *Hill, piano.*
- ARG 11-12/92: 161
+ Fa 9-10/94: 256
+ Gr 9/92: 135

35224. DKP CD 9125: D. SCARLATTI— Late cantatas, vol. 4. *Eckersley, Van Evera, sopranos; Sharman, cello; Roberts, harpsichord.*
- Fa 5-6/93: 311

35225. DKP CD 9126: CROTCH— Symphonies in F and E♭ (fragment); Organ concerto in A; Overture in G. *Lumsden, organ; Milton Keynes Chamber Orch.; Wetton, cond.*
+ ARG 9-10/92: 95
- Fa 11-12/92: 222
+ Gr 1/93: 39

35226. DKP CD 9127: GRAINGER—Piano music. *Thwaites, piano.*
+ ARG 5-6/93: 87
+ Gr 3/93: 71

35227. DKP CD 9128: TELEMANN— Concertos for oboe, strings and continuo: in E♭; in E minor; in D "Concerto gratioso"; in F minor; Concerto in G for oboe d'amore, strings and continuo. *Francis, oboe & oboe d'amore, cond.; London Harpsichord Ensemble.*
+ Fa 5-6/93: 341
+ Gr 4/93: 82

35228. DKP CD 9129: GOEHR—Sing, Ariel; The mouse metamorphosed into a maid. *Shelton, Hulse, Leonard, sopranos; Instrumental Ensemble; Knussen, cond.*
+ ARG 7-8/93: 96
+ Gr 9/93: 98

35229. DKP CD 9130: CALDARA— Madrigals and cantatas. *Wren Baroque Soloists; Elliot, cond.*
• Fa 7-8/93: 122
+ Gr 2/93: 64

35230. DKP CD 9131: TELEMANN—Oboe concertos, vol. 2. *Francis, oboe & oboe d'amore; London Harpsichord Ensemble.*
+ Fa 3-4/94: 109
+ Gr 8/94: 62

35231. DKP CD 9132: KUHLAU—Elf hill: overture and ballet music; Three overtures. *Odense Symphony Orch.; Maga, Serov, conds.*
+ ARG 5-6/93: 100

• Fa 7-8/93: 164
+ Gr 5/93: 47

35232. DKP CD 9133: DEBUSSY—Songs. *Leblanc, soprano; Tryon, piano.*
+ ARG 7-8/93: 80
+ Gr 4/93: 106

35233. DKP CD 9134: ARENSKY— Variations on a theme of Tchaikovsky. TCHAIKOVSKY—Souvenir de Florence; String quartet no. 1: Andante cantabile. *Primavera Chamber Orch.; Manley, cond.*
+ Gr 3/93: 33

35234. DKP CD 9137: DVOŘÁK—Theme and variations; Poetic tone pictures. *Kvapil, piano.*
• ARG 9-10/93: 115
+ Gr 8/93: 58

35235. DKP CD 9138: BRITTEN—Cabaret songs. PORTER—Songs. *Gomez, soprano; M. Jones, piano.*
+ ARG 1-2/94: 85
+ Gr 9/93: 95

35236. DKP CD 9139: SMETANA—Czech dances; Bagatelles and impromptus. *Kvapil, piano.*
+ Gr 10/93: 86

35237. DKP CD 9140: MARTINŮ—Piano music. *Kvapil, piano.*
+ Gr 12/93: 89

35238. DKP CD 9142: CAPLET—Songs. *LeBlanc, soprano; Sharon, piano.*
+ ARG 1-2/95: 95
+ Fa 7-8/95: 148

35239. DKP CD 9143: LUMBYE— Orchestra music. *Odense Symphony Orch.; Guth, cond.*
+ Fa 5-6/94: 182
+ Gr 2/94: 44

35240. DKP CD 9144: MESSIAEN—Pièce pour le tombeau de Paul Dukas; Fantaisie burlesque; Rondeau; Petites esquisses d'oiseaux; Visions de l'amen. *Hill, Frith, pianos.*
+ Fa 9-10/94: 256
+ Gr 6/94: 83

35241. DKP CD 9145: VORISEK— Impromptus, op. 7; Fantasia, op. 12; Variations in B♭, op. 19; Piano sonata in B♭ minor, op. 20. *Kvapil, piano.*
+ Fa 5-6/94: 276
+ Gr 6/94: 88

35242. DKP CD 9146: GOEHR—The death of Moses. *Leonard, Chance, Rangarajan, Richardson; choirs; instrumental ensemble; Cleobury, cond.*
+ Fa 7-8/95: 191
+ Gr 12/93: 99

35243. DKP CD 9147/8 (2 discs): CHOPIN—Nocturnes, Fantaisie

impromptu; Barcarolle. *Stott, piano.*
+ Gr 7/94: 79

35244. DKP CD 9149: FIBICH—Piano music. *Kvapil, piano.*
+ ARG 11-12/94: 111
+ Fa 7-8/95: 184
+ Gr 10/94: 158

35245. DKP CD 9150: CAMILLERI—Piano concertos no. 1-3. *A. de Groote, piano; Bournemouth Symphony Orch.; Laus, cond.*
+ ARG 11-12/94: 88
+ Fa 7-8/95: 147
+ Gr 9/94: 50

35246. DKP CD 9151: CAMILLERI—Organ works. *Bowyer, organ.*
+ Fa 7-8/95: 148
+ Gr 11/95: 124

35247. DKP CD 9152: SMETANA—Piano music. *Kvapil, piano.*
+ ARG 5-6/95: 179
+ Fa 7-8/95: 325
+ Gr 2/95: 75

35248. DKP CD 9153: HANDEL—Oboe concertos and sonatas. *Francis, oboe & cond.; London Harpsichord Ensemble; Dodd, harpsichord; Richards, cello; Stevens, Wallace, violins.*
● Fa 3-4/95: 181
+ Gr 8/95: 72

35249. DKP CD 9154: JANÁČEK—Moravian folk poetry in songs (excerpts). *Kloubová, soprano; Vodička, tenor; Kvapil, piano.*
+ ARG 9-10/95: 161
+ Fa 7-8/95: 213
+ Gr 4/95: 98

35250. DKP CD 9155: *Les charmes de la vie.* MILHAUD—Piano music. SATIE—Cinq grimaces. *Sharon, piano.*
+ ARG 5-6/95: 140
+ Fa 7-8/95: 246
+ Gr 5/95: 84

35251. DKP CD 9156: JANÁČEK—On an overgrown path, books 1-2; I X 1905: piano sonata; In the mist. *Kvapil, piano.*
● ARG 1-2/96: 126
+ Fa 11-12/95: 281
+ Gr 11/95: 124

35252. DKP CD 9157: CAMILLERI—Choral works. *Colston, tenor; Rees-Jones, baritone; Joyful Company of Singers; Broadbent, cond.*
+ Fa 7-8/95: 148
+ Gr 3/95: 82

35253. DKP CD 9158: CHABRIER—Pièces pittoresques; Pièces posthumes; Impromptu in C major; Trois valses romantiques. *Stott, Burley, pianos.*
● ARG 9-10/95: 123
● Fa 9-10/95: 172
+ Gr 5/95: 79

35254. DKP CD 9159: SUK—Piano music. *Kvapil, piano.*
+ ARG 5-6/96: 207
+ Fa 5-6/96: 295
+ Gr 2/96: 78

35255. DKP CD 9160: *Saxophone song book.* Music of Rachmaninoff, Dowland, Nyman, Ives, and others. *Leonard, soprano; Harle, Haram, Roach, saxophones; Tunstall, harp; Lenehan, harpsichord, piano.*
● Gr 2/96: 70

35256. DKP CD 9161: *Nuccia Focile: sole e amore.* Songs of Verdi, Puccini, and Donizetti. *Focile, soprano; Pollock, piano.*
+ ARG 11-12/96: 228
● Fa 9-10/96: 367
● Gr 9/96: 100

35257. DKP CD 9162: LISZT—Songs. *Langridge, tenor; Constable, piano.*
+ ARG 5-6/96: 138
+ Fa 5-6/96: 192
+ Gr 2/96: 90

UNITED RECORDINGS

35258. 88001-2: SHOSTAKOVICH—Hypothetically murdered; Fragments, op. 42; Suite no. 1 for jazz band; Songs, op. 46. *Kharitonov, bass; City of Birmingham Symphony Orch.; Elder, cond.*
● Gr 1/94: 54

35259. 88002-2: *My beloved spake.* Music of Handel, Purcell, Blow, Humfrey, and Arne. *Bowman, Ainsley, George; Winchester College Quiristers; King's Consort; King, cond.*
+ Gr 12/93: 111

35260. 88005-2: SCARLATTI—Sonatas. SOLER—Sonatas. *Black, harpsichord.*
+ Gr 8/94: 76

35261. 88006-2: Cello sonatas by Prokofiev, Schnittke, and Shostakovich. *Marleyn, cello; Morley, piano.*
● Gr 1/94: 68

35262. 88016-2: *Dweller in my deathless dreams.* Songs by Warlock, Ireland, Howells, Bridge, and Holst. *Leonard, soprano; Martineau, piano.*
+ Gr 3/95: 98

35263. 88019-2: MESSIAEN—Piano music. *Hind, piano.*
+ Gr 12/94: 128

35264. 88023-2: TAVENER—Ikons. Thunder entered her; The lamb; The tiger; Hymns to the mother of God; Responsorium; others. *Kirk, MacKenzie, tenors; Andrews, Feaviour, sopranos; Harris, mezzo-soprano; Simcock, handbells.*
● ARG 5-6/95: 232
+ Gr 4/95: 109

35265. 88033-2: HOWELLS—Requiem; Take him, earth, for cherishing. MARTIN—Mass. *Barber, Field, Johnstone, Angus; Vasari; Backhouse, cond.*
+ Gr 12/94: 138

UPBEAT

35266. URCD 115: ELGAR—Violin concerto. BRUCH—Violin concerto no. 1. *Chen, violin; Arnhem Phil. Orch.; Menuhin, Benzi, conds.*
+ Fa 11-12/95: 248
● Gr 11/95: 80

35267. URCD 116: *Recital opus 1.* Music of Sichler, Poulenc, Debussy, Saint-Saëns, Messiaen, Rutter, Boulanger, and Feld. *Milan, flute; Brown, piano.*
+ Fa 11-12/95: 465

USK RECORDINGS

35268. USK 1216: Music of Musgrave, Harvey, Hoddinott, Maconchy, and others. *Ionian Singers; Salter, cond.*
+ Gr 3/96: 92

VAI

35269. VAIA 1003-2: Nyiregyházi at the opera. *Nyireghazi, piano.*
● ARG 7-8/92: 268
+ Fa 7-8/94: 197
+ Gr 12/93: 91

35270. VAIA 1005-2 (2 discs): *Eleanor Steber in concert 1956-58.* Music of Mozart, Berlioz, Bellini, Strauss, Barber, Verdi, Biltcliffe, Charpentier, Puccini, Schubert, Wolf, Canteloube, Menotti, Copland, and Davis . *Steber, soprano.*
+ ARG 9-10/92: 208
+ ON 3/27/93: 35

35271. VAIA 1006-2 (3 discs): BERLIOZ—The Trojans. *Steber, Resnik, Cassilly, Singher, vocalists; orchestra; Lawrence, cond.*
+ ARG 9-10/92: 86
- ON 3/27/93: 35

35272. VAIA 1007-2 (2 discs): SCHUBERT—Winterreise. *Vickers, tenor; Schaaf, piano.* Recorded live 1983.
● Gr 1/93: 56

35273. VAIA 1010-2 (2 discs): DITTERSDORF—Archifanfano. *Steber, Russell, Rehfuss, Smith; Clarion Music Society; Jenkins, cond.* Reissue.
+ ARG 1-2/93: 91
+ Fa 1-2/93: 142
+ ON 3/27/93: 35

35274. VAIA 1011-2: Operatic scenes by Strauss and Wagner. *Lear, soprano; Stewart, baritone; with orch. accomp.*
+ ARG 1-2/93: 196

35275. VAIA 1012-2: STRAUSS—Die Frau ohne Schatten: Excerpts; Four last songs. BEETHOVEN—Ah, perfido! *Steber,*

soprano; Munich Opera; Böhm, cond.; Cleveland Institute of Music Orch.; Levine, cond. Recorded 1953, 1970.
+ ARG 1-2/93: 195
+ Fa 1-2/93: 249
+ ON 3/27/93: 35

35276. VAIA 1016-2: *Jon Vickers: Italian opera arias.* Music of Ponchielli, Flotow, Verdi, Cilea, Leoncavallo, Giordano, and Puccini. *Vickers, tenor; Rome Opera Orch.; Serafin, cond.* Reissue.
+ ARG 9-10/93: 255
+ Fa 9-10/93: 343

35277. VAIA 1018-2: *Ossip Gabrilowitsch: his issued and unissued recordings.* Music of Arensky, Schutt, Bach, Gluck, Moszkowski, Glazunov, Gabrilowitsch, Delibes, Grainger, and Schumann. *Gabrilowitsch, piano; in part with assisting instrumentalists.*
+ ARG 7-8/93: 214
+ Fa 3-4/93: 373

35278. VAIA 1019-2: Strauss piano transcriptions. *Various pianists.* Recorded 1920-70.
+ ARG 7-8/93: 211

35279. VAIA 1020-2: *The complete Josef Hofmann, vol. 2.* Music of Brahms, Rubinstein, Chopin, Hofmann, Mendelssohn, Rachmaninoff, Beethoven, and Moszkowski. *Hofmann, piano; Curtis Institute Orch.; Reiner, Hilsberg, conds.* Recorded live 1937 & 1945.
+ ARG 7-8/93: 215
+ Fa 3-4/93: 371
+ Gr 5/93: 121

35280. VAIA 1021-2: BEETHOVEN—Piano concerto no. 4; Sonata no. 27; 32 variations in C minor. *Moravec, piano; Vienna Musikverein Orch.; Turnovsky, cond.* Reissue.
+ ARG 3-4/93: 56
+ Fa 5-6/93: 151

35281. VAIA 1022-2: Music of Poulenc, Muczynski, Debussy, Franck, and Fauré. *Baker, flute; Logan, piano.*
+ ARG 5-6/93: 163

35282. VAIA 1023-2: First recordings. *Steber, soprano; with piano accomp.* Recorded 1940.
+ ARG 7-8/93: 217

35283. VAIA 1024-2: Music of Bach, Mendelssohn, Schubert, and Brahms. *Tureck, piano.* Recorded live 1992.
+ Gr 8/93: 64

35284. VAIA 1025-2 (2 discs): Music of Gounod, Mozart, Verdi, Puccini, Boito, Massenet, and others. *Angeles, soprano; with orch. and piano acc.* Recorded 1952-60.
+ ARG 9-10/93: 266
+ Fa 9-10/93: 340

+ ON 1/8/94: 34
+ ON 3/19/94: 32

35285. VAIA 1027-2: RACHMANINOFF—Piano concerto no. 3. KHACHATURIAN—Piano concerto. *Kapell, piano; Toronto Symphony Orch.; MacMillan, cond.; NBC Symphony Orch.; Black, cond.* Recorded live 1948, 1945.
+ Fa 9-10/93: 242

35286. VAIA 1029-2: BACH—Goldberg variations. *Tureck, piano.* Reissue.
- ARG 11-12/93: 75

35287. VAIA 1030-2: Music of Piccinni, Falconieri, Schubert, Mussorgsky, and Niles. *London, baritone; Newmark, piano.*
+ ARG 9-10/93: 256

35288. VAIA 1031-2: MOZART—Arias. *Steber, soprano; with orch. acc.* Recorded 1946-60.
● ARG 9-10/93: 158
+ ON 3/19/94: 32

35289. VAIA 1032-2: Music of Handel, Scarlatti, Purcell, Schumann, and Dvořák. *Vickers, tenor; Woitach, piano.*
+ ARG 9-10/93: 256
+ ON 3/19/94: 32

35290. VAIA 1033-2: *Julius Baker in recital, vol. 2.* Music of Mozart, Bach, Sancan, Gieseking, Kuhlau, and Gershwin. *Baker, flute; Wingreen, piano.*
+ ARG 1-2/94: 178
+ Fa 3-4/94: 395

35291. VAIA 1034-2 (3 discs): BRITTEN—Billy Budd. *Uppman, Pears, Dalberg, Evans; Royal Opera House Covent Garden; Britten, cond.* Recorded 1951.
+ Fa 3-4/94: 149
+ ON 2/19/94: 32
+ Op 1/94: 122

35292. VAIA 1036-2 (2 discs): The complete Josef Hofmann, vol. 3. *Hofmann, piano.* Recorded 1918-20.
+ ARG 5-6/94: 211
+ Fa 3-4/94: 409

35293. VAIA 1038-2: Lotte Lehmann: the New York farewell recital 1951. *Lehmann, soprano; Ulanowsky, piano.*
+ ARG 5-6/94: 216
+ Fa 3-4/94: 369

35294. VAIA 1039-2: CHOPIN—Preludes; Scherzo no. 1; Barcarolle; Etude op. 25, no. 7. *Moravec, piano.*
+ ARG 1-2/94: 91
+ Fa 3-4/94: 164

35295. VAIA 1040—1041-2 (2 separate discs): BACH—Rosalyn Tureck plays Bach. *Tureck, harpsichord.* Reissues.
+ Fa 3-4/94: 112

35296. VAIA 1042-2: REFICE—Cecilia (abridged). *Scotto, Theyard, Fourié; chorus & orch.; Campori, cond.* Recorded live 1976.
+ ARG 5-6/94: 129
● Fa 5-6/94: 224

35297. VAIA 1043-2 (2 discs): *Ivan Moravec: French keyboard masterpieces.* Music of Franck, Ravel, and Debussy. *Moravec, piano.*
+ ARG 5-6/94: 184
+ Fa 5-6/94: 325

35298. VAIA 1045-2: HANDEL(ARR. BEECHAM)—The gods go a-begging; The origin of design; The faithful shepherd; short pieces. *London Phil. Orch.; Beecham Symphony Orch.; Leeds Festival Choir; Beecham, cond.*
● ARG 3-4/94: 228
+ Fa 5-6/94: 160
+ Gr 6/94: 128

35299. VAIA 1046-2: *Spanish orchestral favorites.* Music of Falla, Granados, Arbós, Breton, Turina, and Albéniz. *Madrid Symphony Orch.; Arbós, cond.*
+ ARG 3-4/94: 228
● Fa 5-6/94: 357

35300. VAIA 1047-2: *Josef Hofmann, vol. 4.* Music of Scarlatti-Tausig, Gluck-Brahms, Beethoven-Rubinstein, Rubinstein, Hofmann, Rachmaninoff, Wagner-Brassin, Chopin, Chopin-Liszt, and Liszt. *Hofmann, piano.*
+ ARG 5-6/94: 211
+ Fa 5-6/94: 325

35301. VAIA 1048-2: *William Kapell, vol. 2.* Music of Bach, Mozart, Debussy, Liszt, and Mussorgsky. *Kapell, piano.*
+ ARG 5-6/94: 212
+ Fa 5-6/94: 328
- Gr 11/94: 184

35302. VAIA 1049-2: *Evelyn Lear: a celebration of 20th-century song.* Music of Villa-Lobos, Barber, Ravel, and Berg. *Lear, soprano; orch. acc.; Zillig, Montgomery, conds.* Recorded live.
+ ARG 5-6/94: 197
+ Fa 5-6/94: 290

35303. VAIA 1051-2: BACH—The great solo works, vol. 2. *Tureck, piano.* Recorded live.
+ Fa 7-8/94: 46

35304. VAIA 1052-2 (2 discs): MUSSORGSKY (ORCH. RIMSKY-KORSAKOV)—Khovanshchina. *Christoff, Petri, Companez, Berdini, Picchi; unnamed orchestra; Rodzinski, cond.* Sung in Italian. Recorded live 1958.
- Fa 9-10/94: 277

35305. VAIA 1054-2 (2 discs): PUCCINI—Madama Butterfly. *Kirsten, Barioni, Nadell; New Orleans Opera; Cellini, cond.* Recorded 1960.

+ ARG 11-12/94: 258
• Fa 1-2/95: 230

35306. VAIA 1055-2 (2 discs): SAINT-SAËNS—Samson et Dalila. *Vinay, Stevens, Mordino, A. Berberian; New Orleans Opera; Cellini, cond.* Recorded 1960.
• ARG 5-6/95: 162
+ ON 2/18/95: 37

35307. VAIA 1056-2 (2 discs): VERDI—Falstaff. *Warren, Della Chiesa, Torigi, Pritchet; New Orleans Opera; Cellini, cond.* Recorded 1956.
• ARG 5-6/95: 241
+ ON 2/18/95: 37

35308. VAIA 1057-2: *Songs my mother taught me.* Music of Rachmaninoff, Tchaikovksy, Glière, Stravinsky, and Grechaninov. *Lear, soprano; Stewart, baritone; Jansen, Roessner, piano.*
+ ARG 9-10/94: 261
+ Fa 9-10/94: 389

35309. VAIA 1058-2: *The Rosalyn Tureck collection I.* Music of Mendelssohn, Paganini, Debussy, Graun, A. Scarlatti, Paradies, and Brahms. *Tureck, piano.*
+ Fa 9-10/94: 422

35310. VAIA 1059-2: SCHUMANN—Symphony no. 4. WAGNER—Overtures. *Mozart Festival Orch., Paris; Royal Phil. Orch.; British Symphony Orch.; Walter, cond.* Recorded 1928, 1925.
• ARG 9-10/94: 266
• Fa 9-10/94: 334

35311. VAIA 1061-2: MAHLER—Des Knaben Wunderhorn; Es sungen drei Engel; Urlicht. *Lear, soprano; Stewart, baritone; with orch. accomp.* Recorded 1962-83.
+ ARG 11-12/94: 149
+ Fa 11-12/94: 285
+ ON 10/94: 52

35312. VAIA 1062-2 (2 discs): *Celebrated death scenes.* Music from Mefistofele, Adriana Lecouvreur, La Wally, and Iris. *Olivero, soprano; with orch. accomp.* Recorded live 1973, 1966.
+ ARG 11-12/94: 253
• Fa 1-2/95: 315

35313. VAIA 1063-2: Music of Grétry, Fauré, Debussy, Britten, Hahn, and Strauss. *Teyte, soprano; Ranck, Reeves, piano.* Recorded 1935, 1948.
+ ARG 11-12/94: 261
+ Fa 11-12/94: 435

35314. VAIA 1064-2 (3 discs): GOUNOD—Roméo et Juliette (complete opera and excerpts). *Gall, Affre, Journet, Boyer; Opéra-Comique de Paris; Rühlmann, cond.* (complete opera); *Endrèze, Norena, Vezzani, Villabella, Thill, Féraldy* (excerpts). Recorded 1912 (complete opera) and 1932 (excerpts).

+ Fa 11-12/94: 242
+ ON 11/95: 48

35315. VAIA/IPA 1065-2: *Jeanne-Marie Darré.* Music of Chopin, Saint-Saëns, J. Strauss, Bach, Weber, Schumann, Mendelssohn, Liszt, Philipp, Rachmaninoff, and Jary. *Darré, piano; Paris Conservatory Orch.; Cluytens, cond.; Orch. of the Colonne Concerts; Paray, cond.*
+ Fa 1-2/95: 356

35316. VAIA 1067-2 (2 discs): *Sir Adrian Boult conducts English music.* Music of Bliss, Butterworth, Elgar, Vaughan Williams, and Walton. *BBC Symphony Orch.; Hallé Orch.; Boult, cond.* Recorded 1934-1942.
+ Fa 11-12/94: 504

35317. VAIA 1068-2: LECLAIR—Flute sonatas op. 2, no. 1, 3, 11; op. 9, no. 2, 7. *Stallman, harpsichord; Swanborn, flute; Bennion, cello.*
+ Fa 11-12/94: 276

35318. VAIA 1069-2: BEETHOVEN—Piano sonatas no. 8, 14, 23, 26. *Moravec, piano.* Recorded 1962-70.
+ ARG 5-6/95: 84
+ Gr 1/96: 79

35319. VAIA 1071-2: Music of Mascagni, Leoncavallo, Puccini, and others. *Favero, soprano.* Reissues.
+ ARG 11-12/95: 292

35320. VAIA 1072-2: Eleanor Steber, vol. 1: 1938-51. *Steber, soprano.*
+ ARG 3-4/95: 278
+ ON 9/95: 59

35321. VAIA 1073-2: RAVEL—L'Heure espagnole. *Krieger, Arnoult, Gilles, Dufranne; Truc, cond.* Recorded 1929.
+ ARG 3-4/95: 272
+ Gr 9/95: 127
+ ON 4/1/95: 42

35322. VAIA 1074-2: RAVEL—Daphnis et Chloé: Suite no. 2; Alborada del gracioso. DEBUSSY—Afternoon of a faun. ROUSSEL—Spider's feast. IBERT—Escales . *Concerts Straram Orch.; Gaubert, Straram, conds.*
+ ARG 3-4/95: 266

35323. VAIA 1075-2: CHARPENTIER—Impressions d'Italie. RABAUD—Marouf: La procession nocturne. GAUBERT—Chants de la mer; Voiles blanches et crepuscules; Calme de soin. *Orchestras; Charpentier, Rabaud, Gaubert, Cebron, conds.*
+ ARG 3-4/95: 266

35324. VAIA 1076-2 (2 discs): PUCCINI—Tosca. *Melis, Pauli, Granforte; Teatro La Scala; Sabajno, cond.* Recorded 1929.
• ARG 3-4/95: 272

+ Gr 4/95: 140
• ON 5/95: 47

35325. VAIA 1080-2: STRAUSS—Songs. *Lear, soprano; Werba, piano.* Recorded 1964.
• ARG 9-10/95: 222

35326. VAIA 1083-2 (2 discs): VERDI—Aida. *Arangi Lombardi, Lindi, Capuana, Borgioli; Teatro La Scala; Molajoli, cond.* Recorded 1928.
• ARG 7-8/95: 273
+ ON 10/96: 40

35327. VAIA 1084-2: Arias from Aida, Lohengrin, Tannhäuser, and Tristan. *Bampton, soprano.* Recorded 1940.
+ ARG 7-8/95: 276
+ ON 3/2/96: 41

35328. VAIA 1087-2: Arias from La traviata, Tosca, Madame Butterfly, and others. *Kirsten, soprano.* Recorded 1946-65.
+ ARG 11-12/95: 272
+ ON 10/95: 44

35329. VAIA 1088-2: BEETHOVEN—Piano sonatas no. 17, 21, 23, 28; Bagatelle op. 33 no. 3. *Gieseking, piano.* Recorded 1938-39.
+ ARG 11-12/95: 284

35330. VAIA 1091-2: HANDEL—Flute sonatas, op. 1: no. 1-2, 4-5, 7, 9, 11. *Stallman, flute; Bennion, cello; Swanborn, harpsichord.*
+ Gr 7/95: 78

35331. VAIA 1092-2: CHOPIN—Ballades; Mazurkas. *Moravec, piano.* Recorded 1966-69.
+ Gr 12/95: 113

35332. VAIA 1093-2: DEBUSSY—Pelléas et Mélisande (excerpts). *Panzéra, Maguenat, Brothier, Nespoulous, other vocalists; orch.; Coppola, Truc, conds.* Recorded 1927-28.
+ ARG 1-2/96: 242
+ ON 1/6/96: 38

35333. VAIA 1096-2: Music of Mozart, Brahms, and Beethoven. *Moravec, piano.* Recorded 1967-70.
+ ARG 1-2/96: 219

35334. VAIA 1097-2 (2 discs): VERDI—Rigoletto. *L. Piazza, Pagliughi, Folgar, Baccaloni; Teatro La Scala; Sabajno, cond.* Recorded 1928.
• ARG 11-12/95: 287
• Gr 6/96: 114
• ON 10/96: 40

35335. VAIA 1104-2: Music of Bach, Schubert, Strauss, and Liszt. *K. Oldham, piano.*
• ARG 11-12/95: 256

35336. VAIA 1107-2: FLOYD—Markheim. *Treigle, Crofoot, Daird,*

VALOIS

35368. V 4629: Schumann—Kreisleriana;
Nachtstücke; Gesang der Frühe. *Cabasso,
piano.*
+ Fa 9-10/89: 319

35369. V 4638: Marais—Pièces en trio.
Ensemble Fitzwilliam.
• EM 8/92: 512
+ Fa 7-8/92: 210
• Gr 11/92: 141

35370. V 4639: Music of Ligeti, Villa-
Lobos, Barber, Hindemith, and
Stockhausen. *Moragues Wind Quintet.*
• Fa 11-12/92:
• Fa 11-12/92

35371. V 4641: Merula—Canzoni,
Motetti, Sonate. *Ensemble Fitzwilliam.*
+ ARG 11-12/90: 80
+ Fa 7-8/90: 201

35372. V 4644: Ravel— Ravel—Air
d'Alcyone; Deux mélodies hébraïques;
Chansons madécasses; Trois poèmes de
Mallarmé. Debussy (orch. Roger-
Ducasse)—Proses lyriques. *Atger,
soprano; Monte Carlo Phil. Orch.;
Constant, cond.*
+ ARG 9-10/92: 147
+ Gr 4/92: 125

35373. V 4645: *Historic Spanish organ,
vol. 1.* Music of Cabezon, Narvaez,
Jannequin, and Anon. *Marshall, organ.*
+ ARG 11-12/92: 243
• EM 2/93: 143
+ Gr 7/92: 82

35374. V 4646: *The historic Spanish
organ, vol. 2.* Correa de Arauxo—
Thirteen pieces. *Foccroulle, organ.*
+ ARG 11-12/92: 243
• EM 2/93: 143
+ Fa 9-10/92: 422

35375. V 4647: *Historic Spanish organ,
vol. 3.* Music of Cabanilles. *García
Banegas, organ.*
+ ARG 11-12/92: 243

35376. V 4648: *Historic Spanish organ,
vol. 4.* Music of Cabezon, Bruna,
Aguilera de Heredia, Rogg, and Araujo.
Rogg, organ.
+ ARG 11-12/92: 243
+ EM 2/93: 143
+ Gr 7/92: 84

35377. V 4649: *The historic Spanish
organ, vol. 5.* Music of Aquilera de
Heredia, De Sola, Ximénez, Xarava y
Bruna, Nassarre, Durón, and Anon.
González Uriol, organ.
+ ARG 11-12/92: 243
• EM 2/93: 143
+ Fa 9-10/92: 422

35378. V 4650: *The historic Spanish
organ, vol. 6.* Music of Cabezón, De
Sancta Maria, Clavijo del Castillo,
Jiménez, Lidón, Hervás, and Bovet.
Bovet, organ.

+ ARG 11-12/92: 243
+ EM 2/93: 143
+ Fa 9-10/92: 422

35379. V 4651—4652 (2 separate discs):
Historic Spanish organ, vol. 7-8. *Mas i
Bonet, Torrent, organs.*
+ ARG 11-12/92: 243
• EM 2/93: 143 (4651)
+ Fa 11-12/92: 441
+ Gr 7/92: 84

35380. V 4653: *Historic Spanish organs,
vol. 9.* Music of Cabezon, Peraza, Lopez,
Cabanilles, and others. *Chapelet, organ.*
+ ARG 9-10/93: 235

35381. V 4654: *Historic Spanish organ,
vol. 10.* Music of Viola, Lopez, Elias,
Prieto, Baguer, Sese, Lidon, Larranago,
Pedro, Anon. *Freixo, organ.*
+ ARG 11-12/92: 243
+ EM 2/93: 143

35382. V 4655: Prokofiev—Piano
sonatas no. 2, 7; Visions fugitives.
Cabasso, piano.
• Fa 11-12/92: 322
+ Gr 11/92: 156

35383. V 4656: Fauré—Violin sonata no.
1. Franck—Violin sonata. *Nicolas,
violin; Petrov, piano.*
• Fa 11-12/92: 231
• Gr 10/92: 127

35384. V 4657: Saint-Saëns—Fantasia
for violin and harp; Suite for cello and
piano; Piano quartet. *Various performers.*
+ ARG 7-8/92: 210
+ Fa 7-8/92: 264

35385. V 4658: Hahn—Complete music
for two pianos, vol. 1. *Sermet, Paik,
pianos and piano 4-hands.*
+ ARG 9-10/92: 114
+ Fa 9-10/92: 249

35386. V 4659: Alkan—Toccatina;
Twelve preludes; Six esquisses;
Barcarolle, op. 65, no. 6. *Sermet, piano.*
- ARG 7-8/92: 82
- Fa 9-10/92: 161

35387. V 4660: Gerhard—Don Quixote;
Pedrelliana; Albada, interludi, i dansa.
*Orquesta Sinfonica de Tenerife; Pérez,
cond.*
+ Fa 1-2/93: 153
+ Gr 10/92: 61

35388. V 4661: Albéniz—Piano concerto
no. 1 "Concierto fantástico." Albéniz-
Arbós—Iberia suite. *Pérez de Guzmán,
piano; Orch. of Valencia; Galduf, cond.*
• Fa 1-2/93: 92
• Gr 10/92: 53

35389. V 4663 (2 discs): Albéniz—Iberia;
Cantos de España. *Orozco, piano.*
• Fa 1-2/93: 92
+ Gr 11/92: 149

35390. V 4664: Mozart—Piano
concertos no. 20-21. *Badura-Skoda,
piano & cond.; Prague Chamber Orch.*
+ Fa 1-2/93: 200

35391. V 4666: Prokofiev—Cello sonata;
Ballade; Adagio. Shostakovich—Cello
sonata. *Wieder-Atherton, cello; Cabasso,
piano.*
+ Gr 4/94: 64

35392. V 4667: Hummel—Twenty-four
etudes, op. 125; Piano sonata no. 5.
Laval, piano.
+ Fa 3-4/93: 194

35393. V 4669: Mozart—Concertos for
piano and orchestra no. 22, 27. *Badura-
Skoda, piano & cond.; Prague Chamber
Orch.*
• Fa 3-4/93: 236

35394. V 4670: Ravel—L'Enfant et les
sortileges. *Mahe, soprano; Bordeaux
Opera; Lombard, cond.*
+ ARG 9-10/93: 174
• Fa 11-12/93: 357
• Gr 9/93: 113

35395. V 4671: Chopin—Piano sonatas,
no. 2-3. *Badura-Skoda, piano.*
+ ARG 9-10/93: 109
+ Fa 9-10/93: 146
• Gr 6/93: 72

35396. V 4672: Chopin—Ballades;
Fantasie; Barcarolle; Nocturne in C♯
minor. *Badura-Skoda, piano.*
• Fa 9-10/93: 146

35397. V 4673: Paganini—The 24
caprices for solo violin, op. 1. *Pasquier,
violin.*
+ Fa 3-4/93: 246

35398. V 4677: Lalo—Namouna: Suites
no. 1-2. *Monte Carlo Phil. Orch.;
Robertson, cond.*
+ ARG 3-4/93: 103
+ Fa 5-6/93: 243
+ Gr 5/94: 52

35399. V 4678: Indy—String quartet no.
2; Trio no. 2 in the form of a suite; Sextet
for 2 violins, 2 violas and 2 cellos. *Prat
Quartet; Depouy, viola; Michel, cello;
Prat, violin; Gaugué, cello; Paik, piano.*
• ARG 7-8/93: 105
+ Fa 5-6/93: 231

35400. V 4679: Schmitt—Sonate libre;
Trois rapsodies; Hasards. *R. Pasquier,
violin; Sermet, Paik, Greif, piano; B.
Pasquier, viola; Pidoux, cello.*
+ ARG 7-8/93: 149
+ Fa 7-8/93: 227
+ Gr 9/93: 82

35401. V 4680: Alkan—Cello sonata;
Grand duo concertant. *Henkel, cello;
Papavrami, violin; Sermet, piano.*
• ARG 7-8/93: 56
+ Fa 9-10/93: 102

35402. V 4683: Schubert—Piano sonata D. 960; Wanderer fantasy. *Orozco, piano.*
- Fa 5-6/94: 244
+ Gr 8/93: 60

35403. V 4684: Mozart—Serenades no. 11-12 (arr.). *Moragues Quintet.*
- Gr 11/93: 94

35404. V 4685 (2 discs): Falla— Atlántida. *Estes, Bayo, Berganza; National Youth Orch. of Spain; Colomer, cond.*
+ Fa 11-12/93: 233
+ Gr 7/93: 86
+ ON 2/17/96: 40

35405. V 4686: Indy—Symphony no. 3; Saugefleurie; Souvenirs. *Strasbourg Phil. Orch.; Guschlbauer, cond.*
+ ARG 11-12/93: 130
+ Fa 1-2/94: 209
+ Gr 9/93: 51

35406. V 4687: Schmitt—Symphonie concertante; Rêves; Soirs. *Sermet, piano; Phil. Orch. of Monte-Carlo; Robertson, cond.*
+ Fa 9-10/94: 322
+ Gr 9/94: 62

35407. V 4688: Saint-Saëns—Javotte; Rapsodie Bretonne; Andromacque: Selections; Suite algérienne. *Monte Carlo Phil. Orch.; Robertson, cond.*
+ ARG 9-10/94: 187

35408. V 4692: Rachmaninoff—Cello sonata. Strauss—Cello sonata. *Gastinel, cello; Aimard, piano.*
+ Gr 12/93: 84

35409. V 4693: Beethoven—Flute sonatas; Serenade. *Pahud, flute; Le Sage, piano.*
+ Gr 9/93: 70

35410. V 4695 (2 discs): Bach—Suites for solo cello. *Claret, cello.*
+ Gr 3/95: 70

35411. V 4697: Bach—Violin concertos; Concertos for violin and oboe. *Walter, Nicolas, violins; Moglia, oboe; Toulouse National Chamber Orch.; Malgoire, cond.*
- Gr 6/94: 43

35412. V 4698: Rota—Piano music. *Laval, piano.*
+ Gr 1/94: 77

35413. V 4700: Ravel—Mélodies. *Kruysen, baritone; Lee, piano.*
+ Fa 11-12/93: 357

35414. V 4702: Borodin—Piano quintet. Shostakovich—Piano quintet, op. 57. *Quintette Pro Arte de Monte Carlo.*
+ Fa 7-8/94: 242
- Gr 10/94: 131

35415. V 4704: Joplin—Rags. *Chojnacka, harpsichord.*
- ARG 11-12/94: 138

35416. V 4710 (2 discs): Vives—Doña Francisquita. *Bayo, Kraus, Pierotti; Tenrife Orch.; Ros-Marbá, cond.*
+ ARG 9-10/94: 219
+ ARG 5-6/95: 192
+ Fa 9-10/94: 370
- Gr 9/94: 118
+ ON 10/94: 51

35417. V 4711: Vives—Bohemios. *Bayo, Lima, Jerico, Alvarez; Choruses; Tenerife Symphony Orch.; Ros-Marbá, cond.*
+ ARG 5-6/95: 192
+ Fa 11-12/94: 416
+ Gr 3/95: 106
+ ON 4/1/95: 45

35418. V 4712: Mozart—Violin concerto no. 5; Sinfonia concertante, K. 364/320d. *R. Pasquier, violin; B. Pasquier, viola; Liège Phil. Orch.; Bartholomée, cond.*
- Gr 7/95: 62

35419. V 4715 (2 discs): Beethoven— Piano quartets no. 1-3. *Oleg, violin; Silva, viola; Coppey, cello; Cassard, piano.*
+ Gr 5/95: 67

35420. V 4716: Kodály—Duo for violin and cello, op. 7. Martinů—Duos for violin and cello no. 1-2. *Oleg, violin; Wieder-Atherton, cello.*
+ Fa 3-4/96: 192

35421. V 4719: Mendelssohn—String quartets no. 1-2 (transcribed for woodwind quintet). *Quintet Moragues.*
+ Fa 3-4/96: 222
+ Gr 11/95: 108

35422. V 4720: Schubert—Piano music, four hands. *Badura-Skoda, Bonatta, piano.*
+ ARG 11-12/95: 195

35423. V 4724: Falla—Noches en los jardines de España; Fantasia baetica; Quatre pièces espagnoles; Homenajes: Pour le tombeau de Claude Debussy; Pour le tombeau de Paul Dukas. *Orozco, piano; Spanish National Youth Orch.; Colomer, cond.*
- Gr 7/95: 48

35424. V 4725: Bretón—La verbena de la paloma. *Bayo, Domingo, Piero, Tro, R. Castejon, J. Castejon, Amangual, Martin, Baquerizo, Rodriguez, Rios; Chorus of the Comunidad de Madrid; Orquesta Sinfonica de Madrid; Ros-Marbá, cond.*
+ ARG 5-6/95: 192
+ Fa 7-8/95: 136
+ Gr 9/95: 100
+ ON 8/95: 37

35425. V 4727: *Romances et danses pour violon.* Music of Brahms, Suk, Kreisler, Castelnuovo-Tedesco, Wagner,

Rachmaninoff, Wieniawski, Szymanowski, Rubinstein, Sibelius, Granados, and Tchaikovsky. *Bushkov, violin; Dedieu-Vidal, piano.*
+ Fa 3-4/96: 368

35426. V 4728: Gerhard—Symphonies no. 1, 3. *Tenerife Symphony Orch.; Pérez, cond.*
+ Gr 9/95: 55

35427. V 4729: Mendelssohn—Preludes and fugues, op. 35; Rondo capriccioso, op. 14; Variations sérieuses, op. 54; String quartet no. 1: Canzonetta. *Laval, piano.*
+ Gr 7/95: 86

35428. V 4730: Debussy—String quartet. Menu—Sonatine. Ravel—String quartet. *Parisii Quartet.*
+ Gr 10/95: 81

35429. V 4731: Barbieri—El barbarillo de Lavapiés. *Lanza, Casariego, Bayo, Sempere, Pons, Palatchi; Coro Polifonico Universitario; Rondalla de Tenerife; Orquesta Sinfonica de Tenerife; Perez, cond.*
- ARG 11-12/95: 79
+ Fa 11-12/95: 194
+ Gr 2/96: 100
- ON 6/96: 43

35430. V 4733: *In memoriam Pau Casals.* Music of Bach, Cervello, Casals, Fauré, Falla, and others. *Claret, cello; Violoncellistes de Barcelona; Myong, piano.*
+ ARG 5-6/95: 204

35431. V 4734: Bizet—Carmen. *Uria-Monzon, Papis, Vaduva, Le Texier; Bordeaux Theatre Chorus; Bordeaux Aquitaine Orch.; Lombard, cond.*
- Gr 10/95: 131

35432. V 4738: H. Jadin—String quartets op. 3, no. 1; op. 2, no. 1. L.E. Jadin— String quartet no. 2. *Quatuor Mosaïques.*
+ Fa 5-6/96: 176
+ Gr 3/96: 63

35433. V 4747: Fauré—Mélodies: a selection. *Le Texier, baritone; Biros, piano.*
- Fa 5-6/96: 151

35434. V 4748: Janáček—Pohádka. Kodály—Cello sonata, op. 4. Liszt— Elegies no. 1-2; La lugubre gondola. *Gastinel, cello; Aimard, piano.*
+ Gr 9/95: 76

35435. V 4749: Onslow—String quartet no. 23. Dancla—String quartet no. 8. Rode—Quatuor à cordes brillant no. 2. *Quatuor Debussy.*
+ Fa 3-4/96: 242

35436. V 4750: Scarlatti—Sonatas. *Schmidt, guitar.*
+ Fa 7-8/96: 283

VALOIS

35437. V 4751: Weber—Flute sonatas, op. 10, 39. *Pahud, flute; Le Sage, piano.*
+ ARG 7-8/96: 223
+ Fa 5-6/96: 315

35438. V 4752 (2 discs): Nebra—Viento es la dicha de amor. *Arruabarrena, Almajano, Pierotti, Jurado; Limoges Baroque Ensemble; Coin, cond.*
+ ARG 9-10/96: 173
+ EM 11/96: 718
+ Fa 11-12/96: 323
+ Gr 8/96: 94
+ ON 1/11/97: 40
+ Op 1/97: 72

35439. V 4754: Saint-Saëns—Cello concerto no. 1. Lalo—Cello concerto. Fauré—Elegie. *Gastinel, cello; Orch. National de Lyon; Krivine, cond.*
+ ARG 7-8/96: 144
+ Fa 5-6/96: 255
• Gr 2/96: 50

35440. V 4755: Ravel—Gaspard de la nuit; Prélude; Menuet sur le nom de Haydn; Jeux d'eau; Le tombeau de Couperin. *Sermet, piano.*
+ Gr 7/96: 78

35441. V 4757: Tournemire—Symphony no. 6. *Phil. Orch. of Liège and of the French Community; Bartholomée, cond.*
+ Fa 7-8/96: 325

35442. V 4759: Moreno Torroba—Luisa Fernanda. *Villarroel, Domingo, Pons; Coro de la Universidad Politécnica de Madrid; Orquesta Sinfónica de Madrid; Ros-Marbá, cond.*
+ Fa 7-8/96: 245
+ Gr 4/96: 114
+ ON 6/96: 43
+ Op 4/96: 424

35443. V 4761: Vachon—String quartet, op. 5, no. 1. Saint-Georges—String quartet, op. 14, no. 6. Cambini—String quartets, book 13, no. 2; book 20, no. 6. *Quatuor Les Adieux.*
+ Fa 7-8/96: 329

35444. V 4765: Viva la zarzuela! *Various performers.*
+ ARG 7-8/96: 282

35445. V 4962: Rachmaninoff—Cello sonata. Strauss—Cello sonata. *Gastinel, cello; Aimard, piano.*
+ Fa 3-4/94: 286

VANGUARD

35446. OVC 2: Mahler—Symphony no. 2. *Sills, Kopleff; University of Utah Chorale; Utah Symphony Orch.; Abravanel, cond.* Reissue.
• ARG 3-4/95: 132

35447. OVC 3: Copland—Piano concerto. Menotti—Piano concerto. *Wild, piano; Symphony of the Air; Copland,*

Mester, conds. Reissues.
+ ARG 7-8/95: 103

35448. OVC 4: *Fiddle faddle.* Music of Leroy Anderson. *Utah Symphony Orch.; Abravanel, cond.*
- ARG 7-8/95: 236

35449. SVC 5/6 (2 discs): Haydn—Symphonies no. 44-49. *Zagreb Radio Orch.; Janigro, cond.* Reissues.
+ ARG 7-8/95: 123
• Fa 9-10/95: 223

35450. OVC 7: Vaughan Williams—Symphony no. 6; Dona nobis pacem. *Christensen, soprano; Metcalf, baritone; Utah Civic Chorale; Utah Symphony Orch.; Abravanel, cond.* Reissue.
• ARG 11-12/95: 223

35451. SVC 9: Gottschalk—A night in the tropics; Grand tarantelle for piano and orchestra. Gould—Latin American symphonette. *Nibley, piano; Utah Symphony Orch.; Abravanel, cond.* Reissue.
+ Fa 11-12/95: 264

35452. OVC 10: Goldmark—Rustic wedding symphony. Enesco—Romanian rhapsodies. *Utah Symphony Orch.; Abravanel, cond.; Vienna State Opera Orch.; Golschmann, cond.* Reissues.
+ ARG 5-6/96: 116

35453. OVC 11 (3 discs): Beethoven—Symphonies no. 3, 5-7; Overtures. *London Phil. Orch.; Boult, cond.* Recorded 1956.
• ARG 9-10/95: 106

35454. SVC 14/16 (3 discs): Haydn—Symphonies no. 99-104. *Vienna State Opera Orch.; Wöldike, cond.* Recorded 1956.
• ARG 9-10/95: 154
+ Fa 1-2/96: 224
+ Fi 3/96: 115

35455. VBD 15: Vivaldi—The four seasons. *Tomasow, violin; I Solisti di Zagreb; Janigro, cond.*
+ ARG 11-12/88: 208

35456. OVC 34 (2 discs): Haydn—The creation. *Stich-Randall, Felbermeyer, Dermota, Guthrie; Vienna State Opera; Wöldike, cond.* Recorded 1958.
+ ARG 5-6/96: 122

35457. VBD 35: Bach—Organ concertos BWV 592-94, 596. *Heiller, organ.*
+ ARG 9-10/88: 16
• Fa 1-2/89: 105

35458. SVC 40: Varèse—Amériques; Ecuatorial; Nocturnal. Honegger—Pacific 231. *Utah Symphony Orch.; Abravanel, cond.* Reissue.
+ ARG 7-8/96: 219

35459. SVC 44: Cherubini—Missa solemnis. *Wells, Forrester, Shirley, Díaz; Clarion Concerts; Jenkins, cond.* Reissue.
+ ARG 9-10/96: 107

35460. SVC 45: Grieg—Holberg suite; Last spring. Wirén—Serenade. Britten—Simple symphony. *English Chamber Orch.; Somary, cond.* Recorded 1968, 1973.
+ ARG 11-12/96: 132

35461. SVC 46: Boyce—Symphonies. *I Solisti di Zagreb; Janigro, cond.* Reissue.
+ ARG 1-2/97: 79

35462. VBD 175: Bach—Goldberg variations. *Leonhardt, harpsichord.*
• Fa 11-12/88: 119

35463. VBD 363: Music of Vivaldi, Corelli, and Bach. *Kipnis, harpsichord; Stokowski Orch.; Stokowski, cond.*
+ ARG 9-10/88: 116
+ Fa 11-12/88: 350

35464. VBD 385: Thomson—The river: Suite; The plow that broke the plains: Suite. *Symphony of the Air; Stokowski, cond.*
+ ARG 7-8/88: 63
+ Fa 3-4/88: 220

35465. VBD 389: Beethoven—Piano sonatas no. 8, 14, 21. *Hungerford, piano.*
+ Fa 11-12/88: 137

35466. VBD 394: J. Strauss, Jr.—Voices of spring; The blue Danube; Tales from the Vienna Woods; Artist's life; Annen polka; Wine, women and song; Tritsch-tratsch polka; Emperor waltz; Pizzicato polka. *Vienna State Opera Orch.; Paulik, cond.*
+ Fa 3-4/88: 207

35467. VTC 1634: *Bonbons aus Wien.* Music of J. Strauss, Sr., Lanner, Mozart, Schubert, and J. Strauss, Jr. *Boskovsky Ensemble; Boskovsky, violin & director.*
+ Fa 11-12/91: 492

35468. OVC 2002 (2 discs): Purcell—Songs and airs. *Deller, countertenor; Cantelo, soprano; Bevan, baritone.* Reissues.
+ ARG 5-6/93: 121

35469. OVC 2007: Gabrieli—Processional and ceremonial music. *Gabrieli Festival Choir and Orch.; Appia, cond.* Recorded 1958.
• ARG 9-10/93: 123

35470. OVC 2011 (2 discs): Bach—Art of fugue. *Leonhardt, harpsichord.* Recorded 1953.
+ ARG 9-10/93: 261
+ Gr 10/93: 76

35471. OVC 2013: Cantigas de Santa Maria. *Waverly Consort.* Reissue.
+ ARG 9-10/93: 245

35472. SVC 2030 (11 discs): MAHLER—Symphonies no. 1-9; Symphony no. 10: Adagio. *Utah Symphony Orch.; Abravanel, cond.* Reissue.
+ ARG 1-2/96: 136
+ Fi 3/96: 115

35473. OVC 2517: PURCELL—Dioclesian. *Sheppard, Le Sage, Deller, Todd; Concentus Musicus Wien.* Recorded 1965.
• ARG 5-6/94: 126

35474. OVC 2518: HAYDN—Mass in time of war. *Davrath, Rössl-Majdan, Dermota, Berry; Heiller, organ; Vienna State Opera; Wöldike, cond.*
+ ARG 3-4/94: 107

35475. OVC 2519: MONTEVERDI—Madrigals, book 8. *Deller Consort.*
- ARG 3-4/94: 124

35476. OVC 2520: RAMEAU—Pièces de clavecin en concerts. *Frydén, violin; Harnoncourt, viola da gamba; Leonhardt, harpsichord.* Reissue.
+ ARG 1-2/95: 160
+ Gr 3/94: 74

35477. OVC 2523 (2 discs): BACH—Harpsichord concertos. *Heiller, harpsichord; I Solisti di Zagreb; Janigro, cond.* Reissue.
+ ARG 7-8/95: 75

35478. OVC 2525: TALLIS—Lamentations of Jeremiah. COUPERIN—Tenebrae lessons. *Deller Consort.* Recorded 1960.
• ARG 7-8/95: 208

35479. OVC 2533 (2 discs): English madrigal school. *Deller Consort; Deller, cond.* Reissues.
+ ARG 7-8/95: 257

35480. SVC 3133 (3 discs): SIBELIUS—Symphonies (complete). *Utah Symphony Orch.; Abravanel, cond.* Reissue.
- ARG 3-4/96: 185
• Fi 5/96: 132

35481. OVC 4001: MOZART—Flute quartets. *Robison, flute; Members of the Tokyo String Quartet.* Reissue.
+ ARG 7-8/91: 94
+ Fa 9-10/91: 287

35482. OVC 4002: RAVEL—Alborada del grazioso; Boléro; Concerto for piano left-hand; Rapsodie espagnole. *Fleisher, piano; Baltimore Symphony Orch.; Comissiona, cond.*
+ ARG 9-10/91: 112
+ Fa 11-12/91: 453

35483. OVC 4003: MAHLER—Symphony no. 1. *Utah Symphony Orch.; Abravanel,* *cond.* Reissue.
• Fa 9-10/91: 261

35484. OVC 4004: MAHLER—Symphony no. 2. *University of Utah Civic Chorale; Utah Symphony Orch.; Abravanel, cond.* Reissue.
- Fa 9-10/91: 261

35485. OVC 4007: MAHLER—Symphony no. 4. *Davrath, soprano; Utah Symphony Orch.; Abravanel, cond.* Reissue.
- Fa 9-10/91: 261

35486. OVC 4015: MOZART—Piano concertos no. 9, 14. *Brendel, piano; I Solisti di Zagreb; Janigro, cond.* Reissue.
+ Fa 9-10/91: 279

35487. OVC 4016: BARBER—Hand of bridge; Essay no. 2; Music for a scene from Shelley; A stopwatch and an ordnance map; Serenade for string orchestra; Adagio for strings; Let down the bars, o Death! *Symphony of the Air; Golschmann, cond.; Neway, Alberts, Lewis, Maero; I Solisti di Zagreb; Janigro, cond.*
+ Fa 11-12/91: 253
+ Gr 8/92: 69

35488. OVC 4018/19 (2 discs): HANDEL—Messiah. *Price, Minton, Young, Díaz; Amor Artis Chorale; English Chamber Orch.; Somary, cond.* Reissue.
• Fa 9-10/91: 228

35489. OVC 4023: CHOPIN—Piano music. *Brendel, piano.*
+ Fa 9-10/91: 256

35490. OVC 4024: LISZT—Hungarian rhapsodies: nos. 2, 3, 8, 13, 15, 17; Csárdás obstiné. *Brendel, piano.* Reissue.
+ Fa 9-10/91: 256

35491. OVC 4025: MOZART—Piano sonata no. 8; Fantasy, K. 396; Rondo, K. 511; Variations, K. 573. *Brendel, piano.*
+ Fa 9-10/91: 296

35492. OVC 4026: SCHUBERT—Piano sonatas, D. 840; D. 958; German dances, D. 783. *Brendel, piano.*
+ Fa 9-10/91: 346

35493. OVC 4027: SCHUMANN—Fantasia in C, op. 17; Symphonic etudes, op. 13. *Brendel, piano.*
- Fa 9-10/91: 352

35494. OVC 4028: *Solid gold Strauss.* J. STRAUSS JR.—Waltzes and polkas. J. STRAUSS SR. AND JOSEF STRAUSS—Pizzicato polka. *Vienna State Opera Orch.; Paulik, cond.* Reissue.
- Fa 11-12/91: 492

35495. OVC 4030: SATIE—Ballets and orchestral transcriptions. *Utah Symphony Orch.; Abravanel, cond.* Reissues.
+ Gr 5/92: 47

35496. OVC 4031: VARÈSE—Amériques; Nocturnal; Ecuatorial. HONEGGER—Pacific 231. *Utah Symphony Orch.; Abravanel, cond.* Reissue.
+ Fa 11-12/91: 512

35497. OVC 4033: *The virtuoso piano.* Music of Herz, Godowsky, Rubinstein, Thalberg, Hummel, and Paderewski. *Wild, piano.* Reissue.
+ Fa 1-2/92: 401
+ Gr 8/92: 55

35498. OVC 4038: HONEGGER—Le roi David. *Singher, Davrath, Preston, Sorenson, M. Milhaud; University of Utah Chorus; Utah Symphony Orch.; Abravanel, Maurice.* Reissue.
• Fa 11-12/91: 355

35499. OVC 4039/40 (2 discs): GLUCK—Orfeo ed Euridice. *Forrester, Stich-Randall, Steffek; Vienna State Opera; Mackerras, cond.* Reissue.
• Gr 12/92: 135

35500. OVC 4044: PURCELL—Four suites for string orchestra; Harpsichord music. *Malcolm, harpsichord; Hartford Chamber Orch.; F. Mahler, cond.* Reissues.
+ Fa 7-8/92: 251

35501. OVC 4045: MAHLER—Des Knaben Wunderhorn. *Forrester, alto; Rehfuss, baritone; Vienna Festival Orch.; Prohaska, cond.*
+ Fa 3-4/92: 235

35502. OVC 4046: BLOCH—Violin concerto; Trois poèmes juifs. BARTÓK—Rhapsody for violin and orchestra no. 1. *Totenberg, violin; Vienna State Opera Orch.; Golschmann, cond.; Hartford Symphony Orch.; F. Mahler, cond.* Reissue.
+ Fa 5-6/92: 126

35503. OVC 4047: BLOCH—Schelomo; Israel symphony. *Nelsova, cello; Utah Symphony Orch.; Abravanel, cond.* Reissues.
+ Fa 5-6/92: 126

35504. OVC 4050—4051 (2 separate discs): GOTTSCHALK—Piano works, vol. 1-2. *List, Lewis, Werner, Nibley, piano; Utah Symphony Orch.; Abravanel, cond.* Reissues.
+ ARG 11-12/92: 127
+ Gr 5/93: 62

35505. OVC 4052: BLOCH—Concerto symphonique. *Mitchell, piano; Vienna State Opera Orch.; Golschmann, cond.*
□ ARG 11-12/92: 91

35506. OVC 4065: MUSSORGSKY—Pictures at an exhibition. STRAVINSKY—Petrushka. *Philharmonia Orch.; London Symphony Orch.; Mackerras, cond.* Reissue.
+ ARG 11-12/92: 163

VANGUARD

35507. OVC 4068: Schubert—
Impromptus. *L. Kraus, piano.* Recorded
1967.
+ ARG 1-2/93: 145

35508. OVC 4071 (2 discs): Handel—
Judas Maccabeus. *Harper, Watts, Young,
Shirley-Quirk; Amor Artis Chorale;
English Chamber Orch.; Somary, cond.*
+ ARG 11-12/92: 129
+ Gr 7/93: 75
+ ON 3/19/94: 31

35509. OVC 4073: Handel—Judas
Maccabeus (highlights). *Harper, Watts,
Young, Shirley-Quirk; Amor Artis
Chorale; English Chamber Orch.;
Somary, cond.*
+ ARG 11-12/92: 129

35510. OVC 4074 (2 discs): Handel—
Theodora. *Harper, Forrester, Young,
Lawrenson; English Chamber Orch.;
Somary, cond.* Reissue.
+ ARG 5-6/93: 91
+ Gr 7/93: 75
+ ON 6/93: 42

35511. OVC 4076: Harris—Folksong
symphony. Creston—Gregorian chant for
strings. *Orch.; Golschmann, cond.*
Reissue.
□ ARG 5-6/93: 91
- Fa 3-4/94: 168

35512. OVC 4080 (3 discs): Music of
Prokofiev, Beethoven, Franck,
Rachmaninoff, Leclair, and others. *D.
Oistrakh, violin; Oborin, Yampolsky,
piano.* Recorded 1953-54.
+ ARG 5-6/94: 188

35513. OVC 4083: Bach—Solo cello
suites no. 2, 5; Air for the G string;
Adagio from Toccata in C. *Rostropovich,
cello.*
+ ARG 3-4/94: 67

35514. OVC 5000: Haydn—Symphonies
no. 60, 70, 81. *Esterhazy Orch. Blum,
cond.* Reissue.
+ ARG 1-2/93: 102

35515. OVC 5001: Beethoven—Piano
sonatas no. 30-32. *Hungerford, piano.*
+ ARG 7-8/93: 65

35516. OVC 5002: Goldmark—Rustic
wedding symphony. Enesco—Roumanian
rhapsodies. *Utah Symphony Orch.;
Abravanel, cond; Vienna Opera Orch.;
Golschmann, cond.* Reissues.
+ ARG 1-2/93: 99

35517. OVC 5003: Beethoven—String
quartets no. 15-16. *Yale Quartet.* Reissue.
+ ARG 3-4/93: 57

35518. OVC 5004: Music of Albeniz,
Granados, Falla, Malats, Segovia, Turina,
Torroba, and Sainz de la Maza. *Diaz,
guitar.*
+ ARG 5-6/93: 164

35519. OVC 5006: Music of Mudarra,
Narvaez, Sanz, Scarlatti, Sor, Tarrega,
and others. *Diaz, guitar.* Reissue.
+ ARG 7-8/93: 193

35520. OVC 5007: Liszt—Hungarian
rhapsodies. *Vienna State Opera Orch.;
Fistoulari, cond.* Reissue.
+ ARG 5-6/93: 102

35521. OVC 5010: Ippolitov-Ivanov—
Caucasian sketches. Kabalevsky—The
comedians. Khachaturian—Gayne: Suite.
*Utah Symphony Orch.; Abravanel, cond.;
Vienna State Opera Orch.; Golschmann,
cond.* Reissue.
+ ARG 5-6/93: 96

35522. OVC 5011: Mozart—Concerto
for flute and harp. Telemann—Suite in A
minor. *Baker, flute; Jelinek, harp; I
Solisti di Zagreb; Janigro, cond.* Reissue.
+ ARG 7-8/93: 130

35523. OVC 6008: Anderson—Orchestra
music. *Utah Symphony Orch.; Abravanel,
cond.* Reissue.
+ Fa 11-12/91: 236

35524. OVC 6009: German university
songs. *Kunz, baritone; Vienna State
Opera Orch.; Litschauer, cond.* Reissue.
+ ARG 9-10/94: 261

35525. OVC 6010: German university
songs, vol. 2. *Kunz, tenor; Vienna State
Opera; Paulik, cond.* Reissue.
+ ARG 5-6/96: 256

35526. OVC 6022: Favorite spirituals.
Hayes, tenor; Boardman, piano.
Reissues.
+ ARG 9-10/95: 288

35527. OVC 7001: Mozart—Sinfonie
concertante, K. 364; Violin concertos no.
2-3. *Kakuska, viola; Suk Chamber Orch.;
Suk, violin, cond.*
- ARG 11-12/91: 104
+ Fa 9-10/91: 294
+ Gr 6/91: 46

35528. OVC 7002/03 (2 discs): Bach—
The Brandenburg concertos (complete);
Suite no. 2. *Laniar, cello; Paterova,
harpsichord; Suk Chamber Orch.; Suk,
violin & cond.*
- ARG 9-10/91: 37
+ Fa 9-10/91: 144

35529. VBD 10016: *Fiddle faddle: the
music of Leroy Anderson.* Sleigh ride;
Bleu tango; Trumpeter's lullaby; The
belle of the ball; Bugler's holiday;
Forgotten dream; Syncopated clock;
Plink, plank, plunk; Fiddle faddle;
Sandpaper ballet; Typewriter; Sarabande;
Song of the bells; Jazz pizzicato;
Serenata. *Utah Symphony Orch.;
Abravanel, cond.*
+ ARG 7-8/88: 9
● Fa 3-4/88: 61

35530. VBD 71176: Handel—Music for
the royal fireworks; Water music suite in
F. *English Chamber Orch.; Somary,
cond.*
+ ARG 9-10/88: 49
● Fa 3-4/88: 121

35531. VCD 72008: Weber—
Symphonies no. 1-2. Beethoven—
Coriolan overture; Leonore overture no.
3. *Academy of St. Martin-in-the-Fields;
Phil. Promenade Orch.; Marriner, Boult,
conds.*
+ Fa 1-2/88: 239

35532. VCD 72010: *Showpieces for
piano.* Music of Herz, Thallberg,
Godowsky, and Liszt. *Wild, piano.*
+ Fa 1-2/88: 262

35533. VCD 72011: Franck—Symphony
in D minor. Debussy—Nocturnes for
orchestra. *Women of the Houston
Symphony Chorale; Houston Symphony
Orch.; Comissiona, cond.*
● Fa 1-2/88: 122

35534. VCD 72012: Music of
Tchaikovsky, Wiren, Arensky, and
Borodin. *English Chamber Orch.;
Somary, cond.*
+ Fa 7-8/89: 335

35535. VCD 72013: Purcell—Ode for
St. Cecilia's day; Rejoice in the Lord
alway. *Soloists; Ambrosian Singers;
Kalmar Chamber Orch.; Oriana
Chamber Orch.; Tippett, Deller, conds.*
+ ARG 9-10/88: 73
+ DA 7/88: 54
+ Fa 1-2/88: 193

35536. VCD 72014: *Great Bach organ
works.* Toccata and fugue BWV 565;
Fantasia and fugue BWV 542; Liebster
Herr Jesu BWV 730-31; Prelude and
fugue BWV 536, 548; Passacaglia BWV
582; Fantasia BWV 572. *Heiller, organ.*
● Fa 1-2/88: 79

35537. VCD 72016: *Viennese bonbons.*
Music of J. Strauss, Sr., Lanner, J.
Strauss, Jr., Mayer, and others. *Willi
Boskovsky Ensemble; Boskovsky, cond.*
+ Fa 1-2/88: 278

35538. VCD 72019: Music of Rimsky-
Korsakov, Ippolitov-Ivanov, Glière, and
Tchaikovsky. *Utah Symphony Orch.;
Abravanel, cond.*
+ Fa 1-2/88: 200

35539. VCD 72020: *Paul Roveson live at
Carnegie Hall.* Music of Alexandrov,
Clutsam, Kern, Dvořák, Mussorgsky, and
others. *Robeson, bass; Booth, piano.*
Recorded live 1958.
+ Fa 1-2/88: 252

35540. VCD 72021: *English keyboard
music.* Music of Byrd, Tallis, Gibbons,
Dowland, Farnaby, and others. *Pinnock,*

harpsichord & virginal.
  - Fa 9-10/88: 329 m.f.

35541. VCD 72022: Mozart—Piano concertos no. 9, 14; Fantasia in C minor K. 396. *Brendel, piano; I Solisti di Zagreb; Janigro, cond.*
  + Fa 1-2/89: 212

35542. VCD 72023: Music of Debussy, Ravel, and Respighi. *Baltimore Symphony Orch.; Houston Symphony Orch.; Comissiona, cond.*
  • Fa 9-10/88: 349

35543. VCD 72025: *A sonata recital by Bela Bartók and Joseph Szigeti.* Music of Bartók, Beethoven, and Debussy. *Szigeti, violin; Bartók, piano.*
  + ARG 1-2/89: 21
  + Fa 11-12/88: 130

35544. VCD 72026: *The world of Louis Moreau Gottschalk.* Grand tarantelle for piano and orchestra; Symphony no. 1; Piano music: The banjo; The dying poet; Souvenir de Porto Rico; Le bananier; Ojos criollos; The maiden's blush; The last hope; Pasquinade Tournament galop; Bamboula. *List, Nibley, pianos; Utah Symphony Orch.; Abravanel, cond.*
  + ARG 3-4/89: 39
  • Fa 5-6/89: 205

35545. VCD 72027: Music of Mozart, Schumann, Chopin, and Liszt. *Brendel, piano.*
  • ARG 5-6/89: 118

35546. VCD 72028: Dvořák—Piano quintet no. 2. Mozart—Piano quartet no. 1, K. 478. *Serkin, piano; Schneider, Galimir, violins; Tree, viola; Soyer, cello.*
  + ARG 3-4/89: 31
  + Fa 5-6/89: 183

35547. VCD 72029: Music of Tchaikovsky, Berlioz, and Rimsky-Korsakov. *Baltimore Symphony Orch.; Comissiona, cond.*
  • ARG 5-6/89: 96

35548. VCD 72030: Ives—Symphonies no. 3-4; The circus band march; Set for theater orchestra. *Ambrosian Singers; New Philharmonia Orch.; Royal Phil. Orch.; Farberman, cond.*
  + DA 4/89: 60
  • Fa 5-6/89: 205

35549. VCD 72031: Bloch—Israel symphony; Concerto symphonique for piano and orchestra. *Mitchell, piano; Vienna State Opera Orch.; Utah Symphony Orch.; Golschmann, Abravanel, conds.*
  + ARG 5-6/89: 24
  + Fa 5-6/89: 140

35550. OVC 8001/02 (2 discs): Canteloube—Songs of the Auvergne. Canteloube-Kingsley—New songs of the Auvergne. *Davrath, soprano; orchestra;*

La Roche, Kingsley, conds. Reissue.
  + Fa 11-12/91: 292
  + Gr 10/91: 153

35551. OVC 8003: Dvořák—Piano quintet, op. 81. *P. Serkin, piano; Schneider, Galimir, violins; Tree, viola; Soyer, cello.*
  + ARG 7-8/91: 54
  + Fa 9-10/91: 205

35552. OVC 8007: Mozart—Piano quartets no. 1-2. *Serkin, piano; Schneider, violin; Tree, viola; Soyer, cello.*
  + ARG 7-8/91: 95
  + Fa 9-10/91: 288

35553. OVC 8008: *Szigeti and Bartók in recital.* Beethoven—Violin sonata no. 9 Bartók—Violin sonata no. 2; Rhapsody no. 1. Debussy—Violin sonata. *Bartók, piano; Szigeti, violin.* Recorded 1940.
  + Fa 11-12/91: 266

35554. OVC 8012: Tchaikovsky—Symphony no. 4. Scriabin—Etude in C♯ minor, op. 2, no. 1. *American Symphony Orch.; Stokowski, cond.* Reissue.
  • ARG 5-6/92: 146

35555. OVC 8013: Thomson—The River: Suite; The Plow that broke the plains: Suite. Stravinsky—Histoire du soldat: Suite. *Symphony of the Air; Stokowski, cond.* Reissue.
  + Fa 11-12/91: 510

35556. OVC 8014: Bloch—America: an epic rhapsody. *Symphony of the Air; Stokowski, cond.* Recorded 1960.
  + ARG 5-6/94: 70
  + Fa 11-12/92: 202

35557. OVC 8016: *The charm of old Vienna.* Music of J. Strauss Sr., Mayer, Haydn, Lanner, and Beethoven. *Willi Boskovsky and ensemble.* Reissue.
  + Fa 3-4/92: 330

35558. OVC 8021/22 (2 discs): Bach—Six sonatas and partitas for solo violin, BWV 1001-1006. *Szigeti, violin.* Mono.
  + Fa 3-4/92: 138

35559. OVC 8023: The holly and the ivy: Christmas carols of old England. *Deller Consort.*
  + ARG 11-12/92: 268

35560. OVC 8024/25 (2 separate discs): Mozart—String quintets, no. 2-6; Adagio & fugue, K. 546. *Griller Quartet; Primrose, viola.* Reissues.
  + Fa 3-4/92: 264

35561. OVC 8027: Purcell—Birthday ode "Come ye sons of art away"; The bell anthem "Rejoice in the Lord alway"; My beloved spake; St. Cecilia's Day ode "Welcome to all the pleasures". *Deller Consort; Oriana Concert Choir & Orch.; Kalmar Chamber Orch. of London;*

Bergmann, harpsichord; Deller, alto & cond. Reissue.
  • Gr 7/95: 104

35562. OVC 8031/2 (2 discs): Tchaikovsky—Symphony no. 5; Piano concerto no. 1; Romeo and Juliet. *Ogdon, piano; London Symphony Orch.; Monteux, cond.* Recorded 1963.
  + ARG 9-10/92: 172
  + Gr 3/95: 56

35563. OVC 8043/5 (3 discs): Rossini—La pietra del paragone. *Wolff, Carreras, Reardon, Díaz; Clarion Concerts Orch.; Jenkins, cond.* Reissue.
  • ARG 3-4/93: 130
  + Fa 3-4/93: 264
  + Gr 12/92: 140

35564. OVC 8046 (2 discs): Bach—Well-tempered clavier book 1. *Horszowski, piano.*
  + ARG 7-8/93: 60
  + Gr 12/93: 91

35565. OVC 8048: Krenek—Jonny spielt auf. *Blankenship, Lear, Popp, Stewart; Vienna State Opera; Hollreiser, cond.*
  • ARG 11-12/93: 137

35566. OVC 8049: Brahms—Serenade no. 1. *Chelsea Chamber Ensemble; American Symphony Orch.; Botstein, cond.*
  • ARG 5-6/94: 75

35567. OVC 8054: Arias from Meistersinger, Parsifal, Vespri siciliani, and others. *Schoeffler, bass.* Recorded 1955.
  + ARG 11-12/96: 304

35568. OVC 8055: Stravinsky—Concerto for string orchestra; Dumbarton Oaks. Bartók—Divertimento. *Zürich Chamber Orch.; Stoutz, cond.* Reissue.
  □ ARG 9-10/96: 210

35569. OVC 8056: Rzewski—The people united will never be defeated. *Oppens, piano.* Reissue.
  + ARG 1-2/94: 154

35570. OVC 8060 (4 discs): Beethoven—Violin sonatas (complete). *Szigeti, violin; Arrau, piano.* Recorded 1944.
  + ARG 5-6/94: 202

35571. OVC 8067: Milhaud—Pacem in terris; L'homme et son désir. *Kopleff, Quilico, Christensen, Chartland; Utah Symphony Orch.; Abravanel, cond.* Reissue.
  + ARG 7-8/94: 133
  • Gr 11/93: 130

35572. OVC 8069: Castelnuovo-Tedesco—Guitar concerto no. 1. Music of Vivaldi. Diaz, and Kohaut. *Diaz, guitar; I Solisti di Zagreb; Janigro, cond.*

VANGUARD

Recorded 1965.
    + ARG 11-12/96: 110

35573. OVC 8072: Beethoven—Piano sonatas no. 14, 26, 32. *Novaes, piano.*
    • ARG 5-6/95: 84

35574. OVC 8073: Beethoven—Bagatelles (complete). *Matthews, piano.* Reissue.
    + ARG 7-8/95: 81

35575. OVC 8074: Beethoven—Eroica variations; 32 variations in C minor; Variations, op. 34. *Matthews, piano.* Reissue.
    + ARG 7-8/95: 81

35576. OVC 8075: Charpentier—Te Deum; Magnificat. *Jeunesses Musicales; J.-F. Paillard Chamber Orch.; Paillard, cond.* Reissue.
    + ARG 7-8/96: 98

35577. OVC 8076: *Richter in recital.* Music of Haydn, Debussy, and Prokofiev. *Richter, piano.* Recorded live 1961.
    + ARG 1-2/95: 228

35578. OVC 8077: Shostakovich—Piano quintet; String quartet no. 2. *Shostakovich, piano; Beethoven Quartet.* Recorded 1951, 1961.
    + ARG 1-2/95: 178
    + Fa 1-2/95: 269

35579. OVC 8078 (3 discs): Strauss family—Dance music. *Vienna State Opera Orch.; Paulik, cond.* Reissues.
    + ARG 3-4/95: 193

35580. OVC 8082 (2 discs): J. Strauss, Jr.—The gypsy baron. *Schriever, Loose, Rössl-Majdan, Kmentt, Wächter; Wiener Volksoper; Paulik, cond.* Recorded 1956.
    + ARG 5-6/96: 204

35581. OVC 8084 (2 discs): Beethoven—Egmont; Creatures of Prometheus: Excerpts. Schubert—Rosamunde. *Davrath, soprano; Utah Symphony Orch.; Abravanel, cond.* Reissue.
    • ARG 7-8/95: 83

35582. OVC 8087: Bartók—Piano music. *Kraus, piano.*
    + ARG 7-8/95: 80

35583. OVC 8090: Music of Krommer, Weber, Wagner, and Debussy. *Brymer, clarinet; Vienna State Opera Orch.; Prohaska, cond.* Reissues.
    • ARG 11-12/95: 248

35584. OVC 8091: Purcell—Fantasias for viols. *Concentus Musicus Wien; Harnoncourt, cond.* Recorded 1965.
    • ARG 9-10/95: 106

35585. OVC 8100: Monteverdi—Ballo delle ingrate; Lamento d'Arianna. *Deller,*

countertenor; Deller Consort. Reissue.
    • ARG 7-8/96: 156

35586. OVC 8101: William Byrd and his age. *Deller, countertenor; Wenzinger Consort of Viols.* Recorded 1956.
    + ARG 7-8/96: 265

35587. OVC 8102: *Alfred Deller edition, vol. 3.* Elizabethan and Jocobean airs. *Deller, countertenor; Dupré, lute; Leonhardt, harpsichord; Harnoncourt Consort of Viols.* Reissue.
    + ARG 9-10/96: 259

35588. OVC 8103: *Alfred Deller edition, vol. 4.* The silver swan. *Deller, countertenor; Deller Consort.* Reissue.
    + ARG 9-10/96: 259

35589. OVC 8200 (3 discs): Schubert—Impromptus; Sonatas, D. 664, 845, 960; Wanderer fantasy. *Kraus, piano.* Reissue.
    + ARG 1-2/96: 168
    + Fi 9/96: 132

35590. OVC 9008: Bartók—Concerto for orchestra. Kodály—Psalmus hungaricus. *Houston Symphony Orch.; Stokowski, cond.; Nilsson, tenor; London Phil. Orch. & Chorus; Ferencsik, cond.*
    + ARG 3-4/95: 71

35591. VBD 10017: Gershwin—Piano concerto in F; An American in Paris; Rhapsody in blue. *Lownthal, piano; Utah Symphony Orch.; Abravanel, cond.*
    - ARG 1-2/89: 52
    + Fa 11-12/88: 187

35592. VBD 10025: Vaughan Williams—Fantasia on a theme by Thomas Tallis; Five variants on Dives and Lazarus; Flos campi; Fantasia on Greensleeves. *Lentz, viola; University of Utah Chamber Choir; Utah Symphony Orch.; Abravanel, cond.*
    + ARG 9-10/88: 90
    • DA 4/89: 67
    • Fa 11-12/88: 298

35593. VBDS 10090 (2 discs): Handel—Messiah. *Price, Minton, Young, Díaz; Amor Artis Chorale; English Chamber Orch.; Somary, cond.*
    + ARG 3-4/89: 44

35594. VDB2 10138 (2 discs): Bach—Well-tempered clavier bk. 1. *Horszowski, piano.*
    • DA 11/89: 64
    + Fa 9-10/89: 125

35595. VBD 25002: Ravel—Sonatine en trio (arr. Salzedo). Fauré—Impromptu, op. 86. Debussy—Syrinx; Sonata for flute, viola, and harp. Devienne—Duo no. 3 for flute and viola. *Orpheus Trio.*
    • Fa 3-4/88: 264

35596. VBD 25003: Music of Schubert, Bach, Haydn, and Mozart. *Kraus, piano.*
    - Fa 3-4/88: 190

35597. VBD 25007: Haydn—Symphonies no. 100, 103. *Mostly Mozart Orch.; Somary, cond.*
    • Fa 11-12/88: 198

35598. VBD 25009: Debussy—String quartet op. 10. Ravel—String quartet. *Galimir Quartet.*
    + Fa 11-12/88: 167

35599. 99087: Locatelli—Trio sonatas, op. 5. *Musica ad Rhenum.*
    + Gr 7/96: 71

35600. 99091: Rachmaninoff—Piano concertos no. 3-4. *Lugansky, piano; Russian State Symphony Orch.; Shpiller, cond.*
    • Gr 6/96: 52

VARESE SARABANDE

35601. VSD 5257: Waxman—Film music, vol. 2. *Queensland Symphony; Mills, cond.*
    • ARG 3-4/92: 164

35602. VSD 5311: Korngold—Sinfonietta, op. 5. *Berlin Radio Symphony Orch.; Albrecht, cond.*
    + Gr 10/91: 80

35603. VSD 5346: Korngold—Symphony in F♯, op. 40. *Munich Phil. Orch.; Kempe, cond.* Reissue.
    + Gr 6/92: 44

35604. VSD 5600: Herrmann—Vertigo. *Scottish National Orch.; McNeely, cond.*
    + ARG 7-8/96: 182
    + Fi 9/96: 124

35605. VCD 47214: Korngold—Sinfonietta op. 5. *Berlin Radio Symphony Orch.; Albrecht, cond.* Issued also as LP: 704.200.
    + Fa 5-6/86: 165
    + Gr 6/86: 54
    + HF 2/87: 60

35606. VCD 47232: Saint-Saëns—Symphony no. 3. Mendelssohn—Hebrides overture. *Rawsthorne, organ; Royal Liverpool Phil. Orch.; Tjeknavorian, cond.*
    - ARG 1-2/87: 56
    + DA 7/87: 63
    + Fa 1-2/87: 168

35607. VCD 47239: Menotti—Violin concerto in A minor. Barber—Violin concerto op. 14. *Ricci, violin; Pacific Symphony Orch.; Clark, cond.*
    + Fa 9-10/86: 186
    + HF 3/87: 63
    + SR 1/87: 141

35608. VCD 47245: Harris—Symphony no. 6. Copland—Songs on poems of Emily Dickinson. *Nixon, soprano; Pacific Symphony Orch.; Clark, cond.*
    + ARG 1-2/87: 35

+ Fa 5-6/87: 130
+ MA 11/87: 61

35609. VCD 47253: Music of Ligeti, Takemitsu, Xenakis, and Ichiyanagi. *Takahashi, piano; Yomiuri Nihon Symphony Orch.; Ozawa, cond.*
☐ Fa 1-2/87: 257

35610. VCD 47257: Villa-Lobos—Bachianas brasileiras no. 7; Chôros no. 6. *Berlin Radio Symphony Orch.; Villa-Lobos, cond.*
+ ARG 11-12/87: 80
+ Fa 3-4/87: 231
+ Ov 4/87: 38

35611. VCD 47259: Stravinsky—Symphony in 3 movements. Prokofiev—Gypsy fantasia; Symphonic suite of waltzes. *Vienna Phil. Orch.; Kansas City Phil. Orch.; Furtwängler, Schwieger, conds.*
+ ARG 1-2/87: 50
+ Fa 3-4/87: 217

704.200 see VCD 47214.

VENGO

35612. 354.402/03 (2 discs): Martin—Golgotha. *Bargen, Hungerbühler, Decker, Gebhardt, Blasius; Chorus of the Erlöserkirche, Bad Homburg; Frankfurter Bläservereingung; Offenbacher Chamber Orch.; Siemens, cond.*
• Fa 1-2/90: 220

35613. 354.404: Music of Janáček, Martinů, and Prokofiev. *Panke, cello; Mokrosch, piano.*
+ Fa 7-8/90: 359

VEPS

35614. VEPS-CD 012-89: *Norwegian guitar music.* Music of Hvoslef, Kvandal, Bibalo, Sommerfeldt, and Evensen. *Stenstadvold, guitar.*
+ ARG 1-2/90: 119
+ Fa 11-12/89: 464

35615. VEPS-CD 028-90: Music of Gershwin, Brouwer, Terzi, Dyens, Brattland, Barrios, and Grieg. *Brattland, Taylor, guitars.*
• ARG 1-2/92: 154

VERDA

35616. 1: *Be thou my vision.* Music of Schubert, Bach, Montani, Dobici, Day, Tchaikovsky, Attwood, Gottschalk, Verdi, Gregorian chant, and Anon. *Henjum, soprano; Hartman, piano; Boschker, organ; Fay, English horn & oboe; Storhaug, horn.*
+ Fa 9-10/96: 367

VERNISSAGE

35617. VR 1019: Music of Mozart, Faith, Khachaturian, and Milhaud. *Ensemble da Camera of Washington.*
+ ARG 5-6/95: 207
+ Fa 5-6/95: 427

35618. VR 1020: Prokofiev—Violin sonata no. 1. Music of Tchaikovsky, and Frolov. *Rylatko, violin; Balakerskaia, piano.*
+ ARG 7-8/96: 170
+ Fa 7-8/96: 265

VERONA

35619. 2701: Schubert—Die schöne Müllerin. *Wunderlich, tenor; Giesen, piano.* Recorded live 1965.
• ARG 5-6/90: 101
+ DA 9/90: 58
- Fa 3-4/90: 284

35620. 2702: Schubert—Winterreise. *Fischer-Dieskau, baritone; Reutter, piano.* Recorded live 1952.
• Fa 3-4/90: 287

35621. 2704/05 (2 discs): Bellini—La sonnambula. *Callas, Angioletti, Monti, Zaccaria; Teatro alla Scala Chorus & Orch.; Votto, cond.* Recorded live 1957 in Cologne.
+ Fa 3-4/90: 146

35622. 2706: Bellini—Il pirata: Col sorriso d'innocenza. Verdi—Don Carlo: Tu che la vanità; I vespri siciliani overture. *Callas, soprano; Concertgebouw Orch.; Rescigno, cond.*
+ Fa 3-4/90: 347 m.f.

35623. 2707/08 (2 discs): Bizet—Pêcheurs de perles. *Spoorenberg, Vanzo, Joris, Hoekman; Netherlands Radio Phil. Orch.; Fournet, cond.* Recorded live 1963.
• ARG 5-6/90: 32
☐ Fa 3-4/90: 150

35624. 2709/10 (2 discs): Donizetti—Lucia di Lammermoor. *Callas, Di Stefano, Panerai, Zaccaria; Teatro alla Scala Chorus; Berlin Radio Orch.; Karajan, cond.* Recorded live 1955.
+ Fa 3-4/90: 171

35625. 27011/13 (3 discs): Handel—Alcina. *Sutherland, Dijck, Procter, Wunderlich, Monti, Hemsley; Cologne Radio Choir; Capella Coloniensis; Leitner, cond.* Recorded live 1959.
+ ARG 9-10/90: 70
+ Fa 3-4/90: 185

35626. 27014/15 (2 discs): Mascagni—Iris. *Olivero, Ottolini, Capecchi, Clabassi; Netherlands Radio Chorus & Orch.; Vernizzi, cond.* Recorded live 1963.
• ARG 5-6/90: 73
• Fa 3-4/90: 226

35627. 27016/17 (2 discs): Gluck—Orfeo ed Euridice. *Ferrier, Koeman, Duval; Netherlands Opera Chorus & Orch.; Bruck, cond.*
+ ARG 5-6/90: 55 (Ferrier)
• ARG 5-6/90: 55 (otehrs)
+ Fa 3-4/90: 184 (Ferrier)
- Fa 3-4/90: 184 (others)

35628. 27018/20 (3 discs): Bellini—Norma. *Callas, Stignani, Southerland, Picchi, Vaghi; Royal Opera House Covent Garden Chorus & Orch.; Gui, cond.*
+ Fa 3-4/90: 145

35629. 27021: *Elisabeth Schwarzkopf recital.* Music of Wolf, Mozart, Schubert, and Strauss. *Schwarzkopf, soprano; Nobel, piano.* Recorded live 1957, 1962.
+ ARG 5-6/90: 152
+ Fa 3-4/90: 345

35630. 27022: *Recital.* Music of Beach, Strauss, Leoncavallo, Kremser, and others. *Björling, tenor; unidentified orchestras & conds.* Recorded live 1939-1952.
+ ARG 5-6/90: 145
• Fa 3-4/90: 347

35631. 27023/24 (2 discs): Donizetti—Don Pasquale. *D'Angelo, Kraus, Capecchi, Corena; Teatro San Carlo, Naples Chorus & Orch.; Erede, cond.* Recorded live 1963.
+ DA 11/90: 74
+ Fa 9-10/90: 228

35632. 27027/28 (2 discs): Puccini—Tosca. *Callas, Cioni, Gobbi; Royal Opera House Covent Garden Chorus & Orch.; Cillario, cond.* Recorded live 1964.
• Fa 9-10/90: 339

35633. 27032/34 (3 discs): Handel—Xerxes. *Cook, Hallstein, Töpper, Wunderlich, Pöld, Köhn, Probstl; Bavarian Radio Chorus & Orch.; Kubelik, cond.* Recorded live 1962.
• ARG 11-12/90: 64
+ DA 1/91: 70
• Fa 9-10/90: 257

35634. 27035/37 (3 discs): Handel—Giulio Cesare. *Popp, Ludwig, Wunderlich, Berry; Bavarian Radio Chorus; Munich Phil. Orch.; Leitner, cond.* Sung in German; recorded live 1966.
+ ARG 11-12/90: 64
+ Fa 9-10/90: 257 m.f.

35635. 27038/39 (2 discs): Mozart—Idomeneo. *Janowitz, Tarres, Pavarotti, Lewis; Glyndebourne Festival Chorus; London Phil. Orch.; Pritchard, cond.* Recorded live 1964.
+ Fa 9-10/90: 306

35636. 27040/41 (2 discs): Verdi—Jérusalem. *Gencer, Aragall, Guelfi;*

VERONA

Teatro la Fenice, Venice Chorus & Orch.; Gavazzeni, cond. Recorded live 1963.
+ DA 11/90: 74
• Fa 9-10/90: 418

35637. 27042/43 (2 discs): VERDI—Alzira. DONIZETTI—Maria di Rohan: Cupa fatal mestizia; Avvi un Dio; Anna Bolena: Piangete voi. *Zeani, Cecchele, MacNeil, Cava; Rome Opera Chorus & Orch.; Capuana, cond.* Recorded live 1967.
• DA 1/91: 68
• Fa 9-10/90: 415

35638. 27044/45 (2 discs): BEETHOVEN—Fidelio. *Flagstad, Schwarzkopf, Patzak, Schöffler, Greindl; Vienna State Opera Chorus; Vienna Phil. Orch.; Furtwängler, cond.* Recorded live 1950.
+ ARG 11-12/90: 26
+ DA 11/90: 74
+ Fa 9-10/90: 168

35639. 27046/47 (2 discs): DONIZETTI—Fille du régiment. *Freni, Stasio, Pavarotti, Ganzarolli; Teatro alla Scala Chorus & Orch.; Sanzogno, cond.* Recorded live 1969.
+ DA 11/90: 74
+ Fa 9-10/90: 229

35640. 27048/49 (2 discs): DONIZETTI—Belisario. *Gencer, Pecile, Grilli, Taddei, Zaccaria; Teatro La Fenice Chorus & Orch.; Gavazzeni, cond.* Recorded live 1969.
+ Fa 9-10/90: 227

35641. 27050/51 (2 discs): CORNELIUS—Der Barbier von Bagdad. *Jurinac, Schock, Frick; Vienna Radio Chorus & Orch.; Hollreiser, cond.* Recorded live 1952.
+ Fa 9-10/90: 217

35642. 27052/53 (2 discs): MASSENET—Manon. *Freni, Pavarotti, Panerai, Zerbini; Teatro alla Scala; Maag, cond.* Sung in Italian; recorded live 1969.
• ARG 11-12/90: 78
- Fa 9-10/90: 289

35643. 27054/55 (2 discs): VERDI—La traviata. *Callas, Valletti, Zanasi; Royal Opera House Covent Garden; Rescigno, cond.* Recorded live 1958.
+ Fa 9-10/90: 423

35644. 27056: VERDI—Il trovatore: Tacea la notte; D'amor sull'ali rose; Un ballo in maschera: Che v'agita cosi; Ecco L'orrido campo; Teco io sto; Forza del destino: Pace, pace mio Dio; Aida: Titorna vincitor; La fatal pietra; Otello: Dio ti giocondi. *Brouwenstijn, soprano; various orchs. & conds.* Recorded live 1950s.
+ Fa 9-10/90: 447

35645. 27058/59 (2 discs): Music of Wagner, Bellini, Verdi, Donizetti,

Delibes, and others. *Callas, soprano; various orchs. & conds.* Recorded live.
+ Fa 9-10/90: 451

35646. 27060/61 (2 discs): VERDI—Requiem. ROSSINI—Stabat Mater. *Price, Cossotto, Pavarotti, Ghiaurov, Zylis-Gara, Verrett, Zaccaria; Teatro alla Scala Chorus & Orch.; Italian Radio and Television Rome Chorus & Symphony Orch.; Karajan, Giulini, conds.* Recorded live 1967.
+ Fa 9-10/90: 421

35647. 27064: SCHUBERT—Schwanengesang; Der Kreuzzug; Rastlose Liebe; Der Zwerg; Winterreise; Gute Nacht; Frühlingstraum; Die Post; Der Leiermann. *Fischer-Dieskau, baritone; Billing, piano.*
+ Fa 9-10/90: 372

35648. 27065/67 (3 discs): MOZART—Don Giovanni. *Price, Güden, Sciutti, Wunderlich, Wächter, Berry, Panerai; Vienna Phil. Orch.; Karajan, cond.* Recorded live 1963.
+ Fa 11-12/90: 289

35649. 27068: Recital, vol. 2. Music of Verdi, Handel, Niedermeyer, Alfvén, Sibelius, and others. *Björling, tenor; various orchs. & conds.* Recorded live.
• Fa 9-10/90: 461

35650. 27069: Recitals, vol. 2. Music of Rossini, Massenet, Verdi, Puccini, and Spontini. *Callas, soprano; various orchs. & conds.* Recorded live.
• Fa 9-10/90: 451

35651. 27070/72 (3 discs): BACH—St. Matthew passion. *Seefried, Ferrier, Ludwig, Schöffler, Edelmann; Wiener Singverein; Vienna Phil. Orch.; Karajan, cond.* Recorded live 1950.
• Fa 9-10/90: 150 m.f.

35652. 27073/74 (2 discs): BACH—Mass in B minor. *Schwarzkopf, Ferrier, Ludwig, Poell, Schöffler; Wiener Singverein; Vienna Phil. Orch.; Karajan, cond.* Recorded live 1950.
• Fa 9-10/90: 150 m.f.

35653. 27075: Elisabeth Schwarzkopf sings. Music of Schubert, Brahms, Mahler, and strauss. *Schwarzkopf, soprano; various accs.* Recorded live 1960, 1962, 1964.
• Fa 9-10/90: 449

35654. 27076: BACH—St. Matthew Passion: excerpts; Mass in B minor: excerpts. MAHLER—Symphony no. 2: Urlicht. *Ferrier, Seefried, Schwarzkopf; Vienna Phil. Orch.; Concertgebouw Orch.; Karajan, Klemperer, conds.* Recorded live.
+ Fa 9-10/90: 150

VERRA

35655. 101 (LP): REKASIUS—Symphony no. 5; Metaphony; Violin concerto; String quartet no. 3. *Katilius, violin; Lithuanian State Phil. Symphony Orch.; Domarkas, cond.; Vilnius String Quartet.*
+ Fa 7-8/86: 212

VEST-NORSK

35656. VNP 0090-0019: BERGH—String quartet no. 1; String quintet. *Norwegian Quartet; Konstantynovicz, viola.*
+ ARG 1-2/92: 31

35657. VNP 0091-0020: GRIEG—4 Hymns; Album for male choir. *Bjørkøy, baritone; Bergen Cathedral Choir; Mangersnes, cond.*
+ ARG 11-12/91: 70

35658. VNP 0093-0024: GRIEG—Ballade, op. 24; Norwegian folk tunes, op. 66. *Kayser, piano.* Reissue.
- ARG 9-10/93: 127
+ Fa 7-8/93: 145

VESTIGE

35659. 04: CONSTANTINIDES—Hymn to the human spirit; Reflections IV; Intimations; Four Sappho songs; Mutability; Four Greek songs. *Poole, tenor; Petros, Straley, DeVerger, sopranos; Louisiana State Symphony Orch.; Yestadt, cond.; New Music Ensemble; Constantinides, cond.*
+ ARG 3-4/96: 104

VICTORIA

35660. VCD 19001: Marianne Hirsti in recital. Music of Mendelssohn, Mozart, Grieg, Mahler, and Britten. *Hirsti, soprano; Jansen, piano.*
+ ARG 3-4/90: 152
• Fa 3-4/90: 344

35661. VCD 19002: Geir Henning Braaten in recital. Music of Bach (arr. Liszt), Beethoven, Bibalo, and Alkan. *Braaten, piano.*
+ Fa 9-10/90: 477

35662. VCD 19005: Music of Grieg, Sibelius, Müllenbach, and Strauss. *Lund, mezzo-soprano; Müllenbach, piano.*
+ Fa 9-10/90: 455

35663. VCD 19006: GRIEG—Violin sonata in C minor. BRUSTAD—Eventyrsuite; Capricci. HALVORSEN—Passacaglia; Sarabande con variazioni. *Tonnesen, violin; Tomter, viola; Askeland, piano.*
+ ARG 11-12/91: 71
+ Fa 3-4/91: 226
+ Gr 10/91: 122

35664. VCD 19007: Anne Gjevang in recital. Music of Sibelius, Wolf, Liszt, Grieg, and Falla. *Gjevang, contralto;*

Nökleberg, piano.
+ Fa 9-10/90: 454
+ Gr 11/91: 148

35665. VCD 19009: BRUCKNER—Ave Maria; Locus iste; Os justi; Christus factus est; Virga Jesse. BRAHMS—Est ist das Heil; Geistliches Lied; Warum ist das Licht; Fest und Gedenksprüche; Ich aber bin elend. *Oslo Cathedral Choir; Kvam, cond.*
+ Fa 3-4/90: 161

35666. VCD 19010: BEETHOVEN—Piano sonata no. 29, op. 106 "Hammerklavier"; 6 Bagatelles, op. 126. *Smebye, piano.*
• Fa 3-4/92: 151
+ Gr 9/92: 128

35667. VCD 19011: BEETHOVEN—Piano sonatas no. 8, 14, 23. *Steen-Nøkleberg, piano.*
• ARG 3-4/92: 31
• Fa 1-2/92: 161

35668. VCD 19012: *Song recital.* Music of Mussorgsky, Sibelius, and Wagner. *Berntsen, soprano; Smebye, piano.*
+ Fa 3-4/91: 437
+ Gr 11/91: 148

35669. VCD 19013: *The harpsichord 1689-1789.* Music of Handel, Purcell, Bach, F. Couperin, Scarlatti and others. *Henry, harpsichord.*
+ Gr 10/92: 157

35670. VCD 19014: HALLGRIMSON—Poemi. NORDHEIM—Rendezvous; Boomerang. *Larsen, oboe; Norwegian Chamber Orch.; Eggen, Tonnesen, violins.*
+ Fa 3-4/91: 229
+ Gr 10/91: 124

35671. VCD 19015: *Sweet love doth now invite.* Music of Dowland, Monteverdi, Sor, and Schubert. *Hirsti, soprano; Lislevand, lute, theorbo, guitar.*
+ ARG 7-8/95: 262

35672. VCD 19017: BERG—Vier Lieder, op. 2. KVANDAL—Norwegian folk-songs, op. 40. SHOSTAKOVICH—Seven romances, op. 127. *Berntsen, soprano; Tonnesen, violin; Kvalbein, cello; Smebye, piano.*
+ Gr 11/91: 148

35673. VCD 19018: GRIEG—Songs with orchestra. *Hirsti, soprano; Borkoy, baritone; Trondheim Symphony Orch.; Ruud, cond.*
• Gr 4/92: 126

35674. VCD 19020: DVOŘÁK—Piano trio in B minor, B. 166 "Dumky." SCHUMANN—Piano trio no. 1, op. 63. *Oslo Trio.*
+ Fa 3-4/91: 373
+ Gr 10/91: 124

35675. VCD 19022: Music of Nystedt, Johansson, Schoenberg, and Brahms.

Norwegian Soloists Choir; Baekkelund, Levin, pianos; Nystedt, cond.
+ Fa 5-6/91: 344

35676. VCD 19025: GRIEG—Complete piano music, vol. 1. *Braaten, piano.*
• ARG 7-8/92: 138
+ Fa 3-4/92: 201

35677. VCD 19025—19029 (5 separate discs): GRIEG—Piano music, vol. 1-5. *Braaten, piano.*
+ ARG 9-10/93: 127 (v.2-5)
+ Gr 6/93: 75 (v.1-4)

35678. VCD 19031—19032 (2 separate discs): GRIEG—*Complete piano music, vol. 7-8.* Lyric pieces, op. 57, 62, 65, 68; Norwegian folk songs, op. 66. *Braaten, piano.*
+ ARG 3-4/94: 102
+ Gr 4/94: 70

35679. VCD 19034: GRIEG—Moods, op. 73; Larvik's polka; 23 small piano pieces. *Braaten, piano.*
+ ARG 3-4/94: 102

35680. VCD 19035: GRIEG—Complete piano music, vol. 12. *Braaten, piano.*
+ Fa 1-2/95: 166

35681. VCD 19036: Music of Schumann, Madsen, Britten, and Reizensten. *Hoff, oboe; Ornung, piano.*
- Fa 5-6/91: 371

35682. VCD 19037: *Encores for oboe.* Music of Bach, Pergolesi, Cui, Holford, Saint-Saëns, and others. *Hoff, oboe; Levin, piano.*
+ ARG 7-8/91: 161
+ Fa 5-6/91: 372

35683. VCD 19038: GRIEG—*Songs, vol. 1.* Op. 15, 23, 49, 60. *Hirsti, soprano; Sandve, tenor; Skram, baritone; Jansen, piano.*
+ ARG 3-4/93: 83

35684. VCD 19039: GRIEG—Complete songs, vol. 2. *Skram, baritone; Jansen, piano.*
+ ARG 7-8/93: 97
+ Gr 6/93: 84

35685. VCD 19040: GRIEG—Songs, vol. 3. *Hirsti, soprano; Skram, baritone; Jansen, piano.*
+ ARG 5-6/94: 97
+ Gr 2/94: 79

35686. VCD 19041: GRIEG—Songs, vol. 4. *Hirsti, soprano; Pfeiler, mezzo-soprano; Sandve, tenor; Skram, baritone; Jansen, piano.*
• Gr 8/93: 69

35687. VCD 19043—19044 (2 separate discs): GRIEG—Songs, vol. 6-7. *Hirsti, soprano; Sandve, tenor; Skram, baritone; Jansen, piano.*
• ARG 9-10/94: 136

35688. VCD 19045: STRAUSS—Suite for 13 winds, op. 4; Sonatina no. 1 for winds. *Norwegian Winds; Oskamp, cond.*
+ ARG 5-6/92: 141
+ Fa 3-4/92: 335
+ Gr 8/92: 41

35689. VCD 19048: GRIEG—Complete string quartets. *Norwegian String Quartet.*
+ ARG 5-6/92: 65
+ Fa 3-4/92: 201
+ Gr 8/92: 45

35690. VCD 19049: HAUG—Symphony no. 2; String quartet no. 1; Sonata elegica for cello solo; Dialogue for two harps. *Norwegian Youth Symphony Orch.; Andersen, cond.; Norwegian String Quartet; Kvalbein, cello; Walstad, Postma, harps.*
+ ARG 3-4/92: 70
+ Fa 1-2/92: 232

35691. VCD 19050: NORDHEIM—Rendezvous; Boomerang; Spur. *Larsen, oboe; Norwegian Chamber Orch.; Eggen, cond.; Ellegaard, accordion; Royal Phil. Orch.; Dreier, cond.* Reissue.
+ Fa 1-2/92: 288

35692. VCD 19051: LISZT—Piano sonata. SCHUBERT—Four impromptus, op. 90. *Bratlie, piano.*
• Fa 1-2/92: 252

35693. VCD 19052: *Music for a nordic summer night.* Music of Jarnefeld, Henriques, Nielsen, Aulin, Sibelius, Sinding, and others. *Nilsson, violin; Gimse, piano.*
+ ARG 7-8/93: 183

35694. VCD 19057: SAMMARTINI—Cello sonata in G. DEBUSSY—Cello sonata. FRANCK—Cello sonata. *Kvalbein, cello; Askeland, piano.*
- Fa 1-2/92: 314

35695. VCD 19058: *Music from the top of the world.* Music of Vea, Stromholm, Germeten, Monrad-Johansen, Nordheim and Grieg. *Stodle, piano.*
+ Fa 3-4/92: 406

35696. VCD 19059: GLAZUNOV—Saxophone quartet. O. BERG—Saxophone quartet. LACOUR—Saxophone quartet. *Harald Bergersen's Saxophone Quartet.*
• Fa 3-4/92: 194

35697. VCD 19060: SHOSTAKOVICH—Chamber symphony, op. 110a. JOHANSEN—Concerto for 2 violins and strings. BJORKLUND—Sarek. *Trondheim Soloists; Fiskum, cond.*
+ Fa 3-4/92: 234

35698. VCD 19061: *Organ works on Gregorian themes.* Music of Nielsen, Olsson, and Duruflé. *Rise, organ.*
• ARG 9-10/93: 236

VICTORIA

35699. VCD 19062: Vierne—Organ symphonies no. 2, 5. *Rise, organ.*
+ ARG 9-10/94: 217

35700. VCD 19063: Music of Am, Ashelm, Ginastera, Berio, and Britten. *Vindenes, guitar.*
• ARG 7-8/94: 210

35701. VCD 19066: Grieg—Music for strings. *Trondheim Soloists; Fiskum, cond.*
+ ARG 1-2/94: 104
+ Gr 3/93: 40

35702. VCD 19069: *Mahler, Mahler, and friends.* Music of A. Mahler, G. Mahler, Zemlinsky, and Pfitzner. *Gjevang, alto; Steen-Nøkleberg, piano.*
+ ARG 9-10/96: 156
- Fa 7-8/96: 232

35703. VCD 19070: Grieg—Violin sonatas. *Tonnesen, violin; Smebye, piano.*
• ARG 9-10/94: 136

35704. VCD 19071: Grieg—Intermezzo; Andante con moto; Cello sonata; Holberg suite. *Kvalbein, cello; Askeland, piano; Oslo Trio; Trondheim Soloists; Fiskum, cond.*
+ ARG 11-12/93: 113
+ Gr 11/93: 93

35705. VCD 19072: Grieg—Chamber music, vol. 2. *Hirsti, soprano; Skram, baritone; Hoff, oboe; Solum, horn; Trondheim Soloists; Fiskum, cond.*
• ARG 9-10/94: 136

35706. VCD 19073: Music of Brahms, Schumann, Schubert, and Mussorgsky. *Carlsen, bass; Steen-Nøkleberg, piano.*
+ ARG 1-2/95: 239

35707. VCD 19074: Nielsen—Piano music. *Eggen, piano.*
+ ARG 7-8/95: 163
+ Fa 5-6/95: 276

35708. VCD 19078: Vivaldi—Flautino concerto RV 443; Recorder concerto RV 441. Sammartini—Recorder concerto in F major. Telemann—Recorder concerto in C major. *Brochmann, recorders; Trondheim Soloists; Fiskum, cond.*
+ Fa 3-4/95: 330

35709. VCD 19079: Martin—Piano trio. Tchaikovsky—Piano trio. Grieg—Andante con moto. *Oslo Trio.*
+ ARG 5-6/94: 111
+ Gr 10/93: 71

35710. VCD 19083: Music of Albinoni, Bach, Cimarosa, Handel, and Pergolesi. *Hoff, oboe; English Chamber Orch.; Watson, cond.*
+ ARG 3-4/94: 206

35711. VCD 19084—19086 (3 separate discs): Saevarud—Piano music. *Smebye, piano.*
+ ARG 11-12/94: 181

35712. VCD 19087: *Great twentieth century sonatas.* Berg—Piano sonata, op. 1. Valen—Piano sonata no. 2. Barber—Piano sonata, op. 26. Dutilleux—Piano sonata. *Larsen, piano.*
+ Fa 3-4/95: 383

35713. VCD 19088: Schoenberg—Pierrot lunaire; String quartet no. 2. *Berntsen, soprano; Borealis Ensemble; Eggen, cond.*
• ARG 1-2/95: 167
• Fa 1-2/95: 256

35714. VCD 19095: Dvořák—Wind serenade. Gounod—Petite symphonie. Mendelssohn—Nocturne. Enescu—Dixtuor. *Norwegian Winds; Oskamp, cond.*
+ ARG 11-12/96: 118

35715. VCD 19096: Björkland—Actos; Carmina; Cantos; Per la strada; Sarek. *Thorsen, violin; Trondheim Soloists; Fiskum, cond.; Chilingirian String Quartet.*
+ ARG 9-10/95: 302

35716. VCD 19106: Music of Brahms, Heise, Grieg, and Ravel. *Traesdal, mezzo-soprano; Smebye, piano.*
• ARG 5-6/96: 259

35717. VCD 19107: L. Nielsen—Organ music. *Rise, organ.*
• ARG 11-12/96: 173

VICTORIE

35718. 290212, 290232, 290222, 290232, 290242, 290252, 290262 (6 separate discs): Victorie "Great interpreters" series. *Vocalists from the New York Metropolitan, Covent Garden, Paris Opera, Berlin Staatsoper, Bayreuth, and La Scala.*
- Fa 1-2/95: 336

35719. 290382: Bach—Brass music (arr.). *Quintette Magnifica.*
+ Fa 3-4/95: 116

35720. 290402: Haydn—Cello concertos, H. VIIb, 1-2. *Yang, cello; Zürich Chamber Orch.; Stoutz, cond.*
+ Fa 1-2/95: 171

35721. 291182: A. Gabrieli—Per cantor e sonar. *Innocenti, organ & cond.; Coro della Radiotelevisione della Svizera Italiana; Theatrum Instrumentorum, Milano.*
+ Fa 1-2/95: 160

VIENNA MODERN MASTERS

35722. VMM CD 2001: Van de Vate—Music for viola, percussion and piano; Nine preludes for piano; Piano trio; Viola sonata; Quartet no. 1. *Johnson, viola; Wiley, percussion; Zuckerman, Platt, piano; Ridge Quartet.*
+ ARG 1-2/92: 132

35723. VMM CD 2002: *American piano music.* Music of Diemer, Shaffer, Bazelon, Bell, Greenberg, De la Vega, Strunk and Quilling. *Lifchitz, piano.*
+ ARG 3-4/92: 191

35724. VMM CD 2004: Josephs—Violin sonatas, no. 1, 3; Solo violin sonata; Chacony; Siesta. *Davis, violin; Harper, piano.*
• ARG 11-12/93: 134

35725. VMM CD 2005: *Art songs by women.* Music of Boulanger, Holmes, Viardot-Garcia, Malibran, Vieu, Chaminade, Robinson, Howe, Hall, and Donceanu. *Eberle, mezzo-soprano; Guy, piano; Pederson Thelander, horn.*
+ ARG 3-4/94: 226

35726. VMM CD 2006: Van de Vate—Adagio for orchestra; Variations for chamber orchestra; String trio; Suite for violin solo; Letter to a friend's loneliness; Piano sonata no. 2. *Slovak Radio Symphony Orch.; Koszalin State Phil.; Kawalla, cond.; Martinů Phil. String Trio; Girardi, soprano; Davis, violin; Hirashima, piano.*
+ ARG 7-8/94: 183
+ Fa 3-4/94: 350

35727. VMM CD 2007: Music of Schulze, Ebenhöh, Hueber, Bottcher, Johansen, and Alterhaug. *Trondheim Wind Quintet.*
+ ARG 5-6/96: 279

35728. VMM CD 2008: *Music from six continents.* Music of Fortuin, Loeb, Rabushka, and Polishook. *Various performers.*
+ ARG 1-2/95: 214

35729. VMM CD 2009: Ireland—Violin sonatas no. 1-2; Bagatelle. *Davis, violin; Harper, piano.*
+ ARG 9-10/94: 146

35730. VMM CD 2010: Hueber—Piano sonata; Cello sonta; Solo cello sonata; Capriccio for cello. Füssl—Duo; Five tones, five fingers. *A. Chitta, cello; S. Chitta, piano.*
- ARG 7-8/95: 127

35731. VMM CD 2011: Tanaka—Chamber music, vol. 1. *Chomei, cello; Horino, soprano; Matsuyama, piano; Takeda, clarinet; Yamaguchi, percussion; Yasuda, violin.*
+ ARG 1-2/96: 249

35732. VMM CD 2012: Music of Trojanowski, Rabushka, Yasinitsky, Sukegawa, and Snyder. *Hirashima, Flajsinova, Berthiaume, Herbener, piano; Yasnitsky, flute; McMullen, oboe; Kašný, viola; Wharton, cello; Bohuslav*

Martinù Phil. Orch.; Machek, cond.
   □ ARG 3-4/96: 217

35733. VMM CD 2013: KALIMULLIN—
Piano sonata no. 2. BERKELEY—
Introduction and allegro. DAVIS—
Sonatina. ACKER—Cantus gemellus.
JOLIVET—Chant de Linos. HINDEMITH—
Violin sonata, op. 31, no. 2. *Matsunaga,
piano; Davis, Schubert, violins; Duo
Gelland.*
   + ARG 3-4/96: 227

35734. CMM CD 2017: Music of
Schoeck, Burkhard, Jelinek, and others.
Gelland, violin; Wallin, piano.
   + ARG 9-10/96: 250

35735. VMM CD 2019: D. HANDEL—
Poems of our climate; Trio; Flute city;
The tyger; Guitar recitative; Scherzo;
Barge music. *Woods, Henderson,
sopranos; Weinstock, piano; Ensembles;
Samuel, Zimmerman, conds.*
   + ARG 1-2/97: 117

35736. VMM CD 3001—3005 (5
separate discs): *Music from six
continents.* Music of Wolff, Schulze,
Jones, Mageau, Biggs, Dembski,
Jazwinski, Saunway, Reichel, Fortuin,
Constantinides, Hofmann-Engl, Wallach,
Van Appledorn, Fleischer, Tanner,
McKinley, and Kelly. *Various
performers.*
   □ ARG 7-8/92: 245

35737. VMM CD 3005: McKINLEY—New
York overture; Symphony no. 5. P.
KELLY—Symphony no. 1. *Warsaw
National Phil. Orch.; R. Black, cond.*
   □ ARG 7-8/92: 245
   • ARG 3-4/93: 109
   + Fa 7-8/92: 215

35738. VMM CD 3006: SUKEGAWA—The
eternal morning 1945.8.6. VAN DE
VATE—Pura besakih. LOEB—Unkei. D.
HANDEL—Kyushu. *Hiroshima Symphony
Orch.; Kuroiwa, cond.; Slovak Radio
Symphony Orch. of Bratislava; Kawalla,
cond.; Loeb, shinobue; Cincinnati
Philharmonia Orch.; Samuel, cond.*
   + Fa 3-4/93: 393

35739. VMM CD 3007: Music of
Martinù, Constantinides, Waggoner,
Snyder and Shaffer. *Bohuslav Martinù
Phil. Zlin; Macek, cond.*
   + Fa 1-2/93: 315
   + Fa 3-4/93: 393

35740. VMM CD 3009: Music of
Lorentzen, Ovens, Verrando,
Constantinides, and J. Fortner. *B.
Kawalla, piano; Girardi, mezzo-soprano;
Bratislava Radio Orch.; S. Kawalla,
cond.*
   □ ARG 11-12/93: 224

35741. VMM CD 3011: *Music from six
continents.* HEARD—Elegy for our time.
CRONIN—Piano concerto. D. HANDEL—

Acquainted with the night. CARBON—
Hommage a trois. *Bratislava Radio
Symphony Orch.; Kawalla, cond.; Power,
piano; Berlin, mezzo-soprano; Cincinnati
Philharmonia Orch.; Samuel, cond.*
   + ARG 3-4/93: 158

35742. VMM CD 3013: *Music from six
continents.* FLEISCHER—Oratorio 1492-
1992. TANNER—Fragrant harbor. VAN DE
VATE—Four somber songs. SHAFFER—
Concerto for orchestra. *Various
performers.*
   + ARG 7-8/93: 186

35743. VMM CD 3014: ROOMAN—
Prelude, aria, and sinfonia. *Amadeus
Chamber Orch.; Duczmal, cond.*
   + ARG 11-12/93: 179

35744. VMM CD 3015: SCHOENBERG—
Survivor from Warsaw. VAN DE VATE—
Katyn; Krakow concerto. PENDERECKI—
Dies irae. *Vocal soloists; Cracow Radio
Symphony Orch.; Kawalla, cond.*
   + ARG 7-8/93: 187

35745. VMM CD 3016: *Music from six
continents.* Music of Moravec, Silsbee,
Tanner, and Bell. *Bratislava Radio
Symphony Orch.; Kawalla, cond.*
   + ARG 7-8/94: 197

35746. VMM CD 3017: *Music from six
continents.* Music of Konowalski, Steen,
Yasinitsky, Hobson, Loeb, Myers, and
Snyder. *Koszalin State Phil. Orch.;
Bratislava Radio Symphony Orch.;
Kawalla, cond.; Pro Musica Nipponia;
Iimori, cond.; Martinù Symphony Orch.;
Machek, cond.*
   + ARG 7-8/94: 197

35747. VMM CD 3018: *Music from six
continents.* Music of Lutosławski,
Schulze, Myers, Dobbins, and Gordon.
*Koszalin State Phil. Orch.; Kawalla,
cond.; Studio da Camera; Rainer, cond.;
Martinù Symphony Orch.; Machek,
cond.; Polish Radio Symphony Orch.;
Florêncio, cond.*
   + ARG 7-8/94: 197

35748. VMM CD 3019: *Music from six
continents.* Music of Iannaccone, Myers,
and Redmann. *Polish Radio Symphony
Orch.; Florêncio, cond.*
   + ARG 7-8/94: 197

35749. VMM CD 3021: *Music from six
continents.* Music of Perron, Peel, Cleary,
Loeb, Rooman, and Lieuwen. *Polish
Radio Symphony Orch. ; Florêncio,
cond.; Martinù Phil. Orch.; Machek,
cond.; Bratislava Radio Orch.; Koszalin
Phil. Orch.; Kawalla, cond.*
   + ARG 9-10/94: 226

35750. VMM CD 3022: *Music from six
continents.* Music of Yu, Fortner, Scott,
Nakamura, and Van de Vatre. *Girardi,
mezzo-soprano; Silesian University
Choir; Koszalin State Phil. Orch.;*

Kawalla, cond.
   • ARG 9-10/94: 226

35751. VMM CD 3023: *Music from six
continents.* Music of Husa, Weiss,
Penderecki, Perron, and Van de Vate.
Various performers.
   + ARG 1-2/95: 213

35752. VMM CD 3024: *Music from six
continents.* Music of Fortner, Hobson,
Jazwinski, Moss, and Jaffe. *Various
performers.*
   + ARG 1-2/95: 213

35753. VMM CD 3025: VAN DE VATE—
Piano concerto; Adagio and rondo; The
pond; How fares the night? An American
essay. *Various performers.*
   • ARG 3-4/95: 208

35754. VMM CD 3026: McLEOD—
Gokstad ship; Whispered name; A
dramatic landscape; Lieder der Jugend.
Various performers.
   + ARG 11-12/95: 298

35755. VMM CD 3027: BERLINSKI—
Prayer of Bonhoeffer. ZIMMERMANN—New
Year's song. HELMSCHROTT—Cross and
freedom. *Various performers.*
   + ARG 9-10/95: 302

35756. VMM CD 3028: Music of
Gallagher, Pelinka, Ocker, Eyser, and
Wolking. *Various performers.*
   + ARG 11-12/95: 298

35757. VMM CD 3029: *I am an
American woman.* Music of Hershey,
Bell, Mageau, and Pierce. *Girardi,
mezzo- soprano; Szwajgier, soprano;
Spindler, piano; Polish Radio Symphony;
Koszalin State Phil.; Kawalla, cond.*
   + ARG 1-2/96: 249

35758. VMM CD 3030: *Music from six
continents: 1994 series.* Music of Kiraly,
Gallagher, Myers, Heifetz, Carl, and
Wolking. *Pécs Symphony Orch.;
Williams, cond.; Polish Radio and TV
Orch. of Krakow; Koszalin State Phil.
Orch.; Kawalla, cond.; Hartt Symphony
Orch.; Young, cond.; Krieger, electronic
cello.*
   + ARG 3-4/96: 268
   - Fa 3-4/96: 387

35759. VMM CD 3031: *Music from six
continents.* Music of Davis, Beath,
Fetherolf, and Vazzana. *Jiang, cello;
Moravian Phil. Orch.; Silva, cond.; USC
Symphony Orch.; Lewis, cond.*
   • ARG 7-8/96: 238

VIRGIN CLASSICS

35760. CDC 5 45000-2: BONONCINI—
Cantate e duetti; Sonata for cello and
continuo; Trio sonata for 2 violins and
continuo. *Lesne, alto; Seminario
musicale.*
   + ARG 9-10/94: 105

VIRGIN CLASSICS

+ Fa 7-8/94: 84
+ Gr 12/94: 137

35761. CDC 7 45001-2: BEETHOVEN—Violin concerto; Romances for violin and orchestra no. 1-2. *Sitkovetsky, violin; Academy of St. Martin-in-the-Fields; Marriner, cond.*
  + ARG 7-8/94: 67
  + Fa 5-6/94: 104
  • Gr 3/94: 42

35762. CDC 7 45003-2: Music of Davies, Jolivet, Nyman, Henze, Berio, and Fenton. *Ashton, trumpet; Lenehan, piano; Knowles, percussion.*
  + ARG 7-8/94: 218
  + Gr 4/94: 66

35763. CDC 7 45005-2: DOWLAND—Lachrymae. *Fretwork.*
  + ARG 9-10/94: 124
  + Fa 9-10/94: 183
  + Gr 7/94: 71

35764. CDC 7 45006-2: BRAHMS—Symphony no. 3; Alto rhapsody. *Vejzovic, alto; Houston Symphony Orch.; Eschenbach, cond.*
  - ARG 5-6/94: 79
  + Fa 7-8/94: 99
  • Gr 6/94: 44

35765. VC 5 45007-2: *A play of passion songs and dances for the Elizabethan stage.* Music of Holborne, Alberti, Farranti, Johnson, and others. *Budd, treble; Chance, alto; Fretwork.*
  + Gr 7/94: 105

35766. CDC 7 45010-2: MOZART—Violin concertos no. 1-2, 5. *Huggett, violin & cond.; Orch. of the Age of Enlightenment.*
  + ARG 7-8/94: 140
  + Gr 9/94: 56

35767. VC 5 45011-2: BACH—Easter oratorio; Christ lag in Todesbanden. *Van Evera, Trevor, Daniels, Thomas; Taverner Consort; Parrott, cond.*
  + Gr 7/94: 91

35768. CDC 5 45012-2: MOZART—Piano concertos no. 9, 27. *Tan, fortepiano; New Mozart Ensemble.*
  - Fa 7-8/94: 189

35769. VC 5 45014-2: HAYDN—Cello concertos, H. VIIb 1-2. *Mørk, cello; Norwegian Chamber Orch.; Brown, cond.*
  + Fa 9-10/94: 204
  + Gr 6/94: 48

35770. CDC 7 45015-2: DOHNÁNYI—Serenade for string trio. KODÁLY—Intermezzo. MARTINŮ—Madrigals; String trio no. 2. *Domus.*
  + ARG 9-10/94: 123
  + Fa 9-10/94: 181

35771. VC 5 45016-2: RAVEL—Sonata for violin and cello; Trois poèmes de

Stéphane Mallarmé; Chansons madécasses; Piano trio. *Nash Ensemble; Walker, soprano.*
  • ARG 1-2/95: 160
  + Fa 9-10/94: 307
  + Gr 6/94: 76

35772. CDC 5 45017-2: SCHUBERT—Octet D. 803. *Nash Ensemble.* Reissue.
  • Gr 10/94: 144

35773. CDC 5 45018-2: DEBUSSY—Prélude à l'après-midi d'un faune; Jeux; Printemps; Khamma. *Finnish Radio Symphony Orch.; Saraste, cond.*
  • ARG 9-10/94: 121
  + Fa 5-6/94: 132
  + Gr 4/94: 44

35774. CDC 7 45019-2: Four-hand music by Marsh, J.C. Bach, Wesley, Tomkins, Carleton, Mozart, and Handel. *Moroney, Baumont, harpsichord.*
  + ARG 11-12/94: 225
  + EM 5/95: 329

35775. CDC 5 45020-2: TELEMANN—Paris quartets, vol. 2. *Hazelzet, flute; Trio Sonnerie.*
  + ARG 9-10/94: 212
  + Fa 7-8/94: 263
  + Gr 11/94: 104

35776. CDC 5 45022-2: DVOŘÁK—Violin concerto, op. 53. LALO—Symphonie espagnole. *Tetzlaff, violin; Czech Phil. Orch.; Pešek, cond.*
  + ARG 11-12/94: 105
  • Fa 9-10/94: 184
  + Gr 7/94: 42

35777. CDC 5 45023-2: TAVENER—The last sleep of the Virgin; The hidden treasure. PÄRT—Summa; Fratres. *Chilingirian String Quartet; Simcock, handbells.*
  + ARG 1-2/95: 152
  + Fa 9-10/94: 350
  + Gr 5/94: 74

35778. CDC 7 45024-2 : Music of Walton, MacCombie, Gershwin, Tower, Duarte, and Britten. *Isbin, guitar.*
  + ARG 9-10/94: 233
  + Gr 7/94: 84

35779. CDC 5 45029-2: MOZART—String quartets no. 14-15. *Smithson String Quartet.*
  + Fa 11-12/94: 315

35780. CDC 5 45030-2: GALUPPI—Confitebor; Arripe alpestri ad vallem. *Lesne, countertenor; Gens, soprano; Harvey, bass; Il seminario musicale.*
  + ARG 11-12/94: 115
  + Fa 9-10/94: 193
  + Gr 10/94: 168

35781. VC 7 45031-2: BYRD—Consort music. *Fretwork.*
  + EM 2/95: 166
  + ARG 11-12/94: 87

35782. CDC 5 45032-2: STRAVINSKY—Firebird; Symphonies of wind instruments. *London Symphony Orch.; Nagano, cond.*
  + ARG 1-2/95: 186
  + Fa 1-2/95: 280
  + Gr 8/94: 58

35783. VC 5 45033-2: BARBER—Vocal and chamber works. *Allen, baritone; Vignoles, piano; Endellion Quartet.*
  + ARG 7-8/95: 79
  + Gr 10/94: 167

35784. VC 5 45034-2: GRIEG—Cello sonata; Intermezzo. SIBELIUS—Malinconia; Pieces op. 78. *Mørk, cello; Thibaudet, piano.*
  + ARG 5-6/95: 115
  • Gr 10/94: 138

35785. VC 5 45035-2: TAVENER—*Thunder entered her.* Angels; Annunciation; The lament of the mother of God; Thunder entered her; Hymns of paradise; God is with us. *Westminster Cathedral Choir; Hill, cond.; Dunnett, organ.*
  + ARG 5-6/95: 232

35786. VC 5 45036-2: *Psalms, vol. 2.* Music of Bairstow, Lloyd, Lang, Alcock, Peasgood, Parratt, Neary, Buck, Whitlock, Walford Davies, Rose, Purcell, Goss, Stanford, and Atkins. *Westminster Abbey Choir; Neary, cond.*
  + Gr 7/95: 108

35787. VC 5 45038-2: BACH—Cantatas no. 51, 82, 199. *Argenta, soprano; Ensemble Sonnerie; Huggett, cond.*
  • ARG 5-6/95: 70
  + EM 5/95: 338
  + Gr 12/94: 136

35788. VCD 5 45039-2 (2 discs): FLOYD—Susannah. *Studer, Ramey, Hadley; Opéra de Lyon; Nagano, cond.*
  + ARG 3-4/95: 100
  + Fa 1-2/95: 156
  + Gr 10/94: 189
  + ON 12/24/94: 32
  + Op 11/94: 1354

35789. VCD 5 45039-2 (2 discs): FLOYD—Susannah. *Studer, Hadley, Ramey, Chester; Opéra de Lyon; Nagano, cond.*
  + Gr 10/94: 189

35790. VC 5 45042-2: TCHAIKOVSKY—Seasons; Pieces, op. 21. *Pletnev, piano.*
  • ARG 5-6/95: 185
  + Gr 12/94: 132

35791. VC 5 45049-2: BACH—Cantatas no. 84, 202, 209. *Argenta, soprano; Ensemble Sonnerie; Huggett, cond.*
  • ARG 11-12/95: 70

35792. VC 5 45050-2: DUFAY—Missa Ecce ancilla Domini; Proprium de Angelis Dei officium. *Gilles Binchois*

Ensemble; Vellard, cond.
+ ARG 3-4/95: 95
+ EM 2/95: 165
• Gr 11/94: 130

35793. VC 5 45051-2: GRIEG—Bergljot; Olav Trygvason; Funeral march for Rikard Nordraak. *Vocal soloists; Trondheim Symphony Orch. & Chorus; Ruud, cond.*
+ Gr 4/95: 98

35794. VC 5 45053-2: FAURÉ—Songs. POULENC—Le travail du peintre. RAVEL—Songs. *Allen, baritone; Vignoles, piano.*
+ Gr 5/95: 92

35795. VC 5 45054-2: BACH—Concertos for two harpsichords. *Leonhardt, Asperen, harpsichord & cond.; Melante Amsterdam.*
+ ARG 9-10/95: 96
• Gr 10/95: 47

35796. CDC 5 45056-2: WEILL—Concerto for violin and wind orchestra. HINDEMITH—Septet for winds. TOCH—Five pieces for winds and percussion. *Tetzlaff, violin; Deutsche Kammerphilharmonie.*
+ Fa 11-12/95: 427
+ Gr 7/95: 52

35797. CDC 5 45057-2: SUK—A summer tale. *Royal Liverpool Phil. Orch.; Pešek, cond.*
+ ARG 11-12/95: 215
+ Fa 11-12/95: 395
+ Gr 8/95: 86

35798. VC 5 45059-2: BACH—Cantatas no. 84, 202, 209. *Argenta, soprano; Ensemble Sonnerie; Huggett, cond.*
+ Fa 11-12/95: 178
+ Gr 6/95: 86

35799. VC 5 45060-2: MOZART—Violin concertos no. 3-4; Adagio; Rondo. *Huggett, violin & cond.; Orch. of the Age of Enlightenment.*
+ Gr 3/95: 50

35800. CDC 5 45061-2: PURCELL—Selections. *Taverner Consort; Taverner Players; Parrott, cond.*
+ ARG 11-12/95: 179
+ Fa 11-12/95: 334
+ Gr 6/95: 95

35801. VC 5 45062-2: PURCELL—The fantazias and In nomines. *Fretwork.*
+ ARG 11-12/95: 174
+ Fa 9-10/95: 280
+ Gr 5/95: 75

35802. CDC 5 45065-2: ELGAR—Violin concerto, op. 61. *Sitkovetsky, violin; Royal Phil. Orch.; Menuhin, cond.*
+ ARG 11-12/94: 108
+ Fa 11-12/94: 223

35803. VC 5 45066-2: JEHANNOT DE L'ESCUREL—Fontaine de grace. *Gilles Binchois Ensemble; Vellard, cond.*

+ EM 2/96: 177
+ Gr 8/95: 112

35804. VC 5 45075-2: CHARPENTIER—Leçcons de Ténèbres du Jeudi Saint. *Piau, soprano; Lesne, alto; Honeyman, tenor; Harvey, bass; Il Seminario Musicale.*
+ Gr 9/95: 88

35805. VC 5 45076-2: CHOPIN—Piano sonata no. 2; Piano music. *Pletnev, piano.* Reissue.
+ ARG 9-10/95: 125
+ Gr 3/95: 70

35806. CDC 7 45086-2 (2 discs): BACH—Cello suites. *Kirshbaum, cello.*
+ ARG 11-12/94: 67
+ Fa 11-12/94: 156
+ Gr 4/95: 89

35807. VC 5 45089-2 (2 discs): BACH—Sonatas and partitas for violin. *Tetzlaff, violin.*
• ARG 1-2/96: 75

35808. VC 5 45095-2: BACH—Violin and oboe concertos BWV 1052, 1055, 1056, 1060. *Wallfisch, violin; Robson, oboe; Orch. of the Age of Enlightenment.*
+ ARG 3-4/95: 67
+ EM 2/95: 171
+ Gr 11/94: 63

35809. VCD 5 45096-2 (2 discs): BACH—St. John passion. *Covey-Crump, Thomas, Bonner, Van Evera, Trevor; Taverner Consort; Parrott, cond.* Recorded 1990.
• ARG 3-4/96: 83
• Fa 11-12/95: 188

35810. VC 5 45103-2: A. SCARLATTI—Infirmata, vulnerata; De tenebroso lacu; Salve Regina; Totus amore languens. *Gens, soprano; Lesne, alto; Seminario Musicale.*
+ Gr 6/95: 98

35811. VC 5 45104-2: MENDELSSOHN—String quartet no. 2; String quintet no. 2. *Hausmusik.*
+ Gr 5/95: 70

35812. CDC 5 45107-2: CHARPENTIER—Leçons de Ténèbres: Mercredi Saint. *Il Seminario Musicale; Lesne, cond.*
+ ARG 9-10/95: 124
+ Fa 9-10/95: 173
+ Gr 9/95: 88

35813. VC 5 45114-2: SEIXAS—Harpsichord concerto; Sinfonia; Sonatas. *Haugsand, harpsichord & cond.; Norwegian Baroque Orch.*
+ Gr 3/96: 52

35814. CDC 5 45116-2: PURCELL—The pocket Purcell: a suite of theatre music. *Taverner Consort, Choir, & Players; Parrott, cond.* Reissues.

+ ARG 11-12/95: 181
+ Fa 11-12/95: 336

35815. CDC 5 45118-2: BARTÓK—Violin concertos no. 1-2. *Sitkovetsky, violin; Philharmonia Orch.; Pešek, cond.*
+ Fa 11-12/95: 196

35816. VC 5 45119-2: RACHMANINOFF—Cello sonata. MIASKOVSKY—Cello sonata. *Mørk, cello; Thibaudet, piano.*
+ ARG 1-2/97: 201
+ Gr 11/96: 110

35817. VC 5 45121-2: BRITTEN—Lachrymae; Elegy; Prelude and fugue, op. 29; Simple symphony; Variations on a theme of Frank Bridge. *Tomter, viola; Norwegian Chamber Orch.; Brown, cond.*
+ ARG 11-12/95: 99
+ Fa 11-12/95: 221
+ Gr 10/95: 50

35818. CDC 45122-2: *Violin sonatas.* Music of Janáček, Debussy, Ravel, and Nielsen. *Tetzlaff, violin; Andsnes, piano.*
• ARG 1-2/96: 221
+ Fa 1-2/96: 401
• Gr 11/95: 105

35819. VC 5 45123-2 (2 discs): SCARLATTI—Keyboard sonatas. *Pletnev, piano.*
+ Gr 3/96: 72

35820. CDC 5 45124-2: RACHMANINOFF—Vespers. *Swedish Radio Choir; Kaljuste, cond.*
• ARG 3-4/96: 170
- Fa 3-4/96: 255
+ Gr 9/95: 94

35821. VC 5 45125-2: ZEMLINSKY—Ländliche Tänze, op. 1; Balladen; Fantasien über Gedichte von Richard Dehmel; Albumblatt; Skizze; Fugue in G minor. *Mauser, piano.*
+ Gr 9/95: 85

35822. VC 5 45127-2: DVOŘÁK—Symphony no. 2; My home. *Czech Phil. Orch.; Pešek, cond.*
+ ARG 7-8/96: 107
+ Fa 7-8/96: 161
• Gr 4/96: 44

35823. VC 5 45128-2: SVENDSEN—Orchestra music. *Trondheim Symphony Orch.; Ruud, cond.*
+ ARG 11-12/96: 218

35824. VC 5 45129-2: NIELSEN—Piano music. *Andsnes, piano.*
• ARG 1-2/97: 146
+ Gr 8/96: 76

35825. VC 5 45130-2: MOZART—Piano concertos no. 9, 20. *Pletnev, piano & cond.; Deutsche Kammerphilharmonie.*
+ ARG 11-12/96: 168
+ Gr 6/96: 50

35826. VC 5 45133-2: Music of Bernstein, Hyman, Corea, Kusby, Rimelis, Kaplin, and Schickele. *Greene Quartet.*
  □ ARG 3-4/96: 268

35827. CDC 5 45134-2: *1812.* Music of Rossini, Henry VIII, Debussy, Lennon-McCartney, Rene-Scott, Gershwin, Sondheim, Mancini, and Tchaikovsky. *Swingle Singers.*
  + ARG 3-4/96: 250
  + Fa 1-2/96: 370

35828. VC 5 45135-2 : 11th-century organa and tropes. *Ensemble Gilles Binchois; Vellard, cond.*
  + ARG 9-10/96: 254
  + EM 2/97: 145
  + Gr 12/96: 129

35829. VC 5 45139-2: BACH—Musical offering. *Ensemble Sonnerie.*
  + ARG 9-10/96: 83
  + Fi 10/96: 147
  + Gr 7/96: 69

35830. VC 5 45143-2: MONTEVERDI—Primo libro de madrigali; Settimo libro de madrigali: Tempro la cetra, Tirsi e Clori. *Consort of Musicke; Rooley, cond.*
  + Gr 8/96: 84

35831. VC 5 45145-2: SHOSTAKOVICH—Cello concertos no. 1-2. *Mørk, cello; London Phil. Orch.; Jansons, cond.*
  + Gr 2/96: 59

35832. VC 5 45147-2: LAWES—Concord is conquor'd. *Bott, soprano; Boothby, lyra viol; Nicholson, organ; Fretwork.*
  + EM 2/97: 152
  + Gr 10/95: 84

35833. VC 5 45148-2 (2 discs): NAUMANN—Gustaf Wasa. *Andersson, Gedda, Wallström, Nordin; Royal Opera Stockholm; Brunelle, cond.*
  + Gr 3/96: 97

35834. VC 5 45159-2: PURCELL—Welcome to all pleasures; Funeral sentences; Come ye sons of art away; Funeral music. *Taverner Consort; Parrott, cond.* Reissue.
  + Gr 12/95: 131

35835. VC 5 45160-2: PURCELL—Hail! Bright Cecilia. *Taverner Consort; Parrott, cond.* Reissue.
  + Gr 12/95: 131

35836. CDC 5 45166-2: *The Purcell manuscript.* Keyboard works by Purcell, Gibbons, and Draghi. *Maroney, virginal & harpsichords.*
  + ARG 11-12/95: 178
  + Fa 11-12/95: 337
  + Gr 5/95: 84

35837. CDC 5 45173-2: RACHMANINOFF—Piano concerto no. 3. Etudes-tableaux. *Andsnes, piano; Oslo Phil. Orch.; Berglund, cond.* Live recording.
  • ARG 7-8/96: 175
  • Fa 5-6/96: 244
  • Gr 1/96: 60

35838. VC 5 45174-2: HANDEL—Organ concertos op. 4. *Asperen, organ; Orch. of the Age of Enlightenment.*
  + ARG 9-10/96: 131
  • Gr 7/96: 50

35839. VC 5 45175-2: STRADELLA—Motets. *Piau, soprano; Lesne, alto & cond.; Il Seminario Musicale.*
  + Gr 4/96: 96

35840. VC 5 45183-2: WILLAN—Sacred choral music. *Vancouver Chamber Choir; Washburn, cond.*
  + ARG 5-6/96: 222
  + Fa 3-4/96: 320

35841. VC 5 45184-2: BRAHMS—Piano trios no. 1-2. *Grieg Trio.*
  + Gr 4/96: 61

35842. CDC 5 45192-2: BACH—Organ trio sonatas, transcribed for recorder, violin, and continuo. *Musica Pacifica.*
  + ARG 1-2/97: 65
  + Fa 11-12/96: 176
  + Gr 12/96: 92

35843. VC 5 45196-2: HAYDN—Piano concertos, H. XVIII 4, 7, 11. *Pletnev, piano & cond.; Deutsche Kammerphilharmonie.*
  + ARG 3-4/97: 152
  • Fa 1-2/97: 176

35844. CDC 5 45254-2: HAYDN—Variations, H. XVII, 6; Piano sonatas no. 33, 60, 62. *Pletnev, piano.* Reissue.
  + ARG 3-4/97: 152
  • Fa 1-2/97: 176

35845. VC 5 54035-2: TAVENER—Choral pieces. *Winchester Cathedral Choir; Hill, cond.*
  + Gr 8/94: 98

35846. CDC 5 55083-2: CORIGLIANO—Troubadours. FOSS—American landscapes. SCHWANTNER—From afar. *Isbin, guitar; St. Paul Chamber Orch.; Wolff, cond.*
  + ARG 1-2/96: 98
  + Gr 8/96: 44

35847. VC 7 56232-2: VIVALDI—Sacred music for soloist and double orchestra. *Biondi, violin; Il Seminario musicale; Lesne, countertenor & cond.*
  + Fa 7-8/93: 264

35848. CDC 7 59042-2: VICTORIA—Tenebrae responses. *The Sixteen; Christophers, cond.*
  + ARG 3-4/93: 152

35849. CDC 7 59052-2: TAVENER—The protecting veil; Thrinos. BRITTEN—Cello suite no. 3. *Isserlis, cello; London Symphony Orch.; Rozhdestvensky, cond.*
  + ARG 3-4/93: 146

35850. CDC 7 59059-2: C.P.E. BACH—Auferstehung und Himmelfahrt Jesu. *Martinpelto, Prégardien, Harvey; Collegium Vocale; Orch. of the Age of Enlightenment; Herreweghe, cond.*
  • ARG 3-4/93: 49

35851. CDC 7 59075-2: MOZART—Flute concertos; Flute and harp concerto. *Coles, flute; Yoshino, harp; English Chamber Orch.; Menuhin, cond.*
  + ARG 3-4/93: 116

35852. VC 7 59152-2: POULENC—Figure humaine; Quatre motets pour un temps de pénitence; Laudes de Saint Antoine de Padoue; Quatre motets pour le temps de Noël; Quatres petites prières de Saint François d'Assise. *The Sixteen; Christophers, cond.*
  + Fa 1-2/94: 260

35853. VC 7 59154-2: RAMEAU—Pièces de clavecin en concerts. *Trio Sonnerie.* Reissue.
  + ARG 9-10/94: 180
  + Fa 3-4/94: 287

35854. CDC 7 59192-2: POULENC—Figure humaine; Penitence motets; Christmas motets; Lauds of St. Anthony; Prayers of St. Francis of Assisi. *The Sixteen; Christophers, cond.*
  + ARG 3-4/94: 135

35855. CDC 7 59197-2: PACHELBEL—Organ music. *Jacob, organ.*
  + ARG 9-10/94: 171

35856. VC 7 59220-2: BEETHOVEN—Trios for fortepiano, violin, and cello no. 2, 4, WoO 38. *Castle Trio.*
  + Fa 7-8/93: 108
  + Gr 11/92: 118

35857. VC 7 59221-2: WOLF—Lieder. *Allen, baritone; Parsons, piano.*
  + ARG 11-12/93: 221
  + Fa 11-12/93: 451
  + Gr 10/92: 170

35858. VC 7 59222-2: LISZT—An Italian recital. *Hough, piano.*
  + ARG 7-8/93: 116
  • Fa 7-8/93: 170
  + Gr 10/92: 140

35859. VC 7 59223-2: BRAHMS—Symphony no. 1; Academic festival overture. *Houston Symphony Orch.; Eschenbach, cond.*
  • ARG 7-8/93: 72
  + Fa 7-8/93: 116
  • Gr 10/92: 55

35860. VCD 7 59227-2 (2 discs): POULENC—Les dialogues des Carmelites. *Dubosc, Yakar, Gorr, Dam, Sénéchal; Lyon Opera; Nagano, cond.*

+ ARG 5-6/93: 119
+ Fa 11-12/94: 329
+ Gr 9/92: 162
+ ON 5/93: 52
+ Op 7/93: 872

35861. VC 7 59230-2: TCHAIKOVSKY—Manfred symphony. *Bournemouth Symphony Orch.; Litton, cond.*
  • ARG 9-10/93: 202
  + Fa 9-10/93: 308
  + Gr 3/93: 56

35862. VC 7 59231-2: D'INDIA—Music for solo voice. *Rogers, tenor; O'Dette, chitarrone; Lawrence-King, harp, organ, harpsichord.*
  + ARG 7-8/93: 104
  + EM 8/93: 493
  + Fa 5-6/93: 231
  + Gr 4/93: 108

35863. VC 7 59232-2: VIVALDI—Salve regina, RV 616, 618; Introductions to RV 641, 637; Concerto, RV 581. *Lesne, countertenor; Bondi, violin; Seminario Musicale.*
  + ARG 9-10/93: 216
  + Gr 6/93: 92

35864. VC 7 59233-2: RAVEL—Piano music, vol. 1. *Queffélec, piano.*
  + ARG 7-8/93: 141
  + Fa 7-8/93: 213
  • Gr 4/93: 95

35865. VC 7 59234-2: STRAUSS—Don Quixote; Don Juan; Till Eulenspiegels lustige Streiche. *Minnesota Orch.; Waart, cond.*
  - ARG 7-8/93: 163
  + Fa 5-6/93: 333
  • Gr 1/93: 44

35866. VC 7 59235-2: RAVEL—Alborada del gracioso; Shéhérazade; Vocalise en forme de habanera; La valse; Pavane pour une infant défunte; Boléro. *Augér, soprano; Philharmonia Orch.; Pešek, cond.*
  - ARG 7-8/93: 141
  • Fa 5-6/93: 289
  • Gr 3/93: 82
  + ON 2/5/94: 39

35867. VC 7 59236-2: MARTIN—Sechs Monologe aus Jedermann. RAVEL—Don Quichotte à Dulcinée. IBERT—Quatre chansons de Don Quichotte. POULENC—Le bal masqué. *Dam, baritone; Lyon Opera Orch.; Nagano, cond.*
  + ARG 7-8/93: 204
  + Fa 7-8/93: 184
  + Gr 2/93: 72
  + ON 2/5/94: 39

35868. VC 7 59237-2: BACH—Cantatas: Aus der Tiefen rufe ich, Herr, zu dir, BWV 131; Herr, wie du willt, so schicks mit, BWV 73; Herr, gehe nicht ins Gericht mit deinem Knecht, BWV 105. *Schlick, Lesne, Crook, Kooy; Collegium Vocale, Ghent; Herreweghe, cond.*

+ ARG 9-10/93: 85
+ EM 8/93: 504
+ Fa 7-8/93: 92
+ Gr 5/93: 76

35869. CDC 7 59238-2: Le Puy manuscript. *Ensemble Gilles Binchois; Veillard, cond.*
  + ARG 11-12/93: 246

35870. VC 7 59238-2: Le manuscrit Du Puy. *Ensemble Gilles Binchois; Vellard, cond.*
  + Fa 7-8/93: 288
  + EM 8/93: 489
  + Gr 5/93: 92

35871. VC 7 59239-2: TCHAIKOVSKY—Symphony no. 6; Romeo and Juliet. *Bournemouth Symphony Orch.; Litton, cond.*
  + ARG 9-10/93: 208
  + Fa 9-10/93: 310
  + Gr 5/93: 52

35872. VC 7 59243-2: PURCELL—Odes for Queen Mary: Now does the glorious day appear; Love's goddess sure was blind; Come ye sons of art. *Vocalists; Orch. of the Age of Enlightenment; Leonhardt, cond.*
  • ARG 9-10/93: 170
  - EM 11/93: 645
  + Fa 7-8/93: 207

35873. CDC 7 59245-2: SUK—Quartet, op. 1. DVOŘÁK—Five bagatelles, op. 47. MARTINŮ—Piano quartet. *Domus.*
  + ARG 3-4/94: 162
  + Fa 11-12/93: 224

35874. VC 7 59266-2: HAYDN—Sinfonia concertante, H. I, 5; Concertos for violin and orchestra, H. VIIa, 4; H. VIIa, 1. *Wallfisch, violin; Watkin, cello; Robson, oboe; Warnock, bassoon; Orch. of the Age of Enlightenment.*
  + ARG 7-8/93: 99
  • Fa 7-8/93: 150
  + Gr 11/92: 61 (as VC 7 91186 2)

35875. VC 7 59268-2 (2 discs): HAYDN—The seasons. *Laki, Wildhaber, Lika; La Petite Bande; Flanders Opera Choir; S. Kuijken, cond.*
  • ARG 9-10/93: 132

35876. VC 7 59271-2: CARTER—Three occasions for orchestra; Violin concerto; Concerto for orchestra. *Bohn, violin; London Sinfonietta; Knussen, cond.*
  + ARG 7-8/93: 75
  + Fa 7-8/93: 123

35877. VC 7 59272-2: BACH—Italian concerto; Prelude, fugue and allegro; Duets, BWV 802-805; French overture. *Moroney, harpsichord.*
  + ARG 7-8/93: 58
  • Fa 7-8/93: 95

35878. VC 7 59273-2: SCHUBERT—Symphonies no. 5, 8; Rosamunde: Ballet

music. *Orch. of the Age of Enlightenment; Mackerras, cond.*
  + ARG 7-8/93: 154
  + Fa 7-8/93: 235

35879. CDC 7 59277-2: C.P.E. BACH—Organ music. *Danby, organ.*
  + Gr 5/93: 70

35880. VC 7 59278-2: PROKOFIEV—Romeo and Juliet (excerpts). *Royal Liverpool Phil. Orch.; Pešek, cond.*
  • ARG 9-10/93: 169
  + Gr 10/93: 48

35881. VC 7 59280-2: MOZART—Piano concertos no. 23-24. *Pletnev, piano & cond.; Deutsche Kammerphilharmonie.*
  • ARG 9-10/93: 159
  + Fa 9-10/93: 219
  • Gr 6/93: 51

35882. VC 7 59281-2: SHOSTAKOVICH—String quartets no. 2, 12. *Borodin Quartet.*
  + ARG 9-10/93: 190
  - Fa 9-10/93: 287
  + Gr 6/93: 70

35883. CDC 7 59282-2: MONTEVERDI—The second book of madrigals. *Consort of Musicke; Rooley, cond.*
  + ARG 11-12/93: 152
  + Fa 11-12/93: 327
  + Gr 10/93: 94

35884. CDC 7 59283-2: MONTEVERDI—The third book of madrigals. *Consort of Musicke; Rooley, cond.*
  + ARG 11-12/93: 152
  + Fa 11-12/93: 327
  + Gr 10/93: 94

35885. CDC 7 59285-2: Music of Smetana, Dvořák, Fučík, and Nedbal. *Royal Liverpool Phil. Orch.; Pešek, cond.*
  + ARG 9-10/94: 222
  + Gr 11/94: 90

35886. VC 7 59286-2: POULENC—Gloria; Stabat mater; Litanies à la Vierge noire. *Dubosc, soprano; Westminster Singers; City of London Sinfonia; Hickox, cond.*
  + ARG 9-10/93: 168
  + Fa 9-10/93: 235
  + Gr 2/93: 70

35887. VC 7 59287-2: CRUSELL—Clarinet concertos no. 1-3. *Pay, clarinet & cond.; Orch. of the Age of Enlightenment.*
  + Gr 12/93: 67

35888. VCD 7 59289-2 (2 discs): RACHMANINOFF—Preludes op. 23, 32; Selected pieces. *Alexeev, piano.*
  + Gr 5/94: 83

35889. VC 7 59294-2: MARSCHNER—Der Vampyr: highlights. *O'Neill, Shepherdson, Salmon, Ebrahim, Allan; Britten Singers; BBC Phil. Orch.; Parry, cond.*

VIRGIN CLASSICS

+ Fa 7-8/93: 175
• Gr 4/93: 118

35890. VC 7 59295-2: CHARPENTIER—
Leçons de Ténèbres du Vendredi Saint.
*Mellon, soprano; Lesne, alto; Honeyman,
tenor; Bona, baritone; Il Seminario
musicale.*
+ Gr 9/95: 88

35891. CDC 7 59295-2: CHARPENTIER—
Leçons de ténèbres. *Il Seminario
musicale; Mellon, Lesne, Honeyman,
Bona, vocalists.*
+ ARG 11-12/93: 92
+ Fa 11-12/93: 206

35892. VC 7 59296-2: SATIE—Piano
works, vol. 2. *Queffélec, C. Collard,
pianos.*
+ Fa 11-12/93: 371
+ Gr 8/93: 60

35893. CDC 7 59297-2: TCHAIKOVSKY—
Piano concerto no. 1. RACHMANINOFF—
Piano concerto no. 2. *Pommier, piano;
Hallé Orch.; Foster, cond.*
- ARG 11-12/93: 207
+ Fa 11-12/93: 416
• Gr 10/93: 50

35894. CDC 7 59300-2: GRIEG—Piano
sonata, op. 7; Poetic tone-pictures, op. 3,
no. 4-6; Album leaves, op. 28, no. 1, 4;
Agitato; Lyric pieces, op. 43, 54.
Andsnes, piano.
+ ARG 3-4/94: 102
+ Fa 11-12/93: 252
+ Gr 6/93: 76

35895. CDC 7 59301-2: GRIEG—
Symphony in C minor; Symphonic
dances. *Bergen Phil. Orch.; Kitaenko,
Dmitri.*
• Gr 9/93: 50

35896. CDC 7 59303-2: SCHUBERT—Piano
trio no. 2; Sonata movement for piano
trio. *Castle Trio.*
+ Fa 11-12/93: 385
+ Gr 11/93: 96

35897. CDC 7 59304-2: *Piano album no.
2.* Music of Czerny, Levitzki,
Schumann-Tausig, Rubinstein, and
others. *Hough, piano.*
+ ARG 1-2/94: 181

35898. CDCB 7 59305-2 (2 discs):
BRITTEN—A midsummer night's dream.
*Bowman, Watson, Hall, Herford; City of
London Sinfonia; Hickox, cond.*
+ ARG 1-2/94: 85
+ Fa 1-2/94: 144
+ Gr 8/93: 79
• ON 2/19/94: 32
+ Op 10/93: 1256

35899. CDC 7 59308-2: KNUSSEN—Songs
without voices; Whitman settings; Hums
and songs of Winnie the Pooh;
Variations; Four late poems and and
epigram; Sonya's lullaby; Océan de terre.
*Chamber Music Society of Lincoln
Center; Knussen, cond.*
+ ARG 3-4/94: 113
+ Fa 3-4/94: 226
+ Gr 10/93: 90

35900. CDC 7 59309-2: BRAHMS—Viola
sonatas. SCHUMANN—Märchenbilder.
Tomter, viola; Andsnes, piano.
+ ARG 5-6/94: 76
+ Fa 3-4/94: 146
+ Gr 11/93: 92

35901. CDC 7 59310-2: FORQUERAY—
Pièces de clavecin, suites 3, 5. *Meyerson,
harpsichord.*
+ ARG 3-4/94: 96
+ Fa 5-6/94: 146
+ Gr 5/94: 79

35902. VC 7 59311-2: POULENC—*Choral
works, vol. 2.* Salve Regina; Ave verum
corpus; Exultate Deo; Mass in G; Un soir
de neige; Chansons françaises; Chanson à
boire; Sept chansons. *The Sixteen;
Christophers, cond.* Reissue.
+ ARG 3-4/94: 135
+ Fa 1-2/94: 261
+ Gr 12/93: 106

35903. VC 7 59312-2: SHOSTAKOVICH—
Piano quintet; Piano trio no. 2; Waltzes.
Nash Ensemble.
• ARG 3-4/94: 155
• Fa 3-4/94: 320

35904. CDC 7 59313-2 (2 discs):
BUSONI—Arlecchino; Turandot. *Vocal
soloists; Opéra de Lyon; Nagano, cond.*
+ ARG 7-8/94: 87
+ Fa 3-4/94: 155
+ Gr 11/93: 139
+ ON 5/94: 50
+ Op 3/94: 373

35905. CDC 7 59316-2: *American piano
sonatas, vol. 2.* Sonatas by Griffes,
Sessions, and Ives. *Lawson, piano.*
• ARG 3-4/94: 209
+ Fa 3-4/94: 411
+ Gr 2/94: 74

35906. CDC 7 59318-2: SUK—Ripening;
Praga. *Royal Liverpool Phil. Orch. &
Choir; Pešek, cond.*
+ ARG 5-6/94: 151
+ Gr 1/94: 59

35907. VC 7 59319-2: BACH—Violin
concertos no. 1-2; Concertos for 2 and 3
violins. *Wallfisch, violin & cond.; Bury,
Beznosiuk, Mackintosh, violins; Orch. of
the Age of Enlightenment.*
+ ARG 7-8/94: 64
+ Fa 5-6/94: 100

35908. CDC 7 59320-2: BACH—Cantatas:
Brich dem Hungrigen dein Brot, BWV
39; Wen nur den lieben Gott lässt walten,
BWV 93; Was willst du dich betrüben,
BWV 107. *Mellon, soprano; Brett,
countertenor; Crook, tenor; Kooy, bass;
Collegium Vocale, Ghent; Herreweghe,
cond.*
+ Fa 7-8/94: 46
+ Gr 3/94: 86

35909. CDC 7 59321-2: *Shakespeare's
lutenist.* JOHNSON—Lute songs. *Kirkby,
soprano; Thomas, bass; Rooley, lute.*
+ ARG 9-10/94: 250
+ Gr 4/94: 80

35910. CDC 7 59322-2: RAVEL—Piano
music, vol. 2. *Queffélec, piano.*
• ARG 7-8/94: 157
+ Fa 7-8/94: 210
• Gr 3/94: 83

35911. CDC 7 59324-2: *O solitude.*
PURCELL—Songs and airs. *Argenta,
soprano; North, archlute & Baroque
guitar; Boothby, viola da gamba;
Nicholson, harpsichord, chamber organ.*
+ ARG 9-10/94: 177
+ Fa 7-8/94: 205
+ Gr 6/94: 100

35912. CDC 7 59325-2: DVOŘÁK—Cello
concerto no. 2. TCHAIKOVSKY—Variations
on a rococo theme. *Mørk, cello; Oslo
Phil. Orch.; Jansons, cond.*
+ ARG 7-8/94: 97
• Fa 5-6/94: 141
+ Gr 1/94: 44

35913. CDC 7 59326-2: VIVALDI—Gloria;
Magnificat. *Van Evera, Argenta, Place,
King, Cable; Taverner Choir & Players;
Parrott, cond.*
+ ARG 3-4/95: 219
+ Fa 1-2/95: 298
+ Gr 1/95: 93

35914. CDC 7 59602-2: MAHLER—
Symphony no. 5. *Finnish Radio
Symphony Orch.; Saraste, cond.*
+ ARG 3-4/93: 107

35915. VJ 7 59686-2: Concertos by
Strauss, Bach, Marcello; Sinfonias from
Bach cantatas. *Still, oboe; Academy of
London; Stamp, cond.* Reissue.
+ ARG 9-10/93: 235

35916. VJ 7 59688-2: BACH—
Brandenburg concertos no. 1-2, 4;
Concerto for violin & oboe. *Rees, violin;
Scottish Ensemble.*
- ARG 9-10/93: 85

35917. VJ 7 59689-2: WAGNER—
Overtures. *Radio France Phil. Orch.;
Janowski, cond.*
+ ARG 3-4/94: 180

35918. VJ 7 59690-2: STRAVINSKY—
Petrushka. BARTÓK—Concerto for
orchestra. *Melbourne Symphony Orch.;
Iwaki, cond.* Reissue.
+ Fa 9-10/93: 303

35919. VJ 7 59691-2: Music for viols by
Dowland, Byrd, and Lawes. *Fretwork.*
+ ARG 9-10/93: 250

35920. VJ 7 59692-2: Mozart—Symphonies no. 29, 40; Eine kleine Nachtmusik. *Northern Sinfonia Orch.; H. Schiff, cond.*
- ARG 9-10/93: 163
+ Fa 9-10/93: 223

35921. VC 7 59693-2: Gershwin—Cuban overture; Rhapsody in blue; Piano concerto. *Minnesota Orch.; Waart, cond.; Marshall, piano; London Sinfonia; Hickox, cond.; Bournemouth Symphony Orch.; Litton, cond.* Reissues.
• ARG 7-8/93: 93

35922. VJ 7 59694-2: Schubert—Piano sonatas D. 959-960. *D. Levine, piano.*
• ARG 9-10/93: 184
- Fa 9-10/93: 270

35923. VJ 7 59695-2: Ravel—Introduction and allegro; Le tombeau de Couperin. Fauré—Pavane. Debussy—Danse sacrée et danse profane. Ibert—Divertissement. *McKeand, harp; other instrumentalists.*
+ Fa 9-10/93: 381

35924. VMT 7 59699-2 (3 discs): Tchaikovsky—*Symphonies, vol. 1.* Symphonies no. 1-4; Capriccio italien; Serenade for strings; Eugene Onegin polonaise. *Bournemouth Symphony Orch.; Litton, cond.* Reissues.
• ARG 3-4/94: 169

35925. VJ 7 61100-2: Berlioz—Symphonie fantastique; Roman carnival overture. *Royal Phil. Orch.; Menuhin, cond.*
• ARG 3-4/94: 76

35926. VJ 7 61101-2: Mozart—Sonatas no. 8, 11, 14; Fantasy in C minor. *Pommier, piano.* Reissue.
- ARG 3-4/94: 127

35927. VJ 7 61103-2: Vivaldi—Concertos for strings, RV 121, 151, 199, 424, 519, 522, and 547. *Scottish Ensemble; Rees, cond.*
+ ARG 3-4/94: 178

35928. VJ 7 61104-2: Prokofiev—Symphony no. 1; Sinfonietta. Debussy—Sarabande; Danse. Milhaud—La creation du monde. *Lausanne Chamber Orch.; Zedda, cond.*
- ARG 3-4/94: 136

35929. VJ 7 61105-2: Vaughan Williams—Symphony no. 5; 2-piano concerto. *Markham, Broadway, pianos; Royal Phil. Orch.; Menuhin, cond.*
+ ARG 3-4/94: 176

35930. VJ 7 61106-2: Bartók—The miraculous mandarin. Stravinsky—Apollon musagete. *Melbourne Symphony Orch.; Iwaki, cond.; Scottish Chamber Orch.; Saraste, cond.*
• ARG 3-4/94: 70

35931. VJ 7 61107-2: Stravinsky—Pulcinella; Danses concertantes. *Murray, soprano; Hill, tenor; Thomas, bass; City of London Sinfonia; Hickox, cond.*
• ARG 3-4/94: 161

35932. VJ 7 61108-2: Mozart—Flute concertos; Flute and harp concerto. *Coles, flute; Yoshino, harp; English Chamber Orch.; Menuhin, cond.*
+ ARG 3-4/94: 124

35933. VJ 7 61109-2: *French connections.* Music of Debussy, Fauré, Pierné, Satie, Massenet, Saint-Saëns, and Tortelier. *English Chamber Orch.; P. Tortelier, cond.*
+ ARG 3-4/94: 193

35934. CUV 5 61117-2: Beethoven—Violin concerto; Coriolan overture. *Seiler, violin; City of London Sinfonia; Hickox, cond.* Reissue.
- ARG 7-8/95: 82

35935. CUV 5 61122-2: Britten—Noye's fludde; Serenade. *Maxwell, Ormiston; Coull String Quartet; Endymion Ensemble; Salisbury and Chester Singers; Hill, tenor; Lloyd, horn; City of London Sinfonia; Hickox, cond.*
+ ARG 3-4/95: 82

35936. CUV 5 61128-2: Humperdinck—Hansel and Gretel: Overture; The bluebird; The king's children; Sleeping beauty. *Bamberg Symphony Orch.; Rickenbacher, cond.* Reissue.
+ ARG 3-4/95: 116

35937. VJ 5 61129-2: Liszt—Piano music. *Hough.* Reissue.
+ ARG 11-12/94: 145

35938. CUV 5 61130-2: Mahler—Symphony no. 5. *Finnish Radio Symphony Orch.; Saraste, cond.* Reissue.
+ ARG 3-4/95: 133

35939. CUV 5 61134-2: Shostakovich—Symphony no. 10; Festive overture. *London Phil. Orch.; Litton, cond.* Reissue.
• ARG 3-4/95: 190

35940. VJ 5 61136: Nielsen—Violin concerto; Symphony no. 4. *Tellefsen, violin; Royal Phil. Orch.; Menuhin, cond.* Reissues.
+ ARG 11-12/94: 164

35941. VJ 5 61142-2: Strauss—Sinfonia domestica; Suite for winds, op. 4. *Minnesota Orch.; Waart, cond.* Reissue.
+ ARG 1-2/95: 185

35942. CUV 5 61153-2: Bach—Goldberg variations. *Cole, harpsichord.* Reissue.
+ ARG 9-10/95: 100

35943. CUV 5 61154-2 (2 discs): Bach—Brandenburg concertos; Musical offering. *Linde Consort; Linde, cond.*

Reissues.
+ ARG 11-12/95: 69

35944. CUV 5 61157-2 (2 discs): Bach—English suites. *Leonhardt, harpsichord.* Reissue.
• ARG 9-10/95: 98

35945. VER 5 61162-2: Handel—Concerti grossi, op. 3. *Linde Consort; Linde, cond.* Reissue.
+ ARG 1-2/96: 120

35946. VER 5 61163-2: Haydn—Divertimenti. *Linde Consort; Linde, cond.* Reissue.
+ Gr 2/96: 48

35947. VJ 5 61166-2: Lasso—Motets; Chansons. *Hilliard Ensemble; Hillier, cond.* Reissue.
+ ARG 3-4/96: 142

35948. VER 5 61167-2: Mozart—Mass in C minor "Great"; Kyrie in D minor. *Schlick, Frimmer, Prégardien, Mertens, vocalists; Cologne Chamber Choir; Collegium Cartusianum; Neumann, cond.* Reissue.
• Gr 7/95: 101

35949. VJ 5 61168-2 (2 discs): Palestrina—Song of songs; Vergine cycle. *Hilliard Ensemble; Hillier, cond.* Reissue; recorded 1986.
• ARG 3-4/96: 163

35950. VJ 5 61171-2: Vivaldi—Sonatas and trio sonatas, RV 14, 42, 63, 73, 78, 130, 169. *London Baroque; Medlam, cond.*
+ ARG 3-4/96: 205

35951. CUV 5 61172-2: Vivaldi—Violin concertos, op. 8: no. 1-6, 10-11. *Huggett, violin; Raglan Baroque Players; Kraemer, cond.* Reissue.
+ ARG 1-2/96: 193

35952. CUV 5 61174-2 : Libre vermell of Montserrat. *Hespèrion XX; Savall, cond.* Reissue.
+ ARG 9-10/95: 278

35953. CUV 5 61182-2: C.P.E. Bach—Symphonies Wq 183; Wq 182 no. 5. *Orch. of the Age of Enlightenment; Leonhardt, cond.* Reissue.
+ ARG 9-10/95: 94

35954. CUV 5 61183-2: Mendelssohn—Symphony no. 4; Midsummer night's dream: Excerpts. *Orch. of the Age of Enlightenment; Mackerras, cond.* Reissue.
+ ARG 9-10/95: 174

35955. CUV 5 61197-2: Debussy—Piano music. *Pommier, piano.*
+ ARG 1-2/96: 100

35956. CDM 5 61210-2: Corelli—Trio sonatas; Violin sonata, op. 5/3; Concerto

VIRGIN CLASSICS

grosso, op. 6/5. *London Baroque;
Medlam, cond.* Reissue.
- ● ARG 7-8/96: 101
- - Fa 7-8/96: 148

35957. CUV 5 61223-2: SMETANA—Ma
vlast. *Liverpool Phil. Orch.; Pešek, cond.*
- ● ARG 1-2/96: 177

35958. CUV 5 61235-2: HAYDN—Horn
concerto no. 1; Symphonies no. 45, 94.
*Thompson, horn; London Chamber
Orch.; Warren-Green, cond.* Reissue.
- ● ARG 3-4/96: 125
- ● Fa 1-2/96: 219

35959. CDC 5 61239-2: BOCCHERINI—
Cello concertos no. 1, 7, 9. *Möller, cello;
Linde Consort; Linde, cond.* Reissue.
- ● ARG 7-8/96: 84

35960. CDC 5 61240-2 : HANDEL—Water
music. *Linde Consort; Linde, cond.*
Reissue.
- ● ARG 7-8/96: 124

35961. VM 5 61243-2: GERSHWIN—Piano
concerto; Porgy and Bess: symphonic
suite; Second rhapsody. *Marshall, piano
& cond.; Aalborg Symphony Orch.*
- + Gr 4/96: 46

35962. CDM 5 61247-2: GERSHWIN—
Strike up the band: Medley; Rhapsody in
blue; Girl crazy: Medley; An American in
Paris; I got rhythm variations; Cuban
overture. *Marshall, piano & cond.;
Aalborg Symphony Orch.*
- ● ARG 1-2/96: 111
- + Fa 1-2/96: 203

35963. ZDMB 5 61249-2 (2 discs):
STRAVINSKY—Le sacre du printemps;
Perséphone. *Fournet, narrator; Rolfe
Johnson, tenor; London Phil. Orch.;
Tiffin School Boys' Choir; Nagano, cond.*
Reissue.
- ● Fa 9-10/96: 337

35964. CUV 5 61257-2: HOLST—The
planets; The perfect fool. *Royal Liverpool
Phil. Orch.; Mackerras, cond.*
- + ARG 5-6/96: 128

35965. CUV 5 61260-2: MOZART—
Requiem. *Kenny, Hodgson, Davies,
Howell; London Symphony Chorus;
Northern Sinfonia Orch. & Chorus;
Hickox, cond.* Reissue.
- ● ARG 5-6/96: 156

35966. VM 5 61281-2: STRAVINSKY—
Baiser de la fée. Bluebird pas de deux.
TCHAIKOVSKY—Sleeping beauty: excerpts
(orch. Stravinsky). *Hong Kong Phil.
Orch.; Atherton, cond.*
- + Gr 4/96: 57

35967. CUV 5 61288-2: *Monteverdi's
contemporaries.* Music of Donati, Grandi,
India, Porta, and others. *Early Music
Consort of London; Munrow, cond.*
Reissue.

- + ARG 1-2/97: 218
- ● Gr 9/96: 94

35968. CUV 5 61291-2: BACH—Viola da
gamba sonatas. *Savall, gamba; Koopman,
harpsichord.* Reissue.
- + ARG 1-2/97: 64

35969. CUV 5 61292-2 (2 discs):
BACH—Partitas. *Leonhardt, harpsichord.*
Reissue.
- + ARG 1-2/97: 64

35970. VC 7 90700-2: LISZT—Mephisto
waltz no. 1; Années de pèlerinage, Italie:
Tarantella; Rapsodie espagnole;
Harmonies poétiques et religeuses:
Pensée des morts; Deus legendes: St.
Francois d'Assise, la predication aux
oiseaux; Bénédiction de Dieu dans la
solitude. *Hough, piano.*
- + ARG 1-2/89: 62
- - Fa 9-10/88: 184
- + Gr 6/88: 51
- □ Ov 2/89: 50
- + SR 1/89: 129

35971. VC 7 90701-2: TIPPETT—Concerto
for double string orchestra; Fantasia
concertante on a theme of Corelli; Songs
for Dov. *Robson, tenor; Scottish
Chamber Orch.; Tippett, cond.*
- + Fa 9-10/88: 283
- + Gr 6/88: 39

35972. VC 7 90702-2: MOZART—
Symphonies no. 32, 35-36. *Scottish
Chamber Orch.; Saraste, cond.*
- - ARG 1-2/89: 73
- + Fa 9-10/88: 219
- + Gr 6/88: 32
- + SR 12/88: 152

35973. VC 7 90703-2: MAHLER—
Symphony no. 1; Lieder eines fahrenden
Gesellen. *Murray, mezzo-soprano; Royal
Phil. Orch.; Litton, cond.*
- + ARG 9-10/89: 72
- + Fa 9-10/88: 192 (Symphony)
- ● Fa 9-10/88: 192 (Gesellen)
- ● Gr 6/88: 28
- + St 12/89: 157

35974. VC 7 90704-2: Music of Berio,
Cage, Pousseur, and Berberian. *Hirst,
mezzo-soprano; London Sinfonietta;
Masson, cond.*
- + ARG 1-2/89: 121
- + Fa 9-10/88: 313
- + Gr 7/88: 192
- + MA 5/89: 76

35975. VC 7 90706-2: *Heart's ease:
music for viol consort from the late Tudor
and early Stuart age.* Music of Holborne,
Byrd, Dowland, Ferrabosco, and others.
*Fretwork; Wilson, lutes; Nicholson,
organ.*
- + ARG 3-4/89: 112

35976. VC 7 90707-2: *French
impressions.* Music of Debussy, Fauré,
Pierné, Massenet, Satie, and others.

*English Chamber Orch.; Tortelier, cello
& cond.*
- + ARG 1-2/89: 109
- + DA 4/89: 67
- + Fa 9-10/88: 343
- + Gr 7/88: 172
- + SR 12/88: 164

35977. VC 7 90708-2: SCHUBERT—
Symphony no. 9. *Orch. of the Age of
Enlightenment; Mackerras, cond.*
- + ARG 1-2/89: 87
- ● Fa 9-10/88: 253
- ● Gr 6/88: 35
- + HPR 3/89: 64
- + SR 2/89: 144

35978. VC 7 90709-2: BRAHMS—Piano
quartets no. 1, 3. *Domus.*
- + ARG 3-4/89: 26 (no. 1)
- ● ARG 3-4/89: 26 (no. 3)
- + DA 4/89: 68
- + Fa 9-10/88: 119
- ● Gr 6/88: 40

35979. VC 7 90710-2 (2 discs):
BRITTEN—Paul Bunyan. *Soloists;
Plymouth Music Series Chorus & Orch.;
Brunelle, cond.*
- ● ARG 1-2/89: 41
- + Fa 11-12/88: 153
- + Gr 8/88: 330
- + HF 12/88: 59
- + ON 12/24/88: 45
- + Op 10/88: 1252
- + Ov 11/88: 36
- + St 1/89: 209

35980. VC 7 90712-2: BACH—Fantasy
and fugue in D minor BWV 903; Partita
no. 1 BWV 825; Toccata, adagio and
fugue in G BWV 916; Prelude, fugue and
allegro in E♭ BWV 998; Italian concerto
BWV 971. *Cole, harpsichord.*
- + ARG 9-10/89: 20
- + Fa 7-8/89: 72
- + Gr 1/89: 1182
- + St 8/89: 171

35981. VC 7 90713-2: BEETHOVEN—
String quartets no. 9, 11. *Borodin String
Quartet.*
- + ARG 1-2/89: 19
- + Fa 11-12/88: 135
- + Gr 8/88: 311

35982. VC 7 90714-2: CANTELOUBE—
Chants d'Auvergne: Selections. *Augér,
soprano; English Chamber Orch.;
Tortelier, cond.*
- ● ARG 3-4/89: 28
- + Fa 11-12/88: 159
- + Gr 8/88: 322

35983. VC 7 90715-2: WALTON—
Symphony no. 1; Portsmouth Point
overture. *London Phil. Orch.; Slatkin,
cond.*
- + ARG 3-4/89: 104
- ● Fa 11-12/88: 310
- + Gr 8/88: 302
- + SR 12/88: 164
- ● St 12/88: 197

35984. VC 7 90717-2: BACH—Lute suites (complete). *Isbin, guitar.*
+ DA 1/90: 63
+ Fa 7-8/90: 75

35985. VC 7 90718-2: FINZI—Dies natalis; Farewell to arms, Introduction and aria for tenor and strings; Concerto for clarinet and strings. *Hill, tenor; Collins, clarinet; City of London Sinfonia; Hickox, cond.*
+ ARG 1-2/89: 50
+ Fa 11-12/88: 185
+ Gr 8/88: 284

35986. VC 7 90719-2: HAYDN—String quartets op. 54 no. 1-3. *Endellion String Quartet.*
+ ARG 9-10/89: 62
+ Fa 5-6/89: 214
• Gr 11/88: 803

35987. VC 7 90720-2: WEBER—Clarinet concertos (complete); Clarinet concertino op. 26. *Pay, clarinet; Orch. of the Age of Enlightenment.*
+ ARG 9-10/89: 116
+ Fa 5-6/89: 360
+ Fa 9-10/89: 374
+ Gr 10/88: 618
+ MA 1/90: 73
+ St 4/89: 209

35988. VC 7 90721-2: RAVEL—Introduction and allegro. DEBUSSY—Danses sacrée et profane. CAPLET—Conte fantastique. PIERNÉ—Voyage au pays du tendre. SAINT-SAËNS—Morceau de concert, op. 154. *McKeand, harp; Wincenc, flute; Campbell, clarinet; Allegri String Quartet; English Chamber Orch.; Colomer, cond.*
+ ARG 1-2/90: 119
+ Au 5/90: 72
+ Fa 11-12/89: 462

35989. VC 7 90722-2: *Armada.* Music of Byrd, Cabezon, Lopez, Fuenllana, Bevin, and others . *Chance, countertenor; Fretwork.*
+ ARG 7-8/89: 126
+ Fa 5-6/89: 378
+ Gr 11/88: 812
+ St 9/89: 177

35990. VC 7 90723-2: DVOŘÁK—Symphony no. 9; American suite. *Royal Liverpool Phil. Orch.; Pešek, cond.*
• ARG 11-12/89: 56
+ Fa 5-6/89: 181
• Gr 12/88: 996
• St 4/89: 193

35991. VC 7 90724-2: RACHMANINOFF—Piano concerto no. 1; Rhapsody on a theme of Paganini op. 43. *Pletnev, piano; Philharmonia Orch.; Pešek, cond.*
+ ARG 11-12/89: 98
+ DA 10/89: 94
+ Fa 5-6/89: 282
+ Gr 12/88: 1008

35992. VC 7 90725-2: MENDELSSOHN—Symphony no. 4; Midsummer night's dream: Incidental music. *Orch. of the Age of Enlightenment; Mackerras, cond.*
+ Fa 5-6/89: 233 (2 reviews)
• Gr 2/89: 1284

35993. VC 7 90726-2: DOWLAND—Songs for tenor and lute. *Rogers, tenor; O'Dette, lute.*
+ ARG 7-8/89: 39
+ Fa 7-8/89: 134
+ Gr 11/88: 836

35994. VC 7 90727-2: ELGAR—Enigma variations; In the south; Serenade for string orchestra in E minor, op. 20. *Royal Phil. Orch.; Litton, cond.*
+ ARG 9-10/89: 53
+ Fa 5-6/89: 191
+ Gr 12/88: 996
+ HF 7/89: 58
+ MA 11/89: 54

35995. VC 7 90728-2: BRITTEN—A boy was born; Hymn to St. Cecilia; A.M.D.G.; A shepherd's carol. *London Sinfonietta Chorus; St. Paul's Cathedral Choir; London Sinfonietta Voices; Edwards, cond.*
+ ARG 11-12/89: 47
+ Fa 5-6/89: 151
+ Gr 10/88: 652
+ NYT 7/23/89: H25

35996. VC 7 90729-2: RIMSKY-KORSAKOV—Scheherazade. RAVEL—Boléro. *Nolan, violin; London Phil. Orch.; Litton, cond.*
• ARG 7-8/89: 81
+ DA 10/89: 80
• Fa 5-6/89: 288
• Fa 7-8/89: 226
+ Gr 1/89: 1161
• HF 7/89: 58

35997. VC 7 90730-2: SCHUBERT—Songs. *White, tenor; Johnson, piano.*
+ ARG 1-2/90: 91
• Fa 7-8/90: 250

35998. VC 7 90731-2: SCHUBERT—Octet in F major, D. 803. *Nash Ensemble.*
• ARG 1-2/90: 85
+ Fa 11-12/89: 346
+ NYT 9/17/89: H34
+ St 8/89: 185

35999. VC 7 90732-2: *The piano album.* Music of MacDowell, Chopin (arr. Liszt), Dohnányi, Paderewski, and others. *Hough, piano.*
+ Fa 11-12/89: 454

36000. VC 7 90733-2: VAUGHAN WILLIAMS—Symphony no. 5; Concerto for 2 pianos. *Markham, Broadway, pianos; Royal Phil. Orch.; Menuhin, cond.*
• ARG 7-8/89: 102
+ Fa 5-6/89: 340
+ Gr 1/89: 1160
+ MA 9/89: 77

36001. VC 7 90734-2: PROKOFIEV— Violin concertos no. 1-2. *Sitkovetsky, violin; London Symphony Orch.; Davis, cond.*
+ ARG 11-12/89: 95
+ DA 9/89: 58
• Fa 5-6/89: 270
+ Gr 12/88: 1007
+ SR 6/89: 96

36002. VC 7 90735-2: ELGAR—Cello concerto. BLOCH—Schelomo. *Isserlis, cello; London Symphony Orch.; Hickox, cond.*
+ ARG 3-4/90: 47
+ Gr 7/89: 172

36003. VC 7 90736-2: DVOŘÁK—Piano trio no. 4; Piano quintet no. 2. *Nash Ensemble.*
+ ARG 11-12/89: 56
+ Fa 11-12/89: 195
• Gr 7/89: 199
+ St 8/89: 177

36004. VC 7 90737-2: BEETHOVEN—Piano sonatas no. 14, 21, and 23. *Pletnev, piano.*
+ ARG 1-2/90: 23
□ Fa 11-12/89: 133
• Gr 4/89: 1610
+ SR 12/89: 147

36005. VC 7 90738-2: CHOPIN—Piano sonatas no. 2; Nocturnes no. 5, 13, 18, and 20; Scherzo no. 2; Barcarolle in F#. *Pletnev, piano.*
+ ARG 11-12/90: 45
+ DA 3/91: 44
+ Fa 11-12/90: 202 m.f.
• Gr 4/90: 1833
• SR 11/90: 157

36006. VC 7 90739-2: BRAHMS—Piano quartet no. 2. MAHLER—Movement for piano and string trio in A minor. *Domus.*
+ ARG 1-2/90: 34
+ Fa 11-12/89: 154
+ Gr 1/89: 1175
• St 4/90: 193

36007. VC 7 90740-2: MOZART—Flute quartets (complete). *Nash Ensemble.*
+ ARG 9-10/90: 95
+ Fa 7-8/90: 204
• Gr 1/90: 1345

36008. VC 7 90741-2 (2 discs): BACH—Violin sonatas BWV 1014-19, 1021, 1023. *Holloway, violin; Moroney, harpsichord & chamber organ; Sheppard, cello.*
• ARG 3-4/90: 16
+ Fa 11/12/89: 116
+ Gr 6/89: 48

36009. VC 7 90743-2: HAYDN—Symphonies no. 26, 52-53. *La Petite Bande; Kuijken, cond.*
+ ARG 11-12/89: 67
+ Fa 5-6/89: 216
+ Gr 3/89: 1427
+ MA 9/89: 61
+ SR 8/89: 90

VIRGIN CLASSICS

36010. VC 7 90744-2: Bizet—
Symphonies in C. Ravel—Ma mère
l'oye; Pavane pour une infante défunte.
Scottish Chamber Orch.; Saraste, cond.
   • ARG 1-2/90: 33
   - Fa 11-12/89: 279
   • Gr 6/89: 25
   + NYT 11/26/89: H32
   + SR 12/89: 147

36011. VC 7 90746-2: Beethoven—
String quartets op. 18 no. 4; op. 132.
Borodin Quartet.
   + ARG 1-2/90: 22
   + DA 2/90: 59
   • Gr 6/89: 55

36012. VC 7 90747-2 (2 discs): Bach—
Brandenburg concertos (complete). *Orch.
of the Age of Enlightenment.*
   • ARG 1-2/90: 17
   + Fa 11-12/89: 105
   + Gr 7/89: 165
   • St 4/90: 191

36013. VC 7 90749-2: Rameau—Pièces
de clavecin en concerts. *Trio Sonnerie.*
   + DA 1/90: 46
   □ Fa 11-12/89: 326
   + Gr 9/89: 494

36014. VC 7 90750-2: Brahms—Cello
sonatas no. 1-2. *Rose, cello; Pommier,
piano.*
   + Fa 1-2/90: 139
   • MA 9/90: 74

36015. VC 7 90751-2: Saint-Saëns—
Piano trio no. 1; Septet op. 65; Carnival
of the animals. *Nash Ensemble.*
   + Fa 7-8/90: 243

36016. VC 7 90752-2: Rubbra—Four
medieval Latin lyrics; Five Spenser
sonnets; Amoretti; Sinfonietta for large
string orchestra. *Hill, tenor; Wilson-
Johnson, baritone; Endellion String
Quartet; City of London Sinfonia;
Schönzeler, cond.*
   + ARG 7-8/90: 92
   + Fa 9-10/90: 358

36017. VC 7 90753-2: Mozart—A
questo seno deh vieni; Voi avete un cor
fedele; Ah, lo previdi; Bella mia fiamma;
Misero! o sogno; si mostra la sorte;
Clarice cara; Va, dal furor portata; Se al
labbro mio non credi. *Lootens, soprano;
Prégardien, tenor; La Petite Bande;
Kuijken, cond.*
   • ARG 3-4/90: 76
   + Fa 5-6/90: 223
   + Gr 8/89: 355
   + St 10/90: 239

36018. VC 7 90754-2: Satie—Six
gnossiennes; Véritables préludes
flasques; Vieux séquins et vieilles
cuirasses; Chapitres tournés en tous sens;
Trois gymnopédies; Embryons desséchés;
Je te veux; Sonatine bureaucratique;
Heures séculaires et instantanées; Le
Piccadilly; Avant-derniéres pensées;

Sports et divertissements. *Quefféléc,
piano.*
   • ARG 3-4/90: 99
   + Fa 11-12/89: 339
   + SR 1/90: 129
   + St 4/90: 203

36019. VC 7 90755-2: Beethoven—
Serenade op. 25; Trio for strings op. 8.
*Sitkovetsky, violin; Caussé, viola;
Geringas, cello; Adorján, flute.*
   + ARG 3-4/90: 23
   - Gr 8/91: 323

36020. VC 7 90756-2: Dvořák—
Symphonies no. 7-8. *Royal Liverpool
Phil. Orch.; Pešek, cond.*
   + Fa 3-4/90: 174
   + Gr 9/89: 449

36021. VCD 7 90757-2: Bach—Mass in
B minor. *Schlick, Patriasz, Brett, Crook,
Kooy; Collegium Vocale, Ghent Chorus
& Orch.; Herreweghe, cond.*
   + Fa 3-4/90: 115
   + Gr 8/89: 346 m.f.

36022. VC 7 90760-2: Music of Strauss,
Janáček, and Debussy. *Sitkovetsky,
violin; Gililov, piano.*
   • ARG 11-12/90: 121
   + DA 3/90: 74
   + Fa 3-4/90: 311
   + Gr 9/89: 491

36023. VC 7 90761-2: Tchaikovsky—
Symphony no. 3; Capriccio italien;
Eugene Onegin: Polonaise. *Bournemouth
Symphony Orch.; Litton, cond.*
   • ARG 7-8/90: 118
   + Fa 7-8/90: 288
   + Gr 4/90: 1592

36024. VC 7 90763-2: Wert—Seventh
book of madrigals (1581). *Consort of
Musicke; Rooley, cond.*
   + ARG 5-6/90: 132
   + Fa 5-6/90: 346
   + Gr 12/89: 1195

36025. VC 7 90765-2: Bizet—Symphony
in C. Fauré—Pavane. Ravel—Le
tombeau de Couperin. Ibert—
Divertissement. *City of London Sinfonia;
Hickox, cond.*
   - ARG 7-8/90: 30
   + Gr 2/90: 1472

36026. VC 7 90766-2: Music of Barber,
Corpland, and Gershwin. *Gomez,
soprano; Steele-Perkins, trumpet;
McQueen, English horn; Marshall,
piano; City of London Sinfonia; Hickox,
cond.*
   • ARG 7-8/90: 40 m.f.
   + DA 12/90: 92
   + Fa 7-8/90: 80
   • Gr 11/89: 893
   + St 11/90: 217

36027. VC 7 90767-2: Stravinsky—
Pulcinella; Danses concertantes. *Murray,
Hill, Thomas; City of London Sinfonia;*

Hickox, cond.
   + DA 1/91: 72
   + Fa 11-12/90: 368
   • Gr 4/90: 1805

36028. VC 7 90768-2: *The English
Orpheus.* Dowland—Songs for voice and
lute. *Kirkby, soprano; Rooley, lute &
orpharion.*
   + ARG 1-2/91: 47
   + DA 9/90: 58
   + Fa 11-12/90: 217
   + Gr 4/90: 1850

36029. VC 7 90769-2: Dvořák—Czech
suite; Symphony no. 5. *Czech Phil.
Orch.; Pešek, cond.*
   + ARG 1-2/91: 48
   + Fa 1-2/91: 192
   + Gr 7/90: 210
   + SR 1/91: 98

36030. VC 7 90770-2: Schumann—
Davidsbündlertänze; Album für die
Jugend: 3 pieces; Fantasy in C op. 17.
Hough, piano.
   + ARG 7-8/90: 104
   + Fa 7-8/90: 261
   + Gr 11/89: 938

36031. VC 7 90771-2: Mahler—
Blumine; Totenfeier; Symphony no. 10:
Adagio. *Bamberg Symphony Orch.;
Rickenbacher, cond.*
   + ARG 7-8/90: 69
   □ Fa 7-8/90: 189
   + Gr 11/89: 898
   + St 2/92: 259

36032. VC 7 90773-2: Elgar—
Symphony no. 1. *Royal Phil. Orch.;
Menuhin, cond.*
   + ARG 7-8/90: 46
   + Fa 7-8/90: 141
   + Gr 12/89: 1128

36033. VC 7 90774-2: Bartók—String
quartet no. 1, 3; Duos for 2 violins no.
26-35, 36a. *Endellion String Quartet.*
   + ARG 9-10/90: 46
   • Fa 7-8/90: 83
   • Gr 11/89: 910

36034. VCT 7 90775-2 (3 discs):
Monteverdi—L'incoronazione di Poppea.
*Augér, Jones, Bowman, Reinhart; City of
London Baroque Sinfonia; Hickox, cond.*
   + ARG 1-2/90: 66
   + Fa 11-12/90: 285
   • Gr 5/90: 2049
   • MA 9/90: 82
   + NYT 7/1/90: H22
   + ON 3/2/91: 30
   • Op 7/90: 881
   + SR 8/90: 92

36035. VC 7 90779-2: Bach—Magnificat
in D; Ich hatte viel Bekümmernis BWV
21. *Reyghere, Jacobs, Prégardien, Lika;
Netherlands Chamber Choir; La Petite
Bande; Kuijken, cond.*
   + ARG 11-12/90: 16
   + Fa 11-12/90: 148 (Magnificat)

• Fa 11-12/90: 148 (Cantata)
+ Gr 2/90: 1496
+ MA 5/91: 63

36036. VC 7 90780-2: GERSHWIN—Piano concerto. RAVEL—Piano concerto in G. *Litton, piano & cond.; Bournemouth Symphony Orch.*
+ ARG 5-6/91: 59
- Fa 5-6/91: 174
• Gr 9/90: 510 (Gershwin)
+ Gr 9/90: 510 (Ravel)

36037. VCD 7 90781-2 (2 discs): BACH—Weihnachtsoratorium. *Schlick, Chance, Crook, Kooy; Collegium Vocale, Ghent Chorus & Orch.; Herreweghe, cond.*
+ ARG 11-12/90: 14
+ Fa 5-6/90: 104
+ Gr 12/89: 1180
+ NYT 12/3/89: H27

36038. VC 7 90786-2: PROKOFIEV—Peter and the wolf. SAINT-SAËNS—Carnival of the animals. MOZART—Serenade no. 13, K. 525. *Gielgud, Nel, Snell; Academy of London; Stamp, cond.*
• ARG 11-12/90: 98
+ Fa 3-4/90: 262
+ Gr 9/89: 474

36039. VC 7 90787-2: SCHUMANN—Dichterliebe; Liederkreis op. 24; Dein Angesicht; Die beiden Grenadiere; Du bist wie eine Blume. *Allen, baritone; Vignoles, piano.*
+ ARG 1-2/91: 96
+ Fa 7-8/90: 261
• Gr 9/90: 524

36040. VC 7 90788-2: MOZART—Piano concertos no. 21, 23. *Pommier, piano & cond.; Sinfonia Varsovia.*
• ARG 9-10/90: 92 (no. 21)
+ ARG 9-10/90: 92 (no. 23)
+ Fa 7-8/90: 205
+ Gr 9/90: 473

36041. VC 7 90789-2: *In the streets and theatres of London: Elizabethan ballads and theatre music.* Music of Kete, R. Johnson, J. Johnson, Azziaiolo, and others. *Musicians of Swanne Alley.*
+ ARG 3-4/90: 144
+ Fa 3-4/90: 360
+ St 10/90: 253

36042. VC 7 90790-2: FALLA—El amor brujo; El corregidor y la molinera. *Powell, mezzo-soprano; Gomez, soprano; Aquarius; Cleobury, cond.*
• ARG 5-6/90: 51
+ DA 7/90: 54
□ Fa 7-8/90: 142
+ Gr 1/90: 1326

36043. VC 7 90791-2: DVOŘÁK—In nature's realm; Symphony no. 6. *Czech Phil. Orch.; Pešek, cond.*
• ARG 1-2/90: 47
+ Fa 3-4/90: 174
- Gr 9/89: 449

36044. VC 7 90792-2: BRITTEN—Les illuminations; Serenade for tenor, horn & strings; Nocturne. *Hill, tenor; Lloyd, horn; City of London Sinfonia; Hickox, cond.*
+ ARG 7/90: 35
+ Fa 7-8/90: 110
+ Gr 12/89: 1183

36045. VC 7 90793-2: HAYDN—Symphonies no. 82-84. *Orch. of the Age of Enlightenment; Kuijken, cond.*
+ ARG 5-6/90: 59
+ Fa 5-6/90: 187
+ Gr 2/90: 1462
+ MA 9/90: 79

36046. VC 7 90794-2: STRAUSS—Metamorphosen; Songs: Ruhe, meine Seele; Morgen; Meinem Kinde; Befreit; Wiegenlied; Freundliche Vision; Winterweihe; Waldseligkeit; Die Heil'gen drei Königen aus Morgenland. *Janowitz, soprano; Academy of London; Stamp, cond.*
+ ARG 3-4/91: 126
+ Fa 7-8/91: 301
+ Gr 2/91: 1549

36047. VC 7 90795-2: *Nights black bird.* DOWLAND—Lachrimae (1604). BYRD—Fantasies in 6 parts: no. 2-3; Pavan and galliard in 6 parts; Browning in 5 parts; Fantasia in 4 parts no. 1; Pavana Bray; Fantasias in 3 parts no. 1-3. *Fretwork; Wilson, lute.*
+ Fa 5-6/90: 155

36048. VC 7 90796-2: HANDEL—Arias. *White, tenor; City of London Baroque Sinfonia; Bolton, cond.*
+ ARG 3-4/90: 55
+ Fa 7-8/90: 162
+ Gr 1/90: 1345

36049. VC 7 90797-2: DVOŘÁK—Symphony no. 3; Scherzo capriccioso; Carnival. *Royal Liverpool Phil. Orch.; Pešek, cond.*
+ ARG 11-12/90: 52
+ Fa 9-10/90: 236
+ Gr 1/90: 1326

36050. VC 7 90798-2: TCHAIKOVSKY—Symphony no. 4; Serenade for strings. *Bournemouth Symphony Orch.; Litton, cond.*
• ARG 9-10/90: 121
+ Au 12/90: 142
+ Fa 9-10/90: 410
+ Gr 2/90: 1471

36051. VC 7 90799-2: POULENC—Piano concerto; Concert champêtre for harpsichord; Organ concerto. *Pommier, piano; Cole, harpsichord; Weir, organ; City of London Sinfonia; Hickox, cond.*
• ARG 3-4/90: 102
+ Fa 11-12/90: 316 (organ)
• Fa 11-12/90: 316 (others)
• Gr 4/90: 1786 m.f.

36052. VC 7 90800-2: C.P.E. BACH—Concertos for cello and strings Wq. 170-172. *Bylsma, cello; Orch. of the Age of Enlightenment; Leonhardt, cond.*
+ Au 11/90: 132
+ Fa 11-12/90: 141
+ Gr 2/90: 1455

36053. VC 7 90801-2: SCHUBERT—Piano quintet D. 667; Adagio and rondo concertante for piano and strings D. 487. *Domus; Nwanoku, double bass.*
- ARG 7-8/90: 97
+ Fa 7-8/90: 252
• Gr 1/90: 1345

36054. VC 7 90802-2: BYRD—Mass for 5 voices with the gradualia; Propers for the Feast of All Saints; Diliges Dominum; Ad Dominum cum tribularer. *The Sixteen; Christophers, cond.*
+ ARG 9-10/90: 54
+ Fa 11-12/90: 196
+ Gr 9/90: 586
+ NYT 9/2/90: H22

36055. VC 7 90803-2 (2 discs): VIVALDI—Concertos: Op. 8; RV 516, 546. *Huggett, violin; Kraemer, harpsichord & cond.; Raglan Baroque Players.*
+ ARG 3-4/91: 137
+ Fa 11-12/90: 391
+ Gr 4/90: 1806
+ SR 11/90: 165

36056. VC 7 90805-2: BOCCHERINI—Cello concertos, G. 480, G. 482; Cello sonatas no. 2, 5-6. *Isserlis, cello; Cole, harpsichord; Ostrobothnian Chamber Orch.; Kangas, cond.*
+ ARG 3-4/92: 34
+ Fa 3-4/92: 156
+ Gr 7/92: 52

36057. VC 7 90807-2: SMETANA—String quartet no. 1. DVOŘÁK—String quartet no. 12 op. 96. *Endellion String Quartet.*
• ARG 5-6/91: 53
+ Fa 5-6/91: 163
• Gr 6/90: 68

36058. VC 7 90811-2: KABALEVSKY—Cello concerto no. 2. PROKOFIEV—Cello concerto (completed by Rostropovich); Sonata for solo cello. *Isserlis, cello; London Phil. Orch.; Litton, cond.*
+ DA 11/90: 56
+ Fa 9-10/90: 267
+ Gr 3/90: 1609

36059. VC 7 90812-2: DEBUSSY—Cello sonata. POULENC—Cello sonata. FRANCK—Violin sonata (arr. for cello). *Isserlis, cello; Devoyon, piano.*
+ DA 11/90: 56
• Fa 9-10/90: 225
• Gr 3/90: 1609

36060. VC 7 90813-2: STRAUSS—Oboe concerto. BACH—Oboe d'amore concerto, BWV 1055; Sinfonias for oboe and strings BWV 156, 12, 21. A. MARCELLO—Oboe concerto (arr.

VIRGIN CLASSICS

Lauschmann). *Still, oboe; Academy of London; Stamp, cond.*
  + ARG 9-10/90: 142
  + Fa 9-10/90: 397
  + Gr 2/90: 1472

36061. VC 7 90818-2: Mozart—Sinfonia concertante for violin and viola K. 364; Sinfonia concertante for winds K. 297b. *Warren-Green, violin; Chase, viola; Hunt, oboe; Collins, clarinet; Thompson, horn; Alexander, bassoon; London Chamber Orch.*
  + ARG 5-6/90: 83
  • Fa 5-6/90: 231
  + Gr 9/89: 473

36062. VC 7 90819-2: Elgar—Introduction and allegro; Serenade for strings in E minor. Vaughan Williams—Lark ascending; Fantasia on Greensleeves; Fantasia on a theme of Thomas Tallis. *London Chamber Orch.; Warren-Green, cond.*
  • ARG 5-6/90: 123
  + Fa 5-6/90: 163
  + Gr 9/89: 450

36063. VC 7 90821-2: M. Lambert—Leçons de ténèbres. *Rime, Stutzmann, Brett, Crook; ensemble; Piveteau, cond.*
  + ARG 7-8/90: 62
  + Fa 5-6/90: 202

36064. VC 7 90830-2: Rachmaninoff—Symphony no. 1; Isle of the dead. *Royal Phil. Orch.; Litton, cond.*
  + ARG 3-4/91: 104
  + Fa 1-2/91: 281
  + Gr 5/90: 1982
  + SR 12/90: 100

36065. VC 7 90831-2: Rachmaninoff—Symphony no. 2; Vocalise. *Royal Phil. Orch.; Litton, cond.*
  • ARG 3-4/91: 104
  + Fa 1-2/91: 281
  + Gr 5/90: 1982
  + SR 12/90: 100

36066. VC 7 90832-2: Rachmaninoff—Symphony no. 3; Symphonic dances. *Royal Phil. Orch.; Litton, cond.*
  • ARG 3-4/91: 104
  + Fa 1-2/91: 281
  + Gr 5/90: 1982
  + SR 12/90: 100

36067. VC 7 90833-2: Beethoven—String quartets no. 5, 7. *Borodin String Quartet.*
  • ARG 1-2/91: 28
  + Fa 9-10/90: 163
  + Gr 4/90: 1810

36068. VC 7 90834-2: Britten—Sinfonia da requiem; Peter Grimes: Four sea interludes and passacaglia; Young person's guide to the orchestra. *Royal Liverpool Phil.; Pešek, cond.*
  • ARG 11-12/90: 40
  + Gr 4/90: 1772
  + SR 9/90: 120

36069. VC 7 90838-2: Biber—Mystery sonatas. *Holloway, violin; Moroney, chamber organ & harpsichord; Tragicomedia.*
  + ARG 9-10/91: 48
  + Fa 7-8/91: 121
  • HPR v.8, no.3/91: 69
  + MA 7/91: 67

36070. VC 7 90839-2: Haydn—Variation in F minor H. XVII:6; Piano sonatas no. 33, 52 60. *Pletnev, piano.*
  ☐ ARG 7-8/90: 55
  - Fa 7-8/90: 170
  + Gr 11/89: 934

36071. VC 7 90840-2 (2 discs): Corelli—Violin sonatas op. 5. *Trio Sonnerie; North, archlute, theorbo & guitar.*
  + ARG 9-10/90: 58
  + Fa 11-12/90: 205
  + Gr 9/90: 556
  + MA 5/91: 63

36072. VC 7 90842-2: *Danses nobles et sentimentales.* Music of Prokofiev, Dvarák, Brahms, Bartók, Wieniawski, and others. *Sitkovetsky, violin; Gililov, piano.* All works arr. for violin & piano.
  + Fa 9-10/90: 481
  • Gr 3/90: 1636

36073. VC 7 90844-2: Haydn—Symphonies no. 85-87. *Orch. of the Age of Enlightenment; Kuijken, cond.*
  + Fa 1-2/91: 216
  + Gr 5/90: 1976

36074. VC 7 90844-2: Haydn—Symphonies no. 85-87. *Orch. of the Age of Enlightenment; Kuijken, cond.*
  + ARG 11-12/91: 79

36075. VC 7 90846-2: Music of Widor, Fauré, Debussy, Honegger, Roussel, and others. *Snowden, flute; Litton, piano.*
  + Fa 9-10/90: 483
  + Gr 3/90: 1636

36076. VC 7 90847-2: Debussy—Deux arabesques; Children's corner; Estampes; L'isle joyeuse; Pièce pour le vêtement du blessé; La plus que lente; Pour le piano. *Pommier, piano.*
  + Fa 9-10/90: 221
  • Gr 2/90: 1489

36077. VC 7 90849-2: *Cries and fancies.* Gibbons—Fantasias, In nomines and the Cries of London. *Fretwork.*
  + ARG 11-12/90: 59
  + Fa 11-12/90: 233
  + Gr 3/90: 1628

36078. VC 7 90996-2: Morricone—Sestetto; Musica per 11 violini; Tre studi; Ricercare for piano; Quattro pezzi for guitar; Suoni per Dino; Distanze. *Various performers.*
  ☐ Fa 3-4/89: 214
  + HF 7/89: 62

36079. VC 7 91074-2: Mozart—Clarinet trio K. 498; Adagio and rondo for flute, oboe, cello, and piano K. 617; Oboe quartet K. 370; Horn quintet K. 407. *Nash Ensemble.*
  + ARG 3-4/91: 96
  + Fa 1-2/91: 261
  + Gr 4/90: 1824

36080. VC 7 91075-2: Poulenc—Figure humaine; Quatre motets pour un temps de pénitence; Laudes de St. Antoine de Padoue; Quatre motets pour le temps de Noël; Quatre petites prière de Saint François d'Assise. *The Sixteen; Christophers, cond.*
  + ARG 11-12/90: 97
  + Fa 11-12/90: 156
  + Gr 3/90: 1669
  + MA 3/91: 85

36081. VC 7 91077-2: Debussy—String quartet. Ravel—String quartet. *Borodin String Quartet.*
  • ARG 7-8/90: 41
  + DA 2/91: 60
  - Fa 9-10/90: 224
  • Gr 1/90: 1342
  • MA 11/90: 71

36082. VC 7 91078-2: Mozart—Symphonies no. 38-39. *Sinfonia Varsovia; Menuhin, cond.*
  + Fa 9-10/90: 315
  + Gr 3/90: 1614
  + SR 10/90: 114
  + St 1/91: 260

36083. VC 7 91079-2: Nicolai—Symphony no. 2; Lusigen Weiber von Windsor overture; Der Tempelritter overture; Die Heimkehr des Verbannten overture; Christmas overture. *Bamberg Symphony Orch.; Rickenbacher, cond.*
  • ARG 7-8/90: 77
  - Fa 9-10/90: 318
  + Gr 3/90: 1614
  + St 1/91: 260

36084. VC 7 91080-2: Britten—Simple symphony; Prelude and fugue op. 18; Lachrymae. Purcell—Chacony in G minor. *Chase, viola; London Chamber Orch.; Warren-Green, cond.*
  + ARG 11-12/90: 39
  + Fa 5-6/90: 163
  + Gr 9/89: 449

36085. VC 7 91081-2: Music of Vivaldi, Albinoni (arr. Giazotto), and Pachelbel. *Warren-Green, violin; London Chamber Orch.*
  • ARG 5-6/90: 128
  + Fa 5-6/90: 330
  • Gr 9/90: 546

36086. VC 7 91082-2: Mozart—Symphonies no. 40-41. *Sinfonia Varsovia; Menuhin, cond.*
  • ARG 11-12/90: 91
  + DA 9/90: 54
  + Fa 9-10/90: 317

+ Gr 3/90: 1614
+ St 1/91: 260

36087. VC 7 91083-2: BARBER—Cello sonata; Cello concerto; Adagio for strings. *Kirschbaum, cello; Vignoles, piano; Scottish Chamber Orch.; Saraste, cond.*
- • ARG 7-8/90: 18
- • Fa 9-10/90: 162
- + SR 8/90: 87

36088. VCD 7 91084-2 (2 discs): PROKOFIEV—Love for three oranges. *Lagrange, Dubosc, Gautier, Bacquier, Bastin; Lyon Opera Chorus & Orch.; Nagano, cond.*
- + ARG 3-4/90: 88
- + Fa 5-6/90: 249
- + Gr 12/89: 1200
- + NYT 4/29/90: H31
- + ON 3/3/90: 30
- + Op 3/90: 384
- + SR 4/90: 98
- + St 9/90: 197

36089. VC 7 91086-2: HINDEMITH—Symphony Mathis der Maler; Neues vom Tage overture; Symphonic metamorphoses on themes of Carl Maria von Weber. *Bamberg Symphony Orch.; Rickenbacher, cond.*
- • ARG 7-8/90: 57
- - Fa 9-10/90: 264
- • Gr 3/90: 1609

36090. VC 7 91087-2: PACHELBEL—Organ music . *Jacob, organ.*
- + ARG 3-4/91: 100
- + Fa 11-12/90: 305
- + Gr 4/90: 1836
- + MA 5/91: 63

36091. VC 7 91089-2: *L'heure exquise: melodies.* Music of Hahn, Bizet, and Chabrier. *Yakar, soprano; Lavoix, piano.*
- + ARG 9-10/90: 149
- + Fa 9-10/90: 246
- • Gr 3/90: 1676

36092. VC 7 91091-2: MOZART—Piano sonatas no. 1-5. *Pommier, piano.*
- + ARG 3-4/91: 97
- + DA 4/91: 60
- • Fa 3-4/91: 303
- • Gr 9/90: 577

36093. VC 7 91092-2: MOZART—Piano sonatas no. 6-9. *Pommier, piano.*
- + ARG 3-4/91: 97
- + DA 4/91: 60
- • Fa 3-4/91: 303
- • Gr 9/90: 577

36094. VC 7 91093-2: MOZART—Piano sonatas no. 10-12. *Pommier, piano.*
- + ARG 3-4/91: 97
- + DA 4/91: 60
- • Fa 3-4/91: 303
- • Gr 9/90: 577

36095. VC 7 91094-2: MOZART—Piano sonata no. 13; Fantasy and sonata in C

minor K. 475/457. *Pommier, piano.*
- + ARG 3-4/91: 97
- + DA 4/91: 60
- • Fa 3-4/91: 303
- • Gr 9/90: 577

36096. VC 7 91095-2: MOZART—Piano sonatas no. 15-17; Piano sonata K. 533. *Pommier, piano.*
- + ARG 3-4/91: 97
- • Fa 3-4/91: 303
- • Gr 9/90: 577

36097. VC 7 91096-2: MAHLER—Symphony no. 1. *Minnesota Orch.; Waart, cond.*
- + ARG 5-6/91: 78
- • Fa 3-4/91: 262
- • Gr 11/90: 984
- - MA 7/91: 77
- • St 4/91: 257

36098. VC 7 91097-2: HAYDN—String quartets op. 74 no. 1-3. *Endellion String Quartet.*
- + ARG 11-12/90: 67
- + Fa 11-12/90: 293
- + Gr 4/90: 1818

36099. VC 7 91098-2: Music of Prokofiev, Debussy (arr. Ravel), and Milhaud. *Lausanne Chamber Orch.; Zedda, cond.*
- + ARG 11-12/90: 98
- • Fa 11-12/90: 319
- + Gr 5/90: 1972

36100. VC 7 91099-2: MARTINŮ—Double concerto for 2 string orchestras, piano and timpani; Concerto for string quartet; Sinfonia concertante for oboe, bassoon, violin and cello. *Alley, piano; Fullbrook, timpani; Daniel, oboe; Reay, bassoon; Watkinson, violin; Orton, cello; Endellion String Quartet; City of London Sinfonia; Hickox, cond.*
- + ARG 5-6/91: 79
- + Fa 5-6/91: 212

36101. VC 7 91099-2: MARTINŮ—Double concerto; Concerto for string quartet and orchestra; Sinfonia concertante. *Instrumental soloists; City of London Sinfonia; Hickox, cond.*
- + Gr 6/91: 44

36102. VC 7 91101-2: STRAVINSKY—Petrushka (1911 version); Agon; Fireworks. *Melbourne Symphony Orch.; Iwaki, cond.*
- - ARG 1-2/91: 104
- • Fa 1-2/91: 327
- + Gr 9/90: 544

36103. VC 7 91102-2: STRAUSS—Alpine symphony; Serenade for winds op. 7. *Minnesota Orch.; Waart, cond.*
- + ARG 5-6/91: 113
- + Fa 3-4/91: 394
- + Gr 8/91: 382
- • NYT 10/21/90: H36
- + SR 10/90: 118

36104. VC 7 91103-2 (2 discs): BRITTEN—Prince of the pagodas. *London Sinfonietta; Knussen, cond.*
- + ARG 1-2/91: 39
- + Fa 5-6/91: 141
- + Gr 7/90: 208
- + NYT 10/21/90: H36
- + SR 1/91: 94

36105. VC 7 91105-2: *On the idle hill of summer.* Music of Vaughan Williams, Peel, Butterworth, and Quilter. *Allen, baritone; Parsons, piano.*
- • ARG 3-4/91: 168
- + Fa 1-2/91: 371
- • Gr 7/90: 268

36106. VC 7 91107-2: BRITTEN—The company of heaven; Paul Bunyan: Overture; Lullaby of dream shadows; Inkslinger's love song. *Soloists; London Phil. Choir; English Chamber Orch.; Brunelle, cond.*
- + Fa 9-10/91: 179

36107. VC 7 91108-2: WISHART—Vox: no. 1-6. *Electric Phoenix.*
- □ ARG 1-2/91: 125
- + Fa 11-12/90: 405
- + Gr 3/90: 532

36108. VC 7 91110-2: *A Venetian coronation: 1595.* Music of A. Gabrieli, G. Gabrieli, Bendinelli, and Thomsen. *Gabrieli Consort & Players; McCreesh, cond.*
- + ARG 11-12/90: 58
- + Fa 11-12/90: 229
- + Gr 5/90: 2038
- + MA 5/91: 65

36109. VC 7 91111-2: NIELSEN—Violin concerto; Symphony no. 4. *Tellefsen, violin; Royal Phil. Orch.; Menuhin, cond.*
- + ARG 1-2/91: 73 (Concerto)
- - ARG 1-2/91: 73 (Symphony)
- + Fa 1-2/91: 267
- • Gr 9/90: 532

36110. VC 7 91113-2: COPLAND—The tender land. *Comeaux, Hardy, Lehr, Dressen, Bohn; Plymouth Music Series Chorus & Orch.; Brunelle, cond.*
- + ARG 1-2/91: 42
- + DA 10/90: 70
- • Fa 11-12/90: 203
- + Gr 8/90: 407
- + NYT 12/16/90: H35
- + ON 8/90: 40
- + SR 11/90: 159

36111. VC 7 91114-2: MAHLER—Rheinlegendchen; Des heiligen Antonius von Padua Fischpredigy; Nicht widersehen; Lied des Verfolgten im Turm; Zu Strassburg auf der Schabz; Revelge; Der tamboursg'sell'; Ich atmet einen Linden Duft; Liebst du um Schönheit; Blicke mir nicht in die Lieder; Ich bin der Welt abhanden gekommen; Um Mitternacht. *Jerusalem, tenor; Mauser, piano.*

VIRGIN CLASSICS

● ARG 5-6/91: 78
+ Fa 1-2/91: 233
+ Gr 9/90: 590
- MA 3/91: 78

36112. VC 7 91117-2: Goe nightly cares. *Chance, countertenor; Wilson, lute; Fretwork.*
+ ARG 9-10/91: 172
+ Gr 3/91: 1707

36113. VC 7 91118-2: BACH—Masses: in G minor; in A; Sanctus BWV 238. *Mellon, Lesne, Prégardien, Kooy; Collegium Vocale, Ghent Chorus & Orch.; Herreweghe, cond.*
+ ARG 9-10/91: 38
+ Fa 5-6/91: 109
+ Gr 1/91: 1393

36114. VC 7 91118-2: BACH—Masses, BWV 234-235; Sanctus in D, BWV 238. *Collegium vocale, Ghent; Herreweghe, cond.*
+ ARG 9-10/91: 38

36115. VC 7 91119-2: TCHAIKOVSKY— Symphonies no. 1-2. *Bournemouth Symphony Orch.; Litton, cond.*
+ ARG 3-4/91: 130
+ Fa 5-6/91: 301

36116. VC 7 91120-2: SCHUBERT—Octet in F, D. 803. *Atlantis Ensemble.*
+ ARG 7-8/91: 120
+ Fa 7-8/91: 281
+ MA 7/91: 87
+ SR 6/91: 94

36117. VC 7 91122-2: MOZART— Serenades K. 239, 320; Divertimento K. 136; Marches K. 335 . *Chamber Orch. of Lausanne; Menuhin, cond.*
+ ARG 5-6/91: 89
+ Fa 5-6/91: 237

36118. VC 7 91123-2: BRAHMS—Alto rhapsody; Four songs for chorus op. 17. MENDELSSOHN—Infelice; Psalm 42. *Baker, mezzo-soprano; London Symphony Chorus & Orch.; Hickox, cond.*
+ ARG 7-8/91: 37
- Fa 7-8/91: 124 (Rhapsody)
+ Fa 7-8/91: 124 (others)

36119. VC 7 91128-2: *Road to the sun.* Music of Sainz de la Maza, Rodrigo, Barrios, Abreu, Jobim, and others. *Isbin, guitar.*
● ARG 1-2/91: 135
+ Fa 3-4/91: 175
+ Gr 10/90: 795

36120. VC 7 91130-2: BRAHMS—Lieder. *Allen, baritone; Parsons, piano.*
● ARG 3-4/91: 46
+ Fa 1-2/91: 160
+ Gr 9/90: 585

36121. VC 7 91133-2: BYRD—Mass for 4 voices; Propers for the feast of Saints Peter & Paul; Quomodo cantabimus; Tu es pastor ovium; Quodcumque ligaveris;

Hodie Simon Petrus. MONTE—Super flumina Babylonis. *The Sixteen; Christophers, cond.*
+ ARG 3-4/91: 51
+ Fa 5-6/91: 148
● Gr 1/91: 1394

36122. VC 7 91134-2: Music of Tchaikovsky, Glazunov, Rimsky-Korsakov, and Cui. *Isserlis, cello; Chamber Orch. of Europe; Gardiner, cond.*
● ARG 5-6/91: 142
+ Da 5/91: 77
+ Fa 3-4/91: 490
+ Gr 10/90: 751

36123. VC 7 91137-2: BEETHOVEN—Trio for clarinet, cello, and piano; Septet in E♭, op. 20. *Nash Ensemble.*
+ Fa 5-6/91: 129
● Gr 3/91: 1684
+ SR 5/91: 85

36124. VC 7 91138-2: BRAHMS—Piano concerto no. 2 . *Hough, piano; BBC Symphony Orch.; Davis, cond.*
+ ARG 3-4/91: 43
● Fa 1-2/91: 160
● Gr 9/90: 509
+ St 4/91: 252

36125. VC 7 91139-2: BUXTEHUDE— Organ music. *Danby, organ.*
+ ARG 9-10/91: 56
- Fa 7-8/91: 132
+ Gr 2/91: 1530

36126. VC 7 91140-2: TCHAIKOVSKY— Symphony no. 5; The tempest. *Bournemouth Symphony Orch.; Litton, cond.*
● ARG 3-4/91: 131
+ Fa 7-8/91: 306
● Gr 2/91: 1521

36127. VC 7 91141-2: HAYDN— Symphonies no. 90-91. *La Petite Bande; Kuijken, cond.*
+ ARG 11-12/91: 79
+ Fa 5-6/91: 185
+ Gr 2/91: 1506
+ Gr 10/95: 58

36128. VC 7 91141-2: HAYDN— Symphonies 90-91. *La Petite Bande; Kuijken, cond.*
+ ARG 11-12/91: 79

36129. VC 7 91142-2: SCHUBERT—Four impromptus D. 899; Four impromptus D. 935. *Orkis, fortepiano.*
● ARG 7-8/91: 119
+ Fa 7-8/91: 279
+ Gr 12/90: 86
+ Gr 9/92: 136
+ HPR v.8, no.3/91: 83
+ SR 10/91: 76

36130. VC 7 91143-2: SHOSTAKOVICH— Violin concertos no. 1-2. *Sitkovetsky, violin; BBC Symphony Orch.; Davis, cond.*

● ARG 3-4/91: 120
+ Fa 3-4/91: 382
+ Gr 9/90: 540

36131. VC 7 91144-2: DVOŘÁK— Symphony no. 4; Othello. *Czech Phil. Orch.; Pešek, cond.*
+ ARG 5-6/92: 51
+ Fa 7-8/92: 145 (Wiser)
+ Fa 7-8/92: 149 (Hurwitz)
+ Gr 3/92: 43

36132. VC 7 91145-2: *Salve Regina.* MONTEVERDI—Motets for 1, 2, and 3 voices. *G. Lesne, countertenor; Benet, Cabré, B. Lesne; Il Seminario Musicale; Tragicomedia.*
+ Fa 7-8/91: 221

36133. VC 7 91145-2: MONTEVERDI— Sacred motets. *G. Lesne, alto; B. Lesne, mezzo-soprano; Benet, tenor; Cabré, baritone; Il seminario musicale; Tragicomedia.*
+ ARG 5-6/92: 87
+ St 5/92: 199

36134. VC 7 91148-2: DEBUSSY—Violin sonata; Sonata for flute, viola and harp; Syrinx; Cello sonata; Les chansons de Bilitis. *Nash Ensemble.*
● Fa 11-12/91: 310
+ Gr 4/91: 1854

36135. VC 7 91154-2: MONTEVERDI— Sixth book of madrigals. *Consort of Musicke; Rooley, cond.*
+ Fa 3-4/91: 283
+ Gr 12/90: 1246

36136. VC 7 91154-2: MONTEVERDI— Sixth book of madrigals. *Consort of Musicke; Rooley, cond.*
+ ARG 5-6/92: 87

36137. VC 7 91156-2: MONTEVERDI— Madrigali guerrieri (Book 8). *Consort of Musicke.*
+ ARG 11-12/91: 96
+ Fa 11-12/91: 392
+ Gr 3/92: 104

36138. VC 7 91157-2: MONTEVERDI— Madrigali amorosi (Book 8). *Consort of Musicke.*
+ ARG 11-12/91: 96
+ Fa 11-12/91: 392
+ Gr 3/92: 104

36139. VC 7 91158-2: MONTEVERDI— Volgendo il ciel; Combattimento di Tancredi e Clorinda; Il ballo delle ingrate. *Consort of Musicke; Rooley, cond.*
+ Fa 3-4/91: 283
● Gr 12/90: 1246
+ MA 3/91: 65

36140. VC 7 91158-2: MONTEVERDI— Excerpts from Madrigals, book 8. *Consort of Musicke; Rooley, cond.*
+ ARG 5-6/92: 87

36141. VC 7 91162-2: Picker—
Encantadas; Romances and interludes;
Old and lost rivers, for orchestra; Old and
lost rivers, for piano. *Gielgud, speaker;
Atherholt, oboe; Houston Symphony
Orch.; Eschenbach, cond.*
+ ARG 7-8/91: 106
+ Fa 7-8/91: 250
+ Gr 7/90: 56
+ MA 7/91: 83

36142. VC 7 91162-2: Picker—Old and
lost rivers (orch. version); The
Encantadas; Romances and interludes;
Old and lost rivers (piano version).
*Houston Symphony Orch.; Eschenbach,
piano & cond.*
□ Gr 7/91: 56

36143. VC 7 91163-2: *American piano
sonatas, vol. 1.* Copland—Piano sonata.
Ives—Three-page sonata (ed. Cowell).
Carter—Piano sonata. Barber—Piano
sonata, op. 26. *Lawson, piano.*
+ ARG 11-12/91: 191
+ Fa 11-12/91: 547
+ Gr 5/91: 2043

36144. VC 7 91164-2: Berlioz—Les
nuits d'été; La belle voyageuse; La
captive; Zaide. Respighi—La sensitiva.
*Baker, mezzo-soprano; City of London
Sinfonia; Hickox, cond.*
+ ARG 11-12/91: 34
+ Fa 11-12/91: 271
+ Gr 6/91: 70

36145. VC 7 91165-2: Tchaikovsky—
Serenade for strings in C major. Suk—
Serenade for strings in E♭ major.
Dvořák—Serenade for strings in E major.
*London Chamber Orch.; Warren-Green,
cond.*
+ Fa 5-6/91: 298
- Gr 11/90: 975

36146. VC 7 91166-2: Mozart—
Symphony no. 29; Serenade K. 525;
Violin concerto no. 5 K. 219;
Divertimento K. 136. *London Chamber
Orch.; Warren-Green, violin & cond.*
● DA 3/91: 40
+ Fa 3-4/91: 306
● Gr 4/91: 1836

36147. VC 7 91167-2: Vivaldi—
Concertos RV 537, 401, 447, 502, 522,
551, 580 . *London Chamber Orch.;
Warren-Green, violin & cond.*
+ ARG 3-4/91: 135
● DA 3/91: 40
+ Fa 3-4/91: 419
+ Gr 12/91: 1220

36148. VC 7 91168-2: Adams—Shaker
loops. Glass—Façades; Company.
Reich—Eight lines. Heath—The frontier.
*London Chamber Orch.; Warren-Green,
cond.*
+ DA 3/91: 40
+ Fa 3-4/91: 517
+ Gr 11/90: 996

36149. VC 7 91169-2: Mussorgsky—
Pictures at an exhibition. Tchaikovsky—
Sleeping Beauty: Excerpts. *Pletnev,
piano. Arr. Pletnev.*
- Fa 7-8/91: 240 (Mussorgsky)
+ Fa 7-8/91: 240 (Tchaikovsky)
+ SR 9/91: 101

36150. VC 7 91169-2: Mussorgsky—
Pictures at an exhibition. Tchaikovsky—
Sleeping beauty (excerpts). *Pletnev,
piano.*
+ ARG 1-2/92: 80

36151. VC 7 91170-2: Hartmann—Piano
sonata "27 April 1945"; Jazz-toccata and
-fugue; Sonatina; Little suite for piano;
Suite no. 2. *Mauser, piano.*
+ ARG 11-12/91: 76
+ Fa 11-12/91: 342
+ Gr 8/91: 62

36152. VC 7 91171-2: Strauss—Ein
Heldenleben; Don Juan. *Royal Liverpool
Phil. Orch.; Pešek, cond.*
+ ARG 9-10/91: 132
+ Fa 9-10/91: 366
+ Gr 5/91: 2021

36153. VC 7 91172-2: Soler—Sonatas.
Cole, fortepiano & harpsichord.
+ ARG 11-12/91: 148
+ Fa 9-10/91: 362
+ Gr 5/91: 2043

36154. VC 7 91173-2: Schoenberg—
Verklärte Nacht (rev. 1943); Suite for
string orchestra; Chamber symphony no.
2. *Deutsche Kammerphilharmonie;
Venzago, cond.*
● ARG 1-2/92: 104
+ Fa 11-12/91: 470
● Gr 10/91: 109

36155. VC 7 91174-2: Mussorgsky—
Pictures at an exhibition; Night on the
bare mountain. Borodin—Overture and
Polovetsian dances from Prince Igor.
*Royal Liverpool Phil. Orch. & Choir;
Mackerras, cond.*
+ ARG 9-10/91: 101
+ Fa 9-10/91: 303
● Gr 7/91: 56

36156. VC 7 91175-2: Elgar—Pomp and
circumstance and other marches;
Cockaigne. *Royal Phil. Orch.; Menuhin,
cond.*
● ARG 9-10/91: 70
+ Fa 9-10/91: 210
+ Gr 4/91: 1827

36157. VC 7 91179-2: *Au jardin des
aveux: French songs and duets.* Music of
Saint-Saëns, Chausson, Gounod, Fauré,
Messiaen. *Murray, soprano; Langridge,
tenor; Vignoles, piano.*
- ARG 9-10/91: 177
+ Fa 11-12/91: 534
+ Gr 6/91: 78

36158. VC 7 91180-2: Takemitsu—
Riverrun; Water-ways; Rain coming;
Rain spell; Tree line. *Crossley, piano;
London Sinfonietta; Knussen, cond.*
+ ARG 11-12/91: 158
+ Fa 11-12/91: 501
+ Gr 9/91: 74

36159. VC 7 91182-2: Elgar—
Symphony no. 2. *Royal Phil. Orch.;
Menuhin, cond.*
+ ARG 9-10/91: 71
+ Fa 9-10/91: 210
+ Gr 4/91: 1827

36160. VC 7 91183-2: Mendelssohn—
Piano quartets no. 1-3. *Domus.*
+ Fa 9-10/91: 270
+ Gr 6/91: 59

36161. VC 7 91184-2: Argento—
Variations for orchestra; Te Deum. *Jette,
soprano; Plymouth Festival Chorus &
Orch.; Brunelle, cond.*
+ Fa 7-8/91: 96

36162. VC 7 91187-2: Lawes—For ye
violls. *Fretwork; Nicholson, organ.*
+ ARG 9-10/91: 86
+ Fa 9-10/91: 252
+ Gr 8/91: 60

36163. VC 7 91188-2: Smyth—Mass in
D; Mrs. Waters' aria from The
Boatswain's mate; The march of the
women. *Harrhy, Hardy, Dressen, Bohn;
Plymouth Music Series; Brunelle, cond.*
+ ARG 9-10/91: 132
+ Fa 11-12/91: 487
+ Gr 8/91: 68

36164. VC 7 91189-2: Bartók—String
quartets no. 4, 6; Forty-four duos for
violins, Heft I. *Endellion String Quartet.*
+ ARG 3-4/92: 25
+ Fa 1-2/92: 157
● Gr 1/92: 69

36165. VC 7 91190-2: Tchaikovsky—
Piano concerto no. 1; Concert fantasy, op.
56. *Pletnev, piano; Philharmonia Orch.;
Fedoseyev, cond.*
- ARG 7-8/91: 129
+ Fa 11-12/91: 504
+ Gr 4/91: 1846

36166. VC 7 91191-2: Prokofiev—
Sonatas for violin and piano no. 1-2; Five
melodies for violin and piano, op. 35b;
Sonata in D for solo violin. *Sitkovetsky,
violin; Gililov, piano.*
+ ARG 3-4/92: 120
+ Fa 1-2/92: 300
● Gr 11/91: 125
+ St 7/92: 181

36167. VC 7 91192-2: Rodrigo—
Concierto de Aranjuez; Fantasia para un
gentilhombre. Vivaldi—Guitar concerto
in D. *Isbin, guitar; Lausanne Chamber
Orch.; Foster, cond.*
+ ARG 5-6/92: 163
● Fa 3-4/92: 297
+ Gr 11/91: 98

VIRGIN CLASSICS

36168. VC 7 91194-2: Schumann—
Symphonies no. 2, 4. *Bamberg Symphony
Orch.; Eschenbach, cond.*
- ARG 5-6/92: 131
• Fa 1-2/92: 327
• Gr 12/91: 79

36169. VC 7 91195-2: Schubert—Lieder.
Augér, soprano; Orkis, fortepiano.
+ ARG 11-12/91: 144
+ Fa 9-10/91: 343
+ Gr 6/91: 74

36170. VC 7 91196-2: Bridge—String
quartet no. 3. Walton—String quartet in
A minor. *Endellion String Quartet.*
+ ARG 1-2/92: 38
+ Fa 11-12/91: 288
+ Gr 9/91: 84

36171. VC 7 91198-2: Grieg—Piano
concerto; Lyric pieces. Liszt—Piano
concerto no. 2. *Andsnes, piano; Bergen
Symphony Orch.; Kitaenko, cond.*
+ DA 10/91: 66
+ Fa 7-8/91: 166

36172. VC 7 91198-2: Grieg—Piano
concerto; 6 Lyric pieces, op. 65. Liszt—
Piano concerto no. 2. *Andsnes, piano;
Bergen Phil. Orch.; Kitaenko, cond.*
- ARG 9-10/91: 77
- Gr 4/91: 1828

36173. VC 7 91201-2: Bach—French
suites (complete). *Moroney, harpsichord.*
+ ARG 7-8/91: 22
+ DA 8/91: 50
+ Fa 7-8/91: 100
+ SR 7/91: 79

36174. VC 7 91202-2: Tchaikovsky—
Piano concertos no. 2-3. *Pletnev, piano;
Philharmonia Orch.; Fedoseyev, cond.*
- ARG 7-8/91: 129
+ Fa 9-10/91: 370
- Gr 6/91: 52

36175. VC 7 91203-2: Britten—*Piano
music.* Holiday diary; Three character
pieces; Night piece; Sonatina romantica;
Twelve variations on a theme; Five
waltzes; Two lullabies; Mazurka elegiaca;
Introduction and rondo alla burlesca.
Hough, O'Hora, pianos.
+ ARG 11-12/91: 47
+ Fa 1-2/92: 187
+ Gr 8/91: 59

36176. VCD 7 91204-2 (2 discs):
Casken—Golem. *Rozario, soprano; Hall,
baritone; Music Projects, London;
Bernas, cond.*
+ ARG 11-12/91: 51
+ Fa 11-12/91: 293
+ Gr 8/91: 74
+ ON 3/14/92: 35
+ Op 10/91: 1238

36177. VC 7 91206-2: Bruckner—
Symphony no. 4; Overture in G minor.
*French Radio Phil. Orch.; Janowski,
cond.*

+ ARG 5-6/91: 42
• Fa 7-8/91: 130

36178. VC 7 91208-2: Mozart—A
cappella Amadeus. *The Swingle Singers.*
+ ARG 11-12/91: 101

36179. VC 7 91210-2: Nielsen—
Symphonies no. 4-5; Maskarade overture.
BBC Symphony Orch.; Davis, cond.
• ARG 9-10/91: 103
- Fa 11-12/91: 425
+ Gr 4/91: 1840

36180. VC 7 91212-2: Jones—The Muses
garden: songs. *Kirkby, soprano; Rooley,
lute.*
+ ARG 5-6/92: 76
+ Fa 11-12/91: 359
+ Gr 11/91: 140
+ St 10/92: 275

36181. VC 7 91213-2: Bach—Mass in F,
BWV 233; Mass in G, BWV 236.
*Mellon, Lesne, Prégardien, Kooy;
Chorus & Orch. of Collegium Vocale,
Ghent; Herreweghe, cond.*
+ ARG 3-4/92: 20
+ EM 2/92: 187
+ Fa 11-12/91: 250
+ Gr 9/91: 109

36182. VC 7 91214-2: *Joyne hands.*
Music of Thomas Morley: composer,
publisher, arranger. *Red Byrd; Musicians
of Swanne Alley; O'Dette, Nordstrom,
conds.*
+ Gr 1/92: 90

36183. VC 7 91215-2: Haydn—Arianna a
Naxos; Eleven English canzonettas.
*Watkinson, mezzo-soprano; Wilson,
fortepiano.*
• ARG 7-8/92: 145
+ Fa 7-8/92: 176
+ Gr 1/92: 84
- ON 11/92: 47

36184. VC 7 91216-2: *Rosa: Elizabethan
lute music.* Works by J. Johnson,
Taverner, Wilder, Ferrabosco, Danyel,
Cutting, Robinson, Holborne, and
Dowland. *Wilson, lutes.*
+ Fa 11-12/91: 554
+ Gr 11/91: 131

36185. VC 7 91217-2: Ravenscroft—
Songs, rounds, and catches. *Consort of
Musicke; Rooley, cond.*
+ ARG 5-6/92: 115
+ Fa 11-12/91: 457
+ Gr 8/91: 68
+ St 10/92: 275

36186. VCDS 7 91219-2 (2 discs):
Mahler—Symphony no. 9; Symphony
no. 10: Adagio. *Liverpool Phil. Orch.;
Pešek, cond.*
+ ARG 11-12/91: 92
+ Fa 11-12/91: 384
+ Gr 10/91: 89

36187. VC 7 91221-2: Suk—Asrael
symphony. *Royal Liverpool Phil. Orch.;
Pešek, cond.*
+ ARG 1-2/92: 124
+ Fa 1-2/92: 344
+ Gr 9/91: 74

36188. VC 7 91222-2: Janáček—Piano
sonata; In the mist; On an overgrown
path, series 1. *Andsnes, piano.*
- ARG 3-4/92: 78
- Fa 1-2/92: 242
- Gr 10/91: 139
• St 5/93: 179

36189. VC 7 91430-2: Schubert—
Winterreise. *Allen, baritone; Vignoles,
piano.*
+ ARG 1-2/92: 108
• Fa 1-2/92: 323
+ Gr 10/91: 173

36190. VC 7 91431-2: Bernstein—West
side story: Symphonic dances (arr. Ramin
and Kostal); On the town: Three dance
episodes. Gershwin—Rhapsody in blue;
An American in Paris. *Ohlsson, piano;
Minnesota Orch.; Waart, cond.*
+ ARG 9-10/91: 48
- Fa 7-8/91: 121
+ HPR v.8, no.3/91: 68

36191. VC 7 91432-2: Mahler—Des
Knaben Wunderhorn. *Murray, soprano;
Allen, baritone; London Phil. Orch.;
Mackerras, cond.*
+ ARG 3-4/92: 93
+ Fa 3-4/92: 235
+ Gr 11/91: 140

36192. VC 7 91433-2: Bernstein—
Candide: Overture; Symphony no. 2;
Fancy free. *Kahane, piano; Bournemouth
Symphony Orch.; Litton, cond.*
- ARG 1-2/92: 32
+ Fa 1-2/92: 177
+ Gr 9/91: 59
+ St 5/92: 193

36193. VC 7 91434-2: Shostakovich—
Symphony no. 14; Chamber symphony
for string orchestra, op. 110a.
*Kasrashvili, soprano; Lausanne Chamber
Orch.; Lazarev, cond.*
- ARG 1-2/92: 114
- Fa 1-2/92: 332
- Gr 10/91: 110
+ St 5/93: 183

36194. VC 7 91436-2: Schnittke—Piano
quintet; String quartet no. 3. Mahler-
Schnittke—Piano quartet. *Borodin
Quartet; Berlinsky, piano.*
+ Fa 7-8/92: 270
+ Gr 12/91: 94
+ St 10/92: 271

36195. VC 7 91437-2: Shostakovich—
String quartets no. 3, 7-8. *Borodin
Quartet.*
• Gr 12/91: 97
+ St 3/93: 187

36196. VC 7 91440-2: VICTORIA—
Eighteen responsories for Tenebrae. *The
Sixteen; Christophers, cond.*
+ Fa 7-8/92: 318
+ Gr 7/92: 90

36197. VC 7 91441-2: *The Feast of the
Pheasant, 1454.* DUFAY—Ave Regina
caelorum; Je me complains. BINCHOIS—Je
ne vis onquew; Vostre tres doulx regart;
Gloria, laus et honor; Seule esgarée; Deo
gratias. Music of VIDE, FRYE, GRENON AND
FONTAINE. *ENSEMBLE GILLES BINCHOIS;
VELLARD, COND.*
+ ARG 11-12/91: 195
+ EM 2/92: 175
+ Fa 11-12/91: 540
+ Gr 3/92: 106

36198. VC 7 91442-2: BEETHOVEN—Piano
trios, vol. 2. *Castle Trio.*
+ Fa 7-8/92: 119
+ Gr 3/92: 63

36199. VC 7 91444-2: BACH—Goldberg
variations. *Cole, harpsichord.*
+ Fa 7-8/92: 105
+ Gr 2/92: 60

36200. VC 7 91445-2: MAHLER—
Symphony no. 5. *Finnish Radio
Symphony Orch.; Saraste, cond.*
• Fa 7-8/92: 206
- Gr 1/92: 55

36201. VC 7 91446-2: TIPPETT—The ice
break. *Harper, Page, Wilson-Johnson,
Sylvan; London Sinfonietta; Atherton,
cond.*
+ ARG 7-8/92: 239
+ Fa 7-8/92: 312
+ Gr 2/92: 84
+ ON 8/92: 45
+ Op 5/92: 617

36202. VC 7 91447-2: SCHUBERT—String
quartets no. 10, 13; Quartettsatz. *Borodin
Quartet.*
+ ARG 7-8/92: 216
+ Fa 7-8/92: 275

36203. VC 7 91450-2: TELEMANN—Paris
quartets. *Hazelzet, flute; Trio Sonnerie.*
+ ARG 7-8/92: 238
+ EM 8/92: 512
+ Fa 7-8/92: 312
+ Gr 3/92: 71

36204. VC 7 91451-2: *Play this
passionate.* Music of Hume, Kühnel,
Machy, Schenk and, Telemann.
Cunningham, viola da gamba.
+ EM 8/92: 512
+ Gr 4/92: 120

36205. VJ 7 91457-2: HOLST—The
planets; The perfect fool; Ballet music.
*Royal Liverpool Phil. Orch.; Mackerras,
cond.* Reissue.
+ Fa 5-6/92: 174

36206. VJ 7 91458-2: LISZT—Hungarian
rhapsody: Kun Woo Paik plays Liszt.

Paik, piano.
+ Fa 5-6/92: 188

36207. VJ 7 91460-2: MOZART—
Requiem. *Kenny, Hodgson, Davies,
Howell; Northern Sinfonia; Hickox, cond.*
+ Fa 5-6/92: 208

36208. VJ 7 91465-2: *Clair de lune.*
POULENC—Nocturnes no. 1-3;
Improvisations no. 10, 12, 15;
Intermezzo; Trois mouvements
perpetuels. DEBUSSY—Pour le piano; Clair
de lune. SATIE—Piano music. *Paik, piano.*
+ Fa 5-6/92: 320

36209. VJ 7 91466-2: *Fanfare for the
common man.* Music of Copland, Davis,
J. Strauss, Jr., Delius and Brahms.
London Phil. Orch.; Carl Davis, cond.
+ Fa 5-6/92: 341

36210. VC 7 91472-2: MESSIAEN—Trois
petites liturgies de la Présence Divine;
Cinq rechants; O sacrum convivium!
*London Sinfonietta; London Sinfonietta
Chorus; London Sinfonietta Voices;
Edwards, cond.*
• ARG 7-8/92: 176
+ Fa 1-2/92: 267
+ Gr 11/91: 144

36211. VC 7 91474-2: TAVENER—The
protecting veil, for cello and strings;
Thrinos, for solo cello. BRITTEN—Suite
no. 3 for cello, op. 87. *Isserlis, cello;
London Symphony Orch.;
Rozhdestvensky, cond.*
+ Fa 7-8/92: 306
+ Fa 9-10/92: 374
+ Gr 3/92: 56
+ St 4/93: 291

36212. VC 7 91476-2: DVOŘÁK—
Symphony no. 9. TCHAIKOVSKY—
Francesca da Rimini. *Houston Symphony
Orch.; Eschenbach, cond.*
• ARG 5-6/92: 52
+ Fa 5-6/92: 152
• Gr 2/92: 35

36213. VC 7 91477-2 (2 discs):
STRAUSS—Salome. *Huffstodt, Dupouy,
Jossoud, Van Dam; Berlin Phil. Orch.;
Nagano, cond.* Sung in French.
+ ARG 3-4/92: 145
+ Fa 3-4/92: 334
+ Gr 1/92: 94
• ON 2/1/92: 36
+ Op 2/92: 246
• OQ spring 93: 170
+ St 5/92: 199

36214. VC 7 91478-2: SCHOENBERG—
Chamber symphony no. 1; Ode to
Napoleon Buonaparte; Verklärte Nacht.
Nash Ensemble.
+ ARG 7-8/92: 216
+ Fa 3-4/92: 308
+ Gr 11/91: 101

36215. VC 7 91479-2: CALDARA—
Cantatas; Sonatas. *Lesne, countertenor;

Seminario musicale.*
+ ARG 1-2/92: 41
+ EM 5/92: 359
+ Gr 11/91: 139

36216. VC 7 91480-2: HANDEL—
Lucrezia. Solo cantatas. *Lesne,
countertenor; Il Seminario Musicale.*
+ ARG 7-8/92: 141
+ Fa 7-8/92: 173
+ Gr 12/91: 112

36217. VC 7 91481-2: BRUCKNER—Missa
solemnis in B♭ minor; Psalm no. 112;
Psalm no. 150. *Oelze, Schubert,
Dürmüller, Hagen; Bamberg Symphony
Orch. & Chorus; Rickenbacher, cond.*
+ ARG 3-4/92: 38
+ Fa 1-2/92: 190
• Gr 12/91: 106

36218. VC 7 91482-2: MATTHEWS—The
great journey; Fuga; Night's mask.
*Wilson-Johnson, baritone; Kwella,
soprano; Nash Ensemble; Friend, cond.*
□ ARG 7-8/92: 173
+ Fa 1-2/92: 258
+ Gr 3/92: 103

36219. VC 7 91483-2: BARTÓK—Violin
concerto no. 2; Sonata for solo violin.
*Tetzlaff, violin; London Phil. Orch.;
Gielen, cond.*
• ARG 3-4/92: 24
+ Fa 3-4/92: 141
+ Gr 11/91: 82

36220. VC 7 91484-2: ROSSINI—Arias
from L'Assedio di Corinto, Tancredi,
Bianca e Faliero, Elisabetta, Regina
d'Inghilterra, Otello, Guglielmo Tell, and
Semiramide. *Ricciarelli, soprano; Lyon
Opera; Ferro, cond.*
+ ARG 3-4/92: 128
• Fa 3-4/92: 299
• Gr 2/92: 83
• ON 9/92: 51
+ Op 4/92: 489

36221. VC 7 91485-2: MOZART—Piano
quartets; Clarinet trio. *Hosford, clarinet;
Domus.*
+ Gr 1/92: 70

36222. VC 7 91486-2: HONEGGER—
Symphonies, no. 2, 4; Pastorale d'été;
Prélude, arioso et fugue. *Lausanne
Chamber Orch.; López Cobos, cond.*
+ Gr 6/92: 43

36223. VC 7 91487-2: TCHAIKOVSKY—
Symphony no. 6; Marche slave. *Russian
National Orch.; Pletnev, cond.*
- ARG 5-6/92: 147
+ Fa 3-4/92: 346
+ Gr 1/92: 64

36224. VC 7 91489-2: HAYDN—Violin
concertos, no. 1, 3-4. MOZART—Rondo
for violin and orchestra, K. 373. *Tetzlaff,
violin; Northern Sinfonia; Schiff, cond.*
+ ARG 3-4/92: 71

VIRGIN CLASSICS

+ Fa 3-4/92: 210
+ Gr 11/91: 89

36225. VC 7 91492-2: STRAUSS—
Symphonia domestica; Suite for thirteen
winds. *Minnesota Orch.; Waart, cond.*
+ Fa 7-8/92: 297
+ Gr 4/92: 79
+ St 2/93: 195

36226. VC 7 91494-2: HUMPERDINCK—
Fairy-tale music. Hansel and Gretel
overture; The blue bird: Prelude and
Dance of the stars; The king's children
suite; Sleeping beauty suite. *Bamberg
Symphony Orch.; Rickenbacher, cond.*
+ ARG 11-12/92: 137
□ Gr 6/92: 43

36227. VC 7 91495-2: STRAVINSKY—Le
chant du rossignol; Symphony in C;
Symphony in three movements. *Finnish
Radio Symphony Orch.; Saraste, cond.*
- Gr 9/92: 93

36228. VC 7 91496-2: KRAUS—Soliman
II. *Hoel, Örtendahl-Corin, Morgny,
Wallström; Royal Opera of Sweden;
Brunelle, cond.*
+ ARG 5-6/92: 77
+ Fa 7-8/92: 194
+ Gr 5/92: 106
+ ON 9/92: 50
+ St 12/92: 241

36229. VCD 7 91497-2 (2 discs):
HAYDN—The seasons. *Laki, Wildhaber,
Lika; Choir of the Flanders Opera; La
Petite Bande; Kuijken, cond.*
• Fa 7-8/93: 149

36230. VC 7 91498-2: C.P.E. BACH—Die
Auferstehung und Himmelfahrt Jesu.
*Martinpelto, Prégardien, Harvey;
Collegium Vocale, Ghent; Orch. of the
Age of Enlightenment; Herreweghe,
cond.*
+ EM 2/93: 157
+ Fa 7-8/92: 100
+ Gr 9/92: 140

36231. VC 7 91499-2: HAYDN—
Symphonies no. 88-89, 92. *La Petite
Bande; Kuijken, cond.*
+ ARG 3-4/93: 91 (as 59070)
+ Fa 7-8/92: 179
+ Gr 6/92: 43

36232. VC 7 91500-2: *O lusitano:
Portuguese vilancetes, cantigas and
romances.* Music of Cardoso, Escobar,
Machado and Mudarra. *Lesne,
countertenor; Circa 1500; Hadden, cond.*
+ EM 11/92: 685
+ Fa 7-8/92: 339
+ Gr 9/92: 156

36233. VC 7 91501-2 (2 discs):
CHOPIN—Piano music. *Andsnes, piano.*
+ ARG 7-8/92: 118
• Fa 9-10/92: 215
+ Gr 6/92: 67
+ St 10/92: 261

36234. VC 7 91503-2: CARTER—Concerto
for orchestra; Three occasions for
orchestra; Violin concerto. *Böhn, violin;
London Sinfonietta; Knussen, cond.*
+ Gr 7/92: 52

36235. VC 7 91504-2: MOZART—
Concerto for flute and harp, K. 299; Flute
concertos, no. 1-2. *Coles, flute; Yoshino,
harp; English Chamber Orch.; Menuhin,
cond.*
+ Fa 9-10/92: 296

36236. VC 7 91506-2: JANÁČEK—
Sinfonietta; Violin concerto; Taras Bulba;
From the House of the Dead. *Tetzlaff,
violin; Philharmonia Orch.; Pešek, cond.*
+ ARG 1-2/93: 108 (as 59076)
+ Fa 9-10/92: 267
+ Gr 6/92: 44

36237. VC 7 91511-2 (2 discs):
STRAVINSKY—The rite of spring;
Perséphone. *Fournet, Rolfe Johnson;
Tiffin Boys Choir; London Phil. Orch. &
Chorus; Nagano, cond.*
+ ARG 7-8/92: 232
+ Fa 9-10/92: 368
+ Gr 6/92: 49
• St 4/93: 289

36238. VC 7 91514-2: BACH—Four duets;
Overture in B minor; Italian concerto;
Prelude, fugue and allegro. *Moroney,
harpsichord.*
+ Gr 9/92: 128

36239. VC 7 91515-2: SCHUBERT—
Symphonies no. 5, 8 (completed
Newbould); Rosamunde: Excerpts. *Orch.
of the Age of Enlightenment; Mackerras,
cond.*
+ EM 5/93: 324
+ Gr 9/92: 86

36240. VJ 7 91566-2: BRAHMS—
Symphony no. 1; Academic festival
overture. *Royal Phil. Orch.; Litton, cond.*
- Gr 10/92: 55

36241. VJ 7 91567-2: BEETHOVEN—
Symphony no. 3; Serenade op. 8.
*Sitkovetsky, violin; Caussé, viola;
Geringas, cello; Scottish Chamber Orch.;
Saraste, cond.* Reissue.
• Gr 10/92: 54

36242. VC 7 91750-2: Love songs and
lullabies. *Valente, soprano; Allen,
baritone; Isbin, guitar; with flute and
percussion.*
+ ARG 5-6/92: 163
+ Fa 3-4/92: 397
+ Gr 9/92: 158

VIRTUOSO

36243. 2697022: MOZART—Symphonies
no. 36, 39; Serenade no. 13 K. 525. *New
York Phil. Orch.; French National
Orch.; Walter, cond.* Recorded live 1956.
• Fa 5-6/90: 236

VISTA

36244. 942: GERSHWIN—Rhapsody in
blue; Preludes; Song book. *Basaccia,
piano.*
• ARG 9-10/96: 123

VITAL MUSIC

36245. 003: STEUERMANN—Piano sonata.
BRAHMS—Fantasies, op. 116. WAGNER—
Albumleaves. *Brubaker, piano.*
• ARG 9-10/95: 219

VIVACE

36246. G 501: J.C. BACH—Harp
concertos in G, in D. HANDEL—Harp
concerto in B♭. *Klincharova, harp; Sofia
Solisten; Tabakov, cond.*
• Fa 7-8/89: 69

36247. G 503: CHOPIN—Piano concerto
no. 1; Fantasy on Polish melodies op. 13;
Andante spianato and grand polonaise op.
22. *Lima, piano; Philharmonia
Bulgarica; Manolov, cond.*
+ Fa 7-8/89: 123

36248. G 504: CHOPIN—Piano concerto
no. 2 op. 21; Variations on La ci darem la
mano; Krakowiak. *Lima, piano;
Philharmonia Bulgarica; Manolov, cond.*
+ Fa 7-8/89: 123

36249. G 518: HANDEL—Organ concertos
op. 7 no. 5-6, 13-15. *Bucher, organ;
Warsaw Chamber Orch.; Teutsch, cond.*
• Fa 5-6/89: 209

36250. G 531: BRUCH—Violin concerto
no. 1. GLAZUNOV—Violin concerto op. 82.
*Milanova, violin; Philharmonia
Bulgarica; Stefanov, cond.*
• Fa 5-6/89: 125

36251. G 554: VIVALDI—Concertos for
strings op. 3 no. 8, 10-11; in G; R 158;
Sinfonia in C. *I Musici di Zabreb.*
+ ARG 11-12/89: 135

VOCE DELLA LUNA

36252. VL 2011-2 (2 discs):
TCHAIKOVSKY—Eugene Onegin (sung in
German). *Jurinac, Schock, Hasslo, Frick;
Westdeutsche Rundfunk Orch. & Chorus;
Schüchter, cond.* Reissue; recorded 1952.
- Fa 1-2/97: 289

36253. VL 2012-2 (2 discs): WAGNER—
Der fliegende Holländer. *Varnay, Uhde,
Weber, Lustig, Traxel, Schärtel; Bayreuth
Festival; Keilberth, cond.* Recorded 1955.
• Fa 1-2/97: 299

VOGUE

36254. 672 006: BARTÓK—Viola
concerto; The miraculous mandarin:
Suite; Piano concerto no. 2. *Primrose,
viola; Helffer, piano; French Radio and*

Television National Orch.; Bour, cond. Recorded live 1950, 1969.
+ Fa 11-12/88: 128

36255. 672 009: Music of Strauss, Shostakovich (arr. Tsyganov), Prokofiev, and Falla (arr. Kochanski). *Kogan, violin; Mytnik, Valter, pianos.* Recorded live 1959 1964.
+ ARG 5-6/89: 119
+ Fa 3-4/89: 379

36256. 672 010: Music of Beethoven, Brahms, Saint-Saëns, Debussy, and Ravel. *Francescatti, violin; Bagnoli, Casadesus, pianos.* Recorded 1961, 1958, 1963.
+ Fa 3-4/89: 379

VOICE

36257. 115: Music of Beethoven, Wagner, and Berlioz. *Horne, mezzo-soprano; orchs.; Leinsdorf, Lewis, conds.*
+ Fa 1-2/88: 246

VOX ALLEGRETTO

36258. 8154: Music of Scheidt, Weelkes, Simmes, Ferrabosco, Holborne, and others. *Eastman Brass Quintet; Paris Instrumental Ensemble; Holland, cond.* Reissue.
• ARG 1-2/94: 176

36259. 8155: Music of Siegmeister, Bernstein, Gould, Robertson, Nelhybel, Ruggles, Ives, and Copland. *Utah Symphony Orch.; Abravanel, cond.; Buffalo Phil.; Foss, cond.* Reissues.
+ ARG 11-12/93: 197

36260. 8156: Greogrian chant. *Vienna Hofburgkapelle.*
+ ARG 11-12/93: 247

36261. 8157: *Paris in the 1920s.* Music of Milhaud, Poulenc, Satie, Tailleferre, and Honegger. *Marciano, Klien, pianos; Radio Luxembourg Orch.; Froment, cond.; Vienna Pro Musica; Hollreiser, cond.*
+ ARG 11-12/93: 226

36262. 8160: SARASATE—Carmen fantasy; Zigeunerweisen; Spanish dances; Navarra; Caprice basque. *Rosand, violin; Flissler, piano; Southwest German Radio Orch.; Reinhardt, cond.* Reissue.
+ ARG 3-4/94: 147

36263. 8165: PURCELL—Suites from King Arthur, Dido and Aeneas, Dioclesian, Abdelazar, and The fairy queen. *City of London Chamber Orch.; McIntosh, cond.*
• ARG 7-8/94: 152

36264. 8173: GOLDMARK—Violin concerto no. 1; Rustic wedding symphony. *Ricci, violin; Radio Luxembourg Symphony Orch.; Froment, cond.; Westphalian Symphony Orch.; Reichert, cond.*
- ARG 9-10/94: 133

VOX AUSTRALIS

36265. VAST 001-2: Percussion music of Askill, Westlake, Wesley-Smith, Cage, and Kos. *Synergy.*
+ ARG 11-12/93: 240
+ Fa 1-2/93: 310

36266. VAST 003-2: SMALLEY—Piano concerto; Symphony. *Smalley, piano; West Australian Symphony Orch.; Masson, cond.; Sydney Symphony; P. Thomas, cond.*
+ ARG 11-12/93: 198

36267. VAST 006-2: *Modern Australian composers.* Music of Banks, Humble, Kats-Chernin, and Meale. *Judy Bailey Quintet; Sydney Symphony Orch.; Challender, Iwaki, Porcelijn, conds.*
+ ARG 11-12/93: 227

36268. VAST 010-2: WESLEY-SMITH—Boojum. *Sydney Philharmonia Motet Choir; Grundy, cond.*
+ ARG 11-12/93: 220

36269. VAST 015-2: *Forbidden colours.* Music of Smalley, Formosa, Brophy, and Kos. *Crellin, oboe; Olding, violin; Melbourne Symphony Orch.; Schuller, Thomas, conds.; Queensland Symphony Orch.; Fredman, Hopkins, conds.*
+ ARG 1-2/95: 209

36270. VAST 016-2: *Laughter of the mermaids.* Music of Schultz, Whitehead, Ford, Whiticker, and Cronin. *Collins, flute; The Song Company; Peelman, cond.*
+ ARG 9-10/95: 249

36271. VAST 018-2: SCULTHORPE—The stars turn; Eliza Frazier sings. BROADSTOCK—Eheu fugaces. SITSKY—Deep in my hidden country. *Richardson, soprano; Millar, piano; Draeger, flute; Dunlop, clarinet; Ziegler, violin; Blake, cello; Pratt, percussion.*
□ ARG 7-8/96: 195

36272. VAST 020-2: Music of Sitsky, Kerry, Banks, Kos, and Vine. *Australia Ensemble.*
+ ARG 11-12/96: 243

VOX BOX

36284. CDX 3002 (3 discs): RACHMANINOFF—Orchestral works. *St. Louis Symphony Orch.; Slatkin, cond.*
+ ARG 1-2/92: 94

36285. CDX 3004 (3 discs): LISZT—Années de pèlerinage. *Rose, piano.* Reissue.
+ ARG 3-4/92: 86

36286. CDX 3007 (2 discs): *300 years of guitar masterpieces.* Music of Bach, Albeniz, Granados, Scarlatti, Cimarosa, Paganini, Giuliani, Guarnieri, Chavez, and Villa-Lobos. *Barrueco, guitar.*

Reissue.
+ ARG 9-10/92: 191

36287. CDX 3008 (2 discs): BACH—Brandenburg concertos (complete); Three violin concertos. *Lautenbacher, Vorholz, violins; Mainz Chamber Orch.; Kehr, cond.* Reissue; recorded 1958.
+ ARG 7-8/92: 85

36288. CDX 3009 (3 discs): MOZART—String quartets no. 14-19. *Hungarian String Quartet.* Reissue.
• ARG 7-8/92: 187
+ Fa 5-6/92: 207

36289. CDX 3015 (3 discs): BARTÓK—Concerto for orchestra; Dance suite; Miraculous Mandarin: Suite; Wooden Prince: Suite; Music for strings, percussion and celesta; Divertimento for strings. *Minnesota Orch.; Skrowaczewski, cond.* Reissue.
+ ARG 3-4/93: 54

36290. CDX 3017 (3 discs): BEETHOVEN—Variations (Complete); Sonatas no. 4, 20; Piano music. *Brendel, piano.* Reissue.
+ ARG 3-4/93: 58

36291. CDX 3020 (3 discs): *Paganini variations.* Music of Paganini, Brahms, Liszt, Rachmaninoff, and Schumann. *Various performers.* Reissue.
• ARG 9-10/93: 241

36292. CDX 3021 (3 discs): *Russian chamber music.* Music of Tchaikovsky, Mouravieff, Rachmaninoff, Glinka, Arensky, Rimsky-Korsakov, and Shostakovich. *Eastman Trio; Wurttemberg Chamber Orch.; Faerber, cond.; Nieuw Amsterdam Trio.* Reissue.
+ ARG 9-10/93: 227

36293. CDX 3022 (3 discs): Music with guitar, lute or mandolin by Bach, Vivaldi, Logy, Carulli, Fasch, Hoffmann, Beethoven, and others. *Various performers.* Reissue.
+ ARG 7-8/93: 192

36294. CDX 3023, 5087 (5 total discs): TCHAIKOVSKY—Complete piano music. *Ponti, piano.*
• ARG 9-10/93: 205

36295. CDX 3024 (3 discs): TCHAIKOVSKY—Piano trio; String quartets no. 1-3; Souvenir de Florence; Serenade for strings. *Eastman Trio; Copenhagen String Quartet; Hamburg Symphony Orch.; Springer, cond.* Reissue.
+ ARG 11-12/93: 208

36296. CDX 3028 (3 discs): SAINT-SAËNS—Piano concertos (complete). *Tacchino, piano; Radio Luxembourg Symphony Orch.; Froment, cond.* Reissue.
+ ARG 9-10/94: 186

VOX BOX

36297. CDX 3029 (3 discs): BRAHMS—Piano trios. MENDELSSOHN—Piano trios. DVOŘÁK—Piano trio no. 4. *Kalichstein-Laredo-Robinson Trio.* Reissue.
+ ARG 9-10/94: 110

36298. CDX 3032 (3 discs): Music of Debussy, Chabrier, Chausson, d'Indy, Dukas, Franck, Fauré, Milhaud, and others. *Johanessen, piano; Luxembourg Radio Orch.; Kontarsky, Froment, conds.* Reissue.
+ ARG 9-10/94: 241

36299. CDX 3033 (3 discs): GOTTSCHALK—Piano music. *Mandel, piano.* Reissue.
• Fa 9-10/95: 211

36300. CDX 3034 (3 discs): IVES—Piano music. *Mandel, piano.* Reissue.
+ ARG 11-12/95: 139
+ Fa 9-10/95: 234

36301. CDX 3035 (3 discs): *American as apple pie.* Music of Sousa, Gershwin, Rodgers, Kern, Herbert, and others. *Cincinnati Pops Orch.; Kunzel, cond.*
- Fa 9-10/95: 429

36302. CDX 3037 (3 discs): *I hear America singing.* Music of Schuman, Rorem, and Talma. *Gregg Smith Singers; Smith, cond.* Reissues.
+ Fa 11-12/96: 438

36303. CDX 3501 (3 discs): CHOPIN—Twenty nocturnes; Piano sonata no. 2; Etudes, op. 10, 25. *Novaes, piano.* Recorded mid-1950s.
+ Fa 9-10/95: 176

36304. CDX 3502 (3 discs): BEETHOVEN—Piano concertos (complete); Choral fantasy. *Brendel, piano; Vienna Symphony Orch.; Vienna Volksoper Orch.; Stuttgart Phil. Orch.; Walberg, Boettcher, Mehta, conds.* Reissues.
+ Fa 9-10/95: 136

36305. CDX 3503 (3 discs): BEETHOVEN—Violin sonatas (complete). *Rosand, violin; Flissler, piano.* Recorded 1961.
+ Fa 9-10/95: 140

36306. CDX 5021 (2 discs): PROKOFIEV—Lieutenant Kijé: Symphonic suite, op. 60; Alexander Nevsky: Cantata, op. 78; Ivan the Terrible: op. 116. *Voketaitis, bass; Carlson, mezzo-soprano; Timberlake, bass; St. Louis Symphony Orch. & Chorus; Slatkin, cond.*
+ Fa 1-2/92: 297

36307. CDX 5029 (2 discs): *Chamber works by women composers.* Music of C. Schumann, Beach, Tailleferre, Boulanger, Hensel, Carreno, and Chaminade. *Macalester Trio; Roche, Zelnick, violins; Strasser, viola; Heller, cello; Freed, piano.* Reissue.
• Gr 10/94: 152 (as 115845-2)

36308. CDX 5054 (2 discs): PROKOFIEV—Symphonies no. 2, 3, 6; Chout suite. *ORTF Orch; Martinon, cond.*
- ARG 7-8/92: 201

36309. CDX 5057 (2 discs): *Early American string quartets.* Music of Chadwick, Loeffler, Griffes, Foote, Hadley, Mason, and Franklin. *Kohon String Quartet.* Reissue.
☐ ARG 11-12/94: 218

36310. CDX 5064—5069 (6 2-disc sets): The romantic piano concerto. *Various performers.* Reissues.
+ ARG 1-2/93: 182

36311. CDX 5074 (2 discs): *The virtuoso trumpet.* Concertos and sonatas by Telemann, Handel, Stölzel, Biber, Haydn, Purcell, and others. *Various performers.* Reissue.
• ARG 9-10/93: 240

36312. CDX 5075—5076 (2 2-disc sets): GRANADOS—Complete piano music. *Dosse, piano.*
• ARG 9-10/93: 126

36313. CDX 5077 (2 discs): MENDELSSOHN—Songs without words; Variations sérieuses. *Kyriakou, piano.* Reissue.
+ ARG 7-8/93: 124

36314. CDX 5078 (2 discs): Four-hand piano music of Bizet, Debussy, Milhaud, Fauré, Satie, Saint-Saëns, and Chabrier. *Various performers.* Reissue.
+ ARG 9-10/93: 239

36315. CDX 5079 (2 discs): TCHAIKOVSKY—Manfred; Symphonic poems; Overtures. *Various performers.* Reissue.
+ ARG 9-10/93: 203

36316. CDX 5083 (2 discs): Music of Messiaen, Barber, Poulenc, Ibert, Bozza, and Françaix. *J. Casadesus, piano; New York Phil. Chamber Ensemble; Dorian Wind Quintet.*
+ ARG 11-12/93: 244

36317. CDX 5084 (2 discs): SAINT-SAËNS—Violin concertos; Cello concertos. *Ricci, violin; Varga, cello; with accomp.* Reissue.
- ARG 11-12/93: 182

36318. CDX 5085 (2 discs): *Fitzwilliam virginal book.* Music of Byrd, Farnaby, Philips, Bull, Gibbons, and others. *Payne, harpsichord, organ.* Recorded 1965.
• ARG 5-6/94: 176

36319. CDX 5090 (2 discs): *American quartets 1900-1950.* Music of Schuman, Hanson, Ives, Thomson, Gershwin, Sessions, Mennin, Piston, and Copland. *Kohon Quartet.* Reissue.
+ ARG 9-10/94: 228

36320. CDX 5091 (2 discs): HAYDN—Stabat Mater. PERGOLESI—Stabat Mater. VIVALDI—Stabat Mater. *Various performers.* Reissu.
• ARG 9-10/93: 132

36321. CDX 5092 (2 discs): Music of Thomson, Rorem, Schuman, Hanson, Schuller, and MacDowell. *Westphalian Symphony Orch.; Westchester Symphony Orch.; Landau, cond.; Utah Symphony Orch.; Abravanel, cond.; Dallas Symphony Orch.; Johanos, cond.* Reissue.
• ARG 9-10/94: 224

36322. CDX 5098 (2 discs): *Romantic piano concerto, vol. 7.* Music of Weber, Volkmann, Alkan, Schumann, Raff, Alkan, Berwald, and Liszt. *Various performers.* Reissue.
• ARG 9-10/94: 239

36323. CDX 5102 (2 discs): Music of Joachim, Hubay, Enesco, Ernst, Godard, Ysaÿe, Lehár, and Wieniawski. *Rosand, violin; Luxembourg Radio Orch.; Froment, cond.* Reissue.
• ARG 9-10/94: 245

36324. CDX 5103 (2 discs): Piano music of Debussy and Chopin. *Moravec, piano.* Reissue.
+ ARG 9-10/94: 242

36325. CDX 5105 (2 discs): SMETANA—Má vlast. HOLST—The planets. *St. Louis Symphony Orch.; Susskind, cond.* Reissue.
• ARG 1-2/95: 181

36326. CDX 5109 (2 discs): MILHAUD—Orchestra music. *Various performers.* Reissue.
+ ARG 1-2/95: 142

36327. CDX 5110 (2 discs): *French piano concertos.* Music of Boieldieu, Massenet, Pierné, Franck, Lalo, and others. *Various performers.* Reissue.
• ARG 11-12/94: 236

36328. CDX 5107 (2 discs): SATIE—Music for piano, orchestra and voice. *Soloists; Radio Luxembourg Symphony Orch.; Cerha, Froment, conds.* Reissue.
+ ARG 9-10/94: 190

36329. CDX 5108 (3 discs): CHABRIER—Piano music. *Kyriakou, piano.* Reissue.
+ ARG 9-10/94: 116

36330. CDX 5112 (2 discs): BEETHOVEN—Diabelli variations; Bagatelles; Piano pieces. *Brendel, piano.* Recorded 1964.
+ ARG 5-6/96: 82
• Fa 7-8/96: 106

36331. CDX 5114 (2 discs): Music of Berlioz, Lalo, Fauré, Massenet, Chabrier, and Françaix. *Lautenbacher, violin; Koch, viola; Orchs.; Kapp, Cao,*

Froment, Français, conds. Reissue.
+ ARG 9-10/94: 223

36332. CDX 5116 (2 discs): Music of Sibelius, Tchaikovsky, Berlioz, Saint-Saëns, Chausson, Ravel, Tzigane, and Lalo. *Rosand, violin; Southwest German Radio Orch.; Szöke, Reinhardt, conds.* Reissues.
+ ARG 1-2/97: 215
+ Fa 11-12/96: 470

36333. CDX 5123 (2 discs): MAHLER—Symphonies no. 1, 4. *Curry, mezzo-soprano; London Symphony Orch.; Farberman, cond.* Reissue.
+ ARG 5-6/96: 142
• Fa 5-6/96: 199

36334. CDX 5124 (2 discs): Music of Frescobaldi, Fontana, Telemann, Albinoni, and Hertel. *Schwarz, trumpet; with supporting instrumentalists.* Reissue.
+ ARG 9-10/95: 270

36335. CDX 5127 (2 discs): BACH—Cantatas, arias, and choruses. *Bach Aria Group.* Reissues.
• Fa 9-10/95: 133

36336. CDX 5129 (2 discs): *The American composers series: Love's secret and other songs.* Music of Diamond, Persichetti, Luening, Fine, Flanagan, Rorem, Ives, Moore, and others. *Steber, Miller, McCollum, Gramm, vocalists; Biltcliffe, Cumming, piano.* Reissues.
+ ARG 11-12/96: 268
+ Fa 11-12/96: 433

36337. CDX 5131 (2 discs): OFFENBACH—Selections. *Harnoy, cello; Collins, trumpet; Cincinnati Pops Orch.; Kunzel, cond.* Reissue.
- Fa 9-10/95: 270

36338. CDX 5133 (2 discs): BUSONI—Konzertstück, op. 31a; Divertimento, op. 52; Rondò arlecchinesco; Concertino, op. 48. SZYMANOWSKI—Violin sonata, op. 9; Violin concerto no. 2. LUTOSŁAWSKI—Little suite for orchestra; Die Strohkette; Five dance preludes; Overture for string orchestra; Trauermusik. *Various performers.* Recorded 1968-1984.
• ARG 5-6/96: 98
+ Fa 5-6/96: 128

36339. CDX 5134 (2 discs): PFITZNER—Violin concerto; String quartets no. 2-3. HARTMANN—Concerto funèbre. ZIMMERMANN—Violin concerto. *Lautenbacher, violin; Philharmonia Hungarica; Wich, cond.; Württemberg Chamber Orch.; Faerber, cond.; Orch. of Radio Luxembourg; Köhler, cond.; Reger Quartet; Austrian String Quartet.* Reissue.
• ARG 5-6/96: 161
- Fa 5-6/96: 236

36340. CDX 5136 (2 discs): STRAUSS—Metamorphosen; Tod und Verklärung. LUTOSŁAWSKI—Double concerto for oboe, harp, and chamber orchestra. BERG—Lulu suite; Lyric suite. *H. Holliger, oboe; U. Holliger, harp; Battle, soprano; Cincinnati Symphony Orch.; Gielen, cond.* Reissue.
• ARG 11-12/95: 212
+ Fa 11-12/95: 379
+ Fa 11-12/95: 392

36341. CDX 5137 (2 discs): BEETHOVEN—Symphony no. 3. BUSONI—Turandot: Suite; Doktor Faust: Sarabande and cortège. *Women of the May Festival Chorus; Cincinnati Symphony Orch.; Gielen, cond.* Reissues.
+ ARG 11-12/95: 85
• Fa 11-12/95: 351

36342. CDX 5138 : MAHLER—Das Lied von der Erde. MENDELSSOHN—Midsummer night's dream: Excerpts. SCHUBERT—Symphony no. 8. *Cassilly, tenor; Chookasian, contralto; Cincinnati Symphony Orch.; Susskind, Schippers, conds.* Recorded 1976-78.
+ ARG 9-10/95: 170
+ Fa 11-12/95: 294

36343. CDX 5139 (2 discs): SHOSTAKOVICH—Symphonies no. 1, 9. TCHAIKOVSKY—Piano concerto no. 2. MENDELSSOHN—Fantasy, op. 28; Rondo capriccioso, op. 14. LISZT—Liebestraum no. 3; Hungarian rhapsody no. 12. *Cherkassky, piano; Cincinnati Symphony Orch.; Susskind, cond.* Reissue.
• ARG 11-12/95: 217
• Fa 11-12/95: 351

36344. CDX 5140 (2 discs): STRAUSS—Rosenkavalier waltzes; Don Juan; Salome's dance; Till Eulenspiegel. SCHUBERT—Symphony no. 9. *Cincinnati Symphony Orch.; Schippers, cond.* Reissues.
+ ARG 9-10/95: 221
+ Fa 11-12/95: 365

36345. CDX 5141 (2 discs): ROSSINI—Stabat Mater; Overtures. *Lee, Quivar, Riegel, Plishka, vocalists; May Festival Chorus; Cincinnati Symphony Orch.; Schippers, cond.* Reissue.
• ARG 11-12/95: 187
+ Fa 11-12/95: 351

36346. CDX 5143 (2 discs): *American string quartets 1950-1970.* Music of Wolpe, Brown, Cage, Kirchner, Wolff, Crumb, Hiller, Druckman, and Feldman. *Concord String Quartet.* Reissue.
+ ARG 5-6/96: 230
+ Fa 5-6/96: 358

36347. CDX 5144 (2 discs): *Orchestra of our time.* Music of Schoenberg, Dallapiccola, Crumb, Boulez, Pousseur, Dlugoszewski, and Weill-Berio. *Orch. of Our Time; Thome, cond.* Reissue.
+ Fa 5-6/96: 365

36348. CDX 5145 (2 discs): *20th-century voices in America.* Music of Rochberg, Cage, Carter, Crumb, Schuman, Imbrie, Blumenfeld, Smith, Kolb, and Ran. *Various performers.* Reissue.
+ Fa 5-6/96: 323

36349. CDX 5146 (2 discs): CHOPIN—21 nocturnes. *Simon, piano.* Reissue; recorded 1982.
+ ARG 5-6/96: 100
+ Fa 5-6/96: 132

36350. CDX 5157 (2 discs): *American composers series: the Incredible flutist.* Music of Coolidge, Piston, Mason, Still, and Kay. *Westphalian Symphony; Westchester Symphony; Landau, cond.; MIT Symphony; Epstein, cond.* Reissue.
• ARG 9-10/96: 109
• Fa 11-12/96: 488

36351. CDX 5158 (2 discs): *The American composers series: American concertos.* Music of Lees, Starer, Kupferman, Colgrass, Harrison, Piston, and Bergsma. *Various performers.* Reissues.
• ARG 11-12/96: 242
+ Fa 11-12/96: 488

36352. CDX 5165 (2 discs): MENDELSSOHN—Symphonies no. 3-5; A midsummer night's dream incidental music. *Rochester Phil. Orch.; Zinman, cond.* Reissues.
• ARG 1-2/97: 139
- Fa 11-12/96: 306

36353. CDX 5501 (2 discs): *Novaes/Klemperer.* Music of Beethoven, Chopin, Schumann, Bach, Brahms, Gluck, and Saint-Saëns. *Novaes, piano; Vienna Symphony Orch.; Klemperer, cond.* Reissues.
• Fa 9-10/95: 429

36354. CDX 5504 (2 discs): BRUCKNER—Symphony no. 8. LISZT—Faust symphony. WAGNER—Faust overture. *Pro Musica Orch.; Southwest German Radio Symphony; Horenstein, cond.* Reissues.
+ ARG 3-4/93: 188

36355. CDX 5512 (2 discs): *The classical Novaes.* Music of Beethoven and Mozart. *Novaes, piano; Bamberg Symphony Orch.; Perlea, cond.; Vienna Symphony Orch.; Swarowsky, cond.* Reissues.
• Fa 9-10/95: 429

36356. CDX 5513 (2 discs): *The romantic Novaes.* Music of Chopin, Falla, and Grieg. *Novaes, piano; Bamberg Symphony Orch.; Perlea, cond.; Vienna Symphony Orch.; Swarowsky, cond.* Reissues.
• Fa 9-10/95: 430

36357. CDX 5516 (2 discs): MOZART—Piano concertos no. 22, 26; Piano sonatas no. 8, 17; Adagio, K. 540. HAYDN—

VOX BOX

Piano sonata, H. XVI, 37. *Kraus, piano; Vienna Symphony Orch.; Moralt, cond.*
- Fa 5-6/96: 219

36358. CDX 5517 (2 discs): MOZART—Piano concertos no. 14, 18, 21; Music for solo piano. *Klien, piano; Mainz Chamber Orch.; Kehr, cond.; Vienna Symphony Orch.; Angerer, cond.*
- ● ARG 5-6/96: 152
- ● Fa 5-6/96: 219

36359. CDX 5518 (2 discs): MAHLER—Das Lied von der Erde. BRUCKNER—Symphony no. 7. *Hoffman, alto; Melchert, tenor; Symphony Orch. of the Southwest German Radio, Baden-Baden; Rosbaud, cond.* Reissue.
- ● ARG 5-6/96: 97
- + Fa 5-6/96: 197

36360. CDX 5519 (2 discs): BACH—Brandenburg concertos. *Chamber Orch. of the Vienna Symphony Orch.; Horenstein, cond.* Recorded 1954.
- - ARG 5-6/96: 264
- + Fa 5-6/96: 72

36361. CDX 5520 (2 discs): BRUCKNER—Symphony no. 4. MAHLER—Symphony no. 7. *Vienna Symphony Orch.; Klemperer, cond.; Symphony Orch. of Radio Berlin; Rosbaud, cond.* Recorded 1951 and 1952.
- ● Fa 7-8/96: 133

36362. CDX 5523 (2 discs): Music of Bruch, Dvořák, Goldmark, Kreisler, Tartini, Rimsky-Korsakov, Rachmaninoff, and Falla. *Gimpel, violin; Southwest German Radio Orch.; Reinhardt, cond.; Pro Musica Orch., Stuttgart; Cremer, cond.* Reissues.
- + Fa 11-12/96: 213

36363. CDX 5524 (2 discs): MOZART—Symphonies no. 38-39, 41; Mass, K. 317; Vesperae solennes de confessore. *Lipp, Ludwig, Dickie, Berry, vocalists; chorus; Vienna Symphony Orch.; Horenstein, cond.* Reissues.
- + ARG 11-12/96: 171
- ● Fa 11-12/96: 319

36364. CDX 5514 (2 discs): *Piano sonatas, vol. 1.* BEETHOVEN—Piano sonatas no. 1-2, 9-10, 13-14, 21, 24. *Taub, piano.*
- + Fa 7-8/96: 103

36365. CDX 5502 (2 discs): HANDEL—Messiah. *Baird, Lane, Price, Deas; Ama Deus Ensemble; Radu, cond.*
- ● ARG 11-12/95: 129
- + Fa 9-10/95: 217
- ● ON 9/95: 55

36366. CDX 5503 (2 discs): HANDEL—Ezio. *Fortunato, Baird, Lane, Watson, Urrey, Pellerin; Magic Circle Opera Ensemble; Manhattan Chamber Orch.; Clark, cond.*
- ● ARG 11-12/95: 128

+ Fa 9-10/95: 214
+ ON 9/95: 55

36367. CDX 7505 : *Romances for violin and piano.* Music of Bruch, Kreisler, Sibelius, Dvořák, Liszt, Sinding, Vieuxtemps, Wieniawski, C. Schumann, Svendsen, Nielsen, and Janáček. *Rosand, violin; Sung, piano.*
- + ARG 1-2/96: 223
- + Fa 9-10/95: 406

36368. CDX 7506 : Clothed with the rays of the sun. *Nuns of St. Scholastica Priory; Monks of St. Mary's Monastery; Saint-Cyr, cond.* Reissue.
- + Fa 9-10/95: 386

36369. CDX 7518: PURCELL—Dido and Aeneas. *Lane, Brown, Hoffman; Musici di San Cassiano; Brookshire, cond.*
- ● ARG 5-6/96: 168
- ● Fa 5-6/96: 241
- ● ON 7/96: 49

36370. CDX 7519 (2 discs): HANDEL—Acis and Galatea. *Baird, Urrey, Price, Deas; Ama Deus Ensemble; Radu, cond.*
- - ARG 9-10/96: 130
- ● ON 7/96: 48

36371. CDX 7521: FLAGELLO—Piano concertos no. 2-3; Credendum; Overtures. *Rankovich, piano; Oliveira, violin; Kosice Symphony Orch.; Amos, cond.*
- + ARG 7-8/96: 112
- + Fa 7-8/96: 166

VOX CLASSICS

36273. VOX 7502 (2 discs): HANDEL—Acis and Galatea. *Baird, Urrey, Price, Deas; Ama Deus Ensemble; Radu, cond.*
- + Fa 7-8/96: 184

36274. VOX 7504: *Sounds of remembered dreams.* Music of Ravel, Delibes, Fauré, Saint-Saëns, and others. *Lucarelli, oboe; Jolles, harp; Morelli, bassoon.*
- + ARG 9-10/95: 262

36275. VOX 7520: BACH—Chromatic fantasy and fugue; Toccatas, BWV 910-916. *Newman, harpsichord.*
- + ARG 9-10/96: 85
- ● Fa 7-8/96: 90

36276. VOX 7522: BRAHMS—Piano pieces op. 116-118. *Tomšič, piano.*
- ● ARG 9-10/96: 100

36277. VOX 7523: *Arietta 2.* MOZART (ARR. PUKLICKY)—Opera arias in salon concert. *Prague Chamber Ensemble; Puklicky, cond.*
- + Fa 7-8/96: 251

36278. VOX 7524: BACH—Mass in B minor. *Baird, Gratis, Gordon, Deas; Ama Deus Ensemble; Radu, cond.*
- ● ARG 9-10/96: 83
- ● Fa 7-8/96: 185

36279. VOX 7526: MOZART—Piano concertos no. 11-12, 14. *Kagan, piano; Suk Chamber Orch.*
- ● ARG 1-2/97: 145
- + Fa 11-12/96: 314

36280. VOX 7527: HANDEL—Greatest arias. *Baird, Lane, Fortunato, Tsingopoulos, Urrey, Ostendorf, Opalach, vocalists; Brewer Chamber Orch.; Palmer, cond.; Brewer, harpsichord.* Reissue.
- ● ARG 3-4/97: 145
- + Fa 11-12/96: 262

36281. VOX 7529 (2 discs): BEETHOVEN—Piano sonatas no. 5-8, 16, 28. *Taub, piano.*
- ● Fa 11-12/96: 184

36282. VOX 7530 (3 discs): HANDEL—Tolomeo. *Lane, Harris, Matthews, Hart, Castaldi, Brookshire; Manhattan Chamber Orch.; Clark, cond.*
- + ARG 3-4/97: 147
- + Fa 11-12/96: 263
- + ON 7/96: 48

36283. VOX 7531: BACH—Magnificat, BWV 243; Orchestral suite no. 3. *Baird, Gratis, Price, Deas, vocalists; Fix-Keller, harpsichord; Ama Deus Ensemble; Radu, cond.*
- + Fa 11-12/96: 172

VOX CUM LAUDE

36372. MWCD 7153: DVOŘÁK—Symphony no. 7. ELGAR—Variations on an original theme (Enigma). *London Symphony Orch.; Mata, cond.*
- + ARG 5-6/88: 26
- - Fa 5-6/88: 123

36373. MCD 10039: BRAHMS—String quartets no. 1, 3. *Tokyo String Quartet.*
- + Fa 3-4/87: 91
- + Opus 4/87: 33
- + SR 5/87: 80

36374. MCD 10047: FUCHS—Twelve duets op. 60. HANDEL—Passacaglia (arr. Halvorsen); Sarabande con variazione; Chaconne (arr. Vermes). *Ronald Patterson, violin; Roxana Patterson, viola .*
- + Fa 5-6/88: 264

36375. MCD 10050: Music of Boellmann, Kilpinen, and Castelnuovo-Tedesco. *Heled, cello; Zak, piano.*
- + ARG 7-8/88: 83
- + Fa 5-6/88: 88
- + Ov 8/88: 16

36376. MCD 10051: Music of Magnard, Cilea, Tcherepnin, Milhaud, and Castelnuovo-Tedesco. *Heled, cello; Zak, piano.*
- + ARG 7-8/88: 83
- + Fa 5-6/88: 88
- + Ov 8/88: 16

36377. MCD 10063 (2 discs): HANDEL—Imeneo. *Baird, Hoch, Fortunato, Ostendorf, Opalach; Brewer Chamber Chorus & Orch.; Palmer, cond.*
+ Fa 5-6/88: 137
+ Ma 1/88: 60
+ NYT 11/29/87: H27
+ Ov 4/88: 36
+ SR 12/87: 146

36378. 115451-2 (2 discs): HANDEL—Imeneo. *Hoch, Baird, Opalach, Ostendorf; Brewer Chamber Orch.; Palmer, cond.* Reissue.
• Gr 8/93: 79

36379. 115772-2 (2 discs): BEETHOVEN—Piano sonatas, vol. 3. *Brendel, piano.* Reissue.
+ Gr 9/93: 84

VOX TEMPORIS

36380. CD 20 007: WEBER—Piano sonatas no. 1-2. *Vermeulen, piano.*
+ Fa 5-6/93: 355

36381. CD 92 001: *Laudate pueri.* MENDELSSOHN—3 Motets, op. 39. FAURÉ—Messe basse; Cantique de Jean Racine; Maria Mater gratiae; Ave verum corpus natum; Tantum ergo. GYROWETZ—3 Motets. *Capella Concinite; Heyerick, cond.; Termont, organ.*
+ Fa 11-12/91: 538

36382. CD 92 002: KARG-ELERT—Suite pointillistique; Ten caprices; Impressions exotiques. HINDEMITH—Eight pieces for solo flute; Flute sonata. *Dequeker, flute; Bernier, piano.*
+ Fa 7-8/92: 189

36383. CD 92 003: Early Italian recorder music. *Flanders Recorder Quartet.*
+ ARG 5-6/93: 168

36384. CD 92 005: LEKEU—Piano quartet (unfinished); Molto adagio, for string quartet; Meditation; Andante for violin and piano. *Ysaÿe Ensemble.*
+ ARG 9-10/92: 124
+ Fa 7-8/92: 199

36385. CD 92 006: M. HAYDN—St. Leopold mass and vespers for Holy Innocents; German magnificat; Notturno. *Capella Concinite; Collegium Instrumentale Brugense; Heyerick, cond.*
+ ARG 3-4/93: 93
+ Fa 3-4/93: 187

36386. CD 92 008: Music of Giuliani, Mertz, and Pettoletti. *Pieters, Dumortier, terz guitar.*
+ ARG 5-6/93: 164

36387. CD 92 027: SOR—Duets for guitars. *Pieters, Dumortier, guitars.*
- ARG 11-12/96: 213
+ Fa 7-8/96: 312

36388. CD 92 030: MENDES—Chamber music. *Spectra Ensemble; Rathe, cond.*
+ ARG 11-12/96: 161

36389. CD 92 033: *Seicento: early Italian recorder music.* Music of Riccio, Castello, Grillo, Gabrieli, Frescobaldi, Picchi, Porta, Trabaci, Guami, Palestrina, and Merula. *Flanders Recorder Quartet "Vier op'n Rij"; assisting musicians.*
+ Fa 5-6/93: 375

VOX TURNABOUT

36390. PVT 7167: CHOPIN—Piano concerto no. 1; Variations on La ci darem la mano; Krakowiak. *Simon, piano; Hamburg State Phil. Orch.; Beissel, cond.*
+ ARG 11-12/90: 45

36391. PVT 7191: LISZT—Piano concerto no. 1; Spanish rhapsody (arr. Busoni); Totentanz (solo piano version). *Marsh, piano; London Symphony Orch.; Freeman, cond.*
• ARG 11-12/90: 74

36392. PVT 7195: JOACHIM—Violin concerto no. 2. HUBAY—Violin concerto no. 3. *Rosand, violin; Luxembourg Radio Symphony Orch.; Froment, cond.*
+ ARG 11-12/91: 86
+ Fa 1-2/92: 244

36393. PVT 7196: BEACH—Piano concerto, op. 45; Piano quintet, op. 67. *Boehm, piano; Westphalian Symphony Orch.; Laundau, cond.; Kooper, Rogers, violins; Maximoff, viola; Sherry, cello.*
+ ARG 3-4/92: 26
- Fa 1-2/92: 158

36394. PVT 7200: BEETHOVEN—Diabelli variations; Bagatelles, op. 126. *Brendel, piano.* Recorded 1964.
+ ARG 7-8/92: 93

36395. PVT 7201: FAURÉ—Ballade; Fantaisie. SAINT-SAËNS—Piano concerto no. 4. CHAUSSON—Quelques danses. *Johannesen, piano; Luxembourg Radio Symphony Orch.; Froment, cond.*
+ ARG 5-6/92: 59

36396. PVT 7507: *Arietta: Italian opera arias in salon concert.* Music of Puccini and Verdi. *Prague Chamber Ensemble.*
+ ARG 11-12/95: 239
- Fa 11-12/95: 479

36397. PVT 7509: BOLCOM—Piano concerto; Three dance portraits. ADLER—Flute concerto; Sonata for flute solo. *Bolcom, piano; Rochester Phil. Orch.; Hodkinson, Effron, conds.; Snyder, piano; Boyd, flute.* Reissue.
+ ARG 5-6/96: 86
+ Fa 5-6/96: 110

36398. PVT 7511: GÓRECKI—Symphony no. 3. *Kilanowicz, soprano; Polish State Phil. Orch. of Katowice; Swoboda, cond.*

• ARG 1-2/96: 117
+ Fa 1-2/96: 212

36399. PVT 7513: *Bravura trumpet.* Music of Ketting, Suderberg, Chardon, and Hindemith. *Schlueter, trumpet; Suderberg, Emery, piano; Moerschel, cello.*
• ARG 1-2/96: 220
+ Fa 1-2/96: 399

36400. PVT 7514 (2 discs): BEETHOVEN—Piano sonatas no. 1-2, 9-10, 13-14, 21, 24. *Taub, piano.*
- ARG 1-2/96: 83
+ Fa 1-2/96: 144

36401. PVT 7515: SCHUMANN—Davidsbündlertänze; Piano sonata, op. 22. *Rose, piano.*
• ARG 5-6/96: 190
+ Fa 1-2/96: 303

36402. PVT 7516: *Authentic tangos from Argentina.* Music of Pascual, Maffia, Cobián, De Caro, Piazzolla, Villoldo, Mores, Troilo, Binelli, and Pugliese. *Tango 7.*
+ ARG 3-4/96: 225
+ Fa 1-2/96: 407

36403. PVT 8167: FOSTER—Songs. *Gregg Smith Singers; New York Vocal Ensemble.* Reissue.
+ ARG 7-8/94: 102

36404. 30371 0002-2: BEETHOVEN—Missa solemnis. *Steingruber, Schürhoff, Majkut, Wiener; Vienna Academy Choir; Vienna Symphony Orch.; Klemperer, cond.* Reissue; recorded 1953.
- Gr 7/96: 83

36405. 30371 0016-2: MOZART—Piano concertos no. 17, 19. *Brendel, piano; Vienna Volksoper Orch.; Angerer, Boettcher, conds.* Reissue; recorded 1967.
+ Gr 7/96: 58

VOX UNIQUE

36406. VU 9002: GRIEG—Violin sonata in C minor. SIBELIUS—Violin concerto. SVENDSEN—Romance. *Schwartz, violin; Franklin, piano; London Symphony Orch.; Freeman, cond.*
+ ARG 11-12/91: 71

36407. VU 9003: SCHUBERT—Liebesbotschaft; Das Rosenband; Willkommen und Abschied; Fischerweise; Ganymed; Nachtstück; Abschied; Das Fischermädchen; Der Winterabend; Im Frühling; Der Musensohn; Sehnsucht; Die Taubenpost. *Opalach, bass-baritone; Vallecillo, piano.*
+ Fa 1-2/92: 319

36408. VU 9013: PROKOFIEV—Violin sonatas; 5 melodies. *Oliveira, violin;*

VOX UNIQUE

McDonald, piano.
+ ARG 11-12/91: 136

36409. VU 9022: Liszt—Transcendental etudes. *Rose, piano.*
+ ARG 11-12/91: 89

VQR DIGITAL

36410. VQR 2001: Cage—Sonata and interludes for prepared piano. *Rosenberg, piano.*
• Fa 7-8/87: 82

36411. VQR 2011: Vierne—Messe solennelle op. 16; Symphony no. 3. *Ferre, Lewis, Smith, organs; Independent Choir; Schreiber, cond.*
+ Fa 1-2/89: 287

36412. VQR 2031: *The Spirit of Koussevitzky.* Music of Koussevitzky, Glière, Scriabin, and Rachmaninoff (arr. for double bass) . *Karr, double bass; Lewis, piano.*
- ARG 5-6/90: 137

WALSINGHAM

36413. WAL 8000-2 (2 discs): Berlioz—Grande messe des morts. *Hamilton, tenor; Willoughby Symphony Choir; Choirs & Orch. of the Sydney Conservatorium; Hopkins, cond.*
• Fa 11-12/94: 176

36414. WAL 8001-2: *The digital dance.* Music of Memo, Anon., Attaignant, Newman, Gardane, Facoli, Byrd, Bach, Rameau, and Handel. *Kinsela, virginals & harpsichord; Atherton, percussion.*
• Fa 11-12/94: 496

36415. WAL 8002-2: *Grand music for great occasions.* Music of Farnham, Elgar, Ross, Proulx, Karg-Elert, Alcock, Joulain, Fleury, Vann, Smart, Floyd, Willan, and Saint-Martin. *Nixon, organ.*
- Fa 11-12/94: 488

36416. WAL 8003-2: *The muses' gift. Renaissance Players; Evans, cond.*
• Fa 11-12/94: 464

36417. WAL 8004-2: *Venus' fire. Renaissance Players; Evans, cond.*
• Fa 11-12/94: 464

36418. WAL 8005-2: The ring of creation. *The Renaissance Players.*
+ Fa 7-8/95: 411

36419. WAL 8006-2: *Garland dances.* Music of Guillaume d'Amiens, Gui, Li Chestelain de Couci, Audefrois le Bastars, and Anon. *Renaissance Players; Evans, cond.*
- Fa 1-2/96: 382

36420. WAL 8010-2: Delany—Mass in A♭; Ave Maria. *St. Mary's Cathedral Choir; Jubilee Choir; Sydney Conservatory Choir and Chorale; Jubilee*

Orch.; Russell, cond.
- ARG 11-12/94: 98
+ Fa 11-12/94: 213

36421. WAL 8011-2 (3 discs): Gounod—Messe solenelle no. 3. *Choirs; Jubilee Orch.; Russell, cond.*
+ ARG 11-12/94: 120
+ Fa 11-12/94: 241

36422. WAL 8012-2: *Celebrating the eightieth anniversary of the Sydney Male Choir.* Music of Handel, Welsh, Trad.; Kosma, Lloyd Webber, Heyman, Malotte, and Schoenberg. *Sydney Male Choir; Thrift, cond.; McQueen, acc.*
- Fa 11-12/94: 460

36423. WAL 8013-2: *The Sydney International Piano Competition series.* Music of Schubert, Mozart, Brahms, Liszt, and Grainger. *Kong, piano.*
+ Fa 11-12/94: 489
+ Gr 8/96: 78

36424. WAL 8014-2: *Sing joyfully.* Music of Byrd, Drury, Gibbons, Langlais, Palestrina, Bach, Duruflé, Vaughan Williams, Britten, Stanford, Rutter, Ward, and Mathias. *Choir of Christ Church, St. Laurence; McEwan, cond.; Drury, organ.*
+ Fa 11-12/94: 459

36425. WAL 8015-2: *Strings attached: music for two guitars.* Music of D. Scarlatti, Giuliani, Castelnuovo- Tedesco, Piazzolla, Houghton, and Gnattali. *S. & C. Strano, guitars.*
+ Fa 7-8/95: 418

36426. WAL 8016-2 (2 discs): Debussy—Préludes, books 1-2. *Gifford, piano.*
+ Fa 7-8/95: 168

36427. WAL 8017-2: *Clarinet collection.* Music of Febland, Horowitz, Arnold, Holloway, Berkeley, Easton, Williamson, Banks, Hyde, Vorster, Atkinson, Bozza, Debussy, Tailleferre, and Templeton. *Graff, clarinet; Vorster, piano.*
+ Fa 7-8/95: 414

36428. WAL 8018-2: *Flute impressions: romantic music for flute and piano.* Music of Boulanger, Ropartz, Bloch, Pijper, Binet, and Holmès. *Chislett, flute; Miller, piano.*
+ Fa 7-8/95: 418

36429. WAL 8019-2: Beethoven—Piano sonata no. 21; Andante favori. Schubert—Piano sonata, D. 960. *Bolla, Saver, Cazal, pianos.*
• Fa 7-8/95: 118

36430. WAL 8020-2: *Lauda Jerusalem Dominum.* Music of Charpentier, Dunstable, Josquin, Byrd, Lassus, Tallis, Parsons, Palestrina, Monteverdi, G. Gabrieli, Lalande, Moreau, Duruflé, Poston, Herbeck, and Anon. *St. Mary's*

Cathedral Choir, Sydney; Russell, cond.
+ Fa 7-8/95: 404

36431. WAL 8021-2: *Masterworks at St. Matthew's.* Music of Bach, Byrd, Drury, Mozart, Vierne, Mendelssohn, and Valente. *Drury, organ.*
+ Fa 11-12/95: 468

36432. WAL 8022-2: *Bouquet of melodies.* Music of Gounod, Franck, Bizet, Fauré, Duparc, Ravel, Hahn, and Satie. *Kenny, soprano; Martineau, piano.*
+ Fa 3-4/96: 326

36433. WAL 8023-2: *Historic organs of Sydney: 29 imported and indigenous organs.* Music of Mendelssohn, S. Wesley, Schumann, Franck, Titelouze, Bach, Boëly, Boëllmann, Saint-Saëns, Clérambault, Chavet, Pachelbel, Arne, Avison, Corette, L. Couperin, C. Wesley, Pasquini, Buxtehude, Alain, and Langlais. *Dudman, organ.*
+ Fa 1-2/96: 389

36434. WAL 9000-2: *Colonial brass: The Hawthorn Band, Australia's champions.* Music of Curnow, Grainger, Rimmer, Puccini, Gershwin, C.-M. Schonberg, Sparke, Rive, Wilcocks, Saint-Saëns, Rose, Van der Roost, and Elfman. *Hawthorn Band; MacDonald, cond.*
+ Fa 7-8/95: 440

WARM ARTS

36435. WCD 80022: *Baroque music for trumpet and organ.* Music of Martini, Tartini, Corelli, Purcell, Boyce, Greene, Krebs, Telemann, and Handel. *Fleet, trumpet; Adams, organ.*
+ ARG 1-2/94: 183
+ Fa 11-12/93: 499

WARNER BROTHERS

36436. 9 45846-2: O'Connor—The fiddle concerto for violin and orchestra; Quartet for violin, viola, cello, and double bass. *O'Connor, violin; Phillips, viola; Brey, cello; Meyer, double bass; Concordia Orch.; Alsop, cond.*
+ Fa 9-10/95: 270

WATER LILY ACOUSTICS

36437. 07: Bach—Partita no. 2 for solo violin. Kreisler—Recitative and scherzo. Ysaÿe—Sonata no. 2 for solo violin. *Delmoni, violin.*
+ ARG 11-12/90: 160

WATT

36438. 835 580-2 : Mantler—Many have no speech. *Bruce, Faithfull, Wyatt, vocalists; Mantler, trumpet; Fenn, guitar; Dnanish Radio Concert Orch.; Kragerup, cond.*
+ Fa 11-12/88: 220

WELL-TEMPERED

36439. 5160: BACH—Cantata arias, duets, and choruses. *Geisler, computers.*
+ ARG 1-2/94: 69

36440. 5164: JAFFE—Grass Valley fire; American miniatures; Ellis Island sonata; Silicon Valley breakdown. *Various performers and electronics.*
□ ARG 7-8/94: 117

36441. 5168: SCARLATTI—Sonatas. *Drake, harp.*
+ ARG 5-6/95: 164

36442. 5169: TELEMANN—Oboe partitas. *Lucarelli, oboe; Ranck, harpsichord; Brown, bassoon.*
+ ARG 3-4/95: 204

36443. 5172: EWAZEN—Frost fire; To cast a shadow again; Trumpet quintet; Horn sonata. *American Brass Quintet; Sharp, baritone; Gekker, trumpet; Valentine, Ewazen, piano; Brubaker, horn; St. Luke's Chamber Ensemble.*
+ ARG 1-2/96: 249

36444. 5180: BACH—Partita no. 2; Sonata no. 3. *St. John, violin.*
+ ARG 11-12/96: 84

WELTBILD

36445. 703769 (14 discs): WAGNER—Der Ring des Nibelungen. *Polke, Uhl, McKee, Kniplová; Czech Phil. Orch.; Prague National Theater Orch.; Swarowsky, cond.* Reissue; recorded 1968.
+ ARG 11-12/96: 231

WERGO

36446. SM 1022-2: M. MONK—Songs from the hill; Tablet. *Monk, vocals.*
+ Fa 3-4/90: 234

36447. SM 1058-2: M. MONK—Our lady of late. *Monk, voice & glass; Walcott, percussion & glass .*
+ Fa 7-8/89: 188

36448. SM 1067-2 (2 discs): HENCK—Improvisation IV. *Henck, piano.*
+ Fa 11-12/88: 199

36449. WER 2012-2: CHOWNING—Phoné; Tuenas; Stria; Sabelithe. *Electronic sounds.*
□ Fa 9-10/88: 128
□ MA 3/89: 58

36450. WER 2013-2: RISSET—Songes; Passages; Little boy: Computer suite; Sud. *Artaud, flute; Electronic sounds.*
□ Fa 9-10/88: 129
□ MA 3/89: 58

36451. WER 2015-2: McNABB—Invisible cities. *McNabb, soprano saxophone & synthesizers; Wodehouse, piano.*
□ Fa 1-2/90: 227

36452. WER 2017-2: TRUAX—The bland man; Aerial; Wave edge; Solar ellipse; Riverrun. *Electronic sounds.*
+ Fa 9-10/88: 129
□ MA 3/89: 58

36453. WER 2018-2: DASHOW—Archimedes: Scene II; Mnemonics, for violin and computer; Oro, arento and legno, for flute and computer. *Buffa, violin; Conti, flutes.*
+ Fa 7-8/90: 127

36454. WER 2019-2: VIÑAO—Music with computers: Son entero, for 4 voices and computer; Triple concerto for flute, cello, piano and computer. *Singcircle; Lucas, flute; Mitchell, cello; Mead, piano; electronic music .*
+ ARG 1-2/91: 120
+ Fa 1-2/91: 344

36455. WER 2021-2: *Computer music currents, 1.* SAVOURET—Don Quixote corporation. LINDWALL—Points. OPPENHEIM—Round the corners of purgatory. *Computer compositions.*
□ Fa 3-4/90: 395

36456. WER 2022-2: *Computer music currents, 2.* Music of Davidovsky, Koenig, Lorrain, Ghent, Arfib, and Rush. *Computer compositions.*
□ Fa 3-4/90: 395

36457. WER 2023-2: *Computer music currents, 3.* Music of Bayle, Karpen, Schottstaedt, and Goebel. *Computer compositions.*
□ Fa 3-4/90: 395

36458. WER 2024-2: *Computer music currents, 4.* Music of Jones, Decoust, Dodge, Barrier, Wishart, and Reynolds. *University of Illinois Chamber Singers; Brooks, cond.; computer compositions.*
□ Fa 3-4/90: 395

36459. WER 2025-2: *Computer music currents, 5.* Music of Smally, Maiguashca, Loy, Saariaho, and Harvey. *Schumacher, cello; Klinkenberg, percussion; electronic music.*
□ Fa 1-2/91: 344

36460. WER 2026-2: *Computer music currents, 6.* Music of Vaggione, Kessler, Smalley, Wolman, and Chafe. *Kientzy, bass saxophone; Nicolet, flute; Heaton, clarinet; Fobes, bass clarinet; electronic music.*
□ Fa 1-2/91: 344

36461. WER 2027-2: *Computer music currents, 7.* Music of Karpen, Risset, Bodin, Petersen, White, and Yuasa. *Bettina, Jarsky, sopranos; electronic music.*
□ Fa 1-2/91: 344

36462. WER 2030-2—2031-2 (2 separate discs): *Computer music currents 10-11.* Music of Motz, Wessel, Nelson, Stroppa;

Viñao, Kropowicz, Dodge, Fulton, and Lansky.
□ Fa 11-12/92: 453

36463. WER 4008-2: REUTER—Abendangelus; Die Passion in 9 Inventionen; Cinco caprichos sobre Cervantes; Drei Nachstücke aus Fantasiestücke op. 28. *Turnagoel, guitar.*
• Fa 11-12/86: 200

36464. WER 6009-2: STOCKHAUSEN—Kontakte. *Tudor, piano & percussion; Caskel, percussion; Stockhausen, Koenig, electronic tape.*
+ Fa 3-4/93: 303

36465. WER 6011-2: BOULEZ—Structures. *A. & A. Kontarsky, pianos.* Reissue.
+ Gr 6/93: 58

36466. WER 6021-2: BERIO—Circles; Sequenza I: for flute; Sequenza III: for voice; Sequenza V: for trombone. *Various performers.*
+ ARG 3-4/92: 33
+ Fa 3-4/92: 154

36467. WER 6074-2: CAGE—Sonata 13 for prepared piano; Music for Marcel Duchamp; Songbooks 1-2; Empty words 3. *Roggenkamp, piano; Schola Cantorum Stuttgart.*
□ ARG 3-4/92: 40
□ Fa 3-4/92: 169
• Gr 9/92: 142

36468. WER 6087-2: FRANÇAIX—Concerto for two pianos; Variations sur un thème plaisant; Cinq portraits de jeunes filles. *J. & C. Françaix; Mainz Wind Ensemble; Schöll, cond.; Southwest German Radio Symphony Orch.; Stoll, cond.* Reissue.
+ Gr 1/92: 52

36469. WER 6152-2 (3 discs): CAGE—Etudes australes. *Sultan, piano.*
+ Gr 7/93: 65

36470. WER 6158-2: CAGE—*Piano and prepared piano music, vol. 3.* Suite for toy piano; The seasons ballet; Music for amplified toy pianos; A book of music. *Pierce, Ajemian, Crispell, Kubera, pianos & toy pianos.*
+ ARG 7-8/92: 114
+ Fa 11-12/91: 291

36471. WER 60045-2: LIGETI—Requiem; Aventures; Nouvelles aventures. *Poli, Ericson, Charlent, Cahn, Pearson; Bavarian Radio Chorus; Hessian Radio Symphony Orch.; International Chamber Ensemble of Darmstadt; Gielen, Maderna, conds.*
□ Fa 11-12/88: 214

36472. WER 6168/69-2 (2 discs): NANCARROW—Studies for player piano, vol. 2 and 1. *Performed on Nancarrow's modified 1927 Ampico reproducing*

WERGO

pianos.
+ Fa 11-12/91: 424
+ Gr 3/92: 80

36473. WER 6170/71 (2 discs): LIGETI—Le grand macabre. *Weller, Walmsley-Clark, Fredricks, Haage; ORF- Chor; Arnold Schönberg-Chor; Gumpoldskirchner Spatzen; ORF-Symphonie-Orch.; Howarth, cond.* Reissue.
+ ARG 1-2/92: 71
+ Fa 11-12/91: 368
+ Gr 12/91: 126

36474. WER 6173-2: ADORNO—Orchestral, chamber and choral works. *Frankfurt Opera House and Museum Orch.; Bertini, cond.*
□ Gr 6/91: 37

36475. WER 6178-2: XENAKIS—Palimpsest; Epei; Dikhthas; Akanthos. *Arditti, violin; Helffer, piano; Walmsley-Clark, soprano; Spectrum; Protheroe, cond.*
+ ARG 1-2/92: 141
+ Fa 7-8/91: 330

36476. WER 6181-2: HINDEMITH—*Das Klavierwerk, vol. 1.* In einer Nacht, op. 15; Suite für Klavier, op. 26. *Mauser, piano.*
+ Fa 9-10/91: 237

36477. WER 6186-2: SATIE—Socrate. CAGE—Cheap imitation. *Helling, alto; Richards, Henck, piano.*
+ ARG 7-8/92: 211

36478. WER 6192/93-2 (2 discs): HINDEMITH—Neues vom Tage. *Werres, Nicolai, Pries, Hiestermann; Cologne Radio Orch.; Latham-Koenig, cond.*
+ ARG 7-8/92: 150

36479. WER 6197-2: HINDEMITH—Clarinet quintet; Minimax; [Flying Dutchman parody for string quartet]. *Löffler, clarinet; Buchberger Quartet.*
+ ARG 7-8/92: 150
• Fa 7-8/92: 182

36480. WER 6198-2: FRANÇAIX—Harpsichord concerto; Piano trio; Guitar concerto. *Françaix, harpsichord; Saarbrücken Radio Symphony Orch.; Naoumoff, cond.; Gawriloff, violin; Goritzki, cello; Havenith, piano; Segre, guitar; SWDR Chamber Orch.; H. Richter, cond.*
+ ARG 11-12/92: 120
+ Fa 9-10/92: 234

36481. WER 6202-2: HINDEMITH—Piano music, vol. 2. *Mauser, piano.*
- ARG 11-12/92: 136
+ Fa 11-12/92: 260

36482. WER 6203-2: CAGE—Works for percussion. *Hêlios Quartet.*
+ Fa 3-4/92: 168
+ Gr 9/92: 105

36483. WER 6204-2 (2 discs): HENZE—The English cat. *Vocalists of the Hans Werner Henze Summer Academy, Gütersloh; Parnassus Orch., London; Stenz, cond.*
+ ARG 7-8/92: 148
• Fa 1-2/92: 236
+ Gr 12/92: 136

36484. WER 6207-2: ROSLAVETS—In the house of the new moon; Violin concerto no. 1. *Grindenko, violin; Saar Radio Symphony Orch.; Holliger, cond.*
+ ARG 1-2/94: 139

36485. WER 6208-2: WANEK—Tableau symphonique; Duo sonetti; String quartet; Musique concertante. *Berlin Radio Symphony Orch.; Rögner, cond.; Naidu, mezzo-soprano; Kiss, Martin, harpsichords; Sonare Quartet.*
+ Fa 3-4/93: 330

36486. WER 6209-2: ZEMLINSKY—Die Seejungfrau; Sinfonische Gesänge, op. 20. *Wenkel, alto; Symphony Orch. of Southwest German Radio, Baden-Baden; Peskó, Neumann, conds.*
+ Fa 9-10/93: 334

36487. WER 6210-2: TURINA—Guitar music. *Uriarte, piano.*
+ ARG 9-10/93: 210

36488. WER 6211-2 : COPLAND—Piano music. *Tichman, piano.*
+ ARG 1-2/94: 92

36489. WER 6212-2: COPLAND—Piano music. *Tichman, piano.*
• ARG 1-2/95: 96

36490. WER 6213-2: PETERSEN—Grand mass. *Vocal soloists; Choir of St. Martin's, Mainz; Orch. of Mainz; Breitschaft, cond.*
+ ARG 3-4/93: 123

36491. WER 6214-2: HINDEMITH—The piano works, vol. 3. *Mauser, piano.*
+ Fa 1-2/94: 203

36492. WER 6216-2 : CAGE—Concert for piano & orchestra; Atlas eclipticalis. *Kubera, piano; S.E.M. Ensemble; Kotík, cond.*
+ Fa 9-10/93: 141
+ Gr 12/93: 64

36493. WER 6227 : MESSIAEN—Visions de l'Amen. *Uriarte, Mrongovius, pianos.*
+ ARG 1-2/95: 142

36494. WER 6228-2: STRAVINSKY—Music for two pianos. *A. & A. Kontarsky, pianos.* Recorded 1962.
+ ARG 1-2/94: 160
+ Fa 1-2/94: 325

36495. WER 6229-2: NONO—Canti di vita e d'amore; Per Bastiana; Omaggio a Vedova. *Taskova, soprano; Driscoll, tenor; Sinfonieorch. des Saarländischen Rundfunks; Radio-Symphonie Orch., Berlin; Gielen, cond.* Reissue.
□ ARG 3-4/94: 128
□ Fa 3-4/94: 258

36496. WER 6231/38-2 (8 discs): CAGE—Diary: how to improve the world. *Cage, voice.*
+ Fa 9-10/93: 141

36497. WER 6239-2: HENZE—Piano music. *Francesch, piano.*
+ ARG 9-10/94: 144
+ Fa 9-10/94: 211

36498. WER 6250-2: HINDEMITH—Ludus tonalis. *Mauser, piano.*
• ARG 5-6/95: 120

36499. WER 6255-2 (3 discs): HINDEMITH—Mathis der Maler. *Hermann, Protschka, Rossmanith, Hass; Cologne Radio Symphony Orch.; Albrecht, cond.*
+ ARG 1-2/95: 117
+ Gr 9/94: 112
+ ON 7/95: 46

36500. WER 6259-2 (2 discs): HARTMANN—Simplicius simplicissimus. *Donath, Buchner, König, Brinkmann, Scholze; Munich Concert Choir; Bavarian Radio Orch.; Fricke, cond.*
+ ARG 3-4/96: 121
• Gr 11/95: 155

36501. WER 6261-2: PENDERECKI—Choral music. *Warsaw Phil. Choir; Warsaw Phil. Orch.; Penderecki, cond.*
+ ARG 9-10/95: 190

36502. WER 6273-2: FELDMAN—For Franz Kline; O'Hara songs; De Kooning; Piano piece for Philip Gustan; 4 instruments; For Frank O'Hara. *Klein, soprano; Köhler, bass; Ensemble Avantgarde.*
+ ARG 1-2/97: 105

36503. WER 6275-2 (3 discs): ORFF—Trionfi: Carmina Burana; Catulli carmina; Trionfo di Afrodite. *Griffith, Roberts, Ress, Dewald, Mohr; Flanders Phil. Orch.; Tang, Schäfer, conds.*
• ARG 9-10/95: 186
• Gr 8/95: 117

36504. WER 6301-2: HENRY—La ville. *Electronics.*
• ARG 1-2/95: 115

36505. WER 6303-2: CAGE—Roaratorio; Writing for the second time through Finnegan's Wake. *Various performers; Cage, narrator.*
□ ARG 11-12/94: 88

36506. WER 6401-2: MESSIAEN—Turangalîla-symphonie. *Loriod, piano; G. Martenot, ondes Martenot; Southwest German Radio Symphony Orch., Baden-Baden; Rosbaud, cond.* Recorded 1951.
+ Fa 7-8/93: 182

36507. WER 6403-2 (2 discs): SCHOENBERG—Five orchestral pieces, op. 16; Ode to Napoleon Bonaparte; Pierrot Lunaire. *Olsen, reciter; Héricard, Sprechstimme; Southwest German Radio Symphony Orch. Baden-Baden; Rosbaud, cond.* Recorded 1958, 53, 57.
+ Fa 3-4/94: 305

36508. WER 6603-2: HINDEMITH—Das Unaufhörliche. *Sonntag, Wörle, Lorenz, Korn, vocalists; Chorus & Symphony Orch. of Radio Berlin; Zagrosek, cond.*
+ ARG 3-4/97: 157
+ Fa 1-2/97: 179

36509. WER 60054-2: *Magnificathy: the many voices of Cathy Berberian.* Music of Monteverdi, Debussy, Cage, Bussotti, Weill, and others. *Berberian, soprano; Canino, piano & cembalo.*
+ ARG 3-4/89: 122
+ Fa 3-4/89: 350
+ Gr 7/89: 226
+ MA 5/89: 76
+ Ov 7/89: 59

36510. WER 60080-2: IVES—Piano sonata no. 2. *Henck, piano; Georgiev, viola; Klemeyer, flute.*
- Fa 9-10/88: 173

36511. WER 60100 (LP): LIGETI—Trio for violin, horn and piano; Passacaglia ungherese; Ungarian rock; Continuum; Monument-Selbstportrait-Bewegung. *Gawriloff, violin; Baumann, horn; Besch, Ballista, Canino, pianos; Chojnacka, harpsichord.*
+ Fa 11-12/86: 159

36512. WER 60105 (LP): *Guitar music of our time.* Music of Villa-Lobos, Vogel, Zehm, Mittergradnegger, Smith- Brindle, and Dohl. *Ragossnig, guitar.*
- Fa 5-6/87: 229

36513. WER 60106-2: HINDEMITH— Sancta Susanna op. 21; Drei gesänge op. 9. *Donath, Schnaut, Martin; Berlin Radio Symphony Orch.; Albrecht, cond.*
+ Fa 11-12/86: 153 m.f.
+ Fa 1-2/87: 125

36514. WER 60108 (LP): SCHNEBEL— Schubert-Phantasie; In moto proprio, Kanon à 13; Diapason, Kanon à 13. *Musica Negativa; Southwest German Radio Symphony Orch.; Riehn, Peskó, Bour, conds.*
+ Fa 11-12/86: 208

36515. WER 60114/15-2 (2 discs): HENZE—String quartets no. 1-5. *Arditti String Quartet.*
+ ARG 11-12/87: 37
+ Fa 5-6/87: 136

36516. WER 60117 (LP): HINDEMITH— Die junge Magd; Des Todes Tod. *Schnaut, Schreckenbach, altos; Berlin Radio Symphony Orch.; Albrecht, cond.*

+ ARG 1-2/88: 35
+ Gr 2/89: 1324

36517. WER 60119-2: *Music & graphic: organ improvisations.* Music of Szathmáry, Vetter, Cage, Matsushita, and Haubenstock-Ramati. *Szathmáry, organ.*
□ Fa 3-4/89: 370

36518. WER 60123-2: *Percussion today.* Music of Regner, Brouwer, Henze, Heider, and Hiller. *Hochschule-Percussion Trossingen; Gschwendtner, cond.*
• Fa 11-12/86: 281
+ Fa 3-4/87: 272

36519. WER 60126-2: HENZE—Royal winter music. *Kres, guitar.*
• Fa 5-6/87: 136

36520. WER 60127-2: SCELSI—Canti del Capricorno 1-19. *Hirayama, voice; Curran, thai-gong; Nakagawa, saxophone; Yoshihara, Yamaguchi, percussions.*
+ Fa 1-2/90: 291

36521. WER 60128-2: HILLER—Expo 85; String quartet no. 4; Computer music for percussion and tape; Persiflage, for flute, oboe, and percussion; An avalanche for pitchman, prima donna, player piano, percussionist, and pre-recorded playback. *Williams, Rosen, percussion; Dick, flute; Post, oboe; MacDonald, voice; Harder, soprano; Hiller, synthesizers; Ritscher, audio technician; Composition String Quartet of the University of Illinois.*
+ ARG 1-2/91: 56
+ Fa 5-6/87: 138
□ Fa 11-12/90: 249

36522. WER 60129/30-2 (2 discs): HENZE—La Cubana order Ein Leben für die Kunst. *Silja, Anders, Schmidt, Büchner; Hamburg Choir & Chamber Orch.; Latham-Koenig, cond.*
+ Fa 9-10/89: 219

36523. WER 60131-2: LIGETI—Musica ricercata; Capriccio no. 1-2; Invention; Monument-Selbstportrait- Bewegung. *Uriarte, Mrongovius, pianos.*
+ Fa 3-4/88: 133

36524. WER 60132-2: HINDEMITH— Mörder, Hoffnung der Fraune; Der Dämon. *Schnaut, Grundheber; Verstärkter RIAS Chamber Choir; Berlin Radio Symphony Orch.; Albrecht, cond.*
+ Fa 3-4/88: 127

36525. WER 60133-2: EGK—La tentation de St. Antoine; Die Nachtigall; Polonaise, Adagio, und Finale. *Walker, alto; Clement, oboe; Rodenhäuser, clarinet; Ritzkowsky, horn; Marschall, bassoon; Booz, double bass; Werner Egk Quartet.*
+ Fa 5-6/88: 121

36526. WER 60135/36-2 (2 discs): STOCKHAUSEN—Klavierstücke I-XI.

Henck, piano.
+ ARG 1-2/88: 64
+ Fa 11-12/87: 119

36527. WER 60137-2: KOECHLIN—Les heures persanes. *Henck, piano.*
+ ARG 7-8/88: 32
+ DA 8/88: 42
+ Fa 5-6/88: 150

36528. WER 60138-2: *The dream of heaven: new music from china.* Music of Ho, Shang, Ding, L. Wang, C. Wang, Li, Lo, and Quan. *Liao, piano.*
+ Fa 11-12/89: 452

36529. WER 60139-2: *Toccaten.* Music of Widor, Boellmann, Gigout, Duruflé, Reger, and others. *Haas, organ.*
• Fa 3-4/88: 258

36530. WER 60140-2: RAVEL—Valses nobles et sentimentales; La valse; Prélude; Menuet sur le nom de Haydn; Jeux d'eau; Frontispice; Gaspard de la nuit. *Mrongovius, Uriarte, pianos.*
+ Fa 9-10/89: 297

36531. WER 60141-2: KILLMAYER—3 piano pieces. RIHM—Piano pieces no. 1, 7. *Mauser, piano.*
+ Fa 9-10/88: 176
+ HPR 3/89: 78
□ MA 5/89: 78

36532. WER 60142-2: Music of Linde, Terzakis, Brindle, Stockhausen, Sehm, and others. *Linde, recorder; Ragossnig, guitar.*
+ Fa 1-2/90: 403

36533. WER 60143 (LP): FRANÇAIX— Variations on a theme of Haydn; Mozart new-look; Musique pour faire plaisir; Hommage à l'ami Papageno; Quasi improvvisando; Danses exotiques. *Blaser Ensemble Mainz; Schöll, cond.*
+ ARG 3-4/88: 35
□ Fa 1-2/88: 121

36534. WER 60144-2: HINDEMITH—Cello sonata op. 11 no. 3; Three pieces for cello and piano op. 8. *Berger, cello; Mauser, piano.*
• Fa 7-8/89: 162

36535. WER 60145-2: HINDEMITH—Cello sonata (1948); Three easy pieces; Little sonata for cello; A frog he want a-courting. *Berger, cello; Mauser, piano.*
+ ARG 11-12/90: 69
• Fa 11-12/90: 249
+ Gr 9/90: 556

36536. WER 60146-2: HINDEMITH—Das Nusch-nuschi op. 20. *Stamm; Berlin Radio Symphony Orch.; Albrecht, cond.*
□ ARG 3-4/89: 46
+ Fa 3-4/89: 183
+ Gr 7/89: 230
+ MA 11/89: 56

WERGO

36537. WER 60148/49-2 (2 discs):
HINDEMITH—Cardillac. *Schweizer,
Schunk, Nimsgern, Stamm; RIAS
Chamber Choir; Berlin Radio Symphony
Orch.; Albrecht, cond.*
+ Fa 7-8/89: 162
+ Gr 7/89: 230

36538. WER 60150-2: HINDEMITH—
Lustige Sinfonietta in D minor; Rag time.
*Berlin Radio Symphony Orch.; Albrecht,
cond.*
+ Fa 9-10/89: 220
+ Gr 9/89: 454

36539. WER 60151-2: CAGE—A room;
She is asleep l; In a landscape; Seven
Haiku; Totem Ancestor; 2 pastorales;
And the earth shall bear again; Waiting
for M. C. and D. T. *Pierce, piano &
prepared piano; Clayton, voice; Paul
Price Percussion Ensemble.*
• Fa 7-8/89: 120

36540. WER 60152/55 (2 LPs): CAGE—
Etudes australes. *Sultan, piano.*
+ Fa 11-12/87: 119

36541. WER 60156-50: CAGE—Sonatas
and interludes for prepared piano. *Pierce,
piano.*
+ ARG 5-6/90: 39
+ Fa 11-12/91: 291

36542. WER 60157-2: CAGE—Mysterious
adventure; TV Köln; Daughters of the
lonesome isle; Dream; The perilous night;
Nocturne; Three dances. *Pierce, Jonas,
pianos; Almond, violin.*
• Fa 7-8/89: 120

36543. WER 60160-2: RAVEL—Sérénade
grotesque; Sites auriculaire; Pavane pour
une infante défunte; Rapsodie espagnole;
Miroirs; Boléro. *Uriarte, Mrongovius,
pianos.*
- Fa 3-4/90: 270

36544. WER 60162-2: LIGETI—Chamber
concerto; Ramifications (string orchestra
version and solo strings version); Lux
aeterna; Atmosphères. *Ensemble "Die
Reihe"; Southwest Symphony Orch.,
Baden-Baden; Saarland Radio Chamber
Orch.; Schola Cantorum Stuttgart;
Cerha, Bour, Janigro, Gottwald, conds.*
+ ARG 7-8/89: 52
+ DA 8/89: 58
+ Fa 3-4/89: 200
• Gr 10/89: 558
+ HF 4/89: 74

36545. WER 60163-2: LIGETI—Cello
concerto; Lontano; Double concerto for
flute and oboe; San Francisco polyphony.
*Palm, cello; Bahr, flute; Lännerholm,
oboe; Hessian Radio Symphony Orch.;
Southwest Symphony Orch., Baden-
Baden; Swedish Radio Symphony Orch.;
Gielen, Bour, Howarth, conds.*
+ ARG 7-8/89: 52
+ DA 8/89: 58

+ Fa 3-4/89: 200
+ HF 4/89: 74

36546. WER 60164-2: BIALAS—Lament;
Autumn; String quartet no. 4. *Mauser,
piano; Altenburger, violin; Westphal,
viola; Berger, cello; Auryn Quartet.*
+ Fa 3-4/91: 156

36547. WER 60165-2: NANCARROW—
Studies for player piano, v. 5. *Performed
on Nancarrow's modified 1927 Ampico
reproducing piano.*
+ Fa 9-10/89: 271
□ Gr 8/89: 342

36548. WER 60166/67-2 (2 discs):
NANCARROW—Studies for player piano:
Selections from vols. 3-4. *Performed on
Nancarrow's modified 1927 Ampico
reproducing piano.*
+ Fa 5-6/91: 240
+ Gr 7/91: 87

36549. WER 60172-2: PENDERECKI—
Viola concerto; Capriccio for oboe and
11 strings; Strophes for soprano, speaking
voice and 10 instruments; Intermezzo for
24 strings; Three pieces in antique style.
*Zimmermann, viola; Pedzialek, oboe;
Szwajgier, soprano; Amadeus Chamber
Orch., Posen; Duczmal, cond.*
+ ARG 7-8/90: 84
• Fa 7-8/90: 221
+ Gr 9/90: 532

36550. WER 60173-2: ADORNO—Two
pieces for string quartet; Six short
orchestral pieces; Three poems of
Theodor Däuber; Two songs with
orchestra from a planned Singspiel on
Mark Twain's The treasure of Indian Joe;
Kinderjahr. *Kiener, Neiser, vocalists;
Buchberger Quartet, Frankfurt;
Frankfurt Chamber Choir; Frankfurt
Opera House and Museum Orch.;
Bertini, cond.*
□ Fa 7-8/91: 94

36551. WER 60174-2: ORFF—Kleines
Konzert after lute pieces of the sixteenth
century; Carmina burana: Five pieces for
10 winds (arr. Wanek); Der Mond: Three
dances and finale; Die Kluge: Scene of
the 3 tramps. *Mainz Wind Ensemble;
Schöll, cond.*
+ Fa 5-6/91: 244

36552. WER 60176-2: NAOUMOFF—Four
préludes; Anecdotes; Impasse; Sonata.
Naoumoff, piano.
• Fa 9-10/89: 272

36553. WER 60179-50: EGK—
Divertissement for winds; Die
Zaubergeige: Overture. MOZART (ARR.
EGK)—Sinfonia concertante, K. 297b.
Mainz Wind Ensemble; Schöll, cond.
+ Fa 7-8/90: 139
• Gr 9/91: 84

36554. WER 60180-2: ZIMMERMANN—
Requiem for a young poet. *Bryn-Julson,*

Hermann; Manfred School Quintet;
North German Radio Chorus; Cologne
Radio Chorus & Symphony Orch.;
Bertini, cond.
□ Fa 7-8/90: 321

36555. WER 60183-2: REIMANN—
Kinderlieder; Nine sonnets of Louize
Labe; Night spaces. *Schäfer, soprano;
Himmelheber, mezzo-soprano; Bauni,
Reimann, pianos.*
+ Fa 11-12/90: 328
+ Gr 9/90: 591

36556. WER 60185-2: SCHOENBERG—Five
pieces for orchestra op. 16; Cello
concerto, freely adapted from the
concerto for clavicembalo by M. G.
Monn; Modern psalm op. 50c; Variations
for orchestra op. 31. *Schiff, cello; Reich,
speaker; Slovak Phil. Chorus; Southwest
German Radio Symphony Orch.; Gielen,
cond.*
+ Fa 9-10/90: 194

36557. WER 60501-2: PLATE—Moon a
pale imitation; Greasy luck; The sting.
Various performers.
□ Fa 5-6/89: 268

36558. WER 60502-2: FEBEL—Variations
for orchestra; Das Unendliche; String
quartet no. 1. *Bair-Ivenz, mezzo-
soprano; Anlauf, bass; Arditti String
Quartet; Saarbrücken Radio Symphony
Orch.; Stuttgart Radio Symphony Orch.;
Zilm, Mercier, conds.*
+ Fa 3-4/89: 162

36559. WER 60503-2: MÜLLER-
SIEMENS—Variationen über einen Ländler
von Schubert; Under neonlight I; Piano
concerto. *Banfield, piano; Ensemble 13;
Basel Radio Symphony Orch.; Southwest
German Radio Symphony Orch., Baden-
Baden; Reichert, Carewe, Kord, conds.*
+ Fa 3-4/89: 229

36560. WER 60504-2: SCHWEINITZ—
Messe op. 21. *Studer, Schreckenbach,
Pell, Carmelli; Italian Radio and
Television Chamber Choir; Berlin Radio
Symphony Orch.; Albrecht, cond.*
+ Fa 3-4/89: 162

36561. WER 60507-2: LEYENDECKER—
Cello concerto; String quartet no. 1;
Piano concerto; Canto. *Faust, cello;
Havenith, piano; Brahms Quartet; North
German Radio Symphony Orch.; Berlin
Radio Symphony Orch.; Carewe, Gülke,
Dörnburg, conds.*
+ Fa 11-12/89: 263

WESTERN WIND

36562. 1800: The Passover story. *The
Western Wind.*
+ ARG 3-4/93: 182

36563. 1818: The Chanukkah story. *The
Western Wind.*
+ ARG 3-4/93: 182

36564. 1836: Mazal bueno: the Spanish Jews. *Western Wind.*
+ ARG 5-6/93: 172

36565. 2002: An almost a cappella songbook. *Western Wind.*
+ ARG 9-10/94: 256

36566. 9201: Buhr—Akasha; Jyotir; The cycle of spring; Lure of the fallen seraphim. *Perillo, soprano; Winnipeg Singers; Winnipeg Symphony Orch.; Tovey, cond.*
+ ARG 3-4/93: 66

WHAT NEXT?

36567. 0015: Hunt—Haramand plane: three transition links. *Hunt, acoustics.*
+ ARG 9-10/95: 302

36568. 0016: Trance gong. *Gamelan Pacifica.*
+ ARG 9-10/95: 302

WHITE LABEL

36569. HRC 071: Haydn—Sonatas for violin and viola H. VI:1-6. *Kovács, violin; Németh, viola.*
+ Fa 9-10/88: 168

36570. HRC 072: Mozart—Divertimento for string trio K. 563; Duos for violin and viola K. 423-24. *Kovács, violin; Németh, viola; Banda, cello.*
- Fa 9-10/88: 210

36571. HRC 074: Vivaldi—Stabat Mater; Longe mala umbrae terrores; Nisi Dominus. *Takács, mezzo-soprano; Budai, alto; Franz Liszt Chamber Orch.; Hungarian State Orch.; Sándor, Szekeres, conds.*
• Fa 9-10/88: 295

36572. HRC 075: Mahler—Des Knaben Wunderhorn; Lieder eines fahrenden Gesellen. *Andor, soprano; Gáti, Sólyom-Nagy, baritones; Budapest Symphony Orch.; Lehel, cond.*
- Fa 9-10/88: 191
• Gr 11/88: 842

36573. HRC 076: Mozart—Serenade for winds K. 361. *Hungarian State Opera Wind Ensemble; Lukács, cond.*
- Fa 9-10/88: 210

36574. HRC 077: Mahler—Symphony no. 1 in D (with Blumine movement). *Hungarian State Orch.; Fischer, cond.*
• Fa 9-10/88: 191

36575. HRC 079: *The Fitzwilliam virginal book: excerpts.* Music of Byrd, Dowland, Bull, Tomkins, Mundy, and others. *Pertis, harpsichord.*
+ Fa 9-10/88: 330
+ Gr 11/88: 830

36576. HRC 081: Strauss—Don Quixote; Salome: Dance of the seven veils. *Perényi, cello; Bársony, viola; Hungarian State Orch.; Ferencsik, cond.*
• Fa 9-10/88: 272

36577. HRC 082: Strauss—Till Eulenspiegels lustige Streiche; Don Juan; Duet-Concertino for clarinet, and bassoon. *Berkes, clarinet; Fülemile, bassoon; Budapest Symphony Orch.; Budapest Phil. Orch.; Kobayashi, Kórodi, conds.*
- Fa 9-10/88: 271

36578. HRC 083: *The baroque and classical bassoon.* Music of Fasch, Vivaldi, Boismotier, Zachow, Stamitz, and Mozart. *Hara, bassoon; Tatrai Quartet; Hungarian Baroque Trio; Hungarian State Orch.; Ferencsik, cond.*
+ ARG 11-12/88: 102
+ Fa 11-12/88: 342

36579. HRC 084: Chopin—Piano concertos no. 1-2. *Falvai, piano; Budapest Phil. Orch.; Kórodi, cond.*
+ Fa 9-10/88: 127

36580. HRC 085: Mozart—String quintets K. 515, 174. *Tátrai String Quartet; Mauthner, 2nd viola.*
+ ARG 1-2/89: 71
• Fa 11-12/88: 234

36581. HRC 087: Telemann—Quartets for flute, violin, viola da gamba and continuo no. 1, 3-5 . *Kovács, violin; Hungarian Baroque Trio.*
• Fa 9-10/88: 283
• Gr 3/89: 1451
• HPR 12/88: 87

36582. HRC 088: Haydn—Harpsichord concerto in D; Concerto for violin and harpsichord in F; Symphony no. 31. *Pertis, harpsichord; Rolla, violin & cond.; Franz Liszt Chamber Orch.*
- Fa 9-10/88: 164

36583. HRC 090: Haydn—Symphony no. 27, 88, 100. *Hungarian Chamber Orch.; Hungarian State Orch.; Tatrai, Fischer, conds.*
+ ARG 9-10/88: 53
- Fa 1-2/89: 179

36584. HRC 092: Clementi—Piano sonatas op. 23 no. 3; op. 25 no. 6; op. 37 no. 1-2. *Failoni, piano.*
+ Fa 3-4/89: 138

36585. HRC 094: Bach—St. John passion: Excerpts. *Franz Liszt Chamber Chorus & Orch.; Lehel, cond.*
+ ARG 11-12/88: 10
- Fa 11-12/88: 122

36586. HRC 095: Liszt—Tu es Petrus; Weimars Volkslied; Ora pro nobis; Salve Regina; Ave maris stella; Angelus; Am Grabe Richard Wagners; Praeludium; Gebet; Andante maestoso: Slavimo slavno, Slaveni; Rosario; Missa pro organo. *Margittay, Kovács, Lehotka, organs.*
+ Fa 11-12/88: 215

36587. HRC 096: Mozart—String quintets K. 593, 614. *Tátrai String Quartet; Mauthner, 2nd viola.*
+ ARG 5-6/89: 71
+ Fa 3-4/89: 224

36588. HRC 098: Haydn—Symphonies no. 92, 101. *Hungarian State Orch.; Lukács, cond.*
• Fa 9-10/88: 167

36589. HRC 099: Handel—Organ concertos op. 4 no. 1, 4-5; op. 7 no. 3. *Lehotka, organ; Franz Liszt Chamber Orch.; Sándor, cond.*
• ARG 1-2/89: 55
+ Fa 11-12/88: 198

36590. HRC 100: M. Haydn—Serenade; Symphony in D. *Budapest Phil. Orch.; Sándor, cond.*
+ ARG 3-4/89: 46
□ Fa 5-6/89: 217

36591. HRC 101: Haydn—Symphonies no. 6-8. *Hungarian Chamber Orch.; Tátrai, cond.*
+ ARG 3-4/89: 46
- Fa 3-4/89: 182

36592. HRC 102: Haydn—Symphonies no. 26, 44-45. *Hungarian Chamber Orch.; Tátrai, cond.*
+ ARG 3-4/89: 46
• Fa 3-4/89: 182

36593. HRC 103: Haydn—Symphonies no. 49, 59, 73. *Hungarian Chamber Orch.; Tátrai, cond.*
+ ARG 3-4/89: 46
• Fa 3-4/89: 183

36594. HRC 104: Schumann—Symphony no. 2. Schubert—Rosamunde: Excerpts. *Hungarian State Orch.; Fischer, Patanè, conds.*
• Fa 3-4/89: 270

36595. HRC 105: Beethoven—Violin sonatas no. 5, 9. *Kovács, violin; Bächer, piano.*
+ ARG 1-2/90: 24
+ Fa 3-4/89: 97

36596. HRC 106: Lalo—Symphonie espagnole. Indy—Symphony on a French mountain air. *Szenthelyi, violin; Hungarian State Orch.; Budapest Phil. Orch.; Lukács, Pál, cond.*
- Fa 11-12/88: 211

36597. HRC 107: Mozart—Flute concertos (complete). M. Haydn—Flute concerto in D. *Kovács, flute; Hungarian State Orch.; Győr Phil. Orch.; Lukács, Sándor, conds.*
+ ARG 3-4/89: 59
- Fa 3-4/89: 216

36598. HRC 108: Brahms—Symphony no. 4; Academic festival overture; Tragic overture. *Budapest Symphony Orch.; Lehel, cond.*
- Fa 3-4/89: 124

36599. HRC 110: Beethoven— Symphonies no. 1-2. *Hungarian State Orch.; Ferencsik, cond.*
+ ARG 3-4/89: 22
- Fa 3-4/89: 98

36600. HRC 111: Beethoven— Symphony no. 3. *Hungarian State Orch.; Ferencsik, cond.*
+ ARG 3-4/89: 22
- Fa 3-4/89: 98

36601. HRC 113: Beethoven— Symphony no. 6; Egmont overture. *Hungarian State Orch.; Ferencsik, cond.*
+ ARG 3-4/89: 22
- Fa 3-4/89: 98

36602. HRC 114: Beethoven— Symphonies no. 7-8. *Hungarian State Orch.; Ferencsik, cond.*
+ Fa 11-12/88: 139

36603. HRC 115: Beethoven— Symphony no. 9. *Andor, Szirmay, Korondi, Sólyom-Nagy; Budapest Chorus; Hungarian State Orch.; Ferencsik, cond.*
+ Fa 1-2/88: 139

36604. HRC 117: C.P.E. Bach—Cello concertos Wq. 171-172. Cherubini— Thirteen contredanses. *Onczay, cello; Franz Liszt Chamber Orch.*
- ARG 11-12/89: 16
- Fa 1-2/90: 89

36605. HRC 118: Beethoven—King Stephan: Excerpts; Ruins of Athens: Excerpts; Creatures of Prometheus: Overture. *László, soprano; Sólyom-Nagy, baritone; Hungarian Radio and Television Chorus; Budapest Phil. Orch.; Hungarian State Orch.; Oberfrank, Kórodi, conds.*
+ ARG 9-10/89: 24
+ Fa 11-12/89: 129

36606. HRC 119: Bach—Flute sonatas BWV 1020, 1031, 1033-35. *Kovács, flute; Sebestyén, harpsichord; Banda, cello.*
- Fa 11-12/89: 113

36607. HRC 120: Franck—Pièce héroïque; Final; Grande pièce symphonique; Prelude, fugue & variation; L'organiste: Andantino in A♭. *Lehotka, Gergely, organs.*
- Fa 11-12/89: 208

36608. HRC 121: Dohnányi—Ruralia hungarica; Variations on a nursery song; Serenade for string trio in C. *Kovács, violin; Bársony, viola; Botvay, cello; Lantos, piano; Budapest Symphony Orch.; Lehel, cond.*
- Fa 11-12/89: 189

36609. HRC 122: Dvořák—String quartet no. 12. Debussy—String quartet. Ravel—String quartet. *Bartók Quartet.*
+ Fa 11-12/89: 196

36610. HRC 123: Haydn—Symphonies no. 43, 82, 94. *Hungarian Chamber Orch.; Tátrai, cond.*
+ ARG 11-12/89: 67
- ARG 9-10/90: 74
+ Fa 11-12/89: 237

36611. HRC 124: Bach—Komm, du süsse Todesstunde, BWV 161; Gott soll allein mein Herze haben, BWV 169. *Hamari, alto; Réti, tenor; Ferenc Liszt Academy of Music Chamber Chorus & Orch.; Sándor, cond.*
+ ARG 11-12/89: 20
+ Fa 11-12/89: 107

36612. HRC 125: Beethoven—String quartets op. 127, 131. *Bartók Quartet.*
+ ARG 11-12/89: 35

36613. HRC 126: Beethoven—String quartets op. 132, 135. *Bartók Quartet.*
+ ARG 11-12/89: 35

36614. HRC 127: Vivaldi—Flute concertos op. 10. *Kovács, flute; Franz Liszt Chamber Orch.; Rolla, cond.*
+ ARG 11-12/89: 134
+ Fa 11-12/89: 398

36615. HRC 128: Mozart—Flute quartets K. 285, 285a-285b, 298; Trio for piano, clarinet & viola K. 498. *Szebenyi, flute; Kiss, violin; Bársony, viola; Botvay, cello; Rados, piano; Kovács, clarinet; Németh, viola.*
+ ARG 9-10/89: 85
- Fa 11-12/89: 292

36616. HRC 129: Mozart—String quartets no. 14-15. *Bartók Quartet.*
+ ARG 11-12/89: 88
- Fa 11-12/89: 292

36617. HRC 130: Kuhnau—Biblical sonatas no. 1-3, 6. *Horváth, harpsichord.*
□ ARG 11-12/89: 73
+ Fa 11-12/89: 256

36618. HRC 133: Handel—Concerti grossi op. 6 no. 4, 6, 9, 11. *Rolla, violin & cond.; Franz Liszt Chamber Orch.*
+ ARG 9-10/89: 58
+ Fa 11-12/89: 225

36619. HRC 136: Beethoven—String quartet no. 13; Grosse Fuge. *Bartók Quartet.*
- ARG 3-4/90: 22
+ Fa 3-4/90: 127

36620. HRC 137: Mozart—String quartets no. 16-17. *Bartók Quartet.*
- ARG 3-4/90: 79
- Fa 3-4/90: 244

36621. HRC 138: Mozart—String quartets no. 18-19. *Bartók Quartet.*
- ARG 3-4/90: 79
- Fa 3-4/90: 245

36622. HRC 139: Brahms—Violin sonatas no. 1-3. *Szenthelyi, violin; Schiff, piano.*
+ ARG 3-4/90: 33

36623. HRC 140: Haydn—Symphonies no. 55, 67-68. *Hungarian Chamber Orch.; Tátrai, cond.*
+ ARG 3-4/90: 59
- Fa 3-4/90: 194

36624. HRC 141: Haydn—Symphonies no. 39, 47, 54. *Hungarian Chamber Orch.; Tátrai, cond.*
+ ARG 3-4/90: 59
- Fa 3-4/90: 194

36625. HRC 142: Kodály—Méditation sur un motif de Claude Debussy; Nine pieces op. 3; Seven pieces op. 11; Marosszék dances. *Zempléni, piano.*
+ ARG 3-4/90: 65
+ Fa 3-4/90: 208

36626. HRC 143: Mozart—Symphonies no. 39, 41. *Hungarian State Orch.; Ferencsik, cond.*
- Fa 3-4/90: 248

36627. HRC 144: Haydn (attrib.)— Erwählung eines Kapellmeisters. Paisiello (attrib.)—Il maestro ed' i suoi due scolari. *Takács, Szőkefalvi-Nagy; Budapest Madrigal Choir; Hungarian State Orch.; Szekeres, cond.*
□ ARG 3-4/90: 58
- Fa 3-4/90: 189

36628. HRC 145: Liszt—Mass for male voices and organ (revised version); Via crucis. *Réti, Palcsó, Melis, Gregor, Marton, Andor, Csengery, Komlóssy, Sólyom-Nagy; Male Chorus of the Hungarian People's Army; Budapest Chorus; Lehotka, organ; Kis, Szabó, conds.*
- Fa 5-6/90: 204

36629. HRC 146: Music of Schubert, Bach, Terzi, Tarrega, Vinas, and Falla. *Szendrey-Karper, guitar; Jeney, flute; Lukács, viola; Banda, cello.*
+ ARG 7-8/90: 97

36630. HRC 147: Beethoven—Violin concerto op. 61; Romances for violin no. 1-2. *Kovács, violin; Hungarian State Orch.; Budapest Symphony Orch.; Ferencsik, Lehel, conds.*
- Fa 9-10/90: 167

36631. HRC 148: Hindemith— Schwanendreher; Cello concerto. *Bársony, viola; Perényi, cello; Hungarian State Orch.; Budapest Symphony Orch.; Erdélyi, Lehel, conds.*
+ ARG 9-10/90: 77
+ Fa 7-8/90: 173

36632. HRC 149: CIMAROSA—Piano sonatas. MENDELSSOHN—Songs without words: no. 14, 17, 21, 25, 30, 38. *Failoni, Nemes, pianos.*
- Fa 9-10/90: 214

36633. HRC 150: MOZART—Clarinet quintet K. 581; Clarinet concerto K. 622. *Kovács, clarinet; Tátrai Quartet; Budapest Phil. Orch.; Kórodi, cond.*
• Fa 9-10/90: 310

36634. HRC 152: SCHUBERT— Symphonies no. 5, 8. *Hungarian State Orch.; Ferencsik, cond.*
- Fa 9-10/90: 377

36635. HRC 154: MOZART—Violin concertos no. 3-5. *Kovács, violin; Budapest Phil. Orch.; Budapest Symphony Orch.; Németh, Lehel, conds.*
+ ARG 1-2/91: 69
• Fa 9-10/90: 167

36636. HRC 155: HAYDN— Divertimentos: H. II: 7, 15, 23, D18. *Pongrácz, Hock, oboes; Medveczky, Mesterházy, horns; Fülemile, Nagy, bassoons.*
- Fa 9-10/90: 259

36637. HRC 156—157 (2 separate discs): BEETHOVEN—String quartets op. 18. *Bartók Quartet.*
- ARG 11-12/90: 28
+ Fa 11-12/90: 162

36638. HRC 158: BEETHOVEN—String trio op. 3; String quartet no. 11. *Dénes, violin; Németh, viola; Banda, cello; Bartók Quartet.*
• Fa 11-12/90: 162

36639. HRC 159: MOZART—Sinfonia concertante K. 297b; Serenade for winds K. 375. *Hungarian Chamber Orch.; Tátrai, cond.*
• Fa 11-12/90: 298

36640. HRC 160: LISZT—Les préludes; Mazeppa; Mephisto waltz; Hungaria. *Hungarian State Orch.; Ferencsik, cond.*
• Fa 11-12/90: 258

36641. HRC 161: MENDELSSOHN— Symphonies no. 3-4. *Budapest Phil. Orch.; Hungarian State Orch.; Kórodi, Németh, conds.*
• Fa 11-12/90: 274

36642. HRC 162: GOLDMARK—Violin concerto. PAGANINI—Violin concerto no. 1. *Kocsis, violin; Savaria Symphony Orch.; Petró, cond.; Bálint, violin; Budapest Symphony Orch.; Lehel, cond.*
• Fa 11-12/90: 306
+ Gr 3/94: 52

36643. HRC 163: LISZT—Piano concertos no. 1-2; Totentanz. *Kiss, Jandó, pianos; Hungarian State Orch.; Ferencsik, cond.*
- Fa 11-12/90: 256

36644. HRC 164: HAYDN—Divertimentos H.XIV: 4, 7-9, 13. *Tátrai, Konrád, violins; Banda, cello; Sebestyén, harpsichord.*
+ Fa 1-2/91: 213

36645. HRC 165: BEETHOVEN—Duets for clarinet and bassoon WoO 27 no. 1,3; Trio for 2 oboes and English horn op. 87. *Kovács, clarinet; Fülemile, bassoon; Pongrácz, Tóth, oboes; Eisenbacher, English horn.*
+ ARG 1-2/91: 28
- Fa 11-12/90: 161

36646. HRC 166: HANDEL—Concerti grossi op. 6: no. 7, 8, 10, 12. *Franz Liszt Chamber Orch.; Rolla, cond.*
+ Fa 3-4/91: 231

36647. HRC 167: CORELLI—Violin sonatas op. 5 no. 1-6. *Kovács, violin; Sebestyén, harpsichord; Banda, cello.*
- ARG 5-6/91: 48
• Fa 3-4/91: 272

36648. HRC 168: MENDELSSOHN— Hebrides overture. RESPIGHI—Pines of Rome. MUSSORGSKY—Night on Bald Mountain. TCHAIKOVSKY—Romeo and Juliet. *Budapest Phil. Orch.; Budapest Symphony Orch.; Gardelli, cond.*
+ Fa 3-4/91: 509

36649. HRC 169: MOZART—Quintet for piano and winds K. 452. BEETHOVEN— Quintet for piano and winds op. 16. *Falvai, piano; Hungarian Wind Quartet.*
+ ARG 5-6/91: 29
• Fa 3-4/91: 295

36650. HRC 170: MOZART—Piano quartets no. 1-2. *Kiss, piano; Tátrai Trio.*
+ Fa 3-4/91: 295

36651. HRC 171: CHOPIN—Cello sonata. FAURÉ—Cello sonatas no. 1-2. *Perényi, cello; Wehner, Szűcs, pianos.*
+ ARG 3-4/91: 64
+ Fa 3-4/91: 188

36652. HRC 172: GRIEG—Peer Gynt suites no. 1-2. SIBELIUS—Finlandia; Swan of Tuonela; Karelia suite. *Debrecen Phil. Orch.; Budapest Phil. Orch.; Szabó, Medveczky, conds.*
• Fa 3-4/91: 225

36653. HRC 173: SCHUBERT—Piano trio D. 898; Trio movement D. 897. *Rados, piano; Kovács, violin; Banda, cello.*
+ Fa 3-4/91: 369

36654. HRC 174: MOZART—String quartets no. 21-22; Horn quintet K. 407. *Tarjáni, horn; Kodály Quartet; Eder Quartet.*
+ Fa 3-4/91: 295

36655. HRC 175: MENDELSSOHN—Violin concertos in E minor, in D minor. *Kovács, Kocsis, violins; Hungarian State Orch.; Savaria Symphony Orch.; Németh,*

Petró, conds.
• Fa 3-4/91: 272

36656. HRC 176: RAVEL—Boléro; Rapsodie espagnole; Pavane pour une infante défunte; Ma mère l'oye: Suite. *Budapest Phil. Orch.; Kórodi, cond.*
• Fa 11-12/91: 453

36657. HRC 178: HANDEL—Water music. *Franz Liszt Chamber Orch.; Sándor, cond.* Reissue.
• Fa 11-12/91: 342

36658. HRC 180: *The virtuoso violin.* Works by Debussy, Ravel, Sarasate and Wieniawski. *Szabadi, violin; Gulyás, piano.*
+ ARG 11-12/91: 194
+ Fa 11-12/91: 558

36659. HRC 181: RAVEL—Piano concerto in G. GRIEG—Piano concerto. *Jandó, piano; Budapest Symphony Orch.; Jancsovics, cond.*
• Fa 11-12/91: 455

36660. HRC 184/86 (3 discs): LISZT— Christus. *Andor, Németh, Réti, Sólyom Nagy, Gregor; Margittay, organ; Budapest Choir; Budapest Kodály Female Choir; Hungarian State Orch.; Forrai, cond.* Reissue.
+ Fa 11-12/91: 370

WILDBOAR

36661. WLBR 8503: *English virginal music.* Music of Tallis, Byrd, Bull, Gibbons, P. Philips, and Tomkins. *Fitch, harpsichord & virginals.*
+ Fa 9-10/88: 330

36662. WLBR 9101 (2 discs): BACH— Partitas. *Parmentier, harpsichord.*
+ Fa 11-12/92: 184

36663. WLBR 9102: *Musik as befitts a quene: English virginal music, 1570-1650.* Music of Gibbons, Byrd, Inglot, Anon., Philips, Farnaby, Tomkins, Tisdall, and Bull. *Parmentier, harpsichord.*
+ ARG 3-4/95: 245
+ Fa 11-12/94: 481

36664. WLBR 9201: FORQUERAY— Harpsichord music. DU PHLY—La Forqueray. RAMEAU—La Forqueray. *Hass, harpsichord.*
+ ARG 11-12/94: 111
+ Fa 11-12/94: 226

36665. WLBR 9203: CORELLI—Trio sonatas for 2 recorders and continuo. *Lynn, Stern, recorders; Parmentier, harpsichord; Sutherland, cello.*
+ Fa 1-2/93: 133

36666. WLBR 9501: BACH—Harpsichord music. *Smith, harpsichord.*
+ ARG 5-6/96: 72

WILDBOAR

+ Fa 9-10/96: 134
+ Fi 6/96: 133

36667. WLBR 9512: *In stile moderno.* Music of Fontana, Frescobaldi, Leonarda, Marini, and others. *Matthews, violin; Schenkman, harpsichord.*
+ ARG 7-8/96: 266
• Fa 9-10/96: 416

WILDMAN

36668. 2010: Music of Babin, Bach, Harvey, Osborne, and Giampieri. *Pope, clarinet; Moss, piano.*
+ ARG 11-12/96: 245

WILLIAM GRANT STILL MUSIC

36669. WGSM 1001 (LP): STILL—Suite for violin and piano; Pastorale for violin and piano; Ennanga, for harp and piano quintet; Danzas de Panama, for string quartet. *Kaufman, violin; Kaufman, piano; Craft, harp; Kaufman String Quartet.*
□ Fa 3-4/89: 285

36670. WGSM 1002 (LP): STILL—Bells; Three visions; The blues; Seven traceries. *Dominguez, piano.*
• Fa 3-4/89: 285

WILLIAMSBURG FOUNDATION

36671. 120: *Nottingham ale.* Tavern music from Colonial Williamsburg. *Various drunkards.*
- ARG 9-10/94: 255

WILSON AUDIO

36672. W 8416 (LP): DVOŘÁK—Piano trio op. 90. *Francesco Trio.*
+ HF 11/86: 77

36673. W 9231: GERSHWIN—Porgy and Bess fantasy; Rhapsody in blue; Songs. *Knight, piano.*
+ ARG 11-12/93: 107

WOODMANSTERNE

36674. WOODM 002-2: *Songs, dances and laments from the Age of Elizabeth I.* Music of Byrd, Gibbons, and Holborne. *Tysall, soprano; Rose Consort of Viols.*
+ Gr 10/93: 106

WORK MUSIC

36675. 001: NYMAN—Taking a line for a second walk; Lady in the red hat; Water dance 1-5. *The Zoo II.*
□ ARG 11-12/95: 168

WORLD MUSIC LIBRARY

36676. KICC 5110: Art of the sitar. *Parvez, sitar; Barodekar, tabla.*
+ Fa 5-6/93: 416

WSA

36677. 191: MASSENET—Meditation from Thaïs. ELGAR—Violin sonata. HOOTEN—Cantata per Kym; Cantata per Divino. PONCE—Cancion de Otoño. HORNE—Sonata. *Scobie, violin; Cooper, piano.*
+ ARG 5-6/92: 170

WVH

36678. 165: Music of Schubert, Schumann, and Spohr. *Midas Ensemble.*
• ARG 1-2/96: 234

XI

36679. 112: CAMERON—Raw sangudo; Runa; Gibbous moon; Chamber of statues; Blank sheet of metal. *Various performers.*
□ ARG 5-6/96: 279

XLNT MUSIC

36680. 18003: SMETANA—Piano trio, op. 15. MARTINŮ—Trio. SHOSTAKOVICH—Piano trio no. 2. *Leonardo Trio.*
+ Fa 3-4/89: 385

36681. 18004: WEBER—Clarinet quintet in B♭; Grand duo concertante for clarinet and piano; Introduction, theme and variations for clarinet and strings; Seven variations for clarinet and piano op. 33. *Manasse, clarinet; Manhattan String Quartet; Sanders, piano.*
+ ARG 1-2/90: 105
+ Fa 9-10/89: 377

36682. 18005: WEBER—Clarinet concertos (complete); Concertino for clarinet op. 26; Andante and Hungarian rondo (arr. Cohn). *Manasse, clarinet; Brooklyn Phil. Orch.; Foss, cond.*
+ ARG 3-4/90: 125
+ Fa 3-4/90: 337
+ MA 9/90: 91

36683. 18006: COHN—Chamber music. *Various performers.*
+ ARG 3-4/92: 48

36684. 18007: COHN—Concerto da camera, op. 20; Quintet no. 2 for winds; Serenade for flute, violin, and cello, op. 68; Trio for piano, violin, and cello, op. 66; Mount Gretna suite. *Leonardo Trio; Quintet of the Americas; XLNT Sinfonietta.*
□ ARG 7-8/93: 78
• Fa 7-8/93: 126

36685. 18008: Music for wind quintet by Bernstein, Gershwin, Barber and others. *Quintet of the Americas.*
+ ARG 3-4/93: 178
+ Fa 5-6/93: 404

36686. 18009: Music of Mozart, Spohr, Gershwin, and Cohn. *Manasse, clarinet; Shanghai String Quartet.*

+ ARG 9-10/94: 230
+ Fa 9-10/94: 415

YALE UNIVERSITY LIBRARY

36687. CD no. 1 (2 discs): Treasures from the Yale collection of historical sound recordings. *Various artists and accompanists.*
+ Fa 7-8/94: 300

YELLOW TAIL

36688. 101: Music of Morel, Villa-Lobos, Ponce, and Albéniz. *Field, guitar.*
• ARG 1-2/94: 179

YORK

36689. 110: SAINT-SAËNS—Breton rhapsodies; Preludes and fugues, op. 109; Fantasies. *Phillips, organ.*
• ARG 5-6/96: 181

36690. 111: Organ music of C., S., and S.S. Wesley. *Phillips, organ.*
+ ARG 3-4/96: 210

36691. 112: Music of Widor, Dupré, Langlais, Vierne, Alain, and Litaize. *Harris, organ.*
+ ARG 1-2/96: 216

36692. 117: SAINT-SAËNS—Bénédiction nuptiale; Improvisations; Preludes and fugues, op. 99. LEFÉBURE- WÉLY—Organ pieces. DUBOIS—Toccata in G. *Phillips, organ.*
• ARG 5-6/96: 181

36693. 127: PEETERS—Missa festiva. LANGLAIS—Messe solennelle. WALTON—Missa brevis. *Canterbury Cathedral Choir; Flood, cond.; Harris, organ.*
+ ARG 3-4/96: 164

Z PRESS

36694. PS-1333 (2 LPs): PASATIERI—Three sisters. *Wells, Telese, Cariaga; Opera Columbus Orch.; Kellogg, cond.*
+ Fa 11-12/87: 192
+ ON 5/87: 59
+ Op 3/88: 377
- OQ Winter 87-88: 124
• Ov 4/88: 42

ZUK

36695. 070379: *Horn dessous: French music for horn and orchestra.* Music of Françaix, Chabrier, Dukas, Ravel, Saint-Saëns, Bozza, d'Indy, and Koechlin. *Zuk, horn; Katowice Radio Symphony Orch.; Szostak, cond.*
• ARG 1-2/97: 209
+ Fa 11-12/96: 456

36696. 071088: *Horn obsession.* Music of Schoeck, Dauprat, Hindemith, and Rosetti. *Zuk, horn; Wroclaw Chamber Orch. Leopoldinum; Stanienda, cond.*

+ ARG 1-2/97: 209
+ Fa 11-12/96: 458

36697. 100955: Music of Weber, Kiel, Schumann, and Strauss. *Zuk, horn; Cracow Radio Orch.; Höltzel, cond.*
+ ARG 7-8/96: 245
• Fa 11-12/96: 208

36698. 160114: Mozart—Horn concertos no. 3-4. L. Mozart—Horn concerto; Concerto for 2 horns and orchestra. *Zuk, Muzyk, horns; Wroclaw Chamber Orch. Leopoldinum; Stanienda, cond.*
+ Fa 11-12/96: 314

36699. 160528: *Il corno italiano: Italian music for horn and orchestra.* Music of Vivaldi, Mercadante, Donizetti, Belloli, Cherubini, Bellini, and Rota. *Zuk, horn; Wroclaw Chamber Orch. Leopoldinum; Stanienda, cond.*
+ Fa 11-12/96: 456

36700. 191122: *Horn expression.* Music of Jevtic, Arnold, Turner, Ristori, Plog, and Koetsier. *Zuk, horn; Polish Radio Orch.; Stanienda, cond.*
+ Fa 11-12/96: 456

36701. 310355: Music of Rossini, Telemann, Mann, Haydn, and Mozart. *Zuk, horn; Baltic Virtuosi; Dalinkevicius, cond.*
+ ARG 7-8/96: 245
+ Fa 11-12/96: 314

ZUMA RECORDS

36702. ZMA 101: *Halt.* Cimarosa—Seven sonatas. Scriabin—Piano sonata, op. 64, no. 7 "White mass". Messiaen—Vingt regards sur l'Enfant Jésus (four selections). Crumb—A little suite for Christmas A.D. 1979. *Moltisanti, piano.*
+ ARG 5-6/95: 214
+ Fa 3-4/95: 385

36703. ZMA 102: Crumb—Vox balaenae. Napoli—Songs; Variations on Alessandro Scarlatti's La follia. *Zoerning, cello; Schlefer, flute; Moltisanti, Guidici, piano; Donatella, soprano.*
+ Fa 7-8/95: 162

36704. ZMA 104: *Shards of glass.* Music of Gubaidulina, Segall, Melby, Ives, and Nielsen. *Lane, flute; Wimunc- Pearson, piano.*
+ ARG 5-6/95: 207
+ Fa 5-6/95: 406

ZYODE

36705. 1014: Jacobs—Ambassadors of fortune; Sand castles; Bookends; Canopy of dreams; Night covers all. *Various performers.*
+ ARG 7-8/95: 132